Psychological Testing and Assessment

An Introduction to Tests and Measurement

NINTH EDITION

D0841934

Ronald Jay Cohen
RJ COHEN CONSULTING

Mark E. Swerdlik
ILLINOIS STATE UNIVERSITY

McGraw Hill Education

PSYCHOLOGICAL TESTING AND ASSESSMENT:
AN INTRODUCTION TO TESTS AND MEASUREMENT, NINTH EDITION

Published by McGraw-Hill Education, 2 Penn Plaza, New York, NY 10121. Copyright © 2018 by McGraw-Hill Education. All rights reserved. Printed in the United States of America. Previous editions © 2013, 2010, and 2005. No part of this publication may be reproduced or distributed in any form or by any means, or stored in a database or retrieval system, without the prior written consent of McGraw-Hill Education, including, but not limited to, in any network or other electronic storage or transmission, or broadcast for distance learning.
Some ancillaries, including electronic and print components, may not be available to customers outside the United States.
This book is printed on acid-free paper.

1 2 3 4 5 6 7 8 9 LWI 21 20 19 18 17

ISBN 978-1-259-92208-4
MHID 1-259-92208-1

All credits appearing on page or at the end of the book are considered to be an extension of the copyright page.

The Internet addresses listed in the text were accurate at the time of publication. The inclusion of a website does not indicate an endorsement by the authors or McGraw-Hill Education, and McGraw-Hill Education does not guarantee the accuracy of the information presented at these sites.

mheducation.com/highered

This book is dedicated with love to the memory of Edith and Harold Cohen.

© 2017 Ronald Jay Cohen. All rights reserved.

Contents

PART **II** *The Science of Psychological Measurement*

5 Reliability   141

PART **III** *The Assessment of Intelligence*

9   Intelligence and Its Measurement   273

PART **IV** *The Assessment of Personality*

12   Personality Assessment Methods   401

PART **V** *Testing and Assessment in Action*

13   Clinical and Counseling Assessment   448

Preface

We are proud to welcome instructors of a measurement course in psychology to this ninth edition of *Psychological Testing and Assessment*. Thank you for the privilege of assisting in the exciting task of introducing the world of tests and measurement to your students. In this preface, we impart our vision for a measurement textbook, as well as the philosophy that has driven, and that continues to drive, the organization, content, writing style, and pedagogy of this book. We'll briefly look back at this book's heritage and discuss what is new and distinctive about this ninth edition. Of particular interest to instructors, this preface will overview the authors' general approach to the course content and distinguish how that approach differs from other measurement textbooks. For students who happen to be curious enough to read this preface (or ambitious enough to read it despite the fact that it was not assigned), we would hope that your takeaway from it has to do with the authors' genuine dedication to making this book the far-and-away best available textbook for your measurement course.

Our Vision for a Textbook on Psychological Testing and Assessment

First and foremost, let's get out there that the subject matter of this course is *psychological testing and assessment*—a fact that is contrary to the message conveyed by an array of would-be competitor books, all distinguished by their anachronistic "psychological testing" title. Of course we cover tests and testing, and no available textbook does it better or more comprehensively. But it behooves us to observe that we are now well into the twenty-first century and it has long been recognized that tests are only one tool of assessment. Psychological testing is a process that can be—perhaps reminiscent of those books with the same title—impersonal, noncreative, uninspired, routine, and even robotic in nature. By contrast, psychological assessment is a very human, dynamic, custom, creative, and collaborative enterprise. These aspects of the distinction between *psychological testing* and *psychological assessment* are not trivial.

Paralleling important differences between our book's title and that of other books in this area are key differences in the way that the subject matter of the course is approached. In routine writing and through a variety of pedagogical tools, we attempt to draw students into the world of testing and assessment by *humanizing* the material. Our very human approach to the course material stands in stark contrast to the "by-the-numbers" approach of some of our competitors; the latter approach can easily alienate readers, prompting them to "tune out." Let's briefly elaborate on this critical point.

Although most of our competitors begin by organizing their books with an outline that for the most part mimics our own—right down to the inclusion of the Statistics Refresher that we innovated some 30 years ago—the way that they cover that subject matter, and the pedagogical tools they rely on to assist student learning, bear only cosmetic resemblance to our approach. We take every opportunity to illustrate the course material by putting a human face to it, and by providing practical, "every day" examples of the principles and procedures at work. This approach differs in key ways from the approach of other books in the area, where a "practical approach" may instead be equated with the intermingling of statistical or other exercises within every chapter of the book. Presumably, according to the latter vision, a textbook is a simultaneous delivery system for both course-related information and course-related exercises. Students are expected to read their textbooks until such time that their reading is interrupted by an exercise. After the completion of the exercise, students are expected to go back to the reading, but only until they happen upon another exercise. It is thus the norm to interrupt absorption in assigned reading on a relatively random (variable ratio) schedule in order to have students complete general, one-size-fits-all exercises. Students using such a book are not encouraged to concentrate on assigned reading; they may even be tacitly encouraged to do the opposite. The emphasis given to students having to complete exercises scattered within readings seems especially misplaced when, as is often the case with such one-size-fits-all tasks, some of the exercises will be way too easy for students in some classes and way too difficult for students in others. This brings to mind our own experience with testing-related exercises being assigned to varied groups of introductory students.

For several years and through several editions, our textbook was published with a supplementary exercises workbook. After extensive feedback from many instructors, some of whom used our book in their classes and some of whom did not, we determined that matters related to the choice, content, and level of supplementary exercises were better left to individual instructors as opposed to textbook authors. In general, instructors preferred to assign their own supplementary exercises, which could be custom-designed for the needs of their particular students and the goals of their particular course. A workbook of exercises, complete with detailed, step-by-step, illustrated solutions of statistical and psychometric problems, was determined by us to add little value to our textbook and it is therefore no longer offered. What we learned, and what we now believe, is that there is great value to supplementary, ancillary exercises for students taking an introductory course in measurement. However, these exercises are of optimal use to the student when they are custom-designed (or selected) by the instructor based on factors such as the level and interest of the students in the class, and the students' in-class and out-of-class study schedule. To be clear, supplemental exercises randomly embedded in a textbook work, in our view, not to facilitate students' immersion and concentration in assigned reading, but to obliterate it.[1]

Given the fact that decisions regarding supplementary exercises are best left to individual instructors, the difference between our own approach to the subject matter of the course and that of other approaches are even more profound. In this ninth edition, we have concentrated our attention and effort to crafting a textbook that will immerse and involve students in assigned readings and motivate them to engage in critical and generative thinking about what they have read. Contrast that vision with one in which author effort is divided between writing text and writing nonsupplementary exercises. Could the net result of the latter approach be a textbook that divides student attention between assigned readings and assigned (or unassigned) exercises? Seasoned instructors may concur with our view that most students will skip the intrusive and distracting exercises when they are not specifically assigned for completion by the instructor. In the case where the exercises *are* assigned, students may well skim the reading to complete the exercises.

No available textbook is more focused on being practical, timely, and "real-life" oriented than our's. Further, no other textbook provides students in an introductory course with a more readable or more comprehensive account of how psychological tests and assessment-related procedures are used in practice. That has been the case for some 30 years and it most certainly is the case today. With that as background, let's briefly sum up some of our concerns with regard to certain members of the current community of "psychological testing" books. In our view, red flags rise when books equate "practical" with the systematic burdening of readers with obstacles to immersion in assigned readings. Red flags rise when what appears to be

---

1. We urge any instructors curious about this assertion to informally evaluate it by asking a student or two how they feel about the prospect of scattering statistical exercises in their assigned reading. If the assigned reading is at all immersive, the modal response may be something like "maddening."

well-intentioned pedagogy, perhaps paradoxically, frustrates rather than advances student learning. Red flags rise when randomly placed, one-size-fits-all exercises are used to ostensibly compensate for an apparent inability to write in a way that involves, teaches, and inspires.

Especially with regard to a textbook at the introductory level, what is critical is the breadth and depth of coverage of how tests and other tools of assessment are actually used in practice. Practice-level proficiency and hands-on experience are always nice, but may in some cases be too ambitious. For example, a practical approach to factor analysis in a textbook for an introductory measurement course need not equip the student to conduct a factor analysis. Rather, the coverage ideally provides the student with a sound grounding in what this widely used set of techniques are, as well as how and why they are used. Similarly a practical approach to test utility, as exemplified in Chapter 7, provides students with a sound grounding in what that construct is, as well as how and why it is applied in practice.

Of course when it comes to breadth and depth of coverage of how tests and other tools of assessment are actually used in practice, we have long been the standard by which other books are measured. Consider in this context a small sampling of what is new, timely, and relevant in this ninth edition. The subject of our Chapter 1 *Close-Up* is behavioral assessment using smart phones. The subject of our *Everyday Psychometrics* in Chapter 7 on utility is the utility of police use of body cameras.[2] Terrorism is a matter of worldwide concern and in Chapter 11, the professional profiled in our *Meet an Assessment Professional* feature is Colonel Rick Malone of the United States Army's Criminal Investigation Command. Dr. Malone shares some intriguing insights regarding his area of expertise: threat assessment. New to this ninth edition is a section of online-only boxes, apps, and links or "OOBALs." Among the OOBALs presented online for chapter-specific, supplementary work are a group of original essays, apps, and podcasts, as well as links to stories, videos, or articles from the popular press or the scholarly literature. After reading Chapter 10 (Assessment of Education), for example, students may wish to check out OOBAL-10-B1, which is an original essay that was written especially for this book by guest author Daniel Teichman. In his essay entitled "Educational Evaluation in the Age of the MOOC," Teichman discusses the challenge of educational evaluation when conducting a massive open online class (MOOC) for some 200,000 students. Much more about our vision for this textbook and its supplements, as well as more previews of what is new and exciting in this ninth edition, is presented in what follows.

Organization

From the first edition of our book forward, we have organized the information to be presented into five major sections. Part I, *An Overview*, contains two chapters that do just that. Chapter 1 provides a comprehensive overview of the field, including some important definitional issues, a general description of tools of assessment, and related important information couched as answers to questions regarding the *who*, *what*, *why*, *how*, and *where* of the enterprise.

The foundation for the material to come continues to be laid in the second chapter of the overview, which deals with historical, cultural, and legal/ethical issues. The material presented

---

2. This essay is an informative and timely discussion of the utility of police-worn body cameras in reducing use-of-force complaints. Parenthetically, let's share our view that the concept of *utility* seems lost in, or at least given inadequate coverage in other measurement books. It seems that we may have caught many of those "psychological testing" books off-guard by devoting a chapter to this construct beginning with our seventh edition—this at a time when *utility* was not even an indexed term in most of them. Attempts to compensate have ranged from doing nothing at all to doing near nothing at all by equating "utility" with "validity." For the record, although utility is related to validity, much as reliability is related to validity, we believe it is misleading to even intimate that "utility" and "validity" are synonymous.

in Chapter 2 clearly sets a context for everything that will follow. To relegate such material to the back of the book (as a kind of elective topic, much like the way that legal/ethical issues are treated in some books), or to ignore presentation of such material altogether (as most other books have done with regard to cultural issues in assessment), is, in our estimation, a grave error. "Back page infrequency" (to borrow an MMPI-2 term) is too often the norm, and relegation of this critically important information to the back pages of a textbook too often translates to a potential shortchanging of students with regard to key cultural, historical, and legal/ethical information. The importance of exposure early on to relevant historical, cultural, and legal/ethical issues cannot be overemphasized. This exposure sets a context for succeeding coverage of psychometrics and creates an essential lens through which to view and process such material.

Part II, *The Science of Psychological Measurement*, contains Chapters 3 through 8. These six chapters were designed to build—logically and sequentially—on the student's knowledge of psychometric principles. Part II begins with a chapter reviewing basic statistical principles and ends with a chapter on test construction. In between, there is extensive discussion of assumptions inherent in the enterprise, the elements of good test construction, as well as the concepts of norms, correlation, inference, reliability, and validity. All of the measurement textbooks that came before us were written based on the assumption that every student taking the course was up to speed on all of the statistical concepts that would be necessary to build on learning about psychometrics. In theory, at least, there was no reason not to assume this; statistics was a prerequisite to taking the course. In practice, a different picture emerged. It was simply not the case that all students were adequately and equally prepared to begin learning statistics-based measurement concepts. Our remedy for this problem, some 30 years ago, was to include a "Statistics Refresher" chapter early on, just prior to building on students' statistics-based knowledge. The rest, as they say, is history...

Our book forever changed for the better the way the measurement course was taught and the way all subsequent textbooks for the course would be written. Our unique coverage of the assessment of intelligence and personality, as well as our coverage of assessment for various applications (ranging from neuropsychological to business and organizational applications), made relics of the typical "psychological testing" course outline as it existed prior to the publication of our first edition in 1988.

In our seventh edition, in response to increasing general interest in test utility, we added a chapter on this important construct right after our chapters on the constructs of reliability and validity. Let's note here that topics such as utility and utility analysis can get extremely complicated. However, we have never shied away from the presentation of complicated subject matter. For example, we were the first introductory textbook to present detailed information related to factor analysis. As more commercial publishers and other test users have adopted the use of item response theory (IRT) in test construction, our coverage of IRT has kept pace. As more test reviews have begun to evaluate tests not only in terms of variables such as reliability and validity but in terms of *utility*, we saw a need for the inclusion of a chapter on that topic.

Of course, no matter how "difficult" the concepts we present are, we never for a moment lose sight of the appropriate level of presentation. This book is designed for students taking a first course in psychological testing and assessment. Our objective in presenting material on methods such as IRT and utility analysis is simply to acquaint the introductory student with these techniques. The depth of the presentation in these and other areas has always been guided and informed by extensive reviews from a geographically diverse sampling of instructors who teach measurement courses. For users of this textbook, what currently tends to be required is a conceptual understanding of commonly used IRT methods. We believe our presentation of this material effectively conveys such an understanding. Moreover, it does so without unnecessarily burdening students with level-inappropriate formulas and calculations.

Part III of this book, *The Assessment of Abilities and Aptitudes*, contains two chapters, one on intelligence and its assessment, and the other on assessment in schools and other educational settings. In past editions of this book, two chapters were devoted to the assessment of intelligence. To understand why, it is instructive to consider what the coverage of intelligence testing looked like in the then available introductory measurement textbooks three decades ago. While the books all covered tests of intelligence, they devoted little or no attention to defining and discussing the construct of intelligence. We called attention to this problem and attempted to remedy it by differentiating our book with a chapter devoted to imparting a conceptual understanding of intelligence. Although revolutionary at the time, the logic of our approach had widespread appeal. Before long, the typical "psychological testing" course of the 1980s was being restructured to include conceptual discussions of concepts such as "intelligence" and "personality" before proceeding to discuss their measurement. The "psychological testing" textbooks of the day also followed our lead. And so, to the present day, two-chapter-coverage of the assessment of intelligence (with the first chapter providing a discussion of the construct of intelligence) has become the norm. That is, of course, until the publication of this ninth edition; more on the news there in just a moment.

In retrospect, it seems reasonable to conclude that our addition of a chapter on the nature of intelligence, much like our addition of a statistics refresher, did more than remedy a serious drawback in existing measurement textbooks; it forever revolutionized the way that the measurement course was taught in classrooms around the world. It did this first of all by making the teaching of the course more logical. This is so because the logic of our guiding principle—fully define and discuss the psychological construct being measured before discussing its measurement—had wide appeal. In our first edition, we also extended that logic to the discussion of the measurement of other psychological constructs such as personality. Another benefit we saw in adding the conceptual coverage was that such coverage would serve to "humanize" the content. After all, "Binet" was more than just the name of a psychological test; it was the name of a living, breathing person.

Also, since our first edition, we have revolutionized textbook coverage of psychological tests—this by a philosophy of "less is more" when it comes to such coverage. Back in the 1980s, the "psychological testing" books of the day had elements reminiscent of *Tests in Print*. They provided reliability, validity, and related psychometric data on dozens of psychological tests. But we raised the question, "Why duplicate in a textbook information about dozens of tests that is readily available from reference sources?" We further resolved to limit detailed coverage of psychological tests to a handful of representative tests. Once again, the simple logic of our approach had widespread appeal, and other textbooks in the area—both then, and to the present day—all followed suit.

There is another trend in textbook coverage of the measurement course that also figured prominently in our decision to cover the assessment of intelligence in a single chapter. This trend has to do with the widespread availability of online resources to supplement coverage of a specific topic. We have long taken advantage of this fact by making available various supplementary materials online to our readers, or by supplying links to such materials.

Some three decades after we revolutionized the organization of textbook coverage of the measurement course in so many significant ways, it was time to re-evaluate whether two chapters to cover the subject of intelligence assessment was still necessary. We gave thoughtful consideration to this question and sought-out the opinion of trusted colleagues. In the end, we determined that coverage of the construct and assessment of intelligence could be accomplished in a single chapter. And so, in the interest of streamlining this book in length, Chapter 9 in this ninth edition incorporates text formerly in Chapters 9 and 10 of the eighth edition. By the way, some of the text from each of these eighth edition chapters has been preserved in the Chapter 9 supplementary package of online-only boxes, apps, and links (OOBALs). See, for example, OOBAL-9-B2 for an essay entitled "Nature versus Nurture in Measured Intelligence."

Part IV, *The Assessment of Personality*, contains two chapters, which respectively overview how personality assessments are conducted, and the various methods used.

Part V, *Testing and Assessment in Action*, is designed to convey to students a sense of how a sampling of tests and other tools of assessment are actually used in clinical, counseling, business, and other settings.

Content

In addition to a logical organization that sequentially builds on student learning, we view *content* selection as another key element of our appeal. The multifaceted nature and complexity of the discipline affords textbook authors wide latitude in terms of what material to elaborate on, what material to ignore, and what material to highlight, exemplify, or illustrate. In selecting content to be covered for chapters, the primary question for us was most typically "What do students need to know?" So, for example, since the publication of previous editions of this book, the field of educational evaluation has been greatly influenced by the widespread implementation of the *Common Core Standards*. Accordingly, we take cognizance of these changes in the K-through-12 education landscape and their implications for evaluation in education. Students of educational assessment *need* to know about the *Common Core Standards* and relevant coverage of these standards can be found in this ninth edition in our chapter on educational assessment.

While due consideration is given to creating content that students need to know, consideration is also given to relevant topics that will engage interest and serve as stimuli for critical or generative thinking. In the area of neuropsychological assessment, for example, the topic of Alzheimer's disease is one that generates a great deal of interest. Most students have seen articles or feature stories in the popular media that review the signs and symptoms of this disease. However, while students are aware that such patients are typically referred to a neurologist for formal diagnosis, many questions remain about how a diagnosis of Alzheimer's disease is clinically made. The *Close-Up* in our chapter on neuropsychological assessment addresses those frequently asked questions. It was guest-authored by an experienced neurologist and written especially for students of psychological assessment reading this textbook.

Let's note here that in this ninth edition, more than in any previous edition of this textbook, we have drawn on the firsthand knowledge of psychological assessment experts from around the world. Specifically, we have asked these experts to guest-author brief essays in the form of *Close-Up, Everyday Psychometrics,* or *Meet an Assessment Professional* features. For example, in one of our chapters that deal with personality assessment, two experts on primate behavior (including one who is currently working at Dian Fossey's research center in Karisoke, in Rwanda) prepared an essay on evaluating the personality of gorillas. Written especially for us, this *Close-Up* makes an informative contribution to the literature on cross-species personality assessment. In our chapter on test construction, an Australian team of behavioral scientists guest-authored a *Close-Up* entitled "Adapting Tools of Assessment for Use with Specific Cultural Groups." This essay recounts some of the intriguing culture-related challenges inherent in the psychological assessment of clients from the Aboriginal community.

Sensitivity to cultural issues in psychological testing and assessment is essential, and this textbook has long set the standard for coverage of such issues. Coverage of cultural issues begins in earnest in Chapter 2, where we define culture and overview the importance of cultural considerations in everything from test development to standards of evaluation. Then, much like an identifiable musical theme that recurs throughout a symphony, echoes of the importance of culture repeat in various chapters throughout this book. For example, the echo is heard in Chapter 4 where, among other things, we continue a long tradition of acquainting students with the "do's and don'ts" of culturally informed assessment. In Chapter 13, our chapter on assessment in clinical and counseling settings, there is a discussion of acculturation and culture as these issues pertain to clinical assessment. Also in that chapter, students will find a thought-provoking *Close-Up* entitled, "PTSD in Veterans and the Idealized Culture of Warrior Masculinity." Guest-authored especially for us by Duncan M. Shields, this timely contribution to the clinical literature sheds light on the diagnosis and treatment of post-traumatic stress disorder (PTSD) from a new and novel, cultural perspective.

It is important to note that our presentation of culture-related issues (as well as most other issues relevant to measurement in psychology) does not end with the final page of the final chapter of this book. The breadth and depth of our coverage has been greatly extended by this book's supplementary package of "OOBALs" (our acronym for online-only boxes, apps and links) available at *mhhe.cohentesting9/OOBALS*. In the Chapter 9 OOBAL, for example, students will find an original essay that explores the nature of intelligence from an Eastern perspective. By way of background, this contribution stemmed from an invited presentation on psychological assessment made by the senior author of this textbook (RJC) to the students and faculty of the School of Psychology at Shaanxi Normal University (SNNU) in China, in December, 2015. After the presentation, Cohen was a guest at a dinner hosted by the SNNU faculty and administration. The dinner was memorable not only for an array of tantalizing delicacies, but for the intriguing cultural insights advanced by the SNNU scholars with respect to measurement-related issues. During the course of the evening, Cohen proposed that Dean Xuqun You and Vice Dean Ning He collaborate on brief essays contrasting Eastern versus Western perspectives on topics such as the measurement of intelligence and educational assessment. Professors You and He, along with some of their colleagues, accepted Cohen's invitation. One of the resulting "Eastern Perspective" essays can be found herein as the *Close-Up* in our chapter on educational assessment. This essay, guest-authored by Chengting Ju, Ning He, and Xuqun You is entitled, "Educational Assessment: An Eastern Perspective." The other original essay, guest-authored by Yuanbo Gu, Ning He, and Xuqun is "Intelligence: An Eastern Perspective." This informative essay supplements our coverage of the assessment of intelligence as OOBAL-9-B12. Of course, whether published in the textbook as a *Close-Up* or published in the online supplementary package as an "OOBAL," each of these "Eastern perspective" essays are well worth reading for their valuable contribution to the literature on cross-cultural considerations in psychological assessment.

In addition to standard-setting content related to cultural issues, mention must also be made of our leadership role with respect to coverage of historical and legal/ethical aspects of measurement in psychology. Our own appreciation for the importance of history is emphasized by the listing of noteworthy historical events that is set within the front and back covers of this textbook. As such, readers may be greeted with some aspect of the history of the enterprise on every occasion that they open the book. Although historical vignettes are distributed throughout the book to help set a context or advance understanding, formal coverage begins in Chapter 2. Important historical aspects of testing and assessment may also be found in *Close-Ups*. See, for example, the fascinating account of the controversial career of Henry Goddard found in Chapter 2. In a *Close-Up* in Chapter 15, students will discover what contemporary assessment professionals can learn from World War II-vintage assessment data collected by the Office of Strategic Services (OSS). In this engrossing essay, iconic data meets contemporary data analytic methods with brilliant new insights as a result. This *Close-Up* was guest-authored by Mark F. Lenzenweger, who is a State University of New York (SUNY) Distinguished Professor in the Department of Psychology at The State University of New York at Binghamton.

Much like content pertaining to relevant historical and culture-related material, our discussion of legal–ethical issues, from our first edition through to the present day, has been standard-setting. Discussion of legal and ethical issues as they apply to psychological testing and assessment provides students not only with context essential for understanding psychometric principles and practice, but another lens through which to filter understanding of tests and measurement. In the first edition, while we got the addition of this pioneering content right, we could have done a better job in terms of placement. In retrospect, the first edition would have benefitted from the discussion of such issues much earlier than the last chapter. But in response to the many compelling arguments reviewers and users of that book, discussion of legal/ethical issues was prioritized in Chapter 2 by the time that our second edition was published. The move helped ensure that students were properly equipped to appreciate the role of legal and ethical issues in the many varied settings in which psychological testing and assessment takes place.[3]

Another element of our vision for the content of this book has to do with the art program; that is, the photos, drawings, and other types of illustrations used in a textbook. Before the publication of our ground-breaking first edition, what passed for an art program in the available "psychological testing" textbooks were some number-intensive graphs and tables, as well as photos of test kits or test materials. In general, photos and other illustrations seemed to be inserted more to break up text than to complement it. For us, the art program is an important element of a textbook, not a device for pacing. Illustrations can help draw students into the narrative, and then reinforce learning by solidifying meaningful visual associations to the written words. Photos can be powerful tools to stir the imagination. See, for example, the photo of Army recruits being tested in Chapter 1, or the photo of Ellis Island immigrants being tested in Chapter 2. Photos can bring to life and "humanize" the findings of measurement-related research. See, for example, the photo in Chapter 3 regarding the study that examined the relationship between grades and cell phone use in class. Photos of many past and present luminaries in the field (such as John Exner, Jr. and Ralph Reitan), and photos accompanying the persons featured in our *Meet an Assessment Professional* boxes all serve to breathe life into their respective accounts and descriptions.

In the world of textbooks, photos such as the sampling of the ones described here may not seem very revolutionary. However, in the world of *measurement* textbooks, our innovative art program has been and remains quite revolutionary. One factor that has always distinguished us from other books in this area is the extent to which we have tried to "humanize" the course subject matter; the art program is just another element of this textbook pressed into the service of that objective.

"Humanization" of Content   This ninth edition was conceived with a commitment to continuing our three-decade tradition of exemplary organization, exceptional writing, timely content, and solid pedagogy. Equally important was our desire to spare no effort in making this book as readable and as involving for students as it could possibly be. Our "secret sauce" in accomplishing this is, at this point, not much of a secret. We have the highest respect for the students for whom this book is written. We try to show that respect by never underestimating their capacity to become immersed in course-relevant narratives that are presented clearly and

---

3. Apparently, some of those "psychological testing" books were so enamored with our first edition table of contents that they failed to revise with the times. For example, to date, they still present legal/ethical issues at the end of the book, instead of where it will do students the most good (i.e., near the beginning of the book). Also, in the faded footsteps of an Appendix to our first edition, one can still find in the current edition of a "psychological testing" book a hard copy Appendix that lists test publishers along with contact information. But in the age of the Internet, and in the rare circumstance that current contact information for a test publisher was required, the Appendix of a textbook would not be the first (or best) choice to find such information. Today, there really is no defensible reason to weight down a textbook with these extra, thoroughly unnecessary pages. In all probability, some of the information in the Appendix was out-of-date even before it went to press. So, while imitation is the sincerest form of flattery, and we are flattered by attempts to emulate our first edition (circa 1988), those "psychological testing" books that still have that Appendix, need to have it removed.

straightforwardly. With the goal of further drawing the student into the subject matter, we make every effort possible to "humanize" the presentation of topics covered. So, what does "humanization" in this context actually mean?

While other authors in this discipline impress us as blindly intent on viewing the field as Greek letters to be understood and formulas to be memorized, we view an introduction to the field to be about *people* as much as anything else. Students are more motivated to learn this material when they can place it in a human context. Many psychology students simply do not respond well to endless presentations of psychometric concepts and formulas. In our opinion, to *not* bring a human face to the field of psychological testing and assessment, is to risk perpetuating all of those unpleasant (and now unfair) rumors about the course that first began circulating long before the time that the senior author himself was an undergraduate.

Our effort to humanize the material is evident in the various ways we have tried to bring a face (if not a helping voice) to the material. The inclusion of *Meet an Assessment Professional* is a means toward that end, as it quite literally "brings a face" to the enterprise. Our inclusion of interesting biographical facts on historical figures in assessment is also representative of efforts to humanize the material. Consider in this context the photo and brief biographical statement of MMPI-2 senior author James Butcher in Chapter 11 (p. 389). Whether through such images of historical personages or by other means, our objective has been made to truly involve students via intriguing, real-life illustrations of the material being discussed. See, for example, the discussion of life-or-death psychological assessment and the ethical issues involved in the *Close-Up* feature of Chapter 2. Or check out the candid "confessions" of a behavior rater in the *Everyday Psychometrics* feature in Chapter 12.

So how has our "humanization" of the material in this discipline been received by some of its more "hard core" and "old school" practitioners? Very well, thank you—at least from all that we have heard, and the dozens of reviews that we have read over the years. What stands out prominently in the mind of the senior author (RJC) was the reaction of one particular psychometrician whom I happened to meet at an APA convention not long after the first edition of this text was published. Lee J. Cronbach was quite animated as he shared with me his delight with the book, and how refreshingly different he thought that it was from anything comparable that had been published. I was so grateful to Lee for his encouragement, and felt so uplifted by that meeting, that I subsequently requested a photo from Lee for use in the second edition. The photo he sent was indeed published in the second edition of this book—this despite the fact that at that time, Lee had a measurement book that could be viewed as a direct competitor to ours. Regardless, I felt it was important not only to acknowledge Lee's esteemed place in measurement history, but to express my sincere gratitude in this way for his kind, inspiring, and motivating words, as well as for what I perceived as his most valued "seal of approval."

Pedagogical Tools

The objective of incorporating timely, relevant, and intriguing illustrations of assessment-related material is furthered by several *pedagogical tools* built into the text. One pedagogical tool we created several editions ago is *Everyday Psychometrics*. In each chapter of the book, relevant, practical, and "everyday" examples of the material being discussed are highlighted in an *Everyday Psychometrics* box. For example, in the *Everyday Psychometrics* presented in Chapter 1 ("Everyday Accommodations"), students will be introduced to accommodations made in the testing of persons with handicapping conditions. In Chapter 4, the *Everyday Psychometrics* feature ("Putting Tests to the Test") equips students with a working overview of the variables they need to be thinking about when reading about a test and evaluating how satisfactory the test really is for a particular purpose. In Chapter 5, the subject of the *Everyday Psychometrics* is how the method used to estimate diagnostic reliability may affect the obtained estimate of reliability.

A pedagogical tool called *Meet an Assessment Professional* was first introduced in the seventh edition. This feature provides a forum through which everyday users of psychological tests from various fields can share insights, experiences, and advice with students. The result is that in each chapter of this book, students are introduced to a different test user and provided with an intriguing glimpse of their professional life—this in the form of a *Meet an Assessment Professional (MAP)* essay. For example, in Chapter 4, students will meet a team of test users, Drs. Steve Julius and Howard Atlas, who have pressed psychometric knowledge into the service of professional sports. They provide a unique and fascinating account of how application of their knowledge of was used to improve the on-court of achievement of the Chicago Bulls. A MAP essay from Stephen Finn, the well-known proponent of therapeutic assessment is presented in Chapter 13. Among the many MAP essays that are new to this edition are essays from two mental-health professionals serving in the military. Dr. Alan Ogle introduces readers to aspects of the work of an Air Force psychologist in Chapter 1. In Chapter 11, army psychiatrist Dr. Rick Malone shares his expertise in the area of threat assessment. In other MAPs new to this edition, the senior author of an oft-cited meta-analysis that was published in *Psychological Bulletin* shares her insights on meta-analytic methods in Chapter 3, while a psychiatrist who specializes in cultural issues introduces himself to students in Chapter 2.

Our use of the pedagogical tool referred to as a "*Close-Up*," is reserved for more in-depth and detailed consideration of specific topics related to those under discussion. The *Close-Up* in our chapter on test construction, for example, acquaints readers with the trials and tribulations of test developers working to create a test to measure asexuality. The *Close-Up* in one of our chapters on personality assessment raises the intriguing question of whether it is meaningful to speak of general (*g*) and specific (*s*) factors in the diagnosis of personality disorders.

There are other pedagogical tools that readers (as well as other textbook authors) may take for granted—but we do not. Consider, in this context, the various tables and figures found in every chapter. In addition to their more traditional use, we view tables as space-saving devices in which a lot of information may be presented. For example, in the first chapter alone, tables are used to provide succinct but meaningful comparisons between the terms *testing* and *assessment*, the *pros* and *cons* of computer-assisted psychological assessment, and the *pros* and *cons* of using various sources of information about tests.

Critical thinking may be defined as "the active employment of judgment capabilities and evaluative skills in the thought process" (Cohen, 1994, p. 12). *Generative thinking* may be defined as "the goal-oriented intellectual production of new or creative ideas" (Cohen, 1994, p. 13). The exercise of both of these processes, we believe, helps optimize one's chances for success in the academic world as well as in more applied pursuits. In the early editions of this textbook, questions designed to stimulate critical and generative thinking were raised "the old-fashioned way." That is, they were right in the text, and usually part of a paragraph. Acting on the advice of reviewers, we made this special feature of our writing even more special beginning with the sixth edition of this book; we raised these critical thinking questions in the margins with a *Just Think* heading. Perhaps with some encouragement from their instructors, motivated students will, in fact, give thoughtful consideration to these (critical and generative thought-provoking) *Just Think* questions.

In addition to critical thinking and generative thinking questions called out in the text, other pedagogical aids in this book include original cartoons created by the authors, original illustrations created by the authors (including the model of memory in Chapter 14), and original acronyms created by the authors.[4] Each chapter ends with a *Self-Assessment* feature that students may use to test themselves with respect to key terms and concepts presented in the

_____

4. By the way, our use of the French word for black (*noir*) as an acronym for levels of measurement (nominal, ordinal, interval, and ratio) now appears in other textbooks.

text. Also at the end of each chapter is a reminder to students to check out the supplementary package of online-only boxes, apps, and links (OOBALs). And speaking of online resources...

Connect Logo

connect The 9th edition of *Psychological Testing and Assessment* is now available online with Connect, McGraw-Hill Education's integrated assignment and assessment platform. Connect also offers SmartBook for the new edition, which is the first adaptive reading experience proven to improve grades and help students study more effectively. All of the title's website and ancillary content is also available through Connect, including:

- An Instructor's Manual for each chapter.
- A full Test Bank of multiple choice questions that test students on central concepts and ideas in each chapter.
- Lecture Slides for instructor use in class.

Writing Style

What type of *writing style* or author *voice* works best with students being introduced to the field of psychological testing and assessment? Instructors familiar with the many measurement books that have come (and gone) may agree with us that the "voice" of too many authors in this area might best be characterized as humorless and academic to the point of arrogance or pomposity. Students do not tend to respond well to textbooks written in such styles, and their eagerness and willingness to spend study time with these authors (and even their satisfaction with the course as a whole) may easily suffer as a consequence.

In a writing style that could be characterized as somewhat informal and—to the extent possible, given the medium and particular subject being covered—"conversational," we have made every effort to convey the material to be presented as clearly as humanly possible. In practice, this means:

- keeping the vocabulary of the presentation appropriate (without ever "dumbing-down" or trivializing the material);
- presenting so-called difficult material in step-by-step fashion where appropriate, and always preparing students for its presentation by placing it in an understandable context;
- italicizing the first use of a key word or phrase and then bolding it when a formal definition is given;
- providing a relatively large glossary of terms to which students can refer;
- supplementing material where appropriate with visual aids, tables, or other illustrations.
- supplementing material where appropriate with intriguing historical facts (as in the Chapter 12 material on projectives and the projective test created by B. F. Skinner);
- incorporating timely, relevant, and intriguing illustrations of assessment-related material in the text as well as in the online materials.

In addition, we have interspersed some elements of humor in various forms (original cartoons, illustrations, and vignettes) throughout the text. The judicious use of humor to engage and maintain student interest is something of a novelty among measurement textbooks. Where else would one turn for pedagogy that employs an example involving a bimodal distribution of test scores from a new trade school called *The Home Study School of Elvis Presley Impersonators*? As readers learn about face validity, they discover why it "gets no respect" and how it has been characterized as "the Rodney Dangerfield of psychometric variables."

©Hero Images/Getty Images RF

Required=Results

McGraw-Hill Connect®
Learn Without Limits

Connect is a teaching and learning platform that is proven to deliver better results for students and instructors.

Connect empowers students by continually adapting to deliver precisely what they need, when they need it, and how they need it, so your class time is more engaging and effective.

> 73% of instructors who use **Connect** require it; instructor satisfaction **increases** by 28% when **Connect** is required.

Connect's Impact on Retention Rates, Pass Rates, and Average Exam Scores

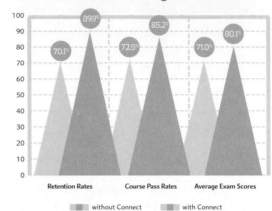

without Connect | with Connect

> Using **Connect** improves retention rates by **19.8%**, passing rates by **12.7%**, and exam scores by **9.1%**.

Analytics

Connect Insight®

Connect Insight is Connect's new one-of-a-kind visual analytics dashboard—now available for both instructors and students—that provides at-a-glance information regarding student performance, which is immediately actionable. By presenting assignment, assessment, and topical performance results together with a time metric that is easily visible for aggregate or individual results, Connect Insight gives the user the ability to take a just-in-time approach to teaching and learning, which was never before available. Connect Insight presents data that empowers students and helps instructors improve class performance in a way that is efficient and effective.

Impact on Final Course Grade Distribution

without Connect		with Connect
22.9%	A	31.0%
27.4%	B	34.3%
22.9%	C	18.7%
11.5%	D	6.1%
15.4%	F	9.9%

> Students can view their results for any **Connect** course.

Mobile

Connect's new, intuitive mobile interface gives students and instructors flexible and convenient, anytime–anywhere access to all components of the Connect platform.

Adaptive

THE **ADAPTIVE** **READING EXPERIENCE** DESIGNED TO TRANSFORM THE WAY STUDENTS READ

More students earn **A's** and **B's** when they use McGraw-Hill Education **Adaptive** products.

SmartBook®

Proven to help students improve grades and study more efficiently, SmartBook contains the same content within the print book, but actively tailors that content to the needs of the individual. SmartBook's adaptive technology provides precise, personalized instruction on what the student should do next, guiding the student to master and remember key concepts, targeting gaps in knowledge and offering customized feedback, and driving the student toward comprehension and retention of the subject matter. Available on tablets, SmartBook puts learning at the student's fingertips—anywhere, anytime.

Over **5.7 billion questions** have been answered, making McGraw-Hill Education products more intelligent, reliable, and precise.

www.mheducation.com

STUDENTS WANT

SMARTBOOK®

95% of students reported **SmartBook** to be a more effective way of reading material.

100% of students want to use the Practice Quiz feature available within **SmartBook** to help them study.

100% of students reported having reliable access to off-campus wifi.

90% of students say they would purchase **SmartBook** over print alone.

95% of students reported that **SmartBook** would impact their study skills in a positive way.

McGraw Hill Education

*Findings based on 2015 focus group results administered by McGraw-Hill Education

Numerous other illustrations could be cited here. But let's reserve those smiles as a pleasant surprise when readers happen to come upon them.

Acknowledgments

Thanks to the members of the academic community who have wholeheartedly placed their confidence in this book through all or part of its nine-edition life-cycle to date. Your trust in our ability to help your students navigate the complex world of measurement in psychology is a source of inspiration to us. We appreciate the privilege of assisting you in the education and professional growth of your students, and we will never take that privilege for granted.

Every edition of this book has begun with blueprinting designed with the singular objective of making this book far-and-away best in the field of available textbooks in terms of organization, content, pedagogy, and writing. Helping the authors to meet that objective were developmental editor Erin Guendelsberger and project supervisor Jamie Laferrera along with a number of guest contributors who graciously gave of their time, talent, and expertise. To be the all-around best textbook in a particular subject area takes, as they say, "a village." On behalf of the authors, a hearty "thank you" is due to many "villagers" in the academic and professional community who wrote or reviewed something for this book, or otherwise contributed to it. First and foremost, thank you to all of the following people who wrote essays designed to enhance and enrich the student experience of the course work. In order of appearance of the ninth edition chapter that their essay appeared in, we say thanks to the following contributors of guest-authored *Meet an Assessment Professional*, *Everyday Psychometrics*, *Close-Up*, or *OOBAL* essays:

Alan, D. Ogle of the 559th Medical Group, Military Training Consult Service of the United States Air Force;

Dror Ben-Zeev of the Department of Psychiatry of the Geisel School of Medicine at Dartmouth;

Neil Krishan Aggarwal of the New York State Psychiatric Institute;

Joni L. Mihura of the Department of Psychology of the University of Toledo;

Michael Chmielewski of the Department of Psychology of Southern Methodist University;

Jason M. Chin of the University of Toronto Faculty of Law;

Ilona M. McNeill of the University of Melbourne (Australia);

Patrick D. Dunlop of the University of Western Australia;

Delphine Courvoisier of Beau-Séjour Hospital, Geneva, Switzerland;

Alex Sutherland of RAND Europe, Cambridge, United Kingdom;

Barak Ariel of the Institute of Criminology of the University of Cambridge (United Kingdom);

Lori A. Brotto of the Department of Gynaecology of the University of British Columbia;

Morag Yule of the Department of Gynaecology of the University of British Columbia;

Sivasankaran Balaratnasingam of the School of Psychiatry and Clinical Neurosciences of the University of Western Australia;

Zaza Lyons of the School of Psychiatry and Clinical Neurosciences of the University of Western Australia;

Aleksander Janca of the School of Psychiatry and Clinical Neurosciences of the University of Western Australia;

Yuanbo Gu of the School of Psychology of Shaanxi Normal University (China);

Ning He of the School of Psychology of Shaanxi Normal University (China);

Xuqun You of the School of Psychology of Shaanxi Normal University (China);

Chengting Ju of the School of Psychology of Shaanxi Normal University (China);

Rick Malone of the U.S. Army Criminal Investigation Command, Quantico, VA;

Winnie Eckardt of The Dian Fossey Gorilla Fund International, Atlanta, GA;

Alexander Weiss of the Department of Psychology of the University of Edinburgh (UK);

Monica Webb Hooper of the Case Comprehensive Cancer Center at Case Western Reserve University;

Carla Sharp of the Department of Psychology at the University of Houston (TX);

Liliana B. Sousa of the Faculty of Psychology and Educational Sciences of the University of Coimbra (Portugal);

Duncan M. Shields of the Faculty of Medicine of the University of British Columbia;

Eric Kramer of Medical Specialists of the Palm Beaches, (Neurology), Atlantis, Florida;

Jed Yalof of the Department of Graduate Psychology of Immaculata University;

Mark F. Lenzenweger of the Department of Psychology of the State University of New York at Binghamton;

Jessica Klein of the Department of Psychology of the University of Florida (Gainesville);

Anna Taylor of the Department of Psychology of Illinois State University;

Suzanne Swagerman of the Department of Biological Psychology of Vrije Universiteit (VU), Amsterdam, The Netherlands;

Eco J.C. de Geus of the Department of Biological Psychology of Vrijc Universiteit (VU), Amsterdam, The Netherlands;

Kees-Jan Kan of the Department of Biological Psychology of Vrije Universiteit (VU), Amsterdam, The Netherlands;

Dorret I. Boomsma of the Department of Biological Psychology of Vrije Universiteit (VU), Amsterdam, The Netherlands;

Faith Miller of the Department of Educational Psychology of the University of Minnesota; and, Daniel Teichman formerly of the Department of Computer and Information Science and Engineering of the University of Florida (Gainesville).

For their enduring contribution to this and previous editions of this book, we thank Dr. Jennifer Kisamore for her work on the original version of our chapter on test utility, and Dr. Bryce Reeve who not only wrote a Meet an Assessment Professional essay, but another informative essay on item response theory (see OOBAL-5-B2). Thanks to the many assessment professionals who, whether in a past or the current edition, took the time to introduce students to what they do. For being a potential source of inspiration to the students who they "met" in these pages, we thank the following assessment professionals: Dr. Rebecca Anderson, Dr. Howard W. Atlas, Dr. Scott Birkeland, Dr. Anthony Bram, Dr. Stephen Finn, Dr. Chris Gee, Dr. Joel Goldberg, Ms. Eliane Hack, Dr. Steve Julius, Dr. Nathaniel V. Mohatt, Dr. Barbara C. Pavlo, Dr. Jeanne P. Ryan, Dr. Adam Shoemaker, Dr. Benoit Verdon, Dr. Erik Viirre, and Dr. Eric A. Zillmer. Thanks also to Dr. John Garruto for his informative contribution to Chapter 10.

Special thanks to two student assistants whose help was invaluable to Ronald Jay Cohen in the preparation of this book and its supplementary package of OOBALs. Jessica Klein of the University of Florida (Gainesville) and Anna Taylor of Illinois State University helped gather publications that were needed for updating this ninth edition. They both also helped in identifying OOBALs that would be of particular interest and value to fellow students. As if that were not enough, Jessica and Anna each also authored OOBALs designed to welcome fellow students to a course in measurement in psychology (see OOBAL-1-B1 and OOBAL-1-B2).

While thanking all who contributed in many varied ways, including Susan Cohen who assisted with keyboarding, we remind readers that the present authorship team takes sole responsibility for any possible errors that may have somehow found their way into this ninth edition.

Meet the Authors

Ronald Jay Cohen, Ph.D., ABPP, ABAP, is a Diplomate of the American Board of Professional Psychology in Clinical Psychology, and a Diplomate of the American Board of Assessment Psychology. He is licensed to practice psychology in New York and Florida, and a "scientist-practitioner" and "scholar-professional" in the finest traditions of each of those terms. During a long and gratifying professional career in which he has published numerous journal articles and books, Dr. Cohen has had the privilege of personally working alongside some of the luminaries in the field of psychological assessment, including David Wechsler (while Cohen was a clinical psychology intern at Bellevue Psychiatric Hospital in New York City) and Doug Bray (while working as an assessor for AT&T in its Management Progress Study). After serving his clinical psychology internship at Bellevue, Dr. Cohen was appointed Senior Psychologist there, and his clinical duties entailed not only psychological assessment but the supervision and training of others in this enterprise. Subsequently, as an independent practitioner in the New York City area, Dr. Cohen taught various courses at local universities on an adjunct basis, including undergraduate and graduate courses in psychological assessment. Asked by a colleague to conduct a qualitative research study for an advertising agency, Dr. Cohen would quickly become a sought-after qualitative research consultant with a client list of major companies and organizations—among them Paramount Pictures, Columbia Pictures, NBC Television, the Campbell Soup Company, Educational Testing Service, and the College Board. Dr. Cohen's approach to qualitative research, referred to by him as *dimensional qualitative research*, has been emulated and written about by qualitative researchers around the world. Dr. Cohen is a sought-after speaker and has delivered invited addresses at the Sorbonne in Paris, Peking University in Beijing, and numerous other universities throughout the world. It was Dr. Cohen's work in the area of qualitative assessment that led him to found the scholarly journal *Psychology & Marketing*. Since the publication of the journal's first issue in 1984, Dr. Cohen has served as its Editor-in-Chief.

Mark E. Swerdlik, Ph.D., ABPP, is Professor of Psychology at Illinois State University, where he has taught the undergraduate psychological measurement course, conducted professional seminars addressing legal/ethical issues in assessment, and supervised practicum students in assessment. He has served as an editorial board member of several journals, written test reviews for several journals, reviewed test-scoring software for a major test publisher, and served as a reviewer for the *Mental Measurements Yearbook*. In various professional capacities, he has participated in the standardization of many psychological tests, including, for example, the WISC-R, the WISC-III, the Kaufman Assessment Battery for Children (K-ABC), the Stanford-Binet IV, the Peabody Picture Vocabulary Test (PPVT), the Kaufman Test of Educational Achievement, the Vineland Adaptive Behavior Scale, the Psychological Processing Checklist (PPC), and the Psychological Processing Checklist-Revised (PPC-R). As a licensed clinical psychologist, a nationally certified school psychologist, independent practitioner, and consultant, Dr. Swerdlik administers and interprets psychological tests, and conducts seminars to train fellow professionals in proper test administration, scoring, and interpretation procedures. He has also served as a program evaluator for many programs, a partial listing of which would include the Heart of Illinois Low Incidence Association (HILA), the Autism/Pervasive Developmental Delays Training and Technical Assistance Project, and the Illinois National

Guard Statewide Reintegration Program for Combat Veterans (for veterans who served in Iraq and Afghanistan, from 2006 to the present).

And on a Personal Note . . .

I think back to the time when we were just wrapping up work on the sixth edition of this book. At that time, I received the unexpected and most painful news that my mother had suffered a massive and fatal stroke. It is impossible to express the sense of sadness and loss experienced by myself, my brother, and my sister, as well as the countless other people who knew this gentle, loving, and much-loved person. To this day, we continue to miss her counsel, her sense of humor, and just knowing that she's there for us. We continue to miss her genuine exhilaration, which in turn exhilarated us, and the image of her welcoming, outstretched arms whenever we came to visit. Her children were her life, and the memory of her smiling face, making each of us feel so special, survives as a private source of peace and comfort for us all. She always kept a copy of this book proudly displayed on her coffee table, and I am very sorry that a copy of more recent editions did not make it to that most special place. My dedication of this book is one small way I can meaningfully acknowledge her contribution, as well as that of my beloved, deceased father, to my personal growth. As in the sixth edition, I am using my parents' wedding photo in the dedication. They were so good together in life. And so there Mom is, reunited with Dad. Now, that is something that would make her very happy.

As the reader might imagine, given the depth and breadth of the material covered in this textbook, it requires great diligence and effort to create and periodically re-create an instructional tool such as this that is timely, informative, and readable. Thank you, again, to all of the people who have helped through the years. Of course, I could not do it myself were it not for the fact that even through nine editions, this truly Herculean undertaking remains a labor of love.

Ronald Jay Cohen, Ph.D., ABPP, ABAP
Diplomate, American Board of Professional Psychology (Clinical)
Diplomate, American Board of Assessment Psychology

1

Psychological Testing and Assessment

All fields of human endeavor use measurement in some form, and each field has its own set of measuring tools and measuring units. For example, if you're recently engaged or thinking about becoming engaged, you may have learned about a unit of measure called the carat. If you've been shopping for a computer, you may have learned something about a unit of measurement called a byte. As a student of psychological measurement, you need a working familiarity with some of the commonly used units of measure in psychology as well as knowledge of some of the many measuring tools employed. In the pages that follow, you will gain that knowledge as well as an acquaintance with the history of measurement in psychology and an understanding of its theoretical basis.

Testing and Assessment

The roots of contemporary psychological testing and assessment can be found in early twentieth-century France. In 1905, Alfred Binet and a colleague published a test designed to help place Paris schoolchildren in appropriate classes. Binet's test would have consequences well beyond the Paris school district. Within a decade an English-language version of Binet's test was prepared for use in schools in the United States. When the United States declared war on Germany and entered World War I in 1917, the military needed a way to screen large numbers of recruits quickly for intellectual and emotional problems. Psychological testing provided this methodology. During World War II, the military would depend even more on psychological tests to screen recruits for service. Following the war, more and more tests purporting to measure an ever-widening array of psychological variables were developed and used. There were tests to measure not only intelligence but also personality, brain functioning, performance at work, and many other aspects of psychological and social functioning.

Psychological Testing and Assessment Defined

The world's receptivity to Binet's test in the early twentieth century spawned not only more tests but more test developers, more test publishers, more test users, and the emergence of what, logically enough, has become known as a testing enterprise. "Testing" was the term used to refer to everything from the administration of a test (as in "Testing in progress") to the interpretation of a test score ("The testing indicated that . . ."). During World War I, the term "testing" aptly described the group screening of thousands of military recruits. We suspect that it was then that the term gained a powerful foothold in the vocabulary of professionals and laypeople. The use of "testing" to denote everything from test administration to test interpretation can be found in postwar textbooks (such as Chapman, 1921; Hull, 1922; Spearman, 1927) as well as in various test-related writings for decades thereafter. However, by World War II a semantic distinction between testing and a more inclusive term, "assessment," began to emerge.

During World War II the U.S. Office of Strategic Services (OSS), a predecessor to today's Central Intelligence Agency (CIA), used a variety of procedures and measurement tools—psychological tests among them—in selecting military personnel for highly specialized positions involving espionage, intelligence gathering, and the like. For example, one of the tools employed was a very uncomfortable, group-on-one interview technique to evaluate how well candidates might respond to Gestapo-like interrogation. With a light harshly pointed at their face, interviewees would have to draw on their own creativity, persuasive abilities, and other resources to satisfactorily defend and explain a given scenario to a group of increasingly hostile interviewers. Candidates might have to explain why they were in a particular building that was off-limits to them, and doing something that they were not authorized to do, such as looking at or removing classified files. Candidates were evaluated on a number of variables, such as their ability to maintain noncontradictory responses. Today, such an assessment method, or any assessment method that has potential for harming the persons being assessed, would be likely to raise serious ethical concerns.

As summarized in *Assessment of Men* (OSS Assessment Staff, 1948) and elsewhere (Murray & MacKinnon, 1946), the assessment data generated were subjected to thoughtful integration and evaluation by highly trained assessment center staff. The OSS model—using an innovative variety of evaluative tools along with data from the evaluations of highly trained assessors—would later inspire what is now referred to as the **assessment center** approach to personnel evaluation (Bray, 1982).

Military, clinical, educational, and business settings are but a few of the many contexts that entail behavioral observation and active integration by assessors of test scores and other data. In such situations, the term *assessment* may be preferable to *testing*. In contrast to testing, assessment acknowledges that tests are only one type of tool used by professional assessors (along with other tools, such as the interview), and that the value of a test, or of any other tool of assessment, is intimately linked to the knowledge, skill, and experience of the assessor.

The semantic distinction between psychological testing and psychological assessment is blurred in everyday conversation. Somewhat surprisingly, the distinction between the two terms still remains blurred in some published "psychological testing" textbooks. Yet the distinction is important. Society at large is best served by a clear definition of and differentiation between these two terms as well as related terms such as *psychological test user* and *psychological assessor*. Clear distinctions between such terms may also help avoid the turf wars now brewing between psychology professionals and members of other professions seeking to use various psychological tests. In many psychological evaluation contexts, conducting an assessment requires greater education, training, and skill than simply administering a test.

> **JUST THINK . . .**
>
> Describe a situation in which testing is more appropriate than assessment. By contrast, describe a situation in which assessment is more appropriate than testing.

We define **psychological assessment** as the gathering and integration of psychology-related data for the purpose of making a psychological evaluation that is accomplished through the use of tools such as tests, interviews, case studies, behavioral observation, and specially designed apparatuses and measurement procedures. We define **psychological testing** as the process of measuring psychology-related variables by means of devices or procedures designed to obtain a sample of behavior. Some of the differences between these two processes are presented in Table 1–1.[1]

---

1. Especially when discussing general principles related to the creation of measurement procedures, as well as the creation, manipulation, or interpretation of data generated from such procedures, the word *test* (as well as related terms, such as *test score*) may be used in the broadest and most generic sense; that is, "test" may be used in shorthand fashion to apply to almost any procedure that entails measurement (including, for example, situational performance measures). Accordingly, when we speak of "test development" in Chapter 8, many of the principles set forth will apply to the development of other measurements that are not, strictly speaking, "tests" (such as situational performance measures, as well as other tools of assessment). Having said that, let's reemphasize that a real and meaningful distinction exists between the terms *psychological testing* and *psychological assessment,* and that effort should continually be made not to confuse the meaning of these two terms.

Table 1–1
Testing in Contrast to Assessment

In contrast to the process of administering, scoring, and interpreting psychological tests (psychological testing), psychological assessment may be conceived as a problem-solving process that can take many different forms. How psychological assessment proceeds depends on many factors, not the least of which is the reason for assessing. Different tools of evaluation—psychological tests among them— might be marshaled in the process of assessment, depending on the particular objectives, people, and circumstances involved as well as on other variables unique to the particular situation.

Admittedly, the line between what constitutes testing and what constitutes assessment is not always as clear as we might like it to be. However, by acknowledging that such ambiguity exists, we can work to sharpen our definition and use of these terms. It seems useful to distinguish the differences between testing and assessment in terms of the objective, process, and outcome of an evaluation and also in terms of the role and skill of the evaluator. Keep in mind that, although these are useful distinctions to consider, exceptions can always be found.

Testing	Assessment
Objective	
Typically, to obtain some gauge, usually numerical in nature, with regard to an ability or attribute.	Typically, to answer a referral question, solve a problem, or arrive at a decision through the use of tools of evaluation.
Process	
Testing may be individual or group in nature. After test administration, the tester will typically add up "the number of correct answers or the number of certain types of responses . . . with little if any regard for the how or mechanics of such content" (Maloney & Ward, 1976, p. 39).	Assessment is typically individualized. In contrast to testing, assessment more typically focuses on how an individual processes rather than simply the results of that processing.
Role of Evaluator	
The tester is not key to the process; practically speaking, one tester may be substituted for another tester without appreciably affecting the evaluation.	The assessor is key to the process of selecting tests and/or other tools of evaluation as well as in drawing conclusions from the entire evaluation.
Skill of Evaluator	
Testing typically requires technician-like skills in terms of administering and scoring a test as well as in interpreting a test result.	Assessment typically requires an educated selection of tools of evaluation, skill in evaluation, and thoughtful organization and integration of data.
Outcome	
Typically, testing yields a test score or series of test scores.	Typically, assessment entails a logical problem-solving approach that brings to bear many sources of data designed to shed light on a referral question.

Varieties of assessment   The term *assessment* may be modified in a seemingly endless number of ways, each such modification referring to a particular variety or area of assessment. Sometimes the meaning of the specialty area can be readily discerned just from the word or term that modifies "assessment." For example, the term "therapeutic psychological assessment" refers to assessment that has a therapeutic component to it. Also intuitively obvious, the term **educational assessment** refers to, broadly speaking, the use of tests and other tools to evaluate abilities and skills relevant to success or failure in a school or pre-school context. Intelligence tests, achievement tests, and reading comprehension tests are some of the evaluative tools that may spring to mind with the mention of the term "educational assessment." But what springs to mind with the mention of other, less common assessment terminology? Consider, for example, terms like *retrospective assessment*, *remote assessment*, and *ecological momentary assessment*.

For the record, the term **retrospective assessment** may be defined as *the use of evaluative tools to draw conclusions about psychological aspects of a person as they existed at some point in time prior to the assessment.* There are unique challenges and hurdles to be overcome when conducting retrospective assessments regardless if the subject of the evaluation is deceased (Reyman et al., 2015) or alive (Teel et al., 2016). **Remote assessment** refers to *the use of tools of psychological evaluation to gather data and draw conclusions about a subject who is not in physical proximity to the person or people conducting the evaluation.* One example of how psychological assessments may be conducted remotely was provided in this chapter's *Close-Up* feature. In each chapter of this book, we will spotlight one topic for "a closer look." In this chapter, the *Close-Up* box explored how the smartphone revolution in communication may also signal a revolution in the way that psychological assessments are conducted.

Psychological assessment by means of smartphones also serves as an example of an approach to assessment called **ecological momentary assessment (EMA)**. EMA refers to the "in the moment" evaluation of specific problems and related cognitive and behavioral variables at the very time and place that they occur. Using various tools of assessment, EMA has been used to help tackle diverse clinical problems including post-traumatic stress disorder (Black et al., 2016), problematic smoking (Ruscio et al., 2016), and chronic abdominal pain in children (Schurman & Friesen, 2015).

The process of assessment   In general, the process of assessment begins with a referral for assessment from a source such as a teacher, school psychologist, counselor, judge, clinician, or corporate human resources specialist. Typically one or more referral questions are put to the assessor about the assessee. Some examples of referral questions are: "Can this child function in a general education environment?," "Is this defendant competent to stand trial?," and "How well can this employee be expected to perform if promoted to an executive position?"

The assessor may meet with the assessee or others before the formal assessment in order to clarify aspects of the reason for referral. The assessor prepares for the assessment by selecting the tools of assessment to be used. For example, if the assessment occurs in a corporate or military setting and the referral question concerns the assessee's leadership ability, the assessor may wish to employ a measure (or two) of leadership. Typically, the assessor's own past experience, education, and training play a key role in the specific tests or other tools to be employed in the assessment. Sometimes an institution in which the assessment is taking place has prescribed guidelines for which instruments can and cannot be used. In most every assessment situation, particularly situations that are relatively novel to the assessor, the tool selection process may be informed by some research in preparation for the assessment. For example, in the assessment of leadership, the tool selection procedure might be informed by publications dealing with behavioral studies of leadership (Derue et al., 2011), psychological studies of leaders (Kouzes & Posner, 2007), cultural issues in leadership (Byrne & Bradley, 2007), or whatever aspect of leadership the assessment will be focused on (Carnevale et al., 2011; Elliott, 2011; Rosenman et al., 2015).

Subsequent to the selection of the instruments or procedures to be employed, the formal assessment will begin. After the assessment, the assessor writes a report of the findings that is

JUST THINK . . .

What qualities makes a good leader? How might these qualities be measured?

Behavioral Assessment Using Smartphones*

Much like the state of one's physical health, the state of one's mental health and functioning is changing and fluid. Varied internal factors (such as neurochemistry and hormonal shifts), external factors (such as marital discord and job pressures), or combinations thereof may affect mental health and functioning. This is as true for people with no diagnosis of mental disorder as it is for patients suffering from chronic psychiatric illnesses.

Changes in people's mental health status rarely come "out of the blue" (or, without warning). Behavioral signs that someone is experiencing increased stress and mental health difficulties may include changes in sleep patterns, social engagement, and physical activity. Because these changes may emerge gradually over time, they can go unnoticed by family members, close friends, or even the affected individuals themselves. By the time most people seek support or professional care, their mental health and functioning may have deteriorated substantially. Identifying behavioral patterns that are associated with increased risk for underlying mental health difficulties is a first step toward more efficient treatment, perhaps even prevention.

Dr. Dror Ben-Zeev and his colleagues are attempting to identify problematic behavioral patterns using a device that is already in the hands of billions: the smartphone. The smartphone (or, a mobile phone that features computational capacity) comes equipped with multiple embedded sensors that measure variables such as acoustics, location, and movement. Ben-Zeev's team uses sophisticated smartphone software that enables them to repurpose these sensors and capture an abundance of information about the smartphone user's environment and behavior. Their program activates the smartphone's microphone every few minutes to capture ambient sound. If the software detects human conversation, it remains active for the duration of the conversation. To protect user's privacy, the speech detection system does not record raw audio. It processes the data in real-time to extract and store conversation-related data while actual conversations cannot be reconstructed. The software calculates both the number of conversations and the average length of a conversation engaged in during a 24-hour period.

In addition to re-purposing the microphone in a cell phone, Ben-Zeev's system repurposes the smartphone's global positioning system (GPS). When the user is outdoors, the GPS

© Maciej Frolow/Getty Images RF

generates geospatial coordinates helpful in determining the daily distance covered, as well as the amount of time spent at specific locations. When the research team conducts studies with individuals who do not move from one location to another, such as hospitalized patients in closed psychiatric units, they place microbluetooth beacons in different rooms throughout the venue. As the subject moves from one room to another, the smartphone's bluetooth sensor receives signals sent by the beacons, and records the subject's precise position in the unit.

A typical smartphone also comes equipped with *accelerometers;* these devices are designed to detect motion. Ben-Zeev's monitoring system collects the accelerometer data to determine whether the individual is or is not active.

The smartphone system collects and stores all of the sensor data and transmits it periodically to a secure study server. There, the information is processed and displayed on a digital dashboard. By means of this system, multidimensional data from faraway places can be viewed online to help clinicians and researchers better understand experiences that cause changes in stress level and general mental health. One smartphone-sensing study conducted with college undergraduate and graduate student subjects over a 10-week period included pre- and post-measures of depression. The data suggested that social engagement (as measured by the

*This *Close-Up* was guest-authored by Dror Ben-Zeev of the Department of Psychiatry of the Geisel School of Medicine at Dartmouth.

(continued)

Behavioral Assessment Using Smartphones *(continued)*

speech detection software) and daily geospatial activity (as measured by GPS) were significantly related to changes in level of depression (Ben-Zeev et al., 2015a).

Of course, tracking someone via their smartphone without their awareness and consent would be unethical. However, for people who may be at risk for mental health problems, or for those who already struggle with psychiatric conditions and need support, this unobtrusive approach may have value. Explaining to patients (or their representatives) what the technology is, how it works, and how data from it may be used for patient benefit, may well allay any privacy concerns. Preliminary research has suggested that even patients with severe mental illness can understand and appreciate the potential benefits of remote assessment by means of the smartphone tracking system. Most of the subjects studied stated that they would have no objection to using a system that could not only passively detect when they

were not doing well, but offer them helpful and timely suggestions for improving their mental state (Ben-Zeev et al., 2015b). Patients and mental health professionals alike appreciate the promise of this potentially useful method for detecting emerging high-risk patterns that require preventative or immediate treatment.

As technology evolves, one can imagine a future in which at-risk individuals derive benefit from smartphones repurposed to serve as objectively scalable measures of behavior. Used in a clinically skilled fashion and with appropriate protections of patient privacy, these ubiquitous devices, now repurposed to yield behavioral data, may be instrumental in creating meaningful diagnostic insights and profiles. In turn, such minute-to-minute assessment data may yield highly personalized and effective treatment protocols.

Used with permission of Dror Ben-Zeev.

designed to answer the referral question. More feedback sessions with the assessee and/or interested third parties (such as the assessee's parents and the referring professional) may also be scheduled.

Different assessors may approach the assessment task in different ways. Some assessors approach the assessment with minimal input from assessees themselves. Other assessors view the process of assessment as more of a collaboration between the assessor and the assessee. For example, in one approach to assessment, referred to (logically enough) as **collaborative psychological assessment,** the assessor and assessee may work as "partners" from initial contact through final feedback (Finello, 2011; Fischer, 1978, 2004, 2006). One variety of collaborative assessment includes an element of therapy as part of the process. Stephen Finn and his colleagues (Finn, 2003, 2011; Finn & Martin, 1997; Finn & Tonsager, 2002; Fischer & Finn, 2014) have described a collaborative approach to assessment called **therapeutic psychological assessment.** In that approach, therapeutic self-discovery and new understandings are encouraged throughout the assessment process.

Another approach to assessment that seems to have picked up momentum in recent years, most notably in educational settings, is referred to as *dynamic assessment* (Poehner & van Compernolle, 2011). The term *dynamic* may suggest that a psychodynamic or psychoanalytic approach to assessment is being applied. However, that is not the case. As used in the present context, *dynamic* is used to describe the interactive, changing, or varying nature of the assessment. In general, **dynamic assessment** refers to an interactive approach to psychological assessment that usually follows a model of (1) evaluation, (2) intervention of some sort, and (3) evaluation. Dynamic assessment is most typically employed in educational settings, although it may be employed in correctional, corporate, neuropsychological, clinical, and most any other setting as well.

Intervention between evaluations, sometimes even between individual questions posed or tasks given, might take many different forms, depending upon the purpose of the dynamic assessment (Haywood & Lidz, 2007). For example, an assessor may intervene in the course of an evaluation of an assessee's abilities with increasingly more explicit feedback or hints. The purpose of the intervention may be to provide assistance with mastering the task at hand. Progress in mastering the same or similar tasks is then measured. In essence, dynamic assessment provides a means for evaluating how the assessee processes or benefits from some type of intervention (feedback, hints, instruction, therapy, and so forth) during the course of evaluation. In some educational contexts, dynamic assessment may be viewed as a way of measuring not just learning but "learning potential," or "learning how to learn" skills. Computers are one tool used to help meet the objectives of dynamic assessment (Wang, 2011). There are others . . .

The Tools of Psychological Assessment

The Test

A **test** may be defined simply as a measuring device or procedure. When the word *test* is prefaced with a modifier, it refers to a device or procedure designed to measure a variable related to that modifier. Consider, for example, the term *medical test,* which refers to a device or procedure designed to measure some variable related to the practice of medicine (including a wide range of tools and procedures, such as X-rays, blood tests, and testing of reflexes). In a like manner, the term **psychological test** refers to a device or procedure designed to measure variables related to psychology (such as intelligence, personality, aptitude, interests, attitudes, or values). Whereas a medical test might involve analysis of a sample of blood, tissue, or the like, a psychological test almost always involves analysis of a sample of behavior. The behavior sample could range from responses to a pencil-and-paper questionnaire, to oral responses to questions related to the performance of some task. The behavior sample could be elicited by the stimulus of the test itself, or it could be naturally occurring behavior (observed by the assessor in real time as it occurs, or recorded).

Psychological tests and other tools of assessment may differ with respect to a number of variables, such as content, format, administration procedures, scoring and interpretation procedures, and technical quality. The *content* (subject matter) of the test will, of course, vary with the focus of the particular test. But even two psychological tests purporting to measure the same thing—for example, personality—may differ widely in item content. This is so because two test developers might have entirely different views regarding what is important in measuring "personality"; different test developers employ different definitions of "personality." Additionally, different test developers come to the test development process with different theoretical orientations. For example, items on a psychoanalytically oriented personality test may have little resemblance to those on a behaviorally oriented personality test, yet both are personality tests. A psychoanalytically oriented personality test might be chosen for use by a psychoanalytically oriented assessor, and an existentially oriented personality test might be chosen for use by an existentially oriented assessor.

The term **format** pertains to the form, plan, structure, arrangement, and layout of test items as well as to related considerations such as time limits. *Format* is also used to refer to the form in which a test is administered: computerized, pencil-and-paper, or some other form. When making specific reference to a computerized test, the format may also involve the form of the software: PC- or Mac-compatible. The term *format* is not confined to tests. *Format* is also used to denote the form or structure of other evaluative tools and processes, such as the guidelines for creating a portfolio work sample.

JUST THINK . . .

Imagine you wanted to develop a test for a personality trait you termed "goth." How would you define this trait? What kinds of items would you include in the test? Why would you include those kinds of items?

Tests differ in their *administration procedures.* Some tests, particularly those designed for administration on a one-to-one basis, may require an active and knowledgeable test administrator. The test administration may involve demonstration of various kinds of tasks demanded of the assessee, as well as trained observation of an assessee's performance. Alternatively, some tests, particularly those designed for administration to groups, may not even require the test administrator to be present while the testtakers independently complete the required tasks.

Tests differ in their *scoring and interpretation procedures.* To better understand how and why, let's define *score* and *scoring.* Sports enthusiasts are no strangers to these terms. For them, these terms refer to the number of points accumulated by competitors and the process of accumulating those points. In testing and assessment, we may formally define **score** as a code or summary statement, usually but not necessarily numerical in nature, that reflects an evaluation of performance on a test, task, interview, or some other sample of behavior. **Scoring** is the process of assigning such evaluative codes or statements to performance on tests, tasks, interviews, or other behavior samples. In the world of psychological assessment, many different types of scores exist. Some scores result from the simple summing of responses (such as the summing of correct/incorrect or agree/disagree responses), and some scores are derived from more elaborate procedures.

Scores themselves can be described and categorized in many different ways. For example, one type of score is the *cut score.* A **cut score** (also referred to as a *cutoff score* or simply a *cutoff*) is a reference point, usually numerical, derived by judgment and used to divide a set of data into two or more classifications. Some action will be taken or some inference will be made on the basis of these classifications. Cut scores on tests, usually in combination with other data, are used in schools in many contexts. For example, they may be used in grading, and in making decisions about the class or program to which children will be assigned. Cut scores are used by employers as aids to decision making about personnel hiring, placement, and advancement. State agencies use cut scores as aids in licensing decisions. There are probably more than a dozen different methods that can be used to formally derive cut scores (Dwyer, 1996). If you're curious about what some of those different methods are, stay tuned; we cover that in an upcoming chapter.

Sometimes no formal method is used to arrive at a cut score. Some teachers use an informal "eyeball" method to proclaim, for example, that a score of 65 or more on a test means "pass" and a score of 64 or below means "fail." Whether formally or informally derived, cut scores typically take into account, at least to some degree, the values of those who set them. Consider, for example, two teachers who teach the same course at the same college. One teacher might set a cut score for passing the course that is significantly higher (and more difficult for students to attain) than the other teacher. There is also another side to the human equation as it relates to cut scores, one that is seldom written about in measurement texts. This phenomenon concerns the emotional consequences of "not making the cut" and "just making the cut" (see Figure 1–1).

Tests differ widely in terms of their guidelines for scoring and interpretation. Some tests are self-scored by the testtakers themselves, others are scored by computer, and others require scoring by trained examiners. Some tests, such as most tests of intelligence, come with test manuals that are explicit not only about scoring criteria but also about the nature of the interpretations that can be made from the scores. Other tests, such as the Rorschach Inkblot Test, are sold with no manual at all. The (presumably qualified) purchaser buys the stimulus materials and then selects and uses one of many available guides for administration, scoring, and interpretation.

JUST THINK . . .

How might one test of intelligence have more utility than another test of intelligence in the same school setting?

Tests differ with respect to their **psychometric soundness** or technical quality. Synonymous with the antiquated term *psychometry,* **psychometrics** may be defined as the science of psychological measurement. Variants of these words include the adjective *psychometric* (which refers to measurement that is psychological in nature) and the nouns **psychometrist** and **psychometrician** (both terms referring to a professional who uses, analyzes, and interprets psychological test data). One speaks of the psychometric soundness of a test when referring to how consistently and how accurately a psychological test measures what it purports to measure. Assessment professionals also speak of the psychometric *utility* of a particular test or assessment method. In this context,

Figure 1–1
Emotion Engendered by Categorical Cutoffs

People who just make some categorical cutoff may feel better about their accomplishment than those who make the cutoff by a substantial margin. But those who just miss the cutoff may feel worse than those who miss it by a substantial margin. Evidence consistent with this view was presented in research with Olympic athletes (Medvec et al., 1995; Medvec & Savitsky, 1997). Bronze medalists were—somewhat paradoxically—happier with the outcome than silver medalists. Bronze medalists might say to themselves "at least I won a medal" and be happy about it. By contrast, silver medalists might feel frustrated that they tried for the gold and missed winning it.
© Jean Catuffe/Getty Images

utility refers to the usefulness or practical value that a test or other tool of assessment has for a particular purpose. These concepts are elaborated on in subsequent chapters. Now, returning to our discussion of tools of assessment, meet one well-known tool that, as they say, "needs no introduction."

The Interview

In everyday conversation, the word *interview* conjures images of face-to-face talk. But the interview as a tool of psychological assessment typically involves more than talk. If the interview is conducted face-to-face, then the interviewer is probably taking note of not only the content of what is said but also the way it is being said. More specifically, the interviewer is taking note of both verbal and nonverbal behavior. Nonverbal behavior may include the interviewee's "body language," movements, and facial expressions in response to the interviewer, the extent of eye contact, apparent willingness to cooperate, and general reaction to the demands of the interview. The interviewer may also take note of the way the interviewee is dressed. Here, variables such as neat versus sloppy, and appropriate versus inappropriate, may be noted.

Because of a potential wealth of nonverbal information to be gained, interviews are ideally conducted face-to-face. However, face-to-face contact is not always possible and interviews may be conducted in other formats. In an interview conducted by telephone, for example, the

JUST THINK . . .

What type of interview situation would you envision as ideal for being carried out entirely through the medium of text-messaging?

interviewer may still be able to gain information beyond the responses to questions by being sensitive to variables such as changes in the interviewee's voice pitch or the extent to which particular questions precipitate long pauses or signs of emotion in response. Of course, interviews need not involve verbalized speech, as when they are conducted in sign language. Interviews may also be conducted by various electronic means, as would be the case with online interviews, e-mail interviews, and interviews conducted by means of text messaging. In its broadest sense, then, we can define an **interview** as a method of gathering information through direct communication involving reciprocal exchange.

Interviews differ with regard to many variables, such as their purpose, length, and nature. Interviews may be used by psychologists in various specialty areas to help make diagnostic, treatment, selection, or other decisions. So, for example, school psychologists may use an interview to help make a decision about the appropriateness of various educational interventions or class placements. A court-appointed psychologist may use an interview to help guide the court in determining whether a defendant was insane at the time of a commission of a crime. A specialist in head injury may use an interview to help shed light on questions related to the extent of damage to the brain that was caused by the injury. A psychologist studying consumer behavior may use an interview to learn about the market for various products and services, as well as how best to advertise and promote them. A police psychologist may instruct eyewitnesses to serious crimes to close their eyes when they are interviewed about details related to the crime. This is so because there is suggestive evidence that the responses will have greater relevance to the questions posed if the witness's eyes are closed (Vredeveldt et al., 2015).

An interview may be used to help professionals in human resources to make more informed recommendations about the hiring, firing, and advancement of personnel. In some instances, what is called a **panel interview** (also referred to as a *board interview*) is employed. Here, more than one interviewer participates in the assessment. A presumed advantage of this personnel assessment technique is that any idiosyncratic biases of a lone interviewer will be minimized (Dipboye, 1992). A disadvantage of the panel interview relates to its utility; the cost of using multiple interviewers may not be justified (Dixon et al., 2002).

Some interviewing, especially in the context of clinical and counseling settings, has as its objective not only the gathering of information from the interviewee, but a targeted change in the interviewee's thinking and behavior. A therapeutic technique called *motivational interviewing*, for example, is used by counselors and clinicians to gather information about some problematic behavior, while simultaneously attempting to address it therapeutically (Bundy, 2004; Miller & Rollnick, 2002). **Motivational interviewing** may be defined as a therapeutic dialogue that combines person-centered listening skills such as openness and empathy, with the use of cognition-altering techniques designed to positively affect motivation and effect therapeutic change. Motivational interviewing has been employed to address a relatively wide range of problems (Hoy et al., 2016; Kistenmacher & Weiss, 2008; Miller & Rollnick, 2009; Pollak et al., 2016; Rothman & Wang, 2016; Shepard et al., 2016) and has been successfully employed in intervention by means of telephone (Lin et al., 2016), Internet chat (Skov-Ettrup et al., 2016), and text messaging (Shingleton et al., 2016).

JUST THINK . . .

What types of interviewing skills must the host of a talk show possess to be considered an effective interviewer? Do these skills differ from those needed by a professional in the field of psychological assessment? If so, how?

The popularity of the interview as a method of gathering information extends far beyond psychology. Just try to think of one day when you were not exposed to an interview on television, radio, or the Internet! Regardless of the medium through which it is conducted, an interview is a reciprocal affair in that the interviewee reacts to the interviewer and the interviewer reacts to the interviewee. The quality, if not the quantity, of useful information produced by an interview depends in no small part on the skills of the interviewer. Interviewers differ in many ways: their pacing of interviews, their rapport with interviewees, and their ability to convey genuineness, empathy, and humor. Keeping these differences firmly in mind, consider Figure 1–2. How might the distinctive personality attributes of these two celebrities affect responses of interviewees? Which of these two interviewers do you think is better at interviewing? Why?

The Portfolio

Students and professionals in many different fields of endeavor ranging from art to architecture keep files of their work products. These work products—whether retained on paper, canvas, film, video, audio, or some other medium—constitute what is called a **portfolio.** As samples of one's ability and accomplishment, a portfolio may be used as a tool of evaluation. Employers of commercial artists, for example, will make hiring decisions based, in part, on the impressiveness of an applicant's portfolio of sample drawings. As another example, consider the employers of on-air radio talent. They, too, will make hiring decisions that are based partly upon their judgments of (audio) samples of the candidate's previous work.

The appeal of portfolio assessment as a tool of evaluation extends to many other fields, including education. Some have argued, for example, that the best evaluation of a student's writing skills can be accomplished not by the administration of a test, but by asking the student to compile a selection of writing samples. Also in the field of education, portfolio assessment has

JUST THINK . . .

If you were to prepare a portfolio representing "who you are" in terms of your educational career, your hobbies, and your values, what would you include in your portfolio?

Figure 1–2
On Interviewing and Being Interviewed

Different interviewers have different styles of interviewing. How would you characterize the interview style of Jimmy Fallon as compared to that of Howard Stern?

© Theo Wargo/Getty Images

been employed as a tool in the hiring of instructors. An instructor's portfolio may consist of various documents such as lesson plans, published writings, and visual aids developed expressly for teaching certain subjects. All of these materials can be extremely useful to those who must make hiring decisions.

Case History Data

Case history data refers to records, transcripts, and other accounts in written, pictorial, or other form that preserve archival information, official and informal accounts, and other data and items relevant to an assessee. Case history data may include files or excerpts from files maintained at institutions and agencies such as schools, hospitals, employers, religious institutions, and criminal justice agencies. Other examples of case history data are letters and written correspondence, photos and family albums, newspaper and magazine clippings, home videos, movies, audiotapes, work samples, artwork, doodlings, and accounts and pictures pertaining to interests and hobbies. Postings on social media such as Facebook or Twitter may also serve as case history data. Employers, university admissions departments, healthcare providers, forensic investigators, and others may collect data from postings on social media to help inform inference and decision making (Lis et al., 2015; Pirelli et al., 2016).

Case history data is a useful tool in a wide variety of assessment contexts. In a clinical evaluation, for example, case history data can shed light on an individual's past and current adjustment as well as on the events and circumstances that may have contributed to any changes in adjustment. Case history data can be of critical value in neuropsychological evaluations, where it often provides information about neuropsychological functioning prior to the occurrence of a trauma or other event that results in a deficit. School psychologists rely on case history data for insight into a student's current academic or behavioral standing. Case history data is also useful in making judgments concerning future class placements.

The assembly of case history data, as well as related data, into an illustrative account is referred to by terms such as *case study* or *case history*. We may formally define a **case study** (or **case history**) as a report or illustrative account concerning a person or an event that was compiled on the basis of case history data. A case study might, for example, shed light on how one individual's personality and a particular set of environmental conditions combined to produce a successful world leader. A case study of an individual who attempted to assassinate a high-ranking political figure could shed light on what types of individuals and conditions might lead to similar attempts in the future. Work on a social psychological phenomenon referred to as *groupthink* contains rich case history material on collective decision making that did not always result in the best decisions (Janis, 1972). **Groupthink** arises as a result of the varied forces that drive decision-makers to reach a consensus (such as the motivation to reach a compromise in positions).

Case history data along with other Intelligence (informative data) can play an important role in the increasingly important area of threat assessment (Bolante & Dykeman, 2015; Borum, 2015; Dietz et al., 1991; Gardeazabal & Sandler, 2015; Malone, 2015; Mrad et al., 2015). The United States Secret Service has long relied on such information to help protect the President as well its other protectees (Coggins et al., 1998; Institute of Medicine, 1984; Takeuchi et al., 1981; Vossekull & Fein, 1997).

> **JUST THINK . . .**
>
> What are the pros and cons of using case history data as a tool of assessment?

Behavioral Observation

If you want to know how someone behaves in a particular situation, observe his or her behavior in that situation. Such "down-home" wisdom underlies at least one approach to evaluation. **Behavioral observation,** as it is employed by assessment professionals, may be defined as monitoring the actions of others or oneself by visual or electronic means while recording quantitative and/or qualitative information regarding those actions. Behavioral observation is often used as a diagnostic aid in various settings such as inpatient facilities, behavioral research laboratories, and classrooms. Behavioral observation may be used for purposes of selection or placement in corporate or organizational settings. In such instances, behavioral observation may be used as an aid in identifying personnel who best demonstrate the abilities required to perform a particular task or job. Sometimes researchers venture outside of the confines of clinics, classrooms, workplaces, and research laboratories in order to observe behavior of humans in a natural setting—that is, the setting in which the behavior would typically be expected to occur. This variety of behavioral observation is referred to as **naturalistic observation.** So, for example, to study the socializing behavior of autistic children with same-age peers, one research team opted for natural settings rather than a controlled, laboratory environment (Bellini et al., 2007).

Behavioral observation as an aid to designing therapeutic intervention has proven to be extremely useful in institutional settings such as schools, hospitals, prisons, and group homes. Using published or self-constructed lists of targeted behaviors, staff can observe firsthand the behavior of individuals and design interventions accordingly. In a school situation, for example, naturalistic observation on the playground of a culturally different child suspected of having linguistic problems might reveal that the child does have English language skills but is unwilling—for reasons of shyness, cultural upbringing, or whatever—to demonstrate those abilities to adults.

JUST THINK . . .

What are the pros and cons of naturalistic observation as tools of assessment?

In practice, behavioral observation, and especially naturalistic observation, tends to be used most frequently by researchers in settings such as classrooms, clinics, prisons, and other types of facilities where observers have ready access to assessees. For private practitioners, it is typically not practical or economically feasible to spend hours out of the consulting room observing clients as they go about their daily lives. Still, there are some mental health professionals, such as those in the field of assisted living, who find great value in behavioral observation of patients outside of their institutional environment. For them, it may be necessary to accompany a patient outside of the institution's walls to learn if that patient is capable of independently performing activities of daily living. In this context, a tool of assessment that relies heavily on behavioral observation, such as the Test of Grocery Shopping Skills (see Figure 1–3), may be extremely useful.

Role-Play Tests

Role play may be defined as acting an improvised or partially improvised part in a simulated situation. A **role-play test** is a tool of assessment wherein assessees are directed to act as if they were in a particular situation. Assessees may then be evaluated with regard to their expressed thoughts, behaviors, abilities, and other variables. (Note that *role play* is hyphenated when used as an adjective or a verb but not as a noun.)

Role play is useful in evaluating various skills. So, for example, grocery shopping skills (Figure 1–3) could conceivably be evaluated through role play. Depending upon how the task is set up, an actual trip to the supermarket could or could not be required. Of course, role play may not be as useful as "the real thing" in all situations. Still, role play is used quite extensively, especially in situations where it is too time-consuming, too expensive, or simply too inconvenient to assess in a real situation. So, for example, astronauts in training may be required to role-play many situations "as if" in outer space. Such "as if" scenarios for training purposes result in truly "astronomical" savings.

JUST THINK . . .

What are the pros and cons of role play as a tool of assessment? In your opinion, what type of presenting problem would be ideal for assessment by role play?

Figure 1–3
Price (and Judgment) Check in Aisle 5

Designed primarily for use with persons with psychiatric disorders, the context-based Test of Grocery Shopping Skills (Hamera & Brown, 2000) may be very useful in evaluating a skill necessary for independent living.
© Blend Images/Dave and Les Jacobs/Getty Images RF

Individuals being evaluated in a corporate, industrial, organizational, or military context for managerial or leadership ability may routinely be placed in role-play situations. They may be asked, for example, to mediate a hypothetical dispute between personnel at a work site. The format of the role play could range from "live scenarios" with live actors, or computer-generated simulations. Outcome measures for such an assessment might include ratings related to various aspects of the individual's ability to resolve the conflict, such as effectiveness of approach, quality of resolution, and number of minutes to resolution.

Role play as a tool of assessment may be used in various clinical contexts. For example, it is routinely employed in many interventions with substance abusers. Clinicians may attempt to obtain a baseline measure of abuse, cravings, or coping skills by administering a role-play test prior to therapeutic intervention. The same test is then administered again subsequent to completion of treatment. Role play can thus be used as both a tool of assessment and a measure of outcome.

Computers as Tools

We have already made reference to the role computers play in contemporary assessment in the context of generating simulations. They may also help in the measurement of variables that in the past were quite difficult to quantify. But perhaps the more obvious role as a tool of assessment is their role in test administration, scoring, and interpretation.

As test administrators, computers do much more than replace the "equipment" that was so widely used in the past (a number 2 pencil). Computers can serve as test administrators (online or off) and as highly efficient test scorers. Within seconds they can derive not only test scores but patterns of test scores. Scoring may be done on-site (**local processing**) or conducted at some central location (**central processing**). If processing occurs at a central location, test-related data may be sent to and returned from this central facility by means of phone lines (**teleprocessing**), mail, or courier. Whether processed locally or centrally, an account of a testtaker's performance can range from a mere listing of a score or scores (a **simple scoring report**) to the more detailed **extended scoring report,** which includes statistical analyses of the testtaker's performance. A step up from scoring reports is the **interpretive report,** which is distinguished by its inclusion of numerical or narrative interpretive statements in the report. Some interpretive reports contain relatively little interpretation and simply call attention to certain high, low, or unusual scores that need to be focused on. At the high end of interpretive reports is what is sometimes referred to as a **consultative report.** This type of report, usually written in language appropriate for communication between assessment professionals, may provide expert opinion concerning analysis of the data. Yet another type of computerized scoring report is designed to integrate data from sources other than the test itself into the interpretive report. Such an **integrative report** will employ previously collected data (such as medication records or behavioral observation data) into the test report.

The acronym **CAPA** refers to the term *computer-assisted psychological assessment.* By the way, here the word *assisted* typically refers to the assistance computers provide to the test user, not the testtaker. One specific brand of CAPA, for example, is *Q-Interactive.* Available from Pearson Assessments, this technology allows test users to administer tests by means of two iPads connected by bluetooth (one for the test administrator and one for the testtaker). Test items that require a verbal response may be recorded, as may be written notes using a stylus with the iPad. Scoring is immediate. Sweeney (2014) reviewed Q-Interactive and was favorably impressed. He liked the fact that it obviated the need for many staples of paper-and-pencil test administration (including test kits and a stopwatch). However, he did point out that only a limited number of tests are available to administer, and that no Android or Windows edition of the software has been made available. Also, despite the publisher's promise of freedom from test kits, the reviewer often found himself "going back to the manual" (Sweeney, 2014, p. 19).

JUST THINK . . .

Describe a test that would be ideal for computer administration. Then describe a test that would not be ideal for computer administration.

Another acronym you may come across is **CAT,** this for *computer adaptive testing.* The *adaptive* in this term is a reference to the computer's ability to tailor the test to the testtaker's ability or test-taking pattern. So, for example, on a computerized test of academic abilities, the computer might be programmed to switch from testing math skills to English skills after three consecutive failures on math items. Another way a computerized test could be programmed to adapt is by providing the testtaker with score feedback as the test proceeds. Score feedback in the context of CAT may, depending on factors such as intrinsic motivation and external incentives, positively affect testtaker engagement as well as performance (Arieli-Attali & Budescu, 2015).

CAPA opened a world of possibilities for test developers, enabling them to create psychometrically sound tests using mathematical procedures and calculations so complicated that they may have taken weeks or months to use in a bygone era. It opened a new world to test users, enabling the construction of tailor-made tests with built-in scoring and interpretive capabilities previously unheard of. For many test users, CAPA was a great advance over the past, when they had to personally administer tests and possibly even place the responses in some other form prior to analysis (such as by manually using a scoring template or other device). And even after doing all of that, they would then begin the often laborious tasks of scoring and interpreting the resulting data. Still, every rose has its thorns; some of the pros and cons of CAPA are summarized in Table 1–2. The number of tests in this format is burgeoning, and test users must take extra care in selecting the right test given factors such as the objective of the testing and the unique characteristics of the test user (Zygouris & Tsolaki, 2015).

Table 1-2
CAPA: Some Pros and Cons

Pros	Cons
CAPA saves professional time in test administration, scoring, and interpretation.	Professionals must still spend significant time reading software and hardware documentation and even ancillary books on the test and its interpretation.
CAPA results in minimal scoring errors resulting from human error or lapses of attention or judgment.	With CAPA, the possibility of software or hardware error is ever present, from difficult-to-pinpoint sources such as software glitches or hardware malfunction.
CAPA ensures standardized test administration to all testtakers with little, if any, variation in test administration procedures.	CAPA leaves those testtakers at a disadvantage who are unable to employ familiar test-taking strategies (previewing test, skipping questions, going back to previous question, etc.).
CAPA yields standardized interpretation of findings due to elimination of unreliability traceable to differing points of view in professional judgment.	CAPA's standardized interpretation of findings based on a set, unitary perspective may not be optimal; interpretation could profit from alternative viewpoints.
Computers' capacity to combine data according to rules is more accurate than that of humans.	Computers lack the flexibility of humans to recognize the exception to a rule in the context of the "big picture."
Nonprofessional assistants can be used in the test administration process, and the test can typically be administered to groups of testtakers in one sitting.	Use of nonprofessionals leaves diminished, if any, opportunity for the professional to observe the assessee's test-taking behavior and note any unusual extra-test conditions that may have affected responses.
Professional groups such as APA develop guidelines and standards for use of CAPA products.	Profit-driven nonprofessionals may also create and distribute tests with little regard for professional guidelines and standards.
Paper-and-pencil tests may be converted to CAPA products with consequential advantages, such as a shorter time between the administration of the test and its scoring and interpretation.	The use of paper-and-pencil tests that have been converted for computer administration raises questions about the equivalence of the original test and its converted form.
Security of CAPA products can be maintained not only by traditional means (such as locked filing cabinets) but by high-tech electronic products (such as firewalls).	Security of CAPA products can be breached by computer hackers, and integrity of data can be altered or destroyed by untoward events such as introduction of computer viruses.
Computers can automatically tailor test content and length based on responses of testtakers.	Not all testtakers take the same test or have the same test-taking experience.

The APA Committee on Psychological Tests and Assessment was convened to consider the pros and cons of computer-assisted assessment, and assessment using the Internet (Naglieri et al., 2004). Among the advantages over paper-and-pencil tests cited were (1) test administrators have greater access to potential test users because of the global reach of the Internet, (2) scoring and interpretation of test data tend to be quicker than for paper-and-pencil tests, (3) costs associated with Internet testing tend to be lower than costs associated with paper-and-pencil tests, and (4) the Internet facilitates the testing of otherwise isolated populations, as well as people with disabilities for whom getting to a test center might prove a hardship. We might add that Internet testing tends to be "greener," as it may conserve paper, shipping materials, and so forth. Further, there is probably less chance for scoring errors with Internet-based tests as compared to paper-and-pencil tests.

Although Internet testing appears to have many advantages, it is not without potential pitfalls, problems, and issues. One basic issue has to do with what Naglieri et al. (2008) termed "test-client integrity." In part this refers to the verification of the identity of the testtaker when a test is administered online. It also refers, in more general terms, to the sometimes varying interests of the testtaker versus that of the test administrator. Depending upon the conditions of the administration, testtakers may have unrestricted access to notes, other Internet resources, and other aids in test-taking—this despite the guidelines for the test administration. At least with regard to achievement tests, there is some evidence that unproctored Internet testing leads to "score inflation" as compared to more traditionally administered tests (Carstairs & Myors, 2009).

A related aspect of test-client integrity has to do with the procedure in place to ensure that the security of the Internet-administered test is not compromised. What will prevent other testtakers from previewing past—or even advance—copies of the test? Naglieri et al. (2008) reminded their readers of the distinction between testing and assessment, and the importance of recognizing that Internet testing is just that—*testing,* not assessment. As such, Internet test users should be aware of all of the possible limitations of the source of the test scores.

JUST THINK . . .

What cautions should Internet test users keep in mind regarding the source of their test data?

Other Tools

The next time you have occasion to stream a video, fire-up that Blu-ray player, or even break-out an old DVD, take a moment to consider the role that video can play in assessment. In fact, specially created videos are widely used in training and evaluation contexts. For example, corporate personnel may be asked to respond to a variety of video-presented incidents of sexual harassment in the workplace. Police personnel may be asked how they would respond to various types of emergencies, which are presented either as reenactments or as video recordings of actual occurrences. Psychotherapists may be asked to respond with a diagnosis and a treatment plan for each of several clients presented to them on video. The list of video's potential applications to assessment is endless. The next generation of video assessment is the assessment that employs virtual reality (VR) technology. Assessment using VR technology is fast finding its way into a number of psychological specialty areas (Morina et al., 2015; Sharkey & Merrick, 2016).

Many items that you may not readily associate with psychological assessment may be pressed into service for just that purpose. For example, psychologists may use many of the tools traditionally associated with medical health, such as thermometers to measure body temperature and gauges to measure blood pressure. Biofeedback equipment is sometimes used to obtain measures of bodily reactions (such as muscular tension) to various sorts of stimuli. And then there are some less common instruments, such as the penile plethysmograph. This instrument, designed to measure male sexual arousal, may be helpful in the diagnosis and treatment of sexual predators. Impaired ability to identify odors is common in many disorders in which there is central nervous system involvement, and simple tests of smell may be administered to help determine if such impairment is present. In general, there has been no shortage of innovation on the part of psychologists in devising measurement tools, or adapting existing tools, for use in psychological assessment.

JUST THINK . . .

When is assessment using video a better approach than using a paper-and-pencil test? What are the pitfalls, if any, to using video in assessment?

To this point, our introduction has focused on some basic definitions, as well as a look at some of the "tools of the (assessment) trade." We now raise some fundamental questions regarding the who, what, why, how, and where of testing and assessment.

Who, What, Why, How, and Where?

Who are the parties in the assessment enterprise? In what types of settings are assessments conducted? Why is assessment conducted? How are assessments conducted? Where does one go for authoritative information about tests? Think about the answer to each of these important questions before reading on. Then check your own ideas against those that follow.

Who Are the Parties?

Parties in the assessment enterprise include developers and publishers of tests, users of tests, and people who are evaluated by means of tests. Additionally, we may consider society at large as a party to the assessment enterprise.

The test developer   Test developers and publishers create tests or other methods of assessment. The American Psychological Association (APA) has estimated that more than 20,000 new psychological tests are developed each year. Among these new tests are some that were created for a specific research study, some that were created in the hope that they would be published, and some that represent refinements or modifications of existing tests. Test creators bring a wide array of backgrounds and interests to the test development process.[2]

Test developers and publishers appreciate the significant impact that test results can have on people's lives. Accordingly, a number of professional organizations have published standards of ethical behavior that specifically address aspects of responsible test development and use. Perhaps the most detailed document addressing such issues is one jointly written by the American Educational Research Association, the American Psychological Association, and the National Council on Measurement in Education (NCME). Referred to by many psychologists simply as "the Standards," *Standards for Educational and Psychological Testing* covers issues related to test construction and evaluation, test administration and use, and special applications of tests, such as special considerations when testing linguistic minorities. Initially published in 1954, revisions of the *Standards* were published in 1966, 1974, 1985, 1999, and 2014. The *Standards* is an indispensable reference work not only for test developers but for test users as well.

The test user   Psychological tests and assessment methodologies are used by a wide range of professionals, including clinicians, counselors, school psychologists, human resources personnel, consumer psychologists, experimental psychologists, and social psychologists. In fact, with respect to the job market, the demand for psychologists with measurement expertise far outweighs the supply (Dahlman & Geisinger, 2015). Still, questions remain as to who exactly is qualified to use psychological tests.

The *Standards* and other published guidelines from specialty professional organizations have had much to say in terms of identifying just who is a qualified test user and who should have access to (and be permitted to purchase) psychological tests and related tools of psychological assessment. Still, controversy exists about which professionals with what type of training should have access to which tests. Members of various professions, with little or no psychological training, have sought the right to obtain and use psychological tests. In many countries, no ethical or legal regulation of psychological test use exists (Leach & Oakland, 2007).

So who are (or should be) test users? Should occupational therapists, for example, be allowed to administer psychological tests? What about employers and human resources executives with no formal training in psychology?

So far, we've listed a number of controversial *Who?* questions that knowledgeable assessment professionals still debate. Fortunately, there is at least one *Who?* question about which there is very little debate: the one regarding who the testtaker or assessee is.

JUST THINK . . .

In addition to psychologists, who should be permitted access to, as well as the privilege of using, psychological tests?

The testtaker   We have all been testtakers. However, we have not all approached tests in the same way. On the day a test is to be administered, testtakers may vary with respect to numerous variables, including these:

- The amount of test anxiety they are experiencing and the degree to which that test anxiety might significantly affect their test results
- The extent to which they understand and agree with the rationale for the assessment

---

2. For an intriguing glimpse at biographical information on a sampling of test developers, navigate to the "Test Developer Profiles" section found in the Instructor Resources within Connect.

- Their capacity and willingness to cooperate with the examiner or to comprehend written test instructions

- The amount of physical pain or emotional distress they are experiencing

- The amount of physical discomfort brought on by not having had enough to eat, having had too much to eat, or other physical conditions

- The extent to which they are alert and wide awake as opposed to nodding off

- The extent to which they are predisposed to agree or disagree when presented with stimulus statements

- The extent to which they have received prior coaching

- The importance they may attribute to portraying themselves in a good (or bad) light

- The extent to which they are, for lack of a better term, "lucky" and can "beat the odds" on a multiple-choice achievement test (even though they may not have learned the subject matter).

In the broad sense in which we are using the term "testtaker," anyone who is the subject of an assessment or an evaluation can be a testtaker or an assessee. As amazing as it sounds, this means that even a deceased individual can be considered an assessee. True, this is the exception to the rule, but there is such a thing as a *psychological autopsy*. A **psychological autopsy** may be defined as a reconstruction of a deceased individual's psychological profile on the basis of archival records, artifacts, and interviews previously conducted with the deceased assessee or people who knew him or her. For example, using psychological autopsies, Townsend (2007) explored the question of whether suicide terrorists were indeed suicidal from a classical psychological perspective. She concluded that they were not. Other researchers have provided fascinating postmortem psychological evaluations of people from various walks of life in many different cultures (Bhatia et al., 2006; Chan et al., 2007; Dattilio, 2006; Fortune et al., 2007; Foster, 2011; Giner et al., 2007; Goldstein et al., 2008; Heller et al., 2007; Knoll & Hatters-Friedman, 2015; McGirr et al., 2007; Owens et al., 2008; Palacio et al., 2007; Phillips et al., 2007; Pouliot & DeLeo, 2006; Rouse et al., 2015; Sanchez, 2006; Thoresen et al., 2006; Vento et al., 2011; Zonda, 2006).

JUST THINK . . .

What recently deceased public figure would you like to see a psychological autopsy done on? Why? What results might you expect?

Society at large

> The uniqueness of individuals is one of the most fundamental characteristic facts of life. . . . At all periods of human history men have observed and described differences between individuals. . . . But educators, politicians, and administrators have felt a need for some way of organizing or systematizing the many-faceted complexity of individual differences. (Tyler, 1965, p. 3)

The societal need for "organizing" and "systematizing" has historically manifested itself in such varied questions as "Who is a witch?," "Who is schizophrenic?," and "Who is qualified?" The specific questions asked have shifted with societal concerns. The methods used to determine the answers have varied throughout history as a function of factors such as intellectual sophistication and religious preoccupation. Proponents of palmistry, podoscopy, astrology, and phrenology, among other pursuits, have argued that the best means of understanding and predicting human behavior was through the study of the palms of the hands, the feet, the stars, bumps on the head, tea leaves, and so on. Unlike such pursuits, the assessment enterprise has roots in science. Through systematic and replicable means that can produce compelling evidence, the assessment enterprise responds to what Tyler (1965, p. 3) described as society's demand for "some way of organizing or systematizing the many-faceted complexity of individual differences."

Society at large exerts its influence as a party to the assessment enterprise in many ways. As society evolves and as the need to measure different psychological variables emerges, test developers respond by devising new tests. Through elected representatives to the legislature, laws are enacted that govern aspects of test development, test administration, and test interpretation. Similarly, by means of court decisions, as well as less formal means (see Figure 1–4), society at large exerts its influence on various aspects of the testing and assessment enterprise.

Other parties Beyond the four primary parties we have focused on here, let's briefly make note of others who may participate in varied ways in the testing and assessment enterprise. Organizations, companies, and governmental agencies sponsor the development of tests for various reasons, such as to certify personnel. Companies and services offer test-scoring or interpretation services. In some cases these companies and services are simply extensions of test publishers, and in other cases they are independent. There are people whose sole responsibility is the marketing and sales of tests. Sometimes these people are employed by the test publisher; sometimes they are not. There are academicians who review tests and evaluate their psychometric soundness. All of these people, as well as many others, are parties to a greater or lesser extent in the assessment enterprise.

Having introduced you to some of the parties involved in the *Who?* of psychological testing and assessment, let's move on to tackle some of the *What?* and *Why?* questions.

In What Types of Settings Are Assessments Conducted, and Why?

Educational settings You are probably no stranger to the many types of tests administered in the classroom. As mandated by law, tests are administered early in school life to help identify children who may have special needs. In addition to school ability tests, another type of test commonly given in schools is an **achievement test,** which evaluates accomplishment or the degree of learning that has taken place. Some of the achievement tests you have taken in school were constructed by your teacher. Other achievement tests were constructed for more widespread use by educators working with measurement professionals. In the latter category, acronyms such as SAT and GRE may ring a bell.

Figure 1–4
Public Feedback Regarding an Educational Testing Program

In recent years there have been many public demonstrations against various educational testing programs. Strident voices have called for banishing such programs, or for parents to "opt out" of having their children tested. As you learn more about the art and science of testing, assessment, and measurement, you will no doubt develop an informed opinion about whether tests do more harm than good, or vice versa.
© Shutterstock RF

You know from your own experience that a **diagnosis** may be defined as a description or conclusion reached on the basis of evidence and opinion. Typically this conclusion is reached through a process of distinguishing the nature of something and ruling out alternative conclusions. Similarly, the term **diagnostic test** refers to a tool of assessment used to help narrow down and identify areas of deficit to be targeted for intervention. In educational settings, diagnostic tests of reading, mathematics, and other academic subjects may be administered to assess the need for educational intervention as well as to establish or rule out eligibility for special education programs.

Schoolchildren receive grades on their report cards that are not based on any formal assessment. For example, the grade next to "Works and plays well with others" is probably based more on the teacher's *informal evaluation* in the classroom than on scores on any published measure of social interaction. We may define **informal evaluation** as a typically nonsystematic assessment that leads to the formation of an opinion or attitude.

JUST THINK . . .

What tools of assessment could be used to evaluate a student's social skills?

Informal evaluation is, of course, not limited to educational settings; it is very much a part of everyday life. In fact, many of the tools of evaluation we have discussed in the context of educational settings (such as achievement tests, diagnostic tests, and informal evaluations) are also administered in various other settings. And some of the types of tests we discuss in the context of the settings described next are also administered in educational settings. So please keep in mind that the tools of evaluation and measurement techniques that we discuss in one context may well be used in other contexts. Our objective at this early stage in our survey of the field is simply to introduce a sampling (not a comprehensive list) of the types of tests used in different settings.

Clinical settings   Tests and many other tools of assessment are widely used in clinical settings such as public, private, and military hospitals, inpatient and outpatient clinics, private-practice consulting rooms, schools, and other institutions. These tools are used to help screen for or diagnose behavior problems. What types of situations might prompt the employment of such tools? Here's a small sample.

- A private psychotherapy client wishes to be evaluated to see if the assessment can provide any nonobvious clues regarding his maladjustment.

- A school psychologist clinically evaluates a child experiencing learning difficulties to determine what factors are primarily responsible for it.

- A psychotherapy researcher uses assessment procedures to determine if a particular method of psychotherapy is effective in treating a particular problem.

JUST THINK . . .

What kinds of issues do psychologists have to consider when assessing prisoners in contrast to assessing workplace managers?

- A psychologist-consultant retained by an insurance company is called on to give an opinion as to the reality of a client's psychological problems; is the client really experiencing such problems or just malingering?

- A court-appointed psychologist is asked to give an opinion as to a defendant's competency to stand trial.

- A prison psychologist is called on to give an opinion regarding the extent of a convicted violent prisoner's rehabilitation.

The tests employed in clinical settings may be intelligence tests, personality tests, neuropsychological tests, or other specialized instruments, depending on the presenting or suspected problem area. The hallmark of testing in clinical settings is that the test or measurement technique is employed with only one individual at a time. Group testing is used primarily for screening—that is, identifying those individuals who require further diagnostic evaluation.

Counseling settings   Assessment in a counseling context may occur in environments as diverse as schools, prisons, and governmental or privately owned institutions. Regardless of the particular tools used, the ultimate objective of many such assessments is the improvement of the assessee in terms of adjustment, productivity, or some related variable. Measures of social and academic skills and measures of personality, interest, attitudes, and values are among the many types of tests that a counselor might administer to a client. Referral questions to be answered range from "How can this child better focus on tasks?" to "For what career is the client best suited?" to "What activities are recommended for retirement?" Having mentioned retirement, let's hasten to introduce another type of setting in which psychological tests are used extensively.

Geriatric settings   In the United States, more than 12 million adults are currently in the age range of 75 to 84; this is about 16 times more people in this age range than there were in 1900. Four million adults in the United States are currently 85 years old or older, which is a 33-fold increase in the number of people of that age since 1900. People in the United States are living longer, and the population as a whole is getting older.

Older Americans may live at home, in special housing designed for independent living, in housing designed for assisted living, or in long-term care facilities such as hospitals and hospices. Wherever older individuals reside, they may at some point require psychological assessment to evaluate cognitive, psychological, adaptive, or other functioning. At issue in many such assessments is the extent to which assessees are enjoying as good a *quality of life* as possible. The definition of quality of life has varied as a function of perspective in different studies. In some research, for example, quality of life is defined from the perspective of an observer; in other research it is defined from the perspective of assessees themselves and refers to an individual's own self-report regarding lifestyle-related variables.

JUST THINK . . .

Tests are used in geriatric, counseling, and other settings to help improve quality of life. But are there some aspects of quality of life that a psychological test just can't measure?

However defined, what is typically assessed in **quality of life** evaluations are variables related to perceived stress, loneliness, sources of satisfaction, personal values, quality of living conditions, and quality of friendships and other social support.

Generally speaking, from a clinical perspective, the assessment of older adults is more likely to include screening for cognitive decline and *dementia* than the assessment of younger adults (Gallo & Bogner, 2006; Gallo & Wittink, 2006). **Dementia** is a loss of cognitive functioning (which may affect memory, thinking, reasoning, psychomotor speed, attention, and related abilities, as well as personality) that occurs as the result of damage to or loss of brain cells. Perhaps the best known of the many forms of dementia that exist is Alzheimer's disease. The road to diagnosis by the clinician is complicated by the fact that severe depression in the elderly can contribute to cognitive functioning that mimics dementia, a condition referred to as **pseudodementia** (Madden et al., 1952). It is also true that the majority of individuals suffering from dementia exhibit depressive symptoms (Strober & Arnett, 2009). Clinicians rely on a variety of different tools of assessment to make a diagnosis of dementia or pseudodementia.

Business and military settings   In business, as in the military, various tools of assessment are used in sundry ways, perhaps most notably in decision making about the careers of personnel. A wide range of achievement, aptitude, interest, motivational, and other tests may be employed in the decision to hire as well as in related decisions regarding promotions, transfer, job satisfaction, and eligibility for further training. For a prospective air traffic controller, successful performance on a test of sustained attention to detail may be one requirement of employment. For promotion to the rank of officer in the military, successful performance on a series of leadership tasks may be essential.

Another application of psychological tests involves the engineering and design of products and environments. Engineering psychologists employ a variety of existing and specially devised tests in research designed to help people at home, in the workplace, and in the military. Products ranging from home computers to office furniture to jet cockpit control panels benefit from the work of such research efforts.

Using tests, interviews, and other tools of assessment, psychologists who specialize in the marketing and sale of products are involved in taking the pulse of consumers. They help corporations predict the public's receptivity to a new product, a new brand, or a new advertising or marketing campaign. Psychologists working in the area of marketing help "diagnose" what is wrong (and right) about brands, products, and campaigns. On the basis of such assessments, these psychologists might make recommendations regarding how new brands and products can be made appealing to consumers, and when it is time for older brands and products to be retired or revitalized.

JUST THINK . . .

Assume the role of a consumer psychologist. What ad campaign do you find particularly effective in terms of pushing consumer "buy" buttons? What ad campaign do you find particularly ineffective in this regard? Why?

Have you ever wondered about the variety of assessments conducted by a psychologist in the military? In this chapter's *Meet an Assessment Professional* (MAP) feature, we meet U.S. Air Force psychologist, Lt. Col. Alan Ogle, Ph.D., and learn about his wide range of professional duties. Note that each chapter of this book contains a "MAP" feature allowing readers unprecedented access to the "real world life" of a mental health professional who uses psychological tests and other tools of psychological assessment. Each of the featured assessment professionals were asked to write a brief essay in which they shared a thoughtful and educational perspective on their assessment-related activities.

Governmental and organizational credentialing   One of the many applications of measurement is in governmental licensing, certification, or general credentialing of professionals. Before they are legally entitled to practice medicine, physicians must pass an examination. Law school graduates cannot present themselves to the public as attorneys until they pass their state's bar examination. Psychologists, too, must pass an examination before adopting the official title "psychologist."

Members of some professions have formed organizations with requirements for membership that go beyond those of licensing or certification. For example, physicians can take further specialized training and a specialty examination to earn the distinction of being "board certified" in a particular area of medicine. Psychologists specializing in certain areas may be evaluated for a diploma from the American Board of Professional Psychology (ABPP) to recognize excellence in the practice of psychology. Another organization, the American Board of Assessment Psychology (ABAP), awards its diploma on the basis of an examination to test users, test developers, and others who have distinguished themselves in the field of testing and assessment.

Academic research settings   Conducting any sort of research typically entails measurement of some kind, and any academician who ever hopes to publish research should ideally have a sound knowledge of measurement principles and tools of assessment. To emphasize this simple fact of research life, imagine the limitless number of questions that psychological researchers could conceivably raise, and the tools and methodologies that might be used to find answers to those questions. For example, Thrash et al. (2010) wondered about the role of inspiration in the writing process. Herbranson and Schroeder (2010) raised the question "Are pigeons smarter than mathematicians?" Milling et al. (2010) asked whether one's level of hypnotizability predicts responses to pain-lessening hypnotic suggestions. Angie et al. (2011) explored whether the potential for violence of an ideological group can be assessed by studying the group's website.

JUST THINK . . .

What research question would *you* like to see researched? What tools of assessment might be used in that research?

Other settings   Many different kinds of measurement procedures find application in a wide variety of settings. For example, the

Meet Dr. Alan Ogle

arrived at my first duty station on 8th September, 2001, having completed doctoral training at a civilian university followed by an internship at Wright-Patterson Air Force Medical Center. An amazing, challenging, and rewarding career has ensued, with assignments at various bases in the United States, the United Kingdom, and Afghanistan.

As a clinical psychologist for the Air Force, I provide assessment and treatment to military personnel and their families, as well as consultation to military commanders regarding psychological health, substance abuse prevention, and combat and operational stress control. A postdoctoral fellowship and additional military coursework has qualified me to also support various other military activities such as high-risk survival, evasion, resistance, and escape (SERE) training, reintegration support services for military and civilians returning from isolation or captivity, human performance optimization, and the evaluation and selection of personnel for special assignments.

The use of clinical assessment measures in the military is comparable to civilian practice. Commonly used measures include brief symptom screeners (such as the Patient Health Questionnaire-9 and the Generalized Anxiety Disorder scale-7). We also administer, as indicated, measures of personality and cognitive functioning (such as the current versions of the MMPI and Wechsler tests) to identify treatment needs, monitor progress, and/or assess fitness for military service.

Unlike many other military selection assignments, assessment of military personnel for special missions may entail both "select-in" as well as "select-out" options. Here, the tools of assessment are used to identify psychological or psychosocial concerns that would indicate risk to job candidates (or their families) if selected for a challenging assignment as well as to identify areas that might make a challenging assignment as well as to identify areas that might make a candidate a liability to a mission. Beyond helping to "select out" candidates deemed to be at risk, psychologists assist in helping to "select in" candidates deemed to be the best for a particular unit and mission. Here, the "best fit" would be those

Alan Ogle, Ph.D., Lieutenant Colonel, US Air Force
© Alan Ogle

candidates who not only are free of vulnerabilities in psychological health and psychosocial circumstances that might impair performance and possess the requisite qualifications but also excel in job-relevant skills and characteristics for success in a specific unit and mission set.

One example of psychological assessment for a special duty is the program developed and utilized for selection of Military Training Instructors (MTIs) for USAF Basic Military Training (BMT). Called drill instructors or drill sergeants in other services, these are noncommissioned officers (NCOs) with seven or more years of service in their primary career field (e.g., aircraft maintenance, security forces, intelligence) selected for this special duty assignment. This is a position of challenge and tremendous trust, tasked with engaging and transforming young civilian volunteers from diverse backgrounds and motivations through a highly intensive training regimen into capable military members. Training can devolve dangerously when not well managed by the instructor—intense training coupled with the power differential between MTI and recruits may lead to errors in decision making, overly affective responses, maltreatment, or maltraining. Assigning the right instructors, those best skilled and suited for this special duty, is paramount to the success and safety of the training.

I had the opportunity to serve on a working group of psychologists to develop an empirically derived, standardized psychological screening protocol of candidates for entry into MTI duty. Job analytic studies were conducted to identify knowledge, skills, abilities, and other characteristics (KSAOs) important to serving successfully in MTI duty, with emphasis on both identification of factors important to safe, effective performance, as well as potential "red flag" warning signs for this position of trust and power over a vulnerable population of trainees. An assessment protocol was developed including an interview by a mental health provider meeting with the MTI candidate and their significant other (if partnered). With awareness that a large body of research indicates clinicians are at risk to overestimate clinical judgment's accuracy for predicting behavior and job success, the interview is structured by behaviorally anchored rating scales for each of the job-critical areas. Ratings for the domain of judgment/self-control, for instance, include consideration of history of childhood delinquency behaviors (such as skipping school, or fighting), adult discipline and legal issues, and interview questions such as "What are some choices or mistakes that you particularly regret?" Assessment of Family Stability/ Support includes interview of the candidate and partner regarding questions such as "What would be the most challenging changes for your family in this assignment?" Cognitive screening is required and a brief screening tool is used for time efficiency.

An additional component of the assessment protocol we developed is the Multidimensional 360 Assessment (MD360), which collects input from a candidate's coworkers regarding MTI-relevant work performance behaviors and potential "red flags." As examples, subordinates, peers, and supervisors provide ratings about the candidate on items such as, "Remains focused, on task, and decisive in stressful situations," "Leads others in a fair and consistent manner," and, "Avoids inappropriate personal relationships (such as flirting or fraternization)." Responses are confidential and not released to the candidate or other coworkers.

There is also a component of the MD360 completed by the candidate that includes self-assessment of relevant skills, personality and attitude scales, and a situational judgment test developed specific to types of challenges faced in MTI duty. A concurrent validation study of the self-assessment measures found significant relationships of several attitudes to performance in leadership, mentorship, and risk for maltreatment by MTIs. Based on results of the interview and MD360, a recommendation is made regarding strengths and any concerns regarding suitability for MTI duty, including nonrecommend (select out) as well as recommend with sufficient characterization of skills for prioritization of candidates.

At least equally important to "getting the right people" are efforts to sufficiently train, supervise, and support MTIs through their challenging duties. A team titled the USAF BMT Military Training Consult Service was established, providing ongoing assessment and support to serving MTIs, as well as training in appropriate use of stress inoculation training of recruits. Additionally, training and command consultation is provided to mitigate risks of behavioral drift inherent to the positional power dynamics of the instructor–recruit relationship. The goal is to support safe, effective training of new military members as well as excellence in instructor staff.

Students considering service in the military are encouraged to research opportunities, either in uniform or civilian positions. The US Air Force, Army, and Navy each offer APA-approved internships at multiple sites, for those meeting medical and other requirements, then requiring completion of one assignment. I have been honored to remain in service beyond the initial obligation, thoroughly enjoying the opportunities for training, broad responsibilities from early on in my psychology career, and service with national purpose.

Used with permission of Alan Ogle.

courts rely on psychological test data and related expert testimony as one source of information to help answer important questions such as "Is this defendant competent to stand trial?" and "Did this defendant know right from wrong at the time the criminal act was committed?"

Measurement may play an important part in program evaluation, whether it is a large-scale government program or a small-scale, privately funded one. Is the program working? How can the program be improved? Are funds being spent in the areas where they ought to be spent? How sound is the theory on which the program is based? These are the types of general questions that tests and measurement procedures used in program evaluation are designed to answer.

Tools of assessment can be found in use in research and practice in every specialty area within psychology. For example, consider **health psychology,** a discipline that focuses on understanding the role of psychological variables in the onset, course, treatment, and prevention of illness, disease, and disability (Cohen, 1994). Health psychologists are involved in teaching, research, or direct-service activities designed to promote good health. Individual interviews, surveys, and paper-and-pencil tests are some of the tools that may be employed to help assess current status with regard to some disease or condition, gauge treatment progress, and evaluate outcome of intervention. One general line of research in health psychology focuses on aspects of personality, behavior, or lifestyle as they relate to physical health. The methodology employed may entail reporting on measurable respondent variables as they change in response to some intervention, such as education, therapy, counseling, change in diet, or change in habits. Measurement tools may be used to compare one naturally occurring group of research subjects to another such group (such as smokers compared to nonsmokers) with regard to some other health-related variable (such as longevity). Many of the questions raised in health-related research have real, life-and-death consequences. All of these important questions, like the questions raised in other areas of psychology, require that sound techniques of evaluation be employed.

How Are Assessments Conducted?

If a need exists to measure a particular variable, a way to measure that variable will be devised. As Figure 1–5 just begins to illustrate, the ways in which measurements can be taken are limited only by imagination. Keep in mind that this figure illustrates only a small sample of the many methods used in psychological testing and assessment. The photos are not designed to illustrate the most typical kinds of assessment procedures. Rather, their purpose is to call attention to the wide range of measuring tools that have been created for varied uses.

Responsible test users have obligations before, during, and after a test or any measurement procedure is administered. For purposes of illustration, consider the administration of a paper-and-pencil test. Before the test, ethical guidelines dictate that when test users have discretion with regard to the tests administered, they should select and use only the test or tests that are most appropriate for the individual being tested. Before a test is administered, the test should be stored in a way that reasonably ensures that its specific contents will not be made known to the testtaker in advance. Another obligation of the test user before the test's administration is to ensure that a prepared and suitably trained person administers the test properly.

The test administrator (or examiner) must be familiar with the test materials and procedures and must have at the test site all the materials needed to properly administer the test. Materials needed might include a stopwatch, a supply of pencils, and a sufficient number of test *protocols.* By the way, in everyday, non-test-related conversation, *protocol* refers to diplomatic etiquette. A less common use of the word is a synonym for the first copy or rough draft of a treaty or other official document before its ratification. With reference to testing and assessment, **protocol** typically refers to the form or sheet or booklet on which a testtaker's responses are entered. The term may also be used to refer to a description of a set of test- or assessment-related procedures, as in the sentence "The examiner dutifully followed the complete protocol for the stress interview."

Test users have the responsibility of ensuring that the room in which the test will be conducted is suitable and conducive to the testing. To the extent possible, distracting conditions such as excessive noise, heat, cold, interruptions, glaring sunlight, crowding, inadequate ventilation, and so forth should be avoided. Of course, creating an ideal testing environment is not always something every examiner can do (see Figure 1–6).

During test administration, and especially in one-on-one or small-group testing, *rapport* between the examiner and the examinee can be critically important. In this context, **rapport** may be defined as a working relationship between the examiner and the examinee. Such a working relationship can sometimes be achieved with a few words of small talk when examiner

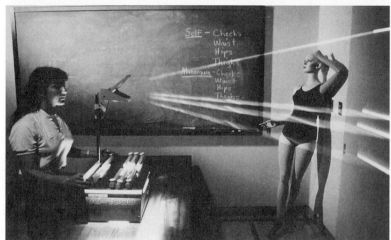

At least since the beginning of the nineteenth century, military units throughout the world have relied on psychological and other tests for personnel selection, program validation, and related reasons (Hartmann et al., 2003). In some cultures where military service is highly valued, students take preparatory courses with hopes of being accepted into elite military units. This is the case in Israel, where rigorous training such as that pictured here prepares high-school students for physical and related tests that only 1 in 60 military recruits will pass.
© Gil Cohen-Magen/AFP/Getty Images

Evidence suggests that some people with eating disorders may actually have a self-perception disorder; that is, they see themselves as heavier than they really are (Thompson & Smolak, 2001). J. Kevin Thompson and his associates devised the adjustable light-beam apparatus to measure body image distortion. Assessees adjust four beams of light to indicate what they believe is the width of their cheeks, waist, hips, and thighs. A measure of accuracy of these estimates is then obtained.
© Joel Thompson

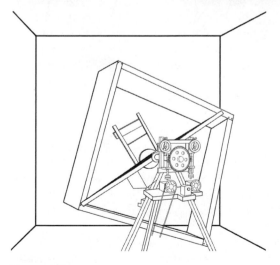

Herman Witkin and his associates (Witkin & Goodenough, 1977) studied personality-related variables in some innovative ways. For example, they identified field (or context)-dependent and field-independent people by means of this specially constructed tilting room–tilting chair device. Assessees were asked questions designed to evaluate their dependence on or independence of visual cues.

Figure 1–5
The Wide World of Measurement

Pictures such as these sample items from the Meier Art Judgment Test might be used to evaluate people's aesthetic perception. Which of these two renderings do you find more aesthetically pleasing? The difference between the two pictures involves the positioning of the objects on the shelf.
© Norman C. Meier Papers, University of Iowa Libraries, Iowa City, Iowa

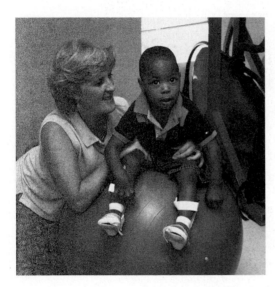

Impairment of certain sensory functions can indicate neurological deficit. For purposes of diagnosis, as well as measuring progress in remediation, the neurodevelopment training ball can be useful in evaluating one's sense of balance.
© Fotosearch/Getty Images RF

Some college admissions officers are evaluating the notebook doodles of applicants in their search for "authentic and imperfect" (as opposed to "ideal") candidates for admission (Gray, 2016). As a result, profiles created on social media platforms such as ZeeMee may increasingly be used by applicants to convey "a side of themselves that might not come through in the typical mix of transcripts, essays and teacher recommendations" (Gray, 2016, p. 48).

Figure 1–6
Less-Than-Optimal Testing Conditions

In 1917, new Army recruits sat on the floor as they were administered the first group tests of intelligence—not ideal testing conditions by current standards.
© Time Life Pictures/US Signal Corps/The LIFE Picture Collection/Getty Images

and examinee are introduced. If appropriate, some words about the nature of the test and why it is important for examinees to do their best may also be helpful. In other instances—for example, with a frightened child—the achievement of rapport might involve more elaborate techniques such as engaging the child in play or some other activity until the child has acclimated to the examiner and the surroundings. It is important that attempts to establish rapport with the testtaker not compromise any rules of the test administration instructions.

After a test administration, test users have many obligations as well. These obligations range from safeguarding the test protocols to conveying the test results in a clearly understandable fashion. If third parties were present during testing or if anything else that might be considered out of the ordinary happened during testing, it is the test user's responsibility to make a note of such events on the report of the testing. Test scorers have obligations as well. For example, if a test is to be scored by people, scoring needs to conform to pre-established scoring criteria. Test users who have responsibility for interpreting scores or other test results have an obligation to do so in accordance with established procedures and ethical guidelines.

JUST THINK . . .

What unforeseen incidents could conceivably occur during a test session? Should such incidents be noted on the report of that session?

Assessment of people with disabilities   People with disabilities are assessed for exactly the same reasons people with no disabilities are assessed: to obtain employment, to earn a professional credential, to be screened for psychopathology, and so forth. A number of laws have been enacted that affect the conditions under which tests are administered to people with disabling conditions. For example, one law mandates the development and implementation of "alternate assessment" programs for children who, as a result of a disability, could not otherwise participate in state- and district-wide assessments. Defining exactly what "alternate assessment" meant was left to the individual states or their local school districts. These authorities define who requires alternate assessment, how such assessments are to be conducted, and how meaningful inferences are to be drawn from the assessment data.

In general, alternate assessment is typically accomplished by means of some *accommodation* made to the assessee. The verb *to accommodate* may be defined as "to adapt, adjust, or make suitable." In the context of psychological testing and assessment, **accommodation** may be defined as the adaptation of a test, procedure, or situation, or the substitution of one test for another, to make the assessment more suitable for an assessee with exceptional needs.

At first blush, the process of accommodating students, employees, or other testtakers with special needs might seem straightforward. For example, the individual who has difficulty reading the small print of a particular test may be accommodated with a large-print version of the same test or with a specially lit test environment. A student with a hearing impairment may be administered the test in sign language. An individual with ADHD might have an extended evaluation time, with frequent breaks during periods of evaluation. Although this may all seem simple at first, it can actually become quite complicated.

Consider, for example, the case of a student with a visual impairment who is scheduled to be given a written, multiple-choice test. There are several possible alternate procedures for test administration. For example, the test could be translated into Braille and administered in that form, or the test could be administered by means of audiotape. However, some students may do better with a Braille administration and others with audiotape. Students with superior short-term attention and memory skills for auditory stimuli would seem to have an advantage with the audiotaped administration. Students with superior haptic (sense of touch) and perceptual-motor skills might have an advantage with the Braille administration. And so, even in this relatively simple example, it can be readily appreciated that a testtaker's performance (and score) on a test may be affected by the manner of the alternate administration of the test. This reality of alternate assessment raises important questions about how equivalent such methods really are. Indeed, because the alternate procedures have been individually tailored, there is seldom compelling research to support equivalence. Governmental guidelines for alternate assessment will evolve to include ways of translating measurement procedures from one format to another. Other guidelines may suggest substituting one assessment tool for another. Currently there are many ways to accommodate people with disabilities in an assessment situation (see this chapter's *Everyday Psychometrics*), and many different definitions of *alternate assessment.* For the record, we offer our own, general definition of that elusive term. **Alternate assessment** is *an evaluative or diagnostic procedure or process that varies from the usual, customary, or standardized way a measurement is derived, either by virtue of some special accommodation made to the assessee or by means of alternative methods designed to measure the same variable(s).*

◆
JUST THINK . . .

Are there some types of assessments for which no alternate assessment procedure should be developed?

Having considered some of the *who, what, how,* and *why* of assessment, let's now consider sources for more information with regard to all aspects of the assessment enterprise.

Where to Go for Authoritative Information: Reference Sources

Many reference sources exist for learning more about published tests and assessment-related issues. These sources vary with respect to detail. Some merely provide descriptions of tests, others provide detailed information on technical aspects, and still others provide critical reviews complete with discussion of the pros and cons of usage.

Test catalogues Perhaps one of the most readily accessible sources of information is a catalogue distributed by the publisher of the test. Because most test publishers make available

Everyday Accommodations

It has been estimated that as many as one in seven Americans has a disability that interferes with activities of daily living. In recent years society has acknowledged more than ever before the special needs of citizens challenged by physical and/or mental disabilities. The effects of this ever-increasing acknowledgment are visibly evident: special access ramps alongside flights of stairs, captioned television programming for the hearing-impaired, and large-print newspapers, books, magazines, and size-adjustable online media for the visually impaired. In general, there has been a trend toward altering environments to make individuals with handicapping conditions feel less challenged.

Depending on the nature of a testtaker's disability and other factors, modifications—referred to as accommodations—may need to be made in a psychological test (or measurement procedure) in order for an evaluation to proceed. Accommodation may take many different forms. One general type of accommodation involves the form of the test as presented to the testtaker, as when a written test is set in larger type for presentation to a visually impaired testtaker. Another general type of accommodation concerns the way responses to the test are obtained. For example, a speech-impaired individual might be allowed to write out responses in an examination that would otherwise be administered orally. Students with learning disabilities may be accommodated by being permitted to read test questions aloud (Fuchs et al., 2000).

Modification of the physical environment in which a test is conducted is yet another general type of accommodation. For example, a test that is usually group-administered at a central location may on occasion be administered individually to a disabled person in his or her home. Modifications of the interpersonal environment in which a test is conducted is another possibility (see Figure 1).

Which of many different types of accommodation should be employed? An answer to this question is typically approached by consideration of at least four variables:

1. the capabilities of the assessee;
2. the purpose of the assessment;
3. the meaning attached to test scores; and
4. the capabilities of the assessor.

The Capabilities of the Assessee

Which of several alternate means of assessment is best tailored to the needs and capabilities of the assessee? Case history data, records of prior assessments, and interviews with friends, family,

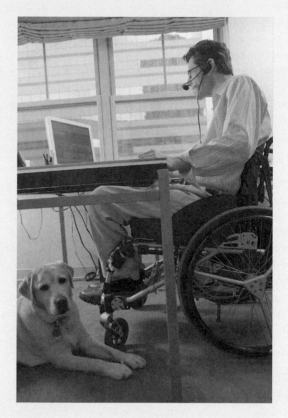

Figure 1
Modification of the Interpersonal Environment

An individual testtaker who requires the aid of a helper or service dog may require the presence of a third party (or animal) if a particular test is to be administered. In some cases, because of the nature of the testtaker's disability and the demands of a partic ular test, a more suitable test might have to be substituted for the test usually given if a meaningful evaluation is to be conducted.
© Huntstock/Getty Images

teachers, and others who know the assessee all can provide a wealth of useful information concerning which of several alternate means of assessment is most suitable.

The Purpose of the Assessment

Accommodation is appropriate under some circumstances and inappropriate under others. In general one looks to the purpose of the assessment and the consequences of the accommodation in order to judge the appropriateness of modifying a test to accommodate a person with a disability. For example, modifying

(continued)

Everyday Accommodations *(continued)*

a written driving test—or a road test—so a blind person could be tested for a driver's license is clearly inappropriate. For their own as well as the public's safety, the blind are prohibited from driving automobiles. On the other hand, changing the form of most other written tests so that a blind person could take them is another matter entirely. In general, accommodation is simply a way of being true to a social policy that promotes and guarantees equal opportunity and treatment for all citizens.

The Meaning Attached to Test Scores

What happens to the meaning of a score on a test when that test has not been administered in the manner that it was designed to be? More often than not, when test administration instructions are modified (some would say "compromised"), the meaning of scores on that test becomes questionable at best. Test users are left to their own devices in interpreting such data. Professional judgment, expertise, and, quite frankly, guesswork can all enter into the process of drawing inferences from scores on modified tests. Of course, a precise record of just how a test was modified for accommodation purposes should be made on the test report.

The Capabilities of the Assessor

Although most persons charged with the responsibility of assessment would like to think that they can administer an assessment professionally to almost anyone, this is actually not the case. It is important to acknowledge that some assessors may experience a level of discomfort in the presence of people with particular disabilities, and this discomfort may affect their evaluation. It is also important to acknowledge that some assessors may require additional training prior to conducting certain assessments, including supervised experience with members of certain populations. Alternatively, the assessor may refer such assessment assignments to another assessor who has had more training and experience with members of a particular population.

A burgeoning scholarly literature has focused on various aspects of accommodation, including issues related to general policies (Burns, 1998; Nehring, 2007; Shriner, 2000; Simpson et al., 1999), method of test administration (Calhoon et al., 2000; Danford & Steinfeld, 1999), score comparability (Elliott et al., 2001; Johnson, 2000; Pomplun & Omar, 2000, 2001), documentation (Schulte et al., 2000), and the motivation of testtakers to request accommodation (Baldridge & Veiga, 2006). Before a decision about accommodation is made for any individual testtaker, due consideration must be given to issues regarding the meaning of scores derived from modified instruments and the validity of the inferences that can be made from the data derived (Guthmann et al., 2012; Reesman et al., 2014; Toner et al., 2012).

---

catalogues of their offerings, this source of test information can be tapped by a simple telephone call, e-mail, or note. As you might expect, however, publishers' catalogues usually contain only a brief description of the test and seldom contain the kind of detailed technical information that a prospective user might require. Moreover, the catalogue's objective is to sell the test. For this reason, highly critical reviews of a test are seldom, if ever, found in a publisher's test catalogue.

Test manuals Detailed information concerning the development of a particular test and technical information relating to it should be found in the test manual, which usually can be purchased from the test publisher. However, for security purposes the test publisher will typically require documentation of professional training before filling an order for a test manual. The chances are good that your university maintains a collection of popular test manuals, perhaps in the library or counseling center. If the test manual you seek is not available there, ask your instructor how best to obtain a reference copy. In surveying the various test manuals, you are likely to see that they vary not only in the details of how the tests were developed and deemed psychometrically sound but also in the candor with which they describe their own test's limitations.

Professional books Many books written for an audience of assessment professionals are available to supplement, re-organize, or enhance the information typically found in the manual of a very widely used psychological test. So, for example, a book that focuses on a particular test may contain useful information about the content and structure of the test, and how and why that content and structure is superior to a previous version or edition of the test. The book might shed new light on how or why the test may be used for a particular assessment purpose, or administered to members of some special population. The book might provide helpful guidelines for planning a pre-test interview with a particular assessee, or for drawing conclusions from, and making inferences about, the data derived from the test. The book may alert potential users of the test to common errors in test administration, scoring, or interpretation, or to well-documented cautions regarding the use of the test with members of specific cultural groups. In sum, books devoted to an in-depth discussion of a particular test can systematically provide students of assessment, as well as assessment professionals, with the thoughtful insights and actionable knowledge of more experienced practitioners and test users.

Reference volumes   The Buros Center for Testing provides "one-stop shopping" for a great deal of test-related information. The initial version of what would evolve into the *Mental Measurements Yearbook* series was compiled by Oscar Buros in 1938. This authoritative compilation of test reviews is currently updated about every three years. The Buros Center also publishes *Tests in Print,* which lists all commercially available English-language tests in print. This volume, which is also updated periodically, provides detailed information for each test listed, including test publisher, test author, test purpose, intended test population, and test administration time.

Journal articles   Articles in current journals may contain reviews of the test, updated or independent studies of its psychometric soundness, or examples of how the instrument was used in either research or an applied context. Such articles may appear in a wide array of behavioral science journals, such as *Psychological Bulletin, Psychological Review, Professional Psychology: Research and Practice, Journal of Personality and Social Psychology, Psychology & Marketing, Psychology in the Schools, School Psychology Quarterly,* and *School Psychology Review.* There are also journals that focus more specifically on matters related to testing and assessment. For example, take a look at journals such as the *Journal of Psychoeducational Assessment, Psychological Assessment, Educational and Psychological Measurement, Applied Measurement in Education,* and the *Journal of Personality Assessment.* Journals such as *Psychology, Public Policy, and Law* and *Law and Human Behavior* frequently contain highly informative articles on legal and ethical issues and controversies as they relate to psychological testing and assessment. Journals such as *Computers & Education, Computers in Human Behavior,* and *Cyberpsychology, Behavior, and Social Networking* frequently contain insightful articles on computer and Internet-related measurement.

Online databases   One of the most widely used bibliographic databases for test-related publications is that maintained by the Educational Resources Information Center (ERIC). Funded by the U.S. Department of Education and operated out of the University of Maryland, the ERIC website at *www.eric.ed.gov* contains a wealth of resources and news about tests, testing, and assessment. There are abstracts of articles, original articles, and links to other useful websites. ERIC strives to provide balanced information concerning educational assessment and to provide resources that encourage responsible test use.

The American Psychological Association (APA) maintains a number of databases useful in locating psychology-related information in journal articles, book chapters, and doctoral dissertations. PsycINFO is a database of abstracts dating back to 1887. ClinPSYC is a database derived from PsycINFO that focuses on abstracts of a clinical nature. PsycSCAN: Psychopharmacology contains abstracts of articles concerning psychopharmacology. PsycARTICLES is a database of full-length articles dating back to 1894. Health and Psychosocial Instruments (HAPI) contains a listing of measures created or modified for specific research studies but not commercially available; it is available at many college libraries through BRS Information Technologies and also on CD-ROM (updated twice a year). PsycLAW is a free database, available to everyone, that contains discussions of selected topics involving psychology and law. It can be accessed at *www.apa.org/psyclaw.* For more information on any of these databases, visit APA's website at *www.apa.org.*

The world's largest private measurement institution is Educational Testing Service (ETS). This company, based in Princeton, New Jersey, maintains a staff of some 2,500 people, including about 1,000 measurement professionals and education specialists. These are the folks who bring you the Scholastic Aptitude Test (SAT) and the Graduate Record Exam (GRE), among many other tests. Descriptions of these and the many other tests developed by this company can be found at their website, *www.ets.org*.

Other sources   A source for exploring the world of unpublished tests and measures is the *Directory of Unpublished Experimental Mental Measures* (Goldman & Mitchell, 2008). Also, as a service to psychologists and other test users, ETS maintains a list of unpublished tests. This list can be accessed at *http://www.ets.org/testcoll/*. Some pros and cons of the various sources of information we have listed are summarized in Table 1–3.

Table 1–3
Sources of Information About Tests: Some Pros and Cons

Information Source	Pros	Cons
Test catalogue available from the publisher of the test as well as affiliated distributors of the test	Contains general description of test, including what it is designed to do and who it is designed to be used with. Readily available to most anyone who requests a catalogue.	Primarily designed to sell the test to test users and seldom contains any critical reviews. Information not detailed enough for basing a decision to use the test.
Test manual	Usually the most detailed source available for information regarding the standardization sample and test administration instructions. May also contain useful information regarding the theory the test is based on, if that is the case. Typically contains at least some information regarding psychometric soundness of the test.	Details regarding the test's psychometric soundness are usually self-serving and written on the basis of studies conducted by the test author and/or test publisher. A test manual itself may be difficult for students to obtain, as its distribution may be restricted to qualified professionals.
Professional books	May contain one-of-a-kind, authoritative insights of a highly experienced assessment professional regarding the structure and content of the test, as well as more practical insights regarding the administration, scoring, and interpretation of the test.	Be on the lookout for a professional book author who is strongly allied with a unique theoretical perspective with regard to the test. Although useful to know, this theoretical perspective may not be widely accepted. Also, caution is advised when an author expresses strong but idiosyncratic views about the value of a test (or its lack thereof) with assessees who are members of a particular cultural group.
Reference volumes such as the *Mental Measurements Yearbook,* available in bound book form or online	Much like *Consumer Reports* for tests, contain descriptions and critical reviews of a test written by third parties who presumably have nothing to gain or lose by praising or criticizing the instrument, its standardization sample, and its psychometric soundness.	Few disadvantages if reviewer is genuinely trying to be objective and is knowledgeable, but as with any review, can provide a misleading picture if this is not the case. Also, for very detailed accounts of the standardization sample and related matters, it is best to consult the test manual itself.
Journal articles	Up-to-date source of reviews and studies of psychometric soundness. Can provide practical examples of how an instrument is used in research or applied contexts.	As with reference volumes, reviews are valuable to the extent that they are informed and, as far as possible, unbiased. Reader should research as many articles as possible when attempting to learn how the instrument is actually used; any one article alone may provide an atypical picture.
Online databases	Widely known and respected online databases such as the ERIC database are virtual "gold mines" of useful information containing varying amounts of detail. Although some legitimate psychological tests may be available for self-administration and scoring online, the vast majority are not.	Consumer beware! Some sites masquerading as databases for psychological tests are designed more to entertain or to sell something than to inform. These sites frequently offer tests you can take online. As you learn more about tests, you will probably become more critical of the value of these self-administered and self-scored "psychological tests."

Many university libraries also provide access to online databases, such as PsycINFO, and electronic journals. Most scientific papers can be downloaded straight to one's computer using such an online service. This is an extremely valuable resource to students, as non-subscribers to such databases may be charged hefty access fees for such access.

Armed with a wealth of background information about tests and other tools of assessment, we'll explore historical, cultural, and legal/ethical aspects of the assessment enterprise in the following chapter.

Self-Assessment

Test your understanding of elements of this chapter by seeing if you can explain each of the following terms, expressions, and abbreviations:

accommodation
achievement test
alternate assessment
behavioral observation
CAPA
case history
case history data
case study
central processing
collaborative psychological
   assessment
consultative report
cut score
dementia
diagnosis
diagnostic test
dynamic assessment
ecological momentary assessment
educational assessment
extended scoring report
format

groupthink
health psychology
informal evaluation
integrative report
interpretive report
interview
local processing
motivational interviewing
naturalistic observation
panel interview
portfolio
protocol
pseudodementia
psychological assessment
psychological autopsy
psychological test
psychological testing
psychometrician
psychometrics
psychometric soundness
psychometrist

Q-Interactive
quality of life
rapport
remote assessment
retrospective assessment
role play
role-play test
score
scoring
scoring report
simple scoring report
social facilitation
teleprocessing
test
test catalogue
test developer
test manual
testtaker
test user
therapeutic psychological assessment
utility

2

Historical, Cultural, and Legal/Ethical Considerations

We continue our broad overview of the field of psychological testing and assessment with a look backward, the better to appreciate the historical context of the enterprise. We also present "food for thought" regarding cultural and legal/ethical matters. Consider this presentation only as an appetizer; material on historical, cultural, and legal/ethical considerations is interwoven where appropriate throughout this book.

A Historical Perspective

Antiquity to the Nineteenth Century

It is believed that tests and testing programs first came into being in China as early as 2200 B.C.E. (DuBois, 1966, 1970). Testing was instituted as a means of selecting who, of many applicants, would obtain government jobs. In a culture with a long tradition of one's social position being determined solely by the family into which one was born, the fact that one could improve one's lot in life by scoring high on an examination was a significant step forward. In reality, passing the examinations required knowledge that usually came from either long hours of study or work with a tutor. Given those facts of life, it was likely that only the land-owning gentry could afford to have their children spend the time necessary to prepare for the tests. Still, tales emerged of some people who were able to vastly improve their lot in life by passing the state-sponsored examinations. Just imagine the feeling of anticipation experienced by these men—the tests were only open to men, with the exception of a brief period in the 1800s—as the grades were released and posted.

What were applicants for jobs in ancient China tested on? As might be expected, the content of the examination changed over time and with the cultural expectations of the day—as well as with the values of the ruling dynasty. In general, the tests examined proficiency in subjects like music, archery, horsemanship, writing, and arithmetic, as well as agriculture, geography, civil law, and military strategy. Knowledge of and skill in the rites and ceremonies of public and social life were also evaluated. During the Song (or Sung) dynasty, which ran from 960 to 1279 C.E., tests emphasized knowledge of classical literature. Testtakers who demonstrated their command of the classics were perceived as having acquired the wisdom of the past and were therefore entitled to a government position. During some dynasties, testing was virtually suspended and government positions were given to family members or friends, or simply sold.

In dynasties with state-sponsored examinations for official positions (referred to as *imperial examination*), the privileges of making the grade varied. During some periods, those who passed the examination were entitled not only to a government job but also to wear special garb; this entitled them to be accorded special courtesies by anyone they happened to meet. In some dynasties, passing the examinations could result in exemption from taxes. Passing the examination might even exempt one from government-sponsored interrogation by torture if the individual was suspected of committing a crime. Clearly, it paid to do well on these difficult examinations.

JUST THINK . . .

What parallels in terms of privileges and benefits can you draw between doing well on examinations in ancient China and doing well on modern-day civil service examinations?

Also intriguing from a historical perspective are ancient Greco-Roman writings indicative of attempts to categorize people in terms of personality types. Such categorizations typically included reference to an overabundance or deficiency in some bodily fluid (such as blood or phlegm) as a factor believed to influence personality. During the Middle Ages, a question of critical importance was "Who is in league with the Devil?" and various measurement procedures were devised to address this question. It would not be until the Renaissance that psychological assessment in the modern sense began to emerge. By the eighteenth century, Christian von Wolff (1732, 1734) had anticipated psychology as a science and psychological measurement as a specialty within that science.

JUST THINK . . .

Among the most critical "diagnostic" questions during the Middle Ages was "Who is in league with the Devil?" What is one of the most critical diagnostic questions today?

In 1859, the book *On the Origin of Species by Means of Natural Selection* by Charles Darwin (1809–1882) was published. In this important, far-reaching work, Darwin argued that chance variation in species would be selected or rejected by nature according to adaptivity and survival value. He further argued that humans had descended from the ape as a result of such chance genetic variations. This revolutionary notion aroused interest, admiration, and a good deal of enmity. The enmity came primarily from religious individuals who interpreted Darwin's ideas as an affront to the biblical account of creation in Genesis. Still, the notion of an evolutionary link between human beings and animals conferred a new scientific respectability on experimentation with animals. It also raised questions about how animals and humans compare with respect to states of consciousness—questions that would beg for answers in laboratories of future behavioral scientists.[1]

History records that it was Darwin who spurred scientific interest in individual differences. Darwin (1859) wrote:

> The many slight differences which appear in the offspring from the same parents . . . may be called individual differences. . . . These individual differences are of the highest importance . . . [for they] afford materials for natural selection to act on. (p. 125)

Indeed, Darwin's writing on individual differences kindled interest in research on heredity by his half cousin, Francis Galton. In the course of his efforts to explore and quantify individual differences between people, Galton became an extremely influential contributor to the field of measurement (Forrest, 1974). Galton (1869) aspired to classify people "according to their natural gifts" (p. 1) and to ascertain their "deviation from an average" (p. 11). Along the way, Galton would be credited with devising or contributing to the development of many contemporary tools of psychological assessment, including questionnaires, rating scales, and self-report inventories.

Galton's initial work on heredity was done with sweet peas, in part because there tended to be fewer variations among the peas in a single pod. In this work Galton pioneered the use of a statistical concept central to psychological experimentation and testing: the coefficient of

---

1. The influence of Darwin's thinking is also apparent in the theory of personality formulated by Sigmund Freud. In this context, Freud's notion of the primary importance of instinctual sexual and aggressive urges can be better understood.

correlation. Although Karl Pearson (1857–1936) developed the product-moment correlation technique, its roots can be traced directly to the work of Galton (Magnello & Spies, 1984). From heredity in peas, Galton's interest turned to heredity in humans and various ways of measuring aspects of people and their abilities.

At an exhibition in London in 1884, Galton displayed his Anthropometric Laboratory, where for a few pence you could be measured on variables such as height (standing), height (sitting), arm span, weight, breathing capacity, strength of pull, strength of squeeze, swiftness of blow, keenness of sight, memory of form, discrimination of color, and steadiness of hand. Through his own efforts and his urging of educational institutions to keep anthropometric records on their students, Galton excited widespread interest in the measurement of psychology-related variables.

Assessment was also an important activity at the first experimental psychology laboratory, founded at the University of Leipzig in Germany by Wilhelm Max Wundt (1832–1920), a medical doctor whose title at the university was professor of philosophy. Wundt and his students tried to formulate a general description of human abilities with respect to variables such as reaction time, perception, and attention span. In contrast to Galton, Wundt focused on how people were similar, not different. In fact, Wundt viewed individual differences as a frustrating source of error in experimentation, and he attempted to control all extraneous variables in an effort to reduce error to a minimum. As we will see, such attempts are fairly routine in contemporary assessment. The objective is to ensure that any observed differences in performance are indeed due to differences between the people being measured and not to any extraneous variables. Manuals for the administration of many tests provide explicit instructions designed to hold constant or "standardize" the conditions under which the test is administered. This is so that any differences in scores on the test are due to differences in the testtakers rather than to differences in the conditions under which the test is administered. In Chapter 4, we will elaborate on the meaning of terms such as *standardized* and *standardization* as applied to tests.

In spite of the prevailing research focus on people's similarities, one of Wundt's students at Leipzig, an American named James McKeen Cattell (Figure 2–1), completed a doctoral dissertation that dealt with individual differences—specifically, individual differences in reaction time. After receiving his doctoral degree from Leipzig, Cattell returned to the United

◆

JUST THINK . . .

Which orientation in assessment research appeals to you more, the Galtonian orientation (researching how individuals differ) or the Wundtian (researching how individuals are the same)? Why? Do you think researchers arrive at similar conclusions despite these two contrasting orientations?

Figure 2–1
James McKeen Cattell (1860–1944)

The psychologist who is credited with coining the term "mental test" is James McKeen Cattell. Among his many accomplishments, Cattell was a founding member of the American Psychological Association and that organization's fourth president.

© JHU Sheridan Libraries/Gado/Archive Photos/Getty Images

States, teaching at Bryn Mawr and then at the University of Pennsylvania, before leaving for Europe to teach at Cambridge. At Cambridge, Cattell came in contact with Galton, whom he later described as "the greatest man I have known" (Roback, 1961, p. 96).

Inspired by his interaction with Galton, Cattell returned to the University of Pennsylvania in 1888 and coined the term *mental test* in an 1890 publication. Boring (1950, p. 283) noted that "Cattell more than any other person was in this fashion responsible for getting mental testing underway in America, and it is plain that his motivation was similar to Galton's and that he was influenced, or at least reinforced, by Galton." Cattell went on to become professor and chair of the psychology department at Columbia University. Over the next 26 years, he not only trained many psychologists but also founded a number of publications (such as the *Psychological Review, Science,* and *American Men of Science*). In 1921, Cattell was instrumental in founding the Psychological Corporation, which named 20 of the country's leading psychologists as its directors. The goal of the corporation was the "advancement of psychology and the promotion of the useful applications of psychology."[2]

Other students of Wundt at Leipzig included Charles Spearman, Victor Henri, Emil Kraepelin, E. B. Titchener, G. Stanley Hall, and Lightner Witmer. Spearman is credited with originating the concept of test reliability as well as building the mathematical framework for the statistical technique of factor analysis. Victor Henri is the Frenchman who would collaborate with Alfred Binet on papers suggesting how mental tests could be used to measure higher mental processes (e.g., Binet & Henri, 1895a, 1895b, 1895c). Psychiatrist Emil Kraepelin was an early experimenter with the word association technique as a formal test (Kraepelin, 1892, 1895). Lightner Witmer received his Ph.D. from Leipzig and went on to succeed Cattell as director of the psychology laboratory at the University of Pennsylvania. Witmer has been cited as the "little-known founder of clinical psychology" (McReynolds, 1987), owing at least in part to his being challenged to treat a "chronic bad speller" in March of 1896 (Brotemarkle, 1947). Later that year Witmer founded the first psychological clinic in the United States at the University of Pennsylvania. In 1907 Witmer founded the journal *Psychological Clinic.* The first article in that journal was entitled "Clinical Psychology" (Witmer, 1907).

The Twentieth Century

Much of the nineteenth-century testing that could be described as psychological in nature involved the measurement of sensory abilities, reaction time, and the like. Generally the public was fascinated by such testing. However, there was no widespread belief that testing for variables such as reaction time had any applied value. But all of that would change in the early 1900s with the birth of the first formal tests of intelligence. These were tests that were useful for reasons readily understandable to anyone who had school-age children. Public receptivity to psychological tests would shift from mild curiosity to outright enthusiasm as more and more instruments that purportedly quantified mental ability were introduced. Soon there would be tests to measure sundry mental characteristics such as personality, interests, attitudes, values, and widely varied mental abilities. It all began with a single test designed for use with young Paris pupils.

The measurement of intelligence   As early as 1895, Alfred Binet (1857–1911) and his colleague Victor Henri published several articles in which they argued for the measurement of abilities such as memory and social comprehension. Ten years later, Binet and collaborator Theodore Simon published a 30-item "measuring scale of intelligence" designed to help

---

2. Today, many of the products and services of what was once known as the Psychological Corporation have been absorbed under the "PsychCorp" brand of a corporate parent, Pearson Assessment, Inc.

JUST THINK . . .

In the early 1900s, the Binet test was being used worldwide for various purposes far beyond identifying exceptional Paris schoolchildren. What were some of the other uses of the test? How appropriate do you think it was to use this test for these other purposes?

identify Paris schoolchildren with intellectual disability (Binet & Simon, 1905). The Binet test would subsequently go through many revisions and translations—and, in the process, launch both the intelligence testing movement and the clinical testing movement. Before long, psychological tests were being used with regularity in such diverse settings as schools, hospitals, clinics, courts, reformatories, and prisons (Pintner, 1931).

In 1939 David Wechsler, a clinical psychologist at Bellevue Hospital in New York City, introduced a test designed to measure adult intelligence. For Wechsler, intelligence was "the aggregate or global capacity of the individual to act purposefully, to think rationally, and to deal effectively with his environment" (Wechsler, 1939, p. 3). Originally christened the Wechsler-Bellevue Intelligence Scale, the test was subsequently revised and renamed the Wechsler Adult Intelligence Scale (WAIS). The WAIS has been revised several times since then, and versions of Wechsler's test have been published that extend the age range of testtakers from early childhood through senior adulthood.

JUST THINK . . .

Should the definition of *intelligence* change as one moves from infancy through childhood, adolescence, adulthood, and late adulthood?

A natural outgrowth of the individually administered intelligence test devised by Binet was the *group* intelligence test. Group intelligence tests came into being in the United States in response to the military's need for an efficient method of screening the intellectual ability of World War I recruits. This same need again became urgent as the United States prepared for entry into World War II. Psychologists would again be called upon by the government service to develop group tests, administer them to recruits, and interpret the test data.

After the war, psychologists returning from military service brought back a wealth of applied testing skills that would be useful in civilian as well as governmental applications. Psychological tests were increasingly used in diverse settings, including large corporations and private organizations. New tests were being developed at a brisk pace to measure various abilities and interests as well as personality.

The measurement of personality Public receptivity to tests of intellectual ability spurred the development of many other types of tests (Garrett & Schneck, 1933; Pintner, 1931). Only eight years after the publication of Binet's scale, the field of psychology was being criticized for being too test oriented (Sylvester, 1913). By the late 1930s, approximately 4,000 different psychological tests were in print (Buros, 1938), and "clinical psychology" was synonymous with "mental testing" (Institute for Juvenile Research, 1937; Tulchin, 1939).

World War I had brought with it not only the need to screen the intellectual functioning of recruits but also the need to screen for recruits' general adjustment. A governmental Committee on Emotional Fitness chaired by psychologist Robert S. Woodworth was assigned the task of developing a measure of adjustment and emotional stability that could be administered quickly and efficiently to groups of recruits. The committee developed several experimental versions of what were, in essence, paper-and-pencil psychiatric interviews. To disguise the true purpose of one such test, the questionnaire was labeled as a "Personal Data Sheet." Draftees and volunteers were asked to indicate *yes* or *no* to a series of questions that probed for the existence of various kinds of psychopathology. For example, one of the test questions was "Are you troubled with the idea that people are watching you on the street?"

The Personal Data Sheet developed by Woodworth and his colleagues never went beyond the experimental stages, for the treaty of peace rendered the development of this and other tests less urgent. After the war, Woodworth developed a personality test for civilian use that was based on the Personal Data Sheet. He called it the Woodworth Psychoneurotic Inventory. This instrument was the first widely used *self-report* measure of personality. In general, **self-report** refers to a process whereby assessees themselves supply assessment-related information by responding to questions, keeping a diary, or self-monitoring thoughts or behaviors.

J U S T   T H I N K . . .

Describe an ideal situation for obtaining personality-related information by means of self-report. In what type of situation might it be inadvisable to rely solely on an assessee's self-report?

Personality tests that employ self-report methodologies have both advantages and disadvantages. On the face of it, respondents are arguably the best-qualified people to provide answers about themselves. However, there are also compelling arguments *against* respondents supplying such information. For example, respondents may have poor insight into themselves. People might honestly believe some things about themselves that in reality are not true. And regardless of the quality of their insight, some respondents are unwilling to reveal anything about themselves that is very personal or that could put them in a negative light. Given these shortcomings of the self-report method of personality assessment, there was a need for alternative types of personality tests.

Various methods were developed to provide measures of personality that did not rely on self-report. One such method or approach to personality assessment came to be described as *projective* in nature. A **projective test** is one in which an individual is assumed to "project" onto some ambiguous stimulus his or her own unique needs, fears, hopes, and motivation. The ambiguous stimulus might be an inkblot, a drawing, a photograph, or something else. Perhaps the best known of all projective tests is the Rorschach, a series of inkblots developed by the Swiss psychiatrist Hermann Rorschach. The use of pictures as projective stimuli was popularized in the late 1930s by Henry A. Murray, Christiana D. Morgan, and their colleagues at the Harvard Psychological Clinic. When pictures or photos are used as projective stimuli, respondents are typically asked to tell a story about the picture they are shown. The stories told are then analyzed in terms of what needs and motivations the respondents may be projecting onto the ambiguous pictures. Projective and many other types of instruments used in personality assessment will be discussed in Chapter 12.

J U S T   T H I N K . . .

What potential problems do you think might attend the use of picture story-telling tests to assess personality?

The academic and applied traditions   Like the development of its parent field, psychology, the development of psychological measurement can be traced along two distinct threads: the academic and the applied. In the tradition of Galton, Wundt, and other scholars, researchers at universities throughout the world use the tools of assessment to help advance knowledge and understanding of human and animal behavior. Yet there is also an applied tradition, one that dates at least back to ancient China and the examinations developed there to help select applicants for various positions on the basis of merit. Today, society relies on the tools of psychological assessment to help answer important questions. Who is best for this job? What class should this child be placed in? Who is competent to stand trial? Tests and other tools of assessment, when used in a competent manner, can help provide answers.

Contemporary test users hold a keen appreciation for the role of culture in the human experience. So, whether in academic or applied settings, assessment professionals recognize the need for cultural sensitivity in the development and use of the tools of psychological assessment. In what follows, we briefly overview some of the issues that such cultural sensitivity entails.

Culture and Assessment

Culture may be defined as "the socially transmitted behavior patterns, beliefs, and products of work of a particular population, community, or group of people" (Cohen, 1994, p. 5). As taught to us by parents, peers, and societal institutions such as schools, culture prescribes many behaviors and ways of thinking. Spoken language, attitudes toward elders, and techniques of child rearing are but a few critical manifestations of culture. Culture teaches specific rituals to be performed at birth, marriage, death, and other momentous occasions. Culture imparts much about what is to be valued or prized as well as what is to be rejected or despised. Culture teaches a point of view about what it means to be born of one or another gender, race, or ethnic background. Culture teaches us something about what we can expect from other people and what we can expect from ourselves. Indeed, the influence of culture on an individual's thoughts and behavior may be a great deal stronger than most of us would acknowledge at first blush.

◆ JUST THINK . . .

Can you think of one way in which you are a product of your culture? How about one way this fact might come through on a psychological test?

Professionals involved in the assessment enterprise have shown increasing sensitivity to the role of culture in many different aspects of measurement. This sensitivity is manifested in greater consideration of cultural issues with respect to every aspect of test development and use, including decision making on the basis of test data. Unfortunately, it was not always that way.

Evolving Interest in Culture-Related Issues

Soon after Alfred Binet introduced intelligence testing in France, the U.S. Public Health Service began using such tests to measure the intelligence of people seeking to immigrate to the United States (Figure 2–2). Henry H. Goddard, who had been highly instrumental in getting Binet's test adopted for use in various settings in the United States, was the chief researcher assigned to the project. Early on, Goddard raised questions about how meaningful such tests are when used with people from various cultural and language backgrounds. Goddard (1913) used interpreters in test administration, employed a bilingual psychologist, and administered mental tests to selected immigrants who appeared to have intellectual disability to trained observers. Although seemingly sensitive to cultural issues in assessment, Goddard's legacy with regard to such sensitivity is, at best, controversial. Goddard found most immigrants from various nationalities to be mentally deficient when tested. In one widely quoted report, 35 Jews, 22 Hungarians, 50 Italians, and 45 Russians were selected for testing among the masses of immigrants being processed for entry into the United States at Ellis Island. Reporting on his findings in a paper entitled "Mental Tests and the Immigrant," Goddard (1917) concluded that, in this sample, 83% of the Jews, 80% of the Hungarians, 79% of the Italians, and 87% of the Russians were feebleminded. Although Goddard had written extensively on the genetic nature of mental deficiency, it is to his credit that he did not summarily conclude that these test findings were the result of hereditary. Rather, Goddard (1917) wondered aloud whether the findings were due to "hereditary defect" or "apparent defect due to deprivation" (p. 243). In reality, the findings were largely the result of using a translated Binet test that overestimated mental deficiency in native English-speaking populations, let alone immigrant populations (Terman, 1916).

◆ JUST THINK . . .

What safeguards must be firmly in place before meaningful psychological testing with immigrants can take place?

Goddard's research, although leaving much to be desired methodologically, fueled the fires of an ongoing nature–nurture debate about what intelligence tests actually measure. On one

Figure 2–2
Psychological Testing at Ellis Island

Immigrants coming to America via Ellis Island were greeted not only by the Statue of Liberty, but also by immigration officials ready to evaluate them with respect to physical, mental, and other variables. Here, a block design test, one measure of intelligence, is administered to a would-be American. Immigrants who failed physical, mental, or other tests were returned to their country of origin at the expense of the shipping company that had brought them. Critics would later charge that at least some of the immigrants who had fared poorly on mental tests were sent away from our shores not because they were actually mentally deficient but simply because they did not understand English well enough to follow instructions. Critics also questioned the criteria on which these immigrants from many lands were being evaluated.
© akg-images/The Image Works

side were those who viewed intelligence test results as indicative of some underlying native ability. On the other side were those who viewed such data as indicative of the extent to which knowledge and skills had been acquired. More details about the highly influential Henry Goddard and his most controversial career are presented in this chapter's *Close-Up.*

If language and culture did indeed have an effect on mental ability test scores, then how could a more unconfounded or "pure" measure of intelligence be obtained? One way that early test developers attempted to deal with the impact of language and culture on tests of mental ability was, in essence, to "isolate" the cultural variable. So-called **culture-specific tests,** or tests designed for use with people from one culture but not from another, soon began to appear on the scene. Representative of the culture-specific approach to test development were early versions of some of the best-known tests of intelligence. For example, the 1937 revision of the Stanford-Binet Intelligence Scale, which enjoyed widespread use until it was revised in 1960, included no minority children in the research that went into its formulation. Similarly, the

The Controversial Career of Henry Herbert Goddard *(continued)*

and other social causes. Goddard classified many people as feebleminded based on undesirable social status, illegitimacy, or "sinful" activity. This fact has left some scholars wondering how much Goddard's own religious upbringing—along with biblical teachings linking children's problems with parents' sins—may have been inappropriately emphasized in what was supposed to be strictly scientific writing.

After 12 years at Vineland, Goddard left under conditions that have been the subject of some speculation (Wehmeyer & Smith, 2006). From 1918 through 1922, Goddard was director of the Ohio Bureau of Juvenile Research. From 1922 until his retirement in 1938, Goddard was a psychology professor at the Ohio State University. In 1947 Goddard moved to Santa Barbara, California, where he lived until his death at the age of 90. His remains were cremated and interred at the Vineland school, along with those of his wife, who had predeceased him in 1936.

Goddard's accomplishments were many. It was largely through his efforts that state mandates requiring special education services first became law. These laws worked to the benefit of many mentally deficient as well as many gifted students. Goddard's introduction of Binet's test to American society attracted other researchers, such as Lewis Terman, to see what they could do in terms of improving the test for various applications. Goddard's writings certainly had a momentous heuristic impact on the nature–nurture question. His books and papers stimulated many others to research and write, if only to disprove Goddard's conclusions. Goddard advocated for court acceptance of intelligence test data into evidence and for the limitation of criminal responsibility in the case of mentally defective defendants, especially with respect to capital crimes. He personally contributed his time to military screening efforts during World War I. Of more dubious distinction, of course, was the Ellis Island intelligence testing program he set up to screen immigrants. Although ostensibly well intentioned, this effort resulted in the misclassification and consequential repatriation of countless would-be citizens.

Despite an impressive list of career accomplishments, the light of history has not shone favorably on Henry Goddard. Goddard's (1912) recommendation for segregation of the

mentally deficient and his calls for their sterilization tend to be viewed as, at best, misguided. The low esteem in which Goddard is generally held today is perhaps compounded by the fact that Goddard's work has traditionally been held in very *high* esteem by some groups with radically offensive views, such as the Nazi party. During the late 1930s and early 1940s, more than 40,000 people were euthanized by Nazi physicians simply because they were deemed mentally deficient. This action preceded the horrific and systematic mass murder of more than 6 million innocent civilians by the Nazi military. The alleged "genetic defect" of most of these victims was that they were Jewish. Clearly, eugenicist propaganda fed to the German public was being used by the Nazi party for political means. The purported goal was to "purify German blood" by limiting or totally eliminating the ability of people from various groups to reproduce.

It is not a matter of controversy that Goddard used ill-advised research methods to derive many of his conclusions; he himself acknowledged this sad fact in later life. At the very least Goddard could be criticized for being too easily influenced by the (bad) ideas of others, for being somewhat naive in terms of how his writings were being used, and for not being up to the task of executing methodologically sound research. Goddard focused on the nature side of the nature–nurture controversy not because he was an ardent eugenicist at heart but rather because the nature side of the coin was where researchers at the time all tended to focus. Responding to a critic some years later, Goddard (letter to Nicolas Pastore dated April 3, 1948, quoted in J. D. Smith, 1985) wrote, in part, that he had "no inclination to deemphasize environment . . . [but] in those days environment was not being considered."

The conclusion of Leila Zenderland's relatively sympathetic biography of Goddard leaves one with the impression that he was basically a decent and likable man who was a product of his times. He harbored neither evil intentions nor right-wing prejudices. For her, a review of the life of Henry Herbert Goddard should serve as a warning not to reflexively jump to the conclusion that "bad science is usually the product of bad motives or, more broadly, bad character" (1998, p. 358).

Wechsler-Bellevue Intelligence Scale, forerunner of a widely used measure of adult intelligence, contained no minority members in the samples of testtakers used in its development. Although "a large number" of Blacks had, in fact, been tested (Wechsler, 1944), that data had been omitted from the final test manual because the test developers "did not feel that norms derived by mixing the populations could be interpreted without special provisos and reservations." Hence, Wechsler (1944) stated at the outset that the Wechsler-Bellevue norms could not be used for "the colored populations of the United States." In like fashion, the inaugural edition of the Wechsler Intelligence Scale for Children (WISC), first published in 1949 and not revised until 1974, contained no minority children in its development.

Even though many published tests were purposely designed to be culture-specific, it soon became apparent that the tests were being administered—improperly—to people from different cultures. Perhaps not surprisingly, testtakers from minority cultures tended to score lower as a group than people from the group for whom the test was developed. Illustrative of the type of problems encountered by test users was this item from the 1949 WISC: "If your mother sends you to the store for a loaf of bread and there is none, what do you do?" Many Hispanic children were routinely sent to the store for tortillas and so were not familiar with the phrase "loaf of bread."

JUST THINK . . .

Try your hand at creating one culture-specific test item on any subject. Testtakers from what culture would probably succeed in responding correctly to the item? Testtakers from what culture would not?

Today test developers typically take many steps to ensure that a major test developed for national use is indeed suitable for such use. Those steps might involve administering a preliminary version of the test to a tryout sample of testtakers from various cultural backgrounds, particularly from those whose members are likely to be administered the final version of the test. Examiners who administer the test may be asked to describe their impressions with regard to various aspects of testtakers' responses. For example, subjective impressions regarding testtakers' reactions to the test materials or opinions regarding the clarity of instructions will be noted. All of the accumulated test scores from the tryout sample will be analyzed to determine if any individual item seems to be biased with regard to race, gender, or culture. In addition, a panel of independent reviewers may be asked to go through the test items and screen them for possible bias. A revised version of the test may then be administered to a large sample of testtakers that is representative of key variables of the latest U.S. Census data (such as age, gender, ethnic background, and socioeconomic status). Information from this large-scale test administration will also be used to root out any identifiable sources of bias. More details regarding the contemporary process of test development will be presented in Chapter 8.

Some Issues Regarding Culture and Assessment

Communication between assessor and assessee is a most basic part of assessment. Assessors must be sensitive to any differences between the language or dialect familiar to assessees and the language in which the assessment is conducted. Assessors must also be sensitive to the degree to which assessees have been exposed to the dominant culture and the extent to which they have made a conscious choice to become assimilated. Next, we briefly consider assessment-related issues of communication, both verbal and nonverbal, in a cultural context.

Verbal communication Language, the means by which information is communicated, is a key yet sometimes overlooked variable in the assessment process. Most obviously, the examiner and the examinee must speak the same language. This is necessary not only for the assessment to proceed but also for the assessor's conclusions regarding the assessment to be reasonably accurate. If a test is in written form and includes written instructions, then the testtaker must be able to read and comprehend what is written. When the language in which the assessment is conducted is not the assessee's primary language, he or she may not fully comprehend the instructions or the test items. The danger of such misunderstanding may increase as infrequently used vocabulary or unusual idioms are employed in the assessment. All of the foregoing presumes that the assessee is making a sincere and well-intentioned effort to respond to the demands of the assessment. Although this is frequently presumed, it is not always the case. In some instances, assessees may purposely attempt to use a language deficit to frustrate evaluation efforts (Stephens, 1992).

JUST THINK . . .

What might an assessor do to make sure that a prospective assessee's competence in the language a test is written in is sufficient to administer the test to that assessee?

When an assessment is conducted with the aid of a translator, different types of problems may emerge. Depending upon the translator's skill and professionalism, subtle nuances of meaning may be lost in translation, or unintentional hints to the correct or more desirable response may be conveyed. Whether translated "live" by a translator or in writing, translated items may be either easier or more difficult than the original. Some vocabulary words may change meaning or have dual meanings when translated.

Interpreters may have limited understanding of mental health issues. In turn, an assessor may have little experience in working with a translator. So in some cases, where possible, it may be desirable to have some pretraining for interpreters on the relevant issues, and some pretraining for assessors on working with translators (Searight & Searight, 2009).

In interviews or other situations in which an evaluation is made on the basis of an oral exchange between two parties, a trained examiner may detect through verbal or nonverbal means that the examinee's grasp of a language or a dialect is too deficient to proceed. A trained examiner might not be able to detect this when the test is in written form. In the case of written tests, it is clearly essential that the examinee be able to read and comprehend what is written. Otherwise the evaluation may be more about language or dialect competency than whatever the test purports to measure. Even when examiner and examinee speak the same language, miscommunication and consequential effects on test results may result owing to differences in dialect (Wolfram, 1971).

In the assessment of an individual whose proficiency in the English language is limited or nonexistent, some basic questions may need to be raised: What level of proficiency in English must the testtaker have, and does the testtaker have that proficiency? Can a meaningful assessment take place through a trained interpreter? Can an alternative and more appropriate assessment procedure be devised to meet the objectives of the assessment? In addition to linguistic barriers, the contents of tests from a particular culture are typically laden with items and material—some obvious, some very subtle—that draw heavily from that culture. Test performance may, at least in part, reflect not only whatever variables the test purports to measure but also one additional variable: the degree to which the testtaker has assimilated the culture.

Nonverbal communication and behavior   Humans communicate not only through verbal means but also through nonverbal means. Facial expressions, finger and hand signs, and shifts in one's position in space may all convey messages. Of course, the messages conveyed by such body language may be different from culture to culture. In American culture, for example, one who fails to look another person in the eye when speaking may be viewed as deceitful or having something to hide. However, in other cultures, failure to make eye contact when speaking may be a sign of respect.

If you have ever gone on or conducted a job interview, you may have developed a firsthand appreciation of the value of nonverbal communication in an evaluative setting. Interviewees who show enthusiasm and interest have the edge over interviewees who appear to be drowsy or bored. In clinical settings, an experienced evaluator may develop hypotheses to be tested from the nonverbal behavior of the interviewee. For example, a person who is slouching, moving slowly, and exhibiting a sad facial expression may be depressed. Then again, such an individual may be experiencing physical discomfort from any number of sources, such as a muscle spasm or an arthritis attack. It remains for the assessor to determine which hypothesis best accounts for the observed behavior.

Certain theories and systems in the mental health field go beyond more traditional interpretations of body language. For example, in **psychoanalysis,** a theory of personality and psychological treatment developed by Sigmund Freud, symbolic significance is assigned to many nonverbal acts. From a psychoanalytic perspective, an interviewee's fidgeting with a wedding band during an interview may be interpreted as a message regarding an unstable marriage. As evidenced by his thoughts on "the first chance actions" of a patient during a therapy session, Sigmund Freud believed he could tell much about motivation from nonverbal behavior:

> The first . . . chance actions of the patient . . . will betray one of the governing complexes of the neurosis. . . . A young girl . . . hurriedly pulls the hem of her skirt over her exposed ankle; she has betrayed the kernel of what analysis will discover later; her narcissistic pride in her bodily beauty and her tendencies to exhibitionism. (Freud, 1913/1959, p. 359)

This quote from Freud is also useful in illustrating the influence of culture on diagnostic and therapeutic views. Freud lived in Victorian Vienna. In that time and in that place, sex was not a subject for public discussion. In many ways Freud's views regarding a sexual basis for various thoughts and behaviors were a product of the sexually repressed culture in which he lived.

An example of a nonverbal behavior in which people differ is the speed at which they characteristically move to complete tasks. The overall pace of life in one geographic area, for example, may tend to be faster than in another. In a similar vein, differences in pace of life across cultures may enhance or detract from test scores on tests involving timed items (Gopaul-McNicol, 1993). In a more general sense, Hoffman (1962) questioned the value of timed tests of ability, particularly those tests that employed multiple-choice items. He believed such tests relied too heavily on testtakers' quickness of response and as such discriminated against the individual who is characteristically a "deep, brooding thinker."

JUST THINK . . .

Play the role of a therapist in the Freudian tradition and cite one example of a student's or an instructor's public behavior that you believe may be telling about that individual's private motivation. No naming names!

JUST THINK . . .

What type of test is best suited for administration to people who are "deep, brooding thinkers"? How practical for group administration would such tests be?

Culture exerts effects over many aspects of nonverbal behavior. For example, a child may present as noncommunicative and having only minimal language skills when verbally examined. This finding may be due to the fact that the child is from a culture where elders are revered and where children speak to adults only when they are spoken to—and then only in as short a phrase as possible. Clearly, it is incumbent upon test users to be knowledgeable about aspects of an assessee's culture that are relevant to the assessment.

Standards of evaluation   Suppose that master chefs representing nations around the globe entered a contest designed to crown "the best chicken soup in the world." Who do you think would win? The answer to that question hinges on the evaluative standard to be employed. If the sole judge of the contest was the owner of a kosher delicatessen on the Lower East Side of Manhattan, it is conceivable that the entry that came closest to the "Jewish mother homemade" variety might well be declared the winner. However, other judges might have other standards and preferences. For example, soup connoisseurs from Arabic cultures might prefer chicken soup with fresh lemon juice in the recipe. Judges from India might be inclined to give their vote to a chicken soup flavored with curry and other Asian spices. For Japanese and Chinese judges, soy sauce might be viewed as an indispensable ingredient. Ultimately, the judgment of which soup is best will probably be very much a matter of personal preference and the standard of evaluation employed.

Somewhat akin to judgments concerning the best chicken soup recipe, judgments related to certain psychological traits can also be culturally relative. For example, whether specific patterns of behavior are considered to be male- or female-appropriate will depend on the prevailing societal standards regarding masculinity and femininity. In some societies, for example, it is role-appropriate for women to fight wars and put food on the table while the men are occupied in more domestic activities. Whether specific patterns of behavior are considered to be psychopathological also depends on the prevailing societal standards. In Sudan, for example, there are tribes that live among cattle because they regard the animals as sacred. Judgments as to who might be the best employee, manager, or leader may differ as a function of culture, as might judgments regarding intelligence, wisdom, courage, and other psychological variables.

Cultures differ from one another in the extent to which they are *individualist* or *collectivist* (Markus & Kitayama, 1991). Generally speaking, an **individualist culture** (typically associated with the dominant culture in countries such as the United States and Great Britain) is characterized by value being placed on traits such as self-reliance, autonomy, independence, uniqueness, and competitiveness. In a **collectivist culture** (typically associated with the dominant culture in many countries throughout Asia, Latin America and Africa), value is placed on traits such as conformity, cooperation, interdependence, and striving toward group goals. As a consequence of being raised in one or another of these types of cultures, people may develop certain characteristic aspects of their sense of self. Markus and Kitayama (1991) believe that people raised in Western culture tend to see themselves as having a unique constellation of traits that are stable over time and through situations. The person raised in an individualist culture exhibits behavior that is "organized and made meaningful primarily by reference to one's own internal repertoire of thoughts, feelings, and action, rather than by reference to the thoughts, feelings, and actions of others" (Markus & Kitayama, 1991, p. 226). By contrast, people raised in a collectivist culture see themselves as part of a larger whole, with much greater connectedness to others. And rather than seeing their own traits as stable over time and through situations, the person raised in a collectivist culture believes that "one's behavior is determined, contingent on, and, to a large extent organized by what the actor perceives to be the thoughts, feelings, and actions of *others* in the relationship" (Markus & Kitayama, 1991, p. 227, emphasis in the original).

JUST THINK . . .

When considering tools of evaluation that purport to measure the trait of assertiveness, what are some culture-related considerations that should be kept in mind?

Consider in a clinical context, for example, a psychiatric diagnosis of dependent personality disorder. To some extent the description of this disorder reflects the values of an individualist culture in deeming overdependence on others to be pathological. Yet the clinician making such a diagnosis would, ideally, be aware that such a belief foundation is contradictory to a guiding philosophy for many people from a collectivist culture wherein dependence and submission may be integral to fulfilling role obligations (Chen et al., 2009). In the workplace, individuals from collectivist cultures may be penalized in some performance ratings because they are less likely to attribute success in their jobs to themselves. Rather, they are more likely to be self-effacing and self-critical (Newman et al., 2004). The point is clear: cultural differences carry with them important implications for assessment.

A challenge inherent in the assessment enterprise concerns tempering test- and assessment-related outcomes with good judgment regarding the cultural relativity of those outcomes. In practice, this means raising questions about the applicability of assessment-related findings to specific individuals. It therefore seems prudent to supplement questions such as "How intelligent is this person?" or "How assertive is this individual?" with other questions, such as: "How appropriate are the norms or other standards that will be used to make this evaluation?" "To what extent has the assessee been assimilated by the culture from which the test is drawn, and what influence might such assimilation (or lack of it) have on the test results?" "What research has been done on the test to support the applicability of findings with it for use in evaluating this particular asssessee?" These are the types of questions that are being raised by responsible test users such as this chapter's guest assessment professional, Dr. Neil Krishan Aggarwal (see *Meet an Assessment Professional*). They are also the types of questions being increasingly raised in courts of law.

Meet Dr. Neil Krishan Aggarwal

Cultural assessment informs every aspect of my work, from the medical students and psychiatry resident trainees whom I teach at C.U., the mental health clinicians whom I train to conduct culturally competent interviews with patients for my research at N.Y.S.P.I., and the patients I treat in private practice. The fact that an understanding of culture is essential to understand all aspects of mental health has been recognized increasingly over the years by the American Psychiatric Association in its *Diagnostic and Statistical Manual* (DSM).

In my subspecialty of cultural psychiatry, it has long been recognized that culture influences when, where, how, and to whom patients narrate their experiences of distress, the patterning of symptoms recognized as illnesses, and the models clinicians use to interpret symptoms through diagnoses (Kirmayer, 2006; Kleinman, 1988). Culture also shapes perceptions of care such as expectations around appropriate healers (medical or non-medical), the duration and types of acceptable treatments, and anticipated improvements in quality of life (Aggarwal, Pieh, et al., 2016). The American Psychiatric Association and the American Psychological Association now have professional guidelines that encourage cultural competence training for all clinicians with the recognition that all patients—not just those from racial or ethnic minority groups—have cultural concerns that impact diagnosis and treatment. Despite the growing appreciation that cultural competence training for clinicians can reduce disparities in treatment (Office of the Surgeon General, 1999), many well-intentioned clinicians are too often trained only in making a diagnosis, developing a treatment plan, or administering therapies without systematically reflecting on a patient's cultural needs.

Mental health clinicians need an assessment tool that comprehensively accounts for all relevant cultural factors in sufficient depth, and can be used in a standardized way in diverse clinical settings with different populations. Ideally, such an instrument would be focused on the cultural identity of the individual patient, the better to avoid the risk of stereotyping patients based on group identities (such as race or ethnicity). The tool of assessment that I use in clinical practice is the DSM-5 core Cultural Formulation

Neil Krishan Aggarwal, M.D., M.A., Assistant Professor of Clinical Psychiatry at Columbia University (C.U.), Research Psychiatrist at the New York State Psychiatric Institute (N.Y.S.P.I.), and psychiatrist in private practice.

© Neil Krishan Aggarwal, M.D., M.A.

Interview (CFI). The CFI consists of 16 questions, and is based on a comprehensive literature review of 140 publications in seven languages. Field tested with 321 patients by 75 clinicians in six countries, the CFI has been revised through patient and clinician feedback (Lewis-Fernández et al., 2016). The 16 questions cover topics of enduring interest in mental health such as patients' explanations of illness (definitions for their presenting problem, preferred idiomatic terms, level of severity, causes), perceived social stressors and supports, the role of cultural identity in their lives and in relation to the presenting problem, individual coping mechanisms, past help-seeking behaviors, personal barriers to care, current expectations of treatment, and potential differences between patients and clinicians that can impact rapport. In recognition of this instrument's scientific value, the American Psychiatric Association has made the CFI available to all users. It may be accessed, free-of-charge, at *http://www. psychiatry.org/File%20Library/Psychiatrists/Practice/ DSM/APA_D.S.M.5_Cultural-Formulation-Interview.pdf.*

The data derived from a CFI administration can introduce clinicians to very fundamental ways that culture and mental health interrelate for the individual patient. Responses can yield important clinical insights

(continued)

Meet Dr. Neil Krishan Aggarwal
(continued)

as to when, where, how, and to whom patients narrate experiences of illness, and the healers whom they approach for care. It can provide useful information regarding the duration and types of treatments that the individual patient would find acceptable. On average, the complete interview takes about 15–20 minutes—well within the time typically allotted for an initial intake session (Aggarwal, Jiménez-Solomon, et al., 2016). The use of the CFI can improve health communication as it provides patients with an open-ended opportunity to narrate what is most at stake for them during illness in an open-ended way (Aggarwal et al., 2015).

Several versions of the CFI, all based on the core format, are available. These alternative versions are variously designed for use with informants and caregivers, and for use with children, adolescents, older adults, and immigrants and refugees (Lewis-Fernández et al., 2016). I particularly find useful the CFI supplementary interviews on level of functioning, cultural identity, and spirituality, religion, and moral traditions because they help me better situate patients in their environment.

Consistent with recommendations from the latest version of the DSM (the DSM-5), I use the CFI with all patients whenever I do an initial intake interview. A patient's responses to the questions can be particularly helpful in formulating a diagnosis when the presenting symptoms seem to differ from formal DSM criteria. The data may also be instructive with regard to judging impairments in academic, occupational, and social functioning, and in negotiating a treatment plan around the length and types of treatments deemed necessary. Additionally, the data may have value in formulating a treatment plan that is devoid of approaches to therapy, including certain medications, that an individual patient is not predisposed to respond to favorably. In cases where patients develop resistance to therapy protocols, it may be useful to revisit CFI data as a way of reminding patients of what was previously agreed upon, or open a door to renegotiation of the therapeutic contract.

No tool of assessment is perfect, and the CFI certainly has its shortcomings. First, the DSM-5 encourages the use of all 16 questions. The questions are to be raised, in order, during the initial intake interview (prior to taking the medical or psychiatric history). Sometimes this feels too rigid, especially when a patient's responses to CFI questions seem to naturally lead to questions about the medical or psychiatric history. Second, some patients in acute illness cannot answer the questions. For example, people with acute substance intoxication, psychosis, or cognition-impairing conditions such as Alzheimer's or Parkinson's disease cannot always answer questions directly. Finally, the CFI builds from the meaning-centered approach to culture in medical anthropology that mostly relies on patient interviews (Lewis-Fernández et al., 2016). The CFI thus has all of the drawbacks one would expect from a self-report instrument that lacks a behavioral component. Accordingly, the CFI is perhaps best viewed as a beginning, and not an end, to a conversation about culture and mental health with new patients.

The CFI builds from and contributes to an ongoing movement across the health disciplines that patient care should be culturally competent and individually tailored. Today, all clinical stakeholders—patients, clinicians, administrators, families, and health advocates—recognize that cultural assessment is one of the few ways to emphasize the patient's own narrative of suffering within a health care environment that has too often prioritized diagnostic assessment and billing considerations. Budding psychiatrists and psychologists can help advance the science and practice of cultural assessments in mental health by using, critiquing, and refining standardized instruments such as the CFI. In the continued absence of confirmatory laboratory or radiological tests that we can order, diagnosis and treatment planning are acts of interpretation in mental health: patients must first interpret their symptoms through the use of language and we must interpret their colloquial language in scientific terms (Kleinman, 1988). Cultural assessments such as the CFI can remind psychiatrists and psychologists that our own professional cultures—systems of knowledge, concepts, rules, and practices that are learned and transmitted across generations—mold our scientific interpretations that may not reflect the realities of health and illness in our patients' lives.

Used with permission of Neil Krishan Aggarwal.

Tests and Group Membership

Tests and other evaluative measures administered in vocational, educational, counseling, and other settings leave little doubt that people differ from one another on an individual basis and also from group to group on a collective basis. What happens when groups systematically differ in terms of scores on a particular test? The answer, in a word, is *conflict*.

On the face of it, questions such as "What student is best qualified to be admitted to this school?" or "Which job candidate should get the job?" are rather straightforward. On the other hand, societal concerns about fairness both to individuals and to groups of individuals have made the answers to such questions matters of heated debate, if not lawsuits and civil disobedience. Consider the case of a person who happens to be a member of a particular group—cultural or otherwise—who fails to obtain a desired outcome (such as attainment of employment or admission to a university). Suppose it is further observed that most other people from that same group have also failed to obtain that same prized outcome. What may well happen is that the criteria being used to judge attainment of the prized outcome becomes the subject of intense scrutiny, sometimes by a court or a legislature.

In vocational assessment, test users are sensitive to legal and ethical mandates concerning the use of tests with regard to hiring, firing, and related decision making. If a test is used to evaluate a candidate's ability to do a job, one point of view is that the test should do just that—regardless of the group membership of the testtaker. According to this view, scores on a test of job ability should be influenced only by job-related variables. That is, scores should not be affected by variables such as group membership, hair length, eye color, or any other variable extraneous to the ability to perform the job. Although this rather straightforward view of the role of tests in personnel selection may seem consistent with principles of equal opportunity, it has attracted charges of unfairness and claims of discrimination. Why?

Claims of test-related discrimination made against major test publishers may be best understood as evidence of the great complexity of the assessment enterprise rather than as a conspiracy to use tests to discriminate against individuals from certain groups. In vocational assessment, for example, conflicts may arise from disagreements about the criteria for performing a particular job. The potential for controversy looms over almost all selection criteria that an employer sets, regardless of whether the criteria are physical, educational, psychological, or experiential.

The critical question with regard to hiring, promotion, and other selection decisions in almost any work setting is: "What criteria must be met to do this job?" A state police department may require all applicants for the position of police officer to meet certain physical requirements, including a minimum height of 5 feet 4 inches. A person who is 5 feet 2 inches tall is therefore barred from applying. Because such police force evaluation policies have the effect of systematically excluding members of cultural groups where the average height of adults is less than 5 feet 4 inches, the result may be a class-action lawsuit charging discrimination. Whether the police department's height requirement is reasonable and job related, and whether discrimination actually occurred, are complex questions that are usually left for the courts to resolve. Compelling arguments may be presented on both sides, as benevolent, fair-minded, knowledgeable, and well-intentioned people may have honest differences about the necessity of the prevailing height requirement for the job of police officer.

Beyond the variable of height, it would seem that variables such as appearance and religion should have little to do with what job one is qualified to perform. However, it is precisely such factors that keep some group members from entry into many jobs and careers. Consider in this context observant Jews. Their appearance and dress is not mainstream. The food they eat must be kosher. They are unable to work or travel on

JUST THINK . . .

What might be a fair and equitable way to determine the minimum required height, if any, for police officers in your community?

weekends. Given the established selection criteria for many positions in corporate America, candidates who are members of the group known as observant Jews are effectively excluded, regardless of their ability to perform the work (Korman, 1988; Mael, 1991; Zweigenhaft, 1984).

General differences among groups of people also extend to psychological attributes such as measured intelligence. Unfortunately, the mere suggestion that such differences in psychological variables exist arouses skepticism if not charges of discrimination, bias, or worse. This is especially true when the observed group differences are deemed responsible for blocking one or another group from employment or educational opportunities.

JUST THINK . . .

What should be done if a test adequately assesses a skill required for a job but is discriminatory?

If systematic differences related to group membership were found to exist on job ability test scores, then what, if anything, should be done? One view is that nothing needs to be done. According to this view, the test was designed to measure job ability, and it does what it was designed to do. In support of this view is evidence suggesting that group differences in scores on professionally developed tests do reflect differences in real-world performance (Gottfredson, 2000; Halpern, 2000; Hartigan & Wigdor, 1989; Kubiszyn et al., 2000; Neisser et al., 1996; Schmidt, 1988; Schmidt & Hunter, 1992).

A contrasting view is that efforts should be made to "level the playing field" between groups of people. The term **affirmative action** refers to voluntary and mandatory efforts undertaken by federal, state, and local governments, private employers, and schools to combat discrimination and to promote equal opportunity for all in education and employment (American Psychological Association, 1996a, p. 2). Affirmative action seeks to create equal opportunity actively, not passively. One impetus to affirmative action is the view that "policies that appear to be neutral with regard to ethnicity or gender can operate in ways that advantage individuals from one group over individuals from another group" (Crosby et al., 2003, p. 95).

In assessment, one way of implementing affirmative action is by altering test-scoring procedures according to set guidelines. For example, an individual's score on a test could be revised according to the individual's group membership (McNemar, 1975). While proponents of this approach view such remedies as necessary to address past inequities, others condemn manipulation of test scores as introducing "inequity in equity" (Benbow & Stanley, 1996).

JUST THINK . . .

What are your thoughts on the manipulation of test scores as a function of group membership to advance certain social goals? Should membership in a particular cultural group trigger an automatic increase (or decrease) in test scores?

As sincerely committed as they may be to principles of egalitarianism and fair play, test developers and test users must ultimately look to society at large—and, more specifically, to laws, administrative regulations, and other rules and professional codes of conduct—for guidance in the use of tests and test scores.

Psychology, tests, and public policy Few people would object to using psychological tests in academic and applied contexts that obviously benefit human welfare. Then again, few people are aware of the everyday use of psychological tests in such ways. More typically, members of the general public become acquainted with the use of psychological tests in high-profile contexts, such as when an individual or a group has a great deal to gain or to lose as a result of a test score. In such situations, tests and other tools of assessment are portrayed as instruments that can have a momentous and immediate impact on one's life. In such situations, tests may be perceived by the everyday person as tools used to deny people things they very much want or need. Denial of educational advancement, dismissal from a job, denial of parole, and denial of custody are some of the more threatening consequences that the public may associate with psychological tests and assessment procedures.

Members of the public call upon government policy-makers to protect them from perceived threats. Legislators pass laws, administrative agencies make regulations, judges hand down rulings, and citizens call for referenda regarding prevailing public policies. In the section that follows, we broaden our view of the assessment enterprise beyond the concerns of the profession. Legal and ethical considerations with regard to assessment are a matter of concern to the public at large.

Legal and Ethical Considerations

Laws are rules that individuals must obey for the good of the society as a whole—or rules thought to be for the good of society as a whole. Some laws are and have been relatively uncontroversial. For example, the law that mandates driving on the right side of the road has not been a subject of debate, a source of emotional soul-searching, or a stimulus to civil disobedience. For safety and the common good, most people are willing to relinquish their freedom to drive all over the road. Even visitors from countries where it is common to drive on the other side of the road will readily comply with this law when driving in the United States.

Although rules of the road may be relatively uncontroversial, there are some laws that are very controversial. Consider in this context laws pertaining to abortion, capital punishment, euthanasia, affirmative action, busing . . . the list goes on. Exactly how laws regulating matters like these should be written and interpreted are issues of heated controversy. So too is the role of testing and assessment in such matters.

Whereas a body of laws is a body of rules, a body of **ethics** is a body of principles of right, proper, or good conduct. Thus, for example, an ethic of the Old West was "Never shoot 'em in the back." Two well-known principles subscribed to by seafarers are "Women and children leave first in an emergency" and "A captain goes down with his ship."[3] The ethics of journalism dictate that reporters present all sides of a controversial issue. A principle of ethical research is that the researcher should never fudge data; all data must be reported accurately.

To the extent that a **code of professional ethics** is recognized and accepted by members of a profession, it defines the *standard of care* expected of members of that profession. In this context, we may define **standard of care** as the level at which the average, reasonable, and prudent professional would provide diagnostic or therapeutic services under the same or similar conditions.

Members of the public and members of the profession have not always been on "the same side of the fence" with respect to issues of ethics and law. Let's review how and why this has been the case.

JUST THINK . . .

List five ethical guidelines that you think should govern the professional behavior of psychologists involved in psychological testing and assessment.

The Concerns of the Public

The assessment enterprise has never been well understood by the public, and even today we might hear criticisms based on a misunderstanding of testing (e.g., "The only thing tests measure is the ability to take tests"). Possible consequences of public misunderstanding include fear, anger, legislation, litigation, and administrative regulations. In recent years, the testing-related provisions of the *No Child Left Behind Act of 2001* (re-authorized in 2015 as the *Every Student Succeeds Act* or ESSA) and the 2010 *Common Core State Standards* (jointly drafted and released by the National Governor's Association Center for Best Practices and the Council of Chief State School Officers) have generated a great deal of controversy. The *Common Core State Standards* was the product of a state-led effort to bring greater interstate uniformity to

---

3. We leave the question of what to do when the captain of the ship is a woman to some more contemporary volume of seafaring ethics.

what constituted proficiency in various academic subjects. To date, however, *Common Core* has probably been more at the core of public controversy than anything else. Efforts to dismantle these standards have taken the form of everything from verbal attacks by politicians, to local demonstrations by consortiums of teachers, parents, and students. In Chapter 10, *Educational Assessment*, we will take a closer look at the pros and cons of *Common Core*.

Concern about the use of psychological tests first became widespread in the aftermath of World War I, when various professionals (as well as nonprofessionals) sought to adapt group tests developed by the military for civilian use in schools and industry. Reflecting growing public discomfort with the burgeoning assessment industry were popular magazine articles featuring stories with titles such as "The Abuse of Tests" (see Haney, 1981). Less well known were voices of reason that offered constructive ways to correct what was wrong with assessment practices.

The nationwide military testing during World War II in the 1940s did not attract as much popular attention as the testing undertaken during World War I. Rather, an event that took place on the other side of the globe had a far more momentous effect on testing in the United States: the launching of a satellite into space by the country then known as the Union of Soviet Socialist Republics (USSR or Soviet Union). This unanticipated action on the part of a cold-war enemy immediately compounded homeland security concerns in the United States. The prospect of a Russian satellite orbiting Earth 24 hours a day was most unsettling, as it magnified feelings of vulnerability. Perhaps on a positive note, the Soviet launch of Sputnik (the name given to the satellite) had the effect of galvanizing public and legislative opinion around the value of education in areas such as math, science, engineering, and physics. More resources would have to be allocated toward identifying the gifted children who would one day equip the United States to successfully compete with the Soviets.

About a year after the launch of *Sputnik,* Congress passed the National Defense Education Act, which provided federal money to local schools for the purpose of testing ability and aptitude to identify gifted and academically talented students. This event triggered a proliferation of large-scale testing programs in the schools. At the same time, the use of ability tests and personality tests for personnel selection increased in government, the military, and business. The wide and growing use of tests led to renewed public concern, reflected in magazine articles such as "Testing: Can Everyone Be Pigeonholed?" (*Newsweek,* July 20, 1959) and "What the Tests Do Not Test" (*New York Times Magazine,* October 2, 1960). The upshot of such concern was congressional hearings on the subject of testing (Amrine, 1965).

The fires of public concern about testing were again fanned in 1969 when widespread media attention was given to the publication of an article, in the prestigious *Harvard Educational Review,* entitled "How Much Can We Boost IQ and Scholastic Achievement?" Its author, Arthur Jensen, argued that "genetic factors are strongly implicated in the average Negro–white intelligence difference" (1969, p. 82). What followed was an outpouring of public and professional attention to nature-versus-nurture issues in addition to widespread skepticism about what intelligence tests were really measuring. By 1972 the U.S. Select Committee on Equal Education Opportunity was preparing for hearings on the matter. However, according to Haney (1981), the hearings "were canceled because they promised to be too controversial" (p. 1026).

The extent of public concern about psychological assessment is reflected in the extensive involvement of the government in many aspects of the assessment process in recent decades. Assessment has been affected in numerous and important ways by activities of the legislative, executive, and judicial branches of federal and state governments. A sampling of some landmark legislation and litigation is presented in Table 2–1.

Legislation Although the legislation summarized in Table 2–1 was enacted at the federal level, states also have passed legislation that affects the assessment enterprise. In the 1970s numerous states enacted **minimum competency testing programs:** formal testing programs

Table 2–1
Some Significant Legislation and Litigation

Legislation	Significance
Americans with Disabilities Act of 1990	Employment testing materials and procedures must be essential to the job and not discriminate against persons with handicaps.
Civil Rights Act of 1964 (amended in 1991), also known as the Equal Opportunity Employment Act	It is an unlawful employment practice to adjust the scores of, use different cutoff scores for, or otherwise alter the results of employment-related tests on the basis of race, religion, sex, or national origin.
Family Education Rights and Privacy Act (1974)	Parents and eligible students must be given access to school records, and have a right to challenge findings in records by a hearing.
Health Insurance Portability and Accountability Act of 1996 (HIPAA)	New federal privacy standards limit the ways in which health care providers and others can use patients' personal information.
Education for All Handicapped Children (PL 94-142) (1975 and then amended several times thereafter, including IDEA of 1997 and 2004)	Screening is mandated for children suspected to have mental or physical handicaps. Once identified, an individual child must be evaluated by a professional team qualified to determine that child's special educational needs. The child must be reevaluated periodically. Amended in 1986 to extend disability-related protections downward to infants and toddlers.
Individuals with Disabilities Education Act (IDEA) Amendments of 1997 (PL 105-17)	Children should not be inappropriately placed in special education programs due to cultural differences. Schools should accommodate existing test instruments and other alternate means of assessment for the purpose of gauging the progress of special education students as measured by state- and district-wide assessments.
Every Student Succeeds Act (ESSA) (2015)	This reauthorization of the Elementary and Secondary Education Act of 2001 was designed to "close the achievement gaps between minority and nonminority students and between disadvantaged children and their more advantaged peers" by, among other things, setting strict standards for school accountability and establishing periodic assessments to gauge the progress of school districts in improving academic achievement. The "battle cry" driving this legislation was "Demographics are not destiny!" However, by 2012, it was clear that many, perhaps the majority of states, sought or will seek waivers to opt out of NCLB and what has been viewed as its demanding bureaucratic structure, and overly ambitious goals.
Hobson v. Hansen (1967)	U.S. Supreme Court ruled that ability tests developed on Whites could not lawfully be used to track Black students in the school system. To do so could result in resegregation of desegregated schools.
Tarasoff v. Regents of the University of California (1974)	Therapists (and presumably psychological assessors) must reveal privileged information if a third party is endangered. In the words of the Court, "Protective privilege ends where the public peril begins."
Larry P. v. Riles (1979 and reaffirmed by the same judge in 1986)	California judge ruled that the use of intelligence tests to place Black children in special classes had a discriminatory impact because the tests were "racially and culturally biased."
Debra P. v. Turlington (1981)	Federal court ruled that minimum competency testing in Florida was unconstitutional because it perpetuated the effects of past discrimination.
Griggs v. Duke Power Company (1971)	Black employees brought suit against a private company for discriminatory hiring practices. The U.S. Supreme Court found problems with "broad and general testing devices" and ruled that tests must "fairly measure the knowledge or skills required by a particular job."
Albemarle Paper Company v. Moody (1976)	An industrial psychologist at a paper mill found that scores on a general ability test predicted measures of job performance. However, as a group, Whites scored better than Blacks on the test. The U.S. District Court found the use of the test to be sufficiently job related. An appeals court did not. It ruled that discrimination had occurred, however unintended.
Regents of the University of California v. Bakke (1978)	When Alan Bakke, who had been denied admission, learned that his test scores were higher than those of some minority students who had gained admission to the University of California at Davis medical school, he sued. A highly divided U.S. Supreme Court agreed that Bakke should be admitted, but it did not preclude the use of diversity considerations in admission decisions.
Allen v. District of Columbia (1993)	Blacks scored lower than Whites on a city fire department promotion test based on specific aspects of firefighting. The court found in favor of the fire department, ruling that "the promotional examination . . . was a valid measure of the abilities and probable future success of those individuals taking the test."

(continued)

Table 2–1
Some Significant Legislation and Litigation *(continued)*

Legislation	Significance
Adarand Constructors, Inc. v. Pena et al. (1995)	A construction firm competing for a federal contract brought suit against the federal government after it lost a bid to a minority-controlled competitor, which the government had retained instead in the interest of affirmative action. The U.S. Supreme Court, in a close (5–4) decision, found in favor of the plaintiff, ruling that the government's affirmative action policy violated the equal protection clause of the 14th Amendment. The Court ruled, "Government may treat people differently because of their race only for the most compelling reasons."
Jaffee v. Redmond (1996)	Communication between a psychotherapist and a patient (and presumably a psychological assessor and a client) is privileged in federal courts.
Grutter v. Bollinger (2003)	In a highly divided decision, the U.S. Supreme Court approved the use of race in admissions decisions on a time-limited basis to further the educational benefits that flow from a diverse student body.
Mitchell v. State, 192 P.3d 721 (Nev. 2008)	Does a court order for a compulsory psychiatric examination of the defendant in a criminal trial violate that defendant's Fifth Amendment right to avoid self-incrimination? Given the particular circumstances of the case (see Leahy et al., 2010), the Nevada Supreme Court ruled that the defendant's right to avoid self-incrimination was not violated by the trial court's order to have him undergo a psychiatric evaluation.
Ricci v. DeStefano (2009)	The ruling of the U.S. Supreme Court in this case had implications for the ways in which government agencies can and cannot institute race-conscious remedies in hiring and promotional practices. Employers in the public sector were forbidden from e-hiring or promoting personnel using certain practices (such as altering a cutoff score to avoid adverse impact) unless the practice has been demonstrated to have a "strong basis in evidence."

designed to be used in decisions regarding various aspects of students' education. The data from such programs was used in decision making about grade promotions, awarding of diplomas, and identification of areas for remedial instruction. These laws grew out of grassroots support for the idea that high-school graduates should have, at the very least, "minimal competencies" in areas such as reading, writing, and arithmetic.

Truth-in-testing legislation was also passed at the state level beginning in the 1980s. The primary objective of these laws was to give testtakers a way to learn the criteria by which they are being judged. To meet that objective, some laws mandate the disclosure of answers to postsecondary and professional school admissions tests within 30 days of the publication of test scores. Some laws require that information relevant to a test's development and technical soundness be kept on file. Some truth-in-testing laws require providing descriptions of (1) the test's purpose and its subject matter, (2) the knowledge and skills the test purports to measure, (3) procedures for ensuring accuracy in scoring, (4) procedures for notifying testtakers of errors in scoring, and (5) procedures for ensuring the testtaker's confidentiality. Truth-in-testing laws create special difficulties for test developers and publishers, who argue that it is essential for them to keep the test items secret. They note that there may be a limited item pool for some tests and that the cost of developing an entirely new set of items for each succeeding administration of a test is prohibitive.

Some laws mandate the involvement of the executive branch of government in their application. For example, Title VII of the Civil Rights Act of 1964 created the Equal Employment Opportunity Commission (EEOC) to enforce the act. The EEOC has published sets of guidelines concerning standards to be met in constructing and using employment tests. In 1978 the EEOC, the Civil Service Commission, the Department of Labor, and the Justice Department jointly published the *Uniform Guidelines on Employee Selection Procedures.* Here is a sample guideline:

JUST THINK . . .

How might truth-in-testing laws be modified to better protect both the interest of testtakers and that of test developers?

The use of any test which adversely affects hiring, promotion, transfer or any other employment or membership opportunity of classes protected by Title VII constitutes discrimination unless (a) the test has been validated and evidences a high degree of utility as hereinafter described, and (b) the person giving or acting upon the results of the particular test can demonstrate that alternative suitable hiring, transfer or promotion procedures are unavailable for . . . use.

Note that here the definition of discrimination as exclusionary coexists with the proviso that a valid test evidencing "a high degree of utility" (among other criteria) will not be considered discriminatory. Generally, however, the public has been quick to label a test as unfair and discriminatory regardless of its utility. As a consequence, a great public demand for proportionality by group membership in hiring and college admissions now coexists with a great lack of proportionality in skills across groups. Gottfredson (2000) noted that although selection standards can often be improved, the manipulation of such standards "will produce only lasting frustration, not enduring solutions." She recommended that enduring solutions be sought by addressing the problems related to gaps in skills between groups. She argued against addressing the problem by lowering hiring and admission standards or by legislation designed to make hiring and admissions decisions a matter of group quotas.

In Texas, state law was enacted mandating that the top 10% of graduating seniors at each Texas high school be admitted to a state university regardless of SAT scores. This means that, regardless of the quality of education in any particular Texas high school, a senior in the top 10% of the graduating class is guaranteed college admission regardless of how he or she might score on a nationally administered measure. In California, the use of skills tests in the public sector decreased following the passage of Proposition 209, which banned racial preferences (Rosen, 1998). One consequence has been the deemphasis on the Law School Admissions Test (LSAT) as a criterion for being accepted by the University of California at Berkeley law school. Additionally, the law school stopped weighing grade point averages from undergraduate schools in their admission criteria, so that a 4.0 from any California state school "is now worth as much as a 4.0 from Harvard" (Rosen, 1998, p. 62).

Gottfredson (2000) makes the point that those who advocate reversal of achievement standards obtain "nothing of lasting value by eliminating valid tests." For her, lowering standards amounts to hindering progress "while providing only the illusion of progress." Rather than reversing achievement standards, society is best served by action to reverse other trends with deleterious effects (such as trends in family structure). In the face of consistent gaps between members of various groups, Gottfredson emphasized the need for skills training, not a lowering of achievement standards or an unfounded attack on tests.

State and federal legislatures, executive bodies, and courts have been involved in many aspects of testing and assessment. There has been little consensus about whether validated tests on which there are racial differences can be used to assist with employment-related decisions. Courts have also been grappling with the role of diversity in criteria for admission to colleges, universities, and professional schools. For example, in 2003 the question before the U.S. Supreme Court in the case of *Grutter v. Bollinger* was "whether diversity is a compelling interest that can justify the narrowly tailored use of race in selecting applicants for admission to public universities." One of the questions to be decided in that case was whether or not the University of Michigan Law School was using a **quota system,** a selection procedure whereby a fixed number or percentage of applicants from certain backgrounds were selected.[4]

Many of the cases brought before federal courts under Title VII of the Civil Rights Act are employment *discrimination* cases. In this context, **discrimination** may be defined as the

> ◆
>
> **JUST THINK . . .**
>
> How can government and the private sector address problems related to gaps in skills between groups?

---

4. A detailed account of *Grutter v. Bollinger* is presented in the Instructor Resources within Connect.

practice of making distinctions in hiring, promotion, or other selection decisions that tend to systematically favor members of a majority group regardless of actual qualifications for positions. Discrimination may occur as the result of intentional or unintentional action on the part of an employer. As an example of unintentional discrimination, consider the hiring practice of a municipal fire department that required applicants to weigh not less than 135 pounds, and not more than 225 pounds. This job requirement might unintentionally discriminate against, and systematically screen-out, applicants from members of cultural groups whose average weight fell below the required minimum. In all likelihood, the fire department would be challenged in a court of law by a member of the excluded cultural group. Accordingly, the municipality would be required to document why weighing a minimum of 135 pounds should be a requirement for joining that particular fire department.

Typically, when a Title VII charge of discrimination in the workplace is leveled at an employer, a claim is made that hiring, promotion, or some related employment decisions are systematically being made not on the basis of job-related variables, but rather on the basis of some non-job-related variable (such as race, gender, sexual orientation, religion, or national origin). Presumably, the selection criteria favors members of the majority group. In some instances, however, it is members of the majority group who are compelled to make a claim of *reverse discrimination*. In this context, **reverse discrimination** may be defined as the practice of making distinctions in hiring, promotion, or other selection decisions that systematically tend to favor members of a minority group regardless of actual qualifications for positions.

In both discrimination and reverse discrimination cases, the alleged discrimination may occur as the result of intentional or unintentional employer practices. The legal term **disparate treatment** refers to the consequence of an employer's hiring or promotion practice that was intentionally devised to yield some discriminatory result or outcome. Possible motivations for disparate treatment include racial prejudice and a desire to maintain the status quo. By contrast, the legal term **disparate impact** refers to the consequence of an employer's hiring or promotion practice that unintentionally resulted in a discriminatory result or outcome. Because disparate impact is presumed to occur unintentionally, it is not viewed as the product of motivation or planning.

As you will discover as you learn more about test construction and the art and science of testing, a job applicant's score on a test or other assessment procedure is, at least ideally, a reflection of that applicant's underlying ability to succeed at the job. Exactly how well that score actually reflects the job applicant's underlying ability depends on a number of things. One thing it surely depends on is the quality of the test or selection procedure. When a claim of discrimination (or reverse discrimination) is made, an evaluation of the quality of a test or selection procedure will typically entail scrutiny of a number of variables including, for example: (a) the competencies actually assessed by the test and how related those competencies are to the job; (b) the differential weighting, if any, of items on the test or the selection procedures; (c) the psychometric basis for the cutoff score in effect (is a score of 65 to pass, for example, really justified?); (d) the rationale in place for rank-ordering candidates; (e) a consideration of potential alternative evaluation procedures that could have been used; and (f) an evaluation of the statistical evidence that suggests discrimination or reverse discrimination occurred.

Many large companies and organizations, as well as government agencies, hire experts in assessment to help make certain that their hiring and promotion practices result in neither disparate treatment nor disparate impact. This is so because the mere allegation of discrimination can be a source of great expense for any private or public employer. An employer accused of discrimination under Title VII will typically have to budget for a number of expenses including the costs of attorneys, consultants, and experts, and the retrieval, scanning, and storage of records. The consequences of losing such a lawsuit can add additional, sometimes staggering, costs. Included here, for examples, are the costs of the plaintiff's attorney fees, the costs attendant to improving and restructuring hiring and promotion protocols, and the costs of monetary damages to all present and past injured parties. Additionally, new hiring may be halted and pending promotions may be delayed until the court is satisfied that the new practices put into place by the offending employer do not and will not result in disparate treatment or impact. In some cases, a lawsuit will be momentous not merely for the number of dollars spent, but for the number of changes in the law that are a direct result of the litigation.

Litigation Rules governing citizens' behavior stem not only from legislatures but also from interpretations of existing law in the form of decisions handed down by courts. This is why law resulting from **litigation** (the court-mediated resolution of legal matters of a civil, criminal or administrative nature) can impact our daily lives. Examples of some court cases that have affected the assessment enterprise were presented in Table 2–1 under the "Litigation" heading. It is also true that litigation can result in bringing an important and timely matter to the attention of legislators, thus serving as a stimulus to the creation of new legislation. This is exactly what happened in the cases of *PARC v. Commonwealth of Pennsylvania* (1971) and *Mills v. Board of Education of District of Columbia* (1972). In the PARC case, the Pennsylvania Association for Retarded Children brought suit because children with intellectual disability in that state had been denied access to public education. In *Mills,* a similar lawsuit was filed on behalf of children with behavioral, emotional, and learning impairments. Taken together, these two cases had the effect of jump-starting similar litigation in several other jurisdictions and alerting Congress to the need for federal law to ensure appropriate educational opportunities for children with disabilities.

Litigation has sometimes been referred to as "judge-made law" because it typically comes in the form of a ruling by a court. And although judges do, in essence, create law by their rulings, these rulings are seldom made in a vacuum. Rather, judges typically rely on prior rulings and on other people—most notably, expert witnesses—to assist in their judgments. A psychologist acting as an expert witness in criminal litigation may testify on matters such as the competence of a defendant to stand trial, the competence of a witness to give testimony, or the sanity of a defendant entering a plea of "not guilty by reason of insanity." A psychologist acting as an expert witness in a civil matter could conceivably offer opinions on many different types of issues ranging from the parenting skills of a parent in a divorce case to the capabilities of a factory worker prior to sustaining a head injury on the job. In a malpractice case, an expert witness might testify about how reasonable and professional the actions taken by a fellow psychologist were and whether any reasonable and prudent practitioner would have engaged in the same or similar actions (Cohen, 1979).

The issues on which expert witnesses can be called upon to give testimony are as varied as the issues that reach courtrooms for resolution. And so, some important questions arise with respect to expert witnesses. For example: Who is qualified to be an expert witness? How much weight should be given to the testimony of an expert witness? Questions such as these have themselves been the subject of litigation.

A landmark case heard by the U.S. Supreme Court in June 1993 has implications for the admissibility of expert testimony in court. The case was *Daubert v. Merrell Dow Pharmaceuticals.* The origins of this case can be traced to Mrs. Daubert's use of the prescription drug Bendectin to relieve nausea during pregnancy. The plaintiffs sued the manufacturer of this drug, Merrell Dow Pharmaceuticals, when their children were born with birth defects. They claimed that Mrs. Daubert's use of Bendectin had caused their children's birth defects.

Attorneys for the Dauberts were armed with research that they claimed would prove that Bendectin causes birth defects. However, the trial judge ruled that the research failed to meet the criteria for admissibility. In part because the evidence the Dauberts wished to present was not deemed admissible, the trial judge ruled against the Dauberts.

The Dauberts appealed to the next higher court. That court, too, ruled against them and in favor of Merrell Dow. Once again, the plaintiffs appealed, this time to the U.S. Supreme Court. A question before the Court was whether the judge in the original trial had acted properly by not allowing the plaintiffs' research to be admitted into evidence. To understand whether the trial judge acted properly, it is important to understand (1) a ruling that was made in the 1923 case of *Frye v. the United States* and (2) a law subsequently passed by Congress, Rule 702 in the *Federal Rules of Evidence* (1975).

In *Frye,* the Court held that scientific research is admissible as evidence when the research study or method enjoys general acceptance. General acceptance could typically be established by the testimony of experts and by reference to publications in peer-reviewed journals. In short, if an expert witness claimed something that most other experts in the same field would agree with then, under *Frye,* the testimony could be admitted into evidence. Rule 702 changed that by allowing more experts to testify regarding the admissibility of the original expert testimony. Beyond expert testimony indicating that some research method or technique enjoyed general acceptance in the field, other experts were now allowed to testify and present their opinions with regard to the admissibility of the evidence. So, an expert might offer an opinion to a jury concerning the acceptability of a research study or method regardless of whether that opinion represented the opinions of other experts. Rule 702 was enacted to assist juries in their fact-finding by helping them to understand the issues involved.

Presenting their case before the Supreme Court, the attorneys for the Dauberts argued that Rule 702 had wrongly been ignored by the trial judge. The attorneys for the defendant, Merrell Dow Pharmaceuticals, countered that the trial judge had ruled appropriately. The defendant argued that high standards of evidence admissibility were necessary to protect juries from "scientific shamans who, in the guise of their purported expertise, are willing to testify to virtually any conclusion to suit the needs of the litigant with resources sufficient to pay their retainer."

The Supreme Court ruled that the *Daubert* case be retried and that the trial judge should be given wide discretion in deciding what does and does not qualify as scientific evidence. In effect, federal judges were charged with a *gatekeeping* function with respect to what expert testimony would or would not be admitted into evidence. The *Daubert* ruling superseded the long-standing policy, set forth in *Frye,* of admitting into evidence only scientific testimony that had won general acceptance in the scientific community. Opposing expert testimony, whether or not such testimony had won general acceptance in the scientific community, would be admissible.

… the Ancients measured facial beauty by the millihelen, *a unit equal to that necessary to launch one ship….*

Copyright 2016 by Ronald Jay Cohen. All rights reserved.

In *Daubert,* the Supreme Court viewed factors such as general acceptance in the scientific community or publication in a peer-reviewed journal as only some of many possible factors for judges to consider. Other factors judges might consider included the extent to which a theory or technique had been tested and the extent to which the theory or technique might be subject to error. In essence, the Supreme Court's ruling in *Daubert* gave trial judges a great deal of leeway in deciding what juries would be allowed to hear.

Subsequent to *Daubert,* the Supreme Court has ruled on several other cases that in one way or another clarify or slightly modify its position in *Daubert.* For example, in the case of *General Electric Co. v. Joiner* (1997), the Court emphasized that the trial court had a duty to exclude unreliable expert testimony as evidence. In the case of *Kumho Tire Company Ltd. v. Carmichael* (1999), the Supreme Court expanded the principles expounded in *Daubert* to include the testimony of *all* experts, whether or not the experts claimed scientific research as a basis for their testimony. Thus, for example, a psychologist's testimony based on personal experience in independent practice (rather than findings from a formal research study) could be admitted into evidence at the discretion of the trial judge (Mark, 1999).

Whether or not *Frye* or *Daubert* will be relied on by the court depends on the individual jurisdiction in which a legal proceeding occurs. Some jurisdictions still rely on the *Frye* standard when it comes to admitting expert testimony, and some subscribe to *Daubert.* As an example, consider the Missouri case of *Zink vs. State* (2009). After David Zink rear-ended a woman's car in traffic, Zink kidnapped the woman, and then raped, mutilated, and murdered her. Zink was subsequently caught, tried, convicted, and sentenced to death. In an appeal proceeding, Zink argued that the death penalty should be set aside because of his mental disease. Zink's position was that he was not adequately represented by his attorney, because during the trial, his defense attorney had failed to present "hard" evidence of a mental disorder as indicated by a PET scan (a type of neuro-imaging tool that will be discussed in Chapter 14). The appeals court denied Zink's claim, noting that the PET scan failed to meet the *Frye* standard for proving mental disorder (Haque & Guyer, 2010).

The implications of *Daubert* for psychologists and others who might have occasion to provide expert testimony in a trial are wide-ranging (Ewing & McCann, 2006). More specifically, discussions of the implications of *Daubert* for psychological experts can be found in cases involving mental capacity (Frolik, 1999; Poythress, 2004; Bumann, 2010), claims of emotional distress (McLearen et al., 2004), personnel decisions (Landy, 2007), child custody and termination of parental rights (Bogacki & Weiss, 2007; Gould, 2006; Krauss & Sales, 1999), and numerous other matters (Grove & Barden, 1999; Lipton, 1999; Mossman, 2003; Posthuma et al., 2002; Saldanha, 2005; Saxe & Ben-Shakhar, 1999; Slobogin, 1999; Stern, 2001; Tenopyr, 1999). One concern is that *Daubert* has not been applied consistently across jurisdictions and within jurisdictions (Sanders, 2010).

The Concerns of the Profession

As early as 1895 the American Psychological Association (APA), in its infancy, formed its first committee on mental measurement. The committee was charged with investigating various aspects of the relatively new practice of testing. Another APA committee on measurement was formed in 1906 to further study various testing-related issues and problems. In 1916 and again in 1921, symposia dealing with various issues surrounding the expanding uses of tests were sponsored (*Mentality Tests,* 1916; *Intelligence and Its Measurement,* 1921). In 1954, APA published its *Technical Recommendations for Psychological Tests and Diagnostic Tests,* a document that set forth testing standards and technical recommendations. The following year, another professional organization, the National Educational Association (working in collaboration with the National Council on Measurements Used in Education—now known as the National Council on Measurement) published its *Technical Recommendations for Achievement Tests.*

Collaboration between these professional organizations led to the development of rather detailed testing standards and guidelines that would be periodically updated in future years.

Expressions of concern about the quality of tests being administered could also be found in the work of several professionals, acting independently. Anticipating the present-day *Standards,* Ruch (1925), a measurement specialist, proposed a number of standards for tests and guidelines for test development. He also wrote of "the urgent need for a fact-finding organization which will undertake impartial, experimental, and statistical evaluations of tests" (Ruch, 1933). History records that one team of measurement experts even took on the (overly) ambitious task of attempting to rank all published tests designed for use in educational settings. The result was a pioneering book (Kelley, 1927) that provided test users with information needed to compare the merits of published tests. However, given the pace at which test instruments were being published, this resource required regular updating. And so, Oscar Buros was not the first measurement professional to undertake a comprehensive testing of the tests. He was, however, the most tenacious in updating and revising the information.

The APA and related professional organizations in the United States have made available numerous reference works and publications designed to delineate ethical, sound practice in the field of psychological testing and assessment.[5] Along the way, these professional organizations have tackled a variety of thorny questions, such as the questions cited in the next *Just Think.*

◆

JUST THINK . . .

Who should be privy to test data? Who should be able to purchase psychological test materials? Who is qualified to administer, score, and interpret psychological tests? What level of expertise in psychometrics qualifies someone to administer which types of test?

Test-user qualifications Should just anyone be allowed to purchase and use psychological test materials? If not, then who should be permitted to use psychological tests? As early as 1950 an APA Committee on Ethical Standards for Psychology published a report called *Ethical Standards for the Distribution of Psychological Tests and Diagnostic Aids.* This report defined three levels of tests in terms of the degree to which the test's use required knowledge of testing and psychology.

Level A: Tests or aids that can adequately be administered, scored, and interpreted with the aid of the manual and a general orientation to the kind of institution or organization in which one is working (for instance, achievement or proficiency tests).

Level B: Tests or aids that require some technical knowledge of test construction and use and of supporting psychological and educational fields such as statistics, individual differences, psychology of adjustment, personnel psychology, and guidance (e.g., aptitude tests and adjustment inventories applicable to normal populations).

Level C: Tests and aids that require substantial understanding of testing and supporting psychological fields together with supervised experience in the use of these devices (for instance, projective tests, individual mental tests).

The report included descriptions of the general levels of training corresponding to each of the three levels of tests. Although many test publishers continue to use this three-level classification, some do not. In general, professional standards promulgated by professional organizations state that psychological tests should be used only by qualified persons. Furthermore, there is an ethical mandate to take reasonable steps to prevent the misuse of the tests and the information they provide. The obligations of professionals to testtakers are set forth in a document called the *Code of Fair Testing Practices in Education.* Jointly authored and/or sponsored by the Joint Committee of Testing Practices (a coalition of APA, AERA, NCME, the American

---

5. Unfortunately, although organizations in many other countries have verbalized concern about ethics and standards in testing and assessment, relatively few organizations have taken meaningful and effective action in this regard (Leach & Oakland, 2007).

Association for Measurement and Evaluation in Counseling and Development, and the American Speech-Language Hearing Association), this document presents standards for educational test developers in four areas: (1) developing/selecting tests, (2) interpreting scores, (3) striving for fairness, and (4) informing testtakers.

Beyond promoting high standards in testing and assessment among professionals, APA has initiated or assisted in litigation to limit the use of psychological tests to qualified personnel. Skeptics label such measurement-related legal action as a kind of jockeying for turf, done solely for financial gain. A more charitable and perhaps more realistic view is that such actions benefit society at large. It is essential to the survival of the assessment enterprise that certain assessments be conducted by people qualified to conduct them by virtue of their education, training, and experience.

A psychologist licensing law designed to serve as a model for state legislatures has been available from APA since 1987. The law contains no definition of psychological testing. In the interest of the public, the profession of psychology, and other professions that employ psychological tests, it may now be time for that model legislation to be rewritten—with terms such as *psychological testing* and *psychological assessment* clearly defined and differentiated. Terms such as *test-user qualifications* and *psychological assessor qualifications* must also be clearly defined and differentiated. It seems that legal conflicts regarding psychological test usage partly stem from confusion of the terms *psychological testing* and *psychological assessment.* People who are not considered professionals by society may be qualified to use psychological tests (psychological testers). However, these same people may not be qualified to engage in psychological assessment. As we argued in Chapter 1, psychological assessment requires certain skills, talents, expertise, and training in psychology and measurement over and above that required to engage in psychological testing. In the past, psychologists have been lax in differentiating psychological testing from psychological assessment. However, continued laxity may prove to be a costly indulgence, given current legislative and judicial trends.

JUST THINK . . .

Why is it essential for the terms *psychological testing* and *psychological assessment* to be defined and differentiated in state licensing laws?

Testing people with disabilities Challenges analogous to those concerning testtakers from linguistic and cultural minorities are present when testing people with disabling conditions. Specifically, these challenges may include (1) transforming the test into a form that can be taken by the testtaker, (2) transforming the responses of the testtaker so that they are scorable, and (3) meaningfully interpreting the test data.

The nature of the transformation of the test into a form ready for administration to the individual with a disabling condition will, of course, depend on the nature of the disability. Then, too, some test stimuli do not translate easily. For example, if a critical aspect of a test item contains artwork to be analyzed, there may be no meaningful way to translate this item for use with testtakers who are blind. With respect to any test converted for use with a population for which the test was not originally intended, choices must inevitably be made regarding exactly how the test materials will be modified, what standards of evaluation will be applied, and how the results will be interpreted. Professional assessors do not always agree on the answers to such questions.

Another complex issue—this one, ethically charged—has to do with a request by a terminally ill individual for assistance in quickening the process of dying. In Oregon, the first state to enact "Death with Dignity" legislation, a request for assistance in dying may be granted only contingent on the findings of a psychological evaluation; life or death literally hangs in the balance of such assessments. Some ethical and related issues surrounding this phenomenon are discussed in greater detail in this chapter's *Everyday Psychometrics.*

JUST THINK . . .

If the form of a test is changed or adapted for a specific type of administration to a particular individual or group, can the scores obtained by that individual or group be interpreted in a "business as usual" manner?

Life-or-Death Psychological Assessment

The state of Oregon has the distinction—dubious to some people, depending on one's values—of having enacted the nation's first aid-in-dying law. Oregon's Death with Dignity Act (ODDA) provides that a patient with a medical condition thought to give that patient 6 months or less to live may end his or her own life by voluntarily requesting a lethal dose of medication. The law requires that two physicians corroborate the terminal diagnosis and stipulates that either may request a psychological evaluation of the patient by a state-licensed psychologist or psychiatrist in order to ensure that the patient is competent to make the life-ending decision and to rule out impaired judgment due to psychiatric disorder. Assistance in dying will be denied to persons "suffering from a psychiatric or psychological disorder, or depression causing impaired judgement" (ODDA, 1997). Since 1997, similar legislation has been enacted in other states (California, Montana, New Mexico, Vermont, and Washington), and a number of other states are actively considering such "death with dignity" (otherwise known as "physician-aid-in-dying") legislation. Although our focus here is on the ODDA as it affects psychological assessors who are called upon to make life-and-death evaluations, many of the complex issues surrounding such legislation are the same or similar in other jurisdictions. More detailed coverage of the complex legal and values-related issues can be found in sources such as S.M. Johnson, et al. (2014, 2015), Reynolds (2014), Smith et al. (2015), and White (2015).

The ODDA was hotly debated prior to its passage by referendum, and it remains controversial today. Critics of the law question whether suicide is ever a rational choice under any circumstances, and they fear that state-condoned aid in dying will serve to destigmatize suicide in general (Callahan, 1994; see also Richman, 1988). It is argued that the first duty of health and mental health professionals is to do no harm (Jennings, 1991). Some fear that professionals willing to testify to almost anything (so-called **hired guns**) will corrupt the process by providing whatever professional opinion is desired by those who will pay their fees. Critics also point with concern to the experience of the Dutch death-with-dignity legislation. In the Netherlands, relatively few individuals requesting physician-assisted suicide are referred for psychological assessment. Further, the highest court of that land ruled that "in rare cases, physician-assisted suicide is possible even for individuals suffering only from mental problems rather than from physical illnesses" (Abeles & Barlev, 1999, p. 233). On moral and religious grounds, it has been argued that death should be viewed as the province solely of Divine, not human, intervention.

Sigmund Freud (1856–1939)

It has been said that Sigmund Freud made a "rational decision" to end his life. Suffering from terminal throat cancer, having great difficulty in speaking, and experiencing increasing difficulty in breathing, the founder of psychoanalysis asked his physician for a lethal dose of morphine. For years it has been debated whether a decision to die, even made by a terminally ill patient, can ever truly be "rational." Today, in accordance with death-with-dignity legislation, the responsibility for evaluating just how rational such a choice is falls on mental health professionals.
© Max Halberstadt/Pictures From History/The Image Works

Supporters of death-with-dignity legislation argue that life-sustaining equipment and methods can extend life beyond a time when it is meaningful and that the first obligation of health and mental health professionals is to relieve suffering (Latimer, 1991; Quill et al., 1992; Weir, 1992). Additionally, they may point to the dogged determination of people intent on dying and to stories of how many terminally ill people have struggled to end their lives using all kinds of less-than-sure methods, enduring even greater suffering in the process. In marked contrast to such horror stories, the first patient to die under the ODDA is said to have described how the family "could relax and say what a wonderful life we had. We could look back at all the lovely things because we knew we finally had an answer" (cited in Farrenkopf & Bryan, 1999, p. 246).

Professional associations such as the American Psychological Association and the American Psychiatric Association have long promulgated codes of ethics requiring the prevention of suicide. The enactment of the law in Oregon has placed clinicians in that state in a uniquely awkward position. Clinicians who for years have devoted their efforts to suicide prevention have been thrust into the position of being a potential party to, if not a facilitator of, physician-assisted suicide—regardless of how the aid-in-dying process is referred to in the legislation. Note that the Oregon law scrupulously denies that its objective is the legalization of physician-assisted suicide. In fact, the language of the act mandates that action taken under it "shall not, for any purpose, constitute suicide, assisted suicide, mercy killing or homicide, under the law." The framers of the legislation perceived it as a means by which a terminally ill individual could exercise some control over the dying process. Couched in these terms, the

sober duty of the clinician drawn into the process may be made more palatable or even ennobled.

The ODDA provides for various records to be kept regarding patients who die under its provisions. Each year since the Act first took effect, the collected data is published in an annual report. So, for example, in the 2010 report we learn that the reasons most frequently cited for seeking to end one's life were loss of autonomy, decreasing ability to participate in activities that made life enjoyable, loss of dignity, and loss of control of bodily functions. In 2010, 96 prescriptions for lethal medications were prescribed and 59 people had opted to end their life by ingesting the medications.

Psychologists and psychiatrists called upon to make death-with-dignity competency evaluations may accept or decline the responsibility (Haley & Lee, 1998). Judging from one survey of 423 psychologists in clinical practice in Oregon (Fenn & Ganzini, 1999), many of the psychologists who could be asked to make such a life-or-death assessment might decline to do so. About one-third of the sample responded that an ODDA assessment would be outside the scope of their practice. Another 53% of the sample said they would either refuse to perform the assessment and take no further action or refuse to perform the assessment themselves and refer the patient to a colleague.

Guidelines for the ODDA assessment process were offered by Farrenkopf and Bryan (1999), and they are as follows.

The ODDA Assessment Process

1. Review of Records and Case History
With the patient's consent, the assessor will gather records from all relevant sources, including medical and mental health records. A goal is to understand the patient's current functioning in the context of many factors, ranging from the current medical condition and prognosis to the effects of medication and substance use.

2. Consultation with Treating Professionals
With the patient's consent, the assessor may consult with the patient's physician and other professionals involved in the case to better understand the patient's current functioning and current situation.

3. Patient Interviews
Sensitive but thorough interviews with the patient will explore the reasons for the aid-in-dying request, including the pressures and values motivating the request. Other areas to explore include: (a) the patient's understanding of his or her medical condition, the prognosis, and the treatment alternatives; (b) the patient's experience of physical pain, limitations of functioning, and changes over time in cognitive, emotional, and perceptual functioning; (c) the patient's characterization of his or her quality of life, including exploration of related factors including personal identity, role functioning, and self-esteem; and (d) external

pressures on the patient, such as personal or familial financial inability to pay for continued treatment.

4. Interviews with Family Members and Significant Others
With the permission of the patient, separate interviews should be conducted with the patient's family and significant others. One objective is to explore from their perspective how the patient has adjusted in the past to adversity and how the patient has changed and adjusted to his or her current situation.

5. Assessment of Competence
Like the other elements of this overview, this aspect of the assessment is complicated, and only the barest of guidelines can be presented here. In general, the assessor seeks to understand the patient's reasoning and decision-making process, including all information relevant to the decision and its consequences. Some formal tests of competency are available (Appelbaum & Grisso, 1995a, 1995b; Lavin, 1992), but the clinical and legal applicability of such tests to an ODDA assessment has yet to be established.

6. Assessment of Psychopathology
To what extent is the decision to end one's life a function of pathological depression, anxiety, dementia, delirium, psychosis, or some other pathological condition? This is a question the assessor addresses using not only interviews but formal tests.

(continued)

Life-or-Death Psychological Assessment *(continued)*

Examples of the many possible instruments the assessor might employ include intelligence tests, personality tests, neuropsychological tests, symptom checklists, and depression and anxiety scales; refer to the appendix in Farrenkopf and Bryan (1999) for a complete list of these tests.

7. Reporting Findings and Recommendations
Findings, including those related to the patient's mental status and competence, family support and pressures, and anything else relevant to the patient's aid-in-dying request, should be reported. If treatable conditions were found, treatment recommendations relevant to those conditions may be made. Nontreatment types of recommendations may include recommendations for legal advice, estate planning, or other resources. In Oregon, a Psychiatric/Psychological Consultant's Compliance Form with the consultant's recommendations should be completed and sent to the Oregon Health Division.

Computerized test administration, scoring, and interpretation Computer-assisted psychological assessment (CAPA) has become more the norm than the exception. An ever-growing number of psychological tests can be purchased on disc or administered and scored online. In many respects, the relative simplicity, convenience, and range of potential testing activities that computer technology brings to the testing industry have been a great boon. Of course, every rose has its thorns.

For assessment professionals, some major issues with regard to CAPA are as follows.

- *Access to test administration, scoring, and interpretation software.* Despite purchase restrictions on software and technological safeguards to guard against unauthorized copying, software may still be copied. Unlike test kits, which may contain manipulatable objects, manuals, and other tangible items, a computer-administered test may be easily copied and duplicated.

- *Comparability of pencil-and-paper and computerized versions of tests.* Many tests once available only in a paper-and-pencil format are now available in computerized form as well. In many instances the comparability of the traditional and the computerized forms of the test has not been researched or has only insufficiently been researched.

- *The value of computerized test interpretations.* Many tests available for computerized administration also come with computerized scoring and interpretation procedures. Thousands of words are spewed out every day in the form of test interpretation results, but the value of these words in many cases is questionable.

- *Unprofessional, unregulated "psychological testing" online.* A growing number of Internet sites purport to provide, usually for a fee, online psychological tests. Yet the vast majority of the tests offered would not meet a psychologist's standards. Assessment professionals wonder about the long-term effect of these largely unprofessional and unregulated "psychological testing" sites. Might they, for example, contribute to more public skepticism about psychological tests?

Imagine being administered what has been represented to you as a "psychological test," only to find that the test is not bona fide. The online availability of myriad tests of uncertain quality that purport to measure psychological variables increases the possibility of this happening. To help remedy such potential

JUST THINK . . .

What differences in the test results may exist as a result of the same test being administered orally, online, or by means of a paper-and-pencil examination? What differences in the testtaker's experience may exist as a function of test administration method?

problems, a Florida-based organization called the International Test Commission developed the "International Guidelines on Computer-Based and Internet-Delivered Testing" (Coyne & Bartram, 2006). These guidelines address technical, quality, security, and related issues. Although not without limitations (Sale, 2006), these guidelines clearly are a step forward in nongovernmental regulation. Other guidelines are written to inform the rendering of professional services to members of certain populations.

Guidelines with respect to certain populations   From time to time, the American Psychological Association (APA) has published special guidelines for professionals who have occasion to assess, treat, conduct research with, or otherwise consult with members of certain populations. In general, the guidelines are designed to assist professionals in providing informed and developmentally appropriate services. Note that there exists a distinction between APA *guidelines* and *standards*. Although standards must be followed by all psychologists, guidelines are more aspirational in nature (Reed et al., 2002). In late 2015, for example, APA published its *Guidelines for Psychological Practice with Transgender and Gender Nonconforming (TGNC) People.* The document lists and discusses 16 guidelines. To get a sense of what these guidelines say, the first guideline is: "Psychologists understand that gender is a non-binary construct that allows for a range of gender identities and that a person's gender identity may not align with sex assigned at birth." The last guideline, Guideline 16, is: "Psychologists seek to prepare trainees in psychology to work competently with TGNC people."

Various other groups and professional organizations also publish documents that may be helpful to mental health professionals vis-à-vis the provision of services to members of specific populations. For example, the Intercollegiate Committee of the Royal College of Psychiatrists publishes a list of "good practices" for the assessment and treatment of people with gender dysphoria (Wylie et al., 2014). Other groups have their own "best practices" (Goodrich et al., 2013) or simply "practices" (Beek et al., 2015; Bouman et al., 2014; de Vries et al., 2014; Dhejne et al., 2016; Sherman et al., 2014) that may inform professional practice. Additional practice-related resources that may be of particular interest to assessment professionals include special issues of journals devoted to the topic of interest (such as Borden, 2015), and publications that specifically focus on the topic from an assessment perspective (da Silva et al., 2016; Dèttore et al., 2015; Johnson et al., 2004; Luyt, 2015; Rönspies et al., 2015).

The Rights of Testtakers

As prescribed by the *Standards* and in some cases by law, some of the rights that test users accord to testtakers are the right of informed consent, the right to be informed of test findings, the right to privacy and confidentiality, and the right to the least stigmatizing label.

The right of informed consent   Testtakers have a right to know why they are being evaluated, how the test data will be used, and what (if any) information will be released to whom. With full knowledge of such information, testtakers give their **informed consent** to be tested. The disclosure of the information needed for consent must, of course, be in language the testtaker can understand. Thus, for a testtaker as young as 2 or 3 years of age or an individual who has an intellectual disability with limited language skills, a disclosure before testing might be worded as follows: "I'm going to ask you to try to do some things so that I can see what you know how to do and what things you could use some more help with" (APA, 1985, p. 85).

Competency in providing informed consent has been broken down into several components: (1) Being able to evidence a choice as to whether one wants to participate; (2) demonstrating a factual understanding of the issues; (3) being able to reason about the facts of a study, treatment, or whatever it is to which consent is sought, and (4) appreciating the nature of the situation (Appelbaum & Roth, 1982; Roth et al., 1977).

Competency to provide consent may be assessed informally, and in fact many physicians engage in such informal assessment. Marson et al. (1997) cautioned that informal assessment of competency may be idiosyncratic and unreliable. As an alternative, many standardized instruments are available (Sturman, 2005). One such instrument is the MacArthur Competence Assessment Tool-Treatment (Grisso & Appelbaum, 1998). Also known as the MacCAT-T, it consists of structured interviews based on the four components of competency listed above (Grisso et al., 1997). Other instruments have been developed that are performance based and yield information on decision-making competence (Finucane & Gullion, 2010).

Another consideration related to competency is the extent to which persons diagnosed with psychopathology may be incompetent to provide informed consent (Sturman, 2005). So, for example, individuals diagnosed with dementia, bipolar disorder, and schizophrenia are likely to have competency impairments that may affect their ability to provide informed consent. By contrast, individuals with major depression may retain the competency to give truly informed consent (Grisso & Appelbaum, 1995; Palmer et al., 2007; Vollmann et al., 2003). Competence to provide informed consent may be improved by training (Carpenter et al., 2000; Dunn et al., 2002; Palmer et al., 2007). Therefore, clinicians should not necessarily assume that patients are not capable of consent based solely on their diagnosis.

If a testtaker is incapable of providing an informed consent to testing, such consent may be obtained from a parent or a legal representative. Consent must be in written rather than oral form. The written form should specify (1) the general purpose of the testing, (2) the specific reason it is being undertaken in the present case, and (3) the general type of instruments to be administered. Many school districts now routinely send home such forms before testing children. Such forms typically include the option to have the child assessed privately if a parent so desires. In instances where testing is legally mandated (as in a court-ordered situation), obtaining informed consent to test may be considered more of a courtesy (undertaken in part for reasons of establishing good rapport) than a necessity.

One gray area with respect to the testtaker's right of fully informed consent before testing involves research and experimental situations wherein the examiner's complete disclosure of all facts pertinent to the testing (including the experimenter's hypothesis and so forth) might irrevocably contaminate the test data. In some instances, deception is used to create situations that occur relatively rarely. For example, a deception might be created to evaluate how an emergency worker might react under emergency conditions. Sometimes deception involves the use of confederates to simulate social conditions that can occur during an event of some sort.

For situations in which it is deemed advisable not to obtain fully informed consent to evaluation, professional discretion is in order. Testtakers might be given a minimum amount of information before the testing. For example, "This testing is being undertaken as part of an experiment on obedience to authority." A full disclosure and debriefing would be made after the testing. Various professional organizations have created policies and guidelines regarding deception in research. For example, the APA *Ethical Principles of Psychologists and Code of Conduct* (2002) provides that psychologists (a) do not use deception unless it is absolutely necessary, (b) do not use deception at all if it will cause participants emotional distress, and (c) fully debrief participants.[6]

JUST THINK . . .

Describe a scenario where knowledge of the experimenter's hypotheses would probably invalidate the data gathered.

The right to be informed of test findings In a bygone era, the inclination of many psychological assessors, particularly many clinicians, was to tell testtakers as little as possible

---

6. A detailed presentation of exactly how APA's *Ethical Principles of Psychologists* impacts the professional conduct of users of tests and measurements can be accessed through the Instructor Resources within Connect.

about the nature of their performance on a particular test or test battery. In no case would they disclose diagnostic conclusions that could arouse anxiety or precipitate a crisis. This orientation was reflected in at least one authoritative text that advised testers to keep information about test results superficial and focus only on "positive" findings. This was done so that the examinee would leave the test session feeling "pleased and satisfied" (Klopfer et al., 1954, p. 15). But all that has changed, and giving realistic information about test performance to examinees is not only ethically and legally mandated but may be useful from a therapeutic perspective as well. Testtakers have a right to be informed, in language they can understand, of the nature of the findings with respect to a test they have taken. They are also entitled to know what recommendations are being made as a consequence of the test data. If the test results, findings, or recommendations made on the basis of test data are voided for any reason (such as irregularities in the test administration), testtakers have a right to know that as well.

Because of the possibility of untoward consequences of providing individuals with information about themselves—ability, lack of ability, personality, values—the communication of results of a psychological test is a most important part of the evaluation process. With sensitivity to the situation, the test user will inform the testtaker (and the parent or the legal representative or both) of the purpose of the test, the meaning of the score relative to those of other testtakers, and the possible limitations and margins of error of the test. And regardless of whether such reporting is done in person or in writing, a qualified professional should be available to answer any further questions that testtakers (or their parents or legal representatives) have about the test scores. Ideally, counseling resources will be available for those who react adversely to the information presented.

The right to privacy and confidentiality   The concept of the **privacy right** "recognizes the freedom of the individual to pick and choose for himself the time, circumstances, and particularly the extent to which he wishes to share or withhold from others his attitudes, beliefs, behavior, and opinions" (Shah, 1969, p. 57). When people in court proceedings "take the Fifth" and refuse to answer a question put to them on the grounds that the answer might be self-incriminating, they are asserting a right to privacy provided by the Fifth Amendment to the Constitution. The information withheld in such a manner is termed *privileged;* it is information that is protected by law from disclosure in a legal proceeding. State statutes have extended the concept of **privileged information** to parties who communicate with each other in the context of certain relationships, including the lawyer–client relationship, the doctor–patient relationship, the priest–penitent relationship, and the husband–wife relationship. In most states, privilege is also accorded to the psychologist–client relationship.

Privilege is extended to parties in various relationships because it has been deemed that the parties' right to privacy serves a greater public interest than would be served if their communications were vulnerable to revelation during legal proceedings. Stated another way, it is for the social good if people feel confident that they can talk freely to their attorneys, clergy, physicians, psychologists, and spouses. Professionals such as psychologists who are parties to such special relationships have a legal and ethical duty to keep their clients' communications confidential.

Confidentiality may be distinguished from *privilege* in that, whereas "confidentiality concerns matters of communication outside the courtroom, privilege protects clients from disclosure in judicial proceedings" (Jagim et al., 1978, p. 459). Privilege is not absolute. There are occasions when a court can deem the disclosure of certain information necessary and can order the disclosure of that information. Should the psychologist or other professional so ordered refuse, he or she does so under the threat of going to jail, being fined, and other legal consequences.

JUST THINK . . .

Psychologists may be compelled by court order to reveal privileged communications. What types of situations might result in such a court order?

Privilege in the psychologist–client relationship belongs to the client, not the psychologist. The competent client can direct the psychologist to disclose information to some third party (such as an attorney or an insurance carrier), and the psychologist is obligated to make the disclosure. In some rare instances the psychologist may be ethically (if not legally) compelled to disclose information if that information will prevent harm either to the client or to some endangered third party. An illustrative case would be the situation where a client details a plan to commit suicide or homicide. In such an instance the psychologist would be legally and ethically compelled to take reasonable action to prevent the client's intended outcome from occurring. Here, the preservation of life would be deemed an objective more important than the nonrevelation of privileged information. Matters of ethics are seldom straightforward; questions will inevitably arise, and reasonable people may differ as to the answers to those questions. One such assessment-related ethics question has to do with the extent to which third-party observers should be allowed to be part of an assessment (see Figure 2–3). Some have argued that third parties are necessary and should be allowed, while others have argued that the presence of the third party changes the dynamics of the assessment by a social influence process that may result in spurious increases or decreases in the assessee's observed performance (Aiello & Douthitt, 2001; Gavett et al., 2005; McCaffrey, 2007; McCaffrey et al., 2005;

Figure 2–3
Ethical Issues when Third-Parties Observe or Participate in Assessments

Two necessary parties to any assessment are an assessor and an assessee. A third party might be an observer/supervisor of the assessor, a friend or relative of the assessee, a legal representative of the assesse or the institution in which the assessment is being conducted, a translator, or someone else. Ethical questions have been raised regarding the extent to which assessment data gathered in the presence of third parties is compromised due to a process of social influence (Duff & Fischer, 2005).
© Thomas Barwick/Getty Images

Vanderhoff et al., 2011; Yantz & McCaffrey, 2005, 2009). Advocates of the strict enforcement of a policy that prohibits third-party observers during psychological assessment argue that alternatives to such observation either exist (e.g., unobtrusive electronic observation) or must be developed.

Another important confidentiality-related issue has to do with what a psychologist must keep confidential versus what must be disclosed. A wrong judgment on the part of the clinician regarding the revelation of confidential communication may lead to a lawsuit or worse. A landmark U.S. Supreme Court case in this area was the 1974 case of *Tarasoff v. Regents of the University of California*. In that case, a therapy patient had made known to his psychologist his intention to kill an unnamed but readily identifiable girl two months before the murder. The Court held that "protective privilege ends where the public peril begins," and so the therapist had a duty to warn the endangered girl of her peril. Clinicians may have a duty to warn endangered third parties not only of potential violence but of potential AIDS infection from an HIV-positive client (Buckner & Firestone, 2000; Melchert & Patterson, 1999) as well as other threats to physical well-being.

Another ethical mandate with regard to confidentiality involves the safekeeping of test data. Test users must take reasonable precautions to safeguard test records. If these data are stored in a filing cabinet, then the cabinet should be locked and preferably made of steel. If these data are stored in a computer, electronic safeguards must be taken to ensure only authorized access. The individual or institution should have a reasonable policy covering the length of time that records are stored and when, if ever, the records will be deemed to be outdated, invalid, or useful only from an academic perspective. In general, it is not a good policy to maintain all records in perpetuity. Policies in conformance with privacy laws should also be in place governing the conditions under which requests for release of records to a third party will be honored. Some states have enacted law that describes, in detail, procedures for storing and disposing of patient records.

JUST THINK . . .

Describe key features of a model law designed to guide psychologists in the storage and disposal of patient records.

Relevant to the release of assessment-related information is the Health Insurance Portability and Accountability Act of 1996 (HIPAA), which took effect in April 2003. These federal privacy standards limit the ways that health care providers, health plans, pharmacies, and hospitals can use patients' personal medical information. For example, personal health information may not be used for purposes unrelated to health care.

In part due to the decision of the U.S. Supreme Court in the case of *Jaffee v. Redmond* (1996), HIPAA singled out "psychotherapy notes" as requiring even more stringent protection than other records. The ruling in *Jaffee* affirmed that communications between a psychotherapist and a patient were privileged in federal courts. The HIPAA privacy rule cited *Jaffee* and defined privacy notes as "notes recorded (in any medium) by a health care provider who is a mental health professional documenting or analyzing the contents of conversation during a private counseling session or a group, joint, or family counseling session and that are separated from the rest of the individual's medical record." Although "results of clinical tests" were specifically *excluded* in this definition, we would caution assessment professionals to obtain specific consent from assessees before releasing assessment-related information. This is particularly essential with respect to data gathered using assessment tools such as the interview, behavioral observation, and role play.

The right to the least stigmatizing label   The *Standards* advise that the least stigmatizing labels should always be assigned when reporting test results. To better appreciate the need for this standard, consider the case of Jo Ann Iverson.[7] Jo Ann was 9 years old and suffering from

7. See *Iverson v. Frandsen,* 237 F. 2d 898 (Idaho, 1956) or Cohen (1979), pp. 149–150.

claustrophobia when her mother brought her to a state hospital in Blackfoot, Idaho, for a psychological evaluation. Arden Frandsen, a psychologist employed part-time at the hospital, conducted an evaluation of Jo Ann, during the course of which he administered a Stanford-Binet Intelligence Test. In his report, Frandsen classified Jo Ann as "feeble-minded, at the high-grade moron level of general mental ability." Following a request from Jo Ann's school guidance counselor, a copy of the psychological report was forwarded to the school—and embarrassing rumors concerning Jo Ann's mental condition began to circulate.

Jo Ann's mother, Carmel Iverson, brought a libel (defamation) suit against Frandsen on behalf of her daughter.[8] Mrs. Iverson lost the lawsuit. The court ruled in part that the psychological evaluation "was a professional report made by a public servant in good faith, representing his best judgment." But although Mrs. Iverson did not prevail in her lawsuit, we can certainly sympathize with her anguish at the thought of her daughter going through life with a label such as "high-grade moron"—this despite the fact that the psychologist had probably merely copied that designation from the test manual. We would also add that the Iversons may have prevailed in their lawsuit had the cause of action been breach of confidentiality and had the defendant been the guidance counselor; there was uncontested testimony that it was from the guidance counselor's office, and not that of the psychologist, that the rumors concerning Jo Ann first emanated.

While on the subject of the rights of testtakers, let's not forget about the rights—of sorts—of students of testing and assessment. Having been introduced to various aspects of the assessment enterprise, you have the right to learn more about technical aspects of measurement. Exercise that right in the succeeding chapters.

Self-Assessment

Test your understanding of elements of this chapter by seeing if you can explain each of the following terms, expressions, abbreviations, events, or names in terms of their significance in the context of psychological testing and assessment:

affirmative action
Albemarle Paper Company v. Moody
Alfred Binet
James McKeen Cattell
Charles Darwin
Code of Fair Testing Practices in Education
code of professional ethics
collectivist culture
confidentiality
culture
culture-specific test
Debra P. v. Turlington
discrimination
disparate impact
disparate treatment
ethics
eugenics

Francis Galton
Henry H. Goddard
Griggs v. Duke Power Company
HIPAA
hired gun
Hobson v. Hansen
individualist culture
informed consent
Jaffee v. Redmond
Larry P. v. Riles
laws
litigation
minimum competency testing programs
Christiana D. Morgan
Henry A. Murray
ODDA
Karl Pearson

privacy right
privileged information
projective test
psychoanalysis
Public Law 105-17
quota system
reverse discrimination
Hermann Rorschach
self-report
Sputnik
standard of care
Tarasoff v. Regents of the University of California
truth-in-testing legislation
David Wechsler
Lightner Witmer
Robert S. Woodworth
Wilhelm Max Wundt

---

8. An interesting though tangential aspect of this case was that Iverson had brought her child in with a presenting problem of claustrophobia. The plaintiff questioned whether the administration of an intelligence test under these circumstances was unauthorized and beyond the scope of the consultation. However, the defendant psychologist proved to the satisfaction of the Court that the administration of the Stanford-Binet was necessary to determine whether Jo Ann had the mental capacity to respond to psychotherapy.

3

A Statistics Refresher

F rom the red-pencil number circled at the top of your first spelling test to the computer printout of your college entrance examination scores, tests and test scores touch your life. They seem to reach out from the paper and shake your hand when you do well and punch you in the face when you do poorly. They can point you toward or away from a particular school or curriculum. They can help you to identify strengths and weaknesses in your physical and mental abilities. They can accompany you on job interviews and influence a job or career choice.

In your role as a student, you have probably found that your relationship to tests has been primarily that of a testtaker. But as a psychologist, teacher, researcher, or employer, you may find that your relationship with tests is primarily that of a test user—the person who breathes life and meaning into test scores by applying the knowledge and skill to interpret them appropriately. You may one day create a test, whether in an academic or a business setting, and then have the responsibility

JUST THINK . . .

For most people, test scores are an important fact of life. But what makes those numbers so meaningful? In general terms, what information, ideally, should be conveyed by a test score?

for scoring and interpreting it. In that situation, or even from the perspective of one who would take that test, it's essential to understand the theory underlying test use and the principles of test-score interpretation.

Test scores are frequently expressed as numbers, and statistical tools are used to describe, make inferences from, and draw conclusions about numbers.[1] In this statistics refresher, we cover scales of measurement, tabular and graphic presentations of data, measures of central tendency, measures of variability, aspects of the normal curve, and standard scores. If these statistics-related terms look painfully familiar to you, we ask your indulgence and ask you to remember that overlearning is the key to retention. Of course, if any of these terms appear unfamiliar, we urge you to learn more about them. Feel free to supplement the discussion here with a review of these and related terms in any good elementary statistics text. The brief review of statistical concepts that follows can in no way replace a sound grounding in basic statistics gained through an introductory course in that subject.

---

1. Of course, a test score may be expressed in other forms, such as a letter grade or a pass–fail designation. Unless stated otherwise, terms such as *test score, test data, test results,* and *test scores* are used throughout this book to refer to numeric descriptions of test performance.

Scales of Measurement

We may formally define **measurement** as the act of assigning numbers or symbols to characteristics of things (people, events, whatever) according to rules. The rules used in assigning numbers are guidelines for representing the magnitude (or some other characteristic) of the object being measured. Here is an example of a measurement rule: *Assign the number 12 to all lengths that are exactly the same length as a 12-inch ruler.* A **scale** is a set of numbers (or other symbols) whose properties model empirical properties of the objects to which the numbers are assigned.[2]

JUST THINK . . .

What is another example of a measurement rule?

There are various ways in which a scale can be categorized. One way of categorizing a scale is according to the type of variable being measured. Thus, a scale used to measure a continuous variable might be referred to as a *continuous scale,* whereas a scale used to measure a discrete variable might be referred to as a *discrete scale.* A continuous scale exists when it is theoretically possible to divide any of the values of the scale. A distinction must be made, however, between what is theoretically possible and what is practically desirable. The units into which a continuous scale will actually be divided may depend on such factors as the purpose of the measurement and practicality. In measurement to install venetian blinds, for example, it is theoretically possible to measure by the millimeter or even by the micrometer. But is such precision necessary? Most installers do just fine with measurement by the inch.

As an example of measurement using a discrete scale, consider mental health research that presorted subjects into one of two discrete groups: (1) previously hospitalized and (2) never hospitalized. Such a, categorization scale would be characterized as *discrete* because it would not be accurate or meaningful to categorize any of the subjects in the study as anything other than "previously hospitalized" or "not previously hospitalized."

JUST THINK . . .

The *scale* with which we are all perhaps most familiar is the common bathroom scale. How are a psychological test and a bathroom scale alike? How are they different? Your answer may change as you read on.

JUST THINK . . .

Assume the role of a test creator. Now write some instructions to users of your test that are designed to reduce to the absolute minimum any error associated with test scores. Be sure to include instructions regarding the preparation of the site where the test will be administered.

Measurement always involves *error.* In the language of assessment, **error** refers to the collective influence of all of the factors on a test score or measurement beyond those specifically measured by the test or measurement. As we will see, there are many different sources of error in measurement. Consider, for example, the score someone received on a test in American history. We might conceive of part of the score as reflecting the testtaker's knowledge of American history and part of the score as reflecting error. The error part of the test score may be due to many different factors. One source of error might have been a distracting thunderstorm going on outside at the time the test was administered. Another source of error was the particular selection of test items the instructor chose to use for the test. Had a different item or two been used in the test, the testtaker's score on the test might have been higher or lower. Error is very much an element of all measurement, and it is an element for which any theory of measurement must surely account.

Measurement using continuous scales always involves error. To illustrate why, let's go back to the scenario involving venetian

---

2. David L. Streiner reflected, "Many terms have been used to describe a collection of items or questions—*scale, test, questionnaire, index, inventory,* and a host of others—with no consistency from one author to another" (2003a, p. 217, emphasis in the original). Streiner proposed to refer to questionnaires of theoretically like or related items as scales and those of theoretically unrelated items as *indexes.* He acknowledged that counterexamples of each term could readily be found.

blinds. The length of the window measured to be 35.5 inches could, in reality, be 35.7 inches. The measuring scale is conveniently marked off in grosser gradations of measurement. Most scales used in psychological and educational assessment are continuous and therefore can be expected to contain this sort of error. The number or score used to characterize the trait being measured on a continuous scale should be thought of as an approximation of the "real" number. Thus, for example, a score of 25 on some test of anxiety should not be thought of as a precise measure of anxiety. Rather, it should be thought of as an approximation of the real anxiety score had the measuring instrument been calibrated to yield such a score. In such a case, perhaps the score of 25 is an approximation of a real score of, say, 24.7 or 25.44.

It is generally agreed that there are four different levels or scales of measurement. Within these levels or scales of measurement, assigned numbers convey different kinds of information. Accordingly, certain statistical manipulations may or may not be appropriate, depending upon the level or scale of measurement.[3]

The French word for black is *noir* (pronounced "'nwăre"). We bring this up here only to call attention to the fact that this word is a useful acronym for remembering the four levels or scales of measurement. Each letter in *noir* is the first letter of the succeedingly more rigorous levels: *N* stands for *nominal, o* for *ordinal, i* for *interval,* and *r* for *ratio* scales.

JUST THINK . . .

Acronyms like *noir* are useful memory aids. As you continue in your study of psychological testing and assessment, create your own acronyms to help remember related groups of information. Hey, you may even learn some French in the process.

Nominal Scales

Nominal scales are the simplest form of measurement. These scales involve classification or categorization based on one or more distinguishing characteristics, where all things measured must be placed into mutually exclusive and exhaustive categories. For example, in the specialty area of clinical psychology, a nominal scale in use for many years is the *Diagnostic and Statistical Manual of Mental Disorders*. Each disorder listed in that manual is assigned its own number. In a past version of that manual, the version really does not matter for the purposes of this example, the number 303.00 identified alcohol intoxication, and the number 307.00 identified stuttering. But these numbers were used exclusively for classification purposes and could not be meaningfully added, subtracted, ranked, or averaged. Hence, the middle number between these two diagnostic codes, 305.00, did *not* identify an intoxicated stutterer.

Individual test items may also employ nominal scaling, including *yes/no* responses. For example, consider the following test items:

Instructions: Answer either *yes* or *no*.

Are you actively contemplating suicide? _____

Are you currently under professional care for a psychiatric disorder? _____

Have you ever been convicted of a felony? _____

In each case, a *yes* or *no* response results in the placement into one of a set of mutually exclusive groups: suicidal or not, under care for psychiatric disorder or not, and felon or not. Arithmetic operations that can legitimately be performed with

JUST THINK . . .

What are some other examples of nominal scales?

---

3. For the purposes of our statistics refresher, we present what Nunnally (1978) called the "fundamentalist" view of measurement scales, which "holds that 1. there are distinct types of measurement scales into which all possible measures of attributes can be classified, 2. each measure has some 'real' characteristics that permit its proper classification, and 3. once a measure is classified, the classification specifies the types of mathematical analyses that can be employed with the measure" (p. 24). Nunnally and others have acknowledged that alternatives to the "fundamentalist" view may also be viable.

nominal data include counting for the purpose of determining how many cases fall into each category and a resulting determination of proportion or percentages.[4]

Ordinal Scales

Like nominal scales, **ordinal scales** permit classification. However, in addition to classification, rank ordering on some characteristic is also permissible with ordinal scales. In business and organizational settings, job applicants may be rank-ordered according to their desirability for a position. In clinical settings, people on a waiting list for psychotherapy may be rank-ordered according to their need for treatment. In these examples, individuals are compared with others and assigned a rank (perhaps 1 to the best applicant or the most needy wait-listed client, 2 to the next, and so forth).

Although he may have never used the term *ordinal scale,* Alfred Binet, a developer of the intelligence test that today bears his name, believed strongly that the data derived from an intelligence test are ordinal in nature. He emphasized that what he tried to do with his test was not to *measure* people (as one might measure a person's height), but merely to *classify* (and rank) people on the basis of their performance on the tasks. He wrote:

> I have not sought . . . to sketch a method of measuring, in the physical sense of the word, but only a method of classification of individuals. The procedures which I have indicated will, if perfected, come to classify a person before or after such another person, or such another series of persons; but I do not believe that one may measure one of the intellectual aptitudes in the sense that one measures a length or a capacity. Thus, when a person studied can retain seven figures after a single audition, one can class him, from the point of his memory for figures, after the individual who retains eight figures under the same conditions, and before those who retain six. It is a classification, not a measurement . . . we do not measure, we classify. (Binet, cited in Varon, 1936, p. 41)

Assessment instruments applied to the individual subject may also use an ordinal form of measurement. The Rokeach Value Survey uses such an approach. In that test, a list of personal values—such as freedom, happiness, and wisdom—are put in order according to their perceived importance to the testtaker (Rokeach, 1973). If a set of 10 values is rank ordered, then the testtaker would assign a value of "1" to the most important and "10" to the least important.

Ordinal scales imply nothing about how much greater one ranking is than another. Even though ordinal scales may employ numbers or "scores" to represent the rank ordering, the numbers do not indicate units of measurement. So, for example, the performance difference between the first-ranked job applicant and the second-ranked applicant may be small while the difference between the second- and third-ranked applicants may be large. On the Rokeach Value Survey, the value ranked "1" may be handily the most important in the mind of the testtaker. However, ordering the values that follow may be difficult to the point of being almost arbitrary.

Ordinal scales have no absolute zero point. In the case of a test of job performance ability, every testtaker, regardless of standing on the test, is presumed to have *some* ability. No testtaker is presumed to have zero ability. Zero is without meaning in such a test because the number of units that separate one testtaker's score from another's is simply not known. The scores are ranked, but the actual number of units separating one score from the next may be many, just a few, or practically none. Because there is no zero point on an ordinal scale, the ways in which data from such scales can be analyzed statistically are limited. One cannot average the qualifications of the

> **JUST THINK . . .**
>
> What are some other examples of ordinal scales?

---

4. Other ways to analyze nominal data exist (Gokhale & Kullback, 1978; Kranzler & Moursund, 1999). However, let's leave the discussion of these advanced methods for another time (and another book).

first- and third-ranked job applicants, for example, and expect to come out with the qualifications of the second-ranked applicant.

Interval Scales

In addition to the features of nominal and ordinal scales, **interval scales** contain equal intervals between numbers. Each unit on the scale is exactly equal to any other unit on the scale. But like ordinal scales, interval scales contain no absolute zero point. With interval scales, we have reached a level of measurement at which it *is* possible to average a set of measurements and obtain a meaningful result.

Scores on many tests, such as tests of intelligence, are analyzed statistically in ways appropriate for data at the interval level of measurement. The difference in intellectual ability represented by IQs of 80 and 100, for example, is thought to be similar to that existing between IQs of 100 and 120. However, if an individual were to achieve an IQ of 0 (something that is not even possible, given the way most intelligence tests are structured), that would not be an indication of zero (the total absence of) intelligence. Because interval scales contain no absolute zero point, a presumption inherent in their use is that no testtaker possesses none of the ability or trait (or whatever) being measured.

JUST THINK . . .

What are some other examples of interval scales?

Ratio Scales

In addition to all the properties of nominal, ordinal, and interval measurement, a **ratio scale** has a true zero point. All mathematical operations can meaningfully be performed because there exist equal intervals between the numbers on the scale as well as a true or absolute zero point.

In psychology, ratio-level measurement is employed in some types of tests and test items, perhaps most notably those involving assessment of neurological functioning. One example is a test of hand grip, where the variable measured is the amount of pressure a person can exert with one hand (see Figure 3–1). Another example is a timed test of perceptual-motor ability that requires the testtaker to assemble a jigsaw-like puzzle. In such an instance, the time taken to successfully complete the puzzle is the measure that is recorded. Because there is a true zero point on this scale (or, 0 seconds), it is meaningful to say that a testtaker who completes the assembly in 30 seconds has taken half the time of a testtaker who completed it in 60 seconds. In this example, it is meaningful to speak of a true zero point on the scale—but in theory only. Why? *Just think . . .*

No testtaker could ever obtain a score of zero on this assembly task. Stated another way, no testtaker, not even The Flash (a comic-book superhero whose power is the ability to move at superhuman speed), could assemble the puzzle in zero seconds.

JUST THINK . . .

What are some other examples of ratio scales?

Measurement Scales in Psychology

The ordinal level of measurement is most frequently used in psychology. As Kerlinger (1973, p. 439) put it: "Intelligence, aptitude, and personality test scores are, *basically and strictly speaking,* ordinal. These tests indicate with more or less accuracy not the amount of intelligence, aptitude, and personality traits of individuals, but rather the rank-order positions of the individuals." Kerlinger allowed that "most psychological and educational scales approximate interval equality fairly well," though he cautioned that if ordinal measurements are treated as if they were interval measurements, then the test user must "be constantly alert to the possibility of *gross* inequality of intervals" (pp. 440–441).

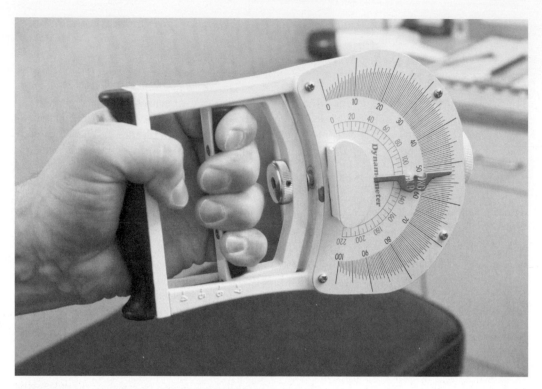

Figure 3–1
Ratio-Level Measurement in the Palm of One's Hand

*Pictured above is a **dynamometer,** an instrument used to measure strength of hand grip. The examinee is instructed to squeeze the grips as hard as possible. The squeezing of the grips causes the gauge needle to move and reflect the number of pounds of pressure exerted. The highest point reached by the needle is the score. This is an example of ratio-level measurement. Someone who can exert 10 pounds of pressure (and earns a score of 10) exerts twice as much pressure as a person who exerts 5 pounds of pressure (and earns a score of 5). On this test it is possible to achieve a score of 0, indicating a complete lack of exerted pressure. Although it is meaningful to speak of a score of 0 on this test, we have to wonder about its significance. How might a score of 0 result? One way would be if the testtaker genuinely had paralysis of the hand. Another way would be if the testtaker was uncooperative and unwilling to comply with the demands of the task. Yet another way would be if the testtaker was attempting to malinger or "fake bad" on the test. Ratio scales may provide us "solid" numbers to work with, but some interpretation of the test data yielded may still be required before drawing any "solid" conclusions.*

© BanksPhotos/Getty Images RF

Why would psychologists want to treat their assessment data as interval when those data would be better described as ordinal? Why not just say that they are ordinal? The attraction of interval measurement for users of psychological tests is the flexibility with which such data can be manipulated statistically. "What kinds of statistical manipulation?" you may ask.

In this chapter we discuss the various ways in which test data can be described or converted to make those data more manageable and understandable. Some of the techniques we'll describe, such as the computation of an average, can be used if data are assumed to be interval- or ratio-level in nature but not if they are ordinal- or nominal-level. Other techniques, such as those involving the creation of graphs or tables, may be used with ordinal- or even nominal-level data.

Describing Data

Suppose you have magically changed places with the professor teaching this course and that you have just administered an examination that consists of 100 multiple-choice items (where 1 point is awarded for each correct answer). The distribution of scores for the 25 students enrolled in your class could theoretically range from 0 (none correct) to 100 (all correct). A **distribution** may be defined as a set of test scores arrayed for recording or study. The 25 scores in this distribution are referred to as *raw scores*. As its name implies, a **raw score** is a straightforward, unmodified accounting of performance that is usually numerical. A raw score may reflect a simple tally, as in *number of items responded to correctly on an achievement test*. As we will see later in this chapter, raw scores can be converted into other types of scores. For now, let's assume it's the day after the examination and that you are sitting in your office looking at the raw scores listed in Table 3–1. What do you do next?

One task at hand is to communicate the test results to your class. You want to do that in a way that will help students understand how their performance on the test compared to the performance of other students. Perhaps the first step is to organize the data by transforming it from a random listing of raw scores into something that immediately conveys a bit more information. Later, as we will see, you may wish to transform the data in other ways.

JUST THINK . . .

In what way do most of your instructors convey test-related feedback to students? Is there a better way they could do this?

Frequency Distributions

The data from the test could be organized into a distribution of the raw scores. One way the scores could be distributed is by the frequency with which they occur. In a **frequency distribution,** all scores are listed alongside the number of times each score occurred. The scores might be listed in tabular or graphic form. Table 3–2 lists the frequency of occurrence of each score in one column and the score itself in the other column.

Often, a frequency distribution is referred to as a *simple frequency distribution* to indicate that individual scores have been used and the data have not been grouped. Another kind of

Table 3–1

Data from Your Measurement Course Test

Student	Score (number correct)
Judy	78
Joe	67
Lee-Wu	69
Miriam	63
Valerie	85
Diane	72
Henry	92
Esperanza	67
Paula	94
Martha	62
Rill	61
Homer	44
Robert	66
Michael	87
Jorge	76
Mary	83
"Mousey"	42
Barbara	82
John	84
Donna	51
Uriah	69
Leroy	61
Ronald	96
Vinnie	73
Bianca	79

Table 3–2

Frequency Distribution of Scores from Your Test

Score	f (frequency)
96	1
94	1
92	1
87	1
85	1
84	1
83	1
82	1
79	1
78	1
76	1
73	1
72	1
69	2
67	2
66	1
63	1
62	1
61	2
51	1
44	1
42	1

frequency distribution used to summarize data is a *grouped frequency distribution.* In a **grouped frequency distribution,** test-score intervals, also called *class intervals,* replace the actual test scores. The number of class intervals used and the size or *width* of each class interval (or, the range of test scores contained in each class interval) are for the test user to decide. But how?

In most instances, a decision about the size of a class interval in a grouped frequency distribution is made on the basis of convenience. Of course, virtually any decision will represent a trade-off of sorts. A convenient, easy-to-read summary of the data is the trade-off for the loss of detail. To what extent must the data be summarized? How important is detail? These types of questions must be considered. In the grouped frequency distribution in Table 3–3, the test scores have been grouped into 12 class intervals, where each class interval is equal to 5 points.[5] The highest class interval (95–99) and the lowest class interval (40–44) are referred to, respectively, as the upper and lower limits of the distribution. Here, the need for convenience in reading the data outweighs the need for great detail, so such groupings of data seem logical.

Frequency distributions of test scores can also be illustrated graphically. A **graph** is a diagram or chart composed of lines, points, bars, or other symbols that describe and illustrate

Table 3–3

A Grouped Frequency Distribution

Class Interval	f (frequency)
95–99	1
90–94	2
85–89	2
80–84	3
75–79	3
70–74	2
65–69	5
60–64	4
55–59	0
50–54	1
45–49	0
40–44	2

---

5. Technically, each number on such a scale would be viewed as ranging from as much as 0.5 below it to as much as 0.5 above it. For example, the "real" but hypothetical width of the class interval ranging from 95 to 99 would be the difference between 99.5 and 94.5, or 5. The true upper and lower limits of the class intervals presented in the table would be 99.5 and 39.5, respectively.

data. With a good graph, the place of a single score in relation to a distribution of test scores can be understood easily. Three kinds of graphs used to illustrate frequency distributions are the histogram, the bar graph, and the frequency polygon (Figure 3–2). A **histogram** is a graph

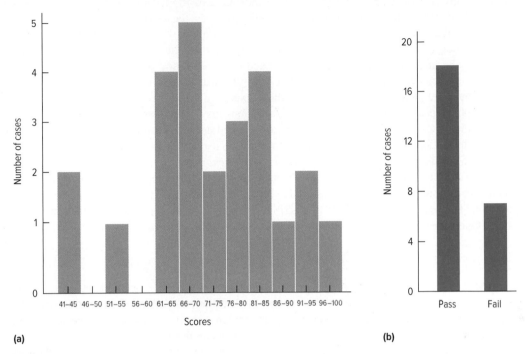

(a)

(b)

Figure 3–2
Graphic Illustrations of Data from Table 3–3

A histogram (a), a bar graph (b), and a frequency polygon (c) all may be used to graphically convey information about test performance. Of course, the labeling of the bar graph and the specific nature of the data conveyed by it depend on the variables of interest. In (b), the variable of interest is the number of students who passed the test (assuming, for the purpose of this illustration, that a raw score of 65 or higher had been arbitrarily designated in advance as a passing grade).

Returning to the question posed earlier—the one in which you play the role of instructor and must communicate the test results to your students—which type of graph would best serve your purpose? Why?

As we continue our review of descriptive statistics, you may wish to return to your role of professor and formulate your response to challenging related questions, such as "Which measure(s) of central tendency shall I use to convey this information?" and "Which measure(s) of variability would convey the information best?"

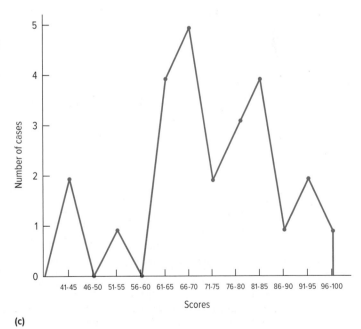

(c)

with vertical lines drawn at the true limits of each test score (or class interval), forming a series of contiguous rectangles. It is customary for the test scores (either the single scores or the midpoints of the class intervals) to be placed along the graph's horizontal axis (also referred to as the *abscissa* or *X*-axis) and for numbers indicative of the frequency of occurrence to be placed along the graph's vertical axis (also referred to as the *ordinate* or *Y*-axis). In a **bar graph,** numbers indicative of frequency also appear on the *Y*-axis, and reference to some categorization (e.g., yes/no/maybe, male/female) appears on the *X*-axis. Here the rectangular bars typically are not contiguous. Data illustrated in a **frequency polygon** are expressed by a continuous line connecting the points where test scores or class intervals (as indicated on the *X*-axis) meet frequencies (as indicated on the *Y*-axis).

Graphic representations of frequency distributions may assume any of a number of different shapes (Figure 3–3). Regardless of the shape of graphed data, it is a good idea for the consumer of the information contained in the graph to examine it carefully—and, if need be, critically. Consider, in this context, this chapter's *Everyday Psychometrics*.

As we discuss in detail later in this chapter, one graphic representation of data of particular interest to measurement professionals is the *normal* or *bell-shaped curve*. Before getting to that, however, let's return to the subject of distributions and how we can describe and characterize them. One way to describe a distribution of test scores is by a measure of central tendency.

Measures of Central Tendency

A **measure of central tendency** is a statistic that indicates the average or midmost score between the extreme scores in a distribution. The center of a distribution can be defined in different ways. Perhaps the most commonly used measure of central tendency is the *arithmetic mean* (or, more simply, **mean**), which is referred to in everyday language as the "average." The mean takes into account the actual numerical value of every score. In special instances, such as when there are only a few scores and one or two of the scores are extreme in relation to the remaining ones, a measure of central tendency other than the mean may be desirable. Other measures of central tendency we review include the *median* and the *mode*. Note that, in the formulas to follow, the standard statistical shorthand called "summation notation" (*summation* meaning "the sum of") is used. The Greek uppercase letter sigma, Σ, is the symbol used to signify "sum"; if X represents a test score, then the expression ΣX means "add all the test scores."

The arithmetic mean The **arithmetic mean,** denoted by the symbol $\overline{X}$ (and pronounced "X bar"), is equal to the sum of the observations (or test scores, in this case) divided by the number of observations. Symbolically written, the formula for the arithmetic mean is $\overline{X} = \Sigma(X/n)$, where n equals the number of observations or test scores. The arithmetic mean is typically the most appropriate measure of central tendency for interval or ratio data when the distributions are believed to be approximately normal. An arithmetic mean can also be computed from a frequency distribution. The formula for doing this is

$$\overline{X} = \frac{\Sigma(fX)}{n}$$

where $\Sigma(fX)$ means "multiply the frequency of each score by its corresponding score and then sum." An estimate of the arithmetic mean may also be obtained from a grouped frequency distribution using the same formula, where X is equal to the midpoint of the class interval. Table 3–4 illustrates a calculation of the mean from a grouped frequency distribution. After doing the math you will find that, using the grouped data, a mean of 71.8 (which may be rounded to 72) is calculated. Using the raw scores, a mean of 72.12 (which also may be rounded to 72) is

JUST THINK . . .

Imagine that a thousand or so engineers took an extremely difficult pre-employment test. A handful of the engineers earned very high scores but the vast majority did poorly, earning extremely low scores. Given this scenario, what are the pros and cons of using the mean as a measure of central tendency for this test?

Consumer (of Graphed Data), Beware!

One picture is worth a thousand words, and one purpose of representing data in graphic form is to convey information at a glance. However, although two graphs may be accurate with respect to the data they represent, their pictures—and the impression drawn from a glance at them—may be vastly different. As an example, consider the following hypothetical scenario involving a hamburger restaurant chain we'll call "The Charred House."

The Charred House chain serves very charbroiled, microscopically thin hamburgers formed in the shape of little triangular houses. In the 10-year period since its founding in 1993, the company has sold, on average, 100 million burgers per year. On the chain's tenth anniversary, The Charred House distributes a press release proudly announcing "Over a Billion Served."

Reporters from two business publications set out to research and write a feature article on this hamburger restaurant chain. Working solely from sales figures as compiled from annual reports to the shareholders, Reporter 1 focuses her story on the differences in yearly sales. Her article is entitled "A Billion Served—But Charred House Sales Fluctuate from Year to Year," and its graphic illustration is reprinted here.

Quite a different picture of the company emerges from Reporter 2's story, entitled "A Billion Served—And Charred House Sales Are as Steady as Ever," and its accompanying graph. The latter story is based on a diligent analysis of comparable data for the same number of hamburger chains in the same areas of the country over the same time period. While researching the story, Reporter 2 learned that yearly fluctuations in sales are common to the entire industry and that the annual fluctuations observed in the Charred House figures were—relative to other chains—insignificant.

Compare the graphs that accompanied each story. Although both are accurate insofar as they are based on the correct numbers, the impressions they are likely to leave are quite different.

Incidentally, custom dictates that the intersection of the two axes of a graph be at 0 and that all the points on the *Y*-axis be in equal and proportional intervals from 0. This custom is followed in Reporter 2's story, where the first point on the ordinate is 10 units more than 0, and each succeeding point is also 10 more units away from 0. However, the custom is violated in Reporter

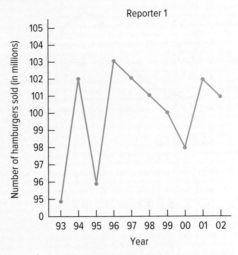

(a)   The Charred House Sales over a 10-Year Period

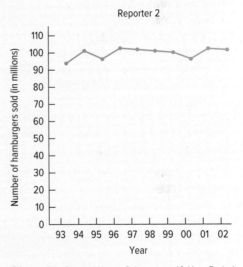

(b)   The Charred House Sales over a 10-Year Period

1's story, where the first point on the ordinate is 95 units more than 0, and each succeeding point increases only by 1. The fact that the custom is violated in Reporter 1's story should serve as a warning to evaluate pictorial representations of data all the more critically.

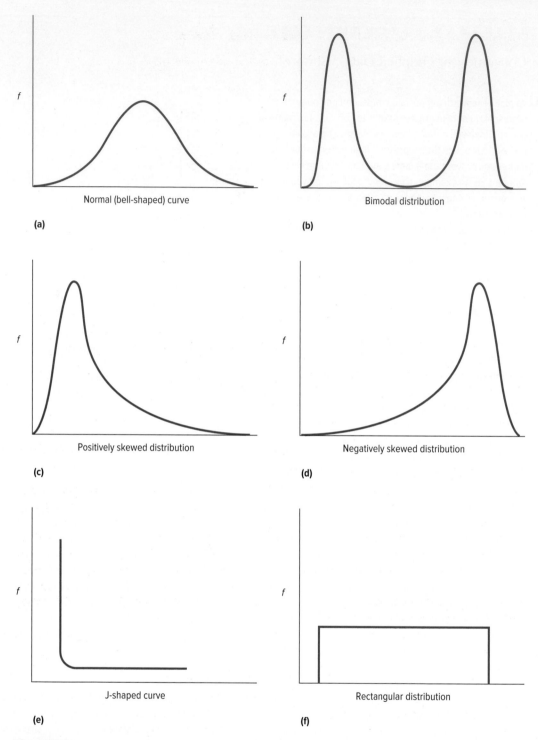

Figure 3–3
Shapes That Frequency Distributions Can Take

Table 3–4
Calculating the Arithmetic Mean from a Grouped Frequency Distribution

Class Interval	f	X (midpoint of class interval)	fX
95–99	1	97	97
90–94	2	92	184
85–89	2	87	174
80–84	3	82	246
75–79	3	77	231
70–74	2	72	144
65–69	5	67	335
60–64	4	62	248
55–59	0	57	000
50–54	1	52	52
45–49	0	47	000
40–44	2	42	84
	$\Sigma f = 25$		$\Sigma (fX) = 1{,}795$

To estimate the arithmetic mean of this grouped frequency distribution,

$$\bar{X} = \frac{\sum (fX)}{n} = \frac{1795}{25} = 71.80$$

To calculate the mean of this distribution using raw scores,

$$\bar{X} = \frac{\sum X}{n} = \frac{1803}{25} = 72.12$$

calculated. Frequently, the choice of statistic will depend on the required degree of precision in measurement.

The median   The **median,** defined as the middle score in a distribution, is another commonly used measure of central tendency. We determine the median of a distribution of scores by ordering the scores in a list by magnitude, in either ascending or descending order. If the total number of scores ordered is an odd number, then the median will be the score that is exactly in the middle, with one-half of the remaining scores lying above it and the other half of the remaining scores lying below it. When the total number of scores ordered is an even number, then the median can be calculated by determining the arithmetic mean of the two middle scores. For example, suppose that 10 people took a preemployment word-processing test at The Rochester Wrenchworks (TRW) Corporation. They obtained the following scores, presented here in descending order:

66

65

61

59

53

52

41

36

35

32

The median of these data would be calculated by obtaining the average (or, the arithmetic mean) of the two middle scores, 53 and 52 (which would be equal to 52.5). The median is an appropriate measure of central tendency for ordinal, interval, and ratio data. The median may be a particularly useful measure of central tendency in cases where relatively few scores fall at the high end of the distribution or relatively few scores fall at the low end of the distribution.

Suppose not 10 but rather tens of thousands of people had applied for jobs at The Rochester Wrenchworks. It would be impractical to find the median by simply ordering the data and finding the midmost scores, so how would the median score be identified? For our purposes, the answer is simply that there are advanced methods for doing so. There are also techniques for identifying the median in other sorts of distributions, such as a grouped frequency distribution and a distribution wherein various scores are identical. However, instead of delving into such new and complex territory, let's resume our discussion of central tendency and consider another such measure.

The mode The most frequently occurring score in a distribution of scores is the **mode.**[6] As an example, determine the mode for the following scores obtained by another TRW job applicant, Bruce. The scores reflect the number of words Bruce word-processed in seven 1-minute trials:

43   34   45   51   42   31   51

It is TRW policy that new hires must be able to word-process at least 50 words per minute. Now, place yourself in the role of the corporate personnel officer. Would you hire Bruce? The most frequently occurring score in this distribution of scores is 51. If hiring guidelines gave you the freedom to use any measure of central tendency in your personnel decision making, then it would be your choice as to whether or not Bruce is hired. You could hire him and justify this decision on the basis of his modal score (51). You also could *not* hire him and justify this decision on the basis of his mean score (below the required 50 words per minute). Ultimately, whether Rochester Wrenchworks will be Bruce's new home away from home will depend on other job-related factors, such as the nature of the job market in Rochester and the qualifications of competing applicants. Of course, if company guidelines dictate that only the mean score be used in hiring decisions, then a career at TRW is not in Bruce's immediate future.

Distributions that contain a tie for the designation "most frequently occurring score" can have more than one mode. Consider the following scores—arranged in no particular order—obtained by 20 students on the final exam of a new trade school called the Home Study School of Elvis Presley Impersonators:

51   49   51   50   66   52   53   38   17   66
33   44   73   13   21   91   87   92   47   3

These scores are said to have a **bimodal distribution** because there are two scores (51 and 66) that occur with the highest frequency (of two). Except with nominal data, the mode tends not to be a very commonly used measure of central tendency. Unlike the arithmetic mean, which has to be calculated, the value of the modal score is not calculated; one simply counts and determines which score occurs most frequently. Because the mode is arrived at in this manner, the modal score may be totally atypical—for instance, one at an extreme end of the distribution—which nonetheless occurs with the greatest frequency. In fact, it is theoretically possible for a bimodal distribution to have two modes, each of which falls at the high or the low end of the distribution—thus violating the expectation that a measure of central tendency should be . . . well, central (or indicative of a point at the middle of the distribution).

---

6. If adjacent scores occur equally often and more often than other scores, custom dictates that the mode be referred to as the average.

Even though the mode is not calculated in the sense that the mean is calculated, and even though the mode is not necessarily a unique point in a distribution (a distribution can have two, three, or even more modes), the mode can still be useful in conveying certain types of information. The mode is useful in analyses of a qualitative or verbal nature. For example, when assessing consumers' recall of a commercial by means of interviews, a researcher might be interested in which word or words were mentioned most by interviewees.

The mode can convey a wealth of information *in addition to* the mean. As an example, suppose you wanted an estimate of the number of journal articles published by clinical psychologists in the United States in the past year. To arrive at this figure, you might total the number of journal articles accepted for publication written by each clinical psychologist in the United States, divide by the number of psychologists, and arrive at the arithmetic mean. This calculation would yield an indication of the average number of journal articles published. Whatever that number would be, we can say with certainty that it would be more than the mode. It is well known that most clinical psychologists do not write journal articles. The mode for publications by clinical psychologists in any given year is zero. In this example, the arithmetic mean would provide us with a precise measure of the average number of articles published by clinicians. However, what might be lost in that measure of central tendency is that, proportionately, very few of all clinicians do most of the publishing. The mode (in this case, a mode of zero) would provide us with a great deal of information at a glance. It would tell us that, regardless of the mean, most clinicians do not publish.

Because the mode is not calculated in a true sense, it is a nominal statistic and cannot legitimately be used in further calculations. The median is a statistic that takes into account the order of scores and is itself ordinal in nature. The mean, an interval-level statistic, is generally the most stable and useful measure of central tendency.

JUST THINK . . .

Devise your own example to illustrate how the mode, and not the mean, can be the most useful measure of central tendency.

Measures of Variability

Variability is an indication of how scores in a distribution are scattered or dispersed. As Figure 3–4 illustrates, two or more distributions of test scores can have the same mean even though differences in the dispersion of scores around the mean can be wide. In both distributions A and B, test scores could range from 0 to 100. In distribution A, we see that the mean score was 50 and the remaining scores were widely distributed around the mean. In distribution B, the mean was also 50 but few people scored higher than 60 or lower than 40.

Statistics that describe the amount of variation in a distribution are referred to as **measures of variability.** Some measures of variability include the range, the interquartile range, the semi-interquartile range, the average deviation, the standard deviation, and the variance.

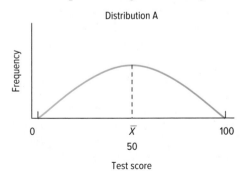
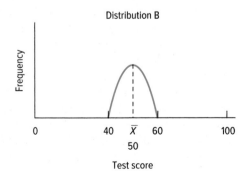

Figure 3–4
Two Distributions with Differences in Variability

JUST THINK . . .

Devise two distributions of test scores to illustrate how the range can overstate or understate the degree of variability in the scores.

The range   The **range** of a distribution is equal to the difference between the highest and the lowest scores. We could describe distribution B of Figure 3–3, for example, as having a range of 20 if we knew that the highest score in this distribution was 60 and the lowest score was 40 (60 − 40 = 20). With respect to distribution A, if we knew that the lowest score was 0 and the highest score was 100, the range would be equal to 100 − 0, or 100. The range is the simplest measure of variability to calculate, but its potential use is limited. Because the range is based entirely on the values of the lowest and highest scores, one extreme score (if it happens to be the lowest or the highest) can radically alter the value of the range. For example, suppose distribution B included a score of 90. The range of this distribution would now be equal to 90 − 40, or 50. Yet, in looking at the data in the graph for distribution B, it is clear that the vast majority of scores tend to be between 40 and 60.

As a descriptive statistic of variation, the range provides a quick but gross description of the spread of scores. When its value is based on extreme scores in a distribution, the resulting description of variation may be understated or overstated. Better measures of variation include the interquartile range and the semi-interquartile range.

The interquartile and semi-interquartile ranges   A distribution of test scores (or any other data, for that matter) can be divided into four parts such that 25% of the test scores occur in each quarter. As illustrated in Figure 3–5, the dividing points between the four quarters in the distribution are the **quartiles.** There are three of them, respectively labeled Q_1, Q_2, and Q_3. Note that *quartile* refers to a specific point whereas *quarter* refers to an interval. An individual score may, for example, fall *at* the third quartile or *in* the third quarter (but *not* "in" the third quartile or "at" the third quarter). It should come as no surprise to you that Q_2 and the median are exactly the same. And just as the median is the midpoint in a distribution of scores, so are quartiles Q_1 and Q_3 the *quarter-points* in a distribution of scores. Formulas may be employed to determine the exact value of these points.

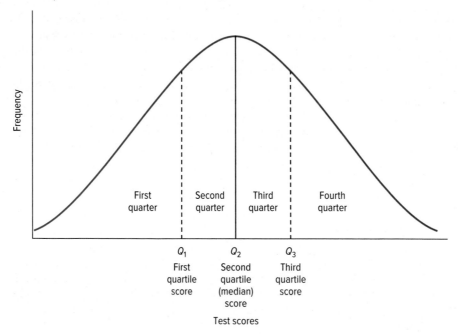

Figure 3–5
A Quartered Distribution

The **interquartile range** is a measure of variability equal to the difference between Q_3 and Q_1. Like the median, it is an ordinal statistic. A related measure of variability is the **semi-interquartile range,** which is equal to the interquartile range divided by 2. Knowledge of the relative distances of Q_1 and Q_3 from Q_2 (the median) provides the seasoned test interpreter with immediate information as to the shape of the distribution of scores. In a perfectly symmetrical distribution, Q_1 and Q_3 will be exactly the same distance from the median. If these distances are unequal then there is a lack of symmetry. This lack of symmetry is referred to as *skewness,* and we will have more to say about that shortly.

The average deviation   Another tool that could be used to describe the amount of variability in a distribution is the **average deviation,** or AD for short. Its formula is

$$AD = \frac{\sum |x|}{n}$$

The lowercase italic x in the formula signifies a score's deviation from the mean. The value of x is obtained by subtracting the mean from the score ($X -$ mean $= x$). The bars on each side of x indicate that it is the *absolute value* of the deviation score (ignoring the positive or negative sign and treating all deviation scores as positive). All the deviation scores are then summed and divided by the total number of scores (n) to arrive at the average deviation. As an exercise, calculate the average deviation for the following distribution of test scores:

85   100   90   95   80

Begin by calculating the arithmetic mean. Next, obtain the absolute value of each of the five deviation scores and sum them. As you sum them, note what would happen if you did not ignore the plus or minus signs: All the deviation scores would then sum to 0. Divide the sum of the deviation scores by the number of measurements (5). Did you obtain an AD of 6? The AD tells us that the five scores in this distribution varied, on average, 6 points from the mean.

The average deviation is rarely used. Perhaps this is so because the deletion of algebraic signs renders it a useless measure for purposes of any further operations. Why, then, discuss it here? The reason is that a clear understanding of what an average deviation measures provides a solid foundation for understanding the conceptual basis of another, more widely used measure: the *standard deviation.* Keeping in mind what an average deviation is, what it tells us, and how it is derived, let's consider its more frequently used "cousin," the standard deviation.

> **JUST THINK . . .**
>
> After reading about the standard deviation, explain in your own words how an understanding of the *average deviation* can provide a "stepping-stone" to better understanding the concept of a *standard deviation.*

The standard deviation   Recall that, when we calculated the average deviation, the problem of the sum of all deviation scores around the mean equaling zero was solved by employing only the absolute value of the deviation scores. In calculating the standard deviation, the same problem must be dealt with, but we do so in a different way. Instead of using the absolute value of each deviation score, we use the square of each score. With each score squared, the sign of any negative deviation becomes positive. Because all the deviation scores are squared, we know that our calculations won't be complete until we go back and obtain the square root of whatever value we reach.

We may define the **standard deviation** as a measure of variability equal to the square root of the average squared deviations about the mean. More succinctly, it is equal to the square root of the *variance.* The **variance** is equal to the arithmetic mean of the squares of the differences between the scores in a distribution and their mean. The formula used to calculate the variance (s^2) using deviation scores is

$$s^2 = \frac{\sum x^2}{n}$$

Simply stated, the variance is calculated by squaring and summing all the deviation scores and then dividing by the total number of scores. The variance can also be calculated in other ways. For example: From raw scores, first calculate the summation of the raw scores squared, divide by the number of scores, and then subtract the mean squared. The result is

$$s^2 = \frac{\sum X^2}{n} - \overline{X}^2$$

The variance is a widely used measure in psychological research. To make meaningful interpretations, the test-score distribution should be approximately normal. We'll have more to say about "normal" distributions later in the chapter. At this point, think of a normal distribution as a distribution with the greatest frequency of scores occurring near the arithmetic mean. Correspondingly fewer and fewer scores relative to the mean occur on both sides of it.

For some hands-on experience with—and to develop a sense of mastery of—the concepts of variance and standard deviation, why not allot the next 10 or 15 minutes to calculating the standard deviation for the test scores shown in Table 3–1? Use both formulas to verify that they produce the same results. Using deviation scores, your calculations should look similar to these:

$$s^2 = \frac{\sum x^2}{n}$$

$$s^2 = \frac{\sum (X - \text{mean})^2}{n}$$

$$s^2 = \frac{[(78 - 72.12)^2 + (67 - 72.12)^2 + \cdots + (79 - 72.12)^2]}{25}$$

$$s^2 = \frac{4972.64}{25}$$

$$s^2 = 198.91$$

Using the raw-scores formula, your calculations should look similar to these:

$$s^2 = \frac{\sum X^2}{n} - \overline{X}^2$$

$$s^2 = \frac{[(78)^2 + (67)^2 + \cdots + (79)^2)}{25} - 5201.29$$

$$s^2 = \frac{135005}{25} - 5201.29$$

$$s^2 = 5400.20 - 5201.29$$

$$s^2 = 198.91$$

In both cases, the standard deviation is the square root of the variance (s^2). According to our calculations, the standard deviation of the test scores is 14.10. If $s = 14.10$, then 1 standard deviation unit is approximately equal to 14 units of measurement or (with reference to our example and rounded to a whole number) to 14 test-score points. The test data did not provide a good normal curve approximation. Test professionals would describe these data as "positively skewed." *Skewness,* as well as related terms such as *negatively skewed* and *positively skewed,* are covered in the next section. Once you are "positively familiar" with terms like *positively skewed,* you'll appreciate all the more the section later in this chapter entitled "The Area Under the Normal Curve." There you will find a wealth of information about test-score interpretation in the case when the scores are *not* skewed—that is, when the test scores are approximately normal in distribution.

The symbol for standard deviation has variously been represented as *s, S,* SD, and the lowercase Greek letter sigma (σ). One custom (the one we adhere to) has it that *s* refers to the sample standard deviation and σ refers to the population standard deviation. The number of observations in the sample is *n,* and the denominator $n - 1$ is sometimes used to calculate what is referred to as an "unbiased estimate" of the population value (though it's actually only *less* biased; see Hopkins & Glass, 1978). Unless *n* is 10 or less, the use of *n* or $n - 1$ tends not to make a meaningful difference.

Whether the denominator is more properly *n* or $n - 1$ has been a matter of debate. Lindgren (1983) has argued for the use of $n - 1$, in part because this denominator tends to make correlation formulas simpler. By contrast, most texts recommend the use of $n - 1$ only when the data constitute a sample; when the data constitute a population, *n* is preferable. For Lindgren (1983), it doesn't matter whether the data are from a sample or a population. Perhaps the most reasonable convention is to use *n* either when the entire population has been assessed or when no inferences to the population are intended. So, when considering the examination scores of one class of students—including all the people about whom we're going to make inferences—it seems appropriate to use *n*.

Having stated our position on the *n* versus $n - 1$ controversy, our formula for the population standard deviation follows. In this formula, $\overline{X}$ represents a sample mean and *M* a population mean:

$$\sqrt{\frac{\Sigma(X - M)^2}{n}}$$

The standard deviation is a very useful measure of variation because each individual score's distance from the mean of the distribution is factored into its computation. You will come across this measure of variation frequently in the study and practice of measurement in psychology.

Skewness

Distributions can be characterized by their **skewness,** or the nature and extent to which symmetry is absent. Skewness is an indication of how the measurements in a distribution are distributed. A distribution has a **positive skew** when relatively few of the scores fall at the high end of the distribution. Positively skewed examination results may indicate that the test was too difficult. More items that were easier would have been desirable in order to better discriminate at the lower end of the distribution of test scores. A distribution has a **negative skew** when relatively few of the scores fall at the low end of the distribution. Negatively skewed examination results may indicate that the test was too easy. In this case, more items of a higher level of difficulty would make it possible to better discriminate between scores at the upper end of the distribution. (Refer to Figure 3–3 for graphic examples of skewed distributions.)

The term *skewed* carries with it negative implications for many students. We suspect that *skewed* is associated with *abnormal,* perhaps because the skewed distribution deviates from the symmetrical or so-called normal distribution. However, the presence or absence of symmetry in a distribution (skewness) is simply one characteristic by which a distribution can be described. Consider in this context a hypothetical Marine Corps Ability and Endurance Screening Test administered to all civilians seeking to enlist in the U.S. Marines. Now look again at the graphs in Figure 3–3. Which graph do you think would best describe the resulting distribution of test scores? (No peeking at the next paragraph before you respond.)

No one can say with certainty, but if we had to guess, then we would say that the Marine Corps Ability and Endurance Screening Test data would look like graph C, the positively skewed distribution in Figure 3–3. We say this assuming that a level of difficulty would have been built into the test to ensure that relatively few assessees would score at the high end of the distribution. Most of the applicants would probably score at the low end of the distribution. All of this is quite consistent with the advertised objective of the Marines, who are only looking for a *few* good men. You know: *the few, the proud.* Now, a question regarding this positively skewed distribution: Is the skewness a good thing? A bad thing? An abnormal thing? In truth, it is probably none of these things—it just *is*. By the way, although they may not advertise it as much, the Marines are also looking for (an unknown quantity of) good women. But here we are straying a bit too far from skewness.

Various formulas exist for measuring skewness. One way of gauging the skewness of a distribution is through examination of the relative distances of quartiles from the median. In a positively skewed distribution, $Q_3 - Q_2$ will be greater than the distance of $Q_2 - Q_1$. In a negatively skewed distribution, $Q_3 - Q_2$ will be less than the distance of $Q_2 - Q_1$. In a distribution that is symmetrical, the distances from Q_1 and Q_3 to the median are the same.

Kurtosis

The term testing professionals use to refer to the steepness of a distribution in its center is **kurtosis.** To the root *kurtic* is added to one of the prefixes *platy-*, *lepto-*, or *meso-* to describe the peakedness/flatness of three general types of curves (Figure 3–6). Distributions are generally described as **platykurtic** (relatively flat), **leptokurtic** (relatively peaked), or—somewhere in the middle—**mesokurtic.** Distributions that have high kurtosis are characterized by a high peak and "fatter" tails compared to a normal distribution. In contrast, lower kurtosis values indicate a distribution with a rounded peak and thinner tails. Many methods exist for measuring kurtosis. According to the original definition, the normal bell-shaped curve (see graph A from Figure 3–3) would have a kurtosis value of 3. In other methods of computing kurtosis, a normal distribution would have kurtosis of 0, with positive values indicating higher kurtosis and negative values indicating lower kurtosis. It is important to keep the different methods of calculating kurtosis in mind when examining the values reported by researchers or computer programs. So, given that this can quickly become an advanced-level topic and that this book is of a more introductory nature, let's move on. It's time to focus on a type of distribution that happens to be the standard against which all other distributions (including all of the kurtic ones) are compared: the normal distribution.

JUST THINK . . .

Like skewness, reference to the kurtosis of a distribution can provide a kind of "shorthand" description of a distribution of test scores. Imagine and describe the kind of test that might yield a distribution of scores that form a platykurtic curve.

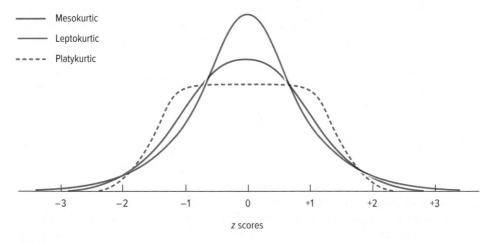

Figure 3–6
The Kurtosis of Curves

The Normal Curve

Before delving into the statistical, a little bit of the historical is in order. Development of the concept of a normal curve began in the middle of the eighteenth century with the work of Abraham DeMoivre and, later, the Marquis de Laplace. At the beginning of the nineteenth century, Karl Friedrich Gauss made some substantial contributions. Through the early nineteenth century, scientists referred to it as the "Laplace-Gaussian curve." Karl Pearson is credited with being the first to refer to the curve as the *normal curve,* perhaps in an effort to be diplomatic to all of the people who helped develop it. Somehow the term *normal curve* stuck—but don't be surprised if you're sitting at some scientific meeting one day and you hear this distribution or curve referred to as *Gaussian.*

Theoretically, the **normal curve** is a bell-shaped, smooth, mathematically defined curve that is highest at its center. From the center it tapers on both sides approaching the *X*-axis *asymptotically* (meaning that it approaches, but never touches, the axis). In theory, the distribution of the normal curve ranges from negative infinity to positive infinity. The curve is perfectly symmetrical, with no skewness. If you folded it in half at the mean, one side would lie exactly on top of the other. Because it is symmetrical, the mean, the median, and the mode all have the same exact value.

Why is the normal curve important in understanding the characteristics of psychological tests? Our *Close-Up* provides some answers.

The Area Under the Normal Curve

The normal curve can be conveniently divided into areas defined in units of standard deviation. A hypothetical distribution of National Spelling Test scores with a mean of 50 and a standard deviation of 15 is illustrated in Figure 3–7. In this example, a score equal to 1 standard deviation above the mean would be equal to 65 $(\overline{X} + 1s = 50 + 15 = 65)$.

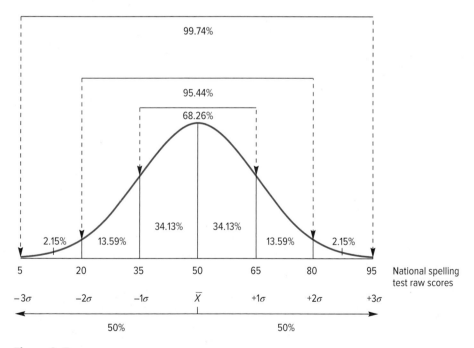

Figure 3–7
The Area Under the Normal Curve

The Normal Curve and Psychological Tests

Scores on many psychological tests are often approximately normally distributed, particularly when the tests are administered to large numbers of subjects. Few, if any, psychological tests yield precisely normal distributions of test scores (Micceri, 1989). As a general rule (with ample exceptions), the larger the sample size and the wider the range of abilities measured by a particular test, the more the graph of the test scores will approximate the normal curve. A classic illustration of this was provided by E. L. Thorndike and his colleagues (1927). They compiled intelligence test scores from several large samples of students. As you can see in Figure 1, the distribution of scores closely approximated the normal curve.

Following is a sample of more varied examples of the wide range of characteristics that psychologists have found to be approximately normal in distribution.

- The strength of handedness in right-handed individuals, as measured by the Waterloo Handedness Questionnaire (Tan, 1993).

- Scores on the Women's Health Questionnaire, a scale measuring a variety of health problems in women across a wide age range (Hunter, 1992).

- Responses of both college students and working adults to a measure of intrinsic and extrinsic work motivation (Amabile et al., 1994).

- The intelligence-scale scores of girls and women with eating disorders, as measured by the Wechsler Adult Intelligence Scale–Revised and the Wechsler Intelligence Scale for Children–Revised (Ranseen & Humphries, 1992).

- The intellectual functioning of children and adolescents with cystic fibrosis (Thompson et al., 1992).

- Decline in cognitive abilities over a one-year period in people with Alzheimer's disease (Burns et al., 1991).

- The rate of motor-skill development in developmentally delayed preschoolers, as measured by the Vineland Adaptive Behavior Scale (Davies & Gavin, 1994).

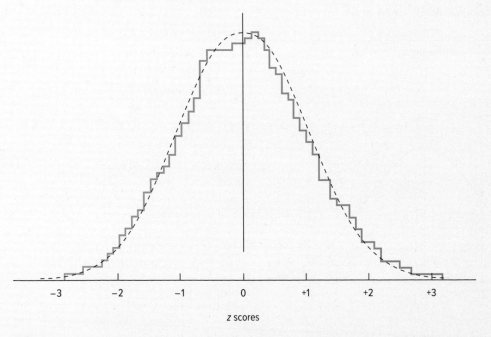

z scores

Figure 1
Graphic Representation of Thorndike et al. Data

The solid line outlines the distribution of intelligence test scores of sixth-grade students (N = 15,138). The dotted line is the theoretical normal curve (Thorndike et al., 1927).

- Scores on the Swedish translation of the Positive and Negative Syndrome Scale, which assesses the presence of positive and negative symptoms in people with schizophrenia (von Knorring & Lindstrom, 1992).

- Scores of psychiatrists on the Scale for Treatment Integration of the Dually Diagnosed (people with both a drug problem and another mental disorder); the scale examines opinions about drug treatment for this group of patients (Adelman et al., 1991).

- Responses to the Tridimensional Personality Questionnaire, a measure of three distinct personality features (Cloninger et al., 1991).

- Scores on a self-esteem measure among undergraduates (Addeo et al., 1994).

In each case, the researchers made a special point of stating that the scale under investigation yielded something close to a normal distribution of scores. Why? One benefit of a normal distribution of scores is that it simplifies the interpretation of individual scores on the test. In a normal distribution, the mean, the median, and the mode take on the same value. For example, if we know that the average score for intellectual ability of children with cystic fibrosis is a particular value and that the scores are normally distributed, then we know quite a bit more. We know that the average is the most common score and the score below and above which half of all the scores fall. Knowing the mean and the standard deviation of a scale and that it is approximately normally distributed tells us that (1) approximately two-thirds of all testtakers' scores are within a standard deviation of the mean and (2) approximately 95% of the scores fall within 2 standard deviations of the mean.

The characteristics of the normal curve provide a ready model for score interpretation that can be applied to a wide range of test results.

Before reading on, take a minute or two to calculate what a score exactly at 3 standard deviations below the mean would be equal to. How about a score exactly at 3 standard deviations above the mean? Were your answers 5 and 95, respectively? The graph tells us that 99.74% of all scores in these normally distributed spelling-test data lie between ±3 standard deviations. Stated another way, 99.74% of all spelling test scores lie between 5 and 95. This graph also illustrates the following characteristics of all normal distributions.

- 50% of the scores occur above the mean and 50% of the scores occur below the mean.

- Approximately 34% of all scores occur between the mean and 1 standard deviation above the mean.

- Approximately 34% of all scores occur between the mean and 1 standard deviation below the mean.

- Approximately 68% of all scores occur between the mean and ±1 standard deviation.

- Approximately 95% of all scores occur between the mean and ±2 standard deviations.

A normal curve has two *tails*. The area on the normal curve between 2 and 3 standard deviations above the mean is referred to as a **tail.** The area between −2 and −3 standard deviations below the mean is also referred to as a tail. Let's digress here momentarily for a "real-life" tale of the tails to consider along with our rather abstract discussion of statistical concepts.

As observed in a thought-provoking article entitled "Two Tails of the Normal Curve," an intelligence test score that falls within the limits of either tail can have momentous consequences in terms of the tale of one's life:

> Individuals who are mentally retarded or gifted share the burden of deviance from the norm, in both a developmental and a statistical sense. In terms of mental ability as operationalized by tests of intelligence, performance that is approximately two standard deviations from the mean (or, IQ of 70–75 or lower or IQ of 125–130 or higher) is one key element in identification. Success at life's tasks, or its absence, also plays a defining role, but the primary classifying feature of both gifted and retarded groups is intellectual deviance. These individuals are out of sync with more average people, simply by their difference from what is expected for their age

and circumstance. This asynchrony results in highly significant consequences for them and for those who share their lives. None of the familiar norms apply, and substantial adjustments are needed in parental expectations, educational settings, and social and leisure activities. (Robinson et al., 2000, p. 1413)

Robinson et al. (2000) convincingly demonstrated that knowledge of the areas under the normal curve can be quite useful to the interpreter of test data. This knowledge can tell us not only something about where the score falls among a distribution of scores but also something about a *person* and perhaps even something about the people who share that person's life. This knowledge might also convey something about how impressive, average, or lackluster the individual is with respect to a particular discipline or ability. For example, consider a high-school student whose score on a national, well-respected spelling test is close to 3 standard deviations above the mean. It's a good bet that this student would know how to spell words like *asymptotic* and *leptokurtic*.

Just as knowledge of the areas under the normal curve can instantly convey useful information about a test score in relation to other test scores, so can knowledge of standard scores.

Standard Scores

Simply stated, a **standard score** is a raw score that has been converted from one scale to another scale, where the latter scale has some arbitrarily set mean and standard deviation. Why convert raw scores to standard scores?

Raw scores may be converted to standard scores because standard scores are more easily interpretable than raw scores. With a standard score, the position of a testtaker's performance relative to other testtakers is readily apparent.

Different systems for standard scores exist, each unique in terms of its respective mean and standard deviations. We will briefly describe *z* scores, *T* scores, stanines, and some other standard scores. First for consideration is the type of standard score scale that may be thought of as the *zero plus or minus one scale*. This is so because it has a mean set at 0 and a standard deviation set at 1. Raw scores converted into standard scores on this scale are more popularly referred to as *z* scores.

z Scores

A *z* **score** results from the conversion of a raw score into a number indicating how many standard deviation units the raw score is below or above the mean of the distribution. Let's use an example from the normally distributed "National Spelling Test" data in Figure 3–7 to demonstrate how a raw score is converted to a *z* score. We'll convert a raw score of 65 to a *z* score by using the formula

$$z = \frac{X - \overline{X}}{s} = \frac{65 - 50}{15} = \frac{15}{15} = 1$$

In essence, a *z* score is equal to the difference between a particular raw score and the mean divided by the standard deviation. In the preceding example, a raw score of 65 was found to be equal to a *z* score of +1. Knowing that someone obtained a *z* score of 1 on a spelling test provides context and meaning for the score. Drawing on our knowledge of areas under the normal curve, for example, we would know that only about 16% of the other testtakers obtained higher scores. By contrast, knowing simply that someone obtained a raw score of 65 on a spelling test conveys virtually no usable information because information about the context of this score is lacking.

In addition to providing a convenient context for comparing scores on the same test, standard scores provide a convenient context for comparing scores on different tests. As an example, consider that Crystal's raw score on the hypothetical Main Street Reading Test was 24 and that her raw score on the (equally hypothetical) Main Street Arithmetic Test was 42. Without knowing anything other than these raw scores, one might conclude that Crystal did better on the arithmetic test than on the reading test. Yet more informative than the two raw scores would be the two z scores.

Converting Crystal's raw scores to z scores based on the performance of other students in her class, suppose we find that her z score on the reading test was 1.32 and that her z score on the arithmetic test was -0.75. Thus, although her raw score in arithmetic was higher than in reading, the z scores paint a different picture. The z scores tell us that, relative to the other students in her class (and assuming that the distribution of scores is relatively normal), Crystal performed above average on the reading test and below average on the arithmetic test. An interpretation of exactly how much better she performed could be obtained by reference to tables detailing distances under the normal curve as well as the resulting percentage of cases that could be expected to fall above or below a particular standard deviation point (or z score).

T Scores

If the scale used in the computation of z scores is called a *zero plus or minus one scale,* then the scale used in the computation of T **scores** can be called a *fifty plus or minus ten scale;* that is, a scale with a mean set at 50 and a standard deviation set at 10. Devised by W. A. McCall (1922, 1939) and named a T score in honor of his professor E. L. Thorndike, this standard score system is composed of a scale that ranges from 5 standard deviations below the mean to 5 standard deviations above the mean. Thus, for example, a raw score that fell exactly at 5 standard deviations below the mean would be equal to a T score of 0, a raw score that fell at the mean would be equal to a T of 50, and a raw score 5 standard deviations above the mean would be equal to a T of 100. One advantage in using T scores is that none of the scores is negative. By contrast, in a z score distribution, scores can be positive and negative; this can make further computation cumbersome in some instances.

Other Standard Scores

Numerous other standard scoring systems exist. Researchers during World War II developed a standard score with a mean of 5 and a standard deviation of approximately 2. Divided into nine units, the scale was christened a **stanine,** a term that was a contraction of the words *standard* and *nine.*

Stanine scoring may be familiar to many students from achievement tests administered in elementary and secondary school, where test scores are often represented as stanines. Stanines are different from other standard scores in that they take on whole values from 1 to 9, which represent a range of performance that is half of a standard deviation in width (Figure 3–8). The 5th stanine indicates performance in the average range, from 1/4 standard deviation below the mean to 1/4 standard deviation above the mean, and captures the middle 20% of the scores in a normal distribution. The 4th and 6th stanines are also 1/2 standard deviation wide and capture the 17% of cases below and above (respectively) the 5th stanine.

Another type of standard score is employed on tests such as the Scholastic Aptitude Test (SAT) and the Graduate Record Examination (GRE). Raw scores on those tests are converted to standard scores such that the resulting distribution has a mean of 500 and a standard deviation of 100. If the letter A is used to represent a standard score from a college or graduate school admissions test whose distribution has a mean of 500 and a standard deviation of 100, then the following is true:

$$(A = 600) = (z = 1) = (T = 60)$$

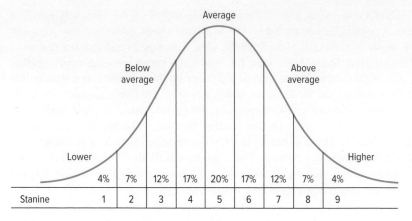

Figure 3–8
Stanines and the Normal Curve

Have you ever heard the term *IQ* used as a synonym for one's score on an intelligence test? Of course you have. What you may not know is that what is referred to variously as IQ, deviation IQ, or deviation intelligence quotient is yet another kind of standard score. For most IQ tests, the distribution of raw scores is converted to IQ scores, whose distribution typically has a mean set at 100 and a standard deviation set at 15. Let's emphasize *typically* because there is some variation in standard scoring systems, depending on the test used. The typical mean and standard deviation for IQ tests results in approximately 95% of deviation IQs ranging from 70 to 130, which is 2 standard deviations below and above the mean. In the context of a normal distribution, the relationship of deviation IQ scores to the other standard scores we have discussed so far (*z, T,* and *A* scores) is illustrated in Figure 3–9.

Standard scores converted from raw scores may involve either linear or nonlinear transformations. A standard score obtained by a **linear transformation** is one that retains a direct numerical relationship to the original raw score. The magnitude of differences between such standard scores exactly parallels the differences between corresponding raw scores. Sometimes scores may undergo more than one transformation. For example, the creators of the SAT did a second linear transformation on their data to convert *z* scores into a new scale that has a mean of 500 and a standard deviation of 100.

A **nonlinear transformation** may be required when the data under consideration are not normally distributed yet comparisons with normal distributions need to be made. In a nonlinear transformation, the resulting standard score does not necessarily have a direct numerical relationship to the original, raw score. As the result of a nonlinear transformation, the original distribution is said to have been *normalized.*

Normalized standard scores Many test developers hope that the test they are working on will yield a normal distribution of scores. Yet even after very large samples have been tested with the instrument under development, skewed distributions result. What should be done?

One alternative available to the test developer is to normalize the distribution. Conceptually, **normalizing a distribution** involves "stretching" the skewed curve into the shape of a normal curve and creating a corresponding scale of standard scores, a scale that is technically referred to as a **normalized standard score scale.**

Normalization of a skewed distribution of scores may also be desirable for purposes of comparability. One of the primary advantages of a standard score on one test is that it can readily be compared with a standard score on another test. However, such comparisons are appropriate only when the distributions from which they derived are the same. In most instances,

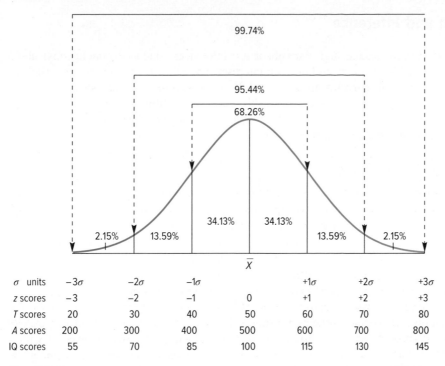

σ units	−3σ		−2σ		−1σ			+1σ		+2σ		+3σ
z scores	−3		−2		−1		0	+1		+2		+3
T scores	20		30		40		50	60		70		80
A scores	200		300		400		500	600		700		800
IQ scores	55		70		85		100	115		130		145

Figure 3–9
Some Standard Score Equivalents

Note that the values presented here for the IQ scores assume that the intelligence test scores have a mean of 100 and a standard deviation of 15. This is true for many, but not all, intelligence tests. If a particular test of intelligence yielded scores with a mean other than 100 and/or a standard deviation other than 15, then the values shown for IQ scores would have to be adjusted accordingly.

they are the same because the two distributions are approximately normal. But if, for example, distribution A were normal and distribution B were highly skewed, then z scores in these respective distributions would represent different amounts of area subsumed under the curve. A z score of −1 with respect to normally distributed data tells us, among other things, that about 84% of the scores in this distribution were higher than this score. A z score of −1 with respect to data that were very positively skewed might mean, for example, that only 62% of the scores were higher.

For test developers intent on creating tests that yield normally distributed measurements, it is generally preferable to fine-tune the test according to difficulty or other relevant variables so that the resulting distribution will approximate the normal curve. That usually is a better bet than attempting to normalize skewed distributions. This is so because there are technical cautions to be observed before attempting normalization. For example, transformations should be made only when there is good reason to believe that the test sample was large enough and representative enough and that the failure to obtain normally distributed scores was due to the measuring instrument.

JUST THINK . . .

Apply what you have learned about frequency distributions, graphing frequency distributions, measures of central tendency, measures of variability, and the normal curve and standard scores to the question of the data listed in Table 3–1. How would you communicate the data from Table 3–1 to the class? Which type of frequency distribution might you use? Which type of graph? Which measure of central tendency? Which measure of variability? Might reference to a normal curve or to standard scores be helpful? Why or why not?

Correlation and Inference

Central to psychological testing and assessment are inferences (deduced conclusions) about how some things (such as traits, abilities, or interests) are related to other things (such as behavior). A **coefficient of correlation** (or **correlation coefficient**) is a number that provides us with an index of the strength of the relationship between two things. An understanding of the concept of correlation and an ability to compute a coefficient of correlation is therefore central to the study of tests and measurement.

The Concept of Correlation

Simply stated, **correlation** is an expression of the degree and direction of correspondence between two things. A coefficient of correlation (r) expresses a linear relationship between two (and only two) variables, usually continuous in nature. It reflects the degree of concomitant variation between variable X and variable Y. The *coefficient of correlation* is the numerical index that expresses this relationship: It tells us the extent to which X and Y are "co-related."

The meaning of a correlation coefficient is interpreted by its sign and magnitude. If a correlation coefficient were a person asked "What's your sign?," it wouldn't answer anything like "Leo" or "Pisces." It would answer "plus" (for a positive correlation), "minus" (for a negative correlation), or "none" (in the rare instance that the correlation coefficient was exactly equal to zero). If asked to supply information about its magnitude, it would respond with a number anywhere at all between -1 and $+1$. And here is a rather intriguing fact about the magnitude of a correlation coefficient: It is judged by its absolute value. This means that to the extent that we are impressed by correlation coefficients, a correlation of $-.99$ is every bit as impressive as a correlation of $+.99$. To understand why, you need to know a bit more about correlation.

"Ahh . . . a perfect correlation! Let me count the ways." Well, actually there are only *two* ways. The two ways to describe a perfect correlation between two variables are as either $+1$ or -1. If a correlation coefficient has a value of $+1$ or -1, then the relationship between the two variables being correlated is perfect—without error in the statistical sense. And just as perfection in almost anything is difficult to find, so too are perfect correlations. It's challenging to try to think of any two variables in psychological work that are perfectly correlated. Perhaps that is why, if you look in the margin, you are asked to "just think" about it.

JUST THINK . . .

Can you name two variables that are perfectly correlated? How about two *psychological* variables that are perfectly correlated?

If two variables simultaneously increase or simultaneously decrease, then those two variables are said to be *positively* (or directly) correlated. The height and weight of normal, healthy children ranging in age from birth to 10 years tend to be positively or directly correlated. As children get older, their height and their weight generally increase simultaneously. A positive correlation also exists when two variables simultaneously decrease. For example, the less a student prepares for an examination, the lower that student's score on the examination. A *negative* (or inverse) correlation occurs when one variable increases while the other variable decreases. For example, there tends to be an inverse relationship between the number of miles on your car's odometer (mileage indicator) and the number of dollars a car dealer is willing to give you on a trade-in allowance; all other things being equal, as the mileage increases, the number of dollars offered on trade-in decreases. And by the way, we all know students who use cell phones during class to text, tweet, check e-mail, or otherwise be engaged with their phone at a questionably appropriate time and place. What would you estimate the correlation to be between such daily, in-class cell phone use and test grades? See Figure 3–10 for one such estimate (and kindly refrain from sharing the findings on Facebook during class).

Figure 3–10
Cell Phone Use in Class and Class Grade

This may be the "wired" generation, but some college students are clearly more wired than others. They seem to be on their cell phones constantly, even during class. Their gaze may be fixed on Mech Commander when it should more appropriately be on Class Instructor. Over the course of two semesters, Chris Bjornsen and Kellie Archer (2015) studied 218 college students, each of whom completed a questionnaire on their cell phone usage right after class. Correlating the questionnaire data with grades, the researchers reported that cell phone usage during class was significantly, negatively correlated with grades.
© Caia Image/Glow Images RF

If a correlation is zero, then absolutely no relationship exists between the two variables. And some might consider "perfectly no correlation" to be a third variety of perfect correlation; that is, a perfect noncorrelation. After all, just as it is nearly impossible in psychological work to identify two variables that have a perfect correlation, so it is nearly impossible to identify two variables that have a zero correlation. Most of the time, two variables will be fractionally correlated. The fractional correlation may be extremely small but seldom "perfectly" zero.

As we stated in our introduction to this topic, correlation is often confused with causation. It must be emphasized that a correlation coefficient is merely an index of the relationship between two variables, *not* an index of the causal relationship between two variables. If you were told, for example, that from birth to age 9 there is a high positive correlation between hat size and spelling ability, would it be appropriate to conclude that hat size causes spelling ability? Of course not. The period

JUST THINK . . .

Bjornsen & Archer (2015) discussed the implications of their cell phone study in terms of the effect of cell phone usage on student learning, student achievement, and post-college success. What would you anticipate those implications to be?

JUST THINK . . .

Could a correlation of zero between two variables also be considered a "perfect" correlation? Can you name two variables that have a correlation that is exactly zero?

from birth to age 9 is a time of maturation in *all* areas, including physical size and cognitive abilities such as spelling. Intellectual development parallels physical development during these years, and a relationship clearly exists between physical and mental growth. Still, this doesn't mean that the relationship between hat size and spelling ability is causal.

Although correlation does not imply causation, there *is* an implication of prediction. Stated another way, if we know that there is a high correlation between X and Y, then we should be able to predict—with various degrees of accuracy, depending on other factors—the value of one of these variables if we know the value of the other.

The Pearson r

Many techniques have been devised to measure correlation. The most widely used of all is the **Pearson r,** also known as the *Pearson correlation coefficient* and the *Pearson product-moment coefficient of correlation.* Devised by Karl Pearson (Figure 3–11), r can be the statistical tool of choice when the relationship between the variables is linear and when the two variables being correlated are continuous (or, they can theoretically take any value). Other correlational techniques can be employed with data that are discontinuous and where the relationship is nonlinear. The formula for the Pearson r takes into account the relative position of each test score or measurement with respect to the mean of the distribution.

A number of formulas can be used to calculate a Pearson r. One formula requires that we convert each raw score to a standard score and then multiply each pair of standard scores. A mean for the sum of the products is calculated, and that mean is the value of the Pearson r. Even from this simple verbal conceptualization of the Pearson r, it can be seen that the sign of the resulting r would be a function of the sign and the magnitude of the standard scores used. If, for example, negative standard score values for measurements of X always corresponded with negative standard score values for Y scores, the resulting r would be positive (because the product of two negative values is positive). Similarly, if positive standard score values on X always corresponded with positive standard score values on Y, the resulting correlation would also be positive. However, if positive standard score values for X corresponded with negative

Figure 3–11
Karl Pearson (1857–1936)

Karl Pearson's name has become synonymous with correlation. History records, however, that it was actually Sir Francis Galton who should be credited with developing the concept of correlation (Magnello & Spies, 1984). Galton experimented with many formulas to measure correlation, including one he labeled r. *Pearson, a contemporary of Galton's, modified Galton's* r, *and the rest, as they say, is history. The Pearson* r *eventually became the most widely used measure of correlation.*

© TopFoto/Fotomas/The Image Works

standard score values for Y and vice versa, then an inverse relationship would exist and so a negative correlation would result. A zero or near-zero correlation could result when some products are positive and some are negative.

The formula used to calculate a Pearson r from raw scores is

$$r = \frac{\Sigma(X - \overline{X})(Y - \overline{Y})}{\sqrt{[\Sigma(X - \overline{X})^2][\Sigma(Y - \overline{Y})^2]}}$$

This formula has been simplified for shortcut purposes. One such shortcut is a deviation formula employing "little x," or x in place of $X - \overline{X}$, and "little y," or y in place of $Y - \overline{Y}$:

$$r = \frac{\Sigma xy}{\sqrt{(\Sigma x^2)(\Sigma y^2)}}$$

Another formula for calculating a Pearson r is

$$r = \frac{N\Sigma XY - (\Sigma X)(\Sigma Y)}{\sqrt{N\Sigma X^2 - (\Sigma X)^2}\sqrt{N\Sigma Y^2 - (\Sigma Y)^2}}$$

Although this formula looks more complicated than the previous deviation formula, it is easier to use. Here N represents the number of paired scores; ΣXY is the sum of the product of the paired X and Y scores; ΣX is the sum of the X scores; ΣY is the sum of the Y scores; ΣX^2 is the sum of the squared X scores; and ΣY^2 is the sum of the squared Y scores. Similar results are obtained with the use of each formula.

The next logical question concerns what to do with the number obtained for the value of r. The answer is that you ask even more questions, such as "Is this number statistically significant, given the size and nature of the sample?" or "Could this result have occurred by chance?" At this point, you will need to consult tables of significance for Pearson r—tables that are probably in the back of your old statistics textbook. In those tables you will find, for example, that a Pearson r of .899 with an $N = 10$ is significant at the .01 level (using a two-tailed test). You will recall from your statistics course that significance at the .01 level tells you, with reference to these data, that a correlation such as this could have been expected to occur merely by chance only one time or less in a hundred if X and Y are not correlated in the population. You will also recall that significance at either the .01 level or the (somewhat less rigorous) .05 level provides a basis for concluding that a correlation does indeed exist. Significance at the .05 level means that the result could have been expected to occur by chance alone five times or less in a hundred.

The value obtained for the coefficient of correlation can be further interpreted by deriving from it what is called a **coefficient of determination,** or r^2. The coefficient of determination is an indication of how much variance is shared by the X- and the Y-variables. The calculation of r^2 is quite straightforward. Simply square the correlation coefficient and multiply by 100; the result is equal to the percentage of the variance accounted for. If, for example, you calculated r to be .9, then r^2 would be equal to .81. The number .81 tells us that 81% of the variance is accounted for by the X- and Y-variables. The remaining variance, equal to $100(1 - r^2)$, or 19%, could presumably be accounted for by chance, error, or otherwise unmeasured or unexplainable factors.[7]

---

7. On a technical note, Ozer (1985) cautioned that the actual estimation of a coefficient of determination must be made with scrupulous regard to the assumptions operative in the particular case. Evaluating a coefficient of determination solely in terms of the variance accounted for may lead to interpretations that underestimate the magnitude of a relation.

Before moving on to consider another index of correlation, let's address a logical question sometimes raised by students when they hear the Pearson *r* referred to as the *product-moment coefficient of correlation.* Why is it called that? The answer is a little complicated, but here goes.

In the language of psychometrics, a *moment* describes a deviation about a mean of a distribution. Individual deviations about the mean of a distribution are referred to as *deviates.* Deviates are referred to as the *first moments* of the distribution. The *second moments* of the distribution are the moments squared. The *third moments* of the distribution are the moments cubed, and so forth. The computation of the Pearson *r* in one of its many formulas entails multiplying corresponding standard scores on two measures. One way of conceptualizing standard scores is as the first moments of a distribution. This is because standard scores are deviates about a mean of zero. A formula that entails the multiplication of two corresponding standard scores can therefore be conceptualized as one that entails the computation of the *product* of corresponding *moments.* And there you have the reason *r* is called *product-moment correlation.* It's probably all more a matter of psychometric trivia than anything else, but we think it's cool to know. Further, you can now understand the rather "high-end" humor contained in the cartoon (below).

The Spearman Rho

The Pearson *r* enjoys such widespread use and acceptance as an index of correlation that if for some reason it is not used to compute a correlation coefficient, mention is made of the statistic that was used. There are many alternative ways to derive a coefficient of correlation. One commonly used alternative statistic is variously called a **rank-order correlation coefficient,** a **rank-difference correlation coefficient,** or simply **Spearman's rho.** Developed by Charles Spearman, a British psychologist (Figure 3–12), this coefficient of correlation is frequently used when the sample size is small (fewer than 30 pairs of measurements) and especially when both sets of measurements are in ordinal (or rank-order) form. Special tables are used to determine whether an obtained rho coefficient is or is not significant.

YOU STANDARD SCORES ARE A BUNCH OF DEVIATES ABOUT A MEAN OF ZERO!

Copyright 2016 by Ronald Jay Cohen. All rights reserved.

Figure 3–12
Charles Spearman (1863–1945)

Charles Spearman is best known as the developer of the Spearman rho statistic and the Spearman-Brown prophecy formula, which is used to "prophesize" the accuracy of tests of different sizes. Spearman is also credited with being the father of a statistical method called factor analysis, discussed later in this text.

© Atlas Archive/The Image Works

Graphic Representations of Correlation

One type of graphic representation of correlation is referred to by many names, including a **bivariate distribution,** a **scatter diagram,** a **scattergram,** or—our favorite—a **scatterplot.** A *scatterplot* is a simple graphing of the coordinate points for values of the *X*-variable (placed along the graph's horizontal axis) and the *Y*-variable (placed along the graph's vertical axis). Scatterplots are useful because they provide a quick indication of the direction and magnitude of the relationship, if any, between the two variables. Figures 3–13 and 3–14 offer a quick course in eyeballing the nature and degree of correlation by means of scatterplots. To distinguish positive from negative correlations, note the direction of the curve. And to estimate the strength of magnitude of the correlation, note the degree to which the points form a straight line.

Scatterplots are useful in revealing the presence of *curvilinearity* in a relationship. As you may have guessed, **curvilinearity** in this context refers to an "eyeball gauge" of how curved a graph is. Remember that a Pearson *r* should be used only if the relationship between the variables is linear. If the graph does not appear to take the form of a straight line, the chances are good that the relationship is not linear (Figure 3–15). When the relationship is nonlinear, other statistical tools and techniques may be employed.[8]

---

8. The specific statistic to be employed will depend at least in part on the suspected reason for the nonlinearity. For example, if it is believed that the nonlinearity is due to one distribution being highly skewed because of a poor measuring instrument, then the skewed distribution may be statistically normalized and the result may be a correction of the curvilinearity. If—even after graphing the data—a question remains concerning the linearity of the correlation, a statistic called "eta squared" (η^2) can be used to calculate the exact degree of curvilinearity.

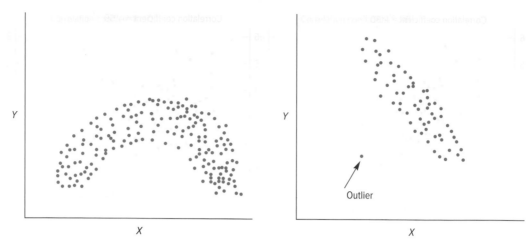

Figure 3–15
Scatterplot Showing a Nonlinear Correlation

Figure 3–16
Scatterplot Showing an Outlier

A graph also makes the spotting of outliers relatively easy. An **outlier** is an extremely atypical point located at a relatively long distance—an outlying distance—from the rest of the coordinate points in a scatterplot (Figure 3–16). Outliers stimulate interpreters of test data to speculate about the reason for the atypical score. For example, consider an outlier on a scatterplot that reflects a correlation between hours each member of a fifth-grade class spent studying and their grades on a 20-item spelling test. And let's say that one student studied for 10 hours and received a failing grade. This outlier on the scatterplot might raise a red flag and compel the test user to raise some important questions, such as "How effective are this student's study skills and habits?" or "What was this student's state of mind during the test?"

In some cases, outliers are simply the result of administering a test to a very small sample of testtakers. In the example just cited, if the test were given statewide to fifth-graders and the sample size were much larger, perhaps many more low scorers who put in large amounts of study time would be identified.

As is the case with very low raw scores or raw scores of zero, outliers can sometimes help identify a testtaker who did not understand the instructions, was not able to follow the instructions, or was simply oppositional and did not follow the instructions. In other cases, an outlier can provide a hint of some deficiency in the testing or scoring procedures.

People who have occasion to use or make interpretations from graphed data need to know if the range of scores has been restricted in any way. To understand why this is so necessary to know, consider Figure 3–17. Let's say that graph A describes the relationship between Public University entrance test scores for 600 applicants (all of whom were later admitted) and their grade point averages at the end of the first semester. The scatterplot indicates that the relationship between entrance test scores and grade point average is both linear and positive. But what if the admissions officer had accepted only the applications of the students who scored within the top half or so on the entrance exam? To a trained eye, this scatterplot (graph B) appears to indicate a weaker correlation than that indicated in graph A—an effect attributable exclusively to the restriction of range. Graph B is less a straight line than graph A, and its direction is not as obvious.

Meta-Analysis

Generally, the best estimate of the correlation between two variables is most likely to come not from a single study alone but from analysis of the data from several studies. One option to

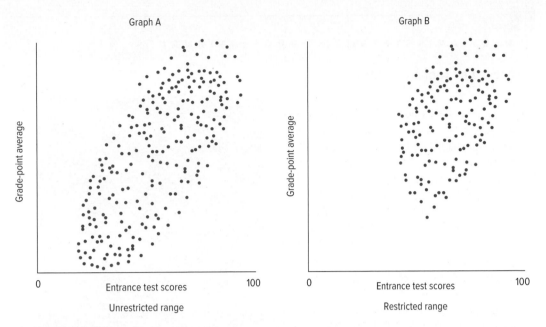

Graph A

Graph B

Grade-point average

Grade-point average

0   Entrance test scores   100

0   Entrance test scores   100

Unrestricted range

Restricted range

Figure 3–17
Two Scatterplots Illustrating Unrestricted and Restricted Ranges

facilitate understanding of the research across a number of studies is to present the range of statistical values calculated from a number of different studies of the same phenomenon. Viewing all of the data from a number of studies that attempted to determine the correlation between variable X and variable Y, for example, might lead the researcher to conclude that "The correlation between variable *X* and variable *Y* ranges from .73 to .91." Another option might be to combine statistically the information across the various studies; that is what is done using a statistical technique called *meta-analysis.* Using this technique, researchers raise (and strive to answer) the question: "Combined, what do all of these studies tell us about the matter under study?" For example, Imtiaz et al. (2016) used meta-analysis to draw some conclusions regarding the relationship between cannabis use and physical health. Colin (2015) used meta-analysis to study the correlations of use-of-force decisions among American police officers.

Meta-analysis may be defined as a family of techniques used to statistically combine information across studies to produce single estimates of the data under study. The estimates derived, referred to as **effect size,** may take several different forms. In most meta-analytic studies, effect size is typically expressed as a correlation coefficient.[9] Meta-analysis facilitates the drawing of conclusions and the making of statements like, "the typical therapy client is better off than 75% of untreated individuals" (Smith & Glass, 1977, p. 752), there is "about 10% increased risk for antisocial behavior among children with incarcerated parents, compared to peers" (Murray et al., 2012), and "GRE and UGPA [undergraduate grade point average] are generalizably valid predictors of graduate grade point average, 1st-year graduate grade point average, comprehensive examination scores, publication citation counts, and faculty ratings" (Kuncel et al., 2001, p. 162).

9. More generally, *effect size* refers to an estimate of the strength of the relationship (or the size of the differences) between groups. In a typical study using two groups (an experimental group and a control group) effect size, ideally reported with confidence intervals, is helpful in determining the effectiveness of some sort of intervention (such as a new form of therapy, a drug, a new management approach, and so forth). In practice, many different procedures may be used to determine effect size, and the procedure selected will be based on the particular research situation.

Meet Dr. Joni L. Mihura

Hi, my name is Joni Mihura, and my research expertise is in psychological assessment, with a special focus on the Rorschach. To tell you a little about me, I was the only woman* to serve on the Research Council for John E. Exner's Rorschach Comprehensive System (CS) until he passed away in 2006. Due to the controversy around the Rorschach's validity, I began reviewing the research literature to ensure I was teaching my doctoral students valid measures to assess their clients. That is, the controversy about the Rorschach has *not* been that it is a completely invalid test—the critics have endorsed several Rorschach scales as valid for their intended purpose—the main problem that they have highlighted is that only a small proportion of its scales had been subjected to "meta-analysis," a systematic technique for summarizing the research literature. To make a long story short, I eventually published my review of the Rorschach literature in the top scientific review journal in psychology (*Psychological Bulletin*) in the form of systematic reviews and meta-analyses of the 65 main Rorschach CS variables (Mihura *et al.,* 2013), therefore making the Rorschach the psychological test with the *most* construct validity meta-analyses for its scales!

My meta-analyses also resulted in two other pivotal events. They formed the backbone for a new scientifically based Rorschach system of which I am a codeveloper—the *Rorschach Performance Assessment System* (*R-PAS*; Meyer *et al.,* 2011), and they resulted in the Rorschach critics removing the "moratorium" they had recommended for the Rorschach (or, Garb, 1999) for the scales they deemed had solid support in our meta-analyses (Wood *et al.,* 2015; also see our reply, Mihura *et al.,* 2015).

I'm very excited to talk with you about meta-analysis. First, to set the stage, let's take a step back and look at what you might have experienced so far when reading about psychology. When

Joni L. Mihura, Ph.D. is Associate Professor of Psychology at the University of Toledo in Toledo, Ohio

© Joni L. Mihura, Ph.D.

students take their first psychology course, they are often surprised how much of the field is based on research findings rather than just "common sense." Even so, because undergraduate textbooks have numerous topics about which they cannot cite all of the research, it can appear that the textbook is relying on just one or two studies as the "proof." Therefore, you might be surprised just how many psychological research studies actually exist! Conducting a quick search in the PsycINFO database shows that over a million psychology journal articles are classified as empirical studies—and that *excludes* chapters, theses, dissertations, and many other studies not listed in PsycINFO.

But, good news or bad news, a significant challenge with many research studies is how to summarize results. The classic example of such a dilemma and the eventual solution is a fascinating one that comes from the psychotherapy literature. In 1952, Hans Eysenck published a classic article entitled

---

*I have also edited the *Handbook of Gender and Sexuality in Psychological Assessment* (Brabender & Mihura, 2016).

"The Effects of Psychotherapy: An Evaluation," in which he summarized the results of a few studies and concluded that psychotherapy doesn't work! Wow! This finding had the potential to shake the foundation of psychotherapy and even ban its existence. After all, Eysenck had cited research that suggested that the longer a person was in therapy, the worse-off they became. Notwithstanding the psychotherapists and the psychotherapy enterprise, Eysenck's publication had sobering implications for people who had sought help through psychotherapy. Had they done so in vain? Was there really no hope for the future? Were psychotherapists truly ill-equipped to do things like reduce emotional suffering and improve peoples' lives through psychotherapy?

In the wake of this potentially damning article, several psychologists—and in particular Hans H. Strupp—responded by pointing out problems with Eysenck's methodology. Other psychologists conducted their own reviews of the psychotherapy literature. Somewhat surprisingly, after reviewing the *same* body of research literature on psychotherapy, various psychologists drew widely different conclusions. Some researchers found strong support for the efficacy of psychotherapy. Other researchers found only modest support for the efficacy of psychotherapy. Yet other researchers found no support for it at all.

How can such different conclusions be drawn when the researchers are reviewing the same body of literature? A comprehensive answer to this important question could fill the pages of this book. Certainly, one key element of the answer to this question had to do with a lack of systematic rules for making decisions about including studies, as well as lack of a widely acceptable protocol for statistically summarizing the findings of the various studies. With such rules and protocols absent, it would be all too easy for researchers to let their preexisting biases run amok. The result was that many researchers "found" in their analyses of the literature what they believed to be true in the first place.

A fortuitous bi-product of such turmoil in the research community was the emergence of a research technique called "meta-analysis." Literally, "an analysis of analyses," meta-analysis is a tool used to systematically review and statistically summarize the research findings for a particular topic. In 1977, Mary Lee Smith and Gene V. Glass published the first meta-analysis of psychotherapy outcomes. They found strong support for the efficacy of psychotherapy. Subsequently, others tried to challenge Smith and Glass' findings. However, the systematic rigor of their meta-analytic technique produced findings that were consistently replicated by others. Today there are thousands of psychotherapy studies, and many meta-analysts ready to research specific, therapy-related questions (like "What type of psychotherapy is best for what type of problem?").

What does all of this mean for psychological testing and assessment? Meta-analytic methodology can be used to glean insights about specific tools of assessment, and testing and assessment procedures. However, meta-analyses of information related to psychological tests brings new challenges owing, for example, to the sheer number of articles to be analyzed, the many variables on which tests differ, and the specific methodology of the meta-analysis. Consider, for example, that multiscale personality tests may contain over 50, and sometimes over 100, scales that each need to be evaluated separately. Furthermore, some popular multiscale personality tests, like the MMPI-2 and Rorschach, have had over a thousand research studies published on them. The studies typically report findings that focus on varied aspects of the test (such as the utility of specific test scales, or other indices of test reliability or validity). In order to make the meta-analytic task manageable, meta-analyses for multiscale tests will typically focus on one or another of these characteristics or indices.

In sum, a thoughtful meta-analysis of research on a specific topic can yield important insights of both theoretical and applied value. A meta-analytic review of the literature on a particular psychological test can even be instrumental in the formulation of revised ways to score the test and interpret the findings (just ask Meyer et al., 2011). So, the next time a question about psychological research arises, students are advised to respond to that question with their own question, namely "Is there a meta-analysis on that?"

Used with permission of Joni L. Mihura.

A key advantage of meta-analysis over simply reporting a range of findings is that, in meta-analysis, more weight can be given to studies that have larger numbers of subjects. This weighting process results in more accurate estimates (Hunter & Schmidt, 1990). Some advantages to meta-analyses are: (1) meta-analyses can be replicated; (2) the conclusions of meta-analyses tend to be more reliable and precise than the conclusions from single studies; (3) there is more focus on effect size rather than statistical significance alone; and (4) meta-analysis promotes **evidence-based practice,** which may be defined as professional practice that is based on clinical and research findings (Sánchez-Meca & Marin-Martinez, 2010). Despite these and other advantages, meta-analysis is, at least to some degree, art as well as science (Hall & Rosenthal, 1995). The value of any meta-analytic investigation is very much a matter of the skill and ability of the meta-analyst (Kavale, 1995), and use of an inappropriate meta-analytic method can lead to misleading conclusions (Kisamore & Brannick, 2008).

It may be helpful at this time to review this statistics refresher to make certain that you indeed feel "refreshed" and ready to continue. We will build on your knowledge of basic statistical principles in the chapters to come, and it is important to build on a rock-solid foundation.

Self-Assessment

Test your understanding of elements of this chapter by seeing if you can explain each of the following terms, expressions, and abbreviations:

arithmetic mean
average deviation
bar graph
bimodal distribution
bivariate distribution
coefficient of correlation
coefficient of determination
correlation
curvilinearity
distribution
dynamometer
effect size
error
evidence-based practice
frequency distribution
frequency polygon
graph
grouped frequency distribution
histogram
interquartile range
interval scale
kurtosis

leptokurtic
linear transformation
mean
measurement
measure of central tendency
measure of variability
median
mesokurtic
meta-analysis
mode
negative skew
nominal scale
nonlinear transformation
normal curve
normalized standard score scale
normalizing a distribution
ordinal scale
outlier
Pearson r
platykurtic
positive skew
quartile

range
rank-order/rank-difference
    correlation coefficient
ratio scale
raw score
scale
scatter diagram
scattergram
scatterplot
semi-interquartile range
skewness
Spearman's rho
standard deviation
standard score
stanine
T score
tail
variability
variance
z score

4

Of Tests and Testing

What is this patient's diagnosis?

Is this person competent to stand trial?

Who should be hired, transferred, promoted, or fired?

Which individual should gain entry to this special program or be awarded a scholarship?

Who shall be granted custody of the children?

Every day, throughout the world, critically important questions like these are addressed through the use of tests. The answers to these kinds of questions are likely to have a significant impact on many lives.

If they are to sleep comfortably at night, assessment professionals must have confidence in the tests and other tools of assessment they employ. They need to know, for example, what does and does not constitute a "good test."

Our objective in this chapter is to overview the elements of a good test. As background, we begin by listing some basic assumptions about assessment. Aspects of these fundamental assumptions will be elaborated later on in this chapter as well as in subsequent chapters.

> **JUST THINK . . .**
>
> What's a "good test"? Outline some elements or features that you believe are essential to a good test before reading on.

Some Assumptions About Psychological Testing and Assessment

Assumption 1: Psychological Traits and States Exist

A **trait** has been defined as "any distinguishable, relatively enduring way in which one individual varies from another" (Guilford, 1959, p. 6). **States** also distinguish one person from another but are relatively less enduring (Chaplin et al., 1988). The trait term that an observer applies, as well as the strength or magnitude of the trait presumed to be present, is based on observing a sample of behavior. Samples of behavior may be obtained in a number of ways, ranging from direct observation to the analysis of self-report statements or pencil-and-paper test answers.

The term *psychological trait,* much like the term *trait* alone, covers a wide range of possible characteristics. Thousands of psychological trait terms can be found in the English language (Allport & Odbert, 1936). Among them are psychological traits that relate to intelligence, specific intellectual abilities, cognitive style, adjustment, interests, attitudes, sexual orientation and preferences, psychopathology, personality in general, and specific personality traits. New concepts or discoveries in research may bring new trait terms to the fore. For example, a trait term seen in the professional literature on human sexuality is *androgynous* (referring to an absence of primacy of male or female characteristics). Cultural evolution may bring new trait terms into common usage, as it did in the 1960s when people began speaking of the degree to which women were *liberated* (or freed from the constraints of gender-dependent social expectations). A more recent example is the trait term *New Age,* used in the popular culture to refer to a particular nonmainstream orientation to spirituality and health.

Few people deny that psychological traits exist. Yet there has been a fair amount of controversy regarding just *how* they exist (McCabe & Fleeson, 2016; Sherman et al., 2015). For example, do traits have a physical existence, perhaps as a circuit in the brain? Although some have argued in favor of such a conception of psychological traits (Allport, 1937; Holt, 1971), compelling evidence to support such a view has been difficult to obtain. For our purposes, a psychological trait exists only as a **construct**—an informed, scientific concept developed or *constructed* to describe or explain behavior. We can't see, hear, or touch constructs, but we can infer their existence from *overt behavior.* In this context, **overt behavior** refers to an observable action or the product of an observable action, including test- or assessment-related responses. A challenge facing test developers is to construct tests that are at least as telling as observable behavior such as that illustrated in Figure 4–1.

The phrase *relatively enduring* in our definition of *trait* is a reminder that a trait is not expected to be manifested in behavior 100% of the time So, for example, we may become more agreeable and conscientious as we age, and perhaps become less prone to "sweat the small stuff" (Lüdtke et al., 2009; Roberts et al., 2003, 2006). Yet there also seems to be rank-order stability in personality traits. This is evidenced by relatively high correlations between trait scores at different time points (Lüdtke et al., 2009; Roberts & Del Vecchio, 2000).

Whether a trait manifests itself in observable behavior, and to what degree it manifests, is presumed to depend not only on the strength of the trait in the individual but also on the nature of the situation. Stated another way, exactly how a particular trait manifests itself is, at least to some extent, situation-dependent. For example, a violent parolee may be prone to behave in a rather subdued way with her parole officer and much more violently in the presence of her family and friends. John may be viewed as dull and cheap by his wife but as charming and extravagant by his business associates, whom he keenly wants to impress.

The context within which behavior occurs also plays a role in helping us select appropriate trait terms for observed behavior. Consider how we might label the behavior of someone who is kneeling and praying aloud. Such behavior might be viewed as either religious or deviant, depending on the context in which it occurs. A person who is doing this inside a church or upon a prayer rug may be described as *religious,* whereas another person engaged in the exact same behavior at a venue such as a sporting event or a movie theater might be viewed as deviant or *paranoid.*

JUST THINK . . .

Give another example of how the same behavior in two different contexts may be viewed in terms of two different traits.

The definitions of *trait* and *state* we are using also refer to *a way in which one individual varies from another.* Attributions of a trait or state term are relative. For example, in describing one person as *shy,* or even in using terms such as *very shy* or *not shy,* most people are making an unstated comparison with the degree of shyness they could reasonably expect the average person to exhibit under the same or similar circumstances. In psychological assessment, assessors may also make such comparisons with respect to the hypothetical average person. Alternatively, assessors may make comparisons among people who, because of their membership in some group or for any number of other reasons, are decidedly not average.

Figure 4–1
Measuring Sensation Seeking

The psychological trait of sensation seeking has been defined as "the need for varied, novel, and complex sensations and experiences and the willingness to take physical and social risks for the sake of such experiences" (Zuckerman, 1979, p. 10). A 22-item Sensation-Seeking Scale (SSS) seeks to identify people who are high or low on this trait. Assuming the SSS actually measures what it purports to measure, how would you expect a random sample of people lining up to bungee jump to score on the test as compared with another age-matched sample of people shopping at the local mall? What are the comparative advantages of using paper-and-pencil measures, such as the SSS, and using more performance-based measures, such as the one pictured here?
© Vitalii Nesterchuk/Shutterstock RF

As you might expect, the reference group with which comparisons are made can greatly influence one's conclusions or judgments. For example, suppose a psychologist administers a test of shyness to a 22-year-old male who earns his living as an exotic dancer. The interpretation of the test data will almost surely differ as a function of the reference group with which the testtaker is compared—that is, other males in his age group or other male exotic dancers in his age group.

JUST THINK . . .

Is the strength of a particular psychological trait the same across all situations or environments? What are the implications of one's answer to this question for assessment?

Assumption 2: Psychological Traits and States Can Be Quantified and Measured

Once it's acknowledged that psychological traits and states do exist, the specific traits and states to be measured and quantified need to be carefully defined. Test developers and researchers, much like people in general, have many different ways of looking at and defining the same phenomenon. Just think, for example, of the different ways a term such as *aggressive* is used. We speak of an aggressive salesperson, an aggressive killer, and an aggressive waiter, to name but a few contexts. In each of these different contexts, *aggressive* carries with it a different meaning. If a personality test yields a score purporting to provide information about how aggressive a testtaker is, a first step in understanding the meaning of that score is understanding how *aggressive* was defined by the test developer. More specifically, what types of behaviors are presumed to be indicative of someone who is aggressive as defined by the test? One test developer may define aggressive behavior as "the number of self-reported acts of physically harming others." Another test developer might define it as the number of observed acts of aggression, such as pushing, hitting, or kicking, that occur in a playground setting. Other test developers may define "aggressive behavior" in vastly different ways. Ideally, the test developer has provided test users with a clear operational definition of the construct under study.

Once having defined the trait, state, or other construct to be measured, a test developer considers the types of item content that would provide insight into it. From a universe of behaviors presumed to be indicative of the targeted trait, a test developer has a world of possible items that can be written to gauge the strength of that trait in testtakers.[1] For example, if the test developer deems knowledge of American history to be one component of intelligence in U.S. adults, then the item *Who was the second president of the United States?* may appear on the test. Similarly, if social judgment is deemed to be indicative of adult intelligence, then it might be reasonable to include the item *Why should guns in the home always be inaccessible to children?*

Suppose we agree that an item tapping knowledge of American history and an item tapping social judgment are both appropriate for an adult intelligence test. One question that arises is: Should both items be given equal weight? That is, should we place more importance on—and award more points for—an answer keyed "correct" to one or the other of these two items? Perhaps a correct response to the social judgment question should earn more credit than a correct response to the American history question. Weighting the comparative value of a test's items comes about as the result of a complex interplay among many factors, including technical considerations, the way a construct has been defined for the purposes of the test, and the value society (and the test developer) attaches to the behaviors evaluated.

JUST THINK . . .

On an adult intelligence test, what type of item should be given the most weight? What type of item should be given the least weight?

Measuring traits and states by means of a test entails developing not only appropriate test items but also appropriate ways to score the test and interpret the results. For many varieties of psychological tests, some number representing the score on the test is derived from the examinee's responses. The test score is presumed to represent the strength of the targeted ability or trait or state and is frequently based on **cumulative scoring.**[2] Inherent in cumulative scoring is the assumption that the more the testtaker responds in a particular direction as keyed by the test manual as correct or consistent with a particular trait, the higher that testtaker is presumed to be on the targeted ability or trait. You were probably first introduced to cumulative scoring early in elementary school when you observed that your score on a weekly spelling test had everything to do with how many words you spelled correctly or incorrectly. The score reflected the extent to which you had successfully mastered the spelling assignment for the week. On the basis of that score, we might predict that you would spell those words correctly if called upon to do so. And in the context of such prediction, consider the next assumption.

---

1. In the language of psychological testing and assessment, the word *domain* is substituted for *world* in this context. Assessment professionals speak, for example, of **domain sampling,** which may refer to either (1) a sample of behaviors from all possible behaviors that could conceivably be indicative of a particular construct or (2) a sample of test items from all possible items that could conceivably be used to measure a particular construct.

2. Other models of scoring are discussed in Chapter 8.

Assumption 3: Test-Related Behavior Predicts Non-Test-Related Behavior

Many tests involve tasks such as blackening little grids with a number 2 pencil or simply pressing keys on a computer keyboard. The objective of such tests typically has little to do with predicting future grid-blackening or key-pressing behavior. Rather, the objective of the test is to provide some indication of other aspects of the examinee's behavior. For example, patterns of answers to true–false questions on one widely used test of personality are used in decision making regarding mental disorders.

The tasks in some tests mimic the actual behaviors that the test user is attempting to understand. By their nature, however, such tests yield only a sample of the behavior that can be expected to be emitted under nontest conditions. The obtained sample of behavior is typically used to make predictions about future behavior, such as work performance of a job applicant. In some forensic (legal) matters, psychological tests may be used not to predict behavior but to *postdict* it—that is, to aid in the understanding of behavior that has already taken place. For example, there may be a need to understand a criminal defendant's state of mind at the time of the commission of a crime. It is beyond the capability of any known testing or assessment procedure to reconstruct someone's state of mind. Still, behavior samples may shed light, under certain circumstances, on someone's state of mind in the past.

JUST THINK . . .

In practice, tests have proven to be good predictors of some types of behaviors and not-so-good predictors of other types of behaviors. For example, tests have *not* proven to be as good at predicting violence as had been hoped. Why do you think it is so difficult to predict violence by means of a test?

Additionally, other tools of assessment—such as case history data or the defendant's personal diary during the period in question—might be of great value in such an evaluation.

Assumption 4: Tests and Other Measurement Techniques Have Strengths and Weaknesses

Competent test users understand a great deal about the tests they use. They understand, among other things, how a test was developed, the circumstances under which it is appropriate to administer the test, how the test should be administered and to whom, and how the test results should be interpreted. Competent test users understand and appreciate the limitations of the tests they use as well as how those limitations might be compensated for by data from other sources. All of this may sound quite commonsensical, and it probably is. Yet this deceptively simple assumption—that test users know the tests they use and are aware of the tests' limitations—is emphasized repeatedly in the codes of ethics of associations of assessment professionals.

Assumption 5: Various Sources of Error Are Part of the Assessment Process

In everyday conversation, we use the word *error* to refer to mistakes, miscalculations, and the like. In the context of assessment, error need not refer to a deviation, an oversight, or something that otherwise violates expectations. To the contrary, *error* traditionally refers to something that is more than expected; it is actually a component of the measurement process. More specifically, *error* refers to a long-standing assumption that factors other than what a test attempts to measure will influence performance on the test. Test scores are always subject to questions about the degree to which the measurement process includes error. For example, an intelligence test score could be subject to debate concerning the degree to which the obtained score truly reflects the examinee's intelligence and the degree to which it was due to factors other than intelligence. Because error is a variable that must be taken account of in any assessment, we often speak of **error variance,** that is, the component of a test score attributable to sources other than the trait or ability measured.

There are many potential sources of error variance. Whether or not an assessee has the flu when taking a test is a source of error variance. In a more general sense, then, assessees themselves are sources of error variance. Assessors, too, are sources of error variance. For example, some assessors are more professional than others in the extent to which they follow the instructions governing how and under what conditions a test should be administered. In addition to assessors and assessees, measuring instruments themselves are another source of error variance. Some tests are simply better than others in measuring what they purport to measure. Some error is random, or, for lack of a better term, just a matter of chance. To illustrate, consider the weather outside, right now, as you are reading this. If it is daytime, would you characterize the weather as unambiguously sunny, unambiguously rainy, or mixed? Now, consider the weather at another random time—the day that happens to be the one that a personality test is being administered. *Might the weather on the day that one takes a personality test affect that person's test scores?* According to Beatrice Rammstedt and her colleagues (2015), the answer is "blowing in the wind" (see Figure 4–2).

Instructors who teach the undergraduate measurement course will occasionally hear a student refer to error as "creeping into" or "contaminating" the measurement process. Yet measurement professionals tend to view error as simply an element in the process of

FIGURE 4–2
Weather and Self-Concept

There is research to suggest that self-reported personality ratings may differ depending upon the weather on the day that the self-report was made (Rammstedt et al., 2015). This research is instructive regarding the extent to which random situational conditions (such as the weather on the day of an assessment) may affect the expression of traits.
© Andrei Mayatnik/Shutterstock RF

measurement, one for which any theory of measurement must surely account. In what is referred to as **classical test theory** (**CTT;** also variously referred to as **true score theory**) the assumption is made that each testtaker has a *true* score on a test that would be obtained but for the action of measurement error. Alternatives to CTT exist, such as a model of measurement based on item response theory (IRT, to be discussed later). However, whether CTT, IRT, or some other model of measurement is used, the model must have a way of accounting for measurement error. There is more on CTT and its alternatives in Chapter 5.

Assumption 6: Testing and Assessment Can Be Conducted in a Fair and Unbiased Manner

If we had to pick the one of these seven assumptions that is more controversial than the remaining six, this one is it. Decades of court challenges to various tests and testing programs have sensitized test developers and users to the societal demand for fair tests used in a fair manner. Today all major test publishers strive to develop instruments that are fair when used in strict accordance with guidelines in the test manual. However, despite the best efforts of many professionals, fairness-related questions and problems do occasionally arise. One source of fairness-related problems is the test user who attempts to use a particular test with people whose background and experience are different from the background and experience of people for whom the test was intended. Some potential problems related to test fairness are more political than psychometric. For example, heated debate on selection, hiring, and access or denial of access to various opportunities often surrounds affirmative action programs. In many cases the real question for debate is not "Is this test or assessment procedure fair?" but rather "What do we as a society wish to accomplish by the use of this test or assessment procedure?" In all questions about tests with regard to fairness, it is important to keep in mind that tests are tools. And just like other, more familiar tools (hammers, ice picks, wrenches, and so on), they can be used properly or improperly.

JUST THINK . . .

Do you believe that testing can be conducted in a fair and unbiased manner?

Assumption 7: Testing and Assessment Benefit Society

At first glance, the prospect of a world devoid of testing and assessment might seem appealing, especially from the perspective of a harried student preparing for a week of midterm examinations. Yet a world without tests would most likely be more a nightmare than a dream. In such a world, people could present themselves as surgeons, bridge builders, or airline pilots regardless of their background, ability, or professional credentials. In a world without tests or other assessment procedures, personnel might be hired on the basis of nepotism rather than documented merit. In a world without tests, teachers and school administrators could arbitrarily place children in different types of special classes simply because that is where they believed the children belonged. In a world without tests, there would be a great need for instruments to diagnose educational difficulties in reading and math and point the way to remediation. In a world without tests, there would be no instruments to diagnose neuropsychological impairments. In a world without tests, there would be no practical way for the military to screen thousands of recruits with regard to many key variables.

JUST THINK . . .

How else might a world without tests or other assessment procedures be different from the world today?

Considering the many critical decisions that are based on testing and assessment procedures, we can readily appreciate the need for tests, especially good tests. And that, of course, raises one critically important question . . .

What's a "Good Test"?

Logically, the criteria for a good test would include clear instructions for administration, scoring, and interpretation. It would also seem to be a plus if a test offered economy in the time and money it took to administer, score, and interpret it. Most of all, a good test would seem to be one that measures what it purports to measure.

Beyond simple logic, there are technical criteria that assessment professionals use to evaluate the quality of tests and other measurement procedures. Test users often speak of the *psychometric soundness* of tests, two key aspects of which are *reliability* and *validity*.

Reliability

A good test or, more generally, a good measuring tool or procedure is *reliable*. As we will explain in Chapter 5, the criterion of reliability involves the *consistency* of the measuring tool: the precision with which the test measures and the extent to which error is present in measurements. In theory, the perfectly reliable measuring tool consistently measures in the same way.

To exemplify reliability, visualize three digital scales labeled A, B, and C. To determine if they are reliable measuring tools, we will use a standard 1-pound gold bar that has been certified by experts to indeed weigh 1 pound and not a fraction of an ounce more or less. Now, let the testing begin.

Repeated weighings of the 1-pound bar on Scale A register a reading of 1 pound every time. No doubt about it, Scale A is a reliable tool of measurement. On to Scale B. Repeated weighings of the bar on Scale B yield a reading of 1.3 pounds. Is this scale reliable? It sure is! It may be consistently inaccurate by three-tenths of a pound, but there's no taking away the fact that it is reliable. Finally, Scale C. Repeated weighings of the bar on Scale C register a different weight every time. On one weighing, the gold bar weighs in at 1.7 pounds. On the next weighing, the weight registered is 0.9 pound. In short, the weights registered are all over the map. Is this scale reliable? Hardly. This scale is neither reliable nor accurate. Contrast it to Scale B, which also did not record the weight of the gold standard correctly. Although inaccurate, Scale B was consistent in terms of how much the registered weight deviated from the true weight. By contrast, the weight registered by Scale C deviated from the true weight of the bar in seemingly random fashion.

Whether we are measuring gold bars, behavior, or anything else, unreliable measurement is to be avoided. We want to be reasonably certain that the measuring tool or test that we are using is consistent. That is, we want to know that it yields the same numerical measurement every time it measures the same thing under the same conditions. Psychological tests, like other tests and instruments, are reliable to varying degrees. As you might expect, however, reliability is a necessary but not sufficient element of a good test. In addition to being reliable, tests must be reasonably accurate. In the language of psychometrics, tests must be *valid*.

Validity

A test is considered valid for a particular purpose if it does, in fact, measure what it purports to measure. In the gold bar example cited earlier, the scale that consistently indicated that the 1-pound gold bar weighed 1 pound is a valid scale. Likewise, a test of reaction time is a valid test if it accurately measures reaction time. A test of intelligence is a valid test if it truly measures intelligence. Well, yes, but . . .

Although there is relatively little controversy about the definition of a term such as *reaction time,* a great deal of controversy exists about the definition of intelligence. Because there is controversy surrounding the definition of intelligence, the validity of any test purporting to measure this variable is sure to be closely scrutinized by critics. If the definition of intelligence on which the test is based is sufficiently different from the definition of intelligence on other accepted tests, then the test may be condemned as not measuring what it purports to measure.

Questions regarding a test's validity may focus on the items that collectively make up the test. Do the items adequately sample the range of areas that must be sampled to adequately measure the construct? Individual items will also come under scrutiny in an investigation of a test's validity. How do individual items contribute to or detract from the test's validity? The validity of a test may also be questioned on grounds related to the interpretation of resulting test scores. What do these scores really tell us about the targeted construct? How are high scores on the test related to testtakers' behavior? How are low scores on the test related to testtakers' behavior? How do scores on this test relate to scores on other tests purporting to measure the same construct? How do scores on this test relate to scores on other tests purporting to measure opposite types of constructs?

JUST THINK . . .

Why might a test shown to be valid for use for a particular purpose with members of one population not be valid for use for that same purpose with members of another population?

We might expect one person's score on a valid test of introversion to be inversely related to that same person's score on a valid test of extraversion; that is, the higher the introversion test score, the lower the extraversion test score, and vice versa. As we will see when we discuss validity in greater detail in Chapter 6, questions concerning the validity of a particular test may be raised at every stage in the life of a test. From its initial development through the life of its use with members of different populations, assessment professionals may raise questions regarding the extent to which a test is measuring what it purports to measure.

Other Considerations

A good test is one that trained examiners can administer, score, and interpret with a minimum of difficulty. A good test is a useful test, one that yields actionable results that will ultimately benefit individual testtakers or society at large. In "putting a test to the test," there are a number of ways to evaluate just how good a test really is (see this chapter's *Everyday Psychometrics*).

If the purpose of a test is to compare the performance of the testtaker with the performance of other testtakers, then a "good test" is one that contains adequate *norms*. Also referred to as *normative data*, norms provide a standard with which the results of measurement can be compared. Let's explore the important subject of norms in a bit more detail.

Norms

We may define **norm-referenced testing and assessment** as a method of evaluation and a way of deriving meaning from test scores by evaluating an individual testtaker's score and comparing it to scores of a group of testtakers. In this approach, the meaning of an individual test score is understood relative to other scores on the same test. A common goal of norm-referenced tests is to yield information on a testtaker's standing or ranking relative to some comparison group of testtakers.

Norm in the singular is used in the scholarly literature to refer to behavior that is usual, average, normal, standard, expected, or typical. Reference to a particular variety of norm may be specified by means of modifiers such as *age,* as in the term *age norm. Norms* is the plural form of norm, as in the term *gender norms.* In a psychometric context, **norms** are the test performance data of a particular group of testtakers that are designed for use as a reference when evaluating or interpreting individual test scores. As used in this definition, the "particular group of testtakers" may be defined broadly (e.g., "a sample representative of the adult

population of the United States") or narrowly (e.g., "female inpatients at the Bronx Community Hospital with a primary diagnosis of depression"). A **normative sample** is that group of people whose performance on a particular test is analyzed for reference in evaluating the performance of individual testtakers.

Whether broad or narrow in scope, members of the normative sample will all be typical with respect to some characteristic(s) of the people for whom the particular test was designed. A test administration to this representative sample of testtakers yields a distribution (or distributions) of scores. These data constitute the *norms* for the test and typically are used as a reference source for evaluating and placing into context test scores obtained by individual testtakers. The data may be in the form of raw scores or converted scores.

The verb *to norm,* as well as related terms such as **norming,** refer to the process of deriving norms. *Norming* may be modified to describe a particular type of norm derivation. For example, **race norming** is the controversial practice of norming on the basis of race or ethnic background. Race norming was once engaged in by some government agencies and private organizations, and the practice resulted in the establishment of different cutoff scores for hiring by cultural group. Members of one cultural group would have to attain one score to be hired, whereas members of another cultural group would have to attain a different score. Although initially instituted in the service of affirmative action objectives (Greenlaw & Jensen, 1996), the practice was outlawed by the Civil Rights Act of 1991. The Act left unclear a number of issues, however, including "whether, or under what circumstances, in the development of an assessment procedure, it is lawful to adjust item content to minimize group differences" (Kehoe & Tenopyr, 1994, p. 291).

Norming a test, especially with the participation of a nationally representative normative sample, can be a very expensive proposition. For this reason, some test manuals provide what are variously known as **user norms** or **program norms,** which "consist of descriptive statistics based on a group of testtakers in a given period of time rather than norms obtained by formal sampling methods" (Nelson, 1994, p. 283). Understanding how norms are derived through "formal sampling methods" requires some discussion of the process of sampling.

Sampling to Develop Norms

The process of administering a test to a representative sample of testtakers for the purpose of establishing norms is referred to as **standardization** or **test standardization.** As will be clear from this chapter's *Close-Up,* a test is said to be *standardized* when it has clearly specified procedures for administration and scoring, typically including normative data. To understand how norms are derived, an understanding of sampling is necessary.

Sampling   In the process of developing a test, a test developer has targeted some defined group as the population for which the test is designed. This population is the complete universe or set of individuals with at least one common, observable characteristic. The common observable characteristic(s) could be just about anything. For example, it might be *high-school seniors who aspire to go to college,* or *the 16 boys and girls in Mrs. Perez's day-care center,* or *all housewives with primary responsibility for household shopping who have purchased over-the-counter headache remedies within the last two months.*

To obtain a distribution of scores, the test developer could have the test administered to every person in the targeted population. If the total targeted population consists of something like the 16 boys and girls in Mrs. Perez's day-care center, it may well be feasible to administer the test to each member of the targeted population. However, for tests developed to be used with large or wide-ranging populations, it is usually impossible, impractical, or simply too expensive to administer the test to everyone, nor is it necessary.

How "Standard" Is *Standard* in Measurement?

The foot, a unit of distance measurement in the United States, probably had its origins in the length of a British king's foot used as a standard—one that measured about 12 inches, give or take. It wasn't so very long ago that different localities throughout the world all had different "feet" to measure by. We have come a long way since then, especially with regard to standards and standardization in measurement . . . haven't we?

Perhaps. However, in the field of psychological testing and assessment, there's still more than a little confusion when it comes to the meaning of terms like *standard* and *standardization.* Questions also exist concerning what is and is not *standardized.* To address these and related questions, a close-up look at the word *standard* and its derivatives seems very much in order.

The word *standard* can be a noun or an adjective, and in either case it may have multiple (and quite different) definitions. As a noun, *standard* may be defined as *that which others are compared to or evaluated against.* One may speak, for example, of a test with exceptional psychometric properties as being "the standard against which all similar tests are judged." An exceptional textbook on the subject of psychological testing and assessment—take the one you are reading, for example—may be judged "the standard against which all similar textbooks are judged." Perhaps the most common use of *standard* as a noun in the context of testing and assessment is in the title of that well-known manual that sets forth ideals of professional behavior against which any practitioner's behavior can be judged: *The Standards for Educational and Psychological Testing,* usually referred to simply as *the Standards.*

As an adjective, *standard* often refers to *what is usual, generally accepted, or commonly employed.* One may speak, for example, of the *standard* way of conducting a particular measurement procedure, especially as a means of contrasting it to some newer or experimental measurement procedure. For example, a researcher experimenting with a new, multimedia approach to conducting a mental status examination might conduct a study to compare the value of this approach to the *standard* mental status examination interview.

In some areas of psychology, there has been a need to create a new *standard unit of measurement* in the interest of better understanding or quantifying particular phenomena. For example, in studying alcoholism and associated problems, many researchers have adopted the concept of a *standard drink.* The notion of a "standard drink" is designed to facilitate communication and to enhance understanding regarding alcohol

Figure 1
Ben's Cold Cut Preference Test (CCPT)

Ben owns a small "deli boutique" that sells 10 varieties of private-label cold cuts. Ben had read somewhere that if a test has clearly specified methods for test administration and scoring, then it must be considered "standardized." He then went on to create his own "standardized test"—the Cold Cut Preference Test (CCPT). The CCPT consists of only two questions: "What would you like today?" and a follow-up question, "How much of that would you like?" Ben scrupulously trains his only employee (his wife—it's literally a "mom and pop" business) on "test administration" and "test scoring" of the CCPT. So, just think: Does the CCPT really qualify as a "standardized test"?
© DreamPictures/Pam Ostrow/Blend Images LLC RF

consumption patterns (Aros et al., 2006; Gill et al., 2007), intervention strategies (Hwang, 2006; Podymow et al., 2006), and costs associated with alcohol consumption (Farrell, 1998). Regardless of whether it is beer, wine, liquor, or any other alcoholic beverage, reference to a "standard drink" immediately conveys information to the knowledgeable researcher about the amount of alcohol in the beverage.

The verb "to standardize" refers to *making or transforming something into something that can serve as a basis of comparison or judgment.* One may speak, for example, of the efforts of researchers to *standardize* an alcoholic beverage that contains 15 milliliters of alcohol as a "standard drink." For many of the variables commonly used in assessment studies, there is an attempt to *standardize* a definition. As an example, Anderson

(continued)

How "Standard" Is *Standard* in Measurement? *(continued)*

(2007) sought to standardize exactly what is meant by "creative thinking." Well known to any student who has ever taken a nationally administered achievement test or college admission examination is the standardizing of tests. But what does it mean to say that a test is "standardized"? Some "food for thought" regarding an answer to this deceptively simple question can be found in Figure 1.

Test developers *standardize* tests by developing replicable procedures for administering the test and for scoring and interpreting the test. Also part of *standardizing* a test is developing norms for the test. Well, not necessarily . . . whether or not norms for the test must be developed in order for the test to be deemed "standardized" is debatable. It is true that almost any "test" that has clearly specified procedures for administration, scoring, and interpretation can be considered "standardized." So even Ben the deli guy's CCPT (described in Figure 1) might be deemed a "standardized test" according to some. This is so because the test is "standardized" to the extent that the "test items" are clearly specified (presumably along with "rules" for "administering" them and rules for "scoring and interpretation"). Still, many assessment professionals would hesitate to refer to Ben's CCPT as a "standardized test." Why?

Traditionally, assessment professionals have reserved the term **standardized test** for those tests that have clearly specified procedures for administration, scoring, and interpretation in addition to norms. Such tests also come with manuals that are as much a part of the test package as the test's items. Ideally, the test manual, which may be published in one or more booklets, will provide potential test users with all of the information they need to use the test in a responsible fashion. The test manual enables the test user to administer the test in the "standardized" manner in which it was designed to be administered; all test users should be able to replicate the test administration as prescribed by the test developer. Ideally, there will be little deviation from examiner to examiner in the way that a standardized test is administered, owing to the rigorous preparation and training that all potential users of the test have undergone prior to administering the test to testtakers.

If a standardized test is designed for scoring by the test user (in contrast to computer scoring), the test manual will ideally contain detailed scoring guidelines. If the test is one of ability that has correct and incorrect answers, the manual will ideally contain an ample number of examples of correct, incorrect, or partially correct responses, complete with scoring guidelines. In

like fashion, if it is a test that measures personality, interest, or any other variable that is *not* scored as correct or incorrect, then ample examples of potential responses will be provided along with complete scoring guidelines. We would also expect the test manual to contain detailed guidelines for interpreting the test results, including samples of both appropriate and inappropriate generalizations from the findings.

Also from a traditional perspective, we think of standardized tests as having undergone a *standardization* process. Conceivably, the term *standardization* could be applied to "standardizing" all the elements of a standardized test that need to be standardized. Thus, for a standardized test of leadership, we might speak of standardizing the definition of leadership, standardizing test administration instructions, standardizing test scoring, standardizing test interpretation, and so forth. Indeed, one definition of standardization as applied to tests is "the process employed to introduce objectivity and uniformity into test administration, scoring and interpretation" (Robertson, 1990, p. 75). Another and perhaps more typical use of *standardization*, however, is reserved for that part of the test development process during which norms are developed. It is for this very reason that the terms *test standardization* and *test norming* have been used interchangeably by many test professionals.

Assessment professionals develop and use standardized tests to benefit testtakers, test users, and/or society at large. Although there is conceivably some benefit to Ben in gathering data on the frequency of orders for a pound or two of bratwurst, this type of data gathering does not require a "standardized test." So, getting back to Ben's CCPT . . . although some writers would staunchly defend the CCPT as a "standardized test" (simply because any two questions with clearly specified guidelines for administration and scoring would make the "cut"), practically speaking this is simply not the case from the perspective of most assessment professionals.

There are a number of other ambiguities in psychological testing and assessment when it comes to the use of the word *standard* and its derivatives. Consider, for example, the term *standard score*. Some test manuals and books reserve the term *standard score* for use with reference to *z* scores. Raw scores (as well as *z* scores) linearly transformed to any other type of standard scoring systems—that is, transformed to a scale with an arbitrarily set mean and standard deviation—are differentiated from *z* scores by the term *standardized*. For these authors, a *z* score would still be referred to as a "standard score" whereas a *T* score, for example, would be referred to as a "standardized score."

For the purpose of tackling another "nonstandard" use of the word *standard,* let's digress for just a moment to images of the great American pastime of baseball. Imagine, for a moment, all of the different ways that players can be charged with an error. There really isn't one type of error that could be characterized as *standard* in the game of baseball. Now, back to psychological testing and assessment—where there also isn't just one variety of error that could be characterized as "standard." No, there isn't one . . . there are lots of them! One speaks, for example, of the *standard error of measurement* (also known as the *standard error of a score*) the *standard error of estimate* (also known as the *standard error of prediction*), the *standard error of the mean,* and the *standard error of the difference*. A table briefly summarizing the main differences between these terms is presented here, although they are discussed in greater detail elsewhere in this book.

Type of "Standard Error"	What Is It?
Standard error of measurement	A statistic used to estimate the extent to which an observed score deviates from a true score
Standard error of estimate	In regression, an estimate of the degree of error involved in predicting the value of one variable from another
Standard error of the mean	A measure of sampling error
Standard error of the difference	A statistic used to estimate how large a difference between two scores should be before the difference is considered statistically significant

We conclude by encouraging the exercise of critical thinking upon encountering the word *standard*. The next time you encounter the word *standard* in any context, give some thought to how standard that "standard" really is. Certainly with regard to this word's use in the context of psychological testing and assessment, what is presented as "standard" usually turns out to be not as standard as we might expect.

The test developer can obtain a distribution of test responses by administering the test to a **sample** of the population—a portion of the universe of people deemed to be representative of the whole population. The size of the sample could be as small as one person, though samples that approach the size of the population reduce the possible sources of error due to insufficient sample size. The process of selecting the portion of the universe deemed to be representative of the whole population is referred to as **sampling.**

Subgroups within a defined population may differ with respect to some characteristics, and it is sometimes essential to have these differences proportionately represented in the sample. Thus, for example, if you devised a public opinion test and wanted to sample the opinions of Manhattan residents with this instrument, it would be desirable to include in your sample people representing different subgroups (or strata) of the population, such as Blacks, Whites, Asians, other non-Whites, males, females, the poor, the middle class, the rich, professional people, business people, office workers, skilled and unskilled laborers, the unemployed, homemakers, Catholics, Jews, members of other religions, and so forth—all in proportion to the current occurrence of these strata in the population of people who reside on the island of Manhattan. Such sampling, termed **stratified sampling,** would help prevent sampling bias and ultimately aid in the interpretation of the findings. If such sampling were *random* (or, if every member of the population had the same chance of being included in the sample), then the procedure would be termed **stratified-random sampling.**

JUST THINK . . .

Truly random sampling is relatively rare. Why do you think this is so?

Two other types of sampling procedures are *purposive sampling* and *incidental sampling.* If we arbitrarily select some sample because we believe it to be representative of the population, then we have selected what is referred to as a **purposive sample.** Manufacturers of products frequently use purposive sampling when they test the appeal of a new product in one city or market and then make assumptions about how that product would sell nationally. For example, the manufacturer might test a product in a market such as Cleveland because, on the basis of experience with this particular product, "how goes Cleveland, so goes the nation." The danger in using such a purposive sample is that the sample, in this case Cleveland residents, may no longer be representative of the nation. Alternatively, this sample may simply not be representative of national preferences with regard to the particular product being test-marketed.

Often a test user's decisions regarding sampling wind up pitting what is ideal against what is practical. It may be ideal, for example, to use 50 chief executive officers from any of the *Fortune 500* companies (or, the top 500 companies in terms of income) as a sample in an experiment. However, conditions may dictate that it is practical for the experimenter only to use 50 volunteers recruited from the local Chamber of Commerce. This important distinction between what is *ideal* and what is *practical* in sampling brings us to a discussion of what has been referred to variously as an *incidental sample* or a *convenience sample.*

Ever hear the old joke about a drunk searching for money he lost under the lamppost? He may not have lost his money there, but that is where the light is. Like the drunk searching for money under the lamppost, a researcher may sometimes employ a sample that is not necessarily the most appropriate but is simply the most convenient. Unlike the drunk, the researcher employing this type of sample is doing so not as a result of poor judgment but because of budgetary limitations or other constraints. An **incidental sample** or **convenience sample** is one that is convenient or available for use. You may have been a party to incidental sampling if you have ever been placed in a subject pool for experimentation with introductory psychology students. It's not that the students in such subject pools are necessarily the most appropriate subjects for the experiments, it's just that they are the most available. Generalization of findings from incidental samples must be made with caution.

If incidental or convenience samples were clubs, they would not be considered very exclusive clubs. By contrast, there are many samples that are exclusive, in a sense, because they contain many exclusionary criteria. Consider, for example, the group of children and adolescents who served as the normative sample for one well-known children's intelligence test. The sample was selected to reflect key demographic variables representative of the U.S. population according to the latest available census data. Still, some groups were deliberately excluded from participation. Who?

- Persons tested on any intelligence measure in the six months prior to the testing
- Persons not fluent in English or who are primarily nonverbal
- Persons with uncorrected visual impairment or hearing loss
- Persons with upper-extremity disability that affects motor performance
- Persons currently admitted to a hospital or mental or psychiatric facility
- Persons currently taking medication that might depress test performance
- Persons previously diagnosed with any physical condition or illness that might depress test performance (such as stroke, epilepsy, or meningitis)

Our general description of the norming process for a standardized test continues in what follows and, to varying degrees, in subsequent chapters. A highly recommended way to supplement this study and gain a great deal of firsthand knowledge about norms for intelligence tests, personality tests, and other tests is to peruse the technical manuals of major standardized instruments. By going to the library and consulting a few of these manuals, you will discover not only the "real life" way that normative samples are described but also the many varied ways that normative data can be presented.

Developing norms for a standardized test   Having obtained a sample, the test developer administers the test according to the standard set of instructions that will be used with the test. The test developer also describes the recommended setting for giving the test. This may be as simple as making sure that the room is quiet and well lit or as complex

JUST THINK . . .

Why do you think each of these groups of people were excluded from the standardization sample of a nationally standardized intelligence test?

as providing a specific set of toys to test an infant's cognitive skills. Establishing a standard set of instructions and conditions under which the test is given makes the test scores of the normative sample more comparable with the scores of future testtakers. For example, if a test of concentration ability is given to a normative sample in the summer with the windows open near people mowing the grass and arguing about whether the hedges need trimming, then the normative sample probably won't concentrate well. If a testtaker then completes the concentration test under quiet, comfortable conditions, that person may well do much better than the normative group, resulting in a high standard score. That high score would not be very helpful in understanding the testtaker's concentration abilities because it would reflect the differing conditions under which the tests were taken. This example illustrates how important it is that the normative sample take the test under a standard set of conditions, which are then replicated (to the extent possible) on each occasion the test is administered.

After all the test data have been collected and analyzed, the test developer will summarize the data using descriptive statistics, including measures of central tendency and variability. In addition, it is incumbent on the test developer to provide a precise description of the standardization sample itself. Good practice dictates that the norms be developed with data derived from a group of people who are presumed to be representative of the people who will take the test in the future. After all, if the normative group is very different from future testtakers, the basis for comparison becomes questionable at best. In order to best assist future users of the test, test developers are encouraged to "provide information to support recommended interpretations of the results, including the nature of the content, norms or comparison groups, and other technical evidence" (*Code of Fair Testing Practices in Education,* 2004, p. 4).

In practice, descriptions of normative samples vary widely in detail. Test authors wish to present their tests in the most favorable light possible. Shortcomings in the standardization procedure or elsewhere in the process of the test's development therefore may be given short shrift or totally overlooked in a test's manual. Sometimes, although the sample is scrupulously defined, the generalizability of the norms to a particular group or individual is questionable. For example, a test carefully normed on school-age children who reside within the Los Angeles school district may be relevant only to a lesser degree to school-age children who reside within the Dubuque, Iowa, school district. How many children in the standardization sample were English speaking? How many were of Hispanic origin? How does the elementary school curriculum in Los Angeles differ from the curriculum in Dubuque? These are the types of questions that must be raised before the Los Angeles norms are judged to be generalizable to the children of Dubuque. Test manuals sometimes supply prospective test users with guidelines for establishing *local norms* (discussed shortly), one of many different ways norms can be categorized.

One note on terminology is in order before moving on. When the people in the normative sample are the same people on whom the test was standardized, the phrases *normative sample* and *standardization sample* are often used interchangeably. Increasingly, however, new norms for standardized tests for specific groups of testtakers are developed some time after the original standardization. That is, the test remains standardized based on data from the original standardization sample; it's just that new normative data are developed based on an administration of the test to a new normative sample. Included in this new normative sample may be groups of people who were underrepresented in the original standardization sample data. For example, with the changing demographics of a state such as California, and the increasing numbers of people identified as "Hispanic" in that state, an updated normative sample for a California-statewide test might well include a higher proportion of individuals of Hispanic origin. In such a scenario, the normative sample for the new norms clearly would not be identical to the standardization sample, so it would be inaccurate to use the terms *standardization sample* and *normative sample* interchangeably.

Types of Norms

Some of the many different ways we can classify norms are as follows: *age norms, grade norms, national norms, national anchor norms, local norms, norms from a fixed reference group, subgroup norms,* and *percentile norms. Percentile norms* are the raw data from a test's standardization sample converted to percentile form. To better understand them, let's backtrack for a moment and review what is meant by *percentiles.*

Percentiles   In our discussion of the median, we saw that a distribution could be divided into quartiles where the median was the second quartile (Q_2), the point at or below which 50% of the scores fell and above which the remaining 50% fell. Instead of dividing a distribution of scores into quartiles, we might wish to divide the distribution into *deciles,* or 10 equal parts. Alternatively, we could divide a distribution into 100 equal parts—100 *percentiles.* In such a distribution, the *x*th percentile is equal to the score at or below which *x*% of scores fall. Thus, the 15th percentile is the score at or below which 15% of the scores in the distribution fall. The 99th percentile is the score at or below which 99% of the scores in the distribution fall. If 99% of a particular standardization sample answered fewer than 47 questions on a test correctly, then we could say that a raw score of 47 corresponds to the 99th percentile on this test. It can be seen that a percentile is a ranking that conveys information about the relative position of a score within a distribution of scores. More formally defined, a **percentile** is an expression of the percentage of people whose score on a test or measure falls below a particular raw score.

Intimately related to the concept of a percentile as a description of performance on a test is the concept of *percentage correct.* Note that *percentile* and *percentage correct* are *not* synonymous. A percentile is a converted score that refers to a percentage of testtakers. **Percentage correct** refers to the distribution of raw scores—more specifically, to the number of items that were answered correctly multiplied by 100 and divided by the total number of items.

Because percentiles are easily calculated, they are a popular way of organizing all test-related data, including standardization sample data. Additionally, they lend themselves to use with a wide range of tests. Of course, every rose has its thorns. A problem with using percentiles with normally distributed scores is that real differences between raw scores may be minimized near the ends of the distribution and exaggerated in the middle of the distribution. This distortion may even be worse with highly skewed data. In the normal distribution, the highest frequency of raw scores occurs in the middle. That being the case, the differences between all those scores that cluster in the middle might be quite small, yet even the smallest differences will appear as differences in percentiles. The reverse is true at the extremes of the distributions, where differences between raw scores may be great, though we would have no way of knowing that from the relatively small differences in percentiles.

Age norms   Also known as **age-equivalent scores, age norms** indicate the average performance of different samples of testtakers who were at various ages at the time the test was administered. If the measurement under consideration is height in inches, for example, then we know that scores (heights) for children will gradually increase at various rates as a function of age up to the middle to late teens. With the graying of America, there has been increased interest in performance on various types of psychological tests, particularly neuropsychological tests, as a function of advancing age.

Carefully constructed age norm tables for physical characteristics such as height enjoy widespread acceptance and are virtually noncontroversial. This is not the case, however, with respect to age norm tables for psychological characteristics such as intelligence. Ever since the introduction of the Stanford-Binet to this country in the early twentieth century, the idea of identifying the "mental age" of a testtaker has had great intuitive appeal. The child of any chronological age whose performance on a valid test of intellectual ability indicated that he or she had intellectual ability similar to that of the average child of some other age was said to have the mental age of the norm group in which his or her test score fell. The reasoning here was that, irrespective of chronological age, children with the same mental age could be expected to read the same level of material, solve the same kinds of math problems, reason with a similar level of judgment, and so forth.

Increasing sophistication about the limitations of the mental age concept has prompted assessment professionals to be hesitant about describing results in terms of mental age. The problem is that "mental age" as a way to report test results is too broad and too inappropriately generalized. To understand why, consider the case of a 6-year-old who, according to the tasks sampled on an intelligence test, performs intellectually like a 12-year-old. Regardless, the 6-year-old is likely not to be very similar at all to the average 12-year-old socially, psychologically, and in many other key respects. Beyond such obvious faults in mental age analogies, the mental age concept has also been criticized on technical grounds.[3]

Grade norms   Designed to indicate the average test performance of testtakers in a given school grade, **grade norms** are developed by administering the test to representative samples of children over a range of consecutive grade levels (such as first through sixth grades). Next, the mean or median score for children at each grade level is calculated. Because the school year typically runs from September to June—10 months—fractions in the mean or median are easily expressed as decimals. Thus, for example, a sixth-grader performing exactly at the average on a grade-normed test administered during the fourth month of the school year (December) would achieve a grade-equivalent score of 6.4. Like age norms, grade norms have great intuitive appeal. Children learn and develop at varying rates but in ways that are in some aspects predictable. Perhaps because of this fact, grade norms have widespread application, especially to children of elementary school age.

Now consider the case of a student in 12th grade who scores "6" on a grade-normed spelling test. Does this mean that the student has the same spelling abilities as the average sixth-grader? The answer is no. What this finding means is that the student and a hypothetical, average sixth-grader answered the same fraction of items correctly on that test. Grade norms do not provide information as to the content or type of items that a student could or could not answer correctly. Perhaps the primary use of grade norms is as a convenient, readily understandable gauge of how one student's performance compares with that of fellow students in the same grade.

One drawback of grade norms is that they are useful only with respect to years and months of schooling completed. They have little or no applicability to children who are not yet in school or to children who are out of school. Further, they are not typically designed for use with adults who have returned to school. Both grade norms and age norms are referred to more

JUST THINK . . .

Some experts in testing have called for a moratorium on the use of grade-equivalent as well as age-equivalent scores because such scores may so easily be misinterpreted. What is your opinion on this issue?

3. For many years, IQ (intelligence quotient) scores on tests such as the Stanford-Binet were calculated by dividing mental age (as indicated by the test) by chronological age. The quotient would then be multiplied by 100 to eliminate the fraction. The distribution of IQ scores had a mean set at 100 and a standard deviation of approximately 16. A child of 12 with a mental age of 12 had an IQ of 100 (12/12 × 100 = 100). The technical problem here is that IQ standard deviations were not constant with age. At one age, an IQ of 116 might be indicative of performance at 1 standard deviation above the mean, whereas at another age an IQ of 121 might be indicative of performance at 1 standard deviation above the mean.

generally as **developmental norms,** a term applied broadly to norms developed on the basis of any trait, ability, skill, or other characteristic that is presumed to develop, deteriorate, or otherwise be affected by chronological age, school grade, or stage of life.

National norms   As the name implies, **national norms** are derived from a normative sample that was nationally representative of the population at the time the norming study was conducted. In the fields of psychology and education, for example, national norms may be obtained by testing large numbers of people representative of different variables of interest such as age, gender, racial/ethnic background, socioeconomic strata, geographical location (such as North, East, South, West, Midwest), and different types of communities within the various parts of the country (such as rural, urban, suburban).

If the test were designed for use in the schools, norms might be obtained for students in every grade to which the test aimed to be applicable. Factors related to the representativeness of the school from which members of the norming sample were drawn might also be criteria for inclusion in or exclusion from the sample. For example, is the school the student attends publicly funded, privately funded, religiously oriented, military, or something else? How representative are the pupil/teacher ratios in the school under consideration? Does the school have a library, and if so, how many books are in it? These are only a sample of the types of questions that could be raised in assembling a normative sample to be used in the establishment of national norms. The precise nature of the questions raised when developing national norms will depend on whom the test is designed for and what the test is designed to do.

Norms from many different tests may all claim to have nationally representative samples. Still, close scrutiny of the description of the sample employed may reveal that the sample differs in many important respects from similar tests also claiming to be based on a nationally representative sample. For this reason, it is always a good idea to check the manual of the tests under consideration to see exactly how comparable the tests are. Two important questions that test users must raise as consumers of test-related information are "What are the differences between the tests I am considering for use in terms of their normative samples?" and "How comparable are these normative samples to the sample of testtakers with whom I will be using the test?"

National anchor norms   Even the most casual survey of catalogues from various test publishers will reveal that, with respect to almost any human characteristic or ability, there exist many different tests purporting to measure the characteristic or ability. Dozens of tests, for example, purport to measure reading. Suppose we select a reading test designed for use in grades 3 to 6, which, for the purposes of this hypothetical example, we call the Best Reading Test (BRT). Suppose further that we want to compare findings obtained on another national reading test designed for use with grades 3 to 6, the hypothetical XYZ Reading Test, with the BRT. An equivalency table for scores on the two tests, or **national anchor norms,** could provide the tool for such a comparison. Just as an anchor provides some stability to a vessel, so national anchor norms provide some stability to test scores by anchoring them to other test scores.

The method by which such equivalency tables or national anchor norms are established typically begins with the computation of percentile norms for each of the tests to be compared. Using the **equipercentile method,** the equivalency of scores on different tests is calculated with reference to corresponding percentile scores. Thus, if the 96th percentile corresponds to a score of 69 on the BRT and if the 96th percentile corresponds to a score of 14 on the XYZ, then we can say that a BRT score of 69 is equivalent to an XYZ score of 14. We should note that the national anchor norms for our hypothetical BRT and XYZ tests must have been obtained on the same sample—each member of the sample took both tests, and the equivalency tables were then calculated on the basis of these data.[4] Although national anchor norms provide an indication of

_____

4. When two tests are normed from the same sample, the norming process is referred to as *co-norming.*

the equivalency of scores on various tests, technical considerations entail that it would be a mistake to treat these equivalencies as precise equalities (Angoff, 1964, 1966, 1971).

Subgroup norms   A normative sample can be segmented by any of the criteria initially used in selecting subjects for the sample. What results from such segmentation are more narrowly defined **subgroup norms.** Thus, for example, suppose criteria used in selecting children for inclusion in the XYZ Reading Test normative sample were age, educational level, socioeconomic level, geographic region, community type, and handedness (whether the child was right-handed or left-handed). The test manual or a supplement to it might report normative information by each of these subgroups. A community school board member might find the regional norms to be most useful, whereas a psychologist doing exploratory research in the area of brain lateralization and reading scores might find the handedness norms most useful.

Local norms   Typically developed by test users themselves, **local norms** provide normative information with respect to the local population's performance on some test. A local company personnel director might find some nationally standardized test useful in making selection decisions but might deem the norms published in the test manual to be far afield of local job applicants' score distributions. Individual high schools may wish to develop their own school norms (local norms) for student scores on an examination that is administered statewide. A school guidance center may find that locally derived norms for a particular test—say, a survey of personal values— are more useful in counseling students than the national norms printed in the manual. Some test users use abbreviated forms of existing tests, which requires new norms. Some test users substitute one subtest for another within a larger test, thus creating the need for new norms. There are many different scenarios that would lead the prudent test user to develop local norms.

Fixed Reference Group Scoring Systems

Norms provide a context for interpreting the meaning of a test score. Another type of aid in providing a context for interpretation is termed a **fixed reference group scoring system.** Here, the distribution of scores obtained on the test from one group of testtakers—referred to as the *fixed reference group*—is used as the basis for the calculation of test scores for future administrations of the test. Perhaps the test most familiar to college students that has historically exemplified the use of a fixed reference group scoring system is the SAT. This test was first administered in 1926. Its norms were then based on the mean and standard deviation of the people who took the test at the time. With passing years, more colleges became members of the College Board, the sponsoring organization for the test. It soon became evident that SAT scores tended to vary somewhat as a function of the time of year the test was administered. In an effort to ensure perpetual comparability and continuity of scores, a fixed reference group scoring system was put into place in 1941. The distribution of scores from the 11,000 people who took the SAT in 1941 was immortalized as a standard to be used in the conversion of raw scores on future administrations of the test.[5] A new fixed reference group, which consisted of the more than 2 million testtakers who completed the SAT in 1990, began to be used in 1995. A score of 500 on the SAT corresponds to the mean obtained by the 1990 sample, a score of 400 corresponds to a score that is 1 standard deviation below the 1990 mean, and so forth. As an example, suppose John took the SAT in 1995 and answered 50 items correctly on a particular scale. And let's say Mary took the test in 2008 and, just like John, answered 50 items correctly. Although John and Mary may have achieved the same raw score, they would not necessarily achieve the same scaled score. If, for example, the 2008 version of the test was judged to be somewhat easier than the

---

5. Conceptually, the idea of a *fixed reference group* is analogous to the idea of a *fixed reference foot,* the foot of the English king that also became immortalized as a measurement standard (Angoff, 1962).

1995 version, then scaled scores for the 2008 testtakers would be calibrated downward. This would be done so as to make scores earned in 2008 comparable to scores earned in 1995.

Test items common to each new version of the SAT and each previous version of it are employed in a procedure (termed *anchoring*) that permits the conversion of raw scores on the new version of the test into *fixed reference group scores*. Like other fixed reference group scores, including Graduate Record Examination scores, SAT scores are most typically interpreted by local decision-making bodies with respect to local norms. Thus, for example, college admissions officers usually rely on their own independently collected norms to make selection decisions. They will typically compare applicants' SAT scores to the SAT scores of students in their school who completed or failed to complete their program. Of course, admissions decisions are seldom made on the basis of the SAT (or any other single test) alone. Various criteria are typically evaluated in admissions decisions.

Norm-Referenced Versus Criterion-Referenced Evaluation

One way to derive meaning from a test score is to evaluate the test score in relation to other scores on the same test. As we have pointed out, this approach to evaluation is referred to as *norm-referenced*. Another way to derive meaning from a test score is to evaluate it on the basis of whether or not some criterion has been met. We may define a **criterion** as a standard on which a judgment or decision may be based.

Criterion-referenced testing and assessment may be defined as a method of evaluation and a way of deriving meaning from test scores by evaluating an individual's score with reference to a set standard. Some examples:

- To be eligible for a high-school diploma, students must demonstrate at least a sixth-grade reading level.
- To earn the privilege of driving an automobile, would-be drivers must take a road test and demonstrate their driving skill to the satisfaction of a state-appointed examiner.
- To be licensed as a psychologist, the applicant must achieve a score that meets or exceeds the score mandated by the state on the licensing test.
- To conduct research using human subjects, many universities and other organizations require researchers to successfully complete an online course that presents testtakers with ethics-oriented information in a series of modules, followed by a set of forced-choice questions.

The criterion in criterion-referenced assessments typically derives from the values or standards of an individual or organization. For example, in order to earn a black belt in karate, students must demonstrate a black-belt level of proficiency in karate and meet related criteria such as those related to self-discipline and focus. Each student is evaluated individually to see if all of these criteria are met. Regardless of the level of performance of all the testtakers, only students who meet all the criteria will leave the *dojo* (training room) with a brand-new black belt.

JUST THINK . . .

List other examples of a criterion that must be met in order to gain privileges or access of some sort.

Criterion-referenced testing and assessment goes by other names. Because the focus in the criterion-referenced approach is on how scores relate to a particular content area or domain, the approach has also been referred to as **domain-** or **content-referenced testing and assessment.**[6]

---

6. Although acknowledging that content-referenced interpretations can be referred to as criterion-referenced interpretations, the 1974 edition of the *Standards for Educational and Psychological Testing* also noted a technical distinction between interpretations so designated: "*Content-referenced* interpretations are those where the score is directly interpreted in terms of performance at each point on the achievement continuum being measured. *Criterion-referenced* interpretations are those where the score is directly interpreted in terms of performance at any given point on the continuum of an *external* variable. An external criterion variable might be grade averages or levels of job performance" (p. 19; footnote in original omitted).

One way of conceptualizing the difference between norm-referenced and criterion-referenced approaches to assessment has to do with the area of focus regarding test results. In norm-referenced interpretations of test data, a usual area of focus is how an individual performed relative to other people who took the test. In criterion-referenced interpretations of test data, a usual area of focus is the testtaker's performance: what the testtaker can or cannot do; what the testtaker has or has not learned; whether the testtaker does or does not meet specified criteria for inclusion in some group, access to certain privileges, and so forth. Because criterion-referenced tests are frequently used to gauge achievement or mastery, they are sometimes referred to as *mastery tests*. The criterion-referenced approach has enjoyed widespread acceptance in the field of computer-assisted education programs. In such programs, mastery of segments of materials is assessed before the program user can proceed to the next level.

"Has this flight trainee mastered the material she needs to be an airline pilot?" This is the type of question that an airline personnel office might seek to address with a mastery test on a flight simulator. If a standard, or criterion, for passing a hypothetical "Airline Pilot Test" (APT) has been set at 85% correct, then trainees who score 84% correct or less will not pass. It matters not whether they scored 84% or 42%. Conversely, trainees who score 85% or better on the test will pass whether they scored 85% or 100%. All who score 85% or better are said to have mastered the skills and knowledge necessary to be an airline pilot. Taking this example one step further, another airline might find it useful to set up three categories of findings based on criterion-referenced interpretation of test scores:

85% or better correct = pass

75% to 84% correct = retest after a two-month refresher course

74% or less = fail

How should cut scores in mastery testing be determined? How many and what kinds of test items are needed to demonstrate mastery in a given field? The answers to these and related questions have been tackled in diverse ways (Cizek & Bunch, 2007; Ferguson & Novick, 1973; Geisenger & McCormick, 2010; Glaser & Nitko, 1971; Panell & Laabs, 1979).

Critics of the criterion-referenced approach argue that if it is strictly followed, potentially important information about an individual's performance relative to other testtakers is lost. Another criticism is that although this approach may have value with respect to the assessment of mastery of basic knowledge, skills, or both, it has little or no meaningful application at the upper end of the knowledge/skill continuum. Thus, the approach is clearly meaningful in evaluating whether pupils have mastered basic reading, writing, and arithmetic. But how useful is it in evaluating doctoral-level writing or math? Identifying stand-alone originality or brilliant analytic ability is *not* the stuff of which criterion-oriented tests are made. By contrast, brilliance and superior abilities are recognizable in tests that employ norm-referenced interpretations. They are the scores that trail off all the way to the right on the normal curve, past the third standard deviation.

Norm-referenced and criterion-referenced are two of many ways that test data may be viewed and interpreted. However, these terms are *not* mutually exclusive, and the use of one approach with a set of test data does not necessarily preclude the use of the other approach for another application. In a sense, all testing is ultimately normative, even if the scores are as seemingly criterion-referenced as pass–fail. This is so because even in a pass–fail score there is an inherent acknowledgment of a continuum of abilities. At some point in that continuum, a dichotomizing cutoff point has been applied. We should also make the point that some so-called norm-referenced assessments are made with subject samples wherein "the norm is hardly the norm." In a similar vein, when dealing with special or extraordinary populations, the criterion level that is set by a test may also be "far from

JUST THINK . . .

For licensing of physicians, psychologists, engineers, and other professionals, would you advocate that your state use criterion- or norm-referenced assessment? Why?

the norm" in the sense of being average with regard to the general population. To get a sense what we mean by such statements, just think of the norm for everyday skills related to playing basketball, and then imagine how those norms might be with a subject sample limited exclusively to players on NBA teams. Now, meet two sports psychologists who have worked in a professional assessment capacity with the Chicago Bulls in this chapter's *Meet an Assessment Professional.*

Culture and Inference

Along with statistical tools designed to help ensure that prediction and inferences from measurement are reasonable, there are other considerations. It is incumbent upon responsible test users not to lose sight of culture as a factor in test administration, scoring, and interpretation.

MEET AN ASSESSMENT PROFESSIONAL

Meet Dr. Steve Julius and Dr. Howard W. Atlas

The Chicago Bulls of the 1990s is considered one of the great dynasties in sports, as witnessed by their six world championships in that decade. . . .

The team benefited from great individual contributors, but like all successful organizations, the Bulls were always on the lookout for ways to maintain a competitive edge. The Bulls . . . were one of the first NBA franchises to apply personality testing and behavioral interviewing to aid in the selection of college players during the annual draft, as well as in the evaluation of goodness-of-fit when considering the addition of free agents. The purpose of this effort was not to rule out psychopathology, but rather to evaluate a range of competencies (e.g., resilience, relationship to authority, team orientation) that were deemed necessary for success in the league, in general, and the Chicago Bulls, in particular.

[The team utilized] commonly used and well-validated personality assessment tools and techniques from the world of business (e.g., 16PF–fifth edition). . . . Eventually, sufficient data was collected to allow for the validation of a regression formula, useful as a prediction tool in its own right. In addition to selection, the information collected on the athletes often is used to assist the coaching staff in their efforts to motivate and instruct players, as well as to create an atmosphere of collaboration.

Read more of what Dr. Atlas and Dr. Julius had to say—their complete essay—through the Instructor Resources within Connect.

Steve Julius, Ph.D., Sports Psychologist, Chicago Bulls
© Steve Julius

Howard W. Atlas, Ed.D., Sports Psychologist, Chicago Bulls
© Howard W. Atlas

So, in selecting a test for use, the responsible test user does some advance research on the test's available norms to check on how appropriate they are for use with the targeted testtaker population. In interpreting data from psychological tests, it is frequently helpful to know about the culture of the testtaker, including something about the era or "times" that the testtaker experienced. In this regard, think of the words of the famous anthropologist Margaret Mead (1978, p. 71), who, in recalling her youth, wrote: "We grew up under skies which no satellite had flashed." In interpreting assessment data from assessees of different generations, it would seem useful to keep in mind whether "satellites had or had not flashed in the sky." In other words, historical context should not be lost sight of in evaluation (Rogler, 2002).

JUST THINK . . .

What event in recent history may have relevance when interpreting data from a psychological assessment?

It seems appropriate to conclude a chapter entitled "Of Tests and Testing" with the introduction of the term *culturally informed assessment* and with some guidelines for accomplishing it (Table 4–1). Think of these guidelines as a list of themes that may be repeated in different ways as you continue to learn about the assessment enterprise. To supplement this list, see the guidelines published by the American Psychological Association (2003). For now, let's continue to build a sound foundation in testing and assessment with a discussion of the psychometric concept of *reliability* in Chapter 5.

Table 4–1
Culturally Informed Assessment: Some "Do's" and "Don'ts"

Do	Do Not
Be aware of the cultural assumptions on which a test is based	Take for granted that a test is based on assumptions that impact all groups in much the same way
Consider consulting with members of particular cultural communities regarding the appropriateness of particular assessment techniques, tests, or test items	Take for granted that members of all cultural communities will automatically deem particular techniques, tests, or test items appropriate for use
Strive to incorporate assessment methods that complement the worldview and lifestyle of assessees who come from a specific cultural and linguistic population	Take a "one-size-fits-all" view of assessment when it comes to evaluation of persons from various cultural and linguistic populations
Be knowledgeable about the many alternative tests or measurement procedures that may be used to fulfill the assessment objectives	Select tests or other tools of assessment with little or no regard for the extent to which such tools are appropriate for use with a particular assessee.
Be aware of equivalence issues across cultures, including equivalence of language used and the constructs measured	Simply assume that a test that has been translated into another language is automatically equivalent in every way to the original
Score, interpret, and analyze assessment data in its cultural context with due consideration of cultural hypotheses as possible explanations for findings	Score, interpret, and analyze assessment in a cultural vacuum

Self-Assessment

Test your understanding of elements of this chapter by seeing if you can explain each of the following terms, expressions, and abbreviations:

age-equivalent scores
age norms
classical test theory (CTT)
construct

content-referenced testing and assessment
convenience sample
criterion

criterion-referenced testing and assessment
cumulative scoring
developmental norms

domain-referenced testing and
    assessment
domain sampling
equipercentile method
error variance
fixed reference group scoring
    system
grade norms
incidental sample
local norms
national anchor norms
national norms

norm
normative sample
norming
norm-referenced testing and
    assessment
overt behavior
percentage correct
percentile
program norms
purposive sampling
race norming
sample

sampling
standardization
standardized test
state
stratified-random sampling
stratified sampling
subgroup norms
test standardization
trait
true score theory
user norms

5

Reliability

In everyday conversation, *reliability* is a synonym for *dependability* or *consistency*. We speak of the train that is so reliable you can set your watch by it. If we're lucky, we have a reliable friend who is always there for us in a time of need.

Broadly speaking, in the language of psychometrics *reliability* refers to consistency in measurement. And whereas in everyday conversation reliability always connotes something positive, in the psychometric sense it really only refers to something that is consistent—not necessarily consistently good or bad, but simply consistent.

It is important for us, as users of tests and consumers of information about tests, to know how reliable tests and other measurement procedures are. But reliability is not an all-or-none matter. A test may be reliable in one context and unreliable in another. There are different types and degrees of reliability. A **reliability coefficient** is an index of reliability, a proportion that indicates the ratio between the true score variance on a test and the total variance. In this chapter, we explore different kinds of reliability coefficients, including those for measuring test-retest reliability, alternate-forms reliability, split-half reliability, and inter-scorer reliability.

The Concept of Reliability

Recall from our discussion of classical test theory that a score on an ability test is presumed to reflect not only the testtaker's true score on the ability being measured but also error.[1] In its broadest sense, error refers to the component of the observed test score that does not have to do with the testtaker's ability. If we use X to represent an observed score, T to represent a true score, and E to represent error, then the fact that an observed score equals the true score plus error may be expressed as follows:

$$X = T + E$$

A statistic useful in describing sources of test score variability is the **variance** (σ^2)—the standard deviation squared. This statistic is useful because it can be broken into components.

---

1. Ability is frequently used for illustrative purposes as a trait being measured. However, unless stated otherwise, the principles to which we refer with respect to ability tests also hold true with respect to other types of tests, such as tests for personality. Thus, according to the true score model, it is also true that the magnitude of the presence of a certain psychological trait (such as extraversion) as measured by a test of extraversion will be due to (1) the "true" amount of extraversion and (2) other factors.

Variance from true differences is **true variance,** and variance from irrelevant, random sources is **error variance.** If σ^2 represents the total variance, the true variance, and the error variance, then the relationship of the variances can be expressed as

$$\sigma^2 = \sigma_{th}^2 + \sigma_e^2$$

In this equation, the total variance in an observed distribution of test scores (σ^2) equals the sum of the true variance (σ_{th}^2) plus the error variance (σ_e^2). The term **reliability** refers to the proportion of the total variance attributed to true variance. The greater the proportion of the total variance attributed to true variance, the more reliable the test. Because true differences are assumed to be stable, they are presumed to yield consistent scores on repeated administrations of the same test as well as on equivalent forms of tests. Because error variance may increase or decrease a test score by varying amounts, consistency of the test score—and thus the reliability—can be affected.

In general, the term **measurement error** refers to, collectively, all of the factors associated with the process of measuring some variable, other than the variable being measured. To illustrate, consider an English-language test on the subject of 12th-grade algebra being administered, in English, to a sample of 12-grade students, newly arrived to the United States from China. The students in the sample are all known to be "whiz kids" in algebra. Yet for some reason, all of the students receive failing grades on the test. Do these failures indicate that these students really are not "whiz kids" at all? Possibly. But a researcher looking for answers regarding this outcome would do well to evaluate the English-language skills of the students. Perhaps this group of students did not do well on the algebra test because they could neither read nor understand what was required of them. In such an instance, the fact that the test was written and administered in English could have contributed in large part to the measurement error in this evaluation. Stated another way, although the test was designed to evaluate one variable (knowledge of algebra), scores on it may have been more reflective of another variable (knowledge of and proficiency in English language). This source of measurement error (the fact that the test was written and administered in English) could have been eliminated by translating the test and administering it in the language of the testtakers.

Measurement error, much like error in general, can be categorized as being either *systematic* or *random.* **Random error** is a source of error in measuring a targeted variable caused by unpredictable fluctuations and inconsistencies of other variables in the measurement process. Sometimes referred to as "noise," this source of error fluctuates from one testing situation to another with no discernible pattern that would systematically raise or lower scores. Examples of random error that could conceivably affect test scores range from unanticipated events happening in the immediate vicinity of the test environment (such as a lightning strike or a spontaneous "occupy the university" rally), to unanticipated physical events happening within the testtaker (such as a sudden and unexpected surge in the testtaker's blood sugar or blood pressure).

JUST THINK . . .

What might be a source of random error inherent in all the tests an assessor administers in his or her private office?

In contrast to random error, **systematic error** refers to a source of error in measuring a variable that is typically constant or proportionate to what is presumed to be the true value of the variable being measured. For example, a 12-inch ruler may be found to be, in actuality, a tenth of one inch longer than 12 inches. All of the 12-inch measurements previously taken with that ruler were systematically off by one-tenth of an inch; that is, anything measured to be exactly 12 inches with that ruler was, in reality, 12 and one-tenth inches. In this example, it is the measuring instrument itself that has been found to be a source of systematic error. Once a systematic error becomes known, it becomes predictable—as well as fixable. Note also that a systematic source of error does not affect score consistency. So, for example, suppose a measuring instrument such as the official weight scale used on *The Biggest Loser* television program consistently underweighed by 5 pounds everyone who stepped on it. Regardless of this (systematic) error, the relative standings of all of the contestants weighed on that scale would remain unchanged. A scale underweighing all contestants by 5 pounds simply amounts to a constant being subtracted from every "score." Although weighing contestants on such a scale would not yield a true (or valid) weight, such a systematic error source would not change the variability of the distribution or affect the measured reliability of the instrument. In the end, the individual crowned "the biggest loser" would indeed be the contestant who lost the most weight—it's just that he or she would actually weigh 5 pounds more than the weight measured by the show's official scale. Now moving from the realm of reality television back to the realm of psychological testing and assessment, let's take a closer look at the source of some error variance commonly encountered during testing and assessment.

JUST THINK . . .

What might be a source of systematic error inherent in all the tests an assessor administers in his or her private office?

Sources of Error Variance

Sources of error variance include test construction, administration, scoring, and/or interpretation.

Test construction   One source of variance during test construction is **item sampling** or **content sampling,** terms that refer to variation among items within a test as well as to variation among items between tests. Consider two or more tests designed to measure a specific skill, personality attribute, or body of knowledge. Differences are sure to be found in the way the items are worded and in the exact content sampled. Each of us has probably walked into an achievement test setting thinking "I hope they ask this question" or "I hope they don't ask that question." If the only questions on the examination were the ones we hoped would be asked, we might achieve a higher score on that test than on another test purporting to measure the same thing. The higher score would be due to the specific content sampled, the way the items were worded, and so on. The extent to which a testtaker's score is affected by the content sampled on a test and by the way the content is sampled (that is, the way in which the item is constructed) is a source of error variance. From the perspective of a test creator, a challenge in test development is to maximize the proportion of the total variance that is true variance and to minimize the proportion of the total variance that is error variance.

Test administration   Sources of error variance that occur during test administration may influence the testtaker's attention or motivation. The testtaker's reactions to those influences are the source of one kind of error variance. Examples of untoward influences during administration of a test include factors related to the *test environment:* room temperature, level of lighting, and amount of ventilation and noise, for instance. A relentless fly may develop a tenacious attraction to an examinee's face. A wad of gum on the seat of the chair may make itself known only after the testtaker sits down on it. Other environment-related variables include the instrument used to enter responses and even the writing surface on which responses are entered. A pencil with a dull or broken point can make it difficult to blacken the little grids. The writing surface on a school desk may be riddled with heart carvings, the legacy of past years' students who felt compelled to express their eternal devotion to someone now long forgotten. External to the test environment in a global sense, the events of the day may also serve as a source of error. So, for example, test results may vary depending upon whether the testtaker's country is at war or at peace (Gil et al., 2016). A variable of interest when evaluating a patient's general level of suspiciousness or fear is the patient's home neighborhood and lifestyle. Especially in patients who live in and must cope daily with an unsafe neighborhood,

An estimate of the reliability of a test can be obtained without developing an alternate form of the test and without having to administer the test twice to the same people. Deriving this type of estimate entails an evaluation of the internal consistency of the test items. Logically enough, it is referred to as an **internal consistency estimate of reliability** or as an **estimate of inter-item consistency.** There are different methods of obtaining internal consistency estimates of reliability. One such method is the *split-half estimate.*

Split-Half Reliability Estimates

An estimate of **split-half reliability** is obtained by correlating two pairs of scores obtained from equivalent halves of a single test administered once. It is a useful measure of reliability when it is impractical or undesirable to assess reliability with two tests or to administer a test twice (because of factors such as time or expense). The computation of a coefficient of split-half reliability generally entails three steps:

Step 1. Divide the test into equivalent halves.

Step 2. Calculate a Pearson *r* between scores on the two halves of the test.

Step 3. Adjust the half-test reliability using the Spearman–Brown formula (discussed shortly).

When it comes to calculating split-half reliability coefficients, there's more than one way to split a test—but there are some ways you should never split a test. Simply dividing the test in the middle is not recommended because it's likely that this procedure would spuriously raise or lower the reliability coefficient. Different amounts of fatigue for the first as opposed to the second part of the test, different amounts of test anxiety, and differences in item difficulty as a function of placement in the test are all factors to consider.

One acceptable way to split a test is to randomly assign items to one or the other half of the test. Another acceptable way to split a test is to assign odd-numbered items to one half of the test and even-numbered items to the other half. This method yields an estimate of split-half reliability that is also referred to as **odd-even reliability.**[4] Yet another way to split a test is to divide the test by content so that each half contains items equivalent with respect to content and difficulty. In general, a primary objective in splitting a test in half for the purpose of obtaining a split-half reliability estimate is to create what might be called "mini-parallel-forms," with each half equal to the other—or as nearly equal as humanly possible—in format, stylistic, statistical, and related aspects.

Step 2 in the procedure entails the computation of a Pearson *r,* which requires little explanation at this point. However, the third step requires the use of the Spearman–Brown formula.

The Spearman–Brown formula The **Spearman–Brown formula** allows a test developer or user to estimate internal consistency reliability from a correlation of two halves of a test. It is a specific application of a more general formula to estimate the reliability of a test that is lengthened or shortened by any number of items. Because the reliability of a test is affected by its length, a formula is necessary for estimating the reliability of a test that has been shortened or lengthened. The general Spearman–Brown (r_{SB}) formula is

$$r_{SB} = \frac{nr_{xy}}{1 + (n - 1)r_{xy}}$$

---

4. One precaution here: With respect to a group of items on an achievement test that deals with a single problem, it is usually desirable to assign the whole group of items to one half of the test. Otherwise—if part of the group were in one half and another part in the other half—the similarity of the half scores would be spuriously inflated. In this instance, a single error in understanding, for example, might affect items in both halves of the test.

where r_{SB} is equal to the reliability adjusted by the Spearman–Brown formula, r_{xy} is equal to the Pearson r in the original-length test, and n is equal to the number of items in the revised version divided by the number of items in the original version.

By determining the reliability of one half of a test, a test developer can use the Spearman–Brown formula to estimate the reliability of a whole test. Because a whole test is two times longer than half a test, n becomes 2 in the Spearman–Brown formula for the adjustment of split-half reliability. The symbol r_{hh} stands for the Pearson r of scores in the two half tests:

$$r_{SB} = \frac{2r_{hh}}{1 + r_{hh}}$$

Usually, but not always, reliability increases as test length increases. Ideally, the additional test items are equivalent with respect to the content and the range of difficulty of the original items. Estimates of reliability based on consideration of the entire test therefore tend to be higher than those based on half of a test. Table 5–1 shows half-test correlations presented alongside adjusted reliability estimates for the whole test. You can see that all the adjusted correlations are higher than the unadjusted correlations. This is so because Spearman–Brown estimates are based on a test that is twice as long as the original half test. For the data from the kindergarten pupils, for example, a half-test reliability of .718 is estimated to be equivalent to a whole-test reliability of .836.

If test developers or users wish to shorten a test, the Spearman–Brown formula may be used to estimate the effect of the shortening on the test's reliability. Reduction in test size for the purpose of reducing test administration time is a common practice in certain situations. For example, the test administrator may have only limited time with a particular testtaker or group of testtakers. Reduction in test size may be indicated in situations where boredom or fatigue could produce responses of questionable meaningfulness.

A Spearman–Brown formula could also be used to determine the number of items needed to attain a desired level of reliability. In adding items to increase test reliability to a desired level, the rule is that the new items must be equivalent in content and difficulty so that the longer test still measures what the original test measured. If the reliability of the original test is relatively low, then it may be impractical to increase the number of items to reach an acceptable level of reliability. Another alternative would be to abandon this relatively unreliable instrument and locate—or develop—a suitable alternative. The reliability of the instrument could also be raised in some way. For example, the reliability of the instrument might be raised by creating new items, clarifying the test's instructions, or simplifying the scoring rules.

Internal consistency estimates of reliability, such as that obtained by use of the Spearman–Brown formula, are inappropriate for measuring the reliability of heterogeneous tests and speed tests. The impact of test characteristics on reliability is discussed in detail later in this chapter.

JUST THINK . . .

What are other situations in which a reduction in test size or the time it takes to administer a test might be desirable? What are the arguments against reducing test size?

Table 5–1

Odd-Even Reliability Coefficients before and after the Spearman-Brown Adjustment*

Grade	Half-Test Correlation (unadjusted r)	Whole-Test Estimate (r_{SB})
K	.718	.836
1	.807	.893
2	.777	.875

*For scores on a test of mental ability

Other Methods of Estimating Internal Consistency

In addition to the Spearman–Brown formula, other methods used to obtain estimates of internal consistency reliability include formulas developed by Kuder and Richardson (1937) and Cronbach (1951). **Inter-item consistency** refers to the degree of correlation among all the items on a scale. A measure of inter-item consistency is calculated from a single administration of a single form of a test. An index of inter-item consistency, in turn, is useful in assessing the **homogeneity** of the test. Tests are said to be homogeneous if they contain items that measure a single trait. As an adjective used to describe test items, *homogeneity* (derived from the Greek words *homos,* meaning "same," and *genos,* meaning "kind") is the degree to which a test measures a single factor. In other words, homogeneity is the extent to which items in a scale are unifactorial.

In contrast to test homogeneity, **heterogeneity** describes the degree to which a test measures different factors. A *heterogeneous* (or nonhomogeneous) test is composed of items that measure more than one trait. A test that assesses knowledge only of ultra high definition (UHD) television repair skills could be expected to be more homogeneous in content than a general electronics repair test. The former test assesses only one area whereas the latter assesses several, such as knowledge not only of UHD televisions but also of digital video recorders, Blu-Ray players, MP3 players, satellite radio receivers, and so forth.

The more homogeneous a test is, the more inter-item consistency it can be expected to have. Because a homogeneous test samples a relatively narrow content area, it is to be expected to contain more inter-item consistency than a heterogeneous test. Test homogeneity is desirable because it allows relatively straightforward test-score interpretation. Testtakers with the same score on a homogeneous test probably have similar abilities in the area tested. Testtakers with the same score on a more heterogeneous test may have quite different abilities.

Although a homogeneous test is desirable because it so readily lends itself to clear interpretation, it is often an insufficient tool for measuring multifaceted psychological variables such as intelligence or personality. One way to circumvent this potential source of difficulty has been to administer a series of homogeneous tests, each designed to measure some component of a heterogeneous variable.[5]

The Kuder–Richardson formulas Dissatisfaction with existing split-half methods of estimating reliability compelled G. Frederic Kuder and M. W. Richardson (1937; Richardson & Kuder, 1939) to develop their own measures for estimating reliability. The most widely known of the many formulas they collaborated on is their **Kuder–Richardson formula 20,** or KR-20, so named because it was the 20th formula developed in a series. Where test items are highly homogeneous, KR-20 and split-half reliability estimates will be similar. However, KR-20 is the statistic of choice for determining the inter-item consistency of dichotomous items, primarily those items that can be scored right or wrong (such as multiple-choice items). If test items are more heterogeneous, KR-20 will yield lower reliability estimates than the split-half method. Table 5–2 summarizes items on a sample heterogeneous test (the HERT), and Table 5–3 summarizes HERT performance for 20 testtakers. Assuming the difficulty level of all the items on the test to be about the same, would you expect a split-half (odd-even) estimate of reliability to be fairly high or low? How would the KR-20 reliability estimate compare with the odd-even estimate of reliability—would it be higher or lower?

We might guess that, because the content areas sampled for the 18 items from this "Hypothetical Electronics Repair Test" are ordered in a manner whereby odd and even items

---

5. As we will see elsewhere throughout this textbook, important decisions are seldom made on the basis of one test only. Psychologists frequently rely on a **test battery**—a selected assortment of tests and assessment procedures—in the process of evaluation. A test battery is typically composed of tests designed to measure different variables.

Item Number	Content Area
1	UHD television
2	UHD television
3	Digital video recorder (DVR)
4	Digital video recorder (DVR)
5	Blu-Ray player
6	Blu-Ray player
7	Smart phone
8	Smart phone
9	Computer
10	Computer
11	Compact disc player
12	Compact disc player
13	Satellite radio receiver
14	Satellite radio receiver
15	Video camera
16	Video camera
17	MP3 player
18	MP3 player

Table 5–3

Performance on the 18-Item HERT by Item for 20 Testtakers

Item Number	Number of Testtakers Correct
1	14
2	12
3	9
4	18
5	8
6	5
7	6
8	9
9	10
10	10
11	8
12	6
13	15
14	9
15	12
16	12
17	14
18	7

tap the same content area, the odd-even reliability estimate will probably be quite high. Because of the great heterogeneity of content areas when taken as a whole, it could reasonably be predicted that the KR-20 estimate of reliability will be lower than the odd-even one. How is KR-20 computed? The following formula may be used:

$$r_{KR20} = \left(\frac{k}{k-1} \right) \left(1 - \frac{\Sigma pq}{\sigma^2} \right)$$

where r_{KR20} stands for the Kuder–Richardson formula 20 reliability coefficient, k is the number of test items, σ^2 is the variance of total test scores, p is the proportion of testtakers who pass the item, q is the proportion of people who fail the item, and $\Sigma\, pq$ is the sum of the pq products over all items. For this particular example, k equals 18. Based on the data in Table 5–3, Σpq can be computed to be 3.975. The variance of total test scores is 5.26. Thus, $r_{KR20} = .259$.

An approximation of KR-20 can be obtained by the use of the 21st formula in the series developed by Kuder and Richardson, a formula known as—you guessed it—KR-21. The KR-21 formula may be used if there is reason to assume that all the test items have approximately the same degree of difficulty. Let's add that this assumption is seldom justified. Formula KR-21 has become outdated in an era of calculators and computers. Way back when, KR-21 was sometimes used to estimate KR-20 only because it required many fewer calculations.

Numerous modifications of Kuder–Richardson formulas have been proposed through the years. The one variant of the KR-20 formula that has received the most acceptance and is in widest use today is a statistic called coefficient alpha. You may even hear it referred to as *coefficient α–20*. This expression incorporates both the Greek letter alpha (α) and the number 20, the latter a reference to KR-20.

Coefficient alpha   Developed by Cronbach (1951) and subsequently elaborated on by others (such as Kaiser & Michael, 1975; Novick & Lewis, 1967), **coefficient alpha** may be thought of as the mean of all possible split-half correlations, corrected by the Spearman–Brown formula. In contrast to KR-20, which is appropriately used only on tests with dichotomous items, coefficient alpha is appropriate for use on tests containing nondichotomous items. The formula for coefficient alpha is

$$r_\alpha = \left(\frac{k}{k-1} \right) \left(1 - \frac{\Sigma \sigma_i^2}{\sigma^2} \right)$$

where r_a is coefficient alpha, k is the number of items, is the variance of one item, Σ is the sum of variances of each item, and σ^2 is the variance of the total test scores.

Coefficient alpha is the preferred statistic for obtaining an estimate of internal consistency reliability. A variation of the formula has been developed for use in obtaining an estimate of test-retest reliability (Green, 2003). Essentially, this formula yields an estimate of the mean of all possible test-retest, split-half coefficients. Coefficient alpha is widely used as a measure of reliability, in part because it requires only one administration of the test.

Unlike a Pearson *r*, which may range in value from −1 to +1, coefficient alpha typically ranges in value from 0 to 1. The reason for this is that, conceptually, coefficient alpha (much like other coefficients of reliability) is calculated to help answer questions about how *similar* sets of data are. Here, similarity is gauged, in essence, on a scale from 0 (absolutely no similarity) to 1 (perfectly identical). It is possible, however, to conceive of data sets that would yield a negative value of alpha (Streiner, 2003b). Still, because negative values of alpha are theoretically impossible, it is recommended under such rare circumstances that the alpha coefficient be reported as zero (Henson, 2001). Also, a myth about alpha is that "bigger is always better." As Streiner (2003b) pointed out, a value of alpha above .90 may be "too high" and indicate redundancy in the items.

In contrast to coefficient alpha, a Pearson *r* may be thought of as dealing conceptually with both dissimilarity and similarity. Accordingly, an *r* value of −1 may be thought of as indicating "perfect dissimilarity." In practice, most reliability coefficients—regardless of the specific type of reliability they are measuring—range in value from 0 to 1. This is generally true, although it is possible to conceive of exceptional cases in which data sets yield an *r* with a negative value.

Average proportional distance (APD)   A relatively new measure for evaluating the internal consistency of a test is the *average proportional distance* (APD) method (Sturman et al., 2009). Rather than focusing on similarity between scores on items of a test (as do split-half methods and Cronbach's alpha), the APD is a measure that focuses on the degree of *difference* that exists between item scores. Accordingly, we define the **average proportional distance method** as a measure used to evaluate the internal consistency of a test that focuses on the degree of difference that exists between item scores.

To illustrate how the APD is calculated, consider the (hypothetical) "3-Item Test of Extraversion" (3-ITE). As conveyed by the title of the 3-ITE, it is a test that has only three items. Each of the items is a sentence that somehow relates to extraversion. Testtakers are instructed to respond to each of the three items with reference to the following 7-point scale: 1 = Very strongly disagree, 2 = Strongly disagree, 3 = Disagree, 4 = Neither Agree nor Disagree, 5 = Agree, 6 = Strongly agree, and 7 = Very strongly agree.

Typically, in order to evaluate the inter-item consistency of a scale, the calculation of the APD would be calculated for a group of testtakers. However, for the purpose of illustrating the calculations of this measure, let's look at how the APD would be calculated for one testtaker. Yolanda scores 4 on Item 1, 5 on Item 2, and 6 on Item 3. Based on Yolanda's scores, the APD would be calculated as follows:

Step 1: Calculate the absolute difference between scores for all of the items.

Step 2: Average the difference between scores.

Step 3: Obtain the APD by dividing the average difference between scores by the number of response options on the test, minus one.

So, for the 3-ITE, here is how the calculations would look using Yolanda's test scores:

Step 1: Absolute difference between Items 1 and 2 = 1
Absolute difference between Items 1 and 3 = 2
Absolute difference between Items 2 and 3 = 1

Step 2: In order to obtain the average difference (AD), add up the absolute differences in Step 1 and divide by the number of items as follows:

$$AD = \frac{1 + 2 + 1}{3} = \frac{4}{3} = 1.33$$

Step 3: To obtain the average proportional distance (APD), divide the average difference by 6 (the 7 response options in our ITE scale minus 1). Using Yolanda's data, we would divide 1.33 by 6 to get .22. Thus, the APD for the ITE is .22. But what does this mean?

The general "rule of thumb" for interpreting an APD is that an obtained value of .2 or lower is indicative of excellent internal consistency, and that a value of .25 to .2 is in the acceptable range. A calculated APD of .25 is suggestive of problems with the internal consistency of the test. These guidelines are based on the assumption that items measuring a single construct such as extraversion should ideally be correlated with one another in the .6 to .7 range. Let's add that the expected inter-item correlation may vary depending on the variables being measured, so the ideal correlation values are not set in stone. In the case of the 3-ITE, the data for our one subject suggests that the scale has acceptable internal consistency. Of course, in order to make any meaningful conclusions about the internal consistency of the 3-ITE, the instrument would have to be tested with a large sample of testtakers.

One potential advantage of the APD method over using Cronbach's alpha is that the APD index is not connected to the number of items on a measure. Cronbach's alpha will be higher when a measure has more than 25 items (Cortina, 1993). Perhaps the best course of action when evaluating the internal consistency of a given measure is to analyze and integrate the information using several indices, including Cronbach's alpha, mean inter-item correlations, and the APD.

Before proceeding, let's emphasize that all indices of reliability provide an index that is a characteristic of a particular group of test scores, not of the test itself (Caruso, 2000; Yin & Fan, 2000). Measures of reliability are estimates, and estimates are subject to error. The precise amount of error inherent in a reliability estimate will vary with various factors, such as the sample of testtakers from which the data were drawn. A reliability index published in a test manual might be very impressive. However, keep in mind that the reported reliability was achieved with a particular group of testtakers. If a new group of testtakers is sufficiently

The Importance of the Method Used for Estimating Reliability *(continued)*

clinical settings. As such, this method does not allow for truly independent ratings and therefore likely results in overestimates of what would be obtained if separate interviews were conducted.

In the test-retest method, separate independent interviews are conducted by two different clinicians, with neither clinician knowing what occurred during the other interview. These interviews are conducted over a time frame short enough that true change in diagnostic status is highly unlikely, making this method similar to the dependability method of assessing reliability (Chmielewski & Watson, 2009). Because diagnostic reliability is intended to assess the extent to which a patient would receive the same diagnosis at different hospitals or clinics—or, alternatively, the extent to which different studies are recruiting similar patients—the test-retest method provides a more meaningful, realistic, and ecologically valid estimate of diagnostic reliability.

Chmielewski et al. (2015) examined the influence of method on estimates of reliability by using both the audio-recording and test-retest methods in a large sample of psychiatric patients. The authors' analyzed *DSM*-5 diagnoses because of the long-standing claims in the literature that they were reliable and the fact that structured interviews had not yet been created for the *DSM*-5. They carefully selected a one-week test-retest interval, based on theory and research, to minimize the likelihood that true diagnostic change would occur while substantially reducing memory effects and patient fatigue which might exist if the interviews were conducted immediately after each other. Clinicians in the study were at least master's level and underwent extensive training that far exceeded the training of clinicians in the vast majority of research studies. The same pool of clinicians and patients was used for the audio-recording and test-retest methods. Diagnoses were assigned using the *Structured Clinical Interview for DSM-IV (SCID-I/P*; First et al.,

2002), which is widely considered the gold-standard diagnostic interview in the field. Finally, patients completed self-report measures which were examined to ensure patients' symptoms did not change over the one-week interval.

Diagnostic (inter-rater) reliability using the audio-recording method was very high (mean kappa = .80) and would be considered "excellent" by traditional standards (Cicchetti, 1994; Fleiss, 1981). Moreover, estimates of diagnostic reliability were equivalent or superior to previously published values for the *DSM*-5. However, estimates of diagnostic reliability obtained from the test-retest method were substantially lower (mean kappa = .47) and would be considered only "fair" by traditional standards. Moreover, approximately 25% of the disorders demonstrated "poor" diagnostic reliability. Interestingly, this level of diagnostic reliability was very similar to that observed in the *DSM*-5 Field Trials (mean kappa = .44), which also used the test-retest method (Regier et al., 2013). It is important to note these large differences in estimates of diagnostic reliability emerged despite the fact that (1) the same highly trained master's-level clinicians were used for both methods; (2) the SCID-I/P, which is considered the "gold standard" in diagnostic interviews, was used; (3) the same patient sample was used; and (4) patients' self-report of their symptoms was very stable (or, patients were experiencing their symptoms the same way during both interviews) and any changes in self-report were unrelated to diagnostic disagreements between clinicians. These results suggest that the reliability of diagnoses is far lower than commonly believed. Moreover, the results demonstrate the substantial influence that method has on estimates of diagnostic reliability even when other factors are held constant.

Used with permission of Michael Chmielewski.

Using and Interpreting a Coefficient of Reliability

We have seen that, with respect to the test itself, there are basically three approaches to the estimation of reliability: (1) test-retest, (2) alternate or parallel forms, and (3) internal or inter-item consistency. The method or methods employed will depend on a number of factors, such as the purpose of obtaining a measure of reliability.

Another question that is linked in no trivial way to the purpose of the test is, "How high should the coefficient of reliability be?" Perhaps the best "short answer" to this question is:

"On a continuum relative to the purpose and importance of the decisions to be made on the basis of scores on the test." Reliability is a mandatory attribute in all tests we use. However, we need more of it in some tests, and we will admittedly allow for less of it in others. If a test score carries with it life-or-death implications, then we need to hold that test to some high standards—including relatively high standards with regard to coefficients of reliability. If a test score is routinely used in combination with many other test scores and typically accounts for only a small part of the decision process, that test will not be held to the highest standards of reliability. As a rule of thumb, it may be useful to think of reliability coefficients in a way that parallels many grading systems: In the .90s rates a grade of A (with a value of .95 higher for the most important types of decisions), in the .80s rates a B (with below .85 being a clear B−), and anywhere from .65 through the .70s rates a weak, "barely passing" grade that borders on failing (and unacceptable). Now, let's get a bit more technical with regard to the purpose of the reliability coefficient.

The Purpose of the Reliability Coefficient

If a specific test of employee performance is designed for use at various times over the course of the employment period, it would be reasonable to expect the test to demonstrate reliability across time. It would thus be desirable to have an estimate of the instrument's test-retest reliability. For a test designed for a single administration only, an estimate of internal consistency would be the reliability measure of choice. If the purpose of determining reliability is to break down the error variance into its parts, as shown in Figure 5–1, then a number of reliability coefficients would have to be calculated.

Note that the various reliability coefficients do not all reflect the same sources of error variance. Thus, an individual reliability coefficient may provide an index of error from test construction, test administration, or test scoring and interpretation. A coefficient of inter-rater reliability, for example, provides information about error as a result of test scoring. Specifically, it can be used to answer questions about how consistently two scorers score the same test items. Table 5–4 summarizes the different kinds of error variance that are reflected in different reliability coefficients.

Figure 5–1
Sources of Variance in a Hypothetical Test

*In this hypothetical situation, 5% of the variance has not been identified by the test user. It is possible, for example, that this portion of the variance could be accounted for by **transient error**, a source of error attributable to variations in the testtaker's feelings, moods, or mental state over time. Then again, this 5% of the error may be due to other factors that are yet to be identified.*

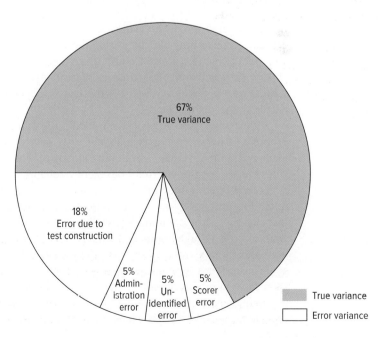

Table 5–4
Summary of Reliability Types

Type of Reliability	Purpose	Typical uses	Number of Testing Sessions	Sources of Error Variance	Statistical Procedures
Test-retest	To evaluate the stability of a measure	When assessing the stability of various personality traits	2	Administration	Pearson *r* or Spearman rho
Alternate-forms	To evaluate the relationship between different forms of a measure	When there is a need for different forms of a test (e.g., makeup tests)	1 or 2	Test construction or administration	Pearson *r* or Spearman rho
Internal consistency	To evaluate the extent to which items on a scale relate to one another	When evaluating the homogeneity of a measure (or, all items are tapping a single construct)	1	Test construction	Pearson *r between equivalent test halves with Spearman Brown correction or Kuder-R-ichardson for dichotomous items, or coefficient alpha for multipoint items or APD*
Inter-scorer	To evaluate the level of agreement between raters on a measure	Interviews or coding of behavior. Used when researchers need to show that there is consensus in the way that different raters view a particular behavior pattern (and hence no observer bias).	1	Scoring and interpretation	Cohen's kappa, Pearson *r* or Spearman rho

The Nature of the Test

Closely related to considerations concerning the purpose and use of a reliability coefficient are those concerning the nature of the test itself. Included here are considerations such as whether (1) the test items are homogeneous or heterogeneous in nature; (2) the characteristic, ability, or trait being measured is presumed to be dynamic or static; (3) the range of test scores is or is not restricted; (4) the test is a speed or a power test; and (5) the test is or is not criterion-referenced.

Some tests present special problems regarding the measurement of their reliability. For example, a number of psychological tests have been developed for use with infants to help identify children who are developing slowly or who may profit from early intervention of some sort. Measuring the internal consistency reliability or the inter-scorer reliability of such tests is accomplished in much the same way as it is with other tests. However, measuring test-retest reliability presents a unique problem. The abilities of the very young children being tested are fast-changing. It is common knowledge that cognitive development during the first months and years of life is both rapid and uneven. Children often grow in spurts, sometimes changing dramatically in as little as days (Hetherington & Parke, 1993). The child tested just before and again just after a developmental advance may perform very differently on the two testings. In such cases, a marked change in test score might be attributed to error when in reality it reflects a genuine change in the testtaker's skills. The challenge in gauging the test-retest reliability of such tests is to do so in such a way that it is not spuriously lowered by the testtaker's actual developmental changes between testings. In attempting to accomplish this, developers of such tests may design test-retest reliability studies with very short intervals between testings, sometimes as little as four days.

Homogeneity versus heterogeneity of test items   Recall that a test is said to be *homogeneous* in items if it is functionally uniform throughout. Tests designed to measure one factor, such as one ability or one trait, are expected to be homogeneous in items. For such tests, it is reasonable to expect a high degree of internal consistency. By contrast, if the test is *heterogeneous* in items, an estimate of internal consistency might be low relative to a more appropriate estimate of test-retest reliability.

Dynamic versus static characteristics   Whether what is being measured by the test is *dynamic* or *static* is also a consideration in obtaining an estimate of reliability. A **dynamic characteristic** is a trait, state, or ability presumed to be ever-changing as a function of situational and cognitive experiences. If, for example, one were to take hourly measurements of the dynamic characteristic of anxiety as manifested by a stockbroker throughout a business day, one might find the measured level of this characteristic to change from hour to hour. Such changes might even be related to the magnitude of the Dow Jones average. Because the true amount of anxiety presumed to exist would vary with each assessment, a test-retest measure would be of little help in gauging the reliability of the measuring instrument. Therefore, the best estimate of reliability would be obtained from a measure of internal consistency. Contrast this situation to one in which hourly assessments of this same stockbroker are made on a trait, state, or ability presumed to be relatively unchanging (a **static characteristic**), such as intelligence. In this instance, obtained measurement would not be expected to vary significantly as a function of time, and either the test-retest or the alternate-forms method would be appropriate.

JUST THINK . . .

Provide another example of both a dynamic characteristic and a static characteristic that a psychological test could measure.

Restriction or inflation of range   In using and interpreting a coefficient of reliability, the issue variously referred to as **restriction of range** or **restriction of variance** (or, conversely, **inflation of range** or **inflation of variance**) is important. If the variance of either variable in a correlational analysis is restricted by the sampling procedure used, then the resulting correlation coefficient tends to be lower. If the variance of either variable in a correlational analysis is inflated by the sampling procedure, then the resulting correlation coefficient tends to be higher. Refer back to Figure 3–17 on page 111 (Two Scatterplots Illustrating Unrestricted and Restricted Ranges) for a graphic illustration.

Also of critical importance is whether the range of variances employed is appropriate to the objective of the correlational analysis. Consider, for example, a published educational test designed for use with children in grades 1 through 6. Ideally, the manual for this test should contain not one reliability value covering all the testtakers in grades 1 through 6 but instead reliability values for testtakers at each grade level. Here's another example: A corporate personnel officer employs a certain screening test in the hiring process. For future testing and hiring purposes, this personnel officer maintains reliability data with respect to scores achieved by job applicants—as opposed to hired employees—in order to avoid restriction of range effects in the data. This is so because the people who were hired typically scored higher on the test than any comparable group of applicants.

Speed tests versus power tests   When a time limit is long enough to allow testtakers to attempt all items, and if some items are so difficult that no testtaker is able to obtain a perfect score, then the test is a **power test.** By contrast, a **speed test** generally contains items of uniform level of difficulty (typically uniformly low) so that, when given generous time limits, all testtakers should be able to complete all the test items correctly. In practice, however, the time limit on a speed test is established so that few if any of the testtakers will be able to complete the entire test. Score differences on a speed test are therefore based on performance speed because items attempted tend to be correct.

A reliability estimate of a speed test should be based on performance from two independent testing periods using one of the following: (1) test-retest reliability, (2) alternate-forms reliability, or (3) split-half reliability from *two separately timed* half tests. If a split-half procedure is used, then the obtained reliability coefficient is for a half test and should be adjusted using the Spearman–Brown formula.

Because a measure of the reliability of a speed test should reflect the consistency of response speed, the reliability of a speed test should not be calculated from a single administration of the test with a single time limit. If a speed test is administered once and some measure of internal consistency, such as the Kuder–Richardson or a split-half correlation, is calculated, the result will be a spuriously high reliability coefficient. To understand why the KR-20 or split-half reliability coefficient will be spuriously high, consider the following example.

When a group of testtakers completes a speed test, almost all the items completed will be correct. If reliability is examined using an odd-even split, and if the testtakers completed the items in order, then testtakers will get close to the same number of odd as even items correct. A testtaker completing 82 items can be expected to get approximately 41 odd and 41 even items correct. A testtaker completing 61 items may get 31 odd and 30 even items correct. When the numbers of odd and even items correct are correlated across a group of testtakers, the correlation will be close to 1.00. Yet this impressive correlation coefficient actually tells us nothing about response consistency.

Under the same scenario, a Kuder–Richardson reliability coefficient would yield a similar coefficient that would also be, well, equally useless. Recall that KR-20 reliability is based on the proportion of testtakers correct (p) and the proportion of testtakers incorrect (q) on each item. In the case of a speed test, it is conceivable that p would equal 1.0 and q would equal 0 for many of the items. Toward the end of the test—when many items would not even be attempted because of the time limit—p might equal 0 and q might equal 1.0. For many, if not a majority, of the items, then, the product pq would equal or approximate 0. When 0 is substituted in the KR-20 formula for $\Sigma\ pq$, the reliability coefficient is 1.0 (a meaningless coefficient in this instance).

Criterion-referenced tests A **criterion-referenced test** is designed to provide an indication of where a testtaker stands with respect to some variable or criterion, such as an educational or a vocational objective. Unlike norm-referenced tests, criterion-referenced tests tend to contain material that has been mastered in hierarchical fashion. For example, the would-be pilot masters on-ground skills before attempting to master in-flight skills. Scores on criterion-referenced tests tend to be interpreted in pass–fail (or, perhaps more accurately, "master-failed-to-master") terms, and any scrutiny of performance on individual items tends to be for diagnostic and remedial purposes.

Traditional techniques of estimating reliability employ measures that take into account scores on the entire test. Recall that a test-retest reliability estimate is based on the correlation between the total scores on two administrations of the same test. In alternate-forms reliability, a reliability estimate is based on the correlation between the two total scores on the two forms. In split-half reliability, a reliability estimate is based on the correlation between scores on two halves of the test and is then adjusted using the Spearman–Brown formula to obtain a reliability estimate of the whole test. Although there are exceptions, such traditional procedures of estimating reliability are usually not appropriate for use with criterion-referenced tests. To understand why, recall that reliability is defined as the proportion of total variance (σ^2) attributable to true variance (σ^2_{th}). Total variance in a test score distribution equals the sum of the true variance plus the error variance (σ_e^2)

$$\sigma^2 = \sigma^2_{th} + \sigma^2_e$$

A measure of reliability, therefore, depends on the variability of the test scores: how different the scores are from one another. In criterion-referenced testing, and particularly in mastery testing, how different the scores are from one another is seldom a focus of interest. In fact, individual differences between examinees on total test scores may be minimal. The critical issue for the user of a mastery test is whether or not a certain criterion score has been achieved.

As individual differences (and the variability) decrease, a traditional measure of reliability would also decrease, regardless of the stability of individual performance. Therefore, traditional ways of estimating reliability are not always appropriate for criterion-referenced tests, though there may be instances in which traditional estimates can be adopted. An example might be a situation in which the same test is being used at different stages in some program—training, therapy, or the like—and so variability in scores could reasonably be expected. Statistical techniques useful in determining the reliability of criterion-referenced tests are discussed in great detail in many sources devoted to that subject (e.g., Hambleton & Jurgensen, 1990).

The True Score Model of Measurement and Alternatives to It

Thus far—and throughout this book, unless specifically stated otherwise—the model we have assumed to be operative is **classical test theory** (**CTT**), also referred to as the true score (or classical) model of measurement. CTT is the most widely used and accepted model in the psychometric literature today—rumors of its demise have been greatly exaggerated (Zickar & Broadfoot, 2009). One of the reasons it has remained the most widely used model has to do with its simplicity, especially when one considers the complexity of other proposed models of measurement. Comparing CTT to IRT, for example, Streiner (2010) mused, "CTT is much simpler to understand than IRT; there aren't formidable-looking equations with exponentiations, Greek letters, and other arcane symbols" (p. 185). Additionally, the CTT notion that everyone has a "true score" on a test has had, and continues to have, great intuitive appeal. Of course, exactly how to define this elusive *true score* has been a matter of sometimes contentious debate. For our purposes, we will define **true score** as a value that according to classical test theory genuinely reflects an individual's ability (or trait) level as measured by a particular test. Let's emphasize here that this value is indeed very test dependent. A person's "true score" on one intelligence test, for example, can vary greatly from that same person's "true score" on another intelligence test. Similarly, if "Form D" of an ability test contains items that the testtaker finds to be much more difficult than those on "Form E" of that test, then there is a good chance that the testtaker's true score on Form D will be lower than that on Form E. The same holds for true scores obtained on different tests of personality. One's true score on one test of extraversion, for example, may not bear much resemblance to one's true score on another test of extraversion. Comparing a testtaker's scores on two different tests purporting to measure the same thing requires a sophisticated knowledge of the properties of each of the two tests, as well as some rather complicated statistical procedures designed to equate the scores.

Another aspect of the appeal of CTT is that its assumptions allow for its application in most situations (Hambleton & Swaminathan, 1985). The fact that CTT assumptions are rather easily met and therefore applicable to so many measurement situations can be advantageous, especially for the test developer in search of an appropriate model of measurement for a particular application. Still, in psychometric parlance, CTT assumptions are characterized as "weak"—this precisely because its assumptions are so readily met. By contrast, the assumptions in another model of measurement, item response theory (IRT), are more difficult to meet. As a consequence, you may read of IRT assumptions being characterized in terms such as "strong," "hard," "rigorous," and "robust." A final advantage of CTT over any other model of measurement has to do with its compatibility and ease of use with widely used statistical techniques (as well as most currently available data analysis software). Factor analytic techniques, whether exploratory or confirmatory, are all "based on the CTT measurement foundation" (Zickar & Broadfoot, 2009, p. 52).

For all of its appeal, measurement experts have also listed many problems with CTT. For starters, one problem with CTT has to do with its assumption concerning the equivalence of all items on a test; that is, all items are presumed to be contributing equally to the score total. This assumption is questionable in many cases, and particularly questionable when doubt exists as to whether the scaling of the instrument in question is genuinely interval level in nature. Another problem has to do with the length of tests that are developed using a CTT model. Whereas test developers favor shorter rather than longer tests (as do most testtakers), the assumptions inherent in CTT favor the development of longer rather than shorter tests. For these reasons, as well as others, alternative measurement models have been developed. Below we briefly describe domain sampling theory and generalizability theory. We will then describe in greater detail, item response theory (IRT), a measurement model that some believe is a worthy successor to CTT (Borsbroom, 2005; Harvey & Hammer, 1999).

Domain sampling theory and generalizability theory The 1950s saw the development of a viable alternative to CTT. It was originally referred to as *domain sampling theory* and is better known today in one of its many modified forms as *generalizability theory*. As set forth by Tryon (1957), the theory of domain sampling rebels against the concept of a true score existing with respect to the measurement of psychological constructs. Whereas those who subscribe to CTT seek to estimate the portion of a test score that is attributable to error, proponents of **domain sampling theory** seek to estimate the extent to which specific sources of variation under defined conditions are contributing to the test score. In domain sampling theory, a test's reliability is conceived of as an objective measure of how precisely the test score assesses the domain from which the test draws a sample (Thorndike, 1985). A *domain* of behavior, or the universe of items that could conceivably measure that behavior, can be thought of as a hypothetical construct: one that shares certain characteristics with (and is measured by) the sample of items that make up the test. In theory, the items in the domain are thought to have the same means and variances of those in the test that samples from the domain. Of the three types of estimates of reliability, measures of internal consistency are perhaps the most compatible with domain sampling theory.

In one modification of domain sampling theory called *generalizability theory*, a "universe score" replaces that of a "true score" (Shavelson et al., 1989). Developed by Lee J. Cronbach (1970) and his colleagues (Cronbach et al., 1972), **generalizability theory** is based on the idea that a person's test scores vary from testing to testing because of variables in the testing situation. Instead of conceiving of all variability in a person's scores as error, Cronbach encouraged test developers and researchers to describe the details of the particular test situation or **universe** leading to a specific test score. This universe is described in terms of its **facets,** which include things like the number of items in the test, the amount of training the test scorers have had, and the purpose of the test administration.

According to generalizability theory, given the exact same conditions of all the facets in the universe, the exact same test score should be obtained. This test score is the **universe score,** and it is, as Cronbach noted, analogous to a true score in the true score model. Cronbach (1970) explained as follows:

> "What is Mary's typing ability?" This must be interpreted as "What would Mary's word processing score on this be if a large number of measurements on the test were collected and averaged?" The particular test score Mary earned is just one out of a universe of possible observations. If one of these scores is as acceptable as the next, then the mean, called the universe score and symbolized here by M_p (mean for person p), would be the most appropriate statement of Mary's performance in the type of situation the test represents.
>
> The universe is a collection of possible measures "of the same kind," but the limits of the collection are determined by the investigator's purpose. If he needs to know Mary's typing ability on May 5 (for example, so that he can plot a learning curve that includes one point for that day), the universe would include observations on that day and on that day only. He probably does want to generalize over passages, testers, and scorers—that is to say, he would like to know Mary's ability on May 5 without reference to any particular passage, tester, or scorer. . . .
>
> The person will ordinarily have a different universe score for each universe. Mary's universe score covering tests on May 5 will not agree perfectly with her universe score for the whole month of May. . . . Some testers call the average over a large number of comparable observations a "true score"; e.g., "Mary's true typing rate on 3-minute tests." Instead, we speak of a "universe score" to emphasize that what score is desired depends on the universe being considered. For any measure there are many "true scores," each corresponding to a different universe.
>
> When we use a single observation as if it represented the universe, we are generalizing. We generalize over scorers, over selections typed, perhaps over days. If the observed scores from a procedure agree closely with the universe score, we can say that the observation is "accurate," or "reliable," or "generalizable." And since the observations then also agree with each other, we say that they are "consistent" and "have little error variance." To have so many terms is confusing, but not seriously so. The term most often used in the literature is "reliability." The author prefers "generalizability" because that term immediately implies "generalization to what?" . . . There is a different degree of generalizability for each universe. The older methods of analysis do not separate the sources of variation. They deal with a single source of variance, or leave two or more sources entangled. (Cronbach, 1970, pp. 153–154)

How can these ideas be applied? Cronbach and his colleagues suggested that tests be developed with the aid of a generalizability study followed by a decision study. A **generalizability study** examines how generalizable scores from a particular test are if the test is administered in different situations. Stated in the language of generalizability theory, a generalizability study examines how much of an impact different facets of the universe have on the test score. Is the test score affected by group as opposed to individual administration? Is the test score affected by the time of day in which the test is administered? The influence of particular facets on the test score is represented by **coefficients of generalizability.** These coefficients are similar to reliability coefficients in the true score model.

After the generalizability study is done, Cronbach et al. (1972) recommended that test developers do a decision study, which involves the application of information from the generalizability study. In the **decision study,** developers examine the usefulness of test scores in helping the test user make decisions. In practice, test scores are used to guide a variety of decisions, from placing a child in special education to hiring new employees to discharging mental patients from the hospital. The decision study is designed to tell the test user how test scores should be used and how dependable those scores are as a basis for decisions, depending on the context of their use. Why is this so important? Cronbach (1970) noted:

> The decision that a student has completed a course or that a patient is ready for termination of therapy must not be seriously influenced by chance errors, temporary variations in performance, or the tester's choice of questions. An erroneous favorable decision may be irreversible and may harm the person or the community. Even when reversible, an erroneous unfavorable decision is unjust, disrupts the person's morale, and perhaps retards his development. Research, too, requires dependable measurement. An experiment is not very informative if an observed difference could be accounted for by chance variation. Large error variance is likely to mask a scientifically important outcome. Taking a better measure improves the sensitivity of an experiment in the same way that increasing the number of subjects does. (p. 152)

Generalizability has not replaced CTT. Perhaps one of its chief contributions has been its emphasis on the fact that a test's reliability does not reside within the test itself. From the perspective of generalizability theory, a test's reliability is very much a function of the circumstances under which the test is developed, administered, and interpreted.

Item response theory (IRT) Another alternative to the true score model is *item response theory* (IRT; Lord & Novick, 1968; Lord, 1980). The procedures of item response theory provide a way to model the probability that a person with *X* ability will be able to perform at a level of *Y*. Stated in terms of personality assessment, it models the probability that a person with *X* amount of a particular personality trait will exhibit *Y* amount of that trait on a personality test designed to measure it. Because so often the psychological or educational construct being measured is physically unobservable (stated another way, is *latent*) and because the construct being measured may be a *trait* (it could also be something else, such as an ability), a synonym for IRT in the academic literature is **latent-trait theory.** Let's note at the outset, however, that IRT is not a term used to refer to a single theory or method. Rather, it refers to a family of theories and methods—and quite a large family at that—with many other names used to distinguish specific approaches. There are well over a hundred varieties of IRT models. Each model is designed to handle data with certain assumptions and data characteristics.

Examples of two characteristics of items within an IRT framework are the *difficulty* level of an item and the item's level of *discrimination;* items may be viewed as varying in terms of these, as well as other, characteristics. "Difficulty" in this sense refers to the attribute of not being easily accomplished, solved, or comprehended. In a mathematics test, for example, a test item tapping basic addition ability will have a lower difficulty level than a test item tapping basic algebra skills. The characteristic of *difficulty* as applied to a test item may also refer to *physical* difficulty—that is, how hard or easy it is for a person to engage in a particular activity. Consider in this context three items on a hypothetical "Activities of Daily Living Questionnaire" (ADLQ), a true–false questionnaire designed to tap the extent to which respondents are physically able to participate in activities of daily living. Item 1 of this test is *I am able to walk from room to room in my home.* Item 2 is *I require assistance to sit, stand, and walk.* Item 3 is *I am able to jog one mile a day, seven days a week.* With regard to difficulty related to mobility, the respondent who answers *true* to item 1 and *false* to item 2 may be presumed to have more mobility than the respondent who answers *false* to item 1 and *true* to item 2. In classical test theory, each of these items might be scored with 1 point awarded to responses indicative of mobility and 0 points for responses indicative of a lack of mobility. Within IRT, however, responses indicative of mobility (as opposed to a lack of mobility or impaired mobility) may be assigned different weights. A *true* response to item 1 may therefore earn more points than a *false* response to item 2, and a *true* response to item 3 may earn more points than a *true* response to item 1.

In the context of IRT, **discrimination** signifies the degree to which an item differentiates among people with higher or lower levels of the trait, ability, or whatever it is that is being measured. Consider two more ADLQ items: item 4, *My mood is generally good;* and item 5, *I am able to walk one block on flat ground.* Which of these two items do you think would be more discriminating in terms of the respondent's physical abilities? If you answered "item 5" then you are correct. And if you were developing this questionnaire within an IRT framework, you would probably assign differential weight to the value of these two items. Item 5 would be given more weight for the purpose of estimating a person's level of physical activity than item 4. Again, within the context of classical test theory, all items of the test might be given equal weight and scored, for example, 1 if indicative of the ability being measured and 0 if not indicative of that ability.

A number of different IRT models exist to handle data resulting from the administration of tests with various characteristics and in various formats. For example, there are IRT models designed to handle data resulting from the administration of tests with **dichotomous test items** (test items or questions that can be answered with only one of two alternative responses, such as *true–false, yes–no,* or *correct–incorrect* questions). There are IRT models designed to handle data resulting from the administration of tests with **polytomous test items** (test items or questions with three or more alternative responses, where only one is scored correct or scored as being consistent with a targeted trait or other construct). Other IRT models exist to handle other types of data.

In general, latent-trait models differ in some important ways from CTT. For example, in CTT, no assumptions are made about the frequency distribution of test scores. By contrast, such assumptions are inherent in latent-trait models. As Allen and Yen (1979, p. 240) have pointed out, "Latent-trait theories propose models that describe how the latent trait influences performance on each test item. Unlike test scores or true scores, latent traits theoretically can take on values from $-\infty$ to $+\infty$ [negative infinity to positive infinity]." Some IRT models have very specific and stringent assumptions about the underlying distribution. In one group of IRT models developed by the Danish mathematician Georg Rasch, each item on the test is assumed to have an equivalent relationship with the construct being measured by the test. A shorthand reference to these types of models is "Rasch," so reference to the **Rasch model** is a reference to an IRT model with very specific assumptions about the underlying distribution.

The psychometric advantages of IRT have made this model appealing, especially to commercial and academic test developers and to large-scale test publishers. It is a model that in recent years has found increasing application in standardized tests, professional licensing examinations, and questionnaires used in behavioral and social sciences (De Champlain, 2010). However, the mathematical sophistication of the approach has made it out of reach for many everyday users of tests such as classroom teachers or "mom and pop" employers (Reise & Henson, 2003). To learn more about the approach that Roid (2006) once characterized as having fostered "new rules of measurement" for ability testing ask your instructor to access the Instructor Resources within Connect and check out OOBAL-5-B2, "Item Response Theory (IRT)." More immediately, you can meet a "real-life" user of IRT in this chapter's *Meet an Assessment Professional* feature.

Meet Dr. Bryce B. Reeve

I use my skills and training as a psychometrician to design questionnaires and studies to capture the burden of cancer and its treatment on patients and their families. . . . The types of questionnaires I help to create measure a person's health-related quality of life (HRQOL). HRQOL is a multidimensional construct capturing such domains as physical functioning, mental well-being, and social well-being. Different cancer types and treatments for those cancers may have different impact on the magnitude and which HRQOL domain is affected. All cancers can impact a person's mental health with documented increases in depressive symptoms and anxiety. . . . There may also be positive impacts of cancer as some cancer survivors experience greater social well-being and appreciation of life. Thus, our challenge is to develop valid and precise measurement tools that capture these changes in patients' lives. Psychometrically strong measures also allow us to evaluate the impact of new behavioral or pharmacological interventions developed to improve quality of life. Because many patients in our research studies are ill, it is important to have very brief questionnaires to minimize their burden responding to a battery of questionnaires.

. . . we . . . use both qualitative and quantitative methodologies to design . . . HRQOL instruments. We use qualitative methods like focus groups and cognitive interviewing to make sure we have captured the experiences and perspectives of cancer patients and to write questions that are comprehendible to people with low literacy skills or people of different cultures. We use quantitative methods to examine how well individual questions and scales perform for measuring the HRQOL domains. Specifically, we use classical test theory, factor analysis, and item response theory (IRT) to: (1) develop and refine questionnaires; (2) identify the performance of instruments across different age groups, males and females, and cultural/racial groups; and (3) to develop item banks which allow for creating standardized questionnaires or administering computerized adaptive testing (CAT).

Bryce B. Reeve, Ph.D., U.S. National Cancer Institute

© Bryce B. Reeve/National Institute of Health

I use IRT models to get an in-depth look as to how questions and scales perform in our cancer research studies. [Using IRT], we were able to reduce a burdensome 21-item scale down to a brief 10-item scale. . . .

Differential item function (DIF) is a key methodology to identify . . . biased items in questionnaires. I have used IRT modeling to examine DIF in item responses on many HRQOL questionnaires. It is especially important to evaluate DIF in questionnaires that have been translated to multiple languages for the purpose of conducting international research studies. An instrument may be translated to have the same words in multiple languages, but the words themselves may have entirely different meaning to people of different cultures. For example, researchers at the University of Massachusetts found Chinese respondents gave lower satisfaction ratings of their medical doctors than non-Chinese. In a review of the translation, the "Excellent" response category translated into Chinese as "God-like." IRT modeling gives me the ability to not only detect DIF items, but the flexibility to correct for bias as well. I can use IRT to look at unadjusted and adjusted IRT scores to see the effect of the DIF item without removing the item from the scale if the item is deemed relevant. . . .

> The greatest challenges I found to greater application or acceptance of IRT methods in health care research are the complexities of the models themselves and lack of easy-to-understand resources and tools to train researchers. Many researchers have been trained in classical test theory statistics, are comfortable interpreting these statistics, and can use readily available software to generate easily familiar summary statistics, such as Cronbach's coefficient α or item-total correlations. In contrast, IRT modeling requires an advanced knowledge of measurement theory to understand the mathematical complexities of the models, to determine whether the assumptions of the IRT models are met, and to choose the model from within the large family of IRT models that best fits the data and the measurement task at hand. In addition, the supporting software and literature are not well adapted for researchers outside the field of educational testing.
>
> *Read more of what Dr. Reeve had to say—his complete essay—through the Instructor Resources within Connect.*
>
> Used with permission of Bryce B. Reeve.

Reliability and Individual Scores

The reliability coefficient helps the test developer build an adequate measuring instrument, and it helps the test user select a suitable test. However, the usefulness of the reliability coefficient does not end with test construction and selection. By employing the reliability coefficient in the formula for the standard error of measurement, the test user now has another descriptive statistic relevant to test interpretation, this one useful in estimating the precision of a particular test score.

The Standard Error of Measurement

The *standard error of measurement,* often abbreviated as *SEM* or SE_M, provides a measure of the precision of an observed test score. Stated another way, it provides an estimate of the amount of error inherent in an observed score or measurement. In general, the relationship between the SEM and the reliability of a test is inverse; the higher the reliability of a test (or individual subtest within a test), the lower the SEM.

To illustrate the utility of the SEM, let's revisit The Rochester Wrenchworks (TRW) and reintroduce Mary (from Cronbach's excerpt earlier in this chapter), who is now applying for a job as a word processor. To be hired at TRW as a word processor, a candidate must be able to word-process accurately at the rate of 50 words per minute. The personnel office administers a total of seven brief word-processing tests to Mary over the course of seven business days. In words per minute, Mary's scores on each of the seven tests are as follows:

52   55   39   56   35   50   54

If you were in charge of hiring at TRW and you looked at these seven scores, you might logically ask, "Which of these scores is the best measure of Mary's 'true' word-processing ability?" And more to the point, "Which is her 'true' score?"

The "true" answer to this question is that we cannot conclude with absolute certainty from the data we have exactly what Mary's true word-processing ability is. We can, however, make an educated guess. Our educated guess would be that her true word-processing ability is equal to the mean of the distribution of her word-processing scores plus or minus a number of points accounted for by error in the measurement process. We do not know how many points are accounted for by error in the measurement process. The best we can do is estimate how much error entered into a particular test score.

The **standard error of measurement** is the tool used to estimate or infer the extent to which an observed score deviates from a true score. We may define the standard error of measurement as the standard deviation of a theoretically normal distribution of test scores obtained by one person on equivalent tests. Also known as the **standard error of a score** and denoted by the symbol σ_{meas}, the standard error of measurement is an index of the extent to which one individual's scores vary over tests presumed to be parallel. In accordance with the true score model, an obtained test score represents one point in the theoretical distribution of scores the testtaker could have obtained. But where on the continuum of possible scores is this obtained score? If the standard deviation for the distribution of test scores is known (or can be calculated) and if an estimate of the reliability of the test is known (or can be calculated), then an estimate of the standard error of a particular score (or, the standard error of measurement) can be determined by the following formula:

$$\sigma_{meas} = \sigma \sqrt{1 - r_{xx}}$$

where σ_{meas} is equal to the standard error of measurement, σ is equal to the standard deviation of test scores by the group of testtakers, and r_{xx} is equal to the reliability coefficient of the test. The standard error of measurement allows us to estimate, with a specific level of confidence, the range in which the true score is likely to exist.

If, for example, a spelling test has a reliability coefficient of .84 and a standard deviation of 10, then

$$\sigma_{meas} = 10 \sqrt{1 - .84} = 4$$

In order to use the standard error of measurement to estimate the range of the true score, we make an assumption: If the individual were to take a large number of equivalent tests, scores on those tests would tend to be normally distributed, with the individual's true score as the mean. Because the standard error of measurement functions like a standard deviation in this context, we can use it to predict what would happen if an individual took additional equivalent tests:

- approximately 68% (actually, 68.26%) of the scores would be expected to occur within $\pm 1\sigma_{meas}$ of the true score;
- approximately 95% (actually, 95.44%) of the scores would be expected to occur within $\pm 2\sigma_{meas}$ of the true score;
- approximately 99% (actually, 99.74%) of the scores would be expected to occur within $\pm 3\sigma_{meas}$ of the true score.

Of course, we don't know the true score for any individual testtaker, so we must estimate it. The best estimate available of the individual's true score on the test is the test score already obtained. Thus, if a student achieved a score of 50 on one spelling test and if the test had a standard error of measurement of 4, then—using 50 as the point estimate—we can be:

- 68% (actually, 68.26%) confident that the true score falls within $50 \pm 1\sigma_{meas}$ (or between 46 and 54, including 46 and 54);
- 95% (actually, 95.44%) confident that the true score falls within $50 \pm 2\sigma_{meas}$ (or between 42 and 58, including 42 and 58);
- 99% (actually, 99.74%) confident that the true score falls within $50 \pm 3\sigma_{meas}$ (or between 38 and 62, including 38 and 62).

The standard error of measurement, like the reliability coefficient, is one way of expressing test reliability. If the standard deviation of a test is held constant, then the smaller the σ_{meas}, the more reliable the test will be; as r_{xx} increases, the σ_{meas} decreases. For example, when a reliability coefficient equals .64 and σ equals 15, the standard error of measurement equals 9:

$$\sigma_{meas} = 15 \sqrt{1 - .64} = 9$$

With a reliability coefficient equal to .96 and σ still equal to 15, the standard error of measurement decreases to 3:

$$\sigma_{meas} = 15\sqrt{1 - .96} = 3$$

In practice, the standard error of measurement is most frequently used in the interpretation of individual test scores. For example, intelligence tests are given as part of the assessment of individuals for intellectual disability. One of the criteria for mental retardation is an IQ score of 70 or below (when the mean is 100 and the standard deviation is 15) on an individually administered intelligence test (American Psychiatric Association, 1994). One question that could be asked about these tests is how scores that are close to the cutoff value of 70 should be treated. Specifically, how high above 70 must a score be for us to conclude confidently that the individual is unlikely to be retarded? Is 72 clearly above the retarded range, so that if the person were to take a parallel form of the test, we could be confident that the second score would be above 70? What about a score of 75? A score of 79?

Useful in answering such questions is an estimate of the amount of error in an observed test score. The standard error of measurement provides such an estimate. Further, the standard error of measurement is useful in establishing what is called a **confidence interval:** a range or band of test scores that is likely to contain the true score.

Consider an application of a confidence interval with one hypothetical measure of adult intelligence. The manual for the test provides a great deal of information relevant to the reliability of the test as a whole as well as more specific reliability-related information for each of its subtests. As reported in the manual, the standard deviation is 3 for the subtest scaled scores and 15 for IQ scores. Across all of the age groups in the normative sample, the average reliability coefficient for the Full Scale IQ (FSIQ) is .98, and the average standard error of measurement for the FSIQ is 2.3.

Knowing an individual testtaker's FSIQ score and his or her age, we can calculate a confidence interval. For example, suppose a 22-year-old testtaker obtained a FSIQ of 75. The test user can be 95% confident that this testtaker's true FSIQ falls in the range of 70 to 80. This is so because the 95% confidence interval is set by taking the observed score of 75, plus or minus 1.96, multiplied by the standard error of measurement. In the test manual we find that the standard error of measurement of the FSIQ for a 22-year-old testtaker is 2.37. With this information in hand, the 95% confidence interval is calculated as follows:

$$75 \pm 1.96\sigma_{meas} = 75 \pm 1.96(2.37) = 75 \pm 4.645$$

The calculated interval of 4.645 is rounded to the nearest whole number, 5. We can therefore be 95% confident that this testtaker's true FSIQ on this particular test of intelligence lies somewhere in the range of the observed score of 75 plus or minus 5, or somewhere in the range of 70 to 80.

In the interest of increasing your SEM "comfort level," consider the data presented in Table 5–5. These are SEMs for selected age ranges and selected types of IQ measurements as reported in the *Technical Manual for the Stanford-Binet Intelligence Scales*, fifth edition (SB5). When presenting these and related data, Roid (2003c, p. 65) noted: "Scores that are more precise and consistent have smaller differences between true and observed scores, resulting in lower SEMs." Given this, *just think:* What hypotheses come to mind regarding SB5 IQ scores at ages 5, 10, 15, and 80+?

The standard error of measurement can be used to set the confidence interval for a particular score or to determine whether a score is significantly different from a criterion (such as the cutoff score of 70 described previously). But the standard error of measurement cannot be used to compare scores. So, how do test users compare scores?

Table 5–5

Standard Errors of Measurement of SB5 IQ Scores at Ages 5, 10, 15, and 80+

IQ Type	Age (in years)			
	5	10	15	80+
Full Scale IQ	2.12	2.60	2.12	2.12
Nonverbal IQ	3.35	2.67	3.00	3.00
Verbal IQ	3.00	3.35	3.00	2.60
Abbreviated Battery IQ	4.24	5.20	4.50	3.00

The Standard Error of the Difference Between Two Scores

Error related to any of the number of possible variables operative in a testing situation can contribute to a change in a score achieved on the same test, or a parallel test, from one administration of the test to the next. The amount of error in a specific test score is embodied in the standard error of measurement. But scores can change from one testing to the next for reasons other than error.

True differences in the characteristic being measured can also affect test scores. These differences may be of great interest, as in the case of a personnel officer who must decide which of many applicants to hire. Indeed, such differences may be hoped for, as in the case of a psychotherapy researcher who hopes to prove the effectiveness of a particular approach to therapy. Comparisons between scores are made using the **standard error of the difference,** a statistical measure that can aid a test user in determining how large a difference should be before it is considered statistically significant. As you are probably aware from your course in statistics, custom in the field of psychology dictates that if the probability is more than 5% that the difference occurred by chance, then, for all intents and purposes, it is presumed that there was no difference. A more rigorous standard is the 1% standard. Applying the 1% standard, no statistically significant difference would be deemed to exist unless the observed difference could have occurred by chance alone less than one time in a hundred.

The standard error of the difference between two scores can be the appropriate statistical tool to address three types of questions:

1. How did this individual's performance on test 1 compare with his or her performance on test 2?

2. How did this individual's performance on test 1 compare with someone else's performance on test 1?

3. How did this individual's performance on test 1 compare with someone else's performance on test 2?

As you might have expected, when comparing scores achieved on the different tests, it is essential that the scores be converted to the same scale. The formula for the standard error of the difference between two scores is

$$\sigma_{\text{diff}} = \sqrt{\sigma_{\text{meas 1}}^2 + \sigma_{\text{meas 2}}^2}$$

where σ_{diff} is the standard error of the difference between two scores, is the squared standard error of measurement for test 1, and is the squared standard error of measurement for test 2. If we substitute reliability coefficients for the standard errors of measurement of the separate scores, the formula becomes

$$\sigma_{\text{diff}} = \sigma\sqrt{2 - r_1 - r_2}$$

where r_1 is the reliability coefficient of test 1, r_2 is the reliability coefficient of test 2, and σ is the standard deviation. Note that both tests would have the same standard deviation because they must be on the same scale (or be converted to the same scale) before a comparison can be made.

The standard error of the difference between two scores will be larger than the standard error of measurement for either score alone because the former is affected by measurement error in both scores. This also makes good sense: If two scores each contain error such that in each case the true score could be higher or lower, then we would want the two scores to be further apart before we conclude that there is a significant difference between them.

The value obtained by calculating the standard error of the difference is used in much the same way as the standard error of the mean. If we wish to be 95% confident that the two scores are different, we would want them to be separated by 2 standard errors of the difference. A separation of only 1 standard error of the difference would give us 68% confidence that the two true scores are different.

As an illustration of the use of the standard error of the difference between two scores, consider the situation of a corporate personnel manager who is seeking a highly responsible person for the position of vice president of safety. The personnel officer in this hypothetical situation decides to use a new published test we will call the Safety-Mindedness Test (SMT) to screen applicants for the position. After placing an ad in the employment section of the local newspaper, the personnel officer tests 100 applicants for the position using the SMT. The personnel officer narrows the search for the vice president to the two highest scorers on the SMT: Moe, who scored 125, and Larry, who scored 134. Assuming the measured reliability of this test to be .92 and its standard deviation to be 14, should the personnel officer conclude that Larry performed significantly better than Moe? To answer this question, first calculate the standard error of the difference:

$$\sigma_{\text{diff}} = 14\sqrt{2 - .92 - .92} = 14\sqrt{.16} = 5.6$$

Note that in this application of the formula, the two test reliability coefficients are the same because the two scores being compared are derived from the same test.

What does this standard error of the difference mean? For any standard error of the difference, we can be:

- 68% confident that two scores differing by $1\sigma_{\text{diff}}$ represent true score differences;
- 95% confident that two scores differing by $2\sigma_{\text{diff}}$ represent true score differences;
- 99.7% confident that two scores differing by $3\sigma_{\text{diff}}$ represent true score differences.

Applying this information to the standard error of the difference just computed for the SMT, we see that the personnel officer can be:

- 68% confident that two scores differing by 5.6 represent true score differences;
- 95% confident that two scores differing by 11.2 represent true score differences;
- 99.7% confident that two scores differing by 16.8 represent true score differences.

The difference between Larry's and Moe's scores is only 9 points, not a large enough difference for the personnel officer to conclude with 95% confidence that the two individuals have true scores that differ on this test. Stated another way: If Larry and Moe were to take a parallel form of the SMT, then the personnel officer could not be 95% confident that, at the next testing, Larry would again outperform Moe. The personnel officer in this example would have to resort to other means to decide whether Moe, Larry, or someone else would be the best candidate for the position (Curly has been patiently waiting in the wings).

JUST THINK . . .

With all of this talk about Moe, Larry, and Curly, please tell us that you have not forgotten about Mary. You know, Mary from the Cronbach quote on page 165—yes, that Mary. Should she get the job at TRW? If your instructor thinks it would be useful to do so, do the math before responding.

As a postscript to the preceding example, suppose Larry got the job primarily on the basis of data from our hypothetical SMT. And let's further suppose that it soon became all too clear that Larry was the hands-down absolute worst vice president of safety that the company had ever seen. Larry spent much of his time playing practical jokes on fellow corporate officers, and he spent many of his off-hours engaged in his favorite pastime, flagpole sitting. The personnel officer might then have very good reason to question how well the instrument called the Safety-Mindedness Test truly measured safety-mindedness. Or, to put it another way, the personnel officer might question the *validity* of the test. Not coincidentally, the subject of test validity is taken up in the next chapter.

Self-Assessment

Test your understanding of elements of this chapter by seeing if you can explain each of the following terms, expressions, and abbreviations:

alternate forms
alternate-forms reliability
average proportional distance (APD)
classical test theory (CTT)
coefficient alpha
coefficient of equivalence
coefficient of generalizability
coefficient of inter-scorer
    reliability
coefficient of stability
confidence interval
content sampling
criterion-referenced test
decision study
dichotomous test item
discrimination
domain sampling theory
dynamic characteristic
error variance
estimate of inter-item consistency
facet

generalizability study
generalizability theory
heterogeneity
homogeneity
inflation of range/variance
information function
inter-item consistency
internal consistency estimate of
    reliability
inter-scorer reliability
item response theory (IRT)
item sampling
Kuder–Richardson formula 20
latent-trait theory
measurement error
odd-even reliability
parallel forms
parallel-forms reliability
polytomous test item
power test
random error

Rasch model
reliability
reliability coefficient
replicability crisis
restriction of range/variance
Spearman–Brown formula
speed test
split-half reliability
standard error of a score
standard error of measurement
standard error of the difference
static characteristic
systematic error
test battery
test-retest reliability
transient error
true score
true variance
universe
universe score
variance

6

Validity

In everyday language we say that something is valid if it is sound, meaningful, or well grounded on principles or evidence. For example, we speak of a valid theory, a valid argument, or a valid reason. In legal terminology, lawyers say that something is valid if it is "executed with the proper formalities" (Black, 1979), such as a valid contract and a valid will. In each of these instances, people make judgments based on evidence of the meaningfulness or the veracity of something. Similarly, in the language of psychological assessment, *validity* is a term used in conjunction with the meaningfulness of a test score— what the test score truly means.

The Concept of Validity

Validity, as applied to a test, is a judgment or estimate of how well a test measures what it purports to measure in a particular context. More specifically, it is a judgment based on evidence about the appropriateness of inferences drawn from test scores.[1] An **inference** is a logical result or deduction. Characterizations of the validity of tests and test scores are frequently phrased in terms such as "acceptable" or "weak." These terms reflect a judgment about how adequately the test measures what it purports to measure.

Inherent in a judgment of an instrument's validity is a judgment of how useful the instrument is for a particular purpose with a particular population of people. As a shorthand, assessors may refer to a particular test as a "valid test." However, what is really meant is that the test has been shown to be valid for a particular use with a particular population of testtakers at a particular time. No test or measurement technique is "universally valid" for all time, for all uses, with all types of testtaker populations. Rather, tests may be shown to be valid within what we would characterize as *reasonable boundaries* of a contemplated usage. If those boundaries are exceeded, the validity of the test may be called into question. Further, to the extent that the validity of a test may diminish as the culture or the times change, the validity of a test may have to be re-established with the same as well as other testtaker populations.

> **JUST THINK . . .**
>
> Why is the phrase *valid test* sometimes misleading?

---

1. Recall from Chapter 1 that the word *test* is used throughout this book in the broadest possible sense. It may therefore also apply to measurement procedures and processes that, strictly speaking, would not be referred to colloquially as "tests."

Validation is the process of gathering and evaluating evidence about validity. Both the test developer and the test user may play a role in the validation of a test for a specific purpose. It is the test developer's responsibility to supply validity evidence in the test manual.

◆
JUST THINK . . .

Local validation studies require professional time and know-how, and they may be costly. For these reasons, they might not be done even if they are desirable or necessary. What would you recommend to a test user who is in no position to conduct such a local validation study but who nonetheless is contemplating the use of a test that requires one?

It may sometimes be appropriate for test users to conduct their own **validation studies** with their own groups of testtakers. Such *local validation studies* may yield insights regarding a particular population of testtakers as compared to the norming sample described in a test manual. **Local validation studies** are absolutely necessary when the test user plans to alter in some way the format, instructions, language, or content of the test. For example, a local validation study would be necessary if the test user sought to transform a nationally standardized test into Braille for administration to blind and visually impaired testtakers. Local validation studies would also be necessary if a test user sought to use a test with a population of testtakers that differed in some significant way from the population on which the test was standardized.

One way measurement specialists have traditionally conceptualized validity is according to three categories:

1. *Content validity.* This is a measure of validity based on an evaluation of the subjects, topics, or content covered by the items in the test.

2. *Criterion-related validity.* This is a measure of validity obtained by evaluating the relationship of scores obtained on the test to scores on other tests or measures

3. *Construct validity.* This is a measure of validity that is arrived at by executing a comprehensive analysis of

   a. how scores on the test relate to other test scores and measures, and

   b. how scores on the test can be understood within some theoretical framework for understanding the construct that the test was designed to measure.

In this classic conception of validity, referred to as the *trinitarian* view (Guion, 1980), it might be useful to visualize construct validity as being "umbrella validity" because every other variety of validity falls under it. Why construct validity is the overriding variety of validity will become clear as we discuss what makes a test valid and the methods and procedures used in validation. Indeed, there are many ways of approaching the process of test validation, and these different plans of attack are often referred to as *strategies.* We speak, for example, of *content validation strategies, criterion-related validation strategies,* and *construct validation strategies.*

Trinitarian approaches to validity assessment are not mutually exclusive. That is, each of the three conceptions of validity provides evidence that, with other evidence, contributes to a judgment concerning the validity of a test. Stated another way, all three types of validity evidence contribute to a unified picture of a test's validity. A test user may not need to know about all three. Depending on the use to which a test is being put, one type of validity evidence may be more relevant than another.

The trinitarian model of validity is not without its critics (Landy, 1986). Messick (1995), for example, condemned this approach as fragmented and incomplete. He called for a unitary view of validity, one that takes into account everything from the implications of test scores in terms of societal values to the consequences of test use. However, even in the so-called unitary view, different elements of validity may come to the fore for scrutiny, and so an understanding of those elements in isolation is necessary.

In this chapter we discuss content validity, criterion-related validity, and construct validity; three now-classic approaches to judging whether a test measures what it purports to measure.

Let's note at the outset that, although the trinitarian model focuses on three types of validity, you are likely to come across other varieties of validity in your readings. For example, you are likely to come across the term *ecological validity*. You may recall from Chapter 1 that the term *ecological momentary assessment* (EMA) refers to the in-the-moment and in-the-place evaluation of targeted variables (such as behaviors, cognitions, and emotions) in a natural, naturalistic, or real-life context. In a somewhat similar vein, the term **ecological validity** refers to a judgment regarding how well a test measures what it purports to measure at the time and place that the variable being measured (typically a behavior, cognition, or emotion) is actually emitted. In essence, the greater the ecological validity of a test or other measurement procedure, the greater the generalizability of the measurement results to particular real-life circumstances.

Part of the appeal of EMA is that it does not have the limitations of retrospective self-report. Studies of the ecological validity of many tests or other assessment procedures are conducted in a natural (or naturalistic) environment, which is identical or similar to the environment in which a targeted behavior or other variable might naturally occur (see, for example, Courvoisier et al., 2012; Lewinski et al., 2014; Lo et al., 2015). However, in some cases, owing to the nature of the particular variable under study, such research may be retrospective in nature (see, for example, the 2014 Weems et al. study of memory for traumatic events).

Other validity-related terms that you will come across in the psychology literature are *predictive validity* and *concurrent validity*. We discuss these terms later in this chapter in the context of *criterion-related validity*. Yet another term you may come across is *face validity* (see Figure 6–1). In fact, you will come across that term right now . . .

Face Validity

Face validity relates more to what a test *appears* to measure to the person being tested than to what the test actually measures. Face validity is a judgment concerning how relevant the

Figure 6–1
Face Validity and Comedian Rodney Dangerfield

Rodney Dangerfield (1921–2004) was famous for complaining, "I don't get no respect." Somewhat analogously, the concept of face validity has been described as the "Rodney Dangerfield of psychometric variables" because it has "received little attention—and even less respect—from researchers examining the construct validity of psychological tests and measures" (Bornstein et al., 1994, p. 363). By the way, the tombstone of this beloved stand-up comic and film actor reads: "Rodney Dangerfield . . . There goes the neighborhood."

© Arthur Schatz/The Life Images Collection/Getty Images

test items appear to be. Stated another way, if a test definitely appears to measure what it purports to measure "on the face of it," then it could be said to be high in face validity. A paper-and-pencil personality test labeled The Introversion/Extraversion Test, with items that ask respondents whether they have acted in an introverted or an extraverted way in particular situations, may be perceived by respondents as a highly face-valid test. On the other hand, a personality test in which respondents are asked to report what they see in inkblots may be perceived as a test with low face validity. Many respondents would be left wondering how what they said they saw in the inkblots really had anything at all to do with personality.

In contrast to judgments about the reliability of a test and judgments about the content, construct, or criterion-related validity of a test, judgments about face validity are frequently thought of from the perspective of the testtaker, not the test user. A test's *lack* of face validity could contribute to a lack of confidence in the perceived effectiveness of the test—with a consequential decrease in the testtaker's cooperation or motivation to do his or her best. In a corporate environment, lack of face validity may lead to unwillingness of administrators or managers to "buy-in" to the use of a particular test (see this chapter's *Meet an Assessment Professional*). In a similar vein, parents may object to having their children tested with instruments that lack ostensible validity. Such concern might stem from a belief that the use of such tests will result in invalid conclusions.

JUST THINK . . .

What is the value of face validity from the perspective of the test user?

In reality, a test that lacks face validity may still be relevant and useful. However, if the test is not perceived as relevant and useful by testtakers, parents, legislators, and others, then negative consequences may result. These consequences may range from poor testtaker attitude to lawsuits filed by disgruntled parties against a test user and test publisher. Ultimately, face validity may be more a matter of public relations than psychometric soundness. Still, it is important nonetheless, and (much like Rodney Dangerfield) deserving of respect.

Content Validity

Content validity describes a judgment of how adequately a test samples behavior representative of the universe of behavior that the test was designed to sample. For example, the universe of behavior referred to as *assertive* is very wide-ranging. A content-valid, paper-and-pencil test of assertiveness would be one that is adequately representative of this wide range. We might expect that such a test would contain items sampling from hypothetical situations at home (such as whether the respondent has difficulty in making her or his views known to fellow family members), on the job (such as whether the respondent has difficulty in asking subordinates to do what is required of them), and in social situations (such as whether the respondent would send back a steak not done to order in a fancy restaurant). Ideally, test developers have a clear (as opposed to "fuzzy") vision of the construct being measured, and the clarity of this vision can be reflected in the content validity of the test (Haynes et al., 1995). In the interest of ensuring content validity, test developers strive to include key components of the construct targeted for measurement, and exclude content irrelevant to the construct targeted for measurement.

With respect to educational achievement tests, it is customary to consider a test a content-valid measure when the proportion of material covered by the test approximates the proportion of material covered in the course. A cumulative final exam in introductory statistics would be considered content-valid if the proportion and type of introductory statistics problems on the test approximates the proportion and type of introductory statistics problems presented in the course.

The early stages of a test being developed for use in the classroom—be it one classroom or those throughout the state or the nation—typically entail research exploring the universe of possible instructional objectives for the course. Included among the many possible sources of information on such objectives are course syllabi, course textbooks, teachers of the course, specialists who

Meet Dr. Adam Shoemaker

In the "real world," tests require buy-in from test administrators and candidates. While the reliability and validity of the test are always of primary importance, the test process can be short-circuited by administrators who don't know how to use the test or who don't have a good understanding of test theory. So at least half the battle of implementing a new testing tool is to make sure administrators know how to use it, accept the way that it works, and feel comfortable that it is tapping the skills and abilities necessary for the candidate to do the job.

Here's an example: Early in my company's history of using online assessments, we piloted a test that had acceptable reliability and criterion validity. We saw some strongly significant correlations between scores on the test and objective performance numbers, suggesting that this test did a good job of distinguishing between high and low performers on the job. The test proved to be unbiased and showed no demonstrable adverse impact against minority groups. However, very few test administrators felt comfortable using the assessment because most people felt that the skills that it tapped were not closely related to the skills needed for the job. Legally, ethically, and statistically, we were on firm ground, but we could never fully achieve "buy-in" from the people who had to administer the test.

On the other hand, we also piloted a test that showed very little criterion validity at all. There were no significant correlations between scores on the test and performance outcomes; the test was unable to distinguish between a high and a low performer. Still . . . the test administrators loved this test because it "looked" so much like the job. That is, it had high face validity and tapped skills that seemed to be precisely the kinds of skills that were needed on the job. From a legal, ethical, and statistical perspective, we knew we could not use this test to select employees, but we continued to use it to provide a "realistic job preview" to candidates. That way, the test continued

Adam Shoemaker, Ph.D., Human Resources Consultant for Talent Acquisition, Tampa, Florida

© Adam Shoemaker

to work for us in really showing candidates that this was the kind of thing they would be doing all day at work. More than a few times, candidates voluntarily withdrew from the process because they had a better understanding of what the job involved long before they even sat down at a desk.

The moral of this story is that as scientists, we have to remember that reliability and validity are super important in the development and implementation of a test . . . but as human beings, we have to remember that the test we end up using must also be easy to use and appear face valid for both the candidate and the administrator.

Read more of what Dr. Shoemaker had to say—his complete essay—through the Instructor Resources within Connect.

Used with permission of Adam Shoemaker.

develop curricula, and professors and supervisors who train teachers in the particular subject area. From the pooled information (along with the judgment of the test developer), there emerges a **test blueprint** for the "structure" of the evaluation—that is, a plan regarding the types of information to be covered by the items, the number of items tapping each area of coverage, the organization of the items in the test, and so forth (see Figure 6–2). In many instances the test blueprint represents the culmination of efforts to adequately sample the universe of content areas that conceivably could be sampled in such a test.[2]

♦

JUST THINK . . .

A test developer is working on a brief screening instrument designed to predict student success in a psychological testing and assessment course. You are the consultant called upon to blueprint the content areas covered. Your recommendations?

For an employment test to be content-valid, its content must be a representative sample of the job-related skills required for employment. Behavioral observation is one technique frequently used in blueprinting the content areas to be covered in certain types of employment tests. The test developer will observe successful veterans on that job, note the behaviors necessary for success on the job, and design the test to include a representative

Figure 6–2
Building a Test from a Test Blueprint

An architect's blueprint usually takes the form of a technical drawing or diagram of a structure, sometimes written in white lines on a blue background. The blueprint may be thought of as a plan of a structure, typically detailed enough so that the structure could actually be constructed from it. Somewhat comparable to the architect's blueprint is the test blueprint of a test developer. Seldom, if ever, on a blue background and written in white, it is nonetheless a detailed plan of the content, organization, and quantity of the items that a test will contain—sometimes complete with "weightings" of the content to be covered (He, 2011; Spray & Huang, 2000; Sykes & Hou, 2003). A test administered on a regular basis may require "item-pool management" to manage the creation of new items and the output of old items in a manner that is consistent with the test's blueprint (Ariel et al., 2006; van der Linden et al., 2000).
© John Rowley/Getty Images RF

---

2. The application of the concept of *blueprint* and of *blueprinting* is, of course, not limited to achievement tests. Blueprinting may be used in the design of a personality test, an attitude measure, an employment test, or any other test. The judgments of experts in the field are often employed in order to construct the best possible test blueprint.

sample of those behaviors. Those same workers (as well as their supervisors and others) may subsequently be called on to act as experts or judges in rating the degree to which the content of the test is a representative sample of the required job-related skills. At that point, the test developer will want to know about the extent to which the experts or judges agree. A description of one such method for quantifying the degree of agreement between such raters can be found "online only" through the Instructor Resources within Connect (refer to OOBAL-6-B2).

Culture and the relativity of content validity   Tests are often thought of as either valid or not valid. A history test, for example, either does or does not accurately measure one's knowledge of historical fact. However, it is also true that what constitutes historical fact depends to some extent on who is writing the history. Consider, for example, a momentous event in the history of the world, one that served as a catalyst for World War I. Archduke Franz Ferdinand was assassinated on June 28, 1914, by a Serb named Gavrilo Princip (Figure 6–3). Now think about how you would answer the following multiple-choice item on a history test:

Gavrilo Princip was

   a.   a poet
   b.   a hero
   c.   a terrorist
   d.   a nationalist
   e.   all of the above

Figure 6–3
Cultural Relativity, History, and Test Validity

Austro-Hungarian Archduke Franz Ferdinand and his wife, Sophia, are pictured (left) as they left Sarajevo's City Hall on June 28, 1914. Moments later, Ferdinand would be assassinated by Gavrilo Princip, shown in custody at right. The killing served as a catalyst for World War I and is discussed and analyzed in history textbooks in every language around the world. Yet descriptions of the assassin Princip in those textbooks—and ability test items based on those descriptions—vary as a function of culture.
© Ingram Publishing RF

JUST THINK . . .

The passage of time sometimes serves to place historical figures in a different light. How might the textbook descriptions of Gavrilo Princip have changed in these regions?

For various textbooks in the Bosnian region of the world, choice "e"—that's right, "all of the above"—is the "correct" answer. Hedges (1997) observed that textbooks in areas of Bosnia and Herzegovina that were controlled by different ethnic groups imparted widely varying characterizations of the assassin. In the Serb-controlled region of the country, history textbooks—and presumably the tests constructed to measure students' learning—regarded Princip as a "hero and poet." By contrast, Croatian students might read that Princip was an assassin trained to commit a terrorist act. Muslims in the region were taught that Princip was a nationalist whose deed sparked anti-Serbian rioting.

A history test considered valid in one classroom, at one time, and in one place will not necessarily be considered so in another classroom, at another time, and in another place. Consider a test containing the true-false item, "Colonel Claus von Stauffenberg is a hero." Such an item is useful in illustrating the cultural relativity affecting item scoring. In 1944, von Stauffenberg, a German officer, was an active participant in a bomb plot to assassinate Germany's leader, Adolf Hitler. When the plot (popularized in the film, *Operation Valkyrie*) failed, von Stauffenberg was executed and promptly villified in Germany as a despicable traitor. Today, the light of history shines favorably on von Stauffenberg, and he is perceived as a hero in Germany. A German postage stamp with his face on it was issued to honor von Stauffenberg's 100th birthday.

Politics is another factor that may well play a part in perceptions and judgments concerning the validity of tests and test items. In many countries throughout the world, a response that is keyed incorrect to a particular test item can lead to consequences far more dire than a deduction in points towards the total test score. Sometimes, even constructing a test with a reference to a taboo topic can have dire consequences for the test developer. For example, one Palestinian professor who included items pertaining to governmental corruption on an examination was tortured by authorities as a result ("Brother Against Brother," 1997). Such scenarios bring new meaning to the term *politically correct* as it applies to tests, test items, and testtaker responses.

JUST THINK . . .

Commercial test developers who publish widely used history tests must maintain the content validity of their tests. What challenges do they face in doing so?

Criterion-Related Validity

Criterion-related validity is a judgment of how adequately a test score can be used to infer an individual's most probable standing on some measure of interest—the measure of interest being the criterion. Two types of validity evidence are subsumed under the heading *criterion-related validity*. **Concurrent validity** is an index of the degree to which a test score is related to some criterion measure obtained at the same time (concurrently). **Predictive validity** is an index of the degree to which a test score predicts some criterion measure. Before we discuss each of these types of validity evidence in detail, it seems appropriate to raise (and answer) an important question.

What Is a Criterion?

We were first introduced to the concept of a criterion in Chapter 4, where, in the context of defining criterion-referenced assessment, we defined a criterion broadly as a standard on which a judgment or decision may be based. Here, in the context of our discussion of criterion-related validity, we will define a **criterion** just a bit more narrowly as the standard against which a test or a test score is evaluated. So, for example, if a test purports to measure the trait of athleticism, we might expect to employ "membership in a health club" or any generally accepted measure of physical fitness as a criterion in evaluating whether the athleticism test truly measures athleticism. Operationally, a criterion can be most anything: *pilot performance in flying a Boeing 767, grade on examination in Advanced Hairweaving, number of days spent in psychiatric hospitalization;* the list is endless. There are no hard-and-fast rules for what constitutes a criterion. It can be a test score, a specific behavior or group of behaviors, an amount of time, a rating, a psychiatric diagnosis, a training cost, an index of absenteeism, an index of alcohol intoxication, and so on. Whatever the criterion, ideally it is relevant, valid, and uncontaminated. Let's explain.

Characteristics of a criterion   An adequate criterion is *relevant*. By this we mean that it is pertinent or applicable to the matter at hand. We would expect, for example, that a test purporting to advise testtakers whether they share the same interests of successful actors to have been validated using the interests of successful actors as a criterion.

An adequate criterion measure must also be *valid* for the purpose for which it is being used. If one test (X) is being used as the criterion to validate a second test (Y), then evidence should exist that test X is valid. If the criterion used is a rating made by a judge or a panel, then evidence should exist that the rating is valid. Suppose, for example, that a test purporting to measure depression is said to have been validated using as a criterion the diagnoses made by a blue-ribbon panel of psychodiagnosticians. A test user might wish to probe further regarding variables such as the credentials of the "blue-ribbon panel" (or, their educational background, training, and experience) and the actual procedures used to validate a diagnosis of depression. Answers to such questions would help address the issue of whether the criterion (in this case, the diagnoses made by panel members) was indeed valid.

Ideally, a criterion is also *uncontaminated.* **Criterion contamination** is the term applied to a criterion measure that has been based, at least in part, on predictor measures. As an example, consider a hypothetical "Inmate Violence Potential Test" (IVPT) designed to predict a prisoner's potential for violence in the cell block. In part, this evaluation entails ratings from fellow inmates, guards, and other staff in order to come up with a number that represents each inmate's violence potential. After all of the inmates in the study have been given scores on this test, the study authors then attempt to validate the test by asking guards to rate each inmate on their violence potential. Because the guards' opinions were used to formulate the inmate's test score in the first place (the predictor variable), the guards' opinions cannot be used as a criterion against which to judge the soundness of the test. If the guards' opinions were used both as a predictor and as a criterion, then we would say that criterion contamination had occurred.

Here is another example of criterion contamination. Suppose that a team of researchers from a company called Ventura International Psychiatric Research (VIPR) just completed a study of how accurately a test called the MMPI-2-RF predicted psychiatric diagnosis in the psychiatric population of the Minnesota state hospital system. As we will see in Chapter 12, the MMPI-2-RF is, in fact, a widely used test. In this study, the predictor is the MMPI-2-RF, and the criterion is the psychiatric diagnosis that exists in the patient's record. Further, let's suppose that while all the data are being analyzed at VIPR headquarters, someone informs these researchers that the diagnosis for every patient in the Minnesota state hospital system was determined, at least in part, by an MMPI-2-RF test score. Should they still proceed with their analysis? The answer is no. Because the predictor measure has contaminated the criterion measure, it would be of little value to find, in essence, that the predictor can indeed predict itself.

When criterion contamination does occur, the results of the validation study cannot be taken seriously. There are no methods or statistics to gauge the extent to which criterion contamination has taken place, and there are no methods or statistics to correct for such contamination.

Now, let's take a closer look at concurrent validity and predictive validity.

Concurrent Validity

If test scores are obtained at about the same time as the criterion measures are obtained, measures of the relationship between the test scores and the criterion provide evidence of concurrent validity. Statements of concurrent validity indicate the extent to which test scores may be used to estimate an individual's present standing on a criterion. If, for example, scores (or classifications) made on the basis of a psychodiagnostic test were to be validated against a criterion of already diagnosed psychiatric patients, then the process would be one of concurrent validation. In general, once the validity of the inference from the test scores is established, the test may provide a faster, less expensive way to offer a diagnosis or a classification decision. A test with satisfactorily demonstrated concurrent validity may therefore be appealing to prospective users because it holds out the potential of savings of money and professional time.

Sometimes the concurrent validity of a particular test (let's call it Test A) is explored with respect to another test (we'll call Test B). In such studies, prior research has satisfactorily demonstrated the validity of Test B, so the question becomes: "How well does Test A compare with Test B?" Here, Test B is used as the *validating criterion*. In some studies, Test A is either a brand-new test or a test being used for some new purpose, perhaps with a new population.

Here is a real-life example of a concurrent validity study in which a group of researchers explored whether a test validated for use with adults could be used with adolescents. The Beck Depression Inventory (BDI; Beck et al., 1961, 1979; Beck & Steer, 1993) and its revision, the Beck Depression Inventory-II (BDI-II; Beck et al., 1996) are self-report measures used to identify symptoms of depression and quantify their severity. Although the BDI had been widely used with adults, questions were raised regarding its appropriateness for use with adolescents. Ambrosini et al. (1991) conducted a concurrent validity study to explore the utility of the BDI with adolescents. They also sought to determine if the test could successfully differentiate patients with depression from those without depression in a population of adolescent outpatients. Diagnoses generated from the concurrent administration of an instrument previously validated for use with adolescents were used as the criterion validators. The findings suggested that the BDI is valid for use with adolescents.

JUST THINK . . .

What else might these researchers have done to explore the utility of the BDI with adolescents?

We now turn our attention to another form of criterion validity, one in which the criterion measure is obtained not concurrently but at some future time.

Predictive Validity

Test scores may be obtained at one time and the criterion measures obtained at a future time, usually after some intervening event has taken place. The intervening event may take varied forms, such as training, experience, therapy, medication, or simply the passage of time. Measures of the relationship between the test scores and a criterion measure obtained at a future time provide an indication of the *predictive validity* of the test; that is, how accurately scores on the test predict some criterion measure. Measures of the relationship between college admissions tests and freshman grade point averages, for example, provide evidence of the predictive validity of the admissions tests.

In settings where tests might be employed—such as a personnel agency, a college admissions office, or a warden's office—a test's high predictive validity can be a useful aid to decision-makers who must select successful students, productive workers, or good parole risks. Whether a test result is valuable in decision making depends on how well the test results improve selection decisions over decisions made without knowledge of test results. In an industrial setting where volume turnout is important, if the use of a personnel selection test can enhance productivity to even a small degree, then that enhancement will pay off year after year and may translate into millions of dollars of increased revenue. And in a clinical context, no price could be placed on a test that could save more lives from suicide or by providing predictive accuracy over and above existing tests with respect to such acts. Unfortunately, the difficulties inherent in developing such tests are numerous and multifaceted (Mulvey & Lidz, 1984; Murphy, 1984; Petrie & Chamberlain, 1985). When evaluating the predictive validity of a test, researchers must take into consideration the base rate of the occurrence of the variable in question, both as that variable exists in the general population and as it exists in the sample being studied. Generally, a **base rate** is the extent to which a particular trait, behavior, characteristic, or attribute exists in the population (expressed as a proportion). In psychometric parlance, a **hit rate** may be defined as the proportion of people a test accurately identifies as possessing or exhibiting a particular trait, behavior, characteristic, or attribute. For example, hit rate could refer to the proportion of people accurately predicted to be able to perform work at the graduate school level or to the proportion of neurological patients accurately identified as having a brain tumor. In like fashion, a **miss rate** may be defined as the proportion of people the test fails to identify as having, or not having, a particular characteristic or attribute. Here, a miss amounts to an inaccurate prediction. The category of misses may be further subdivided. A **false positive** is a miss wherein the test predicted that the testtaker did possess the particular characteristic or attribute being measured when in fact the testtaker did not. A **false negative** is a miss wherein the test predicted that the testtaker did not possess the particular characteristic or attribute being measured when the testtaker actually did.

To evaluate the predictive validity of a test, a test targeting a particular attribute may be administered to a sample of research subjects in which approximately half of the subjects possess or exhibit the targeted attribute and the other half do not. Evaluating the predictive validity of a test is essentially a matter of evaluating the extent to which use of the test results in an acceptable hit rate.

Judgments of criterion-related validity, whether concurrent or predictive, are based on two types of statistical evidence: *the validity coefficient* and *expectancy data.*

The validity coefficient   The **validity coefficient** is a correlation coefficient that provides a measure of the relationship between test scores and scores on the criterion measure. The correlation coefficient computed from a score (or classification) on a psychodiagnostic test and the criterion score (or classification) assigned by psychodiagnosticians is one example of a validity coefficient. Typically, the Pearson correlation coefficient is used to determine the validity between the two measures. However, depending on variables such as the type of data, the sample size, and the shape of the distribution, other correlation coefficients could be used. For example, in correlating self-rankings of performance on some job with rankings made by job supervisors, the formula for the Spearman rho rank-order correlation would be employed.

Like the reliability coefficient and other correlational measures, the validity coefficient is affected by restriction or inflation of range. And as in other correlational studies, a key issue is whether the range of scores employed is appropriate to the objective of the correlational analysis. In situations where, for example, attrition in the number of subjects has occurred over the course of the study, the validity coefficient may be adversely affected.

The problem of restricted range can also occur through a self-selection process in the sample employed for the validation study. Thus, for example, if the test purports to measure something as technical or as dangerous as oil-barge firefighting skills, it may well be that the only people who reply to an ad for the position of oil-barge firefighter are those who are actually highly qualified for the position. Accordingly, the range of the distribution of scores on this test of oil-barge firefighting skills would be restricted. For less technical or dangerous positions, a self-selection factor might be operative if the test developer selects a group of newly hired employees to test (with the expectation that criterion measures will be available for this group at some subsequent date). However, because the newly hired employees have probably already passed some formal or informal evaluation in the process of being hired, there is a good chance that ability to do the job will be higher among this group than among a random sample of ordinary job applicants. Consequently, scores on the criterion measure that is later administered will tend to be higher than scores on the criterion measure obtained from a random sample of ordinary job applicants. Stated another way, the scores will be restricted in range.

Whereas it is the responsibility of the test developer to report validation data in the test manual, it is the responsibility of test users to read carefully the description of the validation study and then to evaluate the suitability of the test for their specific purposes. What were the characteristics of the sample used in the validation study? How matched are those characteristics to the people for whom an administration of the test is contemplated? For a specific test purpose, are some subtests of a test more appropriate than the entire test?

How high should a validity coefficient be for a user or a test developer to infer that the test is valid? There are no rules for determining the minimum acceptable size of a validity coefficient. In fact, Cronbach and Gleser (1965) cautioned against the establishment of such rules. They argued that validity coefficients need to be large enough to enable the test user to make accurate decisions within the unique context in which a test is being used. Essentially, the validity coefficient should be high enough to result in the identification and differentiation of testtakers with respect to target attribute(s), such as employees who are likely to be more productive, police officers who are less likely to misuse their weapons, and students who are more likely to be successful in a particular course of study.

Incremental validity   Test users involved in predicting some criterion from test scores are often interested in the utility of multiple predictors. The value of including more than one predictor depends on a couple of factors. First, of course, each measure used as a predictor should have criterion-related predictive validity. Second, additional predictors should possess **incremental validity,** defined here as the degree to which an additional predictor explains something about the criterion measure that is not explained by predictors already in use.

Incremental validity may be used when predicting something like academic success in college. Grade point average (GPA) at the end of the first year may be used as a measure of academic success. A study of potential predictors of GPA may reveal that time spent in the library and time spent studying are highly correlated with GPA. How much sleep a student's roommate allows the student to have during exam periods correlates with GPA to a smaller extent. What is the most accurate but most efficient way to predict GPA? One approach, employing the principles of incremental validity, is to start with the best predictor: the predictor that is most highly correlated with GPA. This may be time spent studying. Then, using multiple regression techniques, one would examine the usefulness of the other predictors.

Even though time in the library is highly correlated with GPA, it may not possess incremental validity if it overlaps too much with the first predictor, time spent studying. Said another way, if time spent studying and time in the library are so highly correlated with each other that they reflect essentially the same thing, then only one of them needs to be included as a predictor. Including both predictors will provide little new information. By contrast, the variable of how much sleep a student's roommate allows the student to have during exams may have good incremental validity. This is so because it reflects a different aspect of preparing for exams (resting) from the first predictor (studying). Incremental validity has been used to improve the prediction of job performance for Marine Corps mechanics (Carey, 1994) and the prediction of child abuse (Murphy-Berman, 1994). In both instances, predictor measures were included only if they demonstrated that they could explain something about the criterion measure that was not already known from the other predictors.

Construct Validity

Construct validity is a judgment about the appropriateness of inferences drawn from test scores regarding individual standings on a variable called a *construct*. A **construct** is an informed, scientific idea developed or hypothesized to describe or explain behavior. *Intelligence* is a construct that may be invoked to describe why a student performs well in school. *Anxiety* is a construct that may be invoked to describe why a psychiatric patient paces the floor. Other examples of constructs are *job satisfaction, personality, bigotry, clerical aptitude, depression, motivation, self-esteem, emotional adjustment, potential dangerousness, executive potential, creativity,* and *mechanical comprehension,* to name but a few.

Constructs are unobservable, presupposed (underlying) traits that a test developer may invoke to describe test behavior or criterion performance. The researcher investigating a test's construct validity must formulate hypotheses about the expected behavior of high scorers and low scorers on the test. These hypotheses give rise to a tentative theory about the nature of the construct the test was designed to measure. If the test is a valid measure of the construct, then high scorers and low scorers will behave as predicted by the theory. If high scorers and low scorers on the test do not behave as predicted, the investigator will need to reexamine the nature of the construct itself or hypotheses made about it. One possible reason for obtaining results contrary to those predicted by the theory is that the test simply does not measure the construct. An alternative explanation could lie in the theory that generated hypotheses about the construct. The theory may need to be reexamined.

In some instances, the reason for obtaining contrary findings can be traced to the statistical procedures used or to the way the procedures were executed. One procedure may have been more appropriate than another, given the particular assumptions. Thus, although confirming evidence contributes to a judgment that a test is a valid measure of a construct, evidence to the contrary can also be useful. Contrary evidence can provide a stimulus for the discovery of new facets of the construct as well as alternative methods of measurement.

Traditionally, construct validity has been viewed as the unifying concept for all validity evidence (American Educational Research Association et al., 1999). As we noted at the outset, all types of validity evidence, including evidence from the content- and criterion-related varieties of validity, come under the umbrella of construct validity. Let's look at the types of evidence that might be gathered.

Evidence of Construct Validity

A number of procedures may be used to provide different kinds of evidence that a test has construct validity. The various techniques of construct validation may provide evidence, for example, that

- the test is homogeneous, measuring a single construct;
- test scores increase or decrease as a function of age, the passage of time, or an experimental manipulation as theoretically predicted;
- test scores obtained after some event or the mere passage of time (or, posttest scores) differ from pretest scores as theoretically predicted;
- test scores obtained by people from distinct groups vary as predicted by the theory;
- test scores correlate with scores on other tests in accordance with what would be predicted from a theory that covers the manifestation of the construct in question.

A brief discussion of each type of construct validity evidence and the procedures used to obtain it follows.

Evidence of homogeneity   When describing a test and its items, **homogeneity** refers to how uniform a test is in measuring a single concept. A test developer can increase test homogeneity in several ways. Consider, for example, a test of academic achievement that contains subtests in areas such as mathematics, spelling, and reading comprehension. The Pearson r could be used to correlate average subtest scores with the average total test score. Subtests that in the test developer's judgment do not correlate very well with the test as a whole might have to be reconstructed (or eliminated) lest the test not measure the construct *academic achievement*. Correlations between subtest scores and total test score are generally reported in the test manual as evidence of homogeneity.

One way a test developer can improve the homogeneity of a test containing items that are scored dichotomously (such as a true-false test) is by eliminating items that do not show significant correlation coefficients with total test scores. If all test items show significant, positive correlations with total test scores and if high scorers on the test tend to pass each item more than low scorers do, then each item is probably measuring the same construct as the total test. Each item is contributing to test homogeneity.

The homogeneity of a test in which items are scored on a multipoint scale can also be improved. For example, some attitude and opinion questionnaires require respondents to indicate level of agreement with specific statements by responding, for example, *strongly agree, agree, disagree,* or *strongly disagree.* Each response is assigned a numerical score, and items that do not show significant Spearman rank-order correlation coefficients are eliminated. If all test items show significant, positive correlations with total test scores, then each item is most likely measuring the same construct that the test as a whole is measuring (and is thereby contributing to the test's homogeneity). Coefficient alpha may also be used in estimating the homogeneity of a test composed of multiple-choice items (Novick & Lewis, 1967).

As a case study illustrating how a test's homogeneity can be improved, consider the Marital Satisfaction Scale (MSS; Roach et al., 1981). Designed to assess various aspects of married people's attitudes toward their marital relationship, the MSS contains an approximately equal number of items expressing positive and negative sentiments with respect to marriage. For example, *My life would seem empty without my marriage* and *My marriage has "smothered" my personality.* In one stage of the development of this test, subjects indicated how much they agreed or disagreed with the various sentiments in each of 73 items by marking a 5-point scale that ranged from *strongly agree* to *strongly disagree.* Based on the correlations between item scores and total score, the test developers elected to retain 48 items with correlation coefficients greater than .50, thus creating a more homogeneous instrument.

Item-analysis procedures have also been employed in the quest for test homogeneity. One item-analysis procedure focuses on the relationship between testtakers' scores on individual items and their score on the entire test. Each item is analyzed with respect to how high scorers versus low scorers responded to it. If it is an academic test and if high scorers on the entire test for some reason tended to get that particular item wrong while low scorers on the test as a whole tended to get the item right, the item is obviously not a good one. The item should be eliminated in the interest of test homogeneity, among other considerations. If the test is one of marital satisfaction, and if individuals who score high on the test as a whole respond to a particular item in a way that would indicate that they are not satisfied whereas people who tend not to be satisfied respond to the item in a way that would indicate that they are satisfied, then again the item should probably be eliminated or at least reexamined for clarity.

JUST THINK . . .

Is it possible for a test to be *too* homogeneous in item content?

Although test homogeneity is desirable because it assures us that all the items on the test tend to be measuring the same thing, it is not the be-all and end-all of construct validity. Knowing that a test is homogeneous contributes no information about how the construct being measured relates to other constructs. It is therefore important to report evidence of a test's homogeneity along with other evidence of construct validity.

Evidence of changes with age Some constructs are expected to change over time. *Reading rate,* for example, tends to increase dramatically year by year from age 6 to the early teens. If a test score purports to be a measure of a construct that could be expected to change over time, then the test score, too, should show the same progressive changes with age to be considered a valid measure of the construct. For example, if children in grades 6, 7, 8, and 9 took a test of eighth-grade vocabulary, then we would expect that the total number of items scored as correct from all the test protocols would increase as a function of the higher grade level of the testtakers.

Some constructs lend themselves more readily than others to predictions of change over time. Thus, although we may be able to predict that a gifted child's scores on a test of reading skills will increase over the course of the testtaker's years of elementary and secondary education, we may not be able to predict with such confidence how a newlywed couple will score through the years on a test of marital satisfaction. This fact does not relegate a construct such as *marital satisfaction* to a lower stature than *reading ability.* Rather, it simply means that measures of marital satisfaction may be less stable over time or more vulnerable to situational events (such as in-laws coming to visit and refusing to leave for three months) than is reading ability. Evidence of change over time, like evidence of test homogeneity, does not in itself provide information about how the construct relates to other constructs.

Evidence of pretest–posttest changes   Evidence that test scores change as a result of some experience between a pretest and a posttest can be evidence of construct validity. Some of the more typical intervening experiences responsible for changes in test scores are formal education, a course of therapy or medication, and on-the-job experience. Of course, depending on the construct being measured, almost any intervening life experience could be predicted to yield changes in score from pretest to posttest. Reading an inspirational book, watching a TV talk show, undergoing surgery, serving a prison sentence, or the mere passage of time may each prove to be a potent intervening variable.

Returning to our example of the Marital Satisfaction Scale, one investigator cited in Roach et al. (1981) compared scores on that instrument before and after a sex therapy treatment program. Scores showed a significant change between pretest and posttest. A second posttest given eight weeks later showed that scores remained stable (suggesting the instrument was reliable), whereas the pretest–posttest measures were still significantly different. Such changes in scores in the predicted direction after the treatment program contribute to evidence of the construct validity for this test.

We would expect a decline in marital satisfaction scores if a pretest were administered to a sample of couples shortly after they took their nuptial vows and a posttest were administered shortly after members of the couples consulted their respective divorce attorneys sometime within the first five years of marriage. The experimental group in this study would consist of couples who consulted a divorce attorney within the first five years of marriage. The design of such pretest–posttest research ideally should include a control group to rule out alternative explanations of the findings.

> **JUST THINK . . .**
>
> Might it have been advisable to have simultaneous testing of a matched group of couples who did not participate in sex therapy and simultaneous testing of a matched group of couples who did not consult divorce attorneys? In both instances, would there have been any reason to expect any significant changes in the test scores of these two control groups?

Evidence from distinct groups   Also referred to as the **method of contrasted groups,** one way of providing evidence for the validity of a test is to demonstrate that scores on the test vary in a predictable way as a function of membership in some group. The rationale here is that if a test is a valid measure of a particular construct, then test scores from groups of people who would be presumed to differ with respect to that construct should have correspondingly different test scores. Consider in this context a test of depression wherein the higher the test score, the more depressed the testtaker is presumed to be. We would expect individuals psychiatrically hospitalized for depression to score higher on this measure than a random sample of Walmart shoppers.

Now, suppose it was your intention to provide construct validity evidence for the Marital Satisfaction Scale by showing differences in scores between distinct groups. How might you go about doing that?

Roach and colleagues (1981) proceeded by identifying two groups of married couples, one relatively satisfied in their marriage, the other not so satisfied. The groups were identified by ratings by peers and professional marriage counselors. A *t* test on the difference between mean score on the test was significant ($p < .01$)—evidence to support the notion that the Marital Satisfaction Scale is indeed a valid measure of the construct *marital satisfaction.*

In a bygone era, the method many test developers used to create distinct groups was deception. For example, if it had been predicted that more of the construct would be exhibited on the test in question if the subject felt highly anxious, an experimental situation might be designed to make the subject feel highly anxious. Virtually any feeling state the theory called for could be induced by an experimental scenario that typically involved giving the research subject some misinformation. However, given the ethical constraints of contemporary psychologists and the reluctance of academic institutions and other sponsors of research to condone deception in human research, the method of obtaining distinct groups by creating them through the dissemination of deceptive information is frowned upon (if not prohibited) today.

Convergent evidence   Evidence for the construct validity of a particular test may converge from a number of sources, such as other tests or measures designed to assess the same (or a similar) construct. Thus, if scores on the test undergoing construct validation tend to correlate highly in the predicted direction with scores on older, more established, and already validated tests designed to measure the same (or a similar) construct, this would be an example of **convergent evidence.**[3]

Convergent evidence for validity may come not only from correlations with tests purporting to measure an identical construct but also from correlations with measures purporting to measure related constructs. Consider, for example, a new test designed to measure the construct *test anxiety.* Generally speaking, we might expect high positive correlations between this new test and older, more established measures of test anxiety. However, we might also expect more moderate correlations between this new test and measures of general anxiety.

Roach et al. (1981) provided convergent evidence of the construct validity of the Marital Satisfaction Scale by computing a validity coefficient between scores on it and scores on the Marital Adjustment Test (Locke & Wallace, 1959). The validity coefficient of .79 provided additional evidence of their instrument's construct validity.

Discriminant evidence   A validity coefficient showing little (a statistically insignificant) relationship between test scores and/or other variables with which scores on the test being construct-validated should *not* theoretically be correlated provides **discriminant evidence** of construct validity (also known as *discriminant validity*). In the course of developing the Marital Satisfaction Scale (MSS), its authors correlated scores on that instrument with scores on the Marlowe-Crowne Social Desirability Scale (Crowne & Marlowe, 1964). Roach et al. (1981) hypothesized that high correlations between these two instruments would suggest that respondents were probably not answering items on the MSS entirely honestly but instead were responding in socially desirable ways. But the correlation between the MSS and the social desirability measure did not prove to be significant, so the test developers concluded that social desirability could be ruled out as a primary factor in explaining the meaning of MSS test scores.

In 1959 an experimental technique useful for examining both convergent and discriminant validity evidence was presented in *Psychological Bulletin.* This rather technical procedure was called the **multitrait-multimethod matrix.** A detailed description of it, along with an

---

3. Data indicating that a test measures the same construct as other tests purporting to measure the same construct are also referred to as evidence of **convergent validity.** One question that may be raised here concerns the necessity for the new test if it simply duplicates existing tests that measure the same construct. The answer, generally speaking, is a claim that the new test has some advantage over the more established test. For example, the new test may be shorter and capable of being administered in less time without significant loss in reliability or validity. On a practical level, the new test may be less costly.

illustration, can be found in OOBAL-6-B1. Here, let's simply point out that *multitrait* means "two or more traits" and *multimethod* means "two or more methods." The multitrait-multimethod matrix (Campbell & Fiske, 1959) is the matrix or table that results from correlating variables (traits) within and between methods. Values for any number of traits (such as aggressiveness or extraversion) as obtained by various methods (such as behavioral observation or a personality test) are inserted into the table, and the resulting matrix of correlations provides insight with respect to both the convergent and the discriminant validity of the methods used.[4]

Factor analysis   Both convergent and discriminant evidence of construct validity can be obtained by the use of factor analysis. **Factor analysis** is a shorthand term for a class of mathematical procedures designed to identify *factors* or specific variables that are typically attributes, characteristics, or dimensions on which people may differ. In psychometric research, factor analysis is frequently employed as a data reduction method in which several sets of scores and the correlations between them are analyzed. In such studies, the purpose of the factor analysis may be to identify the factor or factors in common between test scores on subscales within a particular test, or the factors in common between scores on a series of tests. In general, factor analysis is conducted on either an exploratory or a confirmatory basis. **Exploratory factor analysis** typically entails "estimating, or extracting factors; deciding how many factors to retain; and rotating factors to an interpretable orientation" (Floyd & Widaman, 1995, p. 287). By contrast, in **confirmatory factor analysis,** researchers test the degree to which a hypothetical model (which includes factors) fits the actual data.

A term commonly employed in factor analysis is **factor loading,** which is "a sort of metaphor. Each test is thought of as a vehicle carrying a certain amount of one or more abilities" (Tyler, 1965, p. 44). Factor loading in a test conveys information about the extent to which the factor determines the test score or scores. A new test purporting to measure bulimia, for example, can be factor-analyzed with other known measures of bulimia, as well as with other kinds of measures (such as measures of intelligence, self-esteem, general anxiety, anorexia, or perfectionism). High factor loadings by the new test on a "bulimia factor" would provide convergent evidence of construct validity. Moderate to low factor loadings by the new test with respect to measures of other eating disorders such as anorexia would provide discriminant evidence of construct validity.

Factor analysis frequently involves technical procedures so complex that few contemporary researchers would attempt to conduct one without the aid of sophisticated software. But although the actual data analysis has become work for computers, humans still tend to be very much involved in the *naming* of factors once the computer has identified them. Thus, for example, suppose a factor analysis identified a common factor being measured by two hypothetical instruments, a "Bulimia Test" and an "Anorexia Test." This common factor would have to be named. One factor analyst looking at the data and the items of each test might christen the common factor an *eating disorder factor.* Another factor analyst examining exactly the same materials might label the common factor a *body weight preoccupation factor.* A third analyst might name the factor a *self-perception disorder factor.* Which of these is correct?

From a statistical perspective, it is simply impossible to say what the common factor should be named. Naming factors that emerge from a factor analysis has more to do with knowledge, judgment, and verbal abstraction ability than with mathematical expertise. There are no hard-and-fast rules. Factor analysts exercise their own judgment about what factor name best communicates the meaning of the factor. Further, even the criteria used to identify a common factor, as well as related technical matters, can be a matter of debate, if not heated controversy.

---

4. For an interesting real-life application of the multitrait-multimethod technique as used to better understand tests, see Storholm et al. (2011). The researchers used this technique to explore construct validity-related questions regarding a test called the Compulsive Sexual Behavior Inventory.

◆
JUST THINK . . .

What might be an example of a valid test
used in an unfair manner?

Factor analysis is a subject rich in technical complexity. Its uses and applications can vary as a function of the research objectives as well as the nature of the tests and the constructs under study. Factor analysis is the subject of our *Close-Up* in Chapter 9. More immediately, our *Close-Up* here brings together much of the information imparted so far in this chapter to provide a "real life" example of the test validation process.

Validity, Bias, and Fairness

In the eyes of many laypeople, questions concerning the validity of a test are intimately tied to questions concerning the fair use of tests and the issues of bias and fairness. Let us hasten to point out that validity, fairness in test use, and test bias are three separate issues. It is possible, for example, for a valid test to be used fairly or unfairly.

Test Bias

For the general public, the term *bias* as applied to psychological and educational tests may conjure up many meanings having to do with prejudice and preferential treatment (Brown et al., 1999). For federal judges, the term *bias* as it relates to items on children's intelligence tests is synonymous with "too difficult for one group as compared to another" (Sattler, 1991). For psychometricians, **bias** is a factor inherent in a test that systematically prevents accurate, impartial measurement.

Psychometricians have developed the technical means to identify and remedy bias, at least in the mathematical sense. As a simple illustration, consider a test we will call the "flip-coin test" (FCT). The "equipment" needed to conduct this test is a two-sided coin. One side ("heads") has the image of a profile and the other side ("tails") does not. The FCT would be considered biased if the instrument (the coin) were weighted so that either heads or tails appears more frequently than by chance alone. If the test in question were an intelligence test, the test would be considered biased if it were constructed so that people who had brown eyes consistently and systematically obtained higher scores than people with green eyes—assuming, of course, that in reality people with brown eyes are not generally more intelligent than people with green eyes. *Systematic* is a key word in our definition of test bias. We have previously looked at sources of *random* or chance variation in test scores. *Bias* implies *systematic* variation.

Another illustration: Let's suppose we need to hire 50 secretaries and so we place an ad in the newspaper. In response to the ad, 200 people reply, including 100 people who happen to have brown eyes and 100 people who happen to have green eyes. Each of the 200 applicants is individually administered a hypothetical test we will call the "Test of Secretarial Skills" (TSS). Logic tells us that eye color is probably not a relevant variable with respect to performing the duties of a secretary. We would therefore have no reason to believe that green-eyed people are better secretaries than brown-eyed people or vice versa. We might reasonably expect that, after the tests have been scored and the selection process has been completed, an approximately equivalent number of brown-eyed and green-eyed people would have been hired (or, approximately 25 brown-eyed people and 25 green-eyed people). But what if it turned out that 48 green-eyed people were hired and only 2 brown-eyed people were hired? Is this evidence that the TSS is a biased test?

Although the answer to this question seems simple on the face of it—"Yes, the test is biased because they should have hired 25 and 25!"—a truly responsible answer to this question would entail statistically troubleshooting the test and the entire selection procedure (see Berk, 1982). One reason some tests have been found to be biased has more to do with the design of the research study than the design of the test. For example, if there are too few testtakers in one of the groups (such as the minority group—literally), this methodological problem will make it appear as if the test is biased when in fact it may not be. A test may justifiably be

The Preliminary Validation of a Measure of Individual Differences in Constructive Versus Unconstructive Worry*

Establishing validity is an important step in the development of new psychological measures. The development of a questionnaire that measures individual differences in worry called the Constructive and Unconstructive Worry Questionnaire (CUWQ; McNeill & Dunlop, 2016) provides an illustration of some of the steps in the test validation process.

Prior to the development of this questionnaire, research on worry had shown that the act of worrying can lead to both positive outcomes (such as increased work performance; Perkins & Corr, 2005) and negative outcomes (such as insomnia; Carney & Waters, 2006). Importantly, findings suggested that the types of worrying thoughts that lead to positive outcomes (which are referred to by the test authors as *constructive worry*) may differ from the types of worrying thoughts that lead to negative outcomes (referred to as *unconstructive worry*). However, a review of existing measures of individual differences in worry suggested that none of the measures were made to distinguish people's tendency to worry constructively from their tendency to worry unconstructively. Since the ability to determine whether individuals are predominantly worrying constructively or unconstructively holds diagnostic and therapeutic benefits, the test authors set out to fill this gap and develop a new questionnaire that would be able to capture both these dimensions of the worry construct.

During the first step of questionnaire development, the creation of an item pool, it was important to ensure the questionnaire would have good content validity. That is, the items would need to adequately sample the variety of characteristics of constructive and unconstructive worry. Based on the test authors' definition of these two constructs, a literature review was conducted and a list of potential characteristics of constructive versus unconstructive worry was created. This list of characteristics was used to develop a pool of 40 items. These 40 items were cross checked by each author, as well as one independent expert, to ensure that each item was unique and concise. A review of the list as a whole was conducted to ensure that it covered the full range of characteristics identified by the literature review. This process resulted in the elimination of 11 of the initial items, leaving a pool of 29 items. Of the 29 items in total, 13 items were expected to measure the tendency to worry constructively, and the remaining 16 items were expected to measure the tendency to worry unconstructively.

*This *Close-Up* was guest-authored by Ilona M. McNeill of The University of Melbourne, and Patrick D. Dunlop of The University of Western Australia.

Next, drawing from the theoretical background behind the test authors' definition of constructive and unconstructive worry, a range of criteria that should be differentially related to one's tendency to worry constructively versus unconstructively were selected. More specifically, it was hypothesized that the tendency to worry unconstructively would be *positively* related to trait-anxiety (State Trait Anxiety Inventory (STAI-T); Spielberger et al., 1970) and amount of worry one experiences (e.g., Worry Domains Questionnaire (WDQ); Stöber & Joormann, 2001). In addition, this tendency to worry unconstructively was hypothesized to be *negatively* related to one's tendency to be punctual and one's actual performance of risk-mitigating behaviors. The tendency to worry constructively, on the other hand, was hypothesized to be *negatively* related to trait-anxiety and amount of worry, and *positively* related to one's tendency to be punctual and one's performance of risk-mitigating behaviors. Identification of these criteria prior to data collection would pave the way for the test authors to conduct an evaluation of the questionnaire's criterion-based construct-validity in the future.

Upon completion of item pool construction and criterion identification, two studies were conducted. In Study 1, data from 295 participants from the United States was collected on the 29 newly developed worry items, plus two criterion-based measures, namely trait-anxiety and punctuality. An exploratory factor analysis was conducted, and the majority of the 29 items grouped together into a two-factor solution (as expected). The items predicted to capture a tendency to worry constructively loaded strongly on one factor, and the items predicted to capture a tendency to worry unconstructively loaded strongly on the other factor. However, 11 out of the original 29 items either did not load strongly on either factor, or they cross-loaded onto the other factor to a moderate extent. To increase construct validity through increased homogeneity of the two scales, these 11 items were removed from the final version of the questionnaire. The 18 items that remained included eight that primarily loaded on the factor labeled as constructive worry and ten that primarily loaded on the factor labeled as unconstructive worry.

A confirmatory factor analysis on these 18 items showed a good model fit. However, this analysis does not *prove* that these two factors actually captured the tendencies to worry constructively and unconstructively. To test the construct validity of these factor scores, the relations of the unconstructive and constructive worry factors with both trait-anxiety (Spielberger et al., 1970)

(continued)

The Preliminary Validation of a Measure of Individual Differences in Constructive Versus Unconstructive Worry (*continued*)

and the tendency to be punctual were examined. Results supported the hypotheses and supported an assumption of criterion-based construct validity. That is, as hypothesized, scores on the constructive worry factor were negatively associated with trait-anxiety and positively associated with the tendency to be punctual. Scores on the Unconstructive Worry factor were positively associated with trait-anxiety and negatively associated with the tendency to be punctual.

To further test the construct validity of this newly developed measure, a second study was conducted. In Study 2, data from 998 Australian residents of wildfire-prone areas responded to the 18 (final) worry items from Study 1, plus two additional items, respectively, capturing two additional criteria. These two additional criteria were (1) the amount of worry one tends to experience as captured by two existing worry questionnaires, namely the Worry Domains Questionnaire (Stöber & Joormann, 2001) and the Penn State Worry Questionnaire (Meyer et al., 1990), and (2) the performance of risk-mitigating behaviors that reduce the risk of harm or property damage resulting from a potential wildfire threat. A confirmatory factor analysis on this second data set supported the notion that constructive worry versus unconstructive worry items were indeed capturing separate constructs in a homogenous manner. Furthermore, as hypothesized, the constructive worry factor was positively associated with the performance of wildfire risk-mitigating behaviors, and negatively associated with the amount of worry one experiences. The unconstructive worry factor,

on the other hand, was negatively associated with the performance of wildfire risk-mitigating behaviors, and positively associated with the amount of worry one experiences. This provided further criterion-based construct validity.

There are several ways in which future studies could provide additional evidence of construct validity of the CUWQ. For one, both studies reported above looked at the two scales' concurrent criterion-based validity, but not at their predictive criterion-based validity. Future studies could focus on filling this gap. For example, since both constructs are hypothesized to predict the experience of anxiety (which was confirmed by the scales' relationships with trait-anxiety in Study 1), they should predict the likelihood of an individual being diagnosed with an anxiety disorder in the future, with unconstructive worry being a positive predictor and constructive worry being a negative predictor. Furthermore, future studies could provide additional evidence of construct validity by testing whether interventions, such as therapy aimed at reducing unconstructive worry, can lead to a reduction in scores on the unconstructive worry scale over time. Finally, it is important to note that all validity testing to date has been conducted in samples from the general population, so the test should be further tested in samples from a clinical population of pathological worriers before test validity in this population can be assumed. The same applies to the use of the questionnaire in samples from non-US/Australian populations.

deemed biased if some portion of its variance stems from some factor(s) that are irrelevant to performance on the criterion measure; as a consequence, one group of testtakers will systematically perform differently from another. Prevention during test development is the best cure for test bias, though a procedure called *estimated true score transformations* represents one of many available *post hoc* remedies (Mueller, 1949; see also Reynolds & Brown, 1984).[5]

Rating error A **rating** is a numerical or verbal judgment (or both) that places a person or an attribute along a continuum identified by a scale of numerical or word descriptors known as a **rating scale.** Simply stated, a **rating error** is a judgment resulting from the intentional or unintentional misuse of a rating scale. Thus, for example, a **leniency error** (also known as a **generosity error**) is, as its name implies, an error in rating that arises from the tendency on the part of the rater to be lenient in scoring, marking, and/or grading. From your own experience during course registration, you might be aware that a section of a particular course will quickly

---

5. Lest you think that there is something not quite right about transforming data under such circumstances, we add that even though *transformation* is synonymous with *change,* the change referred to here is merely a change in form, not meaning. Data may be transformed to place them in a more useful form, not to change their meaning.

be filled if it is being taught by a professor with a reputation for leniency errors in end-of-term grading. As another possible example of a leniency or generosity error, consider comments in the "Twittersphere" after a high-profile performance of a popular performer. Intuitively, one would expect more favorable (and forgiving) ratings of the performance from die-hard fans of the performer, regardless of the actual quality of the performance as rated by more objective reviewers. The phenomenon of leniency and severity in ratings can be found mostly in any setting that ratings are rendered. In psychotherapy settings, for example, it is not unheard of for supervisors to be a bit too generous or too lenient in their ratings of their supervisees.

Reviewing the literature on psychotherapy supervision and supervision in other disciplines, Gonsalvez and Crowe (2014) concluded that raters' judgments of psychotherapy supervisees' competency are compromised by leniency errors. In an effort to remedy the state of affairs, they offered a series of concrete suggestions including a list of specific competencies to be evaluated, as well as when and how such evaluations for competency should be conducted.

JUST THINK . . .

What factor do you think might account for the phenomenon of raters whose ratings always seem to fall victim to the central tendency error?

At the other extreme is a **severity error.** Movie critics who pan just about everything they review may be guilty of severity errors. Of course, that is only true if they review a wide range of movies that might consensually be viewed as good and bad.

Another type of error might be termed a **central tendency error.** Here the rater, for whatever reason, exhibits a general and systematic reluctance to giving ratings at either the positive or the negative extreme. Consequently, all of this rater's ratings would tend to cluster in the middle of the rating continuum.

One way to overcome what might be termed *restriction-of-range rating errors* (central tendency, leniency, severity errors) is to use **rankings,** a procedure that requires the rater to measure individuals against one another instead of against an absolute scale. By using rankings instead of ratings, the rater (now the "ranker") is forced to select first, second, third choices, and so forth.

Halo effect describes the fact that, for some raters, some ratees can do no wrong. More specifically, a halo effect may also be defined as a tendency to give a particular ratee a higher rating than he or she objectively deserves because of the rater's failure to discriminate among conceptually distinct and potentially independent aspects of a ratee's behavior. Just for the sake of example—and not for a moment because we believe it is even in the realm of possibility— let's suppose Lady Gaga consented to write and deliver a speech on multivariate analysis. Her speech probably would earn much higher all-around ratings if given before the founding chapter of the Lady Gaga Fan Club than if delivered before and rated by the membership of, say, the Royal Statistical Society. This would be true even in the highly improbable case that the members of each group were equally savvy with respect to multivariate analysis. We would expect the halo effect to be operative at full power as Lady Gaga spoke before her diehard fans.

Criterion data may also be influenced by the rater's knowledge of the ratee's race or sex (Landy & Farr, 1980). Males have been shown to receive more favorable evaluations than females in traditionally masculine occupations. Except in highly integrated situations, ratees tend to receive higher ratings from raters of the same race (Landy & Farr, 1980). Returning to our hypothetical Test of Secretarial Skills (TSS) example, a particular rater may have had particularly great—or particularly distressing—prior experiences with green-eyed (or brown-eyed) people and so may be making extraordinarily high (or low) ratings on that irrational basis.

Training programs to familiarize raters with common rating errors and sources of rater bias have shown promise in reducing rating errors and increasing measures of reliability and validity. Lecture, role playing, discussion, watching oneself on videotape, and computer simulation of different situations are some of the many techniques that could be brought to bear in such training programs. We revisit the subject of rating and rating error in our discussion of personality assessment later. For now, let's take up the issue of test fairness.

Adjustment of Test Scores by Group Membership: Fairness in Testing or Foul Play? (*continued*)

Table 1
Psychometric Techniques for Preventing or Remedying Adverse Impact and/or Instituting an Affirmative Action Program

Some of these techniques may be preventive if employed in the test development process, and others may be employed with already established tests. Some of these techniques entail direct score manipulation; others, such as banding, do not. Preparation of this table benefited from Sackett and Wilk (1994), and their work should be consulted for more detailed consideration of the complex issues involved.

Technique	Description
Addition of Points	A constant number of points is added to the test score of members of a particular group. The purpose of the point addition is to reduce or eliminate observed differences between groups.
Differential Scoring of Items	This technique incorporates group membership information, not in adjusting a raw score on a test but in deriving the score in the first place. The application of the technique may involve the scoring of some test items for members of one group but not scoring the same test items for members of another group. This technique is also known as *empirical keying by group*.
Elimination of Items Based on Differential Item Functioning	This procedure entails removing from a test any items found to inappropriately favor one group's test performance over another's. Ideally, the intent of the elimination of certain test items is not to make the test easier for any group but simply to make the test fairer. Sackett and Wilk (1994) put it this way: "Conceptually, rather than asking 'Is this item harder for members of Group X than it is for Group Y?' these approaches ask 'Is this item harder for members of Group X with true score Z than it is for members of Group Y with true score Z?'"
Differential Cutoffs	Different cutoffs are set for members of different groups. For example, a passing score for members of one group is 65, whereas a passing score for members of another group is 70. As with the addition of points, the purpose of differential cutoffs is to reduce or eliminate observed differences between groups.
Separate Lists	Different lists of testtaker scores are established by group membership. For each list, test performance of testtakers is ranked in top-down fashion. Users of the test scores for selection purposes may alternate selections from the different lists. Depending on factors such as the allocation rules in effect and the equivalency of the standard deviation within the groups, the separate-lists technique may yield effects similar to those of other techniques, such as the addition of points and differential cutoffs. In practice, the separate list is popular in affirmative action programs where the intent is to overselect from previously excluded groups.
Within-Group Norming	Used as a remedy for adverse impact if members of different groups tend to perform differentially on a particular test, within-group norming entails the conversion of all raw scores into percentile scores or standard scores based on the test performance of one's own group. In essence, an individual testtaker is being compared only with other members of his or her own group. When race is the primary criterion of group membership and separate norms are established by race, this technique is known as *race-norming*.
Banding	The effect of banding of test scores is to make equivalent all scores that fall within a particular range or band. For example, thousands of raw scores on a test may be transformed to a stanine having a value of 1 to 9. All scores that fall within each of the stanine boundaries will be treated by the test user as either equivalent or subject to some additional selection criteria. A *sliding band* (Cascio et al., 1991) is a modified banding procedure wherein a band is adjusted ("slid") to permit the selection of more members of some group than would otherwise be selected.
Preference Policies	In the interest of affirmative action, reverse discrimination, or some other policy deemed to be in the interest of society at large, a test user might establish a policy of preference based on group membership. For example, if a municipal fire department sought to increase the representation of female personnel in its ranks, it might institute a test-related policy designed to do just that. A key provision in this policy might be that when a male and a female earn equal scores on the test used for hiring, the female will be hired.

J U S T   T H I N K . . .

How do *you* feel about the use of various procedures to adjust test scores on the basis of group membership? Are these types of issues best left to measurement experts?

If performance differences are found between identified groups of people on a valid and reliable test used for selection purposes, some hard questions may have to be dealt with if the test is to continue to be used. Is the problem due to some technical deficiency in the test, or is the test in reality too good at identifying people of different levels of ability? Regardless, is the test being used fairly? If so, what might society do to remedy the skill disparity between different groups as reflected on the test?

Our discussion of issues of test fairness and test bias may seem to have brought us far afield of the seemingly cut-and-dried, relatively nonemotional subject of test validity. However, the complex issues accompanying discussions of test validity, including issues of fairness and bias, must be wrestled with by us all. For further consideration of the philosophical issues involved, we refer you to the solitude of your own thoughts and the reading of your own conscience.

Self-Assessment

Test your understanding of elements of this chapter by seeing if you can explain each of the following terms, expressions, and abbreviations:

base rate	exploratory factor analysis	method of contrasted groups
bias	face validity	miss rate
central tendency error	factor analysis	multitrait-multimethod matrix
concurrent validity	factor loading	predictive validity
confirmatory factor analysis	fairness	ranking
construct	false negative	rating
construct validity	false positive	rating error
content validity	generosity error	rating scale
convergent evidence	halo effect	severity error
convergent validity	hit rate	slope bias
criterion	homogeneity	test blueprint
criterion contamination	incremental validity	validation
criterion-related validity	inference	validation study
discriminant evidence	intercept bias	validity
expectancy chart	leniency error	validity coefficient
expectancy data	local validation study	

7

Utility

In everyday language, we use the term *utility* to refer to the usefulness of some thing or some process. In the language of psychometrics, *utility* (also referred to as *test utility*) means much the same thing; it refers to how useful a test is. More specifically, it refers to the practical value of using a test to aid in decision making. An overview of some frequently raised utility-related questions would include the following:

- How useful is this test in terms of cost efficiency?

- How useful is this test in terms of savings in time?

- What is the *comparative utility* of this test? That is, how useful is this test as compared to another test?

- What is the *clinical utility* of this test? That is, how useful is it for purposes of diagnostic assessment or treatment?

- What is the *diagnostic utility* of this neurological test? That is, how useful is it for classification purposes?

- How useful is this medical school admissions test used in assigning a limited number of openings to an overwhelming number of applicants?

- How useful is the addition of another test to the test battery already in use for screening purposes?

- How useful is this personnel test as a tool for the selection of new employees?

- Is this particular personnel test used for promoting middle-management employees more useful than using no test at all?

- Is the time and money it takes to administer, score, and interpret this personnel promotion test battery worth it as compared to simply asking the employee's supervisor for a recommendation as to whether the employee should be promoted?

- How useful is the training program in place for new recruits?

- How effective is this particular clinical technique?

- Should this new intervention be used in place of an existing intervention?

What Is Utility?

We may define **utility** in the context of testing and assessment as the usefulness or practical value of testing to improve efficiency. Note that in this definition, "testing" refers to anything from a single test to a large-scale testing program that employs a battery of tests. For simplicity and convenience, in this chapter we often refer to the utility of one individual test. Keep in mind, however, that such discussion is applicable and generalizable to the utility of large-scale testing programs that may employ many tests or test batteries. *Utility* is also used to refer to the usefulness or practical value of a training program or intervention. We may speak, for example, of the utility of adding a particular component to an existing corporate training program or clinical intervention. Throughout this chapter, however, our discussion and illustrations will focus primarily on utility as it relates to testing.

JUST THINK . . .

Based on everything that you have read about tests and testing so far in this book, how do you think you would go about making a judgment regarding the utility of a test?

If your response to our *Just Think* question about judging a test's utility made reference to the reliability of a test or the validity of a test, then you are correct—well, partly. Judgments concerning the utility of a test are made on the basis of test reliability and validity data as well as on other data.

Factors That Affect a Test's Utility

A number of considerations are involved in making a judgment about the utility of a test. Here we will review how a test's psychometric soundness, costs, and benefits can all affect a judgment concerning a test's utility.

Psychometric soundness By psychometric soundness, we refer—as you probably know by now—to the reliability and validity of a test. A test is said to be psychometrically sound for a particular purpose if reliability and validity coefficients are acceptably high. How can an index of utility be distinguished from an index of reliability or validity? The short answer to that question is as follows: An index of reliability can tell us something about how consistently a test measures what it measures; and an index of validity can tell us something about whether a test measures what it purports to measure. But an index of utility can tell us something about the practical value of the information derived from scores on the test. Test scores are said to have utility if their use in a particular situation helps us to make better decisions—better, that is, in the sense of being more cost-effective (see, for example, Brettschneider et al., 2015; or Winser et al., 2015).

In previous chapters on reliability and validity, it was noted that reliability sets a ceiling on validity. It is tempting to draw the conclusion that a comparable relationship exists between validity and utility and conclude that "validity sets a ceiling on utility." In many instances, such a conclusion would certainly be defensible. After all, a test must be valid to be useful. Of what practical value or usefulness is a test for a specific purpose if the test is not valid for that purpose?

Unfortunately, few things about utility theory and its application are simple and uncomplicated. Generally speaking, the higher the criterion-related validity of test scores for making a particular decision, the higher the utility of the test is likely to be. However, there are exceptions to this general rule. This is so because many factors may enter into an estimate of a test's utility, and there are great variations in the ways in which the utility of a test is determined. In a study of the utility of a test used for personnel selection, for example, the selection ratio may be very high. We'll review the concept of a selection ratio (introduced in the previous chapter) in greater detail later in this chapter. For now, let's simply note that if the selection ratio is very high, most people who apply for the job are being hired. Under such circumstances, the validity of the test may have little to do with the test's utility.

What about the other side of the coin? Would it be accurate to conclude that "a valid test is a useful test"? At first blush this statement may also seem perfectly logical and true. But once again—we're talking about utility theory here, and this can be very complicated stuff—the answer is no; it is *not* the case that "a valid test is a useful test." People often refer to a particular test as "valid" if scores on the test have been shown to be good indicators of how the person will score on the criterion.

An example from the published literature may help to further illustrate how a valid tool of assessment may have questionable utility. One way of monitoring the drug use of cocaine users being treated on an outpatient basis is through regular urine tests. As an alternative to that monitoring method, researchers developed a patch which, if worn day and night, could detect cocaine use through sweat. In a study designed to explore the utility of the sweat patch with 63 opiate-dependent volunteers who were seeking treatment, investigators found a 92% level of agreement between a positive urine test for cocaine and a positive test on the sweat patch for cocaine. On the face of it, these results would seem to be encouraging for the developers of the patch. However, this high rate of agreement occurred only when the patch had been untampered with and properly applied by research participants—which, as it turned out, wasn't all that often. Overall, the researchers felt compelled to conclude that the sweat patch had limited utility as a means of monitoring drug use in outpatient treatment facilities (Chawarski et al., 2007). This study illustrates that even though a test may be psychometrically sound, it may have little utility—particularly if the targeted testtakers demonstrate a tendency to "bend, fold, spindle, mutilate, destroy, tamper with," or otherwise fail to scrupulously follow the test's directions.

Another utility-related factor does not necessarily have anything to do with the behavior of targeted testtakers. In fact, it typically has more to do with the behavior of the test's targeted *users*.

Costs   Mention the word *costs* and what comes to mind? Usually words like *money* or *dollars.* In considerations of test utility, factors variously referred to as *economic, financial,* or *budget-related* in nature must certainly be taken into account. In fact, one of the most basic elements in any utility analysis is the financial cost of the selection device (or training program or clinical intervention) under study. However, the meaning of "cost" as applied to test utility can extend far beyond dollars and cents (see Figure 7–1). Briefly, **cost** in the context of test utility refers to disadvantages, losses, or expenses in both economic and noneconomic terms.

As used with respect to test utility decisions, the term *costs* can be interpreted in the traditional, economic sense; that is, relating to expenditures associated with testing or not testing. If testing is to be conducted, then it may be necessary to allocate funds to purchase (1) a particular test, (2) a supply of blank test protocols, and (3) computerized test processing, scoring, and interpretation from the test publisher or some independent service. Associated

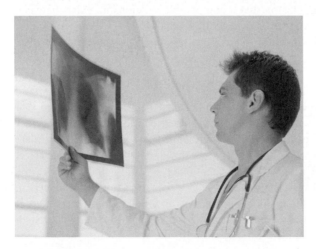

Figure 7–1
Rethinking the "Costs" of Testing—and of Not Testing

The cost of this X-ray might be $100 or so . . . but what is the cost of not having this diagnostic procedure done? Depending on the particular case, the cost of not testing might be unnecessary pain and suffering, lifelong disability, or worse. In sum, the decision to test or not must be made with thoughtful consideration of all possible pros and cons, financial and otherwise.

© Martin Barraud/age fotostock RF

costs of testing may come in the form of (1) payment to professional personnel and staff associated with test administration, scoring, and interpretation, (2) facility rental, mortgage, and/or other charges related to the usage of the test facility, and (3) insurance, legal, accounting, licensing, and other routine costs of doing business. In some settings, such as private clinics, these costs may be offset by revenue, such as fees paid by testtakers. In other settings, such as research organizations, these costs will be paid from the test user's funds, which may in turn derive from sources such as private donations or government grants.

The economic costs listed here are the easy ones to calculate. Not so easy to calculate are other economic costs, particularly those associated with not testing or testing with an instrument that turns out to be ineffective. As an admittedly far-fetched example, what if skyrocketing fuel costs prompted a commercial airline to institute cost-cutting methods?[1] What if one of the cost-cutting methods the airline instituted was the cessation of its personnel assessment program? Now, all personnel—including pilots and equipment repair personnel—would be hired and trained with little or no evaluation. Alternatively, what if the airline simply converted its current hiring and training program to a much less expensive program with much less rigorous (and perhaps ineffective) testing for all personnel? What economic (and noneconomic) consequences do you envision might result from such action? Would cost-cutting actions such as those described previously be prudent from a business perspective?

One need not hold an M.B.A. or an advanced degree in consumer psychology to understand that such actions on the part of the airline would probably not be effective. The resulting cost savings from elimination of such assessment programs would pale in comparison to the probable losses in customer revenue once word got out about the airline's strategy for cost cutting; loss of public confidence in the safety of the airline would almost certainly translate into a loss of ticket sales. Additionally, such revenue losses would be irrevocably compounded by any safety-related incidents (with their attendant lawsuits) that occurred as a consequence of such imprudent cost cutting.

In this example, mention of the variable of "loss of confidence" brings us to another meaning of "costs" in terms of utility analyses; that is, costs in terms of loss. Noneconomic costs of drastic cost cutting by the airline might come in the form of harm or injury to airline passengers and crew as a result of incompetent pilots flying the plane and incompetent ground crews servicing the planes. Although people (and most notably insurance companies) do place dollar amounts on the loss of life and limb, for our purposes we can still categorize such tragic losses as noneconomic in nature.

Other noneconomic costs of testing can be far more subtle. Consider, for example, a published study that examined the utility of taking four X-ray pictures as compared to two X-ray pictures in routine screening for fractured ribs among potential child abuse victims. Hansen et al. (2008) found that a four-view series of X-rays differed significantly from the more traditional, two-view series in terms of the number of fractures identified. These researchers recommended the addition of two more views in the routine X-ray protocols for possible physical abuse. Stated another way, these authors found diagnostic utility in adding two X-ray views to the more traditional protocol. The financial cost of using the two additional X-rays was seen as worth it, given the consequences and potential costs of failing to diagnose the injuries. Here, the (non-economic) cost concerns the risk of letting a potential child abuser continue to abuse a child without detection. In other medical research, such as that described by our featured assessment professional, the utility of various other tests and procedures are routinely evaluated (see this chapter's *Meet an Assessment Professional*).

> ## JUST THINK . . .
>
> How would you describe the non-economic cost of a nation's armed forces using ineffective screening mechanisms to screen military recruits?

---

1. This example may not be all that far-fetched. See *www.usatoday.com/travel/flights/2008-03-06-fine_N.htm*.

Meet Dr. Delphine Courvoisier

My name is Delphine Courvoisier. I hold a Ph.D. in psychometrics from the University of Geneva, Switzerland, and Master's degrees in statistics from the University of Geneva, in epidemiology from Harvard School of Public Health, and in human resources from the University of Geneva. I currently work as a biostatistician in the Department of Rheumatology, at the University Hospitals of Geneva, Switzerland. A typical work day for me entails consulting with clinicians about their research projects. Assistance from me may be sought at any stage in a research project. So, for example, I might help out one team of researchers in conceptualizing initial hypotheses. Another research team might require assistance in selecting the most appropriate outcome measures, given the population of subjects with whom they are working. Yet another team might request assistance with data analysis or interpretation. In addition to all of that, a work day typically includes providing a colleague with some technical or social support—this to counter the concern or discouragement that may have been engendered by some methodological or statistical complexity inherent in a project that they are working on.

Rheumatoid arthritis is a chronic disease. Patients with this disease frequently suffer pain and may have limited functioning. Among other variables, research team members may focus their attention on quality-of-life issues for members of this population. Quality-of-life research may be conducted at different points in time through the course of the disease. In conducting the research, various tools of assessment, including psychological tests and structured interviews, may be used.

The focus of my own research team has been on several overlapping variables, including health-related quality of life, degree of functional disability, and disease activity and progression. We measure health-related quality of life using the Short-Form 36 Health Survey (SF36). We measure functional disability by means of the Health Assessment Questionnaire (HAQ). We assess disease activity and progression by means of a structured interview conducted by a health-care professional. The interview yields a proprietary disease activity score

Delphine Courvoisier, Ph.D., Psychometrician and biostatistician at the Department of Rheumatology at the University Hospitals of Geneva, Switzerland.
© Delphine Courvoisier

(DAS). All these data are then employed to evaluate the effectiveness of various treatment regimens, and adjust, where necessary, patient treatment plans.

Since so much of our work involves evaluation by means of tests or other assessment procedures, it is important to examine the utility of the methods we use. For example, when a research project demands that subjects respond to a series of telephone calls, it would be instructive to understand how compliance (or, answering the phone and responding to the experimenter's questions) versus non-compliance (or, not answering the phone) affects the other variables under study. It may be, for example, that people who are more compliant are simply more conscientious. If that was indeed the case, all the data collected from people who answered the phone might be more causally related to a personality variable (such as conscientiousness) than anything else. Thus, prior to analyzing content of phone interviews, it would be useful to test—and reject—the hypothesis that only patients high on the personality trait of conscientiousness will answer the phone.

We conducted a study that entailed the administration of a personality test (the NEO Personality Inventory-Revised), as well as ecological momentary assessment (EMA) in the form of a series of phone interviews with subjects (Courvoisier et al., 2012). EMA is a tool of assessment that researchers can use to examine behaviors and subjective states in the settings in which they naturally occur, and at a frequency that can capture their variability. Through the use of EMA we learned, among other things, that subject compliance was not attributable to personality factors (see Courvoisier et al., 2012 for full details).

Being a psychometrician can be most fulfilling, especially when one's measurement-related knowledge and expertise brings added value to a research project that has exciting prospects for bettering the quality of life for members of a specific population. Psychologists who raise compelling research questions understand that the road to satisfactory answers is paved with psychometric essentials such as a sound research design, the use of appropriate measures, and accurate analysis and interpretation of findings. Psychometricians lend their expertise in these areas to help make research meaningful, replicable, generalizable, and actionable. From my own experience, one day I might be meeting with a

researcher to discuss why a particular test is (or is not) more appropriate as an outcome measure, given the unique design and objectives of the study. Another day might find me cautioning experimenters against the use of a spontaneously created, "home-made" questionnaire for the purpose of screening subjects. In such scenarios, a strong knowledge of psychometrics combined with a certain *savoir faire* in diplomacy would seem to be useful prerequisites to success.

I would advise any student who is considering or contemplating a career as a psychometrician to learn everything they can about measurement theory and practice. In addition, the student would do well to cultivate the interpersonal skills that will most certainly be needed to interact professionally and effectively with fellow producers and consumers of psychological research. Contrary to what many may hold as an intuitive truth, success in the world of psychometrics cannot be measured by numbers alone.

Used with permission of Delphine Courvoisier.

Benefits Judgments regarding the utility of a test may take into account whether the benefits of testing justify the costs of administering, scoring, and interpreting the test. So, when evaluating the utility of a particular test, an evaluation is made of the costs incurred by testing as compared to the benefits accrued from testing. Here, **benefit** refers to profits, gains, or advantages. As we did in discussing costs associated with testing (and not testing), we can view *benefits* in both economic and noneconomic terms.

From an economic perspective, the cost of administering tests can be minuscule when compared to the economic benefits—or financial returns in dollars and cents—that a successful testing program can yield. For example, if a new personnel testing program results in the selection of employees who produce significantly more than other employees, then the program will have been responsible for greater productivity on the part of the new employees. This greater productivity may lead to greater overall company profits. If a new method of quality control in a food-processing plant results in higher quality products and less product being trashed as waste, the net result will be greater profits for the company.

There are also many potential noneconomic benefits to be derived from thoughtfully designed and well-run testing programs. In industrial settings, a partial list of such noneconomic benefits—many carrying with them economic benefits as well—would include:

- an increase in the quality of workers' performance;
- an increase in the quantity of workers' performance;
- a decrease in the time needed to train workers;
- a reduction in the number of accidents;
- a reduction in worker turnover.

The cost of administering tests can be well worth it if the result is certain noneconomic benefits, such as a good work environment. As an example, consider the admissions program in place at most universities. Educational institutions that pride themselves on their graduates are often on the lookout for ways to improve the way that they select applicants for their programs. Why? Because it is to the credit of a university that their graduates succeed at their chosen careers. A large portion of happy, successful graduates enhances the university's reputation and sends the message that the university is doing something right. Related benefits to a university that has students who are successfully going through its programs may include high morale and a good learning environment for students, high morale of and a good work environment for the faculty, and reduced load on counselors and on disciplinary personnel and boards. With fewer students leaving the school before graduation for academic reasons, there might actually be less of a load on admissions personnel as well; the admissions office will not be constantly working to select students to replace those who have left before completing their degree programs. A good work environment and a good learning environment are not necessarily things that money can buy. Such outcomes can, however, result from a well-administered admissions program that consistently selects qualified students who will keep up with the work and "fit in" to the environment of a particular university.

One of the economic benefits of a diagnostic test used to make decisions about involuntary hospitalization of psychiatric patients is a benefit to society at large. Persons are frequently confined involuntarily for psychiatric reasons if they are harmful to themselves or others. Tools of psychological assessment such as tests, case history data, and interviews may be used to make a decision regarding involuntary psychiatric hospitalization. The more useful such tools of assessment are, the safer society will be from individuals intent on inflicting harm or injury. Clearly, the potential noneconomic benefit derived from the use of such diagnostic tools is great. It is also true, however, that the potential economic *costs* are great when errors are made. Errors in clinical determination made in cases of involuntary hospitalization may cause people who are not threats to themselves or others to be denied their freedom. The stakes involving the utility of tests can indeed be quite high.

JUST THINK . . .

Provide an example of another situation in which the stakes involving the utility of a tool of psychological assessment are high.

How do professionals in the field of testing and assessment balance variables such as psychometric soundness, benefits, and costs? How do they come to a judgment regarding the utility of a specific test? How do they decide that the benefits (however defined) outweigh the costs (however defined) and that a test or intervention indeed has utility? There are formulas that can be used with values that can be filled in, and there are tables that can be used with values to be looked up. We will introduce you to such methods in this chapter. But let's preface our discussion of utility analysis by emphasizing that other, less definable elements—such as prudence, vision, and, for lack of a better (or more technical) term, *common sense*—must be ever-present in the process. A psychometrically sound test of practical value is worth paying for, even when the dollar cost is high, if the potential benefits of its use are also high or if the potential costs of *not* using it are high. We have discussed "costs" and "benefits" at length in order to underscore that such matters cannot be considered solely in monetary terms.

Utility Analysis

What Is a Utility Analysis?

A **utility analysis** may be broadly defined as a family of techniques that entail a cost–benefit analysis designed to yield information relevant to a decision about the usefulness and/or practical value of a tool of assessment. Note that in this definition, we used the phrase "family of techniques." This is so because a utility analysis is not one specific technique used for one specific objective. Rather, *utility analysis* is an umbrella term covering various possible methods, each requiring various kinds of data to be inputted and yielding various kinds of output. Some utility analyses are quite sophisticated, employing high-level mathematical models and detailed strategies for weighting the different variables under consideration (Roth et al., 2001). Other utility analyses are far more straightforward and can be readily understood in terms of answers to relatively uncomplicated questions, such as: "Which test gives us more bang for the buck?"

In a most general sense, a utility analysis may be undertaken for the purpose of evaluating whether the benefits of using a test (or training program or intervention) outweigh the costs. If undertaken to evaluate a test, the utility analysis will help make decisions regarding whether:

- one test is preferable to another test for use for a specific purpose;
- one tool of assessment (such as a test) is preferable to another tool of assessment (such as behavioral observation) for a specific purpose;
- the addition of one or more tests (or other tools of assessment) to one or more tests (or other tools of assessment) that are already in use is preferable for a specific purpose;
- no testing or assessment is preferable to any testing or assessment.

If undertaken for the purpose of evaluating a training program or intervention, the utility analysis will help make decisions regarding whether:

- one training program is preferable to another training program;
- one method of intervention is preferable to another method of intervention;
- the addition or subtraction of elements to an existing training program improves the overall training program by making it more effective and efficient;
- the addition or subtraction of elements to an existing method of intervention improves the overall intervention by making it more effective and efficient;
- no training program is preferable to a given training program;
- no intervention is preferable to a given intervention.

The endpoint of a utility analysis is typically an educated decision about which of many possible courses of action is optimal. For example, in a now-classic utility analysis, Cascio and Ramos (1986) found that the use of a particular approach to assessment in selecting managers could save a telephone company more than $13 million over four years (see also Cascio, 1994, 2000).

Whether reading about utility analysis in this chapter or in other sources, a solid foundation in the language of this endeavor—both written and graphic—is essential. Toward that end, we hope you find the detailed case illustration presented in our *Close-Up* helpful.

How Is a Utility Analysis Conducted?

The specific objective of a utility analysis will dictate what sort of information will be required as well as the specific methods to be used. Here we will briefly discuss two general approaches to utility analysis. The first is an approach that employs data that should actually be quite familiar.

Expectancy data Some utility analyses will require little more than converting a scatterplot of test data to an expectancy table (much like the process described in the previous chapter). An expectancy table can provide an indication of the likelihood that a testtaker will score within some interval of scores on a criterion measure—an interval that may be categorized as "passing," "acceptable," or "failing." For example, with regard to the utility of a new and experimental personnel test in a corporate setting, an expectancy table can provide vital information to decision-makers. An expectancy table might indicate, for example, that the higher a worker's score is on this new test, the greater the probability that the worker will be judged successful. In other words, the test is working as it should and, by instituting this new test on a permanent basis, the company could reasonably expect to improve its productivity.

Utility Analysis: An Illustration *(continued)*

(4) Ensure, to the extent possible, that qualified candidates will be selected and unqualified candidates will be rejected.

This objective can be met by setting a cut score on the FERT that is helpful in (a) selecting for permanent positions those drivers who performed satisfactorily on the OTJSR, (b) eliminating from consideration those drivers who performed unsatisfactorily on the OTJSR, and (c) reducing the miss rate as much as possible. This approach to setting a cut score will yield the highest hit rate while allowing for FERT-related "misses" that may be either of the false-positive or false-negative variety. Here, false positives are seen as no better or worse than false negatives and vice versa.

It is seldom possible to "have it all ways." In other words, it is seldom possible to have the lowest false positive rate, the lowest false negative rate, the highest hit rate, and not incur any costs of testing. Which of the four listed objectives represents the best "fit" with your policies and the company's hiring objectives? Before responding, it may be helpful to review Table 1.

After reviewing Table 1 and all of the material on terms including *hit, miss, false positive,* and *false negative,* Dr. Carlos elects to *continue* and is presented with the following four options from which to choose.

1. Select applicants without using the FERT.

2. Use the FERT to select with the lowest false negative rate.

3. Use the FERT to select with the lowest false positive rate.

4. Use the FERT to yield the highest hit rate and lowest miss rate.

Curious about the outcome associated with each of these four options, Dr. Carlos wishes to explore all of them. She begins by selecting Option 1: *Select applicants without using the FERT.* Immediately, a graph (*Close-Up* Figure 1) and this prompt pop up:

Generally speaking, base rate is defined as the proportion of people in the population that possess a particular trait, behavior, characteristic, or attribute. In this study, base rate refers to the proportion of new hire drivers who would go on to perform satisfactorily on the criterion measure (the OTJSRs) and be deemed "qualified" regardless of whether or not a test such as the FERT existed (and regardless of their score on the FERT if it were administered). The base rate is represented in Figure 1 (and in all subsequent graphs) by the number of drivers whose OTJSRs fall above the dashed horizontal line (a line that refers to minimally acceptable performance on the OTJSR) as compared to the total number of scores. In other words, the base rate is equal to the ratio of qualified applicants to the total number of applicants.

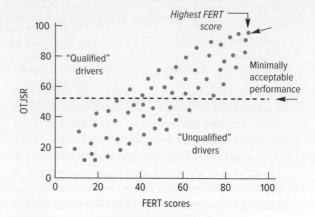

Figure 1
Base Rate Data for Federale Express

Before the use of the FERT, any applicant with a valid driver's license and no criminal record was hired for a permanent position as an FE driver. Drivers could be classified into two groups based on their on-the-job supervisory ratings (OTJSRs): those whose driving was considered to be satisfactory (located above the dashed horizontal line) and those whose driving was considered to be unsatisfactory (below the dashed line). Without use of the FERT, then, all applicants were hired and the selection ratio was 1.0; 60 drivers were hired out of the 60 applicants. However, the base rate of successful performance shown in Figure 1 was only .50. This means that only half of the drivers hired (30 of 60) were considered "qualified" drivers by their supervisor. This also shows a miss rate of .50, because half of the drivers turned out to perform below the minimally accepted level.

Yet because scores on the FERT and the OTJSRs are positively correlated, the FERT can be used to help select the individuals who are likely to be rated as qualified drivers. Thus, using the FERT is a good idea, but how should it be used? One method would entail top-down selection. That is, a permanent position could be offered first to the individual with the highest score on the FERT (top, rightmost case in Figure 1), followed by the individual with the next highest FERT score, and so on until all available positions are filled. As you can see in the figure, if permanent positions are offered only to individuals with the top 20 FERT scores, then OTJSR ratings of the permanent hires will mostly be in the satisfactory performer range. However, as previously noted, such a top-down selection policy can be discriminatory.

Without the use of the FERT, it is estimated that about one-half of all new hires would exhibit satisfactory performance; that is, the base rate would be .50. Without use of the FERT, the miss rate would also be .50—this because half of all drivers hired would be deemed unqualified based on the OTJSRs at the end of the probationary period.

Dr. Carlos considers the consequences of a 50% miss rate. She thinks about the possibility of an increase in customer complaints regarding the level of service. She envisions an increase in at-fault accidents and costly lawsuits. Dr. Carlos is pleasantly distracted from these potential nightmares when she inadvertently leans on her keyboard and it furiously begins to beep. Having rejected Option 1, she "presses on" and next explores what outcomes would be associated with Option 2: *Use the FERT to select with the lowest false negative rate.* Now, another graph (*Close-Up* Figure 2) appears along with this text:

This graph, as well as all others incorporating FERT cut-score data, have FERT (predictor) scores on the horizontal axis (which increase from left to right), and OTJSR (criterion) scores on the vertical axis (with scores increasing from the bottom toward the top). The selection ratio provides an indication of the competitiveness of the position; it is directly affected by the cut score used in selection. As the cut score is set farther to the right, the selection ratio goes down. The practical implication of the decreasing selection ratio is that hiring becomes more selective; this means that there is more competition for a position and that the proportion of people actually hired (from all of those who applied) will be less.[2] As the cut score is set farther to the left, the selection ratio goes up; hiring becomes less selective, and chances are that more people will be hired.[3]

Using a cut score of 18 on the FERT, as compared to not using the FERT at all, reduces the miss rate from 50% to 45% (see Figure 2). The major advantage of setting the cut score this low is that the false negative rate falls to zero; no potentially qualified drivers will be rejected based on the FERT. Use of this FERT cut score also increases the base rate of successful performance from .50 to .526. This means that the percentage of hires who will be rated as "qualified" has increased from 50% without use of the FERT to 52.6% with the FERT. The selection ratio associated with using 18 as the cut score is .95, which means that 95% of drivers who apply are selected.

Dr. Carlos appreciates that the false negative rate is zero and thus no potentially qualified drivers are turned away based on FERT score. She also believes that a 5% reduction in the miss

2. It may help you to remember this if you think: "Selection ratio down, fewer employees around." Of course it works the opposite way when it comes to cut scores: "Cut score low, more employees to know."

3. It may help you to remember this if you think: "Selection ratio high, more employees say 'Hi!'" Of course, it works the opposite way when it comes to cut scores: "Cut score high, bid applicants good-bye."

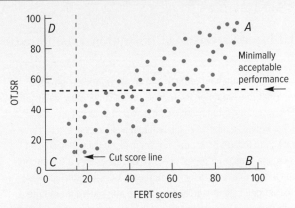

Figure 2
Selection with Low Cut Score and High Selection Ratio

As we saw in Figure 1, without the use of the FERT, only half of all the probationary hires would be rated as satisfactory drivers by their supervisors. Now we will consider how to improve selection by using the FERT. For ease of reference, each of the quadrants in Figure 2 (as well as the remaining Close-Up graphs) have been labeled, A, B, C, or D. The selection ratio in this and the following graphs may be defined as being equal to the ratio of the number of people who are hired on a permanent basis (qualified applicants as determined by FERT score) compared to the total number of people who apply.

The total number of applicants for permanent positions was 60, as evidenced by all of the dots in all of the quadrants. In quadrants A and B, just to the right of the vertical Cut score line (set at 18), are the 57 FE drivers who were offered permanent employment. We can also see that the false positive rate is zero because no scores fall in quadrant D; thus, no potentially qualified drivers will be rejected based on use of the FERT with a cut score of 18. The selection ratio in this scenario is 57/60, or .95. We can therefore conclude that 57 applicants (95% of the 60 who originally applied) would have been hired on the basis of their FERT scores with a cut score set at 18 (resulting in a "high" selection ratio of 95%); only three applicants would not be hired based on their FERT scores. These three applicants would also be rated as unqualified by their supervisors at the end of the probationary period. We can also see that, by removing the lowest-scoring applicants, the base rate of successful performance improves slightly as compared to not using the FERT at all. Instead of having a successful performance base rate of only .50 (as was the case when all applicants were hired), now the base rate of successful performance is .526. This is so because 30 drivers are still rated as qualified based on OTJSRs while the number of drivers hired has been reduced from 60 to 57.

(continued)

Utility Analysis: An Illustration *(continued)*

rate is better than no reduction at all. She wonders, however, whether this reduction in the miss rate is statistically significant. She would have to formally analyze these data to be certain but, after simply "eyeballing" these findings, a decrease in the miss rate from 50% to 45% does not seem significant. Similarly, an increase in the number of qualified drivers of only 2.6% through the use of a test for selection purposes does not, on its face, seem significant. It simply does not seem prudent to institute a new personnel selection test at real cost and expense to the company if the only benefit of the test is to reject the lowest-scoring 3 of 60 applicants—when, in reality, 30 of the 60 applicants will be rated as "unqualified."

Dr. Carlos pauses to envision a situation in which reducing the false negative rate to zero might be prudent; it might be ideal if she were testing drivers for drug use, because she would definitely not want a test to indicate a driver is drug-free if that driver had been using drugs. Of course, a test with a false negative rate of zero would likely also have a high false positive rate. But then she could retest any candidate who received a positive result with a second, more expensive, more accurate test—this to ensure that the initial positive result was correct and not a testing error. As Dr. Carlos mulls over these issues, a colleague startles her with a friendly query: "How's that FERT researching coming?"

Dr. Carlos says, "Fine," and smoothly reaches for her keyboard to select Option 3: *Use the FERT to select with the lowest false positive rate*. Now, another graph (*Close-Up* Figure 3) and another message pop up:

Using a cut score of 80 on the FERT, as compared to not using the FERT at all, results in a reduction of the miss rate from 50% to 40% (see Figure 3) but also reduces the false positive rate to zero. Use of this FERT cut score also increases the base rate of successful performance from .50 to 1.00. This means that the percentage of drivers selected who are rated as "qualified" increases from 50% without use of the FERT to 100% when the FERT is used with a cut score of 80. The selection ratio associated with using 80 as the cut score is .10, which means that 10% of applicants are selected.

Dr. Carlos likes the idea of the "100% solution" entailed by a false positive rate of zero. It means that 100% of the applicants selected by their FERT scores will turn out to be qualified drivers. At first blush, this solution seems optimal. However, there is, as they say, a fly in the ointment. Although the high cut score (80) results in the selection of only qualified candidates, the selection ratio is so stringent that only 10% of those candidates would actually be hired. Dr. Carlos envisions the consequences of this low selection ratio. She sees herself as having to recruit and test at

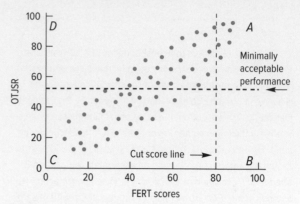

Figure 3
Selection with High Cut Score and Low Selection Ratio

As before, the total number of applicants for permanent positions was 60, as evidenced by all of the dots in all of the quadrants. In quadrants A and B, just to the right of the vertical Cut score line (set at a FERT score of 80), are the 6 FE drivers who were offered permanent employment. The selection ratio in this scenario is 6/60, or .10. We can therefore conclude that 6 applicants (10% of the 60 who originally applied) would have been hired on the basis of their FERT scores with the cut score set at 80 (and with a "low" selection ratio of 10%). Note also that the base rate improves dramatically, from .50 without use of the FERT to 1.00 with a FERT cut score set at 80. This means that all drivers selected when this cut score is in place will be qualified. Although only 10% of the drivers will be offered permanent positions, all who are offered permanent positions will be rated qualified drivers on the OTJSR. Note, however, that even though the false positive rate drops to zero, the overall miss rate only drops to .40. This is so because a substantial number (24) of qualified applicants would be denied permanent positions because their FERT scores were below 80.

least 100 applicants for every 10 drivers she actually hires. To meet her company goal of hiring 60 drivers, for example, she would have to recruit about 600 applicants for testing. Attracting that many applicants to the company is a venture that has some obvious (as well as some less obvious) costs. Dr. Carlos sees her recruiting budget dwindle as she repeatedly writes checks for classified advertising in newspapers. She sees herself purchasing airline tickets and making hotel reservations in order to attend various job fairs, far and wide. Fantasizing about the applicants she will attract at one of those job fairs, she is abruptly brought back to the here-and-now by the friendly voice of a fellow staff member asking her if she wants to go to lunch. Still half-steeped in thought about a potential budget crisis, Dr. Carlos responds, "Yes, just give me ten dollars . . . I mean, ten minutes."

As Dr. Carlos takes the menu of a local hamburger haunt from her desk to review, she still can't get the "100% solution" out of her mind. Although clearly attractive, she has reservations (about the solution, not for the restaurant). Offering permanent positions to only the top-performing applicants could easily backfire. Competing companies could be expected to also offer these applicants positions, perhaps with more attractive benefit packages. How many of the top drivers hired would actually stay at Federale Express? Hard to say. What is not hard to say, however, is that the use of the "100% solution" has essentially brought Dr. Carlos full circle back to the top-down hiring policy that she sought to avoid in the first place. Also, scrutinizing Figure 3, Dr. Carlos sees that—even though the base rate with this cut score is 100%—the percentage of misclassifications (as compared to not using any selection test) is reduced only by a measly 10%. Further, there would be many qualified drivers who would also be cut by this cut score. In this instance, then, a cut score that scrupulously seeks to avoid the hiring of unqualified drivers also leads to rejecting a number of qualified applicants. Perhaps in the hiring of "super responsible" positions—say, nuclear power plant supervisors—such a rigorous selection policy could be justified. But is such rigor really required in the selection of Federale Express drivers?

Hoping for a more reasonable solution to her cut-score dilemma and beginning to feel hungry, Dr. Carlos leafs through the burger menu while choosing Option 4 on her computer screen: *Use the FERT to yield the highest hit rate and lowest miss rate.* In response to this selection, another graph (*Close-Up* Figure 4) along with the following message is presented:

> *Using a cut score of 48 on the FERT results in a reduction of the miss rate from 50% to 15% as compared to not using the FERT (see Figure 4). False positive and false negative rates are both fairly low at .167 and .133, respectively. Use of this cut score also increases the base rate from .50 (without use of the FERT) to .839. This means that the percentage of hired drivers who are rated as "qualified" at the end of the probationary period has increased from 50% (without use of the FERT) to 83.9%. The selection ratio associated with using 48 as the cut score is .517, which means that 51.7% of applicants will be hired.*

Although a formal analysis would have to be run, Dr. Carlos again "eyeballs" the findings and, based on her extensive experience, strongly suspects that these results are statistically significant. Moreover, these findings would seem to be of practical significance. As compared to not using the FERT, use of the FERT with a cut score of 48 could reduce misclassifications from 50% to 15%. Such a reduction in misclassifications would almost certainly have positive cost–benefit implications for FE.

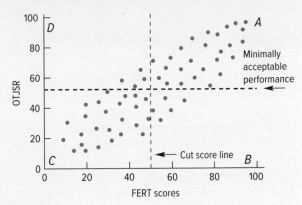

Figure 4
Selection with Moderate Cut Score and Moderate Selection Ratio

Again, the total number of applicants was 60. In quadrants A and B, just to the right of the vertical Cut Score line (set at 48), are the 31 FE drivers who were offered permanent employment at the end of the probationary period. The selection ratio in this scenario is therefore equal to 31/60, or about .517. This means that slightly more than half of all applicants will be hired based on the use of 48 as the FERT cut score. The selection ratio of .517 is a moderate one. It is not as stringent as is the .10 selection ratio that results from a cut score of 80, nor is it as lenient as the .95 selection ratio that results from a cut score of 18. Note also that the cut score set at 48 effectively weeds out many of the applicants who won't receive acceptable performance ratings. Further, it does this while retaining many of the applicants who will receive acceptable performance ratings. With a FERT cut score of 48, the base rate increases quite a bit: from .50 (as was the case without using the FERT) to .839. This means that about 84% (83.9%, to be exact) of the hired drivers will be rated as qualified when the FERT cut score is set to 48 for driver selection.

Also, the percentage of drivers who are deemed qualified at the end of the probationary period would rise from 50% (without use of the FERT) to 83.9% (using the FERT with a cut score of 48). The implications of such improved selection are many and include better service to customers (leading to an increase in business volume), less costly accidents, and fewer costs involved in hiring and training new personnel.

Yet another benefit of using the FERT with a cut score of 48 concerns recruiting costs. Using a cut score of 48, FE would need to recruit only 39 or so qualified applicants for every 20 permanent positions it needed to fill. Now, anticipating real savings in her annual budget, Dr. Carlos returns the hamburger menu to her desk drawer and removes instead the menu from her favorite (pricey) steakhouse.

(continued)

Utility Analysis: An Illustration *(continued)*

Dr. Carlos decides that the moderate cut-score solution is optimal for FE. She acknowledges that this solution doesn't reduce any of the error rates to zero. However, it produces relatively low error rates overall. It also yields a relatively high hit rate; about 84% of the drivers hired will be qualified at the end of the probationary period. Dr. Carlos believes that the costs associated with recruitment and testing using this FERT cut score will be more than compensated by the evolution of a work force that evidences satisfactory performance and has fewer accidents. As she peruses the steakhouse menu and mentally debates the pros and cons of sautéed onions, she also wonders about the dollars-and-cents utility of using the FERT. Are all of the costs associated with instituting the FERT as part of FE hiring procedures worth the benefits?

Dr. Carlos puts down the menu and begins to calculate the company's **return on investment** (the ratio of benefits to costs).

She estimates the cost of each FERT to be about $200, including the costs associated with truck usage, gas, and supervisory personnel time. She further estimates that FE will test 120 applicants per year in order to select approximately 60 new hires based on a moderate FERT cut score. Given the cost of each test ($200) administered individually to 120 applicants, the total to be spent on testing annually will be about $24,000. So, is it worth it? Considering all of the possible benefits previously listed that could result from a significant reduction of the misclassification rate, Dr. Carlos's guess is, "Yes, it would be worth it." Of course, decisions like that aren't made with guesses. So continue reading—later in this chapter, a formula will be applied that will prove Dr. Carlos right. In fact, the moderate cut score shown in Figure 4 would produce a return on investment of 12.5 to 1. And once Dr. Carlos gets wind of these projections, you can bet it will be surf-and-turf-tortilla time at Federale Express.

Tables that could be used as an aid for personnel directors in their decision-making chores were published by H. C. Taylor and J. T. Russell in the *Journal of Applied Psychology* in 1939. Referred to by the names of their authors, the **Taylor-Russell tables** provide an estimate of the extent to which inclusion of a particular test in the selection system will improve selection. More specifically, the tables provide an estimate of the percentage of employees hired by the use of a particular test who will be successful at their jobs, given different combinations of three variables: the test's validity, the selection ratio used, and the base rate.

The value assigned for the test's validity is the computed validity coefficient. The *selection ratio* is a numerical value that reflects the relationship between the number of people to be hired and the number of people available to be hired. For instance, if there are 50 positions and 100 applicants, then the selection ratio is 50/100, or .50. As used here, *base rate* refers to the percentage of people hired under the existing system for a particular position. If, for example, a firm employs 25 computer programmers and 20 are considered successful, the base rate would be .80. With knowledge of the validity coefficient of a particular test along with the selection ratio, reference to the Taylor-Russell tables provides the personnel officer with an estimate of how much using the test would improve selection over existing methods.

A sample Taylor-Russell table is presented in Table 7–1. This table is for the base rate of .60, meaning that 60% of those hired under the existing system are successful in their work. Down the left-hand side are validity coefficients for a test that could be used to help select employees. Across the top are the various selection ratios. They reflect the proportion of the people applying for the jobs who will be hired. If a new test is introduced to help select employees in a situation with a selection ratio of .20 and if the new test has a predictive validity coefficient of .55, then the table shows that the base rate will increase to .88. This means that, rather than 60% of the hired employees being expected to perform successfully, a full 88% can be expected to do so. When selection ratios are low, as when only 5% of the applicants will be hired, even tests with low validity coefficients, such as .15, can result in improved base rates.

One limitation of the Taylor-Russell tables is that the relationship between the predictor (the test) and the criterion (rating of performance on the job) must be linear. If, for example,

Table 7–1

Taylor-Russell Table for a Base Rate of .60

Validity (ρ_{xy})	Selection Ratio										
	.05	.10	.20	.30	.40	.50	.60	.70	.80	.90	.95
.00	.60	.60	.60	.60	.60	.60	.60	.60	.60	.60	.60
.05	.64	.63	.63	.62	.62	.62	.61	.61	.61	.60	.60
.10	.68	.67	.65	.64	.64	.63	.63	.62	.61	.61	.60
.15	.71	.70	.68	.67	.66	.65	.64	.63	.62	.61	.61
.20	.75	.73	.71	.69	.67	.66	.65	.64	.63	.62	.61
.25	.78	.76	.73	.71	.69	.68	.66	.65	.63	.62	.61
.30	.82	.79	.76	.73	.71	.69	.68	.66	.64	.62	.61
.35	.85	.82	.78	.75	.73	.71	.69	.67	.65	.63	.62
.40	.88	.85	.81	.78	.75	.73	.70	.68	.66	.63	.62
.45	.90	.87	.83	.80	.77	.74	.72	.69	.66	.64	.62
.50	.93	.90	.86	.82	.79	.76	.73	.70	.67	.64	.62
.55	.95	.92	.88	.84	.81	.78	.75	.71	.68	.64	.62
.60	.96	.94	.90	.87	.83	.80	.76	.73	.69	.65	.63
.65	.98	.96	.92	.89	.85	.82	.78	.74	.70	.65	.63
.70	.99	.97	.94	.91	.87	.84	.80	.75	.71	.66	.63
.75	.99	.99	.96	.93	.90	.86	.81	.77	.71	.66	.63
.80	1.00	.99	.98	.95	.92	.88	.83	.78	.72	.66	.63
.85	1.00	1.00	.99	.97	.95	.91	.86	.80	.73	.66	.63
.90	1.00	1.00	1.00	.99	.97	.94	.88	.82	.74	.67	.63
.95	1.00	1.00	1.00	1.00	.99	.97	.92	.84	.75	.67	.63
1.00	1.00	1.00	1.00	1.00	1.00	1.00	1.00	.86	.75	.67	.63

Source: Taylor and Russell (1939).

there is some point at which job performance levels off, no matter how high the score on the test, use of the Taylor-Russell tables would be inappropriate. Another limitation of the Taylor-Russell tables is the potential difficulty of identifying a criterion score that separates "successful" from "unsuccessful" employees.

The potential problems of the Taylor-Russell tables were avoided by an alternative set of tables (Naylor & Shine, 1965) that provided an indication of the difference in average criterion scores for the selected group as compared with the original group. Use of the **Naylor-Shine tables** entails obtaining the difference between the means of the selected and unselected groups to derive an index of what the test (or some other tool of assessment) is adding to already established procedures.

Both the Taylor-Russell and the Naylor-Shine tables can assist in judging the utility of a particular test, the former by determining the increase over current procedures and the latter by determining the increase in average score on some criterion measure. With both tables, the validity coefficient used must be one obtained by concurrent validation procedures—a fact that should not be surprising because it is obtained with respect to current employees hired by the selection process in effect at the time of the study.

If hiring decisions were made solely on the basis of variables such as the validity of an employment test and the prevailing selection ratio, then tables such as those offered by Taylor and Russell and Naylor and Shine would be in wide use today. The fact is that many other kinds of variables might enter into hiring and other sorts of personnel selection decisions (including decisions

JUST THINK . . .

In addition to testing, what types of assessment procedures might employers use to help them make judicious personnel selection decisions?

relating to promotion, transfer, layoff, and firing). Some additional variables might include, for example, applicants' minority status, general physical or mental health, or drug use. Given that many variables may affect a personnel selection decision, of what use is a given test in the decision process?

Expectancy data, such as that provided by the Taylor-Russell tables or the Naylor-Shine tables could be used to shed light on many utility-related decisions, particularly those confined to questions concerning the validity of an employment test and the selection ratio employed. Table 7–2 presents a brief summary of some of the uses, advantages, and disadvantages of these approaches. In many instances, however, the purpose of a utility analysis is to answer a question related to costs and benefits in terms of dollars and cents. When such questions are raised, the answer may be found by using the Brogden-Cronbach-Gleser formula.

Table 7–2

Most Everything You Ever Wanted to Know About Utility Tables

Instrument	What It Tells Us	Example	Advantages	Disadvantages
Expectancy table or chart	Likelihood that individuals who score within a given range on the predictor will perform successfully on the criterion	A school psychologist uses an expectancy table to determine the likelihood that students who score within a particular range on an aptitude test will succeed in regular classes as opposed to special education classes.	Easy-to-use graphical display; can aid in decision making regarding a specific individual or a group of individuals scoring in a given range on the predictor	Dichotomizes performance into successful and unsuccessful categories, which is not realistic in most situations; does not address monetary issues such as cost of testing or return on investment of testing
Taylor-Russell tables	Increase in base rate of successful performance that is associated with a particular level of criterion-related validity	A human resources manager of a large computer store uses the Taylor-Russell tables to help decide whether applicants for sales positions should be administered an extraversion inventory prior to hire. The manager wants to increase the portion of the sales force that is considered successful (or, consistently meets sales quota). By using an estimate of the test's validity (e.g., by using a value of .20 based on research by Conte & Gintoft, 2005), the current base rate, and selection ratio, the manager can estimate whether the increase in proportion of the sales force that do successfully meet their quotas will justify the cost of testing all sales applicants.	Easy-to-use; shows the relationships between selection ratio, criterion-related validity, and existing base rate; facilitates decision making with regard to test use and/or recruitment to lower the selection ratio	Relationship between predictor and criterion must be linear; does not indicate the likely average increase in performance with use of the test; difficulty identifying a criterion value to separate successful and unsuccessful performance; dichotomizes performance into successful versus unsuccessful, which is not realistic in most situations; does not consider the cost of testing in comparison to benefits
Naylor-Shine tables	Likely average increase in criterion performance as a result of using a particular test or intervention; also provides selection ratio needed to achieve a particular increase in criterion performance	The provost at a private college estimates the increase in applicant pool (and corresponding decrease in selection ratio) that is needed in order to improve the mean performance of students it selects by 0.50 standardized units while still maintaining its enrollment figures.	Provides information (or, average performance gain) needed to use the Brogden-Cronbach-Gleser utility formula; does not dichotomize criterion performance; useful either for showing average performance gain or to show selection ratio needed for a particular performance gain; facilitates decision making with regard to likely increase in performance with test use and/or recruitment needed to lower the selection ratio	Overestimates utility unless top-down selection is used;[a] utility expressed in terms of performance gain based on standardized units, which can be difficult to interpret in practical terms; does not address monetary issues such as cost of testing or return on investment

[a]Boudreau (1988).

The Brogden-Cronbach-Gleser formula   The independent work of Hubert E. Brogden (1949) and a team of decision theorists (Cronbach & Gleser, 1965) has been immortalized in the **Brogden-Cronbach-Gleser formula,** used to calculate the dollar amount of a *utility gain* resulting from the use of a particular selection instrument under specified conditions. In general, **utility gain** refers to an estimate of the benefit (monetary or otherwise) of using a particular test or selection method. The Brogden-Cronbach-Gleser (BCG) formula is:

$$\text{utility gain} = (N)(T)(r_{xy})(\text{SD}_y)(\overline{Z}_m) - (N)(C)$$

In the first part of the formula, N represents the number of applicants selected per year, T represents the average length of time in the position (or, tenure), r_{xy} represents the (criterion-related) validity coefficient for the given predictor and criterion, SD_y represents the standard deviation of performance (in dollars) of employees, and $\overline{Z}_m$ represents the mean (standardized) score on the test for selected applicants. The second part of the formula represents the cost of testing, which takes into consideration the number of applicants (N) multiplied by the cost of the test for each applicant (C). A difficulty in using this formula is estimating the value of SD_y, a value that is, quite literally, estimated (Hunter et al., 1990). One recommended way to estimate SD_y is by setting it equal to 40% of the mean salary for the job (Schmidt & Hunter, 1998).

The BCG formula can be applied to the question raised in this chapter's *Close-Up* about the utility of the FERT. Suppose 60 Federale Express (FE) drivers are selected per year and that each driver stays with FE for one and a half years. Let's further suppose that the standard deviation of performance of the drivers is about $9,000 (calculated as 40% of annual salary), that the criterion-related validity of FERT scores is .40, and that the mean standardized FERT score for applicants is +1.0. Applying the *benefits* part of the BCG formula, the benefits are $324,000 (60 × 1.5 × .40 × $9,000 × 1.0). When the costs of testing ($24,000) are subtracted from the financial benefits of testing ($324,000), it can be seen that the utility gain amounts to $300,000.

So, would it be wise for a company to make an investment of $24,000 to receive a return of about $300,000? Most people (and corporations) would be more than willing to invest in something if they knew that the return on their investment would be more than $12.50 for each dollar invested. Clearly, with such a return on investment, using the FERT with the cut score illustrated in Figure 4 of the *Close-Up* does provide a cost-effective method of selecting delivery drivers.

By the way, a modification of the BCG formula exists for researchers who prefer their findings in terms of *productivity gains* rather than financial ones. Here, **productivity gain** refers to an estimated increase in work output. In this modification of the formula, the value of the standard deviation of productivity, SD_p, is substituted for the value of the standard deviation of performance in dollars, SD_y (Schmidt et al., 1986). The result

J U S T   T H I N K . . .

When might it be better to present utility gains in productivity terms rather than financial terms?

is a formula that helps estimate the percent increase in output expected through the use of a particular test. The revised formula is:

$$\text{productivity gain} = (N)(T)(r_{xy})(\text{SD}_p)(\overline{Z}_m) - (N)(C)$$

Throughout this text, including in the boxed material, we have sought to illustrate psychometric principles with reference to contemporary, practical illustrations from everyday life. In recent years, for example, there has increasingly been calls for police to wear body cameras as a means to reduce inappropriate use of force against citizens (Ariel, 2015). In response to such demands, some have questioned whether the purchase of such recording systems as well as all of the ancillary recording and record-keeping technology is justified; that is, will it really make a difference in the behavior of police personnel. Stated another way, important questions regarding the *utility* of such systems have been raised. Some answers to these important questions can be found in this chapter's *Everyday Psychometrics*.

The Utility of Police Use of Body Cameras*

Imagine you are walking down a street. You see two police officers approach a man who has just walked out of a shop, carrying a shopping bag. The police stop the man, and aggressively ask him to explain who he is, where he is going, and what he was doing in the shop. Frustrated at being detained in this way, the man becomes angry and refuses to cooperate. The situation quickly escalates as the police resort to the use of pepper spray and handcuffs to effect and arrest. The man being arrested is physically injured in the process. After his release, the man files a lawsuit in civil court against the police force, alleging illegal use of force. Several bystanders come forward as witnesses to the event. Their account of what happened serves to support the plaintiff's claims against the defendant (the defendant being the municipality that manages the police). A jury finds in favor of the plaintiff and orders the defendant city to pay the plaintiff one-million dollars in damages.

Now imagine the same scenario but played through the eyes of the police officer who effected the arrest. Prior to your sighting of the suspect individual, you have heard "be on the lookout" reports over your police radio regarding a man roughly fitting this person's description. The individual in question has reportedly been observed stealing items from shops in the area. Having observed him, you now approach him and take command of the situation, because that is what you have been trained to do. Despite your forceful, no-nonsense approach to the suspect, the suspect is uncooperative to the point of defiance. As the suspect becomes increasingly agitated, you become increasingly concerned for your own safety, as well as the safety of your partner. Now trying to effect an arrest without resorting to the use of lethal force, you use pepper spray in an effort to subdue him. Subsequently, in court, after the suspect has been cleared of all charges, and the municipality that employs you has been hit with a one-million-dollar judgement, you wonder how things could have more effectively been handled.

In the scenarios described above, the police did pretty much what they were trained to do. Unfortunately, all of that training resulted in a "lose-lose" situation for both the citizen wrongly detained for suspicion of being a thief, and the police officer who was just doing his job as best as he could. So, now a question arises, "Is there something that might have been added to the situation that might have had the effect of retarding the citizen's combativeness, and the police's defensive and reflexive use of force in response?"

*This *Everyday Psychometrics* was guest-authored by Alex Sutherland of RAND Europe, and Barak Ariel of Cambridge University and Hebrew University.

© George Frey/Getty Images

More specifically, might the situation have been different if the parties involved knew that their every move, and their every utterance, were being faithfully recorded? Might the fact that the event was being recorded influence the extent to which the wrongfully charged citizen was noncompliant, even combative? Similarly, might the fact that the event was being recorded influence the extent to which the police officer doing his job had to resort to the use of force? The answer to such questions is "yes" according to a study by Ariel et al. (2015). A brief description of that study follows. Readers interested in a more detailed description of the experiment are urged to consult the original article.

The Ariel (2015) Study

Ariel et al.'s (2015) study with the police force in Rialto, California, was the first published experimental evidence on the effectiveness of the body-worn camera (BWC). In order to establish whether or not cameras were actually able to change officer–citizen interactions for the better, a randomized-controlled field trial (RCT) was designed.[1] In nearly every police force around the world, officers work according to a shift pattern. Using a randomization program called the Cambridge Randomizer (Ariel et al., 2012), which is essentially an online coin-flip, the researchers randomly assigned officers of each shift to either a camera or no-camera experimental condition. This meant that every officer on a shift would wear a camera in the *Camera* condition, but not wear a camera in the *No Camera* condition. The relevant behavioral data for analysis was not what one of the 54 police officers on the Rialto police

1. Although RCT entails the use of experimental methods, the laboratory in a field experiment is the "real world." This fact enhances the generalizability of the results. It is also more challenging because there are a lot more things that can go wrong. This is the case for many reasons, not the least of which is the fact that participants do not always do exactly what the experimenter has asked them to do.

force was doing, but what occurred during the 988 randomly assigned shifts over a one-year period.

The research protocol required officers to (i) wear cameras only during *Camera* shifts; (ii) not wear (or use) cameras during *No Camera* shifts; (iii) keep cameras on throughout their entire *Camera* shift; and (iv) issue verbal warnings during the *Camera* shifts to advise citizens confronted that the interaction was being videotaped by a camera attached to the officer's uniform.

Over the course of a year that the experiment ran, data from police reports of arrest as well as data from videos (when available) were analyzed for the presence or absence of "use of force." For the purposes of this experiment, "use of force" was coded as being present on any occasion that a police verbal confrontation with a citizen escalated to the point of physical contact. In addition to the presence or absence of use of force as an outcome measure, another outcome measure was formal complaints of police use of force made by citizens. As clearly illustrated in Figure 7–7, the number of use-of force incidents in shifts significantly decreased beginning at the time of the initiation of this study, as did the number of use-of-force complaints by citizens. Ariel et al. (2015) found that use-of-force rates were more than twice that in the *No Camera* shifts as compared to the *Camera* shifts.

Although this study suggests that body cameras worn by police have utility in reducing use-of-force incidents, as well as use-of-force complaints by citizens, it sheds no light on *why* this might be so. In fact, there are a multitude of variables to consider when analyzing the factors that may influence a police officer's decision to use force (Bolger, 2015). Given the procedures used in this study, the question of whether changes in the participants' behavior is more a function of the camera or the police officer's verbal warning, is an open one ("Cameras on Cops," 2014; Ariel, 2016). It would be useful to explore in future research the extent to which being filmed, or simply being advised that one is being filmed, is causal in reducing use-of-force incidents and use-of-force complaints.

To be sure, use of force by police in some situations is indicated, legitimate, and unquestionably justified. However, in those more borderline situations, cameras may serve as silent reminders of the efficacy of more "civil" interaction—and this may be true for both members of the general public as well as those well-meaning police officers whose dedicated service and whose judicious use of force is integral to the functioning of civilized society.

Used with permission of Alex Sutherland and Barak Ariel.

Figure 1

Use of Force by Police and Use-of-Force Complaints by Citizens Before and During the Rialto Body Camera Experiment

Used with permission of Alex Sutherland and Barak Ariel.

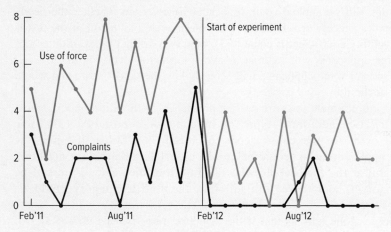

Decision theory and test utility Perhaps the most oft-cited application of statistical decision theory to the field of psychological testing is Cronbach and Gleser's *Psychological Tests and Personnel Decisions* (1957, 1965). The idea of applying statistical decision theory to questions of test utility was conceptually appealing and promising, and an authoritative textbook of the day reflects the great enthusiasm with which this marriage of enterprises was greeted:

> The basic decision-theory approach to selection and placement . . . has a number of advantages over the more classical approach based upon the correlation model. . . . There is no question but that it is a more general and better model for handling this kind of decision task, and we predict that in the future problems of selection and placement will be treated in this context more frequently—perhaps to [the] eventual exclusion of the more stereotyped correlational model. (Blum & Naylor, 1968, p. 58)

Stated generally, Cronbach and Gleser (1965) presented (1) a classification of decision problems; (2) various selection strategies ranging from single-stage processes to sequential analyses; (3) a quantitative analysis of the relationship between test utility, the selection ratio, cost of the testing program, and expected value of the outcome; and (4) a recommendation that in some instances job requirements be tailored to the applicant's ability instead of the other way around (a concept they refer to as *adaptive treatment*).

Let's illustrate decision theory in action. To do so, recall the definition of five terms that you learned in the previous chapter: *base rate, hit rate, miss rate, false positive,* and *false negative.* Now, imagine that you developed a procedure called the Vapor Test (VT), which was designed to determine if alive-and-well subjects are indeed breathing. The procedure for the VT entails having the examiner hold a mirror under the subject's nose and mouth for a minute or so and observing whether the subject's breath fogs the mirror. Let's say that 100 introductory psychology students are administered the VT, and it is concluded that 89 were, in fact, breathing (whereas 11 are deemed, on the basis of the VT, not to be breathing). Is the VT a good test? Obviously not. Because the base rate is 100% of the (alive-and-well) population, we really don't even need a test to measure the characteristic *breathing.* If for some reason we did need such a measurement procedure, we probably wouldn't use one that was inaccurate in approximately 11% of the cases. A test is obviously of no value if the hit rate is higher *without* using it. One measure of the value of a test lies in the extent to which its use improves on the hit rate that exists without its use.

As a simple illustration of decision theory applied to testing, suppose a test is administered to a group of 100 job applicants and that some cutoff score is applied to distinguish applicants who will be hired (applicants judged to have passed the test) from applicants whose employment application will be rejected (applicants judged to have failed the test). Let's further suppose that some criterion measure will be applied some time later to ascertain whether the newly hired person was considered a success or a failure at the job. In such a situation, if the test is a perfect predictor (if its validity coefficient is equal to 1), then two distinct types of outcomes can be identified: (1) Some applicants will score at or above the cutoff score on the test and be successful at the job, and (2) some applicants will score below the cutoff score and would not have been successful at the job.

In reality, few, if any, employment tests are perfect predictors with validity coefficients equal to 1. Consequently, two additional types of outcomes are possible: (3) Some applicants will score at or above the cutoff score, be hired, and fail at the job (the criterion), and (4) some applicants who scored below the cutoff score and were not hired could have been successful at the job. People who fall into the third category could be categorized as *false positives,* and those who fall into the fourth category could be categorized as *false negatives.*

In this illustration, logic alone tells us that if the selection ratio is, say, 90% (9 out of 10 applicants will be hired), then the cutoff score will probably be set lower than if the selection ratio is 5% (only 5 of the 100 applicants will be hired). Further, if the selection ratio is 90%, then it is a good bet that the number of false positives (people hired who will fail on the criterion measure) will be greater than if the selection ratio is 5%. Conversely, if the selection ratio is only 5%, it is a good bet that the number of false negatives (people not hired who could have succeeded on the criterion measure) will be greater than if the selection ratio is 90%.

Decision theory provides guidelines for setting optimal cutoff scores. In setting such scores, the relative seriousness of making false-positive or false-negative selection decisions is frequently taken into account. Thus, for example, it is a prudent policy for an airline personnel office to set cutoff scores on tests for pilots that might result in a false negative (a pilot who is truly qualified being rejected) as opposed to a cutoff score that would allow a false positive (a pilot who is truly unqualified being hired).

In the hands of highly skilled researchers, principles of decision theory applied to problems of test utility have led to some enlightening and impressive findings. For example, Schmidt et al. (1979) demonstrated in dollars and cents how the utility of a company's selection program (and the validity coefficient of the tests used in that program) can play a critical role in the profitability of the company. Focusing on one employer's population of computer programmers, these researchers asked supervisors to rate (in terms of dollars) the value of good, average, and poor programmers. This information was used in conjunction with other information, including these facts: (1) Each year the employer hired 600 new programmers, (2) the average programmer remained on the job for about 10 years, (3) the Programmer Aptitude Test currently in use as part of the hiring process had a validity coefficient of .76, (4) it cost about $10 per applicant to administer the test, and (5) the company currently employed more than 4,000 programmers.

Schmidt et al. (1979) made a number of calculations using different values for some of the variables. For example, knowing that some of the tests previously used in the hiring process had validity coefficients ranging from .00 to .50, they varied the value of the test's validity coefficient (along with other factors such as different selection ratios that had been in effect) and examined the relative efficiency of the various conditions. Among their findings was that the existing selection ratio and selection process provided a great gain in efficiency over a previous situation (when the selection ratio was 5% and the validity coefficient of the test used in hiring was equal to .50). This gain was equal to almost $6 million per year. Multiplied over, say, 10 years, that's $60 million. The existing selection ratio and selection process provided an even greater gain in efficiency over a previously existing situation in which the test had no validity at all and the selection ratio was .80. Here, in one year, the gain in efficiency was estimated to be equal to over $97 million.

By the way, the employer in the previous study was the U.S. government. Hunter and Schmidt (1981) applied the same type of analysis to the national workforce and made a compelling argument with respect to the critical relationship between valid tests and measurement procedures and our national productivity. In a subsequent study, Schmidt, Hunter, and their colleagues found that substantial increases in work output or reductions in payroll costs would result from using valid measures of cognitive ability as opposed to non-test procedures (Schmidt et al., 1986).

> **JUST THINK . . .**
>
> What must happen in society at large if the promise of decision theory in personnel selection is to be fulfilled?

Employers are reluctant to use decision-theory-based strategies in their hiring practices because of the complexity of their application and the threat of legal challenges. Thus, although decision theory approaches to assessment hold great promise, this promise has yet to be fulfilled.

Some Practical Considerations

A number of practical matters must be considered when conducting utility analyses. For example, as we have noted elsewhere, issues related to existing base rates can affect the accuracy of decisions made on the basis of tests. Particular attention must be paid to this factor when the base rates are extremely low or high because such a situation may render the test useless as a tool of selection. Focusing for the purpose of this discussion on the area of personnel selection, some other practical matters to keep in mind involve assumptions about the pool of job applicants, the complexity of the job, and the cut score in use.

The pool of job applicants If you were to read a number of articles in the utility analysis literature on personnel selection, you might come to the conclusion that there exists, "out there," what seems to be a limitless supply of potential employees just waiting to be evaluated and possibly selected for employment. For example, utility estimates such as those derived by Schmidt et al. (1979) are based on the assumption that there will be a ready supply of viable applicants from which to choose and fill positions. Perhaps for some types of jobs and in some economic climates that is, indeed, the case. There are certain jobs, however, that require such unique skills or demand such great sacrifice that there are relatively few people who would even apply, let alone be selected. Also, the pool of possible job applicants for a particular type of position may vary with the economic climate. It may be that in periods of high unemployment there are significantly more people in the pool of possible job applicants than in periods of high employment.

JUST THINK . . .

What is an example of a type of job that requires such unique skills that there are probably relatively few people in the pool of qualified employees?

Closely related to issues concerning the available pool of job applicants is the issue of how many people would actually *accept* the employment position offered to them even if they were found to be a qualified candidate. Many utility models, somewhat naively, are constructed on the assumption that all of the people selected by a personnel test accept the position that they are offered. In fact, many of the top performers on the test are people who, because of their superior and desirable abilities, are also being offered positions by one or more other potential employers. Consequently, the top performers on the test are probably the least likely of all of the job applicants to actually be hired. Utility estimates based on the assumption that all people selected will actually accept offers of employment thus tend to overestimate the utility of the measurement tool. These estimates may have to be adjusted downward as much as 80% in order to provide a more realistic estimate of the utility of a tool of assessment used for selection purposes (Murphy, 1986).

The complexity of the job   In general, the same sorts of approaches to utility analysis are put to work for positions that vary greatly in terms of complexity. The same sorts of data are gathered, the same sorts of analytic methods may be applied, and the same sorts of utility models may be invoked for corporate positions ranging from assembly line worker to computer programmer. Yet as Hunter et al. (1990) observed, the more complex the job, the more people differ on how well or poorly they do that job. Whether or not the same utility models apply to jobs of varied complexity, and whether or not the same utility analysis methods are equally applicable, remain matters of debate.

The cut score in use   Also called a *cutoff score,* we have previously defined a **cut score** as a (usually numerical) reference point derived as a result of a judgment and used to divide a set of data into two or more classifications, with some action to be taken or some inference to be made on the basis of these classifications. In discussions of utility theory and utility analysis, reference is frequently made to different types of cut scores. For example, a distinction can be made between a *relative cut score* and a *fixed cut score.* A **relative cut score** may be defined as a reference point—in a distribution of test scores used to divide a set of data into two or more classifications—that is set based on norm-related considerations rather than on the relationship of test scores to a criterion. Because this type of cut score is set with reference to the performance of a group (or some target segment of a group), it is also referred to as a **norm-referenced cut score.**

As an example of a relative cut score, envision your instructor announcing on the first day of class that, for each of the four examinations to come, the top 10% of all scores on each test would receive the grade of A. In other words, the cut score in use would depend on the performance of the class as a whole. Stated another way, the cut score in use would be *relative* to the scores achieved by a targeted group (in this case, the entire class and in particular the top 10% of the class). The actual test score used to define who would and would not achieve the grade of A on each test could be quite different for each of the four tests, depending upon where the boundary line for the 10% cutoff fell on each test.

In contrast to a relative cut score is the **fixed cut score,** which we may define as a reference point—in a distribution of test scores used to divide a set of data into two or more classifications—that is typically set with reference to a judgment concerning a minimum level of proficiency required to be included in a particular classification. Fixed cut scores may also be referred to as *absolute cut scores.* An example of a fixed cut score might be the score achieved on the road test for a driver's license. Here the performance of other would-be drivers has no bearing upon whether an individual testtaker is classified as "licensed" or "not licensed." All that really matters here is the examiner's answer to this question: "Is this driver able to meet (or exceed) the fixed and absolute score on the road test necessary to be licensed?"

A distinction can also be made between the terms *multiple cut scores* and *multiple hurdles* as used in decision-making processes. **Multiple cut scores** refers to the use of two or more cut scores with reference to one predictor for the purpose of categorizing testtakers. So, for example, your instructor may have multiple cut scores in place every time an examination is administered, and each class member will be assigned to one category (e.g., A, B, C, D, or F) on the basis of scores on that examination. That is, meeting or exceeding one cut score will result in an A for the examination, meeting or exceeding another cut score will result in a B for the examination, and so forth. This is an example of multiple cut scores being used with a single predictor. Of course, we may also speak of multiple cut scores being used in an evaluation that entails several predictors wherein applicants must meet the requisite cut score on every predictor to be considered for the position. A more sophisticated but cost-effective multiple cut-score method can involve several "hurdles" to overcome.

At every stage in a multistage (or **multiple hurdle**) selection process, a cut score is in place for each predictor used. The cut score used for each predictor will be designed to ensure that each applicant possess some minimum level of a specific attribute or skill. In this context, *multiple hurdles* may be thought of as one collective element of a multistage decision-making process in which the achievement of a particular cut score on one test is necessary in order to advance to the next stage of evaluation in the selection process. In applying to colleges or professional schools, for example, applicants may have to successfully meet some standard in order to move to the next stage in a series of stages. The process might begin, for example, with the *written application* stage in which individuals who turn in incomplete applications are eliminated from further consideration. This is followed by what might be termed an *additional materials* stage in which individuals with low test scores, GPAs, or poor letters of recommendation are eliminated. The final stage in the process might be a *personal interview* stage. Each of these stages entails unique demands (and cut scores) to be successfully met, or hurdles to be overcome, if an applicant is to proceed to the next stage. Switching gears considerably, another example of a selection process that entails multiple hurdles is presented in Figure 7–2.

Multiple-hurdle selection methods assume that an individual must possess a certain minimum amount of knowledge, skill, or ability for each attribute measured by a predictor to be successful in the desired position. But is that really the case? Could it be that a very high score in one stage of a multistage evaluation compensates for or "balances out" a relatively low score in another stage of the evaluation? In what is referred to as a

JUST THINK . . .

Can both relative and absolute cut scores be used within the same evaluation? If so, provide an example.

JUST THINK . . .

Many television programs—including shows like *Dancing with the Stars,* and *The Voice*—could be conceptualized as having a multiple-hurdle selection policy in place. Explain why these are multiple-hurdle processes. Offer your suggestions, from a psychometric perspective, for improving the selection process on these or any other show with a multiple-hurdle selection policy.

Figure 7–2
"There She Goes . . ." Over Yet Another Hurdle

Contestants in this pageant must exhibit more than beauty if they are to be crowned. Beyond the swimsuit competition, contestants are judged on talent, responses to interview questions, and other variables. Only by "making the cut" and "clearing each hurdle" in each category of the judging will one of the contestants emerge as the pageant winner.

© James Atoa/Everett Collection/Age Fotostock

JUST THINK . . .

Imagine that you are on the hiring committee of an airline that has a compensatory selection model in place. What three pilot characteristics would you rate as most desirable in new hires? Using percentages, how would you differentially weight each of these three characteristics in terms of importance (with the total equal to 100%)?

JUST THINK . . .

It is possible for a corporate employer to have in place personnel selection procedures that use both cutoff scores at one stage of the decision process and a compensatory approach at another? Can you think of an example?

compensatory model of selection, an assumption is made that high scores on one attribute can, in fact, "balance out" or compensate for low scores on another attribute. According to this model, a person strong in some areas and weak in others can perform as successfully in a position as a person with moderate abilities in all areas relevant to the position in question.

Intuitively, the compensatory model is appealing, especially when post-hire training or other opportunities are available to develop proficiencies and help an applicant compensate for any areas of deficiency. For instance, with reference to the delivery driver example in this chapter's *Close-Up,* consider an applicant with strong driving skills but weak customer service skills. All it might take for this applicant to blossom into an outstanding employee is some additional education (including readings and exposure to videotaped models) and training (role-play and on-the-job supervision) in customer service.

When a compensatory selection model is in place, the individual or entity making the selection will, in general, differentially weight the predictors being used in order to arrive at a total score. Such differential weightings may reflect value judgments made on the part of the test developers regarding the relative importance of different criteria used in hiring. For example, a safe driving history may be weighted higher in the selection formula than is customer service. This weighting might be based on a company-wide "safety first" ethic. It may also be based on a company belief that skill in driving safely is less amenable to education and training than skill in customer service. The total score on all of the predictors will be used to make the decision to select or reject. The statistical tool that is ideally suited for making such selection decisions within the framework of a compensatory model is multiple regression. Other tools, as we will see in what follows, are used to set cut scores.

Methods for Setting Cut Scores

If you have ever had the experience of earning a grade of B when you came oh-so-close to the cut score needed for a grade A, then you have no doubt spent some time pondering the way that cut scores are determined. In this exercise, you are not alone. Educators, researchers, corporate statisticians, and others with diverse backgrounds have spent countless hours questioning, debating, and—judging from the nature of the heated debates in the literature— agonizing about various aspects of cut scores. No wonder; cut scores applied to a wide array of tests may be used (usually in combination with other tools of measurement) to make various "high-stakes" (read "life-changing") decisions, a partial listing of which would include:

- who gets into what college, graduate school, or professional school;
- who is certified or licensed to practice a particular occupation or profession;
- who is accepted for employment, promoted, or moved to some desirable position in a business or other organization;
- who will advance to the next stage in evaluation of knowledge or skills;
- who is legally able to drive an automobile;
- who is legally competent to stand trial;
- who is legally competent to make a last will;
- who is considered to be legally intoxicated;
- who is not guilty by reason of insanity;
- which foreign national will earn American citizenship.

Page upon page in journal articles, books, and other scholarly publications contain writings that wrestle with issues regarding the optimal method of "making the cut" with cut scores. One thoughtful researcher raised the question that served as the inspiration for our next *Just Think* exercise (see Reckase, 2004). So, after you have given due thought to that exercise, read on and become acquainted with various methods in use today for setting fixed and relative cut scores. Although no one method has won universal acceptance, some methods are more popular than others.

> **JUST THINK . . .**
>
> What if there were a "true cut-score theory" for setting cut scores that was analogous to the "true score theory" for tests? What might it look like?

The Angoff Method

Devised by William Angoff (1971), the **Angoff method** for setting fixed cut scores can be applied to personnel selection tasks as well as to questions regarding the presence or absence of a particular trait, attribute, or ability. When used for purposes of personnel selection, experts in the area provide estimates regarding how testtakers who have at least minimal competence for the position should answer test items correctly. As applied for purposes relating to the determination of whether or not testtakers possess a particular trait, attribute, or ability, an expert panel makes judgments concerning the way a person with that trait, attribute, or ability would respond to test items. In both cases, the judgments of the experts are averaged to yield cut scores for the test. Persons who score at or above the cut score are considered high enough in the ability to be hired or to be sufficiently high in the trait, attribute, or ability of interest. This relatively simple technique has wide appeal (Cascio et al., 1988; Maurer & Alexander, 1992) and works well—that is, as long as the experts agree. The Achilles heel of the Angoff method is when there is low inter-rater reliability and major disagreement regarding how certain populations of testtakers should respond to items. In such scenarios, it may be time for "Plan B," a strategy for setting cut scores that is driven more by data and less by subjective judgments.

The Known Groups Method

Also referred to as the *method of contrasting groups,* the **known groups method** entails collection of data on the predictor of interest from groups known to possess, and *not* to possess, a trait, attribute, or ability of interest. Based on an analysis of this data, a cut score is set on the test that best discriminates the two groups' test performance. How does this work in practice? Consider the following example.

A hypothetical online college called Internet Oxford University (IOU) offers a remedial math course for students who have not been adequately prepared in high school for college-level math. But who needs to take remedial math before taking regular math? To answer that question, senior personnel in the IOU Math Department prepare a placement test called the "Who Needs to Take Remedial Math? Test" (WNTRMT). The next question is, "What shall the cut score on the WNTRMT be?" That question will be answered by administering the test to a selected population and then setting a cut score based on the performance of two contrasting groups: (1) students who successfully completed college-level math, and (2) students who failed college-level math.

Accordingly, the WNTRMT is administered to all incoming freshmen. IOU collects all test data and holds it for a semester (or two). It then analyzes the scores of two approximately equal-sized groups of students who took college-level math courses: a group who passed the course and earned credit, and a group who did not earn credit for the course because their final grade was a D or an F. IOU statisticians will now use these data to choose the score that best discriminates the two groups from each other, which is the score at the point of *least* difference between the two groups. As shown in Figure 7–3 the two groups are indistinguishable at a score of 6. Consequently, now and forever more (or at least until IOU conducts another study), the cutoff score on the IOU shall be 6.

The main problem with using known groups is that determination of where to set the cutoff score is inherently affected by the composition of the contrasting groups. No standard set of guidelines exist for choosing contrasting groups. In the IOU example, the university officials could have chosen to contrast just the A students with the F students when deriving a cut score; this would definitely have resulted in a different cutoff score. Other types of problems in choosing scores from contrasting groups occur in other studies. For example, in setting cut scores for a clinical measure of depression, just how depressed do respondents from the depressed group have to be? How "normal" should the respondents in the nondepressed group be?

IRT-Based Methods

The methods described thus far for setting cut scores are based on classical test score theory. In this theory, cut scores are typically set based on tessttakers' performance across all the items

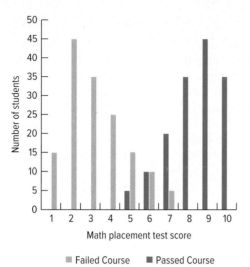

Figure 7–3
Scores on IOU's WMTRMT

■ Failed Course ■ Passed Course

on the test; some portion of the total number of items on the test must be scored "correct" (or in a way that indicates the testtaker possesses the target trait or attribute) in order for the testtaker to "pass" the test (or be deemed to possess the targeted trait or attribute). Within an item response theory (IRT) framework, however, things can be done a little differently. In the IRT framework, each item is associated with a particular level of difficulty. In order to "pass" the test, the testtaker must answer items that are deemed to be above some minimum level of difficulty, which is determined by experts and serves as the cut score.

There are several IRT-based methods for determining the difficulty level reflected by a cut score (Karantonis & Sireci, 2006; Wang, 2003). For example, a technique that has found application in setting cut scores for licensing examinations is the **item-mapping method.** It entails the arrangement of items in a histogram, with each column in the histogram containing items deemed to be of equivalent value. Judges who have been trained regarding minimal competence required for licensure are presented with sample items from each column and are asked whether or not a minimally competent licensed individual would answer those items correctly about half the time. If so, that difficulty level is set as the cut score; if not, the process continues until the appropriate difficulty level has been selected. Typically, the process involves several rounds of judgments in which experts may receive feedback regarding how their ratings compare to ratings made by other experts.

An IRT-based method of setting cut scores that is more typically used in academic applications is the **bookmark method** (Lewis et al., 1996; see also Mitzel et al., 2000). Use of this method begins with the training of experts with regard to the minimal knowledge, skills, and/or abilities that testtakers should possess in order to "pass." Subsequent to this training, the experts are given a book of items, with one item printed per page, such that items are arranged in an ascending order of difficulty. The expert then places a "bookmark" between the two pages (or, the two items) that are deemed to separate testtakers who have acquired the minimal knowledge, skills, and/or abilities from those who have not. The bookmark serves as the cut score. Additional rounds of bookmarking with the same or other judges may take place as necessary. Feedback regarding placement may be provided, and discussion among experts about the bookmarkings may be allowed. In the end, the level of difficulty to use as the cut score is decided upon by the test developers. Of course, none of these procedures are free of possible drawbacks. Some concerns raised about the bookmarking method include issues regarding the training of experts, possible floor and ceiling effects, and the optimal length of item booklets (Skaggs et al., 2007).

Other Methods

Our overview of cut-score setting has touched on only a few of the many methods that have been proposed, implemented, or experimented with; many other methods exist. For example, Hambleton and Novick (1973) presented a decision-theoretic approach to setting cut scores. In his book *Personnel Psychology,* R. L. Thorndike (1949) proposed a norm-referenced method for setting cut scores called the *method of predictive yield.* The **method of predictive yield** was a technique for setting cut scores which took into account the number of positions to be filled, projections regarding the likelihood of offer acceptance, and the distribution of applicant scores. Another approach to setting cut scores employs a family of statistical techniques called **discriminant analysis** (also referred to as *discriminant function analysis*). These techniques are typically used to shed light on the relationship between identified variables (such as scores on a battery of tests) and two (and in some cases more) naturally occurring groups (such as persons judged to be successful at a job and persons judged unsuccessful at a job).

Given the importance of setting cut scores and how much can be at stake for individuals "cut" by them, research and debate on the issues involved are likely to continue—at least until that hypothetical "true score theory for cut scores" alluded to earlier in this chapter is identified and welcomed by members of the research community.

In this chapter, we have focused on the possible benefits of testing and how to assess those benefits. In so doing, we have touched on several aspects of test development and construction. In the next chapter, we delve more deeply into the details of these important elements of testing and assessment.

Self-Assessment

Test your understanding of elements of this chapter by seeing if you can explain each of the following terms, expressions, and abbreviations:

absolute cut score	discriminant analysis	norm-referenced cut score
Angoff method	fixed cut score	productivity gain
benefit (as related to test utility)	item-mapping method	relative cut score
bookmark method	known groups method	return on investment
Brogden-Cronbach-Gleser formula	method of contrasting groups	top-down selection
compensatory model of selection	method of predictive yield	utility (test utility)
cost (as related to test utility)	multiple cut scores	utility analysis
cut score	multiple hurdle (selection process)	utility gain

CHAPTER 8

Test Development

All tests are not created equal. The creation of a good test is not a matter of chance. It is the product of the thoughtful and sound application of established principles of *test development.* In this context, **test development** is an umbrella term for all that goes into the process of creating a test.

In this chapter, we introduce the basics of test development and examine in detail the processes by which tests are assembled. We explore, for example, ways that test items are written, and ultimately selected for use. Although we focus on tests of the published, standardized variety, much of what we have to say also applies to custom-made tests such as those created by teachers, researchers, and employers.

The process of developing a test occurs in five stages:

1. test conceptualization;
2. test construction;
3. test tryout;
4. item analysis;
5. test revision.

Once the idea for a test is conceived (**test conceptualization**), *test construction* begins. As we are using this term, **test construction** is a stage in the process of test development that entails writing test items (or re-writing or revising existing items), as well as formatting items, setting scoring rules, and otherwise designing and building a test. Once a preliminary form of the test has been developed, it is administered to a representative sample of testtakers under conditions that simulate the conditions that the final version of the test will be administered under (**test tryout**). The data from the tryout will be collected and testtakers' performance on the test as a whole and on each item will be analyzed. Statistical procedures, referred to as *item analysis,* are employed to assist in making judgments about which items are good as they are, which items need to be revised, and which items should be discarded. The analysis of the test's items may include analyses of item reliability, item validity, and item discrimination. Depending on the type of test, item-difficulty level may be analyzed as well.

Next in the sequence of events in test development is *test revision.* Here, **test revision** refers to action taken to modify a test's content or format for the purpose of improving the test's effectiveness as a tool of measurement. This action is usually based on item analyses, as well as related information derived from the test tryout. The revised version of the test will then be tried out on a new sample of testtakers. After the results are

JUST THINK . . .

Can you think of a classic psychological test from the past that has never undergone test tryout, item analysis, or revision? What about so-called psychological tests found on the Internet?

analyzed the test will be further revised if necessary—and so it goes (see Figure 8–1). Although the test development process described is fairly typical today, let's note that there are many exceptions to it, both with regard to tests developed in the past, and some contemporary tests. Some tests are conceived of and constructed but neither tried-out, nor item-analyzed, nor revised.

Test Conceptualization

The beginnings of any published test can probably be traced to thoughts—self-talk, in behavioral terms. The test developer says to himself or herself something like: "There ought to be a test designed to measure [fill in the blank] in [such and such] way." The stimulus for such a thought could be almost anything. A review of the available literature on existing tests designed to measure a particular construct might indicate that such tests leave much to be desired in psychometric soundness. An emerging social phenomenon or pattern of behavior might serve as the stimulus for the development of a new test. The analogy with medicine is straightforward: Once a new disease comes to the attention of medical researchers, they attempt to develop diagnostic tests to assess its presence or absence as well as the severity of its manifestations in the body.

The development of a new test may be in response to a need to assess mastery in an emerging occupation or profession. For example, new tests may be developed to assess mastery in fields such as high-definition electronics, environmental engineering, and wireless communications.

In recent years, measurement interest related to aspects of the LGBT (lesbian, gay, bi-sexual, and transgender) experience has increased. The present authors propose that in the interest of comprehensive inclusion, an "A" should be added to the end of "LGBT" so that this term is routinely abbreviated as "LGBTA." The additional "A" would acknowledge the existence of asexuality as a sexual orientation or preference.

Asexuality may be defined as *a sexual orientation characterized by a long-term lack of interest in a sexual relationship with anyone or anything.* Given that some research is conducted with persons claiming to be asexual, and given that asexual individuals must be selected-in or selected-out to participate in such research, Yule et al. (2015) perceived a need for a reliable and valid test to measure asexuality. Read about their efforts to develop and validate their rather novel test in this chapter's *Close-Up.*

JUST THINK . . .

What is a "hot topic" today that developers of psychological tests should be working on? What aspects of this topic might be explored by means of a psychological test?

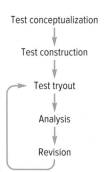

Test conceptualization

↓

Test construction

↓

Test tryout

↓

Analysis

↓

Revision

Figure 8–1
The Test Development Process

Creating and Validating a Test of Asexuality*

In general, and with some variation according to the source, **human asexuality** may be defined as an absence of sexual attraction to anyone at all. Estimates suggest that approximately 1% of the population might be asexual (Bogaert, 2004). Although the concept of asexuality was first introduced by Alfred Kinsey in 1948, it is only in the past decade that it has received any substantial academic attention. Scholars are grappling with how best to conceptualize asexuality. For some, asexuality is thought of as itself, a sexual orientation (Berkey et al., 1990; Bogaert, 2004; Brotto & Yule, 2011; Brotto et al., 2010; Storms, 1978; Yule et al., 2014). Others view asexuality more as a mental health issue, a paraphilia, or human sexual dysfunction (see Bogaert, 2012, 2015).

More research on human asexuality would be helpful. However, researchers who design projects to explore human asexuality face the challenge of finding qualified subjects. Perhaps the best source of asexual research subjects has been an online organization called "AVEN" (an acronym for the Asexuality and Visibility Education Network). Located at *asexuality.org,* this organization had some 120,000 members at the time of this writing (in May, 2016). But while the convenience of these group members as a recruitment source is obvious, there are also limitations inherent to exclusively recruiting research participants from a single online community. For example, asexual individuals who do not belong to AVEN are systematically excluded from such research. It may well be that those unaffiliated asexual individuals differ from AVEN members in significant ways. For example, these individuals may have lived their lives devoid of any sexual attraction, but have never construed themselves to be "asexual." On the other hand, persons belonging to AVEN may be a unique group within the asexual population, as they have not only acknowledged their asexuality as an identity, but actively sought out affiliation with other like-minded individuals. Clearly, an alternative recruitment procedure is needed. Simply relying on membership in AVEN as a credential of asexuality is flawed. What is needed is a validated measure to screen for human asexuality.

In response to this need for a test designed to screen for human asexuality, the Asexuality Identification Scale (AIS) was developed (Yule et al., 2015). The AIS is a 12-item, sex- and gender-neutral, self-report measure of asexuality. The AIS was developed in a series of stages. Stage 1 included development and administration of eight open-ended questions to sexual

*This *Close-Up* was guest-authored by Morag A. Yule and Lori A. Brotto, both of the Department of Obstetrics & Gynaecology of the University of British Columbia.

($n = 70$) and asexual ($n = 139$) individuals. These subjects were selected for participation in the study through online channels (e.g., AVEN, Craigslist, and Facebook). Subjects responded in writing to a series of questions focused on definitions of asexuality, sexual attraction, sexual desire, and romantic attraction. There were no space limitations, and participants were encouraged to answer in as much or as little detail as they wished. Participant responses were examined to identify prevalent themes, and this information was used to generate 111 multiple-choice items. In Stage 2, these 111 items were administered to another group of asexual ($n = 165$) and sexual ($n = 752$) participants. Subjects in this phase of the test development process were selected for participation through a variety of online websites, and also through our university's human subjects pool. The resulting data were then factor- and item-analyzed in order to determine which items should be retained. The decision to retain an item was made on the basis of our judgment as to which items best differentiated asexual from sexual participants. Thirty-seven items were selected based on the results of this item selection process. In Stage 3, these 37 items were administered to another group of asexual ($n = 316$) and sexual ($n = 926$) participants. Here, subjects were selected through the same means as in Stage 2, but also through websites that host psychological online studies. As in Stage 2, the items were analyzed for the purpose of selecting those items that best loaded on the asexual versus the sexual factors. Of the 37 original items subjected to item analysis, 12 items were retained, and 25 were discarded.

In order to determine construct validity, psychometric validation on the 12-item AIS was conducted using data from the same participants in Stage 3. Known-groups validity was established as the AIS total score showed excellent ability to distinguish between asexual and sexual subjects. Specifically, a cut-off score of 40/60 was found to identify 93% of self-identified asexual individuals, while excluding 95% of sexual individuals. In order to assess whether the measure was useful over and above already-available measures of sexual orientation, we compared the AIS to an adaptation of a previously established measure of sexual orientation (Klein Scale; Klein & Sepekoff, 1985). Incremental validity was established, as the AIS showed only moderate correlations with the Klein Scale, suggesting that the AIS is a better predictor of asexuality compared to an existing measure. To determine whether the AIS correlates with a construct that is thought to be highly related to asexuality (or, lack of sexual desire), convergent validity was assessed by correlating total AIS

(continued)

Creating and Validating a Test of Asexuality *(continued)*

scores with scores on the Sexual Desire Inventory (SDI; Spector et al., 1996). As we expected, the AIS correlated only weakly with Solitary Desire subscale of the SDI, while the Dyadic Desire subscale of the SDI had a moderate negative correlation with the AIS. Finally, we conducted discriminant validity analyses by comparing the AIS with the Childhood Trauma Questionnaire (CTQ; Bernstein et al., 1994; Bernstein & Fink, 1998), the Short-Form Inventory of Interpersonal Problems-Circumplex scales (IIP-SC; Soldz et al., 1995), and the Big-Five Inventory (BFI; John et al., 1991; John et al., 2008; John & Srivastava, 1999) in order to determine whether the AIS was actually tapping into negative sexual experiences or personality traits. Discriminant validity was established, as the AIS was not significantly correlated with scores on the CTQ, IIP-SC, or the BFI.

Sexual and asexual participants significantly differed in their AIS total scores with a large effect size. Further, the AIS passed tests of known-groups, incremental, convergent, and discriminant validity. This suggests that the AIS is a useful tool for identifying asexuality, and could be used in future research to identify individuals with a lack of sexual attraction. We believe that respondents need not be self-identified as asexual in order to be selected as asexual on the AIS. Research suggests that the AIS will identify as asexual the individual who exhibits characteristics of a lifelong lack of sexual attraction in the absence of personal distress. It is our hope that the AIS will allow for recruitment of more representative samples of the asexuality population, and contribute toward a growing body of research on this topic.

Used with permission of Morag A. Yule and Lori A. Brotto.

Some Preliminary Questions

Regardless of the stimulus for developing the new test, a number of questions immediately confront the prospective test developer.

- *What is the test designed to measure?* This is a deceptively simple question. Its answer is closely linked to how the test developer defines the construct being measured and how that definition is the same as or different from other tests purporting to measure the same construct.

- *What is the objective of the test?* In the service of what goal will the test be employed? In what way or ways is the objective of this test the same as or different from other tests with similar goals? What real-world behaviors would be anticipated to correlate with testtaker responses?

- *Is there a need for this test?* Are there any other tests purporting to measure the same thing? In what ways will the new test be better than or different from existing ones? Will there be more compelling evidence for its reliability or validity? Will it be more comprehensive? Will it take less time to administer? In what ways would this test *not* be better than existing tests?

- *Who will use this test?* Clinicians? Educators? Others? For what purpose or purposes would this test be used?

- *Who will take this test?* Who is this test for? Who needs to take it? Who would find it desirable to take it? For what age range of testtakers is the test designed? What reading level is required of a testtaker? What cultural factors might affect testtaker response?

- *What content will the test cover?* Why should it cover this content? Is this coverage different from the content coverage of existing tests with the same or similar objectives? How and why is the content area different? To what extent is this content culture-specific?

- *How will the test be administered?* Individually or in groups? Is it amenable to both group and individual administration? What differences will exist between individual and group administrations of this test? Will the test be designed for or amenable to computer administration? How might differences between versions of the test be reflected in test scores?

■ *What is the ideal format of the test?* Should it be true–false, essay, multiple-choice, or in some other format? Why is the format selected for this test the best format?

■ *Should more than one form of the test be developed?* On the basis of a cost–benefit analysis, should alternate or parallel forms of this test be created?

■ *What special training will be required of test users for administering or interpreting the test?* What background and qualifications will a prospective user of data derived from an administration of this test need to have? What restrictions, if any, should be placed on distributors of the test and on the test's usage?

■ *What types of responses will be required of testtakers?* What kind of disability might preclude someone from being able to take this test? What adaptations or accommodations are recommended for persons with disabilities?

■ *Who benefits from an administration of this test?* What would the testtaker learn, or how might the testtaker benefit, from an administration of this test? What would the test user learn, or how might the test user benefit? What social benefit, if any, derives from an administration of this test?

■ *Is there any potential for harm as the result of an administration of this test?* What safeguards are built into the recommended testing procedure to prevent any sort of harm to any of the parties involved in the use of this test?

■ *How will meaning be attributed to scores on this test?* Will a testtaker's score be compared to those of others taking the test at the same time? To those of others in a criterion group? Will the test evaluate mastery of a particular content area?

This last question provides a point of departure for elaborating on issues related to test development with regard to norm- versus criterion-referenced tests.

Norm-referenced versus criterion-referenced tests: Item development issues Different approaches to test development and individual item analyses are necessary, depending upon whether the finished test is designed to be norm-referenced or criterion-referenced. Generally speaking, for example, a good item on a norm-referenced achievement test is an item for which high scorers on the test respond correctly. Low scorers on the test tend to respond to that same item incorrectly. On a criterion-oriented test, this same pattern of results may occur: High scorers on the test get a particular item right whereas low scorers on the test get that same item wrong. However, that is not what makes an item good or acceptable from a criterion-oriented perspective. Ideally, each item on a criterion-oriented test addresses the issue of whether the testtaker—a would-be physician, engineer, piano student, or whoever—has met certain criteria. In short, when it comes to criterion-oriented assessment, being "first in the class" does not count and is often irrelevant. Although we can envision exceptions to this general rule, norm-referenced comparisons typically are insufficient and inappropriate when knowledge of mastery is what the test user requires.

Criterion-referenced testing and assessment are commonly employed in licensing contexts, be it a license to practice medicine or to drive a car. Criterion-referenced approaches are also employed in educational contexts in which mastery of particular material must be demonstrated before the student moves on to advanced material that conceptually builds on the existing base of knowledge, skills, or both.

In contrast to techniques and principles applicable to the development of norm-referenced tests (many of which are discussed in this chapter), the development of criterion-referenced instruments derives from a conceptualization of the knowledge or skills to be mastered. For purposes of assessment, the required cognitive or motor skills may be broken down into component parts. The test developer may attempt to sample criterion-related knowledge with regard to general principles relevant to the criterion being assessed. Experimentation with different items, tests, formats, or measurement procedures will help the test developer discover the best measure of mastery for the targeted skills or knowledge.

◆

JUST THINK . . .

Suppose you were charged with developing a criterion-referenced test to measure mastery of Chapter 8 of this book. Explain, in as much detail as you think sufficient, how you would go about doing that. It's OK to read on before answering (in fact, you are encouraged to do so).

In general, the development of a criterion-referenced test or assessment procedure may entail exploratory work with at least two groups of testtakers: one group known to have mastered the knowledge or skill being measured and another group known *not* to have mastered such knowledge or skill. For example, during the development of a criterion-referenced written test for a driver's license, a preliminary version of the test may be administered to one group of people who have been driving about 15,000 miles per year for 10 years and who have perfect safety records (no accidents and no moving violations). The second group of testtakers might be a group of adults matched in demographic and related respects to the first group but who have never had any instruction in driving or driving experience. The items that best discriminate between these two groups would be considered "good" items. The preliminary exploratory experimentation done in test development need not have anything at all to do with flying, but you wouldn't know that from its name . . .

Pilot Work

In the context of test development, terms such as **pilot work**, *pilot study,* and *pilot research* refer, in general, to the preliminary research surrounding the creation of a prototype of the test. Test items may be pilot studied (or piloted) to evaluate whether they should be included in the final form of the instrument. In developing a structured interview to measure introversion/extraversion, for example, pilot research may involve open-ended interviews with research subjects believed for some reason (perhaps on the basis of an existing test) to be introverted or extraverted. Additionally, interviews with parents, teachers, friends, and others who know the subject might also be arranged. Another type of pilot study might involve physiological monitoring of the subjects (such as monitoring of heart rate) as a function of exposure to different types of stimuli.

In pilot work, the test developer typically attempts to determine how best to measure a targeted construct. The process may entail literature reviews and experimentation as well as the creation, revision, and deletion of preliminary test items. After pilot work comes the process of test construction. Keep in mind, however, that depending on the nature of the test, as well as the nature of the changing responses to it by testtakers, test users, and the community at large, the need for further pilot research and test revision is always a possibility.

Pilot work is a necessity when constructing tests or other measuring instruments for publication and wide distribution. Of course, pilot work need not be part of the process of developing teacher-made tests for classroom use. Let's take a moment at this juncture to discuss selected aspects of the process of developing tests not for use on the world stage, but rather to measure achievement in a class.

Test Construction

Scaling

We have previously defined *measurement* as the assignment of numbers according to rules. **Scaling** may be defined as the process of setting rules for assigning numbers in measurement. Stated another way, scaling is the process by which a measuring device is designed and calibrated and by which numbers (or other indices)—scale values—are assigned to different amounts of the trait, attribute, or characteristic being measured.

Historically, the prolific L. L. Thurstone (Figure 8–2) is credited for being at the forefront of efforts to develop methodologically sound scaling methods. He adapted psychophysical scaling methods to the study of psychological variables such as attitudes and values (Thurstone, 1959; Thurstone & Chave, 1929). Thurstone's (1925) article entitled "A Method of Scaling Psychological and Educational Tests" introduced, among other things, the notion of absolute scaling—a procedure for obtaining a measure of item difficulty across samples of testtakers who vary in ability.

Types of scales   In common parlance, scales are instruments used to measure something, such as weight. In psychometrics, scales may also be conceived of as instruments used to measure. Here, however, that *something* being measured is likely to be a trait, a state, or an ability. When we think of types of scales, we think of the different ways that scales can be categorized. In Chapter 3, for example, we saw that scales can be meaningfully categorized along a continuum of level of measurement and be referred to as nominal, ordinal, interval, or ratio. But we might also characterize scales in other ways.

If the testtaker's test performance as a function of age is of critical interest, then the test might be referred to as an *age-based scale.* If the testtaker's test performance as a function of grade is of critical interest, then the test might be referred to as a *grade-based scale.* If all raw scores on the test are to be transformed into scores that can range from 1 to 9, then the test might be referred to as a *stanine* scale. A scale might be described in still other ways. For example, it may be categorized as *unidimensional* as opposed to *multidimensional.* It may be categorized as *comparative* as opposed to *categorical.* This is just a sampling of the various ways in which scales can be categorized.

Given that scales can be categorized in many different ways, it would be reasonable to assume that there are many different methods of scaling. Indeed, there are; there is no one method of scaling. There is no best type of scale. Test developers scale a test in the manner they believe is optimally suited to their conception of the measurement of the trait (or whatever) that is being measured.

Figure 8–2
L. L. Thurstone (1887–1955)

Among his many achievements in the area of scaling was Thurstone's (1927) influential article "A Law of Comparative Judgment." One of the few "laws" in psychology, this was Thurstone's proudest achievement (Nunnally, 1978, pp. 60–61). Of course, he had many achievements from which to choose. Thurstone's adaptations of scaling methods for use in psychophysiological research and the study of attitudes and values have served as models for generations of researchers (Bock & Jones, 1968). He is also widely considered to be one of the primary architects of modern factor analysis.
© George Skadding/Time LIFE Pictures Collection/Getty Images

Scaling methods   Generally speaking, a testtaker is presumed to have more or less of the characteristic measured by a (valid) test as a function of the test score. The higher or lower the score, the more or less of the characteristic the testtaker presumably possesses. But how are numbers assigned to responses so that a test score can be calculated? This is done through scaling the test items, using any one of several available methods.

For example, consider a moral-issues opinion measure called the Morally Debatable Behaviors Scale–Revised (MDBS-R; Katz et al., 1994). Developed to be "a practical means of assessing what people believe, the strength of their convictions, as well as individual differences in moral tolerance" (p. 15), the MDBS-R contains 30 items. Each item contains a brief description of a moral issue or behavior on which testtakers express their opinion by means of a 10-point scale that ranges from "never justified" to "always justified." Here is a sample.

Cheating on taxes if you have a chance is:

1	2	3	4	5	6	7	8	9	10
never									always
justified									justified

The MDBS-R is an example of a **rating scale,** which can be defined as a grouping of words, statements, or symbols on which judgments of the strength of a particular trait, attitude, or emotion are indicated by the testtaker. Rating scales can be used to record judgments of oneself, others, experiences, or objects, and they can take several forms (Figure 8–3).

On the MDBS-R, the ratings that the testtaker makes for each of the 30 test items are added together to obtain a final score. Scores range from a low of 30 (if the testtaker indicates that all 30 behaviors are never justified) to a high of 300 (if the testtaker indicates that all

Rating Scale Item A
How did you feel about what you saw on television?

Rating Scale Item B
I believe I would like the work of a lighthouse keeper.
True   False   (circle one)

Rating Scale Item C
Please rate the employee on ability to cooperate and get along with fellow employees:
Excellent _____ /_____ /_____ /_____ /_____ /_____ /_____ / Unsatisfactory

Figure 8–3
The Many Faces of Rating Scales

Rating scales can take many forms. "Smiley" faces, such as those illustrated here as Item A, have been used in social-psychological research with young children and adults with limited language skills. The faces are used in lieu of words such as positive, neutral, and negative.

30 situations are always justified). Because the final test score is obtained by summing the ratings across all the items, it is termed a **summative scale.**

One type of summative rating scale, the **Likert scale** (Likert, 1932), is used extensively in psychology, usually to scale attitudes. Likert scales are relatively easy to construct. Each item presents the testtaker with five alternative responses (sometimes seven), usually on an agree–disagree or approve–disapprove continuum. If Katz et al. had used a Likert scale, an item on their test might have looked like this:

Cheating on taxes if you have a chance.

This is (check one):

_____	_____	_____	_____	_____
never justified	rarely justified	sometimes justified	usually justified	always justified

Likert scales are usually reliable, which may account for their widespread popularity. Likert (1932) experimented with different weightings of the five categories but concluded that assigning weights of 1 (for endorsement of items at one extreme) through 5 (for endorsement of items at the other extreme) generally worked best.

The use of rating scales of any type results in ordinal-level data. With reference to the Likert scale item, for example, if the response *never justified* is assigned the value 1, *rarely justified* the value 2, and so on, then a higher score indicates greater permissiveness with regard to cheating on taxes. Respondents could even be ranked with regard to such permissiveness.

JUST THINK . . .

In your opinion, which version of the Morally Debatable Behaviors Scale is optimal?

However, the difference in permissiveness between the opinions of a pair of people who scored 2 and 3 on this scale is not necessarily the same as the difference between the opinions of a pair of people who scored 3 and 4.

Rating scales differ in the number of dimensions underlying the ratings being made. Some rating scales are *unidimensional,* meaning that only one dimension is presumed to underlie the ratings. Other rating scales are *multidimensional,* meaning that more than one dimension is thought to guide the testtaker's responses. Consider in this context an item from the MDBS-R regarding marijuana use. Responses to this item, particularly responses in the low to middle range, may be interpreted in many different ways. Such responses may reflect the view (a) that people should not engage in illegal activities, (b) that people should not take risks with their health, or (c) that people should avoid activities that could lead to contact with a bad crowd. Responses to this item may also reflect other attitudes and beliefs, including those related to documented benefits of marijuana use, as well as new legislation and regulations. When more than one dimension is tapped by an item, multidimensional scaling techniques are used to identify the dimensions.

Another scaling method that produces ordinal data is the **method of paired comparisons.** Testtakers are presented with pairs of stimuli (two photographs, two objects, two statements), which they are asked to compare. They must select one of the stimuli according to some rule; for example, the rule that they agree more with one statement than the other, or the rule that they find one stimulus more appealing than the other. Had Katz et al. used the method of paired comparisons, an item on their scale might have looked like the one that follows.

Select the behavior that you think would be more justified:

a. cheating on taxes if one has a chance
b. accepting a bribe in the course of one's duties

For each pair of options, testtakers receive a higher score for selecting the option deemed more justifiable by the majority of a group of judges. The judges would have been asked to rate the pairs of options before the distribution of the test, and a list of the options selected by the judges would be provided along with the scoring instructions as an answer key. The test score would reflect the number of times the choices of a testtaker agreed with those of the judges. If we use Katz et al.'s (1994) standardization sample as the judges, then the more justifiable option is cheating on taxes. A testtaker might receive a point toward the total score for selecting option "a" but no points for selecting option "b." An advantage of the method of paired comparisons is that it forces testtakers to choose between items.

◆ JUST THINK . . .

Under what circumstance might it be advantageous for tests to contain items presented as a sorting task?

Sorting tasks are another way that ordinal information may be developed and scaled. Here, stimuli such as printed cards, drawings, photographs, or other objects are typically presented to testtakers for evaluation. One method of sorting, **comparative scaling,** entails judgments of a stimulus in comparison with every other stimulus on the scale. A version of the MDBS-R that employs comparative scaling might feature 30 items, each printed on a separate index card. Testtakers would be asked to sort the cards from most justifiable to least justifiable. Comparative scaling could also be accomplished by providing testtakers with a list of 30 items on a sheet of paper and asking them to rank the justifiability of the items from 1 to 30.

Another scaling system that relies on sorting is **categorical scaling.** Stimuli are placed into one of two or more alternative categories that differ quantitatively with respect to some continuum. In our running MDBS-R example, testtakers might be given 30 index cards, on each of which is printed one of the 30 items. Testtakers would be asked to sort the cards into three piles: those behaviors that are never justified, those that are sometimes justified, and those that are always justified.

A **Guttman scale** (Guttman, 1944a,b, 1947) is yet another scaling method that yields ordinal-level measures. Items on it range sequentially from weaker to stronger expressions of the attitude, belief, or feeling being measured. A feature of Guttman scales is that all respondents who agree with the stronger statements of the attitude will also agree with milder statements. Using the MDBS-R scale as an example, consider the following statements that reflect attitudes toward suicide.

Do you agree or disagree with each of the following:

a. All people should have the right to decide whether they wish to end their lives.

b. People who are terminally ill and in pain should have the option to have a doctor assist them in ending their lives.

c. People should have the option to sign away the use of artificial life-support equipment before they become seriously ill.

d. People have the right to a comfortable life.

If this were a perfect Guttman scale, then all respondents who agree with "a" (the most extreme position) should also agree with "b," "c," and "d." All respondents who disagree with "a" but agree with "b" should also agree with "c" and "d," and so forth. Guttman scales are developed through the administration of a number of items to a target group. The resulting data are then analyzed by means of **scalogram analysis**, an item-analysis procedure and approach to test development that involves a graphic mapping of a testtaker's responses. The objective for the developer of a measure of attitudes is to obtain an arrangement of items wherein endorsement of one item automatically connotes endorsement of less extreme positions. It is not always possible to do this. Beyond the measurement of attitudes, Guttman scaling or scalogram analysis (the two terms are used synonymously) appeals to test developers in consumer psychology, where an objective may be to learn if a consumer who will purchase one product will purchase another product.

All the foregoing methods yield ordinal data. The method of equal-appearing intervals, first described by Thurstone (1929), is one scaling method used to obtain data that are presumed to be interval in nature. Again using the example of attitudes about the justifiability of suicide, let's outline the steps that would be involved in creating a scale using Thurstone's equal-appearing intervals method.

1. A reasonably large number of statements reflecting positive and negative attitudes toward suicide are collected, such as *Life is sacred, so people should never take their own lives* and *A person in a great deal of physical or emotional pain may rationally decide that suicide is the best available option.*

2. Judges (or experts in some cases) evaluate each statement in terms of how strongly it indicates that suicide is justified. Each judge is instructed to rate each statement on a scale as if the scale were interval in nature. For example, the scale might range from 1 (the statement indicates that suicide is never justified) to 9 (the statement indicates that suicide is always justified). Judges are instructed that the 1-to-9 scale is being used as if there were an equal distance between each of the values—that is, as if it were an interval scale. Judges are cautioned to focus their ratings on the statements, not on their own views on the matter.

3. A mean and a standard deviation of the judges' ratings are calculated for each statement. For example, if fifteen judges rated 100 statements on a scale from 1 to 9 then, for each of these 100 statements, the fifteen judges' ratings would be averaged. Suppose five of the judges rated a particular item as a 1, five other judges rated it as a 2, and the remaining five judges rated it as a 3. The average rating would be 2 (with a standard deviation of 0.816).

4. Items are selected for inclusion in the final scale based on several criteria, including (a) the degree to which the item contributes to a comprehensive measurement of the variable in question and (b) the test developer's degree of confidence that the items have indeed been sorted into equal intervals. Item means and standard deviations are also considered. Items should represent a wide range of attitudes reflected in a variety of ways. A low standard deviation is indicative of a good item; the judges agreed about the meaning of the item with respect to its reflection of attitudes toward suicide.

5. The scale is now ready for administration. The way the scale is used depends on the objectives of the test situation. Typically, respondents are asked to select those statements that most accurately reflect their own attitudes. The values of the items that the respondent selects (based on the judges' ratings) are averaged, producing a score on the test.

The method of equal-appearing intervals is an example of a scaling method of the *direct estimation* variety. In contrast to other methods that involve *indirect estimation,* there is no need to transform the testtaker's responses into some other scale.

The particular scaling method employed in the development of a new test depends on many factors, including the variables being measured, the group for whom the test is intended (children may require a less complicated scaling method than adults, for example), and the preferences of the test developer.

Writing Items

In the grand scheme of test construction, considerations related to the actual writing of the test's items go hand in hand with scaling considerations. The prospective test developer or item writer immediately faces three questions related to the test blueprint:

- What range of content should the items cover?
- Which of the many different types of item formats should be employed?
- How many items should be written in total and for each content area covered?

When devising a standardized test using a multiple-choice format, it is usually advisable that the first draft contain approximately twice the number of items that the final version of the test will contain.[1] If, for example, a test called "American History: 1940 to 1990" is to have 30 questions in its final version, it would be useful to have as many as 60 items in the item pool. Ideally, these items will adequately sample the domain of the test. An **item pool** is the reservoir or well from which items will or will not be drawn for the final version of the test.

A comprehensive sampling provides a basis for content validity of the final version of the test. Because approximately half of these items will be eliminated from the test's final version, the test developer needs to ensure that the final version also contains items that adequately sample the domain. Thus, if all the questions about the Persian Gulf War from the original 60 items were determined to be poorly written, then the test developer should either rewrite items sampling this period or create new items. The new or rewritten items would then also be subjected to tryout so as not to jeopardize the test's content validity. As in earlier versions of the test, an effort is made to ensure adequate sampling of the domain in the final version of the test. Another consideration here is whether or not alternate forms of the test will be created and, if so, how many. Multiply the number of items required in the pool for one form of the test by the number of forms planned, and you have the total number of items needed for the initial item pool.

How does one develop items for the item pool? The test developer may write a large number of items from personal experience or academic acquaintance with the subject matter. Help may also be sought from others, including experts. For psychological tests designed to be used in clinical settings, clinicians, patients, patients' family members, clinical staff, and others may be interviewed for insights that could assist in item writing. For psychological tests designed to be used by personnel psychologists, interviews with members of a targeted industry or organization will likely be of great value. For psychological tests designed to be used by school psychologists, interviews with teachers, administrative staff, educational psychologists, and others may be invaluable. Searches through the academic research literature may prove fruitful, as may searches through other databases.

Considerations related to variables such as the purpose of the test and the number of examinees to be tested at one time enter into decisions regarding the format of the test under construction.

◆

JUST THINK . . .

If you were going to develop a pool of items to cover the subject of "academic knowledge of what it takes to develop an item pool," how would you go about doing it?

Item format   Variables such as the form, plan, structure, arrangement, and layout of individual test items are collectively referred to as **item format.** Two types of item format we will discuss in detail are the *selected-response format* and the *constructed-response format.* Items presented in a **selected-response format** require testtakers to select a response from a set of alternative responses. Items presented in a **constructed-response format** require testtakers to supply or to create the correct answer, not merely to select it.

If a test is designed to measure achievement and if the items are written in a selected-response format, then examinees must select the response that is keyed as correct. If the test is designed to measure the strength of a particular trait and if the items are written in a selected-response format, then examinees must select the alternative that best answers the question with respect to themselves. As we further discuss item formats, for the sake of simplicity we will confine our examples to achievement tests. The reader may wish to mentally substitute other appropriate terms for words such as *correct* for personality or other types of tests that are not achievement tests.

---

1. Common sense and the practical demands of the situation may dictate that fewer items be written for the first draft of a test. If, for example, the final draft were to contain 1,000 items, then creating an item pool of 2,000 items might be an undue burden. If the test developer is a knowledgeable and capable item writer, it might be necessary to create only about 1,200 items for the item pool.

Three types of selected-response item formats are *multiple-choice, matching,* and *true–false*. An item written in a **multiple-choice format** has three elements: (1) a stem, (2) a correct alternative or option, and (3) several incorrect alternatives or options variously referred to as *distractors* or *foils*. Two illustrations follow (despite the fact that you are probably all too familiar with multiple-choice items).

Item A

Stem	$\longrightarrow$	A psychological test, an interview, and a case study are:
Correct alt.	$\longrightarrow$	a. psychological assessment tools
Distractors	$\longrightarrow$	b. standardized behavioral samples c. reliable assessment instruments d. theory-linked measures

Now consider Item B:

Item B

A good multiple-choice item in an achievement test:

a. has one correct alternative
b. has grammatically parallel alternatives
c. has alternatives of similar length
d. has alternatives that fit grammatically with the stem
e. includes as much of the item as possible in the stem to avoid unnecessary repetition
f. avoids ridiculous distractors
g. is not excessively long
h. all of the above
i. none of the above

If you answered "h" to Item B, you are correct. As you read the list of alternatives, it may have occurred to you that Item B violated some of the rules it set forth!

In a **matching item,** the testtaker is presented with two columns: *premises* on the left and *responses* on the right. The testtaker's task is to determine which response is best associated with which premise. For very young testtakers, the instructions will direct them to draw a line from one premise to one response. Testtakers other than young children are typically asked to write a letter or number as a response. Here's an example of a matching item one might see on a test in a class on modern film history:

Directions: Match an actor's name in Column X with a film role the actor played in Column Y. Write the letter of the film role next to the number of the corresponding actor. Each of the roles listed in Column Y may be used once, more than once, or not at all.

Column X	Column Y
_____ 1. Matt Damon	a. Anton Chigurh
_____ 2. Javier Bardem	b. Max Styph
_____ 3. Stephen James	c. Storm
_____ 4. Michael Keaton	d. Jason Bourne
_____ 5. Charlize Theron	e. Ray Kroc
_____ 6. Chris Evans	f. Jesse Owens
_____ 7. George Lazenby	g. Hugh ("The Revenant") Glass
_____ 8. Ben Affleck	h. Steve ("Captain America") Rogers
_____ 9. Keanu Reeves	i. Bruce (Batman) Wayne
_____ 10. Leonardo DiCaprio	j. Aileen Wuornos
_____ 11. Halle Berry	k. James Bond
	l. John Wick
	m. Jennifer Styph

You may have noticed that the two columns contain different numbers of items. If the number of items in the two columns were the same, then a person unsure about one of the actor's roles could merely deduce it by matching all the other options first. A perfect score would then result even though the testtaker did not actually know all the answers. Providing more options than needed minimizes such a possibility. Another way to lessen the probability of chance or guessing as a factor in the test score is to state in the directions that each response may be a correct answer once, more than once, or not at all.

Some guidelines should be observed in writing matching items for classroom use. The wording of the premises and the responses should be fairly short and to the point. No more than a dozen or so premises should be included; otherwise, some students will forget what they were looking for as they go through the lists. The lists of premises and responses should both be homogeneous—that is, lists of the same sort of thing. Our film school example provides a homogeneous list of premises (all names of actors) and a homogeneous list of responses (all names of film characters). Care must be taken to ensure that one and only one premise is matched to one and only one response. For example, adding the name of actors Sean Connery, Roger Moore, David Niven, Timothy Dalton, Pierce Brosnan, or Daniel Craig to the premise column as it now exists would be inadvisable, regardless of what character's name was added to the response column. Do you know why?

At one time or another, Connery, Moore, Niven, Dalton, Brosnan, and Craig all played the role of James Bond (response "k"). As the list of premises and responses currently stands, the match to response "k" is premise "7" (this Australian actor played Agent 007 in the film *On Her Majesty's Secret Service*). If in the future the test developer wanted to substitute the name of another actor—say, Daniel Craig for George Lazenby—then it would be prudent to review the columns to confirm that Craig did not play any of the other characters in the response list and that James Bond still was not played by any actor in the premise list besides Craig.[2]

A multiple-choice item that contains only two possible responses is called a **binary-choice item.** Perhaps the most familiar binary-choice item is the **true–false item.** As you know, this type of selected-response item usually takes the form of a sentence that requires the testtaker to indicate whether the statement is or is not a fact. Other varieties of binary-choice items include sentences to which the testtaker responds with one of two responses, such as *agree or disagree, yes or no, right or wrong,* or *fact or opinion.*

JUST THINK . . .

Respond either true or false, depending upon your opinion as a student: *In the field of education, selected-response items are preferable to constructed-response items.* Then respond again, this time from the perspective of an educator and test user. Explain your answers.

A good binary choice contains a single idea, is not excessively long, and is not subject to debate; the correct response must undoubtedly be one of the two choices. Like multiple-choice items, binary-choice items are readily applicable to a wide range of subjects. Unlike multiple-choice items, binary-choice items cannot contain distractor alternatives. For this reason, binary-choice items are typically easier to write than multiple-choice items and can be written relatively quickly. A disadvantage of the binary-choice item is that the probability of obtaining a correct response purely on the basis of chance (guessing) on any one item is .5, or 50%.[3] In contrast, the probability of obtaining a correct response by guessing on a four-alternative multiple-choice question is .25, or 25%.

---

2. Here's the entire answer key: 1-d, 2-a, 3-f, 4-e, 5-j, 6-h, 7-k, 8-i, 9-l, 10-g, 11-c.

3. We note in passing, however, that although the probability of guessing correctly on an individual binary-choice item on the basis of chance alone is .5, the probability of guessing correctly on a *sequence* of such items decreases as the number of items increases. The probability of guessing correctly on two such items is equal to $.5^2$, or 25%. The probability of guessing correctly on ten such items is equal to $.5^{10}$, or .001. This means there is a one-in-a-thousand chance that a testtaker would guess correctly on ten true–false (or other binary-choice) items on the basis of chance alone.

Moving from a discussion of the selected-response format to the constructed variety, three types of constructed-response items are the *completion item,* the *short answer,* and the *essay.*

A **completion item** requires the examinee to provide a word or phrase that completes a sentence, as in the following example:

The standard deviation is generally considered the most useful measure of _____.

A good completion item should be worded so that the correct answer is specific. Completion items that can be correctly answered in many ways lead to scoring problems. (The correct completion here is *variability.*) An alternative way of constructing this question would be as a short-answer item:

What descriptive statistic is generally considered the most useful measure of variability?

A completion item may also be referred to as a **short-answer item.** It is desirable for completion or short-answer items to be written clearly enough that the testtaker can respond succinctly—that is, with a short answer. There are no hard-and-fast rules for how short an answer must be to be considered a short answer; a word, a term, a sentence, or a paragraph may qualify. Beyond a paragraph or two, the item is more properly referred to as an essay item. We may define an **essay item** as a test item that requires the testtaker to respond to a question by writing a composition, typically one that demonstrates recall of facts, understanding, analysis, and/or interpretation.

Here is an example of an essay item:

Compare and contrast definitions and techniques of classical and operant conditioning. Include examples of how principles of each have been applied in clinical as well as educational settings.

An essay item is useful when the test developer wants the examinee to demonstrate a depth of knowledge about a single topic. In contrast to selected-response and constructed-response items such as the short-answer item, the essay question not only permits the restating of learned material but also allows for the creative integration and expression of the material in the testtaker's own words. The skills tapped by essay items are different from those tapped by true–false and matching items. Whereas these latter types of items require only recognition, an essay requires recall, organization, planning, and writing ability. A drawback of the essay item is that it tends to focus on a more limited area than can be covered in the same amount of time when using a series of selected-response items or completion items. Another potential problem with essays can be subjectivity in scoring and inter-scorer differences. A review of some advantages and disadvantages of these different item formats, especially as used in academic classroom settings, is presented in Table 8–1.

Writing items for computer administration A number of widely available computer programs are designed to facilitate the construction of tests as well as their administration, scoring, and interpretation. These programs typically make use of two advantages of digital media: the ability to store items in an *item bank* and the ability to individualize testing through a technique called *item branching.*

An **item bank** is a relatively large and easily accessible collection of test questions. Instructors who regularly teach a particular course sometimes create their own item bank of questions that they have found to be useful on examinations. One of the many potential advantages of an item bank is accessibility to a large number of test items conveniently classified by subject area, item statistics, or other variables. And just as funds may be added to or withdrawn from a more traditional bank, so items may be added to, withdrawn from, and even modified in an item bank. A detailed description of the process of designing an item bank can be found through the Instructor Resources within Connect, in OOBAL-8-B1, "How to 'Fund' an Item Bank."

The term **computerized adaptive testing (CAT)** refers to an interactive, computer-administered test-taking process wherein items presented to the testtaker are based in part on the

Table 8–1

Some Advantages and Disadvantages of Various Item Formats

Format of Item	Advantages	Disadvantages
Multiple-choice	• Can sample a great deal of content in a relatively short time. • Allows for precise interpretation and little "bluffing" other than guessing. This, in turn, may allow for more content-valid test score interpretation than some other formats. • May be machine- or computer-scored.	• Does not allow for expression of original or creative thought. • Not all subject matter lends itself to reduction to one and only one answer keyed correct. • May be time-consuming to construct series of good items. • Advantages of this format may be nullified if item is poorly written or if a pattern of correct alternatives is discerned by the testtaker.
Binary-choice items (such as true/false)	• Can sample a great deal of content in a relatively short time. • Test consisting of such items is relatively easy to construct and score. • May be machine- or computer-scored.	• Susceptibility to guessing is high, especially for "test-wise" students who may detect cues to reject one choice or the other. • Some wordings, including use of adverbs such as *typically* or *usually,* can be interpreted differently by different students. • Can be used only when a choice of dichotomous responses can be made without qualification.
Matching	• Can effectively and efficiently be used to evaluate testtakers' recall of related facts. • Particularly useful when there are a large number of facts on a single topic. • Can be fun or game-like for testtaker (especially the well-prepared testtaker). • May be machine- or computer-scored.	• As with other items in the selected-response format, test-takers need only *recognize* a correct answer and not recall it or devise it. • One of the choices may help eliminate one of the other choices as the correct response. • Requires pools of related information and is of less utility with distinctive ideas.
Completion or short-answer (fill-in-the-blank)	• Wide content area, particularly of questions that require factual recall, can be sampled in relatively brief amount of time. • This type of test is relatively easy to construct. • Useful in obtaining picture of what testtaker is able to generate as opposed to merely recognize since testtaker must generate response.	• Useful only with responses of one word or a few words. • May demonstrate only recall of circumscribed facts or bits of knowledge. • Potential for inter-scorer reliability problems when test is scored by more than one person. • Typically hand-scored.
Essay	• Useful in measuring responses that require complex, imaginative, or original solutions, applications, or demonstrations. • Useful in measuring how well testtaker is able to communicate ideas in writing. • Requires testtaker to generate entire response, not merely recognize it or supply a word or two.	• May not sample wide content area as well as other tests do. • Testtaker with limited knowledge can attempt to bluff with confusing, sometimes long and elaborate writing designed to be as broad and ambiguous as possible. • Scoring can be time-consuming and fraught with pitfalls. • When more than one person is scoring, inter-scorer reliability issues may be raised. • May rely too heavily on writing skills, even to the point of confounding writing ability with what is purportedly being measured. • Typically hand-scored.

JUST THINK . . .

If an item bank is sufficiently large, might it make sense to publish the entire bank of items in advance to the testtakers before the test?

testtaker's performance on previous items. As in traditional test administration, the test might begin with some sample, practice items. However, the computer may not permit the testtaker to continue with the test until the practice items have been responded to in a satisfactory manner and the testtaker has demonstrated an understanding of the test procedure. Using CAT, the test administered may be different for each testtaker, depending on the test performance on the items presented. Each item on an achievement test, for example, may have a known difficulty level. This fact as well as other data (such as a statistical allowance for blind guessing) may be factored in when it comes time to tally a final score on the items administered. Note that we do not say "final score on the test" because what constitutes "the test" may well be different for different testtakers.

The advantages of CAT have been well documented (Weiss & Vale, 1987). Only a sample of the total number of items in the item pool is administered to any one testtaker. On the basis of previous response patterns, items that have a high probability of being answered in a particular fashion ("correctly" if an ability test) are not presented, thus providing economy in terms of testing time and total number of items presented. Computerized adaptive testing has been found to reduce the number of test items that need to be administered by as much as 50% while simultaneously reducing measurement error by 50%.

CAT tends to reduce *floor effects* and *ceiling effects.* A **floor effect** refers to the diminished utility of an assessment tool for distinguishing testtakers at the low end of the ability, trait, or other attribute being measured. A test of ninth-grade mathematics, for example, may contain items that range from easy to hard for testtakers having the mathematical ability of the average ninth-grader. However, testtakers who have not yet achieved such ability might fail all of the items; because of the floor effect, the test would not provide any guidance as to the relative mathematical ability of testtakers in this group. If the item bank contained some less difficult items, these could be pressed into service to minimize the floor effect and provide discrimination among the low-ability testtakers.

As you might expect, a **ceiling effect** refers to the diminished utility of an assessment tool for distinguishing testtakers at the high end of the ability, trait, or other attribute being measured. Returning to our example of the ninth-grade mathematics test, what would happen if all of the testtakers answered all of the items correctly? It is likely that the test user would conclude that the test was too easy for this group of testtakers and so discrimination was impaired by a ceiling effect. If the item bank contained some items that were more difficult, these could be used to minimize the ceiling effect and enable the test user to better discriminate among these high-ability testtakers.

JUST THINK . . .

Provide an example of how a floor effect in a test of integrity might occur when the sample of testtakers consisted of prison inmates convicted of fraud.

The ability of the computer to tailor the content and order of presentation of test items on the basis of responses to previous items is referred to as **item branching.** A computer that has stored a bank of achievement test items of different difficulty levels can be programmed to present items according to an algorithm or rule. For example, one rule might be "don't present an item of the next difficulty level until two consecutive items of the current difficulty level are answered correctly." Another rule might be "terminate the test when five consecutive items of a given level of difficulty have been answered incorrectly." Alternatively, the pattern of items to which the testtaker is exposed might be based not on the testtaker's response to preceding items but on a random drawing from the total pool of test items. Random presentation of items reduces the ease with which testtakers can memorize items on behalf of future testtakers.

JUST THINK . . .

Provide an example of a ceiling effect in a test that measures a personality trait.

Item-branching technology may be applied when constructing tests not only of achievement but also of personality. For example, if a respondent answers an item in a way that suggests he or she is depressed, the computer might automatically probe for depression-related symptoms and behavior. The next item presented might be designed to probe the respondents' sleep patterns or the existence of suicidal ideation.

Item-branching technology may be used in personality tests to recognize nonpurposive or inconsistent responding. For example, on a computer-based true–false test, if the examinee responds *true* to an item such as "I summered in Baghdad last year," then there would be reason to suspect that the examinee is responding nonpurposively, randomly, or in some way other

JUST THINK . . .

Try your hand at writing a couple of true–false items that could be used to detect nonpurposive or random responding on a personality test.

than genuinely. And if the same respondent responds *false* to the identical item later on in the test, the respondent is being inconsistent as well. Should the computer recognize a nonpurposive response pattern, it may be programmed to respond in a prescribed way—for example, by admonishing the respondent to be more careful or even by refusing to proceed until a purposive response is given.

Scoring Items

Many different test scoring models have been devised. Perhaps the model used most commonly—owing, in part, to its simplicity and logic—is the cumulative model. Typically, the rule in a cumulatively scored test is that the higher the score on the test, the higher the testtaker is on the ability, trait, or other characteristic that the test purports to measure. For each testtaker response to targeted items made in a particular way, the testtaker earns cumulative credit with regard to a particular construct.

In tests that employ **class scoring** or (also referred to as **category scoring),** testtaker responses earn credit toward placement in a particular class or category with other testtakers whose pattern of responses is presumably similar in some way. This approach is used by some diagnostic systems wherein individuals must exhibit a certain number of symptoms to qualify for a specific diagnosis. A third scoring model, *ipsative scoring,* departs radically in rationale from either cumulative or class models. A typical objective in **ipsative scoring** is comparing a testtaker's score on one scale within a test to another scale within that same test.

Consider, for example, a personality test called the Edwards Personal Preference Schedule (EPPS), which is designed to measure the relative strength of different psychological needs. The EPPS ipsative scoring system yields information on the strength of various needs in relation to the strength of other needs of the testtaker. The test does not yield information on the strength of a testtaker's need relative to the presumed strength of that need in the general population. Edwards constructed his test of 210 pairs of statements in a way such that respondents were "forced" to answer *true* or *false* or *yes* or *no* to only one of two statements. Prior research by Edwards had indicated that the two statements were equivalent in terms of how socially desirable the responses were. Here is a sample of an EPPS-like forced-choice item, to which the respondents would indicate which is "more true" of themselves:

I feel depressed when I fail at something.

I feel nervous when giving a talk before a group.

On the basis of such an ipsatively scored personality test, it would be possible to draw only intra-individual conclusions about the testtaker. Here's an example: "John's need for achievement is higher than his need for affiliation." It would not be appropriate to draw inter-individual comparisons on the basis of an ipsatively scored test. It would be inappropriate, for example, to compare two testtakers with a statement like "John's need for achievement is higher than Jane's need for achievement."

Once the test developer has decided on a scoring model and has done everything else necessary to prepare the first draft of the test for administration, the next step is test tryout.

Test Tryout

Having created a pool of items from which the final version of the test will be developed, the test developer will try out the test. The test should be tried out on people who are similar in critical respects to the people for whom the test was designed. Thus, for example, if a test is designed to aid in decisions regarding the selection of corporate employees with management potential at a certain level, it would be appropriate to try out the test on corporate employees at the targeted level.

Equally important are questions about the number of people on whom the test should be tried out. An informal rule of thumb is that there should be no fewer than 5 subjects and preferably as many as 10 for each item on the test. In general, the more subjects in the tryout the better. The thinking here is that the more subjects employed, the weaker the role of chance in subsequent data analysis. A definite risk in using too few subjects during test tryout comes during factor analysis of the findings, when what we might call phantom factors—factors that actually are just artifacts of the small sample size—may emerge.

The test tryout should be executed under conditions as identical as possible to the conditions under which the standardized test will be administered; all instructions, and everything from the time limits allotted for completing the test to the atmosphere at the test site, should be as similar as possible. As Nunnally (1978, p. 279) so aptly phrased it, "If items for a personality inventory are being administered in an atmosphere that encourages frankness and the eventual test is to be administered in an atmosphere where subjects will be reluctant to say bad things about themselves, the item analysis will tell a faulty story." In general, the test developer endeavors to ensure that differences in response to the test's items are due in fact to the items, not to extraneous factors.

JUST THINK . . .

How appropriate would it be to try out a "management potential" test on a convenience sample of introductory psychology students?

In Chapter 4, we dealt in detail with the important question "What is a good test?" Now is a good time to raise a related question.

What Is a Good Item?

Pseudobulbar affect (PBA) is a neurological disorder characterized by frequent and involuntary outbursts of laughing or crying that may or may not be appropriate to the situation. In one study of veterans with traumatic brain injury, the researchers asked whether the respondents had ever experienced exaggerated episodes of laughing or crying. The subjects' responses to this single item were critically important in identifying persons who required more thorough clinical evaluation for PBA symptoms (Rudolph et al., 2016). By any measure, this single survey item about exaggerated laughing or crying constituted, for the purposes of the evaluation, "a good item."

In the same sense that a good test is reliable and valid, a good test item is reliable and valid. Further, a good test item helps to discriminate testtakers. That is, a good test item is one that is answered correctly (or in an expected manner) by high scorers on the test as a whole. Certainly in the context of academic achievement testing, an item that is answered incorrectly by high scorers on the test as a whole is probably not a good item. Conversely, a good test item is one that is answered incorrectly by low scorers on the test as a whole. By the way, it is also the case that an item that is answered correctly by low scorers on the test as a whole may not be a good item.

How does a test developer identify good items? After the first draft of the test has been administered to a representative group of examinees, the test developer analyzes test scores and responses to individual items. The different types of statistical scrutiny that the test data can potentially undergo at this point are referred to collectively as **item analysis.** Although item analysis tends to be regarded as a quantitative endeavor, it may also be qualitative, as we shall see.

JUST THINK . . .

Well, do a bit more than think: Write one good item in any format, along with a brief explanation of why you think it is a good item. The item should be for a new test you are developing called the American History Test, which will be administered to ninth-graders.

Item Analysis

Statistical procedures used to analyze items may become quite complex, and our treatment of this subject should be viewed as only introductory. We briefly survey some procedures typically used by test developers in their efforts to select the best items from a pool of tryout items. The criteria for the best items may differ as a function of the test developer's objectives. Thus, for example, one test developer might deem the best items to be those that optimally contribute to the internal reliability of the test. Another test developer might wish to design a test with the highest possible criterion-related validity and then select items accordingly. Among the tools test developers might employ to analyze and select items are

- an index of the item's difficulty
- an index of the item's reliability
- an index of the item's validity
- an index of item discrimination

JUST THINK . . .

Apply these item-analysis statistics to a test of personality. Make translations in phraseology as you think about how statistics such as an item-difficulty index or an item-validity index could be used to help identify good items for a personality test (not for an achievement test).

Assume for the moment that you got carried away on the previous *Just Think* exercise and are now the proud author of 100 items for a ninth-grade-level American History Test (AHT). Let's further assume that this 100-item (draft) test has been administered to 100 ninth-graders. Hoping in the long run to standardize the test and have it distributed by a commercial test publisher, you have a more immediate, short-term goal: to select the 50 best of the 100 items you originally created. How might that short-term goal be achieved? As we will see, the answer lies in item-analysis procedures.

The Item-Difficulty Index

Suppose every examinee answered item 1 of the AHT correctly. Can we say that item 1 is a good item? What if no one answered item 1 correctly? In either case, item 1 is not a good item. If everyone gets the item right then the item is too easy; if everyone gets the item wrong, the item is too difficult. Just as the test as a whole is designed to provide an index of degree of knowledge about American history, so each individual item on the test should be passed (scored as correct) or failed (scored as incorrect) on the basis of testtakers' differential knowledge of American history.[4]

An index of an item's difficulty is obtained by calculating the proportion of the total number of testtakers who answered the item correctly. A lowercase italic "p" (p) is used to denote item difficulty, and a subscript refers to the item number (so p_1 is read "item-difficulty index for item 1"). The value of an item-difficulty index can theoretically range from 0 (if no one got the item right) to 1 (if everyone got the item right). If 50 of the 100 examinees answered item 2 correctly, then the item-difficulty index for this item would be equal to 50 divided by 100, or .5 ($p_2 = .5$). If 75 of the examinees got item 3 right, then p_3 would be equal to .75 and we could say that item 3 was easier than item 2. Note that the larger the item-difficulty index, the easier the item. Because p refers to the percent of people passing an item, the higher the p for an item, the easier the item. The statistic referred to as an **item-difficulty index** in the context of achievement testing may be an **item-endorsement index** in other contexts, such as personality testing. Here, the

---

4. An exception here may be a **giveaway item.** Such an item might be inserted near the beginning of an achievement test to spur motivation and a positive test-taking attitude and to lessen testtakers' test-related anxiety. In general, however, if an item analysis suggests that a particular item is too easy or too difficult, the item must be either rewritten or discarded.

statistic provides not a measure of the percent of people passing the item but a measure of the percent of people who said yes to, agreed with, or otherwise endorsed the item.

An index of the difficulty of the average test item for a particular test can be calculated by averaging the item-difficulty indices for all the test's items. This is accomplished by summing the item-difficulty indices for all test items and dividing by the total number of items on the test. For maximum discrimination among the abilities of the testtakers, the optimal average item difficulty is approximately .5, with individual items on the test ranging in difficulty from about .3 to .8. Note, however, that the possible effect of guessing must be taken into account when considering items of the selected-response variety. With this type of item, the optimal average item difficulty is usually the midpoint between 1.00 and the chance success proportion, defined as the probability of answering correctly by random guessing. In a true–false item, the probability of guessing correctly on the basis of chance alone is 1/2, or .50. Therefore, the optimal item difficulty is halfway between .50 and 1.00, or .75. In general, the midpoint representing the optimal item difficulty is obtained by summing the chance success proportion and 1.00 and then dividing the sum by 2, or

JUST THINK . . .

Create an achievement test item having to do with any aspect of psychological testing and assessment that you believe would yield a *p* of 0 if administered to every member of your class.

$$.5 + 1.00 = 1.5$$
$$\frac{1.5}{2} = .60$$

For a five-option multiple-choice item, the probability of guessing correctly on any one item on the basis of chance alone is equal to 1/5, or .20. The optimal item difficulty is therefore .60:

$$.20 + 1.00 = 1.20$$
$$\frac{1.20}{2} = .60$$

The Item-Reliability Index

The **item-reliability index** provides an indication of the internal consistency of a test (Figure 8–4); the higher this index, the greater the test's internal consistency. This index is equal to the product of the item-score standard deviation (s) and the correlation (r) between the item score and the total test score.

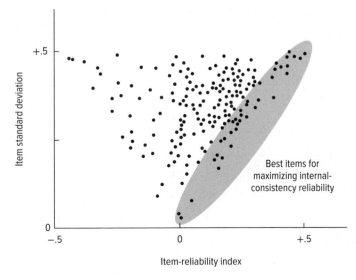

Figure 8–4
Maximizing Internal-Consistency Reliability

Source: Allen and Yen (1979).

JUST THINK . . .

An achievement test on the subject of test development is designed to have two items that load on a factor called "item analysis." Write these two test items.

Factor analysis and inter-item consistency   A statistical tool useful in determining whether items on a test appear to be measuring the same thing(s) is factor analysis. Through the judicious use of factor analysis, items that do not "load on" the factor that they were written to tap (or, items that do not appear to be measuring what they were designed to measure) can be revised or eliminated. If too many items appear to be tapping a particular area, the weakest of such items can be eliminated. Additionally, factor analysis can be useful in the test interpretation process, especially when comparing the constellation of responses to the items from two or more groups. Thus, for example, if a particular personality test is administered to two groups of hospitalized psychiatric patients, each group with a different diagnosis, then the same items may be found to load on different factors in the two groups. Such information will compel the responsible test developer to revise or eliminate certain items from the test or to describe the differential findings in the test manual.

The Item-Validity Index

The **item-validity index** is a statistic designed to provide an indication of the degree to which a test is measuring what it purports to measure. The higher the item-validity index, the greater the test's criterion-related validity. The item-validity index can be calculated once the following two statistics are known:

- the item-score standard deviation
- the correlation between the item score and the criterion score

The item-score standard deviation of item 1 (denoted by the symbol s_1) can be calculated using the index of the item's difficulty (p_1) in the following formula:

$$s_1 = \sqrt{p_1(1 - p_1)}$$

The correlation between the score on item 1 and a score on the criterion measure (denoted by the symbol $r_{1\,C}$) is multiplied by item 1's item-score standard deviation (s_1), and the product is equal to an index of an item's validity ($s_1\, r_{1\,C}$). Calculating the item-validity index will be important when the test developer's goal is to maximize the criterion-related validity of the test. A visual representation of the best items on a test (if the objective is to maximize criterion-related validity) can be achieved by plotting each item's item-validity index and item-reliability index (Figure 8–5).

The Item-Discrimination Index

Measures of item discrimination indicate how adequately an item separates or discriminates between high scorers and low scorers on an entire test. In this context, a multiple-choice item on an achievement test is a good item if most of the high scorers answer correctly and most of the low scorers answer incorrectly. If most of the high scorers fail a particular item, these testtakers may be making an alternative interpretation of a response intended to serve as a distractor. In such a case, the test developer should interview the examinees to understand better the basis for the choice and then appropriately revise (or eliminate) the item. Common sense dictates that an item on an achievement test is not doing its job if it is answered correctly by respondents who least understand the subject matter. Similarly, an item on a test purporting to measure a particular personality trait is not doing its job if responses indicate that people who score very low on the test as a whole (indicating absence or low levels of the trait in

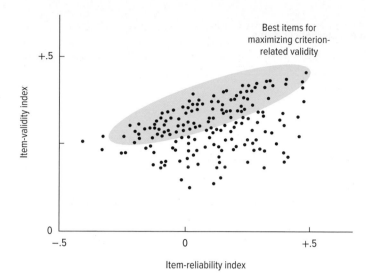

Figure 8–5
Maximizing Criterion-Related Validity

Source: Allen and Yen (1979).

question) tend to score very high on the item (indicating that they are very high on the trait in question—contrary to what the test as a whole indicates).

The **item-discrimination index** is a measure of item discrimination, symbolized by a lowercase italic "d" (*d*). This estimate of item discrimination, in essence, compares performance on a particular item with performance in the upper and lower regions of a distribution of continuous test scores. The optimal boundary lines for what we refer to as the "upper" and "lower" areas of a distribution of scores will demarcate the upper and lower 27% of the distribution of scores—provided the distribution is normal (Kelley, 1939). As the distribution of test scores becomes more platykurtic (flatter), the optimal boundary line for defining upper and lower increases to near 33% (Cureton, 1957). Allen and Yen (1979, p. 122) assure us that "for most applications, any percentage between 25 and 33 will yield similar estimates."

The item-discrimination index is a measure of the difference between the proportion of high scorers answering an item correctly and the proportion of low scorers answering the item correctly; the higher the value of *d*, the greater the number of high scorers answering the item correctly. A negative *d*-value on a particular item is a red flag because it indicates that low-scoring examinees are more likely to answer the item correctly than high-scoring examinees. This situation calls for some action such as revising or eliminating the item.

Suppose a history teacher gave the AHT to a total of 119 students who were just weeks away from completing ninth grade. The teacher isolated the upper (*U*) and lower (*L*) 27% of the test papers, with a total of 32 papers in each group. Data and item-discrimination indices for Items 1 through 5 are presented in Table 8–2. Observe that 20 testtakers in the *U* group answered Item 1 correctly and that 16 testtakers in the *L* group answered Item 1 correctly. With an item-discrimination index equal to .13, Item 1 is probably

JUST THINK . . .

Write two items on the subject of test development. The first item to be one that you will predict will have a very high *d*, and the second to be one that you predict will have a high negative *d*.

a reasonable item because more *U*-group members than *L*-group members answered it correctly. The higher the value of *d*, the more adequately the item discriminates the higher-scoring from the lower-scoring testtakers. For this reason, Item 2 is a better item than Item 1 because Item 2's item-discrimination index is .63. The highest possible value

Table 8–2
Item-Discrimination Indices for Five Hypothetical Items

Item	U	L	U − L	n	d[(U − L)/n]
1	20	16	4	32	.13
2	30	10	20	32	.63
3	32	0	32	32	1.00
4	20	20	0	32	0.00
5	0	32	−32	32	−1.00

of d is +1.00. This value indicates that all members of the U group answered the item correctly whereas all members of the L group answered the item incorrectly.

If the same proportion of members of the U and L groups pass the item, then the item is not discriminating between testtakers at all and d, appropriately enough, will be equal to 0. The lowest value that an index of item discrimination can take is −1. A d equal to −1 is a test developer's nightmare: It indicates that all members of the U group failed the item and all members of the L group passed it. On the face of it, such an item is the worst possible type of item and is in dire need of revision or elimination. However, through further investigation of this unanticipated finding, the test developer might learn or discover something new about the construct being measured.

Analysis of item alternatives   The quality of each alternative within a multiple-choice item can be readily assessed with reference to the comparative performance of upper and lower scorers. No formulas or statistics are necessary here. By charting the number of testtakers in the U and L groups who chose each alternative, the test developer can get an idea of the effectiveness of a distractor by means of a simple eyeball test. To illustrate, let's analyze responses to five items on a hypothetical test, assuming that there were 32 scores in the upper level (U) of the distribution and 32 scores in the lower level (L) of the distribution. Let's begin by looking at the pattern of responses to item 1. In each case, ♦ denotes the correct alternative.

Alternatives

		♦a	b	c	d	e
Item 1	U	24	3	2	0	3
	L	10	5	6	6	5

The response pattern to Item 1 indicates that the item is a good one. More U group members than L group members answered the item correctly, and each of the distractors attracted some testtakers.

Alternatives

		a	b	c	d	♦e
Item 2	U	2	13	3	2	12
	L	6	7	5	7	7

Item 2 signals a situation in which a relatively large number of members of the U group chose a particular distractor choice (in this case, "b"). This item could probably be improved upon revision, preferably one made after an interview with some or all of the U students who chose "b."

Alternatives

Item 3		a	b	♦c	d	e
	U	0	0	32	0	0
	L	3	2	22	2	3

Item 3 indicates a most desirable pattern of testtaker response. All members of the U group answered the item correctly, and each distractor attracted one or more members of the L group.

Alternatives

Item 4		a	♦b	c	d	e
	U	5	15	0	5	7
	L	4	5	4	4	14

Item 4 is more difficult than Item 3; fewer examinees answered it correctly. Still, this item provides useful information because it effectively discriminates higher-scoring from lower-scoring examinees. For some reason, one of the alternatives ("e") was particularly effective—perhaps too effective—as a distractor to students in the low-scoring group. The test developer may wish to further explore why this was the case.

Alternatives

Item 5		a	b	c	♦d	e
	U	14	0	0	5	13
	L	7	0	0	16	9

Item 5 is a poor item because more L group members than U group members answered the item correctly. Furthermore, none of the examinees chose the "b" or "c" distractors.

Before moving on to a consideration of the use of item-characteristic curves in item analysis, let's pause to "bring home" the real-life application of some of what we have discussed so far. In his capacity as a consulting industrial/organizational psychologist, our featured test user in this chapter, Dr. Scott Birkeland, has had occasion to create tests and improve them with item-analytic methods. He shares some of his thoughts in his *Meet an Assessment Professional* essay, an excerpt of which is presented here.

Item-Characteristic Curves

As you may have surmised from the introduction to item response theory (IRT) that was presented in Chapter 5, IRT can be a powerful tool not only for understanding how test items perform but also for creating or modifying individual test items, building new tests, and revising existing tests. We will have more to say about that later in the chapter. For now, let's review how *item-characteristic curves (ICCs)* can play a role in decisions about which items are working well and which items are not. Recall that an **item-characteristic curve** is a graphic representation of item difficulty and discrimination.

Figure 8–6 presents several ICCs with ability plotted on the horizontal axis and probability of correct response plotted on the vertical axis. Note that the extent to which an item discriminates high- from low-scoring examinees is apparent from the slope of the curve. The steeper the slope, the greater the item discrimination. An item may also vary in terms of its difficulty level. An easy item will shift the ICC to the left along the ability axis, indicating that many people will likely get the item correct. A difficult item will shift the ICC to the right along the horizontal axis, indicating that fewer people will answer the item correctly. In other words, it takes high ability levels for a person to have a high probability of their response being scored as correct.

Now focus on the item-characteristic curve for Item A. Do you think this is a good item? The answer is that it is not. The probability of a testtaker's responding correctly is high for

Meet Dr. Scott Birkeland

I also get involved in developing new test items. Given that these tests are used with real-life candidates, I place a high level of importance on a test's face validity. I want applicants who take the tests to walk away feeling as though the questions that they answered were truly relevant for the job for which they applied. Because of this, each new project leads to the development of new questions so that the tests "look and feel right" for the candidates. For example, if we have a reading and comprehension test, we make sure that the materials that the candidates read are materials that are similar to what they would actually read on the job. This can be a challenge in that by having to develop new questions, the test development process takes more time and effort. In the long run, however, we know that this enhances the candidates' reactions to the testing process. Additionally, our research suggests that it enhances the test's predictability.

Once tests have been developed and administered to candidates, we continue to look for ways to improve them. This is where statistics comes into play. We conduct item level analyses of each question to determine if certain questions are performing better than others. I am often amazed at the power of a simple item analysis (or, calculating item difficulty and item discrimination). Oftentimes, an item analysis will flag a question, causing me to go back and re-examine the item only to find something about it to be confusing. An

Scott Birkeland, Ph.D., Stang Decision Systems, Inc.

© Scott Birkeland

item analysis allows us to fix those types of issues and continually enhance the quality of a test.

Read more of what Dr. Birkeland had to say—his complete essay—through the Instructor Resources within Connect.

Used with permission of Scott Birkeland.

testtakers of low ability and low for testtakers of high ability. What about Item B; is it a good test item? Again, the answer is no. The curve tells us that testtakers of moderate ability have the highest probability of answering this item correctly. Testtakers with the greatest amount of ability—as well as their counterparts at the other end of the ability spectrum—are unlikely to respond correctly to this item. Item B may be one of those items to which people who know too much (or think too much) are likely to respond incorrectly.

Item C is a good test item because the probability of responding correctly to it increases with ability. What about Item D? Its ICC profiles an item that discriminates at only one point on the continuum of ability. The probability is great that all testtakers at or above this point will respond correctly to the item, and the probability of an incorrect response is great for testtakers who fall below that particular point in ability. An item such as D therefore has

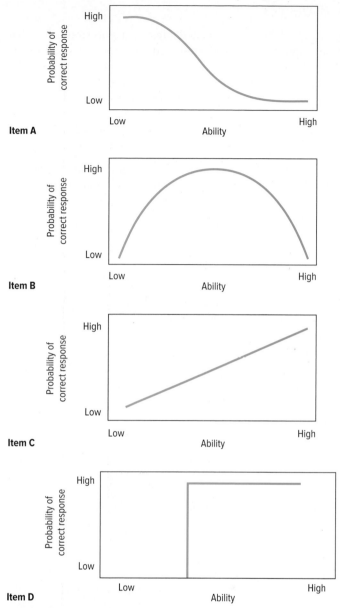

Figure 8–6
Some Sample Item-Characteristic Curves

For simplicity, we have omitted scale values for the axes. The vertical axis in such a graph lists probability of correct response in values ranging from 0 to 1. Values for the horizontal axis, which we have simply labeled "ability," are total scores on the test. In other sources, you may find the vertical axis of an item-characteristic curve labeled something like "proportion of examinees who respond correctly to the item" and the horizontal axis labeled "total test score."

Source: Ghiselli et al. (1981).

excellent discriminative ability and would be useful in a test designed, for example, to select applicants on the basis of some cutoff score. However, such an item might not be desirable in a test designed to provide detailed information on testtaker ability across all ability levels. This might be the case, for example, in a diagnostic reading or arithmetic test.

Other Considerations in Item Analysis

Guessing   In achievement testing, the problem of how to handle testtaker **guessing** is one that has eluded any universally acceptable solution. Methods designed to detect guessing (S.-R. Chang et al., 2011), minimize the effects of guessing (Kubinger et al., 2010), and statistically correct for guessing (Espinosa & Gardeazabal, 2010) have been proposed, but no such method has achieved universal acceptance. Perhaps it is because the issues surrounding guessing are more complex than they appear at first glance. To better appreciate the complexity of the issues, consider the following three criteria that any correction for guessing must meet as well as the other interacting issues that must be addressed:

1. A correction for guessing must recognize that, when a respondent guesses at an answer on an achievement test, the guess is not typically made on a totally random basis. It is more reasonable to assume that the testtaker's guess is based on some knowledge of the subject matter and the ability to rule out one or more of the distractor alternatives. However, the individual testtaker's amount of knowledge of the subject matter will vary from one item to the next.

2. A correction for guessing must also deal with the problem of omitted items. Sometimes, instead of guessing, the testtaker will simply omit a response to an item. Should the omitted item be scored "wrong"? Should the omitted item be excluded from the item analysis? Should the omitted item be scored as if the testtaker had made a random guess? Exactly how should the omitted item be handled?

3. Just as some people may be luckier than others in front of a Las Vegas slot machine, so some testtakers may be luckier than others in guessing the choices that are keyed correct. Any correction for guessing may seriously underestimate or overestimate the effects of guessing for lucky and unlucky testtakers.

In addition to proposed interventions at the level of test scoring through the use of corrections for guessing (referred to as formula scores), intervention has also been proposed at the level of test instructions. Testtakers may be instructed to provide an answer only when they are certain (no guessing) or to complete all items and guess when in doubt. Individual differences in testtakers' willingness to take risks result in problems for this approach to guessing (Slakter et al., 1975). Some people who don't mind taking risks may guess even when instructed not to do so. Others who tend to be reluctant to take risks refuse to guess under any circumstances. This creates a situation in which predisposition to take risks can affect one's test score.

To date, no solution to the problem of guessing has been deemed entirely satisfactory. The responsible test developer addresses the problem of guessing by including in the test manual (1) explicit instructions regarding this point for the examiner to convey to the examinees and (2) specific instructions for scoring and interpreting omitted items.

JUST THINK . . .

The prevailing logic among measurement professionals is that when testtakers guess at an answer on a personality test in a selected-response format, the testtaker is making the best choice. Why should professionals continue to believe this? Alternatively, why might they modify their view?

Guessing on responses to personality and related psychological tests is not thought of as a great problem. Although it may sometimes be difficult to choose the most appropriate alternative on a selected-response format personality test (particularly one with forced-choice items), the presumption is that the testtaker does indeed make the best choice.

Item fairness   Just as we may speak of biased tests, we may speak of biased test items. The term **item fairness** refers to the degree, if any, a test item is biased. A **biased test item** is an item that favors one particular group of examinees in relation to another when differences in group ability are controlled (Camilli & Shepard, 1985). Many different methods may be used to identify biased test items. In fact, evidence suggests that the choice of item-analysis method may affect determinations of item bias (Ironson & Subkoviak, 1979).

Item-characteristic curves can be used to identify biased items. Specific items are identified as biased in a statistical sense if they exhibit differential item functioning. Differential item functioning is exemplified by different shapes of item-characteristic curves for different groups (say, men and women) when the two groups do not differ in total test score (Mellenbergh, 1994). If an item is to be considered fair to different groups of testtakers, the item-characteristic curves for the different groups should not be significantly different:

> The essential rationale of this ICC criterion of item bias is that any persons showing the same ability as measured by the whole test should have the same probability of passing any given item that measures that ability, regardless of the person's race, social class, sex, or any other background characteristics. In other words, the same proportion of persons from each group should pass any given item of the test, provided that the persons all earned the same total score on the test. (Jensen, 1980, p. 444)

Establishing the presence of differential item functioning requires a statistical test of the null hypothesis of no difference between the item-characteristic curves of the two groups. The pros and cons of different statistical tests for detecting differential item functioning have long been a matter of debate (Raju et al., 1993). What is not a matter of debate is that items exhibiting significant difference in item-characteristic curves must be revised or eliminated from the test. If a relatively large number of items biased in favor of one group coexist with approximately the same number of items biased in favor of another group, it cannot be claimed that the test measures the same abilities in the two groups. This is true even though overall test scores of the individuals in the two groups may not be significantly different (Jensen, 1980).

JUST THINK . . .

Write an item that is purposely designed to be biased in favor of one group over another. Members of what group would do well on this item? Members of what group would do poorly on this item?

Speed tests   Item analyses of tests taken under speed conditions yield misleading or uninterpretable results. The closer an item is to the end of the test, the more difficult it may appear to be. This is because testtakers simply may not get to items near the end of the test before time runs out.

In a similar vein, measures of item discrimination may be artificially high for late-appearing items. This is so because testtakers who know the material better may work faster and are thus more likely to answer the later items. Items appearing late in a speed test are consequently more likely to show positive item-total correlations because of the select group of examinees reaching those items.

Given these problems, how can items on a speed test be analyzed? Perhaps the most obvious solution is to restrict the item analysis of items on a speed test only to the items completed by the testtaker. However, this solution is not recommended, for at least three reasons: (1) Item analyses of the later items would be based on a progressively smaller number of testtakers, yielding progressively less reliable results; (2) if the more knowledgeable examinees reach the later items, then part of the analysis is based on all testtakers and part is based on a selected sample; and (3) because the more knowledgeable testtakers are more likely to score correctly, their performance will make items occurring toward the end of the test appear to be easier than they are.

If speed is not an important element of the ability being measured by the test, and because speed as a variable may produce misleading information about item performance, the test developer ideally should administer the test to be item-analyzed

JUST THINK . . .

Provide an example of what, in your opinion is the best, as well as the worst, use of a speed test.

with generous time limits to complete the test. Once the item analysis is completed, norms should be established using the speed conditions intended for use with the test in actual practice.

Qualitative Item Analysis

Test users have had a long-standing interest in understanding test performance from the perspective of testtakers (Fiske, 1967; Mosier, 1947). The calculation of item-validity, item-reliability, and other such *quantitative* indices represents one approach to understanding testtakers. Another general class of research methods is referred to as *qualitative*. In contrast to quantitative methods, **qualitative methods** are techniques of data generation and analysis that rely primarily on verbal rather than mathematical or statistical procedures. Encouraging testtakers—on a group or individual basis—to discuss aspects of their test-taking experience is, in essence, eliciting or generating "data" (words). These data may then be used by test developers, users, and publishers to improve various aspects of the test.

Qualitative item analysis is a general term for various nonstatistical procedures designed to explore how individual test items work. The analysis compares individual test items to each other and to the test as a whole. In contrast to statistically based procedures, qualitative methods involve exploration of the issues through verbal means such as interviews and group discussions conducted with testtakers and other relevant parties. Some of the topics researchers may wish to explore qualitatively are summarized in Table 8–3.

One cautionary note: Providing testtakers with the opportunity to describe a test can be like providing students with the opportunity to describe their instructors. In both cases, there may be abuse of the process, especially by respondents who have extra-test (or extra-instructor) axes to grind. Respondents may be disgruntled for any number of reasons, from failure to prepare adequately for the test to disappointment in their test performance. In such cases, the opportunity to evaluate the test is an opportunity to lash out. The test, the administrator of the test, and the institution, agency, or corporation responsible for the test administration may all become objects of criticism. Testtaker questionnaires, much like other qualitative research tools, must be interpreted with an eye toward the full context of the experience for the respondent(s).

"Think aloud" test administration   An innovative approach to cognitive assessment entails having respondents verbalize thoughts as they occur. Although different researchers use different procedures (Davison et al., 1997; Hurlburt, 1997; Klinger, 1978), this general approach has been employed in a variety of research contexts, including studies of adjustment (Kendall et al., 1979; Sutton-Simon & Goldfried, 1979), problem solving (Duncker, 1945; Kozhevnikov et al., 2007; Montague, 1993), educational research and remediation (Muñoz et al., 2006; Randall et al., 1986; Schellings et al., 2006), clinical intervention (Gann & Davison, 1997; Haaga et al., 1993; Schmitter-Edgecombe & Bales, 2005; White et al., 1992), and jury modeling (Wright & Hall, 2007).

Cohen et al. (1988) proposed the use of **"think aloud" test administration** as a qualitative research tool designed to shed light on the testtaker's thought processes during the administration of a test. On a one-to-one basis with an examiner, examinees are asked to take a test, thinking aloud as they respond to each item. If the test is designed to measure achievement, such verbalizations may be useful in assessing not only if certain students (such as low or high scorers on previous examinations) are misinterpreting a particular item but also *why* and *how* they are misinterpreting the item. If the test is designed to measure personality or some aspect of it, the "think aloud" technique may also yield valuable insights regarding the way individuals perceive, interpret, and respond to the items.

JUST THINK (ALOUD) . . .

How might thinking aloud to evaluate test items be more effective than thinking silently?

Table 8–3

Potential Areas of Exploration by Means of Qualitative Item Analysis

This table lists sample topics and questions of possible interest to test users. The questions could be raised either orally or in writing shortly after a test's administration. Additionally, depending upon the objectives of the test user, the questions could be placed into other formats, such as true–false or multiple choice. Depending upon the specific questions to be asked and the number of testtakers being sampled, the test user may wish to guarantee the anonymity of the respondents.

Topic	Sample Question
Cultural Sensitivity	Did you feel that any item or aspect of this test was discriminatory with respect to any group of people? If so, why?
Face Validity	Did the test appear to measure what you expected it would measure? If not, what was contrary to your expectations?
Test Administrator	Did the behavior of the test administrator affect your performance on this test in any way? If so, how?
Test Environment	Did any conditions in the room affect your performance on this test in any way? If so, how?
Test Fairness	Do you think the test was a fair test of what it sought to measure? Why or why not?
Test Language	Were there any instructions or other written aspects of the test that you had difficulty understanding?
Test Length	How did you feel about the length of the test with respect to (a) the time it took to complete and (b) the number of items?
Testtaker's Guessing	Did you guess on any of the test items? What percentage of the items would you estimate you guessed on? Did you employ any particular strategy for guessing, or was it basically random?
Testtaker's Integrity	Do you think that there was any cheating during this test? If so, please describe the methods you think may have been used.
Testtaker's Mental/Physical State Upon Entry	How would you describe your mental state going into this test? Do you think that your mental state in any way affected the test outcome? If so, how? How would you describe your physical state going into this test? Do you think that your physical state in any way affected the test outcome? If so, how?
Testtaker's Mental/Physical State During the Test	How would you describe your mental state as you took this test? Do you think that your mental state in any way affected the test outcome? If so, how? How would you describe your physical state as you took this test? Do you think that your physical state in any way affected the test outcome? If so, how?
Testtaker's Overall Impressions	What is your overall impression of this test? What suggestions would you offer the test developer for improvement?
Testtaker's Preferences	Did you find any part of the test educational, entertaining, or otherwise rewarding? What, specifically, did you like or dislike about the test? Did you find any part of the test anxiety-provoking, condescending, or otherwise upsetting? Why?
Testtaker's Preparation	How did you prepare for this test? If you were going to advise others how to prepare for it, what would you tell them?

Expert panels   In addition to interviewing testtakers individually or in groups, **expert panels** may also provide qualitative analyses of test items. A **sensitivity review** is a study of test items, typically conducted during the test development process, in which items are examined for fairness to all prospective testtakers and for the presence of offensive language, stereotypes, or situations. Since the 1990s or so, sensitivity reviews have become a standard part of test development (Reckase, 1996). For example, in an effort to root out any possible bias in the Stanford Achievement Test series, the test publisher formed an advisory panel of twelve minority group members, each a prominent member of the educational community. Panel members met with the publisher to obtain an understanding of the history and philosophy of the test battery and to discuss and define the problem of bias. Some of the possible forms of content bias that may find their way into any achievement test were identified as follows (Stanford Special Report, 1992, pp. 3–4).

Status: Are the members of a particular group shown in situations that do not involve authority or leadership?

Stereotype: Are the members of a particular group portrayed as uniformly having certain (1) aptitudes, (2) interests, (3) occupations, or (4) personality characteristics?

Familiarity: Is there greater opportunity on the part of one group to (1) be acquainted with the vocabulary or (2) experience the situation presented by an item?

Offensive Choice of Words: (1) Has a demeaning label been applied, or (2) has a male term been used where a neutral term could be substituted?

Other: Panel members were asked to be specific regarding any other indication of bias they detected.

Expert panels may also play a role in the development of new tools of assessment for members of underserved populations. Additionally, experts on a particular culture can inform test developers on optimal ways to achieve desired measurement ends with specific populations of testtakers. This chapter's *Everyday Psychometrics* provides a unique and fascinating glimpse into the process of developing evaluative tools for use with Aboriginal tribe members.

On the basis of qualitative information from an expert panel or testtakers themselves, a test user or developer may elect to modify or revise the test. In this sense, revision typically involves rewording items, deleting items, or creating new items. Note that there is another meaning of test revision beyond that associated with a stage in the development of a new test. After a period of time, many existing tests are scheduled for republication in new versions or editions. The development process that the test undergoes as it is modified and revised is called, not surprisingly, *test revision.* The time, effort, and expense entailed by this latter variety of test revision may be quite extensive. For example, the revision may involve an age extension of the population for which the test is designed for use—upward for older testtakers and/or downward for younger testtakers—and corresponding new validation studies.

JUST THINK . . .

Is there any way that expert panels might introduce more error into the test development process?

Test Revision

We first consider aspects of test revision as a stage in the development of a new test. Later we will consider aspects of test revision in the context of modifying an existing test to create a new edition. Much of our discussion of test revision in the development of a brand-new test may also apply to the development of subsequent editions of existing tests, depending on just how "revised" the revision really is.

Test Revision as a Stage in New Test Development

Having conceptualized the new test, constructed it, tried it out, and item-analyzed it both quantitatively and qualitatively, what remains is to act judiciously on all the information and mold the test into its final form. A tremendous amount of information is generated at the item-analysis stage, particularly given that a developing test may have hundreds of items. On

Adapting Tools of Assessment for Use with Specific Cultural Groups

Imagine the cultural misunderstandings that may arise when an assessor with a Western perspective evaluates someone from a non-Western culture. As a case in point, consider the potential for serial misinterpretation of signs and symptoms if the assessor is a Caucasian Westerner and the assesse is a member of an Australian Indigenous culture (commonly referred to in Australia and elsewhere as Aboriginal and Torres Strait Islander people) being evaluated for depression.

For Indigenous Australians, health is viewed in a holistic context—one that encompasses not only mental and physical aspects but cultural and spiritual aspects as well. Ill health is often conceived of as a disruption of these interrelated domains. Perhaps consequently, an Indigenous Australian person is more likely to be perceived in the eyes of a Western evaluator, as presenting with vague complaints of illness—this as opposed to more specific symptomatology. Also, shyness is common in the Indigenous Australian population. Shyness during a mental status examination or other evaluation may manifest itself by avoidance of eye contact with the examiner, which, in turn, may be misinterpreted by the examiner as pathological or otherwise suspect behavior. Another potentially misleading sign or symptom of psychopathology could be the respondent's delayed answers and only minimal speech. However, what might otherwise be interpreted as psychomotor retardation or poverty of speech may well have a cultural basis. Traditional Indigenous Australian people are frequently reserved with, and seemingly indifferent to, Caucasian clinicians, especially in a one-on-one assessment situation. Patients who exhibit a blank or unreactive expression may "come alive" with appropriate affect when a family member or two joins the interview.

Knowledge of Aboriginal culture and clinical experience has suggested to us that when interviewing members of this group,

a *yarning* approach works best. Loosely defined, the yarning approach is an interview strategy characterized by the creation of an atmosphere conducive to interviewees conversationally telling their own stories in their own ways. In stark contrast to yarning would be an interview characterized by interrogation, where one direct question is posed after another.

In developing a mental health screening tool for use with members of the Aboriginal culture, a group of clinicians and academic psychiatrists from metropolitan and rural areas of Western Australia and the Northern Territory employed the yarning approach. The interview tool, called the "Here and Now Aboriginal Assessment" (HANAA; see Janca et al., 2015), allows for a traditional story-telling style that involves both family and social yarning. An objective of the design of the instrument was to obtain more meaningful reporting of individual problems while still gathering culturally relevant information about an interviewee's collective identity.

Anhedonia (inability to experience happiness) may be explored by asking questions such as "Have you lost interest in things that you used to like doing?" Engagement in culturally appropriate activities (such as fishing or going out in the bush) may be probed. Reports of a "weak spirit" are met with inquiries designed to elucidate what is meant, and to quantify the extent of a respondent's "weak spirit." For example, the respondent may be asked questions like "Do you have weak spirit all day/every day?" and "What time of the day does your spirit feel the most weak?"

As a screening instrument, the HANAA aims to assist in the determination of when a person should be referred to a mental health professional for further assessment. It provides for the narrative responses to be recorded which can be helpful in-the-moment as well in-the-future when it comes to further discussion of, and "yarning" about, the specific nature of a client's presenting problem.

*This *Everyday Psychometrics* was guest-authored by Sivasankaran Balaratnasingam, Zaza Lyons, and Aleksandar Janca, all of the University of Western Australia, School of Psychiatry and Clinical Neurosciences, Perth, Australia.

Used with permission of Sivasankaran Balaratnasingam, Zaza Lyons, and Aleksandar Janca.

the basis of that information, some items from the original item pool will be eliminated and others will be rewritten. How is information about the difficulty, validity, reliability, discrimination, and bias of test items—along with information from the item-characteristic curves—integrated and used to revise the test?

There are probably as many ways of approaching test revision as there are test developers. One approach is to characterize each item according to its strengths and weaknesses. Some items may be highly reliable but lack criterion validity, whereas other items may be purely unbiased but too easy. Some items will be found to have many weaknesses, making them prime candidates for deletion or revision. For example, very difficult items have a restricted range; all or almost all testtakers get them wrong. Such items will tend to lack reliability and validity because of their restricted range, and the same can be said of very easy items.

Test developers may find that they must balance various strengths and weaknesses across items. For example, if many otherwise good items tend to be somewhat easy, the test developer may purposefully include some more difficult items even if they have other problems. Those more difficult items may be specifically targeted for rewriting. The purpose of the test also influences the blueprint or plan for the revision. For example, if the test will be used to influence major decisions about educational placement or employment, the test developer should be scrupulously concerned with item bias. If there is a need to identify the most highly skilled individuals among those being tested, items demonstrating excellent item discrimination, leading to the best possible test discrimination, will be made a priority.

As revision proceeds, the advantage of writing a large item pool becomes more and more apparent. Poor items can be eliminated in favor of those that were shown on the test tryout to be good items. Even when working with a large item pool, the revising test developer must be aware of the domain the test should sample. For some aspects of the domain, it may be particularly difficult to write good items, and indiscriminate deletion of all poorly functioning items could cause those aspects of the domain to remain untested.

Having balanced all these concerns, the test developer comes out of the revision stage with a better test. The next step is to administer the revised test under standardized conditions to a second appropriate sample of examinees. On the basis of an item analysis of data derived from this administration of the second draft of the test, the test developer may deem the test to be in its finished form. Once the test is in finished form, the test's norms may be developed from the data, and the test will be said to have been "standardized" on this (second) sample. Recall from Chapter 4 that a standardization sample represents the group(s) of individuals with whom examinees' performance will be compared. All of the guidelines presented in that chapter for selecting an appropriate standardization sample should be followed.

◆
JUST THINK . . .

Surprise! An international publisher is interested in publishing your American History Test. You've just been asked which population demographic characteristics you think are most important to be represented in your international standardization sample. Your response?

When the item analysis of data derived from a test administration indicates that the test is not yet in finished form, the steps of revision, tryout, and item analysis are repeated until the test is satisfactory and standardization can occur. Once the test items have been finalized, professional test development procedures dictate that conclusions about the test's validity await a cross-validation of findings. We'll discuss *cross-validation* shortly; for now, let's briefly consider some of the issues surrounding the development of a new edition of an existing test.

Test Revision in the Life Cycle of an Existing Test

Time waits for no person. We all get old, and tests get old, too. Just like people, some tests seem to age more gracefully than others. For example, as we will see when we study projective techniques in Chapter 12, the Rorschach Inkblot Test seems to have held up quite well over the years. By contrast, the stimulus materials for another projective technique, the Thematic Apperception Test (TAT), are showing their age. There comes a time in the life of most tests when the test will be revised in some way or its publication will be discontinued. When is that time?

No hard-and-fast rules exist for when to revise a test. The American Psychological Association (APA, 1996b, Standard 3.18) offered the general suggestions that an existing test be kept in its present form as long as it remains "useful" but that it should be revised "when significant changes in the domain represented, or new conditions of test use and interpretation, make the test inappropriate for its intended use."

Practically speaking, many tests are deemed to be due for revision when any of the following conditions exist.

1. The stimulus materials look dated and current testtakers cannot relate to them.

2. The verbal content of the test, including the administration instructions and the test items, contains dated vocabulary that is not readily understood by current testtakers.

3. As popular culture changes and words take on new meanings, certain words or expressions in the test items or directions may be perceived as inappropriate or even offensive to a particular group and must therefore be changed.

4. The test norms are no longer adequate as a result of group membership changes in the population of potential testtakers.

5. The test norms are no longer adequate as a result of age-related shifts in the abilities measured over time, and so an age extension of the norms (upward, downward, or in both directions) is necessary.

6. The reliability or the validity of the test, as well as the effectiveness of individual test items, can be significantly improved by a revision.

7. The theory on which the test was originally based has been improved significantly, and these changes should be reflected in the design and content of the test.

The steps to revise an existing test parallel those to create a brand-new one. In the test conceptualization phase, the test developer must think through the objectives of the revision and how they can best be met. In the test construction phase, the proposed changes are made. Test tryout, item analysis, and test revision (in the sense of making final refinements) follow. All this sounds relatively easy and straightforward, but creating a revised edition of an existing test can be a most ambitious undertaking. For example, recalling the revision of a test called the Strong Vocational Interest Blank, Campbell (1972) reflected that the process of conceiving the revision started about ten years prior to actual revision work, and the revision work itself ran for another ten years. Butcher (2000) echoed these thoughts in an article that provided a detailed "inside view" of the process of revising a widely used personality test called the MMPI. Others have also noted the sundry considerations that must be kept in mind when conducting or contemplating the revision of an existing instrument (Adams, 2000; Cash et al., 2004; Okazaki & Sue, 2000; Prinzie et al., 2007; Reise et al., 2000; Silverstein & Nelson, 2000; Vickers-Douglas et al., 2005).

Once the successor to an established test is published, there are inevitably questions about the equivalence of the two editions. For example, does a measured full-scale IQ of 110 on the first edition of an intelligence test mean exactly the same thing as a full-scale IQ of 110 on the second edition? A number of researchers have advised caution in comparing results from an original and a revised edition of a test, despite similarities in appearance (Reitan & Wolfson, 1990; Strauss et al., 2000). Even if the content of individual items does not change, the context in which the items appear may change, thus opening up the possibility of significant differences in testtakers' interpretation of the meaning of the items. Simply developing a computerized version of a test may make a difference, at least in terms of test scores achieved by members of different populations (Ozonoff, 1995).

Formal item-analysis methods must be employed to evaluate the stability of items between revisions of the same test (Knowles & Condon, 2000). Ultimately, scores on a test and on its

> **JUST THINK . . .**
>
> Why can the process of creating a revision to an established test take years to complete?

updated version may not be directly comparable. As Tulsky and Ledbetter (2000) summed it up in the context of original and revised versions of tests of cognitive ability: "Any improvement or decrement in performance between the two cannot automatically be viewed as a change in examinee performance" (p. 260).

A key step in the development of all tests—brand-new or revised editions—is cross-validation. Next we discuss that important process as well as a more recent trend in test publishing, *co-validation.*

Cross-validation and co-validation   The term **cross-validation** refers to the revalidation of a test on a sample of testtakers other than those on whom test performance was originally found to be a valid predictor of some criterion. We expect that items selected for the final version of the test (in part because of their high correlations with a criterion measure) will have smaller item validities when administered to a second sample of testtakers. This is so because of the operation of chance. The decrease in item validities that inevitably occurs after cross-validation of findings is referred to as **validity shrinkage.** Such shrinkage is expected and is viewed as integral to the test development process. Further, such shrinkage is infinitely preferable to a scenario wherein (spuriously) high item validities are published in a test manual as a result of inappropriately using the identical sample of testtakers for test standardization and cross-validation of findings. When such scenarios occur, test users will typically be let down by lower-than-expected test validity. The test manual accompanying commercially prepared tests should outline the test development procedures used. Reliability information, including test-retest reliability and internal consistency estimates, should be reported along with evidence of the test's validity. Articles discussing cross-validation of tests are often published in scholarly journals. For example, Bank et al. (2000) provided a detailed account of the cross-validation of an instrument used to screen for cognitive impairment in older adults.

Not to be confused with "cross-validation," **co-validation** may be defined as a test validation process conducted on two or more tests using the same sample of testtakers. When used in conjunction with the creation of norms or the revision of existing norms, this process may also be referred to as **co-norming.** A current trend among test publishers who publish more than one test designed for use with the same population is to co-validate and/or co-norm tests. Co-validation of new tests and revisions of existing tests can be beneficial in various ways to all parties in the assessment enterprise. Co-validation is beneficial to test publishers because it is economical. During the process of validating a test, many prospective testtakers must first be identified. In many instances, after being identified as a possible participant in the validation study, a person will be prescreened for suitability by means of a face-to-face or telephone interview. This costs money, which is charged to the budget for developing the test. Both money and time are saved if the same person is deemed suitable in the validation studies for multiple tests and can be scheduled to participate with a minimum of administrative preliminaries. Qualified examiners to administer the test and other personnel to assist in scoring, interpretation, and statistical analysis must also be identified, retained, and scheduled to participate in the project. The cost of retaining such professional personnel on a per-test basis is minimized when the work is done for multiple tests simultaneously.

Beyond benefits to the publisher, co-validation can hold potentially important benefits for test users and testtakers. Many tests that tend to be used together are published by the same publisher. For example, the fourth edition of the Wechsler Adult Intelligence Scale (WAIS-IV) and the fourth edition of the Wechsler Memory Scale (WMS-IV) might be used together in the clinical evaluation of an adult. And let's suppose that, after an evaluation using these two tests, differences in measured memory ability emerged as a function of the test used. Had these two tests been normed on different samples, then sampling error would be one possible reason for the observed differences in measured memory. However, because the two tests were normed on the same population, sampling error as a causative factor has been virtually eliminated. A clinician might thus look to factors such as differences in the way that the two tests measure memory. One test, for example, might measure short-term memory using the recall of number sequences. The other test might measure the same variable using recalled comprehension of short reading passages. How each test measures the variable under study may yield important diagnostic insights.

On the other hand, consider two co-normed tests that are almost identical in how they measure the variable under study. With sampling error minimized by the co-norming process, a test user can be that much more confident that the scores on the two tests are comparable.

Quality assurance during test revision   Once upon a time, a long time ago in Manhattan, one of this text's authors (Cohen) held the title of senior psychologist at Bellevue Hospital. Among other duties, senior psychologists supervised clinical psychology interns in all phases of their professional development, including the administration of psychological tests:

> One day, in the course of reviewing a test protocol handed in by an intern, something very peculiar caught my eye. On a subtest that had several tasks scored on the basis of number of seconds to completion, all of the recorded times on the protocol were in multiples of 5 (as in 10 seconds, 15 seconds, etc.). I had never seen a protocol like that. All of the completed protocols I had seen previously had recorded completion times with no identifiable pattern or multiple (like 12 seconds, 17 seconds, 9 seconds, etc.). Curious about the way that the protocol had been scored, I called in the intern to discuss it.
>
> As it turned out, the intern had not equipped herself with either a stopwatch or a watch with a second-hand before administering this test. She had ignored this mandatory bit of preparation prior to test administration. Lacking any way to record the exact number of seconds it took to complete each task, the intern said she had "estimated" the number of seconds. Estimating under such circumstances is not permitted because it violates the standardized procedure set forth in the manual. Beyond that, estimating could easily result in the testtaker either earning or failing to earn bonus points for (inaccurately) timed scores. The intern was advised of the error of her ways, and the patient was retested.

Well, that's one "up close and personal" example of quality control in psychological testing at a large municipal hospital. But what mechanisms of quality assurance are put into place by test publishers in the course of standardizing a new test or restandardizing an existing test? Let's take a brief look at some quality control mechanisms for examiners, protocol scoring, and data entry. For the purpose of illustration, we draw some examples from procedures followed by the developers of the Wechsler Intelligence Scale for Children, Fourth Edition (WISC-IV; Wechsler, 2003).

The examiner is the front-line person in test development, and it is critically important that examiners adhere to standardized procedures. In developing a new test or in restandardizing or renorming an existing test, test developers seek to employ examiners who have experience testing members of the population targeted for the test. For example, the developers of the WISC-IV sought to

> recruit examiners with extensive experience testing children and adolescents. Potential examiners completed a questionnaire by supplying information about their educational and professional experience, administration experience with various intellectual measures, certification, and licensing status. Those selected as potential standardization examiners were very familiar with childhood assessment practices. (Wechsler, 2003, p. 22)

Although it might be desirable for every examiner to hold a doctoral degree, this is simply not feasible given that many thousands of tests may have to be individually administered. The professional time of doctoral-level examiners tends to be at a premium—not to mention their fees. Regardless of education or experience, all examiners will be trained to administer the instrument. Training will typically take the form of written guidelines for test administration and may involve everything from classroom instruction to practice test administrations on site to videotaped demonstrations to be reviewed at home. Publishers may evaluate potential examiners by a quiz or other means to determine how well they have learned what they need to know. During the standardization of the WISC-IV, examiners were required to submit a review case prior to testing additional children. And during the course of the test's standardization, all persons selected as examiners received a periodic newsletter advising them of potential problems in test administration. The newsletter was designed to provide an ongoing way to maintain quality assurance in test administration.

In the course of test development, examiners may be involved to greater or lesser degrees in the final scoring of protocols. Regardless of whether it is the examiner or a "dedicated scorer," all persons who have responsibility for scoring protocols will typically undergo training. As with examiner training, the training for scorers may take many forms, from classroom instruction to videotaped demonstrations.

Quality assurance in the restandardization of the WISC-IV was in part maintained by having two qualified scorers rescore each protocol collected during the national tryout and standardization stages of test development. If there were discrepancies in scoring, the discrepancies were resolved by yet another scorer, referred to as a *resolver*. According to the manual, "The resolvers were selected based on their demonstration of exceptional scoring accuracy and previous scoring experience" (Wechsler, 2003, p. 22).

Another mechanism for ensuring consistency in scoring is the *anchor protocol*. An **anchor protocol** is a test protocol scored by a highly authoritative scorer that is designed as a model for scoring and a mechanism for resolving scoring discrepancies. A discrepancy between scoring in an anchor protocol and the scoring of another protocol is referred to as **scoring drift.** Anchor protocols were used for quality assurance in the development of the WISC-IV:

> If two independent scorers made the same scoring error on a protocol, comparison to the anchor score revealed the scoring drift. Scorers received feedback immediately to prevent repetition of the error and to correct for scoring drift. (Wechsler, 2003, p. 23)

Once protocols are scored, the data from them must be entered into a database. For quality assurance during the data entry phase of test development, test developers may employ computer programs to seek out and identify any irregularities in score reporting. For example, if a score on a particular subtest can range from a low of 1 to a high of 10, any score reported out of that range would be flagged by the computer. Additionally, a proportion of protocols can be randomly selected to make certain that the data entered from them faithfully match the data they originally contained.

The Use of IRT in Building and Revising Tests

In the previous chapter, we noted that item response theory (IRT) could be applied in the evaluation of the utility of tests and testing programs. Here, let's briefly elaborate on the possible roles of IRT in test construction, as well as some of its pros and cons vis-à-vis classical test theory (CTT). As can be seen from Table 8–4, one of the *disadvantages* of applying CTT in test development is the extent to which item statistics are dependent upon characteristics (strength of traits or ability level) of the group of people tested. Stated another way, "all CTT-based statistics are sample dependent" (De Champlain, 2010, p. 112). To elaborate, consider a hypothetical "Perceptual-Motor Ability Test" (PMAT), and the characteristics of items on that test with reference to different groups of testtakers. From a CTT perspective, a PMAT item might be judged to be very *high* in difficulty when it is administered to a sample of people known to be very low in perceptual-motor ability. From

Table 8–4

Some Advantages and Disadvantages of Classical Test Theory (CTT) and Item Response Theory (IRT)[*]

Theory	Advantages	Disadvantages
Classical Test Theory	1. Smaller sample sizes are required for testing, so CTT is especially useful if only a small sample of testtakers is available. 2. CTT utilizes relatively simple mathematical models. 3. Assumptions underlying CTT are "weak" allowing CTT wide applicability 4. Most researchers are familiar with this basic approach to test development. 5. Many data analysis and statistics-related software packages are built from a CTT perspective or are readily compatible with it.	1. Item statistics and overall psychometric properties of a test are dependent on the samples which have been administered the test. 2. Tests developed using CTT may be longer (or, require more items) than tests developed using IRT. 3. One often violated assumption is that each item of a test contributes equally to the total test score.
Item Response Theory	1. Item statistics are independent of the samples which have been administered the test. 2. Test items can be matched to ability levels (as in computerized adaptive testing) thus resulting in relatively short tests that are still reliable and valid. 3. IRT models facilitate advanced psychometric tools and methods, holding out the promise of greater precision in measurement under certain circumstances.	1. The techniques used to test item response models are relatively complicated and unfamiliar to most researchers. 2. Sample sizes need to be relatively large to properly test IRT models (200 or more is a good rule-of-thumb). 3. Assumptions for use of IRT are characterized as "hard" or "strong" making IRT inappropriate for use in many applications. 4. As compared to CTT-based statistics-related software, there are much fewer IRT-based packages currently available.

*For a more detailed comparison of CTT to IRT, consult the sources used to synthesize this table (De Champlain, 2010; Hambleton & Jones, 1993; Streiner, 2010; and Zickar & Broadfoot, 2009).

that same perspective, that same PMAT item might be judged to be very *low* in difficulty when administered to a group of people known to be very high in perceptual-motor ability. Because the way that an item is viewed is so dependent on the group of testtakers taking the test, the ideal situation, at least from the CTT perspective, is one in which all testtakers represent a truly random sample of how well the trait or ability being studied is represented in the population. Using IRT, test developers evaluate individual item performance with reference to item-characteristic curves (ICCs). ICCs provide information about the relationship between the performance of individual items and the presumed underlying ability (or trait) level in the testtaker.

Three of the many possible applications of IRT in building and revising tests include (1) evaluating existing tests for the purpose of mapping test revisions, (2) determining measurement equivalence across testtaker populations, and (3) developing item banks.

Evaluating the properties of existing tests and guiding test revision   IRT information curves can help test developers evaluate how well an individual item (or entire test) is working to measure different levels of the underlying construct. Developers can use these information curves to weed out uninformative questions or to eliminate redundant items that provide duplicate levels of information. Information curves allow test developers to tailor an instrument to provide high information (or, precision). As an illustration, refer back to the information curve for a measure of depression in Figure 3 of the OOBAL 5-B2 (page 173). Now suppose the test developer wanted to increase precision so that level of depression could better be measured across all levels of theta. The graph suggests that this could be accomplished by adding more items to the test (or by adding more response options to existing items) that differentiate among people with mild depressive symptoms. Adding appropriate items (or response options) will both broaden the range and increase the height of the curve across the underlying construct—thus reflecting increased precision in measurement.

Determining measurement equivalence across testtaker populations   Test developers often aspire to have their tests become so popular that they will be translated into other languages and used in many places throughout the world. But how do they assure that their tests are tapping into the same construct regardless of who in the world is responding to the test items? One tool to help ensure that the same construct is being measured, no matter what language the test has been translated into, is IRT.

Despite carefully translated test items, it sometimes happens that even though the words may be linguistically equivalent, members of different populations—typically members of populations other than the population for which the test was initially developed—may interpret the items differently. As we saw in Chapter 5, for example, response rates to a measure of depression from people of different cultures may not necessarily depend on how depressed the testtaker is. Rather, response rates may vary more as a function of how much the prevailing culture sanctions outward expression of emotion. This phenomenon, wherein an item functions differently in one group of testtakers as compared to another group of testtakers known to have the same (or similar) level of the underlying trait, is referred to as **differential item functioning (DIF).** Instruments containing such items may have reduced validity for between-group comparisons because their scores may indicate a variety of attributes other than those the scale is intended to measure.

JUST THINK . . .

Create a test item that might be interpreted differently when read by younger Americans (20-something) than when read by older Americans (70-something).

In a process known as **DIF analysis,** test developers scrutinize group-by-group item response curves, looking for what are termed *DIF items.* **DIF items** are those items that respondents from different groups at the same level of the underlying trait have different probabilities of endorsing as a function of their group membership. DIF analysis has been used to evaluate measurement equivalence in item content across groups that vary by culture, gender, and age. It has even been used to explore differential item functioning as a function of different patterns of guessing on the part of members of different groups (DeMars & Wise, 2010). Yet another application of DIF analysis has to do with the evaluation of item-ordering effects, and the effects of different test administration procedures (such as paper-and-pencil test administration versus computer-administered testing).

Developing item banks   Developing an item bank is not simply a matter of collecting a large number of items. Typically, each of the items assembled as part of an item bank, whether taken from an existing test (with appropriate permissions, if necessary) or written especially for the item bank, have undergone rigorous qualitative and quantitative evaluation (Reeve et al., 2007). As can be seen from Figure 8–7, many item banking efforts begin with the collection of appropriate items from existing instruments (Instruments A, B, and C). New items may also be written when existing measures are either not available or do not tap targeted aspects of the construct being measured.

All items available for use as well as new items created especially for the item bank constitute the item pool. The item pool is then evaluated by content experts, potential respondents, and survey experts using a variety of qualitative and quantitative methods. Individual items in an item pool may be evaluated by cognitive testing procedures whereby an

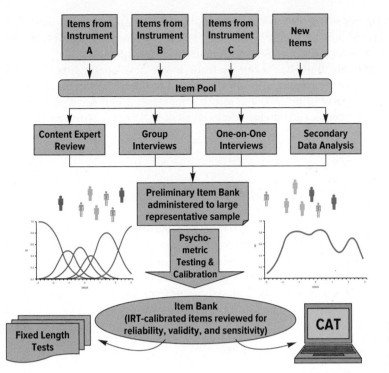

Figure 8–7
The Use of IRT to Create Item Banks

interviewer conducts one-on-one interviews with respondents in an effort to identify any ambiguities associated with the items. Item pools may also be evaluated by groups of respondents, which allows for discussion of the clarity and relevance of each item, among other item characteristics. The items that "make the cut" after such scrutiny constitute the preliminary item bank.

The next step in creating the item bank is the administration of all of the questionnaire items to a large and representative sample of the target population. For ease in data analysis, group administration by computer is preferable. However, depending upon the content and method of administration required by the items, the questionnaire (or portions of it) may be administered individually using paper-and-pencil methods.

After administration of the preliminary item bank to the entire sample of respondents, responses to the items are evaluated with regard to several variables such as validity, reliability, domain coverage, and differential item functioning. The final item bank will consist of a large set of items all measuring a single domain (or, a single trait or ability). A test developer may then use the banked items to create one or more tests with a fixed number of items. For example, a teacher may create two different versions of a math test in order to minimize efforts by testtakers to cheat. The item bank can also be used for purposes of computerized-adaptive testing.

When used within a CAT environment, a testtaker's response to an item may automatically trigger which item is presented to the testtaker next. The software has been programmed to present the item next that will be most informative with regard to the testtaker's standing on the construct being measured. This programming is actually based on near-instantaneous construction and analysis of IRT information curves. The process continues until the testing is terminated.

Because of CAT's widespread appeal, the technology is being increasingly applied to a wide array of tests. It is also becoming available on many different platforms ranging from the Internet to handheld devices to computer-assisted telephone interviewing.

Our survey of how tests are built has taken us from a test developer's first thoughts regarding what new test needs to be created, all the way through to the development of a large item bank. In reading about aspects of professional test development, it may have occurred to you that some parallel types of processes go into the development of less formal, instructor-devised measures for in-class use.

Instructor-Made Tests for In-Class Use

Professors want to give—and students want to take—tests that are reliable and valid measures of student knowledge. Even students who have not taken a course in psychological testing and assessment seem to understand psychometric issues regarding the tests administered in the classroom. As an illustration, consider each of the following pairs of statements in Table 8–5. The first statement in each pair is a criticism of a classroom test you may have heard (or said yourself); the second is that criticism translated into the language of psychometrics.

Addressing Concerns About Classroom Tests

Like their students, professors have concerns about the tests they administer. They want their examination questions to be clear, relevant, and representative of the material covered. They sometimes wonder about the length of their examinations. Their concern is to cover voluminous amounts of material while still providing enough time for students to give thoughtful consideration to their answers.

For most published psychological tests, these types of psychometric concerns would be addressed in a formal way during the test development process. In the classroom, however, rigorous psychometric evaluation of the dozen or so tests that any one instructor may administer during the course of a semester is impractical. Classroom tests are typically created for the purpose of testing just one group of students during one semester. Tests change to reflect changes in lectures and readings as courses evolve. Also, if tests are reused, they are in danger of becoming measures of who has seen or heard about the examination before taking it rather than measures of how well the students know the course material. Of

Table 8–5
Psychometric "Translation" of Student Complaints

Student Complaint	Translation
"I spent all last night studying Chapter 3, and there wasn't one item on that test from that chapter!"	"I question the examination's content validity!"
"The instructions on that essay test weren't clear, and I think it affected my grade."	"There was excessive error variance related to the test administration procedures."
"I wrote the same thing my friend did for this short-answer question—how come she got full credit and the professor took three points off my answer?"	"I have grave concerns about rater error affecting reliability."
"I didn't have enough time to finish; this test didn't measure what I know—only how fast I could write!"	"I wish the person who wrote this test had paid more attention to issues related to criterion-related validity and the comparative efficacy of speed as opposed to power tests!"

course, although formal psychometric evaluation of classroom tests may be impractical, informal methods are frequently used.

Concerns about content validity are routinely addressed, usually informally, by professors in the test development process. For example, suppose an examination containing 50 multiple-choice questions and five short essays is to cover the reading and lecture material on four broad topics. The professor might systematically include 12 or 13 multiple-choice questions and at least one short essay from each topic area. The professor might also draw a certain percentage of the questions from the readings and a certain percentage from the lectures. Such a deliberate approach to content coverage may well boost the test's content validity, although no formal evaluation of the test's content validity will be made. The professor may also make an effort to inform the students that all textbook boxes and appendices and all instructional media presented in class (such as videotapes) are fair game for evaluation.

Criterion-related validity is difficult to establish on many classroom tests because no obvious criterion reflects the level of the students' knowledge of the material. Exceptions may exist for students in a technical or applied program who take an examination for licensure or certification. Informal assessment of something akin to criterion validity may occur on an individual basis in a student–professor chat wherein a student who obtained the lowest score in a class may demonstrate to the professor an unambiguous lack of understanding of the material. It is also true that the criterion validity of the test may be called into question by the same method. A chat with the student who scored the highest might reveal that this student doesn't have a clue about the material the test was designed to tap. Such a finding would give the professor pause.

The construct validity of classroom tests is often assessed informally, as when an anomaly in test performance may call attention to issues related to construct validity. For example, consider a group of students who have a history of performing at an above-average level on exams. Now suppose that all the students in this group perform poorly on a particular exam. If all these students report not having studied for the test or just not having understood the text material, then there is an adequate explanation for their low scores. However, if the students report that they studied and understood the material as usual, then one might explain the outcome by questioning the exam's construct validity.

Aspects of a classroom test's reliability can also be informally assessed. For example, a discussion with students can shed light on the test's internal consistency. Then again, if the test was designed to be heterogeneous, then low internal consistency ratings might be desirable. On essay tests, inter-rater reliability can be explored by providing a group of volunteers with the criteria used in grading the essays and letting them grade some. Such an exercise might clarify the scoring criteria. In the rare instance when the same classroom test is given twice or in an alternate form, a discussion of the test-retest or alternate-forms reliability can be conducted.

Have you ever taken an exam in which one student quietly asks for clarification of a specific question and the professor then announces to the entire class the response to the student's question? This professor is attempting to reduce administration error (and increase reliability) by providing the same experience for all testtakers. When grading short-answer or essay questions, professors may try to reduce rater error by several techniques. For example, they may ask a colleague to help decipher a student's poor handwriting or re-grade a set of essays (without seeing the original grades). Professors also try to reduce administration error and increase reliability by eliminating items that many students misunderstand.

Tests developed for classroom use may not be perfect. Few, if any, tests for any purpose are. Still, most professors much like their professional test developer counterparts, are always on the lookout for ways—to make their tests as psychometrically sound as possible. In the following chapters, we will be exploring various aspects of many different types of tests, beginning with tests of intelligence. But before discussing tests of *intelligence*, reflect for a moment—and once again when you read Chapter 9—on the meaning of that somewhat elusive term.

Self-Assessment

Test your understanding of elements of this chapter by seeing if you can explain each of the following terms, expressions, and abbreviations:

anchor protocol
asexuality
biased test item
binary-choice item
categorical scaling
category scoring
ceiling effect
class scoring
comparative scaling
completion item
computerized adaptive testing
  (CAT)
co-norming
constructed-response format
co-validation
cross-validation
DIF analysis
differential item functioning (DIF)
DIF items
essay item
expert panel

floor effect
giveaway item
guessing
Guttman scale
ipsative scoring
item analysis
item bank
item branching
item-characteristic curve (ICC)
item-difficulty index
item-discrimination index
item-endorsement index
item fairness
item format
item pool
item-reliability index
item-validity index
Likert scale
LGBTA
matching item
method of paired comparisons

multiple-choice format
pilot work
pseudobulbar affect (PBA)
qualitative item analysis
qualitative methods
rating scale
scaling
scalogram analysis
scoring drift
selected-response format
sensitivity review
short-answer item
summative scale
test conceptualization
test construction
test development
test revision
test tryout
"think aloud" test administration
true–false item
validity shrinkage

9

Intelligence and Its Measurement

For as long as there has been a discipline of psychology, psychologists have had differing definitions of intelligence and how best to measure it.

In this chapter we look at the varied ways intelligence has been defined and we survey various approaches to its measurement. Along the way, we will address some of the major issues surrounding how and why intelligence is measured. Before all of that, however, let's consider a question that logically precedes consideration of intelligence measurement issues.

What Is Intelligence?

We may define **intelligence** as a multifaceted capacity that manifests itself in different ways across the life span. In general, intelligence includes the abilities to:

- acquire and apply knowledge
- reason logically
- plan effectively
- infer perceptively
- make sound judgments and solve problems
- grasp and visualize concepts
- pay attention
- be intuitive
- find the right words and thoughts with facility
- cope with, adjust to, and make the most of new situations

As broad as these descriptions are, they are far from the "last word" on the matter. Rather, think of these descriptions as a point of departure for reflection on the meaning of a most intriguing term—one that, as we will see, is paradoxically both simple and complex.

JUST THINK . . .

How do *you* define intelligence?

Young children may define "intelligence" in terms that emphasize positive interpersonal skills (such as acting nice, or being helpful or polite). For older children, more emphasis in the definition will typically be placed on academic skills, such as reading well (Yussen & Kane, 1980). For psychologists, universal agreement as to how intelligence should be defined has been a bit more elusive (Neisser et al., 1996). While most may view it as an abstract construct, some see it as having a more tangible existence at the level of the neuron (Grazioplene, 2015; Kreifelts et al., 2010). There are even highly respected voices in the profession who have questioned the very usefulness of the construct (Das, 2015).

Controversy surrounding the definition of intelligence is not new. In a symposium published in the *Journal of Educational Psychology* in 1921, seventeen of the country's leading psychologists addressed the following questions: (1) *What is intelligence?* (2) *How can it best be measured in group tests?* and (3) *What should be the next steps in the research?* No two psychologists agreed (Thorndike et al., 1921). Six years later, Spearman (1927, p. 14) would reflect: "In truth, intelligence has become . . . a word with so many meanings that finally it has none." And decades after the symposium was first held, Wesman (1968, p. 267) concluded that there appeared to be "no more general agreement as to the nature of intelligence or the most valid means of measuring intelligence today than was the case 50 years ago."

◆ **JUST THINK . . .**

Must professionals agree on a definition of intelligence?

As Neisser (1979) observed, although the *Journal* felt that the symposium would generate vigorous discussion, it generated more heat than light and led to a general increase in exasperation with discussion on the subject. Symptomatic of that exasperation was an unfortunate statement by an experimental psychologist and historian of psychology, Edwin G. Boring. Boring (1923, p. 5), who was not a psychometrician, attempted to quell the argument by pronouncing that "intelligence is what the tests test." Although such a view is not entirely devoid of merit (see Neisser, 1979, p. 225), it is an unsatisfactory, incomplete, and circular definition. In what follows we discuss the thoughts of other behavioral scientists through history and up to contemporary times on the meaning and measurement of intelligence (see Figure 9–1).

Francis Galton (1822–1911)

Figure 9–1
"Intelligence" is. . .

Galton (1883) believed that the most intelligent persons were those equipped with the best sensory abilities. This position was intuitively appealing because, as Galton observed, "The only information that reaches us concerning outward events appears to pass through the avenues of our senses; and the more perceptive the senses are of difference, the larger is the field upon which our judgment and intelligence can act" (p. 27). Following this logic, tests of visual acuity or hearing ability are, in a sense, tests of intelligence. Galton attempted to measure this sort of intelligence in many of the sensorimotor and other perception-related tests he devised. Among his many other accomplishments, Sir Francis Galton is remembered as the first person to publish on the heritability of intelligence, thus anticipating later nature-nurture debates (McGue, 1997).

Alfred Binet (1857–1911)

In papers critical of Galton's approach to intellectual assessment, Binet and a colleague called for more complex measurements of intellectual ability (Binet & Henri, 1895a, 1895b, 1895c). Galton had viewed intelligence as a number of distinct processes or abilities that could be assessed only by separate tests. In contrast, Binet argued that when one solves a particular problem, the abilities used cannot be separated because they interact to produce the solution. For example, memory and concentration interact when a subject is asked to repeat digits presented orally. When analyzing a testtaker's response to such a task, it is difficult to determine the relative contribution of memory and concentration to the successful solution. This difficulty in determining the relative contribution of distinct abilities is the reason Binet called for more complex measurements of intelligence. Although Binet never explicitly defined intelligence, he discussed its components in terms of reasoning, judgment, memory, and abstraction (Varon, 1936).

In Wechsler's (1958, p. 7) definition of intelligence, there is an explicit reference to an "aggregate" or "global" capacity:

> Intelligence, operationally defined, is the aggregate or global capacity of the individual to act purposefully, to think rationally and to deal effectively with his environment. It is aggregate or global because it is composed of elements or abilities which, though not entirely independent, are qualitatively differentiable. By measurement of these abilities, we ultimately evaluate intelligence. But intelligence is not identical with the mere sum of these abilities, however inclusive. . . . The only way we can evaluate it quantitatively is by the measurement of the various aspects of these abilities.

Elsewhere Wechsler added that there are nonintellective factors that must be taken into account when assessing intelligence (Kaufman, 1990). Included among those factors are "capabilities more of the nature of conative, affective, or personality traits [that] include such traits as drive, persistence, and goal awareness [as well as] an individual's potential to perceive and respond to social, moral and aesthetic values" (Wechsler, 1975, p. 136). Ultimately, however, Wechsler was of the opinion that the best way to measure this global ability was by measuring aspects of several "qualitatively differentiable" abilities. Wechsler (1974) wrote of two such "differentiable" abilities, which he conceived as being primarily verbal- or performance-based in nature. Today, the conceptualization of intelligence in terms of these two factors—a verbal factor and a performance factor—is largely a matter of historical interest.

For Piaget (1954, 1971), intelligence may be conceived of as a kind of evolving biological adaptation to the outside world. As cognitive skills are gained, adaptation (at a symbolic level) increases, and mental trial and error replaces physical trial and error. Yet, according to Piaget, the process of cognitive development occurs neither solely through maturation nor solely through learning. He believed that, as a consequence of interaction with the environment, psychological structures become reorganized. Piaget described four stages of cognitive development through which, he theorized, all of us pass during our lifetimes. Although individuals can move through these stages at different rates and ages, he believed that their order was unchangeable. Piaget viewed the unfolding of these stages of cognitive development as the result of the interaction of biological factors and learning. Interested readers will find more about Piaget's theory of cognitive development in OOBAL-9-B1, which can be found in the Instructor Resources within Connect.

David Wechsler (1896–1981)

JUST THINK . . .

What is the role of personality in measured intelligence?

Jean Piaget (1896–1980)

Perspectives on Intelligence

A major thread running through the theories of Binet, Wechsler, and Piaget is a focus on interactionism. **Interactionism** refers to the complex concept by which heredity and environment are presumed to interact and influence the development of one's intelligence. As we will see, other theorists have focused on other aspects of intelligence. For example, Louis L. Thurstone conceived of intelligence as composed of what he termed *primary*

JUST THINK . . .

In everyday living, mental abilities tend to operate in unison rather than in isolation. How useful is it, therefore, to attempt to isolate and measure "primary mental abilities"?

mental abilities (PMAs). Thurstone (1938) developed and published the Primary Mental Abilities test, which consisted of separate tests, each designed to measure one PMA: verbal meaning, perceptual speed, reasoning, number facility, rote memory, word fluency, and spatial relations. Although the test was not widely used, this early model of multiple abilities inspired other theorists and test developers to explore various components of intelligence and ways to measure them.

In **factor-analytic theories,** the focus is squarely on identifying the ability or groups of abilities deemed to constitute intelligence. In **information-processing theories,** the focus is on identifying the specific mental processes that constitute intelligence. Prior to reading about factor-analytic theories of intelligence, some extended discussion of factor analysis may be helpful (see this chapter's *Close-Up*).

Factor-analytic theories of intelligence   Factor analysis is a group of statistical techniques designed to determine the existence of underlying relationships between sets of variables, including test scores. In search of a definition of intelligence, theorists have used factor analysis to study correlations between tests measuring varied abilities presumed to reflect the underlying attribute of intelligence.

As early as 1904, the British psychologist Charles Spearman pioneered new techniques to measure intercorrelations between tests. He found that measures of intelligence tended to correlate to various degrees with each other. Spearman (1927) formalized these observations into an influential theory of general intelligence that postulated the existence of a general intellectual ability factor (denoted by an italic lowercase *g*) that is partially tapped by all other mental abilities. This theory is sometimes referred to as a **two-factor theory of intelligence,** with *g* representing the portion of the variance that all intelligence tests have in common and the remaining portions of the variance being accounted for either by specific components (*s*), or by error components (*e*) of this general factor (Figure 9–2). Tests that

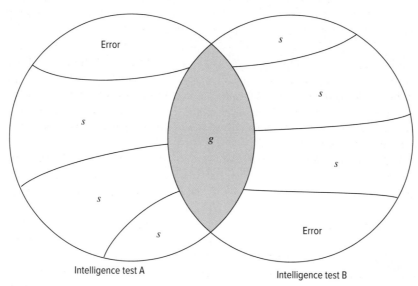

Figure 9–2
Spearman's Two-Factor Theory of Intelligence

Here, g stands for a general intelligence factor and s stands for a specific factor of intelligence (specific to a single intellectual activity only).

Factor Analysis*

To measure characteristics of physical objects, there may be some disagreement about the best methods to use, but there is little disagreement about which dimensions are being measured. We know, for example, that we are measuring length when we use a ruler, and we know that we are measuring temperature when we use a thermometer. Such certainty is not always present in measuring psychological dimensions such as personality traits, attitudes, and cognitive abilities.

Psychologists may disagree about what to name the dimensions being measured and about the number of dimensions being measured. Consider a personality trait that one researcher refers to as *niceness*. Another researcher views *niceness* as a vague term that lumps together two related but independent traits called *friendliness* and *kindness.* Yet another researcher claims that *kindness* is too general and must be dichotomized into *kindness to friends* and *kindness to strangers.* Who is right? Is everybody right? If researchers are ever going to build on each others' findings, there needs to be some way of reaching consensus about what is being measured. Toward that end, factor analysis can be helpful.

An assumption of factor analysis is that things that co-occur tend to have a common cause. Note here that "tend to" does *not* mean "always." Fevers, sore throats, stuffy noses, coughs, and sneezes may *tend to* occur at the same time in the same person, but they do not always co-occur. When these symptoms do co-occur, they may be caused by one thing: the virus that causes the common cold. Although the virus is one thing, its manifestations are quite diverse.

In psychological assessment research, we measure a diverse set of abilities, behaviors, and symptoms and then attempt to deduce which underlying dimensions cause or account for the variations in behavior and symptoms observed in large groups of people. We measure the relations among various behaviors, symptoms, and test scores with correlation coefficients. We then use factor analysis to discover patterns of correlation coefficients that suggest the existence of underlying psychological dimensions.

All else being equal, a simple theory is better than a complicated theory. Factor analysis helps us discover the smallest number of psychological dimensions (or factors) that can account for the various behaviors, symptoms, and test scores we observe. For example, imagine that we create four different tests to measure people's knowledge of vocabulary, grammar, multiplication, and geometry. If the correlations

between all of these tests were zero (or, high scorers on one test are no more likely than low scorers to score high on the other tests), then the factor analysis would suggest to us that we have measured four distinct abilities.

Of course, you probably recognize that it is most unlikely that the correlations between these tests would be zero. Therefore, imagine that the correlation between the vocabulary and grammar tests were quite high (or, high scorers on vocabulary were likely also to score high on grammar, and low scorers on vocabulary were likely to score low on grammar), and suppose also a high correlation between multiplication and geometry. Furthermore, the correlations between the verbal tests and the mathematics tests were zero. Factor analysis would suggest that we have measured not four distinct abilities but two. The researcher interpreting the results of this factor analysis would have to use his or her best judgment in deciding what to call these two abilities. In this case, it would seem reasonable to call them *language ability* and *mathematical ability*.

Now imagine that the correlations between all four tests were equally high—for example, that vocabulary was as strongly correlated with geometry as it was with grammar. In this case, factor analysis suggests that the simplest explanation for this pattern of correlations is that there is just one factor that causes all these tests to be equally correlated. We might call this factor *general academic ability*.

In reality, if you were to actually measure these four abilities, the results would not be so clear-cut. It is likely that all of the correlations would be positive and substantially above zero. It is likely that the verbal subtests would correlate more strongly with each other than with the mathematical subtests. It is likely that factor analysis would suggest that language and mathematical abilities are distinct from but not entirely independent of each other—in other words, that language abilities and mathematics abilities are substantially correlated, suggesting that a general academic (or intellectual) ability influences performance in all academic areas.

Factor analysis can help researchers decide how best to summarize large amounts of information about people by using just a few scores. For example, when we ask parents to complete questionnaires about their children's behavior problems, the questionnaires can have hundreds of items. It would take too long and would be too confusing to review every item. Factor analysis can simplify the information while minimizing the loss of detail. Here is an example of a

*Prepared by W. Joel Schneider.

(continued)

Factor Analysis *(continued)*

short questionnaire that factor analysis can be used to summarize.

> On a scale of 1 to 5, compared to other children his or her age, my child:
>
> 1. gets in fights frequently at school
> 2. is defiant to adults
> 3. is very impulsive
> 4. has stomachaches frequently
> 5. is anxious about many things
> 6. appears sad much of the time

If we give this questionnaire to a large, representative sample of parents, we can calculate the correlations between the items. Table 1 illustrates what we might find.

Note that all of the perfect 1.00 correlations in this table are used to emphasize the fact that each item correlates perfectly with itself. In the analysis of the data, the software would ignore these correlations and analyze only all of the correlations below this diagonal "line of demarcation" of 1.00 correlations.

Using the set of correlation coefficients presented in Table 1, factor analysis suggests that there are two factors measured by this behavior rating scale. The logic of factor analysis suggests that the reason Items 1 through 3 have high correlations with each other is that each has a high correlation with the first factor. Similarly, Items 4 through 6 have high correlations with each other because they have high correlations with the second factor. The correlations of the items with the hypothesized factors are called *factor loadings.* The factor loadings for this hypothetical example are presented in Table 2.

Factor analysis tells us which items *load* on which factors, but it cannot interpret the meaning of the factors. Researchers usually look at all the items that load on a factor and use their intuition or knowledge of theory to identify what the items have in common. In this case, Factor 1 could receive any number of names, such as *Conduct Problems, Acting Out,* or *Externalizing Behaviors.* Factor 2 might also go by various names, such as *Mood Problems, Negative Affectivity,* or *Internalizing Behaviors.* Thus, the problems on this behavior rating scale can be summarized fairly efficiently with just two scores. In this example, a reduction of six scores to two scores may not seem terribly useful. In actual behavior rating scales, factor analysis can reduce the overwhelming complexity of hundreds of different behavior

Table 1
A Sample Table of Correlations

	1	2	3	4	5	6
1. gets in fights frequently at school	1.00					
2. is defiant to adults	.81	1.00				
3. is very impulsive	.79	.75	1.00			
4. has stomachaches frequently	.42	.38	.36	1.00		
5. is anxious about many things	.39	.34	.34	.77	1.00	
6. appears sad much of the time	.37	.34	.32	.77	.74	1.00

Table 2
Factor Loadings for Our Hypothetical Example

	Factor 1	Factor 2
1. gets in fights frequently at school	.91	.03
2. is defiant to adults	.88	−.01
3. is very impulsive	.86	−.01
4. has stomachaches frequently	.02	.89
5. is anxious about many things	.01	.86
6. appears sad much of the time	−.02	.87

problems to a more manageable number of scores that help professionals more easily conceptualize individual cases.

Factor analysis also calculates the correlation among factors. If a large number of factors are identified and if there are substantial correlations among factors, then this new correlation matrix can also be factor-analyzed to obtain *second-order factors.* These factors, in turn, can be analyzed to obtain *third-order factors.* Theoretically, it is possible to have even higher-order factors, but most researchers rarely find it necessary to go beyond third-order factors. The *g* factor from intelligence test data is an example of a third-order factor that emerges because all tests of cognitive abilities are positively correlated. In our previous example, the two factors have a correlation of .46, suggesting that children who have externalizing problems are also at risk of having internalizing problems. It is therefore reasonable to calculate a second-order factor score that measures the overall level of behavior problems.

This example illustrates the most commonly used type of factor analysis: *exploratory factor analysis.* Exploratory factor analysis is helpful when we wish to summarize data efficiently, when we are not sure how many factors are present in our data, or when we are not sure which items load on which factors. In short, when we are exploring or looking for factors, we may use exploratory factor analysis. When we think we have found factors and seek to *confirm* this, we may use another variety of factor analysis.

Researchers can use *confirmatory factor analysis* to test highly specific hypotheses. For example, a researcher might want to know if the two different types of items on the WISC-IV Digit Span subtest measure the same ability or two different abilities. On the Digits Forward type of item, the child must repeat a string of digits in the same order in which they were heard. On the Digits Backward type of item, the child must repeat the string of digits in reverse order. Some researchers believe that repeating numbers verbatim measures auditory short-term memory and that repeating numbers in reverse order measures executive control, the ability to allocate attentional resources efficiently to solve multistep problems. Typically, clinicians add the raw scores of both types of items to produce a single score. If the two item types measure different abilities, then adding the raw scores together is kind of like adding apples and oranges, peaches and pears . . . you get the idea. If, however, the two items measure the same ability, then adding the scores together may yield a more reliable score than the separate scores.

Confirmatory factor analysis may be used to determine whether the two item types measure different abilities. We would need to identify or invent several additional tests that are likely to measure the two separate abilities we believe are measured by the two types of Digit Span items. Usually, three tests per factor is sufficient. Let's call the short-term memory tests STM1, STM2, and STM3. Similarly, we can call the executive control tests EC1, EC2, and EC3.

Next, we specify the hypotheses, or models, we wish to test. There are three of them:

1. *All of the tests measure the same ability.* A graphical representation of a hypothesis in confirmatory factor analysis is called a *path diagram*. Tests are drawn with rectangles, and hypothetical factors are drawn with ovals. The correlations between tests and factors are drawn with arrows. The path diagram for this hypothesis is presented in Figure 1.

2. *Both Digits Forward and Digits Backward measure short-term memory and are distinct from executive control.* The path diagram for this hypothesis is presented in Figure 2.

3. *Digits Forward and Digits Backward measure different abilities.* The path diagram for this hypothesis is presented in Figure 3.

Confirmatory factor analysis produces a number of statistics, called *fit statistics,* that tell us which of the models or hypotheses we tested are most in agreement with the data. Studying the results, we can select the model that provides the best fit with the data or perhaps even generate a new model. Actually, factor analysis can quickly become a lot more complicated than described here, but for now, let's hope this is helpful.

Used with permission of W. Joel Schneider.

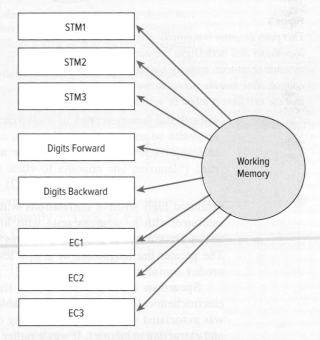

Figure 1
This path diagram is a graphical representation of the hypothesis that All of the tests measure the same ability.

(continued)

Cattell, the theory postulated the existence of two major types of cognitive abilities: crystallized intelligence and fluid intelligence. The abilities that make up **crystallized intelligence** (symbolized *Gc*) include acquired skills and knowledge that are dependent on exposure to a particular culture as well as on formal and informal education (vocabulary, for example). Retrieval of information and application of general knowledge are conceived of as elements of crystallized intelligence. The abilities that make up **fluid intelligence** (symbolized *Gf*) are nonverbal, relatively culture-free, and independent of specific instruction (such as memory for digits). Through the years, Horn (1968, 1985, 1988, 1991, 1994) proposed the addition of several factors: visual processing (*Gv*), auditory processing (*Ga*), quantitative processing (*Gq*), speed of processing (*Gs*), facility with reading and writing (*Grw*), short-term memory (*Gsm*), and long-term storage and retrieval (*Glr*). According to Horn (1989; Horn & Hofer, 1992), some of the abilities (such as *Gv*) are **vulnerable abilities** in that they decline with age and tend not to return to preinjury levels following brain damage. Others of these abilities (such as *Gq*) are **maintained abilities;** they tend not to decline with age and may return to preinjury levels following brain damage.

Another influential multiple-intelligences model based on factor-analytic studies is the **three-stratum theory of cognitive abilities** (Carroll, 1997). In geology, a stratum is a layer of rock formation having the same composition throughout. Strata (the plural of *stratum*) are illustrated in Figure 9–3, along with a representation of each of the three strata in Carroll's theory. The top stratum or level in Carroll's model is *g,* or general intelligence. The second stratum is composed of eight abilities and processes: fluid intelligence (*Gf*), crystallized intelligence (*Gc*), general memory and learning (*Y*), broad visual perception (*V*),

JUST THINK . . .

Moving from an analogy based on geology to one based on chemistry, think of the periodic table, which lists all known elements. Will it ever be possible to develop a comparable, generally agreed-upon "periodic table" of human abilities?

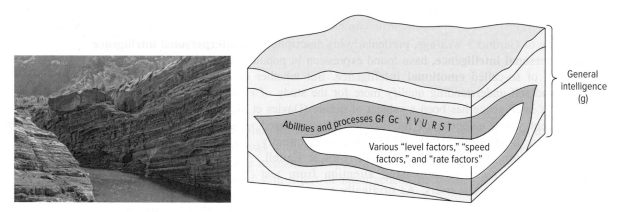

Figure 9–3
Strata in Geology and Carroll's Three-Stratum Theory

Erosion can bare multiple levels of strata on a cliff. In psychology, theory can bare the strata of hypothesized mental structure and function. In Carroll's three-stratum theory of cognitive ability, the first level is g, *followed by a stratum made up of eight abilities and processes, followed by a stratum containing what Carroll refers to as varying "level factors" and "speed factors."*

© Richie Chan/Shutterstock RF

broad auditory perception (U), broad retrieval capacity (R), broad cognitive speediness (S), and processing/decision speed (T). Below each of the abilities in the second stratum are many "level factors" and/or "speed factors"—each different, depending on the second-level stratum to which they are linked. For example, three factors linked to Gf are general reasoning, quantitative reasoning, and Piagetian reasoning. A speed factor linked to Gf is speed of reasoning. Four factors linked to Gc are language development, comprehension, spelling ability, and communication ability. Two speed factors linked to Gc are oral fluency and writing ability. The three-stratum theory is a **hierarchical model,** meaning that all of the abilities listed in a stratum are subsumed by or incorporated in the strata above.

Desire for a comprehensive, agreed-upon conceptualization of human cognitive abilities has led some researchers to try to extract elements of existing models to create a new, more complete model. Using factor analysis as well as other statistical tools, these researchers have attempted to modify and reconfigure existing models to better fit empirical evidence. One such modification that has gained increasing attention blends the Cattell-Horn theory with Carroll's three-stratum theory. Although this blending was not initiated by Cattell or Horn or Carroll, it is nonetheless referred to as the Cattell-Horn-Carroll **(CHC) model** of cognitive abilities.

The Cattell-Horn and Carroll models are similar in several respects, among them the designation of broad abilities (second-stratum level in Carroll's theory) that subsume several narrow abilities (first-stratum level in Carroll's theory). Still, any prospective integration of the Cattell-Horn and Carroll models must somehow account for the differences between these two models. One difference involves the existence of a general intellectual (g) factor. For Carroll, g is the third-stratum factor, subsuming Gf, Gc, and the remaining six other broad, second-stratum abilities. By contrast, g has no place in the Cattell-Horn model. Another difference between the two models concerns whether or not abilities labeled "quantitative knowledge" and "reading/writing ability" should each be considered a distinct, broad ability as they are in the Cattell-Horn model. For Carroll, all of these abilities are first-stratum, narrow abilities. Other differences between the two models include the notation, the specific definitions of abilities, and the grouping of narrow factors related to memory.

An integration of the Cattell-Horn and Carroll models was proposed by Kevin S. McGrew (1997). On the basis of additional factor-analytic work, McGrew and Flanagan (1998) subsequently modified McGrew's initial CHC model. In its current form, the McGrew-Flanagan CHC model features ten "broad-stratum" abilities and over seventy "narrow-stratum" abilities, with each broad-stratum ability subsuming two or more narrow-stratum abilities. The ten broad-stratum abilities, with their "code names" in parentheses, are labeled as follows: fluid intelligence (Gf), crystallized intelligence (Gc), quantitative knowledge (Gq), reading/writing ability (Grw), short-term memory (Gsm), visual processing (Gv), auditory processing (Ga), long-term storage and retrieval (Glr), processing speed (Gs), and decision/reaction time or speed (Gt).

The McGrew-Flanagan CHC model makes no provision for the general intellectual ability factor (g). To understand the reason for this omission, it is important to understand why the authors undertook to create the model in the first place. The model was the product of efforts designed to improve the practice of psychological assessment in education (sometimes referred to as **psychoeducational assessment**) by identifying tests from different batteries that could be used to provide a comprehensive assessment of a student's abilities. Having identified key abilities, the authors made recommendations for **cross-battery assessment** of students, or assessment that employs tests from different test batteries and entails interpretation of data from specified subtests to provide a comprehensive assessment. According to these authors, *g* was not employed in their CHC model because it lacked utility in psychoeducational evaluations. They explained:

> The exclusion of *g* does not mean that the integrated model does not subscribe to a separate general human ability or that *g* does not exist. Rather, it was omitted by McGrew (1997) (and is similarly omitted in the current integrated model) since it has little practical relevance to cross-battery assessment and interpretation. (McGrew & Flanagan, 1998, p. 14)

Other differences between the Cattell-Horn and Carroll models were resolved more on the basis of factor-analytic studies than judgments regarding practical relevance to cross-battery assessment. The abilities labeled "quantitative knowledge" and "reading/writing" were conceived of as distinct broad abilities, much as they were by Horn and Cattell. McGrew and Flanagan drew heavily on Carroll's (1993) writings for definitions of many of the broad and narrow abilities listed and also for the codes for these abilities.

McGrew (2009) called on intelligence researchers to adopt CHC as a consensus model, thus allowing for a common nomenclature and theoretical framework. Toward that end, he established an online archive of over 460 correlation matrices that formed the basis of Carroll's factor-analytic work.[2] This resource was designed to allow researchers to test the CHC model using confirmatory factor analysis, a more powerful statistical technique than the exploratory factor analysis employed by Carroll.

JUST THINK . . .

Do you agree that *g* has little practical relevance in educational settings?

At the very least, CHC theory as formulated by McGrew and Flanagan has great value from a heuristic standpoint. It compels practitioners and researchers alike to think about exactly how many human abilities really need to be measured and about how narrow or how broad an approach is optimal in terms of being clinically useful. Further, it stimulates researchers to revisit other existing theories that may be ripe for reexamination by means of statistical methods like factor analysis. The best features of such theories might then be combined with the goal of developing a clinically useful and actionable model of human abilities.

Another multifactor theory of intelligence we will mention was proposed by psychometrics pioneer, E. L. Thorndike. According to Thorndike (Thorndike et al., 1909; 1921), intelligence can be conceived in terms of three clusters of ability: social intelligence (dealing with people), concrete intelligence (dealing with objects), and abstract intelligence (dealing with verbal and mathematical symbols). Thorndike also incorporated a general mental ability factor (*g*) into the theory, defining it as the total number of modifiable neural connections or "bonds" available in the brain. For Thorndike, one's ability to learn is determined by the number and speed of the bonds that can be marshaled. No major test of intelligence was ever developed based on Thorndike's multifactor theory. And so, to all would-be or future developers of the next great intelligence test: *This is your moment!* Complete the *Just Think* exercise before reading on.

JUST THINK . . .

Outline notes for your very own version of a "Thorndike Test of Intelligence." How will test items be grouped? What types of items would be found in each grouping? What types of summary scores might be reported for each testtaker? What types of interpretations would be made from the test data?

The information-processing view Another approach to conceptualizing intelligence derives from the work of the Russian neuropsychologist Aleksandr Luria (1966a, 1966b, 1970, 1973, 1980). This approach focuses on the mechanisms by which

---

2. The archived data is available through the Woodcock-Muñoz Foundation's Human Cognitive Abilities (WMF HCA) project at *http://www.iapsych.com/wmfhcaarchive/map.htm*

information is processed—*how* information is processed, rather than *what* is processed. Two basic types of information-processing styles, simultaneous and successive, have been distinguished (Das et al., 1975; Luria, 1966a, 1966b). In **simultaneous** (or **parallel**) **processing,** information is integrated all at one time. In **successive** (or **sequential**) **processing,** each bit of information is individually processed in sequence. As its name implies, sequential processing is logical and analytic in nature; piece by piece and one piece after the other, information is arranged and rearranged so that it makes sense. In trying to anticipate who the murderer is while watching television shows like *Law & Order, Criminal Minds,* or *Elementary,* for example, one's thinking could be characterized as *sequential.* The viewer constantly integrates bits of information that will lead to a solution of the "whodunnit?" problem. Memorizing a telephone number or learning the spelling of a new word is typical of the types of tasks that involve acquisition of information through successive processing.

By contrast, *simultaneous* processing may be described as "synthesized." Information is integrated and synthesized at once and as a whole. As you stand before and appreciate a painting in an art museum, the information conveyed by the painting is processed in a manner that, at least for most of us, could reasonably be described as simultaneous. Of course, art critics and connoisseurs may be exceptions to this general rule. In general, tasks that involve the simultaneous mental representations of images or information involve simultaneous processing. Map reading is another task that is typical of such processing.

The strong influence of an information-processing perspective is also evident in the work of others (Das, 1972; Das et al., 1975; Naglieri, 1989, 1990; Naglieri & Das, 1988) who have developed what is referred to as the **PASS model** of intellectual functioning. Here, PASS is an acronym for planning, attention, simultaneous, and successive. In this model, *planning* refers to strategy development for problem solving; *attention* (also referred to as *arousal*) refers to receptivity to information; and *simultaneous* and *successive* refer to the type of information processing employed.

Measuring Intelligence

The measurement of intelligence entails sampling an examinee's performance on different types of tests and tasks as a function of developmental level. At all developmental levels, the intellectual assessment process also provides a standardized situation from which the examinee's approach to the various tasks can be closely observed. It therefore provides an opportunity for an assessment that in itself can have great utility in settings as diverse as schools, the military, and business organizations.

Some Tasks Used to Measure Intelligence

In infancy (the period from birth through 18 months), intellectual assessment consists primarily of measuring sensorimotor development. This includes, for example, the measurement of nonverbal motor responses such as turning over, lifting the head, sitting up, following a moving object with the eyes, imitating gestures, and reaching for a group of objects (Figure 9–4). The examiner who attempts to assess the intellectual and related abilities of infants must be skillful in establishing and maintaining rapport with examinees who do not yet know the meaning of words like *cooperation* and *patience.* Typically, measures of infant intelligence rely to a great degree on information obtained from a structured interview with the examinee's parents, guardians, or other caretakers. For school psychologists and others who have occasion to assess young children, enlisting the participation of parents or other caregivers can, practically

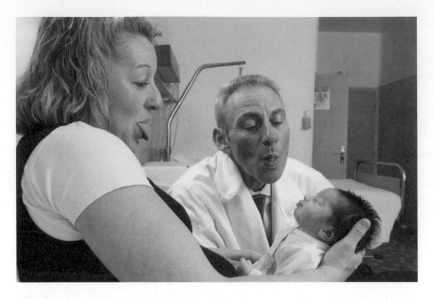

Figure 9–4
Imitation and Cognitive Development

*Researchers such as Susan Fenstemacher of the University of Vermont and Kimberly Saudino of Boston
University (not pictured here) have explored links among imitation, mental development, temperament, and
genetics. Interested readers are referred to their study published in the September–October (2016) issue of*
Infancy.
© Thierry Berrod, Mona Lisa Production/Science Source

speaking, be challenging in its own right. Just ask the consulting psychologist profiled in this
chapter's *Meet an Assessment Professional.*

The focus in evaluation of the older child shifts to verbal and performance abilities. More
specifically, the child may be called on to perform tasks designed to yield a measure of general
fund of information, vocabulary, social judgment, language, reasoning, numerical concepts,
auditory and visual memory, attention, concentration, and spatial visualization. The administration
of many of the items may be preceded, as prescribed by the test manual, with teaching items
designed to provide the examinee with practice in what is required by a particular test item.

According to Wechsler (1958), adult intelligence scales should tap abilities such as
retention of general information, quantitative reasoning, expressive language and memory, and
social judgment. The types of tasks used to reach these measurement objectives on the Wechsler
scale for adults are the same as many of the tasks used on the Wechsler scales for children,
although the content of specific items may vary. For a general description of some past and
present items, see Table 9–1.

Note that tests of intelligence are seldom administered to adults for purposes of educational
placement. Rather, they may be given to obtain clinically relevant information or some measure
of learning potential and skill acquisition. Data from the administration of an adult intelligence
test may be used to evaluate the faculties of an impaired individual (or one suspected of being
senile, traumatized, or otherwise impaired) for the purpose of judging that person's competency
to make important decisions (such as those regarding a will, a
contract, or other legal matter). Insurance companies rely on
such data to make determinations regarding disability. Data from
adult intelligence tests may also be used to help make decisions
about vocational and career decisions and transitions.

JUST THINK . . .

How else might data from adult intelligence
tests be used?

MEET AN ASSESSMENT PROFESSIONAL

Meet Dr. Rebecca Anderson

In my opinion, one of the most important components of an evaluation is generating a report that is reader friendly and provides useful information for parents and teachers who are directly working with the child. A key component of the evaluation is the summary, which should provide a concise picture of the child's strengths and areas of difficulty. Moreover, the recommendations section is a critical element of the report and should provide useful information on ways to support the child's social/emotional and educational success. I try to give recommendations that are accessible to staff and provide tangible tools and suggestions that can be implemented both at home and at school. I often list additional resources (such as books, internet sites, handouts) specific to the child's area of deficiency.

Realistically, when working within the schools, there are strict timelines, which prohibit extensive evaluations. I think one of the biggest challenges relates to the time and effort that goes into a student's evaluation. Schools are often under budget restrictions and want things done quickly. As a rule of thumb, I conduct more thorough evaluations on students who are receiving an initial evaluation in order to determine the nature of the presenting problem. Less time is required for re-evaluation of

Rebecca Anderson, Ph.D., Independent Practice, Consulting School Psychologist

© Rebecca Anderson

students who are already receiving specialized support services. An additional obstacle in the assessment process is accessing parents and staff. I make several efforts to contact parents. If unsuccessful, I note that parental information was unavailable at the time of the evaluation. Ideally, school psychologists would be given ample time and resources and have access to parents and all relevant school personnel, but the reality is that we do the best we can with the time allotted and available resources.

Some Tests Used to Measure Intelligence

As evidenced by reference volumes such as *Tests in Print,* many different intelligence tests exist.[3] From the test user's standpoint, several considerations figure into a test's appeal:

- The theory (if any) on which the test is based
- The ease with which the test can be administered
- The ease with which the test can be scored
- The ease with which results can be interpreted for a particular purpose

---

3. One objective in this and succeeding chapters is not to in any way duplicate the information that can be found in such reference works. Rather, our more modest objective is to supplement discussion of measurement in a particular area with a brief description or overview of sample tests. In each chapter, only a few of the many tests available for the specified measurement purposes are described. The rationale for selecting these illustrative tests had to do with factors such as historical significance, contemporary popularity, or novelty in contrast to other available tools of assessment. Readers are asked not to draw any conclusions about the value of any particular test on the basis of its inclusion in or omission from our discussion.

Table 9–1

Sample Items Used to Measure Intelligence

Subtest	Description
Information	*In what continent is Brazil?* Questions such as these, which are wide-ranging and tap general knowledge, learning, and memory, are asked. Interests, education, cultural background, and reading skills are some influencing factors in the score achieved.
Comprehension	In general, these questions tap social comprehension, the ability to organize and apply knowledge, and what is colloquially referred to as "common sense." An illustrative question is *Why should children be cautious in speaking to strangers?*
Similarities	*How are a pen and a pencil alike?* This is the general type of question that appears in this subtest. Pairs of words are presented to the examinee, and the task is to determine how they are alike. The ability to analyze relationships and engage in logical, abstract thinking are two cognitive abilities tapped by this type of test.
Arithmetic	Arithmetic problems are presented and solved verbally. At lower levels, the task may involve simple counting. Learning of arithmetic, alertness and concentration, and short-term auditory memory are some of the intellectual abilities tapped by this test.
Vocabulary	The task is to define words. This test is thought to be a good measure of general intelligence, although education and cultural opportunity clearly contribute to success on it.
Receptive Vocabulary	The task is to select from four pictures what the examiner has said aloud. This tests taps auditory discrimination and processing, auditory memory, and the integration of visual perception and auditory input.
Picture Naming	The task is to name a picture displayed in a book of stimulus pictures. This test taps expressive language and word retrieval ability.
Digit Span	The examiner verbally presents a series of numbers, and the examinee's task is to repeat the numbers in the same sequence or backward. This subtest taps auditory short-term memory, encoding, and attention.
Letter-Number Sequencing	Letters and numbers are orally presented in a mixed-up order. The task is to repeat the list with numbers in ascending order and letters in alphabetical order. Success on this subtest requires attention, sequencing ability, mental manipulation, and processing speed.
Picture Completion	The subject's task here is to identify what important part is missing from a picture. For example, the testtaker might be shown a picture of a chair with one leg missing. This subtest draws on visual perception abilities, alertness, memory, concentration, attention to detail, and ability to differentiate essential from nonessential detail. Because respondents may point to the missing part, this test provides a good nonverbal estimate of intelligence. However, successful performance on a test such as this still tends to be highly influenced by cultural factors.
Picture Arrangement	In the genre of a comic-strip panel, this subtest requires the testtaker to re-sort a scrambled set of cards with pictures on them into a story that makes sense. Because the testtaker must understand the whole story before a successful re-sorting will occur, this subtest is thought to tap the ability to comprehend or "size up" a situation. Additionally, attention, concentration, and ability to see temporal and cause-and-effect relationships are tapped.
Block Design	A design with colored blocks is illustrated either with blocks themselves or with a picture of the finished design, and the examinee's task is to reproduce the design. This test draws on perceptual-motor skills, psychomotor speed, and the ability to analyze and synthesize. Factors that may influence performance on this test include the examinee's color vision, frustration tolerance, and flexibility or rigidity in problem solving.
Object Assembly	The task here is to assemble, as quickly as possible, a cut-up picture of a familiar object. Some of the abilities called on here include pattern recognition, assembly skills, and psychomotor speed. Useful qualitative information pertinent to the examinee's work habits may also be obtained here by careful observation of the approach to the task. For example, does the examinee give up easily or persist in the face of difficulty?
Coding	If you were given the dot-and-dash equivalents of several letters in Morse code and then had to write out letters in Morse code as quickly as you could, you would be completing a coding task. The Wechsler coding task involves using a code from a printed key. The test is thought to draw on factors such as attention, learning ability, psychomotor speed, and concentration ability.
Symbol Search	The task is to visually scan two groups of symbols, one search group and one target group, and determine whether the target symbol appears in the search group. The test is presumed to tap cognitive processing speed.
Matrix Reasoning	A nonverbal analogy-like task involving an incomplete matrix designed to tap perceptual organizing abilities and reasoning.
Word Reasoning	The task is to identify the common concept being described with a series of clues. This test taps verbal abstraction ability and the ability to generate alternative concepts.
Picture Concepts	The task is to select one picture from two or three rows of pictures to form a group with a common characteristic. It is designed to tap the ability to abstract as well as categorical reasoning ability.
Cancellation	The task is to scan either a structured or an unstructured arrangement of visual stimuli and mark targeted images within a specified time limit. This subtest taps visual selective attention and related abilities.

- The adequacy and appropriateness of the norms
- The acceptability of the published reliability and validity indices
- The test's utility in terms of costs versus benefits

Historically, some tests seem to have been developed more as a matter of necessity than anything else. In the early 1900s, for example, Alfred Binet was charged with the responsibility of developing a test to screen for children with developmental disabilities in the Paris schools. Binet collaborated with Theodore Simon to create the world's first formal test of intelligence in 1905. Adaptations and translations of Binet's work soon appeared in many countries throughout the world. The original Binet-Simon Scale was in use in the United States as early as 1908 (Goddard, 1908, 1910). By 1912 a modified version had been published that extended the age range of the test downward to 3 months (Kuhlmann, 1912). However, it was the work of Lewis Madison Terman at Stanford University that culminated in the ancestor of what we know now as the Stanford-Binet Intelligence Scale.

In what follows, we briefly set the Stanford-Binet in historical context, and describe several aspects of the test in its current form.

The Stanford-Binet Intelligence Scales: Fifth Edition (SB5)   The history of the current version of the Stanford-Binet Intelligence Scales can be traced to Stanford University, and the 1916 publication of an English translation of the Binet-Simon test authored by Lewis Terman (see Figure 9–5).

The result of years of research, Terman's translation and "extension" of the Binet-Simon test featured newly developed test items, and a new methodological approach that included normative studies. Although there were other English translations available, none were as

Figure 9–5
Lewis Madison Terman (1877–1956)

Born on a farm in Indiana, Terman was the 12th of 14 children in the family. After stints at being a teacher and then a school principal, Terman decided to pursue a career in psychology. In 1903 he was awarded a Masters degree. This was followed, two years later, by a doctorate from Clark University. After a few years of teaching child study at Los Angeles State Normal School (a California State teaching college), Terman received an appointment as Assistant Professor in the Education Department at Stanford University. By 1916, largely owing to his revision and refinement of Binet's test, Terman became a prominent figure in the world of psychological testing and assessment. During the first world war, Terman and other leading psychologists were called upon to help the armed forces develop measures that could be used to quickly screen thousands of recruits. Among measurement professionals, Terman is perhaps best remembered for his pioneering innovations in the area of test construction, particularly with regard to standardization. For the larger community, Terman's great contributions to the world of measurement seem to have been overshadowed by his strong, increasingly unpopular views regarding the hereditary nature of intelligence. For example, based on the belief that intelligence is an inherited trait, Terman saw intelligence tests as a tool to identify gifted children, which, in turn could be used as a social tool to identify the best—that is, the most intelligent—leaders (Minton, 2000).
© Atlas Archive/The Image Works

methodologically advanced as Terman's. The publication of the Stanford-Binet had the effect of stimulating a worldwide appetite for intelligence tests (Minton, 1988).

Although the first edition of the **Stanford-Binet** was certainly not without major flaws (such as lack of representativeness of the standardization sample), it also contained some important innovations. It was the first published intelligence test to provide organized and detailed administration and scoring instructions. It was also the first American test to employ the concept of IQ. And it was the first test to introduce the concept of an **alternate item,** an item to be substituted for a regular item under specified conditions (such as the situation in which the examiner failed to properly administer the regular item).

In 1926, Lewis Terman began a project to revise the Stanford-Binet with his former student and subsequent colleague, Maud Merrill (see Figure 9–6). The project would take 11 years to complete. Innovations in the 1937 scale included the development of two equivalent forms, labeled *L* (for Lewis) and *M* (for Maud, according to Becker, 2003), as well as new types of tasks for use with preschool-level and adult-level testtakers.[4] The manual contained many examples to aid the examiner in scoring. The test authors went to then-unprecedented lengths to achieve an adequate standardization sample (Flanagan, 1938), and the test was praised for its technical achievement in the areas of validity and especially reliability. A serious criticism of the test remained: lack of representation of minority groups during the test's development.

Another revision of the Stanford-Binet was well under way at the time of Terman's death at age 79 in 1956. This edition of the Stanford-Binet, the 1960 revision, consisted of only a single form (labeled *L-M*) and included the items considered to be the best from the two forms of the 1937 test, with no new items added to the test. A major innovation, however, was the use of the *deviation IQ* tables in place of the ratio IQ tables. Earlier versions of the Stanford-Binet had employed the *ratio IQ,* which was based on the concept of **mental age** (the age level at which an individual appears to be functioning intellectually as indicated by the level of items

Figure 9–6
Maud Amanda Merrill (1888–1978)

After earning a BA degree from Oberlin College in Minnesota, Merrill was accepted by the Education Department of Stanford University for Masters-level study with Lewis Terman, then a professor in the educational psychology program. Merrill earned a Masters degree in Education in 1920 (Seagoe, 1967) and in 1923 went on to complete a doctorate in psychology, also under Lewis Terman (who had since been promoted to head of the Psychology Department). In her long and distinguished career, Merrill was recognized not only for her expertise on the Stanford-Binet and its administration, but for her expertise in the area of juvenile delinquency (Sears, 1979).

© PF Collection/Alamy Stock Photo

---

4. L. M. Terman left no clue to what initials would have been used for Forms L and M if his co-author's name had not begun with the letter *M.*

responded to correctly). The **ratio IQ** is the ratio of the testtaker's mental age divided by his or her chronological age, multiplied by 100 to eliminate decimals. As illustrated by the formula for its computation, those were the days, now long gone, when an **IQ** (for **intelligence quotient**) really was a quotient:

$$\text{ratio IQ} = \frac{\text{mental age}}{\text{chronological age}} \times 100$$

A child whose mental age and chronological age were equal would thus have an IQ of 100. Beginning with the third edition of the Stanford-Binet, the deviation IQ was used in place of the ratio IQ. The **deviation IQ** reflects a comparison of the performance of the individual with the performance of others of the same age in the standardization sample. Essentially, test performance is converted into a standard score with a mean of 100 and a standard deviation of 16. If an individual performs at the same level as the average person of the same age, the deviation IQ is 100. If performance is a standard deviation above the mean for the examinee's age group, the deviation IQ is 116.

A third revision of the Stanford-Binet was published in 1972. As with previous revisions, the quality of the standardization sample was criticized. Specifically, the manual was vague about the number of minority individuals in the standardization sample, stating only that a "substantial portion" of Black and Spanish-surnamed individuals was included. The 1972 norms may also have overrepresented the West, as well as large urban communities (Waddell, 1980).

The fourth edition of the Stanford-Binet Intelligence Scale (SB:FE; Thorndike et al., 1986) represented a significant departure from previous versions of the Stanford-Binet in theoretical organization, test organization, test administration, test scoring, and test interpretation. Previously, different items were grouped by age and the test was referred to as an **age scale.** The Stanford-Binet: Fourth Edition (SB:FE) was a *point scale.* In contrast to an age scale, a **point scale** is a test organized into subtests by category of item, not by age at which most testtakers are presumed capable of responding in the way that is keyed as correct. The SB:FE manual contained an explicit exposition of the theoretical model of intelligence that guided the revision. The model was one based on the Cattell-Horn (Horn & Cattell, 1966) model of intelligence. A *test composite*—formerly described as a deviation IQ score—could also be obtained. In general, a **test composite** may be defined as a test score or index derived from the combination of, and/or a mathematical transformation of, one or more subtest scores.

The fifth edition of the Stanford-Binet (SB5; Roid, 2003a) was designed for administration to assessees as young as 2 and as old as 85 (or older). The test yields a number of composite scores, including a Full Scale IQ derived from the administration of ten subtests. Subtest scores all have a mean of 10 and a standard deviation of 3. Other composite scores are an Abbreviated Battery IQ score, a Verbal IQ score, and a Nonverbal IQ score. All composite scores have a mean set at 100 and a standard deviation of 15. In addition, the test yields five Factor Index scores corresponding to each of the five factors that the test is presumed to measure (see Table 9–2).

The SB5 was based on the Cattell-Horn-Carroll (CHC) theory of intellectual abilities. In fact, according to Roid (2003c), a factor analysis of the early Forms L and M showed that "the CHC factors were clearly recognizable in the early editions of the Binet scales" (Roid et al., 1997, p. 8). The SB5 measures five CHC factors by different types of tasks and subtests at different levels. The five CHC factor names (with abbreviations) alongside their SB5 equivalents are summarized in Table 9–2.

> **JUST THINK . . .**
>
> The term *IQ* is an abbreviation for "intelligence quotient." Despite the fact that modern expressions of intelligence are no longer quotients, the term *IQ* is very much a part of the public's vocabulary. If what is popularly characterized as "IQ" was to be called by something that is more technically accurate, what would "IQ" be called?

> **JUST THINK . . .**
>
> We live in a society where ability to express oneself in language is highly prized. Should verbal self-expression skills be given more weight on any measure of general ability or intelligence?

Table 9–2

CHC and Corresponding SB5 Factors

CHC Factor Name	SB5 Factor Name	Brief Definition	Sample SB5 Subtest
Fluid Intelligence (*Gf*)	Fluid Reasoning (FR)	Novel problem solving; understanding of relationships that are not culturally bound	Object Series/Matrices (nonverbal) Verbal Analogies (verbal)
Crystallized Knowledge (*Gc*)	Knowledge (KN)	Skills and knowledge acquired by formal and informal education	Picture Absurdities (nonverbal) Vocabulary (verbal)
Quantitative Knowledge (*Gq*)	Quantitative Reasoning (QR)	Knowledge of mathematical thinking including number concepts, estimation, problem solving, and measurement	Verbal Quantitative Reasoning (verbal) Nonverbal Quantitative Reasoning (nonverbal)
Visual Processing (*Gv*)	Visual-Spatial Processing (VS)	Ability to see patterns and relationships and spatial orientation as well as the gestalt among diverse visual stimuli	Position and Direction (verbal) Form Board (nonverbal)
Short-Term Memory (*Gsm*)	Working Memory (WM)	Cognitive process of temporarily storing and then transforming or sorting information in memory	Memory for Sentences (verbal) Delayed Response (nonverbal)

Also provided in that table is a brief definition of the cognitive ability being measured by the SB5 as well as illustrative SB5 verbal and nonverbal subtests designed to measure that ability.

In designing the SB5, an attempt was made to strike an equal balance between tasks requiring facility with language (both expressive and receptive) and tasks that minimize demands on facility with language. In the latter category are subtests that use pictorial items with brief vocal directions administered by the examiner. The examinee response to such items may be made in the form of nonvocal pointing, gesturing, or manipulating.

After about five years in development and extensive item analysis to address possible objections on the grounds of gender, racial/ethnic, cultural, or religious bias, the final standardization edition of the test was developed. Some 500 examiners from all 50 states were trained to administer the test. Examinees in the norming sample were 4,800 subjects from age 2 to over 85. The sample was nationally representative according to year-2000 U.S. Census data stratified with regard to age, race/ethnicity, geographic region, and socioeconomic level. No accommodations were made for persons with special needs in the standardization sample, although such accommodations were made in separate studies. Persons were excluded from the standardization sample (although included in separate validity studies) if they had limited English proficiency, severe medical conditions, severe sensory or communication deficits, or severe emotional/behavior disturbance (Roid, 2003c).

To determine the reliability of the SB5 Full Scale IQ with the norming sample, an internal-consistency reliability formula designed for the sum of multiple tests (Nunnally, 1967, p. 229) was employed. The calculated coefficients for the SB5 Full Scale IQ were consistently high (.97 to .98) across age groups, as was the reliability for the Abbreviated Battery IQ (average of .91). Test-retest reliability coefficients reported in the manual were also high. The test-retest interval was only 5 to 8 days—shorter by some 20 to 25 days than the interval employed on other, comparable tests. Inter-scorer reliability coefficients reported in the SB5 Technical Manual ranged from .74 to .97 with an overall median of .90. Items showing especially poor inter-scorer agreement had been deleted during the test development process.

Content-related evidence of validity for SB5 items was established in various ways, ranging from expert input to empirical item analysis. Criterion-related evidence was presented in the form of both concurrent and predictive data. For the concurrent studies, Roid (2003c) studied correlations between the SB5 and the SB:FE as well as between the SB5 and all three of the then-current major Wechsler batteries (WPPSI-R, WISC-III, and WAIS-III). The correlations were high when comparing the SB5 to the SB:FE and, perhaps as expected, generally less so when comparing to the Wechsler tests. Roid (2003c) attributed the difference in part to the varying extents to which the SB5 and the Wechsler tests were presumed to tap *g*. To establish evidence for predictive validity, correlations with measures of achievement (the Woodcock Johnson III Test of Achievement and the Wechsler Individual Achievement Test, among other tests) were employed and the detailed findings reported in the manual. Roid (2003c) presented a number of factor-analytic studies in support of the construct validity of the SB5. However, exactly how many factors best account for what the test is measuring has been a matter of some debate. Some believe as little as one factor, *g,* best describes what the test measures (Canivez, 2008; DiStefano & Dombrowski, 2006). One study of high-achieving third-graders supported a model with 4 factors (Williams et al., 2010). Using a clinical population in her study, another researcher concluded that "the five factor model on which the SB5 was constructed does not reliably hold true across clinical samples." With regard to her clinical sample, she concluded, "Roid's findings were not generalizable" (Chase, 2005, p. 64). At the very least, it can be said that questions have been raised regarding the utility of the SB-5's five factor model, especially with regard to its applicability to clinical populations.

With regard to the "nuts-and-bolts" of test administration, after the examiner has established a rapport with the testtaker, the examination formally begins with an item from what is called a *routing test.* A **routing test** may be defined as a task used to direct or route the examinee to a particular level of questions. A purpose of the routing test, then, is to direct an examinee to test items that have a high probability of being at an optimal level of difficulty. There are two routing tests on the SB5, each of which may be referred to by either their activity names (Object Series/Matrices and Vocabulary) or their factor-related names (Nonverbal Fluid Reasoning and Verbal Knowledge). By the way, these same two subtests—and only these—are administered for the purpose of obtaining the Abbreviated Battery IQ score.

The routing tests, as well as many of the other subtests, contain **teaching items,** which are designed to illustrate the task required and assure the examiner that the examinee understands. Qualitative aspects of an examinee's performance on teaching items may be recorded as examiner observations on the test protocol. However, performance on teaching items is not formally scored, and performance on such items in no way enters into calculations of any other scores.

Some of the ways that the items of a subtest in intelligence and other ability tests are described by assessment professionals have parallels in your home. For example, there is the *floor.* In intelligence testing parlance, the term **floor** refers to the lowest level of the items on a subtest. So, for example, if the items on a particular subtest run the gamut of ability from *developmentally delayed* at one end of the spectrum to *intellectually gifted* at the other, then the lowest-level item at the former end would be considered the *floor* of the subtest. The highest-level item of the subtest is the **ceiling.** On the Binet, another useful term is *basal level,* which is used to describe a subtest with reference to a specific testtaker's performance. Many Binet subtests have rules for establishing a **basal level,** or a base-level criterion that must be met for testing on the subtest to continue. For example, a rule for establishing a basal level might be "Examinee answers two consecutive items correctly." If and when examinees fail a certain number of items in a row, a **ceiling level** is said to have been reached and testing is discontinued.[5]

For each subtest on the SB5, there are explicit rules for where to *start,* where to *reverse,* and where to *stop* (or *discontinue*). For example, an examiner might start at the examinee's estimated

---

5. Experienced clinicians who have had occasion to test the limits of an examinee will tell you that this assumption is not always correct. **Testing the limits** is a procedure that involves administering test items beyond the level at which the test manual dictates discontinuance. The procedure may be employed when an examiner has reason to believe that an examinee can respond correctly to items at the higher level. On a standardized ability test such as the SB:FE, the discontinue guidelines must be respected, at least in terms of scoring. Testtakers do not earn formal credit for passing the more difficult items. Rather, the examiner would simply note on the protocol that testing the limits was conducted with regard to a particular subtest and then record the findings.

JUST THINK . . .

In what way(s) might an examiner misuse or abuse the obligation to prompt examinees? How could such misuse or abuse be prevented?

present ability level. The examiner might reverse if the examinee scores 0 on the first two items from the start point. The examiner would discontinue testing (stop) after a certain number of item failures after reversing. The manual also provides explicit rules for prompting examinees. If a vague or ambiguous response is given on some verbal items in subtests such as Vocabulary, Verbal Absurdities, or Verbal Analogies, the examiner is encouraged to give the examinee a prompt such as "Tell me more."

Although a few of the subtests are timed, most of the SB5 items are not. The test was constructed this way to accommodate testtakers with special needs and to fit the item response theory model used to calibrate the difficulty of items. Let's also point out that the SB5 has a test administration protocol that could be characterized as *adaptive* in nature.

The SB5 is exemplary in terms of what is called adaptive testing, or testing individually tailored to the testtaker. Other terms used to refer to adaptive testing include tailored testing, sequential testing, branched testing, and response-contingent testing. As employed in intelligence tests, adaptive testing might entail beginning a subtest with a question in the middle range of difficulty. If the testtaker responds correctly to the item, an item of greater difficulty is posed next. If the testtaker responds incorrectly to the item, an item of lesser difficulty is posed. Computerized adaptive testing is in essence designed "to mimic automatically what a wise examiner would do" (Wainer, 1990, p. 10).

Adaptive testing helps ensure that the early test or subtest items are not so difficult as to frustrate the testtaker and not so easy as to lull the testtaker into a false sense of security or a state of mind in which the task will not be taken seriously enough. Three other advantages of beginning an intelligence test or subtest at an optimal level of difficulty are that (1) it allows the test user to collect the maximum amount of information in the minimum amount of time, (2) it facilitates rapport, and (3) it minimizes the potential for examinee fatigue from being administered too many items.

In terms of scoring and interpretation, test manual contains explicit directions for administering, scoring, and interpreting the test in addition to numerous examples of correct and incorrect responses useful in the scoring of individual items. Scores on the individual items of the various subtests are tallied to yield raw scores on each of the various subtests. The scorer then employs tables found in the manual to convert each of the raw subtest scores into a standard score. From these standard scores, composite scores are derived.

When scored by a knowledge test user, an administration of the SB5 may yield much more than a number for a Full Scale IQ and related composite scores: The test may yield a wealth of valuable information regarding the testtaker's strengths and weaknesses with respect to cognitive functioning. This information may be used by clinical and academic professionals in interventions designed to make a meaningful difference in the quality of examinees' lives.

Various methods of profile analysis have been described for use with all major tests of cognitive ability (see, for example, Kaufman & Lichtenberger, 1999). These methods tend to have in common the identification of significant differences between subtest, composite, or other types of index scores as well as a detailed analysis of the factors analyzing those differences. In identifying these significant differences, the test user relies not only on statistical calculations (or tables, if available) but also on the normative data described in the test manual. Large differences between the scores under analysis should be uncommon or infrequent. The SB5 Technical Manual contains various tables designed to assist the test user in analysis. For example, one such table is "Differences Between SB5 IQ Scores and Between SB5 Factor Index Scores Required for Statistical Significance at .05 Level by Age."

In addition to formal scoring and analysis of significant difference scores, the occasion of an individually administered test affords the examiner an opportunity for behavioral observation. More specifically, the assessor is alert to the assessee's **extra-test behavior.** The way the examinee copes with frustration; how the examinee reacts to items considered very easy; the amount of support the examinee seems to require; the general approach to the task; how anxious, fatigued, cooperative, distractible, or compulsive the examinee appears to be—these are the types of behavioral observations that will supplement formal scores. The SB5 record form includes a checklist form of notable examinee behaviors. Included is a brief, yes–no questionnaire with items such as *Examinee's English usage was adequate for testing* and *Examinee was adequately cooperative.* There is also space to record notes and observations regarding the examinee's physical appearance, mood, and activity level, current medications, and related variables. Examiners may also note specific observations during the assessment. For example, when administering Memory for Sentences, there is usually no need to record an examinee's verbatim response. However, if the examinee produced unusual elaborations on the stimulus sentences, good judgment on the part of the examiner dictates that verbatim responses be recorded. Unusual responses on this subtest may also cue the examiner to possible hearing or speech problems.

A long-standing custom with regard to Stanford-Binet Full Scale scores is to convert them into nominal categories designated by certain cutoff boundaries for quick reference. Through the years, these categories have had different names. For the SB5, here are the cutoff boundaries with their corresponding nominal categories:

Measured IQ Range	Category
145–160	Very gifted or highly advanced
130–144	Gifted or very advanced
120–129	Superior
110–119	High average
90–109	Average
80–89	Low average
70–79	Borderline impaired or delayed
55–69	Mildly impaired or delayed
40–54	Moderately impaired or delayed

With reference to this list, Roid (2003b) cautioned that "the important concern is to describe the examinee's skills and abilities in detail, going beyond the label itself" (p. 150). The primary value of such labels is as a shorthand reference in some psychological reports. For example, in a summary statement at the end of a detailed SB5 report, a school psychologist might write, "In summary, Theodore presents as a well-groomed, engaging, and witty fifth-grader who is functioning in the high average range of intellectual ability."

JUST THINK . . .

Not that very long ago, *moron,* a word with pejorative connotations, was one of the categories in use. What, if anything, can test developers do to guard against the use of classification categories with pejorative connotations?

The next revision of the Stanford-Binet will contain not only changes in item content, but changes that will almost certainly relate to its standardization, administration, scoring, and interpretation. Students of psychological testing and assessment would do well to acquaint themselves with these and related issues (such as issues related to the test's psychometric soundness or theoretical basis), using appropriate resources for more information about the test. For now, let's briefly overview some other tests that have been widely used to measure intelligence.

The Wechsler tests   In the early 1930s, psychologist David Wechsler's employer, Bellevue Hospital in Manhattan, needed an instrument for evaluating the intellectual capacity of its multilingual, multinational, and multicultural clients (see Figure 9–7). Dissatisfied with existing intelligence tests, Wechsler began to experiment. The eventual result was a test of his own,

Figure 9–7
David Wechsler (1896–1981)

Born in Romania, David Wechsler came to New York City six years later with his parents and six older siblings. He completed his bachelor's degree in 1916 at City College (New York) and obtained a master's degree at Columbia University the following year. While awaiting induction into the Army at a base in Long Island, Wechsler came in contact with the renowned historian of psychology, E. G. Boring. Wechsler assisted Boring by evaluating the data from one of the first large-scale administrations of a group intelligence test (the Army Alpha test) as the nation geared up for World War I. Wechsler was subsequently assigned to an Army base in Fort Logan, Texas, where his primary duty was administering individual intelligence tests such as the newly published Stanford-Binet Intelligence Scale. Discharged from the Army in 1919, Wechsler spent two years studying in Europe, where he had the opportunity to study with Charles Spearman and Karl Pearson, two brilliant English statisticians known primarily for their work in the area of correlation. Upon his return to New York City, he took a position as a staff psychologist with the Bureau of Child Guidance. In 1935, Wechsler earned a Ph.D. from Columbia University. His dissertation was entitled "The Measurement of Emotional Reactions." By 1932, Wechsler was appointed Chief Psychologist at Bellevue Psychiatric Hospital, a position he held until 1967. An Army private during the first world war, Wechsler served as a measurement consultant to the Armed Forces during the second world war, and as a consultant to the Veterans Administration after the war. Wechsler also assisted in the set-up of a clinic and mental health program for Holocaust survivors in Cyprus in 1947 (Saxon, 1981), and, along with Abraham Maslow, assisted in efforts to launch the Department of Psychology at Hebrew University in Israel ("History of the Department," 2016).

© Atlas Archive/The Image Works

published in 1939. This new test, now referred to as the Wechsler-Bellevue 1 (W-B 1), borrowed from existing tests in format though not in content.

Unlike the most popular individually administered intelligence test of the time, the Stanford-Binet, the W-B 1 was a point scale, not an age scale. The items were classified by subtests rather than by age. The test was organized into six verbal subtests and five performance subtests, and all the items in each test were arranged in order of increasing difficulty. An equivalent alternate form of the test, the W-B 2, was created in 1942 but was never thoroughly standardized (Rapaport et al., 1968). Unless a specific reference is made to the W-B 2, references here (and in the literature in general) to the Wechsler-Bellevue (or the W-B) refer only to the Wechsler-Bellevue 1.

Research comparing the W-B to other intelligence tests of the day suggested that the W-B measured something comparable to what other intelligence tests measured. Still, the test suffered from some problems: (1) The standardization sample was rather restricted; (2) some subtests lacked sufficient inter-item reliability; (3) some of the subtests were made up of items that were too easy; and (4) the scoring criteria for certain items were too ambiguous. Sixteen years after the publication of the W-B, a new Wechsler scale for adults was published: the Wechsler Adult Intelligence Scale (WAIS; Wechsler, 1955).

Like the W-B, the WAIS was organized into Verbal and Performance scales. Scoring yielded a Verbal IQ, a Performance IQ, and a Full Scale IQ. As a result of many improvements over its W-B predecessor, the WAIS would quickly become the standard against which other adult tests were compared. A revision of the WAIS, the WAIS-R, was published in 1981 shortly after Wechsler's death in May of that same year. In addition to new norms and updated materials, the WAIS-R test administration manual mandated the alternate administration of verbal and performance tests. In 1997 the third edition of the test (the WAIS-III) was published.

The WAIS-III contained updated and more user-friendly materials. In some cases, test materials were made physically larger to facilitate viewing by older adults. Some items were added to each of the subtests that extended the test's floor in order to make the test more useful for evaluating people with extreme intellectual deficits. Extensive research was designed to detect and eliminate items that may have contained cultural bias. Norms were expanded to include testtakers in the age range of 74 to 89. The test was co-normed with the Wechsler Memory Scale-Third Edition (WMS-III), thus facilitating

JUST THINK . . .

Why is it important to demonstrate that a new version of an intelligence test is measuring much the same thing as a previous version of the test? Why might it be desirable for the test to measure something that was *not* measured by the previous version of the test?

comparisons of memory with other indices of intellectual functioning when both the WAIS-III and the WMS-III were administered. The WAIS-III yielded a Full Scale (composite) IQ as well as four Index Scores—Verbal Comprehension, Perceptual Organization, Working Memory, and Processing Speed—used for more in-depth interpretation of findings.

At this writing, the WAIS-IV is the current Wechsler adult scale. It is made up of subtests that are designated either as *core* or *supplemental.* A **core subtest** is one that is administered to obtain a composite score. Under usual circumstances, a **supplemental subtest** (also sometimes referred to as an **optional subtest**) is used for purposes such as providing additional clinical information or extending the number of abilities or processes sampled. There are, however, situations in which a supplemental subtest can be used *in place of* a core subtest. The latter types of situation arise when, for some reason, the use of a score on a particular core subtest would be questionable. So, for example, a supplemental subtest might be substituted for a core subtest if:

- the examiner incorrectly administered a core subtest
- the assessee had been inappropriately exposed to the subtest items prior to their administration
- the assessee evidenced a physical limitation that affected the assessee's ability to effectively respond to the items of a particular subtest

The WAIS-IV contains ten core subtests (Block Design, Similarities, Digit Span, Matrix Reasoning, Vocabulary, Arithmetic, Symbol Search, Visual Puzzles, Information, and Coding) and five supplemental subtests (Letter-Number Sequencing, Figure Weights, Comprehension, Cancellation, and Picture Completion). Longtime users of previous versions of the Wechsler series of adult tests will note the absence of four subtests (Picture Arrangement, Object Assembly, Coding Recall, and Coding Copy-Digit Symbol) and the addition of three new subtests (Visual Puzzles, Figure Weights, and Cancellation). Visual Puzzles and Figure Weights are both timed subtests scored on the WAIS-IV Perceptual Reasoning Scale. In Visual Puzzles, the assessee's task is to identify the parts that went into making a stimulus design. In Figure Weights, the assessee's task is to determine what needs to be added to balance a two-sided scale—one that is reminiscent of the "blind justice" type of scale. In Cancellation, a timed subtest used in calculating the Processing Speed Index, the assessee's task is to draw lines through targeted pairs of colored shapes (while not drawing lines through nontargeted shapes presented as distractors).

Improvements in the WAIS-IV over earlier versions of the test include more explicit administration instructions as well as the expanded use of demonstration and sample items—this in an effort to provide assessees with practice in doing what is required, in addition to feedback on their performance. Practice items (or teaching items, as they are also called) are presumed to pay dividends in terms of ensuring that low scores are actually due to a deficit of some sort and not simply to a misunderstanding of directions. As is now customary in the development of most tests of cognitive ability, all of the test items were thoroughly reviewed to root out any possible cultural bias. The WAIS-IV also represents an improvement over its predecessor in terms of its "floor" and "ceiling." The floor of an intelligence test is the lowest level of intelligence the test purports to measure. The WAIS-III had a Full Scale IQ floor of 45; the WAIS-IV has a Full Scale IQ floor of 40. The ceiling of an intelligence test is the highest level of intelligence the test purports to measure. The WAIS-III had a Full Scale IQ ceiling of 155; the WAIS-IV has a Full Scale IQ ceiling of 160. If interest in measuring such extremes in intelligence grows, we can expect to see comparable "home improvements" (in the floors and ceilings) in future versions of this and comparable tests.

Because of longer life expectancies, normative data was extended to include information for testtakers up to age 90 years, 11 months. Other changes in the WAIS-IV as compared to the previous edition of this test reflect greater sensitivity to the needs of older adults. These improvements include:

- enlargement of the images in the Picture Completion, Symbol Search, and Coding subtests
- the recommended nonadministration of certain supplemental tests that tap short-term memory, hand-eye coordination, and/or motor speed for testtakers above the age of 69 (this to reduce testing time and to minimize testtaker frustration)
- an average reduction in overall test administration time from 80 to 67 minutes (accomplished primarily by shortening the number of items the testtaker must fail before a subtest is discontinued)

In a bygone era, testtakers' subtest scores on Wechsler tests were used to calculate a Verbal IQ, a Performance IQ, and a Full Scale IQ; that is not the case with the WAIS-IV. As with its predecessor, the WAIS-III, factor-analytic methods were used to help identify the factors that the test seemed to be loading on. The developers of the WAIS-IV deemed the subtests to be loading on four factors: Verbal Comprehension, Working Memory, Perceptual Reasoning, and Processing Speed.[6] Subtests that loaded heavily on any one of these factors were grouped together, and scores on these subtests were used to calculate corresponding index scores. Subtests that loaded less on a particular factor were designated as supplemental with regard to the measurement of that factor (see Table 9–3). As a result, scoring of subtests yields four index scores: a Verbal Comprehension Index, a Working Memory Index, a Perceptual Reasoning Index, and a Processing Speed Index. There is also a fifth index score, the General Ability Index (GAI), which is a kind of "composite of two composites." It is calculated using the Verbal Comprehension and Perceptual Reasoning indexes. The GAI is useful to clinicians as an overall index of intellectual ability.

Another composite score that has clinical application is the Cognitive Proficiency Index (CPI). Comprised of the Working Memory Index and the Processing Speed Index, the CPI is used to identify problems related to working memory or processing speed (Dumont & Willis, 2001). Some researchers have suggested that it can be used in conjunction with the GAI as an aid to better understanding and identifying various learning disabilities (Weiss et al., 2010). Like the GAI and the Full Scale IQ (FSIQ), the CPI was calibrated to have a mean of 100 and a standard deviation of 15.

The WAIS-IV standardization sample consisted of 2,200 adults from the age of 16 to 90 years, 11 months. The sample was stratified on the basis of 2005 U.S. Census data with regard to variables such as age, sex, race/ethnicity, educational level, and geographic region.

---

6. The WAIS-IV factor called "Perceptual Reasoning" is the same factor that was called "Perceptual Organization" on the WAIS-III.

Table 9–3

WAIS-IV Subtests Grouped According to Indexes

Verbal Comprehension Scale	Perceptual Reasoning Scale	Working Memory Scale	Processing Speed Scale
Similarities[a]	Block Design[a]	Digit Span[a]	Symbol Search[a]
Vocabulary[a]	Matrix Reasoning[a]	Arithmetic[a]	Coding[a]
Information[a]	Visual Puzzles[a]	Letter-Number Sequencing (ages 16–69)[b]	Cancellation (ages 16–69)[b]
Comprehension[b]	Picture Completion[b]		
	Figure Weights (ages 16–69)[b]		

[a]Core subtest.
[b]Supplemental subtest.

Consistent with census data, there were more females than males in the older age bands. As compared to the WAIS-III standardization sample, the WAIS-IV sample is older, more diverse, and has an improved standard of living.

Following a Wechsler tradition, most subtest raw scores for each age group were converted to percentiles and then to a scale with a mean of 10 and a standard deviation of 3. Another Wechsler tradition, beginning with the WAIS-R, called for scaled scores for each subtest to be based on the performance of a "normal" (or, at least, nondiagnosed and nonimpaired) reference group of testtakers 20–34 years old. According to Tulsky et al. (1997), this was done as a consequence of David Wechsler's conviction that "optimal performance tended to occur at these ages" (p. 40). However, the practice was found to contribute to a number of problems in WAIS-R test interpretation, especially with older testtakers (Ivnik et al., 1992; Ryan et al., 1990; Tulsky et al., 1997). Beginning with the WAIS-III and continuing with the WAIS-IV, the practice of deriving norms on a hypothesized "optimal performance" reference group was abandoned. Scores obtained by the testtaker's same-age normative group would serve as the basis for the testtaker's scaled score.[7]

The manual for the WAIS-IV (Coalson & Raiford, 2008) presents data from a number of studies attesting to the reliability, validity, and overall psychometric soundness of the test. For example, high internal consistency reliability estimates were found for all subtests and composite scores for which an estimate of internal consistency is appropriate.[8]

The validity of the WAIS-IV was established by a number of means such as concurrent validity studies and convergent and discriminative validity studies. Additionally, qualitative studies were conducted on the problem-solving strategies testtakers used in responding to questions in order to confirm that they were the same processes targeted for assessment. Independent researchers have noted that although there is comparability between WAIS-IV and SB5 scores in the middle range of intelligence, some discrepancies exist between scores achieved on these tests at the extreme ends of the distribution. For example, in one study, individuals known to be intellectually disabled were found to earn WAIS full scale scores that were roughly 16 points higher than those earned on the SB5 (Silverman et al., 2010).

JUST THINK . . .

Give some thought to your own problem-solving processes. Answer the question "What is the square root of 81?" Now, answer the question "What did you have for dinner last evening?" How are the processes of thought you used to respond to these two questions different? For example, did one of the questions evoke more mental imagery than the other question?

---

7. However, such reference group scores (derived from the performance of adults from age 20 through age 34 years, 11 months) are still published in the WAIS-IV manual. Presumably, these norms are there for research purposes—or for examiners who seek to determine how an individual testtaker's performance compares with adults in this age group.

8. An estimate of internal consistency would not be appropriate for speeded subtests, such as those subtests used to calculate the Processing Speed Index.

The enthusiasm with which the professional community received the Wechsler adult scale prompted a "brand extension" of sorts downward. The result would be a series of Wechsler intelligence tests for children including the Wechsler Intelligence Scale for Children (WISC) first published in 1949 (currently in its fifth edition), and the Wechsler Pre-School and Primary Scale of Intelligence (WPPSI) first published in 1967 (currently in its fourth edition).

A general description of the various types of tasks measured in current as well as past revisions of these tests is presented in Table 9–1. Additionally, taking full advantage of the benefits of computerized test administration, some of the subtests on some of the newer Wechsler revisions (such as the WISC-V) have been specially re-designed for computerized administration.

Traditionally, whether it was the Wechsler adult scale, the child scale, or the preschool scale, an examiner familiar with one Wechsler test would not have a great deal of difficulty navigating any other Wechsler test. Although this is probably still true, the Wechsler tests have shown a clear trend away from such uniformity. For example, there was a time when all Wechsler scales yielded, among other possible composite scores, a Full Scale IQ (a measure of general intelligence), a Verbal IQ (calculated on the basis of scores on subtests categorized as verbal), and a Performance IQ (calculated on the basis of scores on subtests categorized as nonverbal). All of that changed in 2003 with the publication of the fourth edition of the children's scale, a test that dispensed with the long-standing Wechsler dichotomy of Verbal and Performance subtests.

Regardless of the changes instituted to date, there remains a great deal of commonality between the scales. The Wechsler tests are all point scales that yield deviation IQs with a mean of 100 (interpreted as average) and a standard deviation of 15. On each of the Wechsler tests, a testtaker's performance is compared with scores earned by others in that age group. The tests have in common clearly written manuals that provide descriptions of each of the subtests, including the rationale for their inclusion. The manuals also contain clear, explicit directions for administering subtests as well as a number of standard prompts for dealing with a variety of questions, comments, or other contingencies. There are similar starting, stopping, and discontinue guidelines and explicit scoring instructions with clear examples. For test interpretation, all the Wechsler manuals come with myriad statistical charts that can prove very useful when it comes time for the assessor to make recommendations on the basis of the assessment. In addition, a number of aftermarket publications authored by various assessment professionals are available to supplement guidelines presented in the test manuals.

In general, the Wechsler tests have been evaluated favorably from a psychometric standpoint. Although the coefficients of reliability will vary as a function of the specific type of reliability assessed, reported reliability estimates for the Wechsler tests in various categories (internal consistency, test-retest reliability, inter-scorer reliability) tend to be satisfactory and, in many cases, more than satisfactory. Wechsler manuals also typically contain a great deal of information on validity studies, usually in the form of correlational studies or factor-analytic studies.

Short forms of intelligence tests   The term **short form** refers to a test that has been abbreviated in length, typically to reduce the time needed for test administration, scoring, and interpretation. Sometimes, particularly when the testtaker is believed to have an atypically short attention span or other problems that would make administration of the complete test impossible, a sampling of representative subtests is administered. Arguments for such use of Wechsler scales have been made with reference to testtakers from the general population (Kaufman et al., 1991), the elderly (Paolo & Ryan, 1991), and others (Benedict et al., 1992; Boone, 1991; Grossman et al., 1993; Hayes, 1999; Randolph et al., 1993; Ryan & Ward, 1999; Schoop et al., 2001; Sweet et al., 1990).

Short forms of intelligence tests are nothing new. In fact, they have been around almost as long as the long forms. Soon after the Binet-Simon reached the United States, a short form of it was proposed (Doll, 1917). Today, school psychologists with long waiting lists for assessment appointments, forensic psychologists working in an overburdened criminal justice system, and health insurers seeking to pay less for assessment services are some of the groups to whom the short form appeals.

In 1958, David Wechsler endorsed the use of short forms but only for screening purposes. Years later, perhaps in response to the potential for abuse of short forms, he took a much dimmer view of reducing the number of subtests just to save time. He advised those claiming that they did not have the time to administer the entire test to "find the time" (Wechsler, 1967, p. 37).

Some literature reviews on the validity of short forms have tended to support Wechsler's admonition to "find the time." Watkins (1986) concluded that short forms may be used for screening purposes only, not to make placement or educational decisions. From a historical perspective, Smith, McCarthy, and Anderson (2000) characterized views on the transfer of validity from the parent form to the short form as "overly optimistic." In contrast to some critics who have called for the abolishment of short forms altogether, Smith et al. (2000) argued that the standards for the validity of a short form must be high. They suggested a series of procedures to be used in the development of valid short forms. Silverstein (1990) provided an incisive review of the history of short forms, focusing on four issues: (1) how to abbreviate the original test; (2) how to select subjects; (3) how to estimate scores on the original test; and (4) the criteria to apply when comparing the short form with the original. Ryan and Ward (1999) advised that anytime a short form is used, the score should be reported on the official record with the abbreviation "Est" next to it, indicating that the reported value is only an estimate.

From a psychometric standpoint, the validity of a test is affected by and is somewhat dependent on the test's reliability. Changes in a test that lessen its reliability may also lessen its validity. Reducing the number of items in a test typically reduces the test's reliability and hence its validity. For that reason, decisions made on the basis of data derived from administrations of a test's short form must, in general, be made with caution (Nagle & Bell, 1993). In fact, when data from the administration of a short form clearly suggest the need for intervention or placement, the best practice may be to "find the time" to administer the full form of the test.

Against a backdrop in which many practitioners view short forms as desirable and many psychometricians urge caution in their use, the Wechsler Abbreviated Scale of Intelligence (WASI) was published in 1999. The WASI was designed to answer the need for a short instrument to screen intellectual ability in testtakers from 6 to 89 years of age. The test comes in a two-subtest form (consisting of Vocabulary and Block Design) that takes about 15 minutes to administer and a four-subtest form that takes about 30 minutes to administer. The four subtests (Vocabulary, Block Design, Similarities, and Matrix Reasoning) are WISC- and WAIStype subtests that had high correlations with Full Scale IQ on those tests and are thought to tap a wide range of cognitive abilities. The WASI yields measures of Verbal IQ, Performance IQ, and Full Scale IQ. Consistent with many other intelligence tests, the Full Scale IQ was set at 100 with a standard deviation of 15. The WASI was standardized with 2,245 cases including 1,100 children and 1,145 adults. The manual presents evidence for satisfactory psychometric soundness, although some reviewers of this test were not completely satisfied with the way the validity research was conducted and reported (Keith et al., 2001). However, other reviewers have found that the psychometric qualities of the WASI, as well as its overall usefulness, far exceed those of comparable, brief measures of intelligence (Lindskog & Smith, 2001).

A revision of the WASI referred to, logically enough, as the WASI-2 was published in 2011. The test developers had as their goal an increase in linkage and usability with other Wechsler tests, making the test materials more user friendly, and increasing the psychometric soundness of the test. In general, the WASI-2 test developers seem to have accomplished what they set out to do (Irby & Floyd, 2013). Still, users of an abbreviated measure of intelligence are strongly cautioned that reduced clinical accuracy as compared to the use of a full-length test may be expected to result (McCrimmon & Smith, 2013).

Group tests of intelligence   The Stanford revision of the Binet-Simon test was published in 1916, and only one year later, many psychologists were compelled to start thinking about how such a test could be adapted for group administration. To understand why, consider a brief historical look at testing in the military.

On April 6, 1917, the United States entered World War I. On April 7, the president of the American Psychological Association, Robert M. Yerkes, began efforts to mobilize psychologists to help in the war effort. By late May, the APA committee that would develop group tests for the military had their first meeting. There was little debate among the participants about the nature of intelligence, only a clear sense of urgency about developing instruments for the military to identify both the "unfit" and those of "exceptionally superior ability."

Whereas the development of a major intelligence or ability test today might take three to five years, the committee had two tests ready in a matter of weeks and a final form of those tests ready for the printer on July 7. One test became known as the **Army Alpha test.** This test would be administered to Army recruits who could read. It contained tasks such as general information questions, analogies, and scrambled sentences to reassemble. The other test was the **Army Beta test,** designed for administration to foreign-born recruits with poor knowledge of English or to illiterate recruits (defined as "someone who could not read a newspaper or write a letter home"). It contained tasks such as mazes, coding, and picture completion (wherein the examinee's task was to draw in the missing element of the picture). Both tests were soon administered in army camps by teams of officers and enlisted men. By 1919 nearly 2 million recruits had been tested, 8,000 of whom had been recommended for immediate discharge on the basis of the test results. Other recruits had been assigned to various units in the Army based on their Alpha or Beta test results. For example, recruits who scored in the low but acceptable range were likely to draw duty that involved digging ditches or similar kinds of assignments.

If one dream drove the development of the Army Alpha and Beta tests, it was for the Army, other organizations, and society as a whole to run smoothly and efficiently as a result of the proper allocation of human resources—all thanks to tests. Some psychometric scrutiny of the Alpha and Beta tests supported their use. The tests were reliable enough, and they seemed to correlate acceptably with external criteria such as Stanford-Binet Full Scale IQ scores and officers' ratings of men on "practical soldier value." Yerkes (1921) provided this explanation of what he thought the test actually measured:

> The tests give a reliable index of a man's ability to learn, to think quickly and accurately, and to comprehend instructions. They do not measure loyalty, bravery, dependability, or the emotional traits that make a man "carry on." A man's value to the service is measured by his intelligence plus other necessary qualifications. (p. 424)

An original objective of the Alpha and Beta tests was to measure the ability to be a good soldier. However, after the war, that objective seemed to get lost in the shuffle as the tests were used in various aspects of civilian life to measure general intelligence. An Army Alpha or Beta test was much easier to obtain, administer, and interpret than a Stanford-Binet test, and it was also much cheaper. Thousands of unused Alpha and Beta booklets became government surplus that almost anyone could buy. The tests were administered, scored, and interpreted by many who lacked the background and training to use them properly. The utopian vision of a society in which individuals contributed according to their abilities as determined by tests would never materialize. To the contrary, the misuse of tests soured many members of the public and the profession on the use of tests, particularly group tests.

The military's interest in psychological testing during the 1920s and 1930s was minimal. It was only when the threat of a second world war loomed that interest in group intelligence testing reemerged; this led to development of the Army General Classification Test (AGCT). During the course of World War II, the AGCT would be administered to more than 12 million recruits. Other, more specialized tests were also developed by military psychologists. An assessment unit discretely named the Office of Strategic Services (OSS) developed innovative measures for selecting spies and secret agents to work abroad. By the way, the OSS was a predecessor to today's Central Intelligence Agency (CIA).

Today, group tests are still administered to prospective recruits, primarily for screening purposes. In general, we may define a **screening tool** as an instrument or procedure used to identify a particular trait or constellation of traits at a gross or imprecise level. Data derived from the process of screening may be explored in more depth by more individualized methods of assessment. Various types of screening instruments are used in many different settings. For example, in the following chapter we see how screening tools such as behavior checklists are used in preschool settings to identify young children to be evaluated with more individualized, in-depth procedures.

JUST THINK . . .

James Bond aside, what qualities do you think a real secret agent needs to have? How might you measure these qualities in an applicant?

In the military, the long tradition of using data from screening tools as an aid to duty and training assignments continues to this day. Such data also serve to mold the nature of training experiences. For example, data from group testing have indicated a downward trend in the mean intelligence level of recruits since the inception of an all-volunteer army. In response to such findings, the military has developed new weapons training programs that incorporate, for example, simpler vocabulary in programmed instruction.

Included among many group tests used today by the armed forces are the Officer Qualifying Test (a 115-item multiple-choice test used by the U.S. Navy as an admissions test to Officer Candidate School), the Airman Qualifying Exam (a 200-item multiple-choice test given to all U.S. Air Force volunteers), and the Armed Services Vocational Aptitude Battery (ASVAB). The ASVAB is administered to prospective new recruits in all the armed services. It is also made available to high-school students and other young adults who seek guidance and counseling about their future education and career plans.

Annually, hundreds of thousands of people take the ASVAB, making it perhaps the most widely used multiple aptitude test in the United States. It is administered by school counselors and at various walk-in centers at no cost to the testtaker. In the context of a career exploration program, the ASVAB is designed to help testtakers learn about their interests, abilities, and personal preferences in relation to career opportunities in military and civilian settings. Illustrative items from each of the ten subtests are presented in this chapter's *Everyday Psychometrics*.

Through the years, various forms of the ASVAB have been produced, some for exclusive use in schools and some for exclusive use in the military. A set of 100 selected items included in the subtests of Arithmetic Reasoning, Numerical Operations, Word Knowledge, and Paragraph Comprehension make up a measure within the ASVAB called the Armed Forces Qualification Test (AFQT). The AFQT is a measure of general ability used in the selection of recruits. The different armed services employ different cutoff scores in making accept/reject determinations for service, which are based also on such considerations as their preset quotas for particular demographic groups. In addition to the AFQT score, ten aptitude areas are also tapped on the ASVAB, including general technical, general mechanics, electrical, motor-mechanics, science, combat operations, and skill-technical. These are combined to assess aptitude in five separate career areas, including clerical, electronics, mechanics, skill-technical (medical, computers), and combat operations.

The test battery is continually reviewed and improved on the basis of data regarding how predictive scores are of actual performance in various occupations and military training programs. The ASVAB has been found to predict success in computer programming and computer operating roles (Besetsny et al., 1993), multi-tasking in Navy sailors (Hambrick et al., 2011), and grades in military technical schools across a variety of fields (Earles & Ree, 1992; Ree & Earles, 1990). In one study, the ASVAB adequately predicted grades in three United States Air Force courses

The Armed Services Vocational Aptitude Battery (ASVAB): A Test You Can Take

If you would like firsthand experience in taking an ability test that can be useful in vocational guidance, do what about 900,000 other people do each year and take the Armed Services Vocational Aptitude Battery (ASVAB). Uncle Sam makes this test available to you free of charge—along with other elements of a career guidance package, including a workbook and other printed materials and test scoring and interpretation. Although one objective is to get testtakers "into boots" (that is, into the military), taking the test entails no obligation of military service. For more information about how you can take the ASVAB, contact your school's counseling office or a military recruiter. Meanwhile, you may wish to warm up with the following ten sample items representing each of the ten ASVAB subtests.

I. General Science

Included here are general science questions, including questions from the areas of biology and physics.

1. An eclipse of the sun throws the shadow of the
   a. moon on the sun.
   b. moon on the earth.
   c. earth on the sun.
   d. earth on the moon.

II. Arithmetic Reasoning

The task here is to solve arithmetic problems. Testtakers are permitted to use (government-supplied) scratch paper.

2. It costs $0.50 per square yard to waterproof canvas. What will it cost to waterproof a canvas truck that is 15' × 24'?
   a. $6.67
   b. $18.00
   c. $20.00
   d. $180.00

III. Word Knowledge

Which of four possible definitions best defines the underlined word?

3. Rudiments most nearly means
   a. politics.
   b. minute details.
   c. promotion opportunities.
   d. basic methods and procedures.

IV. Paragraph Comprehension

A test of reading comprehension and reasoning.

4. Twenty-five percent of all household burglaries can be attributed to unlocked windows or doors. Crime is the result of opportunity plus desire. To prevent crime, it is each individual's responsibility to
   a. provide the desire.
   b. provide the opportunity.
   c. prevent the desire.
   d. prevent the opportunity.

V. Numerical Operations

This speeded test contains simple arithmetic problems that the testtaker must solve quickly; it is one of two speeded tests on the ASVAB.

5. $6 - 5 =$
   a. 1
   b. 4
   c. 2
   d. 3

VI. Coding Speed

This subtest contains coding items that measure perceptual/motor speed, among other factors.

KEY

| green . . . 2715 | man . . . 3451 | salt . . . 4586 |
| hat . . . 1413 | room . . . 2864 | tree . . . 5927 |

		a.	b.	c.	d.	e.
6.	room	1413	2715	2864	3451	4586

VII. Auto and Shop Information
This test assesses knowledge of automobile shop practice and the use of tools.

7. What tool is shown above?
   a. hole saw
   b. keyhole saw
   c. counter saw
   d. grinding saw

VIII. Mathematics Knowledge
This is a test of ability to solve problems using high-school-level mathematics. Use of scratch paper is permitted.

8. If $3X = -5$, then $X =$
   a. -2
   b. $-5/3$
   c. $-3/5$
   d. $3/5$

IX. Mechanical Comprehension
Knowledge and understanding of general mechanical and physical principles are probed by this test.

9. Liquid is being transferred from the barrel to the bucket by
   a. capillary action.
   b. gravitational forces.
   c. fluid pressure in the hose.
   d. water pressure in the barrel.

X. Electronics Information
Here, knowledge of electrical, radio, and electronics information is assessed.

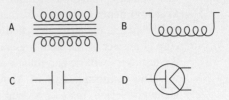

10. Which of the above is the symbol for a transformer?
    a. A
    b. B
    c. C
    d. D

Answer Key

1. b	6. c
2. c	7. a
3. d	8. b
4. d	9. b
5. Why are you looking this one up?	10. a

offered to sensor operators (Carretta et al., 2015).[9] A review of validity studies supports the construct, content, and criterion-related validity of the ASVAB as a device to guide training and selection decisions (Welsh et al., 1990). In general, the test has been deemed quite useful for selection and placement decisions regarding personnel in the armed forces (Chan et al., 1999).

Beyond their applications for military purposes, group tests of intelligence are extensively used in schools and related educational settings. Perhaps no more than a decade or two ago, approximately two-thirds of all school districts in the United States used group intelligence tests on a routine basis to screen 90% of their students. The other 10% were administered individual intelligence tests. Litigation and legislation surrounding the routine use of group intelligence tests have altered this picture somewhat. Still, the group intelligence test, now also referred to as a *school ability test,* is by no means extinct. In many states, legal mandates prohibit the use of group intelligence data alone for class assignment purposes. However, group intelligence test data can, when combined with other data, be extremely useful in developing a profile of a child's intellectual assets.

9. Sensor operators are enlisted aviators who provide a variety of assistance to operators of unmanned, remotely-piloted aircraft.

Group intelligence test results provide school personnel with valuable information for instruction-related activities and increased understanding of the individual pupil. One primary function of data from a group intelligence test is to alert educators to students who might profit from more extensive assessment with individually administered ability tests. The individually administered intelligence test, along with other tests, may point the way to placement in a special class, a program for the gifted, or some other program. Group intelligence test data can also help a school district plan educational goals for all children.

Group intelligence tests in the schools are used in special forms as early as the kindergarten level. The tests are administered to groups of 10 to 15 children, each of whom receives a test booklet that includes printed pictures and diagrams. For the most part, simple motor responses are required to answer items. Oversized alternatives in the form of pictures in a multiple-choice test might appear on the pages, and it is the child's job to circle or place an *X* on the picture that represents the correct answer to the item presented orally by the examiner. During such testing in small groups, the testtakers will be carefully monitored to make certain they are following the directions.

The California Test of Mental Maturity, the Kuhlmann-Anderson Intelligence Tests, the Henmon-Nelson Tests of Mental Ability, and the Cognitive Abilities Test are some of the many group intelligence tests available for use in school settings. The first group intelligence test to be used in U.S. schools was the Otis-Lennon School Ability Test, formerly the Otis Mental Ability Test. In its current edition, the test is designed to measure abstract thinking and reasoning ability and to assist in school evaluation and placement decision-making. This nationally standardized test yields Verbal and Nonverbal score indexes as well as an overall School Ability Index (SAI).

In general, group tests are useful screening tools when large numbers of examinees must be evaluated either simultaneously or within a limited time frame. More specific advantages—and disadvantages—of traditional group testing are listed in Table 9–4. We qualify group testing with *traditional* because more contemporary forms of group testing, especially testing with all testtakers seated at a computer station, might more aptly be termed *individual assessment simultaneously administered in a group* rather than *group testing*.

◆ JUST THINK. . .

How has the dynamics of what has traditionally been referred to as "group testing" changed as a result of the administration of tests to groups of testtakers using personal computers?

Other measures of intellectual abilities   Widely used measures of general intelligence sample only a small realm of the many human abilities that may be conceived of as contributing to an individual's intelligence. There are many known intellectual abilities and talents that are not—or are only indirectly—assessed by popular intelligence tests. There are, for example, tests available to measure very specific abilities such as critical thinking, music, or art appreciation. There is also an evolving knowledge base regarding what are called *cognitive styles*. A **cognitive style** is a psychological dimension that characterizes the consistency with which one acquires and processes information (Ausburn & Ausburn, 1978; Messick, 1976). Examples of cognitive styles include Witkin et al.'s (1977) field dependence versus field independence dimension, the reflection versus impulsivity dimension (Messer, 1976), and the visualizer versus verbalizer dimension (Kirby et al., 1988; Paivio, 1971).

Interestingly, although most intelligence tests do not measure creativity, tests designed to measure creativity may well measure variables related to intelligence. For example, some component abilities of creativity are thought to be originality in problem solving, originality in perception, and originality in abstraction. To the extent that tests of intelligence tap these components, measures of creativity may also be thought of as tools for assessing intelligence. A number of tests and test batteries are available to measure creativity in children and adults. In fact, some universities, such as the University of Georgia and the State University College of New York at Buffalo, maintain libraries containing several hundred of these tests. What types of tasks are featured on these tests? And what do these tests really measure?

Table 9–4
The Pros and Cons of Traditional Group Testing

Advantages of Group Tests	Disadvantages of Group Tests
Large numbers of testtakers can be tested at one time, offering efficient use of time and resources.	All testtakers, regardless of ability, typically must start on the same item, end on the same item, and be exposed to every item on the test. Opportunity for adaptive testing is minimized.
Testtakers work independently at their own pace.	Testtakers must be able to work independently and understand what is expected of them, with little or no opportunity for questions or clarification once testing has begun.
Test items are typically in a format easily scored by computer or machine.	Test items may not be in more innovative formats or any format involving examiner manipulation of materials or examiner–examinee interaction.
The test administrator need not be highly trained, as task may require little beyond reading instructions, keeping time, and supervising testtakers.	Opportunity for assessor observation of testtaker's extra-test behavior is lost.
Test administrator may have less effect on the examinee's score than a test administrator in a one-on-one situation.	Opportunity for learning about assessee through assessor–assessee interaction is lost.
Group testing is less expensive than individual testing on a per-testtaker basis.	The information from a group test may not be as detailed and actionable as information from an individual test administration.
Group testing has proven value for screening purposes.	Instruments designed expressly for screening are occasionally used for making momentous decisions.
Group tests may be normed on large numbers of people more easily than an individual test.	In any test-taking situation, testtakers are assumed to be motivated to perform and follow directions. The opportunity to verify these assumptions may be minimized in large-scale testing programs. The testtaker who "marches to the beat of a different drummer" is at a greater risk of obtaining a score that does not accurately approximate his or her hypothetical true score.
Group tests work well with people who can read, follow directions, grip a pencil, and do not require a great deal of assistance.	Group tests may not work very well with people who cannot read, who cannot grip a pencil (such as very young children), who "march to the beat of a different drummer," or who have exceptional needs or requirements.

Four terms common to many measures of creativity are *originality, fluency, flexibility,* and *elaboration. Originality* refers to the ability to produce something that is innovative or nonobvious. It may be something abstract like an idea or something tangible and visible like artwork or a poem. *Fluency* refers to the ease with which responses are reproduced and is usually measured by the total number of responses produced. For example, an item in a test of word fluency might be *In the next thirty seconds, name as many words as you can that begin with the letter w. Flexibility* refers to the variety of ideas presented and the ability to shift from one approach to another. *Elaboration* refers to the richness of detail in a verbal explanation or pictorial display.

A criticism frequently leveled at group standardized intelligence tests (as well as at other ability and achievement tests) is that evaluation of test performance is too heavily focused on whether the answer is correct. The heavy emphasis on correct response leaves little room for the evaluation of processes such as originality, fluency, flexibility, and elaboration. Stated another way, on most achievement tests the thought process typically required is *convergent thinking.* **Convergent thinking** is a deductive reasoning process that entails recall and consideration of facts as well as a series of logical judgments to narrow down solutions and eventually arrive at one solution. In his structure-of-intellect model, Guilford (1967) drew a distinction between the intellectual processes of *convergent* and *divergent* thinking. **Divergent thinking** is a reasoning process in which thought is free to move in many different directions, making several solutions possible. Divergent thinking requires flexibility of thought, originality, and imagination. There is much less emphasis on recall of facts than in convergent thinking. Guilford's model has served to focus research attention not only on the products but also on the process of creative thought.

Guilford (1954) described several tasks designed to measure creativity, such as Consequences ("Imagine what would happen if . . .") and Unusual Uses (e.g., "Name as many uses as you can think of for a rubber band"). Included in Guilford et al.'s (1974) test battery, the Structure-of-Intellect Abilities, are verbally oriented tasks (such as Word Fluency) and nonverbally oriented tasks (such as Sketches).

A number of other tests are available to tap various aspects of creativity. For example, based on the work of Mednick (1962), the Remote Associates Test (RAT) presents the testtaker with three words; the task is to find a fourth word associated with the other three. The Torrance (1966, 1987a, 1987b) Tests of Creative Thinking consist of word-based, picture-based, and sound-based test materials. In a subtest of different sounds, for example, the examinee's task is to respond with the thoughts that each sound conjures up. Each subtest is designed to measure various characteristics deemed important in the process of creative thought.

◆

JUST THINK . . .

Based on this brief description of the RAT and the Torrance Tests, demonstrate your own creativity by creating a new RAT or Torrance Test item that is unmistakably one from the twenty-first century.

It is interesting that many tests of creativity do not fare well when evaluated by traditional psychometric procedures. For example, the test-retest reliability estimates for some of these tests tend to border on the unacceptable range. Some have wondered aloud whether tests of creativity should be judged by different standards from other tests. After all, creativity may differ from other abilities in that it may be highly susceptible to emotional or physical health, motivation, and related factors—even more so than other abilities. This fact would explain tenuous reliability and validity estimates.

◆

JUST THINK . . .

Should tests of creativity be held to different psychometric standards from other ability tests?

As you read about various human abilities and how they all might be related to that intangible construct *intelligence,* you may have said to yourself, "Why doesn't anyone create a test that measures all these diverse aspects of intelligence?"

Although no one has undertaken that ambitious project, in recent years test packages have been developed to test not only intelligence but also related abilities in educational settings. These test packages, called *psychoeducational batteries,* are discussed in the chapter that follows. For now, let's conclude our introduction to intelligence (and intelligent) testing and assessment with a brief discussion of some important issues associated with such measurement.

Issues in the Assessment of Intelligence

Measured intelligence may vary as a result of factors related to the measurement process. Just a few of the many factors that can affect measured intelligence are a test author's definition of intelligence, the diligence of the examiner, the amount of feedback the examiner gives the examinee (Vygotsky, 1978), the amount of previous practice or coaching the examinee has had, and the competence of the person interpreting the test data. There are many other factors that can cause measured intelligence to vary. In what follows, we briefly discuss the role of culture in measured intelligence, as well as a phenomenon that has come to be called the "Flynn effect."

Culture and Measured Intelligence

A culture provides specific models for thinking, acting, and feeling. Culture enables people to survive both physically and socially and to master and control the world around them (Chinoy, 1967). Because values may differ radically between cultural and subcultural groups, people from different cultural groups can have radically different views about what constitutes intelligence (Super, 1983; Wober, 1974). Because different cultural groups value and promote different types of abilities and pursuits, testtakers from different cultural groups can be expected to bring to a test situation differential levels of ability, achievement, and motivation. These differential levels may even find expression in measured perception and perceptual motor skills.

Consider, for example, an experiment conducted with children who were members of a rural community in eastern Zambia. Serpell (1979) tested Zambian and English research subjects on a task involving the reconstruction of models using pencil and paper, clay, or wire. The English children did best on the paper-and-pencil reconstructions because those were the materials with which they were most familiar. By contrast, the Zambian children did best using wire because that was the medium with which they were most familiar. Both groups of children did about equally well using clay. Any conclusions about the subjects' ability to reconstruct models would have to be qualified with regard to the particular instrument used. This point could be generalized with regard to the use of most any instrument of evaluation or assessment; is it really tapping the ability it purports to tap, or is it tapping something else—especially when used with culturally different subjects or testtakers?

Items on a test of intelligence tend to reflect the culture of the society where the test is employed. To the extent that a score on such a test reflects the degree to which testtakers have been integrated into the society and the culture, it would be expected that members of subcultures (as well as others who, for whatever reason, choose not to identify themselves with the mainstream society) would score lower. In fact, Blacks (Baughman & Dahlstrom, 1968; Dreger & Miller, 1960; Lesser et al., 1965; Shuey, 1966), Hispanics (Gerry, 1973; Holland, 1960; Lesser et al., 1965; Mercer, 1976; Murray, 2007; Simpson, 1970), and Native Americans (Cundick, 1976) tend to score lower on intelligence tests than Whites or Asians (Flynn, 1991). These findings are controversial on many counts—ranging from the great diversity of the people who are grouped under each of these categories, to sampling differences (Zuckerman, 1990), as well as related definitional issues (Daley & Onwuegbuzie, 2011; Sternberg et al., 2005). The meaningfulness of such findings can be questioned further when claims of genetic difference are made owing to the difficulty of separating the effects of genes from effects of the environment. For an authoritative and readable account of the complex issues involved in making such separations see Neisser et al., 1996.

As Gu, He, and Xuqun (2017) have observed, cultural differences with respect to the conceptualization of intelligence extend to culturally appropriate ways of expressing intelligence. In the West, we may be culturally accustomed to expressions of intelligence in the form of writing, speech, debate, and the like. By contrast, in the East, where modesty is culturally valued, such overt demonstrations of one's intellectual prowess may be culturally discouraged. Gu et al. (2017) explained that,

> a component of intelligence in the East has to do with the ability to exhibit culturally appropriate restraint in display of ability. Lao Zi, the philosopher who founded Taoism, states in his work Tao Te Ching, "Whereas the force of words is soon spent, far better is it to keep what is in the heart." This wisdom informs the extent to which a general demeanor of caution and moderation is not only culturally preferable, but seen as the more "intelligent" option. So, all other things being equal, comparing the generally silent person to the generally talkative person, the former may be viewed as the more "intelligent" in the East, while the latter may be viewed as the more "intelligent" in the West.

Alfred Binet shared with many others the desire to develop a measure of intelligence as untainted as possible by factors such as prior education and economic advantages. The Binet-Simon test was designed to separate "natural intelligence from instruction" by "disregarding, insofar as possible, the degree of instruction which the subject possesses" (Binet & Simon, 1908/1961, p. 93). This desire to create what might be termed a **culture-free intelligence test** has resurfaced with various degrees of fervor throughout history. One assumption inherent in the development of such tests is that if cultural factors can be controlled then differences between cultural groups will be lessened. A related assumption is that the effect of culture can be controlled through the elimination

JUST THINK . . .

Is it possible to create a culture-free test of intelligence? Is it desirable to create one?

of verbal items and the exclusive reliance on nonverbal, performance items. Nonverbal items were thought to represent the best available means for determining the cognitive ability of minority group children and adults. However logical this assumption may seem on its face, it has not been borne out in practice (see, for example, Cole & Hunter, 1971; McGurk, 1975).

Exclusively nonverbal tests of intelligence have not lived up to the high expectations of their developers. They have not been found to have the same high level of predictive validity as more verbally loaded tests. This may be due to the fact that nonverbal items do not sample the same psychological processes as do the more verbally loaded, conventional tests of intelligence. Whatever the reason, nonverbal tests tend not to be very good at predicting success in various academic and business settings. Perhaps this is so because such settings require at least some verbal facility.

The idea of developing a truly culture-free test has had great intuitive appeal but has proven to be a practical impossibility. All tests of intelligence reflect, to a greater or lesser degree, the culture in which they were devised and will be used. Stated another way, intelligence tests differ in the extent to which they are *culture-loaded*.

Culture loading may be defined as the extent to which a test incorporates the vocabulary, concepts, traditions, knowledge, and feelings associated with a particular culture. A test item such as "Name three words for snow" is a highly culture-loaded item—one that draws heavily from the Eskimo culture, where many words exist for snow. Testtakers from Brooklyn would be hard put to come up with more than one word for snow (well, maybe two, if you count *slush*).

Soon after it became evident that no test could legitimately be called "culture free," a number of tests referred to as *culture fair* began to be published. We may define a **culture-fair intelligence test** as a test or assessment process designed to minimize the influence of culture with regard to various aspects of the evaluation procedures, such as administration instructions, item content, responses required of testtakers, and interpretations made from the resulting data. Table 9–5 lists techniques used to reduce the culture loading of tests. Note that—in contrast

Table 9–5
Ways of Reducing the Culture Loading of Tests

Culture Loaded	Culture Loading Reduced
Paper-and-pencil tasks	Performance tests
Printed instructions	Oral instructions
Oral instructions	Pantomime instructions
No preliminary practice	Preliminary practice items
Reading required	Purely pictorial
Pictorial (objects)	Abstract figural
Written response	Oral response
Separate answer sheet	Answers written on test itself
Language	Nonlanguage
Speed tests	Power tests
Verbal content	Nonverbal content
Specific factual knowledge	Abstract reasoning
Scholastic skills	Nonscholastic skills
Recall of past-learned information	Solving novel problems
Content graded from familiar to rote	All item content highly familiar
Difficulty based on rarity of content	Difficulty based on complexity of relation education

Source: Jensen (1980).

to the factor-analytic concept of *factor loading,* which can be quantified—the *culture loading* of a test tends to involve more of a subjective, qualitative, nonnumerical judgment.

The rationale for culture-fair test items was to include only those tasks that seemed to reflect experiences, knowledge, and skills common to all different cultures. In addition, all the tasks were designed to be motivating to all groups (Samuda, 1982). An attempt was made to minimize the importance of factors such as verbal skills thought to be responsible for the lower mean scores of various minority groups. Therefore, the culture-fair tests tended to be nonverbal and to have simple, clear directions administered orally by the examiner. The nonverbal tasks typically consisted of assembling, classifying, selecting, or manipulating objects and drawing or identifying geometric designs. Some sample items from the Cattell Culture Fair Test are illustrated in Figure 9–8.

Mazes

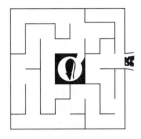

Figure Matrices

Choose from among the six alternatives the one that most logically completes the matrix pattern above it.

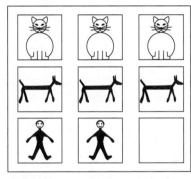

Classification

Pick out the two odd items in each row of figures.

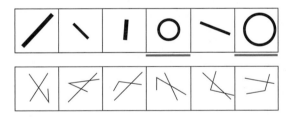

Series

Choose one figure from the six on the right that logically continues the series of three figures at the left.

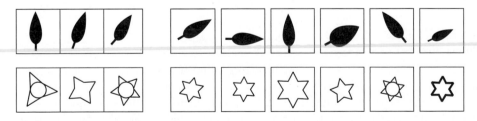

Figure 9–8
Sample "Culture-Fair" and "Culture-Loaded" Items

What types of test items are thought to be "culture-fair"—or at least more culture-fair than other, more culture-loaded items? The items reprinted below from the Culture Fair Test of Intelligence (Cattell, 1940) are a sample. As you look at them, think about how culture-fair they really are. Items from the Culture Fair Test of Intelligence (Cattell, 1940)

Reducing culture loading of intelligence tests seems to lead to a parallel decrease in the value of the test. Culture-fair tests have been found to lack the hallmark of traditional tests of intelligence: predictive validity. Not only that, minority group members still tended to score lower on these tests than did majority group members. Various subcultural characteristics have been presumed to penalize unfairly some minority group members who take intelligence tests that are culturally loaded with American White, middle-class values. Some have argued, for example, that Americans living in urban ghettos share common beliefs and values that are quite different from those of mainstream America. Included among these common beliefs and values, for example, are a "live for today" orientation and a reliance on slang in verbal communication. Native Americans also share a common subculture with core values that may negatively influence their measured intelligence. Central to these values is the belief that individuals should be judged in terms of their relative contribution to the group, not in terms of their individual accomplishments. Native Americans also value their relatively unhurried, present time–oriented lifestyle (Foerster & Little Soldier, 1974).

Frustrated by their seeming inability to develop culture-fair equivalents of traditional intelligence tests, some test developers attempted to develop equivalents of traditional intelligence tests that were culture-specific. Expressly developed for members of a particular cultural group or subculture, such tests were thought to be able to yield a more valid measure of mental development. One culture-specific intelligence test developed expressly for use with African-Americans was the Black Intelligence Test of Cultural Homogeneity (Williams, 1975), a 100-item multiple-choice test. Keeping in mind that many of the items on this test are now dated, here are three samples:[10]

1. *Mother's Day* means

    a. Black independence day.

    b. a day when mothers are honored.

    c. a day the welfare checks come in.

    d. every first Sunday in church.

2. *Blood* means

    a. a vampire.

    b. a dependent individual.

    c. an injured person.

    d. a brother of color.

3. The following are popular brand names. Which one does not belong?

    a. Murray's

    b. Dixie Peach

    c. Royal Crown

    d. Preparation H

As you read the previous items, you may be asking yourself, "Is this really an intelligence test? Should I be taking this seriously?" If you were thinking such questions, you are in good company. At the time, many psychologists probably asked themselves the same questions. In fact, a parody of the BITCH (the test's acronym) was published in the May 1974 issue of *Psychology Today* (p. 101) and was called the "S.O.B. (Son of the Original BITCH) Test." However, the Williams (1975) test was purported to be a genuine culture-specific test of intelligence standardized on 100 Black high-school students in the St. Louis area. Williams was awarded $153,000 by the National Institute of Mental Health to develop the BITCH.

---

10. The answers keyed correct are as follows: 1(c), 2(d), and 3(d).

In what was probably one of the few published studies designed to explore the test's validity, the Wechsler Adult Intelligence Scale (WAIS) and the BITCH were both administered to Black ($n = 17$) and White ($n = 116$) applicants for a job with the Portland, Oregon, police department. The Black subjects performed much better on the test than did the White subjects, with a mean score that exceeded the White mean score by 2.83 standard deviations. The White mean IQ as measured by the WAIS exceeded the Black mean IQ by about 1.5 standard deviations. None of the correlations between the BITCH score and any of the following variables for either the Black or the White testtakers differed significantly from zero: WAIS Verbal IQ, WAIS Performance IQ, WAIS Full Scale IQ, and years of education. Even though the Black sample in this study had an average of more than 2.5 years of college education, and even though their overall mean on the WAIS was about 20 points higher than for Blacks in general, their scores on the BITCH fell below the average of the standardization sample (high-school pupils ranging in age from 16 to 18). What, then, is the BITCH measuring? The study authors, Matarazzo and Wiens (1977), concluded that the test was measuring a variable that could be characterized as *streetwiseness*. This variable, also known by other names (such as "street smarts" or "street efficacy"), has since received serious attention from researchers (see Figure 9–9).

Many of the tests designed to be culture-specific did yield higher mean scores for the minority group for which they were specifically designed. Still, they lacked predictive validity and provided little useful, practical information. The knowledge required to score high on all of the culture-specific and culture-reduced tests has not been seen as relevant for educational purposes within our pluralistic society. Such tests have low predictive validity for the criterion of success in academic as well as vocational settings.

At various phases in the life history of the development of an intelligence test, a number of approaches to reduce cultural bias may be employed. Panels of experts may evaluate the potential bias inherent in a newly developed test, and those items judged to be biased may be eliminated. The test may be devised so that relatively few verbal instructions are needed to administer it or to demonstrate how to respond. Related efforts can be made to minimize any possible language bias. A tryout or pilot testing with ethnically mixed samples of testtakers may be undertaken. If differences in scores emerge solely as a function of ethnic group membership, individual items may be studied further for possible bias.

Major tests of intelligence have undergone a great deal of scrutiny for bias in many investigations. Procedures range from analysis of individual items to analysis of the test's predictive validity. Only when it can be reasonably concluded that a test is as free as it can be of systematic bias is it made available for use. Of course, even if a test is free of bias, other potential sources of bias still exist. These sources include the criterion for referral for assessment, the conduct of the assessment, the scoring of items (particularly those items that are somewhat

Figure 9–9
"Street Smarts"

A person who "knows his (or her) way around the streets" is referred to as "streetwise" or as possessing "street smarts." This characteristic—which has absolutely nothing to do with map-reading ability—was characterized by Sharkey (2006) as street efficacy (or "the perceived ability to avoid violent confrontations and to be safe in one's neighborhood"). Question: Is this characteristic a personality trait, an aspect of intelligence, or something of a "hybrid"?
© Blend Images/SuperStock RF

subjective), and, finally, the interpretation of the findings. Potentially, there are also less obvious sources of systematic bias in scores on intelligence tests. One such source has come to be known as "the Flynn Effect."

The Flynn Effect

James R. Flynn, while at the Department of Political Studies at the University of Otago in Dunedin, New Zealand, published findings that caused those who study and use intelligence tests in the United States to take notice. In his article entitled "The Mean IQ of Americans: Massive Gains 1932 to 1978," Flynn (1984) presented compelling evidence of what might be termed *intelligence inflation*. He found that measured intelligence seems to rise on average, year by year, starting with the year for which the test is normed. The rise in measured IQ is not accompanied by any academic dividend and so is not thought to be due to any actual rise in "true intelligence." The phenomenon has since been well documented not only in the United States but in other countries as well (Flynn, 1988, 2007). The **Flynn effect** is thus a shorthand reference to the progressive rise in intelligence test scores that is expected to occur on a normed test intelligence from the date when the test was first normed. According to Flynn (2000), the exact amount of the rise in IQ will vary as a function of several factors, such as how culture-specific the items are and whether the measure used is one of fluid or crystallized intelligence.

Beyond being a phenomenon of academic interest, the Flynn effect has wide-ranging, real-world implications and consequences. Flynn (2000) sarcastically advised examiners who want the children they test to be eligible for special services to use the most recently normed

JUST THINK . . .

What is your opinion regarding the ethics of Flynn's advice to psychologists and educators who examine children for placement in special classes?

version of an intelligence test. On the other hand, examiners who want the children they test to escape the stigma of any labeling were advised to use "the oldest test they can get away with," which should, according to Flynn, allow for at least 10 points' leeway in measured intelligence. At the very least, examiners who use intelligence tests to make important decisions need to be aware of a possible Flynn effect, especially at the beginning or near the end of the test's norming cycle (Kanaya et al., 2003).

There are numerous other, everyday potential consequences of the Flynn effect ranging from eligibility for special services at school to eligibility for social security benefits. One potential consequence of the Flynn effect has to do with an issue of no less importance than whether one will live or die. Soon after the U.S. Supreme Court ruled it illegal to execute a person who suffers from mental retardation (*Atkins v. Virginia,* 2002), many criminal defense attorneys started familiarizing themselves with the Flynn effect, and investigating whether or not clients accused of capital crimes had been evaluated with an older test—one that spuriously inflated measured intelligence, thereby making such defendants eligible for execution (Fletcher et al., 2010). As might be expected, the ethics of such defense tactics have been questioned, especially because there seems to be sufficient variability in the Flynn effect leading researchers to conclude that not everyone's scores are affected in the same way (Hagan et al., 2010; Zhou et al., 2010).

From a less applied, and more academic perspective, consideration of the Flynn effect can be used to shed light on theories, and to help support or disprove them. For example, Cattell (1971) wrote that fluid intelligence (a product of heredity) formed the basis for crystallized

JUST THINK . . .

In your opinion, are generational gains in measured intelligence due more to factors related more to heredity, environment, or some combination of both?

intelligence (a product of learning and the environment). If Cattell was correct, we might expect generational gains in IQ to be due to increased crystallized intelligence—this as a result of factors such as improvements in education, greater educational opportunities for people, and greater cognitive demands in the workplace (Colom et al., 2007). However, according to Flynn (2009), most of the observed increases in IQ have been in the realm of fluid intelligence. Some research has been designed to address this issue (Rindermann et al., 2010) but the results have been equivocal, with partial support for both Cattell and Flynn.

The Construct Validity of Tests of Intelligence

The evaluation of a test's construct validity proceeds on the assumption that one knows in advance exactly what the test is supposed to measure. For intelligence tests, it is essential to understand how the test developer defined intelligence. If, for example, *intelligence* were defined in a particular intelligence test as Spearman's *g*, then we would expect factor analysis of this test to yield a single large common factor. Such a factor would indicate that the different questions or tasks on the test largely reflected the same underlying characteristic (intelligence, or *g*). By contrast, if intelligence were defined by a test developer in accordance with Guilford's theory, then no one factor would be expected to dominate. Instead, one would anticipate many different factors reflecting a diverse set of abilities. Recall that, from Guilford's perspective, there is no single underlying intelligence for the different test items to reflect. This means that there would be no basis for a large common factor.

In a sense, a compromise between Spearman and Guilford is Thorndike. Thorndike's theory of intelligence leads us to look for one central factor reflecting *g* along with three additional factors representing social, concrete, and abstract intelligences. In this case, an analysis of the test's construct validity would ideally suggest that testtakers' responses to specific items reflected in part a general intelligence but also different types of intelligence: social, concrete, and abstract.

A Perspective

So many decades after the publication of the 1921 symposium, professionals still debate the nature of intelligence and how it should be measured. In the wake of the controversial book *The Bell Curve* (Herrnstein & Murray, 1994), the American Psychological Association commissioned a panel to write a report on intelligence that would carry psychology's official imprimatur. The panel's report reflected wide disagreement with regard to the definition of intelligence but noted that "such disagreements are not cause for dismay. Scientific research rarely begins with fully agreed definitions, though it may eventually lead to them" (Neisser et al., 1996, p. 77).

Another issue that is not going to go away concerns group differences in measured intelligence. Human beings certainly do differ in size, shape, and color, and it is thus reasonable to consider that there is also a physical basis for differences in intellectual ability, so discerning where and how nature can be differentiated from nurture is a laudable academic pursuit. Still, such differentiation remains not only a complex business but one potentially fraught with social, political, and even legal consequences. Claims about group differences can and have been used as political and social tools to oppress religious, ethnic, or other minority group members. This is most unfortunate because, as Jensen (1980) observed, variance attributable to group differences is far less than variance attributable to individual differences. Echoing this sentiment is the view that "what matters for the next person you meet (to the extent that test scores matter at all) is that person's own particular score, not the mean of some reference group to which he or she happens to belong" (Neisser et al., 1996, p. 90).

> **JUST THINK . . .**
>
> In a "real-life" competitive job market, what part—if any—does the "mean of the reference group" play in employment decisions?

The relationship between intelligence and a wide range of social outcomes has been well documented. Scores on intelligence tests, especially when used with other indicators, have value in predicting outcomes such as school performance, years of education, and even social status and income. Measured intelligence is negatively correlated with socially undesirable outcomes such as juvenile crime. For these and related reasons, we would do well to concentrate research attention on the environmental end of the heredity–environment spectrum. We need to find ways of effectively boosting measured intelligence through environmental interventions, the better to engender hope and optimism.

Unfairly maligned by some and unduly worshipped by others, intelligence has endured—and will continue to endure—as a key construct in psychology and psychological assessment. For this reason, professionals who administer intelligence tests have a great responsibility, one for which thorough preparation is a necessity.

Self-Assessment

Test your understanding of elements of this chapter by seeing if you can explain each of the following terms, expressions, and abbreviations:

accommodation
adaptive testing
AFQT
alerting response
alternate item
Army Alpha test
Army Beta test
assimilation
ASVAB
basal level
Binet, Alfred
ceiling effect
ceiling level
CHC model
cognitive style
convergent thinking
cross-battery assessment
crystallized intelligence
culture-fair intelligence test
culture-free intelligence test
culture loading
deviation IQ
divergent thinking
emotional intelligence
extra-test behavior
factor-analytic theories
    (of intelligence)
floor

fluid intelligence
Flynn effect
g (factor of intelligence)
Gf and Gc
giftedness
group factors
hierarchical model
information-processing theories
    (of intelligence)
intelligence
interactionism
interpersonal intelligence
intrapersonal intelligence
IQ (intelligence quotient)
maintained abilities
mental age
nominating technique
optional subtest
parallel processing
PASS model
point scale
predeterminism
preformationism
psychoeducational assessment
RAT
ratio IQ
routing test
schema

schemata
screening tool
sequential processing
s factor (of intelligence)
short form
simultaneous processing
Stanford-Binet
successful intelligence
successive processing
supplemental subtest
teaching item
temperament
Terman, Lewis
Termites
testing the limits
three-stratum theory of cognitive
    abilities
two-factor theory of intelligence
Verbal, Perceptual, and Image
    Rotation (VPR) model
vulnerable abilities
WAIS
WASI
Wechsler, David
Wechsler-Bellevue
WISC
WPPSI

10

Assessment for Education

Whtat word comes to mind first when you think of the word *school?*

If the word *test* came to mind, it would certainly be understandable. Dozens—maybe even hundreds—of tests are administered to students over the course of their academic career. Included are teacher-made tests, state-mandated tests, psychologist-recommended tests, and assorted other tests. Why so many tests?

JUST THINK . . .

How many tests would you estimate you have taken since you first entered preschool or elementary school?

The Role of Testing and Assessment in Education

Educators are interested in answers to diverse questions as students progress through school. A small sampling of those questions might be:

How well have students learned and mastered the subject matter they were taught?

To what extent are students able to apply what they have learned to novel circumstances and situations?

Which students have demonstrated the ability or skills necessary to move on to the next level of learning?

Which students have demonstrated the ability or skills necessary for independent living?

What are the challenges or obstacles that are preventing an individual student from meeting educational objectives, and how can those obstacles best be overcome?

How effective are teachers in assisting students to master specific curriculum goals?

Do passing test scores on a curriculum-specific test genuinely reflect the fact that the testtakers have mastered the curriculum?

Do failing test scores on a curriculum-specific test really reflect the fact that the testtakers have not mastered the content of the curriculum?

In recent years, many such questions have been raised with regard to the states' kindergarten-through-12th-grade (K-through-12) educational systems. Some observers cite generally disappointing answers to such questions. Blame for such dubious educational outcomes has been placed by many on federal legislation such as *No Child Left Behind* (NCLB) legislation. Perhaps the most vocal outcries have been reserved not for NCLB as whole, but certain provisions of NCLB, such as its insistence that educational progress be gauged by standardized tests.

The Case for and Against Educational Testing in the Schools

For all too many parents, teachers, and opinionated third-parties, the "root of all evil" in contemporary education is the standardized test; the blame for any failure of the educational system lies not with the student, the teacher, or the school administration, but with standardized testing (see, for example, García & Thornton, 2015). The logic behind such arguments, questionable as they are, is rooted in the fact that the NCLB legislation mandated improvement in reading and math scores on standardized tests. If an individual state did not meet federal guidelines in this regard, then the result could be the imposition of penalties, such as the withholding of federal funds for education. In the view of some then, the net result of NCLB was undue pressure on teachers to make certain that their students performed satisfactorily on standardized tests. This obligation was seen as forcing teachers to spend valuable classroom time "teaching to the test." The argument of many anti-test advocates could essentially be summed-up as "If there was no pressure to raise students' performance to some federally prescribed level, then teachers would be free to teach in ways designed to promote better, more permanent educational outcomes."

Counter to the arguments of those who rail against standardized tests as the culprit in education is another, more moderate view. Simply stated, this alternative, time-tested position is that standardized tools of assessment, including tests, are not only a desirable element of an educational system, but an absolutely necessary one at that. According to this latter position, tests may serve a variety of critically important needs. For example, standardized educational tests are used for screening purposes. Tests routinely used for screening purposes can alert educators to students who may be at risk for negative, education-related outcomes—outcomes that may be preventable with early, effective intervention. In addition, data from standardized tests may be mined for important diagnostic findings. Diagnostic data may be used to identify areas of weakness that require remediation or other educational intervention. Similarly, diagnostic data may be useful in identifying areas in which a student excels. Knowledge of where a student excels is essential if education resources are to be properly allocated, and not squandered with efforts to teach students what they already know. From the perspective of the student, knowledge derived from diagnostic educational testing is necessary if students are to be increasingly challenged by new and intellectually stimulating subject matter.

In addition to screening and diagnostic purposes, standardized tests are indispensable for purposes of comparison. Data from such tests help educators understand and gauge the rate of progress of a single student, dozens of students, hundreds of students, or thousands of students—all using the same tool of measurement (rather than one idiosyncratic to the preference of an individual teacher or even a particular school district). Students learn at different paces and in different ways, and it is through such comparisons of progress that educators can begin to identify what teaching methods work best for which individual.

So, although there are those who stubbornly cling to what Gerson (2012) called "an ideological opposition to testing as the enemy of educational creativity," standardized testing programs, when judiciously administered, would seem to hold out the promise of more benefit than harm. The logic of those in the education community who focus on testing as the downfall of education seems, at best, flawed. Commenting on teachers who profess such a position, Gerson (2012) reflected, "They love the intangible joys of the profession, without the inconvenience of demonstrating that their work has any effect."

To be fair, when certain negative conditions relevant to the ecology of testing exist, sentiments against tests and testing may well have merit. For example, if a standardized testing program was designed exclusively for alignment with a controversial teaching curriculum, then the controversy surrounding the teaching curriculum could reasonably be expected to "rub off" on (or generalize to) the tests used in conjunction with that curriculum. Also, if individual test items in a standardized test are constructed in a controversial way (such as being widely perceived as age- or grade-inappropriate in terms of content), then—no matter what educational objectives are being served—the standardized test or entire testing program could well be the object of legitimate questions, concerns, and criticism. In fact, each of these examples typify why a relatively new, nationwide program for kindergarten-through-12-grade students is so controversial. A brief explanation of what this program is, as well as why it is so controversial, follows.

The Common Core State Standards

NCLB required, among other mandates, that all children within a state perform at grade-level in reading and math by the end of 2014. However, each of the states set their own definition of what constituted proficiency at each grade level. Given this lack of uniformity in proficiency standards among the states, it would be entirely possible for a student in one state to be deemed proficient in a particular subject (or, performing at grade-level according to that state's standards), while having knowledge and skills that would not be deemed proficient according to another state's standards. Such discrepancies between state standards, as well as myriad other considerations (such as a general lack of sufficient preparation for college-level work) compelled some to consider ways to bring uniformity to state education curriculums for public schools. The result was the creation of a comprehensive set of standards that affects the everyday classroom life of some 50 million K-through-12 students. These standards, which essentially set objectives for what students should know by the end of each school year, are packaged along with a computer-assisted testing program designed to ensure conformity in teachers' teaching as well as students' learning. The program, which currently sets standards for learning in English and math (with standards for more subject areas in development), is called the *Common Core State Standards* (CCSS).

To complement the release of CCSS, in March of 2010, the United States Department of Education offered groups of 15 or more states (referred to as *consortia*) close to $400 million dollars in grant money to develop new K-through-12 tests to be aligned with CCSS (Doorey, 2012/2013). By September of 2010, the funds had been awarded to two consortia, one known as "PARCC" (the Partnership for the Assessment of Readiness for College and Careers), and the other known as "Smarter Balanced" (the Smarter Balanced Assessment Consortium).[1] PARCC and Smarter Balanced were assigned the task of developing a comprehensive assessment system that was qualitatively different in many ways than anything that had preceded it. Doorey (2012/2013) put in perspective some of the challenges inherent in that undertaking:

> K–12 assessment is at the beginning of a sea change. Many of the competencies now considered essential for success in college and the workplace are complex and difficult to measure. The

---

1. Why did the U.S. Department of Education award grants to *two* consortia instead of just one? Although it cannot be stated with certainty, some believe it was "to allay fears of a 'national assessment' and of usurpation of local control over the curriculum" (Doorey, 2012/2013, p. 28).

the world ("Bill and Melinda Gates," 2015). Given the fact that participation in CCSS requires school systems to purchase and perpetually update expensive computer systems and software, the question of whether Gates' contribution is more philanthropy or an investment has been raised (Beck, 2013; "The Case Against Common Core," 2015).

Another reason CCSS is controversial is due to the *en masse,* blind buy-in of so many states with absolutely no evidence that the program works. It seems fair to surmise that the participating states were primarily induced to participate as a result of federal funding incentives for doing so—over four billion dollars in grants was disbursed to the states in return for their participation in CCSS. Thus, although the federal government did not create CCSS, it would seem to own sole responsibility for the states' rapid adoption of the program. By the way, that fact is, in itself, controversial because responsibility for education is Constitutionally left to the states. Holding out huge sums of federal grant money in exchange for the institution of a nationwide set of uniform educational standards has been viewed by some as a quasi-legal way for the federal government to assume greater responsibility and control for education in the states that accept the deal.

Also controversial are the educational credentials of the folks who authored the standards. The Common Core website tells us that the program was developed by teachers and educators from around the country. However, critics of CCSS have disputed that assertion ("The Case Against Common Core," 2015). According to Thornton, CCSS was "written by a small group of individuals and then copyrighted by two Washington lobbyist groups" (the lobbyist groups being The National Governors' Association Center for Best Practices and the Council of Chief State School Officers). Two prominent members of the Common Core Validation Review Panel were James Milgram, professor of mathematics at Stanford University (the panel's math expert), and Sandra Stotsky, *Professor Emerita* at the University of Arkansas and former Senior Associate Commissioner of the Massachusetts Department of Education (the panel's English expert). According to Thornton (2014), both of these experts "refused to give Common Core Math and English standards, respectively, a good recommendation... Both have gone on to testify with a warning voice to state legislatures and school boards about the inadequacy of the standards."

It is also a matter of controversy, if not outright concern, that the CCSS contains recommendations for educational

practices that are not widely supported by the scholarly literature. One such practice is **cold reading**; that is, reading without the benefit of background information or context. So, for example, a student might be asked to study the Gettysburg Address by reading it "cold" (i.e., without the teacher setting the reading material in context or providing any background information on it at all). Commenting on this practice, Anderson (2014) pointed out, "Obviously additional information would help the student become more proficient in the subject, yet Common Core disallows it. The standards cite no research supporting such a practice."

The very content of the CCSS has drawn a great deal of criticism. Part of the problem here is that some of the standards appear to be age- and grade-inappropriate. For example, according to one of the CCSS standards for fifth-grade English, students must be able to demonstrate an understanding of the influence of the perspective of a story's narrator. Similarly, some math standards are arguably ambitious. Enter the search term "inappropriate Common Core math standard" on *Google* (or any comparable computer search engine), and the chances are good the screen will be populated by dozens of entries. One such standard for first-graders is "Understand subtraction as an unknown-addend problem" (for context and an explanation, see Strauss, 2013).

Along with a questioning of the content of the CCSS has come a questioning of the test items used to evaluate teaching outcomes. In some cases, test items have been heavily criticized for being age-inappropriate, or otherwise inappropriate in item content. For example, some of the content in some of the reading passages used to evaluate accomplishment in English has been criticized as being age- and grade-inappropriate. What follows is a sample of one such reading comprehension item represented to have been taken from fourth-grade Common Core classwork (Hope, 2014), and posted online by the student's outraged parent:

Ruby sat on the bed she shared with her husband holding a hairclip. There was something mysterious and powerful about the cheaply manufactured neon clip that she was fondling suspiciously. She didn't recognize the hairclip. It was too big to be their daughter's, and Ruby was sure that it wasn't hers. She hadn't had friends over in weeks but there was this hairclip, little and green with a few long black hair strands caught in it. Ruby ran her fingers through her own blonde hair. She had just been vacuuming when she noticed this small, bright green object under the bed. Now their life would never be the same. She would wait here until Mike returned home.

Why is Ruby so affected by the hairclip?
How has the hairclip affected Ruby's relationship?

Finally, there is the question of the ultimate benefit of subjecting millions of students to an essentially untested program. In this context, critics have raised questions like, "Would it not be more reasonable to model such a new, large-scale, nationwide undertaking after the teaching processes that are known to work?" Why not model the new, nationwide program after a state like Massachusetts, for example?* Why

*In a Wall Street Journal survey, Massachusetts was found to have the best K-through-12 education program (Frohlich & Sauter, 2014).

plunge millions of students and teachers into what is essentially a large-scale educational experiment with an uncertain outcome hanging in the balance?

In sum, since its rather hasty, sight-unseen adoption by so many states, CCSS has been the subject of many important questions, some still in search of satisfactory answers. Skeptics have raised questions having to do with the role of financial profit in the initial development and promulgation of CCSS. Academics have raised questions having to do with the efficacy of the program. Privacy advocates have raised questions about the extensive record-keeping and archiving of educational data that is integral to the administration of CCSS. Until such time that widely acceptable answers to these and related questions have been given, controversy will continue to surround CCSS.

response to scientific, research-based *intervention*" (emphasis added). Although academics had been writing about "response to intervention" in the interim period (see, for example, Dwairy, 2004), all of a sudden the rush to understand and apply this model was on. By 2008 most states had in place legislative or regulatory policies that changed their existing special educations to require RtI (Zirkel & Krohn, 2008).

The RtI model Based on the definition presented on the federally funded website of the National Center on Response to Intervention (2011, p. 2), we may define the **response to intervention model** as a multilevel prevention framework applied in educational settings that is designed to maximize student achievement through the use of data that identifies students at risk for poor learning outcomes combined with evidence-based intervention and teaching that is adjusted on the basis of student responsiveness. A simpler description of this model of teaching and assessment is: (a) Teachers provide evidence-based instruction, (b) student learning of that instruction is regularly evaluated, (c) intervention, if required, occurs in some form of appropriate adjustment in the instruction, (d) reevaluation of learning takes place, and (e) intervention and reassessment occur as necessary.

The model is *multilevel* because there are at least three levels of intervention (or teaching). The first level is the classroom environment wherein all students are being taught whatever it is that the teacher is teaching. The second level of intervention is one in which a small group of learners who have failed to make adequate progress in the classroom have been segregated for special teaching. The third level of intervention is individually tailored and administered instruction for students who have failed to respond to the second level of intervention.

By providing intervention (teaching or remedial instruction, as the case may be) appropriate to the level of the student's needs, the objective of RtI is to accelerate the learning process for all students. In addition, RtI doubles as a process in place that will identify students with learning disabilities. In this sense, RtI is seen by many as superior to the more traditional, referral-based process—which has been characterized as a "wait to fail" process (Fletcher et al., 2002). However, questions regarding the exact nature of a learning disability and the relationship between measured intelligence and academic learning have hardly gone away (Büttner & Hasselhorn, 2011; Collier, 2011; Davis & Broitman, 2011; Goldstein, 2011; Kane et al., 2011; Maehler & Schuchardt, 2009; Swanson, 2011).

Implementing RtI   Owing at least in part to the federal mandate, the RtI-related literature has been burgeoning (see, for example, Fuchs & Fuchs, 2006; Gustafson et al., 2011; Jackson et al., 2009; Johnston, 2011; Mesmer & Duhon, 2011; Petscher et al., 2011; Speece et al., 2011; Tran et al., 2011; Wixon, 2011). Still, because the law left implementation of RtI to the states and school districts, many important questions remain regarding exactly how RtI is to be implemented. Some states and school districts employ what has been referred to as a *problem-solving model.* In this context, **problem-solving model** refers to the use of interventions tailored to students' individual needs that are selected by a multidisciplinary team of school professionals. By contrast, other states and school districts rely more on a more general intervention policy, one selected by the school's administration and designed to address the needs of multiple students. Some schools have put in place a hybrid of these two approaches. That is, some standard school policy is applied to all students, but there are provisions to allow for the problem-solving approach with certain students under certain conditions.

Many critical questions remain regarding exactly how RtI is to be implemented. Some of these questions include: What criteria should be used in moving students from one level to the other in the multilevel model? What tests should be used to assess learning and response to intervention? What are the respective roles of school personnel such as classroom teachers, school psychologists, reading teachers, and guidance counselors in implementing RtI?

Tests and measurement procedures designed to answer RtI-related questions are being developed, and tests already published are being suggested as useful within an RtI model (see, for example, Coleman & Johnsen, 2011; Penner-Williams et al., 2009; Watson et al., 2011; Willcutt et al., 2011). With reference to the question regarding the respective roles of school personnel, it is useful to keep in mind that the same legislation (IDEA) that mandated RtI also encouraged the use of multiple sources of input with regard to the diagnosis of disability. More specifically, IDEA mandated that no single measure be used "as the sole criterion for determining whether a child is a child with a disability." In a comment designed to clarify the intent of the law, the Department of Education wrote that "an evaluation must include a variety of assessment tools and strategies and cannot rely on any single procedure as the sole criterion for determining eligibility for special education and related services." In diagnosing (and treating) disabilities, particularly learning disabilities, it is useful to employ not only various tools of assessment, but input from various school personnel, as well as parents, and other relevant sources of information. The term **integrative assessment** has been used to describe a multidisciplinary approach to evaluation that assimilates input from relevant sources. Judging from the essay written by our guest professional in this chapter, school psychologist Eliane Keyes (see *Meet an Assessment Professional*), integrative assessment is very much a part of the assessment program at her school.

RtI is what has been termed a "dynamic" model. To understand what is meant by that, it is necessary to understand what is meant by "dynamic assessment."

Dynamic Assessment

Although originally developed for use with children, a dynamic approach to assessment may be used with testtakers of any age. It is an approach to assessment that departs from reliance

Meet Eliane Keyes, M.A.

Imagine reading an intriguing mystery novel. The author has laid out the core clues of the case. You, the reader, have your own theories mapped out in your mind. You turn the page to read further, only to discover that the next page is missing. Several pages have been ripped out! You only have one perspective of the story. The solution is therefore incomplete. The same is true for psychoeducational testing that does not incorporate an interdisciplinary approach. In school-based assessments, there will be many team members who contribute vital information in piecing together a child's learning profile. An assessment that does not include multiple measures from various data sources and disciplines is not a full assessment.

With the reauthorization of the *Response to Intervention (RtI)* guidelines in New York State, interdisciplinary testing takes on a whole new meaning. Now, more than ever, the information from classroom and reading teachers holds a great deal of weight in the identification of a specific learning disability. A balance must exist between standardized testing and data supporting response (or nonresponse) to intervention. Whereas school psychologists previously relied more heavily on a discrepancy formula for eligibility into special education, the RtI process urges evaluators to consider external factors that may impede learning. In essence, RtI looks to "even the playing field" by systematically providing intensive levels of intervention before ultimately determining that a disability is "within" a child. Going with the earlier "detective" theme, imagine Sherlock Holmes, or his more modern counterpart, Dr. House. Both used methods of measurement and reasoning to form a hypothesis. They then test the hypothesis to see if it holds weight. To relate this back to the identification of learning disabilities, the interdisciplinary team will focus on a specific target area of intervention. Let's say they are focusing on sight-word recognition. The teacher and interventionists will be responsible for measuring improvement in sight-word vocabulary with additional intervention (either a specific reading program or targeted strategy). After several weeks of intervention and monitoring, results are reviewed. With this information, the team will determine if the same

Eliane Keyes, M.A., School Psychologist, Queensbury Elementary School, Queensbury, NY
© Eliane Keyes

intervention should continue, a new intervention should be introduced, or a higher level of intervention is necessary. After plotting out several data points, it may be evident that the child has not responded to the intervention. At this point, a team can more appropriately discuss the need for a comprehensive psychoeducational evaluation. RtI is an important step in the process of ruling out that a learning difficulty is not due to lack of instruction, or environmental, cultural, or economic disadvantage. Students with these types of disadvantages are oftentimes misidentified as needing special education support, when truly they were in need of specific academic interventions for a more short-term period. RtI seeks to close this gap.

(continued)

Meet Eliane Keyes, M.A. *(continued)*

As an undergraduate school psychology intern, my advisor impressed upon me that the most important skill of a school psychologist is the ability to see the obvious. In a field where children are often represented by test scores and data, it is important to consider the real-world impact for what these scores suggest, and not to lose sight of the fact that a child is more than a set of numbers. Sometimes test scores help explain a deficit, and sometimes they make it more mysterious. One should never underestimate the power of confounding variables! Equally, one should never assume the overall power of a single test score. Interdisciplinary evaluations are a good way to get a more complete picture of a child, but the most indispensable skill for professionals across all education-related fields is to see through to the obvious.

Read more of what school psychologist Eliane Keyes had to say—her complete essay—through the Instructor Resources within Connect.

Used with permission of Eliane Keyes.

---

on, and can be contrasted to, fixed (so-called "static") tests. Dynamic assessment encompasses an approach to exploring learning potential that is based on a test-intervention-retest model. The theoretical underpinnings of this approach can be traced to the work of Budoff (1967, 1987), Feuerstein (1977, 1981), and Vygotsky (1978).

Budoff explored differences between deficits identified by standardized tests that seemed to be due to differences in education versus mental deficiency. He did this by determining whether training could improve test performance. Feuerstein's efforts focused on the extent to which teaching of principles and strategies (or mediated learning) modified cognition. Based on this research, he and his colleagues developed a dynamic system of assessment tasks called The Learning Potential Assessment Device (LPAD; Feuerstein et al., 1979). The LPAD was designed to yield information about the nature and amount of intervention required to enhance a child's performance. Vygotsky (see Figure 10–1) introduced the concept of a **zone of proximal development** or "the distance between the actual developmental level as determined by individual problem-solving, and the level of potential development as determined through problem-solving under adult guidance or in collaboration with more capable peers" (1978, p. 86). The "zone" referred to is, in essence, the area between a testtaker's ability as measured by a formal test and what might be possible as the result of instruction, "guidance," or related intervention. It may be thought of as an index of learning potential that will vary depending upon factors such as the extent of the testtaker's abilities and the nature of the task.

Dynamic assessment procedures differ from more traditional assessment procedures in several key ways. Whereas examiners administering tests in the traditional ways are taught to scrupulously maintain neutrality, dynamic assessors—especially when intervening with teaching, coaching, or other "guidance"—are hardly neutral. To the contrary, their goal may be to do everything in their power to help the testtaker master material in preparation for retesting. Depending upon the assessor's particular approach to dynamic assessment, variations may be introduced into the assessment that are designed to better understand or

Figure 10–1
Lev Semyonovitch Vygotsky (1896–1934)

Now viewed as a celebrated researcher in the history of Soviet psychology and a present-day influence in American education and psychology, Vygotsky was hardly celebrated in his homeland during his lifetime. He labored under strict government regulation and censorship and widespread anti-Semitism (Etkind, 1994). He worked for very little pay, lived in the basement of the institute in which he worked, and suffered ill health—succumbing at the age of 38 from years of living with tuberculosis. Although his political views were Marxist, he was hardly embraced by the authorities. In the end his works were banned by the government and, as Zinchenko (2007) put it, "he was lucky to have managed to die in his own bed."

Vygotsky's impact on the behavioral science community will be long felt years after the relatively brief decade or so that his psychology laboratory was active. His published writings stimulated thought in diverse fields, including educational psychology, developmental psychology, and physiological psychology. A. R. Luria was a contemporary of Vygotsky, and Vygotsky was believed to have had a great influence on Luria's thinking (Radzikhovskii & Khomskaya, 1981). In his own autobiography, Luria referred to Vygotsky as a genius.
© RIA-Novosti/The Image Works

remediate the obstacles to learning. These variations may take any number of different forms, such as clues or prompts delivered in verbal or nonverbal ways. Of course, the great diversity of approaches to dynamic assessment in terms of the goals pursued and the specific techniques and methods used make it difficult to judge the validity of this approach (Beckmann, 2006).

Dynamic assessment is, as you might expect, consistent with the response to intervention model (Wagner & Compton, 2011; Fuchs et al., 2011). For her doctoral dissertation, Emily Duvall (2011) conducted a pilot study with third-graders wherein a state-mandated standardized test was redesigned for purposes of dynamic assessment. She reported that employing dynamic assessment not only facilitated the goal of illuminating the progress that learning disabled children make as a result of intervention, but offered valuable and actionable data to multiple stakeholders (the children being assessed, their parents, teachers, and the school administration).

Of course, before rushing off to convert any standardized tests into a form amenable to dynamic assessment, it is important to acquire a sound understanding of and appreciation for the benefits of such tests as they were developed. Toward that end, we now proceed to describe and survey a small sampling of some standardized (as well as nonstandardized) achievement tests, aptitude tests, and related tools of assessment.

Achievement Tests

Achievement tests are designed to measure accomplishment. An achievement test for a first-grader might have as its subject matter the English language alphabet, whereas an achievement test for a college student might contain questions relating to principles of psychological assessment. In short, achievement tests are designed to measure the degree of learning that has taken place as a result of exposure to a relatively defined learning experience. "Relatively defined learning experience" may mean something as broad as *what was learned from four years of college,* or something much narrower, such as *how to prepare dough for use in making pizza.* In most educational settings, achievement tests are used to gauge student progress toward instructional objectives, compare an individual's accomplishment to peers, and help determine what instructional activities and strategies might best propel the students toward educational objectives.

A test of achievement may be standardized nationally, regionally, or locally, or it may not be standardized at all. The pop quiz on the anatomy of a frog given by your high-school biology teacher qualifies as an achievement test every bit as much as a statewide examination in biology.

Like other tests, achievement tests vary widely with respect to their psychometric soundness. A sound achievement test is one that adequately samples the targeted subject matter and reliably gauges the extent to which the examinees have learned it.

Scores on achievement tests may be put to varied uses. They may help school personnel make decisions about a student's placement in a particular class, acceptance into a program, or advancement to a higher grade level. Achievement test data can be helpful in gauging the quality of instruction in a particular class, school, school district, or state. Achievement tests are sometimes used to screen for difficulties, and in such instances they may precede the administration of more specific tests designed to identify areas that may require remediation. One general way of categorizing achievement tests is in terms of how general their content is in nature.

Measures of General Achievement

Measures of general achievement may survey learning in one or more academic areas. Tests that cover a number of academic areas are typically divided into several subtests and are referred to as *achievement batteries.* Such batteries may be individually administered or group administered. They may consist of a few subtests, as does the Wide Range Achievement Test–4 (Wilkinson & Robertson, 2006) with its measures of reading, spelling, arithmetic, and (new to the fourth edition) reading comprehension. A general measure of achievement may be quite comprehensive, as is the Sequential Tests of Educational Progress (STEP) battery. Used in kindergarten through grade 12, the STEP battery includes achievement subtests in reading, vocabulary, mathematics, writing skills, study skills, science, and social studies, as well as a behavior inventory, an educational environment questionnaire, and an activities inventory. Because it is frequently used to identify gifted children, any of the "five steps" may be administered at or above the testtaker's grade level.

Some batteries, such as the SRA California Achievement Tests, span kindergarten through grade 12, whereas others are grade- or course-specific. Some batteries are constructed to provide both norm-referenced and criterion-referenced analyses. Others are concurrently normed with scholastic aptitude tests to enable a comparison between achievement and aptitude. Some batteries are constructed with practice tests that may be administered several days before actual testing to help students familiarize themselves with test-taking procedures. Other batteries contain **locator tests,** or routing tests, which are pretests administered to determine the level of the actual test most appropriate for administration.

One popular instrument appropriate for use with persons age 4 through adult (age 50 is the age limit) is the Wechsler Individual Achievement Test–Third Edition, otherwise known as the WIAT-III (Psychological Corporation, 2009). Designed for use in the schools as well as clinical and research settings, this battery contains a total of 16 subtests, although not every subtest will be administered to every testtaker. The test was nationally standardized on 3,000 student and adult testtakers, and the manual provides comprehensive normative information. The test has been favorably reviewed regarding its potential to yield actionable data relating to student achievement in academic areas such as reading, writing, and mathematics, as well as skill in listening and speaking (Vaughan-Jensen et al., 2011).

Of the many available achievement batteries, the test most appropriate for use is the one most consistent with the educational objectives of the individual teacher or school system. For a particular purpose, a battery that focuses on achievement in a few select areas may be preferable to one that attempts to sample achievement in several areas. On the other hand, a test that samples many areas may be advantageous when an individual comparison of performance across subject areas is desirable. If a school or a local school district undertakes to follow the progress of a group of students as measured by a particular achievement battery, then the battery of choice will be one that spans the targeted subject areas in all the grades to be tested. If ability to distinguish individual areas of difficulty is of primary concern, then achievement tests with strong diagnostic features will be chosen.

Although achievement batteries sampling a wide range of areas, across grades, and standardized on large, national samples of students have much to recommend them, they also have certain drawbacks. For example, such tests usually take years to develop. In the interim, many of the items, especially in fields such as social studies and science, may become outdated. When selecting such a test, there are certain "musts," as well as certain "desirables," to keep in mind. Psychometric soundness—that is, well-documented reliability and validity data for members of the population to whom the test will be administered—is a must when evaluating the suitability of any nationally standardized test for a local administration. Another "must" is that possible sources of bias in the test have been minimized. In the "desirables" category, it is a plus if the test is relatively easy to administer and score. Further, it is desirable for the content to be up-to-date, as well as engaging and relevant for its targeted audience of testtakers.

Measures of Achievement in Specific Subject Areas

Whereas achievement batteries tend to be standardized instruments, most measures of achievement in specific subject areas are teacher-made tests. Every time a teacher gives a quiz, a test, or a final examination in a course, a test in a specific subject area has been created. Still, there are a number of standardized instruments designed to gauge achievement in specific areas.

At the elementary-school level, the acquisition of basic skills such as reading, writing, and arithmetic is emphasized. Tests to measure achievement in reading come in many different forms. For example, there are tests for individual or group administration and for silent or oral reading. The tests may vary in the theory of cognitive ability on which they are based and in the type of subtest data they yield. In general, the tests present the examinee with words, sentences, or paragraphs to be read silently or aloud, and reading ability is assessed by variables such as comprehension and vocabulary. When the material is read aloud, accuracy and speed are measured. Tests of reading comprehension also vary with respect to the intellectual demands placed on the examinee beyond mere comprehension of the words read. Thus, some tests might require the examinee to simply recall facts from a passage whereas others might require interpretation and the making of inferences.

At the secondary school level, one popular battery is the Cooperative Achievement Test. It consists of a series of separate achievement tests in areas as diverse as English, mathematics, literature, social studies, science, and foreign languages. Each test was standardized on different populations appropriate to the grade level, with samples randomly selected and stratified according to public, parochial, and private schools. In general, the tests tend to be technically sound instruments. Assessment of achievement in high-school students may involve evaluation of minimum competencies, often as a requirement for a high-school diploma.

At the college level, state legislatures are becoming more interested in mandating end-of-major outcomes assessment in state colleges and universities. Apparently taxpayers want confirmation that their education tax dollars are being well spent. Thus, for example, undergraduate psychology students attending a state-run institution could be required in their senior year to sit for a final—in the literal sense—examination encompassing a range of subject matter that could be described as "everything that an undergraduate psychology major should know." And if that sounds formidable to you, be advised that the task of developing such examinations is all the more formidable.

Another use for achievement tests at the college level, as well as for adults, is placement. The advanced placement program developed by the College Entrance Examination Board offers high-school students the opportunity to achieve college credit for work completed in high school. Successful completion of the advanced placement test may result in advanced standing, advanced course credit, or both, depending on the college policy. Since its inception, the advanced placement program has resulted in advanced credit or standing for more than 100,000 high-school students in approximately 2,000 colleges.

Tests of English proficiency or English as a second language are yet another example of a specific variety of achievement test. Data from such tests are currently used in the placement of college applicants in appropriate levels of English as a Second Language (ESL) programs.

Achievement tests at the college or adult level may also assess whether college credit should be awarded for learning acquired outside a college classroom. Numerous programs are designed to systematically assess whether sufficient knowledge has been acquired to qualify for course credit. The College Level Examination Program (CLEP) is based on the premise that knowledge may be obtained through independent study and sources other than formal schooling. The program includes exams in subjects ranging from African American history to tests and measurement. The Proficiency Examination Program (PEP) offered by the American College Testing Program is another service designed to assess achievement and skills learned outside the classroom.

The special needs of adults with a wide variety of educational backgrounds are addressed in tests such as the Adult Basic Learning Examination (ABLE), a test intended for use with examinees age 17 and older who have not completed eight years of formalized schooling. Developed in consultation with experts in the field of adult education, the test is designed to assess achievement in the areas of vocabulary, reading, spelling, and arithmetic.

Achievement tests in nationwide use may test for information or concepts that are not taught within a specific school's curriculum. Some children will do well on such items anyway,

JUST THINK . . .

There have been growing calls for "English only" in some American communities and states. If such demands find their way into legislation, how might that affect the ways English proficiency test results are used?

JUST THINK . . .

Is there an extracurricular life experience for which you should be given college credit? What would a test that measures what you learned from that experience look like?

having been exposed to the concepts or information independently. Performance on a school achievement test therefore does not depend entirely on school achievement. Concern about such issues has led to an interest in **curriculum-based assessment (CBA),** a term used to refer to assessment of information acquired from teachings at school. **Curriculum-based measurement (CBM),** a type of CBA, is characterized by the use of standardized measurement procedures to derive local norms to be used in the evaluation of student performance on curriculum-based tasks.

Before leaving the topic of achievement tests, let's make the point that achievement test items may be characterized by the type of mental processes required by the testtaker to successfully retrieve the information needed to respond to the item. More specifically, there are at least two distinctly different types of achievement test items: *fact-based items* and *conceptual items.* Here is an example of a fact-based test item; that is, one that draws primarily on rote memory:

1. One type of item that could be used in an achievement test is an item that requires
   a. remote memory
   b. rote memory
   c. memory loss
   d. mnemonic loss

Alternatively, achievement test items can require that the respondent not only know and understand relevant facts but also be able to apply them. Because respondents must draw on and apply knowledge related to a particular concept, these types of achievement test items are referred to as *conceptual* in nature. Here's one example of a conceptual type of item on an achievement test designed to measure mastery of the material in this chapter:

2. Which of the following testtakers would be a likely candidate for the CLEP?
   a. an illiterate migrant farmworker
   b. a child factory worker
   c. a learning-disabled third-grader
   d. a carpenter with little formal education

The correct response to item 1 is "b"—an alternative that could be arrived at by rote memory alone. Item 2 requires a bit more than rote memory; it requires *applying* knowledge related to what the CLEP is. Choice "a" can be eliminated because a written test would not be appropriate for administration to an illiterate testtaker. Choices "b" and "c" can be eliminated because the CLEP is administered to adults. A knowledgeable respondent could arrive at the correct alternative, "d," either by the process of elimination or by application of the knowledge of what the CLEP is and with whom it is designed to be used.

Let's move—but not very far—from the subject of achievement tests to the subject of aptitude tests. Before doing so, try your hand (and mind) on this *Just Think* exercise.

> **JUST THINK . . .**
>
> "Achievement tests measure learned knowledge, whereas aptitude tests measure innate potential." Why is this belief a myth?

Aptitude Tests

We are all constantly acquiring information through everyday life experiences and formal learning experiences (such as coursework in school). The primary difference between achievement tests and aptitude tests is that **aptitude tests** tend to focus more on informal learning or life experiences whereas achievement tests tend to focus on the learning that has occurred as a result of relatively structured input. Keeping this distinction in mind, consider the following two items; the first is from a hypothetical achievement test, and the second is from a hypothetical aptitude test.

1. A correlation of .7 between variables X and Y in a predictive validity study accounts for what percentage of the variance?

   a. 7%

   b. 70%

   c. .7%

   d. 49%

   e. 25%

2. o is to O as x is to

   a. /

   b. %

   c. X

   d. Y

At least on the face of it, Item 1 appears to be more dependent on formal learning experiences than does Item 2. The successful completion of Item 1 hinges on familiarity with the concept of correlation and the knowledge that the variance accounted for by a correlation coefficient is equal to the square of the coefficient (in this case, $.7^2$, or .49—choice "d"). The successful completion of Item 2 requires experience with the concept of size as well as the ability to grasp the concept of analogies. The latter abilities tend to be gleaned from life experiences (witness how quickly you determined that the correct answer was choice "c").

Interestingly, the label *achievement* or *aptitude* for a test may depend not simply on the types of items contained in the test but also on the intended *use* of the test. It is possible for two tests containing the same or similar items to be called by different names: one could be labeled an aptitude test while the other is labeled an achievement test. In the preceding examples, a nonverbal analogy item represented an aptitude test item. However, this same item could very well have been used to represent an achievement test item—one administered to test knowledge acquired, for example, at a seminar on conceptual thinking. Similarly, the first item, presented as an illustrative achievement test item, might well be used to assess aptitude (in statistics or psychology, for example) were it included in a test not expressly designed to measure achievement in this area. Whether a test is seen as measuring aptitude or achievement is a context-based judgment—that is, the judgment will be based, at least in part, on whether or not the testtaker is presumed to have prior exposure or formal learning related to the test's content.

> **JUST THINK . . .**
>
> Create an item for an aptitude test that will compel testtakers to draw on life experience rather than classroom learning for a response.

Aptitude tests, also referred to as **prognostic tests,** are typically used to make predictions. Some aptitude tests have been used to measure readiness to:

- enter a particular preschool program
- enter elementary school
- successfully complete a challenging course of study in secondary school
- successfully complete college-level work
- successfully complete graduate-level work, including a course of study at a professional or trade school

Achievement tests may also be used for predictive purposes. For example, an individual who performs well on a first-semester foreign-language achievement test might be considered a good candidate for the second term's work. The operative assumption here is that an individual who was able to master certain basic skills should be able to master more advanced skills. Understanding what students have already mastered can help school authorities better anticipate what content and skills they are ready to learn. When such assumptions are operative, it can be readily understood that achievement tests—as well as test items that tap achievement—are used in ways akin to aptitude tests.

Typically, when measures of achievement tests are used to make predictions, the measures tend to draw on narrower and more formal learning experiences than do aptitude tests. For example, a measure of achievement in a course entitled Basic Conversational French might be used as a predictor of achievement for a course entitled Advanced Conversational French. Aptitude tests tend to draw on a broader fund of information and abilities and may be used to predict a wider variety of variables.

In the following sections, we survey some aptitude tests used from the preschool level through the graduate school level and beyond. Let's note here an "unwritten rule" of terminology regarding reference to aptitude tests. At the preschool and elementary school level, you may hear references to **readiness tests.** Here, "readiness" presumably refers to the physical factors, personality factors, and other factors that are judged necessary for a child to be ready to learn. As the level of education climbs, however, the term *readiness* is dropped in favor of the term *aptitude*—this despite the fact that readiness is very much implied at all levels. So, for example, the Graduate Record Examination (GRE), given in college and used as a predictor of ability to do graduate-level work, might have been called the "GSRE" or "Graduate School Readiness Examination." So—are you ready to learn about readiness for learning at the preschool level?

> **JUST THINK . . .**
>
> Well beyond measuring readiness to participate in higher education, tests such as the SAT and the GRE have been praised as "levelers" that "level the playing field." Scores on these tests are blind to what school the testtakers are from as well as the grades received.

The Preschool Level

The first five years of life—the span of time referred to as the *preschool period*—is a time of profound change. Basic reflexes develop, and the child passes a number of sensorimotor milestones, such as crawling, sitting, standing, walking, running, and grasping. Usually between 18 and 24 months, the child becomes capable of symbolic thought and develops language skills. By age 2, the average child has a vocabulary of more than 200 words. Of course, all such observations about the development of children are of more than mere academic interest to professionals charged with the responsibility of psychological assessment. At the preschool level, such assessment is largely a matter of determining whether a child's cognitive, emotional, and social development is in line with age-related expectations, and whether any problems likely to hamper learning ability are evident.

In the mid-1970s, Congress enacted Public Law (PL) 94-142, which mandated the professional evaluation of children age 3 and older suspected of having physical or mental disabilities in order to determine their special educational needs. The law also provided federal funds to help states meet those needs. In 1986, a set of amendments to PL 94-142 known as PL 99-457 extended downward to birth the obligation of states toward children with disabilities. It further mandated that, beginning with the school year 1990–1991, all disabled children from ages 3 to 5 were to be provided with a free, appropriate education. The law was expanded in scope in 1997 with the passage of PL 105-17. Among other things, PL 105-17 was intended to give greater attention to diversity issues, especially as a factor in evaluation and assignment of special services. PL 105-17 also mandated that infants and toddlers with disabilities must receive services in the home or in other natural settings, and that such services were to be continued in preschool programs.

In 1999, attention deficit hyperactivity disorder (ADHD) was officially listed under "Otherwise Health Impaired" in IDEA as a disabling condition that can qualify a child for special services. This, combined with other federal legislation and a growing movement toward "full-service schools" that dispense health and psychological services in addition to education (Reeder et al., 1997), signaled a growing societal reliance on infant and preschool assessment techniques.

The tools of preschool assessment are, with age-appropriate variations built into them, the same types of tools used to assess school-age children and adults. These tools include, among others, checklists and rating scales, tests, and interviews.

Checklists and rating scales   Checklists and rating scales are tools of assessment commonly used with preschoolers, although their use is certainly not exclusive to this population. In general, a **checklist** is a questionnaire on which marks are made to indicate the presence or absence of a specified behavior, thought, event, or circumstance. The individual doing the "checking" of the boxes on a checklist may be a professional (such as a psychologist or a teacher), an observer (such as a parent or other caretaker), or even the subject of the checklist himself or herself. Checklists can cover a wide array of item content and still be relatively economical and quick to administer.

A *rating scale* is quite similar in definition and sometimes even identical in form to a checklist. The definitional differences between the two terms is technically rather subtle, and for all practical purposes, blurred. The difference involves the degree to which actual rating is involved. For our purposes, we will define a **rating scale** as a form completed by an evaluator (a rater, judge, or examiner) to make a judgment of relative standing with regard to a specified variable or list of variables. As with a checklist, the targeted judgment may have to do with the presence or absence of a particular event or even its frequency.

Have you ever been evaluated by a checklist or rating scale? If you answered no, you are probably incorrect. This is because one of the very first things that most of us are greeted with upon entry to the world is a checklist related to our appearance, behavior, and overall health. The sum total of what might be characterized as "everybody's first test," an **Apgar number.** The Apgar number is a score on a rating scale developed by physician Virginia Apgar (1909–1974), an obstetrical anesthesiologist who saw a need for a simple, rapid method of evaluating newborn infants and determining what immediate action, if any, is necessary.

As first presented in the early 1950s, the Apgar evaluation is conducted at 1 minute after birth to assess how well the infant tolerated the birthing process. The evaluation is conducted again at 5 minutes after birth to assess how well the infant is adapting to the environment. Each evaluation is made with respect to the same five variables; each variable can be scored on a range from 0 to 2; and each score (at 1 minute and 5 minutes) can range from 0 to 10. The five variables are heart rate, respiration, color, muscle tone, and reflex irritability, the last measure being obtained by response to a stimulus such as a mild pinch. For example, with respect to the variable of reflex irritability, the infant will earn a score of 2 for a vigorous cry in response to the stimulus, a score of 1 for a grimace, and a score of 0 if it shows no reflex irritability. Few babies are "perfect 10s" on their 1-minute Apgar; many are 7s, 8s, and 9s. An Apgar score below 7 or 8 may indicate the need for assistance in being stabilized. A very low Apgar score, in the 0-to-3 range, may signal a more enduring problem such as neurological deficit. By the way, a useful acronym for remembering the five variables is the name "APGAR" itself: A stands for activity (or muscle tone), P for pulse (or heart rate), G for grimace (or reflex irritability), A for appearance (or color), and R for respiration.

Moving from the realm of the medical to the realm of the psychological, another evaluation, one far less formal, takes place shortly after birth, by the child's mother (see Figure 10–2). Judith Langlois and colleagues (1995) studied the relationship between infant attractiveness and maternal behavior and attitudes using a sample of 173 mothers and their firstborn infants (86 girls and 87 boys). To gauge attractiveness, the investigators used judges' ratings of photographs taken a standard distance from each infant's face while the child was either sleeping or had an otherwise neutral expression. Maternal behavior during feeding and play was directly observed by trained raters in the hospital. The researchers found that although all of the infants studied received adequate care, the attractive infants received more positive treatment and attitudes from their mothers than did the unattractive infants. The mothers of the attractive infants were more affectionate and playful. The mothers of less attractive infants were more likely to be attentive to other people rather than to their infant. These mothers were also more likely to engage in routine caregiving than in affectionate behavior.

Clearly, from moments after birth and onward, evaluation—both formal and informal—is very much a fact of life. We may define **informal evaluation** as a typically nonsystematic, relatively brief, and "off-the-record" assessment leading to the formation of an opinion or attitude conducted by any person, in any way, for any reason, in an unofficial context that is not subject to the ethics or other standards of an evaluation by a professional. The process of informal evaluation has not received a great deal of attention in the psychological assessment literature. Accordingly, the nature and extent of the influence of informal evaluations by people (such as parents, teachers, supervisors, personnel in the criminal justice system, and others) is largely unknown. On the one hand, considering the need for privacy, perhaps it is best that such private evaluations remain that way. On the other hand, research such as that conducted by Langlois and her colleagues brings to light the everyday implications of such informal evaluations, implications that may ultimately help to improve the quality of life for many people.

Shifting our focus back to *formal* evaluation, assessors have an abundance of options when selecting a checklist or rating scale to use as screening instruments for education-related assessments. Many of these screening instruments, such as the Connors Rating Scales-Revised, come in different versions for use through the life span. Designed for use from preschool through adolescence, the BASC-3 utilizes teacher and parent ratings to identify adaptive difficulties on 16 scales ranging from activities of daily living to study skills. An additional

Figure 10–2
Welcome to the World of Evaluation

Only seconds after birth, a newborn infant is given its first formal evaluation by the hospital staff. The infant's next evaluation, conducted by the mother, may be no less momentous in its consequences especially if the infant is particularly attractive or unattractive (Berkowitz & Frodi, 1979; Dion, 1979; Elder et al., 1985; Parke et al., 1977), and if the newborn infant is physically challenged (Allen et al., 1990; Barden et al., 1989; Field & Vega-Lahr, 1984).
© Amelie-Benoist/BSIP/The Image Works France

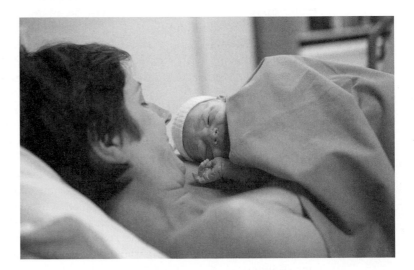

Self-Report of Personality (SRP) may also be administered if the respondents are believed to have sufficient insight into their own behavior with regard to variables such as interpersonal relations, self-esteem, and sensation seeking.

Particularly in preschool assessment, screening tools may be used as a first step in identifying children who are said to be *at risk*. This term came into vogue as an alternative to diagnostic labels that might have a detrimental effect (Smith & Knudtson, 1990). Today, what a child is actually at risk *for* may vary in terms of the context of the discussion and the state in which the child resides. *At risk* has been used to refer to preschool children who may not be ready for first grade. The term has also been applied to children who are believed to be not functioning within normal limits. In a most general sense, **at risk** refers to children who have documented difficulties in one or more psychological, social, or academic areas and for whom intervention is or may be required. The need for intervention may be decided on the basis of a more complete evaluation, often involving psychological assessment. As noted by Faith Miller in an essay that can be found only on our website (*https://mhhe.cohentesting9*), the specific reasons given for an "at risk" designation can be quite varied, Miller (2017) cited a number of possible causal factors, including measured intelligence, temperament, personality, family life, school environment, and environmental hazards (see also Miller et al., 2015).

Psychological tests At the earliest levels, cognitive, emotional, and social attributes are gauged by scales that assess the presence or absence of various developmental achievements through such means as observation and parental (or caretaker) interviews. By age 2, the child enters a challenging period for psychological assessors. Language and conceptual skills are beginning to emerge, yet the kinds of verbal and performance tests traditionally used with older children and adults are inappropriate. The attention span of the preschooler is short. Ideally, test materials are colorful, engaging, and attention-sustaining. Approximately one hour is a good rule-of-thumb limit for an entire test session with a preschooler; less time is preferable. As testing time increases, so does the possibility of fatigue and distraction. Of course, with assessee fatigue and distraction comes a higher potential for an underestimation of the assessee's ability.

JUST THINK . . .

"Especially for very young children, establishing test-retest reliability with an intervening interval of as little as a month or so can be a problem." Do you agree? Why or why not?

Motivation of the young child may vary from one test session to the next, and this is something of which the examiner must be aware. Particularly desirable are tests that are relatively easy to administer and have simple start/discontinue rules. Also very desirable are tests that allow ample opportunity to make behavioral observations. Dual-easel test administration format (Figure 10–3), sample and teaching items for each subtest, and dichotomous scoring (e.g., right/wrong) all may facilitate test administration with very young children.

Data from infant intelligence tests, especially when combined with other information (such as birth history, emotional and social history, health history, data on the quality of the physical and emotional environment, and measures of adaptive behavior) have proved useful to health professionals when questions about developmental disability and related deficits have been raised. Infant intelligence tests have also proved useful in helping to define the abilities—as well as the extent of disability—in older, psychotic children. Furthermore, the tests have been in use for a number of years by many adoption agencies that will disclose and interpret such information to prospective adoptive parents. Infant tests also have wide application in research. They can play a key role, for example, in selecting infants for specialized early educational experiences or in measuring the outcome of educational, therapeutic, or prenatal care interventions.

Figure 10–3
A Dual-Easel Format in Test Administration

Easel format in the context of test administration refers to test materials, usually some sort of book that contains test-stimulus materials and that can be folded and placed on a desk; the examiner turns the pages to reveal to the examinee, for example, objects to identify or designs to copy. When corresponding test administration instructions or notes are printed on the reverse side of the test-stimulus pages for the examiner's convenience during test administration, the format is sometimes referred to as dual easel.
© Mark E. Swerdlik

Tests such as the WPPSI-III and the SB5, as well as others, may be used to gauge developmental strengths and weaknesses by sampling children's performance in cognitive, motor, and social/behavioral content areas. However, the question arises, "What is the meaning of a score on an infant intelligence test?" Whereas some of the developers of infant tests (such as Cattell, 1940; Gesell et al., 1940) claimed that such tests can predict future intellectual ability because they measure the developmental precursors to such ability, others have insisted that performance on such tests at best reflects the infant's physical and neuropsychological intactness. The research literature supports a middle ground between these extreme positions. In general, the tests have not been found to predict performance on child or adult intelligence tests—tests that tap vastly different types of abilities and thought processes. However, the predictive ability of infant intelligence tests does tend to increase with the extremes of the infant's performance. The test interpreter can say with authority more about the future performance of an infant whose performance was either profoundly below age expectancy or significantly precocious. Still, infancy is a developmental period of many spurts and lags, and infants who are slow or precocious at this age might catch up or fall back in later years. Perhaps the great value of preschool tests lies in their ability to help identify children who are in a very low range of functioning and in need of intervention.

Other measures   Many other instruments and assessment techniques are available for use with preschoolers, including interviews, case history methods, portfolio evaluation, and role-play methods. There are instruments, for example, to measure temperament (Fullard et al., 1984; Gagne et al., 2011; McDevitt & Carey, 1978), language skills (Smith, Myers-Jennings, & Coleman, 2000), the family environment in general (Moos & Moos, 1994; Pritchett et al., 2011), and specific aspects of parenting and caregiving (Arnold et al., 1993; Lovejoy et al., 1999). Drawings may be analyzed for insights they can provide with respect to the child's personality. Some techniques are very specialized and would be used only under rather extraordinary conditions or in the context of research with a very specific focus. An example of the latter is the Child Sexual Behavior Inventory (Friedrich et al., 2001), a 38-item behavior checklist that may be helpful in identifying sexually abused children as young as 2 years old. In sum, many different types of instruments are available for use with preschoolers to help evaluate a wide variety of areas related to personal, social, and academic development.

The Elementary-School Level

The age at which a child is mandated by law to enter school varies from state to state. Yet individual children of the same chronological age may vary widely in how ready they are to separate from their parents and begin academic learning. Children entering the educational system come from a wide range of backgrounds and experiences, and their rates of physiological, psychological, and social development also vary widely. School readiness tests provide educators with a yardstick by which to assess pupils' abilities in areas as diverse as general information and sensorimotor skills. How data from such "yardsticks" are actually used will vary from country to country in accordance with many considerations, including cultural traditions (see this chapter's *Close-Up*). One of many instruments designed to assess children's readiness and aptitude for formal education is the Metropolitan Readiness Tests (MRTs).

The Metropolitan Readiness Tests (sixth edition; MRT6)   The MRT6 (Nurss, 1994) is a test battery that assesses the development of the reading and mathematics skills important in the early stages of formal school learning. The test is divided into two levels: Level I (individually administered), for use with beginning and middle kindergarteners, and Level II (group administered), which spans the end of kindergarten through first grade (Table 10–1). There are two forms of the test at each level. The tests are orally administered in several sessions and are untimed, though administration time typically runs about 90 minutes. A practice test (especially useful with young children who have had minimal or no prior test-taking experience) may be administered several days before the actual examination to help familiarize students with the procedures and format.

Normative data for the current edition of the MRTs are based on a national sample of approximately 30,000 children. The standardization sample was stratified according to geographic region, socioeconomic factors, prior school experience, and ethnic background. Data were obtained from both public and parochial schools and from both large and small schools. Split-half reliability coefficients for both forms of both levels of the MRT as well as Kuder-Richardson measures of internal consistency were in the acceptably high range. Content validity was developed through an extensive review of the literature, an analysis of the skills involved in the reading process, and the development of test items that reflected those skills. Items were reviewed by minority consultants in an attempt to reduce, if not eliminate, any potential ethnic bias. The predictive validity of MRT scores has been examined with reference to later school achievement indices, and the obtained validity coefficients have been relatively high.

Educational Assessment:
An Eastern Perspective*

In China, an individual's socioeconomic status is closely linked to their academic achievement. Accordingly, a family's pursuit of academic achievement for the children is of paramount importance. Once a child reaches elementary school, the family strives to provide an environment at home that is conducive for academic success. Parents tend to set the bar for academic performance high, while imbuing children with the value of hard work to meet academic goals and expectations. In general, parents will do their best to instill in their children high ideals regarding academic excellence.

From the view from the East, significant cultural differences seem to exist in terms of the degree to which parents, family, and other members of a community and society-at-large become involved in a child's education. In an individualist, competitive culture like the one that exists in the United States, people are encouraged to take personal responsibility for their actions, their accomplishments, and their struggles. Students are expected to "step up to the plate" and give their personal best to achieve good grades. Parents, teachers, and others can give encouragement, hire tutors, and help in sundry other ways, but ultimately, responsibility for academic success resides squarely with the student. Further, as time goes on, the role of parents, teachers, and others in the community (as well as society-at-large) with regard to the education of the individual, diminishes. In such a system, it is the individual who ultimately takes personal responsibility for academic success or failure.

By contrast, in collective and cooperative cultures, like the ones that exist in China and Japan, family members, teachers, and even other peers are expected to share a good deal of the responsibility for the individual student's learning and achievement. The degree of this shared responsibility tends to grow into mutual obligation as the student progresses through the educational system. The culture encourages individuals to forego personal goals, and to relegate personal ambition to a priority that is secondary to the service of others. In such a system, credit for the success of a single student is shared by the many.

Another contrast may be drawn with regard to Eastern versus Western perspectives on innate ability vice versa academic achievement. The fact that individual differences in innate ability exist is widely acknowledged in all cultures. However, the meaning and implications of such differences would appear to vary. In China, much like other countries that have been deeply influenced by Confucius' teachings in human malleability, the contribution of natural or innate ability in achievement is de-emphasized. The

Chinese choose to focus instead on the role of hard work and effort in learning and training. In general, deficiencies in academic achievement will be attributed not to differences in innate ability, but rather to a lack of motivation, diligence, or perseverance on the part of the student. According to this view, academic success is more the product of effort, perseverance, and motivation, and less the product of a winning combination of genes.

By contrast, Western cultures seem to embrace the more nativist position that not everyone is equally "built" or genetically prepared for academic achievement. This latter view encourages members of the society to pursue paths of self-fulfillment based on their natural gifts, abilities, and aptitudes. From this Western perspective, differential progress in academic mastery is to be expected, and accommodations must be made for both the academically gifted and the academically challenged.

After reviewing the Chinese literature on giftedness, Wu (2005) compared Eastern versus Western theoretical assumptions on that topic. In the Chinese literature, giftedness as an innate ability was de-emphasized. Consistent with a Confucian perspective that places great emphasis on effort and perseverance, giftedness was alternatively conceptualized as "talented performance." At first blush, this difference in conceptualizations may seem to be simply a matter of semantics. Perhaps. But in classrooms throughout China, the performance of students who excel academically tends not to be conceptualized in terms of innate ability, but more the product, say, of higher motivation or greater perseverance. Accordingly, students in the East may not be seen quite as "pigeon-holed" (in the sense of being "on a specific track") as they may be in the West.

China's current educational system, as influenced by Confucian belief, is assessment-oriented. However, it is important to note that psychology, as a scientific and professional discipline, was completely eliminated from mainland China during the Great Cultural Revolution (Han & Yang, 2001). With policy reform beginning in 1978, and the rapid economic development over the decades, China has become increasingly exposed to the rest of the world. It has since adopted and adapted many Western psychological tests for local use (Ryan et al., 1994). Today, China is poised to play an active role in contributing to the future development of the field of psychological assessment in educational, as well as vocational, clinical, and other settings. To what extent Confucian philosophy will influence those contributions in China—and to what extent Confucian philosophy may influence future Western contributions in those fields—remains to be seen.

*This Close-Up was guest-authored by Chengting Ju, Ning He, and Xuqun You, all of the School of Psychology, Shaanxi Normal University (China).

Used with permission of Chengting Ju, Ning He, and Xuqun You.

Table 10–1

The Metropolitan Readiness Tests

Level I

Auditory Memory: Four pictures containing familiar objects are presented. The examiner reads aloud several words. The child must select the picture that corresponds to the same sequence of words that were presented orally.

Rhyming: The examiner supplies the names of each of the pictures presented and then gives a fifth word that rhymes with one of them. The child must select the picture that rhymes with the examiner's word.

Letter Recognition: The examiner names different letters, and the child must identify each from the series presented in the test booklet.

Visual Matching: A sample is presented, and the child must select the choice that matches the sample.

School Language and Listening: The examiner reads a sentence, and the child selects the picture that describes what was read. The task involves some inference making and awareness of relevancy of detail.

Quantitative Language: The test assesses comprehension of quantitative terms and knowledge of ordinal numbers and simple mathematical operations.

Level II

Beginning Consonants: Four pictures representing familiar objects are presented in the test booklet and are named by the examiner. The examiner then supplies a fifth word (not presented), and the child must select the picture that begins with the same sound.

Sound-Letter Correspondence: A picture is presented, followed by a series of letters. The examiner names the picture, and the child selects the choice that corresponds to the beginning sound of the pictured item.

Visual Matching: As in the corresponding subtest at Level I, a model is presented, and the child must select the choice that matches the model.

Finding Patterns: A stimulus consisting of several symbols is presented, followed by a series of representative options. The child must select the option that contains the same sequence of symbols, even though they are presented in a larger grouping with more distractions.

School Language: As in the School Language and Listening Test at Level I, the child must select the picture that corresponds to an orally presented sentence.

Listening: Material is orally presented, and the child must select the picture that reflects comprehension of and drawing conclusions about the stimulus material.

Quantitative Concepts and Quantitative Operations: Two optional tests designed to gauge knowledge of basic mathematical concepts and operations.

The Secondary-School Level

Perhaps the most obvious example of an aptitude test widely used in the schools at the secondary level is the SAT, which until 1993 went by the name Scholastic Aptitude Test. The test has been of value not only in the college selection process but also as an aid to high-school guidance and job placement counselors; it has value in helping students decide whether further academics, vocational training, or some other course of action would be most advisable. SAT data is also used by organizations and government agencies in determining who will receive scholarship grants and other such awards.

What is collectively referred to as "the SAT" is actually a number of tests that consist of (1) a multipart test referred to as the SAT (which contains measures of reading, writing, and mathematics) and (2) SAT subject tests. Reading is measured through reading comprehension tasks as measured by short passages followed by sentence completion items. The mathematics section probes knowledge of subjects such as algebra, geometry, basic statistics, and probability. The writing portion of the exam tests knowledge of grammar, usage, and word choice, and is tested through both multiple-choice items and an essay question. The SAT Subject tests are one-hour-long tests designed to measure achievement in specific subject areas such as English, History and Social Studies, Mathematics, Science, and Languages. Colleges may require or recommend taking a specific subject test for purposes of admission or placement or simply to advise students about course selection.

The SAT always seems to be a "work in progress" with regard to its constantly evolving form and nature. Still, a longstanding controversy exists regarding its developer's claim that SAT scores, combined with a consideration of high-school grade-point average, yields the best available predictor of academic success in college. Critics of the SAT have cited everything from differential functioning of items as a function of race (Santelices & Wilson, 2010) to the effects of daylight savings time (Gaski & Sagarin, 2011) as possible sources of adverse effects on SAT scores. It has also been claimed that SAT scores *over*predict the first-year college grade-point averages of African American and Latino students (Zwick & Himelfarb, 2011).

On the bright side, students who take the test more than once can now decide which institution will receive which results. Prior to 2009, students had no such choice and all test results were forwarded to all of the institutions they listed. For the most current information about the SAT, including sample questions and videos, visit the College Board's informative website at *www.collegeboard.com.*

The ACT Assessment, commonly referred to by its three letters ("A-C-T") and *not* by rhyming it with "fact," serves a purpose that is similar to the SAT's. Formerly known as the American College Testing Program, the ACT was developed at the University of Iowa. This college entrance examination was an outgrowth of the Iowa Tests of Educational Development. The test is curriculum-based, with questions directly based on typical high-school subject areas. One study comparing the ACT with the SAT found that the tests were highly correlated with each other in many respects and that both were highly correlated with general intelligence (Koenig et al., 2008). Scores on the ACT may be predictive of creativity as well as academic success (Dollinger, 2011). Such findings are noteworthy in light of assertions that the lack of creativity-related items on college aptitude tests is a critical omission. In this vein, Kaufman (2010) proposed that the inclusion of creativity items on college aptitude tests may be a way to further reduce possible bias.

Although most colleges and universities in the United States require SAT or ACT scores before an applicant is considered for admission, how much do they really rely on them for making college entrance decisions? Probably less than most people believe. Institutions of higher learning in this country differ widely with respect to their admission criteria. Even among schools that require SAT or ACT test scores, varying weights are accorded to the scores with respect to admission decisions. Scores on the SAT or ACT, along with other criteria (such as grade-point average), are designed to help admissions committees determine which of many candidates will do well at their institution. And given the competition for a finite number of seats at institutions of higher learning, these tests also serve a "gatekeeping" function—serving both to award seats to students with documented academic potential and to preserve an institution's reputation for selectivity. However, SAT and ACT test scores can be balanced by other admissions criteria designed to achieve other goals of admissions committees, such as the encouragement of diversity on campus. Motivation and interest, which are clearly necessary to sustain a student through an undergraduate or graduate course of study, may be judged by less standardized means such as letters written by the candidates themselves, letters of recommendation, and personal interviews.

The College Level and Beyond

If you are a college student planning to pursue further education after graduation, you are probably familiar with the letters G-R-E (which together form an acronym that is very much on the minds of many graduate-school-bound students).

The Graduate Record Examinations (GRE) This long-standing rite of passage for students seeking admission to graduate school has a General Test form as well as specific subject tests. The General Test contains verbal and quantitative sections as well as analytical writing sections. The verbal subtest taps, among other things, the ability to analyze and evaluate written materials as well as the ability to recognize relationships between concepts. The quantitative subtest taps, among other things, knowledge of basic mathematical concepts and the ability to reason quantitatively. The analytical writing subtest taps, among other things, critical thinking and the ability to articulate and argue ideas effectively in standard written English. The General Test may be taken by paper and pencil or by computer at a test center. If it is taken by computer, testtakers use an "elementary word processor" devised by the test developer so that persons familiar with one or another commercially available word-processing programs will not have an advantage. Essays written by respondents may be sent in their entirety to graduate institutions receiving GRE test reports.

Perhaps because of the potentially momentous importance of GRE test results, a number of independent researchers have critically examined the test with regard to various psychometric variables. One comprehensive meta-analysis of the relevant literature focused on the use of the GRE along with undergraduate grade-point average as predictors of graduate success. The researchers concluded that the GRE was a valid predictor of several important criterion measures (ranging from graduate grade-point average to faculty ratings) across disciplines (Kuncel et al., 2001). Other researchers have argued that the GRE has limited utility in predicting other variables related to success in graduate school. These outcomes include the quality of a dissertation, creativity, practical abilities, research skills, and teaching ability (Sternberg & Williams, 1997).

Experience tells us that many readers of this book have more than a casual interest in one specific GRE subject test: *Psychology.* "How do I prepare for it?" is a common question. Here is a four-step preparation program you may wish to consider:

- *Step 1:* Visit the official GRE website maintained by Educational Testing Service (ETS) at *www.ets.org/gre.* Navigate to the *Subject Tests,* and then click on *Psychology.* Use this resource to the fullest to get all the information you can about the current form of the test, even a practice sample of the test.

- *Step 2:* Dust off your introductory psychology textbook and then reread it, review it, do whatever you need to in order to relearn it. If for some reason you no longer have that textbook, or if you took introductory psychology ages ago, ask your instructor to recommend a current text that provides a comprehensive review of the field. Then, read that textbook diligently from cover to cover.

- *Step 3:* Many students have praise for some commercially available review books. There are many available. Spend an evening at your favorite bookstore browsing through the ones available; identify the one that you think will work best for you, and buy it. Typically, these exam preparation books contain a number of sample tests that may be helpful in pinpointing areas that will require extra study.

- *Step 4:* Use all of the resources available to you (textbooks in your personal library, books in your school library, the Internet, etc.) to "fill in the gaps" of knowledge you have identified. Additionally, you may find it helpful to read about effective test preparation and test-taking strategies (see, for example, Loken et al., 2004).

After you have made your best effort to prepare for the test, know that you have the authors' best wishes for luck with it. Or, in psychological and psychometric terms, *may the content sampled on the test match the content you have learned in preparing to take it, and may that information be readily accessed!*

The Miller Analogies Test (MAT)   Another widely used examination is the Miller Analogies Test. This is a 100-item, multiple-choice analogy test that draws not only on the examinee's ability to perceive relationships but also on general intelligence, vocabulary, and academic learning. As an example, complete the following analogy:

Classical conditioning is to *Pavlov* as *operant conditioning* is to

    a. Freud

    b. Rogers

    c. Skinner

    d. Jung

    e. Dr. Phil

Successful completion of this item demands not only the ability to understand the relationship between classical conditioning and Pavlov but also the knowledge that it was B. F. Skinner (choice "c") whose name—of those listed—is best associated with operant conditioning.

The MAT has been cited as one of the most cost-effective of all existing aptitude tests when it comes to forecasting success in graduate school (Kuncel & Hezlett, 2007a). However, as most readers are probably aware, the use of most any aptitude test, even in combination with other predictors, tends to engender controversy (see, for example, Brown, 2007; Kuncel & Hezlett, 2007b; Lerdau & Avery, 2007; Sherley, 2007).

Other aptitude tests   Applicants for training in certain professions and occupations may be required to take specialized entrance examinations. For example, undergraduate students interested in pursuing a career in medicine, including podiatry or osteopathy, will probably be required to sit for the Medical College Admission Test (MCAT). A high rate of attrition among students studying to become physicians in the 1920s was the stimulus for the development of this test in 1928. Since that time, the test has gone through a number of revisions. The various versions of the test "demonstrate that the definition of aptitude for medical education reflects the professional and social mores and values of the time" (McGaghie, 2002, p. 1085). In its present form, the MCAT consists of four sections: Verbal Reasoning, Physical Sciences, Writing Sample, and Biological Sciences. One group of investigators examined the ability of the MCAT to predict performance in medical school and medical licensing examinations in a sample of 7,859 medical school matriculants. The authors concluded that the "obtained predictive validity coefficients are impressive" (Callahan et al., 2011).

Numerous other aptitude tests have been developed to assess specific kinds of academic, professional, and/or occupational aptitudes. Some of the more widely used tests are described briefly in Table 10–2. There are also a number of lesser known (and less widely used) aptitude tests. For example, the Seashore Measures of Musical Talents (Seashore, 1938) is a now-classic measure of musical aptitude administered with the aid of a record (if you can find a record player) or prerecorded tape. The six subtests measure specific aspects of musical talent (e.g., comparing different notes and rhythms on variables such as loudness, pitch, time, and timbre). The Horn Art Aptitude Inventory is a measure designed to gauge various aspects of the respondent's artistic aptitude.

> **JUST THINK . . .**
>
> *"Art is in the eye of the beholder."* Considering this bit of wisdom, how is it possible to determine if someone truly has an aptitude for art?

Table 10–2

Some Entrance Examinations for Professional or Occupational Training

Entrance Examination and Website for More Information	Brief Description
Medical College Admission Test (MCAT) *www.aamc.org*	Designed to assess problem solving, critical thinking, and writing skills, as well as knowledge of science concepts prerequisite to the study of medicine.
Law School Admission Test (LSAT) *www.lsac.org*	A standardized measure of acquired reading and verbal reasoning skills. Includes measures of reading comprehension, analytical reasoning, and logical reasoning, as well as a writing sample.
Veterinary College Admission Test (VCAT) *www.tpcweb.com* (follow links)	Assesses five content areas: biology, chemistry, verbal ability, quantitative ability, and reading comprehension.
Dental Admission Test (DAT) *www.ada.org*	Conducted by the American Dental Association, this test may be computer administered almost any day of the year. Includes four sections: Natural Sciences (biology, general chemistry, organic chemistry), Perceptual Ability (including angle discrimination tasks), Reading Comprehension, and Quantitative Reasoning (including algebra, various conversions, probability and statistics, geometry, trigonometry, and applied mathematics).
Pharmacy College Admission Test (PCAT) *marketplace.psychcorp.com* (follow links)	Contains five subtests: Verbal (including vocabulary with analogies and antonyms), Quantitative (arithmetic, fractions, decimals, percentages, algebra, and reasoning), Biology, Chemistry (basic organic and inorganic), Reading Comprehension (analyze and interpret passages).
Optometry Admission Test (OAT) *www.opted.org*	Contains four subtests: Natural Sciences (tapping knowledge of biology, general chemistry, and organic chemistry), Reading Comprehension, Physics, and Quantitative Reasoning.
Allied Health Professions Admission Test (AHPAT) *www.tpcweb.com* (follow links)	Assesses ability in five content areas: biology, chemistry, verbal ability, quantitative ability, and reading comprehension. Designed for use with aspiring physical and occupational therapists, physician's assistants, and other members of allied health professions.
Entrance Examination for Schools of Nursing (RNEE) *www.tpcweb.com* (follow links)	Voted by the authors of this textbook as "Test with Trickiest Acronym," the RNEE assesses ability in five content areas: physical sciences, numerical ability, life sciences, verbal ability, and reading comprehension.
Accounting Program Admission Test (APAT) *www.tpcweb.com* (follow links)	Measures student achievement in elementary accounting by means of 75 multiple-choice questions, 60% of which deal with financial accounting and the remaining 40% of which deal with managerial accounting.
Graduate Management Admission Test *www.mba.com*	Measures basic verbal and mathematical and analytical writing skills through three subtests: Analytical Writing Assessment, the Quantitative section, and the Verbal section.

Diagnostic Tests

By the early twentieth century, it was recognized that tests of intelligence could be used to do more than simply measure cognitive ability. Binet and Simon (1908/1961) wrote of their concept of "mental orthopedics," whereby intelligence test data could be used to improve learning. Today a distinction is made between tests and test data used primarily for *evaluative* purposes and tests and test data used primarily for *diagnostic* purposes. The term **evaluative,** as used in phrases such as *evaluative purposes* or **evaluative information,** is typically applied to tests or test data that are used to make judgments (such as pass–fail and admit–reject decisions). By contrast, **diagnostic information,** as used in educational contexts (and related phrases such as *diagnostic purposes*) is typically applied to tests or test data used to pinpoint a student's difficulty, usually for remedial purposes. In an educational context, a **diagnostic test** is a tool used to identify areas of deficit to be targeted for intervention.[2]

A diagnostic reading test may, for example, contain a number of subtests. Each subtest is designed to analyze a specific knowledge or skill required for reading. The objective of each of these subtests might be to bring into focus the specific problems that need to be addressed if the testtaker is to read at an appropriate grade level. By the way, the line between "diagnostic" and "evaluative" testing is not carved in stone; diagnostic information can be used for evaluative purposes, and information from evaluative tests can provide diagnostic information. For example, on the basis of a child's performance on a diagnostic reading test, a teacher or an administrator might make a class placement decision.

Diagnostic tests do not necessarily provide information that will answer questions concerning *why* a learning difficulty exists. Other educational, psychological, and perhaps medical examinations are needed to answer that question. In general, diagnostic tests are administered to students who have already demonstrated their problem with a particular subject area through their poor performance either in the classroom or on some achievement test. For this reason, diagnostic tests may contain simpler items than achievement tests designed for use with members of the same grade.

Reading Tests

The ability to read is integral to virtually all classroom learning, so it is not surprising that a number of diagnostic tests are available to help pinpoint difficulties in acquiring this skill. Some of the many tests available to help pinpoint reading difficulties include the Stanford Diagnostic Reading Test, the Metropolitan Reading Instructional Tests, the Diagnostic Reading Scales, and the Durrell Analysis of Reading Test. For illustrative purposes we briefly describe one such diagnostic battery, the Woodcock Reading Mastery Tests.

The Woodcock Reading Mastery Tests-Revised (WRMT-III; Woodcock, 2011) This paper- and-pencil measure of reading readiness, reading achievement, and reading difficulties takes between 15 and 45 minutes to administer the entire battery. It can be used with children as young as 4½, adults as old as 80, and most everyone in between. This edition of the test was standardized on a nationally representative sample totaling over 3,300 testtakers. Users of prior editions of this popular test will recognize many of the subtests on the WRMT-III (with revised artwork to be more engaging), including:

Letter Identification: Items that measure the ability to name letters presented in different forms. Both cursive and printed as well as uppercase and lowercase letters are presented.

Word Identification: Words in isolation arranged in order of increasing difficulty. The student is asked to read each word aloud.

Word Attack: Nonsense syllables that incorporate phonetic as well as structural analysis skills. The student is asked to pronounce each nonsense syllable.

---

2. In a clinical context, the same term may be used to refer to a tool of assessment designed to yield a psychiatric diagnosis.

Word Comprehension: Items that assess word meaning by using a four-part analogy format.

Passage Comprehension: Phrases, sentences, or short paragraphs, read silently, in which a word is missing. The student must supply the missing word.

Three subtests new to the third edition are *Phonological Awareness, Listening Comprehension,* and *Oral Reading Fluency.* All of the subtests taken together are used to derive a picture of the testtaker's reading-related strengths and weaknesses, as well as an actionable plan for reading remediation when necessary. The test comes in parallel forms, useful for establishing a baseline and then monitoring postintervention progress.

Math Tests

The Stanford Diagnostic Mathematics Test, Fourth Edition (SDMT4) and the KeyMath 3 Diagnostic System (KeyMath3-DA) are two of many tests that have been developed to help diagnose difficulties with arithmetic and mathematical concepts. Items on such tests typically test everything from knowledge of basic concepts and operations through applications entailing increasingly advanced problem-solving skills. The KeyMath3-DA (Connolly, 2007) is a standardized test that may be administered to children as young as 4½ and adults as old as 21. According to the website of the test's publisher (Pearson Assessments), the test's development included "a review of state math standards and National Council of Teachers of Mathematics publications," which led to the creation of "a comprehensive blueprint reflecting essential mathematics content, existing curriculum priorities, and national math standards" ("KeyMath," 2011). The test comes in two forms, each containing 10 subtests. Test protocols can either be hand-scored or computer-scored. Because the KeyMath3-DA is individually administered, it is ideally administered by a qualified examiner who is skillful in establishing and maintaining rapport with testtakers and knowledgeable in following the test's standardized procedures.

The SDMT-4 is a standardized test that can provide useful diagnostic insights with regard to the mathematical abilities of children just entering school to just entering college. The test, available in different forms, is amenable for individual or group administration. It contains both multiple-choice and (optional) free-response items. The latter items are designed to provide the examiner with a firsthand understanding of the reasoning, strategies, and methods applied by testtakers to solve different kinds of problems. Test protocols may be hand-scored or centrally scored by the test's publisher. Since 2003 an online version of the SDMT-4 has been available.

Psychoeducational Test Batteries

Psychoeducational test batteries are test kits that generally contain two types of tests: those that measure abilities related to academic success and those that measure educational achievement in areas such as reading and arithmetic. Data derived from these batteries allow for normative comparisons (how the student compares with other students within the same age group), as well as an evaluation of the testtaker's own strengths and weaknesses—all the better to plan educational interventions. Let's begin with a brief look at one psychoeducational battery, the Kaufman Assessment Battery for Children (K-ABC), as well as the extensively revised second edition of the test, the KABC-II.

The Kaufman Assessment Battery for Children (K-ABC) and the Kaufman Assessment Battery for Children, Second Edition (KABC-II)

Developed by a husband-and-wife team of psychologists, the K-ABC was designed for use with testtakers from age 2½ through age 12½. Subtests measuring both intelligence and achievement are included. The K-ABC intelligence subtests are divided into two groups, reflecting the two kinds of information-processing skills identified by Luria and his students (Das et al., 1975; Luria, 1966a, 1966b): *simultaneous skills* and *sequential skills* (see Chapter 9).

Factor-analytic studies of the K-ABC have confirmed the presence of a factor researchers label *simultaneous processing* and a factor labeled *sequential processing*. Perhaps surprisingly, it is an achievement factor that researchers have had difficulty finding. Kaufman (1993) found evidence for the presence of an achievement factor, but independent researchers have different ideas about what that third factor is. Good and Lane (1988) identified the third factor of the K-ABC as *verbal comprehension and reading achievement*. Kaufman and McLean (1986) identified it as *achievement and reading ability*. Keith and Novak (1987) identified it as *reading achievement and verbal reasoning*. Whatever the factor is, the K-ABC Achievement Scale has been shown to predict achievement (Lamp & Krohn, 2001). In addition to questions about what the elusive third factor actually measures, questions have also been raised about whether or not sequential and simultaneous learning are entirely independent (Bracken, 1985; Keith, 1985).

◆

JUST THINK . . .

How realistic is it to expect that children can be taught a variety of subjects by classroom teachers in a way that is individually tailored to each child's unique processing strength as measured by a test?

Recommendations for teaching based on Kaufman and Kaufman's (1983a, 1983b) concept of *processing strength* can be derived from the K-ABC test findings. It may be recommended, for example, that a student whose strength is processing sequentially should be taught using the teaching guidelines for sequential learners. Students who do not have any particular processing strength may be taught using a combination of methods. This model of test interpretation and consequential intervention may engender great enthusiasm on the basis of its intuitive appeal. However, research findings related to this approach have been mixed (Ayres & Cooley, 1986; Good et al., 1989; McCloskey, 1989; Salvia & Hritcko, 1984). Good et al. (1993) concluded that educational decisions based on a child's processing style as defined by the K-ABC did not improve the quality of those decisions.

The next generation of the K-ABC was published in 2004. In the abbreviation for the title of this test, the authors dropped the hyphen between the *K* and the *ABC* and instead inserted a hyphen between the *C* and the roman numeral *II* (KABC-II). But that was only the beginning; there are changes in the age range covered, the structure of the test, and even the conceptual underpinnings of the test.

The age range for the second edition of the test was extended upward (ages 3 to 18) in order to expand the possibility of making ability/achievement comparisons with the same test through high school. Structurally, 10 new subtests were created, 8 of the existing subtests were removed, and only 8 of the original subtests remained. Such significant structural changes in the test must be kept in mind by test users making comparisons between testtaker K-ABC scores and KABC-II scores.

Conceptually, the grounding of the K-ABC in Luria's theory of sequential versus simultaneous processing theory was expanded. In addition, a grounding in the Cattell-Horn-Carroll (CHC) theory was added. This dual theoretical foundation provides the examiner with a choice as to which model of test interpretation is optimal for the particular situation. As stated in the publisher's promotional materials, you can choose the Cattell-Horn-Carroll model for children from a mainstream cultural and language background; if Crystallized Ability would not be a fair indicator of the child's cognitive ability, then you can choose the Luria model, which excludes verbal ability. Administer the same subtests on four or five ability scales. Then, interpret the results based on your chosen model. Either approach gives you a global score that is highly valid and that shows small differences between ethnic groups in comparison with other comprehensive ability batteries.

In general, reviewers of the KABC-II found it to be a psychometrically sound instrument for measuring cognitive abilities. However, few evidenced ease with its new, dual theoretical basis. For example, Thorndike (2007) wondered aloud about assessing two distinct sets of processes and abilities without adequately explaining "how a single test can measure two distinct constructs" (p. 520). Braden and Ouzts (2007) expressed their concern that combining the two interpretive models "smacks of trying to have (and market) it both ways" (p. 519). Bain and Gray (2008) were disappointed that the test manual did not contain sample reports based on each of the models.

Some reviewers raised questions about the variable (or variables) that were actually being measured by the KABC-II. For example, Reynolds et al. (2007) questioned the extent to which certain supplemental tests could best be conceived as measures of specific abilities or measures of multiple abilities. In general, however, they were satisfied that for "school-age children, the KABC-II is closely aligned with the five CHC broad abilities it is intended to measure" (p. 537). Other researchers have confirmed that the KABC-II is indeed tapping the broad CHC abilities (Morgan et al., 2009).

The fourth edition of the Woodcock-Johnson (WJ IV) is another widely known and widely used psychoeducational test battery.

The Woodcock-Johnson IV (WJ IV)

Whereas its predecessor, the WJ III (Woodcock et al., 2000) was a psychoeducational test package consisting of two co-normed batteries (the Tests of Achievement and the Tests of Cognitive Abilities), the WJ IV consists of three co-normed test batteries. Joining the achievement and cognitive abilities tests is a battery of tests designed to measure oral language ability. Included in the latter battery are tests targeting, for example, listening comprehension and speed of lexical access. There are a total of 12 tests in the Tests of Oral Language battery, including nine English language tests, and three parallel tests in Spanish. The battery may be used to gauge proficiency in English or Spanish, and to evaluate various aspects of oral language—the better to assess and understand an assessee's performance on reading, writing, and related tasks.

According to the WJ IV manual, the battery may be used with persons as young as 2, and as old as 90 (or older). Based on the Cattell-Horn-Carroll (CHC) theory of cognitive abilities, the WJ IV yields a multitude of measures including a measure of general intellectual ability (GIA), a measure of fluid abilities (Gf), a measure of crystallized abilities (Gc), and a fluid/crystallized composite (Gf-Gc). Using the Achievement, Cognitive, or Oral Language batteries, the examiner has the flexibility to administer either a standard or extended battery. In general, the extended battery will be used to obtain the most comprehensive and detailed evaluation of an assessee's strengths and weaknesses or educational progress. The standard battery will typically be the measure of choice for brief screenings, periodic re-evaluations, and relatively pinpointed assessments designed to address specific issues related to instruction, performance level, or RtI. In the hands of a skilled assessor, and supplemented by other assessment data (such as data from interviews with parents or other caretakers, RtI data, case history data, data from other standardized measures, and portfolio evaluations), the WJ IV can be a potent tool for diagnostic decision-making, evidence-based intervention, educational planning, and program evaluation.

Tests that rely on the CHC theory can help provide new ways of conceptualizing psychoeducational problems, as well as some novel interventions. Just ask Nationally Certified School Psychologist, Dr. John Garruto (see Figure 10-4).

Other Tools of Assessment in Educational Settings

Beyond traditional achievement, aptitude, and diagnostic instruments lies a wide universe of other instruments and techniques of assessment that may be used in the service of students

Figure 10–4
CHC Theory Applied to Tests: Reflections of a School Psychologist*

Accoring to CHC theory, intelligence can be conceived as being comprised of seven broad abilities, including: crystallized abilities, visual-spatial thinking, auditory processing, processing speed, short-term memory, long-term storage and retrieval, and fluid reasoning. Some of these areas have more to do with certain areas of diagnostic concern than others. For example, fluid reasoning is more important in math than in reading, but auditory processing is more important in reading than in math. Furthermore, although there are seven broad abilities, together they actually account for over seventy different narrow abilities! Now, when I use the WJ-IV (either as my main test or to fill in the gaps for other tests), I always look for those abilities that are related to the problems that the teacher is bringing up. If a child is having problems in reading, I look at skills like crystallized intelligence and auditory processing. If a child is having problems in math, I might look at crystallized intelligence and fluid reasoning . . . learning CHC theory has completely changed now I give assessments.

* This essay was guest-authored by John M. Garruto, Ed.D., NCSP, Nationally Certified School Psychologist.

Used with permission of Dr. John M. Garruto.

© John M. Garruto

and society at large. Let's take a look at a sampling of these approaches, beginning with performance, portfolio, and authentic assessment.

Performance, Portfolio, and Authentic Assessment

For many years the very broad label *performance assessment* has vaguely referred to any type of assessment that requires the examinee to do more than choose the correct response from a small group of alternatives. Thus, for example, essay questions and the development of an art project are examples of performance tasks. By contrast, true–false questions and multiple-choice test items would not be considered performance tasks.

Among testing and assessment professionals, contemporary usage of performance-related terms focuses less on the type of item or task involved and more on the knowledge, skills, and values that the examinee must marshal and exhibit. Additionally, there is a growing tendency to speak of performance tasks and performance assessment in the context of a particular domain of study, where experts in that domain are typically required to set the evaluation standards. For example, a performance task for an architecture student might be to create a blueprint of a contemporary home. The overall quality of the student's work—together with the knowledge, skill, and values inherent in it—will be judged according to standards set by architects acknowledged by the community of architects to have expertise in the construction of contemporary homes. In keeping with these trends, particularly in educational and work settings, we will define a **performance task** as a work sample designed to elicit representative knowledge, skills, and values from a particular domain of study. **Performance assessment** will be defined as an evaluation of performance tasks according to criteria developed by experts from the domain of study tapped by those tasks.

One of many possible types of performance assessment is portfolio assessment. *Portfolio* has many meanings in different contexts. It may refer to a portable carrying case, most typically used to carry artwork, drawings, maps, and the like. Bankers and investors use it as a shorthand reference to one's financial holdings. In the language of psychological and educational assessment, **portfolio** is synonymous with *work sample*. **Portfolio assessment** refers to the evaluation of one's work samples. In many educational settings, dissatisfaction with some more-traditional methods of assessment has led to calls for more performance-based evaluations. *Authentic assessment* (discussed subsequently) is one name given to this trend toward more performance-based assessment. When used in the context of like-minded educational programs, portfolio assessment and authentic assessment are techniques designed to target academic teachings to real-world settings external to the classroom.

JUST THINK . . .

What might your personal portfolio, detailing all that you have learned about psychological testing and assessment to date, look like?

Consider, for example, how students could use portfolios to gauge their progress in a high-school algebra course. They could be instructed to devise their own personal portfolios to illustrate all they have learned about algebra. An important aspect of portfolio assessment is the freedom of the person being evaluated to select the content of the portfolio. Some students might include narrative accounts of their understanding of various algebraic principles. Other students might reflect in writing on the ways algebra can be used in daily life. Still other students might attempt to make a convincing case that they can do some types of algebra problems that they could not do before taking the course. Throughout, the portfolio may be illustrated with items such as gas receipts (complete with algebraic formulas for calculating mileage), paychecks (complete with formulas used to calculate an hourly wage and taxes), and other items limited only by the student's imagination. The illustrations might go from simple to increasingly complex—providing compelling evidence for the student's grasp of the material.

Innovative use of the portfolio method to assess giftedness (Hadaway & Marek-Schroer, 1992) and reading (Henk, 1993), among many other characteristics, can be found in the scholarly literature. Portfolios have also been applied at the college and graduate level as devices to assist students with career decisions (Bernhardt et al., 1993). Benefits of the portfolio approach include engaging students in the assessment process, giving them the opportunity to think generatively, and encouraging them to think about learning as an ongoing and integrated process. A key drawback, however, is the penalty such a technique may levy on the noncreative student. Typically, exceptional portfolios are creative efforts. A person whose strengths do not lie in creativity may have learned the course material but be unable to adequately demonstrate that learning in such a medium. Another drawback, this one from the other side of the instructor's desk, concerns the evaluation of portfolios. Typically, a great deal of time and thought must be devoted to their evaluation. In a lecture class of 300 people, for example, portfolio assessment would be impractical. Also, it is difficult to develop reliable criteria for portfolio assessment, given the great diversity of work products. Hence, inter-rater reliability in portfolio assessment can become a problem.

A related form of assessment is *authentic assessment,* also known as *performance-based assessment* (Baker et al., 1993) as well as other names. We may define **authentic assessment** in educational contexts as evaluation of relevant, meaningful tasks that may be conducted to evaluate learning of academic subject matter but that demonstrate the student's transfer of that study to real-world activities. Authentic assessment of students' writing skills, for example, would therefore be based on writing samples rather than on responses to multiple-choice tests.

Authentic assessment of students' reading would be based on tasks that involve reading—preferably "authentic" reading, such as an article in a local newspaper as opposed to a piece contrived especially for the purposes of assessment. Students in a college-level psychopathology course might be asked to identify patients' psychiatric diagnoses on the basis of videotaped interviews with the patients.

Authentic assessment is thought to increase student interest and the transfer of knowledge to settings outside the classroom. A drawback is that the assessment might assess prior knowledge and experience, not simply what was learned in the classroom. For example, students from homes where there has been a long-standing interest in legislative activities may well do better on an authentic assessment of reading skills that employs an article on legislative activity. Additionally, authentic skill may inadvertently entail the assessment of some skills that have little to do with classroom learning. For example, authentic assessment of learning a cooking school lesson on filleting fish may be confounded with an assessment of the would-be chef's perceptual-motor skills.

Peer Appraisal Techniques

One method of obtaining information about an individual is by asking that individual's peer group to make the evaluation. Techniques employed to obtain such information are termed **peer appraisal** methods. A teacher, a supervisor, or some other group leader may be interested in peer appraisals for a variety of reasons. Peer appraisals can help call needed attention to an individual who is experiencing academic, personal, social, or work-related difficulties—difficulties that, for whatever reason, have not come to the attention of the person in charge. Peer appraisals allow the individual in charge to view members of a group from a different perspective: the perspective of those who work, play, socialize, eat lunch, and walk home with the person being evaluated. In addition to providing information about behavior that is rarely observable, peer appraisals supply information about the group's dynamics: who takes which roles under what conditions. Knowledge of an individual's place within the group is an important aid in guiding the group to optimal efficiency.

Peer appraisal techniques may be used in university settings as well as in grade-school, industrial, and military settings. Such techniques tend to be most useful in settings where the individuals doing the rating have functioned as a group long enough to be able to evaluate each other on specific variables. The nature of peer appraisals may change as a function of changes in the assessment situation and the membership of the group. Thus, for example, an individual who is rated as the shyest in the classroom can theoretically be quite gregarious—and perhaps even be rated the rowdiest—in a peer appraisal undertaken at an after-school center.

One method of peer appraisal that can be employed in elementary school (as well as other) settings is called the Guess Who? technique. Brief descriptive sentences (such as "This person is the most friendly") are read or handed out in the form of questionnaires to the class, and the children are instructed to guess who. Whether negative attributes should be included in the peer appraisal (e.g., "This person is the least friendly") must be decided on an individual basis, considering the potential negative consequences such an appraisal could have on a member of the group.

The *nominating* technique is a method of peer appraisal in which individuals are asked to select or nominate other individuals for various types of activities. A child being interviewed in a psychiatric clinic may be asked, "Who would you most like to go to the moon with?" as a means of determining which parent or other individual is most important to the child. Members of a police department might be asked, "Who would you most like as your partner for your next tour of duty and why?" as a means of finding out which police officers are seen by their peers as especially competent or incompetent.

The results of a peer appraisal can be graphically illustrated. One graphic method of organizing such data is the **sociogram.** Figures such as circles or squares are drawn to represent different individuals, and lines and arrows are drawn to indicate various types of interaction. At a glance, the sociogram can provide information such as who is popular in the group, who tends to be rejected by the group, and who is relatively neutral in the opinion of the group. Nominating techniques have been the most widely researched of the peer appraisal techniques, and they have generally been found to be highly reliable and valid. Still, the careful user of such techniques must be aware that an individual's perceptions within a group are constantly changing. Anyone who has ever watched reality television shows such as *Survivor* or *The Apprentice* is certainly aware of such group dynamics. As some members leave the group and others join it, the positions and roles the members hold within the group change. New alliances form, and as a result, all group members may be looked at in a new light. It is therefore important to periodically update and verify information.

Measuring Study Habits, Interests, and Attitudes

Academic performance is the result of a complex interplay of a number of factors. Ability and motivation are inseparable partners in the pursuit of academic success. A number of instruments designed to look beyond ability and toward factors such as study habits, interests, and attitudes have been published. For example, the Study Habits Checklist, designed for use with students in grades 9 through 14, consists of 37 items that assess study habits with respect to note taking, reading material, and general study practices. In the development of the test, potential items were presented for screening to 136 Phi Beta Kappa members at three colleges. This procedure was based on the premise that good students are the best judges of important and effective study techniques (Preston, 1961). The judges were asked to evaluate the items according to their usefulness to students having difficulty with college course material. Although the judges conceded that they did not always engage in these practices themselves, they identified the techniques they deemed the most useful in study activities. Standardization for the Checklist took place in 1966, and percentile norms were based on a sample of several thousand high-school and college students residing in Pennsylvania. In one validity study, 302 college freshmen who had demonstrated learning difficulties and had been referred to a learning skills center were evaluated with the Checklist. As predicted, it was found that these students demonstrated poor study practices, particularly in the areas of note taking and proper use of study time (Bucofsky, 1971).

If a teacher knows a child's areas of interest, instructional activities engaging those interests can be employed. The What I Like to Do Interest Inventory consists of 150 forced-choice items that assess four areas of interests: academic interests, artistic interests, occupational interests, and interests in leisure time (play) activities. Included in the test materials are suggestions for designing instructional activities that are consonant with the designated areas of interest.

JUST THINK . . .

While we're on the subject of study habits, skills, and attitudes, this seems an appropriate time to raise a question about how these variables are related to another, more global variable: *personality.* Are one's study habits, skills, and attitudes a part of one's personality? Why might it be useful to think about them as such?

Attitude inventories used in educational settings assess student attitudes toward a variety of school-related factors. Interest in student attitudes is based on the premise that "positive reactions to school may increase the likelihood that students will stay in school, develop a lasting commitment to learning, and use the school setting to advantage" (Epstein & McPartland, 1978, p. 2). Some instruments assess attitudes in specific subject areas, whereas others, such as the Survey of School Attitudes and the Quality of School Life Scales, are more general in scope.

The Survey of Study Habits and Attitudes (SSHA) and the Study Attitudes and Methods Survey combine the assessment of attitudes with the assessment of study methods. The SSHA, intended for use in grades 7 through college, consists of 100 items tapping poor study skills and attitudes that could affect academic performance. Two forms are available, Form H for grades 7 to 12 and Form C for college, each requiring 20 to 25 minutes to complete. Students respond to items on the following 5-point scale: *rarely, sometimes, frequently, generally,* or *almost always.* Test items are divided into six areas: Delay Avoidance, Work Methods, Study Habits, Teacher Approval, Education Acceptance, and Study Attitudes. The test yields a study skills score, an attitude score, and a total orientation score.

As you *just think* about the questions raised regarding study and personality, *just know* that you will learn about personality and its assessment in the next two chapters.

Self-Assessment

Test your understanding of elements of this chapter by seeing if you can explain each of the following terms, expressions, names, and abbreviations:

achievement test
Apgar number
aptitude test
at risk
authentic assessment
checklist
Common Core State Standards
cold reading
curriculum-based assessment (CBA)
curriculum-based measurement (CBM)
diagnostic information
diagnostic test

evaluative information
informal evaluation
integrative assessment
K-ABC
KABC-II
LPAD
locator test
peer appraisal
performance assessment
performance task
portfolio
portfolio assessment
problem-solving model

prognostic test
psychoeducational test battery
rating scale
readiness test
response to intervention model
sociogram
specific learning disability (SLD)
syndrome
Vygotsky, Lev
WJ III
zone of proximal development

11

Personality Assessment: An Overview

In a 1950s rock 'n' roll classic song entitled "Personality," singer Lloyd Price described the subject of that song with the words *walk, talk, smile,* and *charm.* In so doing, Price used the term *personality* the way most people tend to use it. For laypeople, *personality* refers to components of an individual's makeup that can elicit positive or negative reactions from others. Someone who consistently tends to elicit positive reactions from others is thought to have a "good personality." Someone who consistently tends to elicit not-so-good reactions from others is thought to have a "bad personality" or, perhaps worse yet, "no personality." We also hear of people described in other ways, with adjectives such as *aggressive, warm,* or *cold.* For professionals in the field of behavioral science, the terms tend to be better-defined, if not more descriptive.

Personality and Personality Assessment

Personality

Dozens of different definitions of personality exist in the psychology literature. Some definitions appear to be all-inclusive. For example, McClelland (1951, p. 69) defined personality as "the most adequate conceptualization of a person's behavior in all its detail." Menninger (1953, p. 23) defined it as "the individual as a whole, his height and weight and love and hates and blood pressure and reflexes; his smiles and hopes and bowed legs and enlarged tonsils. It means all that anyone is and that he is trying to become." Some definitions focus narrowly on a particular aspect of the individual (Goldstein, 1963), whereas others view the individual in the context of society (Sullivan, 1953). Some theorists avoid any definition at all. For example, Byrne (1974, p. 26) characterized the entire area of personality psychology as "psychology's garbage bin in that any research which doesn't fit other existing categories can be labeled 'personality.'"

In their widely read and authoritative textbook *Theories of Personality,* Hall and Lindzey (1970, p. 9) wrote: "It is our conviction that *no substantive definition of personality can be applied with any generality*" and "*Personality is defined by the particular empirical concepts which are a part of the theory of personality employed by the observer*" [emphasis in the original]. Noting that there were important theoretical differences in many theories of personality, Hall and Lindzey encouraged their readers to select a definition of personality from the many presented and adopt it as their own.

For our purposes, we will define **personality** as an individual's unique constellation of psychological traits that is relatively stable over time. We view this definition as one that has the advantage of parsimony yet still is flexible enough to incorporate a wide variety of variables. Included in this definition, then, are variables on which individuals may differ, such as values, interests, attitudes, worldview, acculturation, sense of humor, cognitive and behavioral styles, and personality states.

JUST THINK . . .

Despite great effort, a definition of personality itself—much like a definition of intelligence—has been somewhat elusive. Why do you think this is so?

Personality Assessment

Personality assessment may be defined as the measurement and evaluation of psychological traits, states, values, interests, attitudes, worldview, acculturation, sense of humor, cognitive and behavioral styles, and/or related individual characteristics. In this chapter we overview the process of personality assessment, including different approaches to the construction of personality tests. In Chapter 12, we will focus on various methods of personality assessment, including objective, projective, and behavioral methods. Before all that, however, some background is needed regarding the use of the terms *trait, type,* and *state.*

Traits, Types, and States

Personality traits Just as no consensus exists regarding the definition of personality, there is none regarding the definition of *trait.* Theorists such as Gordon Allport (1937) have tended to view personality traits as real physical entities that are "bona fide mental structures in each personality" (p. 289). For Allport, a trait is a "generalized and focalized neuropsychic system (peculiar to the individual) with the capacity to render many stimuli functionally equivalent, and to initiate and guide consistent (equivalent) forms of adaptive and expressive behavior" (p. 295). Robert Holt (1971) wrote that there "*are* real structures inside people that determine their behavior in lawful ways" (p. 6), and he went on to conceptualize these structures as changes in brain chemistry that might occur as a result of learning: "Learning causes submicroscopic structural changes in the brain, probably in the organization of its biochemical substance" (p. 7). Raymond Cattell (1950) also conceptualized traits as mental structures, but for him *structure* did not necessarily imply actual physical status.

Our own preference is to shy away from definitions that elevate *trait* to the status of physical existence. We view psychological traits as attributions made in an effort to identify threads of consistency in behavioral patterns. In this context, a definition of **personality trait** offered by Guilford (1959, p. 6) has great appeal: "Any distinguishable, relatively enduring way in which one individual varies from another."

This relatively simple definition has some aspects in common with the writings of other personality theorists such as Allport (1937), Cattell (1950, 1965), and Eysenck (1961). The word *distinguishable* indicates that behaviors labeled with different trait terms are actually different from one another. For example, a behavior labeled "friendly" should be distinguishable from a behavior labeled "rude." The *context,* or the situation in which the behavior is displayed, is important in applying trait terms to behaviors. A behavior present in one context may be labeled with one trait term, but the same behavior exhibited in another context may be better described using another trait term. For example, if we observe someone involved in a lengthy, apparently interesting conversation, we would observe the context before drawing any conclusions about the person's traits. A person talking with a friend over lunch may be demonstrating friendliness, whereas that same person talking to that same

JUST THINK . . .

What is another example of how the trait term selected by an observer is dependent both on the behavior emitted as well as the context of that behavior?

friend during a wedding ceremony may be considered rude. Thus, the trait term selected by an observer is dependent both on the behavior itself and on the context in which it appears.

A measure of behavior in a particular context may be obtained using varied tools of psychological assessment. For example, using naturalistic observation, an observer could watch the assessee interact with co-workers during break time. Alternatively, the assessee could be administered a self-report questionnaire that probes various aspects of the assessee's interaction with co-workers during break time.

In his definition of trait, Guilford did not assert that traits represent enduring ways in which individuals vary from one another. Rather, he said *relatively enduring. Relatively* emphasizes that exactly how a particular trait manifests itself is, at least to some extent, dependent on the situation. For example, a "violent" parolee generally may be prone to behave in a rather subdued way with his parole officer and much more violently in the presence of his family and friends. Allport (1937) addressed the issue of cross-situational consistency of traits—or lack of it—as follows:

> Perfect consistency will never be found and must not be expected. . . . People may be ascendant and submissive, perhaps submissive only towards those individuals bearing traditional symbols of authority and prestige; and towards everyone else aggressive and domineering. . . . The ever-changing environment raises now one trait and now another to a state of active tension. (p. 330)

For years personality theorists and assessors have assumed that personality traits are relatively enduring over the course of one's life. Roberts and DelVecchio (2000) explored the endurance of traits by means of a meta-analysis of 152 longitudinal studies. These researchers concluded that trait consistency increases in a steplike pattern until one is 50 to 59 years old, at which time such consistency peaks. Their findings may be interpreted as compelling testimony to the relatively enduring nature of personality traits over the course of one's life. Do you think the physically aggressive hockey player pictured in Figure 11–1 will still be as physically aggressive during his retirement years?

Returning to our elaboration of Guilford's definition, note that *trait* is described as a way in which one individual varies from another. Let's emphasize here that the attribution of a trait term is always a *relative* phenomenon. For instance, some behavior described as "patriotic" may differ greatly from other behavior also described as "patriotic." There are no absolute standards. In describing an individual as patriotic, we are, in essence, making an unstated comparison with the degree of patriotic behavior that could reasonably be expected to be exhibited under the same or similar circumstances.

Classic research on the subject of cross-situational consistency in traits has pointed to a *lack* of consistency with regard to traits such as honesty (Hartshorne & May, 1928), punctuality (Dudycha, 1936), conformity (Hollander & Willis, 1967), attitude toward authority (Burwen & Campbell, 1957), and introversion/extraversion (Newcomb, 1929). These are the types of studies cited by Mischel (1968, 1973, 1977, 1979) and others who have been critical of the predominance of the concept of traits in personality theory. Such critics may also allude to the fact that some undetermined portion of behavior exhibited in public may be governed more by societal expectations and cultural role restrictions than by an individual's personality traits (Barker, 1963; Goffman, 1963). Research designed to shed light on the primacy of individual differences, as opposed to situational factors in behavior, is methodologically complex (Golding, 1975), and a definitive verdict as to the primacy of the trait or the situation is simply not in.

Personality types   Having defined personality as a unique constellation of traits, we might define a **personality type** as a constellation of traits that is similar in pattern to one identified category of personality within a taxonomy of personalities. Whereas traits are frequently discussed as if they were *characteristics* possessed by an individual, types are more clearly

Figure 11–1
Trait Aggressiveness and Flare-ups on the Ice

Bushman and Wells (1998) administered a self-report measure of trait aggressiveness (the Physical Aggression subscale of the Aggression Questionnaire) to 91 high-school team hockey players before the start of the season. The players responded to items such as "Once in a while I cannot control my urge to strike another person" presented in Likert scale format ranging from 1 to 5 (where 1 corresponded to "extremely uncharacteristic of me" and 5 corresponded to "extremely characteristic of me"). At the end of the season, trait aggressiveness scores were examined with respect to minutes served in the penalty box for aggressive penalties such as fighting, slashing, and tripping. The preseason measure of trait aggressiveness predicted aggressive penalty minutes served. The study is particularly noteworthy because the test data were used to predict real-life aggression, not a laboratory analogue of aggression such as the administration of electric shock. The authors recommended that possible applications of the Aggression Questionnaire be explored in other settings where aggression is a problematic behavior.
© Sven Nackstrand/AFP/Getty Images

descriptions of people. So, for example, describing an individual as "depressed" is different from describing that individual as a "depressed type." The latter term has more far-reaching implications regarding characteristic aspects of the individual, such as the person's worldview, activity level, capacity to enjoy life, and level of social interest.

At least since Hippocrates' classification of people into four types (melancholic, phlegmatic, choleric, and sanguine), there has been no shortage of personality typologies through the ages. A typology devised by Carl Jung (1923) became the basis for the Myers-Briggs Type Indicator (MBTI; Myers & Briggs, 1943/1962). An assumption guiding the development of this test was that people exhibit definite preferences in the way that they perceive or become aware of—and judge or arrive at conclusions about—people, events, situations, and ideas. According to Myers (1962, p. 1), these differences in perception and judging result in "corresponding differences in their reactions, in their interests, values, needs, and motivations, in what they do best, and in what they like to do." For example, in one study designed to better understand the personality of chess players, the Myers-Briggs Type Indicator was administered to 2,165 chess players, including players at the masters and senior masters level. The chess players were found to be significantly more introverted, intuitive, and thinking (as opposed to feeling) than members of

> **JUST THINK . . .**
>
> What are the possible benefits of classifying people into types? What possible problems may arise from doing so?

the general population. The investigator also found masters to be more judgmental than the general population (Kelly, 1985).

John Holland (Figure 11–2) argued that most people can be categorized as one of the following six personality types: Artistic, Enterprising, Investigative, Social, Realistic, or Conventional (Holland, 1973, 1985, 1997, 1999). His Self-Directed Search test (SDS; Holland et al., 1994) is a self-administered, self-scored, and self-interpreted aid used to type people according to this system and to offer vocational guidance. Another personality typology, this one having only two categories, was devised by cardiologists Meyer Friedman and Ray Rosenman (1974; Rosenman et al., 1975). They conceived of a **Type A personality,** characterized by competitiveness, haste, restlessness, impatience, feelings of being time-pressured, and strong needs for achievement and dominance. A **Type B personality** has the opposite of the Type A's traits: mellow or laid-back. A 52-item self-report inventory called the Jenkins Activity Survey (JAS; Jenkins et al., 1979) has been used to type respondents as Type A or Type B personalities.

The personality typology that has attracted the most attention from researchers and practitioners alike is associated with scores on a test called the MMPI (as well as all of its successors—discussed later in this chapter). Data from the administration of these tests, as with others, are frequently discussed in terms of the patterns of scores that emerge on the subtests. This pattern is referred to as a *profile*. In general, a **profile** is a narrative description, graph, table, or other representation of the extent to which a person has demonstrated certain targeted characteristics as a result of the administration or application of tools of assessment.[1] In the term **personality profile,** the targeted characteristics are typically traits, states, or types. With specific reference to the MMPI, different profiles of scores are associated with different patterns of behavior. So, for example, a particular MMPI profile designated as "2–4–7" is associated with a type of individual who has a history of alcohol abuse alternating with sobriety and self-recrimination (Dahlstrom, 1995).

Figure 11–2
John L. Holland (1919–2008)

John Holland was well known for the employment-related personality typology he developed, as well as the Self-Directed Search (SDS), a measure of one's interests and perceived abilities. The test is based on Holland's theory of vocational personality. At the heart of this theory is the view that occupational choice has a great deal to do with one's personality and self-perception of abilities. Holland's work was the subject of controversy in the 1970s. Critics asserted that measured differences between the interests of men and women were an artifact of sex bias. Holland argued that such differences reflected valid variance. As the author of Holland's obituary in American Psychologist recalled, "He did not bend willy-nilly in the winds of political correctness" (Gottfredson, 2009, p. 561).
© John Hopkins University

1. The verb *to profile* refers to the creation of such a description. The term **profile analysis** refers to the interpretation of patterns of scores on a test or test battery. Profile analysis is frequently used to generate diagnostic hypotheses from intelligence test data. The noun **profiler** refers to an occupation: one who creates personality profiles of crime suspects to assist law enforcement personnel in capturing the profiled suspects. More on the work of profilers in Chapter 13.

Personality states   The word **state** has been used in at least two distinctly different ways in the personality assessment literature. In one usage, a personality state is an inferred psychodynamic disposition designed to convey the dynamic quality of id, ego, and superego in perpetual conflict. Assessment of these psychodynamic dispositions may be made through the use of various psychoanalytic techniques such as free association, word association, symbolic analysis of interview material, dream analysis, and analysis of slips of the tongue, accidents, jokes, and forgetting.

Presently, a more popular usage of the term *state*—and the one we use in the discussion that follows—refers to the transitory exhibition of some personality trait. Put another way, the use of the word *trait* presupposes a relatively enduring behavioral predisposition, whereas the term *state* is indicative of a relatively temporary predisposition (Chaplin et al., 1988). Thus, for example, your friend may be accurately described as being "in an anxious state" before her midterms, though no one who knows her well would describe her as "an anxious person."

> **JUST THINK . . .**
>
> You experience "butterflies" in your stomach just before asking someone to whom you are attracted to accompany you to the movies. Would this feeling better be characterized as a state or a trait?

Measuring personality states amounts, in essence, to a search for and an assessment of the strength of traits that are relatively transitory or fairly situation specific. Relatively few personality tests seek to distinguish traits from states. Pathbreaking work in this area was done by Charles D. Spielberger and his associates (Spielberger et al., 1980). These researchers developed a number of personality inventories designed to distinguish various states from traits. In the manual for the State-Trait Anxiety Inventory (STAI), for example, we find that state anxiety refers to a transitory experience of tension because of a particular situation. By contrast, trait anxiety or anxiety proneness refers to a relatively stable or enduring personality characteristic. The STAI test items consist of short descriptive statements, and subjects are instructed to indicate either (1) how they feel right now or at this moment (and to indicate the intensity of the feeling), or (2) how they generally feel (and to record the frequency of the feeling). The test-retest reliability coefficients reported in the manual are consistent with the theoretical premise that trait anxiety is the more enduring characteristic, whereas state anxiety is transitory.

Personality Assessment: Some Basic Questions

For what type of employment is a person with this type of personality best suited?

Is this individual sufficiently well adjusted for military service?

What emotional and other adjustment-related factors may be responsible for this student's level of academic achievement?

What pattern of traits and states does this psychotherapy client evince, and to what extent may this pattern be deemed pathological?

How has this patient's personality been affected by neurological trauma?

These questions are a sampling of the kind that might lead to a referral for personality assessment. Collectively, these types of referral questions provide insight into a more general question in a clinical context: Why assess personality?

We might raise the same question in the context of basic research and find another wide world of potential applications for personality assessment. For example, aspects of personality could be explored in identifying determinants of knowledge about health (Beier & Ackerman, 2003), in categorizing different types of commitment in intimate relationships (Frank & Brandstaetter, 2002), in determining peer response to a team's weakest link (Jackson & LePine,

2003), or even in the service of national defense to identify those prone to terrorism. Personality assessment is a staple in developmental research, be it tracking trait development over time (McCrae et al., 2002) or studying some uniquely human characteristic such as moral judgment (Eisenberg et al., 2002). From a health psychology perspective, there are a number of personality variables (such as perfectionism, self-criticism, dependency, and neuroticism) that have been linked to physical and psychological disorders (Flett & Hewitt, 2002; Klein et al., 2011; Kotov et al., 2010; Zuroff et al., 2004; Sturman, 2011). In the corporate world, personality assessment is a key tool of the human resources department, relied on to aid in hiring, firing, promoting, transferring, and related decisions. Perhaps as long as there have been tests to measure people's interests, there have been questions regarding how those interests relate to personality (Larson et al., 2002). In military organizations around the world, leadership is a sought-after trait, and personality tests help identify who has it (see, for example, Bradley et al., 2002; Handler, 2001). In the most general sense, basic research involving personality assessment helps to validate or invalidate theories of behavior and to generate new hypotheses.

Tangentially, let's note that a whole other perspective on the *why* of personality assessment emerges with a consideration of cross-species research. For example, Gosling, Kwan, & John, (2003) viewed their research on the personality of dogs as paving the way for future research in previously uncharted areas such as the exploration of environmental effects on personality. Weiss et al. (2002) viewed cross-species research as presenting an opportunity to explore the heritability of personality. The fascinating research program of Winnie Eckardt and her colleagues at the Dian Fossey Gorilla Fund International is the subject of this chapter's *Close-Up.*

Beyond the *why* of personality assessment are several other questions that must be addressed in any overview of the enterprise. Approaches to personality assessment differ in terms of *who* is being assessed, *what* is being assessed, *where* the assessment is conducted, and *how* the assessment is conducted. Let's take a closer look at each of these related issues.

JUST THINK . . .

What differences in terms of accuracy and reliability of report would you expect when one is reporting on one's own personality as opposed to when another person is reporting about someone's personality?

Who?

Who is being assessed, and who is doing the assessing? Some methods of personality assessment rely on the assessee's own self-report. Assessees may respond to interview questions, answer questionnaires in writing, blacken squares on computer answer forms, or sort cards with various terms on them—all with the ultimate objective of providing the assessor with a personality-related self-description. By contrast, other methods of personality assessment rely on informants other than the person being assessed to provide personality-related information. So, for example, parents or teachers may be asked to participate in the personality assessment of a child by providing ratings, judgments, opinions, and impressions relevant to the child's personality.

The self as the primary referent   People typically undergo personality assessment so that they, as well as the assessor, can learn something about who they are. In many instances, the assessment or some aspect of it requires **self-report,** or a process wherein information about assessees is supplied by the assessees themselves. Self-reported information may be obtained in the form of diaries kept by assessees or in the form of responses to oral or written questions or test items. In some cases, the information sought by the assessor is so private that only the individual assessees themselves are capable of providing it. For example, when researchers investigated the psychometric soundness of the Sexual Sensation Seeking Scale with a sample of college students, only the students themselves could provide the highly personal information needed. The researchers viewed their reliance on self-report as a possible limitation of the study, but noted that this methodology "has been the standard practice in this area of research because no gold standard exists for verifying participants' reports of sexual behaviors" (Gaither & Sellbom, 2003, p. 165).

The Personality of Gorillas*

When he turned 17-years-old, a mountain gorilla named Cantsbee (see Figure 1) took over the leadership of what was to become the largest, ever-observed gorilla group (which included up to 65 members). At this writing, he has held this position for over 20 years, despite challenges from rivals within his group, and from outside attackers. Cantsbee also earned the respect and admiration of the field researchers and assistants who work with him. He leads his group in a sensible way and seems to know when it's time to be supportive, administer discipline, take a strong leadership role, or adopt a laissez-faire approach.

So, what does it take for a gorilla to win such enviable status from gorilla peers and human observers? Apart from morphological traits that quite likely play a role, such as body size, there are personality traits to be considered as well. This and other questions motivated Eckardt et al. (2015) to initiate the first study of mountain gorilla personality.

Perhaps the ideal species for studying personality in wild ape populations is the Virunga mountain gorilla. This is so because over 70% of the remaining 480 gorillas of this species (Gray et al., 2013) are habituated to human presence and known by rangers and researchers individually, most since birth. The Karisoke Research Center in Rwanda is one of the longest-existing primate research field sites with almost 50 years of mountain gorilla monitoring in the Virungas. Well-trained trackers, data technicians, and researchers familiar with gorilla behavior follow about 40% of the population daily. Many years of experience and in-depth knowledge of each gorilla in various contexts make trackers as suitable for assessing the personalities of gorillas as parents are for assessing the personalities of their children.

Between 2007 and 2008, eight of the most experienced Karisoke field staff assessed the personalities of gorillas that they knew well using a version of the Hominoid Personality Questionnaire (HPQ, Weiss et al., 2009). This questionnaire was derived by sampling traits from the human "Big-5," and adapting them so that they are suitable for assessing the personalities of nonhuman primates. Specifically, each of its 54 items is accompanied by a brief description to set the item in the context of gorilla behavior. For example, *dominant* is defined as "Subject is able to displace, threaten, or take food from other gorillas" or "subject may express high status by decisively intervening in social interactions." Another example: *affectionate* is defined as

*This *Close-Up* was guest-authored by Winnie Eckardt who has worked with wild mountain gorillas for over 10 years at the Dian Fossey Gorilla Fund International Karisoke Research Center in Rwanda, and Alexander Weiss of the University of Edinburgh and the Scottish Primate Research Group.

Figure 1
Cantsbee

Cantsbee is the oldest silverback gorilla at the Dian Fossey Gorilla Fund International's Karisoke Research Center in Rwanda. Prior to his birth in 1978, the researchers at Karisoke all thought that his mother was a male, not a female. Dian Fossey's shocked reaction to the birth was encapsulated in her exclamation, "This can't be!" Taking their cue from Fosse, the Rwandan field assistants promptly christened the newborn gorilla, "Cantsbee."

© The Dian Fossey Gorilla Fund International

"subject seems to have a warm attachment or closeness with other gorillas. This may entail frequently grooming, touching, embracing, or lying next to others."

The HPQ was prepared in both English and French since both are official languages of Rwanda. The Rwandan raters were instructed to score gorillas on each trait using a Likert scale ranging from (1) "either total absence or negligible amounts" to (7) "extremely large amounts." A prerating training session with a professional Rwandan translator (who held a Bachelor's degree in French and English) was conducted to ensure that language barriers had a minimal influence on the understanding of the rating procedure and the meaning of each traits. Inter-rater reliability was checked and found to be satisfactory.

Virunga mountain gorillas are folivorous, meaning that they eat mostly leaves, and that they live in what could be described as a "huge salad bowl" (Fossey & Harcourt, 1977; Vedder, 1984; Watts, 1985). The fact that food is plentiful and available all year round is believed to play a role in the lower level of aggression in and between groups of gorillas (Robbins et al., 2005). Other great apes, such as chimpanzees, depend on seasonally available, scattered fruit. As a result, competition for food and

(continued)

The Personality of Gorillas (continued)

levels of aggression can be high in these species (Harcourt & Stewart, 2007).

It is also a fact that gorilla society is hierarchically structured. They live in relatively stable, cohesive social groups with male–female relationships forming the core of their society (Harcourt & Stewart, 2007). Emigration from the natal group is common for both males and females (Robbins et al., 2007; Watts, 1990). Females transfer between groups during intergroup encounters to avoid inbreeding, whereas males become solitary after leaving their natal group to increase breeding opportunities by recruiting females from existing groups.

Because gorillas live in stable and predictable environments with limited food competition, and less vulnerability to the stressors present in the lives of other great apes, the researchers hypothesized that the subjects would be rated as emotionally stable, with generally low levels on traits related to neuroticism. Further, the researchers hypothesized that the subjects would be rated as low in aggression and high in sociability.

As described in greater detail elsewhere (Eckardt et al., 2015), the researchers' hypotheses were confirmed through evaluation of correlations between HPQ scores on personality trait dimensions and corresponding historical behavior of the subjects as noted in archival records. So, for example, in gorilla society, the role of dominant males includes group protection duties as well as the mediation of within-group social conflicts (Schaller, 1963; Watts, 1996). Thus, to ascend the gorilla social hierarchy in dominance, traits such as being *protective, helpful, and sensitive* would seem to be a must. In fact, Eckardt et al. (2015) reported that gorillas with a high social rank scored high

on Dominance. Additionally, rate of intervening to mediate social conflicts in the group was also associated with gorilla Dominance. Another interesting finding was that gorillas high on Dominance stare less at other gorillas. Also, with regard to grooming behavior, gorillas tend to approach and groom group members with higher Dominance scores rather than vice versa.

So, how does Cantsbee's personality compares to other gorillas? Not surprisingly, Cantsbee scored second highest in Dominance. He also scored very high on the Sociability dimension, and his score on the Openness dimension was below average. What is the significance of findings such as these?

Since Darwin (1872), personality research has included the study of personality in species other than our own (Gosling & John, 1999). Darwin believed that behavioral and affective traits evolve just like morphological traits. If that is the case, then we should be able to trace the origins of human personality—and more specifically, personality dimensions such as Openness, Conscientiousness, Extraversion, Agreeableness, and Neuroticism (otherwise known as the "Big-5" or five-factor model; Digman, 1990; Goldberg, 1990). But how do we do that? While fossils can tell us a lot about the evolution of physical features, they tell us nothing about the evolution of personality. Perhaps evolutionary insights can be gleaned by comparing the personality of humans with those of our closest, non-human relatives: the great apes, At the very least, the study of great apes holds the promise of learning how assorted variables (such as differences in ecology, social systems, and life history) may act to shape personality.

Used with permission of Winnie Eckhardt.

Self-report methods are very commonly used to explore an assessee's *self-concept*. **Self-concept** may be defined as one's attitudes, beliefs, opinions, and related thoughts about oneself. Inferences about an assessee's self-concept may be derived from many tools of assessment. However, the tool of choice is typically a dedicated **self-concept measure;** that is, an instrument designed to yield information relevant to how an individual sees him- or herself with regard to selected psychological variables. Data from such an instrument are usually interpreted in the context of how others may see themselves on the same or similar variables. In the Beck Self-Concept Test (BST; Beck & Stein, 1961), named after senior author, psychiatrist Aaron T. Beck, respondents are asked to compare themselves to other people on variables such as looks, knowledge, and the ability to tell jokes.

A number of self-concept measures for children have been developed. Some representative tests include the Tennessee Self-Concept Scale and the Piers-Harris Self-Concept Scale. The latter test contains 80 self-statements (such as "I don't have any friends") to which respondents from grades 3 to 12 respond either *yes* or *no* as the statement applies to them. Factor analysis has suggested that the items cover six general areas of self-concept: behavior, intellectual and school status, physical appearance and attributes, anxiety, popularity, and happiness and satisfaction. The Beck Self-Concept Test was extended down as one component of a series called the Beck Youth Inventories–Second Edition (BYI-II) developed by senior author, psychologist Judith Beck (Aaron T. Beck's daughter). In addition to a self-concept measure, the BYI-II includes inventories to measures depression, anxiety, anger, and disruptive behavior in children and adolescents aged 7 to 18 years.

Some measures of self-concept are based on the notion that states and traits related to self-concept are to a large degree context-dependent—that is, ever-changing as a result of the particular situation (Callero, 1992). The term **self-concept differentiation** refers to the degree to which a person has different self-concepts in different roles (Donahue et al., 1993). People characterized as *highly differentiated* are likely to perceive themselves quite differently in various roles. For example, a highly differentiated businessman in his 40s may perceive himself as motivated and hard-driving in his role at work, conforming and people-pleasing in his role as son, and emotional and passionate in his role as husband. By contrast, people whose concept of self is not very differentiated tend to perceive themselves similarly across their social roles. According to Donahue et al. (1993), people with low levels of self-concept differentiation tend to be healthier psychologically, perhaps because of their more unified and coherent sense of self.

JUST THINK . . .

Highly differentiated or not very differentiated in self-concept—which do *you* think is preferable? Why?

Assuming that assessees have reasonably accurate insight into their own thinking and behavior, and assuming that they are motivated to respond to test items honestly, self-report measures can be extremely valuable. An assessee's candid and accurate self-report can illustrate what that individual is thinking, feeling, and doing. Unfortunately, some assessees may intentionally or unintentionally paint distorted pictures of themselves in self-report measures.

Consider what would happen if employers were to rely on job applicants' representations concerning their personality and their suitability for a particular job. Employers might be led to believe they have found a slew of perfect applicants. Many job applicants—as well as people in contexts as diverse as high-school reunions, singles bars, and child custody hearings—attempt to "fake good" in their presentation of themselves to other people.

JUST THINK . . .

Has anyone you know engaged in "faking good" or "faking bad" behavior (in or out of the context of assessment)? Why?

The other side of the "faking good" coin is "faking bad." Litigants in civil actions who claim injury may seek high awards as compensation for their alleged pain, suffering, and emotional distress—all of which may be exaggerated and dramatized for the benefit of a judge and jury. The accused in a criminal action may view time in a mental institution as preferable to time in prison (or capital punishment) and strategically choose an insanity defense—with accompanying behavior and claims to make such a defense as believable as possible. A homeless person who prefers the environs of a mental hospital to that of the street may attempt to fake bad on tests and in interviews if failure to do so will result in discharge. In the days of the military draft, it was not uncommon for draft resisters to fake bad on psychiatric examinations in their efforts to be deferred.

Some testtakers truly may be impaired with regard to their ability to respond accurately to self-report questions. They may lack insight, for example, because of certain medical or psychological conditions at the time of assessment. By contrast, other testtakers seem blessed with an abundance of self-insight that they can convey with ease and expertise on self-report measures. It is for this latter group of individuals that self-report measures, according to Burisch (1984), will not reveal anything the testtaker does not already know. Of course, Burisch may have overstated the case. Even people with an abundance of self-insight can profit from taking the time to reflect about their own thoughts and behaviors, especially if they are unaccustomed to doing so.

Another person as the referent In some situations, the best available method for the assessment of personality, behavior, or both involves reporting by a third party such as a parent, teacher, peer, supervisor, spouse, or trained observer. Consider, for example, the assessment of a child for emotional difficulties. The child may be unable or unwilling to complete any measure (self-report, performance, or otherwise) that will be of value in making a valid determination concerning that child's emotional status. Even case history data may be of minimal value because the problems may be so subtle as to become evident only after careful and sustained observation. In such cases, the use of a test in which the testtaker or respondent is an informant— but not the subject of study—may be valuable. In basic personality research, this third-party approach to assessment has been found useful, especially when the third-party reporter knows the subject of the evaluation very well. Proceeding under the assumption that spouses should be familiar enough with each other to serve as good informants, one study examined self-versus spouse ratings on personality-related variables (South et al., 2011). Self and spousal ratings were found to be significantly correlated, and this relationship was stronger than that typically found between self- and peer ratings in personality research.

JUST THINK . . .

Do you believe meaningful insights are better derived through self-assessment or through assessment by someone else? Why?

The Personality Inventory for Children (PIC) and its revision, the PIC-2 (pronounced "pick two"), are examples of a kind of standardized interview of a child's parent. Although the child is the subject of the test, the respondent is the parent (usually the mother), guardian, or other adult qualified to respond with reference to the child's characteristic behavior. The test consists of a series of true–false items designed to be free of racial and gender bias. The items may be administered by computer or paper and pencil. Test results yield scores that provide clinical information and shed light on the validity of the testtaker's response patterns. A number of studies attest to the validity of the PIC for its intended purpose (Kline et al., 1992; Kline et al., 1993; Lachar & Wirt, 1981; Lachar et al., 1985; Wirt et al., 1984). However, as with any test that relies on the observations and judgment of a rater, some concerns about this instrument have also been expressed (Achenbach, 1981; Cornell, 1985).

In general, there are many cautions to consider when one person undertakes to evaluate another. These cautions are by no means limited to the area of personality assessment. Rather, in any situation when one individual undertakes to rate another individual, it is important to understand the dynamics of the situation. Although a rater's report can provide a wealth of information about an assessee, it may also be instructive to look at the source of that information.

Raters may vary in the extent to which they are, or strive to be, scrupulously neutral, favorably generous, or harshly severe in their ratings. Generalized biases to rate in a particular direction are referred to in terms such as **leniency error** or **generosity error** and **severity error.** A general tendency to rate everyone near the midpoint of a rating scale is termed an **error of central tendency.** In some situations, a particular set of circumstances may create a certain bias. For example, a teacher might be disposed to judging one pupil very favorably because that pupil's older sister was teacher's pet in a prior class. This variety of favorable response bias is sometimes referred to as a **halo effect.**

Raters may make biased judgments, consciously or unconsciously, simply because it is in their own self-interest to do so (see Figure 11–3). Therapists who passionately believe in the efficacy of a particular therapeutic approach may be more disposed than others to see the benefits of that approach. Proponents of alternative approaches may be more disposed to see the negative aspects of that same treatment.

Numerous other factors may contribute to bias in a rater's ratings. The rater may feel competitive with, physically attracted to, or physically repelled by the subject of the ratings. The rater may not have the proper background, experience, and trained eye needed for the particular task. Judgments may be limited by the rater's general level of conscientiousness and willingness to devote the time and effort required to do the job properly. The rater may harbor

**Figure 11–3
Ratings in One's Own
Self-Interest**

*"Monsters and screamers have
always worked for me; I give
it two thumbs up!"*

biases concerning various stereotypes. Subjectivity based on the rater's own personal preferences
and taste may also enter into judgments. Features that rate a "perfect 10" in one person's
opinion may represent more like a "mediocre 5" in the eyes of another person. If such marked
diversity of opinion occurs frequently with regard to a particular instrument, we would expect
it to be reflected in low inter-rater reliability coefficients. It would probably be desirable to
take another look at the criteria used to make ratings and how specific they are.

When another person is the referent, an important factor to consider with regard to ratings is
the *context* of the evaluation. Different raters may have different perspectives on the individual they
are rating because of the context in which they typically view that person. A parent may indicate
on a rating scale that a child is hyperactive, whereas the same child's teacher may indicate on the
same rating scale that the child's activity level is within normal limits. Can they both be right?

The answer is yes, according to one meta-analysis of 119 articles in the scholarly literature
(Achenbach et al., 1987). Different informants may have different perspectives on the subjects
being evaluated. These different perspectives derive from observing and interacting with the
subjects in different contexts. The study also noted that raters tended to agree more about the
difficulties of young children (ages 6 to 11) than about those of older children and adolescents.
Raters also tended to show more agreement about children exhibiting self-control problems
(such as hyperactivity and mistreating other children) in contrast to "overcontrol" problems
(such as anxiety or depression). The researchers urged professionals to view the differences in
evaluation that arise from different perspectives as something more than error in the evaluation

JUST THINK . . .

Imagining that it was *you* who was being rated, how might you be rated differently on the same variable in different contexts?

process. They urged professionals to employ context-specific differences in treatment plans. Many of their ideas regarding context-dependent evaluation and treatment were incorporated into Achenbach's (1993) Multiaxial Empirically Based Assessment system. The system is an approach to the assessment of children and adolescents that incorporates cognitive and physical assessments of the subject, self-report of the subject, and ratings by parents and teachers. Additionally, performance measures of the child alone, with the family, or in the classroom may be included.

Regardless whether the self or another person is the subject of study, one element of any evaluation that must be kept in mind by the assessor is the cultural context.

The cultural background of assessees   Test developers and users have shown increased sensitivity to issues of cultural diversity. A number of concerns have been raised regarding the use of personality tests and other tools of assessment with members of culturally and linguistically diverse populations (Anderson, 1995; Campos, 1989; Greene, 1987; Hill et al., 2010; Irvine & Berry, 1983; López & Hernandez, 1987; Nye et al., 2008; Sundberg & Gonzales, 1981; Widiger & Samuel, 2009). How fair or generalizable is a particular instrument or measurement technique with a member of a particular cultural group? How a test was developed, how it is administered, and how scores on it are interpreted are all questions to be raised when considering the appropriateness of administering a particular personality test to members of culturally and linguistically diverse populations. We continue to explore these and related questions later in this chapter and throughout this book. In Chapter 13, for example, we consider in detail the meaning of the term *culturally informed psychological assessment.*

What?

What is assessed when a personality assessment is conducted? For many personality tests, it is meaningful to answer this question with reference to the primary content area sampled by the test and to that portion of the test devoted to measuring aspects of the testtaker's general response style.

Primary content area sampled   Personality measures are tools used to gain insight into a wide array of thoughts, feelings, and behaviors associated with all aspects of the human experience. Some tests are designed to measure particular traits (such as introversion) or states (such as test anxiety), whereas others focus on descriptions of behavior, usually in particular contexts. For example, an observational checklist may concentrate on classroom behaviors associated with movement in order to assess a child's hyperactivity. Extended discussion of behavioral measures is presented in Chapter 12.

Many contemporary personality tests, especially tests that can be scored and interpreted by computer, are designed to measure not only some targeted trait or other personality variable but also some aspect of the testtaker's response style. For example, in addition to scales labeled *Introversion* and *Extraversion,* a test of introversion/extraversion might contain other scales. Such additional scales could be designed to shed light on how honestly testtakers responded to the test, how consistently they answered the questions, and other matters related to the validity of the test findings. These measures of response pattern are also known as *measures of response set* or *response style.* Let's take a look at some different testtaker response styles as well as the scales used to identify them.

Testtaker response styles   **Response style** refers to a tendency to respond to a test item or interview question in some characteristic manner regardless of the content of the item or question. For example, an individual may be more apt to respond *yes* or *true* than *no* or *false* on a short-answer test. This particular pattern of responding is characterized as **acquiescent.** Table 11–1 shows a listing of other identified response styles.

Impression management is a term used to describe the attempt to manipulate others' impressions through "the selective exposure of some information (it may be false information) . . . coupled with suppression of [other] information" (Braginsky et al., 1969, p. 51). In the process of personality assessment, assessees might employ any number of impression management strategies for any number of reasons. Delroy Paulhus (1984, 1986, 1990) and his colleagues (Kurt & Paulhus, 2008; Paulhus & Holden, 2010; Paulhus & Levitt, 1987) have explored impression management in test-taking as well as the related phenomena of enhancement (the claiming of positive attributes), denial (the repudiation of negative attributes), and self-deception—"the tendency to give favorably biased but honestly held self-descriptions" (Paulhus & Reid, 1991, p. 307). Testtakers who engage in impression management are exhibiting, in the broadest sense, a response style (Jackson & Messick, 1962).

Some personality tests contain items designed to detect different types of response styles. So, for example, a *true* response to an item like "I summer in Baghdad" would raise a number of questions, such as: Did the testtaker understand the instructions? Take the test seriously? Respond *true* to all items? Respond randomly? Endorse other infrequently endorsed items? Analysis of the entire protocol will help answer such questions.

Responding to a personality test in an inconsistent, contrary, or random way, or attempting to fake good or bad, may affect the validity of the interpretations of the test data. Because a response style can affect the validity of the outcome, one particular type of response style measure is referred to as a *validity scale.* We may define a **validity scale** as a subscale of a test designed to assist in judgments regarding how honestly the testtaker responded and whether observed responses were products of response style, carelessness, deliberate efforts to deceive, or unintentional misunderstanding. Validity scales can provide a kind of shorthand indication of how honestly, diligently, and carefully a testtaker responded to test items. Some tests, such as the MMPI and its revision (to be discussed shortly), contain multiple validity scales. Although there are those who question the utility of formally assessing response styles (Costa & McCrae, 1997; Rorer, 1965), perhaps the more common view is that response styles are themselves important for what they reveal about testtakers. As Nunnally (1978, p. 660) observed: "To the extent that such stylistic variables can be measured independently of content relating to nonstylistic variables or to the extent that they can somehow be separated from the variance of other traits, they might prove useful as measures of personality traits."

JUST THINK . . .

On what occasion did you attempt to manage a particular impression for a friend, a family member, or an acquaintance? Why did you feel the need to do so? Would you consider your effort successful?

Table 11–1
A Sampling of Test Response Styles

Response Style Name	Explanation: A Tendency to . . .
Socially desirable responding	present oneself in a favorable (socially acceptable or desirable) light
Acquiescence	agree with whatever is presented
Nonacquiescence	disagree with whatever is presented
Deviance	make unusual or uncommon responses
Extreme	make extreme, as opposed to middle, ratings on a rating scale
Gambling/cautiousness	guess—or not guess—when in doubt
Overly positive	claim extreme virtue through self-presentation in a superlative manner (Butcher & Han, 1995)

Where?

Where are personality assessments conducted? Traditional sites for personality assessment, as well as other varieties of assessment, are schools, clinics, hospitals, academic research laboratories, employment counseling and vocational selection centers, and the offices of psychologists and counselors. In addition to such traditional venues, contemporary assessors may be found observing behavior and making assessments in natural settings, ranging from the assessee's own home (Marx, 1998; McElwain, 1998; Polizzi, 1998) to the incarcerated assessee's prison cell (Glassbrenner, 1998).

How?

How are personality assessments structured and conducted? Let's look at various facets of this multidimensional question, beginning with issues of scope and theory. We then discuss procedures and item formats that may be employed, the frame of reference of the assessment, and scoring and interpretation.

Scope and theory   One dimension of the *how* of personality assessment concerns its scope. The scope of an evaluation may be very wide, seeking to take a kind of general inventory of an individual's personality. The California Psychological Inventory (CPI 434) is an example of an instrument with a relatively wide scope. This test contains 434 true–false items—but then you knew that from its title—and is designed to yield information on many personality-related variables such as responsibility, self-acceptance, and dominance. It was originally conceived to measure enduring personality traits across cultural groups, and predict the behavior of generally well-functioning people (Boer et al., 2008).

In contrast to instruments and procedures designed to inventory personality as a whole are instruments that are much narrower in terms of what they purport to measure. An instrument may be designed to focus on as little as one particular aspect of personality. For example, consider tests designed to measure a personality variable called *locus of control* (Rotter, 1966; Wallston et al., 1978). **Locus** (meaning "place" or "site") **of control** is a person's perception about the source of things that happen to him or her. In general, people who see themselves as largely responsible for what happens to them are said to have an *internal* locus of control. People who are prone to attribute what happens to them to external factors (such as fate or the actions of others) are said to have an *external* locus of control. A person who believes in the value of seatbelts, for example, would be expected to score closer to the internal than to the external end of the continuum of locus of control as opposed to a nonbuckling counterpart.

> **JUST THINK . . .**
>
> Suppose you would like to learn as much as you can about the personality of an assessee from one personality test that is narrow in scope. On what single aspect of personality do you believe it would be most important to focus?

To what extent is a personality test theory-based or relatively atheoretical? Instruments used in personality testing and assessment vary in the extent to which they are based on a theory of personality. Some are based entirely on a theory, and some are relatively atheoretical. An example of a theory-based instrument is the Blacky Pictures Test (Blum, 1950). This test consists of cartoonlike pictures of a dog named Blacky in various situations, and each image is designed to elicit fantasies associated with various psychoanalytic themes. For example, one card depicts Blacky with a knife hovering over his tail, a scene (according to the test's author) designed to elicit material related to the psychoanalytic concept of castration anxiety. The respondent's task is to make up stories in response to such cards, and the stories are then analyzed according to the guidelines set forth by Blum (1950). The test is seldom used today; we cite it here as a particularly dramatic and graphic illustration of how a personality theory (in this case, psychoanalytic theory) can saturate a test.

The other side of the theory saturation coin is the personality test that is relatively atheoretical. The single most popular personality test in use today is atheoretical: the Minnesota Multiphasic Personality Inventory (MMPI), in both its original and revised forms. Streiner (2003a) referred to this test as "the epitome of an atheoretical, 'dust bowl empiricism' approach to the development of a tool to measure personality traits" (p. 218). You will better appreciate this comment when we discuss the MMPI and its subsequent revisions later in this chapter. For now, let's simply point out one advantage of an atheoretical tool of personality assessment: It allows test users, should they so desire, to impose their own theoretical preferences on the interpretation of the findings.

Pursuing another aspect of the *how* of personality assessment, let's turn to a nuts-and-bolts look at the methods used.

Procedures and item formats   Personality may be assessed by many different methods, such as face-to-face interviews, computer-administered tests, behavioral observation, paper-and-pencil tests, evaluation of case history data, evaluation of portfolio data, and recording of physiological responses. The equipment required for assessment varies greatly, depending upon the method employed. In one technique, for example, all that may be required is a blank sheet of paper and a pencil. The assessee is asked to draw a person, and the assessor makes inferences about the assessee's personality from the drawing. Other approaches to assessment, whether in the interest of basic research or for more applied purposes, may be far more elaborate in terms of the equipment they require (Figure 11–4).

Figure 11–4
Learning About Personality in the Field—Literally

During World War II, the assessment staff of the Office of Strategic Services (OSS) selected American secret agents using a variety of measures. One measure used to assess leadership ability and emotional stability in the field was a simulation that involved rebuilding a blown bridge. Candidates were deliberately supplied with insufficient materials for rebuilding the bridge. In some instances, "assistants" who were actually confederates of the experimenter further frustrated the candidates' efforts. In what was called the "Wall Situation," candidates were thrust into a scenario wherein the structure pictured above was a wall obstructing their escape from enemy forces. The group's task was to get everyone over it. Typically, the first person to survey the situation and devise a plan for completing the task emerged as the group leader.
Courtesy of the National Archives

Measures of personality vary in terms of the degree of *structure* built into them. For example, personality may be assessed by means of an interview, but it may also be assessed by a **structured interview.** In the latter method, the interviewer must typically follow an interview guide and has little leeway in terms of posing questions not in that guide. The variable of structure is also applicable to the tasks assessees are instructed to perform. In some approaches to personality assessment, the tasks are straightforward, highly structured, and unambiguous. Here is one example of the instructions used for such a task: *Copy this sentence in your own handwriting.* Such instructions might be used if the assessor was attempting to learn something about the assessee by handwriting analysis, also referred to as **graphology** (see Figure 11–5). Intuitively appealing as a method of deriving insights into personality, graphology seems not to have lived up to its promise (Dazzi & Pedrabissi, 2009; Fox, 2011; Gawda, 2008; Thiry, 2009).

In other approaches to personality, what is required of the assessee is not so straightforward, not very structured, and intentionally ambiguous. One example of a highly unstructured task is as follows: Hand the assessee one of a series of inkblots and ask, *What might this be?*

Figure 11–5
Three Faces (and Three Handwritings) of Eve

Three Faces of Eve *was a fact-based, 1957 film classic about three of the personalities—there were more over the course of the woman's lifetime—manifested by a patient known as "Eve White," "Eve Black," and "Jane." Prior to making that film, the 20th Century–Fox legal department insisted that the patient on whom the screenplay was based sign three separate contracts, one for each of her personalities. Accordingly, the patient was asked to elicit "Eve White," "Eve Black," and "Jane," and then sign an agreement while manifesting each of these respective personalities. According to Aubrey Solomon, co-author of* The Films of 20th Century–Fox *(Thomas & Solomon, 1989) and commentator on the DVD release of the film, the three signatures on the three separate contracts were all distinctly different—presumably because they were a product of three distinctly different personalities.*
© John Springer Collection/Corbis Historical/Getty Images

The same personality trait or construct may be measured with different instruments in different ways. Consider the many possible ways of determining how *aggressive* a person is. Measurement of this trait could be made in different ways: a paper-and-pencil test; a computerized test; an interview with the assessee; an interview with family, friends, and associates of the assessee; analysis of official records and other case history data; behavioral observation; and laboratory experimentation. Of course, criteria for what constitutes the trait measured—in this case, aggression—would have to be rigorously defined in advance. After all, psychological traits and constructs can and have been defined in many different ways, and virtually all such definitions tend to be context-dependent. For example, *aggressive* may be defined in ways ranging from hostile and assaultive (as in the "aggressive inmate") to bold and enterprising (as in the "aggressive salesperson"). This personality trait, like many others, may or may not be socially desirable; it depends entirely on the context.

JUST THINK . . .

Straightforward or ambiguous? Which approach to personality assessment has more appeal to you in your (future) role as an assessor? Why?

In personality assessment, as well as in assessment of other areas, information may be gathered and questions answered in a variety of ways. For example, a researcher or practitioner interested in learning about the degree to which respondents are field-dependent may construct an elaborate tilting chair/tilting room device—the same one you may recall from Chapter 1 (Figure 1–5). In the interests of time and expense, an equivalent process administered by paper and pencil or computer may be more practical for everyday use. In this chapter's *Everyday Psychometrics,* we illustrate some of the more common item formats employed in the study of personality and related psychological variables. Keep in mind that, although we are using these formats to illustrate different ways that personality has been studied, some are employed in other areas of assessment as well.

Frame of reference   Another variable relevant to the *how* of personality measurement concerns the *frame of reference* of the assessment. In the context of item format and assessment in general, **frame of reference** may be defined as aspects of the focus of exploration such as the time frame (the past, the present, or the future) as well as other contextual issues that involve people, places, and events. Perhaps for most measures of personality, the frame of reference for the assessee may be described in phrases such as *what is* or *how I am right now.* However, some techniques of measurement are easily adapted to tap alternative frames of reference, such as *what I could be ideally, how I am in the office, how others see me, how I see others,* and so forth. Obtaining self-reported information from different frames of reference is, in itself, a way of developing information related to states and traits. For example, in comparing self-perception in the present versus what is anticipated for the future, assessees who report that they will become better people may be presumed to be more optimistic than assessees who report a reverse trend.

Representative of methodologies that can be readily applied in the exploration of varied frames of reference is the **Q-sort technique.** Originally developed by Stephenson (1953), the Q-sort is an assessment technique in which the task is to sort a group of statements, usually in perceived rank order ranging from *most descriptive* to *least descriptive.* The statements, traditionally presented on index cards, may be sorted in ways designed to reflect various perceptions. They may, for example, reflect how respondents see themselves or how they would like to see themselves. Illustrative statements are *I am confident, I try hard to please others,* and *I am uncomfortable in social situations.*

One of the best-known applications of Q-sort methodology in clinical and counseling settings was advocated by the personality theorist and psychotherapist Carl Rogers. Rogers (1959) used the Q-sort to evaluate the discrepancy between the perceived actual self and the ideal self. At the beginning of psychotherapy, clients might be asked to sort cards twice, once

Some Common Item Formats

How may personality be assessed? Here are some of the more typical types of item formats.

ITEM 1

I enjoy being out and among other people.   TRUE   FALSE

This item illustrates the true–false format. Was your reaction something like "been there, done that" when you saw this item?

ITEM 2

Working with fellow community members on organizing and staging a blood drive.   LIKE   DISLIKE

This two-choice item is designed to elicit information about the respondent's likes and dislikes. It is a common format in interest inventories, particularly those used in vocational counseling.

ITEM 3

How I feel when I am out and among other people

Warm	_:_:_:_:_:_	Cold
Tense	_:_:_:_:_:_	Relaxed
Weak	_:_:_:_:_:_	Strong
Brooks Brothers suit	_:_:_:_:_:_	Hawaiian shirt

This item format, called a **semantic differential** (Osgood et al., 1957), is characterized by bipolar adjectives separated by a seven-point rating scale on which respondents select one point to indicate their response. This type of item is useful for gauging the strength, degree, or magnitude of the direction of a particular response and has applications ranging from self-concept descriptions to opinion surveys.

ITEM 4

I enjoy being out and among other people.

or

I have an interest in learning about art.

ITEM 5

I am depressed too much of the time.

or

I am anxious too much of the time.

These are two examples of items written in a **forced-choice format,** where ideally each of the two choices (there may be more than two choices) is equal in social desirability. The Edwards Personal Preference Schedule (Edwards, 1953) is a classic forced-choice test. Edwards (1957a, 1957b, 1966) described in detail how he determined the items in this test to be equivalent in social desirability.

ITEM 6

naughty
needy
negativistic
New Age
nerdy
nimble
nonproductive
numb

This illustrates an item written in an adjective checklist format. Respondents check the traits that apply to them.

ITEM 7

Complete this sentence.

I feel as if I _____.

Respondents are typically instructed to finish the sentence with their "real feelings" in what is called a sentence completion item. The Rotter Incomplete Sentence Blank (Rotter & Rafferty, 1950) is a standardized test that employs such items, and the manual features normative data (Rotter et al., 1992).

ITEM 8

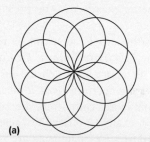

(a)   (b)

Can you distinguish the figure labeled (b) in the figure labeled (a)? This type of item is found in embedded-figures tests. Identifying hidden figures is a skill thought to tap the same field dependence/independence variable tapped by more elaborate apparatuses such as the tilting chair/tilting room illustrated in Figure 1–5.

ITEM 9

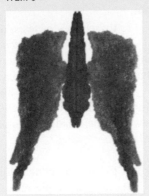

This is an item reminiscent of one of the Rorschach inkblots. We will have much more to say about the Rorschach in the following chapter.

ITEM 10

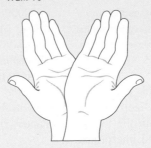

Much like the Rorschach test, which uses inkblots as ambiguous stimuli, many other tests ask the respondent to "project" onto an ambiguous stimulus. This item is reminiscent of one such projective technique called the Hand Test. Respondents are asked to tell the examiner what they think the hands might be doing.

according to how they perceived themselves to be and then according to how they would ultimately like to be. The larger the discrepancy between the sortings, the more goals would have to be set in therapy. Presumably, retesting the client who successfully completed a course of therapy would reveal much less discrepancy between the present and idealized selves.

Beyond its application in initial assessment and reevaluation of a therapy client, the Q-sort technique has also been used extensively in basic research in the area of personality and other areas. Some highly specialized Q-sorts include the Leadership Q-Test (Cassel, 1958) and the Tyler Vocational Classification System (Tyler, 1961). The former test was designed for use in military settings and contains cards with statements that the assessee is instructed to sort in terms of their perceived importance to effective leadership. The Tyler Q-sort contains cards on which occupations are listed; the cards are sorted in terms of the perceived desirability of each occupation. One feature of Q-sort methodology is the ease with which it can be adapted for use with a wide population range for varied clinical and research purposes. Q-sort methodology has been used to measure a wide range of variables (e.g., Bradley & Miller, 2010; Fowler & Westen, 2011; Huang & Shih, 2011). It has been used to measure attachment security with children as young as preschoolers (DeMulder et al., 2000). An adaptation of Q-sort methodology has even been used to measure attachment security in rhesus monkeys (Warfield et al., 2011).

Two other item presentation formats that are readily adaptable to different frames of reference are the *adjective checklist* format and the *sentence completion* format. With the adjective checklist method, respondents simply check off on a list of adjectives those that apply to themselves (or to people they are rating). Using the same list of adjectives, the frame of reference can easily be changed by changing the instructions. For example, to gauge various states, respondents can be asked to check off adjectives indicating how they feel *right now*. Alternatively, to gauge various traits, they may be asked to check off adjectives indicative of how they have felt for the last year or so. A test called, simply enough, the Adjective Check List (Gough, 1960; Gough & Heilbrun, 1980) has been used in a wide range of research studies to study assessees' perceptions of themselves or others. For example, the instrument has been used to study managers' self-perceptions (Hills, 1985), parents' perceptions of their children (Brown, 1972), and clients' perceptions of their therapists (Reinehr, 1969). The sheer simplicity

JUST THINK . . .

Envision and describe an assessment scenario in which it would be important to obtain the assessee's perception of others.

of the measure makes it adaptable for use in a wide range of applications (e.g., Ledesma et al., 2011; Redshaw & Martin, 2009; Tsaousis & Georgiades, 2009).

As implied by the label ascribed to these types of tests, the testtaker's task in responding to an item written in a *sentence completion* format is to complete an incomplete sentence. Items may tap how assessees feel about themselves, as in this sentence completion item: *I would describe my feeling about myself as* _____. Items may tap how assessees feel about others, as in *My classmates are* _____. More on sentence completion methods in the following chapter; right now, let's briefly overview *how* personality tests are scored and interpreted.

Scoring and interpretation Personality measures differ with respect to the way conclusions are drawn from the data they provide. For some paper-and-pencil measures, a simple tally of responses to targeted items is presumed to provide a measure of the strength of a particular trait. For other measures, a computer programmed to apply highly technical manipulations of the data is required for purposes of scoring and interpretation. Yet other measures may require a highly trained clinician reviewing a verbatim transcript of what the assessee said in response to certain stimuli such as inkblots or pictures.

It is also meaningful to dichotomize measures with respect to the *nomothetic* versus *idiographic* approach. The **nomothetic approach** to assessment is characterized by efforts to learn how a limited number of personality traits can be applied to all people. According to a nomothetic view, certain personality traits exist in all people to varying degrees. The assessor's task is to determine what the strength of each of these traits are in the assessee. An assessor who uses a test such as the 16 PF, Fifth Edition (Cattell et al., 1993), probably subscribes to the nomothetic view. This is so because the 16PF was designed to measure the strength of 16 *personality factors* (which is what "PF" stands for) in the testtaker. Similarly, tests purporting to measure the "Big 5" personality traits are very much in the nomothetic tradition.

In contrast to a nomothetic view is the idiographic one. An **idiographic approach** to assessment is characterized by efforts to learn about each individual's unique constellation of personality traits, with no attempt to characterize each person according to any particular set of traits. The idea here is not to see where one falls on the continuum of a few traits deemed to be universal, but rather to understand the specific traits unique to the makeup of the individual. The idiographic orientation is evident in assessment procedures that are more flexible not only in terms of listing the observed traits but also of naming new trait terms.[2] The idiographic approach to personality assessment was described in detail by Allport (1937; Allport & Odbert, 1936). Methods of assessment used by proponents of this view tend to be more like tools such as the case study and personal records rather than tests. Of these two different approaches, most contemporary psychologists seem to favor the nomothetic approach.

Another dimension related to how meaning is attached to test scores has to do with whether inter-individual or intra-individual comparisons are made with respect to test scores. Most common in personality assessment is the *normative* approach, whereby a testtaker's responses and the presumed strength of a measured trait are interpreted relative to the strength of that

---

2. Consider in this context the adjective *New Age* used as a personality trait (referring to a belief in spirituality). A personality assessment conducted with an idiographic orientation would be flexible enough to characterize the assessee as New Age should this trait be judged applicable. Nomothetic instruments developed prior to the emergence of such a new trait term would subsume cognitive and behavioral characteristics of the term under whatever existing trait (or traits) in the nomothetic system were judged appropriate. So, for example, a nomothetic system that included *spiritual* as one of its core traits might subsume "New Age" under "spiritual." At some point, if trends and usage warrant it, an existing nomothetic instrument could be revised to include a new trait term.

trait in a sample of a larger population. However, you may recall that an alternative to the normative approach in test interpretation is the *ipsative* approach. In the ipsative approach, a testtaker's responses, as well as the presumed strength of measured traits, are interpreted relative to the strength of measured traits for that same individual. On a test that employs ipsative scoring procedures, two people with the same score for a particular trait or personality characteristic may differ markedly with regard to the magnitude of that trait or characteristic relative to members of a larger population.

JUST THINK . . .

Place yourself in the role of a human resources executive for a large airline. As part of the evaluation process, all new pilots will be given a personality test. You are asked whether the test should be ipsative or normative in nature. Your response?

Concluding our overview of the *how* of personality assessment, and to prepare for discussing the ways in which personality tests are developed, let's review some issues in personality test development and use.

Issues in personality test development and use Many of the issues inherent in the test development process mirror the basic questions just discussed about personality assessment in general. What testtakers will this test be designed to be used with? Will the test entail self-report? Or will it require the use of raters or judges? If raters or judges are needed, what special training or other qualifications must they have? How will a reasonable level of inter-rater reliability be ensured? What content area will be sampled by the test? How will issues of testtaker response style be dealt with? What item format should be employed, and what is the optimal frame of reference? How will the test be scored and interpreted?

As previously noted, personality assessment that relies exclusively on self-report is a two-edged sword. On the one hand, the information is from "the source." Respondents are in most instances presumed to know themselves better than anyone else does and therefore should be able to supply accurate responses about themselves. On the other hand, the consumer of such information has no way of knowing with certainty which self-reported information is entirely true, partly true, not really true, or an outright lie. Consider a response to a single item on a personality inventory written in a true–false format. The item reads: *I tend to enjoy meeting new people.* A respondent indicates *true.* In reality, we do not know whether the respondent (1) enjoys meeting new people; (2) honestly believes that he or she enjoys meeting new people but really does not (in which case, the response is more the product of a lack of insight than a report of reality); (3) does not enjoy meeting new people but would like people to think that he or she does; or (4) did not even bother to read the item, is not taking the test seriously, and is responding *true* or *false* randomly to each item.

Building validity scales into self-report tests is one way that test developers have attempted to deal with the potential problems. In recent years, there has been some debate about whether validity scales should be included in personality tests. In arguing the case for the inclusion of validity scales, it has been asserted that "detection of an attempt to provide misleading information is a vital and absolutely necessary component of the clinical interpretation of test results" and that using any instrument without validity scales "runs counter to the basic tenets of clinical assessment" (Ben-Porath & Waller, 1992, p. 24). By contrast, the authors of the widely used Revised NEO Personality Inventory (NEO PI-R), Paul T. Costa Jr. and Robert R. McCrae, perceived no need to include any validity scales in their instrument and have been unenthusiastic about the use of such scales in other tests (McCrae & Costa, 1983; McCrae et al., 1989; Piedmont & McCrae, 1996; Piedmont et al., 2000). Referring to validity scales as SD (social desirability) scales, Costa and McCrae (1997) opined:

> SD scales typically consist of items that have a clearly desirable response. We know that people who are trying falsely to appear to have good qualities will endorse many such items, and the creators of SD scales wish to infer from this that people who endorse many SD items are trying

JUST THINK . . .

Having read about some of the pros and cons of using validity scales in personality assessment, where do you stand on the issue? Feel free to revise your opinion as you learn more.

to create a good impression. That argument is formally identical to asserting that presidential candidates shake hands, and therefore people who shake hands are probably running for president. In fact, there are many more common reasons for shaking hands, and there is also a more common reason than impression management for endorsing SD items—namely, because the items are reasonably accurate self-descriptions. (p. 89)

According to Costa and McCrae, assessors can affirm that self-reported information is reasonably accurate by consulting external sources such as peer raters. Of course, the use of raters necessitates certain other precautions to guard against rater error and bias. Education regarding the nature of various types of rater error and bias has been a key weapon in the fight against intentional or unintentional inaccuracies in ratings. Training sessions may be designed to accomplish several objectives, such as clarifying terminology to increase the reliability of ratings. A term like *satisfactory,* for example, may have different meanings to different raters. During training, new raters can observe and work with more experienced raters to become acquainted with aspects of the task that may not be described in the rater's manual, to compare ratings with more experienced raters, and to discuss the thinking that went into the ratings.

To include or not include a validity scale in a personality test is definitely an issue that must be dealt with. What about the language in which the assessment is conducted? At first blush, this would appear to be a non-issue. Well, yes and no. If an assessee is from a culture different from the culture in which the test was developed, or if the assessee is fluent in one or more languages, then language may well become an issue. Words tend to lose—or gain—something in translation, and some words and expressions are not readily translatable into other languages. Consider the following true–false item from a popular personality test: *I am known for my prudence and common sense.* If you are a bilingual student, translate that statement from English as an exercise in test-item translation before reading on.

A French translation of this item is quite close, adding only an extra first-person possessive pronoun ("par ma prudence et *mon* bon sens"); however, the Filipino translation of this item would read *I can be relied on to decide carefully and well on matters* (McCrae et al., 1998, p. 176).

In addition to sometimes significant differences in the meaning of individual items, the traits measured by personality tests sometimes have different meanings as well. Acknowledging this fact, McCrae et al. (1998, p. 183) cautioned that "personality-trait relations reported in Western studies should be considered promising hypotheses to be tested in new cultures."

The broader issue relevant to the development and use of personality tests with members of a culture different from the culture in which the test was normed concerns the applicability of the norms. For example, a number of MMPI studies conducted with members of groups from diverse backgrounds yield findings in which minority group members tend to present with more psychopathology than majority group members (see, for example, Montgomery & Orozco, 1985; Whitworth & Unterbrink, 1994). Such differences have elicited questions regarding the appropriateness of the use of the test with members of different populations (Dana, 1995; Dana & Whatley, 1991; Malgady et al., 1987).

A test may well be appropriate for use with members of culturally different populations. As López (1988, p. 1096) observed, "To argue that the MMPI is culturally biased, one needs to go beyond reporting that ethnic groups differ in their group profiles." López noted that many of the studies showing differences between the groups did not control for psychopathology. Accordingly, there may well have been actual differences across the groups in psychopathology. The size of the sample used in the research and the appropriateness of the statistical analysis are other extracultural factors to consider when evaluating cross-cultural research. Of course, if culture and "learned meanings" (Rohner, 1984, pp. 119–120), as opposed to psychopathology, are found to account for differences in measured psychopathology with members of a particular cultural group, then the continued use of the measures with members of that cultural group must be questioned.

In the wake of heightened security concerns as a result of highly publicized terrorist threats, stalking incidents, and the like, new issues related to privacy have come to the fore. The number of assessments administered in the interest of threat assessment seem ever on the increase—this while professional guidelines and legislative mandates have lagged. The result is that the public's need to know who is a legitimate threat to public safety has been pitted against the individual's right to privacy (among other rights). The topic is delved into by no less than a threat assessment expert in this chapter's *Meet an Assessment Professional*.

Armed with some background information regarding the nature of personality and its assessment, as well as some of the issues that attend the process, let's look at the process of developing instruments designed to assess personality.

Developing Instruments to Assess Personality

Tools such as *logic, theory,* and *data reduction methods* (such as factor analysis) are frequently used in the process of developing personality tests. Another tool in the test development process may be a *criterion group.* As we will see, most personality tests employ two or more of these tools in the course of their development.

Logic and Reason

Notwithstanding the grumblings of skeptics, there is a place for logic and reason in psychology, at least when it comes to writing items for a personality test. Logic and reason may dictate what content is covered by the items. Indeed, the use of logic and reason in the development of test items is sometimes referred to as the *content* or *content-oriented* approach to test development. So, for example, if you were developing a true–false test of extraversion, logic and reason might dictate that one of the items might be something like *I consider myself an outgoing person.*

Efforts to develop such content-oriented, face-valid items can be traced at least as far back as an instrument used to screen World War I recruits for personality and adjustment problems. The Personal Data Sheet (Woodworth, 1917), later known as the Woodworth Psychoneurotic Inventory, contained items designed to elicit self-report of fears, sleep disorders, and other problems deemed symptomatic of a pathological condition referred to then as psychoneuroticism. The greater the number of problems reported, the more psychoneurotic the respondent was presumed to be.

A great deal of clinically actionable information can be collected in relatively little time using such self-report instruments—provided, of course, that the testtaker has the requisite insight and responds with candor. A highly trained professional is not required for administration of the test. A plus in the digital age is that a computerized report of the findings can be available in minutes. Moreover, such instruments are particularly well suited to clinical settings in managed care environments, where drastic cost cutting has led to reductions in orders for assessment, and insurers are reluctant to authorize assessments. In such environments, the preferred use of psychological tests has traditionally been to identify conditions of "medical necessity" (Glazer et al., 1991). Quick, relatively inexpensive tests, wherein assessees report specific problems have won favor with insurers.

A typical companion to logic, reason, and intuition in item development is research. A review of the literature on the aspect of personality that test items are designed to tap will

Meet Dr. Rick Malone

I am Colonel Rick Malone, MD, an active duty military forensic psychiatrist, currently serving as a behavioral science officer with the US Army Criminal Investigation Command (still known by its historical abbreviation, CID). In this capacity I consult with CID Special Agents on a variety of investigations. My work assignments include behavioral analysis of crime scene evidence, the conduct of psychological autopsies, and what I will discuss in more detail here: *threat assessment*.

As its name implies, **threat assessment** may be defined as *a process of identifying or evaluating entities, actions, or occurrences, whether natural or man-made, that have or indicate the potential to harm life, information, operations and/or property* (Department of Homeland Security, 2008). The practice of threat assessment can take many forms depending upon the setting and the organization's mission. In our setting, the mission of threat assessment entails, among other things, the gathering of intelligence designed to protect senior Department of Defense officials (referred to as "principals"). The tool of assessment we tend to rely on most is what is called a *structured professional judgment* (SPJ). The structured professional judgment is an approach that attempts to bridge the gap between actuarial and unstructured clinical approaches to risk assessment. Unstructured clinical approaches are based on the exercise of professional discretion and usually are justified according to the qualifications and experience of the professional who makes them. Of course, given the variance that exists in terms of the qualifications and experience of professionals making such judgments, SPJ as a tool of assessment is vulnerable to criticism on various psychometric grounds such as questionable or unknown reliability and validity. Also, given the wide range of actions that may be launched as a result of such professional discretion, another issue relevant to SPJ is accountability.

In contrast to SPJ as the primary tool of assessment, an actuarial approach employs a fixed set of risk factors that are combined to produce a score. In turn, this score is used to gauge an individual's relative risk compared to a normative group. One of the disadvantages of such strictly "objective" procedures is that they typically prohibit the evaluator

RICKY D. MALONE, MD, MPH, MSSI COL, MC, SFS
Forensic Psychiatry/Behavioral Science Consultant,
U.S. Army Criminal Investigation Command
© Ricky D. Malone

from considering unique, unusual, or context-specific variables that might require intervention.

The SPJ relies on evidence-based guidelines that are directly informed, guided, and structured by the scientific and professional literature, but allows the evaluator discretion in their interpretation. The word "structured" in this term refers to a minimum set of risk factors that should be considered and how to measure them. However, "structured" in this context stops short of requiring that the identified risk factors be combined according to a specific algorithm (Hart & Logan, 2011).

In our setting, we are often asked to assess the threat posed by a person who has demonstrated an "inappropriate direction of interest" toward one of our designated principals. Such an individual will typically come to our attention through attempts to communicate directly with one of these principals by telephone, mail, or e-mail. Occasionally—and even of greater concern—the individual has even directly come in contact or approached a designated principal. In recent years, our attention has been focused on such persons of interest as a result of some posting on social media. Communications of concern may contain anything from an outright threat to a complaint symptomatic of inappropriate or exaggerated anger or blame. Another variety of communication that will get our attention is one that makes an inappropriate plea for help with some personal issue that the writer perceives to be within the public official's sphere of influence. As one might imagine, senior military officials in the public eye can and do receive such inappropriate communications from all over the world. So what is done in response?

In some cases, not very much is done. Given relatively limited resources, we need to pick and choose which communications warrant a response (or a formal investigation) and what the level of that response should be. So what we do for starters is a brief, indirect assessment to estimate the level of concern that the person of interest warrants. If our level of concern is high, a formal law enforcement investigation will be launched. If our level of concern is below the threshold of triggering a formal investigation, we will simply continue to monitor their attempts to communicate and related activities. Useful in this context is Meloy's (2000) biopsychosocial (BPS) model, which identifies individual/psychological factors, social/situational factors, and biological factors that have been shown to be associated with higher rates of interpersonal violence. It avoids the use of numerical scores and assigning ranges for threat levels, but instead recommends that each factor be assessed and weighted according to case-specific circumstances. While the BPS model was not designed specifically for targeted violence towards public figures, it is useful in this context because it relies primarily on readily obtainable information (as opposed to the level of information required for performing a formal investigation).

Perhaps the best source of data for making inferences as to how dangerous persons of interest may be are the communications created by those person themselves. Notes, electronic postings, and other communications frequently contain relevant personal details. These details can provide leads and clues that yield informed insights into the individual's mental state. Hypotheses about the person's mental state and the severity of disorder may be supported or rejected through the examination of other sources such as the individual's social media presence. Often, postings on social media can be quite revealing in terms of things like an individual's daily activities, interests, and political leanings. And looking beyond the obvious, postings on social media may also be revealing in terms of personality and the possible existence of delusional beliefs.

Complementing analysis of material readily found on social media websites is another potential gold mine of relevant information: public records. A search of public records can yield valuable insights into variables as diverse as financial status, residential stability, geographic mobility, and social support systems. The information derived from such publicly available sources is then incorporated into the biopsychosocial assessment and examined for evidence of the warning behaviors (Meloy et al., 2012).

Based on the amount and quality of information we have in hand, as well as the level of concern, the threat management team decides whether to proceed with an investigation and/or take steps to mitigate the threat. In both its investigative capacity, and its efforts to mitigate a threat, the team is challenged to balance the protection of the principal's safety with the need to preserve a citizen's civil rights (including one's right to free speech and privacy, and the right not to be falsely imprisoned). Investigative activities alone can have a significant negative impact on the individual's life. During the investigation, any questionable behavior on the part of a person of interest will be revealed to friends, family, and business associates. One danger here is that the mere revelation of such behavior to third parties will be damaging to the person of interest. From the perspective of the agency, conducting an investigation has its own dangers as it may "tip off" the person of interest and give rise to an escalation in that individual's plans—all before an effective strategy for threat mitigation has been devised or put in place. Alternatively, the "tip off" may serve to impact the person of interest with the reality that it is now time to abandon the suspect activity.

Threat assessment is both an art and a science; it requires the ability to know how to use evidence-based risk factors and to integrate them with relevant insights from the individual narrative. Effective assessment and mitigation of threat further requires the ability to work as part of a multidisciplinary team with a diverse group of professionals such as law enforcement officers, prosecutors, mental health professionals, and corporate security experts. Students who are drawn to this type of work will find indispensable a firm foundation in forensic psychology coursework, and more specifically, coursework in forensic psychological assessment. Beyond formal coursework, read the published works of expert threat assessors such as J. Reid Meloy (e.g., Meloy, 2001; 2011; 2015; Meloy et al., 2008, 2015; Mohandie & Meloy, 2013). Also, consider doing volunteer work, or an internship in a setting where threat assessments are routinely conducted. There, an experienced forensic professional can serve as a model and a mentor in the art and science of unraveling the workings of a mind based on information gathered from a variety of sources.

Used with permission of Ricky D. Malone.

frequently be very helpful to test developers. In a similar vein, clinical experience can be helpful in item creation. So, for example, clinicians with ample experience in treating people diagnosed with antisocial personality disorder could be expected to have their own ideas about which items will work best on a test designed to identify people with the disorder. A related aid in the test development process is correspondence with experts on the subject matter of the test. Included here are experts who have researched and published on the subject matter, as well as experts who have known to have amassed great clinical experience on the subject matter. Yet another possible tool in test development—sometimes even the guiding force—is psychological theory.

Theory

As we noted earlier, personality measures differ in the extent to which they rely on a particular theory of personality in their development as well as their interpretation. If psychoanalytic theory was the guiding force behind the development of a new test designed to measure antisocial personality disorder, for example, the items might look quite different than the items developed solely on the basis of logic and reason. One might find, for example, items designed to tap ego and superego defects that might result in a lack of mutuality in interpersonal relationships. Given that dreams are thought to reveal unconscious motivation, there might even be items probing the respondent's dreams; interpretations of such responses would be made from a psychoanalytic perspective. As with the development of tests using logic and reason, research, clinical experience, and the opinions of experts might be used in the development of a personality test that is theory-based.

Data Reduction Methods

Data reduction methods represent another class of widely used tool in contemporary test development. Data reduction methods include several types of statistical techniques collectively known as factor analysis or cluster analysis. One use of data reduction methods in the design of personality measures is to aid in the identification of the minimum number of variables or factors that account for the intercorrelations in observed phenomena.

Let's illustrate the process of data reduction with a simple example related to painting your apartment. You may not have a strong sense of the exact color that best complements your "student-of-psychology" decor. Your investment in a subscription to *Architectural Digest* proved to be no help at all. You go to the local paint store and obtain free card samples of every shade of paint known to humanity—thousands of color samples. Next, you undertake an informal factor analysis of these thousands of color samples. You attempt to identify the minimum number of variables or factors that account for the intercorrelations among all of these colors. You discover that there are three factors (which might be labeled "primary" factors) and four more factors (which might be labeled "secondary" or "second-order" factors), the latter set of factors being combinations of the first set of factors. Because all colors can be reduced to three primary colors and their combinations, the three primary factors would correspond to the three primary colors, red, yellow, and blue (which you might christen factor *R,* factor *Y,* and factor *B*), and the four secondary or second-order factors would correspond to all the possible combinations that could be made from the primary factors (factors *RY, RB, YB,* and *RYB*).

The paint sample illustration might be helpful to keep in mind as we review how factor analysis is used in test construction and personality assessment. In a way analogous to the factoring of all those shades of paint into three primary colors, think of all personality traits being factored into what one psychologist referred to as "the most important individual differences in human transactions" (Goldberg, 1993, p. 26). After all the factoring is over and the dust has settled, how many personality-related terms do you think would remain? Stated another way, just how many *primary* factors of personality are there?

As the result of a pioneering research program in the 1940s, Raymond Bernard Cattell's answer to the question posed above was "16." Cattell (1946, 1947, 1948a, 1948b) reviewed previous research by Allport and Odbert (1936), which suggested that there were more than 18,000 personality trait names and terms in the English language. Of these, however, only about a quarter were "real traits of personality" or words and terms that designated "generalized and personalized determining tendencies—consistent and stable modes of an individual's adjustment to his environment . . . not . . . merely temporary and specific behavior" (Allport, 1937, p. 306).

Cattell added to the list some trait names and terms employed in the professional psychology and psychiatric literature and then had judges rate "just distinguishable" differences between all the words (Cattell, 1957). The result was a reduction in the size of the list to 171 trait names and terms. College students were asked to rate their friends with respect to these trait names and terms, and the factor-analyzed results of that rating further reduced the number of names and terms to 36, which Cattell referred to as *surface traits*. Still more research indicated that 16 basic dimensions or *source traits* could be distilled. In 1949, Cattell's research culminated in the publication of a test called the Sixteen Personality Factor (16 PF) Questionnaire. Revisions of the test were published in 1956, 1962, 1968, and 1993. In 2002, supplemental updated norms were published (Maraist & Russell, 2002).

Over the years, many questions have been raised regarding (1) whether the 16 factors identified by Cattell do indeed merit the description as the "source traits" of personality, and (2) whether, in fact, the 16 PF measures 16 distinct factors. Although some research supports Cattell's claims, give or take a factor or two depending on the sample (Cattell & Krug, 1986; Lichtenstein et al., 1986), serious reservations regarding these assertions have also been expressed (Eysenck, 1985, 1991; Goldberg, 1993). Some have argued that the 16 PF may be measuring fewer than 16 factors, because several of the factors are substantially intercorrelated.

With colors in the paint store, we can be certain that there are three that are primary. But with regard to personality factors, certainty doesn't seem to be in the cards. Some theorists have argued that the primary factors of personality can be narrowed down to three (Eysenck, 1991), or maybe four, five, or six (Church & Burke, 1994). At least four different five-factor models exist (Johnson & Ostendorf, 1993; Costa & McCrae, 1992a), and Waller and Zavala (1993) made a case for a seven-factor model. Costa and McCrae's five-factor model (with factors that have come to be known as "the Big Five," sometimes also expressed as "the Big 5"). has gained the greatest following. Interestingly, using factor analysis in the 1960s, Raymond Cattell had also derived five factors from his "primary 16" (H. Cattell, 1996). A side-by-side comparison of "Cattell's five" with the Big Five shows strong similarity between the two sets of derived factors (Table 11–2). Still, Cattell believed in the primacy of the 16 factors he originally identified.

The Big Five   The Revised NEO Personality Inventory (NEO PI-R; Costa & McCrae, 1992a) is widely used in both clinical applications and a wide range of research that involves personality assessment. Based on a five-dimension (or factor) model of personality, the NEO PI-R is a measure of five major dimensions (or "domains") of personality and a total of 30 elements or *facets* that define each domain.

The original version of the test was called the NEO Personality Inventory (NEO-PI; Costa & McCrae, 1985), where NEO was an acronym for the first three domains measured: Neuroticism, Extraversion, and Openness. The NEO PI-R provides for the measurement of two additional domains: Agreeableness and Conscientiousness. Stated briefly, the *Neuroticism* domain (now referred to as the *Emotional Stability* factor) taps aspects of adjustment and emotional stability, including how people cope in times of emotional turmoil. The *Extraversion* domain taps aspects

Table 11–2
The Big Five Compared to Cattell's Five

The Big Five	Cattell's Five (circa 1960)
Extraversion	Introversion/Extraversion
Neuroticism	Low Anxiety/High Anxiety
Openness	Tough-Mindedness/Receptivity
Agreeableness	Independence/Accommodation
Conscientiousness	Low Self-Control/High Self-Control

Cattell expressed what he viewed as the source traits of personality in terms of bipolar dimensions. The 16 personality factors measured by the test today are: Warmth (Reserved vs. Warm), Reasoning (Concrete vs. Abstract), Emotional Stability (Reactive vs. Emotionally Stable), Dominance (Deferential vs. Dominant), Liveliness (Serious vs. Lively), Rule-Consciousness (Expedient vs. Rule-Conscious), Social Boldness (Shy vs. Socially Bold), Sensitivity (Utilitarian vs. Sensitive), Vigilance (Trusting vs. Vigilant), Abstractedness (Grounded vs. Abstracted), Privateness (Forthright vs. Private), Apprehension (Self-Assured vs. Apprehensive), Openness to Change (Traditional vs. Open to Change), Self-Reliance (Group-Oriented vs. Self-Reliant), Perfectionism (Tolerates Disorder vs. Perfectionistic), and Tension (Relaxed vs. Tense).

of sociability, how proactive people are in seeking out others, as well as assertiveness. *Openness* (also referred to as the Intellect factor) refers to openness to experience as well as active imagination, aesthetic sensitivity, attentiveness to inner feelings, preference for variety, intellectual curiosity, and independence of judgment. *Agreeableness* is primarily a dimension of interpersonal tendencies that include altruism, sympathy toward others, friendliness, and the belief that others are similarly inclined. *Conscientiousness* is a dimension of personality that has to do with the active processes of planning, organizing, and following through. Each of these major dimensions or domains of personality may be subdivided into individual traits or facets measured by the NEO PI-R. Psychologists have found value in using these dimensions to describe a wide range of behavior attributable to personality (Chang et al., 2011).

The NEO PI-R is designed for use with persons 17 years of age and older and is essentially self-administered. Computerized scoring and interpretation are available. Validity and reliability data are presented in the manual. A more detailed description of this test prepared by the test authors (Costa and McCrae) is presented in the Instructor's Resources within Connect.

Perhaps due to the enthusiasm with which psychologists have embraced "the Big 5," a number of tests other than the NEO PI-R have been developed to measure it. One such instrument is The Big Five Inventory (BFI; John et al., 1991). This test is made publicly available for noncommercial purposes to researchers and students. It consists of only 44 items, which makes it relatively quick to administer. Another instrument, the Ten Item Personality Inventory (TIPI; Gosling, Rentfrow, & Swann, 2003), contains only two items for each of the Big 5 dimensions. Educated on matters of test construction and test validity, you may now be asking yourself how a test with so few items could possibly be valid. And if that is the case, you may want to read an article by Jonason et al. (2011), which actually has some favorable things to say about the construct validity of the TIPI. A nonverbal measure of the Big-5 has also been developed. And once again, educated on matters of test construction as you are, you may be asking yourself something like, "How in blazes did they do that?!" The Five-Factor Nonverbal Personality Questionnaire (FF-NPQ) is administered by showing respondents illustrations of behaviors indicative of the Big-5 dimensions. Respondents are then asked to gauge the likelihood of personally engaging in those behaviors (Paunonen et al., 2004). One study compared the performance of monozygotic (identical) twins on verbal and nonverbal measures of the Big-5. The researchers concluded that the performance of the twins was similar on the measures and that the similarities were attributable to shared genes rather than shared environments (Moore et al., 2010). Such studies fueled speculation regarding the heritability of psychological traits.

We began our discussion of personality test development methods with a note that many personality tests have used two or more of these strategies in their process of development. At this point you may begin to appreciate how, as well as why, two or more tools might be used. A pool of items for an objective personality measure could be created, for example, on the basis of logic or theory, or both logic and theory. The items might then be arranged into scales on the basis of factor analysis. The draft version of the test could be administered to a criterion group and to a control group to see if responses to the items differ as a function of group membership. But here we are getting just a bit ahead of ourselves. We need to define, discuss, and illustrate what is meant by *criterion group* in the context of developing personality tests.

Criterion Groups

A **criterion** may be defined as a standard on which a judgment or decision can be made. With regard to scale development, a **criterion group** is a reference group of testtakers who share specific characteristics and whose responses to test items serve as a standard according to which items will be included in or discarded from the final version of a scale. The process of using criterion groups to develop test items is referred to as **empirical criterion keying** because the scoring or keying of items has been demonstrated empirically to differentiate among groups of testtakers. The shared characteristic of the criterion group to be researched—a psychiatric diagnosis, a unique skill or ability, a genetic aberration, or whatever—will vary as a function of the nature and scope of the test. Development of a test by means of empirical criterion keying may be summed up as follows:

1. Create a large, preliminary pool of test items from which the test items for the final form of the test will be selected.

2. Administer the preliminary pool of items to at least two groups of people:

    Group 1: A criterion group composed of people known to possess the trait being measured.

    Group 2: A randomly selected group of people (who may or may not possess the trait being measured)

3. Conduct an item analysis to select items indicative of membership in the criterion group. Items in the preliminary pool that discriminate between membership in the two groups in a statistically significant fashion will be retained and incorporated in the final form of the test.

4. Obtain data on test performance from a standardization sample of testtakers who are representative of the population from which future testtakers will come. The test performance data for Group 2 members on items incorporated into the final form of the test may be used for this purpose if deemed appropriate. The performance of Group 2 members on the test would then become the standard against which future testtakers will be evaluated. After the mean performance of Group 2 members on the individual items (or scales) of the test has been identified, future testtakers will be evaluated in terms of the extent to which their scores deviate in either direction from the Group 2 mean.

At this point you may ask, "But what about that initial pool of items? How is it created?" The answer is that the test developer may have found inspiration for each of the items from reviews of journals and books, interviews with patients, or consultations with colleagues or known experts. The test developer may have relied on logic or reason alone to write the items, or on other tests. Alternatively, the test developer may have relied on none of these and simply let imagination loose and committed to paper whatever emerged. An interesting aspect of test development by means of empirical criterion keying is that the content of the test items does not have to relate in a logical, rational, direct, or face-valid way to the measurement objective. Burisch (1984, p. 218) captured the essence of empirical criterion keying when he stated flatly, "If shoe size as a predictor improves your ability to predict performance as an airplane pilot, use it."[3] Burisch went on to offer this tongue-in-cheek description of how criterion groups could be used to develop an "M-F" test to differentiate males from females:

> Allegedly not knowing where the differences were, he or she would never dream of using an item such as "I can grow a beard if I want to" or "In a restaurant I tend to prefer the ladies' room to the men's room." Rather, a heterogeneous pool of items would be assembled and administered to a sample of men and women. Next, samples would be compared item by item. Any item discriminating sufficiently well would qualify for inclusion in the M-F test. (p. 214)

Now imagine that it is the 1930s. A team of researchers is keenly interested in devising a paper-and-pencil test that will improve reliability in psychiatric diagnosis. Their idea is to use empirical criterion keying to create the instrument. A preliminary version of the test will be administered (1) to several criterion groups of adult inpatients, each group homogeneous with respect to psychiatric diagnosis, and (2) to a group of randomly selected normal adults. Using item analysis, items useful in differentiating members of the various clinical groups from members of the normal group will be retained to make up the final form of the test. The researchers envision that future users of the published test will be able to derive diagnostic insights by comparing a testtaker's response pattern to that of testtakers in the normal group.

And there you have the beginnings of a relatively simple idea that would, in time, win widespread approval from clinicians around the world. It is an idea for a test that stimulated the publication of thousands of research studies, and an idea that led to the development of a test that would serve as a model for countless other instruments devised through the use of criterion group research. The test, originally called the Medical and Psychiatric Inventory (Dahlstrom & Dahlstrom, 1980), is the MMPI. Years after its tentative beginnings, the test's senior author recalled that "it was difficult to persuade a publisher to accept the MMPI" (Hathaway, cited in Dahlstrom & Welsh, 1960, p. vii). However, the University of Minnesota Press was obviously persuaded, because in 1943 it published the test under a new name, the Minnesota Multiphasic Personality Inventory (MMPI). The rest, as they say, is history.

In the next few pages, we describe the development of the original MMPI as well as its more contemporary progeny, the MMPI-2, the MMPI-2 Restructured Form (the MMPI-2-RF), and the MMPI-A.

The MMPI The MMPI was the product of a collaboration between psychologist Starke R. Hathaway and psychiatrist/neurologist John Charnley McKinley (Hathaway & McKinley, 1940, 1942, 1943, 1951; McKinley & Hathaway, 1940, 1944). It contained 566 true–false items and was designed as an aid to psychiatric diagnosis with adolescents and adults 14 years of age and older. Research preceding the selection of test items included review of textbooks, psychiatric reports, and previously published personality test items. In this sense, the beginnings of the MMPI can be traced to an approach to test development that was based on logic and reason.

A listing of the 10 clinical scales of the MMPI is presented in Table 11–3 along with a description of the corresponding criterion group. Each of the diagnostic categories listed for

---

3. It should come as no surprise, however, that any scale that is the product of such wildly empirical procedures would be expected to be extremely high in heterogeneity of item content and profoundly low in internal consistency measures.

Table 11–3

The Clinical Criterion Groups for MMPI Scales

Scale	Clinical Criterion Group
1. Hypochondriasis (Hs)	Patients who showed exaggerated concerns about their physical health
2. Depression (D)	Clinically depressed patients; unhappy and pessimistic about their future
3. Hysteria (Hy)	Patients with conversion reactions
4. Psychopathic deviate (Pd)	Patients who had histories of delinquency and other antisocial behavior
5. Masculinity-femininity (Mf)	Minnesota draftees, airline stewardesses, and male homosexual college students from the University of Minnesota campus community
6. Paranoia (Pa)	Patients who exhibited paranoid symptomatology such as ideas of reference, suspiciousness, delusions of persecution, and delusions of grandeur
7. Psychasthenia (Pt)	Anxious, obsessive-compulsive, guilt-ridden, and self-doubting patients
8. Schizophrenia (Sc)	Patients who were diagnosed as schizophrenic (various subtypes)
9. Hypomania (Ma)	Patients, most diagnosed as manic-depressive, who exhibited manic symptomatology such as elevated mood, excessive activity, and easy distractibility
10. Social introversion (Si)	College students who had scored at the extremes on a test of introversion/extraversion

Note that these same 10 clinical scales formed the core not only of the original MMPI, but of its 1989 revision, the MMPI-2. The clinical scales did undergo some modification for the MMPI-2, such as editing and reordering, and nine items were eliminated. Still, the MMPI-2 retained the 10 original clinical scale names, despite the fact that some of them (such as "Psychopathic Deviate") are relics of a bygone era. Perhaps that accounts for why convention has it that these scales be referred to by scale numbers only, not their names.

the 10 clinical scales were popular diagnostic categories in the 1930s. Members of the clinical criterion group for each scale were presumed to have met the criteria for inclusion in the category named in the scale. MMPI clinical scale items were derived empirically by administration to clinical criterion groups and normal control groups. The items that successfully differentiated between the two groups were retained in the final version of the test (Welsh & Dahlstrom, 1956). Well, it's actually a bit more complicated than that, and you really should know some of the details . . .

To understand the meaning of *normal control group* in this context, think of an experiment. In experimental research, an experimenter manipulates the situation so that the experimental group is exposed to something (the independent variable) and the control group is not. In the development of the MMPI, members of the criterion groups were drawn from a population of people presumed to be members of a group with a shared diagnostic label. Analogizing an experiment to this test development situation, it is as if the experimental treatment for the criterion group members was membership in the category named. By contrast, members of the **control group** were normal (that is, nondiagnosed) people who ostensibly received no such experimental treatment.

The normal control group, also referred to as the standardization sample, consisted of approximately 1,500 subjects. Included were 724 people who happened to be visiting friends or relatives at University of Minnesota hospitals, 265 high-school graduates seeking precollege guidance at the University of Minnesota Testing Bureau, 265 skilled workers participating in a local Works Progress Administration program, and 243 medical (nonpsychiatric) patients. The clinical criterion group for the MMPI was, for the most part, made up of psychiatric inpatients at the University of Minnesota Hospital. We say "for the most part" because Scale 5 (Masculinity-Femininity) and Scale 0 (Social Introversion) were not derived in this way.

The number of people included in each diagnostic category was relatively low by contemporary standards. For example, the criterion group for Scale 7 (Psychasthenia) contained only

JUST THINK . . .

Applying what you know about the standardization of tests, what are your thoughts regarding the standardization of the original MMPI? What about the composition of the clinical criterion groups? The normal control group?

20 people, all diagnosed as psychasthenic.[4] Two of the "clinical" scales (Scale 0 and Scale 5) did not even use members of a clinical population in the criterion group. The members of the Scale 0 (Social Introversion) clinical criterion group were college students who had earned extreme scores on a measure of introversion-extraversion. Scale 5 (Masculinity-Femininity) was designed to measure neither masculinity nor femininity; rather, it was originally developed to differentiate heterosexual from homosexual males. Due to a dearth of items that effectively differentiated people on this variable, the test developers broadened the definition of Scale 5 and added items that discriminated between normal males (soldiers) and females (airline personnel). Some of the items added to this scale were obtained from the Attitude Interest Scale (Terman & Miles, 1936). Hathaway and McKinley had also attempted to develop a scale to differentiate lesbians from female heterosexuals but were unable to do so.

JUST THINK . . .

Write one true–false item that you believe would successfully differentiate male from female testtakers. Don't forget to provide your suggested answer key.

By the 1930s, research on the Personal Data Sheet (Woodworth, 1917) as well as other face-valid, logic-derived instruments had brought to light problems inherent in self-report methods. Hathaway and McKinley (1943) evinced a keen awareness of such problems. They built into the MMPI three validity scales: the L scale (the Lie scale), the F scale (the Frequency scale—or, perhaps more accurately, the "Infrequency" scale), and the K (Correction) scale. Note that these scales were not designed to measure validity in the technical, psychometric sense. There is, after all, something inherently self-serving, if not suspect, about a test that purports to gauge its own validity! Rather, *validity* here was a reference to a built-in indicator of the operation of testtaker response styles (such as carelessness, deliberate efforts to deceive, or unintentional misunderstanding) that could affect the test results.

The L scale contains 15 items that, if endorsed, could reflect somewhat negatively on the testtaker. Two examples: "I do not always tell the truth" and "I gossip a little at times" (Dahlstrom et al., 1972, p. 109). The willingness of the examinee to reveal *anything* negative of a personal nature will be called into question if the score on the L scale does not fall within certain limits.

The 64 items on the F scale (1) are infrequently endorsed by members of nonpsychiatric populations (that is, normal people) and (2) do not fit into any known pattern of deviance. A response of *true* to an item such as the following would be scored on the F scale: "It would be better if almost all laws were thrown away" (Dahlstrom et al., 1972, p. 115). An elevated F score may mean that the respondent did not take the test seriously and was just responding to items randomly.

JUST THINK . . .

Try your hand at writing a good L-scale item.

Alternatively, the individual with a high F score may be a very eccentric individual or someone who was attempting to fake bad. Malingerers in the armed services, people intent on committing fraud with respect to health insurance, and criminals attempting to cop a psychiatric plea are some of the groups of people who might be expected to have elevated F scores on their profiles.

Like the L score and the F score, the K score is a reflection of the frankness of the testtaker's self-report. An elevated K score is associated with defensiveness and the desire to present a favorable impression. A low K score is associated with excessive self-criticism, desire to detail deviance, or desire to fake bad. A *true* response to the item "I certainly feel useless at times" and a *false* response to "At times I am all full of energy" (Dahlstrom et al., 1972, p. 125) would be scored on the K scale. The K scale is sometimes used to correct scores on

---

4. *Psychasthenia* (literally, *loss of strength* or *weakness* of the *psyche* or *mind)* is a now-antiquated term and psychiatric diagnosis. As used in the 1930s, it referred to an individual unable to think properly or focus concentration owing to conditions such as obsessive thoughts, excessive doubts, and phobias. A person with this diagnosis was said to be *psychasthenic*.

five of the clinical scales. The scores are statistically corrected for an individual's overwillingness or unwillingness to admit deviance.

Another scale that bears on the validity of a test administration is the *Cannot Say* scale, also referred to simply as the ? (question mark) scale. This scale is a simple frequency count of the number of items to which the examinee responded *cannot say* or failed to mark any response. Items may be omitted or marked *cannot say* for many reasons, including respondent indecisiveness, defensiveness, carelessness, and lack of experience relevant to the item. Traditionally, the validity of an answer sheet with a *cannot say* count of 30 or higher is called into question and deemed uninterpretable (Dahlstrom et al., 1972). Even for test protocols with a *cannot say* count of 10, caution has been urged in test interpretation. High *cannot say* scores may be avoided by a proctor's emphasis in the initial instructions to answer *all* items.

The MMPI contains 550 true–false items, 16 of which are repeated on some forms of the test (for a total of 566 items administered). Scores on each MMPI scale are reported in the form of *T* scores which, you may recall, have a mean set at 50 and a standard deviation set at 10. A score of 70 on any MMPI clinical scale is 2 standard deviations above the average score of members of the standardization sample, and a score of 30 is 2 standard deviations below their average score.

In addition to the clinical scales and the validity scales, there are MMPI content scales, supplementary scales, and Harris-Lingoes subscales. As the name implies, the *content scales,* such as the Wiggins Content Scales (after Wiggins, 1966), are composed of groups of test items of similar content. Examples of content scales on the MMPI include the scales labeled Depression and Family Problems. In a sense, content scales "bring order" and face validity to groups of items, derived from empirical criterion keying, that ostensibly have no relation to one another.

Supplementary scales is a catch-all phrase for the hundreds of different MMPI scales that have been developed since the test's publication. These scales have been devised by different researchers using a variety of methods and statistical procedures, most notably factor analysis. There are supplementary scales that are fairly consistent with the original objectives of the MMPI, such as scales designed to shed light on alcoholism and ego strength. And then there are dozens of other supplementary scales, ranging from "Success in Baseball" to—well, you name it![5]

The publisher of the MMPI makes available for computerized scoring only a limited selection of the many hundreds of supplementary scales that have been developed and discussed in the professional literature. One of them, the Harris-Lingoes subscales (often referred to simply as the Harris scales), are groupings of items into subscales (with labels such as Brooding and Social Alienation) that were designed to be more internally consistent than the umbrella scale from which the subscale was derived.

JUST THINK . . .

If you were going to develop a supplementary MMPI scale, what would it be? Why would you want to develop this scale?

Historically administered by paper and pencil, the MMPI is today administered by many methods: online, offline on disk, or by index cards. An audio version for semiliterate testtakers is also available, with instructions recorded on audiocassette. Testtakers respond to items by answering *true* or *false.* Items left unanswered are construed as *cannot say.* In the version of the test administered using individual items printed on cards, testtakers are instructed to sort the cards into three piles labeled *true, false,* and *cannot say.* At least a sixth-grade reading level is required to understand all the items. There are no time limits, and the time required to administer 566 items is typically between 60 and 90 minutes.

It is possible to score MMPI answer sheets by hand, but the process is labor intensive and rarely done. Computer scoring of protocols is accomplished by software on personal computers,

---

5. Here, the astute reader will begin to appreciate just how far from its original intended purpose the MMPI has strayed. In fact, the MMPI in all of its forms has been used for an extraordinarily wide range of adventures that are only tangentially related to the objective of psychiatric diagnosis.

by computer transmission to a scoring service via modem, or by physically mailing the completed form to a computer scoring service. Computer output may range from a simple numerical and graphic presentation of scores to a highly detailed narrative report complete with analysis of scores on selected supplementary scales.

Soon after the MMPI was published, it became evident that the test could not be used to neatly categorize testtakers into diagnostic categories. When testtakers had elevations in the pathological range of two or more scales, diagnostic dilemmas arose. Hathaway and McKinley (1943) had urged users of their test to opt for *configural interpretation* of scores—that is, interpretation based not on scores of single scales but on the pattern, profile, or configuration of the scores. However, their proposed method for profile interpretation was extremely complicated, as were many of the proposed adjunctive and alternative procedures.

Paul Meehl (1951) proposed a 2-point code derived from the numbers of the clinical scales on which the testtaker achieved the highest (most pathological) scores. If a testtaker achieved the highest score on Scale 1 and the second-highest score on Scale 2, then that testtaker's 2-point code type would be 12. The 2-point code type for a highest score on Scale 2 and a second-highest score on Scale 1 would be 21. Because each digit in the code is interchangeable, a code of 12 would be interpreted in exactly the same way as a code of 21. By the way, a code of 12 (or 21) is indicative of an individual in physical pain. An assumption here is that each score in the 2-point code type exceeds an elevation of $T = 70$. If the scale score does not exceed 70, this is indicated by the use of a prime (') after the scale number. Meehl's system had great appeal for many MMPI users. Before long, a wealth of research mounted on the interpretive meanings of the 40 code types that could be derived using 10 scales and two interchangeable digits.[6]

Another popular approach to scoring and interpretation came in the form of **Welsh codes**— referred to as such because they were created by Welsh (1948, 1956), not because they were written in Welsh (although to the uninitiated, they may be equally incomprehensible). Here is an example of a Welsh code:

$$6*\ \underline{78}'''\ 1\text{-}53/4\text{:}2\#\ \underline{90}\ F'L\text{-}/K$$

To the seasoned Welsh code user, this expression provides information about a testtaker's scores on the MMPI clinical and validity scales.

Students interested in learning more about the MMPI need not expend a great deal of effort in tracking down sources. Chances are your university library is teeming with books and journal articles written on or about this multiphasic (many-faceted) instrument. Of course, you may also want to go well beyond this historical introduction by becoming better acquainted with this test's more contemporary revisions, the MMPI-2, the MMPI-2 Restructured Form, and the MMPI-A. A barebones overview of those instruments follows.

The MMPI-2   Much of what has already been said about the MMPI in terms of its general structure, administration, scoring, and interpretation is applicable to the MMPI-2. The most significant difference between the two tests is the more representative standardization sample (normal control group) used in the norming of the MMPI-2. Approximately 14% of the MMPI items were rewritten to correct grammatical errors and to make the language more contemporary, nonsexist, and readable. Items thought to be objectionable to some testtakers were eliminated. Added were items addressing topics such as drug abuse, suicide potential, marital adjustment, attitudes toward work, and Type A behavior patterns.[7] In all, the MMPI-2 contains a total of

---

6. In addition to 2-point coding systems, at least one 3-point coding system was proposed. As you might expect, in that system the first number was the highest score, the second number was the second-highest score, and the third number was the third-highest score.

7. Recall from our discussion of psychological types earlier in this chapter (pages 356 to 358) what constitutes Type A and Type B behavior.

567 true–false items, including 394 items that are identical to the original MMPI items, 66 items that were modified or rewritten, and 107 new items. The suggested age range of testtakers for the MMPI-2 is 18 years and older, as compared to 14 years and older for the MMPI. The reading level required (sixth-grade) is the same as for the MMPI. The MMPI-2, like its predecessor, may be administered online, offline by paper and pencil, or by audiocassette, and it takes about the same length of time to administer.

The 10 clinical scales of the MMPI are identical to those on the MMPI-2, as is the policy of referring to them primarily by number. Content component scales were added to the MMPI-2 to provide more focused indices of content. For example, Family Problems content was subdivided into Family Discord and Familial Alienation content.

The three original validity scales of the MMPI were retained in the MMPI-2, and three new validity scales were added: Back-Page Infrequency (Fb), True Response Inconsistency (TRIN), and Variable Response Inconsistency (VRIN). The Back-Page Infrequency scale contains items seldom endorsed by testtakers who are candid, deliberate, and diligent in their approach to the test. Of course, some testtakers' diligence wanes as the test wears on and so, by the "back pages" of the test, a random or inconsistent pattern of responses may become evident. The Fb scale is designed to detect such a pattern.

The TRIN scale is designed to identify acquiescent and nonacquiescent response patterns. It contains 23 pairs of items worded in opposite forms. Consistency in responding dictates that, for example, a *true* response to the first item in the pair is followed by a *false* response to the second item in the pair. The VRIN scale is designed to identify indiscriminate response patterns. It, too, is made up of item pairs, where each item in the pair is worded in either opposite or similar form.

JUST THINK . . .

To maintain continuity with the original test, the MMPI-2 used the same names for the clinical scales. Some of these scale names, such as *Psychasthenia,* arc no longer used. If you were in charge of the MMPI's revision, what would your recommendation have been for dealing with this issue related to MMPI-2 scale names?

The senior author of the MMPI-2, James Butcher (Figure 11–6),[8] developed yet another validity scale after the publication of that test. The S scale is a validity scale designed to detect self-presentation in a superlative manner (Butcher & Han, 1995; Lanyon, 1993a, 1993b; Lim & Butcher, 1996).

Another proposed validity scale, this one designed to detect malingerers in personal injury claims, was proposed by Paul R. Lees-Haley and his colleagues (1991). Referred to as the FBS or Faking Bad Scale, this scale was originally developed as a means to detect malingerers who submitted bogus personal injury claims. In the years since its development, the FBS Scale has found support from some, most notably Ben-Porath et al. (2009). However, it also has its critics— among them, James Butcher and his colleagues. Butcher et al. (2008) argued that factors other than malingering (such as genuine physical or psychological problems) could contribute to endorsement of items that were keyed as indicative of malingering. They cautioned that the "lack of empirical verification of the 43 items selected by Lees-Haley, including examination of the items' performance across broad categories of people, argues against its widespread dissemination" (pp. 194–195).

A nagging criticism of the original MMPI was the lack of representation of the standardization sample of the U.S. population. This criticism was addressed in the standardization

JUST THINK . . .

Of all of the proposed validity scales for the MMPI-2, which do you think is the best indicator of whether the test scores are truly indicative of the testtaker's personality?

of the MMPI-2. The 2,600 individuals (1,462 females, 1,138 males) from seven states who made up the MMPI-2 standardization sample had been matched to 1980 U.S. Census data on

---

8. Pictured to the right of James Butcher is his buddy, Dale Moss, who was killed in the war. The authors pause at this juncture to remember and express gratitude to all the people in all branches of the military and government who have sacrificed for this country.

Figure 11–6
James Butcher (1933–) and Friend

That's Jim, today better known as the senior author of the MMPI-2, to your right as an Army infantryman at Outpost Yoke in South Korea in 1953. Returning to civilian life, Jim tried various occupations, including salesman and private investigator. He later earned a Ph.D. at the University of North Carolina, where he had occasion to work with W. Grant Dahlstrom and George Welsh (as in MMPI "Welsh code"). Butcher's first teaching job was at the University of Minnesota, where he looked forward to working with Starke Hathaway and Paul Meehl. But he was disappointed to learn that "Hathaway had moved on to the pursuit of psychotherapy research and typically disclaimed any expertise in the test. . . . Hathaway always refused to become involved in teaching people about the test. Meehl had likewise moved on to other venues" (Butcher, 2003, p. 233).
© James Butcher

the variables of age, gender, minority status, social class, and education (Butcher, 1990). Whereas the original MMPI did not contain any non-Whites in the standardization sample, the MMPI-2 sample was 81% White and 19% non-White. Age of subjects in the sample ranged from 18 years to 85 years. Formal education ranged from 3 years to 20+ years, with more highly educated people and people working in the professions overrepresented in the sample. Median annual family income for females in the sample was $25,000 to $30,000. Median annual family income for males in the sample was $30,000 to $35,000.

As with the original MMPI, the standardization sample data provided the basis for transforming the raw scores obtained by respondents into *T* scores for the MMPI-2. However, a technical adjustment was deemed to be in order. The *T* scores used for standardizing the MMPI clinical scales and content scales were linear *T* scores. For the MMPI-2, linear *T* scores were also used for standardization of the validity scales, the supplementary scales, and Scales 5 and 0 of the clinical scales. However, a different *T* score was used to standardize the remaining eight clinical scales as well as all of the content scales; these scales were standardized with uniform *T* scores (*UT* scores). The *UT* scores were used in an effort to make the *T* scores corresponding to percentile scores more comparable across the MMPI-2 scales (Graham, 1990; Tellegen & Ben-Porath, 1992).

Efforts to address concerns about the MMPI did not end with the publication of the MMPI-2. Before long, research was under way to revise the MMPI-2. These efforts were evident in the publication of restructured clinical scales (Tellegen et al., 2003) and culminated more recently in the publication of the MMPI-2 Restructured Form (MMPI-2-RF).

The MMPI-2-RF The need to rework the clinical scales of the MMPI-2 was perceived by Tellegen et al. (2003) as arising, at least in part, from two basic problems with the structure of the scales. One basic problem was overlapping items. The method of test development initially used to create the MMPI, empirical criterion keying, practically ensured there would be some item overlap. But just how much item overlap was there? Per pair of clinical scales, it has been observed that there is an average of more than six overlapping items in the MMPI-2 (Greene, 2000; Helmes & Reddon, 1993). Item overlap between the scales can decrease the distinctiveness and discriminant validity of individual scales and can also contribute to difficulties in determining the meaning of elevated scales.

A second problem with the basic structure of the test could also be characterized in terms of overlap—one that is more conceptual in nature. Here, reference is made to the pervasive influence of a factor that seemed to permeate all of the clinical scales. The factor has been described in different ways with different terms such as anxiety, malaise, despair, and maladjustment. It is a factor that is thought to be common to most forms of psychopathology yet unique to none. Exploring the issue of why entirely different approaches to psychotherapy had comparable results, Jerome Frank (1974) focused on what he viewed as this common factor in psychopathology, which he termed *demoralization:*

> Only a small proportion of persons with psychopathology come to therapy; apparently something else must be added that interacts with their symptoms. This state of mind, which may be termed "demoralization," results from persistent failure to cope with internally or externally induced stresses. . . . Its characteristic features, not all of which need to be present in any one person, are feelings of impotence, isolation, and despair. (p. 271)

Dohrenwend et al. (1980) perpetuated the use of Frank's concept of demoralization in their discussion of a nonspecific distress factor in psychopathology. Tellegen (1985) also made reference to demoralization when he wrote of a factor that seemed to inflate correlations between measures within clinical inventories. Many of the items on all of the MMPI and MMPI-2 clinical scales, despite their heterogeneous content, seemed to be saturated with the demoralization factor. Concern about the consequences of this overlapping has a relatively long history (Welsh, 1952; Rosen, 1962; Adams & Horn, 1965). In fact, the history of efforts to remedy the problem of insufficient discriminant validity and discriminative efficiency of the MMPI clinical scales is almost as long as the long history of the test itself.

One goal of the restructuring was to make the clinical scales of the MMPI-2 more distinctive and meaningful. As described in detail in a monograph supplement to the MMPI-2 administration and scoring manual, Tellegen et al. (2003) attempted to (1) identify the "core components" of each clinical scale, (2) create revised scales to measure these core components (referred to as "seed scales"), and (3) derive a final set of Revised Clinical (RC) scales using the MMPI-2 item pool. Another objective of the restructuring was, in essence, to extract the demoralization factor from the existing MMPI-2 clinical scales and create a new Demoralization scale. This new scale was described as one that "measures a broad, emotionally colored variable that underlies much of the variance common to the MMPI-2 Clinical Scales" (Tellegen et al., 2003, p. 11).

Employing the MMPI-2 normative sample as well as three additional clinical samples in their research, Tellegen et al. (2003) made the case that their restructuring procedures were psychometrically sound and had succeeded in improving both convergent and discriminant validity. According to their data, the restructured clinical (RC) scales were less intercorrelated than the original clinical scales, and their convergent and discriminant validity were greater than those original scales. Subsequent to the development of the RC scales, additional scales were developed. For example, the test authors developed scales to measure clinically significant factors that were not directly assessed by the RC scales, such as suicidal ideation. They also saw a need to develop scales tapping higher-order dimensions to provide a framework for organizing and interpreting findings. These higher-order scales were labeled Emotional/Internalizing Dysfunction, Thought Dysfunction, and Behavioral/Externalizing Dysfunction. The finished product was published in 2008 and called the MMPI-2 Restructured Form (MMPI-2-RF; Ben-Porath & Tellegen, 2008). It contains a total of 338 items and 50 scales, some of which are summarized in Table 11–4.

Table 11–4
Description of a Sampling of MMPI-2-RF Scales

Clinical Scales Group

There are a total of nine clinical scales. The RCd, RC1, RC2, and RC3 scales were introduced by Tellegen et al. (2003). Gone from the original MMPI (and MMPI-2) clinical scales is the Masculinity-Femininity Scale.

Scale Name	Scale Description
Demoralization (RCd)	General malaise, unhappiness, and dissatisfaction
Somatic Complaints (RC1)	Diffuse complaints related to physical health
Low Positive Emotions (RC2)	A "core" feeling of vulnerability in depression
Cynicism (RC3)	Beliefs nonrelated to self that others are generally ill-intentioned and not to be trusted
Antisocial Behavior (RC4)	Acting in violation of societal or social rules
Ideas of Persecution (RC6)	Self-referential beliefs that one is in danger or threatened by others
Dysfunctional Negative Emotions (RC7)	Disruptive anxiety, anger, and irritability
Aberrant Experiences (RC8)	Psychotic or psychotic-like thoughts, perceptions, or experiences
Hypomanic Activation (RC9)	Over-activation, grandiosity, impulsivity, or aggression

Validity Scales Group

There are a total of eight validity scales, which is one more validity scale than in the previous edition of the test. The added validity scale is Infrequent Somatic Response (Fs).

Scale Name	Scale Description
Variable Response Inconsistency-Revised (VRIN-r)	Random responding
True Response Inconsistency-Revised (TRIN-r)	Fixed responding
Infrequent Responses-Revised (F-r)	Infrequent responses compared to the general population
Infrequent Psychopathology Responses-Revised (Fp-r)	Infrequent responses characteristic of psychiatric populations
Infrequent Somatic Responses (Fs)	Infrequent somatic complaints from patients with medical problems
Symptom Validity (aka Fake Bad Scale-Revised; FBS-r)	Somatic or mental complaints with little or no credibility
Uncommon Virtues (aka Lie Scale-Revised; L-r)	Willingness to reveal anything negative about oneself
Adjustment Validity (aka Defensiveness Scale-Revised; K-r)	Degree to which the respondent is self-critical

Specific Problem (SP) Scales Group

There are a total of 20 scales that measure problems. These SP scales are grouped as relating to Internalizing, Externalizing, or Interpersonal issues and are subgrouped according to the clinical scale on which they shed light.

Scale Name	Scale Description
Suicidal/Death Ideation (SUI)[a]	Respondent reports self-related suicidal thoughts or actions
Helplessness/Hopelessness (HLP)[a]	Pervasive belief that problems are unsolvable and/or goals unattainable
Self-Doubt (SFD)[a]	Lack of self-confidence, feelings of uselessness
Inefficacy (NFC)[a]	Belief that one is indecisive or incapable of accomplishment
Cognitive Complaints (COG)[a]	Concentration and memory difficulties
Juvenile Conduct Problems (JCP)[b]	Difficulties at home or school, stealing
Substance Abuse (SUB)[b]	Current and past misuse of alcohol and drugs
Sensitivity/Vulnerability (SNV)[c]	Taking things too hard, being easily hurt by others
Stress/Worry (STW)[c]	Preoccupation with disappointments, difficulty with time pressure
Anxiety (AXY)[c]	Pervasive anxiety, frights, frequent nightmares

Table 11–4

(continued)

Anger Proneness (ANP)[c]	Being easily angered, impatient with others
Behavior-Restricting Fears (BRF)[c]	Fears that significantly inhibit normal behavior
Multiple Specific Fears (MSF)[c]	Various specific fears, such as a fear of blood or a fear of thunder
Juvenile Conduct Problems (JCP)[c]	Difficulties at home or school, stealing
Aggression (AGG)[d]	Physically aggressive, violent behavior
Activation (ACT)[d]	Heightened excitation and energy level

Interest Scales Group

There are two scales that measure interests: the AES scale and the MEC scale.

Scale Name	Scale Description
Aesthetic-Literary Interests (AES)	Interest in literature, music, and/or the theater
Mechanical-Physical Interests (MEC)	Fixing things, building things, outdoor pursuits, sports

PSY-5 Scales Group

These five scales are revised versions of MMPI-2 measures.

Scale Name	Scale Description
Aggressiveness-Revised (AGGR-r)	Goal-directed aggression
Psychoticism-Revised (PSYC-r)	Disconnection from reality
Disconstraint-Revised (DISC-r)	Undercontrolled behavior
Negative Emotionality/Neuroticism-Revised (NEGE-r)	Anxiety, insecurity, worry, and fear
Introversion/Low Positive Emotionality-Revised (INTR-r)	Social disengagement and absence of joy or happiness

Note: Overview based on Ben-Porath et al. (2007) and related materials; consult the MMPI-2-RF test manual (and updates) for a complete list and description of all the test's scales.
[a] Internalizing scale that measures facets of Demoralization (RCd).
[b] Internalizing scale that measures facets of Antisocial Behavior (RC4).
[c] Internalizing scale that measures facets of Dysfunctional Negative Emotions (RC7).
[d] Internalizing scale that measures facets of Hypomanic Activation (RC9).

Since the publication of Tellegen et al.'s (2003) monograph, Tellegen, Ben-Porath, and their colleagues have published a number of other articles that provide support for various aspects of the psychometric adequacy of the RC scales and the MMPI-2-RF. Studies from independent researchers have also provided support for some of the claims made regarding the RC scales' reduced item intercorrelations and increased convergent and discriminant validity (Simms et al., 2005; Wallace & Liljequist, 2005). Other authors have obtained support for the Somatic Complaints RC scale, the Cynicism RC scale, and the VRIN-r and TRIN-r validity scales (Handel et al., 2010; Ingram et al., 2011; Thomas & Locke, 2010). Osberg et al. (2008) compared the MMPI-2 clinical scales with the RC scales in terms of psychometric properties and diagnostic efficiency and reported mixed results.

> **JUST THINK . . .**
>
> What is a scale that you think should have been added to the restructured MMPI-2?

The restructuring of a test as iconic at the MMPI has not made everyone happy. For example, Rogers et al. (2006) and Nichols (2006) took issue with aspects of the logic of the restructuring, the restructuring procedures employed, and the result of the restructuring. One of the concerns expressed by Nichols was that Tellegen and colleagues had gone too far in terms of extracting the demoralization factor (Dem) from the clinical scales. Addressing what he viewed as the overextraction of depressive variance from each of the clinical scales, Nichols

(2006, p. 137) asserted that "the depression-biased Dem was used to extract unwanted variance from the Depression scale (Scale 2), thereby assuring that significant core depressive variance would be lost rather than preserved in a restructured scale (RC2)."

The arguments of Nichols and other critics were rebutted by Tellegen et al. (2006), among others. To appreciate the tenor of some of the rebuttals, consider Weed's (2006) response to Nichols' comments about the restructuring of the depression scale:

> The MMPI-2 Clinical Scales are not models of psychopathology by any conventional sense of the term. No effort was made, for example, to guarantee that the most important features of depression were reflected within Clinical Scale D, let alone in careful balance. Furthermore, no effort was made to prevent the inclusion of items with content that lacked theoretical relevance to Major Depression. . . . Scale D is not a neatly ordered multivariate model of depression; it is a dimensional cacophony, probably overrepresenting facets here and underrepresenting there, and certainly comprising both good items and poorly performing items.
>
> Nichols's characterization thus inaccurately recasts a grave flaw of the MMPI-2 Clinical Scales in a benign or even favorable light. Rather than highlighting their internal chaos, Nichols describes the scales as reflecting "syndromal complexity," a phrase that might sound euphemistic if it were not clear that he is serious. One might as well speak of the Clinical Scales as being "charmingly free of typical psychometric restraints," characterized by "sassy heterogeneity," or filled to the brim with "intrascale insouciance." (p. 218)

Well . . . lest the present authors be accused of being insouciant (or otherwise indifferent) about providing some "nuts-and-bolts" information about the MMPI-2-RF, we hasten to note that the test manual reports evidence of the instrument's psychometric soundness. The MMPI-2-RF technical manual provides empirical correlates of test scores based on various criteria in various settings including clinical and nonclinical samples. The MMPI-2-RF can still be hand-scored and hand-profiled, although computerized score reporting (with or without a computerized narrative report) is available.

The MMPI-A   Although its developers had recommended the original MMPI for use with adolescents, test users had evinced skepticism of this recommendation through the years. Early on it was noticed that adolescents as a group tended to score somewhat higher on the clinical scales than adults, a finding that left adolescents as a group in the unenviable position of appearing to suffer from more psychopathology than adults. In part for this reason, separate MMPI norms for adolescents were developed. In the 1980s, while the MMPI was being revised to become the MMPI-2, the test developers had a choice of simply renorming the MMPI-2 for adolescents or creating a new instrument. They opted to develop a new test that was in many key respects a downward extension of the MMPI-2.

The Minnesota Multiphasic Personality Inventory–Adolescent (MMPI-A; Butcher et al., 1992) is a 478-item, true–false test designed for use in clinical, counseling, and school settings for the purpose of assessing psychopathology and identifying personal, social, and behavioral problems. The individual items of the MMPI-A largely parallel the MMPI-2, although there are 88 fewer items. Some of the MMPI-2 items were discarded, others were rewritten, and some completely new ones were added. In its written (as opposed to audiocassette) form, the test is designed for administration to testtakers in the 14- to 18-year-old age range who have at least a sixth-grade reading ability. As with the MMPI-2, versions of the test are available for administration by computer, by paper and pencil, and by audiocassette. The time required for an administration of all the items typically is between 45 and 60 minutes.

The MMPI-A contains 16 basic scales, including 10 clinical scales (identical in name and number to those of the MMPI-2) and six validity scales (actually, a total of eight validity scales given that the F scale is subdivided into F, F_1, and F_2 scales). The validity scales are Variable Response Inconsistency (VRIN), True Response Inconsistency (TRIN), Infrequency (F), Infrequency 1 (F_1; specifically applicable to the clinical scales), Infrequency 2 (F_2; specifically applicable to the content and supplementary scales), Lie (L), Defensiveness (K), and Cannot Say (?).

In addition to basic clinical and validity scales, the MMPI-A contains six supplementary scales (dealing with areas such as alcohol and drug use, immaturity, anxiety, and repression), 15 content scales (including areas such as conduct problems and school problems), 28 Harris-Lingoes scales, and three scales labeled Social Introversion. As with the MMPI-2, uniform T (UT) scales were employed for use with all the content scales and eight of the clinical scales (Scales 5 and 0 excluded) in order to make percentile scores comparable across scales.

The normative sample for the MMPI-A consisted of 805 adolescent males and 815 adolescent females drawn from schools in California, Minnesota, New York, North Carolina, Ohio, Pennsylvania, Virginia, and Washington. The objective was to obtain a sample that was nationally representative in terms of demographic variables such as ethnic background, geographic region of the United States, and urban/rural residence. Concurrent with the norming of the MMPI-A, a clinical sample of 713 adolescents was tested for the purpose of obtaining validity data. However, no effort was made to ensure representativeness of the clinical sample. Subjects were all drawn from the Minneapolis area, most from drug and alcohol treatment centers.

> **JUST THINK . . .**
>
> Your comments on the norming of the MMPI-A?

In general, the MMPI-A has earned high marks from test reviewers and may well have quickly become the most widely used measure of psychopathology in adolescents. More information about this test can be obtained from an authoritative book entitled *A Beginner's Guide to the MMPI—A* (Williams & Butcher, 2011). Chapters variously introduce readers to the history of the MMPI-A and set the test in the contemporary context of the digital age. The test's scales are described and guidelines for test administration are presented. The book also covers culture-related issues, as well as guidelines for interpreting scores and sharing information with testtakers, parents and others. When supplemented with the insights of others with more "arms length" distance from the test (e.g., Martin & Finn, 2010; Stokes et al., 2009; Zubeidat et al., 2011), the Williams and Butcher *Guide* can be an invaluable reference work for students of the MMPI-A.

The MMPI and its revisions and progeny in perspective　　The MMPI burst onto the psychology scene in the 1940s and was greeted as an innovative, well-researched, and highly appealing instrument by both clinical practitioners and academic researchers. Today, we can look back at its development and be even more impressed, as it was developed without the benefit of high-speed computers. The number of research studies that have conducted on this test number in the thousands, and few psychological tests are better known throughout the world. Through the years, various weaknesses in the test have been discovered, and remedies have been proposed as a consequence. The latest "restructuring" of the MMPI represents an effort not only to improve the test and bring it into the twenty-first century but also to maintain continuity with the voluminous research addressing its previous forms. There can be little doubt that the MMPI is very much a "work in progress" that will be continually patched, restructured, and otherwise re-innovated to maintain that continuity.

> **JUST THINK . . .**
>
> What should the next version of the MMPI look like? In what ways should it be different than the MMPI-2-RF?

Personality Assessment and Culture

Every day, assessment professionals across the United States are routinely called on to evaluate personality and related variables of people from culturally and linguistically diverse populations.

Yet personality assessment is anything but routine with children, adolescents, and adults from Native American, Hispanic, Asian, African American, and other cultures that may have been underrepresented in the development, standardization, and interpretation protocols of the measures used. Especially with members of culturally and linguistically diverse populations, a routine and business-as-usual approach to psychological testing and assessment is inappropriate, if not irresponsible. What is required is a professionally trained assessor capable of conducting a meaningful assessment, with sensitivity to how culture relates to the behaviors and cognitions being measured (López, 2000).

Before any tool of personality assessment—an interview, a test, a protocol for behavioral observation, a portfolio, or something else—can be employed, and before data derived from an attempt at measurement can be imbued with meaning, the assessor will ideally consider some important issues with regard to assessment of a particular assessee. Many of these issues relate to the level of acculturation, values, identity, worldview, and language of the assessee. Professional exploration of these areas is capable of yielding not only information necessary as a prerequisite for formal personality assessment but a wealth of personality-related information in its own right.

Acculturation and Related Considerations

Acculturation is an ongoing process by which an individual's thoughts, behaviors, values, worldview, and identity develop in relation to the general thinking, behavior, customs, and values of a particular cultural group. The process of acculturation begins at birth, a time at which the newborn infant's family or caretakers serve as agents of the culture.[9] In the years to come, other family members, teachers, peers, books, films, theater, newspapers, television and radio programs, and other media serve as agents of acculturation. Through the process of acculturation, one develops culturally accepted ways of thinking, feeling, and behaving.

A number of tests and questionnaires have been developed to yield insights regarding assessees' level of acculturation to their native culture or the dominant culture. A sampling of these measures is presented in Table 11–5. As you survey this list, keep in mind that the amount of psychometric research done on these instruments varies. Some of these instruments may be little more than content valid, if that. In such cases, let the buyer beware. Should you wish to use any of these measures, you may wish to look up more information about it in a resource such as the *Mental Measurements Yearbook*. Perhaps the most appropriate use of many of these tests would be to derive hypotheses for future testing by means of other tools of assessment. Unless compelling evidence exists to attest to the use of a particular instrument with members of a specific population, data derived from any of these tests and questionnaires should not be used alone to make selection, treatment, placement, or other momentous decisions.

A number of important questions regarding acculturation and related variables can be raised with regard to assessees from culturally diverse populations. Many general types of interview questions may yield rich insights regarding the overlapping areas of acculturation, values, worldview, and identity. A sampling of such questions is presented in Table 11–6. As an exercise, you may wish to pose some or all of these questions to someone you know who happens to be in the process of acculturation. Before doing so, however, some caveats are in order. Keep in mind the critical importance of rapport when conducting an interview. Be

---

9. The process of acculturation may begin before birth. It seems reasonable to assume that nutritional and other aspects of the mother's prenatal care may have implications for the newborn infant's tastes and other preferences.

Table 11–5
Some Published Measures of Acculturation

Target Population	Reference Sources
African-American	Baldwin (1984)
	Baldwin & Bell (1985)
	Klonoff & Landrine (2000)
	Obasi & Leong (2010)
	Snowden & Hines (1999)
Asian	Kim et al. (1999)
	Suinn et al. (1987)
Asian-American	Gim Chung et al. (2004)
	Wolfe et al. (2001)
Asian (East & South)	Barry (2001)
	Inman et al. (2001)
Asian Indian	Sodowsky & Carey (1988)
Central American	Wallen et al. (2002)
Chinese	Yao (1979)
Cuban	Garcia & Lega (1979)
Deaf culture	Maxwell-McCaw & Zea (2011)
Eskimo	Chance (1965)
Hawaiian	Bautista (2004)
	Hishinuma et al. (2000)
Iranian	Shahim (2007)
Japanese-American	Masuda et al. (1970)
	Padilla et al. (1985)
Khmer	Lim et al. (2002)
Latino/Latina	Murguia et al. (2000)
	Zea et al. (2003)
Mexican-American	Cuéllar et al. (1995)
	Franco (1983)
	Mendoza (1989)
	Ramirez (1984)
Muslim American	Bagasra (2010)
Native American	Garrett & Pichette (2000)
	Howe Chief (1940)
	Roy (1962)
Puerto Rican	Tropp et al. (1999)
	Cortes et al. (2003)
Vietnamese	Nguyen & von Eye (2002)
Population nonspecific measures	Sevig et al. (2000)
	Smither & Rodriguez-Giegling (1982)
	Stephenson (2000)
	Unger et al. (2002)
	Wong-Rieger & Quintana (1987)

sensitive to cultural differences in readiness to engage in self-disclosure about family or other matters that may be perceived as too personal to discuss (with a stranger or otherwise). Be ready and able to change the wording of these questions should you need to facilitate the assessee's understanding of them or to change the order of these questions should an assessee answer more than one question in the same response. Listen carefully and do not hesitate to probe for more information if you perceive value in doing so. Finally, keep in mind that the relevance of each of these questions will vary with the background and unique socialization experiences of each assessee.

Table 11–6
Some Sample Questions to Assess Acculturation

- Describe yourself.
- Describe your family. Who lives at home?
- Describe roles in your family, such as the role of mother, the role of father, the role of grandmother, the role of child, and so forth.
- What traditions, rituals, or customs were passed down to you by family members?
- What traditions, rituals, or customs do you think it is important to pass to the next generation?
- With regard to your family situation, what obligations do you see yourself as having?
- What obligations does your family have to you?
- What role does your family play in everyday life?
- How does the role of males and females differ from your own cultural perspective?
- What kind of music do you like?
- What kinds of foods do you eat most routinely?
- What do you consider fun things to do? When do you do these things?
- Describe yourself in the way that you think most other people would describe you. How would you say your own self-description would differ from that description?
- How might you respond to the question "Who are you?" with reference to your own sense of personal identity?
- With which cultural group or groups do you identify most? Why?
- What aspect of the history of the group with which you most identify is most significant to you? Why?
- Who are some of the people who have influenced you most?
- What are some things that have happened to you in the past that have influenced you most?
- What sources of satisfaction are associated with being you?
- What sources of dissatisfaction or conflict are associated with being you?
- What do you call yourself when asked about your ethnicity?
- What are your feelings regarding your racial and ethnic identity?
- Describe your most pleasant memory as a child.
- Describe your least pleasant memory as a child.
- Describe the ways in which you typically learn new things. In what ways might cultural factors have influenced this learning style?
- Describe the ways you typically resolve conflicts with other people. What influence might cultural factors have on this way of resolving conflicts?
- How would you describe your general view of the world?
- How would you characterize human nature in general?
- How much control do you believe you have over the things that happen to you? Why?
- How much control do you believe you have over your health? Your mental health?
- What are your thoughts regarding the role of work in daily life? Has your cultural identity influenced your views about work in any way? If so, how?
- How would you characterize the role of doctors in the world around you?
- How would you characterize the role of lawyers in the world around you?
- How would you characterize the role of politicians in the world around you?
- How would you characterize the role of spirituality in your daily life?
- What are your feelings about the use of illegal drugs?
- What is the role of play in daily life?
- How would you characterize the ideal relationship between human beings and nature?
- What defines a person who has power?
- What happens when one dies?
- Do you tend to live your life more in the past, the present, or the future? What influences on you do you think helped shape this way of living?
- How would you characterize your attitudes and feelings about the older people in your family? About older people in society in general?
- Describe your thinking about the local police and the criminal justice system.
- How do you see yourself 10 years from now?

Intimately entwined with acculturation is the learning of *values*. **Values** are that which an individual prizes or the ideals an individual believes in. An early systematic treatment of the subject of values came in a book entitled *Types of Men* (Spranger, 1928), which listed different types of people based on whether they valued things like truth, practicality, and power. The book served as an inspiration for a yet more systematic treatment of the subject (Allport et al., 1951). Before long, a number of different systems for listing and categorizing values had been published.

Rokeach (1973) differentiated what he called *instrumental* from *terminal* values. **Instrumental values** are guiding principles to help one attain some objective. Honesty, imagination, ambition, and cheerfulness are examples of instrumental values. **Terminal values** are guiding principles and a mode of behavior that is an endpoint objective. A comfortable life, an exciting life, a sense of accomplishment, and self-respect are some examples of terminal values. Other value-categorization systems focus on values in specific contexts, such as employment settings. Values such as financial reward, job security, or prestige may figure prominently in decisions regarding occupational choice and employment or feelings of job satisfaction.

Writing from an anthropological/cultural perspective, Kluckhohn (1954, 1960; Kluckhohn & Strodtbeck, 1961) conceived of values as answers to key questions with which civilizations must grapple. So, for example, from questions about how the individual should relate to the group, values emerge about individual versus group priorities. In one culture, the answers to such questions might take the form of norms and sanctions that encourage strict conformity and little competition among group members. In another culture, norms and sanctions may encourage individuality and competition among group members. In this context, one can begin to appreciate how members of different cultural groups can grow up with vastly different values, ranging from views on various "isms" (such as individualism versus collectivism) to views on what is trivial and what is worth dying for. The different values people from various cultures bring to the assessment situation may translate into widely varying motivational and incentive systems. Understanding an individual's values is an integral part of understanding personality.

Also intimately tied to the concept of acculturation is the concept of personal *identity*. **Identity** in this context may be defined as a set of cognitive and behavioral characteristics by which individuals define themselves as members of a particular group. Stated simply, identity refers to one's sense of self. Levine and Padilla (1980) defined **identification** as a process by which an individual assumes a pattern of behavior characteristic of other people, and referred to it as one of the "central issues that ethnic minority groups must deal with" (p. 13). Echoing this sentiment, Zuniga (1988) suggested that a question such as "What do you call yourself when asked about your ethnicity?" might be used as an icebreaker when assessing identification. She went on:

> How a minority client handles their response offers evidence of their comfortableness with their identity. A Mexican-American client who responds by saying, "I am an American, and I am just like everyone else," displays a defensiveness that demands gentle probing. One client sheepishly declared that she always called herself Spanish. She used this self-designation since she felt the term "Mexican" was dirty. (p. 291)

Another key culture-related personality variable concerns how an assessee tends to view the world. As its name implies, **worldview** is the unique way people interpret and make sense of their perceptions as a consequence of their learning experiences, cultural background, and related variables.

Our overview of personality began with a consideration of some superficial, lay perspectives on this multifaceted subject. We made reference to the now-classic rock oldie *Personality* and its "definition" of personality in terms of observable variables such as *walk, talk, smile,* and *charm.* Here, at the end of the chapter, we have come a long way in considering more personal, nonobservable elements of personality in the form of constructs such as *worldview, identification, values,* and *acculturation.* In the chapter that follows, we continue to broaden our perspective regarding tools that may be used to better understand and effectively assess personality.

Self-Assessment

Test your understanding of elements of this chapter by seeing if you can explain each of the following terms, expressions, and abbreviations:

acculturation
acquiescent response style
Big Five
control group
criterion
criterion group
empirical criterion keying
error of central tendency
forced-choice format
frame of reference
generosity error
graphology
halo effect
identification
identity
idiographic approach
impression management

instrumental values
leniency error
locus of control
MMPI
MMPI-2
MMPI-2-RF
MMPI-A
NEO PI-R
nomothetic approach
personality
personality assessment
personality profile
personality trait
personality type
profile
profile analysis
profiler

Q-sort technique
response style
self-concept
self-concept differentiation
self-concept measure
self-report
semantic differential
severity error
state
structured interview
terminal values
Type A personality
Type B personality
validity scale
values
Welsh code
worldview

12

Personality Assessment Methods

Some people see the world as filled with love and goodness, where others see hate and evil. Some people equate *living* with behavioral excess, whereas others strive for moderation in all things. Some people have relatively realistic perceptions of themselves. Other people labor under grossly distorted self-images and inaccurate perceptions of family, friends, and acquaintances. For psychologists and others interested in exploring differences among people with regard to these and other dimensions, many different tools are available. In this chapter, we survey some of the tools of personality assessment, including projective methods of assessment and behavioral approaches to assessment. We begin with a consideration of methods that are typically characterized as "objective" in nature.

Objective Methods

Usually administered by paper-and-pencil means or by computer, **objective methods of personality assessment** characteristically contain short-answer items for which the assessee's task is to select one response from the two or more provided. The scoring is done according to set procedures involving little, if any, judgment on the part of the scorer. As with tests of ability, objective methods of personality assessment may include items written in a multiple-choice, true–false, or matching format.

Whereas a particular response on an objective ability test may be scored *correct* or *incorrect,* a response on an objective personality test is scored with reference to either the personality characteristic(s) being measured or the validity of the respondent's pattern of responses. For example, on a personality test where a *true* response is deemed indicative of the presence of a particular trait, a number of *true* responses to *true–false* items will be interpreted with reference to the presumed strength of that trait in the testtaker. Well, maybe.

If the respondent has also responded *true* to items indicative of the *absence* of the trait as well as to items rarely endorsed as such by testtakers, then the validity of the protocol will be called into question. Scrutiny of the protocol may suggest an irregularity of some sort. For example, the items may have been responded to inconsistently, in random fashion, or with a *true* response to all questions. As we have seen, some objective personality tests are constructed with validity scales or other devices (such as a forced-choice format) designed to detect or deter response patterns that would call into question the meaningfulness of the scores.

Objective personality tests share many advantages with objective tests of ability. The items can be answered quickly, allowing the administration of many items covering varied aspects of the trait or traits the test is designed to assess. If the items on an objective test are well

JUST THINK . . .

What possible explanations exist for someone exhibiting inconsistency on an objective personality test?

written, then they require little explanation; this makes them well suited for both group and computerized administration. Objective items can usually be scored quickly and reliably by varied means, from hand scoring (usually with the aid of a template held over the test form) to computer scoring. Analysis and interpretation of such tests may be almost as fast as scoring, especially if conducted by computer and custom software.

How Objective Are Objective Methods of Personality Assessment?

Although objective personality test items share many characteristics with objective measures of ability, we hasten to add that the adjective *objective* is something of a misnomer when applied to personality testing and assessment. With reference to short-answer items on *ability* tests, the term *objective* gained favor because all items contained only one correct response. Well, that was not always true, either, but that's the way they were designed.

In contrast to the scoring of, say, essay tests, the scoring of objective, multiple-choice tests of ability left little room for emotion, bias, or favoritism on the part of the test scorer. Scoring was dispassionate and—for lack of a better term—objective. But unlike objective ability tests, objective personality tests typically contain no one correct answer. Rather, the selection of a particular choice from multiple-choice items provides information relevant to something about the testtaker—such as the presence, absence, or strength of a personality-related variable. Yes, the scoring of such tests can still be dispassionate and objective. However, the "objectivity" of the score derived from a so-called objective test of personality can be a matter of debate. Consider, for example, a personality test written in an objective test format designed to detect the existence of an unresolved oedipal conflict. The extent to which these test results will be viewed as "objective" is inextricably linked to one's views about the validity of psychoanalytic theory and, more specifically, the construct *oedipal conflict*.

Another issue related to the use of the adjective *objective* with *personality test* concerns self-report and the distinct *lack* of objectivity that can be associated with self-report. Testtakers' self-reports of what they like or dislike, what they agree or disagree with, what they do or do not do, and so forth can be anything but "objective," for many reasons. Some respondents may lack the insight to respond in what could reasonably be described as an objective manner. Some respondents respond in a manner that they believe will place them in the best or worst possible light—depending on the impression they wish to manage and their objectives in submitting to the evaluation. In other words, they can attempt to manage a desired impression by faking good or faking bad.

Ultimately, the term *objective* as applied to most personality tests may be best thought of as a shorthand description for a test format. Objective personality tests are objective in the sense that they employ a short-answer (typically multiple-choice) format, one that provides little, if any, room for discretion in terms of scoring. To describe a personality test as objective serves to distinguish it from projective and other measurement methods rather than to impart information about the reality, tangibility, or objectivity of scores derived from it.

Projective Methods

Suppose the lights in your classroom were dimmed and everyone was told to stare at the clean chalkboard for a minute or so. And suppose everyone was then asked to take out some paper and write down what they thought could be seen on the chalkboard (other than the chalkboard itself). If you examined what each of your fellow students wrote, you might find as many different things as there were students responding. You could assume that the students saw on the chalkboard—or, more accurately, *projected* onto the chalkboard—something that was not really there but rather was in (or on) their own minds. You might further assume that each student's response to the blank chalkboard reflected something very telling and unique about that student's personality structure.

The **projective hypothesis** holds that an individual supplies structure to unstructured stimuli in a manner consistent with the individual's own unique pattern of conscious and unconscious needs, fears, desires, impulses, conflicts, and ways of perceiving and responding. In like manner, we may define the **projective method** as a technique of personality assessment in which some judgment of the assessee's personality is made on the basis of performance on a task that involves supplying some sort of structure to unstructured or incomplete stimuli. Almost any relatively unstructured stimulus will do for this purpose. In a scene in Shakespeare's play *Hamlet,* Polonius and Hamlet discuss what can be seen in clouds. Indeed, clouds could be used as a projective stimulus.[1] But psychologists, slaves to practicality (and scientific methods) as they are, have developed projective measures of personality that are more reliable than clouds and more portable than chalkboards. Inkblots, pictures, words, drawings, and other things have been used as projective stimuli.

JUST THINK . . .

Be creative and name some non-obvious thing that could be used as a projective stimulus for personality assessment purposes. How might a projective test using what you named be administered, scored, and interpreted?

Unlike self-report methods, projective tests are *indirect* methods of personality assessment; assessees aren't being directly asked to disclose information about themselves. Rather, their task is to talk about something else (like inkblots or pictures). Through such indirect responses the assessor draws inferences about the personality of assessees. On such a task, the ability—and presumably the inclination—of examinees to fake is greatly minimized. Also minimized on some projective tasks is the testtaker's need for great proficiency in the English language. For example, minimal language skills are required to respond to or create a drawing. For that reason, and because some projective methods may be less linked to culture than are other measures of personality, proponents of projective testing believe that there is a promise of cross-cultural utility with these tests that has yet to be fulfilled. Proponents of projective measures also argue that a major advantage of such measures is that they tap unconscious as well as conscious material. In the words of the man who coined the term *projective methods,* "the most important things about an individual are what he cannot or will not say" (Frank, 1939, p. 395).[2]

Projective tests were born in the spirit of rebellion against normative data and through attempts by personality researchers to break down the study of personality into the study of specific traits of varying strengths. This orientation is exemplified by Frank (1939), who reflected: "It is interesting to see how the students of personality have attempted to meet the problem of individuality with methods and procedures designed for study of uniformities and norms that ignore or subordinate individuality, treating it as a troublesome deviation which derogates from the real, the superior, and only important central tendency, mode, average, etc." (pp. 392–393).

---

1. In fact, clouds *have* been used as projective stimuli. Wilhelm Stern's Cloud Picture Test, in which subjects were asked to tell what they saw in pictures of clouds, was one of the earliest projective measures.

2. The first published use of the term *projective methods* that we are aware of was in an article entitled "Projective Methods in the Psychological Study of Children" by Ruth Horowitz and Lois Barclay Murphy (1938). However, these authors had read Lawrence K. Frank's (1939) as-yet-unpublished manuscript and credited him for having "applied the term 'projective methods.'"

In contrast to methods of personality assessment that focused on the individual from a statistics-based, normative perspective, projective techniques were once the technique of choice for focusing on the individual from a purely clinical perspective—a perspective that examined the unique way an individual projects onto an ambiguous stimulus "his way of seeing life, his meanings, significances, patterns, and especially his feelings" (Frank, 1939, p. 403). Somewhat paradoxically, years of clinical experience with these tests and a mounting volume of research data have led the interpretation of responses to projective stimuli to become increasingly norm-referenced.

Inkblots as Projective Stimuli

Spill some ink in the center of a blank, white sheet of paper and fold it over. Allow to dry. There you have the recipe for an inkblot. Inkblots are not only used by assessment professionals as projective stimuli, they are very much associated with psychology itself in the public eye. The most famous inkblot test is, of course . . .

The Rorschach   Hermann Rorschach (Figure 12–1) developed what he called a "form interpretation test" using inkblots as the forms to be interpreted. In 1921 he published his monograph on the technique, *Psychodiagnostics.* In the last section of that monograph, Rorschach proposed applications of his test to personality assessment. He provided 28 case studies employing normal (well, undiagnosed) subjects and people with various psychiatric diagnoses (including neurosis, psychosis, and manic-depressive illness) to illustrate his test. Rorschach died suddenly and unexpectedly at the age of 38, just a year after his book was published. A paper co-authored by Rorschach and Emil Oberholzer entitled "The Application of the Form Interpretation Test" was published posthumously in 1923.

Figure 12–1
Hermann Rorschach (1884–1922)

Rorschach was a Swiss psychiatrist whose father had been an art teacher and whose interests included art as well as psychoanalysis— particularly the work of Carl Jung, who had written extensively on methods of bringing unconscious material to light. In 1913, Rorschach published papers on how analysis of a patient's artwork could provide insights into personality. Rorschach's inkblot test was published in 1921, and it was not an immediate success. Rorschach died of peritonitis the following year at the age of 38, unaware of the great legacy he would leave. For more on Hermann Rorschach, read his Test Developer Profile in the Instructor's Resources within Connect.

© akg-images/The Image Works

Like Rorschach, we will refer to his test as just that—a *test*. However, there has been a bit of a controversy about whether the instrument Rorschach created is best referred to as a test, a task, a method, a technique, or something else. For example, Goldfried et al. (1971) view the Rorschach as a structured interview, and Korchin and Schuldberg (1981) regard it as "less of a test" and more "an open and flexible arena for studying interpersonal transactions" (p. 1151). There has also been debate about whether or not the Rorschach is properly considered a projective instrument (Acklin, 1995; Aronow et al., 1995; Moreland et al., 1995b; Ritzler, 1995). For example, Rorschach authority John Exner once argued that the inkblots are "not completely ambiguous," that the task does not necessarily "force projection," and that "unfortunately, the Rorschach has been erroneously mislabeled a projective test for far too long" (1989, pp. 526–527; see also Exner, 1997). Regardless, *Rorschach* remains virtually synonymous with *projective test* among assessment professionals and, no matter how else referred to, it certainly qualifies as a "test."

The Rorschach consists of 10 bilaterally symmetrical (or, mirror-imaged if folded in half) inkblots printed on separate cards. Five inkblots are achromatic (meaning without color, or black-and-white). Two inkblots are black, white, and red. The remaining three inkblots are multicolored. The test comes with the cards only; there is no test manual or any administration, scoring, or interpretation instructions. There is no rationale for why some of the inkblots are achromatic and others are chromatic (with color). Unlike most psychological test kits, which today are published complete with test manual and optional carrying case, this test contains 10 cards packaged in a cardboard box; that's it. For any old-school clinician who uses the Rorschach, a computer-administered version of this test would somehow seem gauche and inappropriate. Of course, that's not to say that it hasn't been tried (Padawer, 2001). But even computerized scoring and interpretation of Rorschach protocols, let alone a computerized administration of the test, may be frowned upon by Rorschach purists (Andronikof, 2005).

To fill the need for a test manual and instructions for administration, scoring, and interpretation, a number of manuals and handbooks set forth a variety of methods (such as Aronow & Reznikoff, 1976, 1983; Beck, 1944, 1945, 1952, 1960; Exner, 1974, 1978, 1986, 2003; Exner & Weiner, 1982; Klopfer & Davidson, 1962; Lerner, 1991, 1996a, 1996b; Meyer et al., 2011; Piotrowski, 1957). The system most widely used is the "comprehensive system" devised by Exner. Before describing Exner's scoring system, however, here is a general overview of the process of administering, scoring, and interpreting the Rorschach.

JUST THINK . . .

Why might a Rorschach purist object to the administration of the test by computer?

Inkblot cards (similar in some respects to the one shown in Figure 12–2) are initially presented to the testtaker one at a time in numbered order from 1 to 10. The testtaker is instructed to tell what is on each of the cards with a question such as "What might this be?" Testtakers have a great deal of freedom with the Rorschach. They may, for example, rotate the cards and vary the number and length of their responses to each card. The examiner records all relevant information, including the testtaker's verbatim responses, nonverbal gestures, the length of time before the first response to each card, the position of the card, and so forth. The examiner does not engage in any discussion concerning the testtaker's responses during the initial administration of the cards. Every effort is made to provide the testtaker with the opportunity to *project,* free from any outside distractions.

After the entire set of cards has been administered once, a second administration, referred to as the **inquiry,** is conducted. During the inquiry, the examiner attempts to determine what features of the inkblot played a role in formulating the testtaker's **percept** (perception of an image). Questions such as "What made it look like [whatever]?" and "How do you see [whatever it is that the testtaker reported seeing]?" are asked in an attempt to clarify what was seen and which aspects of the inkblot were most influential in forming the perception. The inquiry provides information that is useful in scoring and interpreting the responses. The examiner

Figure 12–2
A Rorschach-like Inkblot
© 2017 Ronald Jay Cohen

also learns whether the testtaker remembers earlier responses, whether the original percept is still seen, and whether any new responses are now perceived.

A third component of the administration, referred to as **testing the limits,** may also be included. This procedure enables the examiner to restructure the situation by asking specific questions that provide additional information concerning personality functioning. If, for example, the testtaker has utilized the entire inkblot when forming percepts throughout the test, the examiner might want to determine if details within the inkblot could be elaborated on. Under those conditions, the examiner might say, "Sometimes people use a part of the blot to see something." Alternatively, the examiner might point to a specific area of the card and ask, "What does this look like?"

◆
JUST THINK . . .

Under what conditions would you think it advisable to engage in a testing the limits procedure? Under what conditions would it be inadvisable?

Other objectives of limit-testing procedures are (1) to identify any confusion or misunderstanding concerning the task, (2) to aid the examiner in determining if the testtaker is able to refocus percepts given a new frame of reference, and (3) to see if a testtaker made anxious by the ambiguous nature of the task is better able to perform given this added structure. At least one Rorschach researcher has advocated the technique of trying to elicit one last response from testtakers who think they have already given as many responses as they are going to give (Cerney, 1984). The rationale was that endings have many meanings, and the one last response may provide a source of questions and inferences applicable to treatment considerations.

Hypotheses concerning personality functioning will be formed by the assessor on the basis of all the variables outlined (such as the content of the response, the location of the response, the length of time to respond) as well as many additional ones. In general, Rorschach protocols are scored according to several categories, including location, determinants, content, popularity, and form. *Location* is the part of the inkblot that was utilized in forming the percept. Individuals may use the entire inkblot, a large section, a small section, a minute detail, or white spaces. *Determinants* are the qualities of the inkblot that determine what the individual perceives. Form, color, shading, or movement that the individual attributes to the inkblot are all considered determinants. *Content* is the content category of the response. Different scoring systems vary in some of the categories scored. Some typical content areas include human figures, animal figures, anatomical parts, blood, clouds, X-rays, and sexual responses. *Popularity* refers to the frequency with which a certain response has been found to correspond with a particular inkblot or section of an inkblot. A popular response is one that has frequently been obtained from the general population. A rare response is one that has been perceived infrequently by the general population. The *form* of a response is how accurately the individual's perception matches or fits the corresponding part of the inkblot. Form level may be evaluated as being adequate or inadequate or as good or poor.

The scoring categories are considered to correspond to various aspects of personality functioning. Hypotheses concerning aspects of personality are based both on the number of responses that fall within each category and on the interrelationships among the categories. For example, the number of whole responses (using the entire inkblot) in a Rorschach record is typically associated with conceptual thought process. Form level is associated with reality testing. Accordingly, psychotic patients would be expected to achieve low scores for form level. Human movement has been associated with creative imagination. Color responses have been associated with emotional reactivity.

> **JUST THINK . . .**
>
> How would you expect the responses of a group of people such as abstract artists to differ from a group of matched controls on the Form category?

Patterns of response, recurrent themes, and the interrelationships among the different scoring categories are all considered in arriving at a final description of the individual from a Rorschach protocol. Data concerning the responses of various clinical and nonclinical groups of adults, adolescents, and children have been compiled in various books and research publications.

Rorschach's form interpretation test was in its infancy at the time of its developer's death. The orphaned work-in-progress found a receptive home in the United States, where it was nurtured by various groups of supporters, each with its own vision of how the test should be administered, scored, and interpreted. In this sense, the Rorschach is, as McDowell and Acklin (1996, p. 308) characterized it, "an anomaly in the field of psychological measurement when compared to objective and other projective techniques."

> **JUST THINK . . .**
>
> "If the Rorschach has anything at all going for it, it has great intuitive appeal." Argue this view—pro or con.

Widely referred to simply as "the Rorschach," as if this instrument were a standardized test, Rorschach practitioners and researchers have for many years employed a variety of Rorschach scoring and interpretation systems—on some occasions picking and choosing interpretive criteria from one or more of each. Consider in this context a study by Saunders (1991) that focused on Rorschach indicators of child abuse. Reporting on how he scored the protocols, Saunders wrote: "Rorschach protocols were scored using Rapaport et al.'s (1945–1946) system as the basic framework, but special scores of four different types were added. I borrowed two of these additional measures from other researchers . . . and developed the other two specifically for this study" (p. 55). Given the variation that existed in terminology and in administration and scoring practices, one readily appreciates how difficult it might be to muster consistent and credible evidence for the test's psychometric soundness.[3]

In a book that reviewed several Rorschach systems, John E. Exner Jr. (Figure 12–3) wrote of the advisability of approaching "the Rorschach problem through a research integration of the systems" (1969, p. 251). Exner would subsequently develop such an integration—a **comprehensive system,** as he called it (Exner 1974, 1978, 1986, 1990, 1991, 1993a, 1993b, 2003; Exner & Weiner, 1982, 1995; see also Handler, 1996)—for the test's administration, scoring, and interpretation. Exner's system has been well received by clinicians and is the single system most used and most taught today. However, to inextricably link the fate of the Rorschach to Exner's system would be unfair, at least according to Bornstein and Masling (2005); Exner's system has much to recommend it, but so do several other systems.

---

3 Partly in response to such criticisms of the Rorschach, another inkblot test, the Holtzman Inkblot Technique (HIT; Holtzman et al., 1961), was designed to be more psychometrically sound. A description of Wayne Holtzman's HIT, as well as speculation as to why it never achieved the popularity and acceptance of the Rorschach, can be found in the supplementary material for this chapter presented in the Instructor's Resources within Connect.

Figure 12–3
John Ernest Exner, Jr. (1928–2006)

In their obituary of John E. Exner Jr., Erdberg and Weiner (2007, p. 54) wrote: "Many psychologists bounce around a bit before they lock in on the specialty that becomes the focus of their professional life. That was not the case with John Exner. He first laid hands on a set of blots from the Rorschach Inkblot Test in 1953, and his fascination with the instrument anchored his career from then on. Through five decades, 14 books, more than 60 journal articles, and countless workshop and conference presentations, John Exner and the Rorschach became synonymous." Among other accomplishments, Exner was the founding curator of the Hermann Rorschach Museum and Archives in Bern, Switzerland. One of his last publications before his death at the age of 77 from leukemia was an article entitled "A New U.S. Adult Nonpatient Sample." In that article Exner discussed implications for modifying Comprehensive System interpretive guidelines based on new data (Exner, 2007).

© Rorschach Workshops

Prior to the development of Exner's system and its widespread adoption by clinicians and researchers, evaluations of the Rorschach's psychometric soundness tended to be mixed at best. Exner's system brought a degree of uniformity to Rorschach use and thus facilitated "apples-to-apples" (or "bats-to-bats") comparison of research studies. Yet, regardless of the scoring system employed, there were a number of reasons why the evaluation of the psychometric soundness of the Rorschach was a tricky business. For example, because each inkblot is considered to have a unique stimulus quality, evaluation of reliability by a split-half method would be inappropriate. Of historical interest in this regard is the work of Hans Behn-Eschenburg, who attempted to develop, under Hermann Rorschach's direction (Eichler, 1951), a similar but not alternate form of the test. The need for such an "analogous" set of cards was recognized by Rorschach himself:

> Frequently occasion arises when the test must be repeated with the same subject. Such situations appear when one wishes to test normals in various moods, manic-depressives in different stages, schizophrenics in various conditions, or in testing patients before and after psychoanalysis, etc. Or a control test on a normal may be desired. If the test is repeated with the same plates, conscious or unconscious memory enters to warp the result. Analogous series of plates, different from the usual ones but satisfying the prerequisites for the individual plates of the basic series, are necessary for these situations. (Rorschach, 1921/1942, p. 53)

The "analogous series of plates" was referred to as "the Behn-Rorschach" or simply "the Behn." Some early research studies sought to compare findings on the "classic" Rorschach with findings on the Behn.

As Exner observed, traditional test-retest reliability procedures may be inappropriate for use with the Rorschach. This is so because of the effect of familiarity in response to the cards and because responses may reflect transient states as opposed to enduring traits. Exner (1983) reflected that "some Comprehensive System scores defy the axiom that something cannot be valid unless it is also reliable" (p. 411).

JUST THINK . . .

Do scores on a test such as the Rorschach defy the axiom that the score cannot be valid unless it is reliable?

The widespread acceptance of Exner's system has advanced the cause of Rorschach reliability—well, inter-scorer reliability, anyway. Exner, as well as others, have provided ample evidence that acceptable levels of inter-scorer reliability can be attained with the Rorschach. Using Exner's system, McDowell and Acklin (1996) reported an overall mean percentage agreement of 87% among Rorschach scorers. Still, as these researchers cautioned, "The complex types of data developed by the Rorschach introduce formidable obstacles to the application of standard procedures and canons of test development" (pp. 308–309). Far more pessimistic about such "formidable obstacles" and far less subtle in their conclusions were Hunsley and Bailey (1999). After reviewing the literature on the clinical utility of the Rorschach, they wrote of "meager support from thousands of publications" and expressed doubt that evidence would ever be developed that the Rorschach or Exner's comprehensive system could "contribute, in routine clinical practice, to scientifically informed psychological assessment" (p. 274).

Countering such pessimism were other reviews of the literature that were far more favorable (Bornstein, 1998, 1999; Ganellen, 1996, 2007; Hughes et al., 2007; Meyer & Handler, 1997; Viglione, 1999). One review of several meta-analyses indicated that the Rorschach validity coefficients were similar to those of the MMPI and the WAIS (Meyer & Archer, 2001). In their meta-analysis designed to compare the validity of the Rorschach with that of the MMPI, Hiller et al. (1999) concluded that "on average, both tests work about equally well when used for purposes deemed appropriate by experts" (p. 293). In a similar vein, Stricker and Gold (1999, p. 240) reflected that, "A test is not valid or invalid; rather, there are as many validity coefficients as there are purposes for which the test is used. The Rorschach can demonstrate its utility for several purposes and can be found wanting for several others." Stricker and Gold (1999) went on to argue for an approach to assessment that incorporated many different types of methods:

> Arguably, Walt Whitman's greatest poem was entitled "Song of Myself." We believe that everything that is done by the person being assessed is a song of the self. The Rorschach is one instrument available to the clinician, who has the task of hearing all of the music. (p. 249)

Perhaps in part due to the Rorschach's now iconic status in psychology, as well as its long-standing promise as an aid to diagnosis and the development and confirmation of clinical hypotheses, the Rorschach is still a tool that is enthusiastically used, taught, and researched by many contemporary psychologists. The publication of evidence-based insights regarding the test's clinical utility is now a staple of the scholarly literature in psychology. In 2011, a scoring system called the Rorschach Performance Assessment System (R-PAS) was published to "take advantage of the Rorschach's unique strengths as a highly portable complex behavioral task that provides a means of systematically observing and measuring personality in action" (Meyer et al., 2011, p. 2). The R-PAS manual contains detailed instructions for administering, coding, and interpreting the Rorschach. It is supplemented by an "online scoring program that calculates the summary scores and plots them using standard scores" (Meyer et al., 2011, p. 3). Although viewed by some as a competitor to the Exner system, the R-PAS authors prefer to conceptualize their work as an evolutionary development of that system (Erard et al., 2014).[4]

Decades ago, Jensen (1965, p. 509) opined that "the rate of scientific progress in clinical psychology might well be measured by the speed and thoroughness with which it gets over the Rorschach." If this statement were true, then the rate of scientific progress in clinical psychology could be characterized as a crawl. Publications supporting its use dot the contemporary literature (e.g., Bram, 2010; Callahan, 2015; Hubbard & Hegarty, 2016; Keddy & Erdberg, 2010; Mishra et al., 2010; Muzio, 2016; Weizmann-Henelius et al., 2009), although controversies still rage (e.g., Choca 2013; Del Giudice, 2010a, 2010b; Katsounari & Jacobowitz,

---

4. Interested readers can find more information about the R-PAS in the Instructor's Resources within Connect. Navigate to OOBAL-12-B3.

JUST THINK . . .

Do you count yourself among those assessment professionals who hope that the Rorschach will some day enjoy academic respect? Why or why not?

2011; Khromov & Dubey, 2016; Kottke et al., 2010; Lindh, 2016; Meyer et al., 2015; Mihura et al., 2015; Wood et al., 2015). The Rorschach remains one of the most frequently used and frequently taught psychological tests. It is widely used in forensic work and generally accepted by the courts. One reviewer concluded his evaluation of the status of the Rorschach at age 75 with words that seem applicable many years later: "Widely used and highly valued by clinicians and researchers in many countries of the world, it appears despite its fame not yet to have received the academic respect it deserves and, it can be hoped, will someday enjoy" (Weiner, 1997, p. 17).

Pictures as Projective Stimuli

Look at Figure 12–4. Now make up a story about it. Your story should have a beginning, a middle, and an end. Write it down, using as much paper as you need. Bring the story to class with you and compare it with other students' stories. What does your story reveal about your needs, fears, desires, impulse control, ways of viewing the world—your personality? What do the stories written by your classmates reveal about them? This exercise introduces you to the use of pictures as projective stimuli. Pictures used as projective stimuli may be photos of real people, animals, objects, or anything. They may be paintings, drawings, etchings, or any other variety of picture.

One of the earliest uses of pictures as projective stimuli came at the beginning of the twentieth century. Differences as a function of gender were found in the stories that children gave in response to nine pictures (Brittain, 1907). The author reported that the girls in the study were more interested in religious and moral themes than the boys. Another early experiment using pictures and a storytelling technique investigated children's imagination. Differences in themes as a function of age were observed (Libby, 1908). In 1932, a psychiatrist working at the Clinic for Juvenile Research in Detroit developed the Social Situation Picture

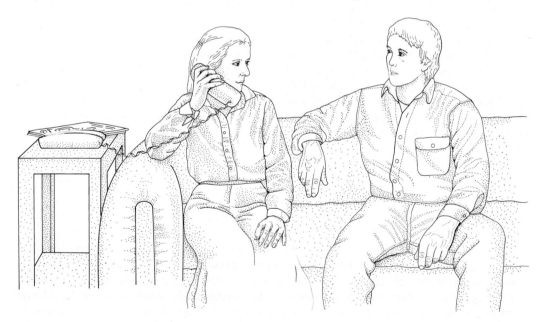

Figure 12–4
Ambiguous Picture for Use in Projective Storytelling Task
© 2017 Ronald Jay Cohen

Test (Schwartz, 1932), a projective instrument designed for use with juvenile delinquents. Working at the Harvard Psychological Clinic in 1935, Christiana D. Morgan (Figure 12–5) and Henry A. Murray (Figure 12–6) published the Thematic Apperception Test (TAT)—pronounced by saying the letters, not by rhyming with *cat*—the instrument that has come to be the most widely used of all the picture storytelling projective tests.

The Thematic Apperception Test (TAT) The TAT was originally designed as an aid to eliciting fantasy material from patients in psychoanalysis (Morgan & Murray, 1935). The stimulus materials consisted, as they do today, of 31 cards, one of which is blank. The 30 picture cards, all black-and-white, contain a variety of scenes designed to present the testtaker with "certain classical human situations" (Murray, 1943). Some of the pictures contain a lone individual, some contain a group of people, and some contain no people. Some of the pictures appear to be almost as real as a photograph; others are surrealistic drawings. Testtakers are introduced to the examination with the cover story that it is a test of imagination in which it is their task to tell what events led up to the scene in the picture, what is happening at that moment, and what the outcome will be. Testtakers are also asked to

Figure 12–5
Christiana D. Morgan (1897–1967)

On the box cover of the widely used TAT and in numerous other measurement-related books and articles, the authorship of the TAT is listed as "Henry A. Murray, Ph.D., and the Staff of the Harvard Psychological Clinic." However, the first articles describing the TAT were written by Christiana D. Morgan (Morgan, 1938) or by Morgan and Murray with Morgan listed as senior author (Morgan & Murray, 1935, 1938). In a mimeographed manuscript in the Harvard University archives, an early version of the test was titled the "Morgan-Murray Thematic Apperception Test" (White et al., 1941). Wesley G. Morgan (1995) noted that, because Christiana Morgan "had been senior author of the earlier publications, a question is raised about why her name was omitted as an author of the 1943 version" (p. 238). Morgan (1995) took up that and related questions in a brief but fascinating account of the origin and history of the TAT images. More on the life of Christiana Morgan can be found in Translate This Darkness: The Life of Christiana Morgan *(Douglas, 1993). Her Test Developer Profile can be found in the Instructor Resources within Connect.*

© Christiana Morgan. HUGFP 97.75.2F (Box 2). Harvard University Archives.

Figure 12–6
Henry A. Murray (1893–1988)

Henry Murray is perhaps best known for the influential theory of personality he developed, as well as for his role as author of the Thematic Apperception Test. Biographies of Murray have been written by Anderson (1990) and Robinson (1992). Murray's Test Developer Profile can be found in the Instructor Resources within Connect.
© John Lindsay/AP Photo

describe what the people depicted in the cards are thinking and feeling. If the blank card is administered, examinees are instructed to imagine that there is a picture on the card and then proceed to tell a story about it.

In the TAT manual, Murray (1943) also advised examiners to attempt to find out the source of the examinee's story. It is noteworthy that the noun *apperception* is derived from the verb **apperceive,** which may be defined as *to perceive in terms of past perceptions.* The source of a story could be a personal experience, a dream, an imagined event, a book, an episode of *Game of Thrones*—really almost anything.

In everyday clinical practice, examiners tend to take liberties with various elements pertaining to the administration, scoring, and interpretation of the TAT. For example, although 20 cards is the recommended number for presentation, in practice an examiner might administer as few as one or two cards or as many as all 31. If a clinician is assessing a patient who has a penchant for telling stories that fill reams of the clinician's notepad, it's probably a good bet that fewer cards will be administered. If, on the other hand, a patient tells brief, one-or two-sentence stories, more cards may be administered in an attempt to collect more raw data with which to work. Some of the cards are suggested for use with adult males, adult females, or both, and some are suggested for use with children. This is so because certain pictorial representations lend themselves more than others to identification and projection by members of these groups. In one study involving 75 males (25 each of 11-, 14-, and 17-year-olds), Cooper (1981) identified the 10 most productive cards for use with adolescent males. In practice, however, any card—be it one recommended for use with males, with females, or with children—may be administered to any subject. The administering clinician selects the cards that are believed likely to elicit responses pertinent to the objective of the testing.

The raw material used in deriving conclusions about the individual examined with the TAT are (1) the stories as they were told by the examinee, (2) the clinician's notes about the

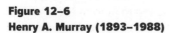

JUST THINK . . .

Describe a picture on a card that would really get *you* talking. After describing the card, imagine what story you might tell in response to it.

way or the manner in which the examinee responded to the cards, and (3) the clinician's notes about extra-test behavior and verbalizations. The last two categories of raw data (test and extra-test behavior) are sources of clinical interpretations for almost any individually administered test. Analysis of the story content requires special training. One illustration of how a testtaker's behavior during testing may influence the examiner's interpretations of the findings was provided by Sugarman (1991, p. 140), who told of a "highly narcissistic patient [who] demonstrated contempt and devaluation of the examiner (and presumably others) by dictating TAT stories complete with spelling and punctuation as though the examiner was a stenographer."

A number of systems for interpreting TAT data exist (e.g., Thompson, 1986; Jenkins, 2008; Westen et al., 1988). Many interpretive systems incorporate, or are to some degree based on, Henry Murray's concepts of **need** (determinants of behavior arising from within the individual), **press** (determinants of behavior arising from within the environment), and **thema** (a unit of interaction between needs and press). In general, the guiding principle in interpreting TAT stories is that the testtaker is identifying with someone (the protagonist) in the story and that the needs, environmental demands, and conflicts of the protagonist in the story are in some way related to the concerns, hopes, fears, or desires of the examinee.

In his discussion of the TAT from the perspective of a clinician, William Henry (1956) examined each of the cards in the test with regard to such variables as *manifest stimulus demand, form demand, latent stimulus demand, frequent plots,* and *significant variations.* To get an idea of how some of these terms are used, look again at Figure 12–5—a picture that is *not* a TAT card—and then review Tables 12–1 and 12–2, which are descriptions of the card and some responses to the card from college-age respondents. Although a clinician may obtain bits of information from the stories told about every individual card, the clinician's final impressions will usually derive from a consideration of the overall patterns of themes that emerge.

As with the Rorschach and many other projective techniques, a debate between academics and practitioners regarding the psychometric soundness of the TAT has been unceasing through the years. Because of the general lack of standardization and uniformity with which administration, scoring, and interpretation procedures tend to be applied in everyday clinical practice, concern on psychometric grounds is clearly justified. However, in experimental tests where trained examiners use the same procedures and scoring systems, inter-rater reliability coefficients can range from adequate to impressive (Stricker & Healy, 1990).

Research suggests that situational factors—including who the examiner is, how the test is administered, and the testtaker's experiences prior to and during the test's administration—may affect test responses. Additionally, transient internal need states such as hunger, thirst, fatigue, and higher-than-ordinary levels of sexual tension can affect a testtaker's responses. Different TAT cards have different stimulus "pulls" (Murstein & Mathes, 1996). Some pictures are more likely than others to elicit stories with themes of despair, for example. Given that the pictures have different stimulus "pulls" or, more technically stated, different latent stimulus demands, it becomes difficult, if not impossible, to determine the inter-item (read "inter-card") reliability of the test. Card 1 might reliably elicit themes of need for achievement, whereas card 16, for example, might not typically elicit any such themes. The possibility of widely variable story lengths in response to the cards presents yet another challenge to the documentation of inter-item reliability.

JUST THINK . . .

Would testtaker identification with the depicted characters or scenes increase if the TAT were redone today in a different media, such as scenes shot on film or video?

JUST THINK . . .

Why are split-half, test-retest, and alternate-form reliability measures inappropriate for use with the TAT?

Table 12–1

A Description of the Sample TAT-Like Picture

Author's Description

A male and a female are seated in close proximity on a sofa. The female is talking on the phone. There is an end table with a magazine on it next to the sofa.

Manifest Stimulus Demand

Some explanation of the nature of the relationship between these two persons and some reason the woman is on the phone are required. Less frequently noted is the magazine on the table and its role in this scene.

Form Demand

Two large details, the woman and the man, must be integrated. Small details include the magazine and the telephone.

Latent Stimulus Demand

This picture may elicit attitudes toward heterosexuality as well as material relevant to the examinee with regard to optimism–pessimism, security–insecurity, dependence–independence, passivity–assertiveness, and related continuums. Alternatively, attitudes toward family and friends may be elicited, with the two primary figures being viewed as brother and sister, the female talking on the phone to a family member, and so on.

Frequent Plots

We haven't administered this card to enough people to make judgments about what constitutes "frequent plots." We have, however, provided a sampling of plots (Table 12–2).

Significant Variations

Just as we cannot provide information on frequent plots, we cannot report data on significant variations. We would guess, however, that most college students viewing this picture would perceive the two individuals in it as being involved in a heterosexual relationship. Were that to be the case, a significant variation would be a story in which the characters are not involved in a heterosexual relationship (e.g., they are employer/employee). Close clinical attention will also be paid to the nature of the relationship of the characters to any "introduced figures" (persons not pictured in the card but introduced into the story by the examinee). The "pull" of this card is to introduce the figure to whom the woman is speaking. What is the phone call about? How will the story be resolved?

Table 12–2

Some Responses to the Sample Picture

Respondent	Story
1. (Male)	This guy has been involved with this girl for a few months. Things haven't been going all that well. He's suspected that she's been seeing a lot of guys. This is just one scene in a whole evening where the phone hasn't stopped ringing. Pretty soon he is just going to get up and leave.
2. (Female)	This couple is dating. They haven't made any plans for the evening, and they are wondering what they should do. She is calling up another couple to ask if they want to get together. They will go out with the other couple and have a good time.
3. (Male)	This girl thinks she is pregnant and is calling the doctor for the results of her test. This guy is pretty worried because he has plans to finish college and go to graduate school. He is afraid she will want to get married, and he doesn't want to get trapped into anything. The doctor will tell her she isn't pregnant, and he'll be really relieved.
4. (Female)	This couple has been dating for about two years, and they're very much in love. She's on the phone firming up plans for a down payment on a hall that's going to cater the wedding. That's a bridal magazine on the table over there. They look like they're really in love. I think things will work out for them even though the odds are against it—the divorce rates and all.
5. (Male)	These are two very close friends. The guy has a real problem and needs to talk to someone. He is feeling really depressed and that he is all alone in the world. Every time he starts to tell her how he feels, the phone rings. Pretty soon he will leave feeling like no one has time for him and even more alone. I don't know what will happen to him, but it doesn't look good.

Conflicting opinions are presented in the scholarly literature concerning the validity of the TAT, including the validity of its assumptions and the validity of various applications (Barends et al., 1990; Cramer, 1996; Gluck, 1955; Hibbard et al., 1994; Kagan, 1956; Keiser & Prather, 1990; Mussen & Naylor, 1954; Ronan et al., 1995; Worchel & Dupree, 1990). Some have argued that as much motivational information could be obtained through much simpler, self-report methods. However, one meta-analysis of this literature concluded that there was little relation between TAT-derived data and that derived from self-report (Spangler, 1992). McClelland et al. (1989) distinguished the products of self-report and TAT-derived motivational information, arguing that self-report measures yielded "self-attributed motives" whereas the TAT was capable of yielding "implicit motives." Drawing partially on McClelland et al. (1989), we may define an **implicit motive** as a nonconscious influence on behavior typically acquired on the basis of experience.

JUST THINK . . .

If someone asked you about your "need to achieve," what would you say? How might what you say differ from the "implicit" measure of need for achievement that would emerge from your TAT protocol?

A study by Peterson et al. (2008) provided partial support not only for the projective hypothesis but also for the value of the TAT in clinical assessment. The research subjects were 126 introductory psychology students (70 female, 56 male) whose average age was about 19½. All subjects completed a demographic questionnaire and were pre-evaluated by self-report measures of personality and mood. Subjects were then exposed to rock music with suicide-related lyrics. The specific songs used were *Dirt, Desperate Now,* and *Fade to Black.* Subjects next completed a memory test for the music they had heard. They also completed self-report measures of personality and mood (again), and a picture storytelling task using three TAT cards. Of particular interest among the many findings was the fact that measured personality traits predicted the level of suicide-related responding in the TAT stories told. Participants who wrote stories with higher levels of suicide-related responding (a) tended to believe that suicidal thinking was valid, and that suicide-related lyrics in songs were potentially harmful, (b) felt more sad, angry, and isolated while listening to the music, and, (c) were more likely to report negative affect states after listening to the music. One unexpected finding from this study was that

> after listening to music with suicide lyrics, many participants wrote projective stories with altruistic themes. . . . There is a vast literature relating exposure to violence in music, video games, and movies to increased aggression but Meier [et al.] 2006 reported that this relationship does not occur for individuals who score high on measures of agreeableness. Indeed, such individuals respond to aggression-related cues by accessing pro-social thoughts. (Peterson et al., 2008, p. 167)

Although the relationship between expression of fantasy stories and real-life behavior is tentative at best, and although the TAT is highly susceptible to faking, the test is widely used by practitioners. The rationale of the TAT, and of many similar published picture story tests (see Table 12–3), has great intuitive appeal. It does make sense that people would project their own motivation when asked to construct a story from an ambiguous stimulus. Another appeal for users of this test is that it is the clinician who tailors the test administration by selecting the cards and the nature of the inquiry—a feature most welcome by many practitioners in an era of computer-adaptive testing and computer-generated narrative summaries. And so it is with the TAT, as it is many other projective tools of assessment, the test must ultimately be judged by a different standard that is more clinically than psychometrically oriented, if its contribution to personality assessment is to be fully appreciated.

Other tests using pictures as projective stimuli Following the publication of the TAT and its subsequent embrace by many clinicians, there has been no shortage of other, TAT-like

Table 12–3
Some Picture-Story Tests

Picture-Story Test	Description
Thompson (1949) modification of the original TAT	Designed specifically for use with African American testtakers, with pictures containing both Black and White protagonists.
TEMAS (Malgady et al., 1984)	Designed for use with urban Hispanic children, with drawings of scenes relevant to their experience.
Children's Apperception Test (CAT; Bellak, 1971) (first published in 1949)	Designed for use with ages 3 to 10 and based on the idea that animals engaged in various activities were useful in stimulating projective storytelling by children.
Children's Apperception Test-Human (CAT-H; Bellak & Bellak, 1965)	A version of the CAT based on the idea that depending on the maturity of the child, a more clinically valuable response might be obtained with humans instead of animals in the pictures.
Senior Apperception Technique (SAT; Bellak & Bellak, 1973)	Picture-story test depicting images relevant to older adults.
The Picture Story Test (Symonds, 1949)	For use with adolescents, with pictures designed to elicit adolescent-related themes such as coming home late and leaving home.
Education Apperception Test (Thompson & Sones, 1973) and the School Apperception Method (Solomon & Starr, 1968)	Two independent tests, listed here together because both were designed to tap school-related themes.
The Michigan Picture Test (Andrew et al., 1953)	For ages 8 to 14, contains pictures designed to elicit various themes ranging from conflict with authority to feelings of personal inadequacy.
Roberts Apperception Test for Children (RATC; McArthur & Roberts, 1982)	Designed to elicit a variety of developmental themes such as family confrontation, parental conflict, parental affection, attitudes toward school, and peer action.
Children's Apperceptive Story-Telling Test (CAST; Schneider, 1989)	Theory-based test based on the work of Alfred Adler.
Blacky Pictures Test (Blum, 1950)	Psychoanalytically based, cartoon-like items featuring Blacky the Dog.
Make a Picture Story Method (Shneidman, 1952)	For ages 6 and up, respondents construct their own pictures from cutout materials included in the test kit and then tell a story.

tests published. The rationale for creating some of these tests has to do with their proposed contribution in terms of greater testtaker identification with the images depicted in the cards. So, for example, one group of TAT-like tests designed for use with the elderly features seniors in the pictures (Bellak & Bellak, 1973; Starr & Weiner, 1979; Wolk & Wolk, 1971). The assumption made by these test authors is that pictures featuring seniors will be more relevant to the elderly and thus elicit verbal responses that more accurately reflect inner conflicts. Verdon (2011) raised some important questions regarding the assumptions inherent in the use of such instruments. One question he raised had to do with the appropriateness of treating the elderly as a group when it comes to measures such as the TAT. He wrote, "We must never forget that these persons too were once children, adolescents, and young adults, and that their past experiences of pleasure and pain, hope and disenchantment are still present in their mental lives. For this reason, we must be careful not to consider the elderly population as a homogeneous clinical entity whose mental characteristics and concerns would have nothing more to do with those of their past" (p. 62). Verdon questioned whether cards shown to elderly testtakers must necessarily depict elderly figures if they are to elicit themes linked to loss or helplessness; the original TAT cards could do that, and may even be more effective at doing so. Verdon cautioned:

if the material does match real life situations too closely, little room is left for fantasy, and the persons' discourse can be taken literally, as supposedly reflecting actual problems of their daily lives. On the other hand . . . if both actor and narrator of the scene are one, we run the risk of attributing a positive value to a story that is in fact conventional, where conflicts are avoided or minimized. (Verdon, 2011, p. 25)

There are other types of projective instruments, not quite like the TAT, that also use pictures as projective stimuli. One such projective technique, the Hand Test (Wagner, 1983), consists of nine cards with pictures of hands on them and a tenth blank card. The testtaker is asked what the hands on each card might be doing. When presented with the blank card, the testtaker is instructed to imagine a pair of hands on the card and then describe what they might be doing. Testtakers may make several responses to each card, and all responses are recorded. Responses are interpreted according to 24 categories such as affection, dependence, and aggression.

Another projective technique, the Rosenzweig Picture-Frustration Study (Rosenzweig, 1945, 1978), employs cartoons depicting frustrating situations (Figure 12–7). The testtaker's task is to fill in the response of the cartoon figure being frustrated. The test, which is based on the assumption that the testtaker will identify with the person being frustrated, is available in forms for children, adolescents, and adults. Young children respond orally to the pictures, whereas older testtakers may respond either orally or in writing. An inquiry period is suggested after administration of all of the pictures in order to clarify the responses.

Test responses are scored in terms of the type of reaction elicited and the direction of the aggression expressed. The direction of the aggression may be *intropunitive* (aggression turned inward), *extrapunitive* (outwardly expressed), or *inpunitive* (aggression is evaded so as to avoid or gloss over the situation). Reactions are grouped into categories such as *obstacle dominance* (in which the response concentrates on the frustrating barrier), *ego defense* (in which attention is focused on protecting the frustrated person), and *need persistence* (in which attention is focused on solving the frustrating problem). For each scoring category, the percentage of responses is calculated and compared with normative data. A group conformity rating (GCR) is derived representing the degree to which one's responses conform to or are typical of those

Figure 12–7
Sample Item from the Rosenzweig Picture-Frustration Study

of the standardization group. This test has captured the imagination of researchers for decades, although questions remain concerning how reactions to cartoons depicting frustrating situations are related to real-life situations.

One variation of the picture story method may appeal to old school clinicians as well as to clinicians who thrive on normative data with all of the companion statistics. The Apperceptive Personality Test (APT; Karp et al., 1990) represents an attempt to address some long-standing criticisms of the TAT as a projective instrument while introducing objectivity into the scoring system. The test consists of eight stimulus cards "depicting recognizable people in everyday settings" (Holmstrom et al., 1990, p. 252), including males and females of different ages as well as minority group members. This, by the way, is in contrast to the TAT stimulus cards, some of which depict fantastic or unreal types of scenes.[5] Another difference between the APT and the TAT is the emotional tone and draw of the stimulus cards. A long-standing criticism of the TAT cards has been their negative or gloomy tone, which may restrict the range of affect projected by a testtaker (Garfield & Eron, 1948; Ritzler et al., 1980). After telling a story about each of the APT pictures orally or in writing, testtakers respond to a series of multiple-choice questions. In addition to supplying quantitative information, the questionnaire segment of the test was designed to fill in information gaps from stories that are too brief or cryptic to otherwise score. Responses are thus subjected to both clinical and actuarial interpretation and may, in fact, be scored and interpreted with computer software.

Every picture tells a story—well, hopefully for the sake of the clinician or researcher trying to collect data by means of a picture-story projective test. Otherwise, it may be time to introduce another type of test, one where words themselves are used as projective stimuli.

JUST THINK . . .

For the purposes of a test such as the TAT, why might the depiction of contemporary "regular" people on the cards work better or worse than the images currently on them?

Words as Projective Stimuli

Projective techniques that employ words or open-ended phrases and sentences are referred to as *semistructured* techniques because, although they allow for a variety of responses, they still provide a framework within which the subject must operate. Perhaps the two best-known examples of verbal projective techniques are *word association tests* and *sentence completion tests.*

Word association tests   **Word association** is a task that may be used in personality assessment in which an assessee verbalizes the first word that comes to mind in response to a stimulus word. A **word association test** may be defined as a semistructured, individually administered, projective technique of personality assessment that involves the presentation of a list of stimulus words, to each of which an assessee responds verbally or in writing with whatever comes immediately to mind first upon first exposure to the stimulus word. Responses are then analyzed on the basis of content and other variables. The first attempt to investigate word association was made by Galton (1879). Galton's method consisted of presenting a series of unrelated stimulus words and instructing the subject to respond with the first word that came to mind. Continued interest in the phenomenon of word association resulted in additional studies. Precise methods were developed for recording the responses given and the length of time elapsed before obtaining a response (Cattell, 1887; Trautscholdt, 1883). Cattell and Bryant (1889) were the first to use cards with stimulus words printed on them. Kraepelin (1895) studied the effect of physical states (such as hunger and fatigue) and of practice on word association. Mounting

---

5. Murray et al. (1938) believed that fantastic or unreal types of stimuli might be particularly effective in tapping unconscious processes.

experimental evidence led psychologists to believe that the associations individuals made to words were not chance happenings but rather the result of the interplay between one's life experiences, attitudes, and unique personality characteristics.

Jung (1910) maintained that, by selecting certain key words that represented possible areas of conflict, word association techniques could be employed for psychodiagnostic purposes. Jung's experiments served as an inspiration to the creators of the Word Association Test developed by Rapaport et al. (1945–1946) at the Menninger Clinic. This test consisted of three parts. In the first part, each stimulus word was administered to the examinee, who had been instructed to respond quickly with the first word that came to mind. The examiner recorded the length of time it took the subject to respond to each item. In the second part of the test, each stimulus word was again presented to the examinee. The examinee was instructed to reproduce the original responses. Any deviation between the original and this second response was recorded, as was the length of time before reacting. The third part of the test was the inquiry. Here the examiner asked questions to clarify the relationship that existed between the stimulus word and the response (e.g., "What were you thinking about?" or "What was going through your mind?"). In some cases, the relationship may have been obvious; in others, however, the relationship between the two words may have been extremely idiosyncratic or even bizarre.

Rapaport et al.'s test consisted of 60 words, some considered neutral by the test authors (e.g., *chair, book, water, dance, taxi*) and some characterized as "traumatic." In the latter category were "words that are likely to touch upon sensitive personal material according to clinical experience, and also words that attract associative disturbances" (Rapaport et al., 1968, p. 257). Examples of words so designated were *love, girlfriend, boyfriend, mother, father, suicide, fire, breast,* and *masturbation.*

Responses on the Word Association Test were evaluated with respect to variables such as popularity, reaction time, content, and test-retest responses. Normative data were provided regarding the percentage of occurrence of certain responses for college students and schizophrenic groups. For example, to the word *stomach,* 21% of the college group responded with "ache" and 13% with "ulcer." Ten percent of the schizophrenic group responded with "ulcer." To the word *mouth,* 20% of the college sample responded with "kiss," 13% with "nose," 11% with "tongue," 11% with "lips," and 11% with "eat." In the schizophrenic group, 19% responded with "teeth," and 10% responded with "eat." The test does not enjoy widespread clinical use today but is more apt to be found in the occasional research application.

JUST THINK . . .

As compared to the 1940s, how emotion-arousing do you think the "traumatic" stimuli on the Word Association Test are by contemporary standards? Why?

The Kent-Rosanoff Free Association Test (Kent & Rosanoff, 1910) represented one of the earliest attempts to develop a standardized test using words as projective stimuli.[6] The test consisted of 100 stimulus words, all commonly used and believed to be neutral with respect to emotional impact. The standardization sample consisted of 1,000 normal adults who varied in geographic location, educational level, occupation, age, and intellectual capacity. Frequency tables based on the responses of these 1,000 cases were developed. These tables were used to evaluate examinees' responses according to the clinical judgment of psychopathology. Psychiatric patients were found to have a lower frequency of popular responses than the normal subjects in the standardization group. However, as it became

---

6. The term **free association** refers to the technique of having subjects relate all their thoughts as they are occurring and is most frequently used in psychoanalysis; the only structure imposed is provided by the subjects themselves. The technique employed in the Kent-Rosanoff is that of **word association** (not free association), in which the examinee relates the first word that comes to mind in response to a stimulus word. The term *free association* in the test's title is, therefore, a misnomer.

JUST THINK . . .

Quick! The first thought that comes into your mind when you hear the term . . . *word association.*

apparent that the individuality of responses may be influenced by many variables other than psychopathology (such as creativity, age, education, and socioeconomic factors), the popularity of the Kent-Rosanoff as a differential diagnostic instrument diminished. Damaging, too, was research indicating that scores on the Kent-Rosanoff were unrelated to other measures of psychotic thought (Ward et al., 1991). Still, the test endures as a standardized instrument of word association responses and, more than 90 years after its publication, continues to be used in experimental research and clinical practice.

Sentence completion tests   Other projective techniques that use verbal material as projective stimuli are *sentence completion tests.* In general, **sentence completion** refers to a task in which the assessee is asked to finish an incomplete sentence or phrase. A **sentence completion test** is a semistructured projective technique of personality assessment that involves the presentation of a list of words that begin a sentence and the assessee's task is to respond by finishing each sentence with whatever word or words come to mind. To obtain some firsthand experience with sentence completion items, how might you complete the following sentences?

I like to _____.

Someday, I will _____.

I will always remember the time _____.

I worry about _____.

I am most frightened when _____.

My feelings are hurt _____.

My mother _____.

I wish my parents _____.

Sentence completion tests may contain items that, like the sample items just presented, are quite general and appropriate for administration in a wide variety of settings. Alternatively, **sentence completion stems** (the part of the sentence completion item that is not blank, but must be created by the testtaker) may be developed for use in specific types of settings (such as school or business) or for specific purposes. Sentence completion tests may be relatively atheoretical or linked very closely to some theory. As an example of the latter, the Washington University Sentence Completion Test (Loevinger et al., 1970) was based on the writings of Loevinger and her colleagues in the area of self-concept development.

A number of standardized sentence completion tests are available to the clinician. One such test, the Rotter[7] Incomplete Sentences Blank (Rotter & Rafferty, 1950) may be the most popular of all. The Rotter was developed for use with populations from grade 9 through adulthood and is available in three levels: high school (grades 9 through 12), college (grades 13 through 16), and adult. Testtakers are instructed to respond to each of the 40 incomplete sentence items in a way that expresses their "real feelings." The manual suggests that responses on the test be interpreted according to several categories: family attitudes, social and sexual attitudes, general attitudes, and character traits. Each response is evaluated on a seven-point scale that ranges from *need for therapy* to *extremely good adjustment.* According to the psychometric studies quoted in the test manual, the Rotter is a reliable and valid instrument.

In general, a sentence completion test may be a useful and straightforward way to obtain information from an honest and verbally expressive testtaker about diverse topics. The tests

---

7. The *o* sound in *Rotter* is long, as in *rote.*

may tap interests, educational aspirations, future goals, fears, conflicts, needs—just about anything the testtaker cares to be candid about. The tests have a high degree of face validity. However, with this high degree of face validity comes a certain degree of transparency about the objective of the test. For this reason, sentence completion tests are perhaps the most vulnerable of all the projective methods to faking on the part of an examinee intent on making a good—or a bad—impression.

> **JUST THINK . . .**
>
> Is there a way that sentence completion tests could be made "less transparent" and thus less vulnerable to faking?

Sounds as Projective Stimuli

Let's state at the outset that this section is included more as a fascinating footnote in the history of projectives than as a description of widely used tests. The history of the use of sound as a projective stimulus is fascinating because of its origins in the laboratory of a then-junior fellow of Harvard University. You may be surprised to learn that it was a behaviorist whose name has seldom been uttered in the same sentence as the term *projective test* by any contemporary psychologist: B. F. Skinner (Figure 12–8). The device was something "like auditory inkblots" (Skinner, 1979, p. 175).

The time was the mid-1930's. Skinner's colleagues Henry Murray and Christiana Morgan were working on the TAT in the Harvard Psychological Clinic. Psychoanalytic theory was very much in vogue. Even behaviorists were curious about Freud's approach, and some were even undergoing psychoanalysis themselves. Switching on the equipment in his laboratory in the biology building, the rhythmic noise served as a stimulus for Skinner to create words that went along with it. This inspired Skinner to think of an application for sound, not only in behavioral

Figure 12–8
Projective Test Pioneer B. F. Skinner . . . *What?!*

Working at the Harvard Psychological Clinic with the blessing of (and even some financial support from) Henry Murray, B. F. Skinner (who today is an icon of behaviorism) evinced great enthusiasm for an auditory projective test he had developed. He believed the technique had potential as "a device for snaring out complexes" (Skinner, 1979, p. 176). A number of well-known psychologists of the day apparently agreed. For example, Joseph Zubin, in correspondence with Skinner, wrote that Skinner's technique had promise "as a means for throwing light on the less objective aspects of the Rorschach experiment" (Zubin, 1939). Of course, if the test really had that much promise, Skinner would probably be getting equal billing in this chapter with Murray and Rorschach.

© Bettmann/The Getty Images

terms but in the elicitation of "latent" verbal behavior that was significant "in the Freudian sense" (Skinner, 1979, p. 175). Skinner created a series of recorded sounds much like muffled, spoken vowels, to which people would be instructed to associate. The sounds, packaged as a device he called a *verbal summator,* presumably would act as a stimulus for the person to verbalize certain unconscious material. Henry Murray, by the way, liked the idea and supplied Skinner with a room at the clinic in which to test subjects. Saul Rosenzweig also liked the idea; he and David Shakow renamed the instrument the *tautophone* (from the Greek *tauto,* meaning "repeating the same") and did research with it (Rutherford, 2003). Their instructions to subjects were as follows:

> Here is a phonograph. On it is a record of a man's voice saying different things. He speaks rather unclearly, so I'll play over what he says a number of times. You'll have to listen carefully. As soon as you have some idea of what he's saying, tell me at once. (Shakow & Rosenzweig, 1940, p. 217)

As recounted in detail by Rutherford (2003), there was little compelling evidence to show that the instrument could differentiate between members of clinical and nonclinical groups. Still, a number of other auditory projective techniques were developed. There was the Auditory Apperception Test (Stone, 1950), in which the subject's task was to respond by creating a story based on three sounds played on a phonograph record. Other researchers produced similar tests, one called an auditory sound association test (Wilmer & Husni, 1951) and the other referred to as an auditory apperception test (Ball & Bernardoni, 1953). Henry Murray also got into the act with his Azzageddi test (Davids & Murray, 1955), named for a Herman Melville character. Unlike other auditory projectives, the Azzageddi presented subjects with spoken paragraphs.

JUST THINK . . .

Are you surprised that early in his career B. F. Skinner experimented with a projective instrument that was psychoanalytically grounded? Why or why not?

So why aren't test publishers today punching out CDs with projective sounds at a pace to match the publication of inkblots and pictures? Rutherford (2003) speculated that a combination of factors conspired to cause the demise of auditory projective methods. The tests proved not to differentiate between different groups of subjects who took it. Responses to the auditory stimuli lacked the complexity and richness of responses to inkblots, pictures, and other projective stimuli. None of the available scoring systems was very satisfactory. Except for use with the blind, auditory projective tests were seen as redundant and not as good as the TAT.

The Production of Figure Drawings

A relatively quick, easily administered projective technique is the analysis of drawings. Drawings can provide the psychodiagnostician with a wealth of clinical hypotheses to be confirmed or discarded as the result of other findings. The use of drawings in clinical and research settings has extended beyond the area of personality assessment. Attempts have been made to use artistic productions as a source of information about intelligence, neurological intactness, visual-motor coordination, cognitive development, and even learning disabilities (Neale & Rosal, 1993). Figure drawings are an appealing source of diagnostic data because the instructions for them can be administered individually or in a group by nonclinicians such as teachers, and no materials other than a pencil and paper are required.

Figure-drawing tests   In general, a **figure drawing test** may be defined as a projective method of personality assessment whereby the assessee produces a drawing that is analyzed on the basis of its content and related variables. The classic work on the use of figure drawings as a projective stimulus is a book entitled *Personality Projection in the Drawing of the Human Figure* by Karen Machover (1949). Machover wrote that

> the human figure drawn by an individual who is directed to "draw a person" [is] related intimately to the impulses, anxieties, conflicts, and compensations characteristic of that individual. In some sense, the figure drawn is the person, and the paper corresponds to the environment. (p. 35)

The instructions for administering the Draw A Person (DAP) test are quite straightforward. The examinee is given a pencil and a blank sheet of 8½-by-11-inch white paper and told to draw a person. Inquiries on the part of the examinee concerning how the picture is to be drawn are met with statements such as "Make it the way you think it should be" or "Do the best you can." Immediately after the first drawing is completed, the examinee is handed a second sheet of paper and instructed to draw a picture of a person of the sex opposite that of the person just drawn.[8] Subsequently, many clinicians will ask questions about the drawings, such as "Tell me a story about that figure," "Tell me about that boy/girl, man/lady," "What is the person doing?" "How is the person feeling?" "What is nice or not nice about the person?" Responses to these questions are used in forming various hypotheses and interpretations about personality functioning.

Traditionally, DAP productions have been formally evaluated through analysis of various characteristics of the drawing. Attention has been given to such factors as the length of time required to complete the picture, placement of the figures, the size of the figure, pencil pressure used, symmetry, line quality, shading, the presence of erasures, facial expressions, posture, clothing, and overall appearance. Various hypotheses have been generated based on these factors (Knoff, 1990a). For example, the *placement* of the figure on the paper is seen as representing how the individual functions within the environment. The person who draws a tiny figure at the bottom of the paper might have a poor self-concept or might be insecure or depressed. The individual who draws a picture that cannot be contained on one sheet of paper and goes off the page is considered to be impulsive. Unusually light pressure suggests character disturbance (Exner, 1962). According to Buck (1948, 1950), placement of drawing on the right of the page suggests orientation to the future; placement to the left suggests an orientation to the past. Placement at the upper right suggests a desire to suppress an unpleasant past as well as excessive optimism about the future. Placement to the lower left suggests depression with a desire to flee into the past.

Another variable of interest to those who analyze figure drawings is the *characteristics* of the individual drawn. For example, unusually large eyes or large ears suggest suspiciousness, ideas of reference, or other paranoid characteristics (Machover, 1949; Shneidman, 1958). Unusually large breasts drawn by a male may be interpreted as unresolved oedipal problems with maternal dependence (Jolles, 1952). Long and conspicuous ties suggest sexual aggressiveness, perhaps overcompensating for fear of impotence (Machover, 1949). Button emphasis suggests dependent, infantile, inadequate personality (Halpern, 1958).

According to Emanuel Hammer (1958, 1981, 2014), people project their self-image or self-concept in figure drawings, as well as in other ways (such as in disguised form in dreams and paintings). For Hammer, figure drawings are both a reflection of, and a window into, an individual's personality. As such, Hammer identified certain commonalities shared in the features of figure drawings rendered by persons from certain diagnostic groups. For example, Hammer noted that in the figure drawings of males who had raped women, common features included simian-like arms, exaggerated shoulders, and features that exaggerate masculinity, such as an inflated chest and arms (see *Drawing A* in Figure 12–9). As also illustrated in *Drawing A*, the rapist's drawing may be so large and imposing, that it practically violates the

---

8. When instructed simply to "draw a person," most people will draw a person of the same sex, so it is deemed clinically significant if the assessee draws a person of the opposite sex when given this instruction. Rierdan and Koff (1981) found that, in some cases, children are uncertain of the sex of the figure drawn. They hypothesized that in such cases "the child has an indefinite or ill-defined notion of sexual identity" (p. 257).

Figure 12–9

The two drawings presented here are figure drawings that represent those rendered by an actual male rapist and an actual male pedophile.

"rules, limits, and boundaries" of an 8½-by-11 sheet of paper. In the drawing, note also that the area below the waist is underemphasized relative to the upper body. According to Hammer (2014), the slightness of the drawing (and presumably of the individual's self-concept) from the waist down may be compensated for by the sheer forcefulness of the upper body. A final observation with respect to the *Drawing A* is that it is devoid of clothing—a fact that itself is ripe for psychodynamic interpretation.

Contrast the drawing produced by a rapist, with a figure drawing produced by an adult male pedophile *(Drawing B)*. According to Hammer (2014), the drawings of male pedophiles may be relatively small and childlike, with features representative of inadequacy. As illustrated in *Drawing B,* there seems to be an incapability of rising to an adult role. Here, inadequacy is represented not only by the size of the self-drawing, but also by specific characteristics of the drawing (such as the fact that each hand has less than five fingers). Also, as Hammer (2014) pointed out, the introduction of the Sun into a figure drawing, while normal for a child, may signify an unmet need for nurturance on the part of a pathologically dependent adult. The excessive shading in the drawing is, according to Hammer (2014), reflective of the great anxiety the pedophile is experiencing.

JUST THINK . . .

Draw a person. Contemplate what that drawing tells about you on the basis of what you have read.

The House-Tree-Person test (HTP; Buck, 1948) is another projective figure-drawing test. As the name of the test implies, the testtaker's task is to draw a picture of a house, a tree, and a person. In much the same way that different aspects of the human figure are presumed to be reflective of psychological functioning, the ways in which an individual represents a house and a tree are considered symbolically significant.

Another test, this one thought to be of particular value in learning about the examinee in relation to her or his family, is the Kinetic Family Drawing (KFD). Derived from Hulse's (1951, 1952) Family Drawing Test, an administration of the KFD (Burns & Kaufman, 1970, 1972) begins with the presentation of an 8½-by-11-inch sheet of paper and a pencil with an eraser. The examinee, usually though not necessarily a child, is instructed as follows:

> Draw a picture of everyone in your family, including you, DOING something. Try to draw whole people, not cartoons or stick people. Remember, make everyone DOING something—some kind of actions. (Burns & Kaufman, 1972, p. 5)

In addition to yielding graphic representations of each family member for analysis, this procedure may yield important information in the form of examinee verbalizations while the drawing is being executed. After the examinee has completed the drawing, a rather detailed inquiry follows. The examinee is asked to identify each of the figures, talk about their relationship, and detail what they are doing in the picture and why. A number of formal scoring systems for the KFD are available. Related techniques include a school adaptation called the Kinetic School Drawing (KSD; Prout & Phillips, 1974); a test that combines aspects of the KFD and the KSD called the Kinetic Drawing System (KDS; Knoff & Prout, 1985); and the Collaborative Drawing Technique (D. K. Smith, 1985), a test that provides an occasion for family members to collaborate on the creation of a drawing—presumably all the better to "draw together."

JUST THINK . . .

How might another creative medium (such as clay modeling) be structured to supply projective information?

Like other projective techniques thought to be clinically useful, figure-drawing tests have had a rather embattled history with regard to their perceived psychometric soundness (Joiner & Schmidt, 1997). In general, the techniques are vulnerable with regard to the assumptions that drawings are essentially self-representations (Tharinger & Stark, 1990) and represent something far more than drawing ability (Swensen, 1968). Although a number of systems have been devised to score figure drawings, solid support for the validity of such approaches has been elusive (Watson et al., 1967). Experience and expertise do not necessarily correlate with greater clinical accuracy in drawing interpretation. Karen Machover (cited in Watson, 1967) herself reportedly had "grave misgivings" (p. 145) about the misuse of her test for diagnostic purposes.

To be sure, the clinical use of figure drawings has its academic defenders (Riethmiller & Handler, 1997a, 1997b). Waehler (1997), for example, cautioned that tests are not foolproof and that a person who comes across as rife with pathology in an interview might well seem benign on a psychological test. He went on to advise that figure drawings "can be considered more than 'tests'; they involve tasks that can also serve as stepping-off points for clients and examiners to discuss and clarify the picture" (p. 486).

Projective Methods in Perspective

Used enthusiastically by many clinicians and criticized harshly by many academics, projective methods continue to occupy a rather unique habitat in the psychological landscape. Lilienfeld et al. (2000) raised serious questions regarding whether that habitat is worth maintaining. These authors focused their criticism on scoring systems for the Rorschach, the TAT, and figure drawings. They concluded that there was empirical support for only a relatively small number of Rorschach and TAT indices. They found even fewer compelling reasons to justify the continued use of figure drawings. Some of their assertions with regard to the Rorschach and the TAT—as well as the response of a projective test user and advocate, Stephen Hibbard (2003)—are presented in Table 12–4. Hibbard commented only on the Rorschach and the TAT because of his greater experience with these tests as opposed to figure drawings.

In general, critics have attacked projective methods on grounds related to the *assumptions* inherent in their use, the *situational variables* that attend their use, and several *psychometric considerations*—most notably, a paucity of data to support their reliability and validity.

Assumptions Bernard Murstein's (1961) criticisms regarding the basic assumptions of projectives are as relevant today as they were when they were first published decades ago. Murstein dismissed the assumption that the more ambiguous the stimuli, the more subjects reveal about their personality. For Murstein the projective stimulus is only one aspect of the "total stimulus situation." Environmental variables, response sets, reactions to

JUST THINK . . .

Suppose a Rorschach card or a TAT card elicited much the same response from *most* people. Would that be an argument for or against the use of the card?

Table 12–4

The Cons and Pros (or Cons Rebutted) of Projective Methods

Lilienfeld et al. (2000) on the Cons	Hibbard (2003) in Rebuttal
Projective techniques tend not to provide incremental validity above more structured measures, as is the argument of proponents of the projective hypothesis as stated by Dosajh (1996).	Lilienfeld et al. presented an outmoded caricature of projection and then proceeded to attack it. Dosajh has not published on any of the coding systems targeted for criticism. None of the authors who developed coding systems that were attacked espouse a view of projection similar to Dosajh's. Some of the criticized authors have even positioned their systems as nonprojective.
The norms for Exner's Comprehensive System (CS) are in error. They may overpathologize normal individuals and may even harm clients.	Evidence is inconclusive as to error in the norms. Observed discrepancies may have many explanations. Overpathologization may be a result of "drift" similar to that observed in the measurement of intelligence (Flynn effect).
There is limited support for the generalizability of the CS across different cultures.	More cross-cultural studies do need to be done, but the same could be said for most major tests.
Four studies are cited to support the deficiency of the test-retest reliability of the CS.	Only three of the four studies cited are in *refereed journals* (for which submitted manuscripts undergo critical review and may be selected or rejected for publication), and none of these three studies are bona fide test-retest reliability studies.
With regard to the TAT, there is no point in aggregating scores into a scale in the absence of applying internal consistency reliability criteria.	This assertion is incorrect because "each subunit of an aggregated group of predictors of a construct could be unrelated to the other, but when found in combination, they might well predict important variance in the construct" (p. 264).
TAT test-retest reliability estimates have been "notoriously problematic" (p. 41).	". . . higher retest reliability would accrue to motive measures if the retest instructions permitted participants to tell stories with the same content as previously" (p. 265).
Various validity studies with different TAT scoring systems can be faulted on methodological grounds.	Lilienfeld et al. (2000) misinterpreted some studies they cited and did not cite other studies. For example, a number of relevant validity studies in support of Cramer's (1991) Defense Mechanism Manual coding system for the TAT were not cited.

Note: Interested readers are encouraged to read the full text of Lilienfeld et al. (2000) and Hibbard (2003), as the arguments made by each are far more detailed than the brief samples presented here.

the examiner, and related factors all contribute to response patterns. In addition, Murstein asserted that projection on the part of the assessee does not increase along with increases in the ambiguity of projective stimuli.

Another assumption inherent in projective testing concerns the supposedly idiosyncratic nature of the responses evoked by projective stimuli. In fact, similarities in the response themes of different subjects to the same stimuli suggest that the stimulus material may not be as ambiguous and amenable to projection as previously assumed. Some consideration of the stimulus properties and the ways they affect the subject's responses is therefore indicated. Also, the assumption that projection is greater onto stimulus material that is similar to the subject (in physical appearance, gender, occupation, and so on) has also been found questionable. This latter point was more recently made by one supporter of projectives and the projective hypothesis, French psychologist Benoît Verdon. Verdon (2011) argued that the latent stimulus demand of projective stimuli such as inkblots and pictures superseded their manifest stimulus demand.

Now consider these assumptions inherent in projective testing:

- Every response provides meaning for personality analysis.
- A relationship exists between the strength of a need and its manifestation on projective instruments.
- Testtakers are unaware of what they are disclosing about themselves.

- A projective protocol reflects sufficient data concerning personality functioning for formulation of judgments.

- There is a parallel between behavior obtained on a projective instrument and behavior displayed in social situations.

Murstein dismissed these assumptions as "cherished beliefs" accepted "without the support of sufficient research validation" (p. 343). Still, proponents of projectives argue that the ambiguous nature of a task such as inkblot interpretation make for test results that are less subject to faking, especially "faking good." This latter assumption is evident in the writings of advocates for the use of the Rorschach in forensic applications (Gacono et al., 2008). The test's presumed utility in bypassing "volitional controls" prompted Weiss et al. (2008) to recommend it for preemployment screening of police personnel. Support for the assumption that the Rorschach test frustrates testtakers' efforts to fake good comes from a study conducted in China with college student subjects (Cai & Shen, 2007). The researchers concluded that the Rorschach was superior to the Tennessee Self-Concept Scale as a measure of self-concept because subjects were unable to manage favorable impressions.

Although studies such as these could be cited to support the use of the Rorschach as a means to lessen or negate the role of impression management in personality assessment, even that assumption remains controversial (Conti, 2007; Fahs, 2004; Ganellen, 2008; Gregg, 1998; Whittington, 1998; Yell, 2008). At the very least, it can be observed that as a measurement method, the Rorschach provides a stimulus that is less susceptible than others to socially conventional responding. It may also be useful in obtaining insights into the respondent's unique way of perceiving and organizing novel stimuli.

Another assumption underlying the use of projective tests is that something called "the unconscious" exists. Though the term *unconscious* is widely used as if its existence were a given, some academicians have questioned whether in fact the unconscious exists in the same way that, say, the liver exists. The scientific studies typically cited to support the existence of the unconscious (or, perhaps more accurately, the efficacy of the construct *unconscious*) have used a wide array of methodologies; see, for example, Diven (1937), Erdelyi (1974), Greenspoon (1955), and Razran (1961). The conclusions of each of these types of studies are subject to alternative explanations. Also subject to alternative explanation are conclusions about the existence of the unconscious based on experimental testing of predictions derived from hypnotic phenomena, from signal detection theory, and from specific personality theories (Brody, 1972). More generally, many interpretive systems for the Rorschach and other projective instruments are based on psychodynamic theory, which itself has no shortage of critics.

Situational variables Proponents of projective techniques have claimed that such tests are capable of illuminating the mind's recesses much like X-rays illuminate the body. Frank (1939) conceptualized projective tests as tapping personality patterns without disturbing the pattern being tapped. If that were true, then variables related to the test situation should have no effect on the data obtained. However, situational variables such as the examiner's presence or absence have significantly affected the responses of experimental subjects. For example, TAT stories written in private are likely to be less guarded, less optimistic, and more affectively involved than those written in the presence of the examiner (Bernstein, 1956). The age of the examiner is likely to affect projective protocols (Mussen & Scodel, 1955), as are the specific instructions (Henry & Rotter, 1956) and the subtle reinforcement cues provided by the examiner (Wickes, 1956).

Masling (1960) reviewed the literature on the influence of situational and interpersonal variables in projective testing and concluded that there was strong evidence for a role of situational and interpersonal influences in projection. Masling concluded that subjects utilized every available cue in the testing situation, including cues related to the actions or the appearance of the examiner. Moreover, Masling argued that examiners also relied on situational cues, in some instances over and above what they were taught. Examiners appeared to interpret projective data with regard to their own needs and expectations, their own subjective feelings about the person being tested, and their own constructions regarding the total test situation. Masling (1965) experimentally demonstrated that Rorschach examiners—through postural, gestural, and facial cues—are capable of unwittingly eliciting the responses they expect.

In any given clinical situation, many variables may be placed in the mix. The interaction of these variables may influence clinical judgments. So it is that research has suggested that even in situations involving objective (not projective) tests or simple history taking, the effect of the clinician's training (Chapman & Chapman, 1967; Fitzgibbons & Shearn, 1972) and role perspective (Snyder et al., 1976) as well as the patient's social class (Hollingshead & Redlich, 1958; Lee, 1968; Routh & King, 1972) and motivation to manage a desired impression (Edwards & Walsh, 1964; Wilcox & Krasnoff, 1967) are capable of influencing ratings of pathology (Langer & Abelson, 1974) and related conclusions (Batson, 1975). These and other variables are given wider latitude in the projective test situation, where the examiner may be at liberty to choose not only the test and extra-test data on which interpretation will be focused but also the scoring system that will be used to arrive at that interpretation.

◆ JUST THINK . . .

Projective tests have been around for a long time because of their appeal to many clinicians. Citing their advantages, argue the case that these tests should be around for a long time to come.

Psychometric considerations The psychometric soundness of many widely used projective instruments has yet to be demonstrated. Critics of projective techniques have called attention to variables such as uncontrolled variations in protocol length, inappropriate subject samples, inadequate control groups, and poor external criteria as factors contributing to spuriously increased ratings of validity. There are methodological obstacles in researching projectives because many test-retest or split-half methods are inappropriate. It is, to say the least, a challenge to design and execute validity studies that effectively rule out, limit, or statistically take into account all of the unique situational variables that attend the administration of such tests.

The debate between academicians who argue that projective tests are not technically sound instruments and clinicians who find such tests useful has been raging ever since projectives came into widespread use. Frank (1939) responded to those who would reject projective methods because of their lack of technical rigor:

> These leads to the study of personality have been rejected by many psychologists because they do not meet psychometric requirements for validity and reliability, but they are being employed in association with clinical and other studies of personality where they are finding increasing validation in the consistency of results for the same subject when independently assayed by each of these procedures. . . .
>
> If we face the problem of personality, in its full complexity, as an active dynamic process to be studied as a *process* rather than as entity or aggregate of traits, factors, or as static organization, then these projective methods offer many advantages for obtaining data on the process of organizing experience which is peculiar to each personality and has a life career. (Frank, 1939, p. 408; emphasis in the original)

Objective Tests and Projective Tests: How Meaningful Is the Dichotomy? So-called objective tests are affected by response styles, malingering and other sources of test bias (Meyer & Kurtz, 2006). Further, testtakers may lack sufficient insight or perspective to respond "objectively" to objective test items. And as Meehl (1945) mused, so-called objective test items may, in a sense, serve as projective stimuli for some testtakers. Too, projective tests, given the vulnerability of some of their assumptions, may not be as projective as they were once thought to be. In fact, many projective tests feature scoring systems that entail rather "objective" coding (Weiner, 2005). And so the question arises: How meaningful is the objective versus projective dichotomy?

Weiner (2005) characterized the objective versus projective dichotomy as misleading. Truth in labeling is not served by characterizing one class of tests as "objective" (in the face of many questions regarding their objectivity), and another class of tests as something "other than objective." Observers might conclude that one group of tests is indeed objective, while the other group of tests must be "subjective."

As an alternative to the objective/projective dichotomy, Weiner (2005) suggested substituting the terms *structured,* in place of objective, and *unstructured,* in place of projective. The more structured a test is, the more likely it is to tap relatively conscious aspects of personality. By contrast, unstructured or ambiguous tests are more likely to access material beyond immediate, conscious awareness (Stone & Dellis, 1960; Weiner & Kuehnle, 1998). As intuitively appealing as Weiner's recommendations are, old habits die hard, and the objective/projective dichotomy remains very much with us today.

Behavioral Assessment Methods

Traits, states, motives, needs, drives, defenses, and related psychological constructs have no tangible existence. They are constructs whose existence must be inferred from behavior. In the traditional approach to clinical assessment, tests as well as other tools are employed to gather data. From these data, diagnoses and inferences are made concerning the existence and strength of psychological constructs. The traditional approach to assessment might therefore be labeled a *sign* approach because test responses are deemed to be signs or clues to underlying personality or ability. In contrast to this traditional approach is an alternative philosophy of assessment that may be termed the *sample* approach. The sample approach focuses on the behavior itself. Emitted behavior is viewed not as a sign of something but rather as a sample to be interpreted in its own right.

The emphasis in **behavioral assessment** is on "what a person *does* in situations rather than on inferences about what attributes he *has* more globally" (Mischel, 1968, p. 10). Predicting what a person will do is thought to entail an understanding of the assessee with respect to both antecedent conditions and consequences of a particular situation (Smith & Iwata, 1997). Upon close scrutiny, however, the trait concept is still present in many behavioral measures, though more narrowly defined and more closely linked to specific situations (Zuckerman, 1979).

To illustrate behavioral observation as an assessment strategy, consider the plight of the single female client who presents herself at the university counseling center. She complains that even though all her friends tell her how attractive she is, she has great difficulty meeting men—so much so that she doesn't even want to try anymore. A counselor confronted with such a client might, among other things, (1) interview the client about this problem, (2) administer an appropriate test to the client, (3) ask the client to keep a detailed diary of her thoughts and behaviors related to various aspects of her efforts to meet men, including her expectations, and (4) accompany the client on a typical night out to a singles bar or similar venue and observe her behavior. The latter two strategies come under the heading of behavioral observation. With regard to the diary, the client is engaging in self-observation. In the scenario of the night out, the counselor is doing the actual observation.

The more traditional administration of a psychological test or test battery to a client such as this single woman might yield signs that then could be inferred to relate to the problem. For example, if a number of the client's TAT stories involved themes of demeaning, hostile, or otherwise unsatisfactory heterosexual encounters as a result of venturing out into the street, a counselor might make an interpretation at a deeper or second level of inference. For example, a counselor, especially one with a psychoanalytic orientation, might reach a conclusion something like this:

> The client's expressed fear of going outdoors, and ultimately her fear of meeting men, might in some way be related to an unconscious fear of promiscuity—a fear of becoming a streetwalker.

Such a conclusion in turn would have implications for treatment. Many hours of treatment might be devoted to uncovering the "real" fear so that it is apparent to the client herself and ultimately dealt with effectively.

In contrast to the sign approach, the clinician employing the sample or behavioral approach to assessment might examine the behavioral diary that the client kept and design an appropriate therapy program on the basis of those records. Thus, for example, the antecedent conditions under which the client would feel most distraught and unmotivated to do anything about the problem might be delineated and worked on in counseling sessions.

An advantage of the sign approach over the sample approach is that—in the hands of a skillful, perceptive clinician—the client might be put in touch with feelings that even she was not really aware of before the assessment. The client may have been consciously (or unconsciously) avoiding certain thoughts and images (those attendant on the expression of her sexuality, for example), and this inability to deal with those thoughts and images may indeed have been a factor contributing to her ambivalence about meeting men.

Behavioral assessors seldom make such deeper-level inferences. For example, if sexuality is not raised as an area of difficulty by the client (in an interview, a diary, a checklist, or by some other behavioral assessment technique), this problem area may well be ignored or given short shrift. Behavioral assessors do, however, tend to be more empirical in their approach, as they systematically assess the client's presenting problem both from the perspective of the client and from the perspective of one observing the client in social situations and the environment in general. The behavioral assessor does not search the Rorschach or other protocols for clues to treatment. Rather, the behaviorally oriented counselor or clinician relies much more on what the client *does* and *has done* for guideposts to treatment. In a sense, the behavioral approach does not require as much clinical creativity as the sign approach. Perhaps for that reason, the behavioral approach may be considered less an art than a science (at least as compared to some other clinical approaches). It is certainly science-based in that it relies on relatively precise methods of proven validity (Haynes & Kaholokula, 2008).

Early on, the shift away from traditional psychological tests by behaviorally oriented clinicians compelled some to call for a way to integrate such tests in behavioral evaluations. This view is typified by the wish that "psychological tests should be able to provide the behavior therapist with information that should be of value in doing behavior therapy. This contention is based on the assumption that the behavior on any psychological test should be lawful" (Greenspoon & Gersten, 1967, p. 849). Accordingly, psychological tests could be useful, for example, in helping the behavior therapist identify the kinds of contingent stimuli that would be most effective with a given patient. For example, patients with high percentages of color or color/form responses on the Rorschach and with IQs over 90 might be most responsive to positive verbal contingencies (such as *good, excellent,* and so forth). By contrast, patients with high percentages of movement or vista (three-dimensional) responses on the Rorschach and IQs over 90 might be most responsive to negative verbal contingencies (such as *no* or *wrong*). Such innovative efforts to narrow a widening schism in the field of clinical assessment have failed to ignite experimental enthusiasm, perhaps because more direct ways exist to assess responsiveness to various contingencies.

JUST THINK . . .

Is there a way to integrate traditional psychological testing and assessment and behavioral assessment?

Differences between traditional and behavioral approaches to psychological assessment exist with respect to several key variables (Hartmann et al., 1979). For example, in traditional approaches to assessment, data is typically used to diagnose and classify, while in behavioral approaches, assessment data is used to describe targeted behaviors and maintaining conditions, usually for the purpose of selecting specific therapeutic techniques and then tracking response to therapeutic intervention. With respect to presumed causes of behavior, traditional assessment is more likely to evaluate the traits and states of the individual (collectively referred to as "personality"), while behavioral assessment is more likely to focus attention on the conditions in the environment that were instrumental in establishing a targeted behavior, as well as the environmental conditions that are currently maintaining the behavior. Rather than drawing inferences about personality from samples of behavior (as in traditional approaches to assessment), behavioral approaches to assessment focus on the meaning (in the sense of purpose, utility, or consequences) of the behavior itself. In traditional assessment, an individual's behavioral history is afforded great weight—almost, but not quite, to the point of being predictive of future behavior. By contrast, in behavioral approaches, behavioral history is important to the extent that it provides baseline information relevant to an individual's learning history. In traditional approaches to assessment, the timing of assessment tends to be pre-, and perhaps post-therapeutic intervention. By contrast, the timing of assessment in behavioral approaches tends to be more ongoing; there are usually peri-intervention assessments conducted in addition to the more traditional pre- and post-interventions. We elaborate on these and related contrasts in the discussion that follows of the "who, what, when, where, why, and how" of behavioral assessment.

The Who, What, When, Where, Why, and How of It

The name says it all: *Behavior* is the focus of assessment in behavioral assessment—not traits, states, or other constructs presumed to be present in various strengths—just behavior. This will become clear as we survey the *who, what, when, where, why,* and *how* of behavioral assessment.

Who? *Who* is the assessee? The person being assessed may be, for example, a patient on a closed psychiatric ward, a client seeking help at a counseling center, or a subject in an academic experiment. Regardless of whether the assessment is for research, clinical, or other purposes, the hallmark of behavioral assessment is the intensive study of individuals. This is in contrast to mass testing of groups of people to obtain normative data with respect to some hypothesized trait or state.

Who is the assessor? Depending on the circumstances, the assessor may be a highly qualified professional or a technician/assistant trained to conduct a particular assessment. Technicians are frequently employed to record the number of times a targeted behavior is exhibited. In this context, the assessor may also be a classroom teacher recording, for example, the number of times a child leaves her or his seat. An assessor in behavioral assessment may also be the assessee. Assessees are frequently directed to maintain behavioral diaries, complete behavioral checklists, or engage in other activities designed to monitor their own behavior.

For example, in one study of 105 Vietnam War veterans with chronic PTSD, the subjects were asked to keep a sleep diary over the course of six weeks. Among the findings was the fact that shorter duration of sleep and greater frequency of nightmares were correlated with severity of PTSD (Gehrman et al., 2015).

Research in the field of health psychology frequently entails measurement by self-report. Practically speaking, it is only through self-report that a researcher can gauge, for example, how many cigarettes (or e-cigarettes) the subjects in the study are smoking. Just ask the psychologist you will meet in this chapter's *Meet an Assessment Professional.*

What? *What* is measured in behavioral assessment? Perhaps not surprisingly, the behavior or behaviors targeted for assessment will vary as a function of the objectives of the assessment. What constitutes a targeted behavior will typically be described in sufficient detail prior to any assessment. For the purposes of assessment, the targeted behavior must be measurable—that is, quantifiable in some way. Examples of such measurable behaviors can range from the number of seconds elapsed before a child calls out in class to the number of degrees body temperature is altered. Note that descriptions of targeted behaviors in behavioral assessment typically begin with the phrase *the number of.* In studies that focus on physiological variables such as muscle tension or autonomic responding, special equipment is required to obtain the behavioral measurements.

When? *When* is an assessment of behavior made? One response to this question is that assessment of behavior is typically made at times when the problem behavior is most likely to be elicited. So, for example, if a pupil is most likely to get into verbal and physical altercations during lunch, a behavioral assessor would focus on lunch hour as a time to assess behavior.

Another way to address the *when* question has to do with the various schedules with which behavioral assessments may be made. For example, one schedule of assessment is referred to as *frequency* or *event recording.* Each time the targeted behavior occurs, it is recorded. Another schedule of assessment is referred to as *interval recording.* Assessment according to this schedule occurs only during predefined intervals of time (e.g., every other minute, every 48 hours, every third week). Beyond merely tallying the number of times a particular behavior occurs, the assessor may also maintain a record of the *intensity* of the behavior. Intensity of a behavior may be gauged by observable and quantifiable events such as the *duration* of the behavior, stated in number of seconds, minutes, hours, days, weeks, months, or years. Alternatively, it may be stated in terms of some ratio or percentage of time that the behavior occurs during a specified interval of time. One method of recording the frequency and intensity of target behavior is **timeline followback (TLFB) methodology** (Sobell & Sobell, 1992, 2000). TLFB was originally designed for use in the context of a clinical interview for the purpose of assessing alcohol abuse. Respondents were presented with a specific calendar time period and asked to recall aspects of their drinking. A feature of TLFB is that respondents are prompted with memory aids (such as memorable dates including birthdays, holidays, events in the news, and events of personal importance) to assist in recall of the targeted behavior during the defined timeline. From the recalled information, patterns regarding the targeted behavior (such as substance abuse versus abstinence) emerge. The technique may be particularly useful in identifying antecedent stimuli that cue the undesired behavior. The method has been used to evaluate problem behaviors as diverse as gambling (Weinstock et al., 2004; Weinstock, Ledgerwood, & Petry, 2007; Weinstock, Whelan, et al., 2007), maternal smoking (Stroud et al., 2009), HIV risk behaviors (Copersino et al., 2010), and alcohol/medication (Garnier et al., 2009), though its utility will vary by situation (Shiffman, 2009). Another assessment methodology entails recording problem behavior-related events (such as drinking, smoking, and so forth) not retrospectively, but as they occur. This is accomplished by means of a handheld computer used to maintain an electronic diary of behavior. Referred to as **ecological**

Meet Dr. Monica Webb Hooper

My name is Monica Webb Hooper and I have a Ph.D. in clinical psychology, with a specialization in health psychology. I am also a licensed clinical psychologist who provides psychotherapy to individuals, families, and groups who are experiencing various forms of psychological distress. My expertise in helping people improve their quality of life and longevity is also applied in my role as a researcher. Research conducted in my laboratory centers on the broad area of health behavior change. One focus of our efforts has been on the intersection where cancer prevention and control meet issues of minority health and disparity elimination. The various studies that I have directed include aspects of clinical health psychology, biobehavioral oncology, public health, and social psychology. Assessment is a critical component of this work, and a thread that is common in past and present research, as well as research yet to be devised. It is only through rigorous measurement that variables targeted in research, and constructs (such as "interest") may be operationalized, quantified, and ultimately, evaluated meaningfully. It is only through rigorous measurement that increases and decreases in specified behaviors can be meaningfully gauged. Ultimately, it is only through rigorous measurement that behavior change can be meaningfully assessed.

One focus of my research program is on tobacco smoking—a behavior which is probably grossly underestimated in terms of its threat to good health. Smoking is responsible for over 400,000 deaths in the United States annually, and worsens or leads to many health problems (such as asthma, respiratory infections, diabetes, heart disease, and cancer). Paramount to public health is developing an understanding why people initiate smoking and how the process of nicotine dependence proceeds. There is also a need for the development of safe and effective methods designed to help people quit smoking...

I offer four recommendations for students of psychological testing and assessment who might be interested in a career as a research psychologist. First, strive to understand the scientific basis for reliable and valid clinical assessment. Second, think about ways that

Monica Webb Hooper, Ph.D., Professor of Oncology and Psychological Sciences, and Director of the Office of Cancer Disparities Research at Case Comprehensive Cancer Center, Case Western Reserve University

© Monica Webb-Hooper

the concepts and techniques you are learning apply to real-world issues or problems. Third, pay special attention to the methods of test administration, scoring, interpretation, and reporting that are covered in your courses. Having this knowledge is also important for accurate interpretation of assessment and related findings (e.g., surveys, polls) delivered through the news media (such as survey or poll data). Finally, think about and practice how best to communicate assessment and research results to fellow professionals and the public. Whether communicating the results of a clinical assessment to a client, or communicating the results of a research project to fellow professionals, a sound grounding in the art and science of psychological testing and assessment is absolutely essential.

Read more of what Dr. Hooper had to say—her complete essay—through the Instructor Resources within Connect.

Used with permission of Monica Webb Hooper.

Chapter 12: Personality Assessment Methods   **433**

JUST THINK . . .

You are a behavior therapist who has a client who is a compulsive gambler. You advise the client to keep a record of his behavior. Do you advise that this self-monitoring be kept on a frequency basis or an interval schedule? Why?

momentary assessment, this methodology was used to analyze the immediate antecedents of cigarette smoking (Shiffman et al., 2002).

Where? *Where* does the assessment take place? In contrast to the administration of psychological tests, behavioral assessment may take place just about anywhere—preferably in the environment where the targeted behavior is most likely to occur naturally. For example, a behavioral assessor studying the obsessive-compulsive habits of a patient might wish to visit the patient at home to see firsthand the variety and intensity of the behaviors exhibited. Does the patient check the oven for gas left on, for example? If so, how many times per hour? Does the patient engage in excessive hand-washing? If so, to what extent? These and related questions may be raised and answered effectively through firsthand observation in the patient's home. In some instances, when virtual reality is deemed preferable to reality, the assessment may involve stimuli created in a laboratory setting, rather than a "real life" setting (see, for example, Bordnick et al., 2008).

Why? *Why* conduct behavioral assessment? In general, data derived from behavioral assessment may have several advantages over data derived by other means. Data derived from behavioral assessment can be used:

- to provide behavioral baseline data with which other behavioral data (accumulated after the passage of time, after intervention, or after some other event) may be compared

- to provide a record of the assessee's behavioral strengths and weaknesses across a variety of situations

- to pinpoint environmental conditions that are acting to trigger, maintain, or extinguish certain behaviors

- to target specific behavioral patterns for modification through interventions

- to create graphic displays useful in stimulating innovative or more effective treatment approaches

In the era of managed care and frugal third-party payers, let's also note that insurance companies tend to favor behavioral assessments over more traditional assessments. This is because behavioral assessment is typically not linked to any particular theory of personality, and patient progress tends to be gauged on the basis of documented behavioral events.

How? *How* is behavioral assessment conducted? The answer to this question will vary, of course, according to the purpose of the assessment. In some situations, the only special equipment required will be a trained observer with pad and pencil. In other types of situations, highly sophisticated recording equipment may be necessary.

Another key *how* question relates to the analysis of data from behavioral assessment. The extent to which traditional psychometric standards are deemed applicable to behavioral assessment is a controversial issue, with two opposing camps. One camp may be characterized as accepting traditional psychometric assumptions about behavioral assessment, including assumptions about the measurement of reliability (Russo et al., 1980) and validity (Haynes, Follingstad, & Sullivan, 1979; Haynes et al., 1981). Representative of this position are statements such as that made by Bellack and

JUST THINK . . .

Imagine that you are a NASA psychologist studying the psychological and behavioral effects of space travel on astronauts. What types of behavioral measures might you employ, and what special equipment would you need—or design—to obtain those measures?

Hersen (1988) that "the reliability, validity, and utility of any procedure should be paramount, regardless of its behavioral or nonbehavioral development" (p. 614).

JUST THINK . . .

Do traditional psychometric standards apply to behavioral assessment?

Cone (1977) championed the traditionalist approach to behavioral assessment in an article entitled "The Relevance of Reliability and Validity for Behavioral Assessment." However, as the years passed, Cone (1986, 1987) would become a leading proponent of an alternative position, one in which traditional psychometric standards are rejected as inappropriate yardsticks for behavioral assessment. Cone (1981) wrote, for example, that "a truly behavioral view of assessment is based on an approach to the study of behavior so radically different from the customary individual differences model that a correspondingly different approach must be taken in evaluating the adequacy of behavioral assessment procedures" (p. 51).

Others, too, have questioned the utility of traditional approaches to test reliability in behavioral assessment, noting that "the assessment tool may be precise, but the behavior being measured may have changed" (Nelson et al., 1977, p. 428). Based on the conceptualization of each behavioral assessment as an experiment unto itself, Dickson (1975) wrote: "If one assumes that each target for assessment represents a single experiment, then what is needed is the scientific method of experimentation and research, rather than a formalized schedule for assessment. . . . Within this framework, each situation is seen as unique, and the reliability of the approach is not a function of standardization techniques . . . but rather is a function of following the experimental method in evaluation" (pp. 376–377).

Varieties of Behavioral Assessment

Behavioral assessment may be accomplished through various means, including behavioral observation and behavior rating scales, analogue studies, self-monitoring, and situational performance methods. Let's briefly take a closer look at each of these as well as related methods.

Behavioral observation and rating scales   *A child psychologist observes a client in a playroom through a one-way mirror. A family therapist views a videotape of a troubled family attempting to resolve a conflict. A school psychologist observes a child interacting with peers in the school cafeteria.* These are all examples of the use of an assessment technique termed **behavioral observation.** As its name implies, this technique involves watching the activities of targeted clients or research subjects and, typically, maintaining some kind of record of those activities. Researchers, clinicians, or counselors may themselves serve as observers, or they may designate trained assistants or other people (such as parents, siblings, teachers, and supervisors) as the observers. Even the observed person can be the behavior observer, although in such cases the term *self-observation* is more appropriate than *behavioral observation.*

In some instances, behavioral observation employs mechanical means, such as a video recording of an event. Recording behavioral events relieves the clinician, the researcher, or any other observer of the need to be physically present when the behavior occurs and allows for detailed analysis of it at a more convenient time. Factors noted in behavioral observation will typically include the presence or absence of specific, targeted behaviors, behavioral excesses, behavioral deficits, behavioral assets, and the situational antecedents and consequences of the observed behaviors. Of course, because the people doing the observing and rating are human themselves, behavioral observation isn't always as cut and dried as it may appear (see this chapter's *Everyday Psychometrics*).

Behavioral observation may take many forms. The observer may, in the tradition of the naturalist, record a running narrative of events using tools such as pencil and paper, video, film, still photography, or a cassette recorder. Mehl and Pennebaker (2003), for example, used

Confessions of a Behavior Rater

In discussions of behavioral assessment, the focus is often placed squarely on the individual being evaluated. Only infrequently, if ever, is reference made to the thoughts and feelings of the person responsible for evaluating the behavior of another. What follows are the hypothetical thoughts of one behavior rater. We say hypothetical because these ideas are not really one person's thoughts but instead a compilation of thoughts of many people responsible for conducting behavioral evaluations.

The behavior raters interviewed for this feature were all on the staff at a community-based inpatient/outpatient facility in Brewster, New York. One objective of this facility is to prepare its adolescent and adult members for a constructive, independent life. Members live in residences with varying degrees of supervision, and their behavior is monitored on a 24-hour basis. Each day, members are issued an eight-page behavior rating sheet referred to as a CDR (clinical data recorder), which is circulated to supervising staff for rating through the course of the day. The staff records behavioral information on variables such as activities, social skills, support needed, and dysfunctional behavior.

On the basis of behavioral data, certain medical or other interventions may be recommended. Because behavioral monitoring is daily and consistent, changes in patient behavior as a function of medication, activities, or other variables are quickly noted and intervention strategies adjusted. In short, the behavioral data may significantly affect the course of a patient's institutional stay—everything from amount of daily supervision to privileges to date of discharge is influenced by the behavioral data. Both patients and staff are aware of this fact of institutional life; therefore, both patients and staff take the completion of the CDR very seriously. With that as background, here are some private thoughts of a behavior rater.

A member receives training in kitchen skills for independent living as a staff member monitors behavior.
© Jessica MacDonald/Syracuse Newspapers/The Image Works

I record behavioral data in the presence of patients, and the patients are usually keenly aware of what I am doing. After I am through coding patients' CDRs for the time they are with me, other staff members will code them with respect to the time they spend with the patient. And so it goes. It is as if each patient is keeping a detailed diary of his or her life; only, it is we, the staff, who are keeping that diary for them.

Sometimes, especially for new staff, it feels odd to be rating the behavior of fellow human beings. One morning, perhaps out of empathy for a patient, I tossed a blank CDR to a patient and jokingly offered to let him rate my behavior. By dinner, long after I had forgotten that incident in the morning, I realized the patient was coding me for poor table manners. Outwardly, I laughed. Inwardly, I was really a bit offended. Subsequently, I told a joke to the assembled company that in retrospect probably was not in the best of taste. The patient coded me for being socially offensive. Now, I was genuinely becoming self-conscious. Later that evening, we drove to a local video store to return a tape we had rented, and the patient coded me for reckless driving. My discomfort level rose to the point where I thought it was time to end the joke. In retrospect, I had experienced firsthand the self-consciousness and discomfort some of our patients had experienced as their every move was monitored on a daily basis by staff members.

Even though patients are not always comfortable having their behavior rated—and indeed many patients have outbursts with staff members that are in one way or another related to the rating system—it is also true that the system seems to work. Sometimes, self-consciousness is what is needed for people to get better. Here, I think of Sandy, a bright young man who gradually became fascinated by the CDR and soon spent much of the day asking staff members various questions about it. Before long, Sandy asked if he could be allowed to code his own CDR. No one had ever asked to do that before, and a staff meeting was held to mull over the consequences of such an action. As an experiment, it was decided that this patient would be allowed to code his own CDR. The experiment paid off. Sandy's self-coding kept him relatively "on track" with regard to his behavioral goals, and he found himself trying even harder to get better as he showed signs of improvement. Upon discharge, Sandy said he would miss tracking his progress with the CDR.

Instruments such as the CDR can and probably have been used as weapons or rewards by staff. Staff may threaten patients with a poor behavioral evaluation. Overly negative evaluations in response to dysfunctional behavior that is particularly upsetting to the staff is also an ever-present possibility. Yet all the time you are keenly aware that the system works best when staff code patients' behavior consistently and fairly.

such a naturalistic approach in their study of student social life. They tracked the conversations of 52 undergraduates across two two-day periods by means of a computerized recorder.

Another form of behavioral observation employs what is called a *behavior rating scale*—a preprinted sheet on which the observer notes the presence or intensity of targeted behaviors, usually by checking boxes or filling in coded terms. Sometimes the user of a behavior rating form writes in coded descriptions of various behaviors. The code is preferable to a running narrative because it takes far less time to enter the data and thus frees the observer to enter data relating to any of hundreds of possible behaviors, not just the ones printed on the sheets. For example, a number of coding systems for observing the behavior of couples and families are available. Two such systems are the Marital Interaction Coding System (Weiss & Summers, 1983) and the Couples Interaction Scoring System (Notarius & Markman, 1981). Handheld data-entry devices are frequently used today to facilitate the work of the observer.

Behavior rating scales and systems may be categorized in different ways. A continuum of *direct* to *indirect* applies to the setting in which the observed behavior occurs and how closely that setting approximates the setting in which the behavior naturally occurs. The more natural the setting, the more direct the measure; the more removed from the natural setting, the less direct the measure (Shapiro & Skinner, 1990). According to this categorization, for example, assessing a firefighter's actions and reactions while fighting a real fire would provide a *direct* measure of firefighting ability. Assessing a firefighter's actions and reactions while fighting a simulated fire would provide a less direct (or more *indirect*) measure of firefighting ability. Still further down the direct-to-indirect continuum would be verbally asking the firefighter about how he or she might react to hypothetical situations that could occur during a fire. Shapiro and Skinner (1990) also distinguished between *broad-band instruments,* designed to measure a wide variety of behaviors, and *narrow-band instruments,* which may focus on behaviors related to single, specific constructs. A broad-band instrument might measure, for example, general firefighter ability, while a narrow-band instrument might measure proficiency in one particular aspect of those abilities, such as proficiency in administering cardiopulmonary resuscitation (CPR).

Self-monitoring   Self-monitoring may be defined as the act of systematically observing and recording aspects of one's own behavior and/or events related to that behavior. Self-monitoring is different from self-report. As noted by Cone (1999, p. 411), self-monitoring

> relies on observations of *the* behavior of clinical interest . . . at the *time* . . . and *place* . . . of its actual occurrence. In contrast, self-report uses stand-ins or surrogates (verbal descriptions, reports) of the behavior of interest that are obtained at a time and place different from the time and place of the behavior's actual occurrence. (emphasis in the original)

Self-monitoring may be used to record specific thoughts, feelings, or behaviors. The utility of self-monitoring depends in large part on the competence, diligence, and motivation of the assessee, although a number of ingenious methods have been devised to assist in the process or to ensure compliance (Barton et al., 1999; Bornstein et al., 1986; Wilson & Vitousek, 1999). For example, just as you may hear a signal in a car if you fail to buckle your seatbelt, handheld computers have been programmed to beep as a cue to observe and record behavior (Shiffman et al., 1997).

Self-monitoring is both a tool of assessment and a tool of intervention. In some instances, the very act of self-monitoring (of smoking, eating, anxiety, and panic, for example) may be therapeutic. Practical issues that must be considered include the methodology employed, the targeting of specific thoughts, feelings, or behaviors, the sampling procedures put in place, the actual self-monitoring devices and procedures, and the training and preparation (Foster et al., 1999).

Any discussion of behavioral assessment, and particularly self-monitoring, would be incomplete without mention of the psychometric issue of *reactivity* (Jackson, 1999). **Reactivity** refers to the possible changes in an assessee's behavior, thinking, or performance that may arise in response to being observed, assessed, or evaluated. For example, if you are on a weight-loss program and are self-monitoring your food intake, you may be more inclined to forgo the cheesecake than to consume it. In this case, reactivity has a positive effect on the assessee's behavior. There are many instances in which reactivity may have a negative effect on an assessee's behavior or performance. For example, we have previously noted how the presence of third parties during an evaluation may adversely effect an assessee's performance on tasks that require memory or attention (Gavett et al., 2005). Education, training, and adequate preparation are some of the tools used to counter the effects of reactivity in self-monitoring. In addition, post-self-monitoring interviews on the effects of reactivity can provide additional insights about the occurrence of the targeted thoughts or behaviors as well as any reactivity effects.

JUST THINK . . .

Create an original example to illustrate how self-monitoring can be a tool of assessment as well as an intervention.

Analogue studies   The behavioral approach to clinical assessment and treatment has been likened to a researcher's approach to experimentation. The behavioral assessor proceeds in many ways like a researcher; the client's problem is the dependent variable, and the factor (or factors) responsible for causing or maintaining the problem behavior is the independent variable. Behavioral assessors may use the phrase *functional analysis of behavior* to convey the process of identifying the dependent and independent variables with respect to the presenting problem. However, just as experimenters must frequently employ independent and dependent variables that imitate those variables in the real world, so must behavioral assessors.

An **analogue study** is a research investigation in which one or more variables are similar or analogous to the real variable that the investigator wishes to examine. This definition is admittedly very broad, and the term *analogue study* has been used in various ways. It has been used, for example, to describe research conducted with white rats when the experimenter really wishes to learn about humans. It has been used to describe research conducted with full-time students when the experimenter really wishes to learn about people employed full-time in business settings. It has been used to describe research on aggression defined as the laboratory administration of electric shock when the experimenter really wishes to learn about real-world aggression outside the laboratory.

More specific than the term *analogue study* is **analogue behavioral observation,** which, after Haynes (2001b), may be defined as the observation of a person or persons in an environment designed to increase the chance that the assessor can observe targeted behaviors and interactions. The person or persons in this definition may be clients (including individual children and adults, families, or couples) or research subjects (including students, co-workers, or any other research sample). The targeted behavior, of course, depends on the objective of the research. For a client who avoids hiking because of a fear of snakes, the behavior targeted for assessment (and change) is the fear reaction to snakes, most typically elicited while hiking. This behavior may be assessed (and treated) in analogue fashion within the confines of a clinician's office, using a backdrop of a scene that might be encountered while hiking, photos of snakes, videos of snakes, live snakes that are caged, and live snakes that are not caged.

JUST THINK . . .

As a result of a car accident, a client of a behavior therapist claims not to be able to get into a car and drive again. The therapist wishes to assess this complaint by means of analogue behavioral observation. How should the therapist proceed?

A variety of environments have been designed to increase the assessor's chances of observing the targeted behavior (see, for example, Heyman, 2001; Mori & Armendariz, 2001; Norton & Hope, 2001; and Roberts, 2001). Questions about how analogous some analogue studies really are have been raised, along with questions regarding their ultimate utility (Haynes, 2001a).

Situational performance measures and role-play measures both may be thought of as analogue approaches to assessment. Let's take a closer look at each.

Situational performance measures   If you have ever applied for a part-time clerical job and been required to take a word processing test, you have had firsthand experience with *situational performance measures.* Broadly stated, a **situational performance measure** is a procedure that allows for observation and evaluation of an individual under a standard set of circumstances. A situational performance measure typically involves performance of some specific task under actual or simulated conditions. The road test you took to obtain your driver's license was a situational performance measure that involved an evaluation of your driving skills in a real car on a real road in real traffic. On the other hand, situational performance measures used to assess the skills of prospective space-traveling astronauts are done in rocket simulators in laboratories firmly planted on Mother Earth. Common to all situational performance measures is that the construct they measure is thought to be more accurately assessed by examining behavior directly than by asking subjects to describe their behavior. If simply asked about how they would perform, some respondents may be motivated to misrepresent themselves to manage a more favorable impression. Also, it is very possible that the respondents really do not know how they will perform under particular circumstances. Verbal speculation about how one would perform under particular circumstances, particularly high stress circumstances, is often quite different than what actually occurs.

The **leaderless group technique** is a situational assessment procedure wherein several people are organized into a group for the purpose of carrying out a task as an observer records information related to individual group members' initiative, cooperation, leadership, and related variables. Usually, all group members know they are being evaluated and that their behavior is being observed and recorded. Purposely vague instructions are typically provided to the group, and no one is placed in the position of leadership or authority. The group determines how it will accomplish the task and who will be responsible for what duties. The leaderless group situation provides an opportunity to observe the degree of cooperation exhibited by each individual group member and the extent to which each is able to function as part of a team.

The leaderless group technique has been employed in military and industrial settings. Its use in the military developed out of attempts by the U.S. Office of Strategic Services (OSS Assessment Staff, 1948) to assess leadership as well as other personality traits. The procedure was designed to aid in the establishment of cohesive military units—cockpit crews, tank crews, and so forth—in which members would work together well and could each make a significant contribution. Similarly, the procedure is used in industrial and organizational settings to identify people who work well together and those with superior managerial skills and "executive potential."

The self-managed work-group approach challenges traditional conceptions of manager and worker. How does one manage a group that is supposed to manage itself? One approach is to try to identify *unleaders,* who act primarily as facilitators in the workplace and are able to balance a hands-off management style with a style that is more directive when necessary (Manz & Sims, 1984).

JUST THINK . . .

You are a management consultant to a major corporation with an assignment: Create a situational performance measure designed to identify an *unleader.* Briefly outline your plan.

Role play   The technique of **role play,** or acting an improvised or partially improvised part in a simulated situation, can be used in teaching, therapy, and assessment. Police departments, for example, routinely prepare rookies for emergencies by having them play roles, such as an officer confronted by a criminal holding a hostage at gunpoint. Part of the prospective police officer's final exam may be successful performance on a role-playing task. A therapist might use role play to help a feuding couple avoid harmful shouting matches and learn more effective methods of conflict resolution. That same couple's successful resolution of role-played issues may be one of a therapist's criteria for terminating therapy.

A large and growing literature exists on role play as a method of assessment. In general, role play can provide a relatively inexpensive and highly adaptable means of assessing various behavior "potentials." We cautiously say "potentials" because of the uncertainty that role-played behavior will then be elicited in a naturalistic situation (Kern et al., 1983; Kolotkin & Wielkiewicz, 1984). Bellack et al. (1990) employed role play for both evaluative and instructional purposes with psychiatric inpatients who were being prepared for independent living. While acknowledging the benefits of role play in assessing patients' readiness to return to the community, these authors cautioned that "the ultimate validity criterion for any laboratory- or clinic-based assessment is unobtrusive observation of the target behavior in the community" (p. 253).

JUST THINK . . .

Describe a referral for evaluation that would ideally lend itself to the use of role play as a tool of assessment.

Psychophysiological methods   The search for clues to understanding and predicting human behavior has led researchers to the study of physiological indices such as heart rate and blood pressure. These and other indices are known to be influenced by psychological factors—hence the term **psychophysiological** to describe these variables as well as the methods used to study them. Whether these methods are properly regarded as *behavioral* in nature is debatable. Still, these techniques do tend to be associated with behaviorally oriented clinicians and researchers.

Perhaps the best known of all psychophysiological methods used by psychologists is *biofeedback*. **Biofeedback** is a generic term that may be defined broadly as a class of psychophysiological assessment techniques designed to gauge, display, and record a continuous monitoring of selected biological processes such as pulse and blood pressure. Depending on how biofeedback instrumentation is designed, many different biological processes—such as heart rate, respiration rate, muscle tone, electrical resistance of the skin, and brain waves—may be monitored and "fed back" to the assessee via visual displays, such as lights and scales, or auditory stimuli, such as bells and buzzers. Perhaps the variety of biofeedback most familiar to students is the electrocardiogram. You may have heard this measure of heart rate referred to in physicians' offices as an "EKG." Less familiar may be varieties of biofeedback that measure brainwaves (the electroencephalogram or EEG), and muscle tone (the electromyogram or EMG).

The use of biofeedback with humans was inspired by reports that animals given rewards (and hence feedback) for exhibiting certain involuntary responses (such as heart rate) could successfully modify those responses (Miller, 1969). Early experimentation with humans demonstrated a capacity to produce certain types of brain waves on command (Kamiya, 1962, 1968). Since that time, different varieties of biofeedback have been experimented with in a wide range of therapeutic and assessment-related applications (Forbes et al., 2011; French et al., 1997; Hazlett et al., 1997; Henriques et al., 2011; Hermann et al., 1997; Lofthouse et al., 2011; Zhang et al., 1997;).

The **plethysmograph** is a biofeedback instrument that records changes in the volume of a part of the body arising from variations in blood supply. Investigators have used this device to explore changes in blood flow as a dependent variable. For example, Kelly (1966) found significant differences in the blood supplies of normal, anxiety-ridden, and psychoneurotic groups (the anxiety group having the highest mean) by using a plethysmograph to measure blood supply in the forearm.

A **penile plethysmograph** is also an instrument designed to measure changes in blood flow, but more specifically blood flow to the penis. Because the volume of blood in the penis increases with male sexual arousal, the penile plethysmograph has found application in the assessment of adolescent and adult male sexual offenders (Clift et al., 2009; Lanyon &

Thomas, 2008). In one study, subjects who were convicted rapists demonstrated more sexual arousal to descriptions of rape and less arousal to consenting-sex stories than did control subjects (Quinsey et al., 1984). Offenders who continue to deny deviant sexual object choices may be confronted with **phallometric data** (the record from a study conducted with a penile plethysmograph) as a means of compelling them to speak more openly about their thoughts and behavior (Abel et al., 1986). Phallometric data also has treatment and program evaluation applications. In one such type of application, the offender—a rapist, a child molester, an exhibitionist, or some other sexual offender—is exposed to visual and/or auditory stimuli depicting scenes of normal and deviant behavior while penile tumescence is simultaneously gauged. Analysis of phallometric data is then used to evaluate improvement as a result of intervention.

Phallometric data have increasingly been introduced into evidence in American and Canadian courts (Purcell et al., 2015). Still, doubts have been raised regarding the reliability and validity of such data. While widely acknowledged to be of value in monitoring the progress in treatment of sex offenders, the value of such data in criminal proceedings and in sentencing is less straightforward. A problem for the methodology is that a defendant's self-interest to avoid incrimination (by demonstrating a lack of deviant sexual urges) co-exists with a known ability to "fake good" on the test (O'Shaughnessy, 2015). Additionally, there is a lack of standardization in phallometrics—this as the result of a plethora of methodologies and scoring systems.

In the public eye, the best-known of all psychophysiological measurement tools is what is commonly referred to as a *lie detector* or **polygraph** (literally, "more than one graph"). Although not commonly associated with psychological assessment, the lie detection industry has been characterized as "one of the most important branches of applied psychology" (Lykken, 1981, p. 4). This is especially true today, given the frequency with which such tests are administered, as well as the potential consequences as a result of such tests.

Based on the assumption that detectable physical changes occur when an individual lies, the polygraph provides a continuous written record (variously referred to as a *tracing,* a *graph,* a *chart,* or a *polygram*) of several physiological indices (typically respiration, galvanic skin response, and blood volume/pulse rate) as an interviewer and instrument operator (known as a *polygrapher* or *polygraphist*) asks the assessee a series of yes–no questions. Judgments of the truthfulness of the responses are made either informally by surveying the charts or more formally by means of a scoring system.

The reliability of judgments made by polygraphers has long been, and today remains, a matter of great controversy (Alpher & Blanton, 1985; Iacono & Lykken, 1997). Different methods of conducting polygraphic examinations exist (Lykken, 1981), and polygraphic equipment is not standardized (Abrams, 1977; Skolnick, 1961). A problem with the method is a high false-positive rate for lying. The procedure "may label more than 50% of the innocent subjects as guilty" (Kleinmuntz & Szucko, 1984, p. 774). In light of the judgments that polygraphers are called upon to make, their education, training, and background requirements seem minimal. One may qualify as a polygrapher after as few as six weeks of training. From the available psychometric and related data, it seems reasonable to conclude that the promise of a machine purporting to detect dishonesty remains unfulfilled.

> **JUST THINK . . .**
>
> Polygraph evidence is not admissible in most courts, yet law enforcement agencies and the military continue to use it as a tool of evaluation. Your thoughts?

Unobtrusive measures   A type of measure quite different from any we have discussed so far is the *nonreactive* or *unobtrusive* variety (Webb et al., 1966). In many instances, an **unobtrusive measure** is a telling physical trace or record. In one study, it was garbage—literally (Cote et al., 1985). Because of their nature, unobtrusive measures do not necessarily require the presence or cooperation of respondents when measurements are being conducted.

In a now-classic book that was almost entitled *The Bullfighter's Beard*,[9] Webb et al. (1966) listed numerous examples of unobtrusive measures, including the following:

- The popularity of a museum exhibit can be measured by examination of the erosion of the floor around it relative to the erosion around other exhibits.

- The amount of whiskey consumption in a town can be measured by counting the number of empty bottles in trashcans.

- The degree of fear induced by session of telling ghost stories can be measured by noting the shrinking diameter of a circle of seated children.

JUST THINK . . .

Webb et al. (1966) argued that unobtrusive measures can usefully complement other research techniques such as interviews and questionnaires. What unobtrusive measure could conceivably be used to complement a questionnaire on student study habits?

One team of researchers used wrappers left on trays at fast-food restaurants to estimate the caloric intake of restaurant patrons (Stice et al., 2004). These researchers had hoped to expand their study by developing a comparably unobtrusive way to gather information on caloric intake in the home. However, they were unable to devise any ethically acceptable way to so. In another innovative use of a "telling record," researchers used college yearbook photos to study the relationship between positive emotional expression and other variables, such as personality and life outcome (see the discussion of this fascinating research online in the Instructor Resources within Connect).

Issues in Behavioral Assessment

The psychometric soundness of tools of behavioral assessment can be evaluated, but how best to do that is debatable. More specifically, questions arise about the appropriateness of various models of measurement. You may recall that classical test theory and generalizability theory conceptualize test-score variation in somewhat different ways. In generalizability theory, rather than trying to estimate a single true score, consideration is given to how test scores would be expected to shift across situations as a result of changes in the characteristic being measured. It is for this and related reasons that generalizability theory seems more applicable to behavioral assessment than to the measurement of personality traits. Behavior changes across situations, necessitating an approach to reliability that can account for those changes. In contrast, personality traits are assumed by many to be relatively stable across situations. Personality traits are therefore presumed to be more appropriately measured by instruments with assumptions that are consistent with the true score model.

Regardless of whether behavioral measures are evaluated in accordance with classical test theory, generalizability theory, or something else (such as a Skinnerian experimental analysis), it would seem there are some things on which everyone can agree. One is that there must be an acceptable level of inter-rater reliability among behavior observers or raters. A potential source of error in behavioral ratings may arise when a dissimilarity in two or more of the observed behaviors (or other things being rated) leads to a more favorable or unfavorable rating than would have been made had the dissimilarity not existed (Maurer & Alexander, 1991). A behavioral rating may be excessively positive (or negative) because a prior rating was excessively negative (or positive). This source of error is referred to as a **contrast effect.**

9. Webb et al. (1966) explained that the provocative, if uncommunicative, title *The Bullfighter's Beard* was a "title drawn from the observation that toreadors' beards are longer on the day of the fight than on any other day. No one seems to know if the toreador's beard really grows faster that day because of anxiety or if he simply stands further away from the blade, shaking razor in hand. Either way, there were not enough American aficionados to get the point" (p. v). The title they finally settled on was *Unobtrusive Measures: Nonreactive Research in the Social Sciences.*

Contrast effects have been observed in interviews (Schuh, 1978), in behavioral diaries and checklists (Maurer et al., 1993), in laboratory-based performance evaluations (Smither et al., 1988), and in field performance evaluations (Ivancevich, 1983). The contrast effect may even be at work in some judgments at the Olympics (see Figure 12–10). In one study of employment interviews, as much as 80% of the total variance was thought to be due to contrast effects (Wexley et al., 1972).

JUST THINK . . .

How might a contrast effect be operative in a university classroom?

To combat potential contrast effects and other types of rating error, rigorous training of raters is necessary. However, such training may be costly in terms of time and labor. For example, teaching professionals how to use the behavior observation and coding system of the Marital Interaction Coding System took "two to three months of weekly instruction and practice to learn how to use its 32 codes" (Fredman & Sherman, 1987, p. 28). Another approach to minimizing error and improving inter-rater reliability among behavioral raters is to employ a **composite judgment,** which is, in essence, an averaging of multiple judgments.

Some types of observer bias cannot practically or readily be remedied. For example, in behavioral observation involving the use of video equipment, it would on many occasions be advantageous if multiple cameras and recorders could be used to cover various angles of the ongoing action, to get close-ups, and so forth. The economic practicality of the situation (let alone other factors, such as the number of hours required to watch footage from multiple views) is that it is seldom feasible to have more than one camera in a fixed position recording the action. The camera is in a sense biased in that one fixed position because in many instances it is recording information that may be quite different from the information that would have been obtained had it been placed in another position—or if multiple recordings were being made.

As we have already noted in the context of self-monitoring, *reactivity* is another possible issue with regard to behavioral assessment; people react differently in experimental than in natural situations. Microphones, cameras, and one-way mirrors may in themselves alter the behavior of persons being observed. For example, some patients under videotaped observation may attempt to minimize the amount of psychopathology they are willing to record for posterity; others under the same conditions may attempt to exaggerate it. One possible solution to the problem of reactivity is the use of hidden observers or clandestine recording techniques, although such methods raise serious ethical issues. Many times, all that is required to solve the problem of reactivity is an adaptation period. People being observed may adjust to the idea

Figure 12–10
The Contrast Effect at the Rink

Figure skating judges, like other behavior raters, are only human. Skaters who give performances worthy of extremely high marks may not always get what they deserve, simply because the skater who performed just before they did excelled by contrast. Ratings may be more favorable when the performance just prior to theirs was very poor. Because of this contrast effect, the points earned by a skater may depend to some degree on the quality of the preceding skater's performance.
© Kevork Djansezian/AP Photo

and begin to behave in their typical ways. Most clinicians are aware from personal experience that a recording device in the therapy room might put off some patients at first, but in only a matter of minutes the chances are good that it will be ignored.

Some of the other possible limitations of behavioral approaches include the equipment costs (some of the electronics can be expensive) and the cost of training behavioral assessors (Kenny et al., 2008). If training is not sufficient, another "cost"—one that few behavioral assessors are willing to pay—may be unwanted variables in their reports such as observer error or bias.

One final issue we will raise has to do with integrating and reconciling behavioral conceptualizations of psychopathology with more traditional conceptualizations, such as those found in the DSM-5. Researchers (such as Woods and Anderson, 2016) are working to develop common ground in the way that members of different theoretical approaches can conceptualize personality and psychopathology. One day, for example, we may be talking about general (g) and specific (s) factors in personality disorders, in a way that is analogous to discussions of g and s with respect to intelligence (see this chapter's *Close-Up*).

A Perspective

More than a half-century ago, Theodor Reik's influential book *Listening with the Third Ear* intrigued clinicians with the possibilities of evaluation and intervention by means of skilled interviewing, active listening, and artful, depth-oriented interpretation. In one vignette, a female therapy patient recounted a visit to the dentist that involved an injection and a tooth extraction. While speaking, she remarked on a book in Reik's bookcase that was "standing on its head"—to which Reik responded, "But why did you not tell me that you had had an abortion?" (Reik, 1948, p. 263). Reflecting on this dazzling exhibition of clinical intuition, Masling (1997) wrote, "We would all have liked to have had Reik's magic touch, the ability to discern what is hidden and secret, to serve as oracle" (p. 259).

Historically, society has called upon mental health professionals to make diagnostic judgments and intervention recommendations, and often on the basis of relatively little information. Early on, psychological tests, particularly in the area of personality assessment, promised to empower clinicians—mere mortals—to play the oracular role society imposed and expected. Soon, two very different philosophies of test design and use emerged. The clinical approach relied heavily on the clinician's judgment and intuition. This approach was criticized for its lack of preset and uniformly applied rules for drawing clinical conclusions and making predictions. By contrast, the statistical or actuarial approach relied heavily on standardization, norms, and preset, uniformly applied rules and procedures. Duels between various members of these two camps were common for many years and have been reviewed in detail elsewhere (Marchese, 1992).

It seems fair to say that in those situations where data are insufficient to formulate rules for decision making and prediction, the clinical approach wins out over the actuarial. For the most part, however, it is the actuarial approach that has been most enthusiastically embraced by contemporary practitioners. This is so for a number of reasons, chief among them a passionate desire to make assessment more a science than an art. And that desire may simply reflect the fact that much as we would like it to be different, most of us are not oracles. Without reliable and valid tools, it is difficult if not impossible to spontaneously and consistently see through to what Reik (1952) characterized as the "secret self." Even with good tools, it's a challenge.

The actuarial approach encourages the retention only of hypotheses and predictions that have proven themselves. Conversely, it enables practitioners to quickly discover and discard untenable hypotheses and predictions (Masling, 1997). Of course, in many instances, skill in clinical assessment can be conceptualized as an internalized, less formal, and more creative version of the actuarial approach.

General (*g*) and Specific (*s*) Factors in the Diagnosis of Personality Disorders*

"**W**hat is borderline personality disorder?" To answer the question authoritatively, a clinician might produce the DSM-5 and define borderline personality disorder by proceeding to quote the nine criteria used to make that diagnosis (see Table 1).

But how meaningful is that DSM-based diagnosis? The short answer to the latter question is "not very," at least according to one review of the available literature (Sheets & Craighead, 2007). Others are of the opinion that personality disorders may more usefully be conceived and diagnosed as psychopathology on a continuum or dimension (Widiger & Trull, 2007). Such a dimensional approach would stand in stark contrast to the present categorical conceptualization (Clark, 2007).

A red flag concerning the unique and "real" existence of a DSM-based diagnosis of a personality disorder is the relatively high co-morbidity rates that have been observed between different varieties of personality disorders, and between personality disorders and other psychiatric disorders (like depression, anxiety, and substance abuse; see Clark, 2007). This means that people who are diagnosed with one variety of personality disorder are frequently diagnosed as having another variety of personality disorder (or some other psychiatric disorder). It may well be that people with multiple diagnoses

TABLE 1
DSM-5 Criteria for the Diagnosis of Borderline Personality Disorder

According to DSM-5 (APA, 2012, p.663) the nine criteria for borderline personality disorder are:

- intense anger,
- affective instability
- chronic feelings of emptiness
- paranoid ideation and dissociation
- identity disturbance
- abandonment fears
- suicidal behaviors
- impulsivity,
- unstable relationships.

In order for a patient to meet criteria for borderline personality disorder, a clinician would interview the patient and determine that at least five of the criteria have been met for at least two years. Further, the symptoms must have been present in a variety of settings. Additionally, this enduring pattern of behavior must not be better explained by any other disorder or the effects of drugs.

*This *Close-Up* was guest-authored by Carla Sharp of the University of Houston.

really are suffering from multiple forms of psychopathology. Then again, it might just be that the diagnostic criteria of the two (or more) conditions overlap to such an extent that it just *appears* as if multiple pathologies are present. If the latter is true, more attention needs to be paid to better understanding the diagnosis of personality disorders. Better understanding may take the form of either sharpening the specificity of existing diagnostic categorizations, or re-conceptualizing them altogether, possibly along a strictly dimensional continuum. This improvement in understanding is especially urgent given the potentially unnecessary cost and expense of treating multiple conditions when in fact, the existence of multiple diagnoses may be an artifact of the diagnostic system.

Another potential problem with the DSM vis-a-vis the categorization of personality disorders is what might be termed the "all-or-none error." Using the DSM diagnostic system, one either has or has not a personality disorder. Here, it is worth noting that longitudinal research suggests that a diagnosis of personality disorder is not very stable (Zanarini et al., 2012). In general, personality disorders may be comprised of some problem thinking and behavior that is acute and transitory in nature, and other such problems that are more lasting and trait-like (Clark, 2007). If that is true, the same individual diagnosed with a particular personality disorder at one point in time may not be diagnosed with that same disorder at another point in time. This fragility of the diagnosis (or, perhaps the unreliability of the diagnosis from a psychometric perspective) has varied implications, including implications for treatment. A patient may be denied much needed treatment by a third-party insurer if as little as one of the necessary diagnostic criteria is, however temporarily, not in evidence.

Based on their review of the prior literature, Carla Sharp and her colleagues (2015) hypothesized that factor analysis of the nine criteria for diagnosing borderline personality would not support the existence of borderline personality disorder as a unique and distinct factor. Sharp et al. further hypothesized that the six other most frequently diagnosed categories of personality disorder (antisocial personality disorder, schizotypal personality disorder, avoidant personality disorder, narcissistic personality disorder, and obsessive-compulsive personality disorder) would be found to be separate and distinct types of personality disorders. Interested readers are referred to Sharp et al. (2015) for the study details, as only the top-line findings will be presented here.

(continued)

General (*g*) and Specific (*s*) Factors in the Diagnosis of Personality Disorders *(continued)*

On the basis of their factor-analytic study with nearly one-thousand psychiatric inpatients, Sharp et al. concluded that the nine criteria cited in the DSM-5 for borderline criteria are in some way analogous to the general factor (*g*) in conceptualizations of intelligence. Rather than defining a separate and distinct variety of personality disorder, these nine criteria, taken together as a whole, seemed to be the "*g*" of personality pathology. The investigators also tested the hypothesis that borderline personality disorder could best be accounted for by two sets of factors, a general factor (*g*), and more disorder-specific (*s*) factors (much like the construct of intelligence, with its overarching *g* factor, and its more individual *s* factors). The results suggested that the borderline criteria loaded most strongly and virtually exclusively, on the general (*g*) factor, with little trace of *s* to be found. By contrast, the other five personality disorders (avoidant personality disorder, obsessive-compulsive personality disorder, narcissistic personality disorder, antisocial personality disorder, and schizotypal personality disorder) all seemed to load on respective, distinct specific (*s*) factors.

The failure of borderline personality disorder to emerge as a distinct factor may be seen by some as challenging the very diagnostic validity of borderline personality disorder. However, Sharp, et al. (2015) interpreted this finding somewhat differently. They suspected that borderline personality disorder actually represents the core features of personality pathology in general.

More specifically, the nine borderline criteria represent some of the basic elemental features that cut across all personality disorders.

An additional explanation for the "disappearance" of the borderline personality disorder into the general factor is the possibility that borderline personality disorder, by its nature, is so severe a personality disorder pathology that it loads exclusively on the general (*g*) factor. Regardless, the results were construed as not supporting the traditional view of borderline personality disorder as a discreet pathological condition.

The limitations of the Sharp et al. (2015) study should be noted. Sharp et al. focused exclusively on the six personality disorders that are described in Section III of the DSM (and not the ten personality disorders described in Section II). Therefore, it is unclear whether the results would hold when all ten personality disorders are factor-analyzed. Also, Sharp et al. used an inpatient sample of subject which may limit the generalizability of the findings exclusively to inpatients.

Despite these limitations, the study was important in that it shed much needed light on how the various categories of personality disorder are—or should be—conceptualized and operationalized. Future replications of this work are encouraged, as are expansions using all ten of the personality disorder categories, and both inpatient and outpatient subjects.

Used with permission of Carla Sharp.

The actuarial approach to personality assessment is increasingly common. Even projective instruments, once the bastion of the "old school" clinical approach, are increasingly published with norms, and scrupulously researched. There have even been efforts—very respectable efforts—to apply sophisticated IRT models to, of all things, TAT data (Tuerlinckx et al., 2002). But swaying long-held opinions about the invalidity of projective assessment will not come easy. There is in academic psychology a climate of opinion that "continues as though nothing has changed and clinicians were still reading tea leaves" (Masling, 1997, p. 263).

If the oracle-like, clinical orientation is characterized as the *third ear approach,* we might characterize the contemporary orientation as a *van Gogh approach;* in a sense, an ear has been dispatched. The day of the all-knowing oracle has passed. Today, it is incumbent upon the responsible clinician to rely on norms, inferential statistics, and related essentials of the actuarial approach. Sound clinical judgment is still desirable, if not mandatory. However, it is required less for the purpose of making off-the-cuff interpretations and predictions and more for the purpose of organizing and interpreting information from different tools of assessment. We'll have more to say on this point as we move to the next chapter.

Self-Assessment

Test your understanding of elements of this chapter by seeing if you can explain each of the following terms, expressions, and abbreviations:

analogue behavioral observation
analogue study
apperceive
behavioral assessment
behavioral observation
biofeedback
composite judgment
comprehensive system (Exner)
contrast effect
ecological momentary assessment
figure drawing test
free association
functional analysis of behavior
implicit motive
inquiry (on the Rorschach)

leaderless group technique
need (Murray)
objective methods of personality
    assessment
penile plethysmograph
percept (on the Rorschach)
phallometric data
plethysmograph
polygraph
press (Murray)
projective hypothesis
projective method
psychophysiological (assessment
    methods)
reactivity

role play
Rorschach test
self-monitoring
sentence completion
sentence completion stem
sentence completion test
situational performance measure
TAT
testing the limits (on the Rorschach)
thema (Murray)
timeline followback (TLFB)
    methodology
unobtrusive measure
word association
word association test

13

Clinical and Counseling Assessment

Clinical psychology is the branch of psychology that has as its primary focus the prevention, diagnosis, and treatment of abnormal behavior. Clinical psychologists receive training in psychological assessment and psychotherapy and are employed in hospitals, public and private mental health centers, independent practice, and academia. Like clinical psychology, **counseling psychology** is a branch of psychology that is concerned with the prevention, diagnosis, and treatment of abnormal behavior. Clinical psychologists tend to focus their research and treatment efforts on the more severe forms of behavior pathology, whereas counseling psychologists focus more on "everyday" types of concerns and problems, such as those related to marriage, family, academics, and career. Members of both professions strive to foster personal growth in their clients. The tools employed in the process of assessment overlap considerably.

All the tests and measures we have covered so far—intelligence, personality, self-concept, cognitive style—would be appropriate for discussion in this chapter, for all have potential application in clinical and counseling contexts. In an introductory text such as this, however, choices must be made as to coverage and organization. We have organized the material in this chapter to best convey to the reader how tools of assessment such as the interview, the case history, and psychological tests are used in clinical contexts. Our discussion will sample some of the many special applications of clinical assessment. We will see, for example, how clinical assessment is useful in forensic work, in custody evaluations, and in evaluations of child abuse and neglect. Interwoven throughout, as has been our custom throughout this book, is attention to cultural aspects of the subjects we discuss. We begin with an overview of psychological assessment, including discussion of some general issues related to the diagnosis of mental disorders.

An Overview

Clinical assessment may be undertaken for various reasons and to answer a variety of important questions. For the clinical psychologist working in a hospital, clinic, or other clinical setting, tools of assessment are frequently used to clarify the psychological problem, make a diagnosis, and/or design a treatment plan. *Does this patient have a mental disorder?* and *If so, what is the diagnosis?* are typical questions that require answers. In many cases, tools of assessment, including an interview, a test, and case history data, can provide those answers. Let's briefly explore how tests and other tools of assessment can be used in clinical settings.

Before or after interviewing a patient, a clinician may administer tests such as a Wechsler intelligence test and the MMPI-2-RF to obtain estimates of the patient's intellectual functioning and level of psychopathology. The data derived may provide the clinician with initial hypotheses about the nature of the individual's difficulties, which will then guide the interview. Alternatively, test data can confirm or refute hypotheses made on the basis of the clinical interview. Interview and test data will be supplemented with case history data, especially if the patient will not or cannot cooperate. The clinician may interview people who know the patient—such as family members, co-workers, and friends—and obtain records relevant to the case.

The tools may be used to address questions such as *What is this person's current level of functioning? How does this level of functioning compare with that of other people of the same age?* Consider the example of an individual who is suspected of suffering from dementia caused by Alzheimer's disease. The patient has experienced a steady and progressive loss of cognitive skills over a period of months. A diagnosis of dementia may involve tracking the individual's performance with repeated administrations of tests of cognitive ability, including memory. If dementia is present, a progressive decline in test performance will be noted. Periodic testing with various instruments may also provide information about the kinds of activities the patient

JUST THINK . . .

Clinicians approach assessment in different ways. Some prefer little more than a referral to begin with (so that their findings will not be shaped in any way by others' impressions or case history data), whereas other clinicians prefer to obtain as much information as they can prior to interviewing and administering any tests. Your preference?

should be advised to pursue as well as the kinds of activities the patient should be encouraged to curtail or give up entirely. Ideally, case history data will provide some way to estimate the patient's level of **premorbid functioning** (or level of psychological and physical performance prior to the development of a disorder, an illness, or a disability).

What type of treatment shall this patient be offered? Tools of assessment can help guide decisions relating to treatment. Patients found to be high in intelligence, for example, tend to make good candidates for insight-oriented methods that require high levels of abstract ability. A person who complains of being depressed may be asked periodically to complete a measure of depression. If such a person is an inpatient, trends in the depth of depression as measured by the instrument may contribute to critical decisions regarding level of supervision within the institution, strength of medication administered, and date of discharge.

How can this person's personality best be described? Gaining an understanding of the individual need not focus on psychopathology. People who do not have any mental disorder sometimes seek psychotherapy for personal growth or support in coping with a difficult set of life circumstances. In such instances, interviews and personality tests geared more to the normal testtaker might be employed.

Researchers may raise a wide variety of other assessment-related questions, including *Which treatment approach is most effective?* or *What kind of client tends to benefit most from a particular kind of treatment?* A researcher may believe, for example, that people with a field-dependent cognitive style would be most likely to benefit from a cognitive-behavioral approach to treatment and that people with a field-independent cognitive style would be most likely to benefit from a humanistic approach to treatment. The researcher would use a variety of assessment tools to combine subjects into treatment groups and then to measure outcome in psychotherapy.

Counseling psychologists who do employment counseling may use a wide variety of assessment tools to help determine not only what occupations a person might enjoy but also which occupations would be sufficiently challenging yet not overwhelming. School psychologists and counseling psychologists working in a school setting may assist students with a wide variety of problems, including those related to studying. Here, behavioral measures, including self-monitoring, might be employed to better understand exactly how, when, and where the student

JUST THINK . . .

Cite another example or two to illustrate how a tool of assessment could be used in a clinical or counseling setting.

engages in study behavior. The answer to related questions such as *Why am I not doing well in school?* may in part be found in diagnostic educational tests, such as those designed to identify problem areas in reading and reading comprehension. Another part of the answer may be obtained through other tools of assessment, including the interview, which may focus on aspects of the student's motivation and other life circumstances.

The Diagnosis of Mental Disorders

Frequently an objective of clinical assessment is to diagnose mental disorders. The reference source used for making such diagnoses is the American Psychiatric Association's *Diagnostic and Statistical Manual (DSM)*.

Now, in its fifth edition, the current version of the DSM (referred to as DSM-5) names and describes all mental disorders. Much like other medical classification and coding systems, such as the tenth edition of the *International Classification of Diseases* (ICD-10) published by the World Health Organization, a DSM diagnosis carries with it summary information about the nature and extent of an individual's psychiatric disorder.

DSM-5 lists all the criteria that have to be met in order to diagnose each of the disorders listed. DSM-5 also contains a listing of conditions that may not be officially named as psychiatric disorders until further research has been completed. DSM-5, much like any other classification or diagnostic system, has many advantages. It permits clinicians and researchers to "speak the same language" by providing a kind of shorthand identification of patients' varied psychological condition. A DSM-5 diagnosis immediately conveys key information about a diagnosed individual's behavior, cognition, and emotions. It conveys information about how extreme, problematic, troubling, odd, or abnormal the individual's behavior is likely to be perceived by others. Also, while there are no treatment plans in the DSM-5, a psychiatric diagnosis provides a starting point for utility-related considerations regarding the therapy, medication, or other intervention that may have the best chance of achieving remission or cure. Also, much like a definitive medical diagnosis, a psychiatric diagnosis may be beneficial in terms of ending (if not solving) the mystery that frequently surrounds the patient with abnormal behavior. The diagnosis provides a name to the disorder—a name that can now be monitored for new details regarding this variety of psychopathology, including new research, new treatments, and ultimately, new hope.

A common diagnostic system affords researchers the ability to compile statistics on the *incidence* and *prevalence* of specific disorders. **Incidence** in this context may be defined as the rate (annual, monthly, weekly, daily, or other) of new occurrences of a particular disorder or condition in a particular population. For example, Zhang et al. (2015) discussed the *incidence* of suicidal ideation in persons diagnosed with depression. **Prevalence** may be defined as the approximate proportion of individuals in a given population at a given point (or range) in time who have been diagnosed or otherwise labeled with a particular disorder or condition. For example, Osborn et al. (2016) researched the *prevalence* of anxiety in patients who had suffered traumatic brain injury.

Data related to the incidence and prevalence of various psychiatric disorders can be useful to clinicians charged with rendering a diagnosis for an individual; clinicians can look, for example, to the known demographics of a particular disorder and note the extent to which there is a match for a particular patient. Incidence and prevalence data are also of value to researchers as a basis for prioritizing their time and resources; the greater the incidence or prevalence, for example, the more compelling the argument may be for a research budget. Incidence and prevalence data can also help guide the plans and regulatory policies of the many companies that are involved in business-related aspects of mental health, such as health insurers and manufacturers of pharmaceuticals (Nelson et al., 2015).

In theory, there would not appear to be much controversy about a diagnostic system that lists, categorizes, and describes all known mental disorders. The fact is that there has been no shortage of controversy surrounding DSM-5—controversy that begins with what may be the most elementary question it raises: "What is a disorder?" This deceptively simple question has generated heated rhetoric (Clark, 1999; Spitzer, 1999). The third edition of the *DSM* was the first edition of that manual to contain a definition of mental disorder, and the definition it offered of *disorder* was criticized by many. As an alternative, Jerome C. Wakefield (1992b) conceptualized mental disorder as a "harmful dysfunction." For Wakefield, a disorder is a harmful failure of internal mechanisms to perform their naturally selected functions. Wakefield's position is an **evolutionary view of mental disorder** because the internal mechanisms that break down or fail are viewed as having been acquired through the Darwinian process of natural selection. For Wakefield, the attribution of disorder entails two things: (1) a scientific judgment that such an evolutionary failure exists; and (2) a value judgment that this failure is harmful to the individual (Wakefield, 1992a).

JUST THINK . . .

Should a diagnostic manual provide clinicians with guidance as to what method of treatment will be optimally effective?

JUST THINK . . .

So, what is a disorder?

In contrast to the evolutionary view of disorder are myriad other views. Klein (1999) argued that "proper evolutionary function" is not known and that behavior labeled "disordered" may be the product of various involuntary causes (such as disease) or even voluntary causes (such as role-playing or malingering). Others have weighed in on this controversial issue by illuminating the role of culture (Kirmayer & Young, 1999) and by championing alternative vantage points, such as focusing on the issue at the level of the neuron (Richters & Hinshaw, 1999).

Some have suggested that the concept of disorder is so broad that it need not have any defining properties (Lilienfeld & Marino, 1995, 1999). Widespread adoption of the view that mental disorders cannot be classified would eclipse the opportunity to perform research that has the potential of advancing treatment outcomes. Also, it is noteworthy but seldom pointed out, that a culturally informed understanding of what is and is not abnormal can have profound consequences for society-at-large. As an example, consider homosexuality, a listed psychiatric disorder from the not-so-distant past.

In a country where the Supreme Court has affirmed the right of its gay and lesbian citizens to marry, some may be surprised to learn that as late as the 1970s, homosexuality had already had a very long history of being a diagnosable psychiatric condition. Patients came to therapists complaining of it, and therapists and researchers were working at ways to treat it. At issue was not whether homosexual behavior was an illness, but rather, whether certain homosexual behavior was more appropriately labeled "perversion" or "spurious" (Bergler, 1947).

In 1973, members of the American Psychiatric Association voted to de-list homosexuality as a mental disorder. The change was the result of neither a scientific breakthrough, nor the formulation of any compelling new theory ("Panel Recalls," 2016). According to Bayer (1981), the action was taken as the result of the political efforts of a small group of gay and lesbian psychiatrists. The group's political lobbying and the reversal of the American Psychiatric Association's longstanding diagnostic position would ultimately result in a global sea change of attitudes towards homosexuality.

Undeniably, the very existence of a psychiatric diagnosis (or lack thereof) can carry with it far-reaching social implications. It is, therefore, all the more imperative for mental health professionals (and others who society charges with the obligation of rendering, creating, and delisting such diagnoses to "get it right." Toward that end, many

JUST THINK . . .

In your opinion, what must the American Psychiatric Association do in terms of future editions of its DSM to "get it right"?

concerned assessment professionals have advocated for diagnostic terminology that is grounded both in behavioral science and informed by contemporary cultural considerations. With regard to the latter point, the DSM-5 is more culturally sensitive than any of its predecessors. There is a section in it which lists cultural concepts of distress. Also included in DSM-5 is a discussion of "cultural formulation," and a 16-item *Cultural Formulation Interview* (CFI) that is recommended for administration at the time of a patient's first session.[1]

In addition to its greater attention to cultural issues in the diagnosis of mental disorders, DSM-5 departs from traditions in other ways—starting with its title. Previous versions of the DSM were titled with Roman numerals (as in DSM-IV). Arabic numerals were used in DSM-5 so that interim editions before the full-fledged DSM-6 was published could easily be titled in increments of tenths (such as DSM-5.1, DSM-5.2, etc.). Some of the most nontraditional departures from previous versions of the DSM have to do with DSM-5's re-conceptualization of certain disorders, as well as some of the new disorders added. For example, in previous versions of the DSM, the diagnosis of schizophrenia could be specified in terms of subtype (such as "paranoid type" or "catatonic type"). In DSM-5, the subtypes of schizophrenia have been eliminated. Essentially, the subtypes have been replaced by a severity rating of core schizophrenic symptoms. Another controversial change in DSM-5 concerns the listing of grief from loss as pathology. In the previous DSM, bereavement as the result of the death of a loved one was excluded from being conceptualized as a mental disorder. In DSM-5, bereavement grief that lasts longer than two weeks may be diagnosed as depression.

Ideally, the terms for classification in any diagnostic system should be so clearly defined that two diagnosticians who are reasonably skilled in psychodiagnostics, and who use the same procedures, should routinely make the same diagnosis when independently presented with the same patient to diagnose. Recall in this context the concept of inter-rater reliability discussed in Chapter 5 (as well as that *Close-Up* on the contribution of method to measures of reliability). For a diagnostic manual to be viable, inter-rater diagnostic reliability between users of that manual must be acceptably high. Of course, disagreements as to diagnosis may derive from other sources of error variance, such as the diagnostic competence of the rater or the specifics of the procedures used. Reasonably competent raters using the same procedures would be expected to arrive at the same diagnosis using the same diagnostic manual. When this is not the case, greater clarity or comprehensiveness in the manual's description of the diagnostic criteria for the disorder may be required for greater reliability in outcomes (McFarlane, 2011; Paris & Phillips, 2013; Pierre, 2013; Thomas et al., 2015).

While the DSM has tended to improve with each successive revision, it is, by its very nature, a work in progress. So, for example, critics of the previous DSM, such as Denton (2007), argued that the manual was insufficiently biopsychosocial in orientation. Does the current version sufficiently remedy past deficiencies in this regard? Readers will be better equipped to respond after a brief explanation of what is meant by *biopsychosocial.*

JUST THINK . . .

Why might it be that the DSM will forever remain a work in progress?

Biopsychosocial assessment   Beginning in 2009, federal mandates required that television broadcasting would not only change from analog to digital in nature but also be broadcast in a "wide screen" format. Likewise, if advocates of the biopsychosocial approach had their way, conceptualizations of mental disorder would be in "wide screen"—providing consumers of such data with the "big picture" view of disorders.

---

1. By the way, back in Chapter 2, you may recall "meeting" Dr. Neil Aggarwal, who described in detail his use of the CFI in clinical practice.

As its name implies, **biopsychosocial assessment** is a multidisciplinary approach to assessment that includes exploration of relevant biological, psychological, social, cultural, and environmental variables for the purpose of evaluating how such variables may have contributed to the development and maintenance of a presenting problem. Rather than being exclusively medical or even psychological in orientation, this approach encourages input from virtually any discipline that can provide relevant insights when such input can be put to use in better understanding the problem and effectively intervening to remedy it (Campbell & Rohrbaugh, 2006; Ingham et al., 2008). Studies focusing on various aspects of physical health, for example, have noted that psychological factors such as **fatalism** (the belief that what happens in life is largely beyond a person's control; Caplan & Schooler, 2003), **self-efficacy** (confidence in one's own ability to accomplish a task) and **social support** (expressions of understanding, acceptance, empathy, love, advice, guidance, care, concern, or trust from friends, family, community caregivers, or others in one's social environment; Keefe et al., 2002) may play key roles. One key tool of biopsychosocial assessment, as with clinical assessment in general, is the interview.

JUST THINK . . .

From your own experience, how has social support been helpful to you in times when you were feeling physically ill? Do you think psychological factors such as social support actually help in feeling better?

The Interview in Clinical Assessment

Except in rare circumstances, such as when an assessee is totally noncommunicative, an interview is likely to be part of every clinician's or counselor's individual assessment. In a clinical situation, for example, an interview may be conducted to arrive at a diagnosis, to pinpoint areas that must be addressed in psychotherapy, or to determine whether an individual will harm himself or others. In a typical counseling application, an interview is conducted to help the interviewee learn more about him- or herself, the better to make potentially momentous life choices. Usually conducted face-to-face, interviewers learn about interviewees not only from *what* they say but also from *how* they say it and from how they present themselves during the interview.

Often, an interview will guide decisions about what else needs to be done to assess an individual. If symptoms or complaints are described by the interviewee in a vague or inconsistent manner, a test designed to screen in a general way for psychopathology may be indicated. If an interviewee complains of memory problems, a standardized memory test may be administered. If the interviewee is unable to describe the frequency with which a particular problem occurs, a period of self-monitoring may be in order. Interviews are frequently used early on in independent practice settings to solidify a **therapeutic contract,** an agreement between client and therapist setting forth goals, expectations, and mutual obligations with regard to a course of therapy.

Seasoned interviewers endeavor to create a positive, accepting climate in which to conduct the interview. They may use open-ended questions initially and then closed questions to obtain specific information. The effective interviewer conveys understanding to the interviewee verbally or nonverbally. Ways of conveying that understanding include attentive posture and facial expression as well as frequent statements acknowledging or summarizing what the interviewee is trying to say. Sometimes interviewers attempt to convey attentiveness by head nodding and vocalizations such as "um-hmm." However, here the interviewer must exercise caution. Such vocalizations and head nodding have been observed to act as reinforcers that increase the emission of certain interviewee verbalizations (Greenspoon, 1955). For example, if a therapist said "um-hmm" every time an interviewee brought up material related to the subject of mother, then—other things being equal—the interviewee might spend more time talking about mother than if not reinforced for bringing up that topic.

JUST THINK . . .

What is another subtle way that an interviewer might inadvertently (or deliberately) encourage an interviewee to spend more time on a particular topic?

Types of interviews Interviews may be typed with respect to a number of different variables. One such variable is *content*. The content of some interviews, such as a general, "getting-to-know-you" interview, can be wide ranging. By contrast, other interviews focus narrowly on particular content. Another variable on which interviews differ is *structure*. A highly structured interview is one in which all the questions asked are prepared in advance. In an interview with little structure, few or no questions are prepared in advance, leaving interviewers the freedom to delve into subject areas as their judgment dictates. An advantage of a structured interview is that it provides a uniform method of exploration and evaluation. A structured interview, much like a test, may therefore be employed as a standardized pre/post measure of outcome. In fact, many research studies that explore the efficacy of a new medication, an approach to therapy, or some other intervention employ structured interviews as outcome measures.

Many structured interviews are available for use by assessment professionals. For example, the Structured Clinical Interview for *DSM*-5 (SCID) is a semistructured interview designed to assist clinicians and researchers in diagnostic decision-making. The Schedule for Affective Disorders and Schizophrenia (SADS) is a standardized interview designed to detect schizophrenia and disorders of affect (such as major depression, bipolar disorder, and anxiety disorders). The Structured Interview of Reported Symptoms-2 (SIRS-2; Rogers et al., 2010) is used primarily in efforts to detect malingering.

In addition to content and structure, interviews may differ in *tone*. In one type of interview—not very common—the interviewer intentionally tries to make the interviewee feel stressed. **Stress interview** is the general name applied to any interview where one objective is to place the interviewee in a pressured state for some particular reason. The stress may be induced to test for some aspect of personality (such as aggressiveness or hostility) that might be elicited only under such conditions. Screening for work in the security or intelligence fields might entail stress interviews if a criterion of the job is the ability to remain cool under pressure. The source of the stress varies as a function of the purpose of the evaluation; possible sources may emanate from the interviewer as disapproving facial expressions, critical remarks, condescending reassurances, relentless probing, or seeming incompetence. Other sources of stress may emanate from the "rules of the game," such as unrealistic time limits for complying with demands.

JUST THINK . . .

Why might it be desirable to subject an interviewee to a stress interview? What ethical constraints are there to stress interviews?

Interviewee *state of consciousness* is another variable related to interview type. Most interviews are conducted with the interviewee in an ordinary, everyday, waking state of consciousness. On occasion, however, a particular situation may call for a very specialized interview in which the state of consciousness of the interviewee is deliberately altered. A **hypnotic interview** is one conducted while the interviewee is under hypnosis. Hypnotic interviews may be conducted as part of a therapeutic assessment or intervention when the interviewee has been an eyewitness to a crime or related situations. In all such cases, the prevailing belief is that the hypnotic state will focus the interviewee's concentration and enhance recall (McConkey & Sheehan, 1996; Reiser, 1980, 1990; Vingoe, 1995).

Critics of hypnotic interviewing suggest that any gains in recall may be offset by losses in accuracy and other possible negative outcomes (Kebbell & Wagstaff, 1998). Hypnotic interview procedures may inadvertently make interviewees more confident of their memories, regardless of their correctness (Dywan & Bowers, 1983; Sheehan et al., 1984). As compared to nonhypnotized interviewees, hypnotized interviewees may be more suggestible to leading questions and thus more vulnerable to distortion of memories (Putnam, 1979; Zelig &

Beidleman, 1981). Some researchers believe that hypnosis of witnesses may inadvertently produce memory distortion that is irreversible (Diamond, 1980; Orne, 1979). As a result, witnesses who have been hypnotized to enhance memory may be banned from testifying (Laurence & Perry, 1988; Perry & Laurence, 1990). A new technique, similar to hypnotic interviewing involves focused meditation with eyes closed (Wagstaff et al., 2011). The researchers reported that their focused meditation technique increased memory yet was resistant to report of misleading information.

An interview procedure designed to retain the best features of a hypnotic interview but without the hypnotic induction has been developed by Fisher and colleagues (Fisher & Geiselman, 1992; Fisher et al., 1987; Fisher et al., 1989; Mello & Fisher, 1996). In the **cognitive interview,** rapport is established and the interviewee is encouraged to use imagery and focused retrieval to recall information. If the interviewee is an eyewitness to a crime, he or she may be asked to shift perspective and describe events from the viewpoint of the perpetrator. Much like what typically occurs in hypnosis, a great deal of control of the interview shifts to the interviewee. And unlike many police interviews, there is an emphasis on open-ended rather than closed questions, and interviewees are allowed to speak without interruption (Kebbell & Wagstaff, 1998). The same term, by the way, has been applied to a questionnaire design procedure whereby draft survey questions are posed to research subjects using a "think aloud" paradigm and the resulting data is analyzed to improve the survey questions (Beatty & Willis, 2007). A meta-analysis of 65 experiments showed that the use of a cognitive interview led to large and significant increases in recalling correct details, although there was also a small increase in erroneous details (Memon et al., 2010). Since 2009, cognitive interviewing has been incorporated into police interview training programs in the United Kingdom.

The **collaborative interview** allows the interviewee wide latitude to interact with the interviewer. It is almost as if the boundary between professional assessor and lay assessee has been diminished and both are participants working closely together—collaborating—on a common mission of discovery, clarification, and enlightenment. In an initial contact prior to a formal assessment by tests and other means, an interviewee might be invited to help frame objectives. What should be accomplished by the assessment? The interviewee is very much an active participant in collaborative assessment. Descriptions of an essentially collaborative assessment process may be found in the writings of Dana (1982), Finn (1996), Fischer (1994), and others. What they have in common is "empowerment of the person through a participatory, collaborative role in the assessment process" (Allen, 2002, p. 221). This, by the way, seems an opportune time to introduce you to Stephen Finn, an architect of collaborative assessment (see *Meet an Assessment Professional*).

JUST THINK . . .

In what innovative way would you like to participate or collaborate in your own clinical or counseling interview, where you are the interviewee?

Regardless of the specific type of interview conducted, certain "standard" questions are typically raised, during the initial intake interview, with regard to several areas. These questions are followed by additional queries as clinical judgment dictates.

Demographic data: Name, age, sex, religion, number of persons in family, race, occupation, marital status, socioeconomic status, address, telephone numbers.

Reason for referral: Why is this individual requesting or being sent for psychological assessment? Who is the referral source?

Past medical history: What events are significant in this individual's medical history?

Present medical condition: What current medical complaints does this individual have? What medications are currently being used?

Familial medical history: What chronic or familial types of disease are present in the family history?

Meet Dr. Stephen Finn

In Therapeutic Assessment, we use a variety of psychological instruments including tests of cognitive functioning (e.g., the WAIS-IV), self-report tests of personality and symptomatology (e.g., the MMPI-2-RF), and performance-based personality tests (e.g., the Rorschach). We select the tests we use based on our initial session with a client. In that meeting, we help clients formulate personalized "assessment questions" they wish to have answered, such as "Why do I have such a difficult time making eye contact?" or "Why have I never been able to have an intimate relationship?" We then select tests that will help address the clients' questions as well as those questions given to us by any referring professionals. For example, with the questions just mentioned, we might propose that a client take the MMPI-2-RF and the Rorschach, because our experience is that the combination of a self-report and performance-based personality test is helpful in helping us understand these types of issues. In our initial session, we would also collect comprehensive background information about the concerns reflected in the client's questions. For example, we would ask about when it is most difficult or easiest for the client to make eye contact, when this problem began, and what the client already has tried to address this problem. We would also ask about previous attempts to have intimate relationships.

We believe that at their best, psychological tests serve as "empathy magnifiers"—helping us to get "in our clients' shoes" and understand puzzles, quandaries, or stuck points in their lives that they have not been able to address in other ways. We administer tests in a standardized fashion early in our assessments, and find that the information they provide yields very useful hypotheses about why clients have the problems they do. Often, through our tests, we are able to help people understand puzzling, even self-destructive or off-putting behaviors that other mental health professionals have not been able to understand or ameliorate. And we consciously use tests to identify people's strengths as well as their struggles.

We involve clients as collaborators and "co-experimenters" during our testing sessions. For example, with the client mentioned above, we might discuss actual MMPI-2 items suggesting that

Stephen Finn, Ph.D., Founder, Center for Therapeutic Assessment, Austin, Texas.
© Stephen Finn

the client felt worthless and ashamed. Or we might ask the client to think with us about the following Rorschach responses: "A bat that is flying with terribly damaged wings—I don't know how it's continuing to fly" and "A mangy dog—the kind no one would ever take home from the animal shelter." We might even ask the client to experiment in session with making more eye contact with the assessor, and to pay attention to what he or she feels. All of these interactions might lead to discussions about the client's feeling inadequate and ashamed, how such feelings came to be, and how this is all related to the client's assessment questions about making eye contact and having intimate relationships.

At the end of the assessment, we would show and talk to the client about the actual test scores, and we would discuss "next steps" the client could take to address the problems in living that were the focus of the assessment. Often a therapeutic assessment is a good entry into further psychological treatment . . .

Read more of what Dr. Finn had to say—his complete essay—through the Instructor Resources within Connect.

Used with permission of Stephen Finn.

Past psychological history: What traumatic events has this individual suffered? What psychological problems (such as disorders of mood or disorders of thought content) have troubled this individual?

Past history with medical or psychological professionals: What similar contacts for assessment or intervention has this individual had? Were these contacts satisfactory in the eyes of the assessee? If not, why not?

Current psychological conditions: What psychological problems are currently troubling this person? How long have these problems persisted? What is causing these problems? What are the psychological strengths of this individual?

Throughout the interview, the interviewer may jot down subjective impressions about the interviewee's general appearance (appropriate?), personality (sociable? suspicious? shy?), mood (elated? depressed?), emotional reactivity (appropriate? blunted?), thought content (hallucinations? delusions? obsessions?), speech (normal conversational? slow and rambling? rhyming? singing? shouting?), and judgment (regarding such matters as prior behavior and plans for the future). During the interview, any chance actions by the patient that may be relevant to the purpose of the assessment are noted.[2]

A parallel to the general physical examination conducted by a physician is a special clinical interview conducted by a clinician called a **mental status examination.** This examination, used to screen for intellectual, emotional, and neurological deficits, typically includes questioning or observation with respect to each area discussed in the following list.

Appearance: Are the patient's dress and general appearance appropriate?

Behavior: Is anything remarkably strange about the patient's speech or general behavior during the interview? Does the patient exhibit facial tics, involuntary movements, difficulties in coordination or gait?

Orientation: Is the patient oriented to person? That is, does he know who he is? Is the patient oriented to place? That is, does she know where she is? Is the patient oriented to time? That is, does he or she know the year, the month, and the day?

Memory: How is the patient's memory of recent and long-past events?

Sensorium: Are there any problems related to the five senses?

Psychomotor activity: Does there appear to be any abnormal retardation or quickening of motor activity?

State of consciousness: Does consciousness appear to be clear, or is the patient bewildered, confused, or stuporous?

Affect: Is the patient's emotional expression appropriate? For example, does the patient (inappropriately) laugh while discussing the death of an immediate family member?

Mood: Throughout the interview, has the patient generally been angry? Depressed? Anxious? Apprehensive?

Personality: In what terms can the patient best be described? Sensitive? Stubborn? Apprehensive?

Thought content: Is the patient hallucinating—seeing, hearing, or otherwise experiencing things that aren't really there? Is the patient delusional—expressing untrue, unfounded

---

2. Tangentially we note the experience of the senior author (RJC) while conducting a clinical interview in the Bellevue Hospital Emergency Psychiatric Service. Throughout the intake interview, the patient sporadically blinked his left eye. At one point in the interview, the interviewer said, "I notice that you keep blinking your left eye"—in response to which the interviewee said, "Oh, this . . ." as he proceeded to remove his (glass) eye. Once he regained his breath, the interviewer noted this vignette on the intake sheet.

beliefs (such as the delusion that someone follows him everywhere)? Does the patient appear to be obsessive—does the patient appear to think the same thoughts over and over again?

Thought processes: Is there under- or overproductivity of ideas? Do ideas seem to come to the patient abnormally slowly or quickly? Is there evidence of loosening of associations? Are the patient's verbal productions rambling or disconnected?

Intellectual resources: What is the estimated intelligence of the interviewee?

Insight: Does the patient realistically appreciate her situation and the necessity for professional assistance if such assistance is necessary?

Judgment: How appropriate has the patient's decision-making been with regard to past events and future plans?

A mental status examination begins the moment the interviewee enters the room. The examiner takes note of the examinee's appearance, gait, and so forth. **Orientation** is assessed by straightforward questions such as "What is your name?" "Where are you now?" and "What is today's date?" If the patient is indeed oriented to person, place, and time, the assessor may note in the record of the assessment "Oriented × 3" (read "**oriented times 3**").

◆
JUST THINK . . .

A clinical interviewer conducts a mental status examination and determines that the interviewee is extremely depressed, possibly to the point of being a danger to himself. How might this clinical impression be validated?

Different kinds of questions based on the individual examiner's own preferences will be asked in order to assess different areas in the examination. For example, to assess intellectual resources, questions may range from those of general information (such as "What is the capital of New York?") to arithmetic calculations ("What is 81 divided by 9?") to proverb interpretations ("What does this saying mean: People who live in glass houses shouldn't throw stones?"). Insight may be assessed, for example, simply by asking the interviewee why he or she is being interviewed. The interviewee who has little or no appreciation of the reason for the interview indicates little insight. An alternative explanation, however, might be that the interviewee is malingering.

As a result of a mental status examination, a clinician might be better able to diagnose the interviewee if, in fact, the purpose of the interview is diagnostic. The outcome of such an examination might be, for example, a decision to hospitalize or not to hospitalize or perhaps a request for a deeper-level psychological or neurological examination.

Psychometric aspects of the interview   After an interview, an interviewer usually reaches some conclusions about the interviewee. Those conclusions, like test scores, can be evaluated for their reliability and validity.

If more than one interviewer conducts an interview with the same individual, inter-rater reliability for interview data could be represented by the degree of agreement between the different interviewers' conclusions. One study explored the diagnosis of schizophrenia through two different types of interviews, one structured and one unstructured. Perhaps not surprisingly, Lindstrom et al. (1994) found that structured interviews yielded higher inter-rater reliability even though the content of the two types of interviews was similar.

Consistent with these findings, the inter-rater reliability of interview data may be increased when different interviewers consider specific issues systematically. Systematic and specific consideration of different interview issues can be fostered in various ways—for instance, by having interviewers complete a scale that rates the interviewee on targeted variables at the conclusion of the interview. In one study, family members were interviewed by several psychologists for the purpose of diagnosing depression. The actual content of the interviews was left to the discretion of the interviewers, although all interviewers completed the same rating scale at the conclusion of the interview. Completion of the post-interview rating scale improved inter-rater reliability (Miller et al., 1994).

In general, when an interview is undertaken for diagnostic purposes, the reliability and validity of the diagnostic conclusions made on the basis of the interview data are likely to increase when the diagnostic criteria are clear and specific. Efforts to increase inter-rater reliability for diagnostic purposes are evident in the third revision of the *Diagnostic and Statistical Manual* (*DSM-III*), published in 1980. Although its predecessor, *DSM-II* (1968), provided descriptive information about the disorders listed, the descriptions were inconsistent in specific detail and in some cases were rather vague. For example, this is the *DSM-II* description of paranoid personality:

> This behavioral pattern is characterized by hypersensitivity, rigidity, unwarranted suspicion, jealousy, envy, excessive self-importance, and a tendency to blame others and ascribe evil motives to them. These characteristics often interfere with the patient's ability to maintain satisfactory interpersonal relations. Of course, the presence of suspicion itself does not justify the diagnosis, because suspicion may be warranted in some cases. (American Psychiatric Association, 1968, p. 42)

A description such as this may be helpful in communicating the nature of the disorder, but because of its nonspecificity and openness to interpretation, it is of only minimal value for diagnostic purposes. In an effort to bolster the reliability and validity of psychiatric diagnoses, the *DSM-III* (American Psychiatric Association, 1980) provided specific diagnostic guidelines, including reference to a number of symptoms that had to be present for the diagnosis to be made. The diagnostic criteria for paranoid personality disorder, for example, listed eight ways in which suspicion might be displayed, at least three of which must be present for the diagnosis to be made. It listed four ways in which hypersensitivity might be displayed, two of which had to be present for the diagnosis to be made. It listed four ways in which restricted affect might be displayed, two of which had to be present for the diagnosis to be made (American Psychiatric Association, 1980). This trend toward increased specificity in diagnostic descriptions continued in an interim revision of *DSM-III* (published in 1987 and referred to as *DSM-III-R*) as well as in the more recent revisions.

Evaluating the consistency of conclusions drawn from two interviews separated by some period of time produces a coefficient of reliability that conceptually parallels a coefficient of test-retest reliability. As an example, consider a study of the reliability of a semi-structured interview for the diagnosis of alcoholism and commonly co-occurring disorders such as substance dependence, substance abuse, depression, and antisocial personality disorder. Bucholz et al. (1994) found that some disorders (substance dependence and depression) were diagnosed with greater test-retest reliability than were other disorders (substance abuse and antisocial personality disorder).

Criterion validity of conclusions made on the basis of interviews concerns psychometricians as much as the criterion validity of conclusions made on the basis of test data. The degree to which an interviewer's findings or conclusions concur with other test results or other behavioral evidence reflects on the criterion-related validity of the conclusions. Consider in this context a study that compared the accuracy of two different tools of assessment in predicting the behavior of probationers: an objective test and a structured interview. Harris (1994) concluded that the structured interview was much more accurate in predicting the criterion (later behavior of probationers) than was the test. In another study, this one having as a criterion the accurate reporting of the subject's drug use, a paper-and-pencil test was also pitted against an interview. The written test was found to be more criterion-valid than the interview, perhaps because people may be more disposed to admit to illegal drug use in writing than in a face-to-face interview (McElrath, 1994).

JUST THINK . . .

Do you think it is true that people are more apt to admit socially disapproved behavior in a written test as opposed to a face-to-face interview? What factors are operative in each situation?

An interview is a dynamic interaction between two or more people. On occasion, interviews may seem to develop lives of their own. Ultimately, the nature and form of any interview is determined by many factors, such as:

- the interview referral question
- the context and setting of the interview (clinic, prison, practitioner's office, etc.)
- the nature and quality of background information available to the interviewer
- time constraints and any other limiting factors
- the interviewee's previous experience, if any, with similar types of interviews
- the motivation, willingness, and abilities of the interviewee
- the motivation, willingness, and abilities of the interviewer
- cultural aspects of the interview

What do we mean by this last point? It will be taken up again shortly in our discussion of *culturally informed assessment.*

Case History Data

Biographical and related data about an assessee may be obtained by interviewing the assessee and/or significant others in that person's life. Additional sources of case history data include hospital records, school records, military records, employment records, and related documents.

JUST THINK . . .

How might the contents of an assessee's home video library be a useful source of information in assembling a case history?

All such data are combined in an effort to obtain an understanding of the assessee, including insights into observed behavior patterns.[3] Case history data may be invaluable in helping a therapist develop a meaningful context in which to interpret data from other sources, such as interview transcripts and reports of psychological testing.

Psychological Tests

Clinicians and counselors may have occasion to use many different tests in the course of their practices, and nearly all of the tests we have described could be employed in clinical or counseling assessment. Some tests are designed primarily to be of diagnostic assistance to clinicians. One such test is the Millon Clinical Multiaxial Inventory–III (MCMI-III; Millon et al., 1994), a 175-item true–false test that yields scores related to enduring personality features as well as acute symptoms. As implied in the name of this *multiaxial* test, it can yield information that can assist clinicians in making diagnoses based on the multiaxial *DSM.*

In addition to tests that are used for general diagnostic purposes, thousands of tests focus on specific traits, states, interests, attitudes, and related variables. Depression is perhaps the most common mental health problem and reason for psychiatric hospitalization. A diagnosis of depression is a most serious matter, as this condition is a key risk factor in suicide. Given the critical importance of depression, many instruments have been developed to measure it and provide insights with respect to it.

---

3. For an example of a case study from the psychology literature, the interested reader is referred to "Socially Reinforced Obsessing: Etiology of a Disorder in a Christian Scientist" (Cohen & Smith, 1976), wherein the authors suggest that a woman's exposure to Christian Science predisposed her to an obsessive disorder. The article stirred some controversy and elicited a number of comments (e.g., Coyne, 1976; Halleck, 1976; London, 1976; McLemore & Court, 1977), including one from a representative of the Christian Science Church (Stokes, 1977)—all rebutted by Cohen (1977, 1979, pp. 76–83).

Perhaps the most widely used test to measure the severity of depression is the Beck Depression Inventory–II (BDI-II; Beck et al., 1996). This is a self-report measure consisting of 21 items, each tapping a specific symptom or attitude associated with depression. For each item, testtakers circle one of four statements that best describes their feelings over the past two weeks. The statements reflect different intensities of feeling and are weighted in their scoring accordingly. Beck et al. (1996) presented data to document their assertion that, on average, patients with mood disorders obtain higher scores on the BDI-II than patients with anxiety, adjustment, or other disorders. Additionally, they presented data to support their claim that, on average, patients with more serious depressive disorders score higher on the BDI-II than patients with less serious forms of depression. However, because the items are so transparent and the test outcome is so easily manipulated by the testtaker, it is usually recommended that the BDI-II be used only with patients who have no known motivation to fake good or fake bad. Further, because the BDI-II contains no validity scales, it is probably advisable to administer it along with other tests that do have validity scales, such as the MMPI-2-RF.

The Center for Epidemiological Studies Depression scale (CES-D) is another widely used self-report measure of depressive symptoms. The CES-D consists of 20 items, although shorter versions of the scale have been developed as screening tools for depression (Andresen et al., 1994; Melchior et al., 1993; Shrout & Yager, 1989; Turvey et al., 1999). Santor et al. (1995) compared the test characteristic curves of the BDI and CES-D and found the CES-D to be more discriminating in determining symptom severity in both a college and a depressed outpatient sample. A revised version of the CESD, the CESD-R, has shown promise as a reliable and valid instrument in a large community sample consisting of 7,389 people (Van Dam & Earleywine, 2011).

JUST THINK . . .

Why is it usually a good idea not to rely on just one test to make any sort of clinical or counseling decision?

Whether assessment is undertaken for general or more specific diagnostic purposes, it is usually good practice to use more than one tool of assessment to meet the assessment objective. Often, more than one test is administered to an assessee. The phrase used to describe the group of tests administered is *test battery.*

The psychological test battery If you are a culinary aficionado, or if you are a fan of *Cupcake Wars* on the Food Network, then you will know that the word *batter* refers to a beaten liquid mixture that typically contains a number of ingredients. Somewhat similar in meaning to this definition of batter is one definition of the word *battery:* an array or grouping of like things to be used together. When psychological assessors speak of a **test battery,** they are referring to a group of tests administered together to gather information about an individual from a variety of instruments.

Personality test battery refers to a group of personality tests. The term *projective test battery* also refers to a group of personality tests, though this term is more specific because it additionally tells us that the battery is confined to projective techniques (such as the Rorschach, the TAT, and figure drawings). In shoptalk among clinicians, if the type of battery referred to is left unspecified, or if the clinician refers to a battery of tests as a **standard battery,** what is usually being referred to is a group of tests including one intelligence test, at least one personality test, and a test designed to screen for neurological deficit (discussed in the following chapter).

Each test in the standard battery provides the clinician with information that goes beyond the specific area the test is designed to tap. Thus, for example, a test of intelligence may yield information not only about intelligence but also about personality and neurological functioning. Conversely, information about intelligence and neurological functioning can be gleaned from personality test data (and here we refer specifically to projective tests rather than personality inventories). The insistence on using a battery of tests and not a single test was one of the many contributions of psychologist David Rapaport in his now-classic work, *Diagnostic Psychological Testing* (Rapaport et al., 1945–1946). At a time when using a battery of tests might mean using more than one projective test, Rapaport argued that assessment would be incomplete if there weren't "right or wrong answers" to at least one of the tests administered. Here, Rapaport was referring to the need for inclusion of at least one test of intellectual ability.

Today, the utility of using multiple measures is a given. However, judging by the lack of attention given to cultural variables that has traditionally been evident in textbooks on assessment other than this one, what is not yet "a given" is attention to the notion of being *culturally informed* when conducting clinical (or other) assessments.

Culturally Informed Psychological Assessment

We may define **culturally informed psychological assessment** as an approach to evaluation that is keenly perceptive of and responsive to issues of acculturation, values, identity, worldview, language, and other culture-related variables as they may impact the evaluation process or the interpretation of resulting data. We offer this definition not as the last word on the subject but rather as a first step designed to promote constructive and scholarly dialogue about what culturally sensitive psychological assessment really is and all that it can be.

When planning an assessment in which there is some question regarding the projected impact of culture, language, or some related variable on the validity of the assessment, the culturally sensitive assessor can do a number of things. One is to carefully read any existing case history data. Such data may provide answers to key questions regarding the assessee's level of acculturation and other factors useful to know about in advance of any formal assessment. Family, friends, clergy, professionals, and others who know the assessee may be able to provide valuable information about culture-related variables prior to the assessment. In some cases, it may be useful to enlist the aid of a local cultural advisor as preparation for the assessment. (One administrative note here: If any such informants are to be used, it will be necessary to have signed permission forms authorizing the exchange of information related to the assessee.)

JUST THINK . . .

Is cultural competence a realistic and achievable goal? If so, what are the criteria for achieving it? Is a culturally competent assessor capable of assessing people from any culture or only those from the culture in which they are "competent"? Would you consider yourself culturally competent to assess someone from the same culture as yourself?

We should also note that assessment experts themselves may disagree on key assessment-related issues regarding individuals who are members of particular groups. Consider, for example, the opinion of two experts regarding one widely used personality test, the MMPI-2. In an article entitled "Culturally Competent MMPI Assessment of Hispanic Populations," Dana (1995, p. 309) advised that "the MMPI-2 is neither better nor worse than [its predecessor] the MMPI for Hispanics." By contrast, Velasquez et al. (1997, p. 111) wrote, *"Counselors should always apply the MMPI-2, and not the MMPI, to Chicano clients"* (emphasis in the original). On the basis of clinical experience, Velasquez et al. (1997) concluded that, as compared to the MMPI, the MMPI-2 "lessens the chances of overpathologization of Chicanos" (p. 111).

We might well consider such factual disagreements as only the tip of the iceberg when it comes to the potential for disagreement about what constitutes culturally competent assessment. It is better (and more realistic), we think, to aspire to culturally informed or culturally sensitive psychological assessment. With specific reference to the disagreement just cited, it would be useful to be informed about, or have a sensitivity to, the possibility of overpathologization of test results. Prior to the formal assessment, the assessor may consider a screening interview with the assessee in which rapport is established and the subject of acculturation, as well as related cultural issues are discussed.

During the formal assessment, the assessor keeps in mind all the cultural information acquired, including any customs regarding personal space, eye contact, and so forth. After the assessment, the culturally sensitive assessor might reevaluate the data and conclusions for any possible adverse impact of culture-related factors. So, for example, with the cautions of Velasquez et al. (1997) firmly in mind, an assessor who happened to have administered the MMPI and not the MMPI-2 to a Chicano client might revisit the protocol and its interpretation with an eye toward identifying any possible overpathologization.

Translators are frequently used in clinic emergency rooms, crisis intervention cases, and other such situations. Whenever a translator is used, the interviewer must be wary not only of the interviewee's translated words but of their intensity as well (Draguns, 1984). Members of the assessee's family are frequently enlisted to serve as translators, although this practice may not be desirable under some circumstances. For example, in some cultures a younger person translating the words of an older person, particularly with regard to certain topics (such as sexual matters), may be perceived as very awkward if not disrespectful (Ho, 1987). Case study and behavioral observation data must be interpreted with sensitivity to the meaning of the historical or behavioral data in a cultural context (Longabaugh, 1980; Williams, 1986). Ultimately, a key aspect of culturally informed psychological assessment is to raise important questions regarding the generalizability and appropriateness of the evaluative measures employed.

If you just happen to be thinking about the *Just Think* question just raised, you are probably not alone. Students frequently are curious about how a culturally informed approach to assessment is acquired. Although there are no hard-and-fast rules, our own view is that formal instruction should occur in the context of a curriculum with three major components: a foundation in basic assessment, a foundation in culture issues in assessment, and supervised training and experience. A more detailed model curriculum, one informed by descriptions of existing programs (Allen, 2002; Hansen, 2002; López, 2002; Dana et al., 2002), as well as other sources (such as Sue & Sue, 2003), is presented in the Instructor Resources within Connect.

JUST THINK . . .

How can culturally informed assessment best be taught?

As you will see in the website presentation of the model curriculum, a subcomponent of both the "foundation in cultural issues in assessment" and the "supervised training and experience" components of the curriculum is **shifting cultural lenses** (Kleinman & Kleinman, 1991). The meaning of this term has been explained and illustrated memorably by Steven Regeser López, who teaches a core course in culturally informed assessment at UCLA. In his course, López (2002) draws on lessons he learned from driving public highways in Mexico, most of which have only two lanes, one in each direction. Frequently, traffic will back up on one lane due to a slow-moving vehicle. Drivers who wish to pass slow-moving vehicles may be assisted by other drivers in front of them, who use their turn signals to indicate when it is safe to pass. A blinking right turn signal indicates that it is *not* safe to pass because of oncoming traffic or visibility issues in the opposing lane. A blinking left turn signal indicates that it *is* safe to pass. Large trucks may have printed on their rear mudflaps the word *siga* ("continue") by the left turn signal light or *alto* ("stop") by the right one. Besides signaling other drivers when it is safe to pass, turn signals have the same meaning as they do in the United States: an indication of an intention to turn.

In a class exercise that uses slides of highway scenes as well as close-ups of turn signals, López asks students to interpret the meaning of a blinking turn signal in different traffic scenarios: Does it mean pass, don't pass, or turning? Students quickly appreciate that the meaning of the blinking signal can be interpreted correctly only from cues in a specific context. López (2002) next builds on this lesson:

> I then translate this concrete example into more conceptual terms. In discerning the appropriate meaning, one must first entertain both sets of meanings or apply both sets of cultural lenses. Then one collects data to test both ideas. Ultimately, one weights the available evidence and then applies the meaning that appears to be most appropriate. It is important to note that

whatever decision is made, there usually exists some degree of uncertainty. By collecting evidence to test the two possible meanings, the psychologist attempts to reduce uncertainty. With multiple assessments over time, greater certainty can be achieved. (pp. 232–233)

The notion of shifting cultural lenses is intimately tied to critical thinking and hypothesis testing. Interview data may suggest, for example, that a client is suffering from some form of psychopathology that involves delusional thinking. A shift in cultural lenses, however, permits the clinician to test an alternative hypothesis: that the observed behavior is culture-specific and arises from long-held family beliefs. The process of culturally informed psychological assessment demands such lens shifting with all forms of gathering information, including the interview.

Cultural Aspects of the Interview

When an interview is conducted in preparation for counseling or psychotherapy, it may be useful to explore a number of culture-related issues. To what extent does the client feel different from other people, and how much of a problem is this? What conflicts, if any, are evident with regard to motivation to assimilate versus commitment to a particular culture? To what extent does the client feel different as an individual vis-à-vis the cultural group with which she or he identifies most? What role, if any, does racism or prejudice play as an obstacle to this client's adjustment? What role, if any, do the dominant culture's standards (such as physical attractiveness) play in this client's adjustment? In what ways have culture-related factors affected this client's feelings of self-worth? What potential exists for cultural loss or feelings of rootlessness and loss of native heritage as a function of efforts to assimilate? Questions regarding physical health may also be appropriate, especially if the client is from a cultural group that has a documented tendency to express emotional distress through physical symptoms (Cheung & Lau, 1982; Kleinman & Lin, 1980).

The misspelled **ADRESSING** is an easy-to-remember acronym that may help the assessor recall various sources of cultural influence when assessing clients. As proposed by Pamela Hays (Hays, 1996; Hays & Iwamasa, 2006; Hays & LeVine, 2001), the letters in ADRESSING stand for *a*ge, *d*isability, *r*eligion, *e*thnicity, *s*ocial status (including variables such as income, occupation, and education), *s*exual orientation, *i*ndigenous heritage, *n*ational origin, and *g*ender. How, for example, might a particular disability affect one's worldview in a particular context? Why might a deeply religious person feel strongly about a particular issue? These are the types of questions that could be raised by considering the ADRESSING acronym in the assessment of clients.

JUST THINK . . .

What other culture-related issues may need to be explored in a clinical or counseling interview?

Whether using an interview, a test, or some other tool of assessment with a culturally different assessee, the assessor needs to be aware of ostensibly psychopathological responses that may be fairly commonplace in a particular culture. For example, claims of spirit involvement are not uncommon among some groups of depressed Native Americans (Johnson & Johnson, 1965) as well as others (Matchett, 1972). Diagnostic conclusions and judgments should attempt to distinguish veritable psychological and behavioral problems from behavior that may be deviant by the standards of the dominant culture but customary by the standards of the assessee's culture. It is important not to lose sight of how culture in the broadest sense may influence presentations and perceptions of pathological behavior. For example, cultural factors have traditionally not been given high priority in evaluations for pathology such as post-traumatic stress disorder (PTSD), especially when both the assessor and the assessee are presumed to be from the same culture (Carvalho et al., 2015; Schumm et al., 2015; Wortmann et al., 2016). However, as suggested in this chapter's thought-provoking *Close-Up*, perhaps greater consideration should be given to understanding cultural factors—and more specifically, *military* cultural factors—in the assessment and treatment of returning veterans with PTSD.

PTSD in Returning Veterans and Military Culture*

An estimated twelve to twenty percent of military veterans and serving military personnel are expected to experience posttraumatic stress injuries either immediately after, or even years after their deployment (U.S. Department of Veterans Affairs, 2016; Veterans Affairs Canada, 2016). Service-related trauma may result in ongoing stress and adjustment difficulties, including substance abuse, depression, social withdrawal or otherwise compromised interpersonal functioning, which increases aggressive behavior, and suicide (Braswell & Kushner, 2012; van der Kolk, Westwood et al., 2010). It is reasonable to assume that to some extent, such harmful conditions are exacerbated when and if the post-traumatic stress is not properly assessed and treated. Here, the focus is on one culture-related aspect of veterans' PTSD that would seem to merit greater attention from the mental health community.

Veterans' Gender and PTSD

Males make up 88% of the veteran population. They experience negative outcomes at proportionally higher rates than their female compatriots. Males also have significantly lower usage rates for trauma therapies, and higher relapse rates and drop-out rates when they do access treatment (Brooks, 2010; Ready et al., 2008; Schnurr & Friedman, 2003; VAC, 2013; van der Kolk et al., 2007; Westwood et al., 2012). In the case of traumatized women, the role of gender socialization in both the experience of trauma and the recovery from trauma has been studied extensively (Burstow, 2003; Herman, 1997). By contrast, relatively little attention has been paid to the influence of gender socialization in both the male experience of trauma, and the experiences associated with being a male veteran of military service (Braswell & Kushner, 2012; Brooks, 2010; Fox & Pease, 2012; Jordan, 2004).

Historically, training for military service entails a kind of re-socialization process. Traditional masculine gender norms of behavior are traded-in for what might be termed "hypermasculine gender norms." The end goal is to infuse recruits—male, female, or otherwise—with a "warrior mentality." This resocialization process, at times subtle and at other times straightforward, is designed to yield an ideal soldier in the image of a strong and stoic male (Barrett, 1996; Fox & Pease, 2012; Hale, 2012; Hinojosa, 2010; Keats, 2010; Keegan, 1994).

*This *Close-Up* was guest-authored by Duncan M. Shields who is an Adjunct Professor at the University of British Columbia, Faculty of Medicine.

Gender, Sex, "Military Masculinity," and the "Warrior Ideal"

It is important to differentiate between the categories of gender and biological sex—two of the most central components of identity. Sex is a term that describes the biological makeup of the body while gender refers to an endless variety of socially constructed roles that are both internalized and enacted and that begin to be imposed on children from the moment at which the sex of the fetus is determined (Brown, 2008). Most of us learn to comply with the dominant gender norms of our reference group at an early age and come to view these norms as a natural and valid set of constructs—if we examine them at all (Barrett, 1996). Gender roles serve as implicit and explicit guideposts that not only provide social valence to certain behaviors and attributes, but influence our behavior throughout the lifespan.

Numerous researchers have observed that aspects of traditional masculine culture are emphasized and exaggerated in military training to prepare soldiers for combat (Brooks, 1999; Fox & Pease, 2012; Westwood et al., 2012; Shields, 2016). All of the armed services reframe masculinity for the purpose of meeting the objectives of a military organization. Hyper-masculine values and behaviors, such as strength, toughness, stoicism, and aggressiveness, are promoted (Alfred et al., 2014; Brooks, 1999, 2010; Duncanson, 2009; Higate, 2007; Lomsky-Feder & Rapoport, 2003; Rosen et al., 2003). This hyper-masculine cultural narrative is instilled and reinforced from basic training, and then through one's military career. Through formal group activities and informal social interactions personnel are taught to embody the warrior ideal (Hinojosa, 2010).

But what is the warrior ideal? Consider a situation of risk or danger that might otherwise trigger biological signals prompting one to run the other way in fear. In such a situation, the positive survival functions of masculine gender ideology involve confronting such biological messages, and suppressing or negating them (Mejía, 2005). In essence, the warrior ideal entails an almost superhuman ability to override and disregard the body's own biological signals. The socialization process in the military helps to build the warrior ideal by placing a premium on values such as stoicism, domination of mind-over-body, little emotional expression, and an emphasis on group identity and self-sacrifice for ones' buddies. Traits attributed to warriors include words like strong, aggressive, dominant, and risk-taker. A trait expressly *not* attributed to warriors is "weak" (or anything that would imply a need for assistance; Brooks, 2010; Gabriel, 1997; Higate, 2007).

(continued)

PTSD in Returning Veterans and Military Culture *(continued)*

DSM-5, PTSD, and Military Masculinity

In DSM-5, the diagnostic category for PTSD is laid out as a grouping of seven events or experiences (American Psychiatric Association, 2013a, pp. 271–272). The trigger for PTSD is identified as exposure to actual or threatened death, serious injury or sexual violation, which leads to later emotional distress and cognitive and behavioral impairment—a loss of agency over world and then self. The diagnostic criteria for PTSD include the presence of four distinct clusters of reactive symptoms: (a) intrusive experiences; (b) avoidance and emotional numbing; (c) negative cognitions and mood; and (d) increased autonomic arousal. The symptoms cause clinically significant distress and impairment in the individual's social interactions, capacity to work or other important areas of functioning (American Psychiatric Association, 2013a, pp. 271–280).

Compare the training objectives of military culture with the DSM-5 definition of PTSD and some stark contrasts immediately become evident (see Table 1). Clearly, the behavioral goals and objectives of training in the military, particularly with respect to the development of a warrior ideal, and the behaviors associated with PTSD, are just about polar opposites. For example, whereas warriors serving in the military have mastery over their environment, thoughts, and emotions, service people with PTSD may be helpless under the same or similar circumstances.

For male and female service people who have been taught to ascribe to military masculine ideals, the detriment in functioning occasioned by PTSD, combined with the physiological "highjacking" of the body from conscious control, may have serious consequences with regard to self-concept and

Table 1
Military Training Objectives and Characteristics of a PTSD Diagnosis

Military Training Objectives	Characteristics of a PTSD Diagnosis
1. Mastery over environment	Helplessness as a result of experienced trauma
2. Mastery over thoughts	Re-experiencing of trauma and intrusive thoughts
3. Mastery over emotions	Numbness, emotional hijacking, or negative mood
4. Mastery over body	Physiological hyper- or hypo-arousal
5. Powerful and capable	Distressed, impaired, and disordered

Used with permission of Duncan M. Shields.

self-esteem. Loss of mastery over one's body and experiences may be equated with revocation of one's warrior identity, and may therefore be a lifelong cause for shame. Thus, the veteran diagnosed with PTSD may see himself or herself going from "hero to zero" in fairly short order. Having been relegated to the ranks of the unfit and the disordered, negative feelings of shame may be further compounded with self-blame. Veterans may blame themselves for being unable to uphold the tenets of their training and for letting their peers and commanding officers down. Perhaps worst of all, by the act of having advised caregivers of the trauma they have suffered, they have violated the warrior norm of remaining silently and honorably stoic in the face of adversity.

Long after their indoctrination to the norms of military service, many veterans retain remnants of a mask of silent stoicism—this as they hide personal struggles from their families, close friends, colleagues, and health professionals (Brooks, 2010; Goldstein, 2001; Oliffe & Phillips, 2008). Recognizing how military culture might inadvertently contribute to under-reporting of PTSD, some military leaders have recommended a re-naming of posttraumatic stress disorder to posttraumatic stress *injury* (American Psychiatric Association, 2013b). The recommendation arose from an acknowledgment that the word "disorder" would serve to discourage members of the military from seeking help. For some, the fact that PTSD continues to be classified as a disorder in the revised DSM-5 raises questions—at least with regard to military veterans— about whether the fundamental right of persons to be diagnosed with the least stigmatizing label is being honored. Indeed, stigma associated with the report of psychological stress seems alive and well within contemporary military culture (Braswell & Kushner, 2012; Greenberg & Brayne, 2007; Keats, 2010). Active duty service men, and probably to some lesser extent service women, who seek out medical attention for PTSD may be viewed by their peers as malingerers or cowards. They may also be referenced with stigmatizing labels such as "moral invalid" or "LMF" ("Lacking Moral Fiber"; Fox & Pease, 2012; Herman, 1997; Whitworth, 2008). From the perspective of many military personnel, admission of, or diagnosis with PTSD is akin to career suicide (Linford, 2013).

Mental health professionals play a key role as gatekeepers to services and benefits for military veterans. Such professionals may be the first (and sometimes the last) significant contact that veterans have with the mental health system. Accordingly, acquaintance with cultural aspects of PTSD is essential— particularly the potential role of culturally inculcated values, such as stoicism, as an obstacle to intervention. Especially when such values are exaggerated during the beginning of one's military career, they may well have the (inadvertent) effect of contributing to feelings of isolation and suffering at the end of that career.

Professionals engaged in assessment and/or treatment may help veterans suffering from PTSD by exploring cultural factors beyond the bounds of the elements of a DSM-5 diagnosis (Brown, 2008). More specifically, assessment professionals may explore the extent to which the norms of "military masculinity" remain operative in the everyday lives of returning male veterans. Equally important is a thorough evaluation of how military indoctrination has affected receptivity of the veteran/civilian to more realistic and "everyday" narratives about being male. Similarly, for returning female veterans suffering from PTSD, an element of assessment might be an evaluation of the extent to which these veterans are still emotionally invested in the doctrines of "military masculinity" and/or the "warrior ideal." For both populations, effective treatment may entail cognitive accommodation of new rules and "marching orders" more consistent with those adhered to by warriors who are surviving and thriving in civilian life. Regardless, an imperative exists for mental health professionals to look more closely than they have in the past at the potential influence of gender and gender-related narratives on traumatic experience. To fail to do so in assessment, in interventions, and in future research, is to ignore a part of the treatment puzzle that must be addressed if veterans who suffer from PTSD are ever to be made "whole again." Key cultural factors in PTSD must be identified in assessment, and taken into consideration in treatment, if veterans are to be provided with the comprehensive and effective service that will finally, and fully, allow them to come home.

Used with permission of Duncan M. Shields.

Special Applications of Clinical Measures

Clinical measures have application in a wide variety of research-related and applied settings. In this chapter, our modest objective is to provide only a small sample of the varied ways that clinical measures are used. Toward that end, let's begin with a brief look at some of the ways that clinicians evaluate various aspects of addiction and substance abuse.

The Assessment of Addiction and Substance Abuse

Assessment for drug addiction and for alcohol and substance abuse has become routine in a number of settings. Whether an individual is seeking outpatient psychotherapy services, being admitted for inpatient services, or even seeking employment, being screened for drug use may be a prerequisite. Such screening can take varied forms, from straightforward physical tests involving the analysis of urine or blood samples to much more imaginative laboratory procedures that involve the analysis of psychophysiological responses (Carter & Tiffany, 1999; Lang et al., 1993; Sayette et al., 2000).

Exploration of personal history with drugs and alcohol may be accomplished by means of questionnaires or face-to-face interviews. However, such direct procedures are highly subject to impression management and all the other potential drawbacks of a self-report instrument. A number of tests and scales have been developed to assist in the assessment of abuse and addiction (see Table 13–1). The MMPI-2-RF, for example, contains three scales that provide information about substance abuse potential. The oldest of these three scales is the MacAndrew Alcoholism Scale (MacAndrew, 1965), since revised and usually referred to simply as the MAC-R. This scale was originally constructed to aid in differentiating alcoholic from nonalcoholic psychiatric patients.

Behavior associated with substance abuse or its potential has also been explored by analogue means, such as role play. The Situational Competency Test (Chaney et al., 1978), the Alcohol Specific Role Play Test (Abrams et al., 1991), and the Cocaine Risk Response Test (Carroll, 1998; Carroll et al., 1999) are all measures that contain audiotaped role-play measures. In

JUST THINK . . .

In your opinion, what are some personality traits that "often serve as pathways to substance abuse"?

Table 13–1

Common Measures of Substance Abuse

Name of Measure	No. Items	Description of Items	Comment
MacAndrew Alcoholism Scale (MAC) and MacAndrew Alcoholism Scale-Revised (MAC-R)	49	Personality and attitude variables thought to underlie alcoholism	The MAC was derived from the MMPI. The MAC-R was derived from the MMPI-2. Neither scale assesses alcoholism directly. Both were designed to differentiate alcoholics from non-alcoholics empirically.
Addiction Potential Scale (APS)	39	Personality traits thought to underlie drug or alcohol abuse	Items were derived from the MMPI-2. Like the MAC-R, it does not assess alcoholism directly.
Addiction Acknowledgment Scale (AAS)	13	Direct acknowledgment of substance abuse	A face-valid, self-report of substance abuse derived from the MMPI-2. Endorsement of items is an admission of drug use.
Addiction Severity Index (ASI)	200	Raters assess severity of addiction in 7 problem areas: medical condition, employment functioning, drug use, alcohol use, illegal activity, family/social relations, and psychiatric functioning	The ASI was first developed by McLellan et al. (1980) and is currently in its 6th edition (ASI-6). It is a semi-structured interview that is useful at intake and follow-up.
Michigan Alcohol Screening Test (MAST)	24	Lifetime alcohol-related problems	Widely used to screen for problem drinking. Shorter versions have been created as well as a 22-item revised version (MAST-R)

the latter test, assessees are asked to orally respond with a description of what they would do under certain conditions—conditions known to prompt cocaine use in regular cocaine users. One scenario involves having had a difficult week followed by cravings for cocaine to reward oneself. Another scenario takes place at a party where people are using cocaine in the next room. Assessees are asked to candidly detail their thinking and behavior in response to these and other situations. Of course, the value of the information elicited will vary as a function of many factors, among them the purpose of the assessment and the candor with which assessees respond. One might expect assessees to be straightforward in their responses if they were self-referred for addiction treatment. On the other hand, assessees might be less than straightforward if, for example, they were court-referred on suspicion of probation violation.

Efforts to reduce widespread substance abuse have led researchers to consider how culture may contribute to the problem and how culturally informed intervention may be part of the solution. Using a wide variety of measures, researchers have explored substance abuse in the context of variables such as cultural identity and generational status (Ames & Stacy, 1998; Chappin & Brook, 2001; Duclos, 1999; Kail & DeLaRosa, 1998; Karlsen et al., 1998; Lessinger, 1998; O'Hare & Van Tran, 1998; Pilgrim et al., 1999), religious beliefs (Corwyn & Benda, 2000; Klonoff & Landrine, 1999), and sexual orientation (Kippax et al., 1998). Recovery from drug addiction has itself been conceptualized as a socially mediated process of **reacculturation** that can result in a new sense of identity (Hurst, 1997).

An important ethical consideration when assessing substance abusers, especially in research contexts, concerns obtaining fully informed consent to assessment. McCrady and Bux (1999) noted that substance abusers may be high or intoxicated at the time of consent and so their ability to attend to and comprehend the requirements of the research might be compromised. Further, because their habit may have thrust them into desperate financial straits, any payment offered to substance abusers for participation in a research study may appear coercive. Procedures to maximize comprehension of consent and minimize the appearance of coercion are necessary elements of the consent process.

JUST THINK . . .

Why is it useful to conceptualize recovery from drug addiction as reacculturation?

Forensic Psychological Assessment

The word *forensic* means "pertaining to or employed in legal proceedings," and the term **forensic psychological assessment** can be defined broadly as the theory and application of psychological evaluation and measurement in a legal context. Psychologists, psychiatrists, and other health professionals may be called on by courts, corrections and parole personnel, attorneys, and others involved in the criminal justice system to offer expert opinion. Expert forensic opinion may be sought in both criminal proceedings as well as civil litigation (Wygant & Lareau, 2015). With respect to criminal proceedings, the opinion may, for example, concern an individual's competency to stand trial or his or her criminal responsibility (or, sanity) at the time a crime was committed. With respect to a civil proceeding, the opinion may involve issues as diverse as the extent of emotional distress suffered in a personal injury suit, the suitability of one or the other parent in a custody proceeding, or the testamentary capacity (capacity to make a last will and testament) of a person before death (Clauhan et al., 2015; Davidson et al., 2015; Honegger, 2015; Zumbach & Koglin, 2015).

JUST THINK . . .

When you envision a psychologist testifying in court, what topic do you see the psychologist speaking on?

Before discussing assessment-related aspects in some of the many areas of forensic psychology, it is important to note that there are major differences between forensic and general clinical practice. Perhaps the biggest difference is that, in the forensic situation, the clinician may be the client of a third party (such as a court) and not of the assessee. This fact, as well as its implications with respect to issues such as confidentiality, must be made clear to the assessee. Another difference between forensic and general clinical practice is that the patient may have been compelled to undergo assessment. Unlike the typical client seeking therapy, for example, the assessee is not highly motivated to be truthful. Consequently, it is imperative that the assessor rely not only on the assessee's representations but also on all available documentation, such as police reports and interviews with persons who may have pertinent knowledge. The mental health professional who performs forensic work would do well to be educated in the language of the law:

> To go into court and render the opinion that a person is not responsible for a crime because he is psychotic is to say nothing of value to the judge or jury. However, to go into the same court and state that a man is not responsible because as a result of a mental disorder, namely, paranoid schizophrenia, "he lacked substantial capacity to conform his behavior to the requirements of the law"—because he was hearing voices that told him he must commit the crime to protect his family from future harm—would be of great value to the judge or jury. It is not because the man had a psychosis that he is not responsible; it is how his illness affected his behavior and his ability to form the necessary criminal intent or to have the *mens rea,* or guilty mind, that is important. (Rappeport, 1982, p. 333)

Forensic assessors are sometimes placed in the role of psychohistorians, especially in cases involving questions of capacity to testify. In such cases, assessors may be called on to offer opinions about people they have never personally interviewed or observed—a situation that seldom if ever arises in nonforensic assessments. Forensic assessment frequently entails rendering opinions about momentous matters such as whether a person is competent to stand trial, is criminally responsible, or is ready for parole. Some have challenged the role of mental health professionals in these and related matters, citing the unreliability of psychiatric diagnosis and the invalidity of various assessment tools for use with such objectives (Faust & Ziskin,

1988a, 1988b; see also Matarazzo, 1990, for a response). Nonetheless, judges, juries, district attorneys, the police, and other members of the criminal justice system rely on mental health professionals to provide them with their best judgments concerning such critical questions. One such question that is raised frequently concerns the prediction of dangerousness (Lally, 2003).

Dangerousness to oneself or others   An official determination that a person is dangerous to self or others is legal cause to deprive that individual of liberty. The individual so judged will, on a voluntary or involuntary basis, undergo psychotherapeutic intervention, typically in a secure treatment facility, until such time that he or she is no longer judged to be dangerous. This is so because the state has a compelling duty to protect its citizens from danger. The duty extends to protecting suicidal people, who are presumed to be suffering from mental disorder, from acting on self-destructive impulses. Mental health professionals play a key role in decisions about who is and is not considered dangerous.

JUST THINK . . .

During the course of a counseling assessment, a counselor learns that an HIV-infected patient is planning to have unprotected sexual contact with an identified party. Is it the counselor's duty to warn that party?

The determination of dangerousness is ideally made on the basis of multiple data sources, including interview data, case history data, and formal testing. When dealing with potentially homicidal or suicidal assessees, the professional assessor must have knowledge of the risk factors associated with such violent acts. Risk factors may include a history of previous attempts to commit the act, drug/alcohol abuse, and unemployment. If given an opportunity to interview the potentially dangerous individual, the assessor will typically explore the assessee's ideation, motivation, and imagery associated with the contemplated violence. Additionally, questions will be raised that relate to the availability and lethality of the method and means by which the violent act would be perpetrated. The assessor will assess how specific and detailed the plan, if any, is. The assessor may also explore the extent to which helping resources such as family, friends, or roommates can prevent violence from occurring. If the assessor determines that a homicide is imminent, the assessor has a legal **duty to warn** the endangered third party—a duty that overrides the privileged communication between psychologist and client. As stated in the landmark 1974 case *Tarasoff v. the Regents of the University of California,* "Protective privilege ends where the public peril begins" (see Cohen, 1979, for elaboration of this and related principles).

Dangerousness manifests itself in sundry ways in varied settings, from the school playground to the post office lobby. Working together, members of the legal and mental health communities strive to keep people reasonably safe from themselves and others while not unduly depriving any citizens of their right to liberty. Toward that end, a rather large literature dealing with the assessment of dangerousness, including suicide, has emerged (see, for example, Baumeister, 1990; Blumenthal & Kupfer, 1990; Catalano et al., 1997; Copas & Tarling, 1986; Gardner et al., 1996; Jobes et al., 1997; Kapusta, 2011; Lewinsohn et al., 1996; Lidz et al., 1993; Monahan, 1981; Olweus, 1979; Pisani et al., 2011; Rice & Harris, 1995; Steadman, 1983; van Praag et al., 1990; Wagner, 1997; Webster et al., 1994) along with a number of tests (Beck et al., 1989; Eyman & Eyman, 1990; Linehan et al., 1983; Patterson et al., 1983; Reynolds, 1987; Rothberg & Geer-Williams, 1992; Williams et al., 1996) and clinical interview guidelines (Sommers-Flanagan & Sommers-Flanagan, 1995; Truant et al., 1991; Wollersheim, 1974). But despite the best efforts of many scholars, the prediction of dangerousness must be considered more an art than a science at present. Historically, clinicians have not been very accurate in their predictions of dangerousness.

Competency   *Competency* in the legal sense has many different meanings. One may speak, for example, of competence to make a will, enter into a contract, commit a crime, waive constitutional rights, consent to medical treatment . . . the list goes on. Before convicted murderer Gary Gilmore was executed in Utah, he underwent an examination designed to determine whether or not he was competent to be executed. That is so because the law mandates that a certain propriety exists with respect to state-ordered executions: It would not be morally proper to execute insane persons. In recent years, with fluctuations in economic conditions, research interest in other competencies, such as competency to choose homelessness has emerged (Wand et al., 2015).

Competence to stand trial has to do largely with a defendant's ability to understand the charges against him and assist in his own defense. As stated in the Supreme Court's ruling in *Dusky v. United States,* a defendant must have "sufficient present ability to consult with his lawyer with a reasonable degree of rational . . . [and] factual understanding of the proceedings against him." This "understand and assist" requirement, as it has come to be called, is in effect an extension of the constitutional prohibition against trials *in absentia;* a defendant must be not only physically present during the trial but mentally present as well.

The competency requirement protects an individual's right to choose and assist counsel, the right to act as a witness on one's own behalf, and the right to confront opposing witnesses. The requirement also increases the probability that the truth of the case will be developed because the competent defendant is able to monitor continuously the testimony of witnesses and help bring discrepancies in testimony to the attention of the court. In general, persons who are mentally retarded, psychotic, or suffering from a debilitating neurological disorder are persons held to be incompetent to stand trial. However, it cannot be overemphasized that any one of these three diagnoses is not in itself sufficient for a person to be found incompetent. Stated another way: It is possible for a person to be mentally retarded, psychotic, or suffering from a debilitating neurological disorder—or all three—and still be found competent to stand trial. The person will be found to be incompetent if and only if she is unable to understand the charges against her and is unable to assist in her own defense.

A number of instruments have been developed as aids in evaluating whether a defendant meets the understand-and-assist requirement. For example, researchers at Georgetown University Law School enumerated 13 criteria of competency to stand trial. Six of the criteria were characterized as "factual," and seven were characterized as "inferential." In general, the factual criteria had to do with clinical judgments regarding the defendant's ability to understand the charges and relevant legal procedures. The inferential criteria focused more on clinical judgments concerning the defendant's ability to communicate with counsel and make informed decisions. Interested readers will find a listing of all 13 criteria as well as a more detailed description of the criteria in Bukatman et al.'s (1971) *American Journal of Psychiatry* article. An earlier volume of that same journal contained a presentation of another instrument used to assess competency to stand trial. The Competency Screening Test (Lipsitt et al., 1971) is a 22-item instrument written in a sentence completion format. The defendant's competency is clinically evaluated by the quality of responses to sentence stems such as "If the jury finds me guilty, I _____." The test is scored on a three-point scale ranging from 0 to 2, with appropriate responses scored 2, marginally appropriate responses scored 1, and clearly inappropriate responses scored 0. For example, consider this item: *When I go to court, the lawyer will . . ."* A 2-point response would be "defend me." Such a response indicates that the assessee has a clear understanding of the lawyer's role. By contrast, a 0-point response might be "have me guillotined," which would be indicative of an inappropriate perception of the lawyer's role. Lipsitt et al. reported the inter-rater reliability among trained scorers of this test to be $r = .93$. They also reported that their test was successful in discriminating seriously disturbed, state-hospitalized men from control groups consisting of students, community adults, club members, and civilly committed hospitalized patients.

Other tests of competency to stand trial include the Fitness Interview Test (FIT; Roesch et al., 1984), the MacArthur Competence Assessment Tool–Criminal Adjudication (MacCAT-CA; Hoge et al., 1999; Poythress et al., 1999) and the Evaluation of Competency to Stand Trial– Revised (ECST-R; Rogers et al., 2004). Although the FIT was developed in accordance with Canadian legal standards it has been widely used in the United States. The FIT is an idiographic measure, thus limiting comparisons between testtakers. By contrast, the MacCAT-CA and

ECST-R both employ a nomothetic approach; scores from defendants on competency to stand trial can be compared to other defendants (Zapf & Roesch, 2011).

Although many measures of competency to stand trial exist, relatively few formal measures exist to measure some other varieties of competency. For example, clinicians have been left largely to their own resources when it comes to the measurement of financial competency. Financial competency may be defined as the capability of people to make reasonably sound decisions regarding day-to-day money matters as well as more global aspects of their personal finances. Financial competency is an essential aspect of independent living. Moreover, when there are decisions involving significant wealth involved, the stakes regarding a determination of financial competency or incompetency can be quite high. Still, up until recently, no standardized tool for evaluating financial competency has existed. However, a new instrument for measuring this competency of everyday living has been developed, and a description of it is presented in this chapter's *Everyday Psychometrics.*

JUST THINK . . .

Should measures of competency ideally be idiographic or nomothetic?

Criminal responsibility "Not guilty by reason of insanity" is a plea to a criminal charge that we have all heard. But stop and think about the meaning of the legal term **insanity** to mental health professionals and the evaluation procedures by which psychological assessors could identify the insane. The insanity defense has its roots in the idea that only blameworthy persons (or, those with a criminal mind) should be punished. Possibly exempt from blame, therefore, are children, mental incompetents, and others who may be irresponsible, lack control of their actions, or have no conception that what they are doing is criminal. As early as the sixteenth century, it was argued in an English court that an offending act should not be considered a felony if the offender had no conception of good and evil. By the eighteenth century, the focus had shifted from good and evil as a criterion for evaluating criminal responsibility to the issue of whether the defendant "doth not know what he is doing no more than . . . a wild beast."

Judicial history was made in nineteenth-century England when in 1843 Daniel M'Naghten was found not guilty by reason of insanity after attempting to assassinate the British prime minister. (He mistakenly shot and killed the prime minister's secretary.) M'Naghten was acquitted. According to the court, he could not be held accountable for the crime if, "at the time of the committing of the act, the party accused was laboring under such a defect of reason from disease of the mind as not to know the nature and quality of the act he was doing, or if he did know it, that he did not know he was doing what was wrong."

The decision in the *M'Naghten* case has come to be referred to as the *right or wrong test,* or the **M'Naghten standard.** To the present day, this test of sanity is used in England as well as in a number of jurisdictions in the United States. However, a problem with the right or wrong test is that it does not provide for the acquitting of persons who know right from wrong yet still are unable to control impulses to commit criminal acts. In 1954, an opinion written by the U.S. Court of Appeal for the District of Columbia in the case of *Durham v. United States* held that a defendant was not culpable for criminal action "if his unlawful act was the product of a mental disease or defect" (the **Durham standard**). Still another standard of legal insanity, set forth by the American Law Institute (ALI) in 1956, has become one of the most widely used throughout the United States (Weiner, 1980). With slight alterations from one jurisdiction to another, the **ALI standard** provides as follows:

> A person is not responsible for criminal conduct, or, [is] insane if, at the time of such conduct, as a result of a mental disease or defect, he lacks substantial capacity either to appreciate the criminality (wrongfulness) of his conduct, or to conform his conduct to the requirements of the law.
>
> As used in this article, the terms "mental disease or defect" do not include an abnormality manifested only by repeated criminal or otherwise antisocial conduct.

Measuring Financial Competency*

Is this person competent to stand trial?

Is this person competent to execute a will?

Is this person competent to consent to medical treatment?

Psychologists and psychiatrists are frequently called upon to provide courts with a professional opinion as to the competency of an individual regarding sundry variables (Franzen, 2008; Grisso, 1986, 2003; Huss, 2009; Levine & Wallach, 2002; Melton et al., 1987; Roesch et al., 2010; Slovenko, 2006). Perhaps one of the most frequently measured varieties of competency is financial competency (Griffith et al., 2003; Hicken et al., 2010; Kershaw & Webber, 2008; Marson & Hebert, 2006).

For our purposes, **financial competency** may be defined as the knowledge and skill required for everything from managing everyday monetary transactions, to hiring a reliable investment firm to manage one's portfolio. At a most basic level, financial knowledge has to do with the ability to accurately identify and appreciate the value of paper currency and coins. At a more advanced level, financial competency may be gauged by one's ability to match potential beneficiaries of one's estate (such as charitable agencies) in a way that is consistent with one's longstanding values.

Evaluating an individual's financial competency can be a complex undertaking that includes consideration of many variables (see Table 1). In order to obtain relevant, reliable, valid, and actionable information, the assessor will typically interview not only the assessee, but knowledgeable informants such as family, friends, relatives, caregivers, work colleagues, and relevant acquaintances in the assessee's everyday world (ranging from local shopkeepers and bankers to stock brokers and other investment professionals). Examination of case study materials, such as family photo albums, video albums, newspaper clippings, diaries, and so forth may also contribute to an assessor's understanding of an assessee's financial competence.

In the past, information pieced together from quite a variety of tests were used to shed light on questions of financial competency. However, unless a test is specifically developed and normed for the purpose of measuring financial competency, its use for such purposes, and its persuasiveness in a court of law will most likely be quite limited (Wadley et al., 2003). Perhaps that is why a number of instruments expressly designed to measure financial competency have been developed (Archer et al., 2006; Heilbronner, 2004). A partial listing of some of the

*This *Everyday Psychometrics* was guest-authored by Liliana B. Sousa, Manuela Vilar, Horácio Firmino, & Mário R. Simões all of the University of Coimbra, Coimbra, Portugal.

Table 1

Some Variables to Consider When Conducting an Examination of a Individual's Financial Competency

- the assessee's pre-morbid functioning (Marson et al., 2012)
- the asessee's past values and preferences (Moye et al., 2005)
- the situational context, including the magnitude and complexity of the finance-related decisions that need to be made (Shulman et al., 2007)
- the presence of any relevant medical or mental illnesses or challenges (Moberg & Rick, 2008)
- performance on standardized, neuropsychological tests and measures such as tests of cognitive functioning (including tests of attention, memory, and executive functioning)
- performance on standardized clinical and personality tests and measures such as measures designed to detect the presence of psychopathology (such as depression or a personality disorder)
- performance on standardized tests and measures of basic to complex functional abilities related to managing one's money and financial affairs
- performance on standardized tests that are specifically designed to measure financial competency

Sousa, L. B., Vilar, M., & Simões, M. R. (2015). *Adults and Older Adults Functional Assessment Inventory [Inventário de Avaliação Funcional de Adultos e Idosos (IAFAI): Manual Técnico].* Coimbra: Psychological Assessment Lab—Faculty of Psychology and Educational Sciences, University of Coimbra.

available instruments includes the Financial Capacity Instrument (Marson et al., 2000), the Financial Competence Assessment Inventory (Kershaw & Webber, 2006), the Financial Assessment & Capacity Test (Black et al., 2007), and the Assessment Capacity for Everyday Decision-Making (Lai & Karlawish, 2007). These instruments, along with their local norms, provide "one-stop shopping" for assessors seeking to gather an abundance of legally relevant information regarding an assessee's finance-related competency.

Much like other jurisdictions, in Portugal, financial competency can be called into question on many grounds. The financial competency of an individual may be challenged, for example, on the grounds that the person is incapable of managing their own affairs due to a psychiatric disorder, substance abuse, or some other debilitating condition (including, for example, deafness or blindness). However, unlike other jurisdictions, no locally developed, comprehensive measure of financial competency had been developed for use in Portugal. Responding to the need in Portugal for such an instrument, Sousa (2014) began by researching Portuguese

(continued)

Measuring Financial Competency *(continued)*

law on the subject of financial competency, as well as similar legislation in several other countries (American Bar Association Commission on Law and Aging & American Psychological Association, 2008; British Psychological Society, 2006; Department of Constitutional Affairs, 2007; Department of Veterans Affairs, 1997; Office of the Public Guardian, 2008; Ontario Capacity Assessment Office, 2005).

In collaboration with colleagues as well as consultations with experts, Sousa's research led to the development of a test that could be used to measure financial competency. The Financial Capacity Assessment Instrument, better known in Portugal as the *Instrumento de Avaliação da Capacidade Financeira* (Sousa et al., 2015a), challenged assessees to demonstrate their knowledge of basic and advanced financial concepts. In addition, the test contained performance-based items by which samples of behavior could be used to evaluate cognitive ability as it related to variables such as monetary transactions in shopping, bill payment, and banking. For information regarding

the reliability and validity of this instrument, interested readers are referred to Sousa et al. (2015b).

Some people defy the odds and live long and prosperous lives relatively unencumbered by any cognitive loss. For others, whether as a result of normal aging, a disease process, drug abuse, head trauma, or some other cause, cognition is negatively impacted, and some deficit in function occurs. Any loss of functional capacity can carry with it many consequences, including, personal consequences (such as depression), social consequences (such as a tendency to be less outgoing), and even financial consequences (such as diminished ability to effectively manage everything from basic shopping transactions to portfolio allocations). When psychologists or psychiatrists are called upon to evaluate the financial competency of an individual, it is heartening to know that more and more instruments are being developed as tools of assessment for that specific purpose.

Used with permission of Liliana B. Sousa, Manuela Vilar, Horácio Firmino, and Mário R. Simões.

In clinical practice, defendants who are mentally retarded, psychotic, or neurologically impaired are likely to be the ones found not guilty by reason of insanity. However, as was the case with considerations of competency to stand trial, the mere fact that a person is judged to be mentally retarded, psychotic, or neurologically impaired is in itself no guarantee that the individual will be found not guilty. Other criteria, such as the ALI standards cited, must be met.

JUST THINK . . .

Should mental health professionals be involved in determining who is not guilty by reason of insanity? Should the insanity plea be eliminated as a legal defense in criminal proceedings?

To help determine if the ALI standards are met, a number of instruments such as the Rogers Criminal Responsibility Assessment Scale (RCRAS) have been developed. Psychologist Richard Rogers and his colleagues (Rogers & Cavanaugh, 1980, 1981; Rogers et al., 1981) designed the RCRAS as a systematic and empirical approach to insanity evaluations. This instrument consists of 25 items tapping both psychological and situational variables. The items are scored with respect to five scales: reliability (including malingering), organic factors, psychopathology, cognitive control, and behavioral control. After scoring, the examiner employs a hierarchical decision model to arrive at a decision concerning the assessee's sanity. Validity studies done with this scale (e.g., Rogers et al., 1983; Rogers et al., 1984) have shown it to be useful in discriminating between sane and insane patients/defendants.

Readiness for parole or probation Some people convicted of a crime will pay their dues to society and go on to lead fulfilling, productive lives after their incarceration. At the other extreme are career criminals who will violate laws at the first opportunity upon their release— or escape—from prison. Predicting who is ready for parole or probation and the possible outcome of such a release has proved to be no easy task. Still, attempts have been made to develop measures that are useful in parole and probation decisions.

A person with a diagnosis of psychopathy (a **psychopath**) is four times more likely than a nonpsychopath to fail on release from prison (Hart et al., 1988). A classic work by Hervey Cleckley (1976; originally published in 1941) entitled *The Mask of Sanity* provided a detailed profile of 15 prototypical psychopaths. Generally speaking, psychopaths are people with few inhibitions who may pursue pleasure or money with callous disregard for the welfare of others. Cleckley's profiles have since been re-evaluated in an effort to provide insights useful in formulating an updated model of psychopathy (Crego & Widiger, 2016).

Based on a factor-analytic study of Cleckley's description of persons with psychopathy, Robert D. Hare (1980) developed a 22-item Psychopathy Checklist (PCL) that reflects personality characteristics as rated by the assessor (such as callousness, impulsiveness, and empathy) in addition to prior history as gleaned from the assessee's records (such as "criminal versatility"). In the revised version of the test, the Revised Psychopathy Checklist (PCL-R; Hare, 1985), two items from the original PCL were omitted because of their relatively low correlation with the rest of the scale, and the scoring criteria for some of the remaining items were modified. Hare et al. (1990) report that the two forms are equivalent.

Diagnosis and evaluation of emotional injury

Emotional injury, or psychological harm or damage, is a term sometimes used synonymously with mental suffering, pain and suffering, and emotional harm. In cases involving charges such as discrimination, harassment, malpractice, stalking, and unlawful termination of employment, psychological assessors may be responsible for evaluating alleged emotional injury. Such an evaluation will be designed to shed light on an individual's functioning prior and subsequent to the alleged injury (Melton et al., 1997). The court will evaluate the findings in light of all of the evidence and make a determination regarding whether the alleged injury exists and, if so, the magnitude of the damage.

Many tools of assessment—including the interview, the case study, and psychological tests—may be used in the process of evaluating and diagnosing claims of emotional injury. Interviews may be conducted with the person claiming the injury as well as with others who have knowledge relevant to the claim. Case study materials include documents such as physician or therapist records, school records, military records, employment records, and police records. The specific psychological tests used in an emotional injury evaluation will vary with the preferences of the assessor. In one study in which 140 forensic psychologists returned a survey dealing with assessment practices, it was found that no two practitioners routinely used exactly the same combination of tests to assess emotional injury (Boccaccini & Brodsky, 1999). The reasons given for the use of specific tests and test batteries most frequently involved established norms, personal clinical experience, the widespread acceptance of the instrument, research support, and content. Greater consistency in test selection would be desirable. Such consistency could be achieved by studying the incremental validity that each test adds to the task of assessing different types of emotional injury in specific contexts.

> **JUST THINK . . .**
>
> Why would greater consistency be desirable in instruments used to evaluate emotional injury?

Profiling

Contemporary films and television shows in the detective genre, not to mention occasional, high profile news stories, have provided many of us with some familiarity with the term *profiling*. Now referred to by the FBI as "criminal investigative analysis," and by some in the mental health field simply as "investigative psychology," **profiling** may be defined as a crime-solving process that draws upon psychological and criminological expertise applied to the study of crime scene evidence.

At the core of profiling is the assumption that perpetrators of serial crimes (usually involving murder, some sort of ritual, and/or sexual violation) leave more than physical evidence at a crime scene; they leave psychological clues about who they are, personality traits they possess, and how they think. The hope is that these behavior-related clues will help investigators effect an arrest. Hypotheses typically made by profilers from crime-scene evidence usually relate to perpetrators' organization and planning skills and to the degrees of control, emotion, and risk that appear evident (O'Toole, 2004). The primary tools of assessment employed in profiling are interviews (both from witnesses and about witnesses) and case study material (such as autopsy reports and crime-scene photos and reports). The Behavioral Science Unit of the FBI (now part of the National Center for the Analysis of Violent Crime) maintains a database of such material.

To date, most of the highly publicized cases for which profilers have been employed have not involved persons with advanced degrees in psychology as the profiler. Rather, the profilers in such cases have tended to be psychologically savvy individuals with a background in law enforcement and/or criminology. Whether or not criminal profiling is more the province of psychologists or criminologists is debatable (Alison & Barrett, 2004; Coupe, 2006; see also Hicks & Sales, 2006). Indeed, some have called for the "professionalization" of what is currently "an ill-formed forensic discipline" (Alison et al., 2004, p. 71). It has further been noted that, to be effective in their work, profilers must have attained a degree of competence in the knowledge of diverse cultures (Palermo, 2002).

Profiling can be viewed with skepticism by behavioral scientists who find aspects of it theoretically and methodologically questionable (Cox, 2006; Snook et al., 2007; Woodworth & Porter, 2000). The process may also be looked at with skepticism by law enforcement officials who question its utility in crime solving (Gregory, 2005). For students who are interested in learning more about psychological evaluation as it has been applied to profiling, a table posted on our companion website presents brief descriptions of a sampling of published work on the subject.

JUST THINK . . .

Should profiling be a specialty area of psychology that is taught in graduate schools within forensic psychology graduate programs? Why or why not?

Custody Evaluations

As the number of divorces in this country continues to climb, so does the number of custody proceedings. Before the 1920s, it was fairly commonplace for the father to be granted custody of the children (Lamb, 1981). The pendulum swung, however, with the widespread adoption of what was referred to as the "tender years" doctrine and the belief that the child's interest would be best served if the mother were granted custody. But with the coming of age of the dual-career household, the courts have begun to be more egalitarian in their custody decisions (McClure-Butterfield, 1990). Courts have recognized that the best interest of the child may be served by father custody, mother custody, or joint custody. Psychological assessors can assist the court in making such decisions through the use of a **custody evaluation**—a psychological assessment of parents or guardians and their parental capacity and/or of children and their parental needs and preferences—usually undertaken for the purpose of assisting a court in making a decision about awarding custody. Ideally, one impartial expert in the mental health field should be responsible for assessing *all* family members and submitting a report to the court (Gardner, 1982). More often than not, however, the husband has his expert, the wife has her expert, and a battle, often bitter in tone, is on (Benjamin & Gollan, 2003).

Evaluation of the parent The evaluation of parental capacity typically involves a detailed interview that focuses primarily on various aspects of child rearing, though tests of intelligence, personality, and adjustment may be employed if questions remain after the interview. The assessor might begin with open-ended questions, designed to let the parent ventilate some of his or her feelings, and then proceed to more specific questions tapping a wide variety of areas, including

- the parent's own childhood: happy? abused?
- the parent's own relationship with parents, siblings, peers
- the circumstances that led up to the marriage and the degree of forethought that went into the decision to have (or adopt) children
- the adequacy of prenatal care and attitudes toward the pregnancy
- the parent's description of the child
- the parent's self-evaluation as a parent, including strengths and weaknesses
- the parent's evaluation of his or her spouse in terms of strengths and weaknesses as a parent
- the quantity and quality of time spent caring for and playing with children
- the parent's approach to discipline
- the parent's receptivity to the child's peer relationships

During the course of the interview, the assessor may find evidence that the interviewee really does not want custody of the children but is undertaking the custody battle for some other reason. For example, custody may be nothing more than another issue to bargain over with respect to the divorce settlement. Alternatively, for example, parents might be embarrassed to admit—to themselves or others—that custody of the children is not desired. Sometimes a parent, emotionally scathed by all that has gone on before the divorce, may be employing the custody battle as a technique of vengeance—to threaten to take away that which is most prized and adored by the spouse. The clinician performing the evaluation must appreciate that such ill-motivated intentions do underlie some custody battles. In the best interest of the children, it is the obligation of the clinician to report such findings.

In certain cases an assessor may deem it desirable to assess any of many variables related to marriage and family life. A wide variety of such instruments is available, including those designed to measure adjustment (Beier & Sternberg, 1977; Epstein et al., 1983; Locke & Wallace, 1959; McCubbin et al., 1985a; McCubbin et al., 1985b; Spanier, 1976; Spanier & Filsinger, 1983; Udry, 1981), assets (Olson et al., 1985), preferences (Price et al., 1982), intimacy (Waring & Reddon, 1983), jealousy (Bringle et al., 1979), communication (Bienvenu, 1978), feelings (Lowman, 1980), satisfaction (Roach et al., 1981; Snyder, 1981), stability (Booth & Edwards, 1983), trust (Larzelere & Huston, 1980), expectancies (Notarius & Vanzetti, 1983; Sabatelli, 1984), parenting ability (Bavolek, 1984), coping strategies (McCubbin et al., 1985a; McCubbin et al., 1985b; Straus, 1979), strength of family ties (Bardis, 1975), family interpersonal environment (Kinston et al., 1985; Moos & Moos, 1981; Robin et al., 1990), children's attitudes toward parents (Hudson, 1982), and overall quality of family life (Beavers, 1985; Olson & Barnes, 1985).

Evaluation of the child   The court will be interested in knowing whether the child in a custody proceeding has a preference with respect to future living and visitation arrangements. Toward that end, the psychological assessor can be of assistance with a wide variety of tests and techniques. Most authorities agree that the preferences of children under the age of 5 are too unreliable and too influenced by recent experiences to be accorded much weight. However, if intelligence test data indicate that the child who is chronologically 5 years old is functioning at a higher level, then those preferences may be accorded greater weight. This is particularly true if evidence attesting to the child's keen social comprehension is presented to the court. Some methods that can be useful in assessing a child's parental preference include structured play exercises with dolls that represent the child and other family members, figure drawings of family members followed by storytelling about the drawings, and the use of projective techniques such as the TAT and related tests.

Specially constructed sentence completion items can also be of value in the assessment of parental preferences. For example, the following items might be useful in examining children's differing perceptions of each parent:

Mothers _____.

If I do something wrong, my father _____.

It is best for children to live with _____.

Fathers _____.

Mommies are bad when _____.

I like to hug _____.

I don't like to hug _____.

Daddies are bad when _____.

The last time I cried _____.

My friends think that my mother _____.

My friends think that my father _____.

Sometimes impromptu innovation on the part of the examiner is required. Years ago, when performing a custody evaluation on a 5-year-old child, one of this text's authors (RJC) noted that the child seemed to identify strongly with the main character in *E.T., The Extraterrestrial.* The child had seen the film three times, came into the test session carrying two *E.T.* bubble-gum cards, and identified as "E.T." the picture he drew when instructed to draw a person. To obtain a measure of parental preference, the examiner took four figures and represented them as "E.T.," "E.T.'s mother," "E.T.'s father," and "E.T.'s sister." An empty cardboard box was then labeled a "spaceship," and the child was told that E.T. (stranded on earth and longing to return to his home planet) had the opportunity to go home but that the spaceship had room for only two other passengers. The child boarded his mother and his sister in addition to "E.T." The child told the examiner that E.T.'s father would "wave goodbye."

The data-gathering process for the evaluation begins the moment the child and the parent(s) come into the office. The assessor takes careful note of the quality of the interaction between the parent(s) and the child. The child will then be interviewed alone and asked about the nature and quality of the relationship. If the child expresses a strong preference for one parent or the other, the assessor must evaluate how meaningful that preference is. For example, a child who sees his rancher father only every other weekend might have a good ol' time on the brief occasions they are together and express a preference for living there—unaware that life in the country would soon become just as routine as life in the city with Mom. If children do not express a preference, insight into their feelings can be obtained by using the tests described earlier combined with skillful interviewing. Included among the topics for discussion will be the child's physical description of the parents and living quarters. Questions will be asked about the routine aspects of life (such as "Who makes breakfast for you?") and about recreation, parental visitation, parental involvement with the children's education, their general well-being, and their siblings and friends.

Before leaving the subject of custody, let's note that children are not the only subject of custody battles. Recent years have witnessed an increasing number of custody disputes over dogs, cats, and other family pets. In most states, pets are considered by law not as living creatures, but simply as property—much like furniture or golf clubs. Many pet lovers would like the legislature and courts to recognize that pets are living entities and that as such, consideration in custody disputes should also be given to what is in the best interest of the pet. Psychologists may find themselves embroiled in this new type of custody battle in the years to come.

JUST THINK . . .

How might hand puppets be used as a tool of assessment with very young children involved in a custody dispute?

Child Abuse and Neglect

A legal mandate exists in most states for many licensed professionals to report *child abuse* and *child neglect* when they have knowledge of it. The legal definitions of child abuse and child neglect vary from state to state. Typically, definitions of **abuse** refer to the creation of conditions that may give rise to abuse of a child (a person under the state-defined age of majority) by an adult responsible for the care of that person. The abuse may be in the form of (1) the infliction or allowing of infliction of physical injury or emotional impairment that is nonaccidental, (2) the creation or allowing the creation of substantial risk of physical injury or emotional impairment that is nonaccidental, or (3) the committing or allowing of a sexual offense to be committed against a child. Typical definitions of **neglect** refer to a failure on the part of an adult responsible for the care of a child to exercise a minimum degree of care in providing the child with food, clothing, shelter, education, medical care, and supervision.

A number of excellent general sources for the study of child abuse and child neglect are currently available (see, for example, Board of Professional Affairs, 1999; Cicchetti & Carlson, 1989; Ellerstein, 1981; Fischer, 1999; Fontana et al., 1963; Helfer & Kempe, 1988; Kelley, 1988; Reece & Groden, 1985). Resources are also available to assist professionals in recognizing specific forms of child abuse such as head injury (Billmire & Myers, 1985), eye injury (Gammon, 1981), mouth injury (Becker et al., 1978), emotional trauma (Brassard et al., 1986), burns (Alexander et al., 1987; Lung et al., 1977), bites (American Board of Forensic Odontology, 1986), fractures (Worlock et al., 1986), poisoning (Kresel & Lovejoy, 1981), sexual abuse (Adams-Tucker, 1982; Faller, 1988; Friedrich et al., 1986; Sanfilippo et al., 1986; Sebold, 1987), and shaken infant syndrome (Dykes, 1986). What follows are some brief, very general guidelines for the assessment of physical and emotional signs of child abuse.

Physical signs of abuse and neglect Although psychologists and other mental health professionals without medical credentials typically do not have occasion to physically examine children, a knowledge of physical signs of abuse and neglect is important.

Many signs of abuse take the form of physical injuries. During an evaluation, these injuries may be described by abused children or abusing adults as the result of an accident. The knowledgeable professional needs a working familiarity with the various kinds of injuries that may signal more ominous causes. Consider, for example, the case of injury to the face. In most veritable accidents, only one side of the face is injured. It may therefore be significant if a child evidences injury on both sides of the face—both eyes and both cheeks. Marks on the skin may be telling. Grab marks made by an adult-size hand and marks that form a recognizable pattern (such as the tines of a fork, a cord or rope, or human teeth) may be especially revealing. Burns from a cigarette or lighter may be in evidence as marks on the soles of the feet, the palms of the hands, the back, or the buttocks. Burns from scalding water may be in evidence as a glove-like redness on the hands or feet. Any bone fracture or dislocation should be investigated, as should head injuries, particularly when a patch of hair appears to be missing. In some instances, the head injury may have resulted from being held by the hair.

Physical signs that may or may not indicate neglect include dress that is inappropriate for the season, poor hygiene, and lagging physical development. Physical signs indicative of sexual abuse are not present in the majority of cases. In many instances, there is no penetration or only partial penetration by the abusing adult, and no physical scars. In young children, physical signs that may or may not indicate sexual abuse include difficulty in sitting or walking; itching or reported pain or discomfort of genital areas; stained, bloody, or torn underclothing; and foreign objects in orifices. In older children, the presence of sexually transmitted diseases or a pregnancy may or may not signal child sexual abuse.

Emotional and behavioral signs of abuse and neglect Emotional and behavioral indicators may reflect something other than child abuse and neglect. Child abuse or neglect is only one of several possible explanations underlying the appearance of such signs. Fear of going home or fear of adults in general and reluctance to remove outer garments may be signs of abuse. Other possible emotional and behavioral signs of abuse include:

- unusual reactions or apprehension in response to other children crying
- low self-esteem
- extreme or inappropriate moods
- aggressiveness
- social withdrawal
- nail biting, thumb sucking, or other habit disorders

Possible emotional and behavioral signs of neglect include frequent lateness to or absence from school, chronic fatigue, and chronic hunger. Age-inappropriate behavior may also be a sign of neglect. Most typically, this is seen as the result of a child taking on many adult roles with younger children owing to the absence of a caregiver at home.

Possible emotional and behavioral signs of sexual abuse in children under 8 years of age may include fear of sleeping alone, eating disorders, enuresis, encopresis, sexual acting out, change in school behavior, tantrums, crying spells, sadness, and suicidal thoughts. These signs may also be present in older children, along with other possible signs such as memory problems, emotional numbness, violent fantasies, hyperalertness, self-mutilation, and sexual concerns or preoccupations, which may be accompanied by guilt or shame.

Interviews, behavioral observation, and psychological tests are all used in identifying child abuse. However, professionals disagree about the appropriate tools for such an assessment, particularly when it involves identifying sexual abuse. One technique involves observing children while they play with **anatomically detailed dolls** (ADDs), which are dolls with accurately represented genitalia. Sexually abused children may, on average, engage ADDs in more sexually oriented activities than other children, but differences between groups of abused and nonabused children tend not to be significant. Many nonabused children play in a sexually explicit way with ADDs, so such play is not necessarily diagnostic of sexual abuse (Elliott et al., 1993; Wolfner et al., 1993).

Human-figure drawings are also used to assess sexual and physical abuse, though their accuracy in distinguishing abused from nonabused children is a subject of debate (Burgess et al., 1981; Chantler et al., 1993; Kelley, 1985). Questionnaires designed for administration to a child who may have been abused (Mannarino et al., 1994) or to adults such as teachers or parents who know that child well (Chantler et al., 1993) have been explored, although no thoroughly validated instruments have been developed to date. In short, no widely accepted, reliable, and valid set of techniques for the assessment of sexual abuse is available. Professionals who have occasion to conduct assessments for sexual abuse have been advised to integrate information from many assessment tools and to select those tools on a case-by-case basis.

Issues in reporting child abuse and neglect Child abuse, when it occurs, is a tragedy. A claim of child abuse when in fact there has been no such abuse is also a tragedy—one that can scar irrevocably an accused but innocent individual for life. It is incumbent on professionals who undertake the weighty obligation of assessing a child for potential abuse not to approach their task with any preconceived notions because such notions can be conveyed to the child and perceived as the right answer to questions (King & Yuille, 1987; White et al., 1988). Children from the ages of about 2 to 7 are highly suggestible, and their

JUST THINK . . .

What obstacles do test developers face as they attempt to develop psychometrically sound instruments to assess sexual abuse in children?

memory is not as well developed as that of older children. It is possible that events that occurred after the alleged incident—including events referred to only in conversations—may be confused with the actual incident (Ceci et al., 1987; Goodman & Reed, 1986; Loftus & Davies, 1984). Related considerations regarding the psychological examination of a child for abuse have been discussed in detail by Weissman (1991). Sensitivity to the rights of all parties in a child abuse proceeding, including the rights of the accused, is critical to making certain that justice is served.

Risk assessment   In an effort to prevent child abuse, test developers have sought to create instruments useful in identifying parents and others who may be at risk for abusing children. The Child Abuse Potential Inventory (CAP; Milner et al., 1986; Milner, 1991) has demonstrated impressive validity in identifying abusers. Another test, the Parenting Stress Index (PSI; Loyd & Abidin, 1985), measures stress associated with the parental role. Parents are asked to reflect on their relationship with one child at a time. Some of the items focus on child characteristics that could engender stress, such as activity level and mood. Other PSI items reflect potentially stressful aspects of the parent's life, such as lack of social support and marital problems (Gresham, 1989). The test's authors report internal consistency reliability coefficients ranging from .89 to .95 for factors and total scores. Test-retest reliability coefficients range from .71 to .82 over three weeks and from .55 to .70 over a one-year interval (Loyd & Abidin, 1985). With respect to the test's validity, parents who physically abuse their children tend to score higher on the PSI than parents who do not (Wantz, 1989).

What are the appropriate uses of measures like the CAP and the PSI? Although positive relationships exist between child abuse and scores on the tests, the tests cannot be used to identify or prosecute child abusers in a legal context (Gresham, 1989). Because child abuse is a low base-rate phenomenon, even the use of highly reliable instruments will produce many false positives. In this instance, a false positive is an erroneous identification of the assessee as an abuser. For some parents, high levels of stress as measured by the PSI may indeed lead to physical abuse; however, for most parents they will not. Some parent–child relationships, such as those involving children with disabilities, are inherently stressful (Innocenti et al., 1992; Orr et al., 1993). Still, most parents manage to weather the relationship without inflicting any harm. Some parents who experience high levels of stress as a result of their relationship with a child may themselves be harmed—and stressed even more—to hear from a mental health official that they are at risk for child abuse. For that reason, great caution is called for in interpreting and acting on the results of a test designed to assess risk for child abuse.

On the other hand, high CAP or PSI scores may well point the way to an abusive situation, and they should alert concerned professionals to be watchful for signs of abuse. A second appropriate use of such scores concerns the allocation of resources designed to reduce parenting stress. Parents who score high on the CAP and the PSI could be given priority for placement in a parenting skills class, individualized parent training, child care assistance, and other such programs. If reducing the stress of the parent will reduce the risk of child abuse, everything that can possibly be done to reduce the parental stress should be attempted.

Elder Abuse and Neglect

Just as psychologists are mandated reporters of child abuse and neglect, they are mandated reporters of *elder abuse and neglect,* also known as elder mistreatment. State statutes vary in language and in the specified age of the person defined as an "elder." So, in very general terms, **elder abuse** may be defined as the intentional affliction of physical, emotional, financial, or other harm on an older individual who meets the statutory age requirement for an elder. **Elder neglect** refers to a failure on the part of a caregiver or service provider to provide for the elder (as defined by statute) what was reasonably needed to prevent physical, emotional, financial, or other harm. Our brief discussion here will focus on elder abuse.

Typically, charges of elder abuse and elder neglect are levied against one who stands in a position of trust with respect to the mistreated person. As such the offender may be a family member or other caregiver, a licensed professional (such as a lawyer or an accountant), an institution (such as a nursing home), a neighbor (who may have been entrusted with access to the elder's home), or a scam artist (such as an unscrupulous and ill-intentioned individual posing as an investment counselor). Elder abuse takes many forms ranging from instances that are physical in nature (including, for example, physical and sexual abuse) to those that are financial in nature (including, for example, efforts to defraud elders or otherwise rob them of their assets).

It has been estimated that as many as 1 in 10 older Americans have been victims of elder abuse (Roberto, 2016). Psychologists who have professional contact with elders and their caregivers should be acquainted with signs suggesting that an elder has been the subject of abuse or mistreatment. Table 13–2 summarizes some of the signs that may contribute to a determination of either (or both) of these circumstances.

Perhaps the most effective way clinicians can assess whether suspected abuse has indeed occurred is through some straightforward questions put directly to the elder. For example, the clinician might pose questions like, "Do you feel that you have been mistreated by anyone for any reason?" If such oral interviewing still leaves the matter unresolved, evaluation by means of adjunctive tools of assessment may help in making a determination. A test such

Table 13–2

Signs Suggesting That an Elder Is Being Abused or Mistreated by a Caregiver

---

• *Elder exhibits a negative change in appearance and/or demeanor.*
Included here are changes in physical appearance (less well groomed, less well fed, less properly medicated), dress (clothes not as fresh as usual), responsiveness (diminished responsiveness, increased lethargy, or reluctance to speak in the presence of the caregiver is noted), and typical mood (elder may be sadder, and more anxious and fearful about the future).

• *Elder's lifestyle has dramatically changed for the better or worse.*
Changes here may impact on everything from the individual's diet (for example, more fast food than would be expected based on prior history or more lavish feasts in luxury restaurants), to the individual's usual and customary mode of transportation (such as a change from driving one's own car to being transported regularly by public bus or private limousine. A red flag is raised by any abrupt and puzzling changes in lifestyle, particularly those changes that are incongruent with the elder's life history, known preferences, or available financial resources.

• *The elder's communication habits have changed markedly from what those habits characteristically were in the past.*
The elder may no longer carry a cell phone or be allowed by the caregiver to speak on the phone alone or operate a computer independently. It is clearly a red flag if the elder no longer answers the phone when at home, speaks on the phone independently, or comes to the door in response to unannounced home visits. Of even greater concern, the elder's responses to e-mail, text messages, or other electronic messages (such as those sent via social media) may seem uncharacteristic or "out of character" for the elder sending them.

• *The elder's physical health or physical appearance has either changed for the worse or been compromised in some visible way.*
The clinician may observe an uncharacteristic gaunt appearance that appears to be the product of things like malnutrition and/or lack of proper rest or sleep. The clinician may observe unexplained or improperly explained injuries, bruises, or pain associated with certain movements. The clinician may observe that the elder does not have a much needed pair of glasses or a hearing aid that is essential if an interview is to be conducted.

• *The elder's financial security has changed for the worse.*
In a change from long-lived life of relative financial stability, there are now a slew of unpaid bills accruing penalty charges. The elder's credit rating may have been downgraded as available funds have been mysteriously depleted. In some cases, the elder's last will and testament may have been revised, a new life insurance policy on the elder may have been purchased by the caregiver, and the elder has signed papers granting power-of-attorney to the caregiver.

• *The elder and the caregiver provide discrepant accounts to explain how and why things have changed under the care of this caregiver.*
If the caregiver allows the elder to be interviewed independently—not the usual case when the caregiver is an elder abuser—the elder and the caregiver may provide widely varying accounts of how and why certain actions were taken. For example, the caregiver may claim that it was the elder's idea to grant the caregiver power-of-attorney—a claim denied by the elder. The elder may assert that the caregiver needed huge sums of money to maintain a drug habit—a claim denied by the caregiver.

---

as the Conflict Tactics Scale (Straus, 1979) may yield actionable information. A newer instrument that has shown promise for work in Adult Protective Services is called the TRIO (an acronym for the *Tool for Risk, Interventions, and Outcomes*). Sommerfeld et al. (2014) described the development of the TRIO, as well as psychometric research related to this test's reliability, validity, and field utility. For use in identifying elder abuse among members of a culture-specific group, such as members of a Native American population, a culture-specific instrument such as the Native Elder Life Scale (NELS) may be the test of choice (Jervis et al., 2014).

Of course, even when certain of these behavioral patterns are present, it may well be the case that no elder abuse has been committed. It is incumbent upon clinicians, as mandatory reporters, to have an understanding of when a critical line has been crossed, and when it is time to report. Toward that end, a number of excellent resources are available (see, for example, DeLiema et al., 2015; Hernandez-Tejada et al., 2013; Iris et al., 2014; Johannesen & LoGiudice, 2013; Lachs & Pillemer, 2015; Lang et al., 2014; Mosqueda & Olsen, 2015; Pisani & Walsh, 2012; Scheiderer, 2012; Sooryanarayana et al., 2013).

Suicide Assessment

While a clinical psychology intern at Bellevue Hospital in New York, the senior author of this book (Cohen) had occasion to conduct therapy under supervision with a number of patients. In the middle of one individual therapy session with a 30-something male outpatient, the patient abruptly went off-topic to say that he had forgotten to take his prescription medication. He then produced his prescription medication from his pocket, swallowed a pill, and then resumed speaking from where he left off.

> **JUST THINK . . .**
>
> Before reading on, state your own opinion about what message this patient might have been telegraphing by this behavior.

Cohen related the incident to his supervisor who, as was the supervisor's custom, asked Cohen for his opinion of what had happened. Cohen opined that the patient's action was a tacit message that the patient required additional help. The supervisor then said thoughtfully, "I would be watchful for suicide." In fact, a couple of weeks thereafter, the patient did attempt (but did not commit) suicide... by overdose.

This vignette was presented to impress readers with the fact that of some 800,000 people annually who die by their own hand (World Health Organization, 2014), there are in many instances tell-tale signs—some more direct than others—that signal suicidal ideation or an impending suicidal gesture or attempt. Three of these signs include:

- *Talking about committing suicide.* It is a myth that "people who actually commit suicide just do it and don't talk about it." In many instances, people who are thinking about suicide float the idea to others, directly or indirectly, in-person, or even through other means such as social media. The trained clinician will pick up on that message, even when that message is disguised or indirect.

- *Making reference to a plan for committing suicide.* Whether in the early stages of formulation, or whether the individual has envisioned the scenario down to the last detail, the existence of a plan for committing suicide should significantly raise the clinician's level of concern.

- One or more past suicide attempts. Unfortunately, the saying "If you don't succeed at first, try, try again" applies to many people who eventually "succeed" at taking their own life.

Red flags are raised when an individual presents with a *combination* of these (and other) risk factors. For example, a person who has attempted suicide in the past and who currently has a plan, along with the means (such as access to a firearm), is at very high risk for suicide. Numerous other variables are also relevant in terms of assessing suicidal risk. A patient's diagnosis must be taken into account as certain diagnoses (such as borderline personality disorder, depression, post-traumatic stress disorder, and alcohol abuse) may place the individual at higher risk for suicide. In addition to evaluating suicidal risk from the perspective of the patient's history, clinician's evaluate risk from the perspective of an individual's current life circumstances. Does the individual look forward to each new day, or dreads getting out of bed in the morning? Is the individual grieving over a loss? Is the individual laboring over the belief that the world has recently changed in some catastrophic and irreversible way? To what extent is the person "connected" to others, and what sources of social support are available? From the perspective of the patient, why might suicide appear to be a viable option?

Clinicians must be vigilant regarding patient communications that convey direct, indirect, or disguised reference to suicidal intent. In some situations, either as routine screening or for supplementary input, the administration of a formal test of suicidality may be in order (see, for example, Adler et al., 2015; Ellis et al., 2016; Fang et al., 2015; Jacobson et al., 2013; LeardMann, 2013; Leslie et al., 2010; Linehan et al., 1983; Liu & Miller, 2014; O'Connor et al., 2015; Peak et al., 2016; Troister et al., 2015). Interpretation of interview, test, or other suicidal assessment data may result in the signing of a "no suicide" agreement by the patient, and the initiation of therapy that is focused on reducing and eliminating the risk of suicide. In other situations, the clinician may judge that it is in the best interest of the patient to be immediately placed in an inpatient therapeutic facility.

JUST THINK . . .

Other than by administering a psychological test, how else might professionals identify parents who are extremely stressed?

As we have seen throughout this book, there are many different tools of assessment and many different ways the tools can be used. If these tools have anything at all in common, it is that their use by a professional will at some time or another culminate in a written report. In clinical and counseling settings, that report is referred to simply as the **psychological report.**

The Psychological Report

A critical component of any testing or assessment procedure is the reporting of the findings. The high reliability or validity of a test or assessment procedure may be cast to the wind if the assessment report is not written in an organized and readable fashion. Of course, what constitutes an organized and readable report will vary as a function of the goal of the assessment and the audience for whom the report is intended. A psychoanalyst's report exploring a patient's unresolved oedipal conflict designed for presentation to the New York Psychoanalytic Society will look and sound quite different from a school psychologist's report to a teacher concerning a child's hyperactive behavior in the classroom.

Psychological reports may be as different as the reasons for undertaking the assessment. Reports may differ on a number of variables, such as the extent to which conclusions rely on one or another assessment procedure and the specificity of recommendations made, if any. Still, some basic elements are common to most psychological reports, and learning how to write one is a necessary skill in educational, organizational, and other settings—any setting where psychological assessment takes place. Figure 13–1 contains a description of sample elements of a report of psychological assessment.

The Barnum Effect

The showman P. T. Barnum is credited with having said, "There's a sucker born every minute." Psychologists, among others, have taken P. T. Barnum's words about the widespread gullibility of people quite seriously. In fact, *Barnum effect* is a term that should be familiar to any psychologist called on to write a psychological report. Before reading on to find out exactly

Figure 13–1
Elements of a Typical Report of Psychological Assessment

Report of Psychological Assessment

Most assessors develop a report-writing style that they believe best suits the specific objectives of the assessment. Generally, however, most clinical reports contain the elements listed and briefly discussed below.

Demographic Data   Included here are all or some of the following: the patient's name, address, telephone number, education, occupation, religion, marital status, date of birth, place of birth, ethnic membership, citizenship, and date of testing. The examiner's name may also be listed with such identifying material.

Reason for Referral   Why was this patient referred for psychological assessment? If all relevant background information is not covered in the *Reason for Referral* section of the report, it may be covered in a separate section labeled *Background* (not illustrated here) or in a later section labeled *Findings*.

Tests Administered   Here the examiner simply lists the names of the tests that were administered, along with the date (or dates) that each test on the list was administered.

Findings   Here the examiner reports not only findings (e.g., "On the WISC-IV Johnny achieved a Verbal IQ of 100 and a Performance IQ of 110, yielding a Full Scale IQ of 106") but also all extra-test considerations, such as observations concerning the examinee's motivation ("the examinee did/did not appear to be motivated to do well on the tests"), the examinee's level of fatigue, the nature of the relationship and rapport with the examiner, indices of anxiety, and method of approach to the task. The section labeled *Findings* may begin with a description that is detailed enough for the reader of the report almost to visualize the examinee. For example:

> *Silas is a 20-year-old college student with brown, shoulder-length, stringy hair and a full beard. He came to the testing wearing a tie-dyed shirt, cutoff and ragged shorts, and sandals. He sat slouched in his chair for most of the test session, tended to speak only when spoken to, and spoke in a slow, lethargic manner.*

Included in this section is mention of any extraneous variables that might in some way have affected the test results.

The *Findings* section of the report is where all the background material, behavioral observations, and test data are integrated to provide an answer to the referral question. Whether or not the examiner makes reference to the actual test data is a matter of personal preference. Thus, for example, one examiner might simply state, "There is evidence of neurological deficit in this record" and stop there. Another examiner might document exactly why this was being asserted:

> *There is evidence of neurological deficit, as indicated by the rotation and perseveration errors in the Bender-Gestalt–2 record. Further, on the TAT, this examinee failed to grasp the situation as a whole and simply enumerated single details. Additionally, this examinee had difficulty abstracting—still another index of neurological deficit—as evidenced by the unusually low score on the WISC-IV Similarities subtest.*

Ideally, the *Findings* section should lead logically into the *Recommendations* section.

Recommendations   On the basis of the psychological assessment, with particular attention to factors such as the personal aspects and deficiencies of the examinee, recommendations addressed to ameliorating the presenting problem are given. The recommendation may be for psychotherapy, a consultation with a neurologist, placement in a special class, short-term family therapy addressed to a specific problem—whatever the examiner believes is required to ameliorate the situation is spelled out here.

Summary   The *Summary* section includes in "short form" a statement concerning the reason for referral, the findings, and the recommendation. This section is usually only a paragraph or two, and it should provide a concise statement of who the examinee is, why the examinee was referred for testing, what was found, and what needs to be done.

what the Barnum effect is, imagine that you have just completed a computerized personality test and that the printout describing the results reads as follows:

> You have a strong need for other people to like you and for them to admire you. You have a tendency to be critical of yourself. You have a great deal of unused capacity that you have not turned to your advantage. Although you have some personality weaknesses, you are generally able to compensate for them. Your sexual adjustment has presented some problems for you. Disciplined and controlled on the outside, you tend to be worrisome and insecure inside. At times you have serious doubts as to whether you have made the right decision or done the right thing. You prefer a certain amount of change and variety and become dissatisfied when hemmed in by restrictions and limitations. You pride yourself on being an independent thinker and do not accept others' opinions without satisfactory proof. You have found it unwise to be too frank in revealing yourself to others. At times you are extraverted, affable, and sociable, whereas at other times you are introverted, wary, and reserved. Some of your aspirations tend to be pretty unrealistic.

Still imagining that the preceding test results had been formulated specifically for you, please rate the accuracy of the description in terms of how well it applies to you personally.

I feel that the interpretation was:

excellent

good

average

poor

very poor

Now that you have completed the exercise, we can say: "Welcome to the ranks of those who have been subject to the Barnum effect." This psychological profile is, as you have no doubt noticed, vague and general. The same paragraph (sometimes with slight modifications) has been used in a number of psychological studies (Forer, 1949; Jackson et al., 1982; Merrens & Richards, 1970; Sundberg, 1955; Ulrich et al., 1963) with similar findings: People tend to accept vague and general personality descriptions as uniquely applicable to themselves without realizing that the same description could be applied to just about anyone.

The finding that people tend to accept vague personality descriptions as accurate descriptions of themselves came to be known as the **Barnum effect** after psychologist Paul Meehl's (1956) condemnation of "personality description after the manner of P. T. Barnum."[4] Meehl suggested that the term *Barnum effect* be used "to stigmatize those pseudo-successful clinical procedures in which personality descriptions from tests are made to fit the patient largely or wholly by virtue of their triviality." Cognizance of this effect and the factors that may heighten or diminish it is necessary if psychological assessors are to avoid making interpretations in the manner of P. T. Barnum.

JUST THINK . . .

Write one paragraph—a vague and general personality description—that could be used to study the Barnum effect. Here's a hint: You may use the daily horoscope column in your local newspaper for assistance in finding the words.

Clinical Versus Mechanical Prediction

Should clinicians review test results and related assessment data and then draw conclusions, make recommendations, and take actions that are based on their own education, training, and clinical experience? Alternatively, should clinicians review test results and related assessment data and then draw conclusions, make recommendations, and take actions on the basis of

---

4. Meehl credited D. G. Patterson with having first used the term *Barnum effect*. The same phenomenon has also been characterized as the *Aunt Fanny effect*. Tallent (1958) originated this term when he deplored the generality and vagueness that plagued too many psychology reports. For example, of the finding that an assessee had "unconscious hostile urges," Tallent wrote, "so has my Aunt Fanny!"

known statistical probabilities, much like an actuary or statistician whose occupation is to calculate risks? A debate regarding the respective merits of what has become known as *clinical versus actuarial prediction* or *clinical versus actuarial assessment* began to simmer more than a half-century ago with the publication of a monograph on the subject by Paul Meehl (1954; see also Dawes et al., 1989; Garb, 1994; Holt, 1970; Marchese, 1992).[5]

The increasing popularity of computer-assisted psychological assessment (CAPA) and computer-generated test interpretation has resurrected the clinical-versus-actuarial debate. The battleground has shifted to the frontier of new technology and questions about actuarial assessment compared to clinical judgment. Contemporary scholars and practitioners tend not to debate whether clinicians should be using actuary-like methods to make clinical judgments; it is more *au courant* to debate whether clinicians should be using software that uses actuary-like methods to make clinical judgments.

Some clarification and definition of terms may be helpful here. In the context of clinical decision-making, **actuarial assessment** and **actuarial prediction** have been used synonymously to refer to the application of empirically demonstrated statistical rules and probabilities as a determining factor in clinical judgment and actions. As observed by Butcher et al. (2000), *actuarial assessment* is not synonymous with *computerized assessment*. Citing Sines (1966), Butcher et al. (2000, p. 6) noted that "a computer-based test interpretation (CBTI) system is actuarial only if its interpretive output is wholly determined by statistical rules that have been demonstrated empirically to exist between the output and the input data." It is possible for the interpretive output of a CBTI system to be determined by things other than statistical rules. The output may be based, for example, not on any statistical formulas or actuarial calculations but rather on the clinical judgment, opinions, and expertise of the author of the software. *Computerized assessment* in such an instance would amount to a computerized application of clinical opinion—that is, the application of a clinician's (or group of clinicians') judgments, opinions, and expertise to a particular set of data as processed by the computer software.

Clinical prediction refers to the application of a clinician's own training and clinical experience as a determining factor in clinical judgment and actions. Clinical prediction relies on clinical judgment, which Grove et al. (2000) characterized as

> the typical procedure long used by applied psychologists and physicians, in which the judge puts data together using informal, subjective methods. Clinicians differ in how they do this: The very nature of the process tends to preclude precise specification. (p. 19)

Grove et al. (2000) proceeded to compare clinical judgment with what they termed **mechanical prediction,** or the application of empirically demonstrated statistical rules and probabilities (as well as computer algorithms) to the computer generation of findings and recommendations. These authors reported the results of a meta-analysis of 136 studies that pitted the accuracy of clinical prediction against mechanical prediction. In some studies, the two approaches to assessment seemed to be about equal in accuracy. On average, however, Grove et al. concluded that the mechanical approach was about 10% more accurate than the clinical approach. The clinical approach fared least well when the predictors included clinical interview data. Perhaps this was so because, unlike computer programs, human clinicians make errors in judgment; for example, by failing to take account of base rates or other statistical mediators of accurate assessment. The researchers also hinted that the cost of mechanical

---

5. Although this debate has traditionally been couched in terms of clinical assessment (or prediction) as compared to statistical or actuarial assessment (or prediction), a parallel debate could pit other applied areas of assessment (including educational, personnel, or organizational assessment, for example) against statistically based methods. At the heart of the debate are questions concerning the utility of a rather subjective approach to assessment that is based on one's training and experience as compared to a more objective and statistically sophisticated approach that is strictly based on preset rules for data analysis.

prediction probably was less than the cost of clinical prediction because the mechanical route obviated the necessity for highly paid professionals and team meetings.

Several studies have supported the use of statistical prediction over clinical prediction. One reason is that some of the methods used in the comparison research seem to tip the scales in favor of the statistical approach. As Karon (2000) observed, "clinical data" in many of the studies was not defined in terms of qualitative information elicited by a clinician but rather in terms of MMPI or MMPI-2 scores. Perhaps many clinicians remain reluctant to place too much trust in CAPA products because, as Karon (1981) argued, variables in the study of personality, abnormal behavior, and other areas of psychology are truly infinite. Exactly which variables need to be focused on in a particular situation can be a very individual matter. Combine these variables with the many other possible variables that may be operative in a situation requiring clinical judgment (such as an assessee's English-speaking ability, cooperativeness, and cultural background), and the size of the software database needed for accurate prediction begins to mushroom. As a result, many clinicians remain willing to hazard their own clinical judgment rather than relying on preprogrammed interpretations.

A compromise of sorts between the two extreme positions in this controversy was proposed by Dana and Thomas (2006). Their review of the literature led them to conclude that clinicians are capable of providing information that computers simply cannot capture in the form of frequency tables, but how such clinical information is used becomes a key question. Dana and Thomas (2006) would rely on mechanical prediction for coming up with the optimal use of such clinical information in the form of decision rules.

Ultimately, it is human hands that are responsible for even the most eloquent computerized narratives, and it is in human hands that the responsibility lies for what further action, if any, will be taken. There is no substitute for good clinical judgment, and the optimal combination of actuarial methods and clinical judgment must be identified for all types of clinical decision making—including clinical decision making that must be made as a result of neuropsychological assessments (not coincidentally, the subject of the following chapter).

◆—————————————————————

JUST THINK . . .

Will clinicians who increasingly rely on computers for test scoring and test interpretation become better or worse clinicians?

Self-Assessment

Test your understanding of elements of this chapter by seeing if you can explain each of the following terms, expressions, and abbreviations:

abuse	*DSM*-5	M'Naghten standard
actuarial assessment	Durham standard	neglect
actuarial prediction	duty to warn	orientation
ADRESSING	emotional and behavioral signs of	oriented times 3
ALI standard	abuse and neglect	physical signs of abuse and neglect
anatomically detailed doll	emotional injury	premorbid functioning
Barnum effect	evolutionary view of mental disorder	profiling
biopsychosocial assessment	fatalism	psychological report
clinical prediction	financial competency	psychopath
clinical psychology	forensic psychological assessment	reacculturation
cognitive interview	hypnotic interview	self-efficacy
collaborative interview	insanity	shifting cultural lenses
competence to stand trial	interview	social support
counseling psychology	MacAndrew Alcoholism Scale	standard battery
culturally informed psychological	(MAC-R)	stress interview
assessment	mechanical prediction	test battery
custody evaluation	mental status examination	therapeutic contract

14

Neuropsychological Assessment

The branch of medicine that focuses on the nervous system and its disorders is **neurology.** The branch of psychology that focuses on the relationship between brain functioning and behavior is **neuropsychology.** Formerly a specialty area within clinical psychology, neuropsychology has evolved into a specialty in its own right, with its own training regimens and certifying bodies. Neuropsychologists study the nervous system as it relates to behavior by using various procedures, including *neuropsychological assessment.* **Neuropsychological assessment** may be defined as the evaluation of brain and nervous system functioning as it relates to behavior. Subspecialty areas within neuropsychology include pediatric neuropsychology, geriatric neuropsychology, forensic neuropsychology, and school neuropsychology. A subspecialty within the medical specialty of neurology that also focuses on brain–behavior relationships (with more biochemical and less behavioral emphasis) is **behavioral neurology** (Feinberg & Farah, 2003; Rizzo & Eslinger, 2004). There are even subspecialty areas within behavioral neurology. For example, **neurotology** is a branch of medicine that focuses on problems related to hearing, balance, and facial nerves.

In what follows, we survey some of the tools and procedures used by clinicians in research and to screen for and diagnose neuropsychological disorders. We begin with a brief introduction to brain–behavior relationships. This material is presented to lay a foundation for understanding how test-taking, as well as other behavior, can be evaluated to form hypotheses about levels of brain intactness and functioning.

The Nervous System and Behavior

The nervous system is composed of various kinds of **neurons** (nerve cells) and can be divided into the **central nervous system** (consisting of the brain and the spinal cord) and the **peripheral nervous system** (consisting of the neurons that convey messages to and from the rest of the body). Viewed from the top, the large, rounded portion of the brain (called the cerebrum) can be divided into two sections, or hemispheres.

Some brain–behavior correlates are summarized in Table 14–1. Each of the two cerebral hemispheres receives sensory information from the opposite side of the body and also controls motor responses on the opposite side of the body—a phenomenon termed **contralateral control.** It is due to the brain's contralateral control of the body that an injury to the right side of the brain may result in sensory or motor defects on the left side of the body. The meeting ground of the two hemispheres is the corpus callosum, although one hemisphere—most frequently the left one—is dominant. It is because the left hemisphere is most frequently

Table 14–1

Some Brain–Behavior Characteristics for Selected Nervous System Sites

Site	Characteristic
Temporal lobes	These lobes contain auditory reception areas as well as certain areas for the processing of visual information. Damage to a temporal lobe may affect sound discrimination, recognition, and comprehension; music appreciation; voice recognition; and auditory or visual memory storage.
Occipital lobes	These lobes contain visual reception areas. Damage to an occipital lobe could result in blindness to all or part of the visual field or deficits in object recognition, visual scanning, visual integration of symbols into wholes, and recall of visual imagery.
Parietal lobes	These lobes contain reception areas for the sense of touch and for the sense of bodily position. Damage to a parietal lobe may result in deficits in the sense of touch, disorganization, and distorted self-perception.
Frontal lobes	These lobes are integrally involved in ordering information and sorting out stimuli. Concentration and attention, abstract-thinking ability, concept-formation ability, foresight, problem-solving ability, and speech, as well as gross and fine motor ability, may be affected by damage to the frontal lobes.
Thalamus	The thalamus is a kind of communications relay station for all sensory information transmitted to the cerebral cortex. Damage to the thalamus may result in altered states of arousal, memory defects, speech deficits, apathy, and disorientation.
Hypothalamus	The hypothalamus is involved in the regulation of bodily functions such as eating, drinking, body temperature, sexual behavior, and emotion. It is sensitive to changes in environment that call for a "fight or flight" response from the organism. Damage to it may elicit a variety of symptoms ranging from uncontrolled eating or drinking to mild alterations of mood states.
Cerebellum	Together with the pons (another brain site in the area of the brain referred to as the hindbrain), the cerebellum is involved in the regulation of balance, breathing, and posture, among other functions. Damage to the cerebellum may manifest as problems in fine motor control and coordination.
Reticular formation	In the core of the brain stem, the reticular formation contains fibers en route to and from the cortex. Because stimulation to this area can cause a sleeping organism to awaken and an awake organism to become even more alert, it is sometimes referred to as the reticular activating system. Damage to this area can cause the organism to sleep for long periods of time.
Limbic system	Composed of the amygdala, the cingulate cortex, the hippocampus, and the septal areas of the brain, the limbic system is integral to the expression of emotions. Damage to this area may profoundly affect emotional behavior.
Spinal cord	Many reflexes necessary for survival (such as withdrawing from a hot surface) are carried out at the level of the spinal cord. In addition to its role in reflex activity, the spinal cord is integral to the coordination of motor movements. Spinal cord injuries may result in various degrees of paralysis or other motor difficulties.

JUST THINK . . .

We take for granted everyday activities such as walking, but imagine the complex mechanics of that simple act with reference to the phenomenon of contralateral control.

dominant that most people are right-handed. The dominant hemisphere leads in such activities as reading, writing, arithmetic, and speech. The nondominant hemisphere leads in tasks involving spatial and textural recognition as well as art and music appreciation. In the normal, neurologically intact individual, one hemisphere complements the other.

Neurological Damage and the Concept of Organicity

Modern-day researchers exploring the link between the brain and the body use a number of varied tools and procedures in their work. Beyond the usual tools of psychological assessment (tests, case studies, etc.), investigators employ high-technology imaging equipment, experimentation involving the electrical or chemical stimulation of various human and animal brain sites, experimentation involving surgical alteration of the brains of animal subjects, laboratory testing and field observation of head-trauma victims, and autopsies of normal and abnormal human and animal subjects. Through these varied means, researchers have learned much about healthy and pathological neurological functioning.

Neurological damage may take the form of a lesion in the brain or any other site within the central or peripheral nervous system. A **lesion** is a pathological alteration of tissue, such as that which could result from injury or infection. Neurological lesions may be physical or chemical in nature, and they are characterized as *focal* (relatively circumscribed at one site) or *diffuse* (scattered at various sites). Because different sites of the brain control various functions, focal and diffuse lesions at different sites will manifest themselves in varying behavioral deficits. A partial listing of the technical names for the many varieties of sensory and motor deficits is presented in Table 14–2.

It is possible for a focal lesion to have diffuse ramifications with regard to behavioral deficits. Stated another way, a circumscribed lesion in one area of the brain may affect many different kinds of behaviors, even variables such as mood, personality, and tolerance to fatigue. It is possible for a diffuse lesion to affect one or more areas of functioning so severely that it masquerades as a focal lesion. With an awareness of these possibilities, neuropsychologists sometimes "work backward" as they try to determine from outward behavior where neurological lesions, if any, may be.

> **JUST THINK . . .**
>
> A patient complains of problems maintaining balance. At what site in the brain might a neuropsychologist "work backward" from this complaint and identify a problem? *Hint:* You may wish to "work backward" yourself and refer back to Table 14–1.

Neurological assessment may also play a critical role in determining the extent of behavioral impairment that has occurred or can be expected to occur as the result of a neurological disorder or injury. Such diagnostic information is useful not only in designing remediation programs but also in evaluating the consequences of drug treatments, physical training, and other therapy. In some instances, the problem at hand entails teasing out the effects of normal aging from pathology or injury (Schmitter-Edgecomb et al., 2014; Wehling et al., 2016).

The terms *brain damage, neurological damage,* and *organicity* have unfortunately been used interchangeably in much of the psychological literature. The term *neurological damage* is the most inclusive because it covers not only damage to the brain but also damage to the spinal cord and to all the components of the peripheral nervous system. The term **brain damage** is a general reference to any physical or functional impairment in the central nervous

Table 14–2
Technical Names for Various Kinds of Sensory and Motor Deficits

Name	Description of Deficit
acalculia	Inability to perform arithmetic calculations
acopia	Inability to copy geometric designs
agnosia	Deficit in recognizing sensory stimuli (e.g., *auditory agnosia* is difficulty in recognizing auditory stimuli)
agraphia	Deficit in writing ability
akinesia	Deficit in motor movements
alexia	Inability to read
amnesia	Loss of memory
amusia	Deficit in ability to produce or appreciate music
anomia	Deficit associated with finding words to name things
anopia	Deficit in sight
anosmia	Deficit in sense of smell
aphasia	Deficit in communication due to impaired speech or writing ability
apraxia	Voluntary movement disorder in the absence of paralysis
ataxia	Deficit in motor ability and muscular coordination

system that results in sensory, motor, cognitive, emotional, or related deficit. The use of the term *organicity* derives from the post–World War I research of the German neurologist Kurt Goldstein. Studies of brain-injured soldiers led Goldstein to conclude that the factors differentiating organically impaired from normal individuals included the loss of abstraction ability, deficits in reasoning ability, and inflexibility in problem-solving tasks. Accordingly, Goldstein (1927, 1939, 1963) and his colleagues developed psychological tests that tapped these factors and were designed to help in the diagnosis of *organic brain syndrome,* or **organicity** for short. In general, the tests included tasks designed to evaluate testtakers' short-term memory and ability to abstract.

In the tradition of Goldstein and his associates, two German psychologists, Heinz Werner and Alfred Strauss, examined brain–behavior correlates in brain-injured children with mental retardation (Werner & Strauss, 1941; Strauss & Lehtinen, 1947). Like their predecessors who had worked with brain-injured adults, these investigators attempted to delineate characteristics common to *all* brain-injured people, including children. Although their work led to a better understanding of the behavioral consequences of brain injury in children, it also led to the presumption that all organically impaired children, regardless of the specific nature or site of their impairment, shared a similar pattern of cognitive, behavioral, sensory, and motor deficits. The unitary concept of organicity that emerged from this work in the 1940s prevailed through much of the 1950s. But by then, researchers such as Birch and Diller (1959) were already beginning to question what they termed the "naïvete of the concept of 'organicity'":

> It is abundantly clear that "brain damage" and "organicity" are terms which though overlapping are not identities and serve to designate interdependent events. "Brain-damage" refers to the fact of an anatomical destruction, whereas "organicity" represents one of the varieties of functional consequences which may attend such destruction. (p. 195)

In fact, the view that organicity and brain damage are nonunitary is supported by a number of observations.

JUST THINK . . .

Can you think of any other diagnostic labels that are routinely used as though they were unitary but that are really nonunitary?

- Persons who have identical lesions in the brain may exhibit markedly different symptoms.

- Many interacting factors—such as the patient's premorbid functioning, the site and diffuseness of the lesion, the cause of the lesion, and its rate of spread—may make one organically impaired individual appear clinically quite dissimilar from another.

- Considerable similarity may exist in the symptoms exhibited by persons who have entirely different types of lesions. Further, these different types of lesions may arise from a variety of causes, such as trauma with or without loss of consciousness, infection, nutritional deficiencies, tumor, stroke, neuronal degeneration, toxins, insufficient cardiac output, and a variety of metabolic disturbances.

- Many conditions that are not due to brain damage produce symptoms that mimic those produced by brain damage. For example, an individual who is psychotic, depressed, or simply fatigued may produce data on an examination for organic brain damage that are characteristically diagnostic of neuropsychological impairment.

- Factors other than brain damage (such as psychosis, depression, and fatigue) influence the responses of brain-damaged persons. Some types of responses are consequences (rather than correlates) of the brain damage. For example, if brain-injured children as a group tend to be described as more aggressive than normals, this may reflect more on the way such children have been treated by parents, teachers, and peers than on the effect of any lesions.

- Persons who are in fact brain-damaged are sometimes able to compensate for their deficits to such an extent that some functions are actually taken over by other, more intact parts of the brain.

With this brief introduction to neuropsychology as background, let's look at the neuropsychological examination, including some possible reasons for referral for an evaluation, as well as some of the tools of assessment that may be employed during such an evaluation.

The Neuropsychological Evaluation

When a Neuropsychological Evaluation Is Indicated

Have you ever had a thorough eye examination by an ophthalmologist (a physician who specializes in disorders of the eye and vision)? How did that compare to the eye examination you received in your general practitioner's office? In all probability, the examination conducted by the specialist was more thorough and quite different in terms of the tools used and the methods employed. The examination in your general practitioner's office may have been relatively superficial, and probably did not take all that long. The examination by the specialist was more complex, and probably took a bit of time. We might characterize the examination of the general practitioner as one designed to screen for problems, whereas the specialist's examination was clearly more diagnostic in nature, and better equipped to understand the precise location of any abnormality, as well as any disease process. In fact, any problems discovered by the general practitioner during a routine screening will surely result in a referral to a specialist for further evaluation.

There is something of a parallel to be drawn with regard to the everyday evaluations of neuropsychological functioning conducted by psychologists who are not specialists in the area, as compared to the evaluations conducted by neuropsychologists. Clinical and counseling psychologists who conduct everyday assessments for a variety of reasons, and school psychologists who conduct everyday assessments with education-related objectives, as well as other mental health professionals who engage in assessment, may all include some sort of neuropsychological evaluation as a component of what they do. However, most typically, what these nonspecialists are trying to do is screen for the presence of a possible neuropsychological problem, rather than definitively diagnose such a problem. If they identify a problem that they believe is neurological in nature, whether through their own examination or through test or case history data, a referral to a specialist ensues.

In some cases, a patient is referred to a psychologist (who is not a neuropsychologist) for screening for suspected neurological problems. In such a case, a battery of tests will typically be administered. This battery at a minimum will consist of an intelligence test, a personality test, and a perceptual-motor/memory test.[1] If suspicious neurological signs are discovered in the course of the evaluation, the patient will be referred for further and more-detailed evaluation. Suspicious signs and symptoms may be documented in case history or test data, or may present themselves in behavior emitted during an interview or test session. Signs of neurological deficit may take the form of troubling episodes (such as a hand tremor or other involuntary movement) that only occur at home, at work, or some other venue. In addition to the presence of signs or symptoms of neurological impairment, the occurrence of various events (such as a concussion sustained as a result of trauma to the head) or the existence of some known pathology (such

---

1. We have listed here what we believe to be the minimum amount of testing for an adequate neuropsychological screening. In the past, however, it was not uncommon for clinicians to administer only a perceptual-motor/memory test—a practice that was strongly a discouraged (Bigler & Ehrenfurth, 1981; Kahn & Taft, 1983).

as any disease known to adversely affect cognition) may prompt a referral for evaluation by a specialist. Table 14–3 lists a sampling of conditions that may prompt such referrals.

The signs signaling that a more thorough neuropsychological or neurological workup by a specialist (such as a neuropsychologist or a neurologist) is advisable are characterized as being "hard" or "soft" depending upon the certainty with which the phenomenon has been known to be related with documented neurological damage. A **hard sign** may be defined as an indicator of definite neurological deficit. Abnormal reflex performance is an example of a hard sign. Cranial nerve damage as indicated by neuroimaging is another example of a hard sign. A **soft sign** is an indicator that is merely suggestive of neurological deficit. One example of a soft sign is an apparent inability to accurately copy a stimulus figure when attempting to draw it. Scores on a test that has verbal and nonverbal components where a significant discrepancy exists between the testtaker's verbal and nonverbal performance is another soft sign. Other soft signs of neurological deficit may take the form of relatively minor sensory or motor deficits.

Although psychologists, neuropsychologists, and other clinicians who are not physicians may refer patients to neurologists for further evaluation, it is also true that neurologists may refer their neurology patients to neuropsychologists for further evaluation. In fact, neurologists as a group represent the largest source of referrals for neuropsychologists (Sweet et al., 2015). A patient may be referred for an in-depth neuropsychological evaluation, for complaints such as headaches or memory loss—this after the neurologist has done a preliminary examination and could find no medical basis for the complaint. In such cases, the hope would be that the tools of neuropsychology could be applied to shed additional light on the medical mystery. A neuropsychologist may be called upon to help more precisely assess the degree of a neurological patient's impairment in functioning. A patient placed on a particular treatment regimen by a neurologist might be referred to a neuropsychologist to monitor subtle cognitive changes that result as a consequence of that treatment. Other common referral sources for neuropsychologists include attorneys, psychiatrists, pediatricians, and school systems (Sweet et al., 2015).

Table 14–3

Some Conditions That May Prompt Referral for Neuropsychological Evaluation

Condition	Possible Reason for Referral
Brain injury resulting from stroke, traumatic brain injury (TBI), concussion, or infection	Differential diagnosis of brain injury and disease from psychiatric disorders such as depression.
	Assessment of current functioning compared to premorbid functioning. Evaluation of treatment progress.
Epilepsy, hydrocephaly, or other known neurological conditions	Assessment of change in functioning. For example, neuropsychological testing may evaluate the effectiveness of drug therapies and possible side effects.
Acquired immune deficiency syndrome (AIDS)	Assessment of cognitive deterioration associated with the disorder and monitoring of changes in cognitive functioning.
Alzheimer's disease and other forms of dementia	Diagnosis and impact of memory loss. Evaluation of drug therapies.
Problems with attention and learning	Diagnosis of ADHD, specific learning disorder, or possible psychological problems that may impair learning. Neuropsychological evaluation often leads to an intervention plan to improve functioning.
Any significant changes from usual sensory, motor, or cognitive functioning	Determine whether the observed deficit is a **functional deficit** (or, a deficit that is psychological or without a known physical or structural cause) or an **organic deficit** (or, a deficit known to have a structural or physical origin).

General Elements of a Neuropsychological Evaluation

The objective of the typical neuropsychological evaluation is "to draw inferences about the structural and functional characteristics of a person's brain by evaluating an individual's behavior in defined stimulus-response situations" (Benton, 1994, p. 1). Exactly how the neuropsychological examination is conducted will vary as a function of a number of factors such as the nature of the referral question, the capabilities of the patient, the availability and nature of records regarding the patient, and practical considerations (such as the time available to conduct the examination). The examination of a patient typically begins with a thorough examination of available, relevant records. Case history data—including medical records, educational records, family reports, employer reports, and prior neuropsychological evaluation records—are all useful to the neuropsychologist in planning the examination.

Preparation for a neuropsychological examination entails making sure that the appropriate tools of assessment will be employed. Neuropsychologists assess persons exhibiting a wide range of physical and psychological disabilities. Some, for example, have known visual or auditory deficits, concentration and attention problems, speech and language difficulties, and so forth. Allowance must be made for such deficits, and a way must be found to administer the appropriate tests so that meaningful results can be obtained. In some cases, neuropsychologists will administer preliminary visual, auditory, memory, perceptual, and problem-solving or cognitive processing tasks, to ensure that patients are appropriate candidates for more extensive and specialized evaluation in these areas. Sometimes during the course of such a preliminary evaluation, a deficit is discovered that in itself may change the plan for the rest of the evaluation. An olfactory (sense of smell) deficit, for example, may be symptomatic of a great variety of neurological and nonneurological problems as diverse as Alzheimer's disease (Serby et al., 1991), Parkinson's disease (Serby et al., 1985), and AIDS (Brody et al., 1991). The discovery of such a deficit by means of a test such as the University of Pennsylvania Smell Identification Test (UPSIT; Doty et al., 1984) might be a stimulus for altering the evaluation plan so as to rule out these other disease processes.

> **JUST THINK . . .**
>
> You are a neuropsychologist evaluating a patient whom you suspect has an olfactory deficit. You do not own a copy of the UPSIT. *Improvise!* Describe what you would do.

Common to all thorough neuropsychological examinations are a history taking, a mental status examination, and the administration of tests and procedures designed to reveal problems of neuropsychological functioning. Throughout the examination, the neuropsychologist's knowledge of neuroanatomy, neurochemistry, and neurophysiology are essential for optimal interpretation of the data. In addition to guiding decisions concerning what to test for and how to test for it, such knowledge will also come into play with respect to the decisions concerning *when* to test. Thus, for example, it would be atypical for a neuropsychologist to psychologically test a stroke victim immediately after the stroke has occurred. Because some recovery of function could be expected to spontaneously occur in the weeks and months following the stroke, testing the patient immediately after the stroke would yield an erroneous picture of the extent of the damage.

Increasingly, neuropsychologists must also have a knowledge of the possible effects of various prescription medications taken by their assessees because such medication can actually cause certain neurobehavioral deficits. For example, certain antipsychotic drugs can cause Parkinsonian-like symptoms such as tremors in the hand. It is also the case that various prescription medications may temporarily mask some of the testtaker's neurobehavioral deficits.

> **JUST THINK . . .**
>
> What types of behavior caused by a drug or prescription medication could present as a neurological problem?

Many of the tools of neuropsychological assessment are tools with which most psychological assessors are quite familiar: the test, the case study, and the interview. Some tools, such as

◆

JUST THINK . . .

Describe a finding from an intelligence test administration that might prompt an assessor to refer the assessee for a thorough neuropsychological evaluation.

sophisticated imaging equipment, are modern marvels of technology with which many readers of this book may be unfamiliar. For our purposes, we will focus primarily on the tools of the more familiar variety—although we will briefly overview some of those modern marvels later in this chapter. Two tools "of the more familiar variety" are history taking and evaluation of case history data. So let's begin there.

History taking, the case history, and case studies Neuropsychologists pay careful attention to patients' histories as told to them by the patients themselves and as revealed in patients' records. Neuropsychologists also study findings from similar cases in order to better understand their assessees. The typical neuropsychological examination begins with a careful history taking, with special attention paid to certain areas:

- The medical history of the patient.

- The medical history of the patient's immediate family and other relatives. A sample question here might be "Have you or any of your relatives experienced dizziness, fainting, blackouts, or spasms?"

- The presence or absence of certain **developmental milestones,** a particularly critical part of the history-taking process when examining young children. A list of some of these milestones appears in Table 14–4.

- Psychosocial history, including level of academic achievement and estimated level of intelligence; an estimated level of adjustment at home and at work or school; observations regarding personality (e.g., "Is this individual hypochondriacal?"), thought processes, and motivation ("Is this person willing and able to respond accurately to these questions?").

- The character, severity, and progress of any history of complaints involving disturbances in sight, hearing, smell, touch, taste, or balance; disturbances in muscle tone, muscle strength, and muscle movement; disturbances in autonomic functions such as breathing, eliminating, and body temperature control; disturbances in speech; disturbances in thought and memory; pain (particularly headache and facial pain); and various types of thought disturbances.

A careful history is critical to the accuracy of the assessment. Consider, for example, a patient who exhibits flat affect, is listless, and doesn't seem to know what day it is or what time it is. Such an individual might be suffering from something neurological in origin (such as a dementia). However, a functional disorder (such as severe depression) might be the problem's true cause. A good history taking will shed light on whether the observed behavior is the result of a genuine dementia or a product of what is referred to as a *pseudodementia* (a

◆

JUST THINK . . .

What else might you like to know about this listless patient with flat affect who doesn't know what day it is or what time it is?

condition that presents *as if* it were dementia but is not). Raising a number of history-related questions may prove helpful when evaluating such a patient. For example: How long has the patient been in this condition, and what emotional or neurological trauma may have precipitated it? Does this patient have a personal or family history of depression or other psychiatric disturbance? What factors appear to be operating to maintain the patient in this state?

The history-taking interview can help shed light on questions of the organic or functional origin of an observed problem and whether the problem is *progressive* (likely to spread or

Table 14–4

Some Developmental Milestones

Age	Development
16 weeks	Gets excited, laughs aloud. Smiles spontaneously in response to people. Anticipates eating at sight of food. Sits propped up for 10 to 15 minutes.
28 weeks	Smiles and vocalizes to a mirror and pats at mirror image. Many vowel sounds. Sits unsupported for brief period and then leans on hands. Takes solids well. When lying on back, places feet to mouth. Grasps objects and transfers objects from hand to hand. When held standing, supports most of own weight.
12 months	Walks with only one hand held. Says "mamma" and "dada" and perhaps two other words. Gives a toy in response to a request or gesture. When being dressed, will cooperate. Plays "peek-a-boo" games.
18 months	Has a vocabulary of some 10 words. Walks well, seldom falls, can run stiffly. Looks at pictures in a book. Feeds self, although spills. Can pull a toy or hug a doll. Can seat self in a small or adult chair. Scribbles spontaneously with a crayon or pencil.
24 months	Walks up and down stairs alone. Runs well, no falling. Can build a tower of six or seven blocks. Uses personal pronouns ("I" and "you") and speaks a three-word sentence. Identifies simple pictures by name and calls self by name. Verbalizes needs fairly consistently. May be dry at night. Can pull on a simple garment.
36 months	Alternates feet when climbing stairs and jumps from bottom stair. Rides a tricycle. Can copy a circle and imitate a cross with a crayon or pencil. Comprehends and answers questions. Feeds self with little spilling. May know and repeat a few simple rhymes.
48 months	Can dry and wash hands, brushes teeth. Laces shoes, dresses and undresses with supervision. Can play cooperatively with other children. Can draw figure of a person with at least two clear body parts.
60 months	Knows and names colors, counts to 10. Skips on both feet. Can print a few letters, can draw identifiable pictures.

Source: Gesell and Amatruda (1947).

worsen) or *nonprogressive*. Data from a history-taking interview may also lead the interviewer to suspect that the presenting problem has more to do with malingering than with neuropsychological deficit.

Beyond the history-taking interview, knowledge of an assessee's history is also developed through existing records. Case history files are valuable resources for all psychological assessors, but they are particularly valuable in neuropsychological assessment. In many instances, the referral question concerns the degree of damage that has been sustained relative to a patient's pre-existing condition. The assessor must determine the level of the patient's functioning and neuropsychological intactness prior to any trauma, disease, or other disabling factors. In making such a determination of premorbid functioning, the assessor may rely on a wide variety of case history data, from archival records to videotapes made with the family video camera.

Supplementing a history-taking interview and historical records in the form of case history data, published case studies on people who have suffered the same or a similar type of neuropsychological deficit may be a source of useful insights. Case study material can provide leads regarding areas of evaluation to explore in depth and can also suggest the course a particular disease or deficit will follow and how observed strengths or weaknesses may change over time. Case study material can also be valuable in formulating plans for therapeutic intervention.

The Interview   A variety of structured interviews and rating forms are available as aids to the neuropsychological screening and evaluation process. Neuropsychological screening devices point the way to further areas of inquiry with more extensive evaluation methods. Such devices can be used economically with members of varied populations who may be at risk for neuropsychological impairment, such as psychiatric patients, the elderly, and alcoholics. Some of these measures, such as the Short Portable Mental Status Questionnaire, are completed by an assessor; others, such as the Neuropsychological Impairment Scale, are self-report instruments.

The Mini-Mental State Exam (MMSE; Folstein et al., 1975) has a very long history as a clinical and research tool used to screen for cognitive impairment. Factor-analytic research suggests that this test primarily measures concentration, language, orientation, memory, and attention (Baños & Franklin, 2003; Jones & Gallo, 2000). In 2010, the second edition of the Mini-Mental State Exam (MMSE-2) was published. This reference work was also published in a brief version (for use in situations with time constraints), as well as an expanded version (designed to be more sensitive to detecting mild cognitive impairment). Another structured interview is the 7 Minute Screen, developed to help identify patients with symptoms characteristic of Alzheimer's disease (Solomon et al., 1998; Ijuin et al., 2008). Tasks on this test tap orientation, verbal fluency, and various aspects of memory. Both the Mini-Mental State Examination and the 7 Minute Screen have value in identifying individuals with previously undetected cognitive impairment (Lawrence et al., 2000), although neither of these screening instruments should be used for the purpose of diagnosis. A useful supplement to a structured interview for screening purposes is the neuropsychological mental status examination.

The neuropsychological mental status examination An outline for a general mental status examination was presented in Chapter 13. The neuropsychological mental status examination overlaps the general examination with respect to questions concerning the assessee's consciousness, emotional state, thought content and clarity, memory, sensory perception, performance of action, language, speech, handwriting, and handedness. The mental status examination administered for the express purpose of evaluating neuropsychological functioning may delve more extensively into specific areas of interest.

Throughout the mental status examination, as well as other aspects of the evaluation (including testing and history taking), the clinician observes and takes note of aspects of the assessee's behavior relevant to neuropsychological functioning. For example, the clinician notes the presence of involuntary movements (such as facial tics), locomotion difficulties, and other sensory and motor problems. The clinician may note, for example, that one corner of the mouth is slower to curl than the other when the patient smiles—a finding suggestive of damage to the seventh (facial) cranial nerve. Knowledge of brain–behavior relationships comes in handy in all phases of the evaluation, including the physical examination.

The Physical Examination

Most neuropsychologists perform some kind of physical examination on patients, but the extent of this examination varies widely as a function of the expertise, competence, and confidence of the examiner. Some neuropsychologists have had extensive training in performing physical examinations under the tutelage of neurologists in teaching hospitals. Such psychologists feel confident in performing many of the same **noninvasive procedures** (procedures that do not involve any intrusion into the examinee's body) that neurologists perform as part of their neurological examination. In the course of the following discussion, we list some of these noninvasive procedures. We precede this discussion with the caveat that it is the physician and not the neuropsychologist who is always the final arbiter of medical questions.

In addition to making observations about the examinee's appearance, the examiner may also physically examine the scalp and skull for any unusual enlargements or depressions. Muscles may be inspected for their tone (soft? rigid?), strength (weak or tired?), and size relative to other muscles. With respect to the last point, the examiner might find, for example, that a patient's right bicep is much larger than his left bicep. Such a finding could indicate muscular dystrophy in the left arm. But it also could reflect the fact that the patient has been working as a shoemaker for the past 40 years—a job that involves constantly hammering nails, thus building up the muscle in his right arm. This patient's case presentation underscores the importance of placing physical findings in historical context, as well as the value of clinical knowledge and experience when it comes to making inferences from observed phenomena.

The clinician conducting a neuropsychological examination may test for simple reflexes. **Reflexes** are involuntary motor responses to stimuli. Many reflexes have survival value for infants but then disappear as the child grows older. One such reflex is the mastication (chewing) reflex. Stroking the tongue or lips will elicit chewing behavior in the normal infant; however, chewing elicited in the older child or adult indicates neurological deficit. In addition to testing for the presence or absence of various reflexes, the examiner might examine muscle coordination by using measures such as those listed in Table 14–5.

The physical examination aspect of the neuropsychological examination is designed to assess not only the functioning of the brain but also aspects of the functioning of the nerves, muscles, and other organs and systems. Some procedures used to shed light on the adequacy and functioning of some of the 12 cranial nerves are summarized in Table 14–6.

Some neurological conditions are most typically diagnosed on the basis of presenting signs and symptoms rather than any formal test. One such neurological condition, second only to dementia as most common neurological disease worldwide (Connolly & Lang, 2014), is described in what follows.

JUST THINK . . .

Do you agree that neuropsychologists should engage in noninvasive physical examinations? Or do you believe that neuropsychologists should avoid physically examining patients and leave that part of the evaluation completely to physicians?

Table 14–5
Sample Tests Used to Evaluate Muscle Coordination

Walking-running-skipping

If the examiner has not had a chance to watch the patient walk for any distance, he or she may ask the patient to do so as part of the examination. We tend to take walking for granted, but neurologically speaking it is a highly complex activity that involves proper integration of many varied components of the nervous system. Sometimes abnormalities in gait may be due to nonneurological causes; if, for example, a severe case of bunions is suspected as the cause of the difficulty, the examiner may ask the patient to remove his or her shoes and socks so that the feet may be physically inspected. Highly trained examiners are additionally sensitive to subtle abnormalities in, for example, arm movements while the patient walks, runs, or skips.

Standing still (technically, the Romberg test)

The patient is asked to stand still with feet together, head erect, and eyes open. Whether patients have their arms extended straight out or at their sides and whether or not they are wearing shoes or other clothing will be a matter of the examiner's preference. Patients are next instructed to close their eyes. The critical variable is the amount of sway exhibited by the patient once the eyes are closed. Because normal persons may sway somewhat with their eyes closed, experience and training are required to determine when the amount of sway is indicative of pathology.

Nose-finger-nose

The patient's task is to touch her nose with the tip of her index finger, then touch the examiner's finger, and then touch her own nose again. The sequence is repeated many times with each hand. This test, as well as many similar ones (such as the toe-finger test, the finger-nose test, the heel-knee test), is designed to assess, among other things, cerebellar functioning.

Finger wiggle

The examiner models finger wiggling (or, playing an imaginary piano or typing), and then the patient is asked to wiggle his own fingers. Typically, the nondominant hand cannot be wiggled as quickly as the dominant hand, but it takes a trained eye to pick up a significant difference in rate. The experienced examiner will also look for abnormalities in the precision of the movements and the rhythm of the movements, "mirror movements" (uncontrolled similar movements in the other hand when instructed to wiggle only one), and other abnormal involuntary movements. Like the nose-finger test, finger wiggling supplies information concerning the quality of involuntary movement and muscular coordination. A related task involves tongue wiggling.

Table 14–6

Sample Tests Used by Neurologists to Assess the Intactness of Some of the 12 Cranial Nerves

Cranial Nerve	Test
I (olfactory nerve)	Closing one nostril with a finger, the examiner places some odoriferous substance under the nostril being tested and asks whether the smell is perceived. Subjects who perceive it are next asked to identify it. Failure to perceive an odor when one is presented may indicate lesions of the olfactory nerve, a brain tumor, or other medical conditions. Of course, failure may be due to other factors, such as oppositional tendencies on the part of the patient or intranasal disease, and such factors must be ruled out as causal.
II (optic nerve)	Assessment of the intactness of the second cranial nerve is a highly complicated procedure, for this is a sensory nerve with functions related to visual acuity and peripheral vision. A Snellen eye chart is one of the tools used by the physician in assessing optic nerve function. If the subject at a distance of 20 feet from the chart is able to read the small numbers or letters in the line labeled "20," then the subject is said to have 20/20 vision in the eye being tested. This is only a standard. Although many persons can read only the larger print at higher numbers on the chart (or, a person who reads the letters on line "40" of the chart would be said to have a distance vision of 20/40), some persons have better than 20/20 vision. An individual who could read the line labeled "15" on the Snellen eye chart would be said to have 20/15 vision.
V (trigeminal nerve)	The trigeminal nerve supplies sensory information from the face, and it supplies motor information to and from the muscles involved in chewing. Information regarding the functioning of this nerve is examined by the use of tests for facial pain (pinpricks are made by the physician), facial sensitivity to different temperatures, and other sensations. Another part of the examination entails having the subject clamp his or her jaw shut. The physician will then feel and inspect the facial muscles for weakness and other abnormalities.
VIII (acoustic nerve)	The acoustic nerve has functions related to the sense of hearing and the sense of balance. Hearing is formally assessed with an audiometer. More frequently, the routine assessment of hearing involves the use of a "dollar watch." Provided the examination room is quiet, an individual with normal hearing should be able to hear a dollar watch ticking at a distance of about 40 inches from each ear (30 inches if the room is not very quiet). Other quick tests of hearing involve placing a vibrating tuning fork on various portions of the skull. Individuals who complain of dizziness, vertigo, disturbances in balance, and so forth may have their vestibular system examined by means of specific tests.

Parkinson's disease   Characterized primarily by disorders of movement (such as tremors, rigidity, slowness, and problems with balance and coordination), **Parkinson's disease** (PD) is a progressive, neurological illness that may also have several nonmotor symptoms associated with it (ranging from depression to dementia).

A description of the symptoms of PD can be found in the 5,000-year-old *Ayurveda,* an age-old system of natural healing that is believed to have originated with the Vedic culture of India. Roughly 2,500 years after that, what we now recognize as PD was described in a Chinese medical textbook called *Huang Di Nei Jing Su Wen.* Although PD is clearly a disease that has been with us since the beginning of recorded history, it was not until 1817 that a British physician named James Parkinson wrote about it in detail. Parkinson's paper was entitled "An Essay on the Shaking Palsy." Subsequently, in one of his lectures in the Salpětrièe amphitheater, the renowned French neurologist, Jean-Martin Charcot, taught his colleagues and students about what he called "Parkinson's disease" (Goetz, 1985). Apparently, the name Charcot used to describe the condition stuck, because it is still referred to as such today.

We now know that PD results from cell loss in a specific area of the brain called the **substantia nigra** (from the Latin for "black substance" because the region appears black under a microscope). The neurons in the substantia nigra are responsible for producing **dopamine,** a **neurotransmitter** (or, a chemical facilitator of communication between neurons) essential for normal movement. PD is a consequence of the compromised function of the substantia nigra to produce adequate levels of dopamine. But what causes that functional compromise?

Unfortunately, to date, no one has come up with a satisfactory answer to the question of *why* one or another person contracts PD. Although there are certain factors (such as age) which would increase one's chances of contracting PD, the fact is that most anyone can contract it (see Figure 14–1). Legendary boxers like Jack Dempsey and Muhammed Ali are thought to have contracted a form of Parkinson's disease (called "pugilistic Parkinson's") as a result of

George H.W. Bush
Library of Congress Prints and Photographs
Division [LC-USZ62-98302]

Muhammad Ali
© Paul Smith/Featureflash/Shutterstock RF

Jack Dempsey
© Library of Congress Prints & Photographs
Division [LC-USZ62-60713]

Pope John Paul II
© Shutterstock RF

**Maurice White (from Earth, Wind,
and Fire)**
© Rob Verhorst/Redferns/Getty Images

Michael J. Fox
© Paul Smith/Shutterstock RF

Johnny Cash
© Hulton Archives/Getty Images

Figure 14–1
Some Famous Faces of Parkinson's Disease

*A short list of famous people who have been diagnosed with Parkinson's
disease would include the 41st President of the United States, George H. W.
Bush, boxing icons Muhammad Ali and Jack Dempsey, actor Michael J.
Fox, and singing legends Maurice White (from* Earth, Wind, and Fire),
Johnny Cash, and Linda Ronstadt.

Linda Ronstadt
© Ron Galella, Ltd./WireImage/Getty Images

the occupational hazard of taking repeated blows to the head. Other varieties of Parkinson's are known to be caused by certain prescription medicines and nonprescription street drugs (such as contaminated heroin). However, the vast majority of diagnoses of PD are characterized in medical jargon as **idiopathic** (of unknown origin). To some as yet-to-be-determined degree, the disease is probably due to hereditary factors (such as a faulty gene), environmental factors (such as neurotoxins in say, pest control products), or some combination thereof.

To the outside observer, PD will look quite different in its various stages. In its earliest stages, PD most typically presents as a disturbance of motor functioning; the motor disturbance may be as slight as a barely noticeable tremor in a finger. As the disease progresses, patients will complain of unwanted nerve-related sensations, sometimes referred to as "internal tremors," primarily on one side of the body. With additional progression, tremors (internal and/or external) may worsen and be experienced at other sites on both sides of the body. Additionally, posture may suffer, and a noticeable loss of swing in the arm (or arms) will be evident when the patient walks.

Beyond tremors and the experience of uncomfortable "nervous energy" in the limbs, head, neck, or elsewhere, a number of other neuromuscular problems may arise. Stiffness or rigidity in the limbs or the facial muscles, slower than usual movement, difficulties associated with gait and balance, and difficulties with fine motor tasks (ranging from word processing to handwriting) are some such symptoms. There may also be issues with swallowing and excessive salivation. Another of the many varied potential consequences of PD is **rapid eye movement sleep behavior disorder** which is a condition characterized by an "acting out" of dreams with vocalizations or gestures. A wide variety of symptoms that are *not* properly neuromuscular in nature may also be evident in patients with PD. These symptoms include sweating (irrespective of temperature or physical activity), excessive fatigue and sleepiness, cognitive difficulties (such as word finding), and various urinary, sexual, and gastrointestinal problems.

Since PD results from dopamine deficiency, pharmacological interventions have been designed to target dopamine levels in the brain. But it's not that simple. The administration of dopamine by various means (such as by mouth, by a skin patch, or by an injection) does not necessarily replenish dopamine at the site where it is needed. Accordingly, medications have been created to work through complicated mechanisms to conserve dopamine levels or mimic the action of dopamine in the brain. To date, no medication or medical procedure cures PD. At best, medication is useful in alleviating some of the troubling symptoms through part or all of the disease's course. Unfortunately, many of the medications available for the treatment of PD come with their own "baggage" in terms of potential side effects. For example, **dyskinesias** (involuntary, jerking-type movements) may result from the long-term use of some of these medications.

In addition to treatment with medication, a number of ancillary treatments for PD may be recommended. Good nutrition is important and the PD patient may be referred to a registered dietician for assistance in menu planning and nutritional supplementation. Nutritional supplementation, especially with antioxidants, has been suggested by some as useful in the treatment of PD (Ebadi et al., 1996; "Powerful class," 2012; Prasad et al., 1999). However, since there have been no large-scale, controlled studies examining the efficacy of supplementation with antioxidants, the value of such supplementation remains anecdotal.

Regular exercise, including strength, endurance, flexibility (stretching), and balance exercises are usually advisable. Patients with PD should be encouraged to consult a physical or occupational therapist who specializes in exercise programs for persons with movement disorders. The physical or occupational therapist will devise an exercise and physical activity schedule that is uniquely tailored to the patient's needs. Some research suggests that the elevation in certain chemicals that occurs during exercise may actually serve a protective function against dopamine depletion and cell loss (Ellis et al., 2016).

Clinical depression is a frequent accompaniment of PD—probably not surprising since PD adversely affects so many spheres of one's public and private life. Accordingly, individual psychotherapy, possibly combined with participation in a local PD support group, may be indicated. Clinicians working with PD patients should be particularly sensitive to issues related to loss of control, and to possible compensatory actions. For example, the PD patient who complains of fine motor loss that makes the process of keyboarding a challenge may be encouraged to adopt word processing software that relies on verbal commands.

In the later stages of PD, adjustments in medication, nutrition, or exercise programs may not be as effective in relieving troubling symptoms as they once were. At the same time, depression or other psychopathology may become more difficult to manage. It is at such times that more invasive interventions may be considered. One invasive intervention is *deep brain stimulation* (DBS). **DBS** is a neurosurgical treatment for use with patients who have advanced PD. The procedure entails the surgical implantation of electrodes at specific sites in the brain. The electrodes are attached to battery-powered pulse generators implanted in the chest (much like cardiac pacemakers) which operate continuously to suppress the motor symptoms of PD. The gain in quality of life as a result of DBS may be substantial. However, like all surgery, the procedure itself carries with it risk. Potentially serious or even fatal events, such as bleeding, infection, stroke, or any of the complications that could arise from the administration of general anesthesia, are possibilities with DBS. While the risks associated with a DBS procedure remain relatively small, they must be weighed against any potential benefits of DBS in terms of the patient's quality of life.

A number of conditions can present like PD, but not be PD. For example, taking certain medications, particularly neuroleptic drugs, can produce tremors as a side effect. Medication-induced tremors, while "Parkinsonian" in appearance, are not necessarily symptomatic of PD. Similarly, the tremors produced by other neurological conditions, such as a disease called *essential tremor*, are not symptomatic of PD. A neurological disease that is closely related to, and can mimic, PD is called *Lewy body dementia* (LBD). First described by Frederick H. Lewy in the early 1900s, what are now known as **Lewy bodies** are clusters of stuck-together proteins that have the effect of depleting available dopamine and other brain substances (such as acetylcholine) critical for normal functioning. **Lewy body dementia** results from the formation of a number of Lewy bodies in the brain stem and cerebral cortex that cause Parkinsonian-like symptoms, Alzheimer-like symptoms, and other symptoms of dementia. Autopsy results of the beloved comedian and actor, Robin Williams, suggest that he was suffering not from PD as first reported at the time of his suicide, but from LBD (Birkinbine, 2015; Olson, 2014).

The vast majority of clinical psychologists and neuropsychologists are not trained to diagnose PD, or to differentially diagnose any of the many conditions that may present like PD. Accordingly, referral to a neurologist with special expertise in such matters is what should be done if PD is suspected by a psychologist or neuropsychologist. Referral sources listing qualified neurologists who are movement disorder specialists can be found at the websites of various PD-related organizations, including, for example, the Michael J. Fox Foundation and the American Parkinson Disease Association.

Once the patient is referred to a neurological specialist in movement disorders, the diagnosis of PD may potentially be made through a combination of case history data and clinical examination. In some cases, the neurologist may order additional tests, such as one called a **DaTscan** (pronounced in a way that rhymes with "cat scan"). A DaTscan entails the use of high-tech imaging equipment to visualize the substantia nigra and gauge the amount of dopamine present. Perhaps because of the relatively limited availability of the highly specialized equipment that is required, DaTscans are currently more a tool of assessment in neurological research as opposed to being an aid to everyday diagnosis.

There is no cure for PD, and there are no known ways to slow its progression. The best practice for managing this disease entails a team approach with knowledgeable specialists from neurology (for medical management) and psychology (for the management of depression and related psychopathology). A social worker knowledgeable in locally available support services may also be invaluable. Ideally, additional members of the team will include a registered dietician (for nutritional counseling) and either a physical or occupational therapist (to help plan and implement a tailored exercise regimen). If problems with swallowing are in evidence, another important member of the treatment team will be a speech therapist who has expertise in teaching patients exercises to help sustain and build-up the muscles associated with swallowing.

PD varies in its aggressiveness from individual to individual. In some people, the severity of symptoms worsens fairly quickly over time. For other people, the severity of symptoms may remain stable for a longer time. But regardless of how aggressive the disease is in terms of severity of symptoms, and the speed of its progression, the formula for treatment remains pretty much the same: medical management by a neurologist who specializes in movement disorders, management of depression and other psychopathology by a clinical psychologist, social support from a local PD support group, and adjunctive nutritional, exercise, and speech counseling as needed.

Neuropsychological Tests

A wide variety of tests are used by neuropsychologists as well as others who are charged with finding answers to neuropsychology-related referral questions. Researchers may employ neuropsychological tests to gauge change in mental status or other variables as a result of the administration of medication or the onset of a disease or disorder. Forensic evaluators may employ tests to gain insight into the effect of neuropsychological factors on issues such as criminal responsibility or competency to stand trial.

In what follows, we present only a sample of the many types of tests used in neuropsychological applications. More-detailed presentations are available in a number of sources (e.g., Golden & Lashley, 2014; Lezak, 2012; Macniven, 2016; Reinstein & Burau, 2014). Current neuropsychology articles can provide another rich source of information on neuropsychological testing and assessment, as can lectures and presentations by speakers with a background in neuropsychology. Speaking of the latter, one neuropsychologist you can learn from is Dr. Jeanne Ryan. The evaluation of people for concussion, particularly participants in contact sports, has been a topic of heightened research interest in recent years (DeMarco & Broshek, 2016; Kelty-Stephen, et al., 2015; Meier et al., 2015; Moser et al., 2015; Murray et al., 2014; Lynall et al., 2013). Read what she had to say about evaluating patients for concussion in this chapter's *Meet an Assessment Professional* feature.

Tests of General Intellectual Ability

Tests of intellectual ability, particularly Wechsler tests, occupy a prominent position among the diagnostic tools available to the neuropsychologist. The varied nature of the tasks on the Wechsler scales and the wide variety of responses required make these tests potentially very useful tools for neuropsychological screening. For example, a clue to the existence of a deficit might be brought to light by difficulties in concentration during one of the subtests. Because certain patterns of test response indicate particular deficits, the examiner looks beyond performance on individual tests to a study of the pattern of test scores, a process termed **pattern analysis.** Thus, for example, extremely poor performance on the Block Design and other performance subtests might be telling in a record that contains relatively high scores on all the verbal subtests. In combination with a known pattern of other data, the poor Block Design performance could indicate damage in the right hemisphere.

Meet Dr. Jeanne P. Ryan

One area in which the need for regular and frequent neuropsychological assessment has been recognized is in sport related concussions. As has been highlighted in the media, athletes with histories of concussion as might occur in the NFL and the NHL have been found to have cognitive problems associated with encephalopathy caused by repeated blows to the head over an extended period of time. This concern is now being directed toward our youth, the amateur athletes in middle school, high school and college. New York State has been very progressive in this regard; every athlete in the public school system is required to have a form of baseline neuropsychological assessment, which can then be compared to the athlete's performance on the same instrument following concussion. Follow-up post-concussion neuropsychological screening provides evidence based information to make return to play decisions or to determine if a more comprehensive evaluation is needed.

Neuropsychological assessment instruments are very effective tools for understanding neurocognitive functioning, but the tests are only as good as the psychologist who uses them. Learning to administer neuropsychological tests is not difficult. Merging test interpretation with multiple sources of information to understand the presenting problem and to develop effective interventions is the challenge. Having a sound understanding of the brain–behavior relationship, knowledge of the strengths and limitations of each test, and an ability to integrate aspects of the individual's inherent features and the environmental contributions are essential. Knowing how to translate the information into meaningful recommendations is imperative. Communicating the

Jeanne P. Ryan, Ph.D., Professor of Psychology at State University of New York (SUNY) at Plattsburgh, and Clinical Director, SUNY–Plattsburgh Neuropsychology Clinic and Psychoeducational Services

© Jeanne P. Ryan

assessment information to the person and the family in understandable terms is necessary so that changes can be made to promote quality of life and well being.

Read more of what Dr. Ryan had to say—her complete essay—in the Instructor Resources within Connect.

Used with permission of Jeanne P. Ryan.

A number of researchers intent on developing a definitive sign of brain damage have devised various ratios and quotients based on patterns of subtest scores. David Wechsler himself referred to one such pattern, called a **deterioration quotient** or DQ (also referred to by some as a *deterioration index*). However, neither Wechsler's DQ nor any other WAIS-based index has performed satisfactorily enough to be deemed a valid, stand-alone measure of neuropsychological impairment.

We have already noted the need to administer standardized tests in strict conformance with the instructions in the test manual. Yet testtaker limitations mean that such "by-the-book" test administrations are not always possible or desirable when testing members of the neurologically impaired population. Because of various problems or potential problems (such as the shortened attention span of some neurologically impaired individuals), the experienced examiner may need to modify the test administration to accommodate the testtaker and still yield clinically useful information. The examiner administering a Wechsler scale may deviate from the prescribed order of test administration when testing an individual who becomes fatigued quickly. In such cases, the more taxing subtests will be administered early in the exam. In the interest of shortening the total test administration time, trained examiners might omit certain subtests that they suspect will fail to provide any information beyond that already obtained. Let us reiterate that such deviations in the administration of standardized tests such as the Wechsler scales can be made—and meaningfully interpreted—by trained and experienced neuropsychologists. For the rest of us, it's by the book!

JUST THINK . . .

Why should deviations from standardized test instructions be made very judiciously, if at all?

Tests to Measure the Ability to Abstract

One symptom commonly associated with neuropsychological deficit, regardless of the site or exact cause of the problem, is inability or lessened ability to think abstractly. One traditional measure of verbal abstraction ability has been the Wechsler Similarities subtest, isolated from the age-appropriate version of the Wechsler intelligence scale. The task in this subtest is to identify how two objects (for instance, a ball and an orange) are alike. Another type of task used to assess ability to think abstractly is proverb interpretation. For example, interpret the following proverb:

A stitch in time saves nine.

If your interpretation of this proverb conveyed the idea that haste makes waste, then you have evinced an ability to think abstractly. By contrast, some people with neurological deficits might have interpreted that proverb more concretely (or, with less abstraction). Here is an example of a concrete interpretation: When sewing, take one stitch at a time—it'll save you from having to do it over nine times. This type of response might (or might not, depending on other factors) betray a deficit in abstraction ability. The Proverbs Test, an instrument specifically designed to test abstraction and related ability, contains a number of proverbs along with standardized administration instructions and normative data. In one form of this test, the subject is instructed to write an explanation of the proverb. In another form of the test, this one multiple-choice, each proverb is followed by four choices, three of which are either common misinterpretations or concrete responses.

Nonverbal tests of abstraction include any of the various tests that require the respondent to sort objects in some logical way. Common to most of these sorting tests are instructions such as "Group together all the ones that belong together" and follow-up questions—for example, "Why did you group those objects together?" Representative of such tests are the Object Sorting Test and the Color-Form Sorting Test (also known as Weigl's Test), which require testtakers to sort objects of different shapes and colors. Another way that sorting tasks are administered is by grouping a few of the stimulus objects together and requiring the testtaker (a) to explain why those objects go together or (b) to select the object that does not belong with the rest.

The Wisconsin Card Sorting Test-64 Card Version (WCST-64; Kongs et al., 2000) requires the testtaker to sort a pack of 64 cards that contain different geometric figures printed in different colors. The cards are to be sorted according to matching rules that must be inferred and that shift as the test progresses. Successful performance on this test requires several abilities associated with frontal lobe functioning, including concentration, planning, organization, cognitive flexibility in shifting set, working memory, and inhibition of impulsive responding. The test may be useful in screening for neurological impairment with or without suspected injury of the frontal lobe. Caution is suggested when using this or similar tests, as some evidence suggests that the test may erroneously indicate neurological impairment when in reality the testtaker has schizophrenia or a mood disorder (Heinrichs, 1990). It is therefore important for clinicians to rule out alternative explanations for a test performance that indicates neurological deficit.

Tests of Executive Function

Sorting tests measure one element of **executive function,** which may be defined as organizing, planning, cognitive flexibility, and inhibition of impulses and related activities associated with the frontal and prefrontal lobes of the brain. One test used to measure executive function is the Tower of Hanoi (Figure 14–2), a puzzle that made its first appearance in Paris in 1883 (Rohl, 1993). It is set up by stacking the rings on one of the pegs, beginning with the largest-diameter ring, with no succeeding ring resting on a smaller one. Probably because the appearance of these stacked rings is reminiscent of a pagoda, the puzzle was christened *La Tour de Hanoi.* The Tower of Hanoi, either in solid form for manipulation by hand or adapted for computerized administration in graphic form, has been used by many researchers to measure various aspects of executive function (Aman et al., 1998; Arnett et al., 1997; Butters et al., 1985; Byrnes & Spitz, 1977; Glosser & Goodglass, 1990; Goel & Grafman, 1995; Goldberg et al., 1990; Grafman et al., 1992; Janssen et al., 2010; Leon-Carrion et al., 1991; Mazzocco et al., 1992; Miller & Ozonoff, 2000; Minsky et al., 1985; Schmand et al., 1992; Spitz et al., 1985).

Performance on mazes is another type of task used to measure executive function. As early as the 1930s, psychologist Stanley D. Porteus became enamored with the potential for psychological assessment of the seemingly simple task of identifying the correct path in a maze and then tracing a line to the end point of that maze. This type of task was originally introduced to yield a quantitative estimate of "prudence, forethought, mental alertness, and power of sustained attention" (Porteus, 1942). Porteus urged colleagues to use mazes for varied research purposes ranging from the exploration of cultural differences (Porteus, 1933) to the study of social inadequacy (Porteus, 1955) to the study of personality traits by means of qualitative analysis of a testtaker's performance (Porteus, 1942). Maze tasks like those in the Porteus Maze Test (Figure 14–3) are used primarily as measures of executive function (Daigneault et al., 1992; Krikorian & Bartok, 1998; Mack & Patterson, 1995). Although useful in measuring

Figure 14–2
The Tower of Hanoi

This version of the Tower of Hanoi puzzle comes with three pegs and eight rings. The puzzle begins with all of the rings on one of the pegs ordered from the bottom up in decreasing size. To solve the puzzle, all of the rings must be transferred to another peg following three rules: (1) only one ring may be moved at a time; (2) the ring is moved from one peg to another; and (3) no ring may ever be placed on a smaller one.
© 2017 Ronald Jay Cohen

Figure 14–3
"Where do we go from here, Charly?"

A Porteus maze–like task is being illustrated by the woman in the white coat to actor Cliff Robertson as "Charly" in the now-classic film of the same name.
© Cinerama/Handout/Moviepix/Getty Images

JUST THINK . . .

How might qualitative analysis of performance on a maze task be telling with regard to the testtaker's personality?

such functioning in adults, its utility for that purpose in children has been questioned. Shum et al. (2000) observed no adverse impact on Porteus maze performance of children with traumatic brain injury.

A test used to quickly screen for certain executive functions is the **clock-drawing test (CDT).** As its name implies, the task in this test is for the patient to draw the face of a clock, usually with the hands of the clock indicating a particular time (such as "ten minutes after eleven"). As used clinically, there are many variations of this test—not only in the time that the clock should indicate but also in the setup of the task (some clinicians begin the test with a pre-drawn circle) and in the scoring of the patient's production (there are more than a dozen scoring systems). Observed abnormalities in the patient's drawing may be reflective of cognitive dysfunction resulting from dementia or other neurological or psychiatric conditions. Poor performance on the CDT has also been associated with visual memory deficits (Takahashi et al., 2008), mild cognitive impairment (Babins et al., 2008), and losses in function that ostensibly result with aging (Bozikas et al., 2008; Hubbard et al., 2008). Parks et al. (2010) examined performance on the clock drawing task in elderly individuals with and without Alzheimer's disease, while observing each group's brain functioning by means of special imaging equipment. It was found that performance on the clock drawing was correlated with a specific pattern of brain activity in the healthy participants that was different from the brain activity of those with Alzheimer's disease.

Representative items for four other types of tasks that may be used in neuropsychological assessment are illustrated in Figure 14–4. Part (a) illustrates a **trail-making item.** The task is

**Figure 14–4
Sample Items Used in
Neuropsychological Assessment**

(a) The Trail Making Test
The testtaker's task is to connect the dots in
a logical fashion.

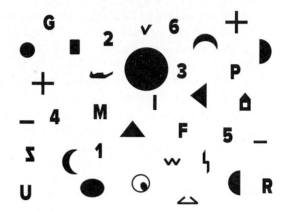

(b) The Field of Search
After being shown a sample stimulus, the
testtaker's task is to locate a match as
quickly as possible.

(c) An Identification Task
A task that involves what is known as
confrontation naming.

(d) A Picture Absurdity
The testtaker answers questions such as
"What's wrong or silly about this picture?"

to connect the circles in a logical way. This type of task is thought to tap many abilities, including visuo-perceptual skills, working memory, and the ability to switch between tasks (Sanchez-Cubillo et al., 2009). In a longitudinal study that followed elderly individuals over the course of 6 years, initial performance on the Trail Making Test was able to predict impairments in mobility and even mortality (Vazzana et al., 2010).

Illustration (b) in Figure 14–4 is an example of a **field-of-search item.** Shown a sample or target stimulus (usually some sort of shape or design), the testtaker must scan a field of various stimuli to match the sample. This kind of item is usually timed. People with right hemisphere lesions may exhibit deficits in visual scanning ability, and a test of field-of-search ability can be of value in discovering such deficits. Field-of-search ability has strong adaptive value and can have life-or-death consequences for predator and prey. Research in field of search has found many applications. For example, it helps us to better understand some everyday activities such as driving (Crundall et al., 1998; Duchek et al., 1998; Guerrier et al., 1999; Recarte & Nunes, 2000; Zwahlen et al., 1998) as well as more specialized activities such as piloting aircraft (Seagull & Gopher, 1997) and monitoring air traffic (Remington et al., 2000).

Illustration (c) is an example of a simple line drawing reminiscent of the type of item that appears in instruments such as the Boston Naming Test. The testtaker's task on the Boston (as it is often abbreviated) is **confrontation naming;** that is, naming each stimulus presented. This seemingly simple task entails three component operations: a perceptual component (perceiving the visual features of the stimulus), a semantic component (accessing the underlying conceptual representation or core meaning of whatever is pictured), and a lexical component (accessing and expressing the appropriate name). Difficulty with the naming task could therefore be due to deficits in any or all of these components. Persons who are neurologically compromised as a result of Alzheimer's disease or other dementia typically experience difficulty with naming tasks.

Illustration (d) in Figure 14–4 is what is called a **picture absurdity item.** The pictorial equivalent of a verbal absurdity item, the task here is to identify what is wrong or silly about the picture. It is similar to the picture absurdity items on the Stanford-Binet intelligence test. As with Wechsler-type Comprehension items, this type of item can provide insight into the testtaker's social comprehension and reasoning abilities. In the event of an emergency, it is imperative that an individual be able to execute certain basic executive functions, such as being able to telephone for help and provide first-responders with emergency-relevant information. To help in the assessment of one's capacity for independent living, a performance-based instrument called the Test of Executive Function in an Emergency (TEFE) was developed. The TEFE was designed to specifically evaluate the ability of cognitively impaired patients to access assistance in the event of an emergency (Wiechmann et al., 2015).

JUST THINK . . .

Picture absurdity items have traditionally been found on tests of intelligence or neuropsychological tests. Describe your own, original, picture absurdity item that you believe could have value in assessing personality.

Tests of Perceptual, Motor, and Perceptual-Motor Function

The term **perceptual test** is a general reference to any of many instruments and procedures used to evaluate varied aspects of sensory functioning, including aspects of sight, hearing, smell, touch, taste, and balance. Similarly, **motor test** is a general reference to any of many instruments and procedures used to evaluate varied aspects of one's ability and mobility, including the ability to move limbs, eyes, or other parts of the body. The term **perceptual-motor test** is a general reference to any of many instruments and procedures used to evaluate the integration or coordination of perceptual and motor abilities. For example, putting together a jigsaw puzzle taps perceptual-motor ability—more specifically, hand–eye coordination. Thousands of tests have been designed to measure various aspects of perceptual, motor, and perceptual-motor functioning. Some of them you may have heard of long before you decided to take a course in assessment. For example, does *Ishihara* sound familiar? The Ishihara (1964) test is used to screen for color blindness. More specialized—and less well-known—instruments are available if rare forms of color perception deficit are suspected.

Among the tests available for measuring deficit in auditory functioning is the Wepman Auditory Discrimination Test. This brief, easy-to-administer test requires that the examiner read a list of 40 pairs of monosyllabic meaningful words (such as *muss/much*) pronounced with lips covered (not muffled, please) by either a screen or a hand. The examinee's task is to determine whether the two words are the same or different. It's quite a straightforward test—provided the examiner isn't suffering from a speech defect, has no heavy accent, and doesn't mutter. The standardization sample for the test represented a broad range within the population, but there is little information available about the test's reliability or validity. The test manual also fails to outline standardized administration conditions, which are particularly critical for this test given the nature of the stimuli (Pannbacker & Middleton, 1992).

A test designed to assess gross and fine motor skills is the Bruininks-Oseretsky Test of Motor Proficiency. Designed for use with children aged 4½ to 14½, this instrument includes subtests that assess running speed and agility, balance, strength, response speed, and dexterity. On a less serious note, the test's box cover could be used as an informal screening device for reading ability by asking colleagues to pronounce the test's name correctly. A test designed to measure manual dexterity is the Purdue Pegboard Test. Originally developed in the late 1940s as an aid in employee selection, the object is to insert pegs into holes using first one hand, then the other hand, and then both hands. Each of these three segments of the test has a time limit of 30 seconds, and the score is equal to the number of pegs correctly placed. Normative data are available, and it is noteworthy that in a population without brain injury, women generally perform slightly better on this task than men do. With brain-injured subjects, this test may help answer questions regarding the lateralization of a lesion.

Once widely used neuropsychological test is the **Bender Visual-Motor Gestalt Test,** usually referred to simply as the Bender-Gestalt or even just "the Bender." As originally conceived by Lauretta Bender (Figure 14–5), the test consisted of nine cards, on each of

Figure 14–5
Lauretta Bender (1896–1987)

Bender (1970) reflected that the objective of her visual-motor test was not to get a perfect reproduction of the test figures but "a record of perceptual motor experience—a living experience unique and never twice the same, even with the same individual" (p. 30).

© Atlas Archive/The Image Works

which was printed one design. The designs had been used by psychologist Max Wertheimer (1923) in his study of the perception of *gestalten* (German for "configurational wholes"). Bender (1938) believed these designs could be used to assess perceptual maturation and neurological impairment. Testtakers were shown each of the cards in turn and instructed "Copy it as best you can." Although there was no time limit, unusually long or short test times were considered to be of diagnostic significance. Average administration time for all nine designs was about five minutes—a fact which also contributed to its wide appeal among test users.

JUST THiNK . . .

Test authors, Lauretta Bender among them, may suggest that their instrument to be scored and interpreted only on the basis of clinical judgment. But users of tests demand otherwise. Why?

Bender (1938, 1970) intended the test to be scored by means of clinical judgment. It was published with few scoring guidelines and no normative information. Still, a number of quantitative scoring systems for this appealingly simple test soon became available for adult (Brannigan & Brunner, 2002; Hutt, 1985; Pascal & Suttell, 1951; Reichenberg & Raphael, 1992) and child (Koppitz, 1963, 1975; Reichenberg & Raphael, 1992) protocols. Some 65 years after the original was published, a "second edition" of the Bender was published, complete with additional test items and norms (Brannigan & Decker, 2003).

Tests of Verbal Functioning

Verbal fluency and fluency in writing are sometimes affected by injury to the brain, and there are tests to assess the extent of the deficit in such skills. In the Controlled Word Association Test (formerly the Verbal Associative Fluency Test), the examiner says a letter of the alphabet and then it is the subject's task to say as many words as he or she can think of that begin with that letter. Each of three trials employs three different letters as a stimulus and lasts one minute; the testtaker's final score on the test reflects the total number of correct words produced, weighted by factors such as the gender, age, and education of the testtaker. Controlled Word Association Test scores are related in the predicted direction to the ability of dementia patients to complete tasks of daily living, such as using the telephone or writing a check (Loewenstein et al., 1992). And although people with dementia tend to do poorly on the test as compared with controls, the differences observed have not been significant enough to justify using the test as an indicator of dementia (Nelson et al., 1993).

Not to be confused with *aphagia,* **aphasia** refers to a loss of ability to express oneself or to understand spoken or written language because of some neurological deficit.[2] A number of tests have been developed to measure aspects of aphasia. For example, the Reitan-Indiana Aphasia Screening Test (AST), available in both a child and an adult form, contains a variety of tasks such as naming common objects, following verbal instructions, and writing familiar words. Factor analysis has suggested that these tasks load on two factors: language abilities and coordination involved in writing words or drawing objects (Williams & Shane, 1986). Both forms of the test were designed to be screening devices that can be administered in 15 minutes or less. Used alone as a screening tool (Reitan, 1984a, 1984b; Reitan & Wolfson, 1992) or in combination with other tests (Tramontana & Boyd, 1986), the AST may be of value in distinguishing testtakers who have brain damage from those who do not. For testtakers of Hispanic descent, a more culturally relevant instrument might be the Multilingual Aphasia Examination. Rey et al. (1999) found the published norms to be comparable to their own data using a sample of Hispanic testtakers. They also discussed specific problems encountered in neuropsychological research with Hispanics and suggested guidelines and directions for future research.

---

2. **Aphagia** is a condition in which the ability to eat is lost or diminished.

Tests of Memory

Memory is a complex, multifaceted cognitive function that has defied simple explanation. To appreciate just how complex it is, consider the following:

> Humans possess an estimated 1 trillion neurons, plus 70 trillion synaptic connections between them. . . . A single neuron may have as many as 10,000 synapses, but during the process of memory formation perhaps only 12 synapses will be strengthened while another 100 will be weakened. The sum of those changes, multiplied neuron by neuron, creates a weighted circuit that amounts to memory. (Hall, 1998, p. 30)

Different models of memory compete for recognition in the scientific community, and no one model has garnered universal acceptance. For our purposes, a sample model is presented in Figure 14–6—along with the caveat that this relatively simple model, which was pieced together from various sources, is incomplete at best and *not* universally accepted. Moreover, the model contains elements that are still very much a matter of debate among contemporary researchers.

Contrary to the popular image of memory as a storehouse of sorts, memory is an active process that is presumed to entail both short-term and long-term components (Atkinson & Shiffrin, 1968). Incoming information is processed in short-term memory, where it is temporarily stored for as little as seconds or as long as a minute or two. Short-term memory has also been characterized by some researchers as virtually synonymous with *working memory* (Daneman & Carpenter, 1980; Newell, 1973). The more traditional view of short-term memory is as a passive buffer in which information is either transferred to long-term memory or dissipated (or, forgotten). Our model allows for both passive and active components of short-term memory, with encoding of long-term memory made from the active, "working" component of short-term memory.

Note in our model the two-way path between short-term memory and conscious awareness. Stimuli from conscious awareness can be fed into short-term memory, and short-term memory can feed stimuli back into conscious awareness. The path to long-term memory is illustrated by a broken line—indicating that not all information in short-term memory is encoded in long-term memory.

With regard to long-term memory, researchers have distinguished between *procedural* and *declarative* memory. **Procedural memory** is memory for things like driving a car, making entries on a keyboard, or riding a bicycle. Most of us can draw on procedural memory with little effort and concentration. **Declarative memory** refers to memory of factual material—such as the differences between procedural and declarative memory. We have compartmentalized the procedural and declarative components of long-term memory for illustrative purposes.

Also illustrated as compartmentalized are what are widely believed to be two components of declarative memory: semantic and episodic memory. **Semantic memory** is, strictly speaking, memory for facts. **Episodic memory** is memory for facts in a particular context or situation. An example of episodic or context-dependent memory might be the recollection of a classmate's name while in class but not at a chance meeting during a social event. Being asked to repeat digits in the context of a memory test is another example of episodic memory because it is linked so intimately to the (testing) context.

> **JUST THINK . . .**
>
> Visualize some remembered image or event. Now, referring to our model of memory, outline how that memory may have been established.

As indicated by the one-way path from long-term memory to consciousness, information stored in long-term memory is available for retrieval. Whether information so retrieved can be restored directly to long-term memory or must instead be processed again through short-term memory is a matter of debate. Also somewhat controversial (and not illustrated in our model) is the concept of *implicit memory*. There is research to suggest that memory exists both within

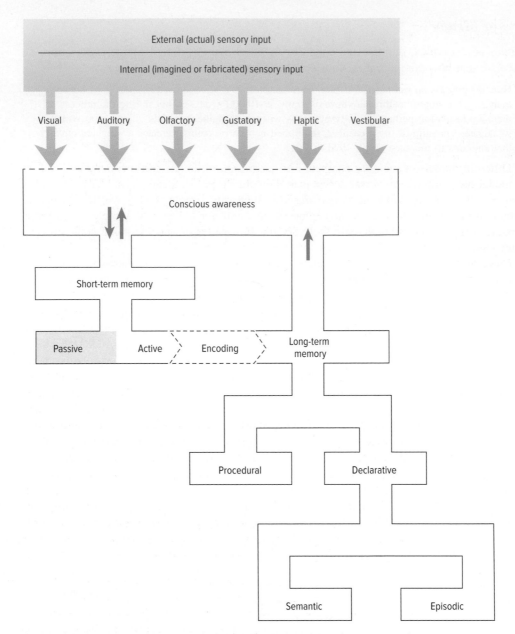

Figure 14–6
A Model of Memory

According to our model, memory results from information processing by the nervous system of external (actual) sensory input, such as sights, sounds, smells, and tastes. Your stored vision of a loved one's face, the song you will never forget, and the smell of freshly mowed grass are examples of memories formed from actual sensory input. Memory of a sort may also result from what one produces internally, in the absence of actual sensation. What one imagines, dreams, and misperceives are all examples of this latter sort of memory. Of course, dominance of imagined or fabricated sorts of memories can become a matter of clinical significance. The line between the sensory input channel and conscious awareness is broken to indicate that not all sensory input automatically makes it into conscious awareness; factors such as attention and concentration play a role in determining which stimuli actually make it into conscious awareness.

conscious awareness and external to conscious control (Greenwald & Banaji, 1995; Richardson-Klavehn & Bjork, 1988; Roediger, 1990; Roediger & McDermott, 1993; Schacter, 1987). The latter variety of memory, which is accessible only by indirect measures and not by conscious recollection, has been referred to as "unconscious memory" or, more recently, **implicit memory.** Support for such proposed divisions of memory can be found in laboratory research and also in the clinical observation of persons with amnesia who exhibit profound compartmentalizations of accessible and nonaccessible memories.

A widely used test of memory (and more) is the California Verbal Learning Test–II (CVLT-II; Dellis et al., 2000). The task is to repeat a list of words that are read by the examiner. A series of trials are administered. The test yields recall and recognition scores as well as information related to learning rate, error types, and encoding strategies. Items administered in a forced-choice format may be useful in the detection of malingering. Norms are provided for testtakers from ages 16 to 89, and there is a short form available for use with testtakers for whom fatigue or related factors must be taken into consideration. Also available is an alternate form of the test for retesting purposes. A child form of the test has also been published.

JUST THINK . . .

What is the relationship, if any, between an *implicit motive* (see Chapter 12) and an *implicit memory?*

The fourth edition of the Wechsler Memory Scale (WMS-IV), published in 2009, is the most recent revision of a brand of memory tests that was preceded by the WMS-III, the WMS-R, and the WMS. Designed for use with testtakers from ages 16 to 90, the materials and tasks in the WMS-IV, much like those in the WAIS-IV, have been revised to be more amenable for use with older testtakers. The WMS provides index scores for Auditory Memory, Visual Memory, Visual Working Memory, Immediate Memory, and Delayed Memory. There is some evidence that the WMS-IV may be a more useful measure of auditory and visual memory than the WMS-III under certain circumstances (Hoelzleet et al., 2011).

Two other approaches to memory testing are illustrated in Figure 14–7. In an approach devised by Milner (1971), tactile nonsense (nonrepresentational) figures are employed to measure immediate tactile (or haptic) memory. Another tactile memory test involves an adaptation of the administration of the Seguin-Goddard Formboard. Halstead (1947a) suggested that the formboard could be used to assess tactile memory if examinees were blindfolded during the test and a recall trial added.

JUST THINK . . .

What methods might you use to evaluate the psychometric soundness of a test of memory? *Note:* You may wish to check your response against the procedures described in the manual of the WMS-IV.

Neuropsychological Test Batteries

On the basis of the mental status examination, the physical examination, and the case history data, the neuropsychologist typically administers a battery of tests for further clinical study. Trained neuropsychologists may administer a prepackaged **fixed battery** of tests, or they may modify a fixed battery for the case at hand. They may choose to administer a **flexible battery,** consisting of an assortment of instruments hand-picked for some purpose relevant to the unique aspects of the patient and the presenting problem.

The clinician who administers a flexible battery has not only the responsibility of selecting the tests to be used but also the burden of integrating all the findings from each of the individual tests—no simple task because each test may have been normed on different populations. Another problem inherent in the use of a flexible battery is that the tests administered frequently overlap with respect to some of the functions tested, and the result is some waste in testing and scoring time. Regardless of these and other drawbacks, the preference of most highly trained neuropsychologists traditionally has been to tailor a battery of tests to

Figure 14–7
Two Tools Used in the Measurement of Tactile Memory

At left, four pieces of wire bent into "nonsense figures" can be used in a tactile test of immediate memory. Examinees are instructed to feel one of the figures with their right or left hand (or with both hands) and then to locate a matching figure. Shown at right is one form of the Seguin-Goddard Formboard. Blindfolded examinees are instructed to fit each of the 10 wooden blocks into the appropriate space in the formboard with each hand separately and then with both hands. Afterward, the examinee may be asked to draw the formboard from memory. All responses are timed and scored for accuracy.

the specific demands of a particular testing situation (Bauer, 2000; Sweet et al., 2002; Sweet et al., 2015). Larrabee (2015) listed a number of tests that in his view comprised a valid flexible battery. The total estimated administration time of the battery was about 4.5 hours, or 5.5 hours if the (optional) MMPI-2-RF was included.

Fixed neuropsychological test batteries are designed to comprehensively sample the patient's neuropsychological functioning. The fixed battery is appealing to clinicians, especially clinicians who are relatively new to neuropsychological assessment, because it tends to be less demanding in many ways. Whereas a great deal of expertise and skill is required to fashion a flexible battery that will adequately answer the referral question, a prepackaged battery represents an alternative that is not tailor-made but is comprehensive. Several tests sampling various areas are included in the battery, and each is supplied with clear scoring methods. One major drawback of the prepackaged tests, however, is that the specific disability of the patient may greatly—and adversely—influence performance on the test. Thus, for example, an individual with a visual impairment may perform poorly on many of the tasks that require visual skills.

A now classic neuropsychological test battery among the many available for use by researchers and clinicians is the **Halstead–Reitan Neuropsychological Battery.** Ward C. Halstead (1908–1969) was an experimental psychologist whose interest in the study of brain–behavior correlates led him to establish a laboratory for that purpose at the University of Chicago in 1935. His was the first laboratory of its kind in the world. During the course of 35 years of research, Halstead studied more than 1,100 brain-damaged persons. From his observations, Halstead (1947a, 1947b) derived a series of 27 tests designed to assess the presence or absence of organic brain damage—the Halstead Neurological Test Battery. A student of Halstead's, Ralph M. Reitan (see Figure 14–8), later elaborated on his mentor's findings. In 1955, Reitan published two papers that dealt with the differential intellectual effects of various brain lesion sites (Reitan, 1955a, 1955b). Fourteen years and much research later, Reitan (1969) privately published a book entitled *Manual for Administration of Neuropsychological Test Batteries for Adults and Children*—the forerunner of the Halstead-Reitan Neuropsychological Test Battery (H-R; see also Reitan & Wolfson, 1993).

Administration of the H-R requires a highly trained examiner conversant with the procedures for administering the various subtests (Table 14–7). Even with such an examiner, the test generally requires a full workday to complete. Subtest scores are interpreted not only with respect to what they mean by themselves but also in terms of their relation to scores on other subtests. Appropriate interpretation of the findings requires the eye of a trained neuropsychologist, though H-R computer interpretation software—no substitute for clinical judgment but an aid to it—is available. Scoring yields a number referred to as the Halstead Impairment Index, and an index of .5 (the cutoff point) or above is indicative of a neuropsychological problem. Data on more than 10,000 patients in the standardization sample were used to establish that cutoff point. Normative information has also been published with respect to special populations. Cultural factors must also be considered when administering this battery (Evans et al., 2000).

Conducting test-retest reliability studies on the H-R is a prohibitive endeavor, given how long it takes to administer and other factors (such as practice effects and effects of memory).

JUST THINK . . .

Just for a moment, don the role of a neuropsychologist who spends the better part of many workdays administering a single neuropsychological test battery to a single assessee. What do you like best about your job? What do you like least about your job?

Figure 14–8
Ralph M. Reitan (1922–2014)

In a distinguished career that spanned six decades, Ralph Reitan earned the distinction of being a "founding father of neuropsychology" (Grant & Heaton, 2015) and a true pioneer of that specialty in psychology (Hom & Nici, 2015a). Through teaching appointments at several universities throughout his career, through countless seminars and workshops, and in over 300 influential publications, Reitan inspired legions of neuropsychologists (Adams, 2015; Dikmen, 2015; Dodrill, 2015; Golden, 2015; Hom & Goldstein, 2015; Hom & Nici, 2015b; Horton & Reynolds, 2015; Janesheski, 2015; Reed & Reed, 2015; Russell, 2015). Interestingly, Reitan shied away from writing textbooks, because he felt that this activity should be reserved for the end of one's career (Finlayson, 2015).
© Jim Hom

Table 14–7
Subtests of the Halstead-Reitan Battery

Category

This is a measure of abstracting ability in which stimulus figures of varying size, shape, number, intensity, color, and location are flashed on an opaque screen. Subjects must determine what principle ties the stimulus figures together (such as color) and indicate their answer among four choices by pressing the appropriate key on a simple keyboard. If the response is correct, a bell rings; if incorrect, a buzzer sounds. The test primarily taps frontal lobe functioning of the brain.

Tactual performance

Blindfolded examinees complete the Seguin-Goddard Formboard (see Figure 14–7) with their dominant and nondominant hands and then with both hands. Time taken to complete each of the tasks is recorded. The formboard is then removed, the blindfold is taken off, and the examinee is given a pencil and paper and asked to draw the formboard from memory. Two scores are computed from the drawing: the memory score, which includes the number of shapes reproduced with a fair amount of accuracy, and the localization score, which is the total number of blocks drawn in the proper relationship to the other blocks and the board. Interpretation of the data includes consideration of the total time to complete this task, the number of figures drawn from memory, and the number of blocks drawn in the proper relationship to the other blocks.

Rhythm

First published as a subtest of the Seashore Test of Musical Talent and subsequently included as a subtest in Halstead's (1947a) original battery, the subject's task here is to discriminate between like and unlike pairs of musical beats. Difficulty with this task has been associated with right temporal brain damage (Milner, 1971).

Speech sounds perception

This test consists of 60 nonsense words administered by means of an audiotape adjusted to the examinee's preferred volume. The task is to discriminate a spoken syllable, selecting from four alternatives presented on a printed form. Performance on this subtest is related to left hemisphere functioning.

Finger-tapping

Originally called the "finger oscillation test," this test of manual dexterity measures the tapping speed of the index finger of each hand on a tapping key. The number of taps from each hand is counted by an automatic counter over five consecutive, 10-second trials with a brief rest period between trials. The total score on this subtest represents the average of the five trials for each hand. A typical, normal score is approximately 50 taps per 10-second period for the dominant hand and 45 taps for the nondominant hand (a 10% faster rate is expected for the dominant hand). Cortical lesions may differentially affect finger-tapping rate of the two hands.

Time sense

The examinee watches the hand of a clock sweep across the clock and then has the task of reproducing that movement from sight. This test taps visual motor skills as well as ability to estimate time span.

Other tests

Also included in the battery is the Trail Making Test (see Figure 14–4), in which the examinee's task is to correctly connect numbered and lettered circles. A strength-of-grip test is also included; strength of grip may be measured informally by a handshake grasp and more scientifically by a dynamometer (in Chapter 3, Figure 3–1).

To determine which eye is the preferred or dominant eye, the Miles ABC Test of Ocular Dominance is administered. Also recommended is the administration of a Wechsler intelligence test, the MMPI (useful in this context for shedding light on questions concerning the possible functional origin of abnormal behavior), and an aphasia screening test adapted from the work of Halstead and Wepman (1959).

Various other sensorimotor tests may also be included. A test called the critical flicker fusion test was once part of this battery but has been discontinued by most examiners. If you have ever been in a disco and watched the action of the strobe light, you can appreciate what is meant by a light that flickers. In the flicker fusion test, an apparatus that emits a flickering light at varying speeds is turned on, and the examinee is instructed to adjust the rate of the flicker until the light appears to be steady or fused.

Still, the test is generally viewed as reliable. A large body of literature attests to the validity of the instrument in differentiating brain-damaged subjects from subjects without brain damage and for assisting in making judgments relative to the severity of a deficit and its possible site (Reitan, 1994a, 1994b; Reitan & Wolfson, 2000). The battery has also been used to identify behavioral deficits associated with particular neurological lesions (Guilmette & Faust, 1991; Guilmette et al., 1990; Heaton et al., 2001).

Many published and unpublished neuropsychological test batteries are designed to probe deeply into one area of neuropsychological functioning instead of surveying for possible behavioral deficit in a variety of areas. Test batteries exist that focus on visual, sensory, memory, and communication problems. The Neurosensory Center Comprehensive Examination of Aphasia (NCCEA) is a battery of tests that focuses on communication deficit. The Montreal Neurological Institute Battery is particularly useful to trained neuropsychologists in locating specific kinds of lesions. The Southern California Sensory Integration Tests make up a battery designed to assess sensory-integrative and motor functioning in children 4 to 9 years of age.

A neuropsychological battery called the Severe Impairment Battery (SIB; Saxton et al., 1990) is designed for use with severely impaired assessees who might otherwise perform at or near the floor of existing tests. The battery is divided into six subscales: Attention, Orientation, Language, Memory, Visuoperception, and Construction. Another specialized battery is the Cognitive Behavioral Driver's Inventory, which was specifically designed to assist in determining whether individuals with brain damage are capable of driving a motor vehicle (Lambert & Engum, 1992).

JUST THINK . . .

The Cognitive Behavioral Driver's Inventory is a neuropsychological battery specially designed to help determine whether an assessee should be driving a motor vehicle. What is another specialized neuropsychological battery that needs to be developed?

Other Tools of Neuropsychological Assessment

Neuropsychologists must be prepared to evaluate persons who are vision-impaired or blind, hearing-impaired or deaf, or suffering from other disabilities. Providing accommodations for such patients while conducting a meaningful assessment can be challenging (Hill-Briggs et al., 2007). As with other evaluations involving accommodation for a disability, due consideration must be given to selection of instruments and to any deviance from standardized test administration and interpretation guidelines. In this context, Miller et al. (2007) described a test of nonverbal reasoning designed for use with the visually impaired and the blind. The test measures nonverbal reasoning primarily through the haptic sense (sense of touch) using a three dimensional matrix. Marinus et al. (2004) described the development of a short scale designed to evaluate motor function in patients with Parkinson's disease. Clinicians must be keen observers of things like a patient's mobility, and Zebehazy et al. (2005) discussed the use of digital video to assess those observational skills.

Perhaps the greatest advances in the field of neuropsychological assessment have come with the advancement of knowledge of genetics and in the application of technologically sophisticated medical equipment for purposes of imaging neurological processes and pathology. Researchers have been exploring the genetic bases of various phenomena related to normal and abnormal neuropsychological functioning, including everyday information processing and decision making (Benedetti et al., 2008; Marcotte & Grant, 2009), attention deficit hyperactivity disorder (Crosbie et al., 2008), and Alzheimer's disease (Borroni et al., 2007). Beyond the level of the gene, more "everyday" miracles in research, diagnosis, and treatment have been brought about through advances in brain imaging technology. One instrument which has shown itself to be very useful in neuropsychological practice and research is the *f*MRI (the functional MRI, usually abbreviated with a lower case, italicized *f*, and the capital letters MRI). "MRI" stands for an imaging procedure called magnetic resonance imaging. The MRI apparatus that many people have some familiarity with (see Figure 3 in this chapter's *Everyday Psychometrics*) is used to create images of structures within the body. The *f***MRI** apparatus creates real-time moving images of internal

Medical Diagnostic Aids
and Neuropsychological Assessment

Data from neuropsychological assessment, combined with data derived from various medical procedures, can in some cases yield a thorough understanding of a neurological problem. For example, certain behavioral indices evident in neuropsychological testing may result in a recommendation to further explore a particular brain site. The suspicion may be confirmed by a diagnostic procedure that yields cross-sectional pictures of the site and clearly reveals the presence of lesions.

The trained neuropsychologist has a working familiarity with the array of medical procedures that may be brought to bear on neuropsychological problems. Here, we take a closer look at a sample of these procedures. Let's begin with a brief description of the medical procedure and apparatus that is perhaps most familiar to us all, whether from experience in a dentist's chair or elsewhere: the X-ray.

To the radiologist, the X-ray photograph's varying shades convey information about the corresponding density of the tissue through which the X-rays have been passed. With front, side, back, and other X-ray views of the brain and the spinal column, the diagnosis of tumors, lesions, infections, and other abnormalities can frequently be made. There are many different types of such neuroradiologic procedures, which range from a simple X-ray of the skull to more complicated procedures. In one procedure, called a **cerebral angiogram,** a tracer element is injected into the bloodstream before the cerebral area is X-rayed.

Perhaps you have also heard or read about another imaging procedure, the **CAT (computerized axial tomography) scan,** also known as a "CT" scan (Figure 1). The CAT scan is superior to traditional X-rays because the structures in the brain may be represented in a systematic series of three-dimensional views, a feature that is extremely important in assessing conditions such as spinal anomalies. The **PET (positron emission tomography) scan** is a tool of nuclear medicine particularly useful in diagnosing biochemical lesions in the brain. Conceptually related to the PET scan is **SPECT (single photon emission computed tomography),** a technology that records the course of a radioactive tracer fluid (iodine) and produces exceptionally clear photographs of organs and tissues (Figure 2).

The term *radioisotope scan* or simply **brain scan** describes a procedure that also involves the introduction of radioactive material into the brain through an injection. The cranial surface is then scanned with a special camera to track the flow of the material. Alterations in blood supply to the brain are noted, including alterations that may be associated with disease such as tumors.

Figure 1
The CT scan is useful in pinpointing the location of tumors, cysts, degenerated tissue, or other abnormalities, and its use may eliminate the need for exploratory surgery or painful diagnostic procedures used in brain or spinal studies.
© Marmaduke St. John/Alamy RF

The **electroencephalograph (EEG)** is a machine that measures the electrical activity of the brain by means of electrodes pasted to the scalp. EEG activity will vary as a function of age, level of arousal (awake, drowsy, asleep), and other factors in addition to varying as a function of brain abnormalities. Electroencephalography is a safe, painless, and noninvasive procedure that can be of significant value in diagnosing and treating seizure and other disorders.

Information about nerve damage and related abnormalities may be obtained by electrically stimulating nerves and then noting movement (or lack of movement) in corresponding muscle tissue. The **electromyograph (EMG)** is a machine that records electrical activity of muscles by means of an electrode inserted directly into the muscle. Abnormalities found in the EMG can be used with other clinical and historical data as an aid in making a final diagnosis. The **echoencephalograph** is a machine that transforms electric energy into sound (sonic) energy. The sonic energy ("echoes") transversing the tissue area under study is then converted back into electric energy and displayed as a printout. This printout is used as an adjunct to other procedures in helping the diagnostician to determine the nature and location of certain types of lesions in the brain. Radio waves in combination with a magnetic field can also be used to create detailed anatomical images, as illustrated in Figure 3.

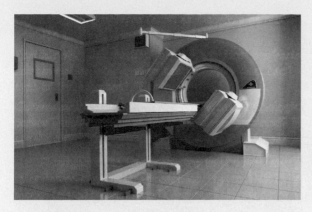

Figure 2

SPECT technology has shown promise in evaluating conditions such as cerebral vascular disease, Alzheimer's disease, and seizure disorders.
© MedicalRF.com RF

Laboratory analysis of bodily fluids such as blood and urine can provide clues about neurological problems and also about nonneurological problems masquerading as neurological problems. Examining cerebrospinal fluid for blood and other abnormalities can yield key diagnostic insights. A sample of the fluid is obtained by means of a medical procedure termed a **lumbar puncture,** or spinal tap. In this procedure, a special needle is inserted into the widest spinal interspace after a local anesthetic has been applied. In addition to providing information

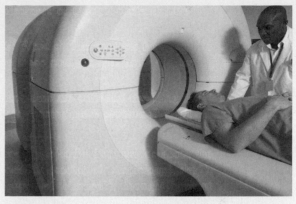

Figure 3

This magnetic resonance system utilizes a magnetic field and radio waves to create detailed images of the body. These and related imaging techniques may be employed not only in the study of neuropsychological functioning but also in the study of abnormal behavior; see, for example, Kellner et al.'s (1991) study of obsessive-compulsive disorder.
© UpperCut Images/SuperStock RF

concerning the chemical normality of the fluid, the test allows the diagnostician to gauge the normality of the intracranial pressure.

Working together, neuropsychologists and medical professionals can help improve the quality of life of many people with neurological problems.

functioning, and is particularly useful in identifying which parts of the brain are active at various times and during various tasks. Countless thousands of *f*MRI studies have been done on sundry topics since this technology first came in to being in 1992 (Blamire, 2011). In recent years, it would seem that research using *f*MRI technology knows no bounds; it is limited only by the imagination (and research budgets) of the researchers. One small sampling of the range of topics explored would include when the brain is prepared to learn (Yoo et al., 2012), how traumatic brain injury impacts the brain network that mediates memory (Kasahara et al., 2011), and how depression moderates reward anticipation (Olino et al., 2011).

As medical technology and instrumentation advances, the hope is that our ability to diagnose, prevent, and effectively treat too common and notoriously devastating disorders like *dementia* will improve. Broadly defined, **dementia** is a neurological disorder characterized by deficits in memory, judgment, ability to concentrate, and other cognitive abilities, with associated changes in personality due to damage to, or disease of brain neurons. In this chapter's *Close-Up*, we are taken for a firsthand look inside the consulting room of a neurologist to learn about what happens when a patient is referred for a neurological evaluation for Alzheimer's Disease or some other dementia.

The tools of neuropsychological assessment, much like many other measuring instruments used by psychologists, can help improve the quality of life of the people who are assessed with them. In the following (final) chapter, we survey how tools of assessment are working to improve, among other things, the quality of *business* life.

A Typical In-Office Dementia Evaluation*

In an outpatient setting, the person coming for an evaluation of dementia would typically be accompanied by a significant other or caregiver. The patient may complain of, or the individual accompanying the patient may have observed, symptoms like forgetfulness, name- or word-finding difficulties, or some other cognition-related compromise in the execution of daily activities.

The in-office evaluation begins with an interview as well as observation. The interview of the patient might begin with an exploration of why the patient is seeking professional assistance at this time. As further light is shed on the nature and extent of the presenting problem, observations are made and recorded regarding the patient's comportment and appearance. It is also during the interview that the patient's ability to comprehend communication and to express thought coherently is assessed.

Additional diagnostic information may come to the fore as a result of a careful history-taking. Certain elements of the history, if present, will be red flags regarding the possible onset of dementia. For example, the individual may have recently received a number of late payment notices. The individual may, of late, forgotten several appointments or other obligations. The individual may have had a recent accident or incident while driving—uncharacteristic of the patient in the past. A patient may report a sudden feeling of being lost in an otherwise familiar locale while driving or being driven.

A thorough neurological assessment for dementia will also typically include the administration of various tests such as the Mini-Mental-Status-Examination and a commercially available or custom-designed neurologic survey. Case history data, if available, will also be evaluated. Prior behavioral and medical records as compared to more current information may be particularly useful in identifying a potentially reversible cause of the observed cognitive dysfunction. Here, the category of "reversible causes" includes pathology related to metabolic disturbances (such as glucose derangements or thyroid abnormalities) and inflammatory or infectious conditions. In this context, blood testing may be suggested to evaluate variables such as the hemoglobin A_{1c} (a three-month gauge of blood sugar), thyroid stimulating hormone and T4 (which both provide information relevant to the status of the thyroid), the ESR and CRP (two indicators of abnormal, inflammatory activity), RPR (a test for prior syphilitic infection), and Vitamin

Eric D. Kramer, M.D., Diplomate, American Board of Psychiatry and Neurology
© Eric D. Kramer, MD

B-12 deficiency, which has the potential to manifest as a dementia (as well as other systemic problems such as a condition called megaloblastic anemia). In cases where pseudodementia is suspected (or, presenting dementia-like symptoms due to some non-neurological cause such as depression), a referral for psychological or neuropsychological assessment would be indicated. Additionally, neuropsychological assessment may be of value in differentially diagnosing dementia in its many varied forms including vascular, frontotemporal, or Alzheimer's type.

In some cases, technologically sophisticated medical tests may provide information critical to making a differential diagnosis. For example, an MRI (magnetic resonance imaging) scan may be ordered for the purpose of obtaining a structural evaluation of the brain. An EEG (electroencephalogram) may be ordered to complement the MRI findings so that data from both a static structural and dynamic functional evaluation is available. One relatively recent tool of assessment employs MRI imaging of a tracer substance with the brand name *AmyVid*. According to its manufacturer, this test can reliably identify a key amyloid that may be accruing in blood vessels and nerve cells. Here,

*This *Close-Up* was guest-authored by Eric D. Kramer of Medical Specialists of the Palm Beaches, Neurology.

"amyloid" refers to any of many varieties of protein deposit; this particular one acts as a marker for senile dementia of the Alzheimer's type.

In sum, a diagnosis of dementia, or senile dementia Alzheimer's type, is made not solely on the basis of something like a reported history of forgetfulness. Cognitive impairment is typically evaluated by, and differential diagnosis is typically accomplished through, the use of various tools of assessment (including the interview, case history data, and medical and neuropsychological tests). Ultimately, it is the application of the knowledge, experience, judgment, and skill of the trained clinician that will result not only in the correct diagnosis, but in the offer of the best treatment options that are currently available to the individual so diagnosed.

Used with permission of Eric D. Kramer, MD.

Self-Assessment

Test your understanding of elements of this chapter by seeing if you can explain each of the following terms, expressions, and abbreviations:

aphagia
aphasia
behavioral neurology
Bender Visual-Motor Gestalt Test
brain damage
brain scan
CAT (computerized axial tomography) scan
central nervous system
cerebral angiogram
clock-drawing test (CDT)
confrontation naming
contralateral control
DaTscan
declarative memory
deterioration quotient
developmental milestone
dopamine
dyskinesia
echoencephalograph
electroencephalograph (EEG)
electromyograph (EMG)
episodic memory

executive function
field-of-search item
fixed battery
flexible battery
ƒMRI
functional deficit
Halstead-Reitan Neuropsychological Battery
hard sign
idiopathic
implicit memory
lesion
lumbar puncture
motor test
neurological damage
neurology
neuron
neuropsychological assessment
neuropsychological mental status examination
neuropsychology
neurotology
neurotransmitter

noninvasive procedure
organic deficit
organicity
Parkinson's disease
pattern analysis
perceptual-motor test
perceptual test
peripheral nervous system
PET (positron emission tomography) scan
picture absurdity item
procedural memory
rapid eye movement sleep behavior disorder
reflex
semantic memory
soft sign
SPECT (single photon emission computed tomography)
substantia nigra
trail-making item

CHAPTER

15

Assessment, Careers, and Business

What do you want to be when you grow up?

It seems just yesterday that we were asked that question . . . For some readers, it really *was* just yesterday.

Questions and concerns about career choice have long occupied the thoughts of people contemplating a transition from student to member of the workforce (Collins, 1998; Murphy et al., 2006). Of course, such questions and concerns are by no means limited to people *entering* the world of work. At any given time, there are millions of people already established in careers who are contemplating career changes.

Professionals involved in career counseling use tools of assessment to help their clients identify the variety of work they might succeed at and would hopefully enjoy doing. In this chapter we survey some of the types of instruments that are used to assist in career choice and career transition. Later in the chapter we'll sample some of the many measures used by businesses, organizations, and the military to serve their various objectives.

JUST THINK . . .

How do you think most people decide on their careers? What factors entered (or will enter) into your own career decision?

Career Choice and Career Transition

A whole world of tests is available to help in various phases of career choice. There are tests, for example, to survey interests, aptitudes, skills, or special talents. There are tests to measure attitudes toward work, confidence in one's skills, assumptions about careers, perceptions regarding career barriers, even dysfunctional career thoughts.

Historically, one variable considered closely related to occupational fulfillment and success is personal interests. It stands to reason that what intrigues, engages, and engrosses would be good to work at. In fact, an individual's interests may be sufficiently solidified by age 15 that they can be useful in career planning (Care, 1996). Further, the odds are that these interests will be fairly stable over time (Savickas & Spokane, 1999).

Measures of Interest

Assuming that interest in one's work promotes better performance, greater productivity, and greater job satisfaction, both employers and prospective employees should have much to gain from methods that can help individuals identify their interests and jobs tailored to those interests. Using such methods, individuals can discover, for example, whether their interests lie in commanding a starship while "seeking new worlds and exploring new civilizations" or something more along the lines of cosmetic dentistry (Figure 15–1). We may formally define an **interest measure** in the context of vocational assessment and pre-employment counseling as an instrument designed to evaluate testtakers' likes, dislikes, leisure activities, curiosities, and involvements in various pursuits for the purpose of comparison with groups of members of various occupations and professions.

Employers can use information about their employees' interest patterns to formulate job descriptions and attract new personnel. For example, a company could design an employment campaign emphasizing job security if job security were found to be the chief interest of the successful workers currently holding similar jobs. Although there are many instruments designed to measure interests, our discussion focuses on the one with the longest history of continuous use, the Strong Interest Inventory (SII).

The Strong Interest Inventory One of the first measures of interest was published in 1907 by psychologist G. Stanley Hall. His questionnaire was designed to assess children's interest in

JUST THINK . . .

Visualize an employer's "want ad" that begins "Wanted: Employees interested in _____." Fill in the blank with a listing of your top three interests. Next, list the possible positions for which this employer might be advertising.

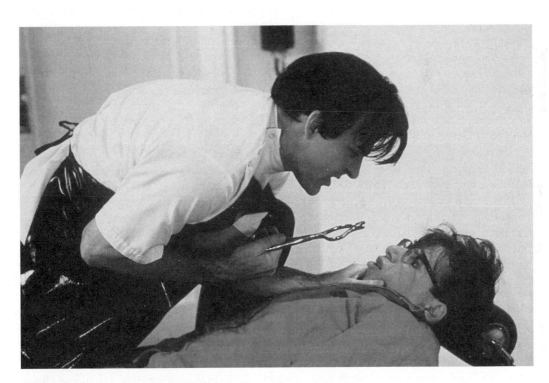

Figure 15–1
It's Not Just a Job, It's an Adventure!

Had Orin Scrivello, D.D.S. (played by Steve Martin) in the now classic comedy Little Shop of Horrors *taken an interest survey, the results might have been quite bizarre. As a child, young Orin's interests leaned toward bashing the heads of pussycats, shooting puppies with a BB gun, and poisoning guppies. He was able to put what his mother described as his "natural tendencies" to use in gainful employment: He became a dentist.*

© AF archive/Alamy

various recreational pursuits. It was not until the early 1920s that Edward K. Strong Jr., inspired by a seminar he attended on the measurement of interest, began a program of systematic investigation in this area. His efforts culminated in a 420-item test he called the Strong Vocational Interest Blank (SVIB).

Originally designed for use with men only, the SVIB was published with a test manual by Stanford University Press in 1928 and then revised in 1938. In 1935, a 410-item SVIB for women was published along with a test manual. The women's SVIB was revised in 1946. The men's and women's SVIBs were again revised in the mid-1960s. Amid concern about sex-specific forms of the test in the late 1960s and early 1970s (McArthur, 1992), a merged form was published in 1974. Developed under the direction of David P. Campbell, the merged form was called the Strong-Campbell Interest Inventory (SCII). The test was revised in 1985, 1994, and again in 2004. This latest version, referred to as the Strong Interest Inventory, Revised Edition (SII; Strong et al., 2004), added new items to reflect contemporary career interests such as those related to computer hardware, software, and programming.

JUST THINK . . .

Are people interested in things they do well? Or do people develop abilities in areas that interest them?

Strong's recipe for test construction was empirical and straightforward: (1) Select hundreds of items that could conceivably distinguish the interests of a person by that person's occupation; (2) administer this rough cut of the test to several hundred people selected as representative of certain occupations or professions; (3) sort out which items seemed of interest to persons by occupational group and discard items with no discriminative ability; and (4) construct a final version of the test that would yield scores describing how an examinee's pattern of interest corresponded to those of people actually employed in various occupations and professions. With such a test, college students majoring in psychology, for example, could see how closely their interests paralleled those of working psychologists. Presumably, if an individual's interests closely match psychologists' (in contrast to the interests of, say, tow-truck operators), that individual would probably enjoy the work of a psychologist.

Test items probe personal preferences in a variety of areas such as occupations, school subjects, and activities. Respondents answer each of these questions on a five-point continuum that ranges from "strongly like" to "strongly dislike." Nine items in a "Your Characteristics" section contain items like "win friends easily"; respondents select an answer on a five-point continuum that ranges from "strongly like me" to "strongly unlike me." Each protocol is computer scored and interpreted, yielding information on the testtaker's personal style, basic interests, and other data useful in determining how similar or dissimilar the respondent's interests are to those of people holding a variety of jobs.

JUST THINK . . .

Why might differential item functioning by gender be expected in interest measures?

Other interest inventories In addition to the SII, many other interest inventories are now in widespread use. You may recall one such inventory from Chapter 11 called The Self-Directed Search (SDS). The SDS explores interests within the context of Holland's (1997) theory of vocational personality types and work environments. According to this theory, vocational choice is an expression of one of six personality types: Realistic, Investigative, Artistic, Social, Enterprising, or Conventional. These personality types are variously referred to simply as the "Big 6" or by the acronym "RIASEC."

Another interest inventory is the Minnesota Vocational Interest Inventory. Empirically keyed, this instrument was expressly designed to compare respondents' interest patterns with those of persons employed in a variety of nonprofessional occupations (such as stock clerks, painters, printers, and truck drivers). Other measures of interest have been designed for use with people who have one or another deficit or disability. For example, interest inventories for testtakers who do not read well will typically employ drawings and other visual media as stimuli (Elksnin & Elksnin, 1993). Brief descriptions of a sampling of various other measures of interest are presented in a table titled, "Some Measures of Interest," available online in the Instructor Resources within Connect.[1]

How well do interest measures predict the kind of work in which individuals will be successful and happy? In one study, interest and aptitude measures were found to correlate in a range of about .40 to .72 (Lam et al., 1993). In another study examining the accuracy with which interest and aptitude tests predict future job performance and satisfaction, Bizot and Goldman (1993) identified people who had been tested in high school with measures of vocational interest and aptitude. Eight years later, these individuals reported on their satisfaction with their jobs, even permitting the researchers to contact their employers for information about the quality of their work. The researchers found that when a good match existed between a subject's aptitude in high school and the level of his or her current job, performance was likely to be evaluated positively by the employer. When a poor match existed, a poor performance rating was more likely. The extent to which employees were themselves satisfied with their jobs was not related to aptitudes as measured in high school. As for predictive validity, the interest tests administered in high school predicted neither job performance nor job satisfaction eight years later. The results of this and related studies (e.g., Jagger et al., 1992) sound a caution to counselors regarding overreliance on interest inventories. Concern has also been expressed about differential item functioning in interest tests (particularly the Strong) as a function of gender (Einarsdóttir & Rounds, 2009). Of course, it has also been well established that, generally speaking, men and women tend to have different interests (Su et al., 2009). Some research suggests that the predictive efficiency of interest measures may be enhanced if they are used in combination with other measures such as measures of confidence and self-efficacy (Chartrand et al., 2002; Rottinghaus et al., 2003), personality (Larson & Borgen, 2002; Staggs et al., 2003), or a portfolio project (Larkin et al., 2002).

Measures of Ability and Aptitude

As we saw in Chapter 10, achievement, ability, and aptitude tests all measure prior learning to some degree, although they differ in the uses to which the test data will be put. Beyond that, aptitude tests may tap a greater amount of informal learning than achievement tests. Achievement tests may be more limited and focused than aptitude tests.

Ability and aptitude measures vary widely in topics covered, specificity of coverage, and other variables. The Wonderlic Personnel Test measures mental ability in a general sense. This brief (12-minute) test includes items that assess spatial skill, abstract thought, and mathematical skill. The test may be useful in screening individuals for jobs that require both fluid and crystallized intellectual abilities (Bell et al., 2002).

The Bennet Mechanical Comprehension Test is a widely used paper-and-pencil measure of a testtaker's ability to understand the relationship between physical forces and various tools (e.g., pulleys and gears) as well as other common objects (carts, steps, and seesaws). Other mechanical tests, such as the Hand-Tool Dexterity Test, blur the lines among aptitude, achievement, and performance tests by requiring the testtaker actually to take apart, reassemble, or otherwise manipulate materials, usually in a prescribed sequence and within a time limit. If a job consists mainly of securing tiny transistors into the inner workings of an electronic

---

1. We parenthetically note a semantic distinction between vocational *interest* and *passion*. According to Vallerand et al. (2003), passion comes in two varieties: *obsessive passion* and *harmonious passion*. Both types derive from internal pressure to engage in activity one likes. However, whereas harmonious passion promotes healthy adaptation, obsessive passion derails it. According to these researchers, obsessive passion leads to rigid persistence, which in turn produces negative affect.

appliance or game, then the employer's focus of interest might well be on prospective employee's perceptual-motor abilities, finger dexterity, and related variables. In such an instance, the O'Connor Tweezer Dexterity Test might be the instrument of choice (Figure 15–2). This test requires the examinee to insert brass pins into a metal plate using a pair of tweezers.

A number of other tests are designed to measure specific aptitudes for a wide variety of occupational fields. For the professions, there are many psychometrically sophisticated assessment programs for screening or selecting applicants by means of aptitude tests (refer back to Table 10-2 on page 344 to view a sampling of such tests). For a while, one of the most widely used aptitude tests was the General Aptitude Test Battery (GATB). A description of that test, as well as the controversy surrounding it, follows.

The General Aptitude Test Battery   The U.S. Employment Service (USES) developed the General Aptitude Test Battery (GATB) and first put it into use in 1947 after extensive research. The GATB (pronounced like "Gatsby" without the *s*) is available for use by state employment services as well as other agencies and organizations, such as school districts and nonprofit organizations, that have obtained official permission from the government to administer it. The GATB is a tool used to identify aptitudes for occupations, and it is a test just about anyone of working age can take. The test is administered regularly at local state offices (referred to by names such as the Job Service, Employment Security Commission, and Labor Security Commission) to people who want the agency to help find them a job. It may also be administered to people who are unemployed and have been referred by a state office of unemployment or to employees of a company that has requested such aptitude assessment.

If you are curious about your own aptitude for work in fields as diverse as psychology, education, and plumbing, you may want to visit your local state employment office and sample the GATB yourself. Be prepared to sit for an examination that will take about three hours if you take the entire test. The GATB consists of 12 timed tests that measure nine aptitudes,

Figure 15–2
The O'Connor Tweezer Dexterity Test

This now classic test is especially useful in evaluating a testtaker's fine motor skills and dexterity. One of the pioneers of the hair transplant industry, cosmetic surgeon Dominic A. Brandy, extolled the benefits of this test when he described its use as a screening tool for hiring surgical hair restoration assistants (Brandy, 1995). Parenthetically, the examiner in this 1940s vintage photo clearly had no need, herself, for such cosmetic intervention.
© SuperStock/SuperStock

which in turn can be divided into three composite aptitudes. About half the time will be spent on psychomotor tasks and the other half on paper-and-pencil tasks. In some instances, depending on factors such as the reason for the assessment, only selected tests of the battery will be administered. The version of the test used to selectively measure aptitudes for a specific line of work is referred to as a Special Aptitude Test Battery, or SATB. SATB data may also be isolated for study from other test data when the entire test is taken.

The GATB has evolved from a test with multiple cutoffs to one that employs regression and *validity generalization* for making recommendations based on test results. The rationale and process by which the GATB has made this evolution has been described by John E. Hunter (1980, 1986), Frank Schmidt, and their associates (Hunter & Hunter, 1984; Hunter & Schmidt, 1983; Hunter et al., 1982). Validity generalization is the subject of this chapter's *Close-Up.*

In the past, recommendations with respect to aptitude for a particular job had been made on the basis of GATB validity studies bearing on specific jobs. For example, if there existed 500 job descriptions covering 500 jobs for which scores on the GATB were to be applied, there would be 500 individual validation studies with the GATB—one validation study for each individual job, typically with a relatively small sample size (many of these single studies containing only 76 subjects on average). Further, there were no validation studies for the other 12,000-plus jobs in the American economy (according to the *Dictionary of Occupational Titles* published by the U.S. Department of Labor, 1991).

Using meta-analysis to cumulate results across a number of validation studies and to correct statistically for errors such as sampling error, Hunter demonstrated that all the jobs could be categorized within five families of jobs, based on the *worker function codes* of the then-current edition of the *Dictionary of Occupational Titles.* The five families of jobs were (1) Setting Up, (2) Feeding and Off-Bearing, (3) Synthesizing and Coordinating, (4) Analyzing, Compiling, and Computing, and (5) Copying and Comparing. Regression equations for each of the families were then developed. Using these equations, Hunter found that recommendations for individual testtakers could be generalized to various jobs.

In the late 1980s the GATB became a center of controversy when it became public knowledge that the test had been race-normed. As described earlier in this book (Chapter 4), *race norming* refers to the process of adjusting scores to show an individual testtaker's standing within his or her own racial group. With the race-normed GATB, high scorers who were categorized within certain groups according to race were recommended for employment. For example, among people being considered for a skilled job, a GATB raw score of 300 was "translated into percentile scores of 79, 62, and 38, respectively, for Blacks, Hispanics, and others" (Gottfredson, 1994, p. 966). Only percentile scores, not raw scores, were reported to employers.

JUST THINK . . .

What are the pros and cons of race-norming an aptitude test?

In an attempt to address the ensuing controversy, the U.S. Department of Labor asked the National Academy of Sciences (NAS) to conduct a study. The NAS issued a report (Hartigan & Wigdor, 1989) that was generally supportive of race norming. The NAS noted that the GATB appeared to suffer from slope bias such that the test correlated more highly with criterion measures for White samples (.19) than for Black samples (.12). Intercept bias was also present, with the result that the performance of Blacks would be more favorably predicted relative to the performance of Whites if the same regression line were used for both groups. The NAS found race norming to be a reasonable method of correcting for the bias of the test.

The NAS report also addressed more general issues concerning the utility of the GATB as a predictor of job performance. Using a database of 755 studies, the NAS noted that the GATB correlated approximately .22 with criteria such as supervisory ratings. Others had estimated the test's validity to be .20 (Vevea et al., 1993) and .21 (Waldman & Avolio, 1989). These relatively small coefficients were viewed by the NAS as modest but acceptable. To understand why they were considered acceptable, recall from Chapter 6 that criterion validity

Validity Generalization and the GATB

Can a test validated for use in personnel selection for one occupation also be valid for use in personnel selection for another occupation? Must the validation of a test used in personnel selection be situation-specific? Stated more generally, can validity evidence for a test meaningfully be applied to situations other than those in which the evidence was obtained? These are the types of questions raised when validity generalization is discussed.

As applied to employment-related decision making on the basis of test scores achieved on the General Aptitude Test Battery (GATB), *validity generalization* means that the same test-score data may be predictive of aptitude for all jobs. The implication is that if a test is validated for a few jobs selected from a much larger cluster of jobs, each requiring similar skills at approximately the same level of complexity, then the test is valid for all jobs in that cluster. For example, if a validation study conclusively indicated that GATB scores are predictive of aptitude for (and ultimately proficiency in) the occupation of assembler in an aircraft assembly plant, then it may not be necessary to conduct an entirely new validation study before applying such data to the occupation of assembler in a shipbuilding plant; if the type and level of skill required in the two occupations can be shown to be sufficiently similar, then it may be that the same or similar procedures used to select aircraft assemblers can profitably be used to select shipbuilders.

Validity generalization (VG) as applied to personnel selection using the GATB makes unnecessary the burden of conducting a separate validation study with the test for every one of the more than 12,000 jobs in the American economy. The application of VG to GATB scores also enables GATB users to supply employers with more precise information about testtakers. To understand why this is so, let's begin by consulting the pie chart in Figure 1.

Note that the inner circle of the chart lists the 12 tests in the General Aptitude Test Battery and the next ring of the circle lists eight aptitudes derived from the 12 tests. Not illustrated here is a ninth aptitude, General Learning Ability, which is derived from scores on the Vocabulary, Arithmetic Reasoning, and Three-Dimensional Space tests. Here is a brief description of each of the eight aptitudes measured by the GATB.

- *Verbal Aptitude* (V): Understanding the meaning of words and their relationships and using words effectively are two of the abilities tapped here. V is measured by Test 4.

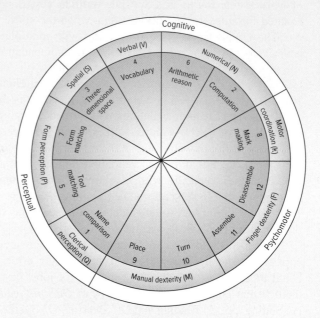

Figure 1
Aptitudes Measured by the General Aptitude Test Battery

- *Numerical Aptitude* (N): N is measured by tasks requiring the quick performance of arithmetic operations. It is measured by Tests 2 and 6.

- *Spatial Aptitude* (S): The ability to visualize and mentally manipulate geometric forms is tapped here. S is measured by Test 3.

- *Form Perception* (P): Attention to detail, including the ability to discriminate slight differences in shapes, shading, lengths, and widths—as well as the ability to perceive pertinent detail—is measured. P is measured by Tests 5 and 7.

- *Clerical Perception* (Q): Attention to detail in written or tabular material, as well as the ability to proofread words and numbers and to avoid perceptual errors in arithmetic computation, is tapped here. Q is measured by Test 1.

- *Motor Coordination* (K): This test taps the ability to quickly make precise movements that require eye–hand coordination. K is measured by Test 8.

- *Finger Dexterity* (F): This test taps the ability to quickly manipulate small objects with the fingers. F is measured by Tests 11 and 12.

- *Manual Dexterity* (M): The ability to work with one's hands in placing and turning motions is measured here. M is measured by Tests 9 and 10.

In the outermost ring of the diagram, note that the three composite aptitudes can be derived from the nine specific aptitudes: a Cognitive composite, a Perceptual composite, and a Psychomotor composite. The nine aptitudes that compose the three composite aptitudes are summarized in the following table.

The Nine GATB Aptitudes		The Three Composite Scores
G	General Learning Ability (also referred to as *intelligence*)	Cognitive
V	Verbal Aptitude	
N	Numerical Aptitude	
S	Spatial Aptitude	Perceptual
P	Form Perception	
Q	Clerical Perception	
K	Motor Coordination	Psychomotor
F	Finger Dexterity	
M	Manual Dexterity	

Traditionally—before the advent of VG—testtakers who sat for the GATB might subsequently receive counseling about their performance in each of the nine aptitude areas. Further, they might have been informed (1) how their own pattern of GATB scores compared with patterns of aptitude (referred to as Occupational Aptitude Patterns, or OAPs) deemed necessary for proficiency in various occupations, and (2) how they performed with respect to any of the 467 constellations of a Special Aptitude Test Battery (SATB) that could potentially be extracted from a GATB protocol. VG provides additional information useful in advising prospective employers and counseling prospective employees, including more precise data on a testtaker's performance with respect to OAPs as well as scores (usually expressed in percentiles) with respect to the five job families.

Research (Hunter, 1982) has indicated that the three composite aptitudes can be used to validly predict job proficiency for all jobs in the U.S. economy. All jobs may be categorized according to five job families, and the aptitude required for each of these families can be described with respect to various contributions of the three composite GATB scores. For example, Job Family 1 (Setup Jobs) is 59% Cognitive, 30% Perceptual, and 11% Psychomotor. GATB scoring is done by computer, as is weighting of scores to determine suitability for employment in each of the five job families.

Proponents of VG as applied to use with the GATB list the following advantages.

1. *The decreased emphasis on multiple cutoffs as a selection strategy has advantages for both prospective employers and prospective employees.* In a multiple cutoff selection model, a prospective employee would have to achieve certain minimum GATB scores in each of the aptitudes deemed critical for proficiency in a given occupation; failure to meet the minimal cutting score in these aptitudes would mean elimination from the candidate pool for that occupation. Using VG, a potential benefit for the prospective employee is that the requirement of a minimum cutting score on any specific aptitude is eliminated. For employers, VG encourages the use of a top-down hiring policy, one in which the best-qualified people (as measured by the GATB) are offered jobs first.

2. *Research has suggested that the relationship between aptitude test scores and job performance is linear (Waldman & Avolio, 1989), a relationship that is statistically better suited to VG than to the multiple cutoff selection model.* The nature of the relationship between scores on a valid test of aptitude and ratings of job performance is illustrated in Figure 2. Given that such a relationship exists, Hunter (1980, 1982) noted that, from a technical standpoint, linear data are better suited to analysis using a VG model than using a model with multiple cutoffs.

3. *More precise information can be reported to employers regarding a testtaker's relative standing in the continuum of aptitude test scores.* Consider in this context Figure 3, and let's suppose that an established and validated cutoff score for selection in a particular occupation using this hypothetical test of aptitude is 155. Examinee X and Examinee Y both meet the cutoff requirement, but Examinee Y is probably better qualified for the job—we say "probably" because there may be exceptions to this general rule, depending on variables such as the specific job's actual demands. Although the score for Examinee X falls below the median score for all testtakers, the score for Examinee Y lies at the high end of the distribution of scores. All other factors being equal, which individual would you prefer to hire if you owned the company? Using a simple cutoff procedure, no distinction with respect to aptitude score would have been made between Examinee X and Examinee Y, provided both scores met the cutoff criterion.

4. *VG better assists employers in their efforts to hire qualified employees.* Studies such as one conducted at the Philip Morris Company suggest that a significant increase in the rate of training success can be expected for employees hired using a selection procedure that uses VG as compared with employees hired by other means (Warmke, 1984).

Is VG the answer to all personnel selection problems? Certainly not. VG is simply one rationale for justifiably avoiding

(continued)

Validity Generalization
and the GATB *(continued)*

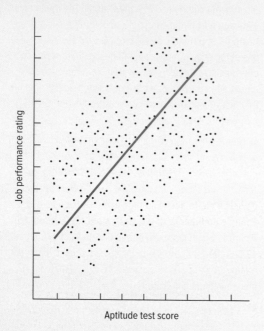

Figure 2
**The Linear Relationship Between Aptitude Test Scores
and Job Performance Ratings**

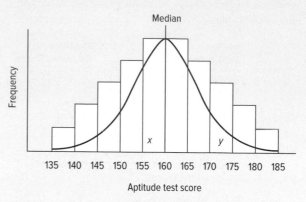

Figure 3
Results of a Hypothetical Aptitude Test

the time and expense of conducting a separate validation study for every single test with every possible group of testtakers under every possible set of circumstances—and usually with too few subjects to achieve meaningful findings. Note, however, that with the convenience of VG come many concerns about the efficacy of the procedures employed. And although we have devoted a fair amount of time to acquainting you with this important concept in the personnel selection literature, it is equally important for you to be aware that a number of technical issues with respect to VG are currently being debated in the professional literature.

You will recall that, in the development of VG as applied to personnel selection, Hunter and his colleagues used a process called meta-analysis to cumulate findings across a number of studies. One important aspect of this work involved statistically correcting for the small sample sizes that occurred in the studies analyzed. The types of procedures used in such a process, and the types of interpretations that legitimately can be made as a result, have been the subject of a number of critical analyses of VG. The amount of unexplained variance that remains even after statistical corrections for differences in sample size (Cascio, 1987), the unknown influence of a

potential restriction-of-range problem with respect to subject self-selection (Cronbach, 1984), objections about using employer ratings as a criterion (Burke, 1984), and the fact that alternative models may explain variation in validity coefficients as well as the cross-situational consistency model (James et al., 1986) are some of the technical issues that have been raised with respect to the use of VG (see also Zedeck & Cascio, 1984). With specific reference to VG as applied to use with the GATB, one might inquire further: What problems arise when more than 12,000 occupations are grouped into five job families? Is it really meaningful to place an occupation such as truck driver in the same job family as secretary?

Clearly, much remains to be learned about how VG can most effectively be brought to bear on problems related to personnel testing. Difficult questions—some psychometric, others that relate more to societal values—will have to be addressed. A detailed critique of VG, beginning with its logic and ending with its application, can be found in Murphy (2003).

Compounding the task of fairly evaluating VG is a litany of variables that are neither psychometric in nature nor directly related to values. Included here are such variables as the strength of the economy, the size of the available labor pool, the experience of the available labor pool, the general desirability of specific jobs, and the salaries offered for various kinds of work. Whether one looks favorably or not at the government's experimentation with VG in personnel selection, it seems reasonable to assume that there is much to be learned in the process, and the field of personnel selection may ultimately profit from the experience.

is limited by the reliability of the measures. Although the GATB had adequate test-retest reliability (around .81), the likely poor reliability of supervisory ratings might very well have depressed the GATB's validity coefficient. Such depression of a validity coefficient could be expected to occur for any test designed to predict job performance that is validated against supervisors' ratings (Hartigan & Wigdor, 1989). Of course, even predictors with modest criterion validity can improve personnel selection decisions. Thus, despite the low criterion validity coefficients, the GATB was widely viewed as a valid means of selecting employees.

The NAS recommendation to continue the practice of race norming the test may have done more to fan the flames of controversy than to quell them. In July 1990, the Department of Labor proposed a two-year suspension in the use of the GATB, during which time the efficacy of the test and its scoring procedures would be further researched. The legality of the practice of race norming had also become a heated topic of debate by that time (Baydoun & Neuman, 1992; Delahunty, 1988). The question of whether race norming of the GATB should continue became moot after Congress passed the Civil Rights Act of 1991, a law that made the practice of race norming illegal.

Today the GATB is still in use by the U.S. Employment Service. Reports to employers are no longer race-normed; the raw scores of people from all racial groups are now converted to interpretable standard scores using the same norms. Still, concerns linger regarding the equity of the test's scoring and cut-score practice as they affect various racial groups (Gardner & Deadrick, 2008). In addition to its potential applied value, the GATB remains a valuable resource for researchers in areas as diverse as rehabilitation counseling (Reid et al., 2007), theory validation (Farrell & McDaniel, 2001), and theory extension (Rashkovky, 2006).

The quest for viable predictors of occupational success has led researchers beyond the study of interests and aptitudes. One area that has been explored quite extensively could be summed up in one word: *personality.*

> **JUST THINK . . .**
>
> Will a person who is outgoing and highly creative find happiness in a career as a data entry technician at a rebate fulfillment center? If not, what type of career is the "best fit" for this type of person? What makes you think so?

Measures of Personality

Just thinking about the questions raised in our *Just Think* compels one to consider the role of personality in career choice. When researchers consider such questions, they may seek answers in a study that includes the administration of a personality test. Let's mention at the outset that the use of personality measures in employment settings is a topic that has generated a fair amount of debate in the scholarly literature. Concern has been expressed about attempts by employees, or prospective employees (i.e., job applicants) to "fake good" on such tests (Birkeland et al., 2006). Such attempts may introduce unanticipated error into the process (Arthur et al., 2001; Mueller-Hanson et al., 2003) and negatively influence selection decisions (Rosse et al., 1998). On the other side of the coin is the view that personality measures are not necessarily fakable (Hogan et al., 2007; Pace & Borman, 2006) and that the collected data is still viable even when attempts at faking occur (Hough, 1998; Ones et al., 1996). Proponents of the use of personality tests in the workplace argue that they have, in some respects, greater utility than cognitive ability tests (Hogan & Roberts, 2001).

Although there are many personality tests, some will be more appropriate for the task at hand than others. For example, the MMPI-2-RF, widely used in clinical settings, may have limited application in the context of career counseling. Other personality tests, such as the Guilford-Zimmerman Temperament Survey and the Edwards Personal Preference Schedule, may be preferred because the measurements they yield tend to be better related to the specific variables under study. Today, two of the most widely used personality tests in the workplace are the NEO PI-R (previously described in Chapter 11 and discussed at length on the companion website to this text) and the Myers-Briggs Type Indicator (MBTI). Following a brief discussion of studies that approach career- and occupation-related questions at the level of the *trait*, we discuss the MBTI and consider such questions at the level of personality *type*.

Measuring personality traits | Personality assessment in the context of employment-related research or counseling might begin with the administration of a test designed to measure Costa and McCrae's (1992b) Big Five, Tellegen's (1985) Big Three, Holland's Big Six, or some other (Big, Little, or Medium) number of traits or types according to a particular conceptualization of personality.[2] The researcher will then analyze the personality test data in terms of how they compare with other job- or career-related variables.

Most of the research cited above employed Costa and McCrae's (1992b) NEO PI-R. In fact, this test probably is the most widely used today. There are, however, more specialized types of instruments that also fall under the general heading of personality test. For example, we may speak of an **integrity test,** specifically designed to predict employee theft, honesty, adherence to established procedures, and/or potential for violence. Such narrowly defined personality tests used in the context of employment-related research and practice have been characterized as *criterion-focused occupational personality scales,* abbreviated as "COPS" (Ones & Viswesvaran, 2001).

Integrity tests may be used to screen new employees as well as to keep honest those already hired. The use of such tests has increased dramatically with the passage of legislation prohibiting the use of polygraphs (lie detectors) in most employment settings. The trend is away from lengthy paper-and-pencil questionnaires toward measures that can be electronically administered quickly and efficiently. One such measure is the Applicant Potential Inventory (API), which can be administered by computer (online or offline), telephone, or fax. Jones et al. (2002) described the development of this test as well as research designed to explore its psychometric soundness.

Sackett et al. (1989) dichotomized integrity tests into *overt integrity tests* (which may straightforwardly ask the examinee questions like "Do you always tell the truth?") and *personality-based measures,* which resemble in many ways objective personality inventories. Items on the latter type of test may be far more subtle than on the former. The lack of face validity in such personality-based measures may work to the advantage of the test user in terms of obtaining integrity test responses that well, "have integrity." After all, how many people that are motivated to get a job would admit to lying, cheating, and stealing? Responses to items on the personality-based measures are likely to be interpreted with reference to the responses of groups of people known to have or lack integrity (as defined by the particular test).

JUST THINK . . .

Do integrity tests and reviews of past records penalize job-seekers who may have recognized that what they did in the past was wrong and have since "changed their ways" for the better?

Whether integrity tests measure what they purport to measure is debatable. Reviews of the validity of such measures have ranged from mixed (American Psychological Association, 1991; Sackett & Harris, 1984; Sackett et al., 1989) to positive (DePaulo, 1994; Honts, 1994; Sackett, 1994; Saxe, 1994). Perhaps the fairest conclusion from this literature is that when the test has been professionally developed, it stands an excellent chance of meeting acceptable standards of validity. *Model Guidelines for Preemployment Integrity Testing Programs,* a document developed by the Association of Personnel Test Publishers (APTP, 1990), addresses many of the issues surrounding integrity tests, including issues relating to test development, administration, scoring, interpretation, confidentiality, public statements regarding the tests, and test-marketing practices. Specific guidelines in these areas are provided, and the responsibilities of test users and publishers are discussed (see Jones et al., 1990, for an overview).

---

2. Holland (1999) made clear that, for him, interest inventories *are* personality inventories. For this reason, it is appropriate to mention Holland's work in discussing interest or personality assessment as an aid to career counseling.

Beyond issues regarding the validity of integrity tests lie broader questions about various aspects of the use of such tests (Camara & Schneider, 1994). For example, is privacy invaded when a prospective employee is asked to sit for such a test? Can such tests be used to support discrimination practices? Should such tests be used alone or in combination with other measurement procedures as a basis for granting or denying employment? It is interesting that White (1984) suggested that preemployment honesty testing may induce negative work-related attitudes. Having to undergo such a test may be interpreted by prospective employees as evidence of high levels of employee theft—paradoxically resulting in a new and higher norm of stealing by employees.

Measuring personality types　How could anyone have foreseen in 1915 that the prospect of having Clarence Myers as a son-in-law would eventually lead Katharine Cook Briggs (see Figure 15–3) down a path that would culminate in the creation of an enduring measure of personality type?

Isabel Briggs Myers and her mother, Katharine Cook Briggs—two women with no formal training in psychology or assessment—were inspired by the writings of Carl Jung (1923) and his ideas about different psychological types. In part, that inspiration was instrumental in the creation of the MBTI (Myers & Briggs, 1943/1962), a test used to classify assessees by psychological type and to shed light on "basic differences in the ways human beings take in information and make decisions" (McCaulley, 2000, p. 117).

From a psychometric perspective, the test has earned mixed reviews. A meta-analysis of published studies did indicate that the test and its scales tended to be internally consistent and stable over time, although some variations were observed (Capraro & Capraro, 2002). Still, many assessment professionals have expressed serious concerns about the MBTI on psychometric and related grounds (Arnau et al., 2003; Girelli & Stake, 1993; Harvey & Murry, 1994; Lorr, 1991; Martin & Bartol, 1986; Pittenger, 1993; Vacha-Haase & Thompson, 2002; Zumbo &

Figure 15–3
Briggs & Myers: A Mother-Daughter Team of Test Developers

Katharine Cook Briggs (left) and Isabel Briggs Myers (right) created the Myers-Briggs Type Indicator. Katharine developed an interest in individual differences in 1915 upon being introduced to her future son-in-law, Clarence Myers. For Katharine, Clarence seemed different in fundamental ways from other members of the Briggs family. Owing in part to her desire to better understand these differences, Katharine created a category of psychological types. Years later, Isabel would put her mother's ideas to the test—literally.
Photos courtesy of the Myers & Briggs Foundation

Taylor, 1993). Regardless of such criticism, the test remains very popular, especially among counselors and organizational consultants.

The relationship between personality and work performance   Most people probably believe that there is a relationship between personality and work performance. However, establishing such a relationship through scholarly research is no easy matter. In fact, owing largely to the methodological obstacles in conducting such research, many researchers have failed to discover a relationship (Barrick et al., 2001). One issue in this kind of research relates to how *work performance* is defined. There is no single metric that can be used for all occupations. For some occupations, such as sales, an objective measure such as "the dollar value of new revenue generated over the course of a calendar year" can be defined. For other occupations, the measure used might not be as objective. For example, the measure relied on might be supervisor ratings—a measure that to varying degrees is idiosyncratic, subjective, and subject to the biases of the supervisors doing the rating.

In addition to issues concerning work performance, there are issues regarding which aspect of personality to measure; different aspects of personality have presumably greater relevance for different occupations. However, studying work performance with regard to Big Five traits has led to some useful findings. Barrick et al. (2001) conducted a **second-order meta-analysis** (a meta-analysis that summarizes other meta-analyses) and determined that in general, high *Conscientiousness* scores were correlated with good work performance, and high *Neuroticism* scores were correlated with poor work performance, *Extraversion* was also positively correlated with good work performance—but why? In follow-up research, Barrick et al. (2002) found that extraverted individuals were more motivated to achieve status, which in turn, predicted higher work performance ratings. Clearly, the relationship between personality and work performance is not straightforward; some personality traits seem helpful with regard to some, but not all types of jobs. Research in the area has increasingly looked at the complex interplay between personality and other variables affecting work performance, such as the perceived work environment (Kacmar et al., 2009; Westerman & Simmons, 2007) and the overall culture of the company (Anderson et al., 2008).

Another intriguing question raised by researchers is: "Does the emotional disposition of children have anything to do with how satisfied they are with their jobs as adults?" If you think the question itself is somewhat surprising, hold on to your hats when we tell you that the answer to the question (a resounding *yes*) is even more surprising. Using data from three separate longitudinal studies, Staw et al. (1986) found that dispositional data obtained in infancy predicted job-related attitudes over a time span of some 50 years. Although the interpretation of the data in this study has been questioned, it generally has received support from other researchers (Arvey et al., 1989; House et al., 1996; Judge et al., 1999, 2002; Motowidlo, 1996). It may be that one's temperament mediates emotionally significant events, including those at work, which in turn influence one's level of job satisfaction (Weiss & Cropanzano, 1996).

The findings cited here—and, more generally, the use of personality tests in any employment-related context—have their critics (see, for example, Ghiselli, 1973; Hollenbeck & Whitener, 1988; Kinslinger, 1966; Schmitt et al., 1984). Still, most researchers would probably concede that valuable job- and career-related information can be developed through the study of the assessment of personality (Fontanna, 2000; Ones et al., 2007; see also Judge & Hurst, 2008; Maurer et al., 2008).

JUST THINK . . .

From the perspective of an employer, might there be a "downside" to seeking one specific *type* of employee for a particular position?

Other Measures

Numerous other tools of assessment may be used in career planning and pre-employment contexts, even though not specifically designed for that purpose. For example, the Checklist of

Adaptive Living Skills (CALS; Morreau & Bruininks, 1991) surveys the life skills needed to make a successful transition from school to work. Organized into four broad domains (Personal Living Skills, Home Living Skills, Community Living Skills, and Employment Skills), this test evaluates 794 life skills. The checklist is designed for use with assessees of any age. According to the manual, the individual completing the checklist must have had the opportunity to observe the assessee for at least three months in natural settings. Assessees are judged to be *independent* with regard to a specific skill if they perform the task with good quality at least 75% of the time when needed and without reminder. This criterion-based instrument may be particularly useful in career and preemployment counseling with members of special populations.

Researchers are interested in the role of culture in various aspects of assessment for employment (Blustein & Ellis, 2000; Hofstede, 1998; Leong & Hartung, 2000; Ponterotto et al., 2000; Rotundo & Sackett, 1999; Ryan et al., 2000; Sandoval et al., 1998; Subich, 1996). According to Meyers (1994), the fact that a new job can sometimes result in a kind of "culture shock" prompted the creation of an instrument called the Cross-Cultural Adaptability Inventory (CCAI; Kelley & Meyers, 1992). The CCAI is a self-administered and self-scored instrument designed to provide information on the testtaker's ability to adapt to other cultures. Testtakers respond to 50 items written in a six-point Likert format. The test yields information about one's readiness to adapt to new situations, tolerate ambiguity, maintain one's personal identity in new surroundings, and interact with people from other cultures. The report is organized into information with regard to four factors thought to be relevant to cross-cultural adaptability: Emotional Resilience, Flexibility/Openness, Perceptual Acuity, and Personal Autonomy. The test may hold value in evaluating readiness to take a job or to be relocated overseas. One study showed that the Emotional Resilience and Personal Autonomy scales were positively related to number of international assignments (Nguyen et al., 2010).

Perhaps one of the most important instruments of assessment relevant to a career decision can be a questionnaire devised by assessees themselves, one that is *not* designed for administration to a prospective employee. Rather, it is written by the assessee and designed for administration to a person established in the career the assessee is contemplating. Laker (2002) proposed that students contemplating a career choice think of more than one career they would like to enter. Students should next identify resource persons already in those careers who can address the students' beliefs and assumptions about the nature of work life in that career. Such resource people can be identified by informal means such as "asking around" as well as more formally by the use of a reference work such as the *Encyclopedia of Associations* (Hunt, 2005). Find the association to which the desired resource person belongs, and then contact that association for help in identifying someone local who is willing to assist. In preparation for the meeting, students list their beliefs and assumptions about the career and then translate that list into questions, such as those presented in Table 15–1.

All the tools of assessment we have discussed so far have application not only in career entry but also in career transition. One test specifically designed for use with people contemplating a career change is the Career Transitions Inventory (CTI; Heppner et al., 1994). The purpose of this test is to assess psychological resources during the process of career transition. For the purposes of the test, *career transition* was operationally defined as *task change* (a shift to other types of tasks but essentially the same job), *position change* (a shift in jobs with the same employer), or *occupation change* (a shift in duties and work settings). The test authors presented evidence for the test's reliability as well as evidence they described as "promising" for the construct validity of this instrument.

Career transition is one variety of what could be referred to as an *exit strategy* for a person in a particular career or business. Another type of exit strategy is retirement. The decision to retire is momentous and multifaceted—and one that has also been explored by means of instruments of assessment. A retirement decision should not be made on the basis of a single criterion such as global satisfaction or financial security (Parnes & Less, 1985). To persons considering retirement, counselors may offer assistance in the form of probing interviews and

Table 15–1

Sample Questions Derived from Students' Beliefs and Assumptions

- What background, both educational and professional, is needed to enter this field?
- Briefly describe your career path and the steps you took to get here.
- What do you do on a typical day?
- In what industries and companies would such careers and jobs exist, or what industries and companies would be best for this career?
- What are the sources of stress in your job?
- If you could, what would you change about your job?
- How does one get started or break into this career or job?
- What kind of lifestyle does such a career or job provide or allow?
- What are the compensation range and benefits for this career or job?
- How often are you required to travel, and for what reasons do you travel?
- Would this type of career or job typically require relocation?
- Do you enjoy your work?
- What advancement opportunities are there for individuals in this field?
- Do you find your job or career satisfying and challenging?
- What special skills are required for a position like yours?
- What is the average number of hours worked in a typical work week?
- What types of skills are necessary to be successful in?
- What should I do or where should I go to acquire these needed skills?
- What is the most challenging aspect of your job?
- What is the most satisfying aspect of your job? What is the least satisfying aspect of your job?
- How would this career impact one's family?
- How important are grades?
- How is your performance evaluated?
- How does your career affect your life outside of work? Spouse? Social? Spiritual?
- What is the job market like in this particular professional area? What do you think it will be like 5–10 years from now?
- What recommendations would you make to me? What would you do if you were me?
- If you were me, who else would you suggest that I talk to? Why would you suggest that person? May I use your name in contacting that person?
- Describe your typical work week.

Source: Laker (2002).

by administering various measures that assess life satisfaction, goal-directedness, leisure satisfaction, and interpersonal support. More specifically, the Goal Instability Scale (Robbins & Patton, 1985), the Life Satisfaction Index A (Neugarten et al., 1961), the Leisure Satisfaction Scale (Beard & Ragheb, 1980), and the Interpersonal Support Evaluations List (Cohen et al., 1985) are some of the instruments that may provide valuable data. Floyd et al. (1992) developed the Retirement Satisfaction Inventory to help assess adjustment to retirement. Of course, Big Five personality traits may also have predictive value when it comes to satisfaction with retirement. In one study, *Extraversion* and *Emotional stability* were found to be positively related to retirement satisfaction (Löckenhoff et al., 2009).

JUST THINK . . .

How might data from personality tests be useful in counseling an individual who is contemplating retirement?

Tests and other tools of assessment may be used by businesses and other organizations to assist in staffing and other personnel-related decisions. Let's now see how.

Screening, Selection, Classification, and Placement

In the context of employment, **screening** refers to a relatively superficial process of evaluation based on certain minimal standards, criteria, or requirements. For example, a municipal fire department may screen on the basis of certain minimal requirements for height, weight, physical health, physical strength, and cognitive ability before admitting candidates to a training program for firefighters. The government may use a group-administered test of intelligence to screen out people unsuited for military service or to identify intellectually gifted recruits for special assignments.

Selection refers to a process whereby each person evaluated for a position will be either accepted or rejected for that position. By contrast, **classification** does not imply acceptance or rejection but rather a rating, categorization, or "pigeonholing" with respect to two or more criteria. The military, for example, classifies personnel with respect to security clearance on the basis of variables such as rank, personal history of political activity, and known associations. As a result of such evaluations, one individual might be granted access to documents labeled *Secret* whereas another individual might be granted access to documents labeled *Top Secret.*

Like classification, *placement* need not carry any implication of acceptance or rejection. **Placement** is a disposition, transfer, or assignment to a group or category that may be made on the basis of one criterion. If, for example, you took a college-level course while still in high school, the score you earned on the advanced placement test in that subject area may have been the sole criterion used to place you in an appropriate section of that college course upon your acceptance to college.

Businesses, academic institutions, the military, and other organizations regularly screen, select, classify, or place individuals. A wide array of tests can be used as aids to decision making. Measures of ability, aptitude, interest, and personality may all be of value, depending on the demands of the particular decision. In the high-profile world of professional sports, where selection errors can be extremely costly, psychological tests may be used to help assess whether a draft choice will live up to his potential (Gardner, 2001) and to measure sundry other aspects of athletic competition (Allen, 2008; Bougard et al., 2008; Brotherhood, 2008; Donohue et al., 2007; Fox, 2008; Gee et al., 2010; Gordon, 2008; Stoeber et al., 2008; Webbe, 2008). Of course, for more everyday types of employment decision making—and especially at the pre-employment stage—some of the most common tools of assessment include the letter of application and the résumé, the job application form, the letter of recommendation, and the interview.

The Résumé and the Letter of Application

There is no single, standard résumé; they can be "as unique as the individuals they represent" (Cohen, 1994, p. 394). Typically, information related to one's work objectives, qualifications, education, and experience is included on a résumé. A companion cover letter to a résumé, called a letter of application, lets a job applicant demonstrate motivation, businesslike writing skills, and his or her unique personality.

Of course, neither a résumé nor a letter of application is likely to be the sole vehicle through which employment is secured. Both of these documents are usually stepping-stones to personal interviews or other types of evaluations. On the other hand, the employer, the personnel psychologist, or some other individual reading the applicant's résumé and cover letter may use these documents as a basis for *rejecting* an application. The cover letter and the résumé may be analyzed for details such as quality of written communication, perceived sincerity, and appropriateness of the applicant's objectives, education, motivation, and prior experience. From the perspective of the evaluator, much the same is true of another common tool of assessment in employment settings, the application form.

The Application Form

Application forms may be thought of as biographical sketches that supply employers with information pertinent to the acceptability of job candidates. In addition to demographic information (such as name and address), details about educational background, military service, and previous work experience may be requested. Application forms may contain a section devoted to contact information in which applicants list, for example, home phone, cell phone, e-mail address, and a website (if applicable). Some classic questions relevant to a traditional application form are presented in Table 15–2. The guiding philosophy is that each item in the form be relevant either to consideration for employment or for contacting the applicant. From the perspective of the employer, the application form is a useful tool for quick screening.

Letters of Recommendation

Another tool useful in the preliminary screening of applicants is the letter of recommendation (Arvey, 1979; Glueck, 1978). Such letters may be a unique source of detailed information about the applicant's past performance, the quality of the applicant's relationships with peers, and so forth. Of course, such letters are not without their drawbacks. It is no secret that applicants solicit letters from those they believe will say only positive things about them. Another possible drawback to letters of recommendation is the variance in the observational and writing skills of the letter writers.

In research that employed application files for admission to graduate school in psychology, it was found that the same applicant might variously be described as "analytically oriented, reserved, and highly motivated" or "free-spirited, imaginative, and outgoing," depending on the letter writer's perspective. As the authors of that study pointed out, "Although favorable recommendations may be intended in both cases, the details of and bases for such recommendations are varied" (Baxter et al., 1981, p. 300). Efforts to minimize the drawbacks inherent in the open-ended letter of recommendation have sometimes taken the form of "questionnaires of recommendation" wherein former employers, professors, and other letter writers respond to structured questions concerning the applicant's prior performance. Some questionnaires employ a forced-choice format designed to force respondents to make negative as well as positive statements about the applicant.

Although originally written to provide a prospective employer with an opinion about an applicant, some letters of reference now serve the function of an archival record—one that provides a glimpse of an unfortunate chapter of American history and the prevailing prejudices of an era. Winston (1996, 1998) documented how letters of reference written by prominent

> **JUST THINK . . .**
>
> Put yourself in the position of an employer. Now discuss how much "weight" you assign letters of recommendation relative to test data and other information about the applicant. Explain the basis of your "weightings."

Table 15–2

Checklist for an Application Form Item

1. Is the item necessary for identifying the applicant?
2. Is it necessary for screening out those who are ineligible under the company's basic hiring policies?
3. Does it help to decide whether the candidate is qualified?
4. Is it based on analysis of the job or jobs for which applicants will be selected?
5. Has it been pretested on the company's employees and found to correlate with success?
6. Will the information be used? How?
7. Is the application form the proper place to ask for it?
8. To what extent will answers duplicate information to be obtained at another step in the selection procedure—for example, through interviews, tests, or medical examinations?
9. Is the information needed for selection at all, or should it be obtained at induction or even later?
10. Is it probable that the applicants' replies will be reliable?
11. Does the question violate any applicable federal or state legislation?

Source: Ahern (1949).

psychologists in the United States for Jewish psychology students and psychologists from the 1920s through the 1950s followed a common practice of identifying the job candidates as Jews. The letters went on to disclose whether or not, in the letter-writer's opinion, the candidate evidenced the "objectionable traits" thought to characterize Jews. These letters support a compelling argument that, although American history tends to treat anti-Semitism as a problem from which European immigrants fled, negative stereotypes associated with being Jewish were very much a part of the cultural landscape in the United States.

Interviews

Interviews, whether individual or group in nature, provide an occasion for the face-to-face exchange of information. Like other interviews, the employment interview may fall anywhere on a continuum from highly structured, with uniform questions being asked to all, to highly unstructured, with the questions left largely to the interviewer's discretion. As with all interviews, the interviewer's biases and prejudices may creep into the evaluation and influence the outcome. The order of interviewing might also affect outcomes by reason of contrast effects. For example, an average applicant may appear better or less qualified depending on whether the preceding candidate was particularly poor or outstanding. Factors that may affect the outcome of an employment interview, according to Schmitt (1976), include the backgrounds, attitudes, motivations, perceptions, expectations, knowledge about the job, and interview behavior of both the interviewer and the interviewee. Situational factors, such as the nature of the job market, may also affect the outcome of the interview.

Portfolio Assessment

In the context of industrial/organizational assessment, portfolio assessment entails an evaluation of an individual's work sample for the purpose of making some screening, selection, classification, or placement decision. A video journalist applying for a position at a new television station may present a portfolio of video clips, including rehearsal footage and outtakes. An art director for a magazine may present a portfolio of art to a prospective employer, including rough drafts and notes about how to solve a particular design-related problem. In portfolio assessment, the assessor may have the opportunity (1) to evaluate many work samples created by the assessee, (2) to obtain some understanding of the assessee's work-related thought processes and habits through an analysis of the materials from rough draft to finished form, and (3) to question the assessee further regarding various aspects of his or her work-related thinking and habits. The result may be a more complete picture of the prospective employee at work in the new setting than might otherwise be available.

JUST THINK . . .

What are some things that a portfolio *fails* to tell an employer about a prospective employee?

Performance Tests

As its name implies, a performance test requires assessees to demonstrate certain skills or abilities under a specified set of circumstances. The typical objective of such an exercise is to obtain a *job-related performance sample*. For example, a word-processing test as a prerequisite for employment as a word processor provides a prospective employer with a job-related performance sample.

Boundaries between performance, achievement, and aptitude tests are often blurred, especially when the work sample entails taking a standardized test of skill or ability. For example, the Seashore Bennett Stenographic Proficiency Test is a standardized measure of stenographic competence. The test materials include a recording in which a voice dictates a series of letters and manuscripts that the assessee must transcribe in shorthand and then type. The recorded directions provide a uniform clarity of voice and rate of dictation. The test protocol may well be viewed as an achievement test, an aptitude test, or a performance sample, depending upon the context of its use.

⬥ JUST THINK . . .

In general, what types of performance assessments lend themselves more to a virtual reality context than to "real-life" reality?

An instrument designed to measure clerical aptitude and skills is the Minnesota Clerical Test (MCT). The MCT comprises two subtests, Number Comparison and Name Comparison. Each subtest contains 200 items, with each item consisting of either a pair of names or a pair of numbers (depending upon the subtest) to be compared. For each item, the assessee's task is to check whether the two names (or numbers) in the pair are the same or different. A score is obtained simply by subtracting the number of incorrect responses from the number of correct ones. Because speed and accuracy in clerical work are important to so many employers, this deceptively simple test has been used for decades as an effective screening tool in the workplace. It can be administered and scored quickly and easily, and the pattern of errors or omissions on this timed test may suggest whether the testtaker values speed over accuracy or vice versa.

The kind of special equipment necessary for performance tests varies widely. During World War II, the assessment staff of the Office of Strategic Services (OSS) was charged with selecting personnel to serve as American secret agents, saboteurs, propaganda experts, and other such job titles for assignments overseas. In addition to interviews, personality tests, and other paper-and-pencil tests, the OSS administered situational performance tests. In this chapter's *Everyday Psychometrics*, we learn that data from that historic and groundbreaking project still has much to teach us today about personnel selection.

A commonly used performance test in the assessment of business leadership ability is the **leaderless group technique.** Communication skills, problem-solving ability, the ability to cope with stress, and other skills can also be assessed economically by a group exercise in which the participants' task is to work together in the solution of some problem or the achievement of some goal. As group members interact, the assessors make judgments with respect to questions such as "Who is the leader?" and "What role do other members play in this group?" The answers to such questions will no doubt figure into decisions concerning the individual assessee's future position in the organization.

Another performance test frequently used to assess managerial ability, organizational skills, and leadership potential is the **in-basket technique.** This technique simulates the way a manager or an executive deals with an in-basket filled with mail, memos, announcements, and various other notices and directives. Assessees are instructed that they have only a limited amount of time, usually two or three hours, to deal with all the items in the basket (more commonly a manila envelope). Through posttest interviews and an examination of the way the assessee handled the materials, assessors can make judgments concerning variables such as organizing and planning, problem solving, decision making, creativity, leadership, and written communication skills.

Testing and assessment for aviators and astronauts Almost from the time that aviation became a reality, a need has existed to research physical and psychological factors in aviation. One of the earliest of such studies was conducted by the British physician Henry Graeme Anderson. Anderson enlisted in the military at the outbreak of World War I and wound up being stationed at the British flying school in Vendome, France, where he held the post of flight surgeon. Although not required to do so, he earned a pilot's license himself. He later would write among the first detailed accounts regarding fitness of recruits to fly, how flying conditions could be improved, and how aerial accidents could be prevented (Anderson, 1919).

The Selection of Personnel for the Office of Strategic Services (OSS): Assessment and Psychometrics in Action*

One of the major turning points in the history of psychological assessment came to pass under conditions far from the university psychometrics laboratory during a time of great world crisis. The psychologists involved in this effort were brought together not by a research funding opportunity or shared academic interest but rather by a forward-thinking U.S. Army General by the name of William "Wild Bill" Donovan (Waller, 2011).

General Donovan, who had served in World War I and was a recipient of the Congressional Medal of Honor, was asked by President Franklin D. Roosevelt to create an intelligence service for the United States. The objectives of the new agency included gathering information about the intentions and activities of this country's World War II (WW II) adversaries, as well as executing operations aimed at disrupting, sabotaging, and otherwise neutralizing enemy actions. In order to fulfill the agency's ambitious and unique objectives, a corps of officers would have to be recruited and trained. Ideally, these newly recruited officers would be intelligent, brave, resourceful, emotionally resilient, and creative. They would have to possess excellent interpersonal skills, as well as leadership potential. Identifying candidates for such positions represented a "real-world" problem that would ultimately be addressed by means of a thoughtfully devised psychological assessment program (Handler, 2001).

The agency that General Donovan created, now viewed as the forerunner to both the Central Intelligence Agency (CIA) and the US Army Special Forces, was the Office of Strategic Services (OSS). The team of psychologists that was assembled to create the OSS's novel assessment program for personnel selection could be characterized as "all-star"; it contained many of the best and brightest minds in clinical psychology at the time. The model of assessment and personnel selection that was ultimately devised by these experts would break new ground then, and survive to the present day.

The Goal of the OSS Assessment Program

The unique, time-pressured charge given to the OSS assessment staff was to develop ". . . a system of procedures which would

*This Everyday Psychometrics was guest-authored by Mark F. Lenzenweger of the Department of Psychology of the State University of New York at Binghamton, and the Department of Psychiatry at Weill Cornell Medical College. Read the complete text of this essay, including Dr. Lenzenweger's firsthand account of an analysis of OSS data using modern methods, in OOBAL-15-B4 at https://mhhe.cohentesting9.

reveal the personalities of OSS recruits to the extent providing ground for sufficiently reliable predictions of their usefulness to the organization during the remaining years of the war" (OSS Assessment Staff, 1948, p. 8). But what would define "usefulness to the organization"? What specific aspects of personality should be the focus of the assessments? What skills were deemed essential for a successful OSS officer? What psychological attributes could reasonably be assessed in the space of a relatively short visit to the assessment facility? And what about the "bottom-line" question of how to go about selecting candidates who were a good fit with the varied demands and complex tasks that would likely be required of OSS intelligence officers?

A number of factors (such as the novelty of the OSS function and the high variability across job descriptions) conspired to make the task of the OSS one of the most complicated behavioral prediction challenges ever encountered in the history of clinical psychology. One alternative considered to meet the challenge was to break down various OSS jobs into their component psychological attributes required for success. In the end, however, the OSS Assessment Staff set what they characterized as **organismic assessment** (evaluation of the total person) as their objective. No single psychological test would measure isolated psychological attributes. Instead, a series of varied tests and tasks would be administered over the course of several sessions. Then candidates would be evaluated on the basis of data derived from the full range of assessments, considered as a whole.

A trip to the country

Beginning in December of 1943, candidates from military bases around the country, recruited by various means, reported to a red brick building in Washington, DC. The converted old schoolhouse contained the Schools and Training Headquarters of the OSS. Each of the candidates had been provided with only minimal detail about why they were being considered for special duty, and what they actually might be doing. Upon arrival, candidates were interviewed, given a code name, and asked to surrender their personal belongings and the uniforms they were wearing in exchange for plain, government-issued civilian attire. Then, it was off to the country (not far from where Dulles International Airport stands today) for three days at a facility

(continued)

The Selection of Personnel for the Office of Strategic Services (OSS): Assessment and Psychometrics in Action *(continued)*

informally referred to as "the farm," and more formally designated by the OSS as "Station S."

The days the candidates spent in the country were anything but a "walk in the park." There, candidates were interviewed by psychologists, completed questionnaires, and sat for paper-and-pencil tests. Less traditionally, assessments also included things like evaluation of their performance in enduring a stressful (mock) interrogation. There were physically demanding challenges that drew on their mental ingenuity and physical stamina. Candidates were also presented with a series of unusual situational performance tasks. For example, in the "Construction Situation," candidates were asked to build a small wooden structure with assistants who (deliberately) provided little assistance. The unhelpful assistants (named "Buster" and "Kippy") were actually members of the assessment team eyeful of the candidates' response to the frustration. In fact, the entire time that candidates spent at the farm, whether involved in an assigned task or just casually interacting with each other, they were almost always being observed and evaluated by the assessors.

The three days of intensive observation of the candidates resulted in mounds of notes and other data about the candidates' psychological strengths and weaknesses, creative problem-solving skills, personality style, frustration tolerance levels, and numerous other attributes. At a staff conference, all such information was reviewed, discussed, and, when necessary,

debated (sometimes in heated fashion). If after such discussion and debate a candidate received "conditional approval," then the staff went on to rate the candidate on the following ten dimensions: Motivation for Assignment, Energy and Initiative, Effective Intelligence, Emotional Stability, Social Relations, Leadership, Physical Ability, Security, Observing and Reporting, and Propaganda Skills. An impressionistic assessment of a candidate's integrity was also formulated. The assessment concluded with the preparation of summary sheet and final report for each candidate and a final report was quickly shipped off to OSS Headquarters in Washington, DC. There, a final decision regarding a candidate's status was made by senior OSS staff officials.

The legacy of the OSS assessment program

The OSS assessment program demonstrated the utility of psychological testing and assessment in the selection of officers to function in the intelligence community. However, the legacy of the pioneering efforts of the OSS program extends well beyond the era of the World War II. The modern day use of assessment centers for personnel selection in corporate, organizational, and government settings worldwide is still informed by, if not modeled after, the program first put in place by "Wild Bill" Donovan and his team of all-star psychologists.

Used with permission of Mark F. Lenzenweger.

As military and commercial aviation matured, psychological testing and assessment would typically be undertaken by the powers that be to evaluate the extent to which prospective pilots and other flight personnel (1) had the ability, skills, and aptitude deemed necessary to perform duties; (2) exhibited personality traits deemed desirable for the specific mission (including, for instance, the ability to function effectively as a team member); and (3) were deemed to be free of psychopathology and pressing distractions that would detract from optimal performance. Specially created performance testing would become the norm for persons who sought the responsibility of piloting aircraft (Retzlaff & Gilbertini, 1988) as well as related employment—including, for example, the job of air traffic controller (Ackerman & Kanfer, 1993).

The dawn of the space age in the 1950s brought with it a new set of demands in terms of personnel selection, particularly with regard to the selection of astronauts. New skills, aptitudes, and tolerances would be required for "crews [who] leave the earth in a fragile vehicle to face a hostile and unforgiving environment" (Helmreich, 1983, p. 445)—one in which weightlessness, isolation, and the absence of an escape option were only the tip of the iceberg in terms of powerful challenges to be met and overcome.

The National Aeronautics and Space Administration (NASA) was formed in 1958. In preparation for a manned mission as part of Project Mercury, NASA administered not only batteries of performance tests to evaluate the physical capabilities of prospective astronauts but also batteries of psychological tests. Psychological tests administered included the MMPI, the Rorschach, the TAT, and the WAIS. In general, NASA was looking for candidates who exhibited promise in terms of operational capabilities (in terms of cognitive and psychomotor functioning), motivation, social abilities, and stress tolerance.

Initially, the selection of astronauts and mission specialists were made from the ranks of male military test pilots. Subsequently, however, the composition of crews became more diverse in many respects; women and people from ethnic minorities were brought on board, and the crews became more multinational in nature. As Helmreich et al. (1979) cautioned, a psychological consideration of the social dynamics of such missions would be critical to their success. Others, such as former NASA psychiatrist Patricia Santy, have been critical of the way that the agency uses—or underutilizes, as the case may be—input from psychologists and psychiatrists. In her book on the subject, *Choosing the Right Stuff: The Psychological Selection of Astronauts and Cosmonauts,* Santy (1994) argued that the culture in the space agency would be well advised to give more weight than it traditionally has to expert psychological and psychiatric opinion. Such arguments rise to the fore when NASA personnel make headlines for the wrong reasons (see Figure 15–4).

By the way, video game enthusiasts may be happy to learn that their experiences with *Flight Simulator* and more sophisticated aviation-related software might be put to good use should they ever pursue a career in aviation. Almost since such software has been available, the industry has taken note of it and employed computer simulations in evaluations (Kennedy et al., 1982). This unique variety of performance assessment permits assessors to evaluate assessees' response to a standardized set of tasks and to monitor precisely the time of response within a safe environment.

Figure 15–4
A High-Profile Employment Screening Failure?

On February 5, 2007, astronaut Lisa Nowak was arrested in a bizarre stalking incident. This prompted NASA to conduct an internal review of its extensive program of psychological evaluations for flight personnel.
© Redd Huber-Pool/Getty Images News/Getty Images

The assessment center   A widely used tool in selection, classification, and placement is the **assessment center.** Although it sounds as if it might be a place, the term actually denotes an organizationally standardized procedure for evaluation involving multiple assessment techniques such as paper-and-pencil tests and situational performance tests. The assessment center concept had its origins in the writings of Henry Murray and his associates (1938). Assessment center activities were pioneered by military organizations both in the United States and abroad (Thornton & Byham, 1982).

In 1956, the first application of the idea in an industrial setting occurred with the initiation of the Management Progress Study (MPS) at American Telephone and Telegraph (Bray, 1964). MPS was to be a longitudinal study that would follow the lives of more than 400 telephone company management and non-management personnel. Participants attended a 3-day assessment center in which they were interviewed for two hours. They then took a number of paper-and-pencil tests designed to shed light on cognitive abilities and personality (e.g., the School and College Ability Test and the Edwards Personal Preference Schedule) and participated in individual and group situational exercises (such as the in-basket test and a leaderless group). Additionally, projective tests such as the Thematic Apperception Test and the Sentence Completion Test were administered. All the data on each of the assessees were integrated at a meeting of the assessors, where judgments on a number of dimensions were made. The dimensions, included areas such as administrative skills, interpersonal skills, and career orientation. A complete description of each of the dimensions is presented in a table entitled "Original Management Progress Study Dimensions" available in the Instructor Resources within Connect.

The use of the assessment center method has mushroomed, with many more business organizations relying on it annually for selection, classification, placement, promotion, career training, and early identification of leadership potential. The method has been subject to numerous studies concerning its validity, and the consensus is that the method has much to recommend it (Cohen et al., 1977; Gaugler et al., 1987; Hunter & Hunter, 1984; McEvoy & Beatty, 1989; Schmitt et al., 1984).

Physical Tests

A lifeguard who is visually impaired is seriously compromised in his or her ability to perform the job. A wine taster with damaged taste buds is of little value to a vintner. An aircraft pilot who has lost the use of an arm . . . the point is clear: Physical requirements of a job must be taken into consideration when screening, selecting, classifying, and placing applicants. Depending on the job's specific requirements, a number of physical subtests may be used. Thus, for example, for a job in which a number of components of vision are critical, a test of visual acuity might be administered along with tests of visual efficiency, stereopsis (distance/depth perception), and color blindness. In its most general sense, a **physical test** may be defined as measurement that entails evaluation of one's somatic health and intactness, and observable sensory and motor abilities.

General physical fitness is required in many jobs, such as police work, where successful candidates might one day have to chase a fleeing suspect on foot or defend themselves against a suspect resisting arrest. The tests used in assessing such fitness might include a complete physical examination, tests of physical strength, and a performance test that meets some determined criterion with respect to running speed and agility. Tasks like vaulting some object, stepping through tires, and going through a window frame could be included to simulate running on difficult terrain.

In some instances, an employer's physical requirements for employment are so reasonable and so necessary that they would readily be upheld by any court if challenged. Other physical requirements for employment, however, may fall into a gray area. In general, the law favors physical standards that are both nondiscriminatory and job related.

Also included under the heading of physical tests are tests of sensory intactness or impairment, including tests to measure color blindness, visual acuity, visual depth perception, and auditory acuity. These types of tests are routinely employed in industrial settings in which the ability to perceive color or the possession of reasonably good eyesight or hearing is essential to the job. Additionally, physical techniques have been applied in the assessment of integrity and honesty, as is the case with the polygraph and drug testing.

JUST THINK . . .

"A police officer must meet certain minimum height requirements." Your thoughts?

Drug testing Beyond concerns about traditional physical, emotional, and cognitive job requirements lies great concern about employee drug use. Personnel and human resource managers are increasingly seeking assurance that the people they hire and the staff they currently employ do not and will not use illegal drugs. The dollar amounts vary by source, but estimates of corporate losses in the workplace that are directly or indirectly due to employee drug or alcohol use run into the tens of billions of dollars. Revenue may be lost because of injury to people or animals, damage to products and the environment, or employee absenteeism, tardiness, or sick leave. And no dollar amount can be attached to the tragic loss of life that may result from a drug- or alcohol-related mishap.

In the context of the workplace, a **drug test** may be defined as an evaluation undertaken to determine the presence, if any, of alcohol or other psychotropic substances, by means of laboratory analysis of blood, urine, hair, or other biological specimens. Testing for drug use is a growing practice in corporate America, with nearly half of all major companies conducting drug testing in some form. Applicants for employment may be tested during the selection process, and current employees may be tested as a condition of maintaining employment. Random drug testing (i.e., testing that occurs with no advance warning) is increasingly common in private companies and organizations, although it has been in use for years in government agencies and in the military.

Methods of drug testing vary. One method, the Immunoassay Test, employs the subject's urine to determine the presence or absence of drugs in the body by identifying the metabolized by-products of the drug (metabolites). Although widely used in workplace settings, the test can be criticized for its inability to specify the precise amount of the drug that was taken, when it was taken, and which of several possible drugs in a particular category was taken. Further, there is no way to estimate the degree of impairment that occurred in response to the drug. The Gas Chromatography/Mass Spectrometry (GCMS) Test also examines metabolites in urine to determine the presence or absence of drugs, but it can more accurately specify which drug was used. GCMS technology cannot, however, pinpoint the time at which the drug was taken or the degree of impairment that occurred as a consequence.

JUST THINK . . .

Generally speaking, is random drug testing in the workplace a good thing?

Many employees object to drug testing as a condition of employment and have argued that such testing violates their constitutional rights to privacy and freedom from unreasonable search and seizure. In the course of legal proceedings, a question that emerges frequently is the validity of drug testing. The consequences of **false positives** (an individual tests positively for drug use when in reality there has been no drug use) and **false negatives** (an individual tests negatively for drug use when in reality there has been drug use) in such cases can be momentous. A false positive may result in, among other things, the loss of one's livelihood. A false negative may result in an impaired person working in a position of responsibility and placing others at risk.

Modern laboratory techniques tend to be relatively accurate in detecting telltale metabolites. Error rates are well under 2%. However, laboratory techniques may not always be used correctly. By one estimate, fully 93% of laboratories that do drug testing failed to meet standards designed to reduce human error (Comer, 1993). Error may also occur in the interpretation of results. Metabolites may be identified accurately, but whether they originated in the abuse of some illicit drug or from over-the-counter medication cannot always be determined. To help prevent such confusion, administrators of the urine test typically ask the subject to compile a list of any medications currently being taken. However, not all subjects are willing or able to remember all medications they may have taken. Further, some employees are reluctant to report some prescription medications they may have taken to treat conditions to which any possible social stigma may be attached, such as depression or epilepsy. Additionally, some foods may also produce metabolites that mimic the metabolites of some illegal drugs. For example, metabolites of opiates will be detected following the subject's ingestion of (perfectly legal) poppy seeds (West & Ackerman, 1993).

Another question related to the validity of drug tests concerns the degree to which drugs identified through testing actually affect job performance. Some drugs leave the body very slowly. For example, a person may test positive for marijuana use up to a month after the last exposure to it. Thus, the residue of the drug remains long after any discernible impairment from having taken the drug. By contrast, cocaine leaves the body in only three days. It is possible for a habitual cocaine user to be off the drug for three days, be highly impaired as a result of cocaine withdrawal, yet still test negative for drug use. Thus, neither a positive nor a negative finding with regard to a drug test necessarily means that behavior has or has not been impaired by drug use (Comer, 1993).

An alternative to drug testing involves using performance tests to directly examine impairment. For example, sophisticated video game–style tests of coordination, judgment, and reaction time are available to compare current performance with baseline performance as established on earlier tests. The advantages of these performance tests over drug testing include a more direct assessment of impairment, fewer ethical concerns regarding invasion of privacy, and immediate information about impairment. The latter advantage is particularly vital in preventing potentially impaired individuals from hurting themselves or others.

Cognitive Ability, Productivity, and Motivation Measures

Beyond their use in pre-employment counseling and in the screening, selection, classification, and placement of personnel, tools of assessment are used to accomplish various goals in the workplace. Let's briefly survey some of these varied uses of assessment tools with reference to measures of cognitive ability, productivity, and motivation.

Measures of Cognitive Ability

Selection decisions regarding personnel, as well as other types of selection decisions such as those regarding professional licensure or acceptance for academic training, are often based (at least in part) on performance on tests that tap acquired knowledge as well as various cognitive skills and abilities. In general, cognitive-based tests are popular tools of selection because they have been shown to be valid predictors of future performance (Schmidt & Hunter, 1998). However, along with that impressive track record come a number of potential considerations with regard to diversity issues.

Personnel selection and diversity issues The continued use of tests that tap primarily cognitive abilities and skills for screening, selection, classification, and placement has become controversial. This controversy stems from a well-documented body of evidence that points to consistent group differences on cognitive ability tests. For example, Asians tend to score higher on average than Whites on mathematical and quantitative ability measures, while Whites score higher than Asians on measures of comprehension and verbal ability. On average, Whites also tend to score higher on cognitive ability tests than Blacks and Hispanics. Given that the test scores may differ by as much as 1 standard deviation (Sackett et al., 2001), such differences may have great impact on who gets what job or who is admitted to an institution of higher learning. Average differences between groups on tests of cognitive ability may contribute to limiting diversity.

It is in society's interest to promote diversity in employment settings, in the professions, and in access to education and training. Toward that end, diversity has, in the past, been encouraged by various means. One approach involved using test cut scores established on the basis of group membership. However, there has been a general trend away from efforts that lead to preferential treatment of any group in terms of test scores. This trend is evident in legislation, court actions, and public referenda. For example, the Civil Rights Act of 1991 made it illegal for employers to adjust test scores as a function of group membership. In 1996, Proposition 209 was passed in California, prohibiting the use of group membership as a basis for any selection decision in that state. In that same year, a federal court ruled that race was not a relevant criterion in selecting university applicants (*Hopwood v. State of Texas,* 1996). In the state of Washington, voters approved legislation that banned the use of race as a criterion in college admissions, contracting, and hiring (Verhovek & Ayres, 1998).

How may diversity in the workplace and other settings be achieved while still using tests known to be good predictors of performance and while not building into the selection criteria a preference for any group? Although no single answer to this complex question is likely to satisfy all concerned, there are jobs waiting to be filled and seats waiting to be occupied at educational and training institutions; some strategy for balancing the various interests must be found. One proposal is for developers and users of cognitive tests in the workplace to place greater emphasis on computer-administered evaluations that minimize verbal content and the demand for verbal skills and abilities (Sackett et al., 2001). These researchers further recommended greater reliance on relevant job or life experience as selection criteria. However, Sackett et al. (2001) cautioned that "subgroup differences are not simply artifacts of paper-and-pencil technologies" (p. 316), and it is incumbent upon society at large to effectively address such extra-test issues.

JUST THINK . . .

In what general ways can society best address these extra-test issues?

Productivity

Productivity may be defined simply as output or value yielded relative to work effort made. The term is used here in its broadest sense and is equally applicable to workers who make products and to workers who provide services. If a business endeavor is to succeed, monitoring output with the ultimate goal of maximizing output is essential. Measures of productivity help to define not only where a business is but also what it needs to do to get where it wants to be. A manufacturer of television sets, for example, might find that the people who manufacture the housing are working at optimal efficiency but the people responsible for installing the screens in the cabinets are working at one-half the expected efficiency. A productivity evaluation can help identify the factors responsible for the sagging performance of the screen installers.

Using techniques such as supervisor ratings, interviews with employees, and undercover employees planted in the workshop, management might determine what—or, in particular, who—is responsible for the unsatisfactory performance. Perhaps the most common method of evaluating worker productivity or performance is through the use of rating and ranking procedures by superiors in the organization. One type of ranking procedure used when large numbers of employees are assessed is the **forced distribution technique.** This procedure involves distributing a predetermined number or percentage of assessees into various categories that describe performance (such as *unsatisfactory, poor, fair, average, good, superior*). Another index of on-the-job performance is number of absences within a given period. It typically reflects more poorly on an employee to be absent on, say, 20 separate occasions than on 20 consecutive days as the result of illness.

The **critical incidents technique** (Flanagan & Burns, 1955) involves the supervisor recording positive and negative employee behaviors. The supervisor catalogues the notations according to various categories (e.g., *dependability* or *initiative*) for ready reference when an evaluation needs to be made. Some evidence suggests that a "honeymoon" period of about three months occurs when a new worker starts a job and that supervisory ratings will more truly reflect the worker's performance once that period has passed.

JUST THINK . . .

What might be the long-range consequences of using evaluation techniques that rely on the use of "undercover employees" in a manufacturing setting?

Peer ratings or evaluations by other workers at the same level have proved to be a valuable method of identifying talent among employees. Although peers have a tendency to rate their counterparts higher than these people would be rated by superiors, the information obtained from the ratings and rankings of peers can be highly predictive of future performance. For example, one study involved 117 inexperienced life insurance agents who attended a three-week training class. At the conclusion of the course, the budding insurance agents were asked to list the three best people in their class with respect to each of 12 situations. From these data, a composite score was obtained for each of the 117 agents. After one year, these peer ratings and three other variables were correlated with job tenure (number of weeks on the job) and with production (number of dollars' worth of insurance sold). As can be seen from Table 15–3, peer ratings had the highest validity in all of the categories. By contrast, a near-zero correlation was obtained between final course grade and all categories.

Is there a downside to peer ratings? Most definitely. Even when peer ratings are carried out anonymously, a person being rated may feel as if some suspected peer rated him or her too low. The reaction of that individual in turn may be to rate the suspected peer extremely low in retaliation. Also, peers do not always have a basis for judging the criteria that the rating scale asks them to judge. But that typically does not stop a rater in the workplace from rating a peer. Instead of rating the peer on the criteria listed on the questionnaire, the rater might use a private "What has this person done for me lately?" criterion to respond to the rating scale.

JUST THINK . . .

Suppose your instructor initiated a peer rating system as the sole determinant of your grade in your measurement class. Would such a system be better than the one in place?

In many organizations, people work in teams. In an organizational or workplace context, a **team** may be defined as two or more people who interact interdependently toward a common and valued goal and who have each been assigned specific roles or functions to perform. For

Table 15–3
Peer Ratings and Performance of Life Insurance Salespeople

	Job Tenure		Production	
	6 months	1 year	6 months	1 year
Peer rating	.18*	.29†	.29†	.30†
Age	.18*	.24†	.06	.09
Starting salary	.01	.03	.13	.26†
Final course grade	.02	.06	−.02	.02

Source: Mayfield (1972).

*$p = .05$ (one-tailed test)

†$p = .01$ (one-tailed test)

a sales team, the division of labor may simply reflect division of sales territories. In the creation of complicated software, the division of labor may involve the assignment of tasks that are too complicated for any one individual. The operation of a cruise ship or military vessel requires a trained team because of the multitude of things that must be done if the ship is to sail. To achieve greater productivity, organizations ask questions such as "What does the team know?" and "How does the collective knowledge of the team differ qualitatively from the individual knowledge and expertise of each of the team members?" These and related questions have been explored with various approaches to the measurement of team knowledge (see, for example, Cannon-Bowers et al., 1998; Cooke et al., 2000; Salas et al., 1998).

Motivation

Why do some people skip lunch, work overtime, and take home work nightly whereas others strive to do as little as possible and live a life of leisure at work? At a practical level, light may be shed on such questions by using assessment instruments that tap the values of the assessee. Dealing with a population of unskilled personnel may require specially devised techniques. Champagne (1969) responded to the challenge of knowing little about what might attract rural, unskilled people to work by devising a motivational questionnaire. As illustrated by the three items in Figure 15–5, the questionnaire used a paired comparison (forced-choice) format that required the subject to make choices about 12 factors used by companies to entice employment applications: fair pay, steady job, vacations and holidays with pay, job extras such as pensions and sick benefits, a fair boss, interesting work, good working conditions, chance for promotion, a job close to home, working with friends and neighbors, nice people to work with, and praise for good work.

The job-seeking factor found to be most important in Champagne's sample of 349 male and female, rural, unskilled subjects was *steady job.* The least important factor was found to be *working with friends and neighbors. Praise for good work* was a close runner-up for least important. In interpreting the findings, Champagne cautioned that "the factors reported here relate to the job-seeking behavior of the unskilled and are not measures of how to retain and motivate the unskilled once employed . . .What prompts a person to accept a job is not necessarily the same as what prompts a person to retain a job or do well in it" (p. 268).

On a theoretical level, an abundance of theories seek to delineate the specific needs, attitudes, social influences, and other factors that might account for differences in motivation. For example, Vroom (1964) proposed an expectancy theory of motivation, which essentially holds that employees expend energy in ways designed to achieve the outcome they want; the greater the expectancy that an action will achieve a certain outcome, the more energy will be expended to achieve that outcome. Maslow (1943, 1970) constructed a theoretical hierarchy of human needs (Figure 15–6) and proposed that, after one category of need is met, people seek to satisfy the next category of need.

Employers who subscribe to Maslow's theory would seek to identify (1) the need level required of the employee by the job and (2) the current need level of the prospective employee. Alderfer (1972) proposed an alternative need theory of motivation that was not hierarchical. Whereas Maslow saw the satisfaction of one need as a prerequisite to satisfaction of the next need in the hierarchy, Alderfer proposed that once a need is satisfied, the organism may strive to satisfy it to an even greater degree. The Alderfer theory also suggests that frustrating one need might channel energy into satisfying a need at another level.

In a widely cited program that undertook to define the characteristics of achievement motivation, McClelland (1961) used as his measure stories written under special instructions about TAT and TAT-like pictures. McClelland described the individual with a high need for achievement as one who prefers a task that is neither too simple nor extremely difficult— something with moderate, not extreme, risks. A situation with little or no risk will not lead to

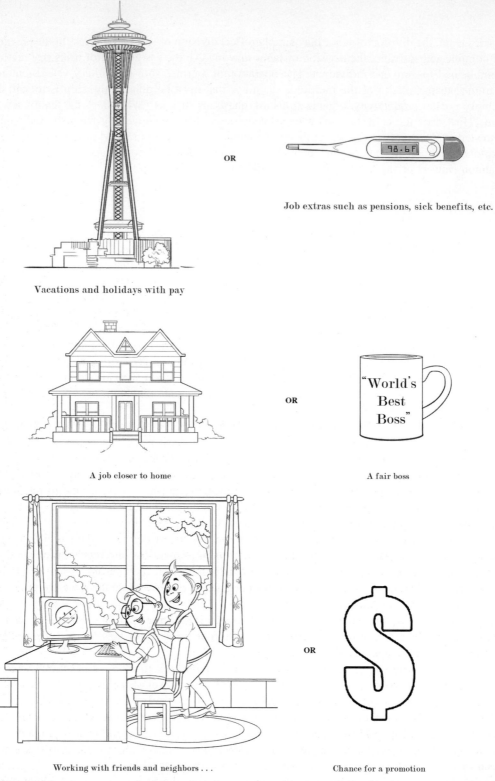

OR

Job extras such as pensions, sick benefits, etc.

Vacations and holidays with pay

OR

A job closer to home

A fair boss

Working with friends and neighbors . . .

OR

Chance for a promotion

Figure 15–5
Studying Values with the Unskilled

Champagne (1969) used pictorial test items reminiscent of those pictured here in a recruitment study with a rural, unskilled population. Subjects had to indicate which of two pictured items they preferred.

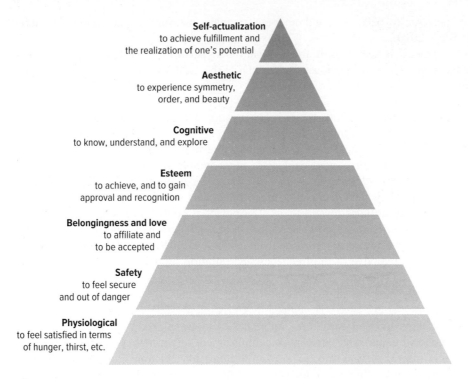

Figure 15–6
Maslow's Hierarchy of Needs (adapted from Maslow, 1970)

feelings of accomplishment if the individual succeeds. On the other hand, an extremely high-risk situation may not lead to feelings of accomplishment owing to the high probability of failure. Persons with a high need for achievement enjoy taking responsibility for their actions because they desire the credit and recognition for their accomplishments. Such individuals also desire information about their performance so they can constantly improve their output. Other researchers have used TAT-like pictures and their own specially devised scoring systems to study related areas of human motivation such as the fear of failure (Birney et al., 1969) and the fear of success (Horner, 1973).

Motivation may be conceptualized as stemming from incentives that are either primarily internal or primarily external in origin. Another way of stating this is to speak of *intrinsic motivation* and *extrinsic motivation.* In **intrinsic motivation,** the primary driving force stems from things such as the individual's involvement in work or satisfaction with work products. In **extrinsic motivation,** the primary driving force stems from rewards, such as salary and bonuses, or from constraints, such as job loss.

A scale designed to assess aspects of intrinsic and extrinsic motivation is the Work Preference Inventory (WPI; Amabile et al., 1994). The WPI contains 30 items rated on a four-point scale based on how much the testtaker believes the item to be self-descriptive. Factor analysis indicates that the test does appear to tap two distinct factors: intrinsic and extrinsic motivation. Each of these two factors may be divided into two subfactors. The intrinsic motivation factor may be divided into subfactors that concern the challenge of work tasks and the enjoyment of work. The extrinsic motivation factor may be divided into subfactors that concern compensation for work and external influences, such as recognition of one's work by others. The WPI has been shown to be internally consistent and to correlate in the predicted

> **JUST THINK . . .**
>
> What motivates you to do what you do? How could that motivation best be measured?

direction with personality, behavioral and other questionnaire measures of motivation (Amabile et al., 1994; Bipp, 2010).

In some instances, it seems as if the motivation to perform a particular job becomes markedly reduced compared to previous levels. Such is the case with a phenomenon referred to as *burnout*.

Burnout and its measurement   *Burnout* is an occupational health problem associated with cumulative occupational stress (Shirom, 2003). **Burnout** has been defined as "a psychological syndrome of emotional exhaustion, depersonalization, and reduced personal accomplishment that can occur among individuals who work with other people in some capacity" (Maslach et al., 1997, p. 192). In this definition, *emotional exhaustion* refers to an inability to give of oneself emotionally to others, and *depersonalization* refers to distancing from other people and even developing cynical attitudes toward them. The potential consequences of burnout range from deterioration in service provided to absenteeism and job turnover. The potential effects of burnout on a worker suffering from it range from insomnia to alcohol and drug use. Burnout has been shown to be predictive of the frequency and duration of sick leave (Schaufeli et al., 2009).

The most widely used measure of burnout is the Maslach Burnout Inventory (MBI), Third Edition (Maslach et al., 1996). Developed by Christina Maslach and her colleagues, this test contains 22 items divided into three subscales: Emotional Exhaustion (nine items), Depersonalization (five items), and Personal Accomplishment (eight items). Testtakers respond on a scale ranging from 0 (*never*) to 6 (*every day*) to items like this one from the Exhaustion scale: *Working all day is really a strain for me.* The MBI manual contains data relevant to the psychometric soundness of the tests. Included is a discussion of discriminant validity in which burnout is conceptually distinguished from similar concepts such as depression and job dissatisfaction.

JUST THINK . . .

Why might it be critically important for some employers to know if their employees are burning out? Besides a test, how else might burnout be gauged?

Using instruments such as the MBI, researchers have found that some occupations are characterized by higher levels of burnout than others. For example, personnel in nursing (Happell et al., 2003) and related fields, including staff in residential homes caring for the elderly (Evers et al., 2002) and children (Decker et al., 2002), seem subject to high levels of stress and burnout. Exactly why is not known. In one study of burnout among student support services personnel, it was found that low levels of job satisfaction led to high levels of the "emotional exhaustion" component of burnout (Brewer & Clippard, 2002). Burnout is a phenomenon that has been studied in diverse occupations throughout the world (see, for example, Ahola et al., 2008; Bellingrath et al., 2008; D'Amato & Zijlstra, 2008; Fahrenkopf et al., 2008; Griffin et al., 2010; Ilhan et al., 2008; Krasner et al., 2009; Narumoto et al., 2008; Ranta & Sud, 2008; Schaufeli et al., 2008; Shanafelt et al., 2010).

Job Satisfaction, Organizational Commitment, and Organizational Culture

An **attitude** may be defined formally as a presumably learned disposition to react in some characteristic manner to a particular stimulus. The stimulus may be an object, a group, an institution—virtually anything. Later in this chapter, we discuss how attitudes toward goods and services are measured. More immediately, however, we focus on workplace-related attitudes. Although attitudes do not necessarily predict behavior (Tittle & Hill, 1967; Wicker, 1969), there has been great interest in measuring the attitudes of employers and employees toward each other and toward numerous variables in the workplace. In what follows, we take a brief look at employee attitudes toward their companies in terms of job satisfaction and organizational commitment. Subsequently, we will briefly explore the attitudes that companies convey toward their employees as reflected by the workplace culture.

Job Satisfaction

Compared with dissatisfied workers, satisfied workers in the workplace are believed to be more productive (Petty et al., 1984), more consistent in work output (Locke, 1976), less likely to complain (Burke, 1970; Locke, 1976), and less likely to be absent from work or to be replaced (Herzberg et al., 1957; Vroom, 1964). Although these assumptions are somewhat controversial (Iaffaldano & Muchinsky, 1985) and should probably be considered on a case-by-case basis, employers, employees, researchers, and consultants have maintained a long-standing interest in the measurement of job satisfaction. Traditionally, **job satisfaction** has been defined as "a pleasurable or positive emotional state resulting from the appraisal of one's job or job experiences" (Locke, 1976, p. 300).

One diagnostic measure of job satisfaction (or, in this case, dissatisfaction) involves video-recording an employee at work and then playing back the video for the employee. The employee clicks on virtual controls to indicate when an unsatisfactory situation arises, and a window of questions automatically opens. According to data from studies of manual workers, analysis of the responses can be useful in creating a more satisfactory work environment (Johansson & Forsman, 2001).

Other measures of job satisfaction may focus on other elements of the job, including cognitive evaluations of the work (Organ & Near, 1985) and the work schedule (Baltes et al., 1999; Barnett & Gareis, 2000), perceived sources of stress (Brown & Peterson, 1993; Vagg & Spielberger, 1998), various aspects of well-being (Daniels, 2000), and mismatches between an employee's cultural background and the prevailing organizational culture (Aycan et al., 2000; Early et al., 1999; Parkes et al., 2001).

In addition to job satisfaction, other job-related constructs that have attracted the attention of theorists and assessment professionals include job involvement, work centrality, organizational socialization, and organizational commitment (Caught et al., 2000; Nystedt et al., 1999; Paullay et al., 1994; Taormina & Bauer, 2000). Let's briefly take a closer look at the latter construct.

Organizational Commitment

Organizational commitment has been defined as "the strength of an individual's identification with and involvement in a particular organization" (Porter et al., 1974, p. 604). This "strength" has been conceptualized and measured in ways that emphasize both its attitudinal and behavioral components (Mathieu & Zajac, 1990). In general, **organizational commitment** refers to a person's feelings of loyalty to, identification with, and involvement in an organization. Presumed correlates of high and low organizational commitment as observed by Randall (1987) are summarized in Table 15–4. The most widely used measure of this construct is the Organizational Commitment Questionnaire (OCQ; Porter et al., 1974), a 15-item Likert scale wherein respondents express their commitment-related attitudes toward an organization. Despite its widespread use, questions have been raised regarding its construct validity (Bozeman & Perrewe, 2001).

As you might expect, the measurement of attitude extends far beyond the workplace. For example, politicians seeking reelection may monitor the attitudes of their constituencies on various issues. We will revisit the subject of attitude measurement in somewhat greater detail when we survey measurement in the area of consumer psychology. However, before leaving the world of work and organizations, let's look at the measurement of organizational culture.

Table 15–4

Consequences of Organizational Commitment Level for Individual Employees and the Organization

	Level of Organizational Commitment		
	Low	**Moderate**	**High**
The Individual Employee	Potentially positive consequences for opportunity for expression of originality and innovation, but an overall negative effect on career advancement opportunities	Enhanced feeling of belongingness and security, along with doubts about the opportunity for advancement	Greater opportunity for advancement and compensation for efforts, along with less opportunity for personal growth and potential for stress in family relationships
The Organization	Absenteeism, tardiness, workforce turnover, and poor quality of work	As compared with low commitment, less absenteeism, tardiness, turnover, and better quality of work, as well as increased level of job satisfaction	Potential for high productivity, but sometimes accompanied by lack of critical/ethical review of employee behavior and by reduced organizational flexibility

Organizational Culture

Organizational culture—or corporate culture, as it is known when applied to a company or corporation—has been defined in many ways. For our purposes, we will follow Cohen (2001) in defining **organizational culture** as the totality of socially transmitted behavior patterns characteristic of a particular organization or company, including: the structure of the organization and the roles within it; the leadership style; the prevailing values, norms, sanctions, and support mechanisms; and the past traditions and folklore, methods of enculturation, and characteristic ways of interacting with people and institutions outside of the culture (such as customers, suppliers, the competition, government agencies, and the general public).

Much like different social groups at different times throughout history, organizations and corporations have developed distinctive cultures. They have distinctive ceremonies, rights, and privileges—formal as well as informal—tied to success and advancement in addition to various types of sanctions tied to failure (Trice & Beyer, 1984). Organizational cultures have observable artifacts, which may be in the form of an annual report or a video of the office Christmas party. Organizational cultures also typically have sets of core values or beliefs that guide the actions of the organization as well as the direction in which it moves.

Just as the term *culture* is traditionally applied to a group of people who share a particular way of life, the term *organizational culture* applies to a *way of work*. An organizational culture provides a way of coping with internal and external challenges and demands. And just as conflicts between ways of thinking and doing things can cause conflicts between groups of people, so conflicts between organizational cultures may develop. Such conflicts are perhaps most evident when a company with one type of corporate culture acquires or merges with a company that has a very different corporate culture (Brannen & Salk, 2000; Veiga et al., 2000). Any effort to remedy such a clash in corporate cultures must be preceded by sober study and understanding of the cultures involved.

JUST THINK . . .

Describe in detail a particular culture you know well. What difficulties do you encounter in trying to capture this culture in a description?

As with any group, the values held by an organization or a corporation represent a key part of the group culture. Various researchers have focused their interest on different aspects of corporate and organizational values (Tang et al., 2016; Kasser & Lin, 2016; Valentine et al., 2016). In this chapter's *Meet an Assessment Professional,* our featured professional shares some thoughts on how aspects of an individual's behavior can clash with the values of an employer or organization.

Meet Dr. Jed Yalof

...There are individuals who might be seen as "poor-fits" by employers, but were not identified as such at the time of hire. Such individuals are not easily screened out by basic self-report measures, and they may be sufficiently well versed in impression management to present themselves in an interview as a potentially good employee. However, in some cases, the individual may have misrepresented their achievements (and past problems) on their resume, and/or had their application supplemented with letters of reference that are not bona fide. A wide range of potential problems with such employees may emerge only after they have settled into the workplace. They might overstep rules, downplay or total disregard feedback, exhibit poor interpersonal skills with coworkers and clients, and in general seem to be in perpetual conflict with authority. They may demonstrate extreme competitiveness with coworkers, prioritizing their own needs ahead of other individuals and the organization at large. Competitiveness might escalate to the point of criticizing or harassing coworkers or inappropriate boasting with regard to one's perceived accomplishments.

Other employees may present with problems that are less serious, but nonetheless problematic. These are employees, for example, who are chronically late, or chronically needy or moody. Some employees may make a habit of bringing their personal problems to work in the hope of resolution, or at the very least, sympathy from coworkers. Unfortunately, their introduction of such problems into the workplace setting will almost surely negatively impact not only their own focus and productivity, but that of those

Jed Yalof, Psy.D., ABPP, ABAP, ABSNP, Professor of Psychology and Chair of the Department of Graduate Psychology at Immaculata University.

© Nadine Desautels, Austen Riggs Center

coworkers around them. Some employees emotionally drain themselves and others with problems that arise in the workplace. Such employees may feel targeted or victimized unfairly and become angered at any perceived slight. Alternatively, other employees may harbor a sense of entitlement that makes them feel as if they are exempt from the rules, regulations, and organizational mandates that govern the behavior of their co-workers...

Read more of what Dr. Yalof had to say—his complete essay—in the Instructor Resources within Connect.

Used with permission of Jed Yalof.

Perhaps because the concept of organizational culture is so multifaceted, obtaining a measure of it is no simple feat. To appreciate just how complex is the task of describing an organizational culture, consider how you would describe any other type of culture—American culture, NASCAR culture, or antiquing culture.

As a qualitative research consultant to many companies, the senior author of this textbook was presented with the challenge of assessing several organizational cultures. Because no satisfactory measure existed for conducting such an assessment, he created an instrument to do so. Interested readers will find sample items from Cohen's (2001) *Discussion of Organizational Culture* in the Instructor Resources within Connect.

Other Tools of Assessment for Business Applications

Psychometric expertise is applied in a wide range of industrial, organizational, and business-related settings. For example, experimental and engineering psychologists use a variety of assessment tools in their ergonomic (work-related) and human factors research as they help develop the plans for everything from household items (Hsu & Peng, 1993) to components for automobiles (Chira-Chavala & Yoo, 1994) and aircraft (Begault, 1993). These researchers may use custom-designed measurement instruments, standardized tests, or both in their efforts to better understand human response to specific equipment or instrumentation in a particular work environment.

Another business-related area in which tests and other tools of assessment are used extensively is consumer psychology.

Consumer Psychology

Consumer psychology is that branch of social psychology that deals primarily with the development, advertising, and marketing of products and services. As is true of almost all other specialty areas in psychology, some consumer psychologists work exclusively in academia, some work in applied settings, and many do both (Tybout & Artz, 1994). In both applied and research studies, consumer psychologists can be found working closely with professionals in fields such as marketing and advertising to help answer questions such as the following:

- Does a market exist for this new product?
- Does a market exist for this new use of an existing product?
- Exactly who—with respect to age, sex, race, social class, and other demographic variables—constitutes the market for this product?
- How can the targeted consumer population be made aware of this product in a cost-effective way?
- How can the targeted consumer population be persuaded to purchase this product in the most cost-effective way?
- What is the best way to package this product?[3]

One area of interest shared by the consumer psychologist and psychologists in other specialty areas is the measurement of attitudes. For the consumer psychologist, however, the attitude of interest is usually one that concerns a particular product or concept.

The Measurement of Attitudes

Attitudes formed about products, services, or brand names are a frequent focus of interest in consumer attitude research. Attitude is typically measured by self-report, using tests and questionnaires. A limitation of this approach is that people differ in their ability to be introspective and in their level of self-awareness. People also differ in the extent to which they are willing to be candid about their attitudes. In some instances, the use of an attitude measure may, in essence, create an attitude where none existed before. In such studies, the attitude measured may be viewed as an artifact of the measurement procedure (Sandelands & Larson, 1985).

Questionnaires and other self-report instruments designed to measure consumer attitudes are developed in ways similar to those previously described for psychological tests in general (see Chapter 8). A more detailed description of the preparation of measures of attitude can be

---

3. Questions concerning packaging and how to make a product stand out on the shelf have been referred to as issues of *shelf esteem* by consumer psychologists with a sense of humor.

found in the now-classic work *The Measurement of Attitude* (Thurstone & Chave, 1929). A monograph entitled "A Technique for the Measurement of Attitudes" (Likert, 1932) provided researchers with a simple procedure for constructing an instrument that would measure attitudes. Essentially, this procedure consists of listing statements (either favorable or unfavorable) that reflect a particular attitude. These statements are then administered to a group of respondents whose responses are analyzed to identify the most discriminating statements (i.e., items that best discriminate people at different points on the hypothetical continuum), which are then included in the final scale. Each statement included in the final scale is accompanied by a five-point continuum of alternative responses. Such a scale may range, for example, from *strongly agree* to *strongly disagree*. Scoring is accomplished by assigning numerical weights of 1 through 5 to each category such that 5 represents the most favorable response and 1 reflects the least favorable response.

Measures of attitude found in the psychological literature run the gamut from instruments devised solely for research and testing of academic theoretical formulations to scales with wide-ranging, real-world applications. In the latter context, we might find sophisticated industrial/organizational measures designed to gauge workers' attitudes toward their work or scales designed to measure the general public's attitudes toward some politician or issue. For example, the Self-Help Agency Satisfaction Scale, which is designed to gauge self-help agency clients' satisfaction with aspects of the support they receive (Segal et al., 2000), is representative of scales designed to measure consumer satisfaction with a product or service. Attitude scales with applied utility may also be found in the educational psychology literature. Consider in this context measures such as the Study Attitudes and Methods Survey (a scale designed to assess study habits) and the Minnesota Teacher Attitude Survey (a scale designed to assess student–teacher relations).

To help answer questions such as those listed in the previous section, consumer psychologists may rely on a variety of methods used individually or in combination. These methods include surveys, "motivation research" (as it is referred to by marketing professionals), and behavioral observation. We discuss these methods following a brief introduction to a relative newcomer on the attitude measurement scene: implicit attitude measurement.

Measuring implicit attitudes   Louis Thurstone's article entitled "Attitudes Can Be Measured" caused a bit of a stir when it was first published in 1928. This was so because the idea of actually measuring an attitude—or describing an attitude by a "single numerical index," to use Thurstone's words—was still quite novel. In some ways, a counterpart to that twentieth-century article is one from the twenty-first century entitled "Implicit Attitudes Can Be Measured" (Banaji, 2001). Although the author of the latter article freely admitted that its content was hardly as original as Thurstone's, it is nonetheless thought-provoking. So, what is meant by an *implicit attitude?*

An **implicit attitude** is a nonconscious, automatic association in memory that produces a disposition to react in some characteristic manner to a particular stimulus. Stated informally, implicit attitudes may be characterized as "gut-level" reactions.

Attempts to measure implicit attitudes have taken many forms, and a number of physiological measures have been tried (Amodio et al., 2006; Phelps et al., 2000; Vanman et al., 1997). But perhaps the measure most enthusiastically embraced by the research community has been the Implicit Attitude Test (IAT), a computerized sorting task by which implicit attitudes are gauged with reference to the testtaker's reaction times. Simply stated, the test is based on the premise that subjects will find it easier—and take less time to make categorizations—when they perceive the stimuli presented to them as being strongly associated (see Greenwald et al., 1998, and Nosek et al., 2007, for more-detailed explanations). So, for example, the speed with which one reacts to the word

> **JUST THINK . . .**
>
> You were previously introduced to an *implicit motive* (Chapter 12) and an *implicit memory* (Chapter 14). What is the relationship, if any, between implicit motives, memories, and attitudes?

did respond are representative of those who did not. People may not respond to a mail questionnaire for many different reasons, and various techniques ranging from incentives to follow-up mailings have been suggested for dealing with various types of nonresponse (Furse & Stewart, 1984).

It is possible to combine the various survey methods to obtain the advantages of each. For example, the survey researcher might mail a lengthy questionnaire to potential respondents and then obtain responses by telephone. Alternatively, those individuals not returning their responses by mail might be contacted by telephone or in person.

Many commercial research firms maintain a list of a large number of people or families who have agreed to respond to questionnaires that are sent to them. The people who make up this list are referred to as a **consumer panel.** In return for their participation, panel members may receive incentives such as cash and free samples of all the products about which they are asked to respond. One special type of panel is called a **diary panel.** Respondents on such a panel must keep detailed records of their behavior. For example, they may be required to keep a record of products they purchased, coupons they used, or radio stations they listened to while in the car. There are also specialized panels that serve to monitor segments of the market, political attitudes, or other variables.

Survey research may employ a wide variety of item types. One approach to item construction, particularly popular for surveys administered in writing, is referred to as the **semantic differential technique** (Osgood et al., 1957). Originally developed as a clinical tool for defining the meaning of concepts and relating concepts to one another in a "semantic space," the technique entails graphically placing a pair of bipolar adjectives (such as *good–bad* or *strong–weak*) on a seven-point scale such as this one:

GOOD _____ / _____ / _____ / _____ / _____ / _____ / _____ BAD

Respondents are instructed to place a mark on this continuum that corresponds to their judgment or rating. In research involving certain consumer applications, the bipolar adjectives may be replaced by descriptive expressions that are more consistent with the research objectives. For example, in rating a new cola-flavored soft drink, the phrase *just another cola* might be at one end of the rating continuum and *a very special beverage* might be at the other.

As with any research, care must be exercised in interpreting the results of a survey. Both the quantity and the quality of the data may vary from survey to survey. Response rates may differ, questions may be asked in different forms, and data collection procedures may vary from one survey to another (Henry, 1984). Ultimately, the utility of any conclusions rests on the integrity of the data and the analytic procedures used.

Occasions arise when research questions cannot be answered through a survey or a poll. Consumers may simply lack the insight to be accurate informants. As an example, consider the hypothetical case of Ralph, who smokes a hypothetical brand of cigarettes we will call "Cowboy." When asked why he chose to smoke Cowboy brand cigarettes, Ralph might reply "taste." In reality, however, Ralph may have begun smoking Cowboy because the advertising for this brand appealed to Ralph's image of himself as an independent, macho type—even though Ralph is employed as a clerk at a bridal boutique and bears little resemblance to the Cowboy image portrayed in the advertising.

JUST THINK . . .

What is another type of question to which consumers may be unwilling or reluctant to respond in a survey or a poll? What means could a consumer psychologist use to obtain an answer to this type of question?

Consumers may also be unwilling or reluctant to respond to some survey or poll questions. Suppose, for example, that the manufacturers of Cowboy cigarettes wished to know where on the product's packaging the Surgeon General's warning could be placed so that it would be *least* likely to be read. How many consumers would be willing to entertain such a question? Indeed, what would even posing such a question do for the public image of the product? It can be seen that if this hypothetical company were interested in obtaining an answer to such a question, it would have to do so through other means, such as motivation research.

Motivation Research Methods

Motivation research in consumer psychology and marketing is so named because it typically involves analyzing motives for consumer behavior and attitudes. **Motivation research methods** include individual interviews and focus groups. These two qualitative research methods are used to examine, in depth, the reactions of consumers who are representative of the group of people who use a particular product or service. Unlike quantitative research, which typically involves large numbers of subjects and elaborate statistical analyses, qualitative research typically involves few respondents and little or no statistical analysis. The emphasis in the latter type of research is not on quantity (of subjects or of data) but on the qualities of whatever is under study. Qualitative research often provides the data from which to develop hypotheses that may then be tested with larger numbers of consumers. Qualitative research also has diagnostic value. The best way to obtain highly detailed information about what a consumer likes and dislikes about a product, a store, or an advertisement is to use qualitative research.

A **focus group** is a group interview led by a trained, independent moderator who, ideally, has a knowledge of group discussion facilitation techniques and group dynamics.[4] As their name implies, *focus groups* are designed to *focus* group discussion on something, such as a particular commercial, a concept for a new product, or packaging for a new product. Focus groups usually consist of 6 to 12 participants who may have been recruited off the floor of a shopping mall or selected in advance to meet some preset qualifications for participation. The usual objective here is for the members of the group to represent in some way the population of targeted consumers for the product or service. Thus, for example, only beer drinkers (defined, for example, as males who drink at least two six-packs per week and females who drink at least one six-pack per week) might be solicited for participation in a focus group designed to explore attributes of a new brand of beer—including such variables as its taste, its packaging, and its advertising. Another attribute of beer not known to most consumers is what is referred to in the industry as its *bar call,* a reference to the ease with which one could order the brew in a bar. Because of the high costs associated with introducing a new product and advertising a new or established product, professionally conducted focus groups, complete with a representative sampling of the targeted consumer population, are a valuable tool in market research.

Depending on the requirements of the moderator's client (an advertiser, a manufacturer, etc.), the group discussion can be relatively structured (with a number of points to be covered) or relatively unstructured (with few points to be covered exhaustively). After establishing a rapport with the group, the moderator may, for example, show some advertising or a product to the group and then pose a general question (such as "What did you think of the beer commercial?") to be followed up by more specific kinds of questions (such as "Were the people in that commercial the kind of people you would like to have a beer with?"). The responses of the group members may build on those of other group members, and the result of the free-flowing discussion may be new information, new perspectives, or some previously overlooked problems with the advertising or product.

Focus groups typically last from one to two hours and are usually conducted in rooms (either conference rooms or living rooms) equipped with one-way mirrors (from which the

---

4. Focus group moderators vary greatly in training and experience. Ideally, a focus group moderator is independent enough to discuss dispassionately the topics with some distance and perspective. Contrary to this caveat, some advertising agencies maintain an in-house focus group moderator staff to test the advertising produced by the agency. Critics of this practice have likened it to assigning wolves to guard the henhouse.

client's staff may observe the proceedings) and audio or video equipment so that a record of the group session will be preserved. Aside from being an active listener and an individual who is careful not to suggest answers to questions or draw conclusions for the respondents, the moderator's duties include (1) following a discussion guide (usually created by the moderator in consultation with the client) and keeping the discussion on the topic; (2) drawing out silent group members so that everyone is heard from; (3) limiting the response time of group members who might dominate the group discussion; and (4) writing a report that not only provides a summary of the group discussion but also offers psychological or marketing insights to the client.

Technology may be employed in focus groups so that second-by-second reaction to stimulus materials such as commercials can be monitored. Cohen described the advantages (1985) and limitations (1987) of a technique whereby respondents watching television commercials pressed a calculator-like keypad to indicate how positive or negative they were feeling on a moment-to-moment basis while watching television. The response could then be visually displayed as a graph and played back for the respondent, who could be asked about the reasons for the spontaneous response.

Focus groups are widely employed in consumer research to

- generate hypotheses that can be further tested quantitatively
- generate information for designing or modifying consumer questionnaires
- provide general background information about a product category
- provide impressions of new product concepts for which little information is available
- obtain new ideas about older products
- generate ideas for product development or names for existing products
- interpret the results of previously obtained quantitative results

In general, the focus group is a highly useful technique for exploratory research, a technique that can be a valuable springboard to more comprehensive quantitative studies. Because so few respondents are typically involved in such groups, the findings from them cannot automatically be thought of as representative of the larger population. Still, many a client (including advertising agency creative staff) has received inspiration from the words spoken by ordinary consumers on the other side of a one-way mirror. Most major commercial test publishers, by the way, employ focus groups with test users to learn more about various aspects of market receptivity to their new test (or new edition of a test).

JUST THINK . . .

For what type of research questions would a focus group probably not be advisable?

Focus groups provide a forum for open-ended probing of thoughts, which ideally stimulates dialogue and discussion among the participants. Although the open-ended nature of the experience is a strength, the lack of any systematic framework for exploring human motivation is not. No two focus group moderators charged with answering the same questions may approach their task in quite the same way. Addressing this issue, Cohen (1999b) proposed a *dimensional* approach to qualitative research. This approach attempts to apply the overlapping psychological modalities or dimensions found so important by clinician Arnold Lazarus (1973, 1989) in his multimodal diagnostic and therapeutic efforts to nonclinical objectives in qualitative research. Specifically, **dimensional qualitative research** is an approach to qualitative research that seeks to ensure a study is comprehensive and systematic from a psychological perspective by guiding the study design and proposed questions for discussion on the basis of "BASIC ID" dimensions. BASIC ID is an acronym for the key dimensions in Lazarus's approach to diagnosis and intervention. The letters stand for *behavior, affect, sensation, imagery, cognition, interpersonal relations,* and *drugs.* Cohen's adaptation of Lazarus's work adds an eighth dimension, a sociocultural one, thus adding an *s* to the acronym and changing it to its plural form (BASIC IDS). Reflecting on this approach, Cohen wrote,

> The dimensions of the BASIC IDS can provide a uniform yet systematic framework for exploration and intervention, yet be flexible enough to allow for the implementation of new techniques and innovation. Anchored in logic, it is an approach that is accessible by nonpsychologists who seek to become more knowledgeable in the ways that psychology can be applied in marketing contexts. . . . Regardless of the specific framework adopted by a researcher, it seems high time to acknowledge that we are all feeling, sensing, behaving, imagining, thinking, socially relating, and biochemical beings who are products of our culture. Once this acknowledgment is made, and once we strive to routinely and systematically account for such variables in marketing research, we can begin to appreciate the added value psychologists bring to qualitative research with consumers in a marketing context. (1999b, p. 365)

In October 2011, the scholarly journal *Psychology & Marketing* devoted a special issue to the subject of dimensional qualitative research. In his guest editorial introducing the articles in that special issue, Haseeb Shabbir (2011) made clear that dimensional qualitative research had applications beyond consumer psychology. He noted that "the application of DQR is by no means limited to marketing or psychology . . . it is worth emphasizing that DQR can be useful in providing a psychologically sophisticated guide to qualitative research in almost any discipline" (p. 977).

Behavioral observation   Why did sales of the pain relievers aspirin, Bufferin, Anacin, and Excedrin rise sharply in October 1982? Was this rise in sales due to the effectiveness of advertising campaigns for these products? No. The sales rose sharply in 1982 when it was learned that seven people had died from ingesting Tylenol capsules laced with cyanide. As Tylenol, the pain reliever with the largest share of the market, was withdrawn from the shelves of stores nationwide, there was a corresponding rise in the sale of alternative preparations. A similar phenomenon occurred in 1986.

Just think what would have happened had market researchers based their judgments concerning the effectiveness of an ad campaign for an over-the-counter pain reliever solely on sales figures during the period of the Tylenol scare. No doubt the data easily could have led to a misinterpretation of what actually occurred. How might market researchers add a quality control component to their research methods? One way is by using multiple methods, such as behavioral observation in addition to survey methods.

It is not unusual for market researchers to station behavioral observers in stores to monitor what really prompts a consumer to buy this or that product at the point of choice. Such an observer at a store selling pain relievers in October 1982 might have observed, for example, a conversation with the clerk about the best alternative to Tylenol. Behavioral observers in a supermarket who studied the purchasing habits of people buying breakfast cereal concluded that children accompanying the purchaser requested or demanded a specific brand of cereal (Atkin, 1978). Hence, it would be wise for breakfast cereal manufacturers to gear their advertising to children, not the adult consumer.

> **JUST THINK . . .**
>
> From your own informal experience, what other types of purchases are probably guided more by input from children than from adults? How could consumer psychologists best test your beliefs regarding this purchase decision?

Other methods   A number of other methods and tools may be brought to bear on marketing and advertising questions. Consumer psychologists sometimes employ projective tests—existing as well as custom designed—as an aid in answering the questions raised by their clients. Special instrumentation, including tachistoscopes and electroencephalographs, have also been used in efforts to uncover consumer motivation. Special computer programs may be used to derive brand names for new products. Thus, for example, when Honda wished to position a new line of its cars as "advanced precision automobiles," a company specializing in the naming of new products conducted a computer search of over 6,900 English-language morphemes to locate word roots that mean or imply "advanced precision." The applicable morphemes were then computer combined in ways that the phonetic rules of English would allow. From the resulting list, the best word (i.e., one that has visibility among other printed words, one that will be recognizable as a brand name, and so forth) was then selected. In this case, that word was *Acura* (Brewer, 1987).

Literature reviews are another method available to consumer psychologists. A literature review might suggest, for example, that certain sounds or imagery in a particular brand tend to be more popular with consumers than other sounds or imagery. Schloss (1981) observed that the sound of the letter *K* was represented better than six times more often than would be expected by chance in the 200 top brand-name products (such as Sanka, Quaker, Nabisco—and, we might add, Acura). Schloss went on to speculate about the ability of the sounds of words to elicit emotional reactions as opposed to rational ones.

And speaking of eliciting reactions, it is the authors of this textbook, Ron Cohen and Mark Swerdlik, who must now pause to *just think* and wonder: What reaction will be elicited from you as the realization sets in that you have come to the last page of the last chapter of *Psychological Testing and Assessment*? Your reaction could range from *extreme sorrow* (you wish there were more pages to turn) to *unbridled ecstasy* (party time!). Whatever, we want you to know that we consider it an honor and a privilege to have helped introduce you to the world of measurement in psychology and education. You have our best wishes for success in your academic and professional development. And who knows? Maybe it will be you and your work that will be presented to a new generation of students in a future edition of this book.

Self-Assessment

Test your understanding of elements of this chapter by seeing if you can explain each of the following terms, expressions, and abbreviations:

assessment center	focus group	organizational commitment
attitude	forced distribution technique	organizational culture
burnout	GATB	physical test
classification	implicit attitude	placement
consumer panel	in-basket technique	poll
consumer psychology	integrity test	productivity
critical incidents technique	interest measure	screening
diary panel	intrinsic motivation	second-order meta-analysis
dimensional qualitative research	job satisfaction	selection
drug test	leaderless group technique	semantic differential technique
extrinsic motivation	MBTI	SII
false negative	motivation research methods	survey
false positive	organismic assessment	team

References

Abel, G. G., Rouleau, J., & Cunningham-Rathner, J. (1986). Sexually aggressive behavior. In W. J. Curran, A. L. McGarry, & S. Shah (Eds.), *Forensic psychiatry and psychology: Perspectives and standards for interdisciplinary practice* (pp. 289–314). Philadelphia: Davis.

Abeles, N., & Barlev, A. (1999). End of life decisions and assisted suicide. *Professional Psychology: Research and Practice, 30,* 229–234.

Abidin, R. R. (1990). *Parenting stress index* (3rd ed.). Odessa, FL: Psychological Assessment Resources.

Abrams, D. B., Binkoff, J. A., Zwick, W. R., et al. (1991). Alcohol abusers' and social drinkers' responses to alcohol-relevant and general situations. *Journal of Studies on Alcohol, 52,* 409–414.

Abrams, S. (1977). *A polygraph handbook for attorneys.* Lexington, MA: Heath.

Achenbach, T. M. (1978). *Child Behavior Profile.* Bethesda, MD: Laboratory of Developmental Psychology, National Institutes of Mental Health.

Achenbach, T. M. (1981). A junior MMPI? *Journal of Personality Assessment, 45,* 332–333.

Achenbach, T. M. (1993). Implications of multiaxial empirically based assessment for behavior therapy with children. *Behavior Therapy, 24,* 91–116.

Achenbach, T. M., McConaughy, S. H., & Howell, C. T. (1987). Child/adolescent behavioral and emotional problems: Implications of cross-informant correlations for situational specificity. *Psychological Bulletin, 101,* 213–232.

Ackerman, M. J. (1995). *Clinician's guide to child custody evaluations.* New York: Wiley-Interscience.

Ackerman, P. L., & Kanfer, R. (1993). Integrating laboratory and field study for improving selection: Development of a battery for predicting air traffic controller success. *Journal of Applied Psychology, 78,* 413–432.

Acklin, M. W. (1995). Avoiding Rorschach dichotomies: Integrating Rorschach interpretation. *Journal of Personality Assessment, 64,* 235–238.

Acklin, M. W. (1996). Personality assessment and managed care. *Journal of Personality Assessment, 66,* 194–201.

Acklin, M. W. (1997). Swimming with sharks. *Journal of Personality Assessment, 69,* 448–451.

Adams, D. K., & Horn, J. L. (1965). Nonoverlapping keys for the MMPI scales. *Journal of Consulting Psychology, 29,* 284.

Adams, K. M. (1984). Luria left in the lurch: Unfulfilled promises are not valid tests. *Journal of Clinical Neuropsychology, 6,* 455–458.

Adams, K. M. (2000). Practical and ethical issues pertaining to test revisions. *Psychological Assessment, 12,* 281–286.

Adams, K. M. (2015). Ralph M. Reitan: A singular career. *Archives of Clinical Neuropsychology, 30*(8), 748–750.

Adams-Tucker, C. (1982). Proximate effects of sexual abuse in childhood: A report on 28 children. *American Journal of Psychiatry, 139,* 1252–1256.

Addeo, R. R., Greene, A. F., & Geisser, M. E. (1994). Construct validity of the Robson Self-Esteem Questionnaire in a sample of college students. *Educational and Psychological Measurement, 54,* 439–446.

Adelman, S. A., Fletcher, K. E., Bahnassi, A., & Munetz, M. R. (1991). The Scale for Treatment Integration of the Dually Diagnosed (STIDD): An instrument for assessing intervention strategies in the pharmacotherapy of mentally ill substance abusers. *Drug and Alcohol Dependence, 27,* 35–42.

Adler, A. (1927/1965). *Understanding human nature.* Greenwich, CT: Fawcett.

Adler, A. (1933/1964). *Social interest: A challenge to mankind.* New York: Capricorn.

Adler, A., Jager-Hyman, S., Green, K. L., et al. (2015). Initial psychometric properties of the Attentional Fixation on Suicide Experiences Questionnaire. *Cognitive Therapy and Research, 39*(4), 492–498.

Adler, T. (1990). Does the "new" MMPI beat the "classic"? *APA Monitor, 20*(4), 18–19.

Aggarwal, N.K., Desilva, R., Nicasio, A. V., et al. (2013). Does the Cultural Formulation Interview for the fifth revision of the Diagnostic and Statistical Manual of Mental Disorders (DSM-5) affect medical communication? A qualitative exploratory study from the New York site. *Ethnicity & Health*, 20, 1–28.

Aggarwal, N. K., DeSilva, R., Nicasio, A. V., Boiler, M., & Lewis-Fernández, R. (2015). Does the Cultural Formulation Interview for the fifth revision of the Diagnostic and Statistical Manual of Mental Disorders (DSM-5) affect medical communication? A qualitative exploratory study from the New York site. *Ethnicity & Health*, 20, 1–28.

Aggarwal, N. K., Jiménez-Solomon, O., Lam, P. C., Hinton, L., & Lewis-Fernández, R. (2016). The core and informant Cultural Formulation Interviews in DSM-5. In R. Lewis-Fernández, N. K. Aggarwal, L. Hinton, D. E. Hinton, & L. J. Kirmayer (Eds.), *DSM-5Handbook on the Cultural Formulation Interview* (pp. 27–44). Arlington, VA: American Psychiatric Association.

Aggarwal, N. K., Pieh, M. C., Dixon, L., Guarnaccia, P., Alegría, M., & Lewis-Fernández, R. (2016). Clinician descriptions of communication strategies to improve treatment engagement by racial/ethnic minorities in mental health services: A systematic review. *Patient Education and Counseling, 99,* 198–209.

Ahern, E. (1949). *Handbook of personnel forms and records.* New York: American Management Association.

Ahola, K., Kivimäki, M., Honkonen, T., et al. (2008). Occupational burnout and medically certified sickness absence: A population-based study of Finnish employees. *Journal of Psychosomatic Research, 64*(2), 185–193.

Aiello, J. R., & Douthitt, E. A. (2001). Social facilitation from Triplett to electronic performance monitoring. *Group Dynamics, 5,* 163–180.

Airasian, P. W., Madaus, G. F., & Pedulla, J. J. (1979). *Minimal competency testing.* Englewood Cliffs, NJ: Educational Technology Publications.

Akamatsu, C. T. (1993–1994). The view from within and without: Conducting research on deaf Asian-Americans. *Journal of the American Deafness and Rehabilitation Association, 27,* 12–16.

Alderfer, C. (1972). *Existence, relatedness and growth: Human needs in organizational settings.* New York: Free Press.

Alderson, J. C., Krahnke, K. J., & Stansfield, C. W. (1987). *Reviews of English language proficiency tests.* Washington, DC: TESOL.

Alessandri, S. M., Bendersky, M., & Lewis, M. (1998). Cognitive functioning in 8- to 18-month-old drug-exposed infants. *Developmental Psychology, 34,* 565–573.

Alexander, R. C., Surrell, J. A., & Cohle, S. D. (1987). Microwave oven burns in children: An unusual manifestation of child abuse. *Pediatrics, 79,* 255–260.

Alfred, G. C., Hammer, J. H., & Good, G. E. (2014). Male student veterans: Hardiness, psychological well-being, and masculine norms. *Psychology of Men & Masculinity, 15,* 95–99.

Alison, L., & Barrett, E. (2004). The interpretation and utilization of offender profiles: A critical review of "traditional" approaches to profiling. In J. R. Adler (Ed.), *Forensic psychology: Concepts, debates and practice* (pp. 58–77). Devon, England: Willan.

Alison, L., West, A., & Goodwill, A. (2004). The academic and the practitioner: Pragmatists' views of offender profiling. *Psychology, Public Policy, and Law, 10,* 71–101.

Allen, J. (2002). Assessment training for practice in American Indian and Alaska native settings. *Journal of Personality Assessment, 79,* 216–225.

Allen, M. J., & Yen, W. M. (1979). *Introduction to measurement theory.* Monterey, CA: Brooks/Cole.

Allen, N. J., & Meyer, J. P. (1990). The measurement and antecedents of affective, continuance, and normative commitment to the organization. *Journal of Occupational Psychology, 63,* 1–18.

Allen, R., Wasserman, G. A., & Seidman, S. (1990). Children with congenital anomalies: The preschool period. *Journal of Pediatric Psychology, 15,* 327–345.

Allen, S. R. (2008). Predicting performance in sport using a portable cognitive assessment device. *Dissertation Abstracts International. Section A. Humanities and Social Sciences, 68*(9-A), 3724.

Allen, T. E. (1994). *Who are the deaf and hard-of-hearing students leaving high school and entering postsecondary education?* (pp. 1–16). U.S. Office of Special Education and Rehabilitative Services: Pelavin Research Institute.

Allport, G. W. (1937). *Personality: A psychological interpretation.* New York: Holt.

Allport, G. W., & Odbert, H. S. (1936). Trait-names: A psycho-lexical study. *Psychological Monographs, 47* (Whole No. 211).

Allport, G. W., Vernon, P. E., & Lindzey, G. (1951). *Study of values* (rev. ed.). Boston: Houghton Mifflin.

Allred, L. J., & Harris, W. G. (1984). *The nonequivalence of computerized and conventional administrations of the Adjective Checklist.* Unpublished manuscript, Johns Hopkins University, Baltimore.

Alpher, V. S., & Blanton, R. L. (1985). The accuracy of lie detection: Why lie tests based on the polygraph should not be admitted into evidence today. *Law & Psychology Review, 9,* 67–75.

Alterman, A. I., McDermott, P. A., Cook, T. G., et al. (2000). Generalizability of the clinical dimensions of the Addiction Severity Index to nonopioid-dependent patients. *Psychology of Addictive Behaviors, 14,* 287–294.

Amabile, T. M., Hill, K. G., Hennessey, B. A., & Tighe, E. M. (1994). The Work Preference Inventory: Assessing intrinsic and extrinsic motivational orientations. *Journal of Personality and Social Psychology, 66,* 950–967.

Amada, G. (1996). You can't please all of the people all of the time: Normative institutional resistances to college psychological services. *Journal of College Student Psychotherapy, 10,* 45–63.

Aman, C. J., Roberts, R. J., & Pennington, B. F. (1998). A neuropsychological examination of the underlying deficit in attention deficit hyperactivity disorder: Frontal lobe versus right parietal lobe theories. *Developmental Psychology, 34,* 956–969.

Ambrosini, P. J., Metz, C., Bianchi, M. D., Rabinovich, H., & Undie, A. (1991). Concurrent validity and psychometric properties of the Beck Depression Inventory in outpatient adolescents. *Journal of the American Academy of Child and Adolescent Psychiatry, 30,* 51–57.

American Association on Mental Retardation. (1992). *Mental retardation: Definition, classification, and systems of supports* (9th ed.). Washington, DC: Author.

American Bar Association Commission on Law and Aging & American Psychological Association. (2008). *Assessment of older adults with diminished capacity: A handbook for psychologists.* Washington, DC: American Bar Association and American Psychological Association.

American Board of Forensic Odontology, Inc. (1986). Guidelines for analysis of bite marks in forensic investigation. *Journal of the American Dental Association, 12,* 383–386.

American Educational Research Association, American Psychological Association, & National Council on Measurement in Education. (1999). *Standards for educational and psychological testing.* Washington, DC: Author.

American Educational Research Association, Committee on Test Standards, and National Council on Measurements Used in Education. (1955). *Technical recommendations for achievement tests.* Washington, DC: American Educational Research Association.

American Law Institute. (1956). *Model penal code.* Tentative Draft Number 4.

American Psychiatric Association. (1968). *Diagnostic and statistical manual of mental disorders* (2nd ed.). Washington, DC: Author.

American Psychiatric Association. (1980). *Diagnostic and statistical manual of mental disorders* (3rd ed.). Washington, DC: Author.

American Psychiatric Association. (1987). *Diagnostic and statistical manual of mental disorders* (3rd ed., rev.). Washington, DC: Author.

American Psychiatric Association. (1994). *Diagnostic and statistical manual of mental disorders* (4th ed.). Washington, DC: Author.

American Psychiatric Association. (2000). *Diagnostic and statistical manual of mental disorders* (4th ed., text rev.). Washington, DC: Author.

American Psychiatric Association. (2001). *Diagnostic and statistical manual of mental disorders* (4th ed., text rev.). [CD-ROM (Windows)]. Washington, DC: Author.

American Psychiatric Association. (2013a). *The diagnostic and statistical manual of mental disorders* (5th ed.). Arlington, VA: American Psychiatric Association.

American Psychiatric Association. (2013b). *Posttraumatic stress disorder. APA Fact Sheet.* Retrieved from www.psychiatry.org/FileLibrary/Practice/DSM/DSM-5/DSM-5-PTSD.pdf

American Psychological Association. (1950). Ethical standards for the distribution of psychological tests and diagnostic aids. *American Psychologist, 5,* 620–626.

American Psychological Association. (1953). *Ethical standards of psychologists.* Washington, DC: Author.

American Psychological Association. (1954). *Technical recommendations for psychological tests and diagnostic techniques.* Washington, DC: Author.

American Psychological Association, American Educational Research Association, & National Council on Measurement in Education. (1966). *Standards for educational and psychological tests and manual.* Washington, DC: Author.

American Psychological Association. (1987). *Casebook on ethical principles of psychologists.* Washington, DC: Author.

American Psychological Association, American Educational Research Association, & National Council on Measurement in Education. (1974). *Standards for educational and psychological tests.* Washington, DC: Author.

American Psychological Association. (1981). Ethical principles of psychologists. *American Psychologist, 36,* 633–638.

American Psychological Association. (1985). *Standards for educational and psychological testing.* Washington, DC: Author.

American Psychological Association. (1967). *Casebook on ethical standards of psychologists.* Washington, DC: Author.

American Psychological Association. (1991). *Questionnaires used in the prediction of trustworthiness in pre-employment selection decisions: An APA Task Force report.* Washington, DC: Author.

American Psychological Association. (1992). Ethical principles of psychologists and code of conduct. *American Psychologist, 47,* 1597–1611.

American Psychological Association. (1993, January). Call for book proposals for test instruments. *APA Monitor, 24,* 12.

American Psychological Association, Committee on Professional Practice and Standards. (1994a). Guidelines for child custody evaluations in divorce proceedings. *American Psychologist, 49,* 677–680.

American Psychological Association. (1994b). C. H. Lawshe. *American Psychologist, 49,* 549–551.

American Psychological Association. (1996a). *Affirmative action: Who benefits?* Washington, DC: Author.

American Psychological Association. (1996b). *Standards for psychological tests.* Washington, DC: Author.

American Psychological Association. (2002). Ethical principles of psychologists and code of conduct. *American Psychologist, 57,* 1060–1073.

American Psychological Association. (2003). Guidelines on multicultural education, training, research, practice, organizational change for psychologists. *American Psychologist, 58,* 377–402.

American Psychological Association. (2015). Guidelines for psychological practice with transgender and gender nonconforming people. *American Psychologist, 70*(9), 832–864.

Ames, S. L., & Stacy, A. W. (1998). Implicit cognition in the prediction of substance use among drug offenders. *Psychology of Addictive Behaviors, 12,* 272–281.

Amodio, D. M., Devine, P. G., & Harmon-Jones, E. (2006). Stereotyping and evaluation in implicit race bias: Evidence for independent constructs and unique effects on behavior. *Journal of Personality and Social Psychology, 91*(4), 652–661.

Amrine, M. (Ed.). (1965). Special issue. *American Psychologist, 20,* 857–991.

Anderson, C., Spataro, S. E., & Flynn, F. J. (2008). Personality and organizational culture as determinants of influence. *Journal of Applied Psychology, 93*(3), 702–710.

Anderson, D. (2007). A reciprocal determinism analysis of the relationship between naturalistic media usage and the development of creative-thinking skills among college students. *Dissertation Abstracts International Section A: Humanities and Social Sciences, 67*(7-A), 2007, 2459.

Anderson, D. V. (2014, October 1). Replacing Common Core with proven standards of excellence. Retrieved May 21, 2016 at https://www.heartland.org/policy-documents/replacing-common-core-proven-standards-excellence

Anderson, G., & Grace, C. (1991). The Black deaf adolescent: A diverse and underserved population. *Volta Review, 93,* 73–86.

Anderson, H. G. (1919). *The medical and surgical aspects of aviation.* London: Oxford Medical.

Anderson, J. W. (1990). The life of Henry A. Murray: 1893–1988. In A. I. Rabin, R. A. Zucker, R. A. Emmons, & S. Frank (Eds.), *Studying persons and lives* (pp. 304–333). New York: Springer.

Anderson, W. P. (1995). Ethnic and cross-cultural differences on the MMPI-2. In J. C. Duckworth & W. P. Anderson (Eds.), *MMPI and MMPI-2: Interpretation manual for counselors and clinicians* (4th ed., pp. 439–460). Bristol, PA: Accelerated Development.

Andresen, E. M., Malmgren, J. A., Carter, W. B., & Patrick, D. L. (1994). Screening for depression in well older adults: Evaluation of a short form of the CES-D. *American Journal of Preventive Medicine, 10*(2), 77–84.

Andrew, G., Hartwell, S. W., Hutt, M. L., & Walton, R. E. (1953). *The Michigan Picture Test.* Chicago: Science Research Associates.

Andronikof, A. (2005). Science and soul: Use and misuse of computerized interpretation. *Rorschachiana, 27*(1), 1–3.

Angie, A. D., Davis, J. L., Allen, M. T., et al. (2011). Studying ideological groups online: Identification and assessment of risk factors for violence. *Journal of Applied Social Psychology, 41,* 627–657.

Angoff, W. H. (1962). Scales with nonmeaningful origins and units of measurement. *Educational and Psychological Measurement, 22,* 27–34.

Angoff, W. H. (1964). Technical problems of obtaining equivalent scores on tests. *Educational and Psychological Measurement, 1,* 11–13.

Angoff, W. H. (1966). Can useful general-purpose equivalency tables be prepared for different college admissions tests? In A. Anastasi (Ed.), *Testing problems in perspective* (pp. 251–264). Washington, DC: American Council on Education.

Angoff, W. H. (1971). Scales, norms, and equivalent scores. In R. L. Thorndike (Ed.), *Educational measurement* (2nd ed., pp. 508–560). Washington, DC: American Council on Education.

Appelbaum, P., & Grisso, T. (1995a). The MacArthur Treatment Competence Study: I. Mental illness and competence to consent to treatment. *Law and Human Behavior, 19,* 105–126.

Appelbaum, P., & Grisso, T. (1995b). The MacArthur Treatment Competence Study: III. Abilities of patients to consent to psychiatric and medical treatments. *Law and Human Behavior, 19,* 149–174.

Appelbaum, P. S., & Roth, L. H. (1982). Competency to consent to research: A psychiatric overview. *Archives of General Psychiatry, 39,* 951–958.

Arbisi, P. A., Ben-Porath, Y. S., & McNulty, J. (2002). A comparison of MMPI-2 validity in African American and Caucasian psychiatric inpatients. *Psychological Assessment, 14,* 3–15.

Archer, R. P., Stredny, R. V., & Zoby, M. (2006). Introduction to forensic uses of clinical assessment instruments. In R. P. Archer (Ed.), *Forensic uses of clinical assessment instruments* (pp. 1–18). London: Lawrence Erlbaum Associates Publishers.

Ariel, A., Van der Linden, W. J., & Veldkamp, B. P. (2006). A strategy for optimizing item-pool management. *Journal of Educational Measurement, 43*(2), 85–96.

Ariel, B., Farrar, W. A., & Sutherland, A. (2015). The effect of police body-worn cameras on use of force and citizens' complaints against the police: A randomized controlled trial. *Journal of Quantitative Criminology, 31*(3), 509–535.

Arieli-Attali, M., & Budescu, D. V. (2015). Effects of score feedback on test-taker behavior in self-adapted testing. *Multivariate Behavioral Research, 50*(6), 724–725.

Arnau, R. C., Green, B. A., Rosen, D. H., et al. (2003). Are Jungian preferences really categorical? *Personality & Individual Differences, 34,* 233–251.

Arnett, P. A., Rao, S. M., Grafman, J., et al. (1997). Executive functions in multiple sclerosis: An analysis of temporal ordering, semantic encoding, and planning abilities. *Neuropsychology, 11,* 535–544.

Arnold, D. S., O'Leary, S. G., Wolff, L. S., & Acker, M. M. (1993). The Parenting Scale: A measure of dysfunctional parenting in discipline situations. *Psychological Assessment, 5,* 137–144.

Aronow, E., & Reznikoff, M. (1976). *Rorschach content interpretation.* Orlando, FL: Grune & Stratton.

Aronow, E., & Reznikoff, M. (1983). *A Rorschach introduction: Content and perceptual approaches.* Orlando, FL: Grune & Stratton.

Aronow, E., Reznikoff, M., & Moreland, K. L. (1995). The Rorschach: Projective technique or psychometric test? *Journal of Personality Assessment, 64,* 213–228.

Aros, S., Mills, J. L., Torres, C., et al. (2006). Prospective identification of pregnant women drinking four or more standard drinks (= 48 g) of alcohol per day. *Substance Use & Misuse, 41*(2), 183–197.

Arthur, W., Jr., Woehr, D. J., & Graziano, W. G. (2001). Personality testing in employment settings: Problems and issues in the application of typical selection practice. *Personnel Review, 30,* 657–676.

Arvey, R. D. (1979). *Fairness in selecting employees.* Reading, MA: Addison-Wesley.

Arvey, R. D., Bouchard, T. J., Segal, N. L., & Abraham, L. M. (1989). Job satisfaction: Environmental and genetic components. *Journal of Applied Psychology, 74,* 187–192.

Asch, S. E. (1951). Effects of group pressure upon the modification and distortion of judgment. In H. Guetzkow (Ed.), *Groups, leadership, and men.* Pittsburgh, PA: Carnegie.

Asch, S. E. (1955). Opinions and social pressure. *Scientific American, 193,* 33–35.

Asch, S. E. (1957a). Studies of independence and conformity: A minority of one against a unanimous majority. *Psychological Monographs, 70* (9, Whole No. 416).

Asch, S. E. (1957b). An experimental investigation of group influence. In Walter Reed Army Institute of Research (Ed.), *Symposium on preventive and social psychiatry.* Washington, DC: U.S. Government Printing Office.

Association of Personnel Test Publishers (APTP). (1990). Model guidelines for preemployment integrity testing programs. Washington, DC: APTP.

ASVAB 18/19 Counselor Manual: The ASVAB career exploration program. (1995). Washington, DC: U.S. Department of Defense.

Atkin, C. K. (1978). Observation of parent–child interaction in supermarket decision making. *Journal of Marketing, 42,* 41–45.

Atkins v. Virginia, 122 S. Ct. 2242 (2002).

Atkinson, J. W. (1981). Studying personality in the context of an advanced motivational psychology. *American Psychologist, 36,* 117–128.

Atkinson, R. C., & Shiffrin, R. M. (1968). A proposed system and its control processes. In K. W. Spence & J. T. Spence (Eds.), *The psychology of learning and motivation: Advances in research and theory* (Vol. 2, pp. 82–90). Oxford: Oxford University Press.

Ausburn, L. J., & Ausburn, F. B. (1978). Cognitive styles: Some information and implications for instructional design. *Educational Communications & Technology Journal, 26,* 337–354.

Aycan, Z., Kanungo, R. N., Mendonca, M., et al. (2000). Impact of culture on human resource management practices: A 10-country comparison. *Applied Psychology: An International Review, 49,* 192–221.

Ayres, R. R., & Cooley, E. J. (1986). Sequential versus simultaneous processing on the K-ABC: Validity in predicting learning success. *Journal of Psychoeducational Assessment, 4,* 211–220.

Babins, L., Slater, M.-E., Whitehead, V., & Chertkow, H. (2008). Can an 18-point clock-drawing scoring system predict dementia in elderly individuals with mild cognitive impairment? *Journal of Clinical and Experimental Neuropsychology, 30*(2), 1–14.

Bagasra, A. (2010). *Development and testing of an acculturation scale for Muslim Americans.* Paper presented at the 119th annual convention of the American Psychological Association, Washington, DC.

Bain, S. K. & Gray, R. (2008). Test reviews: Kaufman Assessment Battery for Children, Second Edition. *Journal of Psychoeducational Assessment, 26*(1), 92–101.

Baker, E. L., O'Neill, H. F., & Linn, R. L. (1993). Policy and validity prospects for performance-based assessment. *American Psychologist, 48,* 1210–1218.

Baldridge, D. C., & Veiga, J. F. (2006). The impact of anticipated social consequences on recurring disability. *Journal of Management, 32*(1), 158–179.

Baldwin, J. A. (1984). African self-consciousness and the mental health of African-Americans. *Journal of Black Studies, 15,* 177–194.

Baldwin, J. A., & Bell, Y. R. (1985). The African Self-Consciousness Scale: An Africentric personality questionnaire. *Western Journal of Black Studies, 9*(2), 65–68.

Ball, J. D., Archer, R. P., Gordon, R. A., & French, J. (1991). Rorschach depression indices with children and adolescents: Concurrent validity findings. *Journal of Personality Assessment, 57,* 465–476.

Ball, T. S., & Bernardoni, L. C. (1953). The application of an auditory apperception test to clinical diagnosis. *Journal of Clinical Psychology, 9,* 54–58.

Baltes, B. B., Briggs, T. E., Huff, J. W., et al. (1999). Flexible and compressed workweek schedules: A meta-analysis of their effects on work-related criteria. *Journal of Applied Psychology, 84,* 496–513.

Banaji, M. R. (2001). Implicit attitudes can be measured. In H. L. Roediger III, J. S. Nairne, I. Neath, & A. M. Surprenant (Eds.), *The nature of remembering: Essays in honor of Robert G. Crowder. Science conference series* (pp. 117–150). Washington, DC: American Psychological Association.

Bank, A. L., MacNeill, S. E., & Lichtenberg, P. A. (2000). Cross validation of the MacNeill-Lichtenberg Decision Tree triaging mental health problems in geriatric rehabilitation patients. *Rehabilitation Psychology, 45,* 193–204.

Baños, J. H., & Franklin, L. M. (2003). Factor structure of the Mini-Mental State Examination in adult psychiatric inpatients. *Psychological Assessment, 14,* 397–400.

Barak, A., & Cohen, L. (2002). Empirical examination of an online version of the Self-Directed Search. *Journal of Career Assessment, 10,* 387–400.

Barden, R. C., Ford, M. E., Jensen, A. G., Rogers-Salyer, M., & Salyer, K. E. (1989). Effects of craniofacial deformity in infancy on the quality of mother-infant interactions. *Child Development, 60,* 819–824.

Bardis, P. D. (1975). The Borromean family. *Social Science, 50,* 144–158.

Barends, A., Westen, D., Leigh, J., Silbert, D., & Byers, S. (1990). Assessing affect-tone of relationship paradigms from TAT and interview data. *Psychological Assessment, 2,* 329–332.

Barker, R. (1963). On the nature of the environment. *Journal of Social Issues, 19,* 17–38.

Barko, N. (1993, August). What's your child's emotional IQ? *Working Mother, 16,* 33–35.

Barnes-Holmes, D., Murtagh, L., Barnes-Holmes, Y., & Stewart, I. (2010). Using the implicit association test and the implicit relational assessment procedure to measure attitudes toward meat and vegetables in vegetarians and meat-eaters. *Psychological Record, 60*(2), Article 6.

Barnett, L. A., Far, J. M., Mauss, A. L., & Miller, J. A. (1996). Changing perceptions of peer norms as a drinking reduction program for college students. *Journal of Alcohol & Drug Education, 41*(2), 39–62.

Barnett, R. C., & Gareis, K. C. (2000). Reduced hours, job-role quality, and life satisfaction among married women physicians with children. *Psychology of Women Quarterly, 24,* 358–364.

Baron, J., & Norman, M. F. (1992). SATs, achievement tests, and high-school class rank as predictors of college performance. *Educational and Psychological Measurement, 52,* 1047–1055.

Barrett, F. J. (1996). The organizational construction of hegemonic masculinity: The case of the US Navy. *Gender, Work and Organization, 3,* 129–142.

Barrick, M. R., Mount, M. K., & Judge, T. A. (2001). Personality and performance at the beginning of the new millennium: What do we know and where do we go next? *International Journal of Selection and Assessment, 9,* 9–30.

Barrick, M. R., Stewart, G. L., & Piotrowski, M. (2002). Personality and job performance: Test of the mediating effects of motivation among sales representatives. *Journal of Applied Psychology, 87,* 43–51.

Barry, D. T. (2001). Development of a new scale for measuring acculturation: The East Asian Acculturation Measure (EAAM). *Journal of Immigrant Health, 3*(4), 193–197.

Barton, K. A., Blanchard, E. B., & Veazy, C. (1999). Self-monitoring as an assessment strategy in behavioral medicine. *Psychological Assessment, 11,* 490–497.

Bartram, D., Beaumont, J. G., Cornford, T., & Dann, P. L. (1987). Recommendations for the design of software for computer based assessment: Summary statement. *Bulletin of the British Psychological Society, 40,* 86–87.

Bass, B. M. (1956). Development of a structured disguised personality test. *Journal of Applied Psychology, 40,* 393–397.

Bass, B. M. (1957). Validity studies of proverbs personality test. *Journal of Applied Psychology, 41,* 158–160.

Bass, B. M. (1958). Famous Sayings Test: General manual. *Psychological Reports, 4,* Monograph No. 6.

Batson, D. C. (1975). Attribution as a mediator of bias in helping. *Journal of Personality and Social Psychology, 32,* 455–466.

Bauer, R. M. (2000). The flexible battery approach to neuropsychological assessment. In R. D. Vanderploeg (Ed.), *Clinician's guide to neuropsychological assessment* (pp. 419–448). Mahwah, NJ: Erlbaum.

Baughman, E. E., & Dahlstrom, W. B. (1968). *Negro and white children: A psychological study in the rural South.* New York: Academic Press.

Bauman, M. K. (1974). Blind and partially sighted. In M. V. Wisland (Ed.), *Psychoeducational diagnosis of exceptional children* (pp. 159–189). Springfield, IL: Charles C Thomas.

Bauman, M. K., & Kropf, C. A. (1979). Psychological tests used with blind and visually handicapped persons. *School Psychology Digest, 8,* 257–270.

Baumeister, A. A., & Muma, J. R. (1975). On defining mental retardation. *Journal of Special Education, 9,* 293–306.

Baumeister, R. F. (1990). Suicide as escape from self. *Psychological Review, 97,* 90–113.

Bautista, D. R. (2004). *Da kine scale: Construction and validation of the Hawaii Local Acculturation Scale.* Unpublished doctoral dissertation, Washington State University.

Bavolek, S. J. (1984). *Handbook for the Adult-Adolescent Parenting Inventory.* Eau Claire, WI: Family Development Associates.

Baxter, J. C., Brock, B., Hill, P. C., & Rozelle, R. M. (1981). Letters of recommendation: A question of value. *Journal of Applied Psychology, 66,* 296–301.

Baydoun, R. B., & Neuman, G. A. (1992). The future of the General Aptitude Test Battery (GATB) for use in public and private testing. *Journal of Business and Psychology, 7,* 81–91.

Bayer, R. (1981). *Homosexuality and American psychiatry: The politics of diagnosis.* Princeton, New York, NY: Basic Books.

Bayley, N. (1955). On the growth of intelligence. *American Psychologist, 10,* 805–818.

Bayley, N. (1959). Value and limitations of infant testing. *Children, 5,* 129–133.

Bayley, N. (1969). *Bayley Scales of Infant Development: Birth to Two Years.* New York: Psychological Corporation.

Bayley, N. (1993). *Bayley Scales of Infant Development (2nd Edition) Manual.* San Antonio: Psychological Corporation.

Beard, J. G., & Ragheb, M. G. (1980). Measuring leisure satisfaction. *Journal of Leisure Research, 12,* 20–33.

Beatty, P. C., & Willis, G. B. (2007). Research synthesis: The practice of cognitive interviewing. *Public Opinion Quarterly, 71*(2), 287–311.

Beavers, R. (1985). *Manual of Beavers-Timberlawn Family Evaluation Scale and Family Style Evaluation.* Dallas, TX: Southwest Family Institute.

Beck, A. T., Brown, G., & Steer, R. A. (1989). Prediction of eventual suicide in psychiatric inpatients by clinical ratings of hopelessness. *Journal of Consulting and Clinical Psychology, 57,* 309–310.

Beck, A. T., Rush, A. J., Shaw, B. F., & Emery, G. (1979). *Cognitive therapy for depression.* New York: Guilford.

Beck, A. T., & Steer, R. A. (1993). *Beck Depression Inventory manual.* San Antonio: Psychological Corporation.

Beck, A. T., Steer, R. A., & Brown, G. K. (1996). *Manual for the Beck Depression Inventory* (2nd ed.). San Antonio: Psychological Corporation.

Beck, A. T., & Stein, D. (1961). *Development of a self-concept test.* Unpublished manuscript, University of Pennsylvania School of Medicine, Center for Cognitive Therapy, Philadelphia.

Beck, A. T., Ward, C. H., Mendelson, M., Mock, J., & Erbaugh, J. (1961). An inventory for measuring depression. *Archives of General Psychiatry, 4,* 561–571.

Beck, G. (2013, September 24). Did Bill Gates admit the real purpose of Common Core? *Youtube* video accessed May 22, 2016 at https://youtu.be/Zrp-Bu2SLp8

Beck, S. J. (1944). *Rorschach's test: Vol. 1. Basic processes.* New York: Grune & Stratton.

Beck, S. J. (1945). *Rorschach's test: Vol. 2. A variety of personality pictures.* New York: Grune & Stratton.

Beck, S. J. (1952). *Rorschach's test: Vol. 3. Advances in interpretation.* New York: Grune & Stratton.

Beck, S. J. (1960). *The Rorschach experiment.* New York: Grune & Stratton.

Becker, H. A., Needleman, H. L., & Kotelchuck, M. (1978). Child abuse and dentistry: Orificial trauma and its recognition by dentists. *Journal of the American Dental Association, 97*(1), 24–28.

Becker, K. A. (2003). *History of the Stanford-Binet intelligence scales: Content and psychometrics.* (Stanford-Binet Intelligence Scales, Fifth Edition, Assessment Service Bulletin No. 1). Itasca, IL: Riverside.

Beckmann, J. F. (2006). Superiority: Always and everywhere? On some misconceptions in the validation of dynamic testing. *Educational and Child Psychology, 23*(3), 35–49.

Beebe, S. A., Casey, R., & Pinto-Martin, J. (1993). Association of reported infant crying and maternal parenting stress. *Clinical Pediatrics, 32,* 15–19.

Beek, T. F.; Kreukels, B. P. C., Cohen–Kettenis, P. T., & Steensma, T. D. (2015). Partial treatment requests and underlying motives of applicants for gender affirming interventions. *Journal of Sexual Medicine, 12*(11), 2201–2205.

Begault, D. R. (1993). Head-up auditory displays for traffic collision avoidance advisories: A preliminary investigation. *Human Factors, 35,* 707–717.

Beier, E. G., & Sternberg, D. P. (1977). Marital communication. *Journal of Communication, 27,* 92–100.

Beier, M. E., & Ackerman, P. L. (2003). Determinants of health knowledge: An investigation of age, gender, abilities, personality, and interests. *Journal of Personality & Social Psychology, 84,* 439–447.

Bell, N. L., Matthews, T. D., Lassiter, K. S., & Leverett, J. P. (2002). Validity of the Wonderlic Personnel Test as a measure of fluid or crystallized intelligence: Implications for career assessment. *North American Journal of Psychology, 4,* 113–120.

Bellack, A. S., & Hersen, M. (Eds.). (1988). *Behavioral assessment: A practical guide* (3rd ed.). Elmsford, NY: Pergamon.

Bellack, A. S., Morrison, R. L., Mueser, K. T., Wade, J. H., & Sayers, S. L. (1990). Role play for assessing the social competence of psychiatric patients. *Psychological Assessment, 2,* 248–255.

Bellak, L. (1971). *The TAT and CAT in clinical use* (2nd ed.). New York: Grune & Stratton.

Bozikas, V. P., Giazkoulidou, A., Hatzigeorgiadou, M., et al. (2008). Do age and education contribute to performance on the clock drawing test? Normative data for the Greek population. *Journal of Clinical and Experimental Neuropsychology, 30*(2), 1–5.

Brabender, V. M., & Mihura, J. L. (Eds.) (2016). *Handbook of gender and sexuality in psychological assessment*. New York, NY: Routledge.

Bracken, B. A. (1985). A critical review of the Kaufman Assessment Battery for Children (K-ABC). *School Psychology Review, 14,* 21–36.

Bracken, B. A., & Barona, A. (1991). State of the art procedures for translating, validating, and using psychoeducational tests in cross-cultural assessment. *School Psychology International, 12,* 119–132.

Braden, J. P. (1985). *Deafness, deprivation, and IQ*. New York: Plenum.

Braden, J. P. (1990). Do deaf persons have a characteristic psychometric profile on the Wechsler Performance Scales? *Journal of Psychoeducational Assessment, 8,* 518–526.

Braden, J. P. (1992). Intellectual assessment of deaf and hard-of-hearing people: A quantitative and qualitative research synthesis. *School Psychology Review, 21,* 82–84.

Braden, J. P., & Ouzts, S. M. (2007). Review of the Kaufman Assessment Battery for Children, Second Edition. In K. F. Geisinger, R. A. Sipes, J. F. Carlson, & B. S. Plake (Eds.), *The 17th Mental Measurements Yearbook* (pp. 517–520). Lincoln: Buros Institute of Mental Measurements, University of Nebraska.

Bradley, J., & Miller, A. (2010). Widening participation in higher education: Constructions of "going to university." *Educational Psychology in Practice, 26*(4), 401–413.

Bradley, J. P., Nicol, A. A., Charbonneau, D., & Meyer, J. P. (2002). Personality correlates of leadership development in Canadian Forces officer candidates. *Canadian Journal of Behavioural Science, 34,* 92–103.

Bradley-Johnson, S. (1994). *Psychoeducational assessment of students who are visually impaired or blind: Infancy through high school*. Austin: PRO-ED.

Bradley-Johnson, S., & Harris, S. (1990). Best practices in working with students with a visual loss. In A. Thomas & J. Grimes (Eds.), *Best practices in school psychology II* (pp. 871–885). Washington, DC: National Association of School Psychologists.

Brady, N. C., & Halle, J. W. (1997). Functional analysis of communicative behaviors. *Focus on Autism and Other Developmental Disabilities, 12*(2), 95–104.

Braginsky, B. M., Braginsky, D. D., & Ring, K. (1969). *Methods of madness*. New York: Holt, Rinehart & Winston.

Bram, A. D. (2010). The relevance of the Rorschach and patient-examiner relationship in treatment planning and outcome assessment. *Journal of Personality Assessment, 92,* 91–115.

Bram, A. D., & Peebles, M. J. (in preparation). *Person- and treatment-focused psychological testing: A psychodynamic approach*. Washington, DC: APA Books.

Brandy, D. A. (1995). The O'Connor Tweezer Dexterity Test as a screening tool for hiring surgical hair restoration assistants. *American Journal of Cosmetic Surgery, 12*(4), 313–316.

Brannen, M. Y., & Salk, J. E. (2000). Partnering across borders: Negotiating organizational culture in a German-Japanese joint venture. *Human Relations, 53,* 451–487.

Brannigan, G. G., & Brunner, N. A. (2002). *Guide to the qualitative scoring system for the modified version of the Bender-Gestalt test*. Springfield, IL: Charles C Thomas.

Brannigan, G. G., & Decker, S. L. (2003). *Bender Visual-Motor Gestalt Test Second Edition, Examiner's Manual*. Itasca, IL: Riverside.

Brassard, M., et al. (Eds.). (1986). *The psychological maltreatment of children and youth*. Elmsford, NY: Pergamon.

Braswell, H., & Kushner, H. I. (2012). Suicide, social integration, and masculinity in the U.S. military. *Social Science & Medicine, 74,* 530–536.

Brauer, B. (1993). Adequacy of a translation of the MMPI into American Sign Language for use with deaf individuals: Linguistic equivalency issues. *Rehabilitation Psychology, 38,* 247–259.

Bray, D. W. (1964). The management progress study. *American Psychologist, 19,* 419–429.

Bray, D. W. (1982). The assessment center and the study of lives. *American Psychologist, 37,* 180–189.

Bresolin, M. J., Jr. (1984). A comparative study of computer administration of the Minnesota Multiphasic Personality Inventory in an inpatient psychiatric setting. *Dissertation Abstracts International, 46,* 295B. (University Microfilms No. 85–06, 377).

Brettschneider, C., Djadran, H., Härter, M., et al. (2015). Cost-utility analyses of cognitive-behavioural therapy of depression: A systematic review. *Psychotherapy and Psychosomatics, 84*(1), 6–21.

Brewer, E. W., & Clippard, L. F. (2002). Burnout and job satisfaction among student support services personnel. *Human Resource Development Quarterly, 13,* 169–186.

Brewer, S. (1987, January 11). A perfect package, yes, but how 'bout the name? *Journal-News* (Rockland County, NY), pp. H-1, H-18.

Bricklin, B. (1984). *The Bricklin Perceptual Scales: Child-Perception-of-Parents-Series*. Furlong, PA: Village.

Bricklin, B., & Halbert, M. H. (2004). Can child custody data be generated scientifically? Part 1. *American Journal of Family Therapy, 32*(2), 119–138.

Bringle, R., Roach, S., Andler, C., & Evenbeck, S. (1979). Measuring the intensity of jealous reactions. *Catalogue of Selected Documents in Psychology, 9,* 23–24.

British Psychological Society (2006). *Assessment of capacity in adults: Interim guidance for psychologists*. Leicester, UK: The British Psychological Society.

Brittain, H. L. (1907). A study in imagination. *Pedagogical Seminary, 14,* 137–207.

Brody, D., Serby, M., Etienne, N., & Kalkstein, D. C. (1991). Olfactory identification deficits in HIV infection. *American Journal of Psychiatry, 148,* 248–250.

Brody, M. L., Walsh, B. T., & Devlin, M. J. (1994). Binge eating disorder: Reliability and validity of a new diagnostic category. *Journal of Consulting and Clinical Psychology, 62,* 381–386.

Brody, N. (1972). *Personality: Research and theory*. New York: Academic Press.

Brodzinsky, D. M. (1993). On the use and misuse of psychological testing in child custody evaluations. *Professional Psychology: Research and Practice, 24,* 213–219.

Brogden, H. E. (1946). On the interpretation of the correlation coefficient as a measure of predictive efficiency. *Journal of Educational Psychology, 37,* 65–76.

Brogden, H. E. (1949). When tests pay off. *Personnel Psychology, 2,* 171–183.

Brooks, G. (1999). A few good men: Military socialization and gender role strain. *Society for the Psychological Study of Men and Masculinity Bulletin, 4,* 9–11.

Brooks, G. R. (2010). *Beyond the crisis of masculinity: A transtheoretical model for male-friendly therapy*. Washington, DC: American Psychological Association.

Brotemarkle, R. A. (1947). Clinical psychology, 1896–1946. *Journal of Consulting and Clinical Psychology, 11,* 1–4.

"Brother Against Brother," (1997, December 7). CBS, *60 Minutes*, reported by Ed Bradley.

Brotherhood, J. R. (2008). Heat stress and strain in exercise and sport. *Journal of Science and Medicine in Sport, 11*(1), 6–19.

Brown, B. (2007). The utility of standardized tests. *Science, 316*(5832), 1694–1695.

Brown, D. C. (1994). Subgroup norming: Legitimate testing practice or reverse discrimination. *American Psychologist, 49,* 927–928.

Brown, G., Nicassio, P. W., & Wallston, K. A. (1989). Pain coping strategies and depression in rheumatoid arthritis. *Journal of Consulting and Clinical Psychology, 57,* 652–657.

Brown, J. M. (1984). Imagery coping strategies in the treatment of migraine. *Pain, 18,* 157–167.

Brown, L. S. (2008). *Cultural competence in trauma therapy.* Washington, DC: American Psychological Association.

Brown, R. D. (1972). The relationship of parental perceptions of university life and their characterizations of their college sons and daughters. *Educational and Psychological Measurement, 32,* 365–375.

Brown, R. T., Reynolds, C. R., & Whitaker, J. S. (1999). Bias in mental testing since *Bias in Mental Testing. School Psychology Quarterly, 14,* 208–238.

Brown, S. P., & Peterson, R. A. (1993). Antecedents and consequences of salesperson job satisfaction: Meta-analysis and assessment of causal effects. *Journal of Marketing Research, 30,* 63–77.

Bryer, J. B., Martines, K. A., & Dignan, M. A. (1990). Millon Clinical Multiaxial Inventory Alcohol Abuse and Drug Abuse scales and the identification of substance-abuse patients. *Psychological Assessment, 2,* 438–441.

Bucholz, K. K., Cadoret, R., Cloninger, C. R., & Dinwiddie, S. H. (1994). A new, semi-structured psychiatric interview for use in genetic linkage studies: A report on the reliability of the SSAGA. *Journal of Studies on Alcohol, 55,* 149–158.

Buck, J. N. (1950). *Administration and interpretation of the H-T-P test: Proceedings of the II-T-P workshop at Veterans Administration Hospital, Richmond, Virginia.* Beverly Hills, CA: Western Psychological Services.

Buckner, F., & Firestone, M. (2000). "Where the public peril begins": 25 years after *Tarasoff. Journal of Legal Medicine, 21,* 187–222.

Bucofsky, D. (1971). Any learning skills taught in the high school? *Journal of Reading, 15*(3), 195–198.

Budoff, M. (1967). Learning potential among institutionalized young adult retardates. *American Journal of Mental Deficiency, 72,* 404–411.

Budoff, M. (1987). Measures of assessing learning potential. In C. S. Lidz (Ed.), *Dynamic assessment* (pp. 173–195). New York: Guilford Press.

Bukatman, B. A., Foy, J. L., & De Grazia, E. (1971). What is competency to stand trial? *American Journal of Psychiatry, 127,* 1225–1229.

Bumann, B. (2010). The Future of Neuroimaging in Witness Testimony. *Virtual Mentor: American Medical Association Journal of Ethics, 12,* 873–878.

Bundy, C. (2004). Changing behaviour: Using motivational interviewing techniques. *Journal of the Royal Society of Medicine, 97,* 43–47.

Burger, J. M., Horita, M., Kinoshita, L., et al. (1997). Effects of time on the norm of reciprocity. *Basic and Applied Social Psychology, 19,* 91–100.

Burgess, A. W., McCausland, M. P., & Wolbert, W. A. (1981, February). Children's drawings as indicators of sexual trauma. *Perspectives in Psychiatric Care, 19,* 50–58.

Burisch, M. (1984). Approaches to personality inventory construction: A comparison of merits. *American Psychologist, 39,* 214–227.

Burke, M. J. (1984). Validity generalization: A review and critique of the correlation model. *Personnel Psychology, 37,* 93–115.

Burke, R. J. (1970). Occupational and life strains, satisfactions, and mental health. *Journal of Business Administration, 1,* 35–41.

Burns, A., Jacoby, R., & Levy, R. (1991). Progression of cognitive impairment in Alzheimer's disease. *Journal of the American Geriatrics Society, 39,* 39–45.

Burns, E. (1998). *Test accommodations for students with disabilities.* Springfield, IL: Charles C Thomas.

Burns, R. C., & Kaufman, S. H. (1970). *Kinetic Family Drawings (K-F-D): An introduction to understanding through kinetic drawings.* New York: Brunner/Mazel.

Burns, R. C., & Kaufman, S. H. (1972). *Actions, styles, and symbols in Kinetic Family Drawings (K-F-D).* New York: Brunner/Mazel.

Buros, O. K. (1938). *The 1938 mental measurements yearbook.* New Brunswick, NJ: Rutgers University Press.

Buros, O. K. (1968). The story behind the mental measurements yearbooks. *Measurement and Evaluation in Guidance, 1*(2), 86–95.

Burstow, B. (2003). Toward a radical understanding of trauma and trauma work. *Violence Against Women, 9,* 1293–1317.

Burwen, L. S., & Campbell, D. T. (1957). The generality of attitudes toward authority and nonauthority figures. *Journal of Abnormal and Social Psychology, 54,* 24–31.

Bushard, P., & Howard, D. A. (Eds.). (1994). *Resource guide for custody evaluators: A handbook for parenting evaluations.* Madison, WI: Association for Family and Conciliation Courts.

Bushman, B. J., & Cantor, J. (2003). Media ratings for violence and sex: Implications for policymakers and parents. *American Psychologist, 58,* 130–141.

Bushman, B. J., & Wells, G. L. (1998). Trait aggressiveness and hockey penalties: Predicting hot tempers on the ice. *Journal of Applied Psychology, 83,* 969–974.

Butcher, J. N. (1987). The use of computers in psychological assessment: An overview of practices and issues. In J. N. Butcher (Ed.), *Computerized psychological assessment: A practitioner's guide* (pp. 3–14). New York: Basic Books.

Butcher, J. N. (1990). *MMPI-2 in psychological treatment.* New York: Oxford University Press.

Butcher, J. N. (1994). Psychological assessment by computer: Potential gains and problems to avoid. *Psychiatric Annals, 24,* 20–24.

Butcher, J. N. (2000). Revising psychological tests: Lessons learned from the revision of the MMPI. *Psychological Assessment, 12,* 263–271.

Butcher, J. N. (2003). Discontinuities, side steps, and finding a proper place: An autobiographical account. *Journal of Personality Assessment, 80,* 223–236.

Butcher, J. N., Gass C. S., Cumella, E., Kally, Z., & Williams, C. (2008). Potential for Bias in MMPI-2 Assessments Using the Fake Bad Scale (FBS). *Psychological Injury and Law, 1*(3), 191–209.

Butcher, J. N., & Han, K. (1995). Development of an MMPI-2 scale to assess the presentation of self in a superlative manner: The *S* Scale. In J. N. Butcher & C. D. Spielberger (Eds.), *Advances in personality assessment* (Vol. 10, pp. 25–50). Hillsdale, NJ: Erlbaum.

Butcher, J. N., Perry, J. N., & Atlis, M. M. (2000). Validity and utility of computer-based test interpretation. *Psychological Assessment, 12,* 6–18.

Butcher, J. N., Williams, C. L., Graham, J. R., et al. (1992). *Minnesota Multiphasic Personality Inventory-Adolescent (MMPI-A): Manual for administration, scoring, and interpretation.* Minneapolis: University of Minnesota Press.

Butters, N., Wolfe, J., Martone, M., et al. (1985). Memory disorders associated with Huntington's disease: Verbal recall, verbal recognition and procedural memory. *Neuropsychologia, 23,* 729–743.

Büttner, G., & Hasselhorn, M. (2011). Learning disabilities: Debates on definitions, causes, subtypes, and responses. *International Journal of Disability, Development and Education, 58*(1), 75–87.

Byrne, D. (1974). *An introduction to personality* (2nd ed.). Englewood Cliffs, NJ: Prentice-Hall.

Chinoy, E. (1967). *Society: An introduction to sociology.* New York: Random House.

Chira-Chavala, T., & Yoo, S. M. (1994). Potential safety benefits on intelligence cruise control systems. *Accident Analysis & Prevention, 26,* 135–146.

Chmielewski, M., Clark, L. A., Bagby, R. M., & Watson, D. (2015). Method matters: Understanding diagnostic reliability in *DSM-IV* and *DSM-5. Journal of Abnormal Psychology, 124*(3), 764–769.

Cho, H., & LaRose, R. (1999). Privacy issues in Internet surveys. *Social Science Computer Review, 17,* 421–434.

Choca, J. P. (2013). *The Rorschach Inkblot Test: An interpretive guide for clinicians.* Washington, DC: American Psychological Association.

Christensen, K. M., & Delgado, G. L. (1993). *Multicultural issues in deafness.* White Plains, NY: Longman.

Christiansen, A. J., Weibe, J. S., Smith, T. W., & Turner, C. W. (1994). Predictors of survival among hemodialysis patients: Effects of perceived family support. *Health Psychology, 13,* 521–525.

Church, A. T., & Burke, P. J. (1994). Exploratory and confirmatory tests of the Big Five and Tellegen's three- and four-dimensional models. *Journal of Personality and Social Psychology, 66,* 93–114.

Cicchetti, D., & Carlson, V. (Eds.). (1989). *Child maltreatment: Theory and research on the causes and consequences of child abuse and neglect.* New York: Cambridge University Press.

Citrin, L. B., & Greenwald, A. G. (1998, April). *Measuring implicit cognition: Psychologists' and entomologists' attitudes toward insects.* Paper presented at the annual meeting of the Midwestern Psychological Association, Chicago.

Cizek, G. J., & Bunch, M. B. (2007). *Standard setting: A guide to establishing and evaluating performance standards on tests.* Thousand Oaks, CA: Sage.

Clarizio, H. F. (1989). *Assessment and treatment of depression in children and adolescents.* Brandon, VT: Clinical Psychological Publishing.

Clark, B. (1979). *Growing up gifted.* Columbus, OH: Merrill.

Clark, L. A. (1999). Introduction to the special section on the concept of disorder. *Journal of Abnormal Psychology, 108,* 371–373.

Clark, L. A. (2007). Assessment and diagnosis of personality disorder: Perennial issues and an emerging reconceptualization. *Annual Review of Psychology, 58,* 227–257.

Cleckley, H. (1976). *The mask of sanity* (5th ed.). St. Louis: Mosby.

Clements, C. B. (1999). Psychology, attitude shifts, and prison growth. *American Psychologist, 54,* 785–786.

Clift, R. J., Rajlic, G., & Gretton, H. M. (2009). Discriminative and predictive validity of the penile plethysmograph in adolescent sex offenders. *Sexual Abuse: Journal of Research and Treatment, 21*(3), 335–362.

Cloninger, C. R., Przybeck, T. R., & Svrakis, D. M. (1991). The Tridimensional Personality Questionnaire: U.S. normative data. *Psychological Reports, 69,* 1047–1057.

Coalson, D. L., & Raiford, S. E. (2008). *WAIS-IV: Technical and interpretive manual.* San Antonio: NCS Pearson.

Code of Fair Testing Practices in Education. (2004). Washington, DC: Joint Committee on Testing Practices.

Coggins, M. H., Pynchon, M. R., & Dvoskin, J. A. (1998). Integrating research and practice in federal law enforcement: Secret Service applications of behavioral science expertise to protect the president. *Behavioral Sciences and the Law, 16,* 51–70.

Cohen, B. M., Moses, J. L., & Byham, W. C. (1977). *The validity of assessment centers: A literature review* (rev. ed., monograph no. 2). Pittsburgh: Development Dimensions.

Cohen, F., & Lazarus, R. S. (1973). Active coping processes, coping dispositions, and recovery from surgery. *Psychosomatic Medicine, 35,* 375–389.

Cohen, J., Marecek, J., & Gillham, J. (2006). Is three a crowd? Clients, clinicians, and managed care. *American Journal of Orthopsychiatry, 76*(2), 251–259.

Cohen, O., Fischgrund, J., & Redding, R. (1990). Deaf children from ethnic, linguistic, and racial minority backgrounds: An overview. *American Annals of the Deaf, 135,* 67–73.

Cohen, R. J. (1977). Socially reinforced obsessing: A reply. *Journal of Consulting and Clinical Psychology, 45,* 1166–1171.

Cohen, R. J. (1979). *Malpractice: A guide for mental health professionals.* New York: Free Press.

Cohen, R. J. (1985). Computer-enhanced qualitative research. *Journal of Advertising Research, 25*(3), 48–52.

Cohen, R. J. (1987). Overview of emerging evaluative and diagnostic methods technologies. In *Proceedings of the fourth annual Advertising Research Foundation workshop: Broadening the horizons of copy research.* New York: Advertising Research Foundation.

Cohen, R. J. (1994). *Psychology & adjustment: Values, culture, and change.* Boston: Allyn & Bacon.

Cohen, R. J. (1999a). *Exercises in psychological testing and assessment.* Mountain View, CA: Mayfield.

Cohen, R. J. (1999b). What qualitative research can be. *Psychology & Marketing, 16,* 351–368.

Cohen, R. J. (2001). *Discussion of Organizational Culture* (DOC). Jamaica, NY: Author.

Cohen, R. J. (2005). *Exercises in psychological testing and assessment.* San Francisco: McGraw-Hill.

Cohen, R. J., Montague, P., Nathanson, L. S., & Swerdlik, M. E. (1988). *Psychological testing: An introduction to tests and measurement.* Mountain View, CA: Mayfield.

Cohen, R. J., & Smith, F. J. (1976). Socially reinforced obsessing: Etiology of a disorder in a Christian Scientist. *Journal of Consulting and Clinical Psychology, 44,* 142–144.

Cohen, S., Nermelstein, R., Karmack, T., & Hoberman, H. (1985). Measuring the functional components of social support. In I. G. Sarason & B. Sarason (Eds.), *Social support: Theory, research, and practice* (pp. 73–94). Dordrecht, Netherlands: Martinus Nijhoff.

Cole, S. T., & Hunter, M. (1971). Pattern analysis of WISC scores achieved by culturally disadvantaged children. *Psychological Reports, 20,* 191–194.

Coleman, M. R., & Johnsen, S. K. (2011). RtI online resources. In M. R. Coleman & S. K. Johnsen (Eds.), *RtI for gifted students: A CEC-TAG educational resource* (pp. 129–134). Waco, TX: Prufrock Press.

Collier, C. (2011). *Seven steps to separating difference from disability.* Thousand Oaks, CA: Corwin Press.

Collins, J. K., Jupp, J. J., Maberly, G. F., et al. (1987). An exploratory study of the intellectual functioning of neurological and myxoedematous cretins in China. *Australia & New Zealand Journal of Developmental Disabilities, 13,* 13–20.

Collins, L. M. (1996). Is reliability obsolete? A commentary on "Are simple gain scores obsolete?" *Applied Psychological Measurement, 20,* 289–292.

Collins, M. (1998, Spring). Great expectations: What students have to say about the process and practice of launching a career. *Journal of Career Planning and Placement,* 41–47.

Colom, R., Flores-Mendoza, C., & Abad, F. J. (2007). Generational changes on the Draw-A-Man Test: A comparison of Brazilian Urban and Rural Children Tested in 1930, 2002, and 2004. *Journal of Biosocial Science, 39,* 79–89.

Comer, D. R. (1993). Workplace drug testing reconsidered. *Journal of Managerial Issues, 5,* 517–531.

Commons, M. (1985, April). How novelty produces continuity in cognitive development within a domain and accounts for unequal development across domains. Toronto: SRCD.

Cone, J. D. (1977). The relevance of reliability and validity for behavioral assessment. *Behavior Therapy, 8,* 411–426.

Cone, J. D. (1981). Psychometric considerations. In M. Hersen & A. S. Bellack (Eds.), *Behavioral assessment: A practical handbook* (2nd ed.). New York: Pergamon.

Cone, J. D. (1986). Idiographic, nomothetic, and related perspectives in behavioral assessment. In R. O. Nelson & S. C. Hayes (Eds.), *Conceptual foundations of behavioral assessment.* New York: Guilford.

Cone, J. D. (1987). Behavioral assessment: Some things old, some things new, some things borrowed? *Behavioral Assessment, 9,* 1–4.

Cone, J. D. (1999). Introduction to the special section on self-monitoring: A major assessment method in clinical psychology. *Psychological Assessment, 11,* 411–414.

Conger, A. J. (1985). Kappa reliabilities for continuing behaviors and events. *Educational and Psychological Measurement, 45,* 861–868.

Connolly, A. J. (2007). *KeyMath 3 Diagnostic Assessment.* San Antonio: Pearson Assessments.

Connolly, B. S., & Lang, A. E. (2014). Pharmacological treatment of Parkinson disease: A review. *JAMA: Journal of the American Medical Association, 311*(16), 1670–1683.

Connolly, J. (1976). Life events before myocardial infarction. *Journal of Human Stress, 3,* 3–17.

Conte, J. M., & Gintoft, J. N. (2005). Polychronicity, big five personality dimensions, and sales performance. *Human Performance, 18*(4), 427–444.

Conte, J. M., & Jacobs, R. R. (2003). Validity evidence linking polychronicity and Big Five personality dimensions to absence, lateness, and supervisory performance ratings. *Human Performance, 16,* 107–129.

Conti, R. P. (2007). The concealment of psychopathology on the Rorschach in criminal forensic investigations. *Dissertation Abstracts International: Section B. Sciences and Engineering, 68* (6-B), 4125.

Cooke, N. J., Salas, E., Cannon-Bowers, J. A., & Stout, R. J. (2000). Measuring team knowledge. *Human Factors, 42,* 151–173.

Cooper, A. (1981). A basic TAT set for adolescent males. *Journal of Clinical Psychology, 37*(2), 411–414.

Copas, J. B., & Tarling, R. (1986). Some methodological issues in making predictions. In A. Blumstein et al. (Eds.), *Criminal careers and "career criminals"* (pp. 291–313). Washington, DC: National Academy.

Copersino, M., Meade, C., Bigelow, G., & Brooner, R. (2010). Measurement of self-reported HIV risk behaviors in injection drug users: Comparison of standard versus timeline follow-back administration procedures. *Journal of Substance Abuse Treatment, 38,* 60–65.

Corish, C. D., Richard, B., & Brown, S. (1989). Missed medication doses in rheumatoid arthritis patients: Intentional and unintentional reasons. *Arthritis Care and Research, 2,* 3–9.

Cornell, D. G. (1985). External validation of the Personality Inventory for Children—Comment on Lachar, Gdowski, and Snyder. *Journal of Consulting and Clinical Psychology, 53,* 273–274.

Cortes, D. E., Deren, S., Andia, J., Colon, H., Robles, R., & Kang, S. (2003). The use of the Puerto Rican biculturality scale with Puerto Rican drug users in New York and Puerto Rico. *Journal of Psychoactive Drugs, 35,* 197–207.

Cortina, J. M. (1993). What is coefficient alpha? An examination of theory and applications. *Journal of Applied Psychology, 78,* 98–104.

Corwyn, R. F., & Benda, B. B. (2000). Religiosity and church attendance: The effects on use of "hard drugs" controlling for sociodemographic and theoretical factors. *International Journal for the Psychology of Religion, 10,* 241–258.

Costa, P. T., Jr., & McCrae, R. R. (1985). *The NEO Personality Inventory manual.* Odessa, FL: Psychological Assessment Resources.

Costa, P. T., Jr., & McCrae, R. R. (1986). Major contributions to personality psychology. In S. Modgil & C. Modgil (Eds.), *Hans Eysenck: Consensus and controversy* (pp. 63–72, 86, 87). Barcombe Lewes, Sussex, England: Falmer.

Costa, P. T., Jr., & McCrae, R. R. (1987). On the need for longitudinal evidence and multiple measures in behavior-genetics studies of adult personality. *Behavioral and Brain Sciences, 10,* 22–23.

Costa, P. T., Jr., & McCrae, R. R. (1992a). Four ways five factors are basic. *Personality and Individual Differences, 13,* 653–665.

Costa, P. T., Jr., & McCrae, R. R. (1992b). Reply to Eysenck. *Personality and Individual Differences, 13,* 861–865.

Costa, P. T., Jr., & McCrae, R. R. (1992c). *Revised NEO Personality Inventory (NEO-PI-R) and NEO Five-Factor Inventory (NEO-FFI) professional manual.* Odessa, FL: Psychological Assessment Resources.

Costa, P. T., Jr., & McCrae, R. R. (1997). Stability and change in personality assessment: The Revised NEO Personality Inventory in the year 2000. *Journal of Personality Assessment, 68,* 86–94.

Cote, J. A., McCullough, J., & Reilly, M. (1985). Effects of unexpected situations on behavior-intention differences: A garbology analysis. *Journal of Consumer Research, 12,* 188–194.

Cotton, P. (1992). Women's health initiative leads way as research begins to fill gender gaps. *Journal of the American Medical Association, 267*(4), 469–470, 473.

Coupe, J. J. (2006). A clinical approach to deductive behavioral profiling. *Dissertation Abstracts International: Section B. Sciences and Engineering, 66*(9-B), 5081.

Courvoisier, D. S., Eid, M., & Lischetzke, T. (2012). Compliance to a cell phone-based ecological momentary assessment study: The effect of time and personality characteristics. *Psychological Assessment, 24*(3), 713–720.

Cox, J. (2006). Review of profiling violent crimes: An investigative tool. *Journal of Investigative Psychology and Offender Profiling, 3*(2), 134–137.

Coyne, I., & Bartram, D. (2006). Design and development of the ITC guidelines on computer-based and internet-delivered testing. *International Journal of Testing, 6*(2), 133–142.

Coyne, J. C. (1976). The place of informed consent in ethical dilemmas. *Journal of Consulting and Clinical Psychology, 44,* 1015–1017.

Cramer, P. (1991). *The development of defense mechanisms: Theory, research, and assessment.* New York: Springer-Verlag.

Cramer, P. (1996). *Storytelling, narrative, and the Thematic Apperception Test.* New York: Guilford.

Crego, C., & Widiger, T. A. (2016). Cleckley's psychopaths: Revisited. *Journal of Abnormal Psychology, 125*(1), 75–87.

Crèvecoeur, M. G. St. J. de (1951). What is an American letter? In H. S. Commager (Ed.), *Living ideas in America.* New York: Harper. (Originally published in *Letters from an American farmer,* 1762.)

Crick, N. R. (1997). Engagement in gender normative versus nonnormative forms of aggression: Links to social-psychological adjustment. *Developmental Psychology, 33,* 610–617.

Crick, N. R., Bigbee, M. A., & Howes, C. (1996). Gender differences in children's normative beliefs about aggression:

How do I hurt thee? Let me count the ways. *Child Development, 67,* 1003–1014.

Crocker, L., Llabre, M., & Miller, M. D. (1988). The generalizability of content validity ratings. *Journal of Educational Measurement, 25,* 287–299.

Cronbach, L. J. (1949). Statistical methods applied to Rorschach scores: A review. *Psychological Bulletin, 46,* 393–429.

Cronbach, L. J. (1951). Coefficient alpha and the internal structure of tests. *Psychometrika, 16,* 297–334.

Cronbach, L. J. (1970). *Essentials of psychological testing* (3rd ed.). New York: Harper & Row.

Cronbach, L. J. (1975). Five decades of public controversy over mental testing. *American Psychologist, 30,* 1–13.

Cronbach, L. J. (1984). *Essentials of psychological testing* (4th ed.). New York: Harper & Row.

Cronbach, L. J., & Gleser, G. C. (1957). *Psychological tests and personnel decisions.* Champaign, IL: University of Illinois.

Cronbach, L. J., & Gleser, G. C. (1965). *Psychological tests and personnel decisions* (2nd ed.). Urbana: University of Illinois.

Cronbach, L. J., Gleser, G. C., Nanda, H., & Rajaratnam, N. (1972). *The dependability of behavioral measurement: Theory of generalizability for scores and profiles.* New York: Wiley.

Crosbie, J., Pérusse, D., Barr, C. L., & Schachar, R. J. (2008). Validating psychiatric endophenotypes: Inhibitory control and attention deficit hyperactivity disorder. *Neuroscience and Biobehavioral Reviews, 32,* 40–55.

Crosby, F. J., Iyer, A., Clayton, S., & Downing, R. A. (2003). Affirmative action: Psychological data and the policy debates. *American Psychologist, 58,* 93–115.

Crowne, D. P., & Marlowe, D. (1964). *The approval motive: Studies in evaluative dependence.* New York: Wiley.

Crundall, D. E., Underwood, G., & Chapman, P. R. (1998). How much do drivers see? The effects of demand on visual search strategies in novice and experienced drivers. In G. Underwood (Ed.), *Eye guidance in reading and scene perception* (pp. 395–417). Oxford, England: Elsevier.

Cuéllar, I., Arnold, B., & Maldonado, R. (1995). Acculturation Rating Scale for Mexican Americans–II: A revision of the original ARSMA scale. *Hispanic Journal of Behavioral Sciences, 17*(3), 275–304.

Cuéllar, I., Harris, I. C., & Jasso, R. (1980). An acculturation scale for Mexican American normal and clinical populations. *Hispanic Journal of Behavioral Science, 2,* 199–217.

Cundick, B. P. (1976). Measures of intelligence on Southwest Indian students. *Journal of Social Psychology, 81,* 151–156.

Cureton, E. E. (1957). The upper and lower twenty-seven percent rule. *Psychometrika, 22,* 293–296.

Cushman, P., & Guilford, P. (2000). Will managed care change our way of being? *American Psychologist, 55,* 985–996.

da Silva, D. C., Schwarz, K., Fontanari, A. M. V., et al. (2016). Whoqol-100 before and after sex reassignment surgery in Brazilian male-to-female transsexual individuals. *Journal of Sexual Medicine, 13*(6), 988–993.

Dahlman, K. A., & Geisinger, K. F. (2015). The prevalence of measurement in undergraduate psychology curricula across the United States. *Scholarship of Teaching and Learning in Psychology, 1*(3), 189–199.

Dahlstrom, W. G. (1995). Pigeons, people, and pigeon holes. *Journal of Personality Assessment, 64,* 2–20.

Dahlstrom, W. G., & Dahlstrom, L. E. (Eds.). (1980). *Basic readings on the MMPI: A new selection on personality measurement.* Minneapolis: University of Minnesota.

Dahlstrom, W. G., & Welsh, G. S. (1960). *An MMPI handbook: A guide to use in clinical practice and research.* Minneapolis: University of Minnesota.

Dahlstrom, W. G., Welsh, G. S., & Dahlstrom, L. E. (1972). *An MMPI handbook: Vol. 1. Clinical interpretation.* Minneapolis: University of Minnesota.

Daigneault, S., Braun, C. M. J., & Whitaker, H. A. (1992). Early effects of normal aging on perseverative and non-perseverative prefrontal measures. *Developmental Neuropsychology, 8,* 99–114.

Daley, C. E., & Onwuegbuzie, A. J. (2011). Race and intelligence. In Sternberg, R. J., & Kaufman, S. B. (Eds.), *The Cambridge Handbook of Intelligence* (pp. 293–307). New York: Cambridge University Press.

D'Amato, A., & Zijlstra, F. R. H. (2008). Psychological climate and individual factors as antecedents of work outcomes. *European Journal of Work and Organizational Psychology, 7*(1), 33–54.

Dana, J., & Thomas, R. (2006). In defense of clinical judgment . . . and mechanical prediction. *Journal of Behavioral Decision Making, 19*(5), 413–428.

Dana, R. H. (1982). *A human science model for personality assessment with projective techniques.* Springfield, IL: Charles C Thomas.

Dana, R. H. (1995). Culturally competent MMPI assessment of Hispanic populations. *Hispanic Journal of Behavioral Sciences, 17,* 305–319.

Dana, R. H., Aguilar-Kitibutr, A., Diaz-Vivar, N., & Vetter, H. (2002). A teaching model for multicultural assessment: Psychological report contents and cultural competence. *Journal of Personality, 79,* 207–215.

Dana, R. H., & Whatley, P. R. (1991). When does a difference make a difference? MMPI scores and African-Americans. *Journal of Clinical Psychology, 47,* 400–406.

Daneman, M., & Carpenter, P. A. (1980). Individual differences in working memory and reading. *Journal of Verbal Learning and Verbal Behavior, 19,* 450–466.

Danford, G. S., & Steinfeld, E. (1999). Measuring the influences of physical environments on the behaviors of people with impairments. In E. Steinfeld & G. S. Danford (Eds.), *Enabling environments: Measuring the impact of environment on disability and rehabilitation* (pp. 111–137). New York: Kluwer Academic/Plenum.

Daniels, K. (2000). Measures of five aspects of affective well-being at work. *Human Relations, 53,* 275–294.

Darwin, C. (1859). *On the origin of species by means of natural selection.* London: Murray.

Darwin, C. R. (1872). *The expression of the emotions in man and animals.* London: John Murray.

Das, J. P. (1972). Patterns of cognitive ability in nonretarded and retarded children. *American Journal of Mental Deficiency, 77,* 6–12.

Das, J. P. (2014). Search for intelligence by PASSing g. *Canadian Psychology/Psychologie Canadienne, 56*(1), 39–45.

Das, J. P., Kirby, J., & Jarman, R. F. (1975). Simultaneous and successive synthesis: An alternative model for cognitive abilities. *Psychological Bulletin, 82,* 87–103.

Dattilio, F. M. (2006). Equivocal death psychological autopsies in cases of criminal homicide. *American Journal of Forensic Psychology, 24*(1), 5–22.

Daubert v. Merrell Dow Pharmaceuticals, 113 S. Ct. 2786 (1993).

Davids, A., & Murray, H. A. (1955). Preliminary appraisal of an auditory projective technique for studying personality and cognition. *American Journal of Orthopsychiatry, 25,* 543–554.

Davidson, F., Kovacevic, V., Cave, M., et al. (2015). Assessing fitness for trial of deaf defendants. *Psychiatry, Psychology and Law, 22*(1), 145–156.

Davidson, H. A. (1949). Malingered psychosis. *Bulletin of the Menninger Clinic, 13,* 157–163.

Davidson, T. N., Bowden, L., & Tholen, D. (1979). Social support as a moderator of burn rehabilitation. *Archives of Physical Medicine and Rehabilitation, 60,* 556.

Davies, M., Stankov, L., & Roberts, R. D. (1998). Emotional intelligence: In search of an elusive construct. *Journal of Personality and Social Psychology, 75,* 989–1015.

Davies, P. L., & Gavin, W. J. (1994). Comparison of individual and group/consultation treatment methods for preschool children with developmental delays. *American Journal of Occupational Therapy, 48,* 155–161.

Davis, J. M., & Broitman, J. (2011). *Nonverbal learning disabilities in children: Bridging the gap between science and practice.* New York: Springer Science and Business Media.

Davison, G. C., Vogel, R. S., & Coffman, S. G. (1997). Think-aloud approaches to cognitive assessment and the articulated thoughts in simulated situations paradigm. *Journal of Consulting and Clinical Psychology, 65,* 950–958.

Dawes, R. M., Faust, D., & Meehl, P. E. (1989, March 31). Clinical versus actuarial judgment. *Science, 243,* 1668–1674.

Day, D. V., & Silverman, S. B. (1989). Personality and job performance: Evidence of incremental validity. *Personnel Psychology, 42,* 25–36.

Dazzi, C., & Pedrabissi, L. (2009). Graphology and personality: An empirical study on validity of handwriting analysis. *Psychological Reports, 105*(3, Pt. 2), 1255–1268.

De Champlain, A. F. (2010). A primer on classical test theory and item response theory for assessments in medical education. *Medical Education, 44*(1), 109–117.

De Corte, W., & Lievens, F. (2005). The risk of adverse impact in selections based on a test with known effect size. *Educational and Psychological Measurement, 65*(5), 643–664.

De Marco, A. P., & Broshek, D. K. (2016). Computerized cognitive testing in the management of youth sports-related concussion. *Journal of Child Neurology, 31*(1), 68–75.

de Vries, A. L. C., McGuire, J. K.. Steensma, T. D., et al. (2014). Young adult psychological outcome after puberty suppression and gender reassignment. *Pediatrics, 134*(4), 696–704.

Deary, I. J., Johnson, W., & Houlihan, L. M. (2009). Genetic foundations of human intelligence. *Human genetics, 126*(1), 215–232.

Decker, J. T., Bailey, T. L., & Westergaard, N. (2002). Burnout among childcare workers. *Residential Treatment for Children & Youth, 19*(4), 61–77.

Del Giudice, M. J. (2010a). What might this be? Rediscovering the Rorschach as a tool for personnel selection in organizations. *Journal of Personality Assessment, 92*(1), 78–89.

Del Giudice, M. J. (2010b). Reply to comment on "What might this be? Rediscovering the Rorschach as a tool for personnel selection in organizations" (Del Giudice, 2010). *Journal of Personality Assessment, 92*(6), 613–615.

Delahunty, R. J. (1988). Perspectives on within-group scoring. *Journal of Vocational Behavior, 33,* 463–477.

DeLiema, M., Navarro, A., Enguidanos, S., & Wilber, K. (2015). Voices from the frontlines: Examining elder abuse from multiple professional perspectives. *Health & Social Work, 40,* 15–24.

Dellis, D. C., Kramer, J. H., Kaplan, E., & Ober, B. A. (2000). *The California Verbal Learning Test–II.* Lutz, FL: PAR.

Deloria, D. J. (1985). Review of the Miller Assessment for Preschoolers. In J. V. Mitchell, Jr. (Ed.), *The ninth mental measurements yearbook.* Lincoln: Buros Institute of Mental Measurements, University of Nebraska.

DeMars, C. E., & Wise, S. L. (2010). Can differential rapid-guessing behavior lead to differential item functioning? *International Journal of Testing, 10*(3), 207–229.

DeMulder, E. K., Denham, S., Schmidt, M., & Mitchell, J. (2000). Q-sort assessment of attachment security during the preschool years: Links from home to school. *Developmental Psychology, 36,* 274–282.

Denton, W. H. (2007). Relational diagnosis: An essential component of biopsychosocial assessment for DSM-V. *American Journal of Psychiatry, 164,* 1146–1147.

Department for Constitutional Affairs. (2007). *Mental Capacity Act 2005 Code of Practice.* London: TSO. Retrieved from http://www3.imperial.ac.uk/pls/portallive/docs/1/51771696.pdf

Department of Health, Education, and Welfare. (1977a). Nondiscrimination on basis of handicap: Implementation of Section 504 of the Rehabilitation Act of 1973. *Federal Register, 42*(86), 22676–22702.

Department of Health, Education, and Welfare. (1977b). Education of Handicapped Children: Implementation of Part B of the Education of the Handicapped Act. *Federal Register, 42*(163), 42474–42518.

Department of Veterans Affairs. (1997). *Assessment of competency and capacity of the older adult: A practice guideline for psychologists.* Milwaukee, W.I.: National Center for Cost Containment, Department of Veterans Affairs.

DePaulo, B. M. (1994). Spotting lies: Can humans learn to do better? *Current Directions in Psychological Science, 3,* 83–86.

Derue, D. S., Nahrgang, J. D., Wellman, N., & Humphrey, S. E. (2011). Trait and behavioral theories of leadership: An integration and meta-analytic test of their relative validity. *Personnel Psychology, 64,* 7–52.

Desrochers, M. N., Hile, M. G., & Williams-Mosely, T. L. (1997). Survey of functional assessment procedures used with individuals who display mental retardation and severe problem behaviors. *American Journal on Mental Retardation, 101,* 535–546.

Dèttore, D., Ristori, J., Antonelli, P., et al. (2015). Gender dysphoria in adolescents: The need for a shared assessment protocol and proposal of the AGIR protocol. *Giornale di Psicopatologia,* [*Journal of Psychopathology*] 21(2), 152–158.

Dhejne, C., Van Vlerken, R., Heylens, G., & Arcelus, J. (2016). Mental health and gender dysphoria: A review of the literature. *International Review of Psychiatry, 28*(1), 44–57.

Diamond, B. L. (1980). Inherent problems in the use of pretrial hypnosis on a prospective witness. *California Law Review, 68,* 313–349.

Dickson, C. R. (1975). Role of assessment in behavior therapy. In P. McReynolds (Ed.), *Advances in psychological assessment* (Vol. 3). San Francisco: Jossey-Bass.

Diebold, M. H., Curtis, W. S., & DuBose, R. F. (1978). Developmental scales versus observational measures for deaf-blind children. *Exceptional Children, 44,* 275–278.

Dietz, P. E., Matthews, D. B., Van Duyne, C., et al. (1991). Threatening and otherwise inappropriate letters to Hollywood celebrities. *Journal of Forensic Sciences, 36,* 185–209.

Digman, J. M. (1990). Personality structure: Emergence of the Five-Factor Model. *Annual Reviews of Psychology, 41*(1), 417–440.

Dikmen, S. (2015). A remembrance: My advisor, Ralph M. Reitan. *Archives of Clinical Neuropsychology, 30*(8), 762–763.

Dimock, P. H., & Cormier, P. (1991). The effects of format differences and computer experience on performance and anxiety on a computer-administered test. *Measurement and Evaluation in Counseling and Development, 24,* 119–126.

Dion, K. K. (1979). Physical attractiveness and evaluation of children's transgressions. *Journal of Personality and Social Psychology, 24,* 207–213.

Dipboye, R. L. (1992). *Selection interviews: Process perspectives.* Cincinnati: South-Western Publishing.

DiStefano, C., & Dombrowski, S. C. (2006). Investigating the theoretical structure of the Stanford-Binet, Fifth Edition. *Journal of Psychoeducational Assessment, 24,* 123–136.

Diven, K. (1937). Certain determinants in the conditioning of anxiety reactions. *Journal of Psychology, 3,* 291–308.

Dixon, M., Wang, S., Calvin, J., et al. (2002). The panel interview: A review of empirical research and guidelines for practice. *Public Personnel Management, 31,* 397–428.

Dohrenwend, B. P., & Shrout, P. E. (1985). Hassles in the conceptualization and measurement of life stresses variables. *American Psychologist, 40,* 780–785.

Dohrenwend, B. P., Shrout, P. E., Egri, G., & Mendelsohn, F. S. (1980). Non-specific psychological distress and other dimensions of psychopathology. *Archives of General Psychiatry, 37,* 1229–1236.

Doll, E. A. (1917). A brief Binet-Simon scale. *Psychological Clinic, 11,* 197–211, 254–261.

Doll, E. A. (1953). *Measurement of social competence: A manual for the Vineland Social Maturity Scale.* Circle Pines, MN: American Guidance Service.

Dollinger, S. J. (2011). "Standardized minds" or individuality? Admissions tests and creativity revisited. *Psychology of Aesthetics, Creativity, and the Arts, 5*(4), 329–341.

Dolnick, E. (1993). Deafness as culture. *Atlantic, 272*(3), 37–53.

Donahue, E. M., Robins, R. W., Roberts, B. W., & John, O. P. (1993). The divided self: Concurrent and longitudinal effects of psychological adjustment and social roles on self-concept differentiation. *Journal of Personality and Social Psychology, 64,* 834–846.

Donders, J. (1992). Validity of the Kaufman Assessment Battery for Children when employed with children with traumatic brain injury. *Journal of Clinical Psychology, 48,* 225–230.

Donohue, B., Silver, N. C., Dickens, Y., et al. (2007). Development and initial psychometric evaluation of the Sport Interference Checklist. *Behavior Modification, 31*(6), 937–957.

Doorey, N. A. (2012/2013). Coming soon: A new generation of assessments. *Educational Leadership, 70*(4), 28–34.

Dosajh, N. L. (1996). Projective techniques with particular reference to inkblot tests. *Journal of Projective Psychology and Mental Health, 3,* 59–68.

Doty, R. L., Shaman, P., & Dann, M. (1984). Development of the University of Pennsylvania Smell Identification Test: A standard microencapsulated test of olfactory dysfunction. *Physiological Behavior, 32,* 489–502.

Douglas, C. (1993). *Translate this darkness: The life of Christiana Morgan.* New York: Simon & Schuster.

Draguns, J. G. (1984). Assessing mental health and disorder across cultures. In P. Pedersen, N. Sartorius, & A. J. Marsella (Eds.), *Mental health services: The cross-cultural context* (pp. 31–57). Beverly Hills, CA: Sage.

Drasgow, F., & Olson-Buchanan, J. B. (Eds.). (1999). *Innovations in computerized assessment.* Mahwah, NJ: Erlbaum.

Dreger, R. M., & Miller, K. S. (1960). Comparative studies of Negroes and Whites in the U.S. *Psychological Bulletin, 51,* 361–402.

Drinkwater, M. J. (1976). Psychological evaluation of visually handicapped children. *Massachusetts School Psychologists Association Newsletter, 6.*

Drotar, D., Olness, K., & Wiznitzer, M., et al. (1999). Neurodevelopmental outcomes of Ugandan infants with HIV infection: An application of growth curve analysis. *Health Psychology, 18,* 114–121.

DuBois, P. H. (1966). A test-dominated society: China 1115 B.C.E–1905 A.D. In A. Anastasi (Ed.), *Testing problems in perspective* (pp. 29–36). Washington, DC: American Council on Education.

DuBois, P. H. (1970). *A history of psychological testing.* Boston: Allyn & Bacon.

Ducharme, F., Levesque, L., Gendron, M., & Legault, A. (2001). Development process and qualitative evaluation of a program to promote the mental health of family caregivers. *Clinical Nursing Research, 10,* 182–201.

Duchek, J. M., Hunt, L., Ball, K., et al. (1998). Attention and driving performance in Alzheimer's disease. *Journal of Gerontology, Series B: Psychological Science & Social Sciences, 53B*(2), 130–141.

Duclos, C. W. (1999). Factors associated with alcohol, drug, and mental health service utilization among a sample of American Indian adolescent detainees. *Dissertation Abstracts International, Section B: The Sciences & Engineering, 40*(4-B), 1524.

Dudycha, G. J. (1936). An objective study of punctuality in relation to personality and achievement. *Archives of Psychology, 204,* 1–319.

Duff, K., & Fisher, J. M. (2005). Ethical dilemmas with third party observers. *Journal of Forensic Neuropsychology, 4*(2), 65–82.

Dumont, R., & Willis, J. (2001). Use of the Tellegen & Briggs formula to determine the Dumont–Willis indexes (DWI–I & DWI–II) for the WISC–IV. http://alpha.fdu.edu/psychology/

Duncanson, C. (2009). Forces for good? Narratives of military masculinity in peacekeeping operations. *International Feminist Journal of Politics, 11,* 63–80.

Duncker, K. (1945). On problem solving. *Psychological Monographs, 5,* 1–13.

Dunham, R. B., Grube, J. A., & Castaneda, M. B. (1994). Organizational commitment: The utility of an integrative definition. *Journal of Applied Psychology, 79,* 370–380.

Dunn, L. B., Lindamer, L. A., Palmer, B. W., et al. (2002). Improving understanding of research consent in middle-aged and elderly patients with psychotic disorders. *American Journal of Geriatric Psychology, 10,* 142–150.

Dunn, L. M., & Dunn, L. M. (1997). *Examiner's manual for the PPVT-III, Peabody Picture Vocabulary Test, Third Edition.* Circle Pines, MN: American Guidance Service.

Duvall, E. D. (2011). No secrets to conceal: Dynamic assessment and a state mandated, standardized 3rd grade reading test for children with learning disabilities. *Dissertation Abstracts International Section A: Humanities and Social Sciences, 2011,* 2401.

Dwairy, M. (2004). Dynamic approach to learning disability assessment: DLD test. *Dyslexia: An International Journal of Research and Practice, 10*(1), 1–23.

Dwyer, C. A. (1996). Cut scores and testing: Statistics, judgment, truth, and error. *Psychological Assessment, 8,* 360–362.

Dykes, L. (1986). The whiplash shaken infant syndrome: What has been learned? *Child Abuse and Neglect, 10,* 211.

Dywan, J., & Bowers, K. (1983). The use of hypnosis to enhance recall. *Science, 22,* 184–185.

Earles, J. A., & Ree, M. J. (1992). The predictive validity of the ASVAB for training grades. *Educational and Psychological Measurement, 52,* 721–725.

Early, P. C., Gibson, C. B., & Chen, C. C. (1999). "How did I do?" versus "How did we do?": Cultural contrasts of performance feedback use and self-efficacy. *Journal of Cross-Cultural Psychology, 30,* 594–619.

Ebadi, M., Srinivasan, S. K., & Baxi, M. D. (1996). Oxidative stress and antioxidant therapy in Parkinson's disease. *Progress in Neurobiology, 48,* 1–19.

Eckardt, W., Steklis, H. D., Gerald-Steklis, N., Fletcher, A. W., Stoinski, T. S., & Weiss, A. (2014). Personality dimensions and their behavioral correlates in wild Virunga mountain gorillas (*Gorilla beringei beringei*). *Journal of Comparative Psychology, 129,* 26–41.

Edens, J. F., Cox, J., S. T., et al. (2015). How reliable are Psychopathy Checklist–Revised scores in Canadian criminal trials? A case law review. *Psychological Assessment, 27*(2), 447–456.

Edwards, A. L. (1953). *Edwards Personal Preference Schedule.* New York: Psychological Corporation.

Edwards, A. L. (1957a). *The social desirability variable in personality assessment and research.* New York: Dryden.

Edwards, A. L. (1957b). *Techniques of attitude scale construction.* New York: Appleton-Century-Crofts.

Edwards, A. L. (1966). Relationship between probability of endorsement and social desirability scale value for a set of 2,824 personality statements. *Journal of Applied Psychology, 50,* 238–239.

Edwards, A. L., & Walsh, J. A. (1964). Response sets in standard and experimental personality scales. *American Education Research Journal, 1,* 52–60.

Edwards, C. P., & Kumru, A. (1999). Culturally sensitive assessment. *Child and Adolescent Psychiatric Clinics of North America, 8,* 409–424.

Eich, E. (2014). Business not as usual. *Psychological Science, 25,* 3–6.

Eichler, R. M. (1951). A comparison of the Rorschach and Behn-Rorschach inkblot tests. *Journal of Consulting Psychology, 15,* 185–189.

Einarsdóttir, S., & Rounds, J. (2009). Gender bias and construct validity in vocational interest measurement: Differential item functioning in the Strong Interest Inventory. *Journal of Vocational Behavior, 74*(3), 295–307.

Eisenberg, N., Guthrie, I. K., Cumberland, A., et al. (2002). Prosocial development in early adulthood: A longitudinal study. *Journal of Personality & Social Psychology, 82,* 993–1006.

Eisman, E. J., Dies, R. R., Finn, S. E., et al. (2000). Problems and limitations in using psychological assessment in the contemporary health care delivery system. *Professional Psychology: Research and Practice, 31,* 131–140.

Elder, G. H., Van Nguyen, T., & Caspi, A. (1985). Linking family hardship to children's lives. *Child Development, 56,* 361–375.

Eldredge, N. (1993). Culturally affirmative counseling with American Indians who are deaf. *Journal of the American Deafness and Rehabilitation Association, 26,* 1–18.

Elksnin, L. K., & Elksnin, N. (1993). A review of picture interest inventories: Implications for vocational assessment of students with disabilities. *Journal of Psychoeducational Assessment, 11,* 323–336.

Ellerstein, N. S. (Ed.). (1981). *Child abuse and neglect: A medical reference.* New York: Wiley.

Elliot, H., Glass, L., & Evans, J. (Eds.). (1987). *Mental health assessment of deaf clients: A practical manual.* Boston: Little, Brown.

Elliott, A. N., O'Donohue, W. T., & Nickerson, M. A. (1993). The use of sexually anatomically detailed dolls in the assessment of sexual abuse. *Clinical Psychology Review, 13,* 207–221.

Elliott, C. D. (1990a). *The Differential Ability Scales.* San Antonio: Psychological Corporation.

Elliott, C. D. (1990b). *Technical handbook: The Differential Ability Scales.* San Antonio: Psychological Corporation.

Elliott, R. (2011). Utilising evidence-based leadership theories in coaching for leadership development: Towards a comprehensive integrating conceptual framework. *International Coaching Psychology Review, 6,* 46–70.

Elliott, S. N. (1988). Acceptability of behavioral treatments in educational settings. In J. C. Witt, S. N. Elliott, & F. M. Greshma (Eds.), *The handbook of behavior therapy education* (pp. 121–150). New York: Plenum.

Elliott, S. N., Katochwill, T. R., & McKevitt, B. C. (2001). Experimental analysis of the effects of testing accommodations on the scores of students with and without disabilities. *Journal of School Psychology, 39,* 3–24.

Elliott, T. R., & Carroll, M. N. (1997). *Issues in psychological assessment for rehabilitation services.* Paper presented at the annual convention of the American Psychological Association, August, Chicago.

Ellis, T., DeAngelis, T. R., Dalton, D., & Venne, J. (2016). *Be active & beyond: A guide to exercise and wellness for people with Parkinson's Disease.* Staten Island, NY: American Parkinson Disease Association.

Ellis, T. E., Rufino, K. A., Green, K. L. (2016). Implicit measure of life/death orientation predicts response of suicidal ideation to treatment in psychiatric inpatients. Archives of Suicide Research, 20(1), 59–68.

Embretson, S. E. (1996). The new rules of measurement. *Psychological Assessment, 8,* 341–349.

Endicott, J., & Spitzer, R. L. (1978). A diagnostic interview: The Schedule for Affective Disorders and Schizophrenia. *Archives of General Psychiatry, 35,* 837–844.

Engin, A., Wallbrown, F., & Brown, D. (1976). The dimensions of reading attitude for children in the intermediate grades. *Psychology in the Schools, 13*(3), 309–316.

Epstein, J. L., & McPartland, J. M. (1978). *The Quality of School Life Scale administration and technical manual.* Boston: Houghton Mifflin.

Epstein, N., Baldwin, L., & Bishop, S. (1983). The McMaster Family Assessment Device. *Journal of Marital and Family Therapy, 9,* 171–180.

Erard, R. E., Meyer, G. J., & Viglione, D. J. (2014). Setting the record straight: Comment on Gurley, Piechowski, Sheehan, and Gray (2014) on the admissibility of the Rorschach Performance Assessment System (R-PAS) in court. *Psychological Injury and Law, 7*(2), 165–177.

Erdberg, P., & Weiner, I. B. (2007). John E. Exner Jr. (1928–2006). *American Psychologist, 62*(1), 54.

Erdelyi, M. H. (1974). A new look at the new look: Perceptual defense and vigilance. *Psychological Review, 81,* 1–25.

Espinosa, M. P., & Gardeazabal, J. (2010). Optimal correction for guessing in multiple-choice tests. *Journal of Mathematical Psychology, 54*(5), 415–425.

Etkind, A. M. (1994). More on L. S. Vygotsky: Forgotten texts and undiscovered contexts. *Journal of Russian & East European Psychology, 32*(6), 6–34.

Evan, W. M., & Miller, J. R. (1969). Differential effects of response bias of computer vs. conventional administration of a social science questionnaire. *Behavioral Science, 14,* 216–227.

Evans, J. D., et al. (2000). Cross-cultural applications of the Halstead-Reitan batteries. In E. Fletcher-Janzen et al. (Eds.), *Handbook of cross-cultural neuropsychology* (pp. 287–303). New York: Kluwer Academic/Plenum.

Evans, M. (1978). Unbiased assessment of locally low incidence handicapped children. In *IRRC practitioners talk to practitioners.* Springfield, IL: Illinois Regional Resource Center.

Evers, W., Tomic, W., & Brouwers, A. (2002). Aggressive behavior and burnout among staff of homes for the elderly. *International Journal of Mental Health Nursing, 11,* 2–9.

Ewing, C. P., and McCann, J. T. (2006). *Minds on trial: Great cases in law and psychology.* New York: Oxford University Press.

Exner, J. E., Jr. (1962). A comparison of human figure drawings of psychoneurotics, character disturbances, normals, and subjects experiencing experimentally induced fears. *Journal of Projective Techniques, 26,* 292–317.

Exner, J. E., Jr. (1969). *The Rorschach systems.* New York: Grune & Stratton.

Exner, J. E., Jr. (1974). *The Rorschach: A comprehensive system.* New York: Wiley.

Exner, J. E., Jr. (1978). *The Rorschach: A comprehensive system: Vol. 2. Current research and advanced interpretations.* New York: Wiley-Interscience.

Exner, J. E., Jr. (1983). Rorschach assessment. In I. B. Weiner (Ed.), *Methods in clinical psychology* (2nd ed.). New York: Wiley.

Exner, J. E., Jr. (1986). *The Rorschach: A comprehensive system: Vol. 1. Basic foundations* (2nd ed.). New York: Wiley.

Exner, J. E., Jr. (1989). Searching for projection in the Rorschach. *Journal of Personality Assessment, 53,* 520–536.

Exner, J. E., Jr. (1990). *Workbook for the comprehensive system* (3rd ed.). Asheville, NC: Rorschach Workshops.

Exner, J. E., Jr. (1991). *The Rorschach: A comprehensive system: Vol. 2. Interpretation* (2nd ed.). New York: Wiley.

Exner, J. E., Jr. (1993). *The Rorschach: A comprehensive system: Vol. 1. Basic foundations* (3rd ed.). New York: Wiley.

Exner, J. E., Jr. (1993). *The Rorschach: A comprehensive system: Vol. 2. Interpretations.* New York: Wiley.

Exner, J. E., Jr. (1997). Critical bits and the Rorschach response process. *Journal of Personality Assessment, 67,* 464–477.

Exner, J. E., Jr. (2003). *The Rorschach: A Comprehensive system: Vol. 1. Basic foundations* (4th ed.). Hoboken, NJ: Wiley.

Exner, J. E., Jr. (2007). A new U.S. adult nonpatient sample. *Journal of Personality Assessment, 89* (Suppl. 1), S154–S158.

Exner, J. E., Jr., & Weiner, I. B. (1982). *The Rorschach: A comprehensive system: Vol. 3. Assessment of children and adolescents.* New York: Wiley.

Exner, J. E., Jr., & Weiner, I. B. (1995). *The Rorschach: A comprehensive system: Vol. 3. Assessment of children and adolescents* (2nd ed.). New York: Wiley.

Exner, J. J. (2003). *The Rorschach: A comprehensive system* (4th ed.). Hoboken, NJ: Wiley.

Eyde, L. D., Kowal, D. M., & Fishburne, F. J., Jr. (1990). The validity of computer-based test interpretations of the MMPI. In S. Wise & T. B. Gutkin (Eds.), *The computer as adjunct in the decision-making process.* Lincoln: Buros Institute of Mental Measurements, University of Nebraska.

Eyde, L. D., Moreland, K. L., Robertson, G. J., Primoff, E. S., & Most, R. B. (1988). Test user qualifications: A data-based approach to promoting good test use. In *Issues in Scientific Psychology: Report of the Test User Qualifications Working Group of the Joint Committee on Testing Practices.* Washington, DC: American Psychological Association.

Eyman, J. R., & Eyman, S. K. (1990). Suicide risk and assessment instruments. In P. Cimbolic & D. A. Jobes (Eds.), *Youth suicide: Issues, assessment, and intervention* (pp. 9–32). Springfield, IL: Charles C Thomas.

Eysenck, H. J. (1952). The effects of psychotherapy: An evaluation. *Journal of Consulting Psychology, 16,* 319–324.

Eysenck, H. J. (1961). The effects of psychotherapy. In H. J. Eysenck (Ed.), *Handbook of abnormal psychology: An experimental approach* (pp. 697–725). New York: Basic Books.

Eysenck, H. J. (1967). Intelligence assessment: A theoretical and experimental approach. *British Journal of Educational Psychology, 37,* 81–98.

Eysenck, H. J. (1985). Can personality study ever be scientific? *Journal of Social Behavior and Personality, 1,* 3–19.

Eysenck, H. J. (1991). Dimensions of personality: 16, 5, or 3?—Criteria for a taxonomic paradigm. *Personality and Individual Differences, 12,* 773–790.

Fahrenkopf, A. M., Sectish, T. C., Barger, L. K., et al. (2008). Rates of medication errors among depressed and burnt out residents: Prospective cohort study. *British Medical Journal, 336,* 488.

Fahs, R. L. (2004). Response bias on the Rorschach: Identifying impression management and self-deception positivity. *Dissertation Abstracts International: Section B. Sciences and Engineering, 65*(5-B), 2621.

Faller, K. C. (1988). *Child sexual abuse.* New York: Columbia University.

Fang, Q., Freedenthal, S., & Osman, A. (2015). Validation of the Suicide Resilience Inventory-25 with American and Chinese college students. *Suicide and Life-Threatening Behavior, 45*(1), 51–64.

Farrell, A. D. (1986). The microcomputer as a tool for behavioral assessment. *Behavior Therapist, 1,* 16–17.

Farrell, J. N., & McDaniel, M. A. (2001). The stability of validity coefficients over time: Ackerman's (1988) model and the General Aptitude Test Battery. *Journal of Applied Psychology, 86,* 60–79.

Farrell, S. F. (1998). Alcohol dependence and the price of alcoholic *beverages. Dissertation Abstracts International: Section B: The Sciences and Engineering, 59*(4-B), 1606.

Farrenkopf, T., & Bryan, J. (1999). Psychological consultation under Oregon's 1994 Death With Dignity Act: Ethics and procedures. *Professional Psychology: Research and Practice, 30,* 245–249.

Faust, D. S., & Ziskin, J. (1988a). The expert witness in psychology and psychiatry. *Science, 241,* 31–35.

Faust, D. S., & Ziskin, J. (1988b). Response to Fowler and Matarrazo. *Science, 242,* 1143–1144.

Federal Rules of Evidence. (1975). Eagan, MN: West Group.

Feinberg, T. E., & Farah, M. J. (Eds.). (2003). *Behavioral neurology and neuropsychology* (2nd ed.). New York: McGraw-Hill.

Feinstein, A. R., Josephy, B. R., & Wells, C. K. (1986). Scientific and clinical problems in indexes of functional disability. *Annals of Internal Medicine, 105,* 413–520.

Feldman, L. B., & Rivas-Vazquez, R. (2003). Assessment and treatment of social anxiety disorder. *Professional Psychology: Research and Practice, 34,* 396–405.

Fenn, D. S., & Ganzini, L. (1999). Attitudes of Oregon psychologists toward physician-assisted suicide and the Oregon Death With Dignity Act. *Professional Psychology: Research and Practice, 30,* 235–244.

Ferguson, R. L., & Novick, M. R. (1973). Implementation of a Bayesian system for decision analysis in a program of individually prescribed instruction. *ACT Research Report,* No. 60.

Feuerstein, R. (1977). Mediated learning experience: A theoretical basis for cognitive modifiability. In P. Mittler (Ed.), *Research to Practice in Mental Retardation.* Baltimore: University Park Press.

Feuerstein, R. (1981). Mediated learning experience in the acquisition of kinesics. In B. L. Hoffer & R. N. St. Clair (Eds.), *Development kinesics: The emerging paradigm.* Baltimore: University Park Press.

Feuerstein, R., Rand, Y., & Hoffman, M. B. (1979). *The dynamic assessment of retarded performers: The Learning Potential Assessment Device.* Baltimore: University Park Press.

Field, T. M., & Vega-Lahr, N. (1984). Early interactions between infants with cranio-facial anomalies and their mothers. *Infant Behavior and Development, 7,* 527–530.

Filsinger, E. (1983). A machine-aided marital observation technique: The Dyadic Interaction Scoring Code. *Journal of Marriage and the Family, 2,* 623–632.

Finding information about psychological tests. (1995). Washington, DC: American Psychological Association, Science Directorate.

Finello, K. M. (2011). Collaboration in the assessment and diagnosis of preschoolers: Challenges and opportunities. *Psychology in the Schools, 48,* 442–453.

Finlayson, M. A. J. (2015). A personal perspective from an appreciative student. *Archives of Clinical Neuropsychology, 30*(8), 764–765.

Finn, S. E. (1996). *Using the MMPI-2 as a therapeutic intervention.* Minneapolis: University of Minnesota Press.

Finn, S. E. (2003). Therapeutic assessment of a man with "ADD." *Journal of Personality Assessment, 80,* 115–129.

Finn, S. E. (2011a). Therapeutic assessment on the front lines: Comment on articles from Westcoast Children's Clinic. *Journal of Personality Assessment, 93*(1), 23–25.

Finn, S. E., & Martin, H. (1997). Therapeutic assessment with the MMPI-2 in managed health care. In J. N. Butcher (Ed.), *Objective psychological assessment in managed health care: A practitioner's guide* (pp. 131–152). New York: Oxford University Press.

Finn, S. E., & Tonsager, M. E. (2002). How therapeutic assessment became humanistic. *Humanistic Psychologist, 30*(1–2), 10–22.

Finucane, M. L., & Gullion, C. M. (2010). Developing a tool for measuring the decision-making competence of older adults. *Psychology and Aging, 25,* 271–288.

Fischer, C. T. (1978). Collaborative psychological assessment. In C. T. Fischer & S. L. Brodsky (Eds.), *Client participation in human services: The Prometheus principle* (pp. 41–61). New Brunswick, NJ: Transaction.

Fischer, C. T. (1994). *Individualizing psychological assessment.* Hillsdale, NJ: Erlbaum.

Fischer, C. T. (2004). In what sense is collaborative psychological assessment collaborative? Some distinctions. *SPA Exchange, 16*(1), 14–15.

Fischer, C. T. (2006). Qualitative psychological research and individualized/collaborative psychological assessment: Implications of their similarities for promoting a life-world orientation. *Humanistic Psychologist, 34*(4), 347–356.

Fischer, C. T., & Finn, S. E. (2014). Developing the life meanings of psychological test data: Collaborative and therapeutic approaches. In R. P. Archer & S. R. Smith (Eds.), *Personality assessment* (2nd ed., pp. 401–431). New York, NY: Routledge/Taylor & Francis.

Fischer, H. (1999). Exemptions from child abuse reporting. *American Psychologist, 54,* 145.

Fisher, R. P., & Geiselman, R. E. (1992). *Memory-enhancing techniques for investigative interviewing.* Springfield, IL: Charles C Thomas.

Fisher, R. P., Geiselman, R. E., & Amador, M. (1989). Field test of the cognitive interview: Enhancing the recollection of actual victims and witnesses of crime. *Journal of Applied Psychology, 74,* 722–727.

Fisher, R. P., Geiselman, R. E., Raymond, D. S., et al. (1987). Enhancing enhanced eyewitness memory: Refining the cognitive interview. *Journal of Police Science & Administration, 15,* 291–297.

Fiske, D. W. (1967). The subjects react to tests. *American Psychologist, 22,* 287–296.

Fitts, W. H. (1965). *Manual for the Tennessee Self-Concept Scale.* Nashville: Counselor Recordings and Tests.

Fitzgibbons, D. J., & Shearn, C. R. (1972). Concepts of schizophrenia among mental health professionals: A factor-analytic study. *Journal of Consulting and Clinical Psychology, 38,* 288–295.

Flanagan, D. P. (2001). *Comparative features of the* WJ III Tests of Cognitive Abilities (Woodcock-Johnson III. Assessment Service Bulletin No. 1). Itasca, IL: Riverside.

Flanagan, D. P., & McGrew, K. S. (1997). A cross-battery approach to assessing and interpreting cognitive abilities: Narrowing the gap between practice and cognitive science. In D. P. Flanagan, J. L. Genshaft, & P. L. Harrison (Eds.), *Contemporary intellectual assessment: Theories, tests, and issues* (pp. 314–325). New York: Guilford.

Flanagan, J. C. (1938). Review of *Measuring Intelligence* by Terman and Merrill. *Harvard Educational Review, 8,* 130–133.

Flanagan, J. C., & Burns, R. K. (1955). The employee business record: A new appraisal and development tool. *Harvard Business Review, 33*(5), 99–102.

Fletcher, J. M., Lyon, G. R., Barnes, M., et al. (2002). Classification of learning disabilities: An evidence-based evaluation. In R. Bradley, L. Danielson, and D. P. Hallahan (Eds.), *Identification of learning disabilities: Research and practice.* Mahwah, NJ: Erlbaum.

Fletcher, J. M., Stuebing, K. K., & Hughes, L. C. (2010). IQ scores should be corrected for the Flynn Effect in high-stakes decisions. *Journal of Psychoeducational Assessment, 28,* 469–473.

Flett, G. L., & Hewitt, P. L. (2002). *Perfectionism: Theory, research and treatment.* Washington: American Psychological.

Flowers, J. H. (1982). Some simple Apple II software for the collection and analysis of observational data. *Behavior Research Methods and Instrumentation, 14,* 241–249.

Floyd, F. J., Haynes, S. N., Doll, E. R., et al. (1992). Assessing retirement satisfaction and perceptions of retirement experiences. *Psychology and Aging, 7,* 609–621.

Floyd, F. J., & Widaman, K. F. (1995). Factor analysis in the development and refinement of clinical assessment instruments. *Psychological Assessment, 7,* 286–299.

Floyd, R. G., Evans, J. J., & McGrew, K. S. (2003). Relations between measures of Cattell-Horn-Carroll (CHC) cognitive abilities and mathematics achievement across the school-age years. *Psychology in the Schools, 40,* 155–171.

Flynn, J. R. (1984). The mean IQ of Americans: Massive gains 1932 to 1978. *Psychological Bulletin, 95,* 29–51.

Flynn, J. R. (1988). Massive IQ gains in 14 nations: What IQ tests really measure. *Psychological Bulletin, 101,* 171–191.

Flynn, J. R. (1991). *Asian-Americans: Achievement beyond IQ.* Hillsdale, NJ: Erlbaum.

Flynn, J. R. (2000). The hidden history of IQ and special education: Can the problems be solved? *Psychology, Public Policy, and Law, 6,* 191–198.

Flynn, J. R. (2007). *What is intelligence? Beyond the Flynn effect.* New York: Cambridge University Press.

Flynn, J. R. (2009). Requiem for nutrition as the cause of IQ gains: Raven's gains in Britain, 1938–2008. *Economics and Human Biology, 7,* 18–27.

Foerster, L. M., & Little Soldier, D. (1974). Open education and native American values. *Educational Leadership, 32,* 41–45.

Folstein, M. F., Folstein, S. E., & McHugh, P. R. (1975). "Mini-Mental State": A practical method for grading the cognitive state of patients for the clinician. *Journal of Psychiatric Research, 12,* 189–198.

Fontana, V. J., Donovan, D., & Wong, R. J. (1963, December 8). The maltreatment syndrome in children. *New England Journal of Medicine, 269,* 1389–1394.

Fontanna, D. (2000). *Personality in the workplace.* Lewiston, NY: Macmillan.

Forbes, P. A., Happee, R., van der Helm, F., & Schouten, A. C. (2011). EMG feedback tasks reduce reflexive stiffness during force and position perturbations. *Experimental Brain Research, 213*(1), 49–61.

Forer, B. R. (1949). The fallacy of personal validation: A classroom demonstration of gullibility. *Journal of Abnormal and Social Psychology, 44,* 118–123.

Forrest, D. W. (1974). *Francis Galton: The life and works of a Victorian genius.* New York: Taplinger.

Fortune, S., Stewart, A., Yadav, V., & Hawton, K. (2007). Suicide in adolescents: Using life charts to understand the suicidal process. *Journal of Affective Disorders, 100*(1–3), 199–210.

Fossey, D., & Harcourt, A. H. (1977). *Feeding ecology of free-ranging mountain gorilla (Gorilla gorilla beringei).* In T. H. Clutton-Brock (Ed.), *Primate ecology: Studies of feeding and ranging behaviour in lemurs, monkeys, and apes* (pp. 415–447). New York, NY: Academic Press.

Foster, S. L., Laverty-Finch, C., Gizzo, D. P., & Osantowski, J. (1999). Practical issues in self-observation. *Psychological Assessment, 11,* 426–438.

Foster, T. (2011). Adverse life events proximal to adult suicide: A synthesis of findings from psychological studies. *Archives of Suicide Research, 15,* 1–15.

Fouad, N. A. (2002). Cross-cultural differences in vocational interests: Between-group differences on the Strong Interest Inventory. *Journal of Counseling Psychology, 49,* 282–289.

Fouad, N. A., & Dancer, L. S. (1992). Cross-cultural structure of interests: Mexico and the United States. *Journal of Vocational Behavior, 40,* 129–143.

Fowler, D. R., Finkelstein, A., & Penk, W. (1986). *Measuring treatment responses by computer interview.* Paper presented at the 94th annual meeting of the American Psychological Association, Washington, DC.

Fowler, K. A., & Westen, D. (2011). Subtyping male perpetrators of intimate partner violence. *Journal of Interpersonal Violence, 26*(4), 607–639.

Fox, B. (2008). A new direction in athletic imagery interventions: The relationship between imagery direction, anxiety, and motor performance. *Dissertation Abstracts International: Section A. Humanities and Social Sciences, 68*(7-A), 2873.

Fox, J., & Pease, B. (2012). Military deployment, masculinity and trauma: Reviewing the connections. *The Journal of Men's Studies, 20,* 16–31.

Fox, S. J. (2011). A correlational analysis between handwriting characteristics and personality type by the Myers-Briggs Type Indicator. *Dissertation Abstracts International: Section B: The Sciences and Engineering,* p. 7773.

Franco, J. N. (1983). An acculturation scale for Mexican-American children. *Journal of General Psychology, 108,* 175–181.

Frank, E., & Brandstaetter, V. (2002). Approach versus avoidance: Different types of commitment in intimate relationships. *Journal of Personality & Social Psychology, 82,* 208–221.

Frank, J. D. (1974). Psychotherapy: The restoration of morale. *American Journal of Psychiatry, 131,* 271–274.

Frank, L. K. (1939). Projective methods for the study of personality. *Journal of Psychology, 8,* 389–413.

Franzen, M. D. (2008). Neuropsychological evaluations in the context of competency decisions. In A. MacNeill & L. C. Hartlage (Eds.), *Handbook of forensic neuropsychology* (pp. 505–518). New York, NY: Springer.

Fredman, N., & Sherman, R. (1987). *Handbook of measurements for marriage & family therapy.* New York: Brunner/Mazel.

Freeman, S. T. (1989). Cultural and linguistic bias in mental health evaluations of deaf people. *Rehabilitation Psychology, 34,* 51–63.

French, C. C., & Beaumont, J. G. (1991). The Differential Aptitude Test (Language Usage and Spelling): A clinical study of a computerized form. *Current Psychology: Research and Reviews, 10,* 31–48.

French, D. J., Gauthier, J. G., Roberge, C., et al. (1997). Self-efficacy in the thermal biofeedback treatment of migraine sufferers. *Behavior Therapy, 28,* 109–125.

Freud, S. (1913/1959). Further recommendations in the technique of psychoanalysis. In E. Jones (Ed.) and J. Riviere (Trans.), *Collected papers* (Vol. 2). New York: Basic Books.

Freund, K. (1963). A laboratory method for diagnosing predominance of homosexual and heterosexual erotic interest in the male. *Behavior Research and Therapy, 1,* 85–93.

Freund, K., Sedlacek, E., & Knob, K. (1965). A simple transducer for mechanical plethysmography of the male genital. *Journal of Experimental Analysis of Behavior, 8,* 169–170.

Friedman, M., & Rosenman, R. H. (1974). *Type A behavior and your heart.* New York: Knopf.

Friedrich, W. N., Fisher, J. L., Dittner, C. A., et al. (2001). Child Sexual Behavior Inventory: Normative, psychiatric, and sexual abuse comparisons. *Child Maltreatment: Journal of the American Professional Society on the Abuse of Children, 6,* 37–49.

Friedrich, W. N., Urquiza, A. J., & Beike, R. (1986). Behavioral problems in sexually abused young children. *Journal of Pediatric Psychiatry, 11,* 47–57.

Friel-Patti, S., & Finitzo, T. (1990). Language learning in a prospective study of otitis media with effusion in the first two years of life. *Journal of Speech and Hearing Research, 33,* 188–194.

Friese, M., Bluemke, M., & Wänke, M. (2007). Predicting voting behavior with implicit attitude measures: The 2002 German parliamentary election. *Experimental Psychology, 54*(4), 247–255.

Frohlich, T. C., & Sauter, M. B. (2014). States with the best (and worst) schools. *24/7 Wall St.* Accessed May 23, 2016 at http://247wallst.com/special-report/2014/01/14/states-with-the-best-and-worst-schools-2/#ixzz49S6ZhZ6j

Frolik, L. A. (1999). Science, common sense, and the determination of mental capacity. *Psychology, Public Policy, and Law, 5,* 41–58.

Frye v. United States, 293 Fed. 1013 (D.C. Cir. 1923).

Fuchs, D., & Fuchs, L. S. (2006). Introduction to responsiveness-to-intervention: What, why, and how valid is it? *Reading Research Quarterly, 41,* 92–99.

Fuchs, L. S., Compton, D. L., Fuchs, D., et al. (2011). Two-stage screening for math problem-solving difficulty using dynamic assessment of algebraic learning. *Journal of Learning Disabilities, 44*(4), 372–380.

Fuchs, L. S., Fuchs, D., Eaton, S. B., et al. (2000). Using objective data sources to enhance teacher judgments about test accommodations. *Exceptional Children, 67,* 67–81.

Fullan, M., & Loubser, J. (1972). Education and adaptive capacity. *Sociology of Education, 45,* 271–287.

Fullard, W., McDevitt, S. C., & Carey, W. B. (1984). Assessing temperament in one- to three-year-old children. *Journal of Pediatric Psychology, 9,* 205–217.

Furnham, A., Petrides, K. V., Jackson, C. J., & Cotter, T. (2002). Do personality factors predict job satisfaction? *Personality & Individual Differences, 33,* 1325–1342.

Furse, D. H., & Stewart, D. W. (1984). Manipulating dissonance to improve mail survey response. *Psychology & Marketing, 1,* 71–84.

Gabriel, R. A. (1997). *No more heroes: Madness and psychiatry in war.* New York, NY: Hill and Wang.

Gacono, C. B., et al. (Eds.). (2008). *The handbook of forensic Rorschach assessment.* New York: Routledge/Taylor & Francis.

Gaddis, B. H., Foster, J. L., & Lemming, M. R. (2015). A comparative review of current practices in personality assessment norming. *International Journal of Selection and Assessment, 23*(1), 14–26.

Gagne, J. R., Van Hulle, C. A., Aksan, N., et al. (2011). Deriving childhood temperament measures from emotion-eliciting behavioral episodes: Scale construction and initial validation. *Psychological Assessment, 23*(2), 337–353.

Gaither, G. A., & Sellbom, M. (2003). The Sexual Sensation Seeking Scale: Reliability and validity within a heterosexual college student sample. *Journal of Personality Assessment, 81,* 157–167.

Gallo, J. J., & Bogner, H. R. (2006). The context of geriatric care. In J. J. Gallo, H. R. Bogner, T. Fulmer, & G. J. Paveza (Eds.), *The handbook of geriatric assessment* (4th ed., pp. 3–13). Sudbury, MA: Jones & Bartlett.

Gallo, J. J., & Wittink, M. N. (2006). Cognitive assessment. In J. J. Gallo, H. R. Bogner, T. Fulmer, & G. J. Paveza (Eds.), *The handbook of geriatric assessment* (4th ed., pp. 105–151). Sudbury, MA: Jones & Bartlett.

Galton, F. (1879). Psychometric experiments. *Brain, 2,* 149–162.

Galton, F. (1883). *Inquiries into human faculty and its development.* London: Macmillan.

Gammon, J. A. (1981). Ophthalmic manifestations of child abuse. In N. S. Ellerstein (Ed.), *Child abuse and neglect: A medical reference* (pp. 121–139). New York: Wiley.

Ganellen, R. J. (1996). Comparing the diagnostic efficiency of the MMPI, MCMI-II, and Rorschach: A review. *Journal of Personality Assessment, 67,* 219–243.

Ganellen, R. J. (2007). Assessing normal and abnormal personality functioning. *Journal of Personality Assessment, 89*(1), 30–40.

Ganellen R. J. (2008). Rorschach assessment of malingering and defensive response sets. In C. Gacono & B. Evans (Eds.), *The handbook of forensic Rorschach assessment.* Hillsdale: Routledge

Gann, M. K., & Davison, G. C. (1997). *Cognitive assessment of reactance using the articulated thoughts in simulated situations paradigm.* Unpublished manuscript, University of Southern California, Los Angeles.

Garb, H. N. (1994). Toward a second generation of statistical prediction rules in psychodiagnosis and personality assessment. *Computers in Human Behavior, 11,* 313–324.

Garb, H. N. (2000a). Introduction to the special section on the use of computers for making judgments and decisions. *Psychological Assessment, 12,* 3–5.

Garb, H. N. (2000b). Computers will become increasingly important for psychological assessment: Not that there's anything wrong with that! *Psychological Assessment, 12,* 31–39.

García, L. E., & Thornton, O. (2015, February 13). "No Child Left Behind" has failed. *The Washington Post.* Accessed online April 12, 2016 at https://www.washingtonpost.com/opinions/no-child-has-failed/2015/02/13/8d619026-b2f8-11e4-827f-93f454140e2b_story.html

Garcia, M., & Lega, L. I. (1979). Development of a Cuban Ethnic Identity Questionnaire. *Hispanic Journal of Behavioral Sciences, 1,* 247–261.

Gardeazabal, J., & Sandler, T. (2015). INTERPOL's surveillance network in curbing transnational terrorism. *Journal of Policy Analysis and Management, 34*(4), 761–780.

Gardner, D., & Deadrick, D. L. (2008). Underprediction of performance for U.S. minorities using cognitive ability measures. *Equal Opportunities International, 27*(5), 455–464.

Gardner, F. L. (2001). Applied sport psychology in professional sports: The team psychologist. *Professional Psychology: Research and Practice, 32,* 34–39.

Gardner, H. (1983). *Frames of mind: The theory of multiple intelligences.* New York: Basic Books

Gardner, H. (1994). Multiple intelligences theory. In R. J. Sternberg (Ed.), *Encyclopedia of human intelligence* (pp. 740–742). New York: Macmillan.

Gardner, R. A. (1971). *The boys' and girls' book about divorce.* New York: Bantam.

Gardner, R. A. (1982). *Family evaluation in child custody litigation.* Cresskill, NJ: Creative Therapeutics.

Gardner, W., Lidz, C. W., Mulvey, E. P., & Shaw, E. C. (1996). Clinical versus actuarial prediction of violence in patients with mental illnesses. *Journal of Consulting and Clinical Psychology, 64,* 602–609.

Garfield, S. L., & Eron, L. D. (1948). Interpreting mood and activity in TAT stories. *Journal of Abnormal and Social Psychology, 43,* 338–345.

Garnier, L. M., Arria, A. M., Caldeira, K. M., et al. (2009). Nonmedical prescription analgesic use and concurrent alcohol consumption among college students. *American Journal of Drug and Alcohol Abuse, 35,* 334–338.

Garrett, H. E., & Schneck, M. R. (1933). *Psychological tests, methods and results.* New York: Harper.

Garrett, M. T. & Pichette, E. F. (2000). Red as an apple: Native American acculturation and counseling with or without reservation. *Journal of Counseling and Development, 78,* 3–13.

Gaski, J. F., & Sagarin, J. (2011). Detrimental effects of daylight-saving times on SAT scores. *Journal of Neuroscience, Psychology, and Economics, 4*(1), 44–53.

Gaugler, B. B., Rosenthal, D. B., Thornton, G. C., III, & Bentson, C. (1987). Meta-analysis of assessment center validity. *Journal of Applied Psychology, 72,* 493–511.

Gavett, B. E., Lynch, J. K., & McCaffrey, R. J. (2005). Third party observers: The effect size is greater than you might think. *Journal of Forensic Neuropsychology, 4*(2), 49–64.

Gavett, B. E., & McCaffrey, R. J. (2007). The influence of an adaptation period in reducing the third party observer effect during a neuropsychological evaluation. *Archives of Clinical Neuropsychology, 22,* 699–710.

Gavzer, B. (1990, May 27). Should you tell all? *Parade Magazine,* pp. 4–7.

Gawda, B. (2008). A graphical analysis of handwriting of prisoners diagnosed with antisocial personality. *Perceptual and Motor Skills, 107*(3), 862–872.

Gawronski, B., & Bodenhausen, G. V. (2007). What do we know about implicit attitude measures and what do we have to learn? In B. Wittenbrink & N. Schwarz (Eds.), *Implicit measures of attitudes* (pp. 265–286). New York: Guilford Press.

Gee, C. J., Marshall, J. C., & King, J. F. (2010). Should coaches use personality assessments in the talent identification process? A 15 year predictive study on professional hockey players. *International Journal of Coaching Science, 4,* 25–34.

Gehrman, P. R., Harb, G. C., Cook, J. M., et al. (2015). Sleep diaries of Vietnam War veterans with chronic PTSD: The relationships among insomnia symptoms, psychosocial stress, and nightmares. *Behavioral Sleep Medicine, 13*(3), 255–264.

Geisenger, K. F., & McCormick, C. M. (2010). Adopting cut scores: Post-standard-setting panel considerations for decision makers. *Educational Measurement: Issues and Practice, 29,* 38–44.

General Electric Co. v. Joiner, 118 S. Ct. 512 (1997).

Gerety, M. B., Mulrow, C. D., Tuley, M. R., et al. (1993). Development and validation of a physical performance instrument for the functionally impaired elderly: The Physical Disability Index (PDI). *Journal of Gerontology, 48,* M33–M38.

Gerry, M. H. (1973). Cultural myopia: The need for a corrective lens. *Journal of School Psychology, 11,* 307–315.

Gerson, M. (2012, July 19). Obama's quiet overturn of *No Child Left Behind. The Washington Post.* Accessed online April 12, 2016 at https://www.washingtonpost.com/opinions/michael-gerson-obamas-quiet-overturn-of-no-child-left-behind/2012/07/19/gJQAbE8hwW_story.html?tid=a_inl

Gesell, A., & Amatruda, C. S. (1947). *Development diagnosis: Normal and abnormal child development* (2nd ed.). New York: Harper & Row.

Ghiselli, E. E. (1973). The variety of aptitude tests in personnel selection. *Personnel Psychology, 26,* 461–477.

Ghiselli, E. E., & Barthol, R. P. (1953). The validity of personality inventories in the selection of employees. *Journal of Applied Psychology, 38,* 18–20.

Ghiselli, E. E., Campbell, J. P., & Zedeck, S. (1981). *Measurement theory for the behavioral sciences.* San Francisco: Freeman.

Gibbins, S. (1988, April). *Use of the K-ABC and WISC-R with deaf children.* Paper presented at the Annual Meeting of the National Association of School Psychologists, Chicago.

Gibbins, S. (1989). The provision of school psychological assessment services for the hearing impaired: A national survey. *Volta Review, 91,* 95–103.

Gil, S., Weinberg, M., Shamai, M. R., et al. (2016). Risk factors for *DSM–5* posttraumatic stress symptoms (PTSS) among Israeli civilians during the 2014 Israel-Hamas war. *Psychological Trauma: Theory, Research, Practice, and Policy, 8*(1), 49–54.

Gilbert, P., & Allan, S. (1998). The role of defeat and entrapment (arrested flight) in depression: An exploration of an evolutionary view. *Psychological Medicine, 28,* 585–598.

Gilch-Pesantez, J. R. (2001). Test-retest reliability and construct validity: The Bricklin Perceptual Scales. *Dissertation Abstracts International: Section B: The Sciences and Engineering, 61*(9-B), 4982.

Gill, C. J., Kewman, D. G., & Brannon, R. W. (2003). Transforming psychological practice and society: Policies that reflect the new paradigm. *American Psychologist, 58,* 305–312.

Gill, J. S., Donaghy, M., Guise, J., & Warner, P. (2007). Descriptors and accounts of alcohol consumption: Methodological issues piloted with female undergraduate drinkers in Scotland. *Health Education Research, 22*(1), 27–36.

Gim Chung, R. H., Kim, B. S. K., & Abreu, J. M. (2004). Asian American Multidimensional Acculturation Scale: Development, factor analysis, reliability, and validity. *Cultural Diversity and Ethnic Minority Psychology, 10*(1), 66–80.

Giner, L., Carballo, J. J., Guija, J. A., et al. (2007). Psychological autopsy studies: The role of alcohol use in adolescent and young adult suicides. *International Journal of Adolescent Medicine and Health, 19*(1), 99–113.

Girelli, S. A., & Stake, J. E. (1993). Bipolarity in Jungian type theory and the Myers-Briggs Type Indicator. *Journal of Personality Assessment, 60,* 290–301.

Glaser, R., & Nitko, A. J. (1971). Measurement in learning and instruction. In R. L. Thorndike (Ed.), *Educational measurement* (2nd ed.). Washington, DC: American Council on Education.

Glassbrenner, J. (1998). Continuity across contexts: Prison, women's counseling center, and home. In L. Handler (Chair), *Conducting assessments in clients' homes: Contexts, surprises, dilemmas, opportunities.* Symposium presented at the Society for Personality Assessment 1998 Midwinter Meeting, February 20.

Glazer, W. M., Kramer, R., Montgomery, J. S., & Myers, L. (1991). Use of medical necessity scales in concurrent review of psychiatric inpatient care. *Hospital and Community Psychiatry, 42,* 1199–1200.

Glosser, G., & Goodglass, H. (1990). Disorders in executive control functions among aphasic and other brain-damaged patients. *Journal of Clinical and Experimental Neuropsychology, 12,* 485–501.

Gluck, M. R. (1955). The relationship between hostility in the TAT and behavioral hostility. *Journal of Projective Techniques, 19,* 21–26.

Glueck, W. F. (1978). *Personnel: A diagnostic approach.* Dallas: Business Publications.

Goddard, H. H. (1908). The Binet and Simon tests of intellectual capacity. *Training School, 5,* 3–9.

Goddard, H. H. (1910). A measuring scale of intelligence. *Training School, 6,* 146–155.

Goddard, H. H. (1913). The Binet tests in relation to immigration. *Journal of Psycho-Asthenics, 18,* 105–107.

Goddard, H. H. (1916). *Feeblemindedness.* New York: Macmillan.

Goddard, H. H. (1917). Mental tests and the immigrant. *Journal of Delinquency, 2,* 243–277.

Goddard, H. H. (1947). A suggested definition of intelligence. *Training School Bulletin, 43,* 185–193.

Goel, V., & Grafman, J. (1995). Are the frontal lobes implicated in "planning" functions? Interpreting data from the Tower of Hanoi. *Neuropsychologia, 33,* 623–642.

Goetz, C. G. (1986). Charcot on Parkinson's disease. *Movement disorders, 1*(1), 27–32.

Goffman, E. (1963). *Behavior in public places.* Glencoe, IL: Free Press.

Gokhale, D. V., & Kullback, S. (1978). *The information in contingency tables.* New York: Marcel Dekker.

Goldberg, I. R. (1990). An alternative "description of personality": The Big-Five factor structure. *Journal of Personality and Social Psychology, 59,* 1216–1229.

Goldberg, L. R. (1993). The structure of phenotypic personality traits. *American Psychologist, 48,* 26–34.

Goldberg, T. E., Gold, J. M., Greenberg, R., et al. (1993). Contrasts between patients with affective disorders and patients with

schizophrenia on a neuropsychological test battery. *American Journal of Psychiatry, 150,* 1355–1362.

Goldberg, T. E., Saint-Cyr, J. A., & Weinberger, D. R. (1990). Assessment of procedural learning and problem solving in schizophrenic patients by Tower of Hanoi type tasks. *Journal of Neuropsychiatry, 2,* 165–173.

Golden, C. J. (2015). The influence of Ralph Reitan on the development of the Luria-Nebraska neuropsychological battery. *Archives of Clinical Neuropsychology, 30*(8), 768–769.

Golden, C. J., & Lashley, L. (2014). *Forensic neuropsychological evaluation of the violent offender.* New York, NY: Springer.

Goldfried, M. R., & Davison, G. C. (1976). *Clinical behavior therapy.* New York: Holt, Rinehart & Winston.

Goldfried, M. R., Stricker, G., & Winer, I. B. (1971). *Rorschach handbook of clinical and research applications.* Englewood Cliffs, NJ: Prentice-Hall.

Golding, S. L. (1975). Flies in the ointment: Methodological problems in the analysis of the percentage of variance due to persons and situations. *Psychological Bulletin, 82,* 278–288.

Golding, S. L., Roesch, R., & Schreiber, J. (1984). Assessment and conceptualization of competency to stand trial. Preliminary data on the interdisciplinary fitness interview. *Law and Human Behavior, 8*(3–4), 321–334.

Goldman, B. A., & Mitchell, D. F. (2008). *Directory of unpublished experimental mental measures* (Vol. 9). Washington, DC: APA Books.

Goldman, B. A., & Mitchell, D. F. (Eds.). (1997). *Directory of unpublished experimental mental measures* (Vol. 7). Dubuque, IA: W. C. Brown.

Goldstein, G. (2015). Ralph Reitan and biological intelligence. *Archives of Clinical Neuropsychology, 30*(8), 733–739.

Goldstein, J. S. (2001). *War and gender: How gender shapes the war system and vice ver*sa. Cambridge: Cambridge University Press.

Goldstein, K. (1927). Die lokalisation in her grosshin rinde. In *Handb. norm. pathol. psychologie.* Berlin: J. Springer.

Goldstein, K. (1939). *The organism.* New York: American Book.

Goldstein, K. (1963a). The modifications of behavior consequent to cerebral lesions. *Psychiatric Quarterly, 10,* 586–610.

Goldstein, K. (1963b). *The organism.* Boston: Beacon Press.

Goldstein, S. (2011). Learning disabilities in childhood. In S. Goldsteein, J. A. Naglieri, & M. DeVries (Eds.), *Learning and attention disorders in adolescence and adulthood: Assessment and treatment* (2nd ed., pp. 31–58). Hoboken, NJ: Wiley.

Goldstein, T. R., Bridge, J. A., & Brent, D. A. (2008). Sleep disturbance preceding completed suicide in adolescents. *Journal of Consulting and Clinical Psychology, 76*(1), 84–91.

Gomez, R., & Hazeldine, P. (1996). Social information processing in mild mentally retarded children. *Research in Developmental Disabilities, 17,* 217–227.

Gonsalvez, C. J., & Crowe, T. P. (2014). Evaluation of psychology practitioner competence in clinical supervision. *American Journal of Psychotherapy, 68*(2), 177–193.

Good, R. H., Chowdhri, S., Katz, L., Vollman, M., & Creek, R. (1989, March). *Effect of matching instruction and simultaneous/ sequential processing strength.* Paper presented at the Annual Meeting of the National Association of School Psychologists, Boston.

Good, R. H., & Lane, S. (1988). *Confirmatory factor analysis of the K-ABC and WISC-R: Hierarchical models.* Paper presented at the Annual Meeting of the American Psychological Association, Atlanta.

Good, R. H., Vollmer, M., Creek, R. J., & Katz, L. (1993). Treatment utility of the Kaufman Assessment Battery for Children: Effects of matching instruction and student processing strength. *School Psychology Review, 22,* 8–26.

Goodman, G. S., & Reed, R. S. (1986). Age differences in eyewitness testimony. *Law and Human Behavior, 10,* 317–332.

Goodman-Delahunty, J. (2000). Psychological impairment under the Americans with Disabilities Act: Legal guidelines. *Professional Psychology: Research and Practice, 31,* 197–205.

Goodman-Delahunty, J., & Foote, W. E. (1995). Compensation for pain, suffering and other psychological injuries: The impact of *Daubert* on employment discrimination claims. *Behavioral Sciences and the Law, 13,* 183–206.

Goodrich, K. M., Harper, A. J., Luke, M., & Singh, A. A. (2013). Best practices for professional school counselors working with LGBTQ youth. *Journal of LGBT Issues in Counseling, 7*(4), 307–322.

Gopaul-McNicol, S. (1993). *Working with West Indian families.* New York: Guilford.

Gordon, R. A. (2008). Attributional style and athlete performance: Strategic optimism and defensive pessimism. *Psychology of Sport and Exercise, 9*(3), 336–350.

Gosling, S. D., & John, O. P. (1999). Personality dimensions in nonhuman animals: a cross-species review. *Current Directions in Psychological Science, 8,* 69–74.

Gosling, S. D., Kwan, V. S., & John, O. P. (2003). A dog's got personality: A cross-species comparative approach to personality judgments in dogs and humans. *Journal of Personality and Social Psychology, 85*(6), 1161–1169.

Gosling, S. D., Rentfrow, P. J., & Swann, W. B., Jr. (2003). A very brief measure of the Big-Five personality domains. *Journal of Research in Personality, 37*(6), 504–528.

Gottfredson, G. D. (2009). John L. Holland (1919–2008). *American Psychologist, 64*(6), 561.

Gottfredson, L. S. (1988). Reconsidering fairness: A matter of social and ethical priorities. *Journal of Vocational Behavior, 33,* 293–319.

Gottfredson, L. S. (1994). The science and politics of race-norming. *American Psychologist, 49,* 955–963.

Gottfredson, L. S. (2000). Skills gaps, not tests, make racial proportionality impossible. *Psychology, Public Policy, and Law, 6,* 129–143.

Gough, H. G. (1960). The Adjective Check List as a personality assessment research technique. *Psychological Reports, 6,* 107–122.

Gough, H. G. (1962). Clinical versus statistical prediction in psychology. In L. Postman (Ed.), *Psychology in the making: Histories of selected research problems* (pp. 526–584). New York: Knopf.

Gough, H. G., & Heilbrun, A. B., Jr. (1980). *The Adjective Checklist manual (Revised).* Palo Alto, CA: Consulting Psychologists Press.

Gould, J. W. (2006). *Conducting scientifically crafted child custody evaluations* (2nd ed.). Sarasota, FL: Professional Resource Press/Professional Resource Exchange.

Grafman, J., Litvan, I., Massaquoi, S., & Stewart, M. (1992). Cognitive planning deficit in patients with cerebellar atrophy. *Neurology, 42,* 1493–1496.

Graham, J. R. (1990). *MMPI-2: Assessing personality and psychopathology.* New York: Oxford University Press.

Granger, C. V., & Gresham, G. E. (Eds.). (1984). *Functional assessment in rehabilitation medicine.* Baltimore: Williams & Wilkins.

Grant, I., & Heaton, R. K. (2015). Ralph M. Reitan: A founding father of neuropsychology. *Archives of Clinical Neuropsychology, 30*(8), 760–761.

Gray, E. (2016). The new college application. *Time, 187*(14), 47–49, 51.

Gray, M., Roy, R., Vigilant, L., Fawcett, K., Basabose, A., Cranfield, M., et al. (2013). Genetic census reveals increased but uneven growth of a critically endangered mountain gorilla population. *Biological Conservation, 158,* 230–238.

Grazioplene, R. G., Ryman, S. G., Gray, J. R., et al. (2015). Subcortical intelligence: Caudate volume predicts IQ in healthy adults. *Human Brain Mapping, 36*(4), 1407–1416.

Greaud, V. A., & Green, B. F. (1986). Equivalence of conventional and computer presentation of speed tests. *Applied Psychological Measurement, 10,* 23–34.

Green, A. (1986). True and false allegations of sexual abuse in child custody disputes. *Journal of the American Academy of Child Psychology, 25,* 449–456.

Green, B. F. (1984). *Computer-based ability testing.* Paper delivered at the 91st annual meeting of the American Psychological Association, Toronto.

Green, S. B. (2003). A coefficient alpha for test-retest data. *Psychological Methods, 8,* 88–101.

Greenberg, N., & Brayne, M. (2007). *Trauma Risk Management (TRiM), the Royal Marines, and the media.* Paper presented at the 2007 Conference of the International Society for Traumatic Stress Studies, Baltimore, MD.

Greene, R. L. (1987). Ethnicity and MMPI performance: A review. *Journal of Consulting and Clinical Psychology, 55,* 497–512.

Greene, R. L. (2000). *The MMPI-2: An interpretive manual* (2nd ed.). Needham Heights, MA: Allyn & Bacon.

Greenfield, D. N. (1999). Psychological characteristics of compulsive Internet use: A preliminary analysis. *CyberPsychology & Behavior, 2,* 403–412.

Greenlaw, P. S., & Jensen, S. S. (1996). Race-norming and the Civil Rights Act of 1991. *Public Personnel Management, 25,* 13–24.

Greenspan, S. (1997). Dead manual walking? Why the AAMR definition needs redoing. *Education & Training in Mental Retardation & Developmental Disabilities, 32,* 179–190.

Greenspoon, J. (1955). The reinforcing effect of two spoken sounds on the frequency of two responses. *American Journal of Psychology, 68,* 409–416.

Greenspoon, J., & Gersten, C. D. (1967). A new look at psychological testing: Psychological testing from the standpoint of a behaviorist. *American Psychologist, 22,* 848–853.

Greenwald, A. G., & Banaji, M. R. (1995). Implicit social cognition: Attitudes, self-esteem, and stereotypes. *Psychological Review, 102,* 4–27.

Greenwald, A. G., & Farnham S. D. (2000). Using the Implicit Association Test to measure self-esteem and self-concept. *Journal of Personality and Social Psychology, 79,* 1022–1038.

Greenwald, A. G., McGhee, D. E., & Schwartz, J. L. K. (1998). Measuring individual differences in implicit cognition: The implicit association test. *Journal of Personality and Social Psychology, 74,* 1464–1480.

Greenwald, A. G., & Nosek, B. A. (2001). Health of the Implicit Association Test at age 3. *Zeitschrift für Experimentelle Psychologie, 48*(2), 85–93.

Gregg, P. A. (1998). The effect of impression management on correlations between Rorschach and MMPI-2 variables. *Dissertation Abstracts International: Section B. Sciences and Engineering, 58*(9-B), 5185.

Gregory, N. (2005). Offender profiling: A review of the literature. *British Journal of Forensic Practice, 7*(3), 29–34.

Gresham, F. M. (1989). Review of the Parenting Stress Index. In J. C. Conoley & J. J. Kramer (Eds.), *The tenth mental measurements yearbook.* Lincoln: Buros Institute of Mental Measurements, University of Nebraska.

Gresham, F. M., MacMillan, D. L., & Siperstein, G. N. (1995). Critical analysis of the 1992 AAMR definition: Implications for school psychology. *School Psychology Quarterly, 10*(1), 1–19.

Grey, R. J., & Kipnis, D. (1976). Untangling the performance appraisal dilemma: The influence of perceived organizational context on evaluative processes. *Journal of Applied Psychology, 61,* 329–335.

Griffin, M. L., Hogan, N. L., Lambert, E. G., Tucker-Gail, K. A., & Baker, D. N. (2010). Job involvement, job stress, job satisfaction, and organizational commitment and the burnout of correctional staff. *Criminal Justice and Behavior, 37,* 239–255.

Griffith, H. R., Belue, K., Sicola, A., Krzywanski, S., Zamrini, E., Harrell, L., & Marson, D. C. (2003). Impaired financial abilities in mild cognitive impairment: A direct assessment approach. *Neurology, 60,* 449–457.

Grisso, T. (1986). *Evaluating competencies: Forensic assessments and instruments.* New York: Plenum.

Grisso T., & Appelbaum, P. S. (1995). MacArthur Treatment Competence Study. *Journal of American Psychiatric Nurses Association, 1,* 125–127.

Grisso, T. (2003). *Evaluating competencies: Forensic assessments and instruments* (2nd ed.). New York: Kluwer Academic.

Grisso, T., & Appelbaum, P. S. (1998). *Assessing competence to consent to treatment: A guide for physicians and other health professionals.* New York: Oxford University Press.

Grisso, T., Appelbaum, P. S., & Hill-Fotouhi, C. (1997). The MacCAT-T: A clinical tool to assess patients' capacities to make treatment decisions. *Psychiatric Services, 48,* 1415–1419.

Groeger, J. A., & Chapman, P. R. (1997). Normative influences on decisions to offend. *Applied Psychology: An International Review, 46,* 265–285.

Groenveld, M., & Jan, J. E. (1992). Intelligence profiles of low vision and blind children. *Journal of Visual Impairment and Blindness, 86,* 68–71.

Grossman, I., Mednitsky, S., Dennis, B., & Scharff, L. (1993). Validation of an "amazingly" short form of the WAIS-R for a clinically depressed sample. *Journal of Psychoeducational Assessment, 11,* 173–181.

Grove, W. M., & Barden, R. C. (1999). Protecting the integrity of the legal system: The admissibility of testimony from mental health experts under *Daubert/Kumho* analyses. *Psychology, Public Policy, and Law, 5,* 224–242.

Grove, W. M., Zald, D. H., Lebow, B. S., et al. (2000). Clinical versus mechanical prediction: A meta-analysis. *Psychological Assessment, 12,* 19–30.

Grutter v. Bollinger, 539 U.S. 306 (2003).

Gu, Y., He, N., & You, X. (2017). Intelligence: An Eastern perspective. In R. J. Cohen (Ed.), *Online-only boxes, apps, & links (OOBALs) to accompany Psychological Testing and Assessment* (9th ed.). Accessed at *www.mhhe.cohentesting9/ OOBAL-9-B12*

Guastello, S. J., & Rieke, M. L. (1990). The Barnum Effect and the validity of computer-based test interpretations: The Human Resource Development Report. *Psychological Assessment, 2,* 186–190.

Guerrier, J. H., Manivannan, P., & Nair, S. N. (1999). The role of working memory, field dependence, visual search, and reaction time in the left turn performance of older female drivers. *Applied Ergonomics, 30,* 109–119.

Guilford, J. P. (1954). A factor analytic study across the domains of reasoning, creativity, and evaluation. I. Hypothesis and description of tests. *Reports from the psychology laboratory.* Los Angeles: University of Southern California.

Guilford, J. P. (1959). *Personality.* New York: McGraw-Hill.

Guilford, J. P. (1967). *The nature of human intelligence.* New York: McGraw-Hill.

Guilmette, T. J., & Faust, D. (1991). Characteristics of neuropsychologists who prefer the Halstead-Reitan Battery or the Luria-Nebraska Neuropsychological Battery. *Professional Psychology: Research and Practice, 22*(1), 80–83.

Guilmette, T. J., Faust, D., Hart, K., & Arkes, H. R. (1990). A national survey of psychologists who offer neuropsychological services. *Archives of Clinical Neuropsychology, 5,* 373–392.

Guion, R. M. (1980). On trinitarian doctrines of validity. *Professional Psychology, 11,* 385–398.

Gulliksen, H., & Messick, S. (Eds.). (1960). *Psychological scaling: Theory and applications.* New York: Wiley.

Gustafson, S., Fälth, L., Svensson, I., et al. (2011). Effects of three interventions on the reading skills of children with reading disabilities in grade 2. *Journal of Learning Disabilities, 44*(2), 123–135.

Guthmann, D., Lazowski, L. E., Moore, D., et al. (2012). Validation of the Substance Abuse Screener in American Sign Language (SAS-ASL). *Rehabilitation Psychology, 57*(2), 140–148.

Guttman, L. (1947). The Cornell technique for scale and intensity analysis. *Educational and Psychological Measurement, 7,* 247–280.

Guttman, L. A. (1944a). A basis for scaling qualitative data. *American Sociological Review, 9,* 139–150.

Guttman, L. A. (1944b). A basis for scaling qualitative data. *American Sociological Review, 9,* 179–190.

Haaga, D. A., Davison, G. C., McDermut, W., Hillis, S. L., & Twomey, H. B. (1993). "State of mind" analysis of the articulated thoughts of ex-smokers. *Cognitive Therapy and Research, 17,* 427–439.

Hadaway, N., & Marek-Schroer, M. F. (1992). Multidimensional assessment of the gifted minority student. *Roeper Review, 15,* 73–77.

Haensly, P. A., & Torrance, E. P. (1990). Assessment of creativity in children and adolescents. In C. R. Reynolds & R. W. Kamphaus (Eds.), *Handbook of psychological and educational assessment of children: Intelligence & achievement* (pp. 697–722). New York: Guilford.

Hafemeister, T. L. (2001, February). Ninth Circuit rejects immunity from liability for mental health evaluations. *Monitor on Psychology, 32.*

Hagan, L. D., Drogin, E. Y., & Guilmette, T. J. (2010). Science rather than advocacy when reporting IQ scores. *Professional Psychology: Research and Practice, 41*(5), 420–423.

Haidt, J., Rosenberg, E., & Horn, H. (2003). Differentiating differences: Moral diversity is not like other kinds. *Journal of Applied Social Psychology, 33,* 1–36.

Haines, M., & Spear, S. F. (1996). Changing the perception of the norm: A strategy to decrease binge drinking among college students. *Journal of American College Health, 45*(3), 134–140.

Hale, H. C. (2012). The role of practice in the development of military masculinities. *Gender, Work and Organization, 19,* 699–722.

Haley, K., & Lee, M. (Eds.). (1998). *The Oregon Death With Dignity Act: A guidebook for health care providers.* Portland: Oregon Health Sciences University, Center for Ethics in Health Care.

Hall, C. I. J. (1997). Cultural malpractice: The growing obsolescence of psychology with the changing U.S. population. *American Psychologist, 52,* 642–651.

Hall, C. S., & Lindzey, G. (1970). *Theories of personality.* New York: Wiley.

Hall, J. A., & Rosenthal, R. (1995). Interpreting and evaluating meta-analysis. *Evaluation and the Health Professions, 18,* 393–407.

Hall, S. S. (1998, February 15). Our memories, our selves. *New York Times Magazine,* pp. 26–33, 49, 56–57.

Halleck, S. L. (1976). Discussion of "Socially Reinforced Obsessing." *Journal of Consulting and Clinical Psychology, 44,* 146–147.

Halpern, A. S., & Fuherer, M. J. (Eds.). (1984). *Functional assessment in rehabilitation.* Baltimore: Paul H. Brookes.

Halpern, D. F. (2000). Validity, fairness, and group differences: Tough questions for selection testing. *Psychology, Public Policy, & Law, 6,* 56–62.

Halpern, F. (1958). Child case study. In E. F. Hammer (Ed.), *The clinical application of projective drawings* (pp. 113–129). Springfield, IL: Charles C Thomas.

Halstead, W. C. (1947a). *Brain and intelligence.* Chicago: University of Chicago.

Halstead, W. C. (1947b). *Brain and intelligence: A quantitative study of the frontal lobes*. Chicago: University of Chicago.

Halstead, W. C., & Wepman, J. M. (1959). The Halstead-Wepman Aphasia Screening Test. *Journal of Speech and Hearing Disorders, 14*, 9–15.

Hambleton, R. K., & Jones, R. W. (1993). Comparison of classical test theory and item response theory and their applications to test development. *Educational Measurement: Issues and Practice, 12*(3), 38–47.

Hambleton, R. K., & Jurgensen, C. (1990). Criterion-referenced assessment of school achievement. In C. R. Reynolds & R. W. Kamphaus (Eds.), *Handbook of psychological and educational assessment of children: Intelligence & achievement* (pp. 456–476). New York: Guilford.

Hambleton, R. K., & Novick, M. R. (1973). Toward and integration of theory and method for criterion-referenced tests. *Journal of Educational Measurement, 15*, 277–290.

Hambleton, R. K., & Swaminathan, H. (1984). *Item response theory: Principles and applications*. Boston: Springer.

Hambleton, S. E., & Swaminathan, H. (1985). *Item response theory: Principles and applications*. Boston: Kluwer Nijoff.

Hambrick, D. Z., Rench, T. A., Poposki, E. M., et al. (2011). The relationship between the ASVAB and multitasking in navy sailors: A process-specific approach. *Military Psychology, 23*(4), 365–380.

Hamera, E., & Brown, C. E. (2000). Developing a context-based performance measure for persons with schizophrenia: The test of grocery shopping skills. *American Journal of Occupational Therapy, 54*, 20–25.

Hammer, E. F. (1958). *The clinical application of projective drawings*. Springfield, IL: Charles C Thomas.

Hammer, E. F. (1981). Projective drawings. In A. I. Rabin (Ed.), *Assessment with projective techniques: A concise introduction* (pp. 151–185). New York: Springer.

Hammitt, J. K. (1990). Risk perceptions and food choice: An exploratory analysis of organic—versus conventional—produce buyers. *Risk Analysis, 10*, 367–374.

Han, M., & Yang, X. W., (2001). Educational assessment in China: Lessons from history and future prospects. *Assessment in Education: Principles, policy & practice, 8*(1), 5–10.

Handel, R. W., Ben-Porath, Y. S., Tellegen, A., & Archer, R. P. (2010). Psychometric functioning of the MMPI-2-RF, VRIN-r, and TRIN-r scales with varying degrees of randomness, acquiescence, and counter-acquiescence. *Psychological Assessment, 22*, 87–95.

Handler, L. (1996). John Exner and the book that started it all: A review of *The Rorschach Systems*. *Journal of Personality Assessment, 66*, 441–471.

Handler, L. (2001). Assessment of men: Personality assessment goes to war by the Office of Strategic Services Assessment Staff. *Journal of Personality Assessment, 76*(3), 558–578.

Haney, W. (1981). Validity, vaudeville, and values: A short history of social concerns over standardized testing. *American Psychologist, 36*, 1021–1034.

Haney, W., & Madaus, G. F. (1978). Making sense of the competency testing movement. *Harvard Educational Review, 48*, 462–484.

Hansen, J. C. (1987). Cross-cultural research on vocational interests. *Measurement and Evaluation in Counseling and Development, 19*, 163–176.

Hansen, K. K., Prince, J. S., & Nixon, G. W. (2008). Oblique chest views as a routine part of skeletal surveys performed for possible physical abuse: Is this practice worthwhile? *Child Abuse & Neglect, 32*(1), 155–159.

Hansen, N. D. (2002). Teaching cultural sensitivity in psychological assessment: A modular approach used in a distance education program. *Journal of Personality, 79*, 200–206.

Hansen, N. D., Pepitone-Arreola-Rockwell, F., & Greene, A. F. (2000). Multicultural competence: Criteria and case examples. *Professional Psychology: Research and Practice, 31*, 652–660.

Happell, B., Pinikahana, J., & Martin, T. (2003). Stress and burnout in forensic psychiatric nursing. *Stress & Health, 19*, 63–68.

Haque, S., & Guyer, M. (2010). Neuroimaging studies in diminished-capacity defense. *Journal of the American Academy of Psychiatry and the Law, 38*(4), 605–607.

Harcourt, A. H., & Stewart, K. J. (2007). *Gorilla society: Conflict, compromise and cooperation between the sexes*. Chicago, IL: University of Chicago Press.

Hare, R. D. (1980). A research scale for the assessment of psychopathy in criminal populations. *Personality and Individual Differences, 1*, 111–119.

Hare, R. D. (1985). *The Psychopathy Checklist*. Unpublished manuscript. University of British Columbia, Vancouver.

Hare, R. D., Harpur, A. R., Hakstian, A. R., Forth, A. E., Hart, S. D., & Newman, J. P. (1990). The Revised Psychopathy Checklist: Reliability and factor structure. *Psychological Assessment, 2*, 338–341.

Harmon, L. W., Hansen, J. C., Borgen, F. H., & Hammer, A. L. (1994). *Strong Interest Inventory: Applications and technical guide*. Palo Alto, CA: Consulting Psychologists Press.

Harris, P. M. (1994). Client management classification and prediction of probation outcome. *Crime and Delinquency, 40*, 154–174.

Harris, S. L., Delmolino, L., & Glasberg, B. A. (1996). Psychological and behavioral assessment in mental retardation. *Child & Adolescent Psychiatric Clinics of North America, 5*, 797–808.

Harrison, P., & Oakland, T. (2000). *Adaptive Behavior Assessment System*. San Antonio: Psychological Corporation.

Harrison, P. L. (1990). *AGS Early Screening Profiles*. Circle Pines, MN: American Guidance Service.

Hart, R. R., & Goldstein, M. A. (1985). Computer-assisted psychological assessment. *Computers in Human Services, 1*, 69–75.

Hart, S. D., Kropp, P. R., & Hare, R. D. (1988). Performance of male psychopaths following conditional release from prison. *Journal of Consulting and Clinical Psychology, 56*, 227–232.

Hart, V. (1992). Review of the Infant Mullen Scales of Early Development. In J. J. Kramer & J. C. Conoley (Eds.), *The eleventh mental measurements yearbook*. Lincoln: Buros Institute of Mental Measurements, University of Nebraska.

Hartigan, J. A., & Wigdor, A. K. (1989). *Fairness in employment testing: Validity generalization, minority issues, and the General Aptitude Test Battery*. Washington, DC: National Academy.

Hartman, D. E. (1986a). Artificial intelligence or artificial psychologist? Conceptual issues in clinical microcomputer use. *Professional Psychology: Research and Practice, 17*, 528–534.

Hartman, D. E. (1986b). On the use of clinical psychology software: Practical, legal, and ethical concerns. *Professional Psychology: Research and Practice, 17*, 462–465.

Hartmann, D. P., Roper, B. L., & Bradford, D. C. (1979). Some relationships between behavioral and traditional assessment. *Journal of Behavioral Assessment, 1*, 3–21.

Hartmann, E., Sunde, T., Kristensen, W., & Martinussen, M. (2003). Psychological measures as predictors of military training performance. *Journal of Personality Assessment, 80*, 87–98.

Hartshorne, H., & May, M. A. (1928). *Studies in the nature of character. Vol. 1: Studies in deceit*. New York: Macmillan.

Harvey, R. J., & Hammer, A. L. (1999). Item response theory. *Counseling Psychologist, 27*, 353–383.

Harvey, R. J., & Murry, W. D. (1994). Scoring the Myers-Briggs Type Indicator: Empirical comparison of preference score versus latent-trait methods. *Journal of Personality Assessment, 62*, 116–129.

Hathaway, S. R., & McKinley, J. C. (1940). A multiphasic personality schedule (Minnesota): 1. Construction of the schedule. *Journal of Psychology, 10*, 249–254.

Hathaway, S. R., & McKinley, J. C. (1942). A multiphasic personality schedule (Minnesota): III. The measurement of symptomatic depression. *Journal of Psychology, 14*, 73–84.

Hathaway, S. R., & McKinley, J. C. (1943). *The Minnesota Multiphasic Personality Inventory* (rev. ed.). Minneapolis: University of Minnesota.

Hathaway, S. R., & McKinley, J. C. (1951). *The MMPI manual.* New York: Psychological Corporation.

Hawkins, M. A. W., Gunstad, J., Calvo, D., & Spitznagel, M. B. (2016). Higher fasting glucose is associated with poorer cognition among healthy young adults. *Health Psychology, 35*(2), 199–202.

Hayden, D. C., Frulong, M. J., & Linnemeyer, S. (1988). A comparison of the Kaufman Assessment Battery for Children and the Stanford-Binet IV for the assessment of gifted children. *Psychology in the Schools, 25*, 239–243.

Hayes, S. C. (1999). Comparison of the Kaufman Brief Intelligence Test and the Matrix Analogies Test-Short Form in an adolescent forensic population. *Psychological Assessment, 11*, 108–110.

Haynes, R. B., Taylor, D. W., & Sackett, D. L. (Eds.). (1979). *Compliance in health care.* Baltimore: Johns Hopkins University.

Haynes, S. N. (2001a). Clinical applications of analogue behavioral observation: Dimensions of psychometric evaluation. *Psychological Assessment, 13*, 73–85.

Haynes, S. N. (2001b). Introduction to the special section on clinical applications of analogue behavioral observation. *Psychological Assessment, 13*, 3–4.

Haynes, S. N., Follingstad, D. R., & Sullivan, J. (1979). Assessment of marital satisfaction and interaction. *Journal of Consulting and Clinical Psychology, 47*, 789–791.

Haynes, S. N., Jensen, B. J., Wise, E., & Sherman, D. (1981). The marital intake interview: A multimethod criterion validity assessment. *Journal of Consulting and Clinical Psychology, 49*, 379–387.

Haynes, S. N., & Kaholokula, J. K. (2008). Behavioral assessment. In M. Hersen & A. M. Gross (Eds.), *Handbook of clinical psychology: Vol. 1. Adults* (pp. 495–522). Hoboken, NJ: Wiley.

Haynes, S. N., Richard, D. R., & Kubany, E. S. (1995). Content validity in psychological assessment: A functional approach to concepts and methods. *Psychological Assessment, 7*, 238–247.

Hays, P. A. (1996). Culturally responsive assessment with diverse older clients. *Professional Psychology: Research and Practice, 27*, 188–193.

Hays, J. R., Reas, D. L., and Shaw, J. B. (2002). Concurrent validity of the Wechsler Abbreviated Scale of Intelligence and the Kaufman Brief Intelligence Test among psychiatric inpatients. *Psychological Reports, 90*(2), 355–59.

Hays, P. A., & Iwamasa, G. Y. (Eds.). (2006). *Culturally responsive cognitive-behavioral therapy: Assessment, practice, and supervision.* Washington, DC: American Psychological Association.

Haywood, H., & Lidz, C. S. (2007). *Dynamic assessment in practice: Clinical and educational applications.* New York: Cambridge University Press.

Hazlett, R. L., Falkin, S., Lawhorn, W., Friedman, E., & Haynes, S. N. (1997). Cardiovascular reactivity to a naturally occurring stressor: Development and psychometric evaluation of psychophysiological assessment procedure. *Journal of Behavioral Medicine, 20*, 551–571.

He, W. (2011). Optimal item pool design for a highly constrained computerized adaptive test. *Dissertation Abstracts International, 72*(1-A), 167.

Heaton, R. K., Temkin, N., Dikmen, S., et al. (2001). Detecting change: A comparison of three neuropsychological methods, using normal and clinical samples. *Archives of Clinical Neuropsychology, 16*, 75–91.

Hedges, C. (1997, November 25). In Bosnia's schools, 3 ways never to learn from history. *New York Times,* pp. A1, A4.

Heilbronner, R. L. (2004). A status report on the practice of forensic neuropsychology. *The Clinical Neuropsychologist, 18*(2), 312–326.

Heinrichs, R. W. (1990). Variables associated with Wisconsin Card Sorting Test performance in neuropsychiatric patients referred for assessment. *Neuropsychiatry, Neuropsychology, and Behavioral Neurology, 3*, 107–112.

Heinze, M. C., & Grisso, T. (1996). Review of instruments assessing parenting competencies used in child custody evaluations. *Behavioral Sciences and the Law, 14*, 293–313.

Helfer, R. E., & Kempe, R. S. (Eds.). (1988). *The battered child* (4th ed.). Chicago: University of Chicago Press.

Heller, T. S., Hawgood, J. L., & De Leo, D. (2007). Correlates of suicide in building industry workers. *Archives of Suicide Research, 11*(1), 105–117.

Helmes, E., & Reddon, J. R. (1993). A perspective on developments in assessing psychopathology: A critical review of the MMPI and MMPI-2. *Psychological Bulletin, 113*, 453–471.

Helmreich, R. L. (1983). Applying psychology in outer space: Unfilled promises revisited. *American Psychologist, 38*(4), 445–450.

Helmreich, R. L., Wilhelm, J. A., Tamer, T. A., et al. (1979, January). A critical review of the life sciences project management at Ames Research Center for the Spacelab Mission Development Test III (NASA Technical Paper 1364).

Henk, W. A. (1993). New directions in reading assessment. *Reading and Writing Quarterly: Overcoming Learning Difficulties, 9*, 103–120.

Henriques, G., Keffer, S., Abrahamson, C., et al. (2011). Exploring the effectiveness of a computer-based heart rate variability biofeedback program in reducing anxiety in college students. *Applied Psychophysiology and Biofeedback, 36*(2), 101–112.

Henry, E. M., & Rotter, J. B. (1956). Situational influences on Rorschach responses. *Journal of Consulting Psychology, 20*, 457–462.

Henry, J. D. (1984). Syndicated public opinion polls: Some thoughts for consideration. *Journal of Advertising Research, 24*, I-5–I-8.

Henry, W. E. (1956). *The analysis of fantasy.* New York: Wiley.

Henson, R. K. (2001). Understanding internal consistency reliability estimates: A conceptual primer on coefficient alpha. *Measurement and Evaluation in Counseling and Development, 34*, 177–189.

Heppner, M. J. (1998). The Career Transitions Inventory: Measuring internal resources in adulthood. *Journal of Career Assessment, 6*, 135–145.

Heppner, M. J., Multon, K. D., & Johnston, J. A. (1994). Assessing psychological resources during career change: Development of the Career Transitions Inventory. *Journal of Vocational Behavior, 44*, 55–74.

Herbranson, W. T., & Schroeder, J. (2010). Are birds smarter than mathematicians? Pigeons (Columba livia) perform optimally on a version of the Monty Hall Dilemma. *Journal of Comparative Psychology, 124*(1), 1–13.

Herman, J. L. (1997). *Trauma and recovery: The aftermath of violence.* New York, NY: Basic Books.

Hermann, C., Blanchard, E. B., & Flor, H. (1997). Biofeedback treatment for pediatric migraine: Prediction of treatment outcome. *Journal of Consulting and Clinical Psychology, 65*, 611–616.

Hernandez, B., Keys, C., & Balcazar, F. (2003). The Americans wth Disabilities Act Knowledge Survey: Strong psychometrics and weak knowledge. *Rehabilitation Psychology, 48*, 93–99.

Hernandez-Tejada, M., Amstadter, A., Muzzy, W., & Acierno, R. (2013). The national elder mistreatment study: Race and ethnicity findings. *Journal of Elder Abuse & Neglect, 25,* 281–293.

Herzberg, F., Mausner, B., Peterson, R. O., & Capwell, D. F. (1957). Job attitudes: Review of research and opinion. *Journal of Applied Psychology, 63,* 596–601.

Hess, E. H. (1965). Attitude and pupil size. *Scientific American, 212,* 46–54.

Hetherington, E. M., & Parke, R. D. (1993). *Child psychology: A contemporary viewpoint* (4th ed.). New York: McGraw-Hill.

Heyman, R. E. (2001). Observation of couple conflicts: Clinical assessment applications, stubborn truths, and shaky foundations. *Psychological Assessment, 13,* 5–35.

History of the Department. (2016). Department of Psychology, The Hebrew University of Jerusalem (Website). Accessed March 30, 2016 at http://psychology.huji.ac.il/en/?cmd=About.112

Hibbard, S. (2003). A critique of Lilienfeld et al.'s (2000). "The scientific status of projective techniques." *Journal of Personality Assessment, 80,* 260–271.

Hibbard, S., Farmer, L., Wells, C., et al. (1994). Validation of Cramer's defense mechanism manual for the TAT. *Journal of Personality Assessment, 63,* 197–210.

Hicken, B. L., Plowhead, A., & Gibson, W. (2010). Values, validity, and ethical angst: Assessment of mental capacity in older adults. In N. A. Pachana, K. Laidlaw, & B. G. Knight (Eds.), *Casebook of clinical geropsychology: International perspectives on practice* (pp. 243–262). New York, NY: Oxford University Press.

Hicks, L. K., Lin, Y., Robertson, D. W., et al. (2001). Understanding the clinical dilemmas that shape medical students' ethical development: Questionnaire survey and focus group study. *British Medical Journal, 322,* 709–710.

Hicks, S. J., & Sales, B. D. (2006). The current models of scientific profiling. In S. J. Hicks & B. D. Sales (Eds.), *Criminal profiling: Developing an effective science and practice* (pp. 71–85). Washington, DC: American Psychological Association.

Higate, P. (2007). Military institutions. In M. Flood, J. K. Gardiner, B. Pease, & K. Pringle (Eds.), *Encyclopedia of men and masculinities* (p. 441). London: Routledge.

Higgins, P. C. (1983). *Outsiders in a hearing world.* Beverly Hills, CA: Sage.

Hill, J. S., Pace, T. M., & Robbins, R. R. (2010). Decolonizing personality assessment and honoring indigenous voices: A critical examination of the MMPI-2. *Cultural Diversity and Ethnic Minority Psychology, 16*(1), 16–25.

Hill-Briggs, F., Dial, J. G., Morere, D. A., & Joyce, A. (2007). Neuropsychological assessment of persons with physical disability, visual impairment or blindness, and hearing impairment or deafness. *Archives of Clinical Neuropsychology, 22*(3), 389–404.

Hiller, J. B., Rosenthal, R., Bornstein, R. F., & Brunell-Neuleib, S. (1999). A comparative meta-analysis of Rorschach and MMPI validity. *Psychological Assessment, 11,* 278–296.

Hills, D. A. (1985). Prediction of effectiveness in leaderless group discussions with the Adjective Check List. *Journal of Applied Psychology, 15,* 443–447.

Hinojosa, R. (2010). Doing hegemony: Military, men, and constructing a hegemonic masculinity. *The Journal of Men's Studies, 18,* 179–194.

Hinrichsen, J. J., & Bradley, L. A. (1974). Situational determinants of personal validation of general personality interpretations: A re-examination. *Journal of Personality Assessment, 38,* 530–534.

Hiscox, M. D. (1983). *A balance sheet for educational item banking.* Paper presented at the annual meeting of the National Council for Measurement in Education, Montreal.

Hiscox, M. D., & Brzezinski, E. (1980). *A guide to item banking in education.* Portland, OR: Northwest Regional Educational Laboratory, Assessment and Education Division.

Hishinuma, E. S., Andrade, N. N., Johnson, R. C., et al. (2000). Psychometric properties of the Hawaiian Culture Scale-Adolescent Version. *Psychological Assessment, 12,* 140–157.

Hiskey, M. S. (1966). *Hiskey-Nebraska Test of Learning Aptitude.* Lincoln, NE: Union College.

Ho, M. K. (1987). *Family therapy with ethnic minorities.* Newbury Park, CA: Sage.

Hodapp, R. M. (1995). Definitions in mental retardation: Effects on research, practice, and perceptions. *School Psychology Quarterly, 10*(1), 24–28.

Hoelzle, J. B., Nelson, N. W., & Smith, C. A. (2011). Comparison of Wechsler Memory Scale–Fourth Edition (WMS–IV) and Third Edition (WMS–III) dimensional structures: Improved ability to evaluate auditory and visual constructs. *Journal of Clinical and Experimental Neuropsychology, 33*(3), 283–291.

Hofer, P. J., & Green, B. F. (1985). The challenge of competence and creativity in computerized psychological testing. *Journal of Consulting and Clinical Psychology, 53,* 826–838.

Hoffman, B. (1962). *The tyranny of testing.* New York: Crowell-Collier.

Hoffman, K. I., & Lundberg, G. D. (1976). A comparison of computer monitored group tests and paper-and-pencil tests. *Educational and Psychological Measurement, 36,* 791–809.

Hofstede, G. (1998). Attitudes, values, and organizational culture: Disentangling the concepts. *Organization Studies, 19,* 477–493.

Hogan, J., Barrett, P., & Hogan, R. (2007). Personality measurement, faking, and employment selection. *Journal of Applied Psychology, 92,* 1270–1285.

Hogan, R., & Roberts, B. W. (2001). Introduction: Personality and industrial and organizational psychology. In B. W. Roberts & R. Hogan (Eds.). *Personality psychology in the workplace* (pp. 3–16). Washington, DC: American Psychological Association.

Hoge, R. D. (1999). An expanded role for psychological assessments in juvenile justice systems. *Criminal Justice and Behavior, 26,* 251–266.

Hoge, S. K., Bonnie, R. J., Poythress, N., & Monahan, J. (1999). *The MacArthur Competence Assessment Tool—Criminal Adjudication.* Odessa, FL: Psychological Assessment Resources.

Holden, G. W., & Edwards, L. A. (1989). Parental attitudes toward child rearing: Instruments, issues, and implications. *Psychological Bulletin, 106,* 29–58.

Holland, A. (1980). *Communicative abilities in daily living: A test of functional communication for aphasic adults.* Baltimore: University Park Press.

Holland, J. L. (1973). *Making vocational choices.* Englewood Cliffs, NJ: Prentice-Hall.

Holland, J. L. (1985). *Manual for the vocational preference inventory.* Odessa, FL: Psychological Assessment Resources.

Holland, J. L. (1997). *Making vocational choices: A theory of vocational personalities and work environments* (3rd ed.). Odessa, FL: Psychological Assessment Resources.

Holland, J. L. (1999). Why interest inventories are also personality inventories. In M. L. Savickas & A. R. Spokane (Eds.), *Vocational interests: Meaning, measurement, and counseling use* (87–101). Palo Alto, CA: Davies-Black.

Holland, J. L., Powell, A. B., & Fritzsche, B. A. (1994). *The Self-Directed Search (SDS) professional user's guide—1994 edition.* Odessa, FL: Psychological Assessment Resources.

Holland, W. R. (1960). Language barrier as an educational problem of Spanish-speaking children. *Exceptional Children, 27,* 42–47.

Hollander, E. P., & Willis, R. H. (1967). Some current issues in the psychology of conformity and nonconformity. *Psychological Bulletin, 68,* 62–76.

Hollenbeck, J. R., & Whitener, E. M. (1988). Reclaiming personality traits for personal selection: Self-esteem as an illustrative case. *Journal of Management, 14,* 81–91.

Hollingshead, A. B., & Redlich, F. C. (1958). *Social class and mental illness: A community study.* New York: Wiley.

Holmstrom, R. W., Silber, D. E., & Karp, S. A. (1990). Development of the Apperceptive Personality Test. *Journal of Personality Assessment, 54,* 252–264.

Holt, R. R. (1958). Clinical and statistical prediction: A reformulation and some new data. *Journal of Abnormal and Social Psychology, 56,* 1–12.

Holt, R. R. (1970). Yet another look at clinical and statistical prediction: Or, is clinical psychology worthwhile? *American Psychologist, 25,* 337–349.

Holt, R. R. (1971). *Assessing personality.* New York: Harcourt Brace Jovanovich.

Holt, R. R. (1978). *Methods in clinical psychology: Vol. 2. Prediction and research.* New York: Plenum.

Holtzman, W. H., Thorpe, J. S., Swartz, J. D., & Herron, E. W. (1961). *Inkblot perception and personality: Holtzman Inkblot Technique.* Austin: University of Texas Press.

Hom, J., & Goldstein, G. (2015). Introduction to the special issue: A tribute to Ralph M. Reitan. *Archives of Clinical Neuropsychology, 30*(8), 721–723.

Hom, J., & Nici, J. (2015a). Ralph M. Reitan: The pioneer of clinical neuropsychology. *Archives of Clinical Neuropsychology, 30*(8), 724–732.

Hom, J., & Nici, J. (2015b). Ralph M. Reitan's bibliography. *Archives of Clinical Neuropsychology, 30*(8), 774–783.

Honaker, L. M. (1988). The equivalency of computerized and conventional MMPI administration: A review. *Clinical Psychology Review, 8,* 561–577.

Honaker, L. M. (1990, August). Recommended guidelines for computer equivalency research (or everything you should know about computer administration but will be disappointed if you ask). In W. J. Camara (Chair), *The state of computer-based testing and interpretation: Consensus or chaos?* Symposium conducted at the Annual Convention of the American Psychological Association, Boston.

Honaker, L. M., & Fowler, R. D. (1990). Computer-assisted psychological assessment. In G. Goldstein & M. Hersen (Eds.), *Handbook of psychological assessment* (2nd ed., pp. 521–546). New York: Pergamon.

Honegger, L. N. (2015). Does the evidence support the case for mental health courts? A review of the literature. *Law and Human Behavior, 39*(5), 478–488.

Honts, C. R. (1994). Psychophysiological detection of deception. *Current Directions in Psychological Science, 3,* 77–82.

Hope, M. (2014, April 20). Fourth grade Common Core reading: "Who's the baby daddy?" *Breitbart.* Accessed online May 20 2016 at http://www.breitbart.com/texas/2014/04/20/fourth-grade-common-core-reading-whos-the-baby-daddy/

Hopkins, K. D., & Glass, G. V. (1978). *Basic statistics for the behavioral sciences.* Englewood Cliffs, NJ: Prentice-Hall.

Hopwood v. State of Texas, 78 F.3d 932, 948 (5th Cir. 1996).

Horn, J. (1988). Thinking about human abilities. In J. R. Nesselroade & R. B. Cattell (Eds.), *Handbook of multivariate psychology.* New York: Plenum.

Horn, J. (2008). Response to Bigler (2007): The sky is not falling. *Archives of Clinical Neuropsychology, 23*(1), 125–128.

Horn, J. L. (1968). Organization of abilities and the development of intelligence. *Psychological Review, 75,* 242–259.

Horn, J. L. (1985). Remodeling old theories of intelligence: *GF-Gc* theory. In B. B. Wolman (Ed.), *Handbook of intelligence* (pp. 267–300). New York: Wiley.

Horn, J. L. (1988). Thinking about human abilities. In J. R. Nesselroade & R. B. Cattell (Eds.), *Handbook of multivariate psychology* (rev. ed., pp. 645–685). New York: Academic Press.

Horn, J. L. (1989). Cognitive diversity: A framework for learning. In P. L. Ackerman et al. (Eds.), *Learning and individual differences* (pp. 61–116). New York: W. H. Freeman.

Horn, J. L. (1991). Measurement of intellectual capabilities: A review of theory. In K. S. McGrew et al. (Eds.), *Woodcock-Johnson technical manual* (pp. 197–232). Chicago: Riverside.

Horn, J. L. (1994). Theory of fluid and crystallized intelligence. In R. J. Sternberg (Ed.), *Encyclopedia of human intelligence* (pp. 443–451). New York, NY: Macmillan Publishing Co, Inc.

Horn, J. L., & Cattell, R. B. (1966). Refinement and test of the theory of fluid and crystallized intelligence. *Journal of Educational Psychology, 57,* 253–270.

Horn, J. L., & Cattell, R. B. (1967). Age differences in fluid and crystallized intelligence. *Acta Psychologica, 26,* 107–129.

Horn, J. L., & Hofer, S. M. (1992). Major abilities and development in the adult period. In R. J. Sternberg & C. A. Berg (Eds.), *Intellectual development* (pp. 44–99). Boston: Cambridge University Press.

Hornby, R. (1993). *Cultural competence for human service providers.* Rosebud, SD: Sinte Gleska University Press.

Horner, M. S. (1973). A psychological barrier to achievement in women: The motive to avoid success. In D. C. McClelland & R. S. Steele (Eds.), *Human motivation* (pp. 222–230). Morristown, NJ: General Learning.

Horowitz, R., & Murphy, L. B. (1938). Projective methods in the psychological study of children. *Journal of Experimental Education, 7,* 133–140.

Horton Jr., A. M., & Reynolds, C. R. (2015). Ralph M. Reitan: Evidenced based before evidence based was cool. *Archives of Clinical Neuropsychology, 30*(8), 740–747.

Horvath, A. O., Del Re, A. C., Flukiger, C., & Symonds, D. (2011). Alliance in individual psychotherapy. *Psychotherapy, 48,* 9–16.

Hough, L. M. (1998). The millennium for personality psychology: New horizons or good ole daze. *Applied Psychology: An International Review, 47,* 233–261.

Hough, L. M., Eaton, N. K., Dunnette, M. D., et al. (1990). Criterion related validities of personality constructs and the effect of response distortion on those validities. *Journal of Applied Psychology, 75,* 581–595.

House, R. J., Shane, S. A., & Herold, D. M. (1996). Rumors of the death of dispositional research are vastly exaggerated. *Academy of Management Review, 20,* 203–224.

Houston, T. K., Cooper, L. A., Vu, H., et al. (2001). Screening the public for depression through the Internet. *Psychiatric Services, 52,* 362–367.

Howard, M. N. (1991). The neutral expert: A plausible threat to justice. *Criminal Law Review, 1991,* 98–105.

Howe Chief, E. (1940). An assimilation study of Indian girls. *Journal of Social Psychology, 11,* 19–30.

Hoy, J., Natarajan, A., & Petra, M. M. (2016). Motivational interviewing and the transtheoretical model of change: Under-explored resources for suicide intervention. *Community Mental Health Journal, 52*(5), 559–567.

Hsu, S.-H., & Peng, Y. (1993). Control/display relationship of the four-burner stove: A re-examination. *Human Factors, 35,* 745–749.

Huang, Y.-C., & Shih, H.-C. (2011). The prosocial and moral character of the spiritual leader. *Social Behavior and Personality, 39*(1), 33–40.

Hubbard, E. J., Santini, V., Blankevoort, C. G., et al. (2008). Clock drawing performance in cognitively normal elderly. *Archives of Clinical Neuropsychology, 23*(3), 295–327.

Hubbard, K., & Hegarty, P. (2016). Blots and all: A history of the Rorschach ink blot test in Britain. *Journal of the History of the Behavioral Sciences, 52*(2), 146–166.

Hudson, W. W. (1982). *The clinical measurement package: A field manual.* Chicago: Dorsey.

Huesmann, L. R., & Guerra, N. G. (1997). Children's normative beliefs about aggression and aggressive behavior. *Journal of Personality and Social Psychology, 72,* 408–419.

Huffcutt, A. I., & Arthur, W., Jr. (1994). Hunter and Hunter (1984) revisited: Interview validity for entry-level jobs. *Journal of Applied Psychology, 79,* 184–190.

Hughes, T. L., Gacono, C. B., & Owen, P. F. (2007). Current status of Rorschach assessment: Implications for the school psychologist. *Psychology in the Schools, 44*(3), 281–291.

Hull, C. L. (1922). *Aptitude testing.* Yonkers, NY: World Book.

Hulse, W. G. (1951). The emotionally disturbed child draws his family. *Quarterly Journal of Child Behavior, 3,* 151–174.

Hulse, W. G. (1952). Childhood conflict expressed through family drawings. *Quarterly Journal of Child Behavior, 16,* 152–174.

Humphreys, L. G. (1996). Linear dependence of gain scores on their components imposes constraints on their use and interpretation: Comment on "Are simple gain scores obsolete?" *Applied Psychological Measurement, 20,* 293–294.

Hunsley, J., & Bailey, J. M. (1999). The clinical utility of the Rorschach: Unfulfilled promises and an uncertain future. *Psychological Assessment, 11,* 266–277.

Hunt, K. N. (2002). *Encyclopedia of associations.* Farmington Hills, MI: Gale Group.

Hunt, K. N. (2005). *Encyclopedia of associations.* Farmington Hills, MI: Gale Group.

Hunter, J. E. (1980). *Validity generalization for 12,000 jobs: An application of synthetic validity and validity generalization to the General Aptitude Test Battery (GATB).* Washington, DC: U.S. Employment Service, Department of Labor.

Hunter, J. E. (1982). *The dimensionality of the General Aptitude Test Battery and the dominance of general factors over specific factors in the prediction of job performance.* Washington, DC: U.S. Employment Service, Department of Labor.

Hunter, J. E. (1986). Cognitive ability, cognitive aptitudes, job knowledge, and job performance. *Journal of Vocational Behavior, 29,* 340–362.

Hunter, J. E., & Hunter, R. (1984). Validity and utility of alternate predictors of job performance. *Psychological Bulletin, 96,* 72–98.

Hunter, J. E., & Schmidt, F. L. (1976). A critical analysis of the statistical and ethical implications of various definitions of "test bias." *Psychological Bulletin, 83,* 1053–1071.

Hunter, J. E., & Schmidt, F. L. (1981). Fitting people into jobs: The impact of personal selection on normal productivity. In M. D. Dunnette & E. A. Fleishman (Eds.), *Human performance and productivity: Vol. 1. Human capability assessment.* Hillsdale, NJ: Erlbaum.

Hunter, J. E., & Schmidt, F. L. (1983). Quantifying the effects of psychological interventions on employee job performance and work-force productivity. *American Psychologist, 38,* 473–478.

Hunter, J. E., & Schmidt, F. L. (1990). *Methods of meta-analysis.* Newbury Park, CA: Sage.

Hunter, J. E., Schmidt, F. L., & Jackson, G. B. (1982). *Meta-analysis: Cumulating research findings across studies.* Beverly Hills, CA: Sage.

Hunter, J. E., Schmidt, F. L., & Judiesch, M. K. (1990). Individual differences in output as a function of job complexity. *Journal of Applied Psychology, 75*(1), 28–42.

Hunter, M. S. (1992). The Women's Health Questionnaire: A measure of mid-aged women's perceptions of their emotional and physical health. *Psychology and Health, 7,* 45–54.

Hurlburt, R. T. (1997). Randomly sampling thinking in the natural environment. *Journal of Consulting and Clinical Psychology, 65,* 941–949.

Hurst, N. H. (1997). A narrative analysis of identity change in treated substance abusers. *Dissertation Abstracts International, Section B: The Sciences & Engineering, 58*(4-B), 2124.

Huss, M. T. (2009). *Forensic psychology: Research, clinical practice, and applications.* Hoboken, NJ: Wiley-Blackwell.

Hwang, S. W. (2006). Homelessness and harm reduction. *Canadian Medical Association Journal, 174*(1), 50–51.

Iacono, W. G., & Lykken, D. T. (1997). The validity of the lie detector: Two surveys of scientific opinion. *Journal of Applied Psychology, 82,* 425–433.

Iaffaldano, M. T., & Muchinsky, P. M. (1985). Job satisfaction and job performance: A meta-analysis. *Psychological Bulletin, 97,* 251–273.

Ijuin, M., Homma, A., Mimura, M., Kitamura, S., et al. (2008). Validation of the 7-minute screen for the detection of early-stage Alzheimer's disease. *Dementia and Geriatric Cognitive Disorders, 25*(3), 248–255.

Ilhan, M. N., Durukan, E., Taner, E., et al. (2008). Burnout and its correlates among nursing staff: Questionnaire survey. *Journal of Advanced Nursing, 61*(1), 100–106.

Illovsky, M. E. (2003). *Mental health professionals, minorities, and the poor.* New York: Brunner-Routledge.

Ilyin, D. (1976). *The Ilyin oral interview.* Rowley, MA: Newbury House.

Impara, J. C., & Plake, B. S. (Eds.). (1998). *The thirteenth mental measurements yearbook.* Lincoln: Buros Institute of Mental Measurements, University of Nebraska.

Imtiaz, S., Shield, K. D., Roerecke, M., et al. (2016). The burden of disease attributable to cannabis use in Canada in 2012. *Addiction, 111*(4), 653–662.

Ingham, B., Clarke, L., & James, I. A. (2008). Biopsychosocial case formulation for people with intellectual disabilities and mental health problems: A pilot study of a training workshop for direct care staff. *British Journal of Developmental Disabilities, 54*(106, Pt. 1), 41–54.

Ingram, P. B., Kelso, K. M., & McCord, D. M. (2011). Empirical correlates and expanded interpretation of the MMPI-2-RF Restructured Clinical Scale 3 (Cynicism). *Assessment, 18,* 95–101.

Inman, A. G., Ladany, N., Constantine, M. G., & Morano, C. K. (2001). Development and preliminary validation of the Cultural Values Conflict Scale for South Asian women. *Journal of Counseling Psychology, 48*(1), 17–27.

Innocenti, M. S., Huh, K., & Boyce, G. C. (1992). Families of children with disabilities: Normative data and other considerations on parenting stress. *Topics in Early Childhood Special Education, 12,* 403–427.

Institute for Juvenile Research. (1937). *Child guidance procedures, methods and techniques employed at the Institute for Juvenile Research.* New York: Appleton-Century.

Institute of Medicine. (1984). *Research and training for the Secret Service: Behavioral science and mental health perspectives: A report of the Institute of Medicine* (IOM Publication No. IOM-84-01). Washington, DC: National Academy Press.

International Test Commission. (1993). *Technical standards for translating tests and establishing test score equivalence.* Amherst, MA: Author. (Available from Dr. Ronald Hambleton, School of Education, University of Massachusetts, Amherst, MA 01003).

Irby, S. M., & Floyd, R. G. (2013). Review of Wechsler Abbreviated Scale of Intelligence, Second Edition. *Canadian Journal of School Psychology, 28*(3), 295–299.

Iris, M., Conrad, K. J., & Ridings, J. (2014). Observational measure of elder self-neglect. *Journal of Elder Abuse & Neglect, 26*(4), 365–397.

Ironson, G. H., & Subkoviak, M. J. (1979). A comparison of several methods of assessing item bias. *Journal of Educational Measurement, 16,* 209–225.

Irvine, S. H., & Berry, J. W. (Eds.). (1983). *Human assessment and cultural factors.* New York: Plenum.

Ishihara, S. (1964). *Tests for color blindness* (11th ed.). Tokyo: Kanehara Shuppan.

Ivancevich, J. M. (1983). Contrast effects in performance evaluation and reward practices. *Academy of Management Journal, 26,* 465–476.

McCloskey, G. W. (1989, March). *The K-ABC sequential simultaneous information processing model and classroom intervention: A report—the Dade County Classroom research study*. Paper presented at the Annual Meeting of the National Association of School Psychologists, Boston.

McClure-Butterfield, P. (1990). Issues in child custody evaluation and testimony. In C. R. Reynolds & R. W. Kamphaus (Eds.), *Handbook of psychological and educational assessment of children: Personality, behavior and context* (pp. 576–588). New York: Guilford.

McConkey, K. M., & Sheehan, P. W. (1996). *Hypnosis, memory, and behavior in criminal investigation*. New York: Guilford.

McCool, J. P., Cameron, L. D., & Petrie, K. J. (2001). Adolescent perceptions of smoking imagery in film. *Social Science & Medicine, 52*, 1577–1587.

McCoy, G. F. (1972). *Diagnostic evaluation and educational programming for hearing impaired children*. Springfield: Office of the Illinois Superintendent of Public Instruction.

McCrady, B. S., & Bux, D. A. (1999). Ethical issues of informed consent with substance abusers. *Journal of Consulting and Clinical Psychology, 67*, 186–193.

McCrae, R. R., & Costa, P. T., Jr. (1983). Social desirability and scales: More substance than style. *Journal of Consulting and Clinical Psychology, 51*, 882–888.

McCrae, R. R., Costa, P. T., Jr., Dahlstrom, W. G., Barefoot, J. C., Siegler, I. C., & Williams, R. B., Jr. (1989). A caution on the use of the MMPI K-correction in research on psychosomatic medicine. *Psychosomatic Medicine, 51*, 58–65.

McCrae, R. R., Costa, P. T., Jr., Del Pilar, G. H., Rolland, J.-P., & Parker, W. D. (1998). Cross-cultural assessment of the five-factor model: The Revised NEO Personality Inventory. *Journal of Cross-Cultural Psychology, 29*, 171–188.

McCrae, R. R., Costa, P. T., Jr., Terracciano, A., et al. (2002). Personality trait development from age 12 to age 18: Longitudinal, cross-sectional and cross-cultural analyses. *Journal of Personality & Social Psychology, 83*, 1456–1468.

McCrimmon, A. W., & Smith, A. D. (2013). Review of Wechsler Abbreviated Scale of Intelligence, Second Edition (WASI-II). *Journal of Psychoeducational Assessment, 31*(3), 337–341.

McCubbin, H., Larsen, A., & Olson, D. (1985a). F-COPES: Family Crisis Oriented Personal Evaluation Scales. In D. H. Olson, H. I. McCubbin, H. L. Barnes, A. S. Larsen, M. Muxen, & M. Wilson (Eds.), *Family inventories* (rev. ed.). St. Paul: Family Social Science, University of Minnesota.

McCubbin, H. I., Patterson, J. M., & Wilson, L. R. (1985b). FILE: Family Inventory of Life Events and Changes. In D. H. Olson, H. I. McCubbin, H. L. Barnes, A. S. Larsen, M. Muxen, & M. Wilson (Eds.), *Family inventories* (rev. ed.). St. Paul: Family Social Science, University of Minnesota.

McCusker, P. J. (1994). Validation of Kaufman, Ishikuma, Kaufman-Packer's Wechsler Adult Intelligence Scale— Revised short forms on a clinical sample. *Psychological Assessment, 6*, 246–248.

McDermott, P. A., Alterman, A. I., Brown, L., et al. (1996). Construct refinement and confirmation for the Addiction Severity Index. *Psychological Assessment, 8*, 182–189.

McDevitt, S. C., & Carey, W. B. (1978). The measurement of temperament in 3- to 7-year-old children. *Journal of Child Psychology & Psychiatry & Allied Disciplines, 19*, 245–253.

McDonald, W. J. (1993). Focus group research dynamics and reporting: An examination of research objectives and moderator influences. *Journal of the Academy of Marketing Science, 21*, 161–168.

McDowell, C., & Acklin, M. W. (1996). Standardizing procedures for calculating Rorschach interrater reliability: Conceptual and empirical foundations. *Journal of Personality Assessment, 66*, 308–320.

McDowell, I., & Newell, C. (1987). *Measuring health: A guide to rating scales and questionnaires*. New York: Oxford University Press.

McElrath, K. (1994). A comparison of two methods for examining inmates' self-reported drug use. *International Journal of the Addictions, 29*, 517–524.

McElwain, B. A. (1998). On seeing Beth at home and in a different light. In L. Handler (Chair), *Conducting assessments in clients' homes: Contexts, surprises, dilemmas, opportunities*. Symposium presented at the Society for Personality Assessment 1998 Midwinter Meeting, February 20.

McEvoy, G. M., & Beatty, R. W. (1989). Assessment centers and subordinate appraisals of managers: A seven-year examination of predictive validity. *Personnel Psychology, 42*, 37–52.

McFarlane, A. C. (2011). Redefining PTSD in DSM-5: Conundrums and potentially unintended risks. In D. J. Stein, M. J. Friedman, & C. Blanco (Eds.), *Post-traumatic stress disorder* (pp. 42–47). New York, NY: Wiley-Blackwell.

McGaghie, W. C. (2002, September 4). Assessing readiness for medical education: Evolution of the Medical College Admission Test. *Journal of the American Medical Association, 288*, p. 1085.

McGirr, A., Renaud, J., Seguin, M., et al. (2007). An examination of DSM-IV depressive symptoms and risk for suicide completion in major depressive disorder: A psychological autopsy study. *Journal of Affective Disorders, 97*(1–3), 203–209.

McGrew, K. S. (1997). Analysis of the major intelligence batteries according to a proposed comprehensive *Gf-Gc* framework. In D. P. Flanagan, J. L. Genshaft, & P. L. Harrison (Eds.), *Contemporary intellectual assessment: Theories, tests, and issues* (pp. 151–180). New York: Guilford.

McGrew, K. S. (2009). Editorial. CHC theory and the human cognitive abilities project. Standing on the shoulders of the giants of psychometric intelligence research, *Intelligence, 37*, 1–10.

McGrew, K. S., & Flanagan, D. P. (1998). *The intelligence test desk reference: Gf-Gc cross-battery assessment*. Boston: Allyn & Bacon.

McGurk, F. J. (1975). Race differences—twenty years later. *Homo, 26*, 219–239.

McKinley, J. C., & Hathaway, S. R. (1940). A multiphasic schedule (Minnesota): II. A differential study of hypochondriases. *Journal of Psychology, 10*, 255–268.

McKinley, J. C., & Hathaway, S. R. (1944). The MMPI: V. Hysteria, hypomania, and psychopathic deviate. *Journal of Applied Psychology, 28*, 153–174.

McKinney, W. R., & Collins, J. R. (1991). The impact on utility, race, and gender using three standard methods of scoring selection examinations. *Public Personnel Management, 20*(2), 145–169.

McLearen, A. M., Pietz, C. A., & Denney, R. L. (2004). Evaluation of psychological damages. In W. T. O'Donohue & E. R. Levensky (Eds.), *Handbook of forensic psychology* (pp. 267–299). Amsterdam: Elsevier.

McLellan, A. T., Luborsky, L., Woody, G. E., & O'Brien, C. P. (1980). An improved diagnostic evaluation instrument for substance abuse patients: The Addiction Severity Index. *Journal of Nervous and Mental Disease, 168*, 26–33.

McLemore, C. W., & Court, J. H. (1977). Religion and psychotherapy—ethics, civil liberties, and clinical savvy: A critique. *Journal of Consulting and Clinical Psychology, 45*, 1172–1175.

McMillen, C., Howard, M. O., Nower, L., & Chung, S. (2001). Positive by-products of the struggle with chemical dependency. *Journal of Substance Abuse Treatment, 20*, 69–79.

McNemar, Q. (1964). Lost: Our intelligence. Why? *American Psychologist, 19*, 871–882.

McNemar, Q. (1975). On so-called test bias. *American Psychologist, 30,* 848–851.

McReynolds, P. (1987). Lightner Witmer: Little-known founder of clinical psychology. *American Psychologist, 42,* 849–858.

McReynolds, P., & Ludwig, K. (1984). Christian Thomasius and the origin of psychological rating scales. *ISIS, 75,* 546–553.

Mead, M. (1978). *Culture and commitment: The new relationship between the generations in the 1970s* (rev. ed.). New York: Columbia University Press.

Meadow, K. P., Karchmer, M. A., Petersen, L. M., & Rudner, L. (1980). *Meadow-Kendall Social-Emotional Assessment Inventory.* Washington, DC: Gallaudet University.

Meadows, G., Turner, T., Campbell, L., Lewis, S. W., Reveley, M. A., & Murray, R. M. (1991). Assessing schizophrenia in adults with mental retardation: A comparative study. *British Journal of Psychiatry, 158,* 103–105.

Mednick, S. A. (1962). The associative basis of the creative process. *Psychological Review, 69,* 220–232.

Mednick, S. A., Higgins, J., & Kirschenbaum, J. (1975). *Psychology.* New York: Wiley.

Medvec, V. H., Madey, S. F., & Gilovich, T. (1995). When less is more: Counterfactual thinking and satisfaction among Olympic medalists. *Journal of Personality and Social Psychology, 69,* 603–610.

Medvec, V. H., & Savitsky, K. (1997). When doing better means feeling worse: The efforts of categorical cutoff points on counterfactual thinking and satisfaction. *Journal of Personality and Social Psychology, 72,* 1284–1296.

Meehl, P. E. (1945), The dynamics of "structured" personality tests. *Journal of Clinical Psychology, 1,* 296–303.

Meehl, P. E. (1951). *Research results for counselors.* St. Paul, MN: State Department of Education.

Meehl, P. E. (1954). *Clinical versus statistical prediction: A theoretical analysis and a review of the evidence.* Minneapolis: University of Minnesota.

Meehl, P. E. (1956). Wanted: A good cookbook. *American Psychologist, 11,* 263–272.

Meehl, P. E., & Rosen, A. (1955). Antecedent probability and the efficiency of psychometric signs, patterns, or cutting scores. *Psychological Bulletin, 52,* 194–216.

Mehl, M. R., & Pennebaker, J. W. (2003). The sounds of social life: A psychometric analysis of students' daily social environments and natural conversations. *Journal of Personality and Social Psychology, 84,* 857–870.

Meier, T. B., Brummel, B. J., Singh, R., et al. (2015). The underreporting of self-reported symptoms following sports-related concussion. *Journal of Science and Medicine in Sport, 18*(5), 507–511.

Mejía, X. (2005). Gender matters: Working with adult male survivors of trauma. *Journal of Counseling & Development, 83,* 29–40.

Melchert, T. P., & Patterson, M. M. (1999). Duty to warn and interventions with HIV-positive clients. *Professional Psychology: Research and Practice, 30,* 180–186.

Melchior, L. A., Huba, G. J., Brown, V. B., & Reback, C. J. (1993). A short depression index for women. *Educational and Psychological Measurement, 53,* 1117–1125.

Melia, R. P., Pledger, C., & Wilson, R. (2003). Disability and rehabilitation research: Opportunities for participation, collaboration, and extramural funding for psychologists. *American Psychologist, 58,* 285–288.

Mellenbergh, G. J. (1994). Generalized linear item response theory. *Psychological Bulletin, 115,* 300–307.

Mello, E. W., & Fisher, R. P. (1996). Enhancing older adult eyewitness memory with the cognitive interview. *Applied Cognitive Psychology, 10,* 403–418.

Melton, G., Petrila, J., Poythress, N. G., & Slobogin, C. (1997). *Psychological evaluations for the courts: A handbook for mental health professionals and lawyers* (2nd ed.). New York: Guilford.

Melton, G. B., Petrila, J., Poythress, N. G., & Slobogin, C. (1987). *Psychological evaluation for the courts: A handbook for mental health professionals and lawyers.* New York, NY: Guilford.

Melton, G. B. (1989). Review of the Child Abuse Protection Inventory, Form VI. In J. C. Conoley & J. J. Kramer (Eds.), *The tenth mental measurements yearbook.* Lincoln: Buros Institute of Mental Measurements, University of Nebraska.

Memon, A., Fraser, J., Colwell, K., Odinot, G., & Mastroberardino, S. (2010). Distinguishing truthful from invented accounts using reality monitoring criteria. *Legal and Criminological Psychology, 15*(2), 177–194.

Mendoza, R. H. (1989). An empirical scale to measure type and degree of acculturation in Mexican-American adolescents and adults. *Journal of Cross-Cultural Psychology, 20,* 372–385.

Menninger, K. A. (1953). *The human mind* (3rd ed.). New York: Knopf.

Mercer, J. R. (1976). A system of multicultural pluralistic assessment (SOMPA). In *Proceedings: With bias toward none.* Lexington: Coordinating Office for Regional Resource Centers, University of Kentucky.

Merrens, M. R., & Richards, W. S. (1970). Acceptance of generalized versus "bona fide" personality interpretation. *Psychological Reports, 27,* 691–694.

Mershon, B., & Gorsuch, R. L. (1988). Number of factors in the personality sphere: Does increase in factors increase predictability of real-life criteria? *Journal of Personality and Social Psychology, 55,* 675–680.

Mesmer, E. M., & Duhon, G. J. (2011). Response to intervention: Promoting and evaluating generalization. *Journal of Evidence-Based Practices for Schools, 12*(1), 75–104.

Messer, S. B. (1976). Reflection-impulsivity: A review. *Psychological Bulletin, 83,* 1026–1052.

Messick, S. (1976). *Individuality in learning: Implications of cognitive style and creativity for human development.* San Franciso: Jossey-Bass.

Messick, S. (1995). Validity of psychological assessment. *American Psychologist, 50,* 741–749.

Meyer, G. J., & Archer, R. P. (2001). The hard science of Rorschach research: What do we know and where do we go? *Psychological Assessment, 13,* 486–502.

Meyer, G. J., & Handler, L. (1997). The ability of the Rorschach to predict subsequent outcome: Meta-analysis of the Rorschach Prognostic Rating Scale. *Journal of Personality Assessment, 69,* 1–38.

Meyer, G. J., & Kurtz, J. E. (2006). Advancing personality assessment terminology: Time to retire "objective" and "projective" as personality test descriptors. *Journal of Personality Assessment, 87,* 223–225.

Meyer, G. J., Shaffer, T. W., Erdberg, P., & Horn, S. L. (2015). Addressing issues in the development and use of the Composite International Reference Values as Rorschach norms for adults. *Journal of Personality Assessment, 97*(4), 330–347.

Meyer, G. J., Viglione, D. J., Mihura, J. L., Erard, R. E., & Erdberg, P. (2011). *Rorschach Performance Assessment System: Administration, coding, interpretation, and technical manual.* Toledo, OH: Author.

Meyers, J. (1994, January/February). Assessing cross-cultural adaptability with the CCAI. *San Diego Psychological Association Newsletter, 3*(1 & 2).

Micceri, T. (1989). The unicorn, the normal curve and other improbable creatures. *Psychological Bulletin, 105,* 156–166.

Midanik, L. T., Greenfield, T. K., & Rogers, J. D. (2001). Reports of alcohol-related harm: Telephone versus face-to-face interviews. *Journal of Studies on Alcohol, 62,* 74–78.

Mihura, J. L., Meyer, G. J., Bombel, G., & Dumitrascu, N. (2015). Standards, accuracy, and questions of bias in Rorschach meta-analyses: Reply to Wood, Garb, Nezworski, Lilienfeld, and Duke (2015). *Psychological Bulletin, 141,* 250–260.

Mihura, J. L., Meyer, G. J., Dumitrascu, N., & Bombel, G. (2013). The validity of individual Rorschach variables: Systematic reviews and meta-analyses of the comprehensive system. *Psychological Bulletin, 139,* 548–605.

Miller, F. (2017). At risk. In R. J. Cohen (Ed.), *Online-only boxes, apps, & links (OOBALs) to accompany Psychological Testing and Assessment,* (9th ed.). Accessed at *www.mhhe. cohentesting9/OOBAL-10-B2*

Miller, F. G., Cohen, D., Chafouleas, S. M., Riley-Tillman, T. C., Welsh, M. E., Fabiano, G. A. (2015). A comparison of measures to screen for social, emotional, and behavioral risk. *School Psychology Quarterly, 30,* 184–196.

Miller, I. W., Kabacoff, R. I., Epstein, N. B., & Bishop, D. S. (1994). The development of a clinical rating scale for the McMaster Model of Family Functioning. *Family Process, 33,* 53–69.

Miller, J. C., Skillman, G. D., Benedetto, J. M., et al. (2007). A three-dimensional haptic matrix test of nonverbal reasoning. *Journal of Visual Impairment and Blindness, 101,* 557–570.

Miller, J. N., & Ozonoff, S. (2000). The external validity of Asperger disorder: Lack of evidence from the domain of neuropsychology. *Journal of Abnormal Psychology, 109,* 227–238.

Miller, N. E. (1969). Learning of visceral and glandular responses. *Science, 163,* 434–445.

Miller, W. R., & Rollnick, S. (2002). *Motivational interviewing: Preparing people for change (2nd ed.).* New York, NY: Guilford Press.

Miller, W. R., & Rollnick, S. (2009). Ten things that motivational interviewing is not. *Behavioural and Cognitive Psychotherapy, 37,* 129–140.

Milling, L. S., Coursen, E. L., Shores, J. S., & Waszkiewicz, J. A. (2010). The predictive utility of hypnotizability: the change in suggestibility produced by hypnosis. *Journal of Consulting and Clinical Psychology, 78*(1), 126–130.

Millman, J., & Arter, J. A. (1984). Issues in item banking. *Journal of Educational Measurement, 21,* 315–330.

Millon, T., Millon, C., & Davis, R. (1994). *MCMI-III manual: Millon Clinical Multiaxial Inventory-III.* Minneapolis: National Computer Systems.

Mills v. Board of Education of the District of Columbia, 348 F. Supp 866 (D. DC 1972).

Mills, C. J. (2003). Characteristics of effective teachers of gifted students: Teacher background and personality styles of students. *Gifted Child Quarterly, 47,* 272–282.

Milner, B. (1971). Interhemispheric differences in the localization of psychological processes in man. *British Medical Bulletin, 27,* 272–277.

Milner, J. S., Gold, R. G., & Wimberley, R. C. (1986). Prediction and explanation of child abuse: Cross-validation of the Child Abuse Protection Inventory. *Journal of Consulting and Clinical Psychology, 54,* 865–866.

Minsky, S. K., Spitz, H. H., & Bessellieu, C. L. (1985). Maintenance and transfer of training by mentally retarded young adults on the Tower of Hanoi problem. *American Journal of Mental Deficiency, 90,* 190–197.

Minton, H. L. (1988). *Lewis M. Terman: Pioneer in psychological testing.* New York: New York University Press.

Minton, H. L. (2000). Terman, Lewis Madison. In A. E. Kazdin (Ed.), *Encyclopedia of Psychology,* (Vol. 8) (pp. 37–39). Washington, DC: American Psychological Association.

Mirka, G. A., Kelaher, D. P., Nay, T., & Lawrence, B. M. (2000). Continuous assessment of back stress (CABS): A new method to quantify low-back stress in jobs with variable biomechanical demands. *Human Factors, 42,* 209–225.

Mischel, W. (1968). *Personality and assessment.* New York: Wiley.

Mischel, W. (1973). Toward a cognitive social learning re-conceptualization of personality. *Psychological Review, 80,* 252–283.

Mischel, W. (1977). On the future of personality measurement. *American Psychologist, 32,* 246–254.

Mischel, W. (1979). On the interface of cognition and personality: Beyond the person-situation debate. *American Psychologist, 34,* 740–754.

Mishra, D., Khalique, A., & Kumar, R. (2010). Rorschach profile of manic patients. *Journal of Projective Psychology & Mental Health, 17*(2), 158–164.

Misiaszek, J., Dooling, J., Gieseke, M., Melman, H., Misiaszek, J. G., & Jorgensen, K. (1985). Diagnostic considerations in deaf patients. *Comprehensive Psychiatry, 26,* 513–521.

Mitchell, J. (1999). *Measurement in psychology: Critical history of a methodological concept.* New York: Cambridge University Press.

Mitchell, J. V., Jr. (Ed.). (1985). *The ninth mental measurements yearbook.* Lincoln: Buros Institute of Mental Measurements, University of Nebraska.

Mitchell, J. V., Jr. (1986). Measurement in the larger context: Critical current issues. *Professional Psychology: Research and Practice, 17,* 544–550.

Mitzel, H. C., Lewis, D. M., Patz, R. J., & Green, D. R. (2000). The bookmark procedure: Cognitive perspectives on standard setting. In G. J. Cizek (Ed.), *Setting performance standards: Concepts, methods, and perspectives,* Mahwah, NJ: Erlbaum.

Moberg, P. J., & Rick, J. H. (2008). Decision-making capacity and competency in the elderly: A clinical and neuropsychological perspective. *NeuroRehabilitation, 23,* 403–413.

Moffitt, T. E., Caspi, A., Krueger, R. F., et al. (1997). Do partners agree about abuse in their relationship? A psychometric evaluation of interpartner agreement. *Psychological Assessment, 9,* 47–56.

Monahan, J. (1981). *The clinical prediction of violent behavior.* Washington, DC: U.S. Government Printing Office.

Montague, M. (1993). Middle school students' mathematical problem solving: An analysis of think-aloud protocols. *Learning Disability Quarterly, 16,* 19–32.

Montgomery, G. T., & Orozco, S. (1985). Mexican Americans' performance on the MMPI as a function of level of acculturation. *Journal of Clinical Psychology, 41,* 203–212.

Moore, M., Schermer, J. A., Paunonen, S. V., & Vernon, P. A. (2010). Genetic and environmental influences on verbal and nonverbal measures of the Big Five. *Personality and Individual Differences, 48*(8), 884–888.

Moore, M. S., & McLaughlin, L. (1992). Assessment of the preschool child with visual impairment. In E. Vasquez Nutall, I. Romero & J. Kalesnik (Eds.), *Assessing and screening pre-schoolers: Psychological and educational dimensions* (pp. 345–368). Boston: Allyn & Bacon.

Moos, R. H. (1986). *Work Environment Scale* (2nd ed.). Palo Alto, CA: Consulting Psychologists Press.

Moos, R. H., & Moos, B. S. (1981). *Family Environment Scale manual.* Palo Alto, CA: Consulting Psychologists Press.

Moos, R. H., & Moos, B. S. (1994). *Family environment manual: Development, applications, research.* Palo Alto, CA: Consulting Psychologists Press.

Moreland, K. L. (1985). Validation of computer-based test interpretations: Problems and prospects. *Journal of Consulting and Clinical Psychology, 53,* 816–825.

Moreland, K. L. (1986). An introduction to the problem of test user qualifications. In R. B. Most (Chair), *Test purchaser qualifications: Present practice, professional needs, and a proposed system.* Symposium presented at the 94th annual convention of the American Psychological Association, Washington, DC.

Moreland, K. L. (1987). Computerized psychological assessment: What's available. In J. N. Butcher (Ed.), *Computerized psychological assessment: A practitioner's guide* (pp. 26–49). New York: Basic Books.

Moreland, K. L., Eyde, L. D., Robertson, G. J., Primoff, E. S., & Most, R. B. (1995a). Assessment of test user qualifications: A research-based measurement procedure. *American Psychologist, 50,* 14–23.

Moreland, K. L., Reznikoff, M., & Aronow, E. (1995b). Integrating Rorschach interpretation by *carefully* placing *more* of your eggs in the content basket. *Journal of Personality Assessment, 64,* 239–242.

Morgan, C. D. (1938). Thematic Apperception Test. In H. A. Murray (Ed.), *Explorations in personality: A clinical and experimental study of fifty men of college age* (pp. 673–680). New York: Oxford University Press.

Morgan, C. D., & Murray, H. A. (1935). A method for investigating fantasies: The Thematic Apperception Test. *Archives of Neurology and Psychiatry, 34,* 289–306.

Morgan, C. D., & Murray, H. A. (1938). Thematic Apperception Test. In H. A. Murray (Ed.), *Explorations in personality: A clinical and experimental study of fifty men of college age* (pp. 530–545). New York: Oxford University Press.

Morgan, K. E., Rothlisberg, B. A., McIntosh, D. E., & Hunt, M. S. (2009). Confirmatory factor analysis of the KABC-II in preschool children. *Psychology in the Schools, 46,* 515–525.

Morgan, W. G. (1995). Origin and history of Thematic Apperception Test images. *Journal of Personality Assessment, 65,* 237–254.

Mori, L. T., & Armendariz, G. M. (2001). Analogue assessment of child behavior problems. *Psychological Assessment, 13,* 36–45.

Morina, N., Ijntema, H., Meyerbröker, K., & Emmelkamp, P. M. G. (2015). Can virtual reality exposure therapy gains be generalized to real-life? A meta-analysis of studies applying behavioral assessments. *Behaviour Research and Therapy, 74,* 18–24.

Morreau, L. E., & Bruininks, R. H. (1991). *Checklist of Adaptive Living Skills.* Itasca, IL: Riverside.

Moser, R. S., Schatz, P., & Lichtenstein, J. D. (2015). The importance of proper administration and interpretation of neuropsychological baseline and post-concussion computerized testing. *Applied Neuropsychology: Child, 4*(1), 41–48.

Moses, S. (1991). Major revision of SAT goes into effect in 1994. *APA Monitor, 22*(1), 35.

Mosier, C. I. (1947). A critical examination of the concepts of face validity. *Educational and Psychological Measurement, 7,* 191–206.

Mosqueda, L., & Olsen, B. (2015). Elder abuse and neglect. In P. Lichtenberg & B. T. Mast (Eds.), *APA handbook of clinical geropsychology, Vol. 2: Assessment, treatment, and issues of later life.* Washington, DC: American Psychological Association. (pp. 667–686).

Moss, K., Ullman, M., Johnsen, M. C., et al. (1999). Different paths to justice: The ADA, employment, and administrative enforcement by the EEOC and FEPAs. *Behavioral Sciences and the Law, 17,* 29–46.

Mossman, D. (2003). *Daubert,* cognitive malingering, and test accuracy. *Law and Human Behavior, 27*(3), 229–249.

Motowidlo, S. J. (1996). Orientation toward the job and organization. In K. R. Murphy (Ed.), *Individual differences and behavior in organizations* (pp. 20–175). San Francisco: Jossey-Bass.

Moye, J., Armesto, J. C., & Karel, M. J. (2005). Evaluating capacity of older adults in rehabilitation settings: Conceptual models and clinical challenges. *Rehabilitation Psychology, 50*(3), 207–214.

Mrad, D. F., Hanigan, A. J. S., & Bateman, J. R. (2015). A model of service and training: Threat assessment on a community college campus. *Psychological Services, 12*(1), 16–19.

Mueller, C. G. (1949). Numerical transformations in the analysis of experimental data. *Psychological Bulletin, 46,* 198–223.

Mueller, J. H., Jacobsen, D. M., & Schwarzer, R. (2000). What are computers good for? A case study in online research. In M. H. Birnbaum (Ed.), *Psychological experiments on the Internet* (pp. 195–216). San Diego: Academic Press.

Mueller-Hanson, R., Heggestad, E. D., & Thornton, G. C., III. (2003). Faking and selection: Considering the use of personality from select-in and select-out perspectives. *Journal of Applied Psychology, 88,* 348–355.

Mulvey, E. P., & Lidz, C. W. (1984). Clinical considerations in the prediction of dangerousness in mental patients. *Clinical Psychology Review, 4,* 379–401.

Muñoz, B., Magliano, J. P., Sheridan, R., & McNamara, D. S. (2006). Typing versus thinking aloud when reading: Implications for computer-based assessment and training tools. *Behavior Research Methods, 38*(2), 211–217.

Murguia, A., Zea, M. C., Reisen, C. A., & Peterson, R. A. (2000). The development of the Cultural Health Attributions Questionnaire (CHAQ). *Cultural Diversity and Ethnic Minority Psychology, 6,* 268–283.

Murphy, G. E. (1984). The prediction of suicide: Why is it so difficult? *American Journal of Psychotherapy, 38,* 341–349.

Murphy, K. A., Blustein, D. L., Bohlig, A., & Platt, M. (2006, August). *College to career transition: An exploration of emerging adulthood.* Paper presented at the 114th Annual Convention of the American Psychological Association, New Orleans.

Murphy, K. M. (1986). When your top choice turns you down: The effect of rejected offers on the utility of selection tests. *Psychological Bulletin, 99,* 133–138.

Murphy, K. R. (Ed.). (2003). *Validity generalization: A critical review.* Mahwah, NJ: Erlbaum.

Murphy, L. L., Conoley, J. C., & Impara, J. C. (1994). *Tests in print IV: An index to tests, test reviews, and the literature on specific tests.* Lincoln: Buros Institute of Mental Measurements, University of Nebraska.

Murphy-Berman, V. (1994). A conceptual framework for thinking about risk assessment and case management in child protective service. *Child Abuse and Neglect, 18,* 193–201.

Murray, C. (2007). The magnitude and components of change in the black-white IQ difference from 1920 to 1991: A birth cohort analysis of the Woodcock-Johnson standardizations. *Intelligence, 35*(4), 305–318.

Murray, H. A. (1943). *Thematic Apperception Test manual.* Cambridge, MA: Harvard University.

Murray, H. A., & MacKinnon, D. W. (1946). Assessment of OSS personnel. *Journal of Consulting Psychology, 10,* 76–80.

Murray, H. A., et al. (1938). *Explorations in personality.* Cambridge, MA: Harvard University.

Murray, N., Salvatore, A., Powell, D., & Reed-Jones, R. (2014). Reliability and validity evidence of multiple balance assessments in athletes with a concussion. *Journal of Athletic Training, 49*(4), 540–549.

Murstein, B. I. (1961). Assumptions, adaptation level, and projective techniques. *Perceptual and Motor Skills, 12,* 107–125.

Murstein, B. I., & Mathes, S. (1996). Projection on projective techniques = pathology: The problem that is not being addressed. *Journal of Personality Assessment, 66,* 337–349.

Mussen, P. H., & Naylor, H. K. (1954). The relationship between overt and fantasy aggression. *Journal of Abnormal and Social Psychology, 49,* 235–240.

Mussen, P. H., & Scodel, A. (1955). The effects of sexual stimulation under varying conditions on TAT sexual responsiveness. *Journal of Consulting and Clinical Psychology, 19,* 90.

Muzio, E. (2016). Inkblots and neurons: Correlating typical cognitive performance with brain structure and function. *Rorschachiana, 37*(1), 1–6.

Myers, I. B. (1962). *The Myers-Briggs Type Indicator: Manual.* Palo Alto, CA: Consulting Psychologists Press.

Myers, I. B., & Briggs, K. C. (1943/1962). *The Myers-Briggs Type Indicator.* Palo Alto, CA: Consulting Psychologists Press.

Myerson, A. (1925). *The inheritance of mental disease.* Oxford, England: Williams & Wilkins.

Nagle, R. J., & Bell, N. L. (1993). Validation of Stanford-Binet Intelligence Scale: Fourth Edition Abbreviated Batteries with college students. *Psychology in the Schools, 30,* 227–231.

Naglieri, J. A. (1985a). Normal children's performance on the McCarthy Scales, Kaufman Assessment Battery and Peabody Individual Achievement Test. *Journal of Psychoeducational Assessment, 3,* 123–129.

Naglieri, J. A. (1985b). Use of the WISC-R and K-ABC with learning disabled, borderline mentally retarded, and normal children. *Psychology in the Schools, 22,* 133–141.

Naglieri, J. A. (1989). A cognitive processing theory for the measurement of intelligence. *Educational Psychologist, 24,* 185–206.

Naglieri, J. A. (1990). *Das-Naglieri Cognitive Assessment System.* Paper presented at the conference "Intelligence: Theories and Practice," Memphis, TN.

Naglieri, J. A. (1997). IQ: Knowns and unknowns, hits and misses. *American Psychologist, 52,* 75–76.

Naglieri, J. A., & Anderson, D. F. (1985). Comparison of the WISC-R and K-ABC with gifted students. *Journal of Psychoeducational Assessment, 3,* 175–179.

Naglieri, J. A., Drasgow, F., Schmit, M., et al. (2004). Psychological testing on the Internet: New problems, old issues. *American Psychologist, 59,* 150–162.

Narumoto, J., Nakamura, K., Kitabayashi, Y., et al. (2008). Relationships among burnout, coping style, and personality: Study of Japanese professional caregivers for elderly. *Psychiatry and Clinical Neurosciences, 62*(2), 174–176.

National Association of School Psychologists. (2000). *Professional conduct manual* (4th ed.). Washington, DC: Author.

National Center on Response to Intervention. (2011). *Essential components of RtI: A closer look at response to intervention.* Document accessed at National Center on Response to Intervention website at www.rti4success.org/pdf/rtiessentialcomponents_042710.pdf

National Council on Disability. (1996). *Cognitive impairments and the application of Title I of the Americans with Disabilities Act.* Washington, DC: Author.

National Joint Committee on Learning Disabilities. (1985). *Learning disabilities and the preschool child: A position paper of the National Joint Committee on Learning Disabilities.* Baltimore: Author.

Naylor, J. C., & Shine, L. C. (1965). A table for determining the increase in mean criterion score obtained by using a selection device. *Journal of Industrial Psychology, 3,* 33–42.

Neale, E. L., & Rosale, M. L. (1993). What can art therapists learn from projective drawing techniques for children? A review of the literature. *The Arts in Psychotherapy, 20,* 37–49.

Neath, J., Bellini, J., & Bolton, B. (1997). Dimensions of the Functional Assessment Inventory for five disability groups. *Rehabilitation Psychology, 42,* 183–207.

Nehring, W. M. (2007). Accommodations for school and work. In C. L. Betz & W. M. Nehring (Eds.), *Promoting health care transitions for adolescents with special health care needs and disabilities* (pp. 97–115). Baltimore: Brookes.

Neisser, U. (1979). The concept of intelligence. *Intelligence, 3,* 217–227.

Nellis, L., & Gridley, B. E. (1994). Review of the Bayley Scales of Infant Development—Second Edition. *Journal of School Psychology, 32,* 201–209.

Nelson, C. A., Wewerka, S., Thomas, K. M., et al. (2000). Neurocognitive sequelae of infants of diabetic mothers. *Behavioral Neuroscience, 114,* 950–956.

Nelson, D. V., Harper, R. G., Kotik-Harper, D., & Kirby, H. B. (1993). Brief neuropsychologic differentiation of demented versus depressed elderly inpatients. *General Hospital Psychiatry, 15,* 409–416.

Nelson, L. D. (1994). Introduction to the special section on normative assessment. *Psychological Assessment, 4,* 283.

Nelson, R. O., Hay, L. R., & Hay, W. M. (1977). Comment on Cone's "The relevance of reliability and validity for behavior assessment." *Behavior Therapy, 8,* 427–430.

Nelson, S. D., Malone, D., & Lafleur, J. (2015). Calculating the baseline incidence in patients without risk factors: A strategy for economic evaluation. *PharmacoEconomics, 33*(9), 887–892.

Nester, M. A. (1993). Psychometric testing and reasonable accommodation for persons with disabilities. *Rehabilitation Psychology, 38,* 75–85.

Neugarten, B., Havighurst, R. J., & Tobin, S. (1961). The measurement of life satisfaction. *Journal of Gerontology, 16,* 134–143.

Nevid, J. S. (2010). Implicit measures of consumer response—The search for the Holy Grail of marketing research: Introduction to the special issue. *Psychology & Marketing, 27*(10), 913–920.

Nevid, J. S., & McClelland, N. (2010). Measurement of implicit and explicit attitudes toward Barack Obama. *Psychology & Marketing, 27*(10), 989–1000.

Newborg, J., Stock, J. R., Wnek, L., et al. (1984). *Battelle Developmental Inventory.* Allen, TX: DLM Teaching Resources.

Newcomb, T. M. (1929). *Consistency of certain extrovert-introvert behavior patterns in 51 problem boys.* New York: Columbia University Bureau of Publications.

Newell, A. (1973). Production systems: Models of control structures. In W. G. Chase (Ed.), *Visual information processing* (pp. 463–526). New York: Academic Press.

Newman, D. A., Kinney, T., & Farr, J. L. (2004). Job performance ratings. In J. C Thomas (Ed.), *Comprehensive handbook of psychological assessment, Volume 4: Industrial and organizational assessment* (pp. 373–389). Hoboken, NJ: Wiley.

Nguyen, H. H., & von Eye, A. (2002). The Acculturation Scale for Vietnamese Adolescents (ASVA): A bidimensional perspective. *International Journal of Behavioral Development, 26*(3), 202–213.

Nguyen, N. T., Biderman, M. D., & McNary, L. D. (2010). A validation study of the cross-cultural adaptability inventory. *International Journal of Training and Development, 14*(2), 112–129.

Nichols, D. S. (2006). The trials of separating bathwater from baby: A review and critique of the MMPI-2 restructured clinical scales. *Journal of Personality Assessment, 87,* 121–138.

Nilsson, J. E., Berkel, L. A., Flores, L. Y., et al. (2003). An 11-year review of *Professional Psychology: Research and Practice:* Content and sample analysis with an emphasis on diversity. *Professional Psychology: Research and Practice, 34,* 611–616.

Nock, M. K., & Banaji, M. R. (2007). Prediction of suicide ideation and attempts among adolescents using a brief performance-based test. *Journal of Consulting and Clinical Psychology, 75*(5), 707–715.

Nordanger, D. (2007). Discourses of loss and bereavement in Tigray, Ethiopia. *Culture, Medicine and Psychiatry, 31*(2), 173–194.

Norton, P. J., & Hope, D. A. (2001). Analogue observational methods in the assessment of social functioning in adults. *Psychological Assessment, 13,* 59–72.

Nosek, B. A., Greenwald, A. G., & Banaji, M. R. (2007). The Implicit Association Test at age 7: Methodological and conceptual review. In J. A. Bargh (Ed.), *Social psychology and the unconscious: The automaticity of higher mental processes. Frontiers of social psychology* (pp. 265–292). New York: Psychology Press.

Notarius, C., & Markman, H. (1981). Couples Interaction Scoring System. In E. Filsinger & R. Lewis (Eds.), *Assessing marriage: New behavioral approaches.* Beverly Hills, CA: Sage.

Notarius, C. I., & Vanzetti, N. A. (1983). The Marital Agendas Protocol. In E. Filsinger (Ed.), *Marriage and family assessment: A sourcebook for family therapy.* Beverly Hills, CA: Sage.

Novick, M. R., & Lewis, C. (1967). Coefficient alpha and the reliability of composite measurements. *Psychometrika, 32,* 1–13.

Nunnally, J. C. (1967). *Psychometric theory.* New York: McGraw-Hill.

Nunnally, J. C. (1978). *Psychometric theory* (2nd ed.). New York: McGraw-Hill.

Nurss, J. R. (1994). *Metropolitan Readiness Tests, Sixth Edition* (MRT6). San Antonio: Pearson Assessments.

Nyborg, H., & Jensen, A. R. (2000). Black–white differences on various psychometric tests: Spearman's hypothesis tested on American armed services veterans. *Personality and Individual Differences, 28,* 593–599.

Nye, C. D., Roberts, B. W. Saucier, G., & Zhou, X. (2008). Testing the measurement equivalence of personality adjective items across cultures. *Journal of Research in Personality, 42*(6), 1524–1536.

Nystedt, L., Sjoeberg, A., & Haegglund, G. (1999). Discriminant validation of measures of organizational commitment, job involvement, and job satisfaction among Swedish army officers. *Scandinavian Journal of Psychology, 40,* 49–55.

Obasi, E. M., & Leong, F. T. L. (2010). Construction and validation of the Measurement of Acculturation Strategies for People of African Descent (MASPAD). *Cultural Diversity and Ethnic Minority Psychology, 16*(4), 526–539.

O'Connor, E. (2001, February). Researchers pinpoint potential cause of autism. *Monitor on Psychology, 32*(2), 13.

O'Connor, M., Dooley, B., & Fitzgerald, A. (2015). Constructing the Suicide Risk Index (SRI): Does it work in predicting suicidal behavior in young adults mediated by proximal factors? *Archives of Suicide Research, 19*(1), 1–16.

O'Donnell, W. E., DeSoto, C. B., & DeSoto, J. L. (1993). Validity and reliability of the Revised Neuropsychological Impairment Scales (NIS). *Journal of Clinical Psychology, 49,* 372–382.

O'Donnell, W. E., DeSoto, C. B., DeSoto, J. L., & Reynolds, D. M. (1993). *The Neuropsychological Impairment Scale (NIS) manual.* Los Angeles: Western Psychological Services.

Office of Strategic Services Assessment Staff. (1948). *Assessment of men: Selection of personnel for the Office of Strategic Services.* New York: Rinehart.

Office of the Public Guardian (2008). *Guide to capacity assessment under the personal directives act.* Alberta: Office of the Public Guardian. Retrieved from http://www.seniors.alberta.ca/opg/personaldirectives/publications/OPG1642.pdf

Office of the Surgeon General, Center for Mental Health Services, National Institute of Mental Health. (2001). *Mental health: Culture, race, and ethnicity: A supplement to mental health: A Report of the Surgeon General.* Rockville, MD: Substance Abuse and Mental Health Services Administration.

O'Hare, T., & Van Tran, T. (1998). Substance abuse among Southeast Asians in the U.S.: Implications for practice and research. *Social Work in Health Care, 26,* 69–80.

Okazaki, S., & Sue, S. (1995). Methodological issues in assessment research with ethnic minorities. *Psychological Assessment, 7,* 367–375.

Okazaki, S., & Sue, S. (2000). Implications of test revisions for assessment with Asian Americans. *Psychological Assessment, 12,* 272–280.

O'Keefe, J. (1993). Disability, discrimination, and the Americans with Disabilities Act. *Consulting Psychology Journal, 45*(2), 3–9.

O'Leary, K. D., & Arias, I. (1988). Assessing agreement of reports of spouse abuse. In G. T. Hotaling, D. Finkelhor, J. T. Kirkpatrick, & M. A. Straus (Eds.), *Family abuse and its consequences* (pp. 218–227). Newbury Park, CA: Sage.

Oliffe, J. L., & Phillips, M. (2008). Depression, men and masculinities: A review and recommendations. *Journal of Men's Health, 5*(3), 194–202.

Olino, T. M., McMakin, D. L., Dahl, R. E., et al. (2011). "I won, but I'm not getting my hopes up": Depression moderates the relationship of outcomes and reward anticipation. *Psychiatry Research: Neuroimaging* (November 11).

Olkin, R., & Pledger, C. (2003). Can disability studies and psychology join hands? *American Psychologist, 58,* 296–304.

Olson, D. H., & Barnes, H. L. (1985). Quality of life. In D. H. Olson, H. I. McCubbin, H. L. Barnes, A. S. Larsen, M. Muxen, & M. Wilson (Eds.), *Family inventories* (rev. ed.). St. Paul: Family Social Science, University of Minnesota.

Olson, D. H., Larsen, A. S., & McCubbin, H. I. (1985). Family strengths. In D. H. Olson, H. I. McCubbin, H. L. Barnes, A. S. Larsen, M. Muxen, & M. Wilson (Eds.), *Family inventories* (rev. ed.). St. Paul: Family Social Science, University of Minnesota.

Olson, S. (2014, November 12). Lewy body dementia: Understanding Robin Williams's battle with a complicated disease. *Medical Daily.* Accessed May 4, 2016 at http://www.medicaldaily.com/lewy-body-dementia-understanding-robin-williamss-battle-complicated-disease-310420

Olweus, D. (1979). Stability of aggressive reaction patterns in males: A review. *Psychological Bulletin, 86,* 852–875.

Ones, D. S., Dilchert, S., Viswesvaran, C., & Judge, T. A. (2007). In support of personality assessment in organizational settings. *Personnel Psychology, 60*(4), 995–1027.

Ones, D. S., & Viswesvaran, C. (2001). Integrity tests and other criterion-focused occupational personality scales (COPS) used in personnel selection. *International Journal of Selection and Assessment, 9,* 31–39.

Ones, D. S., Viswesvaran, C., & Reiss, A. D. (1996). Role of social desirability in personality testing for personnel selection: The red herring. *Journal of Applied Psychology, 81,* 660–670.

Ontario Capacity Assessment Office. (2005). *Guidelines for conducting assessments of capacity.* Ontario: Ontario Ministry of the Attorney Generals. Retrieved from http://www.attorneygeneral.jus.gov.on.ca/english/family/pgt/capacity/2005-06/guide-0505.pdf

Open Science Collaboration. (2015). Estimating the reproducibility of psychological science. *Science, 349,* 943.

Oregon Death With Dignity Act, 2 Ore. Rev. Stat. §§127.800–127.897 (1997).

Organ, D. W., & Near, J. P. (1985). Cognition versus affect in measures of job satisfaction. *International Journal of Psychology, 20,* 241–253.

Orne, M. T. (1979). The use and misuse of hypnosis in court. *International Journal of Clinical and Experimental Hypnosis, 27,* 311–341.

Orr, F. C., DeMatteo, A., Heller, B., Lee, M., & Nguyen, M. (1987). Psychological assessment. In H. Elliott, L. Glass, & J. W. Evans (Eds.), *Mental health assessment of deaf clients* (pp. 93–106). Boston: Little, Brown.

Orr, R. R., Cameron, S. J., Dobson, L. A., & Day, D. M. (1993). Age-related changes in stress experienced by families with a child who has developmental delays. *Mental Retardation, 31,* 171–176.

Osberg, T. M., Haseley, E. N., & Kamas, M. M. (2008). The MMPI-2 Clinical Scales and Restructured Clinical (RC) Scales: Comparative psychometric properties and relative diaganostic efficiency in young adults. *Journal of Personality Assessment, 90*(1), 81–92.

Osborn, A. J., Mathias, J. L., Fairweather-Schmidt, A. K. (2016). Prevalence of anxiety following adult traumatic brain injury: A meta-analysis comparing measures, samples and postinjury intervals. *Neuropsychology, 30*(2), 247–261.

Smith, D. K., & Knudtson, L. S. (1990). *K-ABC and S-B: FE relationships in an at-risk preschool sample.* Paper presented at the Annual Meeting of the American Psychological Association, Boston.

Smith, D. K., Lasee, M. J., & McCloskey, G. M. (1990). *Test-retest reliability of the AGS Early Screening Profiles.* Paper presented at the Annual Meeting of the National Association of School Psychologists, San Francisco.

Smith, D. K., & Lyon, M. A. (1987). *Children with learning difficulties: Differences in ability patterns as a function of placement.* Paper presented at the Annual Meeting of the American Educational Research Association, Washington, DC. (ERIC Document Reproduction Service No. ED 285 317.)

Smith, D. K., St. Martin, M. E., & Lyon, M. A. (1989). A validity study of the Stanford-Binet Fourth Edition with students with learning disabilities. *Journal of Learning Disabilities, 22,* 260–261.

Smith, G. E., Ivnik, R. J., Malec, J. F., Kokmen, E., Tangalos, E. G., & Kurland, L. T. (1992). Mayo's older Americans normative studies (MOANS): Factor structure of a core battery. *Psychological Assessment, 4,* 382–390.

Smith, G. T., McCarthy, D. M., & Anderson, K. G. (2000). On the sins of short form development. *Psychological Assessment, 12,* 102–111.

Smith, J. D. (1985). *Minds made feeble: The myth and legacy of the Kallikaks.* Austin: Pro-Ed.

Smith, K. A., Harvath, T. A., Goy, E. R., & Ganzini, L. (2015). Predictors of pursuit of physician-assisted death. *Journal of Pain and Symptom Management, 49*(3), 555–561.

Smith, M. (1948). Cautions concerning the use of the Taylor-Russell tables in employee selection. *Journal of Applied Psychology, 32,* 595–600.

Smith, M. L., & Glass, G. V. (1977). Meta-analysis of psychotherapy outcome studies. *American Psychologist, 32,* 752–760.

Smith, R. E. (1963). Examination by computer. *Behavioral Science, 8,* 76–79.

Smith, R. G., & Iwata, B. A. (1997). Antecedent influences on behavior disorders. *Journal of Applied Behavior Analysis, 30,* 343–375.

Smith, T. T., Myers-Jennings, C., & Coleman, T. (2000). Assessment of language skills in rural preschool children. *Communication Disorders Quarterly, 21,* 98–113.

Smither, J. W., Reilly, R. R., & Buda, R. (1988). Effect of prior performance information on ratings of present performance: Contrast versus assimilation revisited. *Journal of Applied Psychology, 73,* 487–496.

Smither, R., & Rodriguez-Giegling, M. (1982). Personality, demographics, and acculturation of Vietnamese and Nicaraguan refugees to the United States. *International Journal of Psychology, 17,* 19–25.

Snook, B., Eastwood, J., Gendreau, P., et al. (2007). Taking stock of criminal profiling: A narrative review and meta-analysis. *Criminal Justice and Behavior, 34*(4), 437–452.

Snowden, L. R., & Hines, A. M. (1999). A scale to assess African American acculturation. *Journal of Black Psychology, 25,* 36–47.

Snyder, C. R., Shenkel, R. J., & Lowery, C. R. (1977). Acceptance of personality interpretations: The "Barnum effect" and beyond. *Journal of Consulting and Clinical Psychology, 45,* 104–114.

Snyder, C. R., Shenkel, R. J., & Schmidt, A. (1976). Effect of role perspective and client psychiatric history on locus of problem. *Journal of Consulting and Clinical Psychology, 44,* 467–472.

Snyder, D. K. (1981). *Marital Satisfaction Inventory (MSI) manual.* Los Angeles: Western Psychological Services.

Snyder, D. K. (2000). Computer-assisted judgment: Defining strengths and liabilities. *Psychological Assessment, 12,* 52–60.

Snyder, D. K., Widiger, T. A., & Hoover, D. W. (1990). Methodological considerations in validating computer-based test interpretations: Controlling for response bias. *Psychological Assessment, 2,* 470–477.

Snyder, P., Lawson, S., Thompson, B., Stricklin, S., & Sexton, D. (1993). Evaluating the psychometric integrity of instruments used in early intervention research: The Battelle Developmental Inventory. *Topics in Early Childhood Special Education, 32,* 273–280.

Sobell, L. C., & Sobell, M. B. (1992). Timeline followback: A technique for assessing self-reported alcohol consumption. In R. Z. Litten & J. P. Allen (Eds.), *Measuring alcohol consumption* (pp. 41–71). Totowa, NJ: Humana Press.

Sobell, L. C., & Sobell, M. B. (2000). Alcohol timeline followback (TLFB). In American Psychiatric Association (Ed.), *Handbook of psychiatric measures* (pp. 477–479). Washington, DC: American Psychiatric Association.

Sodowsky, G. R., & Carey, J. C. (1988, July). Relationships between acculturation-related demographics and cultural attitudes of an Asian-Indian immigrant group. *Journal of Multicultural Counseling and Development, 16,* 117–136.

Sokal, M. M. (1991). Psyche Cattell (1893–1989). *American Psychologist, 46,* 72.

Solomon, I. L., & Starr, B. D. (1968). *The School Apperception Method.* New York: Springer.

Solomon, P. R., Hirschoff, A., Kelly, B., et al. (1998). A 7-minute neurocognitive screening battery highly sensitive to Alzheimer's disease. *Archives of Neurology, 55,* 349–355.

Sommerfeld, D. H., Henderson, L. B., Snider, M. A., & Aarons, G. A. (2014). Multidimensional measurement within Adult Protective Services: Design and initial testing of the Tool for Risk, Interventions, and Outcomes. *Journal of Elder Abuse & Neglect, 26*(5), 495–522.

Sommers-Flanagan, J., & Sommers-Flanagan, R. (1995). Intake interviewing with suicidal patients: A systematic approach. *Professional Psychology: Research and Practice, 26,* 41–47.

Sooryanarayana, R., Choo, W. Y., & Hairi, N. N. (2013). A review on the prevalence and measurement of elder abuse in the community. *Trauma, Violence, & Abuse, 14,* 316–325.

Sousa, L. B. (2014). *Functional approach in the determination of Financial and Testamentary Capacity: Guidelines and development of assessment instruments [Abordagem funcional na determinação da Capacidade Financeira e Testamentária: Linhas orientadoras e desenvolvimento de instrumentos de avaliação].* Coimbra: PhD thesis presented to University of Coimbra.

Sousa, L. B., Vilar, M., Firmino, H., & Simões, M. R. (2015a). *Financial Capacity Assessment Instrument [Instrumento de Avaliação da Capacidade Financeira (IACFin): Manual de administração e cotação].* Coimbra: Psychological Assessment Lab – Faculty of Psychology and Educational Sciences, University of Coimbra.(a)

Sousa, L. B., Vilar, M., Firmino, H., & Simões, M. R. (2015b). Financial Capacity Assessment Instrument (IACFin): Development and qualitative study using focus groups. *Psychology, Psychiatry, and Law, 22*(4), 571–585.

South, S. C., Oltmanns, T. F., Johnson, J., & Turkheimer, E. (2011). Level of agreement between self and spouse in the assessment of personality pathology. *Assessment, 18*(2), 217–226.

Spangler, W. D. (1992). Validity of questionnaire and TAT measures of need for achievement: Two meta-analyses. *Psychological Bulletin, 112,* 140–154.

Spanier, G. (1976). Measuring dyadic adjustment: New scales for assessing the quality of marriage and similar dyads. *Journal of Marriage and the Family, 38,* 15–28.

Spanier, G. B., & Filsinger, E. (1983). The Dyadic Adjustment Scale. In E. Filsinger (Ed.), *Marriage and family assessment.* Beverly Hills, CA: Sage.

Sparrow, S. S., Balla, D. A., & Cicchetti, D. V. (1984a). *Vineland Adaptive Behavior Scales, Interview Edition: Expanded form manual.* Circle Pines, MN: American Guidance Service.

Sparrow, S. S., Balla, D. A., & Cicchetti, D. V. (1984b). *Vineland Adaptive Behavior Scales, Interview Edition: Survey form manual.* Circle Pines, MN: American Guidance Service.

Sparrow, S. S., Balla, D. A., & Cicchetti, D. V. (1985). *Vineland Adaptive Behavior Scales, Classroom Edition manual.* Circle Pines, MN: American Guidance Service.

Spearman, C. (1927). *The abilities of man: Their nature and measurement.* New York: Macmillan.

Spearman, C. E. (1904). "General intelligence" objectively determined and measured. *American Journal of Psychiatry, 15,* 201–293.

Spearman, C. E. (1930–1936). Autobiography. In C. Murchison (Ed.), *A history of psychology in autobiography* (3 vols.). Worcester, MA: Clark University Press.

Speece, D. L., Schatschneider, C., Silverman, R., et al. (2011). Identification of reading problems in first grade within a response-to-intervention framework. *Elementary School Journal, 111*(4), 585–607.

Speth, E. B. (1992). *Test-retest reliabilities of Bricklin Perceptual Scales.* Unpublished doctoral dissertation, Hahneman University Graduate School, Philadelphia.

Spiegel, J. S., Leake, B., Spiegel, T. M., et al. (1988). What are we measuring? An examination of self-reported functional status measures. *Arthritis and Rheumatism, 31,* 721–728.

Spielberger, C. D., et al. (1980). *Test Anxiety Inventory: Preliminary professional manual.* Palo Alto, CA: Consulting Psychologists Press.

Spitz, H. H., Minsky, S. K., & Bessellieu, C. L. (1985). Influence of planning time and first-move strategy on Tower of Hanoi problem-solving performance of mentally retarded young adults and non-retarded children. *American Journal of Mental Deficiency, 90,* 46–56.

Spitzer, R. L. (1999). Harmful dysfunction and the *DSM* definition of mental disorder. *Journal of Abnormal Psychology, 108,* 430–432.

Spivack, G., & Spotts, J. (1966). *Devereux Child Behavior Rating Scale manual.* Devon, PA: Devereux Foundation.

Spivack, G., Spotts, J., & Haimes, P. E. (1967). *Devereux Adolescent Behavior Rating Scale.* Devon, PA: Devereux Foundation.

Spokane, A. R., & Decker, A. R. (1999). Expressed and measured interests. In M. L. Savickas & A. R. Spokane (Eds.), *Vocational interests: Meaning, measurement, and counseling use* (pp. 211–233). Palo Alto, CA: Davies-Black.

Spranger, E. (1928). *Types of men* (P. J. W. Pigors, Trans.). Halle, Germany: Niemeyer.

Spray, J. A., & Huang, C.-Y. (2000). Obtaining test blueprint weights from job analysis surveys. *Journal of Educational Measurement, 37*(3), 187–201.

Spreen, O., & Benton, A. L. (1965). Comparative studies of some psychological tests for cerebral damage. *Journal of Nervous and Mental Disease, 140,* 323–333.

Spruill, J., & May, J. (1988). The mentally retarded offender: Prevalence rates based on individual versus group intelligence tests. *Criminal Justice and Behavior, 15,* 484–491.

Spruill, J. A. (1993). Secondary assessment: Structuring the transition process. *Learning Disabilities Research & Practice, 8,* 127–132.

Staggs, G. D., Larson, L. M., & Borgen, F. H. (2003). Convergence of specific factors in vocational interests and personality. *Journal of Career Assessment, 11,* 243–261.

Stahl, P. M. (1995). *Conducting child custody evaluations.* Thousand Oaks, CA: Sage.

Stanczak, D. E., Lynch, M. D., McNeil, C. K., & Brown, B. (1998). The Expanded Trail Making Test: Rationale, development, and psychometric properties. *Archives of Clinical Neuropsychology, 13,* 473–487.

Stanley, J. C. (1971). Reliability. In R. L. Thorndike (Ed.), *Educational measurement* (2nd ed.). Washington, DC: American Council on Education.

Starch, D., & Elliot, E. C. (1912). Reliability of grading of high school work in English. *School Review, 20,* 442–457.

Starr, B. D., & Weiner, M. B. (1979). The Projective Assessment of Aging Method (PAAM). New York: Springer.

Staw, B. M., Bell, N. E., & Clausen, J. A. (1986). The dispositional approach to job attitudes: A lifetime longitudinal test. *Administrative Science Quarterly, 31,* 56–77.

Steadman, H. J. (1983). Predicting dangerousness among the mentally ill: Art, magic, and science. *International Journal of Law and Psychiatry, 6,* 381–390.

Stedman, J. M., Hatch, J. P., & Schoenfeld, L. S. (2000). Pre-internship preparation in psychological testing and psychotherapy: What internship directors say they expect. *Professional Psychology: Research and Practice, 31,* 321–326.

Steinberg, M., Cicchetti, D., Buchanan, J., & Hall, P. (1993). Clinical assessment of dissociative symptoms and disorders: The Structured Clinical Interview for DSM-IV Dissociative Disorders (SCID-D). *Dissociation: Progress in Dissociative Disorders, 6,* 3–15.

Stephens, J. J. (1992). Assessing ethnic minorities. *SPA Exchange, 2*(1), 4–6.

Stephenson, M. (2000). Development and validation of the Stephenson Multigroup Acculturation Scale (SMAS). *Psychological Assessment, 12*(1), 77–88.

Stephenson, W. (1953). *The study of behavior: Q-technique and its methodology.* Chicago: University of Chicago.

Stern, B. H. (2001). Admissability of neuropsychological testimony after Daubert and Kumho. *NeuroRehabilitation, 16*(2), 93–101.

Sternberg, R. J., Grigorenko, E. L., & Kidd, K. K. (2005). Intelligence, race, and genetics. *American Psychologist, 60,* 46–59.

Sternberg, R. J. (1985). *Beyond IQ: A triarchic theory of human intelligence.* Cambridge: Cambridge University Press.

Sternberg, R. J., & Williams, W. M. (1997). Does the Graduate Record Examination predict meaningful success in the graduate training of psychologists? A case study. *American Psychologist, 52,* 630–641.

Stevens, C. D., & Macintosh, G. (2003). Personality and attractiveness of activities within sales jobs. *Journal of Personal Selling & Sales Management, 23,* 23–37.

Stice, E., Fisher, M., & Lowe, M. R. (2004). Are dietary restraint scales valid measures of acute dietary restriction? Unobtrusive observational data suggest not. *Psychological Assessment, 16,* 51–59.

Stillman, R. (1974). *Assessment of deaf-blind children: The Callier-Azusa Scale.* Paper presented at the Intercom '74, Hyannis, MA.

Stinnett, T. A. (1997). "AAMR Adaptive Behavior Scale-School: 2" Test review. *Journal of Psychoeducational Assessment, 15,* 361–372.

Stoeber, J., Stoll, O., Pescheck, E., & Otto, K. (2008). Perfectionism and achievement goals in athletes: Relations with approach and avoidance orientations in mastery and performance goals. *Psychology of Sport and Exercise, 9*(2), 102–121.

Stokes, J., Pogge, D., Sarnicola, J., & McGrath, R. (2009). Correlates of the MMPI—A Psychopathology Five (PSY-5) facet scales in an adolescent inpatient sample. *Journal of Personality Assessment, 91*(1), 48–57.

Stokes, J. B. (1977). Comment on "Socially reinforced obsessing: Etiology of a disorder in a Christian Scientist." *Journal of Consulting and Clinical Psychology, 45,* 1164–1165.

Stone, A. A. (1986). Vermont adopts *Tarasoff:* A real barn-burner. *American Journal of Psychiatry, 143,* 352–355.

Stone, B. J. (1992). Prediction of achievement by Asian-American and White children. *Journal of School Psychology, 30,* 91–99.

Stone, D. R. (1950). A recorded auditory apperception test as a new projective technique. *Journal of Psychology, 29,* 349–353.

Stone, H. K., & Dellis, N. P. (1960). An exploratory investigation into the levels hypothesis. *Journal of Projective Techniques, 24*(3), 333–340.

Storholm, E. D., Fisher, D. G., Napper, L. E., et al. (2011). A psychometric analysis of the Compulsive Sexual Behavior Inventory. *Sexual Addiction & Compulsivity, 18*(2), 86–103.

Stout, C. E., Levant, R. F., Reed, G. M., & Murphy, M. J. (2001). Contracts: A primer for psychologists. *Professional Psychology: Research and Practice, 32,* 89–91.

Straus, M. A. (1979). Measuring intrafamily conflict and violence: The Conflict Tactics (CT) Scales. *Journal of Marriage and the Family, 41,* 75–85.

Straus, M. A. (1979). Measuring intrafamily conflict and violence: The conflict tactics (CT) scales. *Journal of Marriage and the Family, 41,* 75–88.

Strauss, A. A., & Lehtinen, L. E. (1947). *Psychopathology and education of the brain injured child.* New York: Grune & Stratton.

Strauss, E., Ottfried, S., & Hunter, M. (2000). Implications of test revisions for research. *Psychological Assessment, 12,* 237–244.

Strauss, V. (2013, October 31). A ridiculous Common Core test for first graders. *The Washington Post.* Accessed online May 20, 2016 at https://www.washingtonpost.com/news/answer-sheet/wp/2013/10/31/a-ridiculous-common-core-test-for-first-graders/

Streiner, D. L. (2003a). Being inconsistent about consistency: When coefficient alpha does and doesn't matter. *Journal of Personality Assessment, 80,* 217–222.

Streiner, D. L. (2003b). Starting at the beginning: An introduction to coefficient alpha and internal consistency. *Journal of Personality Assessment, 80,* 99–103.

Streiner, D. L. (2010). Measure for measure: New developments in measurement and item response theory. *The Canadian Journal of Psychiatry/La Revue canadienne de psychiatrie, 55*(3), 180–186.

Stricker, G., & Gold, J. R. (1999). The Rorschach: Toward a nomothetically based, idiographically applicable configurational model. *Psychological Assessment, 11,* 240–250.

Stricker, G., & Healey, B. J. (1990). Projective assessment of object relations: A review of the empirical literature. *Psychological Assessment, 2,* 219–230.

Strober, L. B., & Arnett, P. A. (2009). Assessment of depression in three medically ill, elderly populations: Alzheimer's disease, Parkinson's disease, and stroke. *Clinical Neuropsychologist, 23,* 205–230.

Strong, E. K., Jr., Donnay, D. A. C., Morris, M. L., et al. (2004). *Strong Interest Inventory, Second Edition.* Palo Alto, CA: Consulting Psychologists Press.

Strong, E. K., Jr., Hansen, J. C., & Campbell, D. C. (1985). *Strong Vocational Interest Blank. Revised edition of Form T325, Strong-Campbell Interest Inventory.* Stanford, CA: Stanford University. (Distributed by Consulting Psychologists Press.)

Stroud, L. R., Paster, R. L., Papandonatos, G. D., et al. (2009). Maternal smoking during pregnancy and newborn neurobehavior: Effects at 10 to 27 days. *Journal of Pediatrics, 154,* 10–16.

Sturges, J. W. (1998). Practical use of technology in professional practice. *Professional Psychology: Research and Practice, 29,* 183–188.

Sturman, E. D. (2005). The capacity to consent to treatment and research: A review of standardized assessment tools and potentially impaired populations. *Clinical Psychology Review, 25,* 954–974.

Sturman, E. D., Cribbie, R. A., & Flett, G. L. (2009). The average distance between item values: A novel approach for estimating internal consistency. *Journal of Psychoeducational Assessment, 27,* 409–420.

Su, R., Rounds, J., & Armstrong, P. I. (2009). Men and things, women and people: A meta-analysis of sex differences in interests. *Psychological Bulletin, 135*(6), 859–884.

Subich, L. M. (1996). Addressing diversity in the process of career assessment. In M. L. Savickas & W. B. Walsh (Eds.), *Handbook of career counseling: Theory and practice* (pp. 277–289). Palo Alto, CA: Davies-Black.

Suczek, R. F., & Klopfer, W. G. (1952). Interpretation of the Bender-Gestalt Test: The associative value of the figures. *American Journal of Orthopsychiatry, 22,* 62–75.

Sue, D. W., & Sue, D. (2003). *Counseling the culturally diverse: Theory and practice* (4th ed.). New York: Wiley.

Sugarman, A. (1991). Where's the beef? Putting personality back into personality assessment. *Journal of Personality Assessment, 56,* 130–144.

Suinn, R. M., Rickard-Figueroa, K., Lew, S., & Vigil, S. (1987). The Suinn-Lew Asian Self-Identity Acculturation Scale: An initial report. *Educational and Psychological Measurement, 47,* 401–407.

Sullivan, H. S. (1953). *The interpersonal theory of psychiatry.* New York: Norton.

Sullivan, P. M. (1982). Administration modifications on the WISC-R Performance Scale with different categories of deaf children. *American Annals of the Deaf, 127,* 780–788.

Sullivan, P. M., & Brookhouser, P. E. (Eds.). (1996). *Proceedings of the Fourth Annual Conference on the Habilitation and Rehabilitation of Hearing Impaired Adolescents.* Boys Town, NE: Boys Town.

Sullivan, P. M., & Burley, S. K. (1990). Mental testing of the deaf child. In C. Reynolds & R. Kamphaus (Eds.), *Handbook of psychological and educational assessment of children* (pp. 761–788). New York: Guilford.

Sullivan, P. M., & Montoya, L. A. (1997). Factor analysis of the WISC-III with deaf and hard-of-hearing children. *Psychological Assessment, 9,* 317–321.

Sullivan, P. M., & Schulte, L. E. (1992). Factor analysis of WISC-R with deaf and hard-of-hearing children. *Psychological Assessment, 4,* 537–540.

Sundberg, N. D. (1955). The acceptability of "fake" versus "bona fide" personality test interpretations. *Journal of Abnormal and Social Psychology, 50,* 145–147.

Sundberg, N. D., & Gonzales, L. R. (1981). Cross-cultural and cross-ethnic assessment: Overview and issues. In P. McReynolds (Ed.), *Advances in psychological assessment* (Vol. 5, pp. 460–541). San Francisco: Jossey-Bass.

Sundberg, N. D., & Tyler, L. E. (1962). *Clinical psychology.* New York: Appleton-Century-Crofts.

Super, C. M. (1983). Cultural variation in the meaning and uses of children's "intelligence." In J. B. Deregowski, S. Dziurawiec, & R. C. Annis (Eds.), *Explorations in cross-cultural psychology.* Lisse, Netherlands: Swets & Zeitlinger.

Sutton v. United Airlines, 527 U.S. 471, 119 S. Ct. 213 (1999).

Sutton-Simon, K., & Goldfried, M. R. (1979). Faulty thinking patterns in two types of anxiety. *Cognitive Therapy and Research, 3,* 193–203.

Suzuki, L. A., Ponterotto, J. G., & Meller, P. J. (Eds.). (2000). *Handbook of multicultural assessment* (2nd ed.). San Francisco: Jossey-Bass.

Swallow, R. (1981). Fifty assessment instruments commonly used with blind and partially seeing individuals. *Journal of Visual Impairment and Blindness, 75,* 65–72.

Swanson, H. L. (2011). Learning disabilities: Assessment, identification, and treatment. In M. A. Bray, T. J. Kehle, & P. E. Nathan (Eds.), *The Oxford handbook of school psychology* (pp. 334–350). New York: Oxford University Press.

Swanson, J. L. (1992). The structure of vocational interests for African-American college students. *Journal of Vocational Behavior, 40,* 144–157.

Sweeney, C. (2014). Assess: A review of Pearson's Q-Interactive program. *The Ohio School Psychologist, 59*(2), 17–20.

Sweet, J. J., Moberg, P. J., & Tovian, S. M. (1990). Evaluation of Wechsler Adult Intelligence Scale—Revised premorbid IQ formulas in clinical populations. *Psychological Assessment, 2,* 41–44.

Sweet, J. J., Benson, L. M., Nelson, N. W., & Moberg, P. J. (2015). The American Academy of Clinical Neuropsychology, National Academy of Neuropsychology, and Society for Clinical Neuropsychology (APA Division 40) 2015 TCN Professional Practice and "Salary Survey": Professional practices, beliefs, and incomes of U.S. neuropsychologists. *The Clinical Neuropsychologist, 29*(8), 1069–1162.

Sweet, J. J., Peck, E. A., III, Abramowitz, C., & Etzweiler, S. (2002). National Academy of Neuropsychology/Division 40 of the American Psychological Association practice survey of clinical neuropsychology in the United States: Part I: Practitioner and practice characteristics, professional activities, and time requirements. *Clinical Neuropsychologist, 16,* 109–127.

Swensen, C. H. (1968). Empirical evaluations of human figure drawings: 1957–1966. *Psychological Bulletin, 70,* 20–44.

Swerdlik, M. E. (1985). Review of Brigance Diagnostic Comprehensive Inventory of Basic Skills. In J. V. Mitchell, Jr. (Ed.), *The ninth mental measurements yearbook* (pp. 214–215). Lincoln: Buros Institute of Mental Measurements, University of Nebraska.

Swerdlik, M. E. (1992). Review of the Otis-Lennon School Ability Test. In J. J. Kramer & J. C. Conoley (Eds.), *The eleventh mental measurements yearbook.* Lincoln: Buros Institute of Mental Measurements, University of Nebraska.

Swerdlik, M. E., & Dornback, F. (1988, April). *An interpretation guide to the fourth edition of the Stanford-Binet Intelligence Scale.* Paper presented at the annual meeting of the National Association of School Psychologists, Chicago.

Sykes, R. C., & Hou, L. (2003). Weighting constructed-response items in IRT-based exams. *Applied Measurement in Education, 16*(4), 257–275.

Sylvester, R. H. (1913). Clinical psychology adversely criticized. *Psychological Clinic, 7,* 182–188.

Symonds, P. M. (1949). *Adolescent fantasy: An investigation of the picture-story method of personality study.* New York: Columbia University.

Takahashi, M., Sato, A., & Nakajima, K. (2008). Poor performance in Clock-Drawing Test associated with memory deficit and reduced bilateral hippocampal and left temporoparietal regional blood flows in Alzheimer's disease patients. *Psychiatry and Clinical Neurosciences, 62*(2), 167–173.

Takeuchi, J., Solomon, F., & Menninger, W. W. (Eds.). (1981). *Behavioral science and the Secret Service: Toward the prevention of assassination.* Washington, DC: National Academy.

Tallent, N. (1958). On individualizing the psychologist's clinical evaluation. *Journal of Clinical Psychology, 114,* 243–244.

Tamkin, A. S., & Kunce, J. T. (1985). A comparison of three neuropsychological tests: The Weigl, Hooper and Benton. *Journal of Clinical Psychology, 41,* 660–664.

Tan, U. (1993). Normal distribution of hand preference and its bimodality. *International Journal of Neuroscience, 68,* 61–65.

Tang, T. L.-P., Sutarso, T., Ansari, M. A., et al. (2016). Monetary intelligence and behavioral economics: The Enron effect—love of money, corporate ethical values, corruption perceptions index (CPI), and dishonesty across 31 geopolitical entities. *Journal of Business Ethics.*, doi:10.1007/s10551-015-2942-4

Taormina, R. J., & Bauer, T. N. (2000). Organizational socialization in two cultures: Results from the United States and Hong Kong. *International Journal of Organizational Analysis, 8,* 262–289.

Tarasoff v. Regents of the University of California, 17 Cal. 3d 425, 551 P.2d 334, 131 Cal. Rptr. 14 (Cal. 1976).

Tate, D. G., & Pledger, C. (2003). An integrative conceptual framework of disability: New directions for research. *American Psychologist, 58,* 289–295.

Taylor, D. M. (2002). *The quest for identity: From minority groups to Generation Xers.* Westport, CT: Praeger.

Taylor, H. C., & Russell, J. T. (1939). The relationship of validity coefficients to the practical effectiveness of tests in selection. *Journal of Applied Psychology, 23,* 565–578.

Taylor, L. B. (1979). Psychological assessment of neurosurgical patients. In T. Rasmussen & R. Marino (Eds.), *Functional neurosurgery.* New York: Raven.

Taylor, R. L. (1980). Use of the AAMD classification system: A review of recent research. *American Journal of Mental Deficiency, 85,* 116–119.

Teachman, B. A. (2007). Evaluating implicit spider fear associations using the Go/No-go Association Task. *Journal of Behavior Therapy and Experimental Psychiatry, 38*(2), 156–167.

Teague, W. (State Superintendent of Education). (1983). *Basic competency education: Reading, language, mathematics specifications for the Alabama High School Graduation Examination* (Bulletin No. 4). Montgomery: Alabama State Department of Education.

Teel, E., Gay, M., Johnson, B., & Slobounov, S. (2016). Determining sensitivity/specificity of virtual reality-based neuropsychological tool for detecting residual abnormalities following sport-related concussion. *Neuropsychology, 30*(4), 474–483.

Tein, J.-Y., Sandler, I. N., & Zautra, A. J. (2000). Stressful life events, psychological distress, coping, and parenting of divorced mothers: A longitudinal study. *Journal of Family Psychology, 14,* 27–41.

Tellegen, A. (1985). Structures of mood and personality and their relevance to assessing anxiety, with an emphasis on self-report. In A. H. Tuma & J. D. Maser (Eds.), *Anxiety and the anxiety disorders* (pp. 681–706). Hillsdale, NJ: Erlbaum.

Tellegen, A., & Ben-Porath, Y. S. (1992). The new uniform *T* scores for the MMPI-2: Rationale, derivation, and appraisal. *Psychological Assessment, 4,* 145–155.

Tellegen, A., Ben-Porath, Y. S., McNulty, J. L., et al. (2003). *The MMPI-2 Restructured Clinical (RC) scales: Development, validation, and interpretation.* Minneapolis: University of Minnesota Press.

Tellegen, A., Ben-Porath, Y. S., Sellbom, M., et al. (2006). Further evidence on the validity of the MMPI-2 Restructured Clinical (RC) scales: Addressing questions raised by Rogers, Sewell, Harrison, and Jordan and Nichols. *Journal of Personality Assessment, 87*(2), 148–171.

Tenopyr, M. L. (1999). A scientist-practitioner's viewpoint on the admissibility of behavioral and social scientific information. *Psychology, Public Policy, and Law, 5,* 194–202.

Teplin, S. W., et al. (1991). Neurodevelopmental health, and growth status at age 6 years of children with birth weights less than 1001 grams. *Journal of Pediatrics, 118,* 768–777.

Terman, L. M. (1916). *The measurement of intelligence: An explanation of and a complete guide for the use of the Stanford revision and extension of the Binet-Simon Intelligence Scale.* Boston: Houghton Mifflin.

Terman, L. M., & Miles, C. C. (1936). *Sex and personality: Studies in masculinity and femininity.* New York: McGraw-Hill.

The Case Against Common Core. (2015, March 29). *Youtube* video accessed May 23, 2016 at https://youtu.be/1nM8WTBT1lg

Tharinger, D. J., & Stark, K. (1990). A qualitative versus quantitative approach to evaluating the Draw-A-Person and Kinetic Family Drawing: A study of mood- and anxiety-disorder children. *Psychological Assessment, 2,* 365–375.

Tharinger, D. J., Finn, S. E., Wilkinson, A. D., & Schaber, P. (2007). Therapeutic assessment with a child as a family intervention: A clinical and research case study. *Psychology in the Schools, 44*(3), 293–309.

The National Governors' Association Center for Best Practices and the Council of Chief State School Officers. (2010). *Common core state standards.* Retrieved May 20, 2016 from http://www.corestandards.org/

Thiry, B. (2009). Exploring the validity of graphology with the Rorschach test. *Rorschachiana, 30*(1), 26–47.

Thomas, A. D., & Dudek, S. Z. (1985). Interpersonal affect in Thematic Apperception Test responses: A scoring system. *Journal of Personality Assessment, 49,* 30–36.

Thomas, J. J., Eddy, K. T., Murray, H. B., et al. (2015). The impact of revised DSM-5 criteria on the relative distribution and inter-rater reliability of eating disorder diagnoses in a residential treatment setting. *Psychiatry Research, 229*(1–2), 517–523.

Thomas, M. L., & Locke, D. E. C. (2010). Psychometric properties of the MMPI-2-RF Somatic Complaints (RC1) scale. *Psychological Assessment, 22,* 492–503.

Thomas, T., & Solomon, A. (1989). *The films of 20th Century-Fox.* New York: Citadel Press.

Thompson, A. E. (1986). An object relational theory of affect maturity: Applications to the Thematic Apperception Test. In M. Kissen (Ed.), *Assessing object relations phenomena* (pp. 207–224). Madison, CT: International Universities.

Thompson, C. (1949). The Thompson modification of the Thematic Apperception Test. *Journal of Projective Techniques, 13,* 469–478.

Thompson, J. K., & Smolak, L. (Eds.). (2001). *Body image, eating disorders, and obesity in youth: Assessment, prevention, and treatment.* Washington, DC: APA Books.

Thompson, J. K., & Thompson, C. M. (1986). Body size distortion and self-esteem in asymptomatic, normal weight males and females. *International Journal of Eating Disorders, 5,* 1061–1068.

Thompson, J. M., & Sones, R. (1973). *The Education Apperception Test.* Los Angeles: Western Psychological Services.

Thompson, R. J., Gustafson, K. E., Meghdadpour, S., & Harrell, E. S. (1992). The role of biomedical and psychosocial processes in the intellectual and academic functioning of children and adolescents with cystic fibrosis. *Journal of Clinical Psychology, 48,* 3–10.

Thoresen, S., Mehlum, L., Roysamb, E., & Tonnessen, A. (2006). Risk factors for completed suicide in veterans of peacekeeping: Repatriation, negative life events, and marital status. *Archives of Suicide Research, 10*(4), 353–363.

Thorndike, E. L., et al. (1921). Intelligence and its measurement: A symposium. *Journal of Educational Psychology, 12,* 123–147, 195–216.

Thorndike, E. L., Bregman, E. O., Cobb, M. V., Woodward, E., & the staff of the Division of Psychology of the Institute of Educational Research of Teachers College, Columbia University. (1927). *The measurement of intelligence.* New York: Bureau of Publications, Teachers College, Columbia University.

Thorndike, E. L., Lay, W., & Dean, P. R. (1909). The relation of accuracy in sensory discrimination to general intelligence. *American Journal of Psychology, 20,* 364–369.

Thorndike, R. (1985). Reliability. *Journal of Counseling & Development, 63,* 528–530.

Thorndike, R. L. (1949). *Personnel selection.* New York: Wiley.

Thorndike, R. L. (1971). Concepts of cultural fairness. *Journal of Educational Measurement, 8,* 63–70.

Thorndike, R. L., Hagan, E. P., & Sattler, J. P. (1986). *Technical manual for the Stanford-Binet Intelligence Scale, Fourth Edition.* Chicago: Riverside.

Thorndike, R. M. (2007). Review of the Kaufman Assessment Battery for Children, Second Editon. In K. F. Geisinger, R. A. Sipes, J. F. Carlson, & B. S. Plake (Eds.), *The 17th Mental Measurements Yearbook* (pp. 520–522). Lincoln: Buros Institute of Mental Measurements, University of Nebraska.

Thorner, N. (2014, May 20). Thorner: Chilling truth behind Common Core State Standards. The Heartland Institute. Accessed online May 22, 2016 at http://blog.heartland.org/2014/05/thorner-chilling-truth-behind-common-core-state-standards/

Thornton, G. C., & Byham, W. C. (1982). *Assessment centers and managerial performance.* New York: Academic Press.

Thrash, T. M., Maruskin, L. A., Cassidy, S. E., Fryer, J. W., et al. (2010). Mediating between the muse and the masses: Inspiration and the actualization of creative ideas. *Journal of Personality and Social Psychology, 98*(3), 469–487.

Thurstone, L. L. (1925). A method of scaling psychological and educational tests. *Journal of Educational Psychology, 16,* 433–451.

Thurstone, L. L. (1927). A law of comparative judgment. *Psychological Review, 34,* 273–286.

Thurstone, L. L. (1929). Theory of attitude measurement. *Psychological Bulletin, 36,* 222–241.

Thurstone, L. L. (1931). *Multiple-factor analysis.* Chicago: University of Chicago Press.

Thurstone, L. L. (1935). *The vectors of mind.* Chicago: University of Chicago Press.

Thurstone, L. L. (1938). Primary mental abilities. *Psychometric Monographs,* No. 1. Chicago: University of Chicago Press.

Thurstone, L. L. (1947). *Multiple factor analysis.* Chicago: University of Chicago.

Thurstone, L. L. (1959). *The measurement of values.* Chicago: University of Chicago.

Thurstone, L. L., & Chave, E. J. (1929). *The measurement of attitude.* Chicago: University of Chicago.

Tillman, M. H. (1973). Intelligence scale for the blind: A review with implications for research. *Journal of School Psychology, 11,* 80–87.

Timbrook, R. E., & Graham, J. R. (1994). Ethnic differences on the MMPI-2? *Psychological Assessment, 6,* 212–217.

Tinsley, H. E. A., & Weiss, D. J. (1975). Interrater reliability and agreement of subjective judgments. *Journal of Counseling Psychology, 22,* 358–376.

Tittle, C. R., & Hill, R. J. (1967). Attitude measurement and prediction of behavior: An evaluation of conditions and measurement techniques. *Sociometry, 30,* 199–213.

Toner, C. K., Reese, B. E., Neargarder, S., et al. (2012). Vision-fair neuropsychological assessment in normal aging, Parkinson's disease and Alzheimer's disease. *Psychology and Aging, 27*(3),785–790.

Torrance, E. P. (1966). *Torrance Tests of Creative Thinking.* Bensenville, IL: Scholastic Testing Service.

Torrance, E. P. (1987a). *Guidelines for administration and scoring/ Comments on using the Torrance Tests of Creative Thinking.* Bensenville, IL: Scholastic Testing Service.

Torrance, E. P. (1987b). *Survey of the uses of the Torrance Tests of Creative Thinking.* Bensenville, IL: Scholastic Testing Service.

Toscano, M. (2013). The Common Core: Far from home. *Academic Questions, 26*(4), 411–428.

Touliatos, J., Perlmutter, B. F., & Strauss, M. A. (1991). *Handbook of family measurements.* Newbury Park, CA: Sage.

Townsend, E. (2007). Suicide terrorists: Are they suicidal? *Suicide and Life-Threatening Behavior, 37*(1), 35–49.

Tramontana, M. G., & Boyd, T. A. (1986). Psychometric screening of neuropsychological abnormality in older children. *International Journal of Clinical Neuropsychology, 8,* 53–59.

Tran, L., Sanchez, T., Arellano, B., & Swanson, H. L. (2011). A meta-analysis of the RTI literature for children at risk for reading disabilities. *Journal of Learning Disabilities, 44*(3), 283–295.

Trautscholdt, M. (1883). Experimentelle unterschungen uber die association der vorstellungen. *Philosophische Studien, 1,* 213–250.

Trent, J. W. (2001). "Who shall say who is a useful person?" Abraham Myerson's opposition to the eugenics movement. *History of Psychiatry, 12*(45, Pt.1), 33–57.

Trice, H. M., & Beyer, J. M. (1984). Studying organizational cultures through rites and ceremonies. *Academy of Management Review, 9,* 653–669.

Trimble, M. R. (Ed.). (1986). *New brain imaging techniques and psychopharmacology.* Oxford: Oxford University Press.

Troister, T., D'Agata, M. T., & Holden, R. R. (2015). Suicide risk screening: Comparing the Beck Depression Inventory-II, Beck Hopelessness Scale, and Psychache Scale in undergraduates. *Psychological Assessment, 27,* (4), 1500–1506.

Tropp, L. R., Erkut, S., Garcia Coll, C., Alarcon, O., & Vazquez Garcia, H. A. (1999). Psychological acculturation: development of a new measure for Puerto Ricans on the U.S. mainland. *Educational and Psychological Measurement, 59,* 351–367.

Truant, G. S., O'Reilly, R., & Donaldson, L. (1991). How psychiatrists weigh risk factors when assessing suicide risk. *Suicide and Life-Threatening Behavior, 21,* 106–114.

Tryon, R. C. (1957). Reliability and behavior domain validity: Reformulation and historical critique. *Psychological Bulletin, 54,* 229–249.

Tsaousis, I., & Georgiades, S. (2009). Development and psychometric properties of the Greek Personality Adjective Checklist (GPAC). *European Journal of Psychological Assessment, 25*(3), 164–174.

Tuerlinckx, F., De Boeck, P., & Lens, W. (2002). Measuring needs with the Thematic Apperception Test: A psychometric study. *Journal of Personality and Social Psychology, 82,* 448–461.

Tugg v. Towey (1994, July 19). *National Disability Law Reporter, 5,* 999–1005.

Tulchin, S. H. (1939). The clinical training of psychologists and allied specialists. *Journal of Consulting Psychology, 3,* 105–112.

Tulsky, D., Zhu, J., & Ledbetter, M. F. (Project directors). (1997). *WAIS-III, WMS-III Technical manual.* San Antonio: Psychological Corporation.

Tulsky, D. S., & Ledbetter, M. F. (2000). Updating to the WAIS-III and WMS-III: Considerations for research and clinical practice. *Psychological Assessment, 12,* 253–262.

Turvey, C. L., Wallace, R. B., & Herzog, R. (1999). A revised CES-D measure of depressive symptoms and a DSM-based measure of Major Depressive Episodes in the elderly. *International Psychogeriatrics, 11,* 139–148.

Tybout, A. M., & Artz, N. (1994). Consumer psychology. *Annual Review of Psychology, 45,* 131–169.

Tyler, L. E. (1961). Research explorations in the realm of choice. *Journal of Counseling Psychology, 8,* 195–202.

Tyler, L. E. (1965). *The psychology of human differences* (3rd ed.). New York: Appleton-Century-Crofts.

Tyler, R. S. (1993). Cochlear implants and the deaf culture. *American Journal of Audiology, 2,* 26–32.

Tyler, R. W. (1978). *The Florida accountability program: An evaluation of its educational soundness and implementation.* Washington, DC: National Education Association.

Tziner, A., & Eden, D. (1985). Effects of crew composition on crew performance: Does the whole equal the sum of its parts? *Journal of Applied Psychology, 70,* 85–93.

Udry, J. R. (1981). Marital alternatives and marital disruption. *Journal of Marriage and the Family, 43,* 889–897.

Ulrich, R. E., Stachnik, T. J., & Stainton, N. R. (1963). Student acceptance of generalized personality interpretations. *Psychological Reports, 13,* 831–834.

Unger, J. B., et al. (2002). The AHIMSA Acculturation Scale: A new measure of acculturation for adolescents in a multicultural society. *Journal of Early Adolescence, 22*(3), 225–251.

University of Minnesota. (1984). *User's guide for the Minnesota Report: Personal Selection System.* Minneapolis: National Computer Systems.

U.S. Department of Education, Office of Special Education and Rehabilitative Services, National Institute on Disability and Rehabilitation Research. (2000). *Long range plan: 1999–2003.* Washington, DC: Author.

U.S. Department of Labor. (1991). *Dictionary of occupational titles* (4th ed., rev.). Washington, DC: Author.

U.S. Department of Veterans Affairs, (2016). *Epidemiological facts about veterans.* Retrieved April 17, 2016 from www.ptsd.va. gov/professional/PTSD-overview/epidemiological-facts-ptsd.asp

Utley, C. A., Lowitzer, A. C., & Baumeister, A. A. (1987). A comparison of the AAMD's definition, eligibility criteria, and classification schemes with state departments of education guidelines. *Education and Training in Mental Retardation, 22*(1), 35–43.

Vacha-Haase, T., & Thompson, B. (2002). Alternative ways of measuring counselees' Jungian psychological-type preferences. *Journal of Counseling & Development, 80,* 173–179.

Vagg, P. R., & Spielberger, C. D. (1998). Occupational stress: Measuring job pressure and organizational support in the workplace. *Journal of Occupational Health Psychology, 3,* 294–305.

Vale, C. D., & Keller, L. S. (1987). Developing expert computer systems to interpret psychological tests. In J. N. Butcher (Ed.), *Computerized psychological assessment: A practitioner's guide* (pp. 64–83). New York: Basic Books.

Vale, C. D., Keller, L. S., & Bentz, V. J. (1986). Development and validation of a computerized interpretation system for personnel tests. *Personnel Psychology, 39,* 525–542.

Valentine, S., Fleischman, G., & Godkin, L. (2016). Villains, victims, and verisimilitudes: An exploratory study of unethical corporate values, bullying experiences, psychopathy, and selling professionals' ethical reasoning. *Journal of Business Ethics,* doi:10.1007/s10551-015-2993-6

Vallerand, R. J., Blanchard, C., Mageau, G. A., et al. (2003). Les passions de l'âme: On obsessive and harmonious passion. *Journal of Personality and Social Psychology, 85,* 756–767.

Van Dam, N. T., & Earleywine, M. (2011). Validation of the Center for Epidemiologic Studies Depression Scale-Revised (CESD-R): Pragmatic depression assessment in the general population. *Psychiatry Research, 186*(1), 128–132.

van der Kolk, B., McFarlane, A. C., & Weisaeth, L. (2007). *Traumatic stress: The effects of overwhelming experience on mind, body, and society.* New York, NY: Guilford.

Van der Linden, W. J., Veldkamp, B. P., & Reese, L. M. (2000). An integer programming approach to item bank design. *Applied Psychological Measurement, 24*(2), 139–150.

Van der Merwe, A. B., & Theron, P. A. (1947). A new method of measuring emotional stability. *Journal of General Psychology, 37,* 109–124.

Vanderwood, M. L., McGrew, K. S., Flanagan, D. P., & Keith, T. Z. (2001). The contribution of general and specific cognitive abilities to reading achievement. *Learning and Individual Differences, 13,* 159–188.

Vanman, E. J., Paul, B. Y., Ito, T. A., & Miller, N. (1997). The modern face of prejudice and structural features that moderate the effect of cooperation on affect. *Journal of Personality and Social Psychology, 73,* 941–959.

van Praag, H. M., Plutchik, R., & Apter, A. (Eds.). (1990). *Violence and suicidality: Perspectives in clinical and psychobiological research* (pp. 37–65). New York: Brunner/Mazel.

Vander Kolk, C. J. (1977). Intelligence testing for visually impaired persons. *Journal of Visual Impairment & Blindness, 71,* 158–163.

Vanderhoff, H., Jeglic, E. L., & Donovick, P. J. (2011). Neuropsychological assessment in prisons: Ethical and practical challenges. *Journal of Correctional Health Care, 17,* 51–60.

Varon, E. J. (1936). Alfred Binet's concept of intelligence. *Psychological Review, 43,* 32–49.

Vaughan-Jensen, J., Adame, C., McLean, L., & Gámez, B. (2009) Test review of *Wechsler Individual Achievement Test (3rd ed.). Journal of Psychoeducational Assessment, 29*(3), 286–291.

Vause, T., Yu, C. T., & Martin, G. L. (2007). The Assessment of Basic Learning Abilities test for persons with intellectual disability: A valuable clinical tool. *Journal of Applied Research in Intellectual Disabilities, 20*(5), 483–489.

Vazzana, R., Bandinelli, S., Lauretani, F., et al. (2010). Trail making test predicts physical impairment and mortality in older persons. *Journal of the American Geriatrics Society, 58,* 719–723.

Vedder, A. L. (1984). Movement patterns of a group of free-ranging mountain gorillas (*Gorilla gorilla beringei*) and their relation to food availability. *American Journal of Primatology, 7,* 73–88.

Veiga, J., Lubatkin, M., Calori, R., & Very, P. (2000). Measuring organizational culture clashes: A two-nation post-hoc analysis of a cultural compatibility index. *Human Relations, 53,* 539–557.

Velasquez, R. J., Gonzales, M., Butcher, J. N., et al. (1997). Use of the MMPI-2 with Chicanos: Strategies for counselors. *Journal of Multicultural Counseling and Development, 25,* 107–120.

Vento, A. E., Schifano, F., Corkery, J. M., et al. (2011). Suicide verdicts as opposed to accidental deaths in substance-related fatalities (UK, 2001–2007). *Progress in Neuro-Psychopharmacology & Biological Psychiatry, 35,* 1279–1283.

Verdon, B. (2011). The case of thematic tests adapted to older adults: On the importance of differentiating latent and manifest content in projective tests. *Rorschachiana, 32*(1), 46–71.

Verhovek, S. H., & Ayres, B. D., Jr. (1998, November 4). The 1998 elections: The nation—referendums. *New York Times,* p. B2.

Vernon, M. (1989). Assessment of persons with hearing disabilities. In T. Hunt & C. J. Lindley (Eds.), Testing older adults: A reference guide for geropsychological assessments (pp. 150–162). Austin: PRO-ED.

Vernon, M., & Andrews, J. E., Jr. (1990). *Psychology of deafness: Understanding deaf and hard-of-hearing people.* New York: Longman.

Vernon, M., & Brown, D. W. (1964). A guide to psychological tests and testing procedures in the evaluation of deaf and hard-of-hearing children. *Journal of Speech and Hearing Disorders, 29,* 414–423.

Vernon, M., Blair, R., & Lotz, S. (1979). Psychological evaluation and testing of children who are deaf-blind. *School Psychology Digest, 8,* 291–295.

Vernon, P. E. (1950). *The structure of human abilities.* New York: Wiley.

Vernon, P. E. (1964). *Personality assessment: A critical survey.* New York: Wiley.

Veterans Affairs Canada [VAC]. (2013). *General statistics.* Retrieved April 17, 2016 from www.veterans.gc.ca

Vevea, J. L., Clements, N. C., & Hedges, L. V. (1993). Assess the effects of selection bias on validity data for the General Aptitude Test Battery. *Journal of Applied Psychology, 78,* 981–987.

Vickers-Douglas, K. S., Patten, C. A., Decker, P. A., et al. (2005). Revision of the Self-Administered Alcoholism Screening Test (SAAST-R): A pilot study. *Substance Use & Misuse, 40*(6), 789–812.

Vig, S., & Jedrysek, E. (1996). Application of the 1992 AAMR definition: Issues for preschool children. *Mental Retardation, 34,* 244–246.

Viglione, D. J. (1999). A review of recent research addressing the utility of the Rorschach. *Psychological Assessment, 11,* 251–265.

Vingoe, F. J. (1995). Beliefs of British law and medical students compared to expert criterion group on forensic hypnosis. *Contemporary Hypnosis, 12,* 173–187.

Visser, P. S., Krosnick, J. A., & Lavrakas, P. J. (2000). Survey research. In H. T. Reis & C. M. Judd (Eds.), *Handbook of research methods in social and personality psychology* (pp. 223–252). New York: Cambridge University Press.

Volkmar, F. R., Klin, A., Marans, W., & Cohen, D. J. (1996). The pervasive developmental disorders: Diagnosis and assessment. *Child & Adolescent Psychiatric Clinics of North America, 5,* 963–977.

Vollmann, J., Bauer, A., Danker-Hopfe, H., & Helmchen, H. (2003). Competence of mentally ill patients: a comparative empirical study. *Psychological Medicine, 33,* 1463–1471.

von Knorring, L., & Lindstrom, E. (1992). The Swedish version of the Positive and Negative Syndrome Scale (PANSS) for schizophrenia: Construct validity and interrater reliability. *Acta Psychiatrica Scandinavica, 86,* 463–468.

von Wolff, C. (1732). *Psychologia empirica.*

von Wolff, C. (1734). *Psychologia rationalis.*

Vossekuil, B., & Fein, R. A. (1997). *Final report: Secret Service Exceptional Case Study Project.* Washington, DC: U.S. Secret Service, Intelligence Division.

Vredeveldt, A., Tredoux, C. G., Nortje, A., et al. (2015). A field evaluation of the Eye-Closure Interview with witnesses of serious crimes. *Law and Human Behavior, 39*(2), 189–197.

Vroom, V. H. (1964). *Work and motivation.* New York: Wiley.

Vygotsky, L. S. (1978). *Mind in society: The development of higher psychological processes.* Cambridge, MA: Harvard University Press.

Waddell, D. D. (1980). The Stanford-Binet: An evaluation of the technical data available since the 1972 restandardization. *Journal of School Psychology, 18,* 203–209.

Wadley, V. G., Harrell, L. E., & Marson, D. C. (2003). Self- and informant report of financial abilities in patients with Alzheimer's Disease: Reliable and valid? *Journal of the American Geriatrics Society, 51,* 1621–1626.

Waehler, C. A. (1997). Drawing bridges between science and practice. *Journal of Personality Assessment, 69,* 482–487.

Wagner, B. M. (1997). Family risk factors for child and adolescent suicidal behavior. *Psychological Bulletin, 121,* 246–298.

Wagner, E. E. (1983). *The Hand Test.* Los Angeles: Western Psychological Services.

Wagner, R. K., & Compton, D. L. (2011). Dynamic assessment and its implications for RTI models. *Journal of Learning Disabilities, 44*(4), 311–312.

Wagstaff, G. F., Wheatcroft, J. M., Caddick, A. M., Kirby, L. J., & Lamont, E. (2011). Enhancing witness memory with techniques derived from hypnotic investigative interviewing: Focused meditation, eye-closure, and context reinstatement. *International Journal of Clinical and Experimental Hypnosis, 59*(2), 146–164.

Wainer, H. (1990). *Computerized adaptive testing: A primer.* Hillsdale, NJ: Erlbaum.

Wakefield, J. C. (1992a). The concept of mental disorder: On the boundary between biological facts and social values. *American Psychologist, 47,* 373–388.

Wakefield, J. C. (1992b). Disorder as harmful dysfunction: A conceptual critique of DSM-III-R's definition of mental disorder. *Psychological Review, 99,* 232–247.

Wald, A. (1947). *Sequential analysis.* New York: Wiley.

Wald, A. (1950). *Statistical decision function.* New York: Wiley.

Waldman, D. A., & Avolio, B. J. (1989). Homogeneity of test validity. *Journal of Applied Psychology, 74,* 371–374.

Walker, H. M. (1976). *Walker Problem Behavior Identification Checklist.* Los Angeles: Western Psychological Services.

Walker, L. S., & Greene, J. W. (1991). The Functional Disability Inventory: Measuring a neglected dimension of child health status. *Journal of Pediatric Psychology, 16,* 39–58.

Walkup, J. (2000). Disability, health care, and public policy. *Rehabilitation Psychology, 45,* 409–422.

Wallace, A., & Liljequist, L. (2005). A comparison of the correlational structures and elevation patterns of the MMPI-2 Restructured Clinical (RC) and Clinical scales. *Assessment, 12,* 290–294.

Wallace, I. F., Gravel, J. S., McCarton, C. M., & Ruben, R. J. (1988). Otitis media and language development at 1 year of age. *Journal of Speech and Hearing Disorders, 53,* 245–251.

Wallen, G. R., Feldman, R. H., & Anliker, J. (2002). Measuring acculturation among Central American women with the use of a brief language scale. *Journal of Immigrant Health, 4,* 95–102.

Waller, D. (2011). *Wild Bill Donovan: The spymaster who created the OSS and modern American espionage.* New York, NY: Free Press.

Waller, N. G., & Zavala, J. D. (1993). Evaluating the big five. *Psychological Inquiry, 4,* 131–135.

Wallston, K. A., Wallston, B. S., & DeVellis, R. (1978). Development of the Multidimensional Health Locus of Control (MHLC) Scales. *Health Education Monographs, 6,* 160–170.

Wand, A. P. F., Peisah, C., & Hunter, K. L. (2015). Capacity to choose homelessness and assessment of the need for guardianship. *GeroPsych: The Journal of Gerontopsychology and Geriatric Psychiatry, 28*(3), 109–112.

Wang, N. (2003). Use of the Rasch IRT model in standard setting: An item-mapping method. *Journal of Educational Measurement, 40*(3), 231–252.

Wang, T.-H. (2011). Implementation of Web-based dynamic assessment in facilitating junior high school students to learn mathematics. *Computers & Education, 56,* 1062–1071.

Wang, X. M., Brisbin, S., Loo, T., & Straus, S. (2015). Elder abuse: An approach to identification, assessment and intervention. *Canadian Medical Association Journal, 187*(8), 575–581.

Wang, Y. J., & Minor, M. S. (2008). Validity, reliability, and applicability of psychophysiological techniques in marketing research. *Psychology & Marketing, 25*(2), in press.

Wantz, R. A. (1989). Review of the Parenting Stress Index. In J. C. Conoley & J. J. Kramer (Eds.), *The tenth mental measurements yearbook.* Lincoln: Buros Institute of Mental Measurements, University of Nebraska.

Ward, P. B., McConaghy, N., & Catts, S. V. (1991). Word association and measures of psychosis proneness in university students. *Personality and Individual Differences, 12,* 473–480.

Warfield, J. J., Kondo-Ikemura, K., & Waters, E. (2011). Measuring attachment security in rhesus macaques (Macaca mulatta): Adaptation of the attachment Q-set. *American Journal of Primatology, 73*(2), 109–118.

Waring, E. M., & Reddon, J. (1983). The measurement of intimacy in marriage: The Waring Questionnaire. *Journal of Clinical Psychology, 39,* 53–57.

Warmke, D. L. (1984). *Successful implementation of the "new" GATB in entry-level selection.* Presentation at the American Society for Personnel Administrators Region 4 Conference, October 15, Norfolk, VA.

Watkins, C. E., Jr. (1986). Validity and usefulness of WAIS-R, WISC-R, and WPPSI short forms. *Professional Psychology: Research and Practice, 17,* 36–43.

Watkins, C. E., Jr., Campbell, V. L., Nieberding, R., & Hallmark, R. (1995). Contemporary practice of psychological assessment by clinical psychologists. *Professional Psychology: Research and Practice, 26,* 54–60.

Watkins, E. O. (1976). *Watkins Bender-Gestalt Scoring System.* Novato, CA: Academic Therapy.

Watson, C. G. (1967). Relationship of distortion to DAP diagnostic accuracy among psychologists at three levels of sophistication. *Journal of Consulting Psychology, 31,* 142–146.

Watson, C. G., Felling, J., & Maceacherr, D. G. (1967). Objective draw-a-person scales: An attempted cross-validation. *Journal of Clinical Psychology, 23,* 382–386.

Watson, C. G., Thomas, D., & Anderson, P. E. D. (1992). Do computer-administered Minnesota Multiphasic Personality Inventories underestimate booklet-based scores? *Journal of Clinical Psychology, 48,* 744–748.

Watson, S. M. R., Gable, R. A., & Greenwood, C. R. (2011). Combining ecobehavioral assessment, functional assessment, and response to intervention to promote more effective classroom instruction. *Remedial and Special Education, 32*(4), 334–344.

Watts, D. P. (1984). Composition and variability of mountain gorilla diets in the central Virungas. *American Journal of Primatology, 7,* 323–356.

Watts, D. P. (1985). Relations between group size and composition and feeding competition in mountain gorilla groups. *Animal Behaviour, 33,* 72–85.

Watts, D. P. (1990). Ecology of gorillas and its relation to female transfer in mountain gorillas. *International Journal of Primatology, 11,* 21–45.

Weaver, C. B., & Bradley-Johnson, S. (1993). A national survey of school psychological services for deaf and hard-of-hearing students. *American Annals of the Deaf, 138,* 267–274.

Webb, E. J., Campbell, D. T., Schwartz, R. D., & Sechrest, L. (1966). *Unobtrusive measures: Nonreactive research in the social sciences.* Chicago: Rand McNally.

Webbe, F. M. (2008). Sports neuropsychology. In A. M. Horton Jr. & D. Wedding (Eds.), *The neuropsychology handbook* (3rd ed.). New York: Springer.

Webster, C. D., Harris, G. T., Rice, M. E., Cormier, C., & Quinsey, V. L. (1994). *The violence prediction scheme.* Toronto: University of Toronto Centre of Criminology.

Wechsler, D. (1939). *The measurement of adult intelligence.* Baltimore: Williams & Wilkins.

Wechsler, D. (1944). *The measurement of adult intelligence* (3rd ed.). Baltimore: Williams & Wilkins.

Wechsler, D. (1955). *Manual for the Wechsler Adult Intelligence Scale.* New York: Psychological Corporation.

Wechsler, D. (1967). *Manual for the Wechsler Preschool and Primary Scale of Intelligence.* New York: Psychological Corporation.

Wechsler, D. (1974). *Manual for the Wechsler Intelligence Scale for Children—Revised.* New York: Psychological Corporation.

Wechsler, D. (1975). Intelligence defined and undefined: A relativistic appraisal. *American Psychologist, 30,* 135–139.

Wechsler, D. (1981). *Manual for the Wechsler Adult Intelligence Scale—Revised.* New York: Psychological Corporation.

Wechsler, D. (1991). *Manual for the Wechsler Intelligence Scale for Children—Third Edition.* San Antonio: Psychological Corporation.

Wechsler, D. (1997). *Wechsler Adult Intelligence Scale—Third Edition.* San Antonio: Psychological Corporation.

Wechsler, D. (2003). *Wechsler Intelligence Scale for Children— Fourth edition (WISC-IV), Technical and interpretive manual.* San Antonio: Psychological Corporation.

Weed, N. C. (2006). Syndromal complexity, paradigm shifts, and the future of validation research: Comments on Nichols and Rogers, Sewell, Harrison, and Jordan. *Journal of Personality Assessment, 87,* 217–222.

Weed, N. C., Butcher, J. N., McKenna, T., & Ben-Porath, Y. S. (1992). New measures for assessing alcohol and drug abuse with the MMPI-2: The APS and AAS. *Journal of Personality Assessment, 58,* 389–404.

Weems, C. F., Russell, J. D., Banks, D. M., (2014). Memories of traumatic events in childhood fade after experiencing similar less stressful events: Results from two natural experiments. *Journal of Experimental Psychology: General, 143*(5), 2046–2055.

Wehling, E. I., Wollschlaeger, D., Nordin, S., & Lundervold, A. J. (2016). Longitudinal changes in odor identification performance and neuropsychological measures in aging individuals. *Neuropsychology, 30*(1), 87–97.

Wehmeyer, M. L., & Smith, J. D. (2006). Leaving the garden: Henry Herbert Goddard's exodus from the Vineland Training School. *Mental Retardation, 44,* 150–155.

Weiner, B. A. (1980). Not guilty by reason of insanity: A sane approach. *Chicago Kent Law Review, 56,* 1057–1085.

Weiner, I. B. (1966). *Psychodiagnosis in schizophrenia.* New York: Wiley.

Weiner, I. B. (1997). Current status of the Rorschach Inkblot Method. *Journal of Personality Assessment, 68,* 5–19.

Weiner, I. B. (2005). Integrative personality assessments with self-report and performance based measures. In S. Strack (Ed.), *Handbook of personology and psychopathology* (pp. 317–331). Hoboken, NJ: Wiley.

Weiner, I. B., & Kuehnle, K. (1998). Projective assessment of children and adolescents. In M. Hersen & A. Bellack (Eds.), *Comprehensive clinical psychology,* Vol. 3. Tarrytown, NY: Elsevier Science.

Weinstock, J., Ledgerwood, D. M., & Petry, N. M. (2007). The association between post-treatment gambling behavior and harm in pathological gamblers. *Psychology of Addictive Behaviors, 21,* 185–193.

Weinstock, J., Whelan, J. P., & Meyers, A. W. (2004). Behavioral assessment of gambling: An application of the Timeline Followback Method. *Psychological Assessment, 16,* 72–80.

Weinstock, J., Whelan, J. P., Meyers, A. W., & McCausland, C. (2007). The performance of two pathological gambling screens in college students. *Assessment, 14,* 399–407.

Weir, R. F. (1992). The morality of physician-assisted suicide. *Law, Medicine and Health Care, 20,* 116–126.

Weiss, A., Inoue-Murayama, M., Hong, K.-W., et al. (2009). Assessing chimpanzee personality and subjective well-being in Japan. *American Journal of Primatology, 71,* 283–292.

Weiss, A., King, J. E., & Enns, R. M. (2002). Subjective well-being is heritable and genetically correlated with dominance in chimpanzees (*Pan troglodytes*). *Journal of Personality and Social Psychology, 83,* 1141–1149.

Weiss, D. J. (1985). Adaptive testing by computer. *Journal of Consulting and Clinical Psychology, 53,* 774–789.

Weiss, D. J., & Davison, M. L. (1981). Test theory and methods. *Annual Review of Psychology, 32,* 629–658.

Weiss, D. J., & Vale, C. D. (1987). Computerized adaptive testing for measuring abilities and other psychological variables. In J. N. Butcher (Ed.), *Computerized psychological assessment: A practitioner's guide* (pp. 325–343). New York: Basic Books.

Weiss, H. M., & Cropanzano, R. (1996). Affective events theory: A theoretical discussion of the structure, causes, and consequences of affective experiences at work. *Research in Organizational Behavior, 18,* 1–74.

Weiss, L. G., Saklofske, D. H., Prifitera, A., & Holdnack, J. (2006). *WISC-IV Advanced Clinical Interpretation.* San Diego: Elsevier.

Weiss, M. D. (2010). The unique aspects of assessment of ADHD. *Primary Psychiatry, 17,* 21–25.

Weiss, P. A., Weiss, W. U., & Gacono, C. B. (2008). The use of the Rorschach in police psychology: Some preliminary thoughts. In C. B. Gacono et al. (Eds.), *The handbook of forensic assessment* (pp. 527–542). New York: Routledge/Taylor & Francis.

Weiss, R., & Summers, K. (1983). Marital Interaction Coding System III. In E. Filsinger (Ed.), *Marriage and family assessment: A sourcebook of family therapy.* Beverly Hills, CA: Sage.

Weissman, H. N. (1991). Forensic psychological examination of the child witness in cases of alleged sexual abuse. *American Journal of Orthopsychiatry, 6,* 48–58.

Weizmann-Henelius, G., Kivilinna, E., & Eronen, M. (2009). The utility of Rorschach in forensic psychiatric evaluations: A case study. *Nordic Psychology, 62*(3), 36–49.

Welsh, G. S. (1948). An extension of Hathaway's MMPI profile coding system. *Journal of Consulting Psychology, 12,* 343–344.

Welsh, G. S. (1952). A factor study of the MMPI using scales with the item overlap eliminated. *American Psychologist, 7,* 341.

Welsh, G. S. (1956). Factor dimensions A and R. In G. S. Welsh & W. G. Dahlstrom (Eds.), *Basic readings on the MMPI in psychology and medicine* (pp. 264–281). Minneapolis: University of Minnesota Press.

Welsh, G. S., & Dahlstrom, W. G. (Eds.). (1956). *Basic readings on the MMPI in psychology and medicine.* Minneapolis: University of Minnesota Press.

Welsh, J. R., Kucinkas, S. K., & Curran, L. T. (1990). *Armed Services Vocational Aptitude Battery (ASVAB): Integrative review of validity studies* (Rpt 90-22). San Antonio: Operational Technologies Corp.

Werner, H., & Strauss, A. A. (1941). Pathology of figure-background relation in the child. *Journal of Abnormal and Social Psychology, 36,* 236–248.

Wertheimer, M. (1923). Untersuchungen zur Lehre von der Gestalt. *Psychologische Forschung* [Studies in the theory of Gestalt Psychology. *Psychology for Schools*], *4,* 301–303. Translated by Don Cantor in R. J. Herrnstein & E. G. Boring (1965), *A sourcebook in the history of psychology.* Cambridge, MA: Harvard University Press.

West, L. J., & Ackerman, D. L. (1993). The drug-testing controversy. *Journal of Drug Issues, 23,* 579–595.

Westen, D., Barends, A., Leigh, J., Mendel, M., & Silbert, D. (1988). *Manual for coding dimensions of object relations and social cognition from interview data.* Unpublished manuscript, University of Michigan, Ann Arbor.

Westen, D., Silk, K. R., Lohr, N., & Kerber, K. (1985). *Object relations and social cognition: TAT scoring manual.* Unpublished manuscript, University of Michigan, Ann Arbor.

Westerman, J. W., & Simmons, B. L. (2007). The effects of work environment on the personality-performance relationship: An exploratory study. *Journal of Managerial Issues, 19*(2), 288–305.

Westling, D. L. (1996). What do parents of children with moderate and severe mental disabilities want? *Education and Training in Mental Retardation and Developmental Disabilities, 31,* 86–114.

Westwood, M. J., Kuhl, D., & Shields, D. (2012). Counseling military clients: Multicultural challenges, competencies and opportunities. In C. Lee, (Ed.), *Multicultural issues in counseling, Fourth edition.* Thousand Oaks, CA: Sage.

Westwood, M. J., McLean, H. B., Cave, D. G., Borgen, W. A., & Slakov, P. (2010). Coming home: A group-based approach for assisting Canadian military veterans in transition. *Journal for Specialists in Group Work, 35,* 44–68.

Wexley, K. N., Yukl, G. A., Kovacs, S. Z., & Sanders, R. E. (1972). Importance of contrast effects in employment interviews. *Journal of Applied Psychology, 56,* 45–48.

White, C. (2015). Physician aid-in-dying. *Houston Law Review, 53*(2), 595–629.

White, D. M., Clements, C. B., & Fowler, R. D. (1985). A comparison of computer administration with standard administration of the MMPI. *Computers in Human Behavior, 1,* 153–162.

White, J. A., Davison, G. C., Haaga, D. A. F., & White, K. L. (1992). Cognitive bias in the articulated thoughts of depressed and nondepressed psychiatric patients. *Journal of Nervous and Mental Disease, 180,* 77–81.

White, L. T. (1984). Attitudinal consequences of the preemployment polygraph examination. *Journal of Applied Social Psychology, 14,* 364–374.

White, R. W., Sanford, R. N., Murray, H. A., & Bellak, L. (1941, September). *Morgan-Murray Thematic Apperception Test: Manual of directions* [mimeograph]. Cambridge, MA: Harvard Psychological Clinic.

White, S., Santilli, G., & Quinn, K. (1988). Child evaluator's roles in child sexual abuse assessments. In E. B. Nicholson & J. Bulkley (Eds.), *Sexual abuse allegations in custody and visitation cases: A resource book for judges and court personnel* (pp. 94–105). Washington, DC: American Bar Association.

Whittington, M. K. (1998). The Karp inkblot response questionnaire: An evaluation of social desirability responding. *Dissertation Abstracts International: Section B. Sciences and Engineering, 59*(4-B), 1872.

Whitworth, R. H. (1984). Review of Halstead-Reitan Neuropsychological Battery and allied procedures. In D. J. Keyser & R. C. Sweetland (Eds.), *Test critiques* (Vol. 1, pp. 305–314). Kansas City: Test Corporation of America.

Whitworth, R. H., & Unterbrink, C. (1994). Comparison of MMPI-2 clinical and content scales administered to Hispanic and Anglo-Americans. *Hispanic Journal of Behavioral Sciences, 16,* 255–264.

Whitworth, S. (2008). Militarized masculinity and post-traumatic stress disorder. In J. Parpart & M. Zalewski (Eds.), *Rethinking the man question: Sex, gender and violence in international relations.* (pp. 109–126). London: Zed Books.

Wicker, A. W. (1969). Attitudes versus actions: The relationship of verbal and overt behavioral responses to attitude objects. *Journal of Social Issues, 25,* 41–78.

Wickes, T. A., Jr. (1956). Examiner influences in a testing situation. *Journal of Consulting Psychology, 20,* 23–26.

Widiger, T. A., & Samuel, D. B. (2009). Evidence-based assessment of personality disorders. *Personality Disorders: Theory, Research, and Treatment, S*(1), 3–17.

Widiger, T. A., & Trull, T. J. (2007). Plate tectonics in the classification of personality disorder: Shifting to a dimensional model. *American Psychologist, 62*(2), 71–83.

Wiechmann, A., Hall, J., & Azimipour, S. (2015). Test of Executive Functioning in an Emergency (TEFE): A performance-based assessment of safety for geriatric patients with dementia. *Psychology & Neuroscience, 8*(4), 488–494.

Wienstock, J., Whelan, J. P., & Meyers, A. W. (2004). Behavioral assessment of gambling: An application of the timeline followback method. *Psychological Assessment, 16,* 72–80.

Wigdor, A. K., & Garner, W. R. (1982). *Ability testing: Uses, consequences, and controversies.* Washington, DC: National Academy.

Wiggins, N. (1966). Individual viewpoints of social desirability. *Psychological Bulletin, 66,* 68–77.

Wilcox, R., & Krasnoff, A. (1967). Influence of test-taking attitudes on personality inventory scores. *Journal of Consulting Psychology, 31,* 185–194.

Wilkinson, G. S., & Robertson, G. J. (2006). *Wide Range Achievement Test-4 (WRAT-4).* Lutz, FL: Psychological Assessment Resources.

Willcutt, E. G., Boada, R., Riddle, M. W., et al. (2011). Colorado Learning Difficulties Questionnaire: Validation of a parent-report screening measure. *Psychological Assessment, 23*(3), Sep 2011, 778–791.

Williams, A. D. (2000). Fixed versus flexible batteries. In R. J. McCaffrey et al. (Eds.), *The practice of forensic neuropsychology: Meeting challenges in the courtroom* (pp. 57–70). New York: Plenum.

Williams, C. L. (1986). Mental health assessment of refugees. In C. L. Williams & J. Westermeyer (Eds.), *Refugee mental health in resettlement countries* (pp. 175–188). New York: Hemisphere.

Williams, C. L., & Butcher, J. N. (2011). *A beginner's guide to the MMPI–A.* Washington, DC: American Psychological Association.

Williams, J. M., & Shane, B. (1986). The Reitan-Indiana Aphasia Screening Test: Scoring and factor analysis. *Journal of Clinical Psychology, 42,* 156–160.

Williams, R. (1975). The BITCH-100: A culture-specific test. *Journal of Afro-American Issues, 3,* 103–116.

Williams, R. H., & Zimmerman, D. W. (1996a). Are simple gains obsolete? *Applied Psychological Measurement, 20,* 59–69.

Williams, R. H., & Zimmerman, D. W. (1996b). Are simple gain scores obsolete? Commentary on the commentaries of Collins and Humphreys. *Applied Psychological Measurement, 20,* 295–297.

Williams, S. K., Jr. (1978). The Vocational Card Sort: A tool for vocational exploration. *Vocational Guidance Quarterly, 26,* 237–243.

Williams, T. H., McIntosh, D. E., Dixon, F., Newton, J. H., & Youman, E. (2010). A confirmatory factor analysis of the Stanford–Binet Intelligence Scales, Fifth Edition, with a high-achieving sample. *Psychology in the Schools, 47,* 1071–1083.

Williams, T. Y., Boyd, J. C., Cascardi, M. A., & Poythress, N. (1996). Factor structure and convergent validity of the Aggression Questionnaire in an offender population. *Psychological Assessment, 8,* 398–403.

Wilmer, H. A., & Husni, M. (1951, December). An auditory sound association technique. *Science, 114,* 621–622.

Wilson, C., Smith, M. E., Thompson, E., et al. (2016). Context matters: The impact of neighborhood crime and paranoid symptoms on psychosis risk assessment. *Schizophrenia Research, 171*(1–3), 56–61.

Wilson, G. G., & Vitousek, K. M. (1999). Self-monitoring in the assessment of eating disorders. *Psychological Assessment, 11,* 480–489.

Wilson, P. T., & Spitzer, R. L. (1969). A comparison of three current classification systems for mental retardation. *American Journal of Mental Deficiency, 74,* 428–435.

Wilson, S. L., Thompson, J. A., & Wylie, G. (1982). Automated psychological testing for the severely physically handicapped. *International Journal of Man-Machine Studies, 17,* 291–296.

Winser, S. J., Smith, C. M., Hale, L. A. et al. (2015). Systematic review of the psychometric properties of balance measures for cerebellar ataxia. *Clinical Rehabilitation, 29*(1), 69–79.

Winston, A. S. (1996). "As his name indicates": R. S. Woodworth's letters of reference and employment for Jewish psychologists in the 1930s. *Journal of the History of the Behavioral Sciences, 32,* 30–43.

Winston, A. S. (1998). "The defects of his race": E. G. Boring and antisemitism in American psychology, 1923–1953. *History of Psychology, 1,* 27–51.

Wirt, R. D., Lachar, D., Klinedinst, J. K., & Seat, P. D. (1984). *Multidimensional description of child personality: A manual for the Personality Inventory for Children.* (1984 revision by David Lachar.) Los Angeles: Western Psychological Services.

Wish, J., McCombs, K. F., & Edmonson, B. (1980). *Socio-Sexual Knowledge & Attitudes Test.* Chicago: Stoelting.

Witkin, H. A., & Berry, J. W. (1975). Psychological differentiation in cross-cultural perspective. *Journal of Cross-Cultural Psychology, 6,* 4–87.

Witkin, H. A., & Goodenough, D. R. (1977). Field dependence and interpersonal behavior. *Psychological Bulletin, 84,* 661–689.

Witkin, H. A., & Goodenough, D. R. (1981). *Cognitive styles: Essence and origins* (Psychological Issues Monograph 51). New York: International Universities.

Witkin, H. A., Dyk, R. B., Faterson, H. F., Goodenough, D. R., & Karp, S. A. (1962). *Psychological differentiation.* New York: Wiley.

Witkin, H. A., Lewis, H. B., Hertzman, M., Machover, K., Meissner, P. B., & Wapner, S. (1954). *Personality through perception: An experimental and clinical study.* New York: Harper.

Witkin, H. A., Moore, C. A., Goodenough, D. R., & Cox, P. W. (1977). Field-dependent and field-independent cogntive styles and their implications. *Review of Educational Research, 47,* 1–64

Witmer, L. (1907). Clinical psychology. *Psychological Clinic, 1,* 1–9.

Witt, J. C., & Elliott, S. N. (1985). Acceptability of classroom management strategies. In T. R. Kratochwill (Ed.), *Advances in school psychology* (Vol. 4, pp. 251–288). Hillsdale, NJ: Erlbaum.

Wixson, K. (2011). A systematic view of RTI research: Introduction to the special issue. *Elementary School Journal, 111*(4), 503–510.

Wober, M. (1974). Towards an understanding of the Kiganda concept of intelligence. In J. W. Berry & P. R. Dasen (Eds.), *Culture and cognition: Readings in cross-cultural psychology* (pp. 261–280). London: Methuen.

Wolfe, M. M., Yang, P. H., Wong, E. C., & Atkinson, D. R. (2001). Design and development of the European American values scale for Asian Americans. *Cultural Diversity and Ethnic Minority Psychology, 7*(3), 274–283.

Wolfner, G., Fause, D., & Dawes, R. M. (1993). The use of anatomically detailed dolls in sexual abuse evaluations: The state of the science. *Applied and Preventive Psychology, 2,* 1–11.

Wolfram, W. A. (1971). Social dialects from a linguistic perspective: Assumptions, current research, and future directions. In R. Shuy (Ed.), *Social dialects and interdisciplinary perspectives.* Washington, DC: Center for Applied Linguistics.

Wolf-Schein, E. G. (1993). Assessing the "untestable" client: ADLO. *Developmental Disabilities Bulletin, 21,* 52–70.

Wolk, R. L., & Wolk, R. B. (1971). *The Gerontological Apperception Test.* New York: Behavioral Publications.

Wollersheim, J. P. (1974). The assessment of suicide potential via interview methods. *Psychotherapy, 11,* 222–225.

Wong-Rieger, D., & Quintana, D. (1987). Comparative acculturation of Southeast Asians and Hispanic immigrants and sojourners. *Journal of Cross-Cultural Psychology, 18,* 145–162.

Wood, J. M., Garb, H. N., Nezworski, M. T., Lilienfeld, S. O., & Duke, M. C. (2015). A second look at the validity of widely used Rorschach indices: Comment on Mihura, Meyer, Dumitrascu, and Bombel (2013). *Psychological Bulletin, 141,* 236–249.

Woods, S. A., & Anderson, N. R. (2016). Toward a periodic table of personality: Mapping personality scales between the five-factor model and the circumplex model. *Journal of Applied Psychology, 101*(4), 582–604.

Woodcock, R. W. (1990). Theoretical foundations of the WJ-R measures of cognitive ability. *Journal of Psychoeducational Assessment, 8,* 231–258.

Woodcock, R. W. (1997). The Woodcock-Johnson Tests of Cognitive Ability–Revised. In D. P. Flanagan, J. L. Genshaft, & P. L. Harrison (Eds.), *Contemporary intellectual assessment: Theories, tests, and issues* (pp. 230–246). New York: Guilford.

Woodcock, R. W. (2011). *The Woodcock Reading Mastery Tests, Third Edition* (WRMT-III). San Antonio: Pearson Assessments

Woodcock, R. W., & Mather, N. (1989a). *WJ-R Tests of Cognitive Ability—Standard and Supplemental Batteries: Examiner's manual.* In R. W. Woodcock & M. B. Johnson, *Woodcock-Johnson Psychoeducational Battery—Revised.* Allen, TX: DLM Teaching Resources.

Woodcock, R. W., & Mather, N. (1989b, 1990). *WJ-R Tests of Achievement: Examiner's manual.* In R. W. Woodcock & M. B. Johnson, *Woodcock-Johnson Psychoeducational Battery–Revised.* Allen, TX: DLM Teaching Resources.

Woodcock, R. W., McGrew, K. S., & Mather, N. (2000). *Woodcock-Johnson III.* Itasca, IL: Riverside.

Woodward, J. (1972). Implications for sociolinguistics research among the deaf. *Sign Language Studies, 1,* 1–7.

Woodworth, M., & Porter, S. (2000). Historical foundations and current applications of criminal profiling in violent crime investigations. *Expert Evidence, 7*(4), 241–264.

Woodworth, R. S. (1917). *Personal Data Sheet.* Chicago: Stoelting.

Worchel, F. F., & Dupree, J. L. (1990). Projective story-telling techniques. In C. R. Reynolds & R. W. Kamphaus (Eds.), *Handbook of psychological and educational assessment of children: Personality, behavior, & context* (pp. 70–88). New York: Guilford.

World Health Organization. (2001). *International classification of functioning, disability, and health.* Geneva, Switzerland: Author.

World Health Organization. (2014). *Preventing suicide: A global imperative.* Geneva, Switzerland: Author.

Worlock, P., et al. (1986). Patterns of fractures in accidental and non-accidental injury in children. *British Medical Journal, 293,* 100–103.

Wortmann, J. H., Jordan, A. H., Weathers, F. W., et al. (2016). Psychometric analysis of the PTSD Checklist-5 (PCL-5) among treatment-seeking military service members. *Psychological Assessment, 28*(11), 1391–1403.

Wright, B. D., & Stone, M. H. (1979). *Best test design: Rasch measurement.* Chicago: Mesa.

Wright, D. B., & Hall, M. (2007). How a "reasonable doubt" instruction affects decisions of guilt. *Basic and Applied Social Psychology, 29*(1), 91–98.

Wu, E. H. (2005). Factors that contribute to talented performance: A theoretical model from a Chinese perspective. *Gifted Child Quarterly, 49*(3), 231–246.

Wygant, D. B., & Lareau, C. R. (2015). Civil and criminal forensic psychological assessment: Similarities and unique challenges. *Psychological Injury and Law, 8*(1), 11–26.

Wylie, K., Barrett, J., Besser, M., et al. (2014). Good practice guidelines for the assessment and treatment of adults with gender dysphoria. *Sexual and Relationship Therapy, 29*(2), 154–214.

Wylonis, L. (1999). Psychiatric disability, employment, and the Americans with Disabilities Act. *Psychiatric Clinics of North America, 22,* 147–158.

Yañez, Y. T., & Fremouw, W. (2004). The application of the *Daubert* standard to parental capacity measures. *American Journal of Forensic Psychology, 22*(3) 5–28.

Yantz, C. L., & McCaffrey, R. J. (2005). Effects of a supervisor's observation on memory test performance of the examinee: Third party observer effect confirmed. *Journal of Forensic Neuropsychology, 4*(2), 27–38.

Yantz, C. L., & McCaffrey, R. J. (2009). Effects of parental presence and child characteristics on children's neuropsychological test performance: Third party observer effect confirmed. *Clinical Neuropsychologist, 23,* 118–132.

Yao, E. L. (1979). The assimilation of contemporary Chinese immigrants. *Journal of Psychology, 101,* 107–113.

Yarnitsky, D., Sprecher, E., Zaslansky, R., & Hemli, J. A. (1995). Heat pain thresholds: Normative data and repeatability. *Pain, 60,* 329–332.

Yell, N. (2008). A taxometric analysis of impression management and self-deception on the MMPI-2 and Rorschach among a criminal forensic population. *Dissertation Abstracts International: Section B. Sciences and Engineering, 68*(7-B), 4853.

Yerkes, R. M. (Ed.). (1921). *Psychological examining in the United States Army: Memoirs of the National Academy of Sciences* (Vol. 15). Washington, DC: Government Printing Office.

Yin, P., & Fan, X. (2000). Assessing the reliability of Beck Depression Inventory scores: Reliability generalization across studies. *Educational and Psychological Measurement, 60,* 201–223.

Yoo, J. J., Hinds, O., Ofen, N., et al. (2012). When the brain is prepared to learn: Enhancing human learning using real-time *f*MRI. *NeuroImage, 59*(1), 846–852.

Young, K. S., Pistner, M., O'Mara, J., & Buchanan, J. (1999). Cyber disorders: The mental health concern for the new millennium. *CyberPsychology & Behavior, 2,* 475–479.

Younger, J. B. (1991). A model of parenting stress. *Research on Nursing and Health, 14,* 197–204.

Yussen, S. R., & Kane, P. T. (1980). *Children's conception of intelligence.* Madison report for the project on studies of instructional programming for the individual student, University of Wisconsin, Technical Report #546.

Zanarini, M. C., Frankenburg, F. R., Reich, D. B., & Fitzmaurice, G. (2012). Attainment and stability of sustained symptomatic remission and recovery among patients with borderline personality disorder and Axis II comparison subjects: A 16-year prospective follow-up study. *American Journal of Psychiatry, 169*(5), 476–483.

Zapf, P. A., & Roesch, R. (2011). Future directions in the restoration of competency to stand trial. *Current Directions in Psychological Science, 20,* 43–47.

Zea, M. C., Asner-Self, K. K., Birman, D., & Buki, L. P. (2003). The Abbreviated Multidimensional Acculturation Scale: Empirical validation with two Latino/Latina samples. *Cultural Diversity and Ethnic Minority Psychology, 9*(2), 107–126.

Zebehazy, K. T., Zimmerman, G. J., & Fox, L. A. (2005). Use of digital video to assess orientation and mobility observational skills. *Journal of Visual Impairment and Blindness, 99,* 646–658.

Zedeck, S., & Cascio, W. F. (1984). Psychological issues in personnel decisions. *Annual Review of Psychology, 35,* 461–518.

Zedeck, S., Cascio, W. F., Goldstein, I. L., & Outtz, J. (1996). Sliding bands: An alternative to top-down selection. In R. S. Barrett (Ed.), *Fair employment strategies in human resource management* (pp. 222–234). Westport, CT: Quorum Books/Greenwood.

Zelig, M., & Beidleman, W. B. (1981). Investigative hypnosis: A word of caution. *International Journal of Clinical and Experimental Hypnosis, 29,* 401–412.

Zenderland, L. (1998). *Measuring minds: Henry Herbert Goddard and the origins of American intelligence testing.* Cambridge, MA: Cambridge University Press.

Zhang, L.-M., Yu, L.-S., Wang, K.-N., et al. (1997). The psychophysiological assessment method for pilot's professional reliability. *Aviation, Space, & Environmental Medicine, 68,* 368–372.

Zhang, Y., Yip, P. S. F., Chang, S.-S., et al. (2015). Association between changes in risk factor status and suicidal ideation incidence and recovery. *Crisis: The Journal of Crisis Intervention and Suicide Prevention, 36*(6), 390–398.

Zhou, X., Zhu, J., & Weiss, L. G. (2010). Peeking inside the "Black Box" of the Flynn effect: Evidence from three Wechsler instruments. *Journal of Psychoeducational Assessment, 28,* 399–411.

Zickar, M. J., & Broadfoot, A. A. (2009). The partial revival of a dead horse? Comparing classical test theory and item response theory. In C. F. Lance, & R. J. Vandenberg (Eds.), *Statistical and methodological myths and urban legends: Doctrine, verity and fable in the organizational and social sciences* (pp. 37–59). New York: Routledge.

Zieziula, F. R. (Ed.). (1982). *Assessment of hearing-impaired people.* Washington, DC: Gallaudet College.

Zinchenko, V. P. (2007). Thought and word: The approaches of L. S. Vygotsky and G. G. Shpet. In H. Daniels, M. Cole, & J. V. Wertsch (Eds.), *The Cambridge companion to Vygotsky* (pp. 212–245). New York: Cambridge University Press.

Zink v. State, 278 SW 3d 170–Mo: Supreme Court 2009.

Zirkel, P. A., & Krohn, N. (2008). RtI after IDEA: A summary of state laws. *Teaching Exceptional Children, 40*(3), 71–73.

Zonda, T. (2006). One-hundred cases of suicide in Budapest: A case-controlled psychological autopsy study. *Crisis: The Journal of Crisis Intervention and Suicide Prevention, 27*(3), 125–129.

Zubeidat, I., Sierra, J. C., Salinas, J. M., & Rojas-García, A. (2011). Reliability and validity of the Spanish version of the Minnesota Multiphasic Personality Inventory–Adolescent (MMPI-A). *Journal of Personality Assessment, 93*(1), 26–32.

Zubin, J. (1939, November 20). Letter to B. F. Skinner. (B. F. Skinner Papers, Harvard University Archives, Cambridge, MA).

Zubin, J., Eron, L. D., & Schumer, F. (1965). *An experimental approach to projective techniques.* New York: Wiley.

Zucker, S. (1985). *MSCA/K-ABC with high risk pre-schoolers.* Paper presented at the Annual Meeting of the National Association of School Psychologists, Las Vegas.

Zucker, S., & Copeland, E. P. (1987). *K-ABC/McCarthy Scale performance among three groups of "at-risk" pre-schoolers.* Paper presented at the Annual Meeting of the National Association of School Psychologists, Las Vegas.

Zuckerman, M. (1979). Traits, states, situations, and uncertainty. *Journal of Behavioral Assessment, 1,* 43–54.

Zuckerman, M. (1990). Some dubious premises in research and theory on racial differences. *American Psychologist, 45,* 1297–1303.

Zumbach, J., & Koglin, U. (2015). Psychological evaluations in family law proceedings: A systematic review of the contemporary literature. *Professional Psychology: Research and Practice, 46*(4), 221–234.

Zumbo, B. D., & Taylor, S. V. (1993). The construct validity of the Extraversion subscales of the Myers-Briggs Type Indicator. *Canadian Journal of Behavioural Science, 25,* 590–604.

Zuniga, M. E. (1988). Assessment issues with Chicanas: Practice implications. *Psychotherapy, 25,* 288–293.

Zuroff, D. C., Mongrain, M., & Santor, D. A. (2004). Conceptualizing and measuring personality vulnerability to depression: Comment on Coyne and Whiffen (1995). *Psychological Bulletin, 130*(3), 489–511.

Zwahlen, H. T., Schnell, T., Liu, A., et al. (1998). Driver's visual search behaviour. In A. G. Gale et al. (Eds.), *Vision in vehicles–VI* (pp. 3–40). Oxford, England: Elsevier.

Zweigenhaft, R. L. (1984). *Who gets to the top? Executive suite discrimination in the eighties.* New York: American Jewish Committee Institute of Human Relations.

Zwick, R., & Himelfarb, I. (2011). The effect of high school socioeconomic status on the predictive validity of SAT scores and high school grade-point average. *Journal of Educational Measurement, 48*(2), 101–121.

Zygouris, S., & Tsolaki, M. (2015). Computerized cognitive testing for older adults: A review. *American Journal of Alzheimer's Disease and Other Dementias, 30*(1), 13–28.

Zytowski, D. G. (1996). Three decades of interest inventory results: A case study. *Career Development Quarterly, 45,* 141–148.

Name Index

Abel, G. G., 441
Abeles, N., 66
Abelson, R. P., 428
Abidin, R. R., 481
Abrams, D. B., 467
Abrams, S., 441
Achenbach, T. M., 364–366
Ackerman, D. L., 548
Ackerman, P. L., 359, 544
Acklin, M. W., 405, 407, 409
Adams, D. K., 391
Adams, K. M., 263, 517
Adams-Tucker, C., 479
Addeo, R. R., 97
Adelman, S. A., 97
Aggarwal, N. K., 50–52, 452n1
Ahern, E., 540
Ahola, K., 554
Aiello, J. R., 72
Alderfer, C., 551
Alexander, R. A., 226, 442
Alexander, R. C., 479
Alfred, G. C., 465
Ali, M., 500, 501
Alison, L., 476
Allen, J., 455, 463
Allen, M. J., 167, 249, 251
Allen, R., 335
Allen, S. R., 539
Allport, G. W., 115, 116, 355, 356, 374, 381, 399
Alpher, V. S., 441
Amabile, T. M., 96, 553
Aman, C. J., 507
Ambrosini, P. J., 184
Ames, S. L., 468
Amodio, D. M., 559
Amrine, M., 56
Anderson, C., 536
Anderson, D., 127–128
Anderson, D. V., 322
Anderson, H. G., 536, 542
Anderson, J. W., 412
Anderson, K. G., 301
Anderson, N. R., 444
Anderson, R., 287
Anderson, W. P., 366
Andresen, E. M., 461
Andrew, G., 416
Andronikof, A., 405
Angie, A. D., 23
Angoff, W. H., 135, 135n5, 225
Apgar, V., 334
Appelbaum, P., 67, 69
Appelbaum, P. S., 70
Archer, K., 103
Archer, R. P., 409, 473
Arias, I., 145
Ariel, A., 180
Ariel, B., 217–219
Arieli-Attali, M., 15
Armendariz, G. M., 438
Arnau, R. C., 535

Arnett, P. A., 22, 507
Arnold, D. S., 338
Aronow, E., 405
Aros, S., 127
Arthur, W., Jr., 533
Artz, N., 558
Arvey, R. D., 536, 540
Atkin, C. K., 565
Atkinson, J. W., 149n3
Atkinson, R. C., 513
Atlas, H. W., 138
Ausburn, F. B., 306
Ausburn, L. J., 306
Avery, C., 343
Avolio, B. J., 529, 531
Aycan, Z., 555
Ayres, B. D., Jr., 549
Ayres, R. R., 347

Babins, L., 508
Bagasra, A., 397
Bailey, J. M., 409
Bain, S. K., 348
Baker, E. L., 350
Balaratnasingam, S., 261
Baldridge, D. C., 32
Baldwin, J. A., 397
Bales, J. W., 258
Ball, T. S., 422
Baltes, B. B., 554
Banaji, M. R., 515, 559, 560
Bank, A. L., 264
Baños, J. H., 498
Barden, R. C., 63, 335
Bardis, P. D., 477
Barends, A., 415
Barker, R., 356
Barlev, A., 66
Barnes, E., 44
Barnes, H. L., 477
Barnes-Holmes, D., 560
Barnett, R. C., 555
Barnum, P. T., 484, 486
Barrett, E., 476
Barrett, F. J., 465
Barrick, M. R., 536
Barry, D. T., 397
Bartok, J. A., 507
Bartol, K. M., 535
Barton, K. A., 437
Bartram, D., 69
Batson, D. C., 428
Bauer, R. M., 516
Bauer, T. N., 555
Baughman, E. E., 309
Baumeister, R. F., 470
Bautista, D. R., 397
Bavolek, S. J., 477
Baxter, J. C., 540
Baydoun, R. B., 533
Bayer, R., 451
Beard, J. G., 538
Beatty, P. C., 455

Beatty, R. W., 546
Beavers, R., 477
Beck, A. T., 184, 362, 461, 470
Beck, J., 363
Beck, S. J., 405
Becker, H. A., 479
Becker, K. A., 290
Beckman, J. F., 327
Begault, D. R., 558
Behn-Eschenburg, H., 408
Beidleman, W. B., 455
Beier, E. G., 477
Beier, M. E., 359
Bell, N. L., 301, 527
Bell, Y. R., 397
Bellack, A. S., 434–435, 440
Bellak, L., 416
Bellingrath, S., 554
Bellini, S., 13
Benbow, C. P., 54
Benda, B. B., 468
Bender, L., 512
Benedetti, F., 519
Benedict, R. H., 300
Benjamin, G. A. H., 476
Ben-Porath, Y. S., 375, 389–391
Ben-Shakhar, G., 63
Benton, A. L., 495
Ben-Zeev, Dror, 5–6
Bergler, E., 451
Berk, R. A., 192
Berkowitz, L., 335
Berman, N. C., 144
Bernardoni, L. C., 422
Bernhardt, G. R., 350
Bernstein, L., 427
Berrod, T., 286
Berry, J. W., 366
Besetsny, L. K., 303
Beyer, J. M., 556
Bhatia, M. S., 19
Bienvenu, M. J., Sr., 477
Bigler, E. D., 493n1
Billmire, M. G., 479
Binet, A., 1, 39–40, 42, 78, 274, 289, 309, 344
Bipp, T., 554
Birch, H. G., 492
Birkeland, S. A., 253, 254, 533
Birkinbine, J., 503
Birney, R. C., 553
Bizot, E. B., 527
Bjork, R. A., 515
Bjornsen, C., 103
Black, A. C., 4
Black, E. L., 473
Black, H. C., 175
Blamire, A. M., 521
Blanton, R. L., 441
Blum, G. S., 368, 416
Blum, M. L., 219
Blumenthal, S. J., 470
Blustein, D. L., 537
Boccaccini, M. T., 475

Bock, R. D., 235
Bodenhausen, G. V., 560
Boer, D. P., 368
Bogacki, D. F., 63
Bogner, H. R., 22
Bolante, R., 12
Bolger, P. C., 219
Boone, D. E., 300
Booth, A., 477
Bordnick, P. S., 434
Borgen, F. H., 527
Boring, E. G., 39, 274
Borman, W. C., 533
Bornstein, P. H., 437
Bornstein, R. F., 177, 407, 409
Borroni, B., 519
Borsbroom, D., 164
Borum, R., 12
Boudreau, J. W., 216
Bougard, C., 539
Bowers, K., 454
Boyd, T. A., 512
Bozeman, D. P., 555
Bozikas, V. P., 508
Bracken, B. A., 347
Braden, J. P., 348
Bradley, F., 4
Bradley, J., 373
Bradley, J. P., 360
Braginsky, B. M., 367
Bram, A. D., 409
Brandstaetter, V., 359
Brandy, D. A., 528
Brannen, M. Y., 556
Brannick, M. T., 114
Brannigan, G. G., 512
Brassard, M., 479
Braswell, H., 465, 466
Bray, D. W., 2, 546
Brayne, M., 466
Brettschneider, C., 201
Brewer, E. W., 554
Brewer, S., 566
Bricklin, B., 124, 125
Briggs, K. C., 357, 535
Bringle, R., 477
Brittain, H. L., 410
Broadfoot, A. A., 163, 164, 267
Brodsky, S. L., 475
Brody, D., 495
Brody, N., 427
Brodzinsky, D. M., 125
Brogden, H. E., 217
Broitman, J., 324
Brook, J. S., 468
Brooks, G. R., 465, 466
Broshek, D. K., 504
Brotemarkle, R. A., 39
Brotherhood, J. R., 539
Brotto, L. A., 231–232
Brown, 1999, 192
Brown, B., 343
Brown, C. E., 14
Brown, D. C., 197
Brown, L. S., 465
Brown, R. D., 373
Brown, R. T., 194
Brown, S. P., 555
Bruininks, R. H., 537
Brunner, N. A., 512
Bryan, J., 67, 68

Bryant, S., 418
Bucholz, K. K., 459
Buck, J. N., 423
Buckner, F., 73
Bucofsky, D., 352
Budescu, D. V., 15
Budoff, M., 326
Bukatman, B. A., 471
Bumann, B., 63
Bunch, M. B., 137
Burau, D. E., 504
Burgess, A. W., 480
Burisch, M., 363, 384
Burke, M. J., 532
Burke, P. J., 381
Burke, R. J., 555
Burns, A., 96
Burns, E., 32
Burns, R. C., 424
Burns, R. K., 550
Buros, O. K., 33, 40, 64
Burwen, L. S., 356
Bush, G. H. W., 501
Bushman, B. J., 357
Butcher, J. N., 263, 389, 390, 394, 395, 487
Butters, N., 507
Büttner, G., 324
Bux, D. A., 468
Byham, W. C., 546
Byrne, D., 354
Byrne, G. J., 4
Byrnes, M. M., 507

Cai, C.-H., 427
Calhoon, M. B., 32
Callahan, C. A., 343
Callahan, J., 66
Callero, P. L., 363
Camara, W. J., 535
Camilli, G., 256
Campbell, D. P., 263, 526
Campbell, D. T., 191, 356
Campbell, W. H., 453
Campos, L. P., 366
Canivez, G. L., 293
Cannon-Bowers, J. A., 551
Caplan, L. J., 453
Capraro, M. M., 535
Capraro, R. M., 535
Care, E., 524
Carey, J. C., 397
Carey, N. B., 186
Carlson, V., 479
Carnevale, J. J., 4
Carpenter, P. A., 513
Carpenter, W. T., 70
Carroll, J. B., 282–284
Carroll, K. M., 467
Carstairs, J., 16
Carter, B. L., 467
Caruso, J. C., 155
Carvalho, T., 464
Cascio, W. F., 198, 207, 208, 226, 532
Cash, J., 501
Cash, T. F., 263
Cassel, R. N., 373
Catalano, R., 470
Cattell, H. E. P., 381
Cattell, J. M., 38–39, 418

Cattell, P., 314, 337
Cattell, R. B., 281–283, 291, 314, 355, 374, 381
Caught, K., 555
Cavanaugh, J. L., 474
Ceci, S. J., 481
Cerney, M. S., 406
Chamberlain, K., 185
Champagne, J. E., 551, 552
Chan, K.-Y., 305
Chan, R., 282
Chan, S. S., 19
Chance, N. A., 397
Chaney, E. F., 467
Chang, L., 382
Chang, S.-R., 256
Chantler, L., 480
Chaplin, W. F., 115, 359
Chapman, J., 428
Chapman, J. C., 1
Chapman, L., 428
Chappin, S. R., 468
Chartrand, J. M., 527
Chase, D., 293
Chave, E. J., 235, 559
Chawarski, M. C., 202
Chen, Y., 50
Cheung, F. M., 464
Chin, J., 147–148
Chinoy, E., 308
Chira-Chavala, T., 558
Chmielewski, M., 156–158
Cho, H., 561
Church, A. T., 381
Cicchetti, D., 157, 158, 479
Citrin, L. B., 560
Clark, L. A., 445, 451
Cleckley, H., 475
Clift, R. J., 440
Clippard, L. F., 554
Cloninger, C. R., 97
Coalson, D. L., 299
Coggins, M. H., 12
Cohen, B. M., 546
Cohen, J., 546
Cohen, R. J., 26, 42, 61, 62, 460n3, 470, 538, 539, 556, 557, 564–566
Cole, S. T., 310
Coleman, M. R., 324
Coleman, T., 338
Collier, C., 324
Collins, J. R., 208
Collins, L. M., 145
Collins, M., 524
Colom, R., 314
Comer, D. R., 548
Compton, D. L., 327
Condon, C. A., 263
Cone, J. D., 435, 437
Connolly, A. J., 346
Connolly, B. S., 499
Conti, R. P., 427
Cooke, N. J., 551
Cooley, E. J., 347
Cooper, A., 412
Copas, J. B., 470
Copersino, M., 432
Cornell, D. G., 364
Cortes, D. E., 397
Cortina, J. M., 155
Corwyn, R. F., 468

Costa, P. T., Jr., 367, 375, 376, 381, 382, 534
Cote, J. A., 441
Coupe, J. J., 476
Court, J. H., 460n3
Courvoisier, D., 177, 204–205
Cox, J., 476
Coyne, I., 69
Coyne, J. C., 460n3
Craighead, W. E., 445
Cramer, P., 415
Crego, C., 475
Cronbach, L. J., 152, 154, 155, 164–166, 186, 217, 219, 220, 532
Cropanzano, R., 536
Crosbie, J., 519
Crosby, F. J., 54
Crowe, T. P., 195
Crowne, D. P., 190
Crundall, D. E., 510
Cuéllar, I., 397
Cundick, B. P., 309
Cureton, E. E., 251

Dahlman, K. A., 18
Dahlstrom, L. E., 384
Dahlstrom, W. B., 309
Dahlstrom, W. G., 358, 384, 385, 388
Daigneault, S., 507
Daley, C. E., 309
D'Amato, A., 554
Dana, J., 488
Dana, R. H., 376, 455, 462, 463
Daneman, M., 513
Danford, G. S., 32
Dangerfield, R., 177, 178
Daniels, K., 555
Darwin, C., 37, 362
Das, J. P., 273, 285, 347
Dattilio, F. M., 19
Davenport, C., 45
Davids, A., 422
Davidson, F., 469
Davidson, H., 405
Davies, G. M., 481
Davies, M., 281
Davies, P. L., 96
Davis, J. M., 324
Davison, G. C., 258
Dawes, R. M., 487
Dazzi, C., 370
Deadrick, D. L., 397, 533
De Champlain, A. F., 167, 266, 267
Decker, J. T., 512, 554
De Corte, W., 208
Decroly, O., 44
Delahunty, R. J., 533
DeLaRosa, M., 468
De Leo, D., 19
Del Giudice, M. J., 409
Dellis, D. C., 515
Dellis, N. P., 429
DelVecchio, W. F., 116, 356
De Marco, A. P., 504
DeMars, C. E., 268
DeMoivre, A., 95
Dempsey, J., 500, 501
DeMulder, E. K., 373
Denton, W. H., 452
DePaulo, B. M., 534
Derue, D. S., 4

Desautels, N., 557
Diamond, B. L., 455
Dickson, C. R., 435
Dietz, P. E., 12
Digman, J. M., 362
Dikmen, S., 517
Diller, L., 492
Dion, K. K., 335
Dipboye, R. L., 10
DiStefano, C., 293
Diven, K., 427
Dixon, M., 10
Dodrill, C. B., 517
Dohrenwend, B. P., 391
Doll, E. A., 300
Dollinger, S. J., 341
Dombrowski, S. C., 293
Donahue, E. M., 363
Donohue, B., 539
Donovan, W., 543
Doorey, N. A., 319, 319n1
Doty, R. L., 495
Douglas, C., 411
Douthitt, E. A., 72
Draguns, J. G., 463
Dreger, R. M., 309
Dubey, B. L., 410
DuBois, P. H., 36
Duchek, J. M., 510
Duclos, C. W., 468
Dudycha, G. J., 356
Duff, K., 72
Duhon, G. J., 324
Dumont, R., 298
Duncanson, C., 465
Duncker, K., 258
Dunlop, P. D., 193
Dunn, L. B., 70
Dupree, J. L., 415
Duvall, E., 327
Dwairy, M., 323
Dwyer, C. A., 8
Dykeman, C., 12
Dykes, L., 479
Dywan, J., 454

Earles, J. A., 303
Earleywine, M., 461
Early, P. C., 555
Ebadi, M., 502
Eckardt, W., 362
Edens, J. F., 156
Edwards, A. L., 372, 428
Edwards, J., 477
Ehrenfurth, J. W., 493n1
Eich, E., 148
Eichler, R. M., 408
Einarsdóttir, S., 527
Eisenberg, N., 360
Elder, G. H., 335
Elksnin, L. K., 527
Elksnin, N., 527
Ellerstein, N. S., 479
Elliott, A. N., 480
Elliott, E. C., 156
Elliott, J., 4
Elliott, S. N., 32
Ellis, M. V., 537
Ellis, T., 484, 502
Engum, E. S., 519
Epstein, J. L., 352
Epstein, N., 477

Erdberg, P., 408, 409
Erdelyi, M. H., 427
Eron, L. D., 418
Eslinger, P. J., 489
Espinosa, M. P., 256
Etkind, A. M., 327
Evans, J. D., 517
Evers, W., 554
Ewing, C. P., 63
Exner, J. E., Jr., 112–113, 405, 407, 408, 423
Eyman, J. R., 470
Eyman, S. K., 470
Eysenck, H. J., 112–113, 355, 381

Fahrenkopf, A. M., 554
Fahs, R. L., 427
Faller, K. C., 479
Fan, X., 155
Farah, M. J., 489
Farnham, S. D., 560
Farr, J. H., 195
Farrell, J. N., 533
Farrell, S. F., 127
Farrenkopf, T., 67, 68
Faust, D., 519
Faust, D. S., 469
Fein, R. A., 12
Feinberg, T. E., 489
Fenn, D. S., 66
Ferdinand, F., 181
Ferdinand, S., 181
Ferguson, R. L., 137
Feuerstein, R., 326
Field, T. M., 335
Filsinger, E., 477
Finello, K. M., 6
Finlayson, M. A. J., 517
Finn, S. E., 6, 395, 455, 456
Finucane, M. L., 70
Firestone, M., 73
Firmino, H., 474
Fischer, C. T., 6, 455
Fischer, H., 479
Fischer, J. M., 72
Fisher, R. P., 455
Fiske, D. W., 191, 258
Fitzgibbons, D. J., 428
Flanagan, D. P., 284
Flanagan, J. C., 290, 550
Fleeson, W., 116
Fletcher, J. M., 314, 324
Flett, G. L., 360
Floyd, F. J., 191, 538
Floyd, R. G., 301
Flynn, J. R., 309, 314
Foerster, L. M., 312
Follingstad, D. R., 434
Folstein, M. F., 498
Fontana, V. J., 479
Fontanna, D., 536
Forbes, P. A., 440
Forer, B. R., 486
Forrest, D. W., 37
Forsman, M., 555
Fortune, S., 19
Foster, S. L., 437
Foster, T., 19
Fowler, K. A., 373
Fox, B., 539
Fox, J., 465, 466
Fox, M. J., 501

Fox, S. J., 370
Franco, J. N., 397
Frandesen, A., 74
Frandsen, A., 74
Frank, E., 359
Frank, J. D., 391
Frank, L. K., 403, 404, 427, 428
Franklin, L. M., 498
Franzen, M. D., 473
Fredman, N., 443
Fremouw, W., 124
French, D. J., 440
Freud, S., 37n1, 49, 66
Friedman, M., 358
Friedman, M. J., 465
Friedrich, W. N., 338, 479
Friese, M., 560
Friesen, C. A., 4
Frodi, A., 335
Frolik, L. A., 63
Fuchs, D., 324
Fuchs, L. S., 31, 324, 327
Fullard, W., 338
Furse, D. H., 562

Gabriel, R. A., 465
Gacono, C. B., 427
Gagne, J. R., 338
Gaither, G. A., 360
Gallo, J. J., 22, 498
Galton, F., 37–39, 104, 274, 418
Gammon, J. A., 479
Ganellen, R. J., 409, 427
Gann, M. K., 258
Ganzini, L., 66
Garb, H. N., 112, 487
García, L. E., 318
Garcia, M., 397
Gardeazabal, J., 12, 256
Gardner, D., 397, 533
Gardner, F. L., 470, 539
Gardner, H., 281
Gardner, R. A., 476
Gareis, K. C., 555
Garfield, S. L., 418
Garnier, L. M., 432
Garrett, H. E., 40
Garrett, M. T., 397
Gaski, J. F., 341
Gaugler, B. B., 546
Gauss, K. F., 95
Gavett, B. E., 72, 438
Gavin, W. J., 96
Gawda, B., 370
Gawronski, B., 560
Gee, C., 539
Geer-Williams, C., 470
Gehrman, P. R., 432
Geiselman, R. E., 455
Geisenger, K. F., 18, 137
Georgiades, S., 374
Gerry, M. H., 309
Gerson, M., 318
Gersten, C. D., 430
Gesell, A., 337, 497
Ghiselli, E. E., 196n6, 255, 536
Gil, S., 143
Gilbertini, M., 544
Gilch-Pesantez, J. R., 125
Gill, J. S., 127
Gilmore, G., 470–471
Gim Chung, R. H., 397

Giner, L., 19
Girelli, S. A., 535
Glaser, R., 137
Glass, G. V., 93, 111, 113
Glassbrenner, J., 368
Glazer, W. M., 377
Gleser, G. C., 186, 217, 219, 220
Glosser, G., 507
Gluck, M. R., 415
Glueck, W. F., 540
Goddard, H. H., 42–46, 289
Goel, V., 507
Goetz, C. G., 500
Goffman, E., 356
Gokhale, D. V., 78n4
Gold, J. R., 409
Goldberg, I. R., 362
Goldberg, L. R., 380, 381
Goldberg, T. E., 507
Golden, C. J., 504, 517
Goldfried, M. R., 258, 405
Golding, S. L., 356
Goldman, B. A., 34
Goldman, S. H., 527
Goldstein, G., 517
Goldstein, J. S., 466
Goldstein, K., 354, 492
Goldstein, S., 324
Goldstein, T. R., 19
Gollan, J. K., 476
Gonsalves, C. J., 195
Gonzales, L. R., 366
Good, R. H., 347
Goodenough, D. R., 27
Goodglass, H., 507
Goodman, G. S., 481
Gopaul-McNicol, S., 49
Gopher, D., 510
Gordon, R. A., 539
Gosling, S. D., 360, 362, 382
Gottfredson, G. D., 358
Gottfredson, L. S., 54, 59, 197, 529
Gough, H. G., 373
Gould, J. W., 63
Graeme, H., 542
Grafman, J., 507
Graham, J. R., 390
Grant, I., 517, 519
Gray, E., 28
Gray, R., 348
Grazioplene, R. G., 273
Green, R. L., 366, 391
Green, S. B., 154
Greenberg, N., 466
Greenfield, D. N., 561
Greenlaw, P. S., 126
Greenspoon, J., 427, 430, 453
Greenwald, A. G., 515, 559, 560
Gregg, P. A., 427
Gregory, N., 476
Gresham, F. M., 481
Griffin, M. L., 554
Griffith, H. R., 473
Grisso, T., 67, 70, 125, 473
Groden, M. A., 479
Grossman, I., 300
Grove, W. M., 63, 487
Guerrier, J. H., 510
Guilford, J. P., 115, 281, 307, 315, 355
Guilmette, T. J., 519
Guion, R. M., 176
Gullion, C. M., 70

Gustafson, S., 324
Guthmann, D., 32
Guttman, L. A., 238

Haaga, D. A., 258
Hack, E., 324
Hadaway, N., 350
Hagan, L. D., 314
Haidt, J., 197
Halbert, M. H., 125
Hale, H. C., 465
Haley, K., 67
Hall, C. S., 39, 354
Hall, G. S., 44, 525
Hall, J. A., 114
Hall, M., 258
Hall, S. S., 513
Halleck, S. L., 460n3
Halpern, D. F., 54, 196
Halpern, F., 423
Halstead, W. C., 515–518
Hambleton, R. K., 163, 228, 267
Hambrick, D. Z., 303
Hamera, E., 14
Hammer, A. L., 164
Hammer, E. F., 423
Han, K., 389
Handel, R. W., 393
Handler, L., 360, 409, 425, 543
Haney, W., 56
Hansen, K. K., 203
Hansen, N. D., 463
Happell, B., 554
Hare, R. D., 475
Harris, G. T., 470
Harris, M. M., 534
Harris, P. M., 459
Hart, S. D., 475
Hartigan, J. A., 54, 529, 533
Hartmann, D. P., 431
Hartmann, E., 27
Hartshorne, H., 356
Hartung, P. J., 537
Harvey, R. J., 164, 535
Hathaway, S. R., 384, 386, 388
Hatters-Friedman, S., 19
Hawkins, M. A. W., 144
Hayes, S. C., 300
Haynes, S. N., 178, 430, 434, 438
Hays, P. A., 464
Haywood, H., 6
Hazlett, R. L., 440
He, N., 309
He, W., 180
Healy, B. J., 413
Heaton, R. K., 517, 519
Hebert, K. R., 473
Hedges, C., 182
Heilbronner, R. L., 473
Heilbrun, A. B., Jr., 373
Heinrichs, R. W., 507
Heinze, M. C., 125
Helfer, R. E., 479
Heller, T. S., 19
Helmes, E., 391
Helmreich, R. L., 543, 544
Henk, W. A., 350
Henri, V., 39, 274
Henriques, G., 440
Henry, E. M., 427
Henry, J. D., 562
Henry, W., 413

McCarthy, D. M., 301
McCaulley, M. H., 535
McClelland, D. C., 354, 415, 551
McClelland, N., 560
McCloskey, G. W., 347
McClure-Butterfield, P., 476
McConkey, K. M., 454
McCormick, C. M., 137
McCrady, B. S., 468
McCrae, R. R., 360, 367, 375, 376, 381,
    382, 534
McCrimmon, A. W., 301
McCubbin, H. I., 477
McDaniel, M. A., 533
McDermott, K. B., 515
McDevitt, S. C., 338
McDowell, C., 407, 409
McElrath, K., 459
McElwain, B. A., 368
McEvoy, G. M., 546
McFarlane, A. C., 452
McGaghie, W. C., 343
McGirr, A., 19
McGrew, K. S., 283, 284
McGue, M., 274
McGurk, F. J., 310
McKinley, J. C., 384, 386, 388
McKinney, W. R., 208
McLean, J. E., 347
McLearen, A. M., 63
McLemore, C. W., 460n3
McNeill, I. M., 193
McNemar, Q., 54
McPartland, J. M., 352
McReynolds, P., 39
Mead, M., 139
Mednick, S. A., 308
Medvec, V. H., 9
Meehl, P. E., 388, 428, 486, 486n4, 487
Mehl, M. R., 435
Meier, T. B., 504
Mejía, X., 465
Melchert, T. P., 73
Melchior, L. A., 461
Mellenbergh, G. J., 257
Mello, E. W., 455
Meloy, R., 379
Melton, G., 475
Melton, G. B., 473, 475
Memon, A., 455
Menninger, K. A., 354
Mercer, J. R., 309
Merrens, M. R., 486
Merrick, J., 17
Merrill, M., 290
Mesmer, E. M., 324
Messer, S. B., 306
Messick, S., 176, 306, 367
Meyer, G. J., 112–113, 194, 405, 409, 428
Meyers, J., 537
Micceri, T., 96
Michael, W. B., 154
Midanik, L. T., 560
Middleton, G., 511
Mihura, J. L., 112–114, 410
Miles, C. C., 386
Miller, A., 373
Miller, I. W., 459
Miller, J. C., 519
Miller, J. N., 507
Miller, K. S., 309
Miller, N. E., 440

Milling, L. S., 23
Millon, T., 460
Milner, B., 515, 518
Milner, J. S., 481
Minsky, S. K., 507
Minton, H. L., 289, 290
Mischel, W., 356, 429
Mishra, D., 409
Mitchell, D. F., 34
Mitzel, H. C., 227
M'Naghten, D., 472
Moffitt, T. E., 145
Monahan, J., 470
Montague, M., 258
Montgomery, G. T., 376
Moore, M., 382
Moos, B. S., 338, 477
Moos, R. H., 338, 477
Moreland, K. L., 405
Morgan, C. D., 41, 411, 421
Morgan, K. E., 348
Mori, L. T., 438
Morina, N., 17
Morreau, L. E., 537
Moser, R. S., 504
Mosier, C. I., 258
Moss, D., 389n9
Mossman, D., 63
Motowidlo, S. J., 536
Moursund, J., 78n4
Mrad, D. F., 12
Muchinsky, P. M., 555
Mueller, C. G., 194
Mueller, J. H., 561
Mueller-Hanson, R., 533
Mulvey, E. P., 185
Muñoz, B., 258
Murphy, G. E., 185
Murphy, K. A., 524
Murphy, K. M., 222
Murphy, K. R., 532
Murphy, L. B., 403n2
Murphy-Berman, V., 186
Murray, C., 309, 315
Murray, H. A., 2, 41, 411–413, 418n5, 421,
    422, 546
Murray, N., 504
Murry, W. D., 535
Murstein, B. I., 413, 425–427
Mussen, P. H., 415, 427
Muzio, E., 409
Myers, C., 535
Myers, I. B., 357, 535
Myers, P. A., 479
Myers-Jennings, C., 338
Myerson, A., 45–46
Myors, B., 16

Nagle, R. J., 301
Naglieri, J. A., 16, 17, 285
Narumoto, J., 554
Naylor, H. K., 415
Naylor, J. C., 215–216, 219
Neale, E. L., 422
Near, J. P., 555
Nehring, W. M., 32
Neisser, U., 54, 273, 274, 309, 315
Nelson, D. V., 512
Nelson, L. D., 126, 263
Nelson, R. O., 435
Nelson, S. D., 451
Neugarten, B., 538

Neuman, G. A., 533
Nevid, J. S., 560
Newcomb, T. M., 356
Newell, A., 513
Newman, D. A., 50
Nguyen, H. H., 397
Nguyen, N. T., 537
Nichols, D. S., 393, 394
Nici, J., 517
Nitko, A. J., 137
Nock, M. K., 560
Norton, P. J., 438
Nosek, B. A., 559
Notarius, C., 437
Notarius, C. I., 477
Novak, C. G., 347
Novick, M. R., 137, 154, 166, 188,
    197, 228
Nowak, L., 545
Nunes, L. M., 510
Nunnally, J. C., 77n3, 247,
    292, 367
Nurss, J. R., 338
Nye, C. D., 366
Nystedt, L., 555

Oakland, T., 18, 64n5
Obama, B., 560
Obasi, E. M., 397
Oberholzer, E., 404
Odbert, H. S., 115, 374, 381
Ogle, A., 23–25
O'Hare, T., 468
Okazaki, S., 263
O'Leary, K. D., 145
Oliffe, J. L., 466
Olino, T. M., 521
Olson, D. H., 477
Olson, S., 503
Olweus, D., 470
Omar, M. H., 32
Ones, D. S., 533, 534, 536
Onwuegbuzie, A. J., 309
Organ, D. W., 555
Orozco, S., 376
Orr, R. R., 481
Osberg, T. M., 393
Osborn, A. J., 450
Osgood, C. E., 372, 562
O'Shaughnessy, R., 441
Ostendorf, F., 381
O'Toole, M. E., 476
Ouzts, S. M., 348
Owens, C., 19
Ozer, D. J., 105n7
Ozonoff, S., 263, 507

Pace, V. L., 533
Padawer, J. R., 405
Padilla, A., 399
Padilla, A. M., 397
Paivio, A., 306
Palacio, C., 19
Palermo, G. G., 476
Palmer, B. W., 70
Panell, R. C., 137
Pannbacker, M., 511
Paolo, A. M., 300
Paris, J., 452
Parke, R. D., 160, 335
Parkes, L. P., 555
Parkinson, J., 500

anatomically detailed dolls (ADDs): A human figure in doll form with accurately represented genitalia, typically used to assist in the evaluation of sexually abused children, 480

anchor protocol: A test answer sheet developed by a test publisher to check the accuracy of examiners' scoring, 266

Angoff method: A way to set fixed cut scores that entails averaging the judgments of experts, 225–226

anhedonia: Inability to experience happiness, 261

APA. *See* American Psychological Association

APA Committee on Psychological Tests and Assessment, 16

APAT. *See* Accounting Program Admission Test

APD. *See* average proportional distance

Apgar number: A score on a rating scale developed by an obstetrical anesthesiologist who saw a need for a simple, rapid method of evaluating newborn infants and determining what immediate action, if any, is necessary, 334

aphagia: A condition in which the ability to eat is lost or diminished, 512n2

aphasia: A loss of ability to express oneself or to understand spoken or written language due to a neurological deficit, 512

API. *See* Applicant Potential Inventory

apperceive: To perceive in terms of past perceptions (from this verb, the noun apperception is derived), 412

Apperceptive Personality Test (APT), 418

Applicant Potential Inventory (API), 534

application forms, 539–540

application letter, 539

APS. *See* Addiction Potential Scale

APT. *See* Apperceptive Personality Test

aptitude tests: A test that usually focuses more on informal as opposed to formal learning experiences and is designed to measure both learning and inborn potential for the purpose of making predictions about the testtaker's future performance; also referred to as a prognostic test and, especially with young children, a readiness test, 331–344
  career choice/career transition, 527–533
  elementary school level, 338–340
  GRE, 341–342
  MAT, 343
  preschool level, 333–338
  secondary school level, 340–341

APTP. *See* Association of Personnel Test Publishers

arithmetic mean: Also referred to simply as the mean, a measure of central tendency derived by calculating an average of all scores in a distribution, 84

Armed Forces Qualification Test (AFQT), 303

Armed Services Vocational Aptitude Battery (ASVAB), 303–305

Army Alpha test: An intelligence and ability test developed by military psychologists for use in World War I to screen literate recruits; contrast with Army Beta test, 302

Army Beta test: A nonverbal intelligence and ability test developed by military psychologists for use in World War I to screen illiterate and foreign-born recruits; contrast with Army Alpha test, 302

Army General Classification Test (AGCT), 302–303

articles, 33

asexuality: A sexual orientation in which the individual is completely devoid of interest in a sexual relationship with anyone or anything, 230–232

ASI. *See* Addiction Severity Index

assessment center: An organizationally standardized procedure for evaluation involving multiple assessment techniques, 2, 546

Assessment of Men (OSS Assessment Staff), 2

assessor, 2, 4, 6

assessor's role
  behavioral observation, 13–14
  case history data, 12
  clinical (*See* clinical assessment)
  collaborative, 6
  computers as tools, 14–17
  conducting, 26–30
  culture, and, 42–55
  dynamic, 6–7
  educational (*See* educational assessment)
  experience, education, and training, 4
  interview, 9–11
  legal/ethical considerations, 55–74
  life-or-death, 66–68
  neuropsychological (*See* neuropsychological assessment)
  personality (*See* personality assessment)
  portfolio, 11–12
  process of, 6–7
  psychological testing, contrasted, 3
  public policy, and, 54–55
  reference sources, 30–35
  role-play tests, 13–14
  settings, 21–26
  society at large, 19–20
  state licensing laws, 65
  test, 7–9
  test developers, 18
  testtaker, 18–19
  test user, 18
  therapeutic, 6
  tools of, 7–17

Association of Personnel Test Publishers (APTP), 534

astronauts, testing, 542–545

ASVAB. *See* Armed Services Vocational Aptitude Battery

Atkins v. Virginia, 314

at risk: Defined in different ways by different school districts, but in general a reference to functioning that is deficient and possibly in need of intervention, 336

at-risk infant or toddler: According to IDEA, a child under 3 years of age who would be in danger of experiencing a substantial developmental delay if early intervention services were not provided, 336

attention deficit hyperactivity disorder (ADHD), 334

attitude: A presumably learned disposition to react in some characteristic manner to a particular stimulus, 554
  measurement of, 352–353, 558–560

authentic assessment: Also known as performance-based assessment, evaluation on relevant, meaningful tasks that may be conducted to examine learning of academic subject matter but that demonstrates the student's transfer of that study to real-world activities, 350–351

average deviation: A measure of variability derived by summing the absolute value of all the scores in a distribution and dividing by the total number of scores, 91

average proportional distance (APD) method: A measure used to evaluate the internal consistency of a test that focuses on the degree of difference that exists between item scores, 154–156

aviators, testing, 542–545

Back-Page Infrequency (Fb), 389

bar graph: A graphic illustration of data wherein numbers indicative of frequency are set on the vertical axis, categories are set on the horizontal axis, and the rectangle bars that describe the data are typically noncontiguous, 83, 84

Barnum effect: The consequence of one's belief that a vague personality description truly describes oneself when in reality that description may apply to almost anyone; sometimes referred to as the "Aunt Fanny effect" because the same personality might be applied to anyone's Aunt Fanny, 484–486

basal level: A stage in a test achieved by a testtaker by meeting some preset criterion to continue to be tested-for example, responding correctly to two consecutive items on an ability test that contains increasingly difficult items may establish a "base" from which to continue testing; contrast with ceiling level, 293

base rate: An index, usually expressed as a proportion, of the extent to which a particular trait, behavior, characteristic, or attribute exists in a population, 185, 214

BASIC ID (behavior, affect, sensation, imagery, cognition, interpersonal relations, and drugs), 564

Beck Depression Inventory (BDI), 184

Beck Depression Inventory-II (BDI-II), 184, 461

Beck Self-Concept Test, 362

Beck Youth Inventories-Second Edition (BYI-II), 363

Beginner's Guide to the MMPI-A, A (Williams/Butcher), 395

behavior, nonverbal, 48–49

behavioral assessment: An approach to evaluation based on the analysis of samples of behavior, including the antecedents and consequences of the behavior, 429

ceiling level: A stage in a test achieved by a testtaker as a result of meeting some preset criterion to discontinue testing-for example, responding incorrectly to two consecutive items on an ability test that contains increasingly difficult items may establish a presumed "ceiling" on the testtaker's ability; contrast with basal level and testing the limits, 293

Center for Epidemiological Studies Depression scale (CES-D), 461

central nervous system: All of the neurons or nerve cells in the brain and the spinal cord; contrast with the peripheral nervous system, 489

central processing: Computerized scoring, interpretation, or other conversion of raw test data that is physically transported from the same or other test sites; contrast with teleprocessing and local processing, 15

central tendency error: A type of rating error wherein the rater exhibits a general reluctance to issue ratings at either the positive or negative extreme and so all or most ratings cluster in the middle of the rating continuum, 195

cerebral angiogram: A diagnostic procedure in neurology that entails the injection of a tracer element into the bloodstream prior to taking X-rays of the cerebral area, 520

CES-D. *See* Center for Epidemiological Studies Depression scale

CFA. *See* confirmatory factor analysis

CHC model: An abbreviation for the Cattell-Horn-Carroll model of cognitive abilities, 283–284
K-ABC/KABC-II, 347
SB5 and, 291

checklist: A questionnaire formatted to allow a person to mark items indicative of information such as the presence or absence of a specified behavior, thought, event, or circumstance, 334–336

Checklist of Adaptive Living Skills (CALS), 536–537

Chicago Bulls, 138

child abuse: Nonaccidental infliction or creation of conditions that result in a child's physical injury or emotional impairment, or a sexual offense committed against a child, 479–481

Child Abuse Potential Inventory (CAP), 481

child evaluation, custody proceedings, 477–478

Childhood Trauma Questionnaire (CTQ), 232

child neglect: The failure by an adult responsible for a child to exercise a minimum degree of care in providing the child with food, clothing, shelter, education, medical care, and supervision, 479–481

Child Sexual Behavior Inventory, 338

China, historical testing perspective, 36–37

Choosing the Right Stuff: The Psychological Selection of Astronauts and Cosmonauts (Santy), 545

CIIS. *See* Cattell Infant Intelligence Scale

Civil Rights Act (1964), 57, 58–60

Civil Rights Act (1991), 549

Civil Service Commission, 58–59

classical test theory (CTT): Also known as true score theory and the true score model, a system of assumptions about measurement that includes the notion that a test score (and even a response to an individual item) is composed of a relatively stable component that actually is what the test or individual item is designed to measure, as well as a component that is error, 121, 163, 266–267

classification: A rating, categorizing, or "pigeonholing" with respect to two or more criteria; contrast with screening, selection, and placement, 539

class interval, 82

class scoring: Also referred to as category scoring, a method of evaluation in which test responses earn credit toward placement in a particular class or category with other testtakers. Sometimes testtakers must meet a set number of responses corresponding to a particular criterion in order to be placed in a specific category or class; contrast with cumulative scoring and ipsative scoring, 246

CLEP. *See* College Level Examination Program

clinical assessment, 448–488
addiction/substance abuse, 467–469
case history data, 460
child abuse/neglect, 479–481
clinical measures, 467–478
culturally informed psychological assessment, 462–467
custody evaluations, 476–478
emotional injury diagnosis, 475
forensic psychological assessment, 469–475 (*See also* forensic psychological assessment)
interview, 453–460
mental disorder diagnosis, 450–453 (*See also* mental disorders)
profiling, 475–476
psychological report, 484–488
psychological tests, 460–462

clinical measures, 467–478
addiction/substance abuse, 467–469
custody evaluations, 476–478
forensic psychological assessment, 469–475 (*See also* forensic psychological assessment)

clinical prediction: In clinical practice, applying a clinician's own training and clinical experience as a determining factor in clinical judgment and actions; contrast with actuarial prediction and mechanical prediction, 487

clinical psychology: That branch of psychology that has as its primary focus the prevention, diagnosis, and treatment of abnormal behavior, 448

clinical settings, 21

ClinPSYC, 33

clock-drawing test (CDT): A technique used in clinical neuropsychological examinations whereby the testtaker draws the face of a clock, usually indicating a particular time, that is then evaluated for distortions that may be symptomatic of dementia or other neurological or psychiatric conditions, 508

Cocaine Risk Response Test, 467

Code of Fair Testing Practices in Education, 64–65

code of professional ethics: A body of guidelines that sets forth the standard of care expected of members of a profession, 55

coefficient alpha: Also referred to as Cronbach's alpha and alpha, a statistic widely employed in test construction and used to assist in deriving an estimate of reliability; more technically, it is equal to the mean of all split-half reliabilities, 154

coefficient of correlation: Symbolized by r, the correlation coefficient is an index of the strength of the linear relationship between two continuous variables expressed as a number that can range from -1 to 11. Although different statistics may be used to calculate a coefficient of correlation, the most frequently used is the Pearson r, 102

coefficient of determination: A value indicating how much variance is shared by two variables being calculated; this value is obtained by squaring the obtained correlation coefficient, multiplying by 100, and expressing the result as a percentage, which indicates the amount of variance accounted for by the correlation coefficient, 105

coefficient of equivalence: An estimate of parallel-forms reliability or alternate-forms reliability, 149

coefficient of generalizability: In generalizability theory, an index of the influence that particular facets have on a test score, 165

coefficient of inter-scorer reliability: Determines the degree of consistency among scores in the soring of a test, 156

coefficient of stability: An estimate of test-retest reliability obtained during time intervals of six months or longer, 146

Cognitive Abilities Test, 306

cognitive ability measures, 548–549

cognitive interview: A type of hypnotic interview without the hypnotic induction; the interviewee is encouraged to use imagery and focused retrieval to recall information, 455

Cognitive Proficiency Index (CPI), 298

cognitive style: A psychological dimension that characterizes the consistency with which one acquires and processes information, 306

cold reading: A practice recommended by the Common Core State Standards, unsupported by the scholarly literature, which entails having students study reading material in the absence of background information and context, 322. *See also* Common Core State Standards

Collaborative Drawing Technique, 423

collaborative interview: In clinical psychology, a helping, open-ended interview wherein both parties work together on a common mission of discovery, insight, and enlightenment, 455

collaborative psychological assessment: A process of assessment wherein the assessor and assessee work as "partners" from initial contact through final feedback, 6

collectivist culture: A culture in which value is placed on traits such as conformity, cooperation, and striving toward group goals, 50

college level aptitude tests, 341–344

College Level Examination Program (CLEP), 330

Color-Form Sorting Test, 506

Committee on Emotional Fitness, 40

Common Core State Standards: A multistate educational program for kindergarten-through-12th grade education consisting of grade-by-grade objectives for learning (standards), standardized tests to evaluate progress in meeting those objectives, and the means to achieve standardized test data for diagnostic as well as outcome assessment purposes, 319–327
   controversy, 321–323
   dynamic assessment, 324, 326–327
   public concerns and, 55–56
   response to intervention (RtI), 320, 323–324

communication
   nonverbal, 48–49
   verbal, 47–48

comparative scaling: In test development, a method of developing ordinal scales through the use of a sorting task that entails judging a stimulus in comparison with every other stimulus used on the test, 238

compensatory model of selection: A model of applicant selection based on the assumption that high scores on one attribute can balance out low scores on another attribute, 223–224

competence to stand trial: Understanding the charges against one and being able to assist in one's own defense, 471–472

completion item: Requires the examinee to provide a word or phrase that completes a sentence, 243

composite judgment: An averaging of multiple ratings of judgments for the purpose of minimizing rater error, 443

comprehensive system: John Exner's integration of several methods for administering, scoring, and interpreting the Rorschach test, 407

computer assisted psychological assessment. See CAPA

computerized adaptive testing (CAT): An interactive, computer-administered test-taking process wherein items presented to the testtaker are based in part on the testtaker's performance on previous items, 15, 243–246

computerized axial tomography. See CAT

computers as tools, 14–17

conceptual items, 331

concurrent validity: A form of criterion-related validity that is an index of the degree to which a test score is related to some criterion measure obtained at the same time (concurrently), 182, 184

confidence interval: A range or band of test scores that is likely to contain the "true score," 171

confidentiality: The ethical obligation of professionals to keep confidential all communications made or entrusted to them in confidence, although professionals may be compelled to disclose such confidential communications under court order or other extraordinary conditions, such as when such communications refer to a third party in imminent danger; contrast with privacy right, 71–73

configural interpretation of scores, 388

confirmatory factor analysis (CFA): A class of mathematical procedures employed when a factor structure that has been explicitly hypothesized is tested for its fit with the observed relationships between the variables, 191, 279

confrontation naming: Identifying a pictured stimulus in a neuropsychological context, such as in response to administration of items in the Boston Naming Test, 510

Connors Rating Scales-Revised (CRS-R), 335

co-norming: The test norming process conducted on two or more tests using the same sample of testtakers; when used to validate all of the tests being normed, this process may also be referred to as co-validation, 134n4, 264

consent, 69–70

construct: An informed, scientific idea developed or generated to describe or explain behavior; some examples of constructs include "intelligence," "personality," "anxiety," and "job satisfaction," 116, 187

constructed-response format: A form of test item requiring the testtaker to construct or create a response, as opposed to simply selecting a response (e.g., items on essay examinations, fill in the blank, and short-answer tests); contrast with selected-response format, 240

construct validity: A judgment about the appropriateness of inferences drawn from test scores regarding individual standings on a variable called a construct, 187–192
   changes with age, 188–189
   convergent evidence, 190
   defined, 187
   discriminant evidence, 190–191
   factor analysis, 191–192
   homogeneity, 187–188
   instructor-made tests for in-class use, 271
   intelligence tests, 315
   method of contrasted groups, 189–190
   pretest-posttest changes, 189

consultative report: A type of interpretive report designed to provide expert and detailed analysis of test data that mimics the work of an expert consultant, 15

consumer panel: A sample of respondents, selected by demographic and other criteria, who have contracted with a

consumer or marketing research firm to respond on a periodic basis to surveys, questionnaires, and related research instruments regarding various products, services, and/or advertising or other promotional efforts, 562

consumer psychology: The branch of social psychology dealing primarily with the development, advertising, and marketing of products and services, 558

content of test, 7

content-referenced testing and assessment: Also referred to as criterion-referenced or domain-referenced testing and assessment, a method of evaluation and a way of deriving meaning from test scores by evaluating an individual's score with reference to a set standard (or criterion); contrast with norm-referenced testing and assessment, 136

content sampling: The variety of the subject matter contained in the items; frequently referred to in the context of the variation between individual test items in a test or between test items in two or more tests and also referred to as item sampling, 145

content scales, 387

content validity: Describes a judgment of how adequately a test samples behavior representative of the universe of behavior that the test was designed to sample, 178–182, 271

continuous scale, 76

contralateral control: Phenomenon resulting from the fact that each of the two cerebral hemispheres receives sensory information from the opposite side of the body and also controls motor responses on the opposite side of the body; understanding of this phenomenon is necessary in understanding brain-behavior relationships and in diagnosing neuropsychological deficits, 489

contrast effect: A potential source of error in behavioral ratings when a dissimilarity in the observed behaviors (or other things being rated) leads to a more or less favorable rating than would have been made had the dissimilarity not existed, 442

control group: (1) In an experiment, the untreated group; (2) in test development by means of empirical criterion keying, a group of randomly selected testtakers who do not necessarily have in common the shared characteristic of the standardization sample, 385

Controlled Word Association Test, 512

convenience sample. See incidental sampling

convenience sampling: Also referred to as incidental sampling, the process of arbitrarily selecting some people to be part of a sample because they are readily available, not because they are most representative of the population being studied, 130

convergent evidence: With reference to construct validity, data from other measurement instruments designed to measure the same or a similar construct as the test being construct-validated and that all point to the same judgment or conclusion with regard to a test or other tool of measurement; contrast with discriminant evidence, 190

convergent thinking: A deductive reasoning process that entails recall and consideration of facts as well as a series of logical judgments to narrow down solutions and eventually arrive at one solution; contrast with divergent thinking, 307

convergent validity: Data indicating that a test measures the same construct as another test purporting to measure the same construct, 190n3

Cooperative Achievement Test, 330

COPS. *See* criterion-focused occupational personality scales

core subtest: One of a test's subtests that is routinely administered during any administration of the test; contrast with supplemental or optional subtest, 297

corporate culture, 556–557

correlation: An expression of the degree and direction of correspondence between two things, when each thing is continuous in nature, 102–114
  concept of, 102–104
  graphic representation, 107–110
  meta-analysis, 110–114
  Pearson r, 104–106
  Spearman's rho, 106–107

correlation coefficient: Symbolized by r, the correlation coefficient is an index of the strength of the linear relationship between two continuous variables expressed as a number that can range from −1 to 11. Although different statistics may be used to calculate a coefficient of correlation, the most frequently used is the Pearson r, 102

cost: As related to test utility, disadvantages, losses, or expenses in both economic and noneconomic terms, 202–203

counseling psychology: A branch of psychology that has to do with the prevention, diagnosis, and treatment of abnormal behavior, with emphasis on "everyday" types of concerns and problems such as those related to marriage, family, academics, and career, 448

counseling settings, 22

Couples Interaction Scoring System, 437

co-validation: The test validation process conducted on two or more tests using the same sample of testtakers; when used in conjunction with the creation of norms or the revision of existing norms, this process may also be referred to as co-norming, 264

cover letters, 539

CPI. *See* Cognitive Proficiency Index

CPI 434. *See* California Psychological Inventory

cranial nerve damage, 494, 499–500

creativity, 307, 318

criminal responsibility, 472–474

criterion: The standard against which a test or a test score is evaluated; this standard may take many forms, including a specific behavior or set of behaviors, 136, 182–183, 383

criterion contamination: A state in which a criterion measure is itself based, in whole or in part, on a predictor measure, 183

criterion-focused occupational personality scales, 534

criterion group: A reference group of testtakers who share characteristics and whose responses to test items serve as a standard by which items will be included or discarded from the final version of a scale; the shared characteristic of the criterion group will vary as a function of the nature and scope of the test being developed, 383

criterion-referenced testing and assessment: Also referred to as domain-referenced testing and assessment and content-referenced testing and assessment, a method of evaluation and a way of deriving meaning from test scores by evaluating an individual's score with reference to a set standard (or criterion); contrast with norm-referenced testing and assessment, 136–138, 162–163, 233–234

criterion-related validity: A judgment regarding how adequately a score or index on a test or other tool of measurement can be used to infer an individual's most probable standing on some measure of interest (the criterion), 182–186
  concurrent validity, 184
  criterion, defined, 182
  defined, 182
  expectancy data, 185
  incremental validity, 186
  instructor-made tests for in-class use, 271
  predictive validity, 184–186

critical incidents technique: In workplace settings, a procedure that entails recording employee behavior evaluated as positive or negative by a supervisor or other rater, 550

cross-battery assessment: Evaluation that employs tests from different test batteries and entails interpretation of data from specified tests to provide a comprehensive assessment, 283

Cross-Cultural Adaptability Inventory (CCAI), 537

cross-validation: A revalidation on a sample of testtakers other than the testtakers on whom test performance was originally found to be a valid predictor of some criterion, 264–265

CRS-R. *See* Connors Rating Scales-Revised

crystallized intelligence: In Cattell's two-factor theory of intelligence, acquired skills and knowledge that are highly dependent on formal and informal education; contrast with fluid intelligence, 282

CTI. *See* Career Transitions Inventory

CTT. *See* classical test theory

cultural considerations
  assessment, and, 42–55
  of DSM, 51–52
  evaluation standards, 49–50
  evolving interest in, 42–47
  intelligence, and, 308–314

nonverbal communication/behavior, 48–49
  personality assessment, 366, 395–399
  verbal communication, 47–48

Cultural Formulation Interview (CFI) of DSM-V, 51–52

culturally informed psychological assessment: An approach to evaluation that is keenly perceptive about and responsive to issues of acculturation, values, identity, worldview, language, and other culture-related variables as they may affect the evaluation process or the interpretation of resulting data, 138–139, 462–467

culture: The socially transmitted behavior patterns, beliefs, and products of work of a particular population, community, or group of people, 42

culture-fair intelligence test: A test or assessment process designed to minimize the influence of culture on various aspects of the evaluation procedures, such as the administration instructions, the item content, the responses required of the testtaker, and the interpretations made from the resulting data, 310–312

culture-free intelligence test: In psychometrics, the ideal of a test that is devoid of the influence of any particular culture and therefore does not favor people from any culture, 309

culture loading: An index of the magnitude to which a test incorporates the vocabulary, concepts, traditions, knowledge, and feelings associated with a particular culture, 310–313

culture-specific tests: Are tests designed for the use with people from one culture but not from another, 43

cumulative scoring: A method of scoring whereby points or scores accumulated on individual items or subtests are tallied and then, the higher the total sum, the higher the individual is presumed to be on the ability, trait, or other characteristic being measured; contrast with class scoring and ipsative scoring, 118

curriculum-based assessment (CBA): A general term referring to school-based evaluations that clearly and faithfully reflect what is being taught, 331

curriculum-based measurement (CBM): A type of curriculum-based assessment characterized by the use of standardized measurement procedures to derive local norms to be used in the evaluation of student performance on curriculum-based tasks, 331

curvilinearity: Usually with regard to graphs or correlation scatterplots, the degree to which the plot or graph is characterized by curvature, 107

custody evaluation: A psychological assessment of parents or guardians and their parental capacity and/or of children and their parental needs and preferences—usually undertaken for the purpose of assisting a court in making a decision about awarding custody, 476–478

cut score: Also referred to as a cutoff score, a reference point (usually numerical) derived as a result of judgment and used to divide a set of data into two or more classifications, with some action to be taken or some inference to be made on the basis of these classifications
Angoff method, 225–226
defined, 8, 222
fixed, 223
IRT-based methods, 226–227
known groups method, 226
multiple cut scores, 223
norm-referenced, 222
relative, 222
CVLT-II. *See* California Verbal Learning Test-II

DAP test. *See* Draw a Person (DAP) test
DAT. *See* Dental Admission Test
databases, 33–34
data descriptions, 81–94
frequency distributions, 81–84
kurtosis, 94
measure of central tendency, 84–89
skewness, 93–94
variability, 89–93
data reduction methods, 380–383
DaTscan: A high-tech imaging device (pronounced in a way that rhymes with "cat scan") used to visualize the substantia nigra in order to gauge the level of dopamine present, 503
Daubert v. Merrell Dow Pharmaceuticals, 61–63
DBS. *See* deep brain stimulation
"Death with Dignity" legislation, 65–68
Debra P. v. Turlington, 57
decision study: Conducted at the conclusion of a generalizability study, this research is designed to explore the utility and value of test scores in making decisions, 165–166
decision theory: A body of methods used to quantitatively evaluate selection procedures, diagnostic classifications, therapeutic interventions, or other assessment or intervention-related procedures in terms of how optimal they are (most typically from a cost-benefit perspective), 218–220
declarative memory: Memory of factual material; contrast with procedural memory, 513
deep brain stimulation (DBS): Is a neurosurgical treatment for use with patients who have advanced PD, 503
dementia: A neurological disorder characterized by deficits in memory, judgment, ability to concentrate, and other cognitive abilities, with associated changes in personality due to damage to, or disease of brain neurons, 22, 521–523
Dental Admission Test (DAT), 344
deterioration quotient (DQ): Also referred to as a deterioration index, this is a pattern of subtest scores on a Wechsler test that Wechsler himself viewed as suggestive of neurological deficit, 505
developmentally delayed, 293
developmental milestones: Important event during the course of one's life that may be marked by the acquisition, presence, or growth of certain abilities or skills or by the failure, impairment, or cessation of such abilities or skills, 496, 497
developmental norms: Norms derived on the basis of any trait, ability, skill, or other characteristic that is presumed to develop, deteriorate, or otherwise be affected by chronological age, school grade, or stage of life, 134
deviation. *See* average deviation
deviation IQ: A variety of standard score used to report "intelligence quotients" (IQs) with a mean set at 100 and a standard deviation set at 15; on the Stanford-Binet, it is also referred to as a test composite and represents an index of intelligence derived from a comparison between the performance of an individual testtaker and the performance of other testtakers of the same age in the test's standardization sample, 291
diagnosis: A description or conclusion reached on the basis of evidence and opinion through a process of distinguishing the nature of something and ruling out alternative conclusions, 21
Diagnostic and Statistical Manual of Mental Disorders (DSM)
Cultural Formulation Interview (CFI) of DSM-V, 51–52
DSM-II, 459
DSM-III, 459
DSM-III-R, 459
DSM-V, 445–446, 450–451, 454
as nominal scale, 77
diagnostic information: In educational contexts, test or other data used to pinpoint a student's difficulties for the purpose of remediating them; contrast with evaluative information, 345
Diagnostic Psychological Testing (Rapaport), 462
diagnostic test: A tool used to make a diagnosis, usually to identify areas of deficit to be targeted for intervention, 21, 344–346
diary panel: A variety of consumer panel in which respondents have agreed to keep diaries of their thoughts and/or behaviors, 562
dichotomous test item: A test item or question that can be answered with only one of two response options, such as true-false or yes-no, 167
dichotomy, 428–429
Dictionary of Occupational Titles (Dept. of Labor), 529
DIF analysis: In IRT, a process of group-by-group analysis of item response curves for the purpose of evaluating measurement instrument or item equivalence across different groups of testtakers, 268
differential item functioning (DIF): In IRT, a phenomenon in which the same test item yields one result for members of one group and a different result for members of another group, presumably as a result of group differences that are not associated with group differences in the construct being measured, 168, 268
DIF items: In IRT, test items that respondents from different groups, who are presumably at the same level of the underlying construct being measured, have different probabilities of endorsing as a function of their group membership, 268
dimensional qualitative research: An adaptation of Lazarus's multimodal clinical approach for use in qualitative research applications and designed to ensure that the research is comprehensive and systematic from a psychological perspective and is guided by discussion questions based on the seven modalities (or dimensions) named in Lazarus's model, which are summarized by the acronym BASIC ID (behavior, affect, sensation, imagery, cognition, interpersonal relations, and drugs); Cohen's adaptation of Lazarus's work adds an eighth dimension, sociocultural, changing the acronym to BASIC IDS, 564
direct correlation, 102
direct estimation, 239
Directory of Unpublished Experimental Mental Measures (Goldman & Mitchell), 34
disability: As defined in the Americans with Disabilities Act of 1990, a physical or mental impairment that substantially limits one or more of the major life activities of an individual, 29–30, 65, 320, 323–324
discrete scale, 76
discriminant analysis: A family of statistical techniques used to shed light on the relationship between certain variables and two or more naturally occurring groups, 228
discriminant evidence: With reference to construct validity, data from a test or other measurement instrument showing little relationship between test scores or other variables with which the scores on the test being construct-validated should not theoretically be correlated; contrast with convergent evidence, 190–191
discrimination: In IRT, the degree to which an item differentiates among people with higher or lower levels of the trait, ability, or whatever it is that is being measured by a test, 167
discrimination (in Title VII litigation): The practice of making distinctions in hiring, promotion, or other selection decisions that tend to systematically favor members of a majority group regardless of actual qualifications for positions, 59–60
Discussion of Organizational Culture (Cohen), 557
disparate impact: The consequence of an employer's hiring or promotion practice that unintentionally resulted in a discriminatory result or outcome; contrast with disparate treatment, 60
disparate treatment: The consequence of an employer's hiring or promotion practice that was intentionally devised to yield some discriminatory result or outcome; contrast with disparate impact, 60

distribution: In a psychometric context, a set of test scores arrayed for recording or study, 81

divergent thinking: A reasoning process characterized by flexibility of thought, originality, and imagination, making several different solutions possible; contrast with convergent thinking, 307

diversity issues, personnel selection, 548–549

domain-referenced testing and assessment, 136

domain-referenced testing and assessment: Also referred to as criterion-referenced or content-referenced testing and assessment, a method of evaluation and a way of deriving meaning from test scores by evaluating an individual's score with reference to a set standard (or criterion); contrast with norm-referenced testing and assessment, 136

domain sampling: (1) A sample of behaviors from all possible behaviors that could be indicative of a particular construct; (2) a sample of test items from all possible items that could be used to measure a particular construct, 118n1

domain sampling theory: a system of assumptions about measurement that includes the notion that a test score (and even a response to an individual item) consists of a relatively stable component that actually is what the test or individual item is designed to measure as well as relatively unstable components that collectively can be accounted for as error, 164

dopamine: A neurotransmitter essential for normal movement, 500. *See also* neurotransmitter

DQ. *See* deterioration quotient

Draw a Person (DAP) test, 423

drawings, 422–425

drug addiction, 467–469

drug test: In the workplace, an evaluation undertaken to determine the presence, if any, of alcohol or other psychotropic substances, by means of laboratory analysis of blood, urine, hair, or other biological specimens, 547–548

DSM. *See Diagnostic and Statistical Manual of Mental Disorders*

dual-easel format, 337

Durham standard: A standard of legal insanity in Durham v. United States wherein the defendant was not found culpable for criminal action if his unlawful act was the product of a mental disease or defect; contrast with the ALI standard and the M'Naghten standard, 472

Durham v. United States, 472

Dusky v. United States, 471

duty to warn: A legally mandated obligation—to advise an endangered third party of their peril—which may override patient privilege; therapists and assessors may have a legal duty to warn when a client expresses intent to hurt a third party in any way, ranging from physical violence to disease transmission, 470

dynamic assessment: Refers to an interactive approach to psychological assessment that usually follows a model of (1)

evaluation, (2) intervention of some sort, and (3) evaluation, 6, 324, 326–327

dynamic characteristic: A trait, state, or ability presumed to be ever-changing as a function of situational and cognitive experiences; contrast with static characteristic, 161

dynamometer: An instrument used to measure strength of hand grip, 80

dyskinesia: A pathological neurological condition characterized by involuntary, jerking-type muscle movements, 502

easel format, 337

echoencephalograph: In neurology, a machine that transforms electrical energy into sound energy for the purpose of diagnostic studies of brain lesions and abnormalities, 520

ecological momentary assessment (EMA): The in the moment and in the place evaluation of targeted variables, such as behaviors, cognitions, and emotions, in a natural, naturalistic, or real-life context, 4, 432, 434

ecological validity: A judgment regarding how well a test measures what it purports to measure at the time and place that the variable being measured (typically a behavior, cognition, or emotion) is actually emitted, 177

ECST-R. *See* Evaluation of Competency to Stand Trial-Revised

educational assessment: Refers to the use of tests and other tools to evaluate abilities and skills relevant to success or failure in a school or preschool context, 317–353. *See also* Common Core State Standards

achievement tests, 328–331

aptitude tests, 331–344 (*See also* aptitude tests)

authentic assessment, 350–351

defined, 3

diagnostic tests, 344–346

dynamic assessment, 324–327

peer appraisal, 351–352

performance assessment, 349–351

pros and cons, 318–319

psychoeducational test batteries, 346–348 (*See* psychoeducational test batteries)

role of, 317–318

RtI model, 320–324

study habits/interests/attitudes, measuring, 352–353

Educational Resources Information Center (ERIC), 33

educational settings, 20–21

Educational Testing Service (ETS), 34

Education for All Handicapped Children (PL 94-142), 57, 333

Edwards Personal Preference Schedule (EPPS), 246

EEG. *See* electroencephalograph

EEOC. *See* Equal Employment Opportunity Commission

effect size: A statistic used to express the strength of the relationship or the magnitude of the differences in data; in meta-analysis, this statistic is most typically a correlation coefficient, 111

elaboration, 307

elder abuse: The intentional affliction of physical, emotional, financial, or other harm on an older individual who meets the statutory age requirement for an elder, 481–483

elder neglect: A failure on the part of a caregiver or service provider to provide for the elder what was reasonably needed to prevent physical, emotional, financial, or other harm, 481–483

electroencephalograph (EEG): A machine that records electrical activity of the brain by means of electrodes pasted to the scalp, 520, 522

electromyograph (EMG): A machine that records electrical activity of muscles by means of an electrode inserted directly into the muscle, 520

elementary-school level aptitude tests, 338, 340

Ellis Island immigrant testing, 42–43

EMG. *See* electromyograph

emotional injury: A term sometimes used synonymously with mental suffering, emotional harm, and pain and suffering to convey psychological damage, 475

emotional intelligence: A popularization of aspects of Gardner's theory of multiple intelligences, with emphasis on the notions of interpersonal and intrapersonal intelligence, 281

emotional signs of abuse and neglect: Fear of going home or fear of adults in general and reluctance to remove outer garments may be signs of abuse, 480

empirical criterion keying: The process of using criterion groups to develop test items, where the scoring or keying of items has been demonstrated empirically to differentiate among groups of testtakers, 383

employment opportunities. *See* career opportunities

Entrance Examination for Schools of Nursing (RNEE), 344

episodic memory: Memory for facts but only within a particular context or situation; contrast with semantic memory, 513

EPPS. *See* Edwards Personal Preference Schedule

Equal Employment Opportunity Commission (EEOC), 58

Equal Opportunity Employment Act, 57

equipercentile method: A procedure for comparing scores on two or more tests (as in the creation of national anchor norms) that entails calculating percentile norms for each test and then identifying the score on each test that corresponds to the percentile, 134

ERIC. *See* Educational Resources Information Center

error: Collectively, all of the factors other than what a test purports to measure that contribute to scores on the test; error is a variable in all testing and assessment, 76–77, 119–121. *See also* reliability

error of central tendency: Less than accurate rating or evaluation by a rater or judge due to that rater's general tendency to make ratings at or near the midpoint of the scale; contrast with generosity error and severity error, 364

error variance: In the true score model, the component of variance attributable to random sources irrelevant to the trait or ability the test purports to measure in an observed score or distribution of scores; common sources of error variance include those related to test construction (including item or content sampling), test administration, and test scoring and interpretation, 120, 142
  sources of, 143–145

essay item: A test item that requires the testtaker to respond to a question by writing a composition, typically one that demonstrates recall of facts, understanding, analysis, and/or interpretation, 243

estimate of inter-item consistency: An estimate of the reliability of a test obtained from a measure of inter-item consistency, 150

ethical considerations, 55–74. *See also* legal/ethical considerations

Ethical Principles of Psychologists and Code of Conduct (APA), 70

Ethical Standards for the Distribution of Psychological Tests and Diagnostic Aids (APA), 64

ethics: A body of principles of right, proper, or good conduct; contrast with laws, 55

ETS. *See* Educational Testing Service

eugenics: The science of improving qualities of a breed through intervention with factors related to heredity, 45

Evaluation of Competency to Stand Trial-Revised (ECST-R), 471

evaluation standards, 49–50

evaluative information: Test or other data used to make judgments such as class placement, pass-fail, and admit-reject decisions; contrast with diagnostic information, 344

Every Student Succeeds Act (ESSA, 2015), 57

evidence-based practice: Methods, protocols, techniques, and procedures, used by professionals, that have a basis in clinical and research findings, 114

evidence from distinct groups: Provides evidence fot eh validity of a test by demonstrating that scores on the test vary in a predictable way as a function of membership in some group, 189–190

evolutionary view of mental disorder: The view that an attribution of mental disorder requires a scientific judgment (from an evolutionary perspective) that there exists a failure of function as well as a value judgment (from the perspective of social values) that the failure is harmful to the individual, 451

examiner, 26

examiner-related variables, 144

executive function: In neuropsychology, organizing, planning, cognitive flexibility, inhibition of impulses, and other activities associated with the frontal and prefrontal lobes of the brain, 507–510

expectancy chart: Graphic representation of an expectancy table, 185

expectancy data, 185, 207–216

expert panel: In the test development process, a group of people knowledgeable about the subject matter being tested and/or the population for whom the test was designed who can provide input to improve the test's content, fairness, and other related ways, 259–260

expert testimony, 61

exploratory factor analysis, 279

exploratory factor analysis: A class of mathematical procedures employed to estimate factors, extract factors, or decide how many factors to retain, 191

extended scoring report: A type of scoring report that provides not only a listing of scores but statistical data as well, 15

extra-test behavior: Observations made by an examiner regarding what the examinee does and how the examinee reacts during the course of testing (e.g., how the testtaker copes with frustration; how much support the testtaker seems to require; how anxious, fatigued, cooperative, or distractible the testtaker is) that are indirectly related to the test's specific content but of possible significance to interpretations regarding the testtaker's performance, 294–295

extrinsic motivation: A state in which the primary force driving an individual comes from external sources (such as a salary or bonus) and external constraints (such as job loss); contrast with intrinsic motivation, 553

eye contact, 48

facets: In generalizability theory, variables of interest in the universe including, for example, the number of items in the test, the amount of training the test scorers have had, and the purpose of the test administration, 165

face validity: A judgment regarding how well a test or other tool of measurement measures what it purports to measure that is based solely on "appearances," such as the content of the test's items, 177–178

fact-based items, 331

factor analysis: A class of mathematical procedures, frequently employed as data reduction methods, designed to identify variables on which people may differ (or factors), 191–192, 277–280, 281n1, 445–446

factor-analytic theories: A way of looking at intelligence that focuses on identifying the ability or groups of abilities deemed to constitute intelligence, 276, 281

factor loading: In factor analysis, a metaphor suggesting that a test (or an individual test item) carries with it or "loads" on a certain amount of one or more abilities that, in turn, have a determining influence on the test score (or on the response to the individual test item), 191, 278, 310–311

fairness: As applied to tests, the extent to which a test is used in an impartial, just, and equitable way, 196–199

Faking Bad Scale (FBS), 389

false negative: A specific type of miss characterized by a tool of assessment indicating that the testtaker does not possess or exhibit a particular trait, ability, behavior, or attribute when in fact, the testtaker does possess or exhibit this trait, ability, behavior, or attribute, 185, 547

false positive: An error in measurement characterized by a tool of assessment indicating that the testtaker possesses or exhibits a particular trait, ability, behavior, or attribute when in fact the testtaker does not, 185, 547

Family Education Rights and Privacy Act (1974), 57

family environment, 338

fatalism: The belief that what happens in life is largely out of a person's control, 453

FBS. *See* Faking Bad Scale

Federal Rules of Evidence, Rule 702, 62

FF-NPQ. *See* Five-Factor Nonverbal Personality Questionnaire

field (context) dependent people, 27

field independent people, 27

field-of-search item: A type of test item used in ability and neurodiagnostic tests wherein the testtaker's task is to locate a match to a visually presented stimulus, 510

fifty plus or minus ten scale, 99

figure drawing test: A general reference to a type of test in which the testtaker's task is to draw a human figure and/or other figures, and inferences are then made about the testtaker's ability, personality, and/or neurological intactness on the basis of the figure(s) produced, 422–425

financial competency: An area of competency that focuses on the ability of an individual to make reasonably sound decisions regarding day-to-day money matters as well as all aspects of their personal finances, 472–474

first moments of the distribution, 106

Fitness Interview Test (FIT), 471

Five-Factor Nonverbal Personality Questionnaire (FF-NPQ), 382

fixed battery: A prepackaged test battery containing a number of standardized tests to be administered in a prescribed fashion, such as the Halstead-Reitan Neuropsychological Battery; contrast with flexible battery, 515

fixed cut score: Also known as an absolute cut score, a reference point in a distribution of test scores used to divide a set of data into two or more classifications that is typically set with reference to a judgment concerning a minimum level of proficiency required to be included in a particular classification; contrast with relative cut score, 223

fixed reference group scoring system: A system of scoring wherein the distribution of scores obtained on the test from one group of testtakers (the fixed reference group) is used as the basis for the calculation of test scores for future administrations; the SAT and the GRE are scored this way, 135–136

flexibility, 307

flexible battery: Best associated with neuropsychological assessment, a group of tests hand-picked by the assessor to provide an answer to the referral question; contrast with fixed battery, 515

floor: The lowest level of the items on a subtest, 293

floor effect: A phenomenon arising from the diminished utility of a tool of assessment in distinguishing testtakers at the low end of the ability, trait, or other attribute being measured, 245

fluency, 307

fluid intelligence: In Cattell's two-factor theory of intelligence, nonverbal abilities that are relatively less dependent on culture and formal instruction; contrast with crystallized intelligence, 282

Flynn effect: "Intelligence inflation"; the fact that intelligence measured using a normed instrument rises each year after the test was normed, usually in the absence of any academic dividend, 314–315

*f*MRI: An imaging device that creates real-time, moving images of internal functioning (particularly useful in identifying which parts of the brain are active at various times and during various tasks), 519–521

focus group: Qualitative research conducted with a group of respondents who typically have been screened to qualify for participation in the research, 563

forced-choice format: A type of item sometimes used in personality tests wherein each of two or more choices has been predetermined to be equal in social desirability, 372

forced distribution technique: A procedure entailing the distribution of a predetermined number or percentage of assessees into various categories that describe performance (such as categories ranging from "unsatisfactory" to "superior"), 550

forensic psychological assessment: The theory and application of psychological evaluation and management in a legal context, 469–475
  competency to stand trial, 471–472
  criminal responsibility, 472–474
  dangerousness to oneself/others, 470
  emotional injury, 475
  parole/probation readiness, 474–475
  profiling, 475–476

format: A general reference to the form, plan, structure, arrangement, or layout of test items as well as to related considerations such as time limits for test administration, 7

frame of reference: In the context of item format, aspects of the focus of the item such as the time frame (past, present, or future), 371

free association: A technique, most frequently used in psychoanalysis, wherein the subject relates all his or her thoughts as they occur; contrast with word association, 419n5

frequency distribution: A tabular listing of scores along with the number of times each score occurred, 81–84

frequency polygon: A graphic illustration of data wherein numbers indicating frequency are set on the vertical axis, test scores or categories are set on the horizontal axis, and the data are described by a continuous line connecting the points where the test scores or categories meet frequencies, 83, 84

Frye v. the United States, 62

Full Scale IQ (FSIQ), 298

functional analysis of behavior: In behavioral assessment, the process of identifying dependent and independent variables, 438

functional deficit: In neuropsychology, any sensory, motor, or cognitive impairment that is psychological or without a known physical or structural cause; contrast with organic deficit, 494

functional MRI (*f*MRI): An imaging device that creates real-time, moving images of internal functioning (particularly useful in identifying which parts of the brain are active at various times and during various tasks), 519–521

GAI. *See* General Ability Index

Gas Chromatography Mass Spectrometry (GCMS), 547

GATB. *See* General Aptitude Test Battery

GCR. *See* group conformity rating

General Ability Index (GAI), 298

General Aptitude Test Battery (GATB): Is a tool used to identify aptitudes for occupations, and it is a test just about anyone of working age can take, 528–533

General Electric Co. v. Joiner, 63

generalizability study: In the context of generalizability theory, research conducted to explore the impact of different facets of the universe on a test score, 165

generalizability theory: Also referred to as domain sampling theory, a system of assumptions about measurement that includes the notion that a test score (and even a response to an individual item) consists of a relatively stable component that actually is what the test or individual item is designed to measure as well as relatively unstable components that collectively can be accounted for as error, 164

generosity error: Also referred to as leniency error, a less than accurate rating or evaluation by a rater due to that rater's general tendency to be lenient or insufficiently critical; contrast with severity error, 194, 364

geriatric settings, 22

g **factor:** In Spearman's two-factor theory of intelligence, the general factor of intelligence; also, the factor that is measured to greater or lesser degrees by all tests of intelligence; contrast with s factor and group factors, 278, 280, 283, 445–446

Gf-Gc: Fluid-crystallized intelligence as described in the Cattell-Horn model, Carroll's three-stratum theory, and other models, 282–283

giveaway item: A test item, usually near the beginning of a test of ability or achievement, designed to be relatively easy—usually for the purpose of building the testtaker's confidence or lessening test-related anxiety, 248n4

Goal Instability Scale, 538

governmental credentialing, 23

GPA. *See* grade point average

grade-based scale, 235

grade norms: Norms specifically designed as a reference in the context of the grade of the testtaker who achieved a particular score; contrast with age norms, 133–134

grade point average (GPA), 186

Graduate Management Admission Test, 344

Graduate Record Exam (GRE), 34, 341–342

graph: A diagram or chart composed of lines, points, bars, or other symbols that describe and illustrate data, 82, 85

graphology: Handwriting analysis for the purpose of deriving insights into personality, 370

GRE. *See* Graduate Record Exam

Griggs v. Duke Power Company, 57

group conformity rating (GCR), 417–418

grouped frequency distribution: Also referred to as class intervals, a tabular summary of test scores in which the test scores are grouped by intervals, 82–83

group factors: According to Spearman, factors common to a group of activities indicating intelligence, such as linguistic, mechanical, or arithmetic abilities, 280–281

group membership
  public policy, 54–55
  score adjustment, 197–198
  tests and, 53–55

group testing
  military, 302–306
  pros/cons, 307
  schools, 305–306

groupthink: Collective decision-making characterized more by a drive toward consensus than critical analysis and evaluation, which may lead to less reasoned and riskier decisions than those that might have been made by an individual making the same decision, 12

Grutter v. Bollinger, 58, 59

guessing, 256

Guttman scale: Named for its developer, a scale wherein items range sequentially from weaker to stronger expressions of the attitude or belief being measured, 238

halo effect: A type of rating error wherein the rater views the object of the rating with extreme favor and tends to bestow ratings inflated in a positive direction; a set of circumstances resulting in a rater's tendency to be positively disposed and insufficiently critical, 195, 364

Halstead-Reitan Neuropsychological Battery: A widely used fixed neuropsychological test battery based on the work of Ward Halstead and Ralph Reitan, 516–519

HAPI. *See* Health and Psychosocial Instruments

hard sign: In neuropsychological assessment, an indicator of definite neurological deficit, such as an abnormal reflex response; contrast with soft sign, 494

harmonious passion, 527n1

Harris-Lingoes subscales, 387, 395

Health and Psychosocial Instruments (HAPI), 33

Health Insurance Portability and Accountability Act (HIPAA, 1996), 57, 73

health psychology: A specialty area of psychology that focuses on understanding the role of psychological variables in the onset, course, treatment, and prevention of illness, disease, and disability, 26

health-related quality of life (HRQOL), 168

Henmon-Nelson Tests of Mental Ability, 306

heterogeneity: Describes the degree to which a test measures different factors, 152

hierarchical model: A term usually applied to a theoretical model organized into two or more layers, with each layer subsumed by or incorporated in the preceding layer; for example, Carroll's three-stratum theory of cognitive abilities is a hierarchical model with g as the top layer followed by two layers of cognitive abilities and processes, 283

HIPAA. *See* Health Insurance Portability and Accountability Act

hired guns, 66

histogram: A graph with vertical lines drawn at the true limits of each test score (or class interval), forming a series of contiguous rectangles, 83, 84

historical considerations
pre-nineteenth century, 36–39
twentieth century, 39–41

HIT. *See* Holtzman Inkblot Technique

hit rate: The proportion of people who are accurately identified as possessing or not possessing a particular trait, behavior, characteristic, or attribute based on test scores, 185

Hobson v. Hansen, 57

Holtzman Inkblot Technique (HIT), 407n3

homogeneity: Describes the degree to which a test measures a single trait, 152, 187–188

Hopwood v. State of Texas, 549

Horn Art Aptitude Inventory, 343

House-Tree-Person test, 423

HRQOL. *See* health-related quality of life

human asexuality: An absence of sexual attraction to anyone at all, 231

hypnotic interview: An interview conducted after a hypnotic state has been induced in the interviewee, most typically in an effort to enhance concentration, focus, imagery, and recall, 454

IAT. *See* Implicit Attitude Test

ICC. *See* item characteristic curve

IDEA. *See* Individuals with Disabilities Education Act

identification: A process by which an individual assumes a pattern of behavior characteristic of other people, and referred to as one of the "central issues that ethnic minority groups must deal with," 399

identity: A set of cognitive and behavioral characteristics by which individuals define themselves as members of a particular group; one's sense of self, 399

idiographic approach: An approach to assessment characterized by efforts to learn about each individual's unique constellation of personality traits, with no attempt to characterize each person according to any particular set of traits; contrast with nomothetic approach, 374

idiopathic: An adjective that means "of unknown origin" (as in "idiopathic Parkinson's disease"), 502

immigrant psychological testing, 42–43

imperial examination, 37

implicit attitude: A nonconscious, automatic association in memory that produces a disposition to react in some characteristic manner to a particular stimulus, 559

Implicit Attitude Test (IAT), 559

implicit memory: Memory that is outside of conscious control and accessible only by indirect measures, 515

implicit motive: A nonconscious influence on behavior, typically acquired on the basis of experience, 415

impression management: Attempting to manipulate others' opinions and impressions through the selective exposure of some information, including false information, usually coupled with the suppression of other information; in responding to self-report measures of personality, psychopathology, or achievement, impression management may be synonymous with attempts to "fake good" or "fake bad," 367

in-basket technique: A measurement technique used to assess managerial ability and organizational skills that entails a timed simulation of the way a manager or executive deals with an in-basket filled with mail, memos, announcements, and other notices and directives, 542

incidence: The rate (annual, monthly, weekly, daily, or other) of new occurrences of a particular disorder or condition in a particular population; contrast with prevalence, 450

incidental sampling: Also referred to as convenience sampling, the process of arbitrarily selecting some people to be part of a sample because they are readily available, not because they are most representative of the population being studied, 130

incremental validity: Used in conjunction with predictive validity, an index of the explanatory power of additional predictors over and above the predictors already in use, 186

indirect estimation, 239

individualist culture: A culture in which value is placed on traits such as autonomy, self-reliance, independence, uniqueness, and competitiveness, 50

Individuals with Disabilities Education Act (IDEA, 1997), 57, 320

inference: A logical result or a deduction in a reasoning process, 175

inflation of range/variance: Also referred to as inflation of variance, a reference to a phenomenon associated with reliability estimates wherein the variance of either variable in a correlational analysis is inflated by the sampling procedure used and so the resulting correlation coefficient tends to be higher; contrast with restriction of range, 161

informal evaluation: A typically nonsystematic, relatively brief, and "off-the-record" assessment leading to the formation of an opinion or attitude, conducted by any person in any way for any reason, in an unofficial context and not subject to the same ethics or standards as evaluation by a professional; contrast with formal evaluation, 21, 335

information-processing theories: A way of looking at intelligence that focuses on how information is processed rather than what is processed, 276

information-processing view, 284–285

informed consent: Permission to proceed with a (typically) diagnostic, evaluative, or therapeutic service on the basis of knowledge about the service and its risks and potential benefits, 69–70

inheritance, 45

inkblot, 8, 404–410, 407n3

inquiry: A typical element of Rorschach test administration; following the initial presentation of all ten cards, the assessor asks specific questions designed, among other things, to determine what about each card led to the assessee's perceptions, 405

insanity: A legal term denoting an inability to tell right from wrong, a lack of control, or a state of other mental incompetence or disorder sufficient to prevent that person from standing trial, being judged guilty, or entering into a contract or other legal relationship, 472

instructor-made tests for in-class use, 270–271

instrumental values: Guiding principles in the attainment of some objective—for example, honesty and ambition; contrast with terminal values, 399

integrative assessment: A multidisciplinary approach to evaluation that assimilates input from relevant sources, 324

integrative report: A form of interpretive report of psychological assessment, usually computer-generated, in which data from behavioral, medical, administrative, and/or other sources are integrated; contrast with scoring report and interpretive report, 15

integrity test: A screening instrument designed to predict who will and will not be an honest employee, 534

intellectual ability tests, 504–506

intellectually gifted, 293

intelligence: A multifaceted capacity that manifests itself in different ways across the life span but in general includes the abilities and capacities to acquire and apply knowledge, to reason effectively and logically, to exhibit sound judgment, to be perceptive, intuitive, mentally alert, and able to find the right words and

thoughts with facility, and to be able to cope with and adjust to new situations and new types of problems, 273–316
Binet's views, 274
CHC model, 283–284
construct validity of tests, 315
crystallized, 282
culture, 308–314
defined, 273
factor-analysis theories, 276–284
fluid, 282
Flynn effect, 314–315
Galton's views, 274
information-processing view, 284–285
lay public views, 273–274
measuring, 39–40, 285–308
nature *vs.* nurture, 315
Piaget's views, 275
testing for (*See* intelligence testing)
Wechsler's views, 275
intelligence inflation, 314
intelligence quotient (IQ). *See* IQ (intelligence quotient)
intelligence testing. *See also* Stanford-Binet Intelligence Scale; Wechsler intelligence tests
ASVAB, 303–305
cognitive style, 307
factor analysis, 277–280
group administration, tests for, 302–306
short forms for, 301
interactionism: The belief that heredity and environment interact to influence the development of one's mental capacity and abilities, 275
intercept bias: A reference to the intercept of a regression line exhibited by a test or measurement procedure that systematically underpredicts or overpredicts the performance of members of a group; contrast with slope bias, 529
interest measure: In the context of vocational assessment and preemployment counseling, an instrument designed to evaluate testtakers' likes, dislikes, leisure activities, curiosities, and involvements in various pursuits for the purpose of comparison with groups of members of various occupations and professions, 352, 524–527
inter-item consistency: The consistency or homogeneity of the items of a test, estimated by techniques such as the split-half method, 152
internal consistency estimate of reliability: An estimate of the reliability of a test obtained from a measure of inter-item consistency, 150, 160
International Guidelines on Computer-Based and Internet-Delivered Testing, 69
interpersonal intelligence: In Gardner's theory of multiple intelligences, the ability to understand other people, what motivates them, how they work, and how to work cooperatively with them; contrast with intrapersonal intelligence, 281
Interpersonal Support Evaluations List, 538
interpretive report: A formal or official computer-generated account of test performance presented in both numeric and narrative form and including an

explanation of the findings; the three varieties of interpretive report are descriptive, screening, and consultative; contrast with scoring report and integrative report, 15
interquartile range: An ordinal statistic of variability equal to the difference between the third and first quartile points in a distribution that has been divided into quartiles, 91
interrogation, 2
inter-scorer reliability: Also referred to as inter-rater reliability, observer reliability, judge reliability, and scorer reliability, an estimate of the degree of agreement or consistency between two and more scorers (or judges or raters or observers), 156, 160
interval scales: A system of measurement in which all things measured can be rank-ordered into equal intervals, where every unit on the scale is equal to every other and there is no absolute zero point (which precludes mathematical operations on such data), 79
interview: A tool of assessment in which information is gathered through direct, reciprocal communication
assessor's role, 9–11
in clinical assessment, 453–460
cultural aspects of, 464
defined, 10
for employment, 541
for neuropsychological evaluations, 497–498
psychometric aspects of, 458–460
types of, 454–458
intrapersonal intelligence: In Gardner's theory of multiple intelligences, a capacity to form accurate self-perceptions, to discriminate accurately between emotions, and to be able to draw upon one's emotions as a means of understanding and an effective guide; contrast with interpersonal intelligence, 281
intrinsic motivation: A state in which the primary force driving an individual comes from within, such as personal satisfaction with one's work; contrast with extrinsic motivation, 553
Inventory of Interpersonal Problems-Circumplex scales (IIP-SC), 232
ipsative approach, 375
ipsative scoring: An approach to test scoring and interpretation wherein the testtaker's responses and the presumed strength of a measured trait are interpreted relative to the measured strength of other traits for that testtaker; contrast with class scoring and cumulative scoring, 246
IQ (intelligence quotient): A widely used, shorthand reference to intelligence that echoes back from days now long gone when a testtaker's mental age as determined by a test was divided by chronological age and multiplied by 100 to determine the "intelligence quotient." *See also* intelligence
defined, 291
deviation IQ, 291
Flynn effect, 314–315
ratio IQ, 290–291
IRT. *See* item response theory

item analysis: A general term to describe various procedures, usually statistical, designed to explore how individual test items work as compared to other items in the test and in the context of the whole test (e.g., to explore the level of difficulty of individual items on an achievement test or the reliability of a personality test); contrast with qualitative item analysis, 248–260
defined, 248
guessing, 256
item-characteristic curves, 253–255
item-difficulty index, 248–249
item-discrimination index, 250–253
item fairness, 256–257
item-reliability index, 249–250
item-validity index, 250
qualitative, 258–260
speed tests, 257–258
test development, 229
item bank: A collection of questions to be used in the construction of tests
computer test administration, 243
defined, 243
developing, 268–270
item branching: In computerized adaptive testing, the individualized presentation of test items drawn from an item bank based on the testtaker's previous responses, 245
item-characteristic curve (ICC): A graphic representation of the probabilistic relationship between a person's level on a trait (or ability or other characteristic being measured) and the probability for responding to an item in a predicted way; also known as a category response curve, an item response curve, or an item trace line, 253–255, 267
item-difficulty index: In achievement or ability testing and other contexts in which responses are keyed correct, a statistic indicating how many testtakers responded correctly to an item; in contexts where the nature of the test is such that responses are not keyed correct, this same statistic may be referred to as an item-endorsement index, 248–249
item-discrimination index: A statistic designed to indicate how adequately a test item discriminates between high and low scorers, 250–253
item-endorsement index: In personality assessment and other contexts in which the nature of the test is such that responses are not keyed correct or incorrect, a statistic indicating how many testtakers responded to an item in a particular direction; in achievement tests, which have responses that are keyed correct, this statistic is referred to as an item-difficulty index, 248
item fairness: A reference to the degree of bias, if any, in a test item, 256–257. *See also* biased test item
item format: A reference to the form, plan, structure, arrangement, or layout of individual test items, including whether the items require testtakers to select a response from existing alternative responses or to construct a response, 240–243

item-mapping method: An IRT-based method of setting cut scores that entails a histographic representation of test items and expert judgments regarding item effectiveness, 227

item pool: The reservoir or well from which items will or will not be drawn for the final version of the test; the collection of items to be further evaluated for possible selection for use in an item bank, 239

item-reliability index: A statistic designed to provide an indication of a test's internal consistency; the higher the item-reliability index, the greater the test's internal consistency, 249–250

item response theory (IRT): Also referred to as latent-trait theory or the latent-trait model, a system of assumptions about measurement (including the assumption that a trait being measured by a test is unidimensional) and the extent to which each test item measures the trait, 164, 166–169

cutoff scores, setting, 226–227

test revision, 266–270

item sampling: Also referred to as content sampling, the variety of the subject matter contained in the items; frequently referred to in the context of the variation between individual test items in a test or between test items in two or more tests, 145

item-validity index: A statistic indicating the degree to which a test measures what it purports to measure; the higher the item-validity index, the greater the test's criterion-related validity, 250

Iverson v. Frandsen, 73–74, 74n8

Jaffee v. Redmond, 58, 73

Jenkins Activity Survey (JAS), 358

job applicant pool, 221–222

job complexity, 22

job opportunities. *See* career opportunities

job satisfaction: A pleasurable or positive emotional state resulting from the appraisal of one's job or job experience, 555

journal articles: Articles in current journals that may contain reviews of tests, updated or independent studies of psychometric soundness, or examples of how instruments are used in either research or an applied context, 33

J-shaped curve, 86

"judge-made law." *See* litigation

judge reliability, 156

K-ABC. *See* Kaufman Assessment Battery for Children

KABC-II. *See* Kaufman Assessment Battery for Children, Second Edition

Kallikak Family: A Study in the Heredity of Feeble-Mindedness, The (Goddard), 45

Kaufman Assessment Battery for Children, Second Edition (KABC-II), 346–348

Kaufman Assessment Battery for Children (K-ABC), 346–348

KDS. *See* Kinetic Drawing System

Kent-Rosanoff Free Association Test, 419–420

KeyMath 3 Diagnostic System (KeyMath3-DA), 346

Kinetic Drawing System (KDS), 424

Kinetic Family Drawing (KFD), 425

Kinetic School Drawing (KSD), 425

Kline Scale, 231

known groups method: Also referred to as the method of contrasted groups, a system of collecting data on a predictor of interest from groups known to possess (and not to possess) a trait, attribute, or ability of interest, 226

KSD. *See* Kinetic School Drawing

Kuder-Richardson formula 20 (KR-20): A series of equations developed by G. F. Kuder and M. W. Richardson designed to estimate the inter-item consistency of tests, 152–154, 162

Kuhlmann Anderson Intelligence Tests, 306

Kumho Tire Company Ltd v. Carmichael, 63

kurtosis: An indication of the nature of the steepness (peaked versus flat) of the center of a distribution, 94

language, 47–48

Larry P. v. Riles, 57

latent-trait theory: Also referred to as latent-trait model, a system of assumptions about measurement, including the assumption that a trait being measured by a test is unidimensional, and the extent to which each test item measures the trait, 166

laws: Rules that individuals must obey because they are deemed to be good for society as a whole; contrast with ethics, 55

Law School Admissions Test (LSAT), 59, 344

leaderless group technique: A situational assessment procedure wherein an observer/assessor evaluates the performance of assessees in a group situation with regard to variables such as leadership, initiative, and cooperation, 439, 542

Leadership Q-Test, 373

learning disability. *See* specific learning disability

Learning Potential Assessment Device (LPAD), 326

least stigmatizing label, 73–74

legal/ethical considerations, 55–74
   APA guidelines, 69
   computer-assisted psychological assessment, 68–69
   legislation, 56–60
   life-ending decisions, 66–68
   litigation, 61–63
   people with disabilities, testing, 65
   profession, concerns of, 63–69
   public, concerns of, 55–63
   testtakers, rights of, 69–74
   test-user qualifications, 64–65

legislation, 56–61

Leisure Satisfaction Scale, 538

leniency error: Also referred to as a generosity error, a rating error that occurs as the result of a rater's tendency to be too forgiving and insufficiently critical, 194, 364

leptokurtic: A description of the kurtosis of a distribution that is relatively peaked in its center, 94

lesion: A pathological alteration of tissue as might result from injury or infection, 491

letters of recommendation, 540–541

Lewy bodies: Clusters of stuck-together proteins in the brain that have the effect of depleting available dopamine and other brain substances (such as acetylcholine) critical for normal functioning, 503

Lewy body dementia (LBD) A progressive neurological disease that results from the formation of Lewy bodies in the brain stem and cerebral cortex that cause Parkinsonian-like symptoms, Alzheimer-like symptoms, and other symptoms of dementia, 503

LGBTA (lesbian, gay, bisexual, transgender, and asexual), 230

lie detector, 441

life-or-death psychological assessment, 66–68

Life Satisfaction Index A, 538

Likert scale: Named for its developer, a summative rating scale with five alternative responses ranging on a continuum from, for example, "strongly agree" to "strongly disagree," 237

linear transformation: In psychometrics, a process of changing a score such that (a) the new score has a direct numerical relationship to the original score and (b) the magnitude of the difference between the new score and other scores on the scale parallels the magnitude of differences between the original score and the other scores on the scales from which it was derived; contrast with nonlinear transformation, 100

Listening with the Third Ear (Reik), 444

litigation: Law resulting from the court-mediated resolution of legal matters of a civil, criminal, or administrative nature, also referred to as "judge-made law," 61–63

local norms: Normative information about some limited population, frequently of specific interest to the test user, 132, 135

local processing: On-site, computerized scoring, interpretation, or other conversion of raw test data; contrast with central processing and teleprocessing, 15

local validation studies: The process of gathering evidence, relevant to how well a test measures what it purports to measure, for the purpose of evaluating the validity of a test or other measurement tool; typically undertaken in conjunction with a population different from the population for whom the test was originally validated, 176

locator tests: A pretest or routing test, usually for determining the most appropriate level of test, 329

locus of control: The self-perceived source of what happens to oneself, 368

long-term memory, 513

LPAD. *See* Learning Potential Assessment Device

LSAT. *See* Law School Admissions Test

lumbar puncture: A diagnostic procedure typically performed by a neurologist in which spinal fluid is extracted from the spinal column by means of an inserted needle; also referred to as a spinal tap, 521

MacAndrew Alcoholism Scale (MAC), 468
MacAndrew Alcoholism Scale-Revised (MAC-R), 468
MacArthur Competence Assessment Tool-Criminal Adjudication (MacCAT-CA), 471
MacArthur Competence Assessment Tool-Treatment (MacCAT-T), 70
maintained abilities: In the Cattell-Horn model of intelligence, cognitive abilities that do not decline with age and tend to return to pre-injury levels after brain damage; contrast with vulnerable abilities, 282
mall intercept studies, 560–561
Management Progress Study (MPS), 546
Manual for Administration of Neuropsychological Test Batteries for Adults and Children (Reitan), 517
Marital Interaction Coding System, 437
Marital Satisfaction Scale (MSS), 188, 189
Marlowe-Crowne Social Desirability Scale, 190
Maslach Burnout Inventory (MBI), Third Edition, 554
MAST. *See* Michigan Alcohol Screening Test
mastery tests, 137
MAT. *See* Miller Analogies Test
matching item: A testtaker is presented with two columns: *premises* and *responses,* and must determine which response is best associated with which premise, 241
math tests, 346
MBTI. *See* Myers-Briggs Type Indicator
MCAT. *See* Medical College Admission Test
MCMI-III. *See* Million Clinical Multiaxial Inventory-III
MCT. *See* Minnesota Clerical Test
MDBS-R. *See* Morally Debatable Behaviors Scale-Revised
mean: Also called the arithmetic mean, a measure of central tendency derived by calculating an average of all scores in a distribution, 84
"Mean IQ of Americans: Massive Gains 1932 to 1978" (Flynn), 314
measurement: Assigning numbers or symbols to characteristics of people or objects according to rules, 76–77
measurement error: Collectively, all of the factors associated with the process of measuring some variable, other than the variable being measured, 142
Measurement of Attitude, The (Thurstone/Chave), 558–559
measure of central tendency: One of three statistics indicating the average or middlemost score between the extreme scores in a distribution; the mean is a measure of central tendency and a statistic at the ratio level of measurement, the median is a measure of central tendency that takes into account the order of scores and is ordinal in nature, and the mode is a measure of

central tendency that is nominal in nature, 84
measures of variability: A statistic indicating how scores in a distribution are scattered or dispersed; range, standard deviation, and variance are common measures of variability, 89–93
mechanical prediction: The application of computer algorithms together with statistical rules and probabilities to generate findings and recommendations; contrast with clinical prediction and actuarial prediction, 487
median: A measure of central tendency derived by identifying the middlemost score in a distribution, 84, 86–87
Medical College Admission Test (MCAT), 343, 344
Meier Art Judgement Test, 28
memory tests, 513–515
mental age: An index, now seldom used, that refers to the chronological age equivalent of one's performance on a test or subtest; derived by reference to norms indicating the age at which most testtakers can pass or meet some performance criterion with respect to individual or groups of items, 290
mental disorders, 450–460
  biopsychosocial assessment, 452–453
  clinical assessment interview, 453–460
  DSM-V, 454
Mental Measurement Yearbook (MMY, Buros), 33
mental status examination: A specialized interview and observation used to screen for intellectual, emotional, and neurological deficits by touching on areas such as the interviewee's appearance, behavior, memory, affect, mood, judgment, personality, thought content, thought processes, and state of consciousness, 457, 498
mental test, 38
"Mental Tests and the Immigrant" (Goddard), 42
mesokurtic: A description of the kurtosis of a distribution that is neither extremely peaked nor flat in its center, 94
meta-analysis: A family of techniques used to statistically combine information across studies to produce single estimates of the statistics being studied, 111–114
method of contrasted groups: Also referred to as the know groups method, a system of collecting data on a predictor of interest from groups known to possess (and not to possess) a trait, attribute, or ability of interest, 189–190, 226
method of paired comparisons: Scaling method whereby one of a pair of stimuli (such as photos) is selected according to a rule (such as "select the one that is more appealing"), 237
method of predictive yield: A technique for identifying cut scores based on the number of positions to be filled, 228
Metropolitan Readiness Tests-Sixth edition (MRT6), 338, 340
Michigan Alcohol Screening Test (MAST), 468

military testing, 22–23, 27, 56, 302–306
Miller Analogies Test (MAT), 343
Million Clinical Multiaxial Inventory-III (MCMI-III), 460
Mills v. Board of Education of District of Columbia, 61
Mini-Mental State Exam (MMSE), 498
minimum competency testing programs: Formal evaluation program in basic skills such as reading, writing, and arithmetic designed to aid in educational decision making that ranges from remediation to graduation, 56
Minnesota Clerical Test (MCT), 542
Minnesota Multiphasic Personality Inventory (MMPI), 384–388
  assessment structure and, 369
  clinical scales in, 385, 392–393
  criterion groups, 385
  MMPI-2, 388–390, 462–463
  MMPI-A, 394–395
  MMPI-2-RF, 390–394
  restructured clinical (RC) scales, 390–391
  revisions/progeny in perspective, 395
  supplementary scales, 387
  T scores, 390
Minnesota Teacher Attitude Survey, 559
Minnesota Vocational Interest Inventory, 526
miss rate: The proportion of people a test or other measurement procedure fails to identify accurately with respect to the possession or exhibition of a trait, behavior, characteristic, or attribute; a "miss" in this context is an inaccurate classification or prediction; may be subdivided into false positives and false negatives, 185
Mitchell v. State, 58
MMPI. *See* Minnesota Multiphasic Personality Inventory
MMSE. *See* Mini-Mental State Exam
MMY. *See* Mental Measurement Yearbook
M'Naghten standard: Also known as the "right or wrong" test of insanity, a (since replaced) standard that hinged on whether an individual knew right from wrong at the time of commission of a crime; contrast with the Durham standard and the ALI standard, 472
mode: A measure of central tendency derived by identifying the most frequently occurring score in a distribution, 84, 88–89
Model Guidelines for Preemployment Integrity Testing Programs (APTP), 534
Morally Debatable Behaviors Scale-Revised (MDBS-R), 236
moron, 45
motivation, 551–554
motivational interviewing: A therapeutic dialogue that combines person-centered listening skills such as openness and empathy with the use of cognition-altering techniques designed to positively affect motivation and effect therapeutic change, 10
motivation research methods: Tools and procedures (e.g., in-depth interviews and focus groups), typically qualitative, associated with consumer research to explore consumer attitudes, behavior, and motivation, 563–566

motor test: A general reference to a type of instrument or evaluation procedure used to obtain information about one's ability to move one's limbs, eyes, or other parts of the body (psychomotor ability) as opposed to abilities that are more strictly cognitive, behavioral, or sensory in nature, 510

MRI (magnetic resonance imaging) scans, 522

MRT6. *See* Metropolitan Readiness Tests-Sixth edition

MSS. *See* Marital Satisfaction Scale

Multiaxial Empirically Based Assessment system, 366

Multilingual Aphasia Examination, 512

multiple-choice format: Has three elements: (1) a stem, (2) a correct alternative or option, and (3) several incorrect alternatives or options variously referred to as *distractors* or *foils,* 241

multiple cut scores: The use of two or more cut scores with reference to one predictor for the purpose of categorizing testtakers into more than two groups, or the use of a different cut score for each predictor when using multiple predictors for selection, 223

multiple hurdle: A multistage decision-making process in which the achievement of a particular cut score on one test is necessary in order to advance to the next stage of evaluation in the selection process, 223

multiple regression: The analysis of relationships between more than one independent variable and one dependent variable to understand how each independent variable predicts the dependent variable, 225

multitrait-multimethod matrix: A method of evaluating construct validity by simultaneously examining both convergent and divergent evidence by means of a table of correlations between traits and methods, 190–191

muscle coordination tests, 499

Myers-Briggs Type Indicator (MBTI), 357, 533–535

narrow-band instruments, 437

National Aeronautics and Space Administration (NASA), 545

national anchor norms: An equivalency table for scores on two nationally standardized tests designed to measure the same thing, 135

National Council on Measurement in Education (NCME), 18

National Defense Education Act, 56

national norms: Norms derived from a standardization sample that was nationally representative of the population, 134

naturalistic observation: Behavioral observation that takes place in a naturally occurring setting (as opposed to a research laboratory) for the purpose of evaluation and information-gathering, 13

nature *vs.* nurture, 56, 315

Naylor-Shine tables: Statistical tables once widely used to assist in judging the utility of a particular test, 215

NCCEA. *See* Neurosensory Center Comprehensive Examination of Aphasia

NCLB. *See* No Child Left Behind Act

NCME. *See* National Council on Measurement in Education

need: According to personality theorist Henry Murray, determinants of behavior arising from within the individual; contrast with the Murrayan concept of press, 413

negative (inverse) correlation, 102

negatively skewed distribution, 86

negative skew: Relatively few scores in a distribution fall at the low end, 93

neglect: Failure on the part of an adult responsible for the care of another to exercise a minimum degree of care in providing food, clothing, shelter, education, medical care, and supervision; contrast with abuse, 479–481

NEO Personality Inventory (NEO-PI), 381–382

revised (NEO PI-R), 375, 381, 534

nervous system, 489–493

neurodevelopment training ball, 28

neurological damage: Impairment, injury, harm, or loss of function of any part or process of the central or peripheral nervous systems, 491

neurology: A branch of medicine that focuses on the nervous system and its disorders; contrast with neuropsychology, 489

neuron: Nerve cell, 489

neuropsychological assessment: The evaluation of brain and nervous system functioning as it relates to behavior, 489–523

defined, 489

executive function tests, 507–510

general intellectual ability tests, 504–506

medical diagnostic aids, 520–521

memory tests, 513–515

nervous system and behavior, 489–493

neuropsychological evaluation, 493–498

neuropsychological tests, 504–519

perceptual/motor/perceptual-motor tests, 510–512

test batteries, 515–519

verbal functioning tests, 512

neuropsychological mental status examination: A general clinical evaluation designed to sample and check for various possible deficiencies in brain-behavior functioning, 498

neuropsychology: A branch of psychology that focuses on the relationship between brain functioning and behavior; contrast with neurology, 489

Neurosensory Center Comprehensive Examination of Aphasia (NCCEA), 519

neurotology: A branch of medicine that focuses on problems relating to hearing, balance, and facial nerves, 489

neurotransmitter: A chemical facilitator of communication between neurons, 500

No Child Left Behind Act (NCLB, 2001), 55, 317–318

nominal scale: A system of measurement in which all things measured are classified or categorized based on one or more distinguishing characteristics and placed into mutually exclusive and exhaustive categories, 77–78

nominating technique, 351

nomothetic approach: An approach to assessment characterized by efforts to learn how a limited number of personality traits can be applied to all people; contrast with idiographic approach, 374

noninvasive procedures: A method of evaluation or treatment that does not involve intrusion (by surgical procedure, X-ray, or other means) into the body; for example, in a neuropsychological evaluation, observation of the client walking or skipping, 498

nonlinear transformation: In psychometrics, a process of changing a score such that (a) the new score does not necessarily have a direct numerical relationship to the original score and (b) the magnitude of the differences between the new score and the other scores on the scale may not parallel the magnitude of differences between the original score and the other scores on the scales from which the original score was derived; contrast with linear transformation, 100

nonverbal communication, 48–49

normal curve: A bell-shaped, smooth, mathematically defined curve highest at the center and gradually tapered on both sides, approaching but never actually touching the horizontal axis, 86, 95–98

normalized standard score scale: Conceptually, the end product of "stretching" a skewed distribution into the shape of a normal curve, usually through nonlinear transformation, 100–101

normalizing a distribution: A statistical correction applied to distributions meeting certain criteria for the purpose of approximating a normal distribution, thus making the data more readily comprehensible or manipulable, 100

normative approach, 374

normative sample: Also referred to as a norm group, a group of people presumed to be representative of the universe of people who may take a particular test and whose performance data on that test may be used as a reference source or context for evaluating individual test scores, 126, 131–132

norming: The process of deriving or creating norms, 126

norm-referenced cut score: Also referred to as a relative cut score, a reference point in a distribution of test scores used to divide a set of data into two classifications based on norm-related considerations rather than on the relationship of test scores to a criterion, 222

norm-referenced evaluation, 136–138

norm-referenced testing and assessment: A method of evaluation and a way of deriving meaning from test scores by evaluating an individual testtaker's score and comparing it to scores of a group of testtakers on the same test; contrast with criterion-referenced testing and assessment

criterion-referenced testing vs., 136–138

defined, 123

item development issues, 233–234

norms: The test performance data of a group of testtakers, designed as a reference for evaluating, interpreting, or otherwise placing in context individual test scores; also referred to as normative data, 132–135
  age norms, 132–133
  defined, 123
  fixed reference group scoring systems, 135–136
  grade norms, 133–134
  local norms, 126
  national anchor norms, 134–135
  national norms, 134
  percentiles, 132
  sampling and, 126–132
  subgroup norms, 135

OAT. *See* Optometry Admission Test
objective personality test: A test consisting of short-answer items wherein the assessee's task is to select one response from the two or more provided and all scoring is done according to set procedures involving little if any judgment on the part of the scorer, 401–402
observer reliability, 156
obsessive passion, 527n1
O'Connor Tweezer Dexterity Test, 528
ODDA. *See* Oregon's Death with Dignity Act
odd-even reliability: An estimate of split-half reliability of a test, obtained by assigning odd-numbered items to one-half of the test and even-numbered items to the other half, 150
Office of Strategic Services (OSS), 2, 303, 369, 439, 543–544
Officer Qualifying Test, 303
online databases: Bibliographic databases for test-related publications, 33–34
online surveys, 560–561
On the Origin of Species by Means of Natural Selection (Darwin), 37
optional subtest: Also referred to as an optional subtest, one of a test's subtests that may be used either for purposes of providing additional information or in place of a core subtest if, for any reason, the use of a score on a core subtest would be questionable; contrast with core subtest, 297
Optometry Admission Test (OAT), 344
ordinal scales: A system of measurement in which all things measured can be rank-ordered, where the rank-ordering implies nothing about exactly how much greater one ranking is than another and there is no absolute zero point on the scale; most scales in psychology and education are ordinal, 78–79
Oregon's Death with Dignity Act (ODDA), 65–66
organic brain syndrome, 492
organic deficit: in neuropsychology, any sensory, motor, or cognitive impairment known to have a structural or physical origin; contrast with functional deficit, 494
organicity: An abbreviated reference to organic brain damage and to one of the varieties of functional consequences that attends such damage, 492

organismic assessment: Evaluation of the total person through a series of varied tests and tasks over the course of several sessions so candidates can be evaluated on the basis of data derived from the full range of assessments, considered as a whole, 543
organizational commitment: The strength of an individual's identification with and involvement in a particular organization, 555–556
organizational credentialing, 23
organizational culture: The totality of socially transmitted behavior patterns characteristic of an organization or company, including the structure of the organization and the roles within it, the leadership style, the prevailing values, norms, sanctions, and support mechanisms as well as the traditions and folklore, methods of enculturation, and characteristic ways of interacting with people and institutions outside the culture (such as customers, suppliers, competition, government agencies, and the general public), 556–557
orientation: A three-part element of the mental status examination consisting of orientation to self (if the interviewee knows who he or she is), place (where the interview is taking place), and time (the date of the interview); interviewees oriented to person, place, and time are said to be "oriented times 3," 458
originality, 307
OSS. *See* Office of Strategic Services
Otis-Lennon School Ability Test, 306
outlier: (1) An extremely atypical plot point in a scatterplot; (2) any extremely atypical finding in research, 110
overt behavior: An observable action or the product of an observable action, including test-or assessment-related responses, 116
overt integrity tests, 534

panel interview: Also referred to as a board interview, an interview conducted with one interviewee by more than one interviewer at a time, 10
parallel forms: Two or more versions or forms of the same test where, for each form, the means and variances of observed test scores are equal; contrast with alternate forms, 149
parallel-forms reliability: An estimate of the extent to which item sampling and other errors have affected test scores on two versions of the same test when, for each form of the test, the means and variances of observed test scores are equal; contrast with alternate-forms reliability, 149–150
parallel processing: Also called simultaneous processing; based on Luria's writings, a type of information processing whereby information is integrated and synthesized all at once and as a whole; contrast with successive processing, 285
PARC v. Commonwealth of Pennsylvania, 61
parent evaluation, custody proceedings, 476–477
Parenting Stress Index (PSI), 481

Parkinson's disease: A progressive, neurological illness that is characterized by disorders of movement such as tremors, muscle rigidity, slowness of movement, and problems with balance and coordination, 500–504
parole/probation readiness, 474–475
passion, 527n1
PASS model: Information-processing model developed by Luria; PASS stands for planning, attention, simultaneous, and successive, 285
pattern analysis: Study of the pattern of test scores on a Wechsler or other test in order to identify a pattern associated with a diagnosis (e.g., neurological deficit in the right hemisphere), 504
PCAT. *See* Pharmacy College Admission Test
PCL. *See* Psychopathy Checklist
PCL-R. *See* Revised Psychopathy Checklist
Pearson r: Also known as the Pearson coefficient of product-moment correlation and the Pearson correlation coefficient, a widely used statistic for obtaining an index of the relationship between two variables when that relationship is linear and when the two correlated variables are continuous (i.e., theoretically can take any value), 104–106
peer appraisal: A method of obtaining evaluation-related information about an individual by polling that individual's friends, classmates, work colleagues, or other peers, 351–352
peer ratings/evaluations, 550
penile plethysmograph: An instrument, used in the assessment and treatment of male sex offenders, designed to measure changes in penis volume as a function of sexual arousal, 17, 440–441
people with disabilities, 29–30, 65
PEP. *See* Proficiency Examination Program
percentage correct: On a test with responses that are scored correct or incorrect, an expression of the number of items answered correctly, multiplied by 100 and divided by the total number of items; contrast with percentile, 132
percentile: An expression of the percentage of people whose score on a test or measure falls below a particular raw score, or a converted score that refers to a percentage of testtakers; contrast with percentage correct, 132
percentile norms: The raw data from a test's standardization sample converted to percentile form, 132
percept: A perception of an image (typically used with reference to the Rorschach Inkblot Test), 405
perceptual-motor test: A general reference to any of many instruments and procedures used to evaluate the integration or coordination of sensory and motor abilities, 510
perceptual test: A general reference to any of many instruments and procedures used to evaluate varied aspects of sensory functioning, including aspects of sight, hearing, smell, touch, taste, and balance, 510

performance assessment: An evaluation of performance tasks according to criteria developed by experts from the domain of study tapped by those tasks, 349–351

performance-based assessment: Also known as authentic assessment, evaluation on relevant, meaningful tasks that may be conducted to examine learning of academic subject matter but that demonstrates the student's transfer of that study to real-world activities, 350–351

performance task or test: (1) In general, a work sample designed to elicit representative knowledge, skills, and values from a particular domain of study; (2) in employment settings, an instrument or procedure that requires the assessee to demonstrate certain job-related skills or abilities under conditions identical or analogous to conditions on the job, 349–350, 541–542

peripheral nervous system: All of the nerve cells that convey neural messages to and from the body except those nerve cells of the brain and spinal cord; contrast with the central nervous system, 489

Personal Data Sheet, 40, 377, 386

personal interview stage, 223

personality: An individual's unique constellation of psychological traits and states, including aspects of values, interests, attitudes, worldview, acculturation, sense of personal identity, sense of humor, cognitive and behavioral styles, and related characteristics, 40–41, 355, 533–536

personality assessment: The measurement and evaluation of psychological traits, states, values, interests, attitudes, worldview, acculturation, personal identity, sense of humor, cognitive and behavioral styles, and/or related individual characteristics, 354–447
  behavioral assessment methods, 429–444
    (*See also* behavioral assessment methods)
  criterion groups, 383–395
  culture, and, 395–399
  data reduction methods, 380–383
  defined, 355
  dichotomy, 428
  drawings, 422–425
  of gorillas, 361–362
  how?, 368–377, 434–435
  inkblot, 404–410
  logic/reason, 377–380
  objective methods, 401–402
  personality, and, 354–359
  pictures, as projective stimuli, 410–418
  projective methods, 402–429
  sounds, as projective stimuli, 421–422
  TAT, 411–415
  theory, 380
  traits, 355–359
  what?, 366–367, 432
  when?, 432–434
  where?, 368, 434
  who?, 360–366, 431–432
  words, as projective stimuli, 418–421

personality-based measures, 534

Personality Inventory for Children (PIC), 364

personality profile: A description, graph, or table representing the extent to which a person has demonstrated a particular pattern of traits and states, 358

Personality Projection in the Drawing of the Human Figure (Machover), 422–423

personality states, 359

personality test battery, 461

personality trait: Any distinguishable, relatively enduring way in which one individual varies from another, 355–359

personality type: A constellation of traits and states that is similar in pattern to one identified category of personality within a taxonomy of personalities, 356–358

personnel selection, 548–549

PET (positron emission tomography) scan: A tool of nuclear medicine particularly useful in diagnosing biochemical lesions in the brain, 520

phallometric data: the record from a study conducted using a penile plethysmograph with a male testtaker that is indicative of penile tumescense in response to stimuli, 441

Pharmacy College Admission Test (PCAT), 344

physical examination, 498–499

physical signs of abuse and neglect: Take the form of physical injuries, 479

physical test: A measurement that entails evaluation of one's somatic health and intactness, and observable sensory and motor abilities, 546–548

Piaget's stages of cognitive development, 275

PIC. *See* Personality Inventory for Children

picture absurdity item: A type of test item that presents the testtaker with the task of identifying what is wrong or silly about a stimulus image, 510

pictures, as projective stimuli, 410–418

Piers-Harris Self-Concept Scale, 362

pilot work: Also referred to as pilot study and pilot research, the preliminary research surrounding the creation of a prototype test; a general objective of pilot work is to determine how best to measure, gauge, assess, or evaluate the targeted construct(s), 234

PL 94-142, 57, 333

placement: A disposition, transfer, or assignment to a group or category that may be made on the basis of one criterion, 539

platykurtic: A description of the kurtosis of a distribution that is relatively flat in its center, 94

plethysmograph: An instrument that records changes in the volume of a part of the body arising from variations in blood supply, 440

PMAs. *See* primary mental abilities

point scale: A test with items organized into subtests by category of item; contrast with age scale, 291

political correctness, 182

poll: A type of survey used to record votes, usually containing questions that can be answered with a "yes-no" or "for-against" response, typically used to gauge opinion about issues, 560

polygraph: The instrument popularly known as a lie detector, 441

polytomous test item: A test item or question with three or more alternative responses, where only one alternative is scored correct or scored as being consistent with a targeted trait or other construct, 167

portfolio: A work sample; referred to as portfolio assessment when used as a tool in an evaluative or diagnostic process, 11–12, 350

portfolio assessment: The evaluation of one's work samples, 349–351, 541

positive (direct) correlation, 102

positively skewed distribution, 86

positive skew: When relatively few of the scores fall at the high end of the distribution, 93

positron emission tomography scan. *See* PET scan

post-traumatic stress disorder (PTSD), 464–467

power test: A test, usually of achievement or ability, with (1) either no time limit or such a long time limit that all testtakers can attempt all items and (2) some items so difficult that no testtaker can obtain a perfect score; contrast with speed test, 161

predictive validity: A form of criterion-related validity that is an index of the degree to which a test score predicts some criterion measure, 184–186

premorbid functioning: The level of psychological and physical performance prior to the development of a disorder, an illness, or a disability, 449

preschool level aptitude tests, 333–338

press: According to personality theorist Henry Murray, determinants of behavior arising from within the environment; contrast with the Murrayan concept of need, 413

prevalence: The approximate proportion of individuals in a given population at a given point (or range) in time who have been diagnosed or labeled with a particular disorder or condition; contrast with incidence, 450

primary mental abilities (PMAs), 275–276

privacy, 71–73

privacy right: The freedom of people to choose the time, circumstances, and extent to which they wish to share or withhold from others personal beliefs, opinions, and behavior; contrast with confidentiality, 71

privileged information: Data protected by law from disclosure in a legal proceeding; typically, exceptions to privilege are also noted in law; contrast with confidential information, 71

probation/parole readiness, 474–475

problem-solving model: As used in the context of RtI, the use of interventions tailored to students' individual needs that are selected by a multidisciplinary team of school professionals, 324. *See also* response to intervention model

procedural memory: Memory for how to do certain things or perform certain functions; contrast with declarative memory, 513

productivity: Output or value yielded relative to work effort, 549–550

productivity gain: A net increase in work output, which in utility analyses may be estimated through the use of a particular test or other evaluative procedure, 216

product-moment coefficient of correlation, 106

professional books: Are written for an audience of assessment professionals and are available to supplement, reorganize, or enhance the information typically found in the manual of a very widely used psychological test, 32–33

professional concerns, 63–69

Proficiency Examination Program (PEP), 330

profile: A narrative description, graph, table, or other representation of the extent to which a person has demonstrated certain targeted characteristics as a result of the administration or application of tools of assessment; also (a verb) to profile, 358

profile analysis: The interpretation of patterns of scores on a test or test battery, frequently used to generate diagnostic hypotheses from intelligence test data, 358n1

profiler: An occupation associated with law enforcement; one who creates psychological profiles of crime suspects to help law enforcement personnel capture the profiled suspect, 358n1

profiling: Referred to by the FBI as "criminal investigative analysis," a crime-solving process that draws upon psychological and criminological expertise applied to the study of crime-scene evidence, 475–476

prognostic test: A tool of assessment used to predict; sometimes synonymous with aptitude test, 332

program norms. *See* user norms

projective hypothesis: The thesis that an individual supplies structure to unstructured stimuli in a manner consistent with the individual's own unique pattern of conscious and unconscious needs, fears, desires, impulses, conflicts, and ways of perceiving and responding, 403

projective method: A technique of personality assessment in which some judgment of the assessee's personality is made on the basis of his or her performance on a task that involves supplying structure to relatively unstructured or incomplete stimuli, 402–429

assumptions of, 425–427
defined, 403
figure drawings, 422–425
inkblots, 404–410
objective tests and, 428–429
pictures, 410–418
psychometric considerations, 428
situational variables, 427–428
sounds, 421–422
words, 418–421

projective test: When an individual is assumed to "project" onto some ambiguous stimulus his or her own unique needs, fears, hopes, and motivation, 41

projective test battery, 461

Proposition 209, 549

protocol: (1) The form or sheet on which testtakers' responses are entered; (2) a method or procedure for evaluation or scoring, 26

Proverbs Test, 506

pseudobulbar affect (PBA): A neurological disorder characterized by frequent and involuntary outbursts of laughing or crying that may or may not be appropriate to the situation, 247

pseudodementia: A loss of cognitive functioning that mimics dementia but that is not due to the loss or damage of brain cells, 22, 496

PSI. *See* Parenting Stress Index

PsycARTICLES, 33

psychasthenia, 385–386, 386n4

PsychCorp, 39n2

psychoanalysis: A theory of personality and psychological treatment originally developed by Sigmund Freud, 49

Psychodiagnostics (Rorschach), 404

psychoeducational assessment: Psychological evaluation in a school or other setting, usually conducted to diagnose, remedy, or measure academic or social progress or to otherwise enrich a student's education, 283

psychoeducational test battery: A packaged kit containing tests that measure educational achievement and abilities related to academic success, 346–348

defined, 346
K-ABC/KABC-II, 346–348
WJ III, 348

psychological assessment: The gathering and integrating of psychological data for psychological evaluation, through the use of tests, interviews, case studies, behavioral observation, and specially designed apparatuses and measurement procedures; contrast with psychological testing, 1–7. *See also* clinical assessment; educational assessment; neuropsychological assessment; personality assessment

psychological assessor, 2

psychological autopsy: A reconstruction of a deceased individual's psychological profile on the basis of archival records, artifacts, and interviews with the assessee while living or with people who knew the deceased, 19

Psychological Corporation, 39, 39n2

psychological report: An archival document describing findings as a result of psychological testing or assessment, Barnum effect in, 484–488

psychological test: A measuring device or procedure designed to measure psychology-related variables, 7, 95–96, 336–337, 460–462

psychological testing: The measuring of psychology-related variables by means of devices or procedures designed to obtain samples of behavior, 2, 218–219

Psychological Tests and Personnel Decisions (Cronbach & Gleser), 218

psychological test user, 2

psychological trait, 115–116

psychologist–client relationship, 71–72

psychometrician: A professional in testing and assessment who typically holds a doctoral degree in psychology or education and specializes in areas such as individual differences, quantitative psychology, or theory of assessment; contrast with psychometrist, 8

psychometrics: The science of psychological measurement (synonymous with the antiquated term psychometry), 8

psychometric soundness: The technical quality of a test or other tool of assessment

behavioral assessment, 442
burnout measurement, 554
defined, 8
figure-drawing tests, 425
Holtzman Inkblot Technique, 407n3
projective methods of personality assessment, 428
Rorschach, 407–408
SB5, 295
Thematic Apperception Test, 413
utility, 201–202
WAIS-IV, 299

psychometrist: A professional in testing and assessment who typically holds a master's degree in psychology or education and is qualified to administer specific tests; contrast with psychometrician, 8

psychopath: A diagnosis that describes individuals with few inhibitions who may pursue pleasure or money with callous disregard for the welfare of others, 475

Psychopathy Checklist (PCL), 475

psychophysiological methods: Techniques for monitoring physiological changes known to be influenced by psychological factors, such as heart rate and blood pressure, 440–441

PsycINFO: An online electronic database, maintained by the American Psychological Association and leased to institutional users, designed to help individuals locate relevant documents from psychology, education, nursing, social work, law, medicine, and other disciplines, 33

PsycLAW, 33

PsycSCAN: Psychopharmacology, 33

public concerns, 55–63

Public Law (PL), 57, 333

public policy, 54–55

Purdue Pegboard Test, 511

purposive sampling: The arbitrary selection of people to be part of a sample because they are thought to be representative of the population being studied, 130

Q-Interactive, 15

Q-sort technique: An assessment technique in which the task is to sort a group of statements, usually in perceived rank order ranging from "most descriptive" to "least descriptive"; the statements, traditionally presented on index cards, may be sorted in ways that reflect various perceptions, such as how respondents see themselves or would like to see themselves, 371–373

qualitative item analysis: A general term for various nonstatistical procedures designed to explore how individual test items work, both compared to other items in the test and in the context of the whole test; in contrast to statistically based procedures, qualitative methods involve exploration of the issues by verbal means such as interviews and group discussions conducted with testtakers and other relevant parties, 258–260

qualitative methods: Techniques of data generation and analysis that rely primarily on mathematical or statistical rather than verbal procedures, 258

quality assurance, test revision, 265–266

quality of life: In psychological assessment, an evaluation of variables such as perceived stress, loneliness, sources of satisfaction, personal values, quality of living conditions, and quality of friendships and other social support, 22

Quality of School Life Scales, 352

quartile: One of three dividing points between the four quarters of a distribution, each typically labeled Q1, Q2, or Q3, 90

quota system: A selection procedure whereby a fixed number or percentage of applicants with certain characteristics or from certain backgrounds are selected regardless of other factors such as documented ability, 59

race norming: The controversial practice of norming on the basis of race or ethnic background, 126

racial differences in testing, 59

random error: A source of error in measuring a targeted variable, caused by unpredictable fluctuations and inconsistencies of other variables in the measurement process; contrast with systematic error, 142

range: A descriptive statistic of variability derived by calculating the difference between the highest and lowest scores in a distribution, 90

rank-difference correlation coefficient. *See* Spearman's rho

ranking: The ordinal ordering of persons, scores, or variables into relative positions or degrees of value, 195

rank-order correlation coefficient. *See* Spearman's rho

rapid eye movement sleep behavior disorder: A condition characterized by an "acting out" of dreams with vocalizations or gestures, 502

rapport: A working relationship between examiner and examinee in testing or assessment, 26

Rasch model: Is a reference to an IRT model with very specific assumptions about the underlying distribution, 167

RAT. *See* Remote Associates Test

rating: A numerical or verbal judgment that places a person or attribute along a continuum identified by a scale of numerical or word descriptors called a rating scale, 194

rating error: A judgment that results from the intentional or unintentional misuse of a rating scale; two types of rating error are leniency error (or generosity error) and severity error, 194–195

rating scale: A system of ordered numerical or verbal descriptors on which judgments about the presence/absence or magnitude of a particular trait, attitude, emotion, or other variable are indicated by raters, judges, examiners, or (when the rating scale reflects self-report) the assessee, 194, 236, 334

ratio IQ: An index of intelligence derived from the ratio of the testtaker's mental age (as calculated from a test) divided by his or her chronological age and multiplied by 100 to eliminate decimals, 290–291

ratio scale: A system of measurement in which all things measured can be rank-ordered, the rank ordering does imply something about exactly how much greater one ranking is than another, equal intervals exist between each number on the scale, and all mathematical operations can be performed meaningfully because a true or absolute zero point exists; few scales in psychology or education are ratio scales, 79–80

raw score: A straightforward, unmodified accounting of performance, usually numerical and typically used for evaluation or diagnosis, 81

RCRAS. *See* Rogers Criminal Responsibility Assessment Scale

RC scales. *See* restructured clinical scales

reacculturation: Recovery from drug addiction that results in a new sense of identity, 468

reactivity: Changes in an assessee's behavior, thinking, or performance that arise in response to being observed, assessed, or evaluated, 437–438

readiness test: A tool of assessment designed to evaluate whether an individual has the requisites to begin a program or perform a task; sometimes synonymous with aptitude test, 333

reading tests, 345–346

reasonable boundaries, 175

recommendation letters, 540–541

rectangular distribution, 86

reference sources, 30–35

reference volumes: Authoritative compilation of test reviews that is currently updated about every three years and provides detailed information for each test listed, 33

reflex: Involuntary motor response to a stimulus, 499

Regents of the University of California v. Bakke, 57

Reitan-Indiana Aphasia Screening Test (AST), 512

relative cut score: Also referred to as a norm-referenced cut score, a reference point in a distribution of test scores used to divide a set of data into two classifications based on norm-related considerations rather than on the relationship of test scores to a criterion, 222

reliability: The extent to which measurements are consistent or repeatable; also, the extent to which measurements differ from occasion to occasion as a function of measurement error, 141–174

average proportional distance (APD), 154–156

coefficient (*See* reliability coefficient)

coefficient alpha, 154

coefficient of, 158–167

concept of, 141–145

defined, 142

error variance sources, 143–145

individual scores, 169–174

instructor-made tests for in-class use, 271

inter-scorer reliability, 156

Kuder-Richardson formulas, 152–154

parallel-forms/alternate forms reliability estimates, 149–150

split-half reliability estimates, 150–151

test criteria, 122

test-retest reliability, 145–146

reliability coefficient: General term for an index of reliability or the ratio of true score variance on a test to the total variance

classical test theory (CTT), 163

defined, 141

domain sampling theory, 164–166

generalizability theory, 164–166

item response theory, 166–169

nature of test, 160–163

purpose of, 159

remote assessment; The use of tools of psychological evaluation to gather data and draw conclusions about a subject who is not in physical proximity to the person or people conducting the evaluation, 4

Remote Associates Test (RAT), 308

replicability crisis, 147–148

resolver, 266

response-contingent testing, 294

response style: A tendency to respond to a test item or interview question in some characteristic manner regardless of content; for example, an acquiescent response style (a tendency to agree) and a socially desirable response style (a tendency to present oneself in a favorable or socially desirable way), 366–367

response to intervention model (RtI): A multilevel prevention framework applied in educational settings that is designed to maximize student achievement through the use of data that identifies students at risk for poor learning outcomes combined with evidence-based intervention and teaching that is adjusted on the basis of student responsiveness, 320, 323–324. *See also* problem-solving model

restriction of range/variance: Also referred to as restriction of variance, a phenomenon associated with reliability estimates wherein the variance of either variable in a correlational analysis is restricted by the sampling procedure used and so the resulting correlation coefficient tends to be lower; contrast with inflation of range, 161 restructured clinical (RC) scales, 392–393

résumé, 539

retrospective assessment: The use of evaluative tools to draw conclusions about psychological aspects of a person as they existed at some point in time prior to the assessment, 4

return on investment: A ratio of the economic and/or noneconomic benefits derived from expenditures to initiate or improve a particular testing program, training program, or intervention as compared to all of the costs of the initiative or improvements, 214

reverse discrimination (in Title VII litigation): The practice of making distinctions in hiring, promotion, or other selection decisions that systematically tend to favor members of a minority group regardless of actual qualifications for positions, 60

Revised NEO Personality Inventory (NEO PI-R), 375, 381, 534

Revised Psychopathy Checklist (PCL-R), 475

Ricci v. DeStefano, 58

right or wrong test of insanity. *See* M'Naghten standard

rights of testtakers, 69–73

Rogers Criminal Responsibility Assessment Scale (RCRAS), 474

Rokeach Value Survey, 78

role play: Acting an improvised or partially improvised part in a simulated situation, 13, 439–440

role-play test: An assessment tool wherein assessees are instructed to act as if they were placed in a particular situation, 13–14

Romberg test, 499

Rorschach Inkblot Test, 8, 404–410

Rosenzweig Picture-Frustration Study, 417–418

Rotter Incomplete Sentences Blank, 420

routing test: A subtest used to direct or route the testtaker to a suitable level of items, 293

RtI model. *See* response to intervention model

Rule 702 in *Federal Rules of Evidence,* 62

SADS. *See* Schedule for Affective Disorders and Schizophrenia

SAI. *See* School Ability Index

sample: A group of people presumed to be representative of the total population or universe of people being studied or tested, 129

sampling: A general reference to the process of developing a sample, 129

SAT, 34, 135–136, 340–341

SATB. *See* Special Aptitude Test Battery

SB5. *See* Stanford-Binet Intelligence Scale

SB:FE. *See* Stanford-Binet Fourth Edition

scale: (1) A system of ordered numerical or verbal descriptors, usually occurring at fixed intervals, used as a reference standard in measurement; (2) a set of numbers or other symbols whose properties model empirical properties of the objects or traits to which numbers or other symbols are assigned, 76

scales of measurement, 76–80
    interval scales, 79–80
    nominal scales, 77–78
    ordinal scales, 78–79
    in psychology, 79–80
    ratio scales, 79

scaling: (1) In test construction, the process of setting rules for assigning numbers in measurement; (2) the process by which a measuring device is designed and calibrated and the way numbers (or other indices that are scale values) are assigned to different amounts of the trait, attribute, or characteristic measured; (3) assigning numbers in accordance with empirical properties of objects or traits, 234–239
    categorical, 238
    comparative, 238
    defined, 234
    Guttman scale, 238
    Likert scale, 237
    MDBS-R, 236
    methods, 236–239
    scale types, 235

scalogram analysis: An item-analysis procedure and approach to test development that entails a graphic mapping of a testtaker's responses, 238

scattergram. *See* bivariate distribution

scatterplot: Also referred to as a scatter diagram, a graphic description of correlation achieved by graphing the coordinate points for the two variables, 107–110

Schedule for Affective Disorders and Schizophrenia (SADS), 454

Scholastic Aptitude Test (SAT). *See* SAT

School Ability Index (SAI), 306

SCID. *See* Structured Clinical Interview for DSM-IV

SCII. *See* Strong-Campbell Interest Inventory

scope of evaluations, 368–369

score: A code or summary statement— usually but not necessarily numerical—that reflects an evaluation of the performance on a test, task, interview, or other sample of behavior, 8. *See also* test score

scorer reliability, 156

scoring: The process of assigning evaluative codes or statements to performance on tests, tasks, interviews, or other behavior samples, 8

scoring drift: A discrepancy between the scoring in an anchor protocol and the scoring of another protocol, 266

scoring/interpretation procedures, 8, 374–375

scoring items, 246

scoring report: A formal or official computer-generated account of test performance, usually represented numerically; the two varieties are the simple scoring report (containing only a report of the scores) and the extended scoring report (containing item statistics); contrast with interpretive report and integrative report, 15

screening: A relatively superficial process of evaluation based on certain minimal standards, criteria, or requirements; contrast with selection, classification, and placement, 538

screening tool: (1) An instrument or procedure used to identify a particular trait or constellation of traits at a gross or imprecise level, as opposed to a test of greater precision used for more definitive diagnosis or evaluation; (2) in preschool assessment, an instrument or procedure used as a first step in identifying a child who is "at risk" or not functioning within normal limits; (3) in employment settings, an instrument or procedure used as a gross measure to determine who meets minimum requirements set by the employer, 303

SDMT4. *See* Stanford Diagnostic Mathematics Test, Fourth Edition

SDS. *See* Self-Directed Search

Seashore Bennett Stenographic Proficiency Test, 541

Seashore Measures of Musical Talents, 343

secondary-school level aptitude tests, 340–341

second moments of the distribution, 106

second-order factors, 278

second-order meta-analysis: a meta-analysis that summarizes two or more other meta-analyses, 536

selected-response format: A form of test item requiring testtakers to select a response (e.g., true-false, multiple-choice, and matching items) as opposed to constructing or creating one; contrast with constructed-response format, 240

selection: A process whereby each person evaluated for a position is either accepted or rejected; contrast with screening, classification, and placement, 539

selection ratio: A numerical value that reflects the relationship between the number of people to be hired and the number of people available to be hired, 214

self-concept: One's attitudes, beliefs, opinions, and related thoughts about oneself, 362

self-concept differentiation: The degree to which an individual has different self-concepts in different roles, 363

self-concept measure: An instrument designed to yield information about how an individual sees him-or herself with regard to selected psychological variables, the data from which are usually interpreted in the context of how others may see themselves on the same or similar variables, 362

Self-Directed Search (SDS), 526

self-efficacy: Confidence in one's own ability to accomplish a task, 453

Self-Help Agency Satisfaction Scale, 559

self-monitoring: The act of systematically observing and recording aspects of one's own behavior and/or events related to that behavior, 437–438

self-report: The process wherein an assessee supplies personal information in forms such as responding to questions, keeping a diary, or reporting on self-monitored thoughts and/or behaviors, 41, 360

Self-Report of Personality (SRP), 336

SEM. *See* standard error of measurement

semantic differential technique: An item format characterized by bipolar adjectives separated by a seven-point rating scale on which respondents select one point to indicate their response, 372, 562

semantic memory: Memory for facts; contrast with episodic memory, 513

semi-interquartile range: A measure of variability equal to the interquartile range divided by 2, 91

Sensation-Seeking Scale (SSS), 117

sensitivity review: A study of test items, usually during test development, in which items are examined for fairness to all prospective testtakers and for the presence of offensive language, stereotypes, or situations, 259

sentence completion: A task in which the assessee is asked to finish an incomplete sentence or phrase, 420

sentence completion format, 373–374

sentence completion stem: All the words that make up the part of a sentence completion item, not including the blank space to be completed by the testtaker, 420

sentence completion test: A projective tool of assessment that contains a series of incomplete phrases wherein the task of the assessee is to insert a word or words that will make each of the phrases a complete sentence, 420–421

sequential processing: Also referred to as sequential processing; based on Luria's writings, a type of information processing whereby information is processed in a sequential, bit-by-bit fashion and arranged and rearranged until it is logical; contrast with simultaneous processing, 285

sequential testing, 294

Sequential Tests of Educational Progress (STEP) battery, 328

7 Minute Screen, 498

Severe Impairment Battery (SIB), 519

severity error: Less than accurate rating or error in evaluation due to the rater's tendency to be overly critical; contrast with generosity error, 195, 364

Sexual Desire Inventory (SDI), 232

s factor, 435–436

shelf esteem, 558n3

shifting cultural lenses, 463

short-answer item: Requires the examinee to provide a word or phrase that completes a sentence, 243

short form: An abbreviated version of a test that has typically been reduced in number of items from the original, usually to reduce the time needed for test administration, scoring, and/or interpretation, 300–301

Short Portable Mental Status Questionnaire, 498

short-term memory, 513

SIB. See Severe Impairment Battery

SII. See Strong Interest Inventory

simple frequency distribution, 82

simple scoring report: A type of scoring report that provides only a listing of scores, 15

simultaneous processing: Also called parallel processing; based on Luria's writings, a type of information processing whereby information is integrated and synthesized all at once and as a whole; contrast with successive processing, 285

single photon emission computed tomography. See SPECT

SIRS-2. See Structured Interview of Reported Symptoms-2

situational performance measure: A procedure that typically involves the performance of a task by the assessee under actual or simulated conditions while allowing for observation and evaluation by an assessor, 439

Sixteen Personality Factor (16 PF) Questionnaire, 374, 381

skewness: An indication of the nature and extent to which symmetry is absent in a distribution; a distribution is said to be skewed positively when relatively few scores fall at the positive end and skewed negatively when relatively few scores fall at the negative end, 93–94

SLD. See specific learning disability

smartphones, 5–6

S.O.B. (Son of the Original BITCH) Test, 312

Social Situation Picture Test, 410–411

social support: Expressions of understanding, acceptance, empathy, love, advice, guidance, care, concern, or trust from friends, family, community caregivers, or others in one's social environment, 453

sociogram: A graphic representation of peer appraisal data or other interpersonal information, 351

soft sign: In neuropsychological assessment, an indication that neurological deficit may be present; for example, a significant discrepancy between Verbal and Performance subtests on a Wechsler test, 494

Song dynasty, 36–37

sounds, as projective stimuli, 421–422

Southern California Sensory Integration Tests, 519

Spearman-Brown formula: An equation used to estimate internal consistency reliability from a correlation of two halves of a test that has been lengthened or shortened; inappropriate for use with heterogeneous tests or speed tests, 150–151

Spearman's rho: Also referred to as the rank-order correlation coefficient and the rank-difference correlation coefficient, this index of correlation may be the statistic of choice when the sample size is small and both sets of measurements are ordinal, 106–107

Special Aptitude Test Battery (SATB), 529, 531

specific learning disability (SLD): A disorder in one or more of the basic psychological processes involved in understanding or using language, spoken or written, that may manifest itself in the imperfect ability to listen, think, speak, read, write, spell, or perform mathematical calculations, 320

SPECT (single photon emission computed tomography): A technology that records the course of a radioactive tracer fluid (iodine) and produces exceptionally clear photographs of organs and tissues, 520, 521

speed test: A test, usually of achievement or ability, with a time limit; speed tests usually contain items of uniform difficulty level, 161–162, 258

split-half reliability: An estimate of the internal consistency of a test obtained by correlating two pairs of scores obtained from equivalent halves of a single test administered once, 150–151

Sputnik launch, 56

SRA California Achievement Tests, 328

SRP. See Self-Report of Personality

SSHA. See Survey of Study Habits and Attitudes

SSS. See Sensation-Seeking Scale

STAI. See State-Trait Anxiety Inventory

standard, 127–129

standard battery: The administration of a group of at least three different types of tests for the purpose of evaluating different spheres of functioning: Usually an intelligence test, a personality test, and a neuropsychological test, 461

standard deviation: A measure of variability equal to the square root of the averaged squared deviations about the mean; a measure of variability equal to the square root of the variance, 91–93

standard error of a score: In true score theory, a statistic designed to estimate the extent to which an observed score deviates from a true score, 170

standard error of estimate, 129

standard error of measurement (SEM): In true score theory, a statistic designed to estimate the extent to which an observed score deviates from a true score; also called the standard error of a score, 129, 169–172

standard error of the difference: A statistic designed to aid in determining how large a difference between two scores should be before it is considered statistically significant, 129, 172–174

standardization. See test standardization

standardization sample, 131–132

standardize: The verb "to standardize" refers to making or transforming something into something that can serve as a basis of comparison or judgment, 38, 126–129

standardized test: A test or measure that has undergone standardization, 128

standard of care: The level at which the average, reasonable, and prudent professional would provide diagnostic or therapeutic services under the same or similar conditions, 55

standard score: A raw score that has been converted from one scale into another, where the latter scale (1) has some arbitrarily set mean and standard deviation and (2) is more widely used and readily interpretable; examples of standard scores are z scores and T scores, 98–101

Standards for Educational and Psychological Testing (AERA, APA, & NCME), 18, 127

standard unit of measure, 127

Stanford-Binet Fourth Edition (SB:FE), 291

Stanford-Binet Intelligence Scale, 43
  fifth edition, 289–295
  psychometric soundness, 295
  scoring/interpretation, 294
  standardization, 295
  test administration, 291–293

Stanford Diagnostic Mathematics Test, Fourth Edition (SDMT4), 346

stanine: A standard score derived from a scale with a mean of 5 and a standard deviation of approximately 2, 99–100

state: (1) As in personality state, the transitory exhibition of a trait, indicative of a relatively temporary predisposition to behave in a particular way (contrast with trait); (2) in psychoanalytic theory, an inferred psychodynamic disposition designed to convey the dynamic quality of id, ego, and superego in perpetual conflict, 115, 359

State-Trait Anxiety Inventory (STAI), 359

static characteristic: A trait, state, or ability presumed to be relatively unchanging over time; contrast with dynamic characteristic, 161

statistics, 75–114
  correlation, 102–114
  data descriptions, 81–94
  normal curve, 95–98
  scales of measurement, 76–80
  standard scores, 98–101

STEP battery. *See* Sequential Tests of Educational Progress battery

stratified-random sampling: The process of developing a sample based on specific subgroups of a population in which every member has the same chance of being included in the sample, 129

stratified sampling: The process of developing a sample based on specific subgroups of a population, 129

streetwiseness, 313–314

stress interview: An interview purposely designed to pressure or stress the interviewee in order to gauge reaction to that stress, 454

Strong-Campbell Interest Inventory (SCII), 526

Strong Interest Inventory, Revised Edition (SII), 526

Strong Interest Inventory (SII), 525

Strong Vocational Interest Blank (SVIB), 526

Structured Clinical Interview for DSM-IV (SCID), 454

structured interview: Questions posed from a guide with little if any leeway to deviate from the guide, 370

Structured Interview of Reported Symptoms-2 (SIRS-2), 454

Study Attitudes and Methods Survey, 352, 559

Study Habits Checklist, 352–353

subgroup norms: Norms for any defined group within a larger group, 135

substance abuse, 467–469

substantia nigra: A pigmented structure in the brain (literally "black substance") that is responsible for dopamine production, 500

successive processing: Also referred to as sequential processing; based on Luria's writings, a type of information processing whereby information is processed in a sequential, bit-by-bit fashion and arranged and rearranged until it is logical; contrast with simultaneous processing, 285

suicide assessment, 483–484

summation notation, 84

summative scale: An index derived from the summing of selected scores on a test or subtest, 237

supplemental subtest: Also referred to as an optional subtest, one of a test's subtests that may be used either for purposes of providing additional information or in place of a core subtest if, for any reason, the use of a score on a core subtest would be questionable; contrast with core subtest, 297

supplementary scales, 387

survey: In consumer psychology, a fixed list of questions administered to a selected sample of persons, typically to learn about consumers' attitudes, beliefs, opinions, and/or behavior regarding targeted products, services, or advertising, 560–563

Survey of School Attitudes, 352

Survey of Study Habits and Attitudes (SSHA), 352–353

SVIB. *See* Strong Vocational Interest Blank

systematic error : a source of error in measuring a variable that is typically constant and proportionate to what is presumed to be the true value of the variable being measured; contrast with random error, 142

tail: The area on the normal curve between 2 and 3 standard deviations above the mean, and the area on the normal curve between-2 and-3 standard deviations below the mean; a normal curve has two tails, 97

tailored testing, 294

Tarasoff v. Regents of the University of California, 57, 73, 470

TAT. *See* Thematic Apperception Test

tautophone, 422

Taylor-Russell tables: Statistical tables once extensively used to provide test users with an estimate of the extent to which inclusion of a particular test in the selection system would improve selection decisions, 214–215

teaching item: A test item designed to illustrate the task required and assure the examiner that the examinee understands what is required for success on the task, 298

team: Two or more people who interact interdependently toward a common and valued goal and who have each been assigned specific roles or functions to perform, 550–551

Technical Recommendations for Psychological Tests and Diagnostic Tests (APA), 63

telephone surveys, 560–562

teleprocessing: Computerized scoring, interpretation, or other conversion of raw test data sent over telephone lines by modem from a test site to a central location for computer processing; contrast with central processing and local processing, 15

Ten Item Personality Inventory (TIPI), 382

Tennessee Self-Concept Scale, 362

terminal values: Guiding principles and a mode of behavior that are an endpoint objective; for example, "a comfortable life" and "an exciting life"; contrast with instrumental values, 399

test: A measuring device or procedure, 7–9
  See also specific tests

test administration
  for intelligence testing, 302–306
  procedures for, 7–8
  SB5, 291–293
  short form for, 300–301
  "think aloud," 258

test administrators, 26, 143–144

test battery: A selection of tests and assessment procedures typically composed of tests designed to measure different variables but having a common objective; for example, an intelligence test, a personality test, and a neuropsychological test might be used to obtain a general psychological profile of an individual, 152n5, 461–462. *See also specific batteries*

test bias, 192–195

test blueprint: A detailed plan of the content, organization, and quantity of the items that a test will contain, 180

test catalogues: Usually contain brief descriptions of the tests and seldom contain the kind of detailed technical information that a prospective user might require, 30–31

test composite: A test score or index derived from the combination and/or mathematical transformation of one or more test scores, 291

test conceptualization: An early stage of the test development process wherein the idea for a particular test or test revision is first conceived, 229, 230–234

test construction: A stage in the process of test development that entails writing test items (or rewriting or otherwise revising existing items), as well as formatting items, setting scoring rules, and otherwise designing and building a test, 143, 229, 234–247
  scaling, 234–239
  scoring items, 246
  writing items, 239–246 (*See also* writing items)

test developers, 18

test development: An umbrella term for all that goes into the process of creating a test, 229–272

defined, 229

instructor-made tests for in-class use, 270–271

item analysis, 248–260 (*See also* item analysis)

item revision, 260–270

test conceptualization, 230–234

test construction, 234–246 (*See also* test construction)

test tryout, 246–247

test environment, 143

test fairness, 196–199

test findings, right to be informed, 70–71

test homogeneity: The extent to which individual test items measure a single construct; contrast with test heterogeneity, 152, 187–188

testing, 115–140

assumptions of, 115–121

content, 7

criteria for, 122–123

cultural considerations, 42–55

cut score, 8

defined, 1–2

format, 7

historical considerations, 36–41

historical perspective, 36–41

intelligence (*See* intelligence testing)

legal/ethical considerations, 55–74

norms, 123–139

psychological assessment, contrasted, 3

psychometrics, 8

reliability, 122

Rorschach, 8

score, 8

state licensing laws, 65

utility, 8–9

validity, 122–123

testing enterprise: A general reference to the engagement of individuals, organizations, and businesses in aspects of psychological measurement ranging from instrument development through instrument administration and interpretation, 1

testing the limits: Administration of test items beyond the level at which the test manual dictates discontinuance, 293n5, 406

test manual: An archival document in any media (booklet, book, electronic form, etc.) devoted to a detailed description of a test and usually available from the test's publisher, that ideally provides all of the key information prospective test users need to know in order to make an informed decision about whether the test is appropriate for use with a particular testtaker for a particular purpose, 32

Test of Grocery Shopping Skills, 14

test protocols, 26

test-related discrimination, 53

test-retest method, 145–146

test-retest reliability: An estimate of reliability obtained by correlating pairs of scores from the same people on two different administrations of the same test, 145–146, 160

test revision: Action taken to modify a test's content or format for the purpose of improving the test's effectiveness as a tool of measurement, 229

cross-validation/co-validation, 264–265

existing test, 262–266

item response theory (IRT), 266–270

new test development, 260–261

quality assurance, 265–266

test score

central tendency, 84–89

correlation/inference, 102–114

cumulative scoring, 118

frequency distributions, 81–84

kurtosis, 94

measurement scales, 76–80

normal (bell) curve, 94–97

reliability (*See* reliability)

skewness, 93–94

standard score, 98–101

as statistical tool, 75

validity (*See* validity)

variability, 89–93

test scoring/interpretation, 144–145, SB5, 322

test standardization: A process of test development wherein the test is administered to a representative sample of testtakers under clearly specified conditions and the data are scored and interpreted; the results establish a context for future test administrations with other testtakers, 126

testtaker rights, 69–73

testtakers, 18–19

testtaker variables, 144

test tryout: A stage in the process of test development that entails administering a preliminary version of a test to a representative sample of testtakers under conditions that simulate the conditions under which the final version of the test will be administered, 229, 246–247

test user, 18

test-user qualifications, 64–65

test utility. *See* utility

Texas college admission requirements, 59

thema: In the personality theory of Henry Murray, a unit of interaction between need and press, 413

Thematic Apperception Test (TAT), 411–415

Theories of Personality (Hall & Lindzey), 354

theory of personality, 380

therapeutic contract: An agreement made between a therapist and a client regarding various aspects of the therapeutic process, 453

therapeutic psychological assessment: A collaborative approach wherein discovery of therapeutic insights about oneself are encouraged and actively promoted by the assessor throughout the assessment process, 6

"think aloud" test administration: A method of qualitative item analysis requiring examinees to verbalize their thoughts as they take a test; useful in understanding how individual items function in a test and how testtakers interpret or misinterpret the meaning of individual items, 258

third moments of the distribution, 106

third-order factors, 278

threat assessment: As defined by the U.S. Department of Homeland Security, *a process of identifying or evaluating entities, actions, or occurrences, whether natural or man-made, that have or indicate the potential to harm life, information, operations and/or property,* 378

Three Faces of Eve (film), 370

three-stratum theory of cognitive abilities: John B. Carroll's conception of mental abilities and processing classified by three levels or strata, with g at the broadest level followed by eight abilities or processes at the second level and a number of more narrowly defined abilities and processes at the third level, 282

timeline followback (TLFB) methodology: A technique of behavioral observation that involves the recording of the frequency and the intensity of a targeted behavior over time, 432

TIPI. *See* Ten Item Personality Inventory

Tower of Hanoi puzzle, 507

trail-making item: An item that taps visual-conceptual, visual-motor, planning, and other cognitive abilities by means of a task in which the testtaker must connect the circles in a logical fashion; the component of the Halstead-Reitan Neuropsychological Battery called the Trail Making Test is one of the most widely used instruments for the assessment of brain damage, 508–509

Trail Making Test, 510

trait: Any distinguishable, relatively enduring way in which one individual varies from another; contrast with state, 115

transient error: A source of error attributable to variations in the testtaker's feelings, moods, or mental state over time, 159

TRIN. *See* True Response Inconsistency

trinitarian model of validity, 176

true-false item: A sentence that requires the testtaker to indicate whether the statement is or is not a fact, 242

True Response Inconsistency (TRIN), 389

true score: A value that, according to classical test theory, genuinely reflects an individual's ability (or trait) level as measured by a particular test, 163

true score model. *See* classical test theory (CTT)

true score theory: Also referred to as the true score model or classical test theory, a system of assumptions about measurement that includes the notion that a test score (and even a response to an individual item) is composed of a relatively stable component that actually is what the test or individual item is designed to measure as well as a random component that is error, 121

true variance: In the true score model, the component of variance attributable to true differences in the ability or trait being measured that are inherent in an observed score or distribution of scores, 142

truth-in-testing legislation: Which gives testtakers a way to learn the criteria by which they are being judged, 58

T score: Named for Thorndike, a standard score calculated using a scale with a mean set at 50 and a standard deviation set at 10; used by developers of the MMPI, 99, 128–129, 390

two-factor theory of intelligence: Spearman's theory of general intelligence, which postulates the existence of a general intellectual ability factor (g) that is partially tapped by all other mental abilities, 276

Tyler Vocational Classification System, 373

type: As in personality type, a constellation of traits and states similar in pattern to one identified category of personality within a taxonomy of personalities, 358

Type A personality: In Friedman and Rosenman's typology, a personality characterized by competitiveness, haste, restlessness, impatience, feelings of being time-pressured, and strong needs for achievement and dominance, 358

Type B personality: In Friedman and Rosenman's typology, a personality characterized by traits (e.g., "mellow" and "laid-back") that are opposite the Type A personality, 358

Types of Men (Spranger), 398

Uniform Guidelines on Employee Selection Procedures (EEOC, Civil Service Commission, Dept. of Labor, & Justice Dept.), 58–59

uniform T (UT) score: A variety of T score used in the MMPI-2, 390

universe: In generalizability theory, the total context of a particular test situation, including all the factors that lead to an individual testtaker's score, 164–165

universe score: In generalizability theory, a test score corresponding to the particular universe being assessed or evaluated, 165

University of Pennsylvania Smell Identification Test (UPSIT), 495

unobtrusive measure: A type of measure that does not necessarily require the presence or cooperation of respondents, often a telling physical trace or record, 441–442

UPSIT. *See* University of Pennsylvania Smell Identification Test

user norms: Also referred to as program norms, descriptive statistics based on a group of testtakers in a given period of time rather than on norms obtained by formal sampling methods, 126

utility (also test utility): In the context of psychological testing and assessment, a reference to how useful a test or assessment technique is for a particular purpose, 8–9, 200–228. *See also* utility analysis
decision theory, and, 218–220
defined, 201
factors affecting, 201–206

utility analysis: A family of techniques designed to evaluate the costs and benefits of testing and not testing in terms of likely outcomes, 206–225
Brogden-Cronbach-Gleser formula, 216–218
cut score, 222–225
decision theory, 218–220

defined, 206
expectancy data, 207, 215–217
illustration of, 208–214
job applicants pool, 221–222
job complexity, 222

utility gain: An estimate of the benefit, monetary or otherwise, of using a particular test or selection method, 216

UT score. *See* uniform T score

validation: The process of gathering and evaluating validity evidence, 176

validation study: Research that entails gathering evidence relevant to how well a test measures what it purports to measure for the purpose of evaluating the validity of a test or other measurement tool, 176

validity: A general term referring to a judgment regarding how well a test or other measurement tool measures what it purports to measure; this judgment has important implications regarding the appropriateness of inferences made and actions taken on the basis of measurements, 122–123
bias and fairness and, 192–199
concept of, 175–182
construct validity, 187–192 (*See also* construct validity)
content validity, 178–182
criterion-related, 182–186 (*See also* criterion-related validity)
defined, 175
face validity, 177–178
incremental, 186

validity coefficient: A correlation coefficient that provides a measure of the relationship between test scores and scores on a criterion measure, 185–186

validity generalization (VG), 530–532

validity scale: A subscale of a test designed to assist in judgments regarding how honestly the testtaker responded and whether or not observed responses were products of response style, carelessness, deliberate efforts to deceive, or unintentional misunderstanding, 367

validity shrinkage: The decrease in item validities that inevitably occurs after cross-validation, 264

values: That which an individual prizes; ideals believed in, 398

variability: An indication of how scores in a distribution are scattered or dispersed, 89–93

Variable Response Inconsistency (VRIN), 389

variance: A measure of variability equal to the arithmetic mean of the squares of the differences between the scores in a distribution and their mean, 91, 141–142

VCAT. *See* Veterinary College Admission Test

verbal communication, 47–48
verbal functioning tests, 512
verbal summator, 422
Veterinary College Admission Test (VCAT), 344
VG. *See* validity generalization
video, as assessment tool, 17
VRIN. *See* Variable Response Inconsistency

vulnerable abilities: In the Cattell-Horn model of intelligence, cognitive abilities that decline with age and that do not return to pre-injury levels after brain damage; contrast with maintained abilities, 282

WAIS. *See* Wechsler Adult Intelligence Scale
Washington University Sentence Completion Test, 420
WCST-64. *See* Wisconsin Card Sorting Test-64 Card Version (WCST-64)
Wechsler Abbreviated Scale of Intelligence (WASI), 301
Wechsler Adult Intelligence Scale (WAIS)
fourth edition (WAIS-IV), 264, 295–300
general item types, 296
history of, 40
psychometric soundness, 299
standardization/norms, 299
subtests grouped according to indexes, 298
test's heritage, 296
test today, 297–299
third edition (WAIS III), 297–299
Wechsler-Bellevue Intelligence Scale, 40, 47, 295–296
Wechsler Individual Achievement Test—Third Edition (WIAT-III), 329
Wechsler Intelligence Scale for Children, Fourth Edition (WISC-IV), 265–266
Wechsler Intelligence Scale for Children-Revised (WISC-R), 300
Wechsler intelligence tests, 295–300. *See also specific tests*
at a glance, 299
short forms, 300–301
Wechsler Memory Scale—Third Edition (WMS-III), 297
Wechsler Memory Scale (WMS-IV), 264, 515
Wechsler Preschool and Primary Scale of Intelligence—Third Edition (WPPSI-III), 300
Weigl's Test, 506
Welsh codes: A shorthand summary of a testtaker's scores on the MMPI clinical and validity scales, 390
Wepman-Auditory Discrimination Test, 511
What I Like to Do Interest Inventory, 352
WIAT-III. *See* Wechsler Individual Achievement Test—Third Edition
Wiggins Content Scales, 387
WISC. *See* Wechsler Intelligence Scale for Children
WISC-IV. *See* Wechsler Intelligence Scale for Children, Fourth Edition
Wisconsin Card Sorting Test-64 Card Version (WCST-64), 506
WISC-R. *See* Wechsler Intelligence Scale for Children-Revised
WMS-IV. *See* Wechsler Memory Scale
Wonderlic Personnel Test, 527
Woodcock-Johnson III (WJ III), 348
Woodcock Reading Mastery Tests-Revised (WRMT-III), 345–346
Woodworth Psychoneurotic Inventory, 377
word association: A type of task that may be used in personality assessment in which an assessee verbalizes the first word that comes to mind in response to a stimulus word; contrast with free association, 418, 419n5

word association test: A semistructured, individually administered, projective technique of personality assessment that involves the presentation of a list of stimulus words, to each of which an assessee responds verbally or in writing with whatever comes immediately to mind first upon first exposure to the stimulus word, 418–420

words as projective stimuli, 418–421

working memory, 513

work performance, 536

Work Preference Inventory (WPI), 553

worldview: The unique way people interpret and make sense of their perceptions in light of their learning experiences, cultural background, and related variables, 399

WPPSI-III. *See* Wechsler Preschool and Primary Scale of Intelligence—Third Edition

writing items, 239–246
computerized adaptive testing (CAT), 243–246
item format, 240–243

WRMT-III. *See* Woodcock Reading Mastery Tests-Revised

zero plus minus one scale, 98, 99

Zink v. State, 63

zone of proximal development: Lev Vygotsky's concept of the area that exists, in theory, between a testtaker's ability as measured by a formal test and what might be possible as the result of instruction, 326

z score: A standard score derived by calculating the difference between a particular raw score and the mean and then dividing by the standard deviation; a z score expresses a score in terms of the number of standard deviation units that the raw score is below or above the mean of the distribution, 98–99, 128–129

Psychological Testing and Assessment: A Timeline Spanning 2200 B.C.E to the Present

Note: This is a brief, decidedly *non*comprehensive overview of historical events perceived important by the authors. Consult other authoritative historical sources for more detailed and comprehensive descriptions of these and other events.

2200 B.C.E.

Proficiency testing is known to have been conducted in China. The Emperor has public officials evaluated periodically.

1115 B.C.E.

Open and competitive civil service examinations in China are common during the Chang Dynasty. Proficiency is tested in areas such as arithmetic, writing, geography, music, agriculture, horsemanship, and cultural rites and ceremonies.

400 B.C.E.

Plato suggests that people should work at jobs consistent with their abilities and endowments—a sentiment that will be echoed many times through the ages by psychologists, human resource professionals, and parents.

175 B.C.E.

Claudius Galenus (otherwise known as Galen) designs experiments to show that the brain, not the heart, is the seat of the intellect.

200

The so-called Dark Ages begin and society forces science to take a (temporary) backseat to faith and superstition.

1484

Interest in individual differences centers primarily on questions such as "Who is in league with Satan?" and "Are they in *voluntary* or *involuntary* league?" *The Hammer of Witches* is a primitive, diagnostic manual of sorts with tips on interviewing and identifying persons suspected of having strayed from the righteous path.

1550

The Renaissance witnesses a rebirth in philosophy, and German physician Johann Weyer writes that those accused of being witches may have been suffering from mental or physical disorders. For the faithful, Weyer is seen as advancing Satan's cause.

1600

The pendulum begins to swing away from a religion-dominated view of the world to one that is more philosophical and scientific in nature.

1700

The cause of philosophy and science is advanced with the writings of the French philosopher René Descartes, the German philosopher Gottfried Leibniz, and a group of English philosophers (John Locke, George Berkeley, Dave Hume, and David Hartley) referred to collectively as "the British empiricists." Descartes, for example, raised intriguing questions regarding the relationship between the mind and the body. These issues would be explored in a less philosophical and more physical way by Pierre Cabanis, a physiologist. For humanitarian purposes, Cabanis personally observed the state of consciousness of guillotine victims of the French Revolution. He concluded that the mind and body were so intimately linked that the guillotine was probably a painless mode of execution.

1734

Christian von Wolff authors two books, *Psychologia Empirica* [*Empirical Psychology*] (1732) and *Psychologia Rationalis* [*Rational Psychology*] (1734), which anticipate psychology as a science. A student of Gottfried Leibniz, von Wolff also elaborated on Leibniz's idea that there exist perceptions below the threshold of awareness, thus anticipating Freud's notion of the unconscious.

1780

Franz Mesmer "mesmerizes" not only Parisian patients but some members of the European medical community with his use of what he once referred to as "animal magnetism" to effect cures. Mesmerism (or *hypnosis* as we know it today) would go on to become a tool of psychological assessment; the hypnotic interview is one of many alternative techniques for information gathering.

1823

The *Journal of Phrenology* is founded to further the study of Franz Joseph Gall's notion that ability and special talents are localized in concentrations of brain fiber that press outward. Extensive experimentation eventually discredits phrenology, and the journal folds by the early twentieth century. By the mid-twentieth century, evaluation of "bumps" in paper profiles would be preferable to examination of bumps on the head for obtaining information about ability and talents.

1829

In *Analysis of the Phenomena of the Human Mind*, English philosopher James Mill argued that the structure of mental life consists of sensation and ideas. Mill anticipates an approach to experimental psychology called *structuralism*, the goal of which would be to explore the components of the structure of the mind.

1848

In Vermont, an accidental discharge of explosives sends a three-foot iron rod through the skull of railway construction foreman Phineas Gage, destroying much of the front part of the left side of his brain. With medical intervention, Gage survives. However, once viewed as a competent and capable worker, after the accident he is seen as fitful, irreverent, and "no longer Gage." Because his intellect seemed unaffected, the case was significant for calling attention to the role of the brain in personality and its assessment.

1859

The publication of Charles Darwin's *On the Origin of Species by Means of Natural Selection* advances the then-radical notion that humans descended from apes. The work raises questions about how animals and humans compare with regard to variables such as state of consciousness. Darwin also writes of natural selection and the survival of the fittest of the species. These ideas may have greatly influenced Freud, whose psychoanalytic theory of personality emphasized the importance of instinctual sexual and aggressive urges.

1860

The German physiologist Gustav Fechner publishes *Elements of Psychophysics*, in which he explored the way people respond to stimuli such as light and sound. The work prompts experimentation in the areas of human and animal perception.

1869

Sir Francis Galton, half-cousin to Charles Darwin, publishes *Hereditary Genius,* which was noteworthy both for (a) its claim that genius is inherited, and (b) its pioneering use of the statistical technique that Karl Pearson would later call *correlation.* Galton would subsequently make numerous and varied contributions to measurement with his inventions and innovations.

1879

Wilhelm Max Wundt founded the first experimental psychology clinic in Leipzig, Germany; psychology is a science in its own right, not simply a branch of philosophy. A structuralist, Wundt relies heavily on a tool of assessment called *introspection* (wherein subjects verbally try to faithfully describe their conscious experience of a stimulus). The structuralists focus attention on the measurement of sensory-related abilities and reaction time.

1885

Herman Ebbinghaus publishes *Memory: A Contribution to Experimental Psychology*, in which he describes his use of nonsense syllables to research and evaluate human memory. His many keen insights on learning (and forgetting) curves proves that higher order mental processes such as memory—not just reaction time or sensory reaction to stimuli—can be effectively assessed.

1890

American psychologist James McKeen Cattell coins the term *mental test* in a publication. He would go on to found several publications, most notably *Science* and *Psychological Review*. In 1921, he formed the Psychological Corporation with the goal of "useful applications of psychology." Also in 1890, New York became the first state to assume responsibility for its mentally ill citizens. Related legislation changed the name of so called "lunatic asylums" to state hospitals—the place where the indigent mentally ill would be afforded medically supervised evaluation and treatment.

1892

Psychiatrist Emil Kraeplin, who studied with Wundt, publishes research that employed a word association test. Also in 1892, the American Psychological Association (APA) is founded with 31 members, thanks primarily to the efforts of its first president, G. Stanley Hall. For a fascinating account, see Samuel Willis Fernberger's article, "The American Psychological Association: 1892–1942" in the January 1943 issue (volume 50) of the *Psychological Review.*

1895

Alfred Binet and Victor Henri publish articles calling for the measurement of cognitive abilities such as memory, as well as other human abilities such as social comprehension. Interestingly, Binet also wondered aloud about the possible uses of inkblots to study personality.

1896

Lightner Witmer establishes the first psychological clinic in the United States, at the University of Pennsylvania. Subsequently, in 1907, Witmer founded a journal called *Psychological Clinic.* Witmer wrote "Clinical Psychology," the first article in that journal.

1904

Charles Spearman, a student of Wundt at Leipzig, begins to lay the foundation for the concept of test reliability. He also begins building the mathematical framework for factor analysis.

1905

Alfred Binet and Theodore Simon publish a 30-item "measuring scale of intelligence" designed to help identify developmentally disabled Paris schoolchildren. The notion of measuring intelligence would strike a responsive chord globally.

1910

How is your handwriting? If you were a student at this time, you might have had it checked by one of the first standardized tests ever—a test authored by E. L. Thorndike. His article entitled "Handwriting" (*Teachers College Record,* volume 11, issue 2) provides 16 handwriting samples arranged in order of merit.

1912

This was the year that the now-familiar term "IQ" (intelligence quotient) came into being. William Stern devised a formula whereby "mental age" as determined by Binet's test was the dividend, the divisor was the testtaker's chronological age, and the quotient, multiplied by 100 was the IQ. Although "IQ" remains a fixture in the world's vocabulary, contemporary measures of intelligence are no longer devised by such ratios. Also in 1912, there was another IQ-related milestone (of sorts): Henry Herbert Goddard's book, *The Kallikak Family: A Study in the Heredity of Feeble-Mindedness,* was published. Goddard's own life and controversial career is presented in our *Close-up* in Chapter 2.

1913

Swiss psychiatrist Hermann Rorschach, the son of an art teacher, publishes papers on how analysis of patients' artwork can provide insights into personality. In 1921 his now-famous monograph, *Psychodiagnostics,* would evolve into a test that has become an icon for psychological tests in the public eye: the Rorschach Inkblot test. Also in 1913, John Watson's now-famous *Psychological Review* article, "Psychology as the Behaviorist Views It," becomes known as the "behaviorist manifesto." Of course, as the behaviorist views it, behavioral observation is a key tool of assessment.

1914

World War I serves as a boon to the testing movement since thousands of recruits must be quickly screened for intellectual functioning, as well as emotional fitness.

1916

After years of research, Lewis M. Terman, working at Stanford University, publishes the Stanford Revision of the Binet-Simon Intelligence Scale. This American adaptation and revision of the test first developed in France would become widely known as the Stanford-Binet.

1920

Army Mental Tests, edited by then Majors Clarence S. Yoakum and Robert M. Yerkes (both psychologists with distinguished careers), is published by Holt. This edited volume provides detailed information about the Army Alpha and Beta tests developed during the first world war at a time, in their words, "in this supreme struggle [when] it became clear . . . that the proper utilization of man power, and more particularly of mind or brain power, would assure ultimate victory" (p. vii).

1926

The College Board sponsors the development of the Scholastic Aptitude Test (SAT) and administers the test for the first time.

1927

Carl Spearman publishes a two-factor theory of intelligence in which he postulates the existence of a general intellectual ability factor (*g*) and specific (*s*) components of that general ability. Also in 1927, German neurologist Kurt Goldstein begins to develop neurodiagnostic tests on the basis of research with soldiers who suffered brain injury during World War I. Many of these tests tap abstraction ability.

1931

L. L. Thurstone publishes *Multiple Factor Analysis,* a landmark work with impact far beyond statistical analyses; it will have the effect of focusing greater research attention on cognitive abilities.

1933

The first edition of test reviews compiled by Oscar Buros—the reference work that would become known as the *Mental Measurements Yearbook*—is published.

1935

Christiana D. Morgan and Henry A. Murray collaborate on what was originally called the *Morgan-Murray Thematic Apperception Test.* This tool of personality assessment entails showing pictures to assessees who are then prompted to make up stories in response to them. The final version of the test, now best known by the letters, TAT, was published in 1943 with authorship credited to "Henry A. Murray, Ph.D., and the Staff of the Harvard Psychological Clinic."

1938

By this year, mental testing has become big business. According to the *1938 Mental Measurements Yearbook,* at least 4,000 different psychological tests are in print. One of those tests published in this year came in the form of a monograph entitled "A Visual Motor Gestalt Test and Its Clinical Use." Authored by physician Lauretta Bender and commonly referred to as the "Bender-Gestalt" or simply "the Bender," this once widely used paper-and-pencil test consisted of nine designs to be copied.

1939

Working at Bellevue Hospital in New York City, David Wechsler introduces the *Wechsler-Bellevue Intelligence Scale,* designed to measure adult intelligence. The test would subsequently be revised and transformed into the Wechsler Adult Intelligence Scale (WAIS). Additional Wechsler tests for use with children and preschoolers would subsequently be developed and revised periodically.

1940

World War II prompts an accelerated need for a means to screen military recruits. Also in this year, psychologist Starke R. Hathaway and psychiatrist/neurologist John Charnley McKinley publish their first journal article on a new "multiphasic personality schedule" that they have been developing—the test we now know as the *Minnesota Multiphasic Personality Inventory* (MMPI; see the *Journal of Psychology,* volume 10, pages 249–254).

1941

Raymond B. Cattell, with the benefit of factor analysis, introduces a theory of intelligence based on two general factors he calls *fluid intelligence* and *crystallized intelligence.*

1945

With its emphasis on the administration and clinical interpretation of various tests in a coordinated battery, *Diagnostic Psychological Testing,* a book by David Rapaport, Roy Schafer, and Merton Gill, becomes a classic. Although clinically compelling, it is criticized for its lack of statistical rigor.

1948

With authorship attributed to Office of Strategic Services Assessment Staff, the landmark book, *Assessment of Men,* is published. Although the book was about the selection of personnel for wartime spy or espionage missions, the procedures described become the basis for modern-day assessment center methods.

1951

Lee Cronbach develops *coefficient alpha* to measure test reliability. Cronbach's formula is a modification of KR-20 (George Frederic Kuder and Marion Webster Richardson's 20th formula). Conceptually, Cronbach's *alpha* calculates the mean of all possible split-half test correlations, corrected by the Spearman-Brown formula.

1952

The first edition of the American Psychiatric Association's *Diagnostic and Statistical Manual* is published. Revisions—and controversy—would follow.

1954

APA publishes *Technical Recommendations for Psychological Tests and Diagnostic Techniques,* a document that would evolve into the periodically revised *Standards.* Also in this year, Swiss psychologist Jean Piaget publishes an original and influential work on the development of cognition in children.

1957

The Psychology of Careers by psychologist Donald Super compels both professional and lay readers to consider the reciprocal effects of personality and career choice.

1958

The National Aeronautics and Space Administration (NASA) is formed and an evaluation program is launched to select seven astronauts for Project Mercury. Psychological tests administered to candidates would include the MMPI, the Rorschach, the TAT, and the WAIS.

1961

Based on the same underlying premise as the Rorschach, but designed to be an improvement in terms of psychometric soundness, the Holtzman Inkblot Technique (HIT) is published. Old habits die hard and Rorschachers would still prefer the original.

1962

The beginnings of the practical application of biofeedback can be traced back to this year, when research provided evidence that human subjects are capable of producing certain types of brain waves on command. A year later, research would describe the use of the penile plethysmograph as a tool for assessment of male erotic interest. Biofeedback instrumentation is now available in various forms to monitor many different variables, such as muscle tension and skin temperature.

1963

Stanley Milgram publishes "Behavioral Study of Obedience" in the *Journal of Abnormal and Social Psychology* and makes a momentous contribution to psychology. The experimental procedure and measurement methods arouse questioning on ethical grounds and eventually spur the establishment of departmental ethics committees to oversee measurement procedures and other aspects of the design of proposed research.

1965

Fred Kanfer publishes "Behavioral Analysis" in the *Archives of General Psychiatry.* An early example of efforts to apply learning theory to clinical assessment, it attempts to shift the focus of diagnosis away from similarities of symptoms between groups to an understanding of the unique variables affecting an individual.

1968

Walter Mischel's book, *Personality and Assessment,* prompts psychologists to question the extent to which personality traits are consistent across situations.

1973

Arnold A. Lazarus publishes an article entitled "Multimodal Behavior Therapy: Treating the BASIC ID" in the *Journal of Nervous and Mental Disease.* The multimodal approach to diagnosis and treatment was designed to improve clinical care. It also inspired the development of a systematic method of qualitative evaluation called *dimensional qualitative research* (see the entry herein for 1999).

1974

Amid a welter of competing scoring systems for the Rorschach, John E. Exner Jr. publishes what he terms the "comprehensive system" for administering, scoring, and interpreting the now-famous inkblot test.

1975

In his *Manual for the Vocational Preference Inventory,* John Holland proposes a classification system consisting of six personality types based upon corresponding interest patterns.

1976

Paul T. Costa Jr. and Robert R. McCrae embark on a research program that begins with an analysis of the 16PF. The research would lead to their "Big Five" concept and the development of their own test of personality, the NEO-PI-R. Also in this year a book by Michael P. Maloney and Michael P. Ward, *Psychological Assessment: A Conceptual Approach,* is published. The authors cogently argue that the tools of assessment (and more specifically, tests) "have been inappropriately equated with the 'process' of assessment."

It was also in 1976 that a much-discussed article in the *Journal of Consulting and Clinical Psychology* was published. Entitled "Socially Reinforced Obsessing: Etiology of a Disorder in a Christian Scientist," Ronald Jay Cohen (with F. J. Smith) presented a case study of how one group's recommended practice of "demonstrating" over problems might actually compound an obsessional disorder. Cohen wrote the paper, while still a graduate student at State University of New York at Albany, based on his clinical assessment of a patient at Capital District Psychiatric Center (where F. J. Smith was his supervisor).

1978

Alan Bakke was excluded from a medical school despite the fact that he had entrance test scores that were higher than minority students who were admitted. In *Regents of the University of California v. Bakke,* a highly divided Supreme Court ordered Bakke admitted but did not preclude the future use of diversity considerations in school admission procedures.

1979

Ronald Jay Cohen's first-of-its-kind and critically acclaimed book, *Malpractice: A Guide for Mental Health Professionals,* explores in detail the legal and ethical issues attendant to psychological assessment and intervention.

1980

Frederic M. Lord's book *Applications of Item Response Theory to Practical Testing Problems* is published. It brings together much of the earlier, pioneering work in the area such as that by the American psychometrician M. W. Richardson (1891–1965), the Danish psychometrician Georg Rasch (1901–1980), and others.

1984

The scholarly journal *Psychology & Marketing* is founded with a mission of facilitating interdisciplinary communication regarding consumer assessment, as well as other contributions of psychology to marketing.

1985

Writing in the *Journal of Advertising Research*, Ronald Jay Cohen's article, "Computer-Enhanced Qualitative Research" is the first published description of a methodology for gathering second-by-second recordings of qualitative response to various stimuli.

1988

The first edition of the textbook you are reading is published. To help promote the book, the publisher gives away to instructors a ruler that has printed on it the book's title as well as the phrase, "A NEW Standard in Measurement!" As it turned out, the phrase was prophetic. The book's logical organization, judicious balance of breadth and depth of content, and appealing writing and pedagogy quickly make it the standard in the field.

1992

In April of this year, an imaging study of the human visual cortex at Yale University is the first scanning study using f MRI.

1993

APA publishes *Guidelines for Providers of Psychological Services to Ethnic, Linguistic, and Culturally Diverse Populations.*

1998

An article in the *Journal of Personality and Social Psychology* by Anthony Greenwald and associates provides a methodology for measuring implicit cognition by means of their Implicit Association Test.

1999

In a Special Issue of *Psychology & Marketing* on qualitative research, Ronald Jay Cohen describes *dimensional qualitative research* (DQR); a systematic, psychologically sophisticated method of inquiry. Readers who have occasion to conduct qualitative studies are encouraged to learn more about it in "What Qualitative Research Can Be" (volume 16 of *Psychology & Marketing,* pp. 351–368).

2003

In *Grutter v. Bollinger et al.,* the first major affirmative action decision by the U. S. Supreme Court since *Bakke,* the Court upheld the right of the University of Michigan Law School to use diversity considerations as one of many criteria for admission, on a time-limited basis.

2004

The reauthorized Individuals with Disabilities Education Act (IDEA) has the effect of focusing educators' attention on students' *response to intervention* (RtI) as a means of diagnosing learning disabilities.

2010

The Common Core State Standards are released and the educational experience as well as the educational evaluation of some 50 million K-through-12 students will change dramatically.

2017

The ninth edition of *Psychological Testing and Assessment* is published. With its much emulated organization and content, and exceptional, never duplicated writing style and pedagogy, the book continues a long tradition of setting the standard for all other such books. The authors take this opportunity to say "thank you" to the countless instructors and students who have relied on this trusted textbook since its first publication in 1988.

Made in the USA
Monee, IL
16 May 2022

96527909R00266

Nomenclature

a	Separation of variables constant
a_0	Separation of variables constant; wire center temperature, K
A	Hamaker's constant, J; area, m^2
b	Separation of variables constant
B	Bulk modulus, Pa
Bo	Bond number
c	Specific heat, J/kg K
c_f	Friction coefficient or Fanning friction factor
C	Constant
d	Particle diameter, m
D	Tube diameter, m
E	Energy, J
f	Frequency, 1/s; friction factor
F	Helmholtz free energy, J; force, N
g	Gibbs free energy, J/kg; gravitational acceleration, m/s^2
h	Heat transfer coefficient, W/m^2 K; height, m
h_{lv}	Latent heat, J/kg
H	Unit volume latent heat, J/m^3
I	Intensity, W/m^2
k	Thermal conductivity, W/m K
K	Curvature, 1/m; permeability, $1/m^2$
l	Mean free path, m
L	Length, m
m	Mass, kg
$\dot{m}$	Mass flow rate, kg/s
M	Number of angles around one particle
$\overline{M}$	Molecular weight (kg/kmol)
Ma	Mach number

N Number of moles; mesh number; number of edges in one structure; number of particles

N_a Surface active nucleation site density

Nu Nusselt number

p Pressure, N/m^2

P Perimeter, m; dimensionless pressure

p_d Disjoining pressure, N/m^2

q Heat transfer rate, W

q' Heat transfer per unit length, W/m

q'' Heat flux, W/m^2

Pr Prandtl number

r Radius, m

R Ideal gas constant, J/(kg K); resistance

$\overline{R}$ Universal gas constant, 8,314.5 J/(kmol K)

Re Reynolds number

s Distance, m; specific entropy (J/kg, J/m^3, J/kmol); Cartesian coordinate of thin film region surface, m; eigenvalue of the Bessel function

S Entropy, J; crimping factor

t Time, s

T Temperature, K

u Velocity along x direction, m/s

$\bar{u}$ Average velocity, m/s; local velocity, m/s

v Specific volume, m^3/kg; velocity along y direction, m/s

V Volume, m^3

$\overrightarrow{V}$ Momentum, kg m/s

w Work, J; velocity along z direction, m/s; groove width, m

W Weight, N

We Weber number

x Cartesian coordinate, m; quality

X Percentage of the edge of the structure

y Cartesian coordinate, m

Y Percentage of particle

z Cartesian coordinate, m

Greeks

α Contact angle, degrees

δ Film thickness, m

δ_0 Equilibrium film thickness, m

ε Porosity; relative error

ϕ Relative humidity; dimensionless pressure difference

Φ Fraction; filling ratio

γ Angle along thin film region, degrees; ratio of specific heats

γ_a Angle between top of wire and end of equilibrium film, radians

Γ Total mass flow rate per unit width

η Cartesian coordinate of thin film region surface, m; thermal efficiency of an OHP

κ Gas spring constant

λ Womersley number

μ Dynamic viscosity, N s/m^2

ν Kinematic viscosity

θ Titled angle, degrees; start angle, degrees

Θ Dimensionless temperature

ρ Density, kg/m^3

σ Surface tension, N/m

τ Shear stress, N/m^2

ξ Dimensionless length

ζ Oscillating amplitude

∇ Hamiltonian operator

Subscripts

a   Adiabatic; advancing

b   Bulk

c   Condenser; capillary; condensation

cri   Critical

d   Disjoining

e   Evaporator; evaporation

E   East

ent   Entrainment

evp   Evaporative

g   Gravity

h   Hydraulic

hor   Horizontal

i   Structure edge number

in   Inside, inlet

int   Interface

l   Liquid

ls   Liquid–solid interface

lv   Liquid–vapor interface

m   Meniscus; mean

max   Maximum

n   Particle number along the line

N   North

out   Outside; outlet

out, b   Bulk fluid region area

r   Radius; radial; receding

s	Surface; sintered particles; saturation; solid; sonic; steady
S	South
sat	Saturation
sl	Solid–liquid
sv	Solid–vapor
t	Transient
v	Vapor
w	Wire; wall; wick
W	West
δ	Thin film

Chapter 1
Introduction

1.1 What Is a Heat Pipe?

The heat pipe is a heat transfer device that effectively utilizes evaporation and condensation to transfer heat over a long distance. A heat pipe typically consists of a container charged with a working fluid. This sealed container is divided into three sections: (1) the evaporator where heat is added, (2) the adiabatic section where no heat transfer exists, and (3) the condenser where heat is rejected. In a typical conventional heat pipe, the container has a cylindrical pipe-like shape. One pure working fluid exists in this sealed pipe. When heat is added onto the evaporator section, the heat is transferred through the container wall and reaches the working fluid inside. When the temperature achieves the saturation temperature corresponding to the local saturation pressure, the working fluid vaporizes, and vapor is generated in the evaporator section. In the condenser section, the temperature is lower than the evaporator section. The saturation pressure corresponding to the condensation temperature in the condenser is lower than the saturation pressure in the evaporator. The pressure difference caused by the temperature difference between the evaporator and condenser makes vapor flow from the evaporator section to the condenser section. The condensate in the condenser is pumped back by the capillary force, gravitational force, electrostatic force, centrifugal force, or other forces. In this way, the heat is transported from the evaporator to the condenser.

From a thermodynamic point of view, a heat pipe is a small "engine." The evaporator, where the heat is added, has a higher temperature. The condenser, where the heat is rejected, has a lower temperature. The evaporator and condenser can be considered as the high-temperature heat source and the low-temperature heat source, respectively. As described above, when heat is transferred from the evaporator to the condenser, the working fluid in the heat pipe circulates from the evaporator to the condenser and from the condenser to the evaporator. Working fluid flow in the heat pipe produces energy creating a work output due to frictional forces between surfaces and the working fluid. In other words, during the heat

© Springer Science+Business Media New York 2015
H. Ma, *Oscillating Heat Pipes*, DOI 10.1007/978-1-4939-2504-9_1

transfer process from the evaporator to the condenser, some of the thermal energy added to the evaporator section must be converted into work consumed by the frictional forces. Clearly, the heat pipe is a small "steam engine" with a thermal efficiency. Therefore, the heat pipe can more efficiently transport heat than pure heat conduction. Although the heat pipe is a small "engine," all work output has been used to pump the working fluid in the system. There is no net work output from the heat pipe, which differentiates the heat pipe from other two-phase systems such as the mechanical refrigeration system with work input or steam turbine machine with work output. Therefore, the heat pipe is called a "passive" heat transfer system because the heat pipe does not have any work output or input externally. Because the heat pipe effectively utilizes some of its thermal energy to pump the working fluid, the heat pipe can efficiently transport heat.

From a structural point of view, a heat pipe mainly consists of a sealed container and a working fluid, which is very simple. The sealed container can be constructed of material ranging from plastics to metallic materials. Because the heat transfer process in a typical heat pipe is based on phase change heat transfer with its induced fluid flows, a material with a low thermal conductivity can be used to construct the container. Most common materials include aluminum, copper, and stainless steel. Because the operation of a heat pipe is based on vaporization and condensation of the working fluid, the operating temperature of a heat pipe must be between the critical and freezing points. For an application with a given range of operating temperatures, selection of a suitable fluid is very important for a heat pipe design. With a suitable working fluid and the proper material making up the container's composition, a heat pipe can be readily developed, and it can operate from a very low temperature to a very high temperature. In addition to the thermophysical properties of the working fluid and material, the compatibility between working fluid and container material must be considered. For example, water cannot work with aluminum because it generates noncondensable gas.

There are many types of heat pipes. Based on the driven force, the heat pipe can be categorized as capillary driven heat pipes, i.e., conventional heat pipes, thermosyphons, oscillating heat pipes (OHPs), and rotating heat pipes. Based on the size or form factor, there are micro heat pipes, flat-plate heat pipes, and vapor chambers. Based on the temperature, low-temperature or cryogenic heat pipe and high-temperature or metal heat pipe are named. If the vapor flows in the vapor line and the liquid flows in the liquid line, the heat pipe is called a loop heat pipe or capillary pumped loop.

1.2   What Is an OHP?

The OHP is a heat transfer device that functions via thermally excited oscillating motion induced by the cyclic phase change of an encapsulated working fluid. A typical OHP consists of a train of liquid plugs and vapor bubbles which exist in serpentine-arranged, interconnected capillary tubes or channels, as shown in

Fig. 1.1 Schematic of an oscillating heat pipe

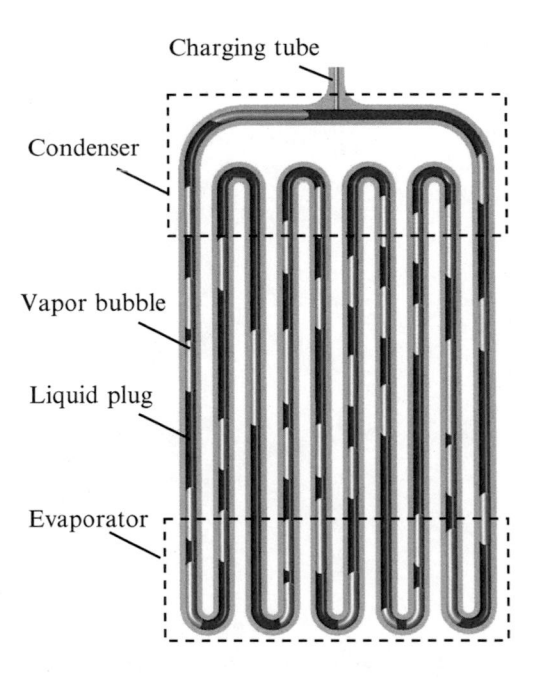

Fig. 1.1. The OHP is partially filled with a working fluid. The internal diameter of the OHP must be small enough so that liquid plugs can be separated by vapor bubbles. Unlike conventional heat pipes (Peterson 1994; Faghri 1995; Reay and Kew 2006), the OHP can function with no wicking structure and has high manufacturability. A typical OHP has three sections: an evaporating section, an adiabatic section, and a condensing section. The OHP functions by meandering its tube/channel to and through a heat reception area (evaporator) and a heat rejection area (condenser). During operation, the continual condensation (in the condenser) and evaporation (in the evaporator) of the working fluid creates a pulsating/nonequilibrium vapor pressure field that drives fluid motion between adjacent tube/channel sections. This results in a complex flow pattern characterized by oscillatory and circulatory liquid/vapor volumes providing for both sensible (convection) and latent (phase change) heat transfer. Although the phase change heat transfer in an OHP helps to generate the oscillating motion, most of the heat is transported by sensible heat transfer. The oscillating flow and heat transfer of single phases play an important role in OHPs.

Oscillating single-phase fluids significantly enhance heat and mass transfer in a channel and have been employed in a number of heat transfer devices (Kaviany 1990; Kaviany and Reckker 1990). The oscillating motions generated by a variable-frequency shaker (Kurzweg 1985; Kurzweg and Zhao 1984) can result in a thermal diffusivity up to 17,900 times higher than those without oscillations in the capillary tubes; however, the use of mechanically driven shakers may limit its application. In 1990, Akachi invented the OHP as shown in Fig. 1.2. In his invention patent (US4921041A), he defined his OHP stating: "A structure of the loop-type heat

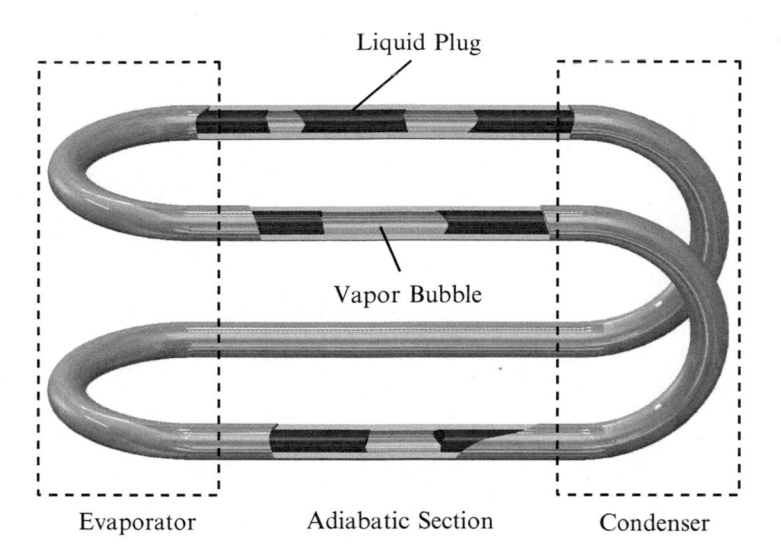

Fig. 1.2 Schematic of an oscillating heat pipe from Akachi's patent (Akachi 1990)

pipe includes the elongate pipe, both ends thereof being air-tightly interconnected to form a loop type container, the heat carrying fluid, at least one heat receiving portion and at least one heat radiating portion... and at least one check valve for limiting a stream direction of the heat carrying fluid." This invention is responsible for the first literature, which describes how an OHP functions. In Akachi's invention, it can be found that the OHP can have different types: closed loop, open loop, check valve, tubular, and flat plate. The heat added in the evaporating section produces vaporization causing vapor volume expansion and the heat removed on the condensation section generates vapor condensation causing vapor volume contraction. The expansion and contraction of vapor volume produces the oscillating motion of liquid plugs and vapor bubbles in the system. In addition to the oscillating motion in the system, the pulsating motions of liquid plugs and vapor bubbles coexist at the same time. For this reason, the OHP is sometimes called a pulsating heat pipe (PHP). The phase change heat transfer in the evaporator and the condenser is the primary driving force for the oscillating/pulsating motion in the system. The thermally excited oscillating/pulsating motion is the primary means used to transport heat from the evaporator to the condenser. The oscillating/pulsating motions in the OHP depend on the surface conditions, dimensions, working fluid, operating temperature, heat flux and total heat load, orientation, number of meandering turns, and, most importantly, the filling ratio.

For an OHP, the evaporator section has a high temperature which is in contact with a high temperature heat source and the condenser section has a low temperature which is in contact with a low temperature heat sink. During the heat transfer process from the high temperature heat source to the low temperature heat sink, the work output is generated mainly to overcome the work done by the frictional force due to the viscous fluid flow. From the thermodynamic point of view, an OHP is an

engine, but the work output is directly used to generate the oscillating motion and phase change heat transfer. Considering this work output, the thermal efficiency of an OHP can be expressed as

$$\eta_{OHP} = \frac{w}{q} \tag{1.1}$$

where q is heat transfer transported by the OHP and w is the work output to produce the oscillating motions of liquid plugs and vapor bubbles in the system, which should be equal to the work done by the viscous frictional forces and irreversible losses during the heat transfer process. For a typical high power OHP, the work produced from an OHP is higher than a typical conventional heat pipe. Clearly, an OHP has a higher thermal efficiency than a conventional wicked heat pipe, which explains why a typical OHP can achieve a higher heat transport capability.

For a typical OHP shown in Fig. 1.1, the flow in the OHP consists of a number of liquid plugs and a number of vapor bubbles. The shear stress acting on the solid wall by the liquid plug is much higher than the shear stress by the vapor bubble. Due to the surface tension and small radius of liquid–vapor interface, the pressure jump takes place across the liquid–vapor interface between the liquid plug and vapor bubble, controls the liquid–vapor interface, and separates fluid into a train of liquid plugs and vapor bubbles. The pressure distribution of working fluid over each liquid plug and vapor bubble could be described by approximately triangular or sawtooth alternating components (Liang and Ma 2004). This triangular or sawtooth alternating component of pressure drop from the evaporating section to the condensing section produces the driving force of the system. When pressure increases or decreases, vapor bubbles can be compressed or expanded, respectively. Vapor bubbles act as springs in the system. From the mechanical vibration point of view, an OHP is a typical mechanical vibration system. This triangular or sawtooth alternating pressure distribution plus the vapor spring constant excites the oscillating motion of a train of liquid plugs and vapor bubbles in an OHP. The heat transport mechanism of an OHP is very different from a conventional heat pipe. If the heat transfer rate of an OHP increases, the thermally excited oscillating motion increases. The velocity increase of liquid plugs and vapor bubbles in the system directly reduces the length of liquid plugs moving in a capillary tube or channel. When vapor velocity is higher than some critical value, vapor penetrates all liquid plugs and produces an annular flow. When this takes place, the mass-spring system consisting of a train of liquid plugs and vapor bubbles disappears. The oscillating motion in the OHP will stop, and the OHP reaches the maximum heat transport capability, which is very different from the operating limits existing in conventional heat pipes.

1.3   Advantages of OHPs

Similar to the conventional heat pipes, the OHP can have a highly effective thermal conductivity resulting in a high level of temperature uniformity from the evaporator to the condenser. The OHP can be operated from a temperature as low as $-195\,°C$ to

a high temperature where liquid and vapor phases can coexist. The OHP can be fabricated into almost any shape. Compared to conventional heat pipes, OHPs have most of the advantages of conventional heat pipes. In addition, the OHPs have several unique operating features: (1) an OHP can convert some of the heat added onto the evaporator section into the kinetic energy of working fluid to initiate and sustain the oscillating/pulsating motion; (2) the liquid flow in an OHP does not interfere with the vapor flow because both phases flow in the same direction; (3) the thermally driven liquid plugs inside the capillary tube or channel effectively produce thin films that significantly enhance evaporating and condensing heat transfer; (4) the oscillating/ pulsating motions in the capillary tube/channel significantly improve forced convection in addition to the phase change heat transfer; (5) as the input power increases, the heat transport capability of an OHP dramatically increases; (6) no wick structures are needed; and (7) the OHP can be designed to not depend on gravity. Due to these characteristics of fluid flow and heat transfer, the OHP has more advantages than conventional heat pipes, which are summarized as follows.

1.3.1   High Heat Transport Capability

An OHP, as shown in Fig. 1.1, utilizes thermally excited oscillating motion to transport the heat from the evaporator to the condenser. The heat transfer process in an OHP mainly consists of the evaporation heat transfer in the evaporator, condensation heat transfer in the condenser, and forced convection caused by the thermally excited oscillating motion of a train of liquid plugs and vapor bubbles. Figure 1.3 illustrates liquid plugs and vapor bubbles moving in a capillary tube or channel occurring in the evaporator section of an OHP. As shown, liquid plugs are separated by vapor bubbles, and thin liquid films are formed on the wall between the liquid plugs. When heat is added onto the heat pipe wall, some of the heat is transferred from the wall to the vapor phase through a thin liquid film and the rest is directly transferred to the oscillating liquid plugs. Because the liquid film formed on the wall between liquid plugs is very thin, the thermal resistance is very small resulting in an extra-high heat transfer coefficient. For oscillating liquid plugs or vapor bubbles as shown in Fig. 1.3, Yin and Ma (2013) show that the oscillating flow

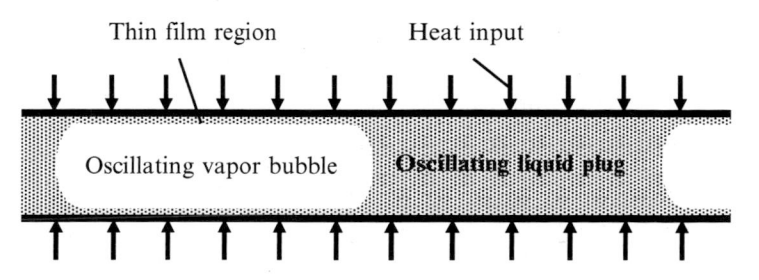

Fig. 1.3 Schematic of liquid plugs and vapor bubbles in an evaporating section of an OHP

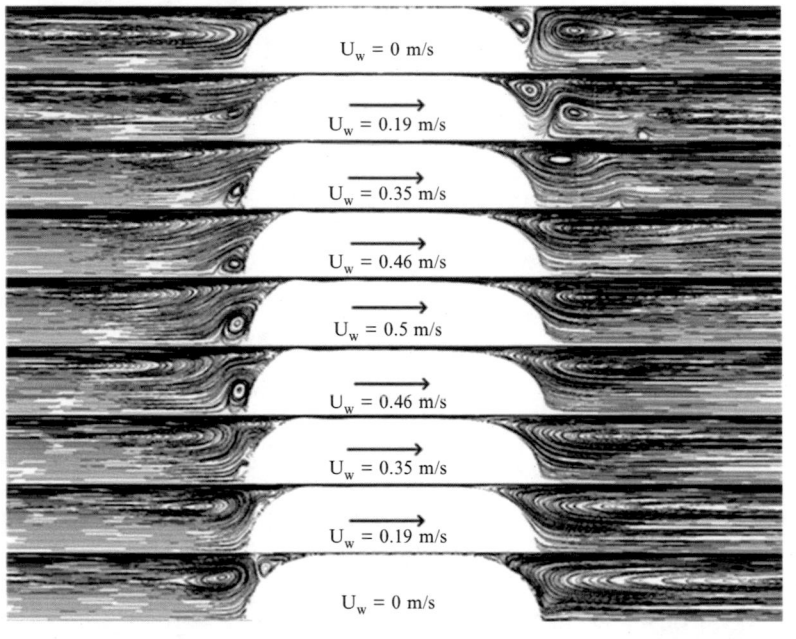

$U_w = 0$ m/s

$\overrightarrow{U_w = 0.19}$ m/s

$\overrightarrow{U_w = 0.35}$ m/s

$\overrightarrow{U_w = 0.46}$ m/s

$\overrightarrow{U_w = 0.5}$ m/s

$\overrightarrow{U_w = 0.46}$ m/s

$\overrightarrow{U_w = 0.35}$ m/s

$\overrightarrow{U_w = 0.19}$ m/s

$U_w = 0$ m/s

Fig. 1.4 Numerical simulation of liquid plugs and vapor bubbles' oscillating motion in a capillary tube (frequency: 10 Hz, tube diameter: 1.0 mm) (Smoot 2013)

with optimum frequencies and amplitudes can have a much higher heat transfer coefficient than a unidirectional flow. In addition, the oscillating flow can produce extensive vortexes, which can further increase the heat transfer coefficient of a thermally excited oscillating flow. Smoot (2013) conducted numerical simulations of liquid plugs and vapor bubbles oscillating in a capillary tube. Due to the axisymmetric tube, Fig. 1.4 illustrates half of the tube with half of one cycle, moving from zero velocity to maximum velocity back down to zero velocity for the dynamics of the system. It can be found that the extensive vortexes have been induced as the liquid plug is oscillating in a capillary tube. For an OHP, liquid plugs are separated by vapor bubbles. The length of individual liquid plugs or vapor bubbles is limited. In other words, these individual liquid plugs and vapor bubbles cannot develop into a fully developed flow. Entrance regions exist in these individual liquid plugs and vapor bubbles oscillating in the tube or channel. It is well known that the heat transfer coefficient in the entrance region is much higher than a fully developed flow. Clearly, the two-phase oscillating flow existing in an evaporating section of an OHP effectively integrates (1) extra-high evaporating heat transfer coefficient of thin liquid film; (2) oscillating flow with extensive vortexes; and (3) high heat transfer coefficient in the entrance region of liquid plugs and vapor bubbles. Due to these heat transfer characteristics, an OHP can result in an extra-high heat transport capability achieving an extra-high effective thermal conductivity.

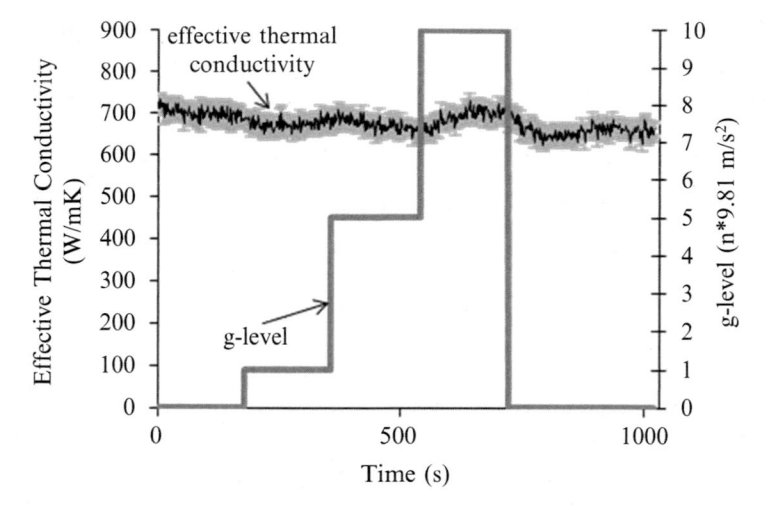

Fig. 1.5 Effective thermal conductivity vs. time at a constant heat input of 95 W and varying gravitational loading (*g*-level) (Thompson et al. 2011b)

1.3.2 Gravity Independence

Due to the hydrothermal coupling in a vertical OHP, its thermal performance can be gravity dependent (Khandekar et al. 2002; Xu et al. 2006; Borgmeyer and Ma 2007; Thompson et al. 2011a; Smoot 2013). However, the degree of gravity effect on the OHP heat transfer performance can be alleviated with appropriate design considerations. Recent investigations (Akachi et al. 1996; Charoensawan et al. 2003; Yang et al. 2009; Lin et al. 2009) indicate that increasing the number of turns and decreasing channel diameter may lessen gravity dependence. Most recently, Thompson et al. (2011b) tested a two-layer miniature flat-plate OHP in a high gravity environment up to 10 g. The gravity was added non-favorably so that it did not assist the return of liquid from the condenser to the evaporator. The experimental results showed that the effective thermal conductivity of the investigated flat-plate OHP was almost independent of the gravity loading up to 10 g as shown in Fig. 1.5. This experiment indicated that an OHP can be independent of gravitational force if the turn number, filling ratio, working fluid, channel dimension, and arrangement are appropriately selected and designed.

1.3.3 Excellent Form Factor and Manufacturing

The OHP size and shape can vary depending on the application. Sizes range from 30 mm × 30 mm (Fig. 1.6) to an OHP with a total length up to 2.0 m (Fig. 1.7) developed for an OHP heat exchanger. OHP shapes range from a flat-plate OHP (Fig. 1.8) for a heat spreader to a U-shaped OHP (Fig. 1.9) for battery cooling.

Fig. 1.6 Photo of 3 mm by
3 mm silicon carbide OHPs
Carbide

Fig. 1.7 Photo of 8-ft long
flat-plate OHP (courtesy of
ThermAvant Technologies,
LLC)

Fig. 1.8 Photo of a 12 in. by 12 in. flat-plate aluminum OHP (courtesy of ThermAvant Technologies, LLC)

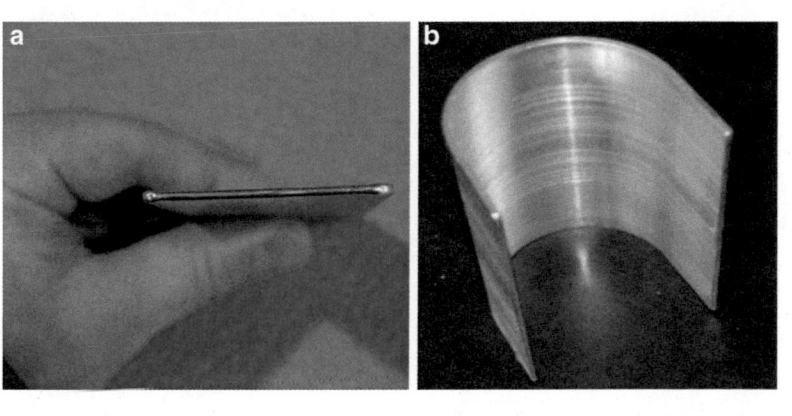

Fig. 1.9 Photos of flat-plate OHPs for battery cooling (**a**) in a flat plate and (**b**) in a U-shaped plate (courtesy of ThermAvant Technologies, LLC)

OHPs can even be flexible. In addition to substantial reductions in the temperature difference and excellent form factors, the use of OHPs normally results in significant decreases in weight because of vapor spaces in OHPs. Because the OHP has no wick structures, it can be readily fabricated. The cost for products shown in Figs. 1.8 and 1.9 is very close to the raw material.

References

Akachi H (1990) Structure of a heat pipe. US Patent #4,921,041
Akachi H, Polasek F, Stulc P (1996) Pulsating heat pipe. In: Proceedings of the 5th international heat pipe symposium, Melbourne, pp 208–217

Borgmeyer B, Ma HB (2007) Experimental investigation of oscillating motions in a flat-plate oscillating heat pipe. J Thermophys Heat Transf 21(2):405–409

Charoensawan P, Khandekar S, Groll M, Terdtoon P (2003) Closed loop pulsating heat pipes— Part A: parametric experimental investigations. Appl Therm Eng 23(16):2009–2020

Faghri A (1995) Heat pipe science and technology. Taylor & Francis, New York

Kaviany M (1990) Performance of a heat exchanger based on enhanced heat diffusion in fluids by oscillation: analysis. ASME J Heat Transf 112:49–55

Kaviany M, Reckker M (1990) Performance of a heat exchanger based on enhanced heat diffusion in fluids by oscillation: experiment. ASME J Heat Transf 112:56–63

Khandekar S, Schneider M, Schäfer P, Kulenovic R, Groll M (2002) Thermofluid dynamic study of flat-plate closed-loop pulsating heat pipes. Microsc Thermophys Eng 6(4):303–317

Kurzweg UH (1985) Enhanced heat conduction in fluids subjected to sinusoidal oscillations. ASME J Heat Transf 107:459–462

Kurzweg UH, Zhao LD (1984) Heat transfer by high-frequency oscillations: a new hydrodynamic technique for achieving large effective thermal conductivities. Phys Fluids 27:2624–2627

Liang SB, Ma HB (2004) Oscillation motions in an oscillating heat pipe. Int Commun Heat Mass Transf 31(3):365–375

Lin YH, Kang SW, Wu TY (2009) Fabrication of polydimethylsiloxane (PDMS) pulsating heat pipe. Appl Therm Eng 29(2–3):573–580

Peterson GP (1994) An introduction to heat pipes. Wiley, New York

Reay DA, Kew PA (2006) Heat pipes, 5th edn. Butterworth-Heinemann, New York

Smoot CD (2013) Factors affecting oscillating motions and heat transfer in an oscillating heat pipe. Ph.D. Dissertation, University of Missouri, Columbia

Thompson SM, Cheng P, Ma HB (2011a) An experimental investigation of a three-dimensional flat-plate oscillating heat pipe with staggered microchannels. Int J Heat Mass Transf 54 (17–18):3951–3959

Thompson SM, Hathaway AA, Smoot CD, Wilson CA, Ma HB, Young RM, Greenberg L, Osick BR, Van Campen S, Morgan BC, Sharar D, Jankowski N (2011b) Robust thermal performance of a flat-plate oscillating heat pipe during high-gravity loading. ASME J Heat Transf 133(11), Article No. 104504

Xu G, Liang S, Vogel M (2006) Thermal characterization of pulsating heat pipes. In: Proceedings of the 10th intersociety conference on thermal and thermomechanical phenomena in electronics systems, San Diego, pp 552–556

Yang H, Khandekar S, Groll M (2009) Performance characteristics of pulsating heat pipes as integral thermal spreaders. Int J Therm Sci 48:815–824

Yin D, Ma HB (2013) Analytical solution of oscillating flow in a capillary tube. Int J Heat Mass Transf 66:699–705

Chapter 2
Fundamentals

2.1 Introduction

The liquid–vapor interface controlled by the surface tension and meniscus radius plays an important role in fluid flow and heat transfer of a heat pipe. In this chapter, the surface tension will be first introduced from three points of view: physical phenomenon, molecular dynamics, and thermodynamics, respectively. The temperature effect on the surface tension will be discussed and its relationship to the Marangoni flow. When the liquid–vapor interface has a curved surface, a pressure difference across the interface exists. This pressure difference can be predicted by the Laplace–Young equation, which will be addressed including the derivation processes and the origin of the capillary force in a heat pipe. The equilibrium vapor pressure of a liquid will be presented including the effects of meniscus radius and electric field on saturation pressure. When the meniscus radius of a bubble decreases, saturation pressure decreases, which can be used to explain the capillary condensation phenomenon. The contact angle, which significantly affects the capillary force, evaporation, and condensation in a heat pipe, will be discussed including the effects of temperature and surface roughness. Following this, advancing and receding contact angles will be addressed including the velocity effect. Finally, this chapter will cover primary factors affecting thin film evaporation which plays a key role in a heat pipe. The goal of this chapter is to provide the fundamentals related to interface surface, surface tension, contact angle, and phase change heat transfer occurring in heat pipes.

2.2 Surface Tension

When liquid flows down in a vertical capillary tube, as shown in Fig. 2.1, a small drop with an almost round shape starts to form and hang from the lower end of the capillary tube. This pendant suspended from the lower end of the capillary caused

© Springer Science+Business Media New York 2015
H. Ma, *Oscillating Heat Pipes*, DOI 10.1007/978-1-4939-2504-9_2

Fig. 2.1 Drops formed
from the lower end of a
vertical capillary

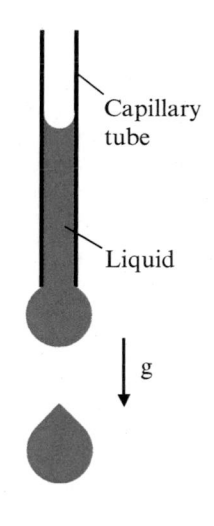

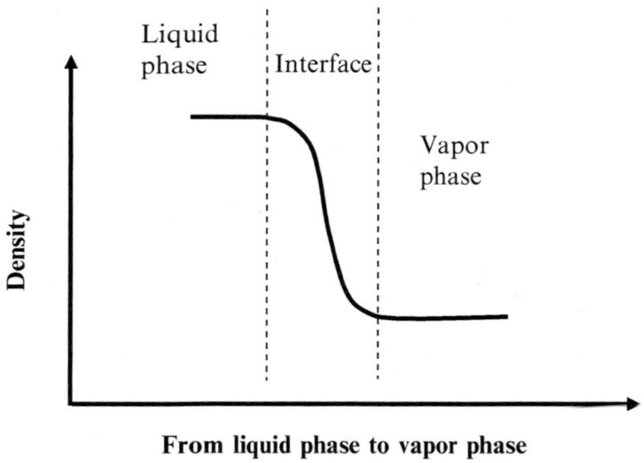

Capillary
tube

Liquid

g

Fig. 2.2 Density variation
across the liquid–vapor
interface

Liquid
phase | Interface |

Vapor
phase

Density

From liquid phase to vapor phase

by the gravity is clearly balanced by a force. As the pendant becomes larger, the
gravitational force acting on this pendant increases. When the gravitational force is
larger than the force holding this pendant, the pendant detaches itself. The falling
liquid is like a rain drop which holds its shape with this force again. This force is
called surface tension. Surface tension is a force that operates on the surface and
acts perpendicularly and inwardly from the boundaries of the surface, which tends
to decrease the area of the interface. As a result, the liquid will form a shape having
a minimum area. In the case of zero gravity in vacuum, the liquid drop will be a
perfect sphere.

Figure 2.2 illustrates the molecule density variation across the liquid–vapor
interface. As shown, the molecule density in the liquid phase is much higher than
that in the vapor phase, and the density change across the liquid–vapor interface is
gradual although the thickness is only several molecules in diameters. It is well

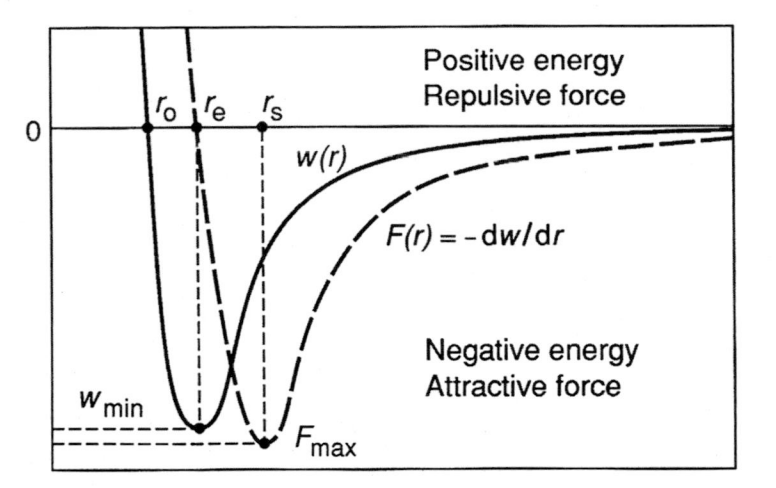

Fig. 2.3 Distance effect on the potential energy (Israelachvili 1992)

known that when two objects or two molecules interact with each other, the potential energy can be described by the Mie Pair Potential, i.e.,

$$w(r) = -\frac{A}{r^n} + \frac{B}{r^m} \tag{2.1}$$

Using Eq. (2.1), the positive energy due to the repulsive forces and the negative energy due to the attractive forces can be predicted as shown in Fig. 2.3. As shown, the distance between two molecules directly affects the repulsive/attractive forces and positive/negative energies between two molecules. From Fig. 2.2, it can be found that the density of the liquid phase is much greater than that of the vapor phase. It means that the distance among molecules in the liquid phase is much smaller than that in the vapor phase, and the distance between two molecules in the interface region varies from that in the liquid phase to the vapor phase. From the molecular point of view, surface tension can be viewed as a consequence of attractive and repulsive forces among molecules near the interface. The origins of intermolecular interactions can be further classified as the van der Waals forces, hydrogen bonding forces, metallic bonds, ionic bonds, hydrophobic interactions, and solvation forces (Israelachvili 1992).

Consider a liquid column in a capillary tube as shown in Fig. 2.4. Due to surface tension, the liquid in the capillary is wicking up with a wicking height of h_w. If the capillary tube is very small, and the liquid is perfectly wetting, i.e., the force due to the surface tension will act along y direction only, then if an external force is added on the top surface of the liquid column, the liquid level of the liquid column with perimeter P will move down by a distance of dL. The total work done by the external force, dw, can be expressed as

Fig. 2.4 Surface tension

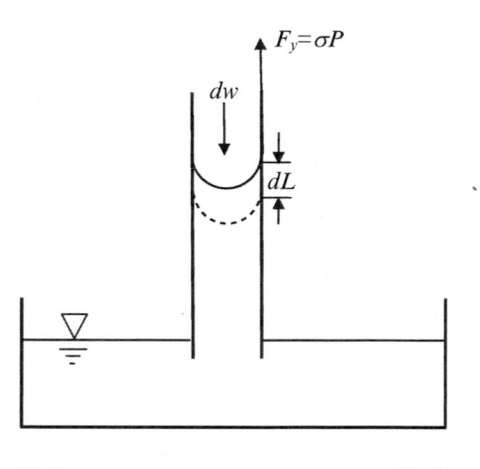

$$dw = \sigma P\, dL \tag{2.2}$$

It shows that this work, dw, is proportional to the product of the tube perimeter and the increase of the distance, $dA = P\, dL$, i.e.,

$$dw = \sigma\, dA \tag{2.3}$$

where the constant σ is the surface tension. By rearranging Eq. (2.3), it can be found that

$$\sigma = \frac{dw}{dA} \tag{2.4}$$

This means that the surface tension is the energy per unit area. From Eq. (2.4), it can be found that the surface tension has the dimension of energy per unit area (J/m^2) or force per unit length (N/m).

Surface tension can be considered as consisting of dispersion forces which make up the most important contribution to the van der Waals forces (Israelachvili 1992) and other specific forces such as metallic or hydrogen bonding, i.e., $\sigma = \sigma_d + \sigma_m$. Surface tension in nonpolar liquids is entirely caused by dispersion forces. In hydrogen-bonded liquids, both dispersion forces and hydrogen bonding contribute to relatively larger values of surface tension. In liquid metals, the metallic force combined with the dispersion force results in higher values of surface tension. What naturally follows is the principle that surface tensions of liquid metals are higher than those of hydrogen-bonded liquids such as water, which in turn are higher than those of nonpolar liquids such as pure hydrocarbons.

Surface tension is significantly dependent on temperature. As temperature increases, the surface tension decreases, and when the temperature is increased to the critical temperature, the surface tension between the liquid and vapor disappears. For example, the surface tension between the liquid and vapor of pure water can be determined by (Carey 1992)

$$\sigma = 0.2358 \left(1 - \frac{T_{sat}}{T_c}\right)^{1.256} \left[1 - 0.625 \left(1 - \frac{T_{sat}}{T_c}\right)\right] \tag{2.5}$$

where the saturation temperature, T_{sat}, and the critical temperature, T_c, are in Kelvin. This expression matches the available data for water within a range of $\pm 0.5 \%$ for $0.01 \leq T \leq 300 \,°C$ or $\pm 13 \%$ for $300 \leq T \leq 374.16 \,°C$. For a given range of temperature, the surface tension decreases linearly as the temperature increases, which can be expressed as

$$\sigma = C_0 - C_1 T \tag{2.6}$$

where T is in degree Celsius. The constants C_0 and C_1 can be found in Table 2.1. It should be noticed that results predicted by Eq. (2.6) are limited in the temperature ranges indicated in Table 2.1. For example, the surface tension of pure water predicted by Eq. (2.5), as shown in Eq. (2.6), agrees very well within a temperature range from 0.01 to 100 °C.

As described above, surface tension depends on temperature. As surface temperature increases, surface tension decreases. If there is a temperature difference between locations A and B for a thin liquid film as shown in Fig. 2.5, the surface tensions between locations A and B will be different. If the surface temperature at location A is higher than that at location B, the surface tension at location B will be higher than that at location A. Because of the surface tension difference between locations A and B, a shear stress at the liquid–vapor interface due the surface tension is produced, i.e.,

$$\tau_\sigma = \frac{d\sigma}{dx} \tag{2.7}$$

Due to this shear stress, the liquid near location A will flow toward location B as shown in Fig. 2.5. This phenomenon where fluid flow is due to the surface tension gradient is known as the Marangoni flow or Marangoni effect (Butt et al. 2013). When temperature changes, surface tension varies resulting in a fluid flow. This flow is also called the thermal capillary flow. The surface tension gradient or the shear stress at the liquid–vapor interface can be obtained by two working fluids with different surface tensions. For example, if the thin liquid film shown in Fig. 2.5 has a uniform temperature, a second fluid with a lower surface tension is generally induced at location A. The surface tension at location A is lower than that at location B. This surface tension difference is due to the composition effect of the working fluids. The liquid with a higher surface tension pulls more strongly on the surrounding liquid than one with a low surface tension. The presence of shear stress at the liquid–vapor interface shown in Eq. (2.7) will naturally cause the liquid to flow away from regions of low surface tension. If some dust or floating particles are

Table 2.1 Constants C_0 and C_1 for some common working fluids

Substance	C_0 (mN/m)	C_1 (mN/m °C)	Temperature range T (°C)	Error (%)
Acetone	25.907	0.1247	−40 to 140	0.59
Acetylene	3.42	0.1935	−90 to −50	
Ammonia	26.23	0.2129	−33 to 117	0.63
Argon	−34.28	0.2493	−189 to −181	
Butane	14.87	0.1206	−70 to 20	
n-Butyl alcohol	27.18	0.08983	10 to 100	
Carbon tetrachloride	29.49	0.1224	15 to 105	
Cesium	72.878	0.0482	227 to 1,227	0.51
Chlorine	19.87	0.1897	−80 to −30	
Dowtherm	39.836	0.0885	100 to 400	0.16
Ethane	1.2159	0.1675	−120 to 0	1.04
Ethanol	25.183	0.1027	0 to 240	2.15
Ethyl alcohol	24.05	0.0832	10 to 70	
Ethylene glycol	50.21	0.0890	20 to 140	
Fluorine	−16.10	0.1646	−202 to −188	
Freon-113	21.338	0.1053	−10 to 70	0.04
Freon-21	21.327	0.1409	−60 to 120	0.18
Freon-22	12.078	0.1575	−100 to 60	0.31
Heptane	22.324	0.0967	20 to 160	0.06
Hydrazine	72.41	0.2407	15 to 40	
Hydrogen peroxide	78.97	0.1549	2 to 20	
Isopropyl alcohol	22.90	0.0789	10 to 80	
Lead	488.81	0.1238	1,127 to 2,227	0.32
Lithium	422.16	0.1381	627 to 1,727	0.11
Mercury	410.18	0.3325	−173 to 427	0.58
Methanol	25.137	0.1009	0 to 220	0.65
Methyl alcohol	24.00	0.0773	10 to 60	
Nitrogen	−31.496	0.2058	−203 to −153	0.57
Octane	23.52	0.09509	10 to 120	
Oxygen	−33.72	0.2561	−202 to −184	
Potassium	116.11	0.0571	327 to 1,227	0.51
Propane	9.22	0.0874	−90 to 10	
Rubidium	96.696	0.0631	227 to 1,227	0.73
Silver	1,072.6	0.1961	1,227 to 2,127	1.18
Sodium	204.85	0.1001	327 to 1,527	0.02
Sulfur dioxide	26.58	0.1948	−50 to 10	
Water	77.703	0.1953	20 to 200	0.03

Notes:
1. The linear relation of the form $\sigma = C_0 - C_1 T$
2. The data of the items with Error (%) shown in the last column are obtained from Faghri (1995, pp. 822 832); The data of items without Error (%) shown in the last column are from Carey (1992, p. 43)

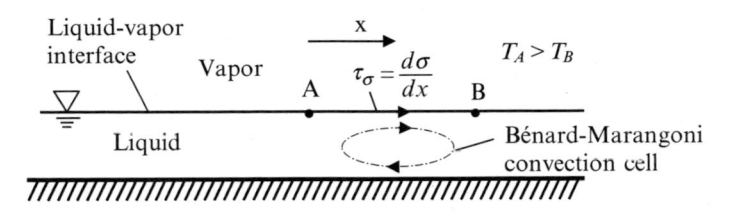

Fig. 2.5 Bénard–Marangoni effect

placed on the surface between locations A and B, it can be found that those dust or floating particles will flow toward location B.

This discussion on the effect of shear stress on liquid does not include the wall temperature effect. If the wall temperature is much higher than the interfacial temperatures T_A or T_B, heat is transferred through a thin liquid film. The liquid temperature near the wall is higher than the interface temperature. This difference directly results in a density difference which produces a buoyancy force. This buoyancy force along with the shear stress near the wall and the surface tension gradient at the liquid–vapor interface produce a convection cell as shown in Fig. 2.5, which is also called the Bénard–Marangoni convection cell (Carey 1992).

2.3   Laplace–Young Equation

When a capillary is plugged into liquid, liquid wicks up. Figure 2.6 shows how surface tension pulls the liquid column up thereby producing a wicking height. If the capillary radius is very small and the meniscus radius at the liquid–vapor interface is constant, the force along y direction (due to surface tension) can be found as

$$F_y = \sigma 2\pi r_0 \cos \alpha \tag{2.8}$$

where α is the contact angle. The weight produced by the liquid column can be determined approximately by

$$W_g \approx \pi r_0^2 h_w \rho_l g \tag{2.9}$$

Based on the force balance, the wicking height can be found by

$$h_w = \frac{2\sigma \cos \alpha}{g \rho_l r_0} \tag{2.10}$$

Fig. 2.6 Wicking height
in a capillary tube

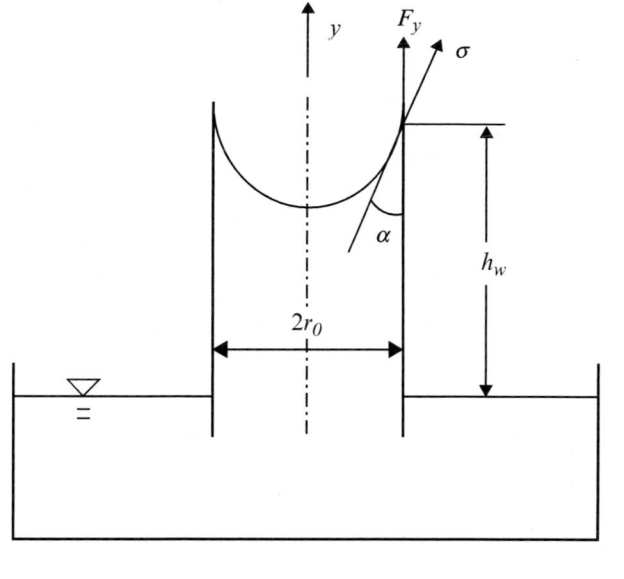

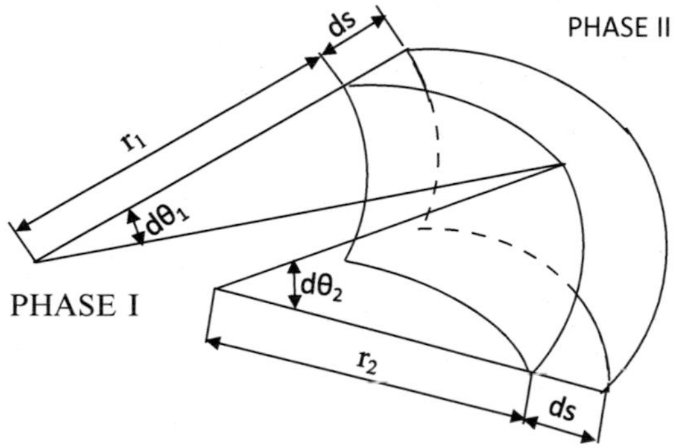

Fig. 2.7 Pressure
difference across the
liquid–vapor interface

As shown in Eq. (2.10), the wicking height depends primarily on the surface tension, contact angle, and capillary radius. If the capillary radius becomes very large or the contact angle is equal to 90°, the meniscus radius of the liquid–vapor interface is equal to infinity and the wicking height descends to zero. In other words, the increase in wicking height can only exist when the liquid–vapor interface has a curved surface.

Consider a curved liquid–vapor interface as shown in Fig. 2.7, which can be characterized by two distinct radii of curvatures, r_1 and r_2 which are oriented perpendicular to each other. For the curved liquid–vapor interface shown in Fig. 2.7, a control volume consisting of the liquid–vapor interface and the regions immediately adjacent to this interface are selected. For this control volume, there are three regions: the region labeled Phase I, the interfacial region, and the region labeled Phase II. The interface region has a thickness of ds. For the selected control

volume, the three regions have the same temperature at a thermodynamic equilibrium. From the basics of classical thermodynamics, at a constant volume condition, the changes in free energy for all three regions can be found as

$$dF_I = -S_I dT + \mu_I dN_I - (p\,dV)_I \tag{2.11}$$

$$dF_{II} = -S_{II} dT + \mu_{II} dN_{II} - (p\,dV)_{II} \tag{2.12}$$

$$dF_{int} = -S_{int} dT + \mu_{int} dN_{int} + \sigma\,dA_{int} \tag{2.13}$$

respectively, where F is the free energy, S is the entropy, μ is the chemical potential, N is the number of moles, p is the pressure, V is the volume, and A is the interfacial area. Hence, total differential energy change for all three regions can be determined by

$$dF = dF_I + dF_{II} + dF_{int} = -S_I dT + \mu_I dN_I - (p\,dV)_I$$
$$- S_{II} dT + \mu_{II} dN_{II} - (p\,dV)_{II} - S_{int} dT + \mu_{int} dN_{int} + \sigma\,dA_{int} \tag{2.14}$$

At a thermodynamic equilibrium with a constant temperature and a constant volume, the total energy is a constant, the total number of moles and the total volume do not change, and the temperature is a constant, i.e.,

$$\begin{aligned} dF &= 0 \\ dV &= dV_I + dV_{II} = 0 \\ dN &= dN_I + dN_{int} + dN_{II} = 0 \\ dT &= 0 \end{aligned} \tag{2.15}$$

Considering Eq. (2.15) and $\mu_I = \mu_{II} = \mu_{int}$, Eq. (2.14) becomes

$$p_I - p_{II} = \sigma \frac{dA_{int}}{dV_{int}} \tag{2.16}$$

where the differential interfacial area, dA_{int}, can be determined by

$$dA_{int} = (r_1 + ds)\delta\theta_1 (r_2 + ds)\delta\theta_2 - r_1\delta\theta_1 r_2\delta\theta_2 = r_2 ds\delta\theta_1\delta\theta_2 + r_1 ds\delta\theta_1\delta\theta_2 \tag{2.17}$$

dV_{int} can be approximately found by

$$dV_{int} = r_1 d\theta_1 r_2 d\theta_2 ds \tag{2.18}$$

Substituting Eqs. (2.17) and (2.18) into Eq. (2.16) yields

$$p_{\text{I}} - p_{\text{II}} = \sigma\left(\frac{1}{r_1} + \frac{1}{r_2}\right) \tag{2.19}$$

Equation (2.19) is the well-known Laplace–Young equation. It indicates that when a liquid–vapor interface has a curved surface characterized with two meniscus radii, r_1 and r_2, which are perpendicular to each other, there is a pressure difference across the liquid–vapor interface.

Example 2.1 When a capillary with a radius of r_0 is plugged into liquid, the liquid wicks up as shown in Fig. 2.6. Use Eq. (2.19) to show that the wicking height can be expressed as $h_{\text{w}} = \frac{2\sigma \cos \alpha}{g \rho_l r_0}$. It is assumed that the capillary radius is very small and the meniscus radius at the liquid–vapor interface is a constant. The contact angle is α.

Solution For the liquid–vapor interface as shown in Fig. 2.6, the pressure difference across the liquid–vapor interface can be found as

$$p_{\text{v}} - p_l = \sigma\left(\frac{1}{r_1} + \frac{1}{r_2}\right) \tag{2.20}$$

For the liquid–vapor interface with a constant meniscus radius in a round capillary tube, the meniscus radius r_1 is equal to the meniscus radius r_2, i.e., $r_1 = r_2 = r$. Equation (2.20) can be expressed as

$$p_{\text{v}} - p_l = \frac{2\sigma}{r} \tag{2.21}$$

Considering the contact angle and the assumption of constant meniscus radius, the meniscus radius, r, can be found as

$$r = \frac{r_0}{\cos \alpha} \tag{2.22}$$

Considering Eq. (2.22), the liquid pressure just across the liquid–vapor interface can be determined as

$$p_l = p_{\text{v}} - \frac{2\sigma \cos \alpha}{r_0} \tag{2.23}$$

As shown, the liquid pressure just across the liquid–vapor interface is $\frac{2\sigma \cos \alpha}{r_0}$ less than the vapor pressure. As a result, this pressure difference will pull the liquid column up resulting in a wicking height. If the vapor density is much smaller than the liquid density, the pressure difference, $\frac{2\sigma \cos \alpha}{r_0}$, will be used to overcome the weight due to the liquid column height, i.e.,

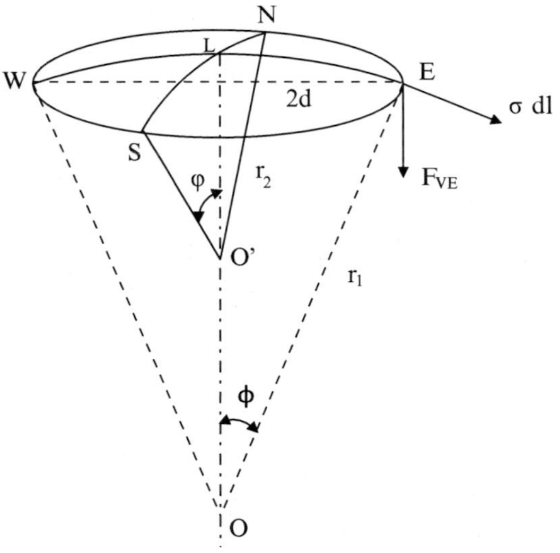

Fig. 2.8 Force balance
analysis of liquid–vapor
interface

$$\frac{2\sigma \cos \alpha}{r_0} = \rho_l g h_w \tag{2.24}$$

The wicking height can be found as $h_w = \frac{2\sigma \cos \alpha}{g \rho_l r_0}$. This wicking height is due to the pressure difference across the liquid–vapor interface produced by the interface meniscus radii, which is called capillary pressure.

Example 2.2 Consider an EW/SN section of liquid–vapor interface for a liquid droplet. The circumference of the selected section, as shown in Fig. 2.8, will have a perfect circle with a diameter of $2d$. Derive the Laplace–Young equation using the force balance.

Solution For the EW/SN section of the liquid droplet, the circumference can be uniformly divided into four elements, i.e., dl_E, dl_W, dl_N, and dl_S. For the element dl_E, the surface tension, σ, produces a force of σdl_E resulting in a resolved downward force, F_E, which can be expressed as

$$F_E = \sigma dl_E \sin \phi \tag{2.25}$$

When the element becomes very small, i.e., $d \to 0$, $\sin \phi = \frac{d}{r_1}$ then Eq. (2.25) becomes

$$F_E = \sigma dl_E \frac{d}{r_1} \tag{2.26}$$

The total downward force acting on four similar elements of dl_E, dl_W, dl_N, and dl_S can be found as

$$F = F_E + F_W + F_S + F_N = \frac{2\sigma\pi d}{4}\left(\frac{2d}{r_1}+\frac{2d}{r_2}\right) = \sigma\pi d^2\left(\frac{1}{r_1}+\frac{1}{r_2}\right) \qquad (2.27)$$

Because the droplet is not in motion, there is an upward force to balance this downward force. This upward force will be due to the pressure difference between the liquid phase and the vapor phase; hence,

$$\pi d^2(p_I - p_{II}) \qquad (2.28)$$

By Newton's third law, this force is equal to the force caused by surface tension, i.e.,

$$\pi d^2(p_I - p_{II}) = \sigma\pi d^2\left(\frac{1}{r_1}+\frac{1}{r_2}\right) \qquad (2.29)$$

and the Laplace–Young equation can be shown as

$$p_I - p_{II} = \sigma\left(\frac{1}{r_1}+\frac{1}{r_2}\right) \qquad (2.30)$$

Example 2.3 As shown in Fig. 2.9, two capillaries with diameters of $D_1 = 1.0$ mm and $D_2 = 2.0$ mm are put into a reservoir filled with saturated water at a temperature of 100 °C. Determine the wicking height difference between two capillaries ($\alpha_1 = 30°$, $\alpha_2 = 105°$, $\sigma = 0.059$ N/m, and $\rho = 958\,\text{kg/m}^3$)

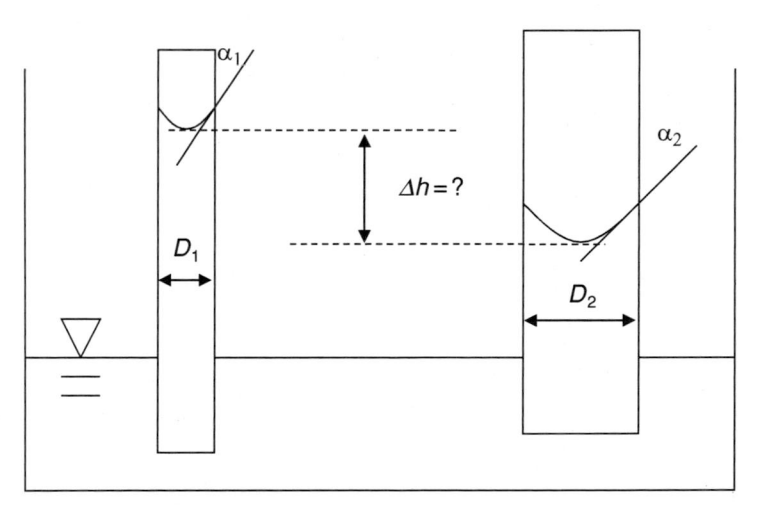

Fig. 2.9 Wicking height calculation

Solution Because the diameters of both capillaries are small, it can be assumed that the meniscus radii of both liquid–vapor interfaces are constant. Considering Eq. (2.10), the wicking height for a capillary with a diameter of 1.0 mm, i.e., $r_{0,1} = D_1/2 = 0.5\,\text{mm} = 0.0005\,\text{m}$, and a contact angle of $\alpha_1 = 30°$ can be found as

$$h_{w,1} = \frac{2\sigma \cos \alpha}{g\rho_l r_{0,1}} = \frac{2 \times 0.059 \times \cos 30°}{9.8 \times 958 \times 0.0005} = 0.0217\,\text{m} = 21.7\,\text{mm}$$

The wicking height for the capillary with a diameter of 2.0 mm, i.e., $r_{0,1} = D_2/2 = 1.0\,\text{mm}$, and a contact angle of $\alpha_1 = 105°$, can be calculated as

$$h_{w,2} = \frac{2\sigma \cos \alpha}{g\rho_l r_{0,2}} = \frac{2 \times 0.059 \times \cos 105°}{9.8 \times 958 \times 0.001} = -0.00325\,\text{m} = -3.25\,\text{mm}$$

The wicking height difference is

$$\Delta h = h_{w,1} - h_{w,2} = 21.7 - (-3.15) = 24.85\,\text{mm}$$

It shows that when the contact angle is higher than $90°$, the wicking height is negative which means the liquid level is below the liquid level of the reservoir.

2.4 Saturation Pressure

For a heat pipe to be functional, a pure working fluid, which has a homogeneous and invariable chemical composition, must be charged inside. The evaporation in the evaporator and the condensation in the condenser play a key role in the heat transfer process of a heat pipe. For a given heat pipe, the total volume is fixed and the internal volume is constant. The evaporation and condensation processes are taking place in a chamber with a constant volume. Let's consider a chamber filled with a pure working fluid, for example, a mixture of water liquid and vapor as shown in Fig. 2.10. If the system has a constant temperature,

Fig. 2.10 Phase change for a pure working fluid in a constant volume

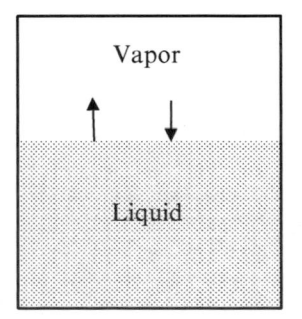

i.e., vapor temperature is equal to liquid temperature, the saturation pressure indicates that the number of molecules leaving the liquid phase is equal to the number of molecules going into the liquid phase from the vapor phase. The liquid and vapor phases are in a thermodynamic equilibrium. Because temperature is a measurement of the molecule movement, the molecule movement varies when the temperature changes. For a given temperature, there is a given saturation pressure corresponding to that temperature. For the system shown in Fig. 2.10, the entropy, pressure, volume, and temperature can be described by one of the Maxwell relations (Wylen and Sonntag 1968), i.e.,

$$\left(\frac{\partial p}{\partial T}\right)_v = \left(\frac{\partial s}{\partial v}\right)_T \tag{2.31}$$

Integrating Eq. (2.31) from the saturated liquid state to saturated vapor state yields

$$\left(\frac{dp}{dT}\right)_{sat} = \frac{s_v - s_l}{v_v - v_l} \tag{2.32}$$

For a constant temperature, the specific entropy difference between the saturated liquid state and saturated vapor state can be found as

$$s_v - s_l = \frac{h_v - h_l}{T} = \frac{h_{lv}}{T} \tag{2.33}$$

where h_v and h_l are the saturated vapor and saturated liquid enthalpies, respectively, and h_{lv} is the latent heat per unit mass. Considering Eq. (2.33), Eq. (2.32) becomes

$$\left(\frac{dp}{dT}\right)_{sat} = \frac{h_{lv}}{(v_v - v_l)T} \tag{2.34}$$

Equation (2.34) is called the Clausius–Clapeyron equation. Using Eq. (2.34), the saturation pressure difference can be calculated for a given saturation temperature difference.

Example 2.4 If the saturation pressure of water at 100 °C is 101,325 Pa, what is the saturation temperature when the pressure increases to 105,325 Pa?

Solution Based on the saturation condition at 100 °C, i.e., $T = 100\,°C = 373.15\,K$, the specific volumes of liquid and vapor can be found as $v_l = 0.001043\,m^3/kg$ and $v_v = 1.6735\,m^3/kg$, respectively, and the latent heat $h_{lv} = 2,256.6\,kJ/kg$. Substituting them into Eq. (2.34) yields

$$\left(\frac{dp}{dT}\right)_{sat} = \frac{h_{lv}}{(v_v - v_l)T} = \frac{2,256,600}{(1.6735 - 0.001043)373.15} = 3,618\,\text{Pa/K}$$

Considering the pressure difference, $dp = 105,325 - 101,325 = 4,000\,\text{Pa}$, the saturation temperature variation due to this pressure difference can be calculated as

$$dT = \frac{dp}{3,618} = \frac{4,000}{3,618} = 1.105\,^\circ\text{C}$$

Therefore, the saturation temperature corresponding to the saturation pressure of 105,325 Pa can be calculated as

$$T = 100 + 1.105 = 101.105\,^\circ\text{C}.$$

If one checks this calculated value with the experimental data, it can be found that the calculated result is acceptable.

   If one is using the saturated condition of water at a temperature of 100 °C and its corresponding pressure of 101,325 Pa to calculate the saturated temperature at the saturated pressure of 202,650 Pa, is the calculated result by Eq. (2.34) still acceptable? In this situation, $\left(\frac{dp}{dT}\right)_{sat}$ is still equal to 3,618 Pa/K; however, the pressure difference becomes

$$dp = 202,650 - 101,325 = 101,325\,\text{Pa}$$

The saturation temperature difference can be found as

$$dT = \frac{dp}{3,618} = \frac{101,325}{3,618} = 28.006\,^\circ\text{C}$$

The calculated saturation temperature corresponding to the saturation pressure of 202,650 Pa will be

$$T = 100 + 28.006 = 128.006\,^\circ\text{C}$$

Checking the experimental data of the saturation temperature at the saturation pressure of 202,660 Pa, it can be found that

$$T = 120.0\,^\circ\text{C}.$$

The difference between the calculated saturation temperature by Eq. (2.34) and the real value is about 8 °C, which is not acceptable. Clearly, it shows that the pressure difference or temperature difference in Eq. (2.34) must be small.

   If the liquid density, ρ_l, is much higher than the vapor density, ρ_v, i.e., $\frac{1}{\rho_l} \ll \frac{1}{\rho_v}$ or $v_l \ll v_v$, Eq. (2.34) becomes

$$\left(\frac{dp}{dT}\right)_{\text{sat}} = \frac{h_{lv}}{v_v T} \qquad (2.35)$$

If vapor is an ideal gas, the specific volume can be expressed as

$$v_v = \frac{RT}{p} \qquad (2.36)$$

R in Eq. (2.36) is the ideal gas constant, which can be found as

$$R = \frac{\overline{R}}{\overline{M}} \qquad (2.37)$$

where $\overline{R}$ is the universal gas constant equal to 8,314.5 kJ/(kmol·K) and $\overline{M}$ is the molar mass (kg/kmol). Substituting Eq. (2.36) into Eq. (2.35), it can be found that

$$\left(\frac{dp}{dT}\right)_{\text{sat}} = \frac{ph_{lv}}{RT^2} \qquad (2.38)$$

Rearranging Eq. (2.38) and integrating from the reference pressure, p_0, and the reference temperature, T_0, to the temperature, T, and the pressure, p, respectively, yields

$$p = p_0 e^{\frac{h_{lv}}{R}\left(\frac{T - T_0}{TT_0}\right)} \qquad (2.39)$$

Equation (2.39) is also called the Clausius–Clapeyron equation. It should be noticed that Eq. (2.39) is valid only when vapor is an ideal gas and the vapor density is much smaller than the liquid density.

Equations (2.34) and (2.39) can be used to find the relationship between the saturation pressure and saturation temperature for which phase change takes place on a flat liquid–vapor interface. When the liquid–vapor interface has a curved surface, the pressure difference across the liquid–vapor interface can be predicted by the Laplace–Young equation as shown in Eq. (2.19). For a system, any change in the Gibbs energy can be described by

$$dg = v\,dp - s\,dT \qquad (2.40)$$

Here, the Gibbs energy changes due to the pressure difference across the liquid–vapor interface for liquid can be found as

$$\Delta g = \int_0^{\Delta p} v\,dp = v\,\Delta p = v\sigma\left(\frac{1}{r_1} + \frac{1}{r_2}\right) \qquad (2.41)$$

If one considers a drop in its vapor, Eq. (2.41) becomes

$$\Delta g = \frac{2\sigma v_l}{r} \tag{2.42}$$

With an assumption of an ideal gas, i.e., $v_v = \frac{RT}{p}$, the Gibbs energy change for the vapor phase can be found as

$$\Delta g = RT \ln \left(\frac{p_k}{p} \right) \tag{2.43}$$

In an equilibrium, Eq. (2.41) or (2.42) is equal to Eq. (2.43), i.e.,

$$RT \ln \left(\frac{p_k}{p} \right) = v\sigma \left(\frac{1}{r_1} + \frac{1}{r_2} \right) \tag{2.44}$$

or

$$RT \ln \left(\frac{p_k}{p} \right) = \frac{2\sigma v_l}{r} \tag{2.45}$$

for a droplet. Rearranging Eq. (2.45) yields

$$p_k = p e^{\frac{2\sigma v_l}{rRT}} \tag{2.46}$$

Equation (2.46) is called the Kelvin equation. As shown in Eq. (2.46), the curvature directly affects the saturation pressure. When the radius of a droplet becomes smaller, the saturation pressure increases. Considering Eq. (2.39), Eq. (2.46) becomes

$$p_k = p_0 e^{\frac{h_{lv}}{R} \left(\frac{T-T_0}{TT_0} \right) + \frac{2\sigma v_l}{rRT}} \tag{2.47}$$

which includes the effects of temperature and curvature on the saturation pressure. Considering the electric field effect, Ma and Peterson (1995) derived an equation, i.e.,

$$p_{e+k} = p_0 e^{\frac{h_{lv}}{R} \left(\frac{T-T_0}{TT_0} \right) + \frac{2\sigma v_l}{rRT} - \frac{v_l \chi \epsilon_0 E^2}{2}} \tag{2.48}$$

As shown, Eq. (2.48) can consider the electric field effect on the saturation pressure in addition to the effects of temperature and curvature for a droplet. As shown in Fig. 2.11, when the strength of the electric field increases, the saturation pressure can be increased, and when the strength of the electric field is higher than a value, the saturation pressure can be significantly increased. Using this equation, it might be better to explain how lightning in the cloud affects rainfall.

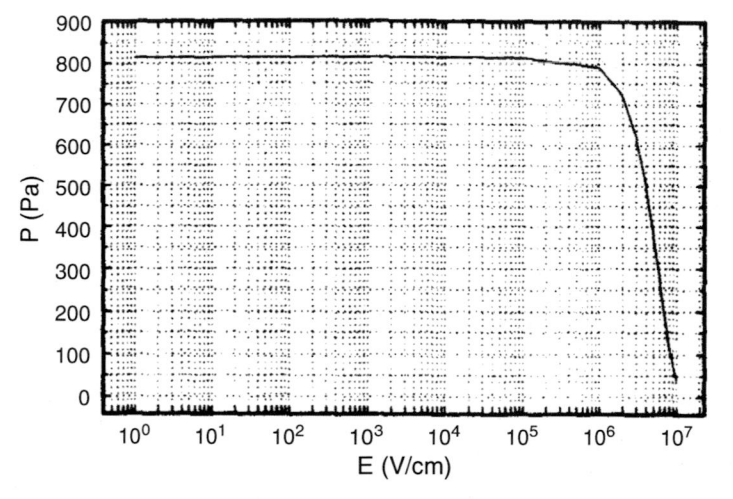

Fig. 2.11 Electric field effect on the saturation pressure ($T = 273.15$ K, $v_l = 0.001093$ m³/kg, $X = 80$, $\varepsilon_0 = 8.845 \times 10^{-12}$ C²/(N·m²)) (Ma and Peterson 1995)

When a droplet is in its vapor, the curvature affects the saturation pressure, and when the radius of the drop decreases, the saturation pressure increases as shown in Eq. (2.46). This effect obviously is due to the pressure difference across the liquid–vapor interface. Now consider a bubble in its liquid with a radius r. Using the Laplace–Young equation, it can be readily found that the pressure difference between the vapor bubble and its liquid is

$$p_l - p_v = -\frac{2\sigma}{r} \tag{2.49}$$

The negative sign is due to the negative curvature of the liquid–vapor interface. As a result, the Kelvin equation for a bubble in its liquid can be found as

$$p_k = p e^{-\frac{2\sigma v_l}{rRT}} \tag{2.50}$$

or

$$p_k = p_0 e^{\frac{h_{lv}}{R}\left(\frac{T-T_0}{TT_0}\right) - \frac{2\sigma v_l}{rRT}} \tag{2.51}$$

As shown in Eq. (2.50) or (2.51), when a bubble is formed in its liquid, the saturation pressure decreases as the bubble radius decreases.

As shown in Eq. (2.50) or (2.51), when a meniscus radius exists, the saturation pressure decreases. For example, if p_∞ is the equilibrium vapor pressure of the liquid for a planar liquid–vapor interface, p_k, the equilibrium vapor pressure of the liquid for a bubble with a meniscus radius of r can be found as

Fig. 2.12 Capillary
evaporation

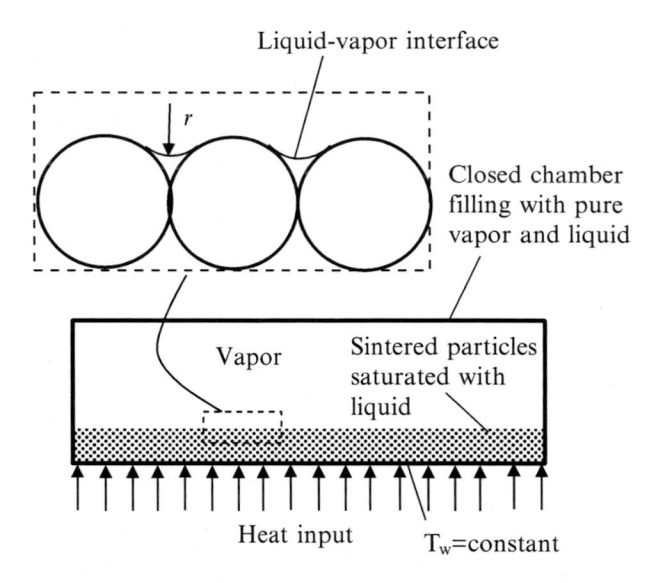

Equation (2.52) can be used to explain the capillary evaporation and capillary condensation phenomena. Consider a surface, for example, coated with sintered particles in a closed chamber and the vapor space is large enough with a constant vapor pressure. When heat is added on the wall which has a constant temperature, evaporation takes place and causes the liquid–vapor interface to recede into the cornered region, and the meniscus radius of the liquid–vapor interface decreases as shown in Fig. 2.12. Due to the curvature variation, the saturation pressure of the working fluid is reduced by

$$\Delta p = p_\infty \left(1 - e^{-\frac{2\sigma v_l}{rRT}} \right) \tag{2.53}$$

The saturation temperature variation due to the saturation pressure variation determined by Eq. (2.53) can be found by Eq. (2.34), i.e.,

$$\Delta T = \Delta p \frac{(v_v - v_l)T}{h_{lv}} \tag{2.54}$$

Substituting Eq. (2.53) into Eq. (2.54), the saturation temperature change can be found as

$$\Delta T = p_\infty \left(1 - e^{-\frac{2\sigma v_l}{rRT}} \right) \frac{(v_v - v_l)T}{h_{lv}} \tag{2.55}$$

Clearly, when the meniscus radius increases, an additional superheat is produced for a given wall temperature, which can enhance the evaporation heat transfer. This phenomenon can be called the capillary evaporation.

Consider air with a relative humidity of ϕ, which is defined as the ratio of the partial pressure, p_{air}, of water vapor in an air–water mixture to the saturated vapor pressure, p_{sat}, of water, i.e.,

$$\phi = \frac{p_{air}}{p_{sat}} \tag{2.56}$$

When a pore or a curved liquid–vapor interface with a meniscus radius of r exists, the saturation pressure can be predicted by Eq. (2.52). Substituting Eq. (2.52) into Eq. (2.56), the relative humidity due to the curvature effect can be found as

$$\phi = \frac{p_{air}}{p_\infty} e^{\frac{2\sigma v_l}{rRT}} \tag{2.57}$$

As shown in Eq. (2.57), the relative humidity is increased by $e^{\frac{2\sigma v_l}{rRT}}$. Clearly, it shows that when a pore or liquid–vapor interface exists, the water vapor in air can easily reach the dew point where condensation takes place. This phenomenon is called the capillary condensation. Using this, for example, it can be readily explained why oatmeal or some other food with porous structures can easily catch moisture.

2.5 Contact Angle

When a liquid drop is on a solid surface, as shown in Fig. 2.13, there is an angle where a liquid–vapor interface meets the solid surface. This measured angle between the liquid–vapor interface and the solid surface starting from point O is known as the contact angle. The contact angle is the result of surface tensions from the interactions among three phases: liquid, solid, and vapor or gas. For the system shown in Fig. 2.13, the surface tension between liquid and vapor is indicated by σ_{lv}, the surface tension between liquid and solid by σ_{ls}, and the surface tension between the vapor and solid by σ_{vs}. Because the liquid drop is not moving and is at equilibrium, the force balance along the x-direction can be found as

Fig. 2.13 Contact angle

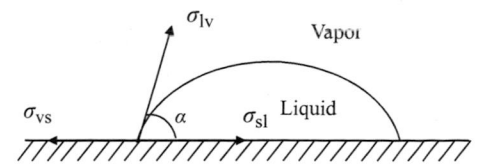

$$\sigma_{ls} + \sigma_{lv} \cos \alpha - \sigma_{vs} = 0 \tag{2.58}$$

Rearranging Eq. (2.58) yields

$$\cos \alpha = \frac{\sigma_{vs} - \sigma_{ls}}{\sigma_{lv}} \tag{2.59}$$

which is called Young's equation. The contact angle can be used to describe the wettability of the liquid. For example, when a water drop on a surface has a contact angle less than 90°, the surface becomes wetting and is called a hydrophilic surface which has an affinity for water. When the contact angle is larger than 90°, the surface is called a hydrophobic surface which tends to repel water. Equation (2.59) is based on the equilibrium state. Therefore, the contact angle defined by Eq. (2.59) is sometimes known as the equilibrium contact angle.

From a thermodynamic point of view, the surface tension may be interpreted in terms of energy stored in the molecules near the interface (Tadmor 2004). Equation (2.59) can be obtained by energy conservation. Consider a small droplet floating in a medium such as in vapor as shown in Fig. 2.14. The droplet has the shape of a sphere with radius r. Due to the surface tension and curvature, the pressure difference between the inside and outside of the droplet can be described by the Laplace–Young equation, i.e.,

$$\Delta p = \frac{2\sigma_{lv}}{r} \tag{2.60}$$

Now this droplet is brought to a surface and stays on this surface as shown in Fig. 2.14. As the droplet touches the surface, the droplet may spread beyond just a point contact depending on the interfacial tensions of σ_{lv}, σ_{ls}, and σ_{vs}. The droplet will form a cap that is part of a sphere with radius R_s as shown in Fig. 2.15. The radius of the sphere, R_s, is much larger than the radius, r, of the droplet before it is placed on the surface. During the spreading process of the droplet, the contact area, A_{sl}, between the liquid and solid surfaces increases, and the contact area, A_{sv}, between the solid and vapor decreases. The change in the contact area, A_{lv}, between

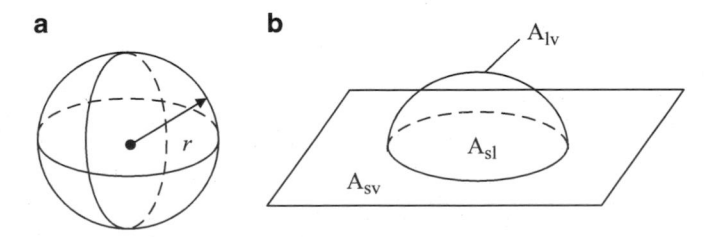

Fig. 2.14   A droplet (**a**) floating in a medium and (**b**) staying on a surface

Fig. 2.15 Schematic of a
small droplet placed on a
flat surface with a uniform
meniscus radius

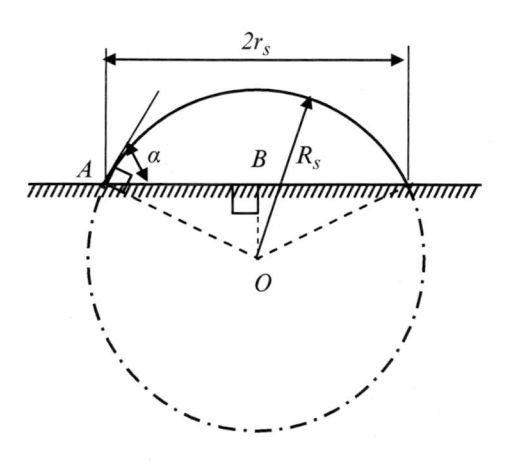

the liquid and vapor of the cap depends on the contact angle the cap makes with the
surface. During the spreading process, the total energy change can be expressed as

$$dF = \sigma_{lv}dA_{lv} + \sigma_{sl}dA_{sl} + \sigma_{sv}dA_{sv} + \Delta p \, dV \tag{2.61}$$

where $\Delta p \, dV$ is the work done by the pressure difference for the volume
change. Because liquid is almost incompressible, $\Delta p dV$ is negligible. Considering
$dA_{sv} = -dA_{sl}$ and $dF = 0$ for an equilibrium state, Eq. (2.61) can be found as

$$0 = \sigma_{lv}dA_{lv} + (\sigma_{sl} - \sigma_{sv})dA_{sl} \tag{2.62}$$

Dividing both sides of Eq. (2.62) by dA_{sl} yields

$$\sigma_{lv}\frac{dA_{lv}}{dA_{sl}} + \sigma_{sl} - \sigma_{sv} = 0 \tag{2.63}$$

To show that $\frac{dA_{lv}}{dA_{sl}} = \cos\alpha$, it is assumed that the droplet is very small, the liquid is
not compressible, and the gravitational force is not considered. The liquid–vapor
interface has a constant meniscus radius when the droplet is either floating in a
vapor or contacting a surface. The droplet with total volume V and radius r contacts
a surface as shown in Fig. 2.15. The droplet forms a cap which can be viewed as part
of a larger sphere with a radius of R_s. It looks as though this spherical cap is cut from
its large sphere by a plane. The total volume of this spherical cap is the same as the
volume of the original droplet. Based on the geometry shown in Fig. 2.15, the total
volume of this spherical cap can be found as

$$V_{cap} = \frac{2}{3}\pi R_s^3 (1 - \cos \alpha) - \frac{1}{3}\pi R_s^3 \sin^2 \alpha \cos \alpha$$

$$= \frac{1}{3}\pi R_s^3 (2 - 3 \cos \alpha + \cos^3 \alpha) \tag{2.64}$$

From Eq. (2.64), the radius of the larger sphere can be expressed as

$$R_s = V_{cap}^{1/3} \left[\frac{\pi}{3}(2 - 3 \cos \alpha + \cos^3 \alpha) \right]^{-1/3} \tag{2.65}$$

The area of the planar surface, A_{sl}, is the circle area, i.e.,

$$A_{sl} = \pi r_s^2 \tag{2.66}$$

Considering

$$r_s = R_s \sin \alpha \tag{2.67}$$

Equation (2.66) can be expressed as

$$A_{sl} = \pi (R_s \sin \alpha)^2 \tag{2.68}$$

Substituting Eq. (2.65) into Eq. (2.68), the area of the planar surface can be found as

$$A_{sl} = \pi V_{cap}^{2/3} \left[\frac{\pi}{3}(2 - 3 \cos \alpha + \cos^3 \alpha) \right]^{-2/3} \sin^2 \alpha \tag{2.69}$$

The area of the cap interface, A_{lv}, can be found as

$$A_{lv} = 2\pi R_s^2 (1 - \cos \alpha) \tag{2.70}$$

Substituting Eq. (2.65) into Eq. (2.70), the area of the cap interface can be expressed as

$$A_{lv} = 2\pi V_{cap}^{2/3} \left[\frac{\pi}{3}(2 - 3 \cos \alpha + \cos^3 \alpha) \right]^{-2/3} (1 - \cos \alpha) \tag{2.71}$$

Because both the surface areas A_{lv} and A_{sl} are from the same constant volume V_{cap}, both the areas should be a function of the contact angle, α, only. Using the chain rule, i.e.,

$$\frac{dA_{lv}}{dA_{sl}} = \frac{dA_{lv}}{d\alpha} \bigg/ \frac{dA_{sl}}{d\alpha} \tag{2.72}$$

where

$$\frac{dA_{lv}}{d\alpha} = 2\pi V_{cap}^{2/3} \left(\frac{\pi}{3}\right)^{-2/3} \frac{d}{d\alpha}\left[(2 - 3\cos\alpha + \cos^3\alpha)^{-2/3}(1 - \cos\alpha)\right]$$

$$= 2\pi V_{cap}^{2/3} \left(\frac{\pi}{3}\right)^{-2/3} \frac{-9\sin\alpha\cos\alpha + 3\sin\alpha\cos^3\alpha + 6\sin\alpha\cos\alpha + 6\cos^2\alpha\sin\alpha - 6\cos^3\alpha\sin\alpha}{3(2 - 3\cos\alpha + \cos^3\alpha)^{5/3}}$$

$$= 2\pi V_{cap}^{2/3} \left(\frac{\pi}{3}\right)^{-2/3} \frac{-\sin\alpha\cos\alpha(1 - 2\cos\alpha + \cos^2\alpha)}{(2 - 3\cos\alpha + \cos^3\alpha)^{5/3}}$$

$$= -2\pi V_{cap}^{2/3} \left(\frac{\pi}{3}\right)^{-2/3} \frac{\sin\alpha\cos\alpha}{(\cos\alpha + 2)(2 - 3\cos\alpha + \cos^3\alpha)^{5/3}}$$

$$(2.73)$$

and

$$\frac{dA_{sl}}{d\alpha} = \pi V_{cap}^{2/3} \left(\frac{\pi}{3}\right)^{-2/3} \frac{d}{d\alpha}\left[(2 - 3\cos\alpha + \cos^3\alpha)^{-2/3}\sin^2\alpha\right]$$

$$= \pi V_{cap}^{2/3} \left(\frac{\pi}{3}\right)^{-2/3} \frac{12\sin\alpha\cos\alpha - 18\sin\alpha\cos^2\alpha + 6\sin\alpha\cos^4\alpha - 6\sin^3\alpha + 6\cos^2\alpha\sin^3\alpha}{3(2 - 3\cos\alpha + \cos^3\alpha)^{5/3}}$$

$$= \pi V_{cap}^{2/3} \left(\frac{\pi}{3}\right)^{-2/3} \frac{2\sin\alpha(-\cos^2\alpha + 2\cos\alpha - 1)}{(2 - 3\cos\alpha + \cos^3\alpha)^{5/3}}$$

$$= -\pi V_{cap}^{2/3} \left(\frac{\pi}{3}\right)^{-2/3} \frac{2\sin\alpha}{(2 - 3\cos\alpha + \cos^3\alpha)^{2/3}}$$

$$(2.74)$$

Substituting Eqs. (2.73) and (2.74) show that

$$\frac{dA_{lv}}{dA_{sl}} = \cos\alpha \tag{2.75}$$

2.5.1 Temperature Effect

Consider a cylindrical liquid column in contact with a solid phase which is surrounded by vapor phase. If the liquid column is separated from the solid column completely, the work done in separation can be found by

$$w_{sl} = \sigma_{lv} + \sigma_{sv} - \sigma_{sl} \tag{2.76}$$

where w_{sl} is called the work of adhesion (Carey 1992). For a liquid–liquid column surrounded by a vapor phase, the work done to separate this liquid–liquid column to a liquid–vapor and vapor–liquid columns can be expressed as

$$w_{ll} = 2\sigma_{lv} \tag{2.77}$$

where w_{ll} is called the work of cohesion. Rearranging Eq. (2.76) yields

$$\sigma_{sl} = \sigma_{lv} + \sigma_{sv} - w_{sl} \tag{2.78}$$

The work of adhesion can be approximately expressed as (Carey 1992)

$$w_{sl} \approx 2(\sigma_{lv}\sigma_{sv})^{1/2} \tag{2.79}$$

Substituting Eq. (2.79) into Eq. (2.78), it can be found that

$$\sigma_{sl} = \sigma_{lv} + \sigma_{sv} - 2(\sigma_{lv}\sigma_{sv})^{1/2} \tag{2.80}$$

Substituting Eq. (2.80) into Young's equation yields

$$\cos \alpha = \frac{\sigma_{vs} - \sigma_{lv} - \sigma_{sv} + 2(\sigma_{lv}\sigma_{sv})^{1/2}}{\sigma_{lv}} = 2\left(\frac{\sigma_{sv}}{\sigma_{lv}}\right)^{1/2} - 1 \tag{2.81}$$

As shown in Eq. (2.81), when the surface tension, σ_{lv}, is going to be infinite, Eq. (2.81) becomes

$$\cos \alpha = -1 \tag{2.82}$$

The contact angle is 180°, which is completely nonwetting. For a given solid surface, the surface tension between the solid and vapor is almost constant. When the temperature increases, the surface tension, σ_{lv}, decreases. From Eq. (2.81), it can be found that when the temperature increases, the contact angle decreases. This can be used to explain why the capillary limitation of some heat pipes increases as the operating temperature increases.

2.5.2 Surface Roughness Effect

Homogenous roughness surface. When the surface has a homogenous roughness as shown in Fig. 2.16, the ratio between the actual surface, A_s, and the projected surface on a horizontal surface, A_{hor}, is

$$\gamma = \frac{A_s}{A_{hor}} \tag{2.83}$$

For the liquid drop placed on the rough surface as shown in Fig. 2.16, neglecting the pressure work, the total free energy for the drop shown in Eq. (2.61) can be expressed as

Fig. 2.16 Wenzel state
contact angle

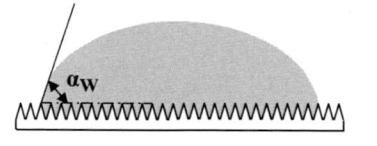

$$dF = \sigma_{lv} dA_{lv} + \sigma_{sl} dA_{sl} + \sigma_{sv} dA_{sv} \tag{2.84}$$

Because the liquid is very small, the droplet forms a cap which can be viewed as a part of a larger sphere with radius R_s. From the geometry and Eq. (2.75), it can be found that

$$dA_{sv} = -dA_{sl} \tag{2.85}$$

$$dA_{lv} = (dA_{sl})_{\text{hor}} \cos \alpha_W \tag{2.86}$$

Considering Eq. (2.83), Eq. (2.86) can be expressed as

$$dA_{lv} = \frac{dA_{sl}}{\gamma} \cos \alpha_W \tag{2.87}$$

Substituting Eqs. (2.85)–(2.87) into Eq. (2.84) yields

$$\frac{dF}{dA_{sl}} = \frac{\sigma_{lv} \cos \alpha_W}{\gamma} + \sigma_{sl} - \sigma_{sv} \tag{2.88}$$

Considering $\frac{dF}{dA_{sl}} = 0$ at equilibrium, Eq. (2.88) becomes

$$\cos \alpha_W = \gamma \frac{\sigma_{sv} - \sigma_{sl}}{\sigma_{lv}} \tag{2.89}$$

Substituting Young's equation, i.e., Eq. (2.59), the Wenzel equation can be obtained as

$$\cos \alpha_W = \gamma \cos \alpha \tag{2.90}$$

where α_W is the contact angle observed by the naked eye or with an optical microscope, which is also called the apparent contact angle. Because the ratio γ between the actual surface and the projected surface on a horizontal surface, A_{hor}, is always greater than one, the parent contact angle decreases for a rough surface for $\alpha < 90°$ When a hydrophobic surface ($\alpha > 90°$) is rough, the apparent contact angle increases. In other words, if a molecularly hydrophobic surface is rough, the surface becomes more hydrophobic. If a hydrophilic surface is roughed, the surface becomes more hydrophilic.

Fig. 2.17 Cassie–Baxter state contact angle

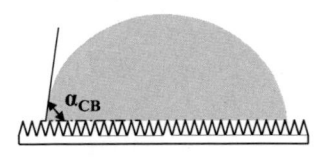

Heterogeneous roughness surface. When a drop lying on a rough surface is trapping air in cavities, as shown in Fig. 2.17, the apparent contact angle is very different from that on the same rough surface without trapped air in cavities as shown in Fig. 2.16 (Whyman et al. 2008). If the rough surface under the drop shown in Fig. 2.17 consists of n sorts of materials randomly distributed over the substrate, each material is characterized by the surface tensions $\sigma_{i,\text{sl}}$ and $\sigma_{i,\text{sv}}$ and the fraction Φ_i. For the drop placed on the rough surface as shown in Fig. 2.17, the total volume and the liquid–vapor interface area can be found by Eqs. (2.64) and (2.70), i.e.,

$$V_{\text{cap}} = \frac{1}{3}\pi R_s^3 \left(2 - 3\cos\alpha_{\text{CB}} + \cos^3\alpha_{\text{CB}}\right) \tag{2.91}$$

$$A_{lv} = 2\pi R_s^2 (1 - \cos\alpha_{\text{CB}}) \tag{2.92}$$

respectively. The total free energy of the drop can be found as

$$F = \sigma_{lv}A_{lv} - \pi(R_s\sin\alpha_{\text{CB}})^2 \sum_{i=1}^{n} \Phi_i(\sigma_{i,\text{sv}} - \sigma_{i,\text{sl}}) \tag{2.93}$$

where

$$\Phi_1 + \Phi_2 + \cdots + \Phi_i + \cdots + \Phi_n = 1 \tag{2.94}$$

Substituting Eq. (2.92) and considering Eqs. (2.91) and (2.65), Eq. (2.93) can be expressed as

$$F = \left[\frac{9\pi V_{\text{cap}}^2}{(1 - \cos\alpha_{\text{CB}})(2 + \cos\alpha_{\text{CB}})^2}\right]^{1/3} \left(2\sigma_{lv} - \sum_{i=1}^{n} \Phi_i(\sigma_{i,\text{sv}} - \sigma_{i,\text{sl}})(1 + \cos\alpha_{\text{CB}})\right) \tag{2.95}$$

The free energy is a function of contact angle. Taking a derivative with the contact angle, it can be found that

$$\frac{dF}{d\alpha_{CB}} = \left[\frac{9\pi V_{cap}^2}{(1 - \cos \alpha_{CB})^4 (2 + \cos \alpha)^5}\right]^{1/3} 2\left(\sum_{i=1}^{n} \Phi_i(\sigma_{i,sv} - \sigma_{i,sl}) - \sigma_{lv} \cos \alpha_{CB}\right) \sin \alpha_{CB}$$

$$(2.96)$$

When $\sum_{i=1}^{n} \Phi_i(\sigma_{i,sv} - \sigma_{i,sl}) - \sigma_{lv} \cos \alpha_{CB} = 0$, $\frac{dF}{d\alpha_{CB}} = 0$ and it can be found that

$$\sigma_{lv} \cos \alpha_{CB} = \sum_{i=1}^{n} \Phi_i(\sigma_{i,sv} - \sigma_{i,sl}) \qquad (2.97)$$

which is the Cassie–Baxter correlation for the Cassie–Baxter contact angle. If there are two kinds of regions with apparent contact angles α_1 and α_2 that occupy the surface ratios Φ_1 and Φ_2, respectively, Eq. (2.97) can be rewritten as

$$\cos \alpha_{CB} = \Phi_1 \cos \alpha_1 + \Phi_2 \cos \alpha_2 \qquad (2.98)$$

If these two kinds of regions consist of a smooth surface with a surface ratio of Φ_1 and air with a surface ratio of Φ_2, Eq. (2.98) becomes

$$\cos \alpha_{CB} = \Phi_1 \cos \alpha_1 + \Phi_1 - 1 \qquad (2.99)$$

where it should be noticed that the droplet in air is a perfect sphere, which results in a contact angle of $\alpha_2 = 180°$ or $\cos \alpha_2 = -1$. From Eq. (2.99), it can be found that the droplets will have a higher apparent contact angle if less area is in contact with the solid substrate. The Cassie–Baxter equation simply indicates that the apparent contact angle can be increased even when the contact angle of a liquid on the original smooth surface is less than 90°. If these two kinds of regions consist of rough surface with a surface ratio of Φ_1 and air with a surface ratio of Φ_2, Eq. (2.98) becomes

$$\cos \alpha_{CB} = \Phi_1 \gamma \cos \alpha_1 + \Phi_1 - 1 \qquad (2.100)$$

If no air is trapped in the cavities, $\Phi_1 = 1$. Then Eq. (2.99) becomes

$$\cos \alpha_{CB} = \gamma \cos \alpha_1 = \cos \alpha_W \qquad (2.101)$$

As shown in Eq. (2.101), when no air or vapor is trapped in the cavities, the Cassie–Baxter contact angle becomes the Wenzel contact angle.

Example 2.5 A rough surface as shown below consists of a smooth surface with a surface ratio of $\Phi_1 = 57\%$ and air trapped in the cavities with a surface ratio of $\Phi_2 = 43\%$. Determine the contact angle (Cassie–Baxter state contact). If no air is trapped in the cavities, determine the contact angle (Wenzel state contact). The contact angle of working fluid on the smooth surface is 60°.

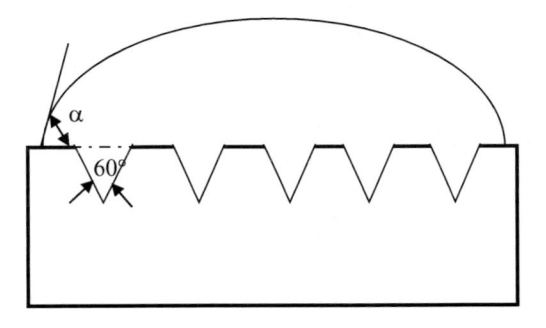

Solution For a rough surface, which consists of two kinds of regions with apparent contact angles α_1 and α_2 that occupy the surface ratios of Φ_1 and Φ_2, respectively, the Cassie–Baxter contact angle can be calculated by Eq. (2.98), i.e., $\cos \alpha_{CB} = \Phi_1 \cos \alpha_1 + \Phi_2 \cos \alpha_2$. Because a droplet in air is a perfect sphere, $\alpha_2 = 180°$ or $\cos \alpha_2 = -1$, the Cassie–Baxter contact angle can be found as

$$\cos \alpha_{CB} = \Phi_1 \cos \alpha_1 + \Phi_2 \cos \alpha_2 = 0.57 \times \cos 60° + 0.43 \times \cos (180°) = -0.145$$

$$\alpha_{CB} = 98.3°$$

If no air is trapped in cavities, the Cassie–Baxter contact angle becomes the Wenzel state contact angle, i.e.,

$$\cos \alpha_{CB} = \cos \alpha_W = \gamma \cos \alpha_1$$

where γ is the ratio between the actual surface, A_s, and the projected surface on a horizontal surface, A_{hor}, which can be calculated by

$$\gamma = \frac{A_s}{A_{hor}} = \frac{0.57 + 0.43 / \sin (30°)}{0.57 + 0.43} = 1.43$$

The Wenzel state contact angle can be found as

$$\cos \alpha_{CB} = \cos \alpha_W = \gamma \cos \alpha_1 = 1.43 \times \cos (60°) = 0.716$$

$$\alpha_W = 44.3°$$

The calculation shows that when air is trapped in the cavities, the contact angle of a rough surface is increased. If air is removed from the cavities, the contact angle is decreased.

2.6   Contact Angle Measurement

There are a number of methods to measure the contact angle. One of the most common methods is to measure the contact angle by observing a sessile microdroplet using a telescope or microscope. When the droplet is very small, it can form a cap which can be viewed as a part of a larger sphere with a radius of R_s. It looks as though this spherical cap is cut from the large sphere by a plane. The meniscus radius of this cap is almost constant as shown in Fig. 2.18. If the meniscus radius, R_s is constant, the height, h, and the radius of the liquid–solid contact circle, r_s, can be measured, the contact angle, α, can be calculated by

$$\tan\left(\frac{\alpha}{2}\right) = \frac{h}{r_s} \tag{2.102}$$

It should be noted that the droplet must be very small. Otherwise, the liquid–vapor interface cannot have a constant meniscus radius, and Eq. (2.102) may result in an inaccurate calculation of the measured contact angle.

Based on Young's equation, i.e., Eq. (2.59), the contact angle depends on the surface tension between the liquid–vapor interface in addition to the surface tensions between liquid and solid and between vapor and solid. As a result, the vapor phase component, or other pollution, will affect the accuracy of the contact angle measurement. Another method, called the sessile bubble, can be used to measure the contact angle. A still microbubble, as shown in Fig. 2.19, is placed at the top of the cell where the liquid is held. High-resolution cameras and software can be used to capture and analyze the contact angle.

Fig. 2.18 A sessile droplet
on a surface

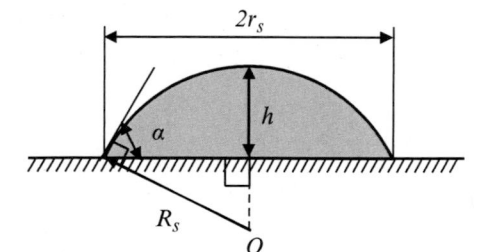

Fig. 2.19 A sessile bubble
in liquid

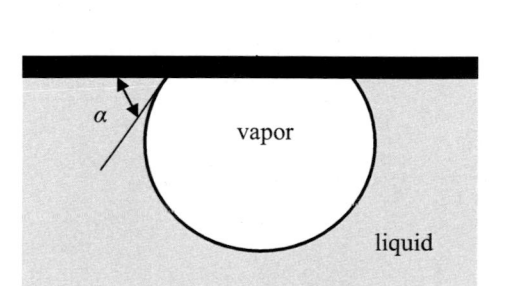

2.7   Dynamic Contact Angle

Figure 2.20a shows a liquid plug placed in a horizontal capillary tube. If the capillary tube is very small, the meniscus radius of the liquid–vapor interface is almost constant. For a still liquid plug shown in Fig. 2.20a, the contact angle on the left side of the liquid plug is equal to that on the right side. When the liquid plug moves, as shown in Fig. 2.20b, the contact angle on the right side increases greater than the equilibrium contact angle. This contact angle is called advancing contact angle, α_a. At the same time, the contact angle on the left side decreases resulting in an angle less than the equilibrium contact angle. The latter is called the receding contact angle, α.

Experiments show that the apparent contact angle depends not only on the speed, viscosity, and surface tension but also on the surface roughness, inhomogeneity, and impurities on the surface. For example, for a droplet on a surface as shown in Fig. 2.21a, when liquid is pumped in from a small hole on the bottom, the volume of the liquid droplet increases and the apparent contact angle increases. Just before the contact line moves, the contact angle reaches its maximum value, which is the advancing contact angle for a still droplet. If liquid is pumped out through the hole as shown in Fig. 2.21b, the liquid volume decreases, and the apparent contact angle decreases. Just before the contact line moves, the apparent contact angle reaches its minimum value, which is called the receding contact angle for a still droplet. Clearly, the receding contact angle is less than the equilibrium contact angle and the advancing contact angle is greater than the equilibrium contact angle. Tadmor (2004) showed that if the advancing and receding contact angles for the droplet shown in Fig. 2.21 are given, the equilibrium contact angle can be determined by

$$\alpha = \arccos\left(\frac{\Gamma_A \cos \alpha_a + \Gamma_R \cos \alpha_r}{\Gamma_A + \Gamma_B}\right) \tag{2.103}$$

Fig. 2.20 Receding and advancing contact angles: (**a**) without movement and (**b**) with movement

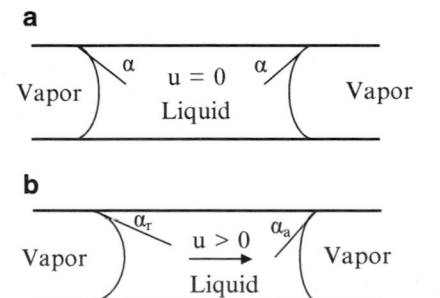

Fig. 2.21 Contact angle
hysteresis: (**a**) advancing
contact angle and (**b**)
receding contact angle

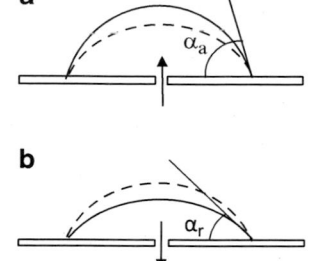

where

$$\Gamma_R = \left(\frac{\sin^3 \alpha_r}{(2 - 3 \cos \alpha_r) + \cos^3 \alpha_r} \right)^{1/3} \tag{2.104}$$

and

$$\Gamma_A = \left(\frac{\sin^3 \alpha_a}{(2 - 3 \cos \alpha_a) + \cos^3 \alpha_a} \right)^{1/3} \tag{2.105}$$

where α_r and α_a are the receding and advancing contact angles, respectively, for the liquid droplet shown in Fig. 2.21.

When the liquid plug in a capillary tube as shown in Fig. 2.20 is moving, the receding and advancing contact angles are very different from when they are still. Consider a liquid plug with a length L moving in a capillary tube with radius r_0, as shown in Fig. 2.22. Because the tube radius is very small, the Bond number is very small. The meniscus radius of curvature at the liquid–vapor interface can be assumed to be constant. The tube surface is smooth. When the liquid plug is moving along the x-direction at a constant velocity as shown in Fig. 2.22, the pressure difference, $p_1 - p_2$, must overcome all pressure drops occurring in the liquid plug (Ma 2012), i.e.,

$$\Delta p_{\text{drive}} = \Delta p_r + \Delta p_f + \Delta p_d + \Delta p_a \tag{2.106}$$

where Δp_r and Δp_a are the pressure differences across the liquid–vapor interface on the left and right sides of the liquid plug, respectively, Δp_f is the pressure drop due to the frictional force, and Δp_d is the dynamic pressure difference.

The driving force acting on the liquid plug, Δp_{drive}, can be expressed as

$$\Delta p_{\text{drive}} = p_1 - p_2 \tag{2.107}$$

The pressure difference across the liquid–vapor interface can be determined by the Laplace equation of capillarity, i.e.,

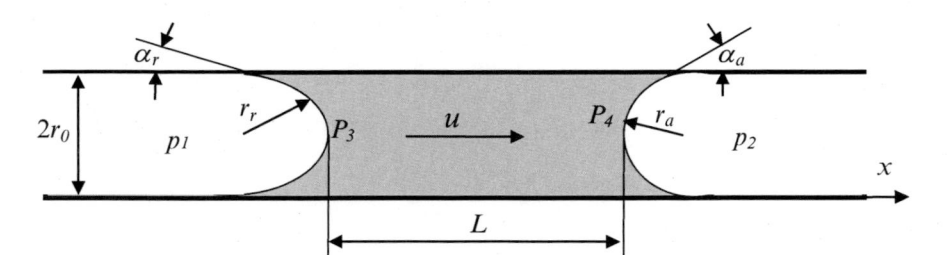

Fig. 2.22 Schematic of a liquid plug moving in a capillary tube

$$p_1 - p_{\mathrm{II}} = \sigma\left(\frac{1}{r_1} + \frac{1}{r_2}\right) \tag{2.108}$$

For a constant meniscus radius of curvature, the pressure difference across the liquid–vapor interface on the left side of the liquid plug can be rewritten as

$$\Delta p_{\mathrm{r}} = p_1 - p_3 = \frac{2\sigma}{r_{\mathrm{r}}} \tag{2.109}$$

where r_{r} is the meniscus radius of curvature at the liquid–vapor interface on the left side of the liquid plug. Considering the receding contact angle, α_{r}, Eq. (2.109) can be written as

$$\Delta p_{\mathrm{r}} = p_1 - p_3 = \frac{2\sigma \cos \alpha_{\mathrm{r}}}{r_0} \tag{2.110}$$

Similarly, the pressure difference across the liquid–vapor interface on the right side of liquid plug shown in Fig. 2.22 can be expressed as

$$\Delta p_{\mathrm{a}} = p_4 - p_2 = -\frac{2\sigma \cos \alpha_{\mathrm{a}}}{r_0} \tag{2.111}$$

The pressure difference due to the frictional force, i.e., Δp_{f}, can be found as

$$\Delta p_{\mathrm{f}} = f\frac{\rho_l L u^2}{4 r_0} \tag{2.112}$$

For a laminar flow in a round tube, the friction factor, f, shown in Eq. (2.112) can be expressed as

$$f = \frac{64}{Re_D} \tag{2.113}$$

where Re_D is Reynolds number. Considering Eq. (2.113), Eq. (2.112) can be rewritten as

$$\Delta p_f = \frac{8\mu Lu}{r_0^2} \tag{2.114}$$

The third item on the right side of Eq. (2.106) is the dynamic pressure difference, which can be expressed as

$$\Delta p_d = \frac{1}{2}\rho u_3^2 - \frac{1}{2}\rho u_4^2 \tag{2.115}$$

For an incompressible fluid with a constant cross-sectional area, the velocity at location 3 is equal to the velocity at location 4. Therefore, the dynamic pressure difference is zero for the liquid plug shown in Fig. 2.22. Considering Eqs. (2.110), (2.111), (2.114), and (2.115), Eq. (2.106) can be rewritten as

$$\Delta p_{\text{drive}} = p_1 - p_2 = \frac{2\sigma(\cos\alpha_r - \cos\alpha_a)}{r_0} + \frac{8\mu Lu}{r_0^2} \tag{2.116}$$

Rearranging Eq. (2.116) yields

$$\cos\alpha_r - \cos\alpha_a = \frac{r_0}{2\sigma}\left(p_1 - p_2 - \frac{8\mu Lu}{r_0^2}\right) \tag{2.117}$$

From Eq. (2.117), it can be found that the receding and advancing contact angles depend on tube radius, surface, driving force, viscosity, liquid plug length, and velocity.

2.8 Thin Film Evaporation

When heat is applied to the evaporating region of a heat pipe, the heat will travel through the wall of a solid container to reach the working fluid. Provided that the fluid level is not above the top surface of the wick, the heat that reaches the top surface of the working fluid in the wick will pass through a thin film region and evaporation will take place at the liquid–vapor interface. In the presence of a thin film, a majority of the heat will be transferred through a very small region (Hanlon and Ma 2003), whereupon thin film evaporation can be compared to boiling heat transfer (Thome 1990; Webb 1994; Kaviany 1995; Bau and Torrance 1982; Liter and Kaviany 2001). It is found that thin film evaporation can provide significantly

higher overall heat transfer coefficients. When evaporation occurs in a pool boiling system, the heat transfer limit at the evaporating surface depends on the mechanisms of liquid supply to and vapor escape from the phase–change interface. To reduce the effects of liquid and vapor flow resistances in the pool boiling system, extensive research on enhanced surfaces such as the machined or etched cavities (Thome 1990), structured surfaces (Webb 1994), low-permeability evaporating surfaces (Bau and Torrance 1982), and coated surfaces (Webb 1994), including modulated porous-layers (Liter and Kaviany 2001), has been conducted. As a result, the heat transfer limit occurring in the pool boiling systems has been continuously pushed. Due to the presence of liquid, however, the resistance to vapor flow still exists and directly limits the further enhancement of boiling heat transfer in the pool boiling systems. Clearly, thin film evaporation occurring only at the top surface of wicks can significantly enhance the evaporation heat transfer.

As early as 1972, Potash and Wayner (1972) expanded the Derjaguin–Landau–Verwey–Overbeek (DLVO) theory (Derjaguin and Zorin 1956) to describe evaporation and fluid flow from an extended meniscus. Following this work, extensive investigations (Wayner et al. 1976; Moosman and Homsy 1980; Holm and Goplen 1979; Mirzamoghadam and Catton 1988; Burelbach et al. 1988; Stephan and Busse 1993; Ma and Peterson 1997; Demsky and Ma 2004; Ma et al. 2008) have been conducted to further understand mechanisms of fluid flow coupled with evaporating heat transfer in thin film region. In this section, the disjoining pressure is introduced first, then the pressure across the liquid–vapor interface is tracked followed by a discussion of thin film profile, interface temperature, and heat transfer through the thin film region.

2.8.1   Disjoining Pressure

When liquid helium is placed in a beaker, it climbs up the wall and down the other side of the wall as shown in Fig. 2.23. Eventually no liquid helium is left in the beaker. Clearly, the liquid pressure, p_δ, in thin film is lower than the bulk pressure, p_l. As a result, liquid helium climbs up the wall. The pressure difference between the liquid pressure, p_δ, in the thin film and the liquid bulk pressure, p_l, i.e.,

$$p_d = p_\delta - p_l \tag{2.118}$$

is called the disjoining pressure. Because the pressure in the liquid film is less than the bulk pressure, the disjoining pressure is negative. The disjoining pressure basically is a function of film thickness, which can be calculated by (Potash and Wayner 1972)

Fig. 2.23 Liquid helium
climbing up the wall
of a beaker

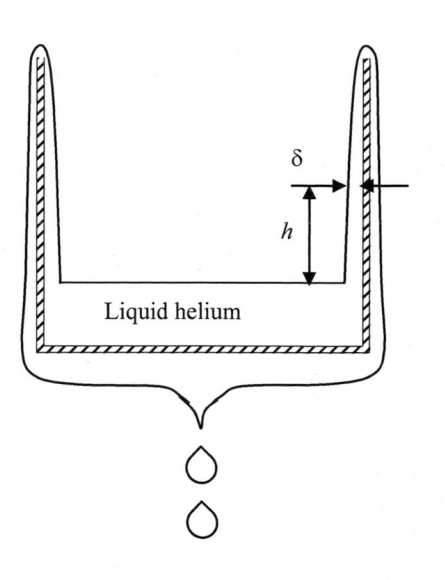

$$p_d = -\frac{A}{6\pi\delta^3} \quad \text{for nonpolar liquid} \tag{2.119}$$

$$p_d = -\frac{A}{6\pi\delta^B}\ln(\delta/\bar{\delta}_0) \quad \text{for polar liquid} \tag{2.120}$$

where A is Hamaker constant (J). Because it is very difficult to find the accurate Hamaker constant, a number of correlations were experimentally obtained. For example, if water is on quartz, the disjoining pressure can be estimated by (Holm and Goplen 1979)

$$p_d = \rho_l RT_{lv}\ln a\delta^b \quad (a = 1.5787, \quad b = 0.0243) \tag{2.121}$$

2.8.2   Pressure Difference Across the Liquid–Vapor Interface

For the control volume which consists of thin liquid film and vapor as shown in Fig. 2.24, the Gibbs–Duhem equations for the liquid phase and vapor phase can be written as

$$dp_l = s_l dT + N_l d\mu_l \tag{2.122}$$

$$dp_v = s_v dT + N_v d\mu_v \tag{2.123}$$

where N_l and N_v are mole numbers of liquid and vapor in the control volume. Considering $\mu_l = \mu_v$ and taking the difference between Eqs. (2.122) and (2.123) for a pure system gives (Wayner 1997)

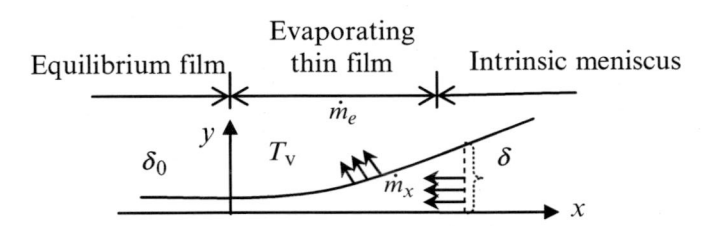

Fig. 2.24 Thin liquid film

$$d(p_v - p_l) = (s_v - s_l)dT + (N_v - N_l)d\mu_v \tag{2.124}$$

For the control volume shown in Fig. 2.24, $N_v - N_l \approx -V_l^{-1}$ and Eq. (2.124) can be expressed as

$$d\mu_v = -V_l d(p_v - p_l) + V_l(s_v - s_l)dT \tag{2.125}$$

Due to the disjoining pressure and curved liquid–vapor interface, the liquid pressure in the liquid film can be found as

$$p_l = p_v + p_d - \sigma_{lv}K \tag{2.126}$$

where p_d is the disjoining pressure, which is negative, and K is the curvature of the liquid–vapor interface which can be found as

$$K = \frac{\frac{d^2\delta}{dx^2}}{\left[1 + \left(\frac{d\delta}{dx}\right)^2\right]^{3/2}} \tag{2.127}$$

Substituting Eq. (2.126) into Eq. (2.125) yields

$$d\mu_v = -V_l d(-p_d + \sigma_{lv}K) + V_l(s_v - s_l)dT \tag{2.128}$$

If the vapor phase is an ideal gas, the chemical potential, μ_v, can be expressed as (Wayner 1997)

$$d\mu_v = \overline{R}T_v d(\ln p_v) \tag{2.129}$$

Substituting Eq. (2.129) into Eq. (2.128) and considering $s_v - s_l = \frac{H_{lv}}{T_{lv}}$, where H_{lv} is the latent heat per unit volume, gives

$$d(\ln p_{\mathrm{v}}) = -\frac{V_l}{\overline{R}T_{\mathrm{v}}} d(-p_{\mathrm{d}} + \sigma_{lv}K) + \frac{V_l H_{lv}}{\overline{R}T_{\mathrm{v}}T_{lv}} dT \qquad (2.130)$$

Integrating from the bulk vapor to the liquid–vapor interface yields

$$\ln\left(\frac{p_{lv}}{p_{\mathrm{v}}}\right) = -\frac{V_l}{\overline{R}T_{\mathrm{v}}}(-p_{\mathrm{d}} + \sigma_{lv}K) + \frac{V_l H_{lv}}{\overline{R}T_{\mathrm{v}}T_{lv}}(T_{lv} - T_{\mathrm{v}}) \qquad (2.131)$$

Using the Taylor series, Eq. (2.131) can be expressed as

$$p_{lv} - p_{\mathrm{v}} = -\frac{p_{\mathrm{v}}V_l}{\overline{R}T_{\mathrm{v}}}(-p_{\mathrm{d}} + \sigma_{lv}K) + \frac{p_{\mathrm{v}}V_l H_{lv}}{\overline{R}T_{\mathrm{v}}T_{lv}}(T_{lv} - T_{\mathrm{v}}) \qquad (2.132)$$

If the thin liquid film with vapor is the isothermal condition, i.e., $T_{lv} = T_{\mathrm{v}}$, Eq. (2.132) becomes

$$p_{lv} - p_{\mathrm{v}} = -\frac{p_{\mathrm{v}}V_l}{\overline{R}T_{\mathrm{v}}}(-p_{\mathrm{d}} + \sigma_{lv}K) \qquad (2.133)$$

Because the disjoining pressure is negative and $\sigma_{lv}K > 0$ for the liquid film shown in Fig. 2.24, the right side of Eq. (2.133) is negative. This means that the pressure at the liquid–vapor interface is less than the vapor pressure, which can help to maintain a thin liquid film as shown in Fig. 2.24. If $p_{lv} \neq p_{\mathrm{v}}$, Eq. (2.132) can be used along with kinetic theory to calculate the rate of evaporation or condensation from a curved thin film. If no heat transfer (no evaporation or condensation) takes place at the liquid–vapor interface, i.e., $p_{lv} = p_{\mathrm{v}}$, Eq. (2.132) can be expressed as

$$\frac{p_{\mathrm{v}}V_l}{\overline{R}T_{\mathrm{v}}}(-p_{\mathrm{d}} + \sigma_{lv}K) = \frac{p_{\mathrm{v}}V_l H_{lv}}{\overline{R}T_{\mathrm{v}}T_{lv}}(T_{lv} - T_{\mathrm{v}}) \qquad (2.134)$$

Under this condition, the temperature at the liquid–vapor interface, T_{lv}, is equal to the wall temperature, T_{w}. Because of no evaporation or condensation, the liquid film should be perfectly flat, i.e., $K = 0$. Equation (2.134) becomes

$$-p_{\mathrm{d}} = \frac{H_{lv}}{T_{\mathrm{w}}}(T_{\mathrm{w}} - T_{\mathrm{v}}) \qquad (2.135)$$

This equation can be used to determine the equilibrium film thickness in the non-evaporating film region.

2.8.3   Analytical Model

Figure 2.24 illustrates a schematic of an evaporating thin film formed on a flat surface. It is assumed that fluid flow in the thin film region is two dimensional and pressure in the liquid film is a function of the x-coordinate only. The wall temperature, T_w, is greater than the vapor temperature, T_v. Because the film thickness is much smaller than the total length of the thin film region, the lubricant theory can be applied to find the total mass flow rate per unit width of the film, $\Gamma(x)$, at a given x, i.e.,

$$\Gamma(x) = -\frac{\delta^3}{3\nu_l}\frac{dp_l}{dx} \tag{2.136}$$

where ν_l is the kinematic viscosity of the liquid phase. Taking a derivative of Eq. (2.136), i.e., $\dot{m}_e = -\frac{d\Gamma(x)}{dx}$, the net evaporative mass transfer per unit area can be obtained as

$$\dot{m}_e = \frac{d}{dx}\left(\frac{\delta^3}{3\nu_l}\frac{dp_l}{dx}\right) \tag{2.137}$$

The heat flux by evaporation occurring at the liquid–vapor interface in the thin film region can be determined by

$$q'' = \dot{m}_e h_{lv} = h_{lv}\frac{d}{dx}\left(\frac{\delta^3}{3\nu_l}\frac{dp_l}{dx}\right) \tag{2.138}$$

Clearly, q'' in Eq. (2.138) is also equal to the heat flux through the liquid thin film, i.e.,

$$q'' = k_l\frac{T_w - T_{lv}}{\delta} \tag{2.139}$$

where T_{lv} is the interface temperature which should be determined first. In the previous section, it has been shown that the vapor pressure difference between the liquid–vapor interface and the bulk vapor can be expressed as

$$p_{lv} - p_v = -\frac{p_v V_l}{\overline{R}T_v}(-p_d + \sigma_{lv}K) + \frac{p_v V_l H_{lv}}{\overline{R}T_v T_{lv}}(T_{lv} - T_v) \tag{2.140}$$

If the bulk flow effect or the thermal resistance due to the vapor flow is not considered, it can be assumed that the vapor pressure at the liquid–vapor interface is equal to the bulk vapor pressure. Equation (2.140) can be expressed as

$$-p_d + \sigma_{lv}K = \frac{H_{lv}}{T_{lv}}(T_{lv} - T_v) \tag{2.141}$$

Rearranging Eq. (2.141) yields

$$T_v = T_{lv}\left(1 - \frac{-p_d + \sigma_{lv}K}{h_{lv}\rho_l}\right) \tag{2.142}$$

where $H_{lv} = h_{lv}\rho_l$. Because the interface temperature, T_{lv}, is very close to the vapor temperature, T_v, $\frac{H_{lv}}{T_{lv}} \approx \frac{H_{lv}}{T_v}$, Eq. (2.141) can be approximately expressed as

$$T_{lv} = T_v\left(1 + \frac{-p_d + \sigma_{lv}K}{h_{lv}\rho_l}\right) \tag{2.143}$$

where the capillary and disjoining pressures can be determined by

$$\sigma K = \frac{\sigma \frac{d^2\delta}{dx^2}}{\left[1 + \left(\frac{d\delta}{dx}\right)^2\right]^{3/2}} \tag{2.144}$$

and

$$p_d = -\frac{A}{6\pi\delta^3} \tag{2.145}$$

respectively. Substituting Eq. (2.143) into Eq. (2.139) and eliminating the interfacial temperature, T_{lv}, the heat flux can be rewritten as

$$q'' = \frac{T_w - T_v\left(1 + \frac{-p_d+\sigma_{lv}K}{\rho_v h_{lv}}\right)}{\frac{\delta}{k_l}} \tag{2.146}$$

Substituting Eq. (2.138) into Eq. (2.146) yields

$$\frac{T_w - \left(1 + \frac{-p_d+\sigma K}{\rho_l h_{lv}}\right)T_v}{\frac{\delta}{k_l}} = h_{lv}\frac{d}{dx}\left(\frac{\delta^3}{3\nu_l}\frac{dp_l}{dx}\right) \tag{2.147}$$

Differentiating Eq. (2.126) with respect to x yields

$$\frac{dp_l}{dx} = -\frac{d(p_d - \sigma K)}{dx} \tag{2.148}$$

where a uniform vapor pressure, p_v, along the meniscus is assumed. Substituting Eq. (2.148) into Eq. (2.147) gives

$$\frac{d}{dx}\left(\frac{\delta^3}{3\nu_l}\frac{d(-p_d+\sigma K)}{dx}\right) = -\frac{1}{h_{lv}}\frac{T_w - \left(1+\frac{-p_d+\sigma_{lv}K}{\rho_l h_{lv}}\right)T_v}{\frac{\delta}{k_l}} \tag{2.149}$$

For the evaporating thin film region, the disjoining pressure is one dominant parameter, which governs the fluid flow in the evaporating thin film region. And in the evaporating thin film region, the absolute disjoining pressure is much larger than the capillary pressure, in particular, when the curvature variation along the meniscus is very small. To find the primary factor affecting the thin film evaporation in the evaporating thin film region, it is assumed that the capillary pressure is neglected. Then Eq. (2.149) becomes

$$\frac{d}{dx}\left(-\frac{\delta^3}{3\nu_l}\frac{dp_d}{dx}\right) = -\frac{1}{h_{lv}}\frac{T_w - \left(1+\frac{-p_d}{\rho_l h_{lv}}\right)T_v}{\frac{\delta}{k_l}} \tag{2.150}$$

Substituting $p_d = -\frac{A}{6\pi\delta^3}$ into Eq. (2.150) and rearranging yields

$$\frac{d}{dx}\left(\frac{1}{\delta}\frac{d\delta}{dx}\right) = \frac{B - C\delta^{-3}}{\delta} \tag{2.151}$$

where $B = \frac{6\pi k_l \nu_l (T_w - T_v)}{A h_{lv}}$ and $C = \frac{k_l \nu_l T_v}{\rho_l h_{lv}^2}$. Solving Eq. (2.151), the slope of the thin film profile is obtained as

$$\frac{d\delta}{dx} = \sqrt{\frac{C}{2\delta^2} - 2B\delta - D\delta^2} \tag{2.152}$$

where D is an integral constant. Using the boundary conditions of $\delta = \delta_0$ and $\frac{d\delta}{dx} = d_0$ at $x = 0$, the constant D can be found as

$$D = \frac{C}{2\delta_0^4} - \frac{2B}{\delta_0} - \frac{d_0^2}{\delta_0^2} \tag{2.153}$$

For the non-evaporating film region, the heat flux is zero. Clearly, the interface temperature is equal to the wall temperature. The equilibrium thickness δ_0 can be readily found by:

$$\delta_0 = \left(\frac{AT_v}{6\pi\rho_l h_{lv}(T_w - T_v)}\right)^{\frac{1}{3}} = \left(\frac{C}{B}\right)^{\frac{1}{3}} \tag{2.154}$$

Considering Eqs. (2.146) and (2.147), the analytical solution of the heat flux, q'', is obtained as

$$q'' = \frac{Ah_{lv}}{6\pi\nu_l}\frac{d}{dx}\left(\frac{1}{\delta}\frac{d\delta}{dx}\right) = \frac{Ah_{lv}}{6\pi\nu_l}\left(\frac{B}{\delta} - \frac{C}{\delta^4}\right) \tag{2.155}$$

Taking a derivative of x for Eq. (2.155), i.e., $\frac{dq''}{dx} = 0$, the optimum thickness of the evaporating thin film $\delta_{q''_{max}}$, where the heat flux reaches its maximum, can be found by

$$\delta_{q''_{max}} = \left(\frac{4C}{B}\right)^{\frac{1}{3}} = 4^{\frac{1}{3}}\delta_0 \tag{2.156}$$

From Eq. (2.156), it can be found that the optimum thickness corresponding to the maximum heat flux through the evaporating thin film region is equal to $4^{\frac{1}{3}}$ times the equilibrium film thickness, δ_0. It does not depend on liquid viscosity, ν_1, conductivity, κ_1, and slope of the thin film profile, d_0, at $x = 0$. Considering Eq. (2.154), Eq. (2.155) can be rewritten as

$$q'' = \frac{Ah_{lv}}{6\pi\nu_l}\frac{B}{\delta}\left(1 - \frac{\delta_0^3}{\delta^3}\right) \tag{2.157}$$

Substituting $B = \frac{6\pi k_l \nu_l (T_w - T_v)}{Ah_{lv}}$ into Eq. (2.157) yields

$$q'' = \frac{k_l(T_w - T_v)}{\delta}\left(1 - \frac{\delta_0^3}{\delta^3}\right) \tag{2.158}$$

To better understand the phenomenon, δ_0 is defined as the characteristic thickness and $q_0'' = \frac{k_l(T_w - T_v)}{\delta_0}$ the characteristic heat flux, where q_0'' is the heat flux at the interface temperature equal to the vapor temperature.

Utilizing the characteristic thickness δ_0, and the characteristic heat flux q_0'', the dimensionless thickness and heat flux are defined as

$$\delta^* = \frac{\delta}{\delta_0} \tag{2.159}$$

and

$$q''^* = \frac{q''}{q_0''} \tag{2.160}$$

respectively. Using Eqs. (2.159) and (2.160), the dimensionless heat flux occurring in the evaporating thin film region can be found as

$$q''^* = \frac{1}{\delta^*} - \frac{1}{\delta^{*4}} \tag{2.161}$$

Considering $\frac{dq''^*}{d\delta^*} = 0$, the maximum dimensionless heat flux q''^*_{max} can be determined. It is found that when the thin film thickness is equal to $4^{\frac{1}{3}}$ times the equilibrium thickness, δ_0, the local heat flux through the evaporating thin film reaches its maximum. Letting $\delta^* = 4^{\frac{1}{3}}$ in Eq. (2.161), the maximum dimensionless heat flux, q''^*_{max}, can be found as

$$q''^*_{max} = \frac{3}{4^{\frac{4}{3}}} \approx 0.47 \tag{2.162}$$

Equation (2.162) indicates that the maximum heat flux occurring in the evaporating thin film region is not greater than 0.47 times the characteristic flux heat, $q''_0 = \frac{k_l(T_w - T_v)}{\delta_0}$. The total heat transfer rate per unit width along the meniscus, q_{tot}, can be calculated by

$$q_{tot} = \int_0^x q'' dx = \int_0^x \frac{Ah_{lv}}{6\pi\nu_l} \frac{d}{dx}\left(\frac{1}{\delta}\frac{d\delta}{dx}\right) dx = \frac{Ah_{lv}}{6\pi\nu_l}\left(\frac{1}{\delta}\frac{d\delta}{dx} - \frac{d_0}{\delta_0}\right) \tag{2.163}$$

Substituting Eqs. (2.152) and (2.153) into Eq. (2.163), the total heat transfer rate per unit width can be found as

$$q_{tot} = \frac{Ah_{lv}}{6\pi\nu_l}\left(\sqrt{\frac{C}{2\delta^4} - \frac{2B}{\delta} + \frac{3B}{2\delta_0} + \frac{d_0^2}{\delta_0^2}} - \frac{d_0}{\delta_0}\right) \tag{2.164}$$

Considering $B = \frac{6\pi k_l \nu_l (T_w - T_v)}{Ah_{lv}}$, $C = \frac{k_l \nu_l T_v}{\rho_l h_{lv}^2}$, Eqs. (2.154), (2.159), and (2.160), Eq. (2.164) becomes

$$q_{tot} = \sqrt{\frac{Ah_{lv}}{6\pi\nu_l}q''_0\left(\frac{1}{2\delta^{*4}} - \frac{2}{\delta^*} + \frac{3}{2}\right) + \frac{d_0^2}{\delta_0^2}\left(\frac{Ah_{lv}}{6\pi\nu_l}\right)^2} - \frac{d_0}{\delta_0}\frac{Ah_{lv}}{6\pi\nu_l} \tag{2.165}$$

Substituting Eq. (2.161) into Eq. (2.165) yields

$$q_{tot} = \sqrt{\frac{Ah_{lv}}{12\pi\nu_l}q''_0\left(3 - \frac{3}{\delta^*} - q''^*\right) + \frac{d_0^2}{\delta_0^2}\left(\frac{Ah_{lv}}{6\pi\nu_l}\right)^2} - \frac{d_0}{\delta_0}\frac{Ah_{lv}}{6\pi\nu_l} \tag{2.166}$$

Using the order analysis, it can be found that $\frac{d_0}{\delta_0}\frac{Ah_{lv}}{6\pi\nu_l}$ is much smaller than other items in Eq. (2.166). Neglecting $\frac{d_0}{\delta_0}\frac{Ah_{lv}}{6\pi\nu_l}$, Eq. (2.166) becomes

$$q_{\text{tot}} = \sqrt{\frac{Ah_{lv}}{12\pi\nu_l} q_0'' \left(3 - \frac{3}{\delta^*} - q''*\right)} \tag{2.167}$$

where q_{tot} is the total heat transfer rate per unit width through the evaporating thin film region from 0 to x. As x increases, the thickness of evaporating thin film increases which directly affects heat flux through the evaporating thin film region. When the liquid film thickness increases, the heat flux through the evaporating thin film decreases quickly. Clearly, at the end of evaporating thin film region where the effect of disjoining pressure can be neglected, $q''* \ll 1.0$ and $\frac{1}{\delta^*} \ll 1$. Equation (2.167) can be rewritten as

$$q_{\text{tot}} \leq \sqrt{\frac{Ah_{lv}}{4\pi\nu_l} q_0''} \tag{2.168}$$

Considering $q_0'' = \frac{k_l(T_w - T_v)}{\delta_0}$ and Eq. (2.154), Eq. (2.168) becomes

$$q_{\text{tot}} \leq \left[\frac{k_l \rho_v^{\frac{1}{3}} A^{\frac{2}{3}} h_{lv}^{\frac{4}{3}} (T_w - T_v)^{\frac{4}{3}}}{4\pi\nu_l T_v^{\frac{1}{3}}}\right]^{1/2} \tag{2.169}$$

The right side of Eq. (2.168) or (2.169) is the maximum heat transfer rate per unit width through the evaporating thin film region. It indicates that the maximum heat transfer rate per unit width is directly proportional to the one-half power of liquid conductivity, one-sixth power of vapor density, one-third power of dispersion constant, two-thirds power of heat of vaporization and superheat, negative one-half power of liquid kinematic viscosity, and negative one-sixth power of vapor temperature.

Considering Eqs. (2.153) and (2.154), Eq. (2.152) becomes

$$\frac{d\delta}{dx} = \sqrt{B\delta\left(\frac{\delta_0^3}{2\delta^3} - 2 + \frac{3\delta}{2\delta_0}\right) + \frac{d_0^2\delta^2}{\delta_0^2}} \tag{2.170}$$

Nondimensionalizing Eq. (2.170) with δ_0, Eq. (2.170) becomes

$$\frac{d\delta^*}{dx^*} = \sqrt{\frac{B\delta_0}{2}\left(\frac{1}{\delta^{*2}} - 4\delta^* + 3\delta^{*2}\right) + d_0^2\delta^{*2}} \tag{2.171}$$

Substituting $B = \frac{k_l \nu_l (T_w - T_v)}{Ah_{lv}}$ into Eq. (2.171) yields

$$\frac{d\delta^*}{dx^*} = \sqrt{\frac{3\pi\nu_l\delta_0^2}{Ah_{lv}}q_0''\left(\frac{1}{\delta^{*2}} - 4\delta^* + 3\delta^{*2}\right) + d_0^2\delta^{*2}} \qquad (2.172)$$

where $x^* = \frac{x}{\delta_0}$ is the dimensionless coordinate. The nondimensional boundary conditions of Eq. (2.172) can be found as

$$\delta^* = 1 \quad \text{at} \quad x^* = 0 \qquad (2.173)$$

When the liquid film thickness is equal to $4^{\frac{1}{3}}\delta_0$ as defined by Eq. (2.156), the maximum heat flux takes place. The location can be found by

$$x = \delta_0 x^* = \delta_0 \int_1^{4^{\frac{1}{3}}} \frac{d\delta^*}{\sqrt{\frac{3\pi\nu_l\delta_0^2}{Ah_{lv}}q_0''\left(\frac{1}{\delta^{*2}} - 4\delta^* + 3\delta^{*2}\right) + d_0^2\delta^{*2}}} \qquad (2.174)$$

Considering the heat transfer coefficient of

$$h = \frac{q''}{T_{lv} - T_v} \qquad (2.175)$$

Substituting Eqs. (2.158) and (2.143) into Eq. (2.175) yields

$$h = \frac{\frac{k_l(T_w - T_v)}{\delta}\left(1 - \frac{\delta_0^3}{\delta^3}\right)}{T_v\left(1 + \frac{-p_d + \sigma_{lv}K}{h_{lv}\rho_l}\right) - T_v} \qquad (2.176)$$

Neglecting the effect of the capillary pressure and considering $p_d = -\frac{A}{6\pi\delta^3}$ with $\delta_0 = \left(\frac{AT_v}{6\pi\rho_l h_{lv}(T_w - T_v)}\right)^{\frac{1}{3}}$ shown in Eq. (2.154) and $\delta^* = \frac{\delta}{\delta_0}$, Eq. (2.176) can be expressed as

$$\frac{\delta h}{k_l} = \delta^{*3} - 1 \qquad (2.177)$$

Rearranging Eq. (2.177) produces

$$\frac{\delta/k_l}{1/h} = \delta^{*3} - 1 \qquad (2.178)$$

As shown in Eq. (2.178), the ratio of the conduction to convection thermal resistance only depends on the dimensionless thin film thickness. It should be noticed that the convection thermal resistance is due to the interface phase change resistance. In addition, it has been demonstrated that the heat flux reaches its maximum

Table 2.2 Liquid properties and operating conditions

Liquid	Water
$A(\text{J})/6\pi$	1.0×10^{-20}
T_v (K)	350
ρ_l (kg/m^3)	973.7
h_{lv} (kJ/kg)	2,382.7
ν_l (m^2/s)	0.5×10^{-6}
k_l (w/(m k))	0.65

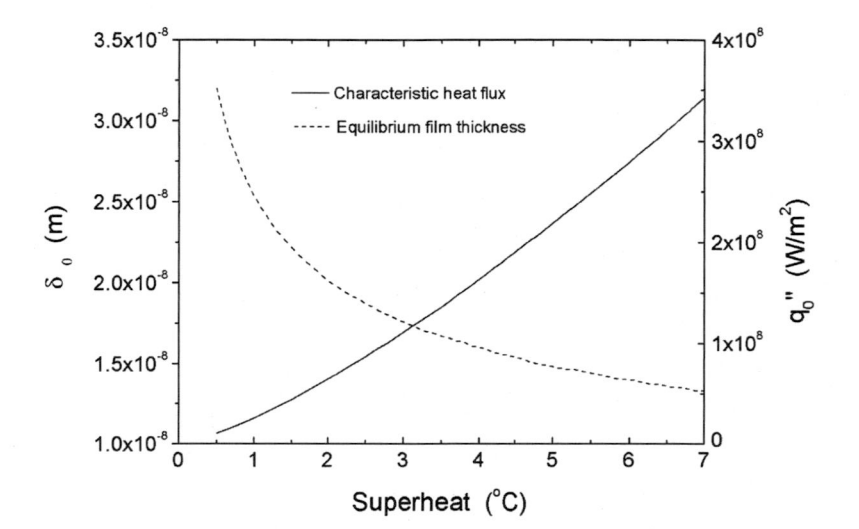

Fig. 2.25 Superheat effect on equilibrium film thickness and characteristic heat flux

when $\delta^* = 4^{\frac{1}{3}}$ as shown in Eq. (2.162). Considering this equation, it can be found that when the ratio of the conduction to convection thermal resistance is equal to 3, the heat flux achieves its maximum.

As presented above, the model can be used to predict the equilibrium film thickness, heat flux distribution, film thickness variation of evaporating film region, maximum total heat transfer rate through the evaporating film region, and ratio of the conduction to convection thermal resistance. Yan and Ma (2013) used the thermal properties and operating conditions shown in Table 2.2 and conducted calculations. Equation (2.172) was solved by the fourth-order Runge–Kutta method using the boundary conditions shown in Eq. (2.173) for the dimensionless thin film profile with a nonzero initial value of the slope $d_0 = 10^{-10}$. Then using Eq. (2.161) the dimensionless heat flux q''^* can be obtained. Substituting δ^* into Eqs. (2.167) and (2.178), the total heat transfer rate q_{tot} at any x along the meniscus and the ratio of the conduction to convection thermal resistance can be obtained.

Figure 2.25 illustrates the superheat effect on the equilibrium film thickness (non-evaporating film thickness) and characteristic heat flux. As shown, the equilibrium film thickness and characteristic heat flux depend on the superheat.

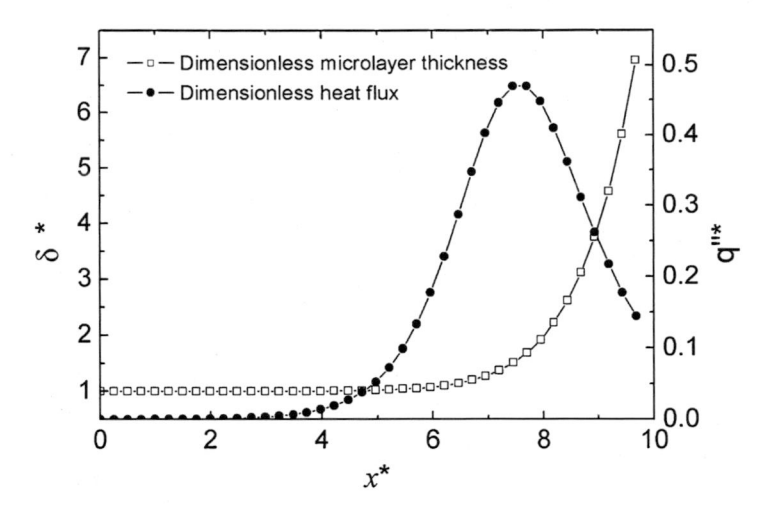

Fig. 2.26 Dimensionless thin film profile and heat flux at a superheat of 2 °C

The equilibrium film thickness decreases as the superheat increases. The characteristic heat flux becomes larger when the superheat is bigger. Figure 2.26 illustrates the variations of the dimensionless thin film profile and heat flux along the nondimensional coordinate. Results show that the heat flux increases very slowly with the increase of film thickness near the equilibrium film. But far from it, the film thickness has a strong effect on the heat flux. Its magnitude increases to the maximum value and then decreases sharply as it reaches the macroregion. In addition, it can be found that $\frac{1}{\delta^*}$ and $q''*$ are very small when x^* is very large, which indicates the assumption obtaining Eq. (2.169) is correct.

Figure 2.27 shows the superheat effect on the dimensionless heat flux through the evaporating thin film region. From Fig. 2.27, it can be found that the maximum dimensionless heat flux is a constant equal to about 0.47, which will not depend on the superheat and is the same as the analytical solution. But the dimensionless location corresponding to the maximum dimensionless heat flux is different, which is a function of the superheat, and the dimensionless heat flux distribution profile shifts to the contact line. Figure 2.28 illustrates variations of the ratio of the conduction to convection thermal resistances and dimensionless heat flux along the dimensionless x^* at a superheat of 2 °C. From Fig. 2.28, it can be clearly found that the convection or interface thermal resistance in the equilibrium film region affects the phase change heat transfer. In the evaporating thin film region near the equilibrium film region, the thermal resistance is primarily due to the interface phase change heat transfer. As it is close to the liquid bulk region, the conduction thermal resistance plays a more and more important role and the interface thermal resistance becomes smaller. The ratio of the conduction-to-convection or interface thermal resistance is a function of dimensionless thickness, $\delta^{*3} - 1$, as shown in Eq. (2.178). Figure 2.29 illustrates the maximum heat transfer rate per unit width

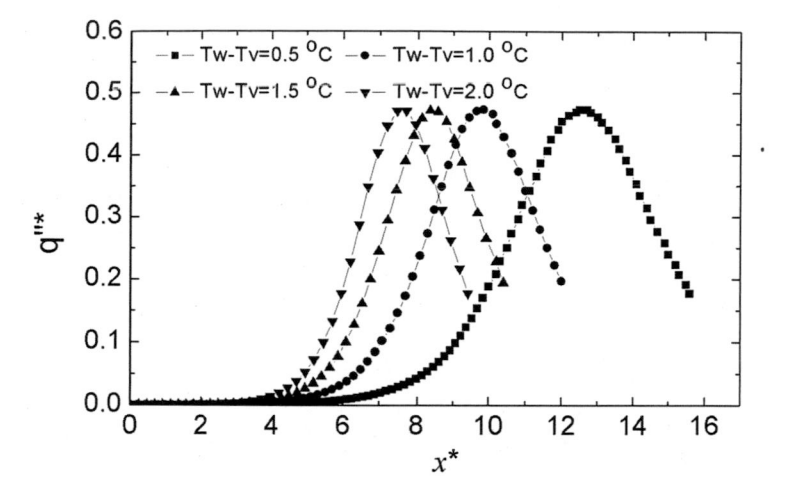

Fig. 2.27 Superheat effect on the nondimensional heat flux

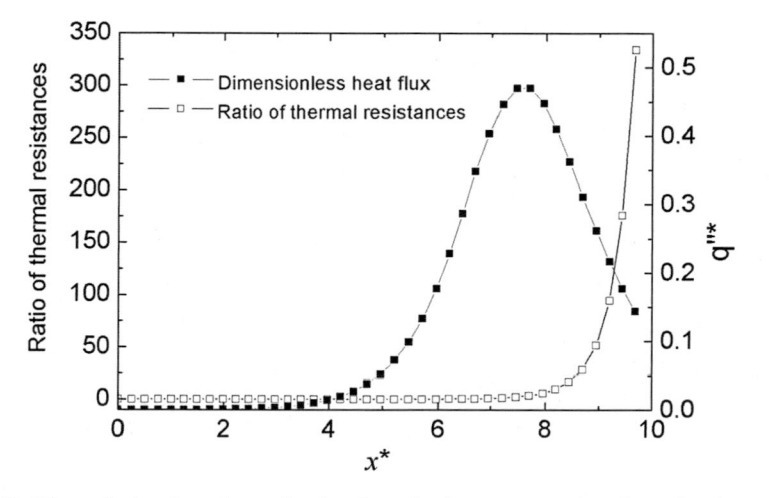

Fig. 2.28 Dimensionless heat flux and ratio of conduction-to-convection thermal resistances

through thin film evaporation calculated by using Eq. (2.168). As shown in Fig. 2.29, the maximum heat transfer rate per unit width increases as the superheat increases.

Example 2.6 For the thin film regions on a flat surface as shown in Fig. 2.24, if the vapor temperature is given, i.e., $T_v = 57$ °C, and the wall temperature $T_w = 60$ °C, determine the equilibrium film thickness (non-evaporating film thinness), optimum film thickness, and maximum heat flux and liquid–vapor interface temperature corresponding to this optimum film thickness (Hamaker constant $A = 10^{-19}$ J, working fluid is water).

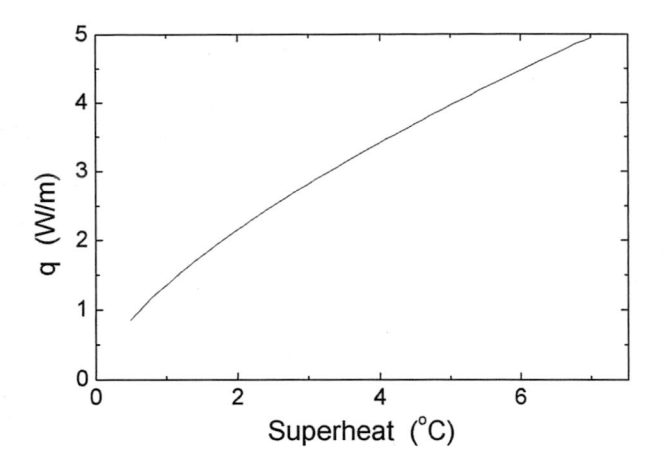

Fig. 2.29 Superheat effect on the maximum heat transfer rate per unit length

Solution For an equilibrium film, there is no heat transfer through the liquid film. The equilibrium film thickness can be calculated by $\delta_0 = \left(\frac{AT_v}{6\pi\rho_l h_{lv}(T_w - T_v)}\right)^{\frac{1}{3}}$. If the water thermal properties at 60 °C, i.e., $\rho_l = 983.28$ kg/m^3, $h_{lv} = 2{,}358.4$ kJ/kg, and $k_l = 0.653$ W/mK, are used, the equilibrium film thickness can be found as

$$\delta_0 = \left(\frac{AT_v}{6\pi\rho_l h_{lv}(T_w - T_v)}\right)^{\frac{1}{3}} = \left(\frac{10^{-19} \times (273.15 + 57)}{6\pi \times 983.28 \times 2{,}358{,}400 \times (60 - 57)}\right)^{\frac{1}{3}}$$

$$= 6.31 \times 10^{-10}\,\text{m}$$

The optimum film thickness where the maximum heat flux takes place can be calculated by Eq. (2.156), i.e.,

$$\delta_{q''_{max}} = 4^{\frac{1}{3}}\delta_0 = 4^{\frac{1}{3}} \times 6.31 \times 10^{-10} = 1.0 \times 10^{-9}\,\text{m}$$

The maximum heat flux occurring at the location of $\delta_{q''_{max}} = 1.0 \times 10^{-9}$ m can be found by Eq. (2.158), i.e.,

$$q'' = \frac{k_l(T_w - T_v)}{\delta}\left(1 - \frac{\delta_0^3}{\delta^3}\right) = \frac{0.653 \times (60 - 57)}{1 \times 10^{-9}} \times \left(1 - \frac{\left(6.31 \times 10^{-10}\right)^3}{\left(1 \times 10^{-9}\right)^3}\right)$$

$$= 1.467 \times 10^9\,\text{W/m}^2$$

The interface temperature of the liquid–vapor interface at this location can be calculated by

$$T_{lv} = T_v \left(1 + \frac{-p_d}{h_{lv}\rho_l}\right) = T_v \left[1 + \frac{-\left(-\dfrac{A}{6\pi\delta^3}\right)}{h_{lv}\rho_l}\right]$$

$$= (273.15 + 57) \times \left[1 + \frac{-\left(-\dfrac{1 \times 10^{-19}}{6\pi \times \left(1.0 \times 10^{-9}\right)^3}\right)}{2,358,400 \times 983.28}\right] = 330.91\,\text{K} = 57.76\,°\text{C}$$

Because the heat transfer rate through the liquid film and liquid–vapor interface is constant, i.e.,

$$q'' = \frac{k_l(T_w - T_v)}{\delta}\left(1 - \frac{\delta_0^3}{\delta^3}\right) = \frac{k_l(T_w - T_{lv})}{\delta} = \frac{(T_{lv} - T_v)}{R_i}$$

where R_i is the interface thermal resistance, the interface temperature can be also found as

$$T_{lv} = T_w - \frac{q''\delta}{k} = 60 - \frac{1.467 \times 10^9 \times 1 \times 10^{-9}}{0.653} = 57.76\,°\text{C}$$

2.8.4 Microscopic Model

When evaporation takes place at the liquid–vapor interface of thin film, liquid becomes vapor at the liquid–vapor interface. The motion of vapor molecules moving away from the interface can be modeled by the kinetic theory (Carey 1992). The evaporation mass flux at the liquid–vapor interface can be predicted by (Wayner 1997)

$$\dot{m} = \hat{\sigma}\left(\frac{M}{2\pi\bar{R}}\right)^{1/2}\left(\frac{p_{lv}}{T_{lv}^{1/2}} - \frac{p_v}{T_v^{1/2}}\right) \qquad (2.179)$$

where $\hat{\sigma}$ is accommodation coefficient. Considering $T_{lv}^{1/2} \approx T_v^{1/2}$, Eq. (2.179) can be expressed as

$$\dot{m} = \hat{\sigma}\left(\frac{M}{2\pi\bar{R}T_v}\right)^{1/2}(p_{lv} - p_v) \qquad (2.180)$$

Substituting Eq. (2.132) into Eq. (2.180) yields

$$\dot{m} = \hat{\sigma} \left(\frac{M}{2\pi \overline{R} T_v}\right)^{1/2} \left(-\frac{p_v V_l}{\overline{R} T_v}(-p_d + \sigma_{lv} K) + \frac{p_v V_l H_{lv}}{\overline{R} T_v T_{lv}}(T_{lv} - T_v)\right) \quad (2.181)$$

The pressure difference between liquid and vapor pressures across the liquid–vapor interface can be expressed as

$$p_l - p_v = p_d - \sigma K \tag{2.182}$$

Substituting Eq. (2.182) into Eq. (2.181), it can be found that

$$\dot{m} = \hat{\sigma} \left(\frac{M}{2\pi \overline{R} T_v}\right)^{1/2} \left(\frac{p_v V_l}{\overline{R} T_v}(p_l - p_v) + \frac{p_v V_l H_{lv}}{\overline{R} T_v T_{lv}}(T_{lv} - T_v)\right) \tag{2.183}$$

or

$$\dot{m} = a(T_{lv} - T_v) + b(p_l - p_v) \tag{2.184}$$

where

$$a = \hat{\sigma} \left(\frac{M}{2\pi \overline{R} T_v}\right)^{1/2} \frac{p_v V_l H_{lv}}{\overline{R} T_v T_{lv}} \tag{2.185}$$

and

$$b = \hat{\sigma} \left(\frac{M}{2\pi \overline{R} T_v}\right)^{1/2} \frac{p_v V_l}{\overline{R} T_v} \tag{2.186}$$

The evaporation mass flux at the liquid–vapor interface is directly related to the heat flux transferred through the thin film region, i.e.,

$$\dot{m} = \frac{q''}{h_{lv}} \tag{2.187}$$

where h_{lv} is the latent heat and q'' is heat flux added on the thin film region as shown in Fig. 2.30, which can be expressed as

$$q'' = \dot{m} h_{lv} = \frac{k_l}{\delta}(T_w - T_{lv}) \tag{2.188}$$

When evaporation takes place, liquid will flow into the evaporating thin film region which directly determines the mass flow rate at a given location and heat flux. Because the film thickness is much smaller than the total length of the thin film region, the lubricant theory can be applied to find the total mass flow rate per unit width of the film, $\Gamma(x)$, at a given x, i.e.,

Fig. 2.30 Thin film region
for microscopic model

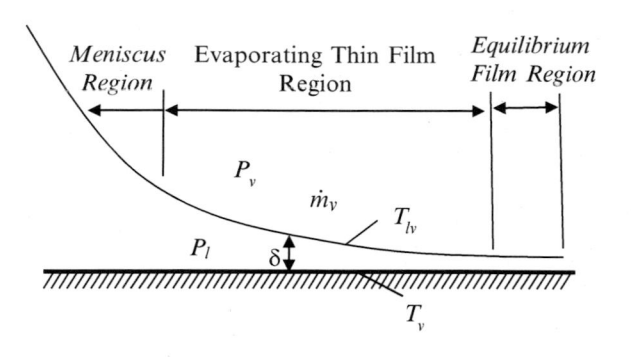

$$\Gamma(x) = -\frac{\delta^3}{3\nu}\frac{dp_l}{dx} \tag{2.189}$$

Taking a derivative with x, the total mass flow rate per unit width of the film, $\Gamma(x)$, can be directly related to the evaporation rate at the liquid–vapor interface, i.e.,

$$\frac{d\Gamma(x)}{dx} = -\frac{d}{dx}\left(\frac{\delta^3}{3\nu}\frac{dp_l}{dx}\right) = -\dot{m} \tag{2.190}$$

Substituting Eq. (2.184) into Eq. (2.190) yields

$$\frac{d}{dx}\left(\frac{\delta^3}{3\nu}\frac{dp_l}{dx}\right) = a(T_{lv} - T_v) + b(p_l - p_v) \tag{2.191}$$

Substituting Eq. (2.188) into Eq. (2.191), the interface temperature, T_{lv}, can be eliminated and Eq. (2.191) can be expressed as (Truong and Wayner 1987)

$$\frac{d}{dx}\left(\frac{\delta^3}{3\nu}\frac{dp_l}{dx}\right) = \frac{1}{1 + \frac{ah_{lv}}{k_l}\delta}[a(T_w - T_v) + b(p_l - p_v)] \tag{2.192}$$

To solve Eq. (2.192), Wayner (1997) conducted a dimensionless analysis. For the equilibrium film, because nonevaporation takes place, the left side of Eq. (2.192) or (2.191) is equal to zero; hence, Eq. (2.192) can be expressed as

$$b(p_l - p_v) = -a(T_w - T_v) \tag{2.193}$$

For the equilibrium film, the film is flat. The pressure difference between the liquid pressure, p_l, and vapor pressure, p_v, is dependent on the film thickness or the disjoining pressure, p_d, i.e.,

$$p_d = p_l - p_v \tag{2.194}$$

If the disjoining pressure in the equilibrium film is defined as Π_0, and Eq. (2.119) is used to determine the value of the disjoining pressure, Eq. (2.193) can be found as

$$\Pi_0 = -\frac{A}{6\pi\delta_0^3} = -\frac{a}{b}(T_{\mathrm{w}} - T_{\mathrm{v}}). \tag{2.195}$$

The dimensionless pressure difference is defined as

$$\phi = \frac{p_l - p_v}{\Pi_0}. \tag{2.196}$$

For the evaporating thin film region, $p_l - p_v$ shown in Eq. (2.196) can be expressed as

$$p_l - p_v = p_{\mathrm{d}} - \sigma K = -\frac{A}{6\pi\delta^3} - \sigma\frac{\frac{d^2\delta}{dx^2}}{\left[1 + \left(\frac{d\delta}{dx}\right)^2\right]^{3/2}} \tag{2.197}$$

The film thickness and dimensionless position are defined as

$$\delta^* = \frac{\delta}{\delta_0} \tag{2.198}$$

and

$$\xi = \frac{x}{l} \tag{2.199}$$

where

$$l = \sqrt{\frac{A}{6\pi a\nu(T_{\mathrm{w}} - T_{\mathrm{v}})}} \tag{2.200}$$

The dimensionless form of Eq. (2.192) can be found as

$$\frac{1}{3}\frac{d}{d\xi}\left(\delta^*\frac{d\phi}{d\xi}\right) = \frac{1}{1 + \kappa\delta^*}(1 + \phi) \tag{2.201}$$

where

$$\phi = -\frac{1}{\delta^3} - \varepsilon\frac{d^2\delta^*}{d\xi^2} \tag{2.202}$$

$$\kappa = \frac{ah_{lv}\delta_0}{k_l}; \quad \varepsilon = \frac{6\pi\sigma\delta_0 b\nu}{A} \tag{2.203}$$

The parameter κ is related to the thermal resistance of the liquid film, and the parameter ε is a measure of the importance of capillary pressure effects relative to the disjoining pressure effect. To solve Eq. (2.201), four boundary conditions are

needed. On the equilibrium film, i.e., at $\xi = 0$, the dimensionless film thickness δ^* is equal to 1 and the curvature K is 0. These are the first two boundary conditions. The last two boundary conditions are met when $\xi \to \infty$, $\delta^* \to \infty$, and $\phi \to$ constant. Using these boundary conditions, Kim and Wayner (1996) solved Eq. (2.201) to determine the equilibrium film thickness, thin film profile, and heat transfer rate through the evaporating thin film. Results demonstrated that when the heat flux increases, the contact angle increases and there is a significant resistance to heat transfer in a small meniscus due to interfacial forces, viscous stresses, and thermal conduction in the liquid.

2.8.5 Momentum Conservation Model

Consider a liquid film placed on a flat surface as illustrated in Fig. 2.31. The wall temperature is kept constant which is equal to T_w and the vapor temperature is equal to T_v. The thin liquid film region consists of three regions: the non-evaporating or equilibrium film region, where the disjoining pressure is dominant and no evaporation takes place; the evaporating thin film region, where a majority of the evaporation occurs; and the meniscus region, where the meniscus radius of curvature is constant. In the non-evaporating (equilibrium) thin film region, the liquid–vapor interfacial temperature approaches and becomes equal to the wall temperature, $T_{lv} = T_w$. The equilibrium film thickness can be determined by Eq. (2.135). Substituting Eq. (2.119) into Eq. (2.135), the equilibrium film thickness can be expressed as

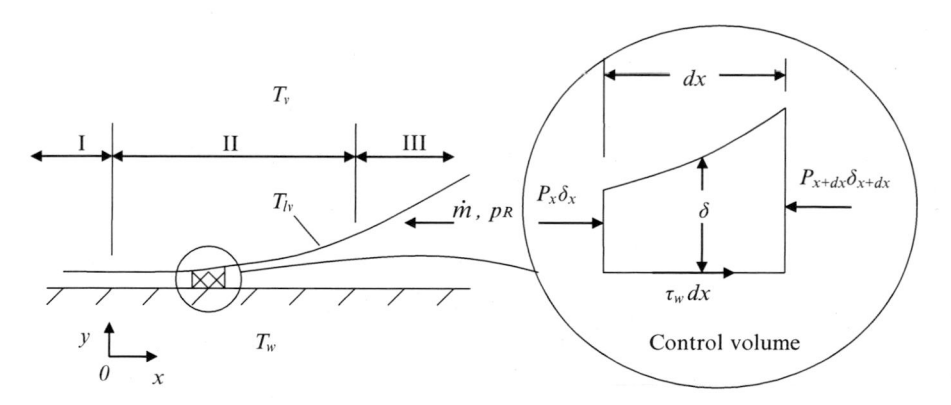

Fig. 2.31 Liquid film on a flat surface with the equilibrium film (*I*), evaporating thin film (*II*), and meniscus (*III*) regions

$$\delta_0 = \left[\frac{A}{6\pi H_{lv}(1 - T_v/T_w)} \right]^{1/3} \tag{2.204}$$

where H_{lv} is the latent heat per unit volume and A is the Hamaker's constant.

To develop the equations governing the fluid flow and heat transfer in the evaporating thin film region, a control volume shown in Fig. 2.31 is taken, and the following assumptions are made, i.e., (1) the temperature on the wall is uniform equal to T_w; (2) the interfacial waves on the fluid flow in the thin film region are neglected; (3) the physical properties are constant at a given temperature; (4) the pressure jump across the liquid–vapor interface is calculated by the Laplace–Young equation; and (5) the disjoining pressure is determined by $p_d = -\frac{A}{6\pi\delta^3}$. For the control volume shown in Fig. 2.31, the pressure in the liquid film can be found as

$$p_l = p_R - \frac{A}{6\pi\delta^3} - \sigma K \tag{2.205}$$

where p_R is the reference pressure, δ is the film thickness, and σ is the surface tension. The meniscus curvature, K, can be directly related to the film thickness by

$$K = \frac{\frac{d^2\delta}{dx^2}}{\left[1 + \left(\frac{d\delta}{dx}\right)^2\right]^{3/2}} \tag{2.206}$$

For the control volume shown in Fig. 2.31, the momentum equation along the x-direction can be expressed as

$$\rho_l \frac{\partial u}{\partial t} + \rho_l u \frac{\partial u}{\partial x} + \rho_l v \frac{\partial u}{\partial y} = \frac{A}{2\pi\delta^4}\frac{\partial \delta}{\partial x} + \sigma \frac{\partial K}{\partial x} + \mu_l \frac{\partial^2 u}{\partial x^2} + \mu_l \frac{\partial^2 u}{\partial y^2} \tag{2.207}$$

If the flow is steady state, the first term in the equation can be neglected, and Eq. (2.207) becomes

$$\rho_l u \frac{\partial u}{\partial x} + \rho_l v \frac{\partial u}{\partial y} = -\frac{A}{2\pi\delta^4}\frac{\partial \delta}{\partial x} + \sigma \frac{\partial K}{\partial x} + \mu_l \frac{\partial^2 u}{\partial x^2} + \mu_l \frac{\partial^2 u}{\partial y^2} \tag{2.208}$$

From the boundary layer theory, it is no question to consider $u \sim 1, y \sim \delta, x \sim 1, v \sim \delta$ for the regular velocity boundary layer, and it is not possible to find whether $\rho_l u \frac{\partial u}{\partial x}$ is larger than $\rho_l v \frac{\partial u}{\partial y}$ shown in Eq. (2.208) for the regular velocity boundary layer. For the thin film flow in the current investigation, the velocity in the non-evaporating region is equal to zero, and the velocity in the bulk region is very small. The velocity in the evaporating film region varies from zero at the non-evaporating film region through the highest value at one location in the evaporation thin film region

to a very low value at the bulk region. Obviously, $\frac{\partial u}{\partial x}$ should have an order of 1. This is very different from the regular boundary layer analysis. As a result, $\rho_l u \frac{\partial u}{\partial x} \gg \rho_l v \frac{\partial u}{\partial y}$.

Based on the order analysis, the momentum equation for the control volume in the thin film evaporating region becomes

$$\rho_l u \frac{\partial u}{\partial x} = -\frac{A}{2\pi\delta^4} \frac{\partial \delta}{\partial x} + \sigma \frac{\partial K}{\partial x} + \mu_l \frac{\partial^2 u}{\partial x^2} + \mu_l \frac{\partial^2 u}{\partial y^2} \tag{2.209}$$

Equation (2.209) can be rewritten as

$$\frac{\rho_l}{2} \frac{\partial u^2}{\partial x} = -\frac{A}{2\pi\delta^4} \frac{\partial \delta}{\partial x} + \sigma \frac{\partial K}{\partial x} + \mu_l \frac{\partial^2 u}{\partial x^2} + \mu_l \frac{\partial^2 u}{\partial y^2} \tag{2.210}$$

Integrating Eq. (2.210) in the y-direction from zero to the film thickness results in

$$\frac{\partial}{\partial x}\left(\frac{\rho_l}{2}\int_0^\delta u^2 dy - \frac{A}{6\pi\delta^3}\int_0^\delta dy - \sigma K\int_0^\delta dy - \mu_l \frac{\partial}{\partial x}\left(\int_0^\delta u\, dy\right)\right)$$
$$= \mu_l\left(\int_0^\delta \frac{\partial^2 u}{\partial y^2} dy\right) \tag{2.211}$$

Assuming that $\int_0^\delta u\, dy = \bar{u}\delta$ and $\int_0^\delta u^2 dy \approx \bar{u}^2\delta$, Eq. (2.211) can be expressed as

$$\frac{\partial}{\partial x}\left(\frac{\rho_l}{2}(\bar{u}^2\delta) - \frac{A}{6\pi\delta^2} - \sigma K\delta - \frac{\partial}{\partial x}(\bar{u}\delta)\right) = \mu_l \left.\frac{\partial u}{\partial y}\right|_0^\delta \tag{2.212}$$

where $\mu_l \left.\frac{\partial u}{\partial y}\right|_0^\delta = -\mu_l \left.\frac{\partial u}{\partial y}\right|_0$ due to free flow at the liquid–vapor interface. Therefore, Eq. (2.212) can be reduced to

$$\frac{\partial}{\partial x}\left(\frac{\rho_l}{2}(\bar{u}^2\delta) - \frac{A}{6\pi\delta^2} - \sigma K\delta - \frac{\partial}{\partial x}(\bar{u}\delta)\right) = -\mu_l \left.\frac{\partial u}{\partial y}\right|_0 \tag{2.213}$$

The mass flow rate across the thin film region is determined by

$$\dot{m} = \bar{u}\rho_l w\delta \tag{2.214}$$

where w is the film width. Evaporation along the interface between liquid and vapor results in a change in mass flow rate in the x-direction based on the superheat and film thickness, which can be expressed

$$\frac{\partial \dot{m}}{\partial x} = \frac{q''}{h_{lv}} = \frac{k_l(T_{\rm w} - T_{lv})}{h_{lv}\delta} \tag{2.215}$$

The shear stress along the wall surface can be expressed as

$$\tau_{\rm w} = \mu_l \frac{\partial u}{\partial y}\bigg|_0 = \frac{(f \cdot Re)\mu_l \bar{u}}{8\delta} \tag{2.216}$$

Considering Eqs. (2.214)–(2.216), Eq. (2.213) becomes

$$\frac{\partial}{\partial x}\left(\frac{1}{2}\dot{m}\bar{u} - \frac{A}{6\pi\delta^2} - \sigma K\delta + \frac{\mu_l}{\rho_l}\frac{\partial \dot{m}}{\partial x}\right) = \frac{(f \cdot Re)\mu_l \dot{m}}{8\rho_l \delta^2} \tag{2.217}$$

From Eqs. (2.214) and (2.215), it could also be obtained that

$$\frac{\partial \bar{u}}{\partial x} = \frac{k_l(T_{\rm w} - T_{lv})}{\rho_l h_{lv}\delta^2} - \frac{\bar{u}}{\delta}\frac{\partial \delta}{\partial x} \tag{2.218}$$

To solve Eq. (2.217), the interface temperature, T_{lv}, must be determined. In the previous section, it has been shown that the vapor pressure difference between the liquid–vapor interface and the bulk vapor can be expressed as

$$p_{lv} - p_{\rm v} = -\frac{p_{\rm v}V_l}{\bar{R}T_{\rm v}}(-p_{\rm d} + \sigma_{lv}K) + \frac{p_{\rm v}V_lH_{lv}}{\bar{R}T_{\rm v}T_{lv}}(T_{lv} - T_{\rm v}) \tag{2.219}$$

If the bulk flow effect or the thermal resistance due to the vapor flow is not considered, it can be assumed that the vapor pressure at the liquid–vapor interface is equal to the bulk vapor pressure. Equation (2.219) can be expressed as

$$-p_{\rm d} + \sigma_{lv}K = \frac{H_{lv}}{T_{lv}}(T_{lv} - T_{\rm v}) \tag{2.220}$$

Rearranging Eq. (2.220) yields

$$T_{\rm v} = T_{lv}\left(1 - \frac{-p_{\rm d} + \sigma_{lv}K}{h_{lv}\rho_l}\right) \tag{2.221}$$

where $H_{lv} = h_{lv}\rho_l$. Because the interface temperature, T_{lv}, is very close to the vapor temperature, $T_{\rm v}$, $\frac{H_{lv}}{T_{lv}} \approx \frac{H_{lv}}{T_{\rm v}}$, and Eq. (2.220) can be approximately expressed as

$$T_{lv} = T_v \left(1 + \frac{-p_d + \sigma_{lv} K}{h_{lv} \rho_l} \right) \tag{2.222}$$

Because the liquid film is very thin, it can be assumed that heat transferred through the liquid film is by conduction, i.e.,

$$q'' = \frac{k_l}{\delta}(T_w - T_{lv}) \tag{2.223}$$

To solve the governing equations presented above, appropriate boundary conditions must be determined. The calculation starts from the non-evaporation region where the boundary conditions satisfy

$$\begin{cases} \dot{m}|_0 = 0, \\ \bar{u}|_0 = 0, \\ K|_0 = 0, \\ T_{lv}|_0 = T_w, \\ \delta|_0 = \delta_0 = \left(\frac{T_v A}{6\pi(T_w - T_v)\rho_l h_{lv}} \right)^{1/3} \\ -\left(\frac{A}{6\pi\delta^3} + \sigma K \right)\delta + \frac{1}{2}\dot{m}\bar{u} + \left. \frac{\mu_l k_l (T_w - T_{lv})}{\rho_l h_{lv}\delta} \right|_0 = -\frac{A}{6\pi\delta_0^2}. \end{cases} \tag{2.224}$$

It is noticed that the boundary condition of $\frac{\partial \delta}{\partial x}$ is not given. If it is assumed that $\frac{\partial \delta}{\partial x} = 0$, then all of the equations should represent the non-evaporation region, and there is no change for each variable solved. On the other hand, in the evaporating region, the boundary condition for $\frac{\partial \delta}{\partial x}$ should be positive, i.e., $\frac{\partial \delta}{\partial x} > 0$, and it should be determined by the superheat, $T_w - T_{lv}$, or heat load and the contact angle.

To solve all of the governing equations, a fourth-order Runge–Kutta method was implemented. If $F = -\left(\frac{A}{6\pi\delta^3} + \sigma K \right)\delta + \frac{1}{2}\dot{m}\bar{u} + \frac{\mu_l k_l (T_w - T_{lv})}{\rho_l h_{lv}\delta}$ and $\frac{\partial \delta}{\partial x} = G$, the governing equations become

$$\frac{\partial F}{\partial x} = \frac{(f \cdot Re)\mu_l \dot{m}}{8\rho_l \delta^2} \tag{2.225}$$

$$\frac{\partial \dot{m}}{\partial x} = \frac{k_l(T_w - T_{lv})}{h_{lv}\delta} \tag{2.226}$$

$$\frac{\partial \bar{u}}{\partial x} = \frac{k_l(T_w - T_{lv})}{\rho_l h_{lv}\delta^2} - \frac{\bar{u}}{\delta}G \tag{2.227}$$

$$\frac{\partial G}{\partial x} = K\left(1 + G^2\right)^{3/2} \tag{2.228}$$

$$\frac{\partial \delta}{\partial x} = G \tag{2.229}$$

At node x_n, the values of F_n, $\dot{m}_n$, $\bar{u}_n$, δ_n, G_n, K_n, and $T_{lv,n}$ are known. By the five first-order PDEs above, F_{n+1}, $\dot{m}_{n+1}$ $\dot{m}_n$, $\bar{u}_{n+1}$, δ_{n+1}, and G_{n+1} were obtained. To determine the two unknowns (K_{n+1} and $T_{lv,n+1}$), the following expression for F is described in discrete form as

$$F_{n+1} = -\left(\frac{A}{6\pi\delta_{n+1}^3} + \sigma K_{n+1}\right)\delta_{n+1} + \frac{1}{2}\dot{m}_{n+1}\bar{u}_{n+1} + \frac{\mu_l}{\rho_l}\frac{k_l(T_w - T_{lv,n+1})}{h_{lv}\delta_{n+1}} \tag{2.230}$$

The numerical form for Eq. (2.222) can be written as

$$T_{lv,n+1} = T_v\left[1 + \frac{\sigma K_{n+1} + \frac{A}{6\pi\delta_{n+1}^3}}{\rho_l h_{lv}}\right] \tag{2.231}$$

Solving these two equations, the two unknown values could be obtained by

$$\left(\delta_{n+1} + \frac{C_T T_v}{h_{lv}\rho_l}\right)\sigma K_{n+1} = -F_{n+1} - \left(\delta_{n+1} + \frac{C_T T_v}{h_{lv}\rho_l}\right)\frac{A}{6\pi\delta_{n+1}^3} + $$
$$\frac{1}{2}\dot{m}_{n+1}\bar{u}_{n+1} + C_T(T_w - T_v) \tag{2.232}$$

where $C_T = \frac{\mu_l k_l}{\rho_l h_{lv}\delta_{n+1}}$.

Using the procedure described above (Ma et al. 2008), the governing equation shown in Eq. (2.217) can be solved with boundary condition shown in Eq. (2.224) and by assuming there is no curvature in the bulk region (disjoining pressure less than 0.01 Pa), i.e., $K = 0$ and $A = 6\pi \times 10^{-19}$ J. Results shown in Figs. 2.32, 2.33, 2.34, 2.35, 2.36, and 2.37 are based on water at a vapor temperature of 305 K. Figure 2.32 illustrates the variation of the temperature at the liquid–vapor interface for various superheats. In the equilibrium thin film region, the interfacial thermal resistance is so large that the temperature at the liquid–vapor interface is equal to the wall temperature and no evaporation occurs in this region. As the location approaches the bulk region, the interfacial thermal resistance reduces, and the temperature at the liquid–vapor interface decreases significantly in the evaporating thin film region and becomes close to the vapor temperature in the meniscus region if the curvature in the meniscus region is small. Figure 2.33 shows the superheat effect on the liquid film profile in the evaporating thin film region. As shown, when the superheat increases, the liquid film thickness in the evaporating thin film region significantly increases as the location approaches the bulk region. In other words, the contact angle significantly increases as the superheat increases. However, the

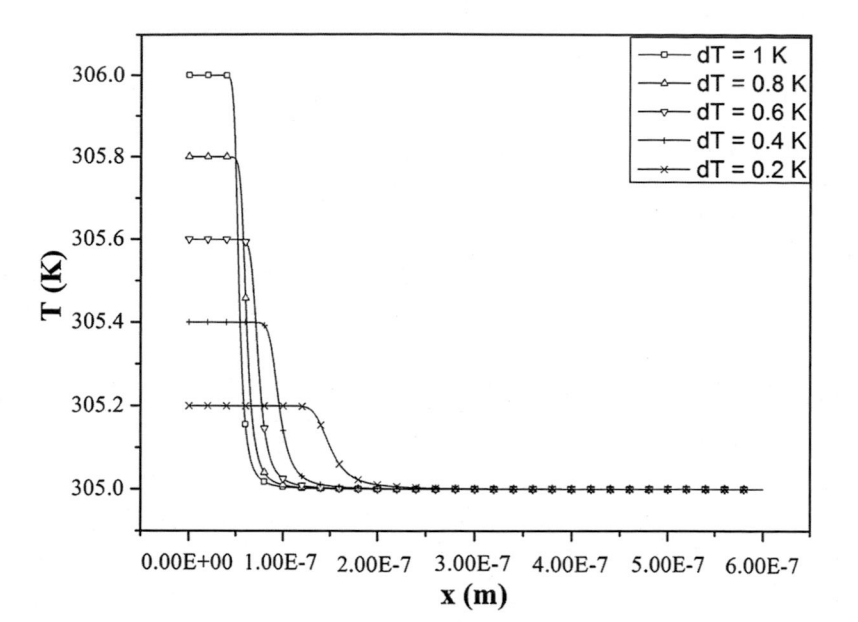

Fig. 2.32 Superheat effect on the liquid–vapor interface temperature

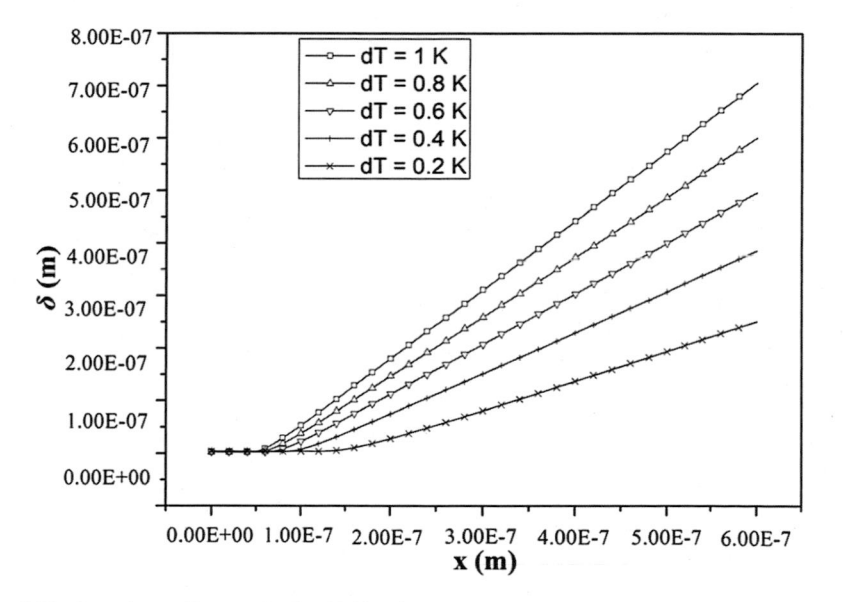

Fig. 2.33 Superheat effect on the liquid film thickness

equilibrium film thickness becomes thinner and the interfacial thermal resistance at the equilibrium film region increases as the superheat increases. Figure 2.34 displays the superheat effect on the heat transfer rate through the evaporating thin film region. When the superheat increases, the heat transfer rate through the evaporating

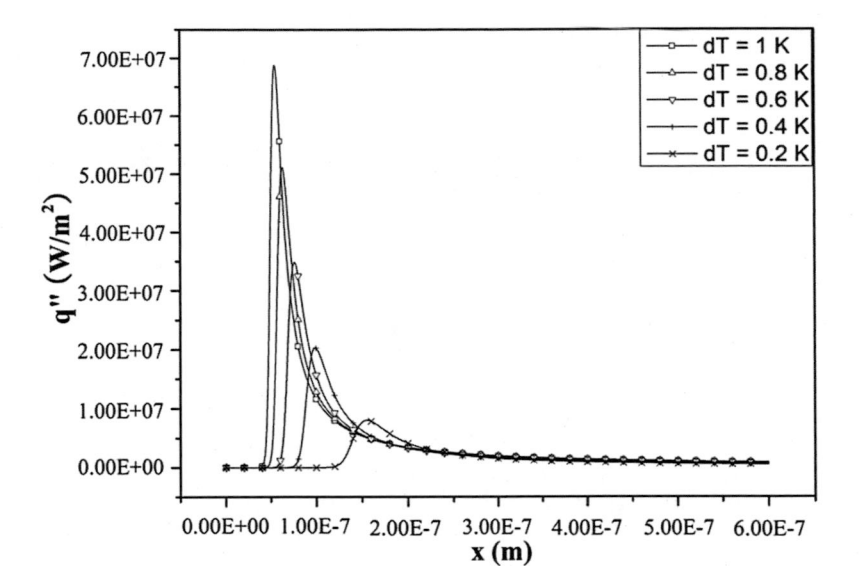

Fig. 2.34 Superheat effect on the heat flux distribution

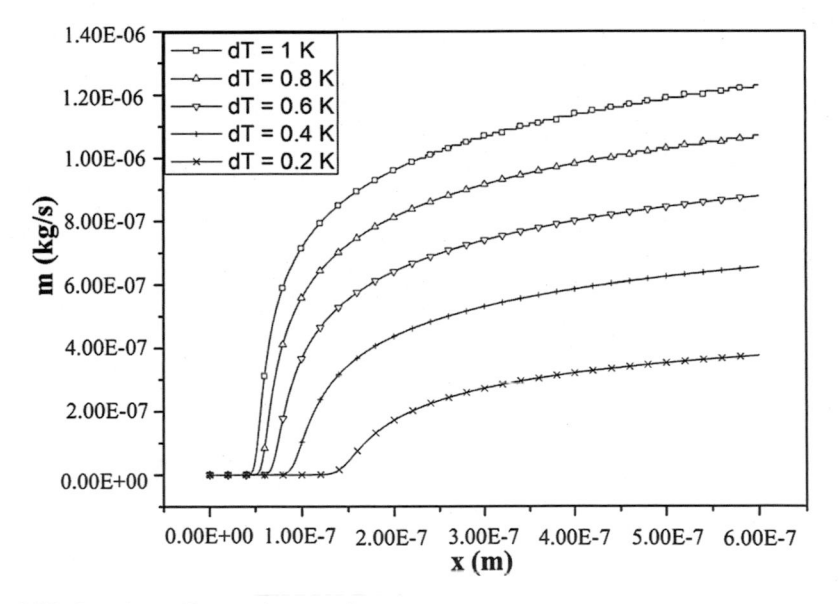

Fig. 2.35 Superheat effect on the mass flow rate

thin film region significantly increases. The model can be used to predict the mass flow rate shown in Fig. 2.35 and the average velocity shown in Fig. 2.36. While the mass flow rate increases as the location approaches the meniscus region, there exists a maximum average velocity in the evaporating thin film region. It can also

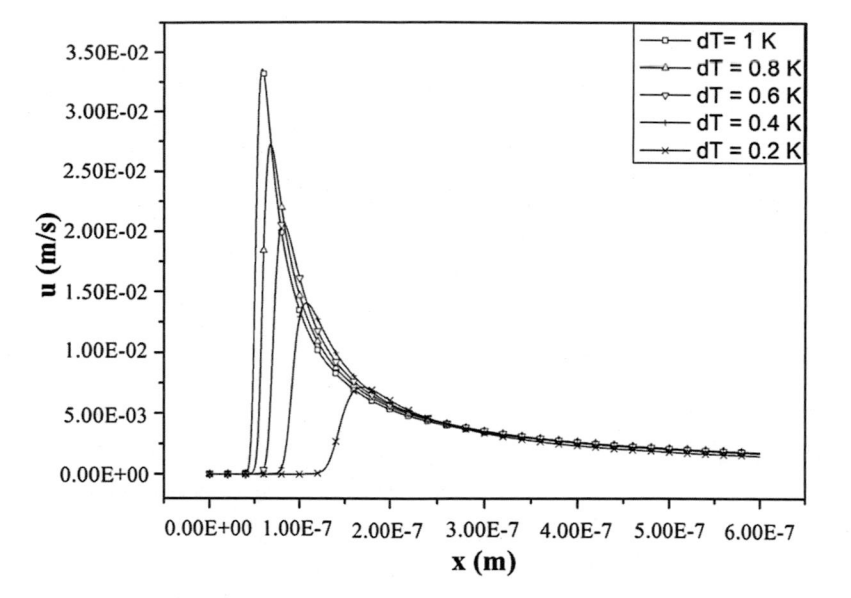

Fig. 2.36 Superheat effect on the average velocity

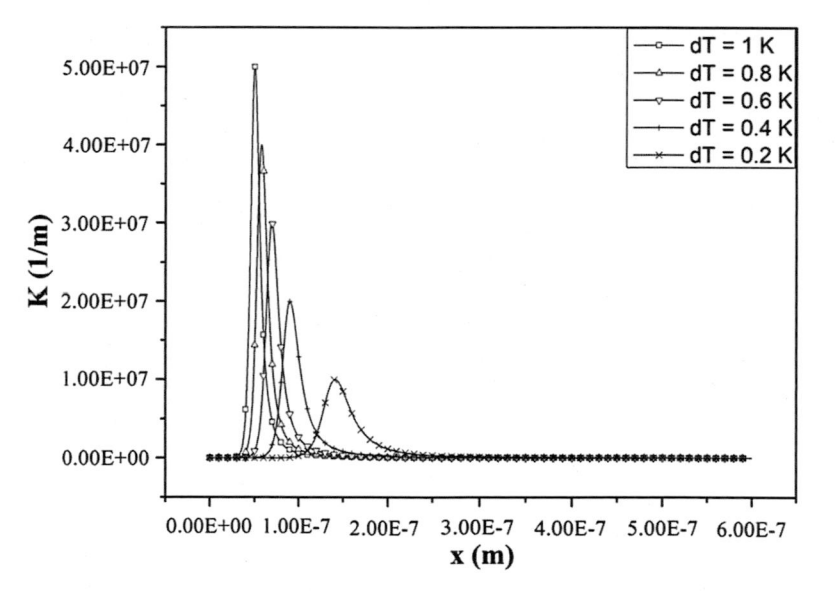

Fig. 2.37 Superheat effect on the curvature

be found that for a given superheat, the location where the maximum average velocity exists is different from that where the maximum heat flux exists. Figure 2.37 shows the superheat effect on the curvature of liquid–vapor interface. As shown, there exists a maximum curvature for a given superheat. The location for

the peak value of curvature is also different from that for the peak value of heat flux through the thin film region. As presented in the model, one feature of this model includes the inertial force effect. Although the prediction shows that the inertial force can affect the thin film profile, interfacial temperature, meniscus radius, heat flux distribution, velocity distribution, and mass flow rate, the effect is very small particularly near the equilibrium film region and can be neglected.

2.8.6   Evaporating Thin Film on a Curved Surface

Consider a miniature flat heat pipe as shown in Fig. 2.38, which consists of two copper plates that sandwich miniature copper wires. The wires are sintered to the plates and the cornered regions formed between the wires and plates are used to pump the working fluid from the condensing section to the evaporating section. As heat is added on the evaporating section, it is transferred through solid regions (plate and wire) and reaches the working fluid. It has been shown that most of the

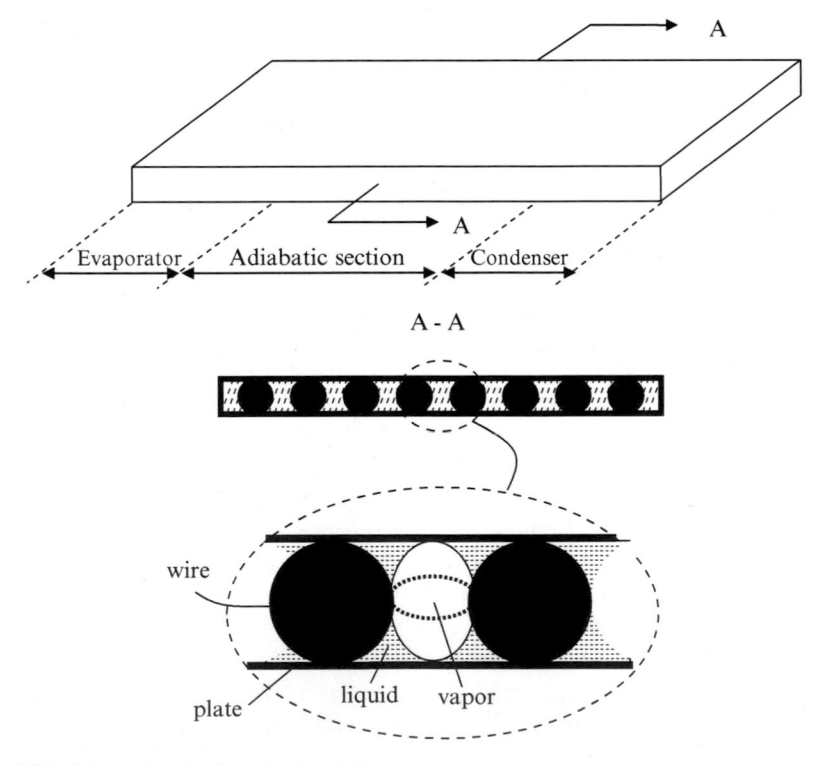

Fig. 2.38   Schematic of a flat-plate heat pipe

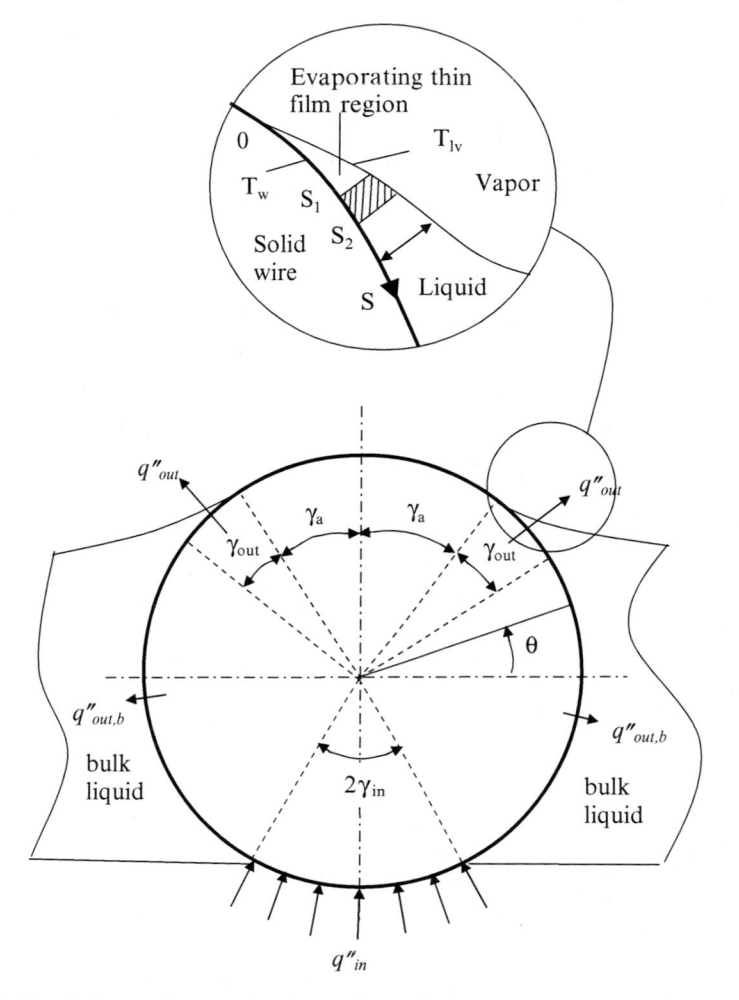

Fig. 2.39 Liquid film on the curved surface and coordinate system

heat is transferred through the thin film formed on the curved surface shown in Fig. 2.38. To simplify the problem and study evaporation and fluid flow in the thin film region formed on a curved surface, a physical model shown in Fig. 2.39 is assumed. When the wires and plates are sintered together, a finite area is formed that the heat flux passes through connecting to the wire from the external plate. It is assumed that the heat added onto the external plate is transferred through this finite area into the solid wire with a constant heat flux. The steady state heat conduction equation governing the temperature distribution on the solid wire can be expressed as

$$\frac{\partial^2 T}{\partial r^2} + \frac{1}{r}\frac{\partial T}{\partial r} + \frac{1}{r^2}\frac{\partial^2 T}{\partial \theta^2} = 0 \tag{2.233}$$

The boundary conditions corresponding to Eq. (2.233) are as follows:

$$-k_w \frac{dT}{dr}\bigg|_{r=r_w} = q_{in}'' = \frac{q_{in}'}{2 r_w \gamma_{in}} \quad \text{at} \quad \frac{3\pi}{2} - \gamma_{in} \le \theta \le \frac{3\pi}{2} + \gamma_{in} \tag{2.234}$$

$$-k_w \frac{dT}{dr}\bigg|_{r=r_w} = \begin{cases} q_{out}'' & \text{at} \quad \dfrac{\pi}{2} - \gamma_a - \gamma_{out} \le \theta \le \dfrac{\pi}{2} - \gamma_a \\[2mm] & \text{and} \quad \dfrac{\pi}{2} + \gamma_a \le \theta \le \dfrac{\pi}{2} + \gamma_a + \gamma_{out} \\[2mm] q_{out,b}'' & \text{at} \quad 0 \le \theta \le \dfrac{\pi}{2} - \gamma_a - \gamma_{out}, \dfrac{\pi}{2} + \gamma_a + \gamma_{out} \le \theta \le \dfrac{3\pi}{2} - \gamma_{in}, \\[2mm] & \text{and} \quad \dfrac{3\pi}{2} + \gamma_{in} \le \theta \le 2\pi \\[2mm] 0 & \text{at} \quad \dfrac{\pi}{2} - \gamma_a \le \theta \le \dfrac{\pi}{2} + \gamma_a \end{cases} \tag{2.235}$$

where q_{in}'' is the heat flux entering the wire from the bottom copper plate, q_{out}'' represents the heat flux through the thin film region, and $q_{out,b}''$ is the heat flux transferred to the bulk fluid region from the wire. The heat flux transferred from the wire to the equilibrium film is considered negligible since no evaporation occurs here. The temperature drop due to conduction across the evaporating thin film can be related to the evaporative heat flux by the following equation:

$$q_{out}'' = k_l \frac{T_w(r_w, \theta) - T_{lv}(\theta)}{\delta(\theta)} \tag{2.236}$$

where one-dimensional heat conduction through the liquid film is assumed, δ is the thin film thickness, and T_w and T_{lv} are, respectively, the wire surface temperature and the liquid–vapor interface temperature at a given arc angle.

Based on the boundary conditions given above, Eq. (2.233) can be solved using separation of variables. The function for the temperature distribution on a given cross section of the wire is found by

$$T_w(r, \theta) = a_0 + \sum_{m=1}^{\infty} \left[\left(\frac{r}{r_w}\right)^m (a_m \cos(m\theta) + b_m \sin(m\theta)) \right] \tag{2.237}$$

where

$$
a_m = \frac{r_w}{\pi m}
\begin{pmatrix}
\displaystyle\int_{\frac{\pi}{2} - \gamma_a - \gamma_{out}}^{\frac{\pi}{2} - \gamma_a} q''_{out}(\theta)\cos(m\theta)d\theta + \int_{\frac{\pi}{2} + \gamma_a}^{\frac{\pi}{2} + \gamma_a + \gamma_{out}} q''_{out}(\theta)\cos(m\theta)d\theta \\[3mm]
+ \displaystyle\int_{\frac{\pi}{2} + \gamma_a + \gamma_{out}}^{\frac{3\pi}{2} - \gamma_{in}} q''_{out,b}(\theta)\cos(m\theta)d\theta + \int_{\frac{3\pi}{2} + \gamma_{in}}^{2\pi} q''_{out,b}(\theta)\cos(m\theta)d\theta \\[3mm]
+ \displaystyle\int_{0}^{\frac{\pi}{2} - \gamma_a - \gamma_{out}} q''_{out,b}(\theta)\cos(m\theta)d\theta + \int_{\frac{3\pi}{2} - \gamma_{in}}^{\frac{3\pi}{2} + \gamma_{in}} q''_{in}(\theta)\cos(m\theta)d\theta
\end{pmatrix}
$$

$$(2.238)$$

and

$$
b_m = \frac{r_w}{\pi m}
\begin{pmatrix}
\displaystyle\int_{\frac{\pi}{2} - \gamma_a - \gamma_{out}}^{\frac{\pi}{2} - \gamma_a} q''_{out}(\theta)\sin(m\theta)d\theta + \int_{\frac{\pi}{2} + \gamma_a}^{\frac{\pi}{2} + \gamma_a + \gamma_{out}} q''_{out}(\theta)\sin(m\theta)d\theta \\[3mm]
+ \displaystyle\int_{\frac{\pi}{2} + \gamma_a + \gamma_{out}}^{\frac{3\pi}{2} - \gamma_{in}} q''_{out,b}(\theta)\sin(m\theta)d\theta + \int_{\frac{3\pi}{2} + \gamma_{in}}^{2\pi} q''_{out,b}(\theta)\sin(m\theta)d\theta \\[3mm]
+ \displaystyle\int_{0}^{\frac{\pi}{2} - \gamma_a - \gamma_{out}} q''_{out,b}(\theta)\sin(m\theta)d\theta + \int_{\frac{3\pi}{2} - \gamma_{in}}^{\frac{3\pi}{2} + \gamma_{in}} q''_{in}(\theta)\sin(m\theta)d\theta
\end{pmatrix}
$$

$$(2.239)$$

respectively. Once the boundary conditions shown in Eqs. (2.234) and (2.235) are determined, Eqs. (2.237)–(2.239) can be used to determine the temperature profile of a given cross section of the mesh wire. The heat transfer through the equilibrium film region along the mesh wire, i.e., $\frac{\pi}{2} - \gamma_a \le \theta \le \frac{\pi}{2} + \gamma_a$, is equal to zero, and the interface temperature, hence, is assumed to be equal to the wall surface temperature of the wire. The equilibrium film thickness depends on the disjoining pressure and the equilibrium film curvature, i.e.,

$$
\delta_0 = \left(\frac{6\pi}{A}\left(\left(1 - \frac{T_w(r_w,\theta)}{T_v}\right)h_{lv}\rho_l + \frac{\sigma}{r_w + \delta_0}\right)\right)^{-\frac{1}{3}} \quad \text{at} \quad \frac{\pi}{2} - \gamma_a \le \theta \le \frac{\pi}{2} + \gamma_a
$$

$$(2.240)$$

Since the film thickness is much smaller than the radius of the solid wire, the film thickness can be neglected in the denominator of the curvature term shown in Eq. (2.240).

Section 2.8.5 shows the inertial force effect to be very small. The fluid flow in the thin film region can be simplified as a force balance, i.e.,

$$(\sigma \cdot K - p_{\mathrm{d}})\big|_{s1}^{s2} = p_l\big|_{s1}^{s2} \tag{2.241}$$

where the momentum variations are neglected. If this control volume is taken to be infinitely small, Eq. (2.241) can be expressed as

$$\sigma \frac{dK}{ds} + K \frac{d\sigma}{ds} - \frac{dp_{\mathrm{d}}}{ds} = \frac{dp_l}{ds} \tag{2.242}$$

where the first term is from curvature variation, the third term is from disjoining pressure effect, and the last term is due to viscous pressure loss. The second term deals with the variation of the surface tension over the evaporating thin film length due to the variation of interface temperature along the evaporating thin film. Surface tension variations with respect to temperature are minimal resulting in this term having negligible effects. With large temperature variations along the interface of the evaporating thin film, this term is significant.

As shown in Fig. 2.39, the evaporating thin film is formed on the curved surface of solid wire. The curvature and pressure terms shown in Eq. (2.242) must be derived in polar coordinates. Using the coordinate transformations

$$s = r \cdot \cos\theta, \quad \eta = r \sin\theta, \quad \text{and} \quad \gamma = \frac{\pi}{2} - \gamma_{\mathrm{a}} - \theta \tag{2.243}$$

Equation (2.242) can be written as

$$\sigma \frac{dK}{d\gamma} + K \frac{d\sigma}{d\gamma} - \frac{dp_{\mathrm{d}}}{d\gamma} = \frac{dp_l}{d\gamma} \tag{2.244}$$

where

$$K = \frac{-\frac{d^2\delta}{d\gamma^2}(\delta + r_{\mathrm{w}}) + 2\left(\frac{d\delta}{d\gamma}\right)^2 + (\delta + r_{\mathrm{w}})^2}{\left(\left(\frac{d\delta}{d\gamma}\right)^2 + (\delta + r_{\mathrm{w}})^2\right)^{3/2}} \tag{2.245}$$

$$\frac{dp_l}{d\gamma} = -\frac{\mu_l \cdot \dot{m}_\delta}{\rho_l\left(\frac{3}{2}\delta^2 + r_{\mathrm{w}}\delta + (r_{\mathrm{w}} + \delta)^2 \ln\left(\frac{r_{\mathrm{w}}}{r_{\mathrm{w}}+\delta}\right)\right)} \tag{2.246}$$

Using the governing equation for the film thickness presented above, the temperature profile of the liquid–vapor interface and the heat flux through the thin film can be determined if the boundary conditions are given. At the equilibrium non-evaporating thin film, the film thickness can be calculated by Eq. (2.240) for a given superheat, $T_{\mathrm{w}} - T_{\mathrm{v}}$, and the curvature of non-evaporating film, i.e.,

$$\delta\big|_{\gamma=0} = \delta_0 \tag{2.247}$$

$$K\big|_{\gamma=0} = K_0 = \frac{1}{r_w + \delta_0} \tag{2.248}$$

Since the film thickness, the curvature of the thin film, and the first and second derivatives of the film thickness with respect to the arc angle are continuous at the end of the equilibrium film or at the beginning of the evaporating thin film, this results in the following boundary conditions:

$$\frac{d\delta}{d\gamma}\bigg|_{\gamma=0} = 0 \quad \text{and} \quad \frac{d^2\delta}{d\gamma^2}\bigg|_{\gamma=0} = 0 \tag{2.249}$$

As presented above, the heat transfer through thin film formed on the curved surface can be modeled using the third-order differential equations, which can be solved using a fourth-order Runge–Kutta method for the interface temperature and a film thickness variation of evaporating thin film. Using the one-dimensional heat conduction shown in Eq. (2.236), the heat flux transferred through the evaporating thin film formed on the curved surface can be determined. However, the heat flux through the thin film region depends on the input heat flux and the temperature distribution on the solid wire, which in turn determines the evaporating heat transfer and the viscous fluid flow in the thin film region. Therefore, an iterative solution technique (Demsky and Ma 2004) must be utilized to solve for the temperature distribution on the solid wire, thin evaporating film profile, interface temperature, and heat flux distribution in the thin film region

Due to the high heat fluxes occurring at the evaporating thin film, the microregions are of significant interest. The temperature difference (superheat) between the solid wire and the vapor, i.e., $T_w - T_v$, drastically affects the evaporating thin film profile, both in length and in shape. As the temperature difference increases, the evaporating thin film profile length begins to decrease. Since at a higher temperature difference, there exists a higher heat flux, the evaporation rate must increase over the microregion. This causes the mass flow rate through the thin film region to increase, resulting in a pressure loss due to viscous forces increasing over a given length. To maintain a steady state evaporating heat transfer over this given length, the pumping pressure due to the disjoining pressure effect must compensate for the viscous pressure loss and the pressure variations due to the curvature effect as the curvature aids in pulling liquid to the bulk fluid region. This causes larger changes in the film profile to produce large disjoining pressure gradients. The trend is similar to thin film evaporation on a flat surface. However, the curvature of the equilibrium film liquid–vapor interface increases the liquid pressure in the thin film region on the curved surface of the solid wire. This adverse curvature results in a larger pressure drop from the equilibrium film to the bulk fluid region, causing the temperature of the equilibrium film on the curved surface of solid wire to be larger than that on a flat surface. This in turn affects the equilibrium film thickness. As a result, the equilibrium film thickness formed on the curved surface of solid wire is smaller than that on the flat surface for the same bulk fluid meniscus radius and interface temperature, as shown in Fig. 2.40.

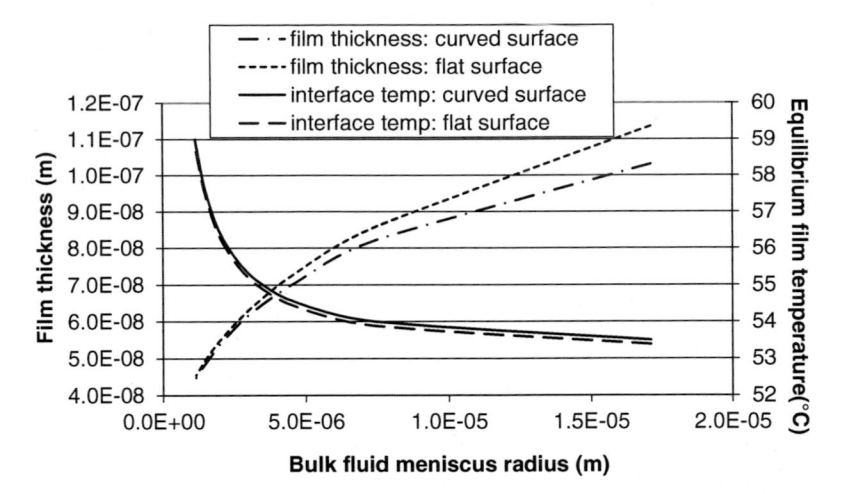

Fig. 2.40 Curvature effect on equilibrium film thickness and equilibrium temperature (Demsky and Ma 2004)

2.8.7   Thin Film Evaporation in a Triangular Groove

In this section, it will be described how heat is transferred in a triangular groove and the role the thin film evaporation plays in the process. Figure 2.41 shows the cross section of one triangular groove in a plate, which is similar to the evaporating heat transfer process in an evaporator of a grooved heat pipe. As shown, when heat is added onto the bottom of the grooved plate, the heat is transferred through the solid region and reaches the liquid where evaporation takes place. Based on the role of the disjoining pressure, the liquid region can be further divided into a thin film region (micro) region and bulk (macro) region. For the microregion, the models presented above can be utilized to find the film profile and heat transfer rate through the thin film region. For the macroregion, the heat transfer process can be described by conventional approaches of heat conduction and heat convection without considering the disjoining pressure effect on fluid flow and heat transfer. To simplify the problem and find the thin film evaporation effect, it can be assumed that (1) the inertial force effect is very small and the momentum effect in the thin film region can be neglected; (2) there is a steady state laminar flow in both the macro- and microregions; (3) there are no slip conditions at the wall; (4) the fluid flow in the microregion is the result of gradients in the disjoining pressure, surface curvature, and surface tension; (5) the convective terms are neglected when solving the energy equations; (6) the vapor pressure and vapor temperature are constant and saturation conditions exist in the liquid and at the interface; (7) the radius of the liquid

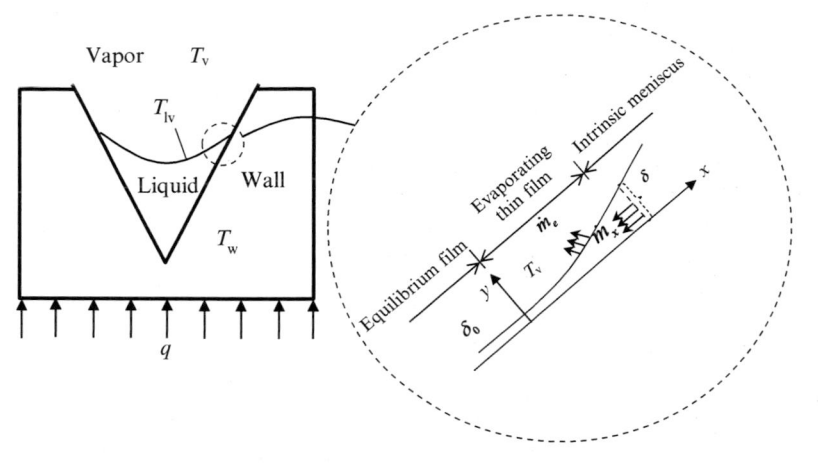

Fig. 2.41 Evaporation in a triangular groove

meniscus in the triangular grooves is given in the macroregion; and (8) there is uniform heat flux at the bottom of the grooved plate. The heat transferred from the wall region between grooves to the saturated vapor region must pass through liquid film regions, which consist of thin film (micro)region and meniscus (macro)region.

Fluid flow and heat transfer in the evaporating thin film. As illustrated in Fig. 2.41, liquid in the triangular groove can be divided into two regions: (1) a microregion, which consists of an equilibrium non-evaporating region and the evaporating thin film region where the disjoining pressure dominates and (2) the macroregion (meniscus) where the meniscus radius of the curvature is constant. Section 2.8.5 shows that the inertial force effect is very small. The fluid flow in the thin film region can be simplified as a force balance:

$$(\sigma \cdot K - p_d)\big|_{s1}^{s2} = p_l\big|_{s1}^{s2} \tag{2.250}$$

where the momentum variations are neglected. If this control volume is taken to be infinitely small, Eq. (2.241) can be expressed as

$$\sigma \frac{dK}{ds} + K \frac{d\sigma}{ds} - \frac{dp_d}{ds} = \frac{dp_l}{ds} \tag{2.251}$$

where K is the curvature of the liquid–vapor interface which can be expressed as

$$K = \frac{\frac{d^2\delta}{dx^2}}{\left[1 + \left(\frac{d\delta}{dx}\right)^2\right]^{3/2}} \tag{2.252}$$

The last term in Eq. (2.251) is due to viscous pressure loss which can be found from lubrication theory, i.e.,

$$\frac{dp_l}{dx} = -\frac{(f \cdot Re)\mu_l \dot{m}}{8\rho_l \delta^3} \tag{2.253}$$

The third term in Eq. (2.251) is from the disjoining pressure effect. The second term in Eq. (2.251) deals with the variation of the surface tension over the evaporating thin film length due to the variation of interface temperature along the evaporating thin film. Surface tension variations with respect to temperature are minimal resulting in this term having negligible effects. With large temperature variations along the interface of the evaporating thin film, this term is significant. Using the governing equation for the film thickness presented above, the temperature profile of the liquid–vapor interface and the heat flux through the thin film can be determined for a given superheat and a given meniscus radius. At the equilibrium non-evaporating thin film, the curvature is equal to zero, and the film thickness can be calculated by Eq. (2.135) for a given superheat, $T_w - T_v$. It should be noticed that the disjoining pressure can be calculated by $p_d = \rho_l RT_{lv} \ln\left(1.5787\,\delta^{0.0243}\right)$ (Holm and Goplen 1979). Since the film thickness, the curvature of the thin film, and the first and second derivatives of the film thickness with respect to x are continuous at the end of the equilibrium film or at the beginning of the evaporating thin film, this results in the following boundary conditions:

$$\left.\frac{d\delta}{dy}\right|_{y=0} = 0 \quad \text{and} \quad \left.\frac{d^2\delta}{dy^2}\right|_{y=0} = 0 \tag{2.254}$$

Using the constant meniscus radius at the macroregion (meniscus), Eq. (2.251) can be solved for film thickness for a given superheat, $T_w - T_v$. Then, using Eq. (2.222), the interface temperature can be calculated and heat flux through the thin film region can be determined by Eq. (2.223).

Heat transfer in the macroregion. The heat transfer passing through the wall of the groove and the liquid film shown in Fig. 2.41 can be described by the two-dimensional heat conduction equation:

$$\nabla \cdot [k_l \nabla (T)] = 0 \tag{2.255}$$

While the temperature distribution resulting from conduction in the wall can be easily determined using a finite difference method, the irregularity of the liquid–vapor interface of the liquid film makes using the finite element method more attractive for this region. In the following analysis, a coordinate transformation is introduced and the irregular geometric shape can be changed into a regular one, allowing the use of the finite difference method for both regions.

   The heat conduction equation shown in Eq. (2.255) when applied to the liquid film shown in Fig. 2.41 can be rewritten as

$$\frac{\partial^2 T}{\partial r^2} + \frac{1}{r}\frac{\partial T}{\partial r} + \frac{1}{r^2}\frac{\partial^2 T}{\partial \theta^2} = 0 \tag{2.256}$$

Applying a coordinate transformation of

$$\Lambda = \frac{\ln(r/r_1)}{\ln(r_2/r_1)} \tag{2.257}$$

Equation (2.256) becomes

$$\frac{\partial^2 T}{\partial \Lambda^2} + \frac{\partial^2 T}{\partial \theta^2}\left(\ln \frac{r_2}{r_1}\right)^2 = 0 \tag{2.258}$$

where r_1 and r_2 can be determined from the following expressions

$$r_1 = r_{w1}\frac{\cos \varphi}{\cos (\varphi - \theta)} \tag{2.259}$$

$$r_2 = r_{w2}\frac{\cos \alpha \cos (\varphi - \theta) - [\sin^2\varphi - \cos^2\alpha \sin (\varphi - \theta)]^{0.5}}{\cos (\alpha + \varphi)} \tag{2.260}$$

respectively. The radius r_1 in Eq. (2.259) is an assumption as shown in Fig. 2.41. When $r_1 \to 0$, the solution corresponds to that obtained for a triangular groove. The boundary conditions corresponding to Eqs. (2.256) and (2.258) can be expressed as

$$\frac{\partial T}{\partial Y}k_s = q''_{in} \quad \text{at} \quad Y = 0 \tag{2.261}$$

$$\frac{\partial T}{\partial n} = 0 \quad \text{at the dry part of the groove} \tag{2.262}$$

$$T = T_{lv} \quad \text{at the liquid} - \text{vapor interface} \tag{2.263}$$

$$\frac{\partial T}{\partial X} = 0 \quad \text{at} \quad X = 0, \quad X = \frac{W}{2} + d \tag{2.264}$$

Using Eqs. (2.251) and (2.258) with corresponding boundary conditions, the heat transfer rate through both micro- and macroregions can be determined including the film thickness of the thin film region and temperature distribution in the bulk liquid region. As shown in Fig. 2.42, when heat is added to the bottom of the grooved plate, most of the heat is transferred through the evaporating thin film region.

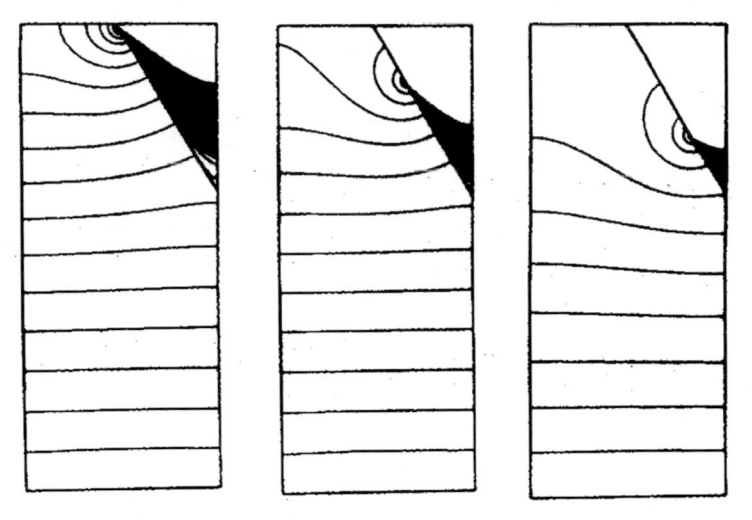

Fig. 2.42 Isotherm in the solid wall and liquid film at different levels of liquid in a triangular groove ($d = 0$ m, $W = 0.000$ m, $H = 0.0015$ m, $\varphi = 30°$, water is 20 °C, and temperature difference between two isotherms is 0.0042 K) (Ma and Peterson 1997)

References

Bau HH, Torrance KE (1982) Boiling in low-permeability porous materials. Int J Heat Mass Transf 25(1):45–55

Burelbach JP, Bankoff SG, Davis SH (1988) Nonlinear stability of evaporating/condensing liquid films. J Fluid Mech 195:463–494

Butt HJ, Craf K, Kappl M (2013) Physics and chemistry of interfaces. Wiley, Weinheim

Carey VP (1992) Liquid-vapor phase-change phenomena. Hemisphere Publishing Corporation, New York

Demsky SM, Ma HB (2004) Thin film evaporation on a curved surface. Microsc Thermophys Eng 8:285–299

Derjaguin BV, Zorin ZM (1956) Optical study of the absorption and surface condensation of vapors in the vicinity of saturation on a smooth surface. In: Proceedings of the 2nd international congress on surface activity, vol 2, London. pp 145–152

Faghri A (1995) Heat pipe science and technology. Taylor & Francis, New York

Hanlon MA, Ma HB (2003) Evaporation heat transfer in sintered porous media. J Heat Transf 125:644–653

Holm FW, Goplen SP (1979) Heat transfer in the meniscus thin film transition region. J Heat Transf 101(3):543–547

Israelachvili JN (1992) Intermolecular and surface forces. Academic, New York

Kaviany M (1995) Principles of heat transfer in porous media. Springer, New York

Kim IY, Wayner PC (1996) Shape of an evaporating completely wetting extended meniscus. J Thermophys Heat Transf 10(2):320–325

Liter SG, Kaviany M (2001) Pool-boiling CHF enhancement by modulated porous-layer coating: theory and experiment. Int J Heat Mass Transf 44:4287–4311

Ma YD (2012) Motion effect on the dynamic contact angles in a capillary tube. Microfluid Nanofluidics 12(1–4):671–675

Ma HB, Peterson GP (1995) Thermodynamic analysis of the influence of electric fields on frost formation. J Thermophys Heat Transf 9(3):562–565

Ma HB, Peterson GP (1997) Temperature variation and heat transfer in triangular grooves with an evaporating film. J Thermophys Heat Transf 11(1):90–97

Ma HB, Cheng P, Borgmeyer B (2008) Fluid flow and heat transfer in the evaporating thin film region. Microfluid Nanofluidics 4(3):237–243

Mirzamoghadam A, Catton I (1988) A physical model of the evaporating meniscus. J Heat Transf 110(1):201–207

Moosman S, Homsy GM (1980) Evaporating menisci of wetting fluids. J Colloid Interface Sci 73 (1):212–223

Potash M, Wayner PC (1972) Evaporation from a two-dimensional extended meniscus. Int J Heat Mass Transf 15:1851–1863

Stephan PC, Busse CA (1993) Analysis of the heat transfer coefficient of grooved heat pipe evaporator walls. Int J Heat Mass Transf 35(2):383–391

Tadmor R (2004) Line energy and the relation between advancing, receding, and Young contact angles. Langmuir 20(18):7659–7664

Thome JR (1990) Enhanced boiling heat transfer. Hemisphere Publishing Corporation, New York

Truong JG, Wayner PC (1987) Effects of capillary and van der Waals dispersion forces on the equilibrium profile of a wetting liquid: theory and experiment. J Chem Phys 87(7):4180–4188

Wayner PC (1997) Interfacial forces and phase changes in thin liquid films. In: Tian CL, Majumdar A, Gerner FM (eds) Microscale transport. Taylor & Francis, Washington, pp 187–229

Wayner PC, Kao YK, LaCroix LV (1976) The interline heat transfer coefficient of an evaporating wetting film. Int J Heat Mass Transf 19(3):487–492

Webb RL (1994) Principles of enhanced heat transfer. Wiley, New York

Whyman G, Bormashenko E, Stein T (2008) The rigorous derivation of Young, Cassie–Baxter and Wenzel equations and the analysis of the contact angle hysteresis phenomenon. Chem Phys Lett 450(4–6):355–359

Wylen GL, Sonntag RE (1968) Fundamentals of classical thermodynamics. Wiley, New York

Yan CJ, Ma HB (2013) Analytical solutions of heat transfer and film thickness in thin-film evaporation. J Heat Transf 135(3), Article No. 031501

Chapter 3
Oscillating Flow and Heat Transfer of Single Phase in Capillary Tubes

3.1 Introduction

For an operating OHP, as shown in Fig. 3.1, when heat is added to the evaporator section, the heat is transferred from the wall to the working fluid inside by evaporation and forced convection. The thermally excited oscillating motion carries the heat to the condenser section where the heat is rejected by condensation and forced convection. During the heat transfer process from the evaporator to the condenser, while some of the heat is transferred through the phase changer heat transfer, i.e., the evaporation heat transfer in the evaporator and the condensation heat transfer in the condenser, most of the heat is transferred by thermally excited convection, i.e., the forced convection heat transfer from the wall to the working fluid in the evaporator and from the working fluid to the wall in the condenser. For an OHP, fluid inside should be formed as a train of liquid plugs and vapor bubbles. Liquid plugs and vapor bubbles are separated distinctly. The heat transfer process due to the thermally excited oscillating motion in an OHP is similar to the forced convection of a single phase oscillating flow either between the liquid phase and wall or between the vapor phase and wall. Therefore, in this chapter, single phase oscillating flow and its heat transfer process will be introduced. First, the concepts of reciprocating and pulsating flow are presented; fluid flow and heat transfer of fully developed and developing laminar oscillating flows in a pipe are then discussed; and finally, fluid flow and heat transfer of turbulent pulsating flow will be introduced.

3.2 Reciprocating Flow

Reciprocating flow is characterized by repeatable back-and-forth action (Zhao and Cheng 1998a). As shown in Fig. 3.2, the average mean velocity of a typical reciprocating flow is zero. In other words, the steady state velocity component,

© Springer Science+Business Media New York 2015
H. Ma, *Oscillating Heat Pipes*, DOI 10.1007/978-1-4939-2504-9_3

Fig. 3.1 Schematic of
an oscillating heat pipe

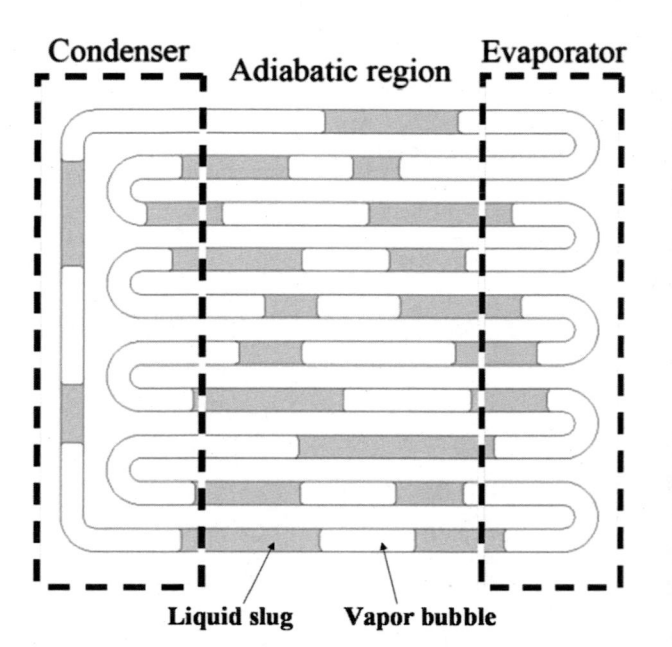

Fig. 3.2 Schematic of a reciprocating flow ($u_s = 0$)

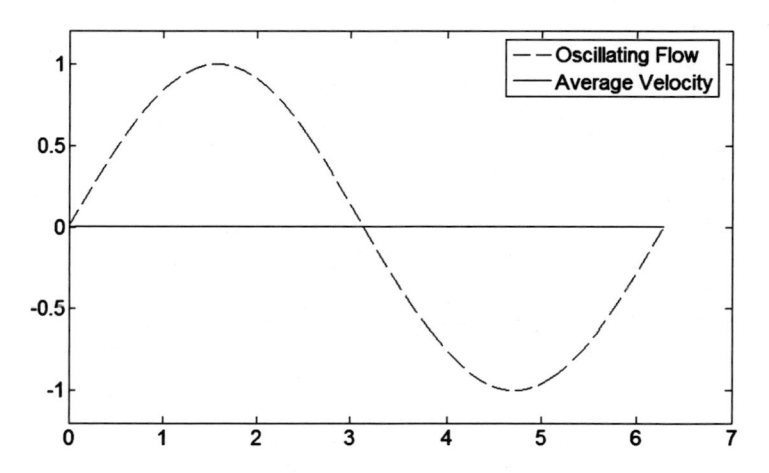

u_s, is equal to zero. Considering a reciprocating incompressible flow in a pipe with
an inner diameter of D, if the reciprocating motion of the fluid is driven by a
sinusoidal oscillator, the fluid displacement, x, can be expressed as

$$x = \frac{x_{max}}{2}(1 - \cos \omega t) \tag{3.1}$$

where ω is the oscillation angular frequency, t is the time, x is the fluid displacement, and x_{max} is the maximum fluid displacement. Differentiating Eq. (3.1) with time gives the velocity, i.e.,

$$u = u_{max} \sin(\omega t) \tag{3.2}$$

where the maximum cross-sectional velocity u_{max} is related to the maximum fluid displacement x_{max}, i.e.,

$$u_{max} = \frac{x_{max}}{2}\omega \tag{3.3}$$

The cross-sectional mean velocity u_m can be obtained by integrating Eq. (3.2) over the cross-sectional area, i.e.,

$$u_m = u_{max,m} \sin(\omega t) \tag{3.4}$$

where u_m is the cross-sectional mean velocity of the transient flow and $u_{max,m}$ is the maximum cross-sectional mean velocity.

3.3 Pulsating Flow

A typical pulsating flow in a capillary tube consists of a steady flow and a transient flow, i.e.,

$$u(r,t) = u_s(r) + u_t(r,t) \tag{3.5}$$

where $u_s(r)$ is the steady flow velocity and $u_t(r,t)$ is the imposed transient velocity component, as shown in Fig. 3.3. The cross-sectional mean velocity u_m can be obtained by integrating Eq. (3.5) over the cross-sectional area, i.e.,

$$u_m = u_{s,m} + u_{t,m} \tag{3.6}$$

where $u_{s,m}$ and $u_{t,m}$ are the cross-sectional mean velocities of the steady state and transient flows. If the transient component is of a sinusoidal variation, Eq. (3.6) can be expressed as

$$u_m = u_{s,m} + u_{max,m} \sin(\omega t) \tag{3.7}$$

If the average steady state mean velocity is equal to zero, i.e., $u_{s,m} = 0$, a pulsating flow becomes a reciprocating flow.

For a unidirectional steady state flow, the Reynolds number defined by

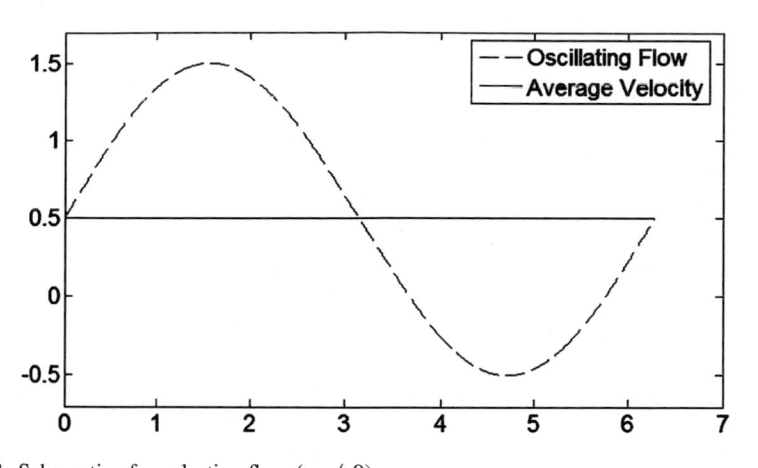

Fig. 3.3 Schematic of a pulsating flow ($u_s \neq 0$)

$$Re = \frac{uD}{\nu} \tag{3.8}$$

is often used to describe fluid flow in a pipe. To better describe the oscillation flow, the kinetic Reynolds number is introduced which is defined as

$$Re_\omega = \frac{\omega D^2}{\nu} \tag{3.9}$$

and the dimensionless oscillation amplitude of fluid in the pipe is defined by

$$A_0 = \frac{x_{max}}{D} \tag{3.10}$$

The Reynolds number defined by Eq. (3.8) can be expressed as

$$Re_{max} = \frac{x_{max}\omega D}{2\nu} \tag{3.11}$$

Considering the kinetic Reynolds number defined by Eq. (3.9), Eq. (3.11) can be expressed as

$$Re_{max} = \frac{A_0}{2}Re_\omega \tag{3.12}$$

Sometime, the Womersley number (Womersley 1955) which is defined by

$$\lambda = \frac{D}{2}\left(\frac{\omega}{v}\right)^{1/2} \tag{3.13}$$

is often employed to describe the oscillating flow effect on fluid flow. The Womersley number is similar to the Reynolds number. They both have the same physical meaning, i.e., the ratio of the inertial force to the viscous force. The difference is that while the Reynolds number is based on velocity, the Womersley number is based on frequency similar to Eq. (3.9).

3.4 Fully Developed Oscillating Pipe Flow

3.4.1 Critical Dimensionless Parameter of Laminar Oscillating Pipe Flow

For a unidirectional flow in a round pipe, when a critical Reynolds number is higher than about 2,300, the transition from laminar to turbulent flow takes place (Bergman et al. 2011). For an oscillating flow, experimental results show that a transition from laminar flow to turbulent flow does exist, but it is very different from a steady state unidirectional flow (Zhao and Cheng 1996a, b, c, 1998a, b). Measurements show that a laminar-like flow exists during the acceleration phase of a half cycle whereas a turbulence-like flow exists during a certain period in the deceleration phase. Figure 3.4 shows two typical examples of the temporal axial velocity variations of a reciprocating flow at the centerline of the pipe and near the wall at the onset of turbulence, which were measured by a hot wire anemometer (Zhao and Cheng 1996b). It is found that periodic turbulent bursts occurred near the wall during the deceleration phase of the cycle, when the values of A_0 and Re_ω were increased to certain values. It should be noted that the velocity fluctuations near the wall are much stronger than those in the centerline of the pipe. It implies that instabilities are generated near the wall. The axial velocity near the wall is higher than the centerline velocity at high kinetic Reynolds numbers, and there exists an inflexion point in the velocity profile near the wall. The fluid flow near the wall may first become unstable and eddies occur near the wall. These eddies cause small fluctuations. It is generally agreed in existing literature that an oscillating flow becomes unstable with increasing either dimensionless fluid displacement, A_0, or kinetic Reynolds number, Re_ω. The critical dimensionless parameter, for which flow transition occurs, is defined by

$$\beta_{\text{cri}} = \left(A_0\sqrt{Re_\omega}\right)_{\text{cri}} = \left(x_{\text{max}}\sqrt{\omega/v}\right)_{\text{cri}} \tag{3.14}$$

Fig. 3.4 Temporal axial velocity variations at the onset of transition turbulence: (**a**) $A_0 = 97.1$ and $Re_\omega = 66.6$ and (**b**) $A_0 = 47.3$ and $Re_\omega = 302.2$ (Zhao and Cheng 1996b)

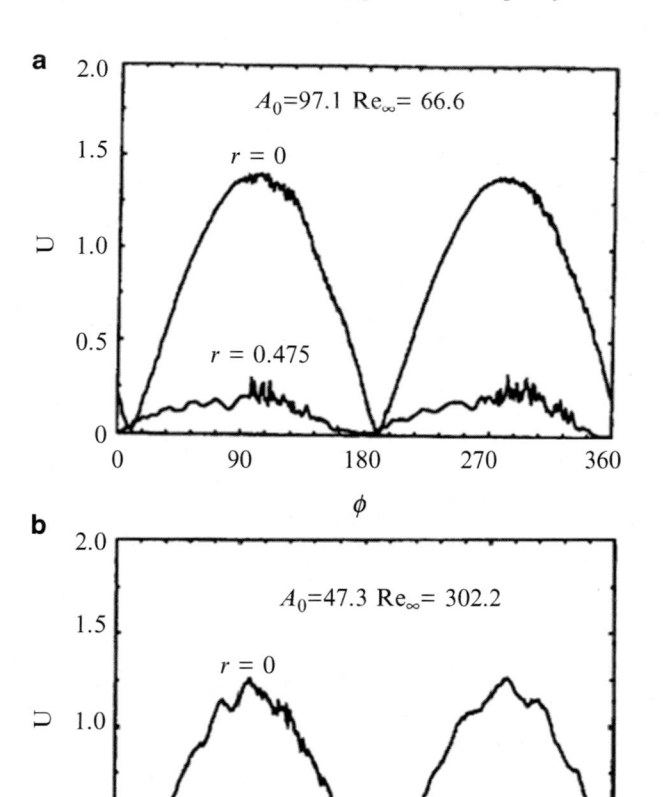

The oscillatory boundary layer or the so-called Stokes layer has a thickness of

$$\delta = \sqrt{2\nu/\omega} \tag{3.15}$$

Substituting Eq. (3.15) into Eq. (3.14) yields

$$\beta_{cri} = \sqrt{2}(Re_\delta)_{cri} \tag{3.16}$$

where $Re_\delta = u_{max}\delta/\nu$. Equation (3.16) indicates that transition from laminar to turbulent flow begins when the Reynolds number, Re_δ, based on the Stokes layer thickness, exceeds a critical value. Critical values of β_{cri} obtained by various investigators are listed in Table 3.1. The discrepancies of critical values may be attributed to the different experimental conditions or measurement methods employed by various researchers. For example, some researchers use flow

Table 3.1 History of critical values of β_{cri} obtained by various investigators for reciprocating pipe flow (Zhao and Cheng 1998a)

n	Authors	Year	β_{cri}
0	Li	1954	800
1	Collins	1963	230
2	Sergeev	1966	700
3	Vincent	1967	160
4	Pelissier	1973	150–420
5	Daneshyar	1973	730
6	Merkli and Tomann	1975	400
7	Hino, Sawamoto, and Takasu	1975	780
8	Ohmi, Iguchi, and Urahata	1982	800
9	Kurzweg, Lindgren, and Lothrop	1989	700
10	Zhao and Cheng	1996	761

Fig. 3.5 Schematic of a fully developed laminar oscillating flow

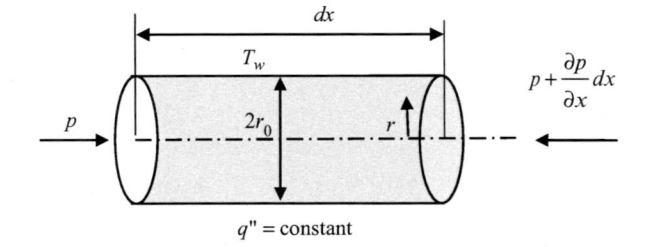

$q'' = \text{constant}$

visualization to determine the onset of turbulence while others rely on velocity measurements by hot wire anemometry or LDA (laser Doppler anemometer).

3.4.2 Laminar Pulsating Pipe Flow

Consider a fully developed oscillating incompressible flow in a capillary round tube with a radius of r_0, as shown in Fig. 3.5. It is assumed that the flow is laminar, i.e., the Reynolds number is less than the critical Reynolds number defined by Eq. (3.16). A uniform heat flux is added on the boundary. The driving force added to the fluid flow is a sinusoidal pressure gradient, i.e.,

$$\frac{\partial p}{\partial x} = \left(\frac{\partial p}{\partial x}\right)_{s} [1 + \zeta \cos(\omega t)] \qquad (3.17)$$

where ζ is a constant that controls the amplitude of the pressure wave form. The equation governing fluid flow of oscillating flow shown in Fig. 3.5 can be written as

$$\frac{\partial u}{\partial \tau} = -\frac{1}{\rho}\frac{\partial p}{\partial x} + v\left(\frac{\partial^2 u}{\partial r^2} + \frac{\partial u}{r\partial r}\right) \tag{3.18}$$

Boundary conditions for governing Eq. (3.18) can be found as

$$\frac{\partial u}{\partial r} = 0 \quad \text{at} \quad r = 0$$

$$u = 0 \quad \text{at} \quad r = r_0 \tag{3.19}$$

respectively. Considering the dimensionless radius,

$$r^* = \frac{r}{r_0} \tag{3.20}$$

dimensionless time,

$$t^* = \frac{vt}{r_0^2} \tag{3.21}$$

dimensionless velocity along the x direction,

$$u^* = \frac{u}{u_m} \tag{3.22}$$

and dimensionless frequency,

$$\omega^* = \frac{\omega r_0^2}{v} \tag{3.23}$$

where ω is the angular pulsation frequency, given by $\omega = 2\pi f$, Eq. (3.18) can be expressed as

$$\frac{\partial u^*}{\partial t^*} = 8\left[1 + \zeta \cos\left(\omega^* t^*\right)\right] + \left(\frac{\partial^2 u^*}{\partial r^{*2}} + \frac{\partial u^*}{r^*\partial r^*}\right) \tag{3.24}$$

and the corresponding boundary conditions defined by Eq. (3.19) become

$$\frac{\partial u^*}{\partial r^*} = 0 \quad \text{at} \quad r^* = 0$$

$$u^* = 0 \quad \text{at} \quad r^* = 1 \tag{3.25}$$

The solution of Eq. (3.24) should consist of the steady state components, $u_s^* = u_s/u_m$, and the instantaneous component, $u_t^* = u_t/u_m$, i.e.,

$$u^*\left(r^*,t^*\right) = u_s^*\left(r^*\right) + u_t^*\left(r^*,t^*\right) \tag{3.26}$$

Substituting Eq. (3.26) into Eq. (3.24) yields

$$\frac{\partial\left[u_s^*\left(r^*\right) + u_t^*\left(r^*,t^*\right)\right]}{\partial t^*} = 8\left[1 + \zeta\cos\left(\omega^*t^*\right)\right]$$

$$+ \frac{\partial^2\left[u_s^*\left(r^*\right) + u_t^*\left(r^*,t^*\right)\right]}{\partial r^{*2}} + \frac{\partial\left[u_s^*\left(r^*\right) + u_t^*\left(r^*,t^*\right)\right]}{r^*\partial r^*} \tag{3.27}$$

Rearranging Eq. (3.27) produces

$$\frac{\partial u_s^*}{\partial t^*} + \frac{\partial u_t^*}{\partial t^*} = 8\left[1 + \zeta\cos\left(\omega^*t^*\right)\right] + \left(\frac{\partial^2 u_s^*}{\partial r^{*2}} + \frac{\partial^2 u_t^*}{\partial r^{*2}} + \frac{\partial u_s^*}{r^*\partial r^*} + \frac{\partial u_t^*}{r^*\partial r^*}\right) \tag{3.28}$$

Equation (3.28) can be separated into two equations of

$$\frac{\partial u_s^*}{\partial t^*} = 8 + \left(\frac{\partial^2 u_s^*}{\partial r^{*2}} + \frac{\partial u_s^*}{r^*\partial r^*}\right) \tag{3.29}$$

$$\frac{\partial u_t^*}{\partial t^*} = 8\zeta\cos\left(\omega^*t^*\right) + \left(\frac{\partial^2 u_t^*}{\partial r^{*2}} + \frac{\partial u_t^*}{r^*\partial r^*}\right) \tag{3.30}$$

respectively. Considering $\frac{\partial u_s^*}{\partial t^*} = 0$, Eqs. (3.29) and (3.30) can be rewritten as

$$\frac{\partial^2 u_s^*}{\partial r^{*2}} + \frac{\partial u_s^*}{r^*\partial r^*} = -8 \tag{3.31}$$

$$\frac{\partial^2 u_t^*}{\partial r^{*2}} + \frac{\partial u_t^*}{r^*\partial r^*} - \frac{\partial u_t^*}{\partial t^*} = -8\zeta\cos\left(\omega^*t^*\right) \tag{3.32}$$

To compare Eq. (3.31) with the steady flow result (Poiseuille solution of steady flow), the solution of Eq. (3.31) can be readily expressed as

$$u_s^* = 2\left(1 - r^{*2}\right) \tag{3.33}$$

Considering a solution of $u_t^* = 8\zeta u_\Delta^*$, Eq. (3.32) becomes

$$\frac{\partial^2 u_\Delta^*}{\partial r^{*2}} + \frac{\partial u_\Delta^*}{r^*\partial r^*} - \frac{\partial u_\Delta^*}{\partial t^*} = -\cos\left(\omega^*t^*\right) \tag{3.34}$$

With the first class Bessel function, Eq. (3.34) can be expressed as

$$J_0 \left[\frac{\partial^2 u_\Delta^*}{\partial r^{*2}} + \frac{\partial u_\Delta^*}{r^* \partial r^*} - \frac{\partial u_\Delta^*}{\partial t^*} \right] = J_0 \left[- \cos \left(\omega^* t^* \right) \right] \tag{3.35}$$

With the following properties of Hankel transform,

$$\left\{ \begin{array}{c} J_0 \left[\frac{\partial^2 f(r)}{\partial r^2} + \frac{\partial f(r)}{r \partial r} \right] = -s^2 J_0 [f(r)] \\[3mm] J_0 \left[\frac{\partial f(r)}{\partial t^*} \right] = \frac{\partial J_0 [f(r)]}{\partial t^*} \\[3mm] J_0 \left[\sin \left((2n-1)\omega^* t^* \right) \right] = \frac{\sin \left((2n-1)\omega^* t^* \right)}{s} J_1 [s] \end{array} \right\} \tag{3.36}$$

Equation (3.35) can be transformed into

$$-s^2 J_0 \left[u_\Delta^* \left(r^*, t^* \right) \right] - \frac{\partial J_0 \left[u_\Delta^* \left(r^*, t^* \right) \right]}{\partial t^*} = \frac{-\cos \left(\omega^* t^* \right)}{s} J_1 [s] \tag{3.37}$$

Defining $J_0 \left[u_\Delta^* \left(r^*, t^* \right) \right] = F \left[s, t^* \right]$, Eq. (3.37) becomes

$$F \left[s, t^* \right] + \frac{1}{s^2} \frac{\partial F \left[s, t^* \right]}{\partial t^*} = \frac{\cos \left(\omega^* t^* \right)}{s^3} J_1 [s] \tag{3.38}$$

If it is assumed that

$$F \left[s, t^* \right] = a \cos \left(\omega^* t^* \right) + b \sin \left(\omega^* t^* \right) \tag{3.39}$$

Equation (3.38) becomes

$$a \cos \left(\omega^* t^* \right) + b \sin \left(\omega^* t^* \right) + \frac{1}{s^2} \frac{\partial \left(a \cos \left(\omega^* t^* \right) + b \sin \left(\omega^* t^* \right) \right)}{\partial t^*}$$
$$= \frac{\cos \left(\omega^* t^* \right)}{s^3} J_1 [s] \tag{3.40}$$

Rearranging Eq. (3.40) yields

$$\left(a + \frac{b\omega^*}{s^2} - \frac{J_1 [s]}{s^3} \right) \cos \left(\omega^* t^* \right) + \left(b - \frac{a\omega^*}{s^2} \right) \sin \left(\omega^* t^* \right) = 0 \tag{3.41}$$

From Eq. (3.41), it can be found that

$$a + \frac{b\omega^*}{s^2} - \frac{J_1[s]}{s^3} = 0 \tag{3.42}$$

$$b - \frac{a\omega^*}{s^2} = 0 \tag{3.43}$$

Solving Eqs. (3.42) and (3.43), the constants a and b can be expressed as

$$a = \frac{sJ_1[s]}{(\omega^{*2} + s^4)} \tag{3.44}$$

$$b = \frac{J_1[s]}{s(\omega^{*2} + s^4)}\omega^* \tag{3.45}$$

respectively. $F[s, t^*]$ can be written as

$$F[s, t^*] = \frac{sJ_1[s]}{(\omega^{*2} + s^4)} \cos\left(\omega^* t^*\right) + \frac{J_1[s]\omega}{s(\omega^{*2} + s^4)} \sin\left(\omega^* t^*\right) \tag{3.46}$$

Rearranging Eq. (3.46) yields

$$F[s, t^*] = \frac{J_1[s]\left(s^2 \cos\left(\omega^* t^*\right) + \omega^* \sin\left(\omega^* t^*\right)\right)}{s(\omega^{*2} + s^4)} \tag{3.47}$$

With the inverse Hankel transform, the velocity distribution can be found as

$$u_t^* = 16\zeta \sum_{n=1}^{\infty} \left(\frac{s^2 \cos\left(\omega^* t^*\right) + \omega^* \sin\left(\omega^* t^*\right)}{sJ_1[s](\omega^{*2} + s^4)} J_0(sr^*)\right) \tag{3.48}$$

where J_0 and J_1 are the Bessel function of the first kind of order 0 and 1, respectively, and s is the eigenvalue of the Bessel function of the first kind of order 0. The total velocity distribution of the pulsating flow driven by Eq. (3.17) can be found as

$$u^* = u_s^* + u_t^* = 2\left(1 - r^{*2}\right) + 16\zeta \sum_{n=1}^{\infty} \left(\frac{s^2 \cos\left(\omega^* t^*\right) + \omega^* \sin\left(\omega^* t^*\right)}{sJ_1[s](\omega^{*2} + s^4)} J_0(sr^*)\right) \tag{3.49}$$

Using Eq. (3.49) the velocity distribution can be readily obtained as shown in Figs. 3.6 and 3.7.

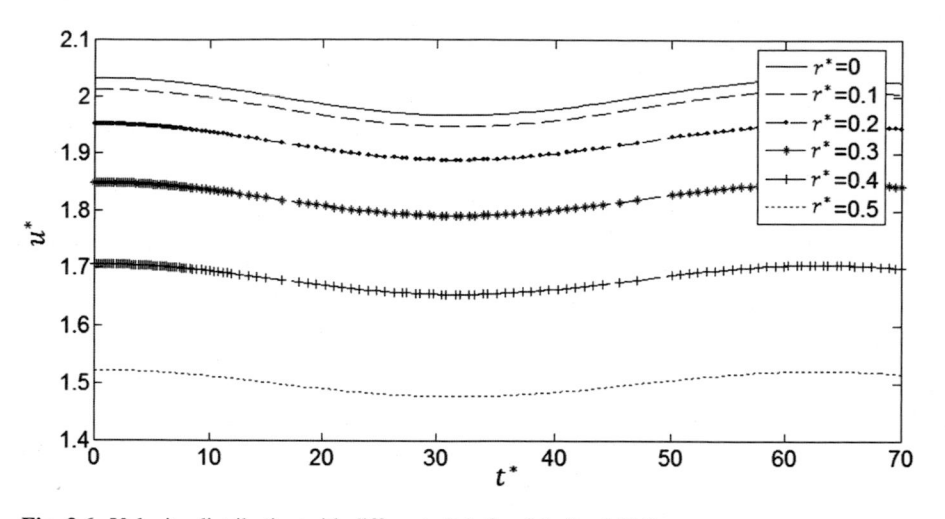

Fig. 3.6 Velocity distribution with different r^* ($\omega^* = 0.1$, $\zeta = 0.015$)

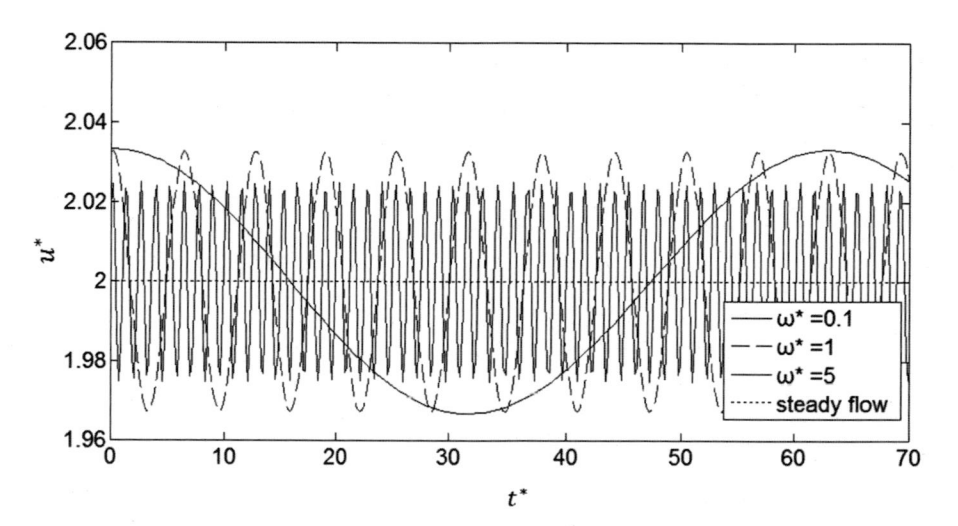

Fig. 3.7 Velocities at $r^* = 0$ with different ω^* ($\zeta = 0.015$)

3.4.3   Richardson's Annular Effect

For the oscillating flow governed by Eq. (3.18), if the driving pressure is determined by

$$-\frac{1}{\rho}\frac{\partial p}{\partial x} = K \cos \omega t \tag{3.50}$$

the oscillating flow is a reciprocating flow, which exhibits a velocity overshoot near the wall. This phenomenon is known as the Richardson annular effect (White 1974).

Equation (3.50) can be expressed as a complex notation, to be considered as the real part only, i.e.,

$$-\frac{1}{\rho}\frac{\partial p}{\partial x} = Ke^{i\omega t} \tag{3.51}$$

Substituting Eq. (3.51) into Eq. (3.18) yields

$$\frac{\partial u}{\partial t} = Ke^{i\omega t} + \nu \left(\frac{\partial^2 u}{\partial r^2} + \frac{\partial u}{r \partial r} \right) \tag{3.52}$$

If the velocity function has a form of

$$u(r,t) = f(r)e^{i\omega t} \tag{3.53}$$

Equation (3.52) becomes

$$\frac{\partial [f(r)e^{i\omega t}]}{\partial t} = Ke^{i\omega t} + \nu \left(\frac{\partial^2 [f(r)e^{i\omega t}]}{\partial r^2} + \frac{\partial [f(r)e^{i\omega t}]}{r \partial r} \right) \tag{3.54}$$

Simplifying Eq. (3.54) yields

$$i\omega \cdot f(r)e^{i\omega t} = Ke^{i\omega t} + \nu \left(\frac{\partial^2 f(r)}{\partial r^2} + \frac{\partial f(r)}{r \partial r} \right) e^{i\omega t} \tag{3.55}$$

Dividing both sides of Eq. (3.55) by $e^{i\omega t}$ and ν, Eq. (3.55) becomes

$$\frac{\partial^2 f(r)}{\partial r^2} + \frac{\partial f(r)}{r \partial r} - \frac{i\omega}{\nu} f(r) = -\frac{K}{\nu} \tag{3.56}$$

Because the terms related to time disappear, Eq. (3.56) can be rewritten as

$$\frac{d^2 f(r)}{dr^2} + \frac{df(r)}{r \, dr} - \frac{i\omega}{\nu} f(r) = -\frac{K}{\nu} \tag{3.57}$$

Assuming that a solution of Eq. (3.57) has a form of

$$f(r) = AJ_0(Br) + C \tag{3.58}$$

and substituting it into Eq. (3.57), it can be found that

$$\frac{d^2(AJ_0(Br) + C)}{dr^2} + \frac{d(AJ_0(Br) + C)}{r\,dr} - \frac{i\omega}{\nu}(AJ_0(Br) + C) = -\frac{K}{\nu} \tag{3.59}$$

Considering the properties of Bessel functions, Eq. (3.59) can be expressed as

$$\frac{ABd(-J_1(Br))}{dr} - \frac{ABJ_1(Br)}{r} - \frac{i\omega}{\nu}AJ_0(Br) - \frac{i\omega}{\nu}C = -\frac{K}{\nu} \tag{3.60}$$

Equation (3.60) can be separated into two equations of a homogeneous integral equation and constant equation, i.e.,

$$\frac{i\omega}{\nu}C = \frac{K}{\nu} \tag{3.61}$$

$$\frac{ABd(-J_1(Br))}{dr} - \frac{ABJ_1(Br)}{r} - \frac{i\omega}{\nu}AJ_0(Br) = 0 \tag{3.62}$$

From Eq. (3.61), it can be found that

$$C = -\frac{iK}{\omega} \tag{3.63}$$

With the properties of Bessel function, Eq. (3.62) can be expressed as

$$B^2 J_0(Br) - \frac{BrJ_1(Br)}{r^2} + \frac{BJ_1(Br)}{r} + \frac{i\omega}{\nu}J_0(Br) = 0 \tag{3.64}$$

Simplifying Eq. (3.64) yields

$$B^2 J_0(Br) = -\frac{i\omega}{\nu}J_0(Br) \tag{3.65}$$

With Eq. (3.65), the constant can be obtained as

$$B = \sqrt{-\frac{i\omega}{\nu}} \tag{3.66}$$

Equation (3.58) can be expressed as

$$f(r) = AJ_0\left(r\sqrt{-\frac{i\omega}{\nu}}\right) - \frac{iK}{\omega} \tag{3.67}$$

Considering the no-slip condition at the wall, i.e., the boundary condition of

$$f(r_0) = 0 \tag{3.68}$$

Equation (3.67) can be expressed as

$$f(r_0) = A J_0\left(r_0\sqrt{-\frac{i\omega}{\nu}}\right) - \frac{iK}{\omega} \tag{3.69}$$

The constant A in (3.67) can be obtained as

$$A = \frac{iK}{\omega} \Big/ J_0\left(r_0\sqrt{-\frac{i\omega}{\nu}}\right) \tag{3.70}$$

The expression of $f(r)$ shown in Eq. (3.58) can be found as

$$f(r) = \frac{iK}{\omega} \Big/ J_0\left(r_0\sqrt{-\frac{i\omega}{\nu}}\right) \cdot J_0\left(r\sqrt{-\frac{i\omega}{\nu}}\right) - \frac{iK}{\omega} \tag{3.71}$$

Rearranging Eq. (3.71) yields

$$f(r) = -i\frac{K}{\omega}\left(1 - \frac{J_0\left(r\sqrt{\frac{-i\omega}{\nu}}\right)}{J_0\left(r_0\sqrt{\frac{-i\omega}{\nu}}\right)}\right) \tag{3.72}$$

Considering Eq. (3.53), the expression of $u(r, t)$ is expressed as

$$u(r,t) = -i\frac{K}{\omega}e^{i\omega t}\left(1 - \frac{J_0\left(r\sqrt{\frac{-i\omega}{\nu}}\right)}{J_0\left(r_0\sqrt{\frac{-i\omega}{\nu}}\right)}\right) \tag{3.73}$$

Considering the Bessel function of

$$J_0(x) = \sum_{m=0}^{\infty} (-1)^m \frac{1}{m!m!}\left(\frac{x}{2}\right)^{2m} \tag{3.74}$$

where it should be noticed that $\Gamma(m+1) = m!$, Eq. (3.73) can be expressed as

$$u(r,t) = -i\frac{K}{\omega}e^{i\omega t}\left(1 - \frac{\sum_{m=0}^{\infty}(-1)^m\frac{1}{m!m!}\left(\frac{r}{2}\sqrt{\frac{-i\omega}{\nu}}\right)^{2m}}{\sum_{m=0}^{\infty}(-1)^m\frac{1}{m!m!}\left(\frac{r_0}{2}\sqrt{\frac{-i\omega}{\nu}}\right)^{2m}}\right) \tag{3.75}$$

Now consider two cases of limitations, i.e., $r\sqrt{\frac{\omega}{\nu}}$ is either very small or very large. If $r\sqrt{\frac{\omega}{\nu}}$ is very small, expanding the Bessel function in a series leads to a solution where

$$J_0(x) \approx 1 - \frac{x^2}{4} \tag{3.76}$$

Using Eq. (3.76), Eq. (3.75) becomes

$$u(r,t) = -i\frac{K}{\omega}e^{i\omega t}\left(1 - \frac{1 + \frac{i\omega}{4\nu}r^2}{1 + \frac{i\omega}{4\nu}r_0^2}\right) \tag{3.77}$$

Rearranging yields

$$u(r,t) = -i\frac{K}{\omega}e^{i\omega t}\left(\frac{i\omega r_0^2 - i\omega r^2}{4\nu + i\omega r_0^2}\right) \tag{3.78}$$

When $r\sqrt{\frac{\omega}{\nu}}$ is very small or $\omega \to 0$, Eq. (3.78) becomes

$$u(r,t) = \lim_{\omega \to 0} Ke^{i\omega t}\left(\frac{r_0^2 - r^2}{4\nu}\right) \tag{3.79}$$

Now return the solution to the real notation, i.e.,

$$u(r,t) = \frac{K}{4\nu}e^{i\omega t}(r_0^2 - r^2) = \frac{K}{4\nu}(r_0^2 - r^2)\cos(\omega t) \tag{3.80}$$

Considering the dimensionless parameters of radius r^* defined by Eq. (3.20), time t^* by Eq. (3.21), velocity u^* by Eq. (3.22), angular velocity ω^* by Eq. (3.23), and $u_{max} = Kr_0/4\nu = 2u_m$, Eq. (3.80) can be expressed as

$$u^* = \frac{1}{2}(1 - r^{*2})\cos(\omega^* t^*) \tag{3.81}$$

From Eq. (3.81), it can be found that for a very small ω^*, the velocity is nearly a quasi-static Poiseuille flow in phase with slowly varying gradient. When $\omega^* = 0$, it should be noted that it is a Poiseuille flow.

For the case of $r_0\sqrt{\frac{\omega}{\nu}}$ which is very large, it can be found that $J_0(x) \rightarrow \sqrt{2/(\pi x)}e^{\frac{1-i}{\sqrt{2}}x}$ and Eq. (3.75) can be expressed as

$$u(r,t) = -i\frac{K}{\omega}e^{i\omega t}\left(1 - \frac{\sqrt{2/\left(\pi r\sqrt{\frac{-i\omega}{\nu}}\right)}e^{\frac{1-i}{\sqrt{2}}r\sqrt{\frac{-i\omega}{\nu}}}}{\sqrt{2/\left(\pi r_0\sqrt{\frac{-i\omega}{\nu}}\right)}e^{\frac{1-i}{\sqrt{2}}r_0\sqrt{\frac{-i\omega}{\nu}}}}\right) \quad (3.82)$$

or

$$u(r,t) = -\frac{K}{\omega}e^{i\omega t}\left(1 - \sqrt{\frac{r_0}{r}}\exp\left[-(1+i)\sqrt{\frac{\omega}{2\nu}}(r_0 - r)\right]\right) \quad (3.83)$$

Rearranging Eq. (3.83) yields

$$u(r,t) = \frac{K}{\omega}\left(-ie^{i\omega t} - (-ie^{i\omega t})\sqrt{\frac{r_0}{r}}\exp\left[-(1+i)\sqrt{\frac{\omega}{2\nu}}(r_0 - r)\right]\right) \quad (3.84)$$

Now return the solution shown in Eq. (3.84) to the real notation, i.e.,

$$u(r,t) = \frac{K}{\omega}\left(\sin(\omega t) - \sqrt{\frac{r_0}{r}}\exp\left(-\sqrt{\frac{\omega}{2\nu}}(r_0 - r)\right)\sin\left(\omega t - \sqrt{\frac{\omega}{2\nu}}(r_0 - r)\right)\right) \quad (3.85)$$

Similarly, with the dimensionless variables of radius r^*, angular velocity ω^*, time t^*, velocity u^*, and $u_{max} = Kr_0/4\nu = 2u_m$, Eq. (3.85) can be expressed as

$$u^* = \frac{2}{\omega^*}\left(\sin(\omega^* t^*) - \frac{1}{\sqrt{r^*}}\exp\left(-\sqrt{\frac{\omega^*}{2}}(1 - r^*)\right)\sin\left(\omega^* t^* - \sqrt{\frac{\omega^*}{2}}(1 - r^*)\right)\right) \quad (3.86)$$

Considering a new variable of $\eta = (1 - r^*)\sqrt{\omega^*/2}$, Eq. (3.86) becomes

$$u^* = \frac{2}{\omega^*}\left(\sin(\omega^* t^*) - \frac{1}{\sqrt{r^*}}\exp(-\eta)\sin(\omega^* t^* - \eta)\right) \quad (3.87)$$

By averaging Eq. (3.87) over one oscillating cycle, the mean square velocity $\overline{u^2}(r^*)$ can be found as

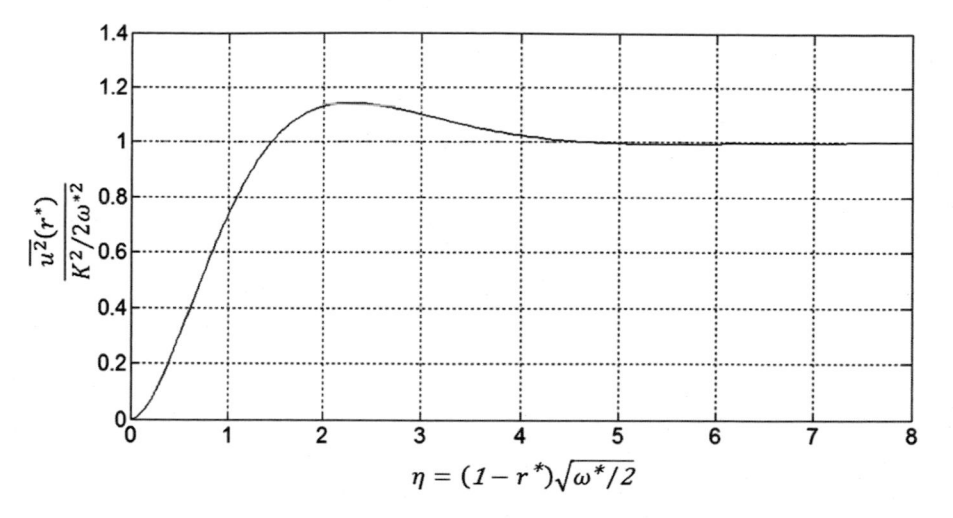

Fig. 3.8 The near-wall velocity overshoot (Richardson's annular effect) due to oscillating pressure gradient

$$\frac{\overline{u^2}\left(r^*\right)}{K^2/2\omega^{*2}} = 1 + \frac{1}{r^*}\exp(-2\eta) - \frac{2}{\sqrt{r^*}}\exp(-\eta)\cos\eta \tag{3.88}$$

Using Eq. (3.88), $\frac{\overline{u^2}\left(r^*\right)}{K^2/2\omega^{*2}}$, variation against η can be readily obtained as shown in Fig. 3.8. As shown, the maximum value does not coincide with the axis of the pipe, but occurs near the wall at the location of $\eta = \left(1 - r^*\right)\sqrt{\omega^*/2} = 2.284$. The flow approximately lags the pressure gradient by 90°, and the centerline square velocity is less than the maximum square velocity. This phenomenon is due to the oscillating flow and was first noticed by Richardson and Tyler (1929) in their tube-flow experiment. This overshoot is called Richardson's annular effect, which was verified theoretically by Sexl (1930).

3.5 Developing Region of Pipe Flow

When an oscillating flow flows into a pipe at the inlet or a stationary flow starts to move in a pipe, the velocity and thermal boundaries start to develop, which is similar to the developing region of a unidirectional flow in a pipe (Szymanski 1932). At $t = 0$, a pressure gradient is added on a stationary flow in a long pipe, fluid in the pipe starts to flow, and an axial pipe flow is formed. If the axial velocity in the pipe is a function of r and t only, i.e., $u = u(r, t)$, the monument equation can be written as

$$\rho \frac{\partial u}{\partial t} = -\frac{dp}{dx} + \mu \left(\frac{\partial^2 u}{\partial r^2} + \frac{1}{r} \frac{\partial u}{\partial r} \right) \tag{3.89}$$

The initial and boundary conditions can be expressed as

$$u(r, 0) = 0 \tag{3.90}$$

$$u(r_0, t) = 0 \tag{3.91}$$

The velocity at a location can be written as

$$u = u_0 - u' \tag{3.92}$$

where u_0 is the steady state velocity component and u' is the imposed unsteady velocity component. Substituting Eq. (3.92) into Eq. (3.89) yields

$$\rho \frac{\partial (u_0 - u')}{\partial t} = -\frac{dp}{dx} + \mu \left(\frac{\partial^2 (u_0 - u')}{\partial r^2} + \frac{1}{r} \frac{\partial (u_0 - u')}{\partial r} \right) \tag{3.93}$$

Simplifying and rearranging Eq. (3.93) produces

$$\rho \frac{\partial u_0}{\partial t} - \rho \frac{\partial u'}{\partial t} = -\frac{dp_0}{dx} - \frac{dp'}{dx} + \mu \left(\frac{\partial^2 u_0}{\partial r^2} + \frac{1}{r} \frac{\partial u_0}{\partial r} - \frac{\partial^2 u'}{\partial r^2} - \frac{1}{r} \frac{\partial u'}{\partial r} \right) \tag{3.94}$$

Because u_0 is the steady state component, $\frac{\partial u_0}{\partial t} = 0$, and similarly $\frac{dp_0}{dx} = 0$. Equation (3.94) becomes

$$\rho \frac{\partial u'}{\partial t} = \frac{dp'}{dx} + \mu \left(\frac{\partial^2 u'}{\partial r^2} + \frac{1}{r} \frac{\partial u'}{\partial r} \right) \tag{3.95}$$

If both sides of Eq. (3.96) are divided by $u_{\max} = \frac{\left(-\frac{dp}{dx} \right) r_0^2}{4\mu}$, Eq. (3.95) becomes

$$\frac{\rho \frac{\partial u'}{\partial t}}{u_{\max}} = \frac{\frac{dp'}{dx}}{u_{\max}} + \frac{\mu \left(\frac{\partial^2 u'}{\partial r^2} + \frac{1}{r} \frac{\partial u'}{\partial r} \right)}{u_{\max}} \tag{3.97}$$

If $dp' \ll dp$, it can be shown that

$$\frac{\frac{dp'}{dx}}{u_{max}} = -\frac{4\mu}{r_0^2} \cdot \frac{\frac{dp'}{dx}}{\frac{dp}{dx}} = -\frac{4\mu}{r_0^2} \cdot \frac{dp'}{dp} \approx 0 \tag{3.98}$$

Equation (3.97) can be rewritten as

$$\rho \frac{\partial \chi}{\partial t} = \mu \left(\frac{\partial^2 \chi}{\partial r^2} + \frac{1}{r}\frac{\partial \chi}{\partial r} \right) \tag{3.99}$$

where $\chi = u'/u_{max}$. Using Bessel function, the solution can be expressed as

$$\chi = \sum_{n=1}^{\infty} \frac{8 J_0\left(\lambda_n\left(\frac{r}{r_0}\right)\right)}{\lambda_n^3 J_1(\lambda_n)} \exp\left(-\lambda_n^2 \frac{\mu \cdot t}{\rho \cdot r_0^2} \right) \tag{3.100}$$

The transient velocity component can be found as

$$u' = u_{max} \sum_{n=1}^{\infty} \frac{8 J_0\left(\lambda_n\left(\frac{r}{r_0}\right)\right)}{\lambda_n^3 J_1(\lambda_n)} \exp\left(-\lambda_n^2 \frac{\mu \cdot t}{\rho \cdot r_0^2} \right) \tag{3.101}$$

Substituting Eq. (3.101) into Eq. (3.92) and considering the expression for the steady state flow, Eq. (3.92) becomes

$$u = u_{max} \left(\left(1 - \left(\frac{r}{r_0}\right)^2 \right) - \sum_{n=1}^{\infty} \frac{8 J_0\left(\lambda_n\left(\frac{r}{r_0}\right)\right)}{\lambda_n^3 J_1(\lambda_n)} \exp\left(-\lambda_n^2 \frac{\mu \cdot t}{\rho \cdot r_0^2} \right) \right) \tag{3.102}$$

Equation (3.102) illustrates how the velocity varies in the developing region, which is similar to an acceleration or deceleration phase of an oscillating flow. This can be used to explain how an oscillating flow can enhance fluid flow and heat transfer.

3.6　Viscous Dissipation Effect in a Capillary Tube

To form a train of liquid plugs and vapor bubbles in an OHP, the channel size must be so small that the surface tension can control the liquid–vapor interface. Heat transport from the evaporator to the condenser in a typical OHP is based on the forced convection and phase change heat transfer. Although phase change heat transfer in an OHP plays a key role in generating the oscillating motion, most of the heat is transferred by the forced convection. In terms of forced convection between liquid plugs or vapor bubbles and wall, fluid flow and heat transfer in an OHP is similar to that in microchannels. Morini (2004, 2005) conducted a detailed

review and found that when the channel dimension becomes smaller, the viscous dissipation plays a more important role. In addition, there exists Richardson's annular effect due to the oscillating flow. The velocity gradient near the wall is high which will make the viscous work term become more important.

The energy equation of a fully developed laminar flow in a capillary tube can be expressed as

$$u\frac{\partial T}{\partial x} + v\frac{\partial T}{\partial r} = \frac{k}{\rho c_p r}\frac{d}{dr}\left(r\frac{dT}{dr}\right) + \frac{\mu}{\rho c_p}\left(\frac{du}{dr}\right)^2 \qquad (3.103)$$

The left side represents the net transport of energy into the control volume, and the right side represents the sum of the net heat conducted out of the control volume and the net viscous work done on the control volume.

To study the effect of viscous dissipation, only the viscous effect is considered and Eq. (3.103) can be expressed as

$$\frac{k}{r}\frac{d}{dr}\left(r\frac{dT}{dr}\right) = -\mu\left(\frac{du}{dr}\right)^2 \qquad (3.104)$$

For a fully developed laminar flow, the velocity distribution can be found as

$$u = \frac{-dp/dx}{4\mu}\left(r_0^2 - r^2\right) \qquad (3.105)$$

Substituting Eq. (3.105) into Eq. (3.104) yields

$$\frac{k}{r}\frac{d}{dr}\left(r\frac{dT}{dr}\right) = -\mu\left(\frac{r\,dp/dx}{2\mu}\right)^2 \qquad (3.106)$$

The mean velocity of the fluid flow in the capillary tube can be found as

$$\bar{u} = \frac{r_0^2(-dp/dx)}{8\mu} \qquad (3.107)$$

Rearranging Eq. (3.107) produces

$$dp/dx = -\frac{8\mu\bar{u}}{r_0^2} \qquad (3.108)$$

Substituting Eq. (3.108) into Eq. (3.106), it can be found that

$$\frac{k}{r}\frac{d}{dr}\left(r\frac{dT}{dr}\right) = -\frac{16\mu\bar{u}^2 r^2}{r_0^4} \qquad (3.109)$$

Integrating Eq. (3.109) and rearranging yields

$$T = -\frac{\mu \bar{u}^2 r^4}{k r_0^4} + C_1 \ln r + C_2 \tag{3.110}$$

Considering the boundary condition at $r = 0$, to avoid a singularity, it can be found that

$$C_1 = 0 \tag{3.111}$$

And substituting the boundary condition of $T = T_w$ at $r = r_0$, the second constant, C_2, can be expressed as

$$C_2 = T_w + \frac{\mu \bar{u}^2}{k} \tag{3.112}$$

Finally, the temperature distribution becomes

$$T = T_w + \frac{\mu \bar{u}^2}{k} \left(1 - \frac{r^4}{r_0^4} \right) \tag{3.113}$$

Using Eq. (3.113), heat transfer from the wall to fluid can be found as

$$q_w'' = k \frac{d \left(T_w + \frac{\mu \bar{u}^2}{k} \left(1 - \frac{r^4}{r_0^4} \right) \right)}{dr} \Bigg|_{r=r_0} \tag{3.114}$$

or

$$q_w'' = -4k \frac{\mu \bar{u}^2}{k} \frac{r_0^3}{r_0^4} = -\frac{4k}{r_0} \frac{\mu \bar{u}^2}{k} \tag{3.115}$$

When $r = 0$, $T_0 = T_w + \frac{\mu \bar{u}^2}{k}$, it can be found that

$$-\frac{\mu \bar{u}^2}{k} = T_w - T_0 \tag{3.116}$$

Substituting Eq. (3.116) into Eq. (3.115) produces

$$q_w'' = 4k(T_w - T_0)/r_0 \tag{3.117}$$

Considering the definition of Nusselt number, i.e.,

$$Nu_t = \frac{2q_w'' r_0}{k(T_w - T_0)} \tag{3.118}$$

and substituting Eq. (3.117) into Eq. (3.118), the Nusselt number due to the viscous dissipation can be found as

$$Nu_t = \frac{2q_w'' r_0}{k(T_w - T_0)} = 8 \qquad (3.119)$$

which is a substantial number. It should be noted that when r_0 is very small, it becomes important and a high q_w'' will be obtained.

3.7 Graetz Question

For a train of liquid plugs and vapor bubbles in an OHP, liquid plugs are separated by vapor bubbles. When an individual liquid plug starts to move, it is similar to a liquid plug moving into a capillary tube. During this movement, a thermal entrance region is formed. Clearly, the thermal entrance region for an oscillating flow of a train of liquid plugs and vapor bubbles plays an important role in the heat transfer process of an OHP. The thermal entrance problem was first solved by Graetz (1883), and later for the Poiseuille flow in 1885, in the form of an infinite series. Graetz' numerical results were crude, but very accurate results were given by Sellars et al. (1956). The problem is a classic one which has been discussed in detail in texts by Shah and London (1978) and Crawford et al. (1980).

Consider a fluid flow flowing into a capillary tube with a tube radius r_0. When the wall temperature has a sudden change, the temperature profile $T(x, r)$ in a pipe is developing. Neglecting dissipation and axial heat conduction, the energy equation shown in Eq. (3.103) is reduced to

$$u \frac{\partial T}{\partial x} \approx \frac{\alpha}{r} \frac{\partial}{\partial r} \left(r \frac{\partial T}{\partial r} \right) \qquad (3.120)$$

where $\alpha = k/\rho c_p$ is the thermal diffusivity. Figure 3.9 illustrates the thermal boundary layer development for the case of a sudden change in wall temperature. The thermal boundary conditions for Eq. (3.120) can be expressed as

$$T = T_0 \quad \text{at} \quad x \leq 0 \qquad (3.121)$$

$$T(r_0, x) = T_w \quad \text{at} \quad x > 0 \qquad (3.122)$$

Because the thermal boundary depends on the velocity boundary, the momentum equation should be provided to solve Eq. (3.120). To simplify the problem, it is assumed that the velocity distribution $u(x, r)$ is given which can have three types of distributions, i.e.,

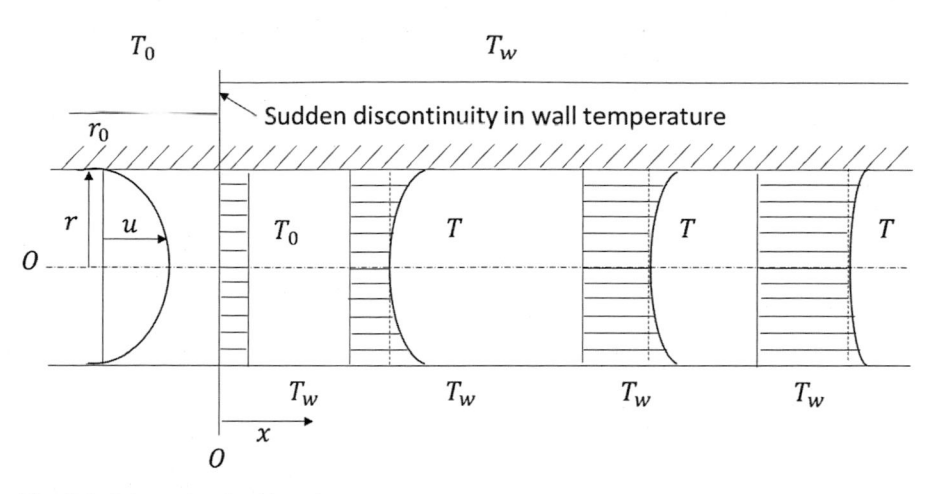

Fig. 3.9 Schematic of a thermal entrance

1. $u = u_m = $ const or slug flow which is appropriate for low Prandtl number fluids such as liquid metals, where T develops much faster than u.
2. $u = 2\bar{u}(1 - r^2/r_0^2)$ or Poiseuille flow which is appropriate for high Prandtl number (oils) or when the thermal entrance is far downstream of the duct entrance.
3. Developing u profiles which is suitable for any Prandtl number when the velocity and temperature entrances are in the same position.

Equation (3.120) with boundary conditions shown in Eqs. (3.121) and (3.122) constitutes a linear boundary value problem, which was successfully solved by Graetz. Figure 3.10 shows results obtained by Goldberg (White 1974) for mean Nusselt number variations in the entrance region starting at $x = 0$. The top curve indicated by uniform velocity is for case 1, i.e., $u = \bar{u} = $ const. For this case, the thermal boundary develops much faster than the velocity boundary, which is typical for low Prandtl number ($Pr \ll 1$). The bottom curve indicated by parabolic velocity is for Poiseuille flow, i.e., case 2 ($Pr \gg 1$ such as oil). Other curves between these two limitations are for case 3, where velocity and temperature develop together. Examining these three cases, it can be found that the Poiseuille flow (case 2) with a discontinuous wall-temperature change provides a lower limit of Nusselt number in thermal entrance which will be discussed in detail in this section.

To obtain a general solution, it is defined that $r^* = \frac{r}{r_0}$, $T^* = \frac{T_w - T}{T_w - T_0}$, $x^* = \frac{x}{2 r_0 Re_m Pr}$, and $Re_m = \frac{2 r_0 \bar{u}}{\nu}$. Using these dimensionless variables, Eq. (3.120) can be expressed as

$$\frac{\partial T^*}{\partial x^*} = \frac{2}{r^*(1 - r^{*2})} \frac{\partial}{\partial r^*}\left(r^* \frac{\partial T^*}{\partial r^*}\right) \qquad (3.123)$$

Fig. 3.10 Finite-difference calculations for log-mean Nusselt number in laminar pipe flow with developing velocity profiles (GoldBerg 1958)

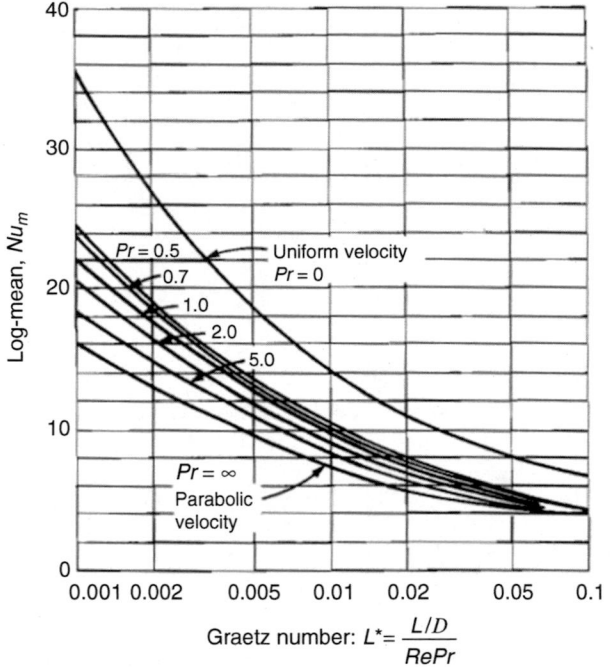

The boundary conditions corresponding to Eq. (3.123) become

$$T^*(r^*,0) = 1 \tag{3.124}$$

$$T^*(1,x^*) = 0 \tag{3.125}$$

Examining Eq. (3.123), it can be found that separation of variable method can be used to solve Eq. (3.123). It is assumed that the solution has a form of

$$T^*(r^*,x^*) = f(r^*)g(x^*) \tag{3.126}$$

Substituting it into Eq. (3.123) yields

$$\frac{g'}{2g} = \frac{r^*f'' + f'}{r^*(1 - r^{*2})f} = -\lambda^2 = \text{const} \tag{3.127}$$

Separating Eq. (3.127) produces

$$\frac{g'}{2g} = -\lambda^2 \tag{3.128}$$

$$\frac{r^* f'' + f'}{r^* (1 - r^{*2}) f} = -\lambda^2 \tag{3.129}$$

respectively. The general solution of Eq. (3.128) can be found as

$$g(x^*) = C \exp(-2\lambda^2 x^*) \tag{3.130}$$

Rearranging Eq. (3.130) yields

$$r^* f'' + f' + \lambda^2 r^* (1 - r^{*2}) f = 0 \tag{3.131}$$

To make the product solution $T^* = f(r^*) g(x^*)$ satisfy the boundary condition of $T^*(r^*, 0) = 1$ for $r*$, the solution can be written as

$$T^*(r^*, x^*) = \sum_{n=0}^{\infty} C_n f_n(r^*) \exp(-2\lambda_n^2 x^*) \tag{3.132}$$

where the function f_n are characteristic solutions to Eq. (3.131), i.e.,

$$r^* f_n'' + f_n' + \lambda_n^2 r^* (1 - r^{*2}) f_n = 0 \tag{3.133}$$

If $f_n(0) = 1$ and $f_n(1) = 0$, the wall-temperature condition of $T^*(1, x^*) = 0$ is satisfied. In addition, the condition shown in Eq. (3.124) should be satisfied; hence,

$$T^*(r^*, 0) = 1 = \sum_{n=0}^{\infty} C_n f_n(r^*) \tag{3.134}$$

When $f_n(0) = 1$ and $f_n(1) = 0$, it showed that the eigenfunctions f_n are orthogonal over the intervals 0–1 with respect to the weighting function. It can be found that

$$C_n = \frac{\displaystyle\int_0^1 r^* (1 - r^{*2}) f_n dr^*}{\displaystyle\int_0^1 r^* (1 - r^{*2}) f_n^2 dr^*} \tag{3.135}$$

Table 3.2 shows the first ten eigenvalues λ_n, the eigenvalues of the Graetz function f_n and their associated constants.

To calculate the Nusselt number at the wall, it is necessary to find the mean temperature, which can be determined by

Table 3.2 Constants in the Graetz problem

n	λ_n	C_n	$-C_n f'_n(1)$
0	2.7043644	+1.46622	1.49758
1	6.679032	−0.802476	1.08848
2	10.67338	+0.587094	0.92576
3	14.67108	−0.474897	0.83036
4	18.66987	+0.404402	0.76474
5	22.67	−0.35535	0.71571
6	26.67	+0.31886	0.67798
7	30.67	−0.29049	0.64711
8	34.67	+0.26769	0.62119
9	38.67	−0.24890	0.59900

$$T_{\mathrm{m}} = \frac{\int T\,dm}{\int dm} = \frac{\int_0^{r_0} T\rho u \cdot 2\pi r\,dr}{\int_0^{r_0} \rho u \cdot 2\pi r\,dr} \tag{3.136}$$

Considering $u = 2u_{\mathrm{m}}\left(1 - r^{*2}\right)$, the mean temperature can be found as

$$T_{\mathrm{m}}^* = 4\int_0^1 T^*\left(1 - r^{*2}\right) r^*\,dr^* \tag{3.137}$$

Substituting Eq. (3.132) into Eq. (3.137) and integrating yields

$$T_{\mathrm{m}}^*\left(x^*\right) = 4\sum_{n=0}^{\infty} \left(-C_n f'_n(1)\right)\lambda_n^{-2}\exp\left(-2\lambda_n^2 x^*\right) \tag{3.138}$$

Finally, the Nusselt number can be expressed as

$$Nu_x = \frac{2r_0 q_{\mathrm{w}}}{k(T_{\mathrm{w}} - T_{\mathrm{m}})} = \frac{\sum C_n f'_n(1)\exp\left(-2\lambda_n^2 x^*\right)}{2\sum C_n \lambda_n^{-2} f'_n(1)\exp\left(-2\lambda_n^2 x^*\right)} \tag{3.139}$$

If $x^* > 0.05$, the first term of the series is dominant, Eq. (3.139) can be approximately written as

$$Nu_x \approx \frac{\lambda_0^2}{2} = 3.66 \tag{3.140}$$

which is the result for the thermally fully developed laminar flow in the pipe. For small x^*, the results can be approximately expressed as

$$Nu_x \approx 1.076x^{*-1/3} - 1.064 \tag{3.141}$$

with an error of less than 1 % if $x^* < 0.0004$.

Considering the definition of the mean Nusselt number, i.e.,

$$Nu_m = \frac{1}{L^*} \int_0^{L^*} Nu_x dx^* \tag{3.142}$$

where $L^* = (L/D)/(Re_m Pr)$, Eq. (3.142) becomes

$$Nu_m = \frac{-1}{4L^*} \ln T_m^* (L^*) \tag{3.143}$$

From the results shown in Fig. 3.10, it can be found that the mean Nusselt numbers for all Prandtl numbers approach 3.66, i.e., $Nu_m = 3.66$ when L^* increases to 0.05, i.e., $L^* \approx 0.05$. Therefore, the thermal entrance length in a pipe flow can be approximately expressed as

$$L \approx 0.05 D Re_m Pr \tag{3.144}$$

For a train of liquid plugs and vapor bubbles moving in an OHP, the developing region plays an important role. For computation purposes, one may curve-fit the bottom curve shown in Fig. 3.10 to a well-known formula developed by Hausen (White 1974), i.e.,

$$Nu_m \approx 3.66 + \frac{0.075/L^*}{1 + 0.05/L^{*2/3}} \tag{3.145}$$

It should be noted that Eq. (3.145) is only for case 2, a Poiseuille flow, i.e., $u = 2\bar{u}(1 - r^2/r_0^2)$.

3.8 Heat Transfer in a Laminar Reciprocating Flow

A laminar flow is oscillating in a pipe with a diameter of D and a finite length of L, as shown in Fig. 3.11. The pipe is connected between two large reservoirs at a constant temperature of T_i. The pipe wall has a constant temperature of T_w. The inlet axial velocity during each half cycle is taken to be uniform over the cross section with a periodical variation as indicated by Eq. (3.2). Considering the dimensionless variables of $X = \frac{x}{D}$, $R = \frac{r}{D}$, $\phi = \omega t$, $U = u/u_{max}$, $P = p/u_{max}^2$, $Re_\omega = \frac{\omega D^2}{\nu}$, and $\theta = (T - T_i)/(T_w - T_i)$, the governing dimensionless conservation equations of mass and momentum for a periodically reciprocating flow can be represented by

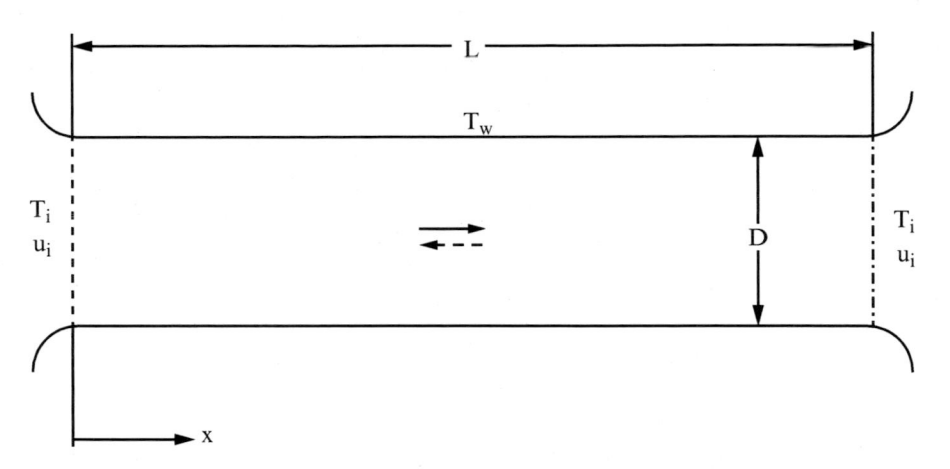

Fig. 3.11 A reciprocating flow in a heated tube at a constant temperature (Zhao and Cheng 1995)

$$\nabla \cdot \vec{V} = 0 \tag{3.146}$$

$$\frac{\partial \vec{V}}{\partial \phi} + \left(\vec{V} \cdot \nabla\right)\vec{V} + \nabla P = \frac{1}{Re_\omega}\nabla^2\vec{V} \tag{3.147}$$

and the energy equation, which is

$$\frac{\partial \theta}{\partial \phi} + \left(\vec{V} \cdot \nabla\right)\theta = \frac{1}{Re_\omega Pr}\nabla^2\theta \tag{3.148}$$

Zhao and Cheng (1995, 1996b) numerically solved Eqs. (3.146)–(3.148) with an oscillating velocity of

$$U(0, R, \phi) = \sin \phi \tag{3.149}$$

and thermal boundary conditions of

$$\text{at} \quad X = 0 \quad 0 \le R \le 0.5 \quad \theta(0, R, \phi) = 0 \tag{3.150}$$

$$\text{at} \quad X = L/D \quad 0 \le R \le 0.5 \quad \theta(L/D, R, \phi) = 0 \tag{3.151}$$

$$\text{at} \quad R = 0 \quad 0 \le X \le L/D \quad \frac{\partial \theta}{\partial R} = 0 \tag{3.152}$$

$$\text{at} \quad R = 0.5 \quad 0 \le X \le L/D \quad \theta(X, 0.5, \phi) = \theta_w = 1 \tag{3.153}$$

Zhao and Cheng (1995, 1996b) also presented these results as functions of dimensionless variables, i.e., Pr, L/D, Re_ω, and A_0 with focuses on $Pr = 0.71$, $L/D = 40$, and, $10 < Re_\omega < 400$ and $5 < A_0 < \frac{761}{\sqrt{Re_\omega}}$ (the onset of turbulence).

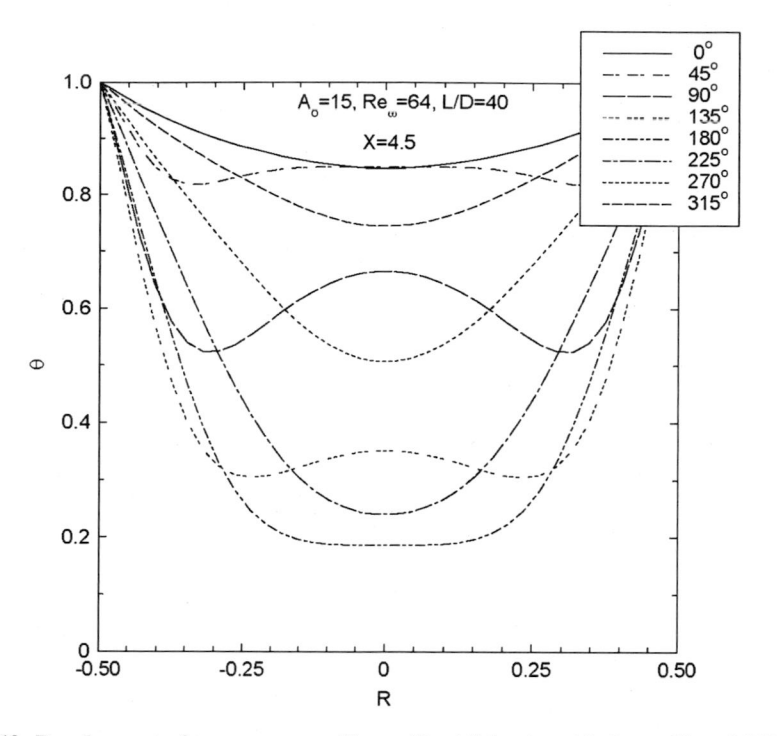

Fig. 3.12 Development of temperature profiles at $X = 4.5$ for $A_0 = 15$, $Re_\omega = 64$, and $L/D = 40$ (Zhao and Cheng 1995)

Figure 3.12 illustrates transient temperature profiles at $X = 4.5$, $A_0 = 15$, and $Re_\omega = 64$, which is near the entrance of the pipe. It is interesting to note that the annular effect exists in the temperature profiles of an oscillatory flow as shown in Fig. 3.12. This annular effect becomes more pronounced as the kinetic Reynolds number is increased; furthermore, the temperature gradients near the wall become steeper when the kinetic Reynolds number is increased.

The local instantaneous Nusselt number along the heated wall for an unsteady flow is defined as

$$Nu_{x,t} = \frac{h(x,t)D}{k} \tag{3.154}$$

where h is the local instantaneous heat transfer coefficient defined as

$$h(x,t) = \frac{q_w(x,t)}{\Delta T(x,t)} = \frac{-k(\partial T/\partial r)_{r=r_0}}{\Delta T} \tag{3.155}$$

ΔT in Eq. (3.155) is the temperature difference between the wall temperature, T_w, and the local instantaneous bulk temperature, T_b, which is defined as

$$T_b = \int_0^R (u(r,x,t)T(r,x,t))r\,dr \Big/ \int_0^R u(r,x,t)r\,dr \tag{3.156}$$

The cross-sectional mean velocity becomes zero twice in each cycle, which gives rise to an infinite value of the bulk temperature twice in a cycle. This will cause anomalies in evaluating the local Nusselt number. For this reason, a temperature difference is defined as $\Delta T = T_w - T_i$ where T_w is the wall temperature and T_i is the inlet or outlet temperature of the fluid flowing through the pipe. Substituting this temperature difference into Eq. (3.155), the local instantaneous Nusselt number can be expressed as

$$Nu_{x,t} = -\left(\frac{\partial \theta}{\partial r}\right)_{R=0.5} \tag{3.157}$$

Figure 3.13 illustrates variations of the local instantaneous Nusselt number $Nu_{x,t}$ at different dimensionless axial locations between $X = 0$ (left side) and $X = L/D$ (right side) of the pipe for a complete cycle with $A_0 = 15$ and $Re_\omega = 64$. It should be noted that the phase difference between the entrance location and the exit location is $180°$. First, focus on the entrance region. Near the inlet at $X = 2$, for example, the instantaneous Nusselt number increases with ϕ until it reaches a maximum value at about $\phi = 90°$. This happens when the colder fluid enters the entrance region with the cross-sectional mean velocity defined by Eq. (3.2) with its maximum velocity at about $\phi = 90°$. Since the colder fluid enters with a decreasing velocity after $\phi > 90°$,

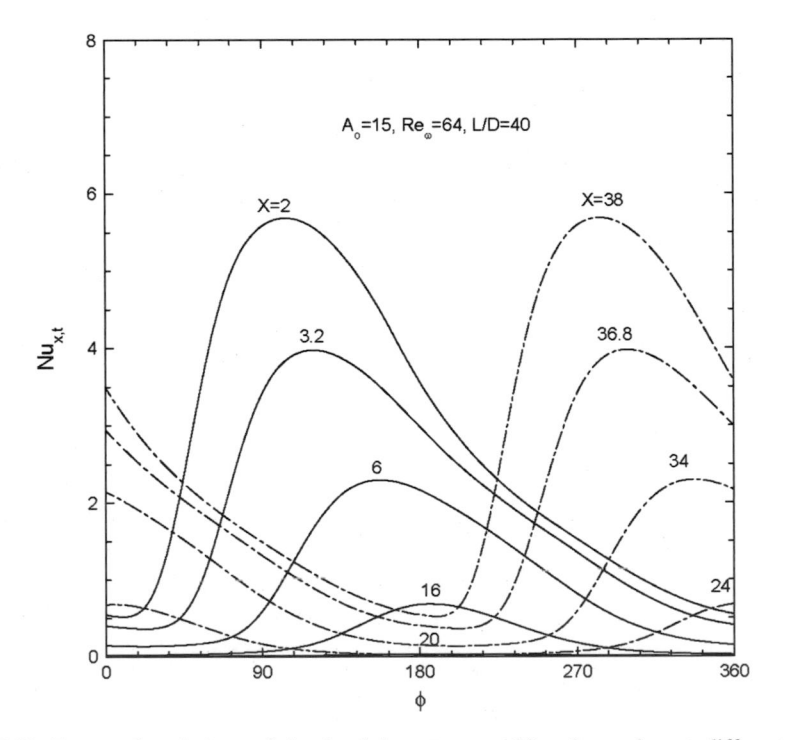

Fig. 3.13 Temporal variations of the local instantaneous Nusselt number at different axial locations for $A_0 = 15$, $Re_\omega = 64$, and $L/D = 40$ (Zhao and Cheng 1995)

the heat transfer rate begins to decrease after $\phi > 90°$. The heat transfer rate continues to decrease as the velocity of the entering fluid decreases to zero at about 180°. Subsequently, the fluid reverses its direction and the warmer fluid passes through the location at $X = 2$; consequently, the heat transfer rate between the fluid and the pipe continues to decrease. The value of $Nu_{x,t}$ decreases as the value of X is increased from the inlet to the middle of the pipe ($X = 20$). Toward the middle of the pipe, the instantaneous Nusselt number becomes vanishingly small. Its value is almost symmetric with respect to ϕ with the maximum value occurring near $\phi = 180°$. And the value of $Nu_{x,t}$ increases as the kinetic Reynolds number is increased.

It should be noted that the value of $Nu_{x,t}$ is a function of the axial location x and time t, i.e.,

$$\overline{Nu} = \frac{1}{t_0 L} \int_0^{t_0} \int_0^L Nu_{x,t} \, dx \, dt \tag{3.158}$$

Using Eq. (3.158), the time-space averaged Nusselt number, $\overline{Nu}$, can be calculated, which can result in a correlation of

$$\overline{Nu} = 0.00495 A_0^{0.9} Re_\omega^{0.656} \tag{3.159}$$

Computations were then carried out for different values of L/D ranging from 10 to 120 for air ($Pr = 0.7$). The effect of L/D can be integrated into Eq. (3.159), i.e.,

$$\overline{Nu} = 0.00495 A_0^{0.9} Re_\omega^{0.656} \left[43.74 (L/D)^{1.18} + 0.06 \right] \tag{3.160}$$

Figure 4.13 illustrates typical temporal temperature variations measured at the left and right mixing chambers during one cycle at the same oscillatory frequency ($Re_\omega = 120.1$) and amplitude ($A_0 = 34.9$). Generally, during the first half cycle ($0° \leq \phi \leq 180°$) as the fluid flow moves from the left to right, the fluid temperature in the left mixing chamber drops due to the cooling effect from the left heat sink while the temperature in the right mixing chamber goes up due to the heating effect from the heated test section. During the second half cycle ($180° \leq \phi \leq 360°$), the fluid flow reverses its flow direction. Results show that A_0 affects the temperature variation for both chambers. When $A_0 = 34.9$, as shown in Fig. 3.14, the fluid temperature in the right mixing chamber increases with the increase of phase angle and reaches a maximum value of about $\phi = 150°$. When A_0 becomes small, however, the fluid temperature in the right mixing chamber increases at the beginning of the cycle, but slowly in comparison with the case of $A_0 = 34.9$. The peak of the temperature is reached as late as at $\phi = 166°$. The reason for the different temporal temperature variations for low and high values of A_0 can be explained as follows: At a high value of A_0 where the maximum cross-sectional mean velocity is high [as can be deduced from Eq. (3.2)], a forced convection effect dominates. Therefore, the fluid temperature in the right mixing chamber rises immediately when the fluid reverses flow direction as hotter fluid enters. However, when A_0 is small, the fluid velocity is low. The axial heat conduction effect dominates at least

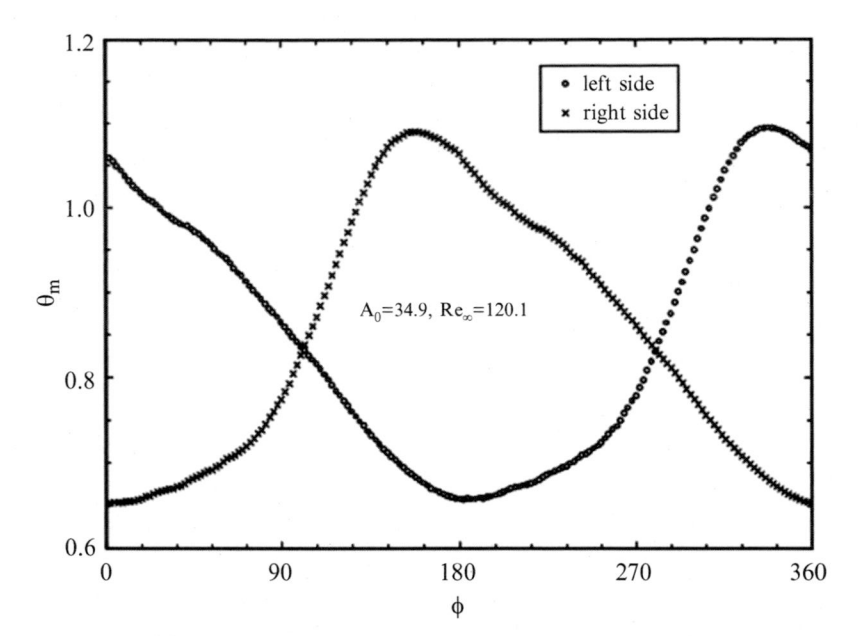

Fig. 3.14 Temporal fluid temperature variations in the left and right mixing chambers for $A_0 = 34.9$, $Re_\omega = 120.1$, and $L/D = 44.8$ (Zhao and Cheng 1996c)

initially, and the fluid temperature in the right mixing chamber responds slowly with respect to velocity.

A cycle-space averaged Nusselt number is defined by Zhao and Cheng (1996c) as follows

$$\overline{Nu} = \frac{qD_i}{k\left(\overline{T}_w - \overline{T}_m\right)} = \frac{1}{k\left(\overline{\theta}_w - \overline{\theta}_m\right)} \tag{3.161}$$

where

$$\overline{\theta}_w = \frac{1}{N}\sum_{i=1}^{N}\overline{\theta}_{w,i} \tag{3.162}$$

$$\overline{\theta}_m = \frac{1}{2\pi}\int_0^{2\pi}\theta_{m,i}d\phi \quad \text{or} \quad \overline{\theta}_m = \frac{1}{2\pi}\int_0^{2\pi}\theta_{m,r}d\phi \tag{3.163}$$

Based on the experimental data, a correlation for the cycle-space averaged Nusselt number in terms of appropriate dimensionless variables for a laminar reciprocating flow of air in a long pipe with constant heat flux is obtained, i.e.,

$$\overline{Nu} = 0.02A_0^{0.85}Re_\omega^{0.58} \tag{3.164}$$

Equation (3.164) with experimental data is presented in Fig. 3.15. The maximum relative error between Eq. (3.164) and the experimental data is about 12.8 %.

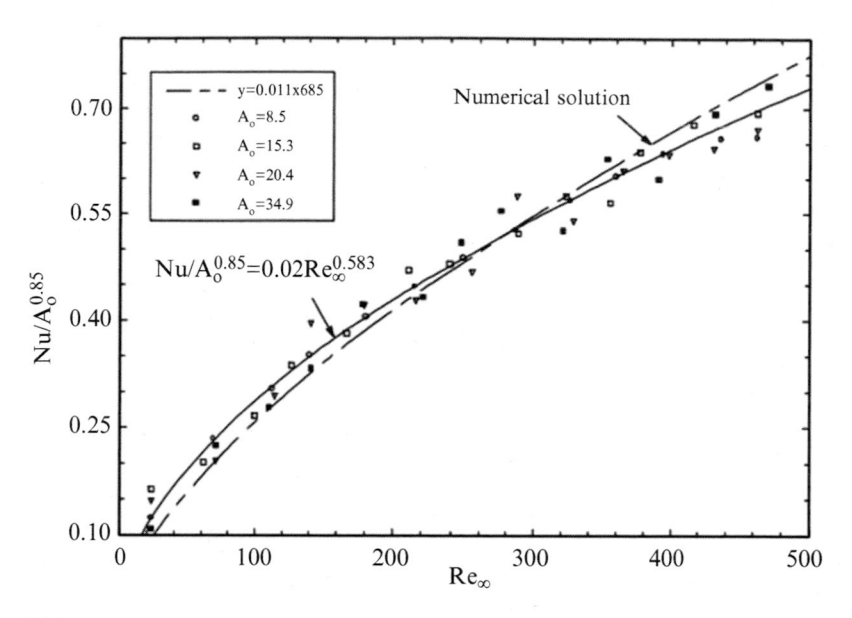

Fig. 3.15 This graph represents a correlation equation based on the experimental data for the cycle-space averaged Nusselt number (Zhao and Cheng 1996c)

The cycle-space averaged Nusselt number $\overline{Nu}$ generated from the numerical simulation is also presented in Fig. 3.15. It shows that the numerical solution (represented by the dashed line) is slightly lower or higher than Eq. (3.164) depending on whether $Re_\omega < 280$ or $Re_\omega > 280$. The maximum relative deviation between the numerical solution and the data is about 7 %. Note that Eq. (3.164) indicates that the heat transfer rate increases with both the dimensionless oscillation amplitude of fluid A_0 and the kinetic Reynolds number Re_ω; the increase in heat transfer is more sensitive to A_0 than to Re_ω because the exponent of A_0 is greater than that of Re_ω. It is also relevant to note that Eq. (3.164) is valid for a long pipe with air as the working fluid medium. Thus, Eq. (3.164) is a conservative estimate of heat transfer rate for a reciprocating flow in a pipe of finite length.

3.9 Heat Transfer in Laminar Pulsating Flow

3.9.1 Pulsating Pipe Flow at Sinusoidal Pressure

For a laminar pulsating flow shown in Fig. 3.5, the energy equation can be written as (Yin and Ma 2013)

$$\frac{\partial T}{\partial t} + u\frac{\partial T}{\partial x} = \alpha\frac{1}{r}\frac{\partial}{\partial r}\left(r\frac{\partial T}{\partial r}\right) \tag{3.165}$$

The corresponding boundary conditions for governing Eq. (3.165) can be expressed as

$$\frac{\partial T}{\partial r} = 0 \text{ at } r = 0$$

$$k\frac{\partial T}{\partial r} = q_w \text{ at } r = r_0$$

$$(3.166)$$

To solve Eq. (3.165) with boundary conditions shown in Eq. (3.166), the momentum equation and driving pressure are needed. In Sect. 3.4.2, the analytical solution of the velocity distribution has been obtained as shown in Eq. (3.49), which can be directly used in the following derivation.

Considering the dimensionless variables of $r^* = \frac{r}{r_0}$, $t^* = \frac{\nu t}{r_0^2}$, $u^* = \frac{u}{u_m}$, $\Theta = \frac{T-T_0}{q_w r_0/k}$, $X = \frac{4x}{Re_m Pr r_0}$, and $Re_m = \frac{2u_m r_0}{\nu}$, Eq. (3.165) can be rewritten as

$$Pr\frac{\partial \Theta}{\partial t^*} + 2u^*\frac{\partial \Theta}{\partial X} = \frac{\partial}{r^*\partial r^*}\left(r^*\frac{\partial \Theta}{\partial r^*}\right) \qquad (3.167)$$

The corresponding boundary conditions shown in Eq. (3.166) become

$$\frac{\partial \Theta}{\partial r^*} = 0 \text{ at } r^* = 0$$

$$\frac{\partial \Theta}{\partial r^*} = 1 \text{ at } r^* = 1$$

$$(3.168)$$

respectively. Following the same approach for the velocity distribution as shown in Eq. (3.49), Eq. (3.167) can be solved for the temperature distribution. Assuming that the dimensionless temperature consists of a steady component and an instantaneous component, i.e.,

$$\Theta = \Theta_s\left(r^*, x^*\right) + \Theta_t\left(r^*, t^*\right) \qquad (3.169)$$

Substituting Eqs. (3.169) and (3.26) into Eq. (3.167) yields

$$Pr\frac{\partial\left(\Theta_s(r^*,x^*) + \Theta_t(r^*,t^*)\right)}{\partial t^*} + 2(u_s^*(r^*) + u_t^*(r^*,t^*))\frac{\partial\left(\Theta_s(r^*,x^*) + \Theta_t(r^*,t^*)\right)}{\partial x^*}$$

$$= \frac{\partial}{r^*\partial r^*}\left(r^*\frac{\partial\left(\Theta_s(r^*,x^*) + \Theta_t(r^*,t^*)\right)}{\partial r^*}\right)$$

$$(3.170)$$

Because $\Theta_s(r^*, x^*)$ is not a function of t^*, Eq. (3.170) can be expressed as

$$
\begin{aligned}
Pr\frac{\partial \Theta_t(r^*, t^*)}{\partial t^*} &+ 2(u_s^*(r^*) + u_t^*(r^*, t^*))\frac{\partial \Theta_s(r^*, x^*)}{\partial X} \\
&= \frac{\partial}{r^*\partial r^*}\left(r^*\frac{\partial \Theta_s(r^*, x^*)}{\partial r^*}\right) + \frac{\partial}{r^*\partial r^*}\left(r^*\frac{\partial \Theta_t(r^*, t^*)}{\partial r^*}\right)
\end{aligned}
\tag{3.171}
$$

Considering the separation of variable method, Eq. (3.171) becomes

$$
2(u_s^*(r^*) + u_t^*(r^*, t^*))\frac{\partial \Theta_s(r^*, x^*)}{\partial X} = \frac{\partial}{r^*\partial r^*}\left(r^*\frac{\partial \Theta_s(r^*, x^*)}{\partial r^*}\right)
\tag{3.172}
$$

$$
Pr\frac{\partial \Theta_t(r^*, t^*)}{\partial t^*} = \frac{\partial}{r^*\partial r^*}\left(r^*\frac{\partial \Theta_t(r^*, t^*)}{\partial r^*}\right)
\tag{3.173}
$$

respectively. If $\Theta_s = f(x^*) + g(r^*)$, Eq. (3.173) can be expressed as

$$
\frac{\partial(f(x^*) + g(r^*))}{\partial X} = \frac{\partial}{2(u_s^*(r^*) + u_t^*(r^*, t^*))r^*\partial r^*}\left(r^*\frac{\partial(f(x^*) + g(r^*))}{\partial r^*}\right)
\tag{3.174}
$$

Because $f(x^*)$ and $g(r^*)$ are functions of x^* and r^*, respectively, Eq. (3.174) can be written as

$$
\frac{\partial(f(x^*))}{\partial x^*} = \frac{\partial}{2(u_s^*(r^*) + u_t^*(r^*, t^*))r^*\partial r^*}\left(r^*\frac{\partial(g(r^*))}{\partial r^*}\right) = c
\tag{3.175}
$$

or

$$
\frac{\partial}{2(u_s^*(r^*) + u_t^*(r^*, t^*))r^*\partial r^*}\left(r^*\frac{\partial(g(r^*))}{\partial r^*}\right) = c
\tag{3.176}
$$

$$
\frac{\partial(f(x^*))}{\partial x^*} = c
\tag{3.177}
$$

Integrating Eq. (3.176) yields

$$
g(r^*) = c \cdot \left(r^{*2} - \frac{r^{*4}}{4}\right) + C_1\ln r^* + C_2
\tag{3.178}
$$

Considering boundary conditions of pipe flow, the constants in Eq. (3.178) can be found as

$$C = 1 \tag{3.179}$$

$$C_1 = 0 \tag{3.180}$$

$$C_2 = 0 \tag{3.181}$$

And the expression of $g(r^*)$ can then be written as

$$g(r^*) = r^{*2} - \frac{r^{*4}}{4} \tag{3.182}$$

Integrating Eq. (3.177) produces

$$f(x^*) = cx^* + C \tag{3.183}$$

Considering the boundary condition shown in Eq. (3.179), Eq. (3.183) becomes

$$f(x^*) = x^* + C \tag{3.184}$$

Considering Eqs. (3.182) and (3.183), the steady state dimensionless temperature, Θ_s, can be written as

$$\Theta_s = x^* + r^{*2} - \frac{r^{*4}}{4} + C \tag{3.185}$$

Based on the constant heat flux boundary condition, it can be found that

$$C = -\frac{7}{24} \tag{3.186}$$

and the steady state dimensionless temperature can be obtained as follows

$$\Theta_s = x^* + r^{*2} - \frac{r^{*4}}{4} - \frac{7}{24} \tag{3.187}$$

Considering Bessel transform, the equation for the instantaneous component can be expressed as

$$J_0\left[\Pr\frac{\partial \Theta_t(r^*,t^*)}{\partial t^*} + 2u_t^*\right] = J_0\left[\frac{\partial}{r^*\partial r^*}\left(r^*\frac{\partial \Theta_t(r^*,t^*)}{\partial r^*}\right)\right] \tag{3.188}$$

Considering $u_t^* = 16\zeta \sum\limits_{n=1}^{\infty} \left(\dfrac{s^2 \cos\left(\omega^* t^*\right) + \omega^* \sin\left(\omega^* t^*\right)}{sJ_1[s]\left(\omega^{*2} + s^4\right)} J_0\left(sr^*\right) \right)$, Eq. (3.188) can be transformed to

$$\mathrm{Pr}\,\frac{\partial F\left(s, t^*\right)}{\partial t^*} + 2J_0\left[u_t^*\right] = -s^2 F\left(s, t^*\right) \tag{3.189}$$

or

$$-\frac{\mathrm{Pr}}{s_n^2}\frac{\partial F\left(s_n, t^*\right)}{\partial t^*} - \sum_{m=1}^{\infty} \frac{16\zeta}{s_n^2}\left(\frac{s_m^2}{s_m\left(\omega^{*2} + s_m^4\right)}\cos\left(\omega^* t^*\right) + \frac{\omega^*}{s_m\left(\omega^{*2} + s_m^4\right)}\sin\left(\omega^* t^*\right)\right)$$

$$\frac{s_n}{s_m^2 - s_n^2}\frac{J_0(s_m)J_1(s_n)}{J_1(s_m)} = F\left(s_n, t^*\right) \tag{3.190}$$

If $F[s_n, t^*]$ is expressed as

$$F\left[s_n, t^*\right] = A\cos\left(\omega^* t^*\right) + B\sin\left(\omega^* t^*\right) \tag{3.191}$$

Equation (3.190) should always be satisfied, i.e.,

$$\left(A + 2\sum_{m=1}^{\infty} \frac{16\zeta}{s_n^2}\left(\frac{s_m^2}{s_m\left(\omega^{*2} + s_m^4\right)}\right)\frac{s_n}{s_m^2 - s_n^2}\frac{J_0(s_m)J_1(s_n)}{J_1(s_m)} + B\frac{\mathrm{Pr}\omega^*}{s_n^2}\right)\cos\left(\omega^* t^*\right) = 0 \tag{3.192}$$

$$\left(2\sum_{m=1}^{\infty} \frac{16\zeta}{s_n^2}\left(\frac{\omega^*}{s_m\left(\omega^{*2} + s_m^4\right)}\right)\frac{s_n}{s_m^2 - s_n^2}\frac{J_0(s_m)J_1(s_n)}{J_1(s_m)} - A\frac{\mathrm{Pr}\omega^*}{s_n^2} + B\right)\sin\left(\omega^* t^*\right) = 0 \tag{3.193}$$

Simplifying Eqs. (3.192) and (3.193) with the properties of Bessel functions yields

$$A + \frac{32\zeta J_1(s_n)s_n}{s_n^2}\sum_{m=1}^{\infty}\left(\frac{s_m^2}{\left(\omega^{*2} + s_m^4\right)\left(s_m^2 - s_n^2\right)}\right) + B\frac{\mathrm{Pr}\omega^*}{s_n^2} = 0 \tag{3.194}$$

$$\frac{32\zeta J_1(s_n)s_n}{s_n^2}\sum_{m=1}^{\infty}\left(\frac{\omega^*}{\left(\omega^{*2} + s_m^4\right)\left(s_m^2 - s_n^2\right)}\right) - A\frac{\mathrm{Pr}\omega^*}{s_n^2} + B = 0 \tag{3.195}$$

respectively. Defining

$$E_{ln} = \sum_{m=1}^{\infty} \left(\frac{s_m^2}{\left(\omega^{*2} + s_m^4\right)\left(s_m^2 - s_n^2\right)} \right) \tag{3.196}$$

$$E_{2n} = \sum_{m=1}^{\infty} \left(\frac{\omega^*}{\left(\omega^{*2} + s_m^4\right)\left(s_m^2 - s_n^2\right)} \right) \tag{3.197}$$

Equations (3.196) and (3.197) can be written as

$$A + \frac{32\zeta J_1(s_n)s_n E_{ln}}{s_n^2} + B \frac{Pr\omega^*}{s_n^2} = 0 \tag{3.198}$$

$$\frac{32\zeta J_1(s_n)s_n E_{2n}}{s_n^2} - A \frac{Pr\omega^*}{s_n^2} + B = 0 \tag{3.199}$$

A and B in Eqs. (3.198) and (3.199) can be found as

$$A = 32\zeta J_1(s_n)s_n \frac{E_{2n}Pr\omega^* - s_n^2 E_{ln}}{Pr^2\omega^{*2} + s_n^4} \tag{3.200}$$

$$B = 32\zeta J_1(s_n)s_n \frac{s_n^2 E_{2n} - E_{ln}Pr\omega^*}{Pr^2\omega^{*2} + s_n^4} \tag{3.201}$$

respectively. The expression of $F[s_n, t^*]$ becomes

$$F\left[s_n, t^*\right] = 32\zeta J_1(s_n)s_n \frac{\left(E_{2n}Pr\omega^* - s_n^2 E_{ln}\right)\cos\left(\omega^* t^*\right) + \left(s_n^2 E_{2n} - E_{ln}Pr\omega^*\right)\sin\left(\omega^* t^*\right)}{Pr^2\omega^{*2} + s_n^4} \tag{3.202}$$

Considering the inverse Bessel transformation, the dimensionless instantaneous temperature can be finally expressed as

$$\Theta_t = 64\zeta \sum_{n=1}^{\infty} \left(\frac{s_n\left(E_{2n}Pr\omega^* - s_n^2 E_{ln}\right)\cos\left(\omega^* t^*\right) + \left(s_n^2 E_{2n} - E_{ln}Pr\omega^*\right)\sin\left(\omega^* t^*\right)}{Pr^2\omega^{*2} + s_n^4} \right) \frac{J_0\left(s_n r^*\right)}{J_1(s_n)} \tag{3.203}$$

where s_m and s_n are the eigenvalues of the Bessel function of the first kind of order 0 and 1.

The Nusselt number is defined as

$$Nu_t = \frac{2q_w r_0}{(T_w - T_{bt})k} \tag{3.204}$$

Considering $\Theta = \frac{T - T_0}{q_w r_0 / k}$, Eq. (3.204) becomes

$$Nu_t = \frac{2}{\Theta_w - \Theta_{bt}} \tag{3.205}$$

where Θ_{bt} is the instantaneous bulk temperature defined by

$$\Theta_{bt} = \frac{\int_0^1 \Theta_t u_t^* dr^*}{\int_0^1 u_t^* dr^*} \tag{3.206}$$

Substituting Eq. (3.203) into Eq. (3.205) and considering the boundary condition ($\Theta_w = 11/24$), the transient Nusselt number can be expressed as

$$Nu_t = 2 \left[\frac{11}{24} - \frac{\int_0^1 64\zeta \sum_{n=1}^{\infty} \left(\frac{s_n\left(E_{2n}Pr\omega^* - s_n^2 E_{In}\right)\cos\left(\omega^* t^*\right) + \left(s_n^2 E_{2n} - E_{In}Pr\omega^*\right)\sin\left(\omega^* t^*\right)}{Pr^2\omega^{*2} + s_n^4} \right) \frac{J_0(s_n r^*)}{J_1(s_n)} 16\zeta \sum_{n=1}^{\infty} \left(\frac{s^2\cos\left(\omega^* t^*\right) + \omega^*\sin\left(\omega^* t^*\right)}{sJ_1[s]\left(\omega^{*2} + s^4\right)} J_0(sr^*) \right) dr^*}{\int_0^1 16\zeta \sum_{n=1}^{\infty} \left(\frac{s^2\cos\left(\omega^* t^*\right) + \omega^*\sin\left(\omega^* t^*\right)}{sJ_1[s]\left(\omega^{*2} + s^4\right)} J_0(sr^*) \right) dr^*} \right]^{-1} \tag{3.207}$$

Using Eq. (3.207), the transient Nusselt numbers can be calculated including the effects of oscillating frequency, oscillating amplitude, and Prandtl number. Results show that for an oscillating flow consisting of both constant and oscillating components, when the constant component or oscillating component is dominant, the average Nusselt number is similar to a steady state constant fully developed laminar flow as shown in Figs. 3.16 and 3.17. When both constant and oscillating components are dominated, the oscillating flow can result in significant heat transfer enhancements as shown in Fig. 3.18. But the Prandtl number significantly affects the Nusselt number. And if the velocity profile of the constant component has a parabolic shape, there exists an optimum Prandtl number for the maximum Nusselt number as shown in Fig. 3.19.

3.9.2 Pulsating Pipe Flow at Triangular Pressure

Consider an oscillating flow driven by a triangular pressure waveform (Yin and Ma 2014) in a capillary round tube with a radius of r_0, as shown in Fig. 3.5. Because the Reynolds number is very small, it is reasonably assumed that the flow is a laminar

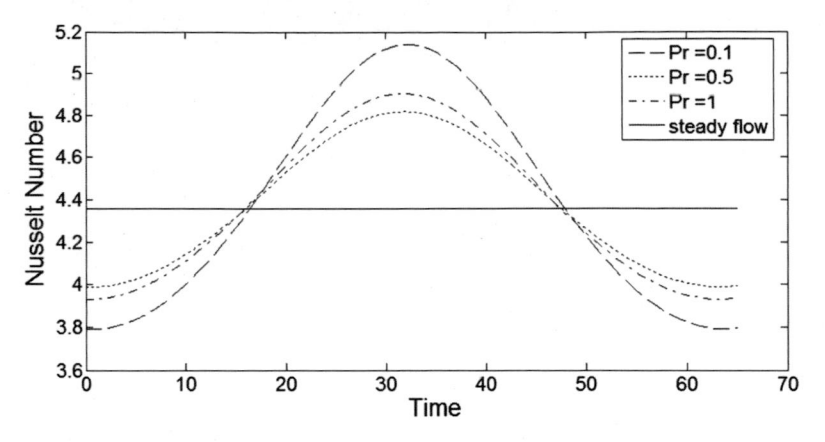

Fig. 3.16 Transient Nusselt numbers for different Prandtl numbers Pr ($\omega^* = 0.1$, $\zeta = 0.01$) (Yin and Ma 2013)

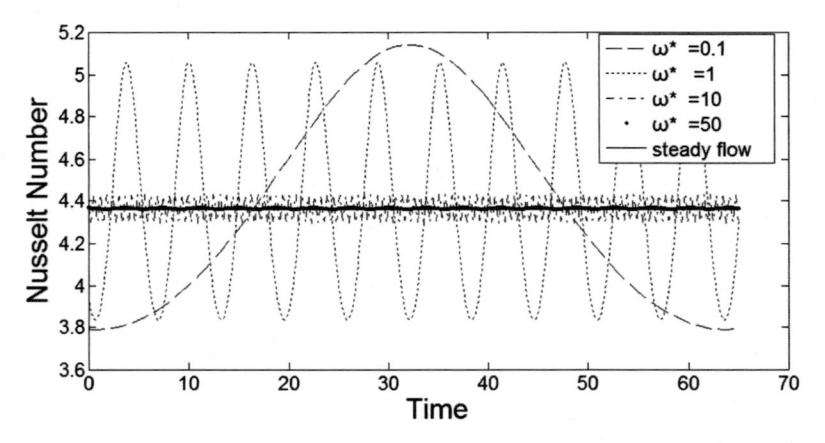

Fig. 3.17 Transient Nusselt numbers for different dimensionless frequencies ω^* ($Pr = 0.1$, $\zeta = 0.01$) (Yin and Ma 2013)

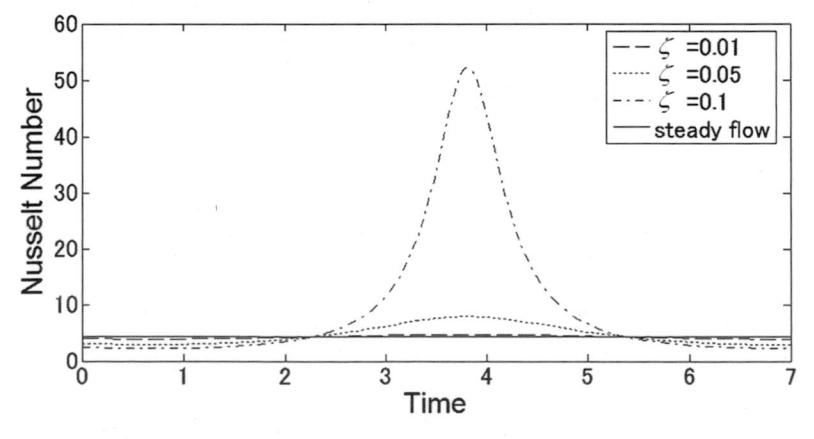

Fig. 3.18 The effect of the oscillating pressure amplitude, ζ, on transient Nusselt numbers ($\omega^* = 1$) (Yin and Ma 2013)

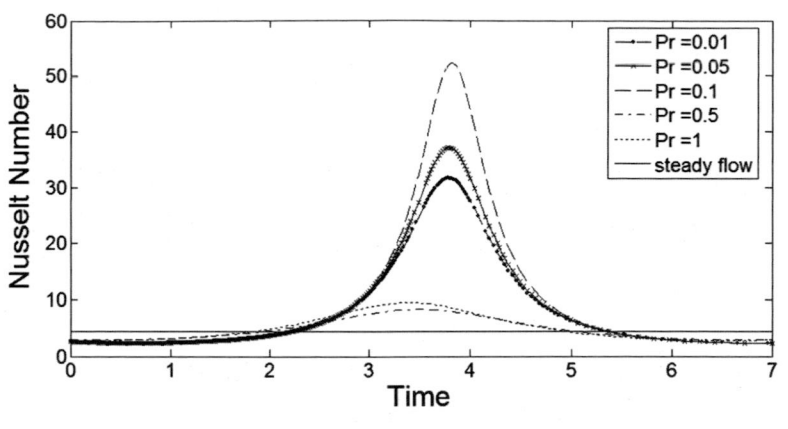

Fig. 3.19 Transient Nusselt numbers for different Prandtl numbers, $Pr = 0.01\text{--}1$ ($\omega^* = 1$, $\zeta = 0.1$) (Yin and Ma 2013)

fully developed flow. In addition, the surface tension effect is not considered. A uniform heat flux is added on the boundary. The triangular pressure waveform for the oscillating flow shown in Fig. 3.5 can be expressed as

$$\frac{\partial p}{\partial x} = \left(\frac{\partial p}{\partial x}\right)_s \left(1 + \zeta_0 \frac{4 \cdot \frac{1}{2f}}{\pi^2} \sum_{n=1}^{\infty} \left(\frac{(-1)^{n-1}}{(2n-1)^2} \sin\left(2(2n-1)f\pi t\right)\right)\right) \tag{3.208}$$

where

$$\zeta_0 = \begin{cases} -\dfrac{1}{2f} - t, & -\dfrac{1}{2f} \le t \le -\dfrac{1}{4f} \\[2mm] t, & -\dfrac{1}{4f} \le t \le \dfrac{1}{4f} \\[2mm] \dfrac{1}{2f} - t, & \dfrac{1}{4f} \le t \le \dfrac{1}{2f} \end{cases} \tag{3.209}$$

Considering $\omega = 2f\pi$, Eq. (3.208) can be rewritten as

$$\frac{\partial p}{\partial x} = \left(\frac{\partial p}{\partial x}\right)_s \left(1 + \zeta_0 \frac{4}{\omega\pi} \sum_{n=1}^{\infty} \left(\frac{(-1)^{n-1}}{(2n-1)^2} \sin\left((2n-1)\omega t\right)\right)\right) \tag{3.210}$$

Considering the driving force shown in Eq. (3.210), the governing equations of momentum and energy equations can be expressed as

$$\frac{\partial u}{\partial t} = -\frac{1}{\rho}\left(\frac{\partial p}{\partial x}\right)_s \left(1 + \zeta_0 \frac{4}{\omega\pi} \sum_{n=1}^{\infty}\left(\frac{(-1)^{n-1}}{(2n-1)^2}\sin\left((2n-1)\omega t\right)\right)\right)$$

$$+ v\left(\frac{\partial^2 u}{\partial r^2} + \frac{\partial u}{r\partial r}\right) \tag{3.211}$$

$$\frac{\partial T}{\partial t} + u\frac{\partial T}{\partial x} = \alpha\frac{1}{r}\frac{\partial}{\partial r}\left(r\frac{\partial T}{\partial r}\right) \tag{3.212}$$

The boundary conditions corresponding to governing Eqs. (3.211) and (3.212) can be found as

$$\frac{\partial u}{\partial r} = 0 \quad\text{and}\quad \frac{\partial T}{\partial r} = 0 \quad\text{at}\quad r = 0 \tag{3.213}$$

$$u = 0 \quad\text{and}\quad k\frac{\partial T}{\partial r} = q_w \quad\text{at}\quad r = r_0 \tag{3.214}$$

respectively. Considering the dimensionless variables of $r^* = \frac{r}{r_0}$, $t^* = \frac{vt}{r_0^2}$, $u^* = \frac{u}{u_m}$, $\Theta = \frac{T-T_0}{q_w r_0/k}$, $X = \frac{4x}{Re_m Pr r_0}$, $\omega^* = \frac{\omega r_0^2}{v}$, and $Re_m = \frac{2u_m r_0}{v}$, Eqs. (3.211) and (3.212) can be rewritten as

$$\frac{\partial u^*}{\partial t^*} = 8\left(1 + \frac{\zeta_0 v}{r_0^2}\frac{4}{\omega^*\pi}\sum_{n=1}^{\infty}\left(\frac{(-1)^{n-1}}{(2n-1)^2}\sin\left((2n-1)\omega^* t^*\right)\right)\right)$$

$$+ \left(\frac{\partial^2 u^*}{\partial r^{*2}} + \frac{\partial u^*}{r^*\partial r^*}\right) \tag{3.215}$$

$$Pr\frac{\partial\Theta}{\partial t^*} + 2u^*\frac{\partial\Theta}{\partial X} = \frac{\partial}{r^*\partial r^*}\left(r^*\frac{\partial\Theta}{\partial r^*}\right) \tag{3.216}$$

respectively. The corresponding boundary conditions shown in Eqs. (3.213) and (3.214) become

$$\frac{\partial u^*}{\partial r^*} = 0 \quad\text{and}\quad \frac{\partial\Theta}{\partial r^*} = 0 \quad\text{at}\quad r^* = 0 \tag{3.217}$$

$$u^* = 0 \quad\text{and}\quad \frac{\partial\Theta}{\partial r^*} = 1 \quad\text{at}\quad r^* = 1 \tag{3.218}$$

The dimensionless velocity u^* can be divided into two components: steady flow velocity and imposed unsteady velocity as shown in Eq. (3.26), and substituting it into Eq. (3.215) produces

$$\frac{\partial u_s^*}{\partial t^*} + \frac{\partial u_t^*}{\partial t^*} = 8\left(1 + \frac{\zeta_0 \nu}{r_0^2}\frac{4}{\omega^* \pi}\sum_{n=1}^{\infty}\left(\frac{(-1)^{n-1}}{(2n-1)^2}\sin\left((2n-1)\omega^* t^*\right)\right)\right)$$
$$+ \left(\frac{\partial^2 u_s^*}{\partial r^{*2}} + \frac{\partial^2 u_t^*}{\partial r^{*2}} + \frac{\partial u_s^*}{r^*\partial r^*} + \frac{\partial u_t^*}{r^*\partial r^*}\right) \tag{3.219}$$

Separating Eq. (3.219) yields

$$\frac{\partial u_s^*}{\partial t^*} = 8 + \left(\frac{\partial^2 u_s^*}{\partial r^{*2}} + \frac{\partial u_s^*}{r^*\partial r^*}\right) \tag{3.220}$$

$$\frac{\partial u_t^*}{\partial t^*} = \frac{8\zeta_0 \nu}{r_0^2}\cdot\frac{4}{\omega^* \pi}\sum_{n=1}^{\infty}\left(\frac{(-1)^{n-1}}{(2n-1)^2}\sin\left((2n-1)\omega^* t^*\right)\right) + \left(\frac{\partial^2 u_t^*}{\partial r^{*2}} + \frac{\partial u_t^*}{r^*\partial r^*}\right) \tag{3.221}$$

respectively. Considering $\frac{\partial u_s^*}{\partial t^*} = 0$ and rearranging, Eqs. (3.220) and (3.221) become

$$\frac{\partial^2 u_s^*}{\partial r^{*2}} + \frac{\partial u_s^*}{r^*\partial r^*} = -8 \tag{3.222}$$

$$\frac{\partial^2 u_t^*}{\partial r^{*2}} + \frac{\partial u_t^*}{r^*\partial r^*} - \frac{\partial u_t^*}{\partial t^*} = -\frac{8\zeta_0 \nu}{r_0^2}\cdot\frac{4}{\omega^* \pi}\sum_{n=1}^{\infty}\left(\frac{(-1)^{n-1}}{(2n-1)^2}\sin\left((2n-1)\omega^* t^*\right)\right) \tag{3.223}$$

respectively. Compared with the well-known Poiseuille solution, the solution of Eq. (3.222) is obtained as shown in Eq. (3.33). Considering $u_t^* = \frac{8\zeta_0 \nu}{r_0^2}\cdot\frac{4}{\pi}\cdot u_\Delta^*$ as the solution of Eq. (3.223) and substituting it into Eq. (3.223) yields

$$\frac{\partial^2 u_\Delta^*}{\partial r^{*2}} + \frac{\partial u_\Delta^*}{r^*\partial r^*} - \frac{\partial u_\Delta^*}{\partial t^*} = -\frac{1}{\omega^*}\sum_{n=1}^{\infty}\left(\frac{(-1)^{n-1}}{(2n-1)^2}\sin\left((2n-1)\omega^* t^*\right)\right) \tag{3.224}$$

With the first class Bessel functions and J_0 Hankel transform, Eq. (3.224) can be expressed as

$$J_0\left[\frac{\partial^2 u_\Delta^*}{\partial r^{*2}} + \frac{\partial u_\Delta^*}{r^*\partial r^*}\right] - J_0\left[\frac{\partial u_\Delta^*}{\partial t^*}\right] = J_0\left[-\frac{1}{\omega^*}\sum_{n=1}^{\infty}\left(\frac{(-1)^{n-1}}{(2n-1)^2}\sin\left((2n-1)\omega^* t^*\right)\right)\right] \tag{3.225}$$

Considering the properties of Bessel transform equation (3.36), Eq. (3.225) becomes

$$-s^2 J_0 \left[u_\Delta^* \left(r^*, t^* \right) \right] - \frac{\partial J_0 \left[u_\Delta^* \left(r^*, t^* \right) \right]}{\partial t^*}$$
$$= J_0 \left[-\frac{1}{\omega^*} \sum_{n=1}^\infty \left(\frac{(-1)^{n-1}}{(2n-1)^2} \frac{\sin \left((2n-1)\omega^* t^* \right)}{s} J_1 [s] \right) \right] \qquad (3.226)$$

Considering $J_0 \left[u_\Delta^* \left(r^*, t^* \right) \right] = F \left[s, t^* \right]$, Eq. (3.226) becomes

$$F \left[s, t^* \right] + \frac{1}{s^2} \frac{\partial F \left[s, t^* \right]}{\partial t^*} = \frac{\frac{1}{\omega^*} \sum_{n=1}^\infty \left(\frac{(-1)^{n-1}}{(2n-1)^2} \sin \left((2n-1)\omega^* t^* \right) \right)}{s^3} J_1 [s] \qquad (3.227)$$

If $F \left[s, t^* \right] = \sum_{n=1}^\infty \left(a_n \cos \left((2n-1)\omega^* t^* \right) + b_n \sin \left((2n-1)\omega^* t^* \right) \right)$ and $N = 2n-1$,
Eq. (3.227) can be expressed as

$$\sum_{n=1}^\infty \left(a_n \cos \left(N\omega^* t^* \right) + b_n \sin \left(N\omega^* t^* \right) \right) + \frac{1}{s^2} \frac{\partial \left(\sum_{n=1}^\infty \left(a_n \cos \left(N\omega^* t^* \right) + b_n \sin \left(N\omega^* t^* \right) \right) \right)}{\partial t^*}$$
$$= \frac{\frac{1}{\omega^*} \sum_{n=1}^\infty \left(\frac{(-1)^{n-1}}{N^2} \sin \left(N\omega^* t^* \right) \right)}{s^3} J_1 [s]$$

$$(3.228)$$

Rearranging yields

$$\sum_{n=1}^\infty \left(a_n \cos \left(N\omega^* t^* \right) + b_n \sin \left(N\omega^* t^* \right) + \frac{\omega^*}{s^2} \left(N \left(-a_n \sin \left(N\omega^* t^* \right) + b_n \cos \left(N\omega^* t^* \right) \right) \right) \right)$$
$$= \frac{\sum_{n=1}^\infty \frac{1}{\omega^*} \frac{(-1)^{n-1}}{N^2} \sin \left(N\omega^* t^* \right)}{s^3} J_1 [s]$$

$$(3.229)$$

or

$$\left(a_n + \frac{\omega^*}{s^2} b_n N \right) \cos \left(N\omega^* t^* \right) + \left(b_n - \frac{\omega^*}{s^2} a_n N - \frac{J_1 [s]}{s^3 \omega^*} \frac{(-1)^{n-1}}{N^2} \right) \sin \left(N\omega^* t^* \right) = 0 \quad (3.230)$$

This means $a_n + \frac{\omega^*}{s^2} b_n N = 0$ and $b_n - \frac{\omega^*}{s^2} a_n N - \frac{J_1 [s]}{s^3 \omega^*} \frac{(-1)^{n-1}}{N^2} = 0$, and the expressions
of a_n and b_n can be obtained as

$$a_n = -\frac{(-1)^{n-1}J_1[s]}{sN(s^4 + \omega^{*2}N^2)} \tag{3.231}$$

$$b_n = \frac{(-1)^{n-1}sJ_1[s]}{\omega^* N^2 (s^4 + \omega^{*2}N^2)} \tag{3.232}$$

respectively. Considering Eqs. (3.231) and (3.232), the expression of $F[s, t^*]$ can be written as

$$F[s, t^*] = \sum_{n=1}^{\infty} \left(\frac{(-1)^{n-1}J_1[s]\left(-N\omega^* \cos\left(N\omega^* t^*\right) + s^2 \sin\left(N\omega^* t^*\right)\right)}{sN(s^4 + \omega^{*2}N^2)} \right) \tag{3.233}$$

The velocity distribution can be expressed as

$$u_t^* = \frac{64\zeta_0 \nu}{r_0^2 \pi} \sum_{m=1}^{\infty} \left(\sum_{n=1}^{\infty} \left(\frac{(-1)^{n-1}\left(-N\omega^* \cos\left(N\omega^* t^*\right) + s_m^2 \sin\left(N\omega^* t^*\right)\right)}{N(s_m^4 + \omega^{*2}N^2)} \right) \frac{J_0\left(s_m r^*\right)}{s_m J_1[s_m]} \right) \tag{3.234}$$

where J_0 and J_1 are the Bessel function of the first kind of order 0 and 1, respectively. s is the eigenvalue of the Bessel function of the first kind of order 0.

Following the same procedure for obtaining the velocity profile, the temperature profile can be obtained similarly. The dimensionless temperature consists of a steady component and an instantaneous component as shown in Eq. (3.169). Substituting Eqs. (3.26) and (3.169) into Eq. (3.216) yields

$$Pr\frac{\partial\left(\Theta_s\left(r^*, x^*\right) + \Theta_t\left(r^*, t^*\right)\right)}{\partial t^*} + 2\left(u_s^*\left(r^*\right) + u_t^*\left(r^*, t^*\right)\right)\frac{\partial\left(\Theta_s\left(r^*, x^*\right) + \Theta_t\left(r^*, t^*\right)\right)}{\partial x^*}$$

$$= \frac{\partial}{\partial r^* \partial r^*}\left(r^*\frac{\partial\left(\Theta_s\left(r^*, x^*\right) + \Theta_t\left(r^*, t^*\right)\right)}{\partial r^*}\right) \tag{3.235}$$

Separating Eq. (3.235) into two equations yields

$$2u_s^*\left(r^*\right)\frac{\partial\Theta_s\left(r^*, x^*\right)}{\partial x^*} = \frac{\partial}{r^*\partial r^*}\left(r^*\frac{\partial\Theta_s\left(r^*, x^*\right)}{\partial r^*}\right) \tag{3.236}$$

$$Pr\frac{\partial\Theta_t\left(r^*, t^*\right)}{\partial t^*} + 2u_t^*\left(r^*, t^*\right)\frac{\partial\Theta_s\left(r^*, x^*\right)}{\partial x^*} = \frac{\partial}{r^*\partial r^*}\left(r^*\frac{\partial\Theta_t\left(r^*, t^*\right)}{\partial r^*}\right) \tag{3.237}$$

respectively. If $\Theta_s = f(x^*) + g(r^*)$, Eq. (3.236) can be expressed as

$$\frac{\partial\left(f\left(x^{*}\right)+g\left(r^{*}\right)\right)}{\partial x^{*}}=\frac{\partial}{2u_{s}^{*}\left(r^{*}\right)\cdot r^{*}\partial r^{*}}\left(r^{*}\frac{\partial\left(f\left(x^{*}\right)+g\left(r^{*}\right)\right)}{\partial r^{*}}\right) \tag{3.238}$$

Separating variables in Eq. (3.238), it can be found that

$$\frac{\partial\left(f\left(x^{*}\right)\right)}{\partial x^{*}}=\frac{\partial}{2u_{s}^{*}\left(r^{*}\right)\cdot r^{*}\partial r^{*}}\left(r^{*}\frac{\partial\left(g\left(r^{*}\right)\right)}{\partial r^{*}}\right)=c \tag{3.239}$$

or

$$\frac{\partial}{2u_{s}^{*}\left(r^{*}\right)\cdot r^{*}\partial r^{*}}\left(r^{*}\frac{\partial\left(g\left(r^{*}\right)\right)}{\partial r^{*}}\right)=c \tag{3.240}$$

$$\frac{\partial\left(f\left(x^{*}\right)\right)}{\partial x^{*}}=c \tag{3.241}$$

Integrating Eq. (3.240) yields

$$g\left(r^{*}\right)=c\cdot\left(r^{*2}-\frac{r^{*4}}{4}\right)+C_{1}\ln r^{*}+C_{2} \tag{3.242}$$

Considering the boundary conditions of Eqs. (3.217) and (3.218), it can be found that $c=1$, $C_{1}=0$, and $C_{2}=0$. Equation (3.242) can be expressed as

$$g\left(r^{*}\right)=r^{*2}-\frac{r^{*4}}{4} \tag{3.243}$$

The solution of Eq. (3.241) can be found as

$$f\left(x^{*}\right)=x^{*}+C \tag{3.244}$$

Considering Eqs. (3.243) and (3.244), the dimensionless steady state temperature distribution, Θ_{s}, can be determined as

$$\Theta_{s}=x^{*}+r^{*2}-\frac{r^{*4}}{4}+C \tag{3.245}$$

Considering the boundary conditions of Eqs. (3.217) and (3.218), it can be found that $C=-\frac{7}{24}$. The dimensionless steady state temperature distribution can be expressed as

$$\Theta_s = x^* + r^{*2} - \frac{r^{*4}}{4} - \frac{7}{24} \tag{3.246}$$

Substituting Eq. (3.246) into Eq. (3.237) and considering J_0 Bessel transform

$$J_0\left[Pr\frac{\partial \Theta_t(r^*,t^*)}{\partial t^*} + 2u_t^*\right] = J_0\left[\frac{\partial}{r^*\partial r^*}\left(r^*\frac{\partial \Theta_t(r^*,t^*)}{\partial r^*}\right)\right] \tag{3.247}$$

it can be found that

$$Pr\frac{\partial F(s,t^*)}{\partial t^*} + 2J_0\left[u_t^*\right] = -s^2 F(s,t^*) \tag{3.248}$$

or

$$-\frac{Pr}{s_k^2}\frac{\partial F(s_k,t^*)}{\partial t^*} - \frac{64\zeta_0\nu}{s_k^3 r_0^2\pi}\sum_{m=1}^{\infty}\left(\begin{array}{c}\left(\sum_{n=1}^{\infty}\left(\dfrac{(-1)^{n-1}\left(-N\omega^*\cos(N\omega^*t^*) + s_m^2\sin(N\omega^*t^*)\right)}{N(s_m^4 + \omega^{*2}N^2)}\right)\right)\\[2mm] \dfrac{s_k}{s_m^2 - s_k^2}\dfrac{J_0(s_m)J_1(s_k r^*)}{s_m J_1(s_m)}\end{array}\right)$$

$$= F(s_n,t^*) \tag{3.249}$$

where $F[s,t^*] = J_0[\Theta_t(r^*,t^*)]$. Considering a solution of

$$F[s,t^*] = \sum_{n=1}^{\infty}(A_n\cos((2n-1)\omega^*t^*) + B_n\sin((2n-1)\omega^*t^*)) \tag{3.250}$$

Equation (3.249) can be expressed as

$$\frac{Pr}{s_k^2}\frac{\partial\left(\sum_{n=1}^{\infty}(A_n\cos(N\omega^*t^*) + B_n\sin(N\omega^*t^*))\right)}{\partial t^*}$$

$$-\frac{128\zeta_0\nu}{s_k^3 r_0^2\pi}\sum_{m=1}^{\infty}\left(\sum_{n=1}^{\infty}\left(\frac{(-1)^{n-1}\left(-N\omega^*\cos(N\omega^*t^*) + s_m^2\sin(N\omega^*t^*)\right)}{N(s_m^4 + \omega^{*2}N^2)}\right)\frac{s_k}{s_m^2 - s_k^2}\frac{J_0(s_m)J_1(s_k r^*)}{s_m J_1(s_m)}\right)$$

$$= \sum_{n=1}^{\infty}(A_n\cos(N\omega^*t^*) + B_n\sin(N\omega^*t^*)) \tag{3.251}$$

Following the same procedure for the velocity distribution as described above, it can be found that

$$\left(\frac{Pr\omega^*N}{s_k^2}A_n - \frac{128\zeta_0\nu}{s_k^3r_0^2\pi}\sum_{m=1}^{\infty}\left(\frac{(-1)^{n-1}s_m^2}{N(s_m^4+\omega^{*2}N^2)\,s_m^2-s_k^2}\frac{s_k}{s_m}\frac{J_0(s_m)J_1(s_kr^*)}{s_mJ_1(s_m)}\right) - B_n\right) = 0$$

$$(3.252)$$

$$\left(-\frac{Pr\omega^*N}{s_k^2}B_n + \frac{128\zeta_0\nu}{s_k^3r_0^2\pi}\sum_{m=1}^{\infty}\left(\frac{(-1)^{n-1}N\omega^*}{(2n-1)(s_m^4+\omega^{*2}N^2)\,s_m^2-s_k^2}\frac{s_k}{s_m}\frac{J_0(s_m)J_1(s_kr^*)}{s_mJ_1(s_m)}\right) - A_n\right) = 0$$

$$(3.253)$$

respectively. Rearranging Eqs. (3.252) and (3.253) produces

$$\frac{Pr\omega^*N}{s_k^2}A_n - \frac{128\zeta_0\nu}{s_k^3r_0^2\pi}\sum_{m=1}^{\infty}\left(\frac{(-1)^{n-1}s_m^2}{N(s_m^4+\omega^{*2}N^2)\,s_m^2-s_k^2}\frac{s_k}{s_m}\frac{J_0(s_m)J_1(s_kr^*)}{s_mJ_1(s_m)}\right) - B_n = 0 \quad (3.254)$$

$$\frac{Pr\omega^*N}{s_k^2}B_n - \frac{128\zeta_0\nu}{s_k^3r_0^2\pi}\sum_{m=1}^{\infty}\left(\frac{(-1)^{n-1}N\omega^*}{(2n-1)(s_m^4+\omega^{*2}N^2)\,s_m^2-s_k^2}\frac{s_k}{s_m}\frac{J_0(s_m)J_1(s_kr^*)}{s_mJ_1(s_m)}\right) + A_n = 0$$

$$(3.255)$$

Solving Eqs. (3.254) and (3.255) it can be found that

$$A_n = \frac{128\zeta_0\nu}{r_0^2\pi}\cdot\frac{E_{1n}Pr\omega^*N + E_{2n}s_k^2}{Pr^2\omega^{*2}N^2}J_1(s_k)$$

$$(3.256)$$

$$B_n = \frac{128\zeta_0\nu}{r_0^2\pi}\cdot\frac{E_{2n}}{Pr\omega^*N}J_1(s_k)$$

$$(3.257)$$

respectively, where

$$E_{1n} = \sum_{m=1}^{\infty}\left(\frac{(-1)^{n-1}s_m^2}{N(s_m^4+\omega^{*2}N^2)(s_m^2-s_k^2)}\right)$$

$$(3.258)$$

$$E_{2n} = \sum_{m=1}^{\infty}\left(\frac{(-1)^{n-1}\omega^*}{(s_m^4+\omega^{*2}N^2)(s_m^2-s_k^2)}\right)$$

$$(3.259)$$

The solution of $F[s_k, t^*]$ is expressed as

$$F[s_k, t^*] = \frac{128\zeta_0\nu}{r_0^2\pi}J_1(s_k)\sum_{n=1}^{\infty}\left(\frac{(E_{1n}Pr\omega^*N + E_{2n}s_k^2)\cos(N\omega^*t^*) + E_{2n}Pr\omega^*N\sin(N\omega^*t^*)}{Pr^2\omega^{*2}N^2}\right)$$

$$(3.260)$$

and the transient temperature distribution

$$\Theta_t = \frac{128\zeta_0\nu}{r_0^2\pi} \sum_{k=1}^{\infty} \left(\sum_{n=1}^{\infty} \left(\frac{\left(E_{In}Pr\omega^*N + E_{2n}s_k^2\right)\cos\left(N\omega^*t^*\right) + E_{2n}Pr\omega^*N\sin\left(N\omega^*t^*\right)}{Pr^2\omega^{*2}N^2} \right) \right) \frac{J_0\left(s_k r^*\right)}{J_1(s_k)}$$

(3.261)

where s_m and s_k are the eigenvalues of the Bessel function of the first kind of order 0 and 1.

Consider the definition of Nusselt number of

$$Nu_t = \frac{2q_w r_0}{(T_w - T_b)\lambda} = \frac{2}{\Theta_w - \Theta_{bt}}$$

(3.262)

where Θ_{bt} is the transient bulk temperature which can be found by

$$\Theta_{bt} = \frac{\int_0^1 \Theta_t u_t^* dr^*}{\int_0^1 u_t^* dr^*}$$

(3.263)

Substituting Eq. (3.263) into Eq. (3.262) and considering $\Theta_w = 11/24$ yields

$$Nu_t = \frac{2}{\dfrac{11}{24} - \dfrac{\displaystyle\int_0^1 \Theta_t u_t^* dr^*}{\displaystyle\int_0^1 u_t^* dr^*}}$$

(3.264)

From Eq. (3.264), it can be found that when the oscillating motion becomes a steady state unidirectional flow, i.e., $\Theta_{bt} = \dfrac{\displaystyle\int_0^1 \Theta_t u_t^* dr^*}{\displaystyle\int_0^1 u_t^* dr^*} = 0$, the Nusselt number calculated by Eq. (3.264) is 4.36 which is the same as the Nusselt number of a steady state unidirectional fully developed laminar flow. Results show that the peak Nusselt number for a triangular pressure waveform is very different from a sinusoidal pressure waveform as shown in Figs. 3.20 and 3.21. For an oscillating flow driven by a triangular waveform, when the oscillating frequency decreases, the oscillating motion can enhance heat transfer. However, when the oscillating frequency is high enough, the pressure waveform effect on heat transfer enhancement disappears.

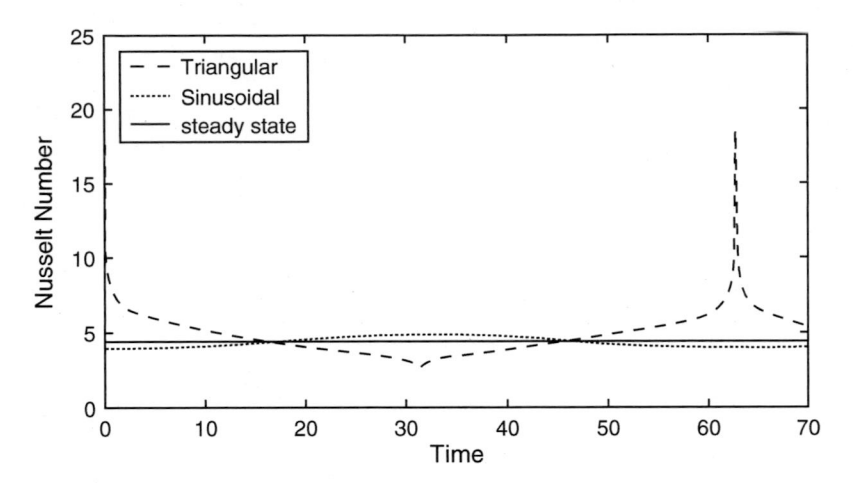

Fig. 3.20 Waveform effect on Nusselt numbers at $\zeta_0 = 0.01$, $\omega^* = 0.1$, and $Pr = 0.1$ (Yin and Ma 2014)

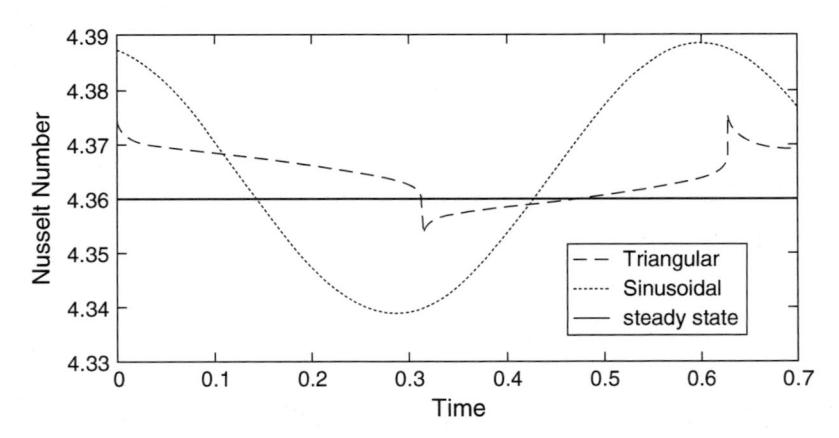

Fig. 3.21 Waveform effect on Nusselt numbers at $\zeta_0 = 0.01$, $\omega^* = 10.0$, and $Pr = 0.1$ (Yin and Ma 2014)

3.10 Heat Transfer in Turbulent Pulsating Flow

Fluid flow and heat transfer of an oscillating flow in a pipe is very complex, in particular, when the oscillating flow becomes turbulent. Several investigators (Wang and Zhang 2005) have numerically investigated fluid flow and heat transfer occurring in an oscillating turbulent pipe flow. But most of investigations (Zhao and Cheng 1998a, b; Baird et al. 1966; Liao and Wang 1985; Mamayev et al. 1976; Gbadebo et al. 1999; Habib et al. 1999, 2004; Havemann and Rao 1954) have been focused on the experimental investigations. Martinelli et al. (1943) experimentally investigated the heat transfer characteristics of pulsating flow in a vertical tube and

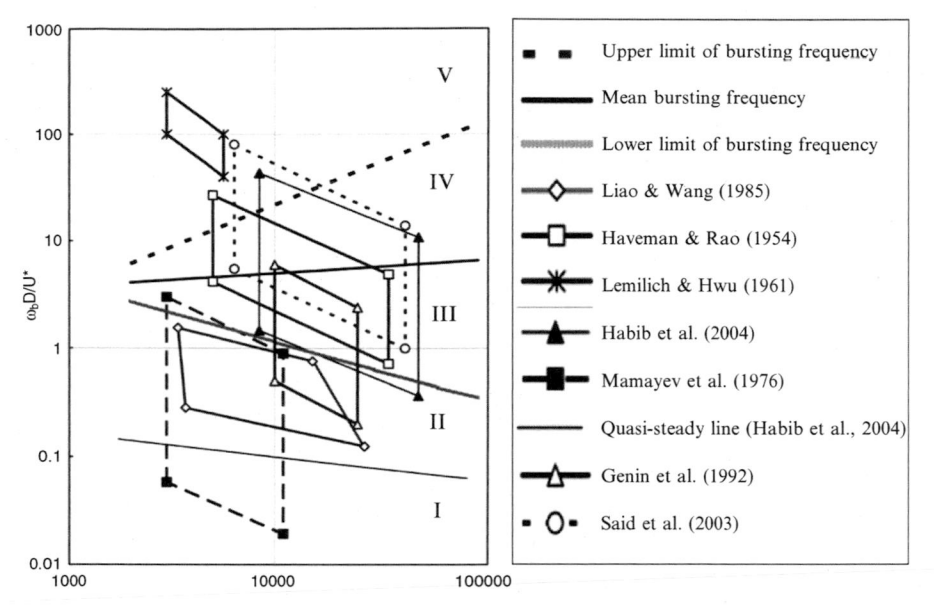

Fig. 3.22 Classification of data of heat transfer with turbulent oscillating flow (Elshafei et al. 2008)

found that the heat transfer rate decreases as compared to that of the unidirectional steady flow for Reynolds numbers higher than 4,500. West and Taylor (1952), however, found an increase of 60–70 % in the heat transfer rate. As presented above, fluid flow and heat transfer of an oscillating even laminar flow depends on many factors including frequency, amplitude, diameter, length, working fluid, and velocity distribution. Due to the complexity of the turbulent fluid flow, studies on heat transfer in oscillating turbulent flow are far from matured. Recently, Habib et al. (2004) and Elshafei et al. (2008) used the dimensionless frequency and Reynolds number to group investigations into five groups, i.e., Regions I, II, III, IV, and V as shown in Fig. 3.22. Regions I and II represent the region which can be modeled by quasi-steady turbulent model in which heat transfer cannot be enhanced (Baird et al. 1966; Liao and Wang 1985). When the dimensionless frequency and Reynolds number increase, there is a bursting phenomenon that occurs in the steady turbulent flow in the form of periodic turbulent bursts, which might be similar to Richardson's annular effect in a laminar oscillating flow. These bursts occur in the boundary layer near the wall, which helps to enhance heat transfer. Regions III and IV are categorized as preferred regions in which the imposed pulsation might make the burst phenomenon take place leading to heat transfer enhancement of turbulent oscillating flow (Liao and Wang 1985; Genin et al. 1992; Mamayev et al. 1976). If the frequency is too high, the burst phenomenon might disappear which is categorized as Region V (Habib et al. 2004). The data of Mamayev et al. (1976), however,

refer to Region V where a heat transfer enhancement of 40 % was obtained. It looks Mamayev et al.'s data do not match the discussion. This means that further investigation is needed to improve the classification shown in Fig. 3.22.

References

Baird MHI, Duncan GJ, Smith JI, Taylor J (1966) Heat transfer in pulsed turbulent flow. Chem Eng Sci 21(2):197–199

Bergman TL, Lavine AS, Incropera FP, Dewitt DP (2011) Introduction to heat transfer. Wiley, Hoboken

Crawford ME, Kay WM, Moffat RJ (1980) Full-coverage film cooling—Part II: heat transfer data and numerical simulation. J Eng Power 102(4):1006–1012

Elshafei EAM, Safwat MM, Mansour H, Sakr M (2008) Experimental study of heat transfer in pulsating turbulent flow in a pipe. Int J Heat Fluid Flow 29(4):1029–1038

Gbadebo SA, Said SAM, Habib MA (1999) Average Nusselt number correlation in the thermal entrance region of steady and pulsating turbulent pipe flows. Heat Mass Transf 35:377–381

Genin LG, Koval AP, Manchkha SP, Sviridow VG (1992) Hydrodynamics and heat transfer with pulsating fluid flow in tubes. Therm Eng 39(5):251–255

GoldBerg P (1958) A digital computer solution for laminar flow: heat transfer in circular tubes. M.S. thesis, Department of Mechanical Engineering, Massachusetts Institute of Technology, Cambridge

Graetz L (1883) Uber die Warmeleitungs fahigkeit van Flussigkeiten. Ann Phys 254(1):79–94

Habib MA, Said SAM, Al-Dini SA, Asghar A, Gbadebo SA (1999) Heat transfer characteristics of pulsated turbulent pipe flow. J Heat Mass Transf 34(5):413–421

Habib MA, Attya AM, Said SAM, Eid AI, Aly AZ (2004) Heat transfer characteristics and Nusselt number correlation of turbulent pulsating air flows. J Heat Mass Transf 40:307–318

Havemann HA, Rao NN (1954) Heat transfer in pulsating flow. Nature 7(4418):41

Liao NS, Wang CC (1985) An investigation of the heat transfer in pulsating turbulent pipe flow. Fundamentals of forced and mixed convection. In: The 23rd National heat transfer conference, Denver, 4–7 Aug, pp 53–59

Mamayev V, Nosov VS, Syromyatnikov NI (1976) Investigation of heat transfer in pulsed flow of air in pipes. Heat Transf Res 8(3):111–116

Martinelli RC, Boelter LMK, Weinberg EB, Yakahi S (1943) Heat transfer to a fluid flowing periodically at low frequencies in a vertical tube. Trans ASME 65:789–798

Morini LG (2004) Single-phase convective heat transfer in microchannels: a review of experimental results. Int J Therm Sci 43:631–651

Morini LG (2005) Viscous heating in liquid flows in micro-channels. Int J Heat Mass Transf 48:3637–3647

Richardson EG, Tyler E (1929) The transverse velocity gradient near the mouths of pipes in which an alternating or continuous air flow is established. In: Proceedings of the Physical Society, London, vol 42, pp 1–15

Said SAM, Habib MA, Iqbal MO (2003) Heat transfer to pulsating flow in an abrupt pipe expansion. Int J Numer Methods Heat Fluid Flow 13(3):286–308

Sellars H, Tribus M, Klein J (1956) Heat transfer to laminar flow in a round tube or flat conduit— the Graetz problem extended. Dept. of Aeronautical and Astronautical Engineering, University of Michigan, Ann Arbor

Sexl T (1930) Uber den von entdeckten Annulareeffekt. Z Phys 61:349–362

Shah RK, London AL (1978) Laminar flow forced convection in ducts. Academic, New York

Szymanski G (1932) Quelques solutions exactes des équations d'hydrodynamique du fluide visqueux dans le cas d'un tube cylindrique. J Math Pures Appl 11:67–108

Wang X, Zhang N (2005) Numerical analysis of heat transfer in pulsating turbulent flow in a pipe. Int J Heat Mass Transf 48(19):3957–3970

West FB, Taylor AT (1952) The effect of pulsation on heat transfer in turbulent flow of water inside tubes. Chem Eng Prog 48(1):39–43

White FM (1974) Viscous fluid flow. McGraw-Hill, New York

Womersley JR (1955) Method for the calculation of velocity, rate of flow and viscous drag in arteries when the pressure gradient is known. J Physiol 127:553–563

Yin D, Ma HB (2013) Analytical solution of oscillating flow in a capillary tube. Int J Heat Mass Transf 66:699–705

Yin D, Ma HB (2014) Analytical solution of heat transfer of oscillating flow at a triangular pressure waveform. Int J Heat Mass Transf 70:46–53

Zhao T, Cheng P (1995) A numerical solution of laminar forced convection in a heated pipe subjected to a reciprocating flow. Int J Heat Mass Transf 38:3011–3022

Zhao TS, Cheng P (1996a) The friction coefficient of a fully-developed laminar reciprocating flow in a circular pipe. Int J Heat Fluid Flow 17:167–172

Zhao TS, Cheng P (1996b) Experimental studies of onset turbulence and frictional losses in an oscillatory turbulent pipe flow. Int J Heat Fluid Flow 17:356–362

Zhao TS, Cheng P (1996c) Oscillatory heat transfer in a pipe subjected a laminar reciprocating flow. ASME J Heat Transf 18:592–598

Zhao TS, Cheng P (1998a) Heat transfer in oscillating flows. Annu Rev Heat Transf 9:359–420

Zhao TS, Cheng P (1998b) A numerical study of laminar reciprocating flow in a pipe of finite length. Appl Sci Res 59:11–25

Chapter 4
Oscillating Motion and Heat Transfer Mechanisms of Oscillating Heat Pipes

4.1 Introduction

An oscillating heat pipe (OHP) consists of interconnected capillary channels or tubes filled with a train of liquid plugs and vapor bubbles. An OHP typically has three sections: evaporator, adiabatic section, and condenser. When heat is added onto the evaporator section, liquid becomes vapor resulting in an increase of both vapor volume and pressure. At the same time, when the heat is removed from the condenser section, vapor condenses into liquid resulting in a decrease of vapor volume and pressure. Due to vapor volume contraction/expansion, and pressure difference, oscillating motion of working fluid inside the OHP is generated. The oscillating motion brings the heat from the evaporator through the adiabatic section into the condenser. Because the heat transfer process is mainly achieved by oscillating motion, the heat pipe is named as the OHP. In order to generate the oscillating motion, a train of liquid plugs and vapor bubbles must be formed, which requires that the diameter of the channels or tubes be small enough to allow separation of liquid plugs by vapor bubbles. If the interconnected capillary channel forms a closed loop, as shown in Fig. 4.1a, the heat pipe is called a looped OHP (Akachi 1990). If the interconnected capillary channels or tubes do not form a closed loop, as shown in Fig. 4.1b, the OHP is called an unlooped OHP (Akachi 1990). For a looped OHP, when the system is not balanced or a Tesla-valve is used, pulsating flows occur, consisting of both steady-state unidirectional and transient oscillating components as indicated by Fig. 3.3 of the previous chapter. Unlooped OHPs do not contain steady-state unidirectional flow; instead, their oscillating flow is a type of reciprocating flow as indicated in Sect. 4.2. For a looped OHP, in addition to reciprocating flows, pulsating flows can take place. For this reason, the OHP is sometimes called a pulsating heat pipe (PHP). Considering typical reciprocating flows in unlooped systems, it is better to name it OHP.

For a train of liquid plugs and vapor bubbles as shown in Fig. 4.1, the flow can be divided into n unit cells if there are n vapor bubbles in an OHP, and each unit cell

© Springer Science+Business Media New York 2015
H. Ma, *Oscillating Heat Pipes*, DOI 10.1007/978-1-4939-2504-9_4

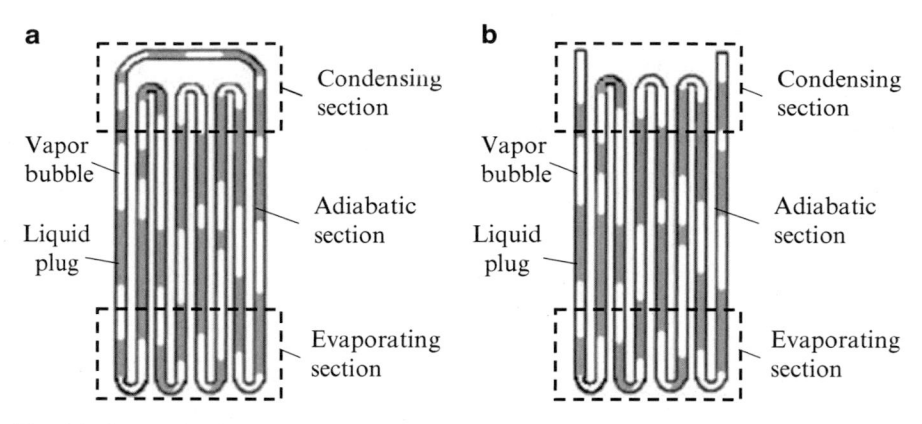

Fig. 4.1 Schematic of an oscillating heat pipe (OHP): (**a**) looped and (**b**) unlooped

contains one vapor bubble and half of a liquid plug from the left side and half of a liquid plug from the right side, as shown in Fig. 4.2. The shear stress acting on the solid wall by the liquid plug is much higher than the shear stress induced by the vapor bubble. Due to the surface tension and small meniscus radius of the liquid–vapor interface, a pressure jump takes place across the liquid–vapor interface between the liquid plug and vapor bubble. This pressure jump serves to control the liquid–vapor interface and separate fluid into a train of liquid plugs and vapor bubbles as shown Figs. 4.1 and 4.2. The pressure distribution of the working fluid over each unit cell alternates forming a somewhat jagged or sawtooth pattern, as shown in Fig. 4.2. This triangular or sawtooth alternating pressure distribution from the evaporating section to the condensing section produces the driving force of the system. When pressure increases or decreases, vapor bubbles can be compressed or expanded, respectively. Vapor bubbles act as springs in the system. From the mechanical vibration point of view, an OHP is a typical mechanical vibration system. This irregular sawtooth-like pattern of alternating pressure distribution along with the vapor spring constant constitutes the basis of the oscillating motion for a train of liquid plugs and vapor bubbles in an OHP.

The oscillating motion in an OHP depends on the dimensions, working fluids, operating temperature, surface conditions, heat flux and total heat load, orientation, turns, and most importantly the filling ratio, V_l/V_t, where V_l is the liquid volume occupied by the liquid in the system and V_t is the total volume. Utilizing phase change heat transfer and oscillating convection, the heat is transferred from the evaporating section to the condensing section. Compared with a conventional heat pipe, OHP has the following unique features: (1) an OHP is an "active" cooling device that converts heat from the heating area into the kinetic energy of liquid plugs to initiate and sustain the oscillating motion; (2) the liquid flow does not interfere with the vapor flow because both phases flow in the same direction; (3) the thermally driven oscillating flow inside the capillary tube effectively produces some free surfaces that significantly enhance evaporating and condensing heat transfer; (4) the oscillating motion in the capillary tube significantly improves the

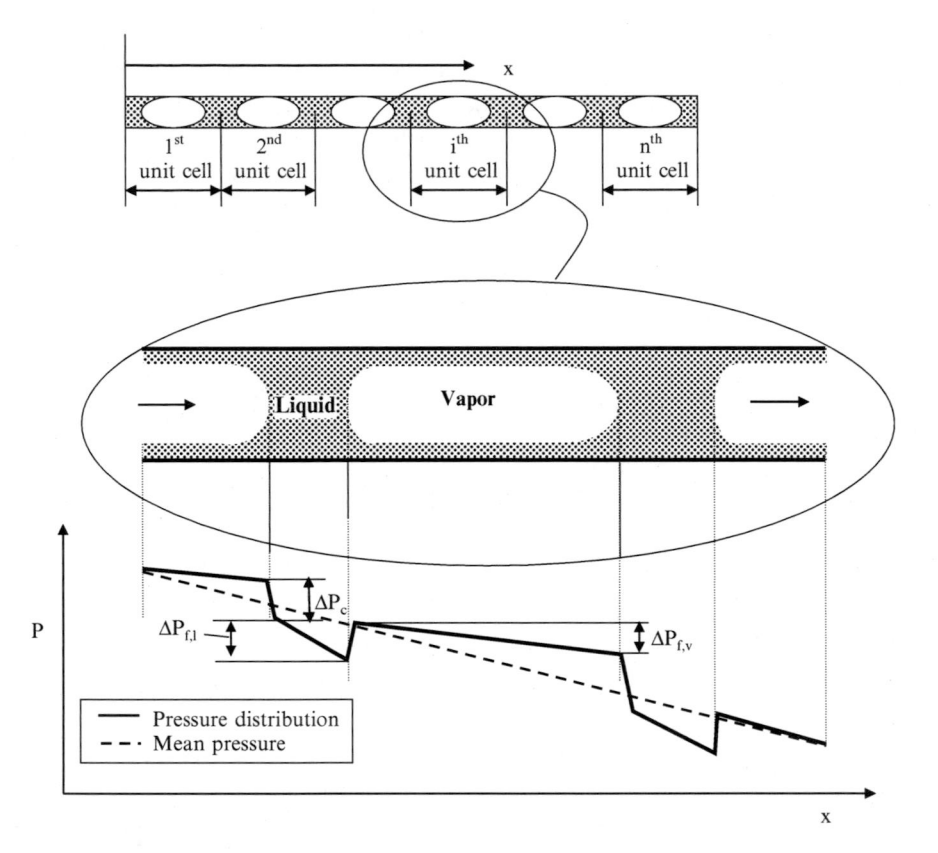

Fig. 4.2 Schematic of pressure distributions in an OHP

forced convection in addition to the phase change heat transfer; and (5) as the input power increases, the heat transport capability of an OHP dramatically increases. This chapter addresses the oscillating and heat transfer mechanisms of a spring-mass system in an OHP.

4.2   Gas Spring Constant

Consider an OHP consisting of a train of liquid plugs and vapor bubbles in a capillary tube with three sections: an evaporator, an adiabatic section, and a condenser. The evaporator section has a temperature higher than the condenser section. When the working fluid flows into the evaporator section, the heat is transferred through the wall and reaches the working fluid. The liquid in the evaporator is vaporized producing vapor volume expansion. At the same time, the heat is removed from the working fluid in the condenser section producing vapor volume contraction. The expansion and contraction of vapor volume generate the

oscillating motion in the OHP. The vapor volume variation acts as a spring in the system, which is the primary start-up factor or reason behind the oscillating motion in an OHP. For any given OHP, the filling ratio is given. In other words, the ratio of the total liquid volume to the total vapor volume is almost constant for an operational OHP. When heat is added to the evaporator section, vapor is generated resulting in an increase of vapor pressure. The vapor pressure increase can be expressed as

$$dp_v = \left(\frac{dp_v}{d\rho_v}\right) d\rho_v \tag{4.1}$$

Based on the mass conservation, i.e., the total vapor mass in the system is a constant, the total vapor mass can be found as

$$m_v = V_v \rho_v = \text{constant} \tag{4.2}$$

Take derivatives on both sides, i.e.,

$$\rho_v dV_v + V_v d\rho_v = 0 \tag{4.3}$$

Rearranging Eq. (4.3) yields

$$\frac{d\rho_v}{\rho_v} = -\frac{dV_v}{V_v} = -\frac{A\,dx}{V_v} \tag{4.4}$$

where A is the cross-sectional area of the working fluid flowing through the tube. The pressure difference due to the volume variation can be found as

$$dp_v = -\rho_v \left(\frac{dp_v}{d\rho_v}\right)\frac{A}{V_v}dx = -\kappa\frac{dx}{A} = -B\frac{A\,\Delta x}{V_v} \tag{4.5}$$

where the gas spring constant, κ, and the bulk modulus, B, of the vapor bubble can be expressed as

$$\kappa = \rho_v \left(\frac{dp_v}{d\rho_v}\right)\frac{A^2}{V_v} \tag{4.6}$$

and

$$B = \rho_v \left(\frac{dp_v}{d\rho_v}\right) \tag{4.7}$$

respectively. If a vapor bubble experiencing an expansion or contraction is an isothermal process, the process can be expressed as

$$\frac{p_v}{\rho_v} = \text{constant} \tag{4.8}$$

Substituting Eq. (4.8) into Eq. (4.7), the bulk modulus, B, can be written as

$$B = B_T \equiv \rho_v \left(\frac{\partial p_v}{\partial \rho_v} \right)_T = p_v \tag{4.9}$$

where B_T is called the isothermal bulk modulus. Considering Eq. (4.6), the gas spring constant for the isothermal process of the vapor bubble can be determined by

$$\kappa = \kappa_T = B_T \frac{A^2}{V_v} = \frac{p_v A^2}{V_v} \tag{4.10}$$

Another typical case is the isotropic condition: In this case, when a vapor bubble experiences an expansion or contraction, no heat is transferred between the bubble and wall and no other losses exist; this process can be described as

$$\frac{p_v}{\rho_v^k} = \text{constant} \tag{4.11}$$

where $k = \frac{c_p}{c_v}$. Considering Eq. (4.11), the bulk modulus, B, can be written as

$$B = B_S \equiv \rho_v \left(\frac{\partial p_v}{\partial \rho_v} \right)_s = k p_v \tag{4.12}$$

where B_s is the isentropic bulk modulus. The effective spring constant, κ_s, of the vapor bubble becomes

$$\kappa = \kappa_s = B_s \frac{A^2}{V_v} = \frac{k p_v A^2}{V_v} \tag{4.13}$$

If the vapor deformation is linear, the restoring force, F, due to the vapor volume expansion or contraction can be found by Hooke's law, i.e.,

$$F = \kappa x \tag{4.14}$$

Clearly, an OHP consisting of a train of liquid plugs and vapor bubbles as shown in Fig. 4.3 is a typical mechanical vibration system as shown in Fig. 4.4.

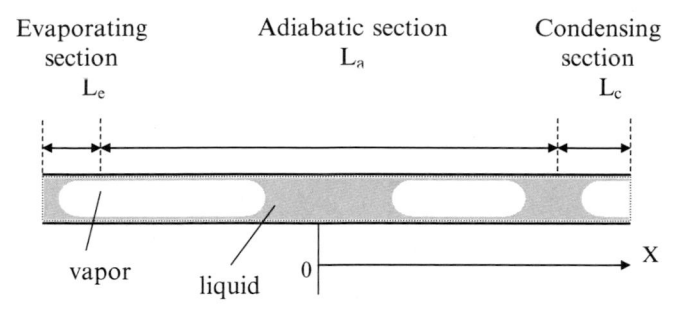

Fig. 4.3 Schematic of a train of liquid plugs and vapor bubbles

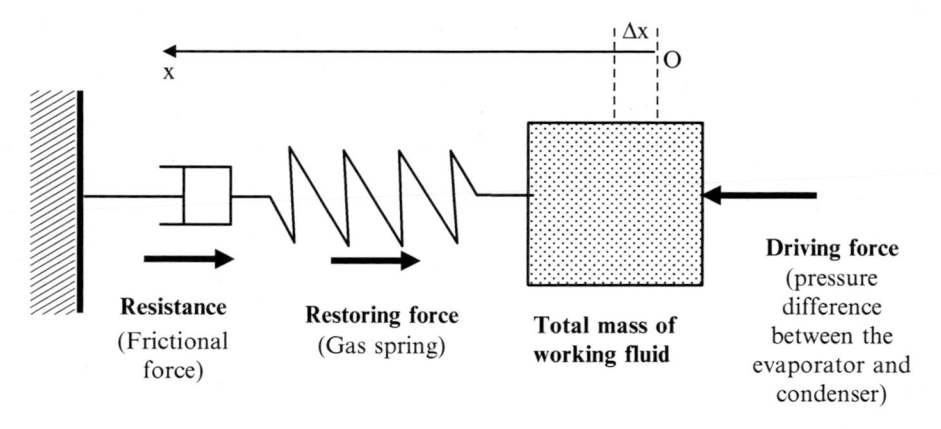

Fig. 4.4 Gas spring model of an OHP

4.3   Maximum Radius of Microchannels in an OHP

The thermally excited oscillating motion of an working fluid in an OHP is due to the spring constant of vapor bubbles in the system. The vapor bubbles in the microchannel of an OHP must be separated by liquid plugs to form the spring-mass system. In other words, the working fluid in the system must exist in a train of liquid plugs and vapor bubbles as shown in Fig. 4.5. The interface formed between liquid phase and vapor phase plays a key role in the separation process. The formation of the liquid–vapor interface depends on the surface tension and channel diameter. When the channel diameter becomes smaller, the surface tension will dominate the liquid–vapor interface. In a gravitational environment, the liquid–vapor interface is characterized by the Bond number, i.e.,

$$Bo = \frac{r_h^2 g (\rho_l - \rho_v)}{\sigma} \tag{4.15}$$

Fig. 4.5 Schematic of an
OHP filling with a train of
liquid plugs and vapor
bubbles

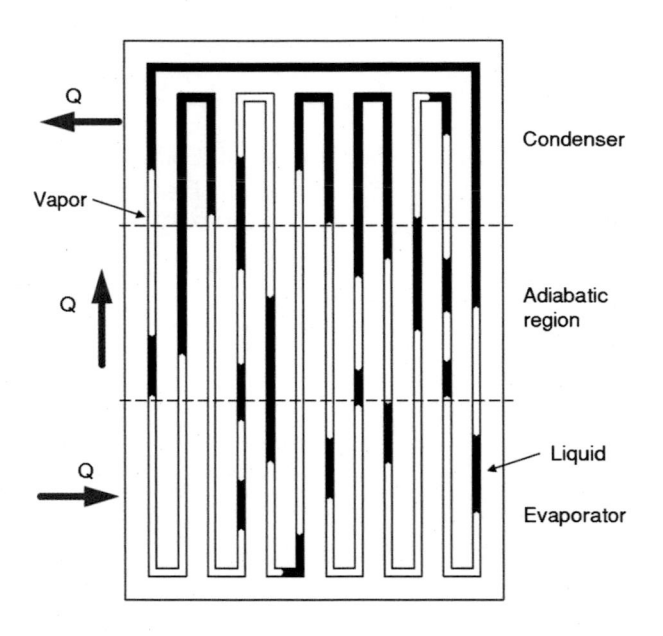

where Bo is the bond number, g is the acceleration, $\rho_l - \rho_v$ is the density difference between the two phases, σ is the surface tension, and r_h is the hydraulic radius of the microchannel. The Bond number is the ratio of the surface tension to the body force. A high Bond number, for example, when $Bo \gg 1$, indicates that the system is relatively unaffected by surface tension. A low number in particular when $Bo < 1$ indicates that the surface tension dominates. Intermediate numbers indicate both forces dominate the interface. Rearranging Eq. (4.15), the maximum hydraulic radius for an OHP can be expressed as

$$r_{h,max} \leq \sqrt{\frac{\sigma Bo}{g(\rho_l - \rho_v)}} \tag{4.16}$$

As shown in Eq. (4.16), the maximum hydraulic radius of the microchannel in an OHP depends on the Bond number only if the working fluid is known for a given gravitational environment. Akachi et al. (1996) suggested that for a one-gravity environment, the Bond number should be equal to 1. But other investigators (Taft et al. 2012) revealed that a Bond number of 0.85 should be used to determine the maximum hydraulic radius for an OHP. If a lower bound of the Bond number, i.e., $Bo = 0.85$ is taken, the maximum radius of the microchannel embedded in an OHP can be found as

$$r_{h,max} \leq 0.92 \sqrt{\frac{\sigma}{g(\rho_l - \rho_v)}} \tag{4.17}$$

As shown in Eq. (4.17), the maximum hydraulic radius, $r_{h,max}$, in an OHP depends on the surface tension, acceleration, and density difference between the liquid and the vapor.

Example 4.1 It is assumed that an interconnected microchannel with a square cross section is used in an OHP. Determine the maximum side length for water, acetone, pentane, and FC72 at a saturation temperature of 60 °C, respectively.

Solution At 60 °C, the surface tensions, liquid and vapor densities for water, acetone, pentane, and FC72 can be found as

	Surface tension (N/m)	Liquid density (kg/m^3)	Vapor density (kg/m^3)
Water	$\sigma = 0.0666$	$\rho_l = 983.3$	$\rho_v = 0.13$
Acetone	$\sigma = 0.0186$	$\rho_l = 744.0$	$\rho_v = 2.37$
Pentane	$\sigma = 0.0117$	$\rho_l = 585.0$	$\rho_v = 6.51$
PP9	$\sigma = 0.0152$	$\rho_l = 1,891.0$	$\rho_v = 0.61$

Substituting these properties into Eq. (4.17), it can be found as

Fluid name	Maximum hydraulic diameter D_{max} (mm)	Side length of each square channel (mm)
Water	4.838	4.838
Acetone	2.939	2.939
Pentane	2.642	2.642
PP9	1.661	1.661

Note: $D_{max} = \frac{4A}{P}$ where A is the cross-sectional area and P is the perimeter.

As shown, the maximum hydraulic diameter significantly depends on the working fluid.

The discussion described above does not consider the momentum effect on the liquid–vapor interface. When the liquid plugs and vapor bubbles in the channel are moving, the inertial force will have an additional effect on the liquid–vapor interface which will directly affect the formation of a train of liquid plugs and vapor bubbles in an OHP. Wang et al. (2013) conducted an experimental investigation of a single water plug moving in a capillary tube to determine the velocity effect on the plug length and vapor penetration through liquid plugs. Using the microscale particle image velocimetry (μPIV) system, the momentum effect on the liquid plug length with an original length of 1.5 mm was measured. The motion of the liquid plug in the capillary tube with an inner diameter of 1.0 mm was controlled by a computer-controlled system, which could produce a velocity ranging from 15 to 80 mm/s. Experimental results show that velocity directly affects the plug length; hence, when velocity increases, the liquid plug length decreases. When the air velocity increases up to 77.5 mm/s, the plug was penetrated and an annular flow was formed as shown in Fig. 4.6. For an OHP, when the power input increases, the oscillating/pulsating motion increases, which is similar to the increase of air

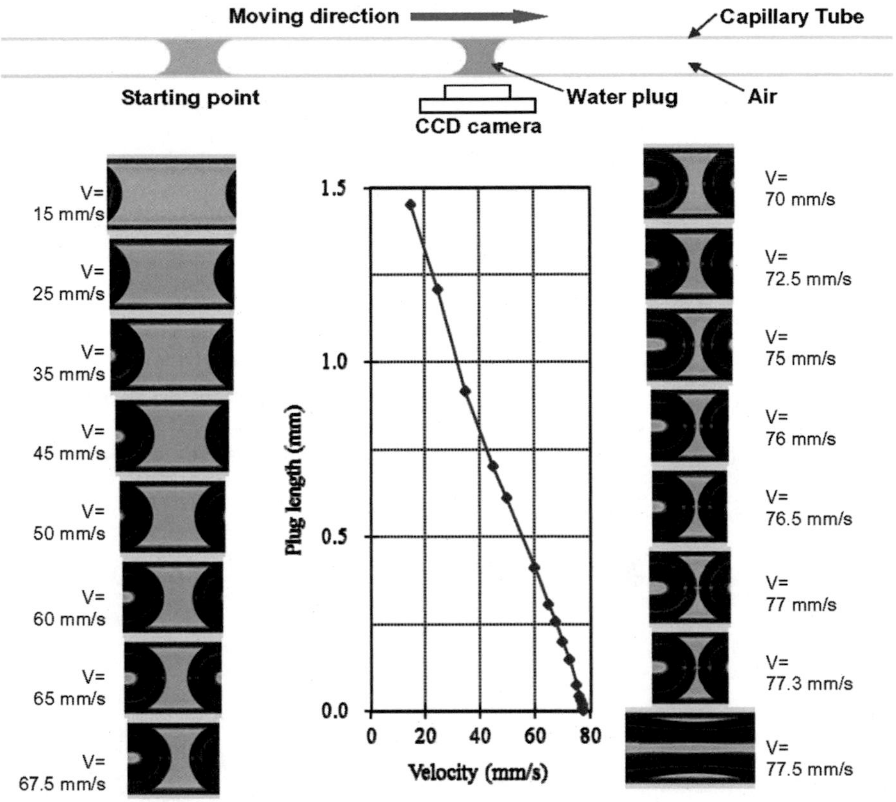

Fig. 4.6 Vapor velocity effect on the liquid plug length (Wang et al. 2013)

velocity investigated by Wang et al. (2013). Too much of an increase in vapor velocity or power input can cause the vapor bubble to penetrate the liquid plug, which means that the liquid plugs are no longer there to separate the vapor phase. In other words, when the power input increases, the maximum diameter of the microchannel in the OHP or the Bond number should decrease. Otherwise, it is not possible to form a train of liquid plugs and vapor bubbles in an OHP. This shows that maximum hydraulic diameter of the OHP depends on the motion or momentum of its working fluid as well.

4.4   Oscillating Motion of One Vapor Bubble and One Liquid Plug

For a typical OHP, the tube diameter must be very small so that the surface tension can make liquid plugs separated by vapor bubbles. The vapor bubbles in the OHP act as springs for the oscillating motion generated in the system. It is assumed that

all liquid plugs behave as one liquid plug and all vapor bubbles as one vapor bubble. When heat is added to the evaporating section, the heat will be transferred through the wall and reach the working fluid. As it does, the saturated liquid will be vaporized into saturated vapor. If the vapor temperature in the evaporator, T_e, is known, the vapor pressure in the evaporating section, p_e, can be determined by the Clapeyron equation, i.e.,

$$p_e = p_0 e^{\left[\frac{h_{lv}}{R} \frac{T_e - T_0}{T_e T_0} \right]} \tag{4.18}$$

where T_0 and p_0 are the reference temperature and reference pressure, respectively. Following the same approach, the vapor pressure, p_c, in the condenser can be determined if the vapor temperature in the condensing section, T_c, is given. The pressure difference between the evaporating section and condensing section can thus be found by

$$\Delta p = p_e - p_c = p_c \left[e^{\left(\frac{h_{lv}}{R} \frac{T_e - T_c}{T_e T_c} \right)} - 1 \right] \tag{4.19}$$

Utilizing a Taylor series and neglecting high-order terms, Eq. (4.19) can be simplified as

$$\Delta p = \Delta T \frac{h_{lv} \rho_{v,c}}{T_c} \tag{4.20}$$

where ΔT is the temperature difference between the evaporating section and condensing section, i.e., $\Delta T = T_e - T_c$. Because the vapor trapped between the liquid slugs is compressible, the volume expansion/contraction in the vapor space causes an oscillating motion that directly affects the saturation temperatures in the evaporating and condensing sections. If the maximum temperature difference between the condensing section and evaporating section is ΔT_{max}, and the minimum temperature difference between the condensing section and evaporating section is ΔT_{min}, the temperature difference between the condensing section and evaporating section would vary between ΔT_{max} and ΔT_{min}. If the system oscillation frequency is ω, the variation of the temperature difference between the evaporating section and condensing section is assumed as

$$\Delta T = \frac{\Delta T_{max} - \Delta T_{min}}{2} [1 + \cos(\omega t)] \tag{4.21}$$

Substituting Eq. (4.21) into Eq. (4.20), the driving force to cause the oscillating motion can be found as

$$F_d = \Delta pA = \left(\frac{Ah_{lv}\rho_{v,c}}{T_c}\right)\left(\frac{\Delta T_{max} - \Delta T_{min}}{2}\right)[1 + \cos{(\omega t)}] \tag{4.22}$$

where A is the cross-sectional area of the channel.

As the working fluid flows through the channel, the frictional force arises from the interaction between the liquid/vapor and the pipe walls, which can be evaluated by

$$\frac{dp_f}{dx} = -\frac{4\tau_s}{D} \tag{4.23}$$

where τ_s is the frictional shear stress at the solid–liquid interface, and D is the hydraulic diameter. The shear stress in Eq. (4.23) may be expressed in terms of the friction factor, f, i.e.,

$$\tau_s = \frac{1}{8}f\rho\left(\frac{dx}{dt}\right)^2 \tag{4.24}$$

Substituting Eq. (4.24) into Eq. (4.23) yields

$$\frac{dp_f}{dx} = -\frac{1}{2D}f\rho\left(\frac{dx}{dt}\right)^2 \tag{4.25}$$

Although the velocity of the working fluid in the OHP is the same for both vapor and liquid phases, the viscosity and density of liquid phase is different from the vapor phase resulting in different pressure drops. The Reynolds numbers for liquid phase and vapor phase can be expressed as

$$Re_l = \frac{\rho_l D}{\mu_l}\frac{dx}{dt} \tag{4.26}$$

$$Re_v = \frac{\rho_v D}{\mu_v}\frac{dx}{dt} \tag{4.27}$$

respectively. Considering Eqs. (4.26) and (4.27) and integrating Eq. (4.25), the total pressure drop due to the frictional shear stress can be determined by

$$\Delta p_f = \left[(f_l \cdot Re_l)\left(\frac{\mu_l L_l}{2D^2}\right) + (f_v \cdot Re_v)\left(\frac{\mu_v L_v}{2D^2}\right)\right]\left(\frac{dx}{dt}\right) \tag{4.28}$$

where L_v and L_l are the total lengths for the vapor bubbles and liquid plugs in the OHP, respectively.

If the total volume occupied by vapor at time t is V_v, i.e., $L_v A$, and vapor is assumed as an ideal gas, the vapor pressure at the time t can be found as

$$p_{v,t} = \frac{m_v RT}{L_v A} \tag{4.29}$$

At time $t + \Delta t$, after heat is added to the evaporating section and evaporation occurs, the increase in the pressure will result in a decrease in the vapor volume by $-xA$. If it is assumed that the vapor temperature is constant during this process, the pressure in the vapor space at time $t + \Delta t$ yields

$$p_{v,t+\Delta t} = \frac{m_v RT}{(L_v - x)A} \tag{4.30}$$

If x is small relative to L_v, the pressure variation at the time interval Δt can be approximately written as

$$\Delta p_v = \frac{\rho_v RT}{L_v} x \tag{4.31}$$

The restoring force due to the vapor volume variation can be found as

$$F_k = A\Delta p_v = A\frac{\rho_v RT}{L_v} x \tag{4.32}$$

or

$$F_k = \kappa x \tag{4.33}$$

where

$$\kappa = \frac{A\rho_v RT}{L_v} \tag{4.34}$$

Considering that the vapor phase is the ideal gas and the vapor volume, V_v, is equal to $L_v A$, Eq. (4.34) can be rewritten as

$$\kappa = \frac{p_v A^2}{V_v} \tag{4.35}$$

which is the gas spring constant for the isothermal process as defined by Eq. (4.10).

According to Newton's Law, i.e., $\sum F = m\frac{d^2 x}{dt^2}$, the equation governing the motion of the working fluid in an OHP can be found as

$$(L_1\rho_1 + L_v\rho_v)A\frac{d^2x}{dt^2} + \left[(f_1 \cdot Re_1)\left(\frac{\mu_1 L_1}{2D^2}\right) + (f_v \cdot Re_v)\left(\frac{\mu_v L_v}{2D^2}\right)\right]$$

$$\cdot A\frac{dx}{dt} + \frac{A\rho_v RT}{L_v}x = \left(\frac{Ah_{lv}\rho_{v,c}}{T_c}\right)\left(\frac{\Delta T_{max} - \Delta T_{min}}{2}\right)[1 + \cos(\omega t)] \tag{4.36}$$

Examining Eq. (4.36), it can be found that Eq. (4.36) is a typical governing equation for forced damped mechanical vibrations, i.e.,

$$\frac{d^2x}{dt^2} + \frac{c}{m}\frac{dx}{dt} + \frac{\kappa}{m}x = \frac{E}{m}[1 + \cos(\omega t)] \tag{4.37}$$

where

$$m = A(\rho_L L_L + \rho_V L_V) \tag{4.38}$$

$$c = A\left[(f_1 \cdot Re_1)\left(\frac{\mu_1 L_1}{2D^2}\right) + (f_v \cdot Re_v)\left(\frac{\mu_v L_v}{2D^2}\right)\right] \tag{4.39}$$

$$\kappa = \frac{p_v A^2}{V_v} \tag{4.40}$$

$$E = \left(\frac{Ah_{lv}\rho_{v,c}}{T_c}\right)\left(\frac{\Delta T_{max} - \Delta T_{min}}{2}\right) \tag{4.41}$$

For the system described by Eq. (4.37), the undamped natural frequency, ω_0, and a damping ratio, ζ, can be written as

$$\omega_0 = \sqrt{\frac{\kappa}{m}} \tag{4.42}$$

and

$$\zeta = \frac{c}{2m\omega_0} \tag{4.43}$$

respectively.

Before heat is added on the evaporator, there is no oscillation movement in the OHP. Thus, the initial conditions for Eq. (4.37) can be found as

$$x = 0 \quad \text{and} \quad \frac{dx}{dt} = 0; \quad \text{at} \quad t = 0 \tag{4.44}$$

Equation (4.37) is simply a nonhomogeneous, second-order ordinary differential equation (ODE) where the exact solution is subject to the boundary conditions

given in Eq. (4.44). Utilizing Laplace transforms, the exact solution can be readily obtained, i.e.,

$$
x(t) = \frac{E}{m} \left[\begin{array}{c} \dfrac{\left(\sqrt{\zeta^2 - 1}\right)\sin\left(\omega t\right) - e^{-\zeta\omega t}\sinh\left[\omega\left(\sqrt{\zeta^2 - 1}\right)t\right]}{2\zeta\omega^2\sqrt{\zeta^2 - 1}} \\[3ex] + \dfrac{1 - e^{-\zeta\omega t}\left[\cosh\left(\left(\sqrt{\zeta^2 - 1}\right)\omega t\right) + \dfrac{\zeta\sinh\left(\left(\sqrt{\zeta^2 - 1}\right)\omega t\right)}{\sqrt{\zeta^2 - 1}}\right]}{\omega^2} \end{array} \right]
$$

$$(4.45)$$

To do the calculation, the OHP configuration and working fluid properties must be given. Using the analysis described above, Ma et al. (2006) studied the effects of the temperature difference, working fluid, operating temperature, dimensions, and filling ratio on the oscillating motion in an OHP. The OHP considered consists of a round tube with an inner diameter of D. The OHP has three sections, i.e., evaporating section, L_e, adiabatic section, L_a, and condensing section, L_c. The total characteristic length of the OHP is equal to the summation of the three sections, i.e.,

$$L = L_e + L_a + L_c \tag{4.46}$$

It is assumed that both liquid and vapor are fully developed laminar flow. The friction factor Reynolds number product for a fully developed laminar flow in a round tube is equal to 64, i.e.,

$$f_1 \cdot Re_1 = f_v \cdot Re_v = 64 \tag{4.47}$$

Considering Eqs. (4.28) and (4.47), the frictional force shown in Eq. (4.36) can be written as

$$F_f = \frac{8P}{D}\left(\mu_1 L_1 + \mu_v L_v\right)\frac{dx}{dt} \tag{4.48}$$

where P is the inner perimeter of the tube.

Ma et al. (2006) used the properties of working fluid (either water or acetone) at 60 °C to conduct an analysis. As heat is added to the evaporating section, the increase of vapor pressure in the evaporating section results in a displacement of the working fluid in the OHP. For the OHP with a total characteristic length of 25.4 cm and a filling ratio of 70 %, the amplitude of this displacement increases for about one second before reaching a steady state oscillation. As the filling ratio decreases, the time needed to reach steady state becomes longer. As shown in Fig. 4.7, the amplitude of the oscillating motion largely depends on the filling ratio. As the filling ratio increases, the amplitude of the oscillating motion becomes smaller. Examining Fig. 4.7, it can be found that increasing the filling ratio causes the

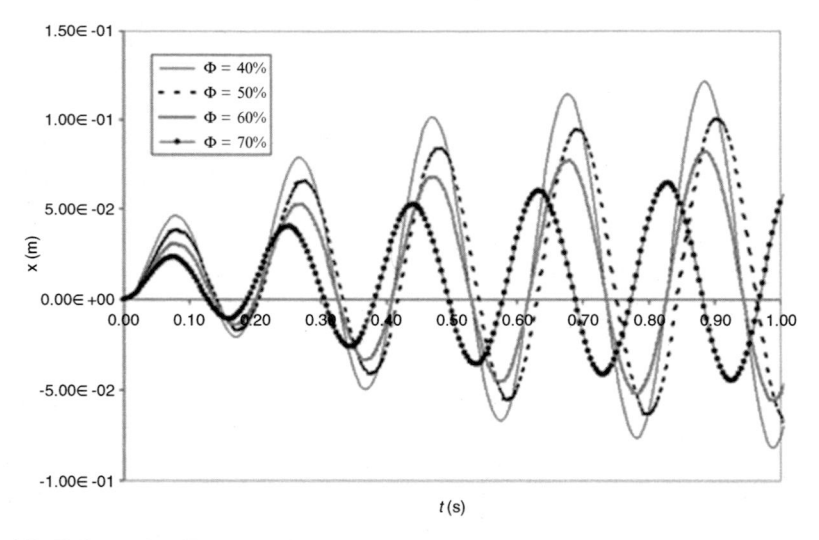

Fig. 4.7 Filling ratio effect on oscillation motion (water at 60 °C, $L = 30.48$ cm, $D = 1.65$ mm)
(Ma et al. 2006)

oscillating frequency to decrease until the filling ratio reaches a value at which point
the oscillating frequency begins to increase, clearly indicating that a minimum
oscillating frequency exists, as shown in Fig. 4.8.

Figure 4.9 illustrates the influence of the total characteristic length on the
oscillating motion. For a given filling ratio, when the total characteristic length
varies from $L = 15.24$ to $L = 30.48$ cm, the time to reach a steady state oscillating
motion will almost be the same. Varying the total characteristic length will not
affect the amplitude of the oscillating motion. Decreasing the total characteristic
length, however, results in an increase in the oscillating frequency. Figure 4.10
illustrates the effect of the hydraulic diameter on the oscillating phenomenon. As
shown, the oscillating frequency is not a function of the hydraulic diameter. The
oscillating amplitude, however, will increase as the hydraulic diameter increases.
Also, as the hydraulic diameter increases, the transient process becomes longer.

As discussed above, the temperature difference between the evaporating section
and condensing section acts as the driving force for the oscillation and transports
the heat from the evaporating section to the condensing section. Clearly, as the heat
flux level increases, the temperature difference between the evaporating section and
condensing section will increase. Figure 4.11 shows the effect of the temperature
difference, i.e., $\Delta T = T_e - T_c$, on the oscillating motion. Results show that increasing the temperature difference will have no effect on the oscillating frequency, but
it will significantly increase the oscillating amplitude. Compared with experimental
results of an actual OHP, it can be found that this conclusion is different from the
measurement. The main reason is an assumption of one liquid plug and one vapor
bubble, which is different from a train of liquid plugs and vapor bubbles existing in
a typical OHP. As the temperature difference increases, the time to reach the steady

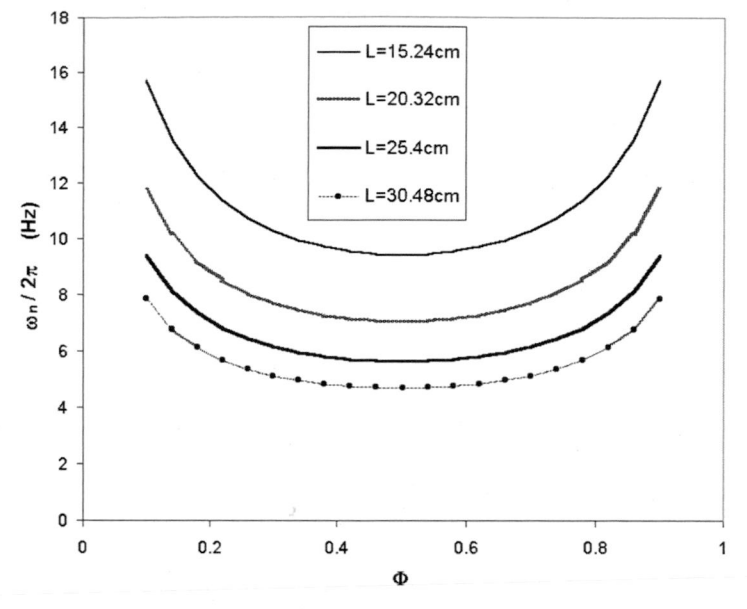

Fig. 4.8 Filling ratio effect on oscillation frequency (water at 60 °C, $D = 1.65$ mm) (Ma et al. 2006)

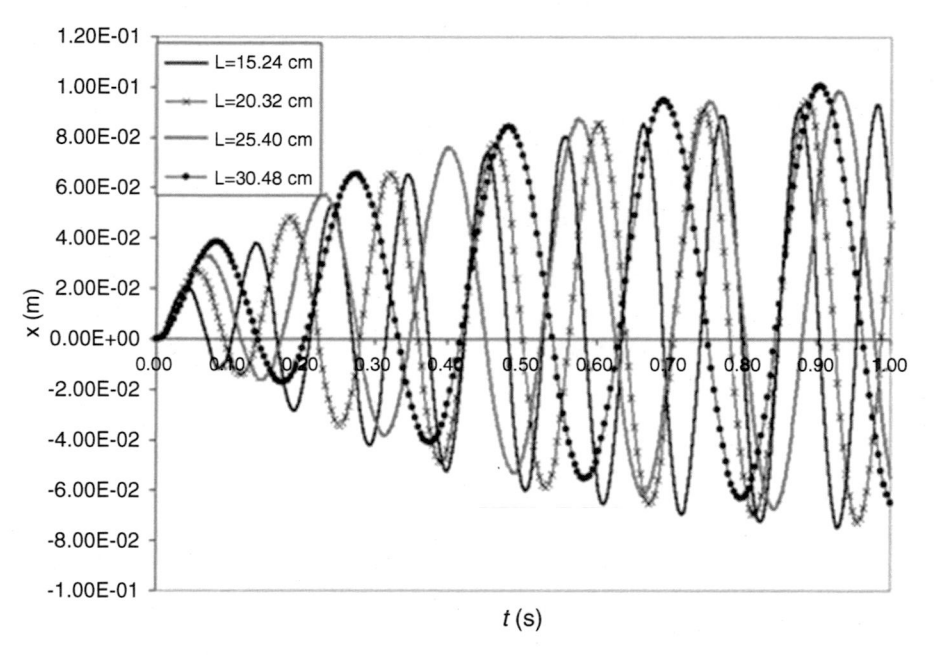

Fig. 4.9 Heat pipe length effect on oscillation motion (water at 60 °C, $\Delta T = 5.0$ K, $D = 1.65$ mm, $\Phi = 50$ %) (Ma et al. 2006)

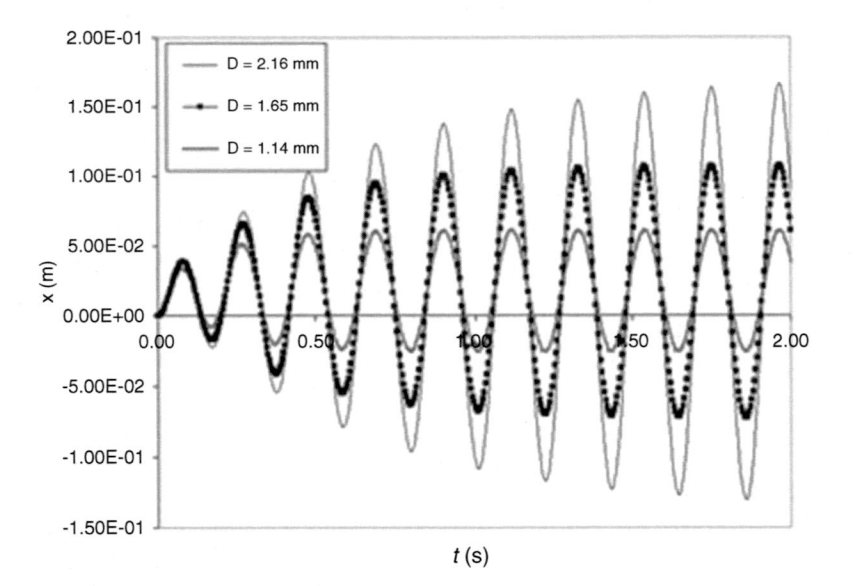

Fig. 4.10 Hydraulic diameter effect on oscillation motion (water at 60 °C, $L = 30.48$ cm, $\Phi = 50$ %, $\Delta T = 5.0$ K) (Ma et al. 2006)

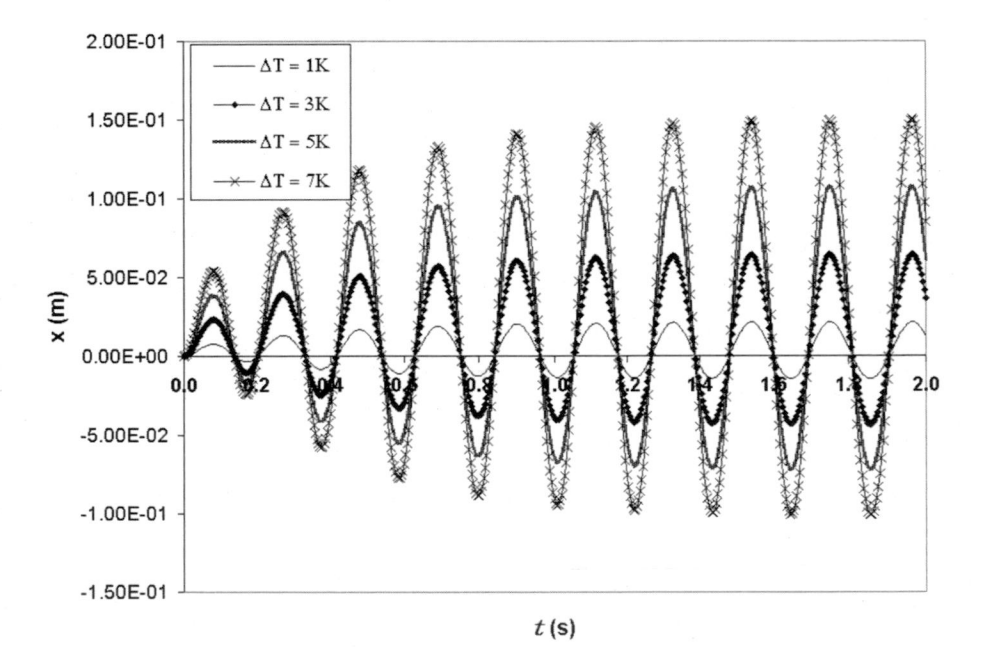

Fig. 4.11 Effect of the superheat temperature difference on oscillation motion (water at 60 °C, $L = 30.48$ cm, $D = 1.65$ mm, $\Phi = 50$ %) (Ma et al. 2006)

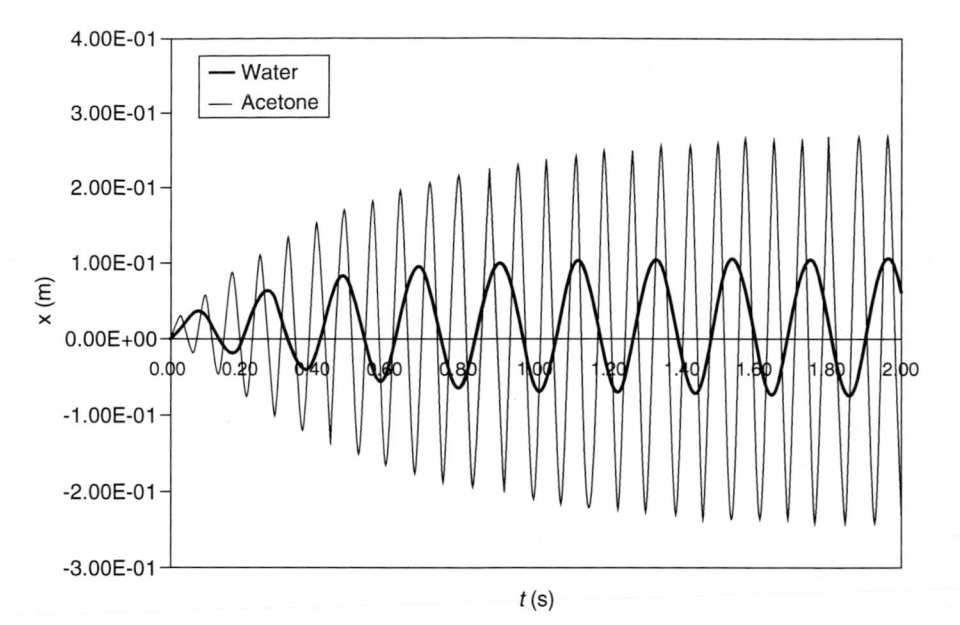

Fig. 4.12 Working fluid effect on oscillation motion ($L = 30.48$ cm, $T = 60$ °C, $D = 1.65$ mm, $\Phi = 50$ %) (Ma et al. 2006)

state becomes longer as well. Because of the expansion and contraction, the pressure in the evaporating and condensing sections will vary and directly affect the saturation temperature in the condensing or evaporating section. Clearly, the temperature difference existing between the evaporating section and condensing section will vary between the maximum temperature difference, ΔT_{max}, and the minimum temperature difference, ΔT_{min}. The results shown in Fig. 4.11 are based on the maximum temperature differences of 1, 3, 5, and 7 °C where the minimum temperature difference is assumed to be zero.

Figure 4.12 illustrates the effect of working fluid on the oscillating motion. As shown, when the working fluid is changed from water to acetone, both the oscillating frequency and amplitude in the system increase significantly. In addition, the working fluid has a significant influence on the transient oscillating motion. It is apparent that the oscillation motion in an OHP depends on the operating temperature. As shown in Fig. 4.13, when the operating temperature increases, both the oscillation frequency and amplitude increase. Because the temperature variation depends on the pressure variation resulting from the oscillating motion in the system, the oscillating frequency of the temperature variation will depend on the natural frequency in the system. As a result, all analyses presented above are based on the assumption that the oscillating frequency of the temperature difference variation is equal to the system's natural frequency. If the frequency of the temperature difference existing between the evaporating section and condensing section can be manipulated, the system's oscillating motion can be modified. As shown in Fig. 4.14, the system frequency and amplitude significantly depend

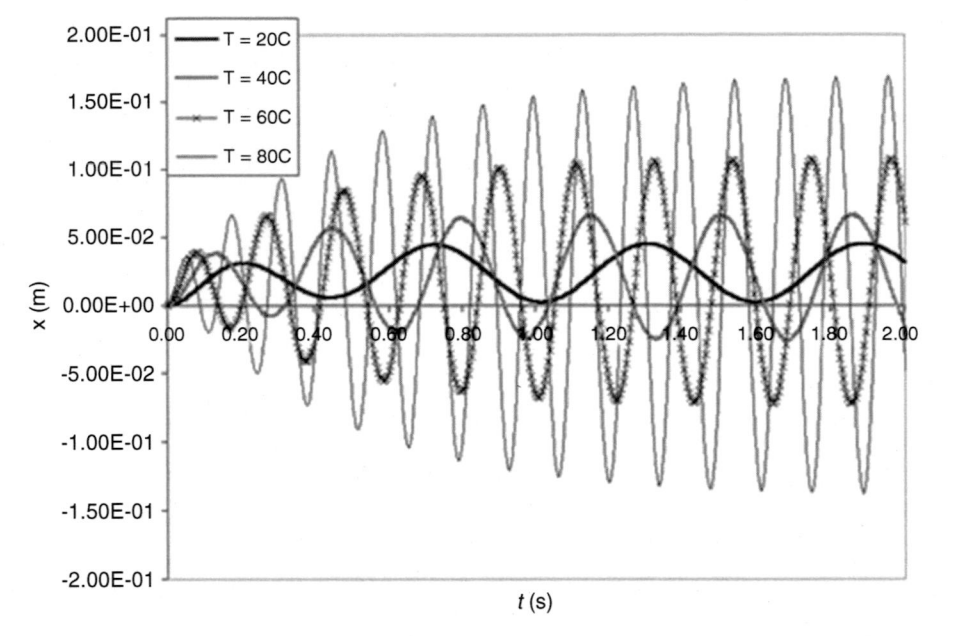

Fig. 4.13 Operating temperature effect on working fluid motion (water, $L = 30.48$ cm, $D = 1.65$ mm, $\Phi = 50$ %) (Ma et al. 2006)

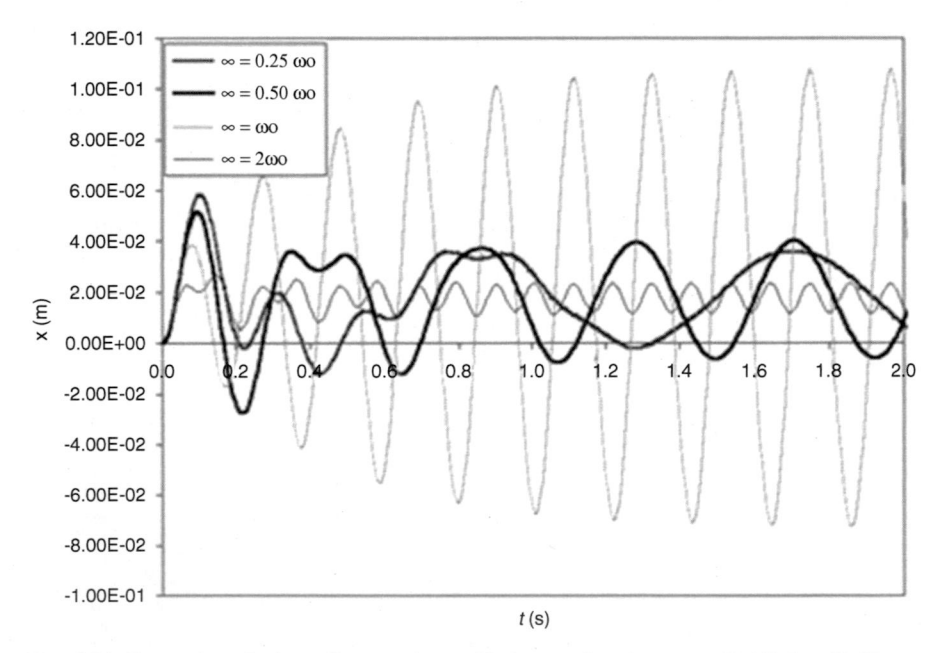

Fig. 4.14 External excitation effect on the oscillation motion (water at 60 °C, $L = 30.48$ cm, $D = 1.65$ mm, $\Phi = 50$ %) (Ma et al. 2006)

on the forced excitation frequency. When the external excitation frequency is equal to the natural frequency, the system can obtain a maximum oscillating motion, which can significantly increase the heat transfer performance. When the external excitation frequency is different from the natural frequency, the oscillating motion in the system can be significantly reduced. Using an external excitation frequency, the fluid flow and heat transfer occurring in an OHP can be readily controlled.

4.5   Oscillating Motion of Two Vapor Bubbles and One Liquid Plug

Consider a U-shaped tube with one vapor bubble at each sealed end of the evaporator section and one liquid plug at the curved condenser section, as shown in Fig. 4.15. The OHP has two sections, i.e., evaporator and condenser only. The evaporator and condenser sections are assumed to have constant wall temperatures, T_e and T_c, and the same length, $2L_e$ and $2L_c$, respectively. Moreover, the averaged liquid plug displacement from the equilibrium position is x. Because the mass density of a vapor plug is only about 0.1 % that of a liquid plug at a saturated

Fig. 4.15 A U-shaped OHP (Pai et al. 2013)

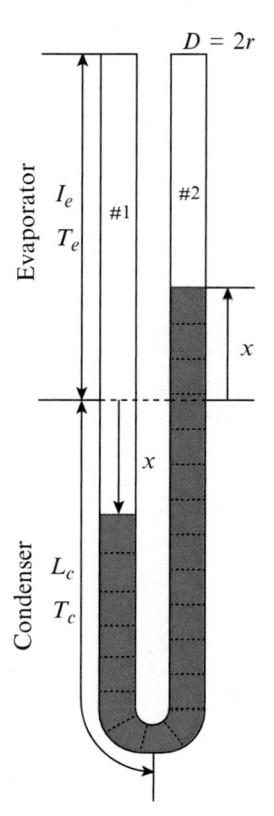

state and the liquid plug is almost incompressible, the length of the liquid plug remains almost constant even if the total vapor condensation rate is different from the total liquid evaporation rate.

When the liquid plug moves up to the left side of the U-shaped tube, the vapor pressure in the left side of the tube increases, and at the same time, the vapor pressure in the right side of the tube deceases. This movement produces a pressure difference between the left side and the right side, which will make the liquid plug move back to the right side. During the movement of the liquid plug, the drag forces due to viscosity and bending always resist the fluid flow. In addition, when the liquid plug moves up and down, the gravitational force resists the fluid flow as well. Considering all forces acting on the liquid plug as shown in Fig. 4.15, the momentum equation of the liquid plug can be derived from Newton's second law as

$$AL_1\rho_1\frac{d^2x}{dt^2} = A(\Delta p_v - \Delta p_b) - 2gA\rho_1 x - L_1 D\pi\tau_s \tag{4.49}$$

where A is the inside cross-sectional area of the tube, L_1 is the length of the liquid plug, D is the diameter of the tube, g is the gravity, and Δp_v is the vapor pressure difference between the left side and the right side, i.e.,

$$\Delta p_v = p_{v,L} - p_{v,R} \tag{4.50}$$

If it is assumed that the liquid plug in the tube is a fully developed flow, the viscous shear stress τ_s can be found as

$$\tau_s = \frac{1}{8}f\rho\left(\frac{dx}{dt}\right)^2 \tag{4.51}$$

where

$$f = \begin{cases} \dfrac{64}{Re} & \text{if } (Re < 2{,}300) \\[2em] \left[\dfrac{1}{2.0\,Log\left(Re\,f^{0.5}\right)-8}\right]^2 & \text{if } Re > 2{,}300 \text{ and the surface is smooth (White 2008)} \\[2em] \left[\dfrac{1}{-2.0\,Log\left(\frac{\epsilon/D}{3.7}+\frac{1}{Re\,f^{0.5}}\right)}\right]^2 & \text{if } Re > 2{,}300 \text{ and the surface has a} \\ & \qquad \text{roughness of } \epsilon \text{ (White 2008)} \end{cases} \tag{4.52}$$

Because the tube diameter for a typical OHP is very small, it is reasonable to assume that the liquid plug is a fully developed laminar flow. The Δp_b in Eq. (4.49) is the pressure loss at the bend, which can be calculated by

$$\Delta p_b = \frac{1}{2} c_b \rho_l \left(\frac{dx}{dt}\right)^2 \tag{4.53}$$

where c_b is the pressure loss coefficient (White 2008). It follows from Eqs. (4.50)–(4.53) that Eq. (4.49) becomes

$$\frac{d^2x}{dt^2} + \frac{32\mu_l}{\rho_l D^2}\frac{dx}{dt} + \frac{g}{L_c}x = \frac{1}{L_l \rho_l}\left[p_{v,L} - p_{v,R} - \frac{1}{2}\text{sign}\left(\frac{dx}{dt}\right)c_b\rho_l\left(\frac{dx}{dt}\right)^2\right] \tag{4.54}$$

For the vapor bubble in an OHP, the oscillating motion excited by the thermal energy added on the OHP produces compression and expansion. During the compression or expansion process, the pressure wave is much faster than the heat transfer process. Therefore, it is assumed that the expansion or compression process of vapor phase occurring in an OHP can be considered an adiabatic process. The relation between the vapor temperature and pressure for both sides shown in Fig. 4.15 can be expressed as

$$T_{v,L} = \frac{A}{C_L R}p_{v,L}^{(k-1)/k} \quad \text{or} \quad p_{v,L} = \left(\frac{C_L R}{A}T_{v,L}\right)^{k/(k-1)} \tag{4.55}$$

$$T_{v,R} = \frac{A}{C_R R}p_{v,R}^{(k-1)/k} \quad \text{or} \quad p_{v,R} = \left(\frac{C_R R}{A}T_{v,R}\right)^{k/(k-1)} \tag{4.56}$$

respectively, where $k = c_p/c_v$ is the heat capacity ratio, c_v and c_p represent the isochoric and isobaric specific heats of the working fluid's vapor, R is the specific gas constant of the working fluid, and finally, $T_{v,L}, p_{v,L}$, and $T_{v,R}, p_{v,R}$ are temperatures and pressures of the left and right vapor bubbles. The integration constants C_L and C_R shown in Eqs. (4.55) and (4.56), respectively, can be obtained through a referential state. If the initial pressure and temperature of both the vapor bubbles are the same, the integration constants C_L and C_R are the same for both the vapor bubbles, i.e.,

$$C_L = C_R = \frac{A}{RT_0}p_0^{(k-1)/k} \tag{4.57}$$

where p_0 and T_0 are set as the vapor bubble's initial pressure and temperature. If the two vapor bubbles are modeled as ideal gas, it can be found that

$$p_{v,L}A(L_c + x) = m_{v,L}RT_{v,L} \tag{4.58}$$

$$p_{v,R}A(L_c - x) = m_{v,R}RT_{v,R} \tag{4.59}$$

where $m_{v,L}$ and $m_{v,R}$ are the mass of the left vapor bubble and right vapor bubble, respectively. x is the displacement of the liquid plug, and L_c is the initial length of the vapor bubble. Substituting Eqs. (4.58) and (4.59) into Eqs. (4.55) and (4.56), respectively, yields the relationship between vapor mass and pressure

$$m_{v,L} = C_L(L_c + x)p_{v,L}^{1/k} \quad \text{or} \quad p_{v,L} = \left(\frac{m_{v,L}}{C_L(L_c + x)}\right)^k \tag{4.60}$$

$$m_{v,R} = C_R(L_c - x)p_{v,R}^{1/k} \quad \text{or} \quad p_{v,R} = \left(\frac{m_{v,R}}{C_R(L_c - x)}\right)^k \tag{4.61}$$

Equations (4.60) and (4.61) show that $p_{v,L}, T_{v,L}, p_{v,R}$, and $T_{v,R}$ are functions of the three dependent variables $x(t), m_{v,L}(t)$, and $m_{v,R}(t)$. Because only a small portion of the liquid plug periodically moves into the evaporator, and the rest of the liquid plug remains at a temperature very close to T_c, the liquid density, ρ_l, and the liquid viscosity, ν_l, can be assumed constant.

If x/L_e is treated as a small parameter, Taylor expansions of Eqs. (4.60) and (4.61) are obtained as

$$p_{v,L} = \hat{p}_{v,L}\left(1 - k\frac{x}{L_e} + \frac{k^2 + k}{2}\frac{x^2}{L_e^2} - \frac{k^3 + 3k^2 + 2k}{6}\frac{x^3}{L_e^3} + \cdots\right), \quad \hat{p}_{v,L} \equiv \left(\frac{m_{v,L}}{C_L L_e}\right)^k \tag{4.62}$$

and

$$p_{v,R} = \hat{p}_{v,R}\left(1 + k\frac{x}{L_e} - \frac{k^2 + k}{2}\frac{x^2}{L_e^2} + \frac{k^3 + 3k^2 + 2k}{6}\frac{x^3}{L_e^3} + \cdots\right), \quad \hat{p}_{v,R} \equiv \left(\frac{m_{v,R}}{C_R L_e}\right)^k \tag{4.63}$$

Considering Eqs. (4.62) and (4.63), Eq. (4.54) can be rewritten as

$$\frac{d^2x}{dt^2} + c\frac{dx}{dt} + \alpha_1 x - \alpha_2 x^2 + \alpha_3 x^3 + \cdots = \frac{\hat{p}_{c,L} - \hat{p}_{v,R}}{L_l \rho_l} \tag{4.64}$$

where

$$c = \frac{32\nu_1}{D^2} + \text{sign}\left(\frac{dx}{dt}\right)\frac{c_b\rho_1}{2L_1\rho_1}\frac{dx}{dt}$$

$$\alpha_1 = \frac{g}{L_c} + \frac{k(\hat{p}_{v,L} + \hat{p}_{v,R})}{L_e L_1 \rho_1}$$

$$\alpha_2 = \frac{(k^2 + k)(\hat{p}_{v,L} + \hat{p}_{v,R})}{2L_e^2 L_1 \rho_1}$$ \hspace{1cm} (4.65)

$$\alpha_3 = \frac{(k^3 + 3k^2 + 2k)(\hat{p}_{v,L} + \hat{p}_{v,R})}{6L_e^3 L_1 \rho_1}$$

Because $m_{v,L}$ and $m_{v,R}$ (hence $\hat{p}_{v,L}$ and $\hat{p}_{v,R}$) change with time due to latent heat transfer, they are functions of $x(t)$. Equation (4.64) clearly reveals that this is a *parametrically excited dynamical system*. However, because $m_{v,L}$ decreases when $m_{v,R}$ increases, $\hat{p}_{v,L} + \hat{p}_{0,R}$ remains about constant. For this weakly nonlinear system with cubic and quadratic nonlinearities, its amplitude-dependent oscillation frequency $\hat{\omega}$ can be estimated using the perturbation solution from the use of the method of multiple scales (Nayfeh and Mook 1979), which can be expressed as

$$\hat{\omega} = \omega + \frac{9\alpha_3\alpha_1 - 10\alpha_2^2}{24\omega^3}A_m^2, \quad \omega \equiv \sqrt{\alpha_1} \hspace{1cm} (4.66)$$

where A_m is the vibration amplitude and ω is the vibration frequency under small-amplitude vibration. Without gravity, from Eq. (4.66), it can be found that

$$\frac{10\alpha_2^2}{9\alpha_3\alpha_1} = \frac{5(k+1)}{3(k+2)} \hspace{1cm} (4.67)$$

If $k = 1.33$, the ratio in Eq. (4.67) yields 1.166. Therefore, $\frac{10\alpha_2^2}{9\alpha_3\alpha_1} = \frac{5(k+1)}{3(k+2)} \approx 1$. In other words, influence of the quadratic nonlinearity will be almost canceled out by that of the cubic nonlinearity. Substituting Eq. (4.65) into Eq. (4.66) yields

$$\hat{\omega} = \omega + \left(\frac{3g\alpha_3}{8L_c\omega^3} - \chi\right)A_m^2, \quad \chi \equiv \frac{(2k-1)(k^3 + k^2)(\hat{p}_{v,L} + \hat{p}_{v,R})^2}{48L_e^4 L_1^2 \rho_1^2 \omega^3} > 0 \hspace{1cm} (4.68)$$

Equation (4.68) shows that the gravity can slightly increase (or decrease) $\hat{\omega}$ if $g > 0$ (or $g < 0$), but the change is very small. Because ω^3 has a big value, both χ and $3g\alpha_3/(8L_c\omega^3)$ have small values, and amplitude A is far less than 1 m in real OHPs; hence, $\hat{\omega} \simeq \omega$. Because $m_{v,L}$ and $m_{v,R}$ in terms of x as shown in Eqs. (4.60) and (4.61) are unknown, $\hat{p}_{v,L} + \hat{p}_{v,R}$ and $\alpha_1(= \omega^2)$ cannot be expanded into

polynomial functions in terms of x. Hence, one can only estimate the oscillation frequency $\hat{\omega} \left(\simeq \sqrt{\alpha_1} \right)$ using the initial values of $m_{v,L}$ and $m_{v,R}$ and then a more accurate estimation can be obtained after the steady state values of $m_{v,L}$ and $m_{v,R}$ are known. Without gravity, the first-order normalized spring constant α_1 can be rewritten as

$$\alpha_1 = \frac{\kappa_L + \kappa_R}{m_1}, \quad m_1 \equiv AL_1\rho_1, \quad \kappa_L \equiv \frac{k\hat{p}_{v,L}A}{L_e}, \quad \kappa_R \equiv \frac{k\hat{p}_{v,R}A}{L_e} \qquad (4.69)$$

Here, κ_L and κ_R are the equivalent linear spring constants of the vapor bubbles.

4.6   Oscillating Motion of Multi Liquid Plugs and Multi Vapor Bubbles

Figure 4.16 shows a typical multi-turn OHP with a bottom heating mode. As shown, the OHP consists of an evaporator, an adiabatic section, and a condenser. The origin of the curvilinear coordinate s is designated with O. The Cartesian coordinate system is placed at the bottom of the OHP with the origin O' at the beginning of the first turn. To study the influence of the inclination effect, the OHP leans backward with an angle of θ. The length from O to the condenser–adiabatic

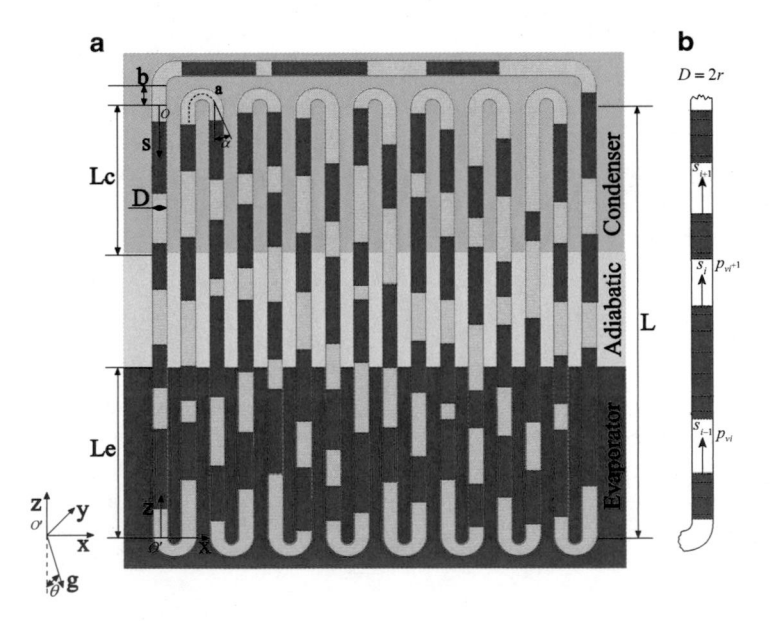

Fig. 4.16 Schematic of a multi-turn OHP: (**a**) coordinate system and (**b**) control volume (Peng et al. 2014)

interface is L_c and from O' to the evaporator–adiabatic interface is L_e. The inner diameter of the capillary tube and the turn radius are denoted as D and a, respectively. Liquid plugs are separated by vapor bubbles and driven by the pressure difference between two adjacent vapor bubbles. The vapor bubbles and liquid plugs are numbered as shown in Fig. 4.16b. Because the pressures of vapor bubbles change with time, motions of liquid plugs are always transient. Gravity pulls a liquid plug forward or backward when the liquid plug moves in the same or opposite direction of the gravity. The gravity effect disappears while the liquid plug moves horizontally. The frictional force between the liquid and wall is the primary contribution to the total pressure loss. The pressure loss at the bending area is significant, particularly when the number of turns is large and, hence, should be included in the physical model.

If n liquid plugs and n vapor bubbles are alternatively distributed along the OHP tube, it can be obtained from Newton's second law that

$$AL_{1,i}\rho_1 \frac{d^2 s_i}{dt^2} = A\left(p_{v,i} - p_{v,i+1} - \Delta p_{b,i}\right) + AL_{1,i}\rho_1 g_i - L_{1,i} P \tau_s, \quad \text{for } i = 1, 2, \ldots, n-1$$

$$AL_{1,n}\rho_1 \frac{d^2 s_n}{dt^2} = A\left(p_{v,n} - p_{v,1} - \Delta p_{b,n}\right) + AL_{1,n}\rho_1 g_n - L_{1,n} P \tau_s, \quad \text{for } i = n$$

$$\text{(4.70)}$$

where A is the cross-sectional area of a liquid plug, $L_{1,i}$ is the length of the ith liquid plug, ρ_1 is the liquid density, P is the inner perimeter of the tube or microchannel, and s_i is the displacement of the ith liquid plug along the tube direction from the initial position of the liquid plug, i.e., s_i is zero for $i = 1, 2, \ldots, n$ at the initial state.

It should be noted that the displacement of each liquid plug is not calculated from O. When a liquid plug moves along the looped capillary tube for a circle and passes the liquid plug's initial position, the displacement of the liquid plug continues to accumulate instead of being set to zero. The vapor pressure difference at two ends of the ith liquid plug is $p_{v,i} - p_{v,i+1}$, and $p_{v,i}$ is the vapor pressure of the ith vapor bubble. The bending pressure loss of the ith liquid plug can be calculated by

$$\Delta p_{bi} = \frac{1}{2} c_b \rho \left(\frac{ds_i}{dt}\right)^2 \tag{4.71}$$

where c_b is the empirical bending pressure loss coefficient. It should be noted that the ith liquid plug length, L_{1i}, is less than the total length of the bending tube, L_{bi}. The empirical bending pressure loss coefficient, c_b, should be further corrected. Because the pressure loss of a vapor bubble is much smaller than a liquid plug, the vapor pressure losses are not considered. Therefore the density, ρ, should be the liquid density of the working fluid. The effective gravity g_i on the ith liquid plug is

defined as the gravity component directing along the positive direction of s_i. If the ith liquid plug is located at the first turn in the condenser area, and the angle between the velocity and the negative z coordinate is α as shown in Fig. 4.16a, the effective gravitational acceleration for the liquid plug can be obtained as

$$g_i = \frac{\cos{(\theta)}g \int_0^{L_{li}} \cos{(\alpha)}ds}{L_{li}} \tag{4.72}$$

where θ is the inclination angle of the OHP. If a liquid plug moves upward along the capillary tube, i.e., $\alpha = 180°$, the effective gravitational acceleration g_i is equal to $-\cos{(\theta)}g$. The shear stress of the ith liquid plug, τ_s, can be obtained through

$$\tau_s = \frac{1}{8}f_1\rho_1\left(\frac{ds}{dt}\right)^2 \tag{4.73}$$

where μ_1 is the dynamic viscosity, and s_i is the displacement of the ith liquid plug. Substituting Eqs. (4.71) and (4.73) into Eq. (4.70) and considering the Reynolds number $Re_1 = \frac{\rho_1 D}{\mu_1}\frac{dx}{dt}$ yields the following governing dynamic equations of the liquid slugs

$$L_{11}\rho_1\frac{d^2s_1}{dt^2} = P_{v1} - P_{v2} - \frac{1}{2}\,c_b\rho_1\left(\frac{ds_1}{dt}\right)^2 + L_{11}\rho_1g_1 - \frac{f_1Re_1P\mu_1L_{11}}{8DA}\frac{ds_1}{dt}$$

$$L_{12}\rho_1\frac{d^2s_2}{dt^2} = P_{v2} - P_{v3} - \frac{1}{2}\,c_b\rho_1\left(\frac{ds_2}{dt}\right)^2 + L_{12}\rho_1g_2 - \frac{f_1Re_1P\mu_1L_{12}}{8DA}\frac{ds_2}{dt} \tag{4.74}$$

$$\vdots$$

$$L_{ln}\rho_1\frac{d^2s_n}{dt^2} = P_{vn} - P_{v1} - \frac{1}{2}\,c_b\rho_1\left(\frac{ds_n}{dt}\right)^2 + L_{ln}\rho_1g_n - \frac{f_1Re_1P\mu_1L_{ln}}{8DA}\frac{ds_n}{dt}$$

Clearly, an OHP is a mass-spring mechanical system.

4.6.1   Modal Analysis

Modal analysis is excellent for understanding a complex system's dynamic characteristics because it provides the system's natural frequencies and modal shapes under small-amplitude free vibrations. Although an OHP is typically taken as a heat transfer device, it is also a multiple DOF (degrees of freedom) mass-spring

mechanical system and, hence, modal analysis is a good way to reveal its dynamic properties. If it is assumed that the flow is a fully developed laminar flow in a round tube, and the bending pressure loss and gravity are neglected, Eq. (4.74) can be simplified as

$$L_{11}\rho_1 \frac{d^2 s_1}{dt^2} + \frac{32\mu_1 L_{11}}{D^2} \frac{ds_1}{dt} = p_{v1} - p_{v2}$$

$$L_{12}\rho_1 \frac{d^2 s_2}{dt^2} + \frac{32\mu_1 L_{12}}{D^2} \frac{ds_2}{dt} = p_{v2} - p_{v3}$$

$$\vdots$$

$$L_{1n}\rho_1 \frac{d^2 s_n}{dt^2} + \frac{32\mu_1 L_{1n}}{D^2} \frac{ds_n}{dt} = p_{vn} - p_{v1}$$

(4.75)

Rewriting Eq. (4.75) in the matrix form yields

$$
\begin{bmatrix} L_{11}\rho_1 & & & 0 \\ & L_{12}\rho_1 & & \\ & & \ddots & \\ 0 & & & L_{1n}\rho_1 \end{bmatrix}
\begin{Bmatrix} \dfrac{d^2 s_1}{dt^2} \\ \dfrac{d^2 s_2}{dt^2} \\ \vdots \\ \dfrac{d^2 s_n}{dt^2} \end{Bmatrix}
+
\begin{bmatrix} \dfrac{32\mu_1 L_{11}}{D^2} & & & 0 \\ & \dfrac{32\mu_1 L_{12}}{D^2} & & \\ & & \ddots & \\ 0 & & & \dfrac{32\mu_1 L_{1n}}{D^2} \end{bmatrix}
\begin{Bmatrix} \dfrac{ds_1}{dt} \\ \dfrac{ds_2}{dt} \\ \vdots \\ \dfrac{ds_n}{dt} \end{Bmatrix}
$$

$$
=
\begin{bmatrix} 1 & -1 & & & \\ & 1 & -1 & & \\ & & \ddots & \ddots & \\ & & & 1 & -1 \\ -1 & & & & 1 \end{bmatrix}
\begin{Bmatrix} p_{v1} \\ p_{v2} \\ \vdots \\ p_{vn-1} \\ p_{vn} \end{Bmatrix}
$$

(4.76)

Equations (4.75) and (4.76) show the relationships between vapor pressures and displacements of liquid plugs. Considering Eq. (4.31), the differential pressure can be expressed as

$$dp_{v1} = \frac{kp_{v1}}{L_{v1}} d(s_n - s_1) \quad \text{for } i = 1$$

$$dp_{vi} = \frac{kp_{vi}}{L_{vi}} d(s_{i-1} - s_i) \quad \text{for } i = 2, 3, \ldots, n$$

(4.77)

where $s_i - s_{i-1} + L_{vi} \approx L_{vi}$ is assumed because modal analysis is under the assumption of small-amplitude vibration. Rewriting Eq. (4.77) in matrix form yields

$$\begin{Bmatrix} dp_{v1} \\ dp_{v2} \\ dp_{v3} \\ \vdots \\ dp_{vn} \end{Bmatrix} = \begin{bmatrix} -kp_{v1}/L_{v1} & 0 & 0 & \cdots & kp_{v1}/L_{v1} \\ kp_{v2}/L_{v2} & -kp_{v2}/L_{v2} & 0 & \cdots & 0 \\ 0 & kp_{v3}/L_{v3} & -kp_{v3}/L_{v3} & & \vdots \\ \vdots & \vdots & \cdots & & 0 \\ 0 & \cdots & 0 & kp_{vn}/L_{vn} & -kp_{vn}/L_{vn} \end{bmatrix} \begin{Bmatrix} ds_1 \\ ds_2 \\ ds_3 \\ \vdots \\ ds_n \end{Bmatrix}$$

(4.78)

or

$$\{dp_v\} = [S]\{ds\}$$

(4.79)

where $[S]$ is the tangential stiffness matrix. Equation (4.78) describes the spring effect of vapor bubbles. Moreover, because p_v and L_v change with time, this liquid–vapor system is an inherently nonlinear dynamical system and its nature frequencies are not constant. Linear modal analysis gives the nature frequencies and modal shapes of the system under the assumption that relationships between vapor pressures and fluid slugs' displacements are linear. If $(\bar{s}_i, \bar{p}_{vi})$ represents an equilibrium state at a specific time, it can be found that

$$s_i \equiv \bar{s}_i + ds_i, \quad p_{vi} \equiv \bar{p}_{vi} + dp_{vi} \quad \text{for } i = 1, \ldots, n$$

(4.80)

Considering Eq. (4.78) and substituting Eq. (4.80) into Eq. (4.76) yields

$$\begin{bmatrix} L_{11}\rho_1 & & & 0 \\ & L_{12}\rho_1 & & \\ & & \ddots & \\ 0 & & & L_{ln}\rho_1 \end{bmatrix} \left\{ \begin{array}{c} d\dfrac{d^2 s_1}{dt^2} \\ d\dfrac{d^2 s_2}{dt^2} \\ \vdots \\ d\dfrac{d^2 s_n}{dt^2} \end{array} \right\} + \begin{bmatrix} \dfrac{32\mu_1 L_{11}}{D^2} & & & 0 \\ & \dfrac{32\mu_1 L_{12}}{D^2} & & \\ & & \ddots & \\ 0 & & & \dfrac{32\mu_1 L_{ln}}{D^2} \end{bmatrix}$$

$$\left\{ \begin{array}{c} d\dfrac{ds_1}{dt} \\ d\dfrac{ds_2}{dt} \\ \vdots \\ d\dfrac{ds_n}{dt} \end{array} \right\} + \begin{bmatrix} -1 & 1 & & & \\ & -1 & 1 & & \\ & & \ddots & \ddots & \\ & & & -1 & 1 \\ 1 & & & & -1 \end{bmatrix}$$

$$\begin{bmatrix} -k p_{v1}/L_{v1} & 0 & 0 & \cdots & k p_{v1}/L_{v1} \\ k p_{v2}/L_{v2} & -k p_{v2}/L_{v2} & 0 & \cdots & 0 \\ 0 & k p_{v3}/L_{v3} & -k p_{v3}/L_{v3} & & \vdots \\ \vdots & \cdots & & & 0 \\ 0 & \cdots & 0 & k p_{vn}/L_{vn} & -k p_{vn}/L_{vn} \end{bmatrix} \left\{ \begin{array}{c} ds_1 \\ ds_2 \\ ds_3 \\ \vdots \\ ds_n \end{array} \right\} = 0$$

$$\tag{4.81}$$

or

$$[M]\left\{ d\dfrac{d^2 s}{dt^2} \right\} + [C]\left\{ d\dfrac{ds}{dt} \right\} + [K]\{ds\} = 0 \tag{4.82}$$

where the mass, damping, and tangent stiffness matrices are given by

$$[M] = \begin{bmatrix} L_{11}\rho_1 & & & 0 \\ & L_{12}\rho_1 & & \\ & & \ddots & \\ 0 & & & L_{ln}\rho_1 \end{bmatrix} \tag{4.83}$$

$$[C] = \begin{bmatrix} \dfrac{32\mu_1 L_{11}}{D^2} & & & & 0 \\ & \dfrac{32\mu_1 L_{12}}{D^2} & & & \\ & & \ddots & & \\ & & & \dfrac{32\mu_1 L_{ln}}{D^2} & \\ 0 & & & & \end{bmatrix} \tag{4.84}$$

$$[K] = \begin{bmatrix} -1 & 1 & & & \\ & -1 & 1 & & \\ & & \ddots & \ddots & \\ & & & -1 & 1 \\ 1 & & & & -1 \end{bmatrix}$$

$$\begin{bmatrix} -kp_{v1}/L_{v1} & 0 & 0 & \cdots & kp_{v1}/L_{v1} \\ kp_{v2}/L_{v2} & -kp_{v2}/L_{v2} & 0 & \cdots & 0 \\ 0 & kp_{v3}/L_{v3} & -kp_{v3}/L_{v3} & \cdots & 0 \\ \vdots & \cdots & \vdots & \ddots & \vdots \\ 0 & \cdots & 0 & kp_{vn}/L_{vn} & -kp_{vn}/L_{vn} \end{bmatrix} \tag{4.85}$$

When a mechanical system is subject to an external excitation, its vibration amplitude becomes excessively large when the excitation frequency is close to some specific values even if the forcing amplitude is small. This phenomenon is known as resonance and the specific frequencies are called resonant frequencies or natural frequencies of the system. When a system is under an excitation at a resonant frequency, the system oscillation tends to exhibit a steady geometric relation among different degrees of freedom. This geometric relation is known as a mode shape, and all DOF move harmonically at a constant frequency with a fixed phase relation. A linear dynamical system's response to an arbitrary excitation is always a combination of many modal vibrations of the system. Modal analysis is used to obtain natural frequencies and modal shapes of a system through eigenvalue analysis. Under free undamped vibration, the slug-flow model becomes a simple mass-spring system governed by

$$[M]\left\{ d\frac{d^2 s}{dt^2} \right\} + [K]\{ds\} = \{0\} \tag{4.86}$$

where the mass matrix $[M]$ and the tangential stiffness matrix $[K]$ are given in Eqs. (4.83) and (4.85). The slug-flow model is nonlinear, and the tangential stiffness matrix $[K]$ may change with time. In linear modal analysis, $[K]$ in Eq. (4.86) is assumed to be the tangential stiffness at a specified time instant. If the liquid plugs oscillate harmonically, it can be expressed as

$$\{ds\} = \{\phi\} \sin (\omega t) \tag{4.87}$$

Substituting Eq. (4.87) into Eq. (4.86) yields

$$\left([K] - \omega^2[M]\right)\{\phi\} = 0 \tag{4.88}$$

Because the eigenvectors $\{\phi\}$ are nonzero vectors, $\left|[K] - \omega^2[M]\right| = 0$ is required for Eq. (4.88), and the natural frequencies of the dynamic system, $\omega (= 2\pi f)$, can be obtained by solving the algebraic equation $\left|[K] - \omega^2[M]\right| = 0$. The mode shapes can be calculated by substituting the natural frequencies back into Eq. (4.88). Modal analysis of an OHP provides its dynamic characteristics, including natural frequencies and mode shapes.

Example 4.2 Consider an 8-turn OHP as shown in Fig. 4.16. The OHP with an inner diameter of $D = 4.0$ mm has three sections with an evaporator length of $L_e = 96.4$ mm, an adiabatic section length of $L_a = 32.1$ mm, and a condenser length of $L_c = 96.4$ mm. It is assumed that there are 48 liquid plugs separated by 48 vapor bubbles with individual lengths shown in Table 4.1. Water is charged into the OHP with a filling ratio $\Phi = 60$ %. The operating temperature is 55 °C. Determine the first seven mode shapes and natural frequencies.

Solution Using the modal analysis discussed above for this specific OHP with properties specified, the mode shapes and natural frequencies can be readily obtained. Shown in Fig. 4.17 are the first seven mode shapes and natural frequencies of an 8-turn OHP. Because the OHP is looped, the liquid slugs can circulate in the capillary tube without restraint. This free-restraint problem is not commonly seen in the analysis of mechanical systems, and it results in the chaotic performance of the slug flow. Figure 4.17a shows the first mode of the OHP. The 48 red points shown in Fig. 4.17a represent the 48 liquid plugs, and the horizontal distribution of the red points indicates that all the liquid plugs move along the same direction and have the same amount of displacement and phase angle. In other words, it is a circulation flow, and it is also called the rigid-body mode for a mechanical system. Because the natural frequency of the first mode is zero, the circulation flow is also called the zero-frequency mode. This circulation of liquid plugs plays an important role in transporting heat from the evaporator to condenser. It shows that the circulation flow exists in a closed loop OHP. Figure 4.17b, c shows the second and third modes and their natural frequencies. Both have two vibration nodes (black dots) and almost the same frequency because the OHP configuration is symmetric. The small discrepancy between the two natural frequencies is caused by a random but asymmetric distribution of the liquid plugs. When the liquid plugs oscillate at the second (or third) natural frequency, liquid plugs around the two vibration nodes are almost stagnant. Similar to the second and third modes, modes having four and six vibration nodes also exist in pairs and have almost the same frequency. Figure 4.17d, e shows the pair of vibration modes with four nodes, and Fig. 4.17f, g shows the pair of vibration modes with six nodes. The actual oscillation amplitude

Table 4.1 Liquid plugs separated by vapor bubbles with individual lengths (liquid plug number 1 starts from O shown in Fig. 4.16 which is followed by the vapor bubble number 1)

Liquid plug number	Liquid plug length (m)	Vapor bubble number	Vapor bubble length (m)
1	0.0522	1	0.0533
2	0.0227	2	0.0150
3	0.0517	3	0.0196
4	0.0526	4	0.0307
5	0.0359	5	0.0193
6	0.0356	6	0.0244
7	0.0613	7	0.0340
8	0.0343	8	0.0395
9	0.0561	9	0.0604
10	0.0256	10	0.0271
11	0.0943	11	0.0531
12	0.0476	12	0.0234
13	0.0403	13	0.0367
14	0.0505	14	0.0472
15	0.0616	15	0.0420
16	0.0427	16	0.0559
17	0.0289	17	0.0625
18	0.0295	18	0.0459
19	0.0831	19	0.0336
20	0.0909	20	0.0381
21	0.0523	21	0.0311
22	0.0411	22	0.0284
23	0.1001	23	0.0214
24	0.0560	24	0.0419
25	0.0273	25	0.0304
26	0.0374	26	0.0169
27	0.0230	27	0.0305
28	0.0305	28	0.0331
29	0.0410	29	0.0163
30	0.0813	30	0.0359
31	0.0438	31	0.0177
32	0.0452	32	0.0133
33	0.0197	33	0.0445
34	0.0689	34	0.0375
35	0.0683	35	0.0364
36	0.0502	36	0.0495
37	0.0512	37	0.0336
38	0.0735	38	0.0251
39	0.0570	39	0.0173
40	0.0644	40	0.0231
41	0.0370	41	0.0409

(continued)

Table 4.1 (continued)

Liquid plug number	Liquid plug length (m)	Vapor bubble number	Vapor bubble length (m)
42	0.0331	42	0.0514
43	0.0619	43	0.0275
44	0.0370	44	0.0140
45	0.0789	45	0.0192
46	0.0300	46	0.0327
47	0.0698	47	0.0233
48	0.0266	48	0.0479

of a high-frequency mode is often small because the vibration energy is proportional to (amplitude × frequency)^2. In other words, the participation of high-frequency modes in an ordinary linear mechanical system is often minor. For a nonlinear system, however, the participation of high-frequency modes may play an important role in system dynamics and stability. For a multi-turn closed loop OHP, the zero-frequency movement plays an important role in its performance. Although the high-frequency modes do not contribute much to the circulation, the liquid plugs' high-frequency and high-velocity oscillations create high temperature gradients to increase the heat transfer between the liquid plugs and the tube wall. Following this line of thinking, one can imagine that an appropriate combination of different modal vibrations by design or control can result in an OHP with high heat transfer capability.

4.6.2   Transient Analysis

Because modal analysis is used to obtain a mechanical system's dynamic characteristics under free undamped vibrations, heat transfer between the tube wall and liquid and vapor slugs, gravity, viscosity-induced damping, and bending-induced pressure drop are not included in the modal analysis of OHPs. The heat transfer between the tube wall and vapor and fluid slugs serves as the driving force for slug oscillation and, therefore, is important for evaluating the heat transfer capability of an OHP. Because the driving force is determined by a complex combination of vapor slug lengths and temperatures, physical properties of the working fluid, fluid filling ratio, the heating mode (top or bottom), and others, transient analysis is necessary to account for all of these factors in evaluating the performance of an OHP. For transient analysis of an OHP, the governing equations of motion need to include all the heat transfer between the tube wall and fluid and vapor slugs, gravity, viscosity-induced damping, and bending-induced pressure drop as

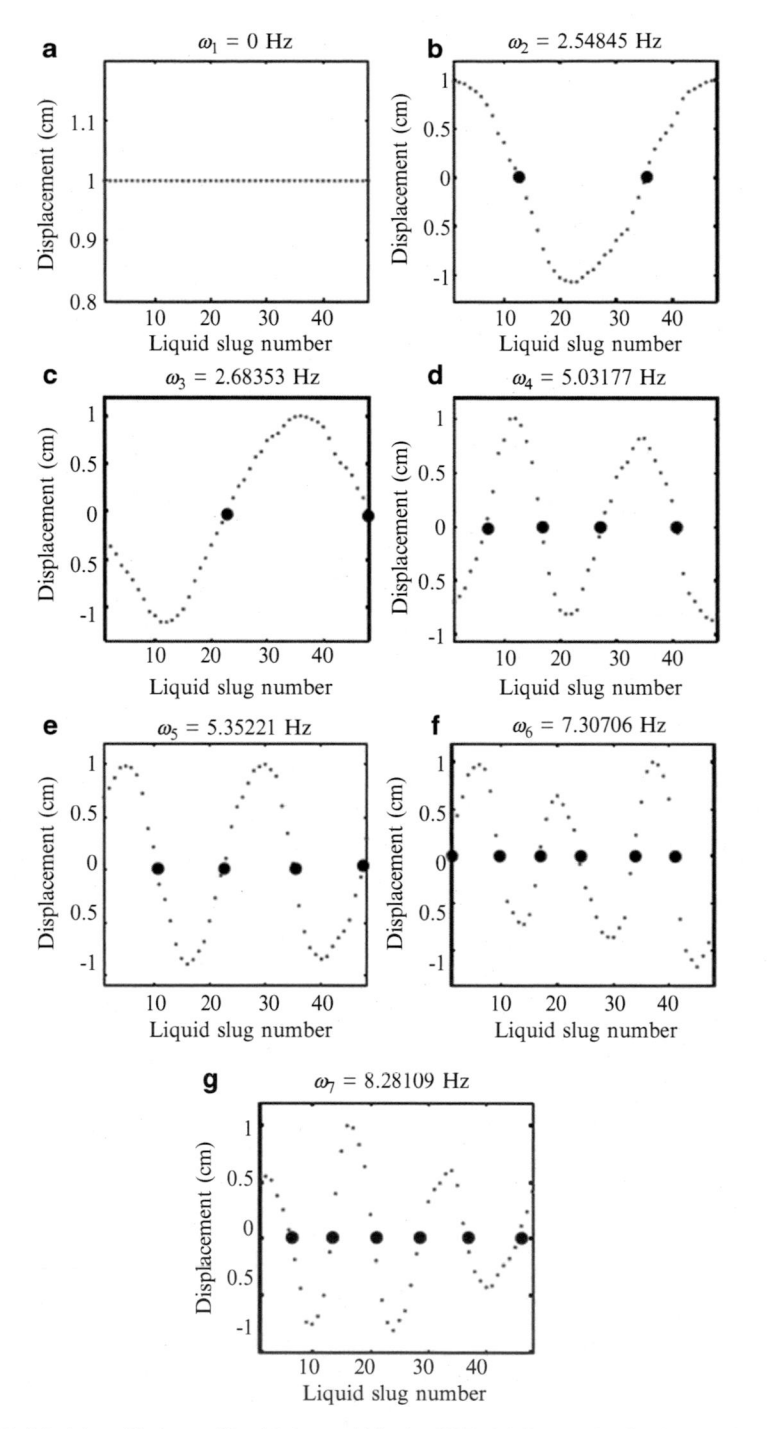

Fig. 4.17 Modal oscillations of liquid slugs within the OHP: (**a**) first mode, (**b, c**) second and third modes, (**d, e**) fourth and fifth modes, and (**f, g**) sixth and seventh modes (Peng et al. 2014)

$$
\begin{bmatrix} L_{11}\rho_1 & & & 0 \\ & L_{12}\rho_1 & & \\ & & \ddots & \\ 0 & & & L_{ln}\rho_1 \end{bmatrix} \begin{Bmatrix} \dfrac{d^2 s_1}{dt^2} \\ \dfrac{d^2 s_2}{dt^2} \\ \vdots \\ \dfrac{d^2 s_n}{dt^2} \end{Bmatrix}
$$

$$
+ \begin{bmatrix} \dfrac{f_1 Re_1 P \mu_1 L_{11}}{8DA} & & & 0 \\ & \dfrac{f_1 Re_1 P \mu_1 L_{12}}{8DA} & & \\ & & \ddots & \\ 0 & & & \dfrac{f_1 Re_1 P \mu_1 L_{ln}}{8DA} \end{bmatrix} \begin{Bmatrix} \dot{s}_1 \\ \dot{s}_2 \\ \vdots \\ \dot{s}_n \end{Bmatrix} + \begin{Bmatrix} P_{v1} - P_{v2} \\ P_{v2} - P_{v3} \\ \vdots \\ P_{vn-1} - P_{vn} \\ P_{vn} - P_{v1} \end{Bmatrix}
$$

$$
= \begin{Bmatrix} -\text{sign}\left(\dfrac{ds_1}{dt}\right) c_b \rho_1 \left(\dfrac{ds_1}{dt}\right)^2 /2 + L_{11}\rho_1 g_1 \\ -\text{sign}\left(\dfrac{ds_2}{dt}\right) c_b \rho_1 \left(\dfrac{ds_2}{dt}\right)^2 /2 + L_{12}\rho_1 g_2 \\ \vdots \\ -\text{sign}\left(\dfrac{ds_n}{dt}\right) c_b \rho_1 \left(\dfrac{ds_n}{dt}\right)^2 /2 + L_{ln}\rho_1 g_n \end{Bmatrix}
$$

$$(4.89)$$

Equation (4.89) can be rewritten in the following form

$$[M]\{\ddot{s}\} + [C]\{\dot{s}\} + [K]\{s\} = \{R\} \tag{4.90}$$

where the mass matrix $[M]$, the damping matrix $[C]$, the stiffness matrix $[K]$, and the load vector $\{R\}$ are defined as

$$
[M] = \begin{bmatrix} L_{11}\rho_1 & & & 0 \\ & L_{12}\rho_1 & & \\ & & \ddots & \\ 0 & & & L_{ln}\rho_1 \end{bmatrix} \tag{4.91}
$$

$$
[C] = \begin{bmatrix} \dfrac{f_1 Re_1 P \mu_1 L_{11}}{8DA} & & & 0 \\ & \dfrac{f_1 Re_1 P \mu_1 L_{12}}{8DA} & & \\ & & \ddots & \\ 0 & & & \dfrac{f_1 Re_1 P \mu_1 L_{ln}}{8DA} \end{bmatrix} \tag{4.92}
$$

$$[K]\{s\} \equiv \left\{ \begin{array}{c} p_{v1} - p_{v2} \\ p_{v2} - p_{v3} \\ \vdots \\ p_{vn-1} - p_{vn} \\ p_{vn} - p_{v1} \end{array} \right\} \tag{4.93}$$

$$\{R\} = \left\{ \begin{array}{c} -\mathrm{sign}\left(\dfrac{ds_1}{dt}\right) c_b \rho_1 \left(\frac{ds_1}{dt}\right)^2 / 2 + L_{11} \rho_1 g_1 \\[2ex] -\mathrm{sign}\left(\dfrac{ds_2}{dt}\right) c_b \rho_1 \left(\frac{ds_2}{dt}\right)^2 / 2 + L_{12} \rho_1 g_2 \\[2ex] \vdots \\[2ex] -\mathrm{sign}\left(\dfrac{ds_n}{dt}\right) c_b \rho_1 \left(\frac{ds_n}{dt}\right)^2 / 2 + L_{ln} \rho_1 g_n \end{array} \right\} \tag{4.94}$$

Note that the explicit form of $[K]$ is not available because the relationships between the vapor bubbles' pressures and the displacements of fluid slugs depend on heat transfer processes between walls and working fluids which are implicit and highly nonlinear. If the heat transfer coefficients between oscillating liquid plugs/vapor bubbles and tube walls are known, Eq. (4.90) can be solved by the Euler Predictor–Corrector method (Peng et al. 2014; Diethelm et al. 2002).

4.7   Exciting Force to Start-Up Oscillating Motions and Maximum Filling Ratio

Vapor bubbles in an OHP play a key role in the oscillating motion. If an OHP is charged with 100 % liquid, i.e., no vapor volume inside, the OHP obviously cannot start up the oscillating motion. Let's consider a system consisting of only one vapor bubble and one liquid plug as shown in Fig. 4.18. As shown, the system is well balanced. From the mechanical vibration point of view, an exciting force is needed to initialize the movement for a mechanical vibration system. Without this exciting force, the system cannot initiate the oscillating motion. When one end of the liquid plug is on the evaporating section, liquid vaporizes and the quantity of vapor increases significantly. Increasing the quantity of vapor directly increases the vapor pressure. Consider the vapor as an ideal gas, i.e.,

$$p_v = \rho_v RT \tag{4.95}$$

Taking derivative on both sides of Eq. (4.95) yields

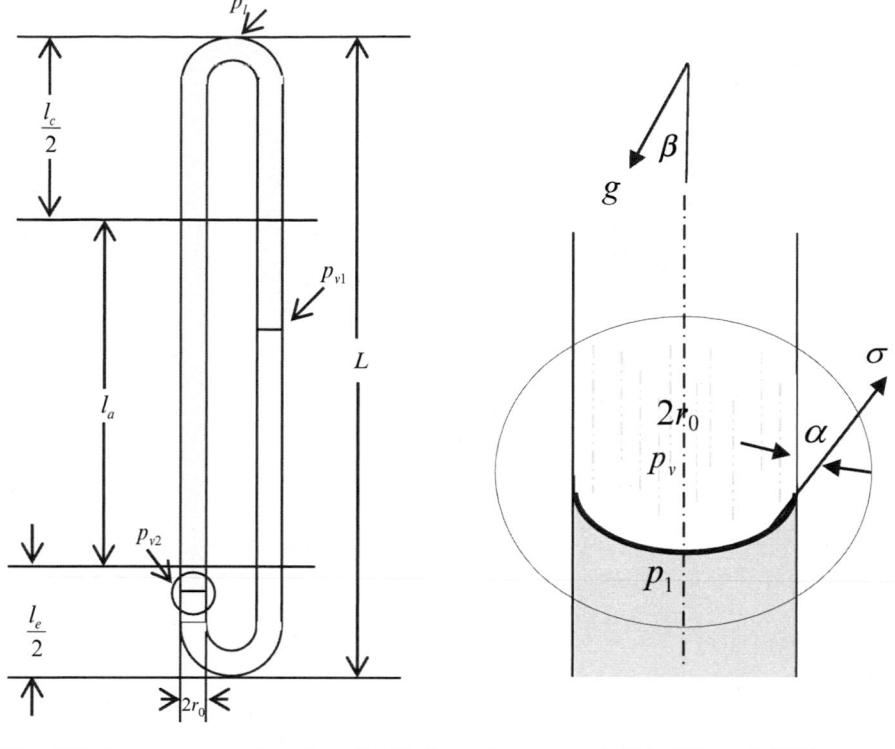

Fig. 4.18 A system consisting of one liquid plug and one vapor bubble (Yin et al. 2014)

$$\frac{dp_v}{dt} = RT\frac{d\rho_v}{dt} + R\rho_v\frac{dT}{dt} \tag{4.96}$$

If the initial vapor density and temperature are $\rho_{v,0}$ and T_0, respectively, the transient density and temperature can be expressed as $\rho_v = \rho_{v,0} + \Delta\rho$ and $T = T_0 + \Delta T$, respectively. Substituting them into Eq. (4.96) yields

$$\frac{dp_v}{dt} = R(T_0 + \Delta T)\frac{d\rho_v}{dt} + R(\rho_{v,0} + \Delta\rho)\frac{dT}{dt} \tag{4.97}$$

Considering that $T_0 \gg \Delta T$ and $\rho_{v,0} \gg \Delta\rho$, Eq. (4.96) can be simplified as

$$\frac{dp_v}{dt} = RT_0\frac{d\rho_v}{dt} + R\rho_{v,0}\frac{dT}{dt} \tag{4.98}$$

For an OHP, the driving force to initiate the oscillating motion is the pressure difference by vapor volume expansion and contraction during the heat addition/rejection processes. To estimate the minimum heat input needed to generate the pressure difference and start the oscillating motion, it is reasonable to assume that

the heat added to the evaporation section will be used to generate vapor just before the oscillating motion takes place, i.e., $q_v = \dot{m}_v h_{lv}$, where $\dot{m}$ is the vapor mass generation per unit time, i.e., $\dot{m}_v = \frac{dm_v}{dt}$. Furthermore, the total vapor mass can be calculated by $m_v = \rho_v V_v$, where $V_v = 2L(1 - \phi)\pi r_0^2$. For a given OHP, the filling ratio is given, and the vapor volume is almost constant. Heat addition can be expressed as

$$q_v = \frac{d\rho_v}{dt} V_v h_{lv} \tag{4.99}$$

Considering Eq. (4.99), Eq. (4.98) becomes

$$\frac{dp_v}{dt} = RT_0 \frac{q_v}{V h_{lv}} + R\rho_{v,0} \frac{dT}{dt} \tag{4.100}$$

Integrating Eq. (4.100) with time t during which heat is added and liquid becomes vapor, it can be found as $\int_0^t \frac{dp_v}{dt} dt = \int_0^t \left(RT_0 \frac{q_v}{V h_{lv}} + R\rho_{v,0} \frac{dT}{dt} \right) dt$ or

$$\Delta p_v = RT_0 \frac{q_v}{V h_{lv}} t + R\rho_{v,0} \Delta T \tag{4.101}$$

As shown in Eq. (4.101), the pressure difference, Δp_v, is due to the heat addition in the evaporator. This pressure difference will be used to drive the oscillating motion in an OHP.

Considering the Laplace–Young equation, the pressure difference across the liquid–vapor interface can be found as

$$\Delta p_{v,1} = p_v - p_1 = \sigma \left(\frac{1}{r_1} + \frac{1}{r_2} \right) \tag{4.102}$$

Because the tube radius, r_0, is very small, the meniscus radius at the liquid–vapor interface can be assumed to be a constant. Consider the pressure difference across the liquid–vapor interface and the hydraulic pressure difference due to the gravitational force; notice that the meniscus radii, r_1 and r_2, can be found as $r_1 = r_2 = \frac{r_0}{\cos \alpha}$, and the pressure difference $p_{v2} - p_{v1}$, can be expressed as

$$p_{v2} - p_{v1} = \frac{2\sigma(\cos \alpha_2 - \cos \alpha_1)}{r_0} + (\rho_1 - \rho_v)g(h_2 - h_1) \cos \beta \tag{4.103}$$

When this total pressure as defined by Eq. (4.103) is equal to or less than the pressure difference defined by Eq. (4.101), the oscillating motion in the system can start. Combining Eqs. (4.101) and (4.103) yields

$$\frac{2\sigma(\cos\alpha_2 - \cos\alpha_1)}{r_0} + (\rho_1 - \rho_v)g(h_2 - h_1)\cos\beta = RT_0\frac{q_v}{Vh_{lv}}t + R\rho_{v,0}\Delta T$$

$$(4.104)$$

When heat is added to the evaporating section, vapor pressure increases. The pressure wave will travel through both vapor and liquid phases. The speed of pressure wave in the vapor phase is different from that in the liquid phase, which results in an exciting pressure difference. The time difference for these two pressure waves reaching another interface can be found as

$$t = \frac{2L(1 - \Phi)}{u_v} - \frac{2L\Phi}{u_l}$$

$$(4.105)$$

where L is the length of the OHP, Φ is the liquid filling ratio, u_v is the pressure wave speed in the vapor phase, and u_l is the pressure wave speed in the liquid phase. For the wave speed in the liquid phase, it is well known that $u_l = \sqrt{\frac{K}{\rho_1}}$, where K is the bulk modulus. The vapor phase can be taken as an ideal gas. The speed of the pressure wave in the vapor phase can be determined by $u_v = \sqrt{kRT}$, where k is the adiabatic coefficient. During this time difference, vapor pressure increases continuously due to the heat addition in the evaporating section, and the pressure waves should travel through both phases continuously. If the heat addition on the evaporating section takes place during this time difference defined by Eq. (4.105), the maximum vapor pressure increase should be equal to that determined by Eq. (4.101). This driving pressure difference will be used to overcome the total pressure drop as shown in Eq. (4.103). Substituting (4.105) into Eq. (4.104), the heat input to generate the oscillating motion can be found as

$$q_v = \frac{(2\sigma(\cos\alpha_2 - \cos\alpha_1) + r_0((\rho_1 - \rho_v)g(h_2 - h_1)\cos\beta - R\rho_{v,0}\Delta T))}{RT_0(u_l - \Phi(u_v + u_l))}(1 - \Phi)\pi r_0 h_{lv}u_lu_v$$

$$(4.106)$$

Equation (4.106) illustrates the minimum heat transfer rate to start up the oscillating motion in an OHP. The start-up of the oscillating motion in an OHP needs an exciting force. Because the pressure travel speed in the vapor phase is different from the liquid phase when a heat addition takes place in the evaporating section, a pressure difference in the system is produced which acts as an exciting force to start up the movement of the liquid plugs and vapor bubbles in the OHP.

Extensive experimental investigations on the filling ratio as it pertains to the heat transfer performance have been investigated (Kim et al. 2003; Im et al. 2004; Cao and Cheng 2004; Qu et al. 2009; 2010; Yuan ct al. 2010; Ji ct al. 2011; Chien et al. 2012; Khandekar et al. 2004; Khandekar and Groll 2008). These studies indicated that an operationally better performing and self-sustained thermally

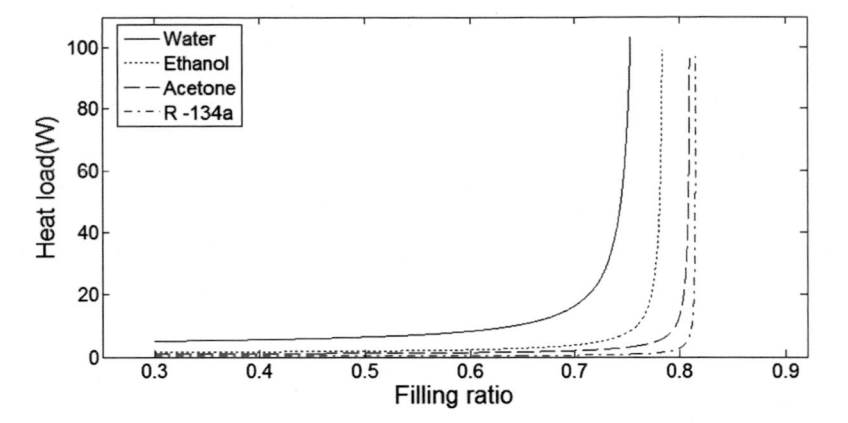

Fig. 4.19   Filling ratio vs. heat input (operation temperature $T = 335$ K) (Yin et al. 2014)

driven pulsating action is only observed when the filling ratio range is between 20 and 80 % depending on the working fluid and gravity. Rearranging Eq. (4.106), the expression of filling ratio (Yin et al. 2014) can be found as

$$\Phi = \frac{\dfrac{\left(2\sigma(\cos\alpha_2 - \cos\alpha_1) + r_0\left((\rho_1 - \rho_v)g(h_2 - h_1)\cos\beta - R\rho_{v,0}\Delta T\right)\right)}{\pi r_0 h_{lv} u_l u_v - q_v R T_0 u_l}}{\dfrac{\left(2\sigma(\cos\alpha_2 - \cos\alpha_1) + r_0\left((\rho_1 - \rho_v)g(h_2 - h_1)\cos\beta - R\rho_{v,0}\Delta T\right)\right)}{\pi r_0 h_{lv} u_l u_v - q_v R T_0 (u_v + u_l)}}$$

$$(4.107)$$

If the heat input becomes infinity, i.e., $q_v \to \infty$, it can be found that $\Phi \to \frac{u_l}{u_v + u_l}$. In other words, when the filling ratio, Φ, is higher than $\frac{u_l}{u_v + u_l}$, the OHP cannot start-up with the oscillating motion even though the heat input becomes infinitely high. This maximum filling ratio can be called the maximum filling limit of an OHP. Combined with the expression of pressure wave speed in the vapor phase and liquid phase, it can be found as

$$\Phi \to \frac{1}{1 + \left(\frac{kRT\rho_1}{K}\right)^{1/2}} \qquad (4.108)$$

As shown in Eq. (4.108), this maximum filling ratio depends on the working fluid and operation temperature. Using Eq. (4.108), the effects of working fluid type on this limitation can be readily predicted. As shown in Fig. 4.19, if the OHP is charged with water, the upper limit is 76.2 % at an operating temperature of 335 K. When using ethanol, this limit is 78.6 % at the same operating temperature. Table 4.2 compares filling ratios in literature with predictions by Eq. (4.108). Groll and Khandekar (2004) conducted a comprehensive review of design rules and modeling strategies in the development of OHP. They found that the maximum

Table 4.2 Comparison with available experimental data of the maximum filling ratio (Yin et al. 2014)

No.	Working fluids	Experimental data from Literature	Prediction by current model (%)	Note
1	–	About 80 % (Groll and Khandekar 2004)	70–85	Depending on the working fluid
2	Water	About 70 % (Khandekar et al. 2004)	75.4	Vertical, operation temperature $T = 335$ K
3	Ethanol	About 75 % (Yang et al. 2009)	78.6	Horizontal, operation temperature $T = 335$ K

filling ratio is about 80 %, which is very close to the prediction shown in Table 4.2. Yang et al. (2009) investigated the possibility of an embedded OHP as an integrated structure or heat spreader, and ethanol was employed as the working fluid so as to render higher overall thermal conductance to the host substrate. It was determined that the maximum filling ratio is about 75 % in the case of horizontal heat orientation, which is almost the same as the prediction obtained by the model based on Eq. (4.108) with a relative difference percentage of about 3.6 %.

4.8   Heat Transfer Model of an OHP

As presented above, the gas spring-mass system consisting of liquid plugs and vapor bubbles is the basis of oscillating motion, and the pressure differences produced in the OHP are the driving forces for the oscillating motion in OHPs. The oscillating motion of liquid plugs and vapor bubbles in an OHP can be predicted if liquid plug and vapor bubble distributions for a given OHP are known with given heat transfer coefficients between liquid plugs or vapor bubbles and walls for both the evaporator and condenser sections. However, the heat transfer process between the working fluid and wall in the OHP is very complicated. It depends on oscillating frequency, oscillating amplitude, liquid plug length, turn number, gravity, and evaporation/condensation heat transfer associated with thermally excited oscillating motion. In addition, the evaporation heat transfer processes in the evaporator section include evaporating heat transfer through liquid film left and/or nucleate boiling on the wall surface, and the condensation heat transfer through condensation film, which is controlled by the surface tension and thermally excited oscillating motion. Therefore, it is not possible to theoretically determine the heat transfer coefficient of a thermally excited oscillating flow of a train of liquid plugs and vapor bubbles in an OHP. In this section, a simplified model will be presented to discuss how the heat transfer process in an OHP can be modeled. In the following analysis, it is assumed that (1) the temperature difference between the evaporator and condenser has a cosine waveform determined by Eq. (4.21) and (2) the vapor phase is considered an ideal gas. The OHP consists of an evaporating

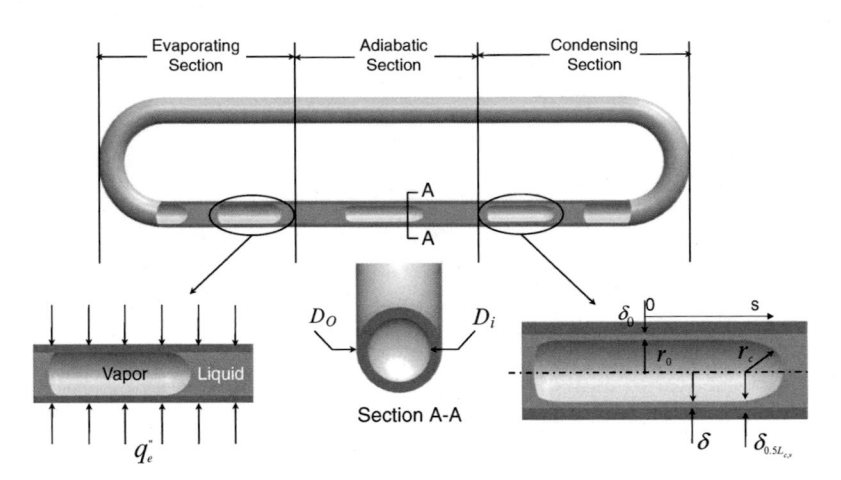

Fig. 4.20 Schematic of an OHP (Ma et al. 2008)

section, an adiabatic section, and a condensing section. Clearly, the heat transfer process in the OHP involves the evaporating heat transfer in the evaporating section, condensing heat transfer in the condensing section, and oscillating motions in the whole heat pipe. Because the oscillating motion has been specified by Eq. (4.21), the focus will be on evaporation and condensation heat transfer as shown below.

4.8.1 Heat Transfer in the Evaporating Section

When applying a heat source to the external circumference of the evaporator section in an OHP, as shown in Fig. 4.20, heat is transported by radial conduction through the evaporator wall and reaches the working fluid, resulting in vaporization. If the tube structuring the evaporating section is smooth, i.e., no wick structures on the inside surface of the tube, the heat transfer process occurring in the evaporating section is similar to convection boiling heat transfer. The heat transfer in the evaporating section of the OHP can be described by a combination of evaporation (microscopic) and bulk convection (macroscopic). The total heat transfer coefficient, h, can be expressed as

$$h = h_{mic} + h_{mac} \qquad (4.109)$$

where h_{mic} is due to the evaporating heat transfer and h_{mac} is due to the bulk convection caused by oscillating motions. Chen (1966) developed a model describing the evaporating heat transfer, where the microscopic evaporation of the heat transfer coefficient could be found by

$$h_{mic} = 0.00122 \left[\frac{k_l^{0.79} c_{pl}^{0.45} \rho_l^{0.49}}{\sigma^{0.5} \mu_l^{0.29} h_{lv}^{0.24} \rho_v^{0.24}} \right] [T_w - T_{sat}(P_l)]^{0.24} [P_{sat}(T_w) - P_l]^{0.75} S$$

(4.110)

where S is a suppression factor and a function of the two-phase Reynolds number, i.e.,

$$S = \left(1 + 2.56 \times 10^{-6} Re_{tp}^{1.17} \right)^{-1}$$

(4.111)

The two-phase Reynolds number in Eq. (4.111) can be determined by

$$Re_{tp} = Re_l [F(X_{tt})]^{1.25}$$

(4.112)

where the liquid Reynolds number and the Martinelli parameter, X_{tt}, are defined by

$$Re_l = \frac{G(1-x)D_i}{\mu_l}$$

(4.113)

$$X_{tt} = \left(\frac{1-x}{x} \right)^{0.9} \left(\frac{\rho_v}{\rho_l} \right)^{0.5} \left(\frac{\mu_l}{\mu_v} \right)^{0.1}$$

(4.114)

respectively. The function $F(X_{tt})$ shown in Eq. (4.112) depends on the Martinelli parameter, i.e.,

$$F(X_{tt}) = 1 \quad \text{for} \quad X_{tt}^{-1} \le 0.1$$

(4.115)

$$F(X_{tt}) = 2.35 \left(0.213 + \frac{1}{X_{tt}} \right)^{0.736} \quad \text{for} \quad X_{tt}^{-1} > 0.1$$

(4.116)

With a given liquid filling ratio, Φ, the quality, x, shown in Eq. (4.113), can be determined by

$$x = \frac{\rho_v - \Phi\rho_v}{\rho}$$

(4.117)

where the average density of the working fluid in the system may be calculated by the following relation:

$$\frac{1}{\rho} = \frac{x}{\rho_v} + \frac{1-x}{\rho_l}$$

(4.118)

Utilizing the Martinelli parameter for a two-phase flow, the heat transfer coefficient due to the forced convection caused by oscillating motions can be readily determined by

$$h_{\text{mac}} = F(X_{tt})h_1 \tag{4.119}$$

where h_1 is the liquid-phase heat transfer coefficient which can be found from Chap. 3.

4.8.2 Heat Transfer in the Condensing Section

The vapor generated in the evaporating section is condensed in the condensing section if the phase change driving force exists, and the condensate in the thin film region will flow into the liquid plug region due to the capillary force. Because the film thickness in the condensing film region is very thin compared with the meniscus thickness in the liquid plug, most of the condensing heat transfer will occur in the thin film region. In this region, as shown in Fig. 4.20, the Reynolds number of the condensate is very small; hence, the inertia terms can be neglected. Therefore, based on conservation of momentum in the thin film, the pressure drop due to the viscous flow can be found as

$$\frac{dP_1}{ds} = \frac{f \cdot Re_\delta \mu_1 D_o q_c'' s}{2\delta^3 D_i \rho_1 h_{1v}} \tag{4.120}$$

where

$$Re_\delta = \frac{\bar{U}_{1,c}\delta\rho_1}{\mu_1} \tag{4.121}$$

where s is the coordinate along the condensing film starting from the middle point of the condensing film and $\bar{U}_{1,c}$ is the average velocity of the condensate. By integrating Eq. (26) from $s = 0$ to $L_{c,v}/2$, the total pressure drop along half of the vapor bubble length can be found as

$$\Delta P_1 = \int_0^{\frac{L_{c,v}}{2}} \left(\frac{f \cdot Re_\delta \mu_1 D_o q_c''}{2\delta^3 D_i \rho_1 h_{1v}}\right) s\, ds \tag{4.122}$$

Numerous vapor bubbles can be found throughout the OHP including the condensing section. Although the vapor bubble distribution, i.e., vapor bubble number, in the OHP is unpredictable, the total vapor space remains constant for a given liquid filling ratio, Φ. It is assumed that all of the vapor bubbles in the condensing region are combined into one large slug with condensation occurring on its perimeter.

4.9 Operating Limitation in an OHP

The heat transport mechanism of an OHP is very different from a conventional heat pipe. The spring-mass system consisting of a train of liquid plugs and vapor bubbles plays a key role in the oscillating motion. When the mass-spring system in the system disappears, the oscillating motion in the OHP will stop. For a given functional OHP, a train of liquid plugs and vapor bubbles must exist in the system. When heat is added to the evaporating section, liquid becomes vapor producing vapor volume expansion. At the same time, when the heat is removed from the condensing section, vapor condenses into liquid producing vapor volume contraction. The pressure differences between the evaporator and condenser are the driving forces for the oscillation motion in the system. It has been shown that when the heat transfer rate increases, the oscillating motion increases and enhances heat transfer. If the heat transfer rate continuously increases, the thermally excited oscillating motion increases. The velocity increase of liquid plugs and vapor bubbles in the system directly reduces the length of liquid plugs moving in a capillary channel. When vapor velocity is higher than some critical value, vapor penetrates all liquid plugs and produces an annular flow. When this takes place, the mass-spring system consisting of a train of liquid plugs and vapor bubbles disappears. The oscillating motion does not exist anymore, and the OHP reaches the maximum heat transport capability, which is called the operating limitation of an OHP.

Consider an OHP with a liquid plug moving into the evaporator section as a control volume (Fig. 4.23). For vapor phase to penetrate the liquid plug, the momentum produced by the vapor phase will be used to overcome the total forces acting on the liquid plug, i.e.,

$$\int_0^{r_0} 2\pi \rho_v u_v^2 r \, dr = (-p_1 + p_2)\pi r_0^2 + 2\pi r_0 \sigma(\cos\alpha_r + \cos\alpha_a)$$

$$+ 2\pi r_0 \left(\int_0^{L_1} \tau_w dx \right) \tag{4.129}$$

where $\int_0^{r_0} 2\pi \rho_v u_v^2 r \, dr$ is the momentum produced by the vapor phase due to the vapor volume expansion, $(-p_1 + p_2)\pi r_0^2$ is due to the pressure difference acting on the liquid plug by vapor bubbles, $2\pi r_0 \sigma(\cos\alpha_r + \cos\alpha_a)$ is due to the surface tensions, and $2\pi r_0 \left(\int_0^{L_1} \tau_w dx \right)$ is due to the shear stress between wall and fluid. The shear stress on the wall can be expressed as

$$\tau_w = \mu \left(-\frac{du_1}{dr} \right)_w \tag{4.130}$$

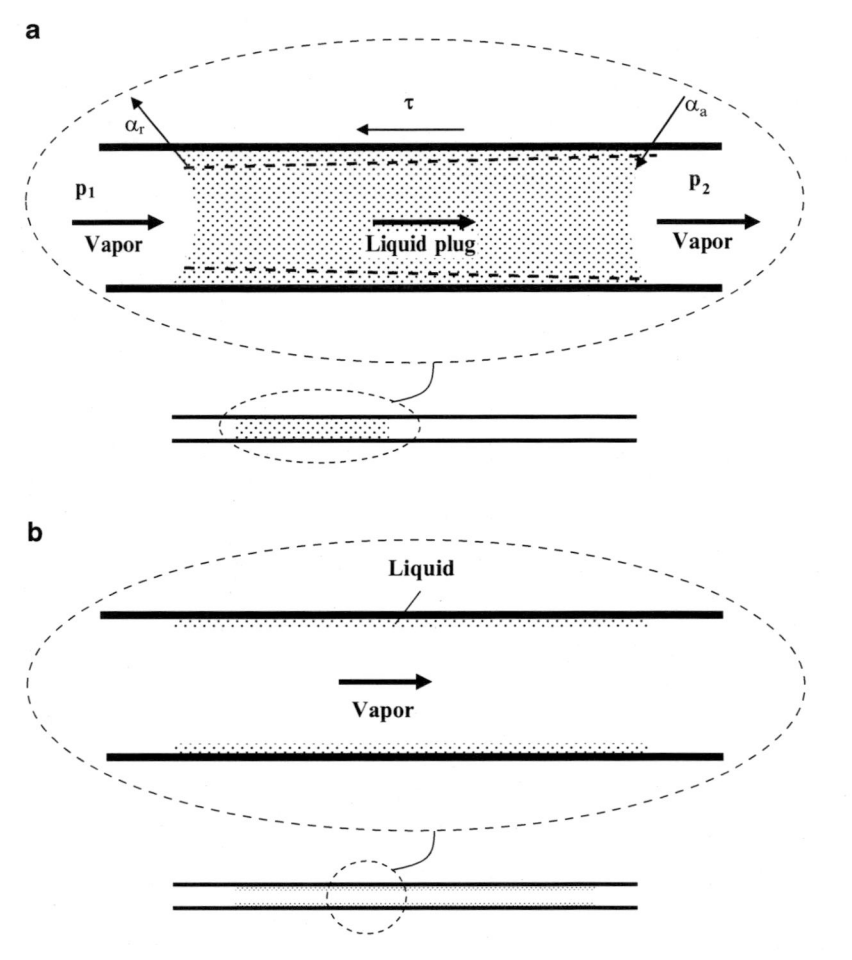

Fig. 4.23 Schematic of a liquid plug moving in the capillary channel of an OHP: (**a**) right before the penetration of vapor through the liquid plug and (**b**) right after the penetration of vapor through the liquid plug (Yin et al. 2015)

When the liquid plug moves to the evaporating section, the heat addition to the evaporating section increases the vapor volume and vapor pressure. Because the pressure wave speed in the liquid phase is different from that in the vapor phase, an exciting force is generated, which helps to start up the oscillating motion (Yin et al. 2014). As a result, when the liquid plug moves to the evaporating section, the liquid plug stops and then starts to move back. The momentum equation can be described by

$$\rho_1 \frac{\partial u_1}{\partial t} = -\frac{dp}{dx} + \mu_1 \left(\frac{\partial^2 u_1}{\partial r^2} + \frac{1}{r} \frac{\partial u_1}{\partial r} \right) \qquad (4.131)$$

with the initial and boundary conditions of

$$u_1(r,0) = 0 \tag{4.132}$$

$$u_1(r_0, t) = 0 \tag{4.133}$$

Consider the expression of fully developed flow

$$u_1(r,t) = \left(-\frac{dp}{dx}\right)(r_0^2 - r^2)/4\mu_1 \tag{4.134}$$

which leads to the solution of the velocity distribution in the developing region and can be obtained as (White 1974),

$$u_1 = u_{1,\max}\left(\left(1 - r^{*2}\right) - \sum_{n=1}^{\infty} \frac{8J_0\left(\lambda_n r^*\right)}{\lambda_n^3 J_1(\lambda_n)} \exp\left(-\lambda_n^2 \frac{\mu_1 \cdot t}{\rho_1 \cdot r_0^2}\right)\right) \tag{4.135}$$

where

$$u_{1,\max} = \left(-\frac{dp}{dx}\right)r_0^2/4\mu_1 \tag{4.136}$$

$$r^* = \frac{r}{r_0} \tag{4.137}$$

If the dimensionless velocity is defined by

$$u^* = \frac{u_1}{u_{1,\max}} \tag{4.138}$$

Equation (4.135) can be expressed as

$$u^* = \left(1 - r^{*2}\right) - \sum_{n=1}^{\infty} \frac{8J_0\left(\lambda_n r^*\right)}{\lambda_n^3 J_1(\lambda_n)} \exp\left(-\lambda_n^2 \frac{\mu_1 \cdot t}{\rho_1 \cdot r_0^2}\right) \tag{4.139}$$

Substituting Eqs. (4.137) and (4.138) into Eq. (4.130) yields

$$\tau_w = \mu_1\left(-\frac{d\left(u_{1,\max}u^*\right)}{dr}\right)_{r^*=1} = \frac{1}{r_0}\mu_1 u_{1,\max}\left(-\frac{du^*}{dr^*}\right)_{r^*=1} \tag{4.140}$$

Considering Eq. (4.140), Eq. (4.129) can be expressed as

$$\int_0^{r_0} 2\pi \rho_v u_v^2 r \, dr = (-p_1 + p_2)\pi r_0^2 + 2\pi r_0 \sigma(\cos \alpha_r + \cos \alpha_a)$$

$$+ 2\pi r_0 \left(\int_0^{L_1} \left(\frac{1}{r_0} \mu_1 u_{1,\max} \left(-\frac{du^*}{dr^*} \right) \right)_{r^*=1} dx \right) \tag{4.141}$$

If $p_1 = p_2$, Eq. (4.141) becomes

$$\int_0^{r_0} 2\pi \rho_v u_v^2 r \, dr = 2\pi r_0 \sigma(\cos \alpha_r + \cos \alpha_a)$$

$$+ 2\pi \left(\int_0^{L_1} \mu_1 u_{1,\max} \left(-\frac{du^*}{dr^*} \right)_{r^*=1} dx \right) \tag{4.142}$$

Recognizing that the vapor phase and the liquid phase share the same velocity at the interface and utilizing Eqs. (4.137) and (4.138), the first term in Eq. (4.142) can be rewritten as

$$\int_0^{r_0} 2\pi \rho_v u_v^2 r \, dr = \rho_v r_0^2 u_{1,\max}^2 \int_0^1 u_1^{*2} r^* \, dr^* \tag{4.143}$$

Substituting it into Eq. (4.143) and simplifying it gives

$$\rho_v r_0^2 u_{1,\max}^2 \int_0^1 u_1^{*2} r^* \, dr^* = r_0 \sigma(\cos \alpha_r + \cos \alpha_a)$$

$$+ \mu_1 \left(-\frac{du^*}{dr^*} \right)_{r^*=1} \int_0^{L_1} u_{1,\max} dx \tag{4.144}$$

To simply the equation, the following parameters are defined as follows

$$A = \int_0^1 u_1^{*2} r^* \, dr^*$$

$$= \int_0^1 \left((1 - r^{*2}) - \sum_{n=1}^{\infty} \frac{8 J_0(\lambda_n r^*)}{\lambda_n^3 J_1(\lambda_n)} \exp\left(-\lambda_n^2 \frac{\mu_1 \cdot t}{\rho_1 \cdot r_0^2} \right) \right)^2 r^* \, dr^* \tag{4.145}$$

$$B = \left(-\frac{du^*}{dr^*} \right)_{r^*=1} = \left(2r^* - \sum_{n=1}^{\infty} \frac{8 J_1(\lambda_n r^*)}{\lambda_n^2 J_1(\lambda_n)} \exp\left(-\lambda_n^2 \frac{\mu_1 \cdot t}{\rho_1 \cdot r_0^2} \right) \right)_{r^*=1}$$

$$= 2 - \sum_{n=1}^{\infty} \frac{8}{\lambda_n^2} \exp\left(-\lambda_n^2 \frac{\mu_1 \cdot t}{\rho_1 \cdot r_0^2} \right) \tag{4.146}$$

$$C = r_0 \sigma(\cos \alpha_r + \cos \alpha_a) \tag{4.147}$$

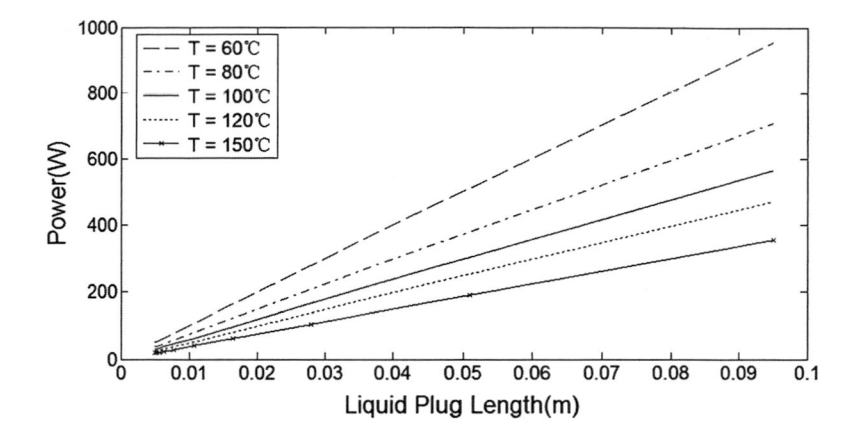

Fig. 4.24 Liquid plug length effect on the operating limitation (water) (Yin et al. 2015)

i.e., the liquid plug velocity reaches the highest and starts to decrease, the acceleration becomes zero. The total force to be overcome by the vapor momentum is the lowest. At this point, the slug flow can easily become annular flow, where the operating limitation takes place. When $t \to \infty$, it can be readily found that

$$\lim_{t \to \infty} A = \frac{1}{6} \tag{4.162}$$

$$\lim_{t \to \infty} B = 2 \tag{4.163}$$

$$\lim_{t \to \infty} D = \frac{1}{4} \tag{4.164}$$

Substituting Eqs. (4.162)–(4.164) into Eq. (4.161) and simplifying it, the operating limitation can be found as

$$q = 3\pi\mu_1 h_{lv} L_1 \tag{4.165}$$

As shown in Eq. (4.165), the operating limitation depends on the liquid plug length in addition to liquid viscosity and latent heat. Yin et al. (2015) used Eq. (4.165) to predict the liquid plug length effect on the operating limitation. When the liquid plug length increases, the operating limitation increases as shown in Fig. 4.24.

For a functional OHP, there are a number of liquid plugs with different lengths. In this case, the liquid plug length, L_1, should correspond to the longest one. If the OHP has a uniform hydraulic diameter of D_h with the filling ratio of Φ, i.e.,

$$\Phi = \frac{V_1}{V_t} = \frac{L_1}{L} \tag{4.166}$$

Table 4.3 Operating limitation with method presented herein

Name	OHP1	OHP2	OHP3	OHP4
Working fluid	HFE7000	HFE7000	HFE7100	Water
Turn numbers	9	14	6	6
Length of OHP (m)	2.79	2.79	1.86	1.86
Liquid viscosity (N/s m^2)	0.000448	0.000448	0.00061	0.000185
Liquid density (kg/m^3)	1,400	1,400	1,520	919.12
Vapor density (kg/m^3)	202.45	202.45	86	2.352
Surface tension force (N/m)	0.0124	0.0124	0.0139	0.0494
Diameter (m)	0.0012	0.00076	0.00165	0.00165
Latent heat (J/kg)	142,000	142,000	125,000	2,123,000
Operating limitation q (W)	148.69	95.59	111.39	573.75

where

$$L = L_l + L_v \tag{4.167}$$

the operating limitation, i.e., Eq. (4.165), can be expressed as a function of filling ratio, i.e.,

$$q = 3\pi\mu_1 h_{lv} L\Phi \tag{4.168}$$

If an OHP has N turns and the liquid plug is uniformly divided into N liquid plugs, the operating limitation can be expressed as

$$q = \frac{3\pi\mu_1 h_{lv} L\Phi}{N} \tag{4.169}$$

For each turn of an OHP, if there are a number of liquid plugs, M, with a uniform distribution, the total operating limitation can be found as

$$q = \frac{3\pi\mu_1 h_{lv} L\Phi}{NM} \tag{4.170}$$

To predict the operating limitation, four OHPs with dimensions, working fluid types, and operating temperatures, as shown in Table 4.3, are considered. It is assumed that each turn has one liquid plug. For example, if an OHP has six turns, there are six liquid plugs. As shown in Table 4.3, when HFE7000 is used as a working fluid, the operating limitation is 148.69 W for a 9-turn OHP. With the same total length and same working fluid at the same filling ratio except the turn number, the operating limitation reduces to 95.59 W for a 14-turn OHP. As shown, if the OHP total tube length is the same, the operating limitation decreases when the turn number increases. Table 4.3 also shows the operating limitations of OHP3 and OHP4. Both OHPs have six turns but with different working fluids. OHP3 is

Table 4.4 Charging ratio effect on the operating limit with method presented herein (W)

Filling ratio (%)	OHP3 (HFE7100)	OHP4 (water)
30	66.83	344.25
40	89.11	459.00
50	111.39	573.75
60	133.67	688.50
70	155.94	803.25

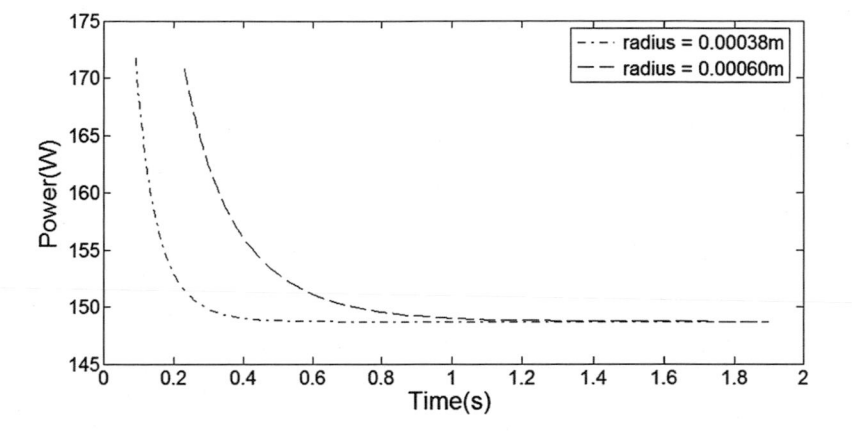

Fig. 4.25 Tube radius effect on the operating limitation (HFE7000, 9 turns) (Yin et al. 2015)

charged with HFE7100 and OHP4 with water, respectively. For the same OHP setup as OHP3, when the working fluid is changed from HFE7100 to water, the operating limitation increases from 111.39 to 573.75 W. It can be concluded that the working fluid significantly affects the operating limitation.

In addition, the operating limitation significantly depends on the filling ratio as shown in Table 4.4. The predictions presented above are based on Eqs. (4.165) and (4.169). If Eq. (4.161) is used to predict the operating limitation, as shown in Figs. 4.25–4.27, it can be found that the operating limitation depends on the oscillating motion. For a given liquid plug, when the oscillating motion starts, the heat input or vapor momentum needed to push the liquid plug is high, which depends on the tube radius (Fig. 4.25), charging ratio (Figs. 4.26 and 4.27), and working fluid (Figs. 4.26 and 4.27). As previously noted, surface tension is not considered. When a liquid plug is moving, the receiving contact angle is different from the advancing contact angle, and the surface tension depends on the temperature. Neglecting the surface tension effect might be one source of prediction error in the model.

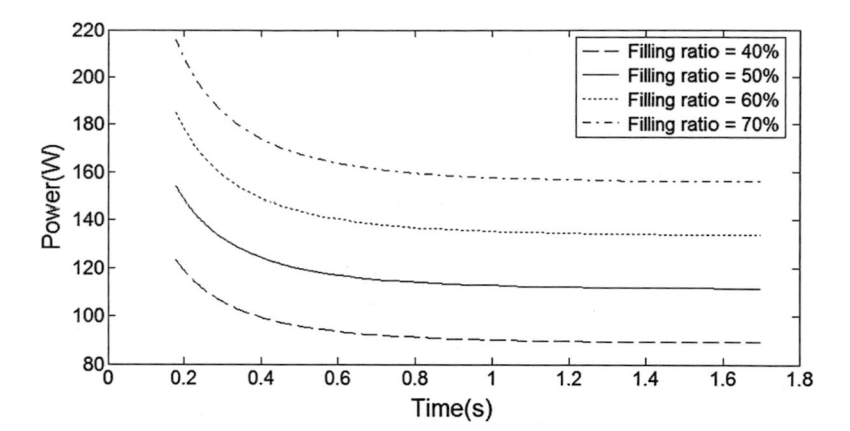

Fig. 4.26   Filling ratio effect on the operating limitation (HFE7100, 6 turns) (Yin et al. 2015)

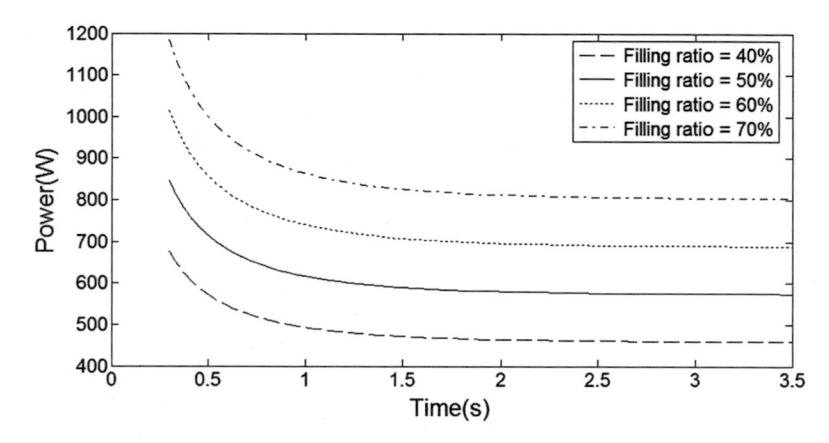

Fig. 4.27   Filling ratio effect on the operating limitation (water, 6 turns) (Yin et al. 2015)

The operating limitation has been experimentally investigated by a number of investigators (Cao and Cheng 2004; Yang et al. 2009; Ji et al. 2014). Cao and Cheng (2004) conducted an experimental investigation of a flat OHP with dimensions of 180 mm × 54 mm × 4 mm charged with FC72 and found that the operating limitation depends on the filling ratio. At filling ratios of 20 and 30 %, which are lower than the typical filling ratio of an OHP, the operating limitations were 60 W and 110 W, respectively. Yang et al. (2009) studied a copper 20-turn OHP with an inner diameter of 2 mm charged with R123 and found that the operating limit was about 540 W with a filling ratio of 50 % and a bottom heated mode. Ji et al. (2014) investigated the operating limitation of a 6-turn OHP as shown in Fig. 4.28.

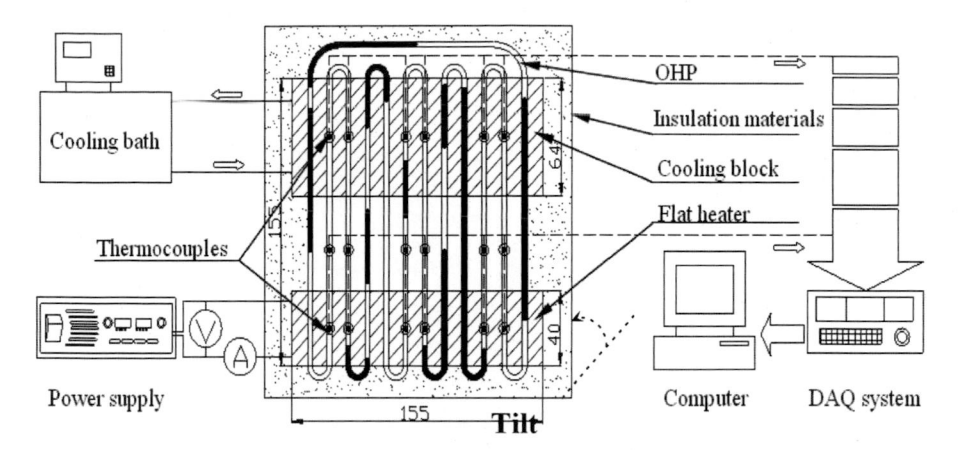

Fig. 4.28 Schematic of a 6-turn OHP and experimental system (units in mm) (Ji et al. 2014)

A copper tube with an inner diameter of 1.65 mm and outer diameter of 3.18 mm was used for the OHP. Figure 4.28 shows six turns and three sections of an evaporator, condenser, and adiabatic section with lengths of 40 mm, 64 mm, and 51 mm, respectively. This OHP was tested at different tilt angles ranging from 0° (horizontal heating mode) to 90° (vertical bottom heating mode). The evaporator was heated by a uniform electrical flat heater. The condenser section was in direct contact with a cooling block which was cooled by a constant-temperature cooling bath. The temperature of the cooling bath (i.e., the operating temperature of the OHP) was set to 20 or 60 °C.

Figure 4.29 shows the working fluid effect on the operating limit. As shown, when the OHP is charged with water, the operating limit is much higher than that charged with HFE7100. Tables 4.5 and 4.6 summarized the experimental results of the effects of tilted angle, filling ratio, and the operating temperature on the operating limitations of this OHP. Working fluid affects the OHP's operating limitation significantly. In addition, it was found that the operating limit of the OHP increases as the filling ratio and tilt angle increase. For a water OHP, the operating limit increases as the operating temperature decreases. However, for an HFE7100 OHP, the operating limit increases as the operating temperature increases.

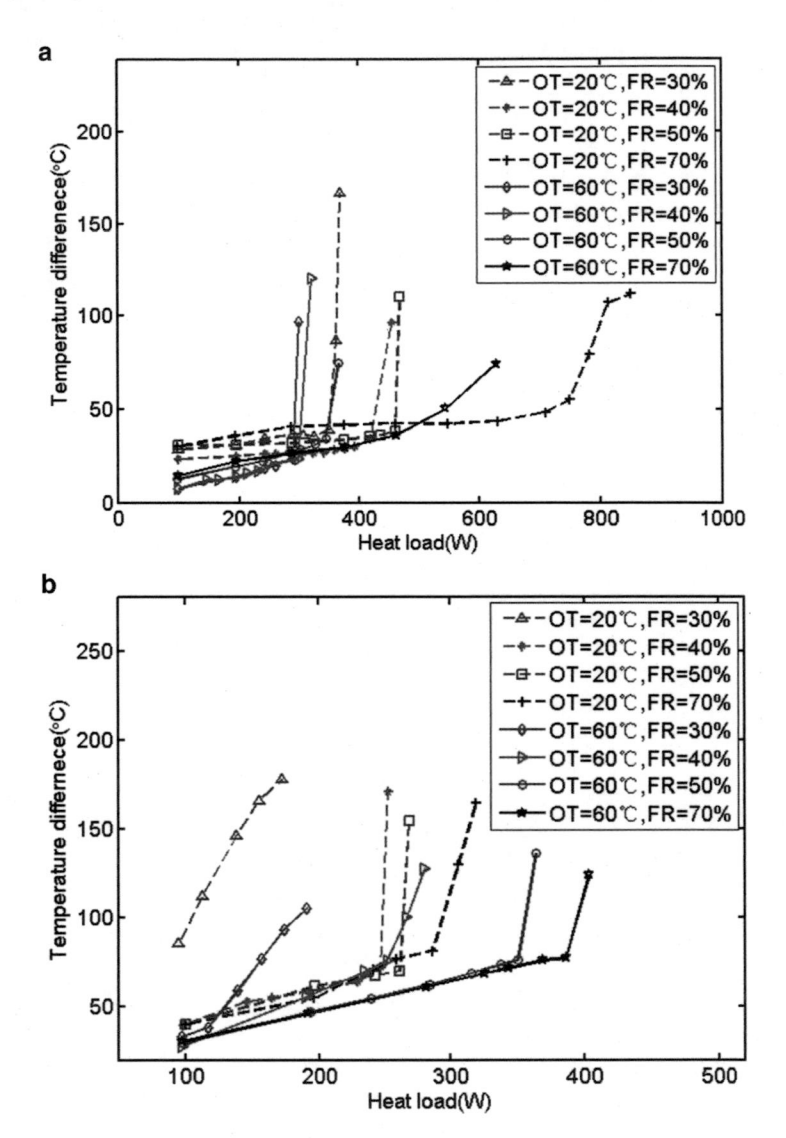

Fig. 4.29 Operating limitations of an OHP charged with (**a**) water in a bottom heating mode and (**b**) HFE7100 in a bottom heating mode (*FR* filling ratio and *OT* operating temperature) (Ji et al. 2014)

Table 4.5 Operating limit of the OHP charged with water (W) (Ji et al. 2014)

Operating temperature (°C)	20				60			
Tilt angle (°)	0	30	60	90	0	30	60	90
Filling ratio 30 %	231.2	311.6	352.7	369.3	215.4	281.0	285.4	298.6
Filling ratio 40 %	310.5	351.7	406.6	455.3	229.7	298.2	313.1	320.5
Filling ratio 50 %	341.5	429.8	444.6	468.6	260.9	318.5	348.5	366.1
Filling ratio 70 %	820.7	827.4	847.1	848.5	587.3	593.2	622.7	628.2

Table 4.6 Operating limit of the OHP charged with HFE7100 (W) (Ji et al. 2014)

Operating temperature (°C)	20				60			
Tilt angle (°)	0	30	60	90	0	30	60	90
Filling ratio 30 %	N	N	112.6	138.3	N	131.8	170.1	190.9
Filling ratio 40 %	N	164.5	241.4	253.0	N	184.2	276.6	280.4
Filling ratio 50 %	N	220.2	247.3	269.3	N	222.9	345.3	364.3
Filling ratio 70 %	N	277.3	318.7	329.4	N	329.5	370.3	403.8

N means OHP did not function

References

Akachi H (1990) Structure of a heat pipe. US Patent No. 4,921,041

Akachi H, Polasek F, Stulc P (1996) Pulsating heat pipes. In: Proceedings of the 5th International heat pipe symposium, Melbourne, pp 208–217

Cao X, Cheng P (2004) A novel design of pulsating heat pipes with improved performance. In: 13th international heat pipe conference.

Chen JC (1966) Correlation for boiling heat transfer to saturated fluids in convective flow. Ind Eng Chem Process Des Dev 5(3):322–339

Chien KH, Lin YT, Chen YR, Yang KS, Wang CC (2012) A novel design of pulsating heat pipe with fewer turns applicable to all orientations. Int J Heat Mass Transf 55:5722–5728

Diethelm K, Ford NJ, Freed AD (2002) A predictor-corrector approach for the numerical solution of fractional differential equations. Nonlinear Dyn 29(1–4):3–22

Groll M, Khandekar S (2004) State of the art on pulsating heat pipes. In: Keynote paper, ASME 2nd international conference of microchannels and minichannels, Rochester, 17–19 June

Im YB, Kim JS, Choi YH (2004) Influence of working fluid to heat transfer characteristics of oscillating heat pipe for low temperature. In: 13th international heat pipe conference, Shanghai, 21–25 Sept

Ji YL, Ma HB, Su FM, Wang GY (2011) Particle size effect on heat transfer performance in an oscillating heat pipe. Exp Therm Fluid Sci 35:724–727

Ji Y, Chang C, Li G, Ma HB (2014) An investigation of operating limits for oscillating heat pipes. In: The 15th international heat transfer conference, IHTC15-9442/HPP-K-424, Kyoto, 10–15 Aug 2014

Khandekar S, Groll M (2008) Roadmap to realistic modeling of closed loop pulsating heat pipes. In: 9th international heat pipe symposium, Kuala Lumpur, Nov 17–20

Khandekar S, Groll M, Charoensawan P, Rittidech S, Terdtoon P (2004) Closed and open loop pulsating heat pipe. In: 13th international heat pipe conference, Shanghai, 21–25 Sept

Kim JS, Bui NH, Jung HS, Lee WH (2003) The study on pressure oscillation and heat transfer characteristics of oscillating capillary tube heat pipe. KSME Int J 17(10):1533–1542

Ma HB, Hanlon MA, Chen L (2006) An investigation of oscillating motions in a miniature pulsating heat pipe. Microfluid Nanofluidics 2:171–179

Ma HB, Borgmeyer B, Cheng P, Zhang Y (2008) Heat transport capability in an oscillating heat pipe. J Heat Transf 130(8). Article No. 081501

Nayfeh AH, Mook DT (1979) Nonlinear oscillations. Wiley, New York

Pai PF, Hao P, Ma HB (2013) Thermomechanical finite-element analysis and dynamics characterization of three-plug oscillating heat pipes. Int J Heat Mass Transf 64:623–635

Peng H, Pai PF, Ma HB (2014) Nonlinear thermomechanical finite-element modeling, analysis and characterization of multi-turn oscillating heat pipes. Int J Heat Mass Transf 69:424–437

Qu J, Wu HY, Cheng P, Wang X (2009) Non-linear analyses of temperature oscillations in a closed-loop pulsating heat pipe. Int J Heat Mass Transf 52:3481–3489

Qu J, Wu HY, Cheng P (2010) Thermal performance of an oscillating heat pipe with Al_2O_3–water nanofluids. Int Commun Heat Mass Transf 37:111–115

Taft BS, Williams AD, Drolen BL (2012) Review of pulsating heat pipe working fluid selection. J Thermophys Heat Transf 26(4):651–656

Wang GY, Zhao NN, Ji YL, Ma HB (2013) Velocity effect on a liquid plug length in a capillary tube. ASME J Heat Transf 135(8). Article No. 080903

White FM (1974) Viscous fluid flow. New York: McGraw-Hill, pp. 138–139

White FM (2008) Fluid mechanics. McGraw Hill Higher Education, New York

Yang HH, Khandekar S, Groll M (2009) Performance characteristics of pulsating heat pipes as integral thermal spreaders. Int J Therm Sci 48(4):815–824

Yin D, Rajab H, Ma HB (2014) Theoretical analysis of maximum filling ratio in an oscillating heat pipe. Int J Heat Mass Transf 74:353–357

Yin D, Wang H, Ma HB, Drolen B (2015) Operating limitation of an oscillating heat pipes. Int J Heat Mass Transf, submitted

Yuan DZ, Qu W, Ma TZ (2010) Flow and heat transfer of liquid plug and neighboring vapor slugs in a pulsating heat pipe. Int J Heat Mass Transf 53:1260–1268

Chapter 5
Factors Affecting Oscillating Motion and Heat Transfer in an OHP

5.1 Introduction

As described in Chap. 4, the gas spring-mass system consisting of vapor bubbles and liquid plugs is the basis that generates the oscillating motion in an OHP. To form a train of liquid plugs and vapor bubbles, the hydraulic diameter of the channels in an OHP must be small. The evaporation and condensation processes must exist at the same time for a functional OHP. The working fluid also plays an important role in the oscillating motion and heat transfer performance. In this chapter, additional factors will be addressed including heat flux level, check valve, channel layer, gravitational force, wall mass, ultrasound, magnetic field, and hydrophobic wetting condition.

5.2 Heat Flux Level Effect

For a typical OHP, when the power input increases, the oscillating motion becomes stronger resulting in higher heat transport capability. Because the heat transport capability of one individual channel is limited, the channel density directly affects the heat transport capability in an OHP. Relative to a tubular OHP, the flat-plate OHP can increase the OHP channel density (channels/unit volume) thereby affecting the thermal performance of the heat pipe at higher heat fluxes. Xu et al. (2006) investigated the effect of heat flux on the heat transfer performance of two aluminum flat-plate OHPs (FP-OHPs). Both OHPs had a width of 5 cm and were charged with either butane or HFC134a. Heating areas were varied by using square copper heat spreaders that had areas of: 9, 16, and 25 cm^2, which directly modified the heat flux level. The heat pipes were dual cooled by submerging the condensing section in a water bath, which created a baseline cooling length of 150 mm. It was found that when the evaporator area of the heat pipe was reduced

© Springer Science+Business Media New York 2015
H. Ma, *Oscillating Heat Pipes*, DOI 10.1007/978-1-4939-2504-9_5

from 25 to 9 cm^2 (64 % reduction) that the thermal resistance of the heat pipe increased by over 340 % while at a heat input of 80 W. However, reduction in thermal resistance was minimal when the heating area was reduced from 50 × 50 mm^2 to 40 × 40 mm^2. The maximum heat flux achieved during this investigation was on the order of 10 W/cm^2.

Charoensawan and Terdtoon (2008) studied the effects of two heating lengths (150 and 50 mm) on horizontal, closed-loop oscillating heat pipes charged with either distilled water or ethanol with a constant condenser length. It was found that the thermal performance was enhanced by decreasing the heating length and increasing the average evaporator temperature. Furthermore, the optimal filling ratio increased as the heating length decreased. Meena et al. (2009) explored the effects of varying the evaporator length on the power limit of an OHP with various working fluids at a filling ratio of 50 %. The heat pipe was made from copper, had an internal diameter of 1.77 mm, and had a total of 10 turns. The evaporator lengths consisted of 15, 10, and 5 cm while the condenser length was varied to have the same length as the evaporator. It was found that when the evaporator length increased, the critical heat flux decreased for all investigated working fluids.

Borgmeyer and Ma (2007) measured the internal fluid oscillation frequencies and velocities for an operating FP-OHP sealed with an acrylic cover. It was found that the oscillation frequencies and amplitudes generally increased with higher heat fluxes. Yang et al. (2009) investigated the applicability of aluminum FP-OHPs filled with ethanol as heat spreaders. They found that FP-OHPs operated in multiple heating orientations and that the OHP which utilized 2 × 2 mm^2 channels as opposed to 1 × 1 mm^2 performed better. It was also found that the average amplitude of thermal oscillations in the evaporator decreased with higher heat inputs. Zuo et al. (1999, 2001) conducted a visualization study of FP-OHPs to observe the pulsating flow behavior. The overall heat pipe consisted of a copper base plate and a glass cover plate. Water was used as the working fluid. It was observed that the fluid pulsating frequency varied from 1 to 10 Hz at various heat input conditions. The experimental results demonstrated that the heat pipe can dissipate over 200 W/cm^2 without showing signs of evaporator dryout, but its performance is sensitive to the filling ratio.

Thompson and Ma (2010) investigated OHPs embedded with two layers of microchannels as shown in Fig. 5.1. The microchannel had dimensions of 0.762 mm × 0.762 mm. Each layer of the OHP had 15 turns and the channels were interconnected to form a single closed loop. The working fluid was allowed to flow perpendicularly at the end of each channel through a circular hole to begin flow within the second layer on the opposite side creating an intertwining flow arrangement. It was found that the FP-OHP embedded with two layers of microchannels can significantly increase the heat transport capability. Thompson and Ma (2010) further investigated the effect of three heating areas of cover-plate-mating heating (31.75 mm × 63.50 mm), OHP-array-mating heating

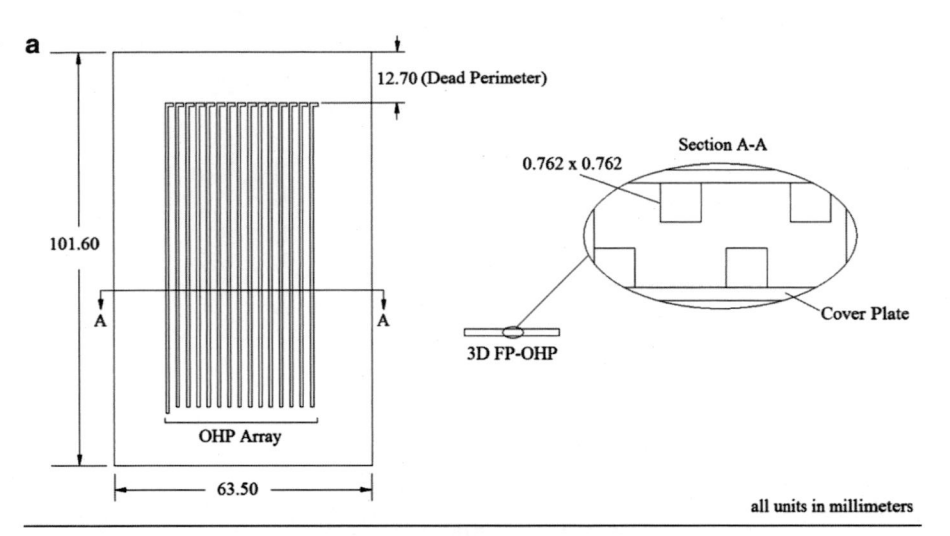

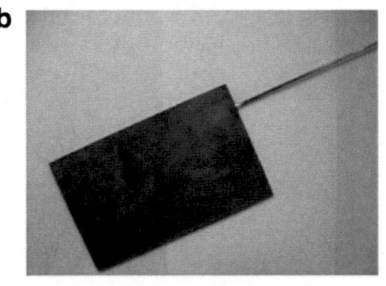

Fig. 5.1 A flat-plate OHP embedded with two layers of microchannels: (**a**) overall dimensions; (**b**) photograph (Thompson and Ma 2010)

(25.40 mm × 44.45 mm), and spot heating (diameter = 11.28 mm) as shown in Fig. 5.2. Cover-plate-mating indicates that the heater width matches that of the FP-OHP, while OHP-array-mating indicates that the heater has a slightly smaller width and spans only the width of the internal channel pattern. Results showed that the thermal resistance and the amplitude of oscillations in the evaporator section increase with the reduction of the heating area. However, it was proved that the FP-OHP can efficiently manage heat fluxes as high as approximately 300 W/cm^2.

5.3   Check Valve Effect

The utilization of check valves on the OHP is desirable for promoting and sustaining pulsating motion making internal flow more predictable as well as increasing thermal performance. A regular check valve normally allows fluid to flow through it in only one direction. If this type of check valve is used in an OHP, it might not

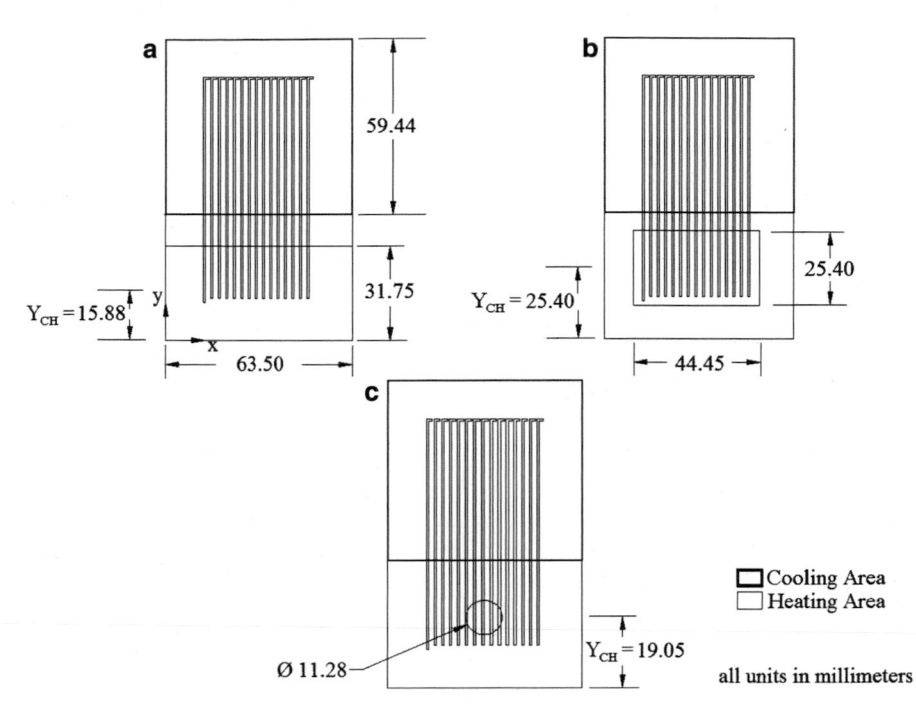

Fig. 5.2 Three heating conditions investigated: (**a**) heating area = 31.75 mm × 63.50 mm; (**b**) heating area = 25.40 mm × 44.45 mm; and (**c**) diameter of spot heating area = 11.28 mm (Thompson and Ma 2010)

enhance oscillating motion and heat transfer. The Tesla valve, first introduced by Tesla (1920), is a "no-moving-parts" valve that connects in-line to a groove/channel containing circulating fluid. The Tesla valve's unique geometry and junctions aid in promoting a net circulatory direction by creating a higher pressure drop in the non-promoted flow direction as shown in Fig. 5.3. The Tesla valve design is characterized by a jet angle, β, an entrance angle, α, and radius, R, as shown in Fig. 5.3. The effectiveness of a Tesla valve is measured via its diodicity expressed as

$$\text{Di}_{\text{valve}} \cong \left. \frac{\Delta P_{r,\text{valve}}}{\Delta P_{f,\text{valve}}} \right|_{\dot{V}} \qquad (5.1)$$

where the diodicity, Di_{valve}, is the ratio of pressure losses for "reverse" (non-promoted) and "forward" (promoted) flow directions for a similar volumetric flow rate, $\dot{V}$. Therefore, effective flow rectification is accomplished with the utilization of Tesla valves that have a diodicity that is greater than unity since a unity diodicity would produce no net flow effect on the implemented flow path. Due to the inconsistency in circulatory direction and accompanying flow reversals

Fig. 5.3 Tesla-type valve
parameters with flow
directions

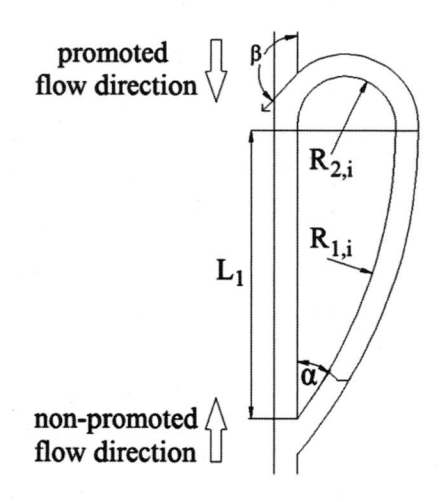

observed in many OHPs, one may assume that the overall diodicity of an unaltered
OHP is unity.

Holley and Faghri (2005) suggested varying the channel diameter for inducing a
bubble pumping action to enhance circulatory motion. It was theoretically demonstrated that this asymmetric flow resistance could aid flow directionality and
improve thermal performance for a 1-turn OHP. Liu et al. (2007) extended the
propositions of Holley and Faghri by conducting a visual/thermal investigation on
glass-tube OHPs each with 4 turns via a high speed camera. One OHP had an
alternating channel diameter and another utilized a single channel section with a
thicker tube. The design modifications enhanced circulatory motion and proved
to increase the thermal performance relative to the standard OHP.
Rittidech et al. (2007) implemented floating-type, ball check valves within the
adiabatic section of a closed-loop, tubular-shaped OHP with 40 total turns in an
effort to promote net directional flow. Using a filling ratio of 50 % and varying the
working fluid (i.e., water, ethanol, R123) and check valve ratio (i.e., number of
OHP turns divided by number of check valves), it was found that optimal thermal
performance occurred with higher check valve ratios, which was attributed to the
effect of gravity on the floating-ball check valves being minimized.

Most recently, Thompson et al. (2011a) explored Tesla-type check valves as
a feasible means to promote circulatory behavior within copper FP-OHPs.
To promote circulation, Thompson et al. (2011a) manufactured two types of copper
flat-plate OHPs: one with Tesla-type check valves (TV FP-OHP) and the other
without Tesla-type check valves (regular FP-OHP) as shown in Fig. 5.4.
Each Tesla-type valve was correctly aligned along the main channel in the
predefined adiabatic section to promote a counterclockwise flow direction as
shown in Fig. 5.4. Using neutron radiography, images of an operating flat-plate
oscillating heat pipe with (TV FP-OHP) and without (FP-OHP) Tesla-type check
valves were analyzed for evidence of circulatory flow rectification and an increase
in thermal performance. It was found that the current implementation of Tesla-type

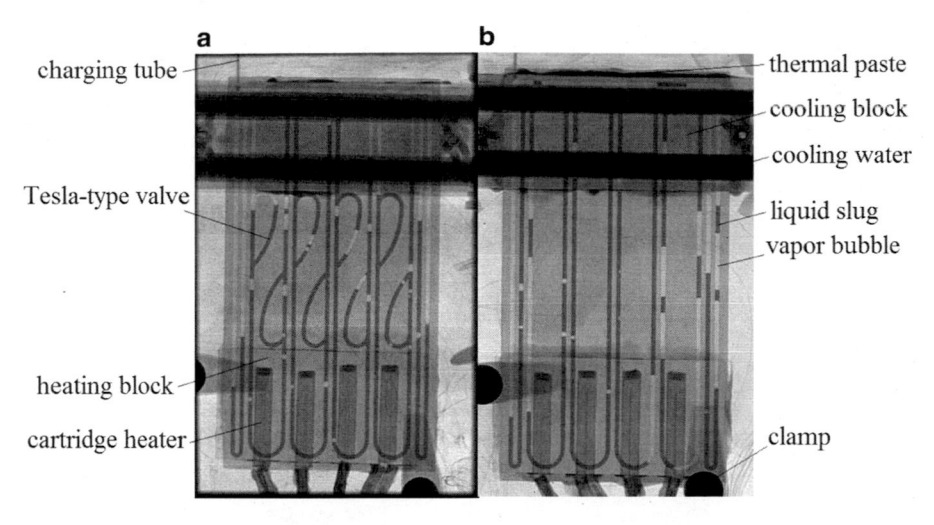

Fig. 5.4 Neutron images of (**a**) TV FP-OHP and (**b**) FP-OHP (Thompson et al. 2011a)

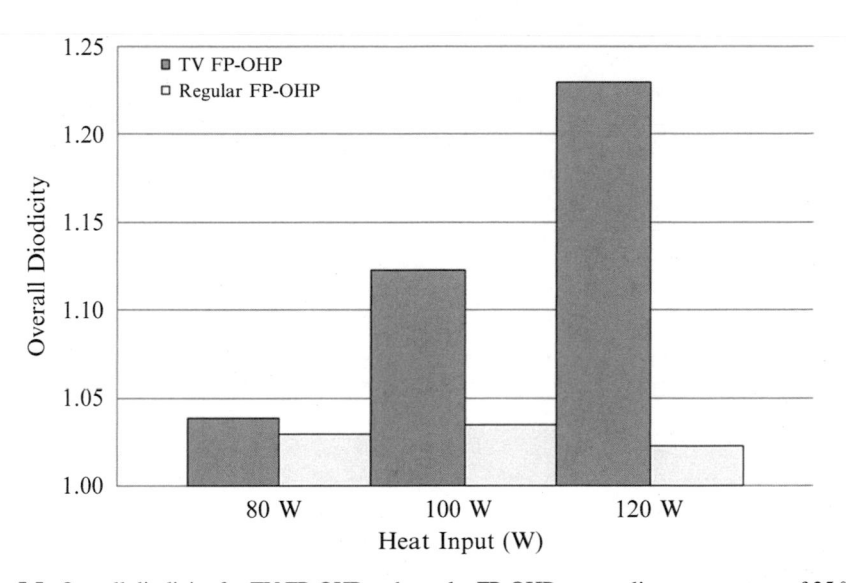

Fig. 5.5 Overall diodicity for TV FP-OHP and regular FP-OHP at a cooling temperature of 35 °C (Thompson et al. 2011a)

valves promoted a circulatory flow direction in the TV FP-OHP and that this circulation was a function of, and increased with, heating power as shown in Fig. 5.5. The increase in diodicity is advantageous for OHP functionality as the thermal resistance of the TV FP-OHP was reduced by approximately 15–25 % as shown in Fig. 5.6. This thermal enhancement is attributed to the Tesla-type valves promoting a common flow direction resulting in more liquid being pumped through

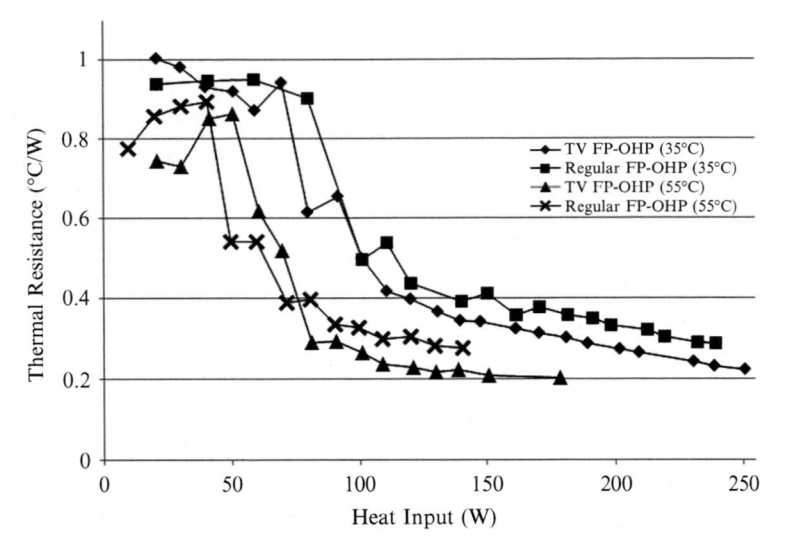

Fig. 5.6 Thermal resistance vs. average heat input for TV FP-OHP and regular FP-OHP at 35 and 55 °C cooling temperatures (Thompson et al. 2011a)

the evaporator turns, fewer periods of static fluid motion, and increased fluid velocities occurring in the non-promoted flow direction. Thompson et al. (2011a) demonstrated that the check valve does enhance heat transfer of an FP-OHP, but the in-depth optimization of geometry, quantity, and alignment of Tesla-type valves for the FP-OHP requires more research. With optimization, future integration of Tesla-type valves into FP-OHPs should prove very advantageous.

5.4   Channel Layer Effect

Single plane (or single layer) OHPs have been widely investigated. Due to channel density for the single layer OHP, the heat flux level is low, and the total power is relatively low as well. To increase heat flux level and total power, interconnected designs with two layers of microchannels or more should be employed. Borgmeyer et al. (2010) conducted an experimental investigation of 20-turn and 10-turn tubular OHPs with two-layer channels as shown in Fig. 5.7. Both OHPs were made of copper tubing (3.175 mm OD, 1.65 mm ID) wrapped in a three-dimensional fashion around two copper spreaders that behaved as the evaporator and condenser. Parameters such as heat input, operating temperature, and filling ratio were varied to determine their effect on overall heat transport. Neutron radiography was simultaneously implemented to create images of the internal fluid flow at a rate of 30 frames per second. It was found that when the number of turns was different, the effect of power input on heat transfer performance varied. It was shown that the temperature difference for the 20-turn OHP decreased or remained steady with increasing power

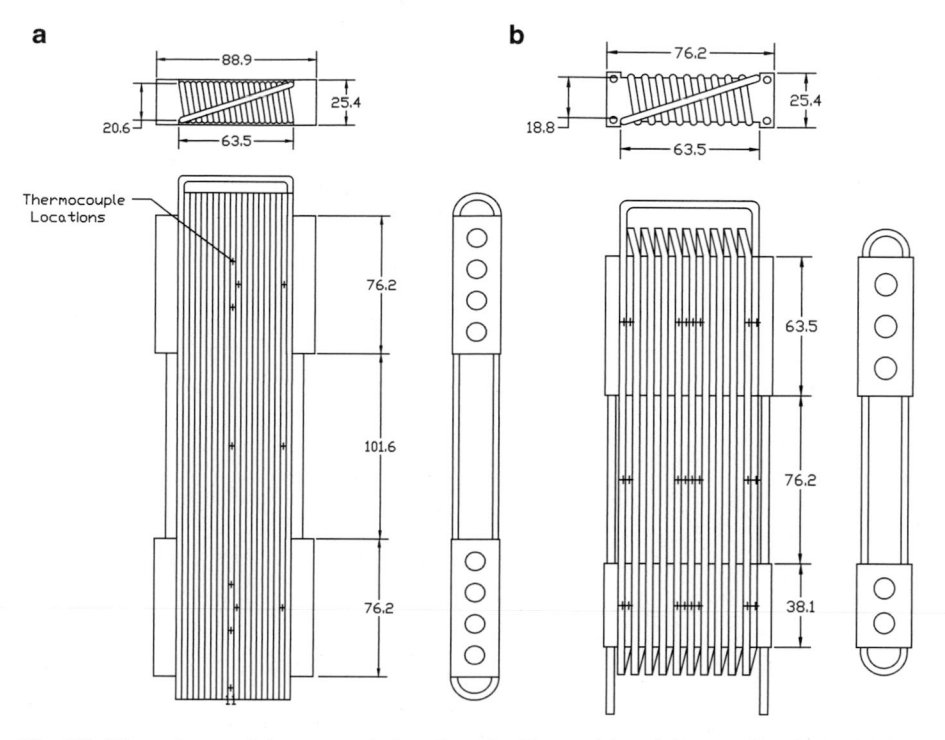

Fig. 5.7 Dimensions and thermocouple locations for 20-turn (**a**) and 10-turn (**b**) tubular OHPs: dimensions in mm (Borgmeyer et al. 2010)

while the 10-turn OHP's temperature drop slightly increased as power increased. The 20-turn OHP was tested up to a power of 400 W with a heat flux of 2.63 W/cm^2. More importantly, it demonstrated that when the turn number increases for an OHP with two-layer channels, the temperature difference between the evaporator and the condenser decreases as the power increases as shown in Fig. 5.8; furthermore, as the operating temperature is increased, the heat transfer performance becomes better. Thompson et al. (2011b) tested small-scale FP-OHPs embedded with two-layer channels. The total dimensions of the heat pipe were $30.0 \times 30.0 \times 2.54$ mm^3 with channel dimensions of 0.76 mm by 0.76 mm. It was demonstrated that the FP-OHP could achieve a total power of 95 W with a heat flux level of 33 W/cm^2.

Yang et al. (2008) determined that using R123-charged tubular OHPs with larger diameter channels results in a better overall performance. The OHPs were tested to their operational limits, which proved to be 540 W in the best case using 2-mm-diameter channels in the bottom heating orientation. This corresponded to 23.7 W/cm^2 radial heat flux, and higher numbers were reported as axial heat flux calculations using the cross-sectional area of the heat pipe rather than the heater area. Thompson and Ma (2010) explored the effect of spot (i.e., localized) heating on the performance of a two-layer FP-OHP and showed that two-layer design can

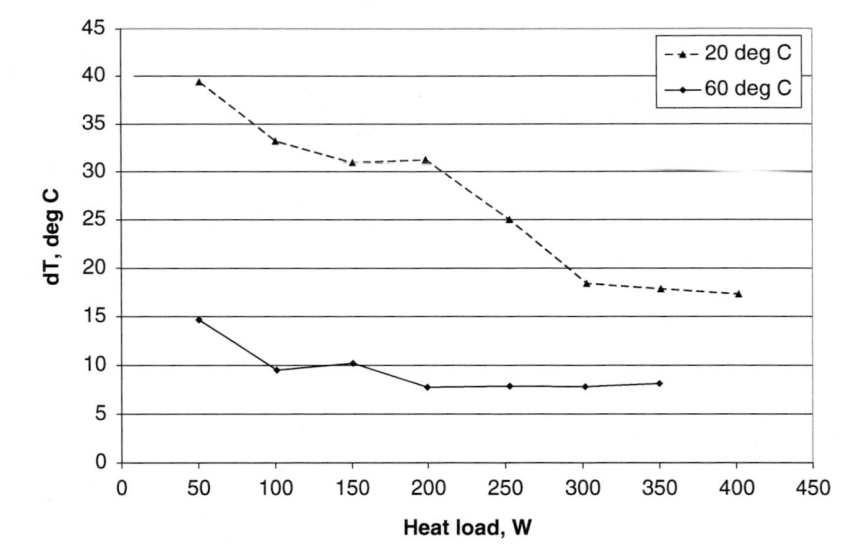

Fig. 5.8 Temperature drop vs. heat load for the 20-turn tubular OHP (Borgmeyer et al. 2010)

increase the heat transport capability. A maximum heat flux of 180 W/cm^2 was achieved with a peak power of 180 W. In another study, Thompson et al. (2011c) studied the effect of larger diameter channels with spot heating and achieved 300 W/cm^2 with a two-layer FP-OHP at a peak power of 300 W.

These previous investigations demonstrated that total power and heat flux level can be increased as the channel layer is increased from single plane to two-layer plane. Most recently, Smoot and Ma (2014) conducted an experimental investigation of channel layer effect on the heat transport capability of a FP-OHP. The FP-OHP was 13 mm thick, 229 mm long, and 76 mm wide. It was embedded with two-independent closed loops forming three layers of channels as shown in Fig. 5.9. The effects of orientation, power input, dryout and heat conduction through the adiabatic section were investigated for one-, two-, and three-layer OHPs. Results showed that when the channel layer number increases, the overall heat transfer performance increases. The largest jump in performance occurred when moving from a single-layer to an interconnected double-layer configuration. The interconnected double-layer configuration demonstrated the least sensitivity to orientation, followed by the three-layer and finally the single-layer configurations. When the OHP switched from one layer of channels to two layers of channels, the highest effective thermal conductivity increased from 5,760 to 26,560 W/m K as shown in Fig. 5.10. At the same time, the dryout limit increased. With three layers of channels, the OHP investigated herein was able to transport a power up to 8 kW with a heat flux level of 103 W/cm^2 while achieving an effective thermal conductivity of 33,170 W/m K.

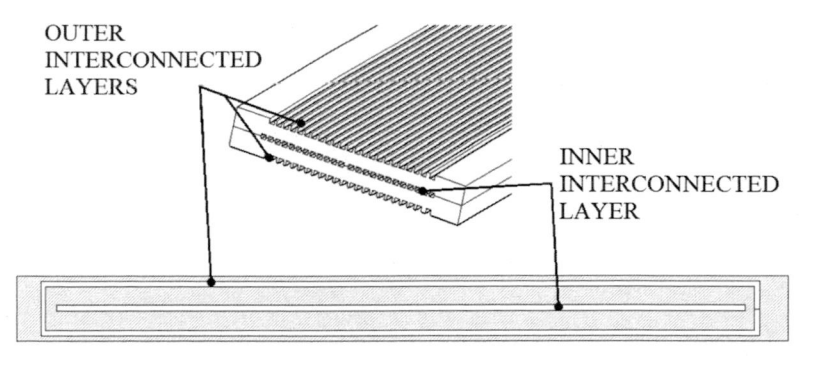

Fig. 5.9 Schematic of a flat-plate OHP embedded with three-layer channels (Smoot and Ma 2014)

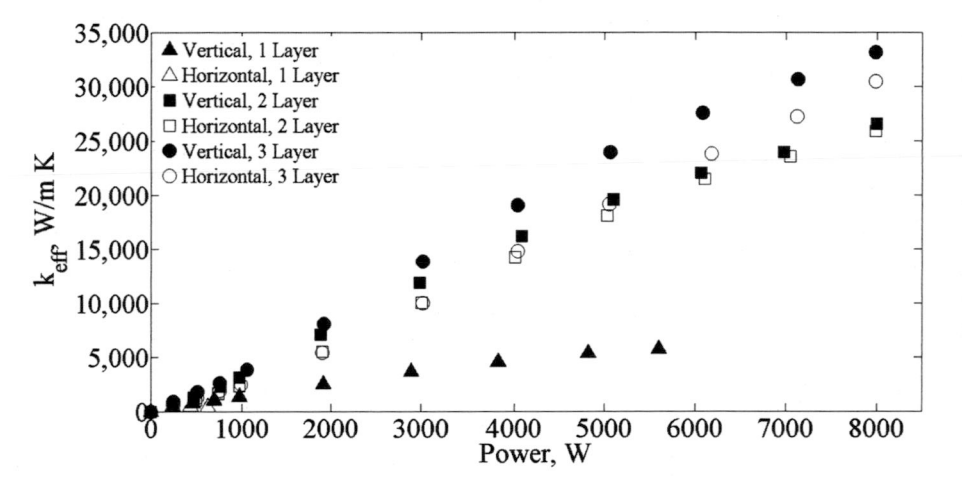

Fig. 5.10 Effects of channel layer and orientation on the effective thermal conductivity (Smoot and Ma 2014)

5.5 Gravity Effect

Due to the hydrothermal coupling of an OHP's functionality, its thermal performance can be gravity dependent (Khandekar et al. 2002; Xu et al. 2006; Borgmeyer and Ma 2007; Thompson et al. 2011c; Smoot and Ma 2014). However, the degree of gravity effect on OHP heat transfer performance can be alleviated with appropriate design considerations. Recent investigations (Akachi et al. 1996; Charoensawan et al. 2003; Yang et al. 2009; Lin et al. 2009) indicate that increasing the number of turns and decreasing the channel diameter may lessen gravity dependence. Kiseev and Zolkin (1999) experimentally investigated the effects of hypergravity (12 *g*) on OHP performance. A stainless steel OHP had a total of 23 turns with an internal diameter of 1.1 mm and was charged with acetone at a filling ratio of 0.6. This OHP was oriented

within a centrifuge so as to allow for a gravity-opposing (or antigravity) operation with regard to liquid return to the evaporator. Results demonstrated that gravity had a strong effect on the heat transfer performance of the OHP. Although dryout was not observed, the evaporator temperature increased from 160 °C at 0 g to 200 °C at 12 g. Gu et al. (2004) investigated the thermal performance of an aluminum FP-OHP under microgravity (~0 g), normal gravity (1 g), and hypergravity (2.5 g) conditions by conducting experiments during parabolic jet trajectories. The heat pipe was charged with refrigerant (R114), and it was found that optimal performance occurred during microgravity conditions. During normal- and high-gravity conditions, the orientation of the heat pipe significantly affected its heat transfer performance. Researchers Van Es and Woering (2000) investigated hypergravity (up to 8.4 g) performance of an open-loop FP-OHP charged with acetone at low heat fluxes. At a gravitational loading of 8.4 g, the investigated heat pipe performed steadily; however, the heat pipe was oriented favorably so as to have gravity assist in the return of liquid to the evaporator.

The investigated OHPs with one-layer channels (Kiseev and Zolkin 1999; Van Es and Woering 2000; Gu et al. 2004) showed that heat transfer performance decreases when gravity increases. Thompson et al. (2011b) tested a two-layer miniature FP-OHP (Fig. 5.11) in a high-gravity environment up to 10 g. The gravity was added unfavorably so that it did not assist the return of liquid from the condenser to the evaporator. Figure 5.12 shows that the effective thermal conductivity of the two-layer FP-OHP was almost independent of gravity loading up to 10 g. At a heat input of 95 W and heat flux of approximately 33 W/cm^2, the effective thermal conductivity reached 729.7 W/m K demonstrating that the FP-OHP embedded with two-layer channels can reduce the gravity effect.

Hathaway et al. (2012) conducted an experimental investigation of a tubular OHP embedded with two-layer channels with uneven turns. In the evaporator, the total turn number was 20 and in the condenser there were 14 full turns and 6 half turns as shown in Fig. 5.13. Experimental results showed that an uneven turn OHP

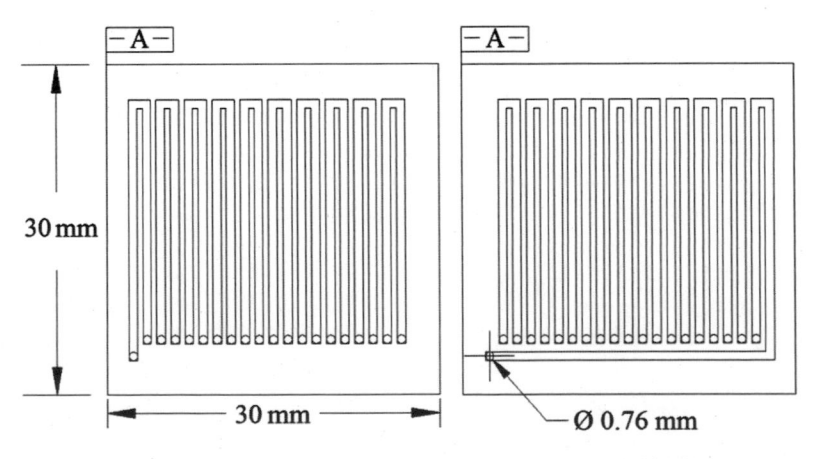

Fig. 5.11 An OHP embedded with two-layer channels (Thompson et al. 2011b)

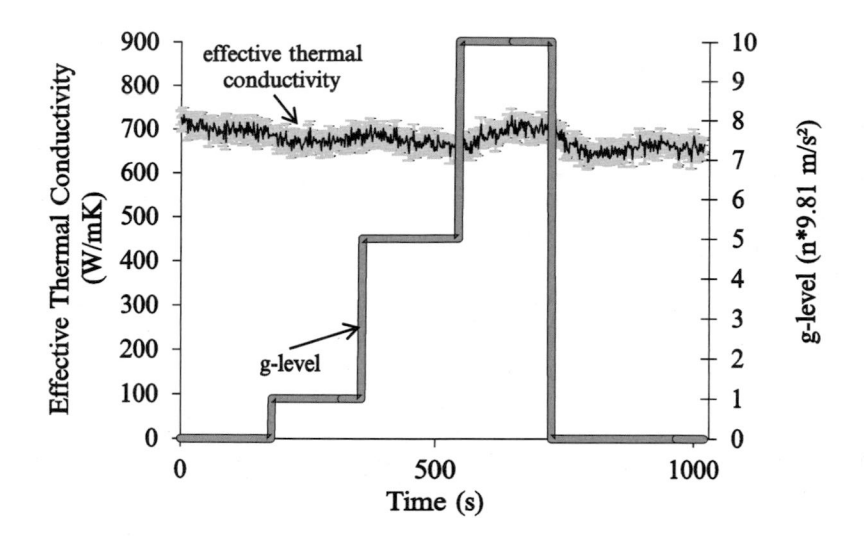

Fig. 5.12 Effective thermal conductivity vs. time at a constant heat input of 95 W and varying gravitational loading (g-level) (Thompson et al. 2011b)

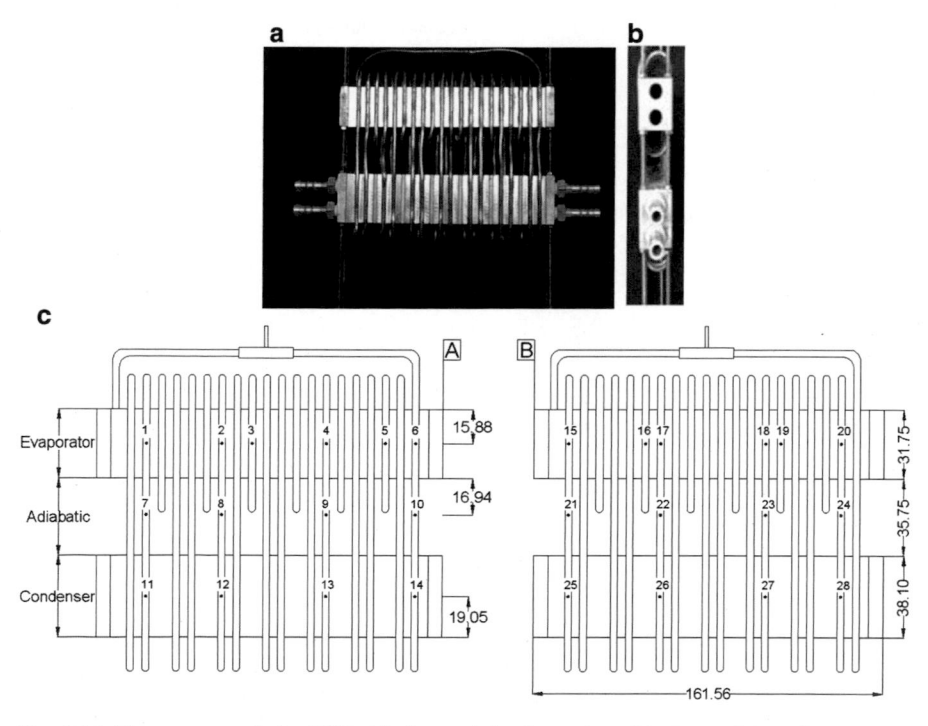

Fig. 5.13 Uneven turn tubular OHP: (**a**) photo of the *front view*; (**b**) photo of the *side view*; and (**c**) schematic (unit: mm) where "A" is the front of the OHP and "B" is the back of the OHP with thermocouple number and locations marked (Hathaway et al. 2012)

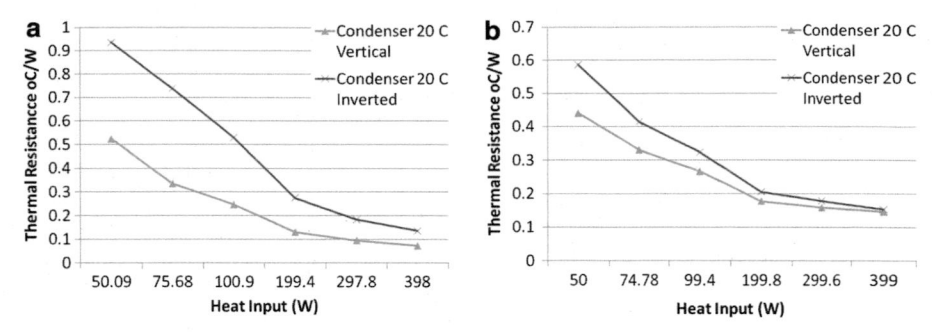

Fig. 5.14 Comparison with the vertical position at cooling bath temperatures of 20 °C for (**a**) water OHP and (**b**) acetone OHP (Hathaway et al. 2012)

with two-layer channels can start the oscillating motion in the negative vertical position (with evaporator located above the condenser) and demonstrated that the uneven turn OHPs can significantly reduce the effect of gravity on the heat transport capability in an OHP. Hathaway et al. (2012) also demonstrated that although at low power inputs, the uneven turn OHP in the negative vertical position did not perform as well as it did in the positive vertical position (with evaporator located below the condenser), at high power inputs, the uneven OHP had similar heat transfer performance as it did in the positive vertical position as shown in Fig. 5.14. Furthermore, at low power inputs the acetone OHP outperformed the water OHP, and at high heat inputs the water OHP outperformed the acetone OHP. With the uneven turn design, both water and acetone OHPs were able to reduce the effect of gravity on heat transport capability in an OHP and achieved a thermal resistance of 0.135 °C/W with a condenser temperature of 20 °C.

5.6   Wall Mass Effect

Many OHP designs have featured small diameter tubing connected between the evaporator and condenser sections. This tube-type OHP basically has a round cross section with a thin wall for all three sections of the evaporator, adiabatic section, and condenser. Due to the limitation of tube curvature, the tube-type OHP cannot produce a high channel density. As a result, this type of OHP cannot remove heat with a higher heat flux. To increase the power density, flat-plate OHPs, which have a potential to remove heat with a higher heat flux, have been studied recently (Thompson and Ma 2014). For a flat-plate-type OHP, the channels are directly fabricated from a flat plate. In addition, the cross-sectional shaped channel, turn radius, and wall mass are very different. While channel shape, turn radius, and channel density affect the oscillating motion and heat transfer performance in an OHP, Smoot et al. (2011) found that the thick wall of a FP-OHP influences its oscillating motion and heat transfer performance.

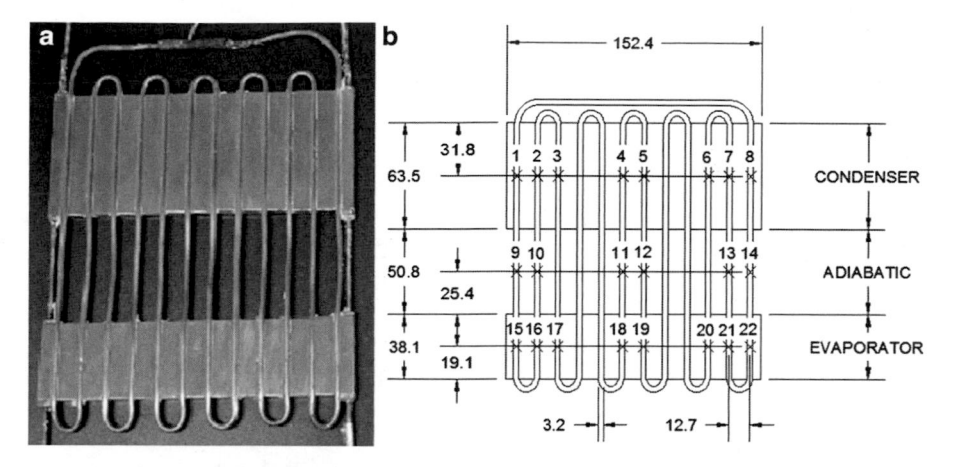

Fig. 5.15 Tube-type OHP—split block design: (**a**) photo and (**b**) dimensions (unit: mm, ×: thermocouple location) (Smoot et al. 2011)

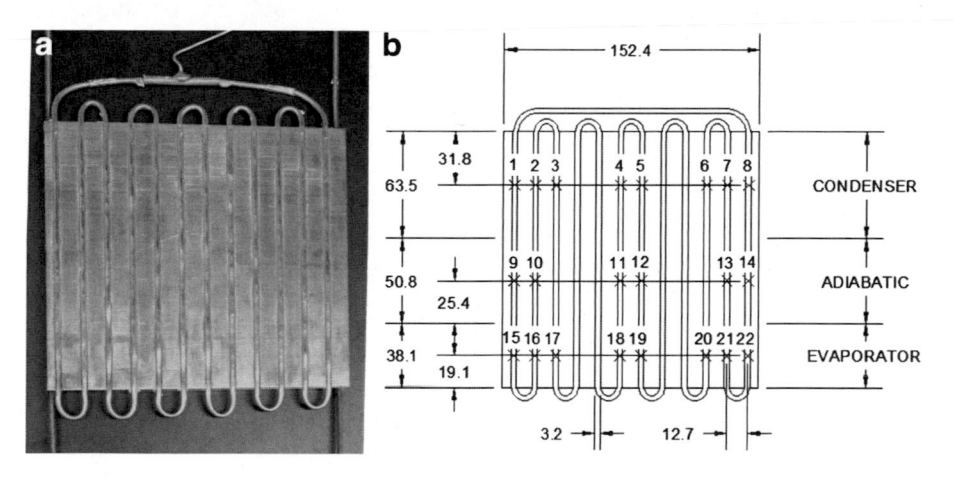

Fig. 5.16 Flat-plate OHP—continuous block design: (**a**) photo and (**b**) dimensions (unit: mm, ×: thermocouple location) (Smoot et al. 2011)

To determine the wall mass effect on the oscillating motion and heat transfer performance in an OHP, Smoot et al. (2011) investigated two 6-turn, closed-loop OHPs, shown in Figs. 5.15 and 5.16. Both OHPs were made of copper tubing with a 3.18 mm outer diameter and a 1.65 mm inner diameter. Figure 5.15 illustrates the typical 6-turn closed-loop copper tube OHP. In this design, a heating plate and a cooling plate were attached to the evaporator and condenser sections, respectively. Figure 5.16 shows the same type flat-plate type OHP design. In this design, a single plate encompasses the evaporator, adiabatic, and condenser sections. To reduce the contact thermal resistance between the plates and tubes of the OHP, all plates with the same thickness of 6.35 mm were machined using a ball end mill with a

radius equal to the tubing; additionally, OMEGATHERM "201" high temperature, high thermal conductivity paste was placed between the plates and tubes. For both OHPs, the evaporating or heating areas of 38 mm by 155 mm were the same and supplied with a heater of the same dimensions. The condensing sections for both OHPs had an area of 64 mm by 155 mm with a cooling block of the same dimensions. The heater was an Omega 300 W strip heater. The cooling block was fabricated from aluminum with three 9.53-mm-diameter channels. Each heat pipe was charged with HPLC grade water or acetone, depending on the test. The filling ratio was about 50 %. Each OHP was fitted with 24 calibrated T-type thermocouples shown in Figs. 5.15 and 5.16. The thermocouples were attached using small pieces of aluminum tape, which allowed direct contact of thermocouples with measured surfaces; this arrangement reduced the heat loss from thermocouples to environment thereby increasing heat measurement accuracy. The heat pipes were wrapped with R19 fiberglass insulation once placed in the test stand. The OHP was placed in an aluminum test stand capable of rotating for both side heating horizontal and bottom heating vertical orientations. Data were collected using a NI SCXI-1600 DAQ at 60 Hz. Power was controlled using a 130 V AC variac. A Fluke 45 DMM was used for resistance and voltage measurements (for power calculation). A Julabo F25 constant temperature cooling bath was used to circulate water through the cooling block at a designed temperature. Data were collected for both the transient and steady state operations at each tested power input. Once steady state operation was established, data were recorded for a minimum of 3 min, which was determined sufficient to capture enough temperature oscillations during normal operation for accurate average temperature calculations.

Using the experimental procedure described, testing was conducted at seven power levels (at 25, 50, 100, 150, 200, 250, and 300 W), three condenser temperatures (20, 40, and 60 °C), two orientations (bottom heating vertical and side heating horizontal), and two working fluids (water and acetone) in both heat pipes. Figure 5.17 illustrates the steady state response of acetone-charged heat pipes at two different power inputs. For the oscillating temperature variation for the evaporator, adiabatic section, or condenser, the averaged temperature from each section cannot be used. To find the temperature variation, a thermocouple indicated by the thermocouple number selected from the evaporator, adiabatic, and condenser sections for each heat pipe and testing condition is displayed to aid visualization of the exact temperature response of the heat pipe. From the temperature data, it can be found that the split design (tube type) appears to be far more "active" at the given power input than the continuous design (flat-plate type). The temperature oscillations were barely visible with the continuous design—even at higher power inputs. Similar results were found at all tested power inputs. The lower temperature oscillation amplitude is believed to be a result of a gradual temperature gradient within the continuous design rather than the sharp hot and cold sections of the split design. Because the adiabatic section includes a substantial mass with a continuous design, evaporation and condensation are likely to occur before reaching each section. Heat conduction directly from the evaporator shell to the adiabatic section and from the adiabatic section to the condenser makes the temperature of the

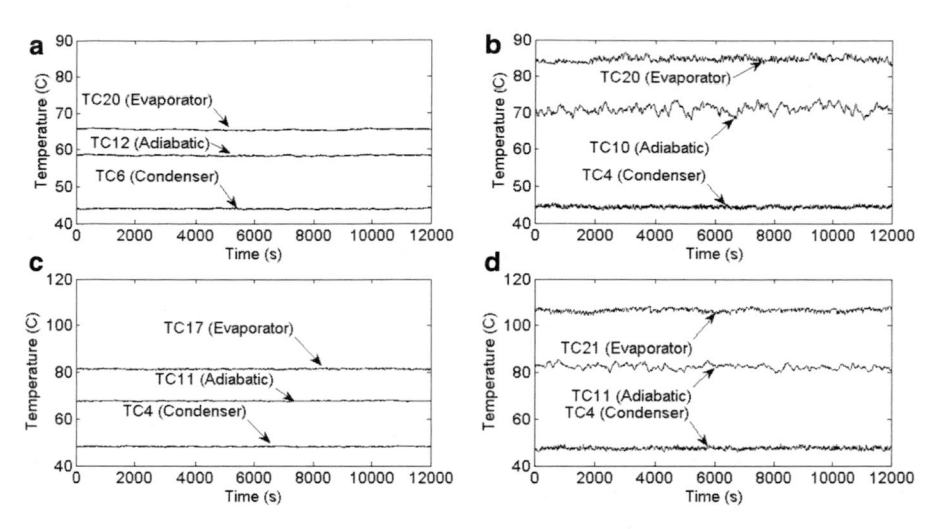

Fig. 5.17 Power input effect on the steady state temperatures of acetone-charged heat pipes in the vertical orientation with 40 °C cooling bath and (**a**) continuous block at 150 W, (**b**) split block at 150 W, (**c**) continuous block at 250 W, and (**d**) split block at 250 W (*TC* thermocouple) (Smoot et al. 2011)

adiabatic section change gradually from the evaporator to the condenser. When the vapor bubble flows through the adiabatic section, heat transfer occurs continuously between the wall and the bubbles in the continuous design of the OHP, which makes bubble expansions or contractions gradual. This process will result in a smaller amplitude of the liquid movement in the heat pipe.

Figure 5.18 illustrates the effect of working fluid on the temperature oscillation occurring in both heat pipes. The same phenomenon also presents itself when water is used as the working fluid, i.e., the temperature oscillation in the continuous design of OHP is much smaller than the split design. Figure 5.18 illustrates the steady state response of both water- and acetone-charged heat pipes at the same power and with a cooling bath temperature. Temperature oscillations have a much higher amplitude with water as the working fluid compared to acetone. Temperature oscillations with water-charged OHP are plainly visible even with the continuous design. However, the water-based continuous design demonstrates significantly reduced temperature oscillations when compared with the water-based split design, echoing the results shown in Fig. 5.17. When acetone is used as the working fluid, the temperature oscillation is much smaller for both designs. It can be concluded that when acetone is used as the working fluid, the continuous design of OHP can result in a higher level of temperature uniformity. In addition to the effects of power input and working fluid, Smoot et al. (2011) experimentally studied the orientation effect. Although the orientation can affect the heat transfer performance, it has almost no effect on the temperature oscillation pattern for both OHPs. It means that

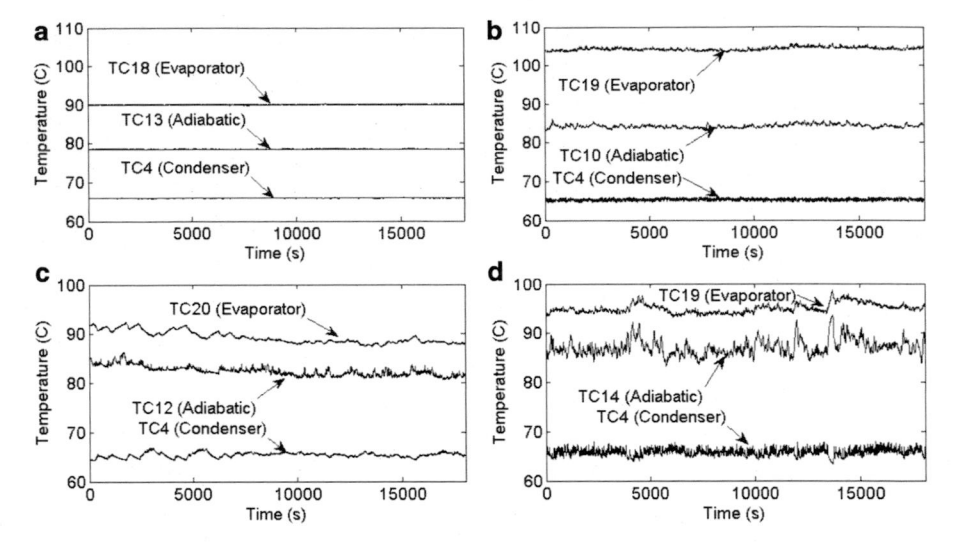

Fig. 5.18 Working fluid effect on the steady state temperatures of both heat pipes in the vertical orientation with 60 °C cooling bath, 200 W input power, and (**a**) continuous block charged with acetone, (**b**) split block charged with acetone, (**c**) continuous block charged with water, and (**d**) split block charged with water (*TC* thermocouple) (Smoot et al. 2011)

when both OHPs were tested vertically (the evaporator was on the bottom), the heat transfer performance of both OHPs was much better than when tested horizontally. But the continuous design of OHP still produces more uniform temperatures on a given location and does not depend on orientation.

Figures 5.19 and 5.20 show the experimental results of the temperature difference between the evaporator and condenser for acetone OHPs including the orientation effect. As illustrated in Figs. 5.19 and 5.20, the acetone-charged heat pipes' performance is very different from that charged with water. When the power input was low, the difference between the split design and continuous design was not big; however, the heat transfer performance of the continuous design OHP was better than the split design OHP. When the power was high as shown in Figs. 5.19 and 5.20, the heat transfer performance of the continuous design was much better than the split design. The presence of additional mass on the adiabatic section and heat conduction directly from the evaporator shell to the adiabatic section and from the adiabatic section to the condenser dampened the temperature oscillations significantly for steady state operation. For the OHP with a continuous design (flat-plate type), the FP-OHP is able to increase the heat transfer performance, and at the same time, it can produce more uniform temperature distribution on the heating or cooling surfaces.

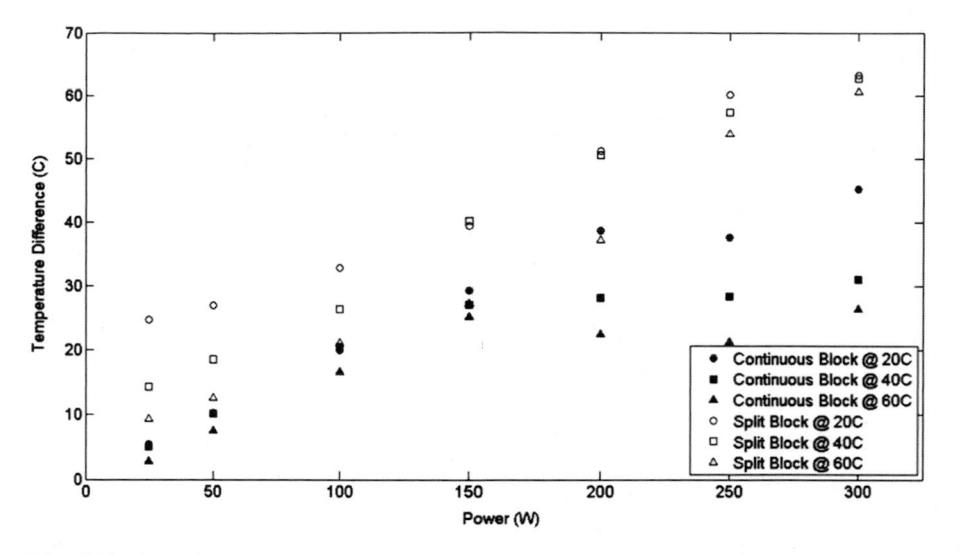

Fig. 5.19 Operating temperature effect on the average evaporator-to-condenser temperature difference for acetone-charged OHPs in bottom heating vertical orientation (Smoot et al. 2011)

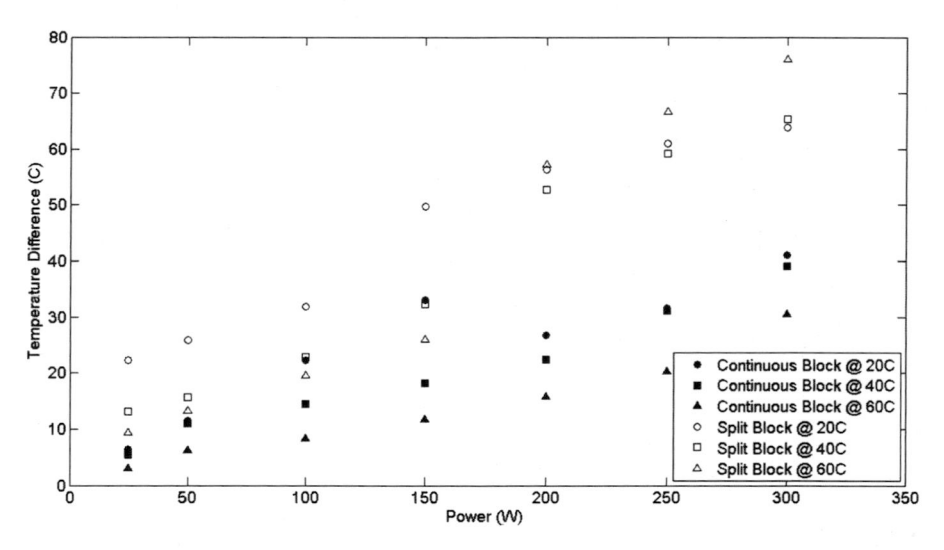

Fig. 5.20 Operating temperature effect on the average evaporator-to-condenser temperature difference for acetone-charged OHPs in the side heating horizontal orientation (Smoot et al. 2011)

5.7 Ultrasound Effect

The piezoelectric effect, which describes the relation between a mechanical stress and an electrical voltage in solids, was discovered in 1880 by two brothers, Jacques and Pierre Curie (Curie and Curie 1880). The converse effect was mathematically deduced from fundamental thermodynamic principles by Gabriel Lippmann in 1881. If an electrical oscillation is applied to piezoelectric materials, they will respond with mechanical vibrations which provide an ultrasonic sound source. Such ultrasound can be used to enhance heat transfer (Laborde et al. 2000; Apfel 1984; Neppiras 1984; Lighthill 1978). The extensive investigation on the ultrasonic effect on boiling heat transfer has been conducted recently and the ultrasonic sound can effectively activate nucleate sites and enhance boiling heat transfer (Bartoli and Baffigi 2011; Kim et al. 2004; Zhou et al. 2002). Most recently, Zhao et al. (2013) investigated the ultrasound effect on the oscillating motion and heat transfer performance in OHPs. The 6-turn OHP has overall dimensions of 155.0 mm by 155.0 mm. As shown in Fig. 5.21, the OHP consisting of the condenser (on the top), adiabatic section (in the middle), and evaporator (at the bottom) was made of copper tubing with an inner diameter of 1.8 mm and an outer diameter of 3.0 mm. Six piezoelectric ceramics made of Pb-based lanthanum-doped lead zirconate titanate (PZT) were placed on the evaporating section. Each piezoelectric ceramic has an inner diameter of 3.0 mm and an outer diameter of 10.0 mm. As shown in Fig. 5.22, when the input power added to the evaporator section was up to 29 W, no oscillating motion (indicated by the temperature) of liquid plugs and vapor bubbles in the OHP was observed without the ultrasonic field. For the same OHP, when an ultrasound was generated from the piezoelectric ceramics by a

Fig. 5.21 Schematic of the interconnected capillary loop with locations of the PZTs and thermocouples (mm) (Zhao et al. 2013)

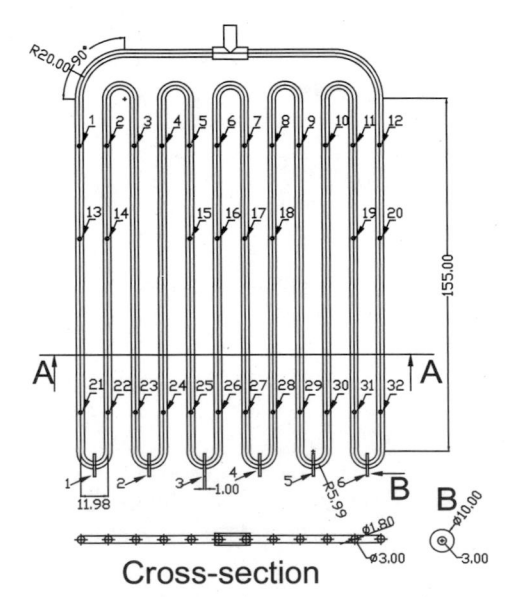

Cross-section

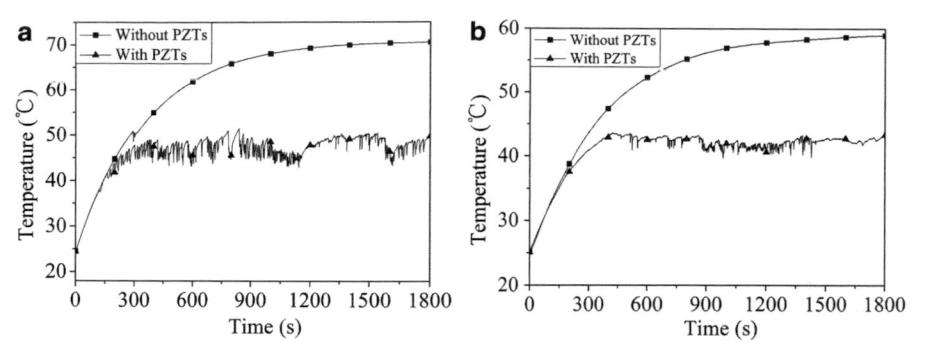

Fig. 5.22 Ultrasonic effect on the oscillating temperature at a heat input of (**a**) 29 W (**b**) 18 W (thermocouple no. 27 on the evaporating section) (Zhao et al. 2013)

voltage of 10 V with applied frequency of 1 kHz, and a total power of 4.48 mW, the oscillating motion of liquid plugs and vapor bubbles started and maintained a steady state oscillating motion. As the oscillating motion started, heat transfer was enhanced resulting in a significant drop of the evaporator temperature from 69.7 to 47.3 °C. A total power of 4.48 mW can activate the oscillating motion of a train of liquid plugs and vapor bubbles in the OHP and enhance heat transfer resulting in a drop of temperature difference between the evaporator and condenser from 48.3 to 25.9 °C and an increase of effective thermal conductivity from 672.8 to 1,254.7 W/mK. In addition, it can be found that when piezoelectric ceramics were supplied with a voltage of 10 V, a frequency of 1 kHz, and a total power of 4.48 mW, the oscillating motion in the OHP could be generated even with a heat input of 18 W. When the oscillating motion started, heat transfer was enhanced resulting in a drop of the evaporator temperature from 58.9 to 42.6 °C. A total power of 4.48 mW could activate the oscillating motion in the OHP and enhance heat transfer resulting in a drop of temperature difference between the evaporator and condenser from 38.9 to 22.6 °C an increase of effective thermal conductivity from 518.5 to 892.5 W/mK. Comparing results shown in Fig. 5.22a, b, it can be found that a very small input of power initiating ultrasonic sound can activate the oscillating motion even when the input power on the evaporator was reduced from 29 to 18 W. In other words, a very small power input of ultrasound can significantly reduce the start-up power of oscillating motion in an OHP and enhance heat transfer resulting in an increase of effective thermal conductivity. Another interesting result obtained by Zhao et al. (2013) is that the ultrasonic effect controlled by piezoelectric ceramics can be used as a switch to turn on the oscillating motion in an OHP. From results shown in Fig. 5.23, it can be found that as soon as an electrical power of 4.48 mW (ultrasonic sound) was added, the oscillating motion was immediately started and a steady state oscillation could be maintained. When the electrical power producing the ultrasonic sound was turned off, the oscillating motion gradually stopped within a few minutes.

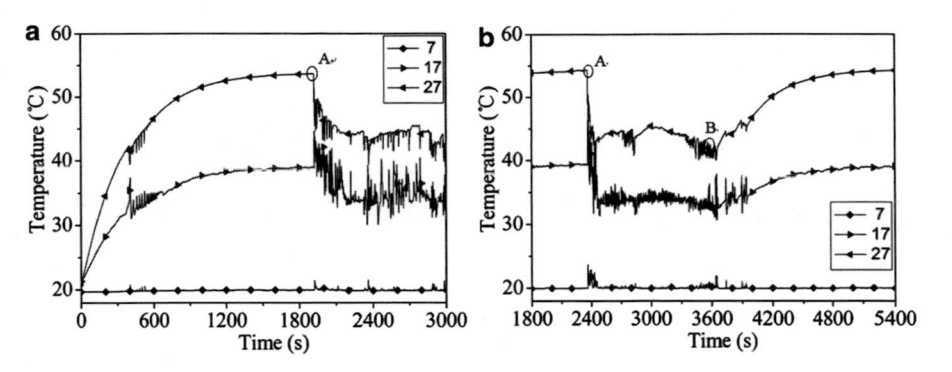

Fig. 5.23 Ultrasonic effect on the oscillating temperatures at a heat input power of 18 W: (**a**) on effect and (**b**) on and off effect (Point *A*: when ultrasonic sound is turned on; and Point *B*: when ultrasonic sound is turned off) (Zhao et al. 2013)

Zhao et al. (2014a, b) further studied the ultrasound effect on bubble formation and heat transfer performance in an OHP charged with nanoparticles. Figure 5.24 shows that when the Dy2O3 nanoparticles were added to the fluid, plenty of bubbles were formed at a heat input of 0.5 W when the ultrasonic effect (at a power input of 0.05 W for the PZTs) was applied. However, only one bubble was generated for the fluid without nanoparticles even when a heating power input of up to 1 W was applied with the same power input of 0.05 W for the PZTs. This demonstrates that when nanoparticles are added to the system, nanoparticles can help initiate the bubble formation, and the ultrasonic effect can further enhance bubble formation. Based on the results of the visualization experiment, Zhao et al. (2014a, b) conducted an OHP experiment to determine the nanoparticle effect on oscillating motion and heat transfer of the nanofluid under the ultrasonic influence. Ultrasound was applied solely to the evaporating section of an OHP with an interconnected capillary loop setup that included PZTs and thermocouples as shown in Fig. 5.21. The ultrasound was generated from the piezoelectric ceramics by a total power of 0.1 W with an applied frequency of 485 kHz.

Figure 5.25 illustrates the nanoparticle effect on the effective thermal conductivity of the nanofluid OHP with and without ultrasonic effect when the operating temperature was 20 °C. As shown, when the nanoparticles and ultrasonic effect are not applied, the heat transfer performance increases as the power input increases. When only ultrasonic effect was added, the heat transfer enhancement took place only in low heat input. When only nanoparticles were added, the heat transfer performance was improved. However, when both nanoparticles and ultrasonic effect were added, as shown in Fig. 5.25b, the heat transfer enhancement was the highest (Enhancement percentage $= \frac{A-B}{B} \times 100\%$, where A is the obtained result, and B is the baseline result, which does not have the effects of nanoparticles and ultrasound). The heat transfer enhancement was able to reach about 47.5 % (based

Water   Nanofluid

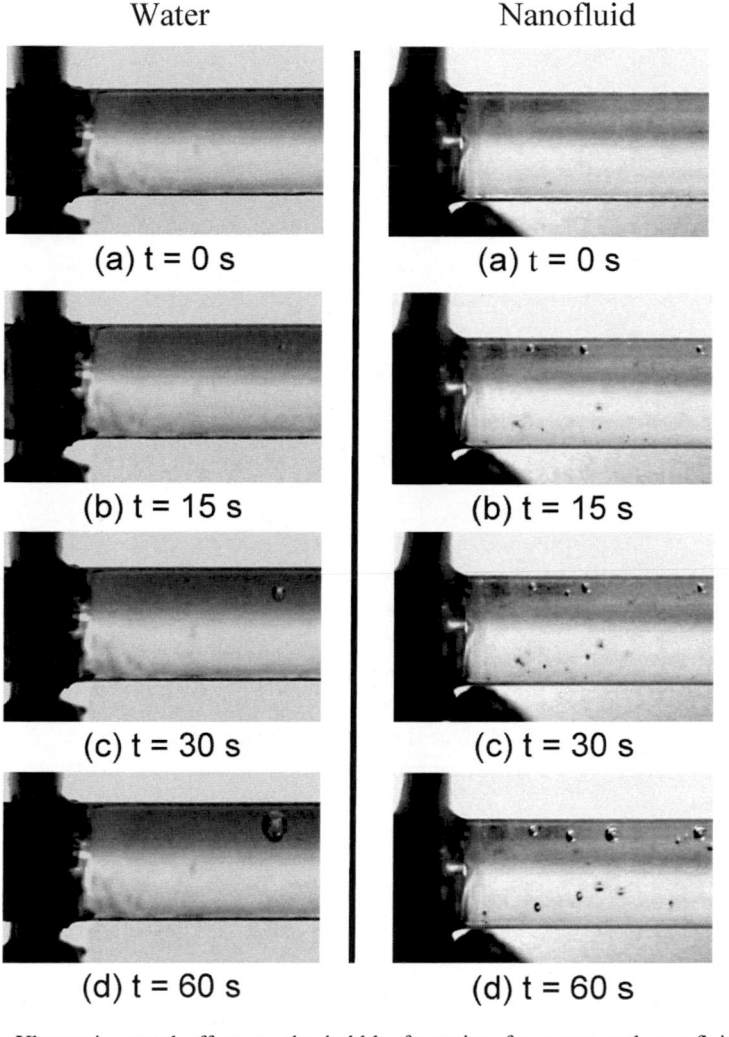

Fig. 5.24 Ultrasonic sound effect on the bubble formation for water and nanofluid (Zhao et al. 2014b)

on the average enhancement percentage of different power inputs). In addition, it was determined that when the nanoparticles were added, the ultrasonic effect can easily start up the thermally excited oscillating motion and enhance heat transfer. The highest enhancement percentage of the thermal conductivity compared to the base line could be up to 71.1 % when the power input was 80 W. Similar results have been achieved with an operating temperature of 60 °C as shown in Fig. 5.26.

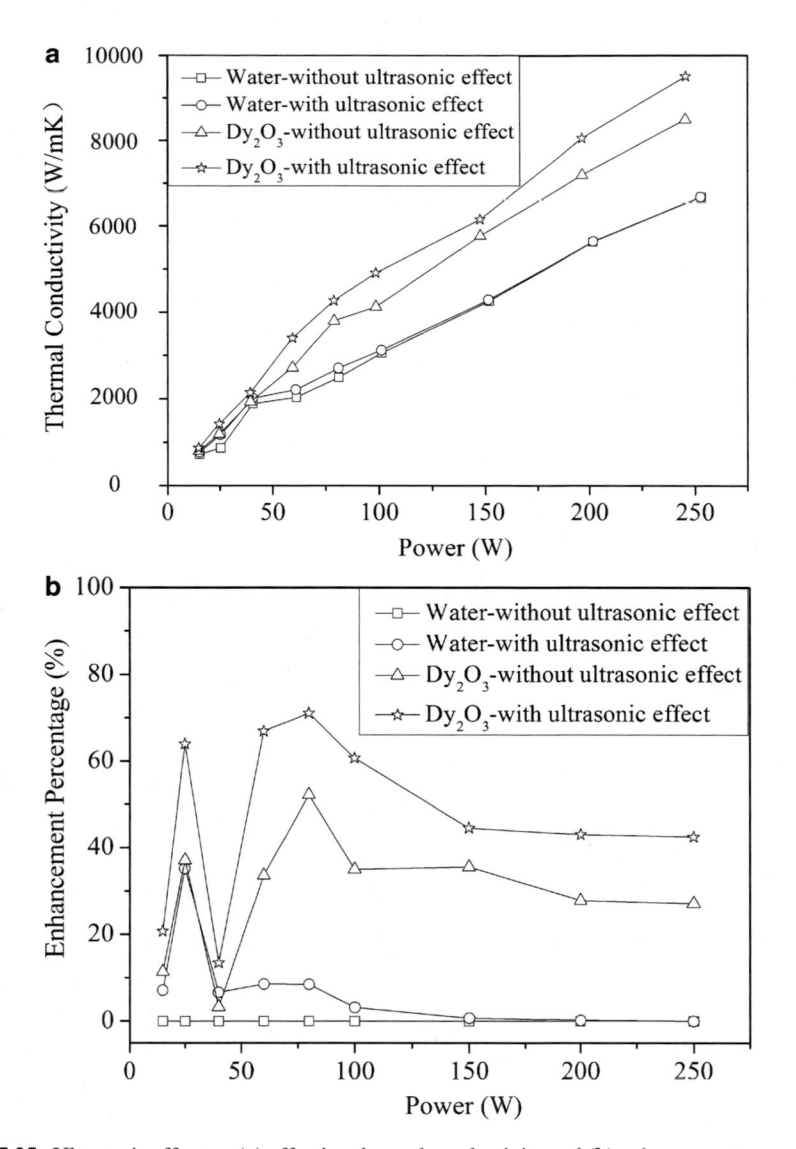

Fig. 5.25 Ultrasonic effect on (**a**) effective thermal conductivity and (**b**) enhancement percentage at an operating temperature is 20 °C (Zhao et al. 2014b)

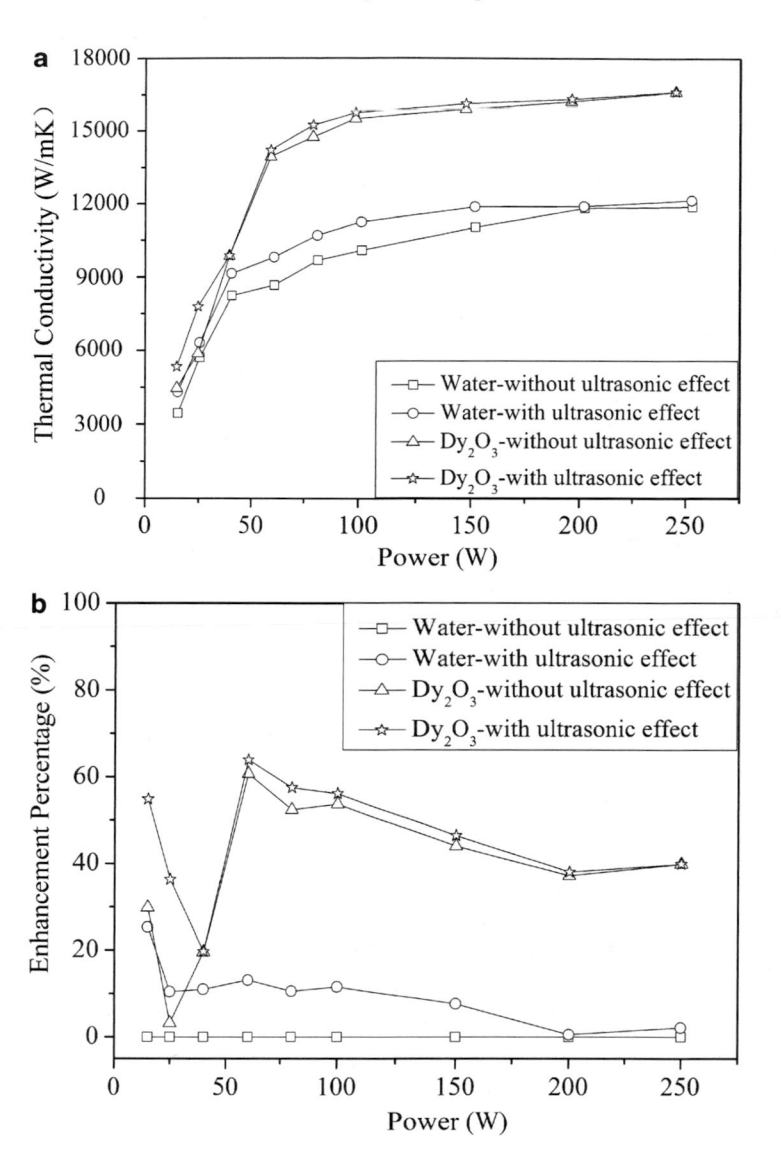

Fig. 5.26 Ultrasonic effect on (**a**) effective thermal conductivity and (**b**) enhancement percentage operating temperature is 60 °C (Zhao et al. 2014b)

5.8 Magnetic Field Effect

The utilization of magnetic field on the magnetic nanofluid OHP is a promising way to affect the oscillating motions and enhance the heat transfer performance of the magnetic nanofluid OHP. Mohammadi et al. (2012) tested the thermal performance of OHPs that are charged with the ferrofluid by applying various magnetic fields; their results showed that applying the magnetic field on the water-based ferrofluid reduced the thermal resistance of OHP in all orientations. Zhao et al. (2013) investigated the magnetic field effect on the oscillating motion and heat transfer in an oscillating heat pipe (OHP) containing dysprosium(III) oxide magnetic nanofluid. The magnetic field was applied to the evaporating section of the OHP by using a permanent magnet. As shown in Fig. 5.27, when the magnetic nanoparticles were not added into the OHP, the magnetic field could not affect the heat transport capability in the OHP. However, when the magnetic dysprosium(III) oxide nanoparticles at a mass ratio of 0.01 % were added in the same OHP, the magnetic nanoparticles in the heat pipe did affect the oscillating motion and heat transport capability. Figure 5.27 shows how heat transfer enhancement is affected by the magnetic field and input power. When the input power is low, the effect of magnetic field on the heat transfer performance of a magnetic nanofluid OHP is significant.

Figure 5.28a, b shows the oscillating temperatures occurring in the evaporator, adiabatic section, and condenser of the magnetic nanofluid OHP at an input power of 50 W without and with the magnetic field, respectively. As shown in Fig. 5.28a, without the magnetic field, the temperature oscillation, which indirectly shows the oscillating motion of liquid plugs and vapor bubbles in the OHP, is not stable. When the magnetic field is applied, the heat pipe can generate steady state oscillating motion as shown in Fig. 5.28b. Due to the steady state oscillation, the temperature difference between the evaporator and condenser is much lower. From the comparison, it is easy to see that the magnetic field can help to generate the steady state oscillation motion and enhance the heat transfer performance occurring in a magnetic nanofluid OHP. As the input power was increased to 250 W, as shown

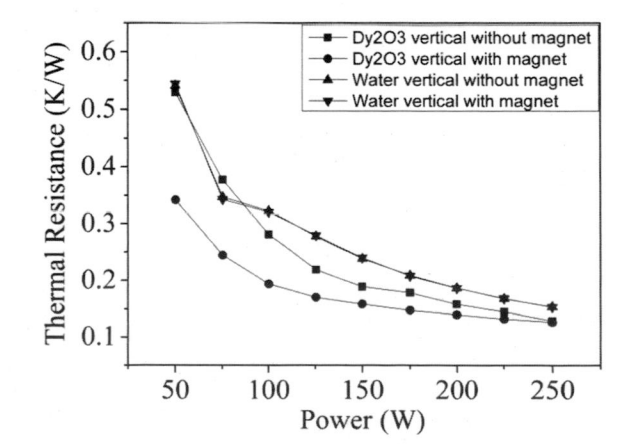

Fig. 5.27 Magnetic nanoparticle effect on the thermal resistance with and without magnetic field (magnetic nanoparticles: Dy2O3; mass ratio: 0.01 %; operating temperature: 20 °C; base fluid: distilled water) (Zhao et al. 2013)

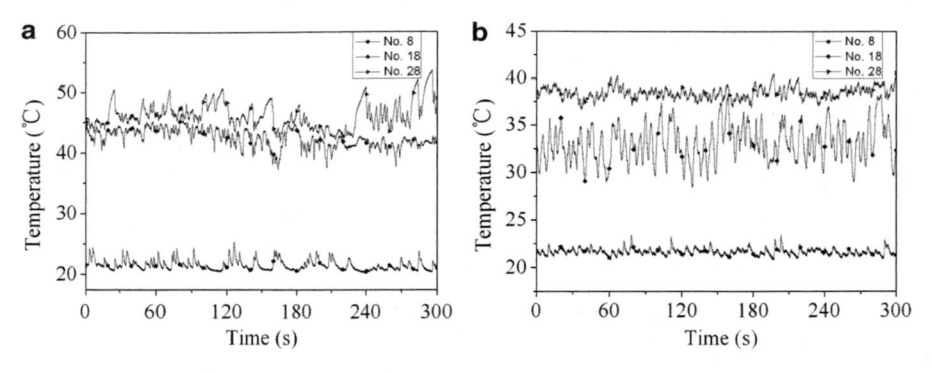

Fig. 5.28 Oscillating temperature of the magnetic nanofluid OHP: (**a**) without the magnetic field and (**b**) with magnetic field (magnetic particles: Dy2O3; mass ratio: 0.01 %; orientation: vertical; power input: 50 W) (Zhao et al. 2013)

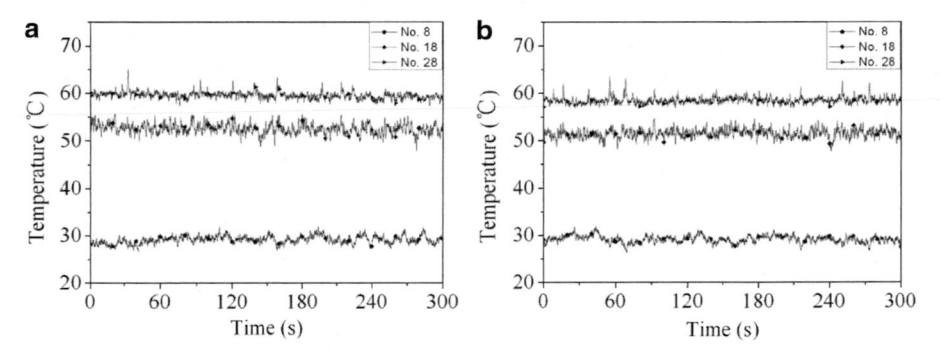

Fig. 5.29 Oscillating temperature of the magnetic nanofluid OHP: (**a**) without the magnetic field and (**b**) with the magnetic field (magnetic particles: Dy2O3; mass ratio: 0.01 %; orientation: vertical; power input: 250 W) (Zhao et al. 2013)

in Fig. 5.29a, b, the heat transfer performance of this heat pipe with the magnetic field is almost the same as that without the magnetic field. As the input power increases, the difference becomes smaller. The primary reason for this is that when the input power increases, the oscillating motion excited by the thermal energy added on the evaporator section becomes stronger. The heat transfer enhancement due to the magnetic field effect on the magnetic nanoparticles decreases relatively compared with the thermal energy effect.

Figure 5.30a–c shows the orientation effect on the thermal resistance of the magnetic nanofluid OHP charged with magnetic dysprosium(III) oxide nanoparticles at a mass ratio of 0.01 %, 0.05 %, and 0.1 %, respectively. As shown in Fig. 5.30a, when the heat pipe was tested in the vertical orientation, the thermal resistance of the OHP with the magnetic field was much lower than that of the OHP without the magnetic field especially in a low input power. In a vertical position, the magnetic nanoparticles of dysprosium(III) oxide added in the OHP were able to enhance the oscillation motion and heat transfer if an external magnetic field was

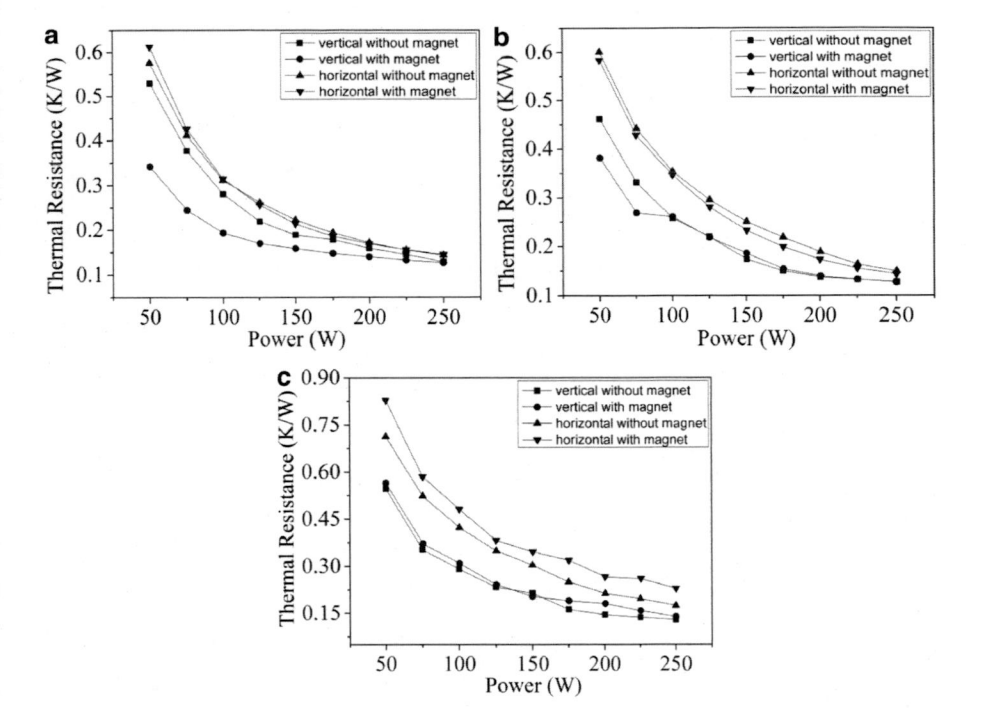

Fig. 5.30 Orientation effect on the thermal resistance of magnetic nanofluid OHP at a mass ratio of (**a**) 0.01 %, (**b**) 0.05 %, and (**c**) 0.1 % (magnetic nanoparticles: Dy2O3; operating temperature: 20 °C) (Zhao et al. 2013)

added on the evaporation section. When the same heat pipe was tested horizontally under the same magnetic field, the heat transfer enhancement was not found. As shown in Fig. 5.30b, c, when the mass ratio of magnetic nanoparticles increases, the heat transfer performance of the magnetic nanoparticle OHP decreases in the same magnetic field. When the mass ratio of magnetic nanoparticles is equal to 0.05 %, the magnetic nanoparticles can enhance heat transfer only when the input power is less than 100 W and in a vertical position. When the mass ratio of magnetic nanoparticles is increased to 0.1 %, the magnetic nanoparticles cannot enhance heat transfer even when OHP is tested vertically under the same magnetic field.

5.9 Hydrophobic Surface Effect

When a surface is hydrophobic, the contact angle is larger than 90°, which significantly increases the meniscus radius in the evaporator section. As a result, the conventional heat pipe, which uses the capillary pressure to pump the condensate

Fig. 5.31 Contact angle
measurements of a liquid
drop on the coated surface
with $CH_{18}H_{37}$ SCu
(Ji et al. 2012)

from the condenser to the evaporator, will not function. For an oscillating heat pipe, heat transfer from the evaporator to condenser is governed by the thermally excited oscillating motion, and most of the heat is transported by the sensible heat. This indicates that even when the inner surface of the OHP is hydrophobic, the OHP might still function. Ji et al. (2012) investigated the superhydrophobic surface effect on the oscillating motion and heat transfer performance in an OHP. In their OHP, the inner surface of the heat pipe was chemically coated with $CH_{18}H_{37}$ SCu. The treated surface significantly increased the contact angle as shown in Fig. 5.31. The heat pipe was charged with water at a filling ratio of 70 %. The OHP was tested vertically, i.e., the evaporator was on the bottom and the condenser was on the top. Figure 5.32 illustrates the temperature oscillations occurring in the evaporator, adiabatic section, and condenser. As shown, the oscillating motion in the hydrophobic OHP can start. In other words, the OHP with a hydrophobic inner surface can function. This is very different from the capillary-force-driven conventional heat pipe, which cannot function if the inner surface is hydrophobic. For an OHP, the gas spring constant of the vapor bubble plays a key role toward initiating and sustaining the oscillating motion. This indicates that the functionality of an OHP is not too sensitive to the surface wetting condition. However, the heat transport capability occurring in the hydrophobic OHP is not as good as that with a hydrophilic inner surface (Wilson et al. 2008). The oscillating motion of liquid plugs and vapor bubbles in the OHP depends on power input. From Fig. 5.32, it can be found that when the power increases, the frequency of temperature oscillation increases, which indirectly shows that the oscillating motion of liquid plugs and vapor bubbles in the OHP increases. Although the frequency of the temperature oscillation occurring in the evaporator and condenser is the same as that in the adiabatic section, the amplitude of temperature oscillation occurring in the condenser and evaporator is smaller than that in the adiabatic section.

Figure 5.33 illustrates the power input effect on thermal resistance. As shown, as the input power increases, the thermal resistance of the OHP with hydrophobic surface decreases. This has the same trend as the one with the hydrophilic inner surface. But, the thermal resistance of the OHP with the hydrophobic surface is

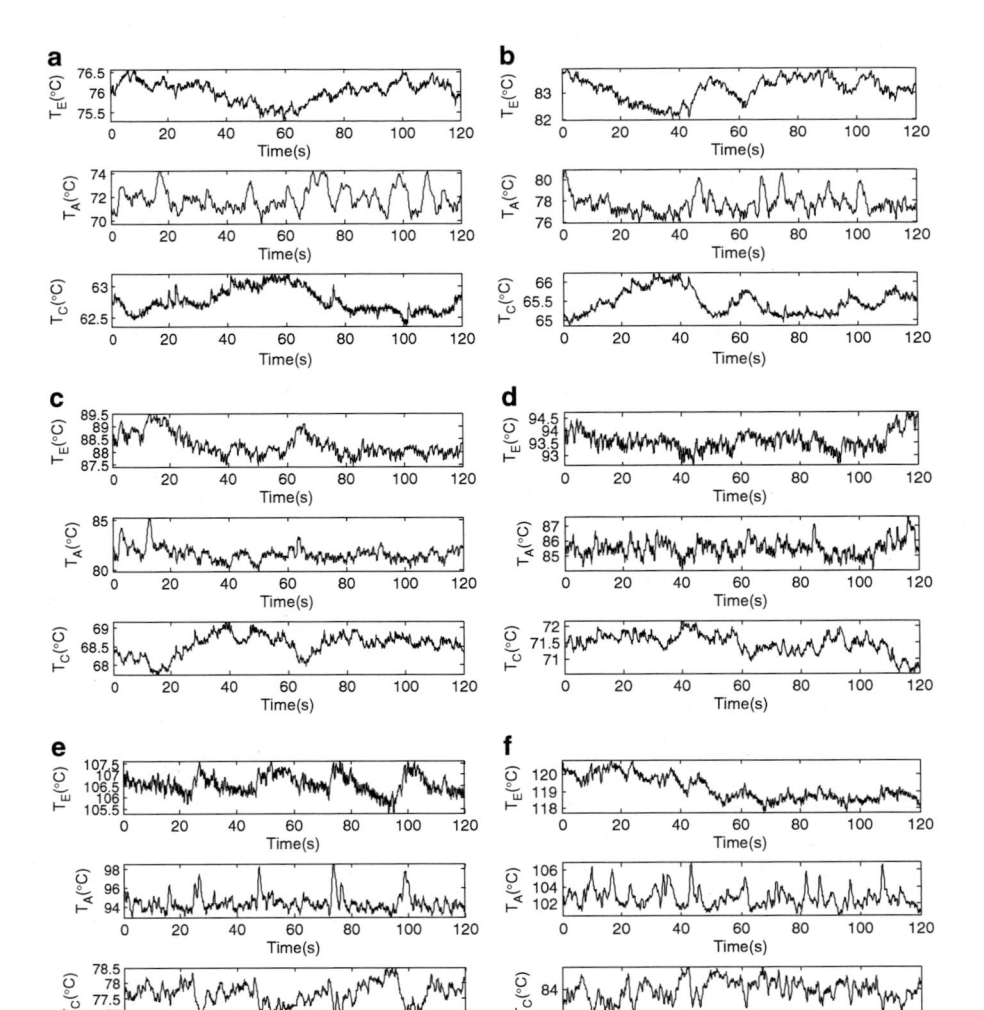

Fig. 5.32 Temperature oscillations of evaporator, adiabatic section, and condenser in an ohp (power input: (**a**) 25 W, (**b**) 50 W, (**c**) 75 W, (**d**) 100 W, (**e**) 150 W, and (**f**) 200 W) (Ji et al. 2012)

larger than that with the hydrophilic inner surface as shown in Fig. 5.33. The primary reason is that when the surface is hydrophobic, thin liquid film cannot be formed in the evaporating section, which significantly increases the thermal resistance. Further investigation is needed to determine the detailed contribution to the increase of the total thermal resistance occurring in the superhydrophobic OHP. It is concluded that when the inner surface of the OHP is superhydrophobic, the oscillating motion of liquid plugs and vapor bubbles in an OHP can be generated, and the OHP can function, which is very different from the conventional wicked heat pipe.

Fig. 5.33 Power input effect on thermal resistance (Ji et al. 2012)

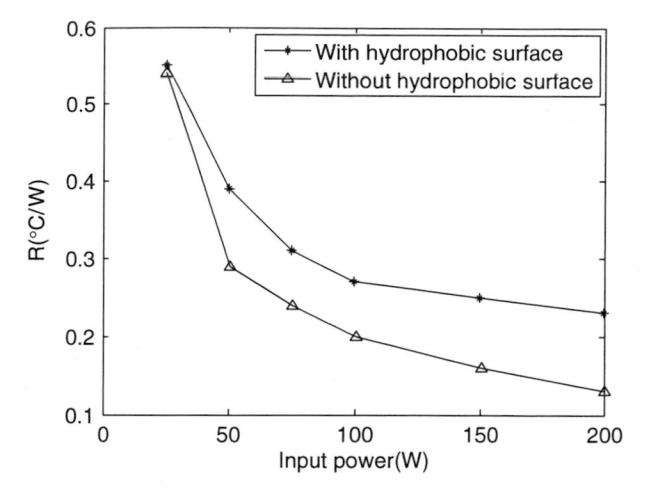

References

Akachi H, Polasek F, Stulc P (1996) Pulsating heat pipe. In: Proceedings of the 5th International heat pipe symposium, Melbourne, pp 208–217

Apfel RE (1984) Acoustic cavitation inception. Ultrasonics 22(4):167–173

Bartoli C, Baffigi F (2011) Effects of ultrasonic waves on the heat transfer enhancement in subcooled boiling. Exp Therm Fluid Sci 35:423–432

Borgmeyer B, Ma HB (2007) Experimental investigation of oscillating motions in a flat-plate oscillating heat pipe. J Thermophys Heat Transf 21(2):405–409

Borgmeyer B, Wilson C, Ma HB (2010) Heat transport capability and fluid flow neutron radiography of a three-dimensional oscillating heat pipes. ASME J Heat Transf 132(6). Article No. 061502

Charoensawan P, Terdtoon P (2008) Thermal performance of horizontal closed-loop oscillating heat pipes. Appl Therm Eng 28(5–6):460–466

Charoensawan P, Khandekar S, Groll M, Terdtoon P (2003) Closed loop pulsating heat pipes—Part A: parametric experimental investigations. Appl Therm Eng 23(16):2009–2020

Curie J, Curie P (1880) Development, via compression, of electric polarization in hemihedral crystals with inclined faces. Bull Soc Mineral 3:90–93

Gu J, Kawaji M, Futamata R (2004) Effects of gravity on the performance of pulsating heat pipes. J Thermophys Heat Transf 18(3):370–378

Hathaway AA, Wilson CA, Ma HB (2012) An experimental investigation of uneven turn water and acetone oscillating heat pipes. J Heat Transf Thermophys 26(1):115–122

Holley B, Faghri A (2005) Analysis of pulsating heat pipe with capillary wick and varying channel diameter. Int J Heat Mass Transf 48(13):2635–2651

Ji Y, Chen H, Kim Y, Yu Q, Ma X, Ma HB (2012) Hydrophobic surface effect on heat transfer performance in an oscillating heat pipe. ASME J Heat Transf 134. Article No. 074502

Khandekar S, Schneider M, Schäfer P, Kulenovic R, Groll M (2002) Thermofluid dynamic study of flat-plate closed-loop pulsating heat pipes. Microsc Thermophys Eng 6(4):303–317

Kim HY, Kim YG, Kang BH (2004) Enhancement of natural convection and pool boiling heat transfer via ultrasonic vibration. Int J Heat Mass Transf 47(12–13):2831–2840

Kiseev VM, Zolkin KA (1999) The influence of acceleration on the performance of oscillating heat pipe. In: Proceedings of 11th international heat pipe conference, Tokyo, vol 2. pp 154–158

Laborde JL, Hita A, Caltagirone JP, Gerard A (2000) Fluid dynamics phenomena induced by power ultrasounds. Ultrasonics 38(1):297–300

Lighthill SJ (1978) Acoustic streaming. J Sound Vib 61(3):391–418

Lin YH, Kang SW, Wu TY (2009) Fabrication of polydimethylsiloxane (PDMS) pulsating heat pipe. Appl Therm Eng 29(2–3):573–580

Lippman G (1881) Principal of the conservation of electricity. Ann Chem Phys 24:145

Liu S, Li J, Dong X, Chen H (2007) Experimental study on flow patterns and improved configurations for pulsating heat pipes. J Therm Sci 16(1):56–62

Meena P, Rittidech S, Tammasaeng P (2009) Effect of evaporator section lengths and working fluids on operational limit of closed loop oscillating heat pipes with check valves (CLOHP/CV). Am J Appl Sci 6(1):133–136

Mohammadi M, Mohammadi M, Shafii MB (2012) Experimental investigation of a pulsating heat pipe using ferrofluid (magnetic nanofluid). ASME J Heat Transf 134. Article No. 014504

Neppiras EA (1984) Acoustic cavitation series: part one. Acoustic cavitation: an introduction. Ultrasonics 22(1):25–28

Rittidech S, Pipatpaiboon N, Terdtoon P (2007) Heat-transfer characteristics of a closed-loop oscillating heat-pipe with check valves. Appl Energy 84(5):565–577

Smoot CD, Ma HB (2014) Experimental investigation of a three-layer oscillating heat pipe. ASME J Heat Transf 136(5). Article No. 051501

Smoot C, Ma HB, Wilson C, Greenberg L (2011) Heat conduction effect on oscillating heat pipe operation. ASME J Therm Sci Eng Appl 3(3). Article No. 024501

Tesla N (1920) Valvular conduit. US Patent #1,329,559

Thompson SM, Ma HB (2010) Effect of localized heating on three-dimensional flat-plate oscillating heat pipe. Adv Mech Eng 2010. Article No. 465153

Thompson SM, Ma HB (2014) Recent advances in two-phase thermal ground planes. Annu Rev Heat Transf 18, accepted for publication

Thompson SM, Ma HB, Wilson C (2011a) Investigation of a flat-plate oscillating heat pipe with Tesla-type check valves. J Exp Therm Fluid Sci 35(7):1265–1273

Thompson SM, Hathaway AA, Smoot CD, Wilson CA, Ma HB, Young RM, Greenberg L, Osick BR, Van Campen S, Morgan BC, Sharar D, Jankowski N (2011b) Robust thermal performance of a flat-plate oscillating heat pipe during high-gravity loading. ASME J Heat Transf 133(11). Article No. 104504

Thompson SM, Cheng P, Ma HB (2011c) An experimental investigation of a three-dimensional flat-plate oscillating heat pipe with staggered microchannels. Int J Heat Mass Transf 54 (17–18):3951–3959

Van Es J, Woering AA (2000) High-acceleration performance of the flat swinging heat pipe. In: Proceedings of the 30th international conference on environmental systems, Toulouse

Wilson C, Borgmeyer B, Winholtz RA (2008) Visual observation of oscillating heat pipes using neutron radiography. J Thermophys Heat Transf 22(3):366–372

Xu G, Liang S, Vogel M (2006) Thermal characterization of pulsating heat pipes. In: Proceedings of the 10th Intersociety conference on thermal and thermomechanical phenomena in electronics, systems, San Diego, pp 552–556

Yang H, Khandekar S, Groll M (2008) Operational limit of closed loop pulsating heat pipes. Appl Therm Eng 28(1):49–59

Yang H, Khandekar S, Groll M (2009) Performance characteristics of pulsating heat pipes as integral thermal spreaders. Int J Therm Sci 48(4):815–824

Zhao N, Zhao D, Ma HB (2013) Experimental investigation of magnetic field effect on the magnetic nanofluid oscillating heat pipe. ASME J Therm Sci Eng Appl 5(1). Article No. 011005

Zhao N, Fu B, Zhao D, Ma HB (2014a) Ultrasonic effect on the oscillating motion and heat transfer in an oscillating heat pipe. ASME J Heat Transf, accepted

Zhao N, Fu B, Ma HB (2014b) Ultrasonic effect on the bubble nucleation and heat transfer of oscillating nanofluid. Appl Phys Lett 104(26). Article No. 263105

Zhou DW, Liu DY, Hu XG, Ma CF (2002) Effect of acoustic cavitation on boiling heat transfer. Exp Therm Fluid Sci 26(8):931–938

Zuo ZJ, North MT, Ray L (1999) Combined pulsating and capillary heat pipe mechanism for cooling of high heat flux electronics. In: Proceedings of the ASME heat transfer device conference

Zuo J, North MT, Wert KL (2001) High heat flux heat pipe mechanism for cooling of electronics. IEEE Trans Compon Packaging Technol 24(1):220–225

Chapter 6
Visualization of Oscillating Heat Pipes

6.1 Introduction

As described in previous chapters, fluid flow and heat transfer in an oscillating heat pipe is very complex. To better understand thermally excited oscillating flow, a number of visualization methods have been used to study fluid flow of liquid plugs and vapor bubbles in OHPs. Three typical visualization methods include visible imaging technique, neutron and proton radiographs (Yoon 2013). Visible imaging technique is the most widely used but is limited due to the fact that the OHP tubes needed for this method must be made of transparent material only such as glass or OHPs covered with transparent materials. Neutron radiography is used to visualize the movements of liquid plugs and vapor bubbles in an OHP made of metallic materials such as copper and aluminum. With neutron imaging, images of liquid plugs and vapor bubbles can be seen through metallic walls. Proton radiography is also used to image the movement of liquid plugs and vapor bubbles of OHPs and can successfully visualize both liquid and vapor motions. In this chapter, these three visualization methods, which have been used to study oscillating flows in OHPs, will be presented including their observation results of oscillating motions in OHPs.

6.2 Visible Light Imaging

Visible light imaging uses visible light, which is a form of electromagnetic wave. Due to its wavelength, an electromagnetic wave is divided into gamma ray, X-ray, ultraviolet, visible light, infrared, microwave, and radio waves. The wavelength of visible light is about 400–700 nm. Using visible light for the visualization of the dynamics of working fluid is a simple system when compared to neutron or proton radiography visualization. Visible light imaging does not need specially prepared devices such as a neutron or proton source and their detectors. Any light source, such

© Springer Science+Business Media New York 2015
H. Ma, *Oscillating Heat Pipes*, DOI 10.1007/978-1-4939-2504-9_6

as a normal lamp, can be used as the light source for imaging the fluid flow in an OHP. The detector can be a high speed camera or a video camera, which is commercially available, to detect and capture an image of reflected or transmitted light from the working fluid in an OHP. Thus, the experimental system for detecting the liquid or liquid plugs in an OHP for visible light imaging technique does not need any special equipment. The liquid plugs in an OHP move or oscillate very fast for an operational OHP. Obviously a high speed camera or video camera is required. There are many commercially available high speed cameras or video cameras with frame rates that typically are set to operate at over 1,000 frames per second, which can cover the movement range of liquid plugs in an OHP thereby capturing detailed interface movement without blurring images. A high-resolution camera can also detect the detailed shape of a liquid plug and vapor bubble in an OHP including its advancing and receding menisci as well as the formation and growth of a bubble during the bubble formations, coalescence of bubbles, breaking up of liquid plugs, accumulation of liquid mass, and liquid film formation.

However, when using visible light imaging, fluid motion in opaque tubes such as copper and aluminum cannot be detected. Hence, the visible light visualization technique has a significant shortcoming because most OHPs are made of metallic material such as copper and aluminum. Because the thermal properties and surface conditions of glass or other transparent material are very different from metallic material such as copper and aluminum, the information obtained in a glass OHP cannot exactly reflect what happens in a metallic OHP. Another disadvantage is that the OHP needs to be placed in an open space. In other words, the test section should not be wrapped or surrounded by any opaque materials such as insulation, which would affect the heat transfer giving an inaccurate measurement and, hence, result in a difference in the movement of liquid plugs and vapor bubbles in an OHP.

6.2.1 Experimental Setup

Experimental results show that the oscillation motion of working fluid in the OHP is very chaotic. The basic experimental setup consists of transparent test sections and a camera. Using visible light, the camera directly catches the movement of liquid plugs and vapor bubbles in OHPs through transparent tubes or windows. Das et al. (2010) performed an experimental investigation on an oscillating flow in a single capillary tube as shown in Fig. 6.1. This tube has an inner diameter of 2.0 mm. The evaporator inserted into a cylindrical copper block had a length of 150.0 mm. The condenser, surrounded by a transparent heat exchanger, has a length of 250.0 mm. Silicon oil was used as the coolant. The adiabatic section between the evaporator and condenser had a length of 10.0 mm. Because the evaporator was surrounded by a copper block, only the condenser region was visible. Using this experimental setup, the displacement of liquid plugs including the meniscus was recorded as shown in Fig. 6.2. As shown, the displacement and meniscus, which

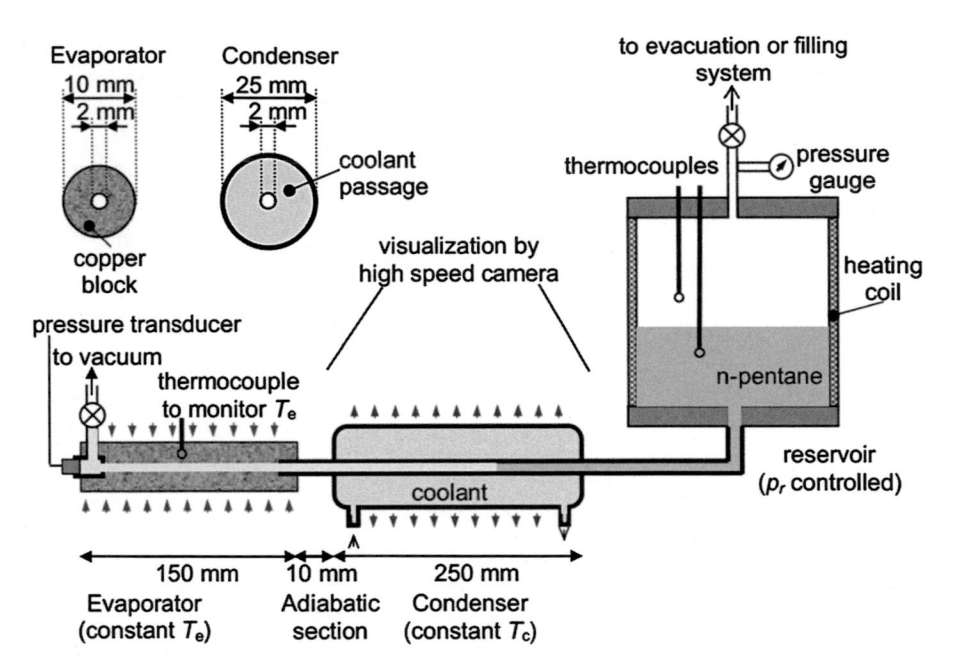

Fig. 6.1 Schematic of an experimental setup for single capillary tube (Das et al. 2010)

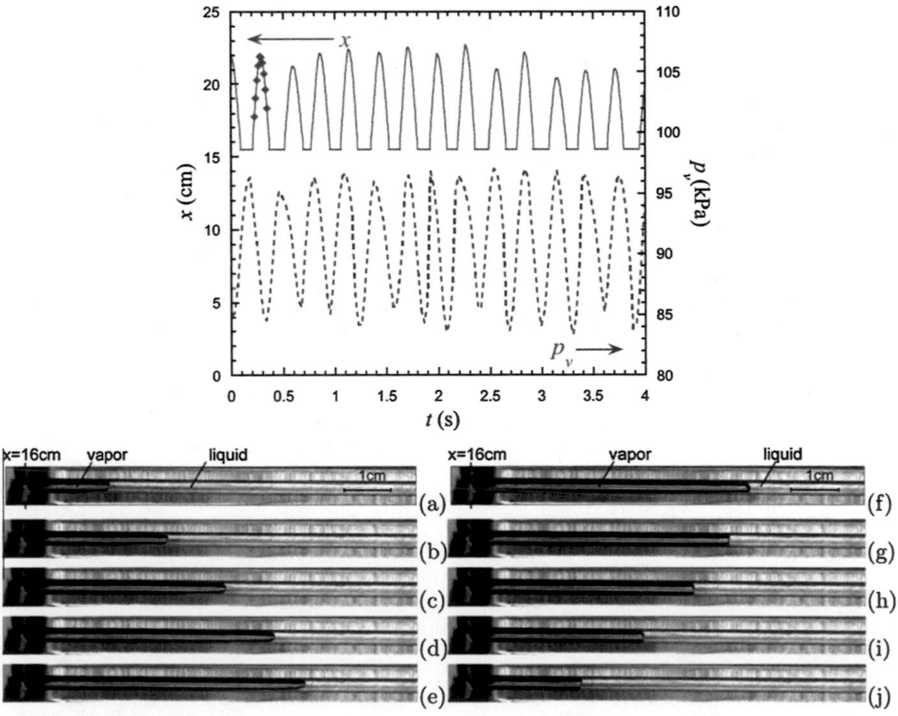

Fig. 6.2 The change of displacement with pressure change due to time change and its corresponding visual image (Das et al. 2010)

Fig. 6.3 An OHP
fabricated by glass tubes
with heating coil at the
evaporator section
(Tong et al. 2001)

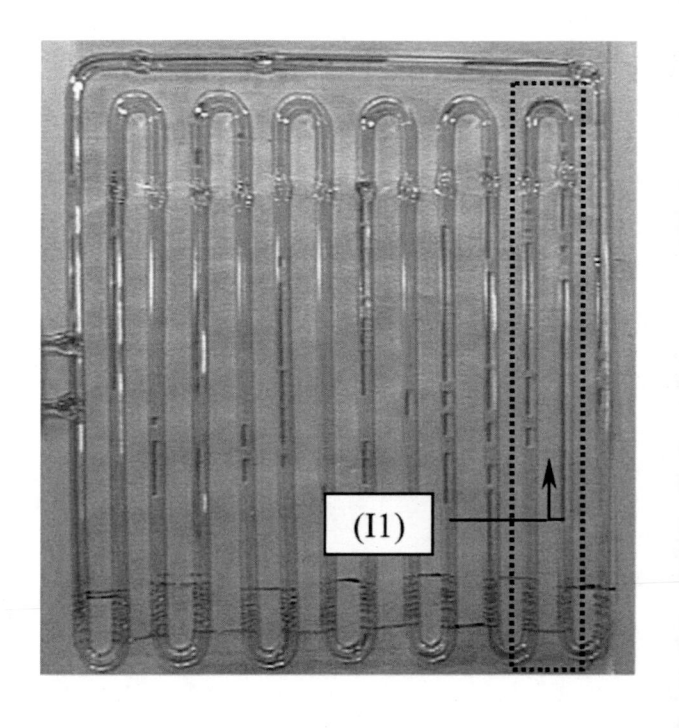

changed over time, can be readily recorded including the pressure variation effect
on the displacement. With this experiment, the effects of the moving direction and
pressure variation on the meniscus were visualized. It should be noted that the
results were for a single tube which is very different from an OHP which has
multiple turns and many liquid plugs and vapor bubbles resulting in different flow
patterns and menisci.

Tong et al. (2001) conducted a visualization experiment of a glass OHP as shown
in Fig. 6.3. To visualize the fluid flow in the evaporator section, a coil heater was
used as shown in Fig. 6.4. The dimension of the OHP was 160×160 mm^2, and the
inner diameter of its tube was 1.8 mm. From Fig. 6.4, it can be found that the coil for
heating wound around tubes in the lower part of the OHP. This helps to visualize the
evaporator while heat is supplied. Figure 6.4 shows a magnified view of the heating
section with coil including the bubble formation and expansion in the tube.

The observation by visible light is usually done for glass OHPs because visible
light can only penetrate transparent materials, but oscillation motion of working
fluid in a glass tube is different from that of a copper tube if the surface condition is
different. Qu and Ma (2002) did a visualization experiment on OHP built with
copper and glass tubes combined as shown in Fig. 6.5. As shown, copper tubes and
glass tubes were connected to one another. Even though this OHP is not totally
made from copper tubes, it gives good insight into how working fluid behaves in
copper tubes.

Borgmeyer and Ma (2007) manufactured an OHP covered with a Lexan sheet as
shown in Fig. 6.6. This OHP consists of a flat plate of copper with a transparent

Fig. 6.4 Magnified view of heating section with heating coil at the lower part of OHP including the bubble formation and growth (Tong et al. 2001).
(**a**) Time = 0 s.
(**b**) Time = 0.0315 s.
(**c**) Time = 0.0676 s

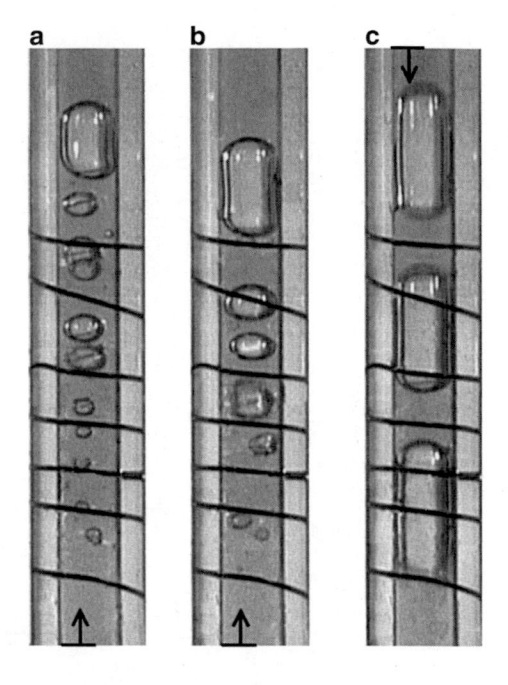

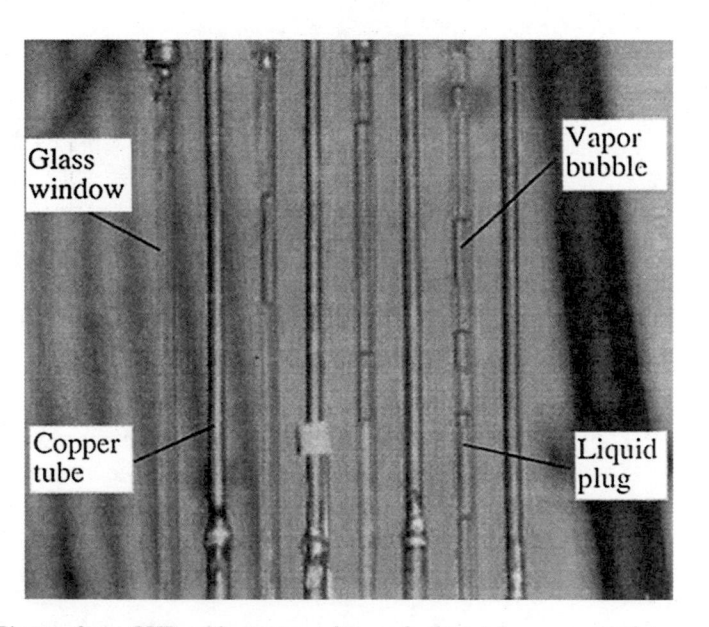

Fig. 6.5 Photo of an OHP with copper tubes and glass tubes connected to one another (Qu and Ma 2002)

a

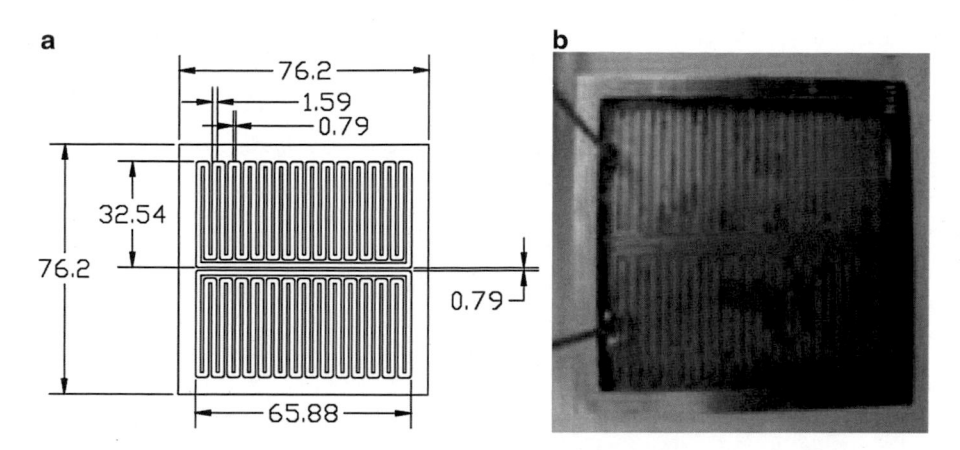

b

Fig. 6.6 A flat-plate OHP: (**a**) schematic and (**b**) photography (Borgmeyer and Ma 2007)

Fig. 6.7 Photos of vapor
bubbles and liquid plugs in
grooved channels
(Borgmeyer and Ma 2007)

cover. The design of this device partially represents the movement of liquid in a copper channel and visualizes the evaporator and condenser. On the flat plate of copper, grooves were made using a carbide end mill with channel dimensions of $1.59 \times 1.59 \text{ mm}^2$ in a square shape. The thickness of the flat plate shown in Fig. 6.6 is 2.54 mm and its area is $76.2 \times 76.2 \text{ mm}^2$. The OHP had two separate closed loops to decrease the length of each channel so that the pressure drop from evaporator to condenser could also be reduced. Using this setup, liquid plugs and vapor bubbles with meniscus interfaces were observed and recorded as shown in Fig. 6.7. Chien et al. (2011) also fabricated an OHP using a grooved copper block, but covered it with a transparent glass. It should also be mentioned that there are a number of studies (Bhuwakietkumjohn and Rittidech 2010; Rittidech and Sangiamsuk 2012)

which enabled visualization of the evaporator and condenser using a glass OHP tube without any opaque obstacles, which was accomplished by attaching tubes to the heater and cooler.

6.2.2   Observations

It has been reported that liquid does not oscillate when the heat input is too low, i.e., a minimum amount of heat input is needed to initiate the oscillation motion. After initiation, oscillation increases as heat input increases. The driving force of this oscillating motion is due to the pressure difference between the evaporator and condenser. It is known that pressure difference is related to temperature difference between evaporator and condenser. As heat input at the evaporator is increased for a typical OHP at a given condenser temperature, the temperature in the evaporator is also increased. When an OHP is charged with a working fluid, the pressure inside is directly related to the temperature. As the temperature increases, it directly increases the pressure inside. For a typical OHP, when the power input increases, the temperature difference between the evaporator and condenser increases, which directly results in an increase in the pressure difference between the evaporator and condenser. This increases the active oscillation movement of fluid. As heat input increases, the oscillating motion occurring in an OHP is accompanied by nucleate boiling, film evaporation, bubble forming and growing, dryout, coalescence of vapor bubbles, circulation of fluid, and/or film condensation. Many experimental results report that the flow pattern of a working fluid in an OHP is changed as heat input increases (Mameli et al. 2011; Qu and Ma 2002; Wilson et al. 2011; Tong et al. 2001).

When an OHP is vertically placed with no heat input, liquid remains in the low section of the heat pipe and vapor stays in the upper section of the heat pipe. When heat is added to the lower section, i.e., evaporator, of the heat pipe, the wall temperature increases. When the wall temperature is higher than the required superheat to activate the nucleate sites, the bubble grows and nucleate boiling takes place, which is similar to a pool boiling in a confined space. Figure 6.8 shows typical nucleate boiling in OHPs (Katpradit et al. 2004; Tong et al. 2001). In Fig. 6.9a, the nucleate boiling is seen at the u-bend section. No electric heater is shown in this figure, but according to the experimental setup, an electric heater was attached to a specific region of the copper thermal conduction plate where OHP was also attached and that region was close to the u-bend sections of OHP. Because u-bend sections are considered to have the highest heat input regions, nucleate sites become more active at these u-bend sections. In Fig. 6.8b, nucleate boiling is shown near the heating coil in the tube indicating that heat input through the coil causes nucleate boiling. For a typical nucleate boiling phenomenon, the bubble formation, growth, and release need a minimum superheat and waiting time. Otherwise, the nucleate boiling cannot take place. Since most reported OHPs for visible observation experiments have been made of glass materials which have low thermal

Fig. 6.8 Nucleate boiling
phenomena in OHPs
observed by (**a**) Katpradit
et al. (2004) and (**b**) Tong
et al. (2001)

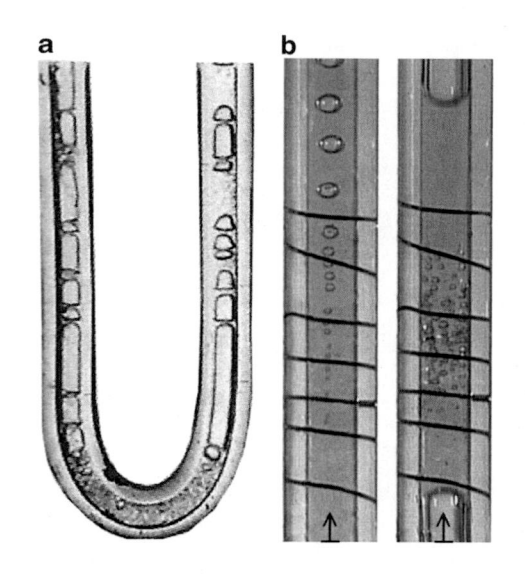

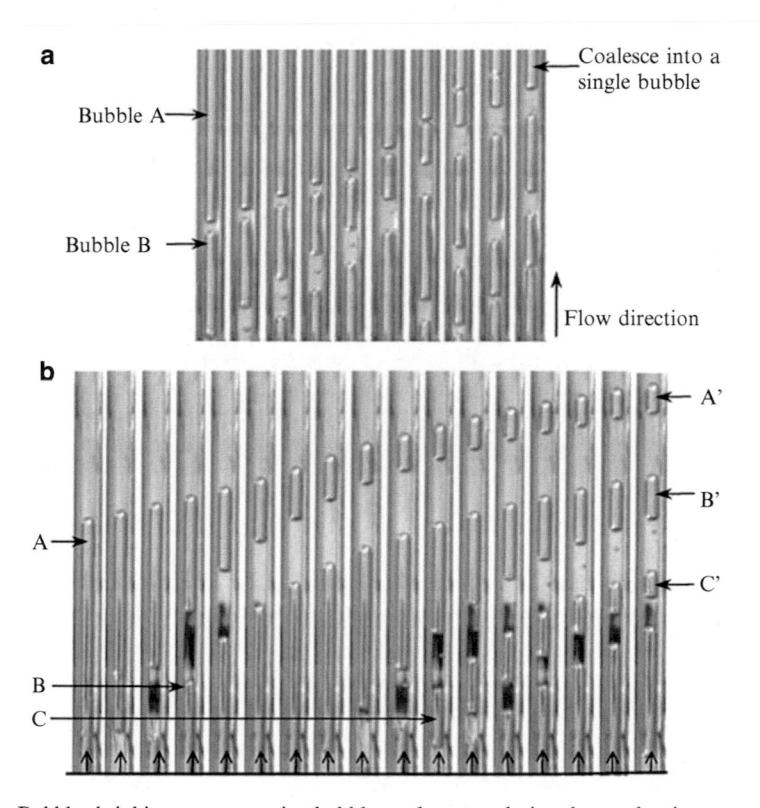

Fig. 6.9 Bubble shrinking accompanying bubble coalescence during the condensing process for a
methanol OHP at the heating power of 30.0 W: (**a**) time step for each successive image = 0.016 s,
time needed for a full process = 0.144 s and (**b**) time step for each successive image = 0.016 s, time
needed for a full process = 0.256 s (Xu et al. 2005)

conductivity, to have a good view, either wired type heaters as shown in Fig. 6.8b or one side heating as shown in Fig. 6.8a was used. This resulted in uneven heating in the evaporator section which can easily make nucleate sites become active. All reported transparent OHPs for visible observations had no fins on condensers, and most of them were just cooled by natural convection. Considering the low thermal conductivity of transparent materials and low heat transfer coefficient in the condenser section, in this condition, nucleate boiling heat transfer can take place. However, when the oscillation motion is stabilized with a high frequency, the waiting time for a bubble to form into a liquid plug is longer than the time it should take for a liquid plug to flow through the evaporating section; hence, nucleate boiling may not occur. In this case, evaporation might be mainly due to thin film evaporation at the liquid–vapor interfaces of a train of liquid plugs and vapor bubbles. When the bubbles formed in the evaporator section move to the condenser section, the bubbles become smaller due to condensation heat transfer accompanying the coalescence as shown in Fig. 6.9.

A vapor bubble is one of the more important objects needed to visualize and analyze fluid flow of an OHP. Equally important is the liquid plug. Besides the bubble formation by nucleate boiling, Das et al. (2010) reported that when the condensation rates are high, secondary bubbles are formed as shown in Fig. 6.10. This can occur during the movement toward or away from the evaporator due to a pinching of the interface resulting in the formation of multiple bubbles. When the velocity is high, unstable liquid film is developed resulting in a bulging toward the central axis of the tube and a coalescing with the bulged liquid film from the opposite wall. These types of secondary bubbles were seen to quickly disappear as they merged into a bigger vapor bubble. When the heat transfer rate increases, the oscillating motion increases resulting in instable liquid film which is a primary contribution to this phenomenon. The instabilities shown in Fig. 6.10 should be directly related to the thermal physical properties of working fluids, tube diameter,

Fig. 6.10 Flow visualization in the condenser section (liquid pentane on right side (*lighter part*), vapor on left side (*dark part*)) shows the meniscus position for a typical cycle using pentane (Das et al. 2010)

and tube surface conditions. Results shown in Fig. 6.10 are based on the tube diameter of 2.0 mm and a pentane working fluid.

For a typical OHP, when heat is added to the evaporator, liquid becomes vapor and vapor volume in the evaporator increases. As the heat is removed from the condenser, the vapor volume in the condenser decreases. Khandekar et al. (2002a, b) summarized bubble formation types observed in transparent OHPs as follows:

- When a train of liquid plugs and vapor bubbles move to the evaporator section, small bubbles are formed by nucleate boiling in addition to bubbles already in existence. If these small bubbles encounter a larger bubble, they merge with the larger bubble as shown in Fig. 6.11a.
- A large bubble will split into two bubbles and one of these two bubbles merges with another large bubble, as shown in Fig. 6.11b.
- In the condenser section, a large bubble becomes small and sometimes smaller than the tube diameter as shown in Fig. 6.11c.
- A couple of large bubbles merge into one larger bubble and sometimes a newly formed larger bubble splits into a few large bubbles shown in Fig. 6.11d.

Bubble flow patterns occurring in transparent OHPs were summarized by Khandekar et al. (2002a, b) as follows:

- Typical vapor bubbles 1 and 2 travel in the same direction with nearly the same velocity taking along the liquid plug which is trapped between them comparable to a piston movement of bubbles as shown in Fig. 6.11e.
- The first vapor bubble (bubble 1) is nearly stationary; however, bubble 2 expands or alternatively travels with a velocity finally merging with bubble 1 to form a bigger vapor bubble 3 which continues to travel. It is clearly observed that vapor bubble 2, instead of acting as a 'piston plug' pushing the liquid plug completely, travels through the liquid slug thereby displacing in-between liquid, which eventually passes through the thin layer around the bubble as shown in Fig. 6.11f.
- Vapor bubbles 1 and 2 are both moving in the same direction, with simultaneous expansion, and finally merge to form a larger vapor bubble 3 which continues to travel in the same direction as shown in Fig. 6.11g.
- Vapor bubbles 1 and 2 both move in the opposite direction, with simultaneous expansion, finally merging together to form a larger bubble 3 that continues to travel in the resultant direction as shown in Fig. 6.11h.

These flow patterns of vapor bubbles summarized above are natural representatives of a typical mass-spring system. For a typical mass-spring system like an OHP with a train of vapor bubbles and liquid plugs, in addition to flow patterns summarized above, a number of other flow patterns can appear depending on the location, liquid plug number/length, vapor bubble number/length, working fluid, and other factors such as driving forces. For example, a vapor bubble may oscillate/vibrate around a mean position due to the unique features of the mass-spring mechanical system.

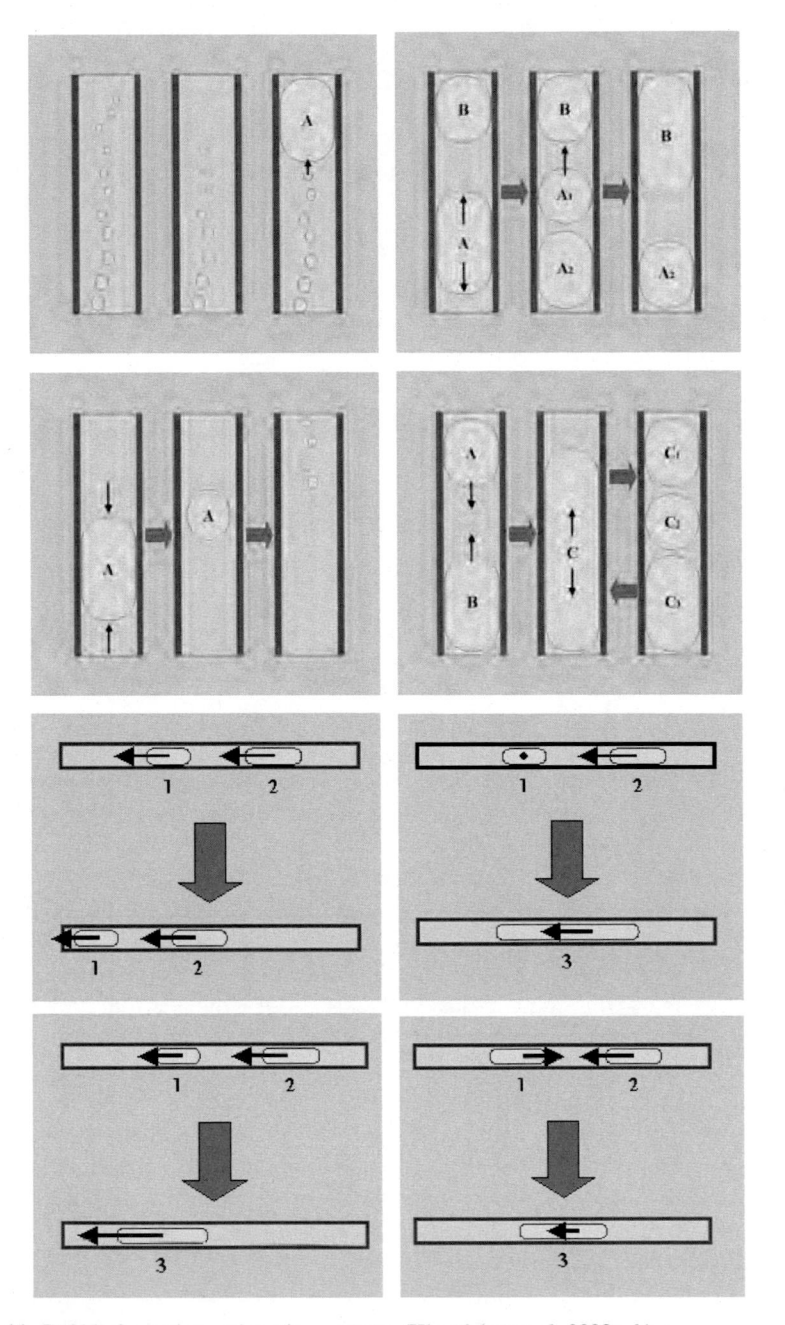

Fig. 6.11 Bubble formation and motion patterns (Khandekar et al. 2002a, b)

Bhuwakietkumjohn and Rittidech (2010) observed that when the heat flux level and the heat source temperature increase for a closed-loop glass OHP with check valves, the slug flow and/or annular flow becomes dispersed bubble flow in the evaporator section as shown in Fig. 6.12. In addition to ethanol, a silver nano-ethanol

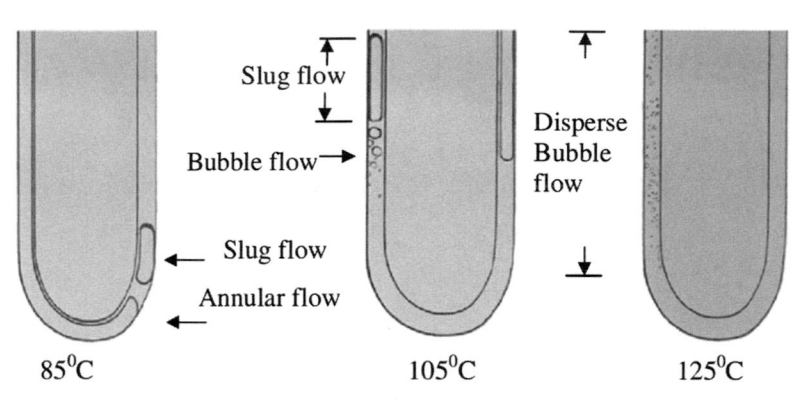

Fig. 6.12 Internal flow patterns for a looped glass OHP with check valves using ethanol (Bhuwakietkumjohn and Rittidech 2010)

mixture was used in the OHP by Bhuwakietkumjohn and Rittidech (2010) who found that the flow pattern in the evaporator section was similar to that with ethanol. As shown, at a heat source temperature of 85 °C with a heat flux of 0.462 kW/m², slug flow and annular flow were dominant in the evaporator section with very few nucleation sites. At a heat source temperature of 105 °C with a heat flux of 0.582 kW/m², slug flow had very few nucleation sites; however, bubble flow with more nucleation sites was observed in the lower part of the evaporator. Bubble flow and slug flow dominated the middle and upper parts of the evaporator. At a heat flux of 0.639 kW/m² with a heat source temperature of 125 °C, dispersed bubble flow with more nucleation sites appearing was observed in the lower part of the evaporator. These vapor dispersed bubbles extended to the middle and upper parts of the evaporator before moving up to the condenser part. Compared to typical convective boiling in a channel (Carey 1992), where the flow pattern starts from a bubbly flow (which has a relatively low heat flux) and goes into an annular flow (with a relatively high heat flux), the flow pattern occurring in the evaporator section of a glass OHP started from the annular flow and/or slug flow at a relatively low heat flux to the bubble flow at a relatively high heat flux. The primary reason for this difference might be due to the constant filling ratio and capillary tube of the OHP. For any OHP, the oscillating motion depends on the vapor spring constant. In other words, the oscillating motion in an OHP is due to the vapor volume expansion in the evaporator and the vapor volume contraction in the condenser. For a glass OHP, glass has a low thermal conductivity. Considering the additional contact thermal resistance and low convection heat transfer coefficient in the condenser section, the vapor in the condenser section could not be effectively condensed into liquid. All these directly limit the heat transfer rates in the condenser and evaporator sections, which result in different flow patterns occurring in a metallic OHP.

Wilson et al. (2011), Thompson et al. (2011), and Smoot and Ma (2014) tested a number of metallic OHPs and they did not reach dryout even when the power reached the heater limit. But intermittent dryout for glass OHPs has been reported in

Fig. 6.13 Dryout seen at
the OHP heating section
(Katpradit et al. 2004)

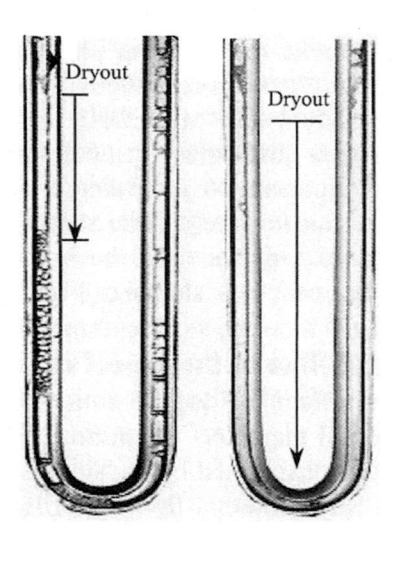

many studies. Katpradit et al. (2004) conducted an experiment of a glass OHP
and reported the existence of an intermittent dryout as shown in Fig. 6.13.
The intermittent dryout time was 0.16–0.4 s at a heat flux of 1,128 W/m², and
when the heat flux was increased to 3,511 W/m², the intermittent dryout time
decreased to 0.86–1.0 s. Therefore, as the power density increases, the intermittent
dryout time increases. At some point, no liquid is returned and a permanent dryout
takes place. Soponpongpipat et al. (2009) conducted an investigation of the start-up
condition of a looped OHP using both a visual study and quantitative experiments;
they found that vapor volume contraction is the key to start up for a steady state
oscillating motion in a looped OHP. If the vapor volume contraction speed is less
than the vapor volume expansion in the condenser, it is highly likely that a looped
OHP will not start up. This investigation indirectly demonstrated that the heat
transfer rate in the condenser section plays a key role in the start-up, steady state
operation, and dryout in an OHP. Tong et al. (2001), however, mentioned that no
permanent dryout occurred because of continuous flow fluid movement by driving
and restoring forces.

   The circulation of working fluid is one of the most common events occurring in
OHP. The circulation direction is random, but by using check valves, the direction
of circulation can be controlled. Bhuwakietkumjohn and Rittidech (2010) reported
circulation in one fixed flow direction using a looped OHP with check valve. On the
contrary, the direction of circulation in a regular OHP without check valve switches
is not controllable. Li et al. (2004) reported that the flow direction will switch a
couple of times at a specific tube before circulation changes its direction, and the
time for each flow direction change is generally less than 0.1 s. They also suggested
that the flow direction for a specific tube may change $2n + 1$ times, and n is
determined by heat input and the type of the working fluid. Tong et al. (2001)
stated that continuous circulation occurs after the start-up of operation.

The circulation direction is consistent once the circulation is initiated. They also reported that the circulation velocity is increased as heat input is increased.

As the liquid flows through the capillary tube, it forms advancing and receding meniscus, as shown in Fig. 6.14 (Lips et al. 2010). When the advancing contact angle is different from the receding angle, the pressure difference due to the curvatures directly increases significantly. Ma (2012) studied the velocity effect on the receding and advancing contact angles of a liquid plug moving in a capillary tube and found that when the liquid plug length is equal to 5 mm at a driving pressure difference of 10 Pa and a tube radius of 500 μm, the flow resistance caused by the dynamic contact angle can be 92 % of the total flow resistance at a temperature of 60 °C. It can be concluded that the effect of the dynamic contact angle on the fluid flow of a liquid plug in a capillary tube should be considered. In addition, it is found that the liquid plug length significantly affects the advancing contact angle and velocity for a given driving pressure difference.

The observation investigations presented above have demonstrated that the nucleate boiling can take place in a glass-type OHP. In addition to nucleate boiling heat transfer, thin liquid film formation and its evaporation plays an important role in oscillating motion and heat transfer in an OHP. Soponpongpipat et al. (2006) reported a photograph (Fig. 6.15) showing a liquid film between the vapor plug and

Fig. 6.14 Advancing and receding meniscus of liquid slug in an OHP tube (Lips et al. 2010)

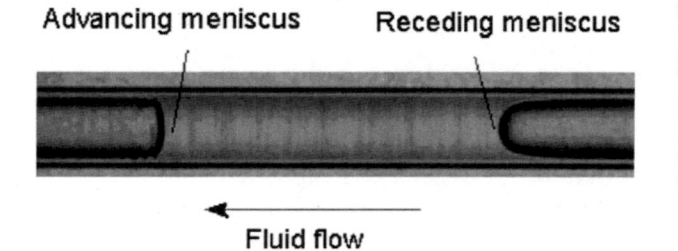

Fig. 6.15 Liquid film between vapor plug and evaporator surface wall (Soponpongpipat et al. 2006)

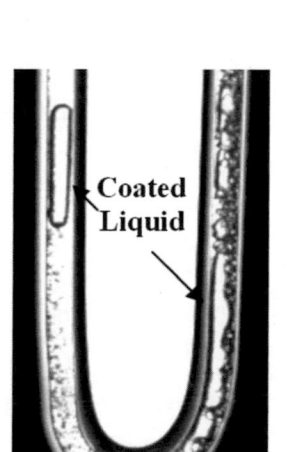

Fig. 6.16 Vapor bubble with increased pressure by liquid film evaporation pushes liquid plug up into the condenser and into the second tube (Mameli et al. 2011)

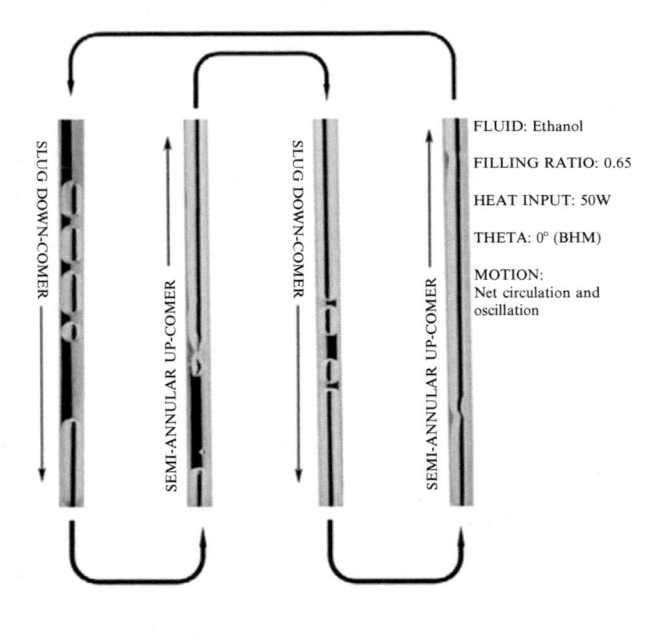

FLUID: Ethanol

FILLING RATIO: 0.65

HEAT INPUT: 50W

THETA: 0° (BHM)

MOTION: Net circulation and oscillation

evaporator surface wall. As shown, liquid film is formed between the vapor and wall of the tube on the left side, and a relatively longer liquid film is formed from the bottom of the u-bend section to the end of the tube on right side.

Mameli et al. (2011) reported that thin film evaporation can help to push liquid plugs. They mentioned that some liquid film evaporates into vapor bubbles causing the increase of vapor pressure within that bubble which pushes its adjacent liquid slug to move to the condenser. Figure 6.16 illustrates this procedure where the liquid film in the u-bend section of the first and second tubes from the left evaporates into vapor, which causes a pressure increase within the vapor bubble. This increased pressure pushes the liquid slug up into the second tube to the condenser. When thin film exists in the evaporating section, the thermal resistance across the thin liquid film is much smaller than the thermal resistance in a typical pool boiling. The low thermal resistance or high evaporating heat transfer coefficient will increase the vapor temperature if the wall temperature of the evaporator is constant. Considering the saturation condition, the vapor pressure in the evaporator section increases which directly increases the pressure difference between the evaporator and condenser. The larger pressure difference helps generate more active oscillation motion of fluid by pushing liquid plugs resulting in a higher heat transfer rate by convection.

To find the primary factors limiting the maximum heat transport capability in an OHP, Wang et al. (2013) established an experimental setup of a single water plug moving in a capillary tube to determine the velocity effect on the plug length as shown in Fig. 6.17. Using the microscale particle image velocimetry (μPIV) system, the velocity effect on the liquid plug length with an original length of 1.5 mm was measured. The motion of the liquid plug in the capillary tube with an

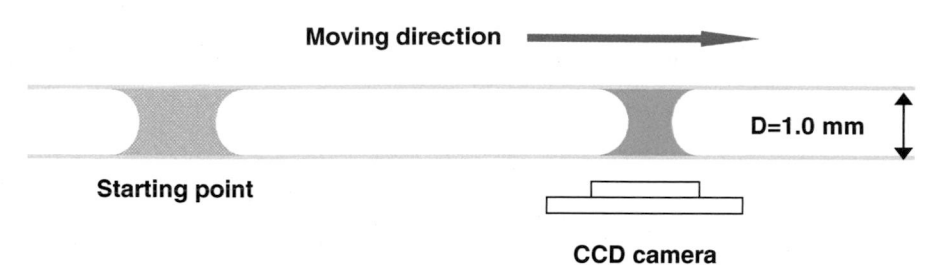

Fig. 6.17   Schematic of an experimental setup of velocity effect on the liquid plug length

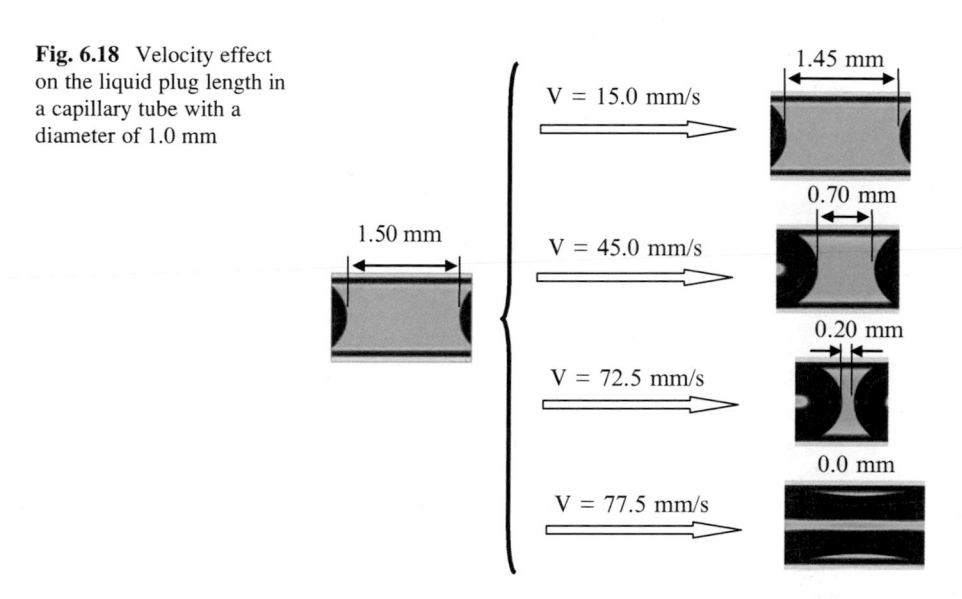

Fig. 6.18   Velocity effect on the liquid plug length in a capillary tube with a diameter of 1.0 mm

inner diameter of 1.0 mm was controlled by a computer-controlled system, which could produce a velocity ranging from 15 to 80 mm/s. Experimental results show that the velocity directly affects the plug length, i.e., when the velocity increases, the liquid plug length decreases. When the air velocity increases up to 77.5 mm/s, the plug becomes penetrated and an annular flow is formed (Fig. 6.18), which might be the mechanism that governs the operating limitation occurring in an OHP.

When the input power is high, a liquid plug in an OHP will be penetrated as shown in Fig. 6.18. A liquid film will be left on the inner wall surface of the heat pipe. When liquid film flows on the inner wall, in particular with the frictional vapor flow effect at the liquid–vapor interface, waves are developed. Tong et al. (2001) reported a photograph of liquid film wave just before entering into the evaporator as shown in Fig. 6.19. When the capillary diameter is small, the wave growth can easily develop into a liquid plug. In addition, Tong et al. (2001) studied turn effect on this type of liquid plug formation as shown in Fig. 6.20. Xu et al. (2005) show that the surface tension and curvature due to the turn contribute to the liquid plug formation in the turn region.

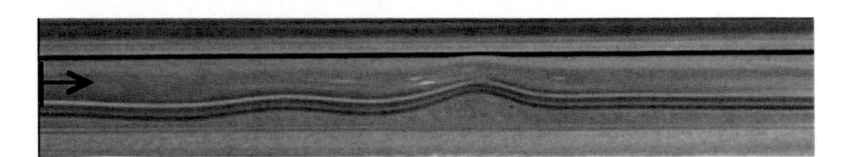

Fig. 6.19 Surface wave transitioning into the evaporator (Tong et al. 2001)

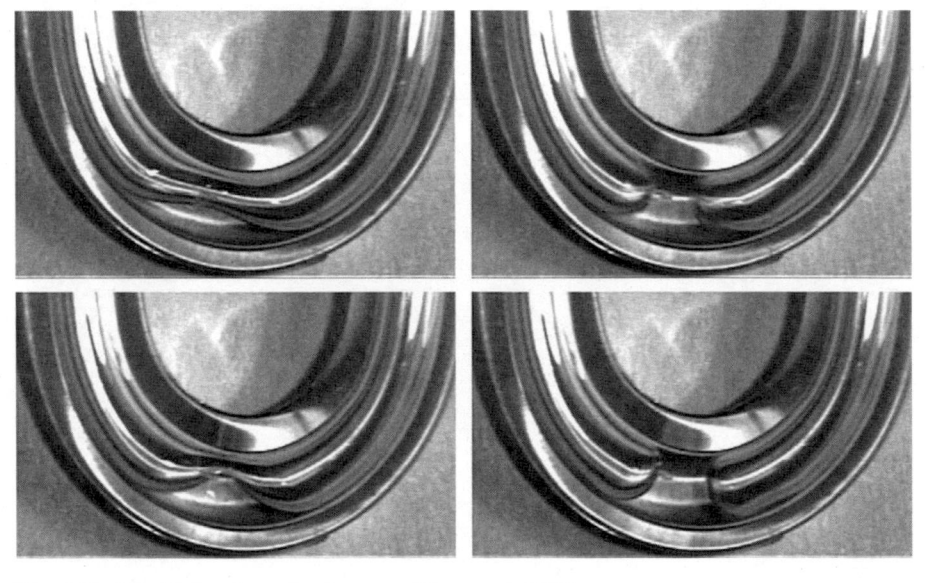

Fig. 6.20 Liquid plug formation in a turn (Tong et al. 2001)

6.3 Neutron Radiography

6.3.1 Experimental Setup

Neutron imaging or neutron radiography is an imaging technique utilizing neutrons as the lighting source. The basic principle of neutron imaging is to utilize its characteristic of penetrating, like X-rays, to look inside specimens where other imaging techniques cannot be used. Neutron imaging equipment is composed mainly of three parts: a neutron beam, specimen or test sample, and detector, as shown in Fig. 6.21. The neutron beam is produced from a neutron source, such as a nuclear reactor, and passes through a collimator to reach the specimen. Then, some of the neutrons are absorbed or scattered when they hit the specimen with the rest of the neutrons penetrating the specimen and reaching the detectors. These penetrating neutrons are then converted into image data by the detector.

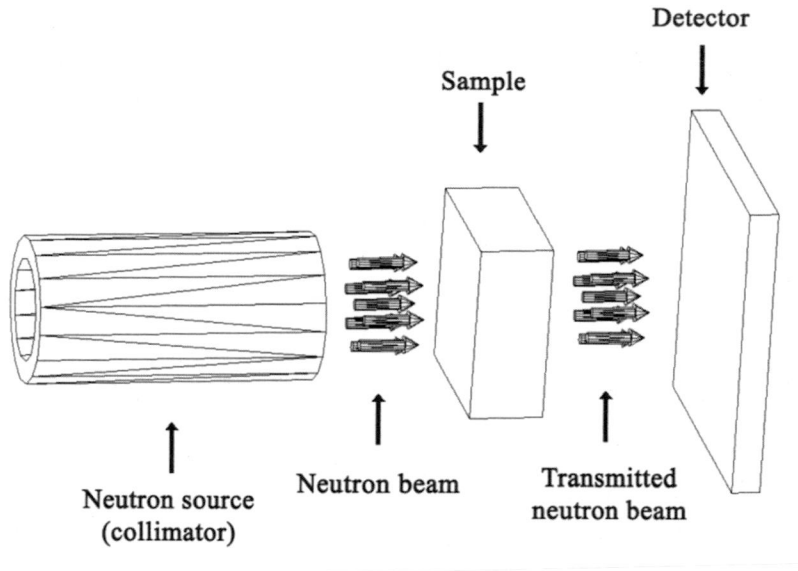

Fig. 6.21 Schematic view of a neutron radiography device

There are several advantages of neutron imaging when investigating fluid dynamics in OHPs. Neutrons have a low attenuation coefficient for copper or aluminum while retaining a high attenuation coefficient for hydrogen. Therefore, when an OHP shell is made of aluminum or copper and charged with a liquid containing hydrogen atoms, such as water or acetone, and exposed to a neutron beam, it will be attenuated by the liquid inside and not the copper or aluminum case. For a functional OHP, there are a train of liquid plugs and vapor bubbles inside. Because the liquid attenuation coefficient is very different from vapor, the vapor bubble length or liquid plug length including the meniscus of liquid–vapor interface can be observed by neutron imaging. Another advantage of neutron imaging for OHP studies is that there is little or no effect from gamma ray radiation (Berger 1970).

Figure 6.22 shows an experimental setup of neutron imaging for the visualization experiment of OHPs (Wilson et al. 2008). The OHP was placed between the camera and the beam. Neutron masks were positioned in front of the OHP to prevent unnecessary irradiation. For the OHP to function, the evaporator section had to be in contact with a heater or a heat source and the condenser had to be cooled. As shown in Fig. 6.22, heat was added by a power supply through a heater and measured by a multimeter. The oscillating motion generated in an OHP directly affects the temperature variations of both evaporator and condenser sections of the OHP. A number of thermocouples were placed on the OHP surface. The condenser was cooled by the coolant flowing through the condenser section via a circulator. Temperature data were acquired with Computer 1 using a data acquisition card

Fig. 6.22 Experimental
setup: (**a**) schematic
and (**b**) photo of neutron
imaging system
(Wilson et al. 2008)

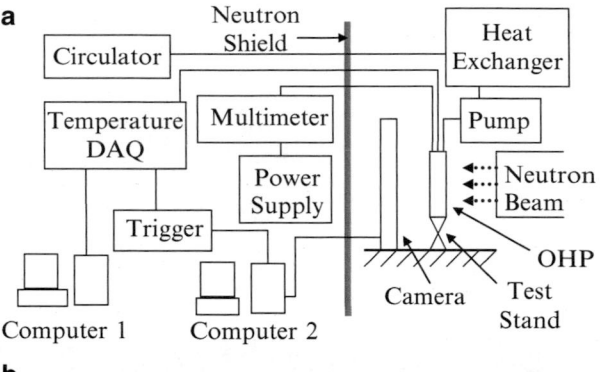

(DAQ). Computer 2 was used to store the digital data of neutron images. The temperature sample rate varied from 50 to 250 Hz depending on the length of the test. At the beginning of each test, the image acquisition software in Computer 2 triggered the temperature DAQ so that the temperature data and images would be synchronized.

Using the experimental setups shown in Fig. 6.22, Wilson et al. (2008) investigated a 12-turn OHP (Fig. 6.23) and an 8-turn OHP (Fig. 6.24). The dimensions of the OHPs are shown in Figs. 6.23 and 6.24. The construction of the 8- and 12-turn OHPs is very similar. Two 0.635-cm-thick copper plates spread heat from the copper tubing to the condensing blocks and the heater. To provide a large contact area between the plates and the 3.2 mm copper tubing, 3.2 mm semicircular grooves were machined into the plates. Omegabond '201' thermal paste was placed between

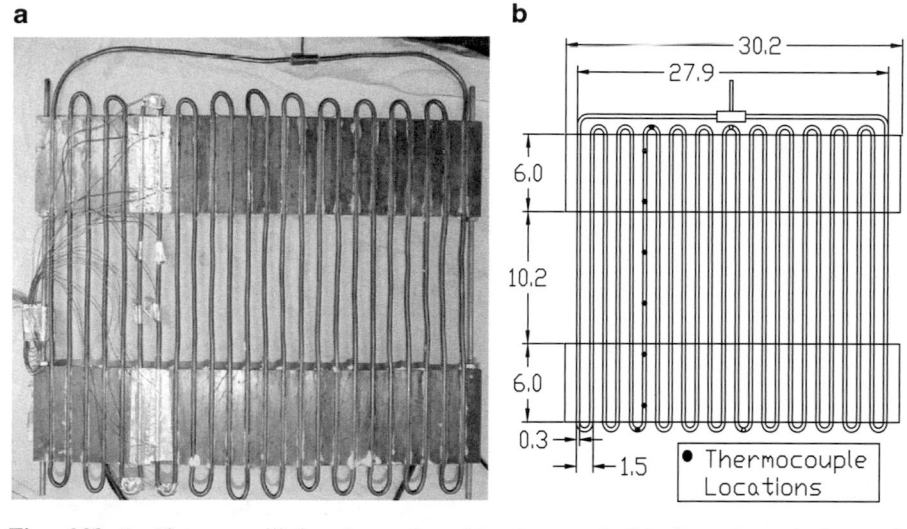

Fig. 6.23 A 12-turn oscillating heat pipe (**a**) photo and (**b**) dimensions (units: cm) (Wilson et al. 2008)

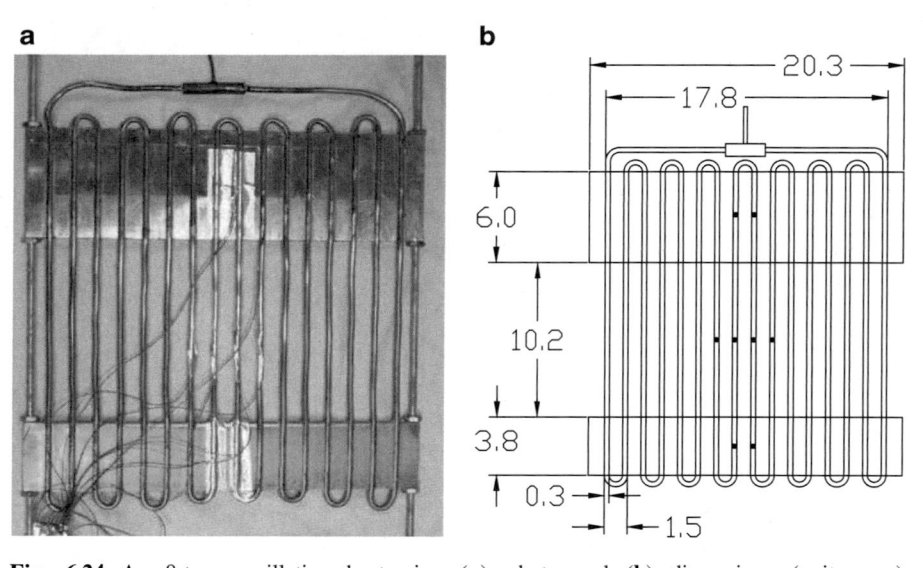

Fig. 6.24 An 8-turn oscillating heat pipe (**a**) photo and (**b**) dimensions (units: cm) (Wilson et al. 2008)

the groove and the tube to reduce the contact resistance. These OHPs were positioned vertically with the evaporator below the condenser. They were insulated with aluminum foil and encased fiberglass insulation (which is assumed to have a similar neutron transmission to silica). The aluminum foil prevented any of the fiberglass from becoming airborne.

Fig. 6.25 Two-layer
OHPs: (**a**) 20 turns and
(**b**) 10 turns (Borgmeyer
et al. 2010)

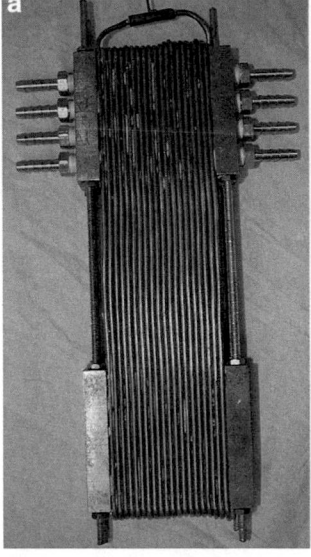

Borgmeyer et al. (2010) investigated the oscillating motion and heat transfer performance of a 10-turn OHP and a 20-turn OHP as shown in Fig. 6.25. Both OHPs were constructed from copper tubing with outer and inner diameters of 3.12 and 1.65 mm, respectively. The evaporator and condenser were constructed from copper blocks. Semicircular channels were milled into the copper blocks to create maximum contact between the two regions and the tubing. The condenser regions had holes drilled through the center for water bath-controlled condenser temperature. Similarly, holes were drilled in the evaporator to hold cylindrical cartridge heaters that would serve as the controlled heat input. The copper tubing was laid in the semicircular channels of the evaporator and condenser blocks. Thermal paste was also added to the grooves to reduce contact resistance. The copper block attached with the copper tubing for the 20-turn OHP has an evaporator section and a condenser section of 7.62 cm × 8.89 cm × 2.54 cm. The length of the adiabatic section was set at 10.16 cm for the 20-turn OHP. To achieve a higher heat flux, the 10-turn OHP was designed to be smaller with dimensions of 3.81 cm × 7.62 cm × 2.54 cm for the evaporator and 6.35 cm × 7.62 cm × 2.54 cm for the condenser. The adiabatic section was set to a length of 7.62 cm. The tubing for the 10-turn OHP was staggered to achieve a clearer image of the fluid flow. Both heat pipes were tested using the experimental setup shown in Fig. 6.22. In addition, Wilson et al. (2011), Hathaway et al. (2012), and Thompson et al. (2011) used the same approach and experimental setup to investigate 6-turn OHPs, uneven-turn OHPs, and check valve OHPs, respectively.

6.3.2   Observations

6.3.2.1   General Observations

Wilson et al. (2008) used the 12-turn OHP with neutron imaging to observe how oscillating motion started in an OHP as shown in Fig. 6.26. Wilson et al. (2008) described the transient process of the 12-turn OHP after a power input of 300 W was added to the evaporating section. After heat was added to the evaporator, the vapor expanded within the evaporator slowly pushing the liquid toward the condenser. Starting at about 15 s, some liquid and vapor portions in the condenser also began slowly and smoothly to move toward the evaporator region. Beginning around 50 s, the movement was characterized by some very slow flow reversals. At about 1 min, there was a sudden transition to a persistent rapid oscillating behavior.

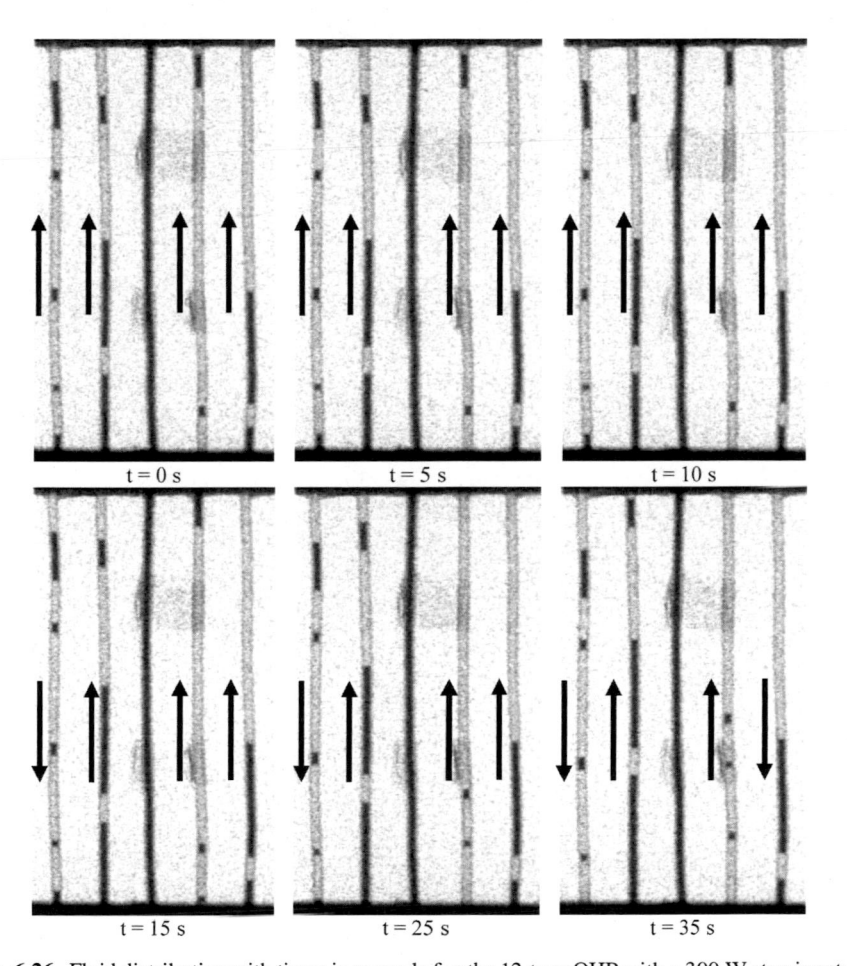

Fig. 6.26 Fluid distribution with times in seconds for the 12-turn OHP with a 300 W step input at $t = 0$ s (Wilson et al. 2008)

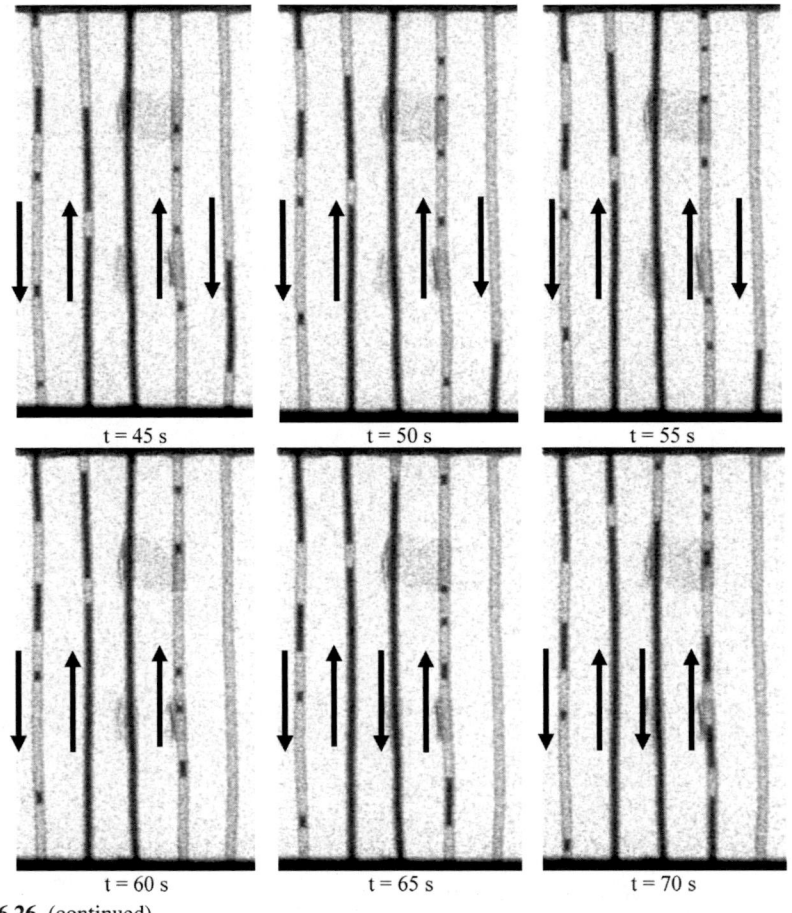

Fig. 6.26 (continued)

This oscillation motion occurred very quickly and appeared to occur throughout the heat pipe. Before the steady state oscillating motion, the temperature response was very smooth and the fluid oscillations were barely noticeable in the temperature measurements. Note that the temperature oscillations did not begin until 125 s, well after significant fluid movements were observed.

For the tubular-type OHPs with 8 or 12 turns, the oscillating movement of fluid inside was highly nonuniform. They were characterized by fast fluid movement at the center turns of the OHP as shown in Fig. 6.27 with very little movement in the outer turns and almost no bulk flow. This flow distribution in the 8- and 12-turn OHPs was likely due to a nonuniform heat flux provided by the strip heater. The outer turns of the OHP received a lower heat flux while the inner turns received a higher heat flux. Besides the nonuniform movement of the OHP, each OHP exhibited slightly different flow patterns. At the same heat load and operating temperature, each heat pipe behaved slightly differently. The 12-turn nanofluid

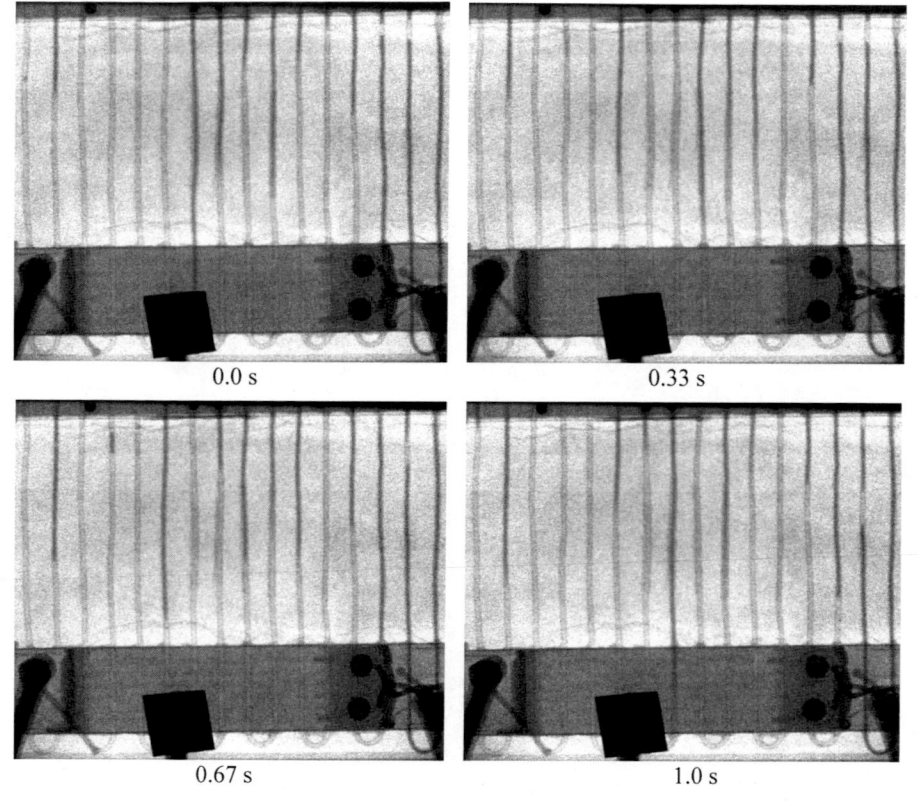

Fig. 6.27 Neutron images of nonuniform oscillating flow in the 8-turn nanofluid OHP at 199.5 W (Wilson et al. 2008)

OHP had the lowest frequency and amplitude temperature oscillations. The heat flux per tube of the 12-turn OHP was lower than the 8-turn OHP, which should be one reason for a lower frequency and amplitude. Also, the 8-turn nanofluid OHP had a lower frequency and amplitude than the 8-turn water OHP. The high heat transport capability of the nanofluid OHP can transfer more heat per liquid slug and, therefore, allowed the OHP to transfer the same amount of heat with less movement. Increasing the heat input of the OHP caused a noticeable increase in fluid velocity and oscillating amplitude. Figure 6.28 illustrates this increase with the 12-turn nanofluid OHP at 50.5 W in which the slugs are relatively stagnant; however, at 199.4 W, Fig. 6.29 shows a marked increase in the slug motion. For the 12-turn nanofluid OHP at 50.5 W, the fluid moved very slowly with only minor movements. At 199.4 W, the fluid movement was much faster as shown by the blurring occurring in these images, caused by an image capture rate of 30 Hz. The blurring is the result of the fluid moving a substantial distance during the data collection time interval for the frame. From a thermal perspective, increasing the condenser temperature significantly reduced the temperature difference between the evaporator and condenser. Visually, the fluid motion for an operating

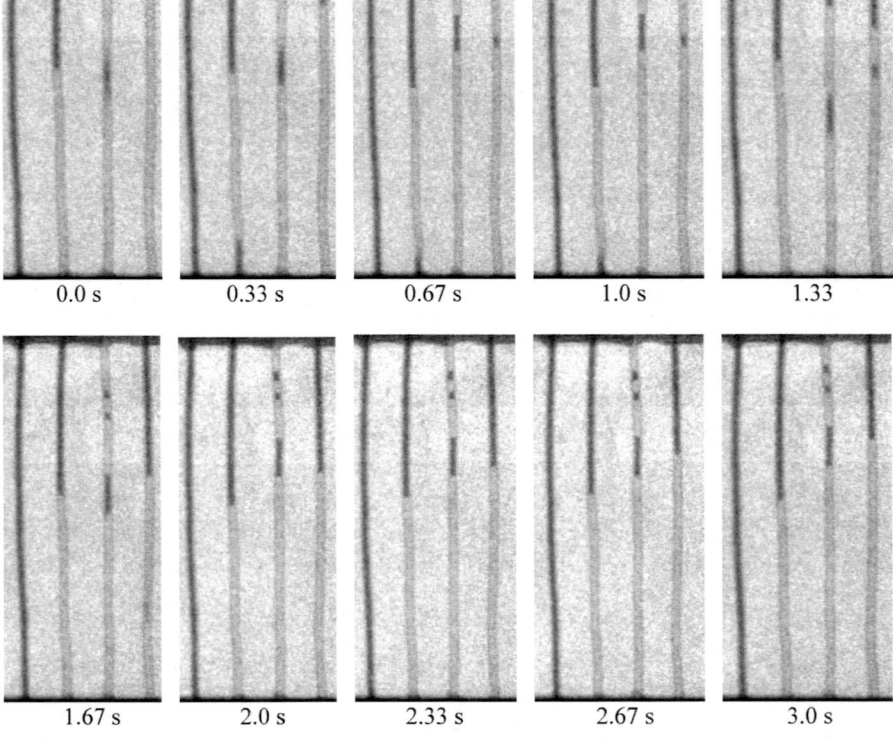

Fig. 6.28 Fluid movement in the center turns of the 12-turn nanofluid OHP at 50.5 W and an operating temperature of 20 °C (Wilson et al. 2008)

temperature of 60 °C had a slightly higher frequency and amplitude than the fluid motion at 20 °C. This is shown by the 12-turn OHP at an operating temperature of 20 and 60 °C in Figs. 6.28 and 6.30, respectively. However, since the fluid velocity change was not as substantial as with increased heat flux, this trend is hard to observe in these figures.

Nucleation has never been observed in the middle of a liquid slug with a low level of heat input where the flow velocity is low and the vapor bubble is easily detectable. When the heat flux level is high, the flow velocity is high. In the Wilson et al. (2008) experiment, the motion blur of the liquid–vapor interface and the low resolution of the video obscured these occurrences preventing proper observation. In addition, the condenser region was not visible, making it impossible to determine if vapor bubbles were completely condensing in this region. Occasionally in the adiabatic region near the condenser, vapor was observed to condense, but vapor bubble collapse was not seen. When the heat input level is low and the flow velocity is low, liquid plugs and vapor bubbles are easily detected. Figures 6.26, 6.27, 6.28, 6.29 and 6.30 show that the liquid plug and vapor bubble pattern did not change

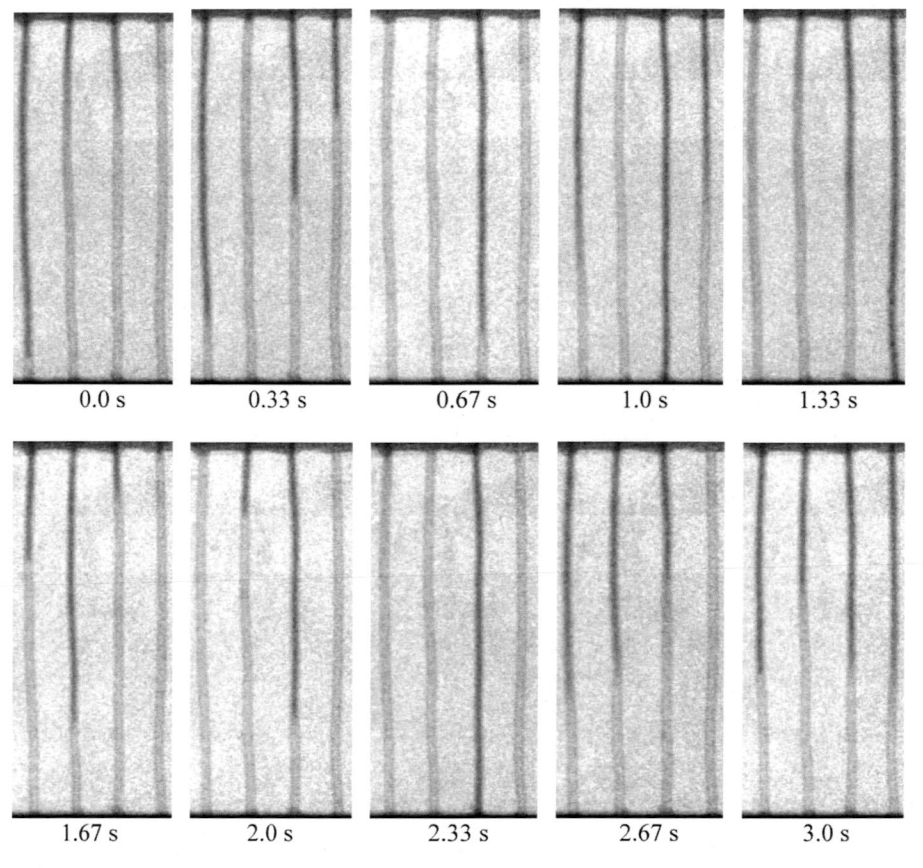

0.0 s   0.33 s   0.67 s   1.0 s   1.33 s

1.67 s   2.0 s   2.33 s   2.67 s   3.0 s

Fig. 6.29 Fluid movement in the center turns of the 12-turn nanofluid OHP at 199.4 W and an operating temperature of 20 °C (Wilson et al. 2008)

with time. It indirectly shows that the vapor bubbles were not collapsed; otherwise, the liquid plug and vapor bubble pattern should be different with time.

Because both fluid flow and temperature data were recorded simultaneously using the experimental setup shown in Fig. 6.22, this combination of data led to more accurate correlations between the neutron images and thermal data; hence, the following general observations were concluded: (1) fluid movement and oscillations started well before temperature oscillations of the OHP; (2) increasing heat load and temperature increased the fluid velocity; (3) the oscillating motion, circulation of liquid plugs, and vapor bubbles were observed; (4) nucleation was never observed at a low level of heat input. However, in this case, when the heat input level was high, nucleation was still not observed, which could have been due to the temporal and spatial limitations of the neutron imaging detector; (5) vapor bubble collapse was not observed; and (6) at a given heat input, the nanofluid oscillating heat pipe produced a lower frequency and amplitude than that charged with pure water.

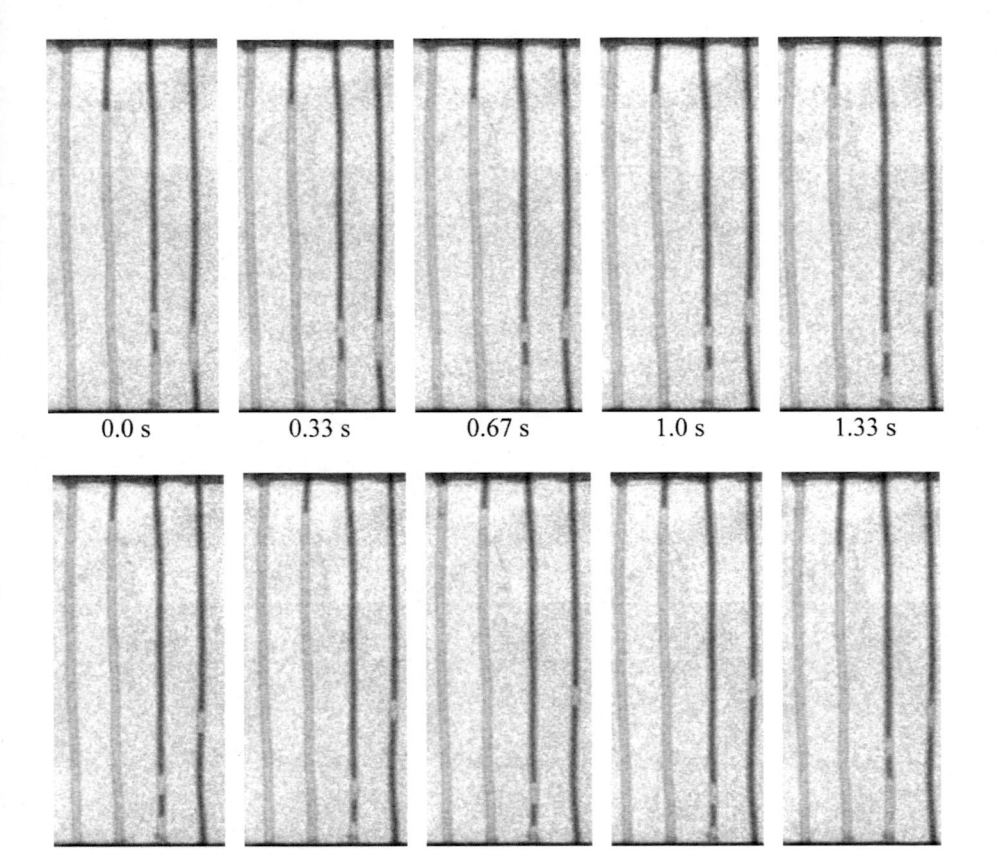

Fig. 6.30 Fluid movement in the center turns of the 12-turn nanofluid OHP at 50.1 W and an operating temperature of 60 °C (Wilson et al. 2008)

6.3.2.2 Working Fluid Effect

Using the experimental setup shown in Fig. 6.22, Wilson et al. (2011) conducted visual and thermal experiments of four 6-turn OHPs (two open loops and two closed loops) as shown in Fig. 6.31. Besides the loop types, the two designs were identical. The overall size of the OHP was dictated by the camera size of the neutron imaging system. Therefore, these 6-turn OHPs had overall dimensions of 155 mm by 155 mm. The OHPs were constructed out of copper tubing with an inner diameter of 1.65 mm and an outer diameter of 3.18 mm with copper condenser and evaporator heat spreaders. The evaporator plate was sized to match the strip heater's dimensions of 39 mm by 155 mm. A deuterium oxide, or heavy water, cooled aluminum block of 64 mm by 155 mm was used to cool the copper condensing plate. The adiabatic region was 53 mm long. The heat pipes were charged with high-performance liquid chromatography (HPLC) grade water or HPLC grade acetone at the filling ratios listed in Table 6.1. Because both the thermal and visual

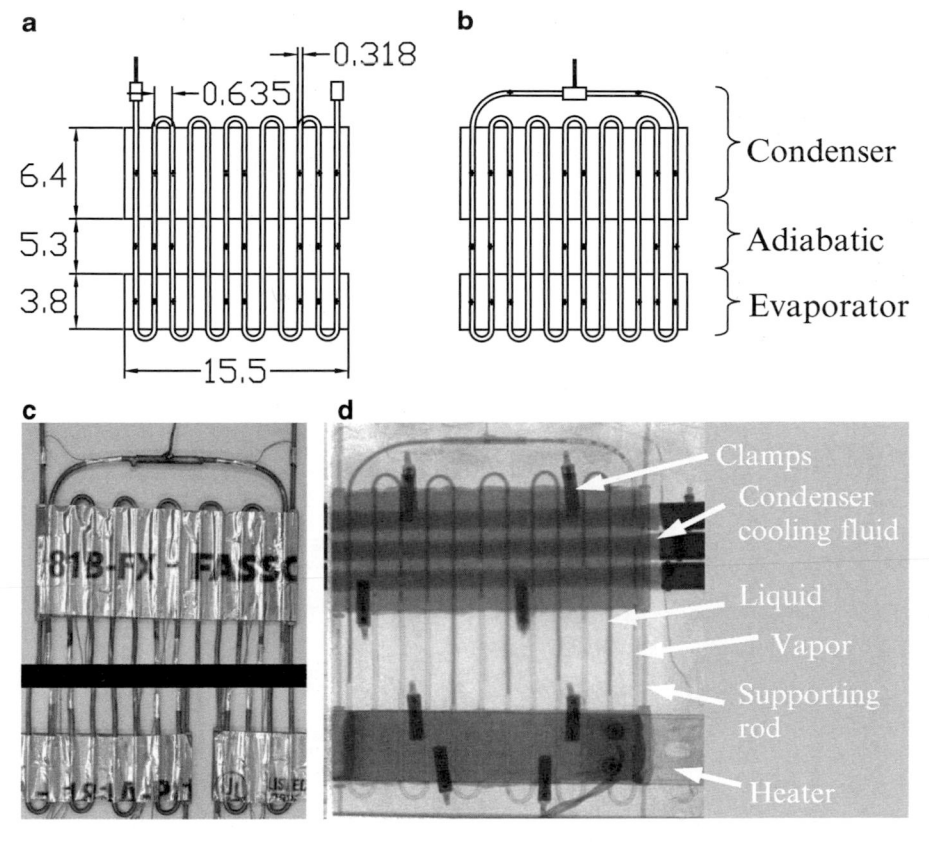

Fig. 6.31 OHPs: (**a**) schematic of the open-loop OHP, (**b**) schematic of the closed-loop OHP, (**c**) photo of the finished OHP, and (**d**) neutron radiography image of the OHP (units in cm) (Wilson et al. 2011)

Table 6.1 Filling ratio of the OHPs

Heat pipe design	Fluid	Filling ratio
Open loop	Acetone	0.45
Open loop	Water	0.46
Closed loop	Acetone	0.48
Closed loop	Water	0.51

data were obtained at the same time, the temperature and video can be directly compared with each other to better understand OHP operation. Because increasing power directly increases fluid velocity within the OHP, the resulting fluid motion in the neutron images at high fluid velocities caused the liquid/vapor interface to blur. Therefore, the power was increased until blurring became too significant, limiting the amount of useful information from the neutron images. For the acetone OHPs, this limit was 100 W and for the water OHPs, this limit was 300 W. Two condenser temperatures of 20 and 60 °C were used during this experiment. Also, two orientations were tested: (1) vertical with the condenser gravitationally above the

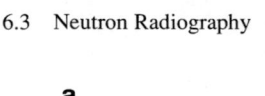

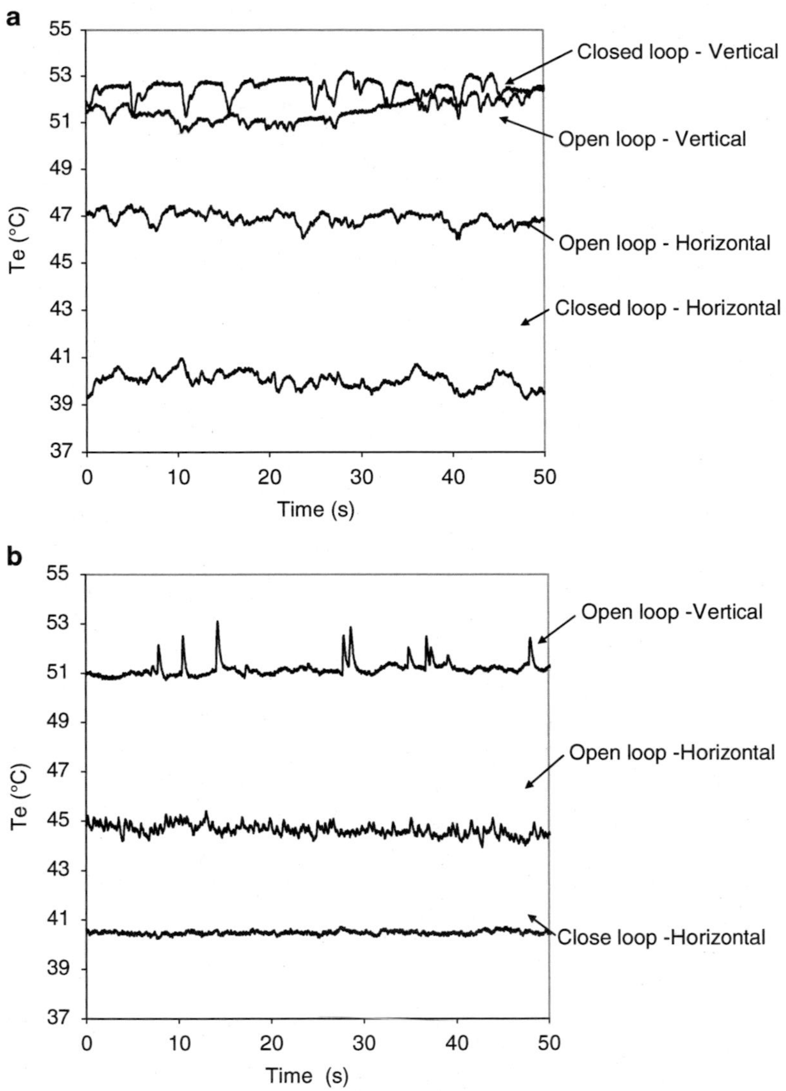

Fig. 6.32 Evaporator temperature oscillations at 100 W and a condenser temperature of 20 °C: (**a**) water OHP and (**b**) acetone OHP (Wilson et al. 2011)

evaporator and (2) horizontal, where the OHP was rotated 90° in the vertical plane, resulting in the evaporator and condenser being side by side. The OHPs could only be tested in the vertical plane due to the neutron beam's orientation.

Figure 6.32 illustrates the temperature variations between a water OHP and an acetone OHP including the effects of orientation and loop type at a condenser temperature of 20 °C and power of 100 W. Using visual data and thermal data as shown in Fig. 6.32a, the frequency and amplitude of the evaporator temperatures of the acetone OHP depended on orientation and loop type. The open-loop vertical

acetone OHP had the highest thermal amplitude and lowest frequency. The open-loop horizontal acetone OHP had a medium frequency and amplitude, while the closed-loop horizontal acetone OHP had the lowest amplitude but highest frequency. The closed-loop vertical acetone OHP was not tested at 100 W due to excessively high fluid velocity. The thermal amplitude for all water OHPs is greater than that for acetone OHPs, and the frequency of all water OHPs is less than that of acetone OHPs as shown in Fig. 6.32b. However, visual data obtained by the neutron images also show that the movement amplitude for all acetone OHPs is greater than all water OHPs at the same power input. While these results are similar to those predicted by Ma et al. (2006), a very different thermal amplitude is shown in Fig. 6.32. This thermal or temperature amplitude represents the temperature variation of the heat pipe wall surface, and the movement amplitude indicates the location variation of the mass center of the total liquid plugs and vapor bubbles in the OHP. Although the thermal amplitude is directly related to the movement amplitude, the thermal amplitude is very different from the movement amplitude meaning that a higher movement amplitude may not result in a higher thermal amplitude. Thermal data are attenuated compared to the movement amplitude because of the thermal mass of the copper tubing. For example, if the time constant of a heat pipe wall is larger, the response time of the wall surface temperature will be less than $1/f$, where f is the frequency of liquid plugs and vapor bubbles in the OHP; hence, the thermal amplitude measured will be smaller than the movement amplitude of the liquid plugs and vapor bubbles in the OHP. Hence, the thermal amplitude cannot truly show the movement amplitude of liquid plugs and vapor bubbles in an OHP.

Due to the thermal mass of the copper tubing, there is a lag and attenuation in amplitude between the thermal and visual data. Figure 6.33 shows a direct comparison of the thermal and visual difference between the water and acetone OHPs at a condenser temperature of 60 °C and input power of 50 W. From the thermal data shown in Fig. 6.33a, the frequency of evaporator temperature in the acetone OHP is much faster than that in the water OHP and the temperature amplitude is much smaller than that of the water OHP at a low power. The neutron visual images shown in Fig. 6.33b also demonstrate that the acetone OHP is oscillating much faster than the water OHP. The higher fluid frequency is visible as high velocity in the figure due to the blurring of the acetone liquid–vapor interface, resulting in gray gradients. The water OHP has a much slower flow, therefore a better defined liquid–vapor interface. The acetone OHP always has a higher frequency. It can be concluded that the acetone OHP can produce higher temperature uniformity in the evaporating section of an OHP at a low power compared to water OHPs.

Figure 6.34 illustrates the effects of power, condensing temperature, and orientation on the temperature difference between the evaporator and condenser in a closed-loop oscillating heat pipe charged with water and acetone, respectively. As shown in Fig. 6.34, when the power increases, the temperature difference between the evaporator and condenser for both OHPs increases. However, the increase rate for the acetone OHP is very different from the water OHP. Figure 6.34 illustrates the general trends of tested OHPs. Vertical OHPs typically have a smaller

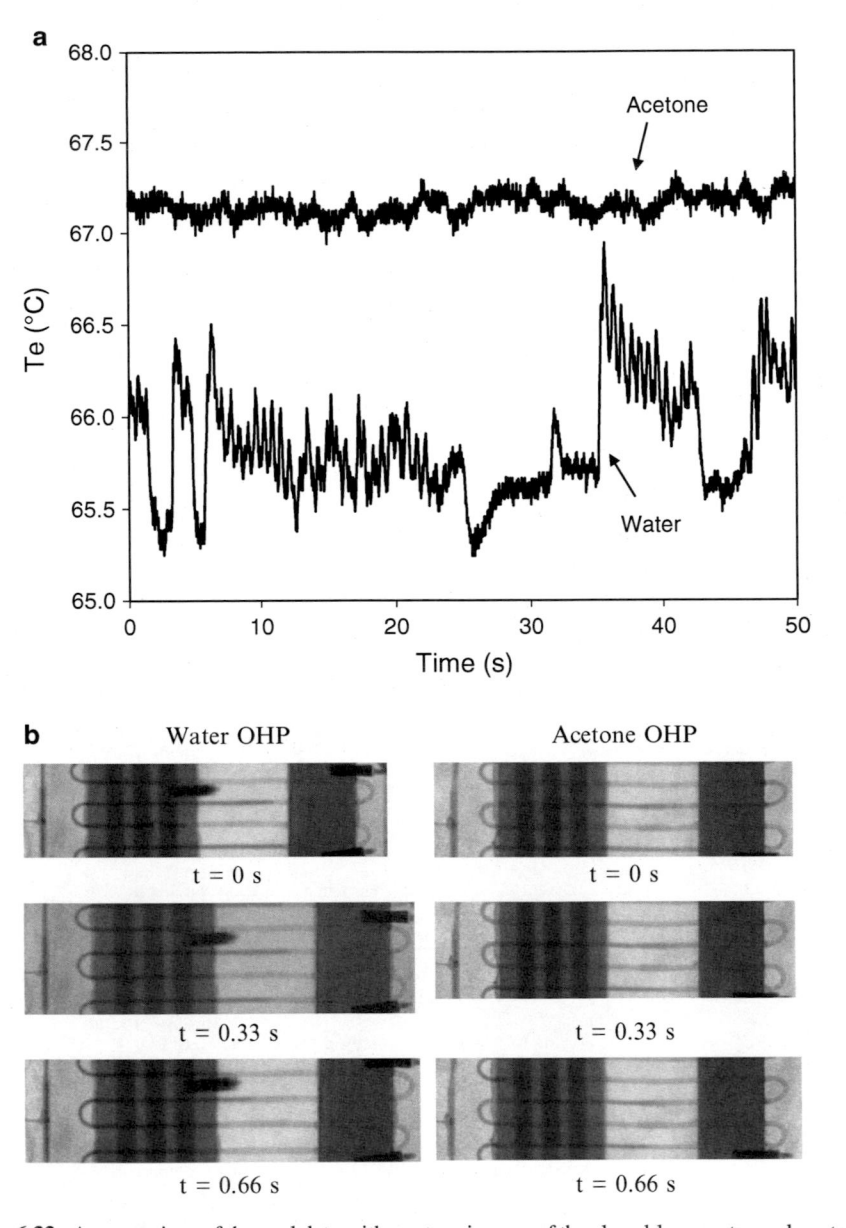

Fig. 6.33 A comparison of thermal data with neutron images of the closed-loop water and acetone OHPs in the horizontal orientation at 50 W with a condenser temperature of 60 °C: (**a**) evaporator temperature and (**b**) neutron images of fluid movement

temperature difference than horizontal OHPs. However, visually the flow patterns were similar. The thermal performance difference is due to gravity assisting in the OHP operation in the vertical orientation but only slightly assisting in the horizontal orientation. The similar visual flow pattern cannot readily be explained but likely

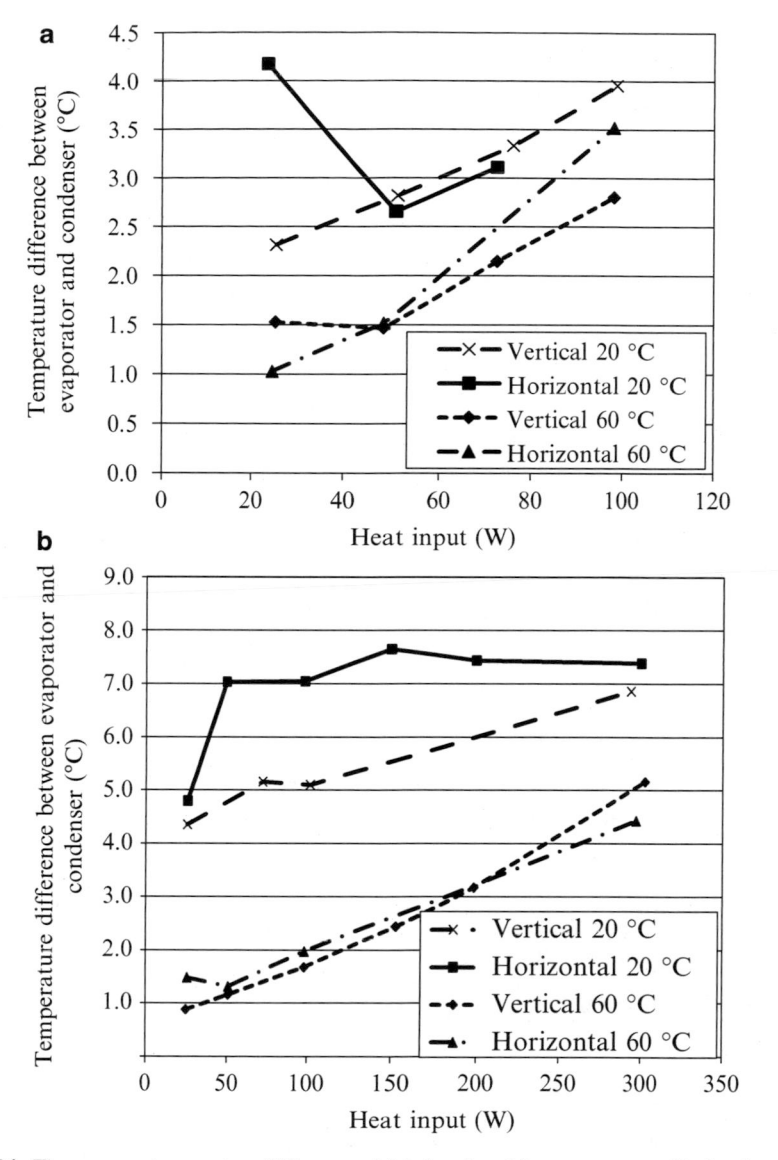

Fig. 6.34 The average temperature difference of (**a**) the closed-loop acetone oscillating heat pipe and (**b**) closed-loop water oscillating heat pipe at a condenser temperature of 20 and 60 °C and in vertical and horizontal orientations (Wilson et al. 2011)

there was a small difference in flow patterns that was not apparent. Another general trend was that higher condenser temperatures always had a lower temperature difference, and visually the only difference was increased fluid velocity. The reduced thermal resistance with increased condenser temperature is due to superior fluid properties at high temperatures. These improved properties include

increased $\left(\frac{\partial P}{\partial T}\right)_{\text{sat}}$ and reduced viscosity. Comparing the acetone and water OHPs as shown in Fig. 6.34, the acetone OHP had a smaller temperature difference at low power input compared to the water OHP. At 25 W, the closed-loop acetone OHP in the vertical orientation and the condenser at 20 °C had an average temperature difference of 2.3 °C, whereas the closed-loop water OHP had an average temperature difference of 4.3 °C. This is primarily due to the higher frequency of the acetone OHP. However, at higher heat fluxes, the water OHP frequency increased and water's superior fluid properties prevailed causing the water OHP to have a smaller average temperature difference than acetone.

Figure 6.35 illustrates flow patterns in both the closed- and open-loop OHPs providing a view of the oscillating motion. Figure 6.35 was made by calculating the standard deviation of each pixel with time during an entire 2-min video.

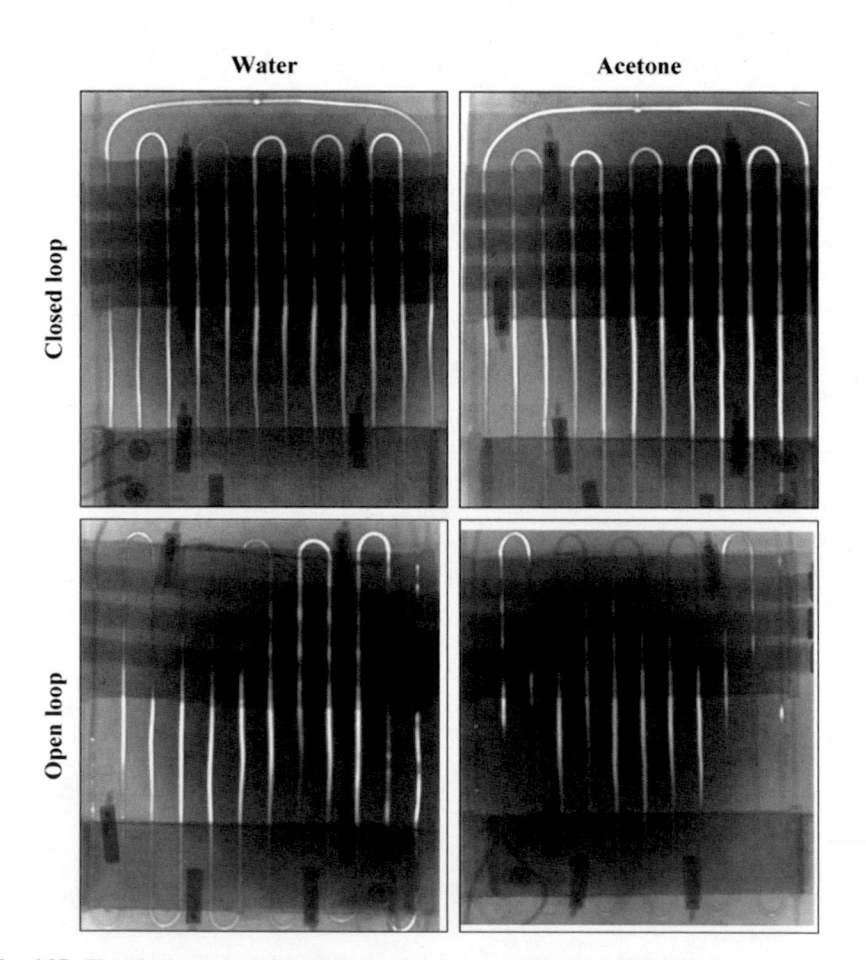

Fig. 6.35 The pixel standard deviation for the open and closed loop of both water and acetone OHPs (vertical orientation had a power input of 50 W and a condenser temperature of 60 °C; the *bright regions* show where the standard deviation was the highest)

In the video, when the interface of the fluid passed across a pixel, the pixel changed from dark to light. This change in intensity resulted in a high standard deviation. In the middle of a liquid plug or vapor bubble, the pixels always had the same intensity and, therefore, had a low standard deviation. In Fig. 6.35 the regions with high standard deviations are light colored and regions with low standard deviations are darker. These results show that closed-loop OHPs have much greater liquid movement throughout compared to open-loop OHPs. Open-loop OHPs experience only localized motion of interfaces, and this is minimal in the outer turns. The reduced flow lowers the heat transport capability of the open-loop design. The advantage of the closed-loop OHP design is that the outer turns are connected, allowing fluid and pressure to transfer between the two sides and throughout the entire OHP. However, it was visually observed that the water in the closed-loop OHP never fully circulated. Therefore, pressure was transferring between the two sides, but not the fluid. In effect, the operation of the closed-loop water OHP was very similar to the open-loop water OHP. Thermally, these two OHPs also performed very similarly. The acetone OHP for the closed-loop design was found to fully circulate but only at high heat flux, and the thermal performance was much better than the open-loop acetone OHP. Therefore, full circulation of fluid is very important to the thermal performance of the OHP. These results are independent of orientation and condenser temperature.

6.3.2.3 Visual Study of Effects of Heat Input and Filling Ratio

Borgmeyer et al. (2010) used a 10-turn OHP and a 20-turn OHP with two-layer channels (Fig. 6.25) with the experimental setup shown in Fig. 6.22 to study the effects of heat input, turn number, operating temperature, and filling ratio on the heat transfer performance. The OHPs performed well overall and the frequency and amplitude of temperature oscillations were very consistent, especially at higher heat fluxes where sustained oscillations and bulk circulation occurred. The consistency of amplitude and frequency of the 20-turn OHP was greater than the 10-turn OHP in general.

Using the thermal data and neutron images, Borgmeyer et al. (2010) found that three stages of fluid flow were evident in an OHP with two-layer channels. The first stage occurred during the start-up. This stage was shown thermally by a gradual increase in evaporator and adiabatic temperature with a steady condenser temperature. The temperature data show a steady curve; however, the neutron images show small movements. Also, at low heat inputs, the growing vapor plugs in the evaporator slowly pushed the liquid plugs to the condenser. Figure 6.36 shows the start-up stage of a 10-turn OHP with two-layer channels, which is similar to that of a 20-turn OHP. The second stage of fluid flow in the OHP was the intermittent flow stage (starting at about 50 W up to 150 W for the 20-turn OHP). This was where the fluid exchange between the evaporator and condenser regions was occasionally hindered. The stoppage in fluid exchange corresponds to a short steady increase in temperature following sustained temperature oscillations. The stoppage in fluid

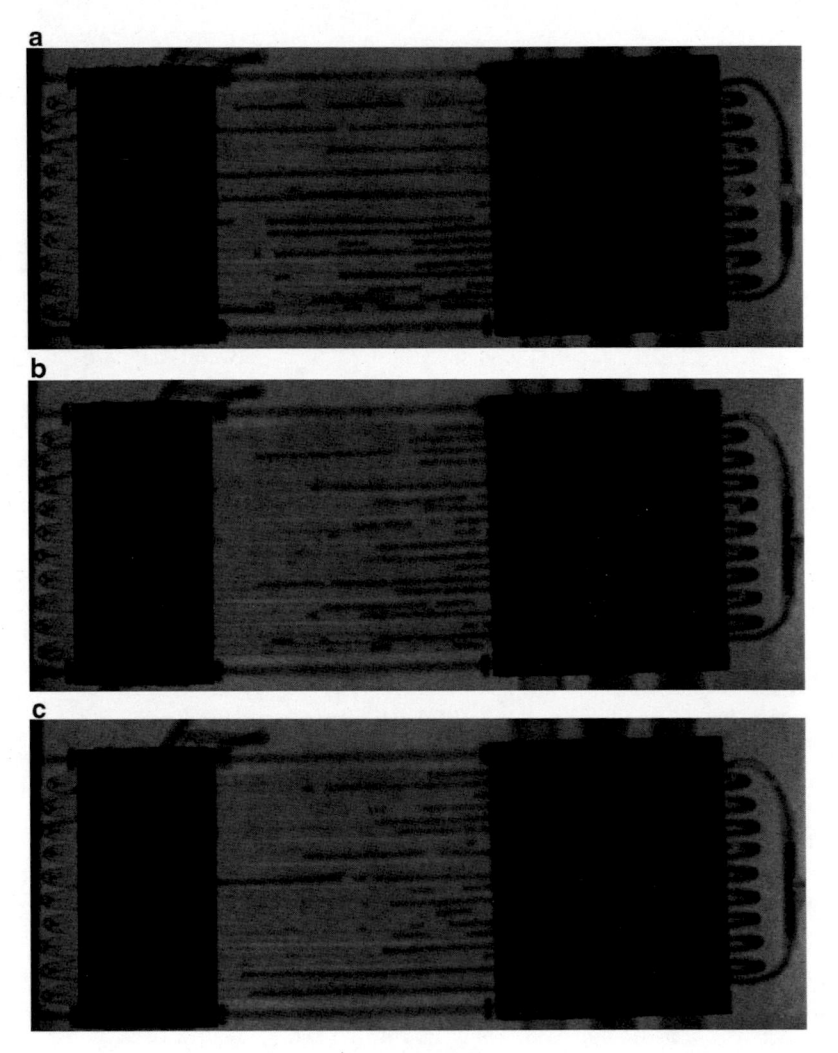

Fig. 6.36 Start-up of the 10-turn OHP at times 0 s (**a**), 400 s (**b**), and 600 s (**c**) (Borgmeyer et al. 2010)

flow resumed once the temperature difference increased enough to provide a driving force sufficient to transfer the fluid. Figure 6.37 shows a large stoppage in fluid motion between 60 and 80 s that corresponds to a large increase in temperature. Results shown in Fig. 6.37 correspond to the 20-turn OHP in a vertical position (bottom heating) maintaining a heat input of 50 W and a condenser temperature of 60 °C. Figure 6.37 shows that the frequency of temperature oscillation is roughly 0.17 Hz with amplitudes ranging from 2 to 7 °C. The majority of the temperature oscillations have amplitudes around 3 °C. Figure 6.38 displays the neutron images at four separate points at times of 70, 75, 80, and 85 s after a heat input of 50 W was added. During this period of temperature increase before 85 s, little movement

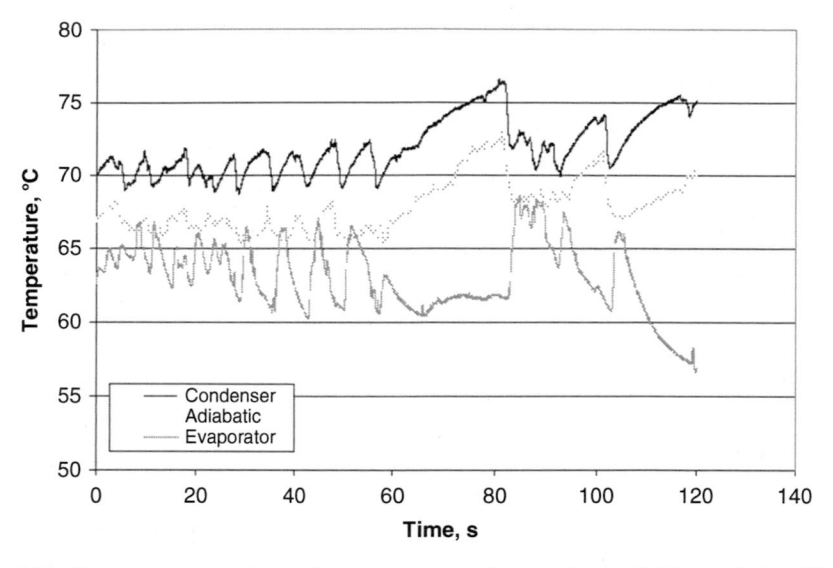

Fig. 6.37 Temperature data for the intermittent stage for the 20-turn OHP (heat input: 50 W, condenser temperature: 60 °C) (Borgmeyer et al. 2010)

occurred. At 85 s (Fig. 6.38) it can be seen where a change in the location of the slugs took place. As heat input was further increased, the intermittent flow became more periodic. The third stage of fluid flow occurred at high heat flux (>150 W) in which there were sustained oscillations and bulk circulation. This stage corresponds to steady fluid flow through the OHP with uniform frequency and amplitude. Figure 6.39 shows the oscillatory temperature readings associated with a 300 W heat input and a condenser setting of 60 °C. At this heat input, consistent bulk circulation was observed from the neutron images. The frequency of temperature oscillation for this heat input was roughly 0.275 Hz. This indicates an increase in frequency with increased heat input. The amplitudes of temperature oscillations ranged from about 2 to 3 °C. The amplitudes of oscillations seemed to become more consistent at higher heat inputs. Figure 6.40 displays the neutron images of this steady state oscillation. The circulating flow tends to match the frequency of the temperature data. It should also be noted that at higher heat inputs, the velocities of the liquid slugs exceeded the capture rate of the detector. The blurring associated with this increase in liquid slug speed made it difficult to track the fluid menisci.

Filling ratio affects both the fluid motion and heat transfer. A filling ratio of 53 % showed good heat transfer as heat input increased. However, at the lower heat input of 50 W, fluid motion was hindered by the large mass of fluid. Figure 6.41b shows increased temperature oscillations for a filling ratio of 35 %. The average evaporator temperature was slightly lower than the higher filling ratio. This may be due to the increase in amplitude and frequency of oscillation. A further decrease in filling ratio to 30 % resulted in a large increase in evaporator temperature

Fig. 6.38 Neutron images of the intermittent stage for the 20-turn OHP (heat input: 50 W, condenser temperature: 60 °C) (Borgmeyer et al. 2010)

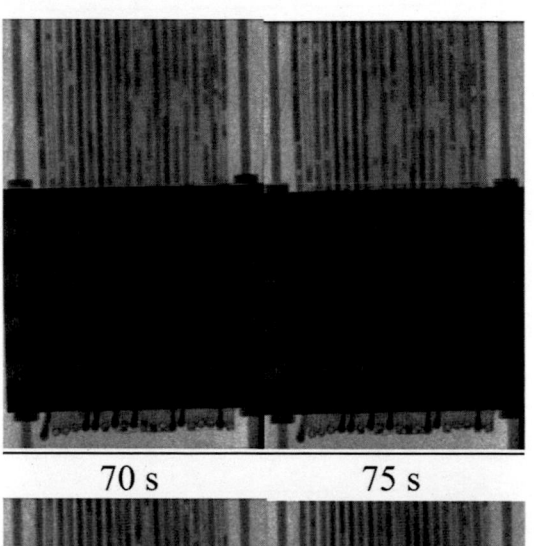

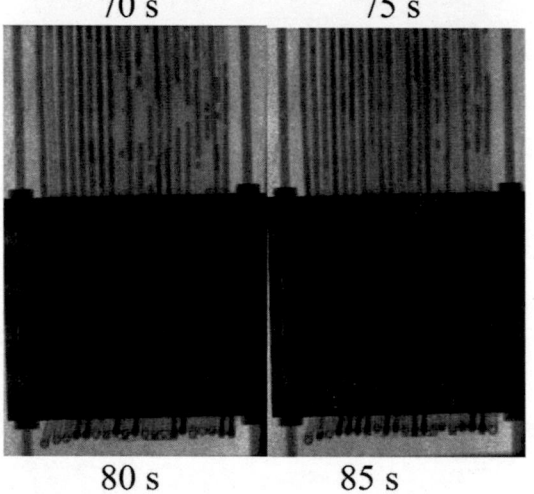

as shown in Fig. 6.41c. Also, a decreased filling ratio was noticed to cause the fluid to run towards gravity. This caused the majority of the liquid to fill only one side of the OHP as shown in Fig. 6.42. Because of this tendency, full circulation through the OHP was hindered and the liquid slug would only oscillate within the same channel or occasionally in an adjacent channel. Figure 6.43 shows the temperature drop vs. heat input for the three filling ratios. An obvious decrease in heat transfer performance occurred with filling ratios of less than 53 %. Although temperature and imaging data show that the oscillating motion for a filling ratio of 35 % was higher than 53 %, the reduction of liquid slugs to carry heat from the evaporator to condenser caused an increase in temperature, which shows that liquid phase plays a key role for an OHP.

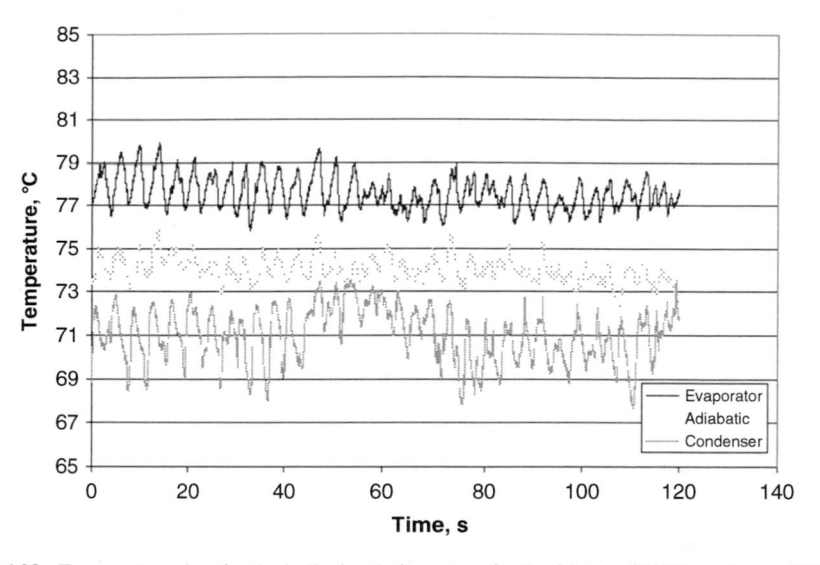

Fig. 6.39 Temperature data for the bulk circulation stage for the 20-turn OHP (heat input: 300 W, condenser temperature: 60 °C) (Borgmeyer et al. 2010)

Fig. 6.40 Neutron images of the circulation stage for the 20-turn OHP (heat input: 300 W, condenser setting: 60 °C) (Borgmeyer et al. 2010)

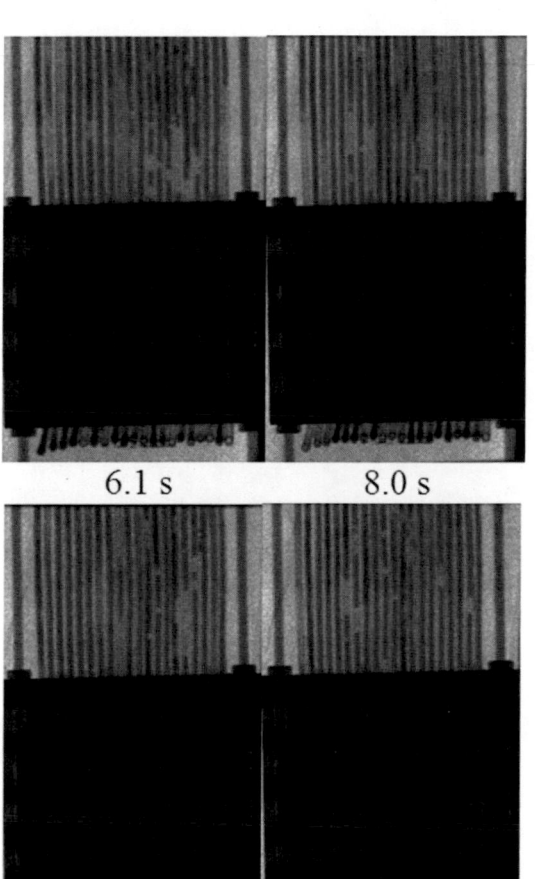

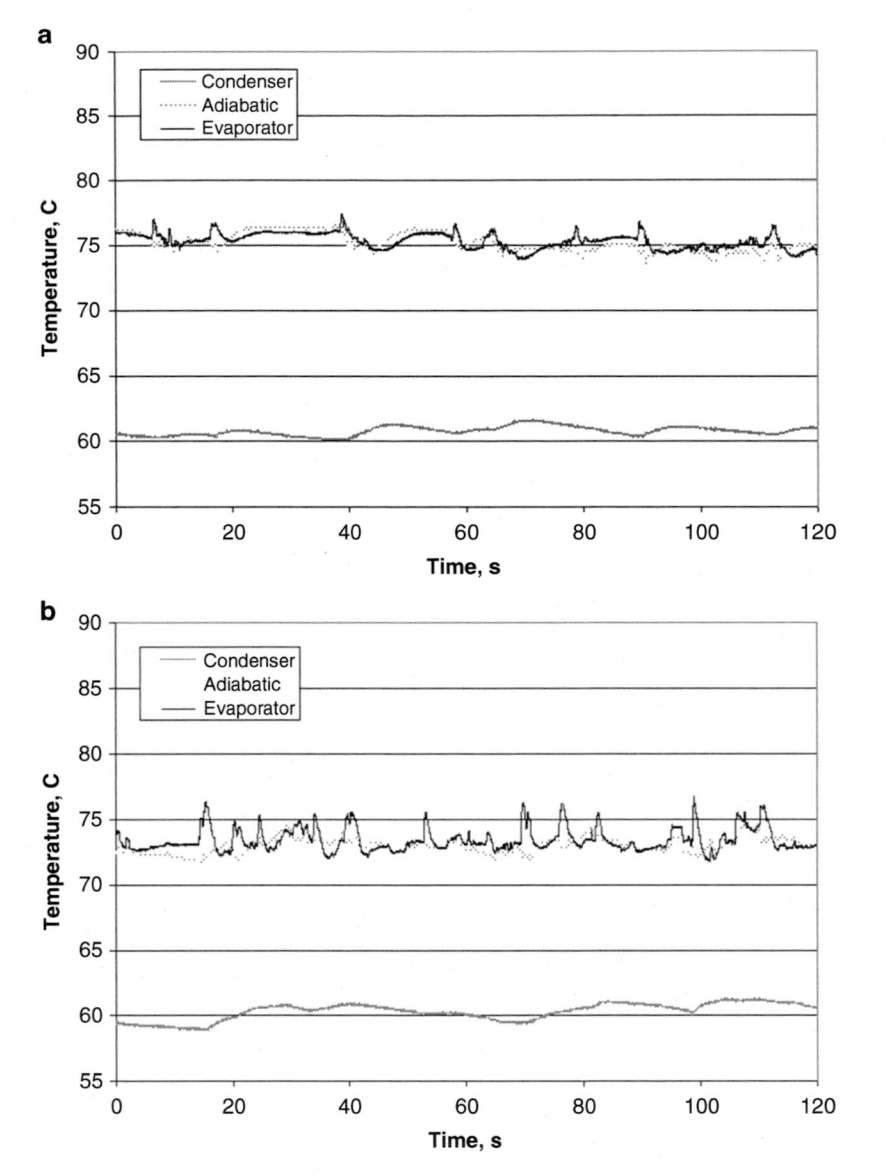

Fig. 6.41 Temperature fluctuations of 10-turn OHP at filling ratios of (**a**) 53 %, (**b**) 35 %, and (**c**) 30 % (Borgmeyer et al. 2010)

6.3.3   Neutron Phase Volumetric Analysis

In an OHP, the thermally excited oscillating motion plays a key role in transferring heat from the evaporator to the condenser. The liquid distribution in the OHP directly affects the heat transfer performance in an OHP. Wilson et al. (2011) and Yoon et al. (2012) used a 6-turn OHP shown in Fig. 6.31 with the experimental

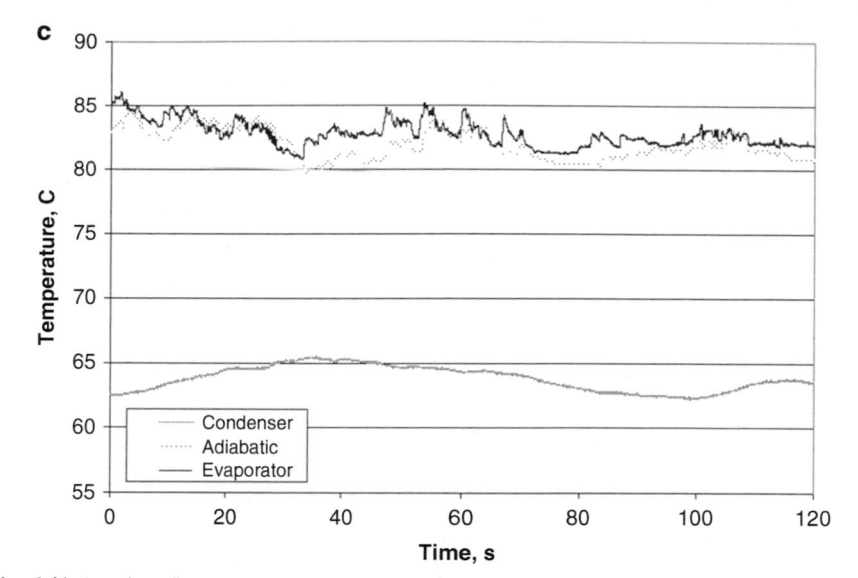

Fig. 6.41 (continued)

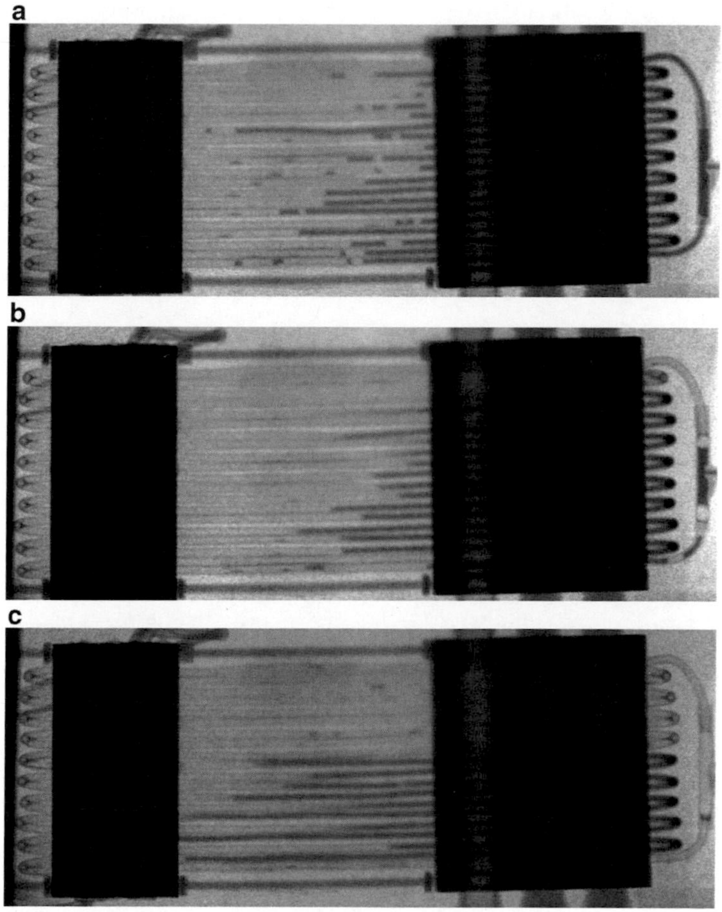

Fig. 6.42 Neutron images of typical fluid distribution at a heat input of 50 W for filling ratios of (**a**) 53 %, (**b**) 35 %, and (**c**) 30 % (Borgmeyer et al. 2010)

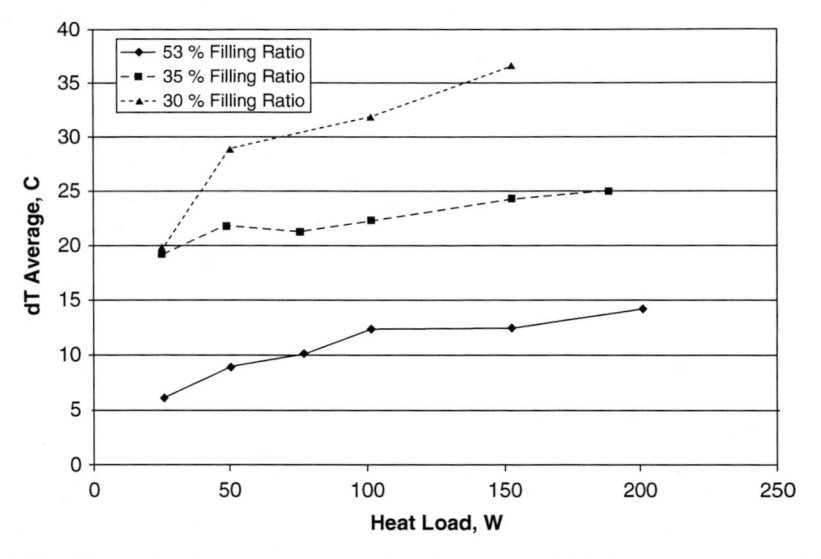

Fig. 6.43 Filling ratio effect on temperature drop for a 10-turn OHP (Borgmeyer et al. 2010)

setup shown in Fig. 6.22 to study the liquid phase distribution and its effect on the temperature variation within an OHP. Because the liquid and vapor phases are nearly three orders of magnitude different in density, there is a high neutron contrast between the liquid and vapor phase distributions in the OHP. If the liquid and vapor phase intensities are determined, the liquid and vapor volume fractions can be found for a given location in the OHP. The liquid and vapor volume fractions along the OHP tubing path within a given section were determined as follows: Three parallel paths along the center of the tubing were drawn by choosing points and connecting them (Yoon 2013). The gaps between the three path lines were about 1 pixel unit. At some points, primarily in curved areas, points on the adjacent path lines were located in the same pixel. In this case, the gap was modified to have a 1.42 pixel distance to avoid locating two separate paths in the same pixel. The total number of points on each path was the same. The line connecting the three points of the same index was roughly perpendicular to the direction of the path at each position. The central path was used for determining distances along the heat pipe's fluid loop.

The intensities in the image can be modeled using the Beer–Lambert law of attenuation, i.e.,

$$I = I_o \exp(-\mu x) \tag{6.1}$$

where I_o is the incident intensity, μ is the attenuation coefficient for the attenuating material, and x is the distance traveled through the attenuating material. It is convenient to take the product of the intensity at the same position on all three paths to give I_{Pr}, which can be modeled as

$$I_{\mathrm{Pr}} = I_1 \times I_2 \times I_3 = I_o \exp\left[-\left(\mu_{\mathrm{ins}}x_{\mathrm{ins}} + \mu_{\mathrm{cb}}x_{\mathrm{cb1}} + \mu_{\mathrm{p}}x_{\mathrm{p1}} + \mu_{\mathrm{v}}f_{\mathrm{v1}}x_1 + \mu_{\mathrm{l}}f_{\mathrm{l1}}x_1\right)\right]$$
$$\times I_o \exp\left[-\left(\mu_{\mathrm{ins}}x_{\mathrm{ins}} + \mu_{\mathrm{cb}}x_{\mathrm{cb2}} + \mu_{\mathrm{p}}x_{\mathrm{p2}} + \mu_{\mathrm{v}}f_{\mathrm{v2}}x_2 + \mu_{\mathrm{l}}f_{\mathrm{l2}}x_2\right)\right]$$
$$\times I_o \exp\left[-\left(\mu_{\mathrm{ins}}x_{\mathrm{ins}} + \mu_{\mathrm{cb}}x_{\mathrm{cb3}} + \mu_{\mathrm{p}}x_{\mathrm{p3}} + \mu_{\mathrm{v}}f_{\mathrm{v3}}x_3 + \mu_{\mathrm{l}}f_{\mathrm{l3}}x_3\right)\right]$$

$$(6.2)$$

where I_1, I_2, and I_3 are the intensities on paths 1, 2, and 3 in the pipe, I_o is the intensity before attenuation, μ_{ins}, μ_{cb}, μ_{p}, μ_{v}, and μ_{l} are the attenuation coefficients for the insulation material, copper block, heat pipe wall, vapor in the pipe, and liquid in the pipe, respectively, x_{ins}, x_{cb}, x_{p}, x_{v}, and x_{l} are the thickness of insulation material, copper block, heat pipe wall, vapor in the pipe, and liquid in the pipe, respectively, and f_{v} and f_{l} are the volume fractions of vapor and liquid, respectively. The subscript numbers 1, 2, and 3 designate the path numbers. The distances x_1, x_2, and x_3 are the distances neutrons travel through the inside of the pipe at the locations of paths 1, 2, and 3, respectively, at each position along the paths. The vapor and liquid volume fractions are defined as

$$f_{\mathrm{v}} = \frac{\displaystyle\int_V\int_t v_{\mathrm{v}}\, dV dt}{V\Delta t} \tag{6.3}$$

$$f_{\mathrm{l}} = \frac{\displaystyle\int_V\int_t v_{\mathrm{l}}\, dV dt}{V\Delta t} \tag{6.4}$$

respectively, where V is the effective volume in the heat pipe seen by a pixel; v_{v} and v_{l} are the volume fraction of vapor and liquid, respectively, at a point within the effective volume; t is the time and Δt is the time increment for which the detector accumulates neutrons for the pixel. It was assumed that the liquid and vapor fractions were equal on each path at a given position, i.e., $f_{\mathrm{l1}} = f_{\mathrm{l2}} = f_{\mathrm{l3}}$ and $f_{\mathrm{v1}} = f_{\mathrm{v2}} = f_{\mathrm{v3}}$. This assumption is justified by the slug flow observed in the images of the operating heat pipes with a small Bond number. Using the assumption that the phase fractions are equal on the three paths and making the substitutions $x_1 + x_2 + x_3 = x$, $x_{\mathrm{cb1}} + x_{\mathrm{cb2}} + x_{\mathrm{cb3}} = x_{\mathrm{cb}}$, and $x_{\mathrm{p1}} + x_{\mathrm{p2}} + x_{\mathrm{p3}} = x_{\mathrm{p}}$, and $f_{\mathrm{l}} = 1 - f_{\mathrm{v}}$, Eq. (6.2) becomes

$$I_{\mathrm{Pr}} = I_o^3 \exp\left[-\left(3\mu_{\mathrm{ins}}x_{\mathrm{ins}} + \mu_{\mathrm{cb}}x_{\mathrm{cb}} + \mu_{\mathrm{p}}x_{\mathrm{p}} + f_{\mathrm{v}}(\mu_{\mathrm{v}}x - \mu_{\mathrm{l}}x) + \mu_{\mathrm{l}}x\right)\right] \tag{6.5}$$

When a position is fully occupied by vapor $f_{\mathrm{v}} = 1$, the vapor intensity can be found as

$$I_{\mathrm{v}} = I_o^3 \exp\left[-\left(3\mu_{\mathrm{ins}}x_{\mathrm{ins}} + \mu_{\mathrm{cb}}x_{\mathrm{cb}} + \mu_{\mathrm{p}}x_{\mathrm{p}} + \mu_{\mathrm{v}}x\right)\right] \tag{6.6}$$

and when $f_{\mathrm{v}} = 0$, the liquid intensity can be determined with

$$I_1 = I_o^3 \exp\left[-\left(3\mu_{\text{ins}}x_{\text{ins}} + \mu_{\text{cb}}x_{\text{cb}} + \mu_p x_p + \mu_1 x\right)\right] \tag{6.7}$$

Using Eqs. (6.5), (6.6), and (6.7), the volume fraction of vapor at a position along the path can be found as

$$f_v = \frac{\ln(I_{\text{Pr}}) - \ln(I_1)}{\ln(I_v) - \ln(I_1)} \tag{6.8}$$

and the volume fraction of liquid, f_1, can be calculated by

$$f_1 = 1 - f_v \tag{6.9}$$

With the volume increments for each path position, the volume fraction of vapor and liquid in a region of the heat pipe (for example the evaporator) can be computed as

$$F_{v,r} = \frac{\text{Volume of vapor in specific region}}{\text{Volume of specific region}} = \frac{\sum_i A\Delta s_{r,i} f_{v,i}}{\sum_i A\Delta s_{r,i}} = \frac{\sum_i \Delta s_{r,i} f_{v,i}}{\sum_i \Delta s_{r,i}} \tag{6.10}$$

$$F_{1,r} = \frac{\text{Volume of liquid in specific region}}{\text{Volume of specific region}} = \frac{\sum_i A\Delta s_{r,i} f_{1,i}}{\sum_i A\Delta s_{r,i}} = \frac{\sum_i \Delta s_{r,i} f_{1,i}}{\sum_i \Delta s_{r,i}} \tag{6.11}$$

where A is the cross-sectional area of the tubing, Δs is an increment of path length associated with position i, and the subscript r stands for path positions along the specific region of interest, e.g., the evaporator.

Using the approach outlined above, neutron images can be analyzed and the liquid and vapor volume fractions determined for the evaporator, adiabatic, and condenser sections of the OHP. Yoon (2013) used the neutron images for the closed-loop water OHP shown in Fig. 6.31 with the method described above to conduct the volumetric analysis in the OHP. Figure 6.44 shows the heat input effect on the liquid and vapor distributions. As shown, a fairly uniform distribution of liquid and vapor is present in the OHP before the application of any heat. With the application of heat, the working liquid (water) is pushed out of the evaporator section and the volume fraction of liquid decreases to near zero. The condenser section experiences an increase in liquid fraction to a near plateau while the adiabatic section shows a slight increase in liquid fraction at 26 W followed by a decrease. Above 50 W heat input, only slight changes in liquid fractions occur. The evaporator and adiabatic sections show slight increases with increased heat input while the condenser section shows a slight decrease. From the observation of the videos, these slight changes can be attributed to an increased motion of the working fluid, which results in liquid entering the evaporator section more often.

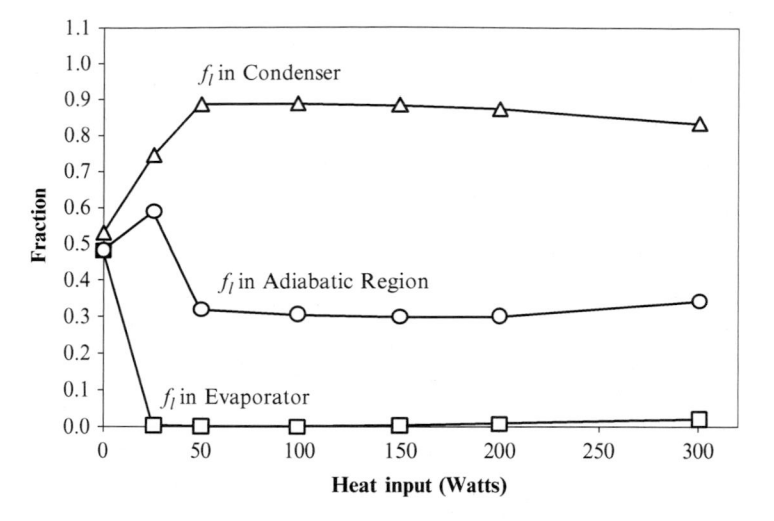

Fig. 6.44 Change in volume fraction of liquid in different regions for the closed-loop water OHP shown in Fig. 6.31 with heat input (Wilson et al. 2011; Yoon et al. 2012)

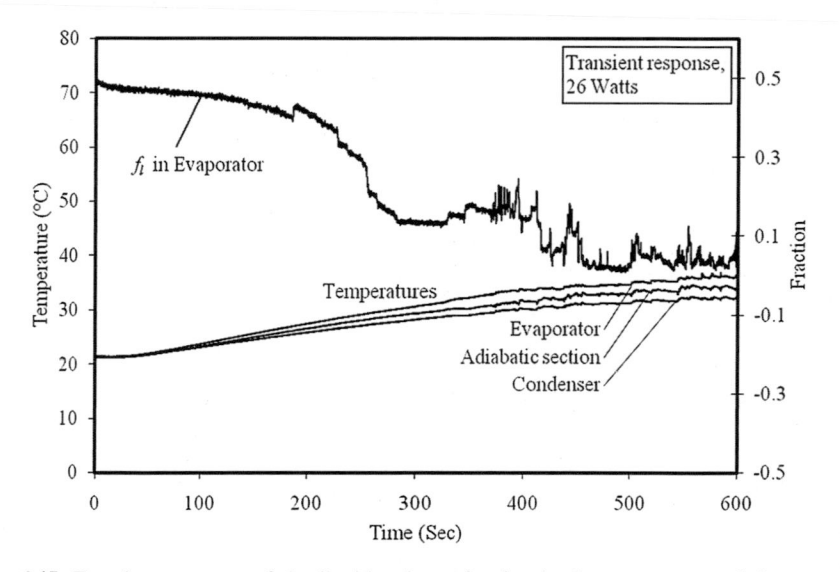

Fig. 6.45 Transient response of the liquid volume fraction in the evaporator and the average temperatures for the evaporator, condenser, and adiabatic region at a heat input of 26 W for the closed-loop water OHP shown in Fig. 6.31 (Yoon et al. 2012)

When a heat input of 26 W was added to the heat pipe shown in Fig. 6.31, the generated vapor pushed the liquid plug to the condenser section. This process is quantitatively described in Fig. 6.45. As shown, the liquid fraction in the evaporator gradually decreased from 55 % to about 15 % over about 300 s. Then, the liquid fraction continued to decrease, but more sporadically with intermittent increases.

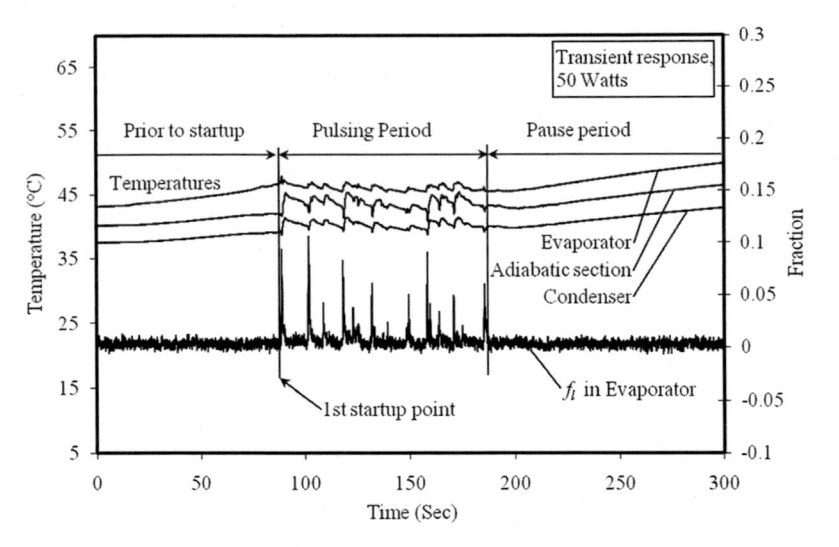

Fig. 6.46 Transient response of the liquid volume fraction in the evaporator and the average temperatures for the evaporator, condenser, and adiabatic regions at a heat input from 26 to 50 W for the closed-loop water OHP shown in Fig. 6.31 (Yoon et al. 2012)

During this process, the temperatures of the evaporator, adiabatic section, and condenser rose slowly because at this heat input without fluid movement the heat transfer rates are always slow.

Figure 6.46 shows the evaporator liquid fraction and average temperatures for the heat input from 26 to 50 W. As shown, the liquid fraction in the evaporator is essentially zero and the average temperatures rise steadily until the 89 s mark where pulses appear in the liquid fraction, and the average temperatures stop their increase and begin to oscillate up and down, as indicated by the sharp temperature spikes corresponding to the pulses in the liquid fraction. The average temperatures during the pulsing period in the evaporator, adiabatic, and condenser sections are 46.8 °C, 41.8 °C, and 39.2 °C, respectively. The observation of the video shows the pulses in the liquid fraction in the evaporator are due to the movement of one or more liquid slugs from the adiabatic section into the evaporator section and rapid exit by reversal of their course. Between the pulses, the fluid in the OHP is relatively still. The pulse/pause behavior continues for about 100 s to the 189-s mark whereupon the pulsing of the liquid slugs stops and the steady temperature rise resumes. Figure 6.47 shows the results from the steady state test at 50 W heat input. When this test started, the pulsing behavior had resumed but stopped at the 46 s mark and resumed at the 154 s mark. The average temperature increased during the pause and decreased after the 154 s mark after the OHP resumed pulsing.

Figure 6.48a shows the results of raising the heat input to 99 W. The heat input was increased during a pause period and the average temperatures rose smoothly until pulsing began at 85 s. From this point through the remainder of the tests, there were no further pause periods where pulsing stopped. As the heat input was

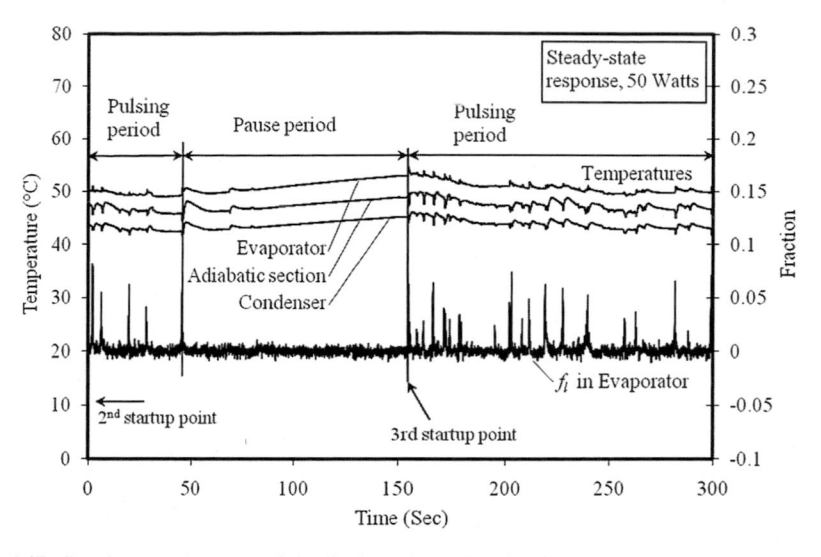

Fig. 6.47 Steady state response of the liquid volume fraction in the evaporator and the average temperatures for the evaporator, condenser and adiabatic regions at a heat input from 26 to 50 W for the closed-loop water OHP shown in Fig. 6.31 (Yoon et al. 2012)

raised above 99 W, the transient and steady state liquid fraction and average temperature responses looked similar to each other except for slight temperature increases during the transient tests and an increase in pulsing frequency with higher heat input. When the heat input increased at 149, 200, and 300 W, the OHP was always in the steady state as shown in Fig. 6.48b–d. No pulsing stops were observed.

When the fluids began to move at low heat input, the video reveals that the motion was intermittent. Liquid slugs would move and then motion would briefly stop as shown in Fig. 6.49, which gives an expanded view of the first pulsing period in Fig. 6.46, which also shows the transient behavior upon application of 50 W of heat input. The peaks in the liquid fraction curve correspond to the entrance of liquid slugs into the evaporator region. It should be noted that a single peak can be the result of more than one liquid slug flowing into the evaporator section in different legs of the OHP. In between these peaks the fluid in the OHP was generally still. Within the pulsing period, evaporator pulses and minor pause periods occurred. Not every pulse movement of fluid generated an evaporator-entrance event shown as a peak in the figure, but this is generally the pattern. To count evaporator pulsing events, a threshold of 0.03 volume fraction of liquid in the evaporator region was chosen to define a pulse event in the data. Figure 6.49 shows this threshold and the 12 pulse events in the first pulsing period observed for the OHP after stepping up to 50 W. As the heat input was increased, the major pauses ceased and the average time between evaporator-entrances decreased. Figure 6.50 shows an individual pulse event from Fig. 6.49 on an expanded time scale.

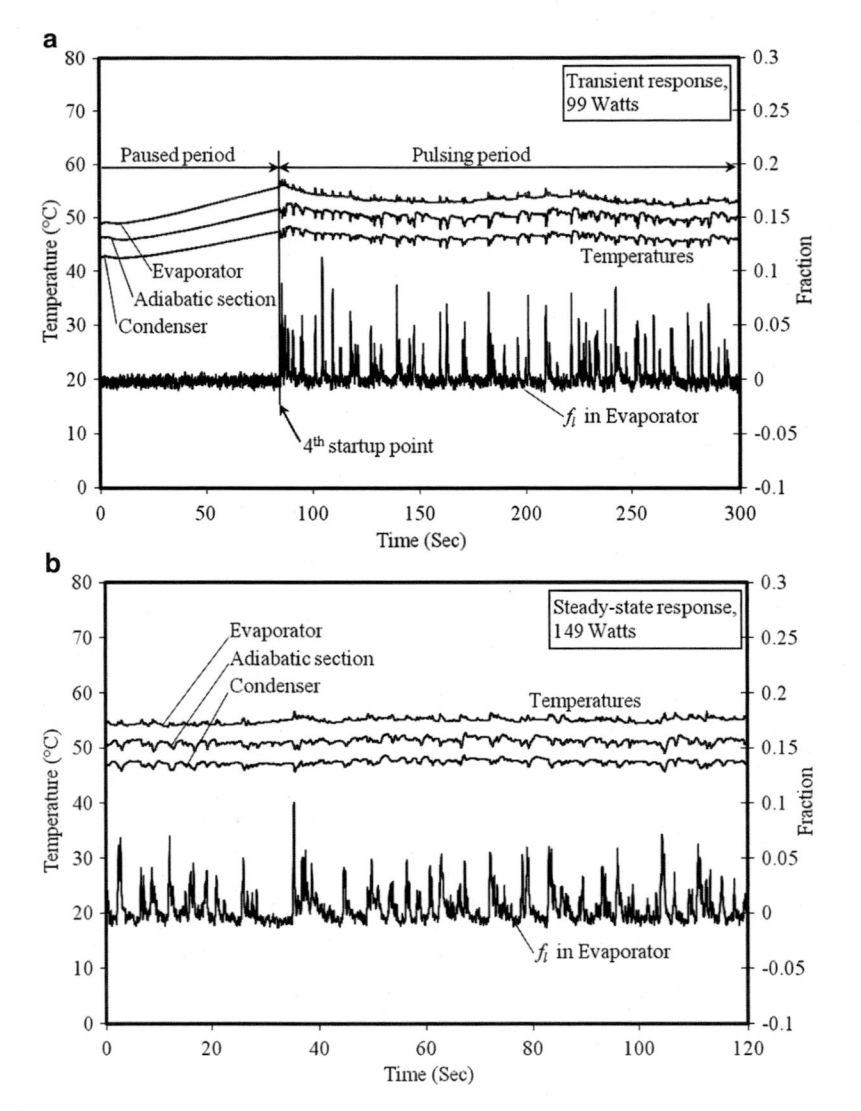

Fig. 6.48 Transient response of the volume fraction of liquid in the evaporator and the average temperatures for the evaporator, condenser, and adiabatic regions for the closed-loop water OHP shown in Fig. 6.31 at heat inputs of (**a**) 99 W, (**b**) 149 W, (**c**) 200 W, and (**d**) 300 W (Wilson et al. 2011; Yoon et al. 2012)

The average temperature responses to a pulse event have the characteristic shape shown in this figure. The condenser and adiabatic regions' average temperature dipped after the beginning of the evaporator-entrance event, followed by a steep rise. The evaporator average temperature, in contrast, did not dip but only rose while the other two temperatures were dipping.

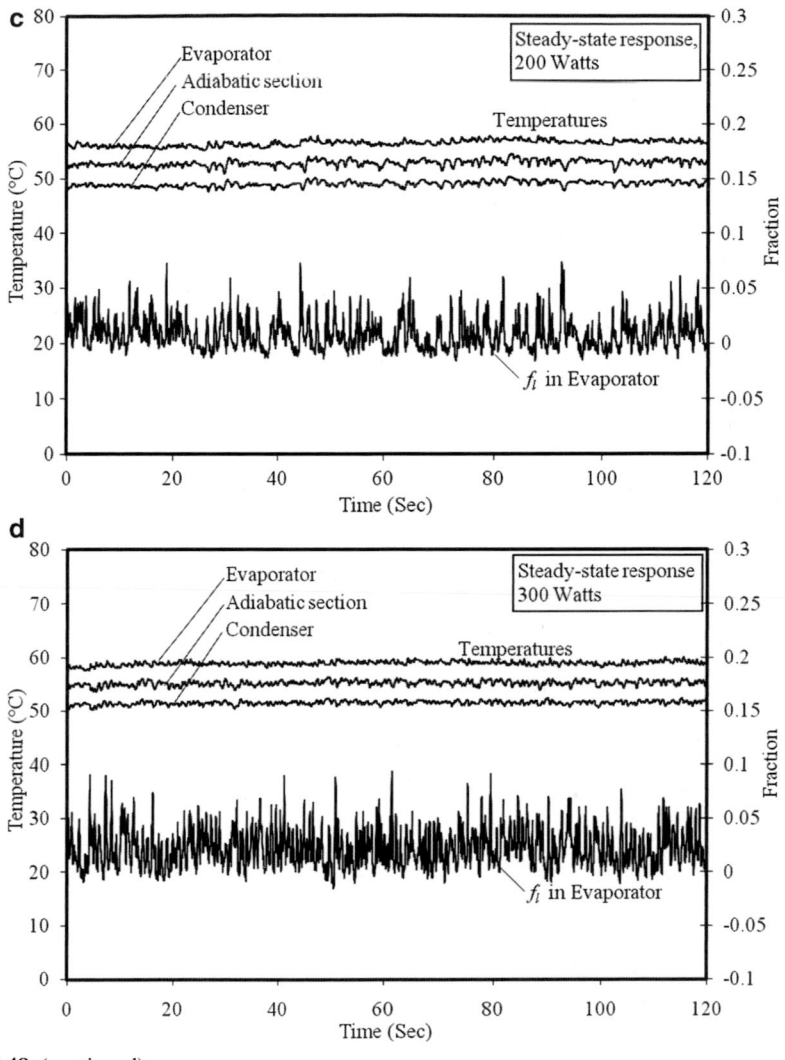

Fig. 6.48 (continued)

Neutron radiography successfully gives visualization information on liquid slug and vapor plug formation in copper tubes and aluminum plate channels. The image data clearly show the dynamics of liquid and vapor. This means they give actual dynamics of the working fluid in copper OHPs unlike the visible imaging technique which works only for transparent OHPs. It also gives better experiment options when the OHP is wrapped with fiber glass or when visualizing the whole area of OHP with an opaque heater and cooler. But, it does not easily give detailed liquid and vapor motion information because of relatively low resolution. Also, it does not give clear

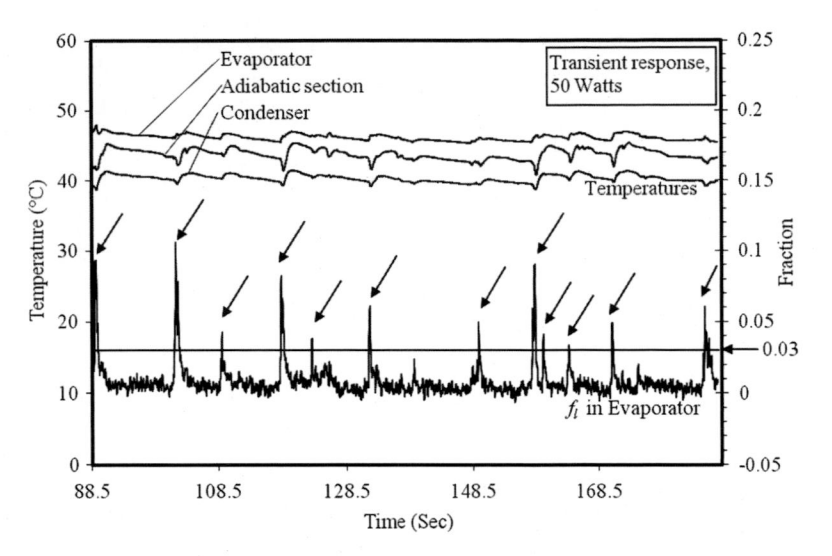

Fig. 6.49 Expanded view of the pulsing period of the initial start-up of fluid motions in the transient behavior test at a heat input of 50 W for the closed-loop water OHP shown in Fig. 6.31 (Wilson et al. 2011; Yoon et al. 2012)

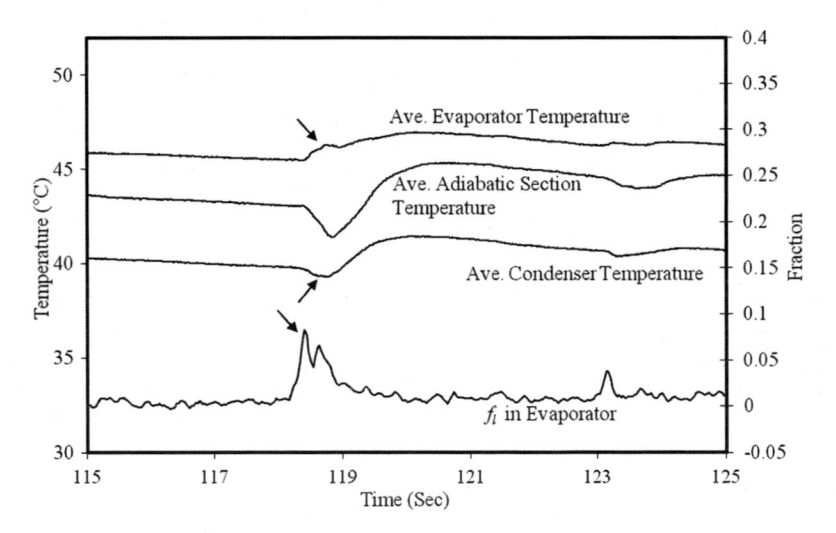

Fig. 6.50 An expanded view of an evaporator-entrance event with the corresponding average temperatures from Fig. 6.49

information on liquid and vapor displacements when they move fast because of relatively slow frame rates in some experiments. The image data from Sugimoto et al. (2009) give good information of meniscus displacement because of a relatively higher frame rate, but it should be noted that the higher frame rate seems to

compromise low resolution; hence, when images are taken at higher frame rates, the resolution is lower. Neutron radiography's setup is much more complex than the visible imaging technique requiring a strong neutron source such as a reactor, a neutron detector, and a protective thick wall to protect technicians and researchers from radiation.

6.4   Proton Radiography

6.4.1   Background

Proton radiography is one of the most nondestructive methods as compared to X-ray radiography or neutron radiography. It is considered analogous to X-ray radiography. For a thick object, X-ray radiography is not successful because of quick attenuation. Neutron radiography also has some problems with thick specimen visualization because of the severe scattering that occurs when neutrons pass through the sample. There are also difficulties in controlling the neutron source. Thus, for an alternative method, proton radiography is suggested (Aufderheide et al. 1999).

Proton radiography has a high penetrating power, high detection efficiency, small scattered background, inherent multipulse capability, and large standoff distances between test objects and detectors. The dominant effects of protons passing through the specimen are absorption, multiple Coulomb scattering, and energy loss. Furthermore, protons are charged particles and have high penetration power, making it possible for a single proton to penetrate multiple thin detection plates to form multiple images (Hogan et al. 1999).

6.4.2   Experimental Consideration and Observation

Kawara et al. (1996) reported some images of OHP made of aluminum with Freon as the working fluid using proton radiography. This study visualized vapor bubbles with diameters of less than 0.6 mm. Example images are shown in Fig. 6.51 with a high speed camera (1,000 frames per second) and Fig. 6.52 with a normal speed camera (60 frames per second). In these figures, the liquid slugs (dark regions) and vapor plugs (bright region) were imaged successfully as well as vapor bubbles (bright small circles). Especially, in Fig. 6.52c, one can see a couple of small vapor bubbles with a diameter of about 0.2 mm, which is significantly smaller than the channel width. The reason for detection of these small vapor bubbles is currently attributed to a high speed frame rate with good resolution. That is, if neutron radiography uses high speed cameras with good resolution, it is reasonable to assume that these small bubbles could also be captured on film while in OHP tubes. This study, however, did not include nucleate boiling, liquid film, and waves

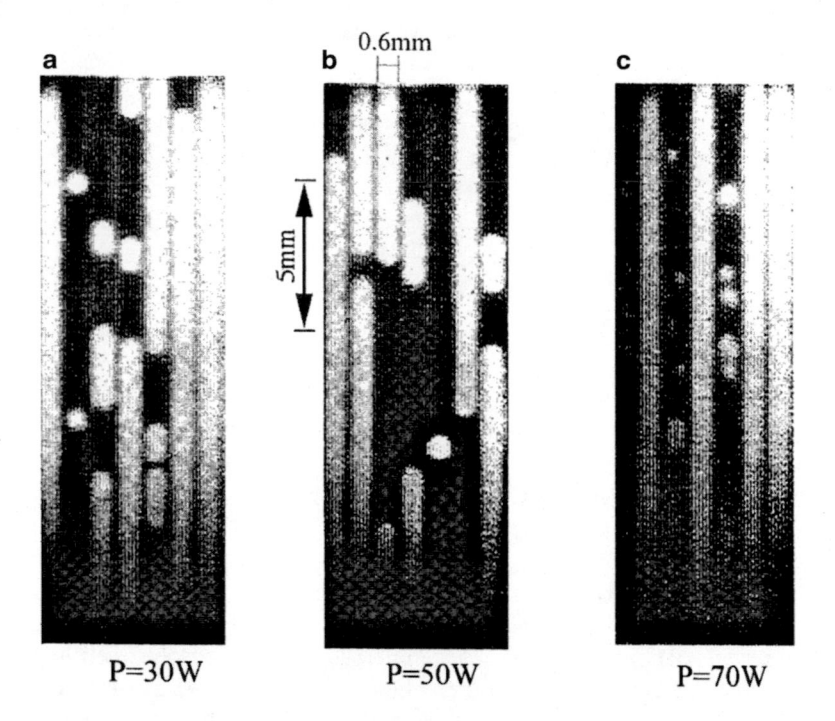

Fig. 6.51 Images of vapor plugs and liquid slugs taken with a high speed camera (1,000 frames per second) (Kawara et al. 1996). (**a**) P = 30 W. (**b**) P = 50 W. (**c**) P = 70 W

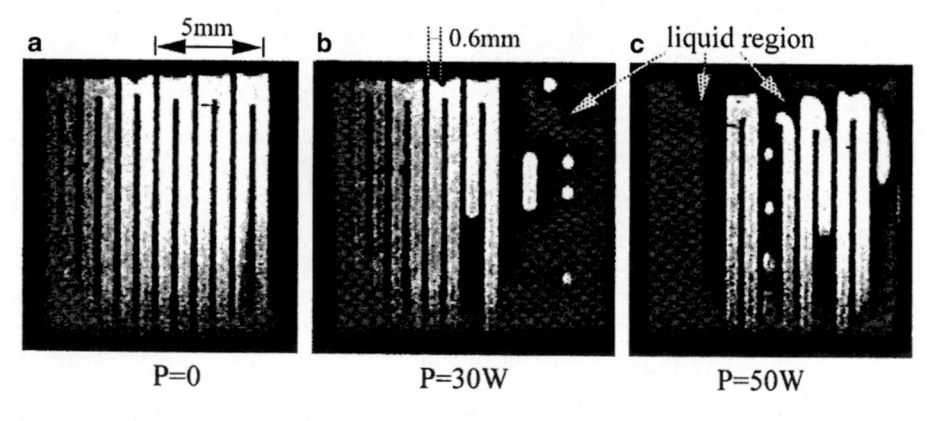

Fig. 6.52 Images of vapor plugs and liquid slugs taken with a normal speed camera (60 frames per second) (Kawara et al. 1996). (**a**) P = 0. (**b**) P = 30 W. (**c**) P = 50 W

on liquid film. Proton radiography imaged vapor plugs and liquid slugs successfully, even visualizing vapor bubbles with diameters significantly smaller than channel width. It also detected the movement of liquid and vapor at high frame rates (1,000 frames per second). This means that the data of displacement and

velocity of menisci can be obtained, even though they are not reported in this study. Thus, proton radiography definitely has advantages for the visualization of fluid in metal-based OHP when compared to traditional visible imaging techniques which are dependent on transparent tubes. However, like neutron radiography, it needs a more complex experimental setup requiring a proton flux source, proton detector, etc.

6.5   Summary

This chapter introduced visualization methods which can be used to investigate the movement of fluids in OHPs and summarized the observation results from each method. The most widely used imaging method is visible light imaging because of its simple experimental setup. The visible imaging method visualizes various patterns of liquid plug and vapor bubbles in transparent OHP tubes with relatively high resolution due to fast frame rates of cameras used to record images capturing details of vapor bubbles and liquid plugs successfully. Visible light imaging's major limitation is that it is only applicable to OHP tubes made mainly of glass. Copper plate OHPs covered with transparent materials were also visualized, but the movement of liquid in copper tubes could not be represented with complete accuracy. Thus, neutron radiography was introduced to visualize liquid motion in copper or aluminum tubes. Neutron radiography successfully imaged the movement of liquid slugs and vapor bubbles in the copper tubes, which the visible light imaging missed. It also required a more complex experimental setup, i.e., insulating OHP with fiber glass and choosing an appropriate heater and cooler. The images of liquid and vapor motion in copper tubes from neutron radiography do not show nucleate boiling, boiling in liquid film, waves on the liquid film, etc., which are shown in glass tubes. This might be due to the characteristic differences of copper and glass. Also, neutron radiography has a relatively low resolution and slow frame rate. So, it does not give detailed images of liquid and vapor and exact displacement of menisci when it moves fast. Proton radiography was also introduced to visualize the motion of liquid and vapor in OHP tubes made of aluminum. It visualized liquid plugs and vapor bubbles successfully even at high frame rates (1,000 frames per second). It also imaged small vapor bubbles with a diameter of about 0.2 mm. But like neutron radiography, proton radiography requires a complex (and expensive) experimental setup. In addition, proton radiography does not report detailed images of liquid and vapor such as nucleate boiling, boiling in liquid film, and waves on liquid film.

References

Aufderheide MB, Park HS, Hartouni EP, Barnes PD, Wright DM, Bionta RM, Zumbro JD, Morris CL (1999) Proton radiography as a means of material characterization. AIP Conf Proc 497(1):706–712

Berger H (1970) Neutron radiography. In: Sharpe RS (ed) Research techniques in nondestructive testing. Academic, New York, pp 269–314

Bhuwakietkumjohn N, Rittidech S (2010) Internal flow patterns on heat transfer characteristics of a closed-loop oscillating heat-pipe with check valves using ethanol and a silver nano-ethanol mixture. Exp Therm Fluid Sci 34(8):1000–1007

Borgmeyer B, Ma HB (2007) Experimental investigation of oscillating motions in a flat plate pulsating heat pipe. J Thermophys Heat Transf 21(2):405–409

Borgmeyer B, Wilson C, Winholtz RA, Ma HB, Jacobson D, Hussey D (2010) Heat transport capability and fluid flow neutron radiography of a three-dimensional oscillating heat pipes. ASME J Heat Transf 132(6), Article Number 061502

Carey VP (1992) Liquid-vapor phase-change phenomena. Hemisphere Publishing Corporation, New York

Chien KH, Chen YR, Lin YT, Wang CC, Yang KS (2011) The experimental studies of flat-plate closed-loop pulsating heat pipes. In: The tenth international heat pipe symposium, Taipei, Taiwan, pp 212–216

Das SP, Nikolayev VS, Lefevre F, Pottier B, Khandekar S, Bonjour J (2010) Thermally induced two-phase oscillating flow inside a capillary tube. Int J Heat Mass Transf 53:3905–3913

Hathaway AA, Wilson CA, Ma HB (2012) An experimental investigation of uneven turn water and acetone oscillating heat pipes. AIAA J Thermophys Heat Transf 26(1):115–122

Hogan GE, Adams KJ, Alrick KR, Amann JF, Boissevain JG, Crow ML, Cushing SB, Eddleman JC, Espinoza CJ, Fife TT, Gallegos RA, Gornez J, Gorman TJ, Gray NT, Holmes VH, Jaramillo SA, King NSP, Knudson JN, London RK, Lopez RP, McClelland JB, Merrill FE, Morley KB, Morris CL, Mottershead CT, Mueller KL, Neri FA, Numkena DM, Pazuchanics PD, Pillai C, Prael RE, Riedel CM, Sarracino JS, Saunders A, Stacy HL, Takala BE, Thiessen HA, Tucker HE, Walstrom PL, Yates GJ, Ziock H-J, Zumbro JD, Ables E, Aufderheide MB, Barnes PD, Bionta RM, Fujino DH, Hartouni EP, Park H-S, Soltz R, Wright DM, Balzer S, Flores PA, Thompson RT, Pendzick A, Prigl R, Scaduto J, Schwaner ET, O'Donnell JM (1999) Proton radiography. In: Proceedings of the 1999 particle accelerator conference, New York, pp 579–583

Katpradit T, Wongratanaphisan T, Terdtoon P, Ritthidech S, Chareonsawan P, Waowaew S (2004) Effect of aspect ratios and bond number on internal flow patterns of closed end oscillating heat pipe at critical state. In: 13th international heat pipe conference (13th IHPC), Shanghai, China, pp 298–303

Kawara Z, Takahashi O, Serizawa A, Kohno M, Kuwabara T (1996) Visualization of flow in heat pipe by proton radiography. Kashika Joho 16(1):23–26

Khandekar S, Groll M, Charoensawan P, Terdtoon P (2002a) Pulsating heat pipes: thermo-fluidic characteristics and comparative study with single phase thermosyphon. In: Proceedings of 12th international heat transfer conference, vol 4. Grenoble, France, pp 459–464

Khandekar S, Schneider M, Schäfer P, Kulenovic R, Groll M (2002b) Thermofluid dynamic study of flat-plate closed-loop pulsating heat pipes. Microscale Thermophys Eng 6:303–317

Li Y, Xu J, Li Y (2004) Study of pulsating heat pipe in GIEC, CAS. In: 13th international heat pipe conference (13th IHPC), vol 1. Shanghai, China, pp 321–328

Lips S, Bensalem A, Bertin Y, Ayel V, Romestant C, Bonjour J (2010) Experimental evidences of distinct heat transfer regimes in pulsating heat pipes (PHP). Appl Therm Eng 30:900–907

Ma HB, Wilson C, Yu Q, Park K, Choi US, Tirumala M (2006) An experimental investigation of heat transport capability in a nanofluid oscillating heat pipe. J Heat Transf 128(11):1213–1216

Ma YD (2012) Motion effect on the dynamic contact angles in a capillary tube. Microfluid Nanofluid 12:671–675

Mameli M, Khandekar S, Marengo M (2011) Flow patterns and corresponding local heat transfer coefficients in a pulsating heat pipe. In: Proceedings of the 29th national heat transfer conference of Italy, Politecnico di Torino, Torino, Italy, pp 1–6

Qu W, Ma T (2002) Experimental investigation on flow and heat transfer of a pulsating heat pipe. In: Proceedings of the 12th international heat pipe conference, Moscow, pp 226–231.

Rittidech S, Sangiamsuk S (2012) Internal flow patterns on heat transfer performance of a closed-loop oscillating heat pipe with check valves. Exp Heat Transf 25(1):48–57

Smoot CD, Ma HB (2014) Experimental investigation of a three-layer oscillating heat pipe. ASME J Heat Transf 136(5), Article No. 051501

Soponpongpipat N, Sakulchangsatjatai P, Saiseub M, Terdtoon P (2006) Time response model of operational mode of closed-loop oscillating heat pipe at normal operating condition. In: Proceedings of the 8th international heat pipe symposium, Kumamoto, Japan, pp 291–296

Soponpongpipat N, Sakulchangsatjaati P, Kammuang-Lue N, Terdtoon P (2009) Investigation of the startup condition of a closed-loop oscillating heat pipe. Heat Transf Eng 30(8):626–642

Sugimoto K, Kamata Y, Yoshida T, Asano H, Murakawa H, Takenaka N, Mochiki K (2009) Flow visualization of refrigerant in a self-vibration heat pipe by neutron radiography. Nucl Instrum Meth Phys Res 605(1):200–203

Thompson SM, Ma HB, Wilson C (2011) Investigation of a flat-plate oscillating heat pipe with tesla-type check valves. Exp Therm Fluid Sci 35:1265–1273

Tong BY, Wong TN, Ooi KT (2001) Closed-loop pulsating heat pipe. Appl Therm Eng 21:1845–1862

Wang GY, Zhao NN, Ji YL, Ma HB (2013) Velocity effect on a liquid plug length in a capillary tube. ASME J Heat Transf 135(8), Article No. 080903

Wilson C, Borgmeyer B, Winholtz RA, Ma HB, Jacobson DL, Hussey DS, Arif M (2008) Visual observation of oscillating heat pipes using neutron radiography. AIAA J Thermophys Heat Transf 22(3):366–372

Wilson C, Borgmeyer B, Winholtz RA, Ma HB, Jacobson D, Hussey D (2011) Thermal and visual observation of water and acetone oscillating heat pipes. J Heat Transf 133, Article No. 061502

Xu JL, Li YX, Wong TN (2005) High speed flow visualization of a closed loop pulsating heat pipe. Int J Heat Mass Transf 48:3338–3351

Yoon I (2013) Oscillating motion study of oscillating heat pipes and its applications to solar water heater. Ph.D. dissertation, University of Missouri, St. Louis, MO

Yoon I, Wilson C, Borgmeyer B, Winholtz BA, Ma HB, Jacobson DL, Hussey DS (2012) Neutron phase volumetry and temperature observations in an oscillating heat pipe. Int J Therm Sci 60:52–60

Chapter 7
Nanofluid Oscillating Heat Pipe

7.1 Introduction

For a typical OHP, forced convection plays a key role in the heat transfer from the evaporator to the condenser sections. In other words, most of the heat transferred from the evaporator to the condenser is by sensible heat. Thermal conductivity, viscosity, and heat capacity of the working fluid play more important roles in an OHP than the surface tension and latent heat in a conventional wicked heat pipe. Many working fluids, such as water (Ma et al. 2006a; Lin et al. 2008), acetone (Qu et al. 2010; Taft et al. 2011), 134a (Taft et al. 2011), and nanofluids (Ma et al. 2006a, b; Qu et al. 2010; Wannapakhe et al. 2010; Qu and Wu 2011), have been investigated. Among these working fluids, nanofluids significantly affect the heat transport capability in an OHP.

By adding a small amount of nanoparticles into the base fluid, the working fluid is defined as a nanofluid. Fabrication technology advancements over the last decade has enabled the production and processing of materials at the nanoscale level, making the use of their novel properties in modern devices a reality. Choi (1995) reported that effective thermal conductivity can be increased by uniformly suspending a very small quantity, preferably less than 1 % by volume, of nanoparticles in conventional coolants. Most recently, an International Nanofluid Property Benchmark Exercise (INPBE) was conducted by over 30 organizations worldwide to measure the thermal conductivity of identical samples of the nanofluids (Buongiorno et al. 2009). They found that the thermal conductivity enhancement afforded by the tested nanofluids increased with increasing particle loading and particle aspect ratio. They also suggested that the effective medium theory was found to be in good agreement with the experimental data and that no anomalous enhancement of thermal conductivity was achieved in the nanofluids tested in their exercise. Nanoparticles cannot produce an anomalous increase of the thermal conductivity; however, when added to the base fluid, they can increase the convection heat transfer (Kalteh et al. 2012; Wen et al. 2009).

© Springer Science+Business Media New York 2015
H. Ma, *Oscillating Heat Pipes*, DOI 10.1007/978-1-4939-2504-9_7

Ma et al. (2006a, b) have demonstrated that when nanofluid is used in an OHP, heat transport capability can be significantly increased. When nanoparticles are added to the base fluid in an OHP, the OHP effectively utilizes (1) the oscillating motion in the OHP to suspend nanoparticles; (2) the higher heat capacity of nanofluid; (3) the higher thermal conductivity; (4) the nanoparticle effect on the fluid field; and (5) the nanoparticle effect on the surface wetting conditions. The unique feature of the oscillating motion fully utilizes the nanofluid features to enhance the heat transport capability in an OHP.

7.2 Nanofluids

7.2.1 Development of Nanofluids

Convection is the key mechanism for convective heat transfer such as flow in the pipes or duct. Convection is divided into two mechanisms: conduction and bulk advection. This means that it is important to use high thermal conductivity liquid for enhancing convective heat transfer when the liquid is used as a working fluid. But, the thermal conductivity of a liquid is always lower than that of a solid. Especially, the thermal conductivity of a metallic solid is much higher than a nonmetallic solid because of the existence of free electrons in a metallic solid.

Because of the high thermal conductivity of metallic materials, adding a metallic particle into a base liquid to enhance the heat transfer rate of that liquid was suggested by Maxwell (1881). Researchers had tried to suspend solids with particle sizes measured in mm or μm to a base liquid to utilize the higher thermal conductivity of solids for enhanced heat transfer. However, the solids did very poorly in the base liquid suspension tests because they were relatively dense, causing uneven dispersion. In addition, the particles' relatively large size caused clogging in the microfluid channel as well as abrasion and pressure drop. Because of these limitations, using solid particles in the base liquid for enhancing heat transfer was not successful.

To overcome these limits, particles smaller than the micrometer scale were needed. The development of nanotechnology solved this problem with its particles ranging from 1 to 100 nm in size. Nanometer-scale particles are suspended in the base liquid and these liquids containing nanoparticles are called nanofluids (Choi 1995). Nanofluids as a heat transfer fluid have significant advantages. Das et al. (2006) described the benefits of nanofluids as high heat conduction, stability, microchannel cooling without clogging, reduced chances of erosion, and reduction in pumping power. It is thought that high heat conduction is achieved by the large surface area of the particles. Because of the large amount of nanoscale-sized particles, a high specific surface area is presented. This, in turn, causes high heat transfer rate by conduction. The mobility of the nanoparticles can also enhance heat transfer by microconvection of the fluid. Stability is achieved by the particles' small size and light weight, which leads to less sedimentation of particles and prevents

particles from settling. Preventing the formation of clogging in the microchannel is another benefit of using nanofluids. The microchannel is usually operated at a high heat load, requiring a good heat transfer fluid to cool down. It is definitely better to use a fluid containing high thermal conductivity particles for better heat transport in the channel. However, the microscale particles could cause clogging in the microchannel because their size would be similar to the size of the channel. Thus, it is useful to use the liquid containing nanoscale particles that are a couple of orders smaller than the size of the microchannel. The reduced chances of erosion are also achieved by the small size and mass of the nanoparticles. Because it has a smaller momentum, component erosion is less likely to happen.

7.2.2   Mechanisms of Nanofluids

Many experiments have reported significantly improved effective thermal conductivity of nanofluids. Despite this improvement, the mechanism of nanofluids has not yet been fully explained. Wang and Mujumdar (2008) suggested two categories of heat transfer mechanisms in nanofluids: The first mechanism consists of conventional static conduction and Brownian motion. The conventional static conduction explains the heat transfer in nanoparticles and base liquids themselves, while the Brownian motion addresses mixing of particles and base liquid. For this mechanism, the particles' size, the volume fraction of particles to the base liquid, thermal conductivities of particles and base liquid, and their operating temperature are important factors used to determine the performance. The second mechanism is a composite theory that a nanoparticle is a core with a nanolayer, which forms a shell around the core. This composite is then immersed in the base liquid. However, the conduction mechanism between the nanoparticle and base liquid is not yet understood.

Keblinski et al. (2002) and Eastman et al. (2004) explained the mechanisms of the increase of the thermal conductivity in more detail. They proposed four possible mechanisms: (1) the nanoparticle motion, (2) liquid layering at the liquid–particle interface, (3) the nature of heat transport in nanoparticles, and (4) the effects of nanoparticle clustering. They only considered heat conduction in the stationary nanofluids. In the theory of nanoparticle motion, the nanoparticles collide with one another and transfer energy from one particle to another, and in turn, enhance the thermal conductivity while traveling in the base liquid. It was also suggested that thermal conductivity might be enhanced just by the Brownian motion of nanoparticles without collision. To confirm that nanoparticle motion can enhance thermal conductivity, they compared the time it takes for a 10 nm nanoparticle to move a distance equal to its diameter by Brownian forces (τ_D) to the time it takes for heat to move the same distance by thermal diffusion in the liquid (τ_H). The result showed that the time ratio (τ_D/τ_H) was about 500 and went down to about 25 when the diameter of a nanoparticle was reduced to 0.5 nm. In other words, the thermal diffusion in the liquid was much faster than the Brownian diffusion of a

Fig. 7.1 Excessive thermal
conductivity enhancement,
κ, as a function
of particle diameter,
d (Keblinski et al. 2002)

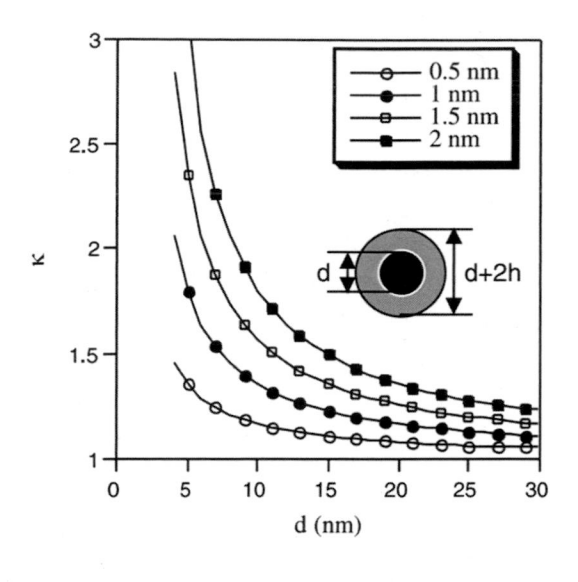

nanoparticle. Thus, the effect of nanoparticle motion for enhancing the thermal conductivity was negligible. However, the nanoparticle motion could indirectly affect the particle clustering, which is one possible explanation for the enhancement of thermal conductivity.

The theory of liquid layering at the liquid–particle interface is based on the well-known fact that liquids tend to form structural ordering at solid–liquid interfaces. A crystalline solid, where the atomic structure is well ordered, has a much higher thermal conductivity than a bulk liquid where the atomic structure is less ordered. Thus, it would be expected that liquid layering at the solid–liquid interface has a higher thermal conductivity than that in the bulk liquid because its atomic structure is better ordered than the bulk liquid. This theory postulates that the thermal conductivity of liquid layering is the same as that of liquid layering at the solid–liquid interface. From this postulation, liquid layering around the solid enlarges the effective volume of the composite, in turn, resulting in enhanced thermal conductivity. Figure 7.1 clearly shows that the larger thickness of layered liquid shows higher thermal conductivity.

Yu and Choi (2003) reached the same conclusion concerning the benefit of liquid layering at a solid–liquid interface. They suggested that a liquid nanolayer structure serves as a thermal bridge, which is a key for enhancing heat transfer between the solid nanoparticle and bulk liquid, because this solid-like nanolayer structure, as shown in Fig. 7.2, is expected to have higher thermal conductivity than a bulk liquid. However, a simulation study by Xue et al. (2004) showed that there is no effect on thermal transport due to liquid layering. Figure 7.3 shows the density profile and the associated temperature profile through a solid–liquid interface. The density profile shows the formation of two layers of significant layering and about three layers of weaker layering. The temperature gradient in the solid is constant, which means the thermal conductivity in the solid is high. However, the

Fig. 7.2 Schematic cross section of nanofluid structure consisting of nanoparticles, bulk liquid, and nanolayers at solid–liquid interface (Yu and Choi 2003)

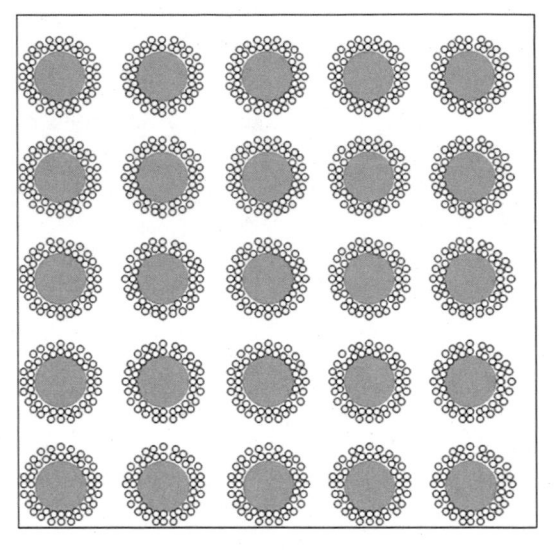

Fig. 7.3 Distribution of number density of atoms (*solid line*) and average temperatures of the atomic layers (*dots*) at the liquid–solid interface for the wetting liquid (Xue et al. 2004)

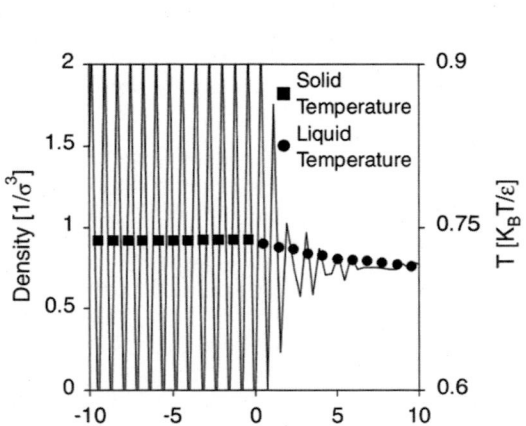

temperature profile through the liquid layering at the solid–liquid interface is similar to the one at the bulk liquid located far from the interface. Thus, the thermal conductivity of the interface is similar to that of the bulk liquid. This means that the thermal conductivity of the liquid layering is much lower than that of the solid and is the same as that of the bulk liquid. However, since this simulation study is done for a simple monoatomic fluid, it cannot claim to have an effect on enhanced thermal conductivity at the liquid layering of more complex molecular liquids.

The enhanced thermal conductivity of a nanofluids also might be explained by the nature of the heat transport in nanoparticles. From the microscopic view, heat is transferred by the phonons in the crystalline solid, which means the energy is propagated by lattice vibration. The mean free path of the phonon is expressed as (Geiger and Poirier 1973)

$$l = \frac{10aT_{\mathrm{m}}}{\gamma T} \tag{7.1}$$

where T_{m} is a melting point, a is a lattice constant, and γ is the Grüneisen parameter (Ashcroft and Mermin 1976). The mean free path, l, of the phonon is too long compared with the size of the nanoparticle to diffuse the energy. For example, the mean free path, l, for a typical nanoparticle, such as alumina (Al_2O_3) is just 35 nm. Thus, the phonon moves in a ballistic motion across the nanoparticle. This means that the heat transport by phonon diffusion is not valid in these nanoparticles. As a result, the heat transport theory in the nanoparticle must be based on the ballistic phonon transport. However, in general, it is not expected that the heat transport by ballistic phonon transport can be more effective than the very fast diffusive phonon transport, causing the significantly enhanced thermal conductivity in nanofluids. One possible explanation would be that a ballistic phonon from one particle passes through the liquid and reaches to the other adjacent particle, resulting in an energy transfer. In this case, the distance between the adjacent particles should be very close, about the order of the thickness of the layered liquid (~1–2 nm), because the mean free path of a phonon in the liquid is very short. This theory is likely to be supported by two facts: (1) the distance between adjacent particles in the nanofluids is very short and (2) the distance could be closer due to the constant Brownian motion.

The effect of nanoparticle clustering is another possible explanation of enhanced thermal conductivity. The heat transfers very fast within the clusters, resulting in high thermal transport. The effective volume of clusters is larger than the physical volume of the particles. This means it forms a path of very low thermal resistance in the clusters, capable of transferring a large amount of heat at a given time with high thermal conductivity. Because larger effective volume of the cluster causes higher thermal conductivity, a loosely packed cluster can have higher thermal conductivity. Even, a cluster that has no physical contact between its particles could have dramatically increased thermal conductivity. This is another possible reason for the highly enhanced thermal conductivity of nanofluids experimentally observed. However, generally, clusters may have a negative effect on heat transport because small particles forming clusters can settle and cause problems outside the base liquid.

7.2.3   Fabrication of Nanofluids

The fabrication of the nanofluids is generally divided into a one-step method and a two-step method. The brief explanation of these two methods for the preparation of nanofluids is described in a review paper by Yu and Xie (2012). In the one-step method, producing nanoparticles and dispersing them into a base liquid is processed simultaneously. By simplifying the procedures, drying, storage, transportation, and dispersion of nanoparticles are avoided. In addition, agglomeration of nanoparticles

is minimized; nanoparticles are suspended more stably in the base liquid, and they are distributed uniformly throughout the liquid. However, this method cannot synthesize the nanofluid on a large scale, and the cost of production is high. Akoh et al. (1978) first introduced this one-step method known as VEROS (vacuum evaporation onto a running oil substrate). Eastman et al. (2011) revised the method so that the nanocrystalline Cu evaporated resistively into the pump oil while the liquid flowed through a rotating cylinder to produce a thin liquid layer above a resistively heated evaporation source.

In the two-step method, two separated procedures are needed to produce the nanofluids. The dry nanopowder is fabricated by the chemical or physical method first, and then this powder is dispersed into the base liquid. In the fabrication process, several techniques are used to prevent particles from aggregating and achieve better dispersion because agglomeration of particles might occur, especially in the process of drying, storage, and transportation, which can cause settlement of particles, clogging, and possibly lowering of thermal conductivity. Preventive techniques include intensive magnetic force agitation, ultrasonic agitation, high-shear mixing, homogenizing, ball milling, and adding surfactants (surface active agents). The two-step method is more economical than the one-step method because in this case, the nanopowder synthesis industry is taking advantage of the economy of scale. Thus, this is the most widely used technique to fabricate nanofluids.

The base fluids for nanofluids include water, ethylene- or tri-ethylene glycols and other coolants, oil and other lubricants, biofluids, polymer solutions, and other common fluids. The materials for nanoparticles can be oxide ceramics (e.g., Al_2O_3 and CuO), metal carbides (SiC), nitrides (AlN and SiN), metals (Al and Cu), nonmetals (graphite, carbon nanotubes (CNTs)), layered materials ($Al + Al_2O_3$ or $Cu + C$), and functionalized nanoparticles.

7.2.4   Enhancement of Thermal Conductivity in Nanofluids

The very reason that the nanofluids have received considerable attention is their ability to enhance thermal conductivity. The significantly increased thermal conductivity of nanofluids compared to the base liquid has been reported by many researchers. Das et al. (2006) reviewed the experimental results of the enhanced thermal conductivity. The nanoparticles used so far are roughly divided into three groups: ceramic particles (e.g., Al_2O_3, CuO, SiC, AlN, and SiN), pure metallic particles (e.g., Al and Cu), and CNTs. The base fluids are divided into four groups: water, ethylene glycol, transformer oil, and toluene.

Lee et al. (1999) investigated ceramic nanofluids consisting of Al_2O_3 and CuO nanoparticles used in a working fluid of water with ethylene glycol as a base liquid to measure thermal conductivity using the transient hot-wire method (THW). Their results clearly indicate that the chosen nanofluids had higher thermal conductivity than non-nanofluid working fluids. The highest increase, about

20 %, was observed from 4 % volume fraction of CuO suspended into ethylene glycol. It also showed higher thermal conductivity when ethylene glycol was used as a base liquid. Wang et al. (1999) also reported thermal conductivity test results using CuO–water and Al_2O_3–water nanofluids, but their nanoparticle sizes were smaller than the ones used by Lee et al. (1999). The results showed different thermal conductivity than that reported by Lee et al. (1999), which means that the size of particle affects the thermal conductivity. It was concluded that the smaller nanoparticles in the base liquid had a higher thermal conductivity. The experimental data from Wang et al. (1999) also showed that the sample preparation method also affects the thermal conductivity of nanofluids. It is remarkable that the oxide ceramic nanofluids show enhanced thermal conductivity, although oxide ceramic materials generally do not have high thermal conductivity. Metallic nanofluids showed higher thermal conductivity when compared to the ceramic nanofluids. Xuan and Li (2000) measured the thermal conductivity of copper nanoparticles suspended into the transformer oil. The nanoparticle size was about 100 nm, which was much larger than the ceramic nanoparticles used by Lee et al. (1999) and Wang et al. (1999); the result was a 55 % increased thermal conductivity compared to that of the base fluid with 5 % volume fraction. Furthermore, Eastman et al. (2001) reported a 40 % increase of thermal conductivity with 0.3 % concentration of 10 nm copper nanoparticles suspended in ethylene glycol. This Eastman et al. (2001) study showed that thermal conductivity is largely affected by nanoparticle size. Another experimental result about the size effect of nanoparticles was reported by Patel et al. (2003). They observed relatively lower thermal conductivity of silver nanoparticles suspended in the water. Even though silver has high thermal conductivity, the silver–water nanofluid did not have much enhancement. This could be because the size of silver nanoparticles is relatively large, about 60–80 nm. This result showed that the size of the nanoparticle is more dominant than the particle conductivity and concentration, which determines the thermal conductivity of nanofluids. Most recently, Buongiorno et al. (2009) found that the thermal conductivity enhancement afforded by the tested nanofluids increased by increasing particle loading, and no anomalous enhancement of thermal conductivity was achieved in the nanofluids tested in their experiments.

7.3 Nanofluid Oscillating Heat Pipe

When nanofluid is used as a working fluid in an OHP, the OHP is called a nanofluid OHP. In other words, the only difference between a nanofluid OHP and a typical OHP is nanofluid. In the fabrication process, success depends on the careful preparation of the nanofluid which includes charging and sealing it into an OHP. Charging and sealing methods and testing procedures could be different for each study. In this chapter, the methods and procedures used by Ma et al. (2006b) are used to represent nanofluid OHP preparation and testing. Similar to a typical OHP, the diameter of the channel for a nanofluid OHP needs to be considered first.

Fig. 7.4 Settlement of nanoparticles at recorded times of (**a**) 0 min, (**b**) 1 min, (**c**) 2 min, (**d**) 3 min, (**e**) 4 min, (**f**) 5 min, and (**g**) 6 min (Ma et al. 2006b)

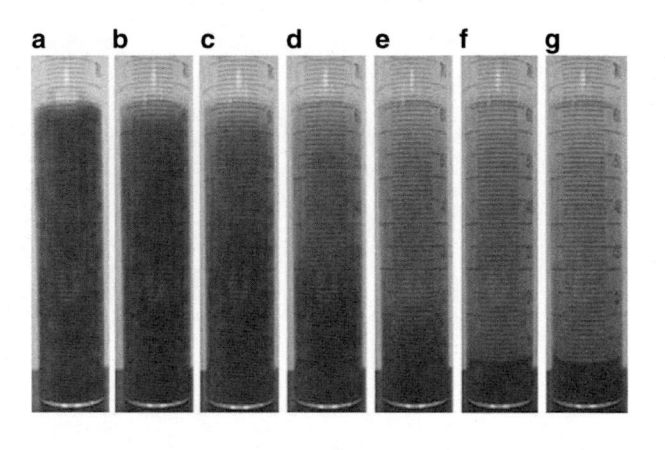

The diameter can be approximately calculated using $r_{h,max} \leq 0.92\sqrt{\frac{\sigma}{g(\rho_l - \rho_v)}}$ as described in Chap. 4, where the surface tension should consider the nanoparticle's effect. In the experiment conducted by Ma et al. (2006b), diamond nanoparticles with HPLC grade water were used. The nanoparticles were fabricated using a 20-kW RF plasma with a high frequency of 13.56 MHz and their sizes ranged from 5 to 50 nm. The fabricated nanoparticles were added into HPLC grade water directly. While most of the nanoparticles settled as shown in Fig. 7.4, some with a size of less than 10 nm remained suspended in the motionless water as shown in Fig. 7.5, photographed by TEM. For charging, the built OHP was placed on the scale and vacuumed. After the air was removed, nanofluid was introduced into the OHP. Once the intended volume percentage was filled, the OHP was sealed. Figure 7.6 shows the experimental setup. A copper plate was used to reduce the thermal contact resistance between the heater and evaporator. The same method was implemented for the condenser. OMEGATHERM "201" thermal paste was placed between the tube and the copper plate to reduce thermal contact resistance. A strip heater was used to supply the heat to the evaporator. Two water cooled aluminum blocks were attached to the condenser plate to dissipate the heat from the OHP. A Julabo F34 circulator was used to control the cooling water temperature and circulation to the condenser. Type T thermocouples were attached on the top surface of the OHP to monitor the temperature change. The entire OHP was wrapped by insulation material to ensure that the heat transfer occurs only at the evaporator and condenser.

Before testing, the OHP system was allowed to achieve equilibrium to reach a steady state. Then, the input power was supplied and increased in small increments. For each power input increment, the OHP was allowed to reach a steady state. The temperature data for each successive power input increment and corresponding steady state were collected. The thermal power and the temperature data were recorded simultaneously.

Fig. 7.5 TEM image of
diamond nanoparticles
suspended in the motionless
water (Ma et al. 2006b)

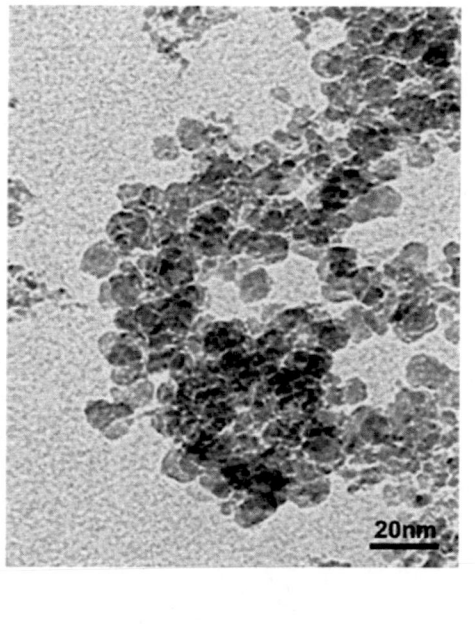

Fig. 7.6 Experimental
setup (Ma et al. 2006b)

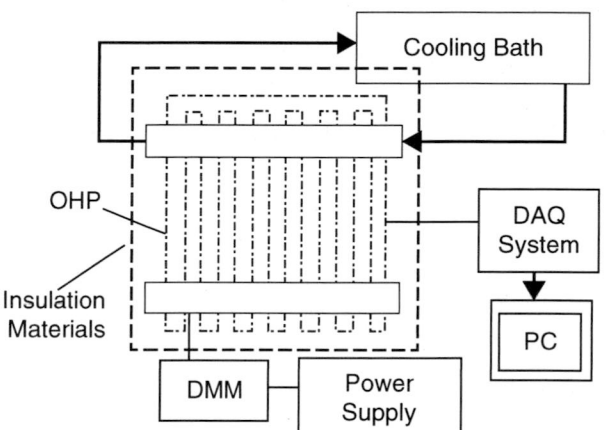

7.4 Parameters Affecting Heat Transfer Performance

The thermal characteristics of nanofluid are suited for the OHP. The improved
thermal properties of the nanofluid aided in the OHP's heat transfer and the motion
helped keep the nanoparticles suspended. Currently the experimental and theoretical understanding of the nanofluid OHP is rudimentary. Because it is new, most
nanofluid OHP experiments are significantly different and only general trends can
be determined from their combined results.

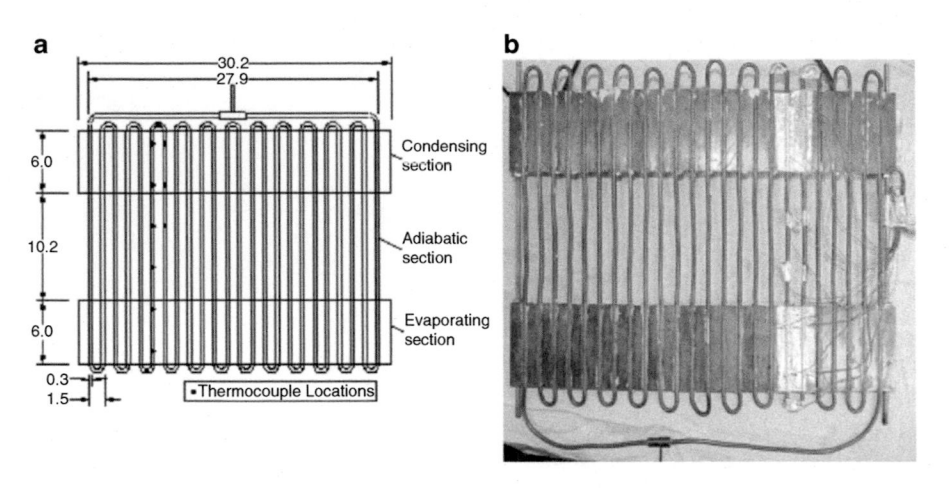

Fig. 7.7 A 12-turn nanofluid oscillating heat pipe (dimensions in cm) (Ma et al. 2006a). (**a**) OHP dimensions and thermocouple locations. (**b**) Photograph

7.4.1 Operating Temperature Effect

Nanofluid was first used as the working fluid in an OHP in 2006 by Ma et al. (2006a) and more extensive tests of the same OHP and fluid were published later (Ma et al. 2006b). In the Ma et al.'s experiment (2006b), alloy 122 copper tubing with an inner diameter of 1.65 mm and outer diameter of 3.18 was used. Figure 7.7 shows this 12-turn OHP with a 59.9 mm × 301.5 mm evaporator and condenser at both ends with the adiabatic section in the middle. The distance between the evaporator and condenser was 101.6 mm. The diamond nanoparticles, 5–50 nm in diameter, were added to pure water at a 1 vol.% concentration. The filling ratio was 50 %. It was tested up to 336 W with a condenser temperatures of 10 °C through 70 °C at 10 °C increments. It was vertically oriented so that the evaporator was gravitationally below the condenser. Figure 7.8 shows a significant improvement when nanofluid was used as the working fluid compared to results where water was used as the base fluid. The improvement is especially significant at low power; however, even at high power the improvement is measurable. It was also found that the thermal resistance decreased with increasing condenser temperature and power input (Fig. 7.9). A minimum resistance of 0.03 °C/W was found at 70 °C and 336 W. Therefore, a nanofluid OHP exhibited improved thermal performance over an OHP using water as the base fluid.

Fig. 7.8 Nanofluid effect
on the heat transport
capability in a 12-turn OHP
(The OHP was vertically
oriented with bottom
heating and circulator
temperature of 20 °C.)
(Ma et al. 2006a)

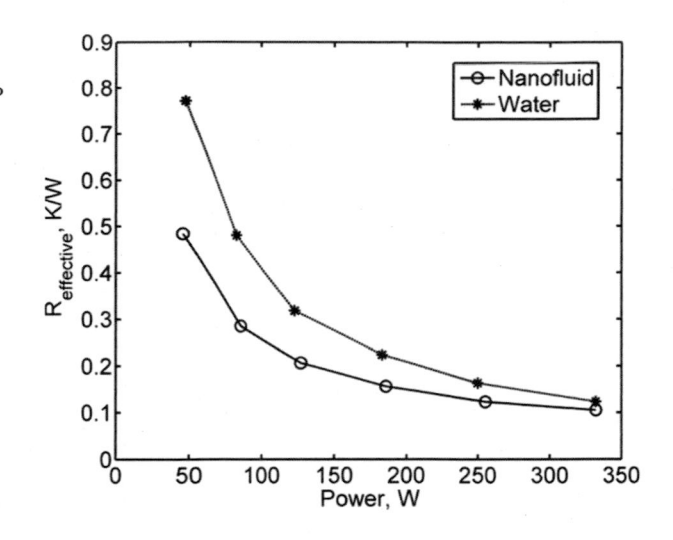

Fig. 7.9 Thermal
resistance at various heat
loads and operating
temperatures of the 12-turn
nanofluid OHP oriented
vertically with bottom
heating (Ma et al. 2006b)

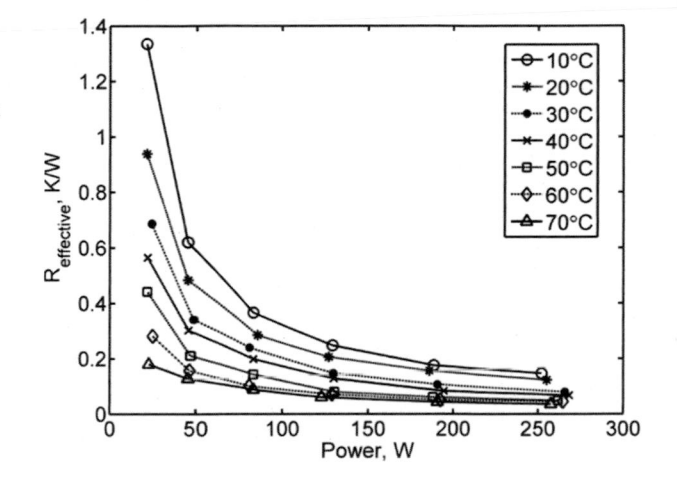

7.4.2   Nanoparticle Effect on the Startup and Nucleation

For a conventional wicked heat pipe, when nucleation occurs and bubbles form in
the wicks, it is well known that the boiling limitation has been reached; this
should be avoided. For an OHP, the heat transport process is mainly due to the
thermally excited oscillating motion. A number of investigators have performed the
visualization experiments using see-through glass OHPs to demonstrate nucleation
taking place in the evaporator section and how it helps the oscillating motion in
an OHP (Khandekar et al. 2002; Katpradit et al. 2004; Nikkanen et al. 2005).
More recently, Li et al. (2011) added nanoparticles in the demonstration OHP to

show how nanoparticles can significantly help the nucleation of bubbles and increase the OHP nucleation site density.

Two factors that affect the boiling heat transfer on a surface are the nucleation of bubbles and the nucleation site density. To successfully initiate the nucleation of a bubble on a surface depends on the cavity pore size and the superheat on the surface. If a vapor bubble to be initiated on a cavity has a meniscus radius of R, the superheat needed to grow the bubble can be found as

$$\Delta T = \frac{2\sigma T_{sat}}{h_{lv}\rho_v R} \tag{7.2}$$

where the meniscus radius R depends on the cavity size. When the cavity size increases, the superheat needed to initialize the bubble decreases. Hsu (1962) developed a semi-theoretical model to predict the effects of the cavity size and superheat on the nucleation of bubbles, bubble growth, and release process. For a given thermal boundary layer thickness of δ_t, the minimum meniscus radius, r_{min}, and the maximum meniscus radius, r_{max}, of the liquid–vapor interfaces of the cavities can be found as

$$\left\{ \begin{matrix} r_{c,max} \\ r_{c,min} \end{matrix} \right\} = \frac{\delta_t}{4} \left[1 - \frac{T_{sat} - T_\infty}{T_w - T_\infty} \left\{ \begin{matrix} + \\ - \end{matrix} \right\} \sqrt{\left(1 - \frac{T_{sat} - T_\infty}{T_w - T_\infty} \right)^2 - \frac{12.8\sigma T_{sat}}{\rho_v h_{lv}\delta_t (T_w - T_\infty)}} \right] \tag{7.3}$$

Equation (7.3) demonstrates that as the superheat, $T_w - T_\infty$, increases starting from zero, the calculated maximum meniscus radius, $r_{c,max}$, and the minimum meniscus radius, $r_{c,min}$, are imaginary, which means that the cavities are not active. When the superheat, $T_w - T_\infty$, increases, the discriminant, $\left(1 - \frac{T_{sat}-T_\infty}{T_w-T_\infty} \right)^2 - \frac{12.8\sigma T_{sat}}{\rho_v h_{lv}\delta_t(T_w-T_\infty)}$, becomes zero, and one solution for the meniscus radius can be obtained. When superheat, $T_w - T_\infty$, further increases, two real values will be obtained from Eq. (7.3), which means that the cavities ranging from $r_{c,min}$ and $r_{c,max}$ will become active sites. In other words, if the surface does not have the cavities in the range between $r_{c,min}$ and $r_{c,max}$, the boiling does not take place for this given superheat. From Eq. (7.3), it can be found that when the superheat becomes larger, the range of active sites increases. It can be summarized that the model developed by Hsu (1962) can result in two important features of the nucleation on heated surfaces with cavities: (1) a certain minimum value of wall superheat is needed to activate the nucleation sites and (2) when the wall superheat is above this minimum value, a finite range of cavities exist and when the superheat increases, this range increases.

Qu and Wu (2011) compared the performance of two different nanofluids in an OHP. They used SiO_2 with a diameter of 30 nm and Al_2O_3 with a diameter of 56 nm; both were spherical in shape and the base fluid was pure water. The nanoparticles were stabilized by adjusting the pH value. The SiO_2–water nanofluid was prepared in 0.1, 0.3, and 0.6 wt% concentrations. The Al_2O_3–water

nanofluid was prepared in 0.1, 0.3, 0.6, 0.9, and 1.2 wt% concentrations. Two 6-turn closed-loop OHPs were manufactured out of stainless steel capillary tubes with an inner diameter of 2 mm and an outer diameter of 3 mm. The lengths of the evaporator, adiabatic, and condenser sections were 50, 105, and 70 mm, respectively. The OHPs were tested in the vertical orientation with the evaporator gravitationally below the condenser. The filling ratio for each nanofluid was 50 %. One of the two OHPs was reserved for the SiO_2–water nanofluid and the other for the Al_2O_3–water nanofluid.

The results showed that the thermal resistance for the Al_2O_3–water nanofluid was lower than that of pure water and had an optimal concentration of 0.9 wt%. The optimal thermal resistance was 0.057 °C/W which was 25.7 % better than pure water. This was similar to previous experiments (Qu et al. 2010). However, the thermal performance of SiO_2–water nanofluid was worse than pure water and became worse with increasing concentration. The worst thermal performance occurred at the thermal resistance of 0.075 °C/W, which was 23.7 % worse than pure water. The suggested reason for the different thermal performance was due to the different deposition patterns of the corresponding nanoparticles at the evaporator and condenser, causing different surface conditions. The enhanced heat transfer caused by using Al_2O_3–water nanofluid is due to the deposition of the nanoparticles, mostly at the evaporator, which increased the surface nucleation site, while the decreased heat transfer caused by using SiO_2–water nanofluid is due to the deposition of the nanoparticles, which decreased the surface nucleation site. Nanofluids' surface effect will be discussed later in a separate section.

Li et al. (2011) conducted visualization experiments of two-phase flows in an OHP charged with deionized (DI) water and a nanofluid (0.268 % v/v). The OHP was made of a quartz glass tube (with an inner diameter of 3.53 mm and an outer diameter of 5.38 mm) and coated with a transparent heating film in its evaporating section. The internal two-phase flows at different heat loads were recorded by a charge-coupled device (CCD) camera. Experimental results demonstrated that when the nanoparticles were added in the OHP, the nucleation of bubbles was easily started as shown in Fig. 7.10. For a quartz glass tube, the surface is very smooth, i.e., the cavity size is very small. The superheat required to activate the nucleation is much larger. When the nanoparticles were added in the OHP as shown in Fig. 7.10, the nanoparticles were deposited on the glass surface to form a number of nanoparticle clusters. Although the individual nanoparticle size was very small, the size of a nanoparticle cluster was much larger, which significantly decreased the superheat required to activate the nucleation of bubbles. When nanoparticles are added in an OHP fabricated with a very smooth wall surface like glass, the nanoparticles added in the OHP can help to increase the nucleation sites.

Ma et al. (2006b) investigated a copper OHP charged with nanofluids. Commercial alloy 122 copper tubing with an inner diameter of 1.65 mm and an outer diameter of 3.18 mm was used for the OHP. The inner surface of the copper tubing had no enhanced cavities. To compare the heat transfer performance of the nanofluid OHP, the heat pipe charged with only HPLC grade water was tested. While the heat transport capability for the OHP charged with nanoparticles was much higher than

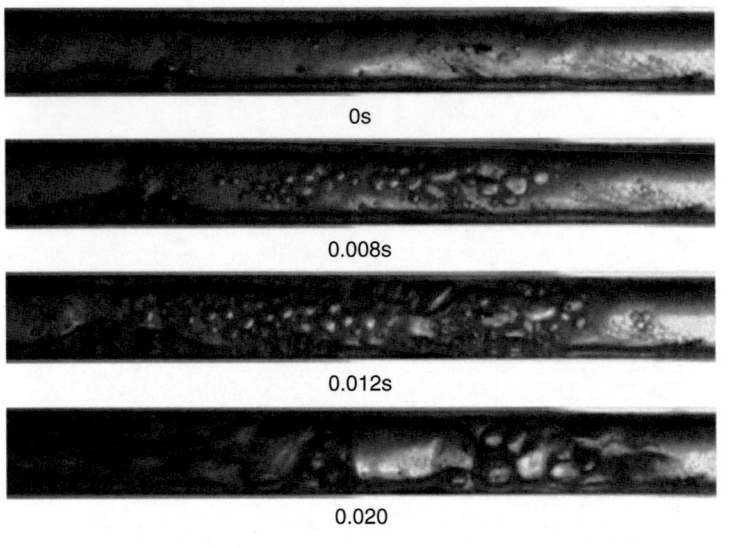

Os

0.008s

0.012s

0.020

Fig. 7.10 Strong boiling in the thick liquid film around a long vapor slug at $Q = 57$ W (Li et al. 2011)

that without nanoparticles, the startup power was significantly decreased. In addition to the increase of both thermal conductivity and higher heat transfer coefficient, the nanoparticles significantly helped to increase the nucleation of the bubbles and site density. As shown, when the input power was 80.0 W, the temperature difference from the evaporator to the condenser could be reduced from 40.9 °C for the one charged only with water to 24.3 °C for the OHP charged with nanofluid. As the heat input increased, the oscillating motion became stronger and stronger. As a result, the temperature difference between the evaporator and the condenser did not increase as the power increased as shown in Fig. 7.11. Due to the strong oscillating motion, the relative contribution of the nucleation site effect on the heat transport capability in the OHP went down. Consequently, the thermal performance difference between the nanofluid OHP and the OHP without nanoparticles became smaller as the power continuously increased.

The difference in thermal performance had to be due to the nanofluid effect on the heat pipe. While the thermal conductivity, heat capacity, and dynamic viscosity of the nanofluid fluid affected the heat transport capability in an OHP, the nanoparticles added in the OHP modified the surface condition in addition to the modification of the nucleation of bubbles. Qu et al. (2010) found that the nanofluid affected the surface of the OHP channel. Scanning electron microscope (SEM) images were taken for the evaporator and condenser sections of the OHP tubing. Both OHPs had deposits of nanoparticles on their surface; however, SiO_2–water nanofluid had larger agglomerations in both the evaporator and condenser sections. In the Al_2O_3–water nanofluid, there were many nanoparticles deposited in the evaporator, but negligible amounts of deposited nanoparticles in the condenser region.

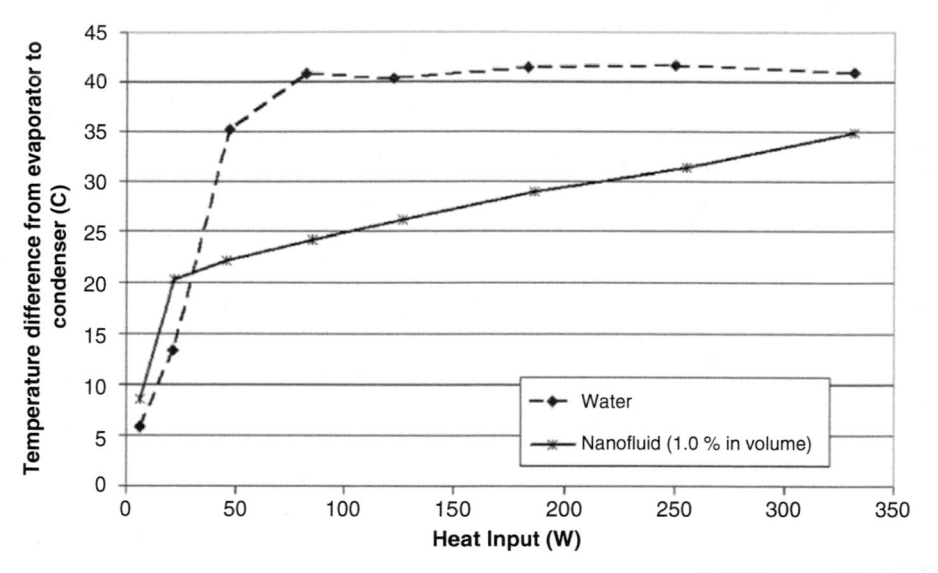

Fig. 7.11 Effect of nanofluid on the heat transport capability in an oscillating heat pipe (vertical position, filled liquid ratio = 50 %, nanoparticles: diamond, 20–50 nm, 1.0 % in volume) (Ma et al. 2006b)

Using the boiling theory, Qu et al. (2010) investigated the parameters relevant to the increase in OHP performance. The resistance of boiling heat transfer is defined as

$$R_{evp} = \frac{1}{hA_e} \qquad (7.4)$$

where h is the boiling heat transfer coefficient and A_e is the surface area of the evaporator. Substituting in Rohsenow's nucleate boiling equation gives

$$R_{evp} = \frac{1}{2N_a D_b^2 A_e \sqrt{f} \sqrt{\pi k \rho c_p}} \qquad (7.5)$$

where N_a is the surface active nucleation site density, D_b is the bubble release diameter, f is the bubble release frequency, k is the liquid thermal conductivity, ρ is the liquid density, and c_p is the liquid specific heat. Comparing the nanofluid properties with the base fluid properties shows that k, ρ, and c_p are negligible. Also, the increase in surface area due to deposited nanoparticles is less than 2.1 %. The nucleate evaporative resistance can be expressed as

$$R_{ev p} \propto \frac{1}{N_a D_b^2 \sqrt{f}} \qquad (7.6)$$

Therefore, the nucleate boiling resistance is only dependent on the number of active sites, the bubble diameter, and the release frequency.

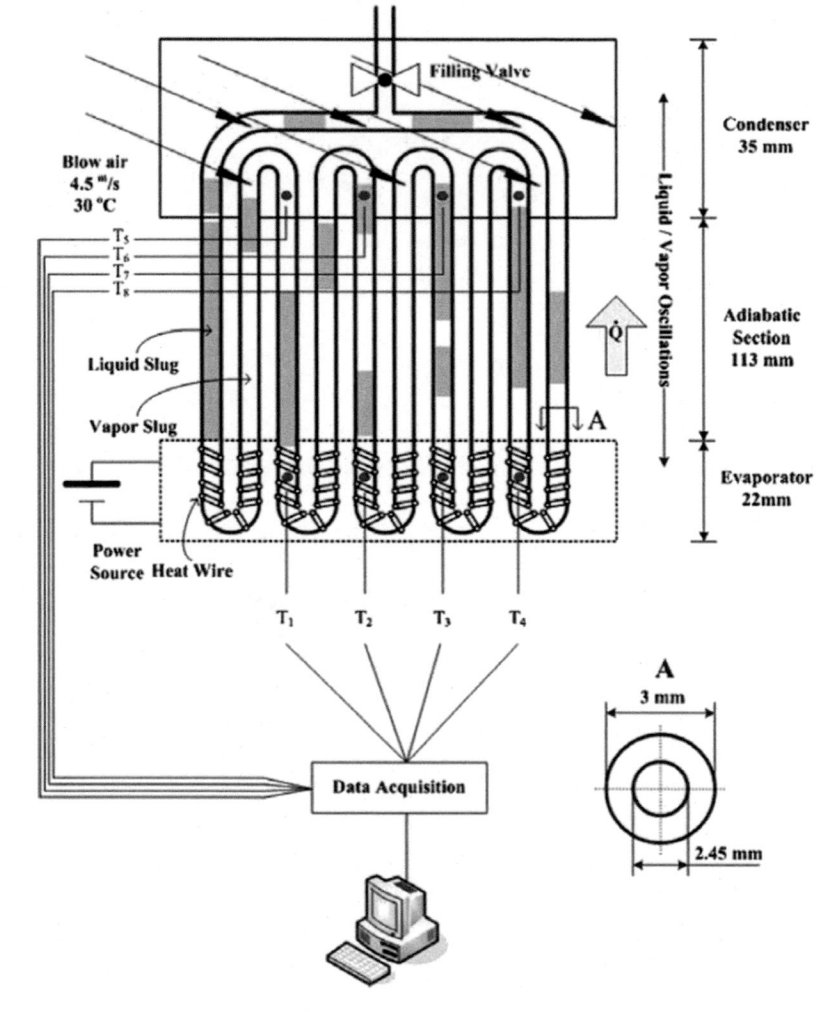

Fig. 7.12 Schematic of the silver nanofluid experiment (Lin et al. 2008)

7.4.3   Effects of Nanoparticle Concentration and Filling Ratio

There are many independent parameters in the nanofluid OHP that should be analyzed for a complete understanding of the device. Lin et al. (2008) analyzed several of these by varying nanofluid concentration, filling ratio, and heating power. They used silver nanofluid as the working fluid in a 5-turn closed-loop OHP built using 2.45 mm inner diameter tubing (Fig. 7.12). The heat pipe was wound with heating wire in the evaporator region and cooled via 4.5 m/s 30 °C forced

convection in the condenser. The OHP was tested at 20, 40, 60, and 80 % filling ratio with pure water, 100, and 450 ppm silver nanofluid. The power was applied from 5 to 85 W at 10 W increments for each case. The same OHP was recharged for all tests.

The silver nanofluid concentration of 100 ppm performed better than the 450 ppm concentration. From this, while it might be expected that a higher concentration nanofluid has better heat transport, the experimental results from this study show that the lower concentration nanofluid has better heat transport. The detailed mechanism on this has not been fully understood. One reason might be due to viscosity, which produces high frictional force increasing the pressure drop. The increase of pressure drop directly affects the oscillating motion in an OHP. Additionally, it was found that 60 % is the best filling ratio with 85 W heating power, and the silver nanofluid thermal resistance was 0.092 °C/W. Thus, it might be concluded that the filling ratio effect of nanofluids is the same as normal heat transfer fluids, but a lower concentration requirement is usually an advantage to higher thermal performance. However, there is a possibility that in some instances, the thermal performance might be poor, which needs to be confirmed by further studies.

A study by Wannapakhe et al. (2010) looked at the effect of evaporator length and orientation with a focus on nanoparticle concentration. Silver nanoparticles with a diameter of less than 100 nm were combined with deionized water at mass concentrations of 0.25, 0.5, 0.75, and 1 % w/v, and sonicated for 5 h. The resulting nanofluid proved to be stable for at least 48 h. The nanofluid was charged into a 40-turn closed-loop OHP with an inner diameter of 2 mm. Two ball check valves were included in the OHP to enhance the flow pattern within the OHP (Fig. 7.13).

The silver nanofluid OHP was heated and cooled by two constant temperature baths flowing at 0.5 L/min. The evaporator temperature was set at 40 °C, 50 °C, and 60 °C, respectively. The angle of the OHP was varied from 0°, 20°, 40°, 60°, 80°, and 90° from the horizontal plane, and the evaporator length ratio was 25, 50, and 75. The evaporator aspect ratio was defined as the evaporator length divided by the OHP tube's inner diameter. The adiabatic length was 100 mm and the condenser length

Fig. 7.13 Check valve design (Wannapakhe et al. 2010)

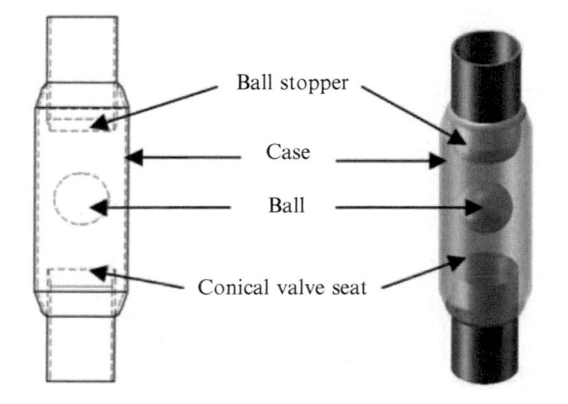

was 150 mm. It was found that the optimal parameters were a vertical orientation (90°) with 0.5 % w/v silver nanoparticles, an evaporator aspect ratio of 25, and an evaporator temperature of 60 °C. This case had a heat transfer rate of 13.19 kW/m^2. The vertical orientation was the best orientation; the performance improved as the evaporator aspect ratio decreased, and the performance improved as the evaporator temperature increased. The experiment also found that nanofluid routinely performed better than pure water at all orientations and aspect ratios. It also showed that the lower concentration generally had a better performance. The optimal concentration was achieved with a 0.5 % w/v silver nanofluid. It was suspected that the increased thermal performance normally seen in higher concentrations was outweighed by the increased viscosity of the silver nanofluid, which worked to provide the opposite effect where a lower concentration is better, which confirms the result by Lin et al. (2008). However, sometimes, the concentration of 0.75 % shows better heat transport than that of the concentration of 0.25 %. Thus, this experimental result shows that, generally, lower concentration is preferred; however, there might be some exceptional cases where a higher concentration is desirable for better performance. More studies are needed theoretically and experimentally to define the nanoparticle concentration effect.

7.4.4   Nanofluid Surface Effect

An experiment by Qu et al. (2010) looked at the surface effects of nanoparticles on the heat transfer performance of OHPs. They used alumina and water (Al$_2$O$_3$–water) nanofluid as their working fluid at weight percentages of 0.1 %, 0.3 %, 0.6 %, 0.6 %, 0.9 %, and 1.2 %, respectively. The nanoparticles had a mean diameter of 56 nm and were stabilized using small amounts of hydrochloric acid to adjust the pH to 4.9 to prevent agglomeration and ensure the solution remained stable for at least 3 days. The OHP had six turns with an inner diameter of 2 mm and an outer diameter of 3 mm. The evaporator, adiabatic, and condenser sections were 50, 105, and 70 mm, respectively. The condenser was held at a constant temperature and the evaporator was heated up to nearly 140 W. The OHP was charged with pure water or nanofluids at filling ratios of 50 %, 60 %, and 70 %, respectively. All tests were conducted in the vertical orientation with the evaporator gravitationally below the condenser. Tube samples were taken from the evaporator and condenser of a nanofluid OHP and from a pure water OHP. The channel surface was observed with a SEM. They found that the pure fluid channel was clean; however, the nanoparticles deposited and agglomerated on both the evaporator and condenser surfaces in the nanofluid OHP. The number of nanoparticle agglomerations on the condenser surface was negligible, but the evaporator had a significant number (see Fig. 7.14).

The nanoparticles on the surface of the evaporator will change the evaporative and boiling properties of the surface. Because nucleation sites are related to surface roughness, the increased surface roughness due to nanoparticles and their

Fig. 7.14 SEM images
of (**a**) a clean substrate
boiled in pure water,
(**b**) a nanoparticle-deposited
substrate at the condenser,
and (**c**) a nanoparticle-
deposited substrate at the
evaporator (Qu et al. 2010)

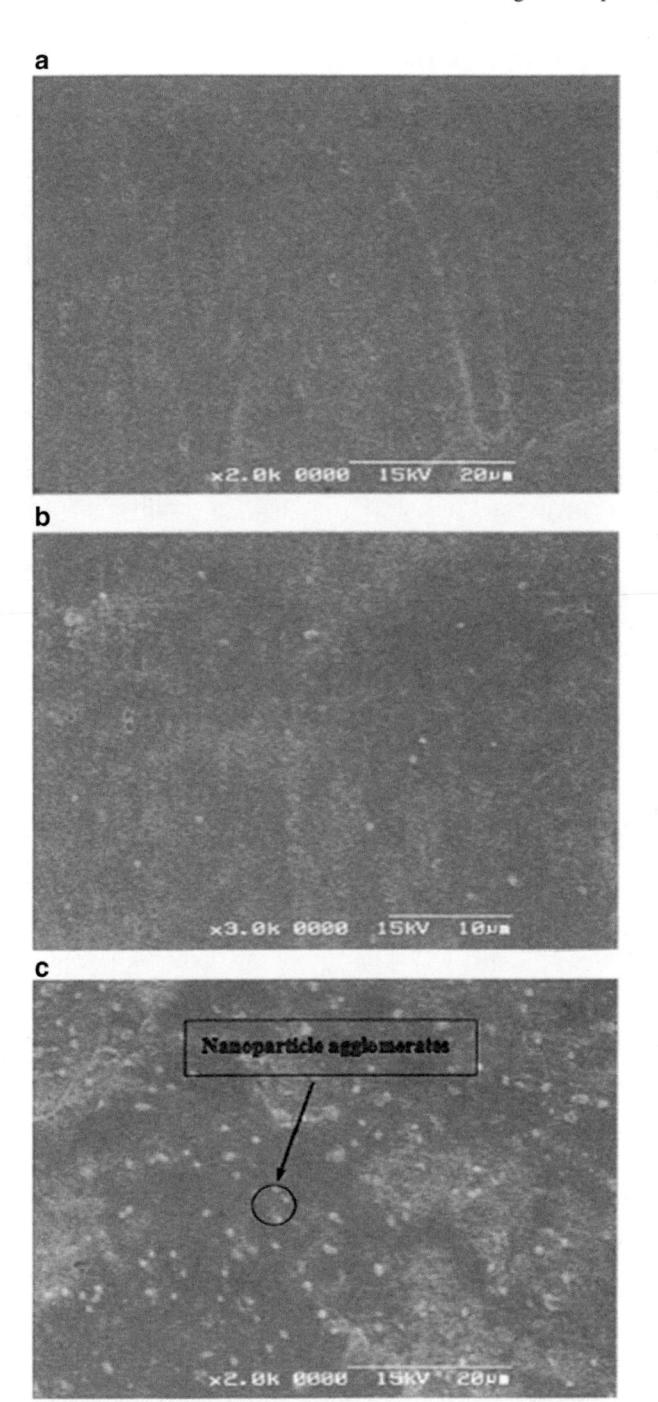

Fig. 7.15 2D atomic force
microscope images of
(**a**) a clean substrate boiled
in pure water and
(**b**) a nanoparticle-deposited
substrate at the evaporator
(Qu et al. 2010)

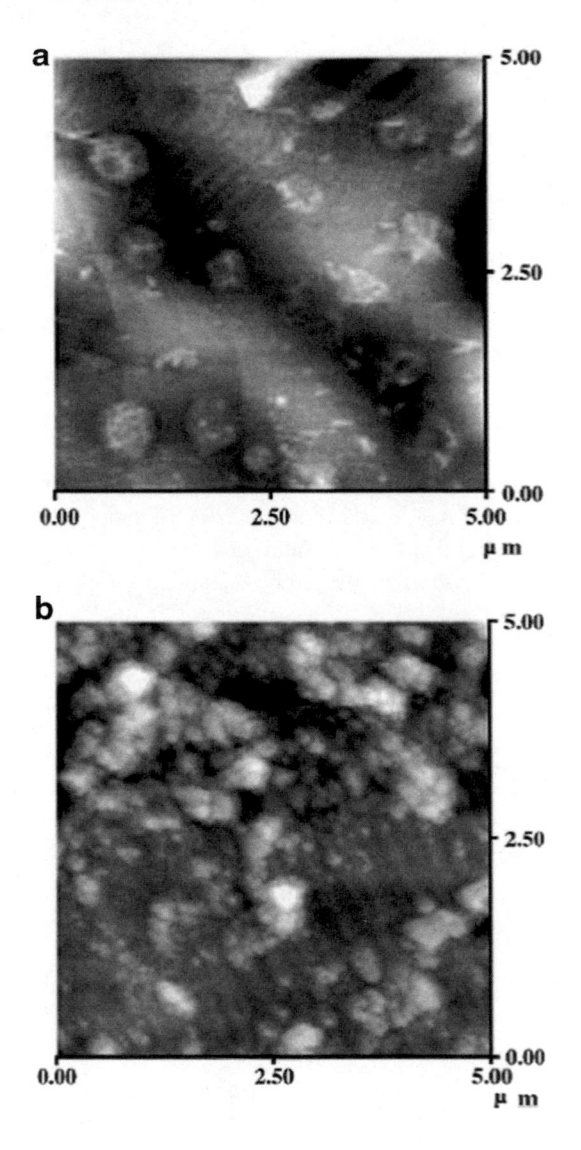

agglomerations will increase bubble generation. The cavities on the clean surface
were observed to be 2–3 μm in diameter (Fig. 7.15). Those cavities in the nanofluid
OHP would fill with nanoparticles, thereby increasing the cavity size and number of
nucleation sites. The increase of nucleation sites and frequency improved the
thermal performance of the nanofluid OHP. It is also suspected that increasing
the concentration of nanoparticles beyond a certain value would fill in the nucleation sites too much, which would decrease the nucleation sites and reduce thermal
performance.

7.4.5   Nanoparticle Size Effect

Ji et al. (2011) investigated the particle size effect on OHP performance. They used a 6-turn closed-loop OHP with copper heat spreading plates in the evaporator and condenser. A copper tube with a 1.65 mm inner diameter and 3.18 mm outer diameter was imbedded into the plates. The OHP had an evaporator length of 40 mm, an adiabatic length of 51 mm, and a condenser length of 64 mm. The OHP was charged with Al_2O_3–water nanofluid with particle sizes of 20 μm, 2.2 μm, 80 nm, and 50 nm, respectively. Each of these particles was mixed with the base fluid at a concentration of 0.5 wt%. All tests were conducted in the vertical orientation with a condenser operating temperature of 25 °C. The heat pipe was tested up to 200 W. First, the optimal filling ratio was determined using pure water. It was found that the thermal performance was improved by decreasing the filling ratio until the optimal filling ratio was accomplished at 50 %. The start-up temperature was compared for the different nanofluids and pure fluid. Start-up temperature is defined as the minimum evaporator temperature at which the OHP will oscillate. Pure water had the highest start-up temperature of 54.2 °C (Fig. 7.16). For the nanofluid OHPs, as nanoparticle size decreased the start-up temperature decreased. Ji et al. (2011) also found that as particle size decreased from 20 μm to 80 nm, thermal resistance decreased; however, the 50 nm nanofluid performed slightly worse than the 80 nm nanofluid. Therefore, the optimal nanofluid size was 80 nm which produced the lowest OHP thermal resistance of 0.113 °C/W at 25 °C and 200 W for the investigated OHP.

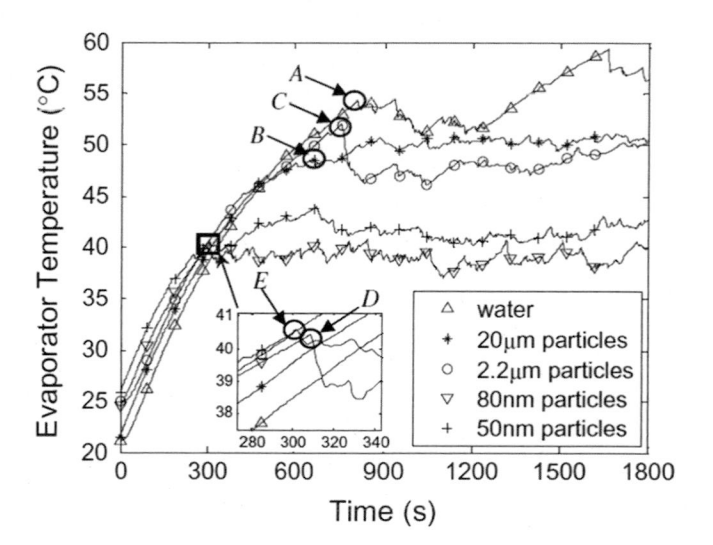

Fig. 7.16   Particle size effect on the start-up temperature (Ji et al. 2011)

References

Akoh H, Tsukasaki Y, Yatsuya S, Tasaki A (1978) Magnetic properties of ferromagnetic ultrafine particles prepared by vacuum evaporation on running oil substrate. J Cryst Growth 45:495–500

Ashcroft NW, Mermin ND (1976) Solid state physics. Holt, Rinehart and Winston, New York

Buongiorno J, Venerus DC, Prabhat N, McKrell T, Townsend J, Christianson R, Tolmachev YV, Keblinski P, Hu L, Alvarado JL, Bang IC, Bishnoi SW, Bonetti M, Botz F, Cecere A, Chang Y, Chen G, Chen H, Chung SJ, Chyu MK, Das SK, Di Paola R, Ding Y, Dubois F, Dzido G, Eapen J, Escher W, Funfschilling D, Galand Q, Gao J, Gharagozloo PE, Goodson KE, Gutierrez JG, Hong H, Horton M, Hwang KS, Iorio CS, Jang SP, Jarzebski AB, Jiang Y, Jin L, Kabelac S, Kamath A, Kedzierski MA, Kieng LG, Kim C, Kim J-H, Kim S, Lee SH, Leong KC, Manna I, Michel B, Ni R, Patel HE, Philip J, Poulikakos D, Reynaud C, Savino R, Singh PK, Song P, Sundararajan T, Timofeeva E, Tritcak T, Turanov AN, Van Vaerenbergh S, Wen D, Witharana S, Yang C, Yeh W-H, Zhao X-Z, Zhou S-Q (2009) A benchmark study on the thermal conductivity of nanofluids. J Appl Phys 106:094312

Choi SUS (1995) Enhancing thermal conductivity of fluids with nanoparticles. In: Singer DA, Wang HP (eds) Developments and applications of non-Newtonian flows. ASME, New York, pp 99–105

Das SK, Choi SUS, Patel HE (2006) Heat transfer in nanofluids—a review. Heat Transf Eng 27(10):3–19

Eastman JA, Choi SUS, Li S, Yu W, Thompson LJ (2001) Anomalously increased effective thermal conductivities of ethylene glycol-based nanofluids containing copper nanoparticles. Appl Phys Lett 78(6):718

Eastman JA, Phillpot SR, Choi SUS, Keblinski P (2004) Thermal transport in nanofluids. Annu Rev Mater Res 34(1):219–246

Eastman JA, Choi US, Li S, Thompson LJ, Lee S (2011) Enhanced thermal conductivity through the development of nanofluids. In: MRS proceedings, pp 457

Geiger GH, Poirier DR (1973) Transport phenomena in metallurgy. Addison-Wesley, Readings

Hsu YY (1962) On the size range of active nucleation cavities on a heating surface. ASME J Heat Transf 84:207–216

Ji Y, Wilson C, Chen H-H, Ma HB (2011) Particle shape effect on heat transfer performance in an oscillating heat pipe. Nanoscale Res Lett 6(1):296

Kalteh M, Abbassi A, Saffar-Avval M, Frijns A, Darhuber A, Harting J (2012) Experimental and numerical investigation of nanofluid forced convection inside a wide microchannel heat sink. Appl Therm Eng 36:260–268

Katpradit T, Worngratanapaisarn T, Terdtoon P, Ritthidech S, Chareonsawan P, Waowaew S (2004) Effect of aspect ratios and bond number on internal flow patterns of closed end oscillating heat pipe at critical state. In: Proceedings of the 13th international heat pipe conference, Shanghai, China

Keblinski P, Phillpot SR, Choi SU, Eastman JA (2002) Mechanisms of heat flow in suspensions of nano-sized particles (nanofluids). Int J Heat Mass Transf 45:855–863

Khandekar S, Schneider M, Schafer P, Kulenovic R, Groll M (2002) Thermofluid dynamic study of flat plate closed loop pulsating heat pipes. Microscale Thermophys Eng 6(4):303–318

Lee S, Choi SU-S, Li S, Eastman JA (1999) Measuring thermal conductivity of fluids containing oxide nanoparticles. J Heat Transf 121(2):280

Li Q-M, Zou J, Yang Z, Duan Y-Y, Wang B-X (2011) Visualization of two-phase flows in nanofluid oscillating heat pipes. J Heat Transf 133(5), Article No. 052901

Lin Y-H, Kang S-W, Chen H-L (2008) Effect of silver nano-fluid on pulsating heat pipe thermal performance. Appl Therm Eng 28(11–12):1312–1317

Ma HB, Wilson C, Borgmeyer B, Park K, Yu Q, Choi SUS, Tirumala M (2006a) Effect of nanofluid on the heat transport capability in an oscillating heat pipe. Appl Phys Lett 88(14):143116

Ma HB, Wilson C, Yu Q, Park K, Choi US, Tirumala M (2006b) An experimental investigation of heat transport capability in a nanofluid oscillating heat pipe. J Heat Transf 128(11):1213–1216

Maxwell JC (1881) A treatise on electricity and magnetism, vol 1. Clarendon, Oxford

Nikkanen K, Lu CG, Kawaji M (2005) Effects of working fluid, fill ratio and orientation on looped and unlooped pulsating heat pipes. In: Proceedings of ASME summer heat transfer conference, San Francisco, CA, USA

Patel HE, Das SK, Sundararajan T, Sreekumaran NA, George B, Pradeep T (2003) Thermal conductivities of naked and monolayer protected metal nanoparticle based nanofluids: manifestation of anomalous enhancement and chemical effects. Appl Phys Lett 83(14):2931

Qu J, Wu H (2011) Thermal performance comparison of oscillating heat pipes with SiO_2/water and Al_2O_3/water nanofluids. Int J Therm Sci 50(10):1954–1962

Qu J, Wu H, Cheng P (2010) Thermal performance of an oscillating heat pipe with Al_2O_3–water nanofluids. Int Commun Heat Mass Transf 37(2):111–115

Taft B, Williams A, Drolen B (2011) Working fluid selection for pulsating heat pipes. In: 42nd AIAA thermophysics conference, Honolulu, Hawaii, pp 1716

Wang XQ, Mujumdar AS (2008) A review on nanofluids—part I: theoretical and numerical investigations. Braz J Chem Eng 25(4):613–630

Wang X, Choi SUS, Xu X (1999) Thermal conductivity of nanoparticle—fluid mixture. J Thermophys Heat Transf 13(4):474–480

Wannapakhe S, Rittidech S, Bubphachot B, Watanabe O (2010) Heat transfer rate of a closed-loop oscillating heat pipe with check valves using silver nanofluid as working fluid. J Mech Sci Technol 23(6):1576–1582

Wen D, Lin G, Vafaei S, Zhang K (2009) Review of nanofluids for heat transfer applications. Particuology 7(2):141–150

Xuan Y, Li Q (2000) Heat transfer enhancement of nanofluids. Int J Heat Fluid Flow 21:58–64

Xue L, Keblinski P, Phillpot S, Choi SUS, Eastman J (2004) Effect of liquid layering at the liquid–solid interface on thermal transport. Int J Heat Mass Transf 47(19–20):4277–4284

Yu W, Choi SUS (2003) The role of interfacial layers in the enhanced thermal conductivity of nanofluids: a renovated Maxwell model. J Nanoparticle Res 5:167–171

Yu W, Xie H (2012) A review on nanofluids: preparation, stability mechanisms, and applications. J Nanomater 2012:1–17

Chapter 8
Experiment and Manufacturing Considerations

8.1 Introduction

The proper construction of an oscillating heat pipe is crucial to achieve a long operating life and optimal performance. Manufacturing an OHP has many considerations. These include material selection, working fluid selection, channel design, charging method, and sealing method. For instance, the OHP envelope must maintain structural integrity when the interior fluid is under vacuum or pressure. This is balanced against optimizing the envelope structure to reduce the overall thermal resistance. OHP materials must also be properly selected so that they do not leak or outgas and are compatible with their working fluid and the exterior environment. If they are not compatible, corrosion can occur and noncondensable gases can be generated, which can interfere with heat transfer. Once the OHP is built it must be accurately tested to verify its performance. The experimental operation of an OHP must account for the effects of gravitational orientation, condensing temperature, evaporator temperature, and heat flux.

8.2 Channel Configuration

For an OHP to function, the OHP must have a train of liquid plugs and vapor bubbles. The formation of the liquid–vapor interface, which plays a key role in the separation of liquid plugs by the vapor bubbles, depends mainly on surface tension and channel diameter. When the channel diameter becomes smaller, the surface tension will dominate the liquid–vapor interface. In a gravitational environment, the liquid–vapor interface is characterized by the Bond number, i.e., $Bo = \frac{r_h^2 g(\rho_l - \rho_v)}{\sigma}$ as described in Chap 4. It is found that when a Bond number, i.e., $Bo = 0.85$, is

© Springer Science+Business Media New York 2015
H. Ma, *Oscillating Heat Pipes*, DOI 10.1007/978-1-4939-2504-9_8

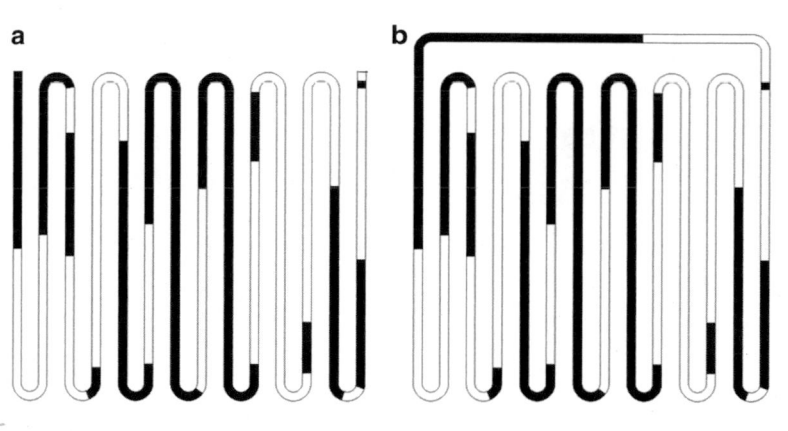

Fig. 8.1 Schematic of OHPs: (**a**) open loop and (**b**) closed loop

taken, the fluid in an OHP with a tube radius determined by $r_{\mathrm{h,max}} \leq 0.92\sqrt{\frac{\sigma}{g(\rho_l - \rho_v)}}$ can form a train of liquid plugs and vapor bubbles. For a given working fluid, the tube radius or channel hydraulic radius should be smaller than that determined by this equation.

The configuration of OHP channels controls fluid flow characteristics and, therefore, the heat transfer performance. Many different designs have been developed to improve the performance of an OHP. This includes minimizing the effect of gravity, increasing bulk flow, and improving heat spreading capabilities. In general, the OHP channel design should have a smaller pressure drop, higher restoring force, higher filling ratio, higher number of channels, etc. But some of these design considerations conflict with each other. For example, heat is transferred by the sensible heat or the forced convection, and the heat transfer coefficient of a liquid phase is much higher than the vapor phase. From this, the filling ratio should be as high as possible. However, the increase of filling ratio directly affects the vapor spring constant. If the liquid filling ratio is too high, the restoring force decreases, and the system cannot produce oscillating motion. Therefore, an optimum channel design must be found for a given heat transfer need. In addition, the following structure factors should be considered.

There are two basic loop configurations: open loop (unlooped) and closed loop (looped) (Fig. 8.1). The open-loop design is a channel that crosses between the condenser and evaporator multiple times but is sealed at each end. The closed-loop design is similar; however, the beginning and end of the channel connect to form a continuous loop. Typically the open-loop OHP is easier to design and manufacture, but there is very little fluid movement near the ends of the channel. The closed-loop design has more uniform movement throughout the OHP and allows for bulk flow through the tube (Wilson et al. 2011). This design can achieve greater fluid movement and, therefore, typically has better thermal performance.

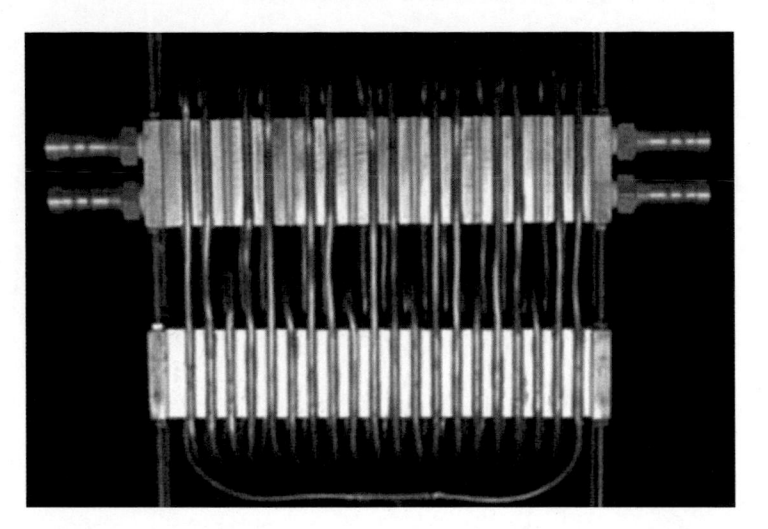

Fig. 8.2 An uneven turn OHP (Hathaway et al. 2012)

The thermal performance of OHP depends on its orientation with respect to gravity. The density of the liquid inside the OHP is significantly higher than the vapor phase. Therefore, the liquid slugs are significantly affected by the orientation of gravity. If the condenser is gravitationally above the evaporator, the liquid plugs will be pulled toward the evaporator. The vapor generated in the evaporator pushes the liquid plug back toward the condenser. This typically improves the OHP start-up process and heat transfer performance. However, if the condenser is gravitationally below the evaporator, gravity will pull the liquid toward the condenser leaving only vapor in the evaporator. The OHP cannot start-up easily when this happens, and if oscillating motion does start, the heat transfer performance is less. By arranging the channels on more than one plane, the gravity effect can be reduced (Charoensawan et al. 2003; Thompson et al. 2011b; Hathaway et al. 2012). The uneven-turn OHP was designed for gravitational orientation independence (Fig. 8.2) (Hathaway et al. 2012). This design utilizes an extra partial turn in the evaporator. This partial turn crosses from the evaporator to the adiabatic region and back into the evaporator.

The check valve and Tesla valve OHPs are designed to encourage unidirectional bulk flow within the OHP. The check valve OHP stops all flow from reversing at the location of the check valve (Fig. 8.3) (Bhuwakietkumjohn and Rittidech 2010). And the Tesla valve OHP introduces a directionally dependent pressure drop at the location of the valves (Fig. 8.4) (Thompson et al. 2011a).

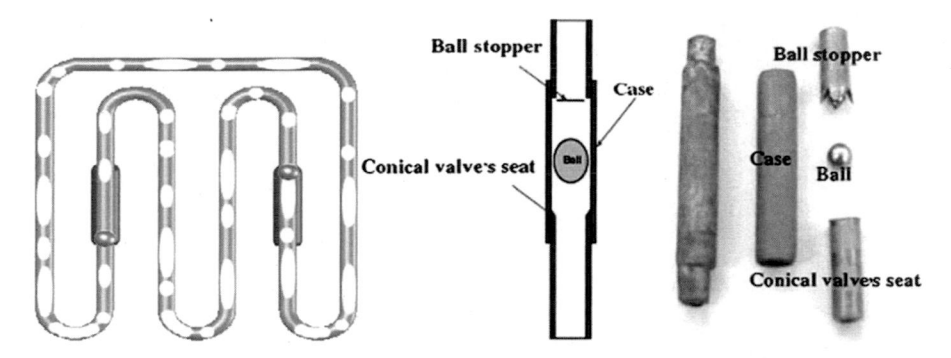

Fig. 8.3 An oscillating heat pipe with check valves (Bhuwakietkumjohn and Rittidech 2010)

Fig. 8.4 A flat-plate OHP
with eight tesla valves
(Thompson et al. 2011a)

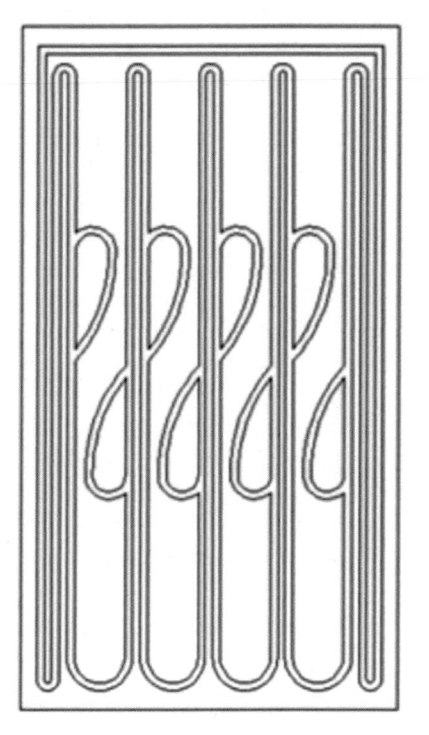

8.3   Working Fluid Selection

Choosing the working fluid is another important factor, which determines OHP performance. When selecting the working fluid, fluid characteristics to consider are as follows: surface tension, thermal conductivity, latent heat, specific heat, and viscosity. Low viscosity reduces the pressure drop; high surface tension increases the maximum channel diameter of the capillary tube; high specific heat of the liquid increases the amount of energy the liquid slugs can transport; high thermal conductivity of the liquid allows the heat to quickly transfer into and out of the liquid; high latent heat increases the amount of energy moved via phase change; low density of the liquid phase reduces the effect of gravity; and high $\partial p/\partial T$ causes increased pressure variations within the OHP. These considerations will increase the oscillation motion and, in turn, transfer high heat for a better performance. While higher surface tension enables a larger channel diameter, which can help to reduce pressure drop due to frictional force, when surface tension increases, the force acting on the wall increases, which will have a negative effect on the oscillating motion and heat transfer in an OHP. Latent heat affects the evaporation rate of the fluid. The oscillation motion of the liquid is started and maintained by the vapor pressure difference between the evaporator and condenser. Thus, to maintain the oscillation motion, higher vapor pressure at the evaporator and lower vapor pressure in the condenser are required. Therefore, a higher $\partial p/\partial T$ can help start up and maintain the oscillation motion. Thermal conductivity directly affects OHP performance because a higher thermal conductivity can help increase both evaporation and condensation heat transfer, and at the same time, it can help the forced convection heat transfer due to the oscillation motion of the bulk fluid (sensible heat). Thus, the fluid that has higher thermal conductivity is preferred for better performance. Specific heat is important in determining the amount of heat transferred from the evaporator to the condenser by forced convection of the bulk liquid. Since forced convection of the bulk liquid (sensible heat) is more responsible than evaporation and condensation (latent heat) to determine the performance of OHP, higher specific heat is preferred to achieve better performance. The viscosity affects the pressure drop in the channel. When the fluid flows in the channel, it encounters shear stress causing pressure drop. To overcome pressure drop and maintain oscillation motion, more powerful pumping power is required by supplying higher heat input. When designing an OHP, it is important to make the working fluid oscillate at a lower temperature difference between the evaporator and condenser. This means that the OHP needs to be designed to work at the lower heat input; otherwise, it will stop working when the heat input does not meet the requirement to maintain oscillation. Thus, low viscosity of the fluid is preferred to achieve higher performance. Filling ratio is the volume ratio of the working fluid to the total volume of the channel. An accurate amount of working fluid needs to be charged because when it is overcharged there might not be enough vapor bubbles to pump the liquid and create oscillations. When it is undercharged, there might not be enough convective liquid to carry the heat from the evaporator to the condenser or

Table 8.1 Fluid thermal properties

	Freezing point (°C)	Boiling point (°C)	Critical temperature (°C)
Acetone	−94[a]	56[a]	235[a]
Ammonia	−78[a]	−33[b]	132[a]
Dowtherm A	12[c]	257.1[c]	497[c]
Ethanol	−114[a]	78[a]	241[a]
FC-72	−90 (pour point)[d]	56[d]	176 (estimated)[d]
Isopropyl alcohol	−88[a]	82[a]	236[a]
Methanol	−97[a]	65[a]	240[a]
R-114	−93[a]	3[a]	145[a]
R-123	−107[e]	27.8[e]	184[a]
R-142b	−131[a]	−10[a]	137[a]
Toluene	−95[a]	111[a]	320[a]
Water	0[a]	100[a]	374[a]

[a]Lemmon et al. (2005)
[b]Arima et al. (2003)
[c]The Dow Chemical Company (2001)
[d]3M (2000)
[e]Arkema Inc. (2004)

all the liquid could evaporate causing dryout. Although Yin et al. (2014) calculated the upper limitation of a filling ratio, no exact equation exists to determine the best filling ratio for a given working fluid and OHP. Some experimental research has offered ways to determine different filling ratios that lead to the best performance. However, each OHP has a different case-by-case experimental setup. Number of turns and the evaporator/condenser size are also important considerations when selecting a working fluid.

Selecting the correct working fluid is an integral to the success of the OHP design process. The selection must balance the properties of the fluid with the desired channel diameter, operating temperature range, material compatibility, and any surface enhancements. In general, the fluid must have a chemically stable liquid and vapor phase and be saturated in the desired operating temperature range (Table 8.1). The OHP working fluid selection is similar to the method used for conventional heat pipes. In addition to the pure fluids, a wide variety of nanofluids have been found to work well in OHPs.

8.4 Material Selection

The materials used in the construction of an oscillating heat pipe are crucial to its thermal performance and operating life. Gas generation can occur when there is an incompatibility between the working fluid and the materials inside of the OHP. This is avoided by selecting compatible materials. For instance, stainless steel and water will typically generate hydrogen gas; however, if the stainless steel is passivated,

then gas will not be generated and is, therefore, compatible. Another common combination that produces hydrogen gas is aluminum and water. The materials in contact with the working fluid must be chemically compatible throughout the required temperature range. Table 8.2 provides a list of compatible fluids and the temperature at which they were tested. If corrosion occurs, this could reduce the integrity of the OHP envelope, generate noncondensable gases inside of the OHP, alter the contact angle, and foul the fluid. The material must also be compatible with the surrounding environment. The material selection requirements for an oscillating heat pipe are similar to those for a conventional heat pipe or heat exchanger. Oscillating heat pipes are typically manufactured from copper or aluminum due to the high thermal conductivity and chemical compatibility with common working fluids.

Outgassing is the release of gas from a material over time. This could be from interstitial molecules or chemical reactions. Interstitial molecules are small molecules that fit within the lattice of the material. In many grades of copper there is a significant amount of interstitial oxygen. This oxygen can slowly flow into the OHP interior. To eliminate this issue, oxygen-free copper must be used to insure a consistent long-term performance of an OHP (Joseph et al. 1999). Outgassing due to chemical reactions is a significant issue especially with adhesives. Many types of adhesives cure by evaporation of a volatile chemical or by chemical reactions that release gases. In addition to this, adhesives and other polymers have a higher leak rate than most metals and ceramics. The use of adhesives in OHPs should be avoided.

8.5   Heat Pipe Fabrication

The two most common designs for the OHP are tubular and flat plate (Fig. 8.5). The tubular OHP is constructed out of a tube that is bent into a serpentine pattern between the evaporator and condenser regions. This design is easy to construct, but it is not compact, and the curved surface of the tube might be difficult to match with the evaporator and/or condenser surface geometries. Therefore, filler material is necessary to provide a thermal contact. In many instances, this is a flat metal plate with the tube embedded in semicircular grooves machined into the surface. This extra material increases the thermal resistance of the OHP and fabrication cost. The flat-plate OHP design is made out of a plate of material. The channels are fabricated into the plate and a cover plate is required to seal the surface of the OHP. The flat plate design is more compact and is easier to match the required surface geometries of the evaporator and condenser.

Table 8.2 Compatibility of working fluids and structural materials

	Acetone	Ammonia	Dowtherm A	Methanol	Toluene	Water
Aluminum	N (80 °C)[a]	Y (excellent)[b]	Y (good, diphenyl oxide, 22 °C)[c]	Y (excellent)[b]	Y (137 °C)[d]	N (227 °C)[e]
Copper	Y[f]	Y[g]	N (200 °C)[d]	Y[f]	Y (excellent)[c]	Y[f]
Mild steel	Y (excellent)[b]	Y (excellent)[b]	Y (240–250 °C)[e] Y (250, 270 °C) N (300 °C)[d]	Y (good)[b]	Y (250 °C)[d]	Y (poor)[b]
Stainless steel 304	Y (good)[b]	Y (good)	Y (253–400 °C)[e]	Y (excellent)[b]	Y (excellent)[b]	Y (with passivation)[f]
Stainless steel 316	Y (excellent)[b]	Y (excellent)[b]	Y (excellent, diphenyl oxide)[c]	Y (excellent)[b]	Y (250 °C)[d]	Y (with passivation)[f]
Titanium	Y (good)[b]	Y (good)[b]	Y (270 °C) N (406 °C)[d]	Y (good)[b]	Y (250 °C)[d]	Y (200, 250 °C)[e]

[a]Hsieh et al. (2014)
[b]Habonim (2013)
[c]Cole-Parner (2014)
[d]Anderson et al. (2013)
[e]Anderson et al. (2007)
[f]Faghri (2014)
[g]UK Copper Board (2014)

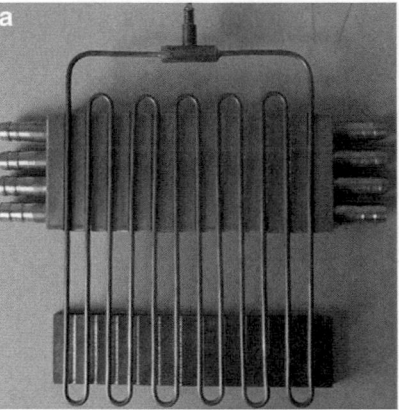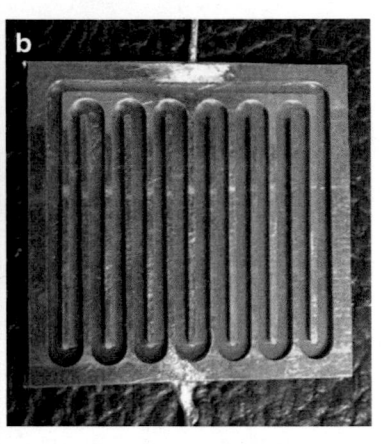

Fig. 8.5 A tubular OHP with (**a**) a single charging tube and (**b**) an interior view of a flat-plate OHP with two charging tubes

8.6 Leak Detection

Oscillating heat pipes are designed for long-term use; therefore, even small leaks, outgassing, and gas generation can eventually alter the performance. After initial charging, oscillating heat pipes do not have a mechanism to remove noncondensable gases. Therefore, the operating life of the OHP is partially determined by the rate at which the noncondensable gasses fill the interior of the OHP. During manufacturing special care must be taken to eliminate all sources of leaks. Several leak testing methods exist that range from finding bulk leaks to miniscule leaks. This can involve either pressurizing the OHP or pulling a vacuum on the OHP. The leaks detected from either positive or negative gauge pressure generally are similar. However, it is possible for the stresses and flexing of the OHP, due to the pressures exerted, to produce leaks that only exist in one of the situations.

Bubble testing is a simple method of detecting a leak in an OHP. The OHP is submerged under water and pressurized with gas. The surface of the OHP is monitored for bubbles. A variation is to put a soapy solution on the outside of a dry OHP while pressurizing it. This method can be used to find bulk leaks.

Gas thermal conductivity leak testing is a more accurate method of finding a leak. The OHP is connected to a vacuum pump with a Pirani vacuum sensor inline between them (Fig. 8.6a). The Pirani vacuum sensor detects pressure by measuring the heat loss from a hot wire. As the pressure decreases, the number of molecules colliding with the hot wire decreases and, therefore, less heat is lost from the wire, and the wire's temperature rises. This sensor is also dependent on the thermal conductivity of the gas in the tube. For detecting a leak in an OHP, the vacuum is applied until the pressure remains constant. Then a gas with significantly different thermal conductivity is blown onto different locations of the OHP. When the gas

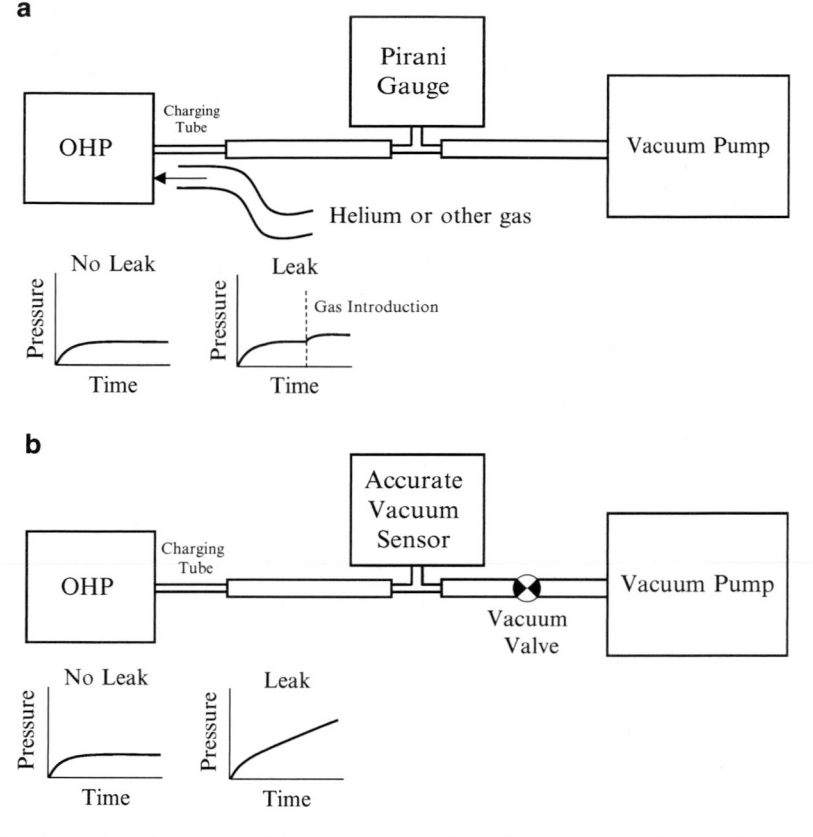

Fig. 8.6 Leak detection using (**a**) Pirani gauge method and (**b**) the pressure rise with time method

arrives at the Pirani sensor, the pressure reading will change substantially. This is an indication that a leak has been detected. This process should be done slowly due to the vacuum conductance between the leak and the Pirani sensor.

Another sensitive method to determine if an OHP is leaking is to monitor the pressure rise with time in the OHP. This is done by placing a sensitive vacuum sensor between the OHP and the vacuum pump (Fig. 8.6b). A high quality vacuum valve is also placed inline between the vacuum sensor and the vacuum pump. First the vacuum is pulled until the pressure is constant. Then the valve is closed. If the system is hermetically sealed, the pressure in the system will rise slightly and then remain constant. If there is a leak, the pressure will continuously rise. This method can be used to determine if the OHP has large or miniscule leaks; however, the location of the leak cannot be determined. And leaks in the vacuum system between the OHP and the valve will be detected as well. Therefore, this method is more difficult to use.

The most accurate method for measuring leaks is via a helium leak detector. A helium leak detector uses a mass spectrometer tuned to only detect helium and is

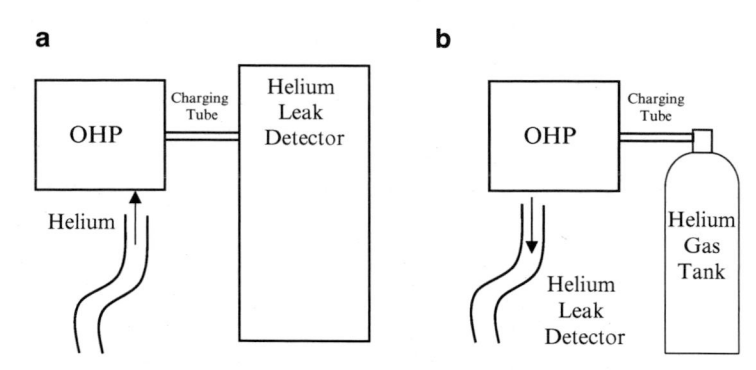

Fig. 8.7 Experimental setup of leak detection with a helium leak detector using (**a**) a vacuum or (**b**) pressure

able to detect very small concentrations of atoms. The detector uses helium as the gas because it is a small inert molecule that has a very small natural abundance in the atmosphere. Two methods for leak detection are generally used (Fig. 8.7). The first method is to use the helium leak detector to pull a high vacuum on the OHP. Helium is blown at the OHP through a tube with a small orifice. The tube is directed at different locations along the OHP to detect the exact location of the leak. This should be done slowly due to the conductance time between the OHP and the helium leak detector. The other method is to pressurize the OHP with helium and direct a small sniffer nozzle at the suspected leak spots of the OHP. The sniffer nozzle is attached to the helium leak detector. As the helium leaks from the OHP, the helium will be pulled into the nozzle and be detected.

8.7   Charging System

Charging an OHP involves removing all fluids from the interior of the OHP and filling it with the desired amount of working fluid. Even trace amounts of noncondensable gases or other fluids can significantly alter the thermal performance of the OHP. To achieve this, a charging system is needed that can

1. Remove all existing liquids and gases from the interior of the OHP
2. Place the required amount of working fluid inside the OHP
3. Verify the correct amount placed inside
4. Permanently seal the OHP

A typical charging system includes a vacuum pump, vacuum gauge, mass balance, container with the working fluid, pinch-off tool, and an attachment mechanism to the OHP (Fig. 8.8). The vacuum pump is used to remove all fluid from the interior of the OHP. Once all fluid is removed, the working fluid is introduced into the evacuated OHP. The mass change is monitored as the working

Fig. 8.8 Photo of a charging system

fluid is added or removed. Once the correct mass has been achieved, the OHP is hermetically sealed.

The charging system and process must be able to evacuate all noncondensable gases, condensable gases, and liquids from the interior of the OHP. It must also be able to handle the presence of liquids in addition to gases. Because a perfect vacuum pump does not exist, a back-filling process (please see below for the detailed procedure) is recommended which can achieve a perfect "vacuum" condition, i.e., only pure working fluid exists in the heat pipe, and at the same time, it can help to degas working fluid. The vacuuming step should have a roughing vacuum of 1×10^{-3} Torr or better for a back-filling process. Liquids and condensable vapors entering the vacuum pump will ruin the ultimate pressure of the vacuum pump, water vapor will rust parts of the vacuum pump, and some hydrocarbons can degrade the seals in the pump. Certain types of vacuum pumps are designed to pump condensable vapors; however, these are more expensive and typically have an ultimate pressure that is significantly less than that of a comparable rotary vane vacuum pump. It is better to place a cold trap between the vacuum pump and the rest of the charging system. By using liquid nitrogen or dry ice, the liquid and vapor is frozen to the cold trap before it arrives at the vacuum pump. The cold trap can also improve the ultimate pressure of the system by capturing oil back streaming from the pump.

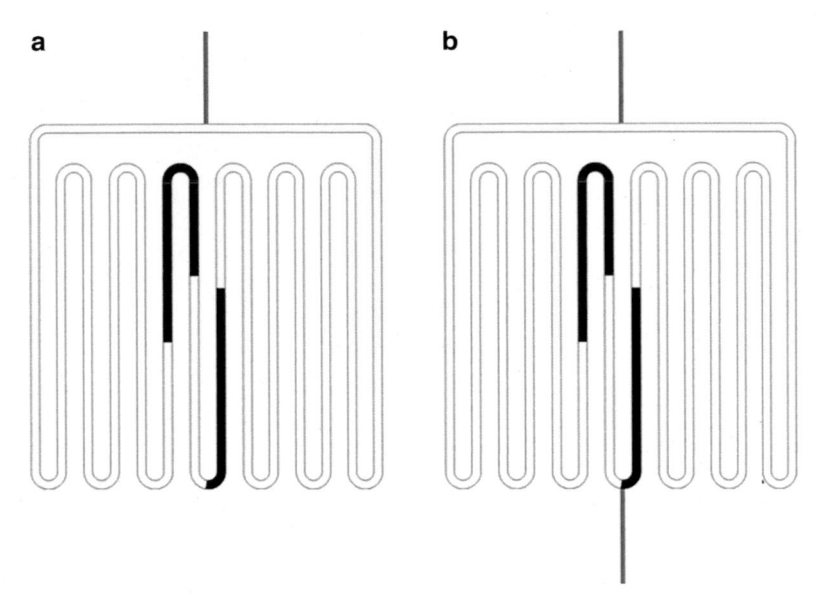

Fig. 8.9 The typical arrangement for the charging tube with (**a**) a single or (**b**) double charging tubes

   The charging tube is typically a small diameter tube used to minimize the internal volume of fluid and to make hermetic sealing easier. This tube is ideally made out of pure copper annealed in a hydrogen atmosphere to remove all oxide. A pinch-off tool is then used to seal the tube by plastically extruding the pinched region and forming a cold weld. The pinched-off tube must be protected from physical damage and not be subject to wide variations in temperature. As an added level of sealing, the tube end can be soldered. In many instances a single charging tube is used in the OHP (Fig. 8.9a). This charging tube is typically located in the condenser section so that it is predominately filled with liquid during the operation of the OHP. A liquid is incompressible and, therefore, does not affect the performance as significantly as a vapor bubble. A single charging tube has the disadvantage that all liquid must be pulled out of the OHP in one restricted location and the ultimate vacuum pressure in the OHP is measured after the constriction of the charging tube. Two charging tubes makes it easier to remove all fluid from the OHP, flush the OHP with a cleaning fluid, and measure the vacuum within the OHP (Fig. 8.9b). One charging tube is connected to the vacuum pump and the other charging tube is connected to the working fluid reservoir and the vacuum sensor. Placing the vacuum sensor across the OHP from the vacuum pump gives a more reliable measurement of the vacuum achieved inside of the OHP. The working fluid can also be pulled through the OHP during charging which is more efficient than the single charging tube method.

   If liquid exists within the OHP, applying a vacuum to the OHP will remove the bulk of the liquid; however, some liquid plugs will remain within the OHP.

Table 8.3 Literature review of vacuum pressures achieved during charging

Source	Vacuum pressure	Bake temperature	Time
Khandekar et al. (2009)	7.5×10^{-5} Torr	N/A	N/A
Song and Xu (2009)	7.5×10^{-4} Torr	150 °C	8 h
Lin et al. (2008)	6×10^{-2} Torr	N/A	N/A
Li and Yan (2008)	37.5 Torr	N/A	N/A
Lin et al. (2009)	7.5 Torr	N/A	N/A
Wang et al. (2009)	>7.5 Torr	N/A	N/A
Xu et al. (2005)	7.5×10^{-4} Torr	100 °C	8 h
Fumoto and Kawaji (2009)	−735.06 Torr (gauge)	N/A	N/A
Tong et al. (2001)	1.0×10^{-5} Torr	N/A	N/A
Kim et al. (2003)	1.0×10^{-3} Torr	N/A	N/A
Hemadri et al. (2011)	7.5×10^{-5} Torr	N/A	N/A
Kumar Saha et al. (2011)	7.5×10^{-5} Torr	N/A	N/A
Mameli et al. (2011)	7.5×10^{-5} Torr	N/A	N/A
Riehl and dos Santos (2012)	7.5×10^{-6} Torr	N/A	24 h

These remaining liquid plugs only leave via evaporation. The capillary nature of the OHP means that the evaporative surface area is only the surface area of the two menisci exposed to the vacuum. In addition, the small size of the charging tube results in a very low vacuum conductance. Therefore, the complete evacuation of an OHP can take a significant amount of time. This amount of time will vary by the OHP geometry, the fluid properties, and temperature. To verify that all liquid has been removed from the OHP, the current weight can be compared to the empty weight of the OHP or the pressure is constant when the OHP is heated. Heating will increase the desorption rate of liquid films on the interior surfaces of the OHP and speed their evacuation from the OHP. In literature, a wide range of ultimate vacuum pressures have been used and few elevate the temperature (Table 8.3).

A mass balance can be used to verify the filling ratio in an OHP. The filling ratio, ϕ, is defined as the percentage of charged liquid volume, V_l, to the total volume, V_t, inside of the OHP, i.e.,

$$\phi = \frac{V_l}{V_t} \qquad (8.1)$$

The volume of the liquid is difficult to determine in an OHP. Therefore, the filling ratio equation can be adapted for mass measurements if the density of the fluid is known at the charging system temperature. First the total volume of the OHP must be determined. This could be determined either from the OHP design specifications or by measuring the volume. Therefore, the total volume of the OHP can be determined by measuring the mass of the empty OHP, m_{empty}, and the mass of a 100 % charged OHP, m_{full}, the known density of the liquid, ρ_{liquid}, i.e.,

$$V_t = \frac{m_{full} - m_{empty}}{\rho_{liquid}} \tag{8.2}$$

The volume of charged liquid can be found in a similar way assuming the mass of the vapor phase is negligible:

$$V_1 = \frac{m_{charged} - m_{empty}}{\rho_{liquid}} \tag{8.3}$$

where $m_{charged}$ is the charged mass of the OHP. A mass balance of sufficient accuracy must be used to determine the filling ratio. It is important to remove all noncondensable gases from the OHP and the working fluid. One way that this can be accomplished is by pulling a vacuum over the working fluid reservoir to initiate boiling. The initial bubbles generated contain the noncondensable gas. After the initial bubbles, the bubble generation rate subsides. This indicates that the noncondensable gas has been removed from the fluid. The charging fluid must then be pushed into the OHP without reintroducing the noncondensable gas.

The typical charging procedure using the back-filling process on a single charging tube OHP with a vacuum flask to degas the fluid (Fig. 8.10a) is summarized in the following steps:

1. Fill the vacuum flask with a sufficient amount of charging fluid.
2. Seal the vacuum flask and insert a stiff tube through the septa or rubber stopper in the top. The tube tip should be in the vapor phase.
3. Close valves 4 and 1 and open valves 2 and 3.
4. Turn the stirring plate on full stirring speed and turn the vacuum pump on.
5. Use a vacuum to remove the gas and lower the pressure within the vacuum flask. Wait for the initial bubbles containing the noncondensable gas to leave the liquid.
6. Close valve 3.
7. Turn off the stirring plate.
8. Lower the stiff tube to the bottom of the flask, well below the fluid surface.
9. Briefly open valve 3 to fill the tubing between the flask and valve 3 with liquid.
10. When the tubing is filled, close valve 3.
11. Wait until the vacuum sensor shows that the system has returned to its ultimate vacuum.
12. Open valve 1 to empty the OHP of noncondensable gas or the previous working fluid.
13. Wait until the OHP is dry by monitoring the vacuum sensor. Heat can be applied to the OHP to accelerate the process.
14. Detach the OHP from the vacuum system.
15. Weigh the OHP to determine the empty mass, m_{empty}. If the mass is different from the expected value, there might be liquid remaining within the OHP and step 13 should be repeated.

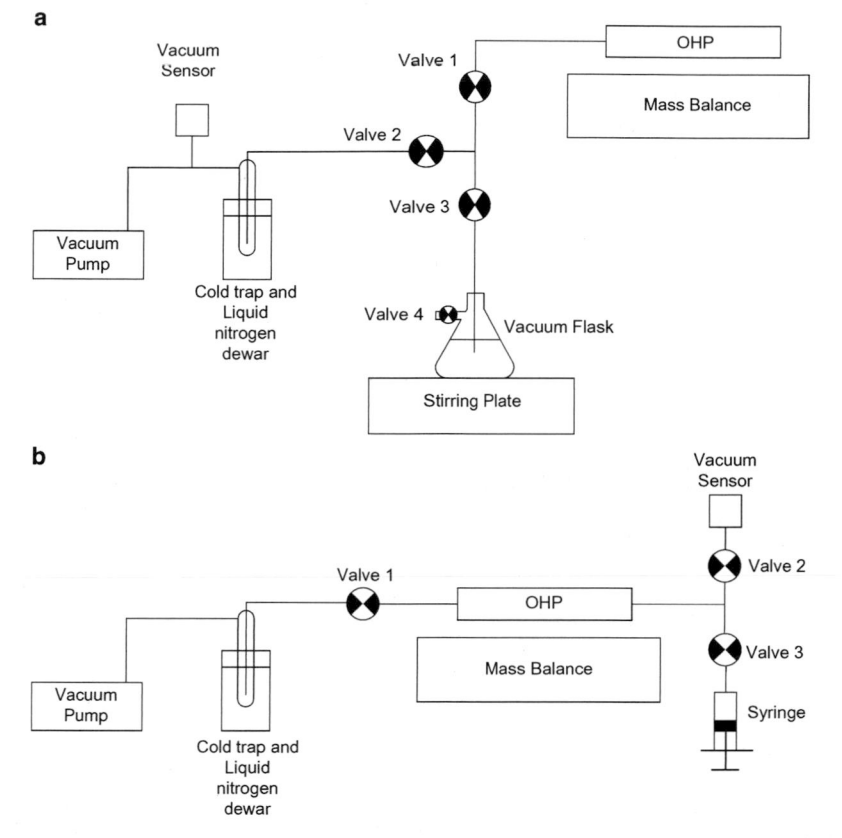

Fig. 8.10 Charging systems for (**a**) a single charging tube OHP and (**b**) a double charging tube OHP

16. Attach the OHP to the vacuum system.
17. Wait until the system returns to its ultimate vacuum.
18. Close valve 2.
19. Open valve 3 slightly for a low flow rate.
20. Monitor the OHP mass.
21. When the OHP reaches the mass of the specified filling ratio, hermetically seal the OHP charging tube.
22. Detach the OHP from the vacuum system.
23. Reweigh the OHP and include any portion of the charging tube that was removed in the sealing process.
24. Apply solder to the pinched-off end of the charging tube to ensure no leakage.

The charging procedure using the back-filling process on a double charging tube OHP with a syringe of the working fluid (Fig. 8.10b) can be accomplished by the following steps:

1. Fill the syringe with a sufficient amount of working fluid
2. Use a vacuum to pull on the fluid in the syringe until all bubbles are removed. The plunger must be held to allow the pressure to drop and the syringe must be vertical with the charging tip up to allow the noncondensable bubbles to escape. It is typically more difficult to remove the bubbles this way than to using the vacuum flask.
3. Close valves 2 and 3 and leave valve 1 open.
4. Turn the vacuum pump on.
5. Briefly open valve 3 to fill the tubing between the syringe and valve 3 with liquid.
6. Close valve 3.
7. Wait until all liquid is gone from the system.
8. Open valve 2 to measure the vacuum.
9. Wait until the vacuum sensor shows that the system and the OHP has returned to its ultimate vacuum. Heat can be applied to the OHP to accelerate the process.
10. Detach the OHP from the vacuum system.
11. Weigh the OHP to determine the empty mass, m_{empty}.
12. Attach the OHP to the vacuum system.
13. Wait until the system returns to its ultimate vacuum.
14. Close valves 1 and 2.
15. Open valve 3 slightly for a low flow rate.
16. Monitor the OHP mass.
17. When the OHP reaches the mass of the specified filling ratio, hermetically seal the OHP charging tubes.
18. Detach the OHP from the vacuum system.
19. Reweigh the OHP and include any portions of the charging tubes that were removed in the sealing process.
20. Apply solder to the pinched-off end of the charging tube to ensure no leakage.

8.8 Experimental Setup and Procedure

OHP performance is determined by testing it over the expected operating temperature range. Most commonly the OHP is tested by applying a constant heat flux to the evaporator region and a constant temperature to the condenser region. Multiple temperature sensors are attached to the OHP, and the OHP is thermally insulated to ensure all heat flows from the evaporator to the condenser. The OHP is also aligned with respect to gravity. The constant heat flux is the easiest to apply using an electric heater. The voltage and current of the heater is measured to determine the heat flux of the OHP. The condenser is kept at a constant temperature using a cold

plate cooled by a temperature-controlled circulator. High thermal conductivity paste is used where necessary to reduce contact resistance. Temperature sensors are attached to the surface of the OHP above the channels. These temperature sensors are typically thermocouples due to their low cost, small size, and fast thermal response. The OHP temperature is nonuniform from turn to turn; therefore, thermocouples should be used to measure multiple turns. Ideally the temperature in the condenser and evaporator of every turn is measured. If there are too many turns for a tubular OHP or for a flat-plate OHP, thermocouple location should be determined by area-weighted calculation.

Both transient and steady state tests should be conducted for a heat pipe. For heat pipes, however, the steady state test is given the highest priority. A typical experimental system for a heat pipe, similar to the one shown in Fig. 8.11, would normally be used. The test facility shown in Fig. 8.11 consists of the heat pipe, a power supply and measuring unit, a cooling unit, a data acquisition unit (DAQ) for the temperature measurements, and a personal computer (PC). The operating temperature of the heat pipe can be controlled by a cooling block connected to a cooling bath, where the temperature of the coolant is maintained at a constant temperature of a designed operating temperature. The heat source is directly connected to the evaporator. Power input can be supplied by an AC or DC power supply and recorded by a multimeter with signals sent directly to a PC which can be used to control the entire system. The heat source should be well insulated to reduce convective losses. A number of temperature sensors are attached to the heat pipe surfaces to measure the temperature distribution and variation with the power

Fig. 8.11 A typical experimental setup of an OHP experiment

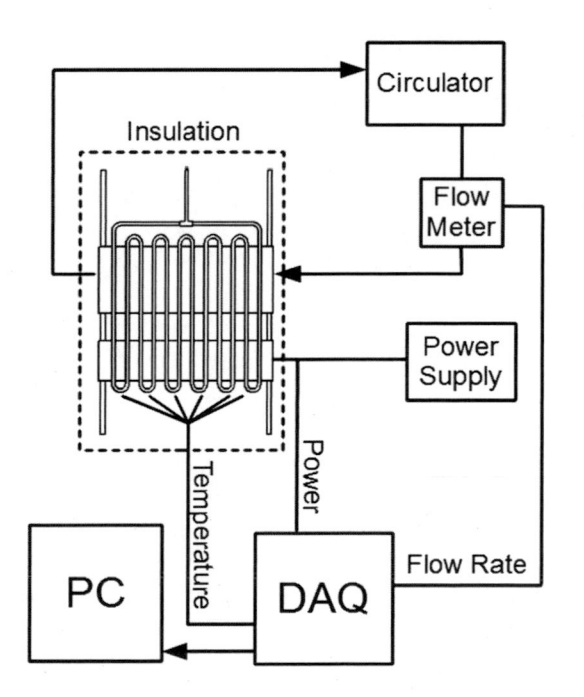

input. All of the measured data are sent to the data acquisition system controlled by a personal computer. Prior to the start of the experiment, the system is allowed to equilibrate and reach steady state such that the temperatures of the cooling media and the heat pipe are constant. When this desired steady state condition is obtained, the input power is then increased in small increments. Tests indicate that a time of approximately 5–30 min is necessary to reach steady state. To obtain the data for the next successive power level, the power is incremented every 5–30 min. During the tests, the power input and the temperature data are simultaneously recorded using a data acquisition system controlled by a personal computer.

References

3M (2000) Fluorinert: electronic liquid FC-72, 3M

Anderson WG, Hartenstine JR, Sarraf DB, Tarau C (2007) Intermediate temperature fluids for heat pipes and loop heat pipes. In: Proceedings of the international energy conversion engineering conference, St. Louis, MO

Anderson WG, Tamanna S, Tarau C, Hartenstine JR, Ellis D (2013) Intermediate temperature heat pipe life tests and analyses. In: 43rd international conference on environmental systems (ICES 2013), Vail, CO

Arima H, Monde M, Mitsutake Y (2003) Heat transfer in pool boiling of ammonia/water mixture. Heat Mass Transf 39(7):535–543

Arkema Inc. (2004) Material safety data sheet. Arkema, Paris

Bhuwakietkumjohn N, Rittidech S (2010) Internal flow patterns on heat transfer characteristics of a closed-loop oscillating heat-pipe with check valves using ethanol and a silver nano-ethanol mixture. Exp Therm Fluid Sci 34(8):1000–1007

Charoensawan P, Khandekar S, Groll M, Terdtoon P (2003) Closed loop pulsating heat pipes part a: parametric experimental investigations. Appl Therm Eng 23(16):2009–2020

Cole-Parmer (2014) Chemical compatibility results. Chemical Compatibility Database

Faghri A (2014) Heat pipes: review, opportunities and challenges. Front Heat Pipes 5(1)

Fumoto K, Kawaji M (2009) Performance improvement in pulsating heat pipes using a self-rewetting fluid. In: 2009 ASME summer heat transfer conference, HT2009, San Francisco, CA, vol 3, pp 359–365

Habonim (2013) Chemical compatibility guide. Habonim

Hathaway AA, Wilson CA, Ma HB (2012) Experimental investigation of uneven-turn water and acetone oscillating heat pipes. J Thermophys Heat Transf 26(1):115–122

Hemadri VA, Gupta A, Khandekar S (2011) Thermal radiators with embedded pulsating heat pipes: infra-red thermography and simulations. Appl Therm Eng 31(6–7):1332–1346

Hsieh J-C, Lin DTW, Huang H-J, Yang T-W (2014) An experimental study on the compatibility of acetone with aluminum flat-plate heat pipes. Heat Mass Transf 50(11):1525–1533

Joseph G, Kundig KJA, I. C. Association (1999) Copper: its trade, manufacture, use, and environmental status. ASM, Materials Park

Khandekar S, Gautam AP, Sharma PK (2009) Multiple quasi-steady states in a closed loop pulsating heat pipe. Int J Therm Sci 48(3):535–546

Kim J-S, Bui N, Kim J-W, Kim J-H, Jung H (2003) Flow visualization of oscillation characteristics of liquid and vapor flow in the oscillating capillary tube heat pipe. J Mech Sci Technol 17(10):1507–1519

Kumar Saha S, Piero Celata G, Kandlikar SG (2011) Thermofluid dynamics of boiling in microchannels. In: Cho YI, Greene GA (eds) Advances in heat transfer, vol 43. Academic, New York, pp 77–226

Lemmon EW, McLinden MO, Friend DG (2005) Thermophysical properties of fluid systems. In: Linstrom PJ, Mallard WG (eds) NIST chemistry WebBook, NIST standard reference database number 69. National Institute of Standards and Technology, Gaithersburg

Li J, Yan L (2008) Experimental research on heat transfer of pulsating heat pipe. J Therm Sci 17 (2):181–185

Lin YH, Kang SW, Chen HL (2008) Effect of silver nano-fluid on pulsating heat pipe thermal performance. Appl Therm Eng 28(11–12):1312–1317

Lin Z, Wang S, Zhang W (2009) Experimental study on microcapsule fluid oscillating heat pipe. Sci China Ser E: Technol Sci 52(6):1601–1606

Mameli M, Khandekar S, Marengo M (2011) Flow patterns and corresponding local heat transfer coefficients in a pulsating heat pipe. In: 29th national heat transfer conference of Italy, Torino, Italy, pp 1–6

Riehl RR, dos Santos N (2012) Water-copper nanofluid application in an open loop pulsating heat pipe. Appl Therm Eng 42:6–10

Song Y, Xu J (2009) Chaotic behavior of pulsating heat pipes. Int J Heat Mass Transf 52 (13–14):2932–2941

The Dow Chemical Company (2001) Dowtherm a: synthetic organic heat transfer fluid-liquid and vapor phase data. The Dow Chemical Company, Midland

Thompson SM, Ma HB, Wilson C (2011a) Investigation of a flat-plate oscillating heat pipe with tesla-type check valves. Exp Therm Fluid Sci 35(7):1265–1273

Thompson SM, Hathaway AA, Smoot CD, Wilson CA, Ma HB, Young RM, Greenberg L, Osick BR, Van Campen S, Morgan BC, Sharar D, Jankowski N (2011b) Robust thermal performance of a flat-plate oscillating heat pipe during high-gravity loading. ASME J Heat Transf 133 (10):1045041–1045045. doi:10.1115/1.4004076

Tong BY, Wong TN, Ooi KT (2001) Closed-loop pulsating heat pipe. Appl Therm Eng 21 (18):1845–1862

UK Copper Board (2014) Guide to the suitability of copper with various chemicals, pp 50

Wang S, Lin Z, Zhang W, Chen J (2009) Experimental study on pulsating heat pipe with functional thermal fluids. Int J Heat Mass Transf 52(21–22):5276–5279

Wilson C, Borgmeyer B, Winholtz RA, Ma HB, Jacobson D, Hussey D (2011) Thermal and visual observation of water and acetone oscillating heat pipes. J Heat Transf 133(6):061502–061505

Xu JL, Li YX, Wong TN (2005) High speed flow visualization of a closed loop pulsating heat pipe. Int J Heat Mass Transf 48(16):3338–3351

Yin D, Rajab H, Ma HB (2014) Theoretical analysis of maximum filling ratio in an oscillating heat pipe. Int J Heat Mass Transf 74:353–357

Chapter 9
Conventional Heat Pipes

9.1 Introduction

The general definition of a heat pipe is defined as a device that utilizes the evaporation heat transfer in its evaporator and the condensation heat transfer in its condenser, in which the vapor flow from the evaporator to condenser is caused by the vapor pressure difference, and the liquid flow from the condenser to the evaporator is produced by capillary force, gravitational force, and/or other forces directly acting on it. The conventional heat pipe basically is referred to as a heat pipe driven by capillary force as shown in Fig. 9.1. A typical conventional heat pipe consists of three sections: an evaporator or heat addition section, an adiabatic section, and a condenser or heat rejection section. When heat is added to the evaporator section of the heat pipe, the heat is transferred through the shell and reaches the liquid. When the liquid in the evaporator section receives enough thermal energy, the liquid vaporizes. The vapor carries the thermal energy through the adiabatic section to the condenser section, where the vapor is condensed into the liquid and releases the latent heat of vaporization. The condensate is pumped back from the condenser to the evaporator by the driving force acting on the liquid.

A number of limitations can affect the return of the working fluid for a typical conventional heat pipe. When the pumping pressure produced by the surface tension cannot overcome the summation of the total pressures, the heat transport occurring in the heat pipe reaches a limit known as the capillary limit. When the heat flux added to the evaporator is sufficiently high, nucleate boiling occurs. The bubbles formed in the wick significantly increase the thermal resistance causing the heat transfer performance to be significantly reduced. More importantly, the bubbles generated in wicks block the return of the working fluid and lead to a dryout of the evaporator, which is known as the boiling limit. The boiling limit plays a key role in a high heat flux heat pipe. When the vapor velocity is high and the cross-sectional area variation of the vapor space in a heat pipe cannot meet the required flow condition, choked flow occurs, and the vapor flow rate will not respond to the amount of heat added in

© Springer Science+Business Media New York 2015
H. Ma, *Oscillating Heat Pipes*, DOI 10.1007/978-1-4939-2504-9_9

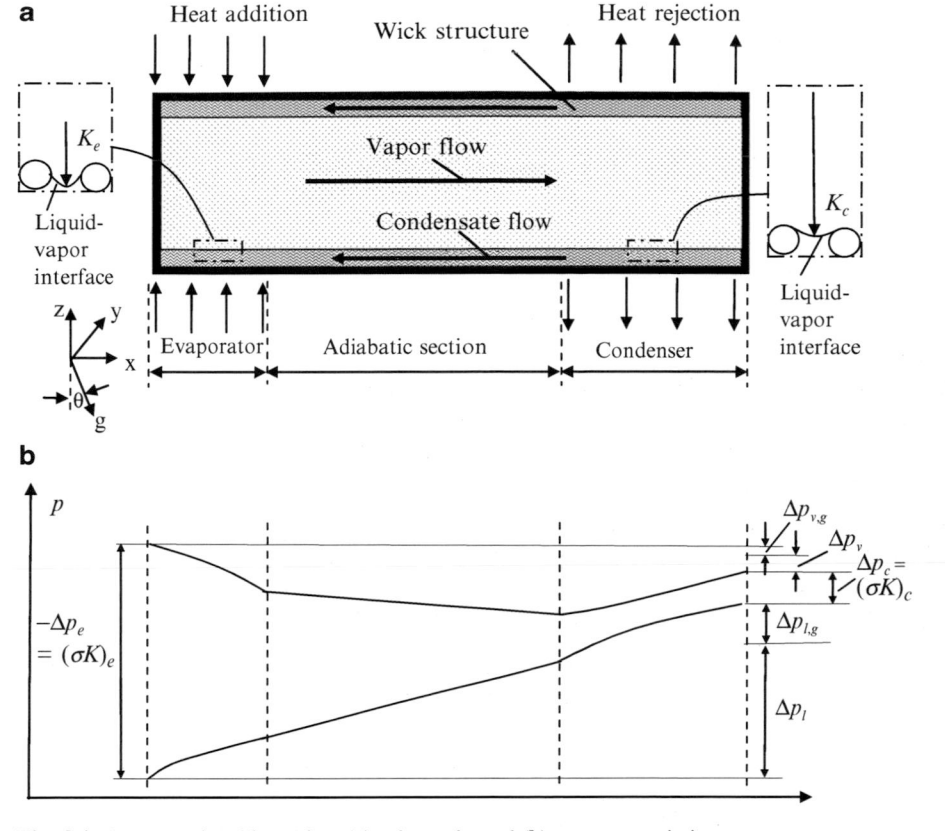

Fig. 9.1 A conventional heat pipe: (**a**) schematic and (**b**) pressure variation

the evaporator. This will lead to a sonic limit. The entrainment limit is due to the frictional shear stresses caused by the vapor flow at the vapor–liquid interface. The viscous limit occurs in a low heat flux heat pipe, where the vapor pressure difference cannot overcome the vapor pressure drop in the vapor phase.

Based on its dimensions, driving force, or structure, the heat pipe can be classified as a micro heat pipe, thermosyphon, loop heat pipe (LHP), high-temperature heat pipe, cryogenic heat pipe, variable conductance heat pipe (VCHP), vapor chamber, rotating heat pipe, and oscillating heat pipe. When the heat pipe dimension becomes very small or the hydraulic radius of the cross section of a heat pipe is similar to the meniscus radius of the liquid–vapor interface, the cornered region can be used to produce the capillary force pumping the condensate from the condenser to the evaporator. This small heat pipe is called a micro heat pipe. When the condensate is pumped back by gravity, the heat pipe is called thermosyphon. If the liquid return is by centrifugal force, the heat pipe is a rotating heat pipe. If the liquid return path is separated from the vapor flow path, the heat pipe is called LHP/capillary pumped loop (CPL). When noncondensable gas is

charged into a heat pipe to achieve a uniform temperature, the heat pipe is called VCHP. A cryogenic heat pipe and a high-temperature heat pipe are named according to the temperature. When a heat pipe has a flat plate shape, it is called a vapor chamber. The oscillation/pulsation motions generated by temperature differences between the evaporator and condenser produce an oscillating heat pipe, which was extensively presented in the preceding chapters of this book. This chapter will present the heat transport limitations of a conventional heat pipe driven by a capillary force followed by an introduction to the basic types of heat pipes and their unique features.

9.2   Capillary Limitation

When heat is added to the evaporator section of a conventional heat pipe, vaporization causes a curvature variation of the liquid–vapor interface, as shown in Fig. 9.1, producing a pressure difference across the liquid–vapor interface in the evaporator, i.e.,

$$\Delta p_e = p_{l,e} - p_{v,e} = -(\sigma K)_e \tag{9.1}$$

where $p_{l,e}$ and $p_{v,e}$ are the liquid pressure and vapor pressure in the evaporator, respectively, and K is the curvature of the liquid–vapor interface in the evaporator, which can be found by

$$K = \frac{1}{r_1} + \frac{1}{r_2} \tag{9.2}$$

where r_1 is the meniscus radius along the x-direction and r_2 is the meniscus radius along the y-direction. The vapor generated in the evaporator flows from the evaporator to the condenser. The pressure variation of the vapor flow from the evaporator to the condenser can be found as

$$\Delta p_v = p_{v,e} - p_{v,c} = f\left(\Delta p_{v,f}, \Delta p_{v,d}\right) \tag{9.3}$$

where $p_{v,c}$ is the vapor pressure in the condenser, $\Delta p_{v,f}$ and $\Delta p_{v,d}$ are the vapor pressure drop and dynamic pressure variation, respectively. Vapor condensation in the condenser makes the curvature of the liquid–vapor interface change, which produces a pressure difference across the liquid–vapor interface in the condenser, i.e.,

$$\Delta p_c = p_{v,c} - p_{l,c} = (\sigma K)_c \tag{9.4}$$

where $p_{l,c}$ is the liquid pressure in the condenser. The condensate flows back from the condenser to the evaporator, which produces a liquid pressure difference from the condenser to the evaporator, i.e.,

$$\Delta p_1 = p_{1,c} - p_{1,e} = f\left(\Delta p_{1,f}, \Delta p_{1,d}\right) \tag{9.5}$$

where $\Delta p_{1,f}$ and $\Delta p_{1,d}$ are the liquid pressure drop and dynamic pressure variation, respectively. If the heat pipe is placed at a titled angle, θ, the gravity directly affects both vapor and liquid flows producing a hydraulic pressure difference, i.e.,

$$\Delta p_g = \Delta p_{v,g} + \Delta p_{1,g} \tag{9.6}$$

For the steady state operation of a heat pipe, the total pressure of the fluid flow in the heat pipe should be equal to zero, i.e.,

$$\sum \Delta p = \Delta p_e + \Delta p_v + \Delta p_1 + \Delta p_c + \Delta p_{v,g} + \Delta p_{1,g} = 0 \tag{9.7}$$

The pressure differences shown in Eqs. (9.1) and (9.4) are due to the curvature variations of liquid–vapor interfaces, which are the driving forces for the fluid flow in the heat pipe. Rearranging Eq. (9.7) yields

$$-\Delta p_e - \Delta p_c = \Delta p_v + \Delta p_1 + \Delta p_g \tag{9.8}$$

Defining

$$\Delta p_C = -\Delta p_e - \Delta p_c \tag{9.9}$$

Equation (9.8) becomes

$$\Delta p_C = \Delta p_v + \Delta p_1 + \Delta p_g \tag{9.10}$$

Considering Eqs. (9.1) and (9.4), Eq. (9.9) can be expressed as

$$\Delta p_C = (\sigma K)_e - (\sigma K)_c \tag{9.11}$$

For a heat pipe to function, the total capillary pressure difference generated by the added heat to the evaporator and removed from the condenser must always be greater than the summation of all pressure losses due to the liquid and vapor flows as shown in Fig. 9.1b. When the heat transfer rate increases, liquid vaporization in the evaporator section makes the liquid recede into the wick structure increasing the capillary pressure. At the same time, when the heat transfer rate increases, pressure losses increase, which will be overcome by the increase of capillary pressure. The continuous increase of the heat transfer rate in a heat pipe will significantly increase pressure losses, and at one heat transfer rate, the total capillary pressure difference is no longer equal or greater than the total pressure losses. This relationship, referred to as the capillary limit, can be expressed mathematically as

$$\Delta p_{C,max} \geq \Delta p_l + \Delta p_v + \Delta p_g \tag{9.12}$$

where $\Delta p_{C,max}$ is the maximum capillary pressure difference generated within the capillary wicking structure. When the maximum capillary pressure difference is equal to or greater than the summation of these pressure drops, the capillary structure is capable of returning an adequate amount of working fluid to prevent dryout of the evaporator wicking structure. This condition varies according to the wicking structure, working fluid, evaporator heat flux, vapor flow channel, and operating temperature.

9.2.1 Capillary Pressure

When the meniscus radius exists at a liquid–vapor interface, there is a pressure difference across the interface, which can be determined by the Laplace–Young equation, i.e.,

$$p_I - p_{II} = \sigma\left(\frac{1}{r_1} + \frac{1}{r_2}\right) \tag{9.13}$$

When a curved surface with a meniscus radius at the liquid–vapor interface takes place, the pressure difference across the liquid–vapor interface exists. For example, when a bubble with a radius of r is formed in liquid (as shown in Fig. 9.2a), the pressure difference between the vapor pressure and liquid pressure across the liquid–vapor interface with a meniscus radius of r can be expressed as

$$p_v - p_l = \sigma\left(\frac{1}{r_1} + \frac{1}{r_2}\right) = \frac{2\sigma}{r} \tag{9.14}$$

where the meniscus radius along the x-direction (on the paper surface), r_1, is equal to the meniscus radius along the y-direction (into the paper), r_2, and both are equal to r. From Eq. (9.14), it can be found that the vapor pressure inside the vapor is higher than the liquid pressure due to the meniscus radius at the liquid–vapor interface. If a round liquid drop with radius r is formed in vapor (as shown in

Fig. 9.2 Pressure differences across liquid–vapor interfaces shown in (**a**) a vapor bubble and (**b**) a liquid drop

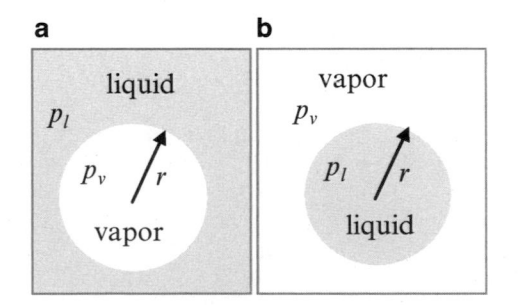

Fig. 9.3 Wicking height
in a capillary tube

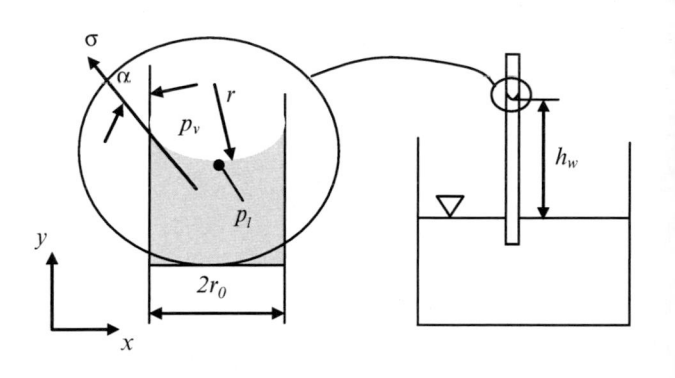

Fig. 9.2b), the pressure difference between the liquid phase and the vapor phase
across the liquid–vapor interface can be found as

$$p_1 - p_v = \sigma\left(\frac{1}{r_1} + \frac{1}{r_2}\right) = \frac{2\sigma}{r} \tag{9.15}$$

When the liquid drop is formed in the vapor phase, the liquid pressure inside the
liquid drop is higher than the vapor pressure.

When a capillary tube with a radius of r_0 is plugged into liquid as shown in
Fig. 9.3, the liquid starts wicking up. If the contact angle is given and the meniscus
radius at the liquid–vapor interface is kept constant, the pressure difference across
the liquid–vapor interface can be found as

$$p_v - p_1 = \sigma\left(\frac{1}{r_1} + \frac{1}{r_2}\right) = \frac{2\sigma}{r} \tag{9.16}$$

where r is the meniscus radius at the liquid–vapor interface. If the meniscus radius
at the liquid–vapor interface is kept constant, the meniscus radius, r, can be directly
related to the radius of the capillary tube, r_0, i.e.,

$$r = \frac{r_0}{\cos \alpha} \tag{9.17}$$

where α is the contact angle. Substituting Eq. (9.17) into Eq. (9.16) yields

$$p_v - p_1 = \frac{2\sigma \cos \alpha}{r_0} \tag{9.18}$$

From Eq. (9.18), it can be found that the liquid pressure at the location indicated by
a black dot in Fig. 9.3 just across the liquid–vapor interface is less than the vapor
pressure, p_v, by $\frac{2\sigma \cos \alpha}{r_0}$. This pressure difference is called the capillary pressure for
this capillary tube. Because the vapor density is much smaller than the liquid

density, the pressure difference due to the vapor weight for the wicking height, h_w, can be neglected. The vapor pressure can be assumed to be uniform. As a result, this pressure difference at the location indicated by the black dot draws liquid up forming a liquid column, which will be used to overcome the weight due to this liquid column, which creates the wicking height, h_w, i.e.,

$$p_v - p_l = \rho_l g h_w \tag{9.19}$$

Combining Eq. (9.18) with Eq. (9.19), the wicking height, h_w, can be found as

$$h_w = \frac{2\sigma \cos \alpha}{r_0 g \rho_l} \tag{9.20}$$

It should be noted that the wicking height determined by Eq. (9.20) is based on an assumption of constant meniscus radius at the liquid–vapor interface. Due to the gravitational force, the meniscus radius at the liquid–vapor interface is not constant. In particular when the tube radius becomes larger, the interface shape will start to vary from a spherical shape, and the interface curvature will be governed by

$$K = \frac{1}{r_1} + \frac{1}{r_2} \tag{9.21}$$

where

$$\frac{1}{r_1} = \frac{\frac{d^2 y}{dx^2}}{\left(1 + \left(\frac{dy}{dx}\right)^2\right)^{3/2}} \tag{9.22}$$

$$\frac{1}{r_2} = \frac{\frac{dy}{dx}}{\left(1 + \left(\frac{dy}{dx}\right)^2\right)^{1/2}} \tag{9.23}$$

Considering Eqs. (9.21), (9.22) and (9.23), the equation governing the wicking height for the capillary tube can be found by

$$\rho_l g y = \sigma \left[\frac{\frac{d^2 y}{dx^2}}{\left(1 + \left(\frac{dy}{dx}\right)^2\right)^{3/2}} + \frac{\frac{dy}{dx}}{\left(1 + \left(\frac{dy}{dx}\right)^2\right)^{1/2}} \right] \tag{9.24}$$

Unfortunately, it has not been possible to obtain an explicit solution to Eq. (9.24) in terms of wick height, which is the usual experimental parameter. However, Adamson (1990) presented an approximate solution with high accuracy compared with experimental data as follows

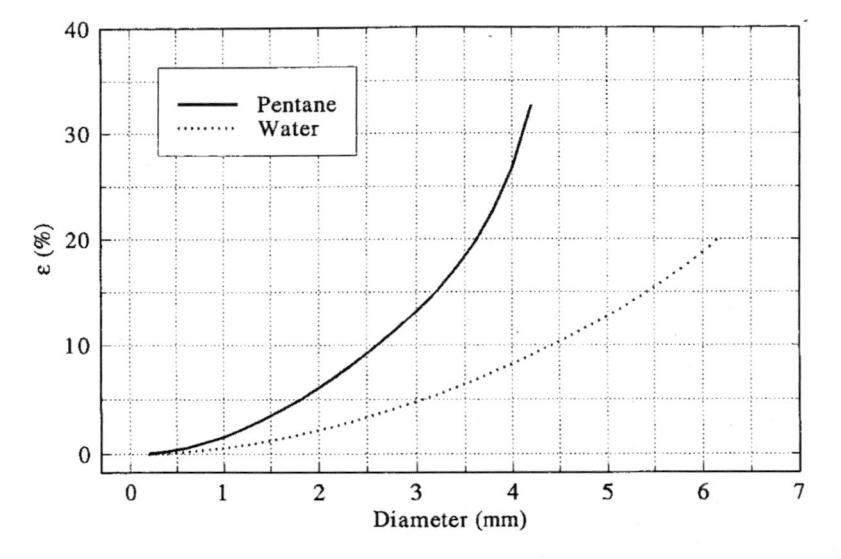

Fig. 9.4 Tube radius effect on the validity of the constant meniscus radius assumption (Ma et al. 1998)

$$\frac{2\sigma}{\rho_l g} = r_0 \left(h_w + \frac{r_0}{3} - \frac{0.1288 r_0^2}{h_w} + \frac{0.1312 r_0^3}{h_w^2} \right) \tag{9.25}$$

where it is assumed that the contact angle is equal to zero. To better illustrate the tube radius effect on the assumption of the constant meniscus radius, let $h_{w,simple}$ express the results predicted by Eq. (9.20) with the assumption of constant meniscus radius and $h_{w,actual}$ be predicted by Eq. (9.25). The relative error can be found as

$$\varepsilon = \frac{h_{w,simple} - h_{w,actual}}{h_{w,actual}} \tag{9.26}$$

As shown in Fig. 9.4, it can be found that when the tube diameter is small, the results obtained by Eq. (9.20), where it is assumed that the meniscus radius of curvature is constant, have very good agreement with the prediction obtained by Eq. (9.25) (Ma et al. 1998), and the largest relative error is less than 5.0 % for liquid pentane at a temperature of 20 °C. Figure 9.4 also shows results for liquid water at a temperature of 20 °C, and for water, the tube diameter can reach up to 3.0 mm with the same relative error of 5.0 %. Obviously, the fluid properties will directly affect the validation of the constant meniscus radius assumption. To generalize the analysis, the Bond number, i.e.,

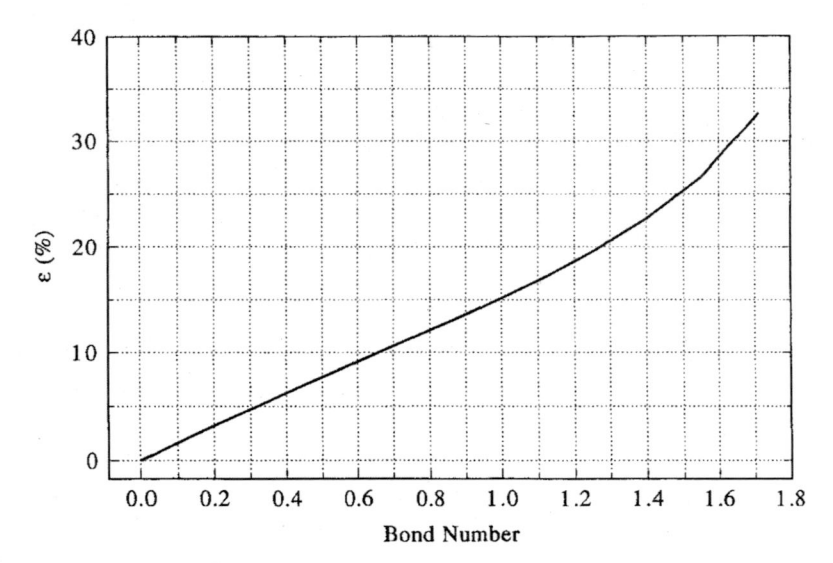

Fig. 9.5 Bond number effect on the validity of the constant meniscus radius assumption (Ma et al. 1998)

$$Bo = \frac{\rho_l g r_0^2}{\sigma} \tag{9.27}$$

should be used to judge the validity of the assumption of constant meniscus radius. Replotting Fig. 9.4 with the Bond number as shown in Fig. 9.5, it can be found that when the Bond number is less than 0.3, the relative error will be less than 5.0 %. It can be concluded that the calculation with a constant meniscus radius assumption can be valid only when the Bond number is less than 0.3 for the calculation of the wicking height in a capillary tube as shown in Fig. 9.3.

For a microgroove as shown in Fig. 9.6, if the meniscus radius at location 0 is r_1 and the meniscus radius at location L is r_2, the pressure differences across the liquid–vapor interfaces at locations 0 and L can be found as

$$p_v - p_{1,0} = \sigma \left(\frac{1}{r_1} + \frac{1}{r_0} \right) \tag{9.28}$$

$$p_v - p_{1,L} = \sigma \left(\frac{1}{r_1} + \frac{1}{r_L} \right) \tag{9.29}$$

respectively, where it is assumed that the vapor pressure is uniform. Because the meniscus radius along the x-direction is infinity, i.e., $r_1 = \infty$, Eqs. (9.28) and (9.29) can be rewritten as

Fig. 9.6 Capillary pressure
in a microgroove

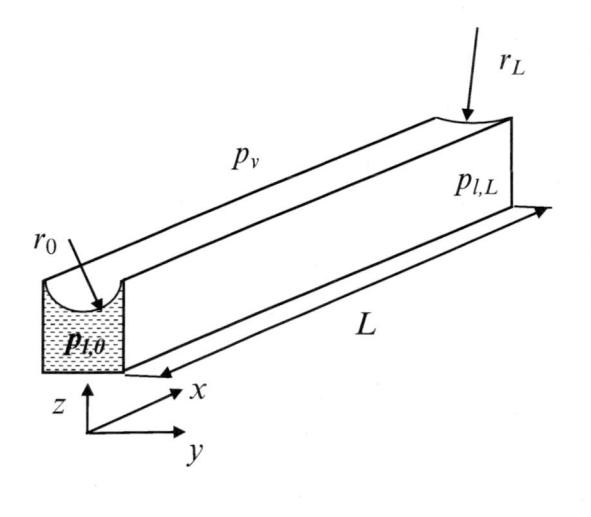

$$p_v - p_{1,0} = \frac{\sigma}{r_0} \tag{9.30}$$

$$p_v - p_{1,L} = \frac{\sigma}{r_L} \tag{9.31}$$

respectively. Equation (9.30) minus Eq. (9.31) yields

$$p_{1,L} - p_{1,0} = \sigma\left(\frac{1}{r_0} - \frac{1}{r_L}\right) \tag{9.32}$$

Because the meniscus radius at location 0 is smaller than that at location L, the term on the left side of Eq. (9.32) is larger than zero producing a positive pumping pressure from location L to location 0, which is known as the capillary pressure for the liquid flow flowing in this microchannel.

9.2.2 Maximum Capillary Pressure

To find the capillary limitation in a heat pipe driven by the capillary force, it has been established that the maximum capillary pressure exists when the meniscus radius in the condenser approaches infinity and the meniscus radius in the evaporator reaches the smallest one. Equation (9.11) becomes

$$\Delta p_{C,\max} = (\sigma K)_e - (\sigma K)_c^{\,0} = (\sigma K)_e \tag{9.33}$$

Table 9.1 Effective capillary radii

Structures	$r_{c,e}$	Note
Capillary tube	r_0	$r_0 =$ tube radius
Rectangular groove	w	$w =$ groove width
Triangular groove	$\frac{w}{\cos \beta}$	$w =$ groove width $\beta =$ half groove angle
Wire screen	$\frac{w+d}{2}$	$d =$ wire diameter $w =$ mesh spacing
Packed or sintered particles	$0.443 r_p$	$r_p =$ particle radius

or

$$\Delta p_{C,\max} = \left[\sigma \left(\frac{1}{r_1} + \frac{1}{r_2} \right) \right]_e = \frac{2\sigma}{r_{c,e}} \tag{9.34}$$

where $r_{c,e}$ is the effective capillary radius depending on the wick structures. As shown in Eq. (9.34), the maximum capillary pressure can be expressed as a function of only the effective meniscus radius of the evaporator wick. In other words, the maximum capillary pressure shown in Eq. (9.34) is the maximum pressure difference across the liquid–vapor interface in the evaporator. From Eq. (9.34), it can be found that

$$\frac{2}{r_{c,e}} = \frac{1}{r_1} + \frac{1}{r_2} \tag{9.35}$$

Using Eq. (9.35) the effective capillary radius can be readily determined. It should be noted that the maximum capillary pressure is based on a contact angle equal to 0. Table 9.1 lists effective capillary radii for capillary tube, parallel wires, rectangular groove, triangular groove, screen mesh, and sintered or packed particles.

For a capillary tube with a radius of r_0, which is similar to the one shown in Fig. 9.3, r_1 is equal to r_2. Considering a zero contact angle, the effective capillary radius can be found as

$$r_{c,e} = r_0 \tag{9.36}$$

For parallel wires or a rectangular groove, the meniscus radius along the axial direction is close to infinity, and the meniscus radius along the radial direction of the groove is equal to $0.5w$. Equation (9.35) can be expressed as

$$\frac{2}{r_{c,e}} = \frac{1}{\frac{w}{2}} + \frac{1}{\cancel{r_2}} \tag{9.37}$$

The effective capillary radius is equal to the groove width, w, i.e.,

$$r_{c,e} = w \tag{9.38}$$

For a triangular groove with an angle of 2β, the effective capillary radius can be found as

$$r_{c,e} = \frac{w}{\cos \beta} \tag{9.39}$$

The effective capillary radius for the screen wires should be equal to half the spacing between the screen wires, i.e., $r_{c,e} = \frac{w}{2}$. For single-layer screen mesh, the effective capillary radius is equal to half of the sum of the screen wire diameter, d, and the spacing between the screen wires, w, (Chi 1976) i.e.,

$$r_{c,e} = \frac{w + d}{2} \tag{9.40}$$

For sintered or packed particles, it is not possible to find the effective radius using the approach presented above. To generalize the definition of the effective capillary radius which is consistent with Eq. (9.35), the effective capillary radius, $r_{c,e}$, is defined as (Cheng and Ma 2007)

$$r_{c,e} = \frac{2A_{proj}}{P_{proj}} \tag{9.41}$$

where A_{proj} is the liquid area trapped by the wick structures. Mathematically, this trapped area is equal to the area projected to the plane perpendicular to the wick wall at the contact line as shown in Fig. 9.7 and p_{proj} is the perimeter of the contact line formed between the liquid and wick structure wall. Figure 9.7 shows a wick structure consisting of rectangular microgrooves with a width of w. For the maximum capillary pressure, the contact angle is equal to zero. For the microgroove

Fig. 9.7 Effective capillary radius of a rectangular groove

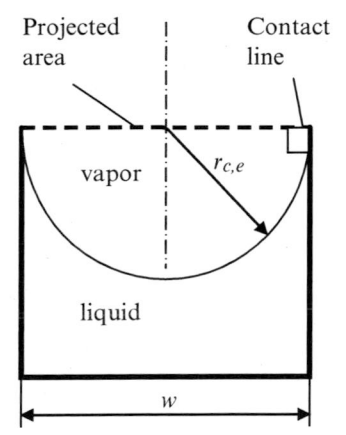

shown in Fig. 9.7, the Bond number is very small; hence, the meniscus radius of the liquid–vapor interface can be a constant. The projected area, A_{proj}, can be expressed as

$$A_{proj} = wL \tag{9.42}$$

where w is the groove width and L is the length. The perimeter, p_{proj}, can be calculated by

$$p_{proj} = 2L + 2w \cong 2L \quad (L \gg w) \tag{9.43}$$

Using Eq. (9.41), the effective capillary radius for the rectangular microgroove can be determined as

$$r_{c,e} = \frac{2wL}{2L} = w \tag{9.44}$$

which is the same as Eq. (9.38). For a capillary tube, $A_{proj} = \pi r_t^2$, $P_{proj} = 2\pi r_t$, the effective capillary radius can be found as $r_{c,e} = r_0$, which is the same as that shown in Eq. (9.36). For a triangular microgroove shown in Fig. 9.8, the projected area, A_{proj}, can be expressed as

$$A_{proj} = \frac{w}{\cos \beta} L \tag{9.45}$$

where w is the groove width, L is the length, and β is the half angle of the triangular groove. The perimeter, p_{proj}, is still $2L$. The effective capillary radius for a triangular groove can be found as $r_{c,e} = \frac{w}{\cos \beta}$, which is the same as that shown in Eq. (9.39).

For the sintered or packed particles, if the trapped liquid area or pore area is known, the effective capillary radius can be easily determined. However, the

Fig. 9.8 Effective capillary radius of a triangular groove

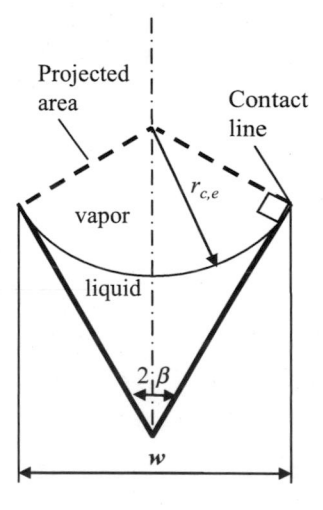

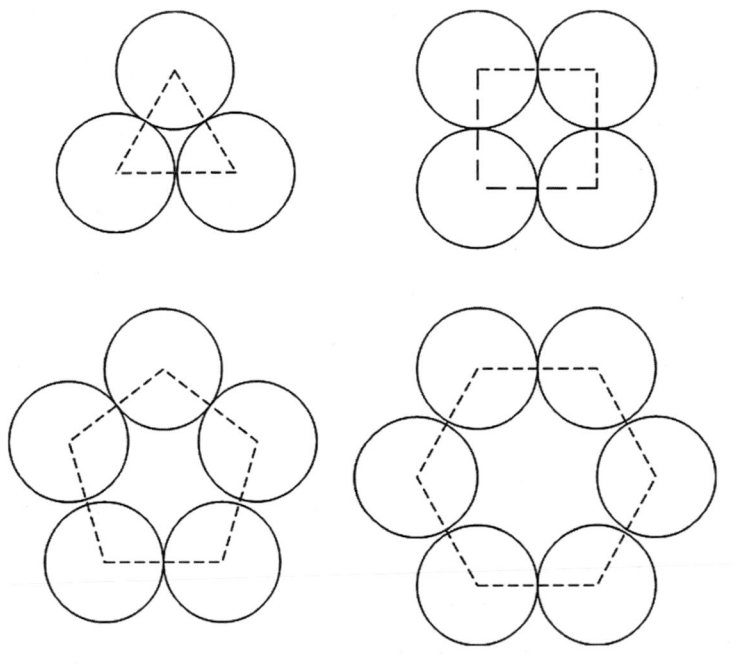

Fig. 9.9 Possible stable structures (Cheng and Ma 2007)

trapped liquid area largely depends on how the structure is formed. To simplify the problem, two assumptions are made: (1) the whole system is in a stable state and (2) the particles are spherical. In the stage of pouring particles, the system of these particles may be unstable and the properties will be different from those in a stable system. During the transition from the unstable system to the stable system, symmetric structures need more energy to have a new structure because the symmetric structures obtained the maximum energy during the pouring process. In other words, once the symmetric structures are formed during the pouring process, it is not easy to be restructured during the sintering process. Based on this assumption, only the triangular, rectangular, and hexagonal structures as shown in Fig. 9.9 can exist in the system. Therefore, it can be concluded that the sintered particles investigated here consist of only these three structures. From viewing one particle, one can see several structures formed around this particle as shown in Fig. 9.10. To determine the percentage of each structure, list all possible arrangements of these structures and consider that each group of these structures has the same possibility. Use A, B, and C to represent triangular, rectangular, and hexagonal structure, respectively. Table 9.2 lists all the possible groups of structures and the number of arrangements for each group. From Table 9.2, it could be found that the percentages for the triangular, rectangular, and hexagonal structures are 45 %, 28 %, and 27 %, respectively. Using Eq. (9.41) the effective capillary radius for these structures can be found as $0.103r$, $0.273r$, and $0.654r$, for triangular,

Fig. 9.10 Angles and
structures formed around
a single particle

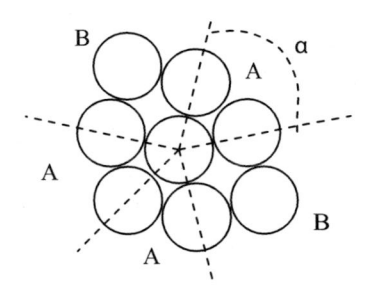

Table 9.2 Possible groups and arrangements

Group	6A	4B	3C	3A + 2B	2A + 2C	4A + 1C	1A + 2B + 1C	Total
Arrangement	1	1	1	2	2	1	2	10

rectangular, and hexagonal structures, respectively. The average effective capillary radius for the sintered particles with a uniform radius can be found by

$$r_{c,e} = 2 \frac{A_{gap,A} \cdot 45\% + A_{gap,B} \cdot 28\% + A_{gap,C} \cdot 27\%}{P_{gap,A} \cdot 45\% + P_{gap,B} \cdot 28\% + P_{gap,C} \cdot 27\%} = 0.443 r_p \qquad (9.46)$$

where r_p is the particle radius. The minimum meniscus radius of $0.443r$ derived here agrees well with the one cited by Ferrell and Alleavitch (1970), which has been accepted by most heat pipe textbooks (Peterson 1994; Faghri 1995; Reay and Kew 2006).

If the size of sintered particles is not uniform, the method described above obviously cannot be used to predict the minimum meniscus radius. To solve this problem, draw a long line linking any two particles, as shown in Fig. 9.11. The line will pass through all of the possible structures, which could be represented by the angles and their relative edges as shown in Fig. 9.11. This can transform a two-dimensional problem into a one-dimensional problem. Considering such a "long-enough" line, it could be found that the number of particles along it is determined by the structures. More structures need more particles to be included. The straight line starts from the center of one particle in one structure and ends at the center of one particle in another structure. The angle, θ, between the long line and the center connecting the line of the first two particles, as shown in Fig. 9.11, is called the start angle, which would also influence the number of the particles along the long line. However, the start angle and structures are independent of each other. With the variation of the start angle, there exists a minimum number, N_0, of particles near the long line, which is directly determined by the structures and could be used to represent the

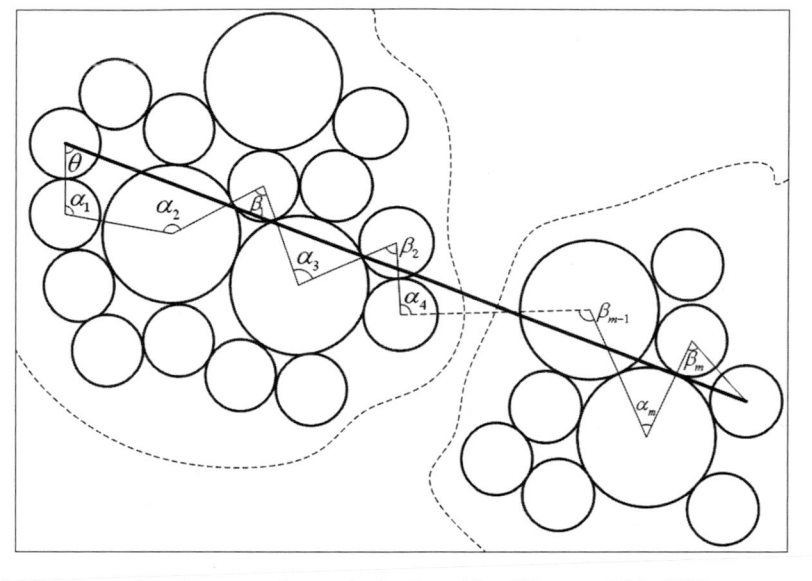

Fig. 9.11 Lines and angles on one layer of mixed particles (Cheng and Ma 2007)

structures. Hence, the number of particles along this long line is a function of start angle θ and N_0, which can be expressed as

$$N = F(N_0, \theta) = f(\theta)N_0 \tag{9.47}$$

In Fig. 9.11 there is another interconnected line connecting the center of particles, which are near the straight line. As discussed above, this interconnected line contains all of the possible angles and edges of structures with their percentage. Angles formed on one side of the straight line are indicated by $\alpha_1, \alpha_2, \alpha_3, \ldots, \alpha_{l-1}$, and α_l and those formed on another side of the straight line by $\beta_1, \beta_2, \beta_3, \ldots, \beta_{m-1}$, and β_m.

The total length of the straight line can be found as

$$
\begin{aligned}
L &= \sum_{n=1}^{N} \left[R_0 \cos\theta + R_n \cos\left(\theta - \sum \alpha_l + \sum \beta_m\right) \right] \\
&= \sqrt{M_1^2 + M_2^2} \cos(\theta + \varphi)
\end{aligned}
\tag{9.48}
$$

where

$$M_1 = R_0 + \sum_{n=1}^{N} \left[R_n \cos\left(-\sum \alpha_l + \sum \beta_m\right) \right] \tag{9.49}$$

$$M_2 = \sum_{n=1}^{N} \left[R_n \sin \left(-\sum \alpha_l + \sum \beta_m \right) \right] \tag{9.50}$$

$$\cos \varphi = M_1 / \sqrt{M_1^2 + M_2^2}$$
$$\sin \varphi = M_2 / \sqrt{M_1^2 + M_2^2} \tag{9.51}$$

Considering Eq. (9.47), the length of the straight line could be expressed as

$$L = \sqrt{f(\theta) N_0 \left[\sum X_i R_i^2 + g(R, \alpha, \beta)/N \right]} \cos (\theta + \varphi) \tag{9.52}$$

where $g(R, \alpha, \beta)$ and sum of $N(N-1)$ terms represent the function of edges and angles.

Imagine one layer of particles placed on a large rectangular surface with each side long enough, and the area of minimum gaps trapped by particles is equal to the difference between the rectangular area and the total area of all of particles. The total length of perimeters of all the minimum gaps trapped by particles in the rectangle is equal to the total length of perimeters of all the particles. Then, the effective capillary radius can be found as

$$r_{c,e} = 2A_{proj}/P_{proj} = \frac{L_1 L_2 - \pi N_0^2 f(\theta) f(\pi/2 - \theta) \sum \left(Y_j r_j^2 \right)}{\pi N_0^2 f(\theta) f(\pi/2 - \theta) \sum \left(Y_j r_j \right)} \tag{9.53}$$

Equation (9.53) can be used to calculate the effective capillary radius occurring in the sintered particles with different sizes.

For example, when the sintered particles consist of two kinds of particles with diameters 100 and 50 μm, respectively, with these given particle sizes, the total length of straight line can be simplified as

$$L \approx k f(\theta) N_0 \sqrt{\sum X_i R_i^2} \tag{9.54}$$

where the constant k considers the angle effect. Then Eq. (9.53) can be expressed as

$$r_{c,e} = \frac{k^2 \sum \left(X_i R_i^2 \right) - \pi \sum \left(Y_j r_j^2 \right)}{\pi \sum \left(Y_j r_j \right)} \tag{9.55}$$

The constant k can be determined from the sintered particles with uniform size, which can be found as

$$k^2 = 1.1333 \tag{9.56}$$

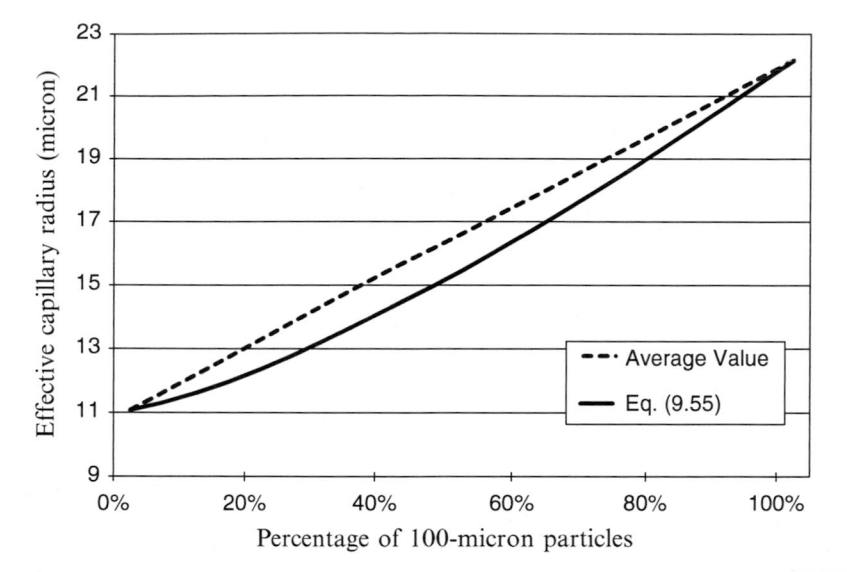

Fig. 9.12 Particle size effect on effective capillary radius meniscus radius predicted by Eq. (9.55) (Cheng and Ma 2007)

Figure 9.12 illustrates the effective capillary radius variation for mixed particles with diameters 100 and 50 μm. As shown, the predicted minimum meniscus radius is smaller than the average one, which has been demonstrated in a heat pipe with sintered mixed particles.

9.2.3 Liquid Pressure Drop

Liquid pressure drop is the result of the combined effect of both viscous and inertial forces. If the flow rate in the wick is very small, the effect of inertial force on pressure drop can be neglected; hence, the pressure difference in the liquid phase is caused only by the frictional forces at the liquid–solid interface and at the liquid–vapor interface due to the vapor flow effect. The total liquid pressure drop can be determined by integrating the pressure gradient over the length of the flow passage, i.e.,

$$\Delta p_1(x) = -\int_0^x \frac{d p_1}{dx} dx \qquad (9.57)$$

where the limits of integration are from the cap end of the evaporator ($x = 0$) to the cap end of the condenser ($x = L$), and dp_1/dx is the gradient of the liquid pressure occurring in the liquid. This pressure gradient can be written as

$$\frac{dp_1}{dx} = -\frac{2\tau_1}{r_{h,1}} \tag{9.58}$$

where τ_1 is the frictional shear stress at the liquid–solid interface and $r_{h,1}$ is the hydraulic radius, which is defined as twice the cross-sectional area divided by the wetted perimeter. Considering the definitions of the Reynolds number, Re_1, and the friction coefficient or Fanning friction factor, $c_{f,1}$, i.e.,

$$Re_1 = \frac{2r_{h,1}\rho_1 u_1}{\mu_1} \tag{9.59}$$

and

$$c_{f,1} = \frac{\tau_1}{\frac{1}{2}\rho_1 u_1^2} \tag{9.60}$$

Equation (9.58) becomes

$$\frac{dp_1}{dx} = -\frac{c_{f,1} \cdot Re_1 u_1 \mu_1}{2r_{h,1}^2} \tag{9.61}$$

It should be noticed that the friction factor shown in Eq. (9.60) is the Fanning friction factor which is four times smaller than the Darcy friction factor. Rearranging Eq. (9.61) yields

$$u_1 = -\frac{2r_{h,1}^2}{c_{f,1} \cdot Re_1 \mu_1} \frac{dp_1}{dx} \tag{9.62}$$

For a given wick structure or flow path, $\frac{2r_{h,1}^2}{c_{f,1} \cdot Re_1}$ is a constant, which can be expressed as

$$K = \frac{2r_{h,1}^2}{c_{f,1} Re_1} \tag{9.63}$$

Equation (9.62) can be rewritten as

$$u_1 = -\frac{K}{\mu_1} \frac{dp_1}{dx} \tag{9.64}$$

where K is the permeability. Clearly, Eq. (9.64) is the well-known Darcy's law. Rewriting Eq. (9.64) yields

$$\frac{dp_1}{dx} = -\frac{\mu_1 u_1}{K} \tag{9.65}$$

It should be noticed that u_1 in Eq. (9.65) is the local liquid velocity which is related to the local heat flux. If $\dot{m}_1$ is the local liquid flow rate, A_w is the wick cross-sectional area, ε is the wick porosity, which is defined as the ratio of the pore volume, V_{por}, to

the total volume, V_{tot}, of the wick structure. Considering the wick porosity, the local liquid velocity in the wick can be written as

$$u_1 = \frac{\dot{m}_1}{\varepsilon A_w \rho_1} \qquad (9.66)$$

Due to evaporation and condensation in the evaporator and condenser, the condensate flow rate in both the evaporator and condenser sections is not constant. But the condensate flow rate through the adiabatic section should be constant because there is no evaporation and condensation, which can be found as

$$u_1 = \frac{q}{\varepsilon A_w \rho_1 h_{lv}} \qquad (9.67)$$

where q is the total heat transfer rate transferred by the heat pipe and h_{lv} is the latent heat of vaporization. Combining Eqs. (9.59), (9.60), (9.61), (9.62), (9.63), (9.64), (9.65) and (9.66), Eq. (9.58) becomes

$$\frac{dp_1}{dx} = -\left(\frac{\mu_1}{K \varepsilon A_w \rho_1}\right) \dot{m}_1 \qquad (9.68)$$

To find the pressure drop of the liquid flow, the permeability, K, shown in Eq. (9.68) must be first determined. For a given wick structure, the permeability, K, defined by Eq. (9.63) depends on the friction coefficient Reynolds number product, i.e., $c_{f,1} \cdot Re_1$, which depends on flow type (laminar or turbulent flow) and passage shape.

Figure 9.13 illustrates the cross section of a typical external artery heat pipe where the liquid flows through a circular channel from the condenser to the evaporator section. For circular passages, i.e., arterial or tunnel wicks, similar to the one shown in Fig. 9.13, if the flow type is given, the friction coefficient Reynolds number product, i.e., $c_{f,1} \cdot Re_1$, can be theoretically or experimentally determined. If the flow through the circular channel is steady and laminar, the friction coefficient Reynolds number product, i.e., $c_{f,1} \cdot Re_1$, can be readily determined theoretically. For a circular channel with a radius of R, the momentum equation governing the fluid flow can be written as

Fig. 9.13 Cross section of a typical external artery heat pipe configuration (Peng and Peterson 1992)

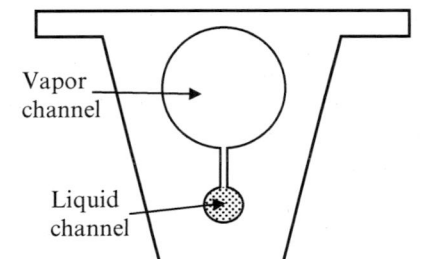

Vapor channel

Liquid channel

$$\frac{d}{dr}\left(r\frac{du_1}{dr}\right) = \frac{r}{\mu_1}\frac{dp_1}{dx} \tag{9.69}$$

With no-slip boundary condition at the wall, the famous solution for a fully developed Hagen–Poiseuille flow can be found as

$$u_1 = \left(-\frac{dp_1}{dx}\right)\frac{1}{4\mu_1}(R^2 - r^2) \tag{9.70}$$

The average velocity can be calculated by

$$
\begin{aligned}
\bar{u}_1 &= \frac{1}{\pi R^2}\int_0^R u_1 2\pi r\, dr = \frac{1}{\pi R^2}\int_0^R \left(-\frac{dp_1}{dx}\right)\frac{1}{4\mu_1}(R^2 - r^2)2\pi r\, dr \\
&= \left(-\frac{dp_1}{dx}\right)\frac{R^2}{8\mu_1} \tag{9.71}
\end{aligned}
$$

Considering the shear stress at the wall, i.e.,

$$\tau_1 = -\mu_1 \left.\frac{du}{dr}\right|_{r=R} \tag{9.72}$$

and the definitions of the friction coefficient shown in Eq. (9.60) and Reynolds number shown in Eq. (9.59), the friction coefficient and Reynolds number product for the fully developed Hagen–Poiseuille flow in a circular channel can be found as

$$c_{f,1}\cdot Re_1 = \left(\frac{-\mu_1\left.\frac{du}{dr}\right|_{r=R}}{\frac{1}{2}\rho_1\bar{u}_1^2}\right)\left(\frac{2r_{h,1}\,\rho_1\bar{u}_1}{\mu_1}\right) \tag{9.73}$$

Substituting Eqs. (9.70) and (9.71) into Eq. (9.73) yields

$$c_{f,1}\cdot Re_1 = 16 \tag{9.74}$$

Considering Eq. (9.63) results in a permeability for a circular passage of

$$K = \frac{R^2}{8} \tag{9.75}$$

Figures 9.14, 9.15, 9.16 and 9.17 show the products of the friction coefficient and Reynolds number, $c_f\cdot Re_1$, of laminar flow for concentric, rectangular, triangular and other shapes of flow passages, respectively. Using Eq. (9.63), the corresponding permeability can then be readily determined. Figure 9.18 shows other types of common wick structures. If the flow is laminar and the flow passage has a regular shape, the product of the friction coefficient and Reynolds number, $c_{f,1}\cdot Re_1$,

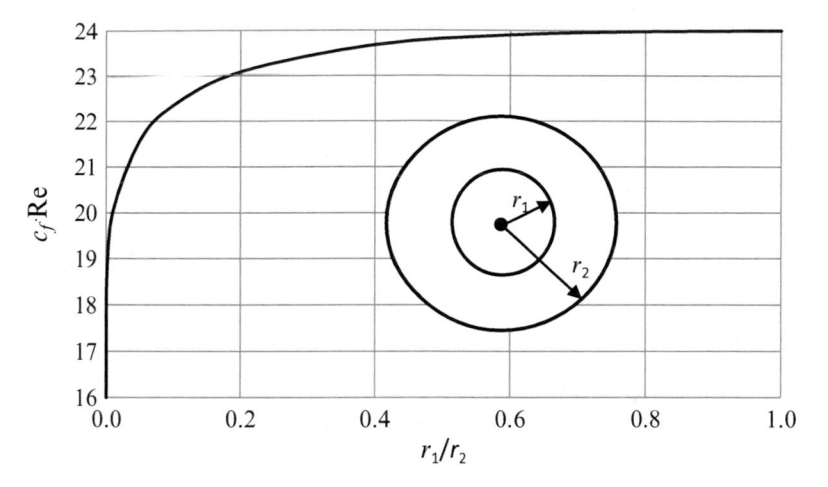

Fig. 9.14 Product of the friction coefficient and Reynolds number of a laminar flow for a concentric annulus

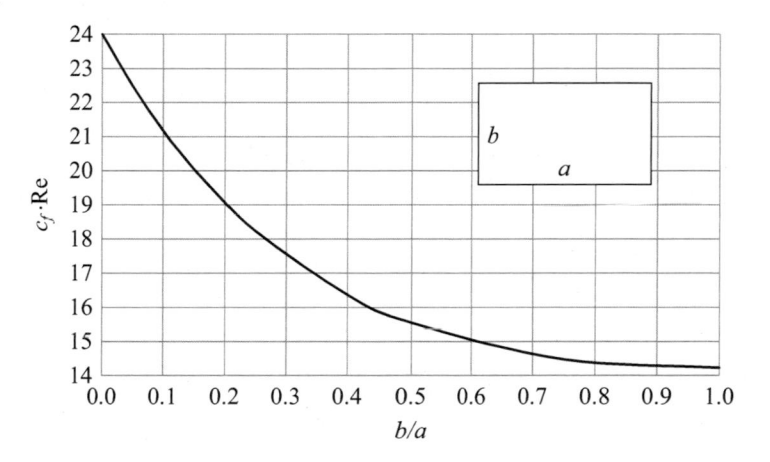

Fig. 9.15 Product of the friction coefficient and Reynolds number of a laminar flow for a rectangular channel

can be readily determined. In many cases, an analytical expression for the product of the friction coefficient and Reynolds number, $c_f \cdot Re_l$, or the permeability, K, shown in Eq. (9.63), is not available. In such a case, semiempirical correlations based on experimental data are usually employed. For example, Marcus (1972) described a method for calculating the permeability of wrapped, screened wicks. This expression, which is a modified form of the Blake–Kozeny equation, can be given as

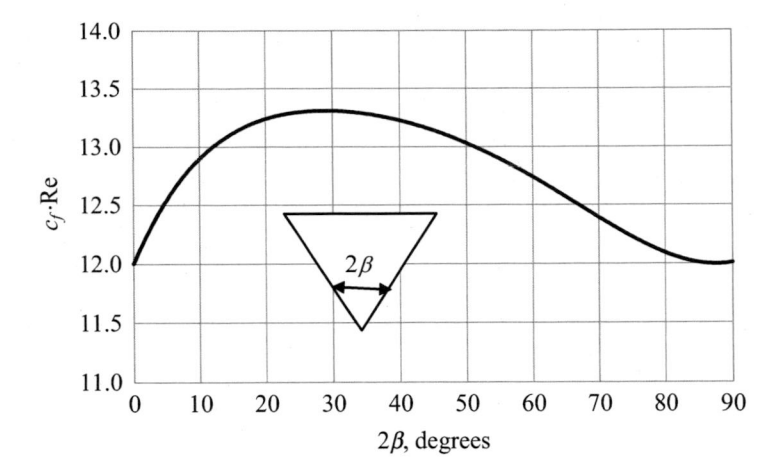

Fig. 9.16 Product of the friction coefficient and Reynolds number of a laminar flow for a triangular channel

$$K = \frac{d^2 \varepsilon^3}{122(1 - \varepsilon)^2} \tag{9.76}$$

In this expression, d is the wire diameter and ε is the wick porosity, which can be determined as

$$\varepsilon = 1 - \frac{1}{4}\pi SNd \tag{9.77}$$

where N is the mesh number per unit length and S is the crimping factor (approximately 1.05) (Peterson 1994). For the sintered particles, this equation takes the form

$$K = \frac{d_s^2 \varepsilon^3}{37.5(1 - \varepsilon)^2} \tag{9.78}$$

where d_s is the average diameter of the sintered particles.

For uniform heat addition and rejection, substituting Eq. (9.68) into Eq. (9.57) yields

$$\Delta p_l = \left(\frac{\mu_l}{K A_w h_{fg} \rho_l}\right) L_{eff} q \tag{9.79}$$

where $q = \dot{m}_l h_{fg}$ and the effective heat pipe length can be found as

$$L_{eff} = 0.5 L_e + L_a + 0.5 L_c \tag{9.80}$$

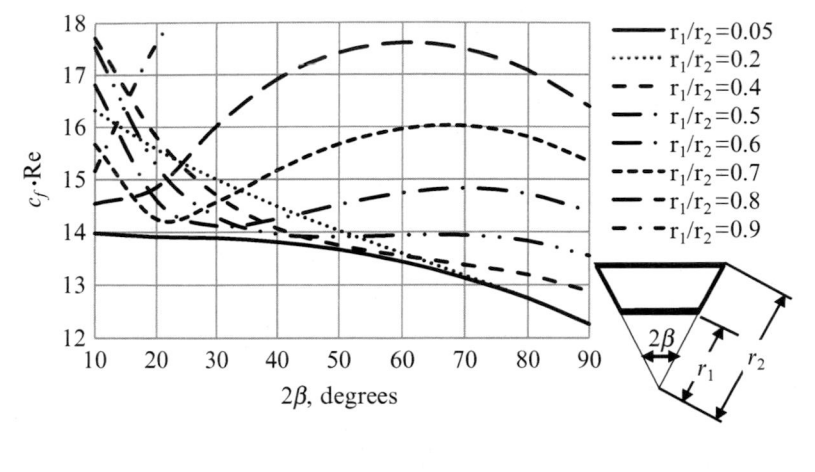

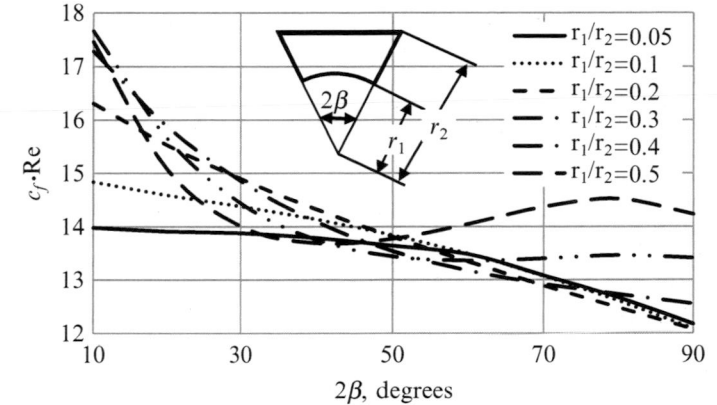

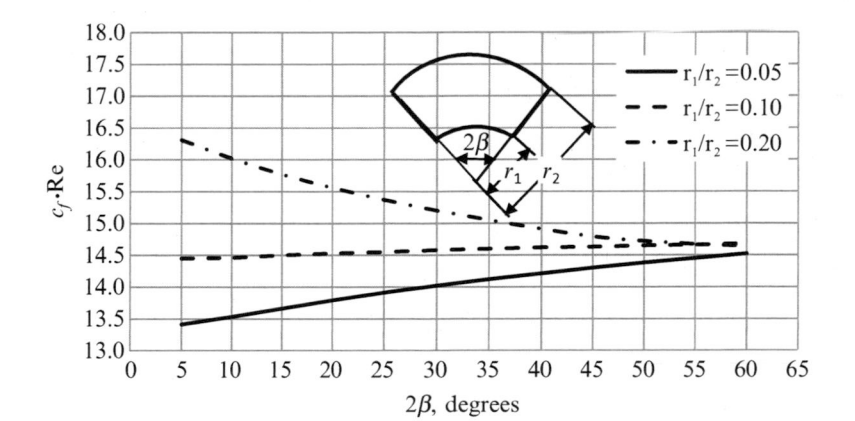

Fig. 9.17 Product of the friction coefficient and Reynolds number of a laminar flow for other special channels

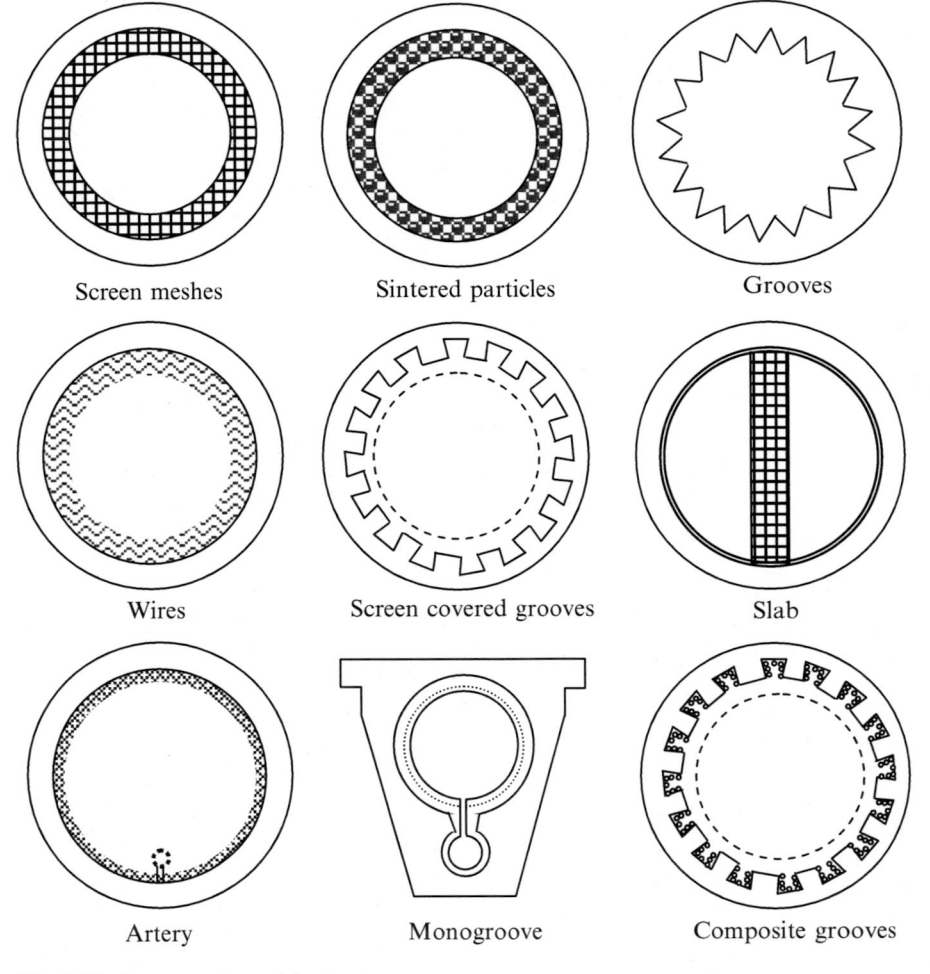

Fig. 9.18 Some common wick structures

9.2.4 Vapor Pressure Drop

9.2.4.1 One-Dimensional Vapor Flow Approximations

The hydraulic diameter of the cross section of a typical heat pipe is much smaller than the length. The vapor flow through the vapor path in the heat pipe can be approximately modeled as a one-directional flow (Peterson 1994). To find equations governing the fluid flow of vapor flow in the heat pipe, a control volume for conservation of momentum shown in Fig. 9.19 is selected, and the equation for the control volume can be found as

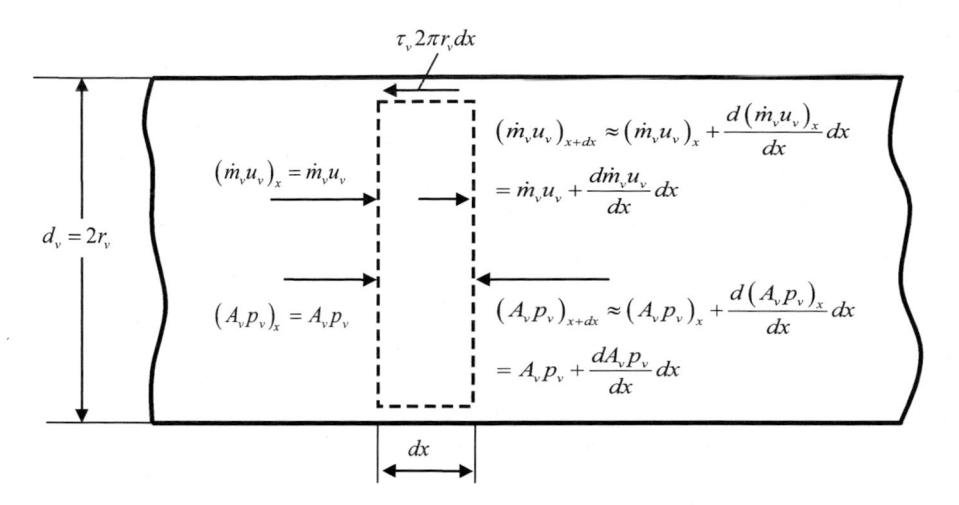

Fig. 9.19 Control volume for conservation of momentum

$$\frac{d\rho_v A_v u_v}{dx} = \begin{cases} q_e'' 2\pi r_v/h_{lv} & \text{evaporator} \\ 0 & \text{adiabatic section} \\ -q_c'' 2\pi r_v/h_{lv} & \text{condenser} \end{cases} \tag{9.81}$$

For the control volume shown in Fig. 9.19, the equation for the conservation of momentum can be expressed as

$$\sum F = \frac{\partial}{\partial t}\left(\iiint_{CV} U\rho_v du_v\right) + \sum(\dot{m}_v u_v)_{x+dx} - \sum(\dot{m}_v u_v)_x \tag{9.82}$$

The term on the left side of Eq. (9.82) is for the total forces acting on the control volume. For a steady state, the first term on the right side of Eq. (9.82) disappears, and Eq. (9.82) becomes

$$\begin{aligned} A_v p_v &- \frac{d(A_v\,p_v)}{dx}dx - A_v\,p_v - \tau_v 2\pi r_v\,dx \\ &= \int_A \rho_v u_v^2(r)\,dA + \frac{d}{dx}\int_A \rho_v u_v^2(r)\,dA\,dx - \int_A \rho_v u_v^2(r)\,dA \end{aligned} \tag{9.83}$$

or

$$-\left(p_v\frac{dA_v}{dx} + A_v\frac{dp_v}{dx}\right)dx - \tau_v 2\pi r_v\,dx = \frac{d}{dx}\int_A \rho_v u_v^2(r)\,dA\,dx \tag{9.84}$$

where τ_v is the shear stress acting on the control volume by the inner surface of the heat pipe. For a constant cross-sectional area, the first term on the left side of Eq. (9.84) is zero. Rearranging Eq. (9.84) yields

$$\frac{dp_v}{dx} = -\frac{\tau_v 2\pi r_v}{A_v} - \frac{1}{A_v}\frac{d}{dx}\int_A \rho_v u_v^2(r)\,dA \qquad (9.85)$$

In Eq. (9.85), the second term on the right side is due to the momentum change. It shows that even when the total flow rate is constant, the velocity change due to the variation of the cross-sectional area will result in a momentum variation. For a heat pipe, when vapor flows through the adiabatic section with a constant cross section of vapor flow, the total flow rate is constant and the velocity through the adiabatic section is constant. Therefore, the momentum is almost constant. The contribution to the local pressure due to the second term on the right side of Eq. (9.85) is almost equal to zero for the adiabatic section. The pressure drop occurring in the adiabatic section is due to frictional force only. For the evaporator or condenser section, the total mass flow rate and vapor velocity at a given location depend on heat addition or rejection, which directly affects the momentum variation and the local vapor pressure. To evaluate the momentum effect on the local pressure in a heat pipe from the cap end of the evaporator to the cap end of the condenser, a momentum correction factor, β, is introduced, i.e.,

$$\beta = \frac{\int_A \rho_v u_v^2(r)\,dA}{\rho_v \bar{u}_v^2 A_v} \qquad (9.86)$$

where $\int_A \rho_v u_v^2(r)\,dA$ is the local actual momentum, and the $\rho_v \bar{u}_v^2 A_v$ is the momentum calculated by the local average velocity, $\bar{u}_v$ which can be determined by

$$\bar{u}_v = \frac{\int_A \rho_v u_v(r)\,dA}{\rho_v A_v} \qquad (9.87)$$

For a viscous flow, the vapor velocity at the center of the flow passage is much higher than the average velocity due to the shear stress at the wall as shown in Fig. 9.20. The actual momentum determined by $\int_A \rho_v u_v^2(r)\,dA$ is not equal to the momentum calculated by $\rho_v \bar{u}_v^2 A_v$ for a viscous flow. For example, β is about 1.33 for a laminar flow and 1.02 for a turbulent flow in a round pipe with a constant flow rate.

Considering Eq. (9.86), the second term on the right side of Eq. (9.85) can be written as

Fig. 9.20 Velocity profile of a laminar flow in a round pile for (**a**) a viscous flow and (**b**) an average velocity of a viscous flow or nonviscous flow

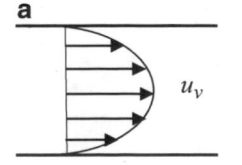
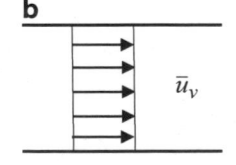

$$\frac{1}{A_v} \frac{d}{dx} \left[\beta \rho_v u_v^2(r) A_v \right] \tag{9.88}$$

Taking a derivative of x, Eq. (9.88) becomes

$$\rho_v u_v^2 \frac{d}{dx}(\beta) + \beta \rho_v \frac{d}{dx}(u_v^2) \tag{9.89}$$

At a given location in a pipe flow, the velocity profile, $u_v(r)$, is a weak function of the position x, which implies that $\frac{d\beta}{dx} \cong 0$. Only the second term in Eq. (9.89) is left. Considering $\dot{m}_v = u_v A_v \rho_v$, Eq. (9.89) becomes

$$\beta \rho_v \frac{d}{dx}(u_v^2) = \beta \rho_v \frac{d}{dx}\left(\frac{\dot{m}_v^2}{\rho_v^2 A_v^2}\right) = \frac{2\beta \dot{m}_v}{\rho_v A_v^2} \frac{d\dot{m}_v}{dx} \tag{9.90}$$

Looking at the first term on the right side of Eq. (9.85)

$$\frac{\tau_v 2\pi r_v}{A_v} \tag{9.91}$$

and recognizing that

$$\tau_v = \frac{1}{2} c_{f,v} \rho_v u_v^2; \quad u_v = \frac{\dot{m}_v}{\rho_v A_v}; \quad Re_v = \frac{2r_v \cdot \rho_v \cdot \bar{u}_v}{\mu_v}; \quad A_v = \pi r_v^2 \tag{9.92}$$

yields after substituting

$$\frac{\tau_v 2\pi r_v}{A_v} = \frac{(c_{f,v} \cdot Re_v)\mu_v \dot{m}_v}{2A_v r_v^2 \rho_v} \tag{9.93}$$

and finally

$$\frac{dp_v}{dx} = -\frac{(c_{f,v} \cdot Re_v)\mu_v \dot{m}_v}{2A_v r_v^2 \rho_v} - \beta \frac{2\dot{m}_v}{\rho_v A_v^2} \frac{d\dot{m}_v}{dx} \tag{9.94}$$

where

$$\beta = \frac{1}{\rho_v u_v^2 A_v} \int_A \rho_v u_v^2(r)\, dA = \frac{\rho_v^2 A_v}{\dot{m}_v^2} \int_A u_v^2(r)\, dA \tag{9.95}$$

Equation (9.95) compensates for variations in the vapor velocity across the cross section. For the vapor flow in a heat pipe, the heat addition in the evaporator section and the heat rejection in the condenser section will significantly increase or reduce the velocity in the evaporator and condenser, respectively, which significantly affects the momentum variation. Determination of the vapor

pressure drop in heat pipes is complicated by the mass addition and removal in the evaporator and condenser, respectively, and by the compressibility of the vapor phase. A mass balance on a section of the adiabatic region of the heat pipe ensures that for continued operation, the liquid mass flow rate and vapor mass flow rate must be equal. Because of the large difference in the density of these two phases, the vapor velocity must be significantly higher than the velocity of the liquid phase. For this reason, in addition to the pressure gradient resulting from frictional drag, the pressure gradient due to variations in the dynamic pressure must also be considered. However, if the cross-sectional area of the vapor flow path in the heat pipe is constant, and the heat addition in the evaporator section and heat rejection in the condenser section is uniform, the total vapor pressure drop can be found by

$$\Delta p_v = -\int_0^L \frac{dp_v}{dx}\, dx = \int_0^L \left(\frac{(C_{f,v} \cdot Re_v)\mu_v \dot{m}_v}{2A_v r_v^2 \rho_v} + \beta \frac{2\dot{m}_v}{\rho_v A_v^2} \frac{d\dot{m}_v}{dx} \right) dx \qquad (9.96)$$

Integrating the second term of Eq. (9.96) shows that the dynamic pressure effects are canceled, and Eq. (9.96) becomes

$$\Delta P_v = \frac{(C_{f,v} \cdot Re_v)\mu_v}{2A_v r_v^2 \rho_v} \int_0^L \dot{m}_v\, dx \qquad (9.97)$$

The vapor flow rate at a given location in the heat pipe depends on the location— whether it is in the evaporator, adiabatic section, or condenser. The local vapor flow rate can be expressed as

$$\dot{m}_v = \begin{cases} \displaystyle\int_0^x \frac{q_e'}{h_{lv}}\, dx & 0 \le x \le L_e \\[3mm] \displaystyle\int_0^{L_e} \frac{q_e'}{h_{lv}}\, dx & L_e \le x \le L_e + L_a \\[3mm] \displaystyle\int_0^{L_e} \frac{q_e'}{h_{lv}}\, dx - \int_{L_e+L_a}^x \frac{q_c'}{h_{lv}}\, dx & L_e + L_a \le x \le L_e + L_a + L_c \end{cases} \qquad (9.98)$$

where q_e' and q_c' are the heat transfer rate per unit length in the evaporator and condenser, respectively, and L_e, L_a, and L_c are the evaporator, adiabatic section, and condenser lengths, respectively.

For a uniform heat addition and rejection, Eq. (9.98) becomes

$$
\dot{m}_v = \begin{cases} \dfrac{q}{h_{lv}} \dfrac{x}{L_e} & 0 \le x \le L_e \\[2mm] \dfrac{q}{h_{lv}} & L_e \le x \le L_e + L_a \\[2mm] \dfrac{q}{h_{lv}} \left(1 - \dfrac{x}{L_c}\right) & L_e + L_a \le x \le L_e + L_a + L_c \end{cases} \tag{9.99}
$$

Integrating Eq. (9.97) yields

$$
\Delta P_v = \frac{(c_{f,v} \cdot Re_v)\mu_v}{2 A_v r_v^2 \rho_v} \frac{q}{h_{lv}} \left(\frac{L_e}{2} + L_a + \frac{L_c}{2}\right) \tag{9.100}
$$

Define

$$
L_{eff} = \frac{L_e}{2} + L_a + \frac{L_c}{2} \tag{9.101}
$$

where L_{eff} is the effective length. Considering Eq. (9.101), Eq. (9.100) becomes

$$
\Delta p_v = \frac{(c_{f,v} \cdot Re_v)\mu_v}{2 A_v r_{h,v}^2 \rho_v h_{lv}} L_{eff} q \tag{9.102}
$$

where $r_{h,v}$ is the hydraulic radius of the vapor space, indicating that although Eq. (9.97) is obtained for a round cross section, Eq. (9.102) can be used for other types of cross sections. Considering the Mach number effect, Eq. (9.102) can be expressed as (Peterson 1994)

$$
\Delta p_v = \left(\frac{C(c_{f,v} \cdot Re_v)\mu_v}{2 A_v r_{h,v}^2 \rho_v h_{lv}}\right) L_{eff} q \tag{9.103}
$$

where C is a constant, which depends on the Mach Number.

During steady state operation, the liquid mass flow rate, $\dot{m}_l$, at the adiabatic section must equal the vapor mass flow rate, $\dot{m}_v$. The vapor flow may be either laminar or turbulent. It is necessary to determine the vapor flow types as a function of the heat flux by evaluating the local axial Reynolds number of the vapor flow, i.e.,

$$
Re_v = \frac{2 r_{h,v} q}{A_v \mu_v h_{lv}} \tag{9.104}
$$

At the same time, it is necessary to determine if the flow should be treated as compressible or incompressible by evaluating the local Mach number of

$$Ma_v = \frac{q}{A_v \rho_v h_{lv} (R_v T_v \gamma_v)^{1/2}} \tag{9.105}$$

where T_v is the vapor temperature, R_v is the gas constant, and γ_v is the ratio of specific heats, which is equal to 1.67, 1.4, and 1.33 for monatomic, diatomic, and polyatomic vapors, respectively (Peterson 1994; Chi 1976). Kraus and Bar-Cohen (1983) have demonstrated that the following combinations of these conditions can be used with reasonable accuracy (Peterson 1994):

$$Re_v < 2,300 \quad \text{and} \quad Ma_v < 0.2$$
$$c_{f,v} \cdot Re_v = \text{constant}, \quad C = 1.0 \tag{9.106}$$

$$Re_v < 2,300 \quad \text{and} \quad Ma_v > 0.2$$
$$c_{f,v} \cdot Re_v = \text{constant}, \quad C = \left[1 + \left(\tfrac{\gamma_v - 1}{2}\right) Ma_v^2\right]^{-1/2} \tag{9.107}$$

$$Re_v > 2,300 \quad \text{and} \quad Ma_v < 0.2$$
$$c_{f,v} \cdot Re_v = 0.038 \left(\frac{2 r_{h,v} q}{A_v \mu_v h_{lv}}\right)^{3/4}, \quad C = 1.0 \tag{9.108}$$

It should be noted that Eq. (9.108) was determined based on a round channel. Because the equations used to evaluate both the Reynolds number and the Mach number are functions of the heat transport capacity, it is first necessary to assume the conditions of the vapor flow, and an iterative procedure must be used to determine the vapor pressure.

If the heat pipe is overcharged and/or the heat pipe is operating at a high cooling rate, only the total pressure drops in the evaporating and adiabatic sections are needed in the calculation of the capillary limitation. Equation (9.103) becomes (Faghri 1995)

$$\Delta p_v = \left(\frac{C(c_{f,v} \cdot Re_v) \mu_v}{2 r_{h,v}^2 A_v \rho_v h_{lv}}\right) q [0.5 L_e (1 + F Re_r) + L_a] \tag{9.109}$$

where the correction factor, F, in Eq. (9.109) can be determined by

$$F = \frac{7}{9} - \frac{1.7 Re_r}{36 + 10 Re_r} \exp\left(-\frac{7.5 L_a}{Re_r L_e}\right) \tag{9.110}$$

The radial Reynolds number, Re_r, in Eqs. (9.109) and (9.110) is defined by

$$Re_r = \frac{\rho_v v_{lv} r_v}{\mu_v} \tag{9.111}$$

where v_{lv} is the interfacial velocity. For evaporation, $v_{lv} > 0$; for condensation, $v_{lv} < 0$.

Since the equations used to evaluate both the Reynolds number and the Mach number are functions of the heat transport capacity, it is necessary to first assume the conditions of the vapor flow. Using these assumptions, an iterative procedure must be used to determine the maximum heat transport capacity. Once the value of the maximum heat transport capability is known, it can then be substituted into expressions for the vapor Reynolds number and Mach number to determine the accuracy of the original assumption. Using this iterative approach, accurate values for the capillary limitation as a function of the operating temperature can be determined.

9.2.4.2 Two-Dimensional Vapor Flow Models

If the cross section of the vapor flow path is rectangular, the approach presented above may not be accurate. Liu and Peterson (1997) conducted a numerical analysis of vapor flow in a flat-plate miniature heat pipe with a vapor flow path as shown in Fig. 9.21. The lengths of the evaporator, adiabatic section, and condensers are L_e, L_a, and L_c, respectively. Because the width is much larger than the thickness of the heat pipe, the vapor flow in the heat pipe can be modeled as a two-dimensional flow. Based on the dimension, power input, and vapor flow velocities, it is reasonable to assume steady, incompressible, two-dimensional laminar vapor flow. The continuity equation and the momentum equations can be found as

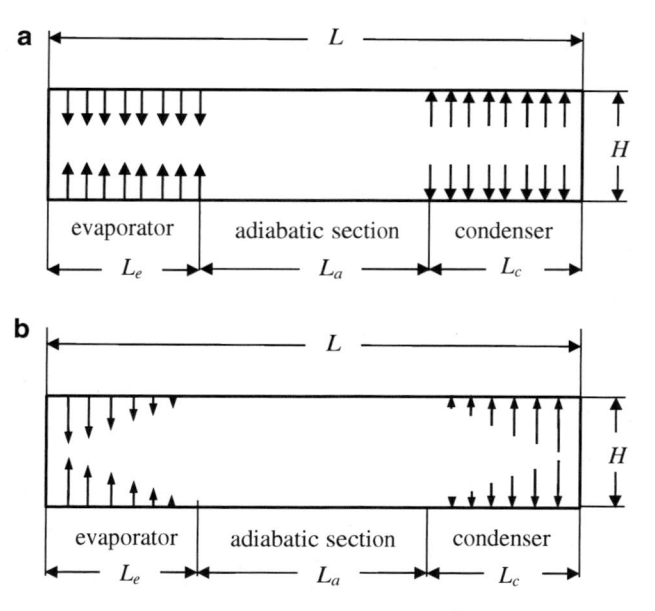

Fig. 9.21 Two-dimensional vapor flow in a flat-plate miniature heat pipe with (**a**) uniform heat addition and rejection and (**b**) linear heat addition and rejection

$$\frac{\partial u}{\partial x} + \frac{\partial v}{\partial y} = 0 \tag{9.112}$$

$$\rho_v \left(u_v \frac{\partial u_v}{\partial x} + v_v \frac{\partial u_v}{\partial y} \right) = -\frac{\partial p_v}{\partial x} + \mu_v \left(\frac{\partial^2 u_v}{\partial x^2} + \frac{\partial^2 u_v}{\partial y^2} \right) \tag{9.113}$$

$$\rho_v \left(u_v \frac{\partial v_v}{\partial x} + v_v \frac{\partial v_v}{\partial y} \right) = -\frac{\partial p_v}{\partial y} + \mu_v \left(\frac{\partial^2 v_v}{\partial x^2} + \frac{\partial^2 v_v}{\partial y^2} \right) \tag{9.114}$$

The boundary conditions are: (1) the velocity u_v will be zero at all surfaces; (2) the velocity v_v can be assumed to be zero at the surfaces of the adiabatic sections and at both far ends of condenser and evaporator; and (3) the evaporation and condensation at the inner wall surface of heat pipes can be modeled as a classical blowing and suction problem, i.e.,

$$
\begin{aligned}
&u_v(0, y) = v_v(0, y) = 0 \\
&u_v(L, y) = v_v(L, y) = 0 \\
&u_v(x, 0) = u_v(x, H) = 0 \\
&v_v(x, 0) = v_v(x), \quad v_v(x, H) = -v_v(x) \quad 0 \le x \le L_e \\
&v_v(x, 0) = 0, \quad v_v(x, H) = 0 \quad L_e \le x \le L_e + L_a \\
&v_v(x, 0) = -v_v(x), \quad v_v(x, H) = v_v(x) \quad L_e + L_a \le x \le L
\end{aligned} \tag{9.115}
$$

Because the heat flux distribution in the evaporator and condenser sections may or may not be uniform, depending on the method of heat addition and rejection, the velocity distribution on the surface of these regions may vary. If the total heat transfer rate of the heat pipe is q with uniform heat addition in the evaporator section and uniform heat rejection in the condenser section, the blowing velocity of vapor flow at the liquid–vapor boundary can be found as

$$
\begin{aligned}
v_e &= -\frac{q}{2\rho_v L_e w h_{lv}} \quad \text{from top surface} \\
v_e &= \frac{q}{2\rho_v L_e w h_{lv}} \quad \text{from bottom surface}
\end{aligned} \tag{9.116}
$$

where w is the heat pipe width. Following the same procedure, the suction velocity in the condenser section can be expressed as

$$v_c = \frac{q}{2\rho_v L_c wh_{lv}} \quad \text{from top surface}$$

$$\hspace{8cm} (9.117)$$

$$v_c = -\frac{q}{2\rho_v L_c wh_{lv}} \quad \text{from bottom surface}$$

Using the finite difference method (Patankar 1980), Eqs. (9.112), (9.113) and (9.114) can be readily solved with required boundary conditions shown in Eqs. (9.115), (9.116) and (9.117).

Liu and Peterson (1997) utilized the approach presented above to analyze the vapor flow occurring in a miniature flat-plate heat pipe with a total length of 60 mm. The evaporator and condenser lengths were each 20 mm. The calculations were carried out for the symmetric case with evaporation and condensation on both the top and bottom plates of the heat pipe with a vapor space height of $H = 3.0$ mm as shown in Fig. 9.21. The working fluid methanol at 65 °C was used as a reference. Figure 9.22 represents the average velocity distribution of the cross sections with both uniform and linear heat fluxes. It should be noted that the total heat transfer for the uniform heat flux is the same as that for the linear heat flux assumption. The only difference is that the uniform heat flux means that the heat is uniformly added on the evaporator section at 20 W/cm^2. For the linear heat flux assumption, the total heat is added to the evaporator or removed from the condenser as shown in Fig. 9.21b. Results show that the average velocity increases gradually in the evaporator section. The average velocity in the adiabatic section is almost constant. At the inlet of the condenser section, the average velocity is the highest for the condenser section. Due to the condensation or suction boundary condition, the average velocity decreases. The velocity distribution is smoother for the linear heat flux condition than for the uniform heat flux conditions around the transition regions. The velocity variation shown in Fig. 9.22 will directly result in local dynamic pressure variation or static pressure variation. From the results shown in Fig. 9.23, it can be found that the local static pressure changes significantly from the evaporator to condenser. But the total

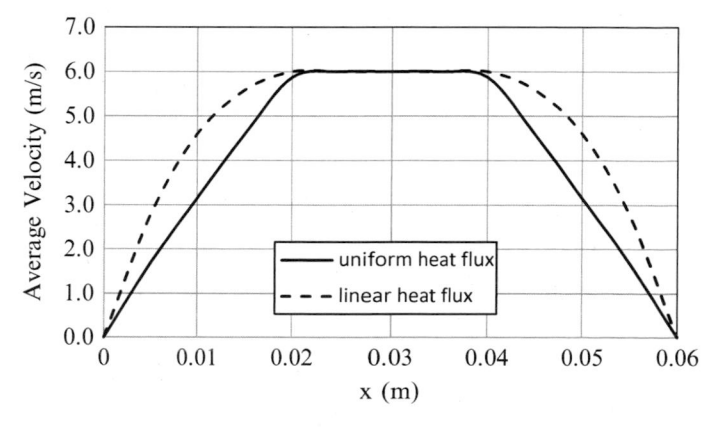

Fig. 9.22 Vapor velocity distribution in a miniature heat pipe (uniform heat flux = 20 W/cm^2)

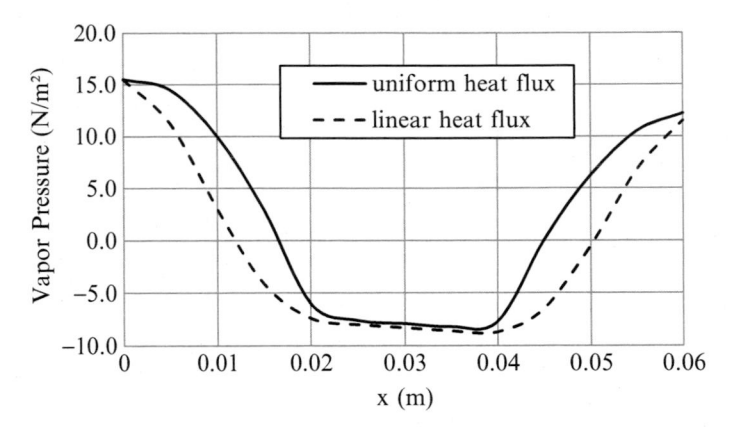

Fig. 9.23 Relative pressure variation in a miniature heat pipe (uniform heat flux $= 20$ W/cm^2 and reference pressure $= 101{,}325$ N/m^2)

pressure drop from the cap end of the evaporator to the cap end of the condenser is small. Although the pressure drop due to the shear stress at the wall is small, the velocity increase from the evaporator to the condenser will result in an additional pressure drop of the condensate flow in wick structures due to the vapor flow effect on the condensate flow at the liquid–vapor interface.

9.2.5 Maximum Capillary Heat Transport

When the maximum capillary pressure cannot overcome the total pressure drops occurring in a heat pipe, the heat pipe reaches the capillary limit as presented in Sect. 9.2. The maximum capillary pressure exists when the capillary radius in the condenser approaches infinity, and the capillary radius in the evaporator reaches the smallest one. If the effective capillary radius for a given wick structure is known, the maximum capillary pressure can be readily determined by Eq. (9.34). The total pressure drop of the liquid flow occurring in the wick structure from the condenser to the evaporator can be found by integrating Eq. (9.68) from the cap end of the condenser to the cap end of the evaporator, i.e.,

$$\Delta p_1 = \int_0^L \left(\frac{\mu_1}{K \varepsilon A_w \rho_1} \right) \dot{m}_1(x) \, dx \qquad (9.118)$$

It should be noticed that the mass flow rate of liquid flow or condensate, $\dot{m}_1$, in the wick is not constant in the evaporator and condenser sections, which depends on how heat is added to the evaporator and how heat is removed from the condenser. For a uniform heat addition in the evaporator and a uniform heat rejection in the condenser with a total heat transfer rate of q, Eq. (9.118) can be expressed as

Eq. (9.79). The total vapor pressure drop occurring in the vapor flow pass can be determined by integrating Eq. (9.96), i.e.,

$$\Delta p_v = \int_0^L \left(\frac{(c_{f,v} \cdot Re_v) \mu_v \dot{m}_v}{2 A_v r_v^2 \rho_v} + \beta \frac{2 \dot{m}_v}{\rho_v A_v^2} \frac{d \dot{m}_v}{dx} \right) dx \qquad (9.119)$$

If the heat pipe is not placed horizontally, the gravitational force will significantly affect the total heat transport capability. When a heat pipe has a tilt angle of θ, as shown in Fig. 9.1, the hydrostatic pressure can be found as

$$\Delta p_g = \rho_l g L \sin \theta \qquad (9.120)$$

Substituting Eqs. (9.34), (9.118), (9.119), and (9.120) into Eq. (9.12) yields

$$\frac{2\sigma}{r_{c,e}} = \int_0^L \left(\frac{\mu_l}{K \varepsilon A_w \rho_l} \right) \dot{m}_l(x) dx$$

$$+ \int_0^L \left(\frac{(c_{f,v} \cdot Re_v) \mu_v \dot{m}_v}{2 A_v r_v^2 \rho_v} + \beta \frac{2 \dot{m}_v}{\rho_v A_v^2} \frac{d \dot{m}_v}{dx} \right) dx - \rho_l g L \sin \theta \qquad (9.121)$$

If all thermal properties are constant and the momentum effect is neglected, Eq. (9.121) can be written as

$$\frac{2\sigma}{r_{c,e}} = \left(\frac{\mu_l}{K A_w h_{lv} \rho_l} \right) L_{\text{eff}} q_{c,\max} + \left(\frac{C (c_{f,v} \cdot Re_v) \mu_v}{2 A_v r_{h,v}^2 \rho_v h_{lv}} \right) L_{\text{eff}} q_{c,\max} - \rho_l g L \sin \theta$$

$$(9.122)$$

Rearranging Eq. (9.122), the maximum capillary heat transport for a heat pipe can be written as

$$q_{c,\max} = \frac{\frac{2\sigma}{r_{c,e}} + \rho_l g L \sin \theta}{\left(\frac{\mu_l}{K A_w h_{lv} \rho_l} + \frac{C (c_{f,v} \cdot Re_v) \mu_v}{2 A_v r_{h,v}^2 \rho_v h_{lv}} \right) L_{\text{eff}}} \qquad (9.123)$$

It should be noticed that L_{eff} shown in Eqs. (9.122) and (9.123) is the effective length depending on the heat flux distributions on the evaporator and condenser sections, which can be expressed as

$$L_{\text{eff}} = \frac{\int_{L_e} \left(\int_0^x q_e' dx \right) dx + L_a q_{c,\max} + \int_{L_c} \left(\int_{L_e + L_a}^x q_e' dx \right) dx}{q_{c,\max}} \qquad (9.124)$$

If the heat addition to the evaporator and heat rejection from the condenser are uniform, i.e.,

$$q'_e = \frac{q_{c,max}}{L_e} \tag{9.125}$$

$$q'_c = \frac{q_{c,max}}{L_c} \tag{9.126}$$

the effective length, L_{eff}, can be found as

$$L_{eff} = \frac{L_e}{2} + L_a + \frac{L_c}{2} \tag{9.127}$$

If the heat flux on both the evaporator and condenser sections has a linear distribution as shown in Fig. 9.21b, i.e.,

$$q'_e = \frac{2q_{c,max}}{L_e}\left(1 - \frac{x}{L_e}\right) \tag{9.128}$$

$$q'_c = \frac{2q_{c,max}}{L_c}\left(\frac{x}{L_c}\right) \tag{9.129}$$

the effective length, L_{eff}, will be

$$L_{eff} = \frac{2}{3}L_e + L_a + \frac{2}{3}L_c \tag{9.130}$$

9.3   Other Heat Transport Limitations

9.3.1   Boiling Limit

When boiling occurs near the evaporating wall in the wick, two consequences result. First, the amount of thin film evaporation at the solid–liquid–vapor interface dramatically decreases as the boiling condition dominates the phase change behavior of the system. Second, the vapor forming at the base of the wick structure forms a blanket of vapor, preventing reentry of the working fluid. Since the vapor conductivity of the working fluid is much lower than the fluid conductivity, the overall conductivity of the wick structure will experience a significant decrease. Obviously, boiling heat transfer in the wick should be avoided as this condition could lead to early dryout of the heat pipe.

   When boiling takes place on a heated surface in a pool, the surface cavity size and superheat play an important role. Hsu (1962) conducted a theoretical analysis and demonstrated that a minimum superheat is needed to activate a cavity and the cavity size affects the superheat. When heat is added on the evaporator section, as

Fig. 9.24 A bubble growth
in a wick

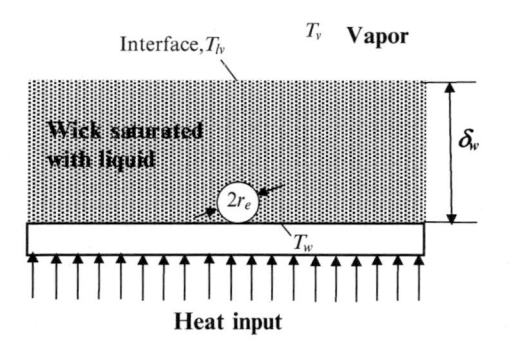

shown in Fig. 9.24, the heat is transferred through the evaporator shell and reaches
the wick saturated with liquid. If no bubble is formed in the wick, i.e., no phase
change heat transfer takes place in the wick, heat is transferred through the wick and
reaches the top surface where the evaporation occurs at the interface, as shown in
Fig. 9.24. If the wall temperature, T_w, the interface temperature, T_{lv}, the wick
thickness, δ_w, and the effective thermal conductivity of the wick, k_{eff}, are given,
the heat flux through the wick can be found as

$$q'' = k_{eff} \frac{T_w - T_{lv}}{\delta_w} \tag{9.131}$$

Rearranging Eq. (9.131) yields

$$T_w - T_{lv} = \frac{q'' \delta_w}{k_{eff}} \tag{9.132}$$

As shown in Eq. (9.132), when the heat flux or wick thickness increases or the
effective thermal conductivity of the wick decreases, the temperature difference,
i.e., $T_w - T_{lv}$, increases. Consider a pore or vapor bubble in the wick structure
with a radius of r_e. If the pore size is small and the wick structure has a higher
effective thermal conductivity, the wick temperature surrounding the bubble is
almost constant equal to the wall temperature, T_w. The pressure difference across
the liquid–vapor interface can be calculated by the Laplace–Young equation, i.e.,

$$p_v - p_l = \frac{2\sigma}{r_e} \tag{9.133}$$

As shown in Eq. (9.133), the vapor pressure is higher than the liquid pressure by
$\frac{2\sigma}{r_e}$. When the temperature increases, the saturation pressure corresponding to
this temperature increases, which can be predicted by the Clausius–Clapeyron
equation, i.e.,

$$\left(\frac{dp}{dT}\right)_{\text{sat}} = \frac{h_{lv}}{(v_v - v_l)T} \tag{9.134}$$

It should be noticed that the unit of temperature, T, in Eq. (9.134) is Kelvin, and $T_w - T_{lv}$ is much smaller than T_w. Therefore, Eq. (9.134) can be further expressed as

$$T_w - T_v = \frac{\Delta p T_w}{h_{lv}}\left(\frac{1}{\rho_v} - \frac{1}{\rho_l}\right) \tag{9.135}$$

where it is assumed that the interface thermal resistance is much smaller than the thermal resistance of the wick, i.e., $T_{lv} \approx T_v$. If the wick is constructed such that the temperature difference between the wall temperature of the evaporator and the saturation temperature, $T_w - T_v$, remains less than the boiling superheat for a given pressure, no bubble(s) will grow near the wall in the wick. The equilibrium state for the bubbles, or the state at which the bubbles no longer collapse, is that thermodynamic state for which the Gibbs free energy between the liquid and vapor phases is minimized. Substituting Eq. (9.133) into Eq. (9.135), the superheat can be found as

$$T_w - T_v = \frac{2\sigma T_w}{h_{lv}r_e}\left(\frac{1}{\rho_v} - \frac{1}{\rho_l}\right) \tag{9.136}$$

If the vapor density is much smaller than the liquid density, Eq. (9.136) may be reduced to

$$T_w - T_v = \frac{2\sigma T_w}{\rho_v h_{lv}r_e} \tag{9.137}$$

where the bubble radius, r_e, in a wick is directly related to the pore size of the wick structure, which can be approximately calculated by Eq. (9.41). According to the theory presented by Hsu (1962), an embryo bubble will grow and a cavity will become an active nucleation site if the equilibrium superheat becomes equaled or exceeded around the perimeter of the embryo bubble. To avoid boiling near the base of the wick structure, the temperature difference between the wall and the saturation temperature must be less than the superheat required for bubble formation. Using the superheat obtained above, the critical heat flux (CHF) related to the boiling limit can be found as

$$q'' = \frac{k_{\text{eff}}}{\delta_w}[T_w - T_v] = \frac{k_{\text{eff}}2\sigma T_w}{\delta_w\rho_v h_{lv}r_e} \tag{9.138}$$

As can be seen, the boiling limit is sensitive to the effective thermal conductivity, k_{eff}, the wick thickness, δ_w, and the meniscus radius of vapor bubble, r_e, at the wick–wall interface. The meniscus radius of the vapor bubble is directly related to the wick pore size and wetting condition.

9.3.2 Sonic Limit

As shown in Figs. 9.22 and 9.23, the mass flow rate increases gradually in the evaporator section. At the evaporating section exit, the mass flow rate is the highest. Starting from this location, the total mass flow at a constant flow rate flows through the adiabatic section, i.e.,

$$\dot{m}_v = \rho_v u_v A_v \tag{9.139}$$

Rewriting Eq. (9.139) in the differential form yields

$$\frac{d\rho_v}{\rho_v} + \frac{du_v}{u_v} + \frac{dA_v}{A_v} = 0 \tag{9.140}$$

Rearranging Eq. (9.140) produces

$$\frac{dA_v}{A_v} = \frac{du_v}{u_v}\left(-\frac{\frac{d\rho_v}{\rho_v}}{\frac{du_v}{u_v}} - 1\right) \tag{9.141}$$

Considering the frictional momentum equation of

$$\frac{dp_v}{\rho_v} + u_v\, du_v = 0 \tag{9.142}$$

and the definition of sound speed of

$$a = \sqrt{\frac{dp_v}{d\rho_v}} \tag{9.143}$$

it can be shown that

$$\frac{\frac{d\rho_v}{\rho_v}}{\frac{du_v}{u_v}} = -Ma^2 \tag{9.144}$$

where Ma is the Mach number, i.e.,

$$Ma = \frac{u_v}{a} \tag{9.145}$$

Considering Eq. (9.144), Eq. (9.141) can be expressed as

$$\frac{dA_v}{A_v} = \frac{du_v}{u_v}\left(Ma^2 - 1\right) \tag{9.146}$$

From Eq. (9.146), it can be found that if the flow is subsonic, i.e., $Ma < 1.0$, the velocity increase must be accompanied with the area decrease. If the flow is

supersonic flow, i.e., $Ma > 1.0$, the velocity increase must be accompanied with the area increase. Clearly, with a constant cross section for a typical vapor path in a heat pipe, the velocity is limited by the local sound speed, i.e., the highest velocity of the vapor flow in a heat pipe cannot be higher than the local sound speed. If the vapor velocity at the evaporating section exit reaches the local sound speed, the vapor flow is choked. As the choked flow occurs, the vapor flow rate will not respond to the amount of heat added in the evaporator. The heat pipe has reached the maximum heat transport, which is called the sonic limit. Based on the energy balance, the maximum heat transport due to the sonic limitation can be expressed as

$$q_{s,\,\mathrm{max}} = A_v \rho_v h_{lv} u_v \tag{9.147}$$

where u_v and ρ_v are the vapor velocity and vapor density at the evaporating section exit, which correspond to the local sound speed. If the vapor flow in the heat pipe can be approximated as one-dimensional flow with assumptions of negligible frictional force and ideal gas, the local sound speed can be found as

$$u_v = (\gamma_v R T_v)^{1/2} \tag{9.148}$$

Substituting Eq. (9.148) into Eq. (9.147) yields

$$q_{s,\,\mathrm{max}} = A_v \rho_v h_{lv} (\gamma_v R T_v)^{1/2} \tag{9.149}$$

It should be noted that the vapor temperature, T_v, shown in Eq. (9.149) is corresponding to the local sound speed as well. For a given heat pipe with a given application, the evaporator temperature is given. Based on the saturation condition, the pressure in the evaporating section can be found. If the evaporator temperature is defined as the stagnation temperature, T_0, and the corresponding saturation pressure is the stagnation pressure, p_0, the vapor pressure, p_v, and the vapor temperature, T_v, at the evaporating section exit, can be found as

$$p_v = \frac{p_0}{1 + \frac{\gamma_v}{2} Ma^2} \tag{9.150}$$

and

$$T_v = \frac{T_0}{1 + \frac{\gamma_v - 1}{2} Ma^2} \tag{9.151}$$

respectively. Considering Eqs. (9.150) and (9.151), Eq. (9.149) can be expressed as

$$q_{s,\,\mathrm{max}} = \frac{A_v h_{lv} p_0 \gamma_v \left(1 + \frac{\gamma_v - 1}{2} Ma^2\right)^{1/2}}{\left(1 + \frac{\gamma_v}{2} Ma^2\right) (\gamma_v R T_0)^{1/2}} \tag{9.152}$$

Considering the ideal gas assumption, i.e.,

$$\rho_0 = \frac{p_0}{RT_0} \tag{9.153}$$

Equation (9.152) can be expressed as

$$q_{s,\max} = \frac{A_v \rho_0 h_{lv} (\gamma_v R T_0)^{1/2} \left(1 + \frac{\gamma_v - 1}{2} Ma^2\right)^{1/2}}{1 + \frac{\gamma_v}{2} Ma^2} \tag{9.154}$$

If $Ma = 1$, Eq. (9.154) becomes

$$q_{s,\max} = 1.41 A_v \rho_0 h_{lv} (\gamma_v R T_0)^{1/2} \frac{(1 + \gamma_v)^{1/2}}{2 + \gamma_v} \tag{9.155}$$

where T_0 and ρ_0 are the stagnation temperature and the stagnation density of vapor flow in the evaporator, respectively. It should be noted that the choked flow might occur at the exit to the evaporator or at any location in the condenser section if the cross-sectional area of the vapor flow path changes.

9.3.3   Entrainment Limit

In an operating heat pipe, when the vapor flow direction is opposite the liquid flow direction, the frictional shear stress occurring at the liquid–vapor interface may slow down the return of liquid to the evaporator. As the vapor velocity increases, the vapor flow effect on the liquid–vapor interface increases depending on surface tension, viscosities, and densities of both the vapor and liquid phases. When the influence caused by the frictional shear stress acting on the liquid–vapor interface by the frictional vapor flow is large enough, the liquid flow cannot flow back to the evaporator. When this occurs, the liquid in the evaporator dries out. At this point the heat pipe reaches a heat transport limit, which is known as the entrainment limit. Based on a Weber number equal to 1, i.e., $We = F_{lv}/F_\sigma = 1$, where F_{lv} is the shear stress at the liquid–vapor interface and F_σ is the surface tension force, Cotter (1967) developed an approximation of the entrainment limit as follows

$$q_{ent} = A_v h_{lv} \left(\frac{\sigma \rho_v}{2 r_{h,w}}\right)^{0.5} \tag{9.156}$$

where $r_{h,w}$ is the hydraulic radius of the wick surface pore.

9.3.4 Viscous Limit

When the vapor pressure from the evaporator to the condenser cannot overcome the vapor pressure drop caused by the viscous forces, the heat pipe reaches a heat transport limit, which is called the viscous limit. Using assumptions of laminar flow, ideal gas, and zero pressure in the cap end of the condenser, the viscous limit can be determined by (Peterson 1994)

$$q_{\text{vis}} = \frac{r_v^2 h_{\text{lv}} \rho_{v,e} p_{v,e} A_v}{c_{f,v} \cdot Re_v \mu_v L_{\text{eff}}} \tag{9.157}$$

where $\rho_{v,e}$ and $p_{v,e}$ are the vapor density and vapor pressure in the cap end of the evaporator, respectively.

9.4 Effective Thermal Conductivity

Utilizing the phase change heat transfer, a heat pipe can effectively increase the heat transport capability. This heat transfer performance can be evaluated by effective thermal resistance or effective thermal conductivity. The effective thermal resistance of a heat pipe, R_{hp}, is defined as the temperature difference between the evaporator and the condenser, $T_e - T_c$, divided by the heat transferred by the heat pipe, q, i.e.,

$$R_{\text{hp}} = \frac{T_e - T_c}{q} \tag{9.158}$$

where T_e and T_c are the average evaporator and average condenser temperatures, respectively. The effective thermal conductivity is defined as

$$k_{\text{eff}} = \frac{q L_{\text{eff}}}{A_c(T_e - T_c)} \tag{9.159}$$

where A_c is the total cross-sectional area of the heat pipe and L_{eff} is the effective length. Compared to the effective thermal resistance, the effective thermal conductivity of a heat pipe can consider the effects of the heat pipe length and cross-sectional area. Examining Eq. (9.159), it can be found that the cross-sectional area of a heat pipe, A_c, the average evaporator temperature, T_e, the average condenser temperatures, T_c, and the input power transferred by the heat pipe, q, can be easily obtained for a given heat pipe. The effective length, L_{eff}, however, depends on how heat is added to the evaporator and how heat is removed from the condenser. If heat is added on the cap end of the evaporator and heat is removed from the cap end of

the condenser, the effective length of the heat pipe is the total length of the heat pipe. But for most applications, the heat is added on the outer surface of the evaporator section and the heat is removed from the outer surface of the condenser. For this situation, the effective length, L_{eff}, should be the length between the location where the average evaporator temperature occurs and the location where the average condenser temperature occurs. The effective length, L_{eff}, can be approximately calculated by Eq. (9.124).

The calculation of the effective thermal conductivity described above is based on the experimental data or the temperature difference between the evaporator and the condenser. If the experimental data or the temperature difference between the evaporator and the condenser is not available, i.e., substituting Eq. (9.158) into Eq. (9.159) and eliminating $\frac{T_e - T_c}{q}$, the effective thermal conductivity can be expressed as

$$k_{\text{eff}} = \frac{L_{\text{eff}}}{A_c R_{\text{hp}}} \tag{9.160}$$

where the total thermal resistance of the heat pipe, R_{hp}, consists of all thermal resistances occurring in the heat transfer processes from the evaporator to the condenser in a heat pipe. Consider a round heat pipe, as shown in Fig. 9.25, with an outer diameter D and a total length L. The heat pipe consists of an evaporator with a length of L_e, an adiabatic section with a length of L_a, and a condenser with a length of L_c. As shown in Fig. 9.25, the total thermal resistance, R_{hp}, can be expressed as

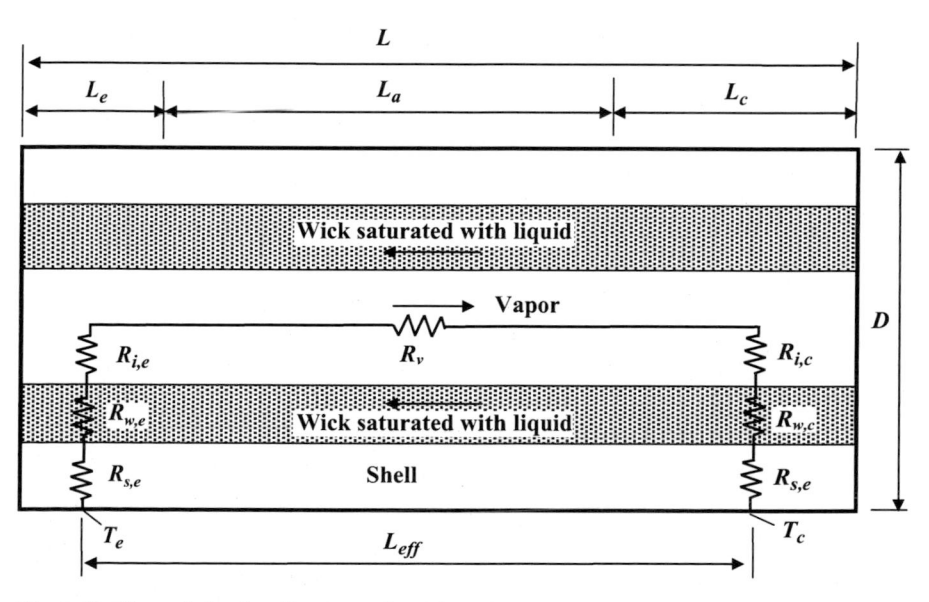

Fig. 9.25 Thermal circuits of a conventional heat pipe

$$R_{hp} = R_{s,e} + R_{w,e} + R_{int,e} + R_v + R_{int,c} + R_{w,c} + R_{s,c} \qquad (9.161)$$

where $R_{s,e}$ and $R_{s,c}$ are the conduction thermal resistances of the evaporator and condenser walls, respectively; $R_{w,e}$ and $R_{w,c}$ are the conduction thermal resistances of the wicks saturated with working fluid at the evaporator and condenser, respectively; $R_{int,e}$ and $R_{int,c}$ are the interfacial thermal resistances of evaporation and condensation occurring at the evaporator and condenser, respectively; and R_v is the thermal resistance of the vapor flow from the evaporator to the condenser.

The thermal resistances of the heat pipe walls at both the evaporator and the condenser can be calculated by

$$R_{s,e} = \frac{\ln\left(\frac{D}{D-2\delta_{s,e}}\right)}{2\pi k_s L_e} \qquad (9.162)$$

and

$$R_{s,c} = \frac{\ln\left(\frac{D}{D-2\delta_{s,c}}\right)}{2\pi k_s L_c} \qquad (9.163)$$

respectively. k_s in Eqs. (9.162) and (9.163) is the thermal conductivity of the heat pipe wall or shell, and $\delta_{s,e}$ and $\delta_{s,c}$ represent the thicknesses of heat pipe wall or shell at the evaporator and condenser, respectively. After heat travels through the wall, the heat reaches the working fluid in the wick. Provided that the wick is saturated with working fluid and no boiling occurs in the wick, the heat will transfer through the wick, and evaporation will only occur at the liquid–vapor–solid interface. The heat transfer across the wick is dominated by heat conduction. The thermal resistances of the wicks at both the evaporator and the condenser can be determined by

$$R_{w,e} = \frac{\ln\left(\frac{D-2\delta_{s,e}}{D-2\delta_{s,e}-2\delta_{w,e}}\right)}{2\pi k_w L_e} \qquad (9.164)$$

and

$$R_{w,c} = \frac{\ln\left(\frac{D-2\delta_{s,c}}{D-2\delta_{s,c}-2\delta_{w,c}}\right)}{2\pi k_w L_c} \qquad (9.165)$$

where k_w is the effective thermal conductivity of the wick, $\delta_{w,e}$ and $\delta_{w,c}$ are the wick thicknesses in the evaporator and condenser, respectively. Table 9.3 lists expressions for determining the effective thermal conductivities of several common wicks. As shown, the effective thermal conductivity of a wick is a function of the solid conductivity, k_s, the working fluid conductivity, k_l, and the porosity, ε. In each of the expressions, it can be found that $\lim_{\varepsilon \to 0} k_{eff} = k_s$ and $\lim_{\varepsilon \to 1} k_{eff} = k_l$, and the manner in which the effective conductivity varies between the limiting cases is

Table 9.3 Expressions for wick effective thermal conductivities for various geometries

Wick condition	Expression for effective thermal conductivity
Sintered	$k_{\text{Sintered}} = \dfrac{k_s[2k_s+k_1-2\varepsilon(k_s-k_1)]}{2k_s+k_1+\varepsilon(k_s-k_1)}$
Packed spheres	$k_{\text{Packed spheres}} = \dfrac{k_1[(2k_1+k_s)-2(1-\varepsilon)(k_1-k_s)]}{(2k_1+k_s)+(1-\varepsilon)(k_1-k_s)}$
Wick and liquid in series	$k_{\text{Series}} = \dfrac{k_1 k_s}{k_s\varepsilon+k_1(1-\varepsilon)}$
Wick and fluid in parallel	$k_{\text{Parallel}} = k_1\varepsilon + k_s(1-\varepsilon)$
Wrapped screens	$k_{\text{Wrapped screen}} = \dfrac{k_1[(k_1+k_s)-(1-\varepsilon)(k_1-k_s)]}{(k_1+k_s)+(1-\varepsilon)(k_1-k_s)}$

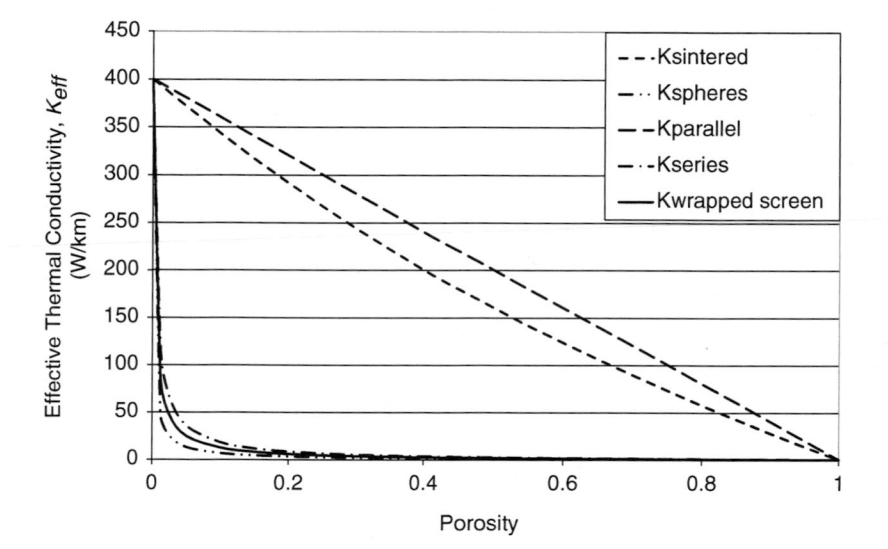

Fig. 9.26 Effective thermal conductivities presented in Table 9.3

drastically different depending upon the type of arrangement of the wick structure. Comparing the various effective conductivity relations, as illustrated in Table 9.3 and Fig. 9.26, it becomes clear that sintering the metallic particles dramatically enhances the effective thermal conductivity.

When heat is transferred through the wick filled with working fluid and reaches the interface between the vapor and the wick, the heat is removed by evaporation. The interfacial thermal resistance of the evaporation can be expressed as

$$R_{i,e} = \frac{1}{L_e\pi(D-2\delta_{s,e}-2\delta_{w,e})h_e} \tag{9.166}$$

where h_e is the evaporation heat transfer coefficient at the interface between the vapor and the wick. Because most of the heat at the interface is removed by thin film evaporation, the interfacial thermal resistance is much smaller than the thermal resistance due to the wick thickness. At a low heat flux, this interface thermal resistance can be neglected.

In the condenser section, vapor is condensed into liquid. At the interface, there is an interfacial thermal resistance, i.e.,

$$R_{i,c} = \frac{1}{L_c \pi (D - 2\delta_{s,c} - 2\delta_{w,c}) h_c} \tag{9.167}$$

where h_c is the condensation heat transfer coefficient at the interface between the vapor and the wick. This interfacial condensation thermal resistance is much smaller than the thermal resistance of the wick, and this interfacial thermal resistance can be neglected.

In a heat pipe, the pure working fluid is charged. Evaporation and condensation processes in a heat pipe are almost in an equilibrium state. In other words, the pressure inside a heat pipe directly affects the saturation temperature. When vapor flows from the cap end of the evaporator through the adiabatic section to the cap end of the condenser, the vapor pressure drop is produced due to the viscous force. If the vapor pressure difference from the evaporator to the condenser in a heat pipe is found as $(\Delta p)_v$, the saturation temperature variation can be expressed as

$$(\Delta T)_v = \frac{T_{v,e}(\Delta p)_v}{h_{lv}} \left(\frac{1}{\rho_v} - \frac{1}{\rho_l}\right) \tag{9.168}$$

The equivalent thermal resistance due to the vapor flow can be expressed as

$$R_v = \frac{(\Delta T)_v}{q} \tag{9.169}$$

9.5 Samples of Heat Transfer Modeling

9.5.1 Heat Transfer Rate Effect on Heat Transfer Performance of a Sintered Heat Pipe

When heat is added to the evaporator section, heat is transferred from the heat pipe wall through the wick saturated with the working fluid to the liquid–vapor–solid interface where thin film evaporation occurs. The vapor flows from the evaporator through the adiabatic section to the condensing section, where the vapor condenses into the condensate and releases the latent heat. The heat is transferred from the condensation film through the wick saturated with the condensate to the heat pipe shell, where the heat is removed by a liquid cooling or forced convection of air flow. During this heat transfer process, thermal resistance in the wick plays an important role in determining the total temperature drop in the heat pipe, in particular, for a high heat flux application. The model described in Sect. 9.4 can be used to predict the effective thermal conductivity or thermal resistance of a heat pipe. This model,

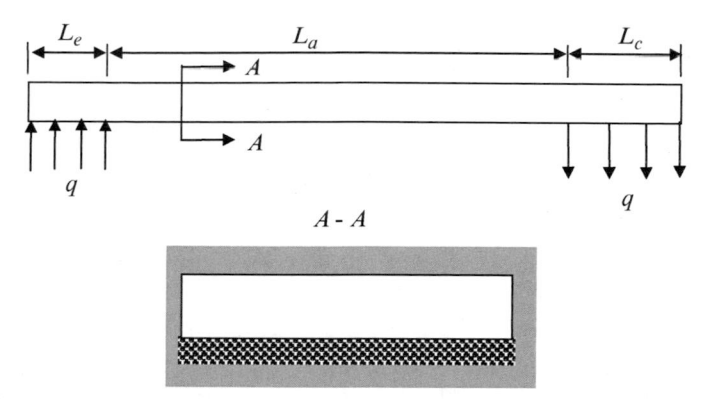

Fig. 9.27 Schematic of a flat-plate heat pipe

however, cannot effectively predict the heat input effect on the thermal resistance of a heat pipe. In other words, when the power input is different, the liquid level in the wick is different, which directly affects the thermal resistance or effective thermal conductivity of a heat pipe (Chang et al. 2008)

Consider a flat-plate heat pipe as shown in Fig. 9.27. As shown, the heat pipe used in this sample has a sandwich structure made up of a lower copper wall, wick layer, vapor space, and upper copper wall. The sintered copper wick with a diameter of 32 μm was placed on the bottom inside wall of the heat pipe. Overall dimensions of the vapor chamber were 130 mm long, 20 mm wide, and 3.3 mm thick. When the power input in an evaporator is increased, the flow rate of the working fluid in the flow path also increases, thereby resulting in the increase of a total pressure drop. To overcome the pressure drop, the driving pressure occurring in the wick must increase. The increase of the capillary pressure is directly related to the meniscus radius of the liquid–vapor interface in the sintered wick. The capillary pressure occurring in the heat pipe can be expressed as

$$\Delta P_{\mathrm{C}} = 2\sigma \left(\frac{1}{r_e} - \frac{1}{r_c} \right) \tag{9.170}$$

where r_e and r_c are the meniscus radii at the liquid–vapor interface in the evaporator and condenser sections, respectively. For the heat pipe investigated herein, r_c can be assumed to be close to infinity. The capillary pressure in the heat pipe will only depend on the meniscus radius of the sintered wick in the evaporator. Cheng and Ma (2007) showed that if the wick consists of sintered particles with a uniform radius, the possible arrangements formed in the wick are triangular, rectangular, and hexagonal structures as shown in Fig. 9.9. By viewing from one particle, there would be several structures formed around this particle. By listing all possible arrangements of these structures and considering that each group of structures has the same possibility, the percentage of each structure can be determined, i.e., the percentages for the triangular, rectangular, and hexagonal structures are 45 %,

28 %, and 27 %, respectively. The minimum meniscus radii of the triangular, rectangular, and hexagonal structures are calculated to be $0.103r_p$, $0.273r_p$, and $0.654r_p$, respectively, where r_p is the particle radius. As a reference case, the average minimum meniscus radius for the sintered particles with a uniform radius is calculated to be $r_{min} = 0.443r_p$, as shown in Eq. (9.46), which agrees well with the one cited by Ferrell and Alleavitch (1970) and most textbooks on heat pipes (Peterson 1994; Faghri 1995; Reay and Kew 2006).

There exist many types of structures with different pore sizes in the wick, and with the increase of power input, the liquid in large pore sizes cannot be held anymore and recede to smaller pore sizes as shown in Fig. 9.28. There are two factors determining the thermal resistance of the wick thickness: one is the expanded liquid–vapor interface and the other is the effective thickness of wick saturated with working fluid. Due to very high heat transfer coefficient of thin film evaporation, the thermal resistance at the expanded liquid–vapor–solid interfaces is much smaller than the thermal resistance of wicks saturated with the working fluid, so the thermal resistance in the wick per unit area can be approximately determined by the effective thickness of wicks saturated with the working fluid, i.e.,

$$R_{w,e}'' = \frac{\delta_{eff}}{k_{eff}} \tag{9.171}$$

where δ_{eff} is the effective thickness of wick saturated with the working fluid depending on power input. From Table 9.3, it can be found that the effective thermal conductivity, k_{eff}, for sintered particles can be determined by

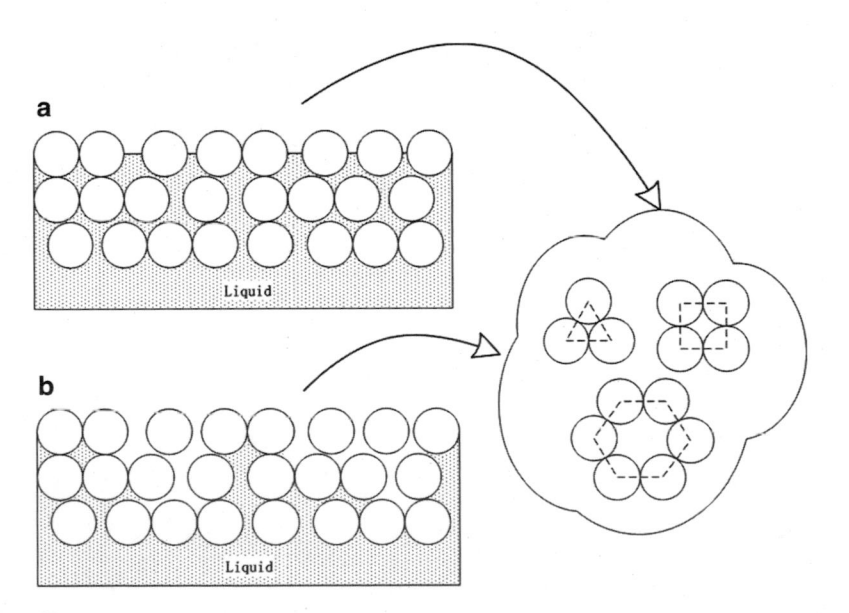

Fig. 9.28 Receding process of liquid in wick and possible particle structures (Chang et al. 2008)

$$k_{\text{eff}} = k_{\text{s}} \left(\frac{2 + k_{\text{l}}/k_{\text{s}} - 2\varepsilon(1 - k_{\text{l}}/k_{\text{s}})}{2 + k_{\text{l}}/k_{\text{s}} + \varepsilon(1 - k_{\text{l}}/k_{\text{s}})} \right) \tag{9.172}$$

When the power input to the heat pipe is zero, the liquid level in the evaporator would not recede into the wick, so the effective thickness of wick, δ_{eff}, is equal to the total thickness of the wick, δ, in the evaporator, as illustrated in Fig. 9.29a.

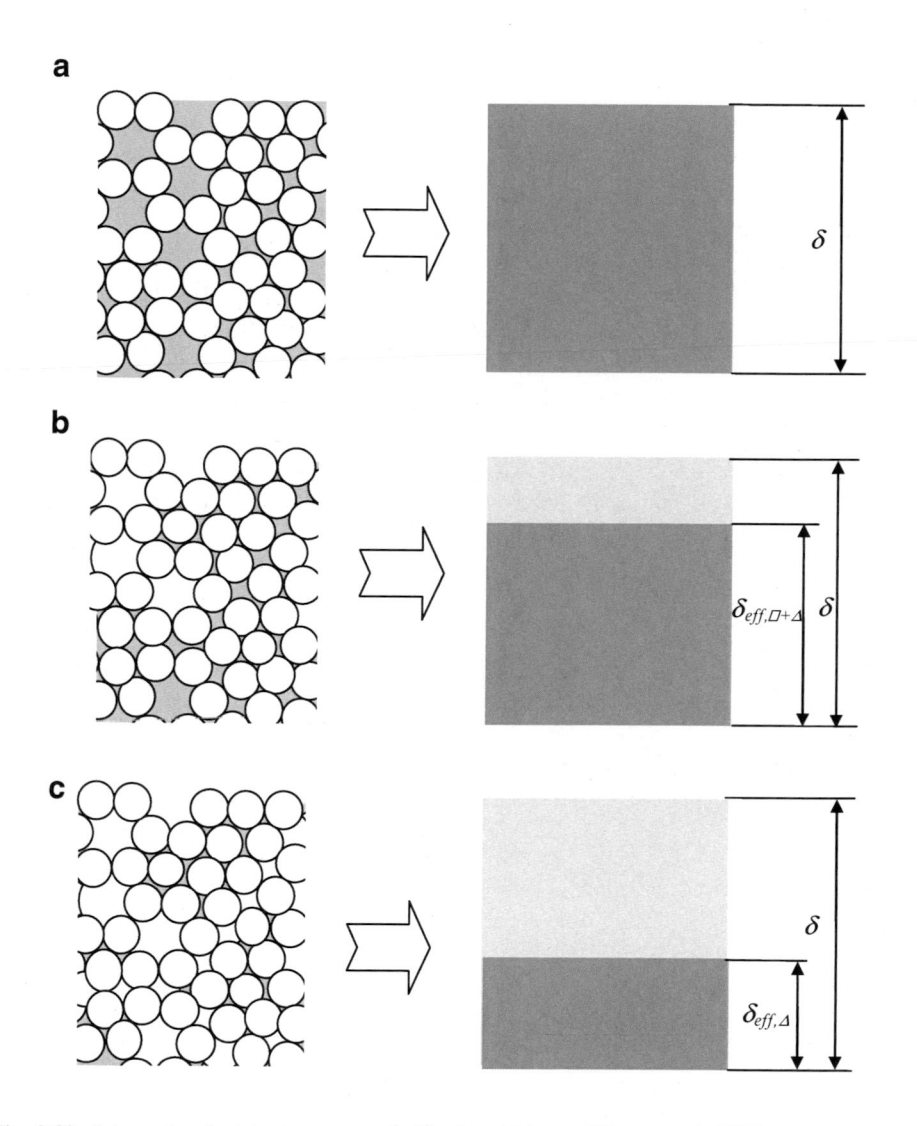

Fig. 9.29 Schematic of wick structures and effective thickness (Chang et al. 2008). (**a**) A wick with particles saturated with liquid at a heat input of 0.0 W. (**b**) As the heat transfer rate is high, larger pores held by hexagonal structures dry out and only rectangular and triangular structures saturated with liquid exist. (**c**) As the heat transfer rate is higher, pores held by hexagonal and rectangular structures dry out and only triangular structures saturated with liquid exist

As the power input to the evaporator is increased, the liquid level recedes into the wick to produce the meniscus radius and the capillary pressure to overcome the liquid pressure drop occurring in the flow path, i.e.,

$$\Delta p_C = \Delta p_l + \Delta p_v + \Delta p_g \tag{9.173}$$

The pumping head due to the capillary pressure, Δp_C, can be determined by Eq. (9.170). The liquid pressure drop, Δp_l, is the result of the combined effect of both viscous and inertial forces. If the flow rate in the wick is very small, the effect of inertial force can be neglected, and the pressure difference in the liquid phase is caused only by frictional forces at the liquid–solid interface and the liquid–vapor interface due to the vapor flow effect. The total liquid pressure drop for uniform heat addition and rejection can be found by integrating Eq. (9.68), i.e.,

$$\Delta p_l = \left(\frac{\mu_l}{KA_w\rho_l h_{lv}}\right)L_{eff}q \tag{9.174}$$

where

$$K = \frac{r_p^2 \varepsilon^3}{37.5(1-\varepsilon)^2} \tag{9.175}$$

and

$$L_{eff} = 0.5L_e + L_a + 0.5L_c \tag{9.176}$$

Based on the one-dimensional vapor flow approximation, the vapor pressure drop can be determined by Eq. (9.103), i.e.,

$$\Delta p_v = \left(\frac{(c_{f,v} \cdot Re_v)\mu_v}{2r_{h,v}^2 A_v \rho_v h_{lv}}\right)L_{eff}q \tag{9.177}$$

As the power input to the evaporator is increased, the meniscus radius decreases, which can be determined by wick structures shown in Fig. 9.28. If the determined meniscus radius is between ∞ and $0.654r_p$, the receding of the liquid level will occur in relatively larger pores, i.e., in the hexagonal structure. When the power input is increased further, the wick structure with larger pores cannot hold liquid and the wick structure with larger pores such as hexagonal structures will dry out, as illustrated in Fig. 9.29b. In this condition, the thermal resistance in the wick will be due to the rectangular and triangular structures saturated with liquid, because the vapor generated at the liquid–vapor interface can easily escape from the opened hexagonal structures as shown in Fig. 9.29b. The thermal resistance per unit area can be expressed as

$$R''_{w,e} = \frac{\delta_{eff,\square+\Delta}}{k_{eff}} \tag{9.178}$$

where $\delta_{\text{eff},\square+\Delta}$ is the effective thickness of the wick consisting of the rectangular and triangular structures saturated with liquid, which can be found by the percentages of the wick structures, i.e.,

$$\delta_{\text{eff},\square+\Delta} = 0.73\delta \tag{9.179}$$

As the power input to the evaporator continues to increase, the liquid level will recede into the wick with relatively smaller pores. If the meniscus radius is smaller than $0.654r_p$, which corresponds to the situation shown in Fig. 9.29b, the liquid–vapor interface will vary in the rectangular structures of the wick. When the power input is higher than that corresponding to the meniscus radius of $0.273r_p$, as illustrated in Fig. 9.29c, the wick structure with rectangular structures cannot hold the liquid and will dry out. If this situation occurs, the thermal resistance in the wick will be primarily attributed to the triangular structures saturated with liquid, because the vapor generated at the liquid–vapor interface can easily escape from the opened hexagonal and rectangular structures, as shown in Fig. 9.29c. In this condition, the thermal resistance per unit area can be expressed as

$$R''_{\text{w,e}} = \frac{\delta_{\text{eff},\Delta}}{k_{\text{eff}}} \tag{9.180}$$

where $\delta_{\text{eff},\Delta}$ is the effective thickness of the wick consisting of the triangular structures saturated with liquid, which can be found by the percentages of the wick structures, i.e.,

$$\delta_{\text{eff},\Delta} = 0.45\delta \tag{9.181}$$

If the power input to the evaporator is increased further, the liquid–vapor interface will further recede and the meniscus radius falls between $0.273r_p$ and $0.103r_p$, which represents the pore size range of the triangular structure. When the power input is higher than that corresponding to the minimum meniscus radius of $0.103r_p$, the whole heat pipe will dry out and reaches the capillary limitation. Clearly, the thermal resistance in the wick section of the evaporator is directly dependent on power input, which determines the meniscus radius variation and liquid distribution in the wick. For a given power input, the meniscus radius can be calculated, and the percentage of hexagonal, rectangular, and/or triangular structures in the wick saturated with liquid can be obtained. Since the effective thickness of wicks saturated with liquid can be determined, the temperature difference across the wick in the evaporator can be calculated. Based on the calculation procedures discussed above, the thermal resistance of the wick per unit area in the evaporator can be expressed as

$$R''_{\text{w,e}} = -C_1 \frac{2\sigma/r_{\text{eff}} - \Delta p_g}{L_{\text{eff}} \left(\dfrac{\mu_l}{KA_w\rho_l h_{lv}} + \dfrac{C\left(c_{f,v}\cdot Re_v\right)\mu_v}{2r_{h,v}^2 A_v\rho_v h_{lv}} \right)} + C_2 \tag{9.182}$$

where the constants C_1 and C_2 depend on the particle size and the meniscus radius at the liquid–vapor interface in the evaporator. Chang et al. (2008) used the approach presented above to successfully predict the thermal resistance occurring in a vapor chamber with heat flux effect, which agreed very well with the experimental data.

9.5.2   Effects of Particle Size and Wick Thickness of Sintered Particles

When the pore size becomes smaller, the capillary pressure can be increased. At the same time, the pore size reduction causes an increase in the liquid pressure drop of the liquid flow in the wick. When the heat flux is high, the boiling limitation plays a more important role than the capillary limitation. The heat conduction resistance, capillary pumping pressure, frictional pressure drop, and onset of bubble formation are primary factors determining the maximum evaporating heat transfer in a sintered wick structure. Hanlon and Ma (2003) considered a two-dimensional flow as shown in Fig. 9.30 and developed a two-dimensional model incorporating all these factors to predict the overall heat transfer capability in the sintered wick structure. The numerical results show that it is possible to promote thin film evaporation from the top surface of a sintered wick by selecting the appropriate particle size, the porosity, and the thickness. By decreasing the average particle radius, the evaporation heat transfer coefficient can be enhanced. Results also indicate that the maximum dryout heat flux is a function of wick thickness and

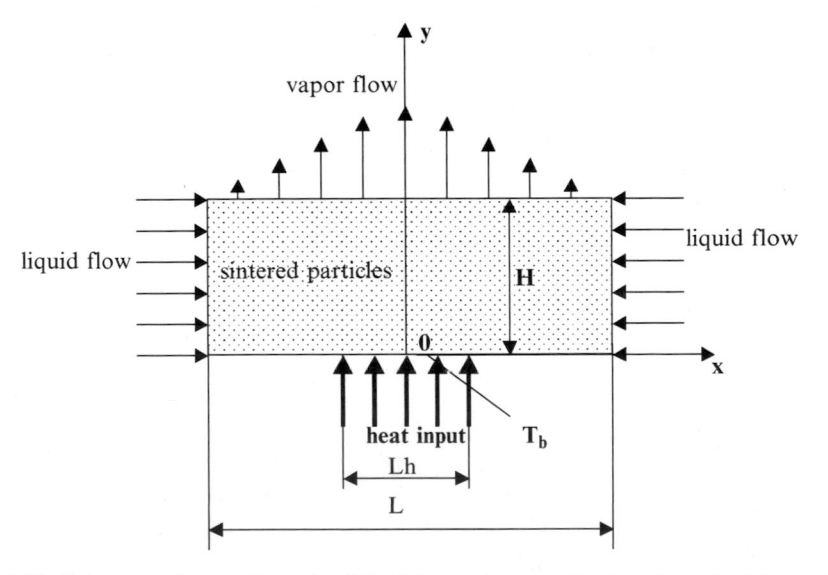

Fig. 9.30 Schematic of a two-dimensional fluid flow and evaporation in a sintered wick structure

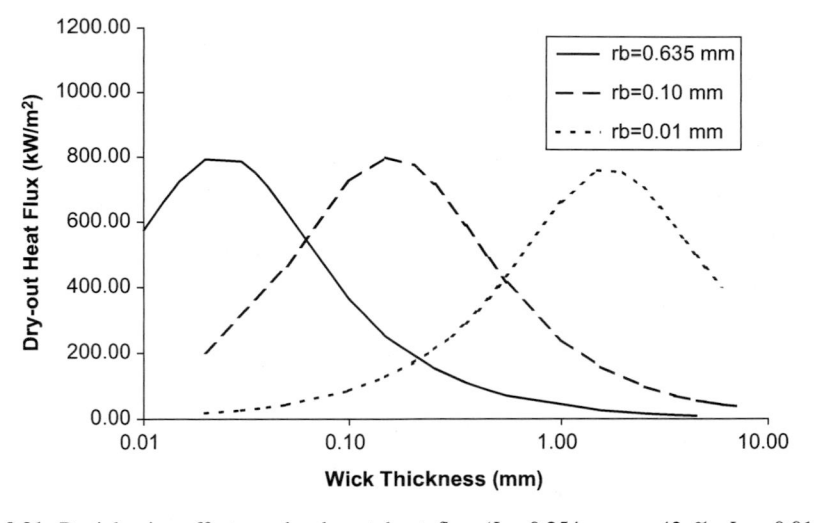

Fig. 9.31 Particle size effect on the dryout heat flux ($L = 0.254$ m; $\varepsilon = 43$ %; $L_h = 0.01$ m; working fluid = water)

particle size as shown in Fig. 9.31, demonstrating that there exists an optimization design in terms of particle size and wick thickness for a given heat flux.

9.6   Thermosyphon

One of the most simple heat pipes is the thermosyphon. A typical thermosyphon is a vertically oriented container with a liquid pool on the bottom as shown in Fig. 9.32. As heat is added to the evaporator section where a liquid pool exists, the liquid vaporizes. The vapor rises and passes through the adiabatic section to the condenser section, where the vapor condenses and releases its latent heat. The condensate is then pumped from the condenser to the evaporator by gravitational force. The initial concept of the thermosyphon can be traced back to the Perkins tube, as shown in Fig. 9.33 (Perkins and Buck 1892). As shown, the tubes charged with liquid were directly placed into a furnace, where the heat was added on. The condensing section which is on top was directly exposed to the ambient air in the room. The heat from the furnace was readily transported to the room. For a typical thermosyphon, heat coming from the bottom section is transferred through the wall and reaches the liquid pool located in the bottom of the thermosyphon. When the temperature difference between the wall temperature and the saturation temperature corresponding to the container pressure is higher than the superheat of the nucleation, pool boiling takes place, which is a typical nucleate boiling heat transfer. The CHF is one of the most important heat transfer limitations occurring in a thermosyphon. The thermosyphon has been widely used in electronics

Fig. 9.32 Schematic
of a thermosyphon

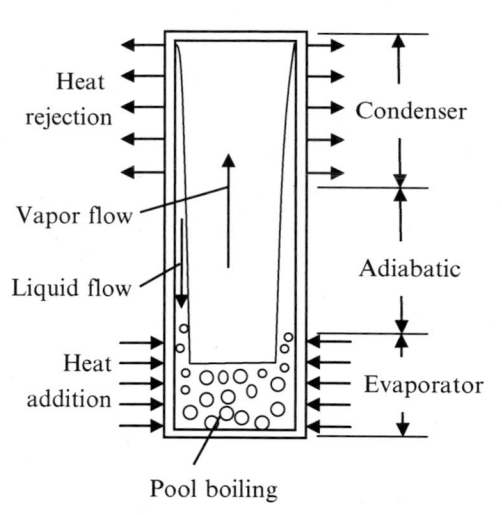

Fig. 9.33 Thermosyphon—original
drawing of Perkins' tubes
(Perkins and Buck 1892)

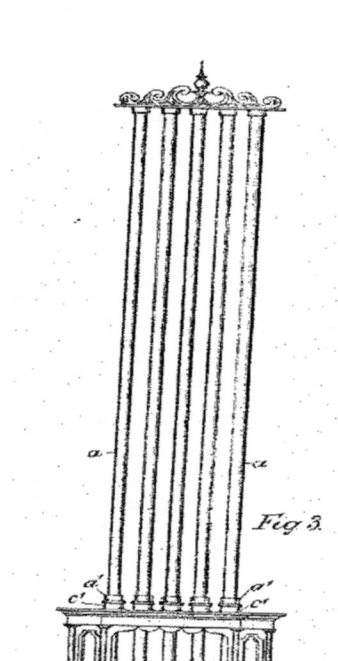

cooling and in the oil industry due to its highly efficient heat transfer performance,
high level of temperature distribution, simplicity, and reliability as well as cost
effectiveness. In a typical thermosyphon, the evaporator must be located below
the condenser for satisfactory operation because the device has to rely on gravity

for condensate return. Therefore, thermosyphons are ineffective in zero gravity or microgravity. In particular, when heat is added on the top section of the container a thermosyphon does not function.

9.7 Loop Heat Pipes/Capillary Pumped Loop

The LHP and CPL utilize the capillary pressure developed in a fine pore wick to circulate the working fluid in a closed loop system. Figure 9.34 shows the schematic of the CPL. The liquid phase flows through the liquid line from the condenser to the evaporator, and the vapor flows from the evaporator to the condenser through the vapor line. The LHP or CPL can significantly reduce or eliminate the liquid pressure drop and vapor flow effect on the liquid flow, resulting in a significant increase in the capillary pumping ability. Because the evaporator in an LHP or a CPL is not only used as a heat sink to remove heat but also used to provide the total capillary pumping pressure, a highly efficient evaporator is the key to success for an LHP or a CPL. Compared to a conventional heat pipe, LHP or CPL systems have the potential to transport large amounts of heat over long distances at various orientations with minimal temperature drops and no external pumping power. Due to this unique feature, the LHP or CPL is especially suitable for the space station program, advanced communication satellite, high powered spacecraft, and electronics cooling, all of which require large heat dissipation. It is anticipated that the CPL or LHP will play an important role in thermal management in space and terrestrial systems in the future.

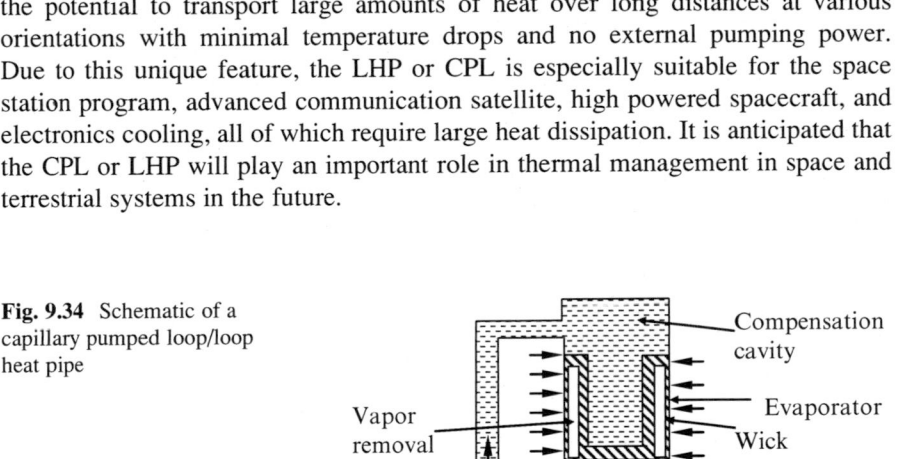

Fig. 9.34 Schematic of a capillary pumped loop/loop heat pipe

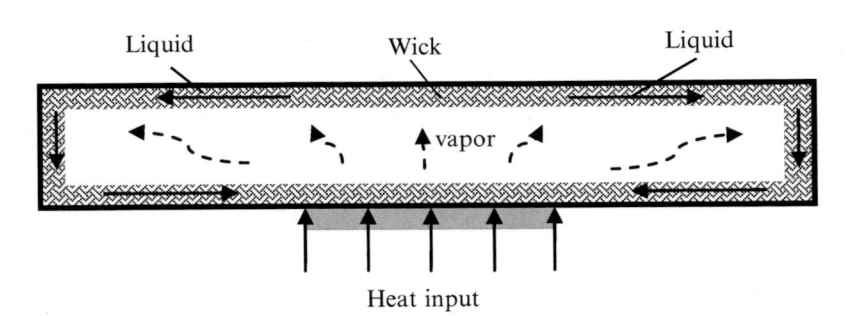

Fig. 9.35 Schematic of the cross-sectional view of a vapor chamber

9.8   Vapor Chamber

Vapor chambers, also known as flat heat pipes, have the same primary components as a typical tubular heat pipe. These components consist of a hermetically sealed hollow chamber, a working fluid, and a wick structure. Compared to a one-dimensional tubular heat pipe, a typical vapor chamber is a two-dimensional heat pipe with a thickness much less than the other two dimensions. The thickness can be as thin as 0.5 mm. Due to this unique dimension feature, the vapor chamber as shown in Fig. 9.35 has been widely used as a heat spreader to spread heat generated from microelectronic components or systems. When the thickness is very small, the cross-sectional area of vapor flow is significantly reduced, which directly limits the heat transport capability. In addition, the thickness reduction makes the wick thickness as thin as possible, which directly limits the capillary pressure in a vapor chamber. A number of new approaches such as nanostructured wicks (Chu et al. 2010; Weibel et al. 2012) have been used to further increase the capillary pressure and enhance heat transfer.

9.9   Micro Heat Pipes

In 1984, Cotter first introduced the concept of very small "micro" heat pipes which were incorporated into semiconductor devices to promote more uniform temperature distributions and improve thermal control. The micro heat pipe (Peterson 1994) is defined as a heat pipe in which the mean curvature of the liquid–vapor interface is comparable in magnitude to the reciprocal of the hydraulic radius of the total flow channel. Based on this definition, the hydraulic diameter of a typical micro heat pipe ranges from 10 to 500 μm. The fundamental operating principle of microheat pipes is essentially the same as that occurring in relatively large conventional heat pipes. A typical micro heat pipe shown in Fig. 9.36 is using the cornered region to pump the condensate from the condenser to the evaporator. As heat is added to the evaporating section, the liquid vaporizes and the vapor brings the heat through the adiabatic section to the condensing section, where the vapor condenses into liquid and releases

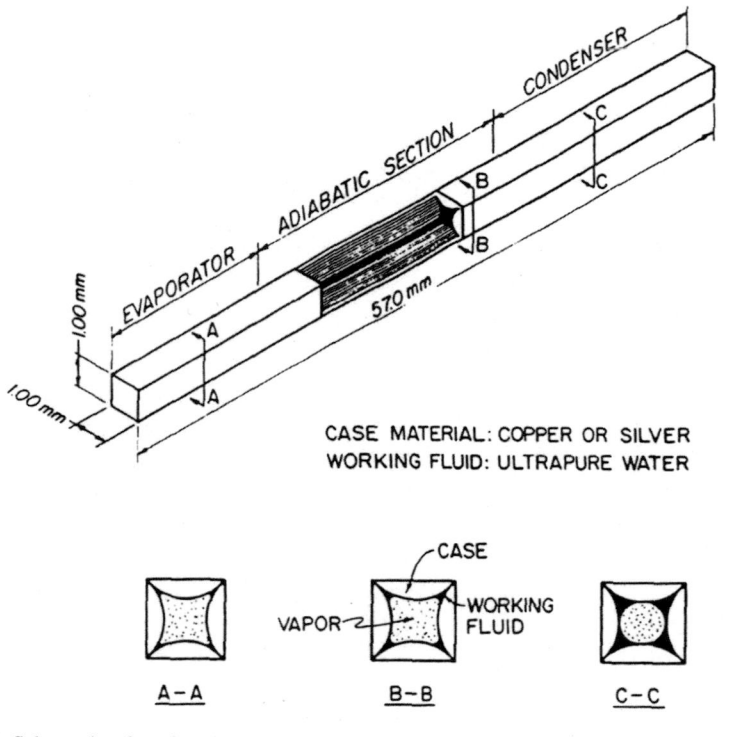

CASE MATERIAL: COPPER OR SILVER
WORKING FLUID: ULTRAPURE WATER

Fig. 9.36 Schematic of a micro heat pipe (Peterson 1994)

latent heat. The heat addition on the evaporating section causes the liquid to recede into the cornered region and directly reduces the meniscus radius at the liquid–vapor interface in the evaporator. This vaporization and condensation process causes the liquid–vapor interface in the liquid arteries to change continually along the pipe and results in a capillary pressure difference between the evaporator and condenser regions. This capillary pressure difference promotes the flow of the working fluid from the condenser back to the evaporator. As the size of the heat pipe decreases, however, the micro heat pipe may encounter vapor continuum limitation. This limitation may prevent the micro heat pipe from working under lower temperatures. In addition to the vapor continuum limitation, the micro heat pipe is also subject to the operating limits occurring in conventional heat pipes. Of those operating limits, the capillary limitation remains the most important for the micro heat pipe. Micro/miniature heat pipes have been widely used in electronics cooling.

9.10   Variable Conductance Heat Pipes

For a typical conventional heat pipe, the operating temperature can be determined by the heat removal rate from the condenser. When the heat load increases, the temperature drop from the evaporator to the condenser increases if the condensing

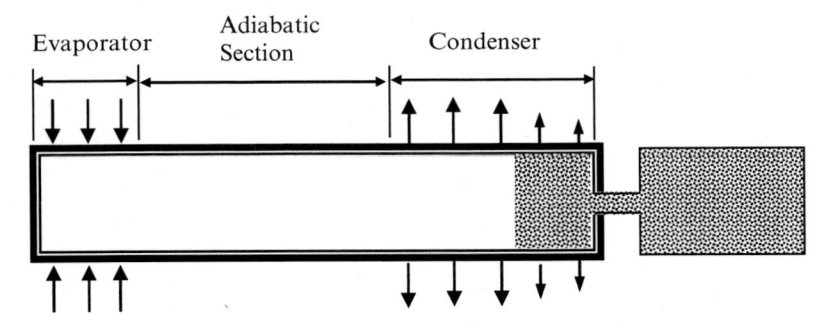

Fig. 9.37 Schematic of a variable conductance heat pipe

area is constant. However, there are some applications where the evaporator or condenser temperature needs to be kept constant with a varying heat input. The VCHP is suitable for this function design and its unique feature is the ability to maintain a device mounted on the evaporator at a near constant temperature, independent of the amount of power being generated by the device. To keep the operating temperature independent of the heat input, the whole conductance of heat pipe should be varied with the heat load. Figure 9.37 illustrates a typical VCHP. Compared to a conventional heat pipe, the VCHP as shown in Fig. 9.37 includes a gas reservoir containing noncondensable gas. When the input power is low, the vapor pressure inside the heat pipe is low. The volume of noncondensable gas expands and reduces the condensing area. When the input power is high, the vapor pressure increases resulting in the contraction of vapor volume and direct increase of the condensing area. As a result, the temperature drop from the evaporator to the condenser is fairly constant. As shown in Fig. 9.37, the noncondensable gas is used to moderate the conductance as the input power is varied, giving the device the name: gas-loaded variable heat pipe. Based on the same principle, several other VCHPs have been developed to moderate the conductance change in the heat pipe; these variations include vapor flow-modulated heat pipes, excess-liquid heat pipes and liquid-flow modulated heat pipes (thermal diodes) (Peterson 1994).

9.11 Rotating Heat Pipes

The rotating heat pipe consists of a sealed hollow shaft which contains a fixed amount of working fluid. The rotating heat pipe can be divided into two types, namely, those with an internal taper and without an internal taper. Compared to a conventional heat pipe, the rotating heat pipe has the following advantages: (1) the condensate in the rotating heat pipe is returned to the evaporator by centrifugal force; (2) the rotational speed plays the most important role in its heat transfer performance; (3) the heat transfer performance is enhanced for a rotating heat pipe with an internal taper because the removal of the condensate from the cooled liquid surface by centrifugal action

helps move the condensate back toward the evaporator; and (4) the sonic, entrainment, boiling, and condensing limits are the primary factors limiting the heat transfer capacity in the rotating heat pipe. For a detailed information related to the rotating heat pipes, see the books written by Peterson (1994) and Faghri (1995).

9.12   High-Temperature Heat Pipes (Metal Heat Pipes)

Because most working fluids in high-temperature heat pipes are metals, a high-temperature heat pipe is also called a metal heat pipe. High-temperature heat pipes can transport a large heat load and reach a very high level of temperature uniformity due to their higher surface tension, higher latent heat of vaporization, and higher thermal conductivity. They have been employed for advanced energy systems such as advanced thermophotovoltaic gas turbine engines and nuclear reactors. However, compared to other heat pipes operating at other temperature ranges, the high-temperature heat pipe possesses some obstructions such as a corrosion and reliability concern, high chemical reactivity, start-up control, and severe working conditions due to too high operating temperatures.

9.13   Cryogenic Heat Pipes

Cryogenic fluids are used in the cryogenic heat pipe. These working fluids are either a chemically pure material such as helium, argon, krypton, nitrogen, and oxygen or a chemical compound such as methane, ethane, and Freon. For cryogenic fluids used at a low temperature, the surface tension, thermal conductivity, and latent heat of vaporization are relatively low and the liquid viscosity is much higher. As a result, the heat pipe optimized for zero-g operation would not properly prime in a one-g environment due to the low surface tension. The very high vapor pressure in the heat pipe during storage and the low operating temperature, where the cooling methods to remove heat from the condenser are limited, are also a concern for those using cryogenic heat pipes. The capillary limit, sonic limit, entrainment limit, and/or boiling limit governs the heat transport limitation. Of those operating limits, the capillary limit from the low surface tension is the primary factor affecting the heat transfer performance in cryogenic heat pipes. For this reason, considerable effort has been made to develop wicking structures that further increase capillary limitation.

References

Adamson AM (1990) Physical chemistry of surfaces, 5th edn. Wiley, New York

Chang JY, Prasher RS, Prstic S, Cheng P, Ma HB (2008) Thermal performance of vapor chambers under hot-spot heating conditions. ASME J Heat Transf 130(12), Article No. 121501

Cheng P, Ma HB (2007) A mathematical model predicting minimum radius occurring in mixed particles. ASME J Heat Transf 129(3):391–394

Chi SW (1976) Heat pipe theory and practice. McGraw-Hill, New York

Chu A, Xiao R, Wang EN (2010) Uni-directional liquid spreading on asymmetric nanostructured surfaces. Nat Mater 9:413–417

Cotter TP (1967) Heat pipe startup dynamics. In: Proceedings of the SAE thermionic conversion specialist conference, Palo Alto, CA

Cotter TP (1984) Principles and prospects of micro heat pipes. In: Proceedings of the 5th international heat pipe conference, Tsukuba, Japan, pp 328–335

Faghri A (1995) Heat pipe science and technology. Taylor & Francis, New York

Ferrell JK, Alleavitch J (1970) Vaporization heat transfer in capillary wick structures. Chem Eng Prog Symp Ser 66(102):82–91

Hanlon MA, Ma HB (2003) Evaporation heat transfer in sintered porous media. ASME J Heat Transf 125:644–653

Hsu YY (1962) On the size range of active nucleation cavities on a heating surface. ASME J Heat Transf 84:207–213

Kraus AD, Bar-Cohen A (1983) Thermal analysis and control of electronic equipment. McGraw-Hill, New York

Liu XQ, Peterson GP (1997) Numerical analysis of vapor flow in a micro heat pipe. In: 34th aerospace sciences, AIAA 96-0475, January 14–18, Reno, Nevada

Ma HB, Peterson GP, Pratt DM (1998) Disjoining pressure effect on the wetting characteristics in a capillary tube. Microscale Thermophys Eng 2(4):283–297

Marcus BD (1972) Theory and design of variable conductance heat pipes. Report no. NASA CR, 2018, NASA, Washington, DC

Patankar SV (1980) Numerical heat transfer and fluid flow. McGraw-Hill, New York

Peng XF, Peterson GP (1992) Convective heat transfer and flow friction for water flow in microchannel structures. Int J Heat Mass Transf 39:2599–2608

Perkins LP, Buck WE (1892) Improvement in devices for the diffusion or transference of heat. UK Patent 22,272, London, England

Peterson GP (1994) An introduction to heat pipes. Wiley, New York

Reay DA, Kew P (2006) Heat pipes. Pergamon, New York

Weibel JA, Kim SS, Fisher TS, Garimella SV (2012) Carbon nanotube coatings for enhanced capillary-fed boiling from porous microstructures. Nanoscale Microscale Thermophys Eng 16:1–17

Appendix A

© Springer Science+Business Media New York 2015
H. Ma, *Oscillating Heat Pipes*, DOI 10.1007/978-1-4939-2504-9

Table A.1 Thermophysical properties at saturation for acetone

Temperature, T (°C)	Saturation pressure, p_v (10^5 Pa)	Latent heat, h_{lv} (kJ/kg)	Liquid density, ρ_l (kg/m³)	Vapor density, ρ_v (kg/m³)	Liquid viscosity, μ_l (10^{-3} N s/m²)	Vapor viscosity, μ_v (10^{-7} N s/m²)	Liquid thermal conductivity, k_l (W/m K)	Vapor thermal conductivity, k_v (W/m K)	Liquid surface tension, σ (10^{-3} N/m)	Liquid specific heat, $c_{p,l}$ (kJ/kg K)	Vapor specific heat, $c_{p,v}$ (kJ/kg K)
−40	0.01	660.0	860.0	0.03	0.800	68.0	0.200		31.0	2.04	1.109
−20	0.03	615.6	845.0	0.10	0.500	73.0	0.189	0.0082	27.6	2.07	1.160
0	0.10	564.0	812.0	0.26	0.395	78.0	0.183	0.0096	26.2	2.11	1.215
20	0.27	552.0	790.0	0.64	0.323	82.0	0.181	0.0110	23.7	2.16	1.271
40	0.60	536.0	768.0	1.05	0.269	86.0	0.175	0.0126	21.2	2.22	1.328
60	1.15	517.0	744.0	2.37	0.226	90.0	0.168	0.0143	18.6	2.29	1.386
80	2.15	495.0	719.0	4.30	0.192	95.0	0.160	0.0161	16.2	2.39	1.444
100	4.43	472.0	689.6	6.94	0.170	98.0	0.148	0.0178	13.4	2.49	1.502
120	6.70	426.1	660.3	11.02	0.148	99.0	0.135	0.0195	10.7	2.61	1.560
140	10.49	394.4	631.8	18.61	0.132	103.0	0.126	0.0215	8.1	2.77	1.616

Acetone, $(CH_3)_2CO$, molecular mass: 58.1 ($T_{sat} = 56.25$ °C; $T_m = -93.15$ °C) (Peterson 1994; Faghri 1995; Faghri and Zhang 2006)

Table A.2 Thermophysical properties at saturation for ammonia

Temperature, T (K)	Saturation pressure, p_v (10^6 Pa)	Latent heat, h_{lv} (kJ/kg)	Liquid density, ρ_l (kg/m^3)	Vapor density, ρ_v (kg/m^3)	Liquid viscosity, μ_l (10^{-6} N s/m^2)	Vapor viscosity, μ_v (10^{-6} N s/m^2)	Liquid thermal conductivity, k_l (W/m K)	Vapor thermal conductivity, k_v (W/m K)	Liquid surface tension, σ (10^{-3} N/m)	Liquid specific heat, $c_{p,l}$ (kJ/kg K)	Vapor specific heat, $c_{p,v}$ (kJ/kg K)
200	0.008646	1,477	728.9	0.08899	407	7.64	0.709		4.606	1.979	
210	0.017746	1,451	717.5	0.1746	369	8.02	0.685		4.375	2.033	
220	0.033811	1,425	705.8	0.3190	334	8.40	0.661	0.0158	4.346	2.083	
230	0.060439	1,398	693.7	0.5489	302	8.78	0.638	0.0171	4.382	2.151	
240	0.10225	1,369	681.4	0.8972	273	9.16	0.615	0.0184	33.9	4.431	2.237
250	0.16496	1,339	668.9	1.404	245	9.54	0.592	0.0199	31.5	4.483	2.343
260	0.25529	1,307	656.1	2.115	220	9.93	0.569	0.0211	29.2	4.539	2.467
270	0.38100	1,273	642.9	3.086	197	10.31	0.546	0.0224	26.9	4.597	2.611
280	0.55077	1,237	629.2	4.380	176	10.70	0.523	0.0239	24.7	4.662	2.776
290	0.77413	1,198	615.0	6.071	157.7	11.07	0.500	0.0256	22.4	4.734	2.963
300	1.0614	1,159	600.2	8.247	141.0	11.45	0.477	0.0277	20.2	4.815	3.180
310	1.4235	1,113	584.6	11.01	126.0	11.86	0.454	0.0302	18.0	4.909	3.428
320	1.8721	1,066	568.2	14.51	113.4	12.29	0.431	0.0332	15.9	5.024	3.725
330	2.4196	1,014	550.9	18.89	101.9	12.74	0.408	0.0368	13.7	5.170	4.088
340	3.0789	958	532.4	24.40	92.1	13.22	0.385	0.0415	11.7	5.366	4.545
350	3.8641	895	512.3	31.34	83.2	13.74	0.361	0.0467	9.60	5.639	5.144
360	4.7902	825	490.3	40.18	75.4	14.35	0.337	0.0536	7.67	6.042	5.978
370	5.8740	745	465.5	51.65	68.5	15.07	0.313	0.0614	5.74	6.677	7.217
380	7.1352	649	436.5	67.16	61.1	15.96	0.286	0.0700	3.98	7.795	9.312
390	8.5977	529	400.2	89.85	50.3	17.14	0.254	0.0800	2.21	10.27	13.86

Ammonia, NH$_3$, molecular mass: 17.0 ($T_{sat} = 239.9$ K; $T_m = 195.5$ K) (Peterson 1994; Faghri 1995; Faghri and Zhang 2006)

Table A.3 Thermophysical properties at saturation for calcium

Temperature, T (K)	Saturation pressure, p_v (10^6 Pa)	Latent heat, h_{lv} (kJ/kg)	Liquid density, ρ_l (kg/m³)	Vapor density, ρ_v (kg/m³)	Liquid viscosity, μ_l (10^{-6} N s/m²)	Vapor viscosity, μ_v (10^{-6} N s/m²)	Liquid thermal conductivity[a], k_l (W/m K)	Vapor thermal conductivity[a], k_v (W/m K)	Liquid surface tension, σ (10^{-3} N/m)	Liquid specific heat[a], $c_{p,l}$ (kJ/kg K)	Vapor specific heat[b], $c_{p,v}$ (kJ/kg K)
1,000	0.000032	3,885	1,392	0.0001549	0.1675	0.135	0.817	0.0135	372	0.973	
1,100	0.000174	3,885	1,370	0.0007674	0.1332	0.146	0.808	0.0151	362	0.929	
1,200	0.000714	3,885	1,348	0.002891	0.1102	0.157	0.799	0.0167	352	0.884	
1,300	0.00236	3,885	1,321	0.0088	0.094	0.168	0.789	0.02325	342	0.840	
1,400	0.00658	3,885	1,293	0.092	0.081	0.179	0.780	0.0298	332	0.795	
1,500	0.01598	3,885	1,265	0.058	0.072	0.19	0.771	0.0266	322	0.751	
1,600	0.03478	3,885	1,248	0.11	0.065	0.201	0.762	0.0234	312	0.707	
1,700	0.06905	3,885	1,220	0.21	0.06	0.212	0.752	0.02485	302	0.662	
1,800	0.127	3,885	1,196	0.37	0.056	0.223	0.743	0.0263	292		0.516
1,900	0.2191	3,885	1,179	0.58	0.0508	0.234	0.734	0.0279	282		0.521
2,000	0.358	3,885	1,165	0.82	0.0467	0.245	0.725	0.0295	272		0.524

Calcium, $_{20}$Ca, molecular mass: 40.078(4) (T_{sat} = 1,757.15 K; T_m = 1,112.15 K) (Peterson 1994; Bentor 2014)
[a]Interpolation from Vargaftik (1975)
[b]Interpolation from Chase (1998)

Table A.4 Thermophysical properties at saturation for carbon dioxide

Temperature, T (K)	Saturation pressure, p_v (10^6 Pa)	Latent heat, h_{lv} (kJ/kg)	Liquid density, ρ_l (kg/m³)	Vapor density, ρ_v (10^{-3} kg/m³)	Liquid viscosity, μ_l (10^{-3} N s/m²)	Vapor viscosity, μ_v (10^{-5} N s/m²)	Liquid thermal conductivity, k_l (W/m K)	Vapor thermal conductivity, k_v (W/m K)	Liquid surface tension, σ (10^{-2} N/m)	Liquid specific heat, $c_{p,l}$ (kJ/kg K)	Vapor specific heat, $c_{p,v}$ (kJ/kg K)
220	0.5991	344.9	1,166	15.82	0.242	10.917	0.176	0.0113	1.6070	1.962	0.903
230	0.8929	328.0	1,129	23.27	0.204	11.456	0.163	0.0122	1.3750	1.997	1.005
240	1.283	309.6	1,089	33.30	0.173	12.025	0.151	0.0133	1.1450	2.051	1.103
250	1.785	289.3	1,046	46.64	0.147	12.642	0.139	0.0146	0.9260	2.132	1.237
260	2.419	266.5	999	64.42	0.124	13.338	0.127	0.0163	0.7160	2.255	1.430
270	3.203	240.1	946	88.37	0.105	14.181	0.115	0.0187	0.5170	2.453	1.731
280	4.161	208.6	884	121.7	0.088	15.288	0.102	0.0225	0.3330	2.814	2.277
290	5.318	168.1	805	172.0	0.071	17.013	0.0895	0.0298	0.1690	3.676	3.614
300	6.713	103.7	679	268.6	0.053	20.884	0.0806	0.0537	0.0349	8.698	11.921
302	7.027		634	308.2	0.048	22.746	0.0845	0.0710	0.0148	1.5787	23.800

Carbon dioxide, CO_2, molecular mass: 44.01 ($T_{sat} = -57\ ^\circ$C; $T_m = -78\ ^\circ$C) (Lienhard and Lienhard 2005; Greenwood and Earnshaw 1997)

Table A.5 Thermophysical properties at saturation for cesium

Temperature, T (K)	Saturation pressure, p_v (10^5 Pa)	Latent heat, h_{lv} (kJ/kg)	Liquid density, ρ_l (10^3 kg/m³)	Vapor density, ρ_v (10^{-3} kg/m³)	Liquid viscosity, μ_l (10^{-4} N s/m²)	Vapor viscosity, μ_v (10^{-5} N s/m²)	Liquid thermal conductivity, k_l (W/m K)	Vapor thermal conductivity, k_v (W/m K)	Liquid surface tension, σ (10^{-3} N/m)	Liquid specific heat, $c_{p,l}$ (kJ/kg K)	Vapor specific heat, $c_{p,v}$ (kJ/kg K)
500	0.0003	544.30	1.723	9.91	3.181	1.460	18.79		61.9	0.232	0.1982
600	0.0056	534.20	1.666	15.50	2.558	1.668	19.02	0.00530	57.1	0.224	0.2344
700	0.0437	523.30	1.609	105.20	2.163	1.893	18.79	0.00631	52.3	0.219	0.2645
800	0.2026	511.60	1.552	433.60	1.890	2.124	18.33	0.00724	47.5	0.217	0.2821
900	0.6580	499.50	1.495	1,275.90	1.690	2.336	17.51	0.00807	42.7	0.222	0.2878
1,000	1.6800	486.50	1.438	2,990.40	1.536	2.567	16.47	0.00878	37.9	0.231	0.2850
1,100	3.6000	472.60	1.377	5,924.10	1.415	2.782	15.49	0.00942	33.1	0.239	0.2776
1,200	6.7700	458.80	1.311	10,364.80	1.316	2.995	13.57	0.01000	28.3	0.248	0.2681
1,300	11.5100	444.60	1.243	16,520.70	1.234	3.198	11.60	0.01060	23.5	0.256	0.2582
1,400	18.0200	429.98	1.174	24,307.20	1.164	3.398	9.39	0.01110	18.0	0.256	0.2582
1,500	26.7200	415.40	1.102	34,048.30	1.104	3.589	7.50	0.01150	14.0		

Cesium, Cs, molecular mass: 132.9 (T_{sat} = 943 K; T_m = 201.6 K) (Faghri 1995; Faghri and Zhang 2006)

Table A.6 Thermophysical properties at saturation for Dowtherm®

Temperature, T (°C)	Saturation pressure, p_v (10^5 Pa)	Latent heat, h_{lv} (kJ/kg)	Liquid density, ρ_l (kg/m³)	Vapor density, ρ_v (kg/m³)	Liquid viscosity, μ_l (10^{-5} N s/m²)	Vapor viscosity, μ_v (10^{-5} N s/m²)	Liquid thermal conductivity, k_l (W/m K)	Vapor thermal conductivity[a], k_v (W/m K)	Liquid surface tension, σ (10^{-3} N/m)	Liquid specific heat[a], $c_{p,l}$ (kJ/kg K)	Vapor specific heat[a], $c_{p,v}$ (kJ/kg K)
100	0.006	345	995	0.035	101.0	0.68	0.126	0.0126	31.6	1.88	1.349
150	0.051	329	953	0.24	60.3	0.77	0.119	0.0160	26.5	2.14	1.512
200	0.245	314	912	0.99	40.7	0.87	0.110	0.0196	21.8	2.34	1.666
250	0.843	291	871	3.20	29.7	0.97	0.104	0.0234	17.3	2.60	1.814
300	2.330	264	825	8.70	22.7	1.07	0.096	0.0275	12.9	2.76	1.961
350	5.200	235	772	20.0	18.2	1.17	0.090	0.0317	8.9	2.89	2.116
400	10.43	207	709	42.0	14.9	1.26	0.083	0.0363	5.0	3.01	2.309

Diphenyl mixture (Dowtherm—Dowtherm is an eutectic mixture of 73.5 % phenyl ether and 26.5 % diphenyl), molecular mass: 166.0 ($T_{sat} = 258$ °C; $T_m = 12$ °C)
(Faghri 1995; Faghri and Zhang 2006)
[a]D. C. C (1997)

Table A.7 Thermophysical properties at saturation for ethane

Temperature, T (°C)	Saturation pressure, p_v (10^5 Pa)	Latent heat, h_{lv} (kJ/kg)	Liquid density, ρ_l (kg/m³)	Vapor density, ρ_v (kg/m³)	Liquid viscosity, μ_l (10^{-7} N s/m²)	Vapor viscosity, μ_v (10^{-7} N s/m²)	Liquid thermal conductivity, k_l (W/m K)	Vapor thermal conductivity, k_v (W/m K)	Liquid surface tension, σ (10^{-3} N/m)	Liquid specific heat, $c_{p,l}$ (kJ/kg K)	Vapor specific heat, $c_{p,v}$ (kJ/kg K)
−120	0.096	530	582	0.230	2,580	49.0	0.149		21.23	2.82	1.297
−100	0.600	506	562	0.921	1,800	55.0	0.137		17.93	2.94	1.349
−80	1.700	480	540	2.600	1,360	61.0	0.125		14.60	3.05	1.401
−60	3.700	450	516	6.200	1,100	67.0	0.113	0.0116	11.30	3.16	1.459
−40	7.200	414	488	12.700	900	73.0	0.100	0.0138	8.00	3.26	1.521
−20	14.000	368	454	25.500	760	79.0	0.088	0.0160	4.60	3.38	1.585
0	25.000	304	414	46.000	660	85.5	0.077	0.0185	1.20	3.48	1.660
20	38.000	200	360	85.000	600	91.0	0.066	0.0209	0.08		1.736

Ethane, C_2H_6, molecular mass: 30.1 ($T_{sat} = -88.6$ °C; $T_m = -183.3$ °C) (Faghri 1995; Faghri and Zhang 2006)

Table A.8 Thermophysical properties at saturation for ethanol

Temperature, T (°C)	Saturation pressure, p_v (10^5 Pa)	Latent heat, h_{lv} (kJ/kg)	Liquid density, ρ_l (10^3 kg/m^3)	Vapor density, ρ_v (kg/m^3)	Liquid viscosity, μ_l (10^{-3} N s/m^2)	Vapor viscosity, μ_v (10^{-5} N s/m^2)	Liquid thermal conductivity, k_l (W/m K)	Vapor thermal conductivity, k_v (W/m K)	Liquid surface tension, σ (10^{-3} N/m)	Liquid specific heat, $c_{p,l}$ (kJ/kg K)	Vapor specific heat, $c_{p,v}$ (kJ/kg K)
0	0.012	1,048.4	0.901	0.036	1.7990	0.774	0.183	0.0117	24.4	2.27	1.34
20	0.058	1,030.0	0.800	0.085	1.1980	0.835	0.179	0.0139	22.8	2.40	1.40
40	0.180	1,011.9	0.789	0.316	0.8190	0.900	0.175	0.0160	21.0	2.57	1.48
60	0.472	988.9	0.770	0.748	0.5880	0.959	0.171	0.0179	19.2	2.78	1.54
80	1.086	960.0	0.757	1.430	0.4320	1.030	0.169	0.0199	17.3	3.03	1.61
100	2.260	927.0	0.730	3.410	0.3180	1.092	0.167	0.0219	15.5	3.30	1.68
120	4.290	885.5	0.710	6.010	0.2430	1.157	0.165	0.0238	13.4	3.61	1.75
140	7.530	834.0	0.680	10.670	0.1900	1.219	0.163	0.0256	11.2	3.96	
160	12.756	772.9	0.650	17.450	0.1500	1.293	0.161	0.0272	9.0		
180	19.600	698.8	0.610	27.650	0.1200	1.369	0.159	0.0288	6.7		
200	29.400	598.3	0.564	44.480	0.0950	1.464	0.57	0.0395	4.3		
220	42.800	468.5	0.510	74.350	0.0725	1.618	0.155	0.0321	2.2		
240	60.200	280.5	0.415	135.500	0.0488	1.948	0.153		0.1		

Ethanol, C_2H_5OH, molecular mass: 46.0 ($T_{sat} = 78.3$ °C; $T_m = -114.5$ °C) (Faghri 1995; Faghri and Zhang 2006)

Table A.9 Thermophysical properties at saturation for Flutec PP2

Temperature, T (°C)	Saturation pressure, p_v (10⁶ Pa)	Latent heat, h_{lv} (kJ/kg)	Liquid density, ρ_l (kg/m³)	Vapor density, ρ_v (10⁻³ kg/m³)	Liquid viscosity, μ_l (10⁻³ N s/m²)	Vapor viscosity, μ_v (10⁻⁵ N s/m²)	Liquid thermal conductivity, k_l (W/m K)	Vapor thermal conductivity, k_v (W/m K)	Liquid surface tension, σ (10⁻² N/m)	Liquid specific heat[a], $c_{p,l}$ (kJ/kg K)	Vapor specific heat, $c_{p,v}$ (kJ/kg K)
−30	0.001	106.2	1,942	0.13	5.200	0.98	0.637		1.90		0.72
−10	0.002	103.1	1,886	0.44	3.500	1.03	0.626		1.71		0.81
10	0.009	99.8	1,829	1.39	2.140	1.07	0.613		1.52		0.92
30	0.022	96.3	1,773	2.96	1.435	1.12	0.601	1.008	1.32	1.017	1.01
50	0.039	91.8	1,716	6.43	1.005	1.17	0.588		1.13	1.038	1.07
70	0.062	87.0	1,660	11.79	0.720	1.22	0.575		0.93	1.059	1.11
90	0.143	82.1	1,599	21.99	0.543	1.26	0.563		0.73	1.080	1.17
110	0.282	76.5	1,558	34.92	0.429	1.31	0.550		0.52		1.25
130	0.483	70.3	1,515	57.21	0.314	1.36	0.537		0.32		1.33
160	0.876	59.1	1,440	103.63	0.167	1.43	0.518		0.01		1.45

Flutec PP2, C_7F_{14}, molecular mass: 350 ($T_{sat} = 76$ °C; $T_m = -37$ °C) (Reay and Kew 2006; F2 Chemicals Ltd 2011)

[a]Interpolation from Yarrington and Kay (1957)

Table A.10 Thermophysical properties at saturation for Flutec PP9

Temperature, T (°C)	Saturation pressure, p_v (10^6 Pa)	Latent heat, h_{lv} (kJ/kg)	Liquid density, ρ_l (kg/m³)	Vapor density, ρ_v (10^{-3} kg/m³)	Liquid viscosity, μ_l (10^{-3} N s/m²)	Vapor viscosity, μ_v (10^{-5} N s/m²)	Liquid thermal conductivity, k_l (W/m K)	Vapor thermal conductivity, k_v (W/m K)	Liquid surface tension, σ (10^{-2} N/m)	Liquid specific heat, $c_{p,l}$ (kJ/kg K)	Vapor specific heat, $c_{p,v}$ (kJ/kg K)
−30	0.000	103.0	2,098	0.01	5.77	0.82	0.060		2.36		0.80
0	0.000	98.4	2,029	0.01	3.31	0.90	0.059		2.08		0.87
30	0.001	94.5	1,960	0.12	1.48	1.06	0.057		1.80		0.94
60	0.003	90.2	1,891	0.61	0.94	1.18	0.056		1.52	1.09	1.02
90	0.012	86.1	1,822	1.93	0.65	1.21	0.054		1.24		1.09
120	0.028	83.0	1,753	4.52	0.49	1.23	0.053		0.95		1.15
150	0.061	77.4	1,685	11.81	0.38	1.26	0.052		0.67		1.23
180	0.158	70.8	1,604	25.13	0.30	1.33	0.051		0.40		1.30
225	0.421	59.4	1,455	63.27	0.21	1.44	0.049		0.01		1.41

Flutec PP9, $C_{11}F_{20}$, molecular mass: 512 ($T_{sat} = 160\ °C$; $T_m = -70\ °C$) (Reay and Kew 2006; F2 Chemicals Ltd 2011)

Table A.11 Thermophysical properties at saturation for Freon®-113

Temperature, T (°C)	Saturation pressure, p_v (10^5 Pa)	Latent heat, h_{lv} (kJ/kg)	Liquid density, ρ_l (10^3 kg/m^3)	Vapor density, ρ_v (kg/m^3)	Liquid viscosity, μ_l (10^{-3} N s/m^2)	Vapor viscosity, μ_v (10^{-7} N s/m^2)	Liquid thermal conductivity, k_l (W/m K)	Vapor thermal conductivity, k_v (W/m K)	Liquid surface tension, σ (10^{-3} N/m)	Liquid specific heat, $c_{p,l}$ (kJ/kg K)	Vapor specific heat, $c_{p,v}$ (kJ/kg K)
−30	0.0283	166.88	1.687	0.2639	1.670	89.4	0.0889		25.3	0.855	0.587
−20	0.0905	161.48	1.643	0.7800	1.130	94.2	0.0867		22.8	0.882	0.597
0	0.1500	158.68	1.621	1.2510	0.948	96.7	0.0822		21.5	0.921	0.621
10	0.2387	155.83	1.598	1.9300	0.780	99.0	0.0799		20.6	0.937	0.627
30	0.5420	149.93	1.554	4.1500	0.590	104.0	0.0754		18.1	0.962	0.647
50	1.0943	143.82	1.508	8.0000	0.475	108.5	0.0709	0.00866	16.0	0.986	0.667
70	2.0120	137.46	1.455	14.3000	0.401	113.0	0.0664		13.9	1.004	0.689

Freon-113, C$_2$F$_3$Cl$_3$, molecular mass: 187.4 ($T_{\mathrm{sat}} = 47.68$ °C; $T_m = -36.6$ °C) (Faghri 1995; Faghri and Zhang 2006)

Table A.12 Thermophysical properties at saturation for Freon®-123

Temperature, T (°C)	Saturation pressure, p_v (10^5 Pa)	Latent heat, h_{lv} (kJ/kg)	Liquid density, ρ_l (10^3 kg/m³)	Vapor density, ρ_v (kg/m³)	Liquid viscosity, μ_l (10^{-3} N s/m²)	Vapor viscosity, μ_v (10^{-7} N s/m²)	Liquid thermal conductivity, k_l (W/m K)	Vapor thermal conductivity, k_v (W/m K)	Liquid surface tension, σ (10^{-3} N/m)	Liquid specific heat, $c_{p,l}$ (kJ/kg K)	Vapor specific heat, $c_{p,v}$ (kJ/kg K)
−60	0.0081	204.20	1.665	0.070	1.383	75.0	0.1020	0.00435	25.78	0.932	0.553
−40	0.0358	196.63	1.620	0.283	0.986	83.1	0.0961	0.00549	23.19	0.948	0.585
−20	0.1200	189.11	1.574	0.880	0.735	90.9	0.0898	0.00661	20.66	0.968	0.617
0	0.3265	181.44	1.526	2.242	0.565	98.4	0.0837	0.00774	18.18	0.990	0.651
20	0.7561	173.44	1.477	4.905	0.443	105.6	0.0778	0.00889	15.77	1.014	0.686
40	1.5447	164.95	1.425	9.629	0.352	112.6	0.0724	0.01008	13.43	1.038	0.724
60	2.8589	155.73	1.370	17.331	0.284	119.4	0.0673	0.01134	11.16	1.066	0.767
80	4.8909	145.54	1.311	29.189	0.231	126.3	0.0626	0.01273	8.97	1.100	0.816

Freon-123, $CHCl_2CF_3$, molecular mass: 152.9 ($T_{sat} = 27.8$ °C; $T_m = -107$ °C) (Faghri 1995; Faghri and Zhang 2006)

Table A.13 Thermophysical properties at saturation for Freon®-134a

Temperature, T (°C)	Saturation pressure, p_v (10^5 Pa)	Latent heat, h_{lv} (kJ/kg)	Liquid density, ρ_l (10^3 kg/m³)	Vapor density, ρ_v (kg/m³)	Liquid viscosity, μ_l (10^{-3} N s/m²)	Vapor viscosity, μ_v (10^{-7} N s/m²)	Liquid thermal conductivity, k_l (W/m K)	Vapor thermal conductivity, k_v (W/m K)	Liquid surface tension, σ (10^{-3} N/m)	Liquid specific heat, $c_{p,l}$ (kJ/kg K)	Vapor specific heat, $c_{p,v}$ (kJ/kg K)
−60	0.1591	237.95	1.474	0.9268	0.663	83.0	0.121	0.00656	20.80	1.223	0.692
−40	0.5121	225.86	1.418	2.769	0.472	91.2	0.111	0.00817	17.60	1.255	0.749
−20	1.3273	212.91	1.358	6.785	0.353	99.2	0.101	0.00982	14.51	1.293	0.816
0	2.9280	198.60	1.295	14.428	0.271	107.3	0.0920	0.01151	11.56	1.341	0.897
20	5.7171	182.28	1.225	27.778	0.211	115.81	0.0833	0.01333	8.76	1.405	1.001
40	10.166	163.02	1.147	50.075	0.163	125.5	0.0747	0.01544	6.13	1.498	1.145
60	16.818	139.13	1.053	81.413	0.124	137.9	0.0661	0.01831	3.72	1.660	1.387

Freon-134a, CF_3CH_2F, molecular mass: 102.0 ($T_{sat} = -26.4$ °C; $T_m = -101$ °C) (Faghri 1995; Faghri and Zhang 2006)

Table A.14 Thermophysical properties at saturation for Freon®-21

Temperature, T (°C)	Saturation pressure, p_v (10^5 Pa)	Latent heat, h_{fv} (kJ/kg)	Liquid density, ρ_l (10^3 kg/m³)	Vapor density, ρ_v (kg/m³)	Liquid viscosity, μ_l (10^{-3} N s/m²)	Vapor viscosity, μ_v (10^{-7} N s/m²)	Liquid thermal conductivity, k_l (W/m K)	Vapor thermal conductivity[a], k_v (W/m K)	Liquid surface tension, σ (10^{-3} N/m)	Liquid specific heat[a], $c_{p,l}$ (kJ/kg K)	Vapor specific heat[a], $c_{p,v}$ (kJ/kg K)
−60	0.0253	269	1.554	0.147	0.849	89	0.132		29.81		0.501
−40	0.0954	262	1.510	0.510	0.597	95	0.123		26.99		0.523
−20	0.2847	253	1.470	1.410	0.444	100	0.116		24.17	0.994	0.545
0	0.7085	243	1.420	3.310	0.345	106	0.109		21.35	1.015	0.566
20	1.5300	232	1.380	6.810	0.272	112	0.102		18.35	1.048	0.588
40	2.955	220	1.330	12.690	0.229	118	0.095	0.0094	15.71	1.093	0.606
60	5.216	206	1.280	21.930	0.200	124	0.087	0.0104	12.89	1.149	0.623
80	8.567	191	1.220	35.710	0.195	130	0.080	0.0113	10.07		0.641
100	13.283	174	1.160	55.860	0.180	136	0.072	0.0122	7.25		0.659
120	19.666	155	1.080	85.470	0.170	142	0.060	0.0132	4.43		0.677

Freon-21, CHFCl₂, molecular mass: 102.9 ($T_{sat} = 8.90$ °C; $T_m = -135$ °C) (Faghri 1995; Faghri and Zhang 2006)

[a] Interpolation from Rohsenow et al. (1985)

Table A.15 Thermophysical properties at saturation for Freon®-22

Temperature, T (°C)	Saturation pressure, p_v (10^5 Pa)	Latent heat, h_{fg} (kJ/kg)	Liquid density, ρ_l (10^3 kg/m³)	Vapor density, ρ_v (kg/m³)	Liquid viscosity, μ_l (10^{-4} N s/m²)	Vapor viscosity, μ_v (10^{-7} N s/m²)	Liquid thermal conductivity, k_l (W/m K)	Vapor thermal conductivity, k_v (W/m K)	Liquid surface tension, σ (10^{-3} N/m)	Liquid specific heat, $c_{p,l}$ (kJ/kg K)	Vapor specific heat, $c_{p,v}$ (kJ/kg K)
−100	0.0199	269.29	1.557	0.1196	6.00	80.0	0.1487	0.00446	28.1	1.075	0.497
−80	0.1034	257.43	1.514	0.561	5.00	87.5	0.1385	0.00525	24.8	1.083	0.528
−60	0.3752	245.42	1.465	1.865	4.14	95.0	0.1283	0.00612	21.5	1.091	0.564
−40	1.0540	232.92	1.412	4.885	3.49	101.7	0.1181	0.00831	18.5	1.105	0.611
−20	2.4560	219.40	1.351	10.821	3.02	110.4	0.1079	0.00929	15.0	1.130	0.654
0	4.9830	204.28	1.285	21.285	2.67	118.7	0.0977	0.01026	11.7	1.171	0.741
20	9.0970	186.89	1.214	38.550	2.40	126.8	0.0875	0.01123	8.7	1.232	0.854
40	15.3150	166.22	1.132	66.225	2.19	134.5	0.0772	0.01221	5.8	1.319	0.994
60	24.2360	139.94	1.030	111.65	2.00	142.1	0.0646	0.01318	3.3	1.526	1.243

Freon-22, CHF_2Cl, molecular mass: 86.5 ($T_{sat} = -40.8$ °C; $T_m = -160$ °C) (Faghri 1995; Faghri and Zhang 2006)

Table A.16 Thermophysical properties at saturation for helium

Temperature, T (°C)	Saturation pressure, p_v (10^5 Pa)	Latent heat, h_{lv} (kJ/kg)	Liquid density, ρ_l (kg/m³)	Vapor density, ρ_v (kg/m³)	Liquid viscosity, μ_l (10^{-7} N s/m²)	Vapor viscosity, μ_v (10^{-8} N s/m²)	Liquid thermal conductivity, k_l (W/m K)	Vapor thermal conductivity, k_v (W/m K)	Liquid surface tension, σ (10^{-3} N/m)	Liquid specific heat, $c_{p,l}$ (kJ/kg K)	Vapor specific heat, $c_{p,v}$ (kJ/kg K)
−271	0.06	22.8	148.3	26.0	390	20	0.0181	0.00393	0.26	5.18	2.045
−270	0.32	23.6	140.7	17.0	370	30	0.0224	0.00607	0.19	2.49	2.699
−269	1.00	20.9	128.0	10.0	290	60	0.0277	0.00803	0.09	3.99	4.619
−268	2.29	4.0	113.8	8.5	134	90	0.0350	0.00962	0.01	11.5	6.642

Helium, He, molecular mass: 4.0 ($T_{sat} = -268$ °C; $T_m = -271$ °C) (Reay and Kew 2006; Faghri 1995; Faghri and Zhang 2006)

Table A.17 Thermophysical properties at saturation for heptane

Temperature, T (°C)	Saturation pressure, p_v (10^5 Pa)	Latent heat, h_{lv} (kJ/kg)	Liquid density, ρ_l (10^3 kg/m³)	Vapor density, ρ_v (10^3 kg/m³)	Liquid viscosity, μ_l (10^{-3} N s/m²)	Vapor viscosity, μ_v (10^{-7} N s/m²)	Liquid thermal conductivity, k_l (W/m K)	Vapor thermal conductivity, k_v (W/m K)	Liquid surface tension, σ (10^{-3} N/m)	Liquid specific heat, $c_{p,l}$ (kJ/kg K)	Vapor specific heat, $c_{p,v}$ (kJ/kg K)
−20	0.003866	383.1	0.7172		0.6890		0.140	0.0084		2.10	0.83
0	0.0152	375.6	0.7005	0.000070	0.5260		0.134	0.0099		2.16	0.87
20	0.0472	366.0	0.6836	0.000200	0.4140		0.129	0.0115	20.86	2.23	0.92
40	0.1230	354.7	0.6665	0.000500	0.3380		0.123	0.0132	18.47	2.30	0.97
60	0.2800	342.6	0.6491	0.001100	0.2810		0.118	0.0151	16.39	2.39	1.02
80	0.5700	330.1	0.6311	0.002000	0.2390		0.113	0.0170	14.35	2.47	1.05
100	1.0606	316.7	0.6124	0.003597	0.1980	73.6		0.0189	12.47	2.57	1.09
120	1.8330	302.9	0.5926	0.006075	0.1672	78.2		0.0207	10.63	2.67	1.16
140	2.9790	287.4	0.5711	0.009785	0.1427	83.4		0.0228	8.87	2.78	
160	4.5990	269.5	0.5481	0.015110	0.1217	89.7		0.0251	7.19	2.89	

Heptane, C_7H_{16}, molecular mass: 100.2 ($T_{sat} = 98.43$ °C; $T_m = -90.59$ °C) (Faghri 1995; Reay and Kew 2006)

Table A.18 Thermophysical properties at saturation for lead

Temperature, T (K)	Saturation pressure, p_v (10^2 Pa)	Latent heat, h_{lv} (kJ/kg)	Liquid density, ρ_l (10^3 kg/m³)	Vapor density, ρ_v (kg/m³)	Liquid viscosity, μ_l (10^{-3} N s/m²)	Vapor viscosity, μ_v (10^{-5} N s/m²)	Liquid thermal conductivity[a], k_l (W/m K)	Vapor thermal conductivity, k_v (W/m K)	Liquid surface tension, σ (10^{-3} N/m)	Liquid specific heat[b], $c_{p,l}$ (kJ/kg K)	Vapor specific heat[b], $c_{p,v}$ (kJ/kg K)
1,400	0.0986	920	9.27	0.147	0.9122	7.46	102.2		347.28	0.136	0.104
1,500	0.2108	920	9.14	0.296	0.8847	7.90	113.0		335.88	0.135	0.105
1,600	0.4200	920	9.01	0.559	0.8586	8.34	123.8		324.48	0.133	0.107
1,700	0.8010	920	8.89	1.011	0.8352	8.78	134.6		313.08	0.131	0.110
1,800	1.3620	920	8.76	1.635	0.8143	9.21	145.4		301.68	0.130	0.112
1,900	2.3100	920	8.63	2.648	0.7958	9.66	156.2		290.28	0.128	0.116
2,000	3.7410	920	8.51	4.106	0.7794	10.10	167.0		278.88	0.127	0.119
2,100	5.5500	920	8.37	5.817	0.7590	10.54	177.8		260.00	0.123	0.123
2,200	8.2000	920	8.25	8.256	0.7410	10.98	188.6		248.00	0.128	0.128
2,300	11.8500	920	8.12	11.480	0.7230	11.42	199.4		237.00	0.132	0.132
2,400	16.7500	920	7.99	15.600	0.7050	11.86	210.2		225.00	0.136	0.136
2,500	22.6000	920	7.86	20.280	0.6870	12.30	221.0		214.00	0.138	0.138

Lead, Pb, molecular mass: 207.2 (T_{sat} = 1,740 °C; T_m = 327.5 °C) (Faghri 1995; Faghri and Zhang 2006)

[a] IAEA (2008)

[b] Interpolation from Weatherford et al. (1961)

Table A.19 Thermophysical properties at saturation for lithium

Temperature, T (K)	Saturation pressure, p_v (10^2 Pa)	Latent heat, h_{lv} (kJ/kg)	Liquid density, ρ_l (kg/m³)	Vapor density, ρ_v (10^{-3} kg/m³)	Liquid viscosity, μ_l (10^{-4} N s/m²)	Vapor viscosity, μ_v (10^{-8} N s/m²)	Liquid thermal conductivity, k_l (W/m K)	Vapor thermal conductivity, k_v (W/m K)	Liquid surface tension, σ (10^{-3} N/m)	Liquid specific heat, $c_{p,l}$ (kJ/kg K)	Vapor specific heat, $c_{p,v}$ (kJ/kg K)
900	0.1256	21,712	472.8	0.012	2.784	890.1	52.75		335.8	4.16	6.956
1,000	0.9680	21,400	462.6	0.085	2.472	975.2	55.10		321.8	4.16	8.171
1,100	5.1200	21,000	452.4	0.415	2.252	1055.0	57.42	0.120	307.8	4.15	9.114
1,200	20.5000	20,740	442.2	1.540	2.072	1128.0	59.62	0.138	293.8	4.14	9.723
1,300	65.8600	20,380	432.0	4.650	1.922	1213.0	61.94	0.156	279.8	4.16	10.019
1,400	179.4000	20,020	421.7	11.960	1.795	1289.0	64.00	0.172	266.0	4.19	10.049
1,500	426.5000	19,670	411.5	26.900	1.685	1368.0	66.50	0.183	252.0	4.20	9.891
1,600	908.4000	19,330	401.3	54.610	1.590	1442.0	68.50	0.192	238.0	4.23	9.611
1,700	1,769.3000	18,990	391.1	101.500	1.506	1518.0	71.00	0.198	226.0	4.25	9.259
1,800	3,190.0000	18,670	380.9	175.100	1.432	1587.0	73.00	0.202	212.0	4.27	8.871
1,900	5,397.0000	18,370	370.0	283.900	1.380	1666.0	75.50	0.207	198.0	4.30	8.481
2,000	8,640.4000	18,080	360.0	436.300	1.300	1746.0	77.00	0.209	182.0	4.32	8.098

Lithium, Li, molecular mass: 6.9 ($T_{sat} = 1,615$ K; $T_m = 453.7$ K) (Faghri 1995; Faghri and Zhang 2006)

Table A.20 Thermophysical properties at saturation for mercury

Temperature, T (K)	Saturation pressure, p_v (10^5 Pa)	Latent heat, h_{lv} (kJ/kg)	Liquid density, ρ_l (kg/m³)	Vapor density, ρ_v (kg/m³)	Liquid viscosity, μ_l (10^{-3} N s/m²)	Vapor viscosity, μ_v (10^{-7} N s/m²)	Liquid thermal conductivity, k_l (W/m K)	Vapor thermal conductivity, k_v (W/m K)	Liquid surface tension, σ (N/m)	Liquid specific heat, $c_{p,l}$ (kJ/kg K)	Vapor specific heat, $c_{p,v}$ (kJ/kg K)
100	0.0003745	303.317	13,351.42	0.00242	1.241	360	9.475		0.4600	0.1371	1.04
200	0.02315	300.056	13,111.97	0.11800	1.039	464	10.64		0.4360	0.1355	1.04
300	0.33015	296.824	12,873.50	1.39100	0.926	562	11.69	0.0043	0.4050	0.1353	1.04
400	2.10240	293.314	12,632.60	7.57200	0.853	662	12.60	0.0058	0.3770	0.1364	1.04
500	8.2220	289.116	12,386.00	26.00000	0.804	762	13.39	0.0073	0.3290	0.1389	1.04
600	23.46000	283.769	12,130.00	66.66000	0.767	862	14.04	0.0090	0.2989	0.1427	1.04
700	54.03000	276.845	11,863.00	140.75000	0.739	961	14.58	0.0107	0.2687	0.1478	1.04

Mercury, Hg, molecular mass: 200.6 ($T_{sat} = 630.1$ K; $T_m = 234.3$ K) (Peterson 1994; Faghri 1995; Faghri and Zhang 2006)

Table A.21 Thermophysical properties at saturation for methanol

Temperature, T (°C)	Saturation pressure, p_v (10^5 Pa)	Latent heat, h_{lv} (kJ/kg)	Liquid density, ρ_l (10^3 kg/m³)	Vapor density, ρ_v (10^3 kg/m³)	Liquid viscosity, μ_l (10^{-3} N s/m²)	Vapor viscosity, μ_v (10^{-7} N s/m²)	Liquid thermal conductivity, k_l (W/m K)	Vapor thermal conductivity, k_v (W/m K)	Liquid surface tension, σ (10^{-3} N/m)	Liquid specific heat, $c_{p,l}$ (kJ/kg K)	Vapor specific heat, $c_{p,v}$ (kJ/kg K)
0	0.0411	1,210.0	0.8100		0.8170	88	0.205		24.5	2.42	1.37
20	0.103	1,191.1	0.7915		0.5780	95	0.204		22.6	2.46	1.44
40	0.358	1,163.9	0.7740		0.4460	101	0.203	0.00157	20.9	2.52	1.50
60	0.861	1,130.4	0.7555	0.0001006	0.3470	108	0.202	0.00178	19.3		1.57
80	1.819	1,084.4	0.7355	0.0020840	0.2710	115	0.200	0.00199	17.5		1.70
100	3.731	1,030.0	0.7140	0.0039840	0.2140	123	0.198	0.00220	15.7		1.86
120	6.551	971.3	0.6900	0.0071420	0.1700	130	0.196	0.00241	13.6		1.92
140	10.810	904.3	0.6640	0.0121600	0.1360	136	0.194	0.00262	11.5		1.92
160	17.609	828.0	0.6340	0.0199400	0.1090	143		0.00283	9.3		
180	16.869	741.1	0.5980	0.0318600	0.0883	150		0.00303	6.9		
200	38.434	636.4	0.5530	0.0507500	0.0716	157		0.00324	4.5		
220	56.728	473.1	0.4900	0.0863500	0.0583	166		0.00344	2.1		
240	79.700		0.2750	0.2750000	0.0460	174					

Methanol, CH_4O, molecular mass: 32.0 ($T_{sat} = 64.7$ °C; $T_m = -98$ °C) (Faghri 1995; Faghri and Zhang 2006; Reay and Kew 2006)

Table A.22 Thermophysical properties at saturation for nitrogen

Temperature, T (K)	Saturation pressure, p_v (10^5 Pa)	Latent heat, h_{fv} (kJ/kg)	Liquid density, ρ_l (10^3 kg/m³)	Vapor density, ρ_v (10^3 kg/m³)	Liquid viscosity, μ_l (10^{-5} N s/m²)	Vapor viscosity, μ_v (10^{-7} N s/m²)	Liquid thermal conductivity, k_l (W/m K)	Vapor thermal conductivity, k_v (W/m K)	Liquid surface tension, σ (10^{-3} N/m)	Liquid specific heat, $c_{p,l}$ (kJ/kg K)	Vapor specific heat, $c_{p,v}$ (kJ/kg K)
70	0.3859	205.7	0.838	0.0019	2.010	48.00	0.1420	0.0066	10.53	1.935	1.08
80	1.3690	194.5	0.790	0.0060	1.390	55.20	0.1280	0.0077	8.27	1.964	1.14
90	3.6000	180.5	0.746	0.0150	1.160	62.00	0.1120	0.0091	6.16	2.028	1.26
100	7.7750	162.2	0.691	0.0320	810	68.80	0.0955	0.0111	4.00	2.176	1.47
110	14.6700	137.0	0.626	0.0620	740	75.60	0.0802	0.0138	2.00	2.566	1.97
120	25.1500	95.7	0.528	0.1245	640	82.10	0.0628	0.0195	0.20		4.14

Nitrogen, N_2, molecular mass: 28.0 ($T_{sat} = -195.65\,^\circ$C; $T_m = 209.85\,^\circ$C) (Faghri 1995; Faghri and Zhang 2006)

Table A.23 Thermophysical properties at saturation for pentane

Temperature, T (°C)	Saturation pressure, p_v (10^6 Pa)	Latent heat, h_{lv} (kJ/kg)	Liquid density, ρ_l (kg/m³)	Vapor density, ρ_v (kg/m³)	Liquid viscosity, μ_l (10^{-3} N s/m²)	Vapor viscosity, μ_v (10^{-5} N s/m²)	Liquid thermal conductivity, k_l (W/m K)	Vapor thermal conductivity[a], k_v (W/m K)	Liquid surface tension, σ (10^{-2} N/m)	Liquid specific heat[b], $c_{p,l}$ (kJ/kg K)	Vapor specific heat, $c_{p,v}$ (kJ/kg K)
−20	0.01	390.0	663.0	0.00001	0.244	0.51	0.149		2.01	2.140	0.825
0	0.024	378.3	664.0	0.00075	0.283	0.53	0.b		1.79	2.212	0.874
20	0.076	366.9	625.5	0.0022	0.242	0.58	0.138		1.58	2.296	0.922
40	0.152	355.5	607.0	0.00435	0.200	0.63	0.133	124.73	1.37		0.971
60	0.228	342.3	585.0	0.00651	0.174	0.69	0.128	131.06	1.17		1.021
80	0.389	329.1	563.0	0.01061	0.147	0.74	0.127	124.90	0.97		1.050
100	0.719	295.7	537.6	0.01654	0.128	0.81	0.124	143.95	0.83		1.088
120	1.381	269.7	509.4	0.0252	0.120	0.90	0.122	150.32	0.68		1.164

Pentane, C_5H_{12}, molecular mass: 72.15 ($T_{sat} = 36.06$ °C; $T_m = -129.67$ °C) (Reay and Kew 2006; Haynes 2014)

[a]Kharin (1985)

[b]Messerly et al. (1967)

Table A.24 Thermophysical properties at saturation for potassium

Temperature, T (K)	Saturation pressure, p_v (10^5 Pa)	Latent heat, h_{lv} (kJ/kg)	Liquid density, ρ_l (kg/m³)	Vapor density, ρ_v (10^{-3} kg/m³)	Liquid viscosity, μ_l (10^{-4} N s/m²)	Vapor viscosity, μ_v (10^{-7} N s/m²)	Liquid thermal conductivity, k_l (W/m K)	Vapor thermal conductivity, k_v (W/m K)	Liquid surface tension, σ (10^{-3} N/m)	Liquid specific heat, $c_{p,l}$ (kJ/kg K)	Vapor specific heat, $c_{p,v}$ (10^{-1} kJ/kg K)
600	0.0009258	2,143	766.9	0.69	2.380		43.85		98.2	0.771	0.8194
700	0.01022	2,108	743.3	6.68	1.981		40.72	0.0142	92.2	0.762	0.9646
800	0.06116	2,068	719.6	36.44	1.707	134	37.58	0.0175	86.2	0.761	1.066
900	0.2441	2,023	695.7	134.80	1.507	148	34.45	0.0205	80.2	0.769	1.116
1,000	0.7322	1,970	671.6	380.20	1.354	163	31.32	0.0228	74.2	0.792	1.121
1,100	1.864	1,924	647.3	871.90	1.233	178	28.19	0.0248	68.2	0.819	1.100
1,200	3.913	1,872	622.9	1,703.00	1.135	196	25.05	0.0266	62.2	0.846	1.064
1,300	7.304	1,820	598.4	2,969.10	1.053	212	22.00	0.0280	56.2	0.873	1.022
1,400	12.44	1,765	573.6	4,768.70	0.984	228	19.00	0.0293	53.0	0.899	0.9796
1,500	20.0	1,711	548.8	7,062.10	0.925	242	16.00	0.0303	47.0	0.924	

Potassium, K, molecular mass: 39.1 (T_{sat} = 1,032.2 K; T_m = 336.4 K) (Faghri 1995; Faghri and Zhang 2006)

Table A.25 Thermophysical properties at saturation for rubidium

Temperature, T (K)	Saturation pressure, p_v $(10^5$ Pa)	Latent heat, h_{lv} (kJ/kg)	Liquid density, ρ_l (kg/m³)	Vapor density, ρ_v (kg/m³)	Liquid viscosity, μ_l $(10^{-4}$ N s/m²)	Vapor viscosity, μ_v $(10^{-4}$ N s/m²)	Liquid thermal conductivity, k_l (W/m K)	Vapor thermal conductivity, k_v (W/m K)	Liquid surface tension, σ $(10^{-3}$ N/m)	Liquid specific heat, $c_{p,l}$ (kJ/kg K)	Vapor specific heat, $c_{p,v}$ (kJ/kg K)
500	0.0001733	889.6	1,386	0.0003585	3.23		29.8		81.6	0.369	0.3353
600	0.003664	870.9	1,340	0.006386	2.58	0.112	27.8	0.0073	75.7	0.362	0.4100
700	0.03174	849.7	1,294	0.04819	2.18	0.135	25.9	0.0089	69.8	0.357	0.4679
800	0.1584	827.3	1,248	0.2145	1.89	0.158	24.1	0.0103	63.9	0.353	0.4979
900	0.5476	804.6	1,202	0.6726	1.69	0.183	22.2	0.0115	58.0	0.353	0.5035
1,000	1.467	782.2	1,156	1.658	1.53	0.208	20.3	0.0125	51.3	0.360	0.4937
1,100	3.295	759.6	1,110	3.437	1.40	0.244	18.5	0.0133	44.5	0.373	0.4762
1,200	6.466	737.0	1,064	6.274	1.30	0.268	16.7	0.0141	37.7	0.385	0.4558
1,300	11.43	714.5	1,018	10.36	1.21	0.289	15.0	0.0149	30.9	0.399	0.4354
1,400	18.6	694.0	972	12.35	1.14	0.314	13.6	0.0156	26.0	0.408	0.4130
1,500	28.5	674.0	926	22.22	1.08	0.336	12.0	0.0160	19.0	0.418	0.3900

Rubidium, Rb, molecular mass: 85.5 ($T_{sat} = 959.2$ K; $T_m = 312.7$ K) (Faghri 1995; Faghri and Zhang 2006)

Table A.26 Thermophysical properties at saturation for silver

Temperature, T (°C)	Saturation pressure, p_v (10^5 Pa)	Latent heat, h_{lv} (kJ/kg)	Liquid density, ρ_l (kg/m³)	Vapor density, ρ_v (kg/m³)	Liquid viscosity, μ_l (10^{-3} N s/m²)	Vapor viscosity, μ_v (10^{-6} N s/m²)	Liquid thermal conductivity, k_l (W/m K)	Vapor thermal conductivity, k_v (W/m K)	Liquid surface tension, σ (10^{-3} N/m)	Liquid specific heat[a], $c_{p,l}$ (kJ/kg K)	Vapor specific heat[a], $c_{p,v}$ (kJ/kg K)
1,500	0.01008	298	8,782	0.0076	2.88	61.69	191.3		827.5	0.291	
1,600	0.02420	298	8,683	0.01698	2.47	64.69	192.7		810.1	0.291	
1,700	0.05300	298	8,585	0.03548	2.08	67.69	194.1		792.1	0.291	
1,800	0.10800	298	8,485	0.06823	1.75	70.69	195.5		775.3	0.291	
1,900	0.20600	298	8,385	0.12300	1.44	73.69	196.9		757.9	0.291	
2,000	0.38300	298	8,289	0.21880	1.17	76.69	198.3		740.5	0.291	
2,100	0.63500	298	8,190	0.35480	0.90	79.69	199.7		723.1	0.291	
2,200	0.86000	298	8,092	0.57540	0.67	82.69			705.7	0.291	
2,300	1.36000	298	8,000	0.87100	0.44	85.69			638.0	0.291	
2,400	2.53000	298	7,894	1.23000	0.24	88.69			680.0	0.291	
2,500	3.84000	298	7,796	1.82000	0.05	91.69			665.0		0.192

Silver, Ag, molecular mass: 107.9 ($T_{\text{sat}} = 2{,}212$ °C; $T_m = 960.5$ °C) (Faghri 1995; Faghri and Zhang 2006)
[a]Interpolation from Kaye and Laby (1995)

Table A.27 Thermophysical properties at saturation for sodium

Temperature, T (K)	Saturation pressure, p_v (10^2 Pa)	Latent heat, h_{lv} (kJ/kg)	Liquid density, ρ_l (kg/m^3)	Vapor density, ρ_v (10^{-3} kg/m^3)	Liquid viscosity, μ_l (10^{-4} N s/m^2)	Vapor viscosity, μ_v (10^{-8} N s/m^2)	Liquid thermal conductivity, k_l (W/m K)	Vapor thermal conductivity, k_v (W/m K)	Liquid surface tension, σ (10^{-3} N/m)	Liquid specific heat, $c_{p,l}$ (kJ/kg K)	Vapor specific heat, $c_{p,v}$ (10^{-1} kJ/kg K)
600	0.047	4,429	873.2	0.022	3.276	1,480	75.17		172.1	1.30	1.793
700	0.951	4,341	849.4	0.396	2.690	1,660	70.53	0.0277	162.1	1.27	2.244
800	8.760	4,237	825.6	3.270	2.298	1,827	65.88	0.0343	152.1	1.26	2.555
900	48.760	4,131	801.8	16.500	2.018	2,010	61.25	0.0406	142.1	1.25	2.700
1,000	192.200	4,026	778.0	59.980	1.809	2,211	56.60	0.0455	132.1	1.26	2.709
1,100	584.280	3,925	754.2	168.100	1.645	2,398	51.96	0.0492	122.1	1.27	2.632
1,200	1,465.400	3,829	730.4	396.600	1.514	2,577	47.00	0.0522	112.1	1.29	2.508
1,300	3,165.000	3,742	706.6	804.500	1.407	2,763	42.50	0.0547	102.1		2.365
1,400	6,097.400	3,656	682.8	1,459.200	1.317	2,938	37.50	0.0570	92.1		2.228
1,500	10,716.600	3,577	658.0	2,424.800	1.240	3,117	33.00	0.0592	82.0		2.095
1,600	17,495.900	3,500	635.2	3,750.900	1.176	3,281	28.50		72.0		
1,700	26,919.900	3,425	611.4	5,482.400	1.117	3,449	24.00		62.0		
1,800	39,350.000	3,353	587.6	7,627.700	1.067	3,620	19.00		52.0		

Sodium, Na, molecular mass: 23.0 (T_{sat} = 1,151.2 K; T_m = 371.0 K) (Faghri 1995; Faghri and Zhang 2006)

Table A.28 Thermophysical properties at saturation for water

Temperature, T (°C)	Saturation pressure, p_v (10^5 Pa)	Latent heat, h_{lv} (kJ/kg)	Liquid density, ρ_l (kg/m³)	Vapor density, ρ_v (kg/m³)	Liquid viscosity, μ_l (10^{-7} N s/m²)	Vapor viscosity, μ_v (10^{-7} N s/m²)	Liquid thermal conductivity, k_l (W/m K)	Vapor thermal conductivity, k_v (W/m K)	Liquid surface tension, σ (10^{-3}/m)	Liquid specific heat, $c_{p,l}$ (kJ/kg K)	Vapor specific heat, $c_{p,v}$ (kJ/kg K)
20	0.023368	2,453.8	999.0	0.01729	10,015	88.5	0.602	0.0188	72.88	4.182	1.874
40	0.073749	2,406.5	993.05	0.05110	6,513	96.6	0.630	0.0201	69.48	4.179	1.894
60	0.199190	2,358.4	983.28	0.13020	4,630	105.0	0.653	0.0216	66.07	4.185	1.924
80	0.473590	2,308.9	971.82	0.29320	3,510	113.0	0.669	0.0231	62.69	4.197	1.969
100	1.013250	2,251.2	958.77	0.59740	2,790	121.0	0.680	0.0248	58.91	4.216	2.034
120	1.985400	2,202.9	943.39	1.12100	2,300	128.0	0.685	0.0267	54.96	4.245	2.124
140	3.613600	2,144.9	925.93	1.96560	1,950	135.0	0.687	0.0288	50.79	4.285	2.245
160	6.180400	2,082.2	907.44	3.25890	1,690	142.0	0.684	0.0313	46.51	4.339	2.406
180	10.02700	2,014.0	887.31	5.15970	1,493	149.0	0.676	0.0341	42.19	4.408	2.615
200	15.55100	1,939.0	865.05	7.86530	1,338	156.0	0.664	0.0375	37.77	4.497	2.883

Water, H_2O, molecular mass: 18.0 ($T_{sat} = 100$ °C; $T_m = 0.0$ °C) (Peterson 1994; Faghri 1995; Faghri and Zhang 2006)

References

Bentor Y (2014) Chemical Element.com—calcium

Chase MW Jr (1998) NIST-JANAF thermochemical tables, 4th edn. J. Phys. Chem. Ref. Data, Monograph 9, pp 1–1951

D. C. C. (1997) DOWTHERM a heat transfer fluid. Dow Chemical Company, Midland

F2 Chemicals Ltd (2011) Safety data sheet FLUTEC PP2. F2 Chemicals Ltd.

Faghri A (1995) Heat pipe science and technologies. Global Digital, New York

Faghri A, Zhang Y (2006) Transport phenomena in multiphase systems. Elsevier, New York

Greenwood NN, Earnshaw A (1997) Chemistry of the elements, 2nd edn. Butterworth-Heinemann, New York

Haynes WM (2014) CRC handbook of chemistry and physics, 97th edn. CRC, Boca Raton, pp 3–438

IAEA (2008) Thermophysical properties of materials for nuclear engineering: a tutorial and collection of data. IAEA, Vienna

Kaye GWC, Laby TH (1995) Tables of physical and chemical constants, 16th edn. Longman, London

Kharin VE (1985) Isobaric heat capacity of n-pentane in the vapor phase. Izv Vyssh Ucheb Zaved Neft Gaz 28:63–66

Lienhard JH IV, Lienhard JH V (2005) A heat transfer textbook, 3rd edn. Phlogiston, Cambridge

Messerly JF, Guthrie GB, Todd SS, Finke HL (1967) Low-temperature thermal data for n-pentane, n-heptadecane, and n-octadecane. J Chem Eng Data 12:338–346

Peterson GP (1994) An introduction to heat pipes modeling, testing and applications. Wiley, New York

Reay DA, Kew PA (2006) Heat pipes: theory, design and applications, 5th edn. Butterworth-Heinemann, New York

Rohsenow WN, Hartnett JP, Ganic EN (1985) Handbook of heat transfer fundamentals. McGraw-Hill, New York

Vargaftik NB (1975) Handbook of physical properties of liquids and gases. Hemisphere, New York

Weatherford WD Jr, Tyler JC, Ku PM (1961) Properties of inorganic energy-conversion and heat-transfer fluids for space applications. Southwest Research Institute, San Antonia

Yarrington RM, Kay WB (1957) The liquid specific heats of some fluorocarbon compounds. J Phys Chem 61:1259–1260

Index

© Springer Science+Business Media New York 2015   425
H. Ma, *Oscillating Heat Pipes*, DOI 10.1007/978-1-4939-2504-9

Contents

effects will help the reader better understand how an OHP can achieve its extra-high heat transport capability. Chapter 4 introduces how oscillating motions are generated in an OHP including gas spring constants, maximum radius of channels, mathematical modeling of a mechanical vibration in an OHP system, exciting forces, and operating limitations. Chapter 5 summarizes important factors affecting oscillating motion and heat transfer in an OHP. To better understand the oscillating motion in an OHP, extensive experimental investigations of OHP observations have been conducted over the last decade. Chapter 6 introduces three observation methods utilized to analyze the oscillating motion in OHPs and also summarizes the OHP observation achievements of the last decade. Chapter 7 presents nanofluid and its effect on fluid flow and heat transfer in OHPs. Information on design, fabrication, and experiments involving OHPs is introduced in Chapter 8. OHP is one type of heat pipe. To show the difference between OHPs and other heat pipes, Chapter 9 presents the fundamentals of conventional heat pipe operation including the heat transfer limitations of conventional heat pipes.

Over the last 16 years, I have conducted research related to OHPs with support from the Office of Naval Research, DARPA, and NSF. In particular, I wanted to thank Dr. Mark Spector of the Office of Naval Research. Dr. Spector has supported my OHP research consistently for many years. Without this kind of support, it would not have been possible for me and my research team to advance the science and engineering of OHPs and it would not have been possible for me to write this book. I am deeply grateful to my students and postdoctoral research associates who have made significant contributions to the results included in this book. Their willingness to examine the text led to valuable comments and contributed greatly to the preparation of this book; hence, I would like to thank Corey Wilson, Peng Cheng, Da Yin, Il Yoon, Scott Thompson, Yulong Ji, Nannan Zhao, Hanwen Lu, Chris Smoot, Fritz Laun, Haijun Li, Aaron Hathaway, Steve Demsky, Brian Borgmeyer, Benwei Fu, Hao Peng, Anjun Jiao, Tom Zhang, Hani Sait, Fengmin Su, Wenbin Cui, Guoyou Wang, Willard Hanson, and many others for their valuable assistance. Their relentless pursuit of knowledge and scientific research helped make the completion of this book possible. My thanks also extend to Ms. Carla Roberts for editing this book. Finally, I wanted to thank my family: Emily, David, and Susan for their love and support.

Columbia, MO, USA   Hongbin Ma

Preface

The main focus of this book is on oscillating heat pipe (OHP) science and technology, which has made tremendous advances in the past 20 years. Heat transfer processes in an OHP are very complex and involve liquid–vapor interfacial phenomenon, surface forces, thermally excited mechanical vibration, evaporation and condensation heat transfer, oscillated forced convection, and heat conduction. The most outstanding feature is that an OHP can effectively integrate the state-of-the-art of heat transfer processes such as thin film evaporation, oscillating flow, thermally excited mechanical vibration, nanoparticles, high heat transfer coefficient of entrance regions, and vortexes induced by the oscillating flow of liquid plugs and vapor bubbles. Therefore, the OHP can achieve an extra high effective thermal conductivity. This book is based on my lecture notes, recent results obtained by my research teams, and outstanding contributions by many other researchers in the field, which made it possible for me to write this book. The book is written for both graduate students and researchers in the field to provide a better understanding of OHP fluid flow and its heat transfer mechanisms.

This book touches on a wide range of topics designed to provide a better understanding of fluid flow and heat transfer mechanisms in an OHP with an emphasis on surface forces, liquid–vapor interface phenomena, thin film evaporation, heat transfer enhancement of oscillating single phase flow, thermally excited mechanical vibration of liquid plugs and vapor bubbles, visualization of two-phase flow, nanoparticle effect, OHP experiment, and fabrication processes. Chapter 2 presents the fundamentals needed to better understand the formation of a liquid–vapor interface as well as fluid flow and heat transfer in an OHP. For an OHP, the working fluid inside forms as a train of liquid plugs and vapor bubbles, which travel together but are distinctly separated. The heat transfer process due to the thermally excited oscillating motion in an OHP is similar to the oscillating flow of a single phase. Therefore, Chapter 3 introduces fundamentals on how an oscillating singe phase flow can enhance heat transfer. For example, the oscillating flow can easily turn a laminar flow into a turbulent flow, and the oscillating flow can develop a near-wall velocity overshoot (Richardson's annular effect). Introduction of these

To my wife Susan and
my children Emily and David

Hongbin Ma
Mechanical and Aerospace Engineering
University of Missouri
Columbia, MO, USA

ISBN 978-1-4939-4523-8   ISBN 978-1-4939-2504-9   (eBook)
DOI 10.1007/978-1-4939-2504-9

Springer New York Heidelberg Dordrecht London
© Springer Science+Business Media New York 2015
Softcover reprint of the hardcover 1st edition 2015

This work is subject to copyright. All rights are reserved by the Publisher, whether the whole or part of
the material is concerned, specifically the rights of translation, reprinting, reuse of illustrations,
recitation, broadcasting, reproduction on microfilms or in any other physical way, and transmission
or information storage and retrieval, electronic adaptation, computer software, or by similar or
dissimilar methodology now known or hereafter developed.
The use of general descriptive names, registered names, trademarks, service marks, etc. in this
publication does not imply, even in the absence of a specific statement, that such names are exempt
from the relevant protective laws and regulations and therefore free for general use.
The publisher, the authors and the editors are safe to assume that the advice and information in this
book are believed to be true and accurate at the date of publication. Neither the publisher nor the
authors or the editors give a warranty, express or implied, with respect to the material contained
herein or for any errors or omissions that may have been made.

Springer Science+Business Media LLC New York is part of Springer Science+Business Media
(www.springer.com)

Hongbin Ma

Oscillating Heat Pipes

 Springer

To: Frank Incropera

Best Regards!

Hongbin Ma

D08Z8930

Oscillating Heat Pipes

DIE NIEMANDSROSE (1963)
THE NO-ONE'S-ROSE

ATEMWENDE (1967)
BREATHTURN

FADENSONNEN (1968)
THREADSUNS

LICHTZWANG (1970)
LIGHT-COMPULSION

SCHNEEPART (1971)
SNOW-PART

ZEITGEHÖFT (1976)
HOMESTEAD OF TIME

ACKNOWLEDGMENTS

Besides the translators of Paul Celan whom I acknowledge in my preface, I've gratefully learned (occasionally borrowing an apt word) from others who have translated or frequented Celan: Jerry Glenn, Luitgard Wundheiler, John Friedmann, Walter Billeter, Rosmarie Waldrop, Brian Lynch and Peter Jankowsky, Ben Friedlander, Esther Cameron, Rosalind Johnston, Michael Roloff. Since *Paul Celan: Poet, Survivor, Jew* appeared in 1995, people from the United States, Germany, Austria, Holland, England, France, and elsewhere have let me know how vitally this writer's work and life matter to them. So have many graduate students and undergraduates. I thank them all for not simply confirming but educating and furthering my sense of Celan's significance. Certain critics and reviewers also gave my book the kind of attentiveness one craves—*Aufmerksamkeit*, Celan called it, "mindfulness." And three friends—Jerry Glenn, Paul Sars, and Amir Eshel—heartened me by their own scholarly devotion. I am glad to thank Eric Celan, once again, for remaining a faithful and gracious custodian of his parents' work. Thanks go to my editor, Jill Bialosky, who welcomed and tended this book, and to Shana Bernstein and Angelica Duran, who typed parts of it. Several organizations generously supported my translation work: the National Endowment for the Arts, National Endowment for the Humanities, Djerassi Resident Artists Program, Stanford Humanities Center, and the Rockefeller Foundation's Bellagio Study and Conference Center.

Finally and foremost, after twenty-plus years of an immersion whose throes did not always make for connubial ease, it's gladdening to thank Mary Lowenthal Felstiner—*ganz, ganz wirklich*, "wholly real." Her own work as a historian, alongside mine in literature, "deepens our depth" (if I may borrow a phrase from Celan).

Would we, if somehow this were possible, trade Anne Frank's diary for her life, give up those salvaged pages to let her survive unscathed, in her seventies now? And would we forgo Charlotte Salomon's *Life or Theater?*, her 1941 autobiography in 760 watercolors, if in exchange she were not to perish in Auschwitz? Would we, in effect, do without such indispensable human documents, relinquish them so as to secure the undeflected lives their creators might have lived?

Why yes! it goes without saying. But the question involves something more. We cherish these creators specifically because of the diary or the paintings that an atrocious history impelled them to create. Undo that history, rewind the reel, and Anne Frank and Charlotte Salomon would not be quite the persons we wish to redeem.

The same question holds for Paul Celan, although he did survive, in his way, the European Jewish catastrophe. Would that he had been spared affliction—the brutal loss of parents and homeland, the re-crudescent neo-Nazism and anti-Semitism in postwar Germany where his poetry was destined, and a vicious plagiarism charge adding insult to injury. Yet Celan's most compelling, inspiriting poems presuppose duress and distress. His body of writing belongs inseparably to its ground, its terrible cost. "For a poem is not timeless," he said in 1958. "Certainly, it lays claim to infinity, it seeks to reach through time—through it [*durch sie hindurch*], not above and beyond it."

Paul Celan's time saw him benignly situated at first, then vulnerable, wounded, unhealing. Born in 1920 to German-speaking Jewish parents in Czernowitz, the chief city of Bukovina and the eastern outpost of the Austrian empire, Celan (born Paul Antschel) grew up like so many other Jews, steeped in the songs and folk tales and classics of German culture. But Goethe and Schiller and Bach and Schubert and his German mother tongue formed no safeguard against what was to come. In 1933, not long before his Bar Mitzvah at age thirteen, the Nazis took power and Hitler's harangues came over the radio to Czernowitz, which along with northern Bukovina had passed to Romania after the Great War.

Nonetheless Celan led his life. A comely, clever boy, an only child fervently attached to his mother, he moved from German to Hebrew to Romanian schools; and later, from a Zionist youth group to an anti-Fascist one whose magazine, *Red Student*, published Marxist texts. In 1936 he rallied to the Spanish republican cause, and always poetry possessed him: Rilke, Verlaine, Shakespeare, his own early Symbolist lyrics and efforts at translating from French, English, Romanian.

After the Hitler-Stalin pact, Soviet troops in 1940 occupied Czernowitz. Besides ridding Celan of any Communist certainties, their presence prompted him to begin learning Russian. Then on July 5, 1941, *Einsatzkommando* 10B entered his homeland. Avidly abetted by Romanian forces, the Germans set about destroying a centuries-old Jewish culture by plunder, burning, murder, the yellow star, ghetto, forced labor, deportation. In late June 1942, his parents were picked up in an overnight raid and sent over the Dniester and Bug Rivers into western Ukraine. Celan, away for the night, came home to find the door sealed—although friends of his underwent deportation and exile alongside their parents. He never recovered from that abrupt loss, however much his words, his voice, might probe it: "Taken off into / the terrain / with the unmistakable trace: // Grass, written asunder... / Read no more—look! / Look no more—go!"

From July 1942 through February 1944, Celan endured forced labor in Romanian camps. He kept a 3″ × 4″ leather notebook for poems, sending copies to a woman he loved back home and aiming distantly, desperately, for a book. Bit by bit he learned his parents' fate: his father had perished from typhus, his mother was shot, sometime in fall and winter 1942–43.

Returning in the wake of the Red Army to his Soviet-occupied homeland in 1944, Celan took up life again, a raw orphan with literally nothing left but his mother tongue. Friends got him a job in a psychiatric hospital tending to Soviet airmen. In a little-known letter of July 1, 1944, he wrote to his Czernowitz boyhood friend Erich Einhorn (the word *Einhorn* appears in a later poem, "Shibboleth"), who'd fled to Russia in 1941 and not come back:

Dear Erich,

I've come to Kiev for two days (on official business) and I'm glad of the chance to write you a letter that will reach you quickly.

Your parents are well, Erich, I talked with them before I came here. That's saying a lot, Erich, you can't imagine *how* much.

My parents were shot by the Germans. In Krasnopolka on the Bug River.

Erich, oh Erich.

There's much to tell. You've seen so much. I've experienced only humiliations and emptiness, endless emptiness. Maybe you can come home.

More nakedly than Celan would later do, this letter expresses the unimaginable loss that grounds all his writing.

Paul's friend Erich did not come home, and Czernowitz did not remain Celan's home for long. Toward the war's end he migrated to Bucharest, then in 1947 fled to Vienna. Finally in July 1948 he settled in Paris and lived the rest of his life there, marrying the graphic artist Gisèle de Lestrange, having a son, Eric, in 1955, earning his livelihood as a German teacher at the École Normale Supérieure, a translator, a poet.

First-person lyrics such as "Black Flakes" and "Nearness of Graves," from 1943, had attested his aching loss: "And can you bear, Mother, as once on a time, / the gentle, the German, the pain-laden rhyme?" Then in late 1944 and early '45, with reports filtering through to Romania and the Polish camps disgorging (or not) their victims, Celan gave a voice to the common trauma:

> Black milk of daybreak we drink you at night
> we drink you at morning and midday we drink you at evening
> we drink and we drink

Black milk, *Schwarze Milch:* How to find words for "that which happened," as Celan called what we call Holocaust or Shoah; how to speak of and through the "thousand darknesses of deathbringing speech" in a mother tongue that had suddenly turned into his mother's murderers' tongue? The cadence and imagery of this ballad, which he named *"Todesfuge"* (Deathfugue), engage atrocity with art, as Celan would go on doing during the next quarter century. Though his rhythms might later compact or rupture, his words grow strange or few, from "Deathfugue" on Celan kept up the wrestle with language that makes him Europe's leading postwar poet.

Testimony to how crucial, how necessary, are Paul Celan and his foremost poem comes from diverse sources across Europe and America. Nobel laureates Heinrich Böll and Günter Grass befriended and supported Celan. Philosophers Martin Heidegger, Theodor Adorno, Hans-Georg Gadamer, and Jürgen Habermas acknowledged his singular importance, as did the French: Emmanuel Levinas, Maurice Blanchot, Jacques Derrida. Numerous German composers have set *"Todesfuge"* to music; its refrain *Der Tod ist ein Meister aus Deutschland* (Death is a master from Germany) has entitled various books and a major TV documentary; in 1988 on the fiftieth anniversary of Kristallnacht, a well-known actress recited *"Todesfuge"* in the Bundestag. Anselm Kiefer has inscribed phrases from the poem—*dein goldenes Haar Margarete, dein aschenes Haar Sulamith*—into some of his most unsettling canvases. The much-prized architect Daniel Libeskind built a Paul Celan Court into Berlin's new Jewish Museum.

Fellow writers—and this is the acid test—acknowledge Celan's vital presence for them. The brilliant Italian witness Primo Levi said about "Deathfugue": "I carry it inside me like a graft." And when I asked whether he'd taken Celan's phrase "a grave in the air" for his book *If Not Now, When?*, Levi replied, "I 'stole' this image from Celan's 'Todesfuge,' which struck me deeply . . . But, as you know, in literature the borderline between stealth and homage is blurred."

Elie Wiesel ranks Celan among "the greatest and most moving Jewish poets of our turbulent time." George Steiner sets him "at the summit of German (perhaps of modern European) poetry." Among poets of the past, says Helen Vendler, Celan is our "greatest poet since Yeats," while Harold Bloom calls him the "astonishing . . . Celan." And no less tellingly, men and women from every walk of life, anywhere from Hurricane, West Virginia, to Thunder Bay, Ontario, have written or telephoned or E-mailed me over the years to say that Paul Celan's writing touches them like no other: clears their vision, fires their hope, braces their pain.

Possibly the most decisive sign that Paul Celan matters essentially comes from the poets, in America and elsewhere. Former Poet Laureate Robert Hass, devoting two syndicated columns to *"Todesfuge"* and the present translation, called this "one of the most indelible poems of the 20th century." For John Hollander, Celan is "genuinely great," and for Denise Levertov, his work forms "at once so inward and such a quintessential artifact of history." Poets as diverse as Adrienne Rich, Michael Palmer, Heather McHugh, Geoffrey Hill, Sharon Olds, Edward Hirsch, Eavan Boland, Rita Dove, and many others all consider Celan a touchstone—for his life-and-death lyric seriousness, his uncompromising verbal honesty, and his courage in exposing his native German, driving language to the verge of unexpected revelation.

Paul Celan is both challenging and exemplary. There can have been only a few modern poets in whom the life and the work cleave so closely, so traumatically.

> Just like the blood that bursts from
> your eye or mouth or ear,
> so your key changes,

> he says to himself,

> Just like the wind that rebuffs you,
> packed round your word is the snow.

> *Je nach dem Wind der dich fortstösst,*
> *ballt um das Wort sich der Schnee.*

At one level, this stifled "word"—Celan's *Wort* shut in between "packed" and "snow"—needs no biographical basis, any more than does Emily Dickinson's mortal vision: "As freezing persons recollect the snow, / First chill, then stupor, then the letting go." Yet what underlies those lines of Celan's, that ars poetica, is the Ukrainian snow where his parents were murdered.

In August 1984 at Cerisy-la-Salle near the Norman coast, shortly after coming to know Gisèle Celan-Lestrange, I asked her (in tentative French): "Is it not that many of your husband's poems arise from his own experience?" *Cent pour cent*, she replied instantly, "One hundred percent." And yet at the same time, if I asked her about Paul Celan's life, Gisèle would urge me to concentrate strictly on his work. So that double focus, or call it a fusing of two lenses, forms the challenge of approaching Celan and of making his life's work and his work's life accessible.

To attend deeply to Paul Celan entails, as Gisèle well knew, studying his own reading habits, since the world's texts in many subjects and languages furnished realia for his writing. She let me peruse his two libraries, in Paris and Normandy. For hours on end I would pull volume after volume from the shelves, to see just what Celan had bought and read, and when and where, and whether he'd made marginal comments or underlinings. Once, for instance, I came upon a poem he'd drafted inside a physiology handbook; this, combined with his multiple markings of Gershom Scholem on the Shechinah, God's radiant presence, guided my rendering of "Near, in the aorta's arch." I also found an offprint of René Char's Résistance notebooks in Celan's German translation. The Frenchman had inscribed it for his translator: "*À Paul Celan, à qui je pensais*" (To Paul Celan, whom I was thinking of)—an uncanny tribute!

Very late one cold night in November '84 at the rue Montorgueil, after Gisèle had gone to bed, I stayed up as long as I could, gripped by this silent private access to the poet's mindwork. Spotting the soft chestnut covers of a frayed, hand-worn volume, I took it down: Kafka's *Erzählungen*. "A Country Doctor," "The Hunter Gracchus," "A Hunger Artist": these stories had been much read. Then on looking into the book's endpapers, I discovered that Celan had this volume with him during a months-long stay in a psychiatric clinic when nervous depression—"the doctor's simplistic formula," he said—was besetting him.

What took my breath away, in the back endpapers, were some terrifying pained scrawlings. Hardly daring to, I nevertheless copied them down: "early afternoon on the 8th of December 1965: It's still quite clear in my head—*Kämen Menschen,* If only people would come, I could almost begin anew, *ich könnte fast neu beginnen."* Along with this heart cry, on the last page I found, in Hebrew: *shaddai shaddai,* the ineffable name of God, and below that, in a distracted Hebrew hand, the Judaic watchword: *Shema Yisrael Adonai Elohenu Adonai Echad,* "Hear, O Israel, the Lord our God, the Lord is One"—the essential profession of faith, which Jewish martyrs have recited over the centuries.

At this moment—3 A.M.? 4 A.M.?—Gisèle happened to come into the living room. Seeing me with this Kafka volume, she asked me to put it back on the shelf. After seven more years of work—research, interviews, translations, conferences, essays—I doubted that I could, or rather that I should, publish those naked scrawlings, however arresting and revealing. Even when I'd finished composing my biographical account of Celan, I kept putting off asking Gisèle for permission. Then, tragically and to my shock, in December 1991 she died of cancer. Fiercely serious about her own art, and loyal to her husband, she had embodied for me the presence of Paul Celan's absence, and now her death deepened that absence.

Finally I decided that a genuine account needed to include Celan's subjunctive *Kämen Menschen,* "If only people would come, I could almost begin anew," and his Hebraic cry, "Hear, O Israel." In 1994, ten years after lighting upon them, I asked the Celans' son, Eric, for permission and he kindly agreed. These utterances belong to the poet's psychic ground, the dark behind the mirror. What's more, in the critical languages of German and Hebrew, they speak for two core motives, the motives that—to my mind, at least—unite in driving Paul Celan's most idiosyncratic writing: *Kämen Menschen,* an uncertain yet urgent hope for human addressability, humane solidarity; and *Shema Yisrael,* a radical imperative—"Listen!"—in the other language that remained "near and not lost," *nah und unverloren,* "in the midst of the losses," as he said in his first major speech, on receiving the Bremen literature prize in 1958.

There he spoke his hope: "A poem . . . can be a message in a bottle, sent out in the—not always greatly hopeful—belief that somewhere and sometime it could wash up on land, on heartland perhaps." Certainly Celan's reader, likewise his translator, can try to inhabit that heartland of intimate appeal.

"Everything is near and unforgotten," Celan wrote in 1944 to Erich Einhorn, meaning the arc of a life, from youth into war and beyond, that might have incurred oblivion. Thus, his life's work, the poems and prose and certain translations, form a continuum in which everything is indeed near and unforgotten. It may help to see Celan's oeuvre evolving from early to middle to late: from 1920 until the summer of 1948, when the State of Israel came into being and when instead of moving there he settled in Paris, "one of the last who must live out to the end the destiny of the Jewish spirit in Europe"; then from 1948, when he took up his living as a poet, translator, and teacher, until late 1962, the completion of *The No-One's-Rose* and his first bout of severe depression; and from 1962, when his poetry was turning spare and dark, until his death in 1970.

Celan closed the 1958 Bremen speech by calling himself one who "goes toward language with his very being, stricken by and seeking reality." Though my last phrase does not quite catch the German's ultimate stresses—*wirklichkeitswund und Wirklichkeit suchend,* "reality-wounded and Reality-seeking," perhaps that closing phrase can chart Paul Celan's poetic phases, a kind of tensile arc: "Stricken . . . Seeking . . . Reality."

Such an arc traverses the entire body of Celan's writing, represented in English translation more fully here than ever before—161 poems, plus much else that also manifests the poet's driving concerns. This anthology opens with his youthful lyrics, scarcely translated until now. Then come chronological selections from the eight books published between 1952 and 1971, and from a further gathering issued after his death. And then follow several poems he never published, found in his private papers. My anthology also presents Celan's major prose, setting it for the first time alongside his poems in translation. These highly unusual prose writings interact with his poetry: the whimsical "Conversation in the Mountains," where Jew Gross and Jew Klein talk about alienation, nature, silence, God, and language itself; Celan's speeches for the Bremen and Büchner prizes, which identify subtly and sharply the state of poetry after "that which happened"; and his half-elated, half-vulnerable words to the Hebrew Writers Association in 1969, shortly before his death.

Also included are photographic reproductions of little-known or hitherto unknown Celan manuscripts, along with Gisèle Celan-Lestrange's graphic art, which accompanied and fortified his own art. As a whole, the anthology reveals someone whose language carved "a Breathcrystal, / your unannullable / witness."

In making these translations, I've consulted the multiple drafts of Celan's poems as well as his notes for the Büchner or "Meridian" speech, all of which expose his shaping process, helping reader and translator alike to come closer to the poet's intentions. I've also listened over and over to recordings of his voice, so as to absorb whatever emphases, rhythmic above all, might aid my task. Even the moments when Celan misspeaks a line (as in *"Todesfuge"* and *"Mit wechselndem Schlüssel"*), utterly rare in so exacting a poet, may possibly open an insight into something crucial happening there. And another unique window on Celan's poetic intentions has become accessible. In 1955 two translators made French versions from his work, and he carefully revised them. Given his nuanced, exact French, these amendations help clarify obscure and enigmatic and ambiguous moments in his German verse. For instance, his poem "Shibboleth" evokes the 1934 workers' uprisings in Vienna and Madrid as *Zwillingsröte*. Originally I rendered that as "twin rednesses"; but since Celan in French suggested *rougeoiements*, I've now opted for "reddenings," which deepens the political image with a sense of dawning. Or in "Praise of Distance," the speaker is "a heart that abode among *Menschen*": the French translator heard this as *hommes*, "men," but Celan made it *humains*, a heart among humans. In the same poem, he replaced *infidèle* (unfaithful) with the stronger *Apostat*, so that the line says "Apostate only am I faithful"—which would provide, by the way, a stimulating but risky motto for translation itself.

Of course there remains one element of Paul Celan's career that cannot figure in a Selected Poems and Prose: namely, his genius as a translator into German. From his teenage years (when he tried Apollinaire, Éluard, Shakespeare, Yeats, Housman, and Sergei Esenin),

Paul CELAN

ELOGE DU LOINTAIN

Aux sources de tes yeux
vivent les filets des pêcheurs ~~en eau trouble~~
Aux sources de tes yeux
la mer tient ses promesses.

C'est là que je ~~rejette~~
coeur ~~qui connaît les hommes,~~
mes ~~haures~~ et le feu d'un serment:
Plus noir, dans le noir, je suis nu davantage.
~~Le reniement seul fait ma foi.~~
Je suis, ~~même~~ moi, même, toi.

Aux sources de tes yeux
je dérive, rêvant de rapine.
Un filet capta un filet :
nous nous séparons enlacés.

Aux sources de tes yeux
un pendu étrangle la corde.

(trad. Denise Naville)

French version of "*Lob der Ferne*," translated by Denise Naville (1955),
edited by Celan.

Paul CELAN

ELOGE DU LOINTAIN

Aux sources de tes yeux
vivent les filets des pêcheurs de la Mer Démente.
Aux sources de tes yeux
La mer tient ses promesses.

C'est là que je jette,
coeur qui a séjourné parmi les humains,
mes vêtements
et me défais de l'éclat d'un serment:

Plus noir dans le noir, je suis nu davantage.
Dans la défection je suis fidèle.
Je suis, étant moi-même, toi.

Aux sources de tes yeux
je dérive, rêvant de rapine.

Un filet capta un filet:
nous nous séparons enlacés.

Aux sources de tes yeux
un pendu étrangle la corde.

(Trad. Denise Naville)

Corrected French version of "*Lob der Ferne*," translated by Denise Naville (1955), edited by Celan.

through the ghetto and forced labor, into his working life where translation also supplemented a teaching income, and up until his death, for Celan the rendering of other poets into German was an essential activity. "All these are encounters," he said, using the word *Begegnung*, which to him meant spiritual recognition; "here too I have gone with my very being toward language." Sometimes translation provided a proving ground, as when he fashioned over five hundred rhymed German alexandrines for Paul Valéry's *La Jeune Parque* because Rilke had said it couldn't be done.

At his most fervent, Celan translated in order to probe the limits of postwar German and to chisel his own truths out of the refractory stone of an other tongue. "I consider translating Mandelshtam into German," he said, "to be as important a task as my own verses." Osip Mandelshtam, to be sure, had perished as poet and Jew—had even (Celan believed for a while) died at Nazi rather than Soviet hands. Yet it did not take that sort of blood brotherhood to evoke penetrating translations. Shakespeare's charged language and themes of time, loss, death, regeneration, as well as of betrayal and bitterness, provoked German versions that appropriate and even sharpen the sonnets.

In Emily Dickinson, vastly removed though she was, Celan found kindred voicings of mortality and theological skepticism:

> I reason, we could die—
> The best Vitality
> Cannot excel decay,
> But, what of that?

Where Dickinson already seems compact and direct, her translator, while keeping meter and slant rhymes, compresses still more and mutates her grammar:

> *Ich denk: Sieh zu, man stirbt,*
> *der Saft, der in dir wirkt,*
> *auch ihm gilt dies: Verdirb—*
> *ja und?*

(I think: Look here, we die,
the sap that works in thee,
it too knows this: Decay—
so what?)

Conditional turns into imperative, abstract into concrete, irony into sar-
casm.

Because the inquiring, illumining process of translation taught me
so much in my book *Translating Neruda: The Way to Macchu Picchu*
(1980), later I thought my work on Paul Celan might be entitled
"Translating Celan: The Strain of Jewishness"—but that smacked a little too much of a mere sequel. Still, *Paul Celan: Poet, Survivor, Jew*
(1995) took its interpretive energy partly from the translator's point of
vantage and disadvantage. Now it feels inevitable to follow that account of Celan's life work with a gathering of his writings, in German
and in English translation.

All too often, it goes without saying that any translator is indebted
to those who have come before—in my case, to the pathbreaking Celan
translators Christopher Middleton and especially Michael Hamburger,
to Jerome Rothenberg, Cid Corman, Joachim Neugroschel. More recently, I've also benefited from the work of Pierre Joris, Heather
McHugh, and Nikolai Popov.*

For this anthology I've revised almost all the poems quoted fully in
my biography of Celan, and completed scores of others cited there
only in part; and I've added fifty more poems to represent him as
broadly as possible. Several poems that I'd bypassed as too enigmatic
or elusive for discussion, such as "Streak," "Dew," "Black," and "King's
rage," I've now translated anyway. Sometimes it's true, as per Franz
Rosenzweig bringing Judah Halevi from Hebrew into German: "I myself fully understand a poem only when I have translated it." But not
always. Now, with inscrutable poems or lines, I gladly pass them along
to the reader within the full stream of Celan's writing. After all, Celan
himself in his recitals refrained utterly from comment, enunciating

---

* Needless to say, because a Celan poem admits of, and indeed often calls for, variant readings, these
will show up in variant translations as well. Surely some misreadings and outright mistakes have also
entered my versions. I would welcome correction.

only the poem's words and lines. His voice was intense, precise, sometimes monotone, grave yet resonant, registering nuance and emotion without excess.

Mostly Celan's lyrics will reach readers who keep their minds peeled, without the sort of interpreting my critical biography offers. I do, though, furnish factual notes for this anthology. With a poem such as "Just Think," responding to Israel's 1967 Six-Day War, it helps to recall the Peat-Bog Soldiers from an early concentration camp protest song, and to recognize Masada, where Jewish zealots held out against Roman siege, then took their own lives rather than surrender. It would also have helped, when Celan tells this poem's addressees *du / erstarkst und / erstarkst*, if I'd originally translated it (as I now do) "you / go from strength / to strength," echoing Psalm 84.

One hears many metaphors for literary and especially poetic translation, most of them pejorative: kissing a bride through her veil; *les belles infidèles* (women beautiful hence unfaithful); the wrong side of a Persian carpet, its design blurred by extra threads; *traduttore, traditore* (translator, traitor); "poetry is what gets lost in translation." Yet some of the hopeful things Celan himself said about poetry, and about love, offer acute figures for translation: "I see no essential difference between a poem and a handshake"; "a poem can be a message in a bottle"; true poems are "making toward something . . . perhaps toward an addressable Thou"; "the poem wants to reach an Other, it needs this Other, it needs an Over-Against." In an early love poem, Celan might also be heard to speak for idiosyncratic translation as strongly as Robert Lowell did: *Ich bin du, wenn ich ich bin*, "I am you when I am I" (or "when I I am"!). And a later poem lets the word for "translate," *übersetzen*, suggest that trauma will inevitably carry over into the process of translation: a ferryboat "bears / wounded readings across," *sie setzt / Wundgelesenes über*.

Celan's poem "Everything is different" (1962) imagines an encounter with Mandelshtam in which, dismembering and remembering, the act of translation could not get much more drastic:

the name Osip comes toward you, you tell him
what he already knows, he takes it, he takes it off you with hands,

you loose the arm from his shoulder, the right one, the left,
you fasten your own in their place . . .
—what ripped apart, grows back together—

Although well shy of anything like Celan's possessings, my own translating practice has occasionally taken small permissions from his. As a
rule, I attempt to be literal yet idiomatic, faithful yet fresh—the rub
coming in that word "yet." For Celan as translator, faithful often did
mean fresh. Vis-à-vis French or Russian or English verse, he was given
to fracturing, contracting, omitting, specifying, intensifying, inventing,
repeating where the original had no repetition, changing nouns into
verbs, indicatives into imperatives or gerunds, and so on.

Now this free hand is not for lesser spirits. Sometimes, though, small
touches or tunings seem right: a biblical or Buberesque "Thou" rather
than "you," even though German *Du* is merely the second-person singular that English has lost; a capital letter when context dictates—
"come with me to Breath / and beyond"—though German nouns take
capitals regularly; an opting for neologism—"Deathfugue"—though
German compounds its words habitually; and a version à la Emily Dickinson for Celan's musing on his mother, *So bist du denn geworden:* "So
you are turned—a Someone / As I had never known."

Too easily, I believe, lyric poetry gets labeled untranslatable, especially in the case of someone whose personal losses rendered his German language at once precarious and privileged, inalienable yet
irreplicable; someone calling himself "whitegravel stutterer"; someone
speaking from his "true- / stammered mouth" about "eternity / blood-
black embabeled," *blutschwarz umbabelt.* But then why not think of
translation as the specific art of loss, and begin from there?

"*Todtnauberg*" (1967), marking his encounter with the philosopher
who decided that "Being speaks German," depicts Celan with Martin
Heidegger in the Black Forest (for this anthology I provide the version
Celan sent to Heidegger; later he deleted *ungesäumt*, "undelayed").
Signing a guest book, the poet wonders,

—*wessen Namen nahms auf*
vor dem meinen?—,

—whose name did it receive
before mine?—

But instead of "receive" for *aufnehmen*, perhaps an ambiguous "take in"—given the philosopher's unacknowledged, unrecanted Hitlerite phase—would make more sense. Such moments in the translator's constant struggle for idiomatic equivalence indicate a possible exchange between loss and gain. For example, Celan's Van Gogh vignette, "Below a Painting" (1955), begins,

Corn wave swarming with ravens.
Which heaven's blue? Below? Above?

Then it ends,

Stärkres Schwirren. Näh'res Glühen. Beide Welten.

Stronger whirring. Nearer glowing. Both worlds.

This does catch Celan's strong cadence, but then botches the last phrase, which wants the same four-syllable on-off beat as *Beide Welten*: not exactly "Both of these worlds," but maybe "Two worlds touching"— or does that add too much?

A certain elation occurs now and then when a translation comes into touch with its original by finding its own rightness. Such elation, inherent to any creative effort, strikes me as slightly suspect, especially touching Paul Celan's "pain-laden" German poems. Unless, perhaps, à la Walter Benjamin, those poems somehow require translation, because they are "making toward . . . something standing open," as Celan put it, "toward an addressable reality." Benjamin said: "Translation takes fire from the endless renewal of languages as they grow to the messianic end of their history."

Paul Celan's poems are astir, albeit thwartedly, with that messianic impulse. Having ventured to Israel in 1969 for the first time, decades later than many compatriots did and he himself possibly should have, Celan wrote a spate of "Jerusalem" lyrics, some elated, some despairing. While there he walked around the Old City, recently liberated in the 1967 Six-Day War, and saw the Temple Mount's Western Wall. One poem speaks of a *Posaunenstelle*, a "trumpet place" or "shofar place / deep in the glowing / text-void," and closes with self-admonition:

> *hör dich ein*
> *mit dem Mund.*

Literally, "hear yourself in / with the mouth." That glowing "text-void," *Leertext*, also puns on *Lehrtext*, "teaching-" or "Torah-text." By holding onto Celan's punctual three-beat utterance, *hör dich ein*, as in the shofar's New Year blast *te-ki-ah*, and letting *dich* deepen the attentiveness called for here, possibly these lines can say

> hear deep in
> with your mouth.

What the poet requires of himself—namely, a voice responding to the text-void after "that which happened"—he asks of his translators and readers alike.

On April 13, 1970, Celan began a poem about the generation of poetry and its listener:

> Vinegrowers dig up
> the dark-houred clock,
> deep upon deep,
>
> you read,

Du liest can also mean "you glean" or "gather." The poem ends by speaking of "Open ones," those now free, in the open, who "carry / the stone behind their eye." Whatever this stone embodies—a blindness or a muteness, paradoxically enabling both vision and speech—

it knows you,
on the Sabbath.

der erkennt dich,
am Sabbath.

This was Celan's last poem. A week later, possibly suffering another depression and dreading the medical treatment for these incurable wounds, he disappeared into the Seine River late at night and drowned himself, unobserved. His closing word, "Sabbath," bespeaks rest and refreshment, anticipating redemption. So possibly Paul Celan's final line, *am Sabbath,* can take a slight spur in translation, a rousing of that stone behind the eye:

it knows you,
come the Sabbath.

SELECTED

POEMS

AND

PROSE

OF PAUL CELAN

EARLY POEMS

1940-1943

DER TOTE

Sterne peitschten seinen Blick:
trat ihr Dorn in sein Geschick,

dass er nach den Gräsern greift
und sein Herz an Winden schleift,

wo Gestrüpp ihn jagt und hält
und sich Nacht zu ihm gesellt?

Grillen setzten sich zur Wehr —
Nun sind keine Grillen mehr . . .

Mohn ritzt Blut aus dem Gesicht:
— knie und trink und säume nicht!

THE DEAD MAN

The stars whipped at his gaze:
have thorns entered his ways

so that he claws at grass,
his heart grasps winds that pass,

where briars pull and rend
and night makes him its friend?

The crickets stand at bay —
Now no more crickets play . . .

Poppies scrape blood from him:
— kneel now and drink it in!

FINSTERNIS

Die Urnen der Stille sind leer.

In Ästen
staut sich schwarz
die Schwüle sprachloser Lieder.

Die Pfähle der Stunden
tasten stumpf nach einer fremden Zeit.

Ein Flügelschlag verwirbelt.

Den Eulen im Herzen
tagt Tod.
In deine Augen stürzt Verrat —

Mein Schatten ringt mit deinem Schrei —

Der Osten raucht nach dieser Nacht . . .
Nur Sterben
sprüht.

DARKNESS

The urns of stillness are empty.

In branches
the swelter of speechless songs
chokes black.

Blunt hourposts
grope toward a strange time.

A wingbeat whirls.

For the owls in the heart
death dawns.
Treason falls into your eyes —

My shadow strives with your scream —

The east smokes after this night . . .
Only dying
sparkles.

NOTTURNO

Schlaf nicht. Sei auf der Hut.
Die Pappeln mit singendem Schritt
ziehn mit dem Kriegsvolk mit.
Die Teiche sind alle dein Blut.

Drin grüne Gerippe tanzen.
Eins reisst die Wolke fort, dreist:
verwittert, verstümmelt, vereist,
blutet dein Traum von den Lanzen.

Die Welt ist ein kreissendes Tier,
das kahl in die Mondnacht schlich.
Gott ist sein Heulen. Ich
fürchte mich und frier.

NOCTURNE

Sleep not. Be on your guard.
The poplars sing and stride
with war troops by their side.
The ditch runs with your blood.

Green skeletons are dancing.
One tears the cloud away:
wind-beaten, battered, icy,
your dream bleeds from the lances.

The world's a laboring beast
creeps stark under night sky.
God is its howling. I
fear for me and freeze.

[WINTER]

Es FÄLLT NUN, MUTTER, Schnee in der Ukraine:
Des Heilands Kranz aus tausend Körnchen Kummer.
Von meinen Tränen hier erreicht dich keine.
Von frühern Winken nur ein stolzer stummer . . .

Wir sterben schon: was schläfst du nicht, Baracke?
Auch dieser Wind geht um wie ein Verscheuchter . . .
Sind sie es denn, die frieren in der Schlacke —
die Herzen Fahnen und die Arme Leuchter?

Ich blieb derselbe in den Finsternissen:
erlöst das Linde und entblösst das Scharfe?
Von meinen Sternen nur wehn noch zerrissen
die Saiten einer überlauten Harfe . . .

Dran hängt zuweilen eine Rosenstunde.
Verlöschend. Eine. Immer eine . . .
Was wär es, Mutter: Wachstum oder Wunde —
versänk ich mit im Schneewehn der Ukraine?

[WINTER]

IT'S FALLING, MOTHER, snow in the Ukraine:
The Savior's crown a thousand grains of grief.
Here all my tears reach out to you in vain.
One proud mute glance is all of my relief . . .

We're dying now: why won't you sleep, you huts?
Even this wind slinks round in frightened rags.
Are these the ones, freezing in slag-choked ruts —
whose arms are candlesticks, whose hearts are flags?

I stayed the same in darknesses forlorn:
Will days heal softly, will they cut too sharp?
Among my stars are drifting now the torn
strings of a strident and discordant harp . . .

On it at times a rose-filled hour is tuned.
Expiring: once. Just once, again . . .
What would come, Mother: wakening or wound —
if I too sank in snows of the Ukraine?

Kennt noch das Wasser des südlichen Bug,
Mutter, die Welle, die Wunden dir schlug?

Weiss noch das Feld mit den Mühlen inmitten,
wie leise dein Herz deine Engel gelitten?

Kann keine der Espen mehr, keine der Weiden,
den Kummer dir nehmen, den Trost dir bereiten?

Und steigt nicht der Gott mit dem knospenden Stab
den Hügel hinan und den Hügel hinab?

Und duldest du, Mutter, wie einst, ach, daheim,
den leisen, den deutschen, den schmerzlichen Reim?

Still do the southerly Bug waters know,
Mother, the wave whose blows wounded you so?

Still does the field with those windmills remember
how gently your heart to its angels surrendered?

Can none of the aspens and none of the willows
allow you their solace, remove all your sorrows?

And does not the god with his blossoming wand
go up in the hills climbing hither and yon?

And can you bear, Mother, as once on a time,
the gentle, the German, the pain-laden rhyme?

DER EINSAME

Mehr als die Taube und den Maulbeerbaum
liebt mich der Herbst. Und mir schenkt er den Schleier.
"Nimm ihn zu träumen", stickt er den Saum.
Und: "Gott ist auch so nahe wie der Geier."

Doch hob ich auf ein ander Tüchlein auch:
gröber als dies und ohne Stickerein.
Rührst du's, fällt Schnee im Brombeerstrauch.
Schwenkst du's, hörst du den Adler schrein.

THE LONELY ONE

More than the dove, more than the mulberry
it's me that autumn loves. Gives me a veil.
"Take this for dreaming," says its stitchery.
And: "God's as nearby as the vulture's nail."

But I have held another cloth instead,
coarser than this, no stitchery or seam.
Touch it and snow falls in the bramble bed.
Wave it and you will hear the eagle scream.

SCHWARZE FLOCKEN

Schnee ist gefallen, lichtlos. Ein Mond
ist es schon oder zwei, dass der Herbst unter mönchischer Kutte
Botschaft brachte auch mir, ein Blatt aus ukrainischen Halden:

"Denk, dass es wintert auch hier, zum tausendstenmal nun
im Land, wo der breiteste Strom fliesst:
Jaakobs himmlisches Blut, benedeiet von Äxten . . .
O Eis von unirdischer Röte — es watet ihr Hetman mit allem
Tross in die finsternden Sonnen . . . Kind, ach ein Tuch,
mich zu hüllen darein, wenn es blinket von Helmen,
wenn die Scholle, die rosige, birst, wenn schneeig stäubt das Gebein
deines Vaters, unter den Hufen zerknirscht
das Lied von der Zeder . . .
Ein Tuch, ein Tüchlein nur schmal, dass ich wahre
nun, da zu weinen du lernst, mir zur Seite
die Enge der Welt, die nie grünt, mein Kind, deinem Kinde!"

Blutete, Mutter, der Herbst mir hinweg, brannte der Schnee mich:
sucht ich mein Herz, dass es weine, fand ich den Hauch, ach des
    Sommers,
war er wie du.
Kam mir die Träne. Webt ich das Tüchlein.

Snow has fallen, with no light. A month
has gone by now or two, since autumn in its monkish cowl
brought tidings my way, a leaf from Ukrainian slopes:

"Remember it's wintry here too, for the thousandth time now
in the land where the broadest torrent flows:
Ya'akov's heavenly blood, blessed by axes . . .
Oh ice of unearthly red — their hetman wades with all
his troop into darkening suns . . . Oh for a cloth, child,
to wrap myself when it's flashing with helmets,
when the rosy floe bursts, when snowdrift sifts your father's
bones, hooves crushing
the Song of the Cedar . . .
A shawl, just a thin little shawl, so I keep
by my side, now you're learning to weep, this anguish,
this world that will never turn green, my child, for your child!"

Autumn bled all away, Mother, snow burned me through:
I sought out my heart so it might weep, I found — oh the summer's
    breath,
it was like you.
Then came my tears. I wove the shawl.

MOHN UND GEDÄCHTNIS

1952

POPPY AND MEMORY

Ein Kranz ward gewunden aus schwärzlichem Laub in der Gegend
  von Akra:
dort riss ich den Rappen herum und stach nach dem Tod mit dem
  Degen.
Auch trank ich aus hölzernen Schalen die Asche der Brunnen von
  Akra
und zog mit gefälltem Visier den Trümmern der Himmel entgegen.

Denn tot sind die Engel und blind ward der Herr in der Gegend von
  Akra,
und keiner ist, der mir betreue im Schlaf die zur Ruhe hier gingen.
Zuschanden gehaun ward der Mond, das Blümlein der Gegend von
  Akra:
so blühn, die den Dornen es gleichtun, die Hände mit rostigen
  Ringen.

So muss ich zum Kuss mich wohl bücken zuletzt, wenn sie beten in
  Akra ...
O schlecht war die Brünne der Nacht, es sickert das Blut durch die
  Spangen!
So ward ich ihr lächelnder Bruder, der eiserne Cherub von Akra.
So sprech ich den Namen noch aus und fühl noch den Brand auf den
  Wangen.

A garland was wound out of blackening leaves in the region of Akra:
I reined my dark stallion around and stabbed out at death with my
    dagger.
From deep wooden vessels I drank of the ashes from wells there at
    Akra,
and charged straight ahead at the ruins of heaven with firmly set
    visor.

The angels are dead and the Lord has gone blind in the region of
    Akra,
and no one will guard for me those who have gone to their sleep and
    are resting.
The moon has been hacked into bits, the flow'r of the region of Akra:
Like dark russet thorntrees they blossom, those hands wearing rings
    that are rusting.

So now at the last I must bend for a kiss when they're praying in
    Akra . . .
O scant was the breastplate of night, the blood through its buckles is
    oozing!
Now I am their brother and smiling, the ironclad cherub of Akra.
And still do I utter the name and still on my cheek feel the blazing.

ESPENBAUM, dein Laub blickt weiss ins Dunkel.
Meiner Mutter Haar ward nimmer weiss.

Löwenzahn, so grün ist die Ukraine.
Meine blonde Mutter kam nicht heim.

Regenwolke, säumst du an den Brunnen?
Meine leise Mutter weint für alle.

Runder Stern, du schlingst die goldne Schleife.
Meiner Mutter Herz ward wund von Blei.

Eichne Tür, wer hob dich aus den Angeln?
Meine sanfte Mutter kann nicht kommen.

ASPEN TREE, your leaves glance white into the dark.
My mother's hair never turned white.

Dandelion, so green is the Ukraine.
My fair-haired mother did not come home.

Rain cloud, do you linger at the well?
My soft-voiced mother weeps for all.

Rounded star, you coil the golden loop.
My mother's heart was hurt by lead.

Oaken door, who hove you off your hinge?
My gentle mother cannot return.

Schimmelgrün ist das Haus des Vergessens.
Vor jedem der wehenden Tore blaut dein enthaupteter Spielmann.
Er schlägt dir die Trommel aus Moos und bitterem Schamhaar;
mit schwärender Zehe malt er im Sand deine Braue.
Länger zeichnet er sie als sie war, und das Rot deiner Lippe.
Du füllst hier die Urnen und speisest dein Herz.

Mould-green is the house of oblivion.
At each of its blowing gates your beheaded minstrel goes blue.
For you he beats on a drum of moss and bitter pubic hair;
with an ulcerous toe he traces your brow in the sand.
Longer than it was he draws it, and the red of your lip.
You fill up the urns here and nourish your heart.

LOB DER FERNE

Im Quell deiner Augen
leben die Garne der Fischer der Irrsee.
Im Quell deiner Augen
hält das Meer sein Versprechen.

Hier werf ich,
ein Herz, das geweilt unter Menschen,
die Kleider von mir und den Glanz eines Schwures:

Schwärzer im Schwarz, bin ich nackter.
Abtrünnig erst bin ich treu.
Ich bin du, wenn ich ich bin.

Im Quell deiner Augen
treib ich und träume von Raub.

Ein Garn fing ein Garn ein:
wir scheiden umschlungen.

Im Quell deiner Augen
erwürgt ein Gehenkter den Strang.

PRAISE OF DISTANCE

In the springs of your eyes
live the Madsea fishermen's nets.
In the springs of your eyes
the sea keeps its promise.

Here, as a heart
that abode among humans,
I throw off my clothes and the glare of an oath:

Blacker in black, am I more naked.
Apostate only am I true.
I am you, when I am I.

In the springs of your eyes
I drift on and dream of spoils.

A net snared a net:
embracing we sever.

In the springs of your eyes
a hanged man strangles the rope.

Boshaft wie goldene Rede beginnt diese Nacht.
Wir essen die Äpfel der Stummen.
Wir tuen ein Werk, das man gern seinem Stern überlässt;
wir stehen im Herbst unsrer Linden als sinnendes Fahnenrot,
als brennende Gäste vom Süden.
Wir schwören bei Christus dem Neuen, den Staub zu vermählen dem
    Staube,
die Vögel dem wandernden Schuh,
unser Herz einer Stiege im Wasser.
Wir schwören der Welt die heiligen Schwüre des Sandes,
wir schwören sie gern,
wir schwören sie laut von den Dächern des traumlosen Schlafes
und schwenken das Weisshaar der Zeit . . .

Sie rufen: Ihr lästert!

Wir wissen es längst.
Wir wissen es längst, doch was tuts?
Ihr mahlt in den Mühlen des Todes das weisse Mehl der Verheissung,
ihr setzet es vor unsern Brüdern und Schwestern —

Wir schwenken das Weisshaar der Zeit.

Ihr mahnt uns: Ihr lästert!
Wir wissen es wohl,
es komme die Schuld über uns.
Es komme die Schuld über uns aller warnenden Zeichen,
es komme das gurgelnde Meer,
der geharnischte Windstoss der Umkehr,
der mitternächtige Tag,
es komme, was niemals noch war!

Es komme ein Mensch aus dem Grabe.

Spiteful like golden speech this night begins.
We eat the apples of the mute.
We do a thing that's gladly left to one's star;
in our lindens' autumn we stand, a flag's pensive red,
ardent guests from the South.
We swear by Christ the New to wed dust to dust,
birds to a wandering shoe,
our hearts to a stair in the water.
We swear to the world the sacred oaths of the sand,
we swear them gladly,
we swear them aloud from the rooftops of dreamless sleep
and flourish the white hair of time . . .

They cry: Blasphemy!

We've known it long since.
Known it long since, but who cares?
You grind in the mills of death the white meal of the Promise,
you set it before our brothers and sisters —

We flourish the white hair of time.

You warn us: Blasphemy!
We know it full well,
let the guilt come on us.
Let the guilt of all forewarning signs come upon us,
let a gurgling sea,
an armored windblast of conversion,
a day of midnights,
let come what never yet was!

Let a man come forth from the grave.

Aus der Hand frisst der Herbst mir sein Blatt: wir sind Freunde.
Wir schälen die Zeit aus den Nüssen und lehren sie gehn:
die Zeit kehrt zurück in die Schale.

Im Spiegel ist Sonntag,
im Traum wird geschlafen,
der Mund redet wahr.

Mein Aug steigt hinab zum Geschlecht der Geliebten:
wir sehen uns an,
wir sagen uns Dunkles,
wir lieben einander wie Mohn und Gedächtnis,
wir schlafen wie Wein in den Muscheln,
wie das Meer im Blutstrahl des Mondes.

Wir stehen umschlungen im Fenster, sie sehen uns zu von der Strasse:
es ist Zeit, dass man weiss!
Es ist Zeit, dass der Stein sich zu blühen bequemt,
dass der Unrast ein Herz schlägt.
Es ist Zeit, dass es Zeit wird.

Es ist Zeit.

CORONA

Autumn nibbles its leaf from my hand: we are friends.
We shell time from the nuts and teach it to walk:
time returns into its shell.

In the mirror is Sunday,
in the dream comes sleeping,
the mouth speaks true.

My eye goes down to my lover's loins:
we gaze at each other,
we speak dark things,
we love one another like poppy and memory,
we slumber like wine in the seashells,
like the sea in the moon's blood-jet.

We stand at the window embracing, they watch from the street:
it's time people knew!
It's time the stone consented to bloom,
a heart beat for unrest.
It's time it came time.

It is time.

TODESFUGE

Schwarze Milch der Frühe wir trinken sie abends
wir trinken sie mittags und morgens wir trinken sie nachts
wir trinken und trinken
wir schaufeln ein Grab in den Lüften da liegt man nicht eng
Ein Mann wohnt im Haus der spielt mit den Schlangen der schreibt
der schreibt wenn es dunkelt nach Deutschland dein goldenes Haar
    Margarete
er schreibt es und tritt vor das Haus und es blitzen die Sterne er pfeift
    seine Rüden herbei
er pfeift seine Juden hervor lässt schaufeln ein Grab in der Erde
er befiehlt uns spielt auf nun zum Tanz

Schwarze Milch der Frühe wir trinken dich nachts
wir trinken dich morgens und mittags wir trinken dich abends
wir trinken und trinken
Ein Mann wohnt im Haus der spielt mit den Schlangen der schreibt
der schreibt wenn es dunkelt nach Deutschland dein goldenes Haar
    Margarete
Dein aschenes Haar Sulamith wir schaufeln ein Grab in den Lüften
    da liegt man nicht eng

Er ruft stecht tiefer ins Erdreich ihr einen ihr andern singet und spielt
er greift nach dem Eisen im Gurt er schwingts seine Augen sind blau
stecht tiefer die Spaten ihr einen ihr andern spielt weiter zum Tanz auf

Schwarze Milch der Frühe wir trinken dich nachts
wir trinken dich mittags und morgens wir trinken dich abends
wir trinken und trinken
ein Mann wohnt im Haus dein goldenes Haar Margarete
dein aschenes Haar Sulamith er spielt mit den Schlangen

• • •

DEATHFUGUE

BLACK milk of daybreak we drink it at evening
we drink it at midday and morning we drink it at night
we drink and we drink
we shovel a grave in the air where you won't lie too cramped
A man lives in the house he plays with his vipers he writes
he writes when it grows dark to Deutschland your golden hair
    Margareta
he writes it and steps out of doors and the stars are all sparkling he
    whistles his hounds to stay close
he whistles his Jews into rows has them shovel a grave in the ground
he commands us play up for the dance

Black milk of daybreak we drink you at night
we drink you at morning and midday we drink you at evening
we drink and we drink
A man lives in the house he plays with his vipers he writes
he writes when it grows dark to Deutschland your golden hair
    Margareta
Your ashen hair Shulamith we shovel a grave in the air
    where you won't lie too cramped

He shouts dig this earth deeper you lot there you others sing up and play
he grabs for the rod in his belt he swings it his eyes are so blue
stick your spades deeper you lot there you others play on for the dancing

Black milk of daybreak we drink you at night
we drink you at midday and morning we drink you at evening
we drink and we drink
a man lives in the house your goldenes Haar Margareta
your aschenes Haar Shulamith he plays with his vipers

                    •   •   •

31

Er ruft spielt süsser den Tod der Tod ist ein Meister aus Deutschland
er ruft streicht dunkler die Geigen dann steigt ihr als Rauch in die Luft
dann habt ihr ein Grab in den Wolken da liegt man nicht eng

Schwarze Milch der Frühe wir trinken dich nachts
wir trinken dich mittags der Tod ist ein Meister aus Deutschland
wir trinken dich abends und morgens wir trinken und trinken
der Tod ist ein Meister aus Deutschland sein Auge ist blau
er trifft dich mit bleierner Kugel er trifft dich genau
ein Mann wohnt im Haus dein goldenes Haar Margarete
er hetzt seine Rüden auf uns er schenkt uns ein Grab in der Luft
er spielt mit den Schlangen und träumet der Tod ist ein Meister aus
    Deutschland

dein goldenes Haar Margarete
dein aschenes Haar Sulamith

He shouts play death more sweetly this Death is a master from
    Deutschland
he shouts scrape your strings darker you'll rise up as smoke to the sky
you'll then have a grave in the clouds where you won't lie too cramped

Black milk of daybreak we drink you at night
we drink you at midday Death is a master aus Deutschland
we drink you at evening and morning we drink and we drink
this Death is ein Meister aus Deutschland his eye it is blue
he shoots you with shot made of lead shoots you level and true
a man lives in the house your goldenes Haar Margarete
he looses his hounds on us grants us a grave in the air
he plays with his vipers and daydreams der Tod ist ein Meister aus
    Deutschland

dein goldenes Haar Margarete
dein aschenes Haar Sulamith

AUF REISEN

Es ist eine Stunde, die macht dir den Staub zum Gefolge,
dein Haus in Paris zur Opferstatt deiner Hände,
dein schwarzes Aug zum schwärzesten Auge.

Es ist ein Gehöft, da hält ein Gespann für dein Herz.
Dein Haar möchte wehn, wenn du fährst — das ist ihm verboten.
Die bleiben und winken, wissen es nicht.

ON A JOURNEY

It is an hour that makes the dust your escort,
your house in Paris an altar for your hands,
your black eyes the blackest of eyes.

It is a farm, a team of horses waits for your heart.
Your hair would blow when you ride — that's forbidden.
They stay there and wave, and know it not.

Du sollst zum Aug der Fremden sagen: Sei das Wasser.
Du sollst, die du im Wasser weisst, im Aug der Fremden suchen.
Du sollst sie rufen aus dem Wasser: Ruth! Noëmi! Mirjam!
Du sollst sie schmücken, wenn du bei der Fremden liegst.
Du sollst sie schmücken mit dem Wolkenhaar der Fremden.
Du sollst zu Ruth und Mirjam und Noëmi sagen:
Seht, ich schlaf bei ihr!
Du sollst die Fremde neben dir am schönsten schmücken.
Du sollst sie schmücken mit dem Schmerz um Ruth, um Mirjam und
  Noëmi.
Du sollst zur Fremden sagen:
Sieh, ich schlief bei diesen!

Thou shalt say to the eye of the woman stranger: Be the water.
Thou shalt seek in the stranger's eye those thou knowest are in the water.
Thou shalt summon them from the water: Ruth! Naomi! Miriam!
Thou shalt adorn them when thou liest with the stranger.
Thou shalt adorn them with the stranger's cloud-hair.
Thou shalt say to Ruth and Miriam and Naomi:
Behold, I sleep with her!
Thou shalt most beautifully adorn the woman stranger near thee.
Thou shalt adorn her with sorrow for Ruth, for Miriam and
   Naomi.
Thou shalt say to the stranger:
Behold, I slept with them!

KRISTALL

Nicht an meinen Lippen suche deinen Mund,
nicht vorm Tor den Fremdling,
nicht im Aug die Träne.

Sieben Nächte höher wandert Rot zu Rot,
sieben Herzen tiefer pocht die Hand ans Tor,
sieben Rosen später rauscht der Brunnen.

CRYSTAL

Do not seek your mouth on my lips,
nor a stranger at the gate,
nor a tear in the eye.

Seven nights higher Red wanders to Red,
seven hearts deeper a hand raps at the gate,
seven roses later the wellspring rushes.

DIE KRÜGE

Für Klaus Demus

An den langen Tischen der Zeit
zechen die Krüge Gottes.
Sie trinken die Augen der Sehenden leer und die Augen der Blinden,
die Herzen der waltenden Schatten,
die hohle Wange des Abends.
Sie sind die gewaltigsten Zecher:
sie führen das Leere zum Mund wie das Volle
und schäumen nicht über wie du oder ich.

THE TANKARDS

For Klaus Demus

At the banquet tables of time
God's tankards are tippling.
They drink till they empty the eyes of the seeing and eyes of the blind,
the hearts of the governing shadows,
the hollow cheek of evening.
It's they are the mightiest tipplers:
they drink deep of emptiness just as of fullness
and never brim over like you or like me.

So bist du denn geworden
wie ich dich nie gekannt:
dein Herz schlägt allerorten
in einem Brunnenland,

wo kein Mund trinkt und keine
Gestalt die Schatten säumt,
wo Wasser quillt zum Scheine
und Schein wie Wasser schäumt.

Du steigst in alle Brunnen,
du schwebst durch jeden Schein.
Du hast ein Spiel ersonnen,
das will vergessen sein.

So you are turned — a Someone
As I had never known —
Your heart a drum that summons
Through Land where Wells once flowed

Where no Mouth drink — and nothing
Will cleave where Shadows form —
Where Water wells to Seeming
And Seeming falls — to Foam

You rise in every Wellspring —
Through every Seeming — run
You've conjured up a Playing
That begs — Oblivion

Deiner Mutter Seele schwebt voraus.
Deiner Mutter Seele hilft die Nacht umschiffen, Riff um Riff.
Deiner Mutter Seele peitscht die Haie vor dir her.

Dieses Wort ist deiner Mutter Mündel.
Deiner Mutter Mündel teilt dein Lager, Stein um Stein.
Deiner Mutter Mündel bückt sich nach der Krume Lichts.

Your mother's soul hovers ahead.
Your mother's soul helps sail around night, reef upon reef.
Your mother's soul lashes the sharks on before you.

This word is your mother's ward.
Your mother's ward shares your bed, stone upon stone.
Your mother's ward stoops for the crumb of light.

LANDSCHAFT

Ihr hohen Pappeln — Menschen dieser Erde!
Ihr schwarzen Teiche Glücks — ihr spiegelt sie zu Tode!

Ich sah dich, Schwester, stehn in diesem Glanze.

LANDSCAPE

You lofty poplars — humans of this earth!
You blackened ponds of happiness — you mirror them toward death!

I saw you, sister, standing in this brilliance.

ZÄHLE die Mandeln,
zähle, was bitter war und dich wachhielt,
zähl mich dazu:

Ich suchte dein Aug, als du's aufschlugst und niemand dich ansah,
ich spann jenen heimlichen Faden,
an dem der Tau, den du dachtest,
hinunterglitt zu den Krügen,
die ein Spruch, der zu niemandes Herz fand, behütet.

Dort erst tratest du ganz in den Namen, der dein ist,
schrittest du sicheren Fusses zu dir,
schwangen die Hämmer frei im Glockenstuhl deines Schweigens,
stiess das Erlauschte zu dir,
legte das Tote den Arm auch um dich,
und ihr ginget selbdritt durch den Abend.

Mache mich bitter.
Zähle mich zu den Mandeln.

COUNT UP the almonds,
count what was bitter and kept you waking,
count me in too:

I sought your eye when you looked out and no one saw you,
I spun that secret thread
where the dew you mused on
slid down to pitchers
tended by a word that reached no one's heart.

There you first fully entered the name that is yours,
you stepped toward yourself on steady feet,
the hammers swung free in the belfry of your silence,
things overheard thrust through to you,
what's dead put its arm around you too,
and the three of you walked through the evening.

Render me bitter.
Number me among the almonds.

VON SCHWELLE
ZU SCHWELLE

———————

1955

FROM THRESHOLD
TO THRESHOLD

ICH HÖRTE SAGEN

Ich hörte sagen, es sei
im Wasser ein Stein und ein Kreis
und über dem Wasser ein Wort,
das den Kreis um den Stein legt.

Ich sah meine Pappel hinabgehn zum Wasser,
ich sah, wie ihr Arm hinuntergriff in die Tiefe,
ich sah ihre Wurzeln gen Himmel um Nacht flehn.

Ich eilt ihr nicht nach,
ich las nur vom Boden auf jene Krume,
die deines Auges Gestalt hat und Adel,
ich nahm dir die Kette der Sprüche vom Hals
und säumte mit ihr den Tisch, wo die Krume nun lag.

Und sah meine Pappel nicht mehr.

I HEARD IT SAID

I heard it said, there is
a stone in the water and a circle
and over the water a word
that lays the circle around the stone.

I saw my poplar descend to the water,
I saw how its arm grasped down in the deep,
I saw its roots pray heavenward for night.

I did not hurry after it,
I picked from the soil that crumb
which has your eye's shape and stature,
I took the chain of judgments from your neck
to frame the table where the crumb now lay.

And saw my poplar no more.

ZU ZWEIEN

Zu zweien schwimmen die Toten,
zu zweien, umflossen von Wein.
Im Wein, den sie über dich gossen,
schwimmen die Toten zu zwein.

Sie flochten ihr Haar sich zu Matten,
sie wohnen einander bei.
Du wirf deinen Würfel noch einmal
und tauch in ein Auge der Zwei.

BY TWOS

By twos the dead are swimming,
by twos in wine they flow.
On you their wine is pouring,
the dead swim two by two.

In matting they've braided their hair,
they dwell near each other here.
So cast down your dice now and you
must dive in an eye of the two.

GRABSCHRIFT FÜR FRANÇOIS

Die beiden Türen der Welt
stehen offen:
geöffnet von dir
in der Zwienacht.
Wir hören sie schlagen und schlagen
und tragen das ungewisse,
und tragen das Grün in dein Immer.

Oktober 1953

EPITAPH FOR FRANÇOIS

Both doors of the world
stand open:
opened by you
in the twinight.
We hear them banging and banging
and bear it uncertainly,
and bear this Green into your Ever.

October 1953

Umbrische Nacht.
Umbrische Nacht mit dem Silber von Glocke und Ölblatt.
Umbrische Nacht mit dem Stein, den du hertrugst.
Umbrische Nacht mit dem Stein.

Stumm, was ins Leben stieg, stumm.
Füll die Krüge um.

Irdener Krug.
Irdener Krug, dran die Töpferhand festwuchs.
Irdener Krug, den die Hand eines Schattens für immer verschloss.
Irdener Krug mit dem Siegel des Schattens.

Stein, wo du hinsiehst, Stein.
Lass das Grautier ein.

Trottendes Tier.
Trottendes Tier im Schnee, den die nackteste Hand streut.
Trottendes Tier vor dem Wort, das ins Schloss fiel.
Trottendes Tier, das den Schlaf aus der Hand frisst.

Glanz, der nicht trösten will, Glanz.
Die Toten — sie betteln noch, Franz.

ASSISI

Umbrian night.
Umbrian night with the silver of bell and olive leaf.
Umbrian night with the stone you hauled here.
Umbrian night with the stone.

Dumb, what climbed into life, dumb.
Refill each jug to the brim.

Earthenware jug.
Earthenware jug, where the potter's hand grew fast.
Earthenware jug that a shadow's hand shut for ever.
Earthenware jug with the shadow's seal.

Stone, where you're gazing, stone.
Let the graybeast in.

Jogtrotting beast.
Jogtrotting beast in snow strewn by the nakedest hand.
Jogtrotting beast facing the word that slammed shut.
Jogtrotting beast that gobbles sleep from your hand.

Brightness that sheds no comfort, brightness.
The dead — they still go begging, Francis.

VOR EINER KERZE

Aus getriebenem Golde, so
wie du's mir anbefahlst, Mutter,
formt ich den Leuchter, daraus
sie empor mir dunkelt inmitten
splitternder Stunden:
deines
Totseins Tochter.

Schlank von Gestalt,
ein schmaler, mandeläugiger Schatten,
Mund und Geschlecht
umtanzt von Schlummergetier,
entschwebt sie dem klaffenden Golde,
steigt sie hinan
zum Scheitel des Jetzt.

Mit nachtverhangnen
Lippen
sprech ich den Segen:

    Im Namen der Drei,
    die einander befehden, bis
    der Himmel hinabtaucht ins Grab der Gefühle,
    im Namen der Drei, deren Ringe
    am Finger mir glänzen, sooft
    ich den Bäumen im Abgrund das Haar lös,
    auf dass die Tiefe durchrauscht sei von reicherer Flut — ,
    im Namen des ersten der Drei,
    der aufschrie,
    als es zu leben galt dort, wo vor ihm sein Wort schon gewesen,
    im Namen des zweiten, der zusah und weinte,
    im Namen des dritten, der weisse
    Steine häuft in der Mitte, —
    sprech ich dich frei

IN FRONT OF A CANDLE

Out of beaten gold, just
as you bade me, mother,
I formed the candlestick from which
she darkens up to me amid
splintering hours:
your
being-dead's daughter.

Slender of build,
slim almond-eyed shadow
with dream fauna dancing around
her mouth and sex,
she floats from the gaping gold,
she climbs
to the crest of the Now.

With nighthung
lips
I speak the blessing:

  In the name of the Three
  who assail each other, till
  heaven plunges to the grave of feeling,
  in the name of the Three whose rings
  glint on my finger whenever
  I loosen the hair from trees in the abyss
  so a fuller tide floods the depths — ,
  in the name of the first of the Three,
  who cried out
  when it came time to live where his word had been before him,
  in the name of the second, who watched and wept,
  in the name of the third, who piles
  white stones in the midst, —
  I speak you free

vom Amen, das uns übertäubt,
vom eisigen Licht, das es säumt,
da, wo es turmhoch ins Meer tritt,
da, wo die graue, die Taube
aufpickt die Namen
diesseits und jenseits des Sterbens:
Du bleibst, du bleibst, du bleibst
einer Toten Kind,
geweiht dem Nein meiner Sehnsucht,
vermählt einer Schrunde der Zeit,
vor die mich das Mutterwort führte,
auf dass ein einziges Mal
erzittre die Hand,
die je und je mir ans Herz greift!

of the Amen that deafens us,
of the icy light that edges it
where it steps tower-high into the sea,
where the gray one, the dove
pecks up names
this side and that side of dying:
You are still, are still, are still
a dead woman's child,
vowed to the No of my longing,
wed to a fissure in time
where the motherword led me,
so that just once
the hand might tremble
that on and on grasps at my heart!

MIT WECHSELNDEM SCHLÜSSEL

Mit wechselndem Schlüssel
schliesst du das Haus auf, darin
der Schnee des Verschwiegenen treibt.
Je nach dem Blut, das dir quillt
aus Aug oder Mund oder Ohr,
wechselt dein Schlüssel.

Wechselt dein Schlüssel, wechselt das Wort,
das treiben darf mit den Flocken.
Je nach dem Wind, der dich fortstösst,
ballt um das Wort sich der Schnee.

WITH A CHANGING KEY

With a changing key
you unlock the house where
the snow of what's silenced drifts.
Just like the blood that bursts from
your eye or mouth or ear,
so your key changes.

Changing your key changes the word
that may drift with the flakes.
Just like the wind that rebuffs you,
packed round your word is the snow.

ANDENKEN

Feigengenährt sei das Herz,
darin sich die Stunde besinnt
auf das Mandelauge des Toten.
Feigengenährt.

Schroff, im Anhauch des Meers,
die gescheiterte
Stirne,
die Klippenschwester.

Und um dein Weisshaar vermehrt
das Vlies
der sömmernden Wolke.

REMEMBRANCE

Nourished by figs be the heart
wherein an hour thinks back
on the deadman's almond eye.
Nourished by figs.

Steep, in the seawind's breath,
the shipwrecked
forehead,
the cliff-sister.

And full-blown by your white hair
the fleece
of the grazing cloud.

NÄCHTLICH GESCHÜRZT

Für Hannah und Hermann Lenz

Nächtlich geschürzt
die Lippen der Blumen,
gekreuzt und verschränkt
die Schäfte der Fichten,
ergraut das Moos, erschüttert der Stein,
erwacht zum unendlichen Fluge
die Dohlen über dem Gletscher:

dies ist die Gegend, wo
rasten, die wir ereilt:

sie werden die Stunde nicht nennen,
die Flocken nicht zählen,
den Wassern nicht folgen ans Wehr.

Sie stehen getrennt in der Welt,
ein jeglicher bei seiner Nacht,
ein jeglicher bei seinem Tode,
unwirsch, barhaupt, bereift
von Nahem und Fernem.

Sie tragen die Schuld ab, die ihren Ursprung beseelte,
sie tragen sie ab an ein Wort,
das zu Unrecht besteht, wie der Sommer.

Ein Wort — du weisst:
eine Leiche.

Lass uns sie waschen,
lass uns sie kämmen,
lass uns ihr Aug
himmelwärts wenden.

NOCTURNALLY PURSED

For Hannah and Hermann Lenz

Nocturnally pursed
the lips of flowers,
crossed and folded
the shafts of spruce,
moss grayed, stone jolted,
jackdaws roused to unending
flight over the glacier:

this is the region where
those we've caught up with are resting:

they will not name the hour,
nor count the flakes,
nor follow water to the weir.

They stand sundered in the world,
each one next to his night,
each one next to his death,
testy, bareheaded, frostbit
with Near and Far.

They pay off the debt that sparked their origin,
they pay it off because of a word
that exists unjustly, like summer.

A word — you know:
a corpse.

Come let us wash it,
come let us comb it,
come let us turn
its eye heavenward.

WELCHEN DER STEINE DU HEBST

Welchen der Steine du hebst —
du entblösst,
die des Schutzes der Steine bedürfen:
nackt,
erneuern sie nun die Verflechtung.

Welchen der Bäume du fällst —
du zimmerst
die Bettstatt, darauf
die Seelen sich abermals stauen,
als schütterte nicht
auch dieser
Äon.

Welches der Worte du sprichst —
du dankst
dem Verderben.

WHICHEVER STONE YOU LIFT

Whichever stone you lift —
you lay bare
those who need the protection of stones:
naked,
now they renew their entwinement.

Whichever tree you fell —
you frame
the bedstead where
souls are stayed once again,
as if this aeon too
did not
tremble.

Whichever word you speak —
you owe to
destruction.

Lege dem Toten die Worte ins Grab,
die er sprach, um zu leben.
Bette sein Haupt zwischen sie,
lass ihn fühlen
die Zungen der Sehnsucht,
die Zangen.

Leg auf die Lider des Toten das Wort,
das er jenem verweigert,
der du zu ihm sagte,
das Wort,
an dem das Blut seines Herzens vorbeisprang,
als eine Hand, so nackt wie die seine,
jenen, der du zu ihm sagte,
in die Bäume der Zukunft knüpfte.

Leg ihm dies Wort auf die Lider:
vielleicht
tritt in sein Aug, das noch blau ist,
eine zweite, fremdere Bläue,
und jener, der du zu ihm sagte,
träumt mit ihm: Wir.

Lay in his grave for the dead man the words
he spoke so as to live.
Cushion his head among them,
let him feel
the tongues of longing,
the tongs.

Lay on the lids of the dead man the word
he denied to that one
who said Thou to him,
the word
his heart's blood skipped past on
when a hand as bare as his own
strung up into trees of the future
the one who said Thou to him.

Lay this word on his lids:
perhaps
in his still-blue eye a second,
stranger blue will enter,
and the one who said Thou to him
will dream with him: We.

SPRICH AUCH DU

Sprich auch du,
sprich als letzter,
sag deinen Spruch.

Sprich —
Doch scheide das Nein nicht vom Ja.
Gib deinem Spruch auch den Sinn:
gib ihm den Schatten.

Gib ihm Schatten genug,
gib ihm so viel,
als du um dich verteilt weisst zwischen
Mittnacht und Mittag und Mittnacht.

Blicke umher:
sieh, wie's lebendig wird rings —
Beim Tode! Lebendig!
Wahr spricht, wer Schatten spricht.

Nun aber schrumpft der Ort, wo du stehst:
Wohin jetzt, Schattenentblösster, wohin?
Steige. Taste empor.
Dünner wirst du, unkenntlicher, feiner!
Feiner: ein Faden,
an dem er herabwill, der Stern:
um unten zu schwimmen, unten,
wo er sich schimmern sieht: in der Dünung
wandernder Worte.

SPEAK YOU TOO

Speak you too,
speak as the last,
say out your say.

Speak —
But don't split off No from Yes.
Give your say this meaning too:
give it the shadow.

Give it shadow enough,
give it as much
as you see spread round you from
midnight to midday and midnight.

Look around:
see how things all come alive —
By death! Alive!
Speaks true who speaks shadow.

But now the place shrinks, where you stand:
Where now, shadow-stripped, where?
Climb. Grope upwards.
Thinner you grow, less knowable, finer!
Finer: a thread
the star wants to descend on:
so as to swim down below, down here
where it sees itself shimmer: in the swell
of wandering words.

ARGUMENTUM E SILENTIO

Für René Char

An die Kette gelegt
zwischen Gold und Vergessen:
die Nacht.
Beide griffen nach ihr.
Beide liess sie gewähren.

Lege,
lege auch du jetzt dorthin, was herauf-
dämmern will neben den Tagen:
das sternüberflogene Wort,
das meerübergossne.

Jedem das Wort.
Jedem das Wort, das ihm sang,
als die Meute ihn hinterrücks anfiel —
Jedem das Wort, das ihm sang und erstarrte.

Ihr, der Nacht,
das sternüberflogne, das meerübergossne,
ihr das erschwiegne,
dem das Blut nicht gerann, als der Giftzahn
die Silben durchstiess.

Ihr das erschwiegene Wort.

Wider die andern, die bald,
die umhurt von den Schinderohren,
auch Zeit und Zeiten erklimmen,
zeugt es zuletzt,
zuletzt, wenn nur Ketten erklingen,
zeugt es von ihr, die dort liegt

ARGUMENTUM E SILENTIO

For René Char

Linked in the chain
between Gold and Forgetting:
Night.
Both grasped at it.
Both had their way.

Link it,
now you too link up what
wants to dawn with each day:
the Word star-overflown,
sea-overflowed.

To each his word.
To each the word that sang to him
when the pack snapped at his heels —
to each the word that sang to him and froze.

To it, to night, the Word
star-overflown, sea-overflowed,
to it the ensilenced Word
whose blood did not clot when a venomed tooth
pierced its syllables.

To Night the ensilenced Word.

Against the others,
enticed by swindlers' ears,
who'll soon climb on time and seasons,
the Word at last testifies,
at last, when only chains ring out,
testifies to Night that lies

zwischen Gold und Vergessen,
beiden verschwistert von je —

Denn wo
dämmerts denn, sag, als bei ihr,
die im Stromgebiet ihrer Träne
tauchenden Sonnen die Saat zeigt
aber und abermals?

between Gold and Forgetting,
their kin for all time —

Then where's
the Word dawning, tell me, if not with Night
in its riverbed of tears,
Night that shows plunging suns the sown seed
over and over again?

DIE WINZER

Für Nani und Klaus Demus

Sie herbsten den Wein ihrer Augen,
sie keltern alles Geweinte, auch dieses:
so will es die Nacht,
die Nacht, an die sie gelehnt sind, die Mauer,
so forderts der Stein,
der Stein, über den ihr Krückstock dahinspricht
ins Schweigen der Antwort —
ihr Krückstock, der einmal,
einmal im Herbst,
wenn das Jahr zum Tod schwillt, als Traube,
der einmal durchs Stumme hindurchspricht, hinab
in den Schacht des Erdachten.

Sie herbsten, sie keltern den Wein,
sie pressen die Zeit wie ihr Auge,
sie kellern das Sickernde ein, das Geweinte,
im Sonnengrab, das sie rüsten
mit nachtstarker Hand:
auf dass ein Mund danach dürste, später —
ein Spätmund, ähnlich dem ihren:
Blindem entgegengekrümmt und gelähmt —
ein Mund, zu dem der Trunk aus der Tiefe emporschäumt, indes
der Himmel hinabsteigt ins wächserne Meer,
um fernher als Lichtstumpf zu leuchten,
wenn endlich die Lippe sich feuchtet.

THE VINTAGERS

For Nani and Klaus Demus

They harvest the wine of their eyes,
they crush out all of the weeping, this also:
thus willed by the night,
the night, which they're leaning against, the wall,
thus forced by the stone,
the stone, over which their crook-stick speaks into
the silence of answers —
their crook-stick, which just once,
just once in fall,
when the year swells to death, swollen grapes,
which just once will speak right through muteness
down into the mineshaft of musings.

They harvest, they crush out the wine,
they press down on time like their eye,
they cellar the seepings, the weepings,
in a sun grave they make ready
with night-toughened hands:
so that a mouth might thirst for this, later —
a latemouth, like to their own:
bent toward blindness and lamed —
a mouth to which the draught from the depth foams upward, meantime
heaven descends into waxen seas,
and far off, as a candle-end, glistens,
at last when the lip comes to moisten.

INSELHIN

Inselhin, neben den Toten,
dem Einbaum waldher vermählt,
von Himmeln umgeiert die Arme,
die Seelen saturnisch beringt:

so rudern die Fremden und Freien,
die Meister vom Eis und vom Stein:
umläutet von sinkenden Bojen,
umbellt von der haiblauen See.

Sie rudern, sie rudern, sie rudern — :
Ihr Toten, ihr Schwimmer, voraus!
Umgittert auch dies von der Reuse!
Und morgen verdampft unser Meer!

ISLANDWARD

Islandward, nearby the dead ones,
wed to a forest dugout,
their arms bound with skyflown vultures,
their souls with Saturnian rings:

the strange ones and free ones are rowing,
the masters of ice and of stone:
are tolled at by foundering buoys,
bayed at by the shark-blue sea.

They're rowing, they're rowing, they're rowing —:
You dead ones, you swimmers, lead on!
These also caged in by the bownet!
Tomorrow our ocean gone dry!

SPRACHGITTER

1959

SPEECH-GRILLE

Stimmen, ins Grün
der Wasserfläche geritzt.
Wenn der Eisvogel taucht,
sirrt die Sekunde:

Was zu dir stand
an jedem der Ufer,
es tritt
gemäht in ein anderes Bild.

*

Stimmen vom Nesselweg her:

Komm auf den Händen zu uns.
Wer mit der Lampe allein ist,
hat nur die Hand, draus zu lesen.

*

Stimmen, nachtdurchwachsen, Stränge,
an die du die Glocke hängst.

Wölbe dich, Welt:
Wenn die Totenmuschel heranschwimmt,
will es hier läuten.

*

Stimmen, vor denen dein Herz
ins Herz deiner Mutter zurückweicht.
Stimmen vom Galgenbaum her,
wo Spätholz und Frühholz die Ringe
tauschen und tauschen.

*

Voices, nicked into
the smooth water's green.
When the kingfisher dives,
that instant buzzes:

What stood by you
on each of the banks
steps
mown into another image.

*

Voices from the nettle path:

Come on your hands to us.
Whoever is alone with the lamp
has only his hand to read from.

*

Voices veined with night, ropes
you hang the bell on.

Grow vaulted, world:
When the deadmen's conch swims up,
there'll be bells pealing here.

*

Voices from which your heart
shrinks back into your mother's heart.
Voices from the gallows tree,
where latewood and springwood
change and exchange their rings.

*

Stimmen, kehlig, im Grus,
darin auch Unendliches schaufelt,
(herz-)
schleimiges Rinnsal.

Setz hier die Boote aus, Kind,
die ich bemannte:

Wenn mittschiffs die Bö sich ins Recht setzt,
treten die Klammern zusammen.

*

Jakobsstimme:

Die Tränen.
Die Tränen im Bruderaug.
Eine blieb hängen, wuchs.
Wir wohnen darin.
Atme, dass
sie sich löse.

*

Stimmen im Innern der Arche:

Es sind
nur die Münder
geborgen. Ihr
Sinkenden, hört
auch uns.

*

Keine
Stimme — ein

Voices, guttural, in the rubble
where endlessness shovels away,
(heart-)
slimy streamlet.

Child, launch the boats here
that I manned:

When a squall sets up amidships,
the clamps will snap shut.

*

Jacob's voice:

The tears.
The tears in a brother's eye.
One stayed clinging, grew.
We dwell inside.
Breathe, that
it come loose.

*

Voices in the bowels of the ark:

It is
only the mouths
are saved. You
sinking ones, hear
us too.

*

*No
voice* — a

Spätgeräusch, stundenfremd, deinen
Gedanken geschenkt, hier, endlich
herbeigewacht: ein
Fruchtblatt, augengross, tief
geritzt; es
harzt, will nicht
vernarben.

late-noise, alien to hours, a
gift for your thoughts, here at last
wakened: a
carpel, eyesize, deeply
nicked; it
resins, will not
scar over.

ZUVERSICHT

Es wird noch ein Aug sein,
ein fremdes, neben
dem unsern: stumm
unter steinernem Lid.

Kommt, bohrt euren Stollen!

Es wird eine Wimper sein,
einwärts gekehrt im Gestein,
von Ungeweintem verstählt,
die feinste der Spindeln.

Vor euch tut sie das Werk,
als gäb es, weil Stein ist, noch Brüder.

CONFIDENCE

There will be one more eye,
a strange one, next to
ours: mute
under a stony lid.

Come drill your shaft!

There will be an eyelash
turned inward in the rock
and steeled by what's unwept,
the thinnest of spindles.

It does its work before you
as if, thanks to stone, there still were brothers.

MIT BRIEF UND UHR

Wachs,
Ungeschriebnes zu siegeln,
das deinen Namen
erriet,
das deinen Namen
verschlüsselt.

Kommst du nun, schwimmendes Licht?

Finger, wächsern auch sie,
durch fremde,
schmerzende Ringe gezogen.
Fortgeschmolzen die Kuppen.

Kommst du, schwimmendes Licht?

Zeitleer die Waben der Uhr,
bräutlich das Immentausend,
reisebereit.

Komm, schwimmendes Licht.

WITH LETTER AND CLOCK

Wax,
to seal what's unwritten
that guessed
your name,
that riddles
your name.

You're coming, are you, downdrifting light?

Fingers, waxen as well,
drawn through
strange and aching rings.
Fingertips melted away.

You're coming, downdrifting light?

Clock's honeycomb empty of time,
bees myriad bridelike,
ready for flight.

Come, downdrifting light.

UNTER EIN BILD

Rabenüberschwärmte Weizenwoge.
Welchen Himmels Blau? Des untern? Obern?
Später Pfeil, der von der Seele schnellte.
Stärkres Schwirren. Näh'res Glühen. Beide Welten.

BELOW A PAINTING

Corn wave swarming with ravens.
Which heaven's blue? Below? Above?
Later arrow, that sped out from the soul.
Stronger whirring. Nearer glowing. Two worlds touching.

SCHLIERE

Schliere im Aug:
von den Blicken auf halbem
Weg erschautes Verloren.
Wirklichgesponnenes Niemals,
wiedergekehrt.

Wege, halb — und die längsten.

Seelenbeschrittene Fäden,
Glasspur,
rückwärtsgerollt
und nun
vom Augen-Du auf dem steten
Stern über dir
weiss überschleiert.

Schliere im Aug:
dass bewahrt sei
ein durchs Dunkel getragenes Zeichen,
vom Sand (oder Eis?) einer fremden
Zeit für ein fremderes Immer
belebt und als stumm
vibrierender Mitlaut gestimmt.

STREAK

Streak in the eye:
Lostness caught sight of
halfway along by the beholder.
Truly spun Never,
come back again.

Ways, half — and the longest.

Soul-stridden threads,
glass trace
rolled backward
and now
filmed white
by the Eyes' Thou on a steady
star above you.

Streak in the eye:
so as to guard
a sign dragged through the dark,
quickened by the sand (or ice?) of a
strange time for a stranger Ever
and tuned as a
mutely vibrating consonant.

TENEBRAE

Nah sind wir, Herr,
nahe und greifbar.

Gegriffen schon, Herr,
ineinander verkrallt, als wär
der Leib eines jeden von uns
dein Leib, Herr.

Bete, Herr,
bete zu uns,
wir sind nah.

Windschief gingen wir hin,
gingen wir hin, uns zu bücken
nach Mulde und Maar.

Zur Tränke gingen wir, Herr.

Es war Blut, es war,
was du vergossen, Herr.

Es glänzte.

Es warf uns dein Bild in die Augen, Herr.
Augen und Mund stehn so offen und leer, Herr.
Wir haben getrunken, Herr.
Das Blut und das Bild, das im Blut war, Herr.

Bete, Herr.
Wir sind nah.

TENEBRAE

Near are we, Lord,
near and graspable.

Grasped already, Lord,
clawed into each other, as if
each of our bodies were
your body, Lord.

Pray, Lord,
pray to us,
we are near.

Wind-skewed we went there,
went there to bend
over pit and crater.

Went to the water-trough, Lord.

It was blood, it was
what you shed, Lord.

It shined.

It cast your image into our eyes, Lord.
Eyes and mouth stand so open and void, Lord.
We have drunk, Lord.
The blood and the image that was in the blood, Lord.

Pray, Lord.
We are near.

BLUME

Der Stein.
Der Stein in der Luft, dem ich folgte.
Dein Aug, so blind wie der Stein.

Wir waren
Hände,
wir schöpften die Finsternis leer, wir fanden
das Wort, das den Sommer heraufkam:
Blume.

Blume — ein Blindenwort.
Dein Aug und mein Aug:
sie sorgen
für Wasser.

Wachstum.
Herzwand um Herzwand
blättert hinzu.

Ein Wort noch, wie dies, und die Hämmer
schwingen im Freien.

FLOWER

The stone.
The stone in the air, which I followed.
Your eye, as blind as the stone.

We were
hands,
we scooped the darkness empty, we found
the word that ascended summer:
Flower.

Flower — a blindman's word.
Your eye and my eye:
they take care
of water.

Growth.
Heartwall by heartwall
adds on petals.

One more word like this, and the hammers
will be swinging free.

SPRACHGITTER

Augenrund zwischen den Stäben.

Flimmertier Lid
rudert nach oben,
gibt einen Blick frei.

Iris, Schwimmerin, traumlos und trüb:
der Himmel, herzgrau, muss nah sein.

Schräg, in der eisernen Tülle,
der blakende Span.
Am Lichtsinn
errätst du die Seele.

(Wär ich wie du. Wärst du wie ich.
Standen wir nicht
unter *einem* Passat?
Wir sind Fremde.)

Die Fliesen. Darauf,
dicht beieinander, die beiden
herzgrauen Lachen:
zwei
Mundvoll Schweigen.

SPEECH-GRILLE

Eyes round between the bars.

Flittering lid
paddles upward,
breaks a glance free.

Iris, the swimmer, dreamless and drab:
heaven, heartgray, must be near.

Aslant, in the iron socket,
a smoldering chip.
By sense of light
you hit on the soul.

(Were I like you. Were you like me.
Did we not stand
under *one* trade wind?
We are strangers.)

The flagstones. On them,
close by each other, both
heartgray puddles:
two
mouthfuls of silence.

MATIÈRE DE BRETAGNE

Ginsterlicht, gelb, die Hänge
eitern gen Himmel, der Dorn
wirbt um die Wunde, es läutet
darin, es ist Abend, das Nichts
rollt seine Meere zur Andacht,
das Blutsegel hält auf dich zu.

Trocken, verlandet
das Bett hinter dir, verschilft
seine Stunde, oben,
beim Stern, die milchigen
Priele schwatzen im Schlamm, Steindattel,
unten, gebuscht, klafft ins Gebläu, eine Staude
Vergänglichkeit, schön,
grüsst dein Gedächtnis.

(Kanntet ihr mich,
Hände? Ich ging
den gegabelten Weg, den ihr wiest, mein Mund
spie seinen Schotter, ich ging, meine Zeit,
wandernde Wächte, warf ihren Schatten — kanntet ihr mich?)

Hände, die dorn-
umworbene Wunde, es läutet,
Hände, das Nichts, seine Meere,
Hände, im Ginsterlicht, das
Blutsegel
hält auf dich zu.

Du
du lehrst
du lehrst deine Hände
du lehrst deine Hände du lehrst
du lehrst deine Hände
           schlafen

MATIÈRE DE BRETAGNE

Gorselight, yellow, the slopes
fester heavenward, a thorn
woos the wound, bells are tolling
inland, it's evening, nothingness
swells its seas to devotions,
the blood sail bears down on you.

Parched, the riverbed
silted behind you, its hour
choked by reeds, up above
near the star, the milky
channels gab in the mud, stone-mussels
tufted below gape into the blue, a bush
of transience, beauteous,
greets your memory.

(Did you know me,
hands? I walked
the forked path you pointed out, my mouth
spat its gravel, I walked, my time,
a wandering snow-wall, cast its shadow — did you know me?)

Hands, thorn
wooing the wound, bells tolling,
hands, nothingness, its seas,
hands, in gorselight, the
blood sail
bears down on you.

You
you teach
you teach your hands
you teach your hands you teach
you teach your hands
             to sleep

KÖLN, AM HOF

Herzzeit, es stehn
die Geträumten für
die Mitternachtsziffer.

Einiges sprach in die Stille, einiges schwieg,
einiges ging seiner Wege.
Verbannt und Verloren
waren daheim.

Ihr Dome.

Ihr Dome ungesehn,
ihr Ströme unbelauscht,
ihr Uhren tief in uns.

COLOGNE, AT THE STATION

Heart time, those
we dreamt stand up for
the midnight cipher.

Something spoke into stillness, something was silent,
something went its way.
Banished and Vanished
were at home.

You cathedrals.

You unseen cathedrals,
you rivers unheard,
you clocks deep in us.

Stummheit, aufs neue, geräumig, ein Haus —:
komm, du sollst wohnen.

Stunden, fluchschön gestuft: erreichbar
die Freistatt.

Schärfer als je die verbliebene Luft: du sollst atmen,
atmen und du sein.

INTO THE DISTANCE

Muteness, afresh, roomy, a house — :
come, you should dwell there.

Hours, fine-tuned like a curse: the asylum
in sight.

Sharper than ever the air remaining: you must breathe,
breathe and be you.

Rundgräber, unten. Im
Viertakt der Jahresschritt auf
den Steilstufen rings.

Laven, Basalte, weltherz-
durchglühtes Gestein.
Quelltuff,
wo uns das Licht wuchs, vor
dem Atem.

Ölgrün, meerdurchstäubt die
unbetretbare Stunde. Gegen
die Mitte zu, grau,
ein Steinsattel, drauf,
gebeult und verkohlt,
die Tierstirn mit
der strahligen Blesse.

SKETCH OF A LANDSCAPE

Round graves, below. In
four-beat the year's pacing
on steep steps around them.

Lava, basalt, worldheart-
red-heated stone.
Wellspring tuff
where light formed for us before
breath.

Oilgreen, an impassable hour
shot through by the sea. Toward
the center, gray,
a rock-saddle and on it,
dented and charred,
the beast's brow with
its radiant blaze.

EIN AUGE, OFFEN

Stunden, maifarben, kühl.
Das nicht mehr zu Nennende, heiss,
hörbar im Mund.

Niemandes Stimme, wieder.

Schmerzende Augapfeltiefe:
das Lid
steht nicht im Wege, die Wimper
zählt nicht, was eintritt.

Die Träne, halb,
die schärfere Linse, beweglich,
holt dir die Bilder.

AN EYE, OPEN

Hours, Maycolor, cool.
What's no more to be named, hot,
hearable in the mouth.

Nobody's voice, again.

Aching depths of an eyeball:
the lid
does not block the way, the lash
does not count what enters.

The tear, half of it,
a sharper lens, nimble,
brings you images.

ENGFÜHRUNG

*

VERBRACHT ins
Gelände
mit der untrüglichen Spur:

Gras, auseinandergeschrieben. Die Steine, weiss,
mit den Schatten der Halme:
Lies nicht mehr — schau!
Schau nicht mehr — geh!

Geh, deine Stunde
hat keine Schwestern, du bist —
bist zuhause. Ein Rad, langsam,
rollt aus sich selber, die Speichen
klettern,
klettern auf schwärzlichem Feld, die Nacht
braucht keine Sterne, nirgends
fragt es nach dir.

*

STRETTO

*

TAKEN OFF into
the terrain
with the unmistakable trace:

Grass, written asunder. The stones, white
with the grassblades' shadows:
Read no more — look!
Look no more — go!

Go, your hour
has no sisters, you are —
are at home. Slowly a wheel
rolls out of itself, the spokes
clamber,
clamber on the blackened field, night
needs no stars, nowhere
are you asked after.

*

                                        Nirgends
                                            fragt es nach dir —

Der Ort, wo sie lagen, er hat
einen Namen — er hat
keinen. Sie lagen nicht dort. Etwas
lag zwischen ihnen. Sie
sahn nicht hindurch.

Sahn nicht, nein,
redeten von
Worten. Keines
erwachte, der
Schlaf
kam über sie.

    *

                                    Kam, kam. Nirgends
                                            fragt es —

Ich bins, ich,
ich lag zwischen euch, ich war
offen, war
hörbar, ich tickte euch zu, euer Atem
gehorchte, ich
bin es noch immer, ihr
schlaft ja.

    *

                                        Bin es noch immer —

Jahre.
Jahre, Jahre, ein Finger
tastet hinab und hinan, tastet

                              Nowhere
                                    are you asked after —

The place where they lay, it has
a name — it has
none. They did not lie there. Something
lay between them. They
did not see through it.

Did not see, no,
spoke of
words. Not one
awoke,
sleep
came over them.

    *

                              Came, came. Nowhere
                                         asked —

I'm the one, I,
I lay between you, I was
open, was
audible, I ticked toward you, your breath
obeyed, I
am still the one, and
you're sleeping.

    *

                                    Am still the one —

Years.
Years, years, a finger
gropes down and up, gropes

umher:
Nahtstellen, fühlbar, hier
klafft es weit auseinander, hier
wuchs es wieder zusammen — wer
deckte es zu?

*

                                        Deckte es
                                            zu — wer?

Kam, kam.
Kam ein Wort, kam,
kam durch die Nacht,
wollt leuchten, wollt leuchten.

Asche.
Asche, Asche.
Nacht.
Nacht-und-Nacht. — Zum
Aug geh, zum feuchten.

*

                            Zum
                                Aug geh,
                                    zum feuchten —

Orkane.
Orkane, von je,
Partikelgestöber, das andre,
du
weissts ja, wir
lasens im Buche, war
Meinung.

                        •   •   •

all around:
sutures, palpable, here
it gapes wide open, here
it grew back together — who
covered it up?

*

                          Covered it
                                up — who?

Came, came.
Came a word, came,
came through the night,
would glisten, would glisten.

Ashes.
Ashes, ashes.
Night.
Night-and-night. — Go
to the eye, to the moist one.

*

                   Go
                    to the eye,
                         to the moist one —

Hurricanes.
Hurricanes, from all time,
particle flurry, the other thing,
you
know this, we
read it in the book, was
opinion.

                 •   •   •

War, war
Meinung. Wie
fassten wir uns
an — an mit
diesen
Händen?

Es stand auch geschrieben, dass.
Wo? Wir
taten ein Schweigen darüber,
giftgestillt, gross,
ein
grünes
Schweigen, ein Kelchblatt, es
hing ein Gedanke an Pflanzliches dran —
grün, ja,
hing, ja,
unter hämischem
Himmel.

An, ja,
Pflanzliches.

Ja.
Orkane, Par-
tikelgestöber, es blieb
Zeit, blieb,
es beim Stein zu versuchen — er
war gastlich, er
fiel nicht ins Wort. Wie
gut wir es hatten:

Körnig,
körnig und faserig. Stengelig,
dicht;
traubig und strahlig; nierig,

Was, was
opinion. How
did we take
hold — hold with
these
hands?

It was also written that.
Where? We
decked it in silence,
poison-hushed, huge,
a
green
silence, a sepal, a
thought of something plantlike hung there —
green, yes,
hung, yes,
under spiteful
skies.

Of, yes,
plantlike.

Yes.
Hurricanes, par-
ticle flurry, there was still
time, still,
to try with the stone — it
was welcoming, it
did not interrupt. How
good we had it:

Grainy,
grainy and stringy. Stalky,
thick;
bunchy and radiate; knobby,

plattig und
klumpig; locker, ver-
ästelt — : er, es
fiel nicht ins Wort, es
sprach,
sprach gerne zu trockenen Augen, eh es sie schloss.

Sprach, sprach.
War, war.

Wir
liessen nicht locker, standen
inmitten, ein
Porenbau, und
es kam.

Kam auf uns zu, kam
hindurch, flickte
unsichtbar, flickte
an der letzten Membran,
und
die Welt, ein Tausendkristall,
schoss an, schoss an.

*

                                        Schoss an, schoss an.
                                                    Dann —

Nächte, entmischt. Kreise,
grün oder blau, rote
Quadrate: die
Welt setzt ihr Innerstes ein
im Spiel mit den neuen
Stunden. — Kreise,
rot oder schwarz, helle

level and
lumpy; crumbling, out-
branching — : the stone, it
did not interrupt, it
spoke,
spoke gladly to dry eyes, before it shut them.

Spoke, spoke.
Was, was.

We
would not let go, stood firm
in the midst, a
framework of pores, and
it came.

Came up to us, came
on through, it mended
invisibly, mended
on the final membrane,
and
the world, thousandfaced crystal,
shot out, shot out.

*

                                    Shot out, shot out.
                                         Then —

Nights, demixed. Circles,
green or blue, red
squares: the
world sets its inmost
at stake with the new
hours. — Circles,
red or black, bright

Quadrate, kein
Flugschatten,
kein
Messtisch, keine
Rauchseele steigt und spielt mit.

*

                                        Stïeigt und
                                            spielt mit —

In der Eulenflucht, beim
versteinerten Aussatz,
bei
unsern geflohenen Händen, in
der jüngsten Verwerfung,
überm
Kugelfang an
der verschütteten Mauer:

sichtbar, aufs
neue: die
Rillen, die

Chöre, damals, die
Psalmen. Ho, ho-
sianna.

Also
stehen noch Tempel. Ein
Stern
hat wohl noch Licht.
Nichts,
nichts ist verloren.

                    •   •   •

squares, no
flight shadow,
no
plane table, no
chimney soul rises and joins in.

*

                                        Rises and
                                            joins in —

At owls' flight, near the
petrified lepra,
near
our fugitive hands, at
the latest rejection,
above the
bullet trap on
the ruined wall:

visible, once
again: the
grooves, the

choirs, back then, the
Psalms. Ho, ho-
sannah.

Therefore
temples still stand. A
star
may still give light.
Nothing,
nothing is lost.

                    •   •   •

Ho-
sianna.

In der Eulenflucht, hier,
die Gespräche, taggrau,
der Grundwasserspuren.

*

                         (— — taggrau,
                                  der
                                      Grundwasserspuren —

Verbracht
ins Gelände
mit
der untrüglichen
Spur:

Gras.
Gras,
auseinandergeschrieben.)

Ho-
sannah.

At owls' flight, here,
the conversations, daygray,
of groundwater traces.

*

                       (— — daygray,
                             of
                             groundwater traces —

Taken off
into the terrain
with
the unmistakable
trace:

Grass.
Grass,
written asunder.)

DIE NIEMANDSROSE

1963

THE NO-ONE'S-ROSE

Es war Erde in ihnen, und
sie gruben.

Sie gruben und gruben, so ging
ihr Tag dahin, ihre Nacht. Und sie lobten nicht Gott,
der, so hörten sie, alles dies wollte,
der, so hörten sie, alles dies wusste.

Sie gruben und hörten nichts mehr;
sie wurden nicht weise, erfanden kein Lied,
erdachten sich keinerlei Sprache.
Sie gruben.

Es kam eine Stille, es kam auch ein Sturm,
es kamen die Meere alle.
Ich grabe, du gräbst, und es gräbt auch der Wurm,
und das Singende dort sagt: Sie graben.

O einer, o keiner, o niemand, o du:
Wohin gings, da's nirgendhin ging?
O du gräbst und ich grab, und ich grab mich dir zu,
und am Finger erwacht uns der Ring.

THERE WAS EARTH INSIDE THEM, and
they dug.

They dug and dug, and so
their day went past, their night. And they did not praise God,
who, so they heard, wanted all this,
who, so they heard, witnessed all this.

They dug and heard nothing more;
they did not grow wise, invented no song,
devised for themselves no sort of language.
They dug.

There came a stillness then, came also storm,
all of the oceans came.
I dig, you dig, and it digs too, the worm,
and the singing there says: They dig.

O one, o none, o no one, o you:
Where did it go then, making for nowhere?
O you dig and I dig, and I dig through to you,
and the ring on our finger awakens.

DAS WORT VOM ZUR-TIEFE-GEHN,
das wir gelesen haben.
Die Jahre, die Worte seither.
Wir sind es noch immer.

Weisst du, der Raum ist unendlich,
weisst du, du brauchst nicht zu fliegen,
weisst du, was sich in dein Aug schrieb,
vertieft uns die Tiefe.

THE WORD ABOUT GOING-TO-THE-DEPTHS
that we once read.
The years, the words since then.
We're still just that.

You know, there's no end of space,
you know, you don't need to fly,
you know, what inscribed itself in your eye
deepens our depth.

BEI WEIN UND VERLORENHEIT, bei
beider Neige:

ich ritt durch den Schnee, hörst du,
ich ritt Gott in die Ferne — die Nähe, er sang,
es war
unser letzter Ritt über
die Menschen-Hürden.

Sie duckten sich, wenn
sie uns über sich hörten, sie
schrieben, sie
logen unser Gewieher
um in eine
ihrer bebilderten Sprachen.

WITH WINE AND LOSTNESS, with
the dregs of both:

I rode through the snow, do you hear,
I rode God into the distance — the nearness, he sang,
it was
our last ride over
human hurdles.

They ducked when
they heard us overhead, they
wrote, they
lied our whinnying
into one of
their painted lingos.

ZÜRICH, ZUM STORCHEN

Für Nelly Sachs

Vom Zuviel war die Rede, vom
Zuwenig. Von Du
und Aber-Du, von
der Trübung durch Helles, von
Jüdischem, von
deinem Gott.

Da-
von.
Am Tag einer Himmelfahrt, das
Münster stand drüben, es kam
mit einigem Gold übers Wasser.

Von deinem Gott war die Rede, ich sprach
gegen ihn, ich
liess das Herz, das ich hatte,
hoffen:
auf
sein höchstes, umröcheltes, sein
haderndes Wort —

Dein Aug sah mir zu, sah hinweg,
dein Mund
sprach sich dem Aug zu, ich hörte:

Wir
wissen ja nicht, weisst du,
wir
wissen ja nicht,
was
gilt.

ZURICH, AT THE STORK

For Nelly Sachs

Our talk was of Too Much, of
Too Little. Of Thou
and Yet-Thou, of
clouding through brightness, of
Jewishness, of
your God.

Of
that.
On the day of an ascension, the
Minster stood over there, it came
with some gold across the water.

Our talk was of your God, I spoke
against him, I let the heart
I had
hope:
for
his highest, death-rattled, his
wrangling word —

Your eye looked at me, looked away,
your mouth
spoke toward the eye, I heard:

We
really don't know, you know,
we
really don't know
what
counts.

SELBDRITT, SELBVIERT

Krauseminze, Minze, krause,
vor dem Haus hier, vor dem Hause.

Diese Stunde, deine Stunde,
ihr Gespräch mit meinem Munde.

Mit dem Mund, mit seinem Schweigen,
mit den Worten, die sich weigern.

Mit den Weiten, mit den Engen,
mit den nahen Untergängen.

Mit mir einem, mit uns dreien,
halb gebunden, halb im Freien.

Krauseminze, Minze, krause,
vor dem Haus hier, vor dem Hause.

BY THREES, BY FOURS

Curly mousetail, mousetail, curly,
here's the housecat, hunting early.

Now's the time, and it's your time now,
time for chatting with my rhyme now.

Here's a mouth and here's its quelling,
here are words, hear them rebelling.

Open spaces, narrow scrapings,
near catastrophes we're facing.

You and me too, then we threesome,
half in fetters, half in freedom.

Curly mousetail, mousetail, curly,
here's the housecat, hunting early.

DEIN
HINÜBERSEIN heute Nacht.
Mit Worten holt ich dich wieder, da bist du,
alles ist wahr und ein Warten
auf Wahres.

Es klettert die Bohne vor
unserm Fenster: denk
wer neben uns aufwächst und
ihr zusieht.

Gott, das lasen wir, ist
ein Teil und ein zweiter, zerstreuter:
im Tod
all der Gemähten
wächst er sich zu.

Dorthin
führt uns der Blick,
mit dieser
Hälfte
haben wir Umgang.

Your
being over there tonight.
I fetched you back with words, here you are,
all things are true and a waiting
for trueness.

The beanstalk climbs
at our window: think
who's growing up near us and
watches it.

God, so we've read, is
one part and a second, dispersed:
in the death
of all who've been reaped
he grows whole.

Our gaze
leads us there,
it's this
half
we deal with.

ZWÖLF JAHRE

Die wahr-
gebliebene, wahr-
gewordene Zeile: ... *dein*
Haus in Paris — zur
Opferstatt deiner Hände.

Dreimal durchatmet,
dreimal durchglänzt.

. . . .

Es wird stumm, es wird taub
hinter den Augen.
Ich sehe das Gift blühn.
In jederlei Wort und Gestalt.

Geh. Komm.
Die Liebe löscht ihren Namen: sie
schreibt sich dir zu.

TWELVE YEARS

The line that
stayed true, that
came true: . . . *your*
house in Paris — an
altar for your hands.

Three times breathed through,
three times shone through.

. . . .

It goes dumb, it goes deaf
behind my eyes.
I see the poison bloom.
In every word and shape.

Go. Come.
Love blots out its name: it
signs on with you.

MIT ALLEN GEDANKEN ging ich
hinaus aus der Welt: da warst du,
du meine Leise, du meine Offne, und —
du empfingst uns.

Wer
sagt, dass uns alles erstarb,
da uns das Aug brach?
Alles erwachte, alles hob an.

Gross kam eine Sonne geschwommen, hell
standen ihr Seele und Seele entgegen, klar,
gebieterisch schwiegen sie ihr
ihre Bahn vor.

Leicht
tat sich dein Schoss auf, still
stieg ein Hauch in den Äther,
und was sich wölkte, wars nicht,
wars nicht Gestalt und von uns her,
wars nicht
so gut wie ein Name?

WITH ALL MY THOUGHTS I went
right out of the world: there you were,
you my gentle one, you my open one, and —
you took us in.

Who
says it all died out for us
when our eye dimmed?
It all awoke, all started up.

Huge, a sun came drifting, bright
against it stood soul and soul, clear,
they forced a silence
in its path.

Easily
your womb opened up, softly
a breath rose into the air
and what turned to cloud — wasn't it,
wasn't it a shape and of our making,
was it not
as good as a name?

DIE SCHLEUSE

Über aller dieser deiner
Trauer: kein
zweiter Himmel.

. . . .

An einen Mund,
dem es ein Tausendwort war,
verlor —
verlor ich ein Wort,
das mir verblieben war:
Schwester.

An
die Vielgötterei
verlor ich ein Wort, das mich suchte:
Kaddisch.

Durch
die Schleuse musst ich,
das Wort in die Salzflut zurück-
und hinaus- und hinüberzuretten:
Jiskor.

THE SLUICE

Over all this
grief of yours: no
second heaven.

. . . .

To a mouth
for which it was a thousandword,
lost —
I lost a word
that was left to me:
Sister.

To
polygoddedness
I lost a word that sought me:
Kaddish.

Through
the sluice I had to go,
to salvage the word back into
and out of and across the salt flood:
Yizkor.

STUMME HERBSTGERÜCHE. Die
Sternblume, ungeknickt, ging
zwischen Heimat und Abgrund durch
dein Gedächtnis.

Eine fremde Verlorenheit war
gestalthaft zugegen, du hättest
beinah
gelebt.

MUTE AUTUMN SMELLS. The
aster, unbent, passed
through your memory
between homeland and chasm.

A strange lostness was
bodily present, you came
near to
living.

EIS, EDEN

Es ist ein Land Verloren,
da wächst ein Mond im Ried,
und das mit uns erfroren,
es glüht umher und sieht.

Es sieht, denn es hat Augen,
die helle Erden sind.
Die Nacht, die Nacht, die Laugen.
Es sieht, das Augenkind.

Es sieht, es sieht, wir sehen,
ich sehe dich, du siehst.
Das Eis wird auferstehen,
eh sich die Stunde schliesst.

ICE, EDEN

There is a land called Lost,
a moon grows in its reeds,
and with us, numbed by frost,
there's something glows and sees.

It sees, for it has eyes,
each eye an earth that's bright.
The night, the night, the lyes.
It sees, this child of sight.

It sees, it sees, we see,
I see you, you see too.
The ice will rise up free
before this hour is through.

PSALM

Niemand knetet uns wieder aus Erde und Lehm,
niemand bespricht unsern Staub.
Niemand.

Gelobt seist du, Niemand.
Dir zulieb wollen
wir blühn.
Dir
entgegen.

Ein Nichts
waren wir, sind wir, werden
wir bleiben, blühend:
die Nichts-, die
Niemandsrose.

Mit
dem Griffel seelenhell,
dem Staubfaden himmelswüst,
der Krone rot
vom Purpurwort, das wir sangen
über, o über
dem Dorn.

PSALM

No one kneads us again out of earth and clay,
no one incants our dust.
No one.

Blessèd art thou, No One.
In thy sight would
we bloom.
In thy
spite.

A Nothing
we were, are now, and ever
shall be, blooming:
the Nothing-, the
No-One's-Rose.

With
our pistil soul-bright,
our stamen heaven-waste,
our corona red
from the purpleword we sang
over, O over
the thorn.

TÜBINGEN, JÄNNER

Zur Blindheit über-
redete Augen.
Ihre — "ein
Rätsel ist Rein-
entsprungenes" — , ihre
Erinnerung an
schwimmende Hölderlintürme, möwen-
umschwirrt.

Besuche ertrunkener Schreiner bei
diesen
tauchenden Worten:

Käme,
käme ein Mensch,
käme ein Mensch zur Welt, heute, mit
dem Lichtbart der
Patriarchen: er dürfte,
spräch er von dieser
Zeit, er
dürfte
nur lallen und lallen,
immer-, immer-
zuzu.

("Pallaksch. Pallaksch.")

Eyes talked in-
to blindness.
Their — "a
riddle, what is pure-
ly arisen" — , their
memory of
floating Hölderlintowers, gull-
enswirled.

Visits of drowned joiners to
these
plunging words:

Came, if there
came a man,
came a man to the world, today, with
the patriarchs'
light-beard: he could,
if he spoke of this
time, he
could
only babble and babble,
ever- ever-
moremore.

("Pallaksch. Pallaksch.")

EINE GAUNER- UND GANOVENWEISE
GESUNGEN ZU PARIS EMPRÈS PONTOISE
VON PAUL CELAN
AUS CZERNOWITZ BEI SADAGORA

Manchmal nur, in dunkeln Zeiten,
Heinrich Heine, An Edom

Damals, als es noch Galgen gab,
da, nicht wahr, gab es
ein Oben.

Wo bleibt mein Bart, Wind, wo
mein Judenfleck, wo
mein Bart, den du raufst?

Krumm war der Weg, den ich ging,
krumm war er, ja,
denn, ja,
er war gerade.

Heia.

Krumm, so wird meine Nase.
Nase.

Und wir zogen auch nach *Friaul.*
Da hätten wir, da hätten wir.
Denn es blühte der Mandelbaum.
Mandelbaum, Bandelmaum.
Mandeltraum, Trandelmaum.
Und auch der Machandelbaum.
Chandelbaum.

Heia.
Aum.

• • •

A ROGUES' AND GONIFS' DITTY
SUNG AT PARIS EMPRÈS PONTOISE
BY PAUL CELAN
FROM CZERNOWITZ NEAR SADAGORA

> *Only now and then, in dark times,*
> Heinrich Heine, "To Edom"

Back then, when they still had gallows,
then — right? — they had
an On High.

Wind, where's my beard got to, where's
my Jew's-patch, where's
my beard you pluck?

Crooked, the path I took was
crooked, yes,
because yes,
it was straight.

Hey-ho.

Hooked, so goes my nose.
Nose.

And we made for *Friuli*.
There we would have, there we would have.
For the almond tree was blossoming.
Almond tree, Talmundree.
Almonddream, Dralmondream.
And the Allemandtree.
Lemandtree.

Hey-ho.
Hum.

          •   •   •

Envoi

Aber,
aber er bäumt sich, der Baum. Er,
auch er
steht gegen
die Pest.

Envoi

Yet,
yet it shoots up, that tree. It,
it too
stands against
the Plague.

Ihr gebet-, ihr lästerungs-, ihr
gebetscharfen Messer
meines
Schweigens.

Ihr meine mit mir ver-
krüppelnden Worte, ihr
meine geraden.

Und du:
du, du, du
mein täglich wahr- und wahrer-
geschundenes Später
der Rosen — :

Wieviel, o wieviel
Welt. Wieviel
Wege.

Krücke du, Schwinge. Wir —— ——

Wir werden das Kinderlied singen, das,
hörst du, das
mit den Men, mit den Schen, mit den Menschen, ja das
mit dem Gestrüpp und mit
dem Augenpaar, das dort bereitlag als
Träne-und-
Träne.

You prayer-, you blasphemy-, you
prayersharp knives
of my
silence.

You my words with me go-
ing crippled, you
my straight ones.

And thou:
thou, thou, thou
my daily true- and more truly
flayed Later
of roses — :

How much, O how much
world. How many
paths.

You crutch, you swingle. We — —

We'll sing the nursery rhyme, the one,
do you hear, the one
with the Men, with the Schen, with the Menschen, yes the one
with the brambles and with
the pair of eyes that lay ready there as
tears-and-
tears.

Wie man zum Stein spricht, wie
du,
mir vom Abgrund her, von
einer Heimat her Ver-
schwisterte, Zu-
geschleuderte, du,
du mir vorzeiten,
du mir im Nichts einer Nacht,
du in der Aber-Nacht Be-
gegnete, du
Aber-Du — :

Damals, da ich nicht da war,
damals, da du
den Acker abschrittst, allein:

Wer,
wer wars, jenes
Geschlecht, jenes gemordete, jenes
schwarz in den Himmel stehende:
Rute und Hode — ?

(Wurzel.
Wurzel Abrahams. Wurzel Jesse. Niemandes
Wurzel — o
unser.)

Ja,
wie man zum Stein spricht, wie
du
mit meinen Händen dorthin
und ins Nichts greifst, so
ist, was hier ist:

.   .   .

RADIX, MATRIX

As one speaks to stone, as
you,
to me from the abyss, from
a homeland con-
Sanguined, up-
Hurled, you,
you of old to me,
you in the Nix of a night to me,
you in Yet-Night en-
Countered, you
Yet-You — :

Back then, when I wasn't there,
back then, when you
paced off the field, alone:

Who,
who was it, that
stock, that murdered one, that one
standing black into heaven:
rod and testis — ?

(Root.
Root of Abraham. Root of Jesse. No One's
root — O
ours.)

Yes,
as one speaks to stone, as
you
with my hands thrust
there and into nothingness, so
it is with what's here:

• • •

auch dieser
Fruchtboden klafft,
dieses
Hinab
ist die eine der wild-
blühenden Kronen.

even this
spore bed gapes,
this
Downward
is one of the wild-
blooming crowns.

EINEM, DER VOR DER TÜR STAND, eines
Abends:
ihm
tat ich mein Wort auf — : zum
Kielkropf sah ich ihn trotten, zum
halb-
schürigen, dem
im kotigen Stiefel des Kriegsknechts
geborenen Bruder, dem
mit dem blutigen
Gottes-
gemächt, dem
schilpenden Menschlein.

Rabbi, knirschte ich, Rabbi
Löw:

Diesem
beschneide das Wort,
diesem
schreib das lebendige
Nichts ins Gemüt,
diesem
spreize die zwei
Krüppelfinger zum heil-
bringenden Spruch.
Diesem.

. . . .

Wirf auch die Abendtür zu, Rabbi.

. . . .

Reiss die Morgentür auf, Ra- —

To one who stood before the door, one
evening:
to him I opened my word — : toward the
clod I saw him trot, toward
the half-
baked
brother born in a
doughboy's dung-caked boot,
him with his god-
like loins all
bloody, the
chittering manikin.

Rabbi, I gnashed, Rabbi
Loew:

For this one —
circumcise his word,
for this one
scribe the living
Nothing on his soul,
for this one
spread your two
cripplefingers in the hale-
making blessing.
For this one.

. . . .

Slam the evening door shut, Rabbi.

. . . .

Fling the morning door open, Ra- —

In der Mandel — was steht in der Mandel?
Das Nichts.
Es steht das Nichts in der Mandel.
Da steht es und steht.

Im Nichts — wer steht da? Der König.
Da steht der König, der König.
Da steht er und steht.

      Judenlocke, wirst nicht grau.

Und dein Aug — wohin steht dein Auge?
Dein Aug steht der Mandel entgegen.
Dein Aug, dem Nichts stehts entgegen.
Es steht zum König.
So steht es und steht.

      Menschenlocke, wirst nicht grau.
      Leere Mandel, königsblau.

MANDORLA

In the almond — what stands in the almond?
The Nothing.
In the almond stands Nothing.
There it stands and stands.

In the Nothing — who stands there? The King.
There stands the King, the King.
There he stands and stands.

    Jewish curls, no gray for you.

And your eye — whereto stands your eye?
Your eye stands opposite the almond.
Your eye, the Nothing it stands opposite.
It stands by the King.
So it stands and stands.

    Human curls, no gray for you.
    Empty almond, kingly blue.

BENEDICTA

Zu ken men aroifgejn in himel arajn
Un fregn baj got zu's darf asoj sajn?
Jiddisches Lied

Ge-
trunken hast du,
was von den Vätern mir kam
und von jenseits der Väter:
— — Pneuma.

Ge-
segnet seist du, von weit her, von
jenseits meiner
erloschenen Finger.

Gesegnet: Du, die ihn grüsste,
den Teneberleuchter.

Du, die du's hörtest, da ich die Augen schloss, wie
die Stimme nicht weitersang nach:
's mus asoj sajn.

Du, die du's sprachst in den augenlosen, den Auen:
dasselbe, das andere
Wort:
Gebenedeiet.

Ge-
trunken.
Ge-
segnet.
Ge-
bentscht.

BENEDICTA

Tsu ken men aroyfgehn in himl arayn
Un fregn bay got tsu s'darf azoy zayn?
Yiddish song

Hast —
thou hast drunken,
what came to me from our fathers
and from beyond our fathers:
— — Pneuma.

Be —
be thou blessed, from afar, from
beyond my
guttering fingers.

Blessed: you that hailed it,
the Tenebrae lamp.

You that heard, when I shut my eyes, how
the voice stopped singing after
's muz azoy zayn.

You that spoke it in the eyeless ones, the pastures:
the same, the other
word:
Blessèd.

Drunk-
en.
Bless-
ed.
Ge-
bentscht.

DIE HELLEN
STEINE gehn durch die Luft, die hell-
weissen, die Licht-
bringer.

Sie wollen
nicht niedergehen, nicht stürzen,
nicht treffen. Sie gehen
auf,
wie die geringen
Heckenrosen, so tun sie sich auf,
sie schweben
dir zu, du meine Leise,
du meine Wahre — :

ich seh dich, du pflückst sie mit meinen
neuen, meinen
Jedermannshänden, du tust sie
ins Abermals-Helle, das niemand
zu weinen braucht noch zu nennen.

THE BRIGHT
STONES ride through the air, bright
white, the light-
bringers.

They want to
not sink, not fall,
not collide. They rise
up,
like slender
dog roses they break open,
they float
toward you, my gentle one,
you, my true one — :

I see you, you pluck them with my
new, my
Everyman's hands, you place them
in Once-Again-Brightness, which no one
need weep for nor name.

EIN WURFHOLZ, auf Atemwegen,
so wanderts, das Flügel-
mächtige, das
Wahre. Auf
Sternen-
bahnen, von Welten-
splittern geküsst, von Zeit-
körnern genarbt, von Zeitstaub, mit-
verwaisend mit euch,
Lapilli, ver-
zwergt, verwinzigt, ver-
nichtet,
verbracht und verworfen,
sich selber der Reim, —
so kommt es
geflogen, so kommts
wieder und heim,
einen Herzschlag, ein Tausendjahr lang
innezuhalten als
einziger Zeiger im Rund,
das eine Seele,
das seine
Seele
beschrieb,
das eine
Seele
beziffert.

A BOOMERANG, on breath paths,
it wanders, being mighty
of wing, being
true. On
star
orbits, by cosmic
splinters kissed, by time
kernels scarred, by time dust, co-
orphaned with you,
Lapilli, out-
weighed, outstripped, out-
done,
played out and thrown out,
itself its own rhyme, —
thus it comes
flying, thus it comes
back home in time,
to pause for
a heartbeat, a thousandyear long,
as the circle's only clockhand
that described
a soul,
its own
soul,
that
numbers
a soul.

HAWDALAH

An dem einen, dem
einzigen
Faden, an ihm
spinnst du — von ihm
Umsponnener, ins
Freie, dahin,
ins Gebundne.

Gross
stehn die Spindeln
ins Unland, die Bäume: es ist,
von unten her, ein
Licht geknüpft in die Luft-
matte, auf der du den Tisch deckst, den leeren
Stühlen und ihrem
Sabbatglanz zu — —

zu Ehren.

HAVDALAH

On the one, the
only
thread, on that
you spin — by that
spun round into
Freeness, out
into Boundness.

The spindles stand
huge
into untilled land, the trees: from
underneath a
light is braided into the airy
matting where you set your table for the empty
chairs and their
Sabbath radiance in — —

in honor.

In Brest, vor den Flammenringen,
im Zelt, wo der Tiger sprang,
da hört ich dich, Endlichkeit, singen,
da sah ich dich, Mandelstamm.

Der Himmel hing über der Reede,
die Möwe hing über dem Kran.
Das Endliche sang, das Stete, —
du, Kanonenboot, heisst "Baobab".

Ich grüsste die Trikolore
mit einem russischen Wort —
Verloren war Unverloren,
das Herz ein befestigter Ort.

AFTERNOON WITH CIRCUS AND CITADEL

In Brest near the flaming rings,
in the tent where the tiger leapt,
there, Finiteness, I heard you sing,
you, Mandelshtam, I saw you there.

The sky hung over the roadstead,
the gull hung over the crane.
What's finite sang, what's steady —
you, gunboat, "Baobab" 's your name.

I saluted the tricolor flag
with a Russian word —
Lost was Not Lost,
our heart a mighty fort.

ICH HABE BAMBUS GESCHNITTEN:
für dich, mein Sohn.
Ich habe gelebt.

Diese morgen fort-
getragene Hütte, sie
steht.

Ich habe nicht mitgebaut: du
weisst nicht, in was für
Gefässe ich den
Sand um mich her tat, vor Jahren, auf
Geheiss und Gebot. Der deine
kommt aus dem Freien — er bleibt
frei.

Das Rohr, das hier Fuss fasst, morgen
steht es noch immer, wohin dich
die Seele auch hinspielt im Un-
gebundnen.

I HAVE CUT BAMBOO:
for you, my son.
I have lived.

This hut, carried off
tomorrow, now
stands.

I did not help build: you've
no idea what sort of
vessels I packed
with the sand around me, years back, at
beck and command. Yours
comes from free ground — it stays
free.

The cane that roots here, tomorrow
will still be standing, wherever your
soul plays you in un-
boundedness.

WAS GESCHAH? Der Stein trat aus dem Berge.
Wer erwachte? Du und ich.
Sprache, Sprache. Mit-Stern. Neben-Erde.
Ärmer. Offen. Heimatlich.

Wohin gings? Gen Unverklungen.
Mit dem Stein gings, mit uns zwein.
Herz und Herz. Zu schwer befunden.
Schwerer werden. Leichter sein.

WHAT HAPPENED? The stone stepped from the mountain.
Who awakened? You and I.
Language, language. Fellow-star. Earth-cousin.
Poorer. Open. Homeland-like.

Where it went? Toward not expiring.
Went with the stone, and with the two of us.
Heart and heart. Weighed and found sinking.
Growing more heavy. Taking on lightness.

HINAUSGEKRÖNT,
hinausgespien in die Nacht.

Bei welchen
Sternen! Lauter
graugeschlagenes Herzhammersilber. Und
Berenikes Haupthaar, auch hier, — ich flocht,
ich zerflocht,
ich flechte, zerflechte.
Ich flechte.

Blauschlucht, in dich
treib ich das Gold. Auch mit ihm, dem
bei Huren und Dirnen vertanen,
komm ich und komm ich. Zu dir,
Geliebte.

Auch mit Fluch und Gebet. Auch mit jeder
der über mich hin-
schwirrenden Keulen: auch sie in eins
geschmolzen, auch sie
phallisch gebündelt zu dir,
Garbe-und-Wort.

Mit Namen, getränkt
von jedem Exil.
Mit Namen und Samen,
mit Namen, getaucht
in alle
Kelche, die vollstehn mit deinem
Königsblut, Mensch, — in alle
Kelche der grossen
Ghetto-Rose, aus der
du uns ansiehst, unsterblich von soviel
auf Morgenwegen gestorbenen Toden.

•   •   •

CROWNED OUT,
spit out into night.

And what
stars! Pure
gray-beaten heart-hammer silver. And
Berenice's head of hair, even here, — I braided,
I braided to bits,
I'm braiding, to bits.
I'm braiding.

Blue gorge, I drive
gold into you. With that too
wasted on whores and wenches,
I come and I come. To you,
beloved.

With curse and prayer too. And with
each bludgeon buzzing away
over me: they too melted
into one, they too
bound phallic to you,
sheaf-and-word.

With names, steeped
in every exile.
With names and seed,
with names dipped
in every
cup brimming with your
kingly blood, O man, — in every
calyx of the great
ghetto rose from which
you gaze on us, deathless from so many
deaths died on morning paths.

               •   •   •

(Und wir sangen die Warschowjanka.
Mit verschilften Lippen, Petrarca.
In Tundra-Ohren, Petrarca.)

Und es steigt eine Erde herauf, die unsre,
diese.
Und wir schicken
keinen der Unsern hinunter
zu dir,
Babel.

(And we sang the Varsovienne.
With reed-ridden lips, Petrarca.
Into tundra ears, Petrarca.)

And an earth arises, ours,
this one.
And we send
none of ours downward
to you,
Babel.

WOHIN MIR das Wort, das unsterblich war, fiel:
in die Himmelsschlucht hinter der Stirn,
dahin geht, geleitet von Speichel und Müll,
der Siebenstern, der mit mir lebt.

Im Nachthaus die Reime, der Atem im Kot,
das Auge ein Bilderknecht —
Und dennoch: ein aufrechtes Schweigen, ein Stein,
der die Teufelsstiege umgeht.

WHERE THE WORD, that was undying, fell:
into heaven's ravine behind my brow,
led by spittle and dreck, there goes
the sevenbranch starflower that lives with me.

Rhymes in the night house, breath in the muck,
the eye a thrall to images —
And yet: an upright silence, a stone
evading the devil's staircase.

HÜTTENFENSTER

Das Aug, dunkel:
als Hüttenfenster. Es sammelt,
was Welt war, Welt bleibt: den Wander-
Osten, die
Schwebenden, die
Menschen-und-Juden,
das Volk-vom-Gewölk, magnetisch
ziehts, mit Herzfingern, an
dir, Erde:
du kommst, du kommst,
wohnen werden wir, wohnen, etwas

— ein Atem? ein Name? —

geht im Verwaisten umher,
tänzerisch, klobig,
die Engels-
schwinge, schwer von Unsichtbarem, am
wundgeschundenen Fuss, kopf-
lastig getrimmt
vom Schwarzhagel, der
auch dort fiel, in Witebsk,

— und sie, die ihn säten, sie
schreiben ihn weg
mit mimetischer Panzerfaustklaue! —,

geht, geht umher,
sucht,
sucht unten,
sucht droben, fern, sucht
mit dem Auge, holt
Alpha Centauri herunter, Arktur, holt
den Strahl hinzu, aus den Gräbern,

TABERNACLE WINDOW

The eye, dark:
as a tabernacle window. It gathers
what was a world and still is: the wander-
East, the
Hovering Ones, the
Humans-and-Jews,
the Cloud Crowd, it pulls
magnetically on you, Earth, with
heart fingers:
you come and you come,
dwell, we shall dwell, something

— a breath? a name? —

goes around orphandom,
dancerish, clumsy,
an angel's
wing with invisibles weighting its
skinstripped foot, trimmed
topheavy with
the black hail that
fell there too, in Vitebsk,

— and those who sowed it, they
write it away
with mimetic antitank claws! — ,

goes, goes around,
looks about,
looks down below,
looks up above, far away, looks
with its eye, fetches
Alpha Centaurus, Arcturus, fetches
a ray of light from the graves,

. . .

geht zu Ghetto und Eden, pflückt
das Sternbild zusammen, das er,
der Mensch, zum Wohnen braucht, hier,
unter Menschen,

schreitet
die Buchstaben ab und der Buchstaben sterblich-
unsterbliche Seele,
geht zu Aleph und Jud und geht weiter,

baut ihn, den Davidsschild, lässt ihn
aufflammen, einmal,

lässt ihn erlöschen — da steht er,
unsichtbar, steht
bei Alpha und Aleph, bei Jud,
bei den andern, bei
allen: in
dir,

Beth, — das ist
das Haus, wo der Tisch steht mit

dem Licht und dem Licht.

• • •

goes to ghetto and Eden, plucks
the constellation that he,
a human, needs so as to dwell here
among humankind,

paces off
the letters and the letters' mortal-
immortal soul,
goes to Aleph and Yud and goes farther,

builds it, the Star of David, lets it
flare up once,

lets it die down—it stands there
invisible, stands
with Alpha and Aleph, with Yud,
with the others, with
them all: in
you,

Beth,—which is
the house where the table stands with

the light and the Light.

DIE SILBE SCHMERZ

Es gab sich Dir in die Hand:
ein Du, todlos,
an dem alles Ich zu sich kam. Es fuhren
wortfreie Stimmen rings, Leerformen, alles
ging in sie ein, gemischt
und entmischt
und wieder
gemischt.

Und Zahlen waren
mitverwoben in das
Unzählbare. Eins und Tausend und was
davor und dahinter
grösser war als es selbst, kleiner, aus-
gereift und
rück- und fort-
verwandelt in
keimendes Niemals.

Vergessenes griff
nach Zu-Vergessendem, Erdteile, Herzteile
schwammen,
sanken und schwammen. Kolumbus,
die Zeit-
lose im Aug, die Mutter-
Blume,
mordete Masten und Segel. Alles fuhr aus,

frei,
entdeckerisch,
blühte die Windrose ab, blätterte
ab, ein Weltmeer
blühte zuhauf und zutag, im Schwarzlicht
der Wildsteuerstriche. In Särgen,

THE SYLLABLE PAIN

It gave itself into your hand:
a Thou, deathless,
on which every I came to itself. Wordfree
voices spun about, void forms, everything
passed into them, mixed
and unmixed
and again
mixed.

And numbers were
woven into the
unnumberable. One and a thousand, and what
was larger than itself
in front and behind, smaller, full
ripened and
back and forth
transformed into a
budding Never.

Forgotten reached
for To-be-Forgotten, land masses, heart masses
swam,
sank and swam. Columbus,
his eye on the meadow
saffron, the mother
flower,
murdered masts and sails. Everything fared forth,

free,
exploringly,
the compass rose faded, its petals
fell, an ocean
bloomed by heaps and bounds in the blacklight
of wild rudder strokes. In coffins,

Urnen, Kanopen
erwachten die Kindlein
Jaspis, Achat, Amethyst — Völker,
Stämme und Sippen, ein blindes

E s s e i

knüpfte sich in
die schlangenköpfigen Frei-
Taue — : ein
Knoten
(und Wider- und Gegen- und Aber- und Zwillings- und Tau-
sendknoten), an dem
die fastnachtsäugige Brut
der Mardersterne im Abgrund
buch-, buch-, buch-
stabierte, stabierte.

urns, canopic jars
little babes awoke:
jasper, agate, amethyst — peoples,
races and tribes, a blind

Let there be

tied into
serpentheaded free-
coils — : a
knot
(and retro- and counter- and over- and double- and Thousand knot) where
a carnival-eyed brood
of weasel stars in the abyss was
book-, book-, book-
stalling and stalling.

Es ist alles anders, als du es dir denkst, als ich es mir denke,
die Fahne weht noch,
die kleinen Geheimnisse sind noch bei sich,
sie werfen noch Schatten, davon
lebst du, leb ich, leben wir.

Die Silbermünze auf deiner Zunge schmilzt,
sie schmeckt nach Morgen, nach Immer, ein Weg
nach Russland steigt dir ins Herz,
die karelische Birke
hat
gewartet,
der Name Ossip kommt auf dich zu, du erzählst ihm,
was er schon weiss, er nimmt es, er nimmt es dir ab, mit Händen,
du löst ihm den Arm von der Schulter, den rechten, den linken,
du heftest die deinen an ihre Stelle, mit Händen, mit Fingern, mit
    Linien,

— was abriss, wächst wieder zusammen —
da hast du sie, da nimm sie dir, da hast du alle beide,
den Namen, den Namen, die Hand, die Hand,
da nimm sie dir zum Unterpfand,
er nimmt auch das, und du hast
wieder, was dein ist, was sein war,

Windmühlen

stossen dir Luft in die Lunge, du ruderst
durch die Kanäle, Lagunen und Grachten,
bei Wortschein,
am Heck kein Warum, am Bug kein Wohin, ein Widderhorn hebt
    dich
— *Tekiah!* —
wie ein Posaunenschall über die Nächte hinweg in den Tag, die
    Auguren
zerfleischen einander, der Mensch

IT'S ALL DIFFERENT from what you think, from what I think,
the flag still waves,
the little secrets are still intact,
they still cast shadows — on this
you live, I live, we live.

The silver shekel melts on your tongue,
it tastes of Tomorrow, of Always, a path
to Russia rises into your heart,
the Karelian birch
is still
waiting,
the name Osip comes toward you, you tell him
what he already knows, he takes it, he takes it off you with hands,
you loose the arm from his shoulder, the right one, the left,
you fasten your own in their place, with hands, fingers, lines,

— what ripped apart, grows back together —
you've got them now, so take them now, so now you've got them both,
the name, the name, the hand, the hand,
so take them and this pledge will stand,
he takes that too and you've got back
what's yours, what was his,

windmills

drive air into your lungs, you're rowing
through channels, lagoons and canals
by wordlight,
no Why at the stern, no Where at the bow, a ram's horn lifts you
— *Tekiah!* —
like a trumpet blast out over nights into day, the soothsayers
tear each other apart, man

hat seinen Frieden, der Gott
hat den seinen, die Liebe
kehrt in die Betten zurück, das Haar
der Frauen wächst wieder,
die nach innen gestülpte
Knospe an ihrer Brust
tritt wieder zutag, lebens-,
herzlinienhin erwacht sie
dir in der Hand, die den Lendenweg hochklomm, —

wie heisst es, dein Land
hinterm Berg, hinterm Jahr?
Ich weiss, wie es heisst.
Wie das Wintermärchen, so heisst es,
es heisst wie das Sommermärchen,
das Dreijahreland deiner Mutter, das war es,
das ists,
es wandert überallhin, wie die Sprache,
wirf sie weg, wirf sie weg,
dann hast du sie wieder, wie ihn,
den Kieselstein aus
der Mährischen Senke,
den dein Gedanke nach Prag trug,
aufs Grab, auf die Gräber, ins Leben,

längst
ist er fort, wie die Briefe, wie alle
Laternen, wieder
musst du ihn suchen, da ist er,
klein ist er, weiss,
um die Ecke, da liegt er,
bei Normandie-Njemen — in Böhmen,
da, da, da,
hinterm Haus, vor dem Haus,
weiss ist er, weiss, er sagt:
Heute — es gilt.

has his peace, God
has his, love
returns to the beds, the hair
of women grows back,
the inturned
bud on their breast
crops up again, on life-
and heartlines it wakes
to your hand that climbed the loins' path —

what is it called, your land
back of the mountain, back of the year?
I know what it's called.
Like the Winter's Tale it's called,
it's called like the Summer's Tale,
your mother's Three Year Land, that was it,
this is it,
it wanders everywhere, like language,
throw it away, throw it away,
then you'll have it again, like
that pebble from
the Moravian Basin
your thought carried to Prague,
on the grave, on the graves, into life,

it's
long gone, like the letters, like all those
lanterns, you must
seek it again, here it is,
it is small, white,
round the corner, it lies here
at Normandy-Niemen — in Bohemia,
here here here
back of the house, front of the house,
white it is white, it says:
Today's the day.

Weiss ist er, weiss, ein Wasser-
strahl findet hindurch, ein Herzstrahl,
ein Fluss,
du kennst seinen Namen, die Ufer
hängen voll Tag, wie der Name,
du tastest ihn ab, mit der Hand:
Alba.

White it is white, a water-
stream courses on through, a heartstream,
a river,
you know its name, the banks
hang heavy with day, like this name,
you run your hand over it:
Alba.

IN DER LUFT, da bleibt deine Wurzel, da,
in der Luft.
Wo sich das Irdische ballt, erdig,
Atem-und-Lehm.

Gross
geht der Verbannte dort oben, der
Verbrannte: ein Pommer, zuhause
im Maikäferlied, das mütterlich blieb, sommerlich, hell-
blütig am Rand
aller schroffen,
winterhart-kalten
Silben.

Mit ihm
wandern die Meridiane:
an-
gesogen von seinem
sonnengesteuerten Schmerz, der die Länder verbrüdert nach
dem Mittagsspruch einer
liebenden
Ferne. Aller-
orten ist Hier und ist Heute, ist, von Verzweiflungen her,
der Glanz,
in den die Entzweiten treten mit ihren
geblendeten Mündern:

der Kuss, nächtlich,
brennt einer Sprache den Sinn ein, zu der sie erwachen, sie — :

heimgekehrt in
den unheimlichen Bannstrahl,
der die Verstreuten versammelt, die
durch die Sternwüste Seele Geführten, die
Zeltmacher droben im Raum
ihrer Blicke und Schiffe,

IN THE AIR your root stays on, there
in the air.
Where earthliness clusters, earthy,
Breath-and-Clay.

Looming
up there, the banned, the
burned: a Pomeranian, at home
in the Maybeetle song that stayed motherly, summerly, bright-
blooded on the edge
of all cragged
cold winterhard
syllables.

With him
the meridians wander:
sucked
up by his
sun-steered pain, which bonds these lands after
the noonday speech of a
loving
distance. Every-
where is Here and Today, is a radiance
made of despairs, that
those who've been sundered step into with their
blinded mouths:

a kiss, at night,
brands the sense of a language they waken to, they — :

gone home again to
uncanny anathema
that gathers the dispersed, those
led through the star-desert soul, the
tentmakers up there in the zone
of their gazings and ships,

die winzigen Garben Hoffnung,
darin es von Erzengelfittichen rauscht, von Verhängnis,
die Brüder, die Schwestern, die
zu leicht, die zu schwer, die zu leicht
Befundenen mit
der Weltenwaage im blut-
schändrischen, im
fruchtbaren Schoss, die lebenslang Fremden,
spermatisch bekränzt von Gestirnen, schwer
in den Untiefen lagernd, die Leiber
zu Schwellen getürmt, zu Dämmen, — die

Furtenwesen, darüber
der Klumpfuss der Götter herüber-
gestolpert kommt — um
wessen
Sternzeit zu spät?

the tiny sheaves of hope
with a rush of archangels' wings, of destiny,
the brothers, the sisters, those
found too light, too heavy,
too light on
cosmic scales in their blood-
defiling
fruitful womb, the lifelong aliens
spermatically crowned with stars, heavily
camped in the shoals, the bodies
embanked in swollen heaps, — the

ford-beings, whom
the clubfoot of the gods
comes stumbling over — by
whose
star time too late?

Gisèle Celan-Lestrange, "*Rencontre-Begegnung*," 1958.

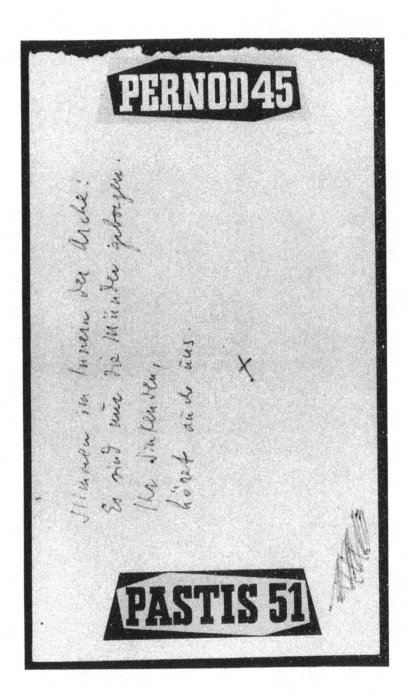

Paul Celan, manuscript draft of "*Stimmen.*"

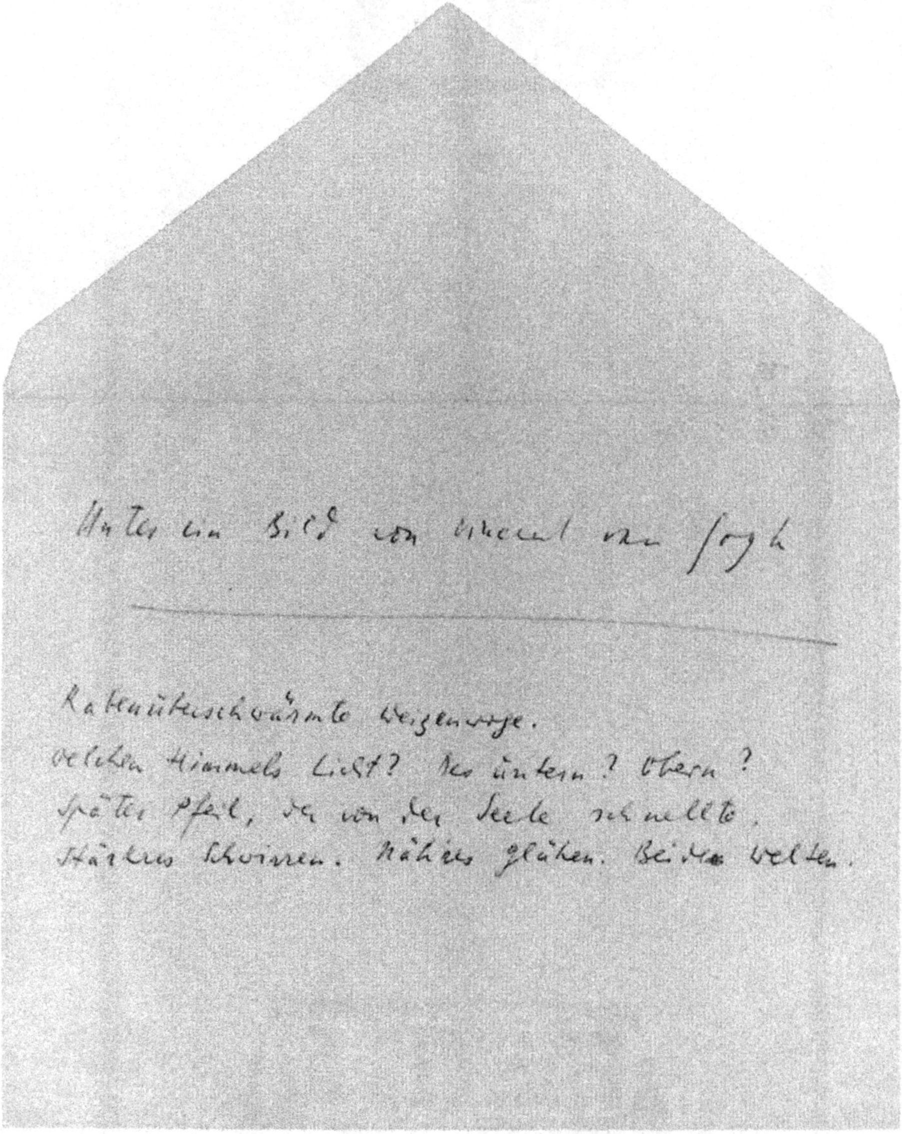

Unter ein Bild von Vincent van Gogh

Rabenüberschwärmte Weizenwoge.
Welchen Himmels Licht? Des untern? Obern?
Später Pfeil, der von der Seele schnellte.
Stärkeres Schwirren. Näheres Glühen. Beide Welten.

Paul Celan, manuscript draft of "*Unter ein Bild.*"

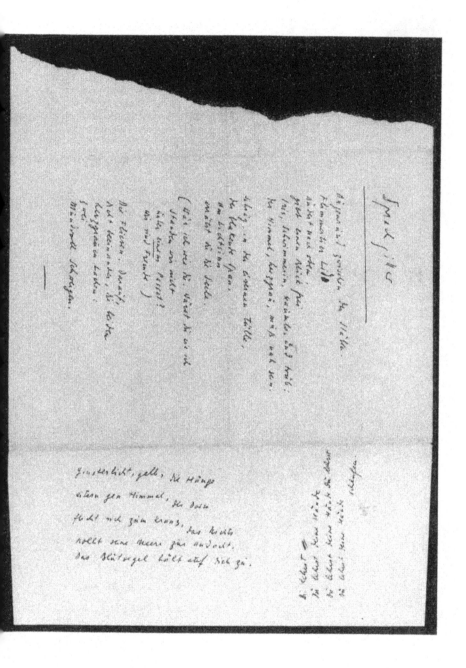

Paul Celan, manuscript drafts of "*Sprachgitter*" and "*Matière de Bretagne*."

ist, bin ich ja, hier, beim Türkenbund und bei der Rapunzel, und hundert Schritt weiter, da drüben, wo ich hinkann, da geht die Lärche zur Zirbelkiefer hinauf, ich seh's, ich seh es und seh's nicht, und mein Stock, der hat gesprochen, hat gesprochen zum Stein, und mein Stock, der schweigt jetzt still, und der Stein, sagst du, der kann sprechen, und in meinem Aug, da hängt der Schleier, der bewegliche, da hängen die Schleier, die beweglichen, da hast du den einen gelüpft, und da hängt schon der zweite, und der Stern – denn ja, der steht jetzt überm Gebirg –, wenn er da hineinwill, so wird er Hochzeit halten müssen und bald nicht mehr er sein, sondern halb Schleier und halb Stern, und ich weiß, ich weiß, Geschwisterkind, ich weiß, ich bin dir begegnet, hier, und geredet haben wir, viel, und die Falten dort, du weißt, nicht für die Menschen sind sie da und nicht für uns, die wir hier gingen und einander trafen, wir hier unterm Stern, wir, die Juden, die da kamen, wie Lenz, durchs Gebirg, du Groß und ich Klein, du, der Geschwätzige, und ich, der Geschwätzige, wir mit den Stöcken, wir mit unsern Namen, den unaussprechlichen, wir mit unserm Schatten, dem eignen und dem fremden, du hier und ich hier –

– ich hier, ich; ich, der ich dir all das sagen kann, sagen hätt können; der ich dirs nicht sag und nicht gesagt hab; ich mit dem Türkenbund links, ich mit der Rapunzel, ich mit der heruntergebrannten, der Kerze, ich mit dem Tag, ich mit den Tagen, ich hier und ich dort, ich, begleitet vielleicht – jetzt! – von der Liebe der Nichtgeliebten, ich auf dem Weg hier zu mir, oben.«

Paris, August 1959

202

Paul Celan, offprint of "*Gespräch im Gebirg*," inscribed to Reinhard Federmann, 1960.

ZU SEI VIE DU, IMMER.

Stant vp Jherosalem inde
erheyff dich,

auch wer das Band zerschnitt zu dir hin,

inde wirt
iluchtet,

knüpfte es neu, in der Gehugnis,

Schlammbrocken schluckt ich, im Turm,
Sprache, Finster-Lisene,

kumi
ori.

91.57.1

Paul Celan, autograph copy of *"Du sei wie du,"* 1969.

ATEMWENDE

───────────

1 9 6 7

BREATHTURN

DU DARFST mich getrost
mit Schnee bewirten:
sooft ich Schulter an Schulter
mit dem Maulbeerbaum schritt durch den Sommer,
schrie sein jüngstes
Blatt.

You may safely
regale me with snow:
whenever shoulder to shoulder
I strode through summer with the mulberry,
its youngest leaf
shrieked.

IN DIE RILLEN
der Himmelsmünze im Türspalt
presst du das Wort,
dem ich entrollte,
als ich mit bebenden Fäusten
das Dach über uns
abtrug, Schiefer um Schiefer,
Silbe um Silbe, dem Kupfer-
Schimmer der Bettel-
Schale dort oben
Zulieb.

INTO THE GROOVES
of heaven's coin in the door crack
you press that word
I unfolded from,
as with quivering fists
I pulled down the roof
above us, slate by slate,
syllable by syllable, for the copper
shimmer's sake
on the begging bowl
up there.

IN DEN FLÜSSEN nördlich der Zukunft
werf ich das Netz aus, das du
zögernd beschwerst
mit von Steinen geschriebenen
Schatten.

IN RIVERS north of the future
I cast the net you
haltingly weight
with stonewritten
shadows.

DIE ZAHLEN, im Bund
mit der Bilder Verhängnis
und Gegen-
verhängnis.

Der drübergestülpte
Schädel, an dessen
schlafloser Schläfe ein irr-
lichternder Hammer
all das im Welttakt
besingt.

THE NUMBERS, in league
with the images' fate
and counter-
fate.

Clapped onto them, the
skull on whose
sleepless temple an ill-
usory hammer
sings the cosmic tempo
of praise.

WEISSGRAU aus-
geschachteten steilen
Gefühls.

Landeinwärts, hierher-
verwehter Strandhafer bläst
Sandmuster über
den Rauch von Brunnengesängen.

Ein Ohr, abgetrennt, lauscht.

Ein Aug, in Streifen geschnitten,
wird all dem gerecht.

WHITEGRAY of a
steeply caved
feeling.

Inland, wind-
driven dunegrass blows
sand patterns over
the smoke of wellsongs.

An ear, severed, listens.

An eye, sliced into strips,
gives all that its due.

MIT ERDWÄRTS GESUNGENEN MASTEN
fahren die Himmelwracks.

In dieses Holzlied
beisst du dich fest mit den Zähnen.

Du bist der liedfeste
Wimpel.

WITH MASTS SUNG EARTHWARD
the heaven wrecks sail.

Into this wood song
you bite fast with your teeth.

You are the songfast
pennant.

SCHLÄFENZANGE,
von deinem Jochbein beäugt.
Ihr Silberglanz da,
wo sie sich festbiss:
du und der Rest deines Schlafs —
bald
habt ihr Geburtstag.

TEMPLE-PINCERS
eyed by your cheekbone.
Their silver gleam
where they bit in:
you and the rest of your sleep —
soon
it's your birthday.

STEHEN, im Schatten
des Wundenmals in der Luft.

Für-niemand-und-nichts-Stehn.
Unerkannt,
für dich
allein.

Mit allem, was darin Raum hat,
auch ohne
Sprache.

To STAND, in the shadow
of a scar in the air.

Stand-for-no-one-and-nothing.
Unrecognized,
for you
alone.

With all that has room within it,
even without
language.

MIT DEN VERFOLGTEN in spätem, un-
verschwiegenem,
strahlendem
Bund.

Das Morgen-Lot, übergoldet,
heftet sich dir an die mit-
schwörende, mit-
schürfende, mit-
schreibende
Ferse.

WITH THE PERSECUTED in late, un-
silenced,
radiant
covenant.

The dawn plummet, gilded,
cleaves to your co-
swearing, co-
scouring, co-
scribbling
heel.

FADENSONNEN
über der grauschwarzen Ödnis.
Ein baum-
hoher Gedanke
greift sich den Lichtton: es sind
noch Lieder zu singen jenseits
der Menschen.

THREADSUNS
over the grayblack wasteness.
A tree-
high thought
strikes the light-tone: there are
still songs to sing beyond
humankind.

IM SCHLANGENWAGEN, an
der weissen Zypresse vorbei,
durch die Flut
fuhren sie dich.

Doch in dir, von
Geburt,
schäumte die andre Quelle,
am schwarzen
Strahl Gedächtnis
klommst du zutag.

IN THE REPTILE-CAR, past
the white cypress,
they drove you
through the flood.

Yet in you, from
birth,
the other wellspring foamed,
on the black
memory beam
you climbed to daylight.

(ICH KENNE DICH, du bist die tief Gebeugte,
ich, der Durchbohrte, bin dir untertan.
Wo flammt ein Wort, das für uns beide zeugte?
Du — ganz, ganz wirklich. Ich — ganz Wahn.)

(I KNOW YOU, you're the one bent over low,
and I, the one pierced through, am in your need.
Where flames a word to witness for us both?
You — wholly real. I — wholly mad.)

WEGGEBEIZT vom
Strahlenwind deiner Sprache
das bunte Gerede des An-
erlebten — das hundert-
zungige Mein-
gedicht, das Genicht.

Aus-
gewirbelt,
frei
der Weg durch den menschen-
gestaltigen Schnee,
den Büsserschnee, zu
den gastlichen
Gletscherstuben und -tischen.

Tief
in der Zeitenschrunde,
beim
Wabeneis
wartet, ein Atemkristall,
dein unumstössliches
Zeugnis.

ETCHED AWAY by the
radiant wind of your speech,
the motley gossip of pseudo-
experience — the hundred-
tongued My-
poem, the Lie-noem.

Whirl-
winded,
free,
a path through human-
shaped snow,
through penitent cowl-ice, to
the glacier's
welcoming chambers and tables.

Deep
in the time crevasse,
by
honeycomb-ice
there waits, a Breathcrystal,
your unannullable
witness.

VOM GROSSEN
Augen-
losen
aus deinen Augen geschöpft:

der sechs-
kantige, absageweisse
Findling.

Eine Blindenhand, sternhart auch sie
vom Namen-Durchwandern,
ruht auf ihm, so
lang wie auf dir,
Esther.

SCOOPED by the
great Eye-
less One
from your eyes:

six-
edged and blanched with refusal,
the foundling stone.

A blindman's hand, starhardened too
from wandering through names,
rests on it
as long as on you,
Esther.

KEINE SANDKUNST MEHR, kein Sandbuch, keine Meister.

Nichts erwürfelt. Wieviel
Stumme?
Siebenzehn.

Deine Frage — deine Antwort.
Dein Gesang, was weiss er?

Tiefimschnee,
   Iefimnee,
     I — i — e.

No more sand art, no sand book, no masters.

Nothing on the dice. How many
mutes?
Seventen.

Your question — your answer.
Your song, what does it know?

Deepinsnow.
      Eepinnow.
            E — i — o.

HOHLES LEBENSGEHÖFT. Im Windfang
die leer-
geblasene Lunge
blüht. Eine Handvoll
Schlafkorn
weht aus dem wahr-
gestammelten Mund
hinaus zu den Schnee-
gesprächen.

HOLLOW HOMESTEAD OF LIFE. In the venthole
the blown-
empty lung
blossoms. A handful of
sleepgrain
wafts from the true-
stammered mouth
out toward snow-
conversations.

SCHWARZ,
wie die Erinnerungswunde,
wühlen die Augen nach dir
in dem von Herzzähnen hell-
gebissenen Kronland,
das unser Bett bleibt:

durch diesen Schacht musst du kommen —
du kommst.

Im Samen-
sinn
sternt dich das Meer aus, zuinnerst, für immer.

Das Namengeben hat ein Ende,
über dich werf ich mein Schicksal.

Black
like memory's wound,
the eyes grub toward you
in a Crownland bitten
bright by heart's teeth —
it remains our bed:

through this shaft you must come —
you come.

In the seed's
sense
the sea stars you out, innermost, for ever.

An end to the granting of names,
over you I cast my fate.

LANDSCHAFT mit Urnenwesen.
Gespräche
von Rauchmund zu Rauchmund.

Sie essen:
die Tollhäusler-Trüffel, ein Stück
unvergrabner Poesie,
fand Zunge und Zahn.

Eine Träne rollt in ihr Auge zurück.

Die linke, verwaiste
Hälfte der Pilger-
muschel — sie schenkten sie dir,
dann banden sie dich —
leuchtet lauschend den Raum aus:

das Klinkerspiel gegen den Tod
kann beginnen.

Landscape with urn beings.
Conversations
from smokemouth to smokemouth.

They eat:
the bedlamite truffle, a piece
of unburied poesy,
found tongue and tooth.

A tear rolls back into its eye.

The orphaned left
half of the pilgrim
shell — they gave you it,
then trussed you up —
illumines the space and listens:

the clinker game against death
can begin.

Der halbe Tod,
grossgesäugt mit unserm Leben,
lag aschenbildwahr um uns her —

auch wir
tranken noch immer, seelenverkreuzt, zwei Degen,
an Himmelssteine genäht, wortblutgeboren
im Nachtbett,

grösser und grösser
wuchsen wir durcheinander, es gab
keinen Namen mehr für
das, was uns trieb (einer der Wieviel-
unddreissig
war mein lebendiger Schatten,
der die Wahnstiege hochklomm zu dir?),

ein Turm,
baute der Halbe sich ins Wohin,
ein Hradschin
aus lauter Goldmacher-Nein,

Knochen-Hebräisch,
zu Sperma zermahlen,
rann durch die Sanduhr,
die wir durchschwammen, zwei Träume jetzt, läutend
wider die Zeit, auf den Plätzen.

IN PRAGUE

The half death,
suckled plump on our life,
lay ash-image-true all around us —

we too
went on drinking, soul-crossed, two daggers,
sewn onto heavenstones, wordblood-born
in the night bed,

larger and larger
we grew through one another, there was
no more name for
what drove us (one of the thirty-
how many
was my living shadow
that climbed the madness stairs up to you?),

a tower
the Half built itself into Whither,
a Hradčany
out of pure goldmakers-No,

Bone Hebrew,
ground down to sperm,
ran through the hourglass
we swam through, two dreams now, tolling
counter time, in the squares.

ASCHENGLORIE hinter
deinen erschüttert-verknoteten
Händen am Dreiweg.

Pontisches Einstmals: hier,
ein Tropfen,
auf
dem ertrunkenen Ruderblatt,
tief
im versteinerten Schwur,
rauscht es auf.

(Auf dem senkrechten
Atemseil, damals,
höher als oben,
zwischen zwei Schmerzknoten, während
der blanke
Tatarenmond zu uns heraufklomm,
grub ich mich in dich und in dich.)

Aschen-
glorie hinter
euch Dreiweg-
Händen.

Das vor euch, vom Osten her, Hin-
gewürfelte, furchtbar.

Niemand
zeugt für den
Zeugen.

Ash-aureole behind
your shaken knotted
hands at the Threeways.

Pontic Once-upon-a-time: here
a drop
on
the drowned oarblade,
deep
in a petrified oath,
it bubbles up.

(On the plumblined
breath cable, back then,
higher than on high,
between two pain knots, while
the gleaming
Tatar moon climbed up to us,
I dug me into you and you.)

Ash-
aureole behind you
Threeways-
hands.

Before you, the easterly
dicethrow, frightful.

No one
bears witness for the
witness.

DAS GESCHRIEBENE höhlt sich, das
Gesprochene, meergrün,
brennt in den Buchten,

in den
verflüssigten Namen
schnellen die Tümmler,

im geewigten Nirgends, hier,
im Gedächtnis der über-
lauten Glocken in — wo nur?,

wer
in diesem
Schattengeviert
schnaubt, wer
unter ihm
schimmert auf, schimmert auf, schimmert auf?

WHAT'S WRITTEN goes hollow, what's
spoken, seagreen,
burns in the bays,

dolphins race
through
liquefied names,

here in forevered Nowhere,
in a memory of out-
crying bells in — but where?,

who
in this
shadow quadrant
is gasping, who
underneath
glimmers up, glimmers up, glimmers up?

Wo?
In den Lockermassen der Nacht.

Im Gramgeröll und -geschiebe,
im langsamsten Aufruhr,
im Weisheitsschacht Nie.

Wassernadeln
nähn den geborstenen
Schatten zusammen — er kämpft sich
tiefer hinunter,
frei.

WHERE?
At night in crumbling rockmass.

In trouble's rubble and scree,
in slowest tumult,
the wisdom-pit named Never.

Water needles
stitch up the split
shadow — it fights its way
deeper down,
free.

KÖNIGSWUT, steinmähnig, vorn.

Und die verrauchten
Gebete —
Hengste, hinzu-
geschmerzt, die
unbezähmbar-gehorsame
Freischar:

psalmhufig, hinsingend über
auf-, auf-, auf-
geblättertes Bibelgebirg,
auf die klaren, mit-
klirrenden,
mächtigen Meerkeime zu.

KING'S RAGE, stone-maned, out front.

And the prayers
up in smoke —
pain-driven
stallions, the
vigilantes
untamable, servile:

psalmhooved, singing out over
o-, o-, o-
penleafed Bible mountains,
toward the clear and
clattering, the
brute buds of the sea.

SOLVE

Entosteter, zu
Brandscheiten zer-
spaltener Grabbaum:

an den Gift-
pfalzen vorbei, an den Domen,
stromaufwärts, strom-
abwärts geflösst

vom winzig-lodernden, vom
freien
Satzzeichen der
zu den unzähligen zu
nennenden un-
aussprechlichen
Namen aus-
einandergeflohenen, ge-
borgenen
Schrift.

SOLVE

Dis-easted, a grave-
tree split into
splintered kindling:

past the poison
palaces, past cathedrals,
floated up-
stream and down

by the tinily flaring, the
free
punctuation of sal-
vaged
Scripture,
fled asunder to the
countlessly
nameable un-
utterable
names.

COAGULA

Auch deine
Wunde, Rosa.

Und das Hörnerlicht deiner
rumänischen Büffel
an Sternes Statt überm
Sandbett, im
redenden, rot-
aschengewaltigen
Kolben.

COAGULA

Also your
wound, Rosa.

And the horns' light of your
Romanian buffaloes
in place of a star above the
sand bed, in the
outspeaking red
ashpotent
alembic.

SCHAUFÄDEN, SINNFÄDEN, aus
Nachtgalle geknüpft
hinter der Zeit:

wer
ist unsichtbar genug,
euch zu sehn?

Mantelaug, Mandelaug, kamst
durch alle die Wände,
erklimmst
dieses Pult,
rollst, was dort liegt, wieder auf —

Zehn Blindenstäbe,
feurig, gerade, frei,
entschweben dem eben
geborenen Zeichen,

stehn
über ihm.

Wir sind es noch immer.

SHOW-FRINGES, SENSE-FRINGES,
knitted from nightgall
well behind time:

who
is invisible enough
to see you?

Mantle eye, almond eye, coming
through each and every wall,
climbing
to this desk,
again scrolling open what lies there —

Ten blindman's sticks,
fiery, upright, free,
soar up from the just-
born sign,

stand
over it.

This is still us.

EIN DRÖHNEN: es ist
die Wahrheit selbst
unter die Menschen
getreten,
mitten ins
Metapherngestöber.

A RUMBLING: it is
Truth itself
walked among
men,
amidst the
metaphor squall.

SCHLICKENDE, dann
krautige Stille der Ufer.

Die eine Schleuse noch. Am
Warzenturm, mit
Brackigem übergossen,
mündest du ein.

Vor dir, in
den rudernden Riesensporangien,
sichelt, als keuchten dort Worte,
ein Glanz.

Oozing, then
weedy stillness on the banks.

Yet one more sluice. At the
wart tower,
bathed in brackishness,
you debouch.

In front of you, among
giant rowing sporangiums,
a brightness sickles as though words
were gasping.

EINMAL,
da hörte ich ihn,
da wusch er die Welt,
ungesehn, nachtlang,
wirklich.

Eins und Unendlich,
vernichtet,
ichten.

Licht war. Rettung.

ONCE,
I heard him,
he was washing the world,
unseen, nightlong,
real.

One and infinite,
annihilated,
they I'ed.

Light was. Salvation.

FADENSONNEN

1968

THREADSUNS

FRANKFURT, SEPTEMBER

Blinde, licht-
bärtige Stellwand.
Ein Maikäfertraum
leuchtet sie aus.

Dahinter, klagegerastert,
tut sich Freuds Stirn auf,

die draussen
hartgeschwiegene Träne
schiesst an mit dem Satz:
"Zum letzten-
mal Psycho-
logie."

Die Simili-
Dohle
frühstückt.

Der Kehlkopfverschlusslaut
singt.

FRANKFURT, SEPTEMBER

Blind, light-
bearded display panel.
A Maybeetle dream
illumines it.

Behind, in mourning halftone,
Freud's brow opens up,

the outward
hard-silenced tear
breaks out with a phrase:
"For the last
time psycho-
logy."

The simulate
jackdaw
breakfasts.

The glottal stop
sings.

DIE SPUR EINES BISSES im Nirgends.

Auch sie
musst du bekämpfen,
von hier aus.

THE TRACE OF A BITE in Nowhere.

It too
you must combat,
from here out.

ALL DEINE SIEGEL ERBROCHEN? NIE.

Geh, verzedere auch
sie, die brief-
häutige, elf-
hufige Tücke:

dass die Welle, die honig-
ferne, die milch-
nahe, wenn
der Mut sie zur Klage bewegt,
die Klage zum Mut, wieder,

dass sie nicht auch
den Elektronen-Idioten
spiegle, der Datteln
verarbeitet für
menetekelnde
Affen.

ALL YOUR SEALS BROKEN? NEVER.

Go on, cedar that away
too, the letter-
skinned, hendeca-
hooved perfidy:

so that the wave, honey-
far, milk-
near, when
mettle stirs it to lament,
lament again to mettle,

that it too not
mirror the electron-
idiot, who fabricates
date fruit for
menetekeling - *warning sign / portent*
apes.

SCHLAFBROCKEN, Keile,
ins Nirgends getrieben:
wir bleiben uns gleich,
der herum-
gesteuerte Rundstern
pflichtet uns bei.

SLEEPSCRAPS, wedges,
driven into Nowhere:
we stay steadfast,
the rounded star
we steer past
concurs with us.

DIE FLEISSIGEN
Bodenschätze, häuslich,

die geheizte Synkope,

das nicht zu enträtselnde
Halljahr,

die vollverglasten
Spinnen-Altäre im alles-
überragenden Flachbau,

die Zwischenlaute
(noch immer?),
die Schattenpalaver,

die Ängste, eisgerecht,
flugklar,

der barock ummantelte,
spracheschluckende Duschraum,
semantisch durchleuchtet,

die unbeschriebene Wand
einer Stehzelle:

hier

leb dich
querdurch, ohne Uhr.

INDUSTRIOUS
mineral resources, domestic,

the heated syncope,

the not-to-be-deciphered
Jubilee year,

the glassed-in
spider altars in a flat, sur-
passing structure,

sliding tones
(even now?),
the shadow palaver,

anxieties fit for ice,
cleared for flight,

the baroquely cloaked
speechswallowing shower room,
semantically X-rayed,

the uninscribed wall
of a stand-up cell:

here

live yourself
right through, with no clock.

WENN ICH NICHT WEISS, NICHT WEISS,
ohne dich, ohne dich, ohne Du,

kommen sie alle,
die
Freigeköpften, die
zeitlebens hirnlos den Stamm
der Du-losen
besangen:

Aschrej,

ein Wort ohne Sinn,
transtibetanisch,
der Jüdin
Pallas
Athene
in die behelmten
Ovarien gespritzt,

und wenn er,

er,

foetal,

karpatisches Nichtnicht beharft,

dann spitzenklöppelt die
Allemande
das sich übergebende un-
sterbliche
Lied.

WHEN I DON'T KNOW, DON'T KNOW,
without you, without you, with no Thou,

then they all come,
those
free beheaded, who
lifelong brainlessly lauded
the tribe of the
Thou-less:

Aschrei,

a word with no meaning,
transtibetan,
squirted into
the Jewess
Pallas
Athena's
helmeted ovaries,

and when he,

he,

fetal,

harps Carpathian Notnot,

then the Allemande
knits lace out of
thrown-up im-
mortal
song.

DU WARST mein Tod:
dich konnte ich halten,
während mir alles entfiel.

You were my death:
you I could hold
while everything slipped from me.

TAU. Und ich lag mit dir, du, im Gemülle,
ein matschiger Mond
bewarf uns mit Antwort,

wir bröckelten auseinander
und bröselten wieder in eins:

der Herr brach das Brot,
das Brot brach den Herrn.

DEW. And I lay with you, you, in the trash,
a mashed-in moon
pelted us with answers,

we crumbled from each other
and crumbed back together:

the Lord broke the bread,
the bread broke the Lord.

ÜPPIGE DURCHSAGE
in einer Gruft, wo
wir mit unsern
Gasfahnen flattern,

wir stehn hier
im Geruch
der Heiligkeit, ja.

Brenzlige
Jenseitsschwaden
treten uns dick aus den Poren,

in jeder zweiten
Zahn-
karies erwacht
eine unverwüstliche Hymne.

Den Batzen Zwielicht, den du uns reinwarfst,
komm, schluck ihn mit runter.

PROFUSE ANNOUNCEMENT
in a grave, where
we with our
gas flags are flapping,

here we stand
in the odor
of sanctity, yeah.

Burnt
fumes of Beyond
leak thick from our pores,

in every other
tooth-
cavity awakes
an undespoilable hymn.

The two bits twilight you tossed in to us,
come, gulp it down too.

NAH, IM AORTENBOGEN,
im Hellblut:
das Hellwort.

Mutter Rahel
weint nicht mehr.
Rübergetragen
alles Geweinte.

Still, in den Kranzarterien,
unumschnürt:
Ziw, jenes Licht.

NEAR, IN THE AORTA'S ARCH,
in bright blood:
the brightword.

Mother Rachel
weeps no more.
Carried across now
all of the weeping.

Still, in the coronary arteries,
unbinded:
Ziv, that light.

WEIL DU DEN NOTSCHERBEN FANDST
in der Wüstung,
ruhn die Schattenjahrhunderte neben dir aus
und hören dich denken:

Vielleicht ist es wahr,
dass hier der Friede zwei Völker besprach,
aus Tongefässen.

Because you found the trouble-shard
in a wilderness place,
the shadow centuries relax beside you
and hear you think:

Perhaps it's true
that peace conjured two peoples here
out of clay vessels.

Denk dir:
der Moorsoldat von Massada
bringt sich Heimat bei, aufs
unauslöschlichste,
wider
allen Dorn im Draht.

Denk dir:
die Augenlosen ohne Gestalt
führen dich frei durchs Gewühl, du
erstarkst und
erstarkst.

Denk dir: deine
eigene Hand
hat dies wieder
ins Leben empor-
gelittene
Stück
bewohnbarer Erde
gehalten.

Denk dir:
das kam auf mich zu,
namenwach, handwach
für immer,
vom Unbestattbaren her.

JUST THINK

Just think:
the Peat-Bog Soldier of Masada
makes a homeland for himself, most
ineffaceably,
against
every barb in the wire.

Just think:
the eyeless ones without shape
lead you free through the tumult, you
go from strength
to strength.

Just think: your
own hand
has held
this piece of
habitable earth,
again suffered
up into life.

Just think:
this came toward me,
name-awake, hand-awake
for ever,
from the unburiable.

LICHTZWANG

1970

LIGHT-COMPULSION

HÖRRESTE, SEHRESTE, im
Schlafsaal eintausendundeins,

tagnächtlich
die Bären-Polka:

sie schulen dich um,

du wirst wieder
er.

Remnants of hearing, of seeing, in
Ward one thousand and one,

daynightly
the Bear Polka:

they're reeducating you,

once more you are
him.

WIR LAGEN
schon tief in der Macchia, als du
endlich herankrochst.
Doch konnten wir nicht
hinüberdunkeln zu dir:
es herrschte
Lichtzwang.

WE LAY
deep in the maquis as you
crawled up at last.
Yet we could not
darken over to you:
the law was
Light-compulsion.

TODTNAUBERG

Arnika, Augentrost, der
Trunk aus dem Brunnen mit dem
Sternwürfel drauf,

in der
Hütte,

die in das Buch
— wessen Namen nahms auf
vor dem meinen? —,
die in dies Buch
geschriebene Zeile von
einer Hoffnung, heute,
auf eines Denkenden
(un-
gesäumt kommendes)
Wort
im Herzen,

Waldwasen, uneingeebnet,
Orchis und Orchis, einzeln,

Krudes, später, im Fahren,
deutlich,

der uns fährt, der Mensch,
der's mit anhört,

die halb-
beschrittenen Knüppel-
pfade im Hochmoor,

Feuchtes,
viel.

TODTNAUBERG

Arnica, Eyebright, the
drink from the well with the
star-die on top,

in the
hut,

into the book
— whose name did it take in
before mine? —
the line written into
this book about
a hope, today,
for a thinker's
(un-
delayed coming)
word
in the heart,

woodland turf, unleveled,
Orchis and Orchis, singly,

crudeness, later, while driving,
clearly,

the one driving us, the man
who hears it too,

the half-
trodden log-
paths on high moorland,

dampness,
much.

KLOPF die
Lichtkeile weg:

das schwimmende Wort
hat der Dämmer.

KNOCK the
light-wedges away:

the floating word
is dusk's.

FAHLSTIMMIG, aus
der Tiefe geschunden:
kein Wort, kein Ding,
und beider einziger Name,

fallgerecht in dir,
fluggerecht in dir,

wunder Gewinn
einer Welt.

WAN-VOICED,
flayed from the depths:
not a word, not a thing,
and of both the single name,

fall-fit in you,
flight-fit in you,

wound-wondrous gain
of a world.

SCHALTJAHRHUNDERTE, Schalt-
sekunden, Schalt-
geburten, novembernd, Schalt-
tode,

in Wabentrögen gespeichert,
bits
on chips,

das Menoragedicht aus Berlin,

(Unasyliert, un-
archiviert, un-
umfürsorgt? Am
Leben?),

Lesestationen im Spätwort,

Sparflammenpunkte
am Himmel,

Kammlinien unter Beschuss,

Gefühle, frost-
gespindelt,

Kaltstart —
mit Hämoglobin.

Leap-centuries, leap-
seconds, leap-
births, novembering, leap-
deaths,

hoarded in comb honey troughs,
bits
on chips,

the menorah poem from Berlin,

(Unasylumed, un-
archived, un-
cared for? A-
live?),

reading stations in the lateword,

pilot-light points
in the sky,

ridgelines under bombardment,

sensations, frost-
spindled,

cold start —
with hemoglobin.

DU SEI WIE DU, immer.

Stant up Jherosalem inde
erheyff dich

Auch wer das Band zerschnitt zu dir hin,

inde wirt
erluchtet

knüpfte es neu, in der Gehugnis,

Schlammbrocken schluckt ich, im Turm,

Sprache, Finster-Lisene,

kumi
ori.

YOU BE LIKE YOU, ever.

Ryse up Ierosalem and
rowse thyselfe

The very one who slashed the bond unto you,

and becum
yllumyned

knotted it new, in myndignesse,

spills of mire I swallowed, inside the tower,

speech, dark-selvedge,

kumi
ori.

WIRK NICHT VORAUS,
sende nicht aus,
steh
herein:

durchgründet vom Nichts,
ledig allen
Gebets,
feinfügig, nach
der Vor-Schrift,
unüberholbar,

nehm ich dich auf,
statt aller
Ruhe.

Do NOT WORK AHEAD,
do not send abroad,
stand
in here:

deep-grounded by Nothingness,
free of all
prayer,
fine-fitted to
the Pre-Script,
unoutstrippable,

you I take up
in place of all
rest.

SCHNEEPART

———

1971

Snow-part

DU LIEGST im grossen Gelausche,
umbuscht, umflockt.

Geh du zur Spree, geh zur Havel,
geh zu den Fleischerhaken,
zu den roten Äppelstaken
aus Schweden ---

Es kommt der Tisch mit den Gaben,
er biegt um ein Eden ---

Der Mann ward zum Sieb, die Frau
musste schwimmen, die Sau,
für sich, für keinen, für jeden ---

Der Landwehrkanal wird nicht rauschen.
Nichts
     stockt.

YOU LIE amid a great listening,
enbushed, enflaked.

Go to the Spree, to the Havel,
go to the meathooks,
the red apple stakes
from Sweden —

Here comes the gift table,
it turns around an Eden —

The man became a sieve, the Frau
had to swim, the sow,
for herself, for no one, for everyone —

The Landwehr Canal won't make a murmur.
Nothing
        stops.

Das angebrochene Jahr
mit dem modernden Kanten
Wahnbrot.

Trink
aus meinem Mund.

THE BROACHED YEAR
with its rotting crust of
madnessbread.

Drink
from my mouth.

UNLESBARKEIT dieser
Welt. Alles doppelt.

Die starken Uhren
geben der Spaltstunde recht,
heiser.

Du, in dein Tiefstes geklemmt,
entsteigst dir
für immer.

ILLEGIBLE this
world. Everything doubled.

Staunch clocks
confirm the split hour,
hoarsely.

You, clamped in your depths,
climb out of yourself
for ever.

ICH HÖRE, DIE AXT HAT GEBLÜHT,
ich höre, der Ort ist nicht nennbar,

ich höre, das Brot, das ihn ansieht,
heilt den Erhängten,
das Brot, das ihm die Frau buk,

ich höre, sie nennen das Leben
die einzige Zuflucht.

I HEAR, THE AXE HAS FLOWERED,
I hear, the place is not nameable,

I hear, the bread that looks at him
heals the hanged man,
the bread his wife baked him,

I hear, they call life
our only refuge.

DIE NACHZUSTOTTERNDE WELT,
bei der ich zu Gast
gewesen sein werde, ein Name,
herabgeschwitzt von der Mauer,
an der eine Wunde hochleckt.

WORLD TO BE STUTTERED AFTER,
in which I'll have been
a guest, a name
sweated down from the wall
where a wound licks up high.

ZUR NACHTORDNUNG Über-
gerittener, Über-
geschlitterter, Über-
gewitterter,

Un-
besungener, Un-
bezwungener, Un-
umwundener, vor
die Irrenzelte gepflanzter

seelenbärtiger, hagel-
äugiger Weisskies-
stotterer.

To NIGHT'S ORDER Over-
ridden, Over-
skidded, Over-
winded,

Un-
sung, un-
wrung, un-
wreathed, and
planted before straying tents

soul-bearded, hail-
eyed whitegravel
stutterer.

FÜR ERIC

Erleuchtet
rammt ein Gewissen
die hüben und drüben
gepestete Gleichung,

später als früh: früher
hält die Zeit sich die jähe
rebellische Waage,

ganz wie du, Sohn,
meine mit dir pfeilende
Hand.

FOR ERIC

Enlightened
a conscience rams through
the Plaguey leveling
on this side and that,

later than soon: sooner
time balances its rashly
rebellious scales,

just like you, son,
my hand arrowing
with you.

EIN BLATT, baumlos,
für Bertolt Brecht:

Was sind das für Zeiten,
wo ein Gespräch
beinah ein Verbrechen ist,
weil es soviel Gesagtes
mit einschliesst?

A LEAF, treeless,
for Bertolt Brecht:

What kind of times are these,
when a conversation
is well nigh a crime
because it includes
so much that is said?

EINKANTER: Rembrandt,
auf du und du mit dem Lichtschliff,
abgesonnen dem Stern
als Bartlocke, schläfig,

Handlinien queren die Stirn,
im Wüstengeschiebe, auf
den Tischfelsen
schimmert dir um den
rechten Mundwinkel der
sechzehnte Psalm.

IN-EDGER: Rembrandt,
intimate with polished light,
bemused by the star
as beardlock, templed,

handlines cross the forehead,
in desert boulders, on
the table-rocks
there glimmers at your
mouth's right corner the
sixteenth psalm.

LEUCHTSTÄBE, deren
Gespräch,
auf Verkehrsinseln,
mit endlich beurlaubten
Wappen-Genüssen,

Bedeutungen
grätschen im aufgerissenen Pflaster,

das Küken
Zeit, putt, putt, putt,
schlüpft in den Kraken-Nerv,
zur Behandlung,

ein Saugarm holt sich
den Jutesack voller
Beschlussmurmeln aus
dem ZK,

die Düngerrinne herauf und herunter
kommt Evidenz.

FLASHLIGHTS, their
palaver
on traffic islands,
with heraldry pleasures
furloughed at last,

meanings
astraddle the torn-up pavestones,

Time, a
chick — cluck cluck cluck —
slips into the octopus nerve
for a cure,

a tentacle clasps
the jute sack full of
decision-murmuring from
the CC,

evidence flows up and down
the dung chute.

ZEITGEHÖFT

1976

HOMESTEAD

OF TIME

Wanderstaude, du fängst dir
eine der Reden,

die abgeschworene Aster
stösst hier hinzu,

wenn einer, der
die Gesänge zerschlug,
jetzt spräche zum Stab,
seine und aller
Blendung
bliebe aus.

Wanderbush, you snare
one of the speeches,

the forsworn aster
thrusts up close,

if the one who
smashed the canticles
spoke now to his rod,
his and everyone's
blinding
would be gone.

MANDELNDE, die du nur halbsprachst,
doch durchzittert vom Keim her,
dich
liess ich warten,
dich.

Und war
noch nicht
entäugt,
noch unverdornt im Gestirn
des Lieds, das beginnt:
Hachnissini.

ALMONDING ONE, you half-spoke only,
though all trembled from the core,
you
I let wait,
you.

And was
not yet
eye-reft,
not yet enthorned in the realm
of the song that begins:
Hachnissini.

ES STAND
der Feigensplitter auf deiner Lippe,

es stand
Jerusalem um uns,

es stand
der Hellkiefernduft
überm Dänenschiff, dem wir dankten,

ich stand
in dir.

THERE STOOD
a splinter of fig on your lip,

there stood
Jerusalem around us,

there stood
the bright pine scent
above the Danish skiff we thanked,

I stood
in you.

DIE GLUT
zählt uns zusammen
im Eselsschrei vor
Absaloms Grab, auch hier,

Gethsemane, drüben,
das umgangene, wen
überhäufts?

Am nächsten der Tore tut sich nichts auf,

über dich, Offene, trag ich dich zu mir.

THE HEAT
counts us together
in the shriek of an ass at
Absalom's Tomb, here as well,

Gethsemane, yonder,
circled around, whom
does it overwhelm?

At the nearest gate nothing opens up,

through you, Open one, I bear you to me.

DAS LEUCHTEN, ja jenes, das
Abu Tor
auf uns zureiten sah, als wir
ineinander verwaisten, vor Leben,
nicht nur von den Handwurzeln her — :

eine Goldboje, aus
Tempeltiefen,
mass die Gefahr aus, die uns
still unterlag.

THAT SHINING, yes, the one that
Abu Tor
saw riding toward us, as we
orphaned into each other, with living,
our hands holding on from the roots — :

a goldbuoy, up from
Temple depths,
marked out the danger that fell
still beneath us.

DIE POSAUNENSTELLE
tief im glühenden
Leertext,
in Fackelhöhe,
im Zeitloch:

hör dich ein
mit dem Mund.

THE SHOFAR PLACE
deep in the glowing
text-void,
at torch height,
in the timehole:

hear deep in
with your mouth.

DIE POLE
sind in uns,
unübersteigbar
im Wachen,
wir schlafen hinüber, vors Tor
des Erbarmens,

ich verliere dich an dich, das
ist mein Schneetrost,

sag, dass Jerusalem i s t,

sags, als wäre ich dieses
dein Weiss,
als wärst du
meins,

als könnten wir ohne uns wir sein,

ich blättre dich auf, für immer,

du betest, du bettest
uns frei.

THE POLES
are within us,
insurmountable
while we're awake,
we sleep across, up to the Gate
of Mercy,

I lose you to you, that
is my snow-comfort,

say, that Jerusalem *is*,

say it, as if I were this
your whiteness,
as if you were
mine,

as if without us we could be we,

I leaf you open, for ever,

you pray, you lay
us free.

DER KÖNIGSWEG hinter der Scheintür,

das vom Gegen-
Zeichen umtodete
Löwenzeichen davor,

das Gestirn, kieloben,
umsumpft,

du, mit der
die Wunde auslotenden
Wimper.

THE KING'S WAY behind the false door,

in front, deathed
round by its counter-
sign, the Lion sign,

the star, keeled over,
beswamped,

you, with your
eyelash
fathoming the wound.

ICH TRINK WEIN aus zwei Gläsern
und zackere an
der Königszäsur
wie Jener
am Pindar,

Gott gibt die Stimmgabel ab
als einer der kleinen
Gerechten,

aus der Lostrommel fällt
unser Deut.

I DRINK WINE from two glasses
and plow away at
the king's caesura
like that one
at Pindar,

God turns in his tuning fork
as one among the least
of the Just,

the lottery drum spills
our two bits.

Es WIRD etwas sein, später,
das füllt sich mit dir
und hebt sich
an einen Mund

Aus dem zerscherbten
Wahn
steh ich auf
und seh meiner Hand zu,
wie sie den einen
einzigen
Kreis zieht

THERE WILL be something, later,
that brims full with you
and lifts up
toward a mouth

Out of a shardstrewn
craze
I stand up
and look upon my hand,
how it draws the one
and only
circle

DAS NICHTS, um unsrer
Namen willen
— sie sammeln uns ein —,
siegelt,

das Ende glaubt uns
den Anfang,

vor den uns
umschweigenden
Meistern,
im Ungeschiednen, bezeugt sich
die klamme
Helle.

NOTHINGNESS, for our
names' sake
— they gather us in — ,
sets a seal,

the end believes we're
the beginning,

in front of
masters
going silent around us,
in the Undivided, there testifies
a binding
brightness.

UMLICHTET die Keime,
die ich in dir
erschwamm,

freigerudert
die Namen — sie
befahren die Engen,

ein Segensspruch, vorn,
ballt sich
zur wetterfühligen
Faust.

CLEARLIT the seeds
I swam unto
in you,

rowed free
the names — they
ply the straits,

a blessing, ahead,
clenches
to a weather-skinned
fist.

KROKUS, vom gastlichen
Tisch aus gesehn:
zeichenfühliges
kleines Exil
einer gemeinsamen
Wahrheit,
du brauchst
jeden Halm.

CROCUS, spotted from a
hospitable table:
small sign-
sensing exile
of a common
truth,
you need
every blade.

REBLEUTE graben
die dunkelstündige Uhr um,
Tiefe um Tiefe,

du liest,

es fordert
der Unsichtbare den Wind
in die Schranken,

du liest,

die Offenen tragen
den Stein hinterm Aug,
der erkennt dich,
am Sabbath.

Vinegrowers dig up
the dark-houred clock,
deep upon deep,

you read,

the Invisible
summons the wind
into bounds,

you read,

the Open ones carry
the stone behind their eye,
it knows you,
come the Sabbath.

Uncollected
Poems

WOLFSBOHNE

... o

Ihr Blüten von Deutschland, o mein Herz wird
Untrügbarer Kristall, an dem
Das Licht sich prüfet, wenn   Deutschland
    Hölderlin, Vom Abgrund nämlich ...*

... wie an den Häusern der Juden (zum Andenken des ruinirten
Jerusalem's), immer etwas u n v o l l e n d e t gelassen werden muss ...
         Jean Paul, Das Kampaner Thal

Leg den Riegel vor: Es
sind Rosen im Haus.
Es sind
sieben Rosen im Haus.
Es ist
der Siebenleuchter im Haus.
Unser
Kind
weiss es und schläft.

(Weit, in Michailowka, in
der Ukraine, wo
sie mir Vater und Mutter erschlugen: was
blühte dort, was
blüht dort? Welche
Blume, Mutter,
tat dir dort weh
mit ihrem Namen?

Mutter, dir,
die du *Wolfsbohne* sagtest, nicht:
Lupine.

Gestern
kam einer von ihnen und

WOLFSBEAN

                                                     . . . Oh
        You flowers of Germany, oh my heart turns
        Unerring crystal, the
        Touchstone of light when   Germany
            Hölderlin, "Vom Abgrund nämlich . . ."

    . . . as in Jewish houses (recalling Jerusalem's destruction),
    something must always be left u n c o m p l e t e d . . .
                    Jean Paul, "Das Kampaner Thal"

Drive the bolt home: There
are roses in the house.
There are
seven roses in the house.
There is
a seven-arm candelabra in the house.
Our
child
knows this and sleeps.

(Far away, in Michailovka, in
the Ukraine, where
they murdered my father and mother: what
blossomed there, what
blossoms there? Which
flower, mother,
hurt you there
with its name?

You, mother,
who said *Wolfsbean*, not:
Lupine.

Yesterday
one of them came and

tötete dich
zum andern Mal in
meinem Gedicht.

Mutter.
Mutter, wessen
Hand hab ich gedrückt,
da ich mit deinen
Worten ging nach
Deutschland?

In Aussig, sagtest du immer, in
Aussig an
der Elbe,
auf
der Flucht.
Mutter, es wohnten dort
Mörder.

Mutter, ich habe
Briefe geschrieben.
Mutter, es kam keine Antwort.
Mutter, es kam eine Antwort.
Mutter, ich habe
Briefe geschrieben an —
Mutter, sie schreiben Gedichte.
Mutter, sie schrieben sie nicht,
wär das Gedicht nicht, das
ich geschrieben hab, um
deinetwillen, um
deines
Gottes
willen.
Gelobt, sprachst du, sei
der Ewige und
gepriesen, drei-

killed you
a second time in
my poem.

Mother.
Mother, whose
hand did I shake
when I went with
your words to
Germany?

At Aussig, you always said, at
Aussig on
the Elbe,
in
flight.
Mother, murderers
lived there.

Mother, I've
written letters.
Mother, no answer came.
Mother, one answer came.
Mother, I've
written letters to —
Mother, they write poems.
Mother, they wouldn't write them
unless the poem
I wrote were for
your sake, for
your
God's
sake.
Blessèd, you said, be
the Eternal and
praised, three

mal
Amen.

Mutter, sie schweigen.
Mutter, sie dulden es, dass
die Niedertracht mich verleumdet.
Mutter, keiner
fällt den Mördern ins Wort.

Mutter, sie schreiben Gedichte.
O
Mutter, wieviel
fremdester Acker trägt deine Frucht!
Trägt sie und nährt
die da töten!

Mutter, ich
bin verloren.
Mutter, wir
sind verloren.
Mutter, mein Kind, das
dir ähnlich sieht.)

Leg den Riegel vor: Es
sind Rosen im Haus.
Es sind
sieben Rosen im Haus.
Es ist
der Siebenleuchter im Haus.
Unser
Kind
weiss es und schläft.

times
Amen.

Mother, they're silent.
Mother, they suffer
vileness to slander me.
Mother, no one
cuts off the murderers' word.

Mother, they write poems.
Oh
mother, how much
alien soil bears your fruit!
Bears it and feeds
those killers there!

Mother, I
am lost.
Mother, we
are lost.
Mother, my child, who
looks like you.)

Drive the bolt home: There
are roses in the house.
There are
seven roses in the house.
There is
a seven-arm candelabra in the house.
Our
child
knows this and sleeps.

FÜLL DIE ÖDNIS in die Augensäcke,
den Opferruf, die Salzflut,

komm mit mir zu Atem
und drüber hinaus.

POUR THE WASTELAND into your eye-sacks,
the call to sacrifice, the salt flood,

come with me to Breath
and beyond.

SCHREIB DICH NICHT
zwischen die Welten,

komm auf gegen
der Bedeutungen Vielfalt,

vertrau der Tränenspur
und lerne leben.

Don't write yourself
in between worlds,

rise up against
multiple meanings,

trust the trail of tears
and learn to live.

GEDICHTZU, GEDICHTAUF:
hier fahren die Farben
zum schutzfremden,
freistirnigen
Juden.
Hier levitiert
der Schwerste.
Hier bin ich.

POEM-CLOSED, POEM-OPEN:
here come the colors
toward a non-defended
freely headed
Jew.
Here the heaviest Levi-
tates.
Here am I.

PROSE

Thinking and thanking in our language are words from one and the same source. Whoever follows out their meaning enters the semantic field of: "recollect," "bear in mind," "remembrance," "devotion." Permit me, from this standpoint, to thank you.

The landscape from which I—by what detours! but are there such things: detours?—the landscape from which I come to you might be unfamiliar to most of you. It is the landscape that was home to a not inconsiderable portion of those Hasidic tales that Martin Buber has retold for us all in German. It was, if I may add to this topographic sketch something that appears before my eyes now from very far away—it was a region in which human beings and books used to live. There in this former province of the Hapsburg monarchy, now fallen into historylessness, I first met the name of Rudolf Alexander Schröder: on reading Rudolf Borchardt's "Ode with Pomegranate." And there Bremen also took shape for me: in the form of publications by the Bremen Press.

Yet Bremen, brought nearer through books and the names of those who wrote books and published books, still had the ring of the unreachable.

What was reachable, if distant enough, what had to be reached was named Vienna. You know how it went then, for years, with this reachability.

Reachable, near and not lost, there remained in the midst of the losses this one thing: language.

It, the language, remained, not lost, yes in spite of everything. But it had to pass through its own answerlessness, pass through frightful muting, pass through the thousand darknesses of deathbringing speech. It passed through and gave back no words for that which happened; yet it passed through this happening. Passed through and could come to light again, "enriched" by all this.

In this language I have sought, during those years and the years since then, to write poems: so as to speak, to orient myself, to find out where I was and where I was meant to go, to sketch out reality for myself.

It was, as you see, event, movement, a being underway, it was an attempt to gain direction. And if I inquire into its meaning, I believe I must tell myself that this question also involves the question of the clockhand's direction.

For a poem is not timeless. Certainly it lays claim to infinity, it seeks to reach through time—through it, not above and beyond it.

A poem, as a manifestation of language and thus essentially dialogue, can be a message in a bottle, sent out in the—not always greatly hopeful—belief that somewhere and sometime it could wash up on land, on heartland perhaps. Poems in this sense too are underway: they are making toward something.

Toward what? Toward something standing open, occupiable, perhaps toward an addressable Thou, toward an addressable reality.

Such realities, I think, are at stake in a poem.

And I also believe that ways of thought like these attend not only my own efforts, but those of other lyric poets in the younger generation. They are the efforts of someone who, overarced by stars that are human handiwork, and who, shelterless in this till now undreamt-of sense and thus most uncannily in the open, goes with his very being to language, stricken by and seeking reality.

One evening when the sun, and not only that, had gone down, then there went walking, stepping out of his cottage went the Jew, the Jew and son of a Jew, and with him went his name, unspeakable, went and came, came shuffling along, made himself heard, came with his stick, came over the stone, do you hear me, you hear me, I'm the one, I, I and the one that you hear, that you think you hear, I and the other one—so he walked, you could hear it, went walking one evening when something had gone down, went beneath the clouds, went in the shadow, his own and alien—because a Jew, you know, now what has he got that really belongs to him, that's not borrowed, on loan and still owed—, so then he went and came, came down this road that's beautiful, that's incomparable, went walking like Lenz through the mountains, he, whom they let live down below where he belongs, in the lowland, he, the Jew, came and he came.

Came, yes, down this road, that's beautiful.

And who do you think came toward him? Toward him came his cousin, his kin and first cousin, older by a quarter of a Jew's lifetime, he came along big, he too came in his shadow, the borrowed one—because I'm asking you, I'm asking, who, if God's made him be a Jew, comes along with something his very own?—, came, came big, came toward the other one, Gross came up to Klein, and Klein, the Jew, bade his stick be silent in front of Jew Gross's stick.

So the stone was silent too, and it was quiet in the mountains where they walked, himself and that one.

So it was quiet, quiet, up there in the mountains. It wasn't quiet for long, because when one Jew comes along and meets another, then it's goodbye silence, even in the mountains. Because the Jew and Nature, that's two very different things, as always, even today, even here.

So there they stand, first cousins, on the left is Turk's-cap in bloom, blooming wild, blooming like nowhere, and on the right, there's some rampion, and Dianthus superbus, the superb pink, growing not far off. But them, the cousins, they've got, God help us, no eyes. More precisely: they've got eyes, even they do, but there's a veil hanging in front, not in front, no, behind, a movable veil; no sooner does an image go in than it catches a web, and right away there's a thread spinning there, it spins itself around the image, a thread in the veil; spins around the image and spawns a child with it, half image and half veil.

Poor Turk's-cap, poor rampion! There they stand, the cousins, standing on a road in the mountains, the stick is silent, the stone is silent, and the silence is no silence, no word's going mute and no phrase, it's merely a pause, it's a word-gap, it's a vacant space, you can see the syllables all standing around; tongue is what they are and mouth, these two, like before, and the veil is hanging in their eyes, and you, you poor things, you're not there and not blooming, you do not exist, and July is no July.

The babblers! They've got, even now, with their tongues bumping dumbly against their teeth and their lips going slack, something to say to each other! Alright, let them talk . . .

"A good ways you've come, you've come all the way here . . ."

"So I have. I've come like you."

"Don't I know it."

"You know it. You know and you see: Up here the earth has folded over, it's folded once and twice and three times, and opened up in the middle, and in the middle there's some water, and the water is green, and the green is white, and the white comes from up farther, comes from the glaciers, now you could say but you shouldn't, that that's the kind of speech that counts here, the green with the white in it, a language not for you and not for me—because I'm asking, who is it meant for then, the earth, it's not meant for you, I'm saying, and not for me—, well then, a language with no I and no Thou, pure He, pure It, d'you see, pure They, and nothing but that."

"I know, I know. Yes I've come a long way, I've come like you."

"I know."

"You know and still ask me: So you've come anyway, you've come here—why, and what for?"

"Why and what for . . . Because maybe I had to talk, to myself or to you, had to talk with my mouth and my tongue and not just with my stick. Because who does it talk to, the stick? It talks to the stone, and the stone—who does it talk to?"

"Who should it talk to, cousin? It doesn't talk, it speaks, and whoever speaks, cousin, talks to no one, he speaks, because no one hears him, no one and No-One, and then he says, he and not his mouth and not his tongue, he and only he says: D'you hear?"

"You hear, says he—I know, cousin, I know . . . You hear, he says, I'm there. I'm there, I'm here, I've come. Come with my stick, I and no other, I and not him, I with my hour, undeserved, I who was touched, I who was not touched, I with my memory, I feeble-memoried, I, I, I . . ."

"Says he, says he . . . You hear, he says . . . And HearestThou, of course, HearestThou, he says nothing, he doesn't answer, because HearestThou, that's the one with the glaciers, the one who folded himself over, three times, and not for humans . . . The Green-and-White there, the one with the Turk's-cap, the one with the rampion . . . But I, cousin, I, I'm standing here, here on this road I don't belong on, today, now, when it's gone down, it and its light, I here with my shadow, my own and alien, I—I, I who can say to you:

—On the stone is where I lay, back then, you know, on the stone slabs; and next to me, they were lying there, the others, who were like me, the others, who were different from me and just the same, the cousins; and they lay there and slept, slept and did not sleep, and they dreamt and did not dream, and they did not love me and I did not love them, because I was just one, and who wants to love just one, and they were many, even more than those lying around me, and who wants to go and love all of them, and—I won't hide it from you—I didn't love them, those who could not love me, I loved the candle that was burning there, to the left in the corner, I loved it because it was burning down, not because *it* was burning down, for *it* was really *his* candle, the candle that he, the father of our mothers, had kindled, because on that evening a day began, a certain one, a day that was the seventh, the seventh, on which the first was to follow, the seventh and not the last, I loved, cousin, not it, I loved its burning down, and you know, I've loved nothing more since then;

nothing, no; or maybe what was burning down like that candle on that day, the seventh and not the last; not the last, no, because after all here I am, here, on this road which they say is beautiful, well I'm near the Turk's-cap and the rampion, and a hundred yards farther, over there, where I can go, the larch climbs up to the stone-pine, I see it, I see it and don't see it, and my stick, it spoke to the stone, and my stick, it's keeping silent now, and the stone, you say, can speak, and in my eye the veil is hanging, the movable one, the veils are hanging, the movable ones, you lift one and the second's already hanging there, and the star— oh yes, it's above the mountains now—, if it wants to go in, it will have to get married and soon not be itself anymore, but half veil and half star, and I know, I know, cousin, I know, I met you, here, and we've talked, a lot, and the folds there, you know, for humans they're not and not for us, who went walking and came on each other, we here under the star, we, the Jews who came here, like Lenz, through the mountains, you Gross and me Klein, you, the babbler, and me, the babbler, we with our sticks, we with our names, unspeakable, we with our shadow, our own and alien, you here and I here—

—I here, I; I, who can say, could have said, all that to you; who don't say and haven't said it to you; I with the Turk's-cap on the left, I with the rampion, I with what burned down, the candle, I with the day, I with the days, I here and I there, I, companioned perhaps—now!—by the love of those not loved, I on the way to myself, up here."

SPEECH ON THE OCCASION OF THE AWARD
OF THE GEORG BÜCHNER PRIZE

Ladies and Gentlemen!

Art, you will recall, is a puppet-like, iambic, five-footed and—mythology confirms this in the reference to Pygmalion and his creature—a childless being.

In this guise art forms the subject of a conversation that takes place in a room, not in the Conciergerie prison, a conversation that could go on endlessly, we feel, if nothing intervened.

Something does intervene.

Art returns. It returns in another work by Georg Büchner, in *Woyzeck*, among other, nameless people and—if I may bring in a phrase coined by Moritz Heimann about *Danton's Death*—in "a thunderstorm's more livid light." The very same art, even in this wholly different age, turns up again, presented by a carnival barker, not linked to the "glowing," "surging," "glittering" creation in that conversation, but alongside the creature and the nada this creature "has on"—art appears this time in the shape of a monkey, but it's the same, we recognize it right away by the "coat and trousers."

And it also comes to us, does art, in a third work of Büchner's, in *Leonce and Lena*. Here time and lighting are not recognizable, we're "on the flight to paradise," "all clocks and calendars" are soon to be "smashed" or "prohibited"—but shortly before this, "two persons, one of each sex," are produced, "two world-renowned robots have arrived," and a man proclaiming himself "perhaps the third and most remarkable of them all" challenges us "in a rasping tone" to marvel at what's before our eyes: "Nothing but art and mechanism, nothing but pasteboard and watch springs."

Art appears here with a larger entourage than before, but visibly among its own kind: it is the same art, the art we already know.—Valerio is just another name for the barker.

Art, ladies and gentlemen, with everything belonging and still to be added to it, is also a problem, indeed an elusive one, tough and long-lived, which is to say eternal.

A problem that allows someone mortal, Camille, and someone understandable only through his death, Danton, to string words onto words. It feels good to talk about art.

But when the talk concerns art, there's always someone who is present and . . . not really listening.

More precisely: someone who hears and listens and looks . . . and then doesn't know what the talk was about. But who hears the speaker, "sees him speak," perceives language and form and, at the same time—who could doubt it, here in the realm of this work—at the same time perceives Breath as well, that is, direction and destiny.

This someone, as you've realized, who is quoted so often and not at all by chance, coming before you in every new year—this someone is Lucile.

What intervened during the conversation pushes heedlessly on, it arrives with us at the Place de la Révolution, "the carts are driven up and stop."

The passengers are there, in full force, Danton, Camille, the others. Even here they all find words, artful words, and put them to good use, they talk of a communal "going-to-our-death" and here Büchner need only quote, Fabre wants to be able to die "twice over," everyone is at his best,—only some voices, "a few"—nameless—"voices" observe that this has all "happened before" and is "tedious."

And here, where everything comes to its end, in longlasting moments as Camille—no, not him, not really him but a co-traveler—, as this Camille theatrically, one might almost say iambically, dies a death that, two scenes later, we only then discern as his own, through a word that's strange to him yet so close; as all around Camille, pathos and proverbialism confirm the triumph of "puppet" and "wire," here comes Lucile, blind to art, the same Lucile for whom language is something personal and perceptible, once again with her sudden "Long live the King!"

After all those words uttered on the rostrum (it's the scaffold)—
what a word!

It is a counter-word, a word that snaps the "wire," a word that no
longer bows to "history's loiterers and parade-horses," it is an act of
freedom. It is a step.

Certainly this sounds—and in view of what I'm venturing to say about
it now, today, there may be no coincidence—this sounds at first like a
profession of faith in the "ancien régime."

But here—you'll allow someone who grew up with the writings of
Peter Kropotkin and Gustav Landauer to stress this explicitly—here
there's no homage to monarchy or to any so preservable Yesterday.

Homage here is to the Majesty of the Absurd, testifying to human
presence.

And that, ladies and gentlemen, has no fixed name once and for all
time, yet it is, I believe . . . poetry.

"—alas, Art!" I'm caught, you see, on this word of Camille's.

I'm fully aware we can read this word one way or another, give it differing accents: the acute of the contemporary, the *grave* accent of history (and literary history too), the circumflex—marking length—of
the eternal.

I give it—there's no other choice left me—, I give it the acute.

Art—"alas, Art": besides its ability to transmute, it has the gift of ubiq-
uity: it can be found in *Lenz* as well, here too—I allow myself to stress
this—as in *Danton's Death*, an episode.

"At table Lenz was again in good spirits: they talked about literature, he
was on his home turf . . ."

" . . . The feeling that what's been created possesses life outweighs
both of these and is the sole criterion in matters of art . . ."

Here I've extracted only two sentences, my bad conscience over the
grave accent forbids my not calling your attention to this right away,—

this passage touches on literary history above all, we must read it together with the conversation from *Danton's Death* cited above, here Büchner's aesthetic finds expression, from here, leaving Büchner's *Lenz* fragment behind, we get to Reinhold Lenz, author of "Notes on Theater," and through him, the historical Lenz, further back to Mercier's "Elargissez l'Art," literarily so fruitful, this passage opens vistas, anticipating Naturalism, Gerhart Hauptmann, here the social and political roots of Büchner's work are to be sought and found.

Ladies and gentlemen, that I don't let this go unmentioned eases my conscience, if only temporarily, but at the same time it also shows you, and thus troubles my conscience afresh,—it shows you I can't free my mind of something that seems linked to art.

I am seeking it here too, in *Lenz*—I'll permit myself to call it to your attention.

Lenz, that is, Büchner, has—"alas, Art"—scornful words for "Idealism" and its "wooden puppets." He sets them off, and here those unforgettable lines on the "life of the humblest" occur, the "quiverings," the "intimations," the "subtle, scarcely discernible play of the features,"—he sets them off against what is natural and creaturely. And this concept of art he illustrates by means of an experience:

"Yesterday, as I was walking up along the valley rim, I saw two girls sitting on a rock: one was doing up her hair, the other helping her; and the golden hair hung down, and the pale serious face, yet so young, and the black dress, and the other girl taking such pains. The Old German School's finest, most intimate pictures can scarcely give an idea of it. At times one might wish to be a Medusa's head, so as to turn such a group into stone and call people over."

Ladies and gentlemen, please take note: "One might wish to be a Medusa's head," so as to . . . grasp the natural as natural by means of art!

One might wish to, it says, not: *I* might.

This means stepping out of what is human, betaking oneself to a realm that is uncanny yet turned toward what's human—the same realm where the monkey, the robots and thereby . . . alas, art too seems to be at home.

This is not the historical Lenz speaking, but Büchner's, here it's Büchner's voice we've heard, here too: art for him retains something uncanny.

Ladies and gentlemen, I have put on the acute accent; I would not deceive you any more than myself, that with my question about art and poetry—one among many questions—that with this question I must have gone to Büchner of my own (if not my free) will, to seek out his question.

But as you can see: Valerio's "rasping tone," whenever art comes forth, cannot be missed.

Probably these are—Büchner's voice forces me to this conjecture—among the oldest forms of the uncanny. That I dwell on them so stubbornly today has likely to do with the air—the air we have to breathe.

Isn't there, I must now ask, in Georg Büchner, the poet of the creature, an only half spoken, perhaps, only half conscious but no less radical—or for that very reason in the most literal sense a radical calling-into-question of art, a calling-into-question from this direction? A calling-into-question that all poetry today must come back to, if it wants to go on questioning? In other words (to leap ahead a little): May we, as happens in many places nowadays, proceed from art as from something already given and implicitly assumed, should we, to put it bluntly, above all—let's say—be thinking Mallarmé through to the end?

I've reached ahead, reached beyond—not far enough, I know—, I'll get back to Büchner's *Lenz*, to that (episodic) conversation carried on "at table" when Lenz "was in good spirits."

Lenz talked a long time, "now smiling, now serious." And now, with the conversation over, it's said about him—that is, about the one concerned with questions of art, but likewise about Lenz the artist: "He had quite forgotten himself."

I think of Lucile when I read that. I read: *He*, he himself.

Whoever keeps art before his eyes and in his mind—here I'm thinking of *Lenz*—has forgotten himself. Art creates I-distantness. Art in a certain direction demands a certain distance, a certain path.

And poetry? Poetry, which still has to take the path of art? Then we'd really have the path to the Medusa's head and the robot.

Now I am not seeking a way out, I'm only questioning further, in the same direction and also, I believe, in the direction of the *Lenz* fragment.

Perhaps—I'm only asking—perhaps poetry, like art, is going with a self-forgotten I toward the uncanny and the strange, and is again—but where? but in what place? but with what? but as what?—setting itself free?

Then art would be the distance poetry must cover—no less, no more.

I know, there are other shorter paths. But poetry too hurries ahead of us at times. La poésie, elle aussi, brûle nos étapes.

I shall leave the self-forgotten man, concerned with art, the artist. I believe I have encountered poetry in Lucile, and Lucile perceives language as form and direction and breath—: I'm seeking the same thing here in this work of Büchner's, I seek Lenz himself, seek him—as a person, I seek his form: for the sake of poetry's place, for the setting free, for the step.

Büchner's Lenz, ladies and gentlemen, remained a fragment. Should we seek out the historical Lenz, to learn what direction this existence had?

"His existence was an urgent burden for him.—So he lived on . . ." Here the story breaks off.

But poetry, like Lucile, does attempt to see the direction form takes, poetry hurries ahead. We know *where* he lives on, how he lives *on*.

"Death," we read in a 1909 book on Jakob Michael Reinhold Lenz published in Leipzig—it comes from the pen of a Moscow lecturer by the name of M. N. Rosanow—"Death the Redeemer did not make him wait long. The night of 23–24 May 1792, Lenz was found lifeless in a

Moscow street. A nobleman paid for his burial. His final resting place remains unknown."

So *he* had lived *on*.

He: the true Lenz, Büchner's, Büchner's figure, the person we perceived on the story's first page, the Lenz who "went walking in the mountains on the 20th of January," he—not the artist and one concerned with questions of art, but he as an I.

Will we now perhaps find the place where the strangeness was, the place where a person was able to set himself free as an—estranged—I? Will we find such a place, such a step?

". . . only it sometimes troubled him that he could not walk on his head."—That is him, Lenz. That is, I believe, him and his step, him and his "Long live the King."

". . . only it sometimes troubled him that he could not walk on his head."

Whoever walks on his head, ladies and gentlemen, whoever walks on his head has heaven as an abyss beneath him.

Ladies and gentlemen, nowadays it's common to blame poetry for its "obscurity."—Allow me here, abruptly—but hasn't something suddenly come open?—allow me to cite a phrase of Pascal's, a phrase I read a little while ago in Leo Shestov: "Ne nous reprochez pas le manque de clarté puisque nous en faisons profession!" That obscurity is, I believe, if not congenital, then the obscurity associated with poetry for the sake of an encounter, by a perhaps self-devised distance or strangeness.

But perhaps, in one and the same direction, there are two kinds of strangeness—chockablock.

Lenz—that is, Büchner—has gone one step further than Lucile. His "Long live the King" is no longer words, it is a frightful falling silent, it takes away his—also our—breath and word.

Poetry: that can signify an *Atemwende*, a Breathturn. Who knows, perhaps poetry follows its path—also the path of art—for the sake of such a breathturn? Perhaps, since strangeness—the abyss *and* the Medusa's head, the abyss *and* the robots—seems to lie in a single direction, perhaps poetry here succeeds in telling strangeness from strangeness, perhaps right here the Medusa's head shrinks, perhaps right here the robots break down—for this unique brief moment? Perhaps here, with the I—the estranged I set free *here* and *in such wise*—here perhaps yet some Other becomes free?

Perhaps from here on the poem is itself . . . and in this art-less, art-free way can now follow its other paths, including the paths of art—again and again?

Perhaps.

Perhaps we may say that every poem has its "20th of January" inscribed? Perhaps what's new for poems written today is just this: that here the attempt is clearest to remain mindful of such dates?

But don't we all date from such dates? And what dates do we ascribe ourselves to?

Yet the poem does speak! It remains mindful of its dates, yet—it speaks. Indeed it speaks only in its very selfmost cause.

But I think—and now this thought can hardly surprise you—I think a hope of poems has always been to speak in just this way in the cause of the *strange*—no, I can't use this word anymore—in just this way to speak *in the cause of an Other*—who knows, perhaps in the cause of a *wholly Other.*

This "who knows" I see I've now arrived at is the only thing I can add, for myself, today and here, to the old hopes.

Perhaps, I must tell myself now—perhaps even a meeting between this "wholly Other"—I'm using a familiar term here—and a not all that distant, a quite near "other" becomes thinkable—thinkable again and again.

A poem's lingerings or longings—a word related to the creature—touch such thoughts.

No one can say how long the breath-pause—the longing and the thought—will last. "Speed," which was always "outside," has gained speed; a poem knows this; but it makes straight for that "Other" which it deems reachable, free-able, perhaps empty and thus turned—let's say, like Lucile—toward it, toward the poem.

Certainly the poem, the poem today shows—and this I think has only indirectly to do with not-to-be-underestimated difficulties of word choice, with the sharper fall of syntax or heightened sense of ellipsis—the poem unmistakably shows a strong bent toward falling silent.

It holds on—after so many extreme formulations, allow me this one too—the poem holds on at the edge of itself; so as to exist, it ceaselessly calls and hauls itself from its Now-no-more back into its Ever-yet.

But this Ever-yet could be only an act of speaking. Not simply language and probably not just verbal "correspondence" either.

But actualized language, set free under the sign of a radical individuation, which at the same time stays mindful of the limits drawn by language, the possibilities opened by language.

This Ever-yet of poems can only be found in a poem by someone who does not forget that he speaks from the angle of inclination of his very being, his creatureliness.

Then a poem would be—even more clearly than before—the language-become-form of a single person and, following its inmost nature, presentness and presence.

The poem is lonely. It is lonely and underway. Whoever writes one stays mated with it.

But in just this way doesn't the poem stand, right here, in an encounter—*in the mystery of an encounter?*

The poem wants to reach an Other, it needs this Other, it needs an Over-against. It seeks it out, speaks toward it.

For the poem making toward an Other, each thing, each human being is a form of this Other.

The attentiveness a poem devotes to all it encounters, with its sharper sense of detail, outline, structure, color, but also of "quiverings" and "intimations"—all this, I think, is not attained by an eye vying (or conniving) with constantly more perfect instruments. Rather, it is a concentration that stays mindful of all our dates.

"Attentiveness"—allow me here to quote a saying by Malebranche from Walter Benjamin's Kafka essay—"Attentiveness is the natural prayer of the soul."

A poem—under what conditions!—becomes the poem of someone (ever yet) perceiving, facing phenomena, questioning and addressing these phenomena; it becomes conversation—often despairing conversation.

What is addressed takes shape only in the space of this conversation, gathers around the I addressing and naming it. But what's addressed and is now become a Thou through naming, as it were, also brings along its otherness into this present. Even in a poem's here and now— the poem itself really has only this one, unique, momentary present— even in this immediacy and nearness it lets the Other's ownmost quality speak: its time.

When we speak with things this way, we are always dealing with the question of their Whence and Whither: with a question "staying open," "coming to no end," pointing into the open and void and free—we are far outside.

A poem, I believe, is searching for this place too.

A poem?

A poem with its images and tropes?

Ladies and gentlemen, what am I really speaking about when I speak from *this* direction, in *this* direction, with *these* words about a poem— no, about *the* poem?

I am speaking about a poem that does not exist!

The absolute poem—no, that certainly doesn't exist, that can't exist!

But there is, with every real poem, with the most undemanding poem, there is this unavoidable question, this unheard-of demand.

And then what would the images be?

Something perceived and to be perceived only now and only here, once, again and again once. And so a poem would be the place where all tropes and metaphors will be carried ad absurdum.

Topos research?
By all means! But in light of what's to be explored: in light of U-topia.
And human beings? And creatures?
In this light.

What questions! What demands!
It is time to turn back.

Ladies and gentlemen, I am at the end—I am back at the beginning.
Élargissez l'Art! With its old, with its new uncanniness, this question steps up to us. I went toward Büchner with it—I thought to find it there again.
I even had an answer ready, a "Lucilesque" counter-word, I wanted to set something opposite, to be there with my contradiction:
Enlarge art?
No. But with art go into your very selfmost straits. And set yourself free.
Here too, in your presence, I've taken this path. It was a circle.
Art, thus also the Medusa's head, the mechanism, the robots, the uncanny strangeness so hard to tell apart, in the end perhaps really only *one* strangeness—art lives on.

Twice, with Lucile's "Long live the King" and when heaven as an abyss opened under Lenz, the *Atemwende* seemed to be there, the Breathturn. Perhaps also when I tried to make toward that occupiable distance which finally became visible only in the figure of Lucile. And once, given the attentiveness devoted to things and creatures, we even got near something open and free. And at last near utopia.

Poetry, ladies and gentlemen—: this speaking endlessly of mere mortality and uselessness!

Ladies and gentlemen, allow me once again, since I'm back at the beginning, to ask the same thing as briefly as possible and from another direction.

Ladies and gentlemen, several years ago I wrote a little quatrain—this is it:

"Voices from the nettle path: / *Come on your hands to us.* / Whoever is alone with the lamp / has only his hand to read from."

And a year ago, in memory of a failed encounter in the Engadin, I set down a little story in which I had a man "like Lenz" walk through the mountains.

In both instances I'd begun writing from a "20th of January," from my "20th of January."

It was . . . myself I encountered.

Then does one, in thinking of poems, does one walk such paths with poems? Are these paths only by-paths, bypaths from thou to thou? Yet at the same time, among how many other paths, they're also paths on which language gets a voice, they are encounters, paths of a voice to a perceiving Thou, creaturely paths, sketches of existence perhaps, a sending oneself ahead toward oneself, in search of oneself . . . A kind of homecoming.

Ladies and gentlemen, I am coming to the end—with the acute accent I had to use, I'm coming to the end of . . . *Leonce and Lena.*

And here, with the last two words of this work, I must take care.

I must guard myself, like Karl Emil Franzos, the editor of that "First Complete Critical Edition of Georg Büchner's Collected Works and Posthumous Manuscripts," published by Sauerländer eighty-one years ago in Frankfurt am Main—I must guard against reading—*like my countryman Karl Emil Franzos whom I've rediscovered here*—the word "accommodating," which is accepted today, as if it were "coming"!

And yet: Doesn't *Leonce and Lena* itself have quotation marks smiling invisibly around the words? Quotation marks to be understood not as goose feet, perhaps, but rather as rabbit ears, not unanxiously listening out beyond themselves and the words?

From this standpoint, from "accommodating," though also in light of utopia, I'll now undertake topos research.

I am seeking the region that Reinhold Lenz and Karl Emil Franzos come from, whom I encountered on my path here and via Georg Büchner. I also seek—for I'm back again where I began—the place of my own origin.

I am seeking all of that with an inexact because uneasy finger on the map—on a children's map, I must admit.

None of these places is to be found, they do not exist, but I know where, especially now, they would have to exist, and . . . I find something!

Ladies and gentlemen, I find something that comforts me a little at having taken, in your presence, this impossible path, this path of the impossible.

I find something that binds and that leads to encounter, like a poem.

I find something—like language—immaterial yet earthly, terrestrial, something circular, returning upon itself by way of both poles and thereby—happily—even crossing the tropics (and tropes): I find . . . a *meridian*.

With you and Georg Büchner and the State of Hesse I believe I've just touched it again.

Ladies and gentlemen, a high honor has been conferred on me today. I shall be able to remember that along with people whose person and work mean an encounter for me, I am the bearer of a prize that commemorates Georg Büchner.

I give you heartfelt thanks for this distinction, heartfelt thanks for this moment and this encounter.

I thank the State of Hesse. I thank the city of Darmstadt. I thank the German Academy of Language and Literature.

I thank the President of the German Academy of Language and Literature, I thank you, my dear Hermann Kasack.

My dear Marie Luise Kaschnitz, I thank you.

Ladies and gentlemen, I thank you for your presence.

I have come to you in Israel because I needed to.

As seldom with such a feeling, I have the strongest sense, after all I've seen and heard, of having done the right thing—not just for me alone, I hope.

I think I have a notion of what Jewish loneliness can be, and I recognize as well, among so many things, a thankful pride in every green thing planted here that's ready to refresh anyone who comes by; just as I take joy in every newly earned, self-discovered, fulfilled word that rushes up to strengthen those who turn toward it—I take that joy in these times of growing self-alienation and mass conformity everywhere. And I find here, in this outward and inward landscape, much of the force for truth, the self-evidentness, and the world-open uniqueness of great poetry. And I believe I've been conversing with those who are calmly, confidently determined to stand firm in what is human.

I am thankful for all that, and I thank you.

NOTES

11 NEARNESS OF GRAVES

Bug River in western Ukraine where Celan's parents were deported in 1942

15 BLACK FLAKES

Ya'akov Jacob, father of the twelve tribes of Israel
Hetman "headman," the Ukrainian Cossack Khmelnitsky, whose massacres in 1648 decimated east European Jewry
Song of the Cedar Anthem of the First Zionist Congress (1897)

19 A SONG IN THE WILDERNESS

Akra Citadel overlooking Jerusalem's Temple Mount, built by Greek tyrant Antiochus

31 DEATHFUGUE

Margareta Faust's beloved in Goethe's drama
Shulamith Hebrew maiden in Song of Songs (the German is *Sulamith*)

57 EPITAPH FOR FRANÇOIS

The Celans' firstborn son, who died shortly after birth

73 IN MEMORIAM PAUL ÉLUARD

In 1950 a Czech Stalinist tribunal condemned Zavis Kalandra, surrealist poet and survivor of Nazi camps. Éluard, who had known Kalandra, was asked to intercede but did not. Kalandra died.

75 SHIBBOLETH

Shibboleth Tribal password used by Gileadites against Ephraimites, who could not pronounce it correctly (Judges 12:4)
Vienna and Madrid Refers to February 1934 Viennese workers' uprising and February 1936, when Spain's Popular Front was elected
No pasaran "They shall not pass": rallying cry of the Republicans in Spanish Civil War (Celan does not use the accent on *pasarán*)
Einhorn Celan's boyhood friend; they supported the Republican cause
Estremadura Spanish province where hard fighting occurred during the Civil War

79 ARGUMENTUM E SILENTIO

Latin: "Argument from silence," the attempt to prove someone's view of a matter by the fact that they do not discuss it

103 TENEBRAE

During the Tenebrae service, in Catholic Holy Week, candles extinguished one by one symbolize the Crucifixion. Cf. Matthew 27.45: *Tenebrae factae sunt*, "there was darkness all over the earth"

105 FLOWER

Fleur (French: "flower") was the Celans' son's first word

109 MATIÈRE DE BRETAGNE

French: "Matter of Brittany," a literary cycle of the Arthurian legends

119 STRETTO

In a fugue, "stretto" denotes intensely overlapping theme entrances. German *Engführung* literally means a "leading narrowly" or "into the straits"

141 ZURICH, AT THE STORK

Zurich hotel where Celan met Nelly Sachs in 1960

Minster Church situated across the Limmat River from the hotel

151 THE SLUICE

Kaddish Aramaic: "Holy"—the Jewish prayer for the dead

Yizkor Hebrew: "May He remember"—Jewish memorial service

159 TÜBINGEN, JANUARY

"a riddle . . ." Cited from the Romantic poet Friedrich Hölderlin's Rhine hymn

Pallaksch A word that Hölderlin, spending his last years in the home of a Tübingen carpenter, was given to uttering in his dementia; it could signify Yes or No.

161 A ROGUES' AND GONIFS' DITTY

Paris emprès Pontoise From a sardonic quatrain by François Villon, reversing the priority of metropolis and nearby town, as in **Czernowitz near Sadagora**

Friuli Region of northeastern Italy, appropriated by German Emperor Maximilian

167 RADIX, MATRIX

Radix Latin: "root"; **matrix** Latin: "womb"

171 TO ONE WHO STOOD BEFORE THE DOOR

Rabbi Loew Sixteenth-century Prague Kabbalist rabbi, said to have fashioned a golem out of clay

173 MANDORLA

Mandorla Italian "almond," designates an oval aureole around paintings of Jesus or Mary

175 BENEDICTA

Tsu ken men . . . "So will you go up into heaven one day, / And question your God should it all be this way?"
Pneuma Greek: "wind," "breath," "spirit"—as in Hebrew *ruach*
's muz azoy zayn Yiddish: "it must be this way"
Ge- / *bentscht* Yiddish: "blessed"

181 HAVDALAH

Havdalah Hebrew: "difference"—closing ritual dividing the Sabbath from the secular week

189 IN ONE

Peuple / de Paris French: "People of Paris"
Shibboleth, No pasarán See note to page 75
"Aurora" Ship that participated in 1917 Russian revolution
Petropolis The name Osip Mandelshtam used for Saint Petersburg
Tuscanly Mandelshtam revered Dante and is said to have recited Petrarch as a prisoner in Siberia
Peace to the cottages Motto from French Revolution, adopted by Georg Büchner in "Der Hessische Landbote"

191 CROWNED OUT

Varsovienne Nineteenth-century Polish workers' song

197 TABERNACLE WINDOW

Vitebsk Marc Chagall's Russian birthplace
Aleph First letter in Hebrew alphabet
Yud Letter that begins the Hebrew word for "Jew"

Beth Hebrew alphabet's second letter, which means "house"—also first letter of the Bible

205　IT'S ALL DIFFERENT

Tekiah Hebrew: "blast"—ceremonial shofar call at the New Year

Three Year Land Celan's mother fled to Bohemia during World War I

Normandy-Niemen The Niemen River is in east Prussia. From his Normandy farmhouse, Celan wrote: "quite near here we recently saw a film on the Normandy-Niemen squadron, which helped in crushing Nazism."

Alba Latin: "white" or "dawn," and the name for the Elbe River

235　TEMPLE-PINCERS

Celan underwent shock therapy in periods of illness

259　IN PRAGUE

Hradčany Prague castle above the Alchemists Lane, where Kafka did his writing

counter time Prague's Jewish Town Hall has a clock with hours numbered in Hebrew letters going counterclockwise

261　ASH-AUREOLE

Pontic Referring to the Black Sea, near where Celan vacationed in 1947

269　SOLVE

The Latin title is an alchemical term: "dissolve"

271　COAGULA

The Latin title is also an alchemical term

Rosa In 1917 the revolutionary Rosa Luxemburg wrote from prison of seeing Romanian water buffaloes brutally beaten by German soldiers

275　SHOW-FRINGES, SENSE-FRINGES

German term referring to tallit, fringed Jewish prayer shawl

285　FRANKFURT, SEPTEMBER

The Frankfurt Book Fair takes place in September; S. Fischer Verlag published Freud and Kafka as well as Celan

"For the last / time . . ." A remark from Kafka

jackdaw *kavka* means "jackdaw" in Czech
Kafka died of tuberculosis of the larynx; his last story was "Josephine the Singer"

295 WHEN I DON'T KNOW, DON'T KNOW
Aschrei Hebrew: "happy," "blessed"—occurs in the Psalms, and opens a familiar prayer
Carpathian Mountain range near Bukovina

303 NEAR, IN THE AORTA'S ARCH
Ziv Hebrew for divine effulgence, a term from Judaic mysticism

307 JUST THINK
Peat-Bog Soldier Cites a 1930s protest song from the Nazi camps
Masada Ancient fortress above the Dead Sea, where Jewish zealots resisted a Roman siege and took their own lives rather than surrender

315 TODTNAUBERG
The poem's title names Martin Heidegger's mountain retreat

323 YOU BE LIKE YOU
Lines 2–3 and 5–6 cite the medieval German of theologian Meister Eckhart, referring to Isaiah
myndignesse Early Middle English: "mindedness," the faculty of memory; cf. German *Gehugnis*, an archaic term for "memory"
kumi ori Hebrew: "arise, shine" (Isaiah 60.1)

329 YOU LIE
Spree, Havel The Spree River flows through Berlin and joins the Havel
Eden Luxury apartments built on the Berlin site where in 1919 Rosa Luxemburg and Karl Liebknecht were assassinated

341 FOR ERIC
Celan's son (b. 1955), with him during the May 1968 Paris uprising

343 A LEAF
Refers to Bertolt Brecht's lines: "What kind of times are these, when / A conversation about trees is almost a crime / Because it omits so many horrors?"

347 FLASHLIGHTS

CC (Communist) Central Committee; the German acronym ZK, reversed, makes KZ, "concentration camp." This poem dates from August 1968, the Soviet invasion of Czechoslovakia

353 ALMONDING ONE

Hachnissini Hebrew: "Bring me in," which opens a 1905 lyric by Chaim Nachman Bialik

355 THERE STOOD

Danish skiff A Jerusalem monument commemorates the Danes' 1943 rescue, in small boats to Sweden, of their Jewish population

357 THE HEAT

nearest gate The Messiah is supposed to enter through the walled-up Gate of Mercy, near Absalom's Tomb

359 THAT SHINING

Abu Tor Jewish-Arab neighborhood outside Jerusalem's walls, overlooking the No Man's Land of Israel's 1948 war—in ancient times, the hell of Gehenna

367 I DRINK WINE

Pindar The Romantic poet Friedrich Hölderlin, in his dementia, translated Pindar's fragments

381 WOLFSBEAN

Aussig In Bohemia; see note to 205 IT'S ALL DIFFERENT

397 CONVERSATION IN THE MOUNTAINS

Gross, Klein German: "big," "little"

Material on Paul Celan can be found in the following books: Ulrich Baer, *Remnants of Song: Trauma and the Experience of Modernity in Charles Baudelaire and Paul Celan* (2000); Haskell M. Block, ed., *The Poetry of Paul Celan* (1991); *Paul Celan, Nelly Sachs: Correspondence* (1995); Israel Chalfen, *Paul Celan: A Biography of His Youth* (1991); Amy Colin, *Paul Celan: Holograms of Darkness* (1991); Adrian Del Caro, *The Early Poetry of Paul Celan* (1997); John Felstiner, *Paul Celan: Poet, Survivor, Jew* (1995); Aris Fioretos, ed., *Word Traces: Readings of Paul Celan* (1994); Jerry Glenn, *Paul Celan* (1973); Bianca Rosenthal, *Pathways to Paul Celan* (1995); Clarise Samuels, *Holocaust Visions: Surrealism and Existentialism in the Poetry of Paul Celan* (1993); Shira Wolosky, *Language Mysticism: The Negative Way of Language in Eliot, Beckett, and Celan* (1995).

ENGLISH INDEX OF TITLES AND FIRST LINES

425

CPSIA information can be obtained
at www.ICGtesting.com
Printed in the USA
BVHW042013210723
667625BV00001B/19

THE POLITICAL MOBILIZATION OF THE EUROPEAN LEFT, 1860–1980

In an in-depth comparative analysis, Stefano Bartolini studies the history of socialism and working-class politics in Western Europe. While examining the social contexts, organizational structures, and political developments of thirteen socialist experiences from the 1880s to the 1980s, he reconstructs the steps through which social conflict was translated and structured into an opposition, as well as how it developed its different organizational and ideological forms and how it managed more or less successfully to mobilize its reference groups politically. Bartolini provides a comparative framework that structures the wealth of material available on the history of each unit and allows him to assess the relative weight of the complex explanatory factors.

Stefano Bartolini is Professor of Comparative Political Institutions at the European University Institute in Florence. He has contributed articles to numerous journals and has edited and written several books, including *Identity, Competition, and Electoral Availability* (Cambridge University Press, 1990), for which he won the UNESCO Stein Rokkan Award.

CAMBRIDGE STUDIES IN COMPARATIVE POLITICS

General Editor

PETER LANGE Duke University

Associate Editors

ROBERT H. BATES Harvard University

ELLEN COMISSO University of California, San Diego

PETER HALL Harvard University

JOEL MIGDAL University of Washington

HELEN MILNER Columbia University

RONALD ROGOWSKI University of California, Los Angeles

SIDNEY TARROW Cornell University

OTHER BOOKS IN THE SERIES

continued after last page of index

THE POLITICAL MOBILIZATION OF THE EUROPEAN LEFT, 1860–1980

The Class Cleavage

STEFANO BARTOLINI

Department of Political and Social Sciences
European University Institute
Florence, Italy

CAMBRIDGE
UNIVERSITY PRESS

CAMBRIDGE UNIVERSITY PRESS
Cambridge, New York, Melbourne, Madrid, Cape Town, Singapore, São Paulo

Cambridge University Press
The Edinburgh Building, Cambridge CB2 2RU, UK

Published in the United States of America by Cambridge University Press, New York

www.cambridge.org
Information on this title: www.cambridge.org/9780521650212

© Cambridge University Press 2000

This publication is in copyright. Subject to statutory exception
and to the provisions of relevant collective licensing agreements,
no reproduction of any part may take place without
the written permission of Cambridge University Press.

First published 2000
This digitally printed first paperback version 2007

A catalogue record for this publication is available from the British Library

Library of Congress Cataloguing in Publication data
Bartolini, Stefano.
    The political mobilization of the European left, 1860–1980 :
    The class cleavage / Stefano Bartolini.
        p.   cm. – (Cambridge studies in comparative politics)
    Includes bibliographical references.
    ISBN 0-521-65021-6 (hardback)
    1. Socialist parties – Europe, Western – History.   2. Socialism –
Europe, Western – History.   I. Title.   II. Series.
JN94.A979B37 2000
324.2'17'094 – dc21   99-33725
                                                          CIP

ISBN-13 978-0-521-65021-2 hardback
ISBN-10 0-521-65021-6 hardback

ISBN-13 978-0-521-03343-5 paperback
ISBN-10 0-521-03343-8 paperback

JN
94
.A979
B37
2000

a Bianca e Duccio,

per il nostro tempo perduto

CONTENTS

FIGURES AND TABLES

FIGURES

TABLES

To predict the presence of such movements was simple; to predict which ones would be strong and which ones weak, which ones unified and which ones split down the middle, required much more knowledge of national conditions and developments and a much more elaborate model of the historical interaction process.

Stein Rokkan, 1970

ACKNOWLEDGMENTS

Almost no part of this work has appeared in published form. Several points in the first chapter are drawn from "On Time and Comparative Research," *Journal of Theoretical Politics,* 5 1993: 131–167. A few others refer to parts in *Identity, Competition and Electoral Availability* (Cambridge University Press, 1990), and I am grateful to Peter Mair for his permission to use and elaborate on them. An early version of part of Chapter 6 was published as a Working Paper of the Juan March Institute in Madrid. Part of Chapter 5 has appeared as a Working Paper of the Institute of Political Science of the University of Barcelona.

The empirical research on which this book is based was made easier by the financial support of the European Union allocated by the Research Council of the European University Institute (Grant No. 36, 1995 and 1996).

I want to thank Simon Dubbins, Gianfranco Miglio, and Stefano Bocconi for their research assistance in data collection; Niki Outhram for her revision of my English; and Mogens Pedersen and Peter Mair for their valuable comments on parts of the manuscript. Hans Peter Kriesi deserves special mention for his thorough reading of and comments on the entire manuscript The same applies to the anonymous readers of Cambridge University Press.

I also want to express my grateful thanks to all the colleagues and members of the three institutions in which this book was written between 1990 and 1998: the Department of Political Sciences of the University of Trieste, the Department of Political Science of the University of Geneva, and the Department of Social and Political Sciences of the European University Institute of Florence.

In the Florentine institution, two friends, whom I have known for a long time, deserve a final and special wholehearted "thank you": Maureen Lechleitner and Marie-Ange Catotti. Maureen offered help that went beyond that usually provided by a secretary; she transformed herself into a research assistant. Marie-Ange, during the three years I served as Head of Department, shielded me from most problems, including those I myself created for her.

INTRODUCTION

With the passing of time, what was regarded in the last quarter of the twentieth century as a troubling problem of limited economic growth will appear as a period of turbulence and social dislocation caused by the transition away from the two-century-old cycle of the Industrial Revolution. This cycle opened with the slow erosion of the agricultural population and culminated in a similar erosion of the industrial working class, because, by the 1970s, in the early industrialized countries, pure manufacturing activities were no longer able to increase employment. A distinct historical period seems to be coming to an end, even if it will take some time before its full effects will be visible everywhere. Even then, however, this is likely to take much less time than it once took for industrialization to spread from the early to the late arrivals in the Western world.

In its various ideological streams, its political organizations, and its social and political battles, the history of socialism is linked closely to this two-century cycle. Indeed, its story, many would argue, now comes to an end with the closing of this period. The passing away of working-class politics, and of class politics as such, leaves open the question of how many of its aims have actually been achieved. This study takes a historical view of socialism and aims to reconstruct the steps through which a social conflict was translated and structured into a political opposition, how it developed its different organizational and ideological forms, and how it managed more or less successfully to mobilize politically its putative reference groups. The theme of this book is the variation in the electoral size, social cohesion, and organizational strength of the left in Western

Europe. The topic is hardly new; indeed, histories of European socialism and the left are too numerous to be cited. What is original about this study, however, is the way in which the theme is approached. The analysis is organized in a strictly comparative framework aimed at the systematic appreciation of the social contexts, the organizational structures, and the political developments of thirteen Western European socialist experiences from the 1880s to the 1980s. In this sense, the goals of the study are methodological as well as substantive.

The methodologically aware comparative social scientist is often subject to fears and doubts and is frequently not self-assured and sometimes even unhappy scholar. Unlike the case-study analyst, the comparativist is not protected by the self-confidence that is generated by an in-depth knowledge of the topic at hand; by the reliance on a large body of literature sharing the same configuration; or by the surrounding conventional wisdom that states that what is done makes sense. She or he needs to argue about diversity without resorting to the sorts of ad hoc hypotheses relating to one case that constitute the forte of the case specialist. Constantly worrying about the combination of an *esprit de finesse* with an *esprit de géométrie*, the comparativist must balance both in the full knowledge of the risk of falling under Pascal's dictum: ". . . les esprits faux ne sont jamais ni fins, ni géomètres." Comparativists, in short, must always justify their research choices.

I take it for granted that large-scale cross-country comparative research is unlikely to make any new discoveries in the history of the units analyzed. The purpose is, first, to provide a comparative framework capable of structuring the wealth of material available on the history of each single unit; second, and on the basis of such a theoretical framework, to arrive at comparative judgments concerning the relative rank ordering of cases along the dimensions of the framework; and third, to assess the relative weight of single or complex explanatory factors. The comparative structure is thus the essential instrument for processing information. The yardstick of relative weight is the specificity of the exercise and the essence of the comparative research design. The testing of existing theses and generalizations, and sometimes the advancement of new ones, is obviously the ultimate goal of this work.

In the study of one country, or even when dealing with a small number of countries, it is possible to refer to a large number of important variables that are relevant to each particular context. Indeed, some would argue that a case-centered strategy is actually the preferred option, and that it is typical of the work of classic authors such as Weber and Tocqueville. However, although case-oriented comparisons attempt to aim at the rep-

resentation of a complex set of interrelations among key variables in different individual settings, I am still not convinced of the merits of this
approach. In fact, I am also quite skeptical about the possibility of a truly
comparative analysis that is not variable-oriented but rather case-oriented.
In any case, I feel unable to carry out such an analysis, because I believe
that cases cannot be compared to one another any more than individuals
can be compared to one another. For in any comparative statement whatsoever, what lies at its heart is not a case, but rather the definition of a
common dimension along which values or status may be attributed to
cases. Hence, what we actually compare are the status and values of individual cases along a theoretically constructed common dimension. In this
sense, the activity of comparison, to my mind, is entirely dependent on the
intellectual and conceptual scheme that guides it. The point here is not to
reopen the enduring debate between nominalists and realists, but simply
to argue that a strategy of comparison based on cases rather than variables
– that is, a strategy of comparison that assumes that it is possible to
compare cases without common abstract properties in the form of variables
– is, for me, difficult to imagine and therefore impossible to perform.

All of this serves to explain why a great deal of energy is devoted in
this work to the development of a set of macrovariables that provides a
common framework of comparison and to the collection of comparable data
and information for each of the thirteen Western European countries
included in the analysis. In the course of this work on the historical
mobilization of the class cleavage, I have processed a wealth of historical
material, and in order to utilize it fully, it would, of course, simply be
easier to deal with one unit at a time, treating similar aspects and problems
in the analysis of each unit. Indeed, to do so would allow the wealth of
material that has been accumulated regarding each unit to be fully presented and, at the same time, for the firm control of each case to be
maintained.

In my opinion, however, this practice is unsatisfactory, because it
leaves too much room for the possibility of sliding into description, for the
temptation of introducing ad hoc aspects, and for the risks of resorting to
systematic justifications about why particular cases and particular experiences should be regarded in one way or another. I have therefore chosen to
follow a different strategy, and, as a result, I have found that even more
energy has been required in order to maintain this framework and its
dimensions. In other words, it has been difficult to avoid adding information, hypotheses, and sheer guesswork about one country or case when the
argument involved could not be generalized conceptually or empirically to
the universe of cases. In consequence, I have often had to sacrifice the

richness of the material at my disposal, for whenever it proved impossible to reconcile particular pieces of information with the overall macrocomparative framework, or to generalize conceptually across the countries those aspects and factors that were fundamental to just one or only some of them, I opted for exclusion. This strategy is costly, but it also has some advantages, several of which are discussed in the chapter that opens this book.

The second major aim of this study is to reach what I have called a "comparative relative weighting" of factors. It is overwhelming to realize how much of the national literature is replete with arguments and statements that are unquestionably comparative in nature but that are expressed, at the same time, without making any explicit comparisons. Arguments concerning the "very radical nature" of a movement; the "early industrialization" of a country; the "high inclusiveness" of a regime; the "late enfranchisement" of another; and so on; as well as terms such as "high," "low," "early," "late," "sudden," "gradual," "strong," and "weak" are all inherently comparative. The problem here is the following: Can the comparativist take the judgment of the national expert, who knows infinitely more about the unit in question, as a solid and grounded comparative assessment? What is in question is obviously not the competence of the scholar, but rather the inevitable need in national accounts to utilize a terminology that is comparative without at the same time having a comparative framework of analysis. In these cases, the comparative judgment is normally arrived at not through any explicit comparative exercise, but rather by reference to the accumulated (and implicit) common knowledge and/or wisdom of a discipline.

The task of the large-scale comparativist is to relativize this information within a comparative perspective. Because, however, explicit comparative research does not exist on many of the relevant concerns, the comparativist must also search for information that is often scattered and unsystematic, organize these materials along various comparative dimensions, and finally come to the sort of rank-ordering or quantitative or qualitative evaluation that is suggested by this analysis. In my experience, this effort has proved to be both arduous and unrewarding. The more we attempt to discover about a set of countries, the more the dimensions of the comparison increase and the more difficult it is to come to a proper evaluation of the comparative position of each country. A factor that is regarded as important by country experts needs to be generalized as an inclusive comparative dimension along which all other cases must be located, even if, for these other cases, this element has not been seen as important and has therefore not been dealt with extensively by the respective country experts.

In principle, this particular work has required the comparative analysis of a very large number of theoretically relevant dimensions: rates and levels of police repression; legislation concerning the recognition of political parties; comparative figures on the average size of industry, types of land tenure, and average land holdings; figures on the territorial organizational strength of parties; and so on. In some cases, this information exists in the form of important monographs or source books. In others, it can be collected only with the enormous effort of trawling through several scattered sources whose level of reliability and standardization is unknown. In still other cases, only indirect qualitative judgments and estimates are available in national accounts. Indeed, this has been the main problem that I have encountered in dealing with the enormous existing historical literature on the parties of the left and the working class: Only rarely does this literature address those questions that appear crucial from a comparative perspective, and even when these questions are considered, the insistence on a national framework of reference makes it difficult to evaluate the real comparative significance of the results. For instance, what may appear to be a strong organizational network when seen within the context of a particular country's history may well turn out to be very weak when placed within a comparative perspective. In other words, the comparative panorama requires a constant reevaluation of national expert judgments and a constant reassessment of what has otherwise been considered with reference to national development to be strong or weak, early or late, or whatever.

The core of this book is the attempt to devise a common comparative framework and to construct a net that allows the maximum available information to be organized as a common dimension of cross-national comparison. Within this general framework, descriptive accounts of the different national experiences are organized along common lines; well-known hypotheses are specified and linked to one another in terms of mutual specifications; finally, and whenever the necessary evidence is available, a comparative test is attempted.

This research lies at the crossroads of two traditions: (1) that of the imprint of stratification and social class, and of "social factors" in general, on mass political behavior and (2) that of the independent effect of specific political and institutional variables. The study of electoral mobilization requires the combination of both perspectives. It invariably turns out, however, that the political data that are required (regarding organization, propaganda, and so on, that is, the list of precisely those political variables that the late Stein Rokkan continuously reminded us we should fill with data) are unavailable; or that they need to be reconstructed and standardized from hundreds of different sources; or that they are scattered and unsystematic. Conversely, and as usual, the socioeconomic data are more easily available. The result is that inevitably, if unwittingly, we end up with a "sociology of politics" rather than a "political sociology," with the socioeconomic aspects as the input and the political and institutional aspects as the output.

For this reason, I have devoted a great deal of attention to the political, organizational, and institutional comparative aspects. Of the four major parts into which this work is divided, the first views the political mobilization of labor mainly as a response to patterns of economic development, industrialization and urbanization; the second part relates these responses to the degree of homogeneity of the national cultural environment; the third part relates them to organizational models and developments; and the fourth part relates them to the patterns of European political and institutional integration. In the concluding section, I have attempted to describe a model of interaction between socioeconomic, cultural, organizational, political, and institutional variables in order to combine these different perspectives into a general interactive model.

The structure of the chapters of this book closely follows the aspects and theoretical framework just sketched.

Chapter 1 discusses the general conceptual framework of the book and the key methodological problems it poses.

Chapter 2 describes the variance in the historical development of the European left from the point of view of electoral size, organizational cohesion, and ideological orientation.

Chapter 3 concerns the structuring of the class cleavage in light of the socioeconomic transformations and conditions that shaped its putative social constituency. Comparative patterns of industrialization and urbanization are related to the cross-country and over-time development of electoral support for the left.

Chapter 4 investigates the level of cultural homogeneity of the class environment. Social mobilization and cultural homogeneity are seen as the two major long-term determinants of the environmental context of class cleavage structuring.

Chapter 5 discusses the historical development of the franchise and its ambiguous role in terms of integration and representation.

Chapter 6 deals with the organizational dimension of cleavage structuring, comparing the conditions of early organizational consolidation as well as the levels of electoral, corporate, and partisan organizational density of different socialist movements.

Chapters 7 and 8 move to the last step of institutional and political integration, discussing respectively the openness/closure of the institutional system and the opportunities for political alliance offered to socialist movements by the cleavage structure of their countries.

Chapter 9 reconsiders all these aspects in specific reference to the issue of organizational cohesion and, in particular, to the question of the strength of communism after World War I and World War II. The problem deserves special attention because communism is both the most conspicuous instance of organizational split *and* the most important ideological innovation and radical version of the post–World War I socialist movement.

Chapter 10 brings together the different threads of the argument, viewing the different configurations of class cleavage structuring as results of particular preconditions, historical sequences, and crucial junctures.

Finally, the notes concerning the data sources and the data problems of this research are presented in the *Appendix*.

A final word about the choice of the spatial and temporal range of this research: thirteen countries across a century. More will follow about the methodological problems of this kind of comparison in the next chapter. Here I want to explain the reasons that pushed me into embarking on a project that I will never consider undertaking again in my future work. In my early doctoral studies, a distinguished economic historian and demographer told me a story. He had asked his professor if he could do a thesis dissertation on the history of world population and was given the demographic history of a small Romagna village during one decade of the seventeenth century to study. The moral of this story is that eventually he became a mature scholar by writing one of the most authoritative histories of world population.[1] The fact that I am now approaching a similarly broad question regarding the mobilization of the left in Western Europe should not mislead the reader. Although a fairly keen reader of history, I am not a professional historian and I have never made a detailed analysis of the mobilization of the left in a small village in my native Tuscany, say from 1870 to 1892. In fact, the story is relevant because in my case it worked the other way round: I actually began in the second half of the 1970s by studying socialism (and communism) in Italy and in Tuscany in particular. I later thought that a comparison with an equivalent French region would be useful, and finally I opted for a general comparison of the socialist–communist split in both of these countries. I probably read most of the available literature on the topic, and I also spent some time in the

---

[1] This was Carlo Cipolla in 1978, telling his personal story to an eager audience of Italian students who were hosted – in the early days of the European University Institute life – by another distinguished Italian scholar, Mauro Cappelletti.

Archives d'Etat in Paris and Rome searching for information about the early penetration of socialism in rural France and Italy. Several years were spent on this project; three boxes of notes were collected; the structure of the book was finally ready, and a few chapters were drafted. However, the book was never completed.

The point here is that while most professional historians would react to a French–Italian comparison by feeling uneasy about overgeneralization, the lack of detailed knowledge, the need to go deeper into local specificities, and so on, I ended up by experiencing the opposite. The more I compared socialism and communism in Florence and Lucca in Tuscany, the more I uncovered variables whose weight could not be evaluated except by broadening the scope of comparison. As yet more information was revealed about the differences between Tuscany and the Veneto in Italy, the more it seemed that these hypotheses needed to be related to the sorts of broader questions that could not be studied at this level in order for them to be validated. Moreover, as the process continued, I began to question whether French and Italian differences and similarities in both explanans and explanandum should not really be tested in an even broader context, a context in which these differences and similarities could take on a different shape. Was it possible to explain the strength of communism without also considering communist movements that were weak or had failed? Why did reformist socialism fail in both countries? Was there something common to France and Italy that could not be perceived without also considering other countries?

This endless chain of questions eventually generated the need for a more general exploration and interpretive study of socialism and communism at a wider level. If anybody feels that in order to understand the history of the world you must first be very familiar with and confident about the history of a village, then in my case the reverse came to pass: In order to be aware of the key question that needs to be asked in your village, you must first start with a broad understanding of the history of the world.

THE CLASS CLEAVAGE:
CONCEPTUAL AND
METHODOLOGICAL
FRAMEWORK

To define what is "left" within the European cultural and political experience, scholars have come up with a variety of focuses.[1] The connotation of "left" may be independent of any school or doctrine and may identify a position of loyalty to the original programs, to the *statu nascenti* doctrine, or to the spirit of the original creed. This conception justifies such terms as "dynastic left" (liberal parliamentarians who installed Luis Philippe [1830] on the throne but later opposed Guizot in the name of the original manifesto); *fascismo di sinistra* (the original radical corporativist and anticapitalist spirit of the fascist movement, as expressed in the San Sepolcro manifesto of 1919 or in the *punti di Verona*); and "Catholic left" (linked closely to the original evangelical message of solidarity and egalitarianism and to the social doctrine stemming from it). More typical of philosophical analysis is to view "left" (and "right," of course) as referring to patterns of thought and behavior that are embedded profoundly and permanently in human nature: "to become" versus "to be"; change versus conservation; the ontological opposition between a right-handed and a left-handed cosmology. Another tradition is to search for the permanent value, or constant guide, of the left – the general principle that it embodies and that differentiates it from any other current of political thinking. The emphasis is most frequently placed on the value of "equality," although this is defined in different ways.[2] Finally, in a more histori-

---

[1] For general overviews, see Laponce (1981) and Cofrancesco (1990: 4th ed., vol. 18, 883–884).

[2] For this line of search, see Bobbio (1994) and Lukes (1995).

cally defined context, "left" is a spatial location, originally linked to the position within the parliamentary hemicycle. This conception of the left has little to do with issues and principles; it is relational and changes over time, just as it also depends on what else defines the spatial continuum.

All these meanings attempt to define the left independently of the name of its historical actor. My aim here is not so ambitious and the left I will be speaking of is identified with a specific set of ideas and political and social organizations stemming from the Industrial Revolution: *social-ism*. From a broad historical perspective, the patterns of industrialization and democratization resulted in the structuring of working-class movements that developed either into a single socialist party or, alternatively, into a socialist party plus a communist party. Later on, this picture was complicated by the emergence of other parties that resulted from splits within the two main tendencies. The class conflict is mostly responsible for the similarity of "party landscapes" across Europe. It was the only social conflict to be politically mobilized in every European country, contributing to the standardization of party systems. The ubiquitous presence of socialist and communist parties is indeed the most visible common feature of European party systems, while most of the variance *among systems* is accounted for by other nonindustrial or preindustrial cleavages, the decisive contrasts of which shaped the individual constellation of each system.[3]

This is a historical identification of the left with no ambition to being a theoretical definition, and I am aware of its shortcomings. Grouping all these parties[4] since the end of the nineteenth century into one category such as the "class left," on the assumption that they all represent and hinge on the class cleavage, is a daring task from ideological, political, and social points of view. First, "other left" parties existed, which were neither official socialists nor official communists and which constituted a far from homogeneous category, including small parties of the extreme left as well as right-wing socialist groups with a more humanitarian or radical flavor. Second, the electoral combination of these parties does not necessarily justify their political combination, as they were often strongly opposed on many issues. Finally, it is equally audacious to regroup these parties according to their connection with the working or lower classes. The classi-

---

[3] Rokkan (1970b: 130).

[4] For a list of the parties that have been included in the left, the reader can consult the Appendix. Beyond the official socialist and communist parties, there are a number of other left parties whose inclusion or exclusion may be more controversial. As indicated in the text, I have included such parties that were originally splinter groups or wings of the historical socialist and communist organizations.

fication of parties that *appeal to, are supported by,* and *represent* such social groups may have little in common across countries.

However, these parties are unquestionably part of the genetic process of lower-class enfranchisement and early political mobilization; they had and have maintained closer contact with the trade unions than any other political family, are generally regarded as being part of one *tendance,*[5] and the literature is rich in hypotheses concerning this political construct, used as a meaningful term of reference for long-term electoral changes. The solution I have chosen is to subsume the three elements of the *social constituency* (support), the *ideological orientation* (appeal), and the *organizational structures* (representation) within the general historical process of class cleavage structuring. By means of a genetic approach, I hope to avoid having to resort to an implicit "class theory" of political representation.

The goal of this chapter is to discuss the nature of the class cleavage that stemmed from the Industrial Revolution and political democratization. In the first section, the concept of cleavage will be discussed and defined; then the peculiarities of the class cleavage compared to other cleavages will be specified; and finally, the macroconstellation of historical processes within which the the class cleavage was structured will be identified. In this process, I will also define my dependent and independent variables more accurately, presenting thereby the general framework for this study. In the second section, the methodological choices that underlay this research are briefly discussed and justified.

CONCEPTUAL FRAMEWORK

POLITICAL MOBILIZATION AND CLASS CLEAVAGE STRUCTURING

"Mobilization" is an ambiguous term. Imported from totalitarian theory and analysis and later used in all sorts of different contexts, it now conveys the meaning of a complex process of self-mobilization and hetero-mobilization – of "being mobilized" and of mobilizing.[6] Mobilization was a multifaceted process of citizen involvement in the (post-)national and

---

[5] The rather telling introduction of this term by André Siegfried should be noted: "Mainly preoccupied with the reality, I therefore concentrate less on parties – superficial and continuously changing categories – than on the basic tendencies"; Siegfried (1913: xxiv).

[6] See Neumann (1956b: 395–421) on "integration" parties addressing themselves to specific social groups that they deliberately try to mobilize, integration being at one and the same time the result of self-interest and organizational enterprise.

industrial phases of modernization. Citizens were progressively mobilized in various nonpolitical spheres: by capitalism and industrialization in the economic sphere through media such as exchange and money; through the extension of the market; geographical and labor mobility; the imposition of tariffs, credit, and capital procedures and techniques; and the availability of services and goods. They were also mobilized by the military and administrative machine of the state, as soldiers, as subjects of administrative agencies, and through traveling and residential restrictions and/or liberalization. They were also mobilized culturally through scripts and other mass media into ideological, religious, and ethnolinguistic movements by socializing agencies of the nationally dominant culture, as well as by dissident intellectuals, missionaries and messages, news, and so on.[7] In the Western experience of the last two centuries, mobilization appears to have acquired a self-sustaining impulse, with spillover effects between one sphere and others. Once started, it became an ongoing process whereby change concerned quantitative growth – new recruits and generation turnover – as well as qualitative structural modifications in the main forms and agencies.

Different phases or waves of (economic/administrative/cultural) political mobilization can be distinguished. However, it was the first wave that was of paramount importance because it not only opened the door to successive waves, it also set the original opportunity structure within which those that followed had to be accommodated. The first political mobilization was *the process by which former subject individuals were initially recruited as active participants in forms of nationwide organizational and electoral activities for the purpose of influencing political decision making;*[8] in order for this to take off, a minimum level of the other forms of mobilization had to be reached. Vertical and downward-first political mobilization was not necessarily monopolized by new actors such as political parties and interest

[7] On the relationship between political and other types of mobilization see Nettl (1967: 115–122).

[8] An analytical discussion of the concept of political mobilization is presented in Nedelmann (1987: 181–191, 199), where the distinction between the three dimensions of mobilization as "formation of interest," "management of emotions," and "development of instrumental capacities" is developed. Nedelmann's general definition of political mobilization as "the actors' attempts to influence the existing distribution of power" is too broad for our purposes. Such a definition is introduced as the result of dissatisfaction with others who limit political mobilization to the processes of authority legitimization (Nettl 1967, cited in footnote 7) or attribute excessive emphasis to the dimension of instrumentality, in the sense of mobilization as "resource control" (as utilized by Tilly [1978]). The emphasis on "recruitment of citizens in active political participation" implies a reference to the three dimensions listed by Nedelmann. However, the main concern and empirical data refer here to the development of instrumental capacities.

organizations. Political and even electoral mobilization was performed by governments, state bureaucracy, charismatic leadership, and so on. In these cases, parties and interest organizations competed with other established agencies that preceded them.[9] However, they remained the most important early mobilization actors. Special attention should be paid to the *specific interaction between the formation of electoral alternatives in the political arena* – that is, the formation of specific political organizations for the mobilization of the vote – *and the structuring of mass organizations in the corporate channel-of-interest organization.* The set of electoral and corporate organizations and their interaction depended on the structure of political opportunity and on the strategic choice of mobilizing actors during the formation and politicization of a given cleavage line.

Drawing on Rokkan's rich contribution to this field,[10] this process can be summarized in a set of analytical steps. I have slightly modified the terminology, as I believe the term "cleavage" should be kept for the politicized dividing line and not applied to the original functional, cultural, or territorial conflict.

1. The initial *generation of oppositions* due to differences of interest and/or *Weltanschauung* generated by the macroprocesses of modernization: monetarization, urbanization, secularization, cultural standardization, industrialization, administrative control, and centralization.
2. The *crystallization of opposition lines into conflicts* over public policy once (and if) the centralization of political decision making became established.
3. The *emergence of alliances of political entrepreneurs* engaged in mobilizing support for one set of policies against others.
4. The *choice of mobilization strategy* made by such entrepreneurs.
   a. Action through and reliance on preestablished community and other association networks.
   b. Action through and reliance on the development of purpose-specific membership organizations.
5. The *choice of arena for the confrontation* of mobilized resources.
   a. Aggregation of votes/members for political/electoral contests.
   b. Direct action (strikes, pressure through public demonstrations, revolt, revolution, etc.).

[9] H. Daalder (1966a: 43–77) directly tackles the issue of the extent to which and the conditions in which parties more or less successfully monopolized such a role vis-à-vis other agencies.
[10] A very large part of Rokkan's work was devoted to the problem of cleavage formation. The classic reference is (1970b: 72–144).

Historically, different alliances of entrepreneurs have chosen dissimilar strategies, both in terms of organizational choice (point 4) and in terms of confrontation-area choice (point 5). Some have relied more intensively on preexisting networks of association, such as occupational, cultural, and religious groups; others have engaged forcefully in the development of their own specific organizational weapons, as distinct and autonomous as possible from others. Some have preferred to concentrate their efforts for demand satisfaction in purely political and electoral strategies; others have resorted to more-direct actions in the market and society. For parties and groups, different strategies in different contexts have yielded different payoffs, ranging from gaining public recognition and legitimacy to substantial success through specific legislation, agreements, and package deals with the state and/or other political forces. In the analysis of historical cases, final payoffs are of great importance. Their evaluation by the actors implied feedback reactions, while any dissatisfaction with existing payoffs and arrangements involved changes in organizational and confrontation-arena strategy.

In his general classification of historical conflicts arising in the course of European modernization, Rokkan simplifies the analysis by concentrating on broad fronts of conflict in the national histories. He distinguishes four critical cleavages that he broadly attributes as the consequences of two revolutions: the national and the industrial. The processes of formation of the nation-state usually provide the potential for two fundamental conflict lines: (1) the dominant cultural group and the nation builders' elite versus the ethnically, linguistically, or religiously distinctive subjected population (i.e., external and internal conflicts concerning cultural and religious identities) and (2) the attempt by the nation-state to centralize, standardize, and mobilize versus the church and its traditional encroachments and privileges in society (e.g., secular versus clerical control of mass education). The Industrial Revolution also produced two lines of conflict: (1) the first between the predominantly rural landed interests and the emerging classes of commercial and industrial entrepreneurs (mainly over tariff policies: free trade versus the protection of agricultural products); (2) the second, *which split the urban milieu*, between the owning classes and the tenants and workers (free enterprise versus state control; rights of workers versus rights of property owners).

The age of Reformation and Counter-Reformation signaled the climax of the conflicts between the center and the periphery. The result of this was generally the strengthening and consolidation of territorial boundaries, as well as that of the linked issue of the cultural and religious identity of the state within these boundaries. In the new polities resulting from national secessions, similar conflicts were postponed and reemerged only later in the nineteenth century. The colossal political mobilization that occurred during the French Revolution and its spread with the Napoleonic wars also determined the emergence of the potential conflict between the mobilization efforts of the state — with its need for system support and legitimacy — and the resistance of the church. The key issue quickly became the control of the growing mass-education and welfare provisions.

The structural conditions for the urban–rural economic conflict developed later. This was the result of the growth in world trade and industrial production during the nineteenth century, and it determined the conflict between the landed and urban interests regarding tariff problems, which in turn were linked to issues of the maintenance of acquired status and the recognition of achievement. These conflicts were not necessarily translated into politics everywhere, and, indeed, they were stronger or weaker according to their contextual situations. In Rokkan's reconstruction, the *roots* of these cleavages all predate the roots of the class cleavage. This point is often overlooked due to the fact that, even if these conflicts had already been present for a long time, their *electoral* mobilization tended to coincide historically with that of the class cleavage. That is, although they were the result of very different and longer lasting conflicts, they were all mobilized at exactly the time that suffrage was extended to the lower classes. Therefore, to fully appreciate the historical sequence of conflict crystallization, one should not concentrate exclusively on electoral politics, but rather on preelectoral forms of organizational developments and political conflict. This clarifies the marked historicity in the formation of basic conflict lines. This aspect of the historical sequence of conflict formation and cleavage structuring is crucial, given that the alliances among insiders at each given historical moment tended to reduce the alliance opportunities for later newcomers.

THE THREE DIMENSIONS OF CLEAVAGE STRUCTURING

Despite his historically creative use of the concept of cleavage, Rokkan never gave a clear definition of what he meant by the term. Its meaning has therefore remained loose,[11] and the concept has been and is used in reference to all sorts of divisions and conflicts. Various authors refer to

[11] See Zuckermann (1975: 231–248) and (1982: 131–144).

cleavages as "political" and define them in terms of political attitudes and behavior, depriving the concept of any link to social structural variables.[12] Others use the term "social cleavages" to indicate nothing more than the divisions implied by social stratification. Still others have identified "cultural cleavages," assuming that "it is a set of beliefs rather than any demographic attribute that defines one's location along the cleavage."[13] Contrary to this reduction of the concept of cleavage to one predominant dimension, more-complex conceptualizations are formulated in Eckstein's concept of "segmental cleavages" and in the distinction made by Allardt and Pesonen between "structural" and "nonstructural" cleavage.[14]

The essential problem with the concept of cleavage lies in its intermediary location between the two main approaches of political sociology: that of social stratification and its impact on institutions and political behavior, on the one hand, and that of political institutions and their impact on social structure and change, on the other.[15] At the theoretical level, the synthesis of these different approaches is difficult; for this reason, the concept of cleavage is often either reduced *down* to that of social cleavage or raised *up* to that of political cleavage. To solve this problem, the concept of cleavage has to be regarded as a link between social structure and political order, and – in much the same way as the Marxist concept of class – it should not be considered as a descriptive concept aimed at the identification of a particular reality.

Within such a perspective, the concept of cleavage can be seen to incorporate three dimensions:[16] an *empirical element*, which identifies the

---

[12] Cf. Dahl (1966b: 448–486).

[13] See Inglehart (1984: 25–69) and Dalton, Flanagan, and Beck (1984: 3–22). Contrasting traditional with new cleavages on these grounds, this line of reasoning neglects the normative-ideological – and therefore cultural – attributes of traditional cleavages such as class. Indeed, by treating a cleavage such as class as primarily socioeconomic – or demographic – such a perspective neglects the fact that ideological or cultural factors lie at the very root of any group definition or sense of self-awareness.

[14] Eckstein (1966) distinguishes "segmental cleavages" from "cultural disagreement" and "specific disagreement." Although in this case the term "cleavage" refers to the link between social structure and political order, the distinction raises problems similar to those of "cultural cleavages" in that the normative element embodied in the second category is in fact also typical of the first. The definition of "structural cleavages" by Allardt and Pesonen (1967: 325–366) is restricted to differentiated social groups that are also characterized by *cohesion* and *solidarity*. As such, in addition to the social attributes (differentiation) on which they focus, they also implicitly introduce organizational (cohesion) and cultural (solidarity) attributes, a combination that strikes me as offering the most fruitful basis on which to build a definition.

[15] See E. Allardt (1968: 66–74).

[16] For this three-dimensional characteristic of theoretical concepts, see the treatment of the

empirical referent of the concept and which we can define in *sociostructural* terms; a *normative* element, that is, the set of values and beliefs that provides a sense of *identity* and role to the empirical element and reflects the self-awareness of the social group(s) involved; and an *organizational/behavioral* element, that is, the set of individual interactions, institutions, and organizations, such as political parties, that develop, as part of the cleavage.[17] The term "cleavage" should, I suggest, be restricted to the indication of a dividing line in a polity that refers to and combines *all* three aspects, and alternative terms should be adopted when referring to objective social distinctions or to ideological, political, and organizational divisions per se. Because the sociostructural, normative/cultural, and political/organizational elements play an inextricable role of mutual reinforcement in shaping individual attitudes and behavior, cleavages can be considered as only one particular kind of division rather than as a concept that exhausts the realm of all possible divisions. For example, it is clear that important lines of social stratification may exist that cannot be identified as cleavages; similarly, there may exist political and ideological divisions that also, however important, cannot be identified as cleavages. Differences in occupation qua occupation, or differences in language qua language, do not produce the respective cleavage, but rather the nature and intensity of the emotions and reactions that can accompany membership in these occupational or linguistic groups, as well as the social and political bonds that organizationally unite the individuals who belong to them. Once achieved, these positions become firmly established, and it is the endurance of this entrenched position in group terms that produces the image of a

concept of class by Aron (1964: chapter 3) and the concept of nation by Lepsius (1985: 43–64). Katznelson (1986; 14–22) has reviewed the problem of the definition of class and class formation, suggesting that class formation is identified by four levels: (1) the structure of capitalist economic development, i.e., class as a constitutive element of every capitalist structure and capitalist transformation, a concept distant from empirical reality; (2) social organization of society as lived by actual people – workplace social relationships, etc., i.e., class-based ways of life; (3) class as formed groups sharing "dispositions"; and (4) collective action. I do not see clear advantages with respect to the structural, normative and behavioral components of the classic distinction between class position, class consciousness, and class action.

[17] These three dimensions of a cleavage should not be confused with the three "types" of cleavage mentioned by Rae and Taylor: "ascriptive" cleavages or "trait" cleavages such as race or caste; "attitudinal" or "opinion" cleavages such as ideology or preference; and "behavioral" or "act" cleavages such as those elicited through voting and/or organizational membership. These authors regard them as mutually exclusive classes of different cleavages rather than as different constitutive aspects of every cleavage. See Rae and Taylor (1970: 1–3).

cleavage becoming stable over and beyond the individuals involved, creating a specific cultural background and a varying propensity to collective action.[18]

From the point of view of its consequences, a cleavage has to be considered primarily as *a form of closure of social relationships*.[19] The concept of cleavage is therefore clearly at quite a remove from any definition of the sociostructural base that provides its reference point, and this approach clarifies the definition of the boundaries and the differences between the two. More concretely, what distinguishes class from the class-based cleavage; religiosity or the community of religious people from the religious-based cleavage; the ethnic group from the ethnolinguistic cleavage? Three key differences are evident, albeit not always to the same degree in each type of cleavage.

First, the sociostructural reference of a cleavage and the cleavage itself are products of different historical phenomena: The former emerges from the processes of state and nation formation and from the development of capitalism and industrialization; the latter emerges by the coupling of these processes with those of politicization, electoral mobilization, and democratization. The social basis of the class cleavage originates in the social stratification produced by industrialization and capitalist development, and these processes establish the structural conditions for group distinctiveness;[20] but it is also clear that the class cleavage derives its special character only in relation to the other, more strictly political processes. A similar argument holds true for religious-based cleavage, whose structural basis is set by the process of the breaking down of Christian European unity in the sixteenth century and the later process of state centralization and secularization. In the same vein, ethnolinguistic groups emerged from the long process of linguistic differentiation, migration, and state boundary creation in European history, but specific cleavages of an ethnolinguistic nature develop only in response to the modern nation builders' attempts to effect cultural and linguistic standardization and when the opportunities to express dissent and to organize opposition become available.

It is only with the development of the modern nation-state and with

---

[18] See Schumpeter (1951).

[19] Cf. M. Weber (1978: 43–47).

[20] The best conceptual reference for the result of such a process is indeed the Weberian idea of "social class" as a group of class situations that are made homogeneous by the existence of a "common possibility of mobility either within the career of the individuals or in the following of successive generation"; cf. Weber (1978: 302–305) and Giddens (1973: 47–48).

the integration of different groups into the central sphere of society that the conflicts between these groups have become centralized. State building brings about a consolidation of military, administrative, and economic boundaries that reduces the possibility of exit for individuals and groups. Nation building and attempts at national cultural standardization bring about, in varying degrees, an ethnically and culturally homogeneous context that sets the stage for the articulation of emerging functional-economic differentiation and conflicts. It is this process – one of "unifying potentially opposing camps, facilitating their society-wide organization, their becoming symbols of social and political identification and their making demands on central political institutions"[21] – that gives rise to the enduring relations between specific social groups, organizational networks, and ideologies. It is, finally, through the historical process of mobilization, politicization, and democratization that voice options are articulated and organized within a bounded territory and any specific cleavage acquires its distinctive normative profile and organizational network. In short, cleavages initially develop on the basis of a social stratification that sets the structural conditions for group identity; only later do they become fully political, particularly with the development of mass democracy.

If a cleavage is regarded as a conflict line or a division line *translated* into politics, the translation is what historically constitutes the linkage between social condition, consciousness, and action. Conflicts and oppositions may not be translated into politics – either repressed, depoliticized, or deflected versus other divisions or channeled into politics in various ways; they may even be generated by politics, activated and reinforced by political processes and institutions. Translation points to the crucial role of the translators and of the mechanisms and conditions of translation, and it implies that there is variance in the capacity to translate the basic preconditions. Therefore, the nature and magnitude of the sociostructural basis of the conflict must be viewed as basic conditions facilitating – to a greater or lesser degree – the translation.

The transition from the early period of politicization to the establishment of a hierarchy of superimposed cleavages, as well as to the creation of close links between cleavage systems and party systems, is complex. The "rationalistic" bias of Marxist class theory was based on a long chain of reasoning. Disciplined by the same conditions and circumstances of their work, brought together in a great multitude where they experienced the community of their status and deprivation, the workers would develop a collective class consciousness. In this phase, Marx expressed and trans-

---

[21] Eisenstadt (1966: 22).

formed into a general philosophy of history the grievances and claims of a segment of the politically aware Western European workers, at that time only a very modest proportion of the proletariat. These grievances were then expressed in the form of the class struggle, that is, as total opposition to the existing system. In this second step, using as a base the psychology of these workers in the transition period, Marx theorized their rejection of capitalism *but not of industrialism.* Workers would have to realize that, although their chains were those of the new industrial system, such a system would have a benevolent long-term effect for them *once its capitalist structure was destroyed.* Finally, the workers should not be distracted from this realization by other nationalistic, religious, ethnic, economic, or other considerations. Only then would social grievances transform themselves into class action. However, at each of these critical junctures, alternatives were possible, and other actors were interested in making these available and credible.

From this point of view, class or class conflict has no special or dominant guaranteed role in politics. Class conflict has dominated the scene of sociology, and its almost mechanical reverberation in politics has led to the idea that class political alignments are the modern and normal form. By the same token, other forms of political division are seen as somehow artificially superimposed on the real and important divisions in the economic functional domain. Sometimes this belief is accompanied by the idea that this is a deliberate attempt by dominant economic circles or classes to conceal the base of domination; sometimes by the idea of false consciousness, that is, the limited capacity of workers and lower classes to see their real interests. This perspective (1) underestimates the ideological nature of the class cleavage itself, (2) exaggerates the simplicity of the political translation of class conditions and identities in class political action, and (3) indulgently disregards the late and often residual nature of such a dividing line with respect to others. The tendency is thus often to see modern mass politics in the light of the class cleavage.

Second, because the relations of individuals to the social basis of a cleavage are defined by certain attributes that can change with relative ease, this social basis represents a grouping and a set of social relationships that are normally much more fluid than those constituted by the cleavage itself. The *cleavage,* on the contrary, thanks to its behavioral and organizational dimension, *is a social relationship that implies a level of external closure* that is always more pronounced than that of the social group. In this sense, it should be noted that there is an important difference between class cleavages, on the one hand, and other cleavages – which may develop on the basis of ethnolinguistic or peripheral communities or even religious identity – on the other. Class conditions are a social stigmata that can be modified by individual or group mobility or by emigration. Ethnic or religious identities are based on characteristics that lead more easily to a wholly closed relationship. This difference, in turn, helps to explain why these kinds of cleavages demonstrate such an impressive capacity to survive over time and to encapsulate their respective communities. Even in the case of social class, it would be a mistake to underestimate the extent to which members of class organizations – both parties and unions – have sought to improve their position through a monopolization of this social relationship and through its closure toward the exterior world. As an illustration of this, one need only recall the debates within the Second International on the "peasant question": the resistance of the skilled working class to the incorporation into the movement of unskilled workers or even the more recent problems experienced by immigrant workers.

The process of political translation was even more complex for class than for other traditional identities. This is because class had left parties to mobilize their constituency in opposition to the individuals' traditional ties of a local, ethnic, and/or religious nature. In every case, they had to induce them to act in a way that was in most cases contrary to and in contradiction with the norms and roles dominant in their geosocial milieu and, in general, against the authority of the consolidated social hierarchy at the local level. The competition among forms of representation based on territorial representation, cultural defense, or functional-economic interest does not easily flow to the advantage of the latter. Territorial forms of representation impose limits on the capacities and possibilities of party conflicts within the localities and tend to reduce or transform politics into a question of external representation, as the whole community is represented to the external world. By contrast, the functional/economic emphasis implies and reflects a type of alliance that crosses local geographical units and undermines the established leadership structure within the community, introducing into it elements of direct-interest conflict. Moreover, territorial and cultural defense need not be linked together, as they tend to be in Rokkan's work. There might be prevalent forms of territorial representation without any cultural defense – as examples from France and the United States in the nineteenth and early twentieth centuries show – as well as a cultural-defense mobilization without a strong territorial basis, which cuts across territory and nationalizes politics, and a cultural defense guaranteed *through* territorial defense – as the Swiss Catholic cantons' experience exemplifies. Thus, in certain circumstances, functional-class interests may be trapped in an uneasy environment in which both cultural and territorial defenses coalesce to make it difficult to appeal to functional identities across territories and across cultural traits.

This problem may be less important for mobilization efforts along other lines, such as for instance religion. Here, there may be less emphasis on abstract ideals and remote collective groups against the local power structure; instead, the emphasis is on well-established identities and on authorities that offer a sense of protection against external authorities. In this sense, the task of mobilizing, already difficult for working-class parties when they had to cut individuals away from these traditional ties, became even more difficult when and where these traditional ties were already mobilized and were the source of very specific political identities.

Third, the social basis of a cleavage is essentially *un*organized. In the case of the class cleavage, for example, the workers' parties, the trade unions, and other agencies of this kind are not the organizations of the social class per se, but are the institutional components of the cleavage. In other words, it can be argued that *the institutional nature of the class cleavage, in terms of both its social membership and its organizational form, is historically and country specific precisely because it does not depend exclusively on social class.* Of course, the model of interaction between the class cleavage and other cleavages is also largely country specific, and it is the sheer complexity of the manner in which the various cleavages become interlinked and super-imposed on one another that makes it particularly difficult to disentangle the process leading from the development of structural prerequisites to the ideological and organizational patterning of the politicization phase. More-over, once cleavages become established and organizationally institutional-ized, they develop their own autonomous strength and, in turn, act as an influence on social, cultural, and political life. Thus, not only do cleavages become more stabilized than social classes or groups, but they are them-selves a means of political stabilization, providing individuals with a con-stellation of preexisting alternatives for their own social and political integration.

Parties, and in general the organizations of the cleavage line, also have the job of creating opportunities and "spaces" in which the feeling of emotional belonging among the members can be created and reinforced. This is more or less necessary, depending on the conditions of environmen-tal hostility that surround the parties. Such spaces become more necessary the more the party has to face severe forms of repression and opposition. Thus, the building of a large, isolated subcultural network of ancillary organizations has often primarily served the function of members' sociali-zation and defense in periods of environmental hostility. Moreover, party subcultural organizational networks reinforce emotional solidarity as well as socializing new members. The way in which such subcultural networks are established in several areas of social life depends on the specific nature of the cleavage and, in particular, on its social basis. Emotional feelings of solidarity are probably more easily shaped and organized by peripheral and ethnolinguistic minorities or by religious groups that are sharply opposed to dominant groups or are simply discriminated against and/or repressed. The homogeneity of the working class, in terms of division of labor, housing conditions, educational levels, workplace, and so on, creates those areas of equality that facilitate the establishment of such subcultural milieus and the development of strong emotional ties within the group. By contrast, such changes as the increasing internal differentiation of labor, workplace heterogeneity, disappearance of specific industrial communities, increasing spatial mobility, and the separation of workplace and residence, as well as growing dependence on impersonal contacts with the party organization and the reduction of daily personal contacts with other members of the group (e.g., through increasing resort to private means of transport), create conditions that weaken the emotional ties of a group. At the same time, however, these subcultural networks are a result not only of favorable social conditions, but also of deliberate efforts by parties to create them and to fight against unfavorable conditions. Once in place, these networks can help to serve the goal of maintaining and even reinforcing group emotional ties with great effectiveness even in periods of rapid change in the earlier structural conditions of similarity.

However difficult the comparative study of these processes might be, it is here that we find the key to understanding the development of different *cleavage systems* characterized by varying levels of organizational fragmentation and social homogeneity across European countries. For example, it is impossible to grasp the difference between the fragmented and socially heterogeneous social basis of the class cleavage in the Southern European countries, on the one hand, and the cohesive and relatively socially homogeneous basis of the class cleavage in the Scandinavian North, on the other, other than by reference to the interplay between the structural, ideological, and organizational aspects of the class cleavage itself *and* between the class cleavage and other cleavages. It follows from this that cleavages have histories of their own that differ substantially from the histories of their social bases and from the histories of their original mobilization and politicization. Such histories, and the strength and hold of traditional or emerging cleavages, can be assessed only in terms of all three constitutive elements, that is, changes in social stratification, changes in the corresponding cultural systems, and changes in sociopolitical organizational forms (not only political parties, but also the networks of social, professional, and other organizations expressive of the cleavage). It also follows that although we define the class cleavage in relation to its genetic origin, this expression does not indicate that the workers, all the workers, or only the workers represent its social constituency. The social membership of the class cleavages may vary considerably over time and across countries.

Any attempt to translate this line of reasoning into an empirical inquiry regarding the modalities of class cleavage structuring necessitates a major attempt to devise indicators and collect data on social structure, attitudes, and organizations. Such an inquiry also needs to be *cross-nationally comparative* and to have a long-term *historical* dimension. It is not surprising that it has rarely been attempted at a comparative level. Rather, most research[22] usually analyzes and privileges a *single* dimension of cleavage structuring (or destructuring) at the national or cross-national level.

Some analysts concentrate mainly on the relationship between the social stratification of European societies and patterns of voting. Through survey data, attempts are made to ascertain the closeness of the relationship between the two, measuring the extent to which social group membership proves an effective predictor of partisan choice and, more broadly, investigating the social, cultural, and psychological characteristics of the left-wing voter.[23] These studies invariably concentrate on the *social homogeneity* of the class cleavage membership. Another research tradition focuses primarily on the changing attitudes and beliefs of the mass public, arguing that the parties of the traditional left face an increasingly complex pattern of competition along a number of other issue dimensions and that a wide selection of new concerns – ranging from neolocalism to environmentalism to welfare problems and law and order – impact on different sections of the population in different ways and thus tend to cut across more-traditional ties based on occupation, income, and status and to undermine the *cultural distinctiveness* of any class alignment.[24] Finally, a separate tradition challenges the view that the political parties of the left *reflect* the identity, interests, and consciousness of the social group. Assuming that

[22] I am not concerned in this context with that tradition of analysis that treats cleavages as an *independent variable* to account for systemic properties such as stability and democratic performance. The starting point of this literature is Simmel (1956). For other key analyses see Eckstein (1966), Nordlingler (1972), and Lijphart (1968: 3–44).

[23] The literature in this area is too large to be quoted in full: Representative of this line of interpretation are Alford (1963); Rawson (1969), Abramson (1971), Goldthorpe, Lockwood, Bechhofer, and Platt (1971: 11–13), and Lipset (1981).

[24] See the sources on cultural cleavage cited in footnote 13. For a good synthesis see Hildebrandt and Dalton (1978: 69–96).

the role of political organization is essential to the creation of the subjective class, this perspective stresses that attention should be focused on the fate of the major left *political organizations* – the trade unions and other agencies and organizations that help to create, reinforce, and transmit group attitudes and attachments. The fate of the class left is thus linked to its capacity to adapt to the new conditions in which it is obliged to reproduce its support and ideology.[25]

These different research traditions tend to give priority to just one of the three constitutive aspects of any cleavage: the reference social group and its possible modifications, the political attitudes and ideological structuring of the group consciousness, and the behavioral element giving rise to the organizational network on which the parties base their strength and of which they are themselves a part. To privilege one dimension or perspective may lead to speculation about the cleavage development that is quite different from that which can be advanced by privileging an alternative dimension. For this reason, in this work I consider them all as constitutive elements of the cleavage structuring. This latter – my dependent variable – is operationalized through different properties, and the cross-country variation of these dimensions is interpreted as resulting from a macroconstellation of systemic factors. The following section outlines the framework as a whole.

DEPENDENT VARIABLES: THE PROPERTY SPACE OF EUROPEAN LEFT VARIATION

Summarizing this discussion, Figure 1.1 graphically presents the structuring of a cleavage in terms of the three dimensions of *social constituency, organizational network*, and *cultural distinctiveness*. Each of the three dimensions changes empirically from cleavage to cleavage, from country to country, and from historical period to historical period. While the cleavage dimensions of social constituency and organizational network have been largely dealt with by the literature, that of cultural "distinctiveness" is more complex. By this term I do not mean the process of "objectivization" of class whereby a third element is introduced between the class as an objective social condition and the class as an expression of observable behavioral patterns of organizational membership and action; nor do I

---

[25] Kitschelt (1994) stresses this point in his interpretive line. In general, the emphasis on the capacity for adaptive change of the established parties is a dominant theme of the work of P. Mair, whose main contributions in this direction are now collected in Mair (1997).

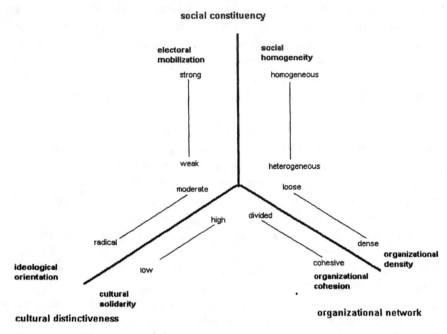

Figure 1.1. Dimensions of cleavage structuring.

mean the "class interest," as this is defined both independently of what individual workers declare it to be and as the political elites and organizational leadership express it. Cultural distinctiveness instead indicates that a certain number of individuals, without any external constraints, react in a similar way to similar situations and absorb *des obligations sociales et des coutumes*, a spontaneous kind of moral behavior within a given group. While the social constituency of a cleavage is ascertained in terms of social homogeneity – that is, a similarity of social conditions – cultural distinctiveness pertains more to the dimension of "community," of a similarity of values and obligations and a sense of belonging. It is difficult to separate this aspect clearly from the communality of the social condition and from the specific pattern of organizational membership and behavior. It refers to something that is similar to what Aron called the "objectivization" of communities when he referred to features that Weber called "ethos," and to the equivalent concept of "habitus" in Bourdieu.[26]

Given that variations in outcomes are used as a key to the comparative search for causes, it is essential to start with an accurate definition of any such variation. The scheme in Figure 1.1 helps to organize the dependent

[26] Aron (1989: 462–471).

variables in a synthetic form. The social constituency dimension points to two aspects of cleavage structuring. (1) *The first is the level of electoral mobilization*, that is, the *electoral strength* of the different left political organizations, meaning the extent to which they were capable of mobilizing support and obtaining the electoral loyalty of sections of the population. From this point of view, there are *strong* and *weak* lefts in electoral terms. At the same time, the structuring of the class cleavage resulted in (2) different *social compositions* of its electoral constituency. From this point of view, class cleavages can be ranked in terms of the extent to which they managed to mobilize the putative social target as well as other social groups. Class cleavages will therefore be characterized by a *higher* or *lower* level of *social homogeneity* of support.

The second important dimension of variation concerns the *organizational network*, which can also be seen from two distinct perspectives. The first perspective concerns *organizational cohesion*, that is, to what extent in their organizational development national lefts were capable of maintaining organizational unity or, alternatively, were faced with processes of internal organizational fragmentation. In this perspective, the European experience sees a *cohesive* and a *divided* left. The second perspective concerns the degree of *organizational density* of the class cleavage, that is, the extent to which such a cleavage rested on a densely organized network of corporate, political, and cultural associations or, at the opposite extreme, consisted mainly of ideological and attitudinal opposition deprived of strong organizational vertebration. The issue is thus the extent to which class cleavages were organizationally encapsulated.

The dimension of cleavage *cultural distinctiveness* also includes two subdimensions. At the level of the political elites and participant activists, the most important element concerns the predominant *ideological orientation* of the movement. The distinction in this case involves different *types of class-left ideologies* (orthodox Marxism, syndicalism, communism, etc.) and the extent to which they are *moderate* or *radical*. Clearly, here I am not interested in the ideological or theoretical schools in themselves, but rather in their spreading and appearing as convincing answers to the problems of the people. The causes and the consequences of the spread of different ideologies are sociological and political questions that have little to do with their exegesis and even less with their success or failure in terms of the accuracy of their historical predictions. At the level of the masses, the important element is the level of *cultural solidarity* that the cleavage structuring is able to create and reproduce within a social constituency. Different class cleavages rest on different levels of class solidarity, on different types of working-class culture, and on the different intensity of feelings of belonging. However, despite its importance, this aspect of cleavage cultural distinctiveness will not be included in this study because I have been unable to conceptualize it, let alone measure it, in any way. Although several historically detailed studies exist at the national level, it is extremely difficult to frame this dimension in a way that allows for grounded comparative statements to be made.[27] Rather than dealing with this aspect unsystematically, I have preferred to omit it from my research. Only indirect indications will therefore be derived on this topic from other dimensions of cleavage structuring.

To sum up, the three dimensions of cleavage structuring are translated into six variables (Figure 1.1), only five of which will be directly dealt with in this study: electoral strength, social homogeneity, organizational cohesion and density, and ideological orientation The study will attempt to explain to what extent and why the class cleavage is electorally strong, socially homogeneous, organizationally cohesive and dense, and ideologically moderate or radical in different historical experiences.

Not only is there cross-country variation, but there is also cross-time variation in each of these properties. That is to say, outcomes are different according to the moment in time at which the study is carried out. On the eve of World War I, for example, the picture would reveal a strong and unified German socialist movement, while in the United Kingdom the working class was organized through unions that were mostly concerned with the marketplace and voted for the Liberals – what we would call today a "catchall party". Thus, the homeland of industrial capitalism had no socialism, while at the same time, "backward" Finland had a strong radical social democratic party with 37% of the vote.[28] Few observers of the time could have guessed accurately where the future of socialist ideology and organization lay. In the early 1920s an evaluation of left radicalism would have pointed to the Norwegian Labor Party as having the most extreme position, given its almost unanimous adhesion to the Third International. Yet, the Norwegian radical takeover was short-lived, and the ensuing history of the party can be more appropriately described as a trend toward consensus.[29] In other words, there is a problem with interpreting

[27] Theoretical discussions of this aspect are not as rare as attempts at comparative evaluation of it. See, for instance, Mann (1973).

[28] Sombart (1905) pointed to the paradox that the United States, the country he regarded as having the most advanced industrial capitalism and representing the direction of future European development, did not have a socialist working class. The question, then, was whether the United States represented an "exceptional" development or just the future European development, and whether the rise of socialism was a necessary and inevitable corollary of the development of capitalism.

[29] See Torgersen (1962).

labor's responses in the short term as against the more permanent long-term features of national labor movements. This is also true when attributing the relative weight to the "states of dynamism" – characterized by a great flexibility of organizational forms and a capacity for qualitative absorption of new groups and strata previously not forming part of the movement. These states of dynamism are typically marked by attitudes and behaviors of a nonconformist nature, as opposed to those of "stabilization" – which are instead characterized by organizational rigidity and by an absorption that is mainly quantitative, that is, by increases in the organization and representation of strata that were already part of the movement.[30] This study is oriented to the interpretation of the more long-term features of the socialist movements. However, these considerations will necessitate a certain amount of contextualization at different points in time if we want to avoid the risk of judging the entire left experience on the basis of its final post–World War II outcome. A certain amount of periodization will therefore be needed.

Let me mention a final insurmountable problem of interpretation of the labor response: Where did the latter originate, and of whom was it the response? Did it emerge from elite groups and social vanguards? From organizational bureaucracies? From the masses and the rank and file? In a Leninist perspective, the political response of national labor movements originated in vanguards, that is, in politically aware groups leading the rank and file. This means that labor's response is the result of a struggle for influence over the whole movement fought by minority groups. From a Michelsean perspective, socialist leaders and functionaries tended to assume a lifestyle and values close to those of the bourgeoisie. Their identification with the labor movement organizations, their defense of the organizations' priorities, and their natural conviction that organizational interests and imperatives were by definition the best embodiment of the class interest in the long run dictated the attitude of the socialist movements as a whole. Thus, progressive socialist integration was neither a conspiracy nor a takeover of the interests of certain sectors of the well-off working class; it was, rather, a natural by-product of the oligarchic tendencies typical of all bureaucratic organizations and of the bureaucratic elites' interest in the status quo.[31] Finally, a third line of argument suggests that the long-term response of the labor movement was the result of a progressive adaptation of the elites to the basic inclinations of the rank and file. The pre–World War I socialist movement was more radical and ideological

[30] Bauman (1972: 324–325).
[31] Cf. Michels (1949).

than the workers themselves. It was directed by ideologues and intellectuals whose sophistication and ideological rigor pushed the ideological stances far beyond the basic claims and interests of the rank-and-file workers. Thus, the post–World War I developments can be seen as the result of the progressive adaptation of such elites to the more moderate and pragmatic approach of the rank-and-file workers, as radical appeals proved unsuccessful almost everywhere.[32] In this case, the response of labor is, in the long run, attributed to the basic orientation and preference of the movement's rank and file, reducing the role of elites and vanguard groups to the early phase of development and leaving little room for organizational imperatives and ends substitution.

These three theories are important. According to whichever one is adopted, the role of elites, intellectuals, vanguards, and rank and file is enhanced or reduced. To a certain extent, the choice of one approach implicitly predisposes the study toward one sort of interpretation of the sources of the long-term response of labor. This, however, does not relieve the scholar of the task of performing a more specific study of the conditions under which the forces evoked were comprehensive and successful.

FRAMEWORK OF INDEPENDENT VARIABLES AND STRUCTURE OF THE BOOK

In the theoretical discussion on cleavage structuring so far, I have discussed a number of theoretical points concerning the process of translation of social oppositions into cleavages through the mobilization efforts of political entrepreneurs. These were framed within the broader processes of state and nation formation and internal democratization that contributed to the specific national interplay of different conflicts and oppositions. It is now necessary to briefly summarize them into a grid of independent explanatory factors; this will also serve as a guide to the structure of the entire book. In Table 1.1, these factors are subdivided into preconditions, sociostructural trends, organizational resources, and politicoinstitutional opportunities. The table starts from the more remote macroconstraining conditions and approaches the conditions of individual, collective, and organizational choices that eventually determine the differentiation of outcomes.

We can imagine preconditions and social inputs as being those general conditions that affect the capacity of a given movement to mobilise – "the basic variables affecting the organizational capacity of a population."[33] The

---

[32] For this position, see the conclusions in Mitchell and Stearns (1971).
[33] Stinchome (1965: 145).

Table 1.1. *Mobilization of the class left: ordering of influencing variables*

preconditions	social inputs	institutional opportunity structure	organizational resources	political opportunity structure	differentiation of outcomes (type of class cleavage structuring)
international status	industrialization and urbanization	stateness: repression vs. toleration	early organizational consolidation	nature of incumbent nation-building alliance	
state - boundary consolidation -bureaucratization/ centralization	working-class constituency formation	regime liberalization	party/trade union relationships	preclass mass antiestablishment traditions and movements	electoral mobilization social homogeneity
cultural homogeneity	education and communication = community formation	electoral incorporation	organizational density: corporate and partisan	preclass or non-class political organization and mobilization	organizational cohesion organizational density
		representation		social and political alliance opportunities	ideological domestication
		executive power access		involvement in international conflicts	

difference between the two is that while the preconditions pertaining to the international status of the polity, its degree of boundary consolidation and internal centralization, and its internal cultural homogeneity are constant for any given polity, sociostructural trends in industrialization, urbanization, working-class constituency formation, education, and community formation have a distinct temporal variation within each polity.

Organizational features and political and institutional opportunities are given a causal role that is closer to the outcomes within a context of given preconditions and sociostructural inputs. They are not exogenous variables but can also be related to preconditions and social inputs. They are also associated with each other, as, for instance, when organizational resources depend considerably on the institutional opportunity structure of the polity. Similarly, the opportunity for political alliance depends on organizational consolidation, as well as on the openness or closure of the institutional structures. The variables listed under the label of "political opportunity structure" include features that clearly lie outside the sphere of choice of the socialist movements – such as the nature of the incumbent dominant alliance or the preexisting traditions of popular movements – as well as features more open to choice opportunity – such as the possibilities of social and political alliances. The last column of Table 1-1 lists the differentiation of outcomes that were presented as independent variables in the previous section.

At this stage, it is premature to discuss details about causal linkages.

In the various sections devoted to each set of features, I introduce and discuss the theories that link them to the mobilization process, and I try to test them as accurately as possible. It is evident, however, that links established between, say, social inputs and the dependent variable also affect intermediate-level variables. In other words, the influence of industrialization levels and working-class constituency size on electoral mobilization can be seen as direct and also indirect, expressing itself through, for instance, trade union organization and recruitment. Moreover, complex interactions between the dependent variable of electoral mobilization and the independent variables of institutional and political opportunity structures are evident. The overcoming of an institutional barrier – for instance, regime liberalization or final enfranchisement – can be seen as something that both affects and is affected by mobilization of the left. These special interactions between potential causes and effects will be dealt with carefully in the specific sections.

The concluding part of this work links these processes together, forming a dynamic model that tries to assess the relative weight of each process. The guidelines for this work can be described here: The more general question concerning class cleavage mobilization is whether this should be regarded primarily as a political response rooted in forms of particularly acute social dislocation and economic alienation or if, by contrast, the main interpretive element should be linked to the idea of "political alienation." Reformulating Huntington's conceptualization of the linkage between social mobilization processes and levels and forms of political stability,[34] we come to the following set of relationships:

$$\frac{social\ mobilization}{economic\ development} = social\ frustration$$

$$social\ frustration \times organizational\ development = political\ mobilization$$

$$\frac{political\ mobilization}{institutional\ integration} = political\ alienation/integration$$

This grid starts from social mobilization (industrialization, urbanization, education and literacy development, and socioprofessional transfor-

---

[34] Huntington's (1968: 54–55) original formulation was mainly concerned with the link between the social mobilization process and the levels and forms of political stability in modernizing countries. His original formulation of the relationship between the two was synthesized in the following formulas: social mobilization / economic development = social frustration; social frustration / mobility opportunities = political participation; political participation / political institutionalization = political instability.

mations) as processes generating rising expectations and demands. The level of satisfaction of these demands – according to certain theories – or the structural conditions of work – according to others – determined by given rates of socioeconomic development foster different levels of social frustration. In this perspective, the historical conditions of *socioeconomic alienation* were favorable to the birth of radical political protest and organized political action. This first part of the scheme, however, says little about how socioeconomic alienation transforms itself into organized political action.

The intervening variable inserted by Huntington to arrive at political participation was "mobility opportunity." An individual's willingness to participate is the result of a ratio between his or her social frustration and the opportunity for mobility. This replicates an individualistic and socially driven process of political mobilization, thereby underestimating the role of political organization in fostering participation (particularly the participation of citizens with few individual sociocultural resources).[35] Moreover, in contrast to the United States, in Europe during the industrialization phase, the mobility opportunity for the lower classes does not seem to have been an important aspect militating against the definition and defense of collective interests. Therefore, *political participation* is seen in my scheme as the result of the combined effect of social frustration and organizational development, which – in the context of socialist history – often took the form of a rapid imitation of political forms of earlycomer by latecomer countries. In the continental context, the spread of organizational forms and techniques of action was relatively fast, faster than the spread of other underlying social and economic processes. Organizational and political leads and lags, therefore, do not correspond to socioeconomic leads and lags.

Finally, Huntington's third equation maintains its importance in this context. The relationship between the levels of participation and the establishment and institutional consolidation of the channels for its expression (institutional integration) gives rise to different levels of political alienation/integration as a result of lack of citizenship and feelings of political exclusion. Political institutionalization must be conceived here mainly in terms of the adaptability of traditional political institutions to the pressures from growing political participation.

There are three positive aspects in this revision of Huntington's scheme. First, it allows dynamic relationships to be established between the macroprocesses of modernization that have so far been considered only

---

[35] See Verba, Nie, and Kim (1978) for their discussion of this role of political institutions.

from a static point of view. Second, it reintroduces the crucial variable of organizational development. Third, it neatly distinguishes the sources of economic alienation from those of political alienation. The last point is particularly important. We can in fact oppose a socioeconomic to a political alienation theory as a source of working-class politics in the period between 1848 and 1920. If one maintains that the sources of class politicization and mobilization were mainly those of socioeconomic alienation, rooted in material conditions and the organization of production, then a set of hypotheses that requires a special emphasis to be given to the socioeconomic conditions of working-class formation and lower-class makeup is in order. If, by contrast, we regard political alienation as an essential feature of the emergence of a class conflict and cleavage, then we need to emphasize the response given to requests for full citizenship, political integration, and representation, that is, to the process of the civic (individual emancipation, freedom of association, etc.) and institutional integration of the lower classes (franchise, liberalization, policy influence, etc.).[36]

By emphasising the opposition between the socioeconomic and politicoinstitutional roots of alienation, one overcomes the implicit equivalence between the two that is not infrequent in the literature on the development of working-class politics. Moreover, this allows us to consider a trade-off between the two spheres; that is, there is the possibility that mutual compensations might occur between political and economic alienation, that higher levels of political alienation might be bearable in exchange for lower levels of social frustration (a Bismarckian strategy), or, alternatively, that higher levels of economic frustration and alienation might be accompanied by, and in part compensated for, higher levels of political representation (a liberal strategy).

---

[36] That working-class politics is mainly a response to political alienation is a thesis that has been discussed by R. Bendix since the time of his early writings. The problem was formulated as follows: Nineteenth-century Europe's problem concerned the way in which societies undergoing industrialization would find a solution to the dilemma of incorporating the newly recruited industrial workforce into the economic and political community of the nation. Bendix's early studies concerned ideologies of management that he felt to be important because they indicated the way each society shaped the answer to this problem of integration. The main reference is Bendix (1974: 436–450). A revision of this piece is found in Bendix (1984b: 70–90). Bendix's thesis that the political movements of the nineteenth century aimed more at citizenship recognition than at economic revolution, and his criticism of Marx's view on the point are in (1984a: 91–107). The problem was also discussed in (1964: 89, 112–122).

METHODOLOGICAL CHOICES

Four methodological issues have been of particular interest to me during the preparation of the research outlined earlier. The first concerns the definition of what needs to be explained about the electoral history of the left. The second concerns the level of spatial variance dealt with in this study and, more precisely, whether a cross-country comparison is too aggregate. The third issue concerns how to deal with the temporal dimension of variation of almost one century and how to relate a comparative synchronic analysis to a comparative historical analysis, that is, how to combine spatial variance with temporal variance to improve control. The fourth and final issue relates to the debate on whether an adequate explanatory attempt necessarily requires a microfoundation anchored to individual motivations, choices, and beliefs. This section delineates the methodological boundaries and ambitions of the research, as well as the methodological biases of the author.

WHICH CASES AND WHAT PROBLEM?

In the history of class cleavage structuring, what needs to be explained and which cases is it worthwhile to consider? These two questions are interlocked because the choice of cases influences what we *can* study, and what we *want* to study influences what cases we should consider. The cases I investigate are thirteen Western European countries for which a sufficiently long period of regular competitive politics and sufficient historical data and studies are available. Spain, Portugal, Greece, Iceland, and Luxembourg are excluded, only because of the difficulty of obtaining reliable and systematic secondary-source historical data on many of the aspects included in this research. For Portugal and Spain, the very long interruption in liberal institutions and democratic elections after World War I is also an important reason for exclusion. However, no country has been excluded for considerations pertaining to size, importance, or peculiarity. The thirteen countries considered are very different in population size, economic strength, and international status. Each of them enters my analysis as a case with the same weight as all the others. This is important, particularly when I base comparative judgments on the yardstick of all-cases average or typical development. If the cases were different, such a comparative yardstick might have to be different.

It is important to bear this in mind because, according to some scholars, the comparative study of domestic internal development should be conducted primarily across countries that are large enough and resourceful enough to enjoy relatively autonomous domestic developments. Barrington Moore has offered this as a reason for his concentrating on major international powers in his study of the social roots of democracy and authoritarianism.[37] I find the reasons for concentrating on large countries unconvincing. Large countries and powers, thanks to their economic and military resources and cultural autonomy, may well show more "autonomous" domestic developments and successfully shelter internal developments from international pressures. However, their high international status may also be a burden that weighs heavily on domestic developments. It may thus entail international interests and/or responsibilities the perceptions of which alter internal political developments. Smaller countries, on the other hand, enjoying less international status, may be less able to avoid external pressures and influences and thus be more prone to institutional imitation. These aspects necessarily have an impact on their internal developments, making them generally less willing to engage in international or military initiatives. In other words, strains on internal domestic politics are not so clearly associated with size. Moreover, international status may change quite rapidly (e.g., the Hapsburg empire into Austria).

In reality, in selecting only large powers, it is not the most important, significant, or autonomous developments that are selected. More simply, these are cases for which one important dimension – that of international status and the strains and responsibilities associated with this status – is turned into a constant. This prevents variance occurring along this dimension, as well as the comparison of cases of high international power and responsibilities with those of a lesser international role. In other words, the international status of a country should not be a criterion for selecting cases, but instead a variable whose different value/status may have an impact. This point is of particular importance for a study of the class cleavage. Class divisions, class ideologies, and class movements were not only forms of internal voice whose nature was particularly divisive for the polity; they were also associated with international movements challenging consolidated state boundaries. It is therefore very likely that the international status and involvement of each country had a strong impact on how the political structuring of the class cleavage was faced and treated.

What needs to be explained is never a neutral question. This is even more true when the issue concerns class politics and the left, on which so many different evaluations exist of what is a success or a failure, and so many analyses have accumulated over time, taking the lead from theories of how objective class positions should translate into politics. For this

[37] See Moore (1966: xii–xiii).

reason, it is worthwhile to devote some time to what needs to be explained in the electoral history of socialism and to the implications of the choice of one explanandum rather than another.

The recent influential works of Przeworski and Przeworski and Sprague[38] about the electoral history of socialism and its predicaments is an excellent and stimulating starting point, as their goal is the exact opposite of the one I have set for myself. Przeworski and Sprague's central question is the following: why has the left (for them the socialist parties) never or only occasionally reached the 50% threshold? Why has the left never obtained the vote of all the workers? Przeworski argues that "by invoking relative standard (i.e., wondering why the Swedish left is stronger than the Dutch, etc.) one often forgets that absolute standards exist as well: One proceeds as if the common fate did not require an explanation. And yet *it is that which different histories have in common that illuminates the limits and historically inherited possibilities*. Before asking why this party has been more successful than that one, we can not ignore the fact that none has been successful in terms of its own dreams and designs, that no one has brought to realization the very purpose of its foundation."[39]

The common feature, the general development that assimilates all such political movements, is said to be a common electoral failure with respect to the left's original purposes and expectations. I disagree with this point of departure on both methodological and substantive grounds. Elsewhere, I have argued[40] that if there is a development common to all units, it is difficult to explain. In any case, the key to the interpretation of a general development or common fate is the variance across cases in the timing, intensity, and so on of this ultimate outcome. Looking at the European experience in its entirety – without excluding embarrassing cases – what strikes me is not that socialism has never reached 50% but rather the striking variance in its strength, between the average 10% of the Irish left and the 45% of the Austrian left. If the focus is on the notion of common failure, both the Irish and the Austrian left have failed, although to different degrees. If instead these two cases are considered in the context of the Europeanwide empirical variance, the first is a dramatic historical failure, ranking on average 25% votes below the Europeanwide mean, while the second is an outstanding success, having around 10% more votes than such a European mean. If the within-group variance can be explained, then this is the key to interpreting the group mean. In other words, the

---

[38] Przeworski (1985) and Przeworski and Sprague (1986).
[39] Przeworski (1985: 103–104); the emphasis is mine.
[40] Bartolini (1993: 158–165).

explanation of the 50% threshold follows as a variant of the former explanation (concerning the appropriate comparative yardstick, see the later
section "Temporal Variation").

The consequences of the choice of the explanandum often extend to
the kind of analysis that is carried out. To justify the relevance of the "why
never above 50%" or "why never all the workers" questions, reference
must be made to the aspirations, desires, and beliefs of the early socialist
thinkers and leaders and therefore to an implicit theory about the relationship between class condition, size, and class action. It is because the people
in a working-class condition were the majority in a given historical period
(and can this really be said to be true?) or were expected to become so over
time that the problem arises as to why this was not reflected in a similar
amount of class consciousness and class action. The 50% question presupposes a model that takes as normal the translation of a class condition into
class consciousness and action and investigates the intervening variables
that make this normal translation more or less successful.[41]

The aspirations and beliefs of the protagonists may be a poor yardstick
for the definition of historical problems. Why have left parties been unable
to realize such aspirations and desires? One could pose the same question
for any other political formation. Why did the liberals never gain the total
support of the rising bourgeoisie, or the religious movements the total
support of religious people, or nationalist movements that of the whole
nation? Catholics, Protestants, and ethnic, liberal, conservative, and agrarian movements all shared the same hopes and aspirations to fully mobilize
their potential electoral constituency, and there are good reasons for claiming that they failed. If it is argued that the socialists were prevented from
reaching their goals by intervening forces, could not the same be said for
all the other political forces? To treat the history of socialism from the
point of view of its failure to mobilize the working-class electorate implies
the assumption that mobilization along functional socioeconomic interests
and identities is normal and that the others are not normal or are exceptional. That class is the dominant factor of political alignment implies the
residual nature of other factors.[42] *If and when* class is politically articulated

---

[41] "It is not necessary to explain at length workers' vote in favour of communist and
socialist parties. Such vote is normal and has its logic, good or bad, which it is not our
job to evaluate"; Dogan (1960: 25).

[42] Przeworski and Sprague (1986: 28, 59, and 78) make this postulate very clear in their
analyses: "The lines of conflict and the modes of individual behaviour that emerge *if and
when* class is not the force guiding the behaviour of workers are beyond the scope of this
analysis"; it "decreases the salience of class as the basis of collective identification. It
leads, therefore, to the *resurgence* of other bases of collective identification, whether they

and appealed to, then it is the force that guides electoral behavior; when it is not, then other forces play a role. Other collective identities, such as religion or language, (re-)emerge only when the class appeal is attenuated or muted.

This way of approaching the problem means prejudging the crucial empirical question of whether class is mobilized before or after other lines of cleavage and which of these other lines are mobilized. It also means simplifying the whole process of competitive mobilization along different fronts and excluding those processes that actually produced the interaction between class and other lines of conflict and that explain when class becomes a strong source of political behavior. The problem cannot be solved from the perspective of the aspiration of one actor; it is the whole pattern of interaction of mobilization efforts by politicized groups and elites that needs to be considered.

Implicit adherence to a model according to which the *true* or *primary* identity is class has a further implication. If class is a normal or natural basis of mobilization, then it will mobilize if somebody cares to mobilize it qua class. If people vote according to their interests if somebody cares to articulate those interests and appeal to them, then the question becomes one of when and why the elites did or did not articulate and appeal to a specific class interest that exists as a reality.[43] Necessarily, the variance in the extent of class mobilization ends up being mainly due to the subjective efforts of the mobilizers. Little room is left for factors that are external to the strategy of the left parties. The explanation of a fate that is defined as common (failure to become majority forces) cannot be found in the external nonhomogeneous environments (institutions, competing forces, etc.). It must be identified within the movement itself, in its common and universal strategic predicament. Przeworski and Sprague's argument is a modern version of a classic tradition that, from a different – historicist – perspec-

were based on the size of revenues, character of work, religion, language, or race"; "workers becomes Catholics." All emphases are mine.

[43] The keystone of every construction based on the naturality of class interests is the belief in the existence of such class interest that is neither the sum of the individual preferences of the workers nor the preferences expressed by their political organizations. If the class interest is identified with the positions articulated by working-class political organizations, then it would be impossible to judge the extent to which such organizations were actually articulating such class interest. By definition, they would do so. If class interest is identified with the empirical preferences of the people in the objective class position, then it would be equally impossible to argue that political organizations do not appeal and articulate such sets of diversified preferences. It is necessary to build the concept of an abstract class interest if one wants to argue about the extent to which political organizations actually appeal to the class qua class. The discussion of this Hegelian class interest is not pursued in this context.

tive, attributes fundamental importance to the role and the choices of elites, that is, to the "historical adequacy" of such choices.

In this study, I do not place any particular importance on the 50% threshold; I do not assume class to be a natural or normal or predominant basis for political mobilization; and I am unable to establish what electoral failure was other than in relative terms. Concentrating on cross-country differences redefines what comparative failure and success is. If one allows that the socialists were not alone in the electoral arena and that competing actors and forces existed, then the 50% threshold loses any significance. Class can be seen as a residual function of other, preceding or parallel, political identities, rather than as a normal source of mobilization, following Finer's acute observation that "class was important in Britain because nothing else was."[44] Without a priori acceptance of any of these positions, I see this work as an investigation of how difficult, complex, and in many ways nonnormal it was to translate objective class positions into a basis for political mobilization against traditional forms of territorial representation, established cultural commitments, the authorities of traditional elites, individual and organizational costs, and other competing mobilizing agencies and actors.

The extent to which this translation was successful and which groups were more receptive to socialist appeals is a matter of empirical investigation. I firmly believe that the mobilization outcomes resulted mainly, but by no means only, from the efforts of class parties. Other actors were involved, and their choices were equally if not more important for the final outcome. I also believe that the history of political and organizational struggles determines what people's interests are, but it can by no means be claimed that such political and organizational struggles were only class struggles; other struggles could also precede, interfere with, or redefine the political significance of class. If one argues that people in the same class condition should in principle have voted left, not because their interests pushed them to do so but only because somebody had convinced them that it would be in their interest to do so, then the possibility that the specific history of political and organizational struggles convinced them that this was *not* in their interest must also be introduced. Any dilemma or electoral predicament disappears in this case. What led a Belgian, Catholic, Flemish worker to decide which of these three social roles and circles should be predominant in the definition of his political identity is a most intriguing historical puzzle. It cannot, however, be solved via assumptions about the

[44] Finer (1970: 142).

normal political translation and about when nonnormal translations come into play.

To consider actors' choices in the reconstruction of historical outcomes becomes extremely difficult indeed when one realizes that the actors involved are many and varied. To reconstruct the information and preferences of the actors, the viable alternatives, the causal structure of the situation of choice when considering socialist leaders, liberal elites, Catholic hierarchies, dynastic circles, and so on (and for each of them, who counts: certain leaders? some hundreds of active militants? some thousands of electors?) yields a very complex matrix. It is understandable that one actor only is chosen and is separated from the others. This has, however, implications and costs. As indicated in the first part of this chapter, the emphasis in this research is placed mainly on the attribution of macroelectoral outcomes to equally macroeconomic, cultural, political, and organizational factors. This tends to subsume the factors of choice, and the consequences of actors' choices, within the framework of constraints posed by the macrofactors. This also has implications and costs. In this strategy, the influences of the environment are as dominant as those of the strategic choices in the actor-centered approach. I believe, however, that for a historical understanding of left electoral mobilization variance, such a macrostructural constellation can offer a richer comparative framework.

SPATIAL VARIATION: ARE CROSS-COUNTRY COMPARISONS TOO AGGREGATE?

Most of my data concern the electoral mobilization of the left at the national level. As a result, other independent variables are necessarily measured at that same level for an election, a period, or a general country mean. The skepticism in regard to widespread geographical research is sometimes argued from the methodological point of view, referring to the "too different experiences" argument and to the "too much is lost in national aggregation" argument. In my opinion, such theses are not justified in terms of variance in independent and dependent variables. The level of spatial aggregation at which research is conducted is crucial only for the definition of those aspects that need to be regarded as constant (those that belong to higher spatial levels than that chosen), those that can be considered as operative variables and are therefore subject to the parameterization controls (those that belong to the same spatial level) and those aspects that cannot be considered in – and are therefore excluded from – the analysis (properties belonging to lower spatial units).

The variance in the dependent variable — for example, the variance in communist electoral strength — is clearly not related to the level of the territorial units of analysis. Whether the territorial units are fifteen countries or fifteen regions of a given country or fifteen cities of a given region or fifteen districts of a given city or even fifteen polling offices of a given district, the variance varies randomly. This is to say that there may be more variance among the Communist electoral strength of fifteen different Florentine districts than among fifteen European countries.

What about variance in independent variables? Moving down the ladder of territorial aggregation, some of the variables that did indeed vary at a higher level of territorial aggregation (e.g., the electoral system, the timing of enfranchisement) become constant and cannot, therefore, be invoked in explaining within-country variations in the dependent variable. At the same time, other independent variables that could not be considered at a higher territorial aggregation level now become potential operational causes of variation. Thus, descending in spatial level, (1) those variables that vary at a higher level of territorial aggregation are transformed into constants; (2) the influence of the specific level variables, which had to be considered as randomly distributed and therefore noninfluential, at the higher level is amplified; and (3) all those potential independent variables that belong to lower territorial levels continue to be excluded. The same logic applies at every level. If the study were to be conducted across the electoral districts in the city of Florence, for example, we would be forced to consider as potential causal conditions district-specific effects such as the 1966 flood having radically changed the social composition of some districts while leaving that of others substantially unchanged. At the same time, every property that can be studied and attributed to the city, the region, or the country necessarily becomes a constant feature across the city districts and cannot be invoked to explain variance among them.

In a comparative study, any changing of the level of territorial analysis produces changes in the variables that can reasonably be considered as potential causal conditions of that level variance. However, while some variables acquire such status at a lower level, others lose this status at the same level, because for each level of spatial unit chosen, we must assume the random distribution of lower-level features and the constant distribution of higher-level features. Once we have listed all the microcontext variables to explain the Communist success in Siena versus its failure in Lucca, how can its success in Tuscany versus its failure in Veneto be explained? Or its success in Italy versus its failure in the Netherlands? There is obviously no way to maintain the status of potential causal conditions for all the variables while descending or climbing the ladder of territorial aggregation. So, for variance-explaining research, the argument that one becomes more specific, context sensitive, accurate, and so on by studying phenomena at a low level of territorial aggregation is *logically* inconsistent.

Therefore, the issue of the level at which we decide to study a given phenomenon has nothing to do with context sensitivity, historical specificity, or level of abstraction. It simply points to different sets of independent variables that we want to consider as potential causal conditions in a situation in which the choice of one set precludes the consideration of other sets. The choice of a spatial level of aggregation is therefore a choice about which sorts of potential sources of variation we can control and which ones we must leave uncontrolled.

The reason some local studies appear to be more appealing and context sensitive is simply that they combine a great deal of local specification with more-general knowledge concerning a higher level of territorial unit: the region, the country, or even the continental context. The latter aspects can, however, only be used as other knowledge and cannot be incorporated into the comparative research design because they do not vary. This is the same case as when, in studying a phenomenon at a given level – for instance, the cross-country level – one adds several subnational aspects, regional or local, to the picture as explanatory elements. It can be done, and it is done, but these cannot be incorporated into the comparative research design properly, and they remain ad hoc interpretations that cannot be submitted to a comparative test.

The manipulation of the variance under examination is achieved only through the selection of cases – either more homogeneous or more different cases – not through the selection of the spatial level of analysis. Selecting cases with the goal of manipulating the sample's variance obviously changes the research design. If one selects, for instance, cases of strong Communist inroads (minimizing the variance in the dependent variable), one is forced to search for the common causes of a common result. In making constant the effect (Communist electoral success), it is necessary to look for features common to all cases that are likely to explain it. If, on the other hand, the aim is to parametrize the causes (for instance, a common state-bureaucratic tradition) through the selection of cases, the search must focus on the differences between the cases that may explain the different outcomes. This is not the place to engage in a discussion of the methodological implications of the different strategies of parameterization of potential causes or effects in comparative research. I am making the point only to underline that the methodological implications of strategies of maximum variance and minimum variance in both the independent and dependent variables have nothing to do with the spatial level at which the research is conducted, as they can be followed at each of these possible levels. My conclusion is, therefore, that the objection that in considering countries as units one cancels internal variation is immaterial from a logical point of view (while it remains important in terms of the selection of independent variables). The question of how much is lost and how much is gained in moving up and down the ladder of spatial unit aggregation is a general methodological question, not a commonsense argument about the presumably more concrete, specific, or context-sensitive quality of local or country studies versus wider comparative research.

This study takes the Western European countries as its main spatial units of analysis. Most of the time, these units are national elections taken as a single piece of data or as a country average. It is clear, therefore, that cross-country variations will be implicated and within-country differentiation will have to be placed to one side. The implication of this choice in terms of which aspects can be submitted to empirical control and which are definitely outside it should by now be clear. It should be added that within the range of thirteen countries and about 370 elections, subsets of cases will often be selected to manipulate variance and to perform more limited comparisons among sets characterized by the maximum and minimum variance in the dependent or independent variables. This, however, will not modify the "systemic properties" framework of the research.

TEMPORAL VARIATION

This study is not a synchronic cross-sectional comparison performed at a given chronological point or functionally equivalent time. It covers almost a century of European politics. This involves temporal variations within countries that are as large as, if not larger than, the cross-country spatial variations. Elsewhere,[45] I have developed my methodological ideas about the difficult relationship between spatial and temporal variance in comparative research, and there is no need to restate them here. The main conclusion is that, for the purpose of advancing causal sequential generalizations, resorting to "history" as the analysis of temporal variance, without the simultaneous analysis of synchronic cross-sectional variance, is far from an ideal solution; rather, it has its own methodological pitfalls. It is pointless to discuss whether the pitfalls of a synchronic analysis deprived of a temporal dimension are more or less intense than those of a longitudinal analysis deprived of synchronic contrasts among different units. For control

[45] Bartolini (1993).

purposes, the safest method is to contrast cross-sectional and cross-temporal results; therefore, research designs should try to observe *both* types of variance.

This research on the political mobilization of the left also has, therefore, methodological objectives. It is an attempt to put into practice these methodological guidelines. I apply a comparative research design that combines variation in both the spatial *and* temporal dimensions, and I hope that the substantive results support the conviction that systematic cross-spatial *and* cross-temporal research designs are feasible and preferable to other strategies of comparative inquiry. My main methodological tool to check sequential generalizations is what I have called the "slides of synchronic comparisons through time," that is, synchronic cross-sectional comparisons made at different points in time and contrasted with the results of general analytical and developmental relationships among the aspects under examination. The relatively limited temporal dimension of this developmental comparison should make it less dependent on general theories and should also make more manageable the crucial problem of defining with sufficient precision the temporal units of the analysis. The absence of any ambition to reach spatial universality allows for a more culturally bounded and less abstract conceptualization, the operationalization and empirical referents of which are easier to identify. The properties that can be considered in this temporally and spatially restricted set of units can thus be made both more numerous and empirically more specific than those usually considered within general development theory, although substantially less numerous than those in the case studies.

Meeting these conditions in the study of the patterns of electoral mobilization of the class left allows for four distinct modes of analysis that guarantee the maximum control over generalizations. These four modes are represented in a simple exemplary form in Figure 1.2, applying them to a set of units for each of which variation over time in two variables (A and B) is considered. I will examine four different types of variance. First, by combining all the spatial units together (countries and elections), relationships among the variables can be established at the general *analytical* level as if they were time nondependent (first graph in the figure). Units enter into the picture according to the value/state of the variables at each different time, and as such, the different temporal units are not logically distinct from the spatial cases. Time is simply a unit-defining parameter. Second, combining all the spatial units along the dimension of time – as in the second graph – allows for the study of the overall temporal variations and the relationships among the historical trends of the variables, which are studied in terms of their *development* over time. In this case, the develop-

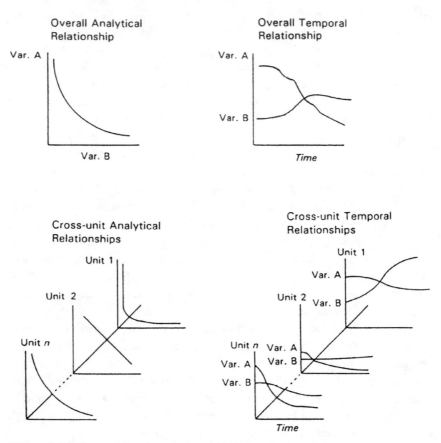

Figure 1.2. Four modes of analysis combining cross-time and cross-space variation.

ment trend is analyzed in terms of its general characteristics or average values (phases of statemaking, party system consolidation, suffrage expansion, etc.). This picture of how and when the relationship between the variables changes over time, or in different periods of time, and the possibility of identifying thresholds of structural change reinforces the understanding of the temporal association and causal priority among the variables.

These two types of variance – analytical and time dependent – can be checked in the history of each unit, so that we can compare whether the general analytical and temporal relationship resulting at the overall level is reproduced in the case of each single unit or whether it results from different patterns. In the third and fourth graphs, cross-unit variance is therefore added. The first two strategies are reproduced in each unit, thus obtaining cross-sectional variance and the possibility of comparison in terms of both the analytical and the temporal relationship between the variables. The analytical and temporal relations studied in the first two graphs constitute the *general reference point* with respect to which the cross-country variance can be identified: both in terms of the differences between units and, what is more important, in terms of the *differences between the country-specific analytical and temporal relationship, on the one hand, and the general analytical and temporal relationship, on the other*. The latter provide the yardstick against which statements of timing, tempo, and mode can be expressed and against which deviant cases can be identified. In other words, the overall analytical relationship and the overall temporal relationship are considered as the yardsticks against which each unit's analytical or temporal relationship can be judged as low or high, strong or weak, early or late. In sum, they provide the reference points for arriving at these comparative statements.

Thus the variance on which I will concentrate is not the difference in any one aspect between unit A and unit B, but the difference of each unit from the overall trend or analytical relation. This point is far from trivial. Assumptions about earliness/lateness, presence/absence, intensity, and so on frequently form part of comparative assessments, but more often than not, the reference point is far from clear. The extension of the suffrage in country X is early – but with respect to what? In a two-country comparison, the answer is simple; but in a twenty-country comparison, it becomes more difficult, and here the yardstick should probably be represented by a general temporal study of suffrage expansion over the whole set of countries. Depending on the nature of the measurement of the variables, such a general study could identify a general trend, or different phases, or different historical thresholds with respect to which national trends, phases, or historical thresholds can be judged. In other words, *a matrix of temporal and spatial variance cannot be identified empirically and systematically solely on the basis of comparisons among individual units, but only by reference to the temporal and analytical relationships that exist more generally*.

This transformation of the variance to be explained is, in my opinion, of paramount importance. Let me clarify further the process involved with an example. Let us assume that the analytical relation between working-class constituency size and left vote is 0.9 in country A and 0.2 in country B. If we concentrate on a direct comparison, then what has to be explained is the difference of 0.7 between the two cases, which may be attributed to any third intervening variable. If, however, we decide to take the overall association as the relative comparative yardstick, the variance to be explained changes drastically. Let us assume that in the entire universe of

400 elections, such an association is 0.55. Thus, both countries are deviating by the same amount (0.35) from the overall association, although in different directions. If, however, the overall association is 0.85, the picture is quite different. Country A is basically in line with the overall association, while country B is an exceptionally deviating case. In this latter example, the variance that interests me is the 0.65 that sets country B apart from the general association. It is thus possible to see that the general analytical and temporal yardsticks not only make comparative statements across many cases more accurate, reliable, and valid intersubjectively, but also redefine the general variance to be explained. In the course of this study, there are many instances in which this redefinition of the variance is surprising and raises unexpected questions.

MICRO VERSUS MACRO: WHAT KIND OF STUDY

Nothwithstanding recent attempts to underline the advantages of "holistic" approaches to the comparative study of political systems,[46] the dominant emphasis in political science in the 1980s and 1990s was different. A "decompositional" approach taken to its extreme consequences − to the fundamental actor, the basic particle of political phenomena: the individual − has recently and aggressively claimed its epistemological superiority and its objective of standardizing social science into a dominant paradigm. The (re)discovery of a few basic propositions has relaunched various versions of the "actor-centred" study of politics, including the idea that individuals have much more control over their own fate than was previously conceded; that therefore attention should be focused on them or, more generally, on the "actor" (collective in this case); that their motivations should be taken seriously, as seriously as their calculation concerning the best way of achieving what they want; and that the outcomes of political processes should hence be seen primarily as the intended or unintended consequence of subjective intentions and actions, interpreted within the framework of rational calculations of alternative costs and advantages.

Differences exist in these rational-choice approaches according to the point of reference for the "rationality" of the actor and the different role attributed to the effect of cognition through and in the process of choice. There is little doubt, however, that these approaches are bound together by the basic idea of assuming individual and collective rationality in pursuing his/her/its interests as the basis of the choice and of regarding as

[46] See Easton (1990).

external constraints of such a choice context the "structures" (in Easton's sense), the "institutions," and that broad and vaguely systematized set of factors usually referred to as "history." Recently, this approach has spread to the field of comparative politics and even that of comparative historical research. In so doing, it has somehow relaxed the set of postulates underlying the more theoretical endeavors, producing works that are both substantially and methodologically challenging.[47]

This book belongs to the opposite tradition. It is mainly concerned with the environmental constraints and macrostructural features of the political system and leaves little room, if any, to the study of the individual or collective actors' motivations, choices, and strategies. The choice of the explicandum – the variation in the left mobilization patterns, the choice of the cross-country spatial dimension, and the choice of a retrospective strategy of identification of crucial historical junctures – is in part responsible for such a design, which overemphasizes constraints on action imposed by structures over the explanation as identification of actors' motivations and choices. However, it is responsible only in part. The other part is simply due to my own preferences.

Those who have a fairly eclectic methodological approach orientation and are convinced that, first, the social sciences will never agree on a superior approach; second, the social sciences will continue to be characterized by cycles in which one approach gains predominance, without dislodging others, until it declines physiologically to the advantage of something else, when the epigones have completely taken over the early original innovators; and, third, that good as well as mediocre studies exist and will exist within each different tradition and approach should not involve themselves to any great extent in an approach debate. However, something should be said against the social science paradigmatic standardization sometimes pursued by rational-choice supporters and the claim made by actor-centered explanations of being the only legitimate approach, together with its correlate claim that macroassociations between collective behavior and historical and structural factors are meaningless unless they specify micromotivations. This is undoubtedly refreshing when it is presented as a new way of restating and reviewing classic problems, but it becomes fatuous when it is presented as the "new paradigm," outside of which old-fashioned, prescientific research persists in the fossilized belief that political action can be interpreted as a response to some sort of external stimulus that can be generalized.

[47] In the comparative party history field, one should mention Przeworski and Sprague (1986) and Kalivas (1996).

The emphasis on individual preferences and rational calculations versus that of the study on constraining conditions – or on "confining conditions," as Kirchheimer once put it[48] – should not be seen in epistemological terms, but more as a question of alternative research strategy. First, to consider collectivities and to study the constraining factors external to them and their collective exposure to similar external stimuli is not to forget factors of choice and individual evaluation in making action decisions. Even in the period of dominant behaviorism, there was a keen awareness of the key role of individual motivations, beliefs, and interests.[49] The issue was not, and is not, whether the action of the actor is or is not a rational adaptation (of some sort) to his or her personal situation in a given system as the actor perceives it subjectively. *From the individual's point of view, this is unquestionably what happens.* Individual action will always be the action of subjective rational adaptation to personal situations. The question is rather whether taking the lead from this subjective perception is the best research strategy from the external point of view of the researcher. This is clearly quite a different question.

The obvious starting point for every approach is the realization and attempt to explain some regularities and conformities in the behavior (or actions, if one prefers) of individuals. In an approach that relates macrophenomena to the aggregate behavior of collectivities, the subjective perceptions of individuals are implicitly thought to be shaped by social characteristics and phenomena that are external to the mind of the actor and that produce the behavioral group conformity and regularity that is observable. It might be methodologically correct and wise to specify the personal motivations that are thought to be produced by a constellation of external stimuli, but it remains obvious that such individual motivations are not and cannot be studied per se and are only *induced* from the influences of the macrofactor.

If, by contrast, the search is initiated at the point of the personal motivations of the individual (or of the interest of the collectivity), it

---

[48] Kirchheimer (1965: 964–974).

[49] For instance, in works like Lazarsfeld, Berelson, and Gaudet (1948) and Berelson, Lazarsfeld, and MacPhee (1954). This quotation is a perfect example of this awareness: "Social-position variables, such as class or place of residence, do not 'cause' any specific behaviour in the sense that they are requisite for, or the immediate antecedent of, given acts. Social conditions. however, do form personalities, beliefs and attitudes which, in turn, do 'cause' (are requisite to) specific acts such as participation in politics. . . . It is a simple matter, then, to find correlational relationship between social position variables and political participation, but the reader should keep in mind that the effect of social position variables must be mediated through personality, beliefs, and opinions." Milbrath (1965: 110).

cannot be said that we know them or study them better. Very simply, we *postulate* them or *reconstruct* them deductively from some general principle such as "self-interest." It seems highly unlikely that either the most radical-rational choice approach or the most deterministic one can know or understand the motivations of individuals, particularly when these number thousands or millions.

To the extent that actions show regularities in groups of individuals, these can be explained by making references to common perceptions, preferences, and situations of choice, but these common personal situations and perceptions can also imply the presence of external influences determining them and external confining conditions shaping and directing them. In a nutshell, if we start from the observation of group regularity in behavior, we may well conclude that this exists because all members of the group have made the same rational adaptation to the situation as they perceive it, but we may also legitimately inquire whether these common situations/perceptions do not come from some external source. If the formation of individual motivations (or preferences) were not somehow shaped by external influences and constraining structures, it would be hard to interpret group behavioral regularities and to escape a total randomness of individual ends.

In this perspective, the issue of individual motivations versus structural constraints is not that of a choice between the "good" and "adequate" approach against the "wrong" one, but more simply the choice between alternative approaches, both of which may have advantages and disadvantages. Basically, by linking macrostructural determinants to aggregate individual behavior, we bypass individual motivations by assuming that aggregate behavioral regularity is an adequate although indirect indicator of regularities in individual motivation formation. By linking micromotivations to aggregate individual behavior, we bypass those forces that can account for the similarity in individual motivations that leads to group regularity and conformity in individual choices. The question is basically where we put the "black box" that seems to be inescapably associated with every human science research approach.[50]

If general processes, outcomes, and institutions are reconstructed as aggregate results of individuals' purposeful rational actions in a given context, it has to be admitted that while the motivations, perceptions, and values of the individuals and groups can be postulated or reconstructed,

---

[50] This is why I find greatly exaggerated the "holistic" paradigm label attributed by Boudon (1979: 187–252) to all approaches that do not take the lead from the motivation of the actor.

their process of formation and actual content is unknown. This is the black box in this case. In contrast, by directly linking the study of macroprocesses and institutions to observable behavior, we assume that somehow these conditions determine a regularity in the productions of goals, perceptions, motivations, and so on that, in turn, leads to behavioral choices. Obviously, in this case, these motivations are not studied directly, nor are they postulated a priori; they disappear into the link that is established between conditions and behaviors.

From this point of view, the accusation in the field of comparative research that macrostructural approaches do not specify the micromotivational foundations of their work is equivalent to the accusation that rational-choice perspectives do not specify the historical, cultural, and institutional constraints that produce and shape individual motivations.

Is it better to examine behavior starting from proximate motivations and leaving aside the processes that structured their formation, or is it better to examine it starting from the more distal point of constraining conditions and postulating their effect on motivations? Is the arbitrariness of postulating motivations and deducing choices within a set of constraining conditions higher or lower than the arbitrariness of inducing motivations and choices from the association between macrofactors and collective behavior? It is, quite honestly, difficult to give an answer to these questions. I am ready to be convinced that the actor-centered perspective is more productive, but this view must derive from the substantive results of comparative research conducted with this paradigm, not from the inappropriate conclusion that, as human history is obviously made up of individuals' choices and actions, scientific research must start with them. As I have been arguing here, the issue of what it is that ultimately constitutes human history, and the question of which is the best paradigm by which to interpret it, are separate questions.

In conclusion, this issue of paradigms – provided that it remains with us long enough before being overshadowed by some new, fashionable rediscovery or comeback – should be treated pragmatically, looking at the quality of the results produced by the different orientations. For this, a comparison of the results of different strategies is necessary. Mutual checking is better than paradigmatic uniformity. As a result of my intellectual training, I have come to believe that collective behaviors and environmental constraints are the visible part of the moon and that individual motivations, beliefs, preferences, perceptions, and eventual choices are its hidden one. If the intellectual climate has changed and it is now viewed as easier and more appropriate to start from the latter, I am ready to accept a definition of the approach followed in this book as traditional. After all, even supposedly disappearing minorities have rights to vindicate; tradition sometimes defends the pluralism facing modernity and checks against the oversized victory of the moderns.

THE EUROPEAN LEFT: SIZE, IDEOLOGICAL ORIENTATION, AND ORGANIZATIONAL COHESION

This chapter is mainly descriptive. Relying on secondary literature and electoral and organizational data, it describes the variation in my dependent variable: the national experiences of the class left in the three main dimensions of *size and electoral development, early ideological orientation,* and *organizational cohesion*.

SIZE AND ELECTORAL DEVELOPMENT

In the 361 national elections held in the thirteen countries between the beginning of the 1880s and the end of the 1980s – almost 110 years – at least one class-left party was present and competed in 347. The fourteen missing cases are concentrated in three countries where free elections were held in the 1880s and 1890s without a socialist-type party taking part: in Sweden between 1887 and 1899 (six elections); in the United Kingdom between 1885 and 1895 (four elections); and in Norway between 1882 and 1891 (four elections). These three countries have, therefore, a late entry of the left into electoral politics with respect to the beginning of competitive elections.

In the twentieth century, socialist, communist, and other splinter parties of the same family collected one-third of the European vote averaged by country (33.2%; see Table 2.1), 30.3% of the vote of the total European electorate (see Table 2.2), and 25.1% of the European valid votes. Table 2.1 reports the country average strength over the whole century and the standard deviation of their results, as well as the number

Table 2.1. *European left average vote by country (% of valid votes, 1880–1989)*

country	mean % of votes	SD	n. of elections
Austria	43.77	8.17	20
Belgium	32.52	9.31	26
Denmark	35.65	14.01	42
Finland	42.16	4.13	30
France	34.10	14.34	25
Germany	32.89	10.42	29
Ireland	11.77	2.78	21
Italy	33.50	13.91	19
Netherlands	24.80	12.60	28
Norway	35.04	16.64	27
Sweden	43.28	13.83	29
Switzerland	23.82	7.23	27
U. Kingdom	33.33	14.68	24
all countries	33.18	14.10	347

Table 2.2. *Average European left vote development (five-year means in thousands)*

period	European electorate	European left votes	left votes as % of the electorate	% rate of electoral growth	number of countries
1881-85	9,235	431	4.7		1
1986-90	10,249	1,097	10.7	6.	2
1891-95	20,648	2,056	9.9	-.8	6
1896-00	24,120	2,809	11.6	1.7	7
1901-05	17,776	3,513	19.8	8.2	7
1906-10	39,647	5,791	14.6	-4.8	10
1911-15	42,959	8,399	19.7	5.1	10
1916-20					
1921-25	99,207	24,292	24.5	4.8	13
1926-30	103,740	30,058	29.0	4.5	12
1931-35	105,328	28,630	27.2	1.8	11
1936-40	31,732	9,219	29.1	1.9	9
1941-45					
1946-50	147,032	49,282	33.5	4.4	13
1951-55	154,513	51,562	33.4	-.1	13
1956-60	162,989	53,632	32.9	-.5	13
1961-65	169,698	57,062	33.6	.7	13
1966-70	176,130	63,257	35.9	2.3	13
1971-75	188,768	66,895	35.4	-.50	13
1976-80	201,721	74,653	36.8	1.4	13
1981-85	211,388	72,442	34.3	-2.5	13

of elections in each country. In a century-long perspective, only three left parties overcome the 40% average barrier: Austria, Finland, and Sweden. The largest group of seven countries averages between 32% and 35% (Belgium, Denmark, France, Germany, Italy, Norway, and the United Kingdom), which is approximately the European mean. Three countries have a very small left – the Netherlands, Switzerland, and Ireland – which are by far the smallest left in Europe. Six countries have a standard deviation (SD) that is much lower than the mean – Ireland and Switzerland, Germany and Belgium, Finland and Austria. In these cases, the electoral scores of the left have remained within a relatively close range, with over-time variations much lower than those in the other countries. If they finally resulted in a strong (Austria and Finland), medium (Germany and Belgium), or small (Switzerland and Ireland) left, they were quite strong, medium, or small from the beginning. The differences in the way in which the electoral performance of the national left is spread over time can be best appreciated in Figure 2.1, where a boxplot of their electoral result is produced.

The boxes in Figure 2.1 include 50% of the values (their top side represents the 75th percentile and their bottom side the 25th percentile), and the line within the boxes is the within-box median value of each distribution. The top and bottom values that are not outliers are shown with lines drawn from the top and the bottom of the box to them. Finally, outlyers are identified with two symbols: o if they are values within a range of 1.5 to 3 box lengths and * if they are values beyond three box lengths (extreme values). The length of the box – the interquartile range – gives a good idea of the variability of the observations. Outliers are located in the lower part of the boxes, indicating in most cases the early elections that the left contested in these countries. However, these outliers are few and are concentrated in those countries with little variation in left electoral results, like Austria, Belgium, Germany, and Ireland. Finland and Austria are impressive for the solid homogeneity of their electoral result over almost a century. Finland does not even have any outlier, and the low position of its median within the box indicates that its electoral history is made up of a very high and historically consistent level of around 40%, with half of the elections ranging between 36% and 42% and the other half spreading from 42% up to 52%. Austria is very similar. The first two elections fought under the constitutional monarchy are deviating; after them, all the Austrian electoral results spread within the narrow range of fourteen points, between 38% and 52%. With a smaller size, Ireland has a variance that is even lower.

In Germany, Belgium, Sweden, and the United Kingdom, the variabil-

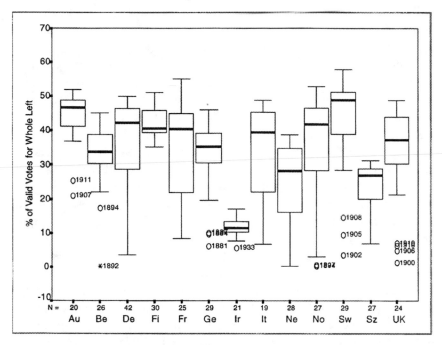

Figure 2.1 Boxplot of total left vote by country (1880–1989).

ity of the electoral results is intermediate. These countries all have outliers
in the first two or three elections, but since then their range has stayed
fairly contained. At the other end of the spectrum, Denmark, France, Italy,
Norway, and the Netherlands evidence the largest spread. The French
distribution is the most striking, standing at about 50 electoral percentage
points. Italy is not far from this extreme, and even in Denmark and
Norway the general spread of values is high, although the bulk of the
50% values in the box is greatly reduced compared with those of France
and Italy. The latter countries are the best examples of stormy electoral
histories, starting with very low levels that, however, do not appear as
outliers, and moving slowly to higher electoral levels, with frequent ups
and downs that cause great variation in their central 50% values. The
median value is more or less the same, but whereas in Italy the top 25%
values are quite compressed in a reduced range, in France the top 25%
of the cases ranges between 40% and 55%. France's left is characterized
by great electoral victories as well as great electoral defeats and probably
by a persistent instability and incapacity to stabilize a solid rock of identified voters. In contrast, the British case is paradigmatic of a normal
electoral development. The few outliers simply indicate the understandably

poor result of the first entry, while the median value is very close to the center of the box and the two top and bottom 25% sections are not too different.

Country median values do not take into account either the different sizes of country electorates or the different number of elections in each country. A better picture of the left mobilization over time is obtained by referring the votes collected by class left parties to the global European electorate. In order to equalize the number of elections, we can take for each country a five-year average vote (Table 2.2). Not all countries are present in every period, so the last column of the table indicates how many countries contribute to the average. Even with the limitation of the different number of countries per period, these figures give a more accurate idea of the overall pattern of European left historical development and rate of growth.

In the 1906–1910 period, the decline in the left vote is due to the large increase in the number of available country results, a step that adds weaker lefts to the picture. With this exception, the left keeps an average positive rate of growth from the end of the nineteenth century to the 1930s. Then the rate of growth begins to diminish. It is again high in the immediate post–World War II five-year period. Following this, for most of the post–World War II period, the European left keeps a stable percentage of the electorate. Throughout the post–World War II period, all countries are present, and although the European electorate passes from 147 million in 1946–1950 to 211 million in 1981–1985, the share of the class left vote tends to remain the same. However, in 1981–1985 for the first time, we observe a negative variation that is quantitatively considerable.

Other aspects of this historical development can be appreciated if, instead of considering five-year averages, we look at the trend of all elections in all countries. Figure 2.2 shows the 347 elections contested by some of the left parties. The set is divided into four periods: the pre–World War I period from 1880 to 1917, the interwars period from 1918 to 1944, the first post–World War II period from 1945 to 1965, and the second postwar period from 1965 to 1985. For each of these periods, a lowess fit line is used that produces a locally weighted regression scatterplot smoothing method to fit a line to a set of points. This method fits a specified number of data points carrying out a specified number of iterations. In Figure 2.2, 70% of the points have been fitted through three iterations.[1]

Figure 2.2 identifies four clearly differentiated patterns of over-time

---

[1] Up to 99% of the points can be fitted. In doing so, the basic trend of the lines does not change, but the lines themselves increasingly approach a pure linear regression.

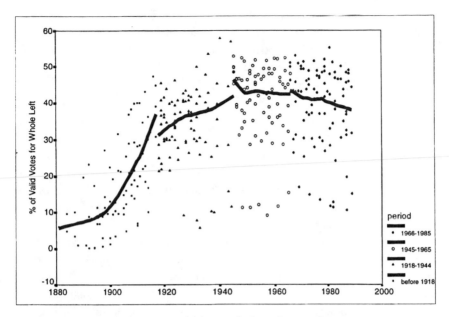

Figure 2.2. Electoral development: lowest fit lines by period.

development, each period characterized by a specific pattern of absolute and relative increases. The data sets that appear in the low part of the figure, starting from about the middle of the 1920s, are the results of the Irish left, deviating from all the other countries and generally very stable over time. The global figure seems to indicate a typical Gompertz function. In the first period before World War I, the European left passes from a *genetic* to a *growth* phase. In the genetic phase, up to the first years of the twentieth century, the developments and rates of growth are minor. This phase was characterized by the first appearances of the class left, generally in contexts of suffrage that were still restricted. By the first decade of the twentieth century, the slope transforms itself into an exponential-growth curve characterized by strong rates of growth and increase. In the period between the two world wars, the left passes to its *maturity* phase, character-ized by declining increments. The trend is still growing, but it has already changed its shape. It becomes linear, with homogeneous increases over time. It is possible that the steepness of this line is reduced by the seven Irish elections between 1927 and 1945, and indeed their impact is visible in the smoothed line in 1927. However, this impact does not modify the radical difference between the lines of the first two decades of the century and that of the second two decades — a difference that highlights the passing from the takeoff phase to the steady-growth phase.

The first post–World War II period corresponds to a phase of *stability*.

In the aftermath of the war, the European left reaches its peak, but immediately afterward, in about 1948, it acquires its period level, which remains more or less stable to the end of the 1960s. The left in this period faced the *saturation of its potential electoral market*. In the last phase, between 1965 and 1985, there are, in fact, signs of *electoral decline*. These are not dramatic, but they are clear. What is more important is that for the entire post–World War II period the European left does not evidence any clear secular trend and thus, historically, it has reached its ceiling. The recent literature that has so strongly emphasized the crisis, and sometimes even the electoral decline of the traditional class left, should be evaluated in the face of this secular trend. At the overall European level, the left had already stopped growing by the late 1940s, and the recent mild signs of decline do not justify the claim of a collapse.

Let us now combine historical development with cross-country differences. Table 2.3 offers a comparative appreciation of national left size by period and its change over time (for the temporal variation by country, see the later discussion). Before the Great War, only the Finnish left had reached the size of a strong, governmental party. It was followed – though at a considerable distance – by the Austrian, Swedish, and German lefts. The German Social Democratic Party could claim to be the oldest in Europe, but even in the pre–World War I period it was not the strongest electorally. At the opposite end, the United Kingdom and the Netherlands had the weakest left parties in Europe at the time (excluding the nonexistent Irish left). In the second period, between the world wars, the generalized pattern of growth reduces the cross-country variation in left size, and weak lefts tend to gain more than strong lefts in a general process of homogenization. The exception is Sweden, whose left – although it was already strong before the end of the Great War – grew more than any other left except the British and became the strongest in Europe in the interwar years. The Dutch and Swiss lefts became the weakest, followed closely by the French, while the British left caught up with all the other countries with an accelerated rate of growth.

In passing from the interwar period to the first post–World War II period, the difference is still positive but greatly reduced. The size of the left grows in all countries except Germany (-3.0%). In two countries – Belgium and Switzerland – the left has clearly stopped growing, although the prewar level of these lefts was not exceptionally high. The same happens to Sweden, but with the difference that it had already become the strongest European left before World War II. It is interesting to note that in 1945–1965 the German left is one of the weakest in Europe, stronger only than the Swiss and, obviously, the Irish. Norway and the United

Table 2.3. *Average electoral strength of the national left by period and differences between periods*

	I before 1918	II 1918-1944	difference II - I	III 1945-1965	difference III - II	IV 1966-1989	difference IV - III
Au	23.2	40.5	+ 17.3	47.3	+6.8	49.0	+1.7
Be	15.5	37.7	+ 22.2	39.4	+1.7	30.5	-8.9
De	17.0	38.1	+ 21.1	46.0	+7.9	46.1	+0.1
Fi	41.3	38.8	- 2.5	47.5	+8.7	42.9	-4.6
Fr	12.7	30.8	+ 18.1	42.8	+12.0	46.1	+3.3
Ge	21.3	37.6	+ 16.3	34.6	- 3.0	41.8	+7.2
Ir	.	10.0	-	11.8	+1.8	13.3	+1.5
It	15.3	32.1	+ 16.8	40.8	+8.7	46.1	+5.3
Ne	7.3	24.8	+ 17.5	35.5	+10.7	34.3	-1.2
No	13.7	36.3	+ 22.6	50.9	+14.6	46.3	-4.6
Sw	23.1	48.5	+25.4	51.1	+2.6	49.8	-1.3
Sz	15.4	27.8	+ 12.4	29.5	+1.7	25.1	-4.4
UK	4.9	34.3	+ 29.0	46.4	+12.1	38.0	-6.4
all elections	18.0	34.2	+16.2	40.6	+6.4	39.1	-1.5

Kingdom experience the highest growth difference between these two periods. The countries with medium growth are those that already had a strong left in the interwar period (Sweden, Finland, Austria, and Denmark). If we exclude the stable lefts and the declining German left, in all the other countries there is a certain inverse proportionality between the prewar size of the left and the electoral increases in the postwar period. On the whole, in the 1945–1965 period, we have two lefts that are on average majoritarian (Sweden and Norway) and four that approach that level (Austria, Denmark, Finland, and the United Kingdom). Three countries have what can be called "intermediate" strength at around 40% of the vote: France, Italy, and Belgium; three others are clearly below the European average, between 30% and 35%: the Netherlands, Germany, and Switzerland. Ireland continues to stand alone as an exceptional case.

In the last period, 1965–1985, few major ranking changes occur. The general level of growth has stopped, as we have seen, and its value is negative. Six countries have positive interperiod differences, and seven have negative ones. The most pronounced change concerns the breakdown of the Belgian left, dramatically affected by the crisis of national politics after the mid-1960s (−8.9%). Other noticeable declines from a previous high occur in the United Kingdom, Norway, and Finland. A less pronounced decline occurs in Sweden. There is no such decline in Austria and Denmark, while France, Italy, and Germany show the most significant increases in electoral support. In general, there are signs that the stronger lefts of the 1945–1965 period tend to have an earlier and more pronounced decline than the weaker lefts, although the Austrian and Danish lefts manage to avoid it. In contrast, some of the medium-sized lefts of the 1945–1965 period still seem to have some margins of growth. Finally, it must be noted that the Dutch and Swiss lefts decline in the last period, although they had never been particularly strong before. In general, therefore, one cannot speak of a uniform and generalized decline since the 1960s.

At the end of the twentieth century, therefore, the picture changes in the relative ranking of countries – apart from the obvious historical failure of the Irish left; also, the Dutch, Swiss, and Belgian lefts appear to be electorally undermobilized. Sweden, Austria, Norway, and Denmark main-tain their historical position as leaders, while Italy and France reach the level of electoral mobilization of the latter two countries in this last phase. Finally, Finland and the United Kingdom fall to around the all-country European average together with Germany. With respect to the beginning of the electoral history of European socialism, this last phase has therefore seen some radical changes in size ranking, the clearest of which are (1) the drastic retrenching of the electorally promising Belgian left; (2) the lack in breakthrough of the early powerful German left; (3) the rising rank position of the relatively late French and Italian lefts; and (4) the parabola of British labor, which in the last phase falls back more or less to the electoral size of the interwar years. The continuous governmental potential of the British left in the context of its party system and electoral rules should not overshadow the fact that in the 1965–1989 period this left is only 4 percentage points stronger than the Dutch left.

Period means by country allow a synthetic appreciation but also con-ceal a great deal of over-time variation. To examine the temporal develop-ment patterns of the thirteen countries, in Figure 2.3 they have been classified into three groups according to the predominant shape of their electoral history. In Figure 2.3a, the United Kingdom, the three Scandi-navian countries, and Finland are charted. These cases demonstrate a com-paratively late entry of the class left into the electoral market. In Norway, the United Kingdom, and Sweden, the left appears only at the beginning of the twentieth century, and, as a consequence, its growth phase is extraordinarily rapid. Denmark has an earlier start and a less rapid growth phase. The Finnish left's appearance is one of the latest in Europe due to the delay of political rights and partisan politics in Finland; but once it appears, its level is extremely high. Finland is the only country in which the left fielded about 40% of the votes before World War I. Consequently, it does not fit the four phases of the overall European development. To begin with, it was an oversized left, and its successive development was therefore less trendy. All cases peak in the middle of the 1940s, all had about 50% of the votes in the 1945–1965 period, and all have tended toward a negative and declining trend since that date, even if such a trend has been more accentuated in the United Kingdom and Finland than in the Scandinavian countries. Note the exceptionally continuous and rapid growth phase of the Swedish left up to the 1940s.

The French, Italian, and Austrian lefts are charted in Figure 2.3b. The growth phase in these countries is less rapid, also because their entry level is higher than that of the previous group: when they first entered the electoral races, they immediately obtained between 10% and 20% of the votes. They therefore tend to grow less rapidly than those in the first group. Moreover, no signs of a ceiling emerge in the middle of the 1940s. In addition, none of these lefts is characterized by a negative electoral trend after 1965. Quite the contrary: They continue to grow even after World War II. Even if the immediate post–World War II election years are peak years, all of them tend to show better electoral performances in the 1970s than in the previous decades. This is particularly evident in Italy, whose trend up to the middle of the 1980s is one of continuous albeit moderate growth. France is interesting because the peak reached in 1945–1946 is followed by a lasting and critical period of decline throughout the Fourth Republic (1945–1958) and by a slow but continuous recovery during the Fifth Republic (1962–1986), which brings it to its highest-ever electoral level. The striking decline of the left during the 1950s is an exclusively French feature. The Austrian left overcomes the 50% voter threshold in the 1970s. Although it was an early strong left, reaching 40% of the votes after World War I, it took another half-century to reach its highest point. Finally, it should be pointed out that in the post–World War II period, it was only in Italy that the electoral growth was constant.

Figure 2.3c regroups the remaining countries. I have included Ireland, which, as I said earlier, is a unique and totally deviating case. The other cases – Germany, Belgium, the Netherlands, and Switzerland – do have something in common, however. First of all, none of these lefts ever approaches the 50% threshold. Second, they tend to be early mobilizers, particularly in Germany and Belgium, but they also reach their maturity level before the other cases. For Germany, Belgium, and Switzerland, the immediate post–World War I years define their maturity level, above which they will never rise. The Netherlands is slightly different because it grows in the interwar period, too, and peaks and reaches maturity in 1945, like the countries of the first group. Its growth is, however, much less marked and rapid, and the overall maturity level reached is much lower.

a)   Scandinavian, Finnish and British lefts

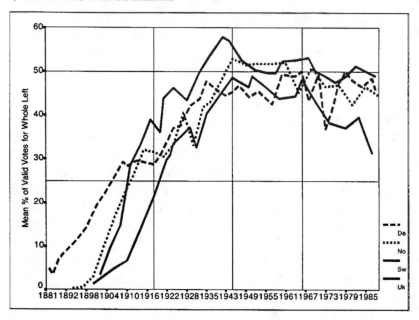

b) French, Italian, and Austrian lefts

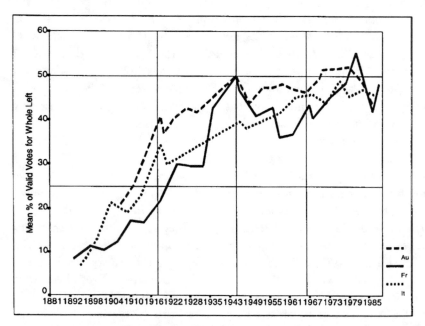

Figure 2.3. National electoral developments (1880–1989).

c: Central European lefts (plus Ireland)

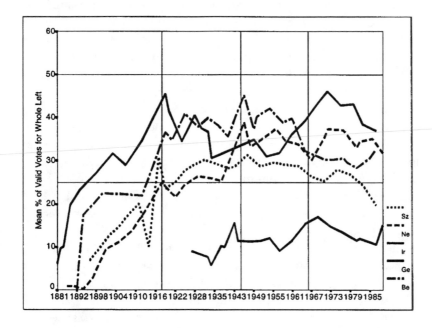

With the partial exception of the Netherlands, then, it can be said that in these countries electoral growth stops between the two world wars at intermediate levels. Switzerland and Ireland are striking for the marked stability of their results; they seem to have been untouched by the huge sociopolitical changes since the end of the First World War. To a certain extent, the Belgian left may also be included in this group, because it remained remarkably stable throughout the long period from 1919 to 1965, changing only when the politicization of ethnic and linguistic cleavages in the latter decade weakened it. These continental cases differ from the Nordic ones in the absence of growth in the interwar period. Germany is noticeable for its unique electoral shape. It starts early – in fact, it was the earliest – and it grows rapidly. By the end of World War I, it has reached an electoral size of about 45%, which is similar to that of the Nordic countries of the first group. However, the German left then enters a long period of decline and stagnation that lasts for almost four decades. It starts to grow again only at the end of the 1950s. The peak reached at the beginning of the 1970s is practically the same level as that reached in 1918.

The four phases of European development discussed in connection with Figure 2.2 were therefore the result of quite different national developments. In terms of general shapes of national development, and irrespective of the general size of the left and the precise dates at which variations occurred in different countries, we can distinguish four patterns. The first is a pattern of rapid growth, a high peak, and an equally accentuated decline, which is epitomized by the United Kingdom but which also characterizes Finland, Sweden, and Belgium quite well. The second is a pattern of less rapid but continuous growth, typical of Italy and also applying to Austria. The third is a more complex pattern, characterizing those countries that experience a period of decline located between two peaks: the typical sine curve of France, but also of Germany and Finland. The fourth and final pattern is that of a growth phase followed by a long stagnation period, a pattern epitomized by Switzerland but also applying to the Netherlands, Norway, and Denmark. After World War II, these lefts have an electoral ceiling around which they oscillate, with no consistent pattern of growth or decline.

On the whole, then, during the postwar period, the European left was generally incapable of improving its level of support among the various national electorates. The increase in support between the pre- and postwar averages was achieved only in the immediate aftermath of the war. Later on, with the exception of Germany and Italy, these increases become marginal. Therefore, in the second half of the 1940s, the European left reached national peaks that later proved difficult to exceed, and it crossed the 50% threshold in only six countries during the entire period: Norway, Sweden, Denmark, Finland, Austria, and France. Even among these countries, it is only in the first two that this phenomenon appears to be a lasting achievement. In the others, it is a more occasional result. In Norway, the left won more than 50% of the votes between 1945 and 1973, while in Sweden this occurred between 1936 and 1956 and again during the 1960s. In the United Kingdom, the left approached this crucial threshold on several occasions. In France and Italy, this has occurred only in recent years.

IDEOLOGICAL ORIENTATION
AND RADICALISM

The European variance in the labor response also includes the predominant ideological orientation of the socialist movements. Slightly more complicated is the possible relationship between radicalism and organizational cohesion. Therefore, some prior clarification of the relationship between *ideological orientation, radicalism,* and *organizational cohesion* is required, as the three phenomena are sometimes inextricably entwined. To approach the question via a general definition of "radicalism" is inadequate because such definitions are in general too broad and rarely useful enough for a historical comparative analysis of several cases.[2] For this reason, the usual strategy used to identify radicalism refers to three phenomena, that are taken as indicators:

1. The spread or strengthening of a *particular ideological version of socialist thought* identified as "radical" or more radical than others.
2. The presence, intensity, and extension of *specific behavioral patterns* regarded as radical – for instance, the frequency, intensity, and adversarial nature of strike activities; the frequency of specific working-class protest activities, confrontations with the forces of order; and revolts and attempted revolutionary actions. In short, the extent to which working-class collective behavior was militant and/or aggressive.
3. The organizational fragmentation of the socialist movement and, in particular, the strength of *specific organizational forms of the socialist movement*. The inability of different groups to live together within broad, organizationally unified movements can be regarded as a sign of internal tension and of radical ideological and organizational strife. In particular for the post–World War II period, the strength of the communist organizations is considered to be the main indicator of a radical orientation.

The degree to which socialism and working-class politics are moderate/radical is usually identified with one of these three aspects, which are not, however, necessarily associated with one another. Finally, they do not coincide historically, as each aspect seems to be particularly important or prominent in a different period. Let me clarify these three points.

---

[2] R. C. Tucker (1967), for instance, defines radicalism by making reference to "attitudes or demands which do imply, request or expect basic and fundamental changes in societal structure." "Attitudes" and "demands" are not the same thing. Radical attitudes in the bulk of the rank and file may be matched by more moderate demands coming from the organizations and the political leadership; alternatively, radical leadership may be non-representative of rank-and-file basic attitude systems. Second, why should radicalism be expressed by or through demands of "societal" change? Radical demands can also concern the state and, more generally, other political aspects. Even if we admit that "attitudes" and "demands" match and that "societal" includes both socioeconomic and political institutional demands, what is "basic and fundamental change"? How can one state that there was more of such demand here than there, now than before? A general definition, even if good, does not serve my purpose because it is not sufficiently denotative to help identify empirical historical variance among cases.

To concentrate attention on the spread and importance of the ideological system guiding the action of the organized part of the socialist movement may focus too heavily on elite conceptualizations and doctrinal debates; it may give too much weight to minor intellectual groups or party bureaucracy; and it may privilege a coherence of thinking and intellectual elaboration on actual class action. Alternatively, to concentrate mainly on mass collective action poses the problem that the radicalization of forms of action may be unrelated to radical goals and strategies. In other words, radical forms of class action do not necessarily indicate radical political socialism. To identify radicalism with the organizational and electoral success of communism is to gainsay too many of the early preconditions for such success.[3] The three aspects do not necessarily covary. Thus, orthodox revolutionary Marxism may combine with the quiescent collective behavior of the socialist movement, just as strong communist organizations may resort to radical collective action regarding events and concerns that are outside the internal dynamics of the national labor movement, and strong anarchist or syndicalist wings may shatter the labor movement without being able to consolidate important political or corporate organisations.

The three aspects are historically separate. If the question of socialist radicalism is raised for the early phase of the consolidation of socialist movements before World War I, the answer to it is likely to emphasize the dominant ideological orientation of the movement. Radicalism was probably associated with the spread of anarchism or revolutionary syndicalism, or even of orthodox Marxism, as opposed to other, more moderate forms or socialist traditions. During the revolutionary post–World War I European crisis, radicalism was mainly identified with the shattering of the traditional socialist political and union organizations by new forms of collective action, by the intensity of the social conflict, and by the existence of the threat of social revolution; that is, it was mainly identified by a pattern of radical class action. The 1920s mark the beginning of the process of organizational fragmentation of the socialist movement after many decades and efforts at political centralization and unification. From the 1930s on and after World War II, the level of "domestication" was judged in reference to the strength of the communist component in each movement and, more generally, to the extent to which the socialist move-

---

[3] The specific identification of communism with radicalism could be subsumed under point (1), that is, communism could be regarded as the spread of a specific ideological current (Leninist doctrines). However, it is better to regard this as a separate case. This is so because the essence of communist radicalism is seen – rightly or wrongly – in its organizational expression, as an organizational weapon.

ment was organizationally unified or divided. Finally, it is important not to characterize radicalism as a secular process according to which the situation crystallizing in the 1950s and 1960s was the final result of a long history whose roots had existed from the beginning. In fact, the countries that *in the long run* are considered the homes of moderate reformist socialism may have had radical labor movements before World War I or in the interwar period.

For this reason, I have decided to organize my description of the internal dynamics of the European left by separating these three aspects into the temporal phases in which they predominated or were the most important feature. I will therefore deal with

1. The *early predominant ideological orientation* of the socialist movement, before World War I (when the movement was organizationally unified or tended toward national political unification);
2. The phase of *collective class action* radicalization between the 1910s and the 1920s – the result of the war and revolutionary crisis;
3. The subsequent process of *organizational fragmentation* of the socialist movement, whose most conspicuous element is the communist split and eventual consolidation.

Early ideological orientation, intermediate militant collective action, and final organizational (communist) fragmentation form specific combinations in each country. Therefore, the poles of the empirical variation can be identified as, on the one hand, an early moderate orientation, lack of revolutionary crisis and mobilization, and absence of organizational fragmentation and communist inroads, and, on the other hand, early radical ideological traits, profound revolutionary crisis, and deep organizational splits. Using this framework, it is possible to remold the inadequate unidimensional opposition between "radical" and "moderate" while maintaining a focus on the ideological, behavioral, and organizational faces of radicalism and, at the same time, detecting historical empirical variance among the cases. The following two sections are devoted to the first two aspects; organizational fragmentation and communist strength will be dealt with separately in the final part of the chapter.

EARLY IDEOLOGICAL ORIENTATION

The starting point for the spread of the ideological tradition that will be taken to represent more or less radical idea systems is the contrast among the United Kingdom, Germany, and France. These three countries are most representative of certain ideological traditions: moderate trade union-ism in the United Kingdom, orthodox revolutionary Marxism in Germany, and a combination of the latter with important anarcho-syndicalist components in France. These variants have also been examined from a normative point of view: While the moderate reformer underlines the realism, pragmatism, and humanitarianism of British Fabianism against the radical, rationalistic continental schemes, the Marxist thinker contrasts the theoretical quality of German socialism with the "adventurousness" and lack of coherence of the French movement and the vulgar pragmatism of the British one. At the same time, the eclectic French socialist criticizes both trade unionism and "bureaucratic state socialism." The experiences of other countries in the historical phase up to the time of the Russian Revolution are interpreted within this triangle of ideological genealogy.

Trade Unionism

The strongest opposition is often thought to be that of the United Kingdom versus the Continent[4] and the connected question of the absence of any Marxist penetration in the British Isles. Without question, of all the theories and ideas that forged British socialism, Marxism played the smallest role. In fact, the initial cultural characterization of the British labor movement was permeated by the liberal culture of its early leaders and organizers. Liberal radicalism was traditionally associated with religious nonconformism, and in the nineteenth century such denominational sects constituted the cultural basis of the labor movement, just as Methodism and its theology of consolation were widespread among the working class. Equally important was the romantic tradition of social criticism, with its strong moral and ethical bases for social protest and change, and the consequent idea that moral reforms were as important as, if not more important than, social ones, and that socialism was fundamentally a process of enlightenment for both workers and employers. At the same time, the origins of the labor tradition of the early trade unions were Owenite and utilitarian, concentrating on reforms within the existing system and redistribution through economic action, that is, by distinguishing between

---

[4] The recent work by S. Berger (1994: 248) denies this opposition and argues that the differences between the British and German parties were more a matter of degree than of substance. He concludes that "the hypothesis that ideological and organisational differences made the Labour party an altogether different type of working-class party from the one to which the SPD belonged can not easily be maintained." This two-country comparison is conducted, however, without an overall comparative framework of reference, and it is based on examples that are selectively drawn from various sources and deliberately emphasize similarities and minimize differences.

fair and unfair competition and good and bad capitalists. These old cultural traditions were unfavorable to the basic tenets of Marxist theory, in particular to the idea of class warfare and the recognition that political and economic power were profoundly related to the question of authority in industry and the state.[5] The fundamental belief in the neutrality of the state machinery caused mainstream laborism to sidestep this feature of continental socialism and Marxism in particular.

Attempts to introduce more politically radical versions of socialist thinking occurred only outside the world of the trade unions. The large middle-class, intellectual composition of the early socialist societies and socialists alike was regarded with suspicion by the unions. Thus, the 1880 Social Democratic Federation of Marxist inspiration was formed by a few intellectuals, whose program of integrating and assimilating the various streams of laborite political thought and movements was a total failure. Any deliberate socialist ideology/program was systematically rebuffed by the unions, and even the formation of a more moderate Independent Labour Party outside a trade union context was unsuccessful (as evidenced by its poor 1895 electoral results).

Radicalization phases were not, however, unknown in the British labor movement. In the 1880s, the original concentration of British trade unionism within the more prosperous and skilled segments of the working class, and its main concern with salary and working hours, was challenged by the rise of "new unionism" and its decisive push toward the unionization of unskilled workers. The conservative character of British trade unionism was shattered but ultimately unaffected by this crucial step (which in other continental countries occurred much later, some time after the Russian Revolution). Rather than causing radicalization along Marxist lines, it produced the two basic streams of British pre–World War I socialism: Fabianism and guild socialism.

Fabianism, notwithstanding its intellectual attitudes and origins, became the dominant theoretical reference for British laborism; in fact, it was more important than the actual number of Fabians may suggest. This was because it concentrated on a theory of political action and programmatic strategy that was compatible with the cultural and organizational traditions of British labor. The Fabian essays of 1889[6] – the same year of the foundation on the Continent of the Second International, dominated by Marxist-oriented parties – were written by various thinkers and incorporated various streams of thought, but virtually none of the themes so

---

[5] See Willis (1977: 417–419) and McKibbin (1984: 297–331).
[6] Webb, Shaw, Wallace, Oliver, Clarke, Besant, and Bland (1962).

typical of Marxism and anarchism were included. The essential tenet was that socialism was simply the fulfillment of democracy in an industrial society; democratic procedures were taken for granted; the transformation was aimed at modifying the attitudes of the large majority of people and therefore had to be gradual; and it was through the state that this would be achieved. In a nutshell, the onset of socialism was constitutional and peaceful.

Guild socialism represented the radicalization of some sectors of the working-class movement before World War I. Its very name linked it to the original anti-industrialism protest, and its anticapitalism was coupled with an antistate attitude, aimed at transforming the state into a coalition of guilds, unions, and professions, each running its own affairs but being held together by some sort of nonstate, which some wanted to call "The Commune" and others "The Industrial Guild Congress." It has been observed that guild socialism echoed elements of the revolutionary radicalization on the Continent, and it is certain that the movement had several points of contact and correspondence with the continental syndicalism of that time, particularly in France, Spain, and Italy.[7] However, while on the continent the end of World War I brought about a further radicalization of the labor movement, in the United Kingdom it saw Fabianism predominate over guild socialism. Unquestionably, British labor developed a local ideological tradition, which Marxism and anarcho-syndicalism influenced only minimally.

Orthodox Marxism

When discussion focuses on British versus continental opposition, it is frequently the British versus German opposition that is meant. Germany is regarded as the homeland of orthodox Marxism and as the "quality side" of socialist theory. Thus, the socialist ideological orientation is mirrored by its programmatic development. The 1869 Eisenach Program of the Social Democratic Worker Party stressed the democratic tradition of the then dominant Saxonian progressives as well as Marxist internationalism. The 1875 Gotha Program of Unification was criticized by Marx and Engels for its Lassallian emphasis on welfare state measures and its progressive stress on the democratization of state and society. Due to the still profound influence of Lassalle in the trade union movement, these early socialist programs favored legalism and a positive attitude to social legislation, although they were more sophisticated than British trade unionism. This tradition did not, however, prove strong enough to guarantee the predom-

[7] See Holton (1985).

inance of ministerial socialism, with its corollary of the acceptance of the state as a positive force and actor.

The 1891 Erfurt Program mirrors the extent to which Marxism had by then become the exclusive theoretical basis and inspiration of the newly named German Socialist Party (SPD). Virtually all the previously mentioned Lassallian elements were eliminated by the new party program. The ideological penetration of Marxism, against the earlier Lassallian and progressive orientation of cooperation with the state while trying to reform it, strengthened during the underground period of repression and suppression. Marxism took over the party and neutralized the unions' positions in the twelve years of repression between 1878 and 1890. Kautsky and Bernstein were the chief popularizers of Marxism in the following period. Their efforts were built on and backed by a socialist press that was impressive for its quantity, diversity, and circulation – a situation unmatched in any other country with the possible exception of Austria (and, to a much lesser extent, Denmark).[8]

If the German labor movement was the homeland of Marxist orthodoxy, it should not be forgotten that its internal intellectual and doctrinaire debate was also so rich that, in addition, it became the homeland of the most coherent and consequent reformist version of Marxism itself. It was Bernstein who represented the alternative political strategy, advocating, first, the need to attract middle-class support in the political struggle against the authoritarian imperial government; second, a more realistic (and not antagonistic) policy on the agrarian question and the peasant problem; and third, the possibility of playing a more effective political role in German policy making and legislation even before the definite political victory of the labor movement.[9] Bernstein's analysis of capitalist development was rejected by the center and the left of the SPD. But while the revisionist theory was rebuffed and the orthodox theory was kept pure, the practical political guidelines of the party met a different fate.

In Germany and in many other European countries influenced by the German debate, the Kautsky–Bernstein dispute opened up two possibilities. The theory could be kept pure and orthodox, in which case it would be necessary to find new and alternative explanations for the socioeconomic

---

[8] On the richness of the Social Democratic press and the immense educational and cultural policy carried over by it, see Hall (1977), whose book provides useful information about the diffusion of different journals and the amount of internal theoretical debate. The author underlines more than once the exceptional number and diffusion of this press in comparison with those of other neighboring countries.

[9] Bernstein (1899). For the analysis of the situation that led to his political conclusions, see Colletti (1972: 61–147).

development identified by Bernstein or to live with a progressively schizo-phrenic split between pure theory and inevitably corrupted and compro-mised practice. Alternatively, the theory could be diluted, softened, and made less important, so that the compromise political tactics would not seem a corrupted and betraying behavior. In this book, I argue that the choice effectively made by the socialist movements in continental countries was largely determined by the response of the political environment of the socialist movement. In Germany, one could interpret the ideological debate within the SPD before World War I as a series of theoretical equilibriums developed in order to save orthodoxy. To offer alternative explanations to trends that Bernstein had interpreted in revisionist terms, Kautsky intro-duced the "relative" element in the theory of working-class impoverish-ment and argued that temporary checks compensated for the general ten-dency toward a worsening of the proletariat's conditions.[10] Luxemburg and the left wing of the party came up with the idea that the capitalist breakdown was not materializing because of the exploitation of colonies, that is, of noncapitalist parts of the world.[11] These new interpretations were compatible with the orthodox theory, but they maximized contradiction and tensions between theory and practice. In conclusion, at least until World War I, in the German socialist movement of Marxist orthodoxy was defended more successfully against moderate revisionism in theory than it was in practice.

Socialist Eclecticism

In France, neither a trade unionist tradition nor orthodox Marxism seems to represent adequately the ideological temperament of the labor movement. In fact, French socialism presents a number of paradoxes. Its political situation and tradition in the second half of the nineteenth cen-tury were the most favorable to socialism development in Western Europe. France had a long tradition of working-class militancy stemming from its long revolutionary tradition. Some of the key reference points for a socialist ideology were identified with French history of the late eighteenth and nineteenth centuries – a history that offered to the birth of socialism a cultural and ideological legitimacy that was absent in most of the other Western European countries. The philosophy of the Enlightenment and Cartesian rationalism were elements of the national culture claimed by the left as its heritage and were the precursor of the founding values of the

---

[10] Kautsky (1899).
[11] Rosa Luxemburg replied immediately to Bernstein's analysis in Luxemburg (1899). For the development of her thinking later on, see the collection of her writings in Luxem-burg (1963).

socialist anthropological vision. The 1789 Revolution[12] was interpreted in the nineteenth century as a popular movement, and the influence over French political culture of works like Lamartine's *Histoire des Girondins*[13] and Michelet's *Histoire de la révolution*[14] contributed to the setting up of a republican tradition as a set of values and political principles (antiauthoritarianism, anticlericalism) that came close to those of socialism. At the moment of consolidation of the socialist movement, the country had already gone through three republics. The brief workers' governments in Paris in 1848, 1870, and 1871 were republican founding experiences that were largely assimilated as positive. Ideas on popular rule were therefore not only theoretical, but had been tried and tested on several occasions. Louis Blanc, Auguste Blanqui, Etienne Cabet, and Pierre-Joseph Proudhon were legendary figures who had spent their lives in the labor movement. Thus, contrary to the cultural isolation of its German counterpart, French socialism was both culturally and politically well integrated into a legitimate and powerful republican and democratic tradition.

However, these conditions created a very complicated ideological scene; a class movement was created that was as rich in cultural traditions and political experience as it was organizationally weak and ideologically eclectic, in which none of the main streams of socialist ideology ever managed to integrate the entire movement. The early socialist thinking of the schools of Saint Simon (1760–1825), Fourier (1772–1837), Blanqui (1805–1881), and Proudhon (1809–1865) shared an incapacity to envisage a reform stemming from mass-organized collective action. In this sense, these thinkers and agitators were all deeply rooted in the mood of the Enlightenment.[15] In reacting against the bureaucratization of modern industry and the modern state, none of them saw, appreciated, or anticipated modern collective action, and thus they provided neither a rationale nor a guide for it. An organized collective movement for the realization of ideas was alien to them and – to a large extent – would remain alien to the entire French political culture.

Any success that Marxism in France had[16] was due largely to Jules Guesde and his review, *L'Egalité* (1877), and was originally confined to

---

[12] Of which the Russian Revolution was seen as a derivative. In his speech at the Congress of Tours in 1920, Cachin considered Lenin a true disciple of the *lumières*.

[13] De La Martine (1895).

[14] Michelet (1847–1853).

[15] That their hope for the reforming philosopher, their search for philanthropists or technocratic state engineering, their belief in insurrection, conspiracy, or a coup d'état had in common the idea that the solution had to be found in favor of or in behalf of the oppressed, more than by the oppressed themselves, is underlined by Ulam (1979: 98–99).

[16] See Dommanget (1969) and Prélot (1939).

this section of the socialist movement. The Guesdesists,[17] although making reference to Marx, maintained a strong anarchist and Blanquist imprint, and the doctrinal formation of the leaders of the Parti Ouvrier Français was the object of frequent complaints by Engels and Marx.[18] But Marxism in its Guesdesist French variant met formidable obstacles along its path to development. At the political level, the Marxist wing was unable to coordinate, and even less to hegemonize, the extremely ideologically, geographically, and organizationally fragmented socialist tradition.[19] The attempts to differentiate French socialism from the German experience – consciously pursued by Lucien Herr, by the municipal socialism of Paul Brousse, and by the intellectual humanitarian and in some ways bourgeois political sensitivity of Jaurès and later by Blum's socialism – represented powerful barriers for a group with very weak inroads into the trade unions. Marxism was perceived as a German doctrine in a country where the memories of the 1870 war had left a persistently anti-German attitude, which was reinforced by the 1914 SPD vote for the war credits.[20] One does not need to accept the radical thesis of Robert Aron, who sees Marxism as a foreign influence with no national roots in France and whose only effect was to ruin the autonomous local traditions,[21] to recognize the deep anti-German feeling of the nationalist tradition of the republican left. In 1882, Brousse criticized Guesde, arguing that "Les ultramontains ne peuvent pas obeir à la loi de leur pays parce que leur chef est à Rome. Les Marxistes peuvent pas obeir aux décisions du Parti et à ses Congrès parce que leur veritable chef est à Londres. . . ."[22] Blum also saw Guesde and his ideas as the French representative of "German collectivism." Many other examples of mistrust in the German origins of Marxism can be found in the early

[17] For the role of the Guesdesists in the formation of the Socialist Party and in the introduction of Marxism, see Perrot (1967: 701–710). Marx's *Das Kapital* was originally translated into French by Jules Roy and was published in 1875. It was not very successful. Far more influential was an abridged version published in 1876 by Gabriel Deville.

[18] The correspondence between Engels and Lafargue, which is a crucial source for the reception of Marxism in France, is full of such complaints; *Correspondance* (1956). Beyond tactical and short-term issues, the fundamental criticism was that Guesde's materialism resembled that of the eighteenth century and had no sense of dialectics.

[19] The piece devoted to socialism by Zeldin (1979: 361–423) clarifies that this fragmentation was geographical and social before being ideological and organizational.

[20] J. Droz's (1973) interpretation attributes to the diffidence originating in 1870 a primordial role in determining the difficult reception of Marxism and, more broadly, the difficult relationship between the German SPD and French socialism..

[21] Marxism is regarded as a foreign graft by Aron (1971). Kriegel (1969) interprets communism in the same vein.

[22] Speech of P. Brousse at the Congress of St. Etienne, where the split between Guesdesists and Broussists occurred. Quoted in Lefranc (1963: 47).

history of French socialism.[23] In the end, the adoption at the political level of more systematic Marxist stands as official party doctrine was always tempered by the influence of many other autonomous local traditions and leadership and remained therefore a surface phenomenon with respect to the broader assimilation of the socialist intelligentsia with radical-democratic values and beliefs.

A further element that prevented Marxism from making significant inroads into France was more overtly political. Initially, Jaurès and then Blum both perceptively pointed out that Marxism, and in general German socialist doctrine, was the result of the forced political *impuissance* of the German SPD in imperial Germany and that the political conditions of France and therefore the political problems of French socialism were fundamentally different.

At the trade union level, the situation was even more difficult. The Guedesists did not manage to penetrate the trade unions, which, indeed, until 1914 constantly affirmed their independence from them. The French trade unions were weaker in organizational terms than their German and British counterparts; they remained non-Marxist, like the British; but unlike the British and the Germans, they placed themselves to the left of the political movement, in the direction of syndicalism. The self-reliance of workers on their direct action qua associations and the mistrust of the professionalized political branch became important features of the movement. The syndicalist tradition, with its emphasis on direct class struggle,

---

[23] For instance, the explicit accusation in the writings and political positions of Lucian Herr that the "solid" and "hard-working" Germans received the ideas from the main French socialist thinkers and had only to systematize them; or the explicit claim of French leadership in the political field mentioned by Blum: "Ce n'est pas le prolétariat allemand qui a conquis le suffrage universel. Il l'a reçu d'en haut" (Conference of Amsterdam of the Second International, 1904, cited in Lefranc [1963 :119]; or the comment of Charles Andler on the 1848 Communist Manifesto: "La thèse du petit livre édité par la Librairie, c'est que, dans Marx, ce qu'il avait de grand c'est la tradition socialiste française et anglaise et qu'auprès d'elle l'originalité de Marx apparaissait moins écrasante" (Andler (1932: 139). The review *Bibliothèque socialiste* was launched in those years as an instrument of research of an original socialist and, above all, French elaboration. Blum, Andler, and other intellectuals of the group close to Herr and Jaurès published in it several articles and studies whose spirit and content was decidedly anti-German and anti-Marxist. This attitude had been fully perceived by Marx himself, as is clear from a letter to Sorge of November 5, 1880; after that, in spring 1881, he elaborated, with Engels and Guesde (with whom he had entered into epistolary contact in 1878), a program in the form of a manifesto published in the *Egalité* that year: "Je n'ai pas besoin de te dire (car tu connais le chauvinisme des français) que les ficelles secrètes à l'aide desquelles leur leaders (Guesde and Malon) ont été mis en mouvement doivent rester entre nous. Il n'en faut rien parler. Quant on veut agir pour MM les français il faut le faire anonymement pour ne pas froisser leur sentiment national"; letter of Marx to Sorge, November 5, 1880, reprinted in Lefranc (1963: 43).

on trade unions as a direct political force, on direct action and the general strike, its polemical attitude toward middle-class and intellectual socialism and socialists, and its antipartitism and antiparliamentarism[24] contributed heavily to preventing the integration of the socialist corporate and political movements.

This combination of factors shaped the French ideological tradition. It was characterized primarily by the unique mixture of elements of Jacobinism, utopianism, anarcho-syndicalism, republicanism, state-technocratic socialism, *and* Marxism. This unusual mix was reflected in the figure of Jaurès, who reconciled the bourgeois and working-class traditions and invented "that sort of sensibility which is typical of the French left,"[25] nurtured of the memories of the Great Revolution, the ideas of utopian thinkers, and those of republican humanists. French socialism was a broad political movement with great cultural legitimacy, but it was organizationally weak and ideologically divided.

A European Map of Early Ideological Orientation

These three paradigmatic cases can serve as a point of reference for the characterization of the other cases. Sometimes they directly influenced neighboring countries. For instance, the United Kingdom successfully screened Ireland from the ideological turmoil of the Continent in the period in which Irish trade unions were effectively part of the British trade union movement until 1894. Similarly, the experiences of Italy and Spain are associated with that of France for the mix of Marxism among political and intellectual elites and of revolutionary syndicalism in the unions and the working-class movement. Indeed, the origins of the socialist movement in Italy and its peculiarities cannot be understood without considering the role played by Michele Bakunin, who arrived in Italy in 1864. Bakunin's influence was decisive in the early orientation toward radical conceptions of the revolutionary action of popular and workers' circles in the peninsula. Much of its prestige, particularly in southern Italy, was also due to the fact that it appeared as the symbol of that glorious, and at the same time mysterious, International under whose colors the Parisian communards had fought.[26] At the beginning of the 1870s, "anarchism, socialism, and inter-

---

[24] For a detailed presentation of the position of French syndicalists, see Lorwin (1954: 30–36). See also Bergounioux and Manin (1979: 66–71).

[25] Bergounioux and Manin (1979: 66). It was customary for historians to criticize the theoretical weakness of French socialism. See in particular Ligou (1962) and Judt (1976: 71–97).

[26] Particularly when Mazzini took an explicitly negative attitude vis-à-vis the Commune,

nationalism were in Italy, if not synonymous, at least equivalent, and the name of Bakunin was far more famous than that of Marx. It was under this influence that the Italian sections of the International multiplied."[27] Malefakis goes far as to argue that the strength of revolutionary syndicalism in Italy (and even more so in Spain) was greater than in France, and that this has been overshadowed by the longevity of French syndicalism, its spread from there to the rest of Europe, its identification with the writing of George Sorel, and its long-standing influence on the largest French trade union organization, the General Confederation of Workers (CGT).[28] Not all scholars share these conclusions, but all agree on the fundamental similarity of these socialist experiences.[29]

The assimilation of the French and Italian experiences is not limited to the role played by revolutionary syndicalism until after World War I, but extends to the unusual – in comparative terms – internal ideological differentiation of the socialist movement. While in Romagna socialism was inserted over a strong republicanism with its patriotic heritage, in Lombardy a worker was ashamed to call himself a republican, and the opposition between Marxist socialism and the Mazzinian democratic vision and ideals was intense.[30] A considerable amount of patriotism was a typical feature that originated from the *Risorgimento* tradition, and it explains in part the yielding of certain socialist groups to interventionist stands that were taken in 1914. A final affinity with the early French socialist tradition was that its character was more popular than working class.[31] The diffusion of Marxist ideas, programmatic lines, and organizational principles was difficult within the socialist party. Marxism in Italy was originally strongly mixed with positivism, and its diffusion and revision in relation to the Italian situation were largely the result of the intellectuals who were external to the party itself, such as Labriola and Mondolfo.[32]

which increased the prestige of Bakunin. Little was known of the violent polemics that were taking place in those years between Bakunin's and Marx's followers within the First International or of the ambivalent attitude that the General Council of the International had initially expressed toward the Commune. See Cole (1954: 176–236).

[27] Procacci (1970: 395)

[28] Malefakis (1974: 7–8).

[29] Lorwin (1954: 36), Judt (1979: 285), Andreasi (1981), Schöttler (1986: 419–476).

[30] Cf. Morandi (1978 (1st ed. 1945): 40).

[31] Morandi (1978: 39–43).

[32] On Italian intellectual Marxism and, in particular, on the role played by Labriola in revising Marxism toward a less fatalistic and more voluntaristic vision of the development of the revolutionary conditions, see Santarelli (1964). For more in general on the Italian Marxist intellectual debate, see Croce (1938). On the poor circulation of the Marxists' basic writings, see Bosio (1951: 268–284, 444–477).

Germany, the quality side of orthodox Marxism, is regarded as the source of the spread of this ideological version of socialism to the Netherlands and Denmark in the north (and through Denmark to the other Scandinavian countries) and Austria and Switzerland in the south. Doubtless, what is called the introduction of Marxism was actually the introduction of Engels's version – or vision – of Marxism after 1883.[33] The correspondence of Engels, and later that of other German leaders, was more politically influential than were the original writings of Marx, most of which were inaccessible outside Germany. Even Marx's famous critique of the Gotha's 1875 SPD Program was actually unknown to German social democrats for almost sixteen years, until it was published in 1891. In the previously mentioned countries, Engels's Marxism penetrated profoundly at the ideological level, but – with the possible exception of Belgium and the Netherlands, where until the end of the century some syndicalist traditions remained important in the unions and workers' societies – in none of them did Marxism have to contend with strong national variants of socialism. The question in these cases is not how Marxism interacted with other ideological streams – amalgamating with them or being rebuffed by them – but, rather, how intensely Marxism orthodoxy permeated these movements and persisted over the forces of ideological or practical revisionism.

In a recent systematic comparison of the reception of Marxism in several countries, Steenson has analyzed in detail Engels's correspondence with foreign party leaders after Marx's death. Instead of relying on theoretical works (as do most other national or international studies of socialism), he has concentrated on party press and party programs in order to judge the Marxist orthodoxy of several socialist movements, in particular the German, Austrian, French, and Italian ones.[34] The conclusions of his work show a clear division between the more eclectic and less orthodox stands of the French and Italian movements versus the orthodox ones of the German and Austrian movements. The Austrian movement was not only Marxist, radical, and orthodox, but also theoretically rich and fertile. The full range of the ideological character and original elements of what is called "Austro-Marxism," represented by the writings and positions of Otto Bauer, were displayed only after World War I, in the conflict between Leninism and Second International socialism. The theoretical work of Otto Bauer, and in general of the Austrian Marxists, interpreted the Russian Revolution and the Bolshevik ideology as a phase of the bourgeois revo-

---

[33] Steenson (1991: 3–46) amply argues and demonstrates this.
[34] Ibid.

lution in Russia and, in particular, as a radical and utopian ideology of the plebeian phases of bourgeois revolutions. Their strategy for the revolutionary forces of the advanced countries centered on the maintenance of democratic political forms, the rejection of the nationalization of the means of production[35] as a strategy that would be dangerous for democracy,[36] and the idea of an economic democracy at the level of the local administration of each enterprise.

It should be added that the Austrian socialists also possessed an unusual ideological-organizational encapsulation and self-reliance. Adler gave a dignified cultural definition of the process of powerlessness and isolation of the movement with the idea of the *poetische Politik*, that is, a policy that concentrated fundamentally on infusing the movement with a strong symbolic content, introducing a sacred aura around its organization and other activities, and emotionally charging the social militancy and participation in order to foster the members' identification with the organization and with each other.[37] No other European socialist movement seems to have succeeded in building such a strong emotional solidarity as the Austrian one. The practical components of this vision were the festivals, celebrations, and political rallies that were staged and the immense effort that was devoted to the development of working-class cultural societies and all sorts of other ancillary organizations. The basic goal was to create a mass psychology of the movement, a strongly distinctive organizational identity of the working class and "the ghetto mentality." The Austrian movement, therefore, is a case of an orthodox radical Marxist movement, which was doctrinaire and theoretically fertile and in which ideology mattered both for the organization and for political action.

In reality, in no other country was Marxist orthodoxy so accentuated or important for organization and action as in Germany and Austria. In the Netherlands, Belgium, Switzerland, and the three Scandinavian coun-

---

[35] "Nationalization" may not be the best word in this case. What was meant was direct state – i.e., state bureaucracy – ownership of the means of production. On the various meanings of the terms relating to the "public" ownership of the means of production in the socialist ideology and jargon, see Waldbrunner (1952: 13–17), who reviews the utilization and meaning of such terms as "socialization," "common ownership," "public ownership," "collectivization," "nationalization," and "state ownership."

[36] The Austrian Marxists and Bauer in particular proposed the socialization of the public economy and, in particular, of big industry. The latter was to be based on expropriation, to be indemnified through a progressive tax hitting the capitalists whose property had not been expropriated. On the programmatic points of Austro-Marxism, see Agnelli (1969).

[37] This cultural and organizational policy of the Austrian movement is discussed at length in McGrath (1974).

tries, Marxism, although widely accepted as the dominant intellectual doctrine, never acquired such an important role for political organization or, above all, for political action. Alongside the Marxist formal orthodoxy a revisionist practice developed early on, but the potential contradiction between the two never exploded into a major political crisis. The experiences of these countries, even if they can be regrouped under this broad characterization, should not, however, be viewed as absolutely similar. Three cases seem to be more ideologically radicalized than the others: those of the Netherlands, Denmark, and Sweden.

Initially, the Dutch socialist movement was revolutionary in nature, although this aspect was progressively curtailed. Until the beginning of the twentieth century, there persisted within the trade union movement a relatively strong syndicalist orientation that was often in conflict with the political wing of the socialist movement. The Social Democratic League, forerunner of the Socialist Party, had basically borrowed its program from Gotha's SPD program. Later, Erfurt's program became the basic inspiration for the Social Democratic Workers Party (SDAP), and at the official ideological level the party followed Kautskyan Marxism quite closely. Even as late as 1913, on the issue of socialist participation in bourgeois governments, Kautsky was consulted.[38] At the ideological and programmatic level, therefore, Dutch socialism was very internationally oriented and particularly focused on the German SPD experience. At the same time, historians have argued that a patriarchal family ideology was accepted by substantial parts of the socialist movement, while it was, of course, the basis for mobilization on religious-ideological grounds of Catholic and Protestant workers against liberalism and socialism. The socialist attempt to counterbalance or neutralize the conservative hegemony failed when it was confronted with the control exerted by bourgeois and religious organizations (state or private) over virtually all aspects of the socialization process: the press, schools, and so on. The socialist organizational pillarization, in this perspective, was defensive, not offensive. It reinforced acquired loyalties but was unable to expand beyond them. Therefore, in its pre–World War I phase, Dutch socialism can be seen as one of the best examples of the maintenance of an official orthodox Marxist doctrine, only slightly adapted to Dutch conditions, and, at the same time, of an increasingly moderate and pragmatic policy pursued by the party majority. It was not that Kautskism was rejected but, quite simply, that practice was separated from theory within the movement.

In the Netherlands, this growing internal tension finally led to organi-

---

[38] Ruitenbeek (1955: 25–26), quoted in Irwin (1989: 40).

zational consequences. At the beginning of the twentieth century, the Marxist stream started to make its voice heard, criticizing the party line for not being Marxist enough. The key issue was indeed party strategy: Predicting a crisis of industrial capitalism, the Marxists argued that until then, the party should limit its support to the relatively small groups of class-conscious workers who were free from conservative religious ideological influences. Theoretical clarity and education of the proletariat would thus be the short-term goals. This debate was transformed into a power struggle within the party that culminated at the 1909 congress, when the parliamentary party expelled the radical left. The latter formed a Social Democratic Party that was later to become the Dutch Communist Party. This turn of events is quite similar to developments in Italy and, to a lesser extent, in Sweden in the same period. Only in these three countries did the socialist movement split into radicals and moderates *before World War I.*

In Sweden (and Norway), Marxism was introduced via Denmark, and cooperation among socialist movements was institutionalized in the Nordic Labor Congress rather than via the Second International. The influence of the German socialist debate was expressed mainly in party programmatic statements but was not accompanied by any profound ideological debate or doctrinaire factionalism. However, a radical minority of the Swedish Social Democratic Party (SAP), which had rejected the moderate and reformist strategy of the majority since the 1890s, acquired greater influence after 1908. This radical wing had identified itself at the beginning of the century with the Young Socialist League (SUF), which advocated more-direct action, general strikes, and no parliamentarism. In 1908, its two most prominent leaders were expelled from the SAP for these antiparliamentary and pro–general strike activities. As a result, they founded the Swedish Young Socialists Party (SUP), which, being antiparliamentary in attitude, did not contest elections. After the bitter confrontation of 1908–1909 and the 1909 general strike (the consequence of a series of strikes in response to lockouts and employers' attempts to lower wages) ended in defeat for both the SAP and the trade union confederation (LO), the Young Socialists managed to push through the foundation of a Swedish Worker's Confederation (SAC) with a syndicalist orientation. Even in Sweden, therefore, the pre–World War I confrontation between radicals and moderates produced organizational splits, even if they had no parliamentary consequences for the main socialist party. This was the beginning of a long history of minor splits in both the communists and socialist left in Sweden.

In Denmark and Norway, the internal ideological strife seems to have been comparatively less and did not produce important organizational splits before the war. Although Danish party programs were directly influenced by the German ones, from the beginning they omitted any references to ideological formulas such as the "iron law of wages," and they included special paragraphs devoted to the agrarian problem. Notwithstanding the early marked internationalism and the intense effort at party publication development (a literature of primarily Marxist orientation),[39] theoretical issues and Marxism did not become a major source of internal conflict. This was even more true of Norway, where such issues were hardly even a source of debate. The approach of the Norwegian socialists to doctrinal issues was instead inherently pragmatic. If some of the party leaders were familiar with the socialist classics, they were never interested in the finer theoretical differences. Different theoretical traditions were seen as equally important (Lassalle as much as Marx). Although the party was represented at the 1889 Paris Labor Congress and although from 1890 onward the First of May was firmly established as a day of international socialist demonstration, the Second International was viewed as fairly unimportant as regards other matters, overshadowed as it was by the role of the Nordic Labor Congress, where the Scandinavian socialist parties cooperated.

It is interesting to note that these early differences in ideological characterization have tended to persist at the programmatic level. After an intense post–World War I radicalization (see later), Norway was the first Scandinavian country to overtly deradicalize its program in 1930. Denmark was slower in programmatic adaptation. Its 1923 program was still Marxist in overtone and remained basically unmodified until 1961, when a new program of total revision and radical deideologization was adopted. Sweden has had the most continuous programmatic development. Successive programs have only slightly adapted official party positions. Indeed, the 1960 and 1975 programs still preserved elements of the original Marxist ideology (e.g., the "third stage of democratic development") and a strong collectivist conception of economic and political democracy.

Finland is a difficult case to classify in a European perspective. In 1903, the Finnish Socialist Party, like so many others, adopted a program that was directly borrowed from Erfurt's German program. However, the impact of Marxist ideas on the development of the party seems to have been minimal before 1905. Socialist literature, particularly Marxist literature, was unavailable in Finnish. It seems that Finnish socialist theory was

---

[39] See Callesen (1990: 142–143) for documentation of this effort to educate the working classes through party publication activities, in many ways similar to the efforts in this field typical of the German and Austrian parties.

relatively rudimentary, and not only did external ideological influences have little impact on it, but few internal ideological debates were launched. However, the party stand on orthodox ground was helped by the fact that in the illiberal climate of Russian domination, the party did not have to face the complex strategic choices and practical decisions that a more liberal political context posed. From this point of view, its position until the end of World War I and independence was similar to that of the German and Austrian socialist movements.

Finally, Switzerland and Belgium are the two clearest cases of socialist movements that formally adopted Marxist elements in their programmatic profile and yet demonstrated a total disjunction between these profiles and moderate and reformist political practice. In Switzerland, prior to the sudden and short period of radicalization at the end of World War I, it is hard to identify any significant radical tendencies, in part because the extreme territorial and cultural fragmentation of the country made it difficult for these groups to forge any solid organizational links. In Belgium, the early ideological matrix of the socialist movement was very complex. The fact is that from the beginning the Belgian Socialist Party was a conglomerate of associations of every kind: professional, economic (cooperatives), social (mutualistic and insurance organizations), cultural (schools, newspapers, libraries, conference centers, local clubs for workers education, *écoles ouvrières superieures*), medical and pharmaceutical (chemists, clinics, nursing homes, kindergartens, assistance to women), political (workers' leagues), sports, travel, dramatic art, "Friends of Nature," and social groups (women, retired workers, young-socialists guards, ex-soldiers, peasants, etc.). Moreover, the need to resist the interference of the state, then in the hands of the Catholics, obliged the early socialists to build a dense network of strongholds at the communal level, where they were in the majority. Communes were traditionally important, numerous, and autonomous entities, and socialists used them to insulate themselves from state influences.

It was hard to give ideological coherence to such an organizationally complex world. Its ideological cement seemed to be that of anticlericalism, free-thinking, and Freemasonry, given the dominant role of the church and Catholics during the nineteenth century. The party concentrated most on winning political reforms − not only universal and equal suffrage, but also the battle for cremation and civic burial, for free and Catholic-emancipated schools − battles that were eventually hegemonized by the rather "Voltaireanian" Belgian bourgeoisie.[40] The party, in a nutshell, was almost en-

---

[40] The trust in the general strike that characterized Belgian socialists concerned the politi-

tirely revisionist and nondoctrinaire, so much so as to elicit the strong criticism of Karl Kautsky: "They have nothing to revise, for they have no theory."[41] However, the moderate and petit bourgeois nature of the Belgian socialists was not only criticized by the father of orthodox Second International Marxism; Sorel also considered Belgian socialism to be one "where the drugstore is erected to sacerdocy,"[42] and one historian has defined it as an "a-political socialism."[43]

A broad classification of the ideologically predominant characterization of pre–World War I socialist movements results, therefore, in a map such as that in Figure 2.4. Opposed to a predominantly trade unionist variant (the United Kingdom and Ireland) is a mixture of a strong anarcho-syndicalist tradition with intellectual Marxism (France and Italy – and Spain – and only to a certain extent Belgium); then there are those countries where theory, organization, and political strategy were based on orthodox Marxism (Germany and Austria), and finally, those where the influence of Marxism was programmatic but accompanied by early revisionist political practices and strategies. It would seem that internal tensions between doctrine and praxis were greatest in the Dutch and Swedish cases, intermediate in the Danish and Norwegian cases, and minor in the Belgian and Swiss cases. It is hard to collapse these different types into a single dimension of radicalism versus revisionism or moderation. If one were forced to do so, the only possibility would be to oppose the basic reformist stand of the British, Irish, Belgian, and Swiss socialist movements to the more radical German, Austrian, French, and Italian movements, leaving in the middle the cases of the Netherlands and Sweden, Denmark, Finland, and Norway.

WAR AND REVOLUTION: THE RADICALIZATION OF WORKING-CLASS ACTION

The pre–World War I characterization of the ideological orientation of different socialist movements is in many cases utterly transformed by the general radicalization of working-class politics on the eve of, during, and

cal strike. Before 1914, the Belgian Socialist Party organized four general strikes, all of which were for political objectives linked to democratization goals.
[41] Letter to Adler quoted by Lorwin (1966: 156).
[42] Quoted in Moulin (1981: 196).
[43] See Liebman (1979: 185, 187) for other colorful descriptions of the same feature: "politics, the party's poor relative"; "theory condemned to ostracism"; "the co-operatives: the small village and the inn."

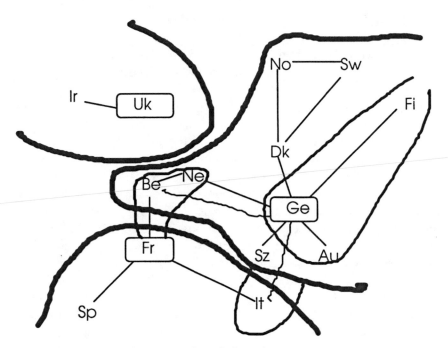

Figure 2.4. A map of early socialist ideological orientation.

immediately after World War I. This radicalization is a Europewide phenomenon and is expressed mainly through growing membership, militantism, and internal ideological strife within labor movements. Its roots can be traced back to four main factors: (1) the broad increase in industrialization and the working classes themselves in many countries in the first decade of the century; (2) the growing problem of integration within the socialist unions and political organizations of new waves of mainly unskilled workers; (3) the Great War mobilization and its consequences; and (4) the impact of the Russian Revolution.

The war and revolution watershed not only fueled and renewed internal ideological and political strife, it also marked the beginning of the organizational divisions of the socialist movement. The results of almost half a century of efforts to organize, unify, and centralize socialist movements suddenly melted away almost everywhere between 1910 and 1920. After World War I, the issue of radicalism must be reinterpreted as the issue of the organizational fragmentation of the socialist movement and, in the final analysis, as the issue of the birth and consolidation of communist parties. A distinction should, however, be maintained between (1) the conditions of generalized radicalization in most European countries; (2) the level of social unrest and turmoil that followed the war; and (3) the ideological strife and organizational fragmentation during the war and its aftermath, with the formation of Third International communist splits. These aspects will be discussed as potential causal conditions in the following chapters, and particularly in the chapter devoted to the political sociology of the communist split (Chapter 9). In this introduction, my aim is limited to a description of their impact and, in particular, of the social turmoil and organizational fragmentation that resulted from them. The most important aspect to highlight remains, as usual, not the general phenomenon but the differences among the cases.

The point is that the accumulation of radicalism and revolutionary potential was unequally distributed across countries as a result of various pre-, during- and postwar national situations. The ideological and organizational strife within national socialist movements after the war was linked to (1) their record of unity and division before the war; (2) the geopolitical war position of each country, that is, its being belligerent or neutral and, if belligerent, its being defeated or victorious, and, if neutral, its being invaded or unaffected by the war; (3) the positions adopted by the national socialist parties during the war with respect to the national war effort; and (4) the national impact of the Russian Revolution and Leninism.

Radicalization and internal ideological strife were already well developed in several, albeit not all, of the socialist movements before the war. Recent historical research on Italy, France, and Germany[44] has shown that after the war, the divisions among socialists took place on the basis of prewar factions of the International, social divisions in the working class, generational gaps, and divisions deriving from previous experiences of the organized socialist movements and other organizations of the working class. Splits would have occurred even without the interference of the Third International, probably in a less mechanical way, with different timings and alliances among the factions.[45] Generalizing this point, it has been argued that "in the political democracies where a left opposition failed to win a strong position in the socialist movement before the rise of international communism, the Communist Party never became a major force of its own."[46] This point attributes the extent of the postwar ideological and organizational fragmentation to the situation of the prewar socialist parties.

We have noted that in three countries – Italy, the Netherlands, and

---

[44] Cortesi (1973: 451) and Lindemann (1977: 451).

[45] In support of this point, see also Schumpter (1976: 358).

[46] Lorwin (1966: 164).

Sweden – important organizational splits along the radical versus moderate dimension had already occurred before the war, even if in the last two countries they had no electoral and parliamentary consequences because the splinter group decided not to stand for elections. In Germany, no organizational split occurred before the war, but the revisionist debate triggered by Bernstein at the end of the 1890s had already split the party profoundly on ideological issues into a revisionist wing, the orthodox Marxist center of Kautsky, and the Luxemburg left wing.[47]

However, it is hazardous to generalize about the relationship between prewar socialist internal divisions and postwar radicalization and socialist splits. All socialist movements experienced some internal ideological fractionalization in this period. Even the moderate British trade unionism in the period 1908–1913 saw an increase in industrial militancy and a growing willingness to strike in sympathy with other workers, indicating a growing class consciousness. But for the declaration of war, it is likely that the spreading anger and the many strikes between 1910 and 1914 – resulting from dissatisfaction with real wages and the deficiences of the collective-bargaining system – may have culminated in a general strike in September 1914. Syndicalism, too, had made inroads in this period. Introduced into the United Kingdom by Tom Mann in the early 1900s, it was present by 1914 in all the major unions, although in a minority position.[48] The radicalization of forms of action was therefore quite generalized, and it was no accident that these actions corresponded to a broader crisis, challenging the intellectual and political base of liberalism, whose rationalistic foundations had come under attack from the philosophies of Bergson and Freud, and whose political theory had been criticized by the theories of Mosca, Ostrogorski, Michels, and Pareto.

The outbreak of war and, in particular, the unanimous vote of the SPD on August 4, 1914, in favor of war credits made it clear that working-class internationalism could not prevent European governments from going to war with each other and that internationalism was a myth. The reaction to this was particularly strong among French and Belgian socialists, who were both directly and immediately involved. However, even socialists of the more distant and neutral areas, such as the Netherlands, Switzerland, and the Scandinavian countries, felt let down, to say the least. The inevitable consequence was that almost all the existing social democratic parties were driven to transform themselves into patriotic defenders of their re-

---

[47] On the characterization of these three ideological wings and on their final split with the coming of the war, see the classic Schorske (1955).

[48] See Holton (1985: 266–282).

spective societies. At the same time, minority groups from the intellectual middle class and the working class were even more radicalized by this "patriotic slaughter" and became completely alienated from and opposed to the liberal tradition and order. The extent of this alienation depended to a large extent on the war position and involvement of each country, that is, whether it was belligerent or neutral, defeated or victorious. In occupied Belgium, "in the long-neutral little nation which, as King Albert said, had been 'driven to heroism,' revolutionary defeatism and post-war recrimination against social patriotism were absurd."[49] The "revolutionary accumulation" was likely to be stronger among countries at war than among neutral countries and stronger among defeated than among victorious ones.[50] Revolutionary potential was clearly associated with the collapse of public order and political control in both belligerant and defeated countries such as Austria, Germany, and Finland,[51] where, indeed, revolutionary defeatism and postwar recrimination found favorable soil.

The third important factor mentioned at the beginning of this section was the extent of the involvement of the socialist movement and leadership in the national war efforts. Internal radical opposition was fed largely by the reaction against socialist and trade union support of the war effort in belligerent countries, particularly in France, Germany, Austria, and Italy. Recriminations against social patriotism and participation in "bourgeois" wartime governments were of course, more or less intense according to the extent of socialist involvement in the "imperialist war." Such involvement was far more open and intense in France and Germany than in Italy and Austria. As a reaction against the early SPD support of what the French regarded as a military aggression, the French Section of the Workers International (SFIO) supported the national coalition. The Austrians were spared the difficult choice of voting for or against war credits thanks to the closing of the parliament by imperial dictum and therefore managed to maintain a more ambivalent position. Thanks to the delay of Italian entry into the conflict, the Italian socialists had more time to oppose the conflict,

---

[49] Lorwin (1966: 164).

[50] Kriegel (1974: 20).

[51] This collapse of public order was probably more acute in Finland than in any other country, even if formally Finland could not be defined as a defeated country. The 1918 civil war was largely the result of the fact that, after the Russian Revolution, the dominant Finnish groups lacked any organized military force. This explains the ease of formation of the Red and White guards in the absence of military and political forces upholding authority. Even in the 1920s, the White-inspired civil guard was far larger than the army (100,000 armed men compared with 25,000 soldiers). Cf. Alapuro and Allardt (1978: 125).

and finally, although with great hesitation, they followed the line of "né aderire né sabotare."[52] This was later very important in explaining why the Livorno communist split in the PSI affected only a minority of the members, while the Tours communist split took with it the majority of the old SFIO (see Chapter 9). An uncompromising "patriotic" socialist alignment in a belligerent and ultimately defeated country was most likely to trigger the highest level of internal criticism, recrimination, and opposition within the socialist leadership and the rank and file. When this was accompanied by the ideological crystallization of different organized ideological factions, the situation became even more explosive.

Finally, the Russian Revolution and Leninism contributed to the fueling of this internal debate. The political and ideological meaning of the Russian Bolshevik Revolution lay not only in the emotional attraction represented by the long-awaited establishment of the first socialist state for the entire socialist movement, but also in the great upheaval of Marxist theory and socialist ideology it produced. Lenin's revolution destroyed the model of historical development based on the Marxist analysis of capitalist society and on the deterministic definition of the conditions of development and revolution as the basis of the socialist understanding of reality and socialist strategy. It proved the bankruptcy of any determinist theory and highlighted the role of organizational and ideological factors with regard to political practice. The fact that a revolution occurred in a country where the socioeconomic conditions were not ripe seemed to prove that revolution was possible under any circumstances. This universal possibility of revolution thereby implied a rejection of, or at least a reconsideration of, any theory of capitalism and, at the same time, a reconsideration of the theory of the development of socialist movements under capitalism. The study of the conditions for the arrival of the revolution now concentrated on the tactical and organizational conditions. A theory was still necessary, but this theory was largely transformed from a theory of capitalist development to a theory of revolution.

The universal possibility of revolution, exemplified by the Russian events, threw the blame for the failure of the revolution in the more advanced European countries on the prewar and wartime socialist leadership, particularly in the larger Western European countries. The idea of

---

[52] Actually, the position of the Italian socialists with regard to the war was less coherently internationalist than the formula implied. The socialists put pressure on the government to avoid intervention in alliance with the central empires, stressing the difference between the two belligerent parties. Cf. Cortesi (1973: 86–87).

party that Lenin progressively developed between the writing of *What Is to Be Done* (1902–1903) and the later revolutionary experience[53] was an effective weapon in an atmosphere of clandestine activity and repression that occurred during political upheavals but was far less so under any other conditions. Similarly, the three propaganda proposals – "land to peasants," "all power to the Soviets," and "stop the war now" – were ideal tactical weapons in a short-term revolutionary situation but hardly an exploitable program under any other condition. The question of the short-versus long-term revolutionary solution has in fact been a vital problem in the development of the international communist movement. The correct evaluation of the nature and possible outcome of the crisis was closely related to the choice of the kind of party and strategy the Third International forces had to organize and follow. If the revolutionary crisis brought about by the war in several countries was to produce a short-term revolutionary outcome, then a leading Bolshevik party was an immediate necessity. If the crisis was leading to restoration rather than to revolution, the new parties had to be able to survive and wait for a new crisis and for a new and favorable conjuncture. In view of the uprising they foresaw, the Bolsheviks considered it essential to drastically change the unitary social democratic parties. It remained to be decided how to organize such a change: the moment of the internal confrontation, the choice of the confrontation line (with whom and against whom), and, if it was the case, the choice of the breaking modality: by minority split or by internal purge.

In conclusion, the prewar socialist divisions, the country's war role, and the socialist attitude to wartime cabinets were the powerful contextual conditions that helped to shape the receptiveness of the Leninist interpretation of the postwar revolutionary potentials and opportunities within the old socialist parties. When by the end of 1921 it became evident that the revolutionary crisis was over, the problem of revolutionary parties working in objectively nonrevolutionary situations became that of settling and organizing the strong extremist nucleus of the early postwar phase. Lenin summed up the problem with this pointed remark addressed to Costantino Lazzari in July 1921: "il faut reculer pour mieux sauter."[54] However, the overestimation of the revolutionary potential in the West was to have far-reaching implications. The main consequence of the political strategy chosen to deal with European socialism was that no communist party would succeed in retaining the majority of the politicized working class.

---

[53] The best account of Lenin's ideas in general, and of his organizational theory in particular, is Lundquist (1982: 297–320).

[54] Sechi (1977: 39).

To what extent was this different accumulation of revolutionary potential in different countries actually mirrored in the radicalization and intensity of class action? The question may be answered by comparing the
intensity of industrial conflict across countries during the war and revolution years and the extent of political turmoil and instability brought about
by them. It is necessary to differentiate between these aspects because
industrial conflict is not by itself a sign of political crisis or revolutionary
potential; that is, it does not necessarily indicate a political radicalization
of the class conflict. Social and industrial unrest and workers' militantism
increased everywhere in this crucial period. To evaluate where such radicalization in collective behavior was stronger, one must rely on information
about protest events and "collective action pursuing an explicit goal by
the use of adversarial, disruptive or even violent means."[55] However, systematic comparative and historical data are difficult to find in this field.[56]
For a global comparison, therefore, the only systematic sources are those
on strikes. Strike actions are composed of three elements that do not
necessarily coincide or covary: The number of strikes launched, the average
number of strikers, and the average length of strikes and country traditions
are very different in this respect.[57] For my purposes, I have combined the
number of strikers and the number of strikes into a multiplicative single
index (see Table 2.4).[58]

The figures in Table 2.4, which cover the period 1901–1940 in five-
years blocks, show how the intensity of the industrial conflict grew steadily
before the war, peaked in the years 1918–1925, and declined rapidly
thereafter up to the Second World War. The high level indicated for the
1936–1940 period is due exclusively to the absolutely exceptional levels of
conflict in France, which is the only European case of industrial conflict
mobilization in the second half of the 1930s. However, even leaving aside
this case, the data show great variation among countries. In five countries

---

[55] Rucht and Ohlemacher (1992: 77).

[56] The pioneering work of Charles Tilly on strikes, collective violence, and "contentious
gatherings" does not allow a synthetic appreciation of differences among our thirteen
countries. See Tilly (1978). Other studies of protest events concentrate on the post–
World War II situation and are less useful for me in this context. See the *World Handbook
of Political and Social Indicators* (1964, 1972, 1983).

[57] See Schorter and Tilly (1974: 306–334).

[58] These data are available in Flora, Alber, Eichenberg, Kohl, Kraus, Pfenning, and Seebohm (1987: 679–753). On the length of strikes, the data are far less complete and
systematic. The data contrast the cases of Norway, Sweden, and the United Kingdom to
all the others. In the former, the relative number of working days lost is far higher, and
systematically higher, than in all other countries, both throughout the forty-year period
from 1901 to 1940 and in the five-year periods immediately preceding and following
the war.

Table 2.4. *Industrial conflict levels (N strikers * N strikes) before and after World War I*

	period							
	1901	1906	1911	1916	1921	1926	1931	1936
Au	.	.	.	.	74488	5440	129	.
Be	3282	6058	7483	111835	17668	7838	4635	4973
De	1650	3085	3451	26176	13392	235.	340	1014
Fi	.	7208	2148	50146	1222	1530	84	263
Fr	3175	7167	3659	13670	6044	6547	646	228435
Ge	5016	8974	6231	22347	51999	1999	.	.
Ir	.	.	.	.	.	1117	3553	8395
It	9192	20419	10683	28508	7920	.	.	.
Ne	4518	4312	13588	27835	14562	3290	3220	444
No	.	.	8323	.	27474	12389	10350	5803
Sw	6625	36637	2387	68325	31870	8650	5164	948
Sz	.	.	632	10685	1098	397	231	124
UK	2285	4446	22344	39743	13239	3699	3332	8699
period average	4448	10923	7357	39927	21748	4426	2880	25910

Note: N of strikes and N of strikers are computed per 100,000 persons of the economically active population.

industrial conflict remained comparatively low, with figures consistently below the European mean levels both before and after the war: Switzerland first of all, but also Denmark, France, Ireland,[59] and the United Kingdom, where strikes tended to be numerous and long but involved few strikers. At the other extreme, the countries that show the highest level of industrial conflict throughout the entire period are Sweden and Norway, both of which remained neutral during the war. The Netherlands and Italy, which we have already singled out as the countries where there was intense ideological strike action and organizational splits in the socialist movement before the war, show levels of industrial conflict that were higher than the mean before the war rather than after it. By contrast, the level of conflict was higher after the war in Austria,[60] Finland, Germany, and Belgium.

The interpretation of these data is not straightforward. The level of industrial disputes does not necessarily mean a corresponding level of social or political tension. According to the ideological tradition and the position

[59] For Ireland, systematic data exist only after 1920; however, there is no indication of particularly intense strike activity before that date in the literature.

[60] For Austria, prewar data are, unfortunately, not available. Between 1921 and 1926, Austria had the highest level of industrial conflict registered (although strikes probably had a short duration).

of trade unions with respect to the political party, each level may acquire a different meaning. The industrial militantism of the British working class after the war years developed within a comparatively liberal political atmosphere and a tradition of relative autonomy between political and industrial action. Although the Irish data are missing for the period, class polarization was not the core issue at that time. Conversely, cases of revolutionary syndicalist trade unions and of orthodox Marxist party–linked trade unions gave a more important political meaning to the industrial disputes. In reality, in only four of our thirteen cases was the postwar high industrial conflict connected to revolutionary threats and political instability (Table 2.5).

In Germany, the military and state collapse of November 9, 1918, triggered a revolutionary phase that carried through the election of the first National Assembly in February 1919; the summer 1919 repression of the Bavarian Council Republic and the workers' agitation in several other parts of the territory; the spring 1920 attempted Kapp Putsch and the following Ruhr workers' rebellion; and, finally, the failed communist upheaval in October 1923. German historians do not agree on the evaluation of this period, namely, whether to consider it as an uninterrupted revolutionary cycle from 1918 to 1923. The majority seems to believe that a revolutionary upheaval would have been possible only in the first phase, before the election of the National Assembly. The developments that followed, with the explosion of the workers' protests in the face of the result of the first phase, are viewed as having been unable to challenge the political equilibrium and the legal and economic choices that were already consolidated.[61] The Bavarian and Spartakist attempts could still be considered as events linked to the collapse of the empire and the war defeat;[62] the Ruhr rebellion has been interpreted as a defensive measure in response to the threat to the Weimar Republic;[63] and the attempted communist revolutions of 1921 and 1923 are judged as less significant challenges and easier for the government to repress than the Ruhr revolt, as they were more clearly minoritarian, insurrectional, and disloyal attempts.[64]

Two other countries witnessed unstable and politically strained postwar development. In Finland, as in Russia, the war slid into a civil war between Reds and Whites, with the eventual military victory of the latter

[61] See Ribeni (1989: 139).
[62] For the Bavarian revolutionary attempt, see A. Mitchell (1965).
[63] Moore (1978: 328, 340).
[64] This is the interpretive conclusion of Angress (1972: 459–461). Actually, the repression that followed was mild, and the Communist Party was made illegal for only a few months.

Table 2.5. *Configurational aspects of the "war and revolution" crisis of the socialist movement*

countries	internal ideological strife before World War I (with or without org. fragm.)	pre-war industrial conflict (1911-915)	war position	war military outcome	socialist party war position	postwar industrial conflict	political conseqences of war	civil war; revolutionary attempts; political instability political violence
Au	low	?	belligerent	defeated	Zimmenwaldian	high	regime collapse/ territorial losses	high organized political violence
Be	low	mid	neutral but invaded	liberated	patriotic	high		
De	low	low	neutral			moderate		
Fi	low	low	belligerent		split: Zimmenwaldian and patriotic	high (repressed by 1919)	regime collapse	civil war
Fr	high; no split	low	belligerent	victorious	patriotic	low		
Ge	high; no split	moderate	belligerent	defeated	patriotic	high	regime collapse, territorial losses	attempted coups and upheavals
Ir	low	(low?)	(belligerent)	(victorious)		(low?)		
It	high; organizational split	high	belligerent	victorious but recriminating	Zimmenwaldian	moderate	territorial vindication	high political and social turmoil
Ne	high; organizational split	high	neutral			moderate		
No		moderate	neutral			high		
Sw	high; organizational split	low	neutral			high		
Sz	low	low	neutral		Zimmenwaldian	low		
UK	low	high	belligerent	victorious	patriotic	low		

setting the terms for a bitter confrontation with the communists, who were forced into a clandestine position and banned in 1923 (the communist-controlled Trade Unions Confederation was banned in 1930). In Austria, the First Republic was proclaimed by the socialists. The communist attempt to penetrate the workers' councils failed completely, and a coalition government of major political forces ran the country from 1918 to 1920. Therefore, the immediate political transition seemed to be under control. However, class warfare was radicalized by the electoral victory and the governmental coalition of the Christian Social Nationals and the German Nationals in autumn 1920. The emergence of armed organizations, such as the Frontkämpfer, the SA, and the Heimwehren on the extreme right led to a corresponding development in the Social Democratic field, with the armed Republikanischer Schutzbund, and to a situation of radical and even violent confrontation. In these three cases, the postwar political instability resulted largely from the collapse of the old prewar authoritarian regime as a consequence of the military defeat it had undergone.

Italy is the fourth European case of high postwar social turmoil and political instability. Although the country fought in the war and was eventually victorious, high social tension permeated the entire post–World War I period until Mussolini came to power. However, to define the Italian situation in 1920 as potentially revolutionary is probably incorrect. The occupation of the factories that took place in September in Turin and in other parts of Italy was in no way a planned revolutionary attempt. It was rather the result of industrial disputes in a period of a rapidly growing political mobilization of the Italian working class and was accompanied by the growth of new working-class institutions: the internal commissions and the factory councils. It was initially a defensive move, that is, a way of protecting workers from the threat of employers' lockout. The interpretation of this period as a failed revolution is usually advanced in reference to the thinking of Antonio Gramsci, who aimed to direct events toward such an outcome.[65] In reality, it was the political skill of Giolitti and the permanent reformist orientation of the General Confederation of Labour (CGL) that limited any revolutionary potential and led the confrontation to a negotiated settlement. The subsequent political threat, which came mainly from the nationalistic groups and the new fascist movement, forced the socialist movement to be permanently on the defensive.

Beyond these four cases, there was no challenge to the political order during the postwar phase in Europe. In an attempt to systematize the experiences discussed so far, we can regroup the factors mentioned in Table 2.5. It was within the resulting configuration that socialist organizations fragmented further that communist splits developed.

ORGANIZATIONAL FRAGMENTATION AND COMMUNIST STRENGTH

The Great War and the crisis that ensued triggered a process of progressive and increasing political fragmentation of the European left. The enormous efforts in almost all countries between 1860 and 1900 to foster the pro-

[65] A typical example of the political situation being interpreted through the lens of Gramsci's thinking is the work by Clark (1977). On the occupation of the factories, see the more sober judgment of Spriano (1964).

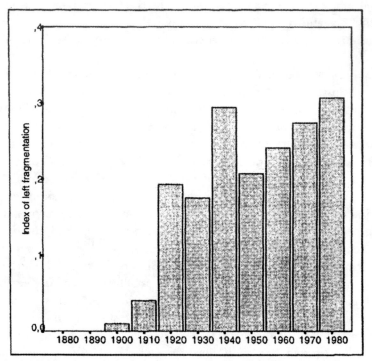

Figure 2.5. Left electoral fragmentation by decade.

gressive unification and centralization of working-class organizations, in both the corporate and electoral channels, evaporated. Under the pressure of powerful internal ideological dissent and international pressures, in most countries the left fell victim to internal ideological and organizational differentiation. In Figure 2.5 this is shown clearly by reporting for each decade Rae's index of fragmentation applied to the total left alone rather than, as usual, to the entire party system.[66] Some fragmentation was already evident before World War I, but the process accelerated from the 1920s to the 1940s. With the electoral stability of the 1950s, fragmentation was again reduced, but afterward it increased progressively in each decade.

Comparing the countries in the four electoral periods that we have discussed, we can observe quite different levels and patterns of electoral fragmentation. In the first period before World War I, most of the left was represented by a single unified socialist party, and other very minor social-

---

[66] That is, having made equal to 100% the size of the total left, the index measures the degree of its internal divisions in electoral terms.

ist formations existed only in France and Italy.[67] After World War I, the general tendency toward growing fragmentation is visible in Belgium, Denmark, Finland, France, Ireland, Italy, and Norway, while the situation is stable in Austria, the Netherlands, Sweden, Switzerland, and the United Kingdom; a clear decline can be seen only in Germany. In Italy and Finland, the interwar period indicates a relatively low index of fragmentation simply because the communist party was outlawed in Finland, and in Italy the only available electoral data refer to the elections of the early 1920s. Germany has the highest electoral fragmentation of the interwar period, but it also shows the sharpest concentration process after World War II and the division of the country. It should perhaps be pointed out that the outlawing of the Communist Party in Germany after World War II was not responsible for this trend; it had been reduced to a tiny proportion of the electoral whole even before it was outlawed.

At the opposite end, four countries are almost immune from politico-organizational fragmentation – Austria, Switzerland, the United Kingdom, and Ireland. Considering the characterization of the early ideological orientation of the left and the "war and revolution" mobilization phase, the capacity of Austrian socialism to maintain its organizational cohesion is somewhat surprising: preconditions seemed favorable to an early and deep ideological-organizational split of the party.

All the other cases fall into a middle position between these extremes, with some change from period to period. In Denmark and Belgium, for instance, the tendency is toward a continuous increase in fragmentation. In the 1966–1985 period, these countries exceed the European mean level and come close to that of Italy, France, and Finland. The Netherlands, Norway, and Sweden instead keep a medium and fairly stable level for the entire period from the end of World War I to the 1980s.

THE MODALITIES OF ORGANIZATIONAL SPLITS

There are three countries in Europe where no serious organizational split occurred after World War I, Ireland, Austria, and the United Kingdom. In Austria, Victor Adler managed to balance the center position of an orthodox Marxist movement between the patriotic tendencies on one side

---

[67] As mentioned before, a split took place in Sweden in 1908 (SVP), but the splinter party did not participate in elections until 1917, when it obtained considerable success with 8% of the votes. In the Netherlands a similar split occurred in 1909, but the radical splinter group (SDP) did not stand for election before or during the war period.

and the antimilitary tendencies on the other (led by Bauer and Renner), and avoided the party split à la Germany. This difficult position was helped by a number of circumstances. First, the restiveness of the various national wings within the socialist movements – in particular, that of the Czechs – helped the center to keep the party united. The dangers of national splits and the centrifugal drives associated with them probably constrained the ideological strife between the moderates and radicals of each national section, and national idiosyncracies prevented them from joining forces cross-nationally. At the same time, to deal with the war, the imperial regime suspended a number of constitutional rights, and by resorting to Article 14 of the constitution, which granted exceptional power to the emperor, the parliament was dissolved. The party fought against this limitation of rights together, while at the same time avoiding the internal debate on the war credits vote (which had triggered the internal conflict in the SPD) and on many other lacerating issues.

The split in the party, created by the extreme antiwar left, occurred as early as November 2, 1918, but it was small and very marginal. This splinter group became involved in an unsuccessful revolutionary coup, initiated in conjunction with the Bavarian one, and from then on remained an ultra-left sectarian group, divided internally by dissidence and factional strife, boycotting the elections and unable to penetrate the social democratic working-class organizations. The Austrian Socialist Party rejected Lenin's twenty-one points, proposed by Zinoviev; but at the same time, they did not return to the Second International, which they accused of having been affected by "social patriotism." Instead, they formed the "Work Community of the Socialist Parties" in 1921, which was immediately defined disparagingly as the "Two-and-a-Half International." They returned to the Second International only in 1923, when the most intense revolutionary crisis was over.

In the British case, one should not speak of a split, as the Communist Party of Great Britain (CPGB) founded in London on August 7, 1920, was rather a fusion of a number of Marxist groups, including the British Socialist Party, the Labour Socialist Party of Glasgow, and other nuclei, none of which can be regarded as a split from the Labour Party. At its second congress, held in Leeds in 1921, other political groups joined, such as the Socialist Federation of Workers and the left of the Independent Labour Party, and the party formally adhered to the Third International.[68] The party tried to affiliate itself with the Labour Party, but it was rejected from the beginning. Following the election of a Communist on the official

[68] Wood (1959).

Labour Ticket in the general election of 1922, the Labour Party decided in 1924 to formally preclude the nomination of CPGB members as Labour candidates in future elections. A year later, in 1925, it finally decided to exclude CPGB members from its constituency branches.[69]

As a result of its electoral weakness – with the few exceptions of small zones like Rhondda East, Motherwell, and North Battersea – British communism has always been considered insignificant, although in the 1920s its influence was considerable in the mining and engineering unions. In some trade councils, such as that of London, relatively strong CPGB cells existed. The CPGB also formed some important organizations like the National Unemployed Workers' Movement (NUWM), whose membership figures are still highly debated by historians. After 1927, its influence in the trade unions was reduced substantially due to the strong attempt to achieve this by the Trade Union Confederation (TUC) reformist leadership and to the CPGB's suicidal policy of attacking moderate trade unions as "social fascists."

The radical split in the Irish Labour Party had few effects. An Irish Communist Party was founded in 1921, but it had already dissolved by 1923 to merge into the League of Irish Workers, its activities limited to the twenty-six Southern counties. Communists continued to work through autonomous structures in the six counties of Northern Ireland until June 1933, when a national congress reunited the Irish Communists across the whole country. This small and politically insignificant group continued to split and reunite until its formal dissolution in 1941. In 1948, the Communists in the South reorganized themselves into the League of Irish Workers. In 1970, the North and South once again united under the name of the Communist Party of Ireland. In Austria, Ireland, and the United Kingdom, therefore, war time and postwar radicalization resolved itself either with no formal split or with the formation of totally insignificant sects.

In the Netherlands and Sweden, the postwar formation of communist parties should be seen in the light of the prewar radical splits in the socialist parties. In both countries, the radical wings had been expelled and had formed new parties of the left: the Social Democratic Party in the Netherlands and the Swedish Young Socialist Party (SUP) in Sweden in 1908 and 1910, respectively. At a congress held in 1918, the Dutch Social Democratic Party changed its name to the Communist Party of the Netherlands. The Swedish development was more complex. The new radical party pushed through the foundation of an anarcho-syndicalist movement

---

[69] For the contact at election times, see Salles (1977: 407–427). On the formation of the Communist Party, see also Mair (1979: 157–182).

in Sweden (SAC). When the Swedish Social Democrats participated in a liberal government in 1917, a second split occurred, with the left wing of the party forming a new party: Sweden's Social Democratic Left Party (SSDLP). This party was the embryo of the various communist parties that would emerge over the following decades. It adhered to the Third International in 1919 and changed its name to the Swedish Communist Party after having reunited various political and unions left-wing groups. What is striking about the fragmentation of the Swedish organizations after World War I is that the formation of a Communist Party was not its end but its beginning. In the following years, continuous confrontation with the Third International led to two right-wing splits: in 1926 the so-called Höglung Communists, who soon returned to the Social Democrats, and in 1929 the Kilborn Communists, who returned to the Social Democrats in 1937. Although there are differences in the process of Communist Party constitution, the Dutch and Swedish cases are similar because the post–World War I birth of a Communist Party resulted from the adherence to the Third International of previously established radical left formations; the original motivations and sources of these groups were independent of the specific push determined by the Russian Revolution and by the initial strategy of the Third International.

Unlike the Netherlands and Sweden, in Belgium, Denmark, and Switzerland the split originated in the last phase of the war and had no specific organizational links with prewar parties. The experiences of the three countries present some variations, but in all cases the split resulted in a minor and nontraumatic separation with a decidedly tiny left-wing minority. In Denmark, where the impact of World War I was minimal thanks to its neutrality, there was little right- or left-wing factionalism. When Thorvald Stauning entered the cabinet as the first Social Democratic minister in 1916, the extraordinary party congress authorized this move by a vote of 291 to only 32,[70] even though the continued governmental cooperation with the Radical Liberals was approved by a much more restricted majority in 1918 (220 to 156).[71] Very minor socialist parties started to organize during 1918.[72] More important was the radical attitude of the Social Democratic Youth organization (the SUF), which adhered to the Zimmerwald left. Having failed to obtain the termination of the socialist participation in government and firmer antimilitarist stances, the SUF

---

[70] Logue (1982: 66).

[71] Ibid. 68.

[72] Namely, a Socialist Workers' Party (SAP) organized by some leaders of the syndicalist opposition unions movement and a second small socialist splinter party. However, they obtained only 2,500 votes of the 920,000 cast in the 1918 election.

broke away from the party and, in November 1919, joined other minor socialist groups to form Denmark's Left Socialist Party, which one year later accepted the Comintern's twenty-one conditions and renamed itself as a Communist Party. Subsequently, in 1921, it merged with the syndicalist trade union opposition (FS).[73] As in Sweden, the Danish Communist Party suffered a major split in 1958, when the wing led by one of its major leaders, Aksel, split to found the People's Socialist Party (SF). In Belgium, the Communist Party was formed in 1921 by the fusion of two left-wing groups that had detached themselves from the Belgian Socialist Party at two different moments. The party was the fusion of two newspapers and of the political groups around them, *L'ouvrier communiste* and *L'exploité*, directed by Joseph Jacquemotte, who was to become the major leader of the new formation. There was a certain amount of continuity between these groups and their internal opposition over the question of the socialist participation in bourgeois government since 1910.[74]

The final outcome of the Swiss radicalization and organizational fragmentation was similar, but the modalities of the split are particularly interesting and merit review. The Swiss Socialist Party is generally portrayed in comparative terms as a moderate movement. However, radicalization had also occurred in Switzerland during the second half of the war, when restricted food and supplies and income reductions accentuated social tensions. This resulted in the general strike of 1918. In the first days, the level of participation was impressive even by non-Swiss standards. However, the strike was unexpectedly stopped by a decision of the executive body of the strike itself and by the Socialist Party. The nine-point set of goals formulated by the strike committee (the Committee of Olten) was abandoned, even though some of the reforms advocated (in particular, proportional representatation and a forty-eight-hour work week) were implemented. This sudden halt produced bitter resentment and opposition among many of the participants and gave dynamic momentum to the radical opposition within the Socialist Party.[75] As a result, a motion in favor of leaving the Second International was approved by 459 delegates and rejected by only 1 in the 1919 Basel Congress. The successive motion

---

[73] On the origins of the Danish Communist Party, see Rohde (1973: 3–33).

[74] The split has been related by some historians to the growing manifestation of a revolutionary syndicalist and radical Marxist left within the Belgian Socialist Party from 1908 on. Steinberg (1971: 3–34), in particular, has underlined these links. Jacquemotte was already the leader of this pre–World War I radical wing, but it was a restricted group of people with only personal links.

[75] On the crucial importance of the 1918 general strike and its interpretation as the high point of working-class protest in Swiss socialist history as a whole, see Stettler (1980: 5–43).

for adherence to the Third International was passed by a majority of 328 to 147. Like the Norwegian and French socialist parties, the Swiss party adhered by majority vote to the new International. However, the minority asked for the decision to be confirmed by a referendum among the members of the party. The surprising result was that the congress's decision to adhere was rejected by 14,612 votes to 8,722. Yet, notwithstanding this burning popular defeat, the supporters of the Third International still numbered more than one-third of the party members. In the extraordinary Congress of Berne in December 1920, the motion to adhere to the Third International was reproposed and this time was defeated by 350 votes to 213. In spite of this result, the left of the party thought that the supporters of the Third International were more numerous than was shown by the vote because the majority of the delegates approved action to obtain modification in the twenty-one conditions of adhesion. It was now their turn to ask for a referendum among the members, but they were again disappointed by the results: The congress decision was confirmed by 25,475 votes to 8,777. Finally, after the sudden and intense resentment had passed, the communist left split in March 1921, when it fused with other older organizations of anarcho-syndicalist tradition.[76]

From the mid-1920s on, the Swiss Communist Party experienced accentuated Bolshevization. The old guard was dismissed and the direction modified *à volonté* until strict Stalinist orthodoxy was granted.[77] In the interwar period, the party was outlawed in some cantons (Geneva, 1932) and, during the war, at the federal level. The bulk of the party's members were in German-speaking Switzerland, and it never succeeded in making inroads into Romandy (although it was moderately successful in Geneva). Federalism and the deeply rooted Swiss traditions of local autonomy were regarded as *vestige bourgeois*; but throughout the 1920s and early 1930s, conflicts between regional committees (particularly Romance ones) and the central committee were frequent. Relationships with the trade unions had been difficult from the beginning and remained so. The Socialist Party took a very hard line against the opposition, reacting strongly against the creation of communist cells. Membership figures show how politically

[76] On this fusion, see Studer (1993: 5–38.) On the historical origins of the Swiss Communist Party, the best source is Stettler (1980).

[77] On the Bolshevization process, see Stettler (1980: 61–92). The party was dominated for a long time by Jules Humbert Droz, who reached the highest echelons of the International. As secretary responsible for the Latin countries and as a member of the executive committee, he spent more than ten years in the service of the Third International. During this period, the Swiss section of the International became an essential support for Droz in its internal dissenting position vis-à-vis Stalin. So, the party probably also suffered from this conflict as well as from Droz's final expulsion.

insignificant Swiss communism was and give some idea of its steadily continuing decline: the 6,356 members were reduced to 3,500 by 1927, to 1,700 by 1933, and to a few hundred in 1938–1939.[78]

In the last group – France, Italy, Germany, Finland, and Norway – the splits were more dramatic, the forces more evenly distributed, and the depth of the divisions more profound. In some cases, such as Norway, Italy, and Germany, the socialist movement split into three major groups. The Norwegian Workers' Party was one of the founders of the Third International, and its original adherence was almost unanimous. However, this was more an act of international solidarity, despite its reflection of the postwar radicalization of the movement. The growing divergence with the Comintern that soon emerged produced the right-wing split of a large group of reformists who founded a Social Democratic Party two years later. An idea of the respective strength of the two groups was given by the election of the same year, when the reformists obtained about 9.2% of the votes compared with 21.3% obtained by the Workers' Party. In other words, a third of the party had split. The resulting growing resistance of the Workers' Party to the Comintern's intrusions into internal party affairs and the skepticism of the trade unions – which had not adhered to the Red Trade Union International – precipitated a withdrawal of the party from the International in November 1923. The pro-Moscow minority immediately founded the Norwegian Communist Party (NKP). As a result, the Norwegian left was split into three separate parties at the 1924 elections, each of them representing a considerable proportion of the vote: 8.8% for the reformist Social Democrats, 18.4% for the "centrist" Workers' Party, and 6.1% for the Communist Party.[79]

The German and Italian experiences produced similar results, even though they took place in a context of more pronounced social turmoil and political instability. The German division into revisionist, orthodox-centrist, and revolutionary groups was an old and well-established internal articulation within the SPD from the beginning of the century, but the war and the war credit vote now precipitated organizational fragmentation. Here the three-party format was the result of successive left-wing splits. In April 1917, the opponents of the patriotic stance of the SPD left the party (after having already constituted an autonomous parliamentary group) to form the Independent Social Democratic Party (USPD), which included both Kautsky and Haase and the radical left Spartakus group led by Karl

---

[78] Studer (1993: 19).
[79] On the stormy 1919–1923 history of the Norwegian labor movement, see Sparre (1981a: 691–704) and (1981b: 393–413).

Liebknecht and Rosa Luxemburg. Between 1918 and 1919, the Spartakus group left the USPD to found the Communist Party of Germany (KPD). The KPD refused to participate in the 1919 election, but in 1920 the socialist movement was electorally divided into a three-party, left-skewed situation: 21.6% of the votes to the "majoritarian" SPD, 17.9% to the Independent Social Democrats, and 2.1% to the Communists. In later years, the Independents were split by the centrifugal attraction of the SPD on the right and the Communists on the left, but they continued to participate in elections up to 1928.

In Italy, the socialist movement had split before the war, when the reformist wing led by Bonomi and Bissolati – which was sensitive to the Bernstein revisionism, as well as to the British model of trade unionism – was expelled from the Socialist Party.[80] During the war, the Italian Socialist Party (PSI) had been an active member of the Zimmerwald (September 1915) and Kienthal (April 1916) Socialist International Conferences and had maintained a pacifist, antimilitarist, and antiwar position, while at the same time trying not to sabotage the military stand taken by the country. The Russian Revolution of 1917 and the end of the war exacerbated the internal divisions of the party. However, under the leadership of the left led by Serrati – within which the intransigent group led by Bordiga and Gramsci started to be noticed – the party seemed capable of maintaining its organizational unity and negotiating its global adherence to the Third International. It was thus only at the beginning of 1921 that the Leninist wing split to found the Communist Party of Italy. The effort to keep the party united while negotiating its entrance into the new International had failed, but the Communist split was not sufficient to safeguard the organizational unity between maximalists and reformists, and the issue of the relationship between socialism and Russian-inspired communism, as well as the interpretation of the Italian political situation and that of the incoming fascist movement, led to a further split of the reformist wing led by Turati and Treves, which founded the Unitary Socialist party (PSU).[81] By 1922, the Socialist Party of 1910 had split into four groups: the majoritarian Socialist Party; the reformists of 1912, who competed autonomously in the elections of 1913 and 1919 (gaining 3.9% and 1.4% of the vote) but not in 1921; the Communist Party, which competed for the

---

[80] It is interesting to note that the left led by Lazzari and Mussolini managed to expel the reformist wing, using as a formal argument the fact that its leaders had violated the socialist tradition, having agreed to be consulted by the king during the previous ministerial crisis. See Arfé (1965: 137–148).

[81] Even in this case, the formal occasion was the fact that Turati had participated in political consultation following the crisis of the Facta government.

first time in 1921, gaining 4.6% of the vote; and the Turati–Treves reformists, who never contested elections. So, from the strictly electoral point of view, the fragmentation was never as sharp as in Germany or Norway, although politically it was similar.

The French split resembled that of Norway: The right wing of the SFIO left the party, while the majority voted for unconditional adherence to the Third International. Although the entry of Guesde into the national defense government met with little internal opposition at the beginning of the war,[82] criticism of the unconditional support for the war and the request for a policy of peaceful conclusion of the conflict started to grow from 1915. As a result, the left fraction established contacts with other European revolutionary socialists, as well as with Lenin at the Kienthal and Zimmerwald congresses. The internal radicalization and factional strife increased to high levels only at the end of the war regarding the issue of adherence to the Third International. The right wing rejected the organizational and political principles of Leninism, the center favored adherence but wanted to negotiate conditions, and the left requested unconditional adherence. In a series of successive votes in the 1919 and 1920 congresses, the unconditional pro-adhesion group gained a strong majority of 67.4% and finally the right and the center abandoned the Tours congress as a minority.[83] A second element that makes the French split very striking is that the communists merged with the syndicalists and even the anarchists. Moreover, the political split was accompanied by a split along the same lines in the trade union movement, leading eventually to the formation of the General Confederation of the United Workers (CGTU).[84] This is virtually a unique phenomenon, as in most cases trade unions resisted

[82] The issue of the socialist participation in bourgeois governments had been highly divisive from 1901, when the participation of Millerand in the government of Waldeck-Rousseau convinced Guesdes to distance himself from the slowly organizing French Socialist Party. This may be regarded as a very early prewar internal split of the socialist movement, but it is true that the Socialist Party was still in a formative period. However, the new condition of foreign attack in 1914 did not create the same tensions. For an account of the episode of the Guesde's sharp opposition to Millerand, see Lefranc (1963: 111–112).

[83] In 1919, the different positions were distributed as follows: right (to stay within the Second International): 757 mandates; center (to stay provisionally within the Second International but to break relations with the German Social Democrats and maintain good relations with Russia): 894 mandates; left (to abandon the Second International for the Third): 270 mandates. In 1920, at Tours, adherence to the Third International was approved with 3,208 votes, while the centrist position obtained 1,002 votes and the right obtained 397 abstentions. A second vote – required by the majority to give the center a second chance to adhere – failed: 3,247 votes to 1,398. See Kriegel (1969: 386).

[84] On the modalities of the trade union movement split and on the extremely heterogeneous nature of the newly founded CGTU, see Robert (1980: 180–182) and Lorwin (1954: 57–58).

internal strife on moderate positions much more successfully. Unquestionably, the formation of the French Communist Party (PCF) – which absorbed the majority of the old SFIO – was the result of political issues concerning the organizational nature of the new political party and its strategy, which were not clearly delineated. This lack of clarity created a larger majority for the Third International, but the extremely heterogeneous nature of the new party led to a more profound and shocking intervention on the part of the Third International later. In Italy, the minority groups of Bordiga and Gramsci had recognized the political and organizational implication of Leninism more clearly, and had proved less inclined toward groups that did not share such implications for the life and organization of the new party.[85]

The Finnish Communist split does not resemble any of these others because of the close link between Finnish and Russian history. Strictly speaking, there was no split, as the Finnish Communist Party (SKP) was founded outside Finland, in Moscow, at the end of August 1918 by the survivors of the defeated Red Guard in the civil war of January–May 1918. Its history was, therefore, from its beginning, intimately linked to that of the Russian Bolsheviks; its culture was that of a clandestine armed group, and it developed outside Finland until its fourth congress in 1920, which was the first held at home. This did not, however, prevent the party from gaining a remarkable 14.8% of the vote at its first appearance in the national electoral competition.

The division with the moderate socialists was particularly deep, as the physical proximity of the Russian Revolution and the national opposition between Finland and the Soviet Union deepened the cleavage between the communists and socialists. One example of this can be found in the contrast that was accentuated by the foundation of the autonomous Soviet Karelia on the Russian side of the Finnish border, which was headed by a number of the central figures of the defeated revolutionary group in 1918. Communists were considered an enduring threat, and the socialists moved to the center even in economic policy. Thus, unlike other Scandinavian socialists, Finnish socialists accepted and went along with classical liberal economic policies that were costly and painful to the working class.

In 1923, three years after its return "home," the Communist Party was dissolved by the Finnish Diet when it held twenty-seven seats. In 1930, the Trade Union Confederation (SAAJ) was also dissolved because it was controlled by the communists.[86] In conclusion, the communist–social-

---

[85] This is the opinion of Galli (1976b: 39–40).
[86] For a general discussion of Finnish communism see Hodgson (1967, 1973), Laulajainen

ist split was more bitter in Finland than in any other country. In fact, even during World War II, which was generally a period of rapprochement for anti-Nazi national coalitions, the two parties remained in opposite camps. This happened as a result of the Finnish–Soviet War that began on November 30, 1939, following the Finnish refusal to yield to the Soviet request for territorial concessions aiming to guarantee the defense of Leningrad. The SKP boycotted the war and established a Soviet government in Terijoki under the direction of the leader Kuusinen. This move was interpreted by the other political forces as a step toward the annexation of Finland to the Soviet Union and precipitated not only the persecution of communists as national traitors, but also the Finno-German alliance of June 1941 and the unique European case of a socialist party cooperating with the Nazis: Vaino Tanner, leader of the Social Democrats, was indeed to participate in all the war governments.

THE ELECTORAL DEVELOPMENT OF THE LEFT'S COMPONENTS

The three main components of the left are represented in this study by, first, the official *socialist, social democratic, or labor parties*, all of which maintained their original affiliation with the socialist International (only in Italy were two socialist parties members of the International at the same time as a result of the 1947 split between socialists and social democrats); second, the *communist parties;* and a third component represented by all those "third" parties that originated as right-wing or left-wing splits from either the official socialists or the official communists. This is a far more heterogeneous group in terms of ideology and organizational orientation. Any further internal differentiation of this group has proved very difficult and I have decided to regroup all these parties into a general category called "other left parties," that is, the left that was neither orthodox communist nor official by socialist.

These three families have varying weights within the overall European left. Socialist parties took part in all the 347 elections that constitute this sample. The average size of their vote was 27.7% with a 12.7% standard deviation. In the frequency distribution of the electoral results of all socialist parties, there is a discontinuity for the values between 30% and 38%. This indicates that this was a point of instability for the socialist performance. Thus, socialist parties reaching this level were either rapidly able

---

(1979), and Haapakoski (1974). For a historical recollection by a former general secretary of the Finnish Communist Party, see Tuominen (1955).

to overcome it, becoming large parties with over 40% of the vote, or rapidly regressed below that level, stabilizing at between 25% and 30%. Few socialist parties managed to stay at that level for a long period of time.

Communist parties participated in only 217 of the 347 elections. A communist party is absent in the Republic of Ireland. In the United Kingdom, the Communist Party (CPGB) consistently won between 0.1% and 0.4% of the vote after 1918, but it has only won three seats in the House of Commons in its history (one in 1922 and two in 1945), and since 1964 most of its candidates have lost their deposits. The distribution of the electoral fortunes of the communist parties is totally skewed. Their mean result was 6.6% but their standard deviation is higher (7.97%), indicating the remarkable cross-country variation and cross-time instability. In more than three-quarters of these elections, Communists scored less than 7% of the vote. In fact, in all elections they have obtained more than 11% of the vote in only four countries: France, Finland, Italy, and interwar Germany. Therefore, Communist parties were either strong or marginal.[87]

Finally, the role of "other left" parties is even less pronounced. Such parties took part in less than one-third of all European elections: 114 of 347. The overall mean across the century is only 4% of the vote, and the standard deviation is as high as that of the Communist parties. Their electoral performance is on the whole modest: In only eleven elections did such parties manage to collect more than 10% of the vote, while 50% of the cases fell below 3.5% of the vote threshold.

The electoral development over time of the three components for all European elections and by country is reported in Figure 2.6. The overall development of the left, discussed in the first section of this chapter, is actually the result of the different trends of the three components. The socialist party electoral record is one of intense growth up to the 1910s, followed by a period of modest increases, which continued up to the 1950s. After this time, the socialist parties tended to stagnate, and by the 1980s a decline is evident. Communist parties, in contrast, grew moderately during the 1920s and 1930s and peaked in the 1940s, particularly in the 1945–1948 period, reaching their maximum of about 10% of the European vote. Since then, they have declined consistently, losing more than half of their percentage points. Finally, "other left" parties showed a third

---

[87] Unfortunately, the exclusion of Spain, Portugal, and Greece for the reasons mentioned in Chapter 1 deprives us not only of three cases in which the communists made considerable electoral inroads, but also of the cases in which such inroads actually represented an intermediate level between the strong and marginal cases. In other words, their inclusion would give a more continuous character to the variance of communist electoral strength.

pattern of historical development. They had their maximum impact in the radicalization phase before and during the First World War, but then they tended to decline considerably and consistently from the 1920s to the 1950s. However, since the 1960s, their electoral performance has been growing again. This growth however, is not sufficient to compensate for the decline of the communists and the stagnation/decline of the socialists. However, it is the only component of the left that has managed to increase its share of the electoral market in the last three decades.

A close look at the graphs in Figure 2.6 is fascinating because it shows the great variety of over-time developments of each component that is concealed behind the overall development of the left in each country (specified in Figure 2.3). Moreover, these figures show how the growth–decline of one component relates to the growth–decline of the others in each country. A detailed descriptive discussion of these figures and data is not necessary and can be left up to the reader. I will limit my comments to a few important and general points.

Given that there is an official Socialist Party in all the countries and an equally official communist party in all of them, with the exception of Ireland, then, *in terms of composition,* the electoral presence of other left parties is the main distinguishing feature between one left and another.[88] No other left party has ever challenged the monopoly of the socialists and communists in Austria and the United Kingdom. Although other left candidates and groups have arisen from time to time, they have been relatively unimportant and can be easily overlooked (although they will be included in the electoral computation). In the United Kingdom, for instance, the British Labour Party never organized in Northern Ireland. Such groups as the Northern Ireland Labor Party, Republican Labour, and the Social Democratic and Labour Party were represented in the Stormont (i.e., the Northern Ireland Parliament) when it functioned and occasionally in Westminster. In the United Kingdom, there is the problem of how to interpret the 1981 split of the Social Democrats. This party was originally considered a truly other left party, which would make the United Kingdom the country with the most recent and late occurrence of left fragmentation. However, the group – consisting of thirteen Labour members and members of Parliament – rapidly merged with the Liberal Party, making their individual identification impossible after the 1983 election. For the

---

[88] I have not taken into consideration the development after 1985. Insisting on electoral presence is crucial. In the history of the socialist movements, there have always been numerous groups, associations, small parties, etc. in each country and in each period, which, however, have not contested the elections autonomously or, if they have, have not been able to gain any significant or measurable support.

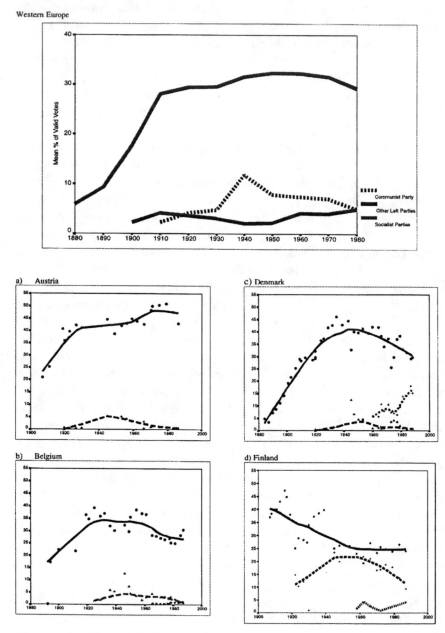

Figure 2.6. Electoral development of the internal components of the left.

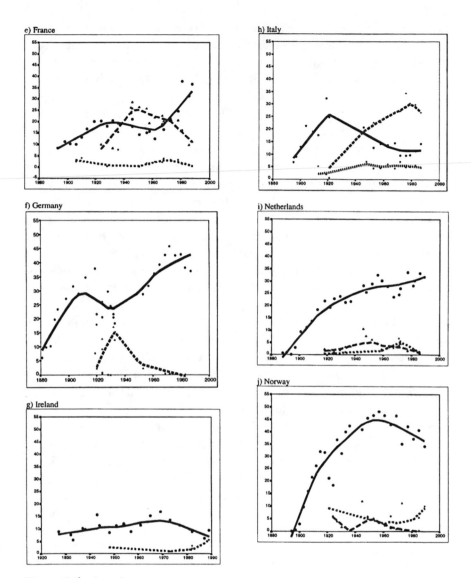

Figure 2.6. (cont.)

purposes of this book, I have decided not to consider the Social Democratic split as a third left party.[89] In Austria, notwithstanding its long experience of a proportional electoral system, a socialist splinter group emerged only once: the Democratic Progressive Party, which was formed from ex-members of the Socialist Party and led by a former minister of the interior. In 1966 it won slightly more than 3% of the vote, but afterward it dissolved immediately.

In all the other European countries, however, the socialist/communist monopoly has always been challenged at one time or another. France is unique in that the class left panorama has always been characterized by the presence of more than one socialist party. However, before the formation of the Unified Socialist Party (PSU) in the 1960s by dissident socialists and Communists, the phenomenon of other left formations can be mainly regarded as an expression of the loosely structured French party system, characterized by the almost continuous presence in parliament of indepen-dent personalities, whose election has been facilitated by the emphasis on uninominal constituencies and the double ballot. Such personalities have regrouped under labels such as Divers Gauche or Indépendents de Gauche. In Italy, too, a third party can be traced back to the pre–World War I period, with a right-wing splinter party gaining 5.2% of the vote in the 1913 elections. In the two elections before the rise of fascism there, loosely organized groups of reformist Socialists were excluded from the official Socialist Party, which was sharply divided by the awkward dilemma of participating in the new International while maintaining the maximum unity compatible with this decision. Since 1945, the presence of third parties in Italy has been continuous as a result of the split of the Social Democratic Party from the PSI in 1947 following the latter's orientation toward the Popular Front. The picture has since been complicated by additional mergers and new splits in the PSI and in the 1970s by the participation in national elections of groups on the extreme left, which combined some of the ideological features of the new left with a somewhat Leninist or pseudo-Leninist vocabulary and ideology.

In the Netherlands, the presence of third parties in the left panorama has been a permanent feature since World War I. For almost the entire interwar period, a Socialist Party (SP, 1918–1925) followed by a Revolu-tionary Socialist Party (RSP, 1929–1933) was present, but only in the 1933 election was the latter able to win more than 1% of the total vote. In the post–World War II period, a left-wing split from the Labor Party, result-

---

[89] The best account of the British SDP is Crewe and King (1995). They finally regard the SDP as a political failure.

ing from disagreement on North Atlantic Treaty Organization policy, gave rise to the Pacifist Socialist Party (PSP, 1959) and provided the opening skirmish in a much larger battle that culminated in what may be considered the highest fragmentation of the left in Europe in terms of the number of parties. In the 1971 election, two more parties were added to the Dutch left. One, the Democratic Socialists 70 (DS, 1970), was a right-wing split from the Labor Party; the other, the Radical Political Party (PPR), which had originally been a left-wing split from the Catholic Party, evolved into a distinct left party and since 1971 has been considered to be a full part of the other left. Even though these parties lost considerably in successive elections, some of them have remained among the largest and most consistent other left forces in the European party systems.

In Sweden and Germany, a three-part division within the class left was limited to the interwar period. In Sweden, as in the Netherlands, the 1908 radical split from the Social Democratic Party generated a Left Socialist Party, which refused to participate in elections until 1917. In 1921, the party joined the Communist International and founded the Swedish Communist Party. However, a minority decided to remain independent and stand for the 1921 election under the earlier label. In 1924, 1932, and 1936, the Swedish other left was composed only of splinter groups from the official Communist Party, sometimes joined by a few dissident left-wing Social Democrats. In Germany, too, the first split occurred during the war years. The split of the SPD into majoritarians and independents was the most profound division of the socialist movement in Europe before the communist splits. However, it lasted for only a decade, and most of the Independent Socialists then provided the electoral basis for the growing German Communist Party. In neither Germany nor Sweden was there another split or a new party after 1945.

It is interesting to note that there is no instance of other left party fragmentation emerging *for the first time* in the first post–World War II period. Either such fragmentation was already a feature of the left or it emerged only beginning in the mid-1960s. In almost half of these countries, the presence of other left parties is mainly or exclusively a feature of the mid-1960s (Denmark, Finland, Norway, and Belgium) or even the 1970s (Ireland and Switzerland). In Denmark, this process was initiated by a right-wing split from the Communist Party, and it later escalated when the Danish Communist Party's leader, Aksel Larsen, who returned from the Twentieth Congress of the CPSU looking for a national road to socialism, was expelled from the party. In 1958, he formed the Socialist People's Party (SF), which was clearly located between the official pro-Soviet Communist Party and the Social Democrats. The left wing of the Danish political spectrum subsequently became crowded with other parties – one stemming from a left-wing split from the Socialist People's Party (the Left Socialists, VS, 1968), the other from a right-wing split from the Social Democratic Party (the Centre Democrats, CD, 1973). In Finland, a left-wing faction of the Social Democrats began to organize itself in 1957, presented some candidates autonomously in the elections of 1958, and finally set up the Social Democratic League (TPSL) in 1959.[90]

The Norwegian picture is more complicated. Strictly speaking, an other left party had been formed in the 1920s. In 1921, a Socialist Democratic Workers' Party (NSA) was formed to the right of the Labor Party when the latter decided to join the Comintern. The situation was unique in that there were thus two official socialist parties, one of which retained its name but was affiliated with the Third International. When this affiliation was terminated two years later, the Norwegian left was for a while divided into three parties – like the German, Italian, and Swedish left in the same period – because a minority of the Labor Party remained in the Comintern. This division lasted for only a short period, however, for in 1927 the Labor Party and the Social Democrats reunited. It was therefore only in the 1924 election that three left parties competed for the Norwegian electorate. A significant and stable presence of third left parties in Norway can thus be dated with the recent rebirth in 1961 of radical socialism with the Socialist People's Party (SF). Its success in the 1973 election, in alliance with the Communist Party, was mainly due to the difficulties experienced by the Labor Party in dealing with such foreign policy issues as membership in the European Economic Community (EEC) and NATO. This has coincided with the particularly strong impact of some typical new left concerns such as Third World ideology, pacifism, and neutralism in a country where proximity to Sweden and the widespread awareness of an ex-colonial periphery constantly recall the advantages of neutrality.

In Belgium, three other left parties emerged when the formidable shattering of the party system occurred due to the linguistic remobilization of the electorate. The first of these parties, the Walloon Workers' Party, competed only in the 1965 and 1968 elections and was regional; the other two emerged in the middle of the 1970s (All Power to the Workers–Labour Party in 1974; Revolutionary Workers–Socialist Workers in 1977) as more permanent and radical left groupings. However, all of these were

---

[90] In 1973, the Social Democratic League of Workers and Small Peasants reunited with the Social Democratic Party. However, a fraction within it repudiated this alliance and founded the Socialist Workers' Party (STP).

electorally insignificant. None ever managed to reach 1% of the vote, and only in 1965 did the Walloon Workers' Party win a parliamentary seat.

Finally, in Ireland and Switzerland, the birth of a new post-1960 left was delayed until the middle of the 1970s. In Ireland, mention should be made of a number of Independent Left representatives elected in the period 1923–1937 and of two others elected in 1977. Moreover, a splinter group of the Labour Party broke away in 1944 as the National Labour Party but reunited with the former in 1950. Also, the National Progressive Democrats, which contested the 1961 election and won two seats with 1% of the vote, is generally regarded by Irish commentators as a socialist formation. It later merged with the Labour Party. Even in this case, however, its participation was intermittent and of very little electoral importance. A continuous and consistent presence of other left parties in Ireland can be identified only in the mid-1970s and early 1980s. In 1973, a Workers' Party began to compete with some success (between 1% and 3% of the vote up to 1985 and between one and three seats). There may, however, be some problem in considering it as a class left party, as it was the official wing of the Sinn Fein. A Socialist Labour Party competed in the 1981 elections (0.4% and one seat). Since 1982, a Democratic Socialist Party has entered the elections, winning about 0.5% of the vote. Both of the latter parties were founded by ex-Labour candidates or independent Labor candidates. In Switzerland, two small other left parties have existed since 1971, when a split from the Communist Party (Progressive Organizations) and a left-wing breakaway from the Ticino Social Democrats (Autonomous Socialist Party) stood for elections.

Table 2.6 sums up the situation and indicates the periods in which other left parties have been present in the party systems. The presence of third parties has generally been intermittent and, in most cases, of little electoral significance over the entire period. Only in Norway, the Netherlands, and Denmark does the total electoral strength of these parties exceed that of the respective communist party in a large number of elections since the 1960s. The only country in which the other left has reached a considerable electoral size is Denmark, where it ranges between 10% and 15%. In the same period, the second strongest other left parties are those of Norway, Sweden, and Italy, all ranging around the 5% threshold.

Therefore, in the period since World War I and in the context of a given national size of the left, the variance in the size of the Communist parties is in large part the result of variance in the size of the socialist parties from which they originated and has been little influenced, so far, by the force of other left parties. This inverse relationship between the size of the Communist and socialist parties, however, presents, a clear discontinuity (see Table 2.7). For a first group of countries, the size of the

Table 2.6. *Electoral presence of left parties other than communist and socialist parties*

always	never	since World War I	only between the wars	only since World War II	only since the 1960s	later than the 1960s
France Italy	Austria Un. Kingdom	Netherlands	Germany Sweden		Denmark Finland Norway Belgium	Ireland Switzerland

communist parties bears no relationship to that of the socialists. Equally small communist parties exist in the Netherlands and Switzerland, as well as in Norway, Sweden, Austria, and the United Kingdom, so that no influence over the size of the socialist support can reasonably be attributed to the Communist split. Moreover, the relatively small changes that took place after 1945 in this group of countries indicate that the problem of the respective size of the parties – whether the communist party was to be large or small – was decided during the 1917–1944 period.

On the other hand, for the remaining countries, it is evident that the greatest variations occurred after 1945. In three cases – France, Finland, and Italy – this change has led to the strongest European Communist parties. In one, Germany, it sharply reduced the size that the Communist Party had reached between the world wars. In only France and Italy did the Communist Party eventually manage to surpass the strength of the socialists. However, the group of countries that developed large Communist parties after World War II was already clearly distinguishable from the other group in the 1917–1944 period. In short, it might seem that the large postwar communist parties were already *in nuce* before World War II. The uncertain case of Italy and that of Germany, however, weaken this conclusion. Because the Italian Communist Party was not as strong as the Finnish or French parties between the world wars, it is difficult to know whether this is due to the fact that Italian Communists participated in only one election against the socialists (1922) before the rise of fascism and the demise of democracy, or wheather it was due to its own weakness. In the second hypothesis, the post–World War II strength of Italian communism can be traced back to the fall of fascism, military defeat, and the resistance movement – that is, to the 1943–1945 period.

The German case is quite the opposite. Communism here was from the beginning a strong political movement, as strong as those in France and Finland; but after the Nazi regime, it fell to an insignificant size. This

Table 2.7. *Electoral size of socialist and communist parties and of the total left (period averages)*

countries	socialist party				communist party		
	1880-17	1918-44	1945-65	1966-89	1918-44	1945-65	1966-89
Au	23.2 (2)	40.0 (5)	42.9 (6)	47.6 (7)	0.7 (4)	4.4 (6)	0.9 (7)
Be	15.5 (4)	35.2 (7)	34.0 (7)	27.3 (8)	3.6 (5)	5.4 (7)	2.5 (8)
De	17.0 (12)	37.4 (11)	39.7 (8)	33.1 (11)	0.8 (9)	4.8 (8)	1.8 (11)
Fi	41.3 (8)	33.1 (9)	24.5 (6)	25.1 (7)	10.4 (5)	22.0 (6)	16.4 (7)
Fr	11.7 (6)	19.6 (5)	17.2 (7)	26.6 (7)	11.2 (4)	24.8 (7)	17.3 (7)
Ge	21.3 (9)	24.5 (9)	33.1 (5)	41.5 (6)	11.4 (8)	4.0 (2)	0.3 (4)
Ir	-	10.0 (7)	11.4 (6)	10.8 (8)	-	-	-
It	14.4 (6)	28.5 (2)	15.4 (4)	11.5 (6)	4.6 (1)	22.4 (4)	29.2 (6)
Ne	7.3 (8)	21.9 (6)	29.0 (6)	29.2 (8)	2.3 (6)	5.7 (6)	2.6 (7)
No	13.7 (8)	31.7 (7)	45.3 (6)	39.4 (6)	2.8 (5)	5.1 (6)	0.5 (4)
Sw	22.0 (7)	41.5 (8)	46.3 (6)	44.8 (8)	5.0 (7)	4.8 (6)	5.0 (8)
Sz	15.4 (8)	26.4 (8)	24.4 (5)	22.8 (6)	1.9 (6)	3.1 (5)	2.0 (6)
UK	4.9 (4)	33.5 (8)	46.2 (6)	35.8 (6)	0.2 (7)	0.2 (6)	0.1 (6)

Note: The number of elections in which the party competed is given in parentheses. The party average electoral size was computed taking into consideration only the elections in which the party actually competed. Corresponding figures for the total left are given in Table 3.3.

major change in the position of the German Communist Party did not produce a corresponding social democratic growth, since after 1945 the SPD simply recovered its Weimar electorate. Even in this case, it is difficult to say whether this is a case of Communist Party electoral failure, notwithstanding its strong electoral inroads in the interwar period, or, alternatively, whether it is the result of the powerful influence of the division of the country and the border with communist Eastern Europe. As a reaction to its uneasy international position, the West Germans played down any potential internal divisions and tended to look "with suspicion at any type of criticism parallel with, even if organizationally independent of, that coming from East Germany" and the Communist world.[91]

The negative statistical correlation between the electoral support of communist and socialist parties increases strongly after World War II (1918–1944 = −.466; 1945–1965 = −.776), thus indicating a closer link between the respective sizes. At first glance, this could lead us to conclude that the postwar stabilization of the total left vote in Europe and the corresponding saturation of the left electoral market necessarily brought about more direct competition between Communists and socialists for this total left constituency. After World War II, these parties were less

[91] Kirchheimer (1966a: 249).

likely to grow together electorally and, in this sense, less likely to develop independently.

A SYNTHETIC MAP

To conclude this descriptive chapter, I will summarize the discussion, offering a general classification of the countries along the three main dimensions discussed so far – size, cohesion, and ideological orientation, that is, the main matrix of European left variance. Table 2.8 derives from the discussion in this chapter and more precisely from Table 2.3 (size), Figure 2.4 (early ideological orientation), Table 2.5 (war and revolutionary radicalization), and Tables 2.6 and 2.7 (Communist size and other left). It goes without saying that this is a very risky exercise. Dichotomizations force intermediate cases. Moreover, given the long time span, countries may belong to different classes in different periods. Nevertheless, it is hoped that a simplified "map"' will be useful to the reader as a guide in the following chapters.

Two points should be underlined. First, I have resorted to a double classification of national experiences only for Germany. Its comparatively different total size before and after World War II and the discontinuity in Communist Party size before and after World War II allow for no other

Table 2.8. *Synthetic map of the European left experiences*

	organizational fragmentation				
	unified		mainly other left or small Communist and other left		Communist fragmentation
early ideological orientation	strong	weak	strong	weak	strong
trade unionist	Britain (low)	Ireland (low)			
reformist Marxism			Denmark (low) Norway (mid) Sweden (mid)	Belgium (low) Netherl. (low) Switz. (low)	
orthodox Marxism	Austria (high)	(Germany) (post–World War II) (high)			Finland (high) Germany (1918-1944) (high)
Marxism-syndicalism					France (low) Italy (high)

Note: Level of "war and revolution" radicalization given in parentheses.

solution. Second, on the ideological orientation dimension it is well known that there is a common historical trend toward a generalized deradicalization of socialist movements and that, therefore, individual national experiences need to be classified differently for different periods. I have tried to solve this problem through time by considering the early ideological orientation of the working-class movement in its genetic phase, from the 1880s to the World War I, by characterizing the war and revolution radicalization between the 1910s and the 1920s, and, finally, by considering communist electoral inroads for the period following this one. After World War II, left radicalism was to a very large extent linked to communist strength.

This division means that one can try to identify more-radical working-class political conditions in each of these three phases while also attempting to characterize the experience of the entire century. In this case, the most radical lefts will be those that fall into the polar type of orthodox Marxist or Marxist-syndicalist early ideological orientation followed by intense radicalization around the time of World War I and by the development of strong communist parties. The polar opposite is represented by lefts with an early trade unionist or pragmatic Marxist orientation, followed by low radicalization after World War I and by the absence of important communist splits.

The main goal of this chapter has been to chart differences. The goal of the following chapters will be to interpret them. The questions that need to be answered are as follows: Why was the overall left mobilization higher in certain countries and lower in others? Why was its electoral development earlier in certain cases than in others? What macrofactors can account for the different patterns of organizational cohesion and division? Why did communism succeed electorally in certain countries and completely fail in others? Is it possible to make a general interpretation of the patterns of genetic ideological orientation and of the radicalization and deradicalization trends?

INDUSTRIALIZATION, URBANIZATION, AND LABOR'S RESPONSE

3

Industrialization and urbanization are regarded as preconditions of working-class political mobilization. These processes create and intensify the social problems and grievances of the working classes and lower classes in general; at the same time, they constitute the structural preconditions for these problems to become sources of organization and mobilization efforts. The resulting social mobilization gives rise to new social groups; it increases the self-awareness of those already existing; and it intensifies existing conflicts and provokes the explosion of latent ones. Linking social mobilization processes with the left's electoral mobilization postulates the following underlying causal chain: that the formation of the working class – in the sense of the creation and spread of given class conditions – impinges directly on the development of class consciousness, which in turn leads to the structuring of the class cleavage. According to this hypothesis, cross-country variance is to be explained by differences in the available proportion of potentially mobilizing voters, the latter in turn resulting from the quantitative spread and qualitative consequences of the formation of working-class conditions. This general hypothesis is the subject of this chapter.

CONCEPTUAL FRAMEWORK

The belief in a relationship between industrialization, working-class formation, and the political response of labor is common to both historical socialist thinking and more recent post–World War II literature. However,

122

the emphasis on what this means is different. The relationship dominated the nineteenth-century debate on the "social question" and was at the heart of the theorizing of socialist thinkers. Marx's analysis of the social consequences of industrialization implied the formation of a new type of worker in large, machine-intensive manufacturing, which he characterized as socially homogeneous, functionally interchangeable, and economically alienated, that is, "abstract labor" potential. For the socialists of the Second International, this discussion took the form of the debate over the "maturity of the socioeconomic conditions" that would allow for the passage to a phase of socialist society building. This was because Second International socialism believed in a long-term "constituency effect" of industrialization. Industrialization and economic development were perceived as benign forces, creating favorable conditions for the development of the labor movement in all its possible conceptions – in terms of quantitative development and the constitution of the critical mass, of ideological education and political consciousness, and of political action.

However, around the turn of the twentieth century, doubts began to be felt about the linear relationship between industrialization, the growth of the working class, and the strengthening of political socialism. More clearly than anybody else, Bernstein suggested that this process was not linear. He envisaged the potential long-term integrative effect of economic growth as having an impact on the quantitative development of the working class, on its internal composition, and the consequent tendency toward political integration. However, opinions of this nature remained in the shadows for a long time. The labor movement's development toward a reformist integration within the existing system was then interpreted in the light of the "aristocracy of labor" phenomenon,[1] which some saw as a sheer and almost deliberate betrayal of "whole" class interest by better-off workers and their leaders and others considered more as a sociological tendency.[2] In this context, the theory explained the "reformist" or integration deviation from a general path that was aimed at linking growing industrialization with the growing strength of radical (if not revolutionary) socialism. What was conceptualized as problematic and in need of an

---

[1] This concept has its origins in Lenin's work on imperialism (1939), although historians have traced it back to an article by Engels in 1885.

[2] For a detailed discussion, see Gray (1981). The thesis had various nuances. Moreover, even in a country like the United Kingdom, where the thesis was meant to explain most, there were convinced supporters and skeptical critics. Although Hobsbown endorsed it, Pelling and Joyce criticized it, arguing that, rather than being moderates, the labor aristocracy (craft and skilled sectors) were exactly the opposite: the most radical and militant sector of the working class. Hobsbawm (1964a), Pelling (1968a), Joyce (1980).

explanatory theory was the failure of radical socialist mobilization of sectors of the working class.[3]

The basic theme of the renewed debate of the 1950s and 1960s can be introduced with a quote: "The growth, the structure and ideology of the labor movement of any country are conditioned by the nature of industrialization process, that is by the character of the tempo and direction of industrial development. This is not to say that political and cultural factors are not important. . . . But the dynamic element . . . appears to be the complex of events subsumed under the concept of Industrialisation."[4] This thesis shows the sophistication of the original link between industrialization and working-class politics. It includes a complex dependent variable: the *growth*, that is, the pattern of quantitative development over time; the *structure*, that is, the internal composition and/or organizational setup; and the *ideology*, that is, the predominant *Weltanschauung* that defines the elements of consciousness, identity, and sense of destiny. There is also an equally complex independent variable: the *character, tempo* and *direction* of industrialization. The possible linkages implied by such a paradigmatic statement have, since the 1950s, been explored by a large number of writers. Most of this debate has been conducted by nonsocialist scholars. It originated in or was largely influenced by the totally different experiences of the labor movement in the United States; it was more systematically comparative and less linked to the experiences of the paradigmatic big-country cases; and finally, it witnessed a less linear conception of economic development and industrialization. While the latter two remained the essential independent variables explaining the development of labor movements,[5] the post–World War II climate changed the conceptualization of the problem or, more precisely, the definition of what is in need of explanation. "Radicalism" became the pathological phenomenon to be explained.

The 1960s witnessed an important debate on the issue of whether economic development and industrialization had a moderating integration effect on working-class politics or the contrary: a radicalizing and nonintegration effect. The question of the response of working-class politics to

---

[3] The influential reconstruction of the paradigmatic case of working-class formation by Thompson (1963) is indicative of the resilience of this conception.

[4] Galenson (1952a: 105).

[5] To the best of my knowledge, Blumer (1960) is the only scholar who has not attributed a specific impact on working-class politics to industrialization. He explicitly considers industrialization a "neutral" process vis-à-vis the working-class response. The latter, he claims, depends on a rather complex interaction of other factors. The list he proposes is rather nonparsimonious and ends with a configurative description of each national experience.

economic development was now posed in more problematic terms, namely, in reference to a typology of different forms of industrialization. The major problem of the debate was now the timing and the tempo of industrialization, that is, its earliness versus lateness and its gradual versus rapid growth and spread. According to Lipset, "economic development producing increased income, greater economic security, and widespread higher education largely determines the form of 'class struggle' by permitting those in lower strata to develop [a] longer time perspective and [a] more complex and gradualist view of politics. A belief in reformist gradualism can be the ideology of only a relatively well-to-do lower class." Successful industrialization had the long-term effect of integration and domestication of the labor movement. Less successful industrialization had different political response outcomes.[6]

This general idea was taken up and developed later by several other authors. Lipset, in particular, introduced the concept of "half-way" industrialization. This industrialization was not "late" in temporal terms, but was instead incomplete and unbalanced in structural terms. In this case, the permanence of traditional family-based small businesses was disadvantageous to the development of strong, stable trade unions. The nonhomogeneity in the class condition prevented full-scale mobilization and integration in reformist movements and, at the same time, created the conditions for political division, with a commitment to radical anarchism, syndicalism, and so on of some sectors of the labor movement.[7] Similar conclusions were advanced by Lorwin about the French labor movement and, in general, about the relationship between forms of economic development and working-class conditions; he attributed similar consequences to sluggish economic growth, small workshops, and lack of entrepreneurial risk taking.[8]

In the 1920s, Edward Bull, contrasting the rapid Norwegian industri-

---

[6] Lipset (1960: 60). Actually, even before World War I, Commons had made a clear distinction based on a then typical comparison between the United Kingdom and the Continent. He distinguished between forms of capitalism characterized by gradual development of the factory system (in the United Kingdom) that were conducive to a reformist, integrated, and politically nonmilitant working class and a form of merchant capitalism, characterized by the definitely minor role of manufacturing, mainly performed in small-scale, scattered workshops (combining masters, journeymen, and apprentices), which tended to foster radical responses of anarchist, syndicalist, radical Marxist militant working classes and labor movements (the French case). He therefore emphasized the type of industrialization and economic development, rather than the quantity. See Commons (1962: 681–685).

[7] See in particular Lipset (1969).

[8] Lorwin (1954) and (1967b).

alization through electrification with the slower and less dislocative industrial development in Denmark (Sweden being an intermediate case), pointed out the extreme radicalizing effect of *late* and *rapid* industrialization.[9] The sudden displacement of workers from rural backgrounds and traditional surroundings to the turbulence of the new industrial surroundings created a working class that was less well versed in the socialist ideas, discipline, and traditions established in the consolidated sectors of the trade union movement. Late and rapid industrialization was thus a vehicle of social disruption and anomie, leading to radical responses and organizational fragmentation of class action.[10] The thesis of the destabilizing force of rapid economic growth was later reasserted and made known internationally by Galenson,[11] in line with the tenets of the literature on mass society and its anomic uprooting.[12] It was later taken up and supported with varying qualifications by other studies, such as those of Halebsky, Mancur Olson, and Dubofsky.[13]

A large group of historical microstudies also tended to support the idea that the enlargement of the socialist movement beyond its original highly conscious craft and specialized workers took place through the recruitment of new workers from relatively homogeneous rural surroundings. Their completely new experience, the sudden breakdown of traditional values, and their great difficulties in adapting to and being integrated into the working-class movement and its organizations, dominated by skilled-craftsman membership and leadership characterized by different status and self-esteem, were significantly correlated with radical feelings and new organizational forms.[14] As usual, dissenting voices can be heard. William Lafferty's very thorough control of Bull's thesis for the Scandinavian countries has offered partial support for this – qualified, however, by a number of intervening variables that refer to the political integration of the working-class movement.[15] R. H. Tilly, on the other hand, directly criticized Bull's thesis in a study of German industrialization.[16]

---

[9] Bull (1922: 329–361).
[10] For a worldwide application of this scheme, see Lipset (1958: 173–192).
[11] See in particular Galenson (1949) and (1952a).
[12] See in particular Kornhauser (1959).
[13] Halebsky (1976), Olson (1963), and Dubofsky (1966).
[14] See, for instance, Stråth (1983: 261–291), who compared the attitudes of the early working class in two Swedish cities (Malmö and Gotheberg) and a German city (Bremen); and Lucas-Busemann (1976), who studied workers' radicalism in two German towns of the Tuhr district.
[15] See the two fundamental works by Lafferty on Norway (1972) and (1974) and on the Scandinavian countries (1971).
[16] Tilly (1980).

The moderation/integration versus dislocation/radicalism interpretations of rapid social change can be reconciled, to some extent, by assuming a nonlinear relationship over time. In their early phase, industrialization and urbanization produce disruptive social effects, raise expectations beyond possible satisfaction, and result in radical responses; in their later phase, adaptation and learning, organizational responses, and the distribution of economic benefits lead to integration and moderate responses. Such a thesis[17] corresponds to an application to working-class politics of a transitional model of political development according to which modernization processes imply the passage from a premodern, relatively steady-state situation to a modern final and again steady-state one after passing through a more or less prolonged transition phase during which social dislocation is at its peak, learning and accommodation processes are not yet effective, and radicalism, anomie, and instability are the likely results.[18]

The previous review points out the multifarious possible ways of operationalizing the process of industrialization. Industrialization sets the structural transformation that creates the phenomenon and the magnitude of the "class condition," which can be seen in both quantitative and qualitative terms. In quantitative terms, industrialization determines the sheer size of the potential constituency for socialist mobilization in terms of sector (industry versus agriculture) and status (dependent versus independent labor) transformations. In qualitative terms, one can emphasize the character or the nature of the class condition, underlining the importance of the size of the workshop, the homogeneity of the composition of the working class, and the disparity between sectors and/or geographical areas. In addition, industrialization can be judged as early versus late in terms of timing and gradual versus rapid in terms of the tempo of the transformation. Both of these dimensions have been considered important factors in explaining labor's response *independent* of the quantitative and qualitative aspects of the class condition formation. So, at each given point in time, the same level of industrialization in terms of structural sector or status transformation can be conceived as the result of a more or less early or late development; of a more or less gradual or rapid growth; and of the predominance of the factory system or of a merchant capitalism with a small amount of manufacturing centered in small, scattered workshops, of half-way, imbalanced, or incomplete industrialization. Table 3.1 summa-

[17] See Soares (1966: 190–199).
[18] Examples of transitional models of political, social, and economic modernization, respectively, are those of Huntington (1968), Lerner (1958), and Fourastié (1963). For a discussion of the characteristics of transitional models of modernization, see Flora (1974). A similar transitional perspective is adopted in the critical analysis by Ulam (1979).

Table 3.1. *Dimensions and indicators of industrialization*

dimensions	conceptualization	possible indicators

quantity	levels: high
	        medium
	        low
		- quantitative indicators of sector and status transformation
		- economic output indicators

character	complete/incompleted balanced/unbalanced halfway	-internal composition of the workers' constituency -size of workshop -weight of manufacturing -geographical unbalance -composition of independents
timing	early/late	-comparative thresholds of preconditions, take-off and maturity attainment
tempo	gradual/rapid	-comparative rates of growth

rizes the possible dimensions of industrialization from the viewpoint of its potential impact on working-class formation and the possible different indicators that each of them implies and requires.

At the conceptual level, the role of urbanization must be kept separate from that of industrialization. The theoretical dimensions of the process of urbanization are, first, the spatial concentration of the population and, second, the growing division and specialization of labor. These two aspects apply to all historical forms of urbanization: ancient as well as medieval urbanism industrial urbanization, and the urbanization of developing countries. From an *economic* point of view, the lessening of the distance among individuals implied by spatial concentration minimizes the spatial "friction" of the market, which was one of the conditions most favorable to economic development (qualification and mobility of labor, decreasing costs of infrastructure, economies of scale).

From a *sociological* perspective, urbanization is mainly seen in light of the growing specialization and division of labor and of the formation of new social relationships, groups, and identities. The concentration of individuals in urban centers multiplies their contacts. It also changes the nature of their contacts, making them briefer and more motivated by specific goals. Urban contacts tend, therefore, to leave aside personal characteristics, and relationships with other people are based on role and function differentiation.[19] Spatial concentration creates social competition,

[19] On this point, see Simmel (1903: 185–206).

which in turn fosters the division of labor and a new type of social solidarity realized through differentiation, that is, through separateness and complementarity. The social consequences of urbanization are also crucial in the formation of new social conditions and the consciousness of them. In the passage from rural communities to urban quarters, loss of contact with the extended family and the soil, weakening of personal social relationships, detachment of place of work from residence, and loss of social and economic security all contribute to the formation of new groups and identities. The spatial concentration of the industrial proletariat tended to foster new forms of group solidarity. Class consciousness or, more generally, socialist ideology has been interpreted as a response to the "casual nature" of social relationships that result from the spatial concentration (workplace as well as residential) of people from very different backgrounds.[20] Ideology and increased group consciousness can be regarded as the natural identity-building mechanism for people who share nothing or have very little in common, as a process that rebuilds a community of shared symbols facing the social dislocation that has destroyed the old community of provenance.

From the *political* point of view, these economic and social characteristics and consequences of urbanization result in three related processes of political change. First, urbanization and urban concentration are the foci of new problem pressures. The articulation of new political demands is linked to the intensity of the socioeconomic problems generated by urban concentration. Second, urbanization indicates higher levels of communication and more sophisticated communication structures. Communication narrows the geographical and social distance between people and facilitates the spread of conformity of behavioral patterns and norms, as well as facilitating propaganda, recruitment, expression of interest, and imitation of organizational forms and experiences. Third, the new socioeconomic conditions of urban life can be conceived as particularly favorable to the "depersonalization" of politics and the passage from predominantly territorial to predominantly functional forms of political representation. Thus, in the nonurban setting, the transition from localism and personalism to modern national politics was slower. For individuals and groups to shift from indifference to political participation, a perception of their involvement in the nation and of the impact of national affairs on persons and localities was required. The latter, in turn, required that they be reached by a flow of information, messages, agitators, and so on.[21]

---

[20] Pizzorno (1962: 41).

[21] But even when this first step was achieved, nonurban politics persisted, sometimes for a long time, in archaic localist and personalized forms. A masterly description of the

Urbanization and the context of urban life are therefore particularly favorable to, and specifically more favorable than, rural or small village settings to the forms of electoral corporate and partisan mobilization that constitute the object of this study. Urbanization can therefore be imagined as an indirect indicator of the formation and concentration of the industrial proletariat that can be considered as complementary to, if not independent of, social stratification data that indicate mainly its quantitative dimension and formation. The extent to which industrialization and urbanization are correlated at different points in time and in different countries is an empirical question to be addressed in the rest of this chapter. Moreover, urbanization points to preconditions facilitating the development of social-ist organizational mobilization, recruitment, and propaganda: The more urbanized the context, the easier it is to recruit organizational membership; the more developed the latter, the stronger the socialist electoral support.[22] Finally, urbanization indicates a set of social relationships and conditions that reduce the weight of traditional forms of social control by established elites and institutions and that build areas of status equality facilitating participation and collective action.[23]

This short review clarifies the wealth of linkages that can be estab-lished between the processes of industrialization and urbanization, on the one hand, and the political responses of labor discussed in Chapter 2, on the other. In this chapter, I concentrate on the relationship between the quantity, character, timing, and tempo of industrialization and urbaniza-tion and the overall electoral mobilization of the class left. The relations between industrialization/urbanization and radicalism/organizational cohe-sion of the labor movement will be discussed separately in Chapter 9.

WORKING-CLASS CONSTITUENCY FORMATION AND SOCIALIST MOBILIZATION

The great transformation that took place in the European economy after the end of the Napoleonic wars and brought about the mature industrial

---

archaism of local politics in rural France can be found in Weber (1979: 241–277). There the gap in political mobilization between countryside and urban centers was particularly wide. Similar accounts can be found in almost all countries. For Italy, see De Sanctis (1876); and for Norway, see Rokkan (1970c). More generally, for the special conditions of national politicization in nonurban settings, see Urwin (1980: 87–110).

[22] See Linz (1959: 346–350).

[23] Hintze (1980: 15) has argued that these elements tended to favor the birth of parties rather than estates. It is therefore worthwhile to investigate the potential autonomous impact of urbanization on political mobilization.

society will be considered here only from the labor allocation point of view.[24] In a discussion of industrialization in reference to the potential mobilization capacity of socialist movements, it is logical to emphasize the changes in social structures that resulted from the rapid growth of industry and to concentrate on socio-occupational consequences. These were expressed in two major processes of labor force displacement: One concerned *sector* shifts; the other, *status* shifts.

In the first case, this structural change was characterized by an accelerating shift of the labor force from agricultural to industrial activity and, later, to services.[25] With its mass production dominated by an increasing use of technology and inanimate energy, industrialization entailed a progressive and continuous shift of the labor force to industry, to the point where mature industrial society was largely dominated by industrial occupations, while both agricultural and traditional service sectors declined. In terms of occupational *status* – rather than sector – the same long-term processes determined a shift of labor from independent to dependent wage- or salary-remunerated positions. Next to the progressive reduction of the employees, particularly the self-employed, status shifts within the dependent labor force strengthened a homogeneous category of workers at the expense of less well defined and less homogeneous groups such as family workers and apprentices and, in a second phase, determined a progressive increase in the number of salaried employees.

THE MATURITY OF INDUSTRIAL SOCIETY

The transformation associated with sector shifts best suits the aim of defining structural conditions for a mature industrial society. It is characterized by three universal trends: the decline of the active population in agriculture; the growth of an active population in industry; and – at a later stage, according to the theory – the growth of the active population in the services. Each of these trends can be looked at comparatively across coun-

---

[24] Other measures refer to productivity, investments, production outputs, or similar economic indicators. The GNP measures are not necessarily a direct indicator of the level of industrialization. On the other hand, indices of sector production are more varied and difficult to compare. Of the various attempts to measure the level of industrialization in terms of output per capita, the most systematic and reliable one concentrates on manufacturing output, excluding not only construction, transport, and utilities, but even mining. Bairoch (1982) reviews all attempts to measure industrial production directly and provides a rich appendix on the method followed and the problems involved in arriving at his estimates.

[25] At the end of the 1950s, Fourastié (1963) and others predicted a further and different long-term sector transformation destined to lead to the final predominance of a new modern service sector.

tries in Table 3.2, where the percentage of the active labor force in each sector is reported by country in the decades between 1880 and 1970 on the basis of census data.[26]

The figures in Table 3.2 help to show comparatively the transformation in each sector. The average level of agricultural occupation in Europe declined from a mean of about 45% of the active population in the decade 1880–1890 to about 12% in the 1970s, a drop of 33 percentage points.[27] In industry, the same time span saw the Western European mean increase from about 25% to about 40% of the active population. In service occupations, the corresponding increase is from about 24% to about 45%. Therefore, of the roughly 35 percentage points lost by agricultural occupations during the century, about 15 have been gained by industry and about 20 by services. So, on average, service occupations have grown more than industrial ones.

The huge disparities in sector occupation before World War I lessened over time, and in the 1970s they were minimal with respect to the starting point. This implies that the rate of change was particularly accelerated or particularly slow for those countries that were further from the European mean value in the early phase. The difference between the highest and lowest percentages of agricultural occupation was about 60% in the 1880s (10% in the United Kingdom; 70% in Finland), and only 20% in the 1970s. In industrial occupation, it was about 30–35% in the 1880s (40% in the United Kingdom and Switzerland; less than 10% in Sweden)[28] and 20% in the 1970s (about 50% in Germany and Switzerland; about 30% in Ireland).[29] In the service sector, the early difference was about 30% in

---

[26] This time span is imposed by the availability of comparable census figures throughout Europe. However, before that date, industrial development had progressed extremely slowly, not only worldwide, but also in Europe. The changes that had begun in English industrial production in the mid-eighteenth century took over half a century to be imitated and followed elsewhere. Considering also that, with the exception of the United Kingdom, Switzerland, and Belgium, the rate of population growth exceeded the rate of growth of industrial output, it is likely that the nature of socio-occupational changes brought about by industrialization before the 1830s was limited. The rate of growth in industrial output in Europe began to speed up after the 1860s and accelerated at an even faster rate after the depression of the 1870s to 1890s. See Bairoch (1982: 272, 274, 290) and Rostow (1978: 111–162).

[27] The decline of the agricultural population in this table, as well as in the following tables of this chapter, is particularly accentuated by the fact that it is expressed as a percentage of the active population or of other groups. The absolute number of people involved did not decline so rapidly, and actually, according to Dovring (1964: 78–98), it may have increased in the early stages of economic development.

[28] No data are available for Ireland and Finland in this period. They probably had an even lower percentage of active population in industry.

[29] This process of leveling off is also underlined by measures of industrial output. Indeed,

Table 3.2. *The European sector transformation (1880–1970)*

a) Active in agriculture

	1880	1890	1900	1910	1920	1930	1940	1950	1960	1970
Au	55.6	64.1	60.9	56.9	45.9	31.9	39.0	32.3	22.8	13.8
Be	30.3	23.1	21.9	22.4	19.1	17.0	12.1	9.7	7.2	4.6
De	50.3	44.8	47.5	40.5	35.2	35.2	29.9	25.6	16.2	10.6
Fi	.	.	.	71.5	70.4	64.5	57.4	46.0	35.5	20.3
Fr	40.3	42.6	42.3	42.1	34.9	35.6	36.5	27.2	17.8	12.2
Ge	43.4	37.5	35.2	32.9	30.5	28.9	26.0	23.2	13.5	7.5
Ir	.	.	.	.	51.3	47.6	45.3	39.6	33.0	25.4
It	56.7	58.1	59.4	55.5	55.7	47.2	43.5	40.0	28.2	16.3
Ne	34.9	30.8	28.4	26.0	23.6	20.6	18.8	14.8	10.7	6.1
No	.	49.6	41.3	39.2	36.8	35.3	29.5	25.9	19.5	11.6
Sw	51.5	53.9	49.8	45.6	40.4	35.4	26.7	20.3	12.8	7.3
Sz	.	37.4	31.0	26.8	27.1	21.3	20.8	16.5	11.2	7.7
UK	.	10.4	7.7	8.1	7.6	6.0	5.6	5.1	3.6	2.5
all countries	45.4	41.1	38.7	39.0	36.8	32.8	30.1	25.1	17.8	11.2

b) Active in industry

	1880	1890	1900	1910	1920	1930	1940	1950	1960	1970
Au	20.5	20.4	21.3	23.5	28.4	33.3	31.7	37.1	40.6	41.6
Be	34.9	37.2	41.3	45.1	45.9	47.8	48.3	47.0	45.7	43.7
De	23.7	25.5	25.0	25.9	26.9	26.8	32.2	34.1	37.5	37.7
Fi	.	.	.	11.1	13.1	14.8	18.5	27.7	31.5	34.3
Fr	26.4	28.5	29.8	29.6	31.3	32.2	29.2	35.7	38.7	34.7
Ge	32.9	36.5	39.0	40.1	41.2	39.8	42.1	42.3	48.2	48.9
Ir	.	.	.	.	14.5	17.9	18.3	24.4	26.9	31.5
It	26.9	25.3	23.7	26.8	23.9	28.4	28.9	30.4	39.4	42.2
Ne	31.2	31.6	32.8	34.2	35.6	36.2	35.0	38.8	42.6	36.2
No	.	22.9	26.9	26.0	27.0	26.6	32.3	36.5	36.5	37.3
Sw	9.9	14.4	19.7	24.7	30.4	30.9	37.0	40.6	44.1	39.1
Sz	.	40.2	43.7	44.2	45.1	43.8	43.6	46.2	50.4	48.2
UK	.	44.5	45.6	44.6	42.0	46.1	47.7	49.2	47.4	42.2
all countries	25.8	29.7	31.7	31.3	31.2	32.7	34.2	37.7	40.7	39.8

c) Active in services

	1880	1890	1900	1910	1920	1930	1940	1950	1960	1970
Au	15.9	13.7	16.3	16.4	24.1	31.8	28.6	29.4	35.4	42.7
Be	22.1	26.9	27.4	30.9	33.0	34.5	34.5	39.3	44.1	49.6
De	17.1	20.8	25.7	31.9	36.6	36.6	37.1	38.3	43.7	48.8
Fi	.	.	.	8.7	11.1	13.4	16.7	24.9	32.8	44.1
Fr	33.4	29.0	28.0	28.3	28.8	32.3	30.3	34.1	41.9	49.3
Ge	22.3	25.0	25.1	26.4	27.6	30.7	31.9	32.3	37.8	43.6
Ir	.	.	.	.	33.3	34.0	35.3	34.9	39.6	42.3
It	16.2	16.6	16.9	17.7	20.4	23.3	23.8	24.3	29.5	36.6
Ne	34.1	35.8	37.9	38.8	39.7	42.2	45.1	45.7	46.2	49.4
No	.	26.4	29.8	32.0	30.6	37.8	37.2	37.1	43.6	50.9
Sw	28.0	24.5	23.2	26.6	27.5	31.3	35.2	38.3	42.8	53.4
Sz	.	21.4	24.8	28.5	26.9	34.1	33.6	36.5	38.0	43.8
UK	.	37.3	41.0	42.9	35.9	47.1	46.2	45.3	48.1	49.4
all countries	23.6	25.2	26.9	27.4	28.9	33.0	33.5	35.4	40.3	46.5

of the countries is not modified in any substantial way in considering industrial output instead of sector occupation.

It is reasonable to expect that the most favorable conditions for social-ist mobilization would emerge in those societies that experienced early attainment and prolonged duration of the occupational structure typical of a mature industrial society. To describe a mature industrial society, we need to use thresholds for defining a prevalently *agricultural* society as opposed to those that are *industrial* or *postindustrial*. Industrial society enters its mature phase when the proportion of the active labor force in industry overtakes the proportion of the labor force in agriculture; postindustrial society begins when the population active in industry is bypassed by the proportion active in providing services. According to the figures on Euro-pean occupational sectors elaborated by Kaeberle (and reported in Figure 3.1), in Western Europe a mature industrial society, as just defined, ap-peared between the 1920s and the 1970s. The industrial sector predomi-nated over the service sector from the beginning of industrialization to the 1970s, but only in the 1920s did industrial occupation bypass agricultural occupation.[31]

With respect to this Europewide picture, national differences con-cerned not only timing but also patterns of structural differences. A mature industrial society was not only reached earlier or later, but could be shorter or longer, not exist at all, or develop with completely different features in some countries. Using the threshold mentioned earlier, in Table 3.4 I have cross-tabulated the countries according to when the industrial societies were reached and according to their duration. The countries that best indicate the European model of sector transformation are undoubtedly the United Kingdom, Belgium, Switzerland, and Germany,[32] because an early decline of the agricultural sector and a very long period of predominance of the industrial sector over the service sector is evident in all of them. In the United Kingdom, industrial society dates back to the 1820s. In this

[31] Kaelble (unpublished manuscript) has argued that the idea of a sequence from agricul-tural to industrial and finally to postindustrial society, and the notion of industrial and postindustrial society make sense only in the European context. For other parts of the world, both developed and underdeveloped, such categories do not have the same significance.

[32] Kaelble, in the previously cited manuscript, produces a similar set of figures and tables for a number of European and non-European countries. My tables are based on different data taken from the cited source of Peter Flora. This produces slight and insignificant differences in the graphs. What is more important is that the conclusions and the classification of individual country experiences are different, as Kaelble concentrates exclusively on the relationship between the service and industrial sectors, leaving aside data about the agricultural one, which from my point of view are essential for the identification of the maturity of industrial society.

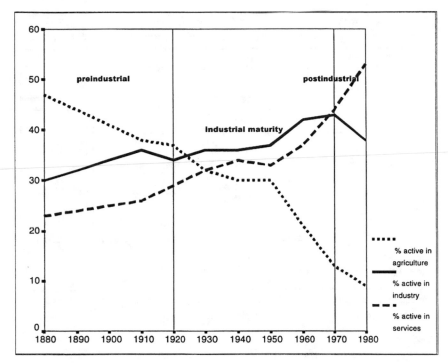

Figure 3.1. Thresholds of mature industrial society in Europe.
Note: Data in this figure are not means of European countries. They represent actual occupation figures summed up for all European countries and computed as a percentage of the Europewide active population.
Source: Kaelbe (unpublished paper: 43).

case, however, by the 1930s the service sector was almost as large as the industrial one. Here, the predominance of industrial occupation over agricultural and service occupations lasted for almost a century.

In a second group of northern countries, the pattern is strikingly different. The beginning of mature industrial society can be identified at different points in time. In the Netherlands, this point was reached very early, in the 1890s[33] (that is, more or less at the same time as the four countries discussed earlier); in Denmark, in 1910; in Sweden, in 1930; in

[33] The Netherlands is slightly different from the other earlycomers. Notwithstanding its advanced sector composition of the labor force, industrialization was not very early nor was it characterized by big factories and industrial concentration: "The Netherlands industrialized relatively late, and until 1914 was typified by extensive agrarian and merchant capitalist sectors. The small firms remained dominant for a long time, while industrial concentration developed only sporadically. These factors explain the birth of a

Table 3.4. *Timing and length of industrial society and left electoral mobilization*

duration of industrial society (more active in industry than in services)	timing of industrial society (more active in industry than in agriculture)			
	1880 - 1965		1900 - 1915	
	early **27.8**	late **31.9**	early **17.5**	late **22.9**
nonexistent **29.7** (1880 - 1965) **23.4** (1900 - 1915)	Ne 21	De 32 Fi 41.9 Ir 10.8 No 31.8 Sw 40.8	Ne 13.3	De 25.6 Fi 39.7 Ir n.a. No 18.1 Sw 20.4
short **32.7** (1880 - 1965) **18.8** (1900 - 1915)		Au 40.9 It 27.7 Fr 29.4		Au 40.9 Fr 29.4 It 27.7
prolonged **29.5** (1880 - 1965) **18.5** (1900 - 1915)	Be 33.4 Ge 30.7 Sz 23.4 UK 30.6		Be 22.3 Ge 31.8 Sz 15 UK 4.9	

Note: Numbers in boldface represent all-countries averages

Norway, in the 1940s; and, finally, in Ireland, in the 1960s. What makes this set of countries an interesting separate group is not the timing of the beginning of mature industrial society, but rather the fact that industrial predominance never really materialized. In all these cases, the service sector *always* remained quantitatively more important than the industrial one. So, while industry eventually predominated over agriculture, both remained quantitatively less important than services. Therefore, these countries therefore do not adhere to the model sector transition since something made them service economies from the beginning.

Finally, in France, Austria, Italy, and Finland, the common feature is the late arrival of industrial maturity: in the 1940s, 1950s, and 1960s, respectively.[34] At the same time, all these cases are characterized by a

movement of artisans from the 1860s onwards when mechanisation began to take place, and also the limited extent of this craftsmen's movement, the relatively late growth of national trade-union organizations, and the weak organizational structure which often did not allow the permanent entrenchment of these organizations. Only at a much later stage, when accelerated industrialisation began and a real industrial working-class started to form, did the artisans' movement begin to change into a workers' movement – if limited in the first instance to a workers' elite – and this was accompanied by changing organizational structures" (Buiting, 1990: 81).

[34] Ireland should be added from this point of view. But, as mentioned, its most striking feature is the dominant role of the services. This aspect differentiates it from the third group.

marked balance between occupation in industry and services, with the result that industrial occupation remained relatively low. In Italy and Austria, the predominance of industry over services is marginal; in Finland and France, it never materialized.[35] As can be expected, the earlycomers to industrial predominance maintained their predominance for a long period, while the latecomers were necessarily characterized by a shorter phase of pure mature industrial society. The most interesting cases are those in the first two rows of Table 3.4: societies that went from an agricultural to a service economy without passing through a clear industrial phase. Three types can be distinguished: early industrializing countries, where industrial predominance never existed (the Netherlands); late industrializing countries, distinguishing in terms of the length of industrial predominance between the group of northern-periphery countries, where such predominance never existed, and a southern-continental group, where such predominance was short (Austria, France, and Italy).

In Table 3.4, I have added to each country the mean level of electoral mobilization for the whole 1880–1965 period and for the early pre–World War I period (to check if it is the earliness of electoral mobilization, rather than its size, that is associated). The data do not correspond to expectations. Each category is nonhomogeneous, and in every period the level of left electoral mobilization is higher in the latecomers to industrial society than in the earlycomers (31.9% versus 27.8% for 1880–1965; 22.9% versus 17.5% in the early period; 38.4% versus 34.6% in the post–World War I period 1918–1965). The mean level of electoral mobilization of the left is not enhanced by the maturity of the industrial society; if anything, it is the opposite. The same can be said for the amount of time that industrial society existed. Whether this period was long, short, or nonexistent does not produce any significant differences in the electoral mobilization potential of the socialist left. In each period, the difference between the two most opposite groups of countries (early and protracted versus late or never-achived industrial society) is always favorable to the latecomers and the service-dominated societies: 27.8% versus 31.4% for the whole period; 18.5% versus 25.9% for the 1900–1915 period).

Let us now look at the sector transformation data from a different perspective. Rather than considering mean levels of mobilization by type of industrial society, let us consider the association between populations active in different sectors and the levels of electoral socialist mobilization

[35] It is interesting to note that this pattern looks rather "southern." In fact, the cases of Spain and Portugal are rather similar to those of France and Italy. Greece is more a case of continuous predominance of the service sector. See the data in Kaelble (unpublished manuscript: 41–42).

for the entire set of elections held in the countries, pooling all the data together, without any reference to particular countries. In Table 3.5 the correlation coefficient is reported by economic sector, by period, and by decade. Over the whole period (1880–1975), the levels of electoral mobilization are associated with the industrial transition as expected: negative association with agricultural occupation and positive association with both industry and service occupations. However, this association concerns data collected over time and with clear trends. The left tends toward secular growth, as well as industrial and service occupation, as we have seen, while agriculture declines sharply. These covariations, therefore, may point to historical multicolinearity rather than to causal linkage. To control for covariation in time, we can look at the associations over shorter periods or even single decades. As the census data are collected on a five-to ten-year basis, within each decade occupational data do not vary much. For each point in time, the association is no longer blurred by potential linear temporal covariation but indicates only the cross-space association. This means that a temporal hypothesis – whether the growth (or decline) of A is associated with the growth (or decline) of B – is transformed into its cross-sectional synchronic equivalent, that is, whether higher (or lower) levels of A are associated with higher (or lower) levels of B at each given point in time.

Looking at the data by period produces a significant change in the picture. In the period from 1880 to 1917 (Ireland is missing), there is a striking positive association between agricultural-sector size and total left vote and a negative association between industrial and service sector size and total left vote. In the following two periods, the situation is reversed and agricultural sector size is not associated with electoral mobilization. However, the association levels are weak or nonexistent. Considering decades, the associations are important up to the 1930s, becoming smaller thereafter. Moreover, in the early phase, higher levels of socialist electoral mobilization are positively associated with high agricultural-sector occupation and negatively associated with the size of industry and service sectors. Only in the period 1930–1960 is a positive association between industrial occupation and left mobilization evident.

In conclusion, whether one considers the *timing* of industrialization, the *length* of the industrial-sector predominance, or *levels* of sector occupation, it does not seem that socialist mobilization was earlier or stronger in the more industrially advanced economies. Only in a global developmental perspective – that is, over the whole period of time covering the occupational transition – does the sector transformation of the labor force seem to influence levels of socialist electoral support. Political mobilization is asso-

Table 3.5. *Correlation between active population in the economic sector and electoral socialist mobilization*

	agriculture	industry	services
whole period	-.268 (294)	.220	.271
1880-1917	.502 (82)	-.421	-.494
1918-1944	-.055 (92)	.180	-.082
1945-1975	-.095 (121)	.148	.006
1890	.190 (20)	.288	-.346
1900	.570 (31)	-.440	-.636
1910	.662 (36)	-.589	-.551
1920	.191 (41)	-.064	-.211
1930	-.190 (33)	.283	-.083
1940	-.212 (28)	.349	-.105
1950	-.187 (38)	.279	.011
1960	-.252 (34)	.245	.130
1970	-.012 (27)	-.105	.153

Note: Number of elections given in parentheses.

ciated over time with the transition from predominantly agricultural economies to industrial and service ones; however, any synchronic control concerning the significance of the early attainment of such a transition, or its more or less protracted nature, fails to offer a clear base of discrimination among national patterns of socialist political mobilization.

STATUS TRANSFORMATION

Status transformation is historically a process of shifting from independent and self-employed status position to dependent ones and, within the dependent labor force, trendy processes of change concerning employees, workers, apprentices, and family workers. Census data concerning the status distribution of the active populations of European countries present problems of comparability represented by the crucial category of "family workers" and their uncertain status.[36] I have chosen to add wives, sons, or

---

[36] Most censuses distinguish family workers from both dependent and independent groups. Some include family workers in the category of independents (as, for instance, the early

close relatives of the self-employed to the "independents" category because this minimizes comparability problems for all those cases in which the two categories are not clearly differentiated in census data; it also makes sense with respect to the specific goal of this analysis.[37] However, to control for differences between the two ways of defining the independent group, in the following analysis I have also reported the data concerning the independents taken in the more restricted sense, that is, excluding family workers. As these data are less interesting in the context of this analysis, I have decided not to present them in table form.

The global picture is the tendency toward the progressive decline of independent labor to the advantage of dependent labor. At the European average level, this trend has progressed at a relatively slow pace and has accelerated only since the 1950s. In the 1940s, more than a third of the average active population in Western European countries was composed of employers, the self-employed, and family workers; from 1880, the decline was only 5–8% in about seventy years. Countries can be classified into four different groups. In the first group, dependent labor prevailed early over independent labor, and the bulk of the historical transformation was accomplished in the 1880s, before electoral enfranchisement and party mobilization. In the United Kingdom, Belgium, and the Netherlands (and, to a lesser extent, in Germany), the over-time trend is almost imperceptible because, since the beginning, dependent labor accounted for 70% or more of the active labor force. Next are Denmark, Norway, and Switzerland, most of whose labor was dependent from the beginning of the period and tended to follow the general European average path of transformation. France and Italy must be considered a third group in which dependent labor was more numerous than independent labor from the 1880s, but the difference was minor and remained so for a long period of time. In these relative latecomers to industrial society, the proportion of independent

censuses of Austria and Italy). In a few cases, some doubt remains about their attribution: in particular in the 1881–1891 French censuses and in the Dutch ones up to the 1930s. Finnish data present different problems. A separate category exists for family workers, but up to the 1940s employees were counted together with the independents. In this case, I have resorted to linear extrapolation from later censuses to deduce the percentage of employees from the independent group. Whether to exclude or include family workers among the independents is an important decision, given that they are often a substantial proportion of the active population, particularly in agriculture. In the censuses of this century, they represent, on average, roughly 26% of the active population in Finland and about 16% in Italy and Austria (at the other extreme, only 0.4% in the United Kingdom).

[37] See Flora, Alber, Eichenberg, Kohl, Kraus, Pfenning, and Seebohm (1987: 445) on the problem of family members in European censuses.

labor remained virtually unchanged until the 1940s–1950s at about 40–45% of the active population. After 1950, these countries caught up rapidly with the others, with higher rates of change. Finally, there is a fourth group of countries in which independents labor was more numerous than dependent labor until well into the twentieth century. In Finland, this was the case up to the 1950s; in Ireland, up to the 1930s; in Austria and Sweden, up to the 1910s.

In Table 3.6 the levels of left political mobilization are related to (a) the four different patterns of status transformation and (b) the levels of dependent/independent occupational status. The results are surprising. From earlycomers to latecomers, passing through two intermediate categories of countries that closely follow the European average pattern, and of those that have minoritarian but stable independent sectors, the left electoral mobilization increases. This overall situation is determined by the earlier period, where the level of left mobilization of latecomers is twice that of all other groups. In the interwar and post–World War II periods, the differences tend to disappear and the four groupings become insignificant. Considering the correlations in part (b) of Table 3.6, significant associations are reported in the expected direction over the entire set of elections in the century. The growth of the left electoral force is associated with the transformation of the status condition of the labor force. Considering that the status transformation trend is less marked than the sector transformation trend, and that rates of change are more muted, these associations appear more significant than those previously reported concerning the sector shift in labor. However, even in this case, such over-time association points to a possible developmental cause that should also be checked by cross-sectional measures. In fact, the period and decade data immediately modify the overall developmental picture. The problem is the first period and the early decades, when the total left vote is associated positively with independent labor and negatively with dependent labor, contrary to the whole developmental association and to what happened in the other two periods. This is because, between the end of the nineteenth century and the first two decades of the twentieth century, the left electoral mobilization was not higher where the percentage of dependent labor was higher – quite the contrary.

The contrast between cross-time and cross-space associations leads to conclusions similar to those reached with sector data. The overall cross-time association is in the expected direction, but the slices of synchronic comparison do not allow us to transform this developmental association into the idea that the early timing or the levels of status transformation were positive preconditions for left mobilization. We can read these results

Table 3.6. *Status transformation and electoral mobilization*

a) mean levels of electoral mobilization by type of status transformation				
	1880-1975	1880-1917	1918-1944	1945-1975
earlycomers (UK, Ge, Be, Ne)	**30.7 (107)**	13.3 (25)	34.1 (30)	38.6 (36)
European average (De, No, Sz)	**32.2 (96)**	15.6 (28)	34.4 (26)	42.0 (29)
protracted-stable independent (Fr, It)	**33.8 (44)**	14.0 (12)	31.2 (7)	42.5 (17)
latecomers (Ir, Fi, Sw, Au)	**36.4 (100)**	31.7 (17)	34.8 (29)	40.8 (37)
all countries	**33.2 (347)**	18.0 (82)	34.2 (92)	40.7 (119)

b) associations between occupational status and left vote			
	independents	independents without family workers	dependants
1880-1975	-.237 (294)	-.506	.264
1880-1917	.523 (81)	-.137	-.195
1918-1944	-.072 (92)	-.195	.137
1945-1975	-.163 (119)	-.243	.239
1890	-.016 (20)	-.222	.002
1900	.484 (31)	.039	-.492
1910	.624 (36)	.045	-.609
1920	.188 (41)	-.184	-.180
1930	-.213 (33)	-.138	.343
1940	-.282 (28)	-.279	.426
1950	-.270 (38)	-.353	.308
1960	-.389 (34)	-.399	.479
1970	-.152 (28)	-.201	.232

Note: Number of elections given in parentheses.

in two different ways. First, this analysis can be read as confirmation of the fact that early left development took place more easily and strongly in countries that were latecomers to the industrial transformation, taking the high proportion of independent labor as a further indicator of such late transformation and leaving aside at this stage the question of why this was the case. Alternatively, the analysis could be read as indicating a more direct causal link between the size of the social group of independent labor and the vote for the left, in the sense that parts of this group, probably to be identified among the agricultural independents and particularly the small farmers, offered direct electoral support to left parties in late-industrializing countries. Some support for this idea comes from considering the category of independents that excludes family workers. Family workers are heavily concentrated in agriculture, and their inclusion in the category of independents makes the latter largely dominated by the agricultural sector. In addition, a large group of family workers points to an agrarian structure characterized by a large number of small independent farmers. When we exclude them, the negative association between independents and left vote is strengthened, doubling over the whole period and becoming more negative with each period and decade (Table 3.6).[38]

WORKING-CLASS CONSTITUENCY

The previous discussion centered on the relative position of individual countries in the industrialization process. In this section, I continue the analysis, considering the size of the *working-class constituency*, which identifies the putative support base of socialist parties. The size of the constituency is not only a presumed quantitative asset; it also produces social and behavioral effects under the thesis that the homogeneity of a social environment – that is, the numerical predominance of a given social group in a community – tends to increase the social pressure of the group on its members toward attitudinal and behavioral conformity. The larger the proportion of a social group in an area, the higher the frequency of social contacts among members of the group; and the higher the frequency of these social interactions, the greater the social pressure that forms and reinforces group identity and organizational behavior, and the greater the sanctions for group nonconformity. Therefore, the more dominant a social group is in the local context, the more uniform its political behaviors are likely to be.[39] Tingsten's argument was developed to explain cross-area differences, and has been mainly used and tested at the level of within-country variance,[40] but there is no reason why it should not be used at the

---

[38] The difference introduced by the exclusion of family workers is enhanced if one considers that the category of independents including family workers is more negatively trendy over time than the category of independents excluding family workers. So, one would expect independents with family workers to correlate more negatively with the growing trend of left electoral development. The reverse is actually the case.

[39] This thesis was formulated and tested explicitly for the first time in Tingsten (1937: 177–180). He based this conclusion on an analysis of district voting in the city of Stockholm in the 1932 elections. Mixed social areas are contrasted with homogeneous ones in terms of the corresponding homogeneity of political behavior, in particular electoral participation and class voting.

[40] For instance, Butler and Stokes (1970: 144–48) find that the support for labor grow in a curvilinear way with the increase in the percentage of workers in the district. Worlunbg (1990: 49–57) has studied the variance in support for the Swedish Social Democratic Party between 1921 and 1940, finding a straight-line relationship rather than a curvilinear one.

cross-country level as well. Working-class size should therefore have both sheer quantitative potential constituency effects as well as qualitative social pressure effects, both of which, in principle, foster socialist political recruitment and mobilization.

Workers can be defined as lower-status dependent laborers or blue-collar personnel, including home workers.[41] The working-class constituency is the result of the combination of status and sector dimensions, and the type of working-class constituency changes according to how many sectors and sub-sectors there are to consider. So the "working class" can be defined as the proportion of lower-status laborers or blue-collar personnel in all sectors of economic activity – industry as well as agriculture and service. Alternatively, the number of sectors can be limited to the industrial ones, thus arriving at a more restricted definition of "industrial working-class." Within industrial subsectors, the key ones, such as manufacturing and mining could also be selected for an even more restricted concept of "core industrial working class,"[42] mainly in reference to large-scale productive units in core industrial sectors.

Notwithstanding the early socialist thinkers' conviction that the working class was already or was soon to become the majoritarian group in society, this was hardly the case in Western Europe, even adopting the broadest possible definition of "worker" so as to include all dependent lower-status and blue-collar workers in all possible sectors of economic activity. Table 3.7 reports the percentage of this social group in the active population in Western European countries between the 1880s and the 1970s. The United Kingdom and Ireland are not included, for up to the

---

[41] The distinction between workers and employees is problematic: Over time and across countries, the census distinction between the two groups may be different, sometimes emphasizing the type of work (in particular, manual versus nonmanual), the place of work (in particular, factory versus office), and finally the legal status (in labor and social security laws). However, for a macrocharacterization of cross-country differences, these problems can be considered minor, and I have therefore relied on the standardization made by Flora and his associates.

[42] The measures of industrialization based on industrial output generally exclude not only transport, building, and services, but also mining (and electrical power). Manufacturing output is regarded as the best indicator. This is based on two arguments. The first is that if one wants to differentiate advanced industrial countries from less developed ones, this is necessary because expansion of the mining industry has been a feature of underdevelopment in the Third World. The second argument is conceptual: If one includes mining in industry, one must also include agriculture, which for a long time was one of the main sources of raw materials for industry. The coal miner is therefore regarded as outside manufacturing even if his work is destined to serve the latter. See the discussion in Bairoch (1982: 321–322). In a homogeneous Western European context and in reference to electoral mobilization problems, it is natural to speak of an "industrial working class" that also includes mining, building, etc.

1960s there prevailed in these countries the tradition of counting "workers" and "employees" together in national censuses (see Appendix); the Dutch figures up to the 1930s are possibly overestimated due to the inclusion among "workers" of other unknown categories, including some family workers (but not assisting spouses, who are kept separate). Nevertheless, it is clear that lower-status dependent labor groups were never as overwhelmingly majoritarian in Europe as has often been implied. In addition their variation over time during the century is modest and, if anything, has a negative trend. The European mean ranges from a starting point of 55% in the 1880s to about 47% in the 1970s, the other half consisting of the independent, the self-employed, family workers, and employees. Even in the group of forerunners of industrialization, the numerical predominance of workers tended to decline over time, and by approximately 1940, workers represented 50% or less of the active population. All the other countries show levels that were clearly below the majority point, and only Sweden (and possibly Ireland) shows any growth. The figures have no historical trend and remain fairly stable, with percentages between 40% and 50%. It is not surprising that the association between this broad conception of the working class and the level of organizational mobilization of the socialist parties is of little significance and actually is systematically negative over time, in each historical period, and in each decade.[43]

The main change over time in the working-class constituency was its internal transformation rather than its increase – that is, the long-term growth of the *industrial working class* (lower-status laborers and blue-collar workers employed in the sectors of mining, manufacturing, utilities [electricity, gas, and steam works and supply], construction and transport) at the expense primarily of the *agricultural working class* (lower-status laborers in agriculture, forestry, and fishing) and, to a lesser extent, of the *service working class* (all other residual categories, ranging from public administration to commerce, banking, and services [restoration, cleaning, domestic services, etc.]). These trends are fairly uniform throughout the set of countries, although at different levels. The only exceptions are Italy and Sweden, where the proportion of the agricultural working class grew remarkably from 1880 to 1910 and from 1880 to 1920, respectively.

For all these reasons, only the industrial working-class constituency is

[43] Exact figures are −.412 for the whole 1880–1975 period; −.382, −.210, and −.330 for the three pre–World War I interwar and post–World War II periods; and .157, −.051, −.270, −.416, −.054, −.234, −.582, −.212, and −.317 for the decades from 1890 to 1970, respectively.

Table 3.7. *Global working-class constituency (workers in all sectors as % of the active population)*

	1880	1890	1900	1910	1920	1930	1940	1950	1960	1970
Au	46.0	45.1	42.6	42.1	47.1	52.9	44.4	44.9	45.0	43.3
Be	59.3	60.7	60.5	57.9	59.6	53.8	52.3	49.5	46.6	44.2
De	60.8	57.1	56.4	54.8	50.0	50.1	53.3	50.6	48.3	44.9
Fi	.	.	.	43.8	39.9	38.1	39.4	42.0	43.3	46.6
Fr	53.0	50.3	48.0	47.0	45.9	43.2	.	.	.	.
Ge	55.3	61.4	57.1	53.7	50.4	34.7	50.8	50.9	50.9	45.6
Ir	.	.	.	.	.	.	.	.	.	.
It	.	45.3	45.3	56.7	51.0	43.9	44.7	47.0	54.1	50.5
Ne	65.0	65.4	62.7	63.0	64.2	62.0	48.3	49.0	49.6	44.9
No	.	48.7	49.0	48.5	52.8	46.2	46.7	51.3	46.2	45.8
Sw	41.7	40.5	43.0	46.4	51.6	53.9	51.0	50.0	48.9	47.5
Sz	.	43.5	51.6	46.7	49.7	53.3	53.8	53.7	55.5	49.9
UK	.	.	.	.	.	.	.	.	.	48.4
all countries	54.4	51.8	51.6	51.0	51.1	48.4	48.5	48.9	48.8	46.5

taken as the reference point for the mobilization capacities of socialist movements. With this restricted definition of the working-class constituency, any perspective on majoritarian size is out of the question. The industrial working class never approached the mythical 50% threshold, and only in the United Kingdom did it come close. Although there was a consistent increase from 1880, industrial workers could never hope by themselves to represent a majority of the active population, and therefore of the population as such. From 1880 to 1960, the industrial working class at the European mean level grew from about one-fifth of the active population to about-one third of it. Moreover, before they reached this level, the process of deindustrialization started to make its effects felt. That is to say, even if the entire social group of the industrial workers had massively supported the socialist movements, it could not have hoped for an electoral takeover.

I will therefore relate the cross-time and cross-country variation in the size of the industrial working class to interpret the variance in electoral support for the European class left. These associations are reported in Table 3.8 for the entire set of elections, by individual country, by broad electoral period, and by decade. Over the whole set of elections, the association between the industrial working class and the total left vote is positive (.257), albeit weaker than might have been expected. Within each country,

Table 3.8. *Industrial working-class size and left political mobilization*

by country		by period		by decade	
Austria	.813 (15)			1890	.194 (20)
Belgium	.715 (21)			1900	-.417 (31)
Denmark	.827 (36)	1880-1917	-.326 (82)	1910	-.547 (36)
Finland	.620 (27)	1918-1944	.171 (92)	1920	-.043 (41)
France	.669 (21)	1945-1975	.183 (119)	1930	.296 (33)
Germany	.468 (25)			1940	.369 (28)
Ireland	.689 (15)			1950	.267 (38)
Italy	.908 (15)			1960	.244 (34)
Netherland	.419 (23)			1970	.025 (25)
Norway	.905 (23)				
Sweden	.908 (24)				
Switzerland	.446 (24)				
Un. Kingdom	-.100 (21)				
all elections 1880-1975			257 (292)		

Note: Number of elections given in parentheses.

however, the association is much higher. This is due in part to the smaller number of cases involved in each country, although the associations are fairly homogeneous. In the three Scandinavian countries and Italy, the levels of association are around .900. Earlycomers to industrialization (the United Kingdom, the Netherlands, Switzerland, and Belgium) have lower associations than the others, because early industrializing countries had high levels of industrial workers relatively early, and such levels tended to vary little over time.

The overall correlation between the industrial working class and the total left (.257 over 292 elections) is the result not only of high individual country associations but also of quite different associations in the three periods. While in the interwar and post–World War II periods the correlation is positive (.171 and .183), in the pre–World War I period it is strongly negative (−.326). This further confirms that it was not in the early industrialized countries that the left grew stronger between 1880 and 1920, but the opposite. Over time, the initial gap in favor of late-industrializing countries is reduced, but initial differences are never completely overcome. A close examination of the plot of elections in the pre–World War I period reveals that the quite marked negative regression line is largely determined by two sets of elections: the Finnish elections between

1907 and 1917 (eight elections) and the United Kingdom elections between 1904 and 1910 (four elections). These two extreme cases in terms of the size of the industrial working class are also extreme cases of, respectively, very strong and very weak left electoral mobilization. This weighs heavily on the overall negative association for the period; if these elections were excluded, the association would become slightly positive, (.166). In the interwar and post–World War II periods, the trends are modestly positive, but the Irish elections are so outlying as to be almost totally responsible for a positive association of this kind. Without the Irish elections, in both periods the association becomes negative ($r = -.123$; $r = -.084$). Finally, in the decade correlations, the same different phases emphasized by the period analysis emerge. In the 1900s, 1910s, and 1920s, the left is stronger where the size of the working class is smaller. In the 1900 and 1910 decades, this result may be due to the disproportionate effect of Finland and the United Kingdom, but this is not the case for the 1920s. From the 1930s to the 1960s the association becomes positive: left mobilization tends to be higher where the size of the working class is also larger.[44]

Figure 3.2 shows the linear regression of each country for all the elections over the whole century. I prefer this graphic presentation to a discussion of regression coefficients, as it clarifies more effectively how the high within-country associations turn into a relatively weak global association. The different starting points of industrial development explain the overall effect of the poor correlation between industrial working class and left vote. The countries can be classified into three clearly distinguishable groups. In the first group, the electoral development of the left started when the level of the industrial working class was around 10–15% of the active population, and this development shows very steep regression lines: Austria, Denmark, France, Italy, Norway, and Sweden. Next is the group of the five early industrialized countries – the United Kingdom, Germany, the Netherlands, Belgium, and Switzerland – which all have a higher starting level of industrial working-class size, a consequent lower internal

---

[44] It may be thought that these associations are overly influenced by the different number of elections in each country, an argument that is particularly true in the first phase, when some countries definitely have more elections than others. Finland, for instance, has eight elections between 1907 and 1917. In the same period, Austria and Belgium have only two. To control for the number of elections, one can conduct the same analysis on a decade base, entering decade averages for each country decade in both left electoral mobilization and working-class size. The correlation coefficient changes, but not the general picture. In the first period, the association remains negative ($-.119$); and in the following two, it is positive (.236 for 1918–1944 and .187 for 1945–1975).

variation, and therefore far less steep regression lines. Finally, the two totally deviant cases of Finland and Ireland should be mentioned. These two countries start with the lowest industrial working-class levels and should therefore resemble more closely the intermediate group of relative latecomers rather than the advanced industrial societies. However, they follow either of the two group patterns: Their regression lines are flatter not because they have little over-time variation in industrialization (quite the contrary) but because they have little over-time variation in the total left vote. In relation to their respective industrial working-class levels, Finland has always had a higher left vote; Ireland, by contrast, has had a disproportionately low left vote.

These data justify a provisional hypothesis: the political left started to organize electorally in European countries at roughly the same time (see the relatively minor difference in early organizational consolidation in Chapter 6) as a result of political imitation and diffusion. When such organization took place in the context of already very large industrial working classes, the political mobilization effect was minor. By contrast, when the left organized politically where there were low levels of industrial working-class development, it was able to fully exploit the subsequent rapid growth of the industrial constituency. In sum, the question seems to be: Was a specific political organization for mobilization already in place when the industrial working class underwent its major growth?

In conclusion, the *developmental* association between the size of the industrial working-class constituency and the levels of left electoral mobilization is strong *within* each country; it is clear – although blurred by different starting points – over the whole set of elections; and it is weak or negative at the *cross-country* level in the first decades and also in successive periods. Finland and the United Kingdom counterbalance each other as deviant cases in the first period; Ireland's deviance in the second and third periods contributes to the slightly positive association. Without these extreme cases, the association would be more homogeneous in the three phases and would be very weak.

WORKING-CLASS HOMOGENEITY

Forms and levels of political mobilization can be linked causally to the more or less *homogeneous* nature of each given working class. That the homogeneity of the working class might be as important as, if not more important than, its sheer size to determine favorable conditions for socialist electoral recruitment is suggested by a number of considerations. On the one hand, the social homogeneity of the environment is essential for

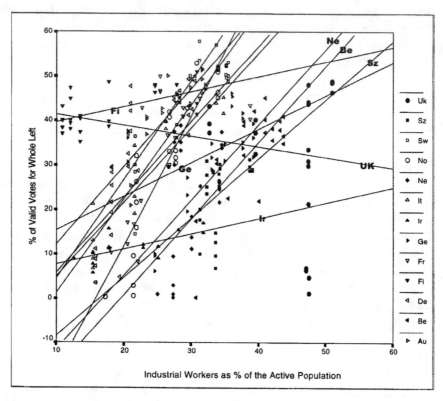

Figure 3.2. Industrial working-class and left vote: regression line by country and period.

building an "equality area" within which political consciousness, mobilization and participation are fostered. On the other hand, a vast literature underlines the job instability of the agrarian proletariat, its inability to exploit certain forms of collective action that are too disruptive and ineffective in the agrarian sector, and its extreme organizational and membership volatility depending on the economic cycle.[45] These points suggest the greater potential for the organized political mobilization of a sector-homogeneous and large-workshop-concentrated working class. Working-class homogeneity can be evaluated through its internal sector composition, that is, whether the working class, independent of its size, is composed of workers concentrated in core industrial-production sectors. A nonhomogeneous or less homogeneous working class, by contrast, is one that is spread more widely across many production sectors, most of which are not core

[45] Malefakis (1974).

industry (agricultural or service workers or workers in non-core industry sectors). This dimension can be approximated in operational terms by considering *the proportion of workers employed in industry (mining, manufacturing, building, transport, utilities)* with respect to those in agriculture and other residual sectors.

Table 3.9 shows the correlation coefficients between the three main internal components of the global working class and the left electoral mobilization level according to the usual scheme: over the whole century, by periods, by decade, and finally by country. The data show in a much clearer form a pattern that has already emerged. Over the whole set of elections, the correlation figures are, as expected, very positive for the industrial component (.455) and clearly negative for both the agricultural and residual other components (−.386 and −.231, respectively). These associations are much stronger than those concerning the size of industrial and agricultural workers' constituencies. When the same data are plotted by country, indicating the regression line of each country as well as of each period, it becomes evident that a small number of outliers sharply reduces the overall temporal association. These outliers are the early Finnish elections (1907–1917) (mentioned earlier) and the early Swiss elections (1899–1914). Excluding these thirteen elections, the overall correlation over time rises to .622. Moreover, the correlation for each country is higher, ranging from .600 to .900, with the single exception of Switzerland (.203), where the proportion of industrial workers in the whole working class remains stable in the twentieth century, having already reached a high level at the turn of the century.[46]

Once again, the picture is different when one looks at analytical and non-time-dependent associations, as the global and within-country pattern is not repeated at the period or decade levels. In each period and decade (with the exception of the first and the last), the association is systematically negative. This indicates that at no point in time was the left electorally stronger where the sector homogeneity of the working class was

---

[46] At least a part of the small variation in the industrial-working-class proportion of the whole working class in Switzerland is due to the rather ambiguous case of the 1941 census figures for the industrial working class and for the working class altogether. The proportion of the first over the latter is 65% in the previous census and 72% in the following one. In 1941, however, the census figures give a proportion of 62%, that is, declining with respect to the 1931 census. This is a doubtful figure. In no other case is such a remarkable drop in working-class constituency found. This is likely to be one of those cases in which some change in accountancy or attribution rules accounts for the change. However, I have accepted the data, avoiding any interpolation. The result is that for almost twenty years the variable remains substantially unchanged, with obvious consequences for its association with the size of the left.

Table 3.9. *Internal composition of the working class and left electoral mobilization*

	industrial working-class proportion of the total working class	agricultural working-class proportion of the total working class	"other sectors" working-class proportion of the total working class
1880-1975	.455 (249)	-.386	-.231
1880-1917	-.105 (78)	.183	-.139
1918-1944	-.023 (77)	.034	-.012
1945-1975	-.074 (94)	.316	-.347
1890	.127 (20)	.081	-.049
1900	-.318 (29)	.413	-.224
1910	-.423 (33)	.363	.161
1920	-.146 (36)	.135	.013
1930	-.171 (27)	.232	.006
1940	-.088 (21)	.203	-.206
1950	-.229 (28)	.387	-.314
1960	-.094 (26)	.537	-.401
1970	.319 (23)	.416	-.511
Austria	.712 (17)	-.810	.074
Belgium	.864 (21)	-.527	-.820
Denmark	.847 (36)	-.788	-.468
Finland	.618 (27)	-.536	-.391
France	.887 (11)	-.807	-.536
Germany	.796 (25)	-.718	-.841
Ireland	n.a.	n.a.	n.a.
Italy	.922 (15)	-.919	-.883
Nether.	.922 (23)	-.923	.453
Norway	.894 (23)	-.890	-.763
Sweden	.839 (24)	-.379	-.927
Switzerland	.203 (24)	-.612	.558
Un.Kingdom	n.a.	n.a.	n.a.

Note: Number of elections given in parentheses.

Table 3.10. *Mean left electoral mobilization by type of working class*

		working-class size	
		small 29.4 (123)	large 36.7 (126)
working-class homogeneity	low 25.5 (107)	26.3 (94)	19.6 (13)
	high 38.8 (142)	39.4 (29)	38.7 (113)

Note: Number of elections given in parentheses.

higher. If anything, quite the contrary: It appeared to be stronger where the latter was weaker. The cases that are missing with respect to the analysis conducted for the size of the working class would have no effect on the general picture. The United Kingdom had an early homogeneous working-class and weak electoral mobilization until the 1930s, while Ireland had a small left and presumably a nonhomogeneous working class.

It may be wondered whether the respective effects of industrial working-class size and working-class homogeneity can be distinguished from one other and which effect is more important. To this end, Table 3.10 presents the mean values of the left vote for the type of working class resulting from the cross-tabulation of size and homogeneity. The axes represent the mean value of the distribution of the two variables (28.5% for the industrial working class as a percentage of the active population and 55.2% for the industrial working class as a percentage of the total working class) and identify four groups of cases: those in which the size of the working class is lower than the mean and where the homogeneity is also lower; those in which, by contrast, both size and homogeneity are above average; and the two mixed groups of high size and low homogeneity and low size and high homogeneity, respectively.

In Table 3.10, the difference in support for the left between the quadrant of small size and low homogeneity (26.3%) and that of large size and high homogeneity (38.7%) reflects the growing temporal trend in both variables. This is not the case for the difference between the quadrant of the small, homogeneous working class (39.4%) versus that of the large heterogeneous one (19.6%). As shown in the discussion of the sector and status transformation of Western European societies, there is no temporal trend moving from a large, heterogeneous working class toward a small, homogeneous one or vice versa. In this case, the remarkable difference in the mobilization of the left (39.4% versus 19.6%) cannot be attributed to over-time temporal association, but instead reflects the weight of homogeneity versus size independent of time. Moreover, it should be noted that in both categories of working-class size, the cases of higher homogeneity show a higher level of electoral mobilization (39.4% versus 26.3%; 38.7% versus 19.6%). Finally, the general effect of size and homogeneity in the entire set is also clearly favorable to the latter: a difference of 7.3 points between small and large size versus a difference of 13.3 points between low and high sector homogeneity.

These data have, however, the problem of large frequency differences among boxes. A second way to search for an impact of homogeneity independent of its over-time association with size is to separate the cases located above the regression line between the two variables from those located below the line. If one imagines the regression line between the two variables as representing the common over-time development, then the cases above the line are those that at each given moment (and independent of overall averages) are characterized by a working-class homogeneity that is higher than one would have expected on the basis of its size. Conversely, the cases below the regression line are those in which, again irrespective of time (represented here by the regression line), the working class is less homogeneous than one would have expected given its size. This analysis is carried out in Figure 3.3. Here, 122 cases fall above the regression line and 127 cases fall below it. The difference between the two groups in terms of average left electoral mobilization is considerable: 38.7% for more homogeneous versus 27.7% for less homogeneous. Considering that in this case no weight can be attributed to over-time variation or to the corresponding concentration of certain cases in certain periods, the conclusion is that homogeneity, in the sense of the predominance of the core industrial working class in the composition of the whole working class, has an effect of its own that appears to be more important than that of the size of the industrial working class.

The data concerning the proportion of agricultural workers within the total working class do not require extended comments, as they point to a pattern that is specular to that discussed for industrial workers: a strong negative over-time association accompanied by a positive association in each of the three periods and in individual decades between 1880 and 1970. Why, then, do the industrial and agricultural components of the working class evidence symmetric and unexpected patterns of influence on the left vote? For the industrial working class, the over-time association is positive, although synchronic associations indicate a stronger left vote in

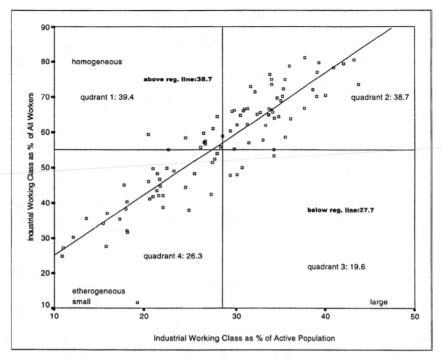

Figure 3.3. Types of working-class structures and left vote.

the context of a weaker industrial component; in contrast, for the agricultural working class, the over-time association is negative, but synchronic associations indicate that the left vote was stronger where this agricultural component was higher. This is a clear example of how misleading it can be to rely exclusively on over-time association among variables. The dyarchic conclusion that the growth of the industrial working class is associated with the growth of the left cannot be transformed into the synchronic statement that the left will be stronger where the industrial working class is higher in number or internal proportion. Two processes coexist, the over-time and the synchronic association, each of which points in a different direction. The fact that positive initial associations for agricultural laborers and negative synchronic associations for industrial workers persist in each period of time, while over time the two processes show a different trend, indicates that these associations *translate* over time without changing. *Whatever initial factors were responsible for the left growing stronger where the working class was less industrial and more agricultural, these initial differences have been maintained through time.* The key problem becomes that of identifying those factors responsible for the initial pattern.

WORKING-CLASS CONCENTRATION

After analyzing sectoral and status transformations, working-class size, and working-class homogeneity, a further approach is to consider working-class *workshop concentration*. It can be argued that the more shop-concentrated (rather than dispersed in a larger number of small workshops) the industrial working class is, the more it leads to social homogeneity and an equality area, which in turn are favorable to ideological and organizational mobilization. This is because, for instance, in large workshops more impersonal relationships between workers and employers predominate, against the more direct face-to-face relationship in small workshops. The latter tend to increase social control, deference, and paternalistic attitudes among the workers and generally strengthen the perception of a common interest of both owners and workers in the fate of the small workshop.

In the absence of direct comparable over-time information on workshop size, an indirect indicator can be devised considering the ratio of employers and the self-employed to those occupied in the core manufacturing industry. Assuming that the number of employers reflects the number of workshop units, this ratio indicates the rate of fragmentation to concentration of the working class in manufacturing. Low rates indicate a higher number of workers per unit; high rates indicate the opposite. Table 3.11 describes the distribution of manufacturing working-class concentration in Western European countries from 1880 to 1970. The figures should be read as indicating the number of employers in manufacturing for every 100 workers occupied in the same sector. As the means of decades indicate, there is a long-term growth trend in the concentration of the manufacturing working class in larger and fewer workshops. At the beginning of the twentieth century there were approximately four workers for one employer/self-employed person in manufacturing; by the 1930s the ratio had risen to seven to one, and in 1970 it was twenty to one.

It is not surprising to find that the British manufacturing working class was the most concentrated, followed at a considerable distance by the Belgian one. In the 1880s, the ratio of British employers to workers was lower or similar to that of all other countries in the 1930s. Yet the differences among the countries do not systematically reflect the differences between earlycomers and latecomers. Notice, in particular, the high manufacturing concentration that always characterized the small Finnish working class. At the opposite end, the most fragmented working classes are those of Italy, followed by France, Denmark, and Norway. In Italy, the process of over-time concentration is less evident than in the other countries. In the 1970s, its level of manufacturing concentration was three

Table 3.11. *Employers/occupied ratio in Western European countries*

	1880	1890	1900	1910	1920	1930	1940	1950	1960	1970	mean
Au	-	-	18.8	18.5	18.2	17.6	14.0	11.2	8.7	6.0	13.2
Be	-	20.6	18.2	14.0	13.0	12.4	13.1	10.6	7.0	4.7	12.0
De	47.5	42.8	35.0	23.1	22.9	19.1	12.9	12.0	8.2	7.0	22.5
Fi	-	-	9.8	13.1	15.5	13.3	11.9	10.3	4.9	2.7	10.9
Fr	-	31.1	30.0	32.8	23.0	23.4	17.3	10.2	7.0	3.4	20.0
Ge	31.9	23.5	16.2	15.1	12.2	12.5	10.8	8.2	5.2	4.5	15.0
Ir	-	-	-	-	25.3	18.1	15.6	9.6	4.7	3.9	12.7
It	-	38.9	37.1	30.0	26.3	21.0	17.0	14.4	12.8	12.8	25.1
Ne	24.0	23.0	19.8	15.8	12.7	12.2	12.5	9.1	5.3	3.1	13.7
No	38.8	34.6	28.0	25.8	17.5	16.1	11.8	9.5	6.2	4.5	20.6
Sw	42.7	38.5	29.7	17.7	10.2	12.4	9.9	6.3	4.0	2.2	17.7
Sz	-	20.4	22.8	24.2	19.0	15.1	13.2	10.7	7.1	6.0	16.4
UK	13.4	13.4	11.0	8.5	7.2	5.7	4.1	2.3	1.1	1.5	6.4
mean	33.7	30.3	24.5	19.5	16.0	14.8	13.2	9.3	6.3	4.5	16.0

Note: Figures are multiplied by 100. They indicate the number of employers for every 100 occupied.

times lower than the average (and eight times lower than in the United Kingdom).

In Table 3.12 the usual correlation analysis is performed on the whole set by periods and decades. Here, not only is the employers/workers ratio in manufacturing strongly associated, as expected, with the left vote over the whole period – .604 (i.e., the smaller the concentration the lower the electoral support) – but this relationship is confirmed across countries as well as within countries. Even the first pre–World War I period shows a strong negative association, while for most other variables discussed so far, it turns out to be quite deviant. In the early mobilization phase, unlike the other aspects discussed so far, the concentration of the working class in large workshops proves advantageous for left mobilization. The same remains true in the interwar period, and the association fades only after World War II. The analysis by decade confirms the consistency of this association and its slow fading away over time. Of all the indicators discussed so far, this is the only one that shows a strong (the strongest) developmental association, as well as a corresponding synchronic association with the left vote,.

RATES OF GROWTH

The last aspect to be considered is the rapidity or tempo of the transformations analyzed so far, as opposed to their earliness or quantity. I use the indicators discussed in the previous sections, and in particular the interde-

Table 3.12. *Working-class concentration and left electoral mobilization*

period		decade		country	
1880-1975	-.604 (292)	1890	-.068 (20)	Austria	-.725 (17)
		1900	-.252 (31)	Belgium	-.501 (21)
1880-1917	-.426 (82)	1910	-.289 (36)	Denmark	-.928 (36)
1918-1944	-.264 (92)	1920	-.310 (41)	Finland	-.326 (27)
1945-1975	.014 (115)	1930	-.167 (33)	France	-.735 (21)
		1940	-.341 (28)	Germany	-.884 (25)
		1950	-.111 (38)	Ireland	-.617 (15)
		1960	.096 (34)	Italy	-.962 (15)
		1970	.028 (25)	Netherlands	-.900 (23)
				Norway	-.858 (23)
				Sweden	-.873 (24)
				Switzerland	-.595 (24)
				Un. Kingdom	-.883 (21)

Note: Number of elections given in parentheses.

cade rate[47] of change, in regard to the following four dimensions: (1) population occupied in industry; (2) dependent labor over the active population; (3) the proportion of manual and lower-status workers in key industrial sectors (mining, manufacturing, building utilities, and transports) over the active population; and (4) the proportion of the global working class constituted by the industrial core workers (defined as belonging to the sectors mentioned in dimension 3). The figures are derived from census data already presented and can be found in the Data Appendix.

The data can lead to several observations on comparative industrialization, but I will limit myself to highlighting some distribution features that appear to be important in this context. Industrial latecomers (Ireland, Finland, Sweden, Austria) experienced high rates of change, while industrial earlycomers (Belgium, the United Kingdom, the Netherlands, Switzerland, and Germany) had comparatively lower rates of change. Looking at the means of each decade, there are some differences in the four dimensions. For the sector transformation, the decades showing a high degree of change were 1890–1900, 1940–1950, and 1950–1960. The period between the end of World War II and the 1960s is the phase of highest growth for all indicators in all countries, Belgium and the United Kingdom exluded. In the interwar decades, the growth of the active population in industry and that of working-class homogenization slow down, and

---

[47] Examining changes between elections produces too much electoral volatility and too little social change (decade census data).

the working-class constituency actually declines (in 1920–1930 by 1.0%). This happens again in the 1970s as deindustrialization occurs in all countries except Ireland and Finland (and, to a lesser extent, Austria). In the same period the working-class constituency declines sharply by 2.3%.

The French industrial development, despite being one of the most advanced in Europe by 1880 in terms of scientific tradition and technical innovation, particularly in the banking and financial sectors, slowed to a virtual standstill thereafter. Between 1890 and 1940 all indicators point to a sluggish development rate, which is unique in a European comparative perspective.[48] The elements that significantly limited the potential for development of the industrial proletariat and the French failure to enter the twentieth century as a mature industrial state have been the subject of considerable debate. The causal factor that appears more consistently in comparative analyses as responsible for this stagnation – and for its correlated continuous predominance of handicraft production,[49] slow growth of factory industry, weak industrial concentration, and little large-scale expansion – is demographic. France had a slow rate of population growth, and no demographic revolution took place. This implies a persistence of regional specialization, of only partially integrated provincial markers, and of the use of local materials.[50] In France, major rates of change in the four dimensions appear only after World War II.

Sweden and Finland experienced the fastest rate of industrial transformation in all its dimensions. From 1870 to 1914, no European country exceeded Sweden in terms of economic growth per capita. The crucial role in creating this situation was played by foreign trade: Swedish raw materials, especially timber and iron ore, were in demand by the growing European economies, and a large share of foreign capital helped to finance industrialization. Large enterprise played a more important role in Sweden than it did in France, for example. Small businesses, by contrast, were less important than in other continental countries.[51] Therefore, the industrial

---

[48] The stagnant nature of the French economy between 1880 and 1930 is underlined by French economic historians. See Dupeux (1964: 170–173); Lévy-Leboyer (1968: 281–298) provides a British–French comparison of the early stages of industrialization; Sauvy (1967: 536) provides a comparison of French industrial production levels with American, British, German, and world levels; see also the classic French–German comparison of Clapham (1936: 53–56 and 402–409).

[49] For the artisan, rather than factory worker, see in particular Sewell (1986: 49).

[50] See the titles in note 48 and Milward and Saul (1977: 125–139); Trebilcock (1981: 140–150, 194); Landes (1969: 245–246).

[51] See Tilton (1974: 561–571). In 1872, the enterprises employing more than 100 people employed 65% of the Swedish industrial working class; Simonson (1990: 86).

working class in Sweden was highly concentrated in terms of industrial units. At the same time, industries were located not in urban centers, but in rural ones (as in Norway). Swedish industrial development was thus not characterized by the rapid growth of urban industry, attracting labor from rural districts. With the exception of the textile industry, industrial workers tended to live outside the large towns. As a consequence, urbanization was scarcely a significant phenomenon (as it was, for example, in Norway).[52]

Although the studies by Bull, Galenson, and Lufferty have singled out Norway as the country with the most accelerated changes, with Sweden coming second and Denmark third, nothing in my data supports this picture: Norway is always clearly characterized by lower rates of change than Sweden (and also Finland). This may, of course, be the result of different types of data.[53] Norwegian industrialization was hampered by a lack of coal until the end of the nineteenth century, but subsequent electrification rapidly overcame this disadvantage. Electrical-energy industrialization was very rapid in terms of output and national product, but some of its features dispersed rather than concentrated industry and the working population. This may explain for Norway (as well as for Switzerland, which also underwent rapid electrification) why rapid rates of change in energy use and output may not be fully reflected in high rates of occupational structural change and (see later) urbanization.[54]

The analysis of the relationship between the tempo of industrialization and left electoral development can be organized on the basis of two hypotheses. The first suggests that cases and periods of higher rates of socioeconomic change are associated with cases and periods of *higher rates of growth in left electoral support*. The second hypothesis argues that cases and periods of higher rates of socioeconomic change are associated with *higher levels of total support*, not with higher levels of change in such support. The two hypotheses have different theoretical meanings. To assume an association between rates of economic change and rates of electoral change postulates a straight and immediate correspondence or translation of economic change into political change. When one relates rates of economic change to levels of left electoral support, the logic of the argument is different.

[52] Simonson (1990: 87).

[53] The data used by Lafferty are indeed different from census data and refer to output indicators of economic development. See Lafferty (1971: 37). On pages 48–51, Lafferty discusses the implications of using different kinds of data to compare the three Scandinavian countries.

[54] A waterfall sufficed to provide cheap energy. Peripheral and rural communities could attract employers, thus favoring high dispersion of industry. On the special features of electrification-led industrialisation see Trede (1992: 204), who sets the Swiss, Norwegian, and Swedish models aside from the rest of the European experiences.

The question is whether left electoral support was higher in countries and periods of rapid economic transformation vis-à-vis countries and periods of less rapid or even sluggish economic transformation. It seems to me that the general theses concerning the rhythm of change are better expressed and tested in this second form. To perform this test in Table 3.13, I report the correlation between the mean electoral size of the left and the mean rates of change in industrialization measures in different periods.

The associations result from a small number of cases, as each country enters with only one average value, and are remarkably high, particularly in the first two periods, 1890–1910 and 1920–1940. Considering the periods 1890–1940 or 1890–1970 still yields systematically positive associations: The working-class constituency effect remains the weakest of all and the working-class homogeneity effect the strongest.[55] These data confirm the hypothesis advanced earlier that the *coincidence* between the organizational development of socialism *and* the rapid growth of the industrial constituency is a far better predictor of electoral mobilization capacity in the industrial society than is the level of development. Industrialization earlycomers had a much larger industrial constituency, which had, however, already experienced the phase of intense growth. Latecomers had a smaller industrial working-class constituency, but in these cases socialism organized precisely during the phase of major industrial society growth rates.

URBANIZATION AND LEFT MOBILIZATION

If one identifies urbanization with concentration in large cities, a threshold of 100,000 inhabitants is adequate. If the intention is to differentiate dispersed settings and microvillages from other settings, a 5,000 or even 2,000 cutoff point might be ideal. However, as in census statistics, the units identified by the threshold do not necessarily correspond to an "urban settlement." The threshold of 20,000 is generally retained as a good approximation between the geographical unit of measurement and the urban settlement. This is because the most important ingredients of urban social life are best guaranteed once the unit size exceeds 20,000 inhabitants. Table 3.14 shows the levels of urbanization by country, taking as a reference point the percentage of the population living in cities larger than 20,000 and 100,000 inhabitants. The lines indicate the point at which a

---

[55] Remember, however, that the United Kingdom and Ireland have no data for this indicator. Ireland, in particular, works as a deviant case, reducing the level of association.

Table 3.13. *Correlation between mean left electoral size and mean rates of change in industrialization measures by periods*

	correlation	between	total left	vote and:
	mean rates of change occupat. in industry	mean rates of change in dependant labor force	mean rates of change in industrial working-class constituency	mean rates of change in industrial working-class homogeneity
1890-1910	.543 (11)	.450 (11)	.005 (12)	.467 (10)
1920-1940	.489 (13)	.235 (13)	.226 (13)	.581 (11)
1950-1970	-.092 (13)	.222 (13)	-.155 (13)	.612 (10)
1890-1940	.532 (13)	.166 (13)	.289 (13)	.781 (11)
1890-1970	.228 (13)	.281 (13)	.019 (13)	.853 (11)

Note: Number of elections given in parentheses.

certain level of urbanization was reached in each country, and they facilitate cross-country comparisons. For the 20,000-inhabitant threshold, the line represents 33% of the population; for the 100,000-inhabitant threshold, the line represents 20% of the population. However, in describing the levels of urbanization of European countries throughout the last century, it is also useful to make some reference to the 2,000- and 5,000-inhabitant thresholds.

Taking the 20,000-inhabitant threshold, the United Kingdom and the Netherlands lead in urbanization, followed by Germany, Belgium, and Italy (the most highly urbanized country following the 2,000 or 5,000 criteria), which show average cross-European levels. Northern countries, including Ireland, remain the least urbanized part of the Continent together with Switzerland (which is one of the most urbanized countries of Western Europe by the 2,000-inhabitant threshold). The 100,000-inhabitant threshold does not substantially modify this picture except for the cases of Austria and Ireland, which both fall into the group of early urbanized countries, although they still are behind the overurbanized cases of the United Kingdom and the Netherlands. After World War I, Austria, Ireland, and, to a certain extent, Denmark are "large-capital" countries, whose urbanization is due to the disproportionate impact of the capital urban center on the whole population. Comparing the different thresholds yields the following characterization: The United Kingdom, the Netherlands, and Germany (to a lesser extent) are homogeneously both early and highly urbanized countries. At the other extreme, the Scandinavian countries are the least urbanized in Europe. France should also be included among the countries with relatively weak and late urbanization irrespective of the threshold chosen. Ireland and Austria would also be in this group,

Table 3.14. *Urbanization rates in Western Europe*

Percentage living in cities with more than 20,000 inhabitants

	Uk	Ne	Ge	It	Be	Au	De	Sw	Fr	Ir	Fi	Sz	No
1880	.	.	16	23	20	.	16	8	24	.	.	.	.
1890	52	36	25	25	25	.	19	11	23	.	.	10	14
1900	57	41	32	27	27	.	26	13	24	.	.	18	18
1910	59	43	36	28	30	17	28	16	26	.	9	21	18
1920	61	45	41	31	30	26	29	20	28	29	11	23	18
1930	70	50	43	37	33	36	30	22	31	22	13	25	17
1940	68	55	44	39	32	36	34	26	31	25	17	29	18
1950	67	57	44	41	33	40	37	34	33	29	22	30	21
1960	.	60	50	47	34	38	37	40	40	33	30	30	22
1970	.	63	51	52	36	38	36	.	42	37	40	32	.

Percentage living in cities with more than 100,000 inhabitants

	Uk	Ne	Ge	De	Au	Ir	Sz	It	Fr	Sw	No	Be
1880	.	.	7	12	.	.	.	8	10	4	.	11
1890	32	22	14	14	.	.	.	8	13	7	7	12
1900	36	24	19	16	.	.	8	9	14	8	10	12
1910	37	24	23	19	11	.	9	11	14	9	10	11
1920	39	24	27	21	21	23	12	13	15	13	10	12
1930	43	29	30	22	32	16	16	15	16	14	9	12
1940	41	30	30	23	32	17	20	19	16	17	13	11
1950	39	31	30	27	33	23	20	20	17	18	17	10
1960	54	33	34	24	32	25	21	25	18	19	16	9
1970	58	29	32	23	32	27	18	29	19	.	.	11

but for the weight of their large capitals. Switzerland is one of the least urbanized countries in terms of medium or large cities, but it had a relatively early level of small-city urbanization. Similarly, Italy is the most and earliest urbanized country in terms of small cities (2,000 to 5,000) but is average or even below average for medium- and large-city levels of urbanization. Consequently, the correlation among these various measures of urbanization is lower than might be expected.[56]

The relationship between urbanisation and levels of left electoral mo-

[56] They are the following:

	U5,000	U20,000	U100,000
U2,000	.9185 (104)	.7232 (104)	.4109 (103)
U5,000		.8942 (104)	.5544 (103)
U20,000			.8749 (111)

bilization is summarized in Table 3.15 following the usual distinction between overall cross-country and cross-time association followed by periods, decades, and country associations. Given the extensive discussion of this type of table in the previous sections, it is no longer necessary to specify the meaning I attribute to the different types of associations. At the overall cross-country and cross-time level, the association between urbanization and left mobilization is positive but weak; it tends to increase systematically with the level of the urban threshold, from .051 for the 2,000-inhabitant threshold to .216 for the 100,000-inhabitant threshold. This suggests that the element of urban settlement that most fosters socialist electoral mobilization efforts is large urbanization. However, even in this case, the picture of developmental association is reversed by cross-sectional synchronic analysis even more clearly than was the case for industrialization. Urbanization levels are negatively associated with left electoral development in almost all temporal units, particularly in the 1890–1917 period and in the first decades in general. The different indicators all behave roughly the same way: For medium- and large-city urbanization the association disappears altogether from the 1930s on, while for small-city urbanization it continues to be consistently negative (if very weak) throughout the entire century. In this case, a more detailed look at scattergrams by periods is not particularly revealing, as no spatially deviant cases can be clearly identified.

The conclusion is that before the 1930s low urbanization contexts proved a more favorable setting for left mobilization. To put it differently, such contexts did not prevent or hamper significantly such mobilization. This conclusion may seem to contradict the widespread assumption that *within each national context* socialist electoral mobilization found more favorable conditions in urban settings. It does not, however: There is no contradiction between this and the finding that *at the cross-national level*, socialism developed earlier and/or faster in less urbanized countries.

A final check concerns the rates of growth in urbanization as opposed to its actual levels, as was done previously for the indicators of industrialization. If the rate of change from one census decade to the next is computed relating the four indicators of urbanization to either the level of the left vote or the rate of change of the vote, no significant associations emerge.[57] When the data are aggregated at the period level (three periods per country), the associations remain weak (around .100), although they become positive. Only when the data are aggregated at the country level does a significant correlation emerge. The average per country rate of

---

[57] The correlation coefficient range between −.065 and .080 over a set of eighty-nine to ninety-eight decades.

Table 3.15. *Electoral mobilization and urbanization levels*

| | % of population living in cities with more than N inhabitants | | | |
	2,000	5,000	20,000	100,000
whole period	.051 (261)	.113	.189 (278)	.216 (285)
before 1918	-.313 (76)	-.354	-.376 (82)	-.339
interwar	-.079 (84)	-.104	-.043 (91)	-.016 (92)
1945-75	-.185 (101)	-.141	.011 (106)	.030 (112)
1890	.013 (19)	-.103	-.002 (20)	.009
1900	-.164 (29)	-.241	-.403 (31)	-.378
1910	-.411 (33)	-.429	-.551 (36)	-.439
1920	-.303 (37)	-.356	-.237 (41)	-.145
1930	.052 (31)	.189	.033 (32)	.016
1940	-.149 (27)	-.068	.002 (28)	.010
1950	-.142 (34)	-.078	.086 (37)	.001
1960	-.168 (30)	-.112	.009 (31)	.038 (33)
1970	-.041 (16)	-.057	.201 (16)	.213 (19)

Note: Number of elections given in parentheses.

urbanization growth (using the 20,000-inhabitant threshold) is linked to the average per country left vote with $r = .495$ and only one deviating case emerges: Norway, with a total left vote that is far higher than expected on the basis of its average urbanization growth rate (without Norway, the association is $r = .625$). In sum, contrary to the case of industrialization measures, there is not enough evidence to confirm that the rates of change in urbanization levels are associated with left electoral mobilization levels.

SOCIAL MOBILIZATION MODEL

Urbanization and industrialization measures are not highly associated with each other. In the global set of census decades considered in this study, the association between different measures of urbanization and the two key measures of industrial society development (the percentage of population employed in industry and the percentage of industrial working class over the active population) ranges between 0.5 and 0.7. Moreover, these associations are stronger in the pre–World War I period and tend to be reduced in the two following periods. This is not surprising considering that in describing patterns of industrialization and urbanization, several differences have emerged. Some of the early and most industrialized countries, like the United Kingdom, are also the most urbanized. Some of the less urbanized countries, like the Scandinavian countries, Finland, and Ireland, are also the latest and least industrially developed. There are, however, some important deviations. Switzerland is an early and strongly industrialized country and is also one of the least urbanized societies of Western Europe; the weak urbanization explains to a certain extent the Swiss peculiarity of early and thorough industrialization occurring without the creation of a proletariat.[58] France is also comparatively more industrialized than urbanized. The exceptional urbanization of the Netherlands does not correspond to similar levels of industrial development.

It might be useful to combine these two processes together into a single *social mobilization* model to see whether their combined effect is a better predictor of left electoral mobilization than its separate elements. Given that (1) the process of growth seems more important than the level of each variable; (2) urbanization and industrialization magnify each other rather than compensate for each other, and (3) the relationship between the two is very different in different countries, the combination of levels of industrialization and urbanization into a common index does not increase the association levels with the overall electoral strength of the left.[59] Rather, we need to consider to what extent the two processes overlap and

[58] For this aspect of the Swiss industrialization see, Biucchi (1976–1977). In 1860, two-thirds of Swiss workers lived in their own houses, and the vast majority were part-time farmers, whose land was often made available by the commune. Cf. Gruner (1968: 94).

[59] The product between the two factors is better than the mean (or the sum) if one assumes that the impact of medium levels of industrialization and urbanization have to be regarded as more significant for a social mobilization syndrome than the combination of high industrialization and low urbanization or the reverse. The major impact of parallel growth processes has been argued, and this would speak for a multiplicative index. However, when dealing with levels rather than rates of change, this argument is less applicable. Actually, the test shows that the way the index is computed does not make much of a difference in terms of association with the left vote. The following table shows both combined indexes of industrialization/urbanization: the additive standardized one and the multiplicative one, taking the natural logarithm of such multiplication. Their association with the left vote is compared with the association of the single processes of urbanization and industrialization.

Social mobilisation and electoral development

	N	industrialization	urbanization	social mobilization	
				ln(I*U)	(ZsI + ZsU)
1880–1975	278	.234	.189	.218	.233
1880–1917	82	−.326	−.376	−.447	−.375
1918–1944	91	.174	−.043	.061	.075
1945–1965	76	.179	−.035	.050	.076
1965–1975	29	.031	.152	.231	.172

Note: Based on the same number of cases for all variables.

reinforce each other or, alternatively, are historically separated. To this end, in Figure 3.4 the countries are represented by their decade values in both industrialization (percentage of industrial working class over the active population) and urbanization (percentage of population living in cities with more than 20,000 inhabitants). They are regrouped into four groups to facilitate the reading of the graphs, but also because different patterns are roughly indicated by each group slope. The relationship between the quantitative scope of the processes of industrialization and urbanization in each country is indicated by the ratio between the increase on the x axis (industrialization) and the y axis (urbanization).

In the top right-hand part of the figure, the United Kingdom, the Netherlands, Switzerland, and Germany show similar ranges in industrialization as earlycomers and highly industrialized countries. At the same time, they have different urbanization starting points, ranging from the highest values for the United Kingdom and the Netherlands to the lowest for Switzerland. They have in common that their twentieth-century transformation is more pronounced in the urbanization level than in the industrialization level. In the second graph (bottom right), Finland, Sweden, and Italy are industrial latecomers that undergo a process of accelerated transformation in both dimensions, but industrialization exceeds urbanization.[60] The transformation pattern of Denmark, Austria, and France is one of relatively balanced but modest growth in both processes. The starting points are neither very low nor very high; the final points have medium values; and, as a result, the paths of transformation are slow and modest in unitary terms, showing no major steps or jumps. The graph in the lower right-hand part of Figure 3.4 groups the three remaining countries: Norway, Belgium, and Ireland. The modest correspondence in the trends of the two processes is determined here by industrialization developments that are far wider in scope than the urbanization changes. Norway is the clearest case of industrialization without urbanization, but the other two countries are also relatively and comparatively flat as far as urbanization growth is concerned.

If one considers (1) that the combination and cumulation of *both* processes of change can be regarded as particularly propitious to early and strong socialist mobilization; (2) that as far as industrialization indicators are concerned, the rates of change were more important than the actual

---

[60] Italy represents a more complicated pattern: After the first three decades (1890–1920) of modest growth in urbanization without important growth in industrial population, the pattern becomes similar to that of Finland and Sweden, with accelerated growth in both dimensions but also with a predominance of industrialization over urbanization.

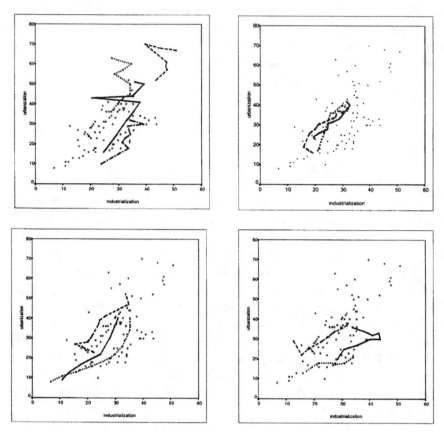

Figure 3.4. Patterns of industrialization and urbanization.

levels; and (3) that for urbanization the same was not true, and the levels
seemed more important than rates of change, it is possible to draw a
number of conclusions about the development of the left in different cases.
It is likely that conditions for left political mobilization are best in cases
of *parallel and combined* significant rates of change in both industrialization
and urbanization, that is, in the countries of the graphs in the top right-
hand and lower left-hand part of the figure. By contrast, I would expect
lower levels of left mobilization in those countries characterized by the
predominance of one aspect over the other: urbanization over industrialization or industrialization over urbanization. The extent to which these
hypotheses are supported by left vote levels is reported in Table 3.16,
where, for each group of countries characterized by a specific historical
pattern of social mobilization, the corresponding mean left vote is reported.

In fact, the countries characterized in the 1890–1960 period by a

Table 3.16. *Patterns of historical social mobilization and left vote*

	mean left vote	
	by decade	by election
accelerated urbanization and industrialization (Sw, Fi, It)	40.0 (27)	40.5 (78)
equilibrated medium growth in both (Au, De, Fr)	36.0 (30)	37.1 (87)
accel. urbanization/small industrialization changes (UK, Ne, Ge, Sz)	28.3 (41)	28.6 (108)
high industrialization changes/small urbanization growth (Ir, Be, No)	28.1 (27)	27.6 (74)
for entire population	32.6 (125)	33.6 (347)

coincidence and a parallel development of industrialization and urbanization show remarkably higher levels of left support than those in which one of the two processes prevails over the other. The idea that modern mass parties, and in particular class parties, are not necessarily the product of higher levels of social mobilization (industrialization and urbanization) – as Duverger wrote in the 1950s[61] – but rather tend to be stronger when both processes are coincident and achieve accelerated parallel growth[62] is supported by these data. Those countries characterized by the decoupling of these processes show much lower left support. Differences with respect to the left vote mean for the entire set of European elections (32.6) are not marginal.

At this stage, one can test the predictive capacity of the social mobilization processes by devising a combined index including all variables that have proved significant in the analysis carried out so far. For the *constituency-size effect*, I consider the weight of the industrial workers on the active population (positive long-term effect) and the weight of the independents without family workers (negative long-term effect). For the *working-class homogeneity* effect, I examine the proportion of industrial workers over the entire working class.[63] For *working-class concentration*, I consider the employ-

---

[61] Duverger (1967).

[62] Pizzorno (1966b) and (1969).

[63] To prevent the indicators of homogeneity from producing the loss of the British and Irish cases and of the French elections after 1945, I have standardized the variables and assigned the value of 0 (i.e., the overall mean) to these cases. This means that in summing up all the indicators, for these cases the missing one is absent and only the remaining three are counted.

ers/occupied ratio. Finally, to consider the variable of the combined coincident rate of growth of industrialization and urbanization, I rank the groups of countries identified in Table 3.16 as those where the two processes do not combine (small growth in one and high or medium growth in the other [value = 1]); those where the processes combine with moderate rates of growth (value = 2); and those with high rates of growth for both industrialization and urbanization (value = 3). The formula of the *combined social mobilization index* is therefore the following sum of standardized values:

Process	Variables	Sign	Index
constituency size	percentage of industrial workers in active population	+	
	percentage of independents in active population	−	
constituency homogeneity	percentage of industrial workers in total workers	+	social mobilization
constituency concentration	employers/occupied ratio	+	
rate of transformation	industrialization/urbanization classification	+	

Figure 3.5 reports the scattergram of this combined social mobilization index and left vote for the whole set of elections from 1880 to 1975. The only group of clearly outlying elections is now represented by the early British elections (the first four elections, 1900–1913). This social mobilization model results in an overall developmental association of .644 over 292 elections, corresponding to an explained variance of 41.4%. The national regression lines in the figure are now much more homogeneous in their slope, with the cited exceptions of Finland, the United Kingdom, and Ireland. The cases of Ireland and Finland are the main novelty of the social mobilization index compared with the various independent indicators of industrialization and urbanization discussed before: Ireland and the Finnish elections no longer appear deviant when set in the overall distribution of elections of Figure 3.5, although it remains true that their over-time variance in left electoral performance is not very closely associated with the over-time growth of social mobilization. In addition, their regression lines are flat compared with those of all the other countries. Nevertheless, their range of values is consistent with the general developmental model. Combining the various indicators of industrialization and urbanization does not entirely dissipate the originality of the Irish and Finnish development, but it does reduce it considerably.

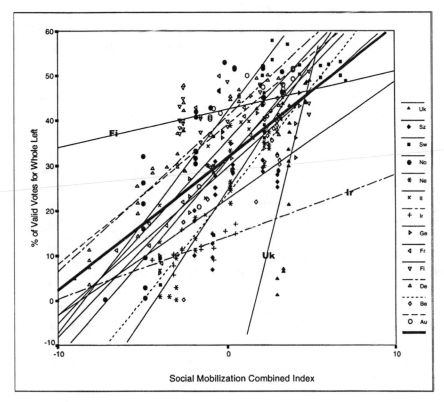

Figure 3.5. Social mobilization and the left vote.

A cumulative index allows for charting of elections and visual control of the structure of the data, but it does not correctly measure the multivariate association. Running a regression between the left vote and the five previously mentioned variables yields an *r* of .755 and an *Rsq* of .570. The variables have the following beta coefficient:

industrial workers as a percentage of the active population (working-class constituency)	.004
independents as a percentage of the active population ("bourgeois" constituency)	−.070
industrial workers as a percentage of all workers (working-class homogeneity)	.259
employers/occupied ratio in manufacturing (working-class concentration)	−.429
urbanization/industrialization coincidence and rates of growth	.490

In these data we find an additional confirmation that the weight of the constituency-size variables is less with respect to the other variables (actually, in a stepwise regression, the two constituency variables do not enter the equation).

Let me finally underline the key difference between this analysis and other similar attempts. The test of the model is not performed *within each country*. The latter strategy normally results in much higher associations (it yields an *Rsq* higher than .800 and in three cases higher than .900), because the number of cases is lower (sometimes simply too low) *and* the historical multicolinearity of social and political processes is maximum. Comparing within-country model performance allows an evaluation whereby the model works better, but it does not allow any identification of deviance from a general European model. Within-country data can be fitted very well by regression lines even if they are totally deviant with respect to the overall model association, or the reverse. In addition, within-country regression cannot incorporate comparative ranking variables, which are obviously constant for each individual country. The purpose of my attempt is to identity a European model and *then* apply it to individual countries to identify their deviation from such a model. For this reason, data are standardized across all the European elections. The consequent variance refers to a fit between social mobilization processes and the left electoral vote, which is established as if country boundaries did not exist. It is thus a truly comparative cross-country variance, according to the logic specified in the introductory methodological notes of Chapter 1.

CONCLUSION: THE LIMITS OF THE SOCIAL MOBILIZATION MODEL

The analysis carried out in this chapter is lengthy and detailed for two reasons. The first is that the relationship between social mobilization processes and left development is often taken implicitly as a matter of fact, and it therefore required thorough investigation. The second is that this relationship takes a variety of forms and versions according to different conceptions of the independent variable. I have tried to explore as many of these varieties as possible.

The discussion has shown that all factors related to industrialization and urbanization are characterized by well-defined temporal trends that are similar across the countries. The same is true of the electoral development of the left, as discussed in Chapter 2. Under these conditions, any analysis of the association among these historical processes is subject to the risk of interpreting a merely historical multicolinearity pattern as a causal link. I have tried to clarify the difference between the two in three main ways. The first way was to apply sequential logic, by reformulating the association between social transformations and left development in terms of relative timing – of earliness versus lateness. The second was through a reformulation of developmental associations to synchronic ones tested at different points in time. The third was a comparison of country levels and trends in socio-occupational transformations with European average trends and levels, with the goal of creating typologies of different paths to be then related to the global left size.

Some of the results are very clear. None of the hypotheses concerning the comparative *timing* of social mobilization can be sustained. The earliness of all possible dimensions of social mobilization is not related either to the earliness of left electoral mobilization or to its average strength over longer periods of time. By contrast, the *tempo* of social mobilization, that is, its rate of growth and its rapidity, have proved to be more significantly related to the patterns of left growth and to left levels. The interplay between the role of timing and tempo explains the more ambiguous results of the data concerning the social constituencies and their homogeneity and concentration. For these variables, a systematic discrepancy between over-time developmental associations and cross-country synchronic ones was reported. The former generally went in the expected direction: The left levels of electoral mobilization were positively associated with all indicators of industrial society, industrial working-class constituency and homogeneity, and urbanization level and were negatively associated with agricultural occupation, independent status groups, agricultural workers, and so on. Some of these variables proved to be more strongly associated than others (the internal homogeneity and concentration of the industrial working class more, for example, than its size).

However, the variables pertaining to urbanization, social constituency size, and homogeneity do not reproduce at the synchronic level their expected over-time association with electoral mobilization. The left tends to be weaker where industrialization levels, industrial working-class size and homogeneity, and urbanization levels are higher. Variables that are associated negatively with left mobilization at the over-time developmental level are associated positively at each point in time, whether a period or a decade. Thus, the agricultural component of the active population and the agricultural component of the working class, both negatively associated over time, tend to be positively associated by period and decade.

The structure of the data that produce this result is shown in Figure 3.6. Positive regression lines exist for each country, and they result in an

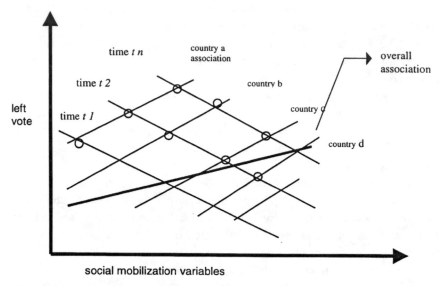

Figure 3.6. Structure of the social mobilization model data (for data that are associated positively over time with the left vote).

overall association that is, however, weakened at this level by the fact that each country enters the period under study with widely diverging starting points for social mobilization levels. However, this "sheaf" of parallel over-time associations for each country is downgraded in such a way as to produce, for each time slice, a negative association. These early differences tend to remain the same over time; they are not reduced. It is as if the early imprint was maintained later within the context of generally growing left movements. A contrasting but symmetrical argument holds for those factors that are negatively associated across time but positively associated across space with the electoral development of the left.

To a certain extent, the discrepancy between over-time and synchronic associations can be explained by the identification of a few country elections that clearly deviate. At different stages, Ireland, Finland, and the United Kingdom deviate drastically from the implicit hypotheses of the social mobilization model, although in different ways. Ireland is one of the least and latest developed industrial economies and has the weakest left mobilization in Europe, which is perfectly consistent with the hypotheses of the model. However, the undermobilization of the Irish left goes well beyond its socioeconomic comparative backwardness. Finland belongs to the same genus in socioeconomic terms but has levels of socialist mobilization that are the highest in Europe in the 1910s and 1920s. The United

Kingdom is the prototype of the early mature society, but its left lags behind that of almost all the other countries before the 1930s. These cases will therefore need special attention to see whether other factors may help to account for their abnormal position. However, their deviance alone is not enough to reconcile the developmental and synchronic associations.

The data structure in Figure 3.6 also helps to show that the different *cross-time, cross-country*, and *within-country* associations between social mobilization and the left vote are not contradictory. Within-country over-time associations are generally very strong, and yet the within-country studies of synchronic associations have produced quite divergent results. While the historical literature of individual countries generally shows that earlier and more intense socialist mobilization took place in the most industrialized and urbanized areas, ecological studies do not systematically confirm this thesis.[64] The coexistence of these different generalizations is possible: (1) at the overall level, left growth is associated with social mobilization growth, while at the synchronic cross-country level, the left is stronger in less industrialized countries; (2) within each country, left growth and social mobilization are associated, while the ecological association is absent or weak.

Therefore, the degree of satisfaction that can be attained with a social mobilization model depends on what one is attempting to explain. If the aim is to explain the general phenomenon of the growth of the left in Europe and within each country, the model performs satisfactorily. Patterns in occupational transformations typically associated with industrial society growth are unable to account for cross-country differences in left voting. The key question then becomes why these early differences in left electoral development existed at time 1 and why they remained stable in the following periods. Additional aspects of a different nature need to be included in the analysis to explain these early differences. General non-country-specific factors need to be found that explain early synchronic differences that later remained as permanent historical patterns.

That social mobilization models explain so few of the differences among the countries at each historical moment is astonishing.[65] If we

---

[64] For instance, Korpi's work about Sweden (1983: 120) shows that support for the left was not only stronger among industrial workers than among agricultural workers, but also that it was stronger in industrial and urban areas than in rural ones. Similarly, Urwin and Aarebrot (1981: 241–273) show that within Germany the left vote correlates positively with industrial employment and negatively with agricultural employment. In France and Italy, however, this was not the case, as shown by Dogan (1967: 135–136) and by Galli (1968: 240–242).

[65] A counterargument, brought to my attention by an early reviewer of this chapter, calls

consider the number of historical national accounts that explain late or early, stronger or weaker left electoral development by levels of industrialization and urbanization, or more generally by the more or less "modern" or "advanced" nature of the social context of one country with respect to others, we must conclude that too much weight is given to these processes. Industrialization and urbanization unquestionably constitute the global context of the *formation of working-class constituencies*. If, however, they fail to explain differences between countries, phases, or periods in the levels of *political mobilization of the class left*, it is exactly *what intervenes between working-class formation and political mobilization* that needs to be investigated.

Marx's *"de te fabula narratur"* in reference to the British social transformation in the eighteenth and nineteenth centuries[66] was an adequate description of the future developments of latecomers *as far as the trends in occupational status and working-class constituencies were concerned*. Their rapid assimilation into the occupational structure of early industrial nations and the global progressive homogenization of such structures was indeed the main structural trend in the century following its forecast.[67] However, the

into question the core hypothesis of the mobilization approach: that the growth of the left should be linked to the social transformation brought about by industrialization and urbanization. According to this argument, it would be wrong in principle to assume an association between left political mobilization and, for instance, the size of the industrial working-class constituency. Actually, left mobilization could have proceeded by progressively acquiring growing proportions of a given industrial working-class constituency without being linked to its size. It would therefore be unnecessary to expect a close association between the growth of the constituency and the growth of its mobilized section. The argument is that a close correspondence between the working class and the growth of the left does not need necessarily to manifest itself in associations between levels of the two processes. On close inspection, the argument seems to me self-defeating; it ends up denying what it seeks to affirm. If socialist electoral mobilization occurred by capturing growing sectors of the national working-class constituency in each country, and if one assumes that such a capturing capacity was independent of the size of the constituency, one must also conclude that this capacity depended on other, non-class-constituency-related factors. The argument implicitly states that industrialization and urbanization, and the class positions they created, were not the essential factors in explaining the increase in class consciousness and political action. This is, in essence, what I conclude, starting from the different premise that, *ceteris paribus*, the mobilization capacity of the socialists should depend on favorable social constituency conditions.

[66] ". . . [T]he industrially more developed country presents to the less developed country a picture of the latter's future"; Marx (1973: 16).

[67] Gerschenkron (1962) has criticized this conclusion in several essays, contending that it is only half-true and that it conceals differences between earlycomers and latecomers. According to his famous analysis, the latter will probably not follow the path of advanced countries, but rather will skip certain stages and substitute for missing prerequisites. His criticism, however, was mainly directed against the uniformity in the stages of development postulated by Rostow (1960): "traditional," "preconditions," takeoff,

earlycomers' *fabula* was not an adequate description of *political developments for latecomers* – quite the contrary. While the United Kingdom was the model for industrial transformation, it was not the model for political mobilization. Instead, latecomers proved more favorable contexts for left electoral development well before they even approached earlycomers' levels of social mobilization. The accelerated rhythm of their industrial development may well be a key to this divergent pattern. When the major push of social and occupational dislocation in the labor force determined by industrialization and urbanization took place in parallel with the organizational development of socialist parties and the granting of the vote, socialist parties were able to capitalize on such transformations. By contrast, when these major social and occupational dislocation effects took place before the socialist organization and before suffrage extension, the mobilization capacity of the socialist parties seems to have been less.

The rapidity of the economic transformation is causally associated with the level of left electoral development. This means that socialists were best able to capitalize on political support where and when the bulk of the industrial and urban transformation was taking place in parallel with the extension of the suffrage and the mobilization efforts it triggered. In this sense, the dynamism of social change was far more important than the level it reached. By contrast, in the case of the earlycomers, the organizational development of socialism and the process of suffrage extension occurred after the bulk of industrial transformation had already taken place. Here, socialism organized politically *after* the *fabula* had already been told. This possible line of interpretation is checked in Chapter 5. Before reaching this stage, however, I discuss the potential impact on a second general model relating to socialist mobilization capacity: the cultural homogeneity of the class environment in which this mobilization had to take place.

"drive to maturity," and "high mass consumption" and in a world perspective, where the latecomers are Third World countries. In a within-Europe perspective, the leveling off in production outputs per capita and in socio-occupational structure is undeniable.

CULTURAL HETEROGENEITY

DIMENSIONS OF CULTURAL HETEROGENEITY

Nation formation is the second macroprocess that sets the context for the development of working-class movements. In particular, the point of interest here is national cultural standardization. Although the nineteenth-century socialist movements were decisively characterized by their international character, that is, they were "anational" when not deliberately "antinational," their successive history showed plenty of evidence of their actually being national movements that were part of and an expression of the formation of a national culture and identity. Where the formation of a relatively homogeneous cultural national context was lacking or weak, working-class movements experienced profound problems of organizational consolidation and spread of appeal. The heterogeneity of the class cultural environment will be regarded in this chapter as a crucial element for the successful establishment and consolidation of a working-class movement and of a class left electoral mobilization.

A class and social group analysis of the political mobilization process rests on a model that links the formation of social position, the development of group solidarity, and uniformity in group political action. Socialist thinkers of the second half of the nineteenth century clearly regarded any social (and political) identities that were not rooted in the social position related to the productive process as supra structural factors amenable to false consciousness. They therefore assumed that the role of such identities was deemed to disappear with time. This position is echoed in recent works that implicitly or explicitly assume that the pro-left party and organizational behavior of workers is normal and that only deviation from this pattern needs to be accounted for. In this sense, other political identities are the result of the failure of the class identity.

This interpretive picture inverts the order of the factors. Preindustrial cleavages created solidarity feelings and identities along several cultural as well as functional lines of conflict well before the class cleavage could acquire sufficient momentum, thanks to the processes of industrialization and concentration in urban environments. Thus, the class cleavage was the outsider striving to establish its domain within a space that was already occupied by strong and consolidated social identities. The distribution and relationships between such preindustrial group identities limited the space for maneuver and the mobilization potential of the class appeal rather than doing the opposite. Obviously, when the social dislocation associated with accelerated processes of social and geographical mobility related to urbanization and industrialization occurred, preindustrial social identities were broken down in certain social milieus, but in no way were they simply erased. The class cleavage did not, therefore, start to recruit and mobilize its potential constituency in a vacuum of solidarity and identity. Therefore, the links postulated by the social-mobilization model between working-class formation and working-class mobilization (via collective identity) should be regarded as more or less valid according to the conditions of contextual cultural homogeneity. "Class in a Culturally Homogeneous Environment"[1] was not the same thing as class in a culturally heterogeneous context.

In this chapter, I analyze those characteristics that pertain to the cultural homogeneity of any given society. Cultural homogeneity is in many ways an essential ingredient for the spread of a nationwide appeal to economic and functional cross-local conflict. My aim is to see to what extent the consideration of these essential preindustrial bases for class mobilization improves the working of the social mobilization model, specifying the best conditions of its application and explaining deviance from it. Cultural heterogeneity (or homogeneity) can be conceptualized along horizontal and vertical dimensions. In the horizontal dimension, we can include those elements of cultural nonhomogeneity that separate segments of the society characterized by clear religious, ethnic, linguistic, or other types of cultural/identity standards and differences. Although to different degrees, each segment is composed of both masses and elites groups.

---

[1] This is the specification made by Schumpeter (1951) in the title of his essay about social classes: *Social Classes in an Ethnically Homogeneous Environment*.

On the vertical dimension, cultural homogeneity refers to the possibility for community development in Toennies's original meaning of the term. The development within a given territory, national in this case, of the possibility for cross-area communication and organization requires the development of links between masses and elites that can be available only under certain conditions made possible by the spread of education, linguistic standardization, and mass media communication development. The spread of ideas, ideologies, organizational forms, and collective cross-cultural identities requires, even in this case, that we identify thresholds above which conditions are equalized and below which basic preconditions are lacking. The formation of the nation, of a national community able to exchange not only goods but also symbols with a shared meaning, seems to be just such a necessary precondition for the development of a class type of cleavage. The spread of both formal education and mediated communication should be considered here (Figure 4.1).

The process of homogenization of religious practices obviously goes back to the dynastic confrontations and religious wars of the sixteenth and early seventeenth centuries. Language as a symbol of national identity became more important, if not dominant, during the period of nationalism following the Napoleonic wars and the expectations they left behind. Dominant versus subject linguistic standards have always existed, but they became dominant elements of identity and of political mobilization only in this relatively recent phase. Finally, the leveling of cultural stratification in terms of cognitive capacities is a third type of process that was accelerated in the nineteenth century in most countries but that can also be traced back to the sixteenth century in the Reformation territories. My goal in this context is not to recall these processes and the differentiated cultural map of Europe they produced.[2] It is rather to consider these processes in terms of their end result – as they were at the moment of the early political mobilization of the class cleavage and in its first decades of development. They will be considered as historical givens that are likely to determine the extent to which the social transformations considered in the previous chapters were more or less likely to result in straight patterns of the political mobilization of the lower classes.

The extent to which cultural standardization within a national territory was extensively achieved or, rather, considerable levels of cultural segmentation and/or cognitive inequalities were left within this territory, influenced the chances of the political mobilization of the left. Why should

---

[2] On this point, see Rokkan and Urwin (1983) and Rokkan, Urwin, Aarobrot, Malaba, and Sande (1987).

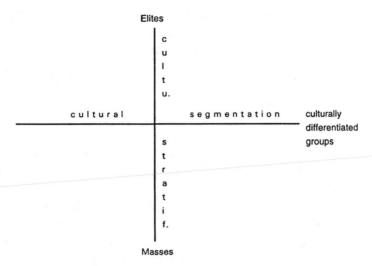

Figure 4.1. Cultural heterogeneity dimensions.

a less homogeneous environment have a negative effect on class mobilization? What are the intermediate steps that link these two macroprocesses?
For linguistic and religious segmentation, the hypothesis is simply that of
the social distance created by group membership. The stronger the boundaries of preexisting group membership, the more difficult the superimposition of new group loyalties. It is reasonable to expect that in contexts
characterized historically by differentiated and often opposing (when not
directly conflicting) religious or linguistic/ethnic group membership, the
social distance (boundary) between these groups was higher than in countries that were largely homogeneous from the same points of view.
Therefore, the superimposition of a new cross-religious or cross-linguistic
group identity could prove more difficult, even in the presence of a rapid
sociostructural transformation of the individuals concerned. With regard
to cognitive stratification, it seems plausible to argue that both organizational recruitment and electoral support in underprivileged groups was
enhanced by the possession or acquisition of basic cognitive instruments.
Without them, not only it is likely that a break with traditional social ties
and social elites was more difficult to achieve, but also that propaganda
and recruitment efforts had to be based almost exclusively on enormous
human resource–intensive organizational efforts. It is not necessary to
postulate that the greater the cognitive competence, the easier the understanding by the people of their "true" interest – even assuming that the
true interest of the lower classes was to vote for the socialists. It is sufficient
to assume that cognitive capacities make it easier for a new and outside

political actor to spread its political message without being obliged to resort to direct, face-to-face intense organizational efforts.

I therefore consider cultural homogeneity as indicated by three variables: (1) the extent of the religious homogeneity of the population, in the sense of adherence to a single religious standard; (2) the extent of linguistic homogeneity of the population, to be understood as adherence to a single common linguistic standard; and (3) the extent of equalization of basic cognitive capacities, such as those of writing and reading. Together, these factors should offer a general picture of the extent of the homogeneity of the social environment in which working-class parties organized their political and electoral activities. I would like to emphasize that the variable taken into consideration here is not religious or linguistic mobilization, that is, the existence, nature, and pervasiveness of political movements built around linguistic or religious identities. I consider cultural heterogeneity in strictly demographic terms, making no reference to political mobilization. In a later chapter, I come back to the question of the extent and the character of political mobilization along different lines, including linguistic and denominational ones. The relevance of this distinction will become clear when we discuss the extent of cultural heterogeneity of different European countries in the next section.

In this chapter, I proceed as in the previous one. First I deal with each individual factor, trying to identify whether it has an impact of its own. I then combine several factors to evaluate the extent of their combined effect, as well as to see if they are independent or autocorrelated. Finally, I discuss a general model of left development as it emerges on the basis of the cultural heterogeneity variable and then relate this model to the social mobilization model discussed previously.

CULTURAL SEGMENTATION

The data on the linguistic and religious composition of the populations of Western European countries are derived from the census.[3] For both religious and linguistic fragmentation, I have decided to consider only the major religious and ethnolinguistic groups in order to avoid inflating fragmentation when many very small cultural minorities are present. This is particularly important because, in order to obtain a single value for linguistic and religious heterogeneity in each decade since the 1880s, I

---

[3] As reported by Flora, Alber, Eichenberg, Kohl, Kraus, Pfenning, and Seebohm (1987: 55–85).

have resorted to the index of fractionalization, which is very sensitive to the number of groups as well as to their respective size.[4] The inclusion of many very small minorities would increase the index considerably, while in reality, the point of interest here is the major cultural divisions. In Table 4.1 the score of the religious and linguistic fractionalization by country and decade is reported. In a few cases, census data were missing for a decade, and I have reported the interpolated value.

Countries tend to divide into two distinct groups. First, there are the clear-cut cases of cultural heterogeneity of Germany, the Netherlands, and Switzerland for religion and Belgium and Switzerland for language; second, there are all the others. Switzerland is the only case of pronounced cultural heterogeneity on both fronts. A few intermediate-level cases also merit further comment. The Finnish case is in an intermediate position, thanks to the persistent presence of a Swedish-speaking minority. Relatively high levels of linguistic fragmentation are also typical of Ireland and the United Kingdom. In these two cases, a common and strong linguistic standard has been observed with regard to the English language for a long time. The data on linguistic heterogeneity, resulting from questions concerning the language that is regarded as the participant's native tongue, may reflect an ideological orientation toward stressing personal identity more than the existence of clearly differentiated linguistic subcommunities. This is evident when we look at the Irish data, where the linguistic heterogeneity that results from the definition of Gaelic as the first language increases slightly over the period from the 1950s to the 1970s. This is less likely to be the result of a renaissance of Gaelic than of a new desire to identify culturally via such a choice.

Another case worth commenting on is the great linguistic homogeneity attributed to Italy and France. Italy is characterized by a large number of minority linguistic groups of small and sometimes minute size. Their inclusion would make for a disproportionately high index of fragmenta-

---

[4] This index is well known. Its formula is the following:

$$F = 1 - \left(\sum_{i=1}^{n} T_i^2 \right)$$

where T_i is each religious or linguistic group's decimal share of the total population. See Rae (1971: 55–58) for a presentation of the index and Pedersen (1980: 387–403) for a critical analysis of its performance. Pedersen rightly underlines the inadequacy of the index to capture the dynamic of over-time changes as it responds to changes in both the number and strength of groups without being able to discriminate between them. This weakness of the index does not concern us in this case. Cultural heterogeneity is fairly stable over time, and I therefore do not want to concentrate attention on over-time variation.

Table 4.1. *Religious and linguistic heterogeneity in Western European countries*

a)   religious heterogeneity

	1880	1890	1900	1910	1920	1930	1940	1950	1960	1970
Austria	.06	.06	.06	.06	18	.18	.18	.20	.20	.20
Belgium	.06	.06	.06	.06	.06	.06	.06	.06	.06	.06
Denmark	.02	.02	.03	.03	.04	.06	.06	.06	.06	.06
Finland	.	.	.	.04	.04	.07	.07	.10	.10	.10
France	.10	.10	.10	.10	.10	.10	.10	.10	.10	.10
Germany	.48	.48	.48	.48	.48	.50	.52	.54	.54	.58
Ireland	.	.	.	.	.14	.11	.11	.11	.12	.12
Italy	.02	.02	.02	.02	.02	.02	.02	.02	.02	.02
Netherlands.	.	.63	.67	.68	.69	.72	.72	.72	.71	.72
Norway	.	.03	.04	.05	.05	.05	.07	.07	.07	.07
Sweden	.03	.05	.05	.09	.08	.06	.09	.09	.09	.09
Switzerland	.	.49	.49	.49	.49	.49	.49	.49	.50	.52
Un. Kingdom	.	.18	.18	.18	.18	.18	.18	.18	.18	.18

b)   linguistic heterogeneity

	1880	1890	1900	1910	1920	1930	1940	1950	1960	1970
Austria	.	.	.	.	.05	.05	.05	.05	.05	.05
Belgium	.61	.61	.65	.65	.65	.68	.68	.68	.68	.68
Denmark	.00	.00	.00	.00	.00	.00	.00	.00	.00	.00
Finland	.	.	.	.21	.21	.18	.18	.18	.15	.13
France	.00	.00	.00	.00	.00	.00	.00	.00	.00	.00
Germany	.15	.15	.15	.15	.14	.14	.14	.00	.00	.00
Ireland	.	.	.	.	.31	.36	.33	.33	.40	.41
Italy	.00	.00	.00	.00	.00	.00	.00	.00	.00	.00
Netherlands	.00	.00	.00	.00	.00	.00	.00	.00	.00	.00
Norway	.00	.00	.00	.00	.00	.00	.00	.00	.00	.00
Sweden	.00	.00	.00	.00	.00	.00	.00	.00	.00	.00
Switzerland	.	.44	.46	.47	.45	.45	.45	.44	.47	.53
Un. Kingdom	.32	.32	.32	.32	.32	.32	.32	.32	.32	.32

tion. A similar picture can be drawn for the French linguistic border minorities, where the Corsican case clearly throws the values of high linguistic homogeneity into some doubt. In this case, however, not much can be done to improve the data, given the fact that Corsica was not given the status of a language or identified separately in census data. On the whole, it is likely that France and Italy[5] should be regarded as far less homogeneous from the linguistic point of view than they actually are according to the figures in Table 4.1.

Religious heterogeneity figures raise fewer problems of reliability and comparability. They do, however, present a problem that is common to all

[5] For all countries, but with particular reference to France and Italy, I should also mention the key question of how language is defined in contrast to dialect. I am unable, however, to take into consideration an alternative distribution of linguistic groups according to any different definition of languages.

countries: in historical statistics, no specific place is left for those who profess to have no creed.[6] In this context, however, this is not a problem that needs to be taken into account. As specified earlier, I am not dealing with the extent or strength of a religious cleavage, which would necessarily require reference to true believers versus nonbelievers. Given that my intention is simply to check whether religious homogeneity versus heterogeneity plays a role in left mobilization, the intensity of the engagement is unimportant, and attention must be centered on the existence of multiple religious choices and groups versus the lack of this pluralism. On the whole, while linguistic heterogeneity – in part as a result of the inadequacy of the data – tends to dichotomize the group of countries between those that are heterogeneous and those that are not, religious heterogeneity is more evenly distributed. It should also be noted, finally, that none of the dimensions of heterogeneity show any temporal trend: They are features that characterize a polity throughout the whole period under examination. Consequently, they will be unable to explain any within-country variation over time, and they should be most important in discriminating cross-country variation. Moreover, no problem of historical multicolinearity arises with left electoral development.

The first simple way of approaching the problem of the influence of religious and linguistic heterogeneity on left political mobilization is to look at the mean level of left support through levels of cultural heterogeneity. To this end, in Table 4.2 I have divided the variance in religious and linguistic fragmentation into low, medium, and high, and I have reported the corresponding mean levels of electoral support for the left in these groups. In order to avoid too skewed a distribution of cases, given the very different distribution of values for the two variables, I have chosen slightly different thresholds, defining as low religious fragmentation those cases that show levels between 0 and .10, medium for those between .10 and .50, and high for those over .50. For linguistic heterogeneity, the corresponding thresholds are 0–0.5, 0.5–0.40, and greater than 0.40 (see the values in Table 4.1).

The figures in Table 4.2 point to a very clear impact of both dimensions of cultural heterogeneity on the mean electoral strength of the left. On average, in both cases there is a difference of about 7 to 8 percentage points between the electoral strength of the left in religious or linguistic homogeneous contexts and those in highly heterogeneous ones. Such a difference represents one quarter of the overall mean of the left vote over

---

[6] Figures on religious denomination, including "no creed," are reported in Taylor and Hudson (1972: 271–274). However, these data have no historical depth.

Table 4.2. *Mean left electoral support by levels of religious and linguistic fragmentation*

	mean left vote by level of religious fragmentation	mean left vote by level of linguistic fragmentation
low	35.6 (173)	34.4 (166)
medium	28.3 (88)	31.7 (79)
high	27.8 (31)	27.6 (47)
all elections	32.6 (292)	32.6 (292)

Note: Number of elections given in parentheses.

the whole set of about 300 elections between roughly 1890 and 1970. In both cases, the medium levels of religious and linguistic heterogeneity produce levels of left electoral strength that fall into the middle of cases of high or low heterogeneity, pointing to the existence of a rather linear effect. The level of cultural heterogeneity of the social environment unquestionably reduces the potential for electoral mobilization of the left.

The next step is to consider the possible interaction effect between these two variables. In reality, both variables could tap the same phenomenon, to the extent that religious and ethno/linguistic heterogeneity coincide. Alternatively, they could be independent factors that cancel each other. Finally, they could both be independent of each other and have a reinforcing effect. The interaction effect can be appreciated by simply dividing our set of elections into four types: (1) those that occur in environments that are both religiously and linguistically heterogeneous and should constitute the most difficult cultural environment for the left; (2) those that occur in both religiously and linguistically homogeneous environments, setting the best conditions for left development; and (3) and (4) those that take place in a split environment, homogeneous with regard to language and religion or the reverse, and that should evidence intermediate levels of left electoral support. In Table 4.3 the mean left vote in these four contexts is reported.

The interaction between the two forms of heterogeneity seems to be virtually uniform and cumulative. Within each category of linguistic cultural heterogeneity, the left vote increases with the homogeneity of the religious context. Similarly, for each category of religious heterogeneity,

Table 4.3. *Mean left vote by types of cultural fragmentation*

religious heterogeneity	linguistic heterogeneity	
	high 26.3 (81)	low 35.0 (211)
high 26.9 (70)	23.8 (24)	28.6 (46)
low 34.3 (222)	27.3 (57)	36.8 (165)

Note: Number of elections given in parentheses.

the left vote increases with the homogeneity of the linguistic context. Thirteen percentage points separate the set of elections taking place in an environment that is both religiously and linguistically heterogeneous (basically, this cell corresponds to the only case of cumulative heterogeneity, that of Switzerland) from those taking place in environments that are homogeneous on both dimensions. This evidence stresses the fact that religious and linguistic heterogeneity has an individual independent effect on left mobilization and that these independent effects can be treated as cumulative with respect to the left vote.[7]

Let us now look at the relationship between cultural heterogeneity and the left vote over time as well as at different points in time. In Table 4.4 Pearson's correlations between the left vote and the index of ethnolinguistic

[7] This analysis by type of social environment has also been performed using the three-category operationalisation of Table 4.2: low, mid and high. Due to the already discussed skewed distribution of cases, this yields a nine-cells typology where, unfortunately, some cells have too low or even null frequencies. However, the results are the same as those discussed with a four-cell scheme if one aggregates the nine cells into three groups: those in the upper right corner with values of high-high, high-mid, and mid-high religious and linguistic heterogeneity; those in the bottom left corner with low-low, low-mid, and mid-low values; and those on the diagonal corresponding to high-low, low-high, or mid-mid values for religious and linguistic heterogeneity. The results are the following:

homogeneous	36.5%	(165)
mixed (diagonal)	28.1%	(101)
heterogeneous	23.2%	(26)

and religious heterogeneity are reported for the whole set of elections, as well as for the usual temporally defined subsets. In addition, the same correlations are computed for a combined index that is the result of the simple sum of the two. The figures in the table add a few other elements. First, all correlations are homogeneously negative throughout the whole period, in each subperiod and for each decade. The only exceptions can be found in the very first phase, and particularly in the 1890s, when positive associations are observable. There can be little doubt, therefore, about the negative impact and very little need to search for period effects. The positive associations of the early decades are understandable if one remembers that cultural heterogeneity does not change over time but remains stable. In the early phases, socialist mobilization was of necessity extremely weak, irrespective of the levels of cultural heterogeneity that were already established. From this derives the lack of association or even the possibility of positive associations.

The second point to be underlined, and that follows from the first one, is that the associations between linguistic and religious heterogeneity indices and the left vote are stronger in each period and decade than generally over time: $-.175$ and $-.187$, respectively, for linguistic and religious heterogeneity are not impressive negative associations, and they are, on the whole, lower than those that can be obtained in each phase or decade. This shows that *cultural-heterogeneity variables discriminate across countries when the temporal variance of the left is somehow controlled, but they are far less important when this temporal variance exists, that is, in the overall bulk of a century's elections.*

The third point worth mentioning is that the negative association of ethnolinguistic fragmentation increases remarkably over time, from the decades around the end of the nineteenth century to those after World War II. In contrast, the negative association of religious heterogeneity remains relatively stable throughout the twentieth century. Cultural heterogeneity is not so negatively associated with left size at the beginning, but as time passes it increasingly becomes a structural barrier to the development of the left. It is thus a constraint that grows in importance after the first beginning phase and that sets definite boundaries on left electoral development.

The negative association of linguistic heterogeneity increases more than that of religious heterogeneity and appears, in the final analysis, to be far more important. If we look at the associations concerning the left vote and the combined index of religious plus linguistic heterogeneity, it is clear that up to the 1920s it is religion that produces negative associations, while from the 1930s on, it is language that plays the more important

Table 4.4. *Religious and linguistic heterogeneity and left vote (Pearson's correlation)*

	ethnolinguistic heterogeneity	religious heterogeneity	ethnolinguistic + religious heterogeneity
all elections	-.175 (292)	-.187	-.248
1880-1917	.040 (80)	-.177	-.096
1918-1944	-.269 (92)	-.269	-.368
1945-1965	-.402 (79)	-.312	-.530
1965-1975	-.713 (41)	-.317	-.724
1890	.115 (19)	.209	.214
1900	.113 (31)	-.142	-.035
1910	-.146 (36)	-.286	-.274
1920	-.095 (41)	-.402	-.348
1930	-.375 (33)	-.227	-.432
1940	-.466 (28)	-.278	-.527
1950	-.347 (38)	-.314	-.481
1960	-.586 (34)	-.315	-.666
1970	-.737 (27)	-.269	-.712

Note: Number of elections given in parentheses.

role. We may have a hint here of the historical sequence of identity mobilization, with religious identity becoming politically important from the beginning of the century and ethnolinguistic (and regional) identity becoming more so after World War II. However, this refers to a feature that belongs to the political mobilization of persons with different identities, and this I have decided to leave aside in this context, where only basic social homogeneity is evaluated. The combined index of the third column of Table 4.4 confirms the additive nature of the interaction that has already been argued: In most cases, it yields higher negative associations than either of the two.

On the whole, these data highlight a pattern this is the opposite of that resulting from the social mobilization analysis. While social mobilization pointed to a long-term positive impact on the left vote over time, but tended to disappear as a cross-country discriminating factor when time was parametrized in different periods and decades, cultural heterogeneity factors worked the opposite way, adding less to the explanation of the temporal development of the left than to the cross-country differences at each given moment in time. This suggests that the combination of these two models may prove a valid way of reducing unexplained variance on both the temporal and spatial dimensions. From a developmental point of view, while social mobilization is a factor of over-time growth, cultural heterogeneity is a factor of over-time containment.

COGNITIVE STRATIFICATION

The third factor to be considered as an indicator of cultural homogeneity/ heterogeneity is the cognitive stratification of a country's population. While cultural segmentation tends to split a society into communities, within which both elites and masses are present, cognitive capacities define strata endowed with different capacities for communication and tend to separate groups along an elite-versus-masses dimension. Cognitive mobilization is the long-term process by which such capacities are equalized through the spread of individual skills, as well as the spread of new means of communication. It involves several features. In political development schemes and theories, it is associated with the idea of rising expectations and therefore of growing demands on the political system. However, cognitive mobilization is also a resource for the system, a "capability" at its disposal.[8] From the point of view of this research, the key aspect is the relationship between participation and the flows of political messages that reach the individual citizen. Generally speaking, the spread of cognitive capacities results in a growing number of individuals who can be reached by a wider variety of sources of political messages, through a larger number of channels of communication, and with potentially longer exposure to them. These changes in sources, channels, and exposition to political messages have progressively transformed the nature of political propaganda. In a context in which the mass media are absent or where their impact is profoundly reduced by the lack of decoding capacities in the public, political propaganda efforts and incentives to activate participation are limited to nonmediated exchanges, that is, direct contact and experience. This requires a form of political organization that is, by necessity, characterized by human capital-intensive techniques.

The spread of decoding capacities has marked the beginning of a long-term process of "privatization" of political information and propaganda,

---

[8] Deutsch (1961) and Coleman (1965b).

leading to a progressive reduction of human capital in the face of a growing capital-intensive technique based on mass media messages. This process reached such an advanced stage in the last quarter of the twentieth century that it has profoundly modified the structural characteristics of political parties. In this context, I am interested in the initial steps of this process. For the early mobilization of the European left, the successive waves of cognitive mobilization of European citizens are probably less important than the first ones, identified with the spread of reading and writing. So, the focus of this section is not the general educational level of a population, but rather the basic preconditions for becoming potential objects of mediated written political messages, as well as the minimum threshold capacity for their interpretation. General education can, and has been considered, as a predominantly conservative institution, transmitting and fostering traditional values and attitudes. At the same time, however, at least minimum levels of education have been regarded as important in fostering socialist propaganda and mobilization capacities, promoting the development of the collective consciousness that is essential to class action and contributing to the creation of individual cultural resources capable of counteracting traditional forces and values in the social environment.

It is difficult to ascertain literacy levels understood as the capacity to read and write. This is in part a result of the fact that the means of ascertaining such skills have been complex and nonuniform through time and space. At the level of census statistics, the most reliable data concern school enrollment in different levels of educational institutions. However, they present some major problems. First of all, they indicate levels of presumed literacy among age groups that are still far from the age of potential political participation, and they say very little about the literacy capacities of their families. Moreover, in addition to representing the cognitive skills of the future adult population, enrollment statistics present a second problem — this time technical. Computing the percentage of people of a given educational level implies the choice of a reference age group that is not necessarily homogeneous across countries. Changes in the length of primary education, for instance, make this type of percentage statistic unreliable for cross-country comparisons, even global ones.

There have been attempts to synthesize and standardize as much as possible the statistics concerning the enrollment of pupils in primary schools as percentages of the 5- to 14-year age group.[9] For the late nineteenth and early twentieth centuries, these statistics may still be able to give a comparative estimate of the extent of primary education in

---

[9] See Flora, Alber, Eichenberg, Kohl, Kraus, Pfenning, and Seebohm (1987: 553–633).

different countries, but as soon as postprimary education in the 11–14 age group develops across European countries, higher levels of education are transformed into declining levels of the index. As many pupils between 11 and 14 go to postprimary school, the percentage of pupils in primary school over the 6–14 age group may decline.[10] Moreover, literacy abilities are by no means linked to school attendance, particularly in Protestant countries.

Alternative indirect indicators of literacy are provided by special groups statistics, such as those reported by Mitchell and taken from marriage registers (which refer to the ability to sign marriage contacts) or statistics based on military recruitment tests of literacy.[11] However, these statistics also refer to special groups rather than to the total population, and, in addition, they are also not systematically available across the thirteen European countries. Therefore, I have decided to rely on the collection of estimates made for literacy levels among global populations by Flora in his work devoted to literacy and urbanization.[12] Such estimates are reported in Table 4.5.

These estimates offer a number of important points that directly concern the question of potential class mobilization. First, with the exception of the high and persisting levels of illiteracy in Italy, which clearly set it apart from the northern and continental model in this field, the bulk of the literacy process was already accomplished in the European countries at

[10] Following is the percentage of pupils enrolled in primary education among the 6–14 age group drawn from the previously mentioned source:

	Au	Be	De	Fi	Fr	Ge	Ir	It	Ne	No	Sw	Sz	Uk
1880	56	.	.	.	82	75	.	35	.	.	72	.	.
1890	63	28	60	.	83	75	.	36	66	65	75	76	56
1900	67	59	60	.	86	73	.	37	70	67	69	72	75
1910	70	62	68	26	76	70	.	43	71	69	68	70	79
1920	74	70	65	36	68	67	83	50	71	69	60	72	79
1930	77	72	67	55	80	75	89	58	74	72	62	70	81
1940	79	70	65	61	79	76	88	43	68	68	63	70	74
1950	76	68	61	62	72	80	87	59	65	67	59	66	67
1960	73	66	71	59	64	69	88	53	62	69	62	69	61
1970	74	65	67	50	54	68	82	56	61	62	59	65	66

[11] See Mitchell (1975).
[12] Flora (1973: 245).

Table 4.5. *Illiteracy rate (% unable to write and to read)*

	1870	1890	1910	1930	1950	1960
Au*	<30	10-15	3-8	1-5	1-2	1-2
Be	35-40	26	13.4	5.9	3.4	1.2
De	5-12	1-8	1-5	1-2	1-2	1-2
Fi	<25	10-15	1.1	1.0	1-2	1-2
Fr	31	18-22	11.9	5.3	3.4	
Ge**	8-13	1-8	1-5	1-2	1-2	1-2
Ir***	25.8	10.1	1.1	3-8	1-2	1-2
It	69	54-56	39.3	23.1	14.5	5-10
Ne	20-25	15-20	5-10	1-5	1-2	1-2
No	5-15	5-10	1-5	1-5	1-2	1-2
Sw	5-10	1-5	1-2	0.1	1-2	1-2
Sz	7-12	1-5	1-2	1-2	1-2	1-2
En. & Wa.	25-30	10-15	7-12	1.5	1-5	1-2
Scotland	15-20	7-12	1-5	1-5	1-2	1-2

*Austria: territory of the Republic
**1950–1960 GDR and GFR rates are the same
***Ireland to 1910; Eire since 1920

the beginning of the period considered here, that is, in the 1890s. This means that in Europe the long-term development of literacy preceded the processes of urbanization and industrialization.[13] In this sense, the basic cognitive mobilization of European citizens can be said to be part of the preceding process of nation building rather than that which followed the Industrial Revolution. This is due to the fact that, in contrast to the processes of urbanization and industrialization, literacy development could be fostered more easily by the nation-state if it was deliberately pursued through cultural agencies and/or by state bureaucracy.

The second important element in the distribution of Table 4.5 is that, given its older origins, the process of basic literacy development tended to be completed by the 1920s. In 1930, with the exception of Italy, almost all the other cases present estimates that are fairly similar. By that date, no trend is present in the data and no significant cross-country differences can be seen. This means that literacy and illiteracy is a dimension that is

[13] The key point in Flora's article (1973: 227) is that literacy development preceded urbanization in Europe, contrary to what has been postulated by modernization theory sequences. The experience of other parts of the world is reversed: Urbanization predates literacy development.

important, if it is important, only for the first part of the period considered here, that is, for the very early mobilization phase up to roughly World War I.

The most obvious characteristic of these data is the sharp difference in literacy levels between Protestant and Catholic countries. The fit is not perfect, but the countries that show earlier and higher levels of literacy are those of Scandinavia, followed by Switzerland and Germany and, very close behind them, Finland. At the other extreme – apart from the already-mentioned Italian case – France, Austria, and Belgium show the highest levels of illiteracy. There are, however, two major exceptions. The levels of illiteracy in England, Wales, and Scotland are far higher than those of the other Protestant countries between 1870 and 1900 and are not much different from those of the Catholic ones. Ireland, although still character-ized by relatively high levels of illiteracy in 1870 (25.8%), rapidly recu-perates: By 1910, its estimates of the illiterate population are among the lowest in Europe. All in all, however, the difference between predomi-nantly Protestant or religiously mixed countries, on the one hand, and homogeneously Catholic ones, on the other, is quite impressive. The stan-dard interpretation takes the lead from the classic theses of Max Weber about Protestantism as the Christian religion with the strongest national language written tradition and, therefore, with the strongest incentive to literacy development among believers and the national population at large. This is confirmed both by the early introduction in Protestant countries of compulsory national primary education and by the more informal role played by Protestant churches in giving incentives to the spread of reading and writing capacities, a feature that is absent in Catholic countries.

Thus, for instance, compulsory-education schemes were introduced in Prussia as early as 1763; in Denmark, as early as 1814 (for children up to seven years of age but for only three days each week; in 1849, this was increased to six days each week); in Norway, between 1848 and 1889. In Sweden, from 1842 to 1848, the parliament introduced an elementary school system lasting for six years for all children. Parishes were responsible for starting and financing elementary schools to teach writing, reading, and arithmetic. However, even before this time, the exigencies of teaching Luther's catechism pushed parishes to enforce educational requirements for marriage and other social occasions. In Finland, institutional thresholds of this type cannot be identified, because the country was not independent until the twentieth century, but it has been reported that in the first 100 years after the Reformation, the Lutheran Church made the ability to read a prerequisite for enjoying certain civil rights, as well as for marriage and communion. Similar forms of incentives are to be found in the history of

Sweden, Norway, Denmark, and even Scotland. Teachers were often recruited from the local community; they were soon to become important local cultural and political figures, often acting as counterweights to the Lutheran national state church, as well as guides and leaders of the popular movements that spread throughout the Scandinavian countries, particularly Norway and Sweden. By 1870, most young workers in these countries were able to write and read.[14] This was a crucial factor for development of the socialist press, as well as for the propaganda published and disseminated by the socialists.

To this religious factor, Flora has added two other hypotheses in order to interpret basic differences in literacy rates: the existence of communal self-government as a further incentive to literacy development and the international status and geopolitical position of the country. In the latter point, he stresses the need for countries at the center of the European system of interstate relationships, concerned with self-defense and self-assertion, to develop efficient bureaucratic machines (both military and civil). This helps to explain the differences between southern peripheral Catholic countries – such as Italy before national unity, Spain and Portugal – and the northern Catholic countries: France, Austria, Belgium, and Ireland. For Ireland, in particular, the accelerated literacy development from the end of the nineteenth century can be interpreted as part of the struggle for national independence and cultural self-expression: "In the nineteenth century, compulsory education became a status symbol of national independence."[15]

The interpretations of the different cross-country levels of literacy need not concern us here except for one reason: They show that literacy development is the product of cultural/bureaucratic incentives and needs that are independent of the development of urbanization and industrialization. Precisely for this reason, around 1910 Finland and Ireland were the most literate countries of Europe while remaining among the least urbanized and certainly the least industrially developed. With the exception of Switzerland, none of the other earlycomers to industrialization and urbanization were characterized by particularly high rates of literacy either. Therefore, even in this case there are no problems of a correlation with social mobilization variables.

To investigate the link between left electoral levels and literacy development it is necessary to interpolate the estimates reported in Table 4.5 for the decades 1880, 1900, 1920, 1940, and 1970 to ensure a complete

---

[14] For this information see Cipolla (1969) and Harvey (1989).
[15] Flora (1973: 230), drawing from MacElligot (1966).

Table 4.6. *Illiteracy and left electoral mobilization*

whole period	-.399 (293)
before 1918	-.308 (81)
interwar	-.194 (92)
1945-1965	.022 (79)
1966-1975	.158 (41)
1890	-.224 (20)
1900	-.134 (31)
1910	-.248 (36)
1920	-.242 (41)
1930	-.496 (33)
1940	.110 (28)
1950	.016 (38)
1960	.115 (34)
1970	.154 (27)

Note: Number of elections given in parentheses.

series of decade values. This is done by taking the mean value between the two. Whenever an estimate was indicated by a range, I have taken the mean value of the range. British decade data have been computed, considering English and Welsh as well as Scottish percentages and computing them in a single percentage for Great Britain that takes into account the relative proportion of each population. With these data modifications, it was possible to calculate the correlation levels between illiteracy and left vote levels in the set of our elections (or decades); the results are reported in Table 4.6.

Over the 293 elections for which data are available, the association reaches −.399, the highest level encountered so far for the whole period. The significance of this association should be underlined because the illiteracy data — like those on cultural segmentation — are not characterized by a strong or clear long-term trend. As stated earlier, any trend disappears around the 1930s. This element became evident when we look at the data by period. The negative association diminishes progressively, disappearing after World War II, when rates of literacy remain virtually unchanged in the European countries. At the same time, the high negative correlation in the 1880–1917 period is of great importance in the context of this discussion. Such a correlation goes in the same direction as the overall developmental one; that is, in each historical period, particularly the first one, the pattern is the same: Higher levels of left electoral support are associated with higher levels of literacy. This is clearly confirmed by the correlation measures at the decade level. In each decade, higher literacy tends to manifest a stronger left.

Illiteracy levels – in contrast to the other two cultural heterogeneity variables, which tended to grow in importance over time – are important factors that help to discriminate among countries in the first early phase of left development. Growing levels of literacy accompanied a growing level of left support, and – more important – the early left movements were stronger where literacy levels were higher.

CULTURAL HETEROGENEITY AND LEFT ELECTORAL DEVELOPMENT

Given that all the aspects of cultural heterogeneity relate as negatively as expected to the left vote, I have summed the standardized values of the two variables of ethnolinguistic and religious fragmentation and those of illiteracy levels. The combined index consistently yields strong negative associations both over time and in each period and decade. As usual, the model works least well in the very early phase of development, and its explanatory power tends to increase with time. Unquestionably, cultural heterogeneity sets limits on the development of the left, and these limits become increasingly clear and strong after the first initial phase of establishment (see Table 4.7).

In a scattergram of cultural heterogeneity and the left vote (Figure 4.2) in the context of a 20% of variance explained over the whole period, several important outliers can be noted. Most of the early Swedish, Danish, and Norwegian elections appear in the bottom left part of the scattergram; given the high level of religious, linguistic, and literacy homogeneity of these countries, the model predicts a far stronger left than was actually observable at the end of the nineteenth and the beginning of the twentieth centuries, when the Scandinavian left was even weaker than the others. Ireland is also a rather deviant case, given its high religious homogeneity and high literacy level, attenuated only in part by linguistic differentiation. In the seventy-nine elections between 1880 and 1917, the model performs poorly, explaining roughly 10% of the variance. This is mainly due to the low left vote of the three Scandinavian countries, compared with their high cultural homogeneity, and to the high Finnish vote for a lower level of cultural heterogeneity. In the periods 1918–1944, 1945–1965, and 1965–

Table 4.7. *Cultural heterogeneity and left vote*

whole period	-.458 (291)
before 1918	-.314 (79)
interwar	-.427 (92)
1945-1965	-.547 (79)
1966-1975	-.728 (41)
1890	-.021 (19)
1900	-.137 (31)
1910	-.406 (36)
1920	-.419(41)
1930	-.489 (33)
1940	-.582 (28)
1950	-.492 (38)
1960	-.672 (34)
1970	-.717 (27)

Note: Number of elections given in parentheses.

1975, the outlying cases are progressively reduced to the Irish elections alone, and the variance explained increases from 10% to 18% to 30% and finally to 50% in the last period.

CONCLUSION: SOCIAL MOBILIZATION AND CULTURAL HETEROGENEITY

Considering the evidence discussed in the previous two chapters, it is possible to recognize three basic patterns at work. The variables pertaining to industrialization and urbanization, which I have called the social mobilization model, have a developmental potential for explanation, that is, they point to a left that increases with the growing level of social mobilization, both within the whole set of elections and within each country. However, they fail to account for differences across countries, particularly in the first formative periods but also in general. In contrast, religious and linguistic fragmentation are deprived of significant power of over-time explanations, both for the whole set and in any country, but they are particularly powerful in explaining cross-country differences in each period; this they do particularly from the 1930s on, although they also are unable

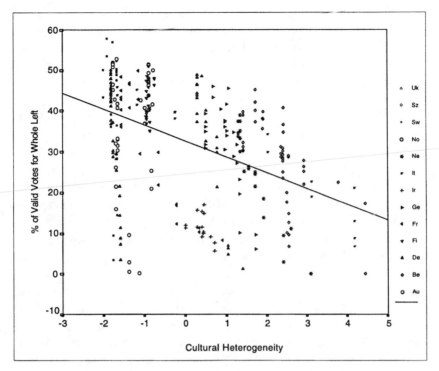

Figure 4.2. Cultural heterogeneity and the left vote (scattergram).

to account for early differences in left mobilization. Finally, levels of illiteracy are significant as a developmental explication in the sense that left votes increased over time as literacy levels increased, and at the same time they discriminate across countries, but only in the first formative periods. Illiteracy is the only variable encountered so far that has some capacity to account for the initial differences in the level of left development.

These different patterns can be combined, as they explain different aspects and different phases of the general phenomenon. We can therefore study the two models of social mobilization and cultural heterogeneity together to see whether their interaction compensates for their respective weaknesses. This interaction can be analyzed, first, by looking at the mean left vote in different types of settings; second, by devising a combined index that subtracts the cultural heterogeneity from the social mobilization levels (social mobilization−cultural heterogeneity); and, finally, by studying their mutual influences, as well as their independent roles, in explaining electoral development via a regression analysis.

In Table 4.8 the interaction between social mobilization and cultural heterogeneity is presented by reporting the mean levels of left support in different sociocultural contexts. I have identified levels of high, medium and low social mobilization and cultural heterogeneity by taking the tertile threshold of the respective frequency distribution of each index. The combination of the two models considerably improves their respective performance. *Within each level of cultural heterogeneity the left vote increases with the growing level of social mobilization and within each level of social mobilization and the left vote declines with the growing level of cultural heterogeneity.* While the difference between cases of low and high mobilization is about 18% and the difference between cases of high and low heterogeneity is about 12%, when the two are crossed, the difference between the context of low social mobilization and high cultural heterogeneity (the worst left mobilization context) and that of high social mobilization and low cultural heterogeneity reaches 35%. One could hardly have expected a clearer interaction between the two macrofeatures.

If we then relate a combined social mobilization and cultural heterogeneity additive index[16] to the size of the left, it shows a strong and positive association, homogeneous through time and space. Over almost a century of elections, the remarkable correlation of .778 is reached. Within each period (before 1918: .419 [79]; interwar period: .706 [91]; 1945–1965: .712 [76]; 1966–1975: .844 [29]) and decade, the association remains positive and significant, although it clearly tends to increase with time. For the first time, through the interaction of social mobilization and cultural heterogeneity, the period before World War I does not appear to be so deviant a phase. Finally, if we regard the same data in a scattergram form (Figure 4.3), we can see that the number of outliers is definitely reduced and that no country now appears as generally and systematically deviant. At this stage, the most deviant cases are the early British, Norwegian, and Swedish elections for their underdeveloped socialist vote and the late Irish elections (i.e., by the 1940s – but no longer the elections of the early 1920s and 1930s) for the same reason; and again the early Finnish elections for a left vote that is still, although to a much smaller extent than before, higher than that predicted by the model.

The model performs less well in the formation period than in any other and is still unable to account for the early original differences in the

---

[16] Given that social mobilization variables are expected to enhance left support and cultural-heterogeneity variables are expected to depress it, the index must be built as social mobilization−cultural heterogeneity. Values are standardized given the different magnitude and range.

Table 4.8. *Mean left vote in different sociocultural contexts*

		cultural heterogeneity		
		high (> .776)	mid (≤ .776 & > -1.188) 34.7 (97)	low (≤ -1.188)
		25.9 (104)		37.6 (100)
social mobilization	low (≤ -1.590) 22.0 (101)	12.6 (22)	23.5 (38)	24.6 (41)
	mid (>-1.590 & ≤ 2.167) 34.9 (99)	28.4 (43)	36.5 (27)	43.2 (29)
	high (> 2.167) 40.1 (101)	31.1 (39)	43.3 (32)	47.4 (30)

Note: Number of elections given in parentheses.

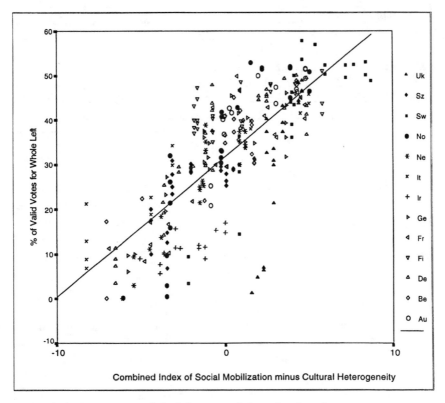

Figure 4.3. Scattergram of the left vote and the sociocultural context.

Table 4.9. *Regression analysis of the sociocultural model*

	Rsq	beta	zero order correlation	partial correlation
whole period				
cultural heterogeneity		-.465	-.454	-.600
social mobilization		.640	.633	.719
	61.6			
1880-1917				
cultural heterogeneity		-.664	-.314	-.413
social mobilization		.338	.180	.331
	19.8			
1918-1944				
cultural heterogeneity		-.628	-.426	-.654
social mobilization		.624	.420	.652
	53.0			
1945-1965				
cultural heterogeneity		-.577	-.547	-.647
social mobilization		.493	.458	.588
	54.1			
1966-1985				
cultural heterogeneity		-.555	-.720	-.697
social mobilization		.471	-.666	.636
	71.3			

socialist vote between the end of the nineteenth century and the beginning of the twentieth. While the total variance accounted for over the whole period is about 60 % – a remarkable result indeed for a model applied *not within each country*, but to the universe of hundreds of elections scattered across thirteen different countries and almost a century – its capacity to explain the pre–World War I variance does not exceed 20%. However, the figures are certainly less puzzling than those discussed for social mobilization alone (Table 4.9).

In the regression, cultural heterogeneity emerges as the more important variable of the two in each subperiod, although not for the whole period. On the whole, it adds the same amount of explained variance as social mobilization alone had over the whole period. Many other factors discussed earlier help us to conclude that this ordering is not a simple computing artifact. Of the two aspects, it is cultural heterogeneity that carries the most weight in determining the cross-country limits of left development and explains most of the early differences among the countries. To some extent, it can be said that cultural heterogeneity sets the conditions of validity of the hypothesis linking left development to the patterns and levels of industrialization and urbanization more than the latter do for the validity of the cultural heterogeneity hypotheses. This is evident when we compare the different orders of correlation. The first order of correlation between social mobilization and the left vote is modest in the first period (.180), but it is almost doubled once the impact of cultural heterogeneity is controlled (.331).

We are still missing a genetic model of left development to account for the wide differences in the starting conditions of political mobilization. Up to now, variables have been limited to the social, prepolitical confining conditions of electoral mobilization. In the following chapters, I add to the scheme other variables that are more political, that is, concerning the institutional conditions and the organizational environment in which electoral mobilization was taking place. The aim is the same as before: to search for general cross-country and cross-time factors capable of defining the macro constellation of left mobilization and restricting the scope and role of more-idiosyncratic factors related to the different structure of opportunity offered in each period and country. The institutional context of electoral participation, that is, the process of political democratization, is the subject of the following chapter.

ENFRANCHISEMENT

THE ROLE OF THE FRANCHISE

The social mobilization and cultural heterogeneity factors are related to the specific historical context and its traditions. It is unlikely that any generalized notion of "industrial society," conceived as a syndrome of structural/cultural features, will help to delineate the contextual political responses of the early phase. Similarly, the inhibiting capacity of cultural heterogeneity on the development of the left is unlikely to make its impact felt clearly in the very early phase of electoral development. It performs better as a limiting condition over the long term or as a potential boundary for mature socialist movements. While the long-term forces of assimilation and standardization may ultimately create similarities and bring about a leveling of both the social structure and cultural attitudes of industrial societies, in the very early phase of mass politics the opposite is more likely: The contextual features of presocial mobilization are more important than long-term developmental forces. Therefore, in the course of this book, I will consider more context-related factors.

The development of political rights, in particular the right to vote, was the end result of a long historical process going back to the eighteenth century and was rooted in the development of civic rights. Civic rights developed primarily in relation to the market as rights of property, contract, unrestricted choice of residence and workplace, and so on. Civic rights also refer to the potential for associability in a society when they touch on freedom of faith, thought, speech, assembly, and association. The combination of these civic rights constituted the point of departure for the opening up of political public space and opinion. The successive development of strictly political rights constituted the decisive push for political mobilization, granting the legal basis for the development of interest groups and political parties.[1]

The development of voting rights should not, however, be seen as a linear development of previous and prerequisite rights of expression, association, and opposition. Even in the second half of the nineteenth century, the combination of all these factors was rather complex. We find that cases of extended voting rights were not accompanied by firmly established rights of association and expression, as well as the reverse. This is due to the ambiguous role that the process of enfranchisement played in the eyes of the ruling elite. From 1848 to the First World War, the level of suffrage granted indicated two quite different situations: suffrage as a device of national integration and suffrage as a device of political representation. In the first case, high levels of suffrage were granted from above as an instrument for integrating social groups nationally, but they were blocked as an instrument of representation by a vast set of inequality devices: from the curia/estate system to plural voting or institutional barriers, from irresponsible government to second-chamber predominance; and so on. Such institutional devices actually prevented suffrage from properly representing the electors and granting them a share of parliamentary and executive power. These inequalities should be incorporated in the analysis of the franchise to avoid drawing false inferences from sheer numbers of the enfranchised population. On the other hand, restricted or enlarged representational suffrage was based on and impinged on already established opposition and association rights and constituted their representational expression. The nature of the suffrage is therefore characterized by other factors that differ from the suffrage itself and that clarify its role and function within the political system. A discussion of this aspect requires a typological cross-tabulation of both *democratization* and *liberalization*, which will be dealt with in Chapter 7. In this chapter, therefore, I concentrate on classifying European experiences in terms of the levels of electorate enfranchisement and turnout.

It is difficult to find a common dimension along which to rank-order national cases.[2] In this chapter, I first distinguish cases along an *early versus*

---

[1] For the waves of developments of rights, see Marshall (1965: 71–134) and Bendix (1964: 89–126).

[2] A separate issue concerns the database. In historical sources, there is little systematic standardization of estimates of enfranchised populations. The electorate is sometimes calculated as a percentage of the total or male population and sometimes as a percentage of the adult (male or total) population, where the latter is defined by the legal standard

late dimension, a *sudden versus gradual* dimension, and a *continuity* dimension (with or without important reversals). Subsequently, I deal with the comparative levels of participation (*turnout*) to ascertain the extent to which the formal right of voting was actually exercised. After describing the cross-country cross-time variance, my analysis concentrates on the relationship with the class left vote, treating the following questions: Were levels of franchise, turnout, and their combination important in determining levels of the left vote? Was the pattern of enfranchisement (tempo and timing) responsible for the earliness or level of left development? Did big jumps count the most, or were step-by-step enlargements more favorable to the left? Was the left definitely launched by universal male suffrage? What was the impact of female enfranchisement?

Finally, at the end of the chapter, I discuss the causal role of the enfranchisement process in the left mobilization model. So far, electoral support for the left has been analyzed as if enfranchisement levels were equal across the countries, which was not the case in the period between 1880 and 1920. In cases of highly restricted and/or particularly unequal franchise, left mobilization is unlikely to be high, whatever the levels of other independent variables. Given the link between suffrage development and left vote development, it may seem surprising that the analysis did not start immediately with this factor. There is, however, a reason for this choice. Social mobilization and cultural heterogeneity are exogenous variables in this model; they represent givens whose origins lie outside the scope and interest of this research. The status of enfranchisement is different and more complex. It is different because it cannot be considered a

---

of the country for adulthood or by the age indicated in the different laws: thirty, twenty-seven, twenty-four, and, later, twenty-one and eighteen years (sometimes independent of and generally higher than the legal age of adulthood for civic rights, as voting was regarded as an especially demanding activity). Sometimes, instead, figures are offered as a percentage of the enfranchised age group, i.e., of the population above the legal age indicated by the electoral law. This makes a rigorous comparison across time and space very difficult. A single measure is necessary that takes the number of people with the legal right to vote as a percentage of a reference group that is relatively stable and homogeneous over time and across countries. Take a simple example to illustrate the problem at its worst: Certain reform acts of the second half of the nineteenth century actually lowered the property, income, capacity, or census requirement for voting, increasing the number of enfranchised people. However, at the same time, the reform modified the age limit for voting by lowering it – for instance, from thirty to twenty-four years. The final result of these sorts of changes is that when the percentage of enfranchised people is computed in reference to the adult population as defined by the electoral law, these reforms can actually result in a decline of the percentage of the enfranchised. I have used a single international source that offers the figure of the electorate as a percentage of the total population (male and female) twenty years of age or older (Flora et al., 1983). This solution has clear advantages.

potential explanation of the vote but rather a necessary precondition: Voters did not choose socialist parties *because* they were allowed to vote but rather *when* they were allowed to vote. It is more complex because enfranchisement cannot be regarded as totally independent of the left vote, nor can it be considered an exogenous variable with regard to social mobilization/cultural heterogeneity. The level of franchise can be seen in three ways:

1. As an endogenous variable in the sense that its level influences left electoral mobilization but is also influenced by social mobilization and cultural heterogeneity. In this case, the relationship between the variables is as indicated in Figure 5.1a. The effect of the franchise on left development includes both a direct component and an indirect one, represented by the effect of social mobilization and cultural heterogeneity on the level of the franchise.

2. As a conditional variable vis-à-vis social mobilization and cultural heterogeneity: The effect of the latter depends on the value of the former, and the possibility of social mobilization (or cultural heterogeneity) having an effect on the left vote is conditional on a certain level of enfranchisement. The conditional variable determines the size of the causal effect of other exogenous variables, as presented in Figure 5.1b.

3. As a reciprocal causation variable: The extension of the franchise may foster left electoral mobilization, but the level of left electoral mobilization may also be responsible for further enlargement of the franchise (as indicated in Figure 5.1c).

EARLINESS

How many individuals were allowed to vote during the nineteenth century? The figures reported in the Appendix are divided into four periods: 1830–1880, 1881–1917, 1918–1944, and 1945–1975. The same data are charted in Figure 5.2 (see later). In the 1848–1880 period, three countries stand out as earlycomers to relatively large suffrage. France, after experimenting with several formulas in the post-Napoleonic period from 1815 to 1846,[3] suddenly introduced universal male suffrage (the suffrage had

[3] In the period immediately after the Restoration (1815–1816), suffrage was kept almost universal and equal for males (dependants were excluded), although this was only for primary elections to elect lifetime members of electoral colleges. It was the latter who elected members of parliament. Between 1824 and 1830, elections became direct, although suffrage was restricted and unequal (the upper 25% of the electorate, paying the

a) direct and indirect effects

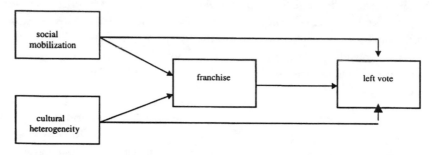

b) conditional effect

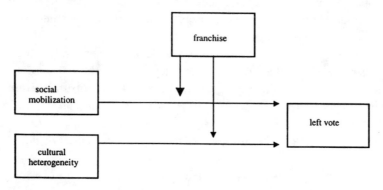

c) reciprocal causation

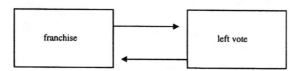

Figure 5.1. Role of the franchise.

already been equal since 1831) for citizens over twenty-one years in 1848, with an increase in the electorate from about 1–2% to 36%. In Switzerland, universal male suffrage for citizens twenty years of age or more was introduced with the constitutional reform that followed the Sonderbund of

highest direct taxes, was made into an additional electoral body) for men over thirty years of age. Between 1831 and 1846, suffrage was equalized for men over twenty-five, but it still remained highly restricted. For detailed information, see Campbell (1958) and Huard (1991).

autumn 1847, bringing the enfranchised electorate to about 30%. Swiss citizens, however, had never really been subjected to any *régime censitaire* and had a long tradition of general voting in the mountain cantons.[4] So, in the Swiss case, there was less of a break with the past. Finally, Denmark introduced equal male suffrage in the wake of the 1848 revolution, and this produced a radical change from autocracy to proto-democracy in the kingdom. The principle, however, was tempered by many more restrictions than in the other two cases[5] and was applied to men over age thirty. This resulted in an smaller enfranchised electorate, standing at about 25%.[6]

The fourth earlycomer to high levels of male suffrage was Germany. The short-lived Frankfurt Assembly of 1848 was elected by universal male suffrage, and after that date many German states could count on a fairly large male electorate. In particular, in the primary elections in the Kingdom of Prussia, every male citizen twenty-four years of age or more was entitled to cast a vote,[7] although the suffrage was not only indirect but also highly unequal.[8] The two elections held in 1867 for the Reichstag of the North Confederation involved universal male suffrage (for citizens twenty-five years of age or more), and the electorate was estimated to be about 35% of the adult population. After 1871, all elections were direct, equal, and male-universal.

In the middle of the nineteenth century, all the other countries had very restrictive suffrage requirements, with electorates ranging between 3% and 8% of the population twenty years old or more; it makes little

---

[4] Electoral inequalities had been intrinsic to the system, however, through the electoral privileges of the cities (of the plateau), against which the 1830 and 1833 "revolutions" had been directed and which had led to the enlargement and equalization of the suffrage. Martin (1980: 252).

[5] Electors had to reside in the electoral district for at least one year; dependent people without a family were excluded, as well as those who received poor relief and those whose patrimony was under bankruptcy proceedings. For details about these limitations, see De Kiriaki (1885: 82–88), which is an invaluable source for the detailed legal aspects of most early-nineteenth-century electoral systems. See also Castairs (1980: 75–77).

[6] On Danish electoral reforms see Elklit (1980: 366–396).

[7] For details about the electoral requirements of Prussia and several other German states, see Nohlen and Schultze (1971).

[8] The primary elections selected grand electors. Primary electors were not subject to any restrictions but were divided into three classes on the basis of the taxes they paid. The total sum of the taxes paid in the constituency was divided into three equal parts. The first class included the biggest taxpayers up to a ceiling of the first one-third of the total tax income. The second and the third classes were determined by the same principle, with obvious inequalities as a result. According to Casertano (1911: 204), in 1893 the proportion of the electorate in the three classes was still 3% in the first, 11% in the second, and 86% in the third. He cites the curious example of the cases of Essen and Frankfurt, where the Krupps and Baron Rothschild respectively, were the only members of the first class.

sense to distinguish between them. One case that can possibly be singled out is that of Norway. The 1814 Norwegian constitution introduced the most liberal voting qualifications of the time, enfranchising about 25% of all men.[9] This corresponded to roughly 10% of the population aged twenty years or more, which, up to 1848, was the highest franchise level in Europe. However, 1848 passed unnoticed in Norway and the electorate remained stable at around 9%, even declining to 8% in the 1870s. By that time, the Norwegian franchise could no longer be regarded as comparatively high.

By the late 1880s in Austria, Sweden, and the United Kingdom, the electorate had passed the 10% threshold. In Austria, the first direct elections to the lower house were held in 1873 (in previous elections, the deputies had been indirectly elected by provincial diets), with an enfranchised electorate of about 10%.[10] Similarly, in Sweden, the establishment of a second chamber and of centrally recorded elections came after 1866, and throughout the 1870s the electorate was about 10%. Finally, in Britain, the electoral reforms of the 1867–1872 period brought the electorate to about 15% of the male population twenty years of age or older.

The 1880–1920 period is the crucial phase of suffrage extension. The first countries to extend the right to vote substantially were Ireland and Great Britain through the reforms of the mid-1880s, which introduced a uniform household franchise, a uniform lodger franchise, and a uniform £10 occupation franchise in every borough and county throughout the country while leaving ownership franchise differentiated. The electorate was increased by 80% by these measures and reached about 30% of the adult population.[11] Three other countries enlarged their electorate to reach a third of the adult population, corresponding roughly to universal male suffrage, before the turn of the century: Belgium (1894 first election),

---

[9] Rokkan (1966a: 247).

[10] The information in the text refers only to the seven provinces carved out of the German-speaking westernmost part of the pre–World War I empire – Cisleithanian Austria – which subsequently became the Republican territory (Treaty of Saint-Germain-en-Laye of September 10, 1919). Burgerland became an Austrian province later in 1921; earlier, it had consisted of the westernmost counties of the three Hungarian provinces of Moson, Sopron, and Vasvar.

[11] Obviously, the series of reforms introduced in this period in the United Kingdom, in particular the Corrupt and Illegal Practices Act (1883), the Representation of the People Act (1884), and the Redistribution of Seats Act (1885), had a number of other political implications. Among the most important ones were an alteration in the balance of representation in favor of urban and industrial areas, the single constituency as a rule (although a few exceptions remained), and a sharp increase in the competitiveness of contests, with a decisive drop in "unopposed" constituencies. See Butler and Cornford (1969: 334). Here we are concerned only with the extension of the electorate.

Austria (1896), and Norway (1900). The Belgian 1893 reform that suddenly increased universal male suffrage was introduced for the national assembly for male citizens age twenty-five or more, increasing the electorate from 3.9% to 37.3%, even though huge inequalities were maintained.[12] In Austria, elections to the lower house (the Abgeordnetenhaus) continued to be held according to a curia system that divided the house into four classes.[13] The total enfranchised electorate was estimated at about 12–13% in the 1890s. The 1896 reform added a fifth curia (72 seats compared to the 353 deputies of the other four), which had a general character and male universal suffrage. This brought the enfranchised population to about 36% of the adult population (see the legend in the Appendix table). Finally, in Norway, the suffrage increased slowly from 10% to 16–17% by the end of the nineteenth century through gradual reforms that extended suffrage from property and occupational requirements to those of citizens paying a minimum tax on income (1885). In 1898, universal suffrage for men aged twenty-five years or more was achieved, bringing the electorate to about 35%.[14] Later, the Norwegian electorate continued to grow by marginal increases and progressive enlargements; thus, in 1907, a proportion of the female electorate (about 48%) was enfranchised; in 1913, universal suffrage for adult women was introduced (it had been preceded by women's universal suffrage at the local level in 1911), bringing the enfranchised adult population to 77%, the second highest level of enfranchisement in Europe at that time after Finland. Overall, the Norwegian pattern of extension was gradual and consistent.

Finland represents the unique case of a relatively late and extremely sudden male universal suffrage (but early female suffrage). Between 1809 and 1867, a four-diet system represented the heads of noble families, the clergy, the city dwellers (one or two representatives for each town or group of towns), and the peasants (one representative by jurisdictional district). From 1872 to 1904, the procedures and qualifications for voting did not change fundamentally, except for allowing school and university teachers and civil servants to vote in the clergy curia. The franchise was probably very restricted in this period. In 1904, an increase of the electorate brought the enfranchised adult population to about 9%. The 1906 reform, follow-

[12] See Gilissen (1980: 338–365).
[13] The first (85 seats) consisted of male landowners who paid at least fifty florins in taxes per year; the second (21 seats), of members of the Chambers of Commerce and Trade; the third (118 seats), of all male urban dwellers twenty-four years of age or more who paid ten florins or more; and the fourth (129 indirectly elected seats), of male rural-commune residents who paid at least ten florins.
[14] For more details, see Rokkan (1970c).

ing the temporary loosening of the Russian hold on Finnish political affairs, suddenly introduced universal male and female suffarage (over twenty-four years of age) direct and secret elections, and even proportional representation. In a single reform, the new Finnish unicameral Parliament (Eduskunta) was elected by 76% of the adult electorate.[15]

The Netherlands, Italy,[16] and Sweden adopted universal male suffrage last. In Italy, the Zanardelli Reform Act of 1882 had significantly increased the electorate to about 13% by lowering the male voting age from twenty-five to twenty-one and by reducing the tax, wealth, and educational requirements. Before this reform, 80% of the electorate was given the right to vote on the basis of tax and property qualifications; after the reform, this percentage dropped to 34.7%, while 63.5% were included due to their intellectual and educational capacities.[17] However, in the period of antisocialist legislation starting in 1894, electoral registers were revised and educational tests were made more stringent, with the result of actual disenfranchisement of almost 5% of the adult population. The electorate fell back to pre-1880 levels until the 1912 electoral reform, which introduced almost universal male suffrage (for men over thirty) and brought the electorate to 42% of the adult population.[18] The Swedish pattern of franchise development resembles the Italian one closely. Although no marked disenfranchisement occurred in Sweden, the electorate remained fairly stable throughout the 1880s and 1890s at around 10% of the adult population and rose to about 15% in the first decade of the twentieth century. In 1909, only a couple of years before Italy, almost universal male suffrage for citizens twenty-four years of age and over was introduced, doubling the electorate from 15.8% to 32.8%. The pattern of the Netherlands differs from those of Italy and Sweden, as the first steps of suffrage enlargement took place earlier and the whole process was more gradual. The reform of 1887 doubled the electorate from 5.7% to almost 12% of the adult population by lowering economic requirements. A second doubling of the electorate from 11% to 20% took place with the reform of 1896,

[15] For Finnish early electoral developments, see Mylly (1984: 9–27).

[16] The referenda (plebiscites) in central and southern regions from 1860 to 1870 for ratifying their annexation to the Italian kingdom were held under almost universal male suffrage. However, this enlarged franchise was an instrument of international legitimation of the new state. By contrast, the first elections of the Italian parliament in 1861 were held under very restricted suffrage, and only about 240,000 people voted (57.2% of the electorate).

[17] See AA. VV. (1955), Shepis (1958), and Ballini (1985) and (1988).

[18] The suffrage was universal for males over age thirty, but certain citizens between twenty-one and thirty had the right to vote if they paid a minimum level of taxes or had completed military service, finished primary school, or exercised official functions.

which enfranchised large parts of the lower middle classes, many highly qualified workers and sections of the rural proletariat, and small farmers and tenants. The electorate grew to almost 28% of the adult population in the last pre–World War I election (1913), and universal male suffrage was introduced after the war in 1918.

The final stage of enfranchisement concerned the female electorate, and in most cases it was a sudden decision. Only two countries had enfranchised women before World War I: Finland in 1907, together with men, and Norway between 1909 (for women whose own or husband's income exceeded a minimum) and 1915. In Austria, Denmark, and Germany, female enfranchisement took place in a single step immediately after the war, between 1918 and 1919. The United Kingdom and Ireland enfranchised women thirty years of age or more (with certain minimal limitations) in 1918, completing the process in Ireland in 1923 and in the United Kingdom in 1928. In both cases, the age limit was brought down to twenty-one years, as for men. The Netherlands and Sweden extended suffrage to women in 1921 and 1922, respectively. Finally, Italy, France, and Belgium granted female suffrage only after Word War II, between 1945 and 1948. Well in the rear came Switzerland, which gave suffrage to women at the national level only in 1971, 123 years after the same right was granted to men.

This brief description shows that a simple and straightforward classification of national experiences is difficult even along a single dimension such as earliness/lateness. Beyond the four clear-cut cases of France, Germany, Switzerland, and Denmark, the relative positions of the other countries has changed from decade to decade. Thus, Switzerland and France, which were in the lead up to the 1860s, formed part of the group at the lowest level by the 1920s; Denmark's early start was followed by a stagnation that allowed several countries to catch up with it by the 1870s and 1880s. Germany is probably the only country that consistently maintained its position in the first ranks.

TEMPO

Considering the same historical data in terms of the rapidity or lengthiness with which suffrage was extended clarifies whether similar levels at a given time were the result of gradual growth or sudden expansions of the electorate. To help the reader follow the discussion, I have reproduced the development of the electorate over time in graphic form for each country (Figure 5.2). Next to the line showing the development of the electorate,

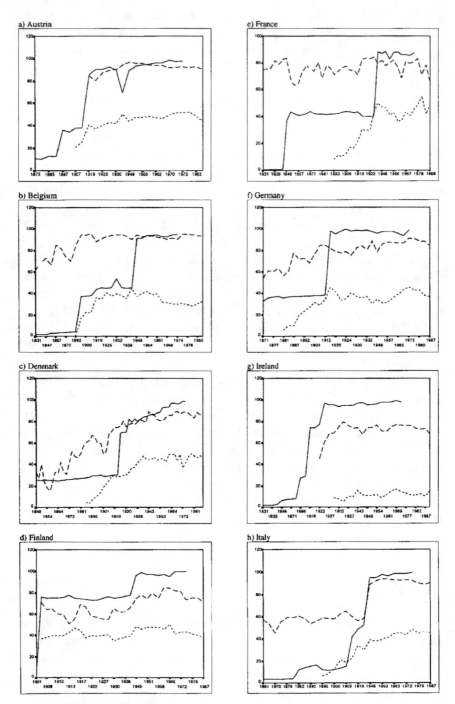

Figure 5.2. Franchise, turnout, and left vote: national developments.

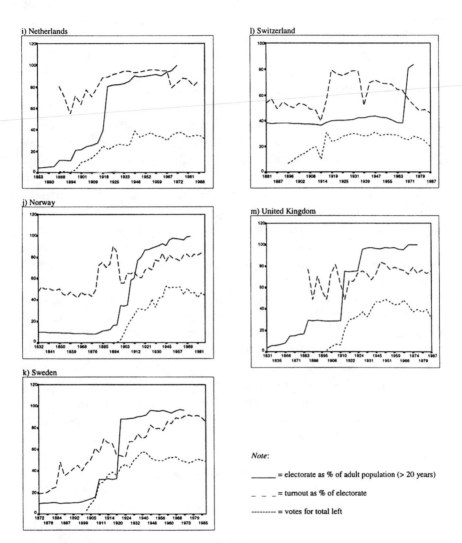

i) Netherlands

j) Norway

k) Sweden

l) Switzerland

m) United Kingdom

Note:

_____ = electorate as % of adult population (> 20 years)

_ _ _ = turnout as % of electorate

-------- = votes for total left

Figure 5.2. (cont.)

there is also the dotted line of the development of the turnout over time (the percentages of valid votes, although occasionally only total votes were available) by the electorate, as well as the percentage of valid votes obtained by the left. These two latter lines will help this discussion later. For the moment, let us concentrate on the sudden versus gradual nature of the electorates' development.

In the vast majority of cases, enlargement of the suffrage proceeded in relatively large steps. Sudden and large changes doubling the electorate occurred where there was female enfranchisement in all but three cases. Only in Norway, Ireland and the United Kingdom did female enfranchisement proceed in two main consecutive steps: in 1909–1915, 1918–1923, and 1918–1929 (I refer, as usual, to the first elections under new rule). Changes in male suffrage were more highly differentiated, but in this case too, jumps predominate over gradual evolution. If a jump is defined as an increase of more than 10%, a change of at least this size is present everywhere except in the four earlycomers (France, Germany, Switzerland, and Denmark), which, after their early sudden enlargement, remained at the same level for almost seventy years, until after World War I. Earlycomers could not have gradual development, so cases of early and gradual enlargement are as impossible as those of late and gradual enlargement. All the other cases were characterized by larger or smaller jumps. Going from the earlier to the later jumps, the cases are the following: The United Kingdom produced the first important jump of about 13% in 1885 and again of about 13% in 1918; Ireland jumped by 18–19% at the same time; Belgium, by 33.4% in 1894; Austria, by 22% in 1896; Norway, by 18.2% in 1900; Finland, by almost 30% in 1907; Sweden, by 16.7% in 1911; Italy, by 27.2% in 1913; and the Netherlands, by almost 12% in 1918. The size of these changes varied. The most sudden increases, affecting a third of the adult population, were no doubt experienced by Belgium at a very early stage and by Finland and Italy later. Austria's sudden increase affected about a fifth of the adult population in 1896. Ireland (1886), Norway (1900), and Sweden (1911) experienced smaller jumps, to around 18% of the adult population. Finally, the Netherlands had only one jump, which came very late, after World War I, and was also the smallest – just above the 10% limit, like the two British increases. Any other changes not mentioned here can safely be considered gradual adaptations due to small modifications in economic and/or capacity requirements and in revisions of the electoral lists.

In Table 5.1, the average yearly increase in (only) the male electorate from the 1860s to the 1920s is reported. Countries are regrouped according to the size of major increases, and the table offers information about

Table 5.1. *Rates of growth per decade in the male electorate*

countries	1860-1870	1870-80	1880-90	1890-1900	1900-10	1910-20
big jumps						
Belgium	0.01	0.02	0.00	**3.38**	0.05	0.33
Finland	stable[a]	stable[a]	0.10[b]	0.10[b]	**2.96**	-0.14
Italy	0.01	0.86	0.31	-0.29	0.27	**2.87**
intermediate jumps						
Austria	n.a.	0.24	0.01	**2.12**	0.39	0.60
Norway	-0.03	0.09	0.32	**2.22**	0.04	0.50
Sweden	n.a.	0.09	-0.03	0.23	**1.98**	0.05
minor jumps						
Ireland	0.10	0.05	**2.07**	stable	n.a	0.33
Britain	0.62	0.15	**1.29**	-0.08	0.02	**1.29**
Netherlands	-0.39	0.07	0.58	0.97	0.64	**1.17**
early and sudden increases						
Denmark	0.07	0.11	0.17	-0.04	0.11	0.44
France	0.25	-0.21	0.02	0.14	0.02	0.00
Germany	stable	0.32	0.12	0.09	0.04	1.02
Switzerland	stable	stable	-0.04	-0.04	-0.09	0.30

[a] Stable: although no precise data are available it is known that no substantial modification of the electoral legislation had taken place in the period.
[b] Data drawn from estimates in secondary literature. n.a.: neither data nor estimations available.

the location and size of the major increases. Following the table from top to bottom, there is a decline in the size of the per annum increases in the case of major enlargements and a growing level of per annum increases in the decades that are not characterized by any major redefinitions of the franchise. The Netherlands shows the most clear-cut case of gradual enlargement. It presents a jump exceeding 10% only in the final phase after World War I. In all the other decades (but one), the average increase is considerably higher than in the other cases, indicating a process of truly progressive enlargement of the electorate. In the three decades preceding the final granting of universal male suffrage after World War I, the electorate was increased by about 6%, 10%, and again 6%, for a total of 22% (see the table in the Appendix and Figure 5.2i). Britain, despite its reputation for very gradual development, presents two peaks, while in other decades the rates of growth are close to zero. Ireland shows a relatively important increase in the 1880s – bigger than that in Great Britain (2.07% versus 1.29%) – but, unfortunately, there are no data for the 1890s and 1900s. Norway is also usually associated with gradual development, but the increase in universal male suffrage in the 1890s was big. Gradual development characterized the pre-1890 and post-1900 periods, but in the 1890s the Norwegian electorate increased by about 20% of the adult population.

Without forcing national cases too much into the comparative framework, I can now provide in Table 5.2 a classification of the Western European enfranchisement process along the two dimensions of its timing and tempo. The most difficult case to classify is that of the Netherlands, whose development is unquestionably gradual, but which in terms of timing is a relative latecomer until the end of the first decade of the twentieth century. We could thus classify it as gradual and intermediate as well as gradual and late. I have, after much thought, placed the Dutch case in the intermediate timing group because the levels of enfranchisement in the 1890s and 1900s were considerably higher than those of Italy and Sweden (classified as latecomers).

REVERSALS

A third dimension of suffrage enlargement is the existence or absence of reversals, that is, the more or less linear nature of the enlargement itself. France is the classic case for which the "early, sudden and followed by reversal" category was originally developed. It is not correct, however, to concentrate on the Restoration reversal vis-à-vis revolutionary times, when the outstanding characteristic of the French pattern remains that of very early universal male suffrage. After 1848, a revision of the electoral lists (the law of May 31, 1850) attempted to restrict the franchise by demanding, as a prerequisite, three years of residence in the voting place. However, this reform had only minor effects: The electorate changed from 9,837,000 in 1849 to 9,836,000 in 1852 to 9,490,00 in 1857, rising again to over 10,000,000 in 1863, which can hardly be regarded as mass disenfranchisement.

In Denmark, the original democratic promises of the 1848 revolution were to some extent muted in the following decade. Confrontation between the king and the conservatives, with their strongholds in the first chamber, and the rurally supported liberals in the second chamber resulted in a minor dedemocratization of the constitution itself. In 1866, suffrage was also restricted, but the impact of such changes was felt particularly in the

Table 5.2. *Comparative enfranchisement: timing and tempo*

		timing		
		early	intermediate	late
tempo	sudden	Fr, De, Ge, Sz	Be	Fi, It
	intermediate		Au, No	Sw
	gradual		Ir, Uk, Ne	

Landsthing (the first chamber), where higher property qualifications were introduced. However, strictly from the point of view of the suffrage, these conflicts were manifested more clearly in the stagnation of a relatively high but not yet universal male suffrage throughout the 1850s and 1860s. No real signs of significant disenfranchisement are evident in the post-1849 figures.[19]

The only case of a franchise reversal that has significant implication for our analysis is that of Italy in the 1890s. The revision of the electoral registers carried out in 1894 reduced the electorate from 2,934,000 in 1892 to 2,121,000 and constituted a clear rupture in the process of growth initiated by the reform law of 1882. Almost a third of the electorate lost its right to vote in 1895. Moreover, this disenfranchisement was without doubt one of a set of measures set up by the government in a clearly anti-socialist operation.[20] The effects of the disenfranchisement lasted for a long time; it took seventeen years and five elections before, in 1909, the electorate reached the same numerical level at which it had been in 1892. This revision was of great political importance because, without it, Italy would show only a very gradual pattern rather than a sudden and late development. So, only in Italy do we find a disenfranchisement that combines size, lasting influence, and a clear antisocialist political orientation.

TURNOUT

During the process of enlargement of the right to vote, the propensity to participate varied remarkably over time and across countries. Here, the interest is not in short-term fluctuations from one election to the next, but rather in systematic cross-time and cross-space differences in levels of

[19] See Svåsand (1980: 398–411).
[20] See Mastropaolo (1980: 97–124).

electoral participation and their relationship to the process of enfranchise-ment.[21] The correlation between the electorate and turnout tends to be weak. It is .583 for the 390 elections between 1831 and 1975, but it is slightly negative in the period before 1880 (−.067) and in the period between the two world wars (−.085), while it is positive in the period 1881–1917 (.138) and in the period following World War I (.439). These data raise some doubts about the validity of the thesis that census- or capacity-restricted electorates have a higher turnout than enlarged elector-ates as the result of the strong propensity of the richest and most highly educated strata of the population to vote. According to this thesis, succes-sive enlargements of the franchise, resulting in granting of the right to vote to citizens of a lower socioeconomic and cultural status, should result in a lowering of the turnout. This would be particularly true with large, sudden increases of the electorate and, I should add, with enfranchisement of women, whose sudden involvement in a political role traditionally associated with and reserved for men should produce a pronounced fall in turnout levels.

However, when we consider the mean level of turnout by decade between 1831 and 1980,[22] the figures offer only modest proof of a curvilin-ear historical effect of franchise development over turnout levels. These levels are no higher during the phase of very restricted suffrage than during the period of suffrage enlargements. This conclusion is strengthened when we examine the mean level of turnout by levels of enfranchised electorate in Table 5-3. The only fall in turnout (from 75.4% to 64.8%) comes in the category of the electorates ranging from 60% to 80% of the adult

[21] There are no systematic *historical* studies of turnout levels and very few solid generaliza-tions about their variation. One of the few generalizations is that turnout tends to correlate historically and cross-sectionally with levels of urbanization – first stated by Thompson (1927). Urwin (1980: 112–123) has argued that the data presented in this research did not fully support the author's conclusion, and he concludes that no clear, systematic "rural lag" in electoral participation can be identified. My data do not concern within-country variance between urban and rural areas but only cross-country differences in levels of urbanization across time. Turnout figures are associated positively with the four different urbanization levels over the entire period and in each decade. The associa-tions are systematically stronger for the 2,000 and 5,000 threshold than for the 20,000 and 100,000 ones. The associations are stronger in the period from the 1910s to the 1950s than in the others. This suggests that turnout levels tend to increase with the increase in urbanization and also that more-urbanized countries tend to have higher levels of turnout than more-rural ones. In short, my data support Thompson's conclusion more than Urwin's. I repeat, however, that they both refer to within-country and not to cross-country variation.

[22] Note that before 1870–1880 the data are far less representative because some countries are missing and others held very few elections (see the table in Appendix for a list of the elections considered).

Table 5.3. *Mean turnout by levels of the enfranchised electorate*

level of the electorate	mean turnout	standard deviation	number of cases
0.1 to 20%	58.8	15.5	39
20.1 to 40%	58.2	17.8	116
40.1 to 60%	75.4	10.6	42
60.1 to 80%	64.8	10.1	29
higher than 80%	81.6	9.3	164
all elections	70.4	17.0	390

population and can be interpreted as the result of female enfranchisement.[23] In conclusion, at the average European level there is no evidence of a long-term curvilinear development in turnout. If anything, it seems that the turnout has experienced a long-term structural growth parallel to that of the franchise. However, national patterns could be more supportive of the curvilinear thesis. Checking the plot of the electorate and turnout figures for each country reveals that this is the case only in Norway. The fact that Rokkan gave a great deal of attention and publicity to this Norwegian pattern has probably turned it into something more than a specific national pattern. However, there is no evidence of its actually being so.

Major enlargements of the suffrage can be accompanied by a fall in turnout even if they do not result in an overall curvilinear historical development. I have checked for each major increase (greater than 10%) in the electorate, as well as the corresponding variation in the turnout level for the same election and the following ones when useful (Table 5.4), separating the major increases resulting from exclusively male, male and

[23] Since I consider the enfranchised population as a percentage of the total population aged twenty years or more, two countries that have both universal male or male/female suffrage but apply different voting ages – for instance, twenty-one and twenty-nine years – result in two different percentages, of which the first is much higher. To avoid this result, one should compute the enfranchised population as a percentage of the enfranchised age group, i.e., the population above the legal voting age. However, to do this would involve even bigger distortions. Given that the voting age in the past was very different from one country to another, I would lose much of the common bases for comparative purposes. How, for instance, can an 80% enfranchised population over thirty years of age vis-à-vis a 70% enfranchised population over twenty years of age be evaluated in comparative terms?

Table 5.4. *Major increases in the electorate and corresponding variations in turnout*

country	year	only male electorate variation	only male turnout variation	year	male & female electorate variation	male & female turnout variation	year	only female electorate variation	only female turnout variation
Austria	1896	+22.8	n.a.*				1919	+47.9	n.a.
Belgium	1894	+33.4	+10.7				1949	+46.0	+4.1
Denmark				1918	+39.1	+1.1			
Finland				1907	–+60	n.a.*			
France	1848	+35.2	1st = +1.4 2nd = -15.4				1945	+48.	-4.6
Germany				1919	+59.2	-3.2			
Ireland	1886	+19.2	n.a.	1918	–+45	n.a.	1923	+19.5	+15.6
Italy	1913	+27.2	-4.6				1946	+42.5	+30.7
Nether.	1897	+9.6	+16.7				1922	+41.4	+0.2
	1918	+12.7	+8.6						
Norway	1900	+18.2	-29.4	1909	+23.2	-0.3	1915	+16.9	-4.1
Sweden	1911	+16.7	-4.3				1921	+54.9	-1-1
Switzer.							1971	+42.6	-7.0
Un.King.	1885	+12.8	n.a.	1918	+46.0	-14.6	1929	+19.9	+2.2

*The turnout differential is missing, as no pre-1907 data are available. However, in the elections following 1907, the turnout dropped drastically.

female, and exclusively female enfranchisement. No general tendency toward a fall in turnout can be ascertained in the case of major enlargements of the franchise. Paradoxically, the most supportive instance of the three listed in the table is that of male enfranchisement. If we consider that the Belgian 1894 and the Dutch 1918 enfranchisements were associated with important increases in turnout because of the introduction of compulsory voting, we are left with three cases of turnout decline at the moment of electorate enlargement (Sweden in 1911, Norway in 1900, and Italy in 1913) and two of turnout stability and even growth (the Netherlands in 1897, +16.7%; France in 1848, stable). In the enlargements involving part of the male and part of the female electorate (middle three columns), the cases of turnout fall still prevail slightly (they all occurred between 1907 and 1918). The most significant, however, is the British drop of 14.6%, while the others are minor changes. Finally, and most surprisingly, no general support for the thesis advanced earlier is offered by the female enlargements, which produce an equal distribution of increases and decreases in turnout. In a nutshell, it is hard to interpret these data in view of a general or predominant tendency; indeed, national contexts seem to dominate and be responsible for individual outcomes. The only two countries where increases in the electorate invariably result in falls in turnout are Sweden and, in particular, Norway.

The last point worth discussing is the comparative cross-country vari-

ation in average levels of turnout before the 1920s. The different levels of
turnout in the European countries can be appreciated by looking at Figure
5.2. A close examination of these graphs shows a great variety of national
patterns. Belgium, Austria, and, to a lesser extent, France and the Netherlands are the prototype of the high-turnout country irrespective of the
level of the electorate. In these cases, the level of the electorate does not
seem to influence significantly the level of turnout, which is always comparatively high. The United Kingdom and Finland have a medium level
of turnout in this period, between 60% and 70%, and it oscillates around
these figures irrespective of electorate development. In Denmark and Germany, turnout grows steadily over time irrespective of the trend in the
electorate. In these two cases, but more clearly in the Danish one, it seems
that electoral mobilization takes place mostly through the progressive
involvement of enfranchised people and that this increase tends to be
gradual over time without being profoundly affected by changes or stability in the electorate. Finally, in Sweden, Italy, and Switzerland, turnout is
comparatively low throughout the entire period. In Italy, it remains stable
below 50–60% until after World War I. In Sweden, it grows over time,
but (see Figure 5.2k) its starting level was so low (only 20% in 1872) that
at the beginning of the twentieth century less than half of the restricted
electorate actually voted. Switzerland has a stable, secular low level of
turnout, with the exception of the jump that occurred in the twenty years
between 1919 and 1939.

ENFRANCHISEMENT AND THE
DEVELOPMENT OF THE EUROPEAN LEFT

Each feature of suffrage development discussed so far – earliness, gradual-
ity, and levels of legal and real participation – may have important consequences for the electoral and/or organizational and/or ideological response
of labor. The effects of these features on organizational and ideological
development will be taken up in later chapters. Here, I will continue to
deal mainly with their effects on electoral developments.

PATTERN OF DEVELOPMENT:
TIMING AND TEMPO

Four fundamental patterns of development can be derived from Table 5.2,
where the countries were classified according to the timing and tempo of
their enfranchisement. At one extreme are those countries that show early

or intermediate timing and a necessarily gradual development (the United Kingdom, Ireland, and the Netherlands); at the other are those that show late or intermediate timing and a rapid tempo (Finland, Italy, and Sweden). In the intermediate cases, one can distinguish between the earlycomers with sudden enlargements (France, Denmark, Germany, Switzerland), on the one hand, and the intermediate cases on both dimensions on the other (Belgium, Austria, and Norway). In Table 5.5 the average left vote for each period and for the whole century for each of these four groups of countries is reported.

The order is quite consistent for each of the four patterns and for the whole period. In all cases, *the left appears to be electorally stronger moving from the cases of early timing to those of late timing and, within each of these groups, moving from gradual to sudden enlargement.* The contrast between the early/gradual and the late/sudden groups is remarkable, and the two intermediate groups always remain within this range of extreme values. The most striking difference is in the first period, when the early/gradual group has an average left vote almost five times smaller than that of the late/sudden group. However, these early differences seem to remain steady through time. In terms of *patterns of development*, the lateness, on the one hand, and the sudden change, on the other — far from being negative aspects for the electoral development of the left — seem to have set conditions that are more favorable, *ceteris paribus*, than very early enfranchisement and more intermediate and gradual developments. In these data, we can see supporting evidence for an argument that has already been advanced for social mobilization processes: It is not the earliness per se or the levels reached that create more or less favorable conditions for political mobilization, but rather the *coincidence* or *lack of coincidence* between such processes and the organizational developments of the socialist movement. The first two groups of countries, those with early timing, had enlarged their suffrage completely or to a great extent before the organizational consolidation of a socialist movement, while in the other two groups the processes tended to be parallel.

LEVELS OF THE ELECTORATE AND OF TURNOUT

In Table 5.6 the relationship between the level of electorate and the level of support for the left is presented with first-order correlation coefficients. At the overall level, the association is positive and high at .678. However, the overall association throughout the century results from two distinct

Table 5.5. *Pattern of enfranchisement and left vote*

franchise development pattern	before 1918	1918-1944	1945-1965	1966-1985	group total
early/intermediate timing; gradual tempo (Uk, Ir, Ne)	6.5	23.5	31.2	28.4	23.9 (72)
early timing; sudden tempo (Fr, Ge, Sz, Dk)	17.0	34.4	39.5	41.0	32.1 (123)
intermediate timing; intermediate/sudden tempo (Be, Au, No)	15.7	37.9	45.5	41.2	36.5 (73)
late/intermediate timing; sudden tempo (Fi, It, Sw)	27.8	42.2	46.8	46.4	40.5 (78)
group total	18.0	34.2	40.6	39.4	33.2 (346)

Note: Number of elections given in parentheses.

Table 5.6. *Electorate and turnout levels and size of the left vote*

period	electorate/left vote	turnout/left vote	country	electorate/left vote	turnout/left vote
all elections	.678 (292)	.419 (292)			
1880-1917	.719 (82)	.012 (80)	Au	.847 (17)	.708 (16)
1918-1944	.118 (92)	-.029 (92)	Be	.498 (21)	.261 (23)
1945-1975	.213 (115)	.304 (115)	De	.886 (36)	.860 (38)
			Fi	.713 (27)	.526 (28)
1880	.888 (6)	-.182 (6)	Fr	.788 (21)	.581 (22)
1890	.702 (20)	-.049 (20)	Ge	.749 (25)	.744 (26)
1900	.644 (31)	.365 (30)	Ir	.752 (15)	.113 (16)
1910	.624 (36)	-.010 (35)	It	.952 (16)	.853 (17)
1920	.210 (41)	-.238 (41)	Ne	.929 (23)	.359 (24)
1930	-.086 (33)	.000 (33)	No	.906 (24)	.683 (26)
1940	0.58 (28)	.204 (28)	Sw	.906 (24)	.683 (26)
1950	.281 (38)	.257 (38)	Sz	.241 (24)	.628 (25)
1960	.282 (34)	.394 (34)	UK	.953 (21)	.550 (22)
1970	.428 (26)	.541 (26)			

Note: Number of elections given in parentheses.

groups. One group can be roughly identified by a level of the electorate that is below 65% and that corresponds to the male or male and part-female enfranchised population. In this group, the regression line is much steeper than in the whole set and the correlation is higher. The second group consists of the fully enfranchised electorates, where, not surprisingly, the association between the electorate and the left vote is weak or nonexistent.[24] The association is maximized in the period before World War I and drops considerably after that date. The minor increase between 1918– 1944 and the post–World War II period should not be regarded as significant, because a closer examination of the graphic form of the data shows that it is due to the outlying position of a few 1946–1967 Swiss elections and to the 1946 Belgian election held with an all-male franchise. These six elections deviate enormously from all the other 109 and therefore contribute to a slightly positive regression line.

The link between turnout levels and left development is less strong (.419). More surprisingly, the association seems to go in the opposite direction than that with the electorate. It is absent in the first phases of electoral mobilization and reaches a significant level only after World War II. In conclusion, the level of the enfranchised electorate is a discriminating variable in the phase of mobilization but ceases to have any important effect once the electorate approaches the saturation level of full mobilization. In contrast, turnout levels appear to be irrelevant in non-fully-mobilized electorates, while they gain some importance when they reach the state of full mobilization. By the 1920s, the level of the enfranchised electorate loses the strong predictive power of the 1880–1919 period, and by the 1940s the importance of turnout levels starts to grow. To sum up, in the first phase, left mobilization rests mainly on enfranchisement; in the later phase, it depends increasingly on turnout levels.

In these data, over-time developmental associations and cross-space synchronic associations are compatible. We can safely transform the development generalization according to which increases in the electorate bring about increases in the left vote (in the first period) into the synchronic generalization that countries with a higher electorate tended to have a higher left vote. Indeed, the decade associations show correlation levels as high as those over time, particularly in the four first decades between 1880 and 1920. The relationships do not result, therefore, from pure temporal covariation. To confirm that this is indeed the case in each period, we can

---

[24] The small number of Irish elections falls into this second group. The sharp drop in the correlation since the 1920s could be due to these elections for their weak left and large electorate. The decade associations computed without Irish elections are substantially higher (1920: .375 [40 elections]; 1930: .296 [29]; 1940: .419 [25]), but are still much smaller than those of the 1890s, 1900s, and 1910s. Moreover, if we want to exclude outliers, the Swiss elections between the 1930s and 1967 should also be left out. Given the nonenfranchisement of women, the Swiss electorate was roughly half that of all the other countries. The presence of these elections increases the positive association; without them, the association between the electorate and the total left vote even becomes negative from the 1940s on: −.184, −.025, and .087 (24). Therefore, the outlying cases of the Irish and Swiss elections compensate for each other to a large extent.

regress each variable – the electoral and the left vote – independently against time and study the association among the residuals of such a regression. A significant association remains among the residuals ($r = .353$ over 293 elections), and this supports the conclusion.

Finally, the strong positive association in the first four decades is important because, in the previous analysis, the "genetic" differences in left mobilization were unexplained by variables concerning the levels of social mobilization and cultural heterogeneity. Here, it is possible to find the first element of the genetic explanation. Early differences in the left vote were due in part to different patterns of enfranchisement. The latter, therefore, should be particularly useful in explaining early genetic cross-country variations.

INCREASES IN THE ELECTORATE AND TURNOUT

Here, the question is whether the major jumps in the electorate corresponding to waves of enfranchisement or major increases in turnout levels were particularly important in determining the electoral growth of the left. A distinction needs to be made between male and female enfranchisement. In Table 5.7, I have synthesized the analysis, showing the level of the electorate, the turnout, and the left vote in the years before and after the main periods of male and female enfranchisement. In the last three columns of the table, I show the increase in the electorate, the turnout, and the left vote between these two elections.[25]

The data show that male enfranchisements were indeed crucial to the initial development of the left, as they are all associated with major jumps in its force in Belgium, Sweden, Finland, and the United Kingdom (and probably in Austria if data were available; in 1907 the Socialist Party recorded a level of support of 21%, while before this date it was judged as electorally unsuccessful by national historians). By contrast, the Netherlands and Norway show smaller increases in left electoral strength. In the Netherlands, this can be explained by the already mentioned fact that the

---

[25] Unfortunately, electoral information is missing for Austria prior to 1907 and the introduction of universal male suffrage. For Ireland, electoral data are available, but the Irish Labor Party deliberately abstained in the first elections during the transition to the Republic. I should also point out that in Finland and the United Kingdom, in 1907 and 1918 respectively, it is impossible to distinguish between male and female enfranchisement because the two were granted together. I have included them in the male table. Finally, the Norwegian case is also complex, as in 1912 only part of the female electorate was enfranchised (the process was completed in 1915) and the enlargement also concerned a section of the male adults.

Table 5.7. *Differentials in electorate, turnout, and left vote before and after male and female enfranchising elections*

a)   male enfranchising election

	year	elect-orate in %	turnout in %	left vote in %	year	elec-torate in %	turnout in %	left vote in %	diff. electorate	diff. turnout	diff. left vote
		election before male franchise				first election male franchise				differences between elections	
Au	n.a										
Be	1892	3.9	83.9	0.2	1894	37.3	94.6	17.4	+ 33.4	+ 10.7	+ 17.2
De	*										
Fi***	1904	~9		0.0	1907	76.2	53.9	37.0	+ 67.2		+ 37.0
Fr	*										
Ge	*										
Ir	**										
It	1909	15.0	65.0	19.0	1913	42.0	64.4	22.8	+ 17.0	- 4.6	+ 3.8
Ne	1913	27.6	80.0	18.5	1918	39.3	86.6	25.0	+ 11.7	+ 6.6	+ 6.5
No	1897	16.6	85.3	0.6	1900	34.8	55.9	3.0	+ 18.2	- 29.4	+ 2.3
Sw	1908	15.8	61.3	14.6	1911	32.5	57.0	28.5	+ 16.7	- 4.3	+ 13.9
Sz	*										
UK***	1910	28.8	63.6	6.4	1918	74.8	49.0	21.4	+ 46.0	- 14,6	+ 15.0

b) female enfranchising election

	year	elect-orate in %	turnout in %	left vote in %	year	elec-torate in %	turnout in %	left vote in %	diff. electorate	diff. turnout	diff. left vote
		election before female franchise				first election female franchise				differences between elections	
Au	1911	38.0		25.4	1919	85.9		40.8	+ 47.9		+ 15.4
Be	1946	45.5	90.3	45.1	1949	91.5	94.4	37.3	+ 46.0	+ 4.1	- 7.8
De	1913	30.1	74.4	29.6	1918	69.1	75.5	28.7	+ 39.0	+ 1.0	- 0.9
Fi*	1904										
Fr	1936	40.1	84.4	42.8	1945	88.3	78.9	49.9	+ 48.2	- 4.6	+ 7.1
Ge	1912	38.7	84.9	34.8	1919	97.9	81.7	45.5	+ 59.2	- 3.2	+ 10.7
Ir**											
It	1921	52.5	58.4	29.9	1946	95.0	89.1	39.6	+ 42.2	+ 30.7	+ 9.7
Ne	1918	39.3	88.6	25.0	1922	80.7	88.8	21.6	+ 41.4	+ 0.2	- 3.4
No***	1906	35.2	64.8	16.0	1909	58.5	64.5	21.6	+ 18.3	- 0.3	+ 5.6
Sw	1920	33.0	55.3	36.1	1921	87.9	54.2	44.0	+ 54.9	- 1.1	+ 7.9
Sz	1967	38.2	63.8	26.4	1971	80.8	56.8	25.3	+ 42.6	- 14.6	- 1.1
UK*	1910										

a)
n.a.: electoral data not available; *: male suffrage reached before socialist party was founded; **: party already founded but not running at election; ***: male and female enlargement
b)
*: impossible to distinguish between male and female enfranchisement; **: party already founded but not running at election; ***: In Norway in 1909, only some women were enfranchised.

final step to universal male suffrage was gradual. In Norway, the final step to male franchise concerned an increase of 18% of the electorate. However, as mentioned before, this increase of the electorate was accompanied by a sharp drop in the levels of electoral participation (turnout dropped from

85.3% to 55.9%), and this may explain why the Socialist Party gained so little (only 2.3%) from this enlargement.[26] The most surprising case is therefore Italy, where male enfranchisement resulted in an increase of 17% of the electorate and only a modest 3.8% strengthening of the socialist forces, while the turnout remained at similar levels.

The cases of female enfranchisement present a different picture. In four cases, they coincided with an electoral decline of the left (Belgium, 1946–1949; the Netherlands, 1918–1922; Switzerland, 1967–1971; Denmark, 1913–1918), while in six there was an increase in the left vote. However, one should consider that in four of the six cases of growth, female enfranchisement coincided with a postwar election and party system restructuring (Austria, 1911–1919; Germany, 1912–1919; France, 1936–1945; Italy, 1921–1946). In these cases, the increases in the left vote cannot be linked to the new female vote. It is far more likely that they instead represent a generally favorable trend arising from the collapse of previous authoritarian or fascist regimes. In the two cases where female enfranchisement occurred under normal conditions, that is, between two consecutive elections that were not separated by long periods, wars, or resistance movements, the left grew (Sweden, 1920–1921; Norway 1906–1909). The conclusion is that female enfranchisement tended to have no impact or a negative impact on left size, because the cases of left growth are more attributable to factors that are independent of new female votes. This conclusion is in line with large survey data evidence that the first female voting practices are more conservative than those of males. Note also that female enfranchisement was more often associated with drops in the level of electoral participation.

If we generalize the argument for the major enfranchising changes in the electorate, we can check whether and when the increments in the electorate were associated with the increments of the left vote (not with its level). In general, this association is quite strong in the first pre–World War I period (.408), declines in the interwar period (.370), and becomes null in the post–World War II period (.085). This association between increments is independent of the level of the electorate, as the partial correlation controlling for the electorate level shows (.414, .380, and .095, respectively). Conversely, the increases and decreases in the levels of participation are not associated with those of the left in any of the three crucial periods (and controlling for levels of turnout does not alter the picture significantly). This suggests that the level of electoral participation should

---

[26] It should also be remembered that Norwegian elections continued to be indirect in this period.

be considered important in only some cases, but that this does not point to a general influence over the levels of left electoral mobilisation.

ROLE OF THE FRANCHISE IN THE MODEL

Before turning to a discussion of the franchise in combination with the sociocultural model, let us comment on the theoretical role of this variable. As mentioned at the beginning of the chapter, the extension of the franchise plays a relatively ambiguous role in any study of the development of mass politics. In Figure 5.1 three models of interaction were presented in which the franchise was first an intermediate, independent, nonexogenous variable; then an intervening conditional variable; and, finally, a dependent/independent variable with respect to the left vote. The association between enfranchisement and the left vote does not resolve the problem of which was the *primum mobile* and what type of relationship it was. In this section, I review the evidence supporting the various positions in regard to these problems.

Let us start with the major issue: reciprocal causation. Was it the force of the left that captured the wider suffrage, or was it the wider suffrage that offered new chances to convert to the left? To test which variable comes first, one can lag both of the two variables and control their level of association with each other. If the level of the electorate has a causal status with respect to left electoral size, it can be expected that lagging it will not modify the association. Conversely, if the strength of the left is the independent variable that explains increases in the electorate, lagging it should increase the level of association, as the association between the left vote and electorate at time t cannot be attributed to the left vote, given that the former is prior to the latter. In Table 5.8, the data concerning the first and crucial period (1880–1917) show that while the lagged values of the level of the electorate maintain roughly the same level of association with the total left vote, the lagged values of the left make the association decline sharply from .703 to .428 to .382. In other words, if we want to explain the levels of the electorate at each election from the strength reached by the left in previous elections, we fare worse than if we do the opposite. The test is also revealing because resorting to an association measure requires exclusion of all those elections in which left parties had not yet competed, that is, all those numerous cases in which the electorate was extended before the left entered political competition; therefore, those

Table 5.8. *Electorate levels and left vote levels: association with lagged variables*
(1880–1917)

a) association between left vote and electorate (electorate at time *t1* and at time *t2*)		
left vote/electorate	left vote/electorate *t1*	left vote/electorate *t2*
.695 (64)	.697 (64)	.665 (64)
b) association between left vote and electorate (left vote at time *t1* and left vote at time *t2*)		
left vote/electorate	left vote *t1*/electorate	left vote *t2*/electorate
.703 (74)	.483 (74)	.382 (74)

Note: Number of elections given in parentheses.

extensions definitely cannot be attributed to the strength of the left.[27] Of
the two possible directions of the association, that going from the level of
the electorate to the strength of the left is much more powerful than that
going from the level of the left support to the extension of the franchise.

Having clarified the direction of the association, we can now consider
the role of the franchise as a conditional intervening variable that is able
to boost the effect of social-mobilization variables. If this hypothesis is
true, once we control for the level reached by the electorate, the association
between social-mobilization indicators and left development should grow.
One way of doing this is by removing the linear effect of electorate levels
from both social-mobilization variables and the left vote. However, the
figures in Table 5.9 show that partial correlations are lower than or equal
to the zero-order correlation for both the whole period and the first period.
Once we control for the effect of the franchise levels, the social-mobilization and the cultural-heterogeneity models work worse rather than better.
This enables us to reject the idea of considering the franchise as an external
conditional variable defining the size of the direct causal effect of the
others.

[27] When the test is repeated for each country, the results are consistent. Where universal
male suffrage was achieved early and before political organization of the class left (France,
Germany, Switzerland, Denmark), no doubt can exist about the direction of the relationship. For the remaining nine cases, in six the pattern is exactly the same as in the bulk
of all the elections; in only three cases, a considerable drop in the association between
the level of the electorate and lagged values of left strength is absent.

Table 5.9. *Association between social mobilization and left vote, controlling for electorate level*

	1880-1985		1880-1917	
	zero order correlation	partial correlation	zero order correlation	partial correlation
correlation between social mobilization and left vote, controlling for the level of franchise	.644 (287)	.427 (286)	.212 (80)	.258 (79)
correlation between cultural heterogeneity and left vote, controlling for the level of franchise	-.345	-.229	-.314 (77)	-.117 (76)

Note: Number of elections given in parentheses.

We are therefore left with the model that assumes that the franchise is an intermediate independent variable standing between social mobilization and cultural heterogeneity on the one hand, and the left vote, on the other. This model assumes that social mobilization and cultural heterogeneity influence the total vote of the left via the extension of the franchise. This view is consistent with the fact that by removing the impact of the franchise on the left vote – as was done in the previous test – we also remove a part of the impact of social mobilization and cultural heterogeneity on the left vote. For this type of interaction to be supported, we would expect a considerably positive impact of social mobilization on the franchise and a considerably negative impact of cultural heterogeneity on the franchise. In reality, controlling for cultural-heterogeneity levels, the association between social mobilization and the franchise increases to a zero-order .568 correlation and a .647 partial correlation. The same is true when we control the association between cultural heterogeneity and franchise for social mobilization levels: a −.272 zero-order correlation and a −.438 partial correlation. In conclusion, the model in Figure 5.1a seems to be the most suitable. The conditional-effect model did not work according to theoretical expectations, and the reciprocal-causation model is not supported by the general data set, although it remains plausible for some individual cases.

ENFRANCHISEMENT PATTERN, SOCIAL MOBILIZATION, AND CULTURAL HETEROGENEITY

In this chapter, we have seen that the aspects of the enfranchisement process that are most significantly associated with the development of left electoral mobilization are the *timing/tempo pattern* and the *level of the enfranchised electorate*, while the increases in the electorate are significant only for the increases in the left vote. Both the levels and the increases in turnout are significant in some cases, but they do not show a systematic or consistent impact.

A specification concerning the role of turnout is, however, in order. A general additive or multiplicative model combining the electorate and the turnout in a single index of electoral mobilization is inadequate to support a general interpretation of left strength. There were cases in which the turnout remained constant at the same high or low levels (Belgium, the Netherlands, Italy, France, and Switzerland), cases in which it tended to grow parallel to the growth of the electorate (Austria, the United Kingdom), cases in which it grew within a constant electorate (Germany and Denmark), and at least two cases (Norway and in part Sweden) in which turnout declined while the electorate increased. It is therefore difficult to identify a systematic effect of turnout. Electoral mobilization through enfranchisement and electoral mobilization through turnout increase have a mixed and varying influence in different cases. The only thing that can be done is to describe the situations in which the two play different roles through a close inspection of the early development of these variables (see Figure 5.2). If we were to maximize the impact of the general process of electoral participation development in each country, we would mix the two dimensions in different ways for each group of countries. We could leave aside turnout in certain countries, consider it as the most important variable in others, and, finally, combine electorate and turnout levels in others.

For these reasons, I have decided not to include turnout in a general index of the enfranchisement process. The latter will therefore be composed only of the levels of the enfranchised electorate and the modality of franchise enlargement. To obtain such an index, I have added the standardized values of the enfranchised electorate to the standardized values of the timing-tempo patterns reported in Table 5.5. Each country has been attributed a rank-order from 1 (early/gradual) to 4 (late/sudden) (see Table 5.5). The index is the following:

franchise levels + *timing/tempo of enfranchisement*
          = *enfranchisement pattern combined index*

Note that the levels of legal franchise and the timing/tempo classification are not associated with each other ($-.021$ over 307 elections). While the franchise level represents an over-time variation across and within countries, the timing-tempo classification represents cross-country differences in sequential patterns.

The improvement of the combined index with respect to the individual variables is shown in the correlation of Table 5.10. While the role of franchise levels is important mainly in the first period and tends to decline later on, the differences in the left vote associated with different timing/tempo models of enlargement tend to persist over time. Combining the two indices into the enfranchisement pattern index, we obtain a more homogeneous association through time, and the total over-time association is also improved. When these data are plotted, no clear subset of outliers emerges.

At this point, it is possible to incorporate the enfranchisement pattern within the general model together with social mobilization and cultural heterogeneity. The result of a stepwise regression of the total left vote against the three indices of social mobilization, cultural heterogeneity, and enfranchisement pattern (see Table 5.11) shows the considerable improvement achieved. Over the century as a whole, this model yields an explained variance of about 70%, each of the three variables maintains a strong impact, and in each of the four periods the model is consistent. The variance explained is now considerable in the first period as well: 56% before World War I, 62% between the wars, and 54% and 71% in the two post–World War II phases.

The relative weights of the different variables change in each period. The role of the enfranchisement pattern is particularly strong before World War I and decreases thereafter, to the advantage of the other two (so much so that it does not enter a stepwise regression equation with standard entry and removal). The weight of cultural heterogeneity is increased constantly from the first period on, while the impact of social mobilization is at its maximum starting from the interwar period. On the whole, the interaction among the three variables guarantees a relatively constant over-time level of explained variance, thanks to their differential impact in each period. Moreover, with this model, one no longer faces the contradiction between over-time and across-space associations. Once the interaction between cultural heterogeneity, social mobilization, and the enfranchisement pattern

Table 5.10. *Enfranchisement pattern: individual and combined index association with the left vote*

	electorate/ left vote	electorate/ timing-tempo type	electorate/ combined index
1880-1985	.678	.400	.742
1880-1917	.719	.500	.709
1918-1944	.118	.607	.603
1945-1965	.189	.532	.536
1966-1989	.342	.541	.594

Table 5.11. *General determinants of the left vote*

variables	1880-1917	1918-1944	1945-1965	1966-1989	whole period
social mobilization	.295	.547	.446	.512	.467
cultural heterogeneity	-.220	-.378	.-491	-.581	-.266
enfranchisement pattern	.636	.390	.155	-.074	.401
Rsquare	56.1%	62.6%	55.6%	71.6	70.9%

is taken into consideration, each of the three variables maintains the same sign of influence and a significant impact in each period as well as across all of them.

Given the type of interaction that emerges among the three factors, we can chart cases using a simple additive index. In Figure 5.3, such an index has been computed and plotted against the left vote. Its predictive capacity is almost the same as that of the regression model (.694 versus .709), which confirms how well the three processes combine in a simple additive manner. In addition, the scatterplot of Figure 5.3 also shows the extent to which the combined index reduces the presence of clear-cut outliers. No country or country–period stands out as a clearly exceptional case; even the Irish elections no longer stand completely alone. At this stage, the bulk of outlying elections in the lower-left part of the plot and below the regression line represent not only Irish elections, but also the early elections in the northern countries of Sweden, Norway, and the

United Kingdom, whose lefts are far below the levels that the model would predict. What is deviating in Ireland is not its early low levels, in line with the general model predictions, but its lack of development over time.

This model can be used to evaluate each country fit, comparing the Europewide predicted left vote with the real national left vote. Applying to each country the general Europewide model, it is possible to evaluate the extent to which each deviates from it. The higher the residuals, the less well the general model performs in fitting the actual national electoral results. It should be emphasized once more that the model is drawn from an all-country analysis, and the country residuals are not the unexplained variance in left vote as predicted by *national* figures of urbanization, industrialization, and enfranchisement, but rather the unexplained variance with respect to European-based predictions.

The analysis of the residuals of national regressions identifies a few experiences as particularly deviating from the general European pattern. The Irish case is no surprise. On the contrary, it is now surprising to see that in the first period, the countries that represent a wider divergence from the model are the Northern European countries of Great Britain, Sweden, and Norway. In the interwar and immediate post–World War II periods, there are fewer marked deviations from the predicted values. In the final period, the cases that stand out for their unexplained variance are Italy, Finland, and Belgium. Note that at this point, with the enfranchisement pattern inserted within the general model, the Finnish left vote no longer appears as deviating. The countries that tend to be best explained by the Europewide model are Austria, the Netherlands, and Switzerland, and to these one should add Belgium except for its last post-1965 phase. The signs of these residuals point to a left that is weaker or stronger than one would have expected on the basis of the general European pattern. What is more important, however, is that in the following chapters, when discussing additional aspects, we should keep in mind that *as far as the electoral size of the left is concerned*, some countries will require the identification of additional potential sources of variation more than others.

In conclusion, the interaction between the processes of social mobilization associated with the patterns of industrialization and urbanization, the early levels and models of enfranchisement, and, finally, the cross-country variation in the extent of cultural homogeneity now constitute a satisfactory general model for the interpretation of the basic differences in the electoral development of the class left across Europe, both at the overall developmental level and at the synchronic cross-country level. With respect to this general Europewide model, more or less important residuals that

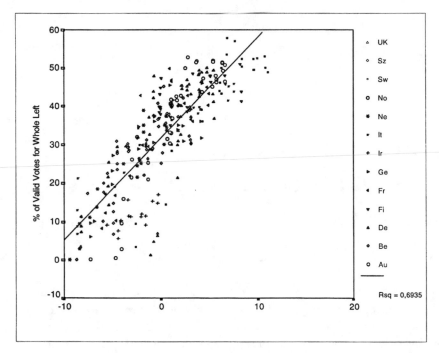

Figure 5.3. Left vote and the combined index of social mobilization, cultural heterogeneity, and enfranchisement pattern.

need to be explained by resorting to aspects other than those analyzed so far exist in some country–periods. In the following chapters, more directly political aspects will be invoked to account for such residuals. Moreover, the general model described so far will be recast and applied to the other aspects of the dimensions of the left that pertain to its organizational development and cohesion and to its more or less radical orientation.

ORGANIZATIONAL STRUCTURING AND MEMBERSHIP MOBILIZATION

In this chapter, attention shifts from the structural conditions of cleavage structuring to the organizational and behavioral dimension. The central questions concern the relationship between organizational development and electoral mobilization; between corporate and political socialism; and between forms of *interest representation* and *political representation*. These themes are discussed along the two dimensions of *organizational consolidation* and *membership mobilization*. The former refers to the establishment and consolidation of specific political organizations into the corporate-group and the electoral-party channels, and to the linkage established between them; the latter refers to the capacity of the same organizations to mobilize individuals into such groups as trade union members, party members, and voters.

This perspective is important for three reasons. First, the levels and patterns of early organizational consolidation and structuring of the cleavage are instrumental in explaining levels and patterns of political mobilization. That is, organizational strength can be translated into both capacity for electoral mobilization and stability of electoral mobilization. Second, once a political organization achieves a certain amount of consolidation, it acquires relative autonomy from the environment, becomes an agent of mobilization of its own, and shapes its environment through ideological and organizational encapsulation and mobilization. In this sense, organization is a way of making the cleavage relatively independent of its socio-structural bases and of strengthening its own ideological and cultural distinctiveness at the same time. Finally, early organizational patterns and the relationship they establish between the party and the environment of corporate interests determine the latitude of action of the party's electoral strategies.

The chapter has three main sections. First, I provide a general framework for the study of the relationship between organizational and electoral mobilization and review the comparative experience of early organizational structuring of working-class movements. Second, I describe and discuss national patterns of membership mobilization in the party and trade union organization domain. Finally, I investigate how these factors relate to different histories of the electoral left, and I determine different types of class cleavages from the organizational/electoral linkage point of view.

EARLY ORGANIZATIONAL CONSOLIDATION

PARTIES AND GROUPS IN THE FIRST POLITICAL MOBILIZATION

A crucial aspect of the early organizational consolidation of every political movement is the *linkage* between the various arenas and types of mobilization bases. Such linkage varies considerably according to the type of interests and/or identities being mobilized, but also according to the general character of the political system environment of the claimant. Table 6.1 systematizes some possible forms of this linkage,[1] separating the two channels – electoral and corporate – of mobilization. Widespread networks may be the only organizational base present in both of them – professional, craft, and other types of organizations, on the one hand, and candidates, caucus, and club-type organizations, on the other. At the other extreme, one can find formal membership organizations in both channels. Electoral and corporate mobilization can, of course, take place without necessarily being dependent on *central* forms of coordination. Only party membership mobilization is necessarily dependent on the consolidation of a central political organization.

The historical experience of Western European parties reveals various modalities.[2] Voters can be mobilized without building on distinctive membership organizations in either the corporate or the political channel, relying instead on widespread networks of professional or other types of

---

[1] The scheme is inspired by a short article in which Rokkan (1977) responded to criticism of his overlooking of the interest group formation process. I have modified it to suit my purpose here. The critique was from Alford and Friedland (1974).

[2] Important analytical considerations concerning the process of party formation are found in Nedelmann (1975), Svåsand (1978), and Panebianco (1982).

Table 6.1. *Type of interlinkage between electoral and corporate mobilization*

organizational base		type of relationship between channels	
electoral channel	corporate channel	cross-linkage	representation mode

-diffuse network
-specific
organization
	- none
	- diffuse network
	-specific
	organization
		- none
		- demand group
		- contingent
		-interlocking
		- dependency
			- corporate
			- fragmented:
			  - segmental
			  - ideological
			  - territorial

organizations. This is usually the case in countries where enfranchisement was early and extended before any decisive waves of urbanization and industrialization, thus predating organizational developments. France during the Second Empire and Third Republic and the United States are examples of this pattern. Where this was the case, the forms of representation tended to be territorial in nature and not easily converted into a cross-local organizational structure. Indeed, the formation of strong corporate and political mass organizations proved very difficult later on. A second model is the early foundation of specific organizations in the electoral channel not matched by and not relying on the support of specific organizations in the corporate channels. This classic model of British liberalism and conservatism proceeds from the electoral caucus to local branches, from registration activities to electioneering to membership and organizational development. This model does not tend to organize support along a single and clearly identifiable cleavage line, but rather across many lines, through a variety of alliances, although none of these are given visible expression in cleavage-specific organizations allied to the party. This modality can be associated with parties that developed in liberalized, but not electorally inclusive, contexts.

"Indirect" parties[3] are the end result of the political mobilization originally taking place through diffuse electoral networks and are the manifestation of specific corporate organizations that preceded the formation of the political organization. The support provided by the corporate organization to the electoral network of candidates and political associations is contingent at first and later progressively interlocking, and it was typical of most of the denominational and agrarian parties, as well as of

---

[3] This terminology was introduced by Duverger (1967).

some socialist ones. In this case, mobilization tended to be along a single and easily recognizable cleavage line, defined by the preexisting corporate organization. A further model is that of the relatively parallel development of specific organizations in both domains, electoral and corporate. The relationship is one of mutual support and reinforcement; representation is more functional than territorial and takes place along well-established cleavage lines.

The relationship between the forms of mobilization in the two channels is represented on the right side of Table 6.1. As can be seen, the *cross-linkage* between corporate and electoral organizations may be *absent or very weak*. Alternatively, it may be of a *demand group* type when organizations in both channels retain full freedom to bargain for support. In this type, they relate to each other in the classic terms of the pluralist model of democracy – each being a "client" of the other in its respective field of action, exchanging electoral for policy support. The relationship may be *contingent* and thus expressed through alliances and coalitions based on interest proximity and goal similarity, but deprived of solid organizational, ideological, and personnel interpenetration. Although closely allied, the two organizations preserve distinct identities and independent latitude of action. The cross-linkage may be *interlocking*, that is, it may be characterized by a profound interpenetrating of corporate and electoral organizations that reinforce each other on the basis of leadership and membership overlap and interchange, support-base coincidence, and a range of common collective activities. Finally, the relationship may be one of *dependency*, in which one of the two forms of central organization tends to direct the second both politically and organizationally.

The *mode of representation* does not depend on the organizational base or the cross-linkage, but instead on the extent to which a one-to-one monopolistic relationship of representation is present in both channels. The *fragmented* mode points to a situation of both corporate and electoral fragmentation. In neither the corporate channel nor the electoral channel does a single or dominant organization exist that can claim a monopoly of the representation of the interests to which it refers. Instead, the link between the interest sector and electoral politics results in a plurality of actors all claiming a representational right. The fragmentation of both channels is often the consequence of mutually reinforcing drives and can be of different types: (1) segmental pluralism, that is, the organization of competing "pillars," with a close interlocking of social movements, interest groups, educational and cultural agencies and activities, *and* political parties divided along culturally distinctive identities (linguistic, religious, or cultural-peripheral);[4] (2) ideological fragmentation along the more classic left – right dimension of competition;[5] and (3) territorial fragmentation. The representation mode labeled "corporate" requires, by definition, a form of interlocking linkage between the two channels. The corporate organization is the only, or the dominant, representative of a well-defined interest population in the interest channel, *and* the electoral organization with which it is interlocked shares the same prerogatives in the electoral-parliamentary channel. A monopoly of representation exists, therefore, in both the corporate and electoral channels.

I will now use these analytical categories to characterize the relationship between corporate and electoral organizations within the class cleavage.

EARLY ORGANIZATIONAL STRUCTURING OF CORPORATE AND ELECTORAL SOCIALISM

Similar to agrarian parties, socialist parties were, in general, the extension of or parallel to organizations that were already active in the corporate channel. The tendency was to start from an economy-based response and to move toward the multiplication of specific cultural and political organizations built around economy-oriented identities in both the corporate and political channels. If one takes as a point of reference *the moment of the formation of a nationally centralized organization in both channels* – that is, the founding of national parties and central national confederations of trade unions – important differences emerge between national contexts concerning opportunities, difficulties, and choices.

The section that follows is a review of the origins of socialist organizations focusing exclusively on the relationship between consolidation in the economic and political spheres of action in the pre–World War I period. The historical information is framed within the conceptual scheme summarized in Table 6.1. A comparative appreciation should pay attention to (1) the organizational sequence of the process, that is, which of the two organizations centralized first, whether it be in the political or the economic sector; (2) the timing of the process, that is, whether, in a comparative European perspective, centralization in the political and economic spheres was early or late; and (3) the length of the process, that is, whether the efforts at national centralization were long and difficult or more rapid. This description, based on threshold points, needs to be complemented by

---

[4] Lorwin (1971: 147–187).
[5] See Sani and Sartori (1983: 307–340).

a discussion of the nature of the relationship between organizations active in corporate and electoral/parliamentary channels, that is, (4) the corporate–electoral cross-linkage and (5) the mode of representation (see Table 6.1). The combination of these five dimensions offers a comparatively perceptive picture of the modalities of organizational consolidation of early European socialist movements.

Organizational Sequence

Raw information concerning organizational consolidation is synthesised in Table 6.2. For each country, a date is suggested that refers to the first push toward the national centralization in trade union and party/political movements. The dates corresponding to the successful formation of a national trade union confederation and socialist party are reported in different columns. When possible, the table indicates in parentheses the length of the process of organizational central consolidation in both channels.

In the majority of cases, the centralization of political organizations took place before a similar process was accomplished in the corporate channel: Denmark[6] and Belgium[7] are the clearest cases of this, followed by less important delays in the Netherlands,[8] Italy,[9] Norway,[10] and Sweden.[11] In Germany,[12] Austria,[13] Finland,[14] and France,[15] the processes were paral-

---

[6] For Denmark, see Galenson (1952b: 104–172), and Foverskov and Johansen (1978). Historians have underlined the importance and the persistent role of craft unionism as a distinctive feature of the Danish labor movement. Its strength is probably due to the slow industrialization of the country. This helped Danish guilds – among the strongest in Europe, and whose privileges were not eroded until 1862 – to transform slowly into unions. By 1895 almost all the former guilds had adopted the trade union organizational format. See Galenson (1952a: 10–32).

[7] My sources for the early organizational history of the Belgian socialist movement are Spitaels (1974: 9–21) and Delsinne (1936).

[8] On the Netherlands see Daalder (1966b), Kossmann (1978: 344–349) and Buiting (1990: 73).

[9] On the party–unions relationship in Italy see Horowitz (1976), Pepe (1971), and Pappalardo (1989). The last author reviews the historians' debate on the issue.

[10] See Galenson (1949: 7–77), Korpi (1983: 107), and Millen (1963).

[11] For Sweden see Galenson (1952b: 104–172) and Carlson (1969: 14–30, 46–50).

[12] For the German party–union early relationships, I have relied on Schorske (1955) and the contributions in Mommsen and Husung (1985). On the close contacts with the political party, see Moses (1982: 67–86).

[13] Sources for the early history of Austrian socialism are Steiner (1964), Knopp (1980), and Klenner (1951).

[14] For the early Finnish labor movement, see Suviranta (1987: para. 275) and Berglund and Lindström (1978: 35–36).

[15] On the French early organizational development, see Zeldin (1979: 210–13, 243), Duveau (1946: 212, 217–231), Lorwin (1954), Goguel (1950: 271–359), and Huard (1996: 268–289).

Table 6.2. *Socialist parties and trade union formation*

country	beginning phase trade union national centralization	foundation of national trade union center		beginning phase of political national centralization	foundation of national political party	
Austria	1867	1893	(26 years)	1874	1889	(15 years)
Belgium	1857-60	1898	(38-41)	1864	1885	(21)
Denmark	1871	1898	(28)	1871	1876-78	(5-7)
Finland	1896-1900	1907	(11-7)	1893	1899	(6)
France	1886	(1895) 1902	(16)	1880	1905	(25)
Germany	1868	1875	(7)	1863-64	1875	(12)
Ireland	(1880)	1894	(14)	1912	1922-30	(10-18)
Italy	(1880)	1906	(20-26)	1880	1892	(10)
Netherlands	1893	1905-6	(12)	1881	1894	(13)
Norway	1874	1899	(25)	1885	1887	(2)
Sweden	1885	1898	(13)	-	1889	(0)
Switzerland	1873	1880	(7)	(1870) 1880	1887	(7-17)
Un. Kingdom	-	1868	-	(1884?-1893?)	1900-06	(10-20)

lel, while in Switzerland[16] and particularly in Great Britain[17] and Ireland,[18] centralization in the trade unions sector preceded that in the political sector. This is paradoxical: There can be no doubt that in most Western European countries, worker mobilization in the corporate channel largely precedes political mobilization in the electoral one. Nevertheless, in almost all cases, the effective *organizational centralization* of a national trade union confederation occurred after a political party was set up at the national level.

According to one line of argument, when industrial revolution preceded the extension of the parliamentary franchise to the working class, the unions organized themselves in the labor market before seeking political representation through political organizations (the British case). By contrast, on the Continent, where unionization took place after the extension of the franchise to the working class, unions tended to be the result of party activity and were more dependent on and subordinated to the political organizations.[19] This interpretation dramatizes the Britain–Continent opposition and reduces excessively the variation among continental

[16] My sources for the Swiss early socialist movement are Balthasar, Gruner, and Hirtner (1988), Garbani and Schmid (1980), Reymond-Sauvain (1966), Gass (1988), and Vuilleumier (1988).

[17] Pelling (1965) and (1976a).

[18] For Ireland, I have used Roche (1990), Berresford Ellis (1972: 167–183), Chubb (1974), Mitchell (1974), and Gallagher (1982).

[19] For this typical Britain-versus-the-Continent interpretation, see Kahn-Freund (1972), in particular the Introduction. On a similar line, broadening the opposition to an Anglo-Saxon (including the United States and the former British colonies) versus continental European interpretation, see also Commons (1962: 681–685).

countries. As we have seen, the British pattern of franchise extension is not very different from some of the continental patterns. A "corporate-first model" is also evident in Ireland, where the precedence of the Industrial Revolution over extension of the franchise is difficult to argue, although in this case, the organizational imitation of neighboring Great Britain could be the explanation. However, in Switzerland, corporate centralization also preceded party centralization, despite the fact that extension of the suffrage to the working class occurred very early.

The following are also probably important factors: (1) the need for centralization was felt more clearly in the political sphere; (2) the cross-country transmission and spread of organizational-political forms was easier in the political sphere; and (3) there were important intrinsic differences in the opportunities for mobilization of the same constituency in different channels. In their original efforts to politically mobilize previously inactive citizens, socialist "agitators" and parties had to motivate individuals to commit themselves emotionally to abstract ideas, abstract categories of individuals, and interpersonal relationships. A feeling of solidarity had to be created among individuals who were physically and socially distant. Individuals' traditional emotional ties to other, more direct primary or territorial groups thus had to be loosened. In every case, socialists had to induce their potential constituency to act in a way that contradicted the norms and roles dominant in their geographical-social milieus and, in general, against the authority of the social hierarchy at the local level.

Compared with these difficulties of electoral and partisan mobilization, corporate mobilization enjoyed the advantage of focusing more on problems of the constituency in the workplace than on abstract ideas. The direct functional-economic interests and direct experiences of common destiny were more easily perceived than broader national political interests; the local factory "enemy" was closer to home than the "capitalist class" and the state. The perception that individual and collective fates could be influenced by remote political decision making demanded higher intellectual sophistication. Corporate recruitment and mobilization took place in a far more socially homogeneous environment than partisan and electoral activities.[20] Therefore, it is not surprising that the first mobilization of labor took place in workers' societies, cooperatives, mutualities, and trade unions rather than in political associations and parties.

However, when one considers the problems of national organizational coordination and consolidation – as opposed to that of early mobilization –

[20] For the significance of the homogeneity of the social context of participation, see the discussion in Chapter 3 and Rokkan (1970d).

some of these advantages fade away and even become liabilities. There were additional difficulties for trade unions. In order to consolidate, national confederations – just like political parties – needed to establish a growing authority over and coordination of local organizations, that is, to overcome territorial fragmentation (chambers of commerce and similar early territorial forms of organizations) that, in several of the cases mentioned, delayed national organizational development. While for political parties this process was facilitated by the obvious centralization of power and decision making in national executives and parliaments, there was nothing similar to foster the central organization of the trade unions. Policy was, of course, decided at the center, but the immediate interests of members were more clearly dealt with at the local factory or branch level. As in the case of the party, it was necessary to add an element of higher solidarity to foster central federal and confederate development. It is not surprising that this stimulus was often produced by the political organization, which by necessity was more center-oriented in its actions.

Moreover, early unionism was craft-based, uniting workers with higher qualifications, higher incomes, and generally greater resources for organizational participation. Such workers were part of a restricted and not very competitive labor market, and their self-identification and status made them a distinct group with a higher tendency toward behavioral conformity. The process of sector integration of different craft traditions, qualifications, and professional figures and the organization of all employees of a given industry, leaving to one side the skills and tasks of the individual employee, was difficult. Similarly difficult was the integration of several sector unions into a single national confederation. In other words, *status differences* within the working class were less important and less damaging to the party than to trade unions, which were highly stratified along craft and professional lines. Within the political sphere, there was an ideological area of equality among members that was far more difficult to achieve in a still highly segmented labor market.[21]

Finally, it is likely that the organizational imitation of earlycomers was easier in the political sphere than in the corporate one. The early formation of the party in Germany, for example, exerted an important influence. The strong influence of the German model and German-born socialist agitators in Denmark (and via Denmark to Norway and Sweden), as well as in Austria, the Netherlands, and Switzerland, is well documented. In addition, the role of the Second International was instrumental

---

[21] On the crucial importance of "areas of equality" in fostering political participation, see Pizzorno (1966b).

almost everywhere on the Continent in fostering the formation of national parties. The most telling cases are probably the Scandinavian countries, where the development of socialist organizations was extremely early and rapid, considering the social background and conditions of these countries. In other countries leading the industrial transformation (Belgium and Switzerland), the tradition of working-class self-organization, mutual societies, cooperatives, unions, and so on was already quite strong, and the external political influence mixed with internal traditions to offer a picture of ideological syncretism and nonhomogeneity. In France, and to a lesser extent in Italy, German and Second International influences were met with considerable opposition from national organizational and ideological streams, which possibly delayed the political unification of the socialist movement. The combination of the three factors discussed earlier may explain why, historically, the mobilization of unions predates forms of political centralization and, with few exceptions, ends up with their national coordination and organization after the parties and often under their auspices.

Timing

There is a small correspondence between the earliness or lateness of central organizational consolidation in the two channels. In the corporate channel, early national coordination characterizes the experiences of the United Kingdom, Germany, and Switzerland, in all of which such a process had already begun before the 1880s. At the other extreme, in Italy, the Netherlands, and France, national central organization was achieved in the first decade of the twentieth century. All other cases fall in between, with the establishment of central national confederations taking place in the 1890s. The pattern is quite different for political organizations. Germany and Denmark had set up central national party headquarters by the 1870s; Austria, Belgium, Norway, Sweden, and Switzerland did so in the 1880s; Finland, Italy, and the Netherlands established theirs in the 1890s; and the latecomers, France, the United Kingdom, and Ireland, did so only in the first quarter of the twentieth century. Germany and France are therefore homogeneous cases of very early and very late organizational consolidation, respectively, in both channels. The Irish experience approaches that of France; the Swiss experience, that of Germany. All the other countries fall between these extreme cases. While Italy and the Netherlands tend to approximate the pattern of France as latecomers in both channels, the United Kingdom stands out as the clearest case of total bifurcation in the development of the two channels: Organizational consolidation in the corporate channel was as early as the corresponding political development was late. Denmark is the clearest case of the reverse pattern: National party formation is astonishingly early compared with its relatively late trade union central organization.

The earliness of the organizational consolidation of the socialist parties is related to the extension of the franchise or to the level of socioeconomic modernization of the country. The hypothesis is that the higher the levels of enfranchisement and social mobilization, the more differentiated the interest representation is in the political system, the greater the need for organization, the greater the potential interparty competition, and therefore, the earlier the development of mass parties. In a recent work, Svåsand has tried to test this thesis with qualitative information concerning the Scandinavian countries.[22] He argues that in order to be supported, the organization of major mass parties should soon follow major extensions of suffrage.

No clear relationship is evident in Table 6.3 among the earlycomers to large franchise (France, Denmark, Switzerland, Germany) and party formation, France being a clearly contradictory case. Among the latecomers to large suffrage (Finland, Italy, Sweden, the Netherlands) party formation was in general late (the 1890s: Italy, Finland, the Netherlands). Sweden had late enfranchisement and relatively early party formation (the 1880s). In the countries where socialist central consolidation was very late – France, the United Kingdom, and Ireland – enfranchisement was early or intermediate. On the whole, therefore, the relationship between level of enfranchisement and socialist party formation is weak. The hypothesis of the short time lag between male suffrage and party formation seems to fit only the British and German cases; in Denmark, Switzerland, and especially France, the time lag is too large to be considered a valid case of confirmation. In almost all other cases, like Belgium, the Netherlands, Finland, Italy, Ireland, and Austria, the parties appear to have formed before major suffrage enlargements occurred.

Considering the level of the enfranchised electorate at the moment of the final consolidation of nationally centralized socialist movements (the third column of Table 6.3), one can see that in seven of the thirteen cases socialist parties were founded with electorates that were enfranchised below the 15% threshold, which can hardly be viewed as a level capable of triggering the organizational consequences of the competitive drives supposed by the thesis. For example, considering the time lag between party formation and male suffrage (the fifth column of Table 6.3) in Germany, the development of the parties and the franchise was almost parallel. In

---

[22] Svåsand (1980). His conclusion is that the thesis does not hold for Sweden and Norway.

Table 6.3. *Socialist party foundation, franchise, and social mobilization levels (cases rank-ordered according to the earliness of national party foundation)*

country	socialist party foundation	level of franchise at foundation	year of manhood suffrage	number of years between foundation and manhood suffrage	universal suffrage	level of social mobilization 1880-1910 (period mean =-3.6)
Germany	1863-1875	36%	1871	+ 4	1918	-2.3
Denmark	1871-1878	27%	1848	+ 23	1918	-6.7
Belgium	1864-1885	4%	1893	- 8	1949	-2.1
Austria	1874-1889	13%	1907	- 18	1919	-1.7
Switzerland	1880-1888	38%	1848	+ 39	1971	-1.1
Norway	1885-1887	12%	1900	- 13	1912-1915	-5.9
Sweden	1889	10%	1911	- 22	1921	-4.7
Italy	1880-1892	16%	1913	- 21	1945	-3.5
Netherlands	1881-1894	11%	1918	- 24	1922	-3.0
Finland	1893-1899	~8%	1907	- 8	1907	-2.8
France	1880-1905	44%	1848	+ 57	1945	-4.6
Un. Kingdom	1900-1906	28%	1918	- 12/- 18	1918	2.6
Ireland	1912-1922/30	78%	1918	- 4	1918-1923	-4.5 *

Note: Cases of very early male suffrage extension are in bold. Cases of late extension are in italics.
*1920s mean value.

Denmark, France, and Switzerland suffrage predated socialist parties by twenty-five to fifty years. In all the other cases, socialist parties organized fifteen to twenty years before universal male suffrage occurred. It is therefore impossible to argue that the formation of socialist parties was closely related to major enfranchisement. Finally, if one considers the combined index of social mobilization (sector and status transformations, working-class size, homogeneity, and concentration; cf. Chapter 3), it is clear that no relation whatsoever can be identified between such a ranking and the timing of party formation.

Length

The length of the process of organizational consolidation is the most difficult factor to evaluate. Any answer depends on the definition of the starting point of political and corporate national consolidation. Three groups of countries can be safely identified as representing very distinctive experiences. The bulk of the northeastern Protestant countries (Denmark, Sweden, Norway, Finland) stand out for their short and apparently nonproblematic process of political centralization. Only six years elapsed in Denmark between the first significant political predecessor – the Danish Federation of the First International (1871) – and the founding of the national political party (1876). Norwegian socialism, which had stayed at the margins of the First

International, founded a Social Democratic Association in 1883, which transformed itself into the Norwegian Workers' Party (DNA, 1885) two years later. The Swedish Social Democratic Workers Party was founded in 1889, and it is difficult to identify a predecessor.[23] In Finland, the first attempt to federate the workers associations, led by the philanthropist industrialist Victor Julius von Wright (1893), preceded by six years the foundation of the Finnish Workers Party (Turku Program, 1899).

By contrast, political centralization proved painfully long and difficult in continental Europe; particularly in Catholic countries like France, Belgium, and Austria but also, to a lesser extent, in religiously mixed countries such as the Netherlands, Switzerland, and Germany. The problems of political coordination were not the same. In Belgium and France, the almost twenty-five year period that elapsed between the first forerunner political organizations and the establishment of identifiable national political parties was characterized by ideological and organizational divisions due to the differentiated initial ideological environment. The difficulties of political coordination of the Belgian socialist movement, notwithstanding early industrial development, have been attributed to several factors: (1) the early diffusion of socialist ideology came from political emigrants – Buonarroti, Proudhom, Rochefort, Marx, and the refugees of the Paris Commune, who gave Belgian socialism an anticlerical spirit, burning rationalism, and several ideological divisions; (2) in its formative period, the movement was divided between a Flemish part, where socialist cooperative associations predominated, and a Walloon part, where anarchic tendencies were strong and opposed to any spread in influence of the political party. In 1885–1890, political initiatives and strikes in Wallony were not controlled by the party but instead by anarchist militants. In France, the SFIO, founded in 1905, was a merger of at least five distinct formations;[24] its formation had been delayed by the strong antagonism and competition

---

[23] One might mention the Almänna Svenska Arbetareföreningen (ASA) founded earlier (1885) at Malmö by August Palm, an émigré tailor who, in Germany and Denmark, had come into contact with Lassallian socialism. Although the ASA was certainly the first socialist association in Sweden, it is improper to regard it as the forerunner of the SAP; the following years did not see the slow process of political unification of different organizations.

[24] The Workers French Party of Jules Guesde (Marxist); the Broussistes, from Paul Brousse, gradualist, reformist, vaguely syndicalist, and open to bourgeois collaboration; the Workers Socialist Party of Jean Allemane, a fundamentally "workerist" party devoted to the revolutionary general strike and to extreme forms of antimilitarism and anticlericalism; the Socialist Revolutionary Party founded by Louis Blanqui and Edouard Vaillant; the Independent Socialists of Millerand and Jaurès.

among these different parties and political organizations[25] and by the long-standing syndicalist hegemony over the workers' vanguard.[26]

In Austria, the difficulties that hampered national political centralization between 1874 – when an Arbeiter-Bildungsverein was founded in Neudörfl – and 1888–1889 – when the process was concluded, under the leadership of Victor Adler, with the formation of the Sozialdemokratische Arbeiterpartei in Oesterreich (SDAPO), were of two types. First of all, there was a strong repressive policy that made the party almost disappear between the middle of the 1870s and the end of the 1880s. Second, there was the serious internal organizational problem of appealing to several nationalities. Not only in the empire, but also in Vienna and all the regions where ethnic Germans were predominant, large sections of the working class were composed of Czech, Polish, and other Slavic groups, often with their own organizations. In the Netherlands between 1881 and 1894, the process leading to the formation of the Dutch Social Democratic Party (SDAP) was characterized by the conflict among socialist leagues. Those leagues that favorably viewed political-parliamentary action were defeated in the League Congress of 1893 and split when founding the SDAP the following year. Thus, Dutch political socialism emerged from a split in the socialist movement, and its dominant position within this movement did not occur until the beginning of the twentieth century, when other forms of socialism – in particular the syndicalist one – suffered important strategic setbacks.

In Switzerland, the major problem was probably territorial fragmentation. The party formed in 1888, eight years after the central Trade Union Confederation and after two failed attempts to do so in 1870 and 1880. Swiss socialism was preoccupied with the issue of centralization against cantonalization, and it remained so throughout its entire history. Linguistic barriers, and its own early almost exclusively Swiss-German roots,[27]

---

[25] "Control by a socialist party might have been endurable. What was unendurable was the competition of rival socialist parties for control of the struggling young unions. The antisocialist current was strengthened when in 1890s a considerable number of anarchists went into the union"; Lorwin (1954: 20–21).

[26] Malefakis (1974) has argued that the internal divisions and the syndicalist role in France should not be exaggerated. France should be assimilated more to the continental experience than to the Southern cases of Italy and Spain. He may be right in stressing more differences than similarities in the role of anarcho-syndicalism in France versus Italy and Spain. However, when the comparison is made between France versus Belgium and the Netherlands – the other two countries in which syndicalism played an important role in the early phase of the labor movement – the picture is reversed. Classification of countries in paired comparisons may differ from classification in a Europewide set.

[27] The German-speaking part of the country offered more favorable conditions for socialist mobilization: higher industrialization, political influence of émigré German-socialist

made it difficult to centralize an organization whose cantonal sections were facing different party systems, alliance opportunities, and power structures. If, in comparison with other Swiss parties, its federal organizations were more important than its cantonal ones, their coordinating capacity and central authority were unimpressive compared with those of other European socialist parties. Notwithstanding all its efforts, the party was best described as a federation of local sections resting on the support of some large unions (in particular the iron metallurgy and building sectors).

The German and Italian cases are more difficult to characterize, as the length of the process of political centralization is less indicative of its difficulty. In Germany, a specific political organization (Sozialdemokratische Arbeiterpartei, SAP) was set up very early in 1875 as a result of the fusion of earlier organizations (in particular, Lassalle's General German Workers' Association [1863] and Bebel's Union of German Workers' Societies). The length of the process should be seen in the context of its remarkable earliness (see the earlier discussion of timing). No imitation advantage – like those that certainly played an important role in the Scandinavian countries – was available in this case. In contrast, the Italian experience resembles the French one in many ways in that the political organization founded in 1892–1893 was the result of difficulties in amalgamating several tendencies and excluding others. Anarchist, "workerist," and radical-republican (in central Italy) tendencies were finally marginalized but did not disappear. The awareness of the need for a specific political organization won over strong resistance. At the beginning, the party (from 1895 on, the Italian Socialist Party) had four presidents to guarantee the autonomy and representation of its various ideological components. Despite this, political centralization was achieved faster in Italy than in France for reasons that are difficult to determine. In all likelihood, the less distinctive ideological and organizational profile of the Italian forerunner organizations, as compared with the French ones, made their amalgamation easier. It is difficult even to clearly identify the beginning of a phase of national political centralization before 1892, although the Workers Italian Party that emerged in the 1880s should be mentioned.[28]

Finally, the experiences of Ireland and the United Kingdom represent a modality differing from those of both continental and Northern Europe. In these two cases, the period between the first predecessor and the final

militants and leaders, and absence of the influence of the historical Radical Party. See Vuilleumier (1988).

[28] The Socialist Revolutionary Party of Andrea Costa was strongly localized in Romagna, and, in addition to having its origins mainly in the peasantry and agricultural laborers, it incorporated a predominantly anarchist component.

party formation is extremely long. The first Irish political organization with a socialist program was the Republican Socialist Party (ISRP), founded in 1896 by the legendary James Connolly, but no organizational continuity can be claimed between this group[29] and the Irish Labour Party (ILP), whose foundation date is still a matter of debate among Irish historians. Some indicate the date of 1912 for an embryonic political organization; in 1914, however, the Irish Trade Union Confederation (ITUC) added "and Labour Party" to its name, indicating at least minimal differentiation between the two. Formally, the party obtained independent existence in 1922, but it was only in 1930 that the true separation between ITUC and ILP occurred.

It is also hard to identify clear predecessors for the British Labour Party, founded officially in 1906 but first formed in 1900. A Marxist Social Democratic Federation had been founded in 1884, but it had remained extremely weak. The Independent Labour Party was founded in 1893; this was less ideologically orthodox than the latter, and it attracted larger numbers of members. Fabian Societies had existed, of course, for many years. All these forces finally joined together, but it is clear that it was the support of the Trade Union Confederation (TUC) that created the crucial momentum for founding the party.[30] Indeed, strictly speaking, the Labour Representation Committee created in 1900, mentioned earlier, was a coalition of organizations and not an institution in its own right. Real organizational separation can be dated only to 1919, when the party began to accept individual members. In both the Irish and British cases, therefore, the process of party formation spread out over time, but the leading position of the trade unions makes this delayed formation different from that of the continental countries.

The four groups of countries discussed in relation to political centralization (northeastern, northwestern, continental Catholic, and mixed) are not so neat when one considers the length of the process of corporate centralization. Certainly in most cases, there is a correspondence between the difficulties of political and corporate centralization; and as the reasons are frequently the same in both cases, no separate discussion is necessary. However, it is interesting to emphasize that the processes of corporate centralization of the three Scandinavian countries are quite long and sharply contrast with their rapid political centralization. There might be special national reasons for this. In the Danish case, for instance, historians

---

[29] Which remained extremely weak and was shattered by the obscure story of its leader's emigration to the United States in 1903.

[30] Pelling (1965: 205).

point to the ongoing presence of craft unionism as a particularly strong impediment to national confederation development. In Sweden and Norway, however, this was not the problem. Rather, the relationship between the party and the trade unions was so close that the party simply operated for a long time as the coordinating body of local and sectoral unions. Between 1885 and 1899, for instance, the Executive Committee of the Norwegian Labor Party functioned as a confederal chamber of the local unions' branches (samorganisasjon), corresponding to the continental chambers of labor. In these two cases at least, the length of the centralization process in the corporate channel simply indicates that this central coordinating function was taken over by and performed within the political party without provoking any significant tension in the socialist movement. Finally, in only three cases is the time lag between the first attempt at national coordination and the setting up of a central confederation very short: Germany, Switzerland, and the United Kingdom.

Cross-linkage

It comes as no surprise that the prevalent cross-linkage between socialist organizations in different channels was interlocking, with overlapping ancillary organizations, leadership, and activities. Even if this was not the case initially, it tended to become so over time. One already familiar example of this is the early organizational, leadership, and activity interpenetration of the Scandinavian cases. Although Austria is similar in its end results, the circumstances in which this took place are not. Even though Austro-Hungarian socialism was ultimately divided by the disintegrating forces of nationalism, the hostile environment and the extensive and protracted governmental repression resulted in a relationship between the party and the unions that was probably closer than anywhere else in continental Europe. Trade unions offered virtually unqualified support to the party; they recognized from the beginning the importance of political action and the role of the party in this field. Unlike the German socialist movement, where unions sympathetic to socialism finally gained the upper hand in matters of tactics (strike decisions in particular) regardless of their initial dependence on the party, Austrian trade unions always developed their strategic decisions in close consultation with the political party.[31]

In Germany, Finland, Great Britain, and Ireland, the relationship between parties and unions was characterized by an initial phase of dependency – trade union dependency on party personnel, political, and ideological guidance in the first two cases and party dependency in the others.

[31] For the German–Austrian comparison on this point, see Steenson (1991: 196–213).

This situation evolved over time in the classic interlocking pattern. However, the idea of "dependency" needs to be qualified here. Germany is regarded as a clear-cut case of a party-led socialist movement. The trade union movement was initially fostered by socialist political agitators who saw them "primarily as recruiting agents for the political labour movement."[32] Once the early unions' national center had centralized to some extent, the movement kept it in a relatively dependant position; this was also due to Bismarck's antisocialist laws (Sozialistengesetz), which severely circumscribed the unions' activity and pushed them to seek political allies. Such dependency did not last, however. The initial silence of the trade unions with regard to the party theoretical debate between reformists and revolutionaries disappeared, and increasingly they cast the decisive vote. Thus, until 1918, the relationship between the two was not one of subordination or equality in the classic sense of a division of labor and independent spheres of competence. Rather, it was a form of convergence dictated by common goals and forms of struggle imposed by the authoritarian system, by the extremely compact working-class culture, and by a basic ideological orientation. All these worked to render the goals, tactics, and strategies of both kinds of organizations inseparable. In this situation, however, it is easy to see the early imprint of political over corporate socialism.

Germany is not the best example of party predominance over the unions; Finland is a more clear-cut case. Here, the dependence of the unions on the party was difficult to overcome because not only had the local as well as central unions been fostered by party political activism, but also because they had remained extremely weak in organizational and membership term for many years. Suffice it to say that still in 1914, while the party enjoyed massive electoral support and claimed 70,000 members, the trade unions claimed only around 30,000.

In Ireland and the United Kingdom dependence of the party on the trade unions is usually found. The Irish case, however, should be differentiated from the British one, not only because this dependence lasted for a longer period of time and was not overcome until World War II, but also because it was different in nature. Moves to broaden the membership of the Irish Labor Party beyond the collectively affiliated unions were regularly defeated throughout the 1920s.[33] Until at least the 1930s, the party

---

[32] Schorske (1955: 9). Lassallistes were particularly active in this job since their founding of the first German trade union in the cigar-makers sector (1865).

[33] Mitchell (1974: 85). It is interesting to recall that the 1914 congress was worried and concerned "to prevent politicians from worming their way into the new party" and ordained that any Labor candidate for public body *must* be a trade union member.

remained trade unionist in personnel and mentality; after 1930, it remained so in spirit.[34] In Britain, the early relationship between the party and the trade unions is not one of pure party dependency. The British Labour Party soon developed into an unusual coalition of forces similar in some ways to the early Belgian Socialist Party. Trade unions played a predominant role through collective affiliation, but they never "colonized" the party in an Irish type of relationship. Various circumstances and features of British trade unionism may explain this: its sense of force, autonomy, and self-awareness; its strong concern with organizational integrity; its attention to the priority of industrial issues; and, finally, a certain sensitivity to party viability and a sense of constitutionality. All this always left a wide range of maneuver to the Labour Party. In many ways, although types of relationships were the same, the difference between this and the Norwegian and Swedish experiences lies in the greater division of labor and in weaker levels of interpenetration.

In contrast to these four cases, even the Belgian socialist movement has sometimes been described as being characterized by early trade union dependence on the political movement. The foundation of the General Confederation of Belgian Workers (CGTB) resulted from party activities. In 1898, at the bidding of the party's twenty original founding local unions, the party had studied the opportunity of forming a Central Trade Union Committee (Commission Syndicale), in fact, the embryo of the CGTB. The committee was appointed by the party executive; it had no independent policy line even if, in principle, it was open to unions of any political tendency. Only in 1907 did the committee obtain its own statutes and congresses. Some experts have claimed that the party brought the unions under its direct control from the beginning. This is correct if one looks at the formal relationship; however, the party continued to draw a large part of its strength from the extraordinary (and absolutely exceptional in European comparative terms) development of the cooperative and mutuality movement, whose organizations were among the elements constituting the party itself. While the party was fostering union centralization, other forms of corporate organization were feeding the party. This original pattern certainly underlines the difficulty of the Belgian unions in organizing autonomously at the center without external coordinating help. Even so, one hesitates to describe the pattern as being party dominated.[35]

---

[34] Gallagher (1982: 4). Until World War II, candidates and party figures were almost exclusively trade unionists. Their explicitly indicated function was to defend trade unions' interests in the Dail. Contrary to most other European experiences, the ILP suffered trade union conflicts and internal strife more than the reverse.

[35] Belgian historians argue that at the national level the development of unionism and

In the French, Italian, and Swiss cases, I regard the cross-linkage between corporate and electoral organizations as predominantly contingent. In these countries, such cross-linkage was organizationally weaker, less stable, and more, conflictual, and had a less clear division of labor. The French situation is the purest from this point of view, and it can be seen in the number of occasions on which political and union socialism have followed conflicting lines on which the political party was obliged to deal with autonomous and previously uncoordinated actions, together with the continuously asserted independence of unions vis-à-vis politics. In this period the French trade union movement was sometimes tempted to become a pure "demand-group" vis-à-vis the party.

In Italy, the Socialist Party remained extremely weak throughout the 1890s and was unable to exercise a dominant role. The relationship with the unions is more akin to the French type than to the German one – close but problematic and without any clear predominance of one over the other. Confusion about the roles of the two organizations persisted for many years, and while the division of labor never prevented the reformist leadership of the trade unions from taking specific political action, sectors of the union movement debated at length the suitability of founding a political organization to be the direct expression of organized labor.[36] As in France, the politicization of the trade union movement was probably the consequence of the internal ideological and organizational fragmentation of the entire socialist movement. The Swiss case is very different. Here, the organizational weakness and the poor centralization of both organizations always meant that differences between party and trade unions were maintained over the national territory while coordination between the two remained very poor, making impossible and nonviable any dependence or strictly interlocking relationships.

Mode of Representation

The nature of the cross-linkage between political and union central organizations needs to be placed within the context of the broader system of interest representation in the polity. The corporate and fragmented modes of representation point to the presence or absence of a one-to-one relationship in the representation of both channels (see Table 6.1 and its discussion). A socialist-inspired trade union organization can be strongly interlocked with the socialist party, but be unable to claim full representation of the organized labor movement. On the political side, ideological

union activities was hindered by an extremely widespread cooperative movement; Spitaels (1974: 9–21).

[36] The Labor Party dreamed of by Rigola; see Cartiglia (1976).

as well as segmental or territorial fragmentation can give rise to organizations competing for political representation of labor. In the corporate channel, this issue can be operationalized in terms of how much of trade-unionized dependent labor is actually represented by the main socialist confederation and, second and less important, whether such a confederation is ideologically divided internally. In the political channel, the issue is whether the political representation of labor is claimed by a single united political party or by a variety of political formations.

Clear examples of a single-organization monopoly of representation in corporate and political channels are those of Sweden, Norway, Denmark, and the United Kingdom. A mode-disputable case is Austria, where both a Catholic-inspired party and a Union Center were founded early on, in direct competition with the socialists, while no important organizational fragmentation within the left occurred. However, superposition of the class and religious cleavage, rather than their cross-cutting, prevailed, with the result that the class alignment tended to coincide with the denominational one to a far greater extent than in other countries with Catholic political and interest organizations. It should also be emphasized that in their formative phase the trade unions had no ideological competition in organization (as mentioned, they faced national splits); thus, nearly all organized workers belonged to unions with close ties to the Socialist Party until the end of World War II. The Austrian experience can, as a result, be assimilated more to the corporate mode of representation than to the fragmented one.

In Italy and the Netherlands, socialist political fragmentation was endemic even before World War I. Eventually, the firmly established link between political and corporate socialism ended a long process of consolidation during which both organizations had finally defeated their left and/ or right wings. At the same time, however, they had seen the parallel development of competing Catholic and Protestant labor organizations,[37] which hindered the development of socialist trade unions and fragmented the representation of dependent labor. In Germany, socialist political fragmentation started during World War I, and political and corporate fragmentation was increased by significant communist splits in France, Italy, Finland, and Germany after World War II.[38] Religious union mobilization

---

[37] The Christian National Federation of Crafts (Protestant) and the Organizational Office of Crafts (Catholic) were founded at about the same time as the Dutch Federation of Trade Unions.

[38] Also, the Norwegian socialist movement was highly radicalized during the First World War and was strongly affected by the Third International split. However, this resulted in minor short-term fragmentation. The Socialist Party moved in a majoritarian and

produced the lack of corporate representation monopoly in Belgium and Germany very early in the nineteenth century and in Switzerland at the beginning of the twentieth century.[39]

In most of these cases, fragmentation of representation in one channel was paralleled by fragmentation in the other. Finland provides the only case of a unified socialist union movement with two political parties espousing socialist and communist principles as a political reference point. The 1918 civil war left the unions' confederation (SAJ) largely dominated by the communists until its final dissolution by court order for subversive activities in 1930. The new Central Organization of Finnish Trade Unions (SAK), founded the same year, was under socialist control; but although it managed to maintain organizational unity until after World War II,[40] internal strife was endemic and profound. To conclude, political representation was fragmented and highly polarized; corporate socialism, although formally unified organizationally, was marked by intense ideological strife.

Table 6.4 summarizes the statuses of each country's experience in the set of five properties of organizational consolidation selected here, distinguishing between corporate and electoral channels. On the basis of this comparative characterization, we can now turn to the central question of the relationship between organizational consolidation and membership mobilization.

MEMBERSHIP MOBILIZATION

In this section, attention is turned from patterns of organizational consolidation to levels of membership mobilization. Data concerning the membership of parties, general trade unions, and socialist trade unions have been collected from a variety of sources documented in the Data Appendix. A comparative analysis based on row figures is obviously misleading for countries with very different total populations. Therefore, it is necessary to

orderly way to the Third International, and in an equally majoritarian and orderly way it came back to the Second three years later. Organizational and ideological fragmentation were in no way comparable to the other cases listed in the text.

[39] In 1906 (Basel Conference), when the socialist-sympathetic Trade Union Confederation (SGB-USS) decided to abandon its principle of political and religious neutrality (codified in 1902) in favor of a class-struggle platform.

[40] When in 1960 – like in France and Italy earlier – moderate Social Democrats split from the SAK and founded their own confederation, which resumed the old name of SAJ. They accused the communists and left-socialist members of the SAK of using the trade union movement for their political purposes. Only in 1969 did the new internal and international situation permit a reunification of the labor movement.

Table 6.4. *Trade unions and parties: organizational consolidation (1880–1940)*

coun-try	sequence	timing		length		cross-linkage	mode of representation
		corporate channel	electoral channel	corporate channel	electoral channel		
Au	parallel	interm.	interm.	long	long	interlocking	corporate/ (segmental fragmentation?)
Be	party first	interm.	early	long	long	interlocking	segmental fragmentation
De	party first	interm.	early	long	short	interlocking	corporate
Fi	parallel	interm.	late	short	short	dependency/ interlocking	ideological fragmentation
Fr	parallel	late	late	long	long	contingent/ demand group	ideological fragmentation
Ge	parallel	early	early	short	med.	dependency/ interlocking	ideological and segmental fragmentation
Ir	corp. first	interm.	late	med.	long	dependency	ideological fragmentation
It	party first	late	late	long	med.	contingent	ideological fragmentation
Ne	party first	late	late	med.	med.	interlocking	segmental fragmentation
No	party first	interm.	interm.	long	short	interlocking	corporate
Sw	party first	interm.	interm.	med.	short	interlocking	corporate
Sz	corp. first	early	interm.	short	short/med.	contingent	ideological, segmental, and territorial fragmentation
UK	corp. first	early	late	short	long	dependency/ interlocking	corporate

use indices that standardize for the size factor, taking as the reference the total dependent labor force, the total vote for the party, and the total electorate. The indices used in the analysis are therefore the following:[41]

1. Partisan mobilization
   a. Membership of socialist parties as a percentage of the national electorate (*socialist partisan density* [SPD])
   b. Membership of socialist parties as a percentage of the socialist vote (*socialist voters' encapsulation* [SVE])
   c. Membership of communist parties as a percentage of the national electorate: (*communist partisan density* [CPD])

---

[41] These indices have been computed on a year-to-year basis. In this chapter, they will be analyzed by decade averages and by election years. When corporate or partisan membership figures are referred to the election year, the actual election year figure is an average of the five years around the election year (two beforehand, the election year, and two afterward).

    d. Membership of Communist parties as a percentage of the Communist vote (*communist voters' encapsulation* [CVE])

    e. Total cumulative membership of socialist and communist parties as a percentage of the electorate (*left partisan density* [LPD])

    f. Total cumulative membership of socialist and communist parties as a percentage of the total left number of votes (*left voters' encapsulation* [LVE])

2. Corporate mobilization

    a. All trade union members as a percentage of the total dependent labor force (*trade union density* [TUD])

    b. Left-oriented trade union members as a percentage of the total dependent labor force (*left trade union density* [LTUD])

    c. Left-oriented trade union members as a percentage of the electorate (*trade union electoral density* [TUED])

The distinction between party organizational *density* and *encapsulation* points to different theoretical meanings of the different indices. When membership figures are computed as percentages of the general electorate, the organizational presence of the party partisan machine is measured within the global electorate. This measure can therefore be viewed as a reliable comparative indirect indicator of the organizational presence within the society. When membership figures are related to the party or party-family *actual vote*, the reference point varies widely from one party to another. What this index can actually indicate is not the absolute partisan density of the given party within the society, but the level of closeness between members and voters. This index, used widely by Duverger in his classic work on parties, is totally inadequate for cross-country or cross-party comparisons, although it may be of some use for cross-temporal comparison.[42]

PARTISAN MOBILIZATION[43]

The entire historical process by which personal experience and group identity were transformed into political choices "could not have got under

---

[42] For this reason, the cross-country voters' encapsulation is not discussed here. A graph with these data can be found in Bartolini (1983: 187).

[43] The levels and rates of corporate and partisan mobilization may depend on the more or less closed nature of the channel in which they operate. Political and corporate mobilization requires association and collective-action rights to be granted; freedom of association is therefore a decisive intervening variable between organizational consolidation and political mobilization. These variables are discussed in the next chapters.

way without the organizational efforts of the parties and their militants, without their educational and promotional activities, and without their tireless drive to mobilize more and more of their clientele."[44] Party members and activists in the pre–mass media era were the protagonists of the scramble for additional support throughout decades of hidden and obscure work on each side of the main cleavage lines. The fact that some socialist parties were preceded by other parties with a mass organization[45] might have facilitated their development in that the legitimacy of this kind of organization had already been recognized. However, in most cases, socialist parties developed as outsiders in hostile environments, needing to mobilize resources in order to overcome the ostracism of the established elites. As such, the organization of a large number of followers was likely to be their answer to the problem of entering into the respective political systems. This led the organizational network to enforce a strong degree of formalization and role differentiation.[46] Members were the most important, if not unique, financial source for the parties and their press; they carried out the work of educating (not only politically) a working population with a low level of class awareness; they provided the party with inexpensive personnel for all kinds of necessary work; in many cases, they also provided medical care, legal assistance, and protection to workers and to groups of potential supporters of the party. Membership entailed militancy. It could be hypothesized that the electoral results of the European socialist parties during the period of their formation and consolidation depended on their increase in membership and their organizational growth.

If one contrasts this early picture with the current situation, it seems that the traditional role of membership in social democratic parties has been severely damaged by the major changes in the post–World War II economy, social structure, and communications. The goals of a high level of involvement and of rank-and-file agitation are incompatible with the socialist parties' massive participation in government. The growing importance of nationwide mass media as channels for political messages has had

[44] Rokkan (1970e: 422).

[45] As in the Netherlands and Belgium, in Great Britain an organization that was truly a mass organization can be dated from the Chamberlain reorganization of the Liberal Party's "Birmingham Caucus"; see Ostrogorski (1970, Vol. 1: 161–203). Even the Conservatives, after much criticism of Chamberlain's system, developed some of the features of an early mass popular party; Cornford (1964).

[46] Neumann (1956a) argues that the "total integration" at which communist parties were aiming was both a function of and a prerequisite for their nondemocratic nature. However, even if, in some of the Western communist parties (although not in all), quantity of membership was sacrificed to quality, the role that members played within the party was not that different.

far-reaching consequences for the communication processes of the parties
and their organizations. The development of the welfare state has inevitably taken over most of the previously mentioned functions of education,
legal aid, medical care, and so on. Finally, even the financial function of
the membership has been challenged by the parties' involvement in business and commercial enterprises and, last but not least, by the introduction
of financial aid from public sources since the 1960s. Paradoxically, such
postwar developments have led some experts to speak about a "contagion
from the right" of the social democratic parties[47] and to emphasize, regret-
fully, the process of growing uniformity among European parties toward a
model implying the "downgrading of the role of individual members."[48]

   We can now look at the historical data in the light of these opposing
perceptions. Three European countries – the United Kingdom, Sweden,
and Norway – have a socialist membership that includes individual card-
carrying members as well as collective affiliation through trade unions, and
this creates problems of comparability that need to be kept in mind. In
the British case, separate figures for individual members are available for
1928 on, and these data are used in the figures and computations.
Therefore, British Labour partisan density and encapsulation are systematically underestimated to an extent that is difficult to guess, corresponding
to the proportion of collective members who would have been individual
members were this the only way of joining the party. No separate figures
for individual members of the Swedish and Norwegian Labour Parties are
available, but in Sweden the collectively affiliated members are estimated
to be about 70% of the total postwar membership and in Norway, about
40%.[49] These partisan densities are therefore systematically overestimated
by the unknown proportion of collective members who would not have
joined the party on an individual basis. Nevertheless, the problem of the
Scandinavian countries is less acute because, particularly in Norway, indirect membership is not channeled through nationwide federations. Rather,
each local union makes a decision on affiliation by majority vote, and
individual members can thus "contract out" fairly easily. For counting
purposes, this kind of affiliation indicates a more serious political involvement in the party than is the case for the United Kingdom.[50]

   In Figure 6.1, the levels of socialist party membership as a percentage

[47] Epstein (1967: 257–261).
[48] Kirchheimer (1966b: 190).
[49] Elvander (1977).
[50] In financial terms, this often does not mean very much, as trade unions support the
   party financially from a common fund without specifying the names of contributors. See
   Rokkan and Valen (1962).

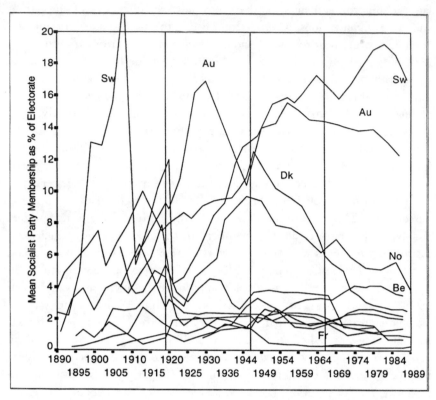

Figure 6.1. Socialist party membership as a percentage of the electorate.

of the total electorate (SPD) from 1890 to 1980 are charted. Between 1890 and 1919, in the context of the still very restricted suffrage, the countries show high levels of partisan density, which for many of them will never be matched later on. When the right to vote was extended to men between 1917 and 1920, the index shows a considerable drop for most countries. In the period between the two world wars, socialist partisan density begin to differentiate across countries. Most of them remain fairly stable at the level reached after World War I, while in the three Scandinavian countries and Austria, socialist partisan density continues to grow during the entire interwar period and reaches a level ranging from 9% to 13% of the electorate. This level is on average three times larger than that of the other countries.

Between 1945 and 1965, two of the four high partisan density countries – Norway and Denmark – start a decline that is remarkable for its sharpness and consistency. Their index shows an impressive parabolic distribution over the twentieth century, peaking in the 1950s. This means that the decline of socialist members in the electorate at large precedes by ten to twenty years the electoral crisis of these parties in the second half of the 1960s. By contrast, in Austria and Sweden, the organizational presence of the socialists continues to grow, both countries reaching an average level of 15 socialist members for every 100 electors. Austria recovers the exceptionally high level reached at the beginning of the 1930s, while Sweden continues to increase steadily. The particularly strong corporate model of Swedish society has allowed the Social Democratic Party to make up through organizational affiliation – which, incidentally, goes well beyond the traditional trade union sectors – what it was losing in individual membership.[51] In Austria, however, membership was, and remained, strictly individual, and the party's attempt to transform every voter into a full party member was linked to the *lager* model of societal development and the necessity within the consociational model to organize the respective subcultures fully.[52]

Among the remaining countries, only three are worth commenting on. In the 1945–1965 period, Switzerland maintained a higher level of partisan density than the other countries simply because its electorate was smaller than that of the others (no female vote). France, by contrast, underwent the organizational demobilization of its socialist party, which became the least densely organized party in Europe. Belgium shows a small but consistently growing trend in the 1945–1965 period,[53] which is surprising, as it occurs in a particularly unfavorable situation of sharp electoral decline and in a political milieu characterized by the relative apathy of the citizens, by elitist values and culture, and by a minor role attributed to militants and members.[54]

In the final period, following 1965, Austria and Sweden show signs of a declining partisan presence. The Norwegian and Danish socialist parties continue to decline at a rapid pace; indeed, the Danish decline amounts to an organizational demobilization, losing two-thirds of its organizational presence in the electorate. The Norwegian decline is similar, although less rapid. Most of the other countries show a declining trend, which is less dramatic given their low starting levels. The only exceptions are Germany

---

[51] Experts have emphasized that if the effects of collective membership are disregarded, there has been a long-term *decrease* in the total number of members since the 1950s; Sjöblom (1978: 66).

[52] Gerlich (1987: 81–83).

[53] The Belgian data are available only for the postwar period; before that time, the party was structured indirectly and federally; see Dewachter (1976: 309). Moreover, the data have been fully reliable only since the increasing efforts to administer the party centrally in the 1960s; see Rowies (1977: 14).

[54] Dewachter (1987: 311–330).

and Finland, which show signs of an increase in the late 1960s and early 1970s and which have since then stagnated. The case of the SPD is worth noting insofar as it challenges conventional wisdom about the development of membership. In clear contrast to all the logical speculation and hypotheses summarized at the beginning of this section, the German SPD experienced a major decline in membership until 1953 under the leadership of Schumacher, that is, during the period in which the party adhered very closely to the "party of mass integration" model and during which the ideological emphasis and the functional uses of the members were still of a classical type.[55] Conversely, after the party began its transformation into a catchall organization, its membership began to increase rapidly. The German SPD kept abreast of the German electorate as it increased – this was no mean achievement – and it even managed to increase its presence after 1965. Finally, there is a striking decrease in the individual membership of the British Labour Party, which is even more pronounced if we consider that in the 1960s "constitutional" amendments were introduced to increase the differentiation between trade union and party members and to encourage people to affiliate individually.[56]

In Figure 6.2 the data concerning the communist parties are reported. In all cases, the over-time development of communist party membership is a normal curve, with a growth phase from 1920 to 1945–1950, with a peak immediately after World War II, and a subsequent generalized tendency to decline. The only exception is that of Finland, where the peak moves to the early 1960s. In eight countries, the partisan density of the communist movement never went beyond 1%, that is, 1 party member for every 100 electors. Only in Italy, France, and Finland has it acquired a higher level; in Belgium and Austria, communist partisan density peaked at a high level for only one or two elections after World War II, and then it rapidly declined to below the 1% level.

A few other points are worth mentioning, as they question widely held assumptions. The French Communist Party is depicted as a large partisan machine in comparison with the other French parties; it looks less impressive, however, in a cross-country perspective. The French communists

---

[55] Hartenstein and Liepelt (1962).

[56] In 1962, a constitutional amendment stated that only trade unionists who were individual members could be trade union delegates to the party conference. In 1965, the same thing was suggested in relation to attendance at constituency meetings. Moreover, in the same period, the Labour Party adopted the rule that local units should affiliate at a minimal membership of 1,000. As it seems that the membership of an average local unit was no more than 500, it follows that the real level of individual membership in the 1970s was much lower than the official figures suggest. See Leonard (1975), Martin and Martin (1977), and Committee on Financing of Political Parties (1976).

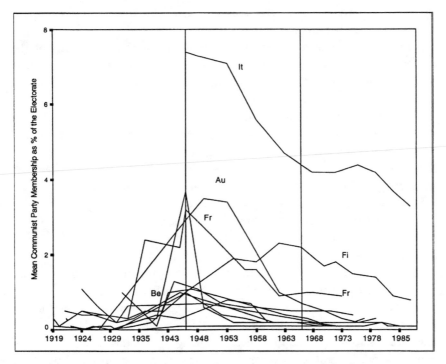

Figure 6.2. Communist party membership as a percentage of the electorate.

strengthened their partisan network only in the 1930s and peaked at about 3% of the electorate after World War II. Immediately after this, their support started to collapse so rapidly that by the 1970s it was only slightly higher than that of the tiny communist parties of other countries. If one compares the partisan mobilization with the electoral support in that period, the conclusion is that the party can hardly be regarded as a powerful partisan network and that its electoral support went far beyond its organizational presence. Again, by social democratic standards, even the Finnish communist movement cannot be characterized as densely partisan, as its social presence never went beyond the 2% threshold. The same argument applies to the German Communist Party at the peak of its electoral fortunes. Only the Italian Communist Party shows a significant level of partisan mobilization after World War II, when there were roughly 8 members for every 100 voters in 1945; this was roughly the same level as the Norwegian Socialist Party in the same period and was well above all the other socialist parties except for the Danish, Austrian, and Swedish ones. Even at the end of the 1980s, shortly before its definitive abandonment of every reference to the communist tradition, the party's partisan density was about 3.5%, still above that of the majority of European socialist parties.[57]

In principle, one might have expected that, within the limits of the partisan mobilization propensity of a country, communists and socialists would share the partisan market in quotas that are somehow related to their electoral size. However, no association exists between the partisan density of communist and socialist parties. Only in Finland does there seem to be an equilibrium among the partisan density of the two parties. A tentative interpretation of the finding that the partisan market is more "monopolistic" than the electoral market is that in the far more ideologically tense world of membership and militant confrontation, one of these two parties necessarily takes a clear lead over the other.

In conclusion, it is worth emphasizing that the overall trend of Communist membership developments since 1945 is similar to that of most socialist parties. If, as is sometimes argued, the Communist parties tried to resist such a tendency and to maintain a mass organization, they failed.

Because they are both expressed as proportions of the electorate, the partisan density of socialist and Communist parties can be summed into a partisan density of the whole left. Considering only the post–World War I data, so as to reduce the influences of changing electorate size, the set of countries can be ranked in terms of average partisan density (Table 6.5). Such a ranking is fairly stable throughout the period and adequately illustrates their differences. I relate these patterns to electoral mobilization later in the chapter. However, a first examination of the main tendencies in Figure 6.1, Figure 6.2, and the averages in Table 6.5 suggests that there are different national propensities toward a card-carrying involvement that should be linked to systemic features and that tend to stay unmodified. A second, and linked, consideration is that, notwithstanding the sharp decline in the memberships of the Danish and Norwegian labor parties, the small countries retain their systematic lead over those with larger populations. In the 1970s, the six countries with the highest ratio between socialist party members and voting population are Sweden, Austria, Norway, Belgium, Denmark, and Finland. Only the Netherlands and Ireland are exceptions. Smallness thus seems to facilitate socialist recruitment and

[57] It is possible to read this information as proof that the Italian communist movement was, at least from the organizational point of view, qualitatively different from the traditional Communist Party from 1945 on. This thesis has always been defended by the party leadership, but it has also been supported by much of the scholarly research on the party. See in particular the collection of essays in Blackmer and Tarrow (1975). See also Tarrow and Ascher (1975).

Table 6.5. *Average partisan left density (1918–1989)*

	sd membership as % of the electorate	cp membership as % of the electorate	left membership as % of the electorate
Sw[a]	**13.8**	.5	14.2
Au	**13.4**	1.1	14,0
De	**7.3**	.3	7.4
No	**6.2**	.4	6.5
It	1.6	**5.1**	5.9
Be	3.4	.4	3.6
Sz[b]	3.4	.5	3.6
Fi	2.3	1.1	3.1
Ge	2.2	.4	2.4
UK[c]	1.7	.1	1.8
Fr	.8	**1.5**	1.9
Ne	1.5	.2	1.7
Ir	.3	.	.3

[a]Limited comparability due to high proportion of collective membership.
[b]Limited comparability due to female enfranchisement in the 1970s.
[c]Only individual members.

penetration, strengthening the old generalization about the negative relationship between size and participation.

The analysis of the data suggests a few concluding considerations and speculations about party membership. The declining fortunes of socialist membership were not compensated for either by the growing membership of other left parties[58] or by the growing membership of the non-left parties.[59] The overall partisan density of the European party system has tended to stagnate or decline since World War II, because it has been

[58] A discussion of radical socialist parties in Scandinavia can be found in Logue (1982: 249–290); membership figures for these parties are available in Katz and Mair (1992: 215, 745, 792).

[59] In some countries, various religious and conservative parties show increases in membership in the 1970s: the Finnish Christian League, the Irish Fianna Fail and Fine Gael, the Parti Chrétien of Luxembourg, the Norwegian Conservative Party and Christian Democratic Party, the Swedish Center Party and Christian Democratic Party, and the German CDU, CSU, and Liberal Party. Katz and Mair document a few other similar cases in the 1980s. See Mair and Katz (1992). However, in no way do these increases compensate for the left secular losses.

unable to keep abreast of the growth of the electorate in these countries. The basic problem thus becomes whether, *from an organizational-resource point of view,* this decline implies a decline in the organizational interest of parties for this type of resource, which in turn determines a corresponding decline in the investment made to promote it, or, *from the individual motivation point of view,* the data point to a decline in the political interest of citizens in this kind of participation and/or a shift toward other channels of participation.

From the *organizational perspective,* party membership should be viewed mainly as a *resource* and as a consequence of the organizational incentives offered by the party leadership and officers.[60] To maintain or increase the levels of membership and activism requires an organizational effort that may or may not be rewarded in terms of money, work, and time. This will thus depend on how party leaders perceive and value the resource of membership and its "by-product," that is, activism. Such an evaluation implies a cost–benefit analysis conducted in terms of politics, ideology, and economics in comparison to the other resources available to the party, which can be strongly dependent on certain institutional characteristics of the political system, as well as on the individual-level phenomena discussed later.[61]

There are three main sources of party interest for partisan density as a resource. The first is party finance. During the 1960s and 1970s, most European democracies introduced some form of public financing for the political parties. Of the many changes that have touched the political parties since their development, this may have had some of the most far-reaching consequences. Public financing tends to decrease the organizational incentive to increase membership, even if much depends on whether alternative financial sources are open to the leadership.[62] This is because

---

[60] Clarke and Wilson (1961), Conway and Fiegert (1968), and Lange (1977).

[61] I have tested a number of hypotheses relating the fluctuation in socialist party membership to conditions of party environmental disturbances: the government/opposition role of the parties, the electoral and postelectoral years as compared with nonelectoral years, and the cases of electoral losses. The results of the test were mixed. More important, however, was the fact that the instances confirming the role of membership as the organizational regulator of the party's relationship with the political environment tended to decline over time, suggesting that parties either renounced efforts at organizational encouragement or lost the capacity to make them effective and rewarding. Cf. Bartolini (1983).

[62] A comparison of the German SPD and the British Labour Party is particularly interesting in this regard. The former has always raised substantial sums from its members. In a sense, it was obliged to do so (despite the fact that some public funds were already given to parties in 1959) by the fact that after World War I the trade union movement was declared to be nonpolitical and, in contrast to the United Kingdom and many other

most of the funds provided by the state are directed toward campaign and research expenses, a factor that could well make the candidates and the party machine more independent of the members.

The second major challenge to the relevance of membership as an organizational resource derives from the postwar changes in the channels of political communication. In literate and urbanized societies, the mass media tend to replace party membership as the key means of conveying the political messages of the parties to the largest possible constituency. The role of traditional campaign and propaganda activities, such as local meetings and speeches by candidates and party representatives and door-to-door propaganda, declines in the face of more-effective techniques of mass propaganda. This thesis was challenged some years ago. It was argued that party leaders may grossly overestimate the capacity of the mass media to convey political messages, as the latter rarely have widespread impact unless they are relayed and reinforced within the innumerable face-to-face environments in each community.[63] However, this criticism preceded the membership decline of the left parties and the further explosion of mediated communication. The environment of political persuasion has been increasingly *privatized* in recent years. This has reduced the role of face-to-face communication and, consequently, the marginal utility of membership and militant activism. The contradiction between membership activism and other forms of party-efforts need not be absolute, but it is difficult to deny that traditional local-party activity today merits less attention from the party leadership.

Leadership attitudes toward membership are also influenced by its role in the formation of party policy. After participating several times in government, leadership groups have learned that their fate is much more closely linked to their responsibility to the electorate at large than to the possibly unrepresentative sample of party members.[64] By increasing its

European countries, was not allowed to give substantial financial support to the Socialist Party. Hence, the SPD emphasis on a dense network of local branches and membership mobilization (about 60% of party income comes from membership fees; cf. Morgan [1969: 38]).

[63] Relying on the pioneering work of Paul Lazarsfeld on the impact of the new mass media on the opinions and tastes of the U.S. public and on his two-step model of communication flow, Rokkan argued that the mass media could reach and influence only active and interested citizen; passive and uncommitted individuals pay little attention to messages that do not fit into their previously established orientation. See Rokkan (1970e: 425). See Seyd and Minkin (1979), who base their analysis on this argument.

[64] Both Pizzorno (1967: 281–283) and Kirchheimer (1966b: 177–200) have stressed this point. They believe that the growing autonomy of political leadership in contemporary political organizations results from the need for all success-oriented organizations to accept conformity to the values held by the society as a whole in selecting their ruling

autonomy and strengthening its position, party leadership becomes a resource in its own right, in the sense of the mass public image of leaders.
Leadership needs visibility and autonomy of action to be exploited as a
resource, whereas increases in membership and militancy for electoral purposes can easily occur at the cost of reducing leadership autonomy both
inside and outside the party.[65]

From the individualistic perspective, membership decline results from
a decline in the positive orientation of individuals toward the specific form
of card-carrying political involvement. This perspective gains importance
whenever collective enthusiasms and mobilizations progressively give way
to phases of "individualistic mobilisation,"[66] when the individual motivations leading to party membership become less stable than those leading
to the party vote.[67]

Individual-level arguments relating party membership fluctuation to
economic cycles or to material return distribution are of little use for
interpreting the data described earlier. Cycle hypotheses cannot explain
secular trends. Material-rewards hypotheses imply that membership increases when parties have more power and greater access to government,

---

groups. Consequently, the success of a leadership rests more on its identification with
the needs and values of the whole society than on the institutional goals and programs
of its own organization.

[65] Associated with this "leadership autonomy" need is the parties' interest in establishing
links with new types of organizations designed to express the interests of new sectors of
society that are not traditionally part of the party network. Parties may reduce their
efforts to increase and strengthen membership in the traditional social units and instead
devote their energy to recruiting from different functional groups in society through the
direct incorporation of their organizational leadership. However, the chance and opportunity for corporate links with various organizations is dependent on the nature of
societal articulation. Moreover, the recognition that other kinds of organizations are
becoming increasingly attractive to politically active people does not necessarily lead to
a reallocation of parties' organizational resources and efforts to establish direct links with
such organizations. The challenge might be regarded as a stimulus to devote more
energy to increasing their own levels of membership and activism.

[66] Pizzorno (1967) and Hirschmann (1982).

[67] Actually, members are more sensitive to internal party life (splits, unifications, leadership
crises) and are more unstable than party voters. An aggregate comparison of the stability
of the socialist electorate with that of the socialist-party membership can be made
through an index — albeit a rather rough one — computed in the following way: (the
difference between the highest and lowest votes of each party divided by the average
vote of the period) (the difference between the highest and lowest membership figure
divided by the average membership of the period). If the index has a negative value, this
means that the electorate of a given party is more stable over time than its membership.
With the marginal exception of a few cases during the pre-1914 period, the clear result
is that party electorates are everywhere more stable than party membership. All the
socialist parties considered can be ranked according to this index, starting with the
Dutch Labor Party, which shows the lowest difference in favor of electoral stability.

and, in the long term, membership is higher in countries with a long-standing socialist participation in government. Neither of these hypotheses, however, is borne out by the data.[68]

It is more promising to focus on the role of *ideological motivations* in stimulating membership, considering the level, intensity, and spread of ideological beliefs in different historical periods as the single most important determinant of fluctuations. In the postwar period, we experienced a decline in the appeal of the traditionally integrative and all-encompassing ideologies that dominated the first half of the twentieth century, even if we have not necessarily witnessed the end of ideology as such. However, the association between the clear decline of ideological tension of citizens' political attitudes, on the one hand, and the long-term decline of partisan density, on the other, retains a distinctively qualitative flavor.

From another point of view, the growth and diversification of leisure, as well as cultural and communal activities, has made membership in political parties, as well as other forms of direct political participation, increasingly marginal and unattractive for those whose membership choice was based on *motivations of solidarity and identity*. A larger and more differentiated number of voluntary associations are currently available, and these are often less demanding in terms of real involvement. Yet another perspective suggests that membership stagnation and decline, rather than being a sign of *depoliticization*, may be attributed to the shift toward *alternative* and competing channels of political participation. Even if it seems that, up to the 1960s, different forms of political participation were not mutually conflicting or exclusive, but rather produced *spillover*,[69] the question remains of whether this has changed with new and unconventional forms of political participation; there is still limited comparative evidence on this problem.[70] However, even individuals' *instrumental moti-*

---

[68] Bartolini (1983: 198–199). This "political economy" argument is certainly not supported by the Norwegian and Danish lefts, whose memberships' secular decline started and was accentuated exactly in the period in which their lefts were enjoying a hegemonic governmental role.

[69] Considerable evidence on the positive relationship between party membership and other forms of political participation (and even of nonpolitical participation) was accumulated in the 1960s: Allardt and Pesonen (1960: 27–39), Barnes (1967: 122), Lane (1959: 166), and Berry (1969: 204).

[70] Two important works on political participation – Verba, Nie, and Kim (1978) and Barnes and Kaase (1979) – do not deal with this problem at all. The former deals only with conventional forms of political participation and, largely influenced by the American conception of and experience with party and party activism, considers membership as a mere indicator (among others) of party identification. The latter, by contrast, studies unconventional participation and protest, but, developing its analysis exclusively at the level of individual attitudes, it rules out the impact of political institutions. These

vations toward party activism have suffered considerably from the changes in the role of party politics. The struggle for collective goals that characterized the period of the structuring of mass politics was based on behaviors largely determined by moral commitments, collective loyalties, and nonspecific participation.

The changes just mentioned have not simply brought about a new politics of "individual possessivism"; they imply a more far-reaching change in the conditions in which various interests can be articulated and represented in the political arenas where parties are confined to exercising an institutional role of mediation. These changes are seen in the growing importance of private, organized interest groups brought about by a type of political behavior that is increasingly influenced by instrumental and selfish calculations coupled with specific forms of participation.[71] The resulting trend is toward the collectively organized representation of specific and limited interests in order to satisfy sectional demands that are articulated autonomously. This behavior is based on the growing awareness among large sectors of the public that the living conditions of individuals are increasingly dependent on specific governmental policies in the welfare state and that they are no longer the result of enduring collective struggles under the leadership of political parties and their ancillary organizations. In facing these new forms of political behavior, parties – and particularly traditional mass parties – are further handicapped by their tendency to be in some way the "captive" of those interests and organizations that led to their initial emergence.[72]

More generally, individual ideological, solidarity, and instrumental sources of party commitment have been challenged by new modalities of political participation such as action groups, local movements, single-issue parties, and so on. Precisely because they concentrate on a narrow range of problems and are not responsible to large electoral constituencies, they can

---

choices are legitimate. However, they weaken the final extrapolations concerning the problems and strains that contemporary institutions of political involvement – namely, parties, interest groups, and mechanisms of representation and election – may undergo as a result of the emergence of the new issues, attitudes, and cleavages documented in the book.

[71] These new phenomena have been very skillfully described by Schmitter (1977). However, this analysis is based to a large extent on the experiences of central and northern European countries, and these phenomena may be less visible and important in Southern European parties. On this point, see Linz (1979: 180).

[72] Offe (1972) elaborates on this point, identifying the "repressive" nature of the modern liberal democratic political systems in this intrinsic selectivity of interest representation. From a different perspective, recent studies on postmaterialist protest come to the conclusion that unconventional forms of behavior emerge as a consequence of inadequate representation; cf. Inglehart (1977) and Barnes and Kaase (1979).

maintain the commitment of their membership, something that is simply not feasible in a larger mass party. In this way, they satisfy the demands that party activism is less suited to meet. It should also be added that the ever-increasing interest in local political issues would seem to favor new kinds of militancy other than that of party membership. Traditional parties, and particularly socialist parties, have tended to nationalize political issues and to place them in a broad perspective, thus finding it difficult to deal with them satisfactorily in purely local terms.

In conclusion, the interpretation of the historical decline of left party membership needs to be framed within three intertwined processes. First, there are *cross-national differences* in partisan mobilization resulting from national systemic properties (historical experiences, the closeness of societal groups to political parties, the role of parties as opposed to other agencies in early mobilization or regime founding, etc.). These elements determine different national propensities toward this form of political participation and explain the main cross-country differences irrespective of time and historical periods of collective mobilization exuberance. Second, the *short-term variation* in partisan mobilization can be referred to as an *organizational* perspective that responds to the party's strategic decisions to foster or dampen this type of mobilization. Finally, *long-term trends* common across countries cannot be interpreted as the result of national systemic features or the strategic choices of the individual parties. Instead, they can be best explained by looking at membership from an individual perspective, as a factor *external to party organization* that influences the propensity to adopt this type of political involvement. Basic changes in individual motivation toward partisan activism, and declining organizational investments in it have combined to determine the post–World War II general decline in or stagnation of membership figures and a corresponding decline in party activism.

UNION MOBILIZATION

Whereas party membership is the result of the creation of a nationalized and centralized political organization, union membership developed before any form of national and centralized union movement occurred. The precondition for party membership was freedom of political association; the precondition for electoral mobilization was the right to vote; and the precondition for corporate mobilization was freedom of economic association. Beyond this, however, the possibility for unions to mobilize potential support rested on their capacity to deliver collective goods for their potential audience. This, in turn, depended mainly on the unions' capacity to provide collective contracts that could benefit an entire group of persons with a single agreement on wages, work conditions, and the like. In this section, I examine the European variation in levels of corporate mobilization by looking at the levels of union membership. I then relate their variation to the modalities of collective-agreement developments.

Data on union membership are more reliable than those on party membership because more research has been devoted to them, and excellent data collections have been produced. However, not all unions were socialist or ideologically linked to left parties, so the latter have to be separated from those of different political orientations. The attribution of unions to one camp or the other has been based on secondary sources and has not posed any major problems (see the Data Appendix for the sources).[73] Figures 6.3 and 6.4 chart the historical trend in overall and left trade union density across the European countries. The difference between Figure 6.3 and Figure 6.1 concerning left party membership is striking. First, there is a secular tendency to growth and no sign of decline in the most recent decades. Second, the over-time development suggests that levels of trade unionization of the dependent labor force were relatively uniform in the pre–1918 period and tended to differentiate later on. Before the turn of the twentieth century, the highest levels of trade unionization (in the United Kingdom and Denmark) stood at about 16–18% of the dependent labor force, while the lowest ranged from 2% to 5%. By the 1980s, the differences between the extremes (even excluding France) are on the order of 50–60%. The period in which cross-country differentiation occurs is therefore the one after World War II. In 1945, the range was still limited to about 30%, and it has doubled since then.

For almost all countries, there are two clear peak periods – 1917–1922 and 1945–1947 – followed by a clear decline in both cases. There was a period of general growth until World War I and a peak after it; then a decline in the 1920s, followed by new growth in the 1930s and a peak immediately after World War II. After this, some countries continued an upward trend: Sweden, Austria, Denmark, Norway, Belgium, and Ireland. Others underwent a decline in the 1950s and then a new growth phase later on: Italy, Finland, and the United Kingdom. Still others remained fairly stable throughout the post–World War II period: the Netherlands and Germany. Finally, there are only two cases of clear and protracted

[73] In Austria, it is more difficult than elsewhere to estimate the percentage of left trade union members over all members. I have based this estimate on the percentage of seats in the Trade Union Confederation governing body, which has been stable at about 77% for the SPO, 20% for the OVP, and 3% for the KPO. A discussion of these figures is available in Gerlich and Müller (1983: 343).

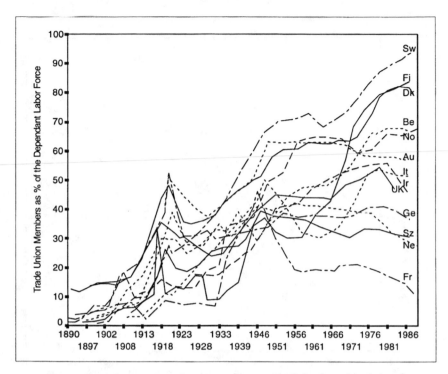

Figure 6.3. All trade union members as a percentage of the dependent labor force.

postwar decline: Switzerland and France. For the latter, it is possible to view this trend in terms of a postwar collapse from which the unions never recovered. In the 1980s, there were some signs of decline in Ireland, the United Kingdom, the Netherlands, Germany, and Austria. However, this trend was not generalized, as it was in the case of party membership. The picture of left union membership (Figure 6.4) is not substantially different, apart from two features. The first concerns the post–World War II period, during which the density of the left unions give an impression of stability rather than growth. Only in Finland, Sweden, and Denmark did left trade unionization grow sharply. This implies that post–World War II trade unionization growth has been greater for non-left unions than for left ones. The second point is that the difference between the Protestant north (Denmark, Sweden, Finland, the United Kingdom, Norway) and the Catholic or religiously mixed center and south of the Continent (Austria, Belgium, Germany, Italy, Switzerland, the Netherlands, France) is far more evident for left trade unionization than it is for overall trade unionization.

The decline in left party membership after 1945 was paralleled by

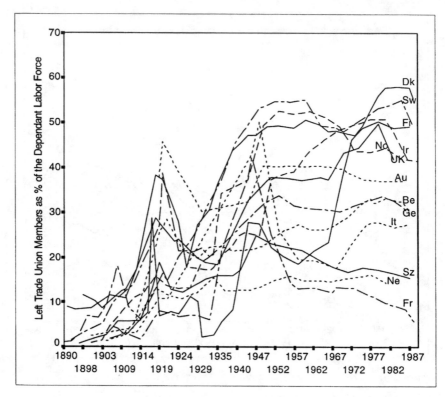

Figure 6.4. Left trade union members as a percentage of the dependent labor force.

increasing levels of trade unionization in European society. Although traditional working-class unionization was generally regarded as supporting
and reinforcing the electoral and membership development of left parties,
the situation became less clear with the new middle-class and public-
employee unionization. Trade unions might well have been seen by many
people as a more effective channel of interest representation than the parties
insofar as they were able to preserve their ideological standpoints and the
defense of their sectional interest more effectively than the parties.

The ratio of left trade union density to total trade union density points
to a varying degree of corporate or fragmented relationship in the interest
channel. This was discussed before and can now be looked at more precisely
for the unions. In Figure 6.5, the lines of total trade union density and left
union density are reported for each country. The difference between the
two is indicated by the gray area, which represents the level of trade
unionization outside the socialist world. In one group of countries –
Austria, Belgium, the Netherlands, Switzerland, and Italy – the union

movement has been historically characterized by the presence of nonsocialist unions; therefore, the mode of representation in the interest channel is historically fragmented.[74] This historical fragmentation has grown over time to the advantage of the nonsocialist unions, which have grown more since World War II.

In another group – France, Germany, and Ireland – there is also the historical tradition of Catholic and/or religious unions, but there is no historical increase in the share of the unionized labor force of this nonsocialist component. Finally, there is the group of the homogeneously Protestant northern countries. In Denmark, Sweden, and Finland, nonsocialist unions were not the result of religious countermobilization, but rather of the unionization of social groups that did not identify politically with social democracy. In these three countries, these unions were weak up to the 1950s, but they exploded from the 1960s on, representing the most dynamic sector of new trade unionization. The same applies to Norway, the only difference being that until the 1950s there were almost no nonsocialist unions there. Britain also belongs to this group but does not show the growth of nonsocialist unionism, as in the other cases. With the exception of Finland, these northern countries provide the clearest historical cases of corporate representation between the political and interest channels. However, more recent developments have broken this pattern: The monopoly of representation of socialist unions disappeared by the end of the 1980s, even if the new nonsocialist unions did not necessarily move closer to other, nonsocialist parties.

Table 6.6 reports a rank ordering of European countries for the period 1918–1986 in terms of the level of general and left trade unionization. Then the average figures for the post-1945 period are reported in order to help judge the extent to which the general ranking for the whole post–World War I period reflects later developments. Sweden and Denmark lead the trade unionization rank ordering, both in general and for the left, with Austria and Norway closely following. The difference between Norway and Austria is that left trade unionization grew more strongly in Norway after World War II, while it was muted in Austria in the same period, also as a result of the success of other nonsocialist unions. Belgium and the United Kingdom follow with slightly lower levels, but in Belgium left trade unionization reaches barely half of the overall trade unionization. On the whole, these are the countries for which it can be safely said that

[74] The figure shows nonsocialist unions appearing only after World War II in Italy. However, even before the rise of fascism, Catholic unions existed, although it is difficult to estimated their membership.

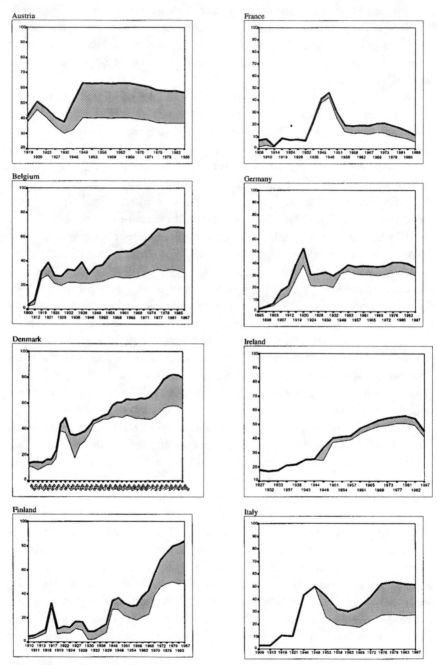

Figure 6.5. Non-left trade unionization by country.

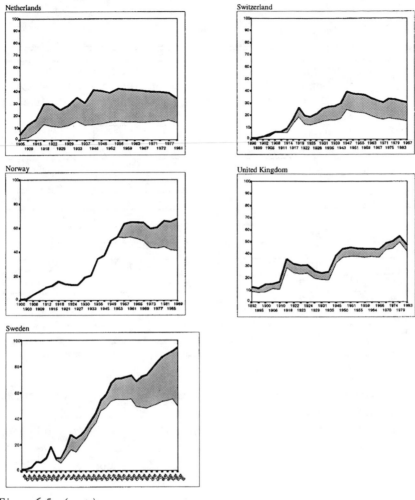

Figure 6.5. (cont.)

Table 6.6. *Trade union and left trade union membership as a percentage of the dependent labor force: country rank ordering*

	trade union density 1918-1986	left trade union density 1918-1986	trade union density 1945-1986	left trade union density 1945-1986
Sw	63.5	44.1	77.8	52.2
De	57.9	44.9	66.7	51.0
Au	55.6	38.4	60.2	38.6
Be	46.4	26.5	52.7	28.2
No	44.5	36.3	59.6	46.6
UK	39.9	33.7	46.2	40.2
Ir	38.6	35.8	48.1	43.8
It	38.8	25.4	43.9	28.0
Fi	36.7	23.0	53.1	34.2
Ge	36.7	28.5	38.2	31.7
Ne	35.3	14.0	37.6	14.8
Sz	30.1	17.6	34.2	19.4
Fr	20.9	16.4	24.5	18.7

there was a comparatively high European level of trade unionization throughout the whole period under consideration.

In Ireland and Finland, by contrast, there is a marked difference between the average for the 1918–1986 period and that for the post–World War II period; in both cases, the period of major growth followed World War II. Switzerland and France stand at opposite ends of the continuum: Their averages were below the European average in both general and left trade unionization. By the 1920s, a general ranking can be said to have been established; and since then, countries have kept their relative levels of overmobilized, medium-mobilized, or decidedly under-mobilized corporate channels. This was less the case in the development of party membership. In other words, if the overall temporal trend is put to one side, in each main period most of the variation is among countries rather than within them.[75]

[75] An analysis of variance for the 1945–1986 period shows that about 70% of the variance is between country groups compared to less than 30% within country groups. For some of the systematic hypotheses concerning these national differences, see Stephens (1979) –

To conclude this section, I shall now deal with the question of the relationship between cross-country and cross-time variation in the levels of mobilization and the unions' incorporation into the industrial-relation system by establishing collective bargaining and agreements. In this area, a cross-country comparison is too crude, as union growth in different sectors should be related to the spread of collective agreements in those sectors, but it does offer some insight into the role that collective agreements played in the development of union strength. To examine the onset of collective bargaining in European countries and to define the point at which it became an established practice is complicated because (1) in some cases, it is difficult to indicate a clear point at which collective bargaining started; (2) the interval between the emergence of a first agreement in a skilled trade and the time when collective bargaining covered a significant section of the working population can be considerable; (3) a general agreement between national employers and trade union confederations did not always lead to formalization of the system; and (4) the date of legal recognition may be misleading, either because it came many years after a system had actually been established (for example, in the Netherlands) or because formal recognition was not matched by practice. Therefore, for a comparative assessment, I have collected information concerning (1) the date at which collective bargaining showed signs of emerging; (2) the date at which laws governing bargaining were enacted; and (3) the point at which collective bargaining became an established practice, that is, the "critical mass" point at which bargaining was widespread and accepted.[76] A comparative overview of these findings is reported in Table 6.7. The table summarizes the development of collective agreements, reporting the date of the first agreement when known, the date of legal recognition and the regulation of such agreements, and the period in which collective agreements spread to become common practice. Together with these three dates, comments are made that add qualitative information.

who emphasizes the degree of concentration of capital as a key explanatory variable – and Rothstein (1992) – who emphasizes the differences in government labor-market institutions, in particular the policies and institutions of unemployment insurance (the Ghent system versus other solutions).

[76] In this section, I have relied on the research assistantship of Simon Dubbins. Only the final results of this comparative analyses are reported here. I have used the following sources: Crouch (1993), Traxler (1992), Vilrokx and Leemput (1992), Scheuer (1992: 172), Skogh (1984), Brunn (1991), Lilja (1992), Goetschy and Rozenblatt (1992: 404–408), Stearns (1971), Neufeld (1974), Ferner and Hyman (1992), Cella and Treu (1989), Windmuller (1969), Galenson (1949), Prodzyznski (1992), Fulcher (1991: 141), Parri (1987), Katzenstein (1984), and Musson (1972).

Table 6.7. *Development of collective bargaining in European countries*

	date of first agreement	date of law for collective bargaining	period of establishment	comments concerning the development
Austria	1870–1880 in some skilled trades	1920	1900–1914	Bargaining seems to have become gradually more widespread in the years between 1900 and 1914, although it only became fully established after the First World War and then following the period of Nazi rule after the Second World War
Belgium	1890–1900	1944	1900–1919	The practice became established between 1900 and 1919 (first joint committees with employers and govt. formed in 1919); however, remained informal until passing of Draft Agreement on Social Solidarity in 1944.
Denmark	1870–1899	1899	1899	Embryonic bargaining in the period 1870–1899 gave way to full-scale bargaining after the signing of the Basic Agreement in 1899. Prior to this, employers resisted strongly and tried to impose their system of bargaining
Finland	1905–1912	1944/5	1944	Some initial bargaining around 1905–1912 followed by complete rejection of bargaining by employers. Although Swedish employers tried to encourage Finnish employers to bargain, nothing developed until after World War II
France	1900	1919 (1936)	1919–1970s	Despite initial agreements around 1900 and some spread until late 1930s, still not a full-fledged system of bargaining until after World War II, and perhaps even as late as the 1970s
Germany	1870s in some skilled trades	1918	1918–1930, 1949	Bargaining in skilled trades prior to 1918, although resisted in heavy industry. After 1918 became more widespread but declined as power of labor weakened in mid-1920s. Fully established after 1949
Italy	1880–1890s in some skilled trades	1948	1948–1970s	Spread of bargaining in some areas around 1880–1890 and increase until 1922; however, never really became fully established. Real growth after World War II, especially from the late 1950s on; move to industry and plant bargaining in late 1960s
Ireland	probably around 1900	1871, 1906	1950–1970s	Although bargaining can be traced to the turn of the century, it did not really become established until the 1950s and afterward
Netherlands	1900–1911	1927	1913–1920	Strong resistance to bargaining gave way after the strikes of 1913 and spread very rapidly in the period until 1920
Norway	1873 Oslo priters	1915	1930s	Some bargaining during the 1880s–1890s but strong employer resistance continued until early 1930s, so no full establishment of bargaining until after 1930s. Rapid spread thereafter
Sweden	1905/6 engineering/ general	1928	1938 -	Some bargaining emerged at beginning of century but fiercely resisted by employers until 1920s and 1930s; full establishment after the Basic Agreement of 1938
Switzerland	1870s in some skilled trades	1911	1890–1900	Very early acceptance of collective bargaining (second only to UK); became effectively established around the turn of the century
United Kingdom	early 1800s in skilled trades	1871, 1906	1880–1890	Bargaining in skilled trades existed by early 1800s; became fully established around 1880–1890, especially after the rise of unskilled unionism around 1890

The various national experiences can be organized along two dimensions, which will now be discussed.

Timing of Development

Three groups can be identified – early, medium, and late. In the early category – 1890–1914 – have been placed Britain, Switzerland, Austria, Denmark, and Belgium, where the critical-mass point was reached either at the end of the nineteenth century or in the first decade of the twentieth century. In the middle category – 1914–1945 – are Germany (excluding the period of Nazi rule), Sweden, Norway, the Netherlands, Ireland, and, to some extent, France. In the late category – after 1945 – are Finland, Italy, and again France. France appears in both categories because bargaining develops between the wars, although it becomes established only much later. Germany is also problematic: While bargaining did develop after World War I, it was accepted only by some employers and was destroyed by the Nazis. Therefore, it may be better to place Germany in the third category.

Types of Development

There seem to be three types of bargaining developments:

1. Steady *evolutionary* developments in which a steadily increasing proportion of the workforce have their terms and conditions regulated by collective agreements. This group includes the United Kingdom, Austria, Switzerland, Germany, Belgium, and Ireland.
2. A more *explosive* style in which bargaining is resisted and then, after intense struggles, gains acceptance spreading rapidly to include large sections of the workforce. This group includes Finland, Norway, Sweden, the Netherlands, and Denmark.
3. An *unbalanced* growth in which bargaining develops for small sections of the population, but with constant reluctance to bargain until very recently. This group includes France and Italy.

These three types of bargaining result in a typology of different national experiences, which is reported in Table 6.8.

From a strictly individualistic perspective, it can be argued that the capacity of an organization to deliver collective goods should lead to stagnation or even decline in its membership.[77] Unions that are unable to force collective agreements may still attract members who desire those

---

[77] Olson (1971).

Table 6.8. *Timing and type of development of collective bargaining*

| | | timing | | |
		early	medium	late
type	*evolutionary*	Britain, Switzerland, Austria, Belgium	Germany (excluding Nazi period), Ireland	
	explosive	Denmark	Netherlands, Norway, Sweden	Finland
	unbalanced			France, Italy

agreements and perceive their additional contribution to the organization as instrumental to such a goal. When the capacity to deliver the collective good is finally achieved, this drastically alters the cost–benefit calculations of potential members and leads to membership stagnation or decline. From a contrasting perspective, collective agreements may be viewed as the sign of the unions' capacity to deliver what their claims promise, that is, as the evidence of unions' claim that organizational mobilization pays. As such, collective agreements may act as a powerful incentive to membership recruitment. In this collective rather than individual perspective, the unions' capacity to win collective concessions actually fosters unionization; therefore, collective agreements mark the turning point in union growth rather than their decline.

We can look at the historical development of union membership discussed before in the light of these two opposite hypotheses. A relationship exists between the earliness of collective agreement institutionalization and the overall unionization rate of the labor force (Table 6.9). Countries where collective agreements developed late tended to have a lower density overall and, in particular, a lower left union density, while the highest density figures are shown by countries with early collective-bargaining practices. However, of the five countries that introduced widespread collective bargaining either early or at an intermediate time, at least two never reached high trade unionization levels: the Netherlands and Switzerland. In contrast, among the latecomers, Ireland, Finland, and Italy have trade unionization levels that are higher than those of Switzerland or the Netherlands.

A more decisive test of the role played by collective bargaining and agreements in relation to trade union growth is performed by comparing the general union density in the *period of the spread* of collective agreements

Table 6.9. *Levels of trade union density by timing of institutionalization of the collective bargaining*

timing of collective bargaining institutionalization	trade union members as % dep. lab. force	cases	left trade union members as % dep. lab. force	cases
late	33.53	74	25.17	74
medium	46.12	78	32.15	75
early	47.25	106	33.30	106
total	42.97	258	30.60	255

(as defined in Table 6.7) with that of the *two decades before* and the *two decades after* this phase. The choice of the two decades rather than a different number of years is arbitrary, but I feel that to evaluate the impact adequately, long periods are necessary. For the same reason, I identify the phase of wide spreading with a long period to avoid identifying the date of collective-agreement institutionalization with that of legal acceptance. In Table 6.10, countries are ranked according to how early collective agreements were institutionalized.[78]

The institutionalization of collective agreements did not start earlier in those countries where the trade unionization level was comparatively higher. This suggests that earlycomers introduced collective agreements not as the result of union growth pressure but because of other institutional or political features of the political system. In these countries, union growth occurred primarily *after* the introduction of collective agreements. This is true even for the United Kingdom, where union density doubled in the two decades after their institutionalization. Even for latecomers, the introduction of collective agreements led to union growth both during and after the introduction, even if, obviously, this introduction occurred when unions were stronger than was the case for the earlycomers.

There are only three cases that lend some support to the idea that collective agreements were the result rather than the cause of union growth and that they were later responsible for union stagnation or decline. Italy

[78] In the final column of Table 6.10, the average trade union density for the entire period *after* collective-agreement institutionalization is reported. This allows a control, particularly for those countries where collective bargaining agreements were established very early in the century, on whether the change in the two decades immediately afterward was major or minor with respect to the overall change in the whole period after the critical-mass phase.

Table 6.10. *Trade union density and development of collective bargaining*

country	period of widespread collective agreements	average trade union density in the two decades before widespread collective agreements	average trade union density during widespread collective agreements	average trade union density in the two decades after widespread collective agreements	average trade union density since widespread collective agreements
UK	1890-1915	n.a.	14.6	28.9	46.2
Sz	1890-1910	n.a.	3.1	19.6	27.5
Au	1898-1912	n.a.	n.a.	43.4	55.6
De	1899-1908	13.7	14.3	35.1	54.4
Be	1900-1918	below 3	5.6	31.9	36.2
Ne	1905-1920	2.5	19.8	29.7	37.6
Ge	1918-1933	9.2	34.6	37.2	38.2
No	1935-1950	11.1	40.3	62.0	63.8
Sw	1938-1950	17.0	59.6	71.3	78.7
Fi	1945-1960	13.3	32.9	60.1	65.7
Ir	1952-1970	25.4	46.7	53.2	53.2
It	1966-1976	39.6	42.7	52.4	52.4
Fr	1970-(1980)	21.1	20.2	14.3	14.3

is a borderline case. Union density had already reached about 40% before collective agreement spread, and there was only a minor increase during the spread itself. Still, the decade following this spread saw a remarkable increase of 10%. In Germany, union density was low before the introduction of collective agreements and increased mainly during the period of their proliferation between the two world wars. In the following period, growth stopped and remained more or less stable. France is the only case in which union density declined both during and after the spread of collective agreements. On the whole, however, it cannot be maintained that in Western Europe the unions' capacity to deliver collective goods to their potential constituency reduced the willingness of employees to join them. Collective agreements appear almost everywhere as a resource for union growth and as a sign of the success and credibility of their representational claims that did nothing to discourage participation.

ORGANIZATIONAL STRUCTURING, MEMBERSHIP MOBILIZATION, AND ELECTORAL DEVELOPMENT

So far, I have discussed (1) the modalities of the early organizational consolidation of the socialist movement in both its political and corporate aspects; (2) the successive levels of partisan mobilization that ensued in the political channel; and (3) the union density levels and growth. In this section, these elements will be related to the electoral developments of socialism. At later stages, they will also be used in reference to other features of the class cleavage. Three issues are discussed in the following sections: (1) to what extent differences in early central organizational consolidation (sequence, timing, length, cross-linkage, representation mode) later influenced membership mobilization capacity; (2) what kind of relationship can be said to exist between corporate, partisan, and electoral mobilization; and (3) whether the combination of the three types of mobilization actually identifies different styles or types of socialist movements and class cleavage mobilization.

ORGANIZATIONAL CONSOLIDATION AND MEMBERSHIP MOBILIZATION

To model the organizational consolidation pattern, I have arranged its dimensions as shown in Figure 6.6. The earliness or lateness of the central consolidation of unions and parties combine to determine the party/union sequence (party first, union first, or parallel). The correlation coefficient of the length-timing classifications indicates the extent to which, for instance, early timing of union development is associated with a resulting pattern of union precedence over the party; similarly, the association between party timing and sequence indicates the extent to which early party formation accompanies a party-led sequence.[79] Party and union length and timing are ordered by giving the highest value to the respectively most favorable situation (early development and short consolidation). This makes it necessary to have two "best sequence" ordinal scales: one for the unions – attributing the highest value to the unions leading over the party – and one for the parties – attributing the highest value to the party leading over unions. This explains why the correlations have double signs but equal value.[80]

---

[79] The correlation in the table results from the following ordering of the organizational-consolidation dimensions.

  Unions' Sequence: 3 = Unions first; 2 = Parallel; 1 = Party first; *Party sequence*: 3 = Party first; 2 = Parallel; 1 = Unions first;

  Unions' timing: 3 = early; 2 = mid; 1 = late; *Party timing*: 3 = early; 2 = mid; 1 = late;

  Unions' length: 3 = short; 2 = mid; 1 = long; *Party length*: 3 = short; 2 = mid; 1 = long;

  Cross-linkage: 3 = interlocking; 1 = contingent; *Mode*: 3 = corporate; 1 = fragmented.

[80] If unions' length ordering is correlated with the sequence for unions (with unions' leading being assigned the highest value), the association is positive. If the same variable

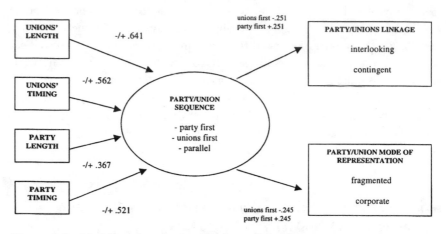

Figure 6.6. Modeling the organizational consolidation process.

If party and union length and timing determine a specific sequence, the latter impacts on the relationship between parties and the unions. Party-led processes of central consolidation should thus more logically result in union dependency or interlocking patterns. At the same time, union-led processes should more often lead to contingent or interlocking relationships. As far as the mode of representation is concerned, union centralization preceding party development is associated more with final fragmented representation in both channels, while the opposite is true for sequential development in which party development clearly precedes union centralization and presumably plays an important role in this process. With this kind of framework, we can investigate the relation between each pattern and the actual mobilization capacity in the different channels of the socialist movement. To this end, Table 6.11 reports the mean levels of the three types of mobilization – left trade union density, left parties' partisan density, and total left vote – by the modalities of organizational consolidation in the period between 1900 and 1940, when all countries had elections and the franchise tended to converge toward universality.

Corporate mobilization is more than twice as high with early or intermediate consolidation than with late consolidation. It is also influenced by the length of the consolidation process in an unexpected direction: higher levels of corporate mobilization with longer centralization processes. Note that factors relating to political centralization and representation have a strong impact on corporate mobilization, which is roughly double (1) in

is associated with the sequence with the party leading the unions, the correlation has the same value but the opposite sign.

Table 6.11. *Pattern of organizational consolidation (1880–1920) and levels of political mobilization (1900–1940)*

	corporate	partisan	electoral
trade union timing			
early	16.0 (35)	3.2 (24)	27.2 (36)
medium	17.4 (78)	7.0 (64)	32.6 (80)
late	8.0 (21)	1.4 (24)	22.1 (25)
party timing			
early	22.1 (36)	6.7 (24)	34.3 (37)
medium	16.1 (44)	6.8 (45)	29.3 (46)
late	10.9 (54)	2.0 (43)	26.2 (58)
trade union length			
short	13.1 (52)	3.2 (49)	31.3 (53)
medium	14.6 (27)	6.2 (23)	24.3 (28)
long	18.5 (55)	5.8 (40)	30.0 (60)
party length			
short	15.4 (59)	6.5 (58)	34.0 (59)
medium	12.8 (37)	2.6 (37)	26.3 (41)
long	18.7 (38)	4.8 (17)	25.8 (41)
sequence			
TU-first	15.0 (29)	3.1 (16)	20.3 (29)
parallel	14.4 (41)	4.2 (36)	35.0 (45)
party-first	16.7 (64)	6.0 (58)	29.5 (67)
linkage			
contingent	8.9 (25)	2.3 (27)	23.2 (28)
interlocking	17.1 (109)	5.8 (85)	30.9 (113)
mode			
fragmented	12.1 (76)	2.6 (61)	28.6 (81)
corporate	20.3 (58)	7.8 (51)	30.3 (60)
mean	15.6 (134)	5.0 (112)	29.3 (114)

Note: Number of elections given in parentheses

cases of early party centralization and (2) in cases of interlocking party–union cross-linkage. A corporate mode of representation is associated with higher levels of corporate mobilization in only a limited way. Finally, sequence – whether party consolidation comes before or after union consolidation – does not influence the membership development of the unions. Although the role of political parties and activists in fostering trade union development is known, it is somehow striking that political and representational factors (the linkage and the mode of representation) have such a strong effect on the levels of union membership mobilization. A similarly notable surprise is that the variables belonging to the process of organizational consolidation do *not* have a significant impact on the levels of *electoral mobilization*. The differences in the means are far lower than for the other forms of mobilization. The only relevant factors are party-related factors:

the early formation, the rapidity of its centralization, and interlocking party–trade union linkage. In contrast, none of the factors relating to trade union consolidation are significantly associated with electoral mobilization. Note that while a fragmented mode of representation is associated with somewhat lower levels of corporate mobilization, it shows little impact on electoral mobilization. *The electoral success of the left parties appear to be quite independent of the modalities of organizational development in the corporate channel. Party organizational and representational factors influence corporate mobilization much more than corporate organizational factors affect electoral mobilization.*[81]

Partisan mobilization is indeed more highly influenced than the other forms by organizational consolidation aspects. Almost all organizational characteristics do have a significant impact on partisan mobilization (the weakest one being the length of party consolidation). Not surprisingly, the factors that play the most important role are the sequence (the party-led sequence is favorable), the timing of party consolidation, and, in particular, the linkage and the mode of representation. Interlocking cross-linkages are associated with two-and-a-half times higher levels of partisan mobilization; corporate monopolistic trade unions and political representation fosters a partisan mobilization that is three times higher than does fragmented representation. Parties that grew in close organizational interpenetration with unified trade union movements gained advantages from the dense network of organizational cross-linkages.

The model in Figure 6.6 can be arranged to create syndromes of the most favorable and most unfavorable sets of conditions for each type of mobilization. For trade union mobilization, one can hypothesize that the most favorable conditions occur when trade unions organize early, within a short period, before the party, with an interlocking or party dependency cross-link with the party and with a corporate mode of representation. The most favorable organizational combination for electoral and partisan mobilization consists of an early and short process of party centralization, a party-led sequence, and again, interlocking linkage with unions and a corporate mode of representation. The opposite combinations should be regarded as the least favorable for each form of participation.

To test this hypothesis, we can run a regression of each type of mobilization against the set of factors that identifies its supposed best conditions and then compare this with a similar analysis in which all the

---

[81] This thesis seems to be valid even for the British case. With a geographical analysis of electoral changes and of unions' density, the important research of Tanner (1990) has shown that the development of the electoral support for the Labour Party does not reflect the areas of union expansion in the 1920s.

organizational variables are included. For each specific form of mobilization, this can identify the most discriminating factor among those discussed here (controlling for the combined effect of all) and the global weight of the whole set. This is reported in Table 6.12. For each type of mobilization, the first column shows the result of a regression performed with only the organizational variables that concern that specific form of mobilization and set the best conditions for it. All the organizational variables are used for the same exercise in the second column.

First, this test confirms that the process of organizational consolidation is far more important for partisan and corporate mobilization than for electoral mobilization, for which it explains little variance (standing at .177 compared with .477 and .311). Second, entering the party consolidation variables into the regression concerning corporate mobilization increases the association considerably, adding about 11 percentage points in explained variance (from .311 to .421). The timing of party development, in particular, takes on an important weight. When the variables concerning union consolidation are added to the regression of electoral mobilization, nothing changes in the overall association (.182 versus .177) and very little in the order and relative weight of the variables. *This confirms that left electoral mobilization does not depend on the forms of corporate-channel organizational consolidation, while corporate mobilization does depend to a considerable extent on the pattern of party consolidation.*[82]

Partisan mobilization lies in an intermediate position, the bulk of the variance being explained by party-related variables. However, the inclusion of the union consolidation variables causes a significant increase in explained variance, as both trade union timing and length appear important. The fragmented or corporate representation model goes a fairly long way toward determining levels of partisan membership. The data indicate that political and organizational divisions impact most strongly on partisan membership participation. By its nature, the latter is an intermediate form of participation that combines the character of voluntary and active adhesion in a way that is appreciably more "expensive" than voting (like corporate mobilization, in this sense) and the character of remoteness from

---

[82] To check this conclusion further, I have performed a regression of each type of mobilization with the variable that, in principle, should have a lower impact on it: that is, corporate mobilization with party consolidation variables and partisan and electoral mobilization with union consolidation variables. While party consolidation variables alone explain more variance in corporate mobilization than do corporate consolidation variables (about 38% compared to 31%), in the other two cases union consolidation variables explain less variance than the party variables (44% versus 48% in partisan consolidation and 14% versus 18% in electoral mobilization).

Table 6.12. *Relative weight of organizational consolidation factors (1900–1940)*

corporate mobilization				partisan mobilization				electoral mobilization			
best condition for corporate mobilization		all organizational variables		best condition for partisan mobilization		all organizational variables		best condition for electoral mobilization		all organizational variables	
Variables	Beta	Variables	Beta	Variables	Beta	Variables	Beta	Variables	Beta	Variables	Beta
Trade Unions-Timing	.403	Trade Unions-Timing	.737	Party Length	.042	Trade Unions-Timing	-1.095	Party Length	.258	Trade Unions-Timing	.291
Cross-linkage	.331	Cross-linkage	.283	Party Timing	.211	Cross-linkage	-.093	Party Timing	.217	Party Length	.185
Mode	.043	Party Length	-.193	Party Sequence	-.062	Party Length	.108	Cross-linkage	.201	Cross-linkage	.149
Trade Unions-Sequence	.241	PartyTiming	.866	Cross-linkage	.052	Mode	1.046	Mode	-.195	Party Timing	.291
Trade Unions-Length	-.611	Mode	.490	Mode	.540	Party Timing	.765			Mode	-.041
		Trade Unions-Length	.196			Party-Sequence	.542			Trade Unions-Sequence	-.056
		Trade Unions-Sequence	.723			Trade Unions-Length	.730			Trade Unions-Length	.208
Rsq	.311		.421	Rsq	.477		.544	Rsq	.177		.182

Note: method = enter; entry .05; removal .10.

functional specific interests and actions, in a way that is appreciably more "abstract" in motivation and incentives than union membership (like electoral mobilization, in this sense). "Costing" more than voting does and being more "remote" from interests than union membership is, partisan mobilization is more strongly affected by organizational and ideological incentives than are corporate and electoral mobilization.

RELATIONSHIP BETWEEN FORMS OF MOBILIZATION

As far as I know, the association between corporate, partisan, and electoral forms of mobilization has never been examined in a comparative perspective. For the period under consideration and for the set of approximately 320 elections, the associations are shown in Figure 6.7, including both left and general trade union density. There are several striking features in these figures. First, they are all very similar. Whether we consider trade union density or left trade union density, the association between partisan and corporate mobilization is basically the same and has a level that comes close to that between partisan and electoral mobilization. Second, the correlation between corporate and electoral mobilization is slightly higher than the others for both total trade union density and left trade union density (.563 versus .491). Moreover, electoral mobilization is associated more strongly with trade union density than with left trade union density. Finally, and most important, these associations appear to be surprisingly low, considering the close historical relationship between the left parties and trade unions and considering the fact that electoral and union developments both show a historically growing trend that should foster their association over time.

Two theses can be used to justify the overall weak association between corporate and electoral socialism in the nineteenth century. The first can be labeled the "learning process thesis." It states that, although both processes show a secular growth trend, in the early days of socialist mobilization workers who were already mobilized in the corporate channel were *not yet* translating this membership into voting practices for class parties due to lack of experience and/or class consciousness, to the habit of abstaining, or to anarcho-syndicalist political or antipolitical stands. It was only over time, and after a long process of apprenticeship and political education, that they came to develop the habit and realize the importance of electoral politics. If this were true, one would expect an increase over time in the association between these forms of political engagement. Thus, a generally weak association should result from weak levels of association in

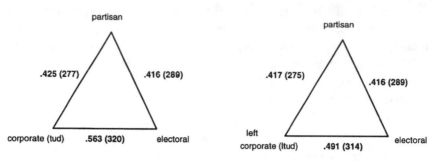

Figure 6.7. Association among partisan, corporate, and electoral mobilization.

the early days of the socialist movement's development, with a growing level in more recent decades, say from the interwar period or from World War II on.

The second thesis can be labeled the "golden age" thesis. Here, the idea is that in the early phase of class mobilization, clearer class alignments and greater social homogeneity of socialist support existed. Later on, goes the argument, the pattern was complicated by several factors, ranging from the progressive abandonment of the class mobilization appeal of socialist parties in favor of broader nonclass appeals, to the social and cultural blurring of class boundaries, to the influence of the countermobilization of religious or nationalist movements, and so on – a long list of explanations of why class is less closely linked with political behavior today than it used to be. In this second case, the overall weak association should result from a temporal pattern that runs in the direction opposite the one described previously: A strong association in the early "golden age" of class alignments should decline over time as other factors impact on the relationship between corporate and electoral socialism.

The learning process and golden age theses can be tested by analyzing the temporal development of the association between the different measures of mobilization. In the first case, we would expect that low association levels in the early formative period become increasingly strong with time. In the second case, the opposite should result: A strong association in the early golden age should become weaker over time. Figure 6.8 reports the values of the correlation between corporate and electoral mobilization, decade by decade, over almost a century of electoral politics. The decade correlations tend to be very low in the period up to the 1920s, peaking in the decade 1930–1940 and tending to decline later to levels roughly similar to those of the first period. This evidence does not fit either the learning process or the golden age thesis. If instead we use the logic of both arguments to interpret the curves, we can argue that the early phase

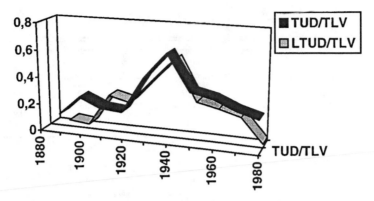

Figure 6.8. Correlation by decade between left votes and trade union density.

was not characterized by strong association because of the delayed translation of corporate membership into political behavior; that the golden age of association between class and electoral behavior is to be located in the decades around the middle of the century; and that the class dealignment factors mentioned previously have tended to make union membership and the left vote increasingly less associated since the 1950s. If there was a period in which left parties became the captive of their own high working-class support, this was in the 1930s to the 1950s. Who voted for the socialists in the early days, then? As far as the class composition of the socialist vote is concerned, the first formative phase should be regarded as being at least as problematic, in terms of class alignment, as the last and most recent phase from the mid-1960s on.

General association measures hide cross-time and cross-country differences. To facilitate the direct *cross-country, cross-time,* and *cross-channel* comparisons of political mobilization processes within the socialist movement, data have been averaged in Table 6.13 by decade, computing left union membership and party membership in percentages of the national electorate. Taking the values of the decade means at the bottom of the table, it is easy to see that in the 1930s there were, on average, 12.6 members of left-oriented trade unions, 5 members of the left parties for every 100 electors, and 34 left voters for every 100 valid votes. Compared with the same figures in the decade of the 1900s, partisan density remained stable, corporate density increased by about 20%, and electoral support increased by 100%. Therefore, in the global experience of European socialism, electoral mobilization lags behind corporate mobilization until approximately the 1890s, but from then on there are far more left voters than left union members. Note also that partisan mobilization is the most stable of all.

Table 6.13. *Levels of corporate, partisan, and electoral mobilization by decade*

		1890	1900	1910	1920	1930	Mean 1920s and 1930s
Austria	corporate	.	.	20.0	22.0	15.9	20.5
	partisan	.	.	7.6	12.0	16.9	13.2
	electoral	.	21.0	33.1	· 40.0	41.7	40.4
Belgium	corporate	.	1.4	15.4	24.3	21.5	22.9
	partisan			n.a.			ab. 2.0
	electoral	8.8	22.5	29.3	37.9	37.9	37.9
Denmark	corporate	33.3	18.1	22.6	16.5	19.3	17.4
	partisan	5.2	6.9	8.7	8.4	9.6	8.7
	electoral	10.5	23.9	28.9	34.9	45.6	38.5
Finland	corporate	.	1.8	3.6	3.8	2.0	2.9
	partisan	.	5.5	4.2	2.0	1.6	1.8
	electoral	.	38.4	42.2	40.2	37.7	38.9
France	corporate	.	1.8	4.6	8.1	14.4	11.2
	partisan	.	.30	.8	1.2	2.8	2.0
	electoral	9.9	11.4	18.6	29.8	36.2	33.0
Germany	corporate	3.2	10.6	16.3	14.3	10.4	12.6
	partisan	.	4.00	4.85	2.9	2.6	2.9
	electoral	23.4	30.4	40.2	37.8	35.4	36.6
Ireland	corporate	.	.	.	6.8	7.8	7.6
	partisan			n.a.			< 1.0
	electoral	.	.	.	9.1	8.4	8.5
Italy	corporate	.	10.0	7.6	9.8	.	9.8
	partisan	1.1	1.2	.60	1.9	.	1.9
	electoral	7.9	17.8	28.6	29.9	.	29.9
Netherl.	corporate	.	3.7	12.7	6.7	7.7	7.1
	partisan	.3	.9	2.3	1.27	2.1	1.6
	electoral	1.4	11.5	21.8	24.2	25.7	24.8
Norway	corporate	.	3.6	8.0	6.7	11.3	9.0
	partisan	2.8	3.6	6.2	4.2	6.6	5.4
	electoral	.5	12.6	30.0	34.9	39.3	37.1
Sweden	corporate	8.2	27.7	11.4	13.9	18.3	15.4
	partisan	5.7	17.0	7.78	7.1	9.3	7.8
	electoral	.	9.2	33.5	42.4	51.8	45.6
Switzer.	corporate	1.6	5.4	14.1	15.6	18.4	17.0
	partisan	.	2.1	3.9	3.6	4.33	4.0
	electoral	8.3	15.1	21.2	27.4	29.3	28.3
U. King.	corporate	17.4	20.6	22.6	18.5	11.8	16.3
	partisan	.	.	.	.8	1.2	1.0
	electoral	.	3.1	11.6	32.9	36.4	34.0
mean	corporate	10.0	10.5	12.0	13.6	12.6	13.2
	partisan	3.6	5.0	4.8	4.9	5.1	5.0
	electoral	9.3	17.9	29.0	34.5	34.1	34.3

n.a. = data are not available

Indeed, between the decade of the 1910s and the 1930s it did not change much, despite the fact that both corporate and electoral mobilization were on the increase.

Moving to national differences, Finland stands out as the only country where early electoral socialism was totally unmatched by corporate mobilization: The Finnish trade unions never had the enormous early success of the Finnish Socialist (and later Communist) Party. France and Italy also stand out as cases of predominantly electoral socialism. The weakness here of the socialist movement in *both* corporate and partisan channels is astonishing when compared with their roughly average electoral development. It is highly unlikely that in this period the considerable electoral strength of these socialist movements lay in their organizational infrastructures.[83] Five countries show a relatively parallel development in the electoral and corporate channels: Austria, Belgium, Switzerland, Denmark, and Sweden. We can therefore come to a second conclusion: Independent of the level of association between corporate and electoral mobilization, the former tended to be higher than the latter in the early decades. After this, the growth in votes began to reflect a higher and more accelerated increase than that of union membership.

Over time the experiences of the different countries tended to become more similar in electoral terms; although converging, they remained more differentiated in corporate mobilization; the profound differences between them in the partisan mobilization channel continued. There is no single instance of a reversal or a recovery in this field. Socialist movements that were weak in partisan mobilization remained in the same class throughout the period. In this context, Austrian socialism provides an impressive image of partisan mobilization: There was one socialist party member for every seven or eight voters. The figure was one for every twelve for Denmark and Sweden and one for every eighteen to twenty for Norway. No other socialist movement even approached these levels of partisan mobilization within the electorate. Intermediate cases, such as Germany and Switzerland, already had one party member for every thirty to forty, voters. To see the contrast, it is interesting to compare these figures with the protracted structural weakness of the French, Italian, Dutch, Belgian, British, and Irish socialist movements; by and large, in these cases, there was one left party member for every 60 to 100 voters. In these cases, therefore, the partisan activities of recruitment, propaganda, social work, and the like were probably concentrated in a few regions or urban areas.

If one directly compares left union members and left voters, considering the ratio between the two (how many left trade union members existed at each moment for 100 left party voters), three countries stand out as clear-cut cases in which socialist mobilization in corporate channels tem-

---

[83] For France, this may reflect the general poverty of association life, which was lamented by Tocqueville and later mentioned by Durkheim in *The Suicide* (1958: 106), Laski (1919: 321), Lerner (1957: 27–32), Kornhauser (1959: 84–87), and many others. However, MacRae (1967: 28–32) and Tilly, Tilly, and Tilly (1975: 40–44) have rejected the thesis of the "underorganization" of French society. Even for Italy, and particularly for southern Italy, it has often been argued that the people are not inclined to create voluntary associations. See Banfield (1958) and the criticism by Pizzorno (1966a: 55–66). For Finland, I have not been able to find any similar complaints about the quantity and quality of association life in the literature.

porally precedes electoral mobilization: Denmark, Sweden, and the United Kingdom. Switzerland, on the other hand, shows an almost one-to-one relation between union members and socialist voters. In all the other cases, electoral socialism at the turn of the twentieth century *was already supported by large sections of previously unmobilized voters.*[84] In Italy, Austria, Belgium, and Germany, there was one member of a left trade union for roughly every two left voters; in Norway and the Netherlands, this number decreases to one for every two and a half; and in France, to one for every three to four.

Differences are more pronounced in terms of the ratio between voters and party members. Sweden, Norway, and Denmark are cases where partisan mobilization preceded electoral mobilization (unfortunately, Austrian Socialist Party membership figures before 1913 are not available). In the first ten years of the century there, were three-and-a-half party members for each voter in Sweden, two-thirds of a party member for each voter in Norway, and one party member for every two voters in Denmark. These early differences tended to decrease over time, but they never disappeared. During the 1900–1940 period, Norway, Denmark, Austria, and Sweden had one socialist member for every two voters. In contrast, Italy, France, Germany, the Netherlands, and the United Kingdom (Belgium and Ireland could be added on the basis of period estimates) had only one member for every six to ten voters.

These data can be seen from two different perspectives. In those cases in which the ratio of members to voters is low, it could be argued that electoral mobilization did not necessitate a strong organizational infrastructure; that electoral socialism had different sources of appeal; and that votes were indeed, from this perspective, organizationally "cheap." Alternatively, one could read the data as indicating the varying strength of the electoral rooting of socialism as deriving from the strong organizational bonds of its electoral constituency. In fact, in the long run, the kind of socialism that was solidly encapsulated proved more electorally stable and more socially hegemonic than weakly encapsulated socialism. This is not to say, however, that it was necessarily stronger in electoral terms.

[84] Shalev and Korpi (1980: 54–55) come to the conclusion that although unions and working-class parties are different things, "unionization may in fact precede and support political organization and mobilization" (p. 55). They argue that this is one of the key explanations of American exceptionalism, i.e., that the weakness of the working-class party in the United States is linked mainly to the weakness of trade unionization. They cite as a counterexample the British case, where the party resulted from the unionized workforce. However, as a general thesis, this is wrong. The authors may have been too strongly influenced by a British-versus-American example, where their thesis works, and also by the experience of the Scandinavian countries, where, as we have seen, trade unionization tended to precede working-class party strength.

TYPES OF SOCIALIST MOVEMENTS

In Figure 6.9, I have tried to summarize the picture discussed so far, charting countries by their mean level of partisan and corporate membership density and indicating their mean left vote for the 1918–1985 period. Those countries that experienced a significant Communist split of the working-class movement are indicated by a large circle; those with the latest collective bargaining development by a smaller circle; and all the others by a square. In Austria, Denmark, and Sweden, mobilization was high in all three channels, the strong electoral support for the socialist movement mirroring strong organizational penetration of the electorate. The Norwegian and German means in each channel are close to the overall means. Germany shows average mobilization in the corporate channel and weak mobilization in the partisan channel. This is interesting, for it is at odds with the usual image of German social democracy as being the most strongly organized and solid socialist example.[85] This was true in the very early phase of socialist development, between the 1860s and 1890s, but it faded at the turn of the century. Perhaps it was based more on strong centralization than on actual levels of partisan mobilization.

The two European early industrialized countries – Belgium, the United Kingdom – show mean corporate mobilization but lower than mean partisan and electoral mobilization. Finland is the opposite, as already noted. At the other extreme are those countries where socialist mobilization remained below the overall European mean level in corporate and partisan as well as electoral mobilization; such as the Netherlands, and Switzerland. What characterizes these countries comparatively is simply their class cleavage undermobilization in all dimensions. The correspondence between organizational density and electoral strength is weakened by the three cases of France, Finland, and Italy, where the left is on average above 40%, although it also shows comparatively low levels of membership density. These are three of the four countries that experienced profound and lasting communist splits. In none of these countries where the communist split was relatively successful was membership density high or collective bargaining an early development.

Several times in this chapter, the different "logics" of corporate versus political socialism, the lack of any strong association between the two, and

---

[85] To quote only one source: "with a membership of more than one million in 1914, the SPD was the largest and best organized Socialist party in Europe." Breitmen (1981: 6).

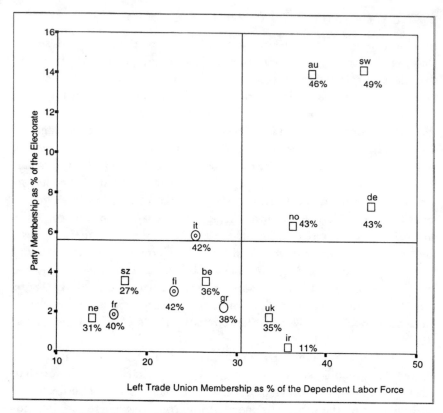

Figure 6.9. Organizational density of the class cleavage (1918–1985).

the preeminence of the latter over the former have been underlined. In reality, these findings point to qualitatively different types of early socialist movements characterized by different mixes of organizational mobilization. I have divided these into four basic types, reported in Table 6.14. *Union lefts* were more highly mobilized in the corporate channel than in the electoral one. *Encapsulated lefts* were densely organized and strongly inter-linked between all the channels. *Ideological lefts* were far more successful electorally than they were organizationally strong. Finally, *undermobilized lefts* simply lagged behind in all the mobilization spheres. Such typological characterizations suggest a number of considerations and point to questions that need to be answered.

First, this research underlines the need to separate interpretations of corporate versus partisan versus electoral mobilization. The form in which the early consolidation of specific organization in both channels of interest representation, and in which voting and direct political action took place,

Table 6.14. *Types of left movements by organizational and electoral mobilization*

	unions' lefts	encapsulated lefts
organizationally overmobilized	Britain Ireland	Sweden Austria Denmark Norway
organizationally undermobilized	undermobilized lefts Belgium Germany Switzerland Netherlands	ideological lefts Italy Finland France
	electorally undermobilized	*electorally overmobilized*

was important for later waves of mass political mobilization. The initial organizational pattern was more influential on corporate and partisan mobilization than it was on electoral mobilization. In most cases, from the beginning, electoral socialism extended far beyond the politically mobilized sectors of the labor movement. The few exceptions to this general picture are, however, important; it is exactly where early corporate and partisan mobilization preceded or paralleled electoral mobilization that socialism proved in the long run to be more successful, more electorally stable, and, in a word, more "hegemonic" than in the other cases. Yet this should not conceal the fact that an electorally large socialist movement was able to develop without building on other forms of preelectoral mobilization; that is to say, it managed to maintain its strength even though it rested on narrow organizational bonds and bases. Particularly in these cases, however, electoral socialism was, from the beginning, "trapped" with large electoral allies – wanted or unwanted – that were linked to socialism for politico-ideological reasons but were deprived of any solid encapsulation in its organizational network. In a nutshell, the explanation of corporate and electoral socialism need not be the same, and a clear distinction between these two channels helps to reconcile the often widely diverging general explanations of socialist development *sub specie* of "economic response" and "political response."

Second, as far as electoral overmobilization is concerned – and, in general, for electoral mobilization greater than corporate mobilization –

this seems to have been particularly true (1) where protracted authoritarian rule forced the socialist movement to give priority to the *political* goals of democratization and liberalization; and, to a lesser extent, (2) where religious and political mobilization were oriented to socialist sections of the electorate that were motivated by rationalistic and anticlerical attitudes. In both instances, electoral socialism was able to attract sections of the middle classes more easily, while, at the same time, it was obliged to relinquish its monopoly over the representation of organized labor. It is important to emphasize that these aspects have traditionally been considered liabilities for socialism, as they have hampered its chances of full mobilization of the working class. However, while these were liabilities for *corporate* socialism, they were not necessarily so for *electoral* socialism. This is because what they lost in terms of organized labor support was compensated for in terms of middle-class ideological support. Of course, this resulted in different kinds of socialist movements: These were different precisely because and according to the relationship between electoral, partisan, and corporate support.

These considerations confirm the need to distinguish clearly the state-bureaucratic environment response from the economy-class environment response in the history of socialism.[86] Patterns of economic and industrial developments – the "maturity of socioeconomic conditions" – were more closely associated with levels of corporate class mobilization than with levels of political class mobilization. For the latter, the relationship appears to be inverted. Electoral socialism profited from the strength of the state/political opposition that it encountered, and grew both earlier and easier in the political sphere where it was forced to fight for goals unattained by infirm or ineffectual liberal-democratic political movements (suffrage extension, parliamentarization, state–church separation, bureaucratic power restriction, antimilitarism, abolition of late feudal remnants, etc.). In contrast, the earlier and easier attainment of these goals, by making mobilization in the interest channel both easier and faster, had the effect, at the same time, of making partisan and electoral mobilization lag behind. When this occurred, the corporate movement did not need to develop a specific political tool rapidly – because it could lend its growing organizational support to other sympathetic candidates or political organizations – and electoral socialism found it difficult to raise support beyond the groups already mobilized in the corporate channel.

Third, reading Table 6.14 along the row of organizational undermobilization, the political fragmentation of the labor movement is seen to

---

[86] On this theme, see the stimulating reflections of Szabo (1982).

associates clearly with weak corporate, but not electoral, mobilization. More specifically, in all those cases in which the Communist split proved to be successful in organizational terms – in particular, in France, Germany, Finland, and Italy – the socialist movement rested on a relatively narrow organizational encapsulation along *both* partisan and corporate dimensions, which was greatly inferior to its electoral mobilization. Does this support the thesis that the prospects for the success of the "international revolution" cleavage were boosted by the weakness of the socialist organizational encapsulation of the working class in the aftermath of World War I? In these cases, the socialist electorate was composed of relatively large sectors that were *not organizationally linked to the socialist party and unions*, and a massive delayed trade unionization took place during the period of maximum appeal of the Russian Revolution. Organizational competition between the socialists and communists did not take place *within* large, established corporate movements, but rather within weak organizations subject to the accelerated recruitment of previously nonmobilized (and mostly unskilled) sectors of the working class.

Finally, a number of more specific questions are left open: What were the nonorganizational sources of the exceptional electoral success of Finnish socialism? Why were the Dutch, Italian, and French movements so undermobilized organizationally? Were there non- or prepolitical networks that made it easier for Scandinavian and Austrian socialism to build extraordinarily dense organizational networks? The national literatures do not lack specific answers; the problem is to make them compatible with a comparative framework. What all these concluding hypotheses call for is a more detailed analysis of institutional developments and political alignments. This will be carried out in the next three chapters.

ORGANIZATIONAL CONSOLIDATION, MEMBERSHIP DEVELOPMENT, AND THE GENERAL MODEL

The three organizational factors that I have found to be most closely associated with left electoral development are (1) the modalities of early party consolidation (those of central union consolidation were not significant); (2) the relationship between party and unions; and, finally, (3) the level of organizational-membership density. These three variables are operationalized as follows. Party organizational consolidation is measured on a seven-point scale ranging from the lowest value of 3 (late founding [*timing*], long centralization process [*length*], and preceded by unions [*se-*

quence]) to the highest value of 9 (early party founding; short centralization; before the unions). The party–unions relationship is a three-point scale ranging from the lowest value (2) when the mode of representation is fragmented and there is no interlocking relation between party and unions, to the intermediate value (4) when the party–union relationship is inter-locking but the mode of representation is fragmented, and, finally, to the highest value (6) when the relationship is based on an interlocking linkage and a corporate mode of representation. The values result from the sum-ming of the individual case ranks on the *linkage* and *mode of representation* variables. Finally, organizational density is measured by the sum of the ratio of left trade union members and party members over the electorate.[87]

When entered into a regression with the left vote, these variables yield a multiple R of .459 corresponding to an Rsq of about 21% (see Table 6.15). The weight of the type of relationship between unions and the parties changes drastically over time. It is negative in the early phase, when corporate representation and an interlocking link were not favorable to electoral development, and becomes equally highly positive after World War II. It is as if parties with this kind of relationship with the unions were late in electoral mobilization. The model of early party consolidation is positively correlated with the left vote in every period, and it is the strongest positive factor in the phase before World War II. Finally, orga-nizational density proves a much weaker predictor for each period than it is for the overall series of elections.

Before entering the organizational variable into the general model, which includes the determinants discussed in previous chapters, let me first briefly report how the organizational aspects relate to social mobiliza-tion and cultural heterogeneity. As expected, the relationship between

---

[87] To avoid losing several cases where membership figures are missing, I have interpolated the missing values. There are only three countries where this is problematic because it concerns not one single missing figure within a series of reliable data but rather an entire period. In Belgium, socialist (but not communist) party membership figures are not available from 1900 to 1939. In the following decades, partisan density ranges from the minimum of 2.2 in 1950 to the maximum of 4.3 in 1978. I have arbitrarily set the level for the 1900–1939 elections at 2%. In Ireland, the same problem applies to the 1927–1961 period. Here, however, partisan density is so low that errors can hardly be made in the estimation. Membership ranges between 0.2% and 0.4% between 1965 and 1989; I have set the level for the 1927–1961 period at 0.2%. Finally, we do not have individual membership figures for the British Labour Party up to 1924. In 1929, partisan density was 0.8%, and it grew to its highest value of 2.7% in 1950. For the few elections between the founding of the party and 1924, I have set the level of partisan density at 0.5%. As is evident, these three are all cases of extremely low and below-European-mean partisan density, and for none of them does the literature offer any reason to believe that this was different in earlier years.

Table 6.15. *Regression of organizational variables on left vote (beta coefficients)*

variables	1880-1917	1918-1944	1945-1965	1966-1985	whole period
party/union relations	-.529	.182	.832	.574	-.027
party organizational consolidation	.308	.446	.463	.400	.168
organizational density	.162	.192	-.444	-.159	.386
Rsq	.238 (70)	.403 (91)	.538 (78)	.482 (92)	.211 (334)

Note: Number of elections given in parentheses.

social mobilization and corporate mobilization is always positive.[88] Social mobilization is a better and more direct predictor of corporate socialism than it is of electoral socialism, while the relationship of social mobilization with partisan density is neither strong nor systematic in sign. Cultural heterogeneity negatively influences all aspects of class cleavage mobilization. As expected, the negative association is higher for left trade union membership than for overall union membership. It is also always extremely high for partisan membership. This supports the idea that in culturally segmented societies partisan mobilization in specific political organizations is either less necessary or more difficult due to the already high and functionally equivalent membership mobilization of all the various subcultural associations and organizations that constitute the bricks and mortar of the cultural pillars of the society.

To enter the significant aspects of the organizational development into this general model, I combined the three factors of membership density, union–party relations, and party organizational consolidation into a single standardized index. I then ran a general regression in which the left vote was predicted on the basis of the four macrofactors discussed so far: the indices of *social mobilization, cultural heterogeneity, enfranchisement pattern,* and *organizational development*

The results are reported in Table 6.16, which should be compared with Table 5.11 in the previous chapter, where the same analysis was performed without the organizational dimension. This new variable does not add to the overall explained variance, which remains at around 70%.

[88] In contrast to this evidence, Wallerstein has found a negative association between the size of the labor force and its degree of unionization, arguing that it is not surprising that the larger the potential constituency of wage earners, the more incomplete is the process of their recruitment. See Wallerstein (1989). However, he does not use, historical data to prove his point.

Table 6.16. *Social mobilization, cultural heterogeneity, enfranchisement, organizational model, and left vote (beta coefficients)*

	before 1917	1918-1944	1945-1965	1966-85	whole period
social mobilization	.260	.409	.328	.484	.432
cultural heterogeneity	-.258	-.109	-.300	-.549	-.178
enfranchisement pattern	.621	.436	.198	.060	.431
organizational model	-.099	.374	.289	.061	.128
Rsq	54.7%	71.1%	60.2%	71.8%	70.1%

It does, however, influence the weight of the other factors and the variance explained in each period. The organizational aspects are quite unimportant in both the first pre–World War I period and the final post-1965 period. However, they do play a significant role in the interwar period and in the first post–World War II period, between 1918 and 1965. In this central phase, they increase the explained variance considerably, from 62.6 to 71.1 and from 55.6 to 60.2. Thus, while the sociostructural variables maintain a constant important role, the enfranchisement pattern is crucial in the first period and declines progressively in the others, the impact of cultural heterogeneity grows over time, and the organizational dimension impacts mainly in the second and third historical periods.

In this chapter, much descriptive space has been devoted to left organizational development, as I believe this to be the least developed field in the comparative history of socialism. However, these conclusions suggest that for further investigation and more accurate control, organizational data need to be complemented by data concerning *the timing, easiness, and modalities of entry* of the socialist movement into the political system. To test macrohypotheses about the historical development of the European class left requires a model that links sociocultural conditions, organizational mobilization instrumentality, and structure of political opportunities. It is to the latter that I turn in the following three chapters, where the argument will acquire a more qualitative flavor.

It is likely that the specific pattern of institutional incorporation in the two channels decisively influenced the extent to which the two paths, corporate and electoral, were separated or remained closely linked. For instance, the earlier collective bargaining, trade union recognition, and so on occurred, the less need there was for unions to rely on politics and the more independent the paths could become in corporate and electoral channels and organizations. At the same time, where the political channel remained closed longer, one would expect a politicization of the organizations in the corporate channel. Generally speaking, the earlier and the more thoroughly the institutional barriers were separated in the two channels, the more we would expect the corporate and electoral paths to be differentiated and less dependent on each other.[89] The respective timing of institutional incorporation may also have had a significant impact on the prevailing ideological orientation of the early socialist movements. The stronger the trade union movement before party development and the smoother its institutional role and development, the less likely it was that an orthodox Marxist orientation would prevail within the party and in the party–union relationship and the more likely a party dependence on trade unions or a strong corporate cross-linkage with a moderate Marxist platform would be. Thus, weak and unrecognized unions may become instrumental in the fragmentation of the political representation of the class left.

[89] See Ebbinghaus (1992: 5–6) for a discussion of this problem.

7

POLITICAL
INTEGRATION

The socialist movement was an outsider for the conservative or liberal groups that controlled the political system in the second half of the nineteenth century. To establish itself, it had to penetrate the system and it faced varying degrees of resistance in this enterprise. The ease with which it came to be recognized as a legitimate political actor and the barriers it had to overcome to achieve this status – in a nutshell, the pattern of *political integration* – influenced its electoral strength, organizational cohesion, and radicalness of stance. Thus, the extent to which working-class political movements felt they could pursue and achieve their goals and values within the existing framework of state and political institutions was shaped by the learning experience deriving from the responses of the dominant groups and established elite when facing their demands.

The goal of this chapter is to assess the European variation in institutional "openness" to the new claimants' demands and organizational efforts, assuming that political alienation was as important as, if not more so than, social dislocation and economic deprivation in setting the context of the political response of new lower-class claimants. I compare the earliness and the level of left institutional integration, concentrating on four institutional obstacles to entry into the dominant pattern of political competition:

1. The extent to which demands made by the political movement of the working class were met by the established elite and institutions' use of nonpolitical means of confrontation, that is, direct legal and administrative repression and harassment. In other words, I consider to what

extent and with what efficacy the state, as an administrative and policing machine, was used against the rising working-class movement.

2. The extent to which the institutional regime was liberalized, that is, the extent to which the resources of power and influence in the administrative and bureaucratic machinery of the state, or in the social and market relationships of the society, were balanced by the parliamentary influence and negotiation based on electoral weight. The parliamentarization of the executive opened a new structure of opportunity, allowing the socialist movement to concentrate part of its resources and efforts on directly influencing the executive, rather than on nonparliamentary confrontation with employers, as well as with administrative, bureaucratic, and legal obstacles.

3. The types of obstacles set up to impede the fair parliamentary representation of the electoral strength of the movement. Even liberalized regimes resisted, with differing styles and vigor, the full transformation of the left movement's electoral force into parliamentary influence by various mechanisms of electoral misrepresentation.

4. The kinds of obstacles that were used to block socialist parties' access to executive responsibilities.

Stateness and repression, responsible government, fair representation, and *executive power access* are linked into a syndrome pattern. In the following pages, I deal with each of them separately, leaving a global description of the pattern of each country for the final section. The losses in case-configuration power resulting from the analytical sectioning of the global process are compensated for by the increased accuracy of the comparative analysis. The qualitative nature of this in the following chapters is due to the type of information and material discussed, *as well as* to the logic of the analysis. Multivariate techniques isolating the role of individual variables are less appropriate when a potential syndrome effect exists: that is, when it is the specific combination that establishes a more or less favorable condition.

STATE RESPONSE

STATENESS

The legal and administrative repression and harassment of the working-class political movement in the nineteenth and early twentieth centuries highlight the role and the resources of the state. Recent literature has emphasized the importance of the state's tradition and role in the process of political modernization, linking it to the alliances between social groups that have determined the liberal, authoritarian, or totalitarian outcomes of the modernization processes,[1] to the sources of revolutions and their outcome,[2] to the process of social group formation,[3] and to collective action.[4] Here, I focus on the state as a set of resources to which established and dominant groups could have recourse in their attempt to obstruct the emerging socialist movement. More precisely, the calculation of the cost of internal repression or tolerance made by dominant groups depended, first of all, on the availability of the means of repression, that is, on the availability of a bureaucratic tradition and bureaucratic machinery that could be exploited to oppose new movements successfully. We can put the question in the following terms: How did the nature of state formation (external challenges, boundary consolidation, centralization, development of apparatuses, army, etc.) influence the relative costs of tolerance and repression of the socialist movement? Levels of administrative and legal harassment are linked to stateness but are not definitely determined by it. Where stateness was weak, a repressive strategy was not available or was likely to be very costly; where it was strong, such a strategy was possible, even if other variables may have influenced the willingness of the established elite to choose it.

The first step is to assess the level of stateness independently of the nature of the institutional and political regime.[5] The second is to evaluate the extent to which existing state resources were actually used against the rising socialist movement. In dealing with the first problem, I will not draw on the ideal type of experience of a few well-known countries (generally France versus Britain versus Prussia). Such ideal or polar types are not effective when dealing with a large comparative design classifying *all* available cases. It is more fruitful to break the concept into a number of constitutive dimensions and to compare individual cases along each of them, and to reconstruct their overall relative positions later.[6]

Stateness indicates the extractive, regulative, and repressive resources that each state holds vis-à-vis society. This accumulation of resources is

[1] Moore (1966).
[2] Skocpol (1979).
[3] Katznelson (1985).
[4] Birnbaum (1988). See also Birnbaum and Badie (1982: 189–190). The third part of the book is devoted to an ideal-type analysis of types of states.
[5] See Nettl (1968).
[6] A decomposition strategy overcomes the criticism that the characterization of stateness at the macrolevel does not take into account possible variations among sectors within a given state; see Atkinson and Coleman (1989: 49).

primarily the result of the pattern of state formation. The latter identifies the process of political, economic, and cultural unification of the central dominant elite. On state formation, the comparative-politics literature generally agrees on the following propositions:

1. If a state-based legal order and a consolidated boundary clearly predate the formation of a strong central bureaucracy, then the repressive powers of the state are more likely to remain fairly independent of the requests and the direct control of the executive.

2. If the consolidation of the state's basic institutions is uncontested or only relatively so, then the pressure for a centralized administration of law-and-order apparatuses will be weaker and the legal tradition will be less likely to be state-centered.

3. If the creation and consolidation of the state structures is early enough and does not involve processes of large-scale political mobilization or violent popular resistance, then the status apparatuses are likely to be less politicized and their repressive means are likely to be more responsible to local judicial bodies.

4. If the central bureaucracy never consolidates, or if it consolidates after representative institutions have been introduced, then the state apparatuses are not a resource for the repression of newcomers.[7]

Taking these points together, European countries can be arranged from a minimum to a maximum of stateness from left to right, as in Table 7.1.

The end result of the state formation process consists technically of the development of the bureaucratic, fiscal, and military apparatuses. Therefore, the final level of stateness of the political processes can be identified along four dimensions:

1. Creation of the organization for the mobilization of resources: bureaucracy and tax burden.

2. External consolidation of the territory: army.

3. Maintenance of internal order: police and judiciary.

4. State activism in regulatory activities and in economic and social intervention.

It is, unfortunately, difficult to assess directly the last of these dimensions (the extent of state intervention in the economy and society). Whereas

[7] I have reformulated theses that have been widely discussed in the literature of state formation and political development. In particular, see the articles in Tilly (1975) and Dahl (1971: 48–49).

Table 7.1. *Modalities of state formation in Europe*

never fully consolidated	early consolidation with little tension and resistance	late and gradual consolidation	early consolidation against considerable resistance	late and violent consolidation
Switzerland	Britain Sweden Denmark	Netherlands Belgium Norway	France	Italy Germany (Prussia) Finland Ireland Austria

it would be relatively easy to build an ideal type placing "Colbertism" and "cameralism" in opposition to "laissez-faire" and "decentralized, amateur-ish public administration," it is impossible to set up a systematic charting of cross-country differences along this dimension.[8] As a result, for the comparative appreciation of each country's *extractive resources*, I propose to look at the following aspects:

1. The tax ratio, that is, the general governmental taxes as a proportion of the gross domestic product.
2. The tax centralization, that is, central governmental taxes as a proportion of general governmental taxes.
3. The general central administration personnel as a percentage of the population.

For an evaluation of the *means of control over external and internal order*, I will examine:

1. The military personnel as a percentage of the male population between twenty-two and forty-four years old (excluding war period figures and post-war demobilization figures in order to account for the belligerent or non-belligerent status of countries during World War I).
2. The police and judiciary personnel as a percentage of the total population (the judiciary calculated as personnel employed by the ministry of justice).

---

[8] Mann (1993: 358–395) provides several tables of data about what he calls the "size" of the state and discusses this dimension to some extent. However this is done for European major powers only.

I have computed the figures for the five indicators, averaging the census decade data of the 1880–1920 period.[9] In Table 7.2, the average value of each dimension is reported, together with the mean of the five indicators as an aggregate index of stateness. Note that figures are expressed in zeta scores of the distribution.[10]

The figures show that the five dimensions are not always homogeneous. Switzerland, Norway, Denmark, and Sweden have values below the Western European mean in all the five dimensions analyzed. Austria and Belgium tend to be homogeneously above the European mean, without, however, reaching very high levels in any of the five dimensions. The United Kingdom oscillates in each dimension close to the European mean, while the Netherlands has medium values in all dimensions with the exception of tax centralization, where it appears to be the most tax-centralized country of Europe at the turn of the twentieth century. Italian stateness, by contrast, looks quite unbalanced. While Italy is more highly bureaucratized than any other country, with an extensive central bureaucratic personnel and high tax centralization, it remains below the mean in other indicators (unfortunately, police and judiciary personnel data are not available). Germany's stateness levels are very high in terms of repressive resources and, in particular, in terms of internal law-and-order means, while they are lower in terms of central resource extraction. French stateness is strong and is above the mean homogeneously along four of the indicators, falling below it only in terms of internal law and order.

In the cumulative stateness index, five countries stand out as characterized by a high level of stateness of their political processes: Italy, France, Austria, Germany, and Belgium. Three countries present intermediate values that come very close to the European mean – the Netherlands, Ireland, and the United Kingdom – and five fall clearly below the European mean level, characterized by weak levels of stateness in their polity: Finland, Denmark, Sweden, Norway, and Switzerland. If we compare these findings with the usual descriptions of the strength of the state, a few surprising points emerge. For example, the ideal type of the weak state, the United Kingdom, does not look so weak when it is merged into a Europewide comparison. It is far weaker than France and Germany, but it is in no way the model of the weak state. Presumably, the impressive

---

[9] Data are elaborated from Flora, Alber, Eichenberg, Kohl, Knaus, Pfenning, and Seebohm (1983).

[10] Note also that not all figures are available for all indicators. In computing the combined index, I have set the missing data at the 0.0 level, that is, to the overall distribution mean.

Table 7.2. *Dimensions of stateness (1880s–1920s) (average standardized scores)*

countries	resource extraction		repressive means			stateness combined index
	tax ratio	tax centralization	central administration personnel	military personnel	police and judiciary personnel	
Italy	2.12	-.97	2.28	-.26	-	3.17
France	(.44)	.94	.62	1.89	-1.02	2.44
Austria	(.0001)	.80	.42	1.06	-.01	2.28
Germany	-.92	-.60	.27	.60	2.61	1.93
Belgium	(.89)	1.08	.20	-.66	.67	1.29
Netherlands	-.03	1.15	-.16	-.48	.04	0.53
United King.	-.11	.09	.47	-.18	-.21	0.07
Ireland	(1.34)	(.68)	-	(-.52)	-	0.01
Finland	(.0001)	.52	-1.02	.27	-70	-0.93
Denmark	-.24	-.18	-.11	-1.23	.16	-1.61
Norway	-.39	-.36	-1.05	-.48	-.70	-2.99
Sweden	-.06	-.22	-1.28	-.55	-.52	-2.63
Switzerland	-.34	-2.25	-.61	-	-.33	-3.35

— = data not available.
(   ) = data refer to the 1920–1940 period.

correspondence of British ranking in all dimensions contributed to forge the image of a weakly state-driven polity.

Beyond the unsurprising case of Switzerland – the real prototype of the low-stateness polity – the low levels of state capacities in the Scandinavian countries are to a certain extent surprising. Sweden and Denmark represent cases of many centuries of dynastic rule and of dynastically driven state and nation building;[11] Denmark, in particular, has often been considered the most "Prussian" of the Scandinavian countries. The countries share deep-rooted traditions of centralized bureaucratic rule that have been inherited from their long-standing absolutist regimes.[12] However, even in Denmark and Sweden, the resources controlled by the state at the end of the nineteenth century were far lower than those of any other European nation.[13]

[11] If the strength of a state is to be seen as resulting from both its capacity to enforce authority and the existence of sentiments of national solidarity – as suggested by Linz (1973: 34–35) – in Scandinavia the identification of the population with the nation-state is high and unchallenged. Even in the peripheral countries that gained independence only in the twentieth century – Finland, Norway, and Iceland – the sense of national identity was fairly consolidated long before.

[12] Rokkan (1966b: 74). See also the various research project reports in Stråth (1988b).

[13] The strong persistence of a relatively independent nobility, the maintenance far longer than anywhere else of older estate principles, the persistence of strong conciliator or collegial forms of rule, and the peculiar bureaucratic separation between policy-making

The intermediate position of the Netherlands comes as no surprise, as state formation in the real sense occurred after 1785; it is only from this time on that one can speak of a central government and direct control over citizens. At the same time, the extent of bureaucratization and centralization brought about by the Napoleonic conquest and reform should probably not be exaggerated in a comparative perspective. In this particular case, the Netherlands may well point to a problem typical of historical systematic comparisons. A process that is unquestionably clear in historical terms with respect to the previous situation in the country – and that is strongly emphasized as such in a developmental perspective by historians – may well remain relatively modest in a cross-national comparison.[14]

Comparing the levels of stateness indicated in Table 7.2 with the modalities of state formation reported in Table 7.1, it is clear that the countries that never consolidated as a unitary state (Switzerland), those with early and unchallenged consolidation (the United Kingdom, Sweden, and Denmark), and those with late and gradual consolidation (the Netherlands and Norway) are all low- or medium-stateness countries. The only exception is Belgium, whose level of stateness is, however, only moderately higher than average. The countries with early consolidation, but with considerable resistance (France and Austria), and those with late and violent consolidation (Italy, Germany, and Austria)[15] all tend to be high-stateness countries also because they were deeply involved in the nineteenth-century continental warfare. In this group, Finland and Ireland are the exceptions, both having low stateness in the context of a late and violent consolidation. This is not surprising considering that we are dealing with peripheries of large empires (the British and the Russian) whose state structures and resources were largely imported externally (and later withdrawn) rather than generated internally.

The process of state formation and its end result in terms of stateness made available potential resources that were not necessarily used or directed against the socialist movement. In a situation of low stateness, the calculus of the established elite regarding the potential costs of repression versus toleration was likely to be negative. That is, dominant groups could hardly embark on a repressive strategy based on the state. Strong stateness

---

boards and executive agencies have been invoked as an explanation of this end result. See Daalder (1995: 119–120) and Anderson (1974: 173–191).

[14] On the debate about the levels of bureaucratization and centralization in the Netherlands after the Napoleonic war, see Daalder (1990: 19–20).

[15] The classification of Austria depends on whether one considers the Hapsburg Empire or the republic.

made a state-repressive strategy available, and this availability may have influenced the calculations of dominant circles. However, in no way was such a strategy either mandatory or without other alternatives. It is therefore necessary to consider the extent to which the state apparatus was *actually* used against the socialist movement.

REPRESSION AND TOLERATION

Some antisocialist hostility and repression existed in all European countries. National accounts, although rich in information about this hostility, rarely make comparative assessments of its relative level.[16] My attempt here is to systematize in relative terms the various kinds of information available in this literature about the fundamental freedoms of the press, association, and the strike.

The achievement of freedom of the press across European countries can be divided into three fundamental steps: the abolition of censorship, the later progressive softening of postpublication prosecution, and, finally, the abandoning of any sort of legal, and possibly insidious, mechanisms by which the socialist press was made less viable and more difficult to circulate. Table 7.3 reports the approximate dates when these barriers were overcome in different countries and indicates if any important setbacks occurred after World War I.

By the end of the Napoleonic wars, Norway was probably the most liberal country in this respect. By the beginning of the 1850s in the United Kingdom, Sweden, the Netherlands, Switzerland, and Belgium, censorship had technically been abolished, although a wide variety of administrative techniques of control and postpublication prosecution were still in existence. At the other end of the continuum, there were still major restrictions on press freedom in Germany, Austria (to a lesser extent), and Finland (to an even lesser extent) on the eve of World War I. In Germany, censorship had first been banned in 1849 in most of its states and again by a press law of 1877 in the Reich, but even so, extensive, severe prosecutions and sanctions continued until the end of the empire.

---

[16] For this reason, in this section I have relied more on comparative sources than on standard national accounts. The only comparative work I am aware of that is devoted to the analysis of political repression in nineteenth-century Europe is Goldstein (1983), which I have used extensively even though Goldstein stresses the commonalities among cases rather than the relative differences. Other works on the history of labor have been very useful: Lafferty (1971), Geary (1989), Abendroth (1965), Kassalow (1963), Castles (1978), Droz (1972), Galli (1976a), Greene (1971), Kendall (1975), Kriegel (1973), Landauer (1959), Lindemann (1974), E.N. Mitchell and Stearns (1971), Piro and Pombeni (1981), and Steenson (1991).

Table 7.3. *Press, association, and strike freedoms: repression and harassment*

	constitutional or legal ban ending prior press censorship	end of severe administration of press restrictions	approximate date of T. U and strikes banning	approximate date of T. U. and strikes legalization	end of severe harassment of T. U. and strikes	date of collective agreement legalization	setbacks	periods of legal repression and strong harassment of political parties
Au	1867	never before 1918	1731, 1852, 1859	1867–1870, 1884–1891	about 1891	1920	1936–1945	illegal in 1860s, 1870s, 1880s; 1911: change of the law of association making the party legal; illegal 1934–1945
Be	1830	1830	1831	1866–1867 1892: eliminated restrictions to the right to strike	1866: relaxed but occasional considerable harassment after	1944		
De	1849	1846	1734,1800,1823	1849	about 1890	1899		socialist organization broken in the early 1870s; 1873: Section of the First International outlawed
Fi	1905?	never before 1918		1906	1919	1944/5	1918–1950 several for Communist press 1930–1945 several for collective bargaining	intermittent legal/illegal status up to civil war and 1945
Fr	1830	1881	1791	1848, 1864, 1884	1884: relaxed but considerable harassment after	1919 (1936)		socialist organizations illegal until 1879, Vichy and German occupation
Ge	1849	never before 1918	1731	1869	1890: relaxed but considerable harassment thereafter	1918	1933–1945	illegal 1878–1889, 1933–1945
Ir	1695	about 1830; successive special restrictive legislation up to W.W.I	1799–1800	1825	1875 (but special legislation thereafter)	1948		
It	1848	about 1900		1859–1889	1900: relaxed	1871, 1906	1924–1945	socialist organizations dissolved and illegal 1893–1895,1898,1924–1943
Ne	1815	1848	1815	1872	1872	1927		
No	1814	1814	never formally outlawed	-	-	1915		
Sw	1809	1838	1739–1770	1846, 1864, 1885	about 1890	1928		police harassment during the 1880s
Sz	1848	about 1830	never formally outlawed	-	-	1911		
UK	1695	about 1830	1799–1800	1825	1875	1871, 1906		

Similarly, Austria abolished press censorship in 1867 but continued to prosecute opposition newspapers with a socialist or nationalist orientation, and the sentences were particularly severe in the 1877–1880 period. Finland remained under the strong censorship regime of Tsarist Russia, softened to some degree by the relative level of its autonomy, but constantly subject to further restrictions whenever the Russian autocracy felt politically menaced or needed to gain a stronger hold on Finnish affairs. France and Italy are located in an intermediate position with respect to the other countries. They formally abandoned censorship in 1830 and 1848, respectively, but in both cases administrative and press restrictions continued to be common practice until near the end of the century. Obviously, in Germany, Austria, and Italy, the collapse of democracy was a sharp setback to this process, bringing about unprecedented levels of censorship. Even in Finland, although to a lesser extent, the political upheavals from the civil war of 1918 to the crisis at the end of World War II led to considerable limitations on the press.

Censorship and postpublication prosecution were not the only forms of harassment for the opposition press and, in particular, for the socialist press. There were several indirect, less insidious, but still effective forms of financial control. For instance, publishers could be asked to pay a security bond and caution money, and newspapers to pay special taxes. The use of these measures, sometimes left to administrative discretion, often damaged the socialist press since they led to higher costs and higher prices. Germany and Austria, once again, used fiscally discriminating measures most frequently and abolished them only as late as 1874 and 1899, respectively. In France, similar provisions also continued until 1881, being imposed and relaxed according to the liberality of the regime. They were not totally abolished in the United Kingdom and the Netherlands until 1861 and 1869, respectively.[17]

In conclusion, the general picture suggests that – apart from the exceptional case of Norway – Sweden, the Netherlands, Belgium, Switzerland, the United Kingdom, and Denmark had abolished strong administrative control of the press by the middle of the nineteenth century and that there were no other major setbacks from then on. The liberalization of the press occurred before the development of early socialist movements, and the latter were therefore free to develop in a fairly liberal press environment. Italy and France were more resistant in giving up forms of press control, particularly those affecting the socialist and anarchist press

[17] Goldstein (1983: 41).

and publications. Finally, in Germany, Austria, and Finland, the early socialist movement had, in contrast, to combat the strong control over the press by the state bureaucracy and to continuously invent methods by which to avoid these restrictions and prosecutions. This is clear from the behavior of the socialist press and publications in these countries: Frequent changes in titles, places of publication, and so on were necessary to enjoy the initial advantages of the formally liberal press law and to delay the hindrance that inevitably followed a certain period of activity.

Almost all Western European states severely limited the freedom of political assembly and association before 1848. The only exceptions were Belgium, under the liberal constitution of 1830; Switzerland, after the canton revolution of 1830 (and again in Switzerland in 1848); and the United Kingdom, where only some kinds of obstruction were practiced up to 1848. After the 1848 revolutions, these freedoms were granted in Piedmont (later Italy, in 1859), the Netherlands, and Denmark. The subsequent constitutional guarantees of these rights were granted in Austria (1867) and Germany (1869). However, constitutional and statutory guarantees of freedom of assembly and association were often suspended or discontinued (Germany in 1878–1890, Austria in the 1880s, and Italy in 1893–1894 and 1898) by the introduction of exceptional legislation in periods of high political tension. Moreover, even after official recognition, actual restrictions of a more administrative and police nature were continued in many cases.

Rather than follow the evolution of constitutional and administrative practices, I concentrate on the actual record of what happened to the basic rights and claims of the socialist movements, in both their political and union components, by investigating the following issues: (1) Were unions, union activities, or political parties ever banned? (2) When, approximately, was this ban repealed in constitutional or legal terms? (3) When did the severe administrative harassment of unions and party activities actually end? (4) When were unions recognized by both the state and the employers as legitimate representatives of employees? (5) Finally, were there any setbacks in these processes? In Table 7.3, all the relevant information has been concisely synthesized. However, some explanation is needed, and the following sections describe the reasons for my choices.

In Norway, a law banning or otherwise making illegal the association activity of the unions never existed. The most serious episode of repression was the Thrane movement in 1851. Once the earlier strong dependence on Denmark was replaced by the milder one on Sweden (in 1814), Norway developed into a fairly liberal, nonviolent state. A few minor confrontations occurred after the 1850s, and historians remind us that during a labor conflict in 1881 one worker was killed,[18] but in general the police and the army remained in the background of social confrontations. During the radicalization phase of the labor movement in the years before and after World War I, renewed nervousness and alertness on the part of the state led to soldiers presiding over various labor conflicts (especially in the northern areas of the country), but this did not lead to any violence. Similarly, the life of the socialist political movement was by any comparative standards relatively easy. There was little obstruction, and no significant cases of repression, conviction of leaders, banning, or other administrative restrictions have been reported by historians.

Switzerland presents more than one similarity with Norway. The canton constitutions of 1830–1831 and the federal constitution of 1848 formally recognized the freedoms of press, association, and political action, and unions were never formally outlawed. In Switzerland, too, the socialist movement had precursors in the so-called democratic movements of the 1860s.[19] At the same time, the early unions and socialist organizations had to deal with a "minimal" state in terms of centralization and resources even after the 1848 and 1874 constitutional revisions. In fact, the army was of a militia type created by conscription, and it was rarely called on to maintain law and order. The executive branch of government was weak, not only at the federal level but also at the canton level as a result of the division of powers between cantons and municipalities. Power was exercised mainly through associations and, above all, through groups of prominent citizens:[20] an oligarchic rule that could not, and probably did not need to, rely on state regulations or state apparatus to defend its socially prominent position. Between 1870 and World War I, unions and socialist parties were harassed rarely, and the episodes of state (canton) direct intervention and repression were unusual and hardly need to be mentioned; casualties resulting from clashes with the police or soldiers were truly exceptional. Most of the repressive measures that did take place focused on anarchists and radical socialist refugees and their activities and resulted from pressure from neighboring major powers (France and Germany in particular) that were eager to persecute internal opponents even outside their national boundaries. The frequency with which such requests were made and the infrequency with which they were complied with by the Swiss authorities indicate the liberal internal climate.

---

[18] Terjesen (1990: 12).
[19] See Schaffner (1982), in particular pp. 144–197, where the author moves from the analysis of the Zurich canton case to that of other cantons.
[20] Jost (1967: 203–219).

The image of a nonrepressive or rarely repressive history of British labor may be misleading, considering the many episodes of sharp clashes and repression in the first half of the nineteenth century. The Combination Acts of 1799 and 1800 forced labor organizations underground. In 1794 and 1817, habeas corpus was twice suspended during the fiercest phases of political confrontation. Even after the repeal of the Combination Acts in 1825, for many years workers remained liable for combination under common law, which prohibited strikes, and unions continued to be harassed. This situation ended only in about 1875, when the Conspiracy and Protection of Property Act removed the taint of conspiracy from trade disputes and ensured that violence or intimidation would be dealt with under the normal course of law. In addition, the Employers and Workmen Act (1875) established equality of contract in the employment relationship, replacing the paternal control of the Master and Servant Law; the Trades Disputes Act (1906), which became known as the "charter of trade union liberties," firmly established the legal immunity of the unions and the right of peaceful picketing; finally, the Trade Union Act (1913) reversed the Osborne judgment of 1909, which had prohibited the use of union funds for political purposes, and thus legalized the financial support of the Labour Party by the unions.[21] Many other legal issues were at the center of union activities and battles in the period 1870–1920. The final decisions concerning trade union support for autonomous and independent labor representation in Parliament was precipitated by a court decision in 1901 that declared the Railwaymen's Union liable for the actions of its members and fined it £40,000.

In Britain, therefore, the fate of labor was regulated by a series of legislative enactments, and the law was historically the central arena of struggle. British labor did dispute the laws that limited, constrained, or repressed its actions, but this was done in most cases by using or addressing the law itself; for this reason, legal issues were often the cause and the occasion of political mobilization.[22] It should be added that the state was mainly identified with Parliament and the law also because bureaucratic centralization was very weak and, until the late nineteenth century, the

---

[21] Price (1990: 7).

[22] The role of the courts needs to be qualified, however. Hattam argues that the difference in U.S. and United Kingdom working-class formation and political strategy has much to do with the role of the courts and the difference in state structure. While the legislative victories of Labour produced significant changes because the courts were less powerful and allowed the government to regulate the labor market, in the United States, where more powerful courts could not be challenged by political power, legislative victories resulted in little change. Hattam (1992: 153–187).

administrative machinery was relatively minor; legislation was administered and enforced by local bodies, and even the police were controlled
locally. The greater bureaucratization of administrative structures, the professionalization of the municipal governments (the ousting of unpaid gentry), the diminishing role of voluntary associations in providing social
needs and their progressive substitution by large insurance companies, and
the state responsibility for education (acts during 1870–1880), and so on –
to sum up, a more interventionist role of the state – developed in parallel
with the labor movement and, not infrequently at labor's own request. In
conclusion, direct repression of the labor movement occurred early, preceding mass political mobilization; it was directed mainly at the market arena
activities (strikes, coalitions); and it was dominated by a liberal ideology
and not by the repressive political fears of the state. The state as an
autonomous apparatus was as invisible in practice as it was underconcep-
tualized in theory. The early socialist movement came to consider existing
institutions mainly in terms of viable channels for its grievances. At the
same time, the absence among the dominant elite of a specific conception
of the state, and of its role and mission, made them perceive such grievances less as a global challenge than as specific requests.

In Sweden, the eighteenth-century laws banning union organization
were dismantled between 1846 and 1864 (together with the restriction on
employers to increase wages). However, no extensive form of labor organization came into being in Sweden before 1870. Legislation affecting workers' organizations and the attitudes of the employers and authorities were
certainly less hostile than in many other European countries. The governing authorities sought to avoid conflict with the socialist movement and
also to reject its most radical demands by a policy of moderate concessions.[23] Unions and socialists were not entirely satisfied with these concessions, but they found it difficult to launch a general mobilization and
attack. The only significant dispute that I have been able to identify took
place in 1876, when a workers' movement at the Sundswall lumberworks,
which had struck for higher pay and better working conditions, was
repressed by military troops. By 1890, the rights of organization and action
were generally recognized, and up to 1931 no worker was ever killed in a
street or workplace dispute. The last and most notable piece of antiunion
legislation was probably the Akarp Law (passed in 1899), which prohibited
striking workers from threatening or physically hindering strikebreakers.

Legislation against workers' organizations was passed with difficulty

---

[23] Examples of these moderate concessions in response to radical requests are presented in
Simonson (1990: 101–102).

because the farmer-dominated lower chamber normally opposed it. At the same time, the apparatus for national control and repression (the police, for instance) was not centralized. Instead, forces were set up through a combination of state police and local constables who were appointed by the local farmers. Courts, too, combined central and local features, with judges appointed by the state and jurymen appointed by the free farmers from among their own ranks. In evaluating the attitude toward the state in Sweden, one should also remember the existence – before the working class started to organize itself – of local institutions allowing for some level of democratic participation, institutions that traditionally resisted any central authority with which it did not seem possible to integrate or be represented. On the other hand, however, it should be pointed out that in Sweden the right to engage in political propaganda and agitation was fought far more fiercely than the right to use corporate activity. Throughout the 1880s, socialist political recruitment and propaganda met with considerable police harassment, and at the beginning of the 1890s there was still substantial official opposition to socialist meetings. In reality, Sweden – like other nonliberalized regimes – tended to recognize, and even to sustain more openly, the corporate representation of workers' interests (in view of the social peace resulting from this recognition and institutionalization) rather than their political representation.

There is some disagreement among scholars of the Danish socialist movement as to the degree of repression it faced.[24] Unions and the right to strike were legalized earlier in Denmark than in Sweden, and their legal status remained unchallenged from 1848. Administrative harassment was suspended at more or less the same time, at the beginning of the 1890s, when the police and the courts softened their considerable hostility to the unions. The state opposition to the political wing of the socialist movement was, however, more pronounced in Denmark than in the other two Scandinavian countries. In the 1870s, the Danish Section of the First International, founded by the Lassallian Louis Pio in 1871, was severely repressed. Its leaders were sentenced to several years in jail in 1872, and in 1873 the supreme court actually banned the International Workers' Association of Denmark (IWAD) and actively persecuted the radical leadership of Pio, Brix, and Geleff. Given this situation, the movement developed in a more moderate direction. Its legitimation was therefore easier, but,

[24] Galenson underlines the similarities among the Scandinavian experiences, arguing that early socialism developed as craft socialism, without any significant state repression and opposition. Lafferty disagrees with this, claiming that repression of the early socialist movement was greater in Denmark than in the other two Scandinavian states. Galenson (1952a) and (1952c) and Lafferty (1971: 146).

according to Lafferty, "the terms of entry were clearly those of the authority."[25]

In the Netherlands and Belgium, the unions and early socialist movements developed in a relatively tolerant, if not fully liberal, climate. Early legislation against strikes and unions existed in both countries from 1815 (the Netherlands) and 1831 (Belgium) on. Belgium slowly legalized union activities in 1866–1867, repealing the provisions of the penal code that had made the combination of workers or employers to influence wage levels illegal. The particularly hostile provision of the compulsory "workbook" (*livret*) for workers – which made it impossible for them to change employers even if they had complied with all the contractual obligations – fell into disuse in the 1870s and was abolished in 1883. The same happened to a law stating that, in a conflict, the employer had to be taken at his word (this was also an article of the penal code). At the same time, it is important to remember that in the 1850s Belgium had instituted a series of Arbitration Councils, the aim of which was to arbitrate and moderate, to judge certain types of conflicts, and to perform certain policing tasks. From 1859 on, workers' representatives gained equal representation on these councils, and the right to vote in these bodies was opened up progressively, first to the more prosperous workers and then to all of them (1896). In Belgium, the key issue of collective action in the period from the 1880s was typically that of electoral reform, and particularly the elimination of the insidious plural voting. In 1912, in connection with this issue, there was considerable rioting and violent demonstrations, which resulted in the death of some of the participants. Again in 1913, the socialists scheduled a general strike for electoral reform; this time, it was peaceful, although it was just as unsuccessful as before.

In the Netherlands, the most violent confrontation occurred during the general strike of 1903, launched by the anarcho-syndicalist groups within the unions against the conservative government and, in particular, against legislation limiting the right to strike in the public service. There was considerable repression of the participants in the strike, and troops were called in to control the railway stations. However, this relatively violent incident – which led to the demise of Dutch anarcho-syndicalism – was isolated. Dutch agitation for suffrage enlargement was far less strained and came into existence somewhat later (1910 and 1912) than in Belgium. In general, socialism developed in a relatively tolerant political climate, which justifies the statement that "the Dutch government yielded to lower

[25] Lafferty (1971: 148).

classes' demands earlier and with considerable more grace."[26] In neither Belgium nor the Netherlands was the political socialist movement ever outlawed, severely persecuted, or repressed.

Ireland is difficult to classify. Formally, it came under British constitutional and legal rule, and its late-developing trade union movement was for many years closely associated with that of the British. While the global environment can be said to have been the same, however, the social problems were different, and by the turn of the century they had begun to be amalgamated with the issues of home rule and independence. Moreover, in sharp contrast to the relative social calm of British politics in the final quarter of the century, Irish society was passing through a period of strong social unrest, to which the British replied with a complex mixture of actions, including repression. For example, the 1881 Coercion Act suspended the right of habeas corpus, authorized detention without trial, prohibited illegal meetings and seditious speeches, and so on. In the same year, Charles Parnell, the leader of the Irish National Land League, was jailed and the league outlawed. In 1882, a new Coercion Act presented by Gladstone introduced three years of martial law. In 1886, the Tory government of Salisbury (1886–1892) responded again to a new upsurge of agrarian disorder with sharply repressive measures. These disturbances continued throughout the 1880s; and when the agrarian issue finally calmed down, new turmoil started to emerge on the issue of home rule, increasingly polarizing both the Protestant and Catholic communities. It was probably only the outbreak of World War I that prevented an escalation in violence.

At the same time, this policy of firm repression was balanced by one of reform. In 1881, the British Parliament passed a major agrarian reform that established dual ownership of land by the landlord and the tenant, fixed the establishment of rent levels by impartial bodies, and limited evictions to cases of nonpayment of rent and other well-defined situations. Each successive wave of repression was accompanied by acts whereby rents would be paid for poor tenants (Arreas Act of 1882) and low interest rates offered so that they could purchase their land (Ashbourne Act of 1885, enlarged and refunded in 1888 and 1891). Thus, the early popular (mostly peasant) movements in Ireland – which were by no means socialist in character – were faced with a stop-and-go policy of repression and appeasement that eventually pacified the agrarian Irish world but left a far from benign image of British rule.

[26] Goldstein (1983: 263).

In Italy, France, Austria, and Germany, the early development of the socialist movement faced strong state opposition and resistance. The established elite resorted to nonpolitical means of confrontation, increasingly relying on the pressure of the state administration, the police, and the army. The similarity of the response of these countries is striking, considering that Austria and Germany were the centers of internationally powerful continental autocracies, while France and Italy were more liberal. At the same time, within a common pattern of relatively violent response, the differences among these countries should not be ignored.

Early attitudes toward the French working-class movement had been relatively tolerant. The 1791 ban on union activities was repealed in 1848, when the right to unite was formally granted. However, the revolution, its drive for mobilization and nationalization, and the Napoleonic reforms had further centralized the French state, making the persistence and development of localized, restricted pluralist traditions in parts of the country difficult and enhancing the local control of the prefects. Later on, this apparatus was used regularly to mobilize supportive voters and to harass the organizational development of the opposition. Old restrictions on clubs, societies, and meetings were restored, and combinations were made subject to legal prosecution. However, in 1864 the ban on combination ended and strikes became legal, although the right to strike was limited and unions remained illegal. This long-standing prohibition against workers' trade associations was finally abolished in 1884 (only a decade after this happened in Britain), and from this date on active state repression perceptively slackened.[27]

There is, however, a history of administrative harassment in France that is almost totally independent of these legal developments and that marked the birth of the working-class movement indelibly between 1864 and 1884. In the late 1860s, the moderate leadership of the French Section of the First International met with strong state opposition, with troops used to end strikes and with extensive arrests and prosecutions. As a result, the section became increasingly less moderate in its views, and more syndicalist and revolutionary.[28] The Commune's repression was by far the most violent military, police, and judicial repression of working-class movements in Europe in the nineteenth century,[29] and it continued to

---

[27] Zeldin (1979: 205–206).
[28] Ibid., 365–369. "The growth of the moderate Trade Unions' movement in the 1860s was cut straight, and the opportunity was given for more violent elements to come to the fore" (Ibid., 381).
[29] According to historical sources, between 20,000 and 25,000 people were summarily

shape the attitude of the established elite to the working-class and socialist movements for many years. Thiers's repressive zeal was resumed during the frequent authoritarian crises: from Marshall MacMahon's attempted "institutional" coup in 1877 to Boulanger's 1886–1889 attempt to overthrow the republican regime; to the 1892 laws against the anarchists (*lois scélérates*) to the casualties of Fourmiers and many others; to the 1905–1908 policies of police provocation and brutal repression that resulted in the definitive break between radicalism and the working class.[30] During this period, and even up to 1936, memories of repression and of violent clashes with the state were repeated by periodic use of the army, which put down strikes, fuelling the workers' antimilitarism and antistate feelings. The strong resistance of the state to recognizing unions was equaled only by that of the employers. As a result, collective bargaining and bilateral negotiation in the Scandinavian style never really gained a foothold (see Chapter 6).[31] In contrast to this strong reaction to the organization of unions, the attitude toward the organization of the political movement was much milder. Its development was comparatively late; but after socialist political organizations were legalized in 1879, no direct attempt to outlaw them was ever made.

In France, therefore, workers' activities and organizations met with strong resistance by the state and with low recognition by the employers. The strong state tradition and its high centralization made resources for repression easily available; at the same time, the politically weak republican liberal and conservative elite was motivated to use such resources. It is difficult to assess to what extent the strong anarcho-syndicalist component in the French working-class movement was a cause, an excuse, or an effect of this intemperate state reaction, even though it is clear that moderate workers' associations and movements were harassed even before the Commune existed.

---

executed and killed; 38,578 were arrested; ten times this number were denounced; and there were large deportations to New Caledonia; (Zeldin 1979: 380).

[30] Kergoat reports that in the 1870s "every year an average of 9% of strikers were brought to justice and sentenced." Kergoat (1990: 165–167). Despite the new style of the Republic of Jules Ferry and Waldeck Rousseau, who instructed the prefects in 1884 not to use the army during strikes, this was largely ignored in the following period. The use of armed forces "which had dropped to 3% in the total number of disputes in 1882 increased to 10% later." Between 1892 and 1895, historians report prison sentences against anarchist and socialist agitators totaling 249 years, three life sentences and forced labor, and five death sentences. In the years 1905–1908, the army intervened against workers, with the following result: 20 killed, 667 wounded, and a total of 104 years of prison sentences.

[31] In 1933, only 7.5% of wage earners had been affected by such agreements. Cf. Zeldin (1979: 207); see also Schorter and Tilly (1974: 35).

Italy lacked the long-standing tradition of dynastic bureaucracy, the old nation building, and the international status of France. Notwithstanding these fundamental differences, the Italian state-building liberal and conservative elite felt as unsafe as its counterpart, the French republican elite, facing strong opposition from the papal state and Italian Catholics, as well as having an uncertain international status and facing strong internal resistance to central control. Legitimation of the socialist movement risked shrinking the flimsy support base of the dominant elite even further. The repressive orientation of the new Italian state was boosted largely to repress the widespread resistance to its establishment, which took the form, among others, of separatist movements in Sicily, pro-Bourbon sentiment in the south, and Mafia and bandits. These created a mood of repressive defense in the state-building elite, in which Bourbonists, clericals, republicans, and internationalists were all considered enemies of the new state. The battle against them was often fought with exceptional legal instruments: preventive arrest, house arrest, limitations on movement, and administrative deportation (*confino*). The legalization of unions and their activities, including strikes, took place over a relatively long period (1859–1889), and the end of severe harassment (but not of administrative nuisances) occurred only at the beginning of the twentieth century. During this period, intense political repression alternated with more-liberal toleration. The coming to power of the liberal left in 1876 coincided with a more moderate use of repressive means;[32] however, repression was renewed after 1885, when socialism started to spread among the agricultural laborers of the Po Valley and the industrial workers of Milan. In 1892–1894, the repression of the *Fasci Siciliani* rebellion led to martial law in Sicily in 1894–1895; Crispi resorted to intense repressive tactics; and in 1897–1898, civil disorders brought about strong military intervention against demonstrators.

Before the time of Giolitti, therefore, the Italian pattern involved frequent use of the army and of administrative and police measures (less of the judiciary), as well as a weak political and legislative response by a largely nonpluralist dominant political elite. Unlike France, however, in Italy the socialist political movement was also repressed strongly. Various socialist political organizations were dissolved during the 1880s, and the Socialist Party, founded in 1893, was made illegal between 1893 and 1895

---

[32] For instance, the use of the "admonition" (*ammonizione*) – the police instrument that was most open to arbitrary political use – was restrained, and the number of *ammoniti* declined from 184,000 to 40,000 between 1876 and 1884. However, a more repressive policy in this field was soon resumed after 1885. Cf. Carocci (1975: 51).

and once again in 1898. In addition, the period after World War I did not mark the legitimation of the socialist movement but, instead, its complete eradication. Unions had to wait until 1945 to regain their previous legality, and up to the end of the 1950s major strikes and political demonstrations maintained a confrontational style with the state and police forces (with frequent casualties). Both the French and Italian liberal regimes rested on a restricted popular base and found it difficult to enlarge. This resulted in a strategy of containment, or even rejection, of the political integration of a considerable portion of their national constituencies (see the following chapter on this point).

Both Austria and Germany banned workers' economic associations from the beginning of the eighteenth century; both formally repealed this legislation at the end of the 1860s; both continued to practice severe administrative harassment until the beginning of the 1890s and continued thereafter with milder forms. In Austria, legal recognition of the unions in 1866 was followed six months later by the prosecution for high treason of those who had signed the request for this recognition. The 1884 emergency introduced a seven-year-long police state in which freedom of the press, the right to meet and assemble, and the protection of postal secrecy were suspended, and arrests could be made without any judicial authorization. A significant easing of control occurred only during the 1900–1905 period. The record is similar in Germany, although here there was also the precedent of the anti-Catholic *Kulturkampf*. In 1871–1876 and in 1878, socialist organizations had been strongly and directly repressed. The "socialist law," in force from 1878 to 1889, was typical of the domineering attitude of the Prussian-German elite toward socialism and, in general, toward democratization and emancipation movements. Social democrats and socialist unions were stigmatized as enemies of the empire and therefore of the state. From the socialist point of view, the anti socialist legislation made it clear that the state had taken the side of dynastic and property interests against the workers and their organizations. The socialist movement, strongly promoted by rapid industrialization, was forced to accept drastic limitations on both its liberty to act and its will to participate in the legal and constitutional systems of the country.[33] In Austria, political rights were regulated by the 1867 law on associations, which prohibited political societies from merging, founding branches, corresponding with each other, or even maintaining contact via a member of the parliament. Strictly speaking, any political activity outside parliament

[33] On the repression of the early German socialist movement and party, see Lidtke (1966: 70–88, 242–253).

and the state institutions could be punished by law.[34] This explains why the Austrian social democratic societies had a strongly cultural character, and educational associations concealed their political commitment and emancipation goals behind a range of cultural and educational activities.

Although unions were never formally recognized by either the state or employers, the autocratic regimes of Germany and Austria tolerated strike and union activities more than political activity.[35] Contrary to the British pattern, economic conflicts and action in the market were more easily accepted than political conflicts and action. This was because the ideal of the autocratic state was one of apolitical corporate representation, which it would probably be willing to recognize, provided that no challenge was made to the political order. The attempt to isolate political socialism from its social base was thus common to both states and was also pursued systematically through the legislation of the early welfare state.[36] In Germany more clearly than in Austria, an exchange of recognition for support occurred when World War I began and the socialists attempted to integrate into the state by supporting its war activities. In a single move, these socialist parties wanted to demonstrate their national reliability and respectability, as well as to rid themselves of the accusation of being antipatriotic enemies of the fatherland.[37] Following this, trade union officials were exempted from military service, state employees were allowed to join the SPD, and the state forced reluctant employers to accept the trade unions as bargaining partners.

Finland is difficult to classify because its late-developing socialist movement was forced to take root in the illiberal climate typical of a subordinate periphery of the Russian Empire. The guild system was abolished by the Trade Acts of 1868 and 1879, which repealed the prohibition on journeymen and employees to associate to further their interests. After this date, no legal restrictions were aimed specifically at the unions, but freedom of association was virtually nonexistent, as governmental approval was necessary to found associations and was granted on a very restrictive basis. Such restrictions were also applied to workingmen's associations when socialism reached Finland in 1890–1900. In 1906, freedom of association was enacted as a constitutional right. The point is that Finland enjoyed relative independence over its internal affairs, which was, however,

---

[34] Mattl (1990: 295).

[35] Several examples of this differentiated attitude of public authorities are documented in Ritter (1963).

[36] On the early welfare measures of authoritarian regimes, see Alber (1982: 119–193) and Flora and Alber (1981).

[37] See the debate on this interpretation in Tenfelde (1981: 216–247).

dependent on Russian attitudes. These were largely determined by the empire's fears of revolutionary movement more than by any specific intention of fostering Finnish employers' interests. The historical record, therefore, is not one of intense socialist movement repression, and when this repression was triggered it was more an attempt by the Russians to repress Finnish autonomy than to repress the socialist movement itself.

Once Finland became an independent state, however, internal social tensions began to prevail. The 1919 constitution embodied a new Association Act, but despite this, in 1922 an Employment Contract Act became necessary to declare unlawful and punishable actions taken by employers to prevent employees from joining or belonging to a lawful association. The Finnish socialist movement had emerged from the civil war under a largely communist leadership, and the political action in which it engaged awoke the suspicion and mistrust of authorities and employers alike (and often of moderate socialists, too). In 1930, the SAJ Confederation was dissolved for subversive activities by a court decision (a unique case in the twentieth century). In 1931 an act for the protection of labor peace included provisions that established punishments for forcing employees to either join or to abandon associations and/or to take part in a strike. It was, of course, easy to turn this act into an antiunion instrument. After the 1918 civil war, mutual distrust concerning collective agreements meant that they ceased to be used, and it was only after World War II that most employer associations were prepared to accept trade unions on an equal footing with themselves (see Chapter 6).

What makes Finland a special case is that the state was weak under Russian rule, with virtually none of its own military or police forces. Again, after independence, there was a situation more of internal social polarization than of state political repression. Thus, Finland between 1914 and 1945 can probably be more appropriately described as a "praetorian society," where a weak state was easily penetrated by the social and political forces that were stronger at any specific moment. If the experience of Finnish socialism cannot be said to be one of early and smooth institutional integration, it should at the same time be kept separate from those of the central European empires.

RESPONSIBLE GOVERNMENT

The political responsibility of the top executive branch adds a third type of resource in the fight for power and influence over decision making. Before this principle is fully implemented, resources are limited to the

influence that individual and political actors have in and over the administrative and bureaucratic machinery of the state, as well as the influence
they have in the market or can mobilize in the society through organizational pressure. Executive political responsibility adds the political resource
of parliamentary influence and negotiation, which are dependent on electioneering and electoral mobilization. When executive elites become dependent on elective bodies, they are forced to take electoral power relationships into consideration. Electoral resources become an element in the
transformation of social and/or administrative influence into executive
dominance. Consequently, elective elites have a greater tendency than
monarchs, bureaucrats, lords, or militaries to see the conflicts and requests
coming from new claimants as political opportunities – to beat and weaken
the adversary or to defend themselves – rather than as political threats.
When this occurs, the political integration of outsiders, that is, their
acceptance of the existing institutional framework as one in which their
values can be fought for and at least in part achieved, is easier and therefore
more likely.

I use the term "responsible government" here in a broad sense to refer
to the process that extends and finally grants to elective chambers control
over the *formation, personnel, duration*, and *legislative activities* of cabinets. In
this broad definition, the process is quite complex. The constitutional
history of European countries offers several cases of ambiguous and intermediate situations.[38] Cabinets might be dependent on the support of the
elective chamber for their continued existence, but their prime ministers
(and ministerial personnel) might be freely chosen by other bodies, such as
the monarch or the nonelective first chamber. Cabinets might depend on
chamber support to be installed, but might still be required to resign by
forces other than those in such a chamber. Cabinets and prime ministers
might be politically responsible to the elective chamber but still face
considerable "legislative" conflicts with other nonrepresentative bodies,
such as the first chamber or the dynastic bureaucracy. Therefore, the
establishment of parliamentary government was often a long process characterized by periods of uncertainty in the distribution of competencies,
mutual veto power among representative and nonrepresentative institutions, steps forward, and setbacks. The analysis of the thirteen countries,
therefore, requires considerable contextual specification, but I propose the
following six yardsticks for comparative evaluation:

---

[38] For a descriptive account of early institutional developments see Anderson and Anderson
(1967).

1. Before the introduction of responsible government, when the elective chamber was unwilling to pass legislation, was parliament dissolved by the crown?
2. At what point in time was the cabinet's responsibility to the elective chamber of parliament accepted or imposed over the monarch's resistance?
3. To what extent and for how long did institutional fights with nonelective or nonrepresentative first chambers persist?
4. Were these conflicts politico-institutional (concerning the powers of the elective chambers toward the executive), or were they mainly legislative (concerning specific legislation veto or rebuttal)?
5. To what extent and how long did the monarchy and its immediate advisers and milieus continue to intruded on the life, personnel, and duration of cabinets?
6. After parliamentary responsibility was introduced, when was a cabinet maintained against the will of the elective chamber for the last time?

Let me begin with the four uncontroversial cases of the United Kingdom, Switzerland, Belgium, and the Netherlands, where parliamentary governments developed slowly and well before the middle of the nineteenth century. No major politico-institutional conflicts concerning the distribution of political power between the two chambers occurred, although conflicts over legislation were frequent. No major monarchical interference in the activities of these governments are reported by historians, and those episodes that are mentioned look marginal in comparison with the remaining cases in our set. Finally, in none of these countries did setbacks in the tradition of responsible government ever occur, and no cabinet was ever kept in power against the explicit will of the elective chamber.

The Belgian case merits little or no discussion. When in January 1831 Great Britain, Austria, Prussia, and Russia ratified the independence of the new Belgian state – the result of a rebellion in the southern provinces of the former Austrian Netherlands – and determined that it would be neutral, the constitutional assembly designed a very liberal constitution. The first chamber was originally elected directly and remained so until 1893. After this, a reform meant that half of it was directly elected and the other half was elected by the provincial government. Neither this chamber nor the crown ever challenged the primacy of the second chamber and the principle of responsible government.

Strictly speaking, in Switzerland the formal principle of government responsibility *at the federal level* was introduced by the further centralizing constitutional revision of 1874. However, this practice made little sense within the loose federation before 1848 and even in the 1848–1874 phase, which followed the Sonderbund canton war of 1848 and the approval of the new federal constitution. In any case, the practice of responsible government was already effective in the cantons well before then, even before 1848 in many cantons. The special character of Swiss cabinet responsibility within the directorate structure of the executive is discussed in more detail in the next section. What matters here is that since that time, federal councilors have always been elected by parliament, and it was unthinkable 150 years ago, just as it is today, that they could challenge the latter. After all, in a republic without a president, the Swiss cabinet had no authority beyond the parliament and the citizens on which to rely or to whom to appeal.

In the Dutch case, a *Whig* interpretation of political development emphasizes the continuity from early corporate pluralism in the seven provinces to modern liberalization. According to this perspective, the early break in the development of a modern absolutist state (under a Burgundian–Hapsburg dynasty) resulted in the weakness of the central institutions (military and bureaucracy), an early and prominent role of the bourgeoisie (given the weakness of the aristocracy), and an emphasis on the right to resist any unlawful action of the sovereign, together with a persistent particularism. As a consequence, the presence of many actors with inherent rights fostered the gradual development from early pluralism to modern democracy. The institutional developments in the nineteenth century, and particularly the constitutional revision of 1848, liberalized the regime, strengthening the parliament and transforming the first chamber from a royally appointed body to one elected by provincial councils.

However, a *radical* interpretation emphasizes the oligarchic and non-democratic character of politics in the pre-Napoleonic period and regards the revolutionary break of the radical Patriots movement of the 1770s and the Bathavian–French period between 1794 and 1813 as crucial for liberalization and democratization. According to this thesis, modern democracy resulted more from these breaks than from any kind of continuity with early pluralism.[39] Whatever the case, by 1848 the practice of parliamentary

---

[39] In reviewing this historiography debate, Daalder argues that the two interpretations refer to two different conceptions of democracy and can to a certain extent be reconciled. While the Whig interpretation concentrates on a vision of democratic development as basically liberalization and contestation, the radicals' interpretation focuses on participation as the key dimension. See Daalder (1990: 4–17).

government was established, and the possible opposition of a first chamber appointed by royalty was eliminated by reform. Conflicts between the crown and the parliament over power attribution were not infrequent between 1848 and 1868, but their nature, frequency, and intensity did not jeopardize basic parliamentary practice.

In the United Kingdom, parliamentary control of the executive occurred comparatively early and gradually, even if there are different opinions about the date when it became fully operational. Some put it as late as 1832, but most argue that the decisive turning point was in the first years of the nineteenth century.[40] The nineteenth century was marked by constant conflicts between the Lords and the Commons over legislative competence and vetoing — which, however, never brought into question the fundamental principle that the prime minister was accountable to the lower elective house. The downgrading of the Lords' powers had started long before, but the final confrontation came in the first decade of the twentieth century and was solved by repeated use of electoral decisions, which consistently (in the two 1910 elections) endorsed the liberal position. Ireland shared the institutional developments of the United Kingdom even though, by the end of the nineteenth century, the issues were different and the growing feeling of nationalism gave rise to violent upheavals (and eventually a civil war in the transition to national independence). In this, the Irish case presents similarities to the Finnish case, on which I will dwell further later on. The important point is that 1922 is the year in which both the new Irish state and the arrival of parliamentary government were achieved, and the key issue that mobilized political forces in Ireland before that date was not so much internal liberalization but home rule.

France and Norway are intermediate cases where parliamentary government was established between the mid-1870s and the mid-1880s. However, the only similarity between them is the timing. While in France the principle and practice of parliamentary government were uncertain for a fairly long period, in Norway the transition was astonishingly smooth. In France, notwithstanding the constitutional provisions of 1871, the practice of parliamentary government did not consolidate until the definitive failure of the reactionary President Marshall MacMahon, who, with the support of a small monarchical majority in the indirectly elected Senate, dissolved the lower chamber and called elections in 1877 under conditions of considerable state administrative pressure. The resulting republican majority introduced the principle of parliamentary responsibility and the curtailing of

---

[40] For the developments up to the 1831 reform, see the documented evaluation of Mackintosh (1977: 35–74).

presidential powers. Given this experience, the mistrust of an active presidency was such that no other parliament was allowed to be dissolved during the Third Republic. However, the principle of parliamentary government was unacceptable to large sections of the public and the bureaucracy and to the end of the century – after the attempt by Boulanger to overthrow the parliamentary regime – the republican majorities remained convinced of the need to defend the system against internal enemies. Moreover, the varying political composition and orientation of a predominantly rural and indirectly elected Senate contributed to the considerable legislative conflicts with the lower chamber until the end of the 1930s, often with significant political consequences. For example, at the end of the 1930s, it was the strong opposition of the Senate to the socioeconomic legislation of the Popular Front governments of Léon Blum that led to the latter's downfall twice, in June 1937 and April 1938.[41]

Norway never faced the problem of curbing the privileges of the upper chamber because the parliament was a unicameral body from the beginning. When it was first established in 1814, during the political void created by the end of Denmark's alliance with Napoleon's France, ideas regarding the use of the upper chamber to represent and secure aristocratic conservative interests were strong everywhere in Europe, particularly in Denmark and Sweden. However, the aristocracy and the ecclesiastic orders were so weak in Norway that eventually the Storing became a unicameral institution.[42] Until 1884, the Norwegian government was not accountable to the Storing, and executive authority was in the hands of nominated governmental officials. In 1884, an alliance of peasants and other groups (mainly doctors, teachers, and lawyers) gained the majority in parliament and founded the first Norwegian political party – the Venstre. This majority impeached, convicted, and removed from office eight members of the

---

[41] The French Senate in the Third Republic – indirectly elected at different points in time than the lower chamber, enjoying the right of censure against the cabinet and considerable control over the timing of the dissolution of parliament, mainly representing the local notables of rural France – acted systematically as an important brake on the consolidation of the French party system and on the powers of cabinets and prime ministers. The fall of Blum's first cabinet (June 1937) is revealing: After the Senate's modification of Blum's fiscal program, the socialist prime minister tried to solve the crisis by resorting to the electorate via dissolution and new elections, that is, following a British style of crisis management by the lower house. Radical ministers in the cabinet and the Senate, which needed to agree on an early dissolution, resisted the request. For a detailed analysis of the role of the Senate in the Popular Front governments, see Lefranc (1963: 339–340, 352–353).

[42] It was composed of two houses (Lagsting and Odelsting), which met separately in the law-making process but were elected at the same time and had a similar composition.

royally appointed government, and this finally forced the Swedish king, Oscar II, to yield to the primacy of parliament, apparently after having carefully considered the advantages and disadvantages of a royal coup. No important internal resistance to this event has been recorded by historians. The absence of a national monarchy, the weakness of the local aristocracy, and the low level of stateness of the political process left the country with few nonparliamentary political resources. Obviously, parliamentarization concerned domestic matters; any control over its own foreign affairs had to wait until 1905, when Norway became formally independent from Sweden.[43]

Denmark, Sweden, Finland, Austria, and Germany can be said to have established the definitive parliamentarization of their governments in the twentieth century; but in addition to differences in timing (from 1901 to 1945), there are also differences in process. Denmark and Sweden had a similar pattern of delayed cabinet responsibility and protracted institutional conflict between an elective lower chamber, on the one hand, and the crown and the upper chamber, on the other. In both cases, final control of the lower house *was not the result of military defeat*. Finland, Austria, and Germany shared protracted autocratic rule curbed only by military defeat, although in Finland this was the defeat of the colonial power rather than of the local dynastic power.

In a broad comparative framework, the Danish and Swedish constitutional developments hardly merit strong differentiation. Both countries had a tradition of dynastic absolutist rule, but whereas in Denmark this tradition was strong and unchallenged until 1834 – when the king was obliged to introduce an "estate constitution" with four different regional assemblies – Sweden is thought to have maintained more continuity in its institutions of representation.[44] In Denmark in 1849 and in Sweden in 1866, constitutional reforms abolished the estate diets and introduced bicameral parliaments that, due to a more restricted franchise or to plural voting systems,[45] were sharply differentiated in social composition (mainly

---

[43] Note that Norway had a tradition of sovereign independence. An autonomous Norwegian kingdom existed from 1163 to 1319, and it was only in 1536 that Norway became a province of Denmark. Even later, during the long period of Danish–Swedish wars for predominance in the area (1563 to 1720), Norway often managed to defend itself by its own efforts. See Derry (1968: 44–67, 89–108).

[44] Even if Denmark is notable for its rapid and peaceful transition from absolutism and a military state to early constitutional liberalism in the first half of the nineteenth century. See Lind (1988: 112–119).

[45] To be more precise, the Swedish upper chamber was indirectly elected after 1866 by an electoral college of members of local governmental bodies. However, the system of

farmers versus officers, landowners, and capitalists). The conflict between the two chambers increasingly came to dominate the politics of the last quarter of the century in Denmark and even longer in Sweden. The lower chamber was probably stronger in Denmark, where it managed to check legislation and even to force the prime minister, Estrup, to resign in 1894. However, there were frequent instances of parliamentary dissolution in this period due to the parliament's recalcitrant attitude to government legislation. The king continued, meanwhile, to rely on conservative ministries drawn from the restricted-suffrage upper house and on government by decree. Finally, in 1901, the king was forced to accept parliamentary responsibility based on the Folketing and to call the Venstre to power, although the resistance of the conservative Landsting continued by systematically blocking measures to reform itself. The last resistance ended in 1914, when all the Danish moderate and left parties agreed to institute universal suffrage of the Landsting, a move that was boycotted and delayed by the upper house until 1915. The Danish king made a last, and unsuccessful, attempt to force his own will on the lower chamber during a cabinet crisis in 1920.

In Sweden, the king resisted the parliamentarization of the executive until 1917. Attempts to introduce parliamentarization had been underway since 1905, however, when the liberals in the second chamber had briefly formed a cabinet. Even before that date, several cabinets had had to resign after losing votes in the parliament, which had already gained power at the expense of the king.[46] However, in 1914, King Gustav forced a liberal prime minister to resign over the issue of increasing military expenditures, and, in an explicit act of rejection of parliamentary democracy, he appointed a conservative ministry that governed throughout the war years by relying on the support of the royal house and the upper chamber. When, in March 1917, a new conservative ministry of this type was appointed, this appeared to be a clear repudiation of parliamentary sovereignty; the ministry was ousted by popular riots and by the lack of reliable army support in repressing them.[47]

Germany, Austria, and Finland introduced the parliamentarization of the executive as a result of the military collapse of their autocratic dynastic rulers at the end of World War I. Until 1809, Finland, as part of Sweden,

---

voting in local elections was characterized by substantial property qualifications linked to plural voting. At the turn of the century, certain people could still cast up to forty votes in this electoral college.

[46] Sannerstedt and Sjölin (1992: 100).

[47] Stjernquist (1966: 117–121).

had had no tradition whatsoever of sovereign independence. When, in that year, Finland was handed over to Russia, it became a grand duchy, maintaining the Swedish constitution of 1770 and displaying some of the characteristics of a sovereign state. For example, it had its own central government, central bank, and customs and postal systems; these national institutions were set up in Norway at a later date.[48] The Finnish four-estate Diet was convened in 1809 but was not reconvened until 1863. From this date on, the Diet met regularly, and there was also a modest degree of liberalization between 1860 and 1894. So, paradoxically, although deprived of a long tradition of nation-state autonomy and subject to the staunchest autocratic power in Europe, Finland did enjoy a certain degree of autonomy under Russian administration.

Finland's relationship with the metropolitan power deteriorated toward the end of the century, when assimilation tendencies gained ascendancy in Russian imperial circles, which clashed with the by now distinctive national structure and identity of the country. By 1894, a new period of absolutism had manifested itself through attempts to russify Finland: Russian was made the official language of the bureaucracy, and Russian personnel were placed in key governmental positions (1902). There were also attempts to conscript Finns into the Russian army. Freedom of the press, of organization, and of assembly were restricted, and the Finnish national opposition was repressed. The series of measures designed to limit Finland's autonomy gave rise to a passive-resistance movement headed by Swedish-speaking liberals and Finnish nationalists. In the period between 1907 and 1913, the tsar continuously blocked legislation and dissolved the Diet almost every year, dissatisfied with the electoral results, which continuously gave power to a body of nationalists among whom the socialists were the strongest. In 1910, a last attempt was made to achieve direct control of Finland through a Russian Duma law that removed a wide range of matters from the jurisdiction of the Finnish Diet. From 1917 to 1919, Finland declared its independence (December 6, 1917), went through a civil war, and appointed a German king (Prince Froedrick Karl of Hesse in October 1918), who was then dropped after the German defeat and surrender. In July 1919, parliamentarization was finally established with a governmental act of secession from Russia.

Finnish cabinet responsibility after 1919, however, requires some clarification because of the special executive dualism of the Finnish consti-

---

[48] Danish rulers allowed the much desired national bank and university to be set up in Norway only in 1813.

tutional model.[49] Notwithstanding the formal inclusion of the principle of responsibility in the constitution, Finnish parliamentarism *does not present or use* any of the three basic mechanisms that usually embody the idea that the cabinet must have the confidence of the parliament: (1) that the president is obliged to find out beforehand if the person he intends to appoint as prime minister enjoys the confidence of the chamber; (2) that the chamber votes to express confidence in the cabinet after its appointment; and (3) that the cabinet invites or initiates such a vote of confidence in presenting its manifesto.[50] Between the world wars, there were several occasions on which the president appointed cabinets against the will of the parliament. For example, in 1924, Ståhlberg dissolved the parliament against the wishes of its majority; and in 1936, a bourgeois minority government was appointed in similar circumstances.[51] Similar cases on the borderline of what is usually regarded as the principle of parliamentary confidence can be mentioned. However, within the Finnish constitutional context and its political practice, it would be misleading to consider these cases as a violation of the constitutional rules. We must in this case accept more-contextual criteria of parliamentary control over the executive, because no major institutional crisis has developed between the president and parliament since the 1919 constitution. Therefore, the latter data can be regarded as the starting point of parlimentary control.

The situation was different in the two central European empires. The German constitution of 1866 was an intricate edifice devised by Bismarck

---

[49] Having failed to get a king, the 1919 constitution makers adopted the statements of the 1917 constitution-drafting commission, opting for writing the principle of parliamentary government into the constitution and, at the same time, giving the presidency of the republic a variety of prerogatives and powers so as to make it a check on purely parliamentary government. As a compromise between the sharply diverging constitutional ideologies of the right – favoring a strong and independent presidency – and the left – favoring a purely parliamentary government – the relationship was finally shaped by practice and conventions, and remained strongly divergent according to the political climate. After the civil war, in the context of continuous minority government, the role of the president in choosing the cabinets and influencing their lives remained crucial. For a discussion of the complex attribution of powers among the parliament, the cabinet, and the presidency in Finland, see Duverger (1986).

[50] For this practice, see Anckar (1992: 154–155).

[51] Anckar mentions a telling episode. When in 1926 the Social Democratic Prime Minister Väinö Tanner presented his program in the parliament after his appointment, arguing that this was the practice parliamentarism implied, the speaker of the chamber did not allow discussion or voting on the matter, arguing that in the parliamentary rule nothing was specified concerning this problem. The speaker's decision was not contested by the parliament's majority, nor was it referred to the Constitutional Committee (Anckar 1992: 155).

as a purely personal invention, intended to permit the chancellor to neutralize his domestic enemies and to facilitate German unification. Each of the twenty-six states retained its theoretical sovereignty. The federal government was, on paper anyway, very restricted in its powers, and its institutions were correspondingly few. They consisted of the emperor and his only minister and executive agent, the chancellor; the high civil servants; military and naval commands; and a parliament whose lower house was elected by universal manhood suffrage. It was in the German states that the residual authority was vested; their delegates composed the upper house of the federal parliament, and they were in a position to dominate the federal government, enjoying veto power on Reichstag legislation. However, there was an element that distorted the imperial constitution: the role of Prussia, which was so dominant as to profoundly influence, if not control, both the imperial regime and the other states too. Prussia accounted for about three-fifths of the territory and population of the German federation. The king of Prussia was also the German emperor; the prime minister of Prussia was, as a matter of custom, also the imperial chancellor; and the Prussian army was the overwhelming majority in the German defense establishment. There was no clear limit to the authority of the emperor, who could appoint and dismiss the chancellor and who considered himself as responsible for forming policy. The government of the state of Prussia was dependent on the Prussian parliament. This body was dominated, thanks to its voting system, by a minority of the Prussian electorate, a minority dominated in turn by the dour, parochial, conservative, and virtually bankrupt landowners of eastern Prussia.

The Prussian roots of the German Empire were important in another respect: It was in Prussia between 1862 and 1866 that an important constitutional conflict took place that defeated the liberal forces and proved crucial for the future of the politico-constitutional equilibrium of the empire. The liberal forces had insisted on having financial control over the army; this was strongly resisted by the king and the army itself. The latter together managed to override several parliamentary vetos, resorting directly to the bureaucracy to find the money necessary to finance the army, and dissolved the parliament three times (in 1861, 1862, and 1863) before the king decided to rule without deferring to it at all.

The chancellor, as prime minister of dominant Prussia, was dependent on the support of that state's decaying aristocracy; as chancellor of Germany, he was also dependent to some extent on the democratic Reichstag; and in both capacities, he was dependent on the hereditary monarchy. Even in the imperial constitution of 1871, executive power was vested more in the Bundesrat, a large, unwieldy body technically presided over by the emperor and accruing to his power.[52] Thus imperial Germany not only did not have the principle of parliamentary responsibility, but even the legislative role of the lower house was restricted, and not only on military and fiscal matters. Still, in the early 1890s, when the Reichstag refused to extend the expiring antisocialist law, Bismarck considered the idea of a coup to restrict the franchise.

The same situation existed in the Hapsburg Empire after Emperor Francis Joseph I recognized the principle of constitutional government through the October Diploma of 1860 and the February Patent of 1861. A similar conservative upper house of aristocratic dignitaries and landowners – chosen and convened by the monarch – existed, and a similar repeated dissolution of the lower chamber occurred between 1861 and 1878, with the emperor requiring different legislation to support his internal and external policies. Finally, parliamentary activities were equally ineffective in controlling the executive and in promoting or controlling legislation. If anything, this latter situation was worse in Austria than in Germany, as the lower house was also paralyzed by its national fragmentation and inability to form cross-national coalitions. Thus, Austria and Germany represent the clearest cases in which not only did executives remain outside the reach of elective chamber control, but legislation also escaped them almost entirely. A growing sense of the powerlessness of elective representatives and of the uselessness of parliamentary activities was inevitably the outcome of such developments. The collapse of democracy in both countries in the 1930s meant that the principle of governmental responsibility and the practice of parliamentary government were not finally consolidated until after World War II.

Finally, Italy has not received in the comparative literature the attention that it deserves as a totally deviant case: Italian liberal democracy collapsed seventy years after the principle and practice of responsible government had been introduced.[53] Although historiographic research has convincingly argued that the Statuto Albertino instituted constitutional government rather than parliamentary government, a wider interpretation was immediately given in practice. Historians tend to regard the *connubio* in the Kingdom of Piedmont – namely, the formation at the beginning of 1852 of an efficient parliamentary majority – as the first step toward

---

[52] Cervelli (1978: 240–245).

[53] In my opinion, Spanish political and constitutional development resembles Italian development more closely than do the German and Austrian cases. A systematic comparison of Italy and Spain in the period 1850–1920/1930 would be particularly revealing in differentiating them from the central empire experience.

ministerial responsibility. "From that moment, once the uncertainties of the Calabiana crisis and of the 1857–1858 period had been overcome, it became consolidated practice that government be formed on the basis of the indications of the Chamber of Deputies. The crown, the upper chamber, and the conservative groups surrounding them actually came to be located in a marginal position as far as the political direction of the country was concerned."[54]

The Italian Senate was nonelective but rarely played an important role in limiting the prerogatives of the lower chamber. In reality, the cabinet soon developed a power of senatorial appointment similar to that of the crown, and several prime ministers made wide use of such power in order to ensure that the Senate's political orientation was compatible with that of the lower chamber.[55] The check to the full parliamentarization of the executive was the persistent influence of the king and the circles around the royal family. Dramatic conflicts never developed, but interventions in the life and composition of the cabinets, particularly in war and foreign affairs and ministries, were frequent.[56] Prime ministers never completely prescinded from the parliamentary situation, and the king never intervened systematically, disregarding the parliamentary orientation, but the role of the monarchy was important and kept alive discussion about a return to the original design of the *Statuto*, that is, to a more constitutional monarchy.[57] The general situation is best described in the following statement: "A [king's] role kept within the limits of a parliamentary regime whenever the political context obliged it to do so; a [king's] role going beyond such limits (and sometime even beyond the limits of a purely constitutional regime) whenever politically possible; in any case, a role *dictated not by the principle and definite acceptance of certain rules of the game, but dictated by the evaluation made in each case of the political convenience to respect them.*"[58] Certainly, it should not be forgotten that the role played by the king was instrumental to the nomination of Mussolini as prime minister in October

[54] Caracciolo (1957: 106) (my translation).

[55] The number of new appointments, called *infornate,* reached 200. The power of appointment of the king and the prime minister was tempered by the autonomous power of the Senate to verify the qualifications of the newly appointed members.

[56] For a list of the interventions of the monarchical circles on the composition of the cabinet and on the resignation of individual ministers disliked by the king, see Fabbri (1991: 103–186). All the conflicts between the king and the ministers are listed. The last one was with De Rudini in 1896.

[57] During the political and institutional crisis at the end of the century, a prominent political personality, Sonnino, called for a return to a constitutional monarchy with the famous slogan "Torniamo allo statuto" ("Let's come back to the statute").

[58] Rotelli (1975: 7–8) (translation and emphasis are mine).

1922 and that he was silent in the face of Mussolini's dismantling of the liberal regime. Thus, the comparative evaluation of the parliamentarization of the executive in Italy is more complex than in the other cases. This process was never really consolidated, but its causes lie more in the weakness of parliament and of the party system than in the objective strength of the royal powers. It was thanks to the lack of structuring of the Italian partisan alignments in the second half of the nineteenth century and to the lack of clear parliamentary majorities that the king maintained his position of strength.

In Table 7.4, I have synthesised most of the information discussed in the previous paragraphs.

FAIR REPRESENTATION

DISREPRESENTATIVE DEVICES

The greatest obstacle to political representation was the restricted franchise. But even when suffrage was extended, diverting mechanisms were often devised or retained to ensure that it had a limited impact on the political process. In the long run, however, these obstacles were likely to arouse a deep, strongly felt sense of injustice among those who were affected because of the clearly discriminating arguments advanced to support them. In defending the class-weighted voting system in Prussia, one minister argued that classes of people had to vote on the basis "of their actual importance in the life of the state."[59] This argument clearly demonstrated the lesser importance of certain individuals and groups and may have created more resentment than exclusion from voting on capacity (cultural and/or economic) grounds.

The obstacles were devices that increased the cost of votes and/or the cost of seats for newcomers. These mechanisms persisted throughout the nineteenth century, distorting the free and direct expression of the voter's choice (*indirect voting* and *open {nonsecret} voting*, which violated the one person, one vote principle, and *plural voting* and *curia/estate voting*) and hindering the fair transformation of electoral strength into parliamentary strength (*disrepresentative* nature of certain electoral formulas).[60]

Oral voting and the *showing of hands* greatly facilitated pressure and

[59] Prussian minister quoted in Anderson and Anderson (1967: 307).
[60] The information concerning open, indirect, and curia voting have been collected mainly from Goldstein (1983) and Flora, Alber, Eichenberg, Kohl, Kraus, Pfenning, and Seebohm (1983).

Table 7.4. *Timing of responsible government development*

country	responsible government	monarchical influences and/or curbing of upper chamber prerogatives	setbacks or last occasion on which a cabinet was kept against the will of the elective chamber
Austria	1818	up to 1918 unlimited appointing power of the monarch in the upper chamber repeated lower chamber dissolution between 1861 and 1879	1834–1845
Belgium	1831	upper chamber: 1831–93 directly elected; after 1893, half directly elected, half elected by provincial governments; major conflict	never
Denmark	1901	upper chamber: 1849–1866 directly elected, conflictual relationship with lower chamber 1866–1901: reform introducing royal appointment of half first chamber, conflictual politico-institutional relationship with lower chamber 1915: upper chamber democratisation lower chamber: frequent dissolution 1876-1894	1920
Finland	1917–1919	upper chamber: up to 1906 unlimited appointing power of the monarch in the higher estate Diet lower chamber: repeated dissolution 1907-13	1924 ?
France	1875–1881	1877–1936: upper chamber indirectly elected 1878–1936: intermittent legislative conflict between first and second chambers	never
Germany	1918	upper chamber: up to 1918 federal council with veto power on Reichstag legislation	1933–1945
Ireland	1922	unicameral	never
Italy	1852, 1945	no major conflict between first and second chambers frequent and important interventions by the monarch on executive life, composition and legislation	1924–1945
Netherl.	1848–1868	since 1848 elected indirectly by lower level governmental bodies no major conflict 1848-1868: lengthy conflict between crown and parliament	never
Norway	1885	unicameral	never
Sweden	(1905) 1917	upper chamber: after 1866 elected indirectly, representation vitiated strong political, institutional and legislative conflicts between chambers up to 1918 upper chamber democratization in 1909, 1920, 1933	never or 1921 ?
Switzerl.	1848–1874	federal; no conflict	never
Un. Kingd.	about 1800	legislative conflicts between chambers up to 1910–1911	never

manipulation by government officials and the local elite, particularly in nonurban settings. During the nineteenth century, these practices were slowly abolished everywhere. This was true in France as early as in 1831, although nonsecrecy remained widespread for a long time and the "secrecy of the ballot was not well preserved until 1914, when voting ballots and envelopes to put the ballot into were instituted."[61] In Germany and the Netherlands, provisions were introduced for protecting secrecy at the end of the 1840s. Italy did this in 1861, but official pressures for voting in public in the rural areas of southern Italy were reported up to the beginning of the twentieth century.[62] A new wave of secret-ballot provisions were introduced in Sweden, Belgium, Switzerland (at the federal level),

[61] E. Weber (1979: 271) offers a number of interesting local examples.
[62] See De Sanctis (1876).

and the United Kingdom (and Ireland) between the end of the 1860s and the beginning of the 1870s. Norway did the same in 1885. The only latecomers were Denmark, Austria, and Finland, which introduced measures to protect secrecy only at the beginning of the twentieth century.

Indirect voting meant that the ballot was cast not for legislative candidates but for "grand electors," who, in turn, selected representatives to parliament. This two-stage process introduced an additional barrier for new movements and for parties that could not rely on an established and visible social elite, particularly at the local level. In reality, indirect voting was conceived as a filter against "dangerous" candidates, and the system was more widespread than is usually thought. France, the Netherlands, and Switzerland had used indirect voting in the early nineteenth century, in the periods 1815–1817 (France), 1815–1848 (the Netherlands), and 1815–1848 (Switzerland); once abandoned they never used it again. By contrast, Austria, Finland, Norway, and Sweden retained some form of indirect voting well in to the twentieth century. In Austria, voting was indirect from 1861 until 1901 in the fourth curia and, from 1897 also in the fifth curia, so that the bulk of the electorate was subject to it. In Finland, the vote was indirect until 1906 for the estate of peasants, who obviously constituted the overwhelming majority of the adult population. Norway and Sweden maintained indirect voting up to 1906 and 1908, respectively, even if, in Sweden, the vote was only partly indirect from 1866 to 1908. In Austria, Finland, Sweden, and Norway, indirect voting may be the key to the very late entrance into parliament of the first socialist representatives. In Sweden, socialists obtained seats in 1902, thirteen years and several elections after their final national centralization. In Norway, seats were obtained only in 1903, after seventeen years of extraparliamentary life. In Finland, the difference was less (eight years) also because the party centralized late (in 1899). In Austria, effective parliamentary entry was also delayed up to the beginning of the nineteenth-century, even though the party had been quite well organized nationally long before this time. However, in the latter two cases, the curia system (about which more will be said later) should also be added to the indirect voting techniques. Indirect voting was not adopted in the imperial elections in Germany, but it was retained in Prussia until 1918.

The *curia* and *estate systems* assigned a disproportionate number of seats to the upper estates, generally representing aristocratic and wealthy families and the clergy, while formally giving the right to vote to everybody or to a small number of people in each major social group. Such systems were retained throughout most of the nineteenth century in four Western European countries: Sweden until the reform of 1866; Prussia until the collapse of the empire; and Austria and Finland until the beginning of the twentieth century, in 1907 and 1906, respectively. The Finnish and Swedish systems were very similar and give a clear idea of how the mechanism worked. The first estate allowed direct representation by the male heads of noble families; the clergy estate allowed it by the higher-ranking clergy and included several elected representatives of the lower-ranking clergy; the burgher estate was composed of representatives elected by plural voting and (see later) by burghers meeting professional and income qualifications; the peasants' estate was elected with indirect voting (see supra) by independent farmers, with tenants and agricultural laborers excluded. This mechanism yielded four houses, each formally endowed with the same powers by which, in 1900, about 150 noble families had the same weight as the 1,083 enfranchised clericals, the 23,469 eligible burghers, and the 10,184 enfranchised peasants.[63]

Finally, throughout the nineteenth century, the practice of *plural voting* – that is, the attribution of extra votes to wealthy and/or well-educated citizens or to representatives of special institutions (churches, universities, etc.) – was continued. This system had the direct effect of separating citizens bureaucratically into voting categories based on class criteria. France had resorted to plural voting only in the 1820s and for a few highly restricted franchise elections. The Swedish eliminated plural voting in the 1866 reform. In the United Kingdom, plural voting continued until well into the twentieth century, when it was drastically reduced in 1914 and eliminated altogether in 1948. However, although in theory it was possible to have up to twenty votes, the weight of extra voting was never overwhelming: In 1911, about 7% of the British electorate cast plural votes as a result of their meeting more than one franchise requirement or of meeting property requirements in more than one constituency. Minor inequalities also persisted in the Irish new state, were progressively removed in 1922, and were completely abolished in 1936. Finland continued to use plural-voting procedures based on professional and income qualification for elections in the burgher estate until 1906.

In Belgium and Austria, plural voting played a more important role because, rather than functioning as a remnant of a gradually fading tradition, it was either introduced or broadened wider to check democratization tendencies. Thus, it acquired a clear political significance that can be described as "anti-newcomers." In Austria, in fact, plural voting was not widely used up to 1897, after which it was widely expanded in the context of the democratization of the franchise. When an additional fifth curia

[63] Goldstein (1983: 13).

with universal and equal suffrage for male citizens over twenty-four years of age was introduced in 1897, the electors of the first four curiae all gained a second vote. Thus, between 1896 and 1907, about 40% of Austrian males cast two votes. Even more clear was the political significance of the introduction of plural voting in Belgium in 1894. Prior to this time, suffrage had been equal but restricted, and the introduction of the universal manhood suffrage brought with it strong inequalities, adding a vote for house owners and owners of real estate that was worth more than a certain value and two extra votes for persons with higher education and certain abilities. When the two qualifications were combined, it was possible to reach a maximum of three extra votes. So, while the franchise was democratized, giving the right to vote to 1.3 millions citizens – in contrast to the previous tax-based 136,000 – the wealthier and more highly educated upper classes were compensated through plural voting. In the 1890s, out of the 1.3 million voters, roughly 850,000 had only one vote, 290,000 had two votes, and 220,000 had three, with the result that 500,000 citizens with more than one vote largely outweighed the 850,000 with a single vote. This explains why the early history of the Belgian socialist movement was largely dominated by heated debates and confrontations concerning the equalization of voting rights.

In Table 7.5 I have synthesized the major representation inequalities discussed so far. I have also added a column indicating the final introduction of proportional (PR) representation, which represents, in all cases but one, the final step in the equalization of the voting right (the exception is Belgium, where PR was introduced very early while the plural voting system was retained). It is difficult to reconcile into a single dimension such a wide array of devices and situations. Taking the onset of the socialist movement as a point of reference, we can say that the obstacles to fair representation were many, significant, and protracted in Austria and Finland; relatively minor and gradually removed in the United Kingdom and Ireland; numerous but removed early in Sweden (long before the socialist movement appeared); limited to one but protracted in Norway (indirect voting) and in Belgium (plural voting); and absent by the time the socialists started to compete in Denmark, France,[64] Germany (although with the important exception of the Prussian state), Italy, the Netherlands, and Switzerland.

---

[64] In France, obstacles to fair representation consisted mainly of widespread governmental gerrymandering in the period 1820–1970s and later of constituency size inequalities that consistently gave extra weight to the countryside and underrepresented the cities and industrial areas; Campbell (1958: 22 and 19–38).

Table 7.5. *Representational inequalities in the lower chambers*

country	introduction of secret voting	indirect voting	curia and estate system	plural voting	PR
Au	1906	1861–1901 (in the Fourth Curia and since 1897 in the Fifth curia)	1861–1907	1861–1896 minor 1897–1907 large	1919
Be	1877			1893–1919	1899
De	1901				1918
Fi	1907	to 1906 (in the estate of peasants)	to 1906	to 1906 (in the estate of burghers)	1907
Fr	1831–1846 (1914)	1815–17		1820–30	1919–1924 1945–1951
Ge	1848	(1849–1918 in Prussia)	(1849–1918 in Prussia)		1919
Ir	1872			1815–1914 1918–1922 (-36) minor inequalities	1921
It	1861				1919–1946
Ne	1849	1815–1848			1918
No	1885	to 1905			1921
Sw	1866	to 1866 1866–1908 partly indirect	to 1866	to 1866	1909
Sz	1872 (federal)	1815–1848			1919
UK	1872			1815–1914 1918–1948 minor	

MAJORITY AND PROPORTIONAL REPRESENTATION

From the point of view of the socialist elite and rank and file, these devices and obstacles to fair representation had two major impacts. First, there were the psychological effects of unfairness and injustice, a tangible institutionalization of the class structural division of society and a sign of the fact that socialists' values and interests could not be defended within the framework of the existing system. Where extensively used, such mechanisms shaped the ideological orientation of the socialist movements toward their state and political system in the formative phase before World War I and influenced the direction of their political action toward this state. The second effect was that of mechanical under representation. These mechanisms delayed the full transformation of the electoral resources of the socialist movement into a direct parliamentary influence. The significance of the first effect can be indicated by the effectiveness of the second. Let us therefore look at the underrepresentation of early socialist parties, considering the difference between the percentage of their votes and the percentage of seats won in the lower elective house.

This picture needs be broken down by type of left party and by country. In Table 7.6 misrepresentation figures are reported by period, type of party, and type of electoral formula.[65] With majority systems socialist parties suffered heavy under-representation in the periods before World War I (-5.5%) and between the wars (-4.35%), enjoying over-representation after World War II. In proportional systems they are, on average, always overrepresented in every period. In contrast, communist parties are, on average, always underrepresented, whatever the period or the electoral system. The situation is fairly similar for the other left parties. Their relatively small size reduced their share of the seats even in PR systems. On the whole, PR offered a premium to the socialists that was basically gained at the expense of communist and other left parties. The most significant figure is the 67% underrepresentation of all left parties and of the whole left in the seventy elections that were held under the majority formula between 1880 and 1944.

In Table 7.7 average misrepresentations are presented by country, with the usual distinction between type of electoral system and type of party. Data concerning the post–World War II period are not reproduced and do not need to be described or commented on. In the period of party founda-tion and consolidation before World War I, socialist parties were severely underrepresented in parliaments in Germany, Switzerland, Italy, Norway, Denmark, and Austria. In the first three cases, underrepresentation was massive, but the Swiss case is different from the Italian and German ones because at the canton level – which was the most important – proportional formulas were predominant. In Germany and Italy, socialist parties gained, on average, 9% fewer seats than their percentage of votes. Taking into consideration their average size in the period, this means that between one-third and one-half of their electoral support was underrepresented. Even the Norwegian socialists suffered from the late introduction of PR, and presumably also as a result of the persistent practice of indirect voting, even if a modified proportional system was introduced for local elections as early as 1896. In Denmark, underrepresentation was less pronounced, but the average of -5% refers to a long electoral history of twelve elections. In Austria, there are data only for 1907 and 1911, when underrepresenta-tion was roughly 5%. In all the other countries, underrepresentation was less pronounced. The Dutch, French, Swedish, and British early socialist parties won fewer seats than votes, but the difference ranged only between 1% and 2%. In Sweden and the United Kingdom, this is likely to be due

---

[65] A detailed discussion of the variety of majority systems utilized before World War I is unnecessary to evaluate the macro-outcome of underrepresentation.

Table 7.6. *Disrepresentation by party and by period (% of seats minus % of votes)*

		socialist parties	communist parties	other left	total left
	maj.	-5.51(68)	-	+0.30 (3)	-5.50 (58)
before 1918	PR	+1.97 (14)	-	-3.20 (1)	1.75 (14)
	all	-4.23 (82)	-	-0.57 (4)	-4.26 (82)
	maj.	-4.35 (12)	-1.96 (10)	-1.01 (6)	-5.65 (12)
1918-1944	PR	+0.44 (80)	-0.90 (57)	-1.06 (23)	-0.51 (80)
	all	-0.18 (92)	-1.06 (67)	-1.05 (29)	-1.18 (92)
	maj.	+3.01 (17)	-3.58 (17)	-2.00 (7)	-1.29 (17)
1944-1980	PR	+1.33 (119)	-0.76 (105)	-0.87 (47)	+0.28 (137)
	all	+1.54 (136)	-1.15 (122)	-1.02 (54)	+0.08 (137)

Note: Number of elections given in parentheses.

to the fact that the socialists entered the competition late and their early small size could not, in any case, bring about high underrepresentation. A similar argument applies to the weak pre–World War I French Socialist Party. A case worth mentioning is that of the Belgian socialists. In the four general elections held before the war,[66] two took place under the majority formula and two under PR. The socialist party was more under-represented under PR than under the majority formula. This is clearly due to the unusual Belgian reform of 1893, which introduced PR but also heavy plural voting.

In the period between the two world wars, PR systems become pre-dominant; of the ninety-two elections held in this period, eighty were held under this formula. The introduction of PR had been easier (that is, less contentious) and earlier where ethnic and/or religious heterogeneity was an issue (e.g., Denmark in the 1850s, with its Schleswig minority; the Swiss cantons at the beginning of the 1890s; Belgium in 1899; Finland, with its Swedish-speaking minority, in 1906). Rokkan has also argued that PR was introduced earlier when the extension of suffrage and the corresponding growth of working-class parties threatened the existence of the traditional regime *censitaire* parties, for which PR became a way to remain in the field (Sweden in 1909 and the Danish lower house in 1915 are the most notable examples).[67] Resistance to PR was stronger in larger polities, where the

[66] More elections took place during this period, but they were partial elections held in different parts of the country to renew half of its parliament. It is misleading to use their results together with those of the general elections. I have therefore considered only the national general elections.

[67] Rokkan (1970f: 147–168).

Table 7.7. *Mean misrepresentation of the left by country, period, and electoral system*

	1880-1917				1918-1944					
	sd parties		other left		sd parties		com. parties		total left	
	maj.	pr.	maj.	pr.	maj.	pr.	maj.	pr.	maj.	pr.
Au	-4.4 (2)					+1.8 (5)		-0.7 (4)		+1.3
Be	+0.4 (2)	-1.2 (2)				+1.8 (7)		-1.1 (5)		+1.0
De	-5.0 (12)					-0.1 (11)		-0.3 (9)		-0.4
Fi	-	+2.7 (8)				+1.6 (9)		-1.6 (5)		+0.7
Fr	-1.2 (6)		+0.4 (2)		+1.5 (3)	-5.7 (2)	-6.3 (3)	-5.3 (1)	-4.1	-8.8
Ge	-9.7 (9)					+0.6 (9)		+0.1 (7)		+0.3
Ir	-		-			-2.5 (7)		-		-2.5
It	-8.3 (6)		+0.1 (1)			-1.7 (2)		-1.8 (1)		-3.1
Ne	-2.3 (8)					+0.6 (6)		0.0 (6)		+0.4
No	-7.3 (8)				-17.3 (1)	+1.4 (6)		-1.6 (5)	-17.3	-1.2
Sw	-1.8 (3)	+2.2 (4)		-3.2 (1)		+3.5 (8)		-2.2 (7)		+0.2
Sz	-9.8 (8)					-1.5 (8)		-0.6 (6)		-1.9
UK	-0.7 (4)				-4.9 (8)	-	-0.1 (7)	-	-4.8	-
All	-5.5 (68)	+2.0 (14)	+0.3 (3)	-3,2 (1)	-4.4 (12)	+0.4 (80)		-0.9 (57)	5.7 (12)	-0.5

Note: Number of elections given in parentheses.

central government was able to mobilize greater resources against the movement demanding PR (the United Kingdom and France, in particular, but also Germany and Austria, where, without the collapse of the empires, resistance to PR would have prevented its adoption for much longer). After World War I, majority systems were used only in France and the United Kingdom and in the single election of 1918 in Norway. In this period, the interesting comparison is instead between the fate of the socialists and the communists.

In the United Kingdom, the Labour Party was, on average, underrepresented by 5%. This, however, was the result of the dispute with the liberals for the position of second party in the British party system and of an alternation of elections with fair representation (1923 and 1924), clear underrepresentation (1918, 1931, and 1935), and equally clear overrepresentation (1929). In France, the majority formula, used three times, did not hit the socialists hard, but instead drastically curtailed the parliamentary representation of the communists (−6.3%). In Norway, the last majority elections of 1918 resulted in the catastrophic underrepresentation of the Norwegian Labor Party parliamentary force (−17.3%). In PR elections, the socialists were in general slightly overrepresented (the exceptions are Italy, Ireland, and Switzerland), and the communist parties were systematically, even if modestly, underrepresented. France is the only significant deviation from this pattern; there, both the communist and the socialist parties continued to be heavily underrepresented under the PR formula, by roughly 5.5% of the seats each, which together made for a substantial average underrepresentation of the left of approximately 9%. This is due to the fact that most of the elections I have classified as involving PR formulas in fact used modified PR, and the alliance premiums that existed were often deliberately devised to penalize the left parties.[68] To the reformist socialists of the SFIO – involved in 1919 in the delicate internal debate with their radical wing on adherence to the Third International – nothing could have been more discouraging than the result of the 1919 elections, the first to be fought with the long-desired PR system. Increasing its electoral strength by almost 5% with respect to the 1914 elections, the SFIO lost 7% of the seats it had previously held and was drastically underrepresented: 20% of the votes and 10% of the seats. The disillusionment among the socialists and the discrediting of the parliamentary road to socialism were enormous.

After World War II, there were only two significant electoral reforms aiming to underrepresent the left: the electoral law of *apparentement* in France in 1951, which was implemented successfully, and the Italian 1953 reform, which failed. Both reforms gave a seats premium to the party coalition that reached a majority threshold. However, while in France alliances could be concluded at the constituency level, where the threshold was applied, in Italy the majority premium was triggered only if the alliance reached more than 50% at the national level. The majority premium was represented by a pool of national sets in Italy, while it consisted of all seats of any given constituency in France. Finally, there was a crucial political difference: The alliance of centrist parties included the socialists in France and was mainly directed against the two extreme parties, the communists and the Gaullists. In contrast, the centrist alliance in Italy excluded the extreme right and both the communist and the socialist parties. These differences explain why the French reform succeeded and the Italian one failed, the 50.1% threshold was not reached, the majority premium was not awarded, and the law was later repealed. In France, no alliances were made in twelve constituencies; in seven, two blocs faced each other with no strong misrepresentation effects; in seventy-six constituencies, one alliance alone was formed, and in two-thirds of them this was an alliance of centrist parties against the extreme parties. The new law deprived the PCF of about seventy-one seats it would probably have gained under the 1946 law. If we add that the left, this time the entire socialist

---

[68] On the continuously changing electoral laws of this period of the Third Republic, see Campbell (1958).

and communist left, was again largely underrepresented under the new majority double-ballot system reintroduced by De Gaulle in 1958 and continued to be so until the 1970s, it is clear that the issue of representative fairness remained central to the politico-institutional debate in this country throughout the century.

ACCESS TO EXECUTIVE POWER

How long did the socialists have to wait before being given cabinet responsibility? For many years, socialist groups debated whether to participate in bourgeois institutions: whether to take part in elections; whether to fill positions of responsibility in the legislative chambers; whether to enter electoral coalitions with bourgeois parties; whether to vote for laws favorable to workers and, in particular, budget or military credit laws; whether to support sympathetic bourgeois governments; whether to formally enter parliamentary majorities; and, finally, whether to accept ministerial responsibility. The debate began with the split of the anarchists on the matter in the First International; it continued with Rosa Luxemburg's critique of "parliamentary cretinism," concerning the real autonomy of the parliament and legislative action; and it was revived after World War I in the early communist movement in Western Europe (for instance, by Bordiga in Italy).

However, whatever the internal dissents and debates and the bargainability of the issues they involved, any socialist inclusion in parliamentary majorities and cabinets depended primarily on the numerical relationships among the parties in parliament and on the reaction of the other political forces. Socialist access to these parliamentary majorities should not be understood as separate from the more general problem of the legitimation of the other political forces, such as extreme right parties, communist parties, and substate nationalist movements. In general, therefore, the chance to participate in government was a function of (1) the extent to which socialists were able to "shrink" the governmental space of the nonsocialist parties. This, in turn, depended on their electoral force but also on the governmental space left once the extreme antisystem forces had been taken away; (2) the level of electoral fragmentation and political division of the nonsocialist forces; (3) the ideological bargainability of policy alternatives; and, finally, (4) the severity of the international environmental pressures that might ease or impede their internal acceptance. In this section, I review the patterns of executive access and the governmental record of the European left, discussing its causes and consequences.

ENTRY PATTERNS

In Table 7.8 I have summarized the basic information about socialist and communist party access to direct cabinet responsibility. Leaving aside the cases of direct socialist support to cabinets in the pre–World War I or war period in neutral Sweden and Denmark and in belligerent France, Finland, and the United Kingdom, the first true executive experiences of the socialists took place in Belgium and Sweden during the war years, and in Denmark, Austria, and Germany immediately afterward. The circumstances of these entries were diverse. In Belgium, the foreign aggression fostered an all-party coalition and led to universal suffrage; this is the clearest case of the role of an external military threat favoring internal democratization.[69] The German invasion was equally important, as the clandestine contacts between leaders of industry and Catholic, socialist, and liberal unions determined the basis of the pact that would be implemented after the war through important advances in social legislation and collective bargaining.[70] In Austria and Germany, the socialists entered cabinet by default, so to speak, as a result of the collapse of the prewar political order and delegitimation of the established political groups and elite. They were thus compelled to inherit the political catastrophe of military defeat associated with the regime's breakdown, and their presence in the cabinet coincided with the introduction of parliamentary responsibility.

Intermediate entries took place during the 1920s in three countries: Finland, Norway, and the United Kingdom. These were normal entries in the sense that no external threat, military event, or regime change fostered them, even if they were all very brief and they were all minority single-party cabinets. The Finnish Tanner cabinet of December 1926, for example, enjoyed the support of 60 out of 200 members of parliament (MPs) and lasted for only four days, while Britain's first MacDonald cabinet in January 1924 had the support of the 191 Labour deputies in a 615-MPs House of Commons[71] and lasted for fourteen days. The January 1928 Hornsrud cabinet in Norway enjoyed the support of 59 MPs out of 150 and lasted for nineteen days. In these cases, strong, rapidly growing labor parties were tested in single-party minority cabinets with which other groups refused to cooperate. They generally presented clear-cut socialist

---

[69] On the "democratizing" role of world wars, see Therborn (1977: 3–41).

[70] Lorwin (1966: 165).

[71] The external and informal support of fifty-nine Liberal deputies was not enough to ensure a majority.

Table 7.8. *Executive entry of socialists and communists*

country	prewar or war support for cabinet	year of entry in cabinet	circumstance	regular governmental party	socialist majority government	year of entry in cabinet	circumstance	regular governmental party
	socialist party					communist party		
Au		1919	regime breakdown coalition	1945 foreign occ./ coalition	1971	1945 (8 months)	postwar military occupation	-
Be		1917	foreign aggression coalition	1919	-	1945 (25 months)	postwar liberation cabinet	-
De	x	1918	coalit. cabinet	1924	. -	-	-	-
Fi	x	1926	minority cab.	1937	-	1945 (41 months)	postwar cabinet	1966
Fr	x	1936	coalition cabinet	1945	1984	1945 (13 months)	postwar liberation cabinet	-
Ge		1919	regime breakdown coalition	1919	-	-	-	-
Ir		1948	coalition cab.	1948	-	-	-	-
It		1945	military defeat/ foreign aggres./ postwar coalition	1963	-	1945 (22 months)	postwar liberation cabinet	-
Ne		1939	external threat/ coalition cab.	1945	-	-	-	-
No		1928	minority cab.	1935	1945	-	-	-
Sw	x	1917	coalition cab.	1933	1941-45	-	-	-
Sz		1943	coalition cab.	1943	-	-	-	-
UK	x	1924	minority cab.	1929	1945	-	-	-

governmental programs and were immediately disposed of once it was evident that they did not accept the constraining conditions of their minority status.

France provides the only example of socialist access to a cabinet in the 1930s.[72] The four Popular Front cabinets between June 1936 and April 1938 (two formed by Blum and two by Chautemps) were coalition cabinets involving socialists and radicals, in which the former accepted a junior-partner role although enjoying a relative majority in the National Assembly. At least three of them were minimum winning coalitions,[73] but

[72] One should not consider as socialist participation in cabinets the entry of independent socialist personalities, such as Alexandre Millerand in the Waldech-Rousseau cabinet. These actions generally embittered the debate within the socialist movement about the usefulness of participating in bourgeois governments rather than opening the way to such participation.

[73] Given the high fluidity of the party and parliamentary group labels of French radical and republican forces even in the late phase of the Third Republic, it is difficult to decide exactly whether a coalition is minimum winning or surplus. Moreover, support of deputies was often granted and withdrawn on a strictly individual base. On the whole, however, Blum's two cabinets and the first of the Chautemps cabinets were the result of a relatively close majority in the lower house.

although they lasted longer than those of other countries in the 1920s (about five-and-a-half months each), they were unstable and ineffective. The main reason for this was politico-institutional: The legislative discipline of the right wing of the radical and republican groups was unreliable,[74] and there was no clear majority in the Senate, which systematically rejected the main legislation of the Popular Front.

Among the socialist latecomers to executive responsibility, participation in the Netherlands and Switzerland was fostered by an external threat. The first Dutch socialist ministers were nominated in August 1939, when the country was preparing to face Hitler. The Swiss Socialist Party, on the other hand, had tried to win one vacant Federal Council seat in 1929 without gaining the majority support of the Federal Assembly. This instead was achieved in the four-party "magic formula" coalition in 1943, in the most delicate period of Swiss World War II neutrality. The Swiss case is, however, exceptional in that (1) socialists had acquired executive responsibility in some cantons long before 1943; (2) the principle of cabinet responsibility is not applicable to the unusual pattern of the Swiss executive–legislative relationship;[75] (3) the executive branch of government was weak as a result of the division of powers between cantons and municipalities; and (4) the forms of popular referendum were powerful counterweights to the role of the cabinet and offered parties and groups not represented in the cabinet (or even in parliament) opportunities to influence legislative decision making.[76] As a consequence, in Switzerland the

[74] The roll-call analysis by Warwich (1977: 154) proves that in legislative behaviors the Marxist–non-Marxist cleavage far outweighed the cabinet–opposition divide.

[75] The peculiarities of the Swiss federal executive are many. Each member of the Conseil Federal is elected individually by the chamber for four years, and there is never a total turnover; each member retires and is substituted for independently of the others. The presidency is rotating. A confidence vote is absent, and if a bill fails in parliament or in a popular referendum, the composition of the council is not affected. When a federal councilor once resigned after the failure in parliament of a major proposal originating from his department, his behavior was regarded as inappropriate by most political and social groups. See Fleiner-Gerstern (1987).

[76] Popular referendums (since 1874 at the federal level but since 1860 at the canton level) and constitutional popular initiatives (since 1891) have been judged by Neidhart (1970: 96–122 and 313–319) as ineffectual in defending the interests of the lower classes. Yet, among the first national laws approved by legislative referendum was an 1877 factory regulation bill setting a maximum eleven hours of work, and banning children's factory work and a 1879 bill abolishing capital punishment. From that time to the socialist entry into the Federal Council in 1943, the amount of legislation passed by popular referendum with socialist support was considerable. Before World War I, socialists actively participated in four constitutional initiative referendums. Only the last, concerning the introduction of PR, was successful, with the help of the Catholic–conservatives. Between 1891 and 1979, of sixty-seven initiatives seven emanated from the PSS or were strongly supported by it.

cabinet was never viewed as the center of power or of state regulation and legislative production, the role of the central executive was less significant, and the outsiders' influence was more important compared with the other typical parliamentary democracies of the period.

The last socialist parties to gain access to cabinet responsibility were those in Italy[77] (1945) and Ireland (1948). Both did so in broad coalitions: the post–World War II antifascist regrouping of liberal, Catholic, and socialist/communist forces in Italy[78] and the anti–Fianna Fail all-party coalition of 1948 in Ireland, whose majority depended, however, on the benevolent support of the independent MPs.

If one compares the moment of first entry with the moment when the socialist parties became a regular governmental party, the biggest time lag is in Austria and Italy. In Austria, the post–World War I socialist cabinet's experience was short and terminated in 1920. From that time to the collapse of democracy, the socialists were given no other chance to share executive power. In Italy, the large 1945–1947 coalition governments were followed by almost two decades of socialist exclusion before the party became a regular coalition partner from 1963.

On the whole, the experience of socialist executive entry falls into three groups:

1. Complete denial: the Austrian case between November 1920 and 1934; in the Netherlands, too, religious parties considered cooperation with the socialists a rare exception; in Italy, of course, fascism ruled it out completely.
2. Introduction to executive responsibility in wide coalitions where socialists played the role of a junior partner or accepted this role even if their electoral strength gave them the right to a more prominent share: Belgium, Germany, Denmark, Switzerland, Netherlands, France, Italy (1963), Ireland.
3. Admission to executive power as minority cabinets during the 1920s: the United Kingdom, Finland, and Norway, and also in Sweden to a certain extent, even if the first Swedish cabinet with socialist ministers was a coalition cabinet with the liberals.

---

[77] In Italy, the Socialist Party split down the middle during the Cold War, giving birth to the Social Democratic Party (PSDI), which continued to participate in the cabinet between 1947 and 1963, while the main socialist party remained in opposition. As it was impossible to combine the cabinet experiences of two socialist parties, in this section the data refer to those of the main and larger one, the PSI.

[78] However, it should be noted that during the liberal period the socialists were offered, and rejected, cabinet office in 1903 and 1911.

Only five socialist parties have managed to exercise single-party majority government since their first cabinet entry: in Norway, Sweden, the United Kingdom (1945), Austria (1971), and France (1984). The Finnish socialists achieved an absolute majority in the Diet in 1916 (51.5% of the seats) but were not able to exercise executive responsibility under the Russian control of the country. Both coalition and minority governments implied controlled access. Thus, socialists were legitimized into an executive responsibility position "under conditions of enforced moderation."[79]

Communist participation in the cabinet was more reduced. If we exclude the very short periods of executive presence of the Danish, Dutch, and Norwegian communists, these parties shared ministerial responsibility in coalition governments in only five countries after World War II, and only in one did they become a regular coalition partner. In Austria, Belgium, Finland, France, and Italy, communist ministers entered coalition governments, remaining there for a minimum of eight months to a maximum of twenty-five. All these experiences terminated with the deterioration of the postwar antifascist coalitions and the beginning of the Cold War. Indeed, by 1948, all the Western European communist parties were in opposition, and only in Finland did they come back as a regular coalition partner after 1966. The brief participation of four communist ministers in the two French Mauroy cabinets for twenty-three months (May 22, 1981 to March 22, 1983), although they should be mentioned, did not mean that the party was a regular coalition partner.

From the point of view of the influence that communist parties had in the cabinet, we can distinguish between (1) Switzerland, Ireland, and the United Kingdom, where the communists exerted no significant influence whatsoever; (2) Belgium and Austria, where the communists formed part of the cabinet for a short time after World War II, to be excluded shortly afterward and to decline in electoral and coalition influence from then on; (3) Sweden, Norway, and Denmark, where communists exercised some strategic influence after World War II, when their votes made the difference between majority and minority social democratic cabinets; (4) France and Germany during the interwar years and France and Italy after World War II, where strong opposition communist parties pushed the socialists into government with centrist and moderate forces, reducing the socialist role to junior partners and, at the same time, preventing the moderating effect of such experience. The presence of a strong left competitor that forced these socialist movements to form coalitions with moderate forces in which they were the junior partner contributed to a schizophrenic

[79] Daalder (1967: 59).

division between their ideological identity and political practice; and (5) Finland, where communists played an important role in coalitions during the 1944–1948 period and again from 1966 on.

DURATION

Once the socialist parties had gained access to cabinet responsibility, did their position as cabinet members last? After 1966, the socialist presence or absence in cabinets was the result of the normal interplay between electoral results and coalition bargaining, and no exclusionary clause or peculiar institutional difficulty of entry is visible. Therefore, in Table 7.9, the length of socialist government is reported in percentages of time and of all cabinets only for the 1918–1966 period. In these forty-nine years, there were 378 cabinets (excluding Switzerland).[80] Of these, 224 (59.3%) did not include socialist or communist party representatives; 11 were not party cabinets, but caretakers cabinets;[81] 143 included socialist ministers and 15 included communist ministers, all of which also held socialists. On the whole, the two main components of the European left participated, respectively, in slightly more than a third of all cabinets (37.9%) and in about 4.0% of them. Of course, these proportions were different in the first (1918–1944) and second (1945–1966) periods: all communist participation took place after World War II, while socialists participated in only 57 of the 216 cabinets between the wars (i.e., 26.4%) and in 86 of the 162 cabinets in the 1945–1966 period (i.e., 53.1%). In the following period, between 1966 and 1985, the socialist presence in cabinets increased only modestly as a result of the decline in the Scandinavian countries and the increase in Italy, Germany, the United Kingdom, and Finland.

With only two exceptions (France and Germany), the length of the

---

[80] The main sources for the elaboration of data in this section are Beyme (1973), Flora, Alber, Eichenberg, Kohl, Kraus, Pfenning, and Seebohm (1983), Woldendorp, Keman, and Budge (1993), and Paloheimo (1984). I have reduced cabinet changes to a minimum: Cabinets persisting throughout elections are counted only once, and minor reshuffles are not considered. External support and parliamentary toleration are not considered, either for the party composition of the cabinet or for the level of parliamentary support of the cabinet. The level of parliamentary support of the cabinet is reckoned in the first chamber at the moment of its installation (even though cabinets may depend on support in both chambers, as in Italy and Sweden up to 1970). Switzerland is excluded because the parliamentary responsibility of the cabinet is not comparable to that of other countries.

[81] One in Denmark and three each in Finland and Sweden. The four no-party cabinets in Germany, however, were the presidential cabinets of 1931–1933 from Brüning to Hitler. Another caretaker cabinet was Churchill's "election-waiting" cabinet of 1945, which was, however, Conservative in its composition and therefore, strictly speaking, not a no-party cabinet.

Table 7.9. *Socialist party presence in cabinets (1918–1966)**

country	percentage of time in cabinet	percentage of cabinets with socialist party
Sw	84.2	66.7
Dk	72.2	72.7
Au	59.3	43.8
No	59.9	38.1
Be	56.4	48.7
Fi	45.5	41.7
Ne	43.0	38.1
UK [a]	39.4	35.0
It	27.9	21.9
Fr [b]	25.1	29.6
Ge	22.3	31.0
Ir	14.3	11.1
Sz	(49.0).	n.a.

*Considering World War II war cabinets.
[a] Including the four months of the second 1931 MacDonald cabinet, which was supported only by parts of the Labour Party.
[b] Considering the SFIO as participating in the Popular Government cabinets.

socialist presence in the cabinet is higher than the percentage of such cabinets over all cabinets. This difference is particularly notable in Sweden, Norway, and Austria. These figures suggest that the entry of socialists into cabinets determined an increase in cabinet duration and a generally higher cabinet stability. While the all-cabinets' average duration was 17.4 months, that of the 162 cabinets that included socialists was 20.6 months and that of the 213 cabinets without socialists was only 14.9 months. In both Sweden and Norway, bourgeois cabinets had, on average, less than half the average tenure of cabinets with socialists.

In Norway between 1919 and 1933, fourteen weak minority governments were formed as the result of a situation in which liberals and the Labor Party were unwilling to govern together, as were the liberals, conservatives, and agrarians. Disputes over agrarian and urban conflicts of interest added to the strong political division between the urban bourgeois classes and the mainly agrarian middle classes. This situation delayed the entry of Labor into the cabinet in Norway, but also exhausted the nonsocialist camp and paved the way for the ensuing cabinet control of the Norwegian socialists, which was both extended and continuous.

Marked stabilization and increased duration were not, however, the outcome of socialist access to executive responsibility everywhere. The Danish Social Democrats formed part of the cabinet several times, but their presence was not as continuous as in the other Scandinavian countries because nonsocialist cabinets – whose tenure was as long as that of the socialist ones – alternated more frequently with socialist cabinets. Thus, while on the one hand most socialist cabinets were minority cabinets in Denmark, dependent on the toleration or external support of other political forces, on the other hand, in contrast to the other two Scandinavian countries, a liberal–conservative coalition remained a viable alternative to the traditional alliance of social democrats and radicals. In the Netherlands, Belgium, and Italy (since the mid-1960s), the possibilities of an alliance switch remained by which liberals could replace socialists as an alternative partner to the religious center parties. Only in Germany and France was the average duration of cabinets, including those of the socialists, shorter than that of cabinets without socialists. The same was true for the United Kingdom between the world wars, while after 1945 there was no considerable difference between Labour and Conservative cabinets. In the four countries where the left was deeply divided down the middle, cabinets with socialist participation were either more unstable than bourgeois cabinets (France and Germany) or the difference was marginal.

COALITION PATTERNS: CABINET FORMAT, STATUS, AND IDEOLOGICAL COMPOSITION

The third relevant question concerns the kinds of cabinets the socialists managed to enter. This question leads to three subquestions. First, how many partners did socialists have in the cabinet, that is, what was the cabinet format? Second, what was the status of the cabinet (i.e., single-party majority cabinet, oversized coalitions)? Third, what was the dominant ideological composition of the cabinet?

Table 7.10 indicates, in percentages the breakdown by country of cabinets with a socialist presence according to the number of parties represented in them. No-party cabinets were formed in only four countries and were numerous and significant only in Finland and Germany. In Finland, only the parties have been counted, although most cabinets also included a number of independent personalities and single-party cabinets in particularly often included experts. In Germany, the four no-party cabinets represent the presidential cabinets of the immediate pre-Nazi period, while in Sweden there were three short caretaker cabinets at the beginning of the 1920s and in 1932. The executives in Ireland, the United

Table 7.10. *Percentage of all cabinets including the socialists by number of parties in cabinet (1918–1966)**

country	1	2	3	4 or more
Au	0%-	46%	100%	-
Be [a]	17%	35%	100%	100%
De	50%	83%	100%	100%
Fi	40%	14%	33%	59%
Fr [b]	100%	0%	89%	52%
Ge	-	29%	57%	27%
Ir [c]	0%	-	100%	100%
It [b]	0%	0%	17%	66%
Ne	-	50%	27%	50%
No	46%	20%	-	33%
Sw	78%	66%	0%	100%
UK	43%	0%	0%	100%

*Excluding no-party/caretaker cabinets (De = 1; Fi = 5; Ge = 4; Sw = 3).
[a] excluding the Delacroix 1918 cabinet.
[b] Only after 1944.
[c] beginning with the Cosgrave cabinet on December 6, 1922.

Kingdom, and Norway were dominated by single-party governments.[82] In the Netherlands, Finland, France, Belgium, Germany, and Switzerland, the dominant executive format was a coalition government, but in Belgium a two-party coalition pattern dominated, with alternation between Catholic–socialist and Catholic–liberal alliances, while in the other countries, coalitions were formed by a larger number of parties. Sweden, Denmark, and Italy (whose data refer only to the post–World War II period) had both single-party governments and coalitions for long periods, and Austria switched from one-party rule until 1934 to a grand postwar coalition until 1966.

The socialists entered 143 of these 378 cabinets. Excluding the cabinets for which the exact number of parties is impossible to calculate,[83] socialists ruled alone in single-party cabinets on only twenty-eight occa-

[82] In Ireland, the association of the Farmer Party with Cumann na nGaedheal from 1927 to 1932 is often regarded as a two-party coalition. Actually, this was a single-party cabinet, as the Farmer Party had only one parliamentary secretary in the government.
[83] The Italian Parri and De Gasperi cabinets and the French De Gaulle cabinet immediately after World War II.

sions, all of which were concentrated almost entirely in the three Scandinavian countries and in Britain. They held executive power in two-party coalitions thirty-four times (23.8% of all socialist cabinets), this pattern of coalition being predominant in Austria and Belgium and sometimes also in Sweden and Denmark. In the other countries, almost all experiences of socialist participation in the cabinet were in large coalitions of three or more parties. Altogether, this pattern represents 55.2% of all the socialist participation in government.

In Table 7.11 all the cabinets of the period and socialist cabinets are classified according to parliamentary status: (1) single-party majority cabinets; (2) minimum-winning coalition (MWC) cabinets;[84] (3) surplus coalition cabinets; (4) single-party minority cabinets; (5) multiparty minority cabinets; and (6) war cabinets. Next to the number of cabinets of each type, the table reports the cumulative duration of this formula for each given country. A comparison of these data with those concerning all cabinets (i.e., those with and without socialists, not reported here) allows an evaluation of the extent to which cabinets with socialists deviated from the general pattern of the country.

Almost half of the socialist governmental experiences were in oversized coalition cabinets (46.2%). In one-quarter, the socialists were part of more vulnerable cabinets: single-party minority (13.3%), minority coalition (4.2%), or war cabinets (6.3%). The remaining one-quarter were cabinets in which the socialist party held a stronger position: single-party majorities (6.3%) and MWC cabinets (21%). Ireland was dominated by single-party cabinets, most but not all of which were majority ones. With a single party approaching the majority-of-seats threshold and with a predominant anticoalition political culture, minority cabinets were often more viable than the necessarily complex coalitions of all the others. Indeed, it was only an alliance of all the other parties against Fianna Fail that enabled the Labour Party to be an indispensable ally in this period. This situation made it difficult, if not impossible, for the weak Labour Party to carve itself out a role of importance in governmental coalition. There were, in fact, only two experiences of coalitions, one MWC and one oversized. Labour was a member of both, but its presence was crucial in only one. In Austria and Italy, socialist parties formed part of surplus coalition cabinets only. In Austria, surplus coalitions were the most popular formula of government, but there were also several single-party and multiparty majority cabinets, MWCs, and single-party minority cabinets, accounting

---

[84] I consider as a minimum winning coalition all those coalitions for which the withdrawal of a partner determines a minority parliamentary status. There are other ways to define MWC. For a complete discussion, see Lijphart (1984: 46–66).

Table 7.11. *Cabinets with socialists, by type and by total months in office*

	single-party majority cabinet		MWC		surplus coalition		single-party minority cabinet		multy-party minority. cabinet.		war cabinet	
	durat.	n.	durat	n.	durat.	n.	durat.	n.	durat.	n.	durat.	n.
Au	-		-	-	283	14	-	-	-	-	-	-
Be	-		166	9	107	8	1	1	-	-	67	1
De	-		197	5	-	-	110	5	48	2	64	4
Fi	-		17	1	222	16	35	2	-	-	8	1
Fr	-		25	6	103	13	1	1	5	1	-	-
Ge	-		12	3	61	4	-	-	18	2	-	-
Ir	-		35	1	-	-	-	-	40	1	-	-
It	-		-	-	87	5	-	-	-	-	-	-
Ne	-		25	1	142	5	-	-	-	-	70	1
No	213	3	25	1	-	-	62	2	-	-	62	1
Sw	74	2	141	3	67	1	234	6	-	-	-	-
UK	143	4	-	-	-	-	36	2	-	-	60	1
all		9 6.3%		30 21.0%		66 46.2%		19 13.3%		6 4.2%		9 6.3%

altogether for almost 60% of all the cabinets and 40% over all time. The socialists entered only surplus coalitions, however. Similarly, the Italian cabinets were of all types except for the single-party majority cabinet, but the socialists entered only surplus coalitions. In both cases, the executive visibility of the socialists was quite weak, even though in the Austrian pattern there was a more balanced relationship with the Christian Democrats than in Italy.

Even in Finland and the Netherlands, most socialist participation in cabinets took place in oversized coalitions. Finland experimented with a large variety of coalition patterns (excluding single-party majorities). It had either minority or large majority cabinets, and in both cases ministerial stability was very precarious. However, the entire socialist experience is concentrated in sixteen surplus coalitions, with only one MWC and two single-party minority cabinets. In contrast, the Netherlands has a straightforward coalition pattern in which the number of surplus coalitions is on a par with MWCs. Once again, socialists have participated in only the latter, with one single exception of an MWC. In Belgium, as in the Netherlands, majority cabinets and the tendency to form them on a very wide basis were prevalent. Because no party approached the 50% threshold, minority governments were unacceptable and attempts to form them were immediately discontinued (there were only three short-lived single-party minority cabinets in Belgium and none in the Netherlands). In Belgium, however, MWCs were more numerous and of longer duration than the surplus ones. Yet, with respect to the dominant pattern in the country, cabinets with socialists were surplus coalitions more frequently and for longer periods.

France shares with Belgium and the Netherlands a dislike for minority cabinets, either single or coalition. Socialist cabinets were surplus coalitions rather than MWCs. The latter six experiences, including three of the four crucial Popular Front cabinets, lasted for only 25 months out of a total of 114 for this type. Germany, too, is totally dominated by coalition cabinets, most of the time majority but also including ten multiparty minority cabinets. The few German socialist cabinet experiences were concentrated in majority coalitions, with an equal distribution between MWCs and oversized formations.

The Scandinavian pattern can be set apart from the continental one because of the absence of surplus coalitions. The predominant formula was either that of single-party majorities (all socialist cabinets in Norway and Sweden), MWCs (the socialists being present in all of them except for one in Norway), or single-party minority cabinets (half of which were socialist). In Denmark, there were a few multiparty minority cabinets, all of which were formed with socialists, while there were none in Norway and Sweden. In a nutshell, then, Scandinavian socialism, although manifesting a clear preference for single-party governments that gave rise to many minority governments, especially but not exclusively in the interwar period, had a more flexible coalition strategy than British socialism. In Sweden, in the 1920–1932 period, none of the parties had a majority, and any coalition between the socialist and other parties was fraught with difficulty. At the end of the 1920s, talks with the liberals failed, the nonsocialist parties were also unable to find ground on which to cooperate, and all the political parties seemed to prefer to stay out of government.[85] Because every election to the lower house turned into a defeat for the governing party, a change of government occurred at least once every year. Although the liberals were in a better position to form a government than the socialists or conservatives, by relying on shifting left or right support, it was not unusual for the conservatives to join forces against the incumbent liberal government. Majority coalition parliamentarism prevailed in the 1933–1941 period as a result of the alliance between social democrats and agrarians. In autumn 1932, the socialists accepted governmental responsibility; they abandoned their previous policy of nationalization and instead emphasized welfare state policies, thereby reducing the antagonism of all the other parties and, in particular, the center-agrarians. In 1941, a period of single-party majority rule began, with the socialists gaining a majority in the lower house (in 1942, they also gained a majority in the upper house).

In Denmark, as in Sweden, the issue was primarily one of cooperation

[85] Stjernquist (1966: 122).

with the center parties, but the formulas experimented with were more varied, the alternation in coalition more frequent, and the cabinet tenure of the socialists less safe than in Sweden and Norway. In Norway, after the radical phase of 1921–1923 and the short-lived 1928 minority cabinet, the party remained divided as to how to interpret the results of its brief governmental experience: that is to say, the impossibility of holding power under capitalism or simply the uselessness of being in government without a solid majority. Its 1930 electoral program was even more radical than that of 1927–1928; it was only in 1930–1933 that the economic crisis and the fascist challenge in Europe triggered a clear process of deradicalization that – together with the 1933 electoral victory on a moderate platform and the 1935 alliance with the agrarians – started the long labor season of almost twenty years of single-party majority cabinet (1945–1963). Throughout the 1919–1935 period, the liberals, agrarians, and conservatives alternated in single-party minority cabinets.[86] Thanks to their electoral strength, the lack of internal division, and the divisions of their adversaries, Scandinavian socialists were also able to hold their own in minority governments (this was also the case in Denmark, although to a lesser extent); this allowed them to escape the dilemma of coalition.

The British Labour Party could compensate for electoral weakness by means of the bonus of the majority system when the electoral climate was favorable; thus, it was able to avoid being forced into coalitions and it managed to form single-party majority cabinets with clear-cut socialist programs. However, these conditions, combined with the cohesion of the conservatives, imposed a price of limited cabinet tenure. It is paradoxical that, notwithstanding a number of favorable conditions (a balanced relationship between the extraparliamentary and parliamentary parties; unwillingness of the unions to engage directly in politics; federal and indirect structure and weak institutionalization of the party organization;[87] internal power structure both congruent with and functional to the parliamentary system), the governmental record of the Labour Party was poor, as can be seen in Table 7.11. After the short-lived MacDonald experience in 1924, a minority Labour government came to power from 1929 to 1931 and from 1976 to 1979. For part of these periods, that is, for almost ten months in 1930–1931 and eighteen in 1978–1979, the Labor government remained in office thanks to an informal agreement with the Liberals. The

---

[86] To be precise, of the twelve bourgeois cabinets before the 1935 Labor–Agrarian alliance, eight were single-party minority cabinets and four were two-party (Conservatives plus National Liberals) minority cabinets.

[87] On this point, see Panebianco (1982: 167–182).

pact was kept secret in 1931–1932; however, in the 1970s, when the same agreement was made public, its importance was diminished by the continuous assertion that no concessions were being made to the liberals. Thus, no real formal coalition was ever formed. Only on two occasions after 1918 did the Labour Party manage to retain a majority large enough to permit the implementation of its policies for an entire legislature: from 1945 to 1950 and from 1966 to 1970, that is, for nine out of almost ninety years. On a number of occasions – from 1930 to 1931, from 1950 to 1951, from 1964 to 1966, and from 1974 to 1979 (eleven years altogether) – there were de facto minority Labour governments or governments whose majorities were so small as to prevent the party from implementing its policies and remaining in charge of the legislature. In other words, for more than half of its entire period of governmental control, the Labour Party did not have a safe majority in the Commons. Leaving aside war governments, it was in power for approximately a third of the period under discussion, and for more than half of this time, it had no majority or one that was unsafe.

In conclusion, the governmental record of the Labour Party is modest and has often been overestimated in a comparative perspective. This poor control was due to the compact nature of the conservative opposition and to the Labour Party's historical unwillingness to enter into formal coalitions with the Liberals,[88] despite the fact that from 1920 to 1931 and again from 1960 to 1970, the latter regarded themselves as a center–left party, generally willing to cooperate with the Labour Party in exchange for a reform guaranteeing more equal representation. At the same time, it cannot be argued that its preference for single-party cabinets and its reluctance to form coalitions was the result of its desire to put its manifesto into practice as it stood, since too often, it was unable to do so without calling on external support. Leaving aside cultural explanations, it remains a mystery why the British Labor Party systematically refused any alliance or coalition with other parties, and in particular with the Liberals, giving rise in this way to a Conservative predominance in the executive.[89]

Finally, let us consider the types of political coalitions in which socialist parties participated. Given the unreliable nature of the pre–World War II cabinet data, I have classified the 378 cabinets between 1918 and 1966 qualitatively rather than resorting to formalized criteria.[90] Cabinets are

---

[88] On the anticoalition attitude of the party, see Marquand (1981: 166–176).

[89] The debate on the payoff of an alliance with the Liberals, based on a few key mutual and tacit withdrawals of candidates, has recently been reopened in a few articles: see Dent (1993: 243–251); and Sharp (1994: 107–131).

[90] The political connotation of a cabinet based on the predominance of its internal left–right orientation has recently been operationalized into a five-point index by scholars

classified as either right-wing or left-wing if their parliamentary support was ensured for more than two-thirds of their tenure by right or left parties; center–right and center–left if centrist forces were represented together with right or left parties, respectively; and balanced when centrist forces were predominant or, alternatively, when both left and right parties joined them in the coalition. I have been able to classify only 311 of the 378 cabinets of the period: The 1919–1922 Italian and the 1919–1939 French cabinets proved impossible to classify precisely. Of the 143 cabinets with socialist ministers, 10 either had no precise characterization (war cabinets) or this kind of description was impossible. Of the remaining 133 cabinets with socialist ministers, a large number of them (45.1%) were balanced, that is, cabinets in which either the center political parties dominated or in which there was an equilibrium between center, left, and right parties. In addition, there were four center–right cabinets (2.8%). The conclusion is that the European socialists participated in center–left or left cabinets in only half of their executive experiences: 29.3% of cases (thirty-nine cabinets) were center–left cabinets; 22.6% (thirty) were predominantly left cabinets.

Table 7.12 ranks the countries, going from the most adversarial left-versus-right to the more centrist pattern. The thirty left cabinets are almost entirely concentrated in Britain and Scandinavia. In these countries, cabinet participation was unlikely to precipitate internal conflicts and divisions, as in all cases it faced an opposition that was almost entirely right-wing. In Belgium, there was only one left cabinet (the minority single-party Spaak cabinet of 1946), but socialists tended to participate in center–left cabinets more often than in balanced ones. This is largely due to the three-party configuration of the party system, in which the socialist–Catholic cabinets should be viewed as center–left (as they excluded the liberals) and the socialist–liberal cabinets as balanced (even if they excluded the Catholics). In all other countries, socialists entered balanced cabinets most of the time. In the countries with denominational parties (Austria, Germany, Italy, and the Netherlands), this was in practice the only possibility.[91]

mostly interested in relating the degree of party control of a cabinet to its policy preference and/or policy performance. For this index, see Castles (1982) and Keman (1988: 192–216). Scores for the ideological makeup of post-1945 cabinets are available in Woldendorp, Keman, and Budge (1993). This analysis has not been done for the interwar period.

[91] Note that the criteria for classifying the ideological completion of cabinets make the Austrian socialist–Catholic coalitions balanced, given that during this period no relevant right of the Catholic Party existed. A similar coalition is classified as center–left in Belgium, given its exclusion of the liberals.

Table 7.12. *Ideological composition and duration (in parentheses) of cabinets with socialist parties (ranked by degree of adversarial coalition pattern)*

	right	center-right	balanced	center-left	left
UK	-	-	-	-	6 - (179)
No	-	-	1 - (62)	-	7 - (305)
Sw	-	-	1 - (67)	3 - (141)	8 - (308)
De	-	-	-	7 - (245	5 - (110)
Fi	-	-	13 - (158)	4 - (81)	2 - (35)
Be	-	-	6 - (176)	12 - (164)	1 - (1)
Au	-	-	11 - (257)	3 - (26)	-
Ge	-	-	8 - (82)	1 - (9)	-
It	-	-	4 - (84)	1 - (3)	-
Ne	-	-	6 - (212)	1 - (25)	-
Ir	-	-	2 - (75)	-	-
Fr	-	4 (33)	8 - (52)	7 - (36)	1 - (1)

Note: excluding war and caretaker cabinets.

In Finland, and also in Italy and France, the division of the left and the post-1947 opposition of the strong Communist Party increased the impossibility of these socialist parties forming left or even center–left cabinets. All the cases of their participation in the cabinet involved bilateral opposition, that is, cabinets that were opposed by strong forces on the right and the left. In particular, in France, the legitimation cleavage that excluded both the communists and forces of the right from the cabinets of the Fourth Republic forced socialists to enter system-defense cabinets that excluded the extremes and in which the moderate right was predominant. In France, Italy, Germany (interwar), and Finland (up to 1966), the internal division of the left prevented the socialists from even thinking of a left or even center–left government; at the same time, their obligation to share power as a junior partner with centrist and sometime conservative forces helped to reinforce the division with the communists and to expose them to criticism and electoral competition with the latter. Where communist parties managed to establish themselves as stable parties with more than 10% of the vote, their strength was sufficient to rule out relatively homogeneous left or center–left coalitions and to push the socialists into tense centrist coalitions. The vicious circle was complete, and the radical-left prophecy of ineffective participation in cabinets with bourgeois forces was therefore self-fulfilling.

SOCIALIST GOVERNMENTAL POWER

This review of left cabinet experiences shows that an evaluation of the socialist executive tenure needs to consider *presence* and *duration* in office, but also to supplement this information with that on the *parliamentary status of the cabinet* (single-party majority, MWC, etc.) to which the socialist party belongs and with the socialist *party cabinet status* (leading, equal, or junior member). The *parliamentary status of a cabinet* results from the intertwining of two dimensions: the number of partners (single-party versus coalition) and majority status (minority versus MWC versus oversized). The *party cabinet status* refers to the weight of the party within the overall coalition, according to its own and its partners' electoral size. In Table 7.13, I propose a scheme based on these four dimensions of governmental power designed to obtain a comprehensive measure of the overall impact of each party on the government. This results from the rank ordering of the different combinations in terms of descending governmental power (last two columns of the table).[92]

The extremes of this rank ordering are represented by the single-party majority and party opposition cases. I have chosen to consider the party-leading role in MWC and oversized coalitions as the closest to the top of the ranking and the party junior position in multiparty minority cabinets and in surplus cabinets as closest to the bottom of the ranking. Equal-partner status in MWC and surplus coalitions come logically before a junior status in these cabinets. The greatest difficulty lies in ranking minority cabinet experiences and, in particular, the single-party and multiparty minority cabinets where a party has a leading or equal status. Finally, it is equally difficult to find the appropriate ranking of necessary external support and necessary abstention.[93] For minority cabinets, the systematic external support of other parties may be of crucial importance. Does such an external-support role point to greater or lesser policy influ-

---

[92] This index of governmental power, as well as that of coalition potential discussed later, is more deeply elaborated and justified in Bartolini (1998: 40–61).

[93] These are situations in which, at the confidence vote and at crucial points in the life of a cabinet, the support or the abstention of a party is necessary without its representation by ministers in the cabinet. I underline "necessary" because, if such external support or abstention is unnecessary for the survival of the cabinet, then the party's influence on such a cabinet is reduced to nothing.

Table 7.13. *Dimension of governmental power*

dimensions				resulting rank ordering	governmental status ranking points
presence/ absence	cabinet status in parliament	party status in cabinet	duration		
in cabinet	single-party majority	leading		single-party majority	13
	minimum winning coalition	leading, equal, junior		leading partner in MWC	12
	surplus coalition	leading. equal, junior		leading partner in surplus coalitions	11
	single-party minority	leading		single-party minority	10
	multiparty minority	leading. equal, junior	N. of months	equal partner in MWC	9
necessary external support				equal partner in surplus coalitions	8
necessary abstention				junior partner in MWC	7
in opposition				leading partner in multiparty minority coalitions	6
				equal partner in multiparty minority coalitions	5
				junior partner in surplus coalitions	4
				junior partner in multiparty minority coalitions	3
				necessary external support (to minority cabinet)	2
				necessary abstention (to minority cabinet)	1
				opposition	0

ence compared with the role of a junior partner within the cabinet? I have chosen the second solution.

Applying to each cabinet the ranking value of Table 7.13 multiplied by its duration (in months), a governmental power index of the socialist parties is produced (a similar index for communist parties is irrelevant, as they shared little cabinet responsibility; see the earlier discussion) that can be cumulative for the whole 1918–1966 period or an average value for all cabinets (378) or for all legislatures (171).[94] In the last column of Table

[94] In comparing a cumulative index (for the whole period) with a mean (by cabinet) index of governmental power, only two differences in ranking appear. Finland and France are slightly more powerful with a cumulative than with a mean index. Belgium is a bit less so. However, with both indexes, Belgium remains ahead of both France and Finland. In the end, the only important change is that with a cumulative index the Finnish socialists appear to be more powerful than the Dutch, while the situation is reversed with a cabinets' mean index.

7.14, the cumulative (by cabinet) governmental power of the socialist parties is reported. The Scandinavian countries are those where the socialists enjoyed by far the highest governmental potential. Britain, and at lower levels the Netherlands, Belgium, and Austria, are intermediate cases, while the large continental countries (France, Germany, Italy) and Ireland have very low indices. If we compare this multidimensional index with that of simple duration in office or the percentage of cabinets (see Table 7.9) some striking differences emerge. For example, Austrian socialists in this period remained in the cabinet about 60% of the time, but in terms of combined governmental power this party was one of the least powerful because it was usually an equal or even junior partner in oversized coalitions with the Christian Democrats. Similarly, in Finland, the socialists were in office for more than 45% of the time (and in 40% of the cabinets), but their global governmental power was much lower than these figures suggest. By contrast, the Dutch and British Labor parties enjoyed more governmental leverage than indicated by their time in office. The British Labour Party stayed in power for only a third of the time and in a third of the cabinets, but it emerges as the party with the highest governmental power after the unmatched Scandinavian cases. The Dutch come after the British; although they began to participate in cabinets late and for about 40% of the time, they did so in a key position and role.

In this way, the descriptive analysis of the governmental experience of the socialist parties in the crucial period of their access to government is completed, and a general description of the moments when they first entered and then became regular governmental partners, as well as the duration of their overall governmental participation in different types of cabinets, is charted (Table 7.14).

After World War I, any further institutional integration of the left into the respective national systems depended on the obstacles it found in translating its electoral and parliamentary weight into executive access and function. Given the European variance discussed so far, two issues are crucial:

1. What is the best predictor of the earliness of cabinet entry of the socialist parties? Was their ideological moderation and the bargainability of their positions more important, or were the favorable circumstances that fostered cabinet access and, consequently, policy and ideological domestication more important?
2. What can be said about the forces, independent of party system format

Table 7.14. *Socialist parties' governmental experiences (countries ranked according to governmental power index)*

	first entry	regular partner	overall duration	format	type	completion	governmental power 1918-1966
Sw	early		long	1 or 2 parties	SP majority, Sp minority, MW	left/center-left	4612
No	early		long	single party	SP majority, SP minority	left	3687
Dk	early		long	1 or 2 parties	MW or SP minority	left/center-left	3304
Be	early		average	2 or 3 parties	MW or surplus	balanced/center-left	2374
UK	early		short	single party	SP majority	left	1981
Au	early	late	long	2 parties	surplus	balanced	1698
Fi	early	late	average	all formats	surplus	balanced/center-left	1887
Ne	late		average	3-4 or more	surplus	balanced	1525
Fr	late		short	3-4 or more	surplus or MW	balanced	816
Ge	early		short	3-4 or more	surplus, MW and MPM	balanced (center-right)	630
Ir	late		short	3-4 or more	MW and MPM	balanced	365
It	late		short	3-4 or more	surplus	balanced	280 ?)
Sz	late		average	4 parties	surplus		-

Note: governmental power = cumulative 1918–1966 governmental power index for all cabinets.

configuration, that fostered or hindered the overall socialist governmental role?

To evaluate the resistance to the translation of socialist parliamentary strength into executive roles, we need to identify the part of the socialist governmental role that derived from the party system format and configuration opportunities from that which derived from other factors. It is necessary to find a comprehensive indicator of the *configuration structure of opportunity* offered to the parties by the party system format and then compare it with the actual governmental role played by that party as measured before. I have measured this potential independently of all other ideological, political, and historical circumstances by resorting to the formula of coalition power within decisional bodies originally developed by Shapley for computing an index of decisional power within committee systems.[95] This is one of the many algorithms developed for measuring decisional power in voting bodies from a game theory perspective,[96] and it can be interpreted as an a priori power index measuring the potential power of an ith member of a certain body (be it a small committee or a

---

[95] Details about the algorithm used are presented in Bartolini (1998).

[96] Shapley (1953). This index is also known and cited as the "Shapley–Shubik index" because of its final formulation by these two authors, with a modification for majority games; Shapley and Shubik (1954).

parliament).[97] Given the percentage of seats of a given party, such a measure computes the number of all the possible majorities above the 50% threshold in which that party is a necessary coalition partner, that is, in how many it is a partner whose withdrawal would lead to the coalition's falling below the 50% threshold.[98] To the best of my knowledge, this index has never been applied to the comparative study of election results across countries and over time.[99]

For each party, its index of coalition potential incorporates all the numerical potentials implicit in a given distribution of strength among actors in a voting body.[100] This "blindness" of the index to any other consideration but numerical ones is an asset. It provides a theoretically adequate description of the situation in which the chances of a party being incorporated into a majority are stripped of all political considerations and are dependent exclusively on the numerical configuration of the party system. It is thus a description of the pure and absolute "coalitionability" of all partners, in which each party is deprived of all its political idiosyncrasies stemming from its past history, previous coalition experiences, or policy preferences. Blindness is, however, also a liability for the same reason that considerations of coalition feasibility are ignored. In this analysis, I have introduced a constraint into the algorithm linked to the spatial positioning of the parties, which forces it to take into consideration only those majority coalitions that are stipulated among spatially connected parties. The coalition potential is computed only in reference to these coalitions.[101]

[97] An alternative way to read the Shapley value is "the probability for the i to deliver the necessary votes for a qualified majority" (Bomsdor 1981: 284). A third definition is the probability that unit i, by casting its votes, establishes a winning majority in any voting sequence or, to put it differently, as the relative frequency with which unit i plays the pivotal role in an infinite number of random majority coalitions among k units (Rattinger 1981: 223).

[98] Attention should be paid to the types of majorities considered by the algorithm itself. These are not the MWCs, but rather all the possible majority coalitions in which the party under discussion is crucial or pivotal. This means that the set of majorities from which the value is finally calculated also includes oversized majorities resulting from the presence of some other party whose withdrawal would still leave them with a majority of seats. The choice of this set of majorities is necessary because the calculation is finalized to the coalition potential of the party in question.

[99] It has frequently been used for the descriptive analysis of the distribution of voting power in specific legislatures. See Frey (1968), Holler and Kellermann (1977), Miller (1973), Guillermo (1975), and De Fraja (1988).

[100] In principle, any of the many theories of coalition formation can be modeled into the algorithm through the introduction of conditions that confine the number and type of coalitions feasible.

[101] For the criteria of left–right ordering of the parties, see the Data Appendix. A second

The theoretical framework summarizes resume the relationship among a *"blind"* *coalition potential*, a *"spatial"* *coalition potential*, and the *actual governmental power* (as measured earlier), as indicated in Figure 7.1. *Configuration and format factors* directly influence the blind coalition potential and only indirectly, through it, governmental power. The blind index should be closely associated with the numerical and distribution conditions of the party system. Traditional *ideological factors* enter the picture, introducing sympathies or compatibility among the parties as a result of past experiences. The spatial rank ordering of the parties can be considered a valid indicator of these historical compatibilities and can be incorporated into the index of coalition potential when it is computed on the basis of left–right-ordered party units. What intervenes between a spatial coalition potential and governmental power can be conceptualized as the black box of "other" *political factors* that are not tapped by any potential index. These factors do not pertain either to the numerical structure of opportunities offered by the party system or to the historical ideological sympathies firmly established among parties. Instead, they include aspects belonging to the *cohesion* of the adversaries (of each given party), to the *issue bargainability* of the party stance, and to the presence of *legitimacy cleavages* concerning that party. Each of these elements may introduce strong deviations in the relations between coalition potential and governmental power by lowering or boosting the governmental role far beyond what would be expected on the basis of the party's coalition potential. Briefly, in principle, one would expect that, if the coalition potential corresponds to governmental power, then the structure of opportunities of the left was basically neutral. Adversaries' coalitionability, socialist policy bargainability, and discontinuities in the space of competition can therefore be conceptualized and measured as otherwise unexplainable discrepancies between the potential and actual governmental role.

We can now interpret the timing of socialist access to government to check whether the prevailing factor was the ideological bargainability of their positions or the party-system configurational features. The hypothesis is that in the absence of specific ideological and/or political factors hampering or favoring socialist access to cabinet responsibility, such access should be entirely a function of the coalition potential resulting from the configuration format of the party system. In Figure 7.2, I have charted the

modification may relax the stringent criteria of perfect connectivity. We can allow only coalition among connected parties, but permitting a "spatial jump," that is, allowing one of the connected parties to be absent. This reduces the problems of the "correct" ordering of parties over the space. Other conditions of coalition feasibility can also be introduced by modifying the set of total feasible coalitions.

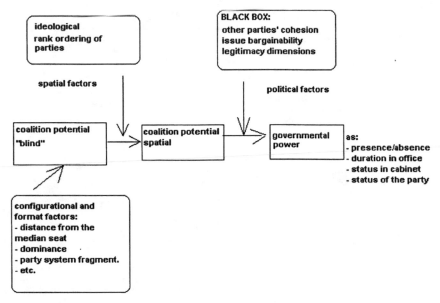

Figure 7.1. A theoretical framework for the analysis of governmental power.

year of first cabinet entry of the socialists against their size and their coalition power at such a moment. For nine out of the thirteen countries (Germany, the United Kingdom, Finland, Norway, France, the Netherlands, Switzerland, Italy, and Ireland), the coalition potential is an almost perfect predictor of the timing of entry. Size represents a far less important factor. In particular, the British, Irish, and Finnish Labor parties entered the cabinet when their coalition potential was much higher than their comparative size. At their entry, the British and Finnish socialists were no stronger in parliamentary terms than their French, Dutch, or Swiss counterparts, which instead entered about fifteen to twenty years later.

Four cases deviate from this pattern: Belgium, Denmark, Austria, and Sweden. These earlycomers to cabinet responsibility did not enjoy a high enough level of coalition potential to justify their executive incorporation, that is, their early entry was due to political factors that were not related to their being highly necessary coalition partners. The strong Austrian socialists had a low coalition potential in 1918, and their entry was due exclusively to the peculiar conditions created by the collapse of the imperial regime and, in particular, to the delegitimation and lack of organization of the conservative forces and their inability to form coalitions with the Catholics. It is not surprising, therefore, that this early entry was a short-lived experience. Given their low coalition potential, the Austrian

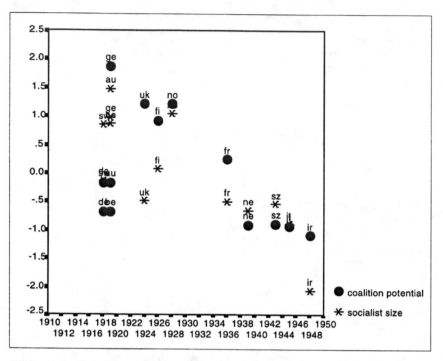

Figure 7.2. Socialist size and coalition potential at their cabinet entry.

socialists were immediately ousted from the cabinet once the Catholic–German nationalist divide was overcome.

In Belgium, the early incorporation of the socialists in coalition making, when their coalition potential was not particularly high with respect to the potential of Catholic predominance or Catholic–liberal alliances, was due to the war and the occupation experience. However, the fact that socialists were not excluded from cabinets later on shows that no stable antisocialist bloc ever developed between the Catholics and liberals. Thus, these latter two parties were sufficiently antagonistic not to consider their alliance as always preferable to one including the socialists, and neither of them regarded the socialists as the main common enemy. This supports the idea that it was the moderation and bargainability of the Belgian socialist positions in this period that allowed them to be coalition partners with both Catholics and liberals (in 1919–1920, 1926, and 1935–1938) or with the Catholics alone (in 1925 and 1939).[102]

---

[102] The total freedom of coalition by which socialists could form cabinets even with the liberals and without the Catholics developed only after World War II.

The Danish and Swedish early entry is more difficult to interpret. Their coalition power was quite low at the time of their entry, although it rose enormously after it. Even in these cases, the best explanation is that their relative moderation, added to the strong divisions within the bourgeois camp, fostered their capacity to enter cabinets beyond their coalition potential. In Denmark, the split of the liberals and the creation of the radicals offered the socialists an early, stable ally that was unavailable in other Western European countries at the time. Between the world wars, the radicals formed a coalition cabinet only with the socialists, never with the liberals or conservatives.[103] For the Swedish Social Democrats, we have seen that the cabinet experiences in the interwar period involved mainly minority cabinets. The key to this formula was, however, that agrarians, liberals, and conservatives could never agree to form a nonsocialist cabinet, and the system only produced either caretaker cabinets or nonsocialist ultraminority cabinets. The Swedish case is the most obvious case of a socialist cabinet experience largely fostered by the division of bourgeois forces.

In conclusion, the good fit between coalition power and timing of entry does not support the idea that it was the more moderate socialist parties that entered first. In reality, it was those socialist parties with the highest coalition potential in their party system that entered first. The relationship between governmental participation and deradicalization seems to go from the former to the latter rather than in the other direction. As I have argued, Austria is no exception to this rule, and it was only in Belgium, Denmark, and Sweden that early socialist ideological moderation and the ideological divisions of the nonsocialist forces played a prevalent role.

Let us now consider the overall picture for the 1918–1966 period rather than the situation at the first cabinet entry. Using the standardized scores in Figure 7.3, the level of coalition potential and the level of governmental power are charted for each country. This allows a clear appreciation of the extent to which either the sheer numerical opportunities offered by a given structure of the party system were actually exploited or some other powerful politico-ideological forces interacted with this relationship, fostering the downgrading of the socialist chances of a governmental role. The Scandinavian countries, Belgium, France, and the Netherlands pose no interpretive problem, as their period average coalition potential is matched by their governmental power. The more interesting cases are those of Austria, Finland, Germany, Britain, Ireland, and Italy,

---

[103] It was only in 1945 that they offered external support to a liberal cabinet for the first time.

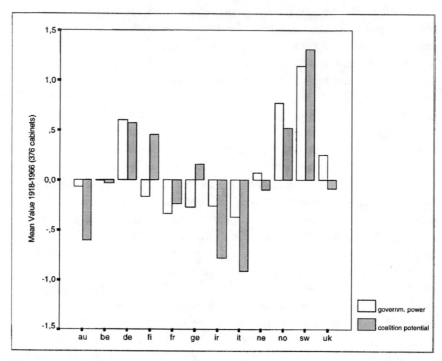

Figure 7.3. Coalition potential and governmental power.

where the ranking in terms of potential and that in terms of actual power differs considerably. In Finland and Germany, the overall high coalition potential of the left was reduced by internal divisions that drastically curtailed the potential for the connected winning coalitions of the socialists. In addition, the ideological "summability" of the center–right forces proved much higher than that of the left, actually contributing to reduce the governmental role of the social democrats with respect to what they could have had if the divide within the left had been less intense or counterbalanced by a similarly strong divide within the right.

   In Austria, surplus coalitions after World War II probably offered the Socialist Party more power than it could possibly have enjoyed if an MWC logic had prevailed in the party system dominated by the central pivotal role of the large Catholic Party. In Britain, where indeed a winner-take-all institutional setting and political culture predominated, the Labour Party enjoyed more actual power than coalition potential, probably thanks to its role in the minority cabinets of the transition period in the late 1920s and 1930s. In Italy and Ireland, the distribution of the forces and the presence of a large, centrally located party offered the Socialist Party very little coalition power. However, the party's actual governmental role, although below the overall mean, was higher than expected because in Ireland the dubious left–right location of the parties allowed for all-party coalitions against the Fianna Fail, while in Italy the unique and simultaneous presence of extreme-left and extreme-right forces pushed the Catholics into preferring oversized coalitions, thereby offering a chance to the socialists.

It is interesting to compare Italy and France. Before World War II, the only difference between them was that the socialists participated, between 1936 and 1938, in the four Popular Front cabinets in France, while the Italian socialists reached cabinet status only after the war. After this, the main difference concerns the fragmentation of the centrist forces, which was very high in France and very low in Italy and which enhanced the coalition potential of the French socialists. However, given that extreme-right antisystem and illegitimate coalition partner forces were far less important and more intermittent in France than in Italy, the need for socialist partners was reduced, as center–right and right cabinets were a more likely and frequent outcome. In these two cases, the difference in coalition potential and the similarity in governmental power resulted more from the cohesion of the center–right forces and from the presence of a legitimacy cleavage in the party system than from opportunity structures linked to electoral size.

This last remark leads me to consider more closely the coalition potential of the communist parties, or more generally of the other left parties, and the issue of the cost of division within the left in terms of cabinet potential. The data for communist parties highlight the enormous difference between the blind coalition potential – depending exclusively on the numerical opportunities created by their size, dominance, and so on – and the spatial coalition potential, which, as a result of their extreme-left position, is curtailed drastically. In Finland, the potential in connected coalitions is, for example, one-tenth of the same potential in unconnected coalitions. The extreme case is Italy: the connected coalition potential of the Communist Party was near zero between 1945 and 1966 because Italian Communists could not attain a majority of seats by allying with neighboring parties on the left or the right. To reach such a majority, their coalition had be extended to the Christian Democrats in a virtually all-party coalition, in which, however, the contribution of the Communists was no longer necessary.

The losses incurred by the left as a result of its internal split can be measured in terms of lost cabinet potential by comparing the cabinet potential of the socialists with the cabinet potential that a unified left would have enjoyed. I have therefore repeated the calculation of the Shapley index, inserting into the party system a fictitious party whose parliamentary size corresponds to the global cumulated parliamentary size of all class left parties (socialists, communists, and others). In the post–World War II period, the Finnish left would have been a necessary partner in 10% more cabinets if it had been united (the same was true after 1966). Losses of some importance were also evident in the Swedish case, where a united left would have been necessary to 16% more cabinets than was the case for the socialists alone, that is, for almost all the cabinets. The major losses were encountered, however, by the French left in the 1945–1966 period. If it had been less politically divided, it would have been a necessary partner for roughly 25% more cabinets than was the case for the socialists. In the two decades after World War II, the Italian left did not incur high cabinet potential losses as a result of its division: If it had been united, it would have been a necessary partner in 12% more cabinets than the socialists were. However, the costs for the Italian left increased dramatically after 1966 with the declining cohesion of the centrist forces. In the period 1966–1985, a united left in Italy would have been a necessary cabinet partner in 30% more cases than the socialists actually were.

This different trend in the costs of divisions in Italy, France, and Finland reflects the history of the communist–socialist cleavage in these countries. The deep divide created by the split was soon reconciled by the common antifascist struggle in Italy, and after World War II the Italian left was the only one in Europe in which the main socialist party aligned in opposition with the communists. Only at the beginning of the 1960s was the ancient cleavage revived with the "autonomist" position of the socialists and their cabinet entry. In Finland, by contrast, the cleavage deriving from the split remained firm until well after World War II and started to decline only in the 1960s, exactly when it was exacerbated in Italy. In France, the rapprochement of the Popular Front was short-lived, and a deep divide remained throughout the whole Fourth Republic and until the beginning of the 1970s.

In a broad historical perspective, the within-left division created the highest cost for the left as a whole, as well as for its internal components in Italy. The socialists' opposition position, and their closeness to the communists in the 1940s and 1950s, deprived them of the possibility of exploiting their coalition opportunities in this period, while their increasing distance from the communists during the 1970s, and even more in the 1980s, boosted their own coalition potential but sharply reduced that of the global left at a moment when the more moderate communist stance made such an alliance conceivable. The Italian socialist–communist relationships went "against history," with a solid, noncompetitive alliance during the Cold War and an increasingly competitive attitude in the 1970s and 1980s.

The consequences of the different governmental experiences of the European left were of great importance. Participation in the cabinet offered leverage on policy making and implementation, as well as the potential for electoral stabilization and strengthening. The capacity of socialist governments to influence macroeconomic and redistributive policies to the advantage of their electoral base has been argued.[104] However, outside the Scandinavian world and Britain, the inferences to be drawn from these data are tenuous for three reasons. The first is documented in the previous sections of this chapter: Clearly left or even center–left-oriented cabinets were rare occurrences, and most of the time socialists in continental Europe entered the cabinet under conditions of enforced moderation of their claims, in broad oversized coalitions or in barely tolerated minority cabinets. Second, in continental Europe the socialists were neither the first nor the only party to foster welfarist, full-employment, and labor-favorable legislation and policies. In the bureaucratic and authoritarian Central European constitutional monarchies, the political elite actively fostered early and advanced social legislation, with the deliberate aim of detaching workers' corporate organizations from their socialist political representation and of achieving political legitimation without resorting to the liberalization of the regime and relying on the electoral-parliamentary channel.[105] Later on, Catholic and denominational parties competed with the socialists, whose cabinet experiences were in most cases carried over in alliances with such forces. However, in Italy, Belgium, the Netherlands, Germany, and Austria, denominational parties governed more frequently and longer than socialists, which makes a case for their claim of having been the main architects of the exceptional development of social policies in the twentieth

---

[104] See the articles in Castles (1982).

[105] In the 1880s, Austria introduced an impressive array of social legislation deliberately aimed at the integration of workers into the state. This legislation was interventionist in the sense that it anticipated workers' requests and was often passed over employers' opposition. For a detailed analysis of Austrian social legislation, see Talos (1981), especially the Introduction and the first chapter, which deals with the early history. In Germany, the situation was similar and responded to the same aim of social integration without political representation for the lower classes. Baldwin (1988) has extended the role of the conservatives in early social policy making beyond the Central European constitutional monarchies. Liberal states could not afford such an interventionist policy in opposition with the capitalists and, at the same time, did not need a different source of legitimation from the one they received from the political-electoral open channel. The paucity of social legislation in liberal France before World War I has been amply demonstrated. A broad social legislation program did not come until the Popular Front in 1936: "a generation later: a generation too late"; Lorwin (1954: 7, 28).

century.[106] A final factor weakening the relation between socialist executive participation and actual policy output is that the thirty-year period between 1930 and 1960 saw the development of welfarist and full-employment policies *anywhere* and *any way*,[107] independently of the composition of governments. That is to say, the political forces that enjoyed control of the executive during this crucial period gained by default the dividends of such growth. This expansion was probably the key factor in the remarkable electoral stabilization that took place after World War II, differentiating the period from the more marked electoral instability of the interwar years and the post-1973 period.[108] The left parties that missed this historical window of opportunity lost the chance of directing such growth to their own and their constituency's advantage forever.

This leads to the consideration that the great opportunities for the left lay not in the actual distribution of the benefits of this growth as such, but rather in the possibility of guiding such growth through regulative policies that would eventually strengthen their electoral and political hegemony in their respective societies. In this lies the exceptionality of the Scandinavian countries. The combination of organizational, institutional, and political factors discussed in the previous chapters made them able to exploit this opportunity fully and allowed them to shape the fabric of their society in a way that was profitable to their continued rule. In the Scandinavian context of high religious homogeneity, the predominance of socioeconomic conflicts (see the next chapter), low stateness (with the state, however, accepted as the regulatory agency of the society),[109] and stable access to power in the 1930s, the labor movement could shape new employment policies; influence social, fiscal, and distributive processes; and deprive employers of friendly governments and favorable state intervention from the beginning. The focus of industrial conflict – which earlier had fallen on the market, where workers confronted capitalists in costly con-

---

[106] This does not mean that the general welfare projects of denominational and socialist parties were not different in general philosophy and also in the relative satisfaction offered to different groups of claimants, in particular dependent versus independent work. For the different political characterization of welfare programs, see Ferrera (1993: 155–200). See also Esping Andersen (1990: Chap. 3).

[107] Growth figures for the countries of Western Europe can be found in Flora, Alber, Eichenberg, Kohl, Kraus, Pfenning, and Seebohm (1987).

[108] Evidence of the striking electoral stability of European party systems in the 1945–1970 period compared with the earlier and later periods is found in Bartolini and Mair (1990: 98–121).

[109] Not necessarily in the statist and paternalist version of Germany and Austria. In Sweden, after the initial influences of Bismarck's reforms, German statism and paternalism were soon rejected in favor of a more emancipatory, radical-liberal, and humanitarian vision. See Olsson (1990).

flicts with uncertain outcomes — switched progressively from the market to the more egalitarian arenas of politics.[110] This helped to avoid risk taking in industrial conflicts and to resort instead to political instruments for redistribution. The early institutionalization of industrial relations and the labor–management pacts outlawing unauthorized strikes and establishing national grievance procedures for resolving disputes over wage contracts changed Sweden from the country with the highest level of labor disputes in Europe to one with a pacified relation pattern. To sum up, governmental control was the key resource for party strategy. Swedish socialists created labor market institutions and policies that strengthened the unions and their recruiting capacity on a continuous basis.[111] Although this slowly but consistently established legal and political context was not the only condition for the development and organizational growth of trade union membership, which was among the strongest in Europe before the socialists gained power (see Chapter 6), it did reinforce their authority over members and their centralized decision-making and bargaining power, as well as the extension of their power in social policy implementation.

The early access to and stability of executive tenure in Scandinavia also fostered the organizational cohesion of socialism, making left criticism and propaganda difficult under the conditions of a firmly controlled Social Democratic government. From the 1930s on, radical wage policies and "outbidding" opposition policies were pursued by communist militants at the grass roots level against those of the socialists even in these cases, but the link between these and real-wage developments was tenuous. The communist wage policy was squeezed between the highly centralized and visible socialist governmental wage negotiations (recognition, etc.) and effective local additions to the central agreements.[112] The gap between the material realities and interpretive ideological schemes in communist propaganda was too wide. In countries where socialists had no firm control over the government, their wage policy was in direct competition with that of the communists only in the ideological and propaganda realm, and no comparison between the material achievements attributable to socialists and the language of radicalism was possible. Only two languages were compared with their possible long-term, abstract consequences, and no gap

---

[110] Korpi (1983: 181).

[111] In particular, the Ghent system's unemployment scheme, by which unions controlled unemployment benefits and workers needed to join unions in order to be eligible for them. Rothstein (1992). The Ghent system is also in use in Denmark, Finland, Iceland, and Belgium (all highly trade-unionized countries), while compulsory state-run systems are in use in all other countries, including Norway.

[112] Stråth (1983: 277).

between reality and communist propaganda was visible. Instead, where communist strength was great enough to make socialist cabinet participation a rare and not particularly effective exercise, the gap opened between the socialists' propaganda and ideological identity and their poor policy achievements. It is likely that the difficult conditions of cabinet participation and/or the perception of the poor results of such participation in countries like Germany, Finland, France, and Austria between the wars, and also in Italy and France after World War II, contributed to the strengthening and maintenance of a verbal radical orthodoxy as a "compensatory myth" for poor policy results and uncertain democratic consolidation.

This use of governmental regulatory initiatives to foster societal development and to consolidate social and political alliances[113] was impractical for the British Labour Party for cultural and political reasons. Not only was the party not in government long enough to enforce such strategies credibly,[114] but the cultural and structural conditions of its relationship with the state made this impossible. The tradition of governmental engineering of civic society remained marginal to, even absent from, the basic ideological orientation of Labour's leaders. Only in 1945, after the exceptional conditions of the war economy and the disruption of the social fabric, was a decisive push in that direction actually achieved.

[113] This is most evident when governmental reform had direct electioneering goals, as in the early 1960s in Sweden and Norway, when both parties faced the issue of maintaining or gaining new middle-class voters while confronting extreme dissent from the left. In Sweden the socialist strategy of breaking down status divisions between manual wage earners and salaried employees, emphasizing issues that united the dependent labor force, concretized in a proposal for a comprehensive, government-administered retirement pension plan based on average earnings during the peak period of work life. In Norway, something very similar was set up at the beginning of the 1960s, in particular in 1963, when, in its radical program, the party proposed a state-administered service pension and a comprehensive plan for investments in the economically backward periphery of the country through capital funds to be created by employers' and employees' contributions toward the pensions. Lipset (1964: 287) and Rokkan (1966b: 103–104) have argued that the socialist plan was based on electoral considerations. Stijernquist (1966: 124–125) is less convinced.

[114] The relevance of long-term government tenure for hegemonic policies is seen in the different outcomes of British and Swedish post–World War II land planning. In Britain, the postwar Labour governments introduced three different systems for taxing the unearned land betterment gains in order to finance public holdings of land. The competitive strategy of the Conservatives was to promise to scrap the legislation and to restore a free-market logic in land, advising landowners to withhold their properties from the market until they were returned to office. Because the landowners expected the Conservatives to come back to office soon, these policies failed. By contrast, in Sweden, the success of the socialists' municipalization of all development land was based largely on the fact that those who controlled the resources in question could hardly hope to repeal such policies in the short term.

In France, the bureaucratic tradition and modernizing role of the state was as old and important as it was resistant to any partisan use of it.[115] Nothing is more telling than the contrast between the conditions of the Scandinavian red–green alliances of the mid-1930s and the French socialist Popular Front of the same years. While, on the one hand, there was a strong, united, and responsible labor movement, on the other hand, the CGT was prey to factional dissension. To the employers' acceptance of limitations on their authority in Scandinavia there was in France no corresponding adjustment to new relations with the labor movement. To the revival of industrial production and to an enduring governmental policy favoring collective bargaining in Scandinavia, there was in France little corresponding economic recovery under Blum's governments and no continuity of governmental social policy after him. Finally, Hitler's March 1936 march into the Rhineland, gambling on the inability of France and the United Kingdom to defend the peace of Versailles and Locarno, deprived the Popular Front and France altogether of the freedom to carry out those social experiments that could not be absorbed without social turmoil.

Only the Scandinavian socialists were able to ensure sufficient, consistent, and high-status tenure of office to mold their respective societies. Large, united socialist parties in Austria and the United Kingdom were confronted with adversaries too strong and cohesive to permit them to even attempt a similar strategy. Where an adversarial logic prevailed, as in the United Kingdom, socialists were offered high power in single-party-majority cabinets, but with little or no continuity. Where a coalescent *grosse Koalition* logic prevailed, as in Austria after World War II, continuity of tenure was achieved at the cost of policy control. In Italy, Germany, France, and Finland, deep cleavage lines both within the left and between the left and the other parties reduced enormously the governmental power of parties supported by 40% to 50% of the voters.

STATENESS, INSTITUTIONAL OPENNESS, AND THE CLASS CLEAVAGE

STATENESS, REPRESSION, AND LABOR RESPONSE

Between 1815 and 1870, most European countries oscillated from phases of internal repression to phases of relative toleration, and these phases were

---

[115] For the modernizing role of the French state, see the work of Legendre (1968) and Brown (1969). The antiparty and antipartisan ideology of the French higher bureaucracy is well documented in Suleiman (1974: 102–108).

uniformly determined by whatever threat was perceived by dynastic rulers. Repression increased almost everywhere in response to the 1820, 1830, and 1848 revolutionary movements, and, in general, revolutionary events in one country were met with preventive repression in the others. Repressive measures were eased in the intermediate periods. The dominant military powers (the Hapsburg Empire, Prussia-Germany, France, Russia) coordinated their efforts to crush national and social movements at home as well as in other countries under the general principle that changes in government and constitutional arrangements in one country actually threatened other European states and legitimized military restorative intervention.[116] Only boundary-safe countries (the United Kingdom) and marginal and strategically less significant areas (Scandinavia, with the partial exception of Denmark) were left free to follow their own development.

After 1870, this pattern of common response stopped, and there was increasing differentiation in the modalities and timing of repression and toleration. Even the response to the French Commune was not uniform. In any case, after 1860, and then after 1890, pure repression was used less and less as a means of social control.[117] Repression became more focused on the most dangerous internal groups and movements. Attempts became more sophisticated, aiming to remove the masses from the influence and leadership of radical groups and adopting ameliorative policies as an alternative form of social control. This change was dependent on the calculation that a purely repressive response was unlikely to solve the problem of lower-class demands and unrest and that the climate of internal turmoil weakened international status and prestige and was increasingly costly and destabilizing. The established European elite thus more frequently admitted and debated in parliaments that reform was necessary to quiet and calm the lower classes and thereby to strengthen the existing regimes. The Austro-Prussian and Franco-German wars had ended any unity of action on the part of major powers and started a new period of large-power continental confrontation during which internal turmoils were seen as possible assets/liabilities to be exploited by these powers, rather than as a challenge to a general and unitary principle of dynastic legitimate law and order.

While this was the general trend, some countries were clearly ahead, while others lagged behind. The variations in institutional openness and

---

[116] Typical of this logic was the Troppau Protocol of November 19, 1820, in which Prussia, Russia, and the Hapsburg Empire coordinated counterrevolutionary intervention to suppress Naples's *carbonari* revolution of the same year.

[117] Goldstein (1983: 345).

the switch in tactics of sociopolitical control were probably determined by the perception of the cost that the upper classes and dynastic rulers would have to pay for delaying reforms and toleration. These costs had an economic as well as a political dimension. Could the dominant economic interests be defended within a political climate of toleration? Politically, could such toleration allow the dominant political elites to retain their security of tenure and their hold on the polity? The other element of the equation was the cost of repression. The issue was, first, whether the means of repression were available and, second, if so, whether dominant elites and circles (king, bureaucracy, upper class) were sufficiently united to pursue that course of action.

Assuming (1) that the resources available for a repressive strategy were mainly represented by the stateness of the political processes, as indicated by the extractive and repressive resources of the dynastic-bureaucratic-political establishment, and (2) that the severity of the economic challenge depended on the homogeneity of economic interests, as indicated by the differentiation of dominant economic groups, we can try to interpret the level of the repression-toleration response as a function of these two aspects. To this end, in Table 7.15 I have cross-tabulated the level of early socialist movement repression to the stateness of the polity and to the level of internal differentiation of dominant economic interests. The latter is based on the strength of industrial and commercial interests, on the basis of the earliness of industrialization, and on the numerical presence of independents in commercial and industrial sectors over the total population of the independents.[118] The thrust of the argument is that the earlier the industrialization, the higher the differentiation of urban commercial and industrial interests versus the rural ones, and, therefore, the less likely a common and uniform dominant group perception of economic challenge. Finally, in Table 7.15, the cases in boldface refer to the early timing of the parliamentarization of the executive, as discussed in the second section of this chapter and presented in Table 7.4.

Bearing in mind the difficult intermediate cases of the United Kingdom, Ireland, and the Netherlands for the level of stateness, and that of Denmark for the introduction of responsible government, we can draw the following conclusions. If we consider, first, the cohesion levels of dominant interests, and therefore the likelihood that they will agree on supporting a

---

[118] I have taken 50% as the cutoff point. The average proportion of commercial and industrial independents over all independents in the 1890–1930 censuses is the following: United Kingdom = 81.5; Switzerland = 54.2; Norway = 35.9; Finland = 22.1; Belgium = 60.6; Denmark = 46.2; Switzerland = 30.3; the Netherlands = 60.3; Austria = 44.3; Ireland = 26.4; Germany = 54.5; France = 38.0; Italy = 25.8.

Table 7.15. *Stateness, strength of commercial/industrial interests, and repression*

		strength of commercial/industrial interests	
		low	high
level of repression	low	No De Sw	Sz UK Ir Ne Be
	high	Fi Fr It Au	Ge
		stateness	
		low	high
level of repression	low	Uk Ir Ne Sz No De Sw	Be
	high	Fi	Ge Fr It Au

Note: Cases of comparative early parliamentarization of the executive in boldface.

repression strategy, we can note that in early industrialized countries with strong industrial and commercial interests, antisocialist repression tended to be low with one exception, that of Germany. By contrast, in countries with later industrialization, where rural interests still tended to be predominant, we can observe two groups. On the one hand, Finland, Austria, France, and Italy showed a relatively high and frequent use of repressive measures. On the other hand, in the three Scandinavian countries – notwithstanding the overwhelming role of rural interests in the 1890–1930 period – no heavily repressive response was mounted against the socialist movement. The fit is far from satisfactory, although in the Scandinavian case one could mention that, much more than in the other late industrializing countries, rural interests were represented here by a very large class of small, independent farmers. The second point to be noted is that the level of repression before World War I is only partially related to the liberalization of the regime. Of the eight cases where we find relative toleration, six are parliamentarized regimes, but the French and Italian parliamentary regimes strongly repressed their internal opposition movements, and in particular the socialist one. In contrast, Denmark and Sweden still had constitutional monarchies that strongly resisted liberalization, but with low levels of internal repression.

The third consideration is that stateness is a much better predictor of the level of repression of early socialism than either the level of differentiation of economic interests or the liberalization of the regime. To be more precise, the role of stateness helps to reconcile the other two factors in explaining the degree of tolerance or repression of dominant groups. Of the five countries that had strong state resources at their disposal, four directed them against internal opposition. Unquestionably, there are important differences between France and Italy, as liberal regimes, and between Austria and Germany, as autocratic regimes, but these differences are less marked than the differences between this cell and the others. Of the eight countries I have classified as having low or modest stateness, only Finland has a pre-1918 history of significant socialist movement repression; Belgium is the only country with relatively high state resources whose political elite did not use them systematically to meet the claims of newcomers. Finland, however, is not really a deviant case because the repressive role was played there not by the Finnish state but by Russia. I have emphasized that the repression of Finnish aspirations (and not only of socialists claims) was due fundamentally to the security imperatives of imperial Russia and to the great political insecurity of its autocratic elite. Actually, in exporting repressive resources to Finland, the Russians inhibited the development of an autonomous Finnish state to such an extent that when the center collapsed, Finland was left with practically no state, but rather with a "praetorian"[119] society that continued for almost thirty more years to see the direct intervention in politics of armed groups and political organizations, with little or no mediating role of state institutions and apparatuses.

If we combine the different dimensions, our understanding of the variation improves and stateness emerges more clearly as the crucial necessary condition for a repressive strategy. Whenever high state resources were available to an established political elite, they were used against newcomers. The exception of Belgium can be explained by the combination of its early liberalization and high internal differentiation of interests between rural groups and powerful urban commercial and industrial interests. On the other hand, countries like Denmark and Sweden, even if they had a conservative and autocratic political structure and a predominance of rural interests, could under no circumstances afford a confrontation strategy against newcomers due to their sheer lack of resources. A typical example of this is the long hesitation of the Swedish crown and its military-aristocratic advisers on whether to yield to the Norwegian request for

---

[119] Huntington (1968: 95).

parliamentarization first and independence later. A repressive reaction was considered at length and was probably the preferred option, but considerations of affordable costs predominated, and in these calculations the low level of stateness in Sweden was probably the crucial variable.

We can therefore conclude that the level of repression tended to be higher (1) the higher the stateness of the polity, which made available the means; (2) the lower the parliamentarization of the regime, which defined the limits of utilization of these resources and also offered possible alternatives for control; and (3) the lower the internal differentiation of dominant interests, which made more likely their perception of a common threat and their agreement on a common response. The level of repression was therefore minimal in countries with little stateness, high interest differentiation, and early parliamentarization of government (the United Kingdom, Switzerland, and the Netherlands). In Austria, low interest differentiation and dynastic autocratic regimes coalesced to make the perception of the socialist challenge unacceptable, while the high stateness of the polity lowered the costs of repression. In autocratic regimes with low stateness (Denmark, Sweden, Finland, and Norway, which, however, had earlier liberalization), repression could be used systematically only if it rested on external resources (Finland); it was too costly if it involved the scanty internal repressive means of the state.

France, Italy, and Germany are more problematic cases. In the first two, high stateness combines with early liberalization and with a weak interest differentiation toward a considerable level of repression. In Germany, higher interest differentiation (concentrated, however, outside politically dominant Prussia) combines with high stateness and no liberalization toward a high repression strategy. The difficult prediction of the French and Italian cases, in particular, suggests a specification of the model. Whether repression or toleration was the outcome may also depend on whether a *political defense* of the dominant interests was possible. In other words, a toleration strategy was more likely if political checks could be expected at the electoral level. This, in turn, depended on something I discuss in the next chapter: the extent to which the structuring of the party system made feasible stable politico-electoral alliances capable of contrasting and checking the electoral influence of the socialists. The hypothesis is that when the lack of structuring of the party system and the persistent threat of illiberal and/or reactionary alternatives made the liberal elite insecure and unsafe, some repressive response was more likely (France and Italy). The same features may also be important in Germany, where industrialization, urbanization, and interest differentiation were considerable. The politico-electoral weakness of industrial and commercial interests can be added to the illiberal regime and the high stateness in explaining its repressive strategy (see the next chapter).

Political repression was one of the main determinants of early socialist movement behaviors and the instrument through which the state shaped the structure and fundamental forms of labor protest.[120] Support for this generalization can be found not only in my general analysis of cross-country differences, but also in a few cases of *within*-country differences. For instance, consider the different socialist ideological position of the 1890s and the defiant attitudes of the southern states of Bavaria and Württemberg – which had universal and equal suffrage, a higher level of respect of civil liberties, and socialist cooperation with the bourgeois parties – and the northern states of Prussia and Saxony – where discriminatory suffrage requirements and repressive controls remained the rule. Other supporting evidence is the sudden transformation of the Austrian Socialist Party in 1890, when the state became more tolerant and the socialists transformed their radical and militant positions almost overnight. Another example is the extreme militant tactics the Belgian socialists used to obtain essentially moderate political reforms, which were therefore soon abandoned once they were achieved. The state response was a decisive influence on the ideological and protest answer of the early socialist movements along the dimensions of moderation/radicalism, militance/acquiescence, and collective action/parliamentary action. The relationship with the states, however, was influenced not only by the timing and level of tolerance of the response, but also by the entire model of institutional integration of national socialism. Such a model can be approached in terms of sequences and levels of institutional integration.

SEQUENCE OF INSTITUTIONAL DEVELOPMENT

The smoothest institutional integration of new political movements is thought to occur when it starts to organize in the context of a liberalized but still undemocratized regime. In this case, the decisive step of suffrage democratization occurs when the party system is already structured and parliamentary control of the executive has been established. The *sequence* of the crucial steps of *suffrage extension, regime liberalization*, and *socialist party foundation* is therefore important. For Germany, Austria, and Italy, we have the usual problem of deciding when to set the date for the establishment of a final responsible government, but only in the case of Italy does this

---

[120] Geary (1981: 60–64).

decision actually modify the sequence. Belgium, the Netherlands, Norway, the United Kingdom (including Ireland), and Italy introduced the principle of cabinet responsibility and parliamentary rule before the decisive extensions of suffrage. Austria, Denmark, Finland, France, Sweden, and Germany introduced manhood suffrage before the effective liberalization and institutionalization of parliamentary rule. Socialist parties were founded and centralized nationally before responsible government was introduced in Austria, Denmark, Finland, Germany, and Sweden, while they were founded after responsible government establishment in Belgium, France, Italy, the Netherlands, and the United Kingdom. In Norway, responsible government and socialist political organization developed at the same time. Ireland is a more difficult case to classify. If one regards the preindependence period as one of colonial rule and considers secession as the crucial final step in Irish liberalization, then the three processes occur at more or less the same time. Finally, the socialist parties were founded before universal suffrage was granted in Austria, Belgium, France, Italy, the Netherlands, and the United Kingdom; in the other cases, they were founded afterward.

Combining these dates (see Tables 6.2 and 6.3, and 7.4) results in five basic sequences that are reported in Table 7.16. The first and fifth sequences represent two polar types in terms of institutional integration patterns. If socialist parties were finally organized within a liberalized government context and had time to consolidate before decisive steps were taken toward manhood suffrage – having time to channel new waves of lower-class voters – their integration into the existing political order was smoother. This should have resulted in a far less radical posture vis-à-vis the political order. It could also result, however, in a weaker mobilization capacity in this early phase. This is not surprising: Smoother institutional integration made it more likely that the working class would be represented by other nonsocialist elites for longer periods of time and made socialist parties less able to capitalize on the representation of demands for liberalization, while the slowly enlarged franchise provided for slower growth of their electoral strength.

In contrast, the fifth sequence can be regarded as the worst combination of integration steps. Socialist parties had to live for long periods under illiberal regimes, carrying the burden of the battle for both liberalization and democratization. This may have contributed to their "total opposition" temperament; but at the same time, it made them more likely to capitalize electorally on such battles, sometimes even beyond their lower-class social base of support. Because it was unlikely that the lower-class groups would find it acceptable to be represented by a liberal and radical elite whose

Table 7.16. *Socialist party foundation and democratization sequences (1880–1918)*

sequence	cases	mean left vote	
I: **RG**, then SPF, then US	Be, (It), Ne, No, Uk	11.4 (30)	12.2 (38)
II: **RG**, then US, then SPF	Ir, Sz	(no Irish data) 15.4 (8)	
III: US, then **RG**, then SPF	Fr	12.7 (6)	15.5 (18)
IV: US, then SPF, then **RG**	De	16.9 (12)	
V: **SPF**, then US, then RG (or **SPF** and US at the same time)	Au, Fi, Ge, Sw (It)	28.1 (26)	28.1 (26)

Note: RG = responsible government; US = universal suffrage (man); SPF = socialist party final foundation. The Italian case appears (in parentheses) in two sequences, according to whether the practice of RG is considered as achieved before fascism or only at its demise.

commitment to liberalization and democratization was, to say the least, ambiguous (see the next chapter), it is not surprising that these socialist parties were much stronger electorally than the first group.

The three intermediate sequences are more difficult to interpret. The Irish and Swiss sequence should be assimilated to that of the first group of countries for the key common feature of early responsible government. The French and Danish experiences have in common very early male suffrage. France is a unique case in which universal suffrage preceded the final (if not complete) liberalization of the regime by about thirty years, and both preceded the late consolidation of a national socialist party. Almost half a century of free and nonfree elections had taken place when the French socialists finally managed to set up a viable national political organization. On the whole, Table 7.16 shows how significant it was for the early electoral development and ideological orientation (see later) of the socialist movement whether the sequence of institutional development started with responsible government, with male universal suffrage, or with the early founding of the socialist party.

LEVELS OF INSTITUTIONAL CLOSURE/OPENNESS

From these data, it can be confirmed that the institutional integration pattern was important for the early ideological orientation and electoral mobilization capacity of the socialists. In other words, the smoother the institutional integration is, the less radical and electorally mobilized the

Table 7.17. *Institutional integration, socialist ideological orientation, and electoral mobilization (1880–1917)*

				repression		
				low	high	all
parlia- menta- rization	high 13.3 (56)	obstacles to representation	low 13.0 (29)	*trade unionism* UK Ir *reformist Marxism* Be Ne 8.7 (16)	*eclectic socialism* Fr 12.7 (6)	9.8 (22)
			high	*reformist Marxism* No Sz De 15.6 (28)	*eclectic socialism* It 15.3 (6)	15.5 (34)
	low 28.1 (26)		low	*reformist Marxism* Sw 23.1 (7)		23.1 (7)
			high 20.7 (53)		*orthodox Marxism* Au Fi Ge 29.9 (19)	29.9 (19)
	all			14.5 (51)	23.8 (31)	18.0 (82)

Note: Number of elections given in parentheses.

class cleavage is. I will pursue this line of argument in looking for further proof and refinement of this basic idea. Specifying the crude sequence pattern with information about the actual level of representation and repression improves our understanding of the differences among cases. To do so, the cases can be classified on the basis of the information discussed so far about the level of *parliamentarization* of the regime with the level of *repression* of the socialist movement and the use of *representational obstacles* against it (this last factor is obtained by combining the level of electoral underrepresentation [Tables 7.6 and 7.7] with the level of unfairness [Table 7.5] of the electoral system).[121] In Table 7.17, I present the cross-tabulation of the three main institutional integration variables. For each cell, row, and column, the average left electoral size is reported. In addition, cases are identified with their early ideological orientation, as discussed in Chapter 2.

The figures in the table point to the role of each variable as being

[121] The two aspects are separate because unfair mechanisms (for instance, indirect, nonsecret, or curia voting) did not necessarily result in underrepresentation. For instance, if the socialist party is very weak electorally, the level of underrepresentation will by definition be minor.

consistent with the theory of institutional integration advanced so far, as well as with a strong, coherent, cumulative interaction effect among the three variables. This justifies the claim that these variables should be considered as additive dimensions of the general problem of institutional integration. The pattern of this integration is strongly related to both the early ideological orientation of the socialist movement and to its early level of electoral mobilization. The cases I have identified as characterized by the persistence of an orthodox Marxist doctrine up to the 1920s and beyond all fall into the category of high-stateness countries, with high levels of state repression combined with low parliamentarization and high obstacles to representation. The socialist movement faced an adversarial state as well as a closed political system, and under these circumstances, the most coherent version of revolutionary Marxism persisted as a convincing interpretation of the relationship between the working-class movement, the state, and the market class conflict. Eclectic socialism, where radical syndicalism survived along with orthodox Marxism and with various forms of reformist socialism (and occasionally even trade unionist visions), was a sort of split answer on the part of the labor movement that was consistent with a contradictory environment. In Italy and France, the repression waged by high-stateness polities against the socialist movement – and in particular against its more radical components – was considerable. At the same time, however, the parliamentarization of the regime and the relatively low representation obstacles (even in Italy) left open within the socialist elite and rank and file the debate about what the best strategy for labor was. In none of the countries where parliamentarization was achieved early and repression was low did these ideological tendencies prevail. Either trade unionism or mild and pragmatic forms of Marxism existed where theoretical lip service to the orthodoxy was accompanied by the domestication of practices. Where, as in Norway or Switzerland, a radicalization phase emerged after World War I, it was short-lived and did not crystallize into long-term features.

At the same time, institutional integration also influenced the level of electoral mobilization of the left. From the end of the nineteenth century to the post–World War I period, in the eighty-two elections fought in Western Europe, the average electoral strength of the left was 18%; it was 14.5% in the fifty-one elections held in countries with low repression and 23.8% in the thirty-one elections fought in countries with high repression. The left had, on average, 13.3% of the vote in highly parliamentarized countries (fifty-six elections) versus 28.1% (twenty-six elections) in the countries that were still autocratic and 13% (twenty-nine elections) in countries with low obstacles to representation versus 20.7% in countries with high obstacles. If we contrast the group of countries/elections held under the best conditions of institutional representation (high parliamentarization, low obstacles to representation, and low political repression) to those held under the worst conditions (low parliamentarization, high obstacles, high repression), the difference ranges from 8.7% to 29.9% of the vote. In situations of low institutional integration, the socialist parties obtained four times more votes than in those of high institutional integration.

What is more striking is the almost perfect interaction effect within the cells of Table 7.17. Cases of high obstacles to representation show a stronger left than cases of low obstacles *for each level of parliamentarization*. The consistency of these data is striking. If the institutional sequence discussed before was a distal precondition of institutional integration, the three variables analyzed here point to concrete aspects of institutional integration, and they work much more effectively. Thus, the consistency of the results greatly strengthens the general hypothesis of the early discriminating role played by the pattern of institutional integration.

A further provisional test (a more thorough analysis will be performed in Chapter 9) of the importance of institutional integration aspects can be made by controlling their impact on the cohesion of the left and communist vote. According to the logic so far described, the class left developing in closed political systems or in mixed environments where regime liberalization was accompanied by persistent bureaucratic harassment should be more highly mobilized electorally, but also more internally radicalized, more prone to strategic and ideological dissent, and therefore more organizationally fragmented than the left developing in more open political systems. We can therefore control this hypothesis in the period between the world wars, when ideological and organizational fragmentation developed within the European left (see Chapter 3).

In the period between the world wars, then, the average communist vote was 8.7% (seventeen elections) in the countries with a history of closed institutional systems, 3.6% (thirty-two elections) in countries in an intermediate position, and 1.9% (eighteen elections) in countries with long periods of institutional openness. In the case of the radical left, and in particular the communists and Third International groups, what had already happened to the socialist family simply occured again: Where integration into the political system was early and good, their development was late and slow, while it was rapid and fast in the opposite cases. Once the socialists had gained a degree of legitimate access after World War I, even in formerly closed systems, memories of past closure and debates about the viability of such integration remained strong, and in many cases institutional-exclusion mechanisms worked against the new radical left in much the same way as they had against the socialists a few decades before.

Finally, let us consider how the institutional-integration setting influences the size of the left in various periods by inserting it into the general model developed for each of the macrofactors discussed in the previous chapters. To do so, I insert the index of *institutional closure*, as measured by the sum of the country ranking in the three dimensions of repression, parliamentarization, and representation obstacles,[122] into a linear regression together with social mobilization, cultural heterogeneity, the enfranchisement pattern, and the organizational variables. In Table 7.18, the beta coefficient and the variance explained by this five-variable model are reported for the whole period and for each phase. These data should be compared with those in similar tables in previous chapters.

I have argued that the more closed the institutional setting, the more likely early mobilization and a higher level of support for socialist movements. The difficulty of the political environment made socialist propaganda more convincing to voters and promoted early and close contacts between corporate and political socialist organizations. In contrast, an open institutional setting made the early political defense of working-class interests less necessary, the corporate and political organizations less closely

[122] The institutional closure rank ordering of countries is as follows:

parliamentarization rank ordering	representative obstacles rank ordering	repression rank ordering	Combined rank ordering
Au 13	Fi 13	Fi 13	Fi 37
Ge 12	Au 12	Ge 12	Au 36
Fi 11	Ge 11	Au 11	Ge 33
Sw 8	No 10	It 10	It 25
Dk 7	It 9	Fr 9	De 19
Ir 6	Sz 8	Be 6	Fr 19
Fr 6	De 6	Dk 6	No 18
It 6	Be 6	Sw 6	Sw 16
No 5	Fr 4	Ne 6	Be 15
Ne 4	Ne 3	Ir 4	Sz 14
Be 3	Sw 2	No 3	Ne 13
Sz 2	Ir 2	Sz 2	Ir 12
Uk 1	Uk 1	Uk 1	Uk 3

Table 7.18. *Social mobilization, cultural heterogeneity, enfranchisement, organizational model, institutional integration, and left vote (beta coefficients)*

	before 1918	1918-1944	1945-1965	1966-1985	whole period
social mobilization	.386012	.560953	.339572	.492554	.499429
cultural heterogeneity	-.239614	-.223145	-.299263	-.511827	-.189052
enfranchisement pattern	.276101	.137948	.154637	-.248677	.303261
organizational model	.048630	.400850	.297639	.127722	.150196
institutional integration	.542343	.384097	.068642	.294689	.173716
Rsq	68.1 %	78.3 %	60.5 %	76.9 %	71.9 %

connected, and the persistence of nonsocialist representation of the enfranchised working-class segments more likely. The figures in Table 7.18 offer new support for this interpretation. On the whole, the inclusion of institutional closure/openness in the model changes only marginally the overall explained variance with respect to the four-variable model discussed in reference to Table 6.16 in the previous chapter (70.1% versus 71.9%). However, its impact in different phases is important. For the period before 1918, the inclusion of institutional closure/openness increases the explained variance of 14% (from 54.7% with four variables to 68.1% with five variables). A considerable impact is also felt during the interwar period (from 71.1% to 78.3%), while this factor loses its weight after World War II, as expected. *In the first period, institutional openness/closure is the single best predictor of the earliness and level of left electoral mobilization.* It gains this role largely at the expense of the enfranchisement pattern. Thus, early cross-national differences in the mobilization capacities of the socialist movement should be related first of all to institutional differences in the liberalization/democratization processes.

The overall picture resulting from this five-macrofactor analysis is the following. The role of social mobilization is enhanced in each period, and this factor now proves to be the most stable systematic influence on the left vote once the other factors are accounted for. Cultural heterogeneity is similarly enhanced in its weight and remains a systematic factor both overall and for each period. The impact of the enfranchisement pattern is maximum at the early stage and declines over time. The organizational-aspects factor is unimportant in the first period, becomes dominant between the wars, and declines thereafter. Finally, institutional openness/ closure is dominant in the first period and is still important in the second, declining thereafter. In the two early periods, *institutional and organizational features determine the conditions of the impact of the underlying structural processes pertaining to social mobilization and cultural heterogeneity.* Finally, with the incorporation of the institutional and organizational aspects linked to the enfranchisement pattern, organizational consolidation, and institutional integration, I have developed a model whose performance is roughly the same in each period, ranging from two-thirds to three-quarters of the explained variance at the overall European level.

HOSTILITY TOWARD THE STATE AND IDEOLOGICAL ORIENTATION

In discussing institutional responses, the primary emphasis can be placed on the compatibility of the economic demands – in other words, on whether the established interests (landed and/or bourgeois) perceived a fatal threat to their economic position, possibly resulting in an alliance of landed and bourgeois interests against the working-class political movement. This line of argument induces a state/institutional response from the compatibility of class interests. It therefore assumes that the state was the guardian of such compatibility and that, by necessity, anticapitalism and antistate attitudes should combine and overlap. To test this view, one should be able to demonstrate that the variance in the repressive response is a function of economic interest compatibility and that in those countries that yielded more gracefully to pressures from below, the conflict of economic interests were more compatible than elsewhere. I have preferred to argue that *the definition of the conflict of interests as compatible or not was shaped by extraeconomic power relationships and bases.* The resources available for repression and the historical pattern of institutional development could be seen as independent variables in the definition and delimitation of the conflict of interests. That is to say, to rely on *state apparatuses*, to rely on *institutional obstacles and privileges* (upper houses, king, etc.), or to rely on *political control* (see the next chapter) was not always a choice.

Birnbaum has related the nature of the state to the development of the ideologies that structured the collective action of the working class: trade unionism, Marxism, and syndicalism.[123] His model is based on the inter-

---

[123] Birnbaum (1988). Katznelson (1985) has followed a similar logic, focusing on the state as a major source of variation in patterns of "class formation." The U.S. versus Britain

action of four variables: (1) the process of political centralization leading to a "minimal" state; (2) the fusion or differentiation between the state and the ruling class; (3) the industrialization coming from below or above; and (4) the open or closed nature of the bargaining process. Birnbaum relates these variables to the ideological response of labor. In Germany, the consolidation of a strong state together with the fission of the state with the dominant aristocratic class and industrialization from above[124] in a nonliberalized regime, produced a dominant Marxist ideology that was stronger than that of anarchism. In France, the state was differentiated from the ruling class and bargaining was open, leading to a predominance of syndicalism over Marxism. Finally, in the United Kingdom, weak structural differentiation of the state and industrialization from below, together with a liberalized regime, tended to produce a predominance of trade unionism as the ideological response of the working class. Anarchism, in this light, established itself in countries ruled by strongly dominant regimes, such as France, Italy, and Spain. The emphasis on selected well-known cases gives Birnbaum's argument an ideal-type flavor. The ideal type of strong state is defined in reference to concepts such as "differentiation," "autonomy," and "institutionalization" that are difficult to operationalize; and in the final analysis, the classification of the British versus the French versus the German experiences is based largely on common knowledge. This makes it difficult to apply the scheme to other European countries, which are not dealt with or are only occasionally mentioned as examples of intermediate or mixed cases.

I have tried to generalize the classic argument of a British versus a continental stereotype to explain within-continental variations. To avoid the tyranny of the large countries and of pattern cases, I have developed indicators to locate the whole range of European experiences along dimensions of a model of institutional integration that can account for the fateful overlap between the class cleavage and the antistate cleavage. Stateness and dominant-interest differentiation represented varying conditions for a possibly repressive response by the dominant classes. The openness/closure of the institutional system was an intervening element that made a repressive strategy possible or not, balanced it in some cases, and reinforced it in others. A further element should be added to this picture: the availability of a political control over the socialist movement that permitted its con-

---

contrast, however, describes the British working-class formation in terms that could apply to the whole European experience and that are therefore of little use in differentiating within Europe.

[124] Industrialization is seen by this author as an intervening variable. Birnbaum (1988: 79).

tainment via politico-electoral parliamentary means (rather than via direct repression or institutional privilege). This required liberalization and favorable conditions of structuring for nonsocialist parties and for the party system in general. Repression and institutional exclusion were more likely the less viable a strategy of political containment was. This last component of the labor environment will be analyzed in the next chapter. The factors I have placed in the picture so far are reported in Table 7.19, together with the ideological outcomes with which they are associated.

The issue raised in this discussion is *the extent to which the class cleavage, whose structural roots were primarily in social antagonisms in the market, came to be ideologically hostile to the state.* It is often argued that "the formation of demands related to the working condition and the organization of various forms of workers' action inevitably pushed the workers into conflict not only against the employers, but also against the state."[125] Marx was, of course, consciously aiming at this combined opposition because he wanted to transform an emancipation movement into a revolutionary movement. However, there was nothing inevitable in this link; it was not necessarily the case that working-class political mobilization would come into conflict with the state. In terms of hostility toward the state, the European experience is far more varied than a British versus continental pattern or a French versus German pattern would indicate. In addition to countries where the state was strong, there were others where it was far less visible or even absent. The use of the state apparatus was also different. The relationship of national movements with their respective national states was therefore different, and the fusion of class feeling with antistate feeling depended on the concrete conditions of state involvement in their emancipation attempt.

The opposition strategies of national dominant forces toward the emerging socialist movements in the last twenty years of the nineteenth century and the first twenty years of the twentieth gave rise to two possible reactions: (1) to help and favor the success of the Marxist identification between the class enemy (the employers) and the state (the class nature of the state) or (2) to recognize that the struggle for socialism was the same as the struggle for a democratic state, that is, for state democratization. The political integration of a social group into an existing political order involves cultural elements and is ultimately expressed through a set of beliefs and attitudes toward the political system. The development of these cultural traits results from organizational activities and the learning experiences concerning the response to these activities. The extent to which the new actors felt they could achieve their aims within the given

[125] Valenzuela (1981: 448).

Table 7.19. *The institutional integration syndrome and predominant ideological orientation*

	state-ness	repres-sion	parliamen-tarization	institutional sequence	representa-tion inequalities	executive entry	average governmen-tal power	early ideological orientation
Au	high	high	late	party formation democratization liberalization	high	early (late)	1698	orthodox revolutionary Marxism
Ge	high	high	late	party formation democratization liberalization	high	early	630	orthodox revolutionary Marxism
Fi	low	high	late	party formation democratization liberalization	high	early (late)	1887	orthodox revolutionary Marxism
It	high	high	early ?	party formation democratization liberalization ?	high	late	280 ?)	ideological eclecticism
Fr	high	high	early	democratization liberalization party formation	low	late	816	ideological eclecticism
Dk	low	low	late ?	democratization party formation liberalization	high	early	3304	nonorthodox moderate Marxism
Sw	low	low	late	party formation democratization liberalization	low	early	4612	nonorthodox moderate Marxism
Be	high	low	early	liberalization party formation democratization	low	early	2374	nonorthodox moderate Marxism
Ne	mid	low	early	liberalization party formation democratization	low	late	1525	nonorthodox moderate Marxism
No	low	low	early	liberalization party formation democratization	high	early	3687	nonorthodox moderate Marxism
Sz	low	low	early	liberalization party formation democratization	high	late	-	nonorthodox moderate Marxism
Ir	mid	low	early	liberalization democratization party formation	low	late	365	trade unionism
UK	mid	low	early	liberalization party formation democratization	low	early	1981	trade unionism

institutional structure has been indirectly deduced in this chapter from the process of the institutional integration of their political movements. Institutional integration influences the extent to which political and corporate movements are inclined to concentrate their pressure on the government and on employers through *electoral, parliamentary, and judicial means* or else to use other resources and conflict arenas that are extrainstitutional. The dominant institutional pattern, therefore, defines a series of opportunities and constraints of the political and social actors and influences their acceptance of the pattern of political competition prevailing within such a structure.

Only when the almost universal economic and ideological conflict with employers overlapped with an equally intense confrontation with the state apparatus and the closed major political institutions did the working-class movement become more radical and revolutionary, concentrate more heavily on extrainstitutional activities, develop its isolationist and conspiratorist nature, and finally find a convincing ideological guide in radical versions of socialism (Marxism and Leninism). The more a closed political system was, characterized by high stateness of its processes, presenting itself as a moral and teleological entity independent of weakly differentiated and weakly self-represented societal interests, the more radical ideologies appeared to be theoretically persuasive, reflecting reality in an appropriate manner and providing convincing strategies to overcome it. Thus, whenever state machinery was used consistently against the socialist movement, opposition feelings were translated directly into deep antistate opposition that combined with the social and economic alienation of the laboring classes to produce the explosive mixture of political and social alienation that is conducive to radical responses and organizational divisions at the same time.

The persistence of nonresponsible government and an executive separated from the parliamentary arena and guarding other traditional institutions, meant that opposition political movements cemented their links with social groups and corporate-interest organizations and that the basic conflict of all of these groups and organizations focused on those extrainstitutional power bases that prevented the parliamentarization of government. When the resources and the willingness to repress the socialist movement made this repression viable, deep divisions usually appeared within the movement – divisions concerning whether the values sought could be achieved within the existing institutional framework – and profound, long-lasting splits of the working-class organizations along radical versus moderate lines occurred. Thus, moderate calls for a peaceful and piecemeal insertion postulated that institutional channels were open enough to allow for democratic changes, while radical arguments for a revolutionary breakthrough assumed that the institutional regime would never allow them to compete fairly. In accepting the costs of repression, the established elite implicitly assumed that the demands of the new claimants could in no way be accommodated within the existing order.

Intermediate cases, where a low differentiation of dominant interests combined with high stateness to foster a repressive strategy and where, at the same time, the openness of the institutional system softened this strategy and seemed to offer alternative future opportunities, tended to result in ideologically divided and eclectic socialist movements, as in Italy and France. In *L'Armée Nouvelle* (1910), Leon Blum dealt with the concept of the state, affirming – in contrast to Marx and the French Guesdesists – that not only did the proletarians have a *patrie* and need to defend it, but also that the state was not the instrument of class domination but a possible arbiter among the classes, which "n'exprime pas une classe: il exprime les rapports de classe, c'est a dire les rapports des leur forces." In so doing, Blum reached a conclusion that was not controversial in many European countries, where verbal agreement with the Marxist programs and orthodoxy had never been fed by profound hostility toward the state. Cases of low or medium interest differentiation and low stateness, unable to afford a cohesive repression response but able to resist the opening up of the institutional system, tended to produce formal Marxist orthodoxy; these cases, however, were accompanied by constant breaks in such orthodoxy in practical everyday political life, as in the Scandinavian countries.

CLEAVAGE STRUCTURES

In addition to resting on repression and institutional closure, opportunities for socialist political control depended on the development of electoral-politico-parliamentary blocs capable of enforcing the political domestication of the socialist movement. Many studies stress the importance of early alliances among major economic and social groups, assuming that the nature of the political regime developed from the logic of the subtending *socioeconomic coalitions*.[1] Instead, I place more emphasis on the logic that *political coalition* results from specific forms of political representation developed by the main social groups during the phase of the party-system structuring. In this view, large social groups do not make coalitions or form alliances unless they are able to develop forms of political self-representation.

This chapter examines the class cleavage in the light of the process of structuring of the national party systems or, more precisely, structuring stable sets of coalitions and alliances among social groups *and* political organizations. Within each national context, I discuss the following:

1. Which other social movement, if any, preceded or accompanied the socialist movement and what its political nature was (antiestablishment, nationalist, popular self-representational, or merely institutional, such as the opposition of the Catholic clergy).
2. What cleavage issues were already politicized when the labor movement entered the electoral race; what kinds of political parties, if any,

---

[1] Moore (1966), Luebbert (1991), and Rueschemeyer, Huber, and Stephens (1992).

were already active in electoral and partisan recruitment; what political alignments and national coalitions were already established among the forerunners and to what extent these reduced the range of options open to the socialists.

3. What relationship the incipient socialist organizations established with these forerunner political movements and parties – forms of delegated political representation, formal alliances, or unstable short-term cooperation.

This chapter is developed on the basis of two central hypotheses. The first is that the earlier and more encompassing the organizational mobilization of most sectors of the community was through *non-* or *pre-socialist* political movements, the earlier the socialist entry was but the lower was its capacity to mobilize. Early nonsocialist political mobilization preempted later socialist mobilization by fixing and strengthening political identities, which progressively narrowed the potential market for the support of the latecomers. The second hypothesis is that the alliance choices and alignments made by the early insiders reduced the alliance alternatives and opportunities available to latecomer outsiders and therefore significantly shaped their choice of allies and adversaries among both social groups and political organizations. To anticipate the main thesis in brief, class mobilization should be regarded as a *residual* process whose coordinates were established by the previous mobilization opportunities and the moves of other social groups and sociopolitical cleavages. Instead of providing the determining factor of political alignments in Western European party systems, class cleavage was dependent on such alignments. Only when circumstances prevented, delayed, or made impossible any form of nonclass mobilization did class become the dominant force and take on predominant importance in elections.

OPPORTUNITIES FOR SOCIAL AND POLITICAL ALLIANCES

In a model of political mobilization in which social position is easily converted into social and political consciousness and collective action, the main social groups would tend toward self-representation and would refuse to be represented indirectly by other sociopolitical elites. When this occurs, the square of social groups and that of the political movement reported in Figure 8.1 tend to coincide, with the peasant world organizing an agrarian

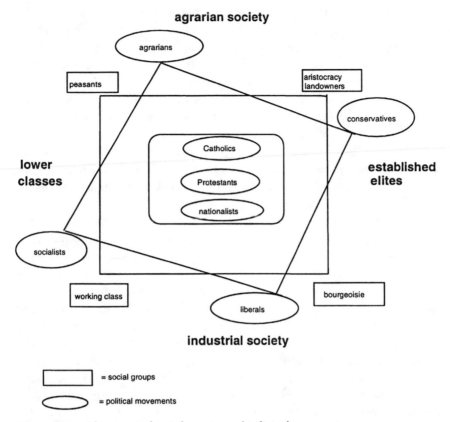

Figure 8.1. Alignment of social groups and political movements.

party; the aristocracy, the landowners, and the dynastic bureaucratic interests organizing a conservative defense of their position; the bourgeoisie expressing its vision of society through a liberal party; and, finally, the working class endowing itself with a socialist movement. In this imaginary case, the working class enters politics in a political world and party system that are already socially well structured.

This perfect coupling is not realistic, however, even in a historical context in which socioeconomic interests tend to predominate and shape the vision of the world. The representation of agrarian interests and society (the upper part of my social group square) against external forces may predominate over the internal division of the agrarian population, and peasants and landowners may find their positions very close in the defense of common interests. On the other side of the square, the working class and the bourgeoisie, who are both representative of the industrial society, may, in an early phase, share interests and forms of representation for quite a while. If we read Figure 8.1 differently, along the axis that opposes the established social and political elite with the lower classes, common interests may exist between parts of the peasantry and the working-class movement, on the one hand, and between the bourgeoisie and the landowners and aristocratic interests, on the other. The picture becomes more complicated if, in the process of political mobilization, forces act with no clear relation to the main agricultural or urban established or emancipationist social groups. Denominational mobilization, as well as nationalist mobilization, had fewer clear social references and were able to drain support from all the most important social groups, as well as to come to represent one of them predominantly.

The diagram in Figure 8.1 is useful, as it simplifies the alliances that were important for the incipient working-class movement. Fundamentally, its political representatives had two social groups and political movements with which to deal. Depending on the circumstances and opportunities, they could establish political links with the liberal bourgeoisie or, alternatively, strengthen their links with the peasants and sectors of the agricultural world. In other cases, they had to come to terms with mobilized denominations. They could also join national independence fronts and coalitions when the problem of national-independence was not solved. Finally, we can envisage a case in which the socialist movement could not establish any stable alliances with other social groups, either because they were not self-representational or because the socialist movement was itself divided on such alliances and was unable to make a stable choice.

The *alliance* of the working class *with liberal forces* against conservatives (1) presupposed a relatively strong, autonomous politically organized urban and/or rural bourgeoisie; (2) had as the main point of its program liberalization of the regime (if this was delayed) and the defense of the rights of the socialist movement and its organizational conquests; and (3) had as its main weakening element the growing industrial conflict (if urban interests predominated).

In contrast, the *alliance with agrarians* (1) presupposed a strong and independent peasantry, capable of self-representation and possessing antiestablishment and countercultural traits; (2) the main points of its program were political liberalization/democratization and the exchange of policy support in respective sectors of interest; and (3) the main problem was the compromise on agricultural protectionism and the defense of small-property owners in the countryside.

The *alliance with religious dissenting movements* (either Catholic or Protestant, where Catholicism was not dominant) (1) required their being sufficiently strong and antiestablishment to offer a basis for such an alliance; (2) the main points of its program were social policies and economic interventionism; and (3) the major problems were state secularization and high competition for lower-class representation.

The *alliance with nationalist movements* (1) presupposed that the mobilization of the left was taking place parallel to the struggle for nation building and national independence; (2) was based on the common interest in national independence from foreign control; and (3) the main problems were the political distinctiveness of the socialist movement within such an alliance and its internal differentiation once independence was achieved.

The *no-alliance option* (1) required either that no real structuring of the party system took place, so that no reference point could be offered to the socialists, or that the party-system structuring would create a political bloc that was strong and cohesive enough to do without the socialists; (2) it helped to maintain doctrinal purism and ideological and organizational unity when this was not a default strategy for movements so internally divided as to be unable to choose alliances or to be credible allies; and (3) its main cost was limited policy influence and, perhaps, delayed executive access.

All alliance options had some advantages and disadvantages. Whether these were based on short-term political goals or on policy exchange, they blurred party images, forced ideological compromise, increased gaps between doctrine and practice, and increased internal divisions and their opportunity costs. They always demanded a high investment in order to keep the socialist movement cohesive and united and, in many cases, were crucial in determining its internal political fragmentation. These choices and opportunities were not fixed permanently and changed substantially between the end of the nineteenth century and the 1930s. No significant changes occurred after that date until the 1970s.

In the following sections, I discuss the European cases and focus attention more on the political movements than on the social groups. Choosing classes or social groups as main actors means overlooking the fact that they are rarely sufficiently united and coherent to allow the recognition of their political preferences without making references to the political elite's interpretation and articulation of them. By the same token, such an approach frequently underestimates the extent to which the organized political elite can contribute to the definition of the preferences, interests, and demands of a social group.

EARLY POLITICAL MOBILIZATION AND THE ROLE OF LIBERALISM AND THE BOURGEOISIE

COOPERATION WITH LIBERALISM

In terms of opportunities for alliance with liberal forces, a clear dividing line separates the northern European countries – Scandinavia and the United Kingdom – from other continental nations. In these countries, (1) the entry of socialism and the final structuring of the party system were preceded by the existence of significant popular, politically conscious movements; (2) although British liberalism was mainly urban, commercial, and industrially based and Scandinavian liberalism was more farmer-based, such middle-class movements were largely self-representational, that is, they did not delegate political representation to other sociopolitical elites; (3) the liberal–labor alliance was a key early feature of party-system formation and lasted for long periods; (4) in all cases, the tensions within liberalism during or immediately after the phase of cooperation with the socialists eventually split the liberals (in 1905 in Denmark; from 1922 to 1923 in Sweden; after World War I in the United Kingdom; with continuous split-ups in the 1930s in Norway); (5) as a consequence, groups with liberal tendencies, even when they opposed socialist-led governments, maintained an internal radical tradition that occasionally surfaced and made their relationships with the respective conservative parties difficult.[2]

In the United Kingdom, Chartism was the most important presocialist movement. Unions began to organize and develop after the Chartist failure between 1830 and 1848 to obtain universal manhood suffrage, annual parliaments, and the secret ballot. Similarly important was the middle-class Anti-Corn Laws League. This movement was so efficient in organizing middle-class opinion and so successful in achieving its representation that "its methods were later adopted by the political parties."[3] In Sweden, the nineteenth century was densely populated with autonomous and self-representational religious, social, and political movements made up of the middle classes and the peasantry. For example, the Free Church Movement wanted to convert individuals to a Christian life and create a Christian society, while the temperance movement fought to save individuals from the excesses of alcohol and to build a sober society. Although the extension

[2] On Scandinavian liberalism, I have relied on Berglund and Lindström (1978).
[3] On the development of early opposition in Great Britain, the best source is Potter (1966: 26).

of their mobilization is subject to debate among Swedish historians, it was very high by any comparative European standard.[4]

Norway also has a long history of dissenting popular movements, particularly peripheral ones, whose development and success demonstrate the low level of repression and high tolerance by the central authorities already discussed.[5] The earliest of these movements was the successful peasant protest against the head tax and in favor of the return of this money by the state (1765). Again, in the first half of the nineteenth century, what was known as "Hauge's movement" successfully mobilized large sectors of the peasant population. Hauge was a lay preacher of peasant parentage who criticized the official, urban-based, secularized clergy; challenged the traditional and conventional doctrines and preachings of the national church; and organized a movement of traveling lay preachers, primitive cooperative ventures, agricultural communities, and colonies in territories still not exploited. His movement established the first elements of a nationwide political organization and raised the political consciousness of the peasantry and rural middle classes, which contributed to the political detachment of the rural groups from the central establishment.[6] Although there are similarities to British Methodism and to the theology of acceptence of German Pietism, Haugianism was much stronger and more aggressive toward the national Norwegian Church, which labeled him a "Jacobin."

Equally important for the lower classes was the Thrane movement. This was not an early or protosocialist movement, but it was certainly a class movement; intellectuals were totally absent from its membership, and its social base was composed of a few industrial workers, peasants working for the rich landowners, and small, impoverished landowners from the west coast. It was a forerunner of the trade union movement, active in organizing strikes, advocating revolutionary aspirations, and making general suffrage claims. Its organizational strength was remarkable for the times; between 1848 and 1854, 273 associations were formed with about 20,854 members. It took the Labor Party twenty-three years to reach the same level of membership that the Thrane movement had at its best. Finally, the "Friends of the Peasants Movement" (1865–1879) was a more periphery-against-the-center movement and was the first modern political move-

---

[4] Stråth (1988a: 32–34) estimates that one-third of the population took part in these movements.
[5] See Lafferty (1971: 117–119).
[6] On Hauge and "Haugism", see Derry (1968: 122–124).

ment in Norway, with a strong press, organization throughout the whole territory, and 21,000 members. It gradually fused with the urban liberals to form the first national Norwegian party (Venstre) to push successfully for parliamentary government (1884).[7]

In Denmark, similar popular movements were less important than in the other two Scandinavian countries because the native landed aristocracy was stronger.[8] However, Danish liberals also organized as an uneasy alliance between urban intellectual radicals and rural interest groups. In the history of the liberal movement, there always had been strong tension between such rural interests and the rather radical urban and intellectual wing, and when the agrarian component became dominant in 1905, the party split, giving rise to an unusually radical "social" version of liberalism, the Radical Liberal Party, which remained a loyal ally of the socialists for a long time.

These movements in Scandinavia had Puritanism, egalitarianism, and antielitism in common; they regrouped both their urban and rural lower- and middle-class sections into an opposition; and their antiestablishment ideology was, if not democratic, at least popular and egalitarian. They offered an ideal basis for alliance and support to the developing working-class movement, which, in the 1880s, thereby joined an already existing popular antiestablishment tradition. Thus, socialists, while making a different political offer, found a receptive audience. In Denmark and Sweden, it was belated liberalization and parliamentarization that fostered close political cooperation and common mobilization between the liberals and the socialists. In Norway, after the repression of the Thrane movement, government officials and the bourgeoisie tended to form labor associations such as labor clubs, cooperative societies, and permanent-assistance funds, with the goal of integrating the working class into the liberal regime. Thus, about half of the industrial workers in 1885 were members of an insurance association.[9] In the 1880s, these associations were rapidly politi-

---

[7] Rokkan (1967) has depicted these and other movements (the *teetotal* movement, the religious layman's movement [mission], and the vernacular [*nynorsk*] movement) movements as mainly territorial and countercultural. An economic explanation can also be advanced, relating to an important inequality dimension between regions: The southern and western regions had a relatively egalitarian agricultural structure. In areas with a more marked inequality structure (the north), conflicts focused on the defense of privilege and inequality (Conservative Party) and the reduction of inequality (Labor Party).

[8] In Finland and Norway, industrial poverty and semicolonial dependence almost completely prevented the formation of a native aristocracy. For a discussion of the strength of the native aristocracy in Scandinavia countries see G. Therborn (1977: 3–41).

[9] Terjesen (1990: 113).

cized and taken over by the Liberal Party, which, in turn, handed them over to the Social Democrats during the following two decades. In 1893, Venstre still had considerable working-class support with twenty-five collectively affiliated unions in Oslo. In the elections of the 1890s, the Norwegian Socialist Party (DNA) polled fewer votes than its members, as most of the enfranchised workers voted for Venstre, whose more liberal-social tendencies had begun to dominate the party in 1891. Not only the franchise enlargement but also the majority of social policies up to 1914 were supported and pushed through by Venstre, as the Social Democratic Party had no influence on policy until that date.[10] On the one hand, the national question and opposition to union with Sweden, which dominated the political debate up to 1905, acted as an obstacle to the early mobilization of the labor movement. On the other hand, many of the reforms carried out – including early universal male suffrage in 1898 – can be regarded as concessions to win the labor vote that Venstre needed to achieve parliamentary power and dissolve the union with Sweden.

However, there is an important difference between the way in which the peasantry in Sweden and Denmark was mobilized and integrated into the national political community and, as a consequence, the way in which the rural middle classes came to relate to the socialist movement. In Denmark, the long-lasting absolutist rule and the early universal male enfranchisement created a profound conflict between the mobilizing peasantry and their landowners (the most powerful in all the Scandinavian countries) and urban-bureaucratic antagonists. In Sweden, instead, the tradition of estate representation eased the entry and domestication of the upper echelons of the peasantry, resulting in a less deep conflict than that of Denmark and more varied alliances between early peasant representatives and other forces. Clearly, the political alliance between Venstre and the socialists was widely discussed and criticized within the Danish Socialist Party. The renewal of the alliance occasionally led to dissent and even splits, although, in the end, it remained a central pillar of the party's strategy. Between 1903 and 1910, the alliance with Venstre became more difficult, as common political goals were limited and growing conflicts over economic policy were emerging. The fact that at that time the agrarian party split and the newly born left-wing (and antimilitarist) Liberal Party became a new potential ally was a great asset for the socialists. In Sweden, the more integrated stratum of the peasantry joined with the urban bourgeoisie to form a moderate or even right-wing protectionist

[10] See Kuhnle (1978: 9–35).

nationalist party. Only later did the peasant component break away to form a specifically agrarian party.[11]

In the United Kingdom, the basis for the alliance was different; it was not based on the request to liberalize the regime, but rather on the defense of the unions.[12] The final separation between labor and liberalism, a long process, was completed only in the 1920s. The early liberal orientation of the British working class and trade unions rested on a structure of social relations that, at the local level, reflected the "paternal and co-operative basis of class relations."[13] The employers influenced the social and political life of their communities and were often voted for and supported by their workers. As the alliance was made among urban social groups, progressive political separation was fostered by economic crises and the harsher employment and wage policies of employers, as well as by the growing strength of trade union strikes. The early liberal political representation of the working class was progressively undermined by the growing number of competing candidates at the local level and in different situations of local compromise or conflict. However, at the national level, the close cooperation of Labour and the Liberals continued until World War I. Indeed, the independent identity of the Labour Party was explicitly declared by the Labour Representative Committee only in 1899, with a close vote and little enthusiasm for it. From 1906 on, Labour MPs acted as a wing of the Liberal Party in Parliament. Until 1910, the Liberal Party was the largest and most representative party of the working class, and up to 1914, when the break with the Liberals at the local level had already been completed, at the national level Labour was unable to win a seat if it was not allied with them.[14]

The final break with liberalism occurred in 1918, when the Labour Party organized itself nationwide and adopted a constitutional commitment to collective ownership. Some authors argue that the decline of liberalism and the rise of Labour should not be attributed to a "class' dynamic." In other words, the fact that Labour was a working-class party did not necessarily imply that, when the working class was given the right to vote, the class cleavage would become dominant and the Liberal vote would inevitably shrink and eventually be swallowed up.[15] Some (liberal) historians have argued that the Liberal Party declined from 1918 on not

[11] For these notes, see Rokkan (1970g: 67–68).
[12] On the British Liberal–Labor relationship in this phase see, Breuilly (1992), which, despite its title, deals exclusively with Britain and Germany.
[13] Price (1990: 19).
[14] For details, see Luebbert (1991: 24).
[15] Matthew, McKibbin, and Kay (1976: 723–752).

because of the inevitable negative social changes and transformations, but due to its internal political divisions and splits during the war period (between Asquith and Lloyd George in 1916), which prevented the party from offering an adequate response to the trade unions' requests.[16] This thesis[17] emphasizes crucial political factors in conjunction with the majority electoral system. The Liberals did not come to believe in proportional representation until the 1920s, when they were on a downward slide, and by then it was too late to make electoral reform a condition of their support for a Lib–Lab governmental coalition.[18] A further Liberal attempt to achieve electoral reform in exchange for governmental support was made between 1929 and 1931 during another minority Labour government. Once again, there was resentment within the Labour rank and file about this, and no agreement could be reached between the two parties.

If proportional representation (PR) had finally become law after World War I, as it had in most other European countries, the Labour Party might well have taken about 20%–30% of the vote and would have failed to establish a corporate relationship with the trade unions and the working class. In the intense electoral period between 1918 and 1931 (six elections), *notwithstanding the plurality formula,* the United Kingdom had a three-party system, with several Liberal splinter groups. Moreover, during the 1920s, nonparty candidates still enjoyed considerable success. On the left, too, the Independent Labour Party and the Communists were not just mere labels. In 1924, the Labour Party became the second party in terms of number of seats, but it surpassed the Liberals in electoral strength only in 1931. Even after World War II, the Liberal resurgence of the 1960s, and later the Social Democratic Party (SDP) and Liberal alliance, and the significant advances of the Scottish and Welsh nationalist parties in the 1970s, are witness to the fact that the two-party structure was and still is maintained by the mechanisms of the electoral-plurality law. In the 1920s, in a comparative perspective, Labour's strength was relatively modest and very much in line with my expectation that early and gradual industrialization, a liberalized context and an open institutional system, and possible political allies for the representation of strong industrial unions are far from favorable conditions for the strong electoral mobilization of the working-class movement. It is therefore not unlikely that the decline of British liberalism was due to its internal divisions following World War I, which

---

[16] For this thesis, see Clarke (1971); for a summary of the historiography debate on this issue, see Ball (1987: 82–86).

[17] Which is not unchallenged in the literature. The historical analysis of British electoral alignments made by Wald (1983) does not support this line of interpretation.

[18] Butler (1990: 457).

prevented it from establishing PR and thus maintaining a longer and larger representation of the working-class world.

In conclusion, the strong industrial trade union movement in the United Kingdom was successful in fighting and isolating independent working-class movements that attempted to define politics in terms of class rather than in terms of union interests, thanks to the political accommodation and representation offered by the Liberals. This helped to shape British socialism in a liberal democratic mood but also made it politically weak. But for the divisions of the Liberal Party in the World War I years and the plurality system, the British Labour Party – deprived of the crucial asset of leading a political battle for the liberalization and democratization of an autocratic regime—would probably have remained a party of medium size and importance.

The lack of ideological rigidity in these northern European socialist movements was therefore due either to an early alliance experience with other popular liberal forces in opposition to the established elite or, more typically in the United Kingdom, to delegation of political representation to these forces until well into the twentieth century. This delegation of political representation helped the movement to concentrate on industrial and typical working-class issues without also having to focus on radicalizing and divisive debates about the goals and tactics of direct political action. The enormous differences between the United Kingdom and Scandinavia in industrial development did not prevent a lasting and profound Lib–Lab alliance in both countries, fostered by experiences of common participation in early popular movements. In the United Kingdom, the Liberals succeeded in integrating their own interests with those of workers' associations until the end of the nineteenth century. In Scandinavia, although the socialist parties organized as an independent political force long before the Labour Party did in the United Kingdom, this alliance lasted even longer. However, the links of the socialists to early liberal forces were broken once the main political goals that held them together (liberalization, dissolution of the union with Sweden, democratization and universal suffrage, and defense of strong union interests) were achieved, and in all these cases this final break led to the fragmentation and restructuring of the liberal forces there.

THE NONCOOPERATION CASES: BELGIUM, THE NETHERLANDS, AND SWITZERLAND

In contrast to the Scandinavian countries, Belgium, the Netherlands, and Switzerland provide the model of an early mismatch between social groups and political movements. The liberalization of their regimes was early (as in the United Kingdom), but in none of these cases can one find any signs of early coalition or delegated representation between the liberals and the socialist movement united against entrenched conservative privileges. Early mobilization soon made the liberals opposed to any forms of denominational mobilization.

In Belgium and the Netherlands, the nineteenth century, and in particular the period between 1848 and 1917, was not a liberal period, but rather one in which the liberal–conservative conflict was dominated by state–church relations and conservatism had a rather traditionalist outlook as a result of the early denominational antiliberal mobilization. Liberals and Catholics had dominated the politics of Belgium since the founding of the nation, first in a grand coalition and later with growing adversarial competition. The 1830 "revolution" against William I, the king of the Dutch–Belgian entity created by the Congress of Vienna, was fought by a pool of Catholics and the liberal opposition; the former were mainly motivated to defend Catholicism from Protestant rule; the latter, although sympathetic to the anticlerical stand of the dominant Dutch circles, were mainly motivated by antiliberal restrictions and by fear of the dominance of the Dutch language over an almost entirely French-speaking Belgian elite. This coalition lasted until 1846, to be followed by the 1846–1884 alternation of liberal and Catholic governments, with liberals generally in a dominant position. The liberal cabinets of this period and the battles on the subject of religion at school between 1878 and 1884 intensified the need for a structured Roman Catholic political party. From 1884 on, there followed thirty years of Catholic cabinets and Catholic supremacy. Consequently, party machines developed early: The liberal–Catholic split of the Unionist Alliance in 1857 had led both the liberals and the Catholics to start canvassing the support of the lower classes. The Catholics started to build a special party structure in the 1860s (as in Germany) and in 1884 formally created the party, although it had already been organized in a loose network since the 1860s. The Liberal Party also already had a precocious national structure by 1846.[19]

The Belgian party system was therefore already consolidated in the 1893–1899 period, much earlier than in all the other European countries.[20] By that time, the dominant position of the local clerical notables, based on the census-restricted suffrage and the majority system, had ended and the

[19] Lorwin (1966: 155).
[20] On the growth of the role of political parties from the time of the 1831 constitution to the electoral reform of 1893, see Witte (1980).

overthrow of the ruling elite had been completed. It was the socialist partisan mobilization that copied, and improved, the organizational model already functioning among the liberals and the Catholics.[21] The country was characterized by an early and particularly strong web of sociopolitical organizations and a corresponding politicization of the social structure.[22] Understandably, trade unions, cooperatives, friendly societies, saving banks, and leisure associations acquired a distinctive political character. The competition between Catholics and socialists, and the challenge of social Catholicism to the allegiance of the working class, provided a further stimulus for the transformation of these agencies into elements of social segregation. The supremacy of the Catholics from 1884 on encouraged closer contact between the liberals and the non-Catholic labor movement, but the basis of this trend was mainly ideological anticlericalism.

The language issue, on the other hand, was not important in the early development phase of mass politics. Around 1860, a Flemish-language movement developed, but this was soon monopolized by the Catholic movement and was used to bolster the development of the Christian Democratic Party. The first election in which parties articulating linguistic demands achieved significant support was in 1919 (with 3% of the vote going to a Flemish nationalist). By the late 1920s and the 1930s, the issue had gained more importance but was still only one of the programmatic concerns of traditional parties (administrative decentralization, cultural autonomy, etc.). Later on, nationalism slowly grew in strength in Flanders, and in the mid-1960s the emergence of Francophone parties led to the current situation of high saliency of linguistic issues.[23]

In conclusion, the first wave of Belgian political mobilization was well advanced before labor entered the game. The Belgian working class faced a complex structure of options: It could found independent socialist political organizations, it could organize itself under the leadership of Catholic clericalism, or it could become part of the liberal movement (even before it could identify with an ethnic linguistic identity). The labor movement was anticlerical, which made for a difficult relationship with traditionalist Catholics; it was antimonarchy and anticapitalist, which made for a difficult relationship with the liberals; it was also alone against the two dominating movements of the nineteenth century in asking for full and complete electoral democratization. No period of close alliance with, or

---

[21] See the review of the debate on early party system consolidation in Belgium in Noiret (1990a).

[22] Particularly well documented by Hill (1974: 40–41). See also De Bakker and Claey-Van Haegendoren (1973: 237–247).

[23] Hill (1974: 30).

delegated representation to, the liberals of the working-class movement can therefore be identified.

A similar lack of consolidated and persistent alliance between early liberalism and socialism is observable in the Dutch and Swiss cases. These two countries' political traditions and structures had several features in common in the nineteenth century. They had both achieved international sovereignty with only minor internal consolidation, and although this independent national existence was achieved by force, no dominant center ever developed. The early weakness of central authority in the Holy Roman Empire, the early development of mercantile cities dominating the surrounding countryside, the multicephalus nature of this network of cities, and the absence of large landowners all made for a nineteenth-century polity with no standing army, no strong national bureaucracy, and a weak national educational system. All this reinforced localism and entrenched pluralism. Yet the Netherlands had fewer barriers to social mobility (given its geography); particularism was broken more easily and earlier (it had a common language) and the national identity was therefore more integrated than in the case of the socioculturally heterogeneous and politically defined national identity of the Swiss. Moreover, the Netherlands was unquestionably more centralized and more internationally involved than federal Switzerland.[24] As a consequence, in the Netherlands, cleavage politicization was nationwide and was dominated, much as in Belgium, by an early liberal–clerical opposition, to which class was added only later. In Switzerland, truly national cleavage and party systems never developed.

The Netherlands was characterized by the very early emergence of an orthodox Protestant movement in reaction to liberalism and religious modernism and in defense of traditional Protestant education. During the nineteenth century, a section of both the elite and the rank and file grew increasingly dissatisfied with the "latitudinarianism" of the Dutch Reformed Church. The leader of this faction, Abraham Kuyper, and his followers founded an Anti-School Law League (1872), the Calvinist newspaper *De Standard* (1872), and a working-class organization called "Patrimonium" (1976); made massive petitions to the king not to accept secularization bills in schools (1878); and formed the Anti-Revolutionary Party (1879), a separate Calvinist University (1880), and, finally, a new Calvinist denomination (the Reformed Church, 1886). Not all orthodox persons joined the Reformed Churches; many remained within the Dutch Reformed Church and later joined the Christian Historical Union Party (1908), which never became a strong mass party, unlike the more militant

[24] For this comparison, see Daalder (1973).

Anti-Revolutionary Party.[25] The founding of the Anti-Revolutionary Party triggered liberal–clerical opposition, stimulated the birth of modern political parties, and determined the upsurge of Catholic political activism.

Catholics were the second group to mobilize politically. By supporting the separation between the dominant Dutch Reformed Church and the state, they had by 1853 achieved the reestablishment of the church hierarchy (the first archbishop in Utrecht) and had started to rebuild their church. Due to long-term discrimination, Catholic organization and mobilization took place largely under the guidance of the church rather than as an explicitly political organization. Thus, the Catholic Party was formed only at the end of the century and remained a weak actor vis-à-vis the reestablished Catholic hierarchy. However, in many ways, the Catholic community had already been reached and densely organized since the middle of the century by the reestablished church organization. By the 1880s, Catholic–Protestant relationships had improved so much that in 1888 a Calvinist–Catholic government (1888–1891) started the first government subsidies to religious elementary schools.[26] In contrast, the socialists and the liberals were the last to mobilize. The liberals, used to being dominant in nineteenth-century politics without any need to resort to much formal organization, developed their party organization late and were never very strong from an organizational point of view. The socialists, too, formed mass organizations late in comparison with other countries.

In Switzerland, in contrast to the Netherlands and Belgium, the local-regional element predominted even after 1848 and strongly affected the degree of politicization of the various cleavages. While in Switzerland no dominant national church existed, and each canton developed a specific and highly territorialized Catholic or Protestant profile, in the Netherlands, national unification and centralization after 1895 brought about the equality of religious groups. Catholic minorities in the non-Catholic parts of the country developed nationwide organizations and solidarity among Dutch Catholics, even in Brabant and Limburg. Consequently, the resulting regional cleavages were successfully subordinated to the religious one. This produced a nationalization of politics: It split mixed religious communities but established strong organizational links among like-minded believers across the country. Strong Calvinist and Catholic organizations meant the segmentation of the nation, with the secular groups as a third section within which class cleavage could develop, but with a much more restricted audience. In Switzerland, regional factors were never subordi-

[25] Daalder (1990: 41).
[26] Ibid., 40, note 22.

nated to cross-national political divisions precisely because religious divisions were essentially regional. Class, religion, language, and territory intersected more profoundly, and none acquired a *national* standardizing role.[27] Very often, the potential for the politicization of any one cleavage line was hampered and minimized by rival claims along other potential lines of division. If accommodation characterized the two countries, this was spread among many arenas and dimensions in Switzerland, while in the Netherlands religion was dominant but class came second and the two subordinated all the others.[28]

Swiss liberalism had two branches. In Protestant cantons, the Liberal Democrats became the majority party and their liberalism was strongly imbued with religious values (as in Scandinavia in the nineteenth century). In Catholic cantons, it instead combined democratic nineteenth-century aspirations with anticlericalism; the nation-building Radical Democratic Party was thus nationalist, populist, and anticlerical and strongly influenced by Mazzini's thinking.[29] The consequence of this structuring of the party system was a lack of uniformity in the party presence across the country. The radicals and the socialists tended to be present in all cantons; the Christian Democrats were virtually nonexistent in Neuchatel and were very weak in Bern and Vaud; and the liberals were very popular in Neuchatel, Vaud, and Geneva, less so in Bale, and unrepresented in other places. In consequence, a pattern was discernible whereby a multipartitism based on the equidistribution of political forces resulted in the highly urbanized and developed cantons (Bale Ville, Bern, Zurich, Geneva, Vaud, Argovie, Thurgovie); a party system *à l'italienne*, with a strong Christian Democratic Party dominating multipartitism, was dominant in Lucerne, St. Gall, Tessin, Soleure, Grisons, and Fribourg; and, finally, a party system *à la belgique*, with three major parties (Catholics, socialists, and radicals) characterized the political situation in the Valais and Zuog cantons. The resulting fragmentation was such that it actually reduced the importance of parties in the federal political process,[30] so that this, even if apparently

---

[27] See Kerr (1987).

[28] According to Kriesi (1990), federalism and pillarization are two different mechanisms for integration of subcultures into a larger national community. See also the contrast between territorial and sectional integration of Switzerland and the "lager," i.e., vertical integration of Austria underlined by Lehmbruch (1966).

[29] It is interesting to recall that, thanks to the early influence of a young left-wing Hegelian, Henry Durney, the party adhered to the First International. Nowadays, the Radicals are the most important antisocialist party in the German-speaking part of the country: the *parti de l'état cantonale* in Romandie and the anticlerical left in the Valais. Swiss liberalism also suffered several splits.

[30] Parties have little voting discipline and little influence over their MPs. Cantonal execu-

related to party politics, retained a low "partisanship." Thus, it can be conlcuded that in Switzerland, federalism (localism) has undercut party loyalties by giving much more weight to territorial loyalties, which, in turn, were based on and reinforced by religious and linguistic identities.[31]

In these three cases – Belgium, the Netherlands, and Switzerland – the socialist movement entered a party system in which important waves of early mobilization had already taken place along preindustrial cleavages of a religious, territorial, and linguistic nature. The socialists' potential electoral market was, therefore, to a large extent already restricted by the competitors' efforts. The basis of the political identities created by this early mobilization was, of course, cultural, and the alliance opportunities were largely shaped by the coalitions and conflicts that the previously mobilized social and political groups had already established. In addition, the early liberalization of the regime made a Lib–Lab anticonservative alliance unnecessary. In none of these cases, although for different reasons, was a lasting and solid alliance between liberalism and early socialism established.

"MALTHUSIAN LIBERALISM": FRANCE AND ITALY

I have grouped France and Italy as cases in which the party system completely failed to structure itself along partisan lines before World War I, and I have chosen the label of "Malthusian liberalism" because the early predominating liberal forces did not engage in party building or expansive competitive drives. Instead, they pursued a defensive and restrictive competition strategy as a result of the continuing menace for them and the regime they were founding that came from forces refusing to accept its legitimacy. The nature of this kind of early liberalism assimilates the two countries despite the crucial difference in the timing of universal manhood suffrage. Nineteenth-century France had a long tradition of revolutionary outbreaks, mainly of an urban nature, whose level of success was determined by the support they obtained in the countryside. However, there

---

tives are generally directly elected by citizens by double ballot majority voting, which weakens the direct role of the parties in the recruitment of executive personnel. Finally, the tradition of widespread direct democracy was not controlled by parties at the beginning and has become less and less so over time. On this latter point, see Libbey (1970).

[31] Kriesi (1990); Scholten (1980) argues that pillarization and federalism are imposed from above and constitute conscious actions by the elite to defend themselves against socialism.

was little growth or consolidation of this early political opposition move-ment, which could be defined as popular, in the sense of incorporating sections of the urban and rural lower and middle classes, and self-representational, in the sense of relying on self-recruitment within these groups. Italian nineteenth-century politics was characterized by narrow intellectual movements and localized popular revolts, both of which were unconnected and unlinked to broader national mobilization processes. The various "political sects" and the Mazzini movements of the first half of the century, the neo-Guelphism of Gioberti, the "moderatism" of Cesare Balbo, the federalist republicanism of Cattaneo, and the democratic radi-calism of Pisacane and Ferrari were all, without exception, intellectual and restricted political movements.[32] Important popular lower- or middle-class movements, capable of fusing different social groups, both elites and rank and file, into a large, mobilizing enterprise were completely absent. The distance of the intellectual elite from the masses could not have been greater than in Italy in this period.

In France as well as in Italy, there were, at the beginning of the period of competitive politics, two dominant dimensions of conflict: On the one hand, the liberal and republican forces were opposed to the confessional and religious-based forces; on the other, conflicts of legitimacy concerned the established constitutional order and opposed the same liberal forces to the reactionary and "legitimist" aspirations of monarchical circles in France and to the staunch refusal of the Catholic hierarchy to accept the new state in Italy. The French Radical Party, the strongest defender of the regime and the political values of the Third Republic, had a social base of notables in the countryside[33] who mixed social, economic, and political power so that they were indistinguishable, occupied positions of local and national authority, and obtained and maintained their power thanks to a network of local and personal relationships; that is, this was a provincial, mainly professional, bourgeoisie that owned a small amount of land, was econom-ically autonomous, relatively well-off, and very close to the small landown-ers and the farmers.[34] As such, these local notables, unless challenged by functionally based and cross-sectional political movements, were neither vote maximizers nor mobilizers. These forces never consolidated politically along organizational partisan lines and neither did any other force. French conservative and monarchical circles held that political parties were ruinous

[32] On these early political movements in Italy, see Morandi (1978: 10–19).
[33] For the classic description of how early manhood suffrage helped the local notables to control rural votes, see Siegfried (1913).
[34] These characteristics emerge in the beautiful portrait of the French local notables by Halévy (1995).

to the country, disliked the word "party" from the outset, and preferred to call their political organizations "movements," "groups," "*rassemblements*," "unions," and so on. The criticism of parties remained one of the key points of conservative platforms and spread well beyond reactionary and conservative circles: parties paralyzed reform and encouraged agitation, sterile quarrels, the feverish unleashing of personal ambitions and ideological passions, and artificial divisions that prevented them from reaching predefined national goals and "missions."[35]

Many explanations have been advanced for these persistent antiparty sentiments in the French political and intellectual circles and for the nonconsolidation of partisan politics in France before World War I.[36] In my view, the most important factor is the separation of the historical processes that give rise to mass political identities and parties, industrialization, urbanization and enfranchisement. The early introduction of enfranchisement long before the processes of industrialization and urbanization meant that the municipalities, the local notables, and the strong state agencies at local levels all maintained an important role in channeling representation. The fact that the French masses, particularly the rural masses, were politicized early in a phase of preparty politics still dominated by localistic and notable networks had strong negative consequences for the ensuing rootness of the party system. New political movements with a functional and cross-sectional profile such as class movements had to fight these early channels and never managed to replace them completely as the main focus of political identity of the people. Industrialization had started early in France but then progressed very slowly and without the major dislocation effects that rapid industrialization produced in other countries. What is more important, the major pushes of the three processes were widely separated in time.

[35] Still, in the 1950s, Goguel complained that parties were exaggerating the role of members and militants at the expense of the voters and depriving them of the possibility to choose their representative directly; Goguel (1950: 352). For a recollection of these antiparty criticisms, see Zeldin (1979: 25–26).

[36] Individualistic and psychocultural explanations underlining the unwillingness of the French mind to compromise and associate different shades of thought: Buell (1920: 1) and Lowell (1896: 100–108); the antiassociation legal tradition going back to the Chapellier law, combined with a renascent Jacobin-republicanism and the use of integrated territorial administration to discourage the rise of party organizations: Tarrow (1977: 54–55); the emphasis on individual personalities making the system to remain in a charismatic mood and thereby delaying the transition to bureaucratized politics through parties: Hoffman (1974: 63–110); the territorial centralization in Paris of everything of importance and the "parisification" of political movements, which rendered the territorial organization of parties unimportant and offered few incentives for the building of national structures: Svåsand (1978: 10).

Even after the 1870s, the high level of personalization of local politics, the fragmentation of the political groups, the existence of parliamentary groups with no corresponding organizational force in the country, the wide freedom of parliamentarians to sustain different governmental coalitions, and the very late recognition of the legitimacy of parliamentary groups in the chambers are probably not enough to assimilate French Third Republic politics to the Italian *trasformismo* of the same period (see later) but instead make the French situation similar to it. Parties started to organize only well after the beginning of the new century, and it was only before World War I that party activities outside parliament began to have some effect on the government and parliamentary life (e.g., party congresses began to have influence the positions taken by the parliamentary group). In 1936, the number of MPs belonging to parties was still a minority in the chamber, not to mention in the Senate.[37] Only at the beginning of the Fourth Republic did parties become key actors in the negotiations for the formation of government and in the definition of the internal rules of the chambers, the parliamentary committees, and so on.

In conclusion, the weak development of French political parties and their failure to establish roots in local and provincial French political life throughout the entire Third Republic are not only the result of the legacy of the Second Empire, with its style of personalistic and populist government and its heavy reliance on state structures and authorities to channel interest representation; equally important was the permanent unwillingness/incapacity of the conservative (and reactionary) right to organize itself into partisan political forms and the aversion of the radical local notables to engagement and compromise in open political and partisan activity.

The structuring of the party system presented a similar picture in Italy and ended by offering a similar constellation to the incipient socialist movement, although for different reasons. An overview of Italian political history between the time of national unification and World War I shows that once the early mobilizing issues of nationalism and national unification were soft-pedaled, the country's political landscape soon became very varied, with a large variety of political organizations and no stabilization or consolidation along important partisan division lines. Even after 1870, the mobilization level of the country remained extremely low; it is not possible to identify political movements with a popular base of a Catholic, peasant, or bourgeois/middle-class nature. The 1860s had already shown the inconsistency of the much desired bipartitism. A single political movement and organization that could claim to be the heir of the Cavour

---

[37] On the development of parliamentary groups, see Goguel (1950: 348–351).

policies did not exist, and programs and groups instead formed around individual leaders (e.g., Ricasoli, Minghetti, Rattazzi). Parliamentary coalitions were formed and dissolved around interests that were very often of a regional character. In other cases, they were formed around purely personal and clientelistic relationships and promises of political positions. Although a few attempts were made to give a new political meaning to the two wings of the chambers, the left and the right, and also to create new forces around a clear program (for instance, this was attempted by Sella with his "young left"), the process of dissolution of the two old preunitary parties continued and the early differences in opinion as to how to solve the problem of national unification faded in the following decades and were dispelled altogether in the era of *trasformismo*.[38]

Trasformismo was a parliamentary praxis that tended to guarantee the cabinet a considerable majority in parliament, either through preliminary negotiation with its most prominent opponents and with their eventual incorporation into the governmental majority or through the occasional exchange of favors with less influential MPs of the centrist *marais*.[39] It was viewed as accepted practice by the entire political class, with the exception of the republican extreme left, and it resulted in limited interelite competition within the broad liberal camp. To sum up, a narrow, closed, and socially and politically homogeneous political class lacked internal cleavages over which to aggregate politico-parliamentary formations that could be less ephemeral than these short-lived personal coalitions.[40] As things stood, the only nonpersonal political coalitions could be of a regional nature (preunitary regions). However, even in this case, these could not go too far because the political class as a whole, while sharing the ideology of the unitary state, was also so aware of the fragility of this state that it was reluctant to risk organizing political conflict along territorial lines. Therefore, the only possibility of organized political conflict and competition was along institutional lines (republicanism versus monarchy) and, later, socioeconomic issues (anarchism and socialism).

It has been argued that this parliamentary practice, essential in preventing the consolidation of clear partisan alternatives in the liberal era, represented a kind of contract between the bourgeoisie of northern Italy and the dominant social groups of the south. The basis of the compromise was a politics of reform and a liberalization of the new unitary state that respected the interests of the dominant Southern social groups. The latter,

[38] See Morandi (1978: 25–33).
[39] Procacci (1970: 407).
[40] On this point, see Caracciolo (1957: 112–113).

as a form of additional guarantee, came to be adequately represented within the government.[41] It is hard to decide whether this was the cause or the consequence of *trasformismo*. The crucial point, in my opinion, is that the political positions adopted by the liberal nation-builders rested on extremely flimsy social bases: The papal *non expedit* had prohibited Catholic intellectuals, organizations, and masses from taking an active part in the new state; the extreme left remained republican and later anarchist and socialist; and the monarchy had not fully abandoned its atempts to intervene directly and needed to be checked continuously.[42] The liberal groups responded to Catholic challenges to their legitimacy with prolonged restriction of the suffrage in order to keep both the Catholic masses and later the socialist masses out of the electoral competition. They responded to the ambivalent monarchical attitude toward parliamentary democracy with a political coalescent behavior whereby certain key issues were silenced. Even the institutional cleavage between republicans and monarchists was somehow muted, as the republicans did not pursue the institutional question vigorously after the *non expedit* of Pius IX. This, however, allowed Catholics and socialists to define themselves as the *pays réel* as against the *pays legal*.[43] The indifference or hostility of all the excluded groups toward the institutions of the new state — in a context in which the means of expressive unification of the society and of consensus building around the modernizing elite were weak due to the high level of illiteracy — made it impossible for the liberals to use the extension of the voting right in a defensive way and brought about their political Malthusianism. The lack of a Catholic political role in support of the conservatives and, at the same time, the lack of an autonomous political organization of the Catholics (as in Belgium, Austria, and the Netherlands) deprived conservatism of the potential support of the Catholic traditionalist masses. For similar reasons, liberalism was deprived of the potential support of early working-class organizations and of the radical middle classes. Both coalesced toward a hostile civic society.

In the pre–World War I period, an Italian radical liberal party similar to the French, Swiss, or Danish variants never developed.[44] The early

---

[41] Procacci (1970: 408–409).

[42] In many cases, the crown deliberately avoided designating as premier a political figure who appeared capable of securing a homogeneous, minimum majority. See Rotelli (1975: 8–9) and Grisalberti (1978).

[43] Galli (1968: 33–35).

[44] For the relationships between Italian radicals and the early socialist movement, see the opinion of Galante Garrone (1973: 197–198). Socialist intellectuals published in radical journals, but few true political connections existed and the relationship remained largely intellectual. This was due fundamentally to the narrowness of Italian radical liberalism,

Socialist Party instead manifested the hope that an alliance with the democratically advanced sectors of the bourgeoisie would be able to break the protectionism and the conservative bloc formed by Southern landowners and Northern steel producers. However, the absence of strong social groups of small farmers or peasant landowners (as there were in France, for example) made it impossible for the radical liberals to obtain support in the countryside and in provincial Italy. The failure of the small liberal bourgeoisie meant that the democratization process depended essentially on the socialist movement. In these circumstances, the liberal and conservative forces, which were not organized as parties, managed to resist thanks only to the restricted suffrage and, after 1913, thanks only to the possibility of obtaining Catholic votes channeled by the secular organization of the Catholic world, which was by then worried about the growing strength of the socialist movement.[45] Subsequently, after World War I, the liberal forces hoped to borrow the support of the growing nationalist movement and, finally, that of the new fascist movement that emerged from it. The latter attempt proved, of course, to be fatal for the Italian liberal regime.

So, in both Italy and France, it can be concluded that parties were organized for parliamentary rather than electoral purposes. Self-representational social movements existed outside parliament, but with few and tenuous linkages to the parliamentary parties. In both systems, religious and institutional issues fragmented representation without achieving expression along clear partisan lines or becoming institutionalized into party formations and alignments. The major difference between Italy and France was that in Italy the delayed extension of the suffrage gave the new mass parties (the socialists, the Catholics, and later the communists) a chance to absorb the masses of *new* voters into party subcultures in the absence of previous experiences of institutional and nonpartisan representation.

In both countries, the first elements of socialism emerged as branches of republicanism, and the first socialist candidates' victories were made possible only by alliances with radical liberals. Despite this, a stable and persistent alliance between socialism and radical liberalism never devel-

---

to its cultural more than its political character, and to its almost nonexistent organizational bases.

[45] The clerical–moderates alliances made before the 1913 elections are known as the "Gentiloni Pact" after the name of the president of the Unione Elettorale Cattolica. In 1904 and 1909, such alliances resulted from local agreements between liberal candidates and Catholic organizations. The situation in 1913 was new, as the papal *non expedit* was suspended in 330 districts and maintained only in 178. See Carocci (1975: 198).

oped. The main reason for this is, perhaps, that in this historical phase neither of the two movements consolidated as strong political organizations capable of strategic choices of alliance. This situation is obvious in Italy; while in France the case is less clear-cut, and there have been different interpretations. Luebbert, for example, has argued that France assimilated to Switzerland and the United Kingdom as a case of "hegemonic role of liberalism" and that in France too, there was close Lib–Lab cooperation.[46] Much of the difference between his and my interpretation derives from his definition of "socialists." While it is true that "socialists" provided essential support for the ministries of Bourgeois and Waldeck-Rousseau and, even more important, for Combes between 1902 and 1905, and while it is true that close cooperation in the defense of republican values was frequent (as, for example, in the Dreyfus affair),[47] the fact is that the rather elitist and personalistic parliamentary socialists of Jaurès represented very little beyond themselves and the local electoral alliances that had brought them to parliament. The formation of the SFIO in 1905 was based on a Guesdesist and Blanquist ideological predominance in opposition to the radical governments. A weak trade union movement was represented politically by a radical Socialist Party in which ideologues predominated over organizational union movements, in contrast to the United Kingdom, where intellectual socialists were defeated and the Labour Party became the mouthpiece of the strong organizational base of the trade unions, with a platform of ministerialism and political integration. If Millerand and his career illustrates the radical foundation on which socialism was built, it does so from the point of view of parliamentary representation only.[48] The early radical–socialist cooperation to defend the liberal and republican order from the menace of clerical, monarchical, and reactionary forces was followed by a sudden radical break between radicalism and socialism at the beginning of the century, when this threat started to evaporate. This profound break between radicalism and the working class is represented in the policy of Clemenceau and the Radical Party in 1905–1908, in its campaign against collectivism, its call for the dissolution of the CGT, and its denunciation of the socialists as antipatriotic.

    In conclusion, political liberalism was a weak, ideologically fragmented, and politically unorganized point of reference for early socialism in both France and Italy. In contrast to Switzerland and the Netherlands,

---

[46] Luebbert (1991: 27–48) argues this point extensively.

[47] For an account of the socialists' positions on the Dreyfus affair, see Noland (1970: 61–85).

[48] Zeldin (1979: 408).

these two countries lacked a consolidated liberal regime, and their defense against antiliberal movements continued well into the 1920s and until the end of World War II. At the same time, given the unstructured party system and the weak institutionalization of partisan alignments, the socialist movement was the first to present modern mass party features and mobilization techniques. As a result, the socialist movement took over a large part of the radical-liberal program and made it part of its complex and composite ideology. These socialist movements remained organizationally weak, and their relationships with the unions were tense, with deep organizational and ideological splits. In this sense, their weakness was simply a reflection of the difficult process of party-system structuring. However, at the same time, this made it easier for them to inherit electorally those radical middle classes, both rural and urban, whose anticlericalism, republicanism, and democratic values were only weakly represented by the organized political forces. In this sense, Malthusian liberalism eventually contributed to the large electoral mobilization of the left, as it did to its composite ideology, organizational divisions, and social heterogeneity.

NONEXISTENT LIBERAL OPTION

Liberalism as an organized political expression of the urban and/or rural middle class and bourgeoisie was nonexistent in Germany and Austria. In Finland and Ireland also, a Lib–Lab alliance option proved to be unavailable in the early phases of national electoral mobilization. This common outcome derives from different factors and contexts, but in all cases there is a common characteristic: the overwhelming role played by early national and nationalistic issues.

Austria is probably the most clear-cut case of the lack of a liberal option for the labor movement. In the Hapsburg Empire, with the monarchy relying on groups from the German, Hungarian, and Polish nobilities, the high Catholic clergy, and the high bureaucracy, the main opposition was formed by liberal groups. These groups, however, were particularly intent on promoting German hegemony, which the monarchy, instead, wanted to limit to a certain extent. After 1879, a year marked by growing internal national tensions, liberalism started to disintegrate organizationally and survived only as an attitude rather than as a movement.[49] Before World War I, obstructive parliamentary practices and national-group divisions and struggles prevented the establishment of any orderly

[49] Engelmann (1966: 260).

or clear government opposition dynamics and fostered (and justified to a certain extent) the practice of ruling by decree of the king and the bureaucracy. However, by the end of the 1880s, both the Social Democratic Party and the Christian Social Party had been formed, and these, thanks to universal and equal suffrage for men, became the two leading parties by 1907. Austria is the most illuminating example of the difficulty of democratizing within nonlegitimate state boundaries. For disaffected national minorities, the aspirations to liberalization and democratization were only partially and instrumentally relevant and were combined with, but more often subordinated to, demands for cultural and political autonomy or total independence.

Thus, the socialist movement was both politically isolated and institutionally unintegrated (see Chapter 7). The socialists were given little support by the liberals in their struggle for democratic reforms. This explains why they were never really concerned with the issue of whether or not to cooperate with bourgeois forces. The clearest example of the impossibility of a Lib–Lab alliance was the 1893 electoral-reform bill prepared by the government. This was a radical reform from above that introduced universal male suffrage, even though, in practice, it included barriers for the lower classes and privileges for the upper classes. Details of the bill are not important here; what counts is that the liberal and bourgeois groups (the so-called left of the Imperial Council) opposed and finally defeated the electoral reform proposal of Taaffe and his government. This was probably due to the fact that their main concern was to keep the national equilibrium that granted German hegemony.

If liberalism and liberal political groups in general remained very weak and offered no option to workers interested in political emancipation and social advancement, no other stable political alliances were available either. For years, the largest populist party was the rather reactionary and openly anti-Semitic Christian Social Party, which gained little support among workers. This resulted in a rather unique European case: a type of isolation in which the Socialist Party had no competitors for the support of the working class on either its left or its right. While this was clearly the cause of its political ineffectiveness and isolation, it also provided the structural context in which the development of orthodox Marxism could be maintained,[50] with maximum advantages in internal cohesion and minimum external costs.

As a result of its involvement in the national question and in the issue of political rights, the Socialist Party was not particularly affected by the

---

[50] On this orthodoxy and its sources, see Steenson (1991: 269).

ideological debate between reformists and radicals. This situation of political isolation did not change substantially after the war. In the 1920s, the two traditional Austrian anti-Marxist groups joined forces to a considerable extent against the socialists, fusing their tickets. Only at the beginning of the 1930s did polarization occur in the non-Marxist camp to produce Austria's three irreconcilable "lagers": the socialists, the proclerical conservatives, and the German nationalists. The issue was, and remained, the possibility of an elite cartel among parties and closely linked organizations that would represent densely organized political subcultures as well as distinct social groups.

In Germany, too, the socialist organizations found it difficult to establish any stable or privileged links with the liberal, or parts of the liberal, forces before World War I. The early general suffrage led to a correspondingly early national political mobilization of the masses. The Catholic population was initially mobilized in opposition to the *Kulturkampf* by the Center Party.[51] A second wave of mobilization was led by the socialists against the antisocialist laws. Finally, political mobilization was enhanced by the government's attempt to transform elections into a plebiscite for its policy and also by the strong development of interest organizations. With an 85% average turnout in the last elections to the Imperial Diet (1912),[52] a strong network of powerful interest organizations, a highly developed central bureaucracy, and a high degree of state intervention in its socioeconomic affairs, Germany was a highly politically mobilized polity before World War I.

However, despite this, there was no national party; with the single exception of the Social Democrats, all the others, including the Zentrum and the two conservative parties, were strongly localized and unable to place candidates in every constituency. The pattern of national unification under Prussian leadership meant that, to a certain extent, regional loyalties were transformed into party divisions, and regional fragmentation was high from 1870 to 1933. Ethnic minorities and a few important regional parties emerged, among which the Bavarian Farmers' League, the Württemberg Farmers' and Wine-Growers' League, and the Guelph Party in the Prussian provinces of Hannover are worth mentioning as the more resilient examples. Again, a wave of regional splinter parties emerged in the 1920s in several states, including Schleswig-Holstein, Braunschweig, Baden,

---

[51] Ritter (1990: 53–55) notes that in 1870 voter participation in Catholic majority constituencies was higher than in Protestant ones.

[52] Ritter (1985: 25) provides figures and comments on the turnout of the 1871–1912 elections.

Württemberg, Hessen, Thuringia, and Bavaria. These parties were generally prominent in the rural areas. More generally, however, in this early phase, almost all the parties displayed strong regional bases, in the sense of the skewed distribution of their support. Catholics were confined to areas of Catholic concentration, while the conservatives and the DNVP were concentrated in the eastern provinces. Even the Social Democrats and Communists were constrained regionally by the uneven distribution of industrialization, urbanization, and Catholic influence. Moreover, the constitutional structure of the Reich encouraged the persistence of regional differences, as the state elections were more important than the national ones. In this context of general and protracted regional fragmentation,[53] it was difficult for a national party to devise strategies of alliance.

Together with the delayed nationalization of political organizations and alignments, the lack of Lib–Lab political cooperation in Germany has been widely discussed in connection with the thesis of the "weakness of the German bourgeoisie"; this discussion provides an opening for the examination of possible links between socialists and liberals. The early abdication of German liberalism on both the socioeconomic and political reform fronts[54] made it unappealing to working-class associations and left the socialists with a relatively easy and early monopoly over electoral and parliamentary working-class representation. This political abdication has traditionally been interpreted as a German peculiarity (*deutscher Sonderweg*). In the assimilation of premodern sociopolitical models by the bourgeoisie, a historiographical tendency has pinpointed its political weakness, the feature explaining the entire historical development of Germany up to the rise of Nazism. The thesis of weak liberalism resulting from an economically weak bourgeoisie with upper-class values and aspirations has also been advanced in regard to Austria and Italy. However, the former – in contrast to the latter – underwent this nineteenth-century bourgeois development, in the sense of its material, cultural, and regulative progression, if not its political liberalization, as a "silent revolution." In the works of Blackbourn and Eley[55] and particularly that of Kocka,[56] the thesis of the economic weakness of the German bourgeoisie, and of its "feudalization"

---

[53] See Ritter (1990: 57–58) and Rokkan, Urwin, Aarebrot, Malaba, and Sande (1987: 129–135). For a more detailed analysis of these regional variations, see the essays in Rohe (1990a), and in particular Niehuss (1990: 83–106), Rohe (1990b: 107–144), and Mintzel (1990: 145–178).

[54] Breuilly (1985: 3–42). Gagel (1958) provides several examples and proofs of the continuous ambivalent position of German liberals on the political-reform front.

[55] Blackbourn and Eley (1984).

[56] Kocka (1989a: 51–55).

and deep assimilation to the nobility, is criticized and rejected, and the differences from the bourgeoisie of other countries such as France and the United Kingdom are reduced. The essays by Tilly and Koeble also both conclude that the weakness was political rather than based on socioeconomic factors, resulting from the weak solidarity among different sectors of the bourgeoisie (i.e., on emerging entrepreneurship versus more traditional sectors that were extraneous and/or inimical to modernization) and by the state intervention that limited the cultural autonomy of the bourgeoisie.[57]

These critiques of the *Deutscher Sonderweg* are convincing, although the interpretation of the political factors in the weakness of the German bourgeoisie still needs to be specified. The problem can be reformulated by emphasizing, on the one hand, the role of the strong state and, on the other, the timing of the mobilization sequence that opened up the phase of political autonomy of the national bourgeoisie. As for the role of the state, it can be argued that in strong, resourceful states with autocratic, dynastic traditions of rule, the controllers of the state machine have ample opportunities through state action and legislation to break the unity of social groups, to gain support from specific sociopolitical groups, and to orchestrate conflict between one sociopolitical group and its adversaries.[58] This was a typical political tool used by dynastic powers and circles in both Germany and Austria. In Germany, the workers' support for the empire was sought in exchange for social policies not supported by the employers. In the context of the *Kulturkampf*, the aspecific support (negative integration) of liberal forces was instead sought through conflict with Catholicism. Before World War I, Social Democratic support and negative integration was attempted by forcing them to support the military commitments of the empire. Rather than view the socioeconomic weakness of a group as resulting in the autonomy of the state, the autonomy of the state can therefore be seen as a resource for curbing and breaking the potential political autonomy of social groups.

In addition, there is a problem of timing among different social developments, and this can foster or reduce the political autonomy of the national bourgeoisie. The identity and autonomous political action of such social groups results from (1) a process of differentiation from aristocratic, dynastic, military, bureaucratic, and landed interests, which requires (1a) the maturation of a sense of diversity in interest and style of life with respect to them and (1b) a growing critique of and detachment from the ancient traditional centers of power and social prestige. At the same time,

---

[57] Tilly (1989) and Koeble (1989).
[58] On the negative integration strategy of the ruling circles, see Lepsius (1973: 72–74).

this historical process interacts with another one that renders the bourgeois and liberal forces (2) antagonistic to the emerging working-class unions and political movements, which also pass through their own (1a) and (1b) phases. From the beginning of the nineteenth century to the beginning of the twentieth century – with differences in timing and tempo – all the national bourgeoisies passed from the predominance of process (1) to the predominance of process (2), accompanied by the progressive fading of the antagonism implicit in process (1).

The timing between these two processes determines the window of opportunity for the autonomous political action of bourgeois liberal forces. The longer the temporal gap between the differentiation of the bourgeois liberal forces from dominant aristocratic and dynastic circles *and* the differentiation of the political movements of the lower classes from the liberal political movement, the more self-conscious and politically autonomous the bourgeois groups and the more profound and protracted the political role of liberalism are likely to be. If such a temporal gap is short or nonexistent, and if the continuing strength of the dominant circles of power overlaps with the early autonomous political mobilization of the lower classes, political liberalism – independent of the socioeconomic strength of the bourgeoisie and middle classes – will be short-lived. In other words, the window of opportunity for liberalism is opened up either by the early curbing of the dynastic–bureaucratic–military–landed aristocracy cluster or by a delay in the effective political mobilization of the socialists. Early socialist mobilization may make Lib–Lab alliances difficult, antagonizing or demobilizing bourgeois liberal forces and eventually making the processes of liberalization and democratization harder. As a result, a delay in the political mobilization of the working class may well be an advantage for the liberalization of the regime and for an extended and autonomous role of liberal forces. In Germany (and also Austria), the protracted power of traditional social and political groups linked to the dynastic power and the early political organization of a socialist challenge greatly reduced the chances of establishing liberalism. Socialism was thus left on its own to represent a potentially large constituency, but it faced the institutional closure of the regime in a situation of political isolation.

NATIONALISM OVERSHADOWING LIBERALISM: THE SPECIAL CASES OF IRELAND AND FINLAND

The mobilization of the left was also affected by nationhood itself and by the timing of nation building. In some countries, left mobilization took place within the long tradition of national identity and state building (the United Kingdom, Denmark, Sweden, France). In others, the issue of the national building of cultural, political, and other identities faded just before the decisive issue of electoral mobilization was initiated (the Netherlands, Switzerland, Belgium, Norway). In Italy and Germany, the two questions overlapped for a long time after unification and nationalism, and national issues continued to play an important role during socialist electoral mobilization. Formally, Austria, Finland, and Ireland achieved independence in the twentieth century, when the socialist mobilization was already well advanced. For Austria, this final change was a *redutio* from a previously nationally heterogeneous empire, while for Ireland and Finland it was a process of political emancipation from a foreign colonial power with high international status.

The Irish and Finnish cases are particularly interesting because from similar geopolitical conditions and a similar predominance of the national independence issue have emerged two completely different party systems and polar types of the left: an early, strong type versus a late, weak one and a persistent ideological trade union orientation versus an orthodox Marxist and a communist orientation. Finland and Ireland both show an absence of liberal forces in the early political mobilization of the masses and a continuous overshadowing of these forces by nationalistic ones in later phases. In both countries, the dominant problem was the relationship with a strong foreign rule exercised by a neighboring imperial power, and – again in both countries – the process of national independence almost ended in civil war. The Irish–Finnish comparison is therefore interesting in view of the relationship that was finally established between the social issue and the class cleavage, on the one hand, and the national issue, on the other.

In Finland, two basic cleavages that were strongly linked to the national question worked as mobilizing forces of the Old Diet (pre-1907) politics:[59] (1) the Finnish nationalist movement against the dominant status of the Swedish language and (2) the russification policy and the attitude toward the tsar and Russia. As for the first issue, a one-seventh minority of the population spoke Swedish, and this language stratification mirrored the status stratification. Swedish was the official language of the affluent, educated upper class, with the exception of the clergy, and gave privileged access to public offices. Early mobilization led by Finnish middle-class nationalists often took the form of nationwide collections of funds

[59] On the early Finnish political conflicts, see Mylly (1984).

and cultural activities favoring the establishment of Finnish-language grammar schools. This was immediately counterbalanced by the formation of a Swedish-speaking political party to defend the privileges of the minority. Thus, the first major political cleavage saw Finnish nationalists, predominant in the clerical and peasant estates, opposing Swedish nationalists, predominant in the nobility and burgher estates.

The second major dividing line saw "constitutionalists" in opposition to "compliers" (that is, those willing to yield to the tsar on nonvital Finnish interests and issues). Progressively, by the end of the nineteenth century and as a result of repeated attempts at russification, the issue of relations with Russia became more important than the linguistic issue and the new focus on political organization.[60] Internal language conflicts were suspended, and a mass national protest movement swept the country (522,931 signatures were collected throughout the country through the churches).[61] Finnish politics, up to then directed internally and focusing on the language issue, suddenly became directed externally against Russian oppression. A new awareness of nationalism was formed, so that in the period around 1894–1906 the political mobilization of a highly literate society combined antiautocratic opposition with that against foreign domination. This perhaps explains the enormous participation of the Finnish electorate in their first election with universal suffrage in 1906.[62]

The attempt to form a liberal party capable of cutting across the crucially salient cleavage between Swedish and Finnish speakers was unsuccessful in the last decades of the nineteenth century, as was the attempt to form a liberal party based on the Finnish-speaking population alone. The issue of russification radicalized Finnish nationalism, and only in 1906 was a party of liberal orientation founded, the Young Finns, although the party that is usually regarded as the expression of Finnish liberalism – the People's Party for Progress – was created only after World War I.[63] At the end of the nineteenth century, with the onset of industrialization, the emergence of a new class cleavage tended to follow and reinforce stratification lines identified by language, estate, and education. This new cleavage line was also congruent with the nationalist divide. In conclusion, the socialist movement was not affected by the linguistic issues that weakened

---

[60] On this first russification process and on the reactions to it, see Wuorinen (1931: 189–205).

[61] Martin and Hopkins (1980: 189).

[62] On the early Finnish popular movements and mass organizations, see Alapuro (1988: 101–110).

[63] Berglund and Lindström (1978: 50).

liberalism and, at the same time, it was able to capitalize on the nationalist mobilization that had preceded its foundation and paralleled its extraordinary partisan organizational development (see Chapter 6).[64]

However, the alliance between the working class and the Finnish constitutionalists did not last. The Russian Revolution of March 1917 opened up the possibility of independence, but Finnish conservatives feared independence with a Social Democratic Party holding the majority in parliament. Moreover, the country faced a crisis in handling political control, as it had no local, autonomous police force or army. Political confrontation began to be organized by the formation of rival armed guards. When the Senate, which was in the hands of the bourgeoisie after the 1917 elections, moved to structure a military and police force at the end of 1917, the Social Democrats interpreted this as a declaration of war against the working class. On January 28, 1918, the party organized a coup to take power. This was successful in Helsinki and southern Finland, while in the north the White Guard began to counterattack. The war between the two sides lasted from January until the final victory of the Whites in May 1918, helped by the intervention of the German army.[65]

The Irish process of nineteenth-century national political mobilization revolves around three issues, which are all interlinked in national resurgence: (1) the land and peasants issue, (2) the Catholic emancipation issue, and (3) the national emancipation issue. The difference with Finland lies in the lower intensity of linguistic issues as a mobilizing factor and the presence of the Catholic emancipation issue. The land and peasants issue and the national emancipation issue are instead fundamentally similar. The crucial difference in explaining the fate of the left thus turns on the way these issues developed sequentially and impinged on each other. The difference in the pattern of sequential solution (typical of Ireland) versus the pattern of sequential cumulation (typical of Finland) is therefore the basis of my comparison.

In Ireland, the Protestants made few real attempts to convert the peasant community, and in the first part of the nineteenth century various Catholic associations began to agitate for Catholic emancipation, home rule, and parliamentary reform. Catholic emancipation was achieved in 1829, and the issue of the position of the Catholic Church began to evolve over the century, with three significant thresholds: in 1869, The Protestant

---

[64] For the structuring of the Finnish party system, see Allardt and Pesonen (1967: 326–329) and Nousiainen (1960: 28–43).

[65] A detailed account of this stormy period is presented in Jutikkala and Pirinen (1962: 254–267) and in Alapuro (1988: 150–196).

Church of Ireland was disestablished; in 1873, Trinity College in Dublin finally abolished its religious entrance test, which usually discriminated against Catholics; and in 1908, a separate Catholic University was established. This ongoing gaining of independence and influence on the part of the Catholic Church resulted in "clerical community leadership" and "hierarchical conservatism."[66]

The peasant and land issue evolved in the second half of the nineteenth century as a result of the large number of economically and legally vulnerable tenants, mainly concentrated in the west and south of the country: not only did they have no title of landownership, but their tenancy was unsafe. As I have already pointed out (see Chapter 7), the tenants' grievances were ultimately resolved before the final nationalist phase began, via a series of successive Land Acts that fostered peasant ownership in 1869, 1881, 1885, 1891, 1896, and 1903. The struggle for land was radical, bitter, and often violent, but the final result was the consolidation of a class of smallholders: There were 3% of these as opposed to 97% of tenants in the 1870s, and they swelled to 97.4% in 1929 as opposed to 2.6% of tenants.[67] This clearly converted the position of the great bulk of the peasantry from radical social protest to social conservatism, thereby neutralizing any potential rural radicalism. The Land League, founded in 1879, was immensely successful and was the first mass movement to mobilize the Irish peasantry into a modern political force. However, it was not a self-representative peasant movement of the Scandinavian type. Neither the Catholic emancipation issue not the peasant and land issues ever gave rise to partisan organizations.

The national issue was the last of the three to be activated and politicized, initially stimulated by a revival of Gaelic culture and Irish literature. In the second half of the nineteenth and early twentieth centuries, about four-fifths of the Irish members in the British House of Commons were members of the Nationalist Party, which was devoted to obtaining home rule by constitutional means and within the framework of a Union. The other fifth was formed by Unionists, who opposed this view. The lack of any concrete results discredited the Nationalist Party and led to the formation of dissenting groups that aimed at achieving independence from the United Kingdom through a wholly Irish administration that would eventually take over from the British. The 1905 foundation of Sinn Fein provided an alternative to the Irish Parliamentary Party. The following two decades of electoral and parliamentary developments are

---

[66] Thornley (1974: 20).
[67] Ibid., 23.

crucial in interpreting the failure of class mobilization in Ireland and need to be reviewed briefly.[68]

The first Irish patriots who set up the Dail were unable to hold their own elections. They accepted the result of the United Kingdom's general election of December 1918 and considered the members of the United Kingdom's Parliament elected from Irish seats to be members of the new Dail. The first Dail, constituted in January 1919, was essentially a revolutionary body; the same was true of the second, constituted on the basis of the acceptance of the May 1921 United Kingdom election, held under the Government of Ireland Act. This resulted in an armed struggle between the Irish nationalists (Sinn Fein) and the British administration, eventually ending in the Anglo-Irish Treaty setting up the Irish Free State as a coequal member of the Commonwealth (1921). Although accepted by a narrow majority of the Sinn Fein deputies sitting in the second Dail (sixty-four in favor and fifty-seven against), the treaty was bitterly resented by the minority, which refused to cooperate and resigned from the Dail, carrying its position to the point of armed civil war against the majority. This split over the terms of the treaty produced the two anti- and protreaty parties that afterward dominated Irish political life. The Third Dail, elected in 1922, worked as a national convention to frame the constitution of the new state. The fourth Dail, elected in August 1923, was the first to be constituted under a purely Irish electoral law. Near independence of the Irish Free State can therefore be dated to 1922, while absolute independence was achieved in various stages between 1933 and 1949, after which the country emerged as the sovereign Republic of Ireland. In 1922–1923, the antitreaty groups continued their policy of absenteeism, ignoring all the institutions of the new state. In 1925, a further split in the antitreaty Sinn Fein was determined by a group of pragmatic members who believed that parliamentary participation was better than total absenteeism. The opposition party, Fianna Fail, was founded in May 1926. In the August 1927 election, antitreaty deputies were voted into parliament, and, in 1932, being the largest parliamentary group, they formed their first cabinet.[69]

How, then, did the working-class and socialist movement enter this series of conflicts and alliances? The urban middle classes were economically weak and numerically limited, and small farmers were originally mobilized by Catholic emancipation, radical land requests, and national

---

[68] None of the British Electoral Reform Acts between 1882 and 1884 were extended to Ireland without substantial dilution. The enfranchised population was 6.5% of the adult population in 1868 and reached 26.9% in 1885. The secret ballot was introduced in 1872.

[69] For a history of the period, see Murphy (1975).

home rule. Under these conditions, the possibility of a delegated representation of the early working-class organizations within a liberal movement was nonexistent, and the labor movement developed with only a weak link to liberal political allies. The rivalry among the three great issues of Catholic emancipation, peasants and land, and home rule sometimes paralyzed Irish development, and their occasional coincidence produced great upheaval. Combined, these issues determined the sporadic and ultimately unsuccessful development of the social-class issues and the proletarian movement. Whenever a choice was to be made about priority among the various issues, socialist and proletarian issues invariably lost out to nationalism, Catholic influence, and peasant conservatism.[70]

In both Ireland and Finland, then, the predominance of the national issue subordinated liberalism to nationalism and negated any form of early Lib–Lab cooperation and support. However, this common feature leaves open the question of why this situation resulted in two opposite outcomes in regard to the strength and ideological orientation of the socialist left. I shall start by discussing the Finnish exceptionalism and shall later test the conclusions against the polar exceptionalism of Ireland.

One interpretive line centers on the socioeconomic conditions fostering status polarization in the agricultural population and how these established favorable conditions for the electoral appeal of Finnish socialism. In 1910, 85% of the Finnish population lived in the countryside; two-thirds of them were engaged in agriculture, particularly small-scale farming; over three-quarters of the farms were less than ten hectares in size, and the few large estates were to be found in the most fertile parts of the south and southwest. As a result, in 1907, nine-tenths of the socialist votes came from the countryside,[71] where the party received most of its support from agricultural workers and the crofters (small leaseholders who paid their rent either by working a number of days for the landowner or by making money payments). Such a high level of agrarian support for the labor movement is unique in Europe. Unlike the peasants in other countries, Finnish peasant communities owned the forests, and as a result of the timber-led industrial development, the effects of capitalism were felt immediately in the countryside; landowners and peasants prospered by entering the market and exploring alternative uses of production factors (e.g., from arable farming to stock raising and dairy farming). This transformation altered the relationship between the landowners and the landless

---

[70] Thornley (1974: 37).
[71] For English sources on early Finnish socialism, see Alapuro (1981), Knoellinger (1960), and Kirby (1971) and (1990).

peasants and crofters, all of whom were increasingly dominated by the market forces (in a country that, it should be remembered, had a low rate of emigration). The commercialization and rising prosperity of landowners and freeholders widened the gap with the landless and tenants. All these factors led to early radicalization of some sectors of the very large agricultural population and to growing class conflicts in the countryside.[72]

The strength of this rural class conflict and the division of the agricultural population into several often antagonistic social groups (the large landowners, the small independent farmers, and a large segment of landless agricultural workers, crofters, and tenants) bring Finland into line with the conditions of large parts of southern Europe, particularly Spain and Italy. On the other hand, the late but rapid and penetrating development of capitalism in the countryside as a result of the forestry economy is a feature almost unique to Finland. The large number of landless or land-eager peasants, the high population pressure over the land, and the forms of sharecropping or crofting are characteristics that can be regarded as favorable to the penetration of socialism in the countryside, because they are important for its ideological orientation and organizational cohesion.

To understand how the Finnish socialist movement managed to exploit this opportunity to the maximum, four additional political conditions need to be added to clarify how this concrete organizational solidarity between the small working-class population and the huge rural proletarian and tenant population became possible. The *first* special condition to be recalled (see Chapter 4) is the exceptionally high level of literacy in Finnish rural society: the extensive network of elementary schools in the countryside and the consequent availability of organizational skills among the rural population, as well as local cultural leadership (the school teacher, the church). The *second* important element is that the Finnish rural communities were exceptionally well organized politically from a comparative point of view.[73] The role played by nineteenth-century linguistic and nationalistic movements in fostering this intense political activism and organization should be considered here. The early, strong local political organization of the Finnish socialists is considered to be as difficult to explain as their strong electoral rural inroads, although the former may be the explanation of the latter.[74]

---

[72] Alapuro (1981).
[73] Quoted by Alapuro (1981: 274) and others.
[74] Alapuro (1981: 274) considers this as a peripheral aspect: "The party was not only strongly supported, but also well organised in the countryside."

A *third* element is the exceptional and unique opportunity for the expansion of the Socialist Party that came about through the sudden mobilization of the 1905 strike and the electoral reform that multiplied by ten the number of those entitled to vote.[75] Until 1905, national electoral politics and the Diet were completely closed to Social Democrats, who consequently concentrated on building their own organizational infrastructure, creating a dense network of extraparliamentary local organizations, centers, and branches, soon supplemented by women's and youth leagues. The party was thus a mobilizing organization for political education and working-class formation and was clearly very efficient organizationally before it had to face any electoral politics issue.[76] Indeed, this concentration on organization and penetration was vital in that it enabled electoral success. Given the traditional nature of the political system, practically no other national political organization existed prior to the granting of universal suffrage, and – in particular – the Finnish nationalists (agrarian and conservative) were ill equipped to contest elections. Thus, the Socialist Party owed much of its success at the polls to the fact that it was organizationally better prepared to contest them.[77] In addition, the national patriotic character of the 1905–1907 mobilization was crucial in cementing the class movement with the nationalistic issue. This phenomenon was absent in Ireland, where the incipient labor movement left the management of the nationalist issues to other partners (see later). Moreover, the revolution of 1905 and the belief in the efficacy of spontaneous mass action strongly influenced the subsequent radical militantism of the socialist movement.[78]

A *fourth* political feature was the specifically political character of the socialist movement in Finland that resulted from the weakness of the trade unions. Party membership outweighed the trade union membership (see the data and discussion in Chapter 6). Unions were concentrated in craft sectors and urban centers, offered little or nothing to the rural proletariat, and had little or no influence on or control over the political organization. As a consequence, the Socialist Party – in sharp contrast with the Irish experience – was not constrained by corporate interlinkages and had great latitude for strategic action. This allowed it to devise appeals to the rural

---

[75] Alapuro (1981: 286–287).
[76] On the lead of the Finnish socialist organization over all the other parties and for its concentration mainly on organizational and recruitment issues, see Nousiainen (1960: 28–43).
[77] Kirby (1990: 526).
[78] On the Red Guard movement mythology of radical protest, see Kirby (1986).

poor and landless or leaseholders without facing internal resistance or constraints.[79]

These Finnish features can be contrasted with the interpretations of the failure of class politics in Ireland. The explanations focusing on economic backwardness, the predominance of the agricultural population, late industrialization, the small size of the working class, and, consequently, low class consciousness[80] do not work comparatively, as these features were present in other countries, too.[81] From an Irish–Finnish perspective, the difference concerns the socialist penetration of the countryside and of the urban middle classes rather than the strength of the working class or the level of industrialization. Another explanation of the failure of class politics[82] is the intense rural conflict throughout the nineteenth century. In reality, this conflict did not radicalize rural laborers or the industrial laborers who had been recently recruited from rural society, as was the case in Finland. This was because the Irish "land war" of 1879–1882 was a struggle between landlords and a land movement (Land League) dominated by larger tenant farmer interests; the dominant purpose of the Land League was to obtain landownership, while radical proposals (e.g., Michael Davitt's proposal to nationalize land) remained peripheral. Class polarization in the countryside along Finnish lines therefore did not develop in Ireland, and by the beginning of the twentieth-century the land reforms had created a class of small, independent peasants for whom landed property (and deep religious feelings) meant that they adopted a conservative political orientation. On the other hand, Irish employers quickly accepted pluralist rules for industrial relations, and apart from some resistance in the 1907–1914 period, no great militancy by employers was registered. Thus, even in the field of industrial conflict, no class radicalization was produced. Finally, the early tradition of popular politics dating from the beginning

[79] An additional element was the fact that the rise of popular mass organizations coincided with the decline of religious observance and a weakening of church authority. This phenomenon primarily concerned factory workers and the rural population. See Kirby (1990: 532–533). Even in Finland, the temperance movement played an important mobilizing role, although it was not comparable to that in other Scandinavian countries.

[80] For instance, Orridge (1975: 484–491) attributes an important role to this factor, combining it with Catholic influence and nationalism.

[81] In rejecting this interpretation, Mair (1992) also provides data about class awareness showing that this is not lower in Ireland than in other countries. The data, however, refer to the end of the 1980s.

[82] A second hypothesis attributes the failure of the Labour Party to the clientelist and individualistic mobilization network set up by Fianna Fail in the countryside. The thesis exaggerates the role of clientelism in Irish politics, lacks comparative reference to other cases, and identifies as responsible for the socialist electoral failure exactly what class politics should have broken down.

of the nineteenth century (the Catholic emancipation issue) established, for some historians, a tradition of cross-class political activism, adding another debilitating factor to class appeal.

A further explanation is often sought in the Catholic influence (particularly in the countryside). Secularization was never a source of political division in Ireland,[83] and this is an important difference from highly secularized and literate Finland, where not only was Catholicism absent, but where there was also a fairly strong (at least for homogeneously Protestant countries) clerical–anticlerical opposition that eased the entry of the socialists into certain milieus. Combining nationalism with Catholicism, Peter Mair[84] has presented a chain of political explanations: (1) cleavage lines dominated by an opposition movement imbued with a nationalistic and Catholic identity; (2) the consequent development of a culture emphasizing solidarity, cohesion, and homogeneity; (3) successful representation by a "national" party that had always insisted on such a role (first Sinn Fein and later Fianna Fail); and (4) reinforcement by the incapacity of the Irish Labour Party to advance a class appeal and a policy line consistently. The last factor is nationalism, whose dominant role did not decline after World War I, as it did in Finland. Yet, by the 1920s and 1930s, the failure of Irish class politics had already become apparent. If, therefore, we take nationalistic mobilization to be important, it must explain both why the potential socialist constituency was captured by nationalist politics before the 1920s in Ireland and why this did not occur in Finland in the same period.

The failure of class politics in Ireland invites, therefore, a host of reasonable explanations. Of these explanations, the weak structural condition of class antagonism in the market combined with the powerful political attraction of two cross-class reinforcing appeals (Catholicism and nationalism) is convincing. Yet, one doubt remains: Why were labor and socialist organizations, intellectuals, and militants so weak in these developments? Why did they not manage (or even try) to shape and build on anticlericalism, as happened in so many Catholic countries on the Continent? Why did they not try to guide or focus the turmoil in the countryside, as was often the case on the Continent in the same period? And why, finally, did they not try to find a place for themselves within the nationalistic movement, infusing it with socialist values and goals and exploiting its mobilization potential, as happened in Finland?

Irish socialism lost a war that it never fought. Its failure to compete is

---

[83] Orridge (1975: 484–491).
[84] Mair (1992: 383–410).

macroscopic. For example, in 1918, Sein Fein worked actively to ensure that class divisions would not disrupt the national revolution, units of the Irish Republic Army being forbidden to take part in land seizure; indeed, they often worked to end radical factory and land actions. This led to a dilemma for the trade unions and the Labour Party: whether or not to contest elections and thus oppose nationalist Sein Fein candidates. Sein Fein obviously sought to dissuade labor from doing so; they suggested that social issues could be dealt with only *after* independence. The contrast with Finland is clear here. Not only did the Finnish Social Democrats not renounce their partisan activities until independence was achieved, but the national issue itself was much more closely linked to the social cleavage there, given that part of the Finnish bourgeoisie was aligned with the tsar. In Ireland, the trade unions and the Labour Party finally decided not to contest the 1918 election, the first under universal adult suffrage. The near civil war that ensued between pro- and antitreaty parties radicalized the country on the one issue on which the working-class constituency was possibly divided, but the Labor Party organization did not try to overcome, contain, or direct such a division; indeed, it abstained. Its involvement in the national revolution in a subordinate and muted position contributed to the containment of working-class militancy, and thus it can be concluded that class conflict was deliberately contained.

It can be argued[85] that the decision of Labour to withdraw from the 1918 general election, in which two out of three voters voted for the first time as a result of the recent enfranchisement, was fatal and that, by not contesting the election, Labour allowed Sinn Fein, the Unionists, and the Irish Parliamentary Party to monopolize the campaign and orient first-time voters, as well as helping to establish the hegemony of nationalist issues and cleavages. However, this damage was not irreparable,[86] given that approximately 55% of the newly enfranchised electorate did not actually vote.[87] More damaging was probably the subsequent inability of the socialists to compete electorally with the other parties. On the treaty and the Free State's relationship to the United Kingdom, Labour's stand was confused and ambiguous in comparison to that of Fianna Fail and Cumann na nGaedheal. It was against the treaty and against the oath of allegiance, but it refused to make these points central parts of its program,

---

[85] Farrell (1970) and (1971: 487–488).
[86] Mair (1978).
[87] In its first elections in 1922, the Irish Labour Party got 21% of the vote, but this percentage is not reliable, as the already exploded institutional conflict between the pro- and antitreaty factions resulted in a very low turnout, a large number of uncontested seats (30%), and muted party competition.

arguing that the economic issue took precedence over constitutional details.[88] On the economic policy dimension, Fianna Fail argued for autarchy and self-sufficiency – trying to attract the support of the small farmers and petit bourgeoisie concentrated mainly in the west and southwest – while the government argued for open economic policy and free trade – defended by the large farmers concentrated in the east and southeast: The Irish Labour Party emphasized welfarist policies oriented to the urban proletariat, which had minimal appeal for the majority of the population. The Irish socialists failed to compete electorally over the salient issues that shaped the party system. As a result, they found themselves in a central position by default, advocating either intermediate positions or different themes on both major issues in a highly polarized context.[89]

In interpreting this situation, it is necessary to stress the importance of Ireland as a periphery of the United Kingdom. The main British contribution to the failure of the socialists was to shield Irish socialism culturally from the continental ideological influences that appeared to be anachronistic in the British context of strong industrial unions but that might have helped Irish socialism to shape its strategic role more effectively. These influences were those of Marxism and anarcho-syndicalism, the peasant and land debate faced by many continental socialist parties, but also the development of the anticlerical themes and feelings of continental socialism. The Irish trade union movement was so deeply influenced by the British model (from which it developed) that it was even incapable of thinking in terms of peasant mobilization and support. Clearly, however, a British craft-style unionism would never manage to radicalize the peasantry.

In Finland, political socialism dominated a very weak trade union movement and directed it according to a competitive electoral logic. This organizational resource made it capable of exploiting the sudden democratization within the context of a national liberation movement. The Irish Labour Party was exactly the opposite: an indirect, trade union–dominated, partisan undermobilized party with no resources and little or no capacity for tactical political maneuvering and strategic behavior. It simply represented the organized trade union stand, which was an extension of the

[88] See Mitchell (1974: 272).
[89] A statistical analysis of swings in these elections shows that the Irish Labour Party lost support to both major parties, particularly to the government party, probably because it alienated the laborers on the big farms in the forefront of the export trade to Britain (and favoring an open economy) and also because it had previously enjoyed the support of antitreaty voters who had expressed their dissatisfaction by voting Labour when Fianna Fail abstained. See Mair (1978: 67–68).

more single-minded unions and as such refused to accept the logic of electoral competition. In Finland, late and sudden political and electoral mobilization had been preceded by the strong organizational development of political socialism. In Ireland, the much earlier popular mobilization and politicization of alternative divisive issues took place in the absence of any autonomous organizational consolidation of political and party socialism. The latter was based on and depended on narrow corporate bases and remained, even ideologically, the inexorable prisoner of a small section of the urban working class.

MOBILIZATION OF THE RELIGIOUS CLEAVAGE AND THE FORMATION OF DENOMINATIONAL PARTIES

In this section, I concentrate on the intertwining issues of religious and class mobilization and, in particular, on

1. Whether and to what extent religious identities were politicized, that is, politically characterized and crystallized by and through conflict over policies that concerned them.
2. Whether religious affiliations and allegiances were not only politicized, but also organized by purpose-specific political organizations in the corporate and electoral/parliamentary channels.
3. The timing of such politicization and organization vis-à-vis class cleavage politicization and organizational mobilization.

Religious issues and religious groups may exist without gaining much political importance, as they are not linked to specific policy alternatives; or they may have political importance without, however, being linked to specific electoral and corporate organizations. Depoliticization versus politicization, the presence or absence of specific organizational mobilization, and the timing of the former with respect to class cleavage development are the three main coordinates of this section.

The structuring of a preindustrial cleavage line such as religion impinges on class mobilization and the formation of the class cleavage in various ways. The Protestant–Catholic dividing line was important because the close relationship between state and church and the incorporation of the church into the state bureaucracy in the Protestant world reduced or eliminated the potential for a state–church conflict. Moreover, the Reformation produced an early nationalization of the territorial culture.

This favored the processes of mobilization from below, also because the early development of literacy aided and encouraged the mobilization of the lower strata into mass politics. In contrast, in Catholic territories, the supranational nature and attitude of the church tended to favor mobilization from above by Catholic hierarchies; the delay of literacy made the mobilization of the lower classes from below more difficult, and the conflict over the control of the educational system and of mass education led to the mobilization of the church against the state.

Class unionism appealed to a wide potential base regardless of other identities; it referred to the workers' interests and conditions in the functional division of labor. However, such an appeal was more successful where other community identities, which could rely on preexisting groups for cultural organizational consolidation, did not exist. So, in general, we may expect the mobilization of religious cleavages to influence the development of class cleavage in all its dimensions: in its electoral potential, insofar as it may reduce its lower-class constituency; on its social composition, insofar as it may lead to radical anticlerical middle-class socialism; in its organizational nature, insofar as it may give a defensive subcultural style to the class cleavage, making it less expansive and more reliant on closed community groups and traditions; and in its organizational cohesion, insofar as the relationship with a religious political movement that is both a competitor and a potential ally may further exacerbate the internal conflicts that lead to organizational divisions. To analyze the variety of political denominational experiences, I use the categories presented in Table 8.1.[90]

"National establishment church" identifies the experience of the dominant and state hegemonic Protestant churches of the Northern European countries that were religiously homogeneous (with the partial exception of Great Britain) and state hegemonic in the sense that they enjoyed territorial dominance, legal privilege, and privileged access to secular rulers. In these countries, the early incorporation of the national church hierarchies within the national bureaucracy, and the absence of the dualism between state and church hierarchies, meant that a church–state cleavage never developed during the phase of nationalization and political democratization. In the United Kingdom, as well as in Scandinavia, dissident religious movements, in particular Methodism, played an important role in raising workers' cultural level and self-respect in the very early phase. The lay preachers enjoyed the confidence of their fellow laborers and won their

---

[90] Labels of these types are inspired by the typology of the church's political attitudes in Latin America by Vallier (1970a) and (1970b).

Table 8.1. *Types of churches*

type	subtype	cases
state hegemonic (national establishment church)		Great Britain, Scandinavia, Finland
political church	monopoly church	Austria under the empire; Ireland after independence
	ideological clericalism	France, Belgium, Italy from 1913, Austria under the Republic
	ghetto church	Germany, Netherlands, Switzerland, Italy until 1908
national emancipation church		Ireland to independence

trust, and this was important for the formation and rise of independent internal protest leadership among workers.[91] In the United Kingdom, however, no independent religiously inspired politico-electoral movement ever emerged, while in Scandinavia small Christian Democratic parties drawing on the Lutheran faith emerged only when the socialist mobilization had been completed.[92] Rather than being an early reaction to the political challenge expressed by liberals or to the social challenge expressed by socialists, denominational mobilization appears more as a late reaction to the accelerated secularization and even the de-Christianization of societies.[93]

The term "political church" can be explained as follows: In continental nations and in Ireland, the churches and denominational movements took clear, active political stands early in the phase of nation formation and mass political mobilization, and religious issues were politicized to a certain extent everywhere, even if not necessarily through the formation of distinct corporate or electoral organizations. The 1864 papal denunciation of liberal doctrines in the *Syllabus of Errors* and the First Vatican Council dogma of papal infallibility in 1870 were motivational steps for the political and electoral organization of Catholic movements. However, the presence of elected representatives of the Catholic communities (excluding the traditional clerical membership of upper houses of parliament) predates

---

[91] See Rimlinger (1960: 333). On the impact of Methodism, see Wearmouth (1937: 221–238). Pelling (1965: 191–192) claims that labor was initially more successful where religious nonconformism had been particularly strong in the past.

[92] Only in Norway does a Christian Party date back to the 1930s, but it managed to poll an average of 10% of the votes and gain national importance only in the late 1950s and early 1960s. The circumstances surrounding the late emergence of these religious parties are described and discussed in Madeley (1977). On the religious dimension in Norwegian politics, see Converse and Valen (1971) and Valen and Rokkan (1974).

[93] Berglund and Lindström (1978: 61).

such documents. As early as 1830, in Belgium, 30 of the 200 members of the assembly were priests. The Austrian Reichstag of 1830 included twenty elected clergymen. In the French Constituent Assembly of 1848, three bishops and twelve priests were elected. Twenty-eight Catholic clergy representatives were present in the Prussian national assembly of 1848, and thirteen Catholic clergy representatives were elected in the Frankfurt Vorparlament of 1848 (representing all of Germany).

The subtype I have labeled the "monopoly church" was characteristic of homogeneous Catholic countries, where the church enjoyed territorial dominance and legal privilege, as well as continuing control of the educational system. In Austria, the Catholic Church had always been one of the pillars of the imperial central establishment, and the state–church relationship and formal concordats – such as that of 1855 – were extremely favorable to the church's dominant and monopolistic position. Even in the years of stronger liberal influence (the 1870s and thereafter), the abolition of the concordat, and the formal separation between state and church, a close link between Catholic interests and state direction was maintained, as were several of the church's privileges. Catholicism and the Catholic hierarchy were so strongly associated with the authoritarian monarchical state and enjoyed such privileged access to the secular rulers that for many years no need for political self-representation was felt, although the conservative political identity of Catholics and Catholic organizations had been well established for a long time.

The Catholic Party was formed by Karl Lueger very late, from 1905 to 1907, and with some reluctance. From the beginning, it was a mass antisocialist political movement, in a country where political liberalism had never developed and where conservative circles rallied around monarchical and bureaucratic institutions, refusing to organize politically for electoral competition. Therefore, after the collapse of the empire, the Catholics inherited the representation of virtually the entire political spectrum from the center to the extreme right. The party was able to combine, if uneasily, dynastic revanchism and state-bureaucratic interests, deep-rooted nationalism (*Heimwehr*), and the peasants' radical wing (which was the least hostile to the socialists). This coalition of interests also explains why, during the 1920s and 1930s, Austrian Catholicism maintained a residual hostility to the new republican political system and an implicit identification with and adherence to traditional state structures and bureaucracies, repeatedly advocating "corporatist" reforms and pressing for constitutional revision in a less liberal direction.

The Catholic political movement, having organized itself against the well-rooted socialist mobilization and having inherited establishment in-

terest representation, had strong class-based social support from the beginning – that is to say, it was strong among the urban middle classes and
the peasants but very weak among the urban proletariat. In contrast to the
other continental cases, Catholic mobilization in Austria did not preempt
or cut across class appeals, but rather reinforced the dividing line of the
latter.[94] This class base and *étatism* made Austrian Catholicism different
from the ideological clerical variant that I consider to be typical of the
French and Belgian experiences and also different from the opposition or
ghetto variants that represent the early experiences of Dutch, Swiss, and
German Catholicism.

The subtype labeled "ideological clericalism" is typical of homogeneously Catholic countries and is characterized by the following elements: (1)
it faced ideological anticlericalism and early attempts to sharply curtail its
position and privileges by strong liberal forces; (2) the Catholic Church
and community aligned with conservatives; (3) it was politically identified
and drawn into partisan conflict at an early stage that preceded the political
organization of the socialist movement. In France and Belgium, the Catholic community developed a political identity early in the nineteenth
century, but the outcomes of this process were very different: early electoral
and political organization in Belgium versus late and failed organization
in France.

As mentioned before, the political role of the Catholic elite is a
constitutive element of the Belgian polity given its role in the secession
from the Netherlands. The Catholics had been the system support group
and party from the beginning. In the mobilization confrontation with the
liberals, they developed an early popular tendency. By 1867, a Federation
of the Catholic Workers Societies existed, and by 1886 the Belgian Democratic League was a coalition of Catholic ancillary organizations in all
fields: trade unions, cooperatives, rural banks, mutualities, and so on.
Therefore, notwithstanding the ongoing internal strife in the Catholic
world between Christian-social and conservative Catholics (the Rexist
Movement) and between the Walloon and Flemish wings, Belgian Catholicism mobilized early, more as an antisecular and antiliberal reaction than
as an antisocialist one, and was never in a monopolistic position, strongly
relying on its own forces as an independent movement. How important
the early political inroads of the Belgian Catholics were for the successive
development of the socialists is indicated by the strong territorial comple-

[94] On this peculiar class base of Austrian political Catholicism, see Houska (1985: 18–124,
163–166).

mentarity of the two movements in the first half of the twentieth century. In Brussels and Walloon, the early electoral impact of socialism was mainly at the expense of the liberals,[95] while in the more rural and less secular Flanders, the strong inroads made by the Catholics and the influence of the church countered the growth of socialist organization from 1910 to 1920.[96] Linguistic differences did not play a role at this stage.

In France, political Catholicism passed through a number of different political experiences. The shock of the 1789 revolution, the 1848 revolution, and the Commune forged its role as an early antiliberal and antisocialist force. Napoleon III enjoyed Catholic support or neutrality,[97] and in this phase the links of the Catholic Church with monarchical sectors and Bonapartists prevented the emergence of autonomous Catholic forces. During the Third Republic, the Catholics supported the moderate, conservative, and monarchical sections. However, after the defeat of the monarchical forces that had formed behind Boulanger, the Catholic conservative forces rallied to the Republic. Even when they confronted widespread anticlericalism and anticlerical legislation in the 1880s and again in 1900–1905,[98] no party was organized. Divided into left and right, as everywhere else, French Catholics were also divided into republicans and monarchists, and attempts to form a Catholic Party failed repeatedly from 1885 on. The Catholic hierarchy could not agree, and the pope often discouraged Catholics' attempts to organize themselves politically for fear of the development of an overly monarchical party. Other internal divisions of a different nature (the relationship of the pope with a nationalistic hierarchy authoritarian and antidemocratic tendencies, the Dreyfus affair, and the Action Française) further complicated the issue, so that no common ground for Catholic alignment was established before World War I or between the world wars.[99] In sum, the clerical guidance in politics was weak and unable to move beyond general indications of tendency.

---

[95] Hill (1974: 37).

[96] Hill (1974: 39, 43).

[97] He gained this support through the 1850 *loi Falloux* – which gave the church extensive rights in secondary education – by sending its troops to crush the Roman Republic and to restore Pius IX to the papal seat, and later by acting as the defender of papal temporal power.

[98] With Catholic schools deprived of all state aid and most religious orders expelled, extensive church property taken over by the state, diplomatic relations with the Vatican broken, and state and church separated.

[99] There were several attempts to build an autonomous political organization of the French Catholics from the 1890s to 1945: 1896 the *Parti démocrate chrétien; le Sillon* of Marc Sangnier in 1910; the *Action Liberale Populaire* between the world wars; and the *Parti*

Attempts to create a "social Catholicism" remained isolated and un-successful, and during the second half of the nineteenth century, no real Catholic political current existed within the working class. From 1894 on, there were several timid attempts to set up mixed trade unions, but only in 1919 was the Confédération Française des Travailleurs Chrétiens (CFTC), the most successful (mildly) Catholic social movement, founded. In France, therefore, the politicization of religious issues and of Catholic identity was originally antiliberal and antirepublican. The repeated failures in organi-zational mobilization and encapsulation were due to the fact that these attempts were led by either right-of-center or left-of-center intellectuals and political elites, in contrast with the bulk of the Catholic-motivated electorate, which existed more in the center. Perhaps for these reasons, the Catholic hierarchy never openly supported any of these parties. French Catholicism therefore remained organizationally "open,"[100] although it was strongly characterized politically, with Catholics supporting mainly con-servative and moderate forces or, less frequently, mildly progressive forces.

The Italian experience has been characterized in two boxes in Table 8.1. First, it can be likened to the experience of a "ghetto church" (see later) for the period between the 1860s and the 1900s. The Catholic Church's break with the liberal and conservative elite, which had unified the country at the direct expense of the papal state territories, was far deeper than in Belgium or France. From the 1900s on, however, the progressive acceptance of the new Italian state transformed this role, so that from 1898 on – five years after the official founding of the Italian Socialist Party – a Catholic union movement started to develop. This was most successful in the areas of Piedmont, Lombardy, and the Veneto, where the influence of the church was stronger and relied on a large number of intermediate Catholic associations and institutions (savings banks, mutual societies, etc.). From 1896 on, the Opera dei Congressi started, in its own words, to prepare "in abstentionism . . . the healthy, educated and orga-nized body of Catholic electors for the moment in which even the conquest of political power will be possible."[101] By 1910, Catholic unions had established a network of trade associations and a general executive was so

---

démocrate populaire in 1924. A similar fate eventually undermined the most successful Christian political experience, the *Mouvement Républicain Populaire* after 1945. On these various experiences, see Vaussard (1956: 86–105). For an analysis of why Catholic party formation failed in France, see Kalivas (1996: 114–165).

[100] The distinction between open and closed Catholicism is drawn by White (1981: 7–8, 147). I use it to indicate the level of organizational encapsulation of the Catholic community and electorate.

[101] Quoted in Galli (1968: 26).

organized in Bergamo in 1909.[102] In 1905, a new papal encyclical (*Il fermo proposito*) finally authorized Catholics to vote in the constituencies where the bishop of the diocese deemed it advisable. Sixteen members of parliament were elected in 1905 with crucial Catholic support, and their number increased progressively until World War I.

For thirty years (from 1870 to about 1900), church opposition in Italy played a clear antisystem role, depriving the liberal and conservative forces of a potentially broader popular base of support and contributing to the delay of suffrage extension. At the same time, the attitude of the church largely helped shape the closed and self-referential political attitude of the Catholic subculture within the liberal state and society. The intransigence of the church against the political participation of Catholics in the new state meant that what was a potentially important political issue remained dormant. The religious cleavage existed, but it was not given political expression until the first decade of the twentieth-century. Thus, socialism developed in this climate for twenty years without any specific Catholic competition. It should, however, be remembered that throughout this period the suffrage was highly restricted.

The level of enfranchisement creates a crucial difference between Italy and France. In France, the attempts by Marc Sangnier in 1909 and by the Parti Démocrate Populaire in 1924 to form a Catholic party met with ambivalent and uncertain support from the Catholic hierarchy. These were not attempts to represent a Catholic world that had hitherto been politically unrepresented and/or excluded, but rather were attempts to detach this world (or part of it) from a representation delegated to moderate and conservative sectors. This switch from consolidated conservative representation to direct Catholic mobilization was more difficult organizationally and electorally, and also less profitable from the point of view of the Catholic Church hierarchy. In Italy, the territorial dimension of the Catholic opposition *and* the restricted suffrage (with the exclusion of the rural masses from electoral competition) meant that Catholics could not be represented by conservative forces. The foundation of a Catholic Party, after World War I, paralleled the introduction of universal suffrage and proportional representation, with no popular conservative representation to defeat and substitute. This offered an exceptionally favorable opportunity to the organizers of the Catholic Party.

These differences in Catholic political representation were important for the nature of the class cleavage that developed in the two countries. Confronted with the late entry of an organizationally closed, subculturally

---

[102] On early Catholic efforts in this domain, see Rossi (1985: 3–49).

encapsulated, and politically autonomous Catholic opposition, Italian socialism (and later on, communism) developed more-pronounced organizational subcultures of their own to contrast with and fight the Catholic one.
In France, strong links between the political parties and civic society never
developed in either the Catholic world or, later, in the class left. With a
less organizationally and subculturally bound electorate, the French socialists and communists never really felt the need to develop a counterculture
or a strong organizational network of party-linked associations. As a result,
they remained ideological currents rather than organizational machines;
that is to say, they relied more on ideological competition than on organizational mobilization.[103]

Catholic political mobilization was very early and organizationally
dense in Belgium, late but also organizationally dense in Italy, and completely absent in France. However, in all three countries, anticlericalism
came to play a crucial role in the ideological identity of radicalism and the
left.[104] If denominational and clerical mobilization tended to be inherently
cross-class, the same is true of its opposite, secularism and anticlericalism.
What denominational appeals subtracted from socialist mobilization potential in terms of lower-class constituency, and therefore in terms of social
homogeneity of support, could be "reimbursed" by radical anticlerical
middle-class support in homogeneous Catholic countries. This contributed
to the shaping of a class cleavage that was not necessarily weaker in terms
of electoral support than that of countries where denominational mobilization was absent, but it was different in terms of social composition,
being less class homogeneous.

The subtype I have labeled the "ghetto church" is characterized in its
early phase by isolation and defensiveness, either because of minority
disadvantages and emancipation demands or because of the will and need
to insulate Catholicism from secular forces or competing denominational
forces. This is typical of Catholic political representation in the religiously
mixed central European countries – Germany, the Netherlands, and Switzerland – where the national and nation-building establishment was predominantly Protestant. In these countries, the Catholic identity was politicized historically in this process of state building and was reinforced by
the emancipation fight within predominantly Protestant contexts.

The Catholic movement in the German Reich (the Catholic Center

---

[103] The tribune role (*function tribunitienne*) that Lavau perceptively sees as a characteristic of
French Communism; Lavau (1968: 445–466).
[104] For Belgium, see Kittell (1973) and Strikwerda (1988).

Party) emerged from a broad tradition of Catholic resistance to the secular state and to the Prussian-led German national unification that excluded Austria. In the overwhelmingly Protestant monarchy and bureaucracy of Prussia, one-third of the population was Catholic, and already in the 1840s there was considerable mobilization on issues concerning national unification (preferred with Austria), civil marriage, and secular education, on which Catholics organizations differentiated their position from that of the liberals. They also diverged from pro-Protestant conservatives. Catholics could, therefore, organize themselves only as a separate group. By 1852, a distinct Catholic Party existed in the Prussian parliament. However, Catholics felt themselves to be a besieged minority even in unified Germany. The *Kulturkampf* started in 1871 and culminated with the laws of May 1873 (control over the formation of the clergy, attribution of seats, limitation of the disciplinary power of the church; institution of a national court for ecclesiastical issues), which were weakened from 1878 on due to the conciliatory intervention of the Vatican and were finally abolished with the 1887 "peace law." By then, the political mobilization of Catholics was already very advanced. It materialized into a network of Catholic associations and into a strong clerical presence in the cadres of the Center Party.

Catholic action in the social field occurred as early as that of the socialists. By the end of the 1860s, Bishop Ketteler was promoting the "social-Christian" associations directed at German workers in competition with the Lassallian union organizations. It is estimated that in the general and universal male suffrage election of 1881, 86% of Catholic voters voted for the Center Party.[105] The later development of the Catholic Party moved in an increasingly conservative direction. In their search for legalism and recognition, the Catholics ended up identifying themselves with the imperialism and colonialism of Wilhelmine Germany, and, like the Social Democrats, believed that the coming of World War I would provide a good occasion to show their patriotism and obtain "national rehabilitation."

In the Netherlands, the two most important religious minorities – the orthodox Calvinists and the Roman Catholics – had first launched a successful emancipation movement some decades before the working class began to respond to the call of socialism. The Roman Catholic minority was heavily concentrated in the southern provinces of Limburg and North Brabant. Strictly speaking, only in 1896 and 1897 did all electoral Catholic associations accept a common political platform (the General Union of

---

[105] Brezzi (1979: 113).

Catholic Electoral Associations), and only in 1904 was the Catholics Political Party finally formed.[106] However, the political action of the Catholics as such went back much further: Since the 1840s, they had fought for the reestablishment of the Catholic hierarchy, which they achieved in 1853. Between 1840 and 1860, Catholics supported liberals and their call for the separation of the state and the (Protestant) church. This alliance was broken in the 1860s and was slowly replaced by an alliance with the Anti-Revolutionary Party, which brought about the electoral defeat of the liberals in 1888.

Throughout this period and later on, electoral associations of the Catholics were active, even though a formal party was lacking. It was, however, the struggle for subsidized private religious schools that provided the first major catalyst for mass action. The liberal Education Act of 1878 had already triggered massive petition movements, and the religious calls for national action and organization eventually resulted in the formation of the Anti-Revolutionary Party in 1879 (the first effective national party, as already mentioned). It was this common Catholic and Calvinist interest in subsidized religious schools that forced the two organizations to cooperate in parliament on the basis of an antiliberal stance.[107] Obviously, the uniqueness of the Dutch case lies in the division of the national Protestant establishment, which led to the very early formation of an orthodox Calvinist opposition. Catholics, instead of facing a common strong Protestant hegemonic establishment, had to strive for recognition and emancipation in a complex multicleavage environment that offered ample opportunities for electoral and political alliances long before the socialists started their political and electoral activities.

In Switzerland, a strong Catholic identity was reinforced and supported by territorial cantonal concentration and identification and by longstanding international issues concerning Swiss alliance politics in international relations. The Sonderbund, defeated in 1847, reinforced this highly territorialized political identity. Confessional rivalries, sometimes masking other conflicts of a territorial, economic, and strategic nature, characterized the post-Sonderbund period from 1874 on, when exceptional measures

---

[106] Righart's comparative study of Catholic mobilization in the Netherlands, Switzerland, Belgium, and Austria (1986) lends support to Daalder's thesis: The development of the Catholic pillar (*zuil*) was mainly due to the effort of Catholics in the diaspora, i.e., of Catholics in territories not dominated by the Catholics. In the more traditional and less developed centers of Catholic domination (Brabant, Limburg, and the Catholic cantons in the central part of Switzerland), they resisted the formation of a Catholic organizational infrastructure in politics and trade unions.

[107] Daalder (1981: 220–222).

were taken by the new federal constitution to limit Jesuit activities, the number of Catholic convents, and so on. Therefore, the Swiss had their own limited *Kulturkampf* on the issue of the 1874–1876 constitutional reform. However, Catholics had a power base in cantons where they were the majority. They were an isolated but territorially represented opposition. This strong territorial concentration and representation delayed the formation of a federal party because, while parties and movements were present at the cantonal level, it was viewed as difficult, and perhaps unnecessary, to coalesce into a national Catholic movement. Thus, the cantonal basis of Swiss Catholicism actually worked against its centralization, blocking attempts at national political unification. When in 1912 a Catholic federal party was finally founded, its formation was accelerated by the growing strength of the socialists.[108]

The Dutch, German, and Swiss Catholic political movements are all characterized by the same features: those of minority movements with a relatively high territorial concentration that mobilized early against state/ nation builders on the emancipation and equality issues. The accumulation of the political challenge, with the social challenge coming from the early socialist movement, may explain why party forms developed earlier in Germany than in Switzerland and the Netherlands. The Dutch division on the Protestant front and the active secularism of the liberals offered Dutch Catholics ample room for political maneuvering without the need to build a specific electoral-parliamentary organization. Similarly, the strong territorial representation of the Swiss Catholics in a federalized state allowed them to defend their autonomy by opposing centralization and national standardization. Neither of these options were available to German Catholics. All these movements took on an early antiestablishment character – which was unknown to ideological clericalism – as the main push toward mobilization was in opposition to the state-dominant Protestant circles; and from the beginning, they tried actively to obtain the support of the lower classes. In all likelihood, the appeal of these subcultural defense movements was more likely to directly affect the lower classes than in the cases of ideological clericalism, and their capacity to inhibit socialist recruitment should be more evident when comparing zones of strong Catholic presence with those of Protestant predominance.

The Irish case is difficult to characterize because of the North–South and pre- and postindependence differences. The emancipation of the Catholic Church in Ireland was one of the key politically mobilizing issues of the nineteenth century, and the Catholic Church and the higher as well as

---

[108] See Girod (1964), Gruner (1977), and Seiler (1977).

lower hierarchies took a clear stand in favor of Irish independence. This is probably the reason why no relevant stream of anti-clericalism developed in Ireland. Catholics never felt any need to organize themselves politically under the umbrella of specific electoral organizations because the entire nationalist movement was imbued with strong Catholic values and orientations. Finally, socialist organization and mobilization was so late and delayed, and so second-rate compared to the national one, that it could hardly challenge the Catholic political defense.

After independence and partition, these characteristics were dramatically accentuated in the Protestant-dominated northern part of the country. However, in the Republic, the Catholic Church suddenly took on the role of a monopoly church, with extensive privileges, direct and special access to rulers, and a limited distinction between the state and the church. It is hard to decide whether Ireland lacked a Catholic Party during the interwar period or whether it was, on the contrary, the only country to have two major Catholic parties. Indeed, for both Fianna Fail and Fine Gael, religious appeals, symbolism, and sensitivity were not inferior to those of most continental Christian parties. Since my major concern here is to inquire into the extent to which Catholic identities were politicized and mobilized *before* the socialists entered the political game, it is safe to regard Ireland as an extreme case of emancipationist ghetto Catholicism, where the combination of the church with the national emancipation movement led to pervasive Catholic political mobilization. Thus, in this case, the absence of the political party should not be regarded as a failure of organizational mobilization, but rather as a sign of its overwhelming victory.

We can organize the information discussed so far on the key dimensions of religious mobilization in Western Europe into a synthetic form. This is laid out in Table 8.2, where each case is classified along the dimension of its religious heterogeneity/homogeneity, religious politicization, religious organization, and timing with respect to the class cleavage organization. This scheme will help the final considerations concerning the interaction between class cleavage and non-class-cleavage structuring.

THE PEASANT ISSUE: MOBILIZATION OF THE PEASANTRY

The question of agrarian society and its transformation was widely debated by socialist thinkers and intellectuals around the turn of the twentieth century. The position of the agricultural workers was likened to that of the industrial working class, and the key problem was felt to be the

Table 8.2. *Patterns of religious mobilization in Western Europe*

religious heterogeneity	religious politicization	type of church	religious electoral organization	approximate date of party foundation	timing compared with socialist electoral mobilization	country	position of the religious organizations
homogeneous Protestant	no	state hegemonic	no or minor		much later	Denmark, Finland, Norway, Sweden	national churches
heterogeneous Protestant	no	state hegemonic	no	n.a.	n.a.	Britain	national churches versus minor opposition Protestants sects
homogeneous Catholic	yes	monopoly	yes	1905-07	late, later	Austria,	conservative proestablishment
homogeneous Catholic	yes	ideological clericalism	failed attempts	1924, 1945	late, later	France	reactionary then conservative
homogeneous Catholic	yes	ideological clericalism	yes yes	1919	late, later	Italy	antinational, reactionary; then conservative opposition
homogeneous Catholic	yes	ideological clericalism	yes	1886	early, before	Belgium	conservative proestablishment
heterogeneous Catholic and Protestant	yes	ghetto	yes (only Catholic)	1870 1870 (cantonal) 1922 (federal)	early, parallel late (territorial before)	Germany, Switzerland	Catholic = antiestablishment opposition Catholic = early antiestablishment, gradual integration
heterogeneous Catholic and Protestant	yes	ghetto	yes (all denominations)	1896-1904	parallel	Netherlands	Catholic = antiestablishment opposition Calvinist = national establishment
heterogeneous Catholic and Protestant	yes	ghetto	no (?)			Ireland (before independence)	nationalist antiestablishment
homogeneous Catholic	yes	monopoly	yes (?)	n.a.	before (?)	Irish Republic	conservative proestablishment

attitude toward the intermediate agricultural groups: the peasantry and particularly small subsistence farmers and the different types of semi-independent peasantry made up of sharecroppers, tenants, and so on. Marx's economic model of capitalist development and capitalist concentration led him to forecast the inevitable economic decline of both farmers and the peasantry, while, at the same time, recognizing the high potential for revolt among the latter in a revolutionary situation.[109] The first question was whether and how fast the small peasantry would disappear, transformed into dependent labor by the mercantilization and capitalist development of agriculture. The second was what policy the socialists would adopt toward it in the transition phase. The importance given to the second question depended on the answer to the first question and, more importantly, on the size of this social group. Orthodox Marxism faced a political predicament in terms of short-term versus long-term political action, the choice of which could lead to a pronounced break between economic analysis and political practice. This was because to protect, defend, and represent poor peasants meant to protect and give incentive to holding private property, and this meant acting politically

---

[109] On Marx and the agrarian question, see Mitrany (1951).

against the law of historical development. Thus, to leave poor peasants to their historical destiny was normally the orthodox response.

To this Marxist position is usually opposed a "socialist-revisionist" solution to the agrarian question, epitomized in the work of Bernstein. Marx and his immediate successors never considered that agrarian concentration could develop differently from industry, or develop with a slower pace and intermediate steps during which the property of small peasants could survive and even grow as a result of the rationalization of the still semifeudal agrarian structures in many countries. In reality, the same intermediate phases could be obtained if the political elite made deliberate efforts to stabilize their political position by supporting the countryside. With an important series of statistical data, Bernstein demonstrated that small productive units did not decline in number and wealth but tended to prosper and increase, both in industry and in agriculture. The revisionists interpreted this evidence as a direct refutation of the Marxist theory of capitalist concentration, rather than as evidence of a short-term postfeudal rationalization of agrarian structure, which was simply postponing agrarian concentration. The perspective of a long-term survival of small properties led to a global revision of the theory of socioeconomic development and the acceptance by revisionists of small family agrarian properties as something that should be helped to survive. Because the only way to organize the small peasants effectively was to help them defend their economic interests, the typical tool that socialists developed to serve this interest was the cooperative society, and this defense often took place at the expense of the radical pushes of other segments of the socialist movement. Clearly, however, if peasants' property was destined to last, to ignore the peasantry meant missing a political opportunity and, what was even more dangerous, leaving an additional chance to the class adversaries.

The third political solution to the agrarian predicament, different from both of those offered by the orthodox Marxists and the socialist-revisionists, was the Leninist solution. Developed in reference to the still semifeudal countryside in which small peasant holdings were not yet consolidated, this solution attempted to exploit the precapitalist revolt potential of land-hungry peasants by jumping directly to a postcapitalist solution of the full socialization of land. This solved the problem by bypassing small peasants' property with a single jump. This theoretical solution (the practical political solution that was adopted during and after the Russian Revolution was very different) was dependent on the existence of a potentially revolutionary situation that would radicalize the peasantry. It was hardly applicable to nonrevolutionary situations and was obviously totally ineffective as an electoral strategy. Thus, this line lost any appeal it ever had for the Western socialist movement, including the Communist parties, once the radicalization period after World War I was over.[110]

This broad characterization of an orthodox-Marxist, a socialist-revisionist, and a Leninist approach to the peasant question captures the essence of the most important streams of socialist theory and thinking. However, it is less clear that it correctly represents the socialist party situation and attitude toward the national peasant and agricultural groups. When specific policies and practical solutions became necessary, political divisions emerged and many socialists started to recognize the basic difference between agriculture and factory industry, to have doubts about the economic superiority of large-scale farming, and, in many cases, to start offering different programmatic tickets for agriculture and industry. The agrarian question in fact posed a different problem-pressure in the different European countries according to (1) the weight of the independent peasantry in their respective agrarian structures; (2) the weight of dependent agricultural labor in the same structures; and (3) the prevalent form of political representation that dominated the peasant world. Not only were agrarian structures highly differentiated throughout Europe, but the peasants were also rarely the "potato sacks" that Marx had spoken of. They actively reacted in defense of their interests and their *Weltanschauung*. Moreover, other political forces had established representational linkages with the peasant world, often before socialists started to face their theoretical dilemmas. In order to understand the variation in the socialist attitude and potential relationship with the agricultural groups, we need to clarify the different types of agrarian structures and the different traditions of pre- and postsocialist political representation of these groups.

AGRARIAN STRUCTURE PROBLEM-PRESSURE: THE PEASANTRY AND AGRICULTURAL LABOR

For a comparative characterization of the numerical weight of the independent peasantry, I have taken the average census values for the decades between the 1900s and the 1930s as a reference (Table 8.3), keeping in mind that the internal distinction within the agricultural employed population is particularly difficult and subject to sudden revision on the basis of different accounting criteria. These figures give a broad idea of the different national weights, but they conceal important qualitative differ-

---

[110] On the different socialist attitudes to the peasantry, see Tarrow (1972: 238–241, 265–267).

Table 8.3. *Independent peasantry in Western Europe: basic features (mean values for the 1900 and 1939 censuses; family workers excluded)*

country	independents in agriculture as % of active population	independents in agriculture as % of active in agriculture	independents in agriculture as % of all independents	man-land ratio (hectares per man)	Gini index of inequality in land distribution
France	25.0	62.7	62.5	9	58.3
Italy	24.4	45.0	68.7	4.5	80.3
Ireland	20.6	41.3	73.3	9.75	59.8
Norway	18.7	43.3	64.0	5	66.9
Finland	16.9	25.8	77.7	5.5	59.9
Sweden	16.3	40.9	68.9	7.5	57.8
Denmark	14.3	37.8	52.7	10	45.8
Austria	13.0	27.5	58.7	6.5	74.0
Switzer.	11.7	45.1	45.6	6.75	49.8
Netherl.	9.2	36.0	40.6	6	60.5
Belgium	9.0	44.8	39.0	4.5	58.7
West Ger.	7.0	23.2	44.8	6.5	67.4
Un. Kingdom	1.2	26.2	17.9	25	71.0

Note: The man-land ratio is calculated by Dovring (1964: 60) as the ratio between male workers in agriculture and the agricultural land in hectares. It therefore does not refer to the independent agricultural labor force but to the total labor force. The figures reported here are the averages of the 1900, 1930, 1950, and 1960 decades. The Gini index of land distribution inequality for the 1960s is from Russett (1964). The index ranges from 0 (maximum equality) to 100 (maximum inequality).

ences in the structure of agricultural society. There are two polar types of agrarian society, labeled by Dahl "traditional peasant society" and "farmer society." The difference lies in the degree of inequality in the distribution of land, which implies, in turn, an inequality of political resources. While the former has a high propensity for inequality, hierarchy, and political hegemony, the second is more egalitarian.[111] The farmer society is characterized by (1) a high weight of independents over the active population; (2) a large number of independents over the active population in agriculture; and (3) patterns of egalitarian distribution of land.

Combining these criteria, the best farmer society candidates are Sweden and Norway, where, since the late Middle Ages, primitive yeomanry had succeeded in holding its right; Denmark, where a profound and successful series of land reforms in the nineteenth century brought about the resurgence of a free peasant class; Belgium and Switzerland in continental Europe; and, to a lesser extent, France and Ireland. At the other extreme, Italy, Austria, and Germany appear to be best characterized as

[111] Dahl (1971: 53–54).

more traditional peasant societies. Finland is an extremely difficult case to characterize with these categories because the estate system, established as a consequence of the military frontier situation, was reinforced during the union with Russia. At the turn of the twentieth century, Finland had some of the features typical of several Eastern European countries, where there was a landlord class. However, after independence between 1921 and 1922, radical land reforms were carried out that quadrupled the number of independent farmers by 1938.[112]

However, even this specification conceals a great variety of different relationships with the land and with types of agrarian contracts. The point is that the differences within rural societies are less functional than those in urban occupations, and they are based on the different types of relationships to the means of production, the foremost among them clearly being the right to own land. Since the conflict of interest is related primarily to the acquisition and distribution of possession, the political expression of such conflicts could not be "oriented to the creation of a new type of society, whatever it may be in modern revolutionary utopias, but to changing the roles in an existing stratification system where the beneficiaries rather than the principles are challenged."[113] Thus, each specific pattern of the right to rural property should be distinguished in a sociological perspective. The independents in agriculture should be clearly differentiated according to whether they are farm owners or tenants, and the latter further differentiated according to whether they pay a rent or share the profits or crops. Both should be distinguished according to the size of the land, the capitalist commercial nature of the enterprise or of the traditional subsistence farms, whether the farmer hired labor or not, and so on, in a long chain of important distinctions that cross-cut each other. In a comprehensive treatment, Sorokin, Zimmerman, and Galpin proposed a stratified hierarchy of thirteen rural social groups, twelve of which concerned the independents.[114] Linz has made a thorough attempt to link this stratification scheme to patterns of electoral behavior, showing how these social groups generally tend to be rather conservatively oriented, but also underlining the potential radical orientation of small farmers and sharecroppers under certain conditions.[115]

From the viewpoint of the integration and mobilization of the socialist movement, Malefakis has proposed a drastic simplification of the issue: In

---

[112] Dovring (1964: 244–246).
[113] Linz (1976: 366).
[114] Sorokin, Zimmerman, and Galpin (1930: 362–370).
[115] See Linz (1976). It excludes, unfortunately, Northern Europe and Scandinavia.

Eastern Europe, the peasantry was simply too large not to become the central concern of the socialist movement; in West-Central Europe, the peasantry was too small to be such a central concern; in Southern Europe the peasantry was large enough to pose important strategic problems to the socialist movement but not large enough to become its dominant concern.[116] The central point concerning the problem-pressure for socialists, which was determined by size, is crucial, but the geographical characterization leaves out the Scandinavian countries and is probably questionable in some important cases. If it is likely that there is a central continental pattern characterized by a small presence of independents in agriculture, France does not belong to it, but instead resembles cases like those of Italy and Ireland, which had the maximum weight of independent peasantry; Scandinavian countries and Finland come next and Central European countries last (the United Kingdom is well known to stand alone in this respect). The weight of the independents in agriculture over the whole category of independents also presents great variations across Western European countries, and although there is some correspondence with the independents over the active population, this correspondence is not perfect (see Table 8.3).

The problem of the role of the peasantry was therefore of minor political relevance in several countries. In the United Kindgom, its weight over the active population was low, the average farming unit was large, the pressure of labor over land consequently was low, and the productivity of the agricultural population was the highest in Europe (see Table 8.4). The agricultural problem did not exist, and the Labour Party was very rarely ever concerned with this issue. The situation was not very different in a number of other countries. In Belgium, Germany, the Netherlands, and Switzerland, the weight of agricultural independents was below 11% of the active population on average, and the gross domestic product (GDP) originating from the agricultural sector was roughly balanced with its numerical weight. In these cases, there were more agricultural independents within the overall group of independents (Table 8.3) than in the United Kingdom, and in Switzerland and the Netherlands there were more agricultural independents in the active agricultural population as such. On the whole, the small bourgeoisie tended to be more rural than was the case in the United Kingdom. These cases show similar levels of weight of the independent peasantry out of the active population, while they differ in the weights of this independent peasantry in the active agricultural population. In Belgium and Switzerland (to a lesser extent), the indepen-

[116] Malefakis (1974).

Table 8.4. *Productivity of the agrarian world (1960s data)*

countries	% of population dependent upon agriculture	% of GDP originating in agriculture	difference
France	21	9	-12
Ireland	37	25	-12
Italy	27	17	-10
Austria	20	11	- 9
Norway	18	12	-6
Finland	25	21	-4
Denmark	18	14	-4
Germany	10	6	-4
Belgium	9	7	-2
Netherlands	12	10	-2
Sweden	17	?	?
Switzerland	14	?	?
Un. Kingdom	5	4	-1

Source: Urwin (1980: 83).

dent peasantry dominated the countryside more than in the Netherlands, Germany, and the United Kingdom. From World War I on, the peasantry in these latter countries was not a major political problem. It is therefore not surprising that the theoretically minded and doctrinaire Germans Social Democrats were long reluctant to renounce some of the key tenets of orthodox Marxism and to expose their urban working-class strongholds to the potential contradiction of a small-peasantry policy and alliance. For a strongly organized, mainly urban, ideologically oriented working-class socialist movement, the cost was probably not worth the potential advantages. Only in 1927 did the party officially accept the thesis that the law of concentration of capital did not operate in agriculture. However, even then, this had little or no impact on party policies and organizational efforts.

The theoretical issue was, however, for outweighed by a pressing practical political problem in the countries where the numerical and economic weight of the peasantry was at least twice that in the previous cases. In the first half of the nineteenth century in Ireland, Italy, and France, the independents in agriculture amounted to approximately one-quarter of the active population, while in Finland, Norway, Sweden, Denmark, and Austria, it ranged from 14% to 20% (Table 8.3). France and Italy made the most strenuous efforts to protect their peasantry and to insulate it from market competition. Particularly in France, protection laws were preserved as a basic creed of the Third Republic. The tariffs on foodstuffs there were the highest in Western Europe, at about 29%, equaled only by those of Austria-Hungary, compared to 24% in Sweden, 22% in Italy and Germany, and 15% in Switzerland.[117] France was so successful that the percentage of agricultural independents over the active population remained more or less unchanged until after World War II. Agricultural independents were protected more than in other countries from falls in agricultural prices, by the maintenance of a higher proportion of labor over the land than would have been otherwise possible, and by the postponement of agricultural modernization throughout the first half of the twentieth century, so that when these issues were faced in the 1950s and early 1960s, there was a strong reaction by the agricultural population.[118] In the other countries, the decline of agricultural independents over the active population is less drastic and, even more important, does not produce a decline in agricultural independents over the active population in agriculture; on the contrary, this proportion tended to increase, not decline, with the development of small property within the population active in agriculture.

In these countries, then (see the third column of Table 8.3), the independents in agriculture represented the majority of all independents in all sectors in this period, in sharp contrast with the situation in the United Kingdom, Germany, Belgium, the Netherlands, and Switzerland. To take the extreme cases, in the United Kingdom and Germany, the agricultural independents represented approximately one-quarter of all independents, while in Ireland, Finland, Italy, Norway, and Sweden they represented more than two-thirds. Finally, these countries have the least productive agricultural economies (see Table 8.4), in particular France, Ireland, Italy, and Austria, where there were particularly significant negative differences between the agricultural population and the agricultural share of the GDP. In conclusion, the socialist movement in the Scandinavian countries, Finland, Ireland, Italy, and France could not afford to avoid the issues of the independent peasantry.

Although the high proportion of the independents in agriculture determined the problem-pressure for an agrarian socialist strategy, the latter did not depend solely on this factor. What the socialists could or could not do with the independent peasantry was also dependent on the size of another agricultural group, whose interests and positions they regarded as

---

[117] For these figures, see Table 1.3 in Tracy (1964: 25).
[118] For this characterization of the French agricultural policies, see Zeldin (1979: 173–185).

more compatible with their class appeal: the *agricultural laborers*. The weight of this category within the global working class of a country was particularly important. In Table 8.5 I report the proportion of agricultural laborers in the national working class for each country and its temporal evolution from the end of the nineteenth century. These figures are not available for the United Kingdom and Ireland, but they can be comparatively estimated as being well below the European mean for both cases. In the United Kingdom, agricultural workers represent two-thirds of the active population in agriculture (64.9%) in the period from 1920 to 1960, but the proportion of the active population in agriculture is so small that the corresponding weight of agricultural workers over the whole working class cannot be higher than 5%. In Ireland, on the other hand, the proportion of the active population in agriculture is very high, although the proportion of agricultural workers active in agriculture is the lowest in Europe (only 17.7% between 1920 and 1960), so that the proportion of agricultural workers over the whole working class is around 20% at most. For France, no data are available for the post–World War II decades, but they have been estimated at about 25% and 22% in the 1940s and 1950s, respectively.[119]

If we look at the average figures for the central period – 1900s to 1930s – we have four quite separate groups. At one extreme, in Belgium, Switzerland, and the United Kingdom, the weight of agricultural workers was insignificant and the working class can be described as urban and industrially integrated. Next come the cases of Germany, the Netherlands, Norway, Sweden, and probably Ireland, where the weight of the agricultural laborers in the total working class was between 15% and 25%; thus, it was not insignificant, although it was minor, and therefore it was not able to create important contradictions in the socialist policy toward the peasantry. Austria and Denmark are intermediate cases. The agricultural working class was around one-third of the total working class, making this group fairly crucial for the electoral and political destiny of the Social Democrats. Finally, in three countries – Italy, Finland, and, to a slightly lesser extent, France – agricultural laborers represented roughly one-third to one-half of the working class. Although, obviously, this agricultural working class was concentrated in the areas of large agricultural enterprises (Paris Basin, Herauld, Normandy, Brittany, the Val de Loire in France; the Po Valley and some southern regions, such as Apulia, Sicily, and Calabria in Italy), it inevitably represented a primary target for socialist recruitment and was such a quantitatively important section of the

[119] See Bourquelot (1972: 533–556).

Table 8.5. *Weight of agricultural workers within the European working class*

countries	1880	1890	1900	1910	1920	1930	1940	1950	1960	1970	country means
Italy		55.9	55.9	52.9	46.6	30.4	29.0	27.4	19.0	13.1	36.7
Finland				51.0	48.3	36.3	26.8	22.1	15.7	6.7	29.6
France	27.0	34.8	38.6	35.2	31.7	26.3	n.a.				(32.2)
Denmark	46.0	39.1	45.7	33.1	23.0	27.2	24.6	20.1	11.4	5.4	27.6
Austria	25.4	46.5	36.2	31.0	26.9	20.9	19.9	15.5	7.4	3.8	23.2
Netherl.	37.0	32.3	27.6	25.7	23.7	19.5	11.3	8.6	5.9	3.3	19.5
Norway		38.3	26.7	22.9	21.5	18.0	14.7	11.4	8.1	6.0	18.6
Germany	29.4	27.4	19.5	17.9	16.2	19.9	12.0	9.7	3.4	2.2	15.8
Sweden	5.5	13.3	13.8	21.4	22.0	19.7	15.1	10.1	8.5	6.0	13.5
Switzerl.		21.6	15.2	12.8	11.9	9.5	9.9	7.0	4.4	2.9	10.6
Belgium	20.6	13.6	12.8	13.5	11.8	6.4	3.2	2.3	1.4	0.8	8.5
Ireland				n.a.							
Un. Kingdom				n.a.							
means for decades	27.2	32.2	29.2	28.2	25.7	21.3	16.7	13.4	8.5	4.8	20.6

working class that the socialist strategy in these cases had to start from this stronghold and then move to address other agricultural groups.

THE REPRESENTATION OF THE AGRARIAN WORLD

Let us now consider the problem-pressure that different agrarian structures created for the theoretical debate of the socialists, and even more so for their alliance strategies and policy initiatives, with the prevailing forms of political representation in the agricultural world. In Table 8.6, I have tried to synthesize the basic features of the political representation of the agrarian world, indicating the cases of successful or failed formation of an autonomous peasants' party, its electoral strength and political orientation, and, finally, in the last column, a comment about how the political representation of the agricultural world was eventually stabilized. In the United Kingdom, the issue was irrelevant. As for Ireland, we have seen that the Irish labor movement, which was dominated by urban working-class unions, adopted what we may call a British perspective toward the agricultural world, although it existed in a country basically made up of relatively small farmers. Whatever one says about the unfavorable conditions that made labor penetration difficult in the countryside, it is a fact that Irish labor history shows no signs of even the slightest ideological or organizational attempt to come to grips with the peasant question.

For the other four countries, where both the working class and the bourgeoisie were predominantly urban (Belgium, the Netherlands, Swit-

Table 8.6. *Self-representational mobilization of the agrarian world*

country	party and approximate date of formation	electoral strength	political orientation	notes
Austria	Landbund (1918)	< 5%	conservative	the bulk of the peasantry remained within the Catholic Party
Belgium	-	-	-	More than 70% of the farmers supported the Catholic Party
Denmark	Venstre (1888)	20-35%	moderate	
Finland	Agrarian (Center) 1906	20-35%	moderate	included 50-70% of all farmers
France	Agrarian (1928)	5-10%	conservative Catholic	50 to 70% of wealthy and large farmers oriented toward the Conservative Party; 40-50% of small farmers oriented toward the Communist Party. No Catholic Party
Germany	several regional parties from the 1890s	all < 5%	all conservative	about 50% of farmers in Catholic Party
Ireland	Farmers (1923)	5-10%	conservative	
Italy	Peasant (1946)	< 5%	moderate	50% of small farmers mobilized by the Catholic Party; sharecroppers and tenants gave significant support to the Communist Party
Netherlands	Agrarian (1920)	< 5%	moderate	about 50% of farmers mobilized by the Catholic Party
Norway	Agrarian (Center) (1920)	10-20 %	moderate	includes 50–70% farmers
Sweden	Agrarian (Center) (1921)	10-20 %	moderate	includes 50–70% farmers
Szitzerland	Farmers', Traders & Citizens (1920)	10-20 %	conservative	includes about 50% of farmers
Un Kingdom	crofters (1885)	< 5%	radical	

Source: Adapted from Table 5.2 and Table 6.1 in Urwin (1980: 138–170).

zerland, and Germany), the problem-pressure for the socialists was relatively minor. Short-lived agrarian parties were founded in the Netherlands and in Germany, while, in Switzerland, a similar political experience lasted longer with the foundation of the Farmers', Traders', and Citizens' Party in 1920. However, in all these countries, the predominant political representation of the peasants was gained by their respective Catholic movements, with about 50% of the peasants supporting the Catholic party.

In Germany, notwithstanding the early and far-reaching theoretical debate about the agrarian question, the SPD never displayed any strong desire to attempt to mobilize rural areas. The revisionists also used the issue of capitalist concentration in the rural economy more as an example and as a tool to modify the urban and industrial strategy of the Social Democrats than as an argument for a clear policy to obtain support from the countryside. All attempts to form peasant parties from the 1890s on were very conservative in orientation, regional in scope, and unsuccessful or short-lived. About half of the German peasantry had been solidly linked to the Catholic Party since its foundation.[120]

---

[120] To explain the failure of the SPD to attract more-extensive rural support, Michels argues that the highly status-conscious nature of both rural and urban workers vis-à-vis each

Among the Central European cases, the question of agrarian support was probably more central in the Netherlands. In the 1897 election, which followed the enlargement of the franchise, the Socialist Party concentrated its campaign in the two northern provinces of Groningen and Friesland, with a program that made far-reaching promises to small peasants and tenants, as well as appealing to agricultural workers. The party's organizational support was particularly strong in these northern rural provinces, perhaps due to the high proportion of nonreligious people among the population. This initial organizational and electoral dependence on the northern regions considerably influenced the party programs and positions later on. The lack of social homogeneity of this support reinforced the idea that parts of the petit bourgeoisie, as well as Protestant and Catholic voters, could be won only by taking a cautious electoral course. This electoral compromise and parliamentary strategy was viewed as conforming to the existing politico-cultural conditions. However, it was exactly this that triggered the internal reaction of the Marxist left wing of the party, which eventually split. The attempt to form a Dutch agrarian party did not succeed in the 1920s, and 50% of the farmers remained loyal to the Catholic Party. In Austria, alongside a larger freeholder peasant groups, there were also regions with some dependent agricultural labor. A *Landbund* party emerged at the collapse of the empire but obtained little support in the 1918 elections. On the whole, Austrian peasants were so deeply and generally supportive of the Catholic Party and so profoundly linked to the Catholic subculture, while the socialist movement was so heavily urban and working class right from the beginning, that there was very little real political or policy debate over attitudes toward the small freeholders.

A large peasantry was therefore mainly a problem of the European southern (France and Italy, but also Spain and Portugal, which are not included in our analysis) and northern periphery (Scandinavia and Finland). While Finland and Southern European countries all had a large agricultural labor force *together with* an urban/rural working class, the former feature was absent in Scandinavian countries. The main difference, however, concerns the pattern of political representation that separates all Northern countries from Southern ones. The Scandinavian peasantry enjoyed both

other made their political alliance impossible; Michels (1906). I lack comparative evidence to test this interpretation. It should be mentioned, however, that for France and Italy the late and sluggish industrialization is thought to have created a smaller cultural gap between the urban working class and the agricultural workers. Large parts of the Italian working class felt very close to their recently abandoned agricultural roots.

economic and political independence in the nineteenth century: Economically, the bases for a landed aristocracy were poor, as a large-scale manorial system was possible in only small parts of southern Sweden and in Denmark. In Norway, two-thirds of the country was owned by the peasants in 1815. The peasants' socioeconomic position was secured through the allodial privilege, which guaranteed the lineage control of the farm. In addition, in large areas of these countries, the prevalent methods of cultivation made the exploitation of peasant labor almost impossible and unprofitable.

The political independence of these peasants was established in Scandinavia very early on, with the presence of a fourth estate of autonomous peasant representation. Of these three countries, only in Denmark did the legal and economic subordination of peasants resemble that of Central Europe. However, fundamental land reform at the end of the eighteenth century multiplied the freeholds and gave rise to a large group of self-reliant small- and medium-sized freeholders. Paradoxically, the Danish peasants rapidly became the best organized and most economically and politically powerful peasant class in Scandinavia. As later imitated by Norwegian and Swedish peasants, they mobilized to different degrees against large landowners (natural enemies seen as the embodiment of the old order), the urban bourgeoisie in commerce, banking and industry (which controlled the basic financial and banking infrastructure, regarded as exploitive), and the bureaucratic elite (the central culture in Norway, which denied them equal status and political influence, as in Denmark and Sweden). The impressive element of the Scandinavian farmers' movements was their astonishing capacity for self-reliance and self-representation, leading to a high degree of independence from the urban financial, commercial, and industrial bourgeoisie (establishing their own network of savings banks, cooperatives, etc.). Cultural and political consciousness should also be seen in the light of the very high level of mass education of the Scandinavian countries. In these conditions, the emergence of a working-class movement was not seen as a challenge. Quite the contrary, in Denmark in particular, the rise of a working-class movement was actually seen as a welcome split in the urban front.

For the Scandinavian Social Democrats, the "agrarian question" was therefore *mainly* a question of political and governmental coalition with a strong, self-representational movement that included the vast majority of farmers. The "predicament" of the agrarian question, if it existed at all, was soon overshadowed by practical considerations concerning the political alliances that could be set up with the freeholder movement. Although the original party policy statements in this policy area ran close to Marxist positions, by the 1890s in Denmark and by 1902 in Norway, party political action had distanced itself from them. In Denmark, the acceptance of small agricultural properties and their defense was qualified only by the idea that the land belonging to the church and other large properties should be handed over to the landless laborers or to the smallholders. In Norway, the party instead outlined an agricultural program in 1902 that openly accepted the existence of independent family farming, along with open-field farming, and from then on attempted to increase its support among agricultural workers and small farmers on the basis of this platform.

Sweden merits a more detailed discussion because of its paradigmatic profile. The Swedish development on the agrarian program issue is indicative of greater theoretical liberty from its beginning. Early Swedish socialists took for granted that large-scale production and land concentration were inevitable. When the issue was rediscussed due to the German debate (around 1894), the party made it equally clear that no expropriation of land was to be envisaged, as socialism did not wish "to separate labor from the means of production." This skillful formulation reconciled the goal of socialism (to avoid alienation by separating capital, land in this case, and labor) with an obviously revisionist stand (to let the peasants own their land). However, the party leadership was still divided about the necessity and feasibility of winning farmers over to socialism. Some of these (led by Hjalmar Branting) did not want to support small farmers against large-scale farming at the cost of delaying or stopping land concentration; others (led by Danielsson Axel) were prepared to make an ideological compromise, arguing that the victory of socialism depended on having the support of the farmers. The dilemma was between having an active reform program in agriculture or supporting small-scale agriculture. From the productive point of view, large-scale agriculture was considered superior, but the idea was advanced that cooperation among small-scale farmers could also work.

Around the end of the century, the party suggested that new small farmers should be encouraged, but that the land should remain the property of the state even if given under hereditary rights to the tenants. The idea that farmers and agricultural workers had the same interests in the face of capitalism spread after the franchise reforms of 1907–1909, but at the same time, it was becoming obvious that the process of concentration in agriculture was not going to take place, at least in the short term. In the 1911 program, formal Marxist ideology was maintained, but at the same time, a clear opening toward the agricultural population was made,[121]

---

[121] A synthesis of the early agricultural debate in the SAP is presented in Simonson (1990: 98–100).

although it seems likely that throughout this period the SAP did not win much small-farmer support anyway (according to survey data from 1950 to 1970,[122] only 10% of farmers voted for the SAP, while 50–70% voted for the Center [ex-Agrarian] Party). When peasant parties started to form in the 1910s,[123] the agrarian question died out and was transformed into the question of what possible policy could be offered to the Agrarian Party in exchange for governmental coalition.

The alliances between urban workers and peasants that gave hegemony to Scandinavian socialism were finalized in the 1930s: Denmark and Sweden in 1933 and Norway in 1935. This compromise between urban and rural interests took the same basic form, involving policy programs organized around (1) the expansion of public employment, support for public works, social welfare programs, unemployment relief, and prohibition or regulation of strikes and lockouts in exchange for (2) reduction of agricultural property taxes, reduction of agricultural interest rates, state help for more-costly loans, debt relief in general for agriculture, and various forms of state subsidies to farmers. In sum, the alliance was based on a common farmer/worker interest in policies to stimulate the economy, and it resulted in urban workers accepting higher food prices in exchange for peasant support for public intervention and public works.[124] It is obvious that the most immediate basis for this alliance was the self-representative character of the Scandinavian peasant movement. If urban workers and peasants had been grouped into different political formations, such an exchange would have been unthinkable, as it would have jeopardized the immediate interest of other groups.

Finland resembles the Scandinavian countries in that it developed an early (1906) and strong self-representational agrarian movement second only to that of Denmark. However, from the beginning, its internal divisions were more pronounced because of the more polarized class relationship in the countryside and also because of the stormy and radical political life of the Finnish republic until 1945. At its birth, the Finnish Socialist Party had been an advocate of smallholder interests, and the well-to-do farm owners had remained within the Conservative Party. In time, however, the party became more conservative and attracted the more prosperous farmers, but, as a consequence, it suffered frequent splits throughout

---

[122] Korpi (1983: 93).

[123] I have taken the date of 1922 for the formation of the Agrarian Party. Note, however, that one agrarian party was founded in 1913 and another one in 1915 and the two parties merged in 1922.

[124] On the economics of these agreements, particularly in Sweden, see Winch (1966: 168–176), Lewin (1988), and Pojas (1991: 64–74).

the 1930s, most of which were characterized by a clear smallholder attraction.[125] A formal Red–Green political alliance like the one in Scandinavia never materialized in Finland. This was due largely to the split of the Finnish left, but also to the fact that in northeast Finland rural support for the Communist Party was high among smallholders and traditionally the socialist and communist left had enjoyed the support of the agricultural laborers.

It is therefore in the countries with a large peasant population, high class polarization of the countryside, and lack of political self-representation that the problem of the attitude to be taken on the agrarian question became crucial and, at the same time, highly divisive for the socialist movement. In Italy and France, the economic independence of the peasantry was weaker; at the same time, their political representation was fragmented and class-polarized.[126] The possibility of forming strong, self-representational agrarian movements is, in general, not linked just to the existence of a large population of independent farmers. Secondary but still important conditions concern the intensity of the urban–rural gap over the territory.[127] For instance, one key characteristic of the Southern European agricultural area is its high degree of urbanization. Settlement patterns of large villages or agro-towns, with peasants working in faraway fields, imply greater urban–rural communication, easier cultural hegemony of the urban elite, easier penetration of urban parties (including clientele politics), generally less stratification in urban–rural terms, and a lack of rural cultural alienation from the urban world. This generally leads to more urban–rural integration and a higher penetration of urban culture in the countryside. In Italy, in particular, the lack of early and radical land reform (the liberals feared the Catholic peasantry) and the piecemeal and delayed reforms up to the 1950s enabled the survival of a strong group of agricultural workers in the large-scale farming of the north; a strong group of tenants and sharecroppers in the smaller agricultural units of central Italy; and an even more complicated structure in the south. During unification, many of the large feudal estates fell into the hands of the Southern urban bourgeoisie, and the provincial middle classes started to take control of large parts of the previous *latifondi*. Professionals and merchants began to buy small

---

[125] Sänkiaho (1971: 27–47) and Berglund and Lindström (1978: 55).

[126] For a synthetic summary of the historical evidence criticizing the myth of the French *paysannerie* as being created by the French Revolution, reinforced and further fragmented by the Napoleonic Code, and representing a solid and largely undifferentiated bloc with common interests and aspirations, see Wright (1964: 2–6).

[127] On the conditions for the formation of agrarian movements, see Urwin (1980: 161–170).

pieces of land, which contributed, on one hand to the low efficiency of agriculture and, on the other, to explosive class relationships.

In France, the attempt to form an agrarian party failed, as it had failed in forming a Catholic party. In 1927, the Agrarian Party, founded by an eccentric lyceum teacher – Gabriel Fleurant, who preferred to be known as Fleurant Agricola – failed to politically unify the rural world, which was torn apart by internal division and competition with other rural organizations such as the Dorgère movement, with its conservative and corporativist flavor. All the attempts made during the 1930s to form a political movement of the peasants were successfully checked by the other political forces, the Radicals *in primis*. Moreover, French farmers never engaged directly in politics. Even in the highest-density areas, their representatives were always village mayors, departmental councillors, deputies, and senators drawn from among the large landowners, the long-established bourgeoisie, or the new elite of the republican period (notaries, doctors, teachers, shopkeepers, civil servants, etc.) rather than working farmers. In France, in the absence of a Catholic point of reference, 50–70% of wealthy and large farmers favored the conservative[128] party (curiously, but revealingly, called the Center of the Independents and of the Peasants), but at the same time, 40–50% of small farmers chose the Communist Party.

The Italian agricultural world never even tried to form an autonomous political movement or achieve political representation. Instead, it delegated representation to other social groups and political elites. The Catholic Party obtained the support of about 50% of the small farmers, but some of these, including significant numbers of tenants and sharecroppers, tended to be socialist and Communist in orientation. In both countries, of course, the large agricultural working class was politically represented predominantly by the left. There was, therefore, substantial rural support for the French and Italian left in general, and in particular for their communist wings. The main difference lay in the fact that, in France, the left took root mainly among small farmers, who were poor but owned their land; in Italy, the left vote grew mainly among tenant farmers (central Italy) and farm laborers.[129]

The socialist agrarian dilemma was increased by the fact that the socioeconomic conditions of the peasants were similar to those of the workers. At the end of the 1960s, the percentage of peasants describing

---

[128] The Radicals, and in part also the socialist tradition of agrarian unionism, regarded the peasantry as a single class from which they excluded only the large landowners. Jollivert (1972: 88–89).

[129] Dogan (1967: 143–151).

their families as living in "somewhat reduced means" was higher than the corresponding percentage among workers' families only in Italy and France.[130] Certainly, in terms of objective economic and educational conditions, they were worse off than the urban working class in these countries. The size of these agricultural groups, combined with their marginal economic position and high status and class polarization, clearly made them potential supporters of radical protest movements. At the same time, it made the question of their support, or at least of their political neutralization, a crucial survival issue for the socialist movement. The problem could not be avoided or put aside on account of its quantitative irrelevance, but neither could it be solved by political agreements and concessions, since these groups lacked any solid political self-representation.

A closer look at the French socialist attitudes makes the point clear. Universal male suffrage and electoral interests pushed French politicians to take care of rural interests, and the electoral power of the peasants was increased by the electoral laws and by the distribution of the population. At least half of the electoral districts for the second chamber were predominantly rural. No more than one deputy in every four could afford to ignore agricultural interests and problems if he wanted electoral victory. The rural weight was even greater in the Senate, whose members were elected in departmental constituencies.[131]

All the French socialist programs and policy documents concerning the rural world, from the early Guesdesist Marxist orthodoxy,[132] to Jaurès's attempt to revise this orientation at the end of the nineteenth century,[133] to the position of the CGT,[134] were characterized by preposterous ambiguities and internal contradictions, confirming the historical fate of small property and, at the same time, presenting socialism as its defender. After the adoption of a more radical program in 1910, signaling the radicalization of the party in this period and a less prominent role for Jaurès in shaping official party policy on agriculture, the party soon reverted to its traditional position.[135] Again, when the socialists were in government in 1936 and 1945, they wanted to adapt agrarian structures to economic

---

[130] Data are from the 1970 European Community Study, as elaborated by Lewis-Beck (1977: 453–452). Unfortunately, no comparable Finnish data are available in this form.

[131] Wright (1964: 213). Each of the small communes had a grand elector for the Senate, while Paris had only thirty.

[132] See Landauer (1961: 212–225).

[133] In the 1890s, Jaurès became the main expert and exponent of agricultural problems. On his programs and positions, which Engels ferociously criticized in an article in the *Neue Zeit* in November 1894, see Wright (1964: 22–23) and Gratton (1972: 165).

[134] Kergoat (1990: 179).

[135] Zeldin (1979: 404–405) and Wright (1964: 217–218).

change without calling into question the foundations of the liberal economy and without touching the peasants' property. They meant to give peasants total control of their economic sector, but policy measures remained marginal, limited to the creation of cooperatives for the collective utilization of machinery.[136]

The Communist Party's position developed differently. In addition to debating different forms of value production in the countryside, the basic aim of the party was to establish an intermediate agrarian regime while waiting for the superiority of collective property and collective land management to be recognized. At the same time, considering the small peasantry as a potential ally of the urban working class in a revolutionary situation, the party continued to support all of its demands and claims vehemently, without overcommitting itself to a risky policy of cooperative development. This attitude was correctly defined as "electoral poujadism deprived of economic viability considerations." It was not significantly modified until the middle of the 1960s.

In France, the problem of the peasantry could not be ignored or set aside, given its considerable indirect political influence. However, this was not a question that could be resolved by bargaining and negotiation with their political representatives. What made the whole issue even more problematic for the class left was the persistence of a large, internally differentiated, and inefficient agricultural sector. Obviously, it was risky to develop comprehensive reform and reorganization policies that might alienate large sections of this world without providing solid political alliance opportunities. However, the presence and weight of this sector still obliged the left to deal with this huge politico-electoral problem as best it could by offering the peasants much more than was envisaged in its doctrine and ideological orientation. This, in turn, weighed enormously on other policy domains. For instance, it continuously prevented the development, ideological use, and policy implementation (when in government) of comprehensive reform policies for the urban working class, all of which required the rationalization and modernization of the agricultural economic system. It can be argued that the problem of a relationship with a large, socially differentiated, and politically divided rural world – typical of the Mediterranean countries, but to which I also assimilate the Finnish situation – is at the root of the reformist policy failure of Southern socialism,[137] of its historical role as a movement more of civic and secular reform than

[136] Tavernier (1972: 127).
[137] On the modest economic achievements of the Popular Front in the field of agrarian policy, see Wright (1955: 75–86).

of economic reform, and of its deep internal divisions. Debates about alternative strategies and alliances, political as well as socioeconomic, were exacerbated by this unmanageable issue. I will come back to this problem in the next chapter where I discuss the organizational cohesion of the European class left.

CONCLUSION: THE RESULTING CLASS CLEAVAGE

In Chapter 7, I divided the response of the established elite to the rising socialist movement into three types. The first response was mainly, if not exclusively, *repressive;* it relied on high stateness resources and implied a high closure of the political system. The most typical examples of this response were the two Central European empires. The second response relied mainly on *institutional obstacles*; was usually pursued by low-stateness polities; and opposed new claimants by postponing regime liberalization and maintaining the institutional privileges of upper political chambers, monarchical intervention, and representational obstacles, although with some minor directly repressive means. This was typical of the Scandinavian countries. Finally, a response based mainly on *political control* was predominant in early liberalized countries such as the United Kingdom, Belgium, Switzerland, and the Netherlands. To a certain extent, a mixture of direct harassment, institutional obtrusion, and political control was present everywhere, but in these three groups the predominance of one type of response was clearer, while in the weakly consolidated liberal regimes, such as those of France and Italy, the various types of responses were all used according to the period and circumstances.

Although level of stateness – interpreted as resource availability – and social interest diversification – interpreted as established elite cohesion – were emphasized as the crucial determinants of the predominance of any one type of response, the latter also depended on the structuring of the party system and on the social and political isolation of the socialists. A purely repressive response required weak political organizations and weak structuring of the party system, just as a political control strategy required the opposite. If, for instance, in Belgium, the Netherlands, or Switzerland, socialists were encountered mainly in the electoral and parliamentary arenas, this was so because the established elite could rely on a variety of cleavages and alliances that granted them considerable control over these arenas. On the other hand, the use of direct repression and institutional intrusion by dominant groups was justified by their fear of being unable or their unwillingness to use political means due to the inadequate political organization of liberal and conservative forces. Therefore, the national pattern of cleavage structuring and party system formation was crucial in shaping both the preferred response of the established elite and the character of the class cleavage. It thus determined different *openings of the electoral market*, different *alliance opportunities*, and different *social bases* for the latter. In turn, these elements were important in determining the levels of radicalization and class polarization of the whole socialist movement. I have focused on four main dimensions of cleavage structuring and party system consolidation: early liberalism and denominational, agricultural, and nationalistic mobilization, examining (1) the extent to which these processes reduced working- and lower-class solidarity and mobilization potential and (2) the conditions in which the choice of available political allies did or did not increase the internal ideological factionalism and organizational unity of the socialists.

The relationship of early socialist movements with liberalism had two major consequences: It reduced or increased the social and political isolation of the socialist movement, and it anticipated or delayed its direct self-representational efforts. In the countries where cooperation with a strong liberal political movement was early and protracted – the United Kingdom and Scandinavia – socialism was not politically isolated from the beginning. This enabled it to be less concerned with defensive organizational mobilization and, eventually, considerably delayed its autonomous entry into the political arena. The latter is particularly evident in Sweden, Norway, and the United Kingdom, where socialists did not enter politics until the beginning of the twentieth century. The same is not true of Denmark, where the early influence of German social democracy and the stormy relationship with the Venstre probably determined earlier efforts to create an autonomous electoral mobilization. Where a liberal ally was not available on the Continent, socialists had no choice but to try to organize their own electoral machine as soon as possible.

However, *liberalism was not a working-class or lower-class unity-dissipating force;* instead, it was an alternative presocialist channel of representation. As such, cooperation with the liberals had no direct impact on the later mobilization capacity of the socialist parties. On the contrary, once this cooperation ended in the first two decades of the twentieth century, the socialist movement grew much more rapidly than in other countries. In reality, the cooperation experience split the liberals more than it damaged the socialists. At the same time, the link between the early relationships with liberal forces and the main ideological orientation and internal ideological and organizational strife of the socialists should be underlined. The long experience of social and political alliances with liberal forces made the integration of the socialists into the political systems easier and earlier; it also avoided political isolation during liberalization and democratization struggles. At the opposite end of the continuum, the typical and early abdication of Austrian and German liberalism, for example, left their socialist movements not only in an authoritarian environment, but also in almost total political isolation. The consequence of this was to reinforce the orthodox doctrinaire stance of these parties. Moderate and reformist groups found very little external political support, and their arguments must have seemed extremely unconvincing given the circumstances. Was it reasonable for the party to face the internal ideological and organizational strife inevitably triggered by moderating and collaborative drives, with little hope that these would be rewarded by the payoff of solid, stable cooperation with disorganized and politically ambiguous potential allies? Retreat to the "centrist" defense of Marxist orthodoxy, was a winning response in a context where institutional closure was accompanied by political isolation.

This argument is also convincing in regard to the eclectic and ideologically variegated nature of French and Italian socialism. In these cases, political liberalism remained weakly organized, divided into many groups and parliamentary factions, and never represented a solid potential ally for the socialist movement. The liberalized nature of the regime offered opportunities for cooperation, but breaks and conflicts were as frequent as rapprochement between the various factions of the liberal and socialist movements. So, relations with liberal forces became a contentious issue within the socialist movement. This ended by increasing the ideological strife within the movement about the pros and cons of cooperation and on several occasions destroyed its ideological and even organizational unity.

The reverse is true of denominational mobilization. Religious political mobilization was the single most important factor reducing lower-class unity and solidarity, and it narrowed the potential electoral support of the socialists. It influenced both the social composition of the class cleavage and its overall mobilization capacity. The greater the politicization of religious identities, the stronger the organizational mobilization of such identities; and the earlier such mobilization occurred with respect to the timing of socialist mobilization, the more it was likely that a religious cleavage would preempt full mobilization along functional class lines, activating competing political alignments and narrowing the potential electoral market of the class cleavage.

The extent of religious politicization in the second half of the nineteenth century and the beginning of the twentieth set the Scandinavian homogeneous Protestant and state-hegemonic church experiences – to which the United Kingdom can be assimilated, notwithstanding its greater heterogeneity – clearly aside from the bulk of continental experiences, where religious identities were politicized everywhere. A second distinction that is relevant here is between the continental experiences characterized by religious heterogeneity, in which Catholic mobilization was of a reactive and emancipationist type, defending equality with other denominations or state denominational neutrality (typically in Germany, the Netherlands, and Switzerland), in contrast to that of homogeneously Catholic countries, where the church was historically associated with one establishment faction at least and where it defended traditional privileges from secular assault (e.g., Belgium, Austria, Italy, and France).

The figures in Table 8.7 clearly show that the absence of politicization of religious issues in Protestant countries was a long-term asset for the electoral development of the left as much as the politicization of competing denominational identities in mixed countries was a liability. The difference between these two groups ranges from 7% to 9% in the periods before World War II and from 15% to 12% in the periods after it, and the size of the difference is systematic through time. In all mixed countries, Catholics started their political organization quite early – before or in parallel with the socialists, from a ghetto church position, and with considerable antiestablishment misgivings. Competition with the socialists for lower-class support was clearly embedded in this position. In the Netherlands, socialist electoral penetration was already regionally differentiated according to the spread of religious feelings in the 1880s: Where religious influence was lower, socialist mobilization was stronger.[138] The rapidly growing mobilization of religious unions in the period after 1906 (see Chapter 6, Figure 6.5) caused the socialists to feel that their trade union movement could not hope, in the foreseeable future, to make any deep inroads into large parts of the religiously organized working class, particularly in the south of the country, or into other Protestant bastions elsewhere. This resulted in an additional push toward a self-moderating position and political course that the party felt was the only one that would attract the religious workers.[139]

---

[138] In particular, in the province of Friesland and in neighboring Groningen. In the 1890s, the center of gravity of early Dutch socialism shifted from the urban regions of the west to the rural ones of the north. Buiting (1990: 65–66) shows membership figures by country regions documenting this shift. The support of agricultural workers in northern agrarian regions was due to the agricultural crisis of the period. But the religious element also was particularly important.

[139] This is a particularly clear-cut case and example – although not the only one – of the fact that the moderating electoral strategy, rather than being responsible for the loss of working-class sections, was often developed precisely to attract working-class nonsocialist sectors. Even the 1913 refusal to accept portfolios in a Lib–Lab government was due

Table 8.7. *Electoral strength by religious composition*

religion	left size				
	1880-1917	1918-1944	1945-1965	1966-1985	whole period
mixed	14.9 (25)	30.8 (23)	33.4 (16)	33.8 (20)	**27.3 (84)**
Catholic	15.4 (18)	29.0 (26)	36.6 (31)	35.9 (36)	**31.1 (111)**
Protestant	21.2 (39)	39.2 (43)	48.2 (32)	45.0 (38)	**37.9 (152)**
period average	**18.0 (82)**	**34.2 (92)**	**40.6 (79)**	**39.1 (94)**	**33.2 (347)**

Note: Number of elections given in parentheses.

In German electoral history, there is equally strong evidence that Catholicism limited socialist electoral expansion dating back to the 1890s. A systematic gap in left support in Catholic regions compared with Protestant ones has been documented by various electoral analyses.[140] In Switzerland, the inhibiting role of religion on class alignments varied markedly as a function of the linguistic community and interacted with the inhibiting role of national versus local identities.[141] However, note in Table 8.8 that the nature of class alignments varied as much within linguistic communities as it did between them (for instance, the three Protestant French-speaking cantons versus the Catholic French-speaking cantons). Therefore, linguistic differences may also be the result of the powerful interaction of religion and language. Whatever the case may be, both muted class mobilization.[142] In conclusion, in countries with a dominant Protestant estab-

---

to the socialist fear of alienating potential workers organized by Catholics and Calvinists (Daalder 1981: 225). The "electoral trade-off" imagined by Przeworski – according to which moderating the working-class appeal in order to attract middle-class voters would eventually lead to the decline of working-class support – was not relevant for Dutch (and other) socialist movements in the pre–World War II periods. They wanted to attract Catholic workers, not the middle classes. It is debatable whether they would have been more successful in attracting Catholic workers with a radical class appeal rather than with a moderate, reformist one.

[140] For ecological data evidence, see Urwin and Aarebrot (1981: 255) and Rokkan, Urwin, Aarebrot, Malaba, and Sande (1987: 148–149).

[141] Ecological research by cantons has shown that the correlation between Christian Democrat support and the percentage of Catholics in the population is incredibly high (.930). Protestantism yields much less significant associations, as the Protestant cantons divided their strength mainly among the other three national parties (radicals, liberals, socialists). The socialist vote is positively associated with Protestantism ($r = .517$) and urbanization ($r = .745$) as a result of the Catholic Party's strength in Catholic cantons and also in rural areas (Catholicism coinciding to a large extent with rural areas); Rokkan, Urwin, Aarebrot, Malaba, and Sande (1987: 261–264).

[142] For further evidence that when language and religion compete with class they preempt the mobilization capacity of the latter see Lijphart (1979: 442–458).

Table 8.8. *Proportion of left support by language and religion and by sense of identity in Switzerland*

	Catholic	Protestant	national identity	linguistic identity	cantonal identity
French speaking	36	53	47	54	28
German speaking	12	28	28	28	21

Note: Identity: national = Swiss; linguistic = Romand or German; cantonal = "*genevois*," etc.
Elaborated from Kerr (1974: 14) and (1987: 153).

lishment, the opposition and the culturally defensive politicization and organization of the Catholic minorities proved a powerful competitor to the socialists for lower-class support.

The situation is more complex in homogeneous Catholic countries. The level of electoral mobilization of the left in these cases is intermediate between that of mixed and Protestant countries, but there is higher within-group variation in mobilization potential than in either of the two other groups. With reference to the timing of organizational mobilization of the Catholic subcultures, a distinction can be made between the cases of Belgium and Ireland and those of Austria, Italy, and France. In the first two, Catholic political mobilization was early, pervasive, and clearly antic-ipated by that of the socialists.[143] Even though one could not formally identify in Ireland – as in Belgium – a "Catholic party," in both countries Catholicism intertwined with nationalistic issues and was an early political mobilizing force because it represented the political identity of the new states as a secession from previous broader and Protestant-dominated poli-ties. In contrast, in Italy and Austria, Catholic political organization was late and its main catalyzing factor was antisocialism. In France, the for-mation of a distinctive Catholic party failed between the world wars and was short-lived after World War II.

In Figure 8.2, I have charted the decade-average level of electoral mobilization of the left continental countries, distinguishing four groups: (1) those that are homogeneously Protestant; (2) those that are religiously mixed; (3) those that are homogeneously Catholic with early Catholic politicization and organizational mobilization; and (4) those that are ho-mogeneously Catholic with late, postsocialist organizational mobilization.

---

[143] Note that Belgium is the only country in which Catholic trade unions were earlier and stronger than the left trade unions.

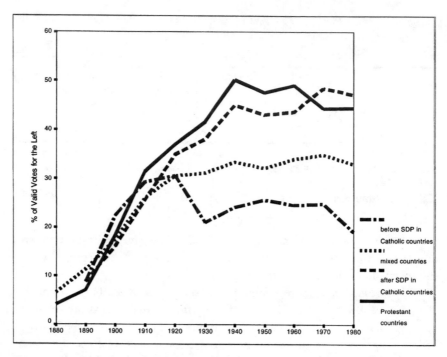

Figure 8.2. Left electoral mobilization by timing and type of religious mobilization.

These groupings best discriminate differential levels of left electoral mobilization. It is interesting to note that between the 1880s and the 1910s, there are only modest differences among the groups *from this point of view* (while, of course, there are differences in the levels of electoral mobilization due to other factors not reflected by these groupings). It is in fact after this that left electoral histories diverge according to denominational context during the late 1920s and the 1930s. Thus, the left stagnates in mixed countries and in the homogeneously Catholic countries where Catholic political mobilization was early. The opposite is true for both Protestant countries and the Catholic countries where Catholic organizational mobilization was late and was an antisocialist reaction, and this is illustrated in the continued growth of the left in the following two to three decades.

Presumably, this is the case for two reasons. On the one hand, this late denominational mobilization in Italy and Austria inherited the political representation of a historically weak political liberalism and also a politically discredited and never well organized conservatism and was thus less well able to challenge the socialist organizational subculture, by then already well rooted. On the other hand, Catholicism in homogeneous Catholic countries was so historically characterized in reactionary, antiliberal, prodynastic terms that its political mobilization determined a fundamental anticlerical political realignment within the middle classes. The Catholic role in politics added radical, anticlerical, middle-class electoral potential to what it subtracted from the working- and lower-class vote. The stronger the religious hierarchies and their links with the masses, the larger the sections of the middle classes and the bourgeoisie that adopted an anticlerical position and were inclined to vote left.[144] In so doing, Catholic political mobilization impinged on the social homogeneity of the class cleavage, and perhaps on the cohesion of the socialist movement, but not on its electoral potential.

By the 1980s, the total left of these Catholic countries tended to be even stronger than that of the Protestant countries. Therefore, while denominational mobilization weakened working-class political homogeneity everywhere, reducing the *social homogeneity* of the class cleavage, it was not always a factor that contained the size of the left. Utilizing both the class-voting index[145] for the 1950s–1960s and an index of "religious voting" constructed with the same logic (percent of churchgoers voting for religious parties − percent of nonchurchgoers voting for religious parties),[146] Figure 8.3 shows that the main dividing line between the northern homogeneous Protestant countries and the mixed and homogeneous Catholic continental ones concerns the social homogeneity of the electoral support of the class left. The left parties that appear more able to attract non-working-class, middle-class votes are those that are also unable to monopolize the representation of working-class constituencies.

Finally, denominational political organizations were not easy partners for socialist movements. The relationship between Catholic parties and socialist parties was, with very few exceptions, highly unstable throughout the period we are discussing. Stable, although intermittent patterns of political alliance developed only in Belgium, the Netherlands, and Switzerland (the "magic formula"). Such alliances either failed completely or were highly unstable and competitive in Italy between 1919 and 1924 and

---

[144] Nor should one assume that this phenomenon is typical only of homogeneously Catholic countries. It is also present in the religiously mixed continental countries; cf. Irwin and Holsteyn (1989: 28).

[145] I take this as an indicator of the social homogeneity of the vote for the left. For a recent and updated discussion of Alford's and Thomsen's indices of class voting and for a detailed analysis of their over-time variation after World War II, see Nieuwbeerta (1995: 12–13, 16–18, 39–56).

[146] The data are drawn from Lijphart (1971).

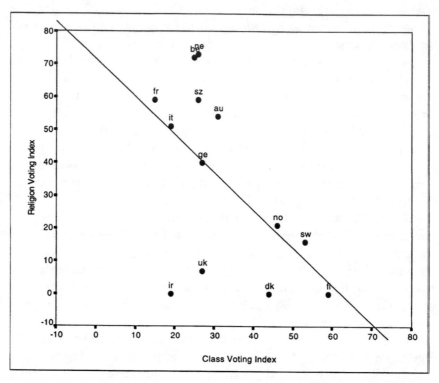

Figure 8.3. Scatterplot of religious and class voting indices (1950s–1960s).

after World War II; in Germany and Austria between the world wars, probably with a fatal outcome for democracy; and in France during the Fourth Republic. The specific cross-class appeal of the Catholic movements created a continuous internal debate and dissension within the socialist camp about the choice between cooperation or adversarial attempts to split this denominational support along class lines.[147]

Concerning the agricultural population and its political representation, the predicament differed according to which agrarian structure the socialist movement was facing and the different forms of its political representation. Where a class of independent freeholders was present and agrarian mobili-

---

[147] There were frequent attempts by the socialists to split their Catholic antagonists along socioeconomic lines. The most explicit attempt was made in Belgium in 1925, when the Flemish laborite wing of the Catholic Party joined the socialists in support of the government. The hopes of breaking the Catholic Party were not unrealistic, given its internal structure organized around corporate membership of several "estates" of Catholic labor, Flemish farmers (Boerenbond), and middle classes. However, the attempt failed. Historically, the socialists proved unable to split Catholic parties everywhere.

zation succeeded in representing the largest proportion of this group, the problem was less one of electoral support than of political alliance. A self-representational agrarian movement was likely to accept Green–Red mutual support. Alliances with peasants were therefore political, based on the exchange of policies among self-representational social groups. Nondoctrinaire socialist parties cooperated with farmers' movements to enact adequate legislation to help them out of the Depression. The socialists found in these movements an early substitute for the previous alliance with more encompassing liberal movements; were less politically isolated; and were not, given the predominantly egalitarian structure, involved in relationships of high class polarization in the rural areas. The social base of the class cleavage tended to be, and to become, even more socially homogeneous.

While the agricultural world was unable to form a unitary self-representational political movement, no political alliance with the left was possible, but the latter was still able to penetrate single sectors of the agrarian world. Doctrinaire socialist parties with rigid Marxist programs hostile to the farmer/owner, strongly antireligious, and overwhelmingly concerned with working-class issues and welfare did not attract farmers, particularly in strongly Catholic countries and regions (Germany, Austria). If the representation of the agrarian world was already ensured by denominational parties (Belgium and the Netherlands are the clearest cases; in Switzerland, representation was shared by Catholics and a noninclusive agrarian party), the socialist movement remained a predominantly urban movement in which political alliances were to be made with Catholic organizations, thus mixing the peasant issues with the denominational one. Although socialist penetration was possible in this case, it was minor and limited to small secular sectors and agricultural laborers.

In other cases, the representation of the agrarian world was split among various forces. When the agrarian social structure was highly differentiated and relationships of class polarization prevailed among different agrarian social groups, Catholic, conservative, and/or agrarian noncomprehensive movements gained the support of about 50% of the peasantry, leaving the representation of other sectors and sections to other political forces. When the class polarization of rural areas was high – separating large owners and small peasants and the latter two from sharecroppers, tenants, and agricultural laborers – it generally produced the deep penetration of the socialist movement. This not only added to the lack of social homogeneity of the class cleavage, but also contributed to its strong radical position. Subsistence farmers (peasant consumption enterprise), tenants, and sharecroppers in nonreligiously committed areas – and where a relatively small peasant owner group coexisted with a number of large farmers – tended to support the radical protest movement of the left, joining their support to that of agricultural workers. In France, Italy, and Finland, the socialists' involvement in the class conflict of the rural areas had momentous consequences for their ideological and organizational developments (see the next chapter) and is the feature that sets these cases more clearly apart from both the Scandinavian and the Central European patterns.

Combining these dimensions, the European experience presents four major patterns from the point of view of the political environment that socialist movements faced between 1880 and 1930. The "most favorable" conditions were the combination of an early, stable, and protracted Lib–Lab alliance, which was then supplanted by an equally long-standing and stable Red–Green alliance with a self-represented peasant movement within a context of little or no political mobilization of religious groups and little or no class conflict in the rural areas. The first-phase alliance was mainly oriented to the liberalization and democratization of the political regime.[148] The later alliance focused mainly on common economic policy interests and set the stage for a pattern of political competition largely dominated by socioeconomic issues and alignments (nationalization in the 1920s, welfare programs in the 1930s and 1950s, sales taxation, etc.). From an ideological point of view, the concrete payoffs of the Lib–Lab alliance, the perceived need to avoid alienating the large rural population (with demands such as the nationalization of land) and to avoid the political and social isolation of the working class and the ideological weakness of laissez-faire and economic individualistic liberalism[149] all favored early and consistent abandonment of an orthodox Marxist revolutionary doctrine and a gradualist position of compromise. At the same time, the absence of strong religious or ethnolinguistic cleavages (and the high level of literacy) made it easier to replicate the class structure in the party structure. This produced the most distinctive and inclusive class cleavage in the Scandinavian countries (see Figure 8.4 for the following discussion), with a political movement that incorporates about 80% of the working-class vote and whose electorate is composed of about 75% of workers.

The United Kingdom's experience is a variation on this pattern; the main difference lies in the nature of the liberalism and its subtending social groups. In the United Kingdom, liberalism was an urban phenome-

---

[148] Also thanks to the fact that Scandinavian liberalism was not historically linked to the laissez-faire ideologies of the urban bourgeoisie, but rather to the social reformist and democratic ethos of the peasant periphery. On these points, see Castles (1977: 25).

[149] It was not only the strong position of the independent peasantry that favored this ideological weakness, but also late industrialization and the strong bureaucratic traditions (in Denmark and Sweden).

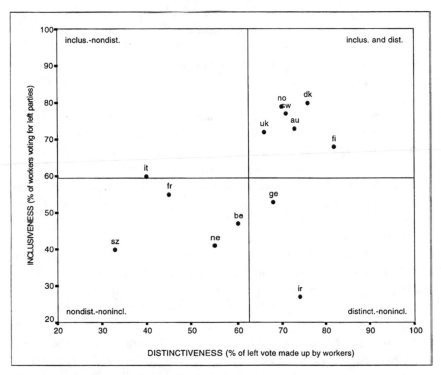

Figure 8.4. Inclusiveness and distinctiveness of the class cleavage.
Note: The figures for inclusiveness and distinctiveness are drawn from
national surveys conducted in the 1950s and 1960s. Because there are
considerable discrepancies among different sources in several cases, when
necessary the different figures have been averaged. Source documentation
is reported in the Data Appendix.

non and could not give birth to an agrarian ally for labor once the original
alliance ended in the first two decades of the twentieth century. Therefore,
while in Scandinavia the opposition of the central nation-building culture
(essentially an urban elite of officials and patricians) to the traditions of the
periphery was reinforced by the opposition between the interests of the
secondary sector and those of the primary sector, in the United Kingdom
the two cut across each other, the central culture being upheld and reinforced by landed families. Labor fought alone against a Conservative Party
that was able to fuse the landed and urban elites in a country deprived of
an influential small peasantry and agricultural labor.[150] The consequence

---

[150] It is important to emphasize that the crucial passage to national politics was more the
result of the Conservatives' efforts. Around 1885, the Conservatives moved into the

was that British labor was unable to achieve ideological and governmental hegemony equal to that of the Scandinavians. While it remains difficult to explain why the British socialists never sought to consolidate a political alliance with the remnants of the liberals (and paid a disproportionate price for this in terms of continuity of governmental tenure), such an alliance would probably not have altered the cleavage structuring to any great extent. Finally, British class cleavage emerged as highly distinctive, similar to that in Scandinavia but considerably less inclusive, involving about 60% of the British working class in the 1950s and 1960s. This lower level of inclusiveness was due to the high working-class deferential vote for the dominant social circles represented *by* and *in* the Conservative Party, whose unblemished historical prestige finds no correspondence on the Continent[151] or in Scandinavia.

By the same token, the more complex conditions of the structuring of the class cleavage occurred in countries where liberalism and the liberal forces were politically weak and disorganized and offered no shield for the rising socialist movement, where denominational mobilization drastically dissipated working-class solidarity and where large agricultural sectors were characterized by deep class polarization in the countryside. The two best examples of this are Italy and France. In both, Catholicism soon acquired a distinct political identity and added to the social heterogeneity of the class cleavage by successfully acquiring the political support of the lower classes while losing, in exchange, the support of the radical anticlerical middle classes. The fragmented social structure of the agricultural world added further elements of social nonhomogeneity, making any dialogue with it as a whole impossible but permitting considerable inroads into some of its more socially radicalized sectors. The political opportunities opened and closed by the instability and divisions of the liberal forces, combined with the great heterogeneity of the social bases, ensured that almost any political strategy would be challenged by sections of the socialist movement and that almost any ideological variety would be present and appear convincing to different sectors of it: from trade unionist tendencies to revolutionary syndicalism, from *ex cathedra* reformism to Leninist. This synthesis was far from unsuccessful in overall electoral terms, but it did mean, of course, that ideological and organizational cohesion was

boroughs, and this led to a gradual merger of the landed interests with the urban business interests. The Conservatives, therefore, produced the crucial shift from a traditional cross-class territorial representation to a new emphasis on cross-local class representation in Britain.

[151] On working-class "Toryism", see McKenzie and Silver (1967) and (1968), Parkin (1967), and Taylor (1978).

impossible to achieve. These class cleavages remained below average in both inclusiveness and distinctiveness. It is, however, the latter – the low distinctiveness – that distinguishes them from the Central European cases. In other words, what is typical is not the inability of the socialist parties to incorporate more than approximately half of the working class, but rather their capacity to attract and recruit *outside* the working class. This was the key to their historical electoral success and, at the same time, the stigma of their being undifferentiated coalitions from the class point of view.

Austria and Germany present a third model. In this model, a liberal option was unavailable in both the early and later stages. Nationalism and the national question continued to agitate and divide the liberal forces, while Catholicism mobilized in both countries and the agrarian world became politically incorporated, to a large extent, within denominational political movements. Yet, compared with Italy and France, the agrarian sectors of Austria and Germany were far less conspicuous and had a less class-polarized internal structure. The two political contexts were similar in terms of both institutional closure and sociopolitical isolation. Under these conditions, any challenge to Marxist orthodoxy presented by cooperation with the bourgeois political forces, or by the need to come to grips with an independent political movement representing the agrarian world, remained unlikely to succeed. By contrast, an orthodox Marxist stand was probably the most effective way of maintaining the organizational and ideological cohesion of the socialist movement, even though, between the world wars, it failed in Germany and was successful in Austria.[152]

The similarity of the cleavage-structuring context in these two countries ends here, however. In Germany, Catholics mobilized politically very early and structured their political organization as an anti-Protestant-establishment ghetto party in direct competition with the socialists for lower-class support. In Austria, monopoly Catholicism organized much later politically, more or less at the collapse of the imperial order. It became the only force of political defense for Catholics against anticlericals, but also for peasant interests as opposed to urban interests, dynastic and bureaucratic circles against republican groups, and the urban bourgeoisie

---

[152] Note that the parties had different responsibilities in interwar politics. The Austrian socialists were ousted from the cabinet in 1920 and never came back, so during this period their opposition role and tactics were quite uncompromising and they could continue their class-based electoral tactics. German socialists were far more deeply involved in governmental cooperation with Catholics and other forces, which continuously fueled internal debate about tactics and strategy.

and independent middle classes against one of the best-organized and most socially cohesive socialist movements. Under these circumstances, all these cleavage lines came to be superimposed on one another in Austria, while in Germany they continued to cut across each other more profoundly, particularly in Catholic areas and regions.[153] Both parties had distinctive working-class profiles, but the level of inclusiveness was considerably different. The Austrian socialist movement included the vast majority of the working class at levels not much lower than those in Scandinavia, while the German socialist movement, which had more-forceful competition, remained at average European levels of inclusiveness, representing about 55% of the working class.

The fourth model is represented by those cases where an early confrontation between liberal-conservative and denominational political groups shaped the political competition in liberalized regimes. The early pluralism within the established elite of countries such as Switzerland, Belgium, and the Netherlands eased the political entry of the socialist movement but did not offer any solid liberal point of reference for political alliances. The weight of the agricultural world and its interests was far less pronounced than in the Scandinavian and Southern European cases, so that socialism remained a primarily urban movement. At the same time, the politicization of denominational identities was early and pervasive in all cases, although with different degrees of territorialization (maximum in Switzerland and less pronounced in Belgium and the Netherlands). Not surprisingly, the class cleavage structuring was very noninclusive in all cases, with the socialists represting only 40–50% of the working class, but the considerable difference in distinctiveness differentiated Swiss socialism from the stronger Dutch and Belgian socialism (up to the 1960s). The combination of religious, linguistic, and cantonal identity as forces dissipating working-class unity and solidarity made the Swiss socialist movement not only the weakest in Europe (after the Irish), but also the least distinctive and inclusive, with around 30% of left voters being workers and around 40% of workers voting left. Belgian and Dutch socialism, facing mainly denominational competition, maintained a more distinctive profile (in the former, this declined sharply when the linguistic cleavage was mobilized organizationally in the late 1960s; my data in Figure 8.4 refer to the situation before this development).

[153] To exemplify the peculiar Austrian overlapping of class and religious feelings and contrast it with the more common continental cutting across pattern, one may recall that the difference between the church attendance of the middle classes and the working classes is +1 in Germany, +7 in the Netherlands, +9 in Belgium, +14 in Italy, +15 in France, and +59 in Austria. See Lewis-Beck (1977: 456) and Houska (1985).

Finland and Ireland remain the more difficult cases to interpret from this perspective. With other cases, they share the absence of a phase of liberal cooperation, but they mix features of different types. Ireland shows an extremely prolonged and pervasive role of nationalistic issues and movements and, at the same time, an equally persistent and pervasive role of Catholic political identity. Rural conflicts were solved with the creation of a large peasantry deprived, however, of any self-representational political organization much before the Socialist Party emerged. Labor was fundamentally unaffected by and uninterested in the agrarian world. The net effect was ludicrously low inclusiveness and extremely high distinctiveness – a working-class party that left the majority of the working class to be represented by other types of political movements, combining a Catholic profile with a clear position on the national issue. Finland combines elements of the Scandinavian and Southern European cleavage-structuring patterns, although the socialist entry was not as easy as in the other Scandinavian countries and the class polarization of the countryside was far higher than in Scandinavia. This meant that the agrarian political movement was less inclusive than its Scandinavian counterpart. At the same time, the socialist movement had, as in Mediterranean France and Italy, considerable early support among sectors of the agrarian world, that is, among the large group of agricultural laborers, as well as tenants and even small farmers. Stable cooperation with the Agrarians Party was impossible in these conditions. Moreover, because the victory in the 1918 civil war was perceived by the Whites as a national liberation war against the Russian influence and by the Reds as a class war, antagonism was strengthened by the superimposition of national feelings over class ones. As a result, the cohesion and unity of the bourgeois forces in Finland between the world wars was far superior to that of the Scandinavian countries. The Finnish left therefore experienced the ideological and organizational tensions associated with this situation, but, at the same time, the absence of cultural identity-dissipating forces made the class cleavage resemble the Scandinavian model in terms of both inclusiveness and distinctiveness.[154]

[154] For the similarity between Finnish and Scandinavian patterns of party support, see Markku (1980: 84–86).

THE COMMUNIST SPLIT: UNITED AND DIVIDED LEFTS

In Chapter 2, the distinction between three different processes was argued: (1) working-class radicalization and revolutionary crisis; (2) short-term socialist organizational and ideological disunity; and (3) long-term communist electoral success. The radicalization of working-class politics during and after World War I, and in some places even before, was a generalized phenomenon, although the organizational and ideological strife and splits affected the national socialist movements differently according to the prewar divisions, the country's position during the war, and the socialist attitudes toward war efforts and governments. In Chapter 2, Tables 2.6, 2.7, and 2.8 have been compiled for comparative purposes, and a descriptive analysis of the level of fragmentation of the socialist movements has been made. Reference to these sections should be kept in mind while reading this chapter, which considers the overall interpretation of the long-term outcome of these processes. The explanation of the consolidation and the long-term electoral success of communism and the general constellation of forces that can explain the difference between united and divided lefts, require, in my view, a broader and more long-term interpretive framework. This problem is the central theme of this chapter.

INTERPRETATION OF COMMUNIST SUCCESS OR FAILURE

The modalities of the communist splits documented in Chapter 2 bear little relation to the more long-term electoral and organizational success of the communist movements, which instead requires a more general analysis. In three out of the four cases where communism made important electoral inroads, this took place in an unstable liberal–democratic environment.[1] Due to the intertwining of the communist question with national integrity and independence, the party was banned in Finland for almost the entire interwar period bracketed by the two civil wars. In Germany, the communist movement was annihilated by Hitler, and after World War II its disappearance in West Germany may well be the result of the partition of the country and the creation of a communist regime in the Eastern part. In Italy, the party remained clandestine during twenty years of fascism, and was resuscitated thanks to the liberation war and the resistance movement. One might say that these are special cases when compared with the less stormy liberal democratic development in other European countries. Consequently, it may be tempting to search for the sources of communist success in these geopolitical situations. However, it should not be forgotten that electoral communism developed in a liberal environment in France, while it failed to do so completely in Austria, in a context as unstable as that of Germany and Finland.

Similarly, it has been argued that the Great War, its development, conditions, and outcomes, had a crucial impact on the chances of a radical Communist movement.[2] Given that all post–World War I and post–World War II radical left oppositions were united in their condemnation of the support and cooperation shown by their bourgeoisies and socialist and trade union movements in the countries at war, the latter forces were not subject to the same recriminations in the countries that were not at war. Indeed, the low success of the communist movements in these countries owed much to the more patriotic stands of their bourgeoisies during the wars and occupations.[3] This contrasts very strongly indeed with the recurring theme of the "betrayal" of the national bourgeoisie that pushed workers and peasants into unnecessary wars without satisfying the requests of those who had sustained the cost of the efforts (typically, France and Italy and, even more so, Germany after World War I) or, worse, leading to defeat and shame (typically again, Italian fascism, France's Vichy regime, German Nazism, and the Finnish alliance with Germany in 1941–1944). The low political and social legitimacy of the bourgeois and domi-

---

[1] On the implications of their adaptation to electoral politics see Greene (1973); and for the role of leadership in this adaptation, see Tannahill (1976).

[2] Kriegel (1969: 184).

[3] A detailed analysis of how war affected the electoral development of communist parties throughout Europe is presented in Timoten (1973). I thank P. Hannivaara for his help in reading this article. See also Rice (1973).

nant circles at the end of the two world wars justified and favored a radical appeal. However, that a warring and victorious country like France experienced radical splits, while a warring and defeated one (with regime change and territorial retrenchment) like Austria did not, requires a more complex set of explaining variables. On the whole, it can be concluded that the role of a country in war is an important intervening factor that added or muted preexisting and more profound socioeconomic, organizational, and politico-institutional preconditions. For these reasons, I will try to place the interpretation within a broader framework, which will not refer to these specific circumstances but will deal with them as instances of more-encompassing underlying processes.

Interpretations of communist strength and success are more numerous than the number of cases on which to test them. The major difference between them lies in those interpretations that refer to individual-level variables and those that refer to systemic or environmental features. Individual and system characteristics can often be translated into each other. Thus, a focus on the distribution of individual motivational, ideological, or social features places the macroprocesses that produced them in the background in the same way that systemic and environmental features need to postulate and induce the individual reactions associated with them that they cannot observe directly.

Let me explain why I have disregarded those interpretations of communism that consider it as a typical mass movement. Sociopsychological interpretations of radicalism, and lower-class left radicalism in particular, have often invoked the variable of "mass society" theory.[4] The argument is that the decline in social and group links in communities, the associated need for new social links, and the personal malaise and frustration associated with the intense, rapid social dislocation at the peak points of industrialization set favorable conditions for lower-class radicalism, and, in particular, for the creation of mass movements such as fascism and communism. The support for radical communist-inclined working-class movements is a typical example of such "mass behavior," characterized more by emotional, noncognitive processes or psychosocial grievances – with extremist, antidemocratic, and intemperate correlates – than by rational responses to class needs and political-action choices.

Within this debate, it is, first, impossible to test these individual-level interpretations with the kind of data utilized here. The test can only be indirect, considering the background variables that identify the condition of a mass society at the structural level. Second, the emphasis on the

---

[4] Kornhauser (1959: 21–113).

psychological and attitudinal characteristics of the supporters of radical and communist movements has produced considerable research and much discussion that, in my opinion, have failed to produce convincing supporting evidence. Kornhauser's specific interpretation of communism and fascism as "mass movements," a typical expression of the social and political alienation of a "mass society,"[5] has been subject to fairly systematic tests in different contexts, and most of the results have been critical of the theory. Studies devoted to communist militants and voters in France, Italy, India, and Chile have come up with results opposite to those expected on the basis of a mass movement interpretation of communism. Studies on Chilean radicalism have also concluded that the most radical left tendencies were not manifested by the socially isolated, least educated, least informed, or low-participating citizens; nor did upwardly or downwardly mobile lower-class individuals or those with status inconsistencies show any greater radical left proclivity. On the contrary, an association between left radicalism and specific social and political cognitive factors has emerged, linked to the perception that the failure to improve an individual's conditions derived from external constraints rather than from her or his weakness or other transcendental factors.[6]

Other research has shown that supporters of radical movements were not necessarily less likely to be involved in local community associations. On the contrary, they took a greater interest in politics and government, had a greater sense of political efficacy, discussed politics more, and were more knowledgeable. Thus, rather than finding an association between radicalism and the lack of ties, estrangement, a sense of helplessness, and ignorance, the reverse seems to be the case.[7] Other criticisms have accumulated in several countries that argue against the "protest" hypotheses that most communist voters in democratic systems are economically deprived, socially isolated, politically vulnerable to extremist parties, and generally alienated from the conventional norms of their society.[8] All these contributions conclude that the Communist labor population is usually not a mass population, and they suggest the limited usefulness of an emphasis on the psychological and expressive roots of working-class radicalism, or on its erratic, irrational, or noninstrumental character.

A certain amount of supporting evidence however, has, also been

---

[5] Kornhauser (1959: 179–180) recognizes a limit to his theory as far as the different class nature of seemingly similar mass movements is concerned.

[6] Portes (1970), (1971a) and (1971b).

[7] Halebsky (1976: 139, 146–147). Similar conclusions were reached for France and Italy: Hamilton (1967: 47 and footnote 10) and Tarrow (1967).

[8] See Greene (1971).

accumulated in favor of some versions of the mass society theory. Lipset devised the category of "working-class authoritarianism," stressing that low levels of education, patterns of family life, and high psychological and economic insecurity foster traits of an authoritarian personality, intolerance, prejudice, and temperamental thinking among the lower classes. Working-class conservatism on cultural issues, combined with their radicalism on economic issues, are not unlikely to make them supporters of antidemocratic movements of the left as well as of the right.[9] For example, the most extensive ecological study of Swedish communist electoral support has emphasized the long-term stability of their strongholds in regions of low religious practice and no farming in the north of the country. The main interpreting factor was "social isolation," by which was meant both geographical isolation (on the spatial periphery outside national communication networks), economic underdevelopment and nonintegration into the national system, and occupational isolation – immigrant labor and nonresidential labor populations.[10]

Again, Allardt, in his classic studies on Finnish communism, distinguishes between (1) traditional communism in the industrial centers of southern and western Finland and (2) "backwoods" communism in rural areas of northern and eastern Finland (after World War II). His interpretation of the latter emphasizes social anomie, alienation from the political system, and legitimacy crises resulting from rapid changes in rural regions. He interprets the communist support more as an emotional protest than as instrumentally oriented political behavior.[11] These arguments have been criticized by Korpi in several works. According to him, some crucial variables interpreted by Lipset as supporting his theory are probably spurious and caused by demographic factors. Korpi's argument also fails to support Allardt's theory of anomie. In his opinion, there are socioeconomic reasons that justify and explain the communist vote, and it is consequently easier to interpret available data on the communist orientation among workers in Western Europe in terms of a simple model that assumes rational, self-interested voters. The communist vote is neither partially nor wholly irrational. Voting is determined by rational choices on the basis of the relative utility of the policies pursued by parties for the workers.[12]

---

[9] Lipset (1959: 482–501).
[10] Rydenfeld (1954). I rely on the summary available in Lafferty (1974: 43–58).
[11] Allardt (1964) and (1970).
[12] Korpi (1971).

The debate is sufficient to justify leaving aside this line of research. I am rather uneasy about arguments concerning rationality versus irrationality of specific political behavior and contrasting emotional reactions to instrumental calculations.[13] In the context of the approach followed so far, I will be looking mainly for a syndrome of system features that best accounts for major cross-system differences in communist development. I will discuss the way in which such differences may have influenced the structure of individual and group beliefs, perceptions, and aspirations, but I will not pursue a direct test of the correspondence of the specific distribution of such beliefs, perceptions, and aspirations and the communist support at the individual level. I will frame the problem by asking the following questions: Under which socioeconomic, organizational, and politico-institutional conditions was an appeal of radical opposition to the dominant economic and political orders most likely to be successful? In other words, when was it most likely to be regarded as a *convincing* explanation of their condition and as a *convincing* perspective for changing such a condition by sections of the lower classes? I will concentrate on the differences among cases, trying to identify which syndrome of systemic factors best account for the successful split of the European left.

The hypotheses are so many and so strongly interlinked that it is difficult to isolate them from each other. At the same time, it is impossible to combine too many of them without falling into a case-specific interpretation that is not applicable outside of its own context. I have, therefore, organized the argument into four subsections before extracting the most convincing factors and linking them together:

1. Interpretations relating communist success or failure to the process, pattern, tempo, and type of social mobilization processes and cultural standardization processes.
2. Interpretations relating communist success or failure to organizational features of the socialist movement.
3. Interpretations relating communist success or failure to the process of institutional and political integration of the socialist movement.
4. Interpretations relating communist success or failure to the development of the cleavage system.

---

[13] Explanations that stress aspects of increased class consciousness or greater solidarity among workers have not been discussed because of their implicit circularity. Cf. Tilly, Tilly, and Tilly (1975: 8).

COMMUNISM, SOCIALISM, AND PATTERNS OF SOCIAL MOBILIZATION AND ECONOMIC DEVELOPMENT

Possibly the oldest of interpretations of the variation in communist support relates it to different patterns of economic development and industrialization. One thesis is that communist support flourishes not in backward but in late-industrializing societies, where the lateness is not absolute but relative to the earlycomers of the Industrial Revolution. At the end of the 1960s, Benjamin and Kautsky discussed communist support in a worldwide perspective, making the distinction between five types of society.[14] According to them, in the two most advanced types, namely, European societies and the United States, communist support was stronger in the (relative) latecomers, where late and slow industrialization had not penetrated the entire economy and the core working class was a minority group. Again, according to them, in this situation the overall weakness of industrial labor and of trade union organizations obliged them to face a solid and majoritarian antilabor coalition of both industrial and preindustrial property groups. In addition, sections of the peasants who were propertyless or propertied (but with relatively small holdings) and sections of the old middle classes (shopkeepers and artisans), threatened by big industry and big commerce, were tempted by defensive anticapitalist stands. Under these conditions, coalitions of sectors of the intelligentsia frustrated by incomplete modernization, sectors of the working class, and sectors of protest voters may be conducive to widespread support for communist movements.[15]

Slightly contradicting with this line of argument are the theses that regard intense radicalization (and Communism as the most stable organizational expression of it) as resulting mainly from situations of rapid and accelerated socioeconomic change and from the social dislocation that follows. This idea was forcefully argued in relation to the Scandinavian countries by Edward Bull in his explanation of why the intense radicalization of the Norwegian Socialist Party was absent in Sweden and Denmark.[16] This general idea is also implicit in Kornhauser's theory: Rapid

---

[14] Benjamin and Kautsky (1968).

[15] In contrast with these characters, one can determine the features of the fifth type, the highly industrialized countries, where the industrial working class is strong and integrated. See Benjamin and Kautsky (1968).

[16] Bull (1922). His analysis includes other factors: (1) the more open and democratic nature of the Norwegian socialist movement compared to the more centralized Swedish and Danish ones; (2) the weaker parliamentary representation of Norwegian labor; and (3)

industrialization and urbanization produce strong support for communist movements because of the difficulty of organizing and socially integrating the new workers coming from the countryside and their difficulties in adapting to industrial and urban life. Neither Bull's nor Kornhauser's generalizations spell out accurately, however, the links between rapid economic development, corresponding intense social dislocation, *and* political radicalism. An explicit hypothesis can be found in Thorstein Veblen's work about the sources of German nationalism.[17] His basic idea is that overly rapid social displacement forces people into what he calls an "obsolescent cultural situation." They find themselves in a new position while, at the same time, they have not forgotten their previous status and have not yet been exposed to the elements of the new situation long enough to assimilate them. This incapacity to forget their previous status and situation, which is linked to the length of exposure to their new position, produces reactions that Veblen identified in radical nationalism. However, one could use this argument as a complement to the theory of the radicalizing effects of rapid social dislocation.

The picture becomes more complicated if one considers Lorwin's propositions on the relationship between economic development and radicalism, largely derived from his studies of the Belgian and French labor movements.[18] He draws the following conclusions: (1) rapid growth and economic development in the early stages of industrialization generate radical protests resulting from dislocations, sacrifices, and difficulty of adaptation. At the same time, (2) continued economic growth leads to the quelling of this protest and satisfaction of needs. However, (3) protest attitudes may persist beyond the economic conditions that provoked them. Finally, (4) sluggish economic growth may generate the most profound and lasting protest as a result of the inability to provide economic well-being and social justice adequate enough to match the aspirations created by the beginning of industrialization and the failure of the economic elite to generate confidence. Interrupted, sluggish, or incomplete industrialization and social transformation seem to be the most favorable conditions for a radical class movement here. We can relate this line of thinking to that of other scholars, too. For example, Schumpeter[19] advanced the thesis that the radicalization of the working class and the birth of strong communist

the lack of a national leadership in Norway like that exercised by Branting in Sweden and by Staunting in Denmark.

[17] Veblen (1994: 21–43, 248–250). This theoretical scheme pervades the entire interpretation of the German imperial experience.

[18] Lorwin (1967b: 58–72).

[19] In Schumpeter (1951).

parties are most likely to occur in the countries and contexts where the urban and rural elites form a coalition against industrial development. Moore's argument is that the alliance of strong noncapitalist rural interests with weak urban industrial interests implies incomplete industrialization, as well as permanent pockets of backwardness and social groups that are weak and politically unstable.[20]

Although they have several interpretive points that can be reconciled, these arguments lead to quite different conclusions. Communism emerged in the 1920s, consolidated in the 1930s, and stabilized – if and where it did – in the 1950s. It makes a great deal of difference whether we argue that it had the best chance of appealing in the *most backward* European economies and social structures or, alternatively, in those that were late-comers but were, at the same time, experiencing high and accelerated rates of change or, alternatively, in those where sluggish and stagnant economic and social change prevailed. These theories agree about one end of the continuum: Early starting, smoothly progressing, and successfully com-pleted industrialization processes generate unfavorable conditions for a radical working-class response. They do not agree about the other end of the continuum – which conditions are more favorable to this response: sheer *backwardness*, late and *rapid socioeconomic change*, or interrupted growth and *sluggish economic development?*

If we relate the characterization of the patterns of industrialization illustrated in Chapter 3 to the strength of communism after World War I (Table 9.1), the cases of strong and persistent communist movements all belong to the group of countries where the industrial society (more active in industry than in agriculture) arrived late and did not permeate the social structure of the society (industrial predominance over the service sector was short or nonexistent). However, two countries where communism never made any inroads (Austria and Ireland) and the Scandinavian coun-tries, where it gained only moderate support, belong to this group too. Moreover, Germany – where communism was important during the Wei-mar Republic – belongs to the countries with both an early and a pro-longed industrial society.

We can look at the same problem from a different perspective by comparing the levels of association between communist and socialist sup-port and the main aspects that define the sociostructural characteristics of the societies. In Table 9.2, these data are reported for the 1918–1980

[20] Moore (1966). Moore applies this argument to the chances of democratic consolidation versus authoritarian rule, but it is indeed applicable at a lower level to the radicalization and communist development problems.

Table 9.1. *Timing and length of industrial society and Communist support*

		timing of industrial society (active in industry greater than active in agriculture)	
		early	late
length of industrial society (how long active in industry greater than active in services)	nonexistent	*Netherlands*	*Denmark* **Finland** *Sweden* Ireland *Norway*
	short		**Italy** **France** Austria
	prolonged	Switzerland *Belgium* Germany Un. Kingdom	

Note:

Normal = insignificant communist movement
Italics = small communist movement
Bold = strong communist movement
Underlined = Germany: strong in interwar years; nonexistent after World War II

Table 9.2. *Social structure and communist/socialist electoral support (1918–1980 elections)*

	Social Democratic vote	Communist vote
active in industry	.303 (207)	-.291 (173)
active in agriculture	-.278 (211)	.339 (173)
independents on active population	-.341 (208)	.364 (174)
dependants on active population	.389 (208)	-.374 (174)
industrial working class on active population	.335 (205)	-.294 (171)
rural working class on active population	-.1225 (206)	.124 (172)
industrial working class on total working class	.152 (167)	-.088 (148)
rural working class on total working class	-.167 (167)	.258 (148)

Note: Number of elections given in parentheses.

elections. Specular associations are systematic. Social democratic strength is associated positively with all the variables that define an industrial and advanced economic structure and negatively with all those that identify a preindustrial or incomplete industrial society. More than was the case for the total left, social democracy appears to be the typical product of industrial society, while communism appears to be the typical product of unsuccessful or delayed industrialization, as a more agrarian and traditional society phenomenon.[21] The association between the social-mobilization model and the left vote discussed in Chapter 3 is the combined result of the different nature of its two components. If applied to the socialist left alone, the social mobilization model performs much better.

The latter considerations point to a characterization of electoral Communism as a phenomenon that finds favorable conditions in the low integration of the working class in two senses: its internal heterogeneity and its low industrial concentration. We can find support for this idea by looking at the communist and socialist support (1) in different subsectors of the working class and (2) in relation to the level of concentration of industry (Table 9.3). In the interwar period, the internal composition of the working class does not seem to be associated with the level of voting for either of the two components of the left. This is probably due to the fact that in this period Germany had both strong communism and a highly homogeneous industrial working class. In the subsequent periods, however, it is clear that socialist support is lower in the context of a large agricultural dependent labor force, while communist support is higher in these cases.

France, Finland, and Italy have the highest proportion of dependent agricultural laborers in their working class. This is not true for Germany, however, and even Denmark and Austria have a slightly higher than average agricultural working class but are not examples of a deep postwar split. Finally, looking at the factory concentration of the industrial sector of the working class in terms of the ratio of employers to employees in industry (Table 3.11 in Chapter 3), one finds that France and Italy are the countries with the lowest industrial concentration by far. On average, in the 1920s and 1930s, there was one employer for every four workers in the industrial sector, while in countries such as the United Kingdom, this ratio ranged from one to fourteen to one to twenty. However, Finland and Germany do not fit into this pattern, while in Denmark, Norway, and

---

[21] These associations are not due to historical multicolinearity. Repeating the correlation analysis by each decade from the 1920s to the 1970s yields higher and similar sign correlations.

Table 9.3. *Working-class composition and support of left parties*

	industrial working class over total working class	rural working class over total working class	other working class over total working class
1918-1944			
Social Democratic vote	-.082 (77)	-.320 (77)	.225 (77)
Communist vote	.005 (60)	.272 (60)	-.439 (60)
1945-1965			
Social Democratic vote	.255 (59)	-.280 (59)	-.022 (59)
Communist vote	-.504 (56)	.667 (56)	-.192 (56)
1965-1985			
Social Democratic vote	.536 (34)	-.304 (34)	-.362 (34)
Communist vote	-.213 (32)	.733 (34	-.206 (32)

Switzerland, industrial plants were on average small and the working class was not highly concentrated in industrial areas.

Let us now turn our attention to the rhythm and tempo of the socioeconomic change rather than to its level. The British case is often cited as a case of early radical working-class responses triggered by the social disturbances of industrialization processes. The social and economic changes of early industrialization certainly stimulated vigorous protests and radical responses, but Luddism and Chartism were defeated or collapsed long before suffrage was granted, and by the time Marxism had developed an articulate theory that could have served the radicalism of the early British working class, the impetus for militancy had abated, that is, the destabilizing period of the Industrial Revolution was over.[22] The British example has given credence to the idea that radical responses are typical of the early and accelerated stages of industrialization; at the same time, if this phase precedes democratization, radical responses are likely to be absorbed and continued growth is likely to channel the newly formed working-class demands differently. This implicitly means that only when democratization and mass organizational and ideological development coincide with the most intense destabilizing social dislocation of the takeoff phase of the Industrial Revolution will the radical responses be channeled into radical communist movements.

Generalizing the argument, it is to be expected that countries experiencing the highest rate of socioeconomic change at the later stage – and

[22] Mair (1979: 162).

particularly at the stage of mass political development between the 1900s and the 1930s – will offer the most favorable opportunities for a political radicalization of the protesters. We can associate the level of the communist vote with the rate of change in the main indicator of socioeconomic transformation by decade. The results are so disappointing for the "rapid socioeconomic change/social dislocation/radical political response" hypothesis that they are not worth reporting in a table. All the correlations are negative with the communist vote and positive with the socialist vote. If the socioeconomic variables are lagged by one unit, so that the level of communist support in the 1920s and 1930s is related to the rate of socioeconomic change in the 1910s and 1920s, the situation does not change: Positive associations with the socialist vote grow, while those with the communist vote remain negative or insignificant. This seems to suggest that rapid change fosters a socialist (moderate) response rather than a communist (radical) response.

If we repeat this analysis at the level of individual countries, relating the mean rate of socioeconomic change to the mean electoral success of the communist splits, as is done in Table 9.4 the data continue to offer little support for the thesis. The most successful communist parties in the 1920s are not to be found in contexts of previous rapid and accelerated socioeconomic transformation. Quite the contrary, Italy, France, and, to a lesser extent, Finland are characterized by the lowest rate of growth in this period. In the second group of periods – the 1930s, 1940s, and 1950s – the situation does not change. Sweden and Austria maintain their position of high-growth countries, but Finland bypasses them in every category except for manufacturing output. The Finnish population employed in industry and the industrial working class grow at a rate either twice or three times higher than the European average in these three decades. France, however, remains the country with the lowest rate of growth, and Italy shows only average figures.

If anything, these data – and particularly those for the first three decades of the century, which are the most important – show that communist electoral strength was highest in the least dynamic societies of Europe. If the United Kingdom is taken as the example of the continuous growth that weakens early radical protest, France and Italy can easily be regarded as good candidates for the thesis that sluggish and incomplete industrialization favors radical reactions and appeal. They are the best examples of the syndrome that links (1) sluggish economic development and little dynamism in economic growth with (2) predominantly small-scale entrepreneurship lacking initiative, Malthusian-oriented, demanding state protection against labor and competition, niggardly in sharing bene-

Table 9.4. *Rate of socioeconomic change and communist strength*

	mean % 1900-1920 rate of change in:			1900/1928 % rate of change in manufacturing output per capita	mean Communist vote, 1920s	mean %1930-1950 rate of change in:			1928/1953 % rate of change in manufacturing output per capita	mean Communist vote, 1930-1950
	active in industry	dependant	industrial working class			active in industry	dependant	industrial working class		
Au	2.66	3.13	2.03	+240	.7	2.90	2.80	2.17	+160	3.4
Be	2.90	.87	4.37	+210	1.8	.37	.60	-1.47	+100	6.1
De	.47	2.06	1.60	+290	.4	2.40	2.87	2.57	+260	5.2
Fi	2.00	-1.30	1.05	+240	12.7	4.86	7.20	4.17	+120	15.0
Fr	.93	-.17	1.50	+210	10.6	1.47	1.97	1.40	+120	20.8
Ge	1.57	.27	2.77	+190	8.6	.37	1.13	-.90	+140	7.4
Ir	n.a.	n.a.	n.a.	n.a.	-	3.30	3.83	3.43	n.a.	-
It	-.47	1.80	.90	+230	4.6	2.17	-.50	1.53	+200	20.8
Ne	1.33	2.00	2.30	+280	2.0	1.07	-1.43	-.87	+160	5.6
No	1.37	2.87	3.37	+230	5.1	3.17	1.63	2.10	+270	4.8
Sw	5.33	6.70	5.63	+210	4.9	3.40	4.13	2.43	+190	4.7
Sz	1.63	4.87	2.87	+130	1.9	.37	3.70	2.13	+190	3.2
UK	-.83	1.90	1.30	+120	.2	2.40	.33	1.17	+170	.3
Mean	1.55	2.28	2.52	+215	4.3	2.17	2,17	1.53	+160	7.7

Note: Cases of strong electoral communism given in italics.

fits, and stubborn to maintain authority in the workplace; with (3) the persistence of large agricultural sectors and high agricultural prices, pockets of backwardness and protectionism, and major inequalities between poorer agricultural areas and industrial regions; and with (4) labor movement pessimism and a persistent sense of injustice, generating little hope for immediate improvements. The result of the French Third Republic's political alliance of the small rural and industrial sectors against the labor movement and big industry, in a country that had originally led early industrial development, is from this point of view not dissimilar to the Italian latecomer situation of asphyxiated capitalism and marked territorial and social inequalities.[23]

The indications derived so far from the discussion of the general hypotheses encourage further investigation of the relation between communist support and the rural population. The ambivalence and dualism of communism to the agrarian world was a constitutive feature for the Bolsheviks. They formed an urban movement, consisting essentially of workers and intellectuals who had never worked in the countryside or among the peasant masses, and among them, antipopulist and antipeasant prejudices and hatred for the *mugik* were widespread. While the Bolsheviks were leading a political revolution of socialist inspiration in Petersburg, with the urban working class as its protagonist, in the countryside a social

[23] For this characterization of the Italian economic elite, see Caracciolo (1957: 92).

revolution was occurring in which the forces of the rural petit bourgeoisie prevailed. Notwithstanding the efforts of Lenin, a true alliance between these two groups never materialized. Within one year of the Russian Revolution, the Bolshevik attempts to penetrate the countryside with class politics based on the poor peasants failed, and the preconditions were set for the future fatal conflict between them and a peasant movement that saw its raison d'être in the private possession of the land. In Western Europe, the relationships between the rural world and the communists were less conflictual, and given that communists were never in a position to implement their economic plans, they could remain ambiguous.

There are some clear-cut cases in which the roots of the communist split were heavily concentrated among the socialist intellectuals and qualified workers – as, for instance in the Netherlands,[24] Belgium, and Germany. However, in many other cases, and particularly those where communism was to prove a lasting feature, the crucial role played by the rural component of society was evident from the beginning. The detailed analysis of party conferences and voting in the Norwegian Socialist Party in the period before the split shows that radical positions and demands were stronger among the representatives of the primary sectors of forestry, fishing, and agriculture.[25] Indeed, at the Congress of Tours (December 1920), the representation of rural and peasant elements was predominant in the majority of the French SFIO that decided to join the Third International.[26] At that congress, many questions were raised by the moderates to the Third International about how they would then deal with the peasant and rural enthusiasm that had turned toward communism.[27] Similarly, it is documented that the Third International faction of the Italian Socialist Party was heavily rural and southern-based and that communist support after the Livorno split was very strong in prevalently rural regions of the country.[28] The organizational and electoral development of the Communist Party of Italy between 1921 and 1924 occurred primarily in southern regions and zones – the traditional bastions of the PSI Third Internationalists.[29]

It is difficult to interpret these common features of Italian, French,

---

[24] Buiting (1990: 71–72).

[25] Lafferty (1971: 257–289).

[26] This role is documented by several detailed reconstructions. See in particular Kriegel (1969: 395) and Judt (1976: 46).

[27] Sembat explicitly asked Cachin and Frossard: "Are you sure that the peasants will be with you in the event that a new Commune will occur?" *Le Congrès de Tours* (1964: 167). See also Lefranc (1963: 233).

[28] See the data provided by Detti (1972: 474).

[29] Detti (1972: 205–206, 499–500 and 500, footnote 137).

and Finnish Communism. The major French historian of the communist Party has extensively argued that the strong propensity of the rural component of the SFIO for Third Internationalism should be related primarily to the strong mobilizing effect of World War I. This war shattered the French countryside, breaking into the social and political isolation of the rural world, placing the peasants in the trenches alongside urban dwellers, making them pay the highest price for the war, and introducing them to politics, orienting them to the more radical and more militant tendencies of the time.[30]

The rural mobilization of the war was important in France, as well as in Italy and Finland (with its civil war), but obviously it does not automatically explain the failure of socialism to channel this phenomenon. The cases of Italy and Finland are more clear-cut because socialism was above all a rural movement to begin with. From the 1890s, Italian socialism grew among the *braccianti* (agricultural workers) of the lower Po Valley and of Emilia. In the provinces around the lower Po River, in this region of large land reclamation projects and newly built villages, often deprived of the familiar presence of a church, the agricultural workers represented a rural proletariat with little resemblance to that of other European countries. Unlike the serfs of the German rural areas to the east of the Elba River, they were a class of recent formation, without a past of subjection and submission, and in many ways more similar in mentality to workers and salaried employees than to peasants. Thanks to the early penetration of socialism in these groups, Italian socialism was rural from the beginning and was never characterized by the distrust of the rural masses typical of other socialist movements. Indeed, sometimes, as in Emilia, it was the "red" countryside that surrounded and went on to conquer the "white" urban settlement.[31] Third Internationalism and communism simply took over this historical support in a phase of intense radicalization and added to it the traditional left-wing orientation of the widespread groups of sharecroppers (*mezzadria*) and tenants in central Italy. This situation of early differentiated social support has always prevented Italian ecological studies from finding any association whatsoever between indicators of industrial development, urbanization, and the communist vote.[32]

In France, by contrast, the agricultural workers were less numerically significant than in Italy and Finland, but also far less concentrated and

---

[30] Kriegel (1969: 395).
[31] For the rural nature of early Italian socialism, see Procacci (1970: 414–415) and Ragionieri (1976: 1774–1785).
[32] Cf. Galli (1968: 161).

politically cohesive.[33] Communism made electoral inroads among them and among the sharecroppers of the *matayage* areas,[34] but also, more significantly than in Italy, among the small peasantry of relatively backward agricultural areas. Linz has summarized the multifaceted sources of communist support in various peasant areas and rural groups in France: from the small owners of the Mediterranean departments – among whom the less well-to-do used to earn part of their income as farm laborers on the large farms of the area – to the small peasant owners of the more backward region around the Central Massif – in an area of widespread agricultural property but also of precapitalist and low-productivity agriculture.[35] The fact that rural support for communism was so socially differentiated[36] and unusually widespread among small owners, plus the fact that in the eyes of intellectuals interpreting the phenomenon it could hardly be attributed to the appeal of the communist rural plans and programs – that from the 1920s to the 1960s oscillated continuously and contradictorily between short-term promises to small owners and long-term transformation plans[37] – has led to the characterization of the rural communist vote as a backward and protest vote, that is, a vote of resistance to change by declining groups. This interpretation probably underestimates both what the Communist Party and militants were actually offering through their organization to these individual and social groups, and the fact that the defense of the status quo was highly appealing for individuals and areas where feelings of economic insecurity were widespread.

The combined appreciation of the comparative role of agricultural independents and laborers helps to characterize the level of class polarization of the countryside. It also clarifies where and when the agrarian question assumed an important role in the internal socialist ideological and policy debate and, finally, how it shaped the profile of the class

[33] Ehrmann (1952: 39).

[34] Linz (1976: 403).

[35] Linz (1976: 390–392). He goes so far as to identify specific historical-tradition factors in given areas, such as the traditional leftism of the Calvinist Protestants that grew out of anti-Catholicism in defense of laicism in departments such as Gard; Ibid., p. 428. This tradition is documented in Schram (1954: 172–218). Relationships between patterns of land tenure and communist support have also been identified in countries like Indonesia, the Philippines, and, to a much lesser extent, India. See the summary of this research in Zagoria (1973: 9–16). For the documentation of the multifaceted social roots of rural communism in France, see Ehrmann (1952: 25–26), Wright (1952: 361–372), and (1964: 185–208), Micaud (1955: 354–366), and Gaborit (1972: 197–222, 467–495).

[36] For the cartographic documentation of this dualism see Goguel (1969) and (1970: 176).

[37] On the French communist rural stands, see Gaborit (1972: 201–208).

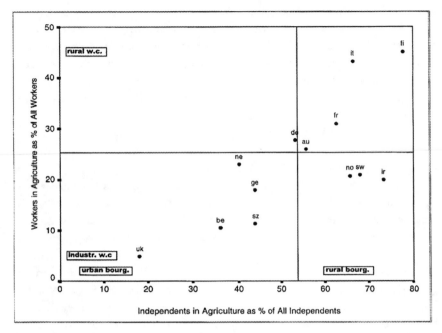

Figure 9.1. Class polarization in the countryside.

cleavage to a considerable extent. Figure 9.1 is a scatterplot for the 1900–
1940 period of the average proportion of agricultural independents over all
the independents and the average proportion of agricultural workers over
all the workers. The *y* axis gives an idea of the extent to which the working
class was either integrated into a predominantly urban and industrial
society or, alternatively, split into an urban and agricultural component.
The *x* axis indicates the extent to which the bourgeoisie (the independents)
were also predominantly urban and industrial or predominantly rural. The
four quadrants identified by the two reference lines of the overall means
single out different agrarian structures. In the bottom left quadrant, we
find cases in which the percentage of agricultural workers out of the whole
working class and the percentage of agricultural independents out of all
the independents are below the European mean. This means that both the
working class and the independent groups were relatively well integrated
into predominantly urban groups. The United Kingdom is the extreme
case in which the independent rural bourgeoisie was as insignificant as the
group of agricultural workers. In Belgium, Switzerland, Germany, and the
Netherlands, this situation is less well clearly delineated because the per-

centage of freeholders in the countryside is much higher than in the United Kingdom. Yet, they are still quite different from all the other European cases precisely because the percentage of agrarian laborers in the working class remains marginal (between 10% and 20%) and the weight of agricultural independents is also limited within the global group of independents. In all these cases, class polarization is mainly a feature of the urban and industrial world.

In the bottom right quadrant, the cases of Norway, Sweden, and Ireland (estimated, see earlier) are located. In these cases, the rural component among the independent groups was strongly dominant. Between 1900 and World War II, about 70% of all independents consisted of agricultural freeholders. At the same time, agricultural laborers formed a small component of the working class, which, whatever its size, was composed of four-fifths of the industrial workers. The combination of these two figures identifies these cases as areas of relatively egalitarian farmers' communities, with strong status equality predominating in the countryside. Denmark and Austria are intermediate cases. More than half of the independents were rural, which gives them some elements of an egalitarian farmers' community. At the same time, about one-quarter of the working class was composed of agricultural workers. In Denmark, this intermediate position was clearly reflected in the polarization of the agrarian independents, which led to the split of the agrarian party into a more radical and egalitarian small peasant movement, on the one hand, and a more conservative large farmer movement, on the other. In Austria, the entire agricultural world remained deprived of autonomous political representation, and – if one excludes the small Landbund of 1918, which never made an electoral breakthrough – the bulk of the peasantry remained within the Catholic Party.

Finally, the most interesting group is represented by the cases in the upper right quadrant. In these countries, the independents were overwhelmingly composed of rural independents, and the working class was, similarly, overwhelmingly composed of agricultural laborers. Particularly in Italy and Finland, and to a lesser extent in France, between one-third and one-half of the working class was represented by rural workers, and this predominantly rural proletariat also faced a predominantly rural group of independents. In these cases, the agrarian question was the *crucial question* for the socialist movement. This movement was, to a large extent, the natural representative of the rural working class, but, at the same time, it could not ignore the problems and requests of the small peasantry. Thus, the working class was not a predominant and homogeneous urban industrial group, but was split down the middle into its agricultural and urban-industrial components. Similarly, the large world of agricultural independents was characterized by strong internal divisions, and class polarization tended to be high in these cases. Peasants' political orientation was divided between rural radicalism and rural conservatism, and the many categories of the rural structure – the large owners, the small peasants, the tenants and sharecroppers, and the agricultural laborers – tended to split their political allegiances. The agricultural question presented a true dilemma for the socialist doctrine and practice. The question was not only about the defense of small agricultural property against the supposed law of economic development, but also about how to reconcile such a defense with the large agricultural worker groups and then how to reconcile both of them with the claims and interests of the urban-industrial working class.

The radicalism and fragmentation of the left seem to be associated with high social nonhomogeneity of both the bourgeoisie and the working class and with the high class polarization of the rural world, with the single exception of Germany, where, in purely sociostructural terms, one would not expect the communist radical left to be strong in the interwar period.[38] The rationale for this association can be identified in a direct and an indirect effect. Strong post–World War II communist parties all managed to add considerably different and sometimes disparate rural groups to the support of sections of the industrial working class. Where communism failed to make inroads into the countryside, either because early industrialization had already reduced the size of these social groups or because other powerful forces – denominational mobilization or self-representational peasant movements – prevented such penetration, it remained an electorally insignificant or modest force. Strong communist movements are therefore "dualistic" movements, combining support from the advanced industrial areas as well as from sectors of "unsafe" agricultural groups.

However, the direct effect of rural support for communism and the radical left is probably less important than the indirect effect created by the predominance of rural components in both the working class and the bourgeoisie. A large proportion of agricultural labor made the self-integration of a cohesive urban and industrial working class difficult, making it difficult to build a stable alliance with the continuously incoming unskilled workers. If the skilled workers' political representatives were unable to find a viable alliance to incorporate the agricultural laborers and sharecroppers (and even tenants and small owners in certain areas), the chances for the spread of radical political alternatives increased. At the

[38] Lipset (1983).

same time, the ongoing predominance of small agricultural property not only contributed to deep internal conflict in the left about strategies, programs, and perspectives toward this social group, it also delayed economic growth and full industrialization and kept agricultural prices high. In a sense, under these conditions socialist parties were obliged to incorporate within their own social base and internal ideological debate the social contradiction of economic development and modernization. In other words, they were driven into the contradiction of simultaneously fostering the social groups that should inherit a fully mature industrial society and those that would be mostly affected by such processes and indeed might have to disappear as a result of it. Therefore, the high percentage of active population in agriculture created continuous problems of internal integration and cohesion for the working class,[39] while the predominantly rural nature of the petit bourgeoisie created problems of system integration for the socialist movements and tended to radicalize the internal debates about short-term and long-term plans, policies, and strategies.

COMMUNISM, LEFT RADICALISM, AND THE ORGANIZATIONAL FEATURES OF THE SOCIALIST MOVEMENT

No strong communist party developed after World War II if it had not already made considerable inroads between the world wars, and only one failed to keep the strength it had achieved prior to World War II. Therefore, the key to communist endurance must be sought in the organizational developments of the 1920s and 1930s. The strength of the communist success between the world wars has been associated with the organizational consolidation of the socialist movement and, in particular, with the links established between trade unions and the socialist parties in the prewar phase. There are several indications in the national literatures about a possible relationship between communism, left radicalism, and the organizational features of the preceding socialist movement. I summarize these into four theses. Communist penetration and the conquest of important positions within both the political and corporate movements were easier and more significant where:

1. A weak and difficult political relationship between the socialist party and the trade unions prevailed. The distance between the party and

[39] Cf. Malefakis (1974: 1–7).

the trade unions allowed radical agitators to penetrate unions without close partisan affilation more easily.

2. Prewar socialism was a narrow movement, both electorally and, more important, organizationally. This occurred where its links with the socialist electorate were organizationally weak; where the party did not enjoy close segmental linkages with society or a *Bund* type of party organization; and where its membership structure was more open (as opposed to the collective membership tradition).

3. Trade unionization was low before the war and a large section of the working classes was still outside the socialist movement and was politically mobilized only during and after World War I. This meant that large numbers of industrial and agricultural workers were not yet solidly bound within the socialist organizational network when the new post–World War I wave of radicalization and political mobilization occurred. Thus they joined the left during the phase of intense communist–socialist strife, offering the communists the possibility of penetrating and even overthrowing working-class organizations that were precluded in other cases.

4. Traditional skilled-worker unions reacted to the new wave of post-war mobilization of agricultural workers and new groups of un-skilled workers with exclusive and noninclusive strategies, which made it possible for new organizations to recruit heavily among these groups.

These "organizational" hypotheses have in common the perception of Communism as a powerful organizational weapon – a perception that pervaded the hostile Western cultural climate of the Cold War in the 1950s and 1960s. Almond, inspired by Duverger and Neumann's insistence on the total integration nature of the party and the control it was able to exercise over "the totality of the militant's existence,"[40] has identified the nature of the communist parties of the West in their special mass–elite relationship. Mass and elite were separated by different models of communication and different levels of information; the communist leader was a "tactician of power," and the mass bases of the parties were instrumental to the leader.[41] Similarly, Selznick has qualified communist parties for their capacity (1) to transform members of voluntary associations into disciplined political ac-tivists; (2) to deploy their members as controlled agents within chosen groups; (3) to use mobilization and indoctrination techniques that

[40] Duverger (1967: 141–149) and Neumann (1956b: 395–421).
[41] Almond (1957: 6–61).

caused members to shift their loyalty away from other groups; and (4) to penetrate and manipulate institutional objectives.[42]

These views of communist parties were justified by the immense tactical flexibility they had shown between 1918 and 1945, a period during which international communism followed at least six different political lines with relatively minor national deviations: the early revolutionary perspective of 1918–1921, the 1921–1923 United Front, the 1923–1934 "anti social-Fascism," the 1934–1939 Popular Front, the 1939–1941 Nazi–Soviet Pact, and the 1941–1947 National Front. Each of them was characterized by different combinations of social and political allies and by different directions of organizational effort. Recognizing the superior organizational skill of communist militants and organizations, as well as their tactical flexibility in penetrating noncommunist organizations, this line of interpretation assumed that the Communist parties were so effective in maintaining control that they were able to mold the preferences and attitudes of their members more than the party machine could be molded by them. In this sense, once Communist parties were established, their organizational and ideological features granted them a high degree of independence from the sociopolitical environment. Once cleansed of the residuals of the Cold War cultural climate, this perspective implies that the communists' capacity for success rested fundamentally on the organizational infrastructure of the preexisting socialist tradition and on the capacity to resist and react to the strategies of organizational penetration of precommunist organizations. Communism could thus penetrate more easily where the organizational consolidation of the socialist movement was weaker. Where the syndicalist traditions had prevented an organic link between the socialist parties and the unions – and where the mystique of the *élan révolutionnaire* was originally seen as a substitute for solidly organized, dues-paying members, and later rationalized into a virtue in itself[43] – unions failed to achieve an early mass base and were more susceptible to communist penetration and organizational take-over.

The paradox of French socialism, discussed earlier, was that the well-established militant and revolutionary traditions of the workers, and the most complex ideological scene, were combined with weak organization, poor recruitment, and low cohesion (see the analysis in Chapter 6). It was perhaps the typical national acceptance and cultural legitimacy of such traditions that caused the lack of cohesiveness of the left's organization and ideology. In contrast to France, the British labor movement established a

[42] Selznick (1960: xiv–xvi).
[43] On this point, see Bowditch (1951: 32–34).

distinctive organizational identity early on, but this may have prevented the development of an equally distinctive ideological identity, as well as of any widespread cultural hegemony. Thus, an organizational split in the working-class movement was avoided in the United Kingdom before World War I and in the 1920s, not because there were fewer conflicts here than elsewhere between radicals and moderates, nationalist and internationalist wings, but because of the organizational features of the Labour Party. The party had only collective membership of affiliated organizations, and the position of each organization, thanks to its internal majority rules, was always clear-cut. Some organizations were antiwar, while others were prowar; some were more radical and others less. As such, whatever internal conflict existed within the party was a conflict among different organizational components. To split the party, a majority had to prevail in a sufficient number of organizations, and very few cross-organizational contacts were available for a minority cross-organizational split.

The British–French contrast also casts light on other cases. In none of the European countries where trade union movements were founded and consolidated before the socialist party's appearance in the last part of the nineteenth century (the United Kingdom, Ireland, and Switzerland; see the discussion in Chapter 6 and Table 6.2) did the radical left, and communism in particular, manage to make any significant inroads. At the same time, in countries where closely interlocking links between the party and the trade unions and collective affiliation prevailed in the socialist movement (as in Norway and Sweden), this may have helped to maintain strong organizational cohesion in both the unions and the party. Extending this argument further, it may be possible to say that indirect socialist party structures or party structures based on strong social pillarization and relying on intense extraparty organizational networks and *Bund*-type organizational affiliations, were also more difficult to radicalize and to split organizationally. In cases of strong organizational pillarization, the leaders of the party could rigorously and efficiently control the internal life of the sections and the activities of their affiliated members. Ideological currents and tendencies find it difficult to emerge unless they can rely on the support of some strong internal organizational component, able to provide financial resources, support, and defenses on which to fall back. In these cases, indirect structures and the indirect control of party resources can counteract the tendency toward ideological internal debate and factionalism.

This argument seems appropriate to cases such as the Belgian, Dutch, and Austrian socialist movements. Belgium, in particular, is a crucial test case, as the ideological and cultural influences of French socialism, the strong anticlerical ideology, and the relatively strong syndicalist traditions

made the Belgian Socialist Party particularly vulnerable to postwar radicalization and splits. However, from the beginning, the party was a mixture
of associations of every kind; and this complex but dense, indirect structure
and network of "communal" and organizational strongholds – held together by the need to resist the interference of the state, which was then
in the hands of Catholic political forces – helped the party to defend itself
from internal ideological factionalism.[44]

The combination of these three features of the relationship between
the party and the corporate channel organizations (respective timing of
corporate and political consolidation, strong versus weak socio-
organizational pillarization, direct versus indirect membership) yields a
classification of our countries, identifying those where the communist
parties became a viable alternative to socialist organizations in the 1920s
and 1930s. Germany, France, Italy, and Finland had all experienced a
consolidation of socialist trade unions that either followed the consolidation of the political party or was parallel to it. In two cases (Germany and
even more clearly Finland), trade union development was directed and
fostered by the party's leadership. In the other two (France and Italy), such
relations were difficult and unstable as a result of the party's attempt to
direct ideologically and politically recalcitrant unions. The strong influences of syndicalism – with its refusal to recognize the reality of politics
and its disdain for parliamentary action – prevented effective working
relationships between unions and socialist parties (Table 9.5).

Let us now consider the other line of argument that relates the narrowness of the pre–World War I socialist movement to its vulnerability to
postwar organizational splits. Narrowness can be conceived in either electoral or organizational membership terms. In the first sense, a narrow
socialist movement is one that is late or below average in its electoral
mobilization capacity. Narrow in organizational terms is a socialist movement that organizes only a small proportion of the labor movement in its
own voluntary organizations. In my opinion, however, narrowness is best
understood in the relationship between the two, that is, a narrow socialist
movement is one whose organizational density is low compared to its own
electoral mobilization.

The link between the fragile establishment of socialism and the communist success can be seen in the fact that between the world wars, narrow
socialist movements were confronted with strong waves of politicization
and mobilization of sectors of the working class that were beyond the reach

---

[44] Moulin was very critical of the role of organizational pillarization in shaping the
moderate petit bourgeois nature of the BSP. See Moulin (1981: 192–202).

Table 9.5. *Socialist movement organization in the early twentieth century*

		strong socio-organizational pillarization (*bund* type party)	weak socio-organizational pillarization
corporate consolidation before party-political consolidation	collective membership		Un. Kingdom Ireland
	individual membership	Switzerland	
party-political consolidation before or parallel to corporate consolidation	collective membership	Belgium	Denmark Norway Sweden
	individual membership	Netherlands Austria	Germany Finland France Italy

of the socialist movement.[45] These sectors were composed mostly of agricultural laborers, unskilled workers, or even small peasants, and they lacked the tradition of the disciplined organizational action of the more skilled and earlier-organized sections of the working class. This rapid mobilization created problems for consolidated socialist organizations. Quite naturally, the reaction was one of exclusiveness, leading to closure of the social relationship in the organizations that, in defending the advantages of the organized members, tended to exclude or only selectively include new groups. When such nonexpansive and noninclusive logic prevails in traditional organizations, the radicalization of the excluded and their incorporation into alternative organizations is more likely.[46] This interpretation has the advantage of linking organizational variables to the sociostructural factors discussed in the first section of this chapter and, in particular, to the internal homogeneity of the working class that resulted from different patterns and tempos of industrialization. The greater the

[45] Kriegel (1969: 431–432) offers a different interpretation of the same association: "a radical foreign experience that proposes abstract goals whose relationship with the real situation are unclear, easily attracts the interest of a sect." This interpretation is consistent with Kriegel's overall interpretation of Western communism as a "grafting," i.e., as the implantation of an external model in an environment different from its own. See Kriegel (1974: 26–27).

[46] Cf. Bendix (1964: 108).

internal homogeneity achieved, the more inclusive the working-class organization will tend to be; the more nonhomogeneous the labor world (artisans, craft unions, a large agricultural sector, agricultural laborers, and
other groups in the countryside), the more likely is a reaction to exclude
some sections of it from the established organizations facing rapid mobilization of new members.

At the empirical level, these theses find support in several national
accounts of trade union history, although few materials are available on the
history of socialist mass organization and membership development.[47] In
cases in which the end of the Great War produced intense radicalization of
working-class politics, historians have related this to massive increases in
the trade-unionized labor force, accompanied by the difficulties of socialist
unions in dealing with this rapid increase. For Germany, the detailed and
specific study by Biader[48] documents how the December 1916 law on
auxiliary service (the forced recruitment of a large number of workers) and
the 1917–1918 strikes led to a large increase in trade union membership
and a rapid change in the social base of these unions through the influx of
unorganized and unqualified workers. This was linked to the development
of an internal trade union opposition. Biader claims that in this period the
German unions reinforced tendencies toward leadership immobilization,
conservatism, and organizational rigidity that were already present before
the war.[49] Such tendencies were emphasized by the unions' support for the
war goals in exchange for concessions that were later nullified by the
beginning of the war. In Norway, it has been shown that postwar radicals
tended to be more concentrated in the areas of explosive membership
growth in the prewar period,[50] while the moderate elements of the labor
movement were concentrated in the guilds and handicraft unions.[51] Sectors
with an old-style organization were gradually overwhelmed and defeated
in the battle for the control of the movement by new unions, which drew
their strength from the rapidly industrializing rural labor force. Similar
accounts are available for the same period in France and Italy.[52]

Generalizing this line of interpretation to all of our cases in Table 9.6,
I have reported the measures of bivariate association between the vote for

[47] See Cronin (1980).
[48] Bieder (1981: 99–108, 778–781).
[49] Tendencies that are also documented by Schönhouver (1980: 333–376). For German
trade union development after 1920 see Potthoff (1979).
[50] See Lafferty (1971: 257–289).
[51] Lafferty (1971: 279).
[52] Detti (1972: xxviii–xxix), Cortesi (1973: 161–162), and Lorwin (1954: 52 and 75–76).
In France, the influence of the communists grew after each membership explosion in the
trade unions; after World War I, during the Popular Front; and after World War II.

Table 9.6. *Correlation between the vote for different components of the left and organizational density indicators (1918–1985)*

	trade union density	left trade union density	left trade union membership as % of the electorate	socialist membership as % of the electorate	socialist membership as % of the socialist vote
socialist vote	.368 (261)	.386 (258)	.431 (258)	.665 (232)	.473 (231)
Communist vote	-.186 (215)	-.216 (213)	-.357 (213)	-.301 (200)	-.208 (199)
other left vote	.459 (108)	.498 (106)	.578 (106)	.135 (105)	.160 (103)
total left vote	.384 (262)	.331 (259)	.299 (259)	.494 (233)	.368 (231)

Note: Number of elections given in parentheses.

different components of the left and the main indicators of organizational density of the left and of the social democrats (for a detailed presentation and discussion of these measures, see Chapter 6 and the Data Appendix). The systematic structure of these data is quite impressive. The Social Democratic vote is always positively associated with trade union density and, quite naturally, with a social democratic organizational presence. The Communist vote, however, is systematically associated in a negative way with these indicators. Communist support tends to be weaker where the trade unionization level is higher and the organizational presence of the socialist parties is stronger. Controlling these associations by decade does not change the picture, so that they do not result from temporal trends but are also valid on a comparative synchronic basis.[53] The association with the total left vote, which was discussed in Chapter 6, is the result of the combined effect of these two phenomena. As was the case with the socio-economic structural variables, but to a much stronger extent, communism and socialism here appear as phenomena of two inherently different environments.

Let us now look more closely at the cross-country variance. The argument presented earlier links communist strength to the narrowness and organizational weakness of the prewar socialist movement and, consequently, to the high rate of growth of trade unionization in the post–

---

[53] Actually, the negative association with the communist vote is much higher on a decade basis. It is also interesting to note that these organizational indicators are associated positively with the other left, i.e., with the strength of left-socialist but noncommunist parties.

World War I period. In Table 9.7, I report the mean value of the prewar (1900–1920) social democrats' vote together with the mean value of the trade union density and social democratic organizational strength. In the last column, I report the communist vote in the following interwar period. The first clear point is that it was not electoral narrowness as such that exposed socialist movements to postwar fragmentation. On the one hand, Finland and Germany had the strongest prewar electoral socialism; on the other, the weakest electoral prewar socialist movements – like the British, Dutch and Swiss, not to speak of Ireland, excluded from the table due to the absence of data before World War I and the absence of a communist party after it – did not experience wide communist splits. As far as socialist organizational density is concerned, three countries are shown to be consistently weak on both indicators: Italy, France, and the Netherlands. In these cases, the organizational presence of socialist members and activists was exceptionally low. Germany and Finland are either intermediate or weak cases. If we turn our attention to the rate of trade unionization (particularly on the left), Italy, France, Finland, the Netherlands, and Norway reveal organizationally narrow bases. Finally, in terms of left trade union membership over the whole electorate and the socialist vote, the weakest cases are again Finland, France, Italy, Germany, and the Netherlands.

It has to be kept in mind that for the prewar period the important differences in the franchise may make it comparatively inappropriate to refer organizational membership to the electorate. To appreciate in a synthetic way the extent to which the prewar socialists encapsulated their electorate organizationally, we can cross-tabulate the level of left trade union density and the level of socialist membership over the socialist votes (partisan density). In Table 9.8, this is done by dividing into "high" and "low" categories the values in Table 9.7. In this arrangement, the organizational encapsulation of the Austrian, Danish, and Swedish socialist movements stands out against the corporate as well as partisan weakness of Finland, Italy, France, and the Netherlands (whether the United Kingdom is high or low on the partisan density dimension depends on how we consider its almost entirely collective membership). For the Netherlands, I have argued that the low level of partisan identity found a functional equivalent in the strong social pillarization of the country and in the host of subcultural organizations surrounding the parties without being formally affiliated to it. All cases of strong communist movements therefore fall into this group, with the exception of Germany, whose level of trade unionization was higher.

The last analysis to be made concerns the extent to which these

Table 9.7. *Pre–World War I (1900–1920) socialist electoral and organizational density and post–World War I communist vote*

country	% valid votes for the socialists (1900-20)	socialist membership as % electorate	socialist membership as % of socialist voters	trade union density	left trade union members as % of the dependent lab. force	left trade union members as % of the electorate	left trade union members as % of left votes	Communist vote 1918-1944
Austria	30.8	8.0	29.2	46.2	41.8	22.0	64.8	.65
Belgium	29.3	.	.	19.5	14.8	15.4	52.9	3.56
Denmark	27.3	7.8	42.5	28.8	22.2	20.2	110.5	.81
Finland	40.9	4.7	18.9	12.1	7.4	3.0	11.0	10.36
France	14.1	0.7	6.2	6.4	3.8	3.9	31.9	11.17
Germany	31.0	4.2	16.8	27.5	19.0	15.1	50.7	11.37
Italy	22.6	1.0	7.7	5.7	5.7	8.4	57.3	4.60
Netherlands	15.0	1.4	11.9	13.4	5.7	8.2	53.7	2.31
Norway	22.8	5.1	42.6	8.8	8.8	6.2	46.8	2.78
Sweden	22.9	11.7	155.2	13.7	10.4	19.0	292.9	4.95
Switzerland	18.5	3.1	35.6	10.2	7.7	10.3	101.2	1.85
Un. Kingdom	9.9	.	.	21.1	15.6	22.8	382.1	.24
Mean	24.7	5.3	43.9	16.9	12.6	12.6	110.4	4.40

Table 9.8. *Pre–World War I organizational density of the socialist movement*

		corporate density (left trade union members as % of dependant labor force)	
		high	low
partisan density (socialist members as % of socialist votes)	high	Austria Denmark Sweden (Britain)	Norway Switzerland
	low	Germany (Belgium)	Netherlands Finland France Italy

countries were characterized by massive trade union membership growth in the post–World War I period. To consider this, I have computed the rate of percentage change in the number of trade union members over the active population in each country by election years. Across the war years, almost all countries experienced significant and rapid changes in trade unionization levels. This happened, in descending order, in Germany between 1912 and 1919 (+17.6%) and 1919 and 1920 (+13.4%); in Belgium between 1912 and 1919 (+23.2%) and 1921 (+7.9%); in Finland between 1916 and 1917 (+22.1%); in Denmark between 1913 and 1918 (+20.8%); in the United Kingdom between 1910 and 1918 (+18.8%);

in the Netherlands between 1913 and 1918 (+13.1%); and in Sweden between 1917 and 1920 (+10.5%). Far less significant increases were experienced by Austria (1919–1920: +9.7%), Switzerland (1914–1919: +7.6% and 1919–1922: +9.6%), Italy (1913–1919: +7.8%), and France (1914–1919: +6.4%). It is possible that, for instance, in Norway, Finland, or Italy, the communist and radical presence was stronger in the more rapidly growing unions, but it is not true that communism was stronger in those countries with a massive explosion in union membership. In France, union membership grew modestly or stagnated throughout the 1930s (as did the economy), and a major increase occurred only in the years of the Popular Front.

Of the countries with massive postwar or cross-war increases, only Finland and Germany saw the growth of a powerful trade union and radical party opposition; this did not happen to any comparable extent in Belgium, Denmark, or the United Kingdom. Germany has the biggest expansion, with an increase of more than 30%. This was immediately followed by an equally massive demobilization, as trade union membership had already declined by 10% in 1924. A similar phenomenon is observable in Finland, where the 22.1% increase in 1917–1919 was followed by a corresponding decline in 1922. On the whole, the evidence of a relationship between rapid growth in union membership and radical left opposition is inconclusive at the comparative level. It can only be mentioned in the cases of Finland and Germany, and even here only in conjunction with the other organizational features discussed previously.

INSTITUTIONAL AND POLITICAL INTEGRATION

A further possible interpretation of radicalism emphasizes the politico-institutional rather than the socioeconomic or organizational conditions. The emphasis therefore switches from an interpretation of radicalism as mainly sociostructurally or organizationally based to one that stresses politico-institutional alienation. There are several examples of this line of reasoning. In a comparison between Disraeli's and Bismarck's governments between the 1860s and 1870s, Schumpeter blames Bismarck for what he regards as a "fatal mistake" that was entirely his own. The attempt to incorporate the proletariat into the state through social legislation, while depriving it of its own organization and leadership in politics and trade unions, was a mistake that produced unforeseen results later on. Schumpeter seems to believe that without such a policy things would have gone differently, and that the antimilitarist, antidynastic, and antibureaucracy attitudes of the socialist leadership in exile, which were obviously unacceptable to the king, would have been avoided.[54] In Lipset's early formulation, "in nations . . . where access was denied for long periods . . . and where force was used to restrict access, the lower strata were alienated from the system and were led to accept extremist ideologies. . . ."[55] Bendix instead insists that the working class felt politically alienated as incomplete or second-rank citizens, a feeling that led to their radical stands and utter rejection of the existing dominant order in early socialist history.[56] Lorwin has made the synthetic but illuminating statement that the labor movements that are most dependent on the state may show the greatest hostility to the state itself.[57]

It is possible to adapt this line of reasoning to the electoral success of European communism. I have already discussed in detail (see Chapters 5, 7, and 8) the patterns of institutional and political response; here it is sufficient to recall and adapt those results. When I commented on the application of this model to the whole left, I concluded that the level of electoral mobilization of the left was higher in those cases where its institutional integration was initially more difficult. On the overall level, when the variables of institutional integration (stateness, parliamentarization, level of repression, obstacles to representation) are related to the vote for the internal components of the left, the variables of level of stateness and level of repression are the ones that best discriminate between the support for the socialists and the Communists (see Table 9.9). The variable of stateness, which was shown to be unrelated to the overall development of the left (see Chapter 7), is instead very effective in discriminating between Communist and socialist support. The stronger the extractive and repressive resources of the state, the stronger the likelihood of a radical Communist movement.

On the basis of this analysis, it can be hypothesized that strong state resources that were directed against the working-class movement enhanced the electoral mobilization of the left, as well as its internal divisions and fragmentation. At the same time, high obstacles to representation and late parliamentarization seem to have damaged the socialist parties more

[54] Schumpeter (1976: 341–344).
[55] Lipset (1963: 541–569).
[56] Bendix (1964: 122–126).
[57] Lorwin (1967b: 58–72).

Table 9.9. *Institutional integration and vote of components of the left*

	stateness	level of repression	representation obstacles	parliamentarization
socialist vote	.111 (264)	.119	-.151	-.357
Communist vote	-.266 (217)	-634	-.066	-.090
other left vote	.305 (110)	.135	-.422	.092
total left vote	-.062 (265)	-262	-.263	-.384

than the communists.[58] This is quite consistent. If communist support is read as a result of poor institutional integration, these aspects are elements of its strength rather than features that hamper its support. If we look at the individual countries rather than at the overall picture (these comments are based on Table 7.19 in Chapter 7), we see that in all the cases where a successful communist party became established after World War I, the level of political repression of the working-class movement had been, and remained for long time, quite high. In none of the countries with a tradition of low repression did communism make any major inroads. Austria is the deviant case in this respect. In the five countries with high stateness traditions, three experienced profound left splits, while Belgium and Austria did not. On the other hand, Finland experienced a split without having a strong state tradition. The combination of the two dimensions points once more to Austria as a deviant case, because a strong communist split that did not occur might have been expected. On the two other dimensions of parliamentarization and representational obstacles, two of the four cases of successful communist splits (Germany and Finland) both have late parliamentarization and high representational obstacles, while Italy and France have modest or low representational obstacles and early (although not fully consolidated) parliamentarization. Even in this case, Austria associates with Finland and Germany without showing a similar electoral split of the left.

In Figure 9.2 the cumulative rank ordering of countries in terms of institutional integration (the higher the rank, the lower the institutional integration; see footnote 122 in Chapter 7) is plotted against the average communist and socialist vote. I have resorted to a longer-term average

[58] The very strong negative association between representational obstacles and other left vote is obviously due to the fact that this vote has always been quite small, suffering particularly from representational threshold of various kinds.

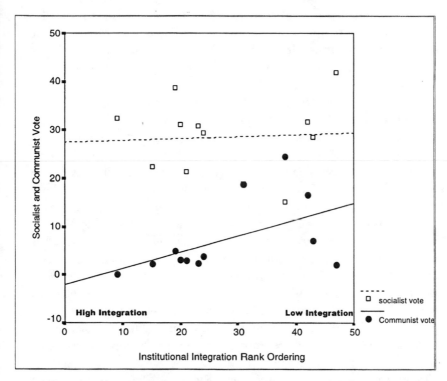

Figure 9.2. Rank ordering of institutional integration and the socialist and communist vote (1918–1985).

(the 1918–1985 period) because the strength of communism is discontinuous in the German and Italian cases. No association exists for socialist parties, whose electoral fortunes are, in the long run, independent of the pattern of institutional closure or openness of the political system. By contrast, communist support appears to be more closely associated with this factor, particularly when the Austrian case, which deviates from the institutional-integration model, is excluded.

Finally, let us consider the problem of left division and cohesion in terms of the variables discussed under the label of *political* integration. Two common features link the countries with a deep left split after World War I. The first is the historical lack of a solid and stable political alliance between the working-class movement and at least one part of the liberal forces, whether representing mainly an urban bourgeoisie or a rural one. The second is the fragmented political representation of the agrarian groups when these groups are both large and polarized along class conflict lines. The presence of a strong religious cleavage that opposed first the church to the state, then secularism to ideological clericalism, and finally the church and the religious community to the rising socialist movement is not a common feature. It is present in several countries that never developed divided lefts (Belgium and Austria among the homogeneous Catholics), and it is absent in Finland.

A Lib–Lab alliance was totally absent in Germany and Austria, where liberal forces remained weak, incapable of autonomous political organization and largely hegemonized by conservative forces, while the rural bourgeoisie was under Catholic hegemony or, at any rate, strong religious influences. The only possible alliance strategy was political and needed to be developed toward the Catholic and religious organizational world. However, it was unstable and unsafe for the socialists from the beginning as it was undermined by a strong clerical-anticlerical tradition of opposition and was therefore likely to increase the internal tension in the socialist movement concerning the possibility, opportunity, goals, and perspectives of such an alliance. In Finland, although the cleavage structure had some of the typical Scandinavian features, its late and stormy independence created divisions within all the political forces concerning the status and nature of the political system to be built, and the high class polarization of the variegated rural world prevented both consistent cooperation with a rural liberal movement and, later, consistent cooperation with the agrarians. In France and Italy, I have argued that liberal forces proved to be Malthusian in both their economic and political strategies. Those parts of these forces that were open to the socialist movement remained in a minority, although they were stronger than in Germany and Austria. Above all, such forces, and in general the large and ideologically heterogeneous *marais*, which in both countries called themselves "liberalism," never consolidated modern political partisan groups capable of providing sufficient discipline, organizational cohesion, and programmatic consistency to offer a safe political, if not governmental, point of reference for the socialist movement. At the same time, the sheer weight of the rural population obliged these parties to compete in a class-polarized countryside that split its support along class lines among socialists, Catholics, and traditional liberal notable representatives.

In all these five cases, the end result was the protracted political isolation of socialism. The unstable nature of any possible political alliance that resulted from the ambiguous democratic record of most liberal forces and the traditional, if not reactionary, attitudes of the Catholic leadership exposed any attempt to increase the bargainability of the socialists' policy goals to high costs and low payoffs. The internal divisions within these

lefts about what could be actually achieved by cooperation with the bourgeois forces were based on the low organizational and ideological reliability
of the opposite camp. Thus, even when socialists accepted executive responsibility under such conditions, coalitions were short and unstable – as in
France in the mid-1930s, in Germany in the 1920s, in Italy in the 1960s,
and in Finland in the early 1920s – and their policy achievement was
generally regarded as minor from the socialist point of view, that is, it was
not comparable in scope and stability of policy orientation to the cases of
long-standing policy cooperation with liberals and agrarians. Where socialists had limited or no control over government, their wage policy was in
direct competition with that of the communists only in the ideological
and propagandistic realm. Only abstract, long-term consequences were
compared. While this did not create a gap between reality and communist
appeals, it did, create a schizophrenic split among socialist doctrine, programs, and political action because of the contradictions between what
they represented in the political alignments of their political systems and
the image that members and militants actually had of them. Where socialists were sufficiently strong and not politically isolated, they could redefine
their identity in terms of performance, avoiding this internal factional
strife based on a clear contradiction between identity and reality.

CONCLUSION: A SYNDROME MODEL

In the preceding discussion, I have definitely rejected some of the generalizations concerning radical political support and found more or less extended support for others. However, it is clear that no one single factor
can account, without exceptions and deviant cases, for the spread of left
radicalism from World War I onward. For this reason, a *syndrome* of various
factors has to be considered. The most elaborate attempt to explain the
more or less radical nature of socialist movements by a syndrome model
has been elaborated by Lipset, who identifies three variables: (1) rigidity of
the status system; (2) extension of the franchise; and (3) de jure and de
facto recognition of trade unions' existence and activities.[59] Of the three
independent variables, the most important is the first. According to Lipset,
"the more rigid the status demarcation lines in a country, the more likely
the emergence of radical working-class based-parties," and "rigid status
systems are conducive to the emergence of radical working-class move-

[59] Lipset (1983).

ments." Such rigidity of status demarcations (or status differentiation) is maintained by "continuation of feudal or aristocratic values," "retention of major post-feudal elements," and "emphasis on status and aristocracy."

My analysis does not support this model. Lipset regards Germany, Austria, Sweden, and Finland as cases of rigid status demarcations and radical working-class movements, with France and Italy as cases of feudal remnants and strong bourgeois concern for status. The United Kingdom, which seems to contradict the association, is dealt with as a confirming case in reference to the Chartists (one century before communism). For Sweden, the supporting evidence for the relationship is that "the strong support obtained by the Social Democrats in Sweden . . . can be related to the strength of *Standenstaat* elements in the most status-bound society in northern Europe";[60] that is, radicalism is defined here as giving strong support to the Social Democrats. However, Norway has a Socialist Party that is just as strong as that of Sweden, but it has no feudalism and aristocratic tradition. Belgium, the Netherlands, Switzerland, and Denmark are grouped together as cases of weak feudal elements that explain moderate working-class movements. My reading of the Danish case is different, much more similar to that of Sweden than to that of the Netherlands.

Lipset's other two independent variables seem less important and receive less attention (particularly the third, de jure and de facto resistance against the labor movement). For the franchise, I have not been able to detect any relation whatsoever supporting the idea that the timing and tempo of the franchise helped to create the most integrated working-class movement. This may be due to the fact that the concept of "franchise" is encompassing in Lipset's treatment. For instance, it is possible to accept his point that political citizenship was early in the United Kingdom only if liberalization and political rights are mixed with strict voting rights. Similarly, in the discussion of Germany and Austria, franchise development and regime liberalization are mixed.

In Table 9.10, I have tried to summarize the factors discussed in connection with the cohesion and division of the European left, classifying cases as precisely as possible. This synthetic table is not only a final summary. It should also identify the syndrome, that is, the set of factors that, when combined, were likely to create the conditions under which radical opposition to the political and economic order appeared as a convincing alternative to large sectors of the lower classes, leading to profound ideological and organizational splits within the working-class movements. A syndrome logic is necessary because these factors impinge on one another

---

[60] Ibid.

Table 9.10. *A syndrome for communist political support*

country	socioeconomic conditions			organizational conditions					political conditions	
	timing of industriali-zation	homogeneity of working class	class polarization of the countryside	timing of corporate versus party consolidation	Strength of socio-organizational pillarization	membership type	corporate density	partisan density	institutional integration	political isolation
UK	early	homo	low	corporate first	weak	collective	high	low/high	high	low
Sz	early	homo	low	corporate first	strong	individual	low	high	high	medium
Sw	late	homo	low	party first	weak	collective	high	high	high	low
Be	early	homo	low	party first	strong	individual	high	low	high	medium
Ne	early	homo	low	party first	strong	individual	low	low	high	medium
No	late	homo	low	party first	weak	collective	low	high	high	low
De	late	hetero	mid	party first	weak	individual	high	high	high	low
Ir	late	homo	low	corporate first	weak	collective	low	low	high	high
Au	late	hetero	mid	party first	strong	individual	high	high	low	high
Ge	early	homo	low	party first	weak	individual	high	low	low	high
Fr	late	hetero	high	party first	weak	individual	low	low	low	high
Fi	late	hetero	high	party first	weak	individual	low	low	low	high
It	late	hetero	high	party first	weak	individual	low	low	low	high

to a large extent. To facilitate this work, the gray areas of the table present all those values that were, according to the theoretical arguments developed in the text, considered to be favorable to the radical outcome.

It is clear that no single variable or set of variables neatly separate the set of strong communist split experiences from those of more cohesive lefts. The first set of variables pertains to the socioeconomic conditions under which socialist movements developed. Delayed and late industrialization tended to produce internally nonhomogeneous working classes with few exceptions. France, Italy, and Finland are the only countries that present the three features together: delayed and late industrialization, a nonhomogeneous working class and high class polarization of the countryside. Austria and Denmark present similar features but with a lower-class polarization of the agrarian world. Germany is totally deviant in terms of socioeconomic conditions. Thus, it is not possible to link communism to socio-economic circumstances too closely. A thesis that links in a causal way the percentage of the agricultural population (and therefore late, uncompleted industrialization) to the lack of self-integration of the working class, to the lower "social integration" of that same working class, and to more radicalism and less organizational cohesion[61] avoids too many intermediate steps and fails to explain why Denmark and Austria did not follow the same pattern as Italy, France, and Finland, and why Germany did in the inter war years. In this set of variables, one finds, however, the only single variable that discriminates the countries with large post–World War II Communist movements from all the others – *the extent of class polarization in the rural world*. If we reason according to Mill's method of concordance – according to which if two or more cases with a common effect have only one circumstance or feature in common, then that feature is the cause of the common effect – we should point to this element as the strongest potential causal condition of communist success.

The second set of variables refers to organizational aspects of prewar and interwar socialism. In this case, the situation is more varied, but only Italy, France, and Finland present systematic features that point to generally low organizational encapsulation of the voter–party links, weak trade unionization and poor party–union linkages, and weak socio-organizational pillarization. The experience of Germany is close to that of these countries, although it tended to have much higher corporate and even partisan density than the latter. The contrast between Belgium, Switzerland, and the Netherlands, on the one hand, and the three Scandinavian countries, on the other, is, however, noteworthy. In the small continental countries,

---

[61] Malefakis (1974: 1–7).

parties tended to precede unions in national organization (with the exception of Switzerland, where, however, the difference in timing is unimportant), and membership tended to be individual, resulting in low corporate and partisan density.

However, in all these cases, societies were strongly pillarized and dense in sociopolitical organizations that, although not necessarily collectively affiliated with the party, offered (not only to the socialists, but to all major parties) a dense network of closely linked and supporting organizations. In the Scandinavian countries, the situation tended to be the reverse: Socio-organizational pillarization was weak, but collective affiliation and high organizational density played an important role (with the exception of Denmark, where membership was predominantly individual, and of Norway, where corporate density was low in the early period). In the first group, the strength of socio-organizational pillarization of the society offered a functional substitute to balance the weak partisan and corporate density, making it less important to establish close voter–party links; in the Scandinavian countries, the strong organizational structuring of both the corporate and partisan channels compensates for the weak societal pillarization.[62]

In this set of variables, we find the elements that set Austria aside from the countries with profound left divisions – the impressive Austrian organizational density in all dimensions and, at the same time, the high level of socio-organizational segmentation resulting from the unique superimposition of the urban–rural, class, and religious cleavages. This, together with the low class polarization in the countryside, seems to provide the main explanation of why the Austrian working class did not eventually split along ideological lines, although it had quite favorable socioeconomic and politico-institutional conditions (see later).

The third set of variables relates to our discussion of institutional integration and political isolation. We again find that Finland, France, and Italy experienced poor institutional integration and political isolation, features that they share with Germany and Austria. These conditions were already at the core of the strategic contradiction of many socialist parties before the Russian Revolution and the development of international communism. After the Great War, the tension between electoral potential and actual achievement created a powerful fissure within the socialist movements, particularly those that could not rely on strong corporate and

---

[62] For this interpretation of the contrast between these two sets of cases in which the functional equivalence between societal segmentation and corporate/partisan density is discussed, see Bartolini and Mair (1990: 234–235).

partisan organizational networks of their own or on strong social pillarization of the respective societies. The fact that the intensity of internal
ideological divisions can be related to the patterns of politico-institutional
integration is best epitomized by the German case, where this variable
probably had great importance, given the weak sociostructural preconditions of radical opposition. The three alternative strategic lines that agitated the pre- and postwar Social Democratic Party can be read as different
responses to different politico-institutional environments. In the German
territories in which the repressive politics of the state yielded to more-
integrative strategies, as was primarily the case in the southern and south-
western areas, the reform-oriented wing of the labor movement predominated. By contrast, in Saxony and in the Prussian regions, where more
severe repression and greater political isolation were common, more radical
politico-theoretical thinking prevailed. This is illustrated not only by the
election results and theoretical positions of elected candidates, but also by
the pragmatic politics at the regional level and by the many reform
proposals of social democrats with regard to the general constitutional
system.[63]

In conclusion, we can summarize our syndrome of the divided left.
Communism was socially the expression of the combined support of advanced sectors of the industrial working class of economically late or
backward societies, of a developmental middle class intelligentsia, and of
considerable sectors of the rural world that resisted and survived its full
transformation in a commercial capitalist direction. This potential base was
able to support a Communist split *only* when the socialist movement was
marked by weak organization, poor institutional integration, and low
political coalition potential. These three elements strongly interacted with
each other. A backward agrarian structure tended to be represented by
political forces that regarded the isolation of socialism as a fundamental
condition of survival. Weak trade unionization weakened the socialist
movement in the market, and organizational weaknesses and poor party–
union relationships could not check the internal tensions generated by
mass mobilization and rank-and-file radical politicization.

Radical political alternatives seemed to provide a convincing way out
of the existing structure of social and political control and market weaknesses. The argument that no substantive goals could be achieved without
radical breakthroughs was convincing. The alternatives proposed to the
combination of high social and cultural control, organizational weakness,
and low institutional and political integration could only be of a long-

[63] Tenfelde (1990: 267).

term ideological and radical nature, achievable only by destroying and overcoming the structure of control: the state *in primis* and the church – the traditional social hierarchies of the rural world. The growth and persistence of a radical left opposition became closely related to the availability of sections of the lower classes that felt dissatisfied in societies in which not only business and capital, but also the state, government, and the church refused to recognize the legitimacy of their organizations, leaders, and demands and where, at the same time, the organizational weakness of the socialist subculture was fueled by the heterogeneity of social groups derived from late and unsuccessful industrialization and by the weak organizational articulation of the civic society. Ideological radicalism of the communist type did not emerge from the class conflict as such, meaning from the opposition in the market with business and employer interests, but only when unsuccessful politico-institutional integration produced the overlapping of such class cleavage (economy) with antistate (politics) (and often antichurch, i.e., cultural) cleavages. The fact that demands directed to employers should have been combined with those directed to the state and other agencies of cultural control into a single coherent ideological alternative – instead of being split and deflected by more powerful integration mechanisms separating the market from politics and both of these from cultural and organizational identities – was not natural, but rather the result of a historically specific syndrome.

Within this syndrome framework, the reader may be surprised by the absence of any reference to the role of syndicalism, which several authors have identified as a crucial factor in protracted radicalism.[64] There are three reasons for this exclusion. First, strong syndicalism was important only in a few of our countries – France, Italy, and, with much less vigor, Belgium and the Netherlands. It was virtually absent in Finland and the Scandinavian countries, as well as in Germany and Austria. The second and more important reason is that the supposed linkage between the ideological role of syndicalism and communist splits is spurious because it is mediated by organizational variables. Syndicalism may have played a separate ideological role, but what is more important is that it resulted in poor party–union relationships, weak unions, and predominantly political movements that were fairly strongly detached from the unions. Syndicalism contributed to the absence of organic relationships between the party and the working-class organizations, to the predominant individual membership and *nonbund* type of socialist political movements, and to the general weak corporate and partisan organizational density of the whole

---

[64] Kornhauser (1959: 156), Lorwin (1954: 38), and Judt (1979: 285–286).

socialist movement. I have decided to give more direct weight to these organizational factors, also because they can be independently assessed in all countries.

Finally, interpretations of why syndicalism gained strongholds in countries like Italy and France normally underline (1) their slow rates of economic development, whereby the spread of industrialization over a long period gave the workforce time to develop and organize in a cooperative defense of its independence; (2) the continued prevalence of small workshops and artisan enterprise, which made it possible to argue that their disappearance was not inevitable and that their defense might have served as a basis for a socialist organization of society; (3) the lack of entrepreneurial flare, harsh and arbitrary shop regulations, and narrow-minded employer attitudes, which led to impatience among workers, who saw little chance of improvement thorough either collective negotiations or personal advancement in the industrial and social hierarchy; and, again, (4) poor, loose, and decentralized union structures. These causal interpretations – which tend to characterize syndicalism as the ideology of a declining group of artisans and partially proletarianized workers – are incorporated into my general plan under the socioeconomic variables. Again, rather than using a variable such as syndicalism, which is strongly idiosyncratic and country-specific, I felt it preferable to operationalize the underlying causal conditions in a way that is generally applicable to all these cases. In this perspective, syndicalism is seen as an ideological mediating factor between specific conditions of industrial development and social structure and corresponding levels of organizational cohesion and density of the corporate and partisan channels of the socialist movement.

In my syndrome model, the single deviating case is Austria, which presents several features that would have made it a suitable candidate for interwar radical splits that never materialized. Within my framework, the explanation for this is that Austria did not have class polarization in the countryside (instead, urban–rural and religious cleavages overlapped) and that it enjoyed one of the most strongly organized and socially pillarized socialist movements. I could stop here, but an additional element deserves mention. The Austrian socialist movement has a unique feature in the history of twentieth-century working-class movements: It was the only movement to develop for a long time in an extremely heterogeneous ethnic environment. Urbanization in the second half of the nineteenth century qualitatively modified the ethnic equilibrium of the empire. This happened particularly in Bohemia and Moravia, seats of the large industrial centers of the empire, where the population was prevalently German, while in the countryside the population was prevalently Czech. Prague, formerly a prevalently German city from a cultural point of view, saw the growing predominance of Czechs in only a few decades. In Vienna, too, the Czech population reached 25%. In Trieste, in the phase of economic growth, there was a massive immigration of Slovene workers that considerably altered the relationship among the ethnic groups.

The working class of the empire thus found itself not only, as usual, socially subordinated to the national bourgeoisie but also encountering ethnic discrimination in the face of the dominant Austro-German nation. This isolated the German workers, pushing them to join ranks in a pan-German nationalism in defense of their relatively privileged position. This weakness within the imperial working-class movement brought it to a national split, but my argument is that, at the same time, it helped the German part of the movement to maintain its own internal cohesion before and after World War I. Ethnic fragmentation limited ideological faction-alism. At the moment of the international crisis of World War I, the party tended to contain its internal debate in order to avoid the splits occurring in Germany, and Adler managed to maintain the center between patriotic pushes, on the one hand, and antimilitary pushes, on the other, thanks also to the skillful play of national tensions.

THE MACROCONSTELLATION
OF CLASS CLEAVAGE
STRUCTURING

The power resources of the lower classes, and wage earners in particular, depended primarily on their willingness and capacity to act collectively in the market and in politics, that is, to create and sustain corporate and political organizations for collective action. This problem can be framed in terms of a collective-action calculation. *Assuming* the existence of a common group interest determined by a common social position, the historical sequences, the institutional setting, and the resulting political opportunities should be regarded as the conditions that shape the individual's cost–benefit analysis and therefore set the incentives for collective-action outcomes. In this case, class consciousness is conceived as the capacity to overcome the free-rider problem in collective action.

The value of this perspective rests entirely on its basic assumption: the possibility of defining some basic or minimal common "interest" for the members of a given social group. This is especially hard when dealing with the long-term processes of formation and transformation of social groups. The fact is that interests, and therefore costs and benefits, cannot be defined unless identity is fixed beforehand, since the former are shaped by the latter. What is regarded as an unbearable cost with one given individual identity may well be seen as an inexpensive benefit with another. In Belgium, at the beginning of the twentieth century, the costs and benefits of any given collective-action choice of a Catholic Flemish worker depended on which of these three possible identities he regarded as predominant. In France, the same worker would not have been embarrassed by a possible subnational ethnolinguistic identity, but could still regard himself primarily as a Catholic or as a member of the working class. In contrast, the Swedish worker of the same period had hardly any chance to identify himself with anything but the political identity of his social reference group. These different opportunities were not *chosen* by individuals, but given to them by the constellation and combination of macrohistorical processes that preceded them and shaped their choices. Identities and, hence, interests were shaped by long-term macroprocesses. The timing of the struggle for nationhood, state–church relationships, and the ethnic composition of territories set limiting conditions for such choices in much the same way that the long-term development of industrialization, urbanization, and capitalism forced structural preconditions on them. The calculation of gains and losses means little if it was not referred to these options.

In this book, I have given great emphasis to the role of these limiting conditions in the context of individual choices. The test of macrohypotheses about the historical development of the European left required a set of models linking sociocultural conditions, organizational mobilization instrumentality, and the structure of political opportunities within the framework of nation- and state-building processes. Extensive theoretical discussions appear at the beginning and at the end of every chapter. Given that each discussion builds on the previous ones and progressively incorporates their conclusions into a broader model, there is only limited need for a general conclusion. These final notes are meant to recast the logic of the exercise and to present the conclusions in a simplified and synthetic form, linking the development of socialist movements back to the macroconstellation of their integration into national mass politics.

THE MACROCONSTELLATION

I will try to organize the range of factors discussed so far into a general analytical layout for the analysis of the variance in class cleavage structuring in terms of electoral mobilization, cohesion and division, social homogeneity, and ideological orientation. This macroconstellation ordering is organized around the effects of the structural restraints on the behaviors of a collectivity.[1] This necessitates reasoning backward, reconstructing the general historical constellation from which the structuring of the class cleavage in each country took on its specific character. Thus, the pattern of left electoral mobilization was part of the global process of competitive

---

[1] See Rokkan (1970d: 19–24) for a discussion of various combinations of micro-macro variables for the explanation of political behaviors.

drives for electoral mobilization along different lines. As such, it was only one of the components in the global process of cleavage system structuring and political party development. The latter was part of an even broader process of mass political nationalization and institutional liberalization and democratization. These modalities of internal-voice articulation and institutionalization were shaped by three preceding or parallel processes:

1. The reduction of external exit options for individuals, groups, and territories, determined by the consolidation of external economic, administrative, and military boundaries of the state.
2. The similar process at the cultural level brought about by the cultural standardization within such boundaries as a result of the development of national loyalties and identities.
3. The powerful social inputs to the definition and redefinition of social group size and internal composition brought about by industrialization, urbanization, and capitalist development.

For the purposes of simplification and schematic representation, these processes are charted in Table 10.1 under four main headings: state (formation), economy (transformation), culture (integration), and politics (democratization). For each of them, the macrovariables dealt with in the chapters are listed. The preconditions that are more or less favorable to class cleavage mobilization must be looked for in (1) the consolidation of territorial units (which allowed centralization of conflicts, stateness, and international status); (2) the growth of capitalism and industrialism (constituency formation and differentiation of dominant interests); and (3) cultural standardization and secularization (cultural homogeneity of the class environment). The process of cleavage structuring is seen as the result of crossing influences from the macrodevelopment in the state as *Herrschaftverbänd*, in the economy as *Wirtschaft-Gesellschaft*, and in culture as *Kultur-Gemeinschaft*.

STATE CONSOLIDATION

State formation indicates the political and economic unification *at the elite level* and, technically, the formation of the fiscal and military state. It involves the creation of an organization for the mobilization of resources: bureaucracy and the tax burden; the consolidation of the territory; the army; and the maintenance of internal order (i.e., the police and the judiciary). There are four ways in which the modalities of state consolida-

Table 10.1. *The macroconstellation of class cleavage structuring*

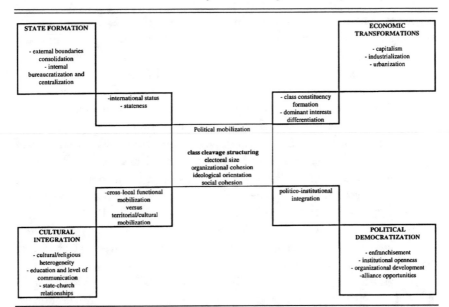

tion impinged on those of electoral mobilization in general and of class cleavage structuring in particular. First, economic-functional conflicts tended to prevail over other divisions with the formation and consolidation of the economic and administrative center. It was only with the development of the modern state and with the integration of different groups into the central sphere of society that the conflicts between these groups became centralized, with the unifying of potentially opposing camps that were not concentrated territorially.

Second, the territorial consolidation of the state's external boundaries can be seen as a facilitating, if not a necessary, condition for the development of functional conflict at the center. Both the timing and the modes of territorial consolidation of the state political *Verbände* influenced types and modes of the conflict articulation "within the *Verbände*."[2] The transition to mass democracy institutionalization was more gradual and less violent in those polities where territorial economic and military exit were less available. Those states that developed in relative isolation from the

---

[2] Generalizing Robert Seeley's dictum that "the degree of political freedom within a state must reasonably be inversely proportional to the military and political pressures on its border," quoted by Hintze (1962: 366).

exit opportunities concentrated in the city-belt continental zone and around it[3] found it easier for their early representative institutions to survive (England, Sweden, and Norway). Where these exit opportunities were higher – at the very edge of the continental city-belt zone – the building of boundaries was the result of constant struggles against the real possibility of exit, and this led to more-profound bureaucratization, militarization, state control, and so on, leading to a higher level of resistance and a more abrupt transition to mass politics and democracy (France, Austria, Prussia, and Denmark). In the continental city-belt zone, the structuring of internal conflicts and voice opportunities depended very much on the inheritance and survival of the traditions of consociational ties within and among cities. Where these consociational ties were strong enough to prevent the development of a centralized state bureaucracy, this structuring was easier (the Netherlands and Switzerland). By contrast, where this tradition was weaker and the city network was only finally and with difficulty incorporated into larger states with an absolutist tradition, the transition was more problematic (Prussia and Piedmont).

Third, external boundary consolidation is also essential in that reduced size and insecure international status may increase or decrease the burden of international politics and external influences. Low international status, on the one hand, calls for more internal cohesion and therefore less conflict and, on the other, for more external dependency. In contrast, high international status and involvement as a primary international actor makes internal dissent harder to accept; at the same time, it allows more autonomous internal developments. The geopolitical location of the state in international affairs is therefore of great importance in the sense that internal evolution is usually "geo-politically assisted."[4]

Finally, there is a fourth way in which external state closure and security impact on internal political voice structuring – by influencing the stateness of the domestic political processes. Bureaucratic development and the consolidation of the center is a key factor in terms of the resources it makes available to the established dominant elites. The insider's perceptions of the costs of repression versus toleration depended on the repressive and extractive resources of the state. The amount of resistance and opposition that newcomer movements encountered, and the willingness of established elites to allow their political incorporation, were influenced by the centralization of state apparatuses, as well as by the extractive and repres-

---

[3] On the concept and characters of the central continental city belt, see Rokkan (1973), (1974), and (1975).

[4] I borrow this inspired expression from Mann (1987).

sive resources these elites could afford to use against them. Territorial fragmentation and low stateness may be seen as the reverse process.

NATION BUILDING

Nation formation is the establishment of direct vertical contacts between the elites and ever larger sectors of the peripheral population, as well as the development of a "national community" whose horizontal exchange concerns not only goods but also symbols. Technically, it is achieved by conscript armies, school education, the mass media, religious and linguistic standardization, the spread of myths, and the feeling of national identity. Under this label are regrouped those system characteristics that pertain to the cultural homogeneity of any given society. Such cultural homogeneity is in many ways an essential ingredient for the spread of a nationwide politicization of economic and functional cross-local conflicts. Without some form of nation formation, the development of cross-local or cross-sectional functional class identities is difficult. In fact, the class conflict and cleavage was more a consequence and a feature of nation building than a force superseding or bypassing it. In principle, we can imagine that the greater the cultural homogeneity of the class environment, the more likely it is that class positions and conflict will be translated into direct political allegiance and action.

Cultural homogeneity has both a vertical and a horizontal dimension. The horizontal dimension includes those elements of cultural nonhomogeneity that separate segments of the society characterized by clear religious, ethnic, linguistic, and other cultural/identity differences. Each segment, although to different degrees, is composed of both mass and elite groups. On the vertical dimension, cultural homogeneity refers to the possibility of community development in Toennies's sense. Within a given national territory, development of the possibility for cross-area communication requires the development of links between the masses and the elites, which are available only with the spread of education and the development of mass media.

Religious and ethnolinguistic homogeneity influenced the basic conditions for the development of mass democracy to a strong degree. The Protestant–Catholic dividing line was important because, on the whole, in those countries where the Protestant Reform produced early "nationalization" of the territorial culture, this favored the processes of mobilization from below, and also because the early development of literacy aided and encouraged the mobilization of the lower classes into mass politics. Moreover, the close relationship between state and church and the incorporation of the church into the state bureaucracy reduced or eliminated the potential for a state–church conflict, which in turn can be said to have helped the clear definition and identification of the center against which the opposition of the outsiders could be directed. By contrast, in Catholic territories, the supranational nature and attitude of the church tended to favor mobilization from above by the Catholic hierarchies, the late spread of literacy made it more difficult to mobilize the lower classes from below, and the conflict over the control of the educational system and of mass education led to mobilization from the church against the state.

The second consideration is the position that churches came to adopt in the process of politicization and mobilization during the nineteenth century. This is of crucial importance and depends more on the degree of pluralism and the strength of the opposition of the churches to the nation-building elites than on the kind of religion – whether Catholic, Protestant, or Calvinist. Religious pluralism was important because it often offered the basis for political resistance against the elites, imposing a recognition of the limitation of state power in certain spheres and affirming the legitimacy of corporate powers and rights. As such, religious pluralism is a forceful factor independent of the religion in question.

In Latin Europe, the dominant Catholic Church (in conflict with nation-building liberal elites over the defense of its vested interests) managed both to mobilize vast sectors of the lower and working classes and, in the same process, to fuel the anticlerical feelings of sections of both the middle and working classes. In so doing, it split and politically weakened both of these social groups. The absence or the lower intensity of this split between nation builders and the Catholic Church in Austria and Belgium resulted in a more pronounced superimposition of the religious and class cleavage, with a strong impact on the social homogeneity of the class support of the socialist parties. Minority opposition Catholicism – of the Dutch type – asking for separation between the (Protestant) church and the state and opposing the established elites was more of an antiestablishment movement and maintained considerable control over lower-class groups.

Even Lutheranism and Calvinism were more aligned with the vested authorities and interests in some countries than in others. For Lutheranism, this was more the case in Prussia-Germany than in Switzerland, where it was more radical and modernist. In Sweden, Lutheranism was, at the same time, the basis for both an official national state religion and a fundamentalist opposition. Calvinism was much more antiestablishment and nonconformist in some countries than in others, depending on its relationship with the dominant elites and on whether there were stronger links with vested interests and the elites or with the lower classes.[5] In conclusion, not only were the type of religion and the extent of the political significance of religious identity important, but also the position that churches and religious groups occupied within each national system of conflicts and oppositions.

Language and ethnic national differences play a similar and equally important role. Whether the class cleavage was structuring before, in parallel with, or after the national issue was settled made an enormous difference to its mobilizing capacity, in its institutional integration, and in its political alliance opportunities. The situation was explosive if mass democracy and general suffrage expansion took place before clear-cut cultural boundaries were defined for the nation. When the channels of mass politics were opened, this easily led to conflict over the national definition of the political unit. The cultural heterogeneity of the class environment proved to be a dissipating force for working-class left support everywhere, but it produced different electoral returns in terms of middle-class support according to the positions that churches adopted toward the liberal-conservative nation-building elites.

ECONOMIC DEVELOPMENT

The idea most frequently referred to in histories and analyses of the working-class movement is that the growth, structure, and ideology of the labor movement of any country were conditioned decisively by the nature of the industrialization process, that is, by the way in which the tempo and direction of industrial development evolved. This general outlook implies that cross-country socioeconomic variation had a direct impact on the variation in the political mobilization process. Under the "economy" label are therefore regrouped those factors pertaining to the development of capitalism – which refer mainly to the spread of the monetary economy and market relationships over the given territory – and those pertaining to industrialization-urbanization – which mainly include its effect on the changing composition and type of the labor force.

The social mobilization produced by these processes is, in a general sense, a precondition for working-class political mobilization. Economic growth, industrialization, and urbanization gave rise to new social groups, determining the spread of certain new social conditions. At the same time, they increased the self-awareness of other social groups, intensifying the

[5] See Daalder (1966a: 47, footnote 4).

social problems and grievances for which the working classes and lower classes in general then demanded political action. They provoked the intensification of existing conflicts and the explosion of latent ones, and they constituted the structural preconditions for these problems to become sources of organization and mobilization efforts. Moreover, in contrast with the original antiindustrialism of the working class, the spread of industrialization brought about the "saturation" of this class with industrial values that helped to overcome forms of traditional socialist consciousness based on the role of the philanthropist, the technocratic state engineer, or conversion through examples and model communities, as well as forms of traditional insurrectional and conspiratorial class action. In this sense, these social processes determined the type of "constituency formation" for class cleavage structuring, impacting on the size, the internal homogeneity, the territorial and workplace concentration, and the cultural distinctiveness of the putative social constituency.

The economic transformation input is crucial to class cleavage structuring in a second way. The timing, tempo, and nature of industrialization and capitalist development determined the level of urban and rural dominant socioeconomic groups and differentiation of interests at the moment of socialist organization and entry into the political system. The more differentiated these economic interests, the less likely the perception of a common threat by the dominant circles and the less likely their possibility of agreeing on a common response to organized labor. On the economic front, therefore, the huge social transformations triggered by industrialization and urbanization created cross-country variation in the interest differentiation of dominant groups and in lower-class constituency formation. Describing the two polar situations, we can imagine a relatively small, socially nonhomogeneous (rural and urban), relatively dispersed working class facing the relatively low interest differentiation of rural and urban dominant circles versus a large, urban-based, and industry-concentrated working class facing well-differentiated and economically conflicting urban and rural dominant circles.

POLITICAL DEMOCRATIZATION

Finally, under the label of "politics," I regroup that set of organizational, institutional, and political developments that are more directly linked to the process of left mobilization but that, at the same time, are influenced by the three previous exogenous macroprocesses. The structuring of a cleavage line is, above all, a translation into politics and through politics. The mechanisms, the path, and the actors of this translation determine the extent to which – within the framework of facilitating or hampering conditions pertaining to state and nation formation and to the social consequences of the economic transformation input – a political movement is built and characterized by a stronger or weaker, organizationally cohesive, socially distinctive, and radical electoral mobilization.

Three main elements have been emphasized: the *organizational consolidation* of the socialist movement; the *institutional openness* of the political system; and the political *alliance opportunities* offered by the mobilization of preclass or nonclass cleavages. These aspects of mass political development are strongly linked to one another and, to a large extent, also result from the kind of combination that occurs among the other three macroprocesses of state and nation formation and economic transformation.

The pattern of organizational consolidation of early socialism (party organizational consolidation, union–party relations, membership density) is far more closely related to the stateness of the polity, to its cultural homogeneity, to the closure of the institutional system, and to the lack of viable early political alliances than it is to any social-input dimension. The organizational features of socialism are more easily interpretable as responses to the state-bureaucratic environment and to the cultural segmentation environment than to any pattern of socioeconomic development.

The institutional closure/openness of the political system can be interpreted as resulting from the combination of stateness levels – making available repressive resources – and the differentiation of dominant interests – creating the political opportunity to use such resources. Combined with the early or delayed partisan structuring of political competition, these variables determine the predominant response the labor movement faced; direct repression, institutional intrusion, or political-electoral control. The level of repression tended to be higher (1) the higher the stateness of the polity, which created the opportunity; (2) the lower the parliamentarization of the regime, which defined how and when these resources would be used and offered possible alternative forms of control; and (3) the lower the internal differentiation of dominant interests, which increased their perception of a common threat and their agreement on a common response. A merely repressive response required a weak structuring of the party system, just as a political-control strategy necessitated the opposite.

If, for instance, in Belgium, the Netherlands, or Switzerland socialists were encountered mainly in the electoral market and in the parliamentary arena, this was so because the established elite could rely on a constellation of cleavages and alliances that granted them considerable control of such arenas. By contrast, the use of direct repression and institutional intrusion by dominant groups was justified by their fear of being unable to handle the socialists or by their unwillingness to combat the socialists politically, given the inadequate political organization of liberal and conservative forces. Therefore, the national pattern of cleavage structuring and party system formation was crucial in shaping both the preferred response of the established elite and the character of the class cleavage. That is to say, it determined different *openings on the electoral market*, different *alliance opportunities*, and different *social bases* for the latter. In turn, these elements were important in determining the level of radicalization and class polarization of the whole socialist movement.

A long tradition of studies of political development stresses the predominant importance of early alliances among major economic and social groups, assuming that the nature of the political regime resulted from the logic of the subtending *socioeconomic coalitions*. In considering the institutional responses to the labor movement, emphasis can be placed on the compatibility of economic demands – in other words, on whether established interests (the landed gentry and/or the bourgeoisie) perceived the socialist movement as a fatal threat to their economic position, which would lead to an alliance of landed and bourgeois interests against it. This line of analysis deduces the state/institutional response from the compatibility of class interests. It therefore assumes that the state was the guardian of such compatibility and that, of necessity, anticapitalism and antistate attitudes should combine and overlap. It also implies that in those countries that yielded more gracefully to pressures from below, the conflict of economic interests was reduced.

Dealing with thirteen cases to avoid the tyranny of large countries and pattern cases, I have developed indicators to locate the European experiences along several dimensions of a model of institutional integration. To interpret the European variation in this outcome, I have preferred to argue that the definition of the conflict of interest as being more or less compatible was shaped by extraeconomic power relationships and bases. First, the possibility of using political power and the state to subordinate labor did not depend only on the willingness of dominant economic circles to do so (on the basis of the perceived threat). We can reverse the argument and assume that such willingness depended ultimately on the availability of politically repressive resources; on the historical stateness legacy, as this was shaped by warfare traditions; and on military challenges in continental Europe. These resources did not exist everywhere; and where they did exist, they not only influenced the response strategy chosen by the dominant economic circles, but they also allowed the survival of more-autonomous dynastic and bureaucratic interests that were able to choose certain economic groups as allies and set up strategies to weaken politically those social groups that they wanted to neutralize. The resources available for repression and the historical pattern of institutional development can be seen as independent variables in the definition and delimitation of the conflict of interests.

To rely on *state apparatuses*, on *institutional obstacles and privileges* (upper houses, king, etc.), or on *political control* was not always a choice made by the dominant economic elites and based purely on an evaluation of interest compatibility. It is clear, in my opinion, that this perspective fits the European experiences of political response far more effectively than any other. It provides a better bit to the German case, where any argument about bourgeois weakness and bourgeois–Junker interest compatibility and differentiation is comparatively untenable. It also describes more accurately the experiences of Denmark and Sweden, where the weak state resources available to curb the political power of the labor movement resulted in nonrepressive strategies, *even though* the dominant economic-interest differentiation was very low.

This leads to another closely related point. I have emphasized somewhat the logic of *political coalition* resulting from the specific forms of political representation that the main social groups develop during the phase of party system structuring. Large social groups do not "make coalitions" and do not "have alliances" unless they establish political self-representation, and the extent to which they represent themselves politically does not depend exclusively on their economic strength or distinctiveness. The early political organization of nonsocialist movements and the degree of structuring along partisan lines of the party system become crucial for checking the potentially autonomous role of dynastic-bureaucratic elites, for using other strategies of political control of socialism, and for easing the institutional integration of the latter. The availability of a political-control strategy of the socialist movement, which permitted its containment by politico-electoral-parliamentary means (rather than by direct repression or institutional privilege), required liberalization *and* favorable conditions for structuring nonsocialist parties and the party system in general. Repression and institutional exclusion was more likely to be used when strategies of political containment were less viable.

The earlier and more encompassing the organizational mobilization of most sectors of the community was through *non-* or *presocialist* political movements, the earlier and easier was the socialist political integration but the lower its resulting mobilization capacity. The alliance choices and alignments made by the early insider forces reduced the alliance alternatives and opportunities available to latecomer outsiders and therefore shaped significantly their choice of allies and adversaries among both social groups and political organizations. It is not surprising that the best alliances for socialist movements were *political alliances* (not social alliances) made along the functional socioeconomic representation axis with politically structured and largely self-representational movements.

Neither early liberalism nor agrarian movements were *working-class or lower-class unity-dissipating forces*. In reality, these cooperation experiences eventually split the liberals and agrarians more than they damaged the socialists. By contrast, denominational mobilization – apart from its forceful role in dissipating lower-class unity and solidarity – weakened political liberalism so as to render it occasionally very weak, occasionally an unviable ally and occasionally an undependable and hostile movement. The impossibility of political alliances with socially characterized political movements and the difficulty of cultural alliances (denominational, ethnolinguistic, nationalistic) forced socialism to adopt a set of complex, politically controversial *social* alliances with sectors of disparate social groups, which proved in most cases to be detrimental to the organizational and ideological cohesiveness of the movement.

THREE MODELS

In the previous chapters, I have slowly built a model explaining variations in the structuring of the class cleavage through the three main dimensions of size, organizational cohesion, and ideological orientation. In a final attempt to further simplify the complex web of connected factors, I have synthesized them in Table 10.2 in relation to the main historical outcomes. From left to right, the table indicates the "distal" and exogenous macrohistorical processes, their specific features directly relevant to our problem, and the intermediate-level variables resulting from combinations of the macrofactors. The following columns present the outcomes in a simplified form.

ELECTORAL SIZE

Electoral mobilization had both a developmental and a cross-sectional component that were difficult to reconcile. Factors explaining over-time change failed to explain cross-country differences in the early stages. The final model, which combined the over-time and cross-space differences into a single explanatory framework, accounting for roughly 70% of the vari-

Table 10.2. *Macroprocesses and variation in outcomes*

macroprocesses	relevant aspects	intermediate variables	configuration 1	2	3	variations	4	variations
nation-state formation — nation formation	- cultural integration - cultural homogeneity		high cultural homogeneity	high	high	medium (Germany)	low	
state formation	- internal stateness - external consolidation		high stateness high external cons. (Fr) low (It)	low stateness high external cons.	high stateness	low stateness (Finland)	low stateness	high (Be) low external consolidation (Ir)
socioeconomic input	- dominant economic interests differentiation		low differentiation	low differentiation	low differentiation	high differentiation (Germany)	high differentiation	low (It)
social mobilization	- class constituency formation - size - internal homogeneity - concentration		nonhomogeneous constituency countryside polarization	homogeneous constituency no countryside class polarization	heterogeneous constituency no countryside class polarization	homogeneous (Germany) countryside class polarization (Finland)	homogeneous constituency no countryside class polarization	
organizational development	- organizational encapsulation - party consolidation - party-union links - socio-organizational pillarization		weak organizational bases	strong organizational encapsulation	weak organizational encapsulation	strong (Austria)	strong organizational encapsulation	weak socio-organizational polarization (UK)
political liberalisation/democratisation	- pattern of enfranchisement - institutional openness - institutional sequence		liberalized (breaks and reversals)	late liberalization	not liberalized	not liberalized	liberalized	liberalized
		dominant circles response: - repression - institutional obtrusion - political control - mix.	mix	institutional obtrusion	repression	repression	political control	
		political alliance opportunities	no liberal alliance no agrarian alliance	Lib-Lab alliance Green-Lab alliance	no liberal alliance no agrarian alliance		Lib-Lab competition no Green-Lab alliance	Lib-Lab alliance (UK)
			denominational polarization (Fr) mobilization (It)	no denominational mobilization	denominational mobilization	no denominational mobilization (Finland)	denominational mobilization	no denominational mobilization (UK)
			electorally strong	electorally strong	electorally strong	medium (Germany after WW2)	weak electoral mobilization	medium (UK); failed mobilization (Fr)
			ideologically eclectic	moderate revisionist Marxism	orthodox Marxism		ideological moderate revisionist Marxism or trade unionism	
			heterogeneous social base	homogeneous social base	homogeneous social base	less so (Germany)	heterogeneous social base	more homogeneous (UK)
			organizationally split	organizationally cohesive	organizationally cohesive	organizationally split (Finland); Germany between world wars	organizationally cohesive	
			France and Italy	Scandinavian	Austria, Finland, Germany		Belgium, Switzerland, Netherlands, Britain, Ireland	

ance along both the time and space dimensions, is summarized in Figure 10.1.

While social mobilization points to a long-term positive impact on the left vote over time, which tended to disappear as a cross-country discriminating factor when time was parametrized into different periods and decades, cultural heterogeneity factors work the opposite way: They add less to the explanation of the temporal development of the left than to the cross-country differences at each moment in time. Because industrialization, urbanization, and the cultural homogeneity of the class context – the global context of the formation of working-class constituencies – fail to account for synchronic differences in levels of electoral mobilization, attention is needed to what intervenes between working-class formation and electoral mobilization. Variation in political translation has been attributed to three sets of variables: the *pattern of franchise extension*, the *level of early organizational consolidation*, and the *closure of the institutional context* in which the left developed.

The pattern of franchise development influenced the ability of the left to mobilize in a rather unexpected way. The left grew stronger moving from the cases of early timing to those of late timing and, within each of these groups, moving from gradual to sudden enlargement. Ceteris paribus, the lateness, on the one hand, and the sudden change, on the other, far from hindering the electoral development of the left, seems to have created conditions that were more favorable than very early enfranchisement or more intermediate and gradual developments. The *coincidence* or *lack of coincidence* between such processes and the early organizational developments of the socialists adds to an interpretation of differences in mobilization capacity. When the major push of social and occupational dislocation of the labor force due to industrialization and urbanization paralleled the organizational development of socialist parties and the development of the franchise, socialist parties were able to capitalize on such a transformation, particularly if the organizational consolidation was party-led rather than union-led.

A similar process is at work with the institutional closure of the political system. Far from being a nuisance to left electoral development, this proved to be a positive factor in general, but particularly in the early period. Before World War I, this is the single most important factor determining the left's level of electoral mobilization. The more open and liberalized the political context, the lower and slower the mobilization of left voters. The institutional sequences that favored the integration of opposition movements (first liberalization, then party organization, and finally universal suffrage) actually reduced the general left's electoral

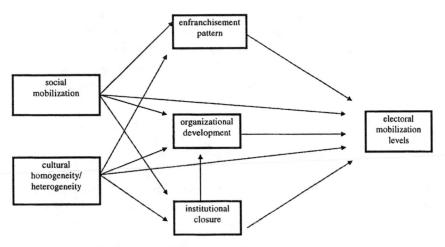

Figure 10.1. The electoral mobilization model.

strength, although it may have favored its long-term organizational cohesion and fostered ideological moderation.

The general picture resulting from the interaction over time of these five factors is the following. Only after the role of all the other factors is controlled for does social mobilization emerge as the most stable and systematic overall force of left development in each period. If social mobilization is the developmental engine of left mobilization, cultural heterogeneity (and, even more, ethnodenominational forms of politicization) represents the long-term limiting condition of left development. The organizational factors are therefore unimportant in both the first pre–World War I period and the post-1965 period. By contrast, they play a significant role between 1918 and 1965. The pattern of enfranchisement is a powerful predictor of early strength or weakness, which tends to fade over time. Finally, including institutional closedness/openness into the model changes only marginally the overall variance explained with respect to the other four variables. However, its impact is decisive in explaining cross-country differences in the early period before World War I, and it is still important up to 1944. Early cross-national differences in socialist electoral mobilization, which tended to persist strongly later on, should, first of all, be related to institutional differences in the liberalization/democratization processes, then to the lateness and sudden nature of suffrage extension, and, finally, particularly between the world wars, to organizational development.

This means that if we concentrate on the long-term general forces of left electoral development, we must look at the socioeconomic and cultural environment of class cleavage structuring. If, however, we focus on the huge cross-country differences in the timing and extent of this mobilization, we should give priority to the institutional and organizational environment of the socialist movement. Given that cross-country differences proved enduring within the context of general historical growth, it could be concluded that the development of national socialist movements in terms of the earliness and scope of electoral mobilization depended more on the state-bureaucratic-political environment than on underlying socio-cultural processes. It is difficult to describe "what socialism was," but if we deduce its nature from the forces underlying its strength, we can conclude that it was more a movement for the national political emancipation of conscious segments of the lower classes than a movement of socioeconomic protest and revolution. Therefore, not only was class not extraneous to the question of citizenship, but the extent (and the nature; see the next section) of class appeal in electoral terms was also dependent on the conditions of citizenship. Socioeconomic positions and their associated grievances created a structural background, but the specific strength and weakness of the political articulation of these grievances was set by the type and number of obstacles blocking their expression through normal (and not even necessarily socialist) corporate, party, and parliamentary channels.

IDEOLOGICAL ORIENTATION

The simple dichotomy between radicalism and reformism that subtends the various ideological orientations of the early socialist movements in Europe was reshaped into four main types in Chapter 2: Orthodox revolutionary Marxism, eclectic socialism, unionism, and moderate reformist "façade" Marxism. In this book, the differential success of these ideological variants has not been analyzed from the viewpoint of the theoretical value of these analyses or from the viewpoint of their success or failure in terms of the accuracy of historical predictions. Instead, the issue is the conditions under which the questions and answers that these theories raise and offer were actually considered important and convincing by sections of the working population and by the socialist rank-and-file and leadership.

The development of the class conflicts in the middle of the nineteenth century was natural. At that time, the sharp contrast was evident between the old agrarian order – maintaining traditions and providing some economic and social security, although little economic well-being – and the new order, with its dynamic, ever changing productive forces, the instability of employment, and the social and economic security it provided, and the resulting necessity for constant adaptation to new habits, skills, and concepts. For newly uprooted peasants and artisans, the clash between these two worlds was very strong, and it is no wonder that it was exactly in this period of transition – in which the two worlds were still potentially viable alternative ways of life for individuals and groups – that the opposition to capitalism/industrialism grew stronger. However, this opposition focused on capitalism/industrialism rather than on simple capitalism as such, which, after all, had existed for some time.

These radical emotions rested on original anti-industrialism feelings. Marxist thinking and political action, adding to this initial emotion the logic of the progressive worship of science and technology and the faith in their limitless possibilities for industrial progress, offered working-class groups a reason and some hope for action *within the industrial society* (inevitable) and *against capitalism* (avoidable). The success of this message rested on the fact that its goal of destroying capitalism coincided with the proletariat's instinctive reaction against industrialism. Without the anti-industrial emotion of a hitherto mainly agrarian and traditional society, early socialism would not have been a revolutionary movement. Equally, if it had had no faith in the potential of industrialism, it would have spent its energy fighting the unavoidable forces of modern life.[6]

However, the progressive saturation of the working class with industrial values tended to deprive radicalism of its implicit revolutionary character and aspirations. Once socialism had helped the working class to become pro-industrialist, it risked losing the emotional basis for its revolutionary goals; that is, anticapitalism feelings, if deprived of an anti-industrialist underpinning, could easily turn into a demand to reform the industrial society without a revolutionary potential. Marxism provided a second source for a radical interpretation of the working-class role, linking anticapitalism and antistate attitudes and action into a coherent theoretical argument. The class cleavage rested on a divide between suppliers and buyers of labor and necessarily implied an opposition between working-class organizations and capitalist or bourgeois interests. However, to assert that the working classes were hoodwinked by the capitalists is one thing; to assert that the state is the "executive committee" of this exploiting class is another. Marxism linked the class cleavage to revolution via the antistate emotion; this provided the basis for a theory that explained why the most conscious sections of the working class could not improve their conditions other than by a political revolution that would destroy the state. However, for this synthesis to become the major source and inspiration of socialist

[6] On this combination of emotion and anti-industrialism, see Ulam (1979: 55).

action and propaganda and a convincing answer to the problems perceived by each national working-class movement, a *theory* linking the state to the defense of capitalism was not enough. A *reality* – that is, an actual situation in which the state defended vested interests, directing its resources to the goal of curbing labor – needed to be added to the everyday experience of the lower classes.

In interpreting the variations of the early ideological orientation of socialist movements, attention must therefore be paid to *the extent to which the class cleavage, whose structural roots were primarily in social antagonisms in the market, came to be ideologically tinted with hostility against the state.* There was nothing compulsory about this link; nothing necessarily implied that working-class political mobilization should come into conflict with the state. In the long run, however, it depended on three fundamental factors: the historical *stateness of the polity*, the degree of *interest differentiation* of the dominant urban and rural groups, and the *partisan structuring* of the party system. The first two provided the terms for the calculations of the costs and benefits of strategies of toleration or repression. The third set, at the same time, the conditions for the presence or absence of political allies for the socialist movements, and the possibility of its political control via partisan competition, available only when non socialists forces were able to organize their electoral defense in the political arenas early on (Figure 10.2).

In terms of hostility toward the state, the European experience is far more varied than a British-versus-continental pattern or a French-versus-German pattern would indicate. In addition to countries where the state was strong, there were others where it was far less visible or even definitely weak. The use of the state apparatus was also different. The relationship of national movements with their respective national states was therefore different, and the fusion of class feeling with antistate feeling depended on the specific nature of state involvement in their emancipation attempt. The opposition strategies of dominant national forces to the emerging socialist movements in the last two decades of the nineteenth century and the first two decades of the twentieth century led to two possible reactions: (1) to help and favor the success of the Marxist identification between the class enemy (the employers) and the state (the class nature of the state) or (2) to the recognition that the struggle for socialism was the same as the struggle for a democratic state, that is, for state democratization.

The political integration of a social group into the existing political order involves cultural elements, and it is ultimately expressed through a set of beliefs and attitudes toward the political system. The development of these cultural traits results from organizational activities and from the learning experiences linked to the response to these activities. The extent

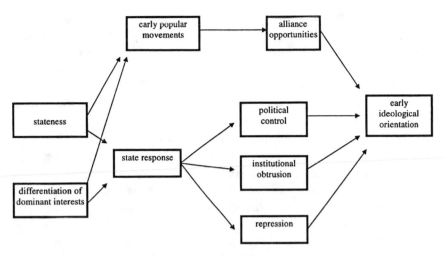

Figure 10.2. The ideological orientation model.

to which new actors feel they can achieve their goals within the institutional structure influences the amount of pressure exerted by the political and corporate movements on the government and the employers through *electoral, parliamentary, and judicial methods* or, rather, the extent to which they are prepared to use other resources and conflict arenas that are extra-institutional.

Thus, the more a closed political system presented itself as a moral entity independent of sectional societal interests, the more theoretically persuasive the radical ideologies appeared to be. There were deep divisions within the movement as to whether their aims would ever be achieved, and profound ideological strife in the working-class organizations occurred along radical versus moderate lines. Moderate calls for a peaceful and piecemeal insertion believed that institutional channels were open enough to allow for democratic change. Radicals, in contrast, arguing for a revolutionary breakthrough, assumed that the regime would never allow them to compete fairly. In accepting the costs of repression, the established elite assumed that the demands of the new claimants could in no way be accommodated within the existing order.

For these reasons, in interpreting variations in early ideological orientations, I have placed greater emphasis on patterns of institutional and political integration, finding little evidence of direct links with socioeconomic, cultural, and organizational features. The countries characterized by the persistence of an orthodox Marxist doctrine up to the 1920s and afterward are all high-stateness countries with a high level of state repression combined with low parliamentarization, high representational obstacles, and political isolation due to a lack or weakness of politically reliable allies. Moderates and reformist groups had very little external political *point de repère*, and their arguments must have appeared quite unconvincing given the circumstances.

Eclectic socialism, in which radical syndicalism survived along with orthodox Marxism and various forms of reformist socialism (and occasionally even trade unionist visions), was the labor force's divided answer consistent with a contradictory environment. In Italy and France, the repression used by high-stateness polities against the socialist movement – and, in particular, against its more radical components – was considerable, but at the same time, the parliamentarization of the regime and the relatively low level of representation obstacles triggered an ongoing debate among the socialist elite and rank-and-file about which was the best strategy for labor. These are cases of weak and late consolidation of the party system, largely because of the weakening of the conservative forces due to the ambivalent attitude of the Catholic masses to the regime, as well as to their unwillingness (or incapacity) to organize politically within a liberal regime framework. This combination of political and institutional circumstances made it likely that almost any political strategy would be challenged by sections of the socialist movement, and for almost any ideological variety to seem available and convincing to different sectors of the movement – from trade unionists to revolutionary syndicalists, from *ex cathedra* reformists to Leninists.

This synthesis was far from unsuccessful in overall electoral terms; but clearly, ideological and organizational cohesion was impossible to achieve. In none of the countries where parliamentarization was achieved early and repression was low did these ideological tendencies exist. Either trade unionism or mild and pragmatic forms of Marxism – where theoretical lip service paid to orthodoxy was often accompanied by a moderation of practices – prevailed.

ORGANIZATIONAL COHESION

The model that best accounts for the cases in which the socialist movement split down the middle permanently requires further specification and additional variables. Sluggish, incomplete, and relatively late industrialization, on the one hand, and low institutional integration and few opportunities for stable social and political alliances, on the other, represent the general context of a deeply divided left. The general background, therefore, shares most of the features of the early orthodox Marxist or eclectic socialist ideological orientation. In reality, communism made no lasting inroads into any country that had no such ideological tradition. However, we should not link communism too closely to these circumstances alone. A thesis that links late and incomplete industrialization in a causal way to the lack of self-integration of the working class, to the lower social integration of the same working class, and to more radicalism and less organizational cohesion leaves out too many intermediate steps and fails to explain why Denmark and Austria did not follow the same pattern as Italy, France, and Finland, and why Germany did so in the interwar years. Similarly, an emphasis on poor institutional integration and political isolation alone is not sufficient. While it may help to include Germany between the world wars – where socioeconomic conditions seemed far from favorable to the organizational division of the socialist movement – it leaves out another deviant case: Austria, where socioeconomic, politico-institutional, and ideological conditions seemed the perfect preconditions for a long-lasting and profound organizational split.

Two further factors need to be added to this background: the *weakness of the organizational web* of the socialist movement in the crucial post–World War I and post–World War II periods, and the intense *class polarization of the countryside* resulting from the conflicts between a large agricultural landless or land-insecure working population and an equally large agricultural bourgeoisie. In countries with successful communist splits, the socialist movement rested on a strong imbalance between the organizational encapsulation of *both* partisan and corporate dimensions, on the one hand, and far stronger electoral mobilization, on the other. In these countries, the socialist electorate was composed of relatively large sectors that were *not organizationally linked to the socialist party and unions*, and a delayed and massive trade union movement occurred precisely during the period of maximum appeal of the Russian Revolution. Organizational competition between the socialists and communists took place not within large, established corporate movements, but within weak organizations subject to the rapidly growing recruitment of previously nonmobilized (and mostly nonspecialized) sectors of the working class.

Italy, France, and Finland all had comparatively low organizational encapsulation of the voter–party links, weak trade unionization, poor party–union linkages, and weak socio-organizational pillarization. The experience of Germany is close to that of these countries, although it tended to have higher corporate and partisan density. The three small continental countries – Belgium, Switzerland, and the Netherlands – had fairly similar organizational features, but they were also strongly pillarized and dense in sociopolitical organizations that, although not necessarily collectively affiliated with the party, offered it (and not only to the socialists, but to all major parties) a dense network of closely linked, supportive organizations. By contrast, in the culturally more homogeneous Scandinavian countries, the socio-organizational pillarization was not high, but the important role of collective affiliation and high organizational density in general placed them in the group of the earliest and more densely organized pre– and post–World War I movements.

In the first group, the strength of the socio-organizational pillarization of the society offered a functional counterbalance to the weak partisan and corporate density, making it less important to establish close voter–party links; in the Scandinavian countries, the strong organizational structuring of both the corporate and partisan channels compensated for the weak societal pillarization. These factors set Austria apart from the countries with profound left divisions – the impressive Austrian organizational density in all dimensions and, at the same time, the high level of socio-organizational segmentation resulting from the unique superimposition of the urban–rural, class, and religious cleavages. Together with the low class polarization in rural areas, this provides the main explanation for why the Austrian working class did not ultimately split along ideological lines, although it had favorable socioeconomic and politico-institutional conditions for doing so.

In conclusion, the syndrome of the divided left is best summarized in Figure 10.3, where background conditions and specific differences are listed. Communism was the social expression of the combined support of advanced sectors of the industrial working class of economically late or backward societies, a developmental middle-class intelligentsia, and considerable sectors of the rural world that resisted their full transformation in a commercial capitalist direction. This potential base became the support for a communist split *only* when the socialist movement had weak organization, poor institutional integration, and little political coalition potential. The three elements interacted strongly with one other. Thus, a backward agrarian structure tended to be represented by political forces that regarded the isolation of socialism as a fundamental condition of survival; weak trade unionization also weakened the socialist movement on the market; and organizational weaknesses and poor party–union relationships could not check the internal tensions generated by phases of mass mobilization and radical politicization of the rank-and-file.

Under these conditions, the alternatives to the combination of high social and cultural control, organizational weakness, and low institutional and political integration required a long-term ideological and radical nature. This was achievable only by destroying structures of control – the

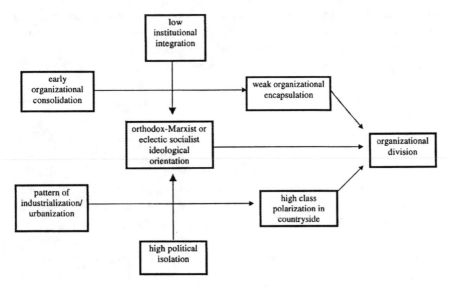

Figure 10.3. The organizational division model.

state *in primis*, but also the church and the traditional social hierarchies of the rural world. The growth and persistence of a radical left opposition was linked to the existence of sections of the lower classes dissatisfied by the societies in which they lived. In these societies, not only business and capital, but also the state, government, and church, refused to recognize the legitimacy of their organizations, leaders, and demands, and, at the same time, the organizational weakness of the socialist subculture was fed by the heterogeneity of social groups deriving from late and unsuccessful industrialization and by the weak organizational development of the civic society. Demands against employers and demands against the state and other agencies of cultural control were combined into a single coherent ideological alternative, rather than being split and deflected by more powerful integration mechanisms separating the market from politics and both of these from cultural and organizational identities. This was the result of this historically specific syndrome.

CONCLUDING CONSIDERATION

The literature has made several attempts to classify the different experiences of national socialism. In the 1920s, Sombart[7] proposed a classification

[7] Sombart (1924: 357–360).

of socialist experiences that identified three basic types of labor movements: the German, the Anglo-Saxon, and the Latin. The German type appeared to be the socialism of the professor, who builds a theory and applies it to reality; this socialism has a strong philosophical and theoretical impact on the elaboration of social and political-action strategies. The Anglo-Saxon variant, by contrast, was the empiricism of the practitioner. The Latin variant was the socialism of the artist, influenced by the role of great personalities and by the idiosyncratic character of the individual. This typology was clearly influenced by reference to the "national character" and to the national collective mentality. Mommsen[8] has, instead, contrasted a stream of Western continental socialism (in which the syndicalist orientation was the dominant element), an Anglo-Saxon labor movement (characterized as a specifically working-class organization and a corporate movement), and a Central, Eastern, and Scandinavian variant (in which the socialist movement was dominated by the Social Democratic parties). His typology refers to both ideological and organizational features, in particular to the relationship with trade unions. M. van der Linden[9] contrasts Western socialist movements (including the German and British variants) as integrated movements versus the Eastern and, in particular, the Russian working-class movement, which are viewed as the least integrated. Valenzuela[10] has developed a five-factor typology of labor movement insertion into the national political process. Three types apply to the Western context: the "Social Democratic" type, characterized by a single union connected with a strong single party (Scandinavia, the United Kingdom, Austria, West Germany, Belgium, the Netherlands); the "contestatory' type," characterized by the communist split of both unions and the party (Italy, France, Finland); and the "pressure group" type, characterized by union links with a preexisting party or fragments of party (as in the United States and also the United Kingdom in the nineteenth century).

None of the efforts to neatly classify the socialist movements in Europe fits well with the schemes or the analysis presented in this book. The reason is probably that each of them selects and privileges one or two main dimensions of differentiation in the Western experience, while I have resorted to a multidimensional characterization of the process of class cleavage structuring, combining electoral mobilization with the social homogeneity of this support, organizational cohesion with the ideological

---

[8] Mommsen (1979: 31).
[9] Linden (1988: 286).
[10] Valenzuela (1992). The "state-sponsored" and "confrontational" integration models refer to authoritarian regimes and are less relevant in this context, although they could be related to the early experiences of some socialist movements.

orientation, and all of them with the pattern of organizational encapsulation. The classifications based on electoral size do not correspond to those based on ideological orientation; those based on organizational cohesion do not correspond to those based on social-support distinctiveness; and so on. The resulting typologies combining two or more of these features are therefore "unstable" in that they depend entirely on which factors are chosen as the primary classification dimension. The frequent attempts to classify in this book were designed mainly to parametrize qualitative variables and cannot be used to obtain a final general typology. My objective was, rather, to see how the processes of state consolidation, national cultural formation, social transformation, and political democratization intertwined with each other, producing different sets of characteristics – strong and socially distinctive movements versus equally strong but socially nondistinctive movements, conditions under which early radicalism preserved organizational cohesion or undermined it, and so on.

Class mobilization and class cleavage structuring was a *residual* process whose coordinates and characteristics were set by the conditions of consolidation of the state-bureaucratic structures and the standardization of the national culture, as well as by the consequent capacity for organization and mobilization of preindustrial or nonindustrial groups, conflicts, and cleavages. If we see socialism as a final step in the broader process of mass nationalization and integration of the lower classes into the national political order, it is natural that the setting for the direct expression of social and economic interests and grievances was fundamentally shaped by the scope of political representation, equality, and citizenship. For this reason, the latter processes proved a far more powerful determinant of the nature of political socialism than the mighty social inputs of economic development and industrialization. This is not to deny the importance of the class cleavage within the alignments of European politics. It simply suggests that the quality and nature of the class cleavage that resulted in each country in terms of mobilization size, internal organizational cohesion, social-support homogeneity, external closure, and ideological orientation can be interpreted as a function of opportunities and constraints set up by more long-standing, and in many ways premodern, forces and structures.

For at least twenty years, empirical evidence and theoretical interpretations have accumulated, pointing to a transformation and/or decline of the class cleavage. Symptoms and signs of this decline have been identified in the quantitative and qualitative changes of the working-class constituency due to deindustrialization and the new division of labor; in the organizational weakening and declining linkages between political organizations, corporate groups, and citizens; in the declining social distinctiveness of social support; in trends toward ideological undifferentiation and the decline of ideological incentives; and in the emergence of competing cleavages and party competition lines.

In this work devoted to the "golden age" of class politics, none of these symptoms have been discussed or need to be discussed. There is a lesson, however, that can be drawn from this work: Such symptoms all point to a new macroconstellation in which the role of the state and the loosening of its economic, administrative, and cultural boundaries, the rebirth and redefinition of cultural identities, the new international military and high diplomacy context, and the new and powerful processes of economic cross-national competition open up new conditions for the definition of group interests and for the direction of their claims toward new decision-making centers. These new conditions modify both the capacities and the modalities of collective organized action, leading to a new macroconstellation of political opposition structuring in loosely bounded territories, in culturally growing heterogeneous populations, and in multiple and nationally displaced decision-making processes. The interpretation of the fate of the class cleavage within this new framework is another story — and, of course, a different book.

DATA APPENDIX

PARTY COMPOSITION OF THE CLASS LEFT BY COUNTRY

Country	Left Parties
Austria	Social Democrats, Communist Party, Democratic Progressives
Belgium	Workers Party/Socialist Party (later Flemish Socialist Party, Francophone Socialist Party), Communist Party, Partij V. de Arbeid, Walloon Workers Party, All Power to Workers/Labor Party, Revolutionary Workers/Socialist Workers
Denmark	Social Democrats, Communist Party, Common Course, Socialist Peoples Party, Left Socialists
Finland	Social Democrats, Socialist Workers Party, Social Democratic League, Democratic Alternative
France	Socialists, Independent Socialists, Communist Party, SFIO, EFD-PSU/Extrême Gauche, Divers Gauche
Germany	Social Democrats, Communist Party, Independent Social Democrats, Action for Democratic Progress
Ireland	Labour, National Labour, Independent Labour, Pro-Labour Independents, National Progressive Democrats, Socialist Labour Party, Workers Party, Democratic Socialist Party
Italy	Independent Socialists, Reformist Socialists, Socialists, Communist Party, PSI, PSIUP, Extreme Left, USI, PSDI

(cont.)

Country	Left Parties
Netherlands	Social Democratic Workers/PVDA, Social Democratic League, Socialist Party, Revolutionary Socialist Party, Communist Party, Pacifist Socialist Party
Norway	Labor Party, Social Democratic Workers Party, Communist Party, Marxist-Leninists, Socialist Peoples Party, Socialist Left Party
Sweden	Social Democrats, Left Socialists, Communist Party, Hoglund Communists, Socialists, Kilbom Communists
Switzerland	Social Democrats, Communist Party, Autonomous Socialist Party
United Kingdom	Labour Party, Independent Labour Party, Communist Party, National Labour, Social Democrats, Social Democratic and Labour Party.

Unless otherwise indicated, my source for electoral and parliamentary data is Mackie and Rose (1974 and following editions). For the early national elections in the nineteenth century, however, more-detailed sources have been used for a number of countries that are documented in Bartolini and Mair (1990: 314–322).

DATA FILES

Census data are normally collected by decade or five-year periods; urbanization data are normally reported by decade; many other data, including those on school enrolment, labor disputes, trade union and party membership, state budgets, and so on, are available on a year-by-year basis. Finally, electoral and cabinet data are available on an irregular basis.

To deal with these different time units, I have created four data files:

1. An election year database. Nonelectoral variables were included, taking the election year as reference. The rule has been to take the nearest census figures, *provided that they were within five years of the election year*. Otherwise, I have interpolated the data. Year-based data have been included in the election file, taking their average value in the four to five preceding years. In a few cases (when data were missing for the first or last election year), I resorted to extrapolations (the Netherlands in 1888; Norway in 1969–1973; Sweden in 1965–1979 for the data concerning WO2AP, WP3AP, WO2WO, and WO3WO; and Sweden

in 1969 for all WO data [see the list of variable names at the end of the Data Appendix]).

2. A census year database. In this case, the other types of data have been considered for periods around the year of the census. Election data, for instance, refer to the two nearest elections, one before and one after the census date. When the census year is also the election year, the number of elections considered becomes three. In a few cases, the single nearest election has been used because it was the only one available.

3. A decade database. In this case, all variables not measured on a decade basis have been averaged for the period concerned (note: the "1910" decade indicates the 1910–1919 period).

4. A cabinet data file, which includes the 378 cabinets formed in the 1918–1966 period.

At the end of this Data Appendix, only the election file codebook is documented.

NOTES CONCERNING THE SOCIOECONOMIC DATA

When not otherwise specified, my main source for the socioeconomic data is Flora, Alber, Eichenberg, Kohl, Knaus, Pfenning, and Seebohn (1983) and (1987). Sometimes the data have been adjusted to my specific needs.

GENERAL

1. "Dependent" refers to employees plus workers.
2. "Workers" are defined as low-status, dependent laborers or blue-collar personnel, including home workers.
3. Unless otherwise stated, "workers" always include the "apprentices," defined as "persons in vocational training in firms."
4. Unless otherwise indicated, "workers in agriculture" exclude "family workers," that is, assisting spouses, children, and relatives.

- *Austria:* Data before World War I refer to the Austrian part of the Hapsburg Empire as defined by the 1867 constitution.

  1880–1990: these censuses combine workers and family workers. I have estimated the figures for the workers on the basis of the 1900 census.

- *Belgium:* 1880–1890: family workers are not included in the labor force

1880: workers and employees are grouped together. I have estimated the respective weight on the basis of the 1890 census. Note, however, that for the core sectors the proportion of employees is very small.

- *Denmark:* 1880–1890: workers and employees are grouped together. I have estimated the relative proportion as indicated for Belgium in 1880. In these two censuses, the category "workers" may be underestimated due to the existence of the category "servants," including people "engaged in domestic work." Moreover, the two categories of "workers" and "servants" must also include "family workers," a category normally kept separate. In fact, family workers are included in the labor force, but with a classification that is unknown. In this case, I was obliged to combine "workers" and "servants," preferring the likely overestimation resulting from the inclusion of the family workers to the underestimation resulting from the global exclusion of servants.

1930: the distinction between "employees," "workers," and "family workers" is available only for some sectors. The figures are reconstructed using interpolation from the previous (1920) and following (1940) censuses.

- *Finland:* 1910–1940: "independent in agriculture" includes "employees." Given the low percentage of employees in agriculture anyway, and in particular in this period (in all countries less than 1%), I have felt no need to modify the data.

1910–1930: "independents as a percentage of the active population" (INDI) and "independents in agriculture as a percentage of total independents" (INAGIN) also include "employees." I have estimated these figures by extrapolation, and I have checked for estimates in alternative source.

- *France:* French data present the greatest problems of comparability, and in many cases I was obliged to resort to missing values.

1881–1891: no category for "family workers" is available. They are probably included in "workers" and in "employers." The category "workers" is therefore inflated compared to the other countries, and I left out all data when it was impossible to exclude the family workers. By contrast, "workers in mining, manufacturing, utilities, construction, and transport" are considered as a percentage of the active population (but not of the overall "workers"), given that the percentage of "family workers" is very small in these sectors.

1881: "workers in construction" are included in the category "manufacturing." The percentage of "workers in mining and manufacturing" on the active population is therefore missed.

1896–1901: employers and workers are classified together. The percentages have been estimated by interpolation of the previous and following census.

1896–1936: a total figure for "family workers," but no breakdown by sector, is available. No agricultural occupation figures can therefore be properly computed. I computed only the percentage statistics for industrial workers, where the weight of family workers could be overlooked.

1901–1936: "casual workers" and "workers" have been summed together.

1946–1980: "employees" and "workers" are included in the same category. The percentages concerning "workers" can be accurately computed only for those cases in which the percentage of employees is marginal with respect to the active population, that is, "workers in agriculture" and "workers in mining and manufacturing." For "workers in construction, utilities, and transport," the proportion of employees to workers is higher, and therefore, statistics are overestimated in this sector.

- *Ireland:* "workers" and "employees" are grouped together. Corresponding statistics concerning workers have not been computed in those cases in which the percentage of employees can be considered irrelevant with respect to active population, that is, "workers in agriculture" and "workers in mining and manufacturing." For "workers in construction, utilities, and transport," see the text for France.

- *Italy:* 1881: separate figures for "family workers" are not available, but they were probably not included in the labor force. Workers and employees are grouped together; the corresponding statistics have been computed only for the cases listed previously under Ireland.

1901–1921: "family workers" are included in the "independents," which, therefore, are comparatively overestimated.

1936: "workers" and "servants" are grouped together.

- *The Netherlands:* 1899–1930: "family workers" are included in part (assisting spouses) in the self-employed status group and in part in other unknown status groups. In this case, statistics concerning "workers" have been retained, even if, particularly in the case of "workers in agriculture," they result in some overestimation compared with other countries.
- *Norway:* 1930–1946: figures concerning "workers in agriculture" are doubtful when compared to those in previous and following censuses. Corresponding statistics have been interpolated from the 1920 and 1950 censuses.

  1930–1950: separate figures for "family workers" in agriculture and services have been derived from the respective status and sector categories.

  1960: "family workers" in agriculture are included within "workers." Their proportion has been estimated by interpolation from the 1950 and 1970 censuses.

  1960: "employees" and "workers" are grouped together. The relative proportion have been derived by extrapolation from the 1946 and 1959 censuses.

  1970: "workers" and "employees" are grouped together; no reliable estimation was possible. Only the proportion of total workers was estimated by extrapolation from the previous census.
- *Sweden:* 1880–1920: the figures for "family workers in agriculture" have been subtracted from the figures for "workers."

  1965–1975: "workers" and "employees" are grouped together. No statistics concerning "workers in agriculture" or "workers in industry" can be accurately calculated. I have extrapolated these data from the 1940 and 1960 censuses. In this case, therefore, the same argument developed for France and Ireland applies to Sweden.
- *Switzerland:* 1888: "employees" and "workers" are grouped together. The percentage of workers has been estimated on the basis of the 1890 census.
- *United Kingdom:* The separate censuses of (1) England and Wales and (2) Scotland have been summed together.

  1891–1901: "family workers" are excluded from the labor force.

  1891–1951: "employees" and "workers" are grouped together. Only those sectors in which the number of employees is small have been considered: agriculture, mining and manufacturing, construction, and transport. As already mentioned, the last sector is the most problematic, and its inclusion in the core working class determines its slight overestimation. No figures are available concerning the whole category of "workers."

1931: an "out of work" category has been deducted from the labor force in order to maintain comparability with other censuses.

1931: "family workers" are included in the labor force, but with an unknown classification.

1931: "managers" are included in "employees and workers," as in previous censuses.

1961–1971: The category "unknown," including "out of work," has been excluded from the labor force.

THE TEMPO OF INDUSTRIALIZATION (DATA DISCUSSED IN CHAPTER 3)

Rates of sector transformation (active in industry as a percentage of the active population)

	1880–1890	1890–1900	1900–1910	1910–1920	1920–1930	1930–1940	1940–1950	1950–1960	1960–1970	country mean
Austria	−0.1	0.9	2.2	4.9	4.9	−1.6	5.4	3.5	1.0	2.3
Belgium	2.3	4.1	3.8	0.8	1.9	0.5	−1.3	−1.3	−2.0	1.0
Denmark	1.8	−0.5	0.9	1.0	−0.1	5.4	1.9	3.4	0.2	1.6
Finland				2.0	1.7	3.7	9.2	3.8	2.8	3.9
France	2.1	1.3	−0.2	1.7	0.9	−3.0	6.5	3.0	−4.0	0.9
Germany	3.6	2.5	1.1	1.1	−1.4	2.3	0.2	5.9	0.7	1.8
Ireland					3.4	0.4	6.1	2.5	4.6	3.4
Italy	−1.6	−1.6	3.1	−2.9	4.5	0.5	1.5	9.0	2.8	1.7
Netherlands	0.4	1.2	1.4	1.4	0.6	−1.2	3.8	3.8	−6.4	0.6
Norway		4.0	−0.9	1.0	−0.4	5.7	4.2	0.0	0.8	1.8
Sweden	4.5	5.3	5.0	5.7	0.5	6.1	3.6	3.5	−5.0	3.2
Switzerland		3.5	0.5	0.9	−1.3	−0.2	2.6	4.2	−2.2	1.0
Un. Kingdom		1.1	−1.0	−2.6	4.1	1.6	1.5	−1.8	−5.2	−0.3
decade mean	1.6	2.0	1.4	1.3	1.5	1.6	3.5	3.0	−0.9	1.7

Rates of status transformation (dependent labor force as a percentage of the active population)

	1880–1890	1890–1900	1900–1910	1910–1920	1920–1930	1930–1940	1940–1950	1950–1960	1960–1970	count mean
Austria	5.8	−1.0	0.4	10.0	11.0	−6.4	3.8	6.1	8.0	4.2
Belgium	1.2	0.5	−2.4	4.5	−2.3	3.1	1.0	1.0	7.9	1.6
Denmark	−3.5	7.2	2.5	−3.5	2.0	6.3	0.3	5.0	4.1	2.3
Finland				−1.3	1.2	6.0	14.4	7.6	13.2	6.9
France	−2.4	−1.0	0.3	0.2	−1.1	−0.3	7.3	8.9	5.5	1.9
Germany	7.4	−1.6	1.2	1.2	1.2	1.1	1.1	6.8	6.4	2.8
Ireland				1.6	5.3	4.6	4.7	5.1	4.3	
Italy	1.1	1.0	8.2	−3.8	−5.5	2.0	2.0	10.4	3.6	2.1
Netherlands		0.6	1.4	4.0	−1.4	−7.7	4.8	3.7	5.8	1.4
Norway		1.3	2.4	4.9	−6.3	4.3	6.9	9.5	2.7	3.2
Sweden	−0.6	3.7	7.4	9.0	1.0	7.0	4.4	7.4	6.0	5.0
Switzerland		11.0	−1.2	4.8	5.9	1.6	3.6	5.9	4.1	4.5
Un. Kingdom		2.4	−2.0	5.3	−11.5	6.3	6.2	−1.1	−3.8	0.2
decade mean	1.3	2.2	1.7	2.9	−0.3	2.2	4.6	5.8	5.3	3.0

Rates of working-class constituency growth (workers in mining, manufacturing, utilities, building, and transport as a percentage of the active population)

	1880–1890	1890–1900	1900–1910	1910–1920	1920–1930	1930–1940	1940–1950	1950–1960	1960–1970	country mean
Austria	1.7	0.9	2.9	2.3	2.3	0.9	3.3	2.3	−0.5	1.8
Belgium	2.4	4.8	4.6	3.7	−0.5	−2.3	−1.6	−1.6	−4.0	0.6
Denmark	−3.5	2.3	2.1	0.4	0.4	6.4	0.9	2.0	−0.7	1.1
Finland			0.9	1.2	1.5	4.2	6.8	3.3	3.0	3.0
France	0.6	−0.8	2.2	3.1	0.1	0.7	3.4	3.9	−1.4	1.3
Germany	4.8	3.6	2.4	2.3	−17.2	14.9	−0.4	4.1	−3.2	1.3
Ireland					2.9	2.3	5.1	3.7	5.2	3.8
Italy	−3.3	−3.4	4.4	1.7	2.3	40.4	1.9	8.6	−1.1	1.3
Netherlands	2.3	2.8	1.6	2.5	0.0	−5.7	3.1	3.0	−7.1	0.3

(*cont.*)

	1880–1890	1890–1900	1900–1910	1910–1920	1920–1930	1930–1940	1940–1950	1950–1960	1960–1970	country mean
Norway		4.1	0.4	5.9	−0.1	4.1	3.2	0.0	0.0	2.1
Sweden	4.2	4.9	5.8	6.2	1.9	2.7	2.7	0.1	0.2	3.2
Switzerland		9.9	−2.3	1.0	2.0	−1.0	5.4	0.4	−5.0	1.3
Un. Kingdom		4.0	−0.5	0.4	−7.9	5.7	5.7	−3.5	−14.8	−1.4
decade mean	1.2	3.0	2.0	2.6	−1.0	2.6	3.0	2.0	−2.3	1.4

Rates of working-class homogenization (workers in mining, manufacturing, utilities, building, and transport as a percentage of the total working class)

	1880–1890	1890–1900	1900–1910	1910–1920	1920–1930	1930–1940	1940–1950	1950–1960	1960–1970	country mean
Austria	4.5	4.3	7.3	−0.6	−0.7	11.4	6.5	5.2	1.4	4.4
Belgium	2.6	8.6	11.8	3.0	7.1	−2.2	1.4	1.4	−4.7	3.2
Denmark	16.0	4.4	4.9	4.2	0.7	9.6	4.4	7.6	2.4	6.0
Finland				5.5	5.4	9.5	13.3	6.1	2.0	7.0
France	1.3	5.3	5.1	5.0	2.8					(3.9)
Germany	3.3	9.9	4.6	4.5	−7.5	10.3	−0.8	8.2	1.7	3.8
Ireland										n.a.
Italy		0.0	0.9	7.1	12.0	0.0	1.6	8.7	2.3	4.1
Netherlands	4.4	5.6	2.7	2.7	1.8	−5.2	9.9	9.8	−8.6	2.6
Norway		8.1	1.2	7.7	5.1	8.5	0.3	7.2	1.4	4.9
Sweden	10.9	9.8	9.6	7.4	1.2	8.4	6.6	2.0	2.7	6.5
Switzerland		10.4	1.8	−1.7	−1.0	−2.1	10.1	−1.8	−4.5	1.4
Un. Kingdom									n.a.	
decade mean	6.1	6.6	5.0	4.1	2.4	4.8	5.3	5.4	−0.4	4.3

It is important to emphasize that the means by decade are country means, that is, they are the mean value of the thirteen (or fewer) European countries.

CULTURAL HETEROGENEITY DATA

RELIGION AND LANGUAGE

The data concerning the religious and linguistic composition of the European population are taken from Flora et al. (1983: 55–85). For some countries the information is not available in census data: for instance, the religious composition of the United Kingdom and the Protestant minorities in France, Belgium, and Italy. Similarly, no statistics about linguistic minorities exist for Italy, France, and Denmark. When this systematic source was not available, I resorted to the estimates provided by Urwin (1980: 193–194).

LITERACY

The ideal statistic for literacy estimation is the percentage of the people able to read (or read and write). Such data are available for only a five countries: Austria, Finland, France, Ireland, and Italy. Other, not strictly comparable, data for Belgium, Germany, the Netherlands, and Sweden concern the literacy level of army recruits and married people. I have utilized the estimates of Flora (1973: 245) on the percentage of the population able to read and write. An alternative source is the statistics concerning the number of pupils enrolled in primary education as a percentage of the 5–14 age group. The comparability problems are described in Flora et al. (1983: 55, 70–85).

Enfranchisement

a. *The electorate as a percentage of the population twenty years of age and older: 1830–1880*

Year	Au	Be	De	Fi	Fr	Ge	Ir	It	Ne	No	Sw	Sz	UK
1831		1.9			0.8		1.7						3.8
1832										9.9			
1833		1.9					2						5.9
1834					0.8								
1835							2.1			9.8			6
1837					0.9								
1838										10			
1839					0.9								

a. *(cont.) The electorate as a percentage of the population twenty years of age and older: 1830–1880*

Year	Au	Be	De	Fi	Fr	Ge	Ir	It	Ne	No	Sw	Sz	UK
1841										9.7			
1842					1								
1844										9.4			
1846					1.1		2.7						6.8
1847		1.8								9.4			
1848		3.1			36.3							~30	
1849			25.7		43.4								
1850										9.3			
1852			25.6		42								
1853			25.1						4.6	9			
1854			25.7										
1856										8.9			
1857		3.3			40.8								
1858			25										
1859										8.9			
1860													
1861			25.3					3.4					
1862										8.8			
1863					41.2								
1864		3.6	24.6										
1865								3.5		8.8			
1866			25.3				6.7						8.3
1866			25.5										
1867						(35)							
1868										8.6			
1869			25.8		42		7.4						14.5
1870		3.7						3.5	5	8.5			
1871					43.7	33	7.7						14.9

a. *(cont.) The electorate as a percentage of the population twenty years of age and older: 1830–188*

Year	Au	Be	De	Fi	Fr	Ge	Ir	It	Ne	No	Sw	Sz	UK
1872			26								9.8		
1873	10.3[1]		26.5							8.4			
1874						36.2		3.6					
1875											10.2		
1876			26.7		42			3.8		8.3			
1877					41.8	36.9							
1878						37.4					10.5		
1879	10.4[1]		26.9							8.3			
1880								3.8	5.4				

b. *The electorate as a percentage of the population twenty years of age and older: 1881–1917*

Year	Au	Be	De	Fi	Fr	Ge	Ir	It	Ne	No	Sw	Sz	UK
1881			27.1		41.6	36.2	8.2				10.7	38.7	16.4
1881			27.1										
1882								12.1		9.4			
1883													16.5
1884		3.9	27.8			36.8					10.9	38	
1885	13[1]				41.3					11.4			29.3
1886							27.4	14.1					29.0
1886/ 1887									5.7				
1887			28.3			37.3					10.1	38.1	
1888									11.8	11.8			
1889					41.8		28.9						
1890		29.4			37.4		15.2			10.4	38.3		
1891	12.9[1]								11.5	12.6			
1892		3.9	29.3			37.8	16.6				10.7		29.3
1893					41.8								
1894		37.3							11.3	16.4			

b. (*cont.*) *The electorate as a percentage of the population twenty years of age and older: 1881–1917*

Year	Au	Be	De	Fi	Fr	Ge	Ir	It	Ne	No	Sw	Sz	UK
1895			29.5					11.8					28.9
1896	13.4/ 35.7[2]										10.8	38.2	
1897								11.7	20.9	16.6			
1898			30.0		42.0	37.8							
1899											11.5	38.0	
1900		37.7						12.3		34.8			28.5
1900/ 1901	14.2/ 34.1[2]												
1901			29.0	8.3					21.2				
1902					43.2						12.7	37.9	
1903			29.1			38.3				34.4			
1904				9				13.5	24.4				
1905											14.0	37.4	
1906					43.7					35.2		28.5	
1907	37.9			76.2		38.3							
1908				75.9							15.8	37.5	
1909			29.8	75.6				15.0	25.7	58.5			
1910			30.1	75.5	43.4								28.7
1911	38.0			75.7							32.5	37.0	
1912		38.2				38.7				60.2			
1913			30.1	77.8				42.0	27.6				
1914					42.8						32.8	36.3	
1915										77.1			
1916				75.4									
1917				74.5							32.3	38.6	

c. *The electorate as a percentage of the population twenty years of age and older: 1918–1944*

Year	Au	Be	De	Fi	Fr	Ge	Ir	It	Ne	No	Sw	Sz	UK
1918			69.1				74.2		39.3	80.4			74.8
1918							74.1						
1919	85.9	43.8		74.1	43.4	97.9		48.8				40.1	
1920	90.1		74.0			95.1					33.0		
1921		45.5						52.5		86.9	87.9		
1922				73.4			77.5		80.7			40.3	74.5
1923	90.0					97							75.1
1924			79.6	73.5	39.9	98.5				87.4	88.2		75.6
1925		45.2							81.8			40.4	
1926			82.0										
1927	92.6			74.8			95.4			88.4			
1928					40.0	97.9					88.5	40.7	
1929		45.3	80.6	76.5					82.1				95.5
1930	89.9			75.5		98.5				89.6			
1931												41.0	97.0
1932		54.0	82.0		39.6	98.4	93.7				89.0		
1933				75.9		97.6	94.9		82.9	91.0			
1934													
1935			83.9									42.4	97.4
1936		45.6		77.1	40.1					92.6	90.1		
1937							95.0		85.2				
1938							95.0						
1939		45.1	84.6	77.8								42.3	
1940										90.6			
1941													
1942													
1943			85.4				96.9					43.4	
1944							97.2				91.8		

d. *The electorate after World War II*

Year	Au	Be	De	Fi	Fr	Ge	Ir	It	Ne	No	Sw	Sz	UK
1945	69.4		86.7	96.5	88.3					91.2			99.6
1946		45.5			88.0			95.0	90.0				
1947			87.0									43.7	
1948					98.9			95.4	95.0	89.2		96.3	
1949	89.3	91.5				95.6				96.0			
1950		91.4	88.2										96.0
1951				97.3	83.0		95.7					42.9	97.6
1952									89.7		95.6		
1953	93.6		90.5			97.3		98.0		97.8			
1954				97.4			96.3						
1955		94.1										42.3	97.0
1956	94.1				87.9				90.5		95.3		
1957			93.1			97.5	97.9			97.3			
1958		93.9		96.7	88.2			96.6		96.0			
1959	95.2								91.3			40.8	97.5
1960			93.2								94.9		
1961		94.4				97.2	97.9			96.9			
1962	96.4			97.3	86.4								
1963								98.7	90.2			38.4	
1964			97.0								93.5		95.7
1965		92.9				95.6	98.2			96.0			
1966	96.4		97.1	95.4									95.3
1967									93.6			38.2	
1968		92.8	96.2		85.5			98.9			95.7		
1969						93.8	99.5			99.0			
1970	98.7			99.8							97.1		99.8
1971	97.3	94.3	97.0						94.7			80.8	
1972				99.8	98.8			98.9	99.8				
1973			99.0		87.5		98.1			99.4	96.3		

d. (cont.) The electorate after World War II

Year	Au	Be	De	Fi	Fr	Ge	Ir	It	Ne	No	Sw	Sz	UK
1974		94.3											99.8
1975	98.0		98.5	99.8								83.5	

Notes on Austria:

[1] The percentage refers to the combined electorate of the Second and Fourth Curiae, whic represented the urban and rural male electorate and can, therefore, be added together. Th electorate of the First and Second Curiae, representing the large landowners and th chambers of commerce and trade, respectively, included only about 5,000 and about 55 electors and can be left out, with no major distortion.

[2] The first figure corresponds to the Third and Fourth Curiae as indicated in note 1. Th second figure corresponds to the electorate of the Fifth Curia added in the 1897 reform In this curia, there was universal and equal suffrage for male citizens over age twenty-fou However, citizens of the first four curiae gained a second vote in the Fifth Curia. The tw figures cannot be summed; instead, they should be subtracted. The total electorate ove the population twenty years of age or more should be between the first and second figures but much closer to the second figure.

SOURCES OF PARTY MEMBERSHIP FIGURES

Membership figures for the left parties are scattered throughout a variety of often conflicting sources. From the 1960s on, a systematic and reliable comparative time series is available, thanks to the research project on party organization directed by Mair and Katz (1992). The database with absolute figures is presented in Katz and Mair (1992). Other data collections are either national (the Dutch collection of Koole and Voerman [1986: 115–176]), limited in comparison (for Scandinavia, Sundberg [1987]), or general collections of secondary sources, such as Beyme, [1985]). See also Katz (1990). For the 1880–1960 period, I have relied both on national experts' advice and on secondary sources. For their help in collecting national data and for their useful suggestions, I would like to thank Wilfried Dewachter, Peter Gerlich, Pertti Pesonen, Gunnar Sjöblom, and Henry Valen.

The following secondary sources were used:

- Austria: 1913–1932 period: Leichter (1964); 1945–1977 period: Be-richte an den Bundesparteitag der SPO (1945 ff.). Systematic, detailed historical data are presented in Maderthaner and Müller (1996), which became available too late to be used in this work.

- *Belgium:* 1951–1963 period: Kendall (1975); 1966–1975 period: Rowies (1977).
- *Denmark:* Data collected by Thomas (1977) from Bertold, Christiansen, and Hansen (1954–1955); personal communications from SD Party Headquarters, *Medlemsudviklingen 1944–1974.*
- *Finland:* Figures provided by Pertti Pesonen.
- *France:* The figures for the membership in the Socialist Party are many and conflicting. I have used the following: 1905–1954 period: Duverger (1967); 1956–1970 period: Hurtig (1971); 1971–1975 period: Criddle (1977) and official figures declared at the Party Conference of Nantes (*Le Point*, June 27, 1977). Different figures are provided by Braunthal (1945 ff.) and by Simmons (1970). *The Socialist International Yearbook* figures, although not coincident with the Duverger-Hurtig figures, are very similar. By contrast, Simmons's figures are consistently lower than the Duverger-Hurtig figures for the postwar period.
- *Germany:* 1906–1931 period: Braunthal (1945 ff.); 1946–1975 period: Paterson (1977) and *Jahrbücher der SPD.*
- *Ireland:* 1964–1978 period: official party figures collected by Peter Mair.
- *Italy:* 1896–1922 period: official party figures in Cannarsa (1950); 1945–1967 period: official party figures in Cazzola (1970); 1970, 1972, and 1973: PSI (1975); 1974 and 1975: official party figures in PSI (1976).
- *The Netherlands:* 1895–1939 period: Vorrink (1945); 1945–1946 period: Braunthal (1945 ff.); 1947–1976 period: Wolinetz (1977); 1977: Daalder (1987b) and Daalder and Schuyt (1986).
- *Norway:* Figures provided by Henry Valen. For nonelection years, the following sources have been used to the extent that they coincided with the figures for election years provided by Valen: Heidar (1977), Duverger (1967), and Torgersen (1962). For the period after 1950, Heidar's figures do not coincide with Valen's figures, and I have used the latter.
- *Sweden:* Official party figures in Scase (1977).
- *Switzerland:* 1902–1954 period: Duverger (1967).
- *United Kingdom:* Annual report of the National Executive Committee of the Labour Party from Pelling (1976b). The party ranks were open to individual members in 1918, but the official party figures for individual members are available only from 1928 on.

In addition to these sources, additional information is drawn from Sworatowski (1973) for a number of small communist parties.

SOURCES OF TRADE UNION MEMBERSHIP FIGURES

Special thanks are due to Jelle Visser, Hans Hirter, and William K. Roche for their help in collecting the trade union membership data. Trade union membership figures come from two main sources: Visser (1987) and Bain and Price (1976). Neither of them covers all countries included in this work. Jelle Visser made available to me his *Trade Union Membership Database* (Amsterdam: Department of Sociology, March 1992), where additional data are available covering Ireland, Finland, and Belgium. Other supplementary information has been drawn from various sources: for Finland, *Työelämän Suhteet* (1990) (made available by Jelle Visser) and Suviranta (1987); for Ireland, Roberts (1958–1959: 95), MacCarthy (1977: 622) and, Roche (1990) and (1992); for Switzerland 1881–1913: Balthasar, Gruner, and Hirter (1988: 66–68, 155, 158).

INDEX OF COALITION POTENTIAL

The index of coalition potential is calculated for the socialist parties, the communist parties, and the combined total left. I have used a modified version of the Shapley formula. The original index and the modifications are documented in Bartolini (1998). I acknowledge the research assistance of Stefano Bocconi, who developed the modified version of the Shapley–Shubik index, and of Massimiliano Miglio, who actually calculated the index.

CLASS CLEAVAGE INCLUSIVENESS AND DISTINCTIVENESS

To estimate how many members of the working class voted for the left parties (INCLUSIVENESS) and how many left voters were members of the working class (DISTINCTIVENESS), I have consulted the survey evidence of the 1950s and 1960s. Survey data normally refer to individual parties and have to be recalculated for the whole left. I have taken the category "workers" or "working class" as defined by each national source, and I have *not* performed any cross-country standardization of the notion. This means that the data are biased for any systematic difference in the survey definition of what a working-class member is. The following notes document my sources and my final choices.

- *Austria:* For 1969, I have taken the percentage of workers voting left (73%) from Haerpfer and Gehmacher (1984) and the percentage of left voters who are workers from Pelinka (1978: 416). For a more detailed analysis of the IFES surveys of 1969, 1972, and 1977, see Haerpfer and Gehmacher (1984) and Gehmacher (1974: 55–75).
- *Belgium:* The level of class inclusiveness in 1968 (47%) is taken from Hill (1974: 83); the value for class distinctiveness (60–61%) is taken from Delruelle, Evalenko, and Fraeys (1970: 49). Dogan (1960: 28–29, Tables 1 and 2) produces different figures for the 1952–1954 period – 63% and 68%, respectively.
- *Denmark:* A 1957 Gallup poll reported in Worre (1979: 68–82) indicates that 80% of workers supported left parties. Dogan (1960) reports 73% for 1953–1955. Berglund and Lindström (1978: 108) report that in the mid-1960s 85% of workers voted for the left (2% for the Communists, 10% for the new radical left, and 73% for the Social Democrats). On the basis of 1971 data, Borre (1980: 253) reports the figure of 75%. I have taken the intermediate figure of 80%. Dogan (1960) estimates the percentage of left voters who are working class as 76% in 1952–1953; Borre (1980: 258) estimates it as 77% in 1971.
- *Finland:* Pesonen (1968) and Allardt and Pesonen (1967: 342) report that about 68% of workers supported left parties in 1958 and that 82% of those supporting left parties were workers. Based on the same survey, however, Dogan (1960) reports widely diverging figures: 80% and 50%, respectively. Berglund and Lindström (1978) estimate that 80% of workers voted left in the mid-1960s. Finally, the 1975 survey analyzed in Pesonen and Sänkiaho (1979: 121) indicated that 60% of workers voted for left parties and 60% of those supporting the latter were workers. I have taken the 1958 figures.
- *France:* Various sources provide different figures, but all within a relatively narrow range. Converse and Pierce (1986: 154–156) estimate between 48% and 51% of workers voting for the left. Their calculations are based on subjective social class and on the manual–nonmanual dichotomy. Stoetzel (1955: 118–119) provides an estimation of about 62%, Dogan (1960) offers the value of 67%, and Adam, Bon, Capdeville, and Mouriaut (1971: 200) give the figure of 57% based on a 1969 survey. I have taken an average value of 55%. An IFOP poll of 1952 (*Sondages,* 1952, n. 3) gives the figure of 48% for the left voters

being workers; a second survey for 1956 (*Sondages*, 1960, n. 4) gives the figure of 48–49%. Dogan (1960) suggests 54–55%. Successive polls in 1967, 1968, and 1973 consistently report figures between 42% and 47% (see Charlot [1973: 55 ff.]). I have chosen the average figure of about 45%.

- *Germany:* A complete list of survey results estimating class inclusiveness is provided by Hildebrandt and Dalton (1978: 72). The figures are 59% for 1953, 61% for 1957, and 58% for 1961. Dogan (1960) offers a lower estimate of 48%, and Urwin (1974: 147) arrives at the same figure. This suggests an average level of 53–54%. As for the distinctiveness of the left, Linz (1959: 195, 200) suggests that between 68% and 70% of manual workers supported the left in the late 1950s, while Dogan (1960) suggests the figure of 66%. A figure of 68% has been used.

- *Ireland:* In 1969, the first Gallup poll indicated that 27% of workers voted for the Labour Party, while 73% of the labor voters were workers. Peter Mair has provided the row data.

- *Italy:* For 1953, Lipset (1966: 415) reported that roughly 69–70% of Italian workers voted for the left. A Doxa survey of 1964 reports a figure of 68%. Dogan (1960) suggests the figure of 65%. Later election surveys give lower estimates, between 55% and 60%, as for instance in Barnes and Pierce (1971), Barnes (1974) and (1977: 59), and Sani (1977: 111). A prudent estimate for the 1950s–1960s should therefore be set at around 60%. The percentage of left voters who are workers is set at about 50–55% by Dogan for 1953 (1960), at 40% by Barnes (1977), and at about 33–35% by Bruschi and Pacini (1978). The figures in this case diverge widely. I have decided to take an intermediate value of 45%.

- *Netherlands:* The survey material reviewed by Andeweg (1982: 93) indicates that in 1966 about a third of the Dutch workers voted for left parties, and this proportion was roughly confirmed in studies in 1971, 1972, and 1977. Dogan (1960), however, reports the figure of 50%. I have used the intermediate value of 41%. Dogan's estimate for the percentage of left voters being workers in the 1950s is 53–54%. The Dutch Parliamentary Election Study of 1971 suggests the figure of 67%. The two surveys of the 1980s (quoted in Daalder [1987b: 226–227]) indicate figures of 53% and 52%, respectively. I have opted for a figure of 55%.

- *Norway:* The 1957 survey analyzed by Rokkan (1967: 427–431) indicated that 79% of Norwegian workers voted Labor, giving, however, no information on the Communist vote. The 1968 survey discussed by

Valen and Rokkan (1974: 334) puts at 76% the workers' vote for the three left parties. Dogan (1960) indicates that 70% of the left parties' support came from working-class voters in the mid-1950s.

- *Sweden:* Dogan (1960) sets at 74% the percentage of workers voting left; Stjerquist (1966: 127) indicates the figure of 68% on the basis of the 1964 survey The 1968 election survey, analyzed in Särlvik (1974: 401–402), reports the figure of 77%. Berglund and Lindström (1978: 108) argue that in the mid-1980s 84% of workers voted left (78% Social Democrats and 6% Communists). I have used the value of 77%. The same three sources offer the following estimation of the percentage of workers within the left electorate: 73%, 71%, and 66%. I have used 71%.
- *Switzerland:* Kerr (1974: 11, 14) indicates that 40% of Swiss workers voted left in 1972 and about 33% of the left vote was cast by workers.
- *United Kingdom:* The large set of British survey studies is difficult to compare due to the different categories used to identify the working class. For the percentage of workers voting left, there are the following estimates: 1955: 75%; 1959: 71% (Goldthorpe, Lockwood, Bechhfer, and Platt [1971: 12]), based on a sample of industrial workers; 1958: 62% (Abrams [1958]); 1963: 72–73% (Butler and Stokes [1970: 76]), based on subjective class assignment; in the period 1945–1965 six surveys have values ranging between 57% and 64%, based on the manual–nonmanual distinction (Heath, Jowell, and Curtice [1985: 30%]); in the period 1964–1966 two survey have values ranging from 70% to 72%, based on a strictly defined working class (Heath, Jowell, and Curtice [1985: 32–33]). I have decided to take a value of 72–73%. As far as the percentage of Labor's vote cast by workers, two sources agree on an estimate of 66–67% for the early 1950s (Bonham [1953: 130] and Abrams and Rose [1961: 18]). Both figures are based on self-reported class.

LIST OF VARIABLES IN THE ELECTION DATA FILE

NUMBER OF CASES (ELECTIONS): 361

COUNTRY
ELECTION YEAR
DECADE
PERIOD:

    1   before 1918
    2   1918–1944
    3   1945–1965
    4   1966–1985

ELECTORAL DATA

ELECTORA	Electorate as % population > 20 years
TURNOUT	Total votes as % population ≥ 20 years
TURNOUTE	Total votes as % of electorate
SDVOTE	% valid votes for Social Democrats
CPVOTE	% valid votes for Communist Party
OLVOTE	% valid votes for other left parties
TLVOTE	% valid votes for whole left
TLSEATS	% of seats for whole left
SDSEATS	% of seats for Social Democrats
CPSEATS	% of seats for Communist Party
OLSEATS	% of seats for other left parties

SOCIOECONOMIC DATA

AGRI	Labor force in agriculture as % of active population
INDU	Labor force in industry as % of active population
SERVI	Labor force in service as % of active population
INDI	Independent, self-employed, and family workers
INDIWFW	Independents without family workers
DEPE	Dependent labor force
DEPAAP	Dependents in public administration as % of active population
INAGAP	Independents in agriculture as % of active population
INAGAA	Independents in agriculture as % of active in agriculture
INAGIN	Independents in agriculture as % of independents
WOAGAP	Workers in agriculture as % of active population
WOAGAA	Workers in agriculture as % of active in agriculture
WOAGWO	Workers in agriculture as % of workers
WO1AP	Workers as % of active population
WO2AP	Workers in mining, manufacturing, construction, utilities, transportation as % of active population
WO3AP	Workers in mining, manufacturing as % of active population

WO2WO	Workers in mining, manufacturing, construction, utilities, transportation as % of workers
WO3WO	Workers in mining manufacturing as % of workers
EMRATE	Employers-self-employed as % of active in manufacturing
RELIGION	Religious F $\times$ 100
LANGUAGE	Linguistic F $\times$ 100
LITERACY	Pupils in primary schools as % of 5–14 age group
ILLITERA	% unable to write and read
U2	Urbanization: % in localities < 2,000 inhabitants
U5	Urbanization: % in localities < 5,000 inhabitants
U20	Urbanization: % in localities < 20,000 inhabitants
U100	Urbanization: % in localities < 100,000 inhabitants

GOVERNMENTAL DATA

MAFTLAST	No. of months elapsed since previous elections
MBEFNEXT	No. of months before next election
LEFT_A	Coalition potential index of the left: blind version
LEFT_B	Coalition potential index of the left: spatial version
LEFT_C	Coalition potential index of the left: spatial version with jump
COMPAR_A	Coalition potential index of the Communist Party: blind version
COMPAR_B	Coalition potential index of the Communist Party: spatial version
COMPAR_C	Coalition potential index of the Communist Party: spatial version with jump
SOCIAL_A	Coalition potential index of the Socialist Party: blind version
SOCIAL_B	Coalition potential index of the Socialist Party: spatial version
SOCIAL_C	Coalition potential index of the Socialist Party: spatial version with jump
GOVPOW	Governmental power of Socialist Party in the legislature. Based on an index comprising: (1) socialist presence in absence form cabinet; (2) parliamentary status of cabinet; (3) socialist status in cabinet; (4) duration in months. This index results from an elaboration done in a different file, taking as a unit all cabinets from 1918 to 1966.

PARTY SYSTEM DATA

FRAC	Index of fractionalization
FRACLEFT	Index of left block fractionalization
TNP	Total number of parties
NUMPART	Number of parties for volatility calculations
MAJORNP	Number of parties over 2%
TLDOMIN	Total left dominance: distance from strongest or second-strongest party
SDDOMIN	SD dominance: distance from strongest or second-strongest party
STRNSOC	% of seats of strongest nonsocialist party
TPSNS	Type of strongest nonsocialist party
NNEWP	No. of parties founded after 1959
VOTENEWP	Vote % of nnewp
SEATNEWP	Seat % of nnewp
NP2PC	No. of parties $\leq$ 2% of votes
VOTEP2PC	Vote % of np2%
SEATP2PC	Seat % of np2%
NP5PC	No. of parties $\leq$ 5% of votes
VOTEP5PC	Vote % of np5%
SEATP5PC	Seat % of np5%
NP10PC	No. of parties $\leq$ 10%
VOTEP10P	Vote % of np10%
SEATP10P	Seat % of np10%
BPVOTE	Vote % of biggest party
BPSEAT	Seat % of biggest (seat) party
IIBPVOTE	Vote % of second-biggest party
IIBPSEAT	Seat % of second-biggest (seat) party
TV	Total volatility by election
BV	Left block volatility
WBV	Within-bloc volatility
PBV	BV as % of TV
PRINROSE	Index of proportionality: Rose
PRIN2	Index of proportionality: %seat − %vote: 2
PRINLIJ	Index of proportionality: Lijphart
RELITYPE	Type of religion
1.00 Heterogeneous	
2.00 Homogeneous Catholic	
3.00 Homogeneous Protestant	
RELIMOB	Type of religious mobilization

1.00   Before socialists in Catholic homogeneous countries (Be, Ir)
2.00   Early before or parallel to socialists in heterogeneous countries (Ge, Ne, Sz)
3.00   Late after socialists in homogeneous Catholic countries (Au, It, Fr)
4.00   Homogeneous Protestant countries (GB, Scan)

PARTY ORGANIZATION DATA

SDMEMELE	Social Democratic Party membership as % of electorate
SDMEMVOT	Social Democratic Party membership as % of Social Democratic Party voters
CPMEMELE	Communist Party membership as % of electorate
CPMEMVOT	Communist Party membership as % of Communist Party voters
PDELE	Sdmemele + cpmemele
PDVOT	Sdmemvot + cpmemvot
TUD	Trade union as % of dependent labor force
LTUD	Left trade union as % of dependent labor force
LTUMELE	Left trade union members as % of electorate
LTUMVOT	Left trade union members as % of left votes
BARG	Bargaining timing

1.00   late
2.00   medium
3.00   early

TUSEQUEN   Party–trade union consolidation sequence

1   party first
2   parallel
3.00   tu first

PASEQUEN   Trade union–party consolidation sequence

1.00   tu first
2.00   parallel
3.00   party first

TUTIMING   Comparative trade union consolidation timing

1.00   tu late
2.00   tu mid
3.00   tu early

PATIMING   Comparative party consolidation timing

1.00   party late
2.00   party mid

3.00   party early

TULENGHT   Length of trade union consolidation

1.00   long

2.00   mid

3.00   short

PALENGHT   Length of party consolidation

1.00   long

2.00   mid

3.00   short

LINKAGE   Party–trade union linkages

1.00   contingent

3.00   interlocking

MODE   Party and trade union mode of representation

1.00   fragmented

3.00   corporate

INSTITUTIONAL VARIABLES

ELECTSYS   Type of electoral system

1   proportional

2   majoritarian

3   mixed

ELSYSCHA   Year of Electoral system change

FRANPATT   Franchise timing/tempo pattern

1.00   early-intermediate/gradual (Ir, Ne, Uk)

2.00   early/sudden (Dk, Fr, Ge, Sz)

3.00   intermediate-sudden/interm. (Au, Be, No)

4.00   late/sudden (Fi, It, Sw)

STATENESS   Z-score sum of tax ratio, tax centralization, central
                administration personnel, military personnel, police,
                and judiciary personnel

REPRESS   Level of repression

01 to 13:   rank ordering of countries

REPOBSTA   Representation obstacles

01 to 13:   rank ordering of countries

PARLA   Parliamentarization (responsible government)

01 to 13:   rank ordering of countries

COMBINED INDICES FOR THE
GENERAL MODEL

INDURB   Pattern of industrialization and urbanization

1.00   uncoupled growth (all other cases)

2.00   medium growth in both (Au, Dk, Fr)

3.00   accelerated growth in both (It, Fi, Sw)

MOBSOC   Combined index (ZSindiwfw + ZSemrate + ZSwo2wo + ZSwo2ap + ZSindurb)

CULTETHE   Country cultural heterogeneity (ZSlanguage + ZSreligion + ZSillitera)

ININ   Institutional integration. Sum of 13 countries rank ordered on three variables (stateness, repression, representation obstacles)

ELEFRAPA   Electorate level and pattern of enfranchisement (ZSelectorat + ZSfranpat)

SEQ   Sequence liberalization, universal suffrage, Socialist Party foundation

1.00   RG-SDF-US

2.00   RG-US-SDF

3.00   US-RG-SDF

4.00   US-SDF-RG

5.00   SDF-US-RG

ORGDEN   Organizational density ltumele + pdele

PAORCON   Party organizational consolidation: paseq + patiming + palength (from 3.00 = low, low, low to 9.00 = high, high, high)

PATURELA   Party–trade union relationship = mode + linkage

2.00   Contingent–noncorporate

4.00   Interlocking-noncorporate/noninterlocking-corporate

6.00   interlocking and corporate

ORGVAR   ZSorgden + ZSpaorcon + ZSpaturela

REFERENCES

Autori, Vari [various] (AA. VV.), 1955. *Compendio dei risultati delle consultazioni popolari dal 1840 al 1954.* Rome: Istituto Poligrafico dello Stato.

Abendroth, W., 1965. *Sozialgeschichte der europäischen Arbeiterbewegung.* Frankfurt am Main: Suhrkamp Verlag.

Abrams, M., 1958. *Class Distinctions in Britain.* In *The Future of the Welfare State.* London: Conservative Political Center.

Abrams, M., and R. Rose, 1961. *Must Labour Lose?* London: Penguin Books.

Abramson, P. R., 1971. Social Class and Political Change in Western Europe: A Cross-National Longitudinal Analysis. *Comparative Political Studies* 4: 131–155.

Adam, G., F. Bon, J. Capdeville, and R. Mouriaut, 1971. *L'ouvrier français en 1970.* Paris: Colin.

Agnelli, A., 1969. *Questione nazionale e socialismo. Contributo allo studio del pensiero di K. Renner e O. Bauer.* Bologna: Il Mulino.

Alapuro, R., 1981. *Origins of Agrarian Socialism in Finland.* In Torsvik (1981: 274–283).

1988. *State and Revolution in Finland.* Berkeley: University of California Press.

Alapuro, R., and E. Allardt, 1978. *The Lapua Movement. The Threat of Rightist Take-over in Finland 1930–32.* In Linz and Stepan (1978: 122–141).

Alber, J., 1982. *Vom Armenhaus zum Wohlfahrtsstaat. Analysen zur Entwicklung der Sozialversicherung in Westeuropa.* Frankfurt: Campus Verlag.

Alford, R., 1963. *Party and Society: The Anglo-American Democracies.* Chicago: Rand McNally.

Alford, R., and R. Friedland, 1974. Nations, Parties and Participation: A Critique of Political Sociology. *Theory and Society* 1: 307–328.

Allardt, E., 1964. *Patterns of Class Conflict and Working Class Consciousness in Finnish Politics.* In Allardt and Littunen (1964: 97–131).

1968. *Past and Emerging Political Cleavages.* In Stammer (1968: 66–74).

1970. *Types of Protest and Alienation.* In Allardt and Rokkan (1970: 45–63).

Allardt, E., and Y. Littunen, eds., 1964. *Cleavages, Ideologies and Party Systems.* Helsinki: Academic Bookstore.

Allardt, E., and P. Pesonen, 1960. Citizens' Participation in Political Life: Finland. *International Social Science Journal* 12: 27–39.

1967. *Cleavages in Finnish Politics.* In Lipset and Rokkan (1967: 325–366).

Allardt, E., and S. Rokkan, eds., 1970. *Mass Politics. Studies in Political Sociology.* New York: Free Press.

Almond, G., 1957. *The Appeals of Communism.* Princeton: Princeton University Press.

Anckar, D., 1992. *Finland: Dualism and Consensus Rule.* In Damgaard (1992: 152–191).

Anderson, E. N., and P. R. Anderson, 1967. *Political Institutions and Social Change in Continetal Europe in the Nineteenth Century.* Berkeley: University of California Press.

Anderson, P., 1974. *Lineage of the Absolutist State.* Thetford (Norfolk, England): Thetford Press.

Andeweg, R. B., 1982. *Dutch Voters Adrift: on Explanations of Electoral Change 1963–1977.* Leyden: Leyden University.

Andler, C., 1932. V*ie de Lucien Herr (1864–1926).* Paris: Rieder.

Andreasi, A., 1981. *L'anarco-sindacalismo in Francia, Italia e Spagna.* Milan: La Pietra.

Angress, W., 1972. *Stillborn Revolution: The Communist Bid for Power in Germany, 1921–1923.* Port Washington, NY: Kennikat Press.

Arfé, G., 1965. *Storia del socialismo italiano (1982–1926).* Turin: Einaudi.

Aron, R., 1964. *La lutte des classes. Nouvelles leçons sur les sociétés industrielles.* Paris: Gallimard.

1971. *Le socialisme français face au marxisme.* Paris: Grasset.

1989. *Leçons sur l'histoire.* Paris: Editions de Fallois.

Atkinson, M. M., and W. G. Coleman, 1989. Strong States and Weak States: Sectoral Policy Networks in Advanced Capitalist Economies. *British Journal of Political Science* 19: 47–67.

Bain, G. S., and R. Price, 1976. *Profiles of Union Growth. A Comparative Statistical Portrait of Eight Countries.* Oxford: Blackwell.

Bairoch, P., 1982. International Industrialisation Levels from 1750 to 1980. *The Journal of European Economic History* 11: 269–333.

Baldwin, P., 1988. How Socialist Is Solidaristic Social Policy? Swedish Post-War Reform as a Case in Point. *International Review of Social History* 33: 121–144.

Ball, A. R., 1987. *British Political Parties: The Emergence of a Modern Party System.* London: Macmillan.

Ballini, P.-L., 1985. Le elezioni politiche nel Regno di Italia. Appunti di bibliografia, legislazione e statistiche. *Quaderni dell'osservatorio elettorale* n. 15: 143–220.

1988. *Le elezioni nella storia d'Italia dall'Unità al Fascismo.* Bologna: Il Mulino.

Balthasar, A., E. Gruner, and H. Hirtner, 1988. *Gewerkschaften und Arbeitgeber auf dem Arbeitsmarkt: Streiks, Kampf ums Recht und Verhältnis zu anderen Interessengruppen*, Band 1 of *Arbeiterschaft und Wirtschaft in der Schweiz 1880–1914.* Bern: Chronos.

Banfield, E. C., 1958. *The Moral Basis of a Backward Society*. Glencoe, IL: Free Press.

Barnes, S. H., 1967. *Party Democracy: Politics in a Socialist Federation*. New Haven: Yale University Press.

1974. *Italy: Religion and Class in Electoral Behaviour*. In Rose (1974: 171–225).

1977. *Representation in Italy: Institutionalised Traditions and Electoral Choice*. Chicago: University of Chicago Press.

Barnes, S. H., and M. Kaase, eds., 1979. *Political Action*. Beverly Hills, CA: Sage.

Barnes, S. H., and R. Pierce, 1971. Public Opinion and Political Preferences in France and Italy. *Midwest Journal of Political Science* 15: 643–660.

Bartolini, S., 1983. *The Membership of the Mass Party: The Social Democratic Experience 1889–1978*. In Daalder and Mair (1983: 177–220).

1993. On Time and Comparative Research. *Journal of Theoretical Politics* 5: 131–167.

1998. *Coalition Potential and Governmental Power*. In Lane and Pennings (1998: 40–61).

Bartolini, S., and P. Mair, 1990. *Identity, Competition and Electoral Availability. The Stabilisation of European Electorates*. Cambridge: Cambridge University Press.

Bauman, Z., 1972. *Between Class and Elites*. Manchester: Manchester University Press.

Bendix, R., 1964. *Nation-Building and Citizenship: Studies of Our Changing Social Order*. Berkeley: University of California Press.

1974. *Work and Authority in Industry*. Berkeley: University of California Press.

1984a. *Citizenship of the Lower Classes*. In Bendix (1984b: 91–107).

1984b. *Force, Fate, and Freedom: On Historical Sociology*. Berkeley: University of California Press.

Bendix, R., and S. M. Lipset, eds., 1966. *Class, Status, and Power: Social Stratification in Contemporary Perspective*. New York: Free Press.

Benjamin, R. W., and J. H. Kautsky, 1968. Communism and Economic Development. *American Political Science Review* 62: 110–123.

Berelson, B., P. F. Lazarsfeld, and W. N. MacPhee, 1954. *Voting*. Chicago: Chicago University Press.

Berger, S., 1994. *The British Labour Party and the German Social Democrats 1900–1931*. Oxford: Clarendon Press.

Berglund, S., and U. Lindström, 1978. *The Scandinavian Party System(s)*. Lund: Studentlitteratur.

Bergounioux, A., and B. Manin, 1979. *La socialdemocratie ou le compromis*. Paris: Presses Universitaires de France.

Bernstein, E., 1899. *Die Voraussetzungen des Sozialismus und die Aufgabe der Sozialdemokratie*. Stuttgart: J. H. W. Dietz.

Berresford Ellis, P., 1972. *A History of the Irish Working Class*. London: Victor Gollancz Ltd.

Berry, D., 1969. Party Membership and Social Participation. *Political Studies* 17: 196–207.

Bertold, O., E. Christiansen, and P. Hansen, 1954–1955. *En bygning vi reyser: Den politiske arbejderbevaegelses historie i Danmark. Socialdemokratiet arsberentninger 1924–1943*. 2 vols. Copenhagen: Fremad.

Beyme, K. von, 1973. *Die parlamentarischen Regierungsysteme in Europa*. Munich: Piper.

—— 1985. *Political Parties in Western Democracies*. Aldershot, England: Gower.

Bieder, H. J., 1981. *Gewerkschaften in Krieg und Revolution. Arbeiterbewegung, Industrie, Staat und Militär in Deutschland 1914–1920*, 2 vols. Hamburg: Hans Christians Verlag.

Birnbaum, P., 1988. *State and Collective Action: The European Experience*. Cambridge: Cambridge University Press.

Birnbaum, P., and B. Badie, 1982. *Sociologie de l'Etat*. Paris: Grasset.

Biucchi, B. M., 1976–1977. *Switzerland, 1700–1914*. In Cipolla (1976–1977: 627–655).

Blackbourn, D., and G. Eley, 1984. *The Peculiarities of German History*. Oxford: Oxford University Press.

Blackmer, D., and S. Tarrow, eds., 1975. *Communism in Italy and France*. Princeton: Princeton University Press.

Blainpain, R., ed., 1987. *International Encyclopedia for Labour Law and Industrial Relations*. Deventer, The Netherlands: Kluwer.

Blumer, H., 1960. Early Industrialism and the Labouring Class. *The Sociological Quarterly* 1: 5–14.

Bobbio, N., 1994. *Destra e sinistra. Ragioni e significati di una distinzione politica*. Rome: Donzelli.

Bomsdor, E., 1981. *The Distribution of Power in Specific Decision-Making Bodies*. In Holler (1981: 283–288).

Bonham, J., 1953. *The Middle Class Vote*. London: Faber and Faber.

Borre, O., 1980. *The Social Bases of Danish Electoral Behaviour*. In Rose (1980: 241–282).

Bosio, G., 1951. La diffusione degli scritti di Marx e di Engels in Italia dal 1871 al 1892. *Società* 7: 268–284, 444–477.

Boudon, R., 1979. *Déterministes sociaux et liberté individuelle*. In *Effets perverses et ordre social*. Paris: Presses Universitaires de France, 187–252.

Bourquelot, F., 1972. *Les salariés agricoles et leurs organisations*. In Tavernier, Gervais, and Servolin (1972: 533–556).

Bowditch, J., 1951. *The Concept of Elan Vital: A Rationalisation of Weakness*. In Earle (1951: 32–43).

Braunthal, J., 1945ff. *Yearbook of the International Socialist Labour Movement*. Amsterdam: Socialist International.

Breitmen, R., 1981. *German Socialism and Weimar Democracy*. Chapel Hill: University of North Carolina Press.

Breuilly, J., 1985. Liberalism or Social Democracy. A Comparison of British and German Labour Politics c. 1850–1875. *European History Quarterly* 15: 3–42.

—— 1992. *Labour and Liberalism in Nineteenth Century Europe: Essays in Comparative History*. Manchester: Manchester University Press.

Brezzi, C., 1979. *I partiti democratici cristiani in Europa*. Milan: Teti.

Brown, B., 1969. The French Experience of Modernization. *World Politics* 21: 366–391.

Brunn, N., 1991. *Law and Society in the Global Village: Toward Collaboration and Comparative Research*. Helsinki: Swedish School of Economics and Business Administration.

Bruschi, A., and M. Pacini, 1978. *Indagine sulle cultura politiche in Italia*. Turin: Fondazione Agnelli.

Bücher, K., ed., 1903. *Die Großstadt*. Dresden: von Zahn und Jaensch.

Buell, R. L., 1920. *Contemporary French Politics*. New York: Appleton.

Buiting, H., 1990. *The Netherlands*. In Linden and Rojahn (1990: 57–84).

Bull, E., 1922. Die Entwicklung der Arbeiterbewegung in den drei skandinavischen Ländern 1914–1920. *Archiv für die Geschichte des Sozialismus und der Arbeiterbewegung* 10: 329–361.

Büsch, O., ed., 1980. *Wählerbewegung in der Europäischen Geschichte*. Berlin: Colloquium Verlag.

Butler, D., 1990. *Electoral Reform and Political Strategy in Britain*. In Noiret (1990b: 451–463).

Butler, D., and J. Cornford, 1969. *United Kingdom*. In Meyriat and Rokkan (1969: 330–351).

Butler, D., and D. Stokes, 1970. *Political Change in Britain*. London: Macmillan.

Callesen, G., 1990. *Denmark*. In Linden and Rojahn (1990: 131–160).

Campbell, P., 1958. *French Electoral Systems and Elections 1789–1957*. London: Faber.

Cannarsa, S., 1950. *Il socialismo ed i XXV congressi nazionali del Partito Socialista Italiano*. Florence: Società Editrice Avanti!.

Caracciolo, A., 1957. *Stato e società civile. Problemi della unificazione italiana*. Turin: Einaudi.

Carlson, B., 1969. *Trade Unions in Sweden*. Stockholm: Tidens Förlag.

Carocci, G., 1975. *Storia d'Italia dall'unità ad oggi*. Milan: Feltrinelli.

Cartiglia, C., 1976. *Rinaldo Rigola e il sindacalismo riformista in Italia*. Milan: Feltrinelli.

Casertano, A., 1911. *Il diritto di voto*. Naples: Pierro.

Castairs, A., 1980. *A Short History of Electoral Systems in Western Europe*. London: Allen & Unwin.

Castles, F. G., 1977. *Scandinavian Social Democracy: Achievements and Origins*. Berlin: ECPR.

—— 1978. *The Social Democratic Image of Society: A Study of the Achievements and Origins of Scandinavian Social Democracy in Comparative Perspective*. London: Routledge & Kegan Paul.

—— ed., 1982. *The Impact of Parties: Politics and Policies in Democratic Capitalist States*. London: Sage.

Cazzola, F., 1970. *Il partito come organizzazione; Studio di un caso – il PSI*. Rome: Edizioni del Tritone.

Cella, G. P., and T. Treu, eds. 1989. *Relazioni industriali: Manuale per l'analisi dell'esperienza italiana*. Bologna: Il Mulino.

Cervelli, I., 1978. *La Germania dell'800. Un caso di modernizzazione conservatrice*. Rome: Editori Riuniti.

Charlot, J., ed., 1973. *Quand la gauche peut gagner . . . Les élections législatives des 4–11 mars 1973*. Paris: Editions Alain Moreau.

Chehabi, H. E., and A. Stepan, eds., 1995. *Politics, Society, and Democracy: Comparative Studies*. Boulder, CO: Westview Press.

Chubb, B., 1974. *The Government and Politics of Ireland*. London: Oxford University Press.

Cipolla, C. M., 1969. *Literacy and Development in the West*. London: Penguin Books.

ed., 1976–1977. *The Emergence of Industrial Society. The Fontana Economic History of Europe*, Vol. 4. Hassocks, Sussex, England: Harvester Press/New York: Barnes & Noble.

Clapham, J. H., 1936. *Economic Development of France and Germany 1815–1915*. London: Cambridge University Press.

Clark, M., 1977. *Antonio Gramsci and the Revolution That Failed*. New Haven: Yale University Press.

Clarke, P., and J. Q. Wilson, 1961. Incentive Systems: A Theory of Organizations. *Administrative Science Quarterly* 6: 126–166.

Clarke, P. F., 1971. *Lancashire and the New Liberalism*. Cambridge: Cambridge University Press.

Cofrancesco, D., 1990. *Sinistra*. In *Grande Dizionario Enciclopedico*, 4th ed., Vol. 18: 883–884. Turin: UTET.

Cole, G. H. D., 1954. *Socialist Thought: Marxism and Anarchism 1850–1890*. London: Macmillan.

Coleman, J. C., 1965a. *Education and Political Development*. Princeton: Princeton University Press.

1965b. *Education and Political Development*. In Coleman (1965a: 3–32).

Colletti, L., 1972. *Bernstein e il marxismo della Seconda Internazionale*. In *Ideologia e società*. Bari: Laterza, 61–147.

Committee on Financing of Political Parties, 1976. *Report*. London: Her Majesty's Stationery Office.

Commons, J., 1962. Labor Movements. In *Encyclopaedia of the Social Sciences*. New York: Macmillan, Vol. 8: 681–685.

Congrès de Tours (décembre 1920). Naissance du parti communiste. Edition critique des principaux débats, 1964. Paris: René Juillard.

Converse, P. E., and E. Pierce, 1986. *Political Representation in France*. Cambridge, MA: Belknap Press of Harvard University Press.

Converse, P. E., and H. Valen, 1971. Dimensions of Cleavage and Perceived Party Distances in Norwegian Voting. *Scandinavian Political Studies* 6: 107–152.

Conway, M. M., and F. B. Fiegert, 1968. Motivations, Incentive Systems and the Political Party Organization. *American Political Science Review* 62: 667–676.

Cornford, J., 1964. *The Adoption of Mass Organization by the British Conservative Party*. In Allardt and Littunen (1964: 400–424).

Correspondance Friedrich Engels et Paul et Laura Lafargue, 1868–1895, 1956. Paris: Editions Sociales.

Cortesi, L., 1973. *Le origini del PCI. Il PSI dalla guerra di Libia alla scissione di Livorno*. Bari: Laterza.

Crewe, I., and A. King, 1995. *The Birth, Life and Death of the Social Democratic Party*. Oxford: Oxford University Press.

Criddle, B., 1977. *The French Parti Socialiste*. In Paterson and Thomas (1977: 25–66).

Croce, B., 1938. *Come nacque e come morì il marxismo teorico in Italia*. Rome: Laterza.

Cronin, J. E., 1980. Labor Insurgency and Class Formation: Comparative Perspectives on the Crisis 1917–1920 in Europe. *Social Science History* 4: 125–152.

Crouch, C., 1993. *Industrial Relations and European State Traditions*. Oxford: Oxford University Press.

Daalder, H., 1966a. *Parties, Elites, and Political Developments in Western Europe*. In La Palombara and Weiner (1966: 43–77).

1966b. *The Netherlands: Opposition in a Segmented Society*. In Dahl (1966a: 188–236).

1967. *Cabinet–Parliament Relations and Party Systems*, unpublished manuscript.

1973. *Building Consociational Nations*. In Eisenstadt and Rokkan (1973: 4–31).

1981. *Consociationalism, Center, and Periphery in the Netherlands*. In Torsvik (1981: 181–240).

ed., 1987a. *Party Systems in Denmark, Austria, Switzerland, the Netherlands and Belgium*. London: Frances Pinter.

1987b. *The Dutch Party System: From Segmentation to Polarization – and Then*. In Daalder (1987a: 193–284).

1990. *Ancient and Modern Pluralism in the Netherlands*: Harvard University: Center for European Studies, Working Paper Series No. 22.

1995. *Paths Towards State Formation in Europe: Democratization, Bureacratization and Politicization*. In Chehabi and Stepan (1995: 113–130).

Daalder, H., and G. A. Irwin, eds., 1989. *Politics in the Netherlands. How Much Change?* London: Frank Cass.

Daalder, H., and P. Mair, eds., 1983. *Western European Party Systems: Continuity and Change*. London: Sage.

Daalder, H., and C. J. M. Schuyt, eds., 1986. *Compendium voor politiek en samenleving in Nederland*. Brussels: Samsom Uitgeverij bv Alphen aan den Rijn.

Dahl, R. A., ed., 1966a. *Political Opposition in Western Democracies*. New Haven: Yale University Press.

1966b. *Some Explanations*. In Dahl (1966a: 448–486).

1971. *Polyarchy, Participation and Opposition*. New Haven: Yale University Press.

Dalton, R. J., P. A. Beck, and S. C. Flanagan, 1984. *Electoral Change in Advanced Industrial Democracies*. In Dalton, Flanagan, and Beck (1984: 3–22).

Dalton, R. J., S. C. Flanagan, and P. A. Beck, eds., 1984. *Electoral Change in Industrial Democracies: Realignment or Dealignment?* Princeton: Princeton University Press.

Damgaard, E., ed., 1992. *Parliamentary Change in the Nordic Countries*. Oslo: Scandinavian University Press.

De Bakker, B., and M. Claeys-Van Haegendoren, 1973. The Socialist Party in the Party System and in Organized Socialism in Belgium. *Res Publica* 15: 237–247.

De Fraja, G., 1988. *Il potere dei partiti italiani. Politeia* 3: 11–17.

De Kiriaki, A. S., 1885. *Della riforma elettorale. Saggio di diritto costituzionale e legislazione comparata*. Rome: Forzano.

De Sanctis, F., 1876. *Viaggio elettorale. Un racconto*. Naples: Morano.

Delruelle, N., R. Evalenko, and W. Fraeys, 1970. *Le comportement politique des électeurs belges*. Brussels: Institut de Sociologie de l' Université Libre de Bruxelles.

Delsinne, L., 1936. *Le mouvement syndical en Belgique*. Brussels: Castaigne.

Dent, M., 1993. The Case for an Electoral Pact between Labour and the Liberal Democrats. *Political Quarterly* 64: 243–251.

Derry, T. K., 1968. *A Short History of Norway*, 2nd ed., London: George Allen & Unwin.

Detti, T., 1972. *Serrati e la formazione del PCI. Storia della frazione terzinternazionalista 1921–1924.* Rome: Editori Riuniti.

Deutsch, K., 1961. Social Mobilization and Political Development. *American Political Science Review* 55: 493–502.

Dewachter, W., 1976. *Politieke Sociologie.* Leuven: Leuven University Press.

     1987. *Changes in the Belgian Party System Since World War Two.* In Daalder (1987a: 311–330).

Diani, M., and R. Eyerman, eds., 1992. *Studying Collective Action.* London: Sage.

Dogan, M., 1960. *Le vote ouvrier en Europe Occidentale. Revue Française de Sociologie* 1: 25–44.

     1967. *Political Cleavages and Social Stratification in France and Italy.* In Lipset and Rokkan (1967: 129–196).

Dommanget, M., 1969. *L'introduction du marxisme en France.* Lausanne: Editions Rencontre.

Dovring, F., 1964. *The Share of Agriculture in a Growing Population.* In Eicher and Witt (1964: 78–98).

Droz, J., 1972. *Socialisme et syndicalisme de 1914 à 1939.* Paris: Centre de Documentation Universitaire.

     1973. *Einfluss der deutschen Sozialdemokratie auf den französischen Sozialismus (1871–1914).* Opladen: Westdeutscher Verlag.

Drucker, H., ed., 1979. *Multi-Party Britain.* London: Macmillan.

Dubofsky, M., 1966. The Origins of Western Working Class Radicalism, 1850–1905. *Labor History* 7: 131–154.

Dupeux, G., 1964. *La société française 1789–1960.* Paris: Colin.

Durkheim, E., 1958. *The Suicide.* Glencoe, IL: Free Press. (1930. *Le suicide.* Paris: Presses Universitaires de France).

Duveau, G., 1946. *La vie ouvrière en France sous le Second Empire.* Paris: Gallimard.

Duverger, M., 1967 (1st ed., 1956). *Les partis politiques.* Paris: Colin.

     1986. *Les régimes semi-présidentiels.* Paris: Presses Universitaires de France.

Earle, E. M., ed., 1951. *Modern France: Problems of the Third and Fourth Republics.* Oxford: Oxford University Press.

Easton, D., 1990. *The Analysis of Political Structures.* London: Routledge.

Ebbinghaus, B., 1992. *The Transformation of Cleavage Structures in Western European Trade Union Systems: Can We Draw Union Diversity in Rokkan's Conceptual Map?* Limerick: ECPR.

Eckstein, H., 1966. *Division and Cohesion in Democracy: A Study of Norway.* Princeton.: Princeton University Press.

Ehrmann, H. W., 1952. French Peasants and Communism. *American Political Science Review* 46: 19–43.

Eicher, C., and L. Witt, eds., 1964. *Agriculture in Economic Development.* New York: McGraw-Hill.

Eisenstadt, S. N., 1966. *Modernization, Protest and Change.* Englewood Cliffs, NJ: Prentice-Hall.

Eisenstadt, S. N., and S. Rokkan, eds., 1973. *Building States and Nations: Models and Data Resources.* London: Sage.

Elklit, J., 1980. *Election Laws and Electoral Behaviour in Denmark until 1920.* In Büsch (1980: 366–396).

Elvander, N., 1977. *Scandinavian Social Democracy: Present Trends and Future Prospects.* Berlin: ECPR.

Engelmann, F. C., 1966. *Austria: The Pooling of Opposition.* In Dahl (1966a: 260–283).

Epstein, L. D., 1967. *Political Parties in Western Democracies.* New York: Praeger.

Esping Andersen, G., 1990. *The Three Worlds of Welfare Capitalism.* New York: Polity Press.

Evans, P. B., D. Rueschemeyer, and T. Skocpol, eds., 1985. *Bringing the State Back In.* Cambridge: Cambridge University Press.

Fabbri, M., 1991. Governo e sovrano nell'Italia liberale. *Rivista Trimestrale di Scienza dell'Amministrazione* no. 3: 103–186.

Farrell, B., 1970. Labour and the Irish Political Party System: A Suggested Approach to Analysis. *The Economic and Social Review* 1: 477–502.

1971. *The Founding of Dáil Eireann.* Dublin: Gill & Macmillan.

Ferner, A., and R. Hyman, 1992. *Italy: Between Political Exchange and Micro-Corporatism.* In Hyman and Ferner (1992: 524–560).

Ferrera, M., 1993. *Modelli di solidarietà. Politica e riforme sociali nelle democrazie.* Bologna: Il Mulino.

Finer, S. E., 1970. *Comparative Government.* London: Allen and Lane.

Fischer, H., ed., 1974. *Das politische System Österreichs.* Vienna: Europa Verlag.

Fleiner-Gerstern, T., 1987. Le conseil Fédéral: Directoire de la Confédération. *Pouvoirs* no. 43: 49–63.

Flora, P., 1973. *Historical Processes of Social Mobilisation: Urbanisation and Literacy 1850–1965.* In Eisenstadt and Rokkan (1973: 213–258).

1974. *Modernisierungforschung. Zur empirischen Analyse der gesellschaftlichen Entwicklung.* Opladen: Westdeutscher Verlag.

Flora, P., and J. Alber, 1981. *Modernization, Democratization, and the Development of Welfare States in Western Europe.* In Flora and Heidenheimer (1981: 37–80).

Flora, P., J. Alber, R. Eichenberg, J. Kohl, F. Kraus, W. Pfenning, and K. Seebohm, 1987. *State, Economy, and Society in Western Europe 1815–1875. A Data Handbook.* Vol. 2: *The Growth of Industrial Societies and Capitalist Economies.* Frankfurt: Campus Verlag.

Flora, P., R. Eichenberg, J. Kohl, F. Kraus, W. Pfenning, and K. Seebohm, 1983. *State, Economy and Society in Western Europe 1815–1975: A Data Handbook.* Vol. 1: *The Growth of Mass Democracies and Welfare States.* Frankfurt: Campus Verlag.

Flora P., and A. J. Heidenheimer, eds., 1981. *The Development of Welfare States in Europe and America.* New Brunswick, NJ: Transaction Books.

Fourastié, J., 1963. *Le grand espoir du XXème siècle.* Paris: Gallimard.

Foverskov, P., and L. N. Johansen, 1978. *The Socialist and Communist Parties in Denmark in a Century: History, Programs and Policy.* Unpublished paper.

Frey, B. S., 1968. Eine spieltheoretische Analyse der Machtverteilung im schweizerischen Bundesrat. *Schweizerische Zeitschrift für Volkswirtschaft und Statistik* 104: 155–169.

Fulcher, J., 1991. *Labour Movements, Employers, and the State.* Oxford: Clarendon.

Gaborit, P., 1972. *Le PCF et les paysans.* In Tavernier, Gervais, and Servolin (1972: 197–222).

Gagel, W., 1958. *Die Wahlrechtsfrage in der Geschichte der deutschen liberalen Parteien, 1848–1918.* Düsseldorf: Droste.

Galante Garrone, A., 1973. *I radicali in Italia 1849–1925.* Milan: Garzanti.

Galenson, W., 1949. *Labour in Norway.* Cambridge, MA: Harvard University Press.

    ed., 1952a. *Comparative Labor Movements.* New York: Prentice-Hall.

    1952b. *Scandinavia.* In Galenson (1952a: 104–172).

    1952c. *The Danish System of Labor Relations.* New York: Russell & Russell.

Gallagher, M., 1982. *The Irish Labour Party in Transition 1957–1982.* Manchester: Manchester University Press.

Galli, G., ed., 1968. *Il comportamento elettorale in Italia:* Bologna: Il Mulino.

    ed., 1976a. *Esperienze riformiste in Europa. Il socialismo tra il 1918 e il 1934.* Naples: Morano.

    1976b. *Storia del Partito Comunista Italiano.* Milan: Il Formichiere.

Garbani, P., and J. Schmid, 1980. *Le syndicalisme suisse. Histoire politique de l'Union Syndicale 1880–1980.* Lausanne: Editions d'en Bas.

Gass, S. 1988. *Les débuts du Parti Socialiste Suisse, 1870–1890.* In *Cent Ans de PSS 1888–1988.* Lausanne: Editions d'en Bas.

Geary, D., 1981. *European Labour Protest 1848–1939.* New York: St. Martin's Press.

    ed., 1989. *Labour and Socialist Movements in Europe Before 1914.* Oxford: Berg.

Gehmacher, E., 1974. *Faktoren des Wählerverhaltens.* In Fischer (1974: 55–75).

Gerlich, P., 1987. *Consociationalism to Competition: The Austrian Party System since 1945.* In Daalder (1987a: 61–106).

Gerlich, P., and W. Müller, eds., 1983. *Zwischen Koalition und Konkurrenz. Österreichs Parteien seit 1945.* Vienna: Braunmüller.

Gerschenkron, A., 1962. *Backwardness in Historical Perspective.* Cambridge, MA: Harvard University Press.

Giddens, A., 1973. *The Class Structure of Advanced Societies.* London: Hutchinson.

Gilissen, J., 1980. *Die Entwicklung des Wahlrechts im Benelux-Raum, 1814 bis 1922.* In Büsch (1980: 338–365).

Girod, R., 1964. Le système des partis en Suisse. *Revue Française de Science Politique* 14: 1114–1133.

Goetschy, J., and P. Rozenblatt, 1992. *France: The Industrial Relations System at a Turning Point?* In Hyman and Ferner (1992: 404–444).

Goguel, F., 1950. *Les partis politiques en France.* In *Encyclopédie Politique de la France et du Monde.* Paris: Editions de l'Encyclopédie Coloniale et Maritime: 271–359.

    1969. *Modernization économique et comportement politique.* Paris: Colin.

    1970. *Géographie des élections françaises sous la Troisième et la Quatrième République.* Paris: Colin.

Goldstein, R. L., 1983. *Political Repression in the Nineteenth Century.* London: Croom Helm.

Goldthorpe, J. H., D. Lockwood, F. Bechhofer, and J. Platt, 1971. *The Affluent Workers: Political Attitudes and Behaviour*. Cambridge, U.K.: Cambridge University Press.

Gratton, P., 1972. *Le mouvement ouvrier et la question agraire de 1870 à 1947*. In Tavernier, Gervais, and Servolin (1972: 111–136).

Graubard, S. R., ed., 1967. *A New Europe? A Timely Appraisal*. Boston: Beacon Press.

Gray, R., 1981. *The Aristocracy of Labour in Nineteenth Century Britain*. London: Studies in Economic and Social History.

Greene, E. N., ed., 1971. *European Socialism since World War I*. Chicago: Quadrangle Books.

Greene, T. H., 1971. The Electorate of Non-Ruling Communist Parties. *Studies in Comparative Communism* 4: 68–103.

——— 1973. Non-Ruling Communist Parties and Political Adaptation. *Studies in Comparative Communism* 6: 331–361.

Grisalberti, C., 1978. *Storia costituzionale d'Italia, 1848–1948*. Bari: Laterza.

Gruner, E., 1968. *Die Arbeit in der Schweiz*. Bern: Franche Verlag.

Gruner, E., 1977. *Die Parteien in der Schweitz*. Bern: Franche Verlag.

Guillermo, O., 1975. Evaluation of a Presidential Election Game. *American Political Science Review* 69: 947–953.

Haapakoski, P., 1974. Breznevism in Finland. *New Left Review* no. 86: 29–49.

Haerpfer, C., 1983. *Nationalrats wahlen und Wählverhalten 1945–1980*. In Gerlich and Müller (1983: 111–150).

Haerpfer, C., and E. Gemacher, 1984. Social Structure and Voting in the Austrian Party System. *Electoral Studies* 2: 25–46.

Halebsky, S., 1976. *Mass Society and Political Conflict: Toward a Reconstruction of Theory*. Cambridge: Cambridge University Press.

Halévy, D., 1995 (1st ed., 1935). *Visites aux paysans du centre: 1907–1934*. Paris: Hachette.

Hall, A., 1977. *Scandals, Sensation and Social Democracy: The SPD Press in Wilhelmine Germany, 1890–1914*. Cambridge: Cambridge University Press.

Hamilton, R. F., 1967. *Affluence and the French Worker in the Fourth Republic*. Princeton: Princeton University Press.

Hartenstein, W., and K. Liepelt, 1962. *Party Members and Party Voters in West Germany*. In Rokkan (1962: 43–52).

Harvey, G.-J., 1989. *Storia dell'alfabetizzazione occidentale*, 3 vols. Bologna: Il Mulino.

Hattam, V. C., 1992. *Institutions and Political Change: Working-Class Formation in England and the United States*. In Steinmo, Thelen, and Lomgstreth (1992: 153–187).

Heath, A., R. Jowell, and J. Curtice, 1985. *How Britain Votes*. Oxford: Pergamon Press.

Heidar, K., 1977. *The Norwegian Labour Party: Social Democracy in a Periphery of Europe*. In Paterson and Thomas (1977: 292–315).

Henig S., and J. Pinder, eds., 1969. *European Political Parties*. London: Allen & Unwin/PEP.

Hildebrandt, K., and R. J. Dalton, 1978. *The New Politics: Political Change or Sunshine Politics?* In Kaase and Von Beyme (1978: 69–96).

Hill, K., 1974. *Belgium: Political Change in a Segmented Society.* In Rose (1974: 29–108).

Hintze, O., 1962. *Soziologie und Geschichte Staat and Vefassung,* edited by G. Oestreich. Göttingen: Vandehhoeck and Ruprecht.

——— 1980. *Stato e società.* Bologna: Zanichelli.

Hirschmann, A., 1982. *Shifting Involvements: Private Interest and Public Action.* Oxford: Robertson.

Hobsbawm, E. J., ed., 1964a. *Labouring Men.* London: Weidenfeld and Nicholson.

——— 1964b. *The Labour Aristocracy in Nineteenth-Century Britain.* In Hobsbown (1964a: 272–315).

Hodgson, H. J., 1967. *Communism in Finland: A History and Interpretation.* Princeton: Princeton University Press.

——— 1973. Finnish Communists and the Opportunism of Conciliation. *Studies in Comparative Communism* 6: 397–404.

Hoffman, S., 1974. *The Rulers: Heroic Leadership in Modern France.* In *Decline or Renewal? France since the 1930s.* New York: Viking Press: 63–110.

Holler, M. J., ed., 1981. *Power, Voting, and Voting Power.* Würzburg: Physica-Verlag.

Holler, M. J., and J. Kellermann, 1977. Power in the European Parliament: What Will Change? *Quality and Quantity* 11: 189–192.

Holton, R. J., 1985. *Revolutionary Syndicalism and the British Labour Movement.* In Mommsen and Husong (1985: 266–282).

Horowitz, D. L., 1976. *Storia del movimento sindacale in Italia.* Bologna: Il Mulino.

Houska, J. J., 1985. *Influencing Mass Political Behavior: Elites and Political Subcultures in the Netherlands and Austria.* Berkeley: Institute of International Studies, University of California.

Huard, R., 1991. *Le suffrage universel en France.* Paris: Aubier.

——— 1996. *La naissance du parti politique en France.* Paris: Presses de la Fondation Nationale des Sciences Politiques.

Huntington, S. P., 1968. *Political Order in Changing Societies.* New Haven: Yale University Press.

Hurtig, S., 1971. *De la SFIO au nouveau parti socialiste.* Paris: Colin.

Hyman, R., and A. Ferner, eds., 1992. *Industrial Relations and the New Europe.* Oxford: Blackwell.

Inglehart, R., 1977. *The Silent Revolution: Changing Values and Political Styles Among Western Publics.* Princeton: Princeton University Press.

——— 1984. *The Changing Cleavage Structure of Political Cleavages in Western Society.* In Dalton, Flanagan, and Beck (1984: 25–69).

Irwin, G. A., and J. J. M. Holsteyn, 1989. *Decline of the Structured Model of Competition.* In Daalder and Irwin (1989: 21–39).

Jollivert, M., 1972. *Sociétés rurales et classes sociales.* In Tavernier, Gervais, and Servolin (1972: 79–106).

Jost, H. U., 1967. Politisches System und Wahlsystem der Schweiz unter dem Aspekt von Integration und Legitimität. *Schweizerisches Jahrbuch für Politische Wissenschaft* 16: 203–219.

Joyce, P., 1980. *Work, Society, and Politics: The Culture of the Factory in Late Victorian England.* New Brunswick, NJ: Rutgers University Press.

Judt, T. R., 1976. *La reconstruction du parti socialiste 1921–1926*. Paris: Presses de la FNSP.

    1979. *Socialism in Provence 1871–1914. A Study in the Origins of the Modern French Left*. Cambridge: Cambridge University Press.

Jutikkala, E., and K. Pirinen, 1962. *A History of Finland*. London: Thames and Hudson.

Kaase, M., and K. Von Beyme, eds., 1978. *Elections and Parties: Socio-Political Change and Participation in the West German Federal Elections of 1976*. London: Sage.

Kaelble, H. *Was Prometheus Most Unbound in Europe? Labor Force in Europe during the late 19th and 20th Century*. Unpublished manuscript.

Kahn-Freund, O., 1972. *Labour and the Law*. London: Stevens.

Kalivas, S. N., 1996. *The Rise of Christian Democracy in Europe*. Ithaca, NY: Cornell University Press.

Kassalow, E. M., ed., 1963. *National Labor Movements in the Post-War World*. Evanston, IL: Northwestern University Press.

Katz, R., 1990. Party as Linkage: A Vestigial Function? *European Journal of Political Research* 18: 143–161.

Katz, R., and P. Mair, eds., 1992. *Party Organization: A Data Handbook*. London: Sage.

Katzenstein, P., 1984. *Corporatism and Change: Austria, Switzerland and the Politics of Industry*. Ithaca, NY: Cornell University Press.

Katznelson, I., 1985. *Working-Class Formation and the State: Nineteenth-Century England in American Perspective*. In Evans, Rueschemeyer, and Skocpol (1985: 257–284).

    1986. *Working Class Formation: Constructing Cases and Comparisons*. In Katznelson and Zolberg (1986: 3–41).

Katznelson, I., and A. R. Zolberg, eds., 1986. *Working Class Formation in Western Europe and the United States*. Princeton: Princeton University Press.

Kautsky, K., 1899. *Bernstein und das Sozialdemokratische Programm: Eine Antikritik*. Berlin: Dietz.

Keman, H., 1988. *The Development Toward Surplus Welfare: Social Democratic Politics and Policies in Advanced Capitalist Democracies (1965–1984)*. Amsterdam: CT Press.

Kendall, W., 1975. *The Labour Movement in Europe*. London: Allen Lane.

Kergoat, J., 1990. *France*. In Linden and Rojahn (1990: 163–190).

Kerr, H., 1974. *Switzerland: Social Cleavages and Partisan Conflict*. London: Sage.

    1987. *The Swiss Party System: Steadfast and Changing*. In Daalder (1987a: 107–192).

Kirby, D., 1971. *The Finnish Social Democratic Party 1903–1918*. London: Ph.D. thesis, London University.

    1986. The Workers' Cause: Rank and File Attitudes in the Finnish Social Democratic Party 1905–1918. *Past and Present* no. 111: 144–164.

    1990. *Finland*. In Linden and Rojahn (1990: 523–540).

Kirchheimer, O., 1965. Confining Conditions and Revolutionary Breakthroughs. *American Political Science Review* 61: 964–974.

    1966a. *Germany: The Vanishing Opposition*. In Dahl (1966a: 237–259).

1966b. *The Transformation of Western European Party Systems*. In La Palombara and Weiner (1966: 177–200).

Kitschelt, H., 1994. *The Transformation of European Social Democracy*. Cambridge: Cambridge University Press.

Kittell, A. K., 1973. Socialist versus Catholic in Belgium: The Role of Anticlericalism in the Development of the Belgian Left. *The Historian* 23: 418–435.

Klenner, F., 1951. *Die Österreichischen Gewerkschaften*, Vol. 1. Vienna: Verlag des ÖGB.

Knoellinger, C. E., 1960. *Labor in Finland*. Cambridge, MA: Harvard University Press.

Knopp, K., 1980. *Austrian Social Democracy 1889–1914*. Washington, DC: University Press of America.

Kocka, J., 1989a. *Borghesia e società borghese nel XIX secolo. Sviluppi europei e peculiarità tedesche*. In Kocka (1989b: 3–67).

    ed., 1989b. *Borghesie Europee del'ottocento*. Venice: Marsilio Editori.

Koeble, H., 1989. *Borghesia francese e borghesia tedesca. 1870–1914*. In Kocka (1989b: 127–159).

Koole, R. A., and G. Voerman, 1986. *Het Lidmaatschap van Politieke Partijen na 1945*. In *Jaarboek 1985*. Groningen: Documentatiecentrum Nederlandse Politieke: 115–176.

Kornhauser, W., 1959. *The Politics of Mass Society*. New York: Free Press.

Korpi, W., 1971. Working Class Communism in Western Europe: Rational or Non-rational. *American Sociological Review* 36: 971–984.

    1983. *The Democratic Class Struggle*. London: Routledge and Kegan Paul.

Kossmann, E. H., 1978. *The Low Countries 1780–1940*. Oxford: Clarendon Press.

Kriegel, A., 1969. *Aux origines du communisme français. Contribution à l'histoire du mouvement ouvrier français*. Paris: Flammarion.

    1973. *Le internazionali operaie (1864–1943)*. Messina and Florence: D'Anna.

    1974. *La crise révolutionnaire (1919–1920): Hypothèses pour la construction d'un modèle'*. In *Communismes au miroir francais. Temps, cultures et sociétés en France devant le communisme*. Paris: Gallimard.

Kriesi, H., 1990. Federalism and Pillarization: The Netherlands and Switzerland Compared. *Acta Politica* 25: 433–450.

Kuhnle, S., 1978. The Beginning of the Nordic Welfare States: Similarities and Differences. *Acta Sociologica Supplement* 21: 9–35.

La Martine, de A., 1895. *Histoire des Girondins*, 4 vols. Paris: Furre.

Lafferty, W., 1971. *Economic Development and the Response of Labor in Scandinavia: A Multi-Level Analysis*. Oslo: Universitetsforlaget.

    1972. Industrialisation and Labor Radicalism in Norway: An Ecological Analysis. *Scandinavian Political Studies* 7: 157–175.

    1974. *Industrialisation, Community Structure and Socialism: An Ecological Analysis of Norway 1875–1924*. Oslo: Universitetsforlaget.

Landauer, C., 1959. *European Socialism*, 2 vols. Berkeley: University of California Press.

    1961. The Guesdists and the Small Farmer: Early Erosion of French Marxism. *International Review of Social History* 6: 212–225.

Landes, D. S., 1969. *The Unbound Prometheus: Technological Change and Industrial*

Development in Western Europe from 1750 to the Present. Cambridge, UK: Cambridge University Press.

Landsberger, H., ed., 1970. *The Church and Social Change in Latin America*. Notre Dame, IN: University of Notre Dame Press.

Lane, J.-E., and P. Pennings, eds., 1998. *Party System Change*. London: Routledge.

Lane, R. E., 1959. *Political Life: Why People Get Involved in Politics*. New York: Free Press.

Lange, P., 1977. La teoria degli incentivi e l'analisi dei partiti politici. *Rassegna Italiana di Sociologia* 18: 501–526.

La Palombara, J., and M. Weiner, eds., 1966. *Political Parties and Political Development*. Princeton: Princeton University Press.

Laponce, L. A., 1981. *Left and Right: The Topography of Political Perceptions*. Toronto: University of Toronto Press.

Laski, H. J., 1919. *Authority in the Modern State*. New Haven: Yale University Press.

Laulajainen, P., 1979. Some Aspects of the Division of the Finnish Working Class Movement after the Civil War: A Research Note. *Scandinavian Political Studies* 2: 53–63.

Lavau, G., 1968. A la recherche d'un cadre théorique pour l'étude du PCF. *Revue Française de Science Politique* 18: 445–466.

Lawson, K., ed., 1980. *Political Parties and Linkage: A Comparative Perspective*. New Haven: Yale University Press.

Lazarsfeld, P. F., B. Berelson, and H. Gaudet, 1948. *The People's Choice*. New York: Columbia University Press.

Lefranc, G., 1963. *Le mouvement socialiste sous la IIIe République 1875–1940*. Paris: Payot.

Legendre, P., 1968. *Histoire de l'administration de 1780 à nos jours*. Paris: Presses Universitaires de France.

Lehmbruch, G., 1966. *Proporzdemokratie*. Tübingen: Mohr.

Leichter, O., 1964. *Glanz und Elend der Ersten Republik*. Vienna: Europa Verlag.

Lenin, V. I., 1939. *Imperialism: The Highest Stage of Capitalism*. New York: International Publishers.

Leonard, D., 1975. *Paying for Parties: The Case of Public Subsidies*. London: Political and Economic Planning.

Lepsius, R., 1973. *Parteien und Sozialstruktur: Zum Problem der Demokratisierung der deutschen Gesellschaft*. In Ritter (1973: 56–80).

⸻ 1985. The Nation and Nationalism in Germany. *Social Research* 52: 43–64.

Lerner, D., 1957. The "Hard-Headed" Frenchman. *Encounter* 8: 27–32.

⸻ 1958. *The Passing of Traditional Societies: Modernizing the Middle East*. New York: Free Press.

Lévy-Leboyer, M., 1968. Le processus d'industrialisation: Le cas de l'Angleterre et de la France. *Revue Historique* n. 230: 281–298.

Lewin, L., 1988. *Ideology and Strategy: A Century of Swedish Politics*. Cambridge: Cambridge University Press.

Lewis-Beck, M. S., 1977. Explaining Peasant Conservatism: The Western European Case. *British Journal of Political Science* 7: 447–464.

Libbey, K. R., 1970. Initiatives, Referenda and Socialism in Switzerland. *Government and Opposition* 5: 307–326.

Lidtke, V. L., 1966. *The Outlawed Party: Social Democracy in Germany 1878–1890.* Princeton: Princeton University Press.

Liebman, M., 1979. *Les socialistes belges, 1885–1914. La révolte et l'organisation.* Brussels: Vie Ouvrière.

Ligou, D., 1962. *Histoire du socialisme en France: 1871–1961.* Paris: Presses Universitaires de France.

Lijphart, A., 1968. Typologies of Democratic Regimes. *Comparative Political Studies* 1: 3–44.

1971. Class Voting and Religious Voting in the European Democracies. *Acta Politica* 6: 158–171.

1979. Religious vs. Linguistic vs. Class Voting: The Crucial Experiment of Comparing Belgium, Canada, South Africa, and Switzerland. *American Political Science Review* 73: 442–458.

1984. *Democracies: Patterns of Majoritarian and Consensus Government in Twenty-One Countries.* New Haven: Yale University Press.

Lilja, K., 1992. *Finland: No Longer the Nordic Exception.* In Hyman and Ferner (1992: 198–217).

Lind, G., 1988. *Military State and Bourgeois Democracy.* In Stråth (1988a: 112–119).

Lindemann, A. S., 1974. *The "Red Years": European Socialism versus Bolshevism, 1919–1921.* Berkeley: University of California Press.

1977. *Socialismo europeo e bolscevismo (1919–1921).* Bologna: Il Mulino.

Linden, van der M., 1988. The National Integration of European Working Classes (1871–1914). *International Review of Social History* 33: 285–311.

Linden, van der M., and J. Rojahn, eds., 1990. *The Formation of Labour Movements, 1870–1914: An International Perspective.* Leiden: E. J. Brill.

Linz, J. J., 1959. *The Social Bases of German Politics.* Ph.D. thesis. New York: Columbia University.

1973. *Early State Building and Late Peripheral Nationalism Against the State: The Case of Spain.* In Eisenstadt and Rokkan (1973: 32–116).

1976. Patterns of Land Tenure, Division of Labor, and Voting Behavior in Europe. *Comparative Politics* 8: 365–412.

1979. Europe's Southern Frontier: Evolving Trends Toward What? *Daedalus* 108: 175–209.

Linz, J. J., and A. Stepan, eds., 1978. *The Breakdown of Democratic Regimes: Europe.* Baltimore: Johns Hopkins University Press.

Lipset, S. M., 1958. Socialism, Left, Right, East and West. *Confluence* 7: 173–192.

1959. Democracy and Working-Class Authoritarianism. *American Sociological Review* 24: 482–501.

1960. *Political Man.* New York: Doubleday.

1963. *Some Social Requisites of Democracy: Economic Development and Political Legitimacy.* In Polsby, Dentler, and Smith (1963: 541–569).

1964. The Changing Class Structure and Contemporary European Politics. *Daedalus* Winter: 271–303.

1966. *Elections: The Expression of Democratic Class Struggle.* In Bendix and Lipset (1966: 413–427).

1969. *Revolution and Counter-Revolution.* London: Heinemann.

1981. Whatever Happened to the Proletariat? An Historical Mission Unfulfilled. *Encounter* 56/6: 18–34.

1983. Radicalism or Reformism: The Sources of Working Class Politics. *International Political Science Review* 77: 1–18.

Lipset, S. M., and S. Rokkan, eds., 1967. *Party Systems and Voter Alignments*. New York: Free Press.

Logue, J., 1982. *Socialism and Abundance: Radical Socialism in the Danish Welfare State*. Minneapolis: University of Minnesota Press.

Lorwin, R. V., 1954. *The French Labour Movement*. Cambridge, MA: Harvard University Press.

1966. *Belgium, Religion, Class, and Language in National Politics*. In Dahl (1966a: 147–187).

ed., 1967a. *Labor and Working Conditions in Modern Europe*. London: Collier-Macmillan.

1967b. *Working Class Politics and Economic Development in Western Europe*. In Lorwin (1967a: 58–72).

1971. Segmented Pluralism, Ideological Cleavages and Political Cohesion in the Smaller European Democracies. *Comparative Politics* 3: 147–187.

Lowell, A. L., 1896. *Governments and Parties in Continental Europe*, 2 vols. Boston: Houghton Mifflin.

Lucas-Busemann, E., 1976. *Zwei Formen von Radikalismus in der deutschen Arbeiterbewegung*. Frankfurt am Main: Verlag Roter Stern.

Luebbert, G., 1991. *Liberalism, Fascism, or Social Democracy. Social Classes and the Political Origins of Regimes in Inter-war Europe*. Oxford: Oxford University Press.

Lukes, S., 1995. *What Is Left?* Florence: European University Institute, unpublished manuscript.

Lundquist, L., 1982. *The Party and the Masses: An Interorganisational Analysis of Lenin's Model for the Bolshevik Revolutionary Movement*. Stockholm: Almqvist & Wiksell International.

Luxemburg, R., 1899. *Sozialreform oder Revolution*. Leipzig: Buchdruckerei und Leipziger Volkszeitung.

1963. *Scritti scelti*, edited by L. Amodio. Milan: Edizioni "Avanti!."

MacCarthy, C., 1977. *Trade Unions in Ireland 1894–1960*. Dublin: Institute of Public Administration.

MacElligot, T. J., 1966. *Education in Ireland*. Dublin: Institute of Public Administration.

Mackie, T. T., and R. Rose, 1974. *The International Almanac of Electoral History*. London: Macmillan.

Mackintosh, J., 1977. *The British Cabinet*. London: Stevens and Sons.

MacRae, D., 1967. *Parliament, Parties and Society in France, 1946–1958*. New York: St. Martin's Press.

Madeley, J. T. S., 1977. Scandinavian Christian Democracy: Throwback or Portent? *European Journal of Political Research* 5: 267–286.

Maderthaner, W., and W. C., Müller, eds., 1996. *Die Organisation der österreichischen Sozialdemokratie 1889–1995*. Vienna: Löcker Verlag.

Mair, P., 1978. Labour and the Irish Party System Revisited: Party Competition in the 1920's. *Economic and Social Review* 9: 59–70.

1979. *The Marxist Left*. In Drucker (1979: 157–182).

1992. Explaining the Absence of Class Politics in Ireland. *Proceedings of the British Academy* 79: 383–410.

1997. *Party System Change*. Oxford: Oxford University Press.

Mair, P., and R. Katz, 1992. The Membership of Political Parties in European Democracies 1960–1990. *European Journal of Political Research* 22: 329–345.

Malefakis, E., 1974. *A Comparative Analysis of Worker Movements in Spain and Italy*. San Francisco: American Historical Association.

Mann, H., 1973. *Consciousness and Action among Western Working Class*. London: Macmillan.

1987. Ruling Class Strategies and Citizenship. *Sociology* 21: 339–354.

1993. *The Sources of Social Power*, Vol. 2: *The Rise of Classes and Nation-States, 1760–1914*. Cambridge: Cambridge University Press.

March, A. J. G., ed., 1965. *Handbook of Organization*. Chicago: Rand McNally College Publishing.

Markku, H., 1980. Dialectics between Occupation and Party Structures: Finland since World War II. *Acta Sociologica* 23: 83–96.

Marquand, D., 1981. *Classe, coalizione e Partito Laburista*. In Piro and Pombeni (1981: 166–176).

Marshall, T. H., 1965. *Class, Citizenship and Social Development*. New York: Anchor Books.

Martin, C., and D. Martin, 1977. The Decline of the Labour Party Membership. *Political Quarterly* 48: 459–471.

Martin, W., 1980 (1st ed., 1928). *Histoire de la Suisse*. Lausanne: Payot.

Martin, W. C., and K. Hopkins, 1980. *Cleavage Crystallization and Party Linkages in Finland, 1900–1918*. In Lawson (1980: 183–203).

Marx, K., 1973. *Il capitale*, 3 vols., *Prefazione*. Rome: Editori Riuniti. (1955–1956. *Capital: A Critique of Political Economy*, 3 vols. London: Lawrence and Wishart.)

Mastropaolo, A., 1980. *Electoral Processes, Political Behaviour, and Social Forces in Italy from the Rise of the Left to the Fall of Giolitti, 1876–1913*. In Büsch (1980: 97–124).

Matthew, C. H., R. I. McKibbin, and J. A. Kay, 1976. The Franchise Factor in the Rise of the Labour Party. *English Historical Review* 91: 723–752.

Mattl, S., 1990. *Austria*. In Linden and Rojahn (1990: 293–320).

McGrath, W. J., 1974. *Dionysian Art and Populist Politics in Austria*. New Haven: and London: Yale University Press.

McKenzie, R. T., and A. Silver, 1967. *The Delicate Experiment: Industrialism, Conservatism and Working-Class Tories*. In Lipset and Rokkan (1967: 115–125).

1968. *Angels of Marble: Working Class Conservatives in Urban England*. Chicago: University of Chicago Press.

McKibbin, R., 1984. Why Was There No Marxism in Great Britain? *English Historical Review* 99: 297–331.

Meyriat, J., and S. Rokkan, eds., 1969. *International Guide to Electoral Statistics. National Elections in Western Europe*. Paris: Mouton.

Micaud, C. A., 1955. The Bases of Communist Strength in France. *Western Political Quarterly* 8: 354–366.

Michelet, J., 1847–1853. *Histoire de la révolution française*. Paris: Chamerot.

Michels, R., 1906. Die Deutsche Sozialdemokratie. I. Parteimitgliederschaft und soziale Zusammensetzung. *Archiv für Sozialwissenschaft und Sozialpolitik.* Tübingen: Mohr, 471–556.

1949. *Political Parties: A Sociological Study of Oligarchical Tendencies of Modern Democracy.* Glencoe, IL: Free Press.

Milbrath, L. W., 1965. *Political Participation.* Chicago: Rand McNally.

Millen, B., 1963. *The Relationship of the Norwegian Labour Party to the Trade Unions.* In Kassalow (1963: 119–141).

Miller, D. R., 1973. A Shapley Value Analysis of the Proposed Canadian Constitutional Amendment Scheme. *Canadian Journal of Political Science* 6: 140–143.

Milward, A. S., and S. B. Saul, 1977. *The Development of the Economies of Continental Europe, 1850–1914.* London: Allen and Unwin.

Mintzel, A., 1990. *Political and Socio-economic Developments in the Post-war Era: The Case of Bavaria, 1945–1989.* In Rohe (1990a: 145–178).

Mitchell, A., 1965. *Revolution in Bavaria: The Eisner Regime and the Soviet Republic, 1918–1919.* Princeton: Princeton University Press.

1974. *Labour in Irish Politics, 1890–1930.* Dublin: Irish University Press.

Mitchell, B. R., 1975. *European Historical Statistics 1750–1975,* 2nd ed. London: Macmillan.

Mitchell, H., and P. Stearns, 1971. *Workers and Protest: The European Labor Movement, the Working Class, and the Origins of Social Democracy 1890–1914.* Ithaca, NY: Peacock.

Mitrany, D., 1951. *Marx Against the Peasants.* Chapel Hill: University of North Carolina Press.

Mommsen, H., 1979. Zum Problem der vergleichenden Behandlung nationaler Arbeiterbewegungen am Beispiel Ost–und Südosttmitteleuropas. *Internationale wissenschaftliche* Korrespondenz zur Geschicht 15: 31–34.

Mommsen, W., and H. G. Husong, eds., 1985. *The Development of Trade Unionism in Great Britain and Germany 1880–1914.* London: Allen and Unwin.

Moore, B. J., Jr., 1966. *Social Origins of Dictatorship and Democracy: Lords and Peasants in the Making of the Modern World.* Boston: Beacon Press.

1978. *Injustice. The Social Bases of Obedience and Revolt.* London: Macmillan.

Morandi, R., 1978 (1st. ed., 1945). *I partiti nella storia d'Italia.* Florence: Le Monnier.

Morgan, R., 1969. *The Federal Republic of Germany.* In Henig and Pinder (1969: 21–67).

Moses, J. A., 1982. *Trade Unionism in Germany from Bismarck to Hitler, 1869–1933.* London: George Prior.

Moulin, L., 1981. *Riflessioni su alcune particolarità del movimento operaio belga.* In Piro and Pombeni (1981: 192–202).

Murphy, J. A., 1975. *Ireland in the Twentieth Century.* Dublin: Gill and Macmillan.

Musson, A. E., 1972. *British Trade Unions 1800–1875.* London: Macmillan.

Mylly, J., 1984. *The Emergence of the Finnish Multi-Party System. A Comparison with Developments in Scandinavia, 1870–1920.* In Mylly and Berry (1984: 9–27).

Mylly, J., and R. M. Berry, eds., 1984. *Political Parties in Finland: Essays in History and Politics.* Turku, Finland: Grafia Oy.

Nedelmann, B., 1975. Handlungsraum politischer Organisationen. *Sozialwissenschaftliches Jahrbuch für Politik* 4: 9–118.

1987. Individuals and Parties: Changes in the Processes of Political Mobilisation. *European Sociological Review* 3: 181–202.

Neidhart, L., 1970. *Plebiszit und pluralitäre Demokratie. Eine Analyse der Funktion des schweizerischen Gesetzesreferendums*. Bern: Francke Verlag.

Nettl, P. J., 1967. *Political Mobilization*. New York: Basic Books.

1968. The State as a Conceptual Variable. *World Politics* 20: 560–592.

Neufeld, M., 1974. *Italy: School for Awakening Countries: The Italian Labour Movement in Its Political, Economic, and Social Setting from 1800–1960*. New York: Greenwood Press.

Neumann, S., ed., 1956a. *Modern Political Parties*. Chicago: University of Chicago Press.

1956b. *Toward a Comparative Study of Political Parties*. In Neumann (1956a: 395–421).

Niehuss, M., 1990. *Party Configurations in State and Municipal Elections in Southern Germany, 1871–1914*. In Rohe (1990a: 83–106).

Nieuwbeerta, P., 1995. *The Democratic Class Struggle in Twenty Countries 1945/1990*. Amsterdam: Thesis Publisher.

Nohlen, D., and R. O. Schultze, 1971. *Wahlen in Deutschland: Theorie – Geschichte– Dokumente, 1848–1970*. Berlin: Walter de Gruyter.

Noiret, S., 1990a. Partiti politici e sistema politico in Belgio (1830–1980). *Ricerche di storia politica* n. 5: 87–128.

ed., 1990b. *Political Strategies and Electoral Reforms: Origins of Voting Systems in Europe in the 19th and 20th Centuries*. Baden-Baden: Nomos Verlagsgesellschaft.

Noland, A., 1970. *The Founding of the French Socialist Party*. New York: Howard Fertig.

Nordlingler, E., 1972. *Conflict Regulation in Divided Societies*. Cambridge, MA: Harvard University Occasional Paper in International Affairs no. 29.

Nousiainen, J., 1960. *The Structure of the Finnish Political Parties*. In *Democracy in Finland: Studies in Politics and Government*. Helsinki: Finnish Political Science Association, 28–43.

Offe, C., 1972. *Strukturprobleme des kapitalistischen Staates: Aufsätzung zur politischen Soziologie*. Frankfurt: Suhrkamp.

Olson, M., 1963. Rapid Growth as a Destabilizing Force. *Journal of Economic History* 23: 529–552.

1971 (1st ed. 1965). *The Logic of Collective Action. Public Goods and the Theory of Groups*. Cambridge: Harvard University Press.

Olsson, S. E., 1990. *Social Policy and Welfare State in Sweden*. Stockholm: Archiv Förlag.

Orridge, A., 1975. The Irish Labour Party. *Journal of Common Market Studies* 13: 484–491.

Ostrogorski, M., 1970 (1st ed., 1902). *Democracy and the Organization of Political Parties*, 2 vols. New York, Haskell House.

Paloheimo, H., 1984. *Governments in Democratic Capitalist States 1950–1983. A Data Handbook*. Turku, Finland: Department of Sociology and Political Science, University of Turku Studies on Political Science no 8.

Panebianco, A., 1982. *Modelli di partito. Organizzazione e potere nei partiti politici.*
   Bologna: Il Mulino. (1988. A. *Political Parties: Organization and Power.*
   Cambridge: Cambridge University Press.)

Pappalardo, A., 1989. *I sindacati prefascisti. Ricostruzione e verifica di ipotesi.* Florence:
   Edizioni Polistampa.

Parkin, F., 1967. Working Class Conservatism: A Theory of Political Deviance.
   British Journal of Sociology 18: 278–290.

Parri, L., 1987. Staat und Gewerkschaften in der Schweiz (1873–1891). *Politische
   Vierteljahreschrift* 28: 35–58.

Paterson, W. E., 1977. *The German Social Democratic Party.* In Paterson and Thomas
   (1977: 176–212)

Paterson, W. E., and A. H. Thomas, eds., 1977. *Social Democratic Parties in Western
   Europe.* London: Croom Helm.

Pedersen, M. N., ed., 1979. *Dansk Politik i 1970'erne.* Copenhagen: Samfundsvi-
   dens-Kabeligt Forlag.

   1980. On Measuring Party System Change: A Methodological Critique and a
   Suggestion. *Comparative Political Studies* 12: 387–403.

Pelinka, A., 1978. *Österreich.* In Raschke (1978: 412–432).

Pelling, H., 1965. *The Origins of the Labour Party.* London: Oxford University
   Press.

   ed., 1968a. *Popular Politics and Society in Late Victorian England.* London:
   Macmillan.

   1968b. *The Concept of Labour Aristocracy.* In Pelling (1968a: 37–61).

   1976a. *A History of British Trade Unionism.* London: Macmillan.

   1976b. *A Short History of the Labour Party.* London: Macmillan.

Penniman, H. R., ed., 1977. *Italy at the Polls. The Parliamentary Elections of 1976.*
   Washington, DC: American Enterprise Institute.

Pepe, G., 1971. *Storia della CGL dalla fondazione alla guerra di Libia 1905–1911.*
   Bari: Laterza.

Perrot, M., 1967. Les guesdesistes: Controverse sur l'introduction du marxisme en
   France. *Annales: Economies, Sociétés, Civilisations* 22: 701–710.

Pesonen, P., 1968. *An Election in Finland: Party Activities and Voters' Reactions.* New
   Haven: Yale University Press.

Pesonen, P., and R. Sänkiaho, 1979. *Kansalaiset ja kansanvalta.* Juva, Finland:
   Söderström.

Piro, F., and P. Pombeni, eds., 1981. *Movimento operaio e società industriale in Europa,
   1870–1970.* Venice: Marsilio.

Pizzorno, A., 1962. Sviluppo economico e urbanizzazione. *Quaderni di sociologia* 11:
   23–51.

   1966a. Amoral Familism and Historical Marginality. *International Review of
   Community Development* 15: 55–66.

   1966b. Introduzione allo studio della partecipazione politica. *Quaderni di
   sociologia* 15: 1–52.

   1967. *The Individualistic Mobilization of Europe.* In Graubard (1967: 281–283).

   1969. *Elementi di uno schema teorico con riferimento i partiti politici in Italia.* In
   Sivini (1969: 5–40).

Pojas, M., 1991. The Swedish Model in Historical Perspective. *Scandinavian Economic History Review* 39: 64–74.

Polsby, N., R. A. Dentler, and P. Smith, 1963. *Politics and Social Life. An Introduction to the Study of Political Behavior*. Boston: Houghton Mifflin.

Portes, A., 1970. Leftist Radicalism in Chile: A Test of Three Hypotheses. *Comparative Politics* 2: 251–274.

1971a. On the Logic of Post-factum Explanation: The Hypothesis of Lower-Class Frustration as the Cause of Leftist Radicalism. *Social Forces* 50: 26–44.

1971b. Political Primitivism, Differential Socialization and Lower Class Leftist Radicalism. *American Sociological Review* 36: 820–835.

Potter, A., 1966. Great Britain: Opposition with a Capital O. In Dahl (1966a: 3–33).

Potthoff, P., 1979. *Gewerkschaften und Politik zwischen Revolution und Inflation*. Düsseldorf: Droste.

Prélot, M., 1939. *L'evolution politique du socialisme français, 1789–1934*. Paris: Spes.

Price, R., 1990. *Britain*. In Linden and Rojahn (1990: 3–24).

Procacci, G., 1970. *Storia degli italiani*, 2 vols. Bari, Italy: Laterza.

Prodzynski, F., 1992. *Ireland Between Centralism and the Market*. In Hyman and Ferner (1992: 69–87).

Przeworski, A., 1985. *Capitalism and Social Democracy*. New York: Cambridge University Press.

Przeworski, A., and J. Sprague, 1986. *Paper Stones: A History of Electoral Socialism*. Chicago: University of Chicago Press.

PSI, 1975. *Il Partito Socialista: Struttura e Organizzazione*. Venice: Marsilio.

1976. *Il partito e il paese: Annuario statistico 1976*. Rome: Quaderni della sezione centrale di organizzazione.

Rae, D. W., 1971. *The Political Consequences of Electoral Laws*. New Haven: Yale University Press.

Rae, D. W., and M. Taylor, 1970. *The Analysis of Political Cleavages*. New Haven: Yale University Press.

Ragionieri, E., 1976. *La storia politico-sociale*. In *Storia d'Italia dall'unità ad oggi*, Vol. 4, Tome 3, 1774–1785. Turin: Einaudi.

Raschke, J., ed., 1978. *Die politischen Parteien in Westeuropa*. Reinbek bei Hamburg: Rowohlt Taschenbuch Verlag.

Rattinger, H., 1981. *Measuring Power in Voting Bodies: Linear Constraints, Spatial Analysis, and a Computer Programme*. In Holler (1981: 222–231).

Rawson, D. W., 1969. The Life-Span of Labour Parties. *Political Studies* 17: 313–333.

Regini, M., ed., 1992. *The Future of Labour Movements*. London: Sage.

Reymond-Sauvain, P., 1966. *Le syndicalisme en Suisse*. Genevá: Editions Générales S.A.

Ribeni, L., 1989. Rivoluzione e democrazia in Germania. La rivoluzione del 1918 nella storiografia tedesco-federale degli anni 80. *Rivista di storia politica* no. 4: 137–154.

Rice, G. W., 1973. The Electoral Prospects of Non-Ruling Communist Parties. *American Journal of Political Science* 17: 597–619.

Righart, H., 1986. *De Katholieke Zuil in Europa*. Amsterdam: Boom.

Rimlinger, G. V., 1960. The Legitimation of Protest. A Comparative Study in Labor History. *Comparative Studies in Society and History* 2: 329–343.

Ritter, G. A., 1963. *Die Arbeiterbewegung im Wilhelminischen Reich. Die sozialdemo-kratische Partei und die freien Gewerkschaften 1890–1900.* Berlin: Collo-quium Verlag.

— ed., 1973. *Deutschen Parteien vor 1918.* Cologne: Kiepenheuer und Witsch.

— 1985. *Die deutschen Parteien 1830–1914. Parteien und Gesellschaft im konstitu-tionellen Regierungssystem.* Göttingen: Vandenhoeck & Ruprecht.

— 1990. *The Electoral Systems of Imperial Germany and Their Consequences for Politics.* In Noiret (1990b: 53–75).

Robert, J. L., 1980. *La scission syndicale de 1921: Essai de reconnaissance des formes.* Paris: Centre de recherches d'histoire des mouvements sociaux et du syndicalisme.

Roberts, R., 1958–1959. Appendix. *Journal of the Statistical and Social Inquiry Society of Ireland* 20.

Roche, W. K., 1990. *A Model Working Class? The Liberal Theory of Industrialization and the Maturation of the Irish Labour Movement.* Oxford: Nuffield College, Conference on the Development of the Industrial Society in Ireland.

— 1992. Modelling Trade Union Growth and Decline in the Republic of Ire-land. *Irish Business and Administrative Research* 13: 86–102.

Rohde, P. P., 1973. *The Communist Party of Denmark.* In Upton (1973: 3–33).

Rohe, K., ed. 1990a. *Elections, Parties and Political Traditions. Social Foundations of German Parties and Party Systems, 1867–1987.* Munich: Berg.

— 1990b. *Political Alignments and Re-alignments in the Ruhr, 1867–1987: Conti-nuity and Change of Political Traditions in an Industrial Region.* In Rohe (1990a: 107–144).

Rokkan, S., ed., 1962. *Approaches to the Study of Political Participation.* Bergen: Chr. Michelson Institute.

— 1966a. *Electoral Mobilization, Party Competition and National Integration.* In La Palombara and Weiner (1966: 241–266).

— 1966b. *Norway: Numerical Democracy and Corporate Pluralism.* In Dahl (1966a: 70–115).

— 1967. *Norway: Geography, Religion and Social Class: Cross Cutting Cleavages in Norwegian Politics.* In Lipset and Rokkan (1967: 367–444).

— 1970a. *Citizens, Elections, Parties.* Oslo: Universitetsforlaget.

— 1970b. *Nation-Building, Cleavage Formation and the Structuring of Mass Politics.* In Rokkan (1970a: 72–144).

— 1970c. *The Mobilization of the Periphery: Data on Turnout, Party Membership and Candidate Recruitment in Norway.* In Rokkan (1970a: 181–225).

— 1970d. *The Comparative Study of Political Participation.* In Rokkan (1970a: 13–45).

— 1970e. *Readers, Viewers, Voters.* In Rokkan (1970a: 417–431).

— 1970f. *Electoral Systems.* In Rokkan (1970a: 147–168).

— 1970g. The Growth and the Structuring of Mass Politics in Europe: Reflec-tions of Possible Models of Explanation. *Scandinavian Political Studies Yearbook* 5: 65–83.

— 1973. *Cities, States, and Nations: A Dimensional Model for the Study of Contrasts in Development.* In Eisenstadt and Rokkan (1973: 73–98).

— 1974. Entries, Voices, Exits: Towards a Possible Generalization of the Hirsch-man Model. *Social Science Information* no. 13: 39–53.

Simmel, G., 1903. *Die Großstadt und das Geisterleben*. In Bücher (1903: 185–206).

1956. *Conflict: The Web of Group Affiliation*. New York: Free Press.

Simmons, H. G., 1970. *French Socialists in Search of a Role 1956–1967*. Ithaca, NY: Cornell University Press.

Simonson, B., 1990. *Sweden*. In Linden and Rojahn (1990: 85–102).

Sivini, G., 1969. *Partiti e partecipazione politica in Italia*. Milan: Giaffré.

Sjöblom, G., 1978. *The Swedish Party System in the Post-War Period*. Florence: European University Institute, Conference on Recent Changes in European Party Systems.

Skocpol, T., 1979. *States and Social Revolutions. A Comparative Analysis of France, Russia and China*. Cambridge: Cambridge University Press.

Skogh, G., 1984. *Employers Associations in Sweden*. In Windmuller and Gladstone (1984: 149–168).

Soares, G. A. D., 1966. *Economic Development and Class Structure*. In Bendix and Lipset (1966: 190–199).

Sombart, W., 1905. Studien zur Entwicklungsgeschichte des nordamerikanischen Proletariats. *Archiv für Sozialwissenschaft und Sozialpolitik* 21: 210–236, 308–346, 556–611.

1924. *Der proletarische Sozialismus*. Jena: G. Fischer.

Sorokin, P. A., C. G. Zimmerman, and C. J. Galpin, 1930. *A Systematic Source Book in Rural Sociology*. Minneapolis: University of Minnesota Press.

Sparre, N. S., 1981a. Factional Strife in the Norwegian Labour Party, 1918–1924. *Journal of Contemporary History* 16: 691–704.

1981b. Labour Insurgencies in Norway: The Crisis of 1917–20. *Social Science History* 5: 393–413.

Spitaels, G., 1974. *Le mouvement sysndicale en Belgique*. Brussels: Editions de l'Université de Bruxelles.

SPO, 1945ff. *Berichte an den Bundesparteitag der SPO*. Vienna.

Spriano, P., 1964. *L'occupazione delle fabbriche. Settembre 1920*. Turin: Einaudi.

Stammer, O., ed., 1968. *Party System, Party Organisation and the Politics of the New Masses*. Berlin: Free University, Institute for Political Science.

Stearns, P., 1971. *Revolutionary Syndicalism and French Labour*. Rutgers: Rutgers University Press.

Steenson, G. P., 1991. *After Marx, Before Lenin. Marxism and Socialist Working-Class Parties in Europe, 1884–1914*. Pittsburgh: University of Pittsburgh Press.

Steinberg, M., 1971. A l'origine du communisme belge: L'extrême gauche révolutionnaire d'avant 1914. *Cahiers Marxistes* 8: 3–34.

Steiner, H., 1964. *Die Arbeiterbewegung Oesterreichs 1867–1889*. Vienna: Europa Verlag.

Steinmo, S., K. Thelen, and F. Longstreth, eds., 1992. *Structuring Politics. Historical Institutionalism in Comparative Analysis*. Cambridge: Cambridge University Press.

Stephens, J. D., 1979. *The Transition from Capitalism to Socialism*. London: Macmillan.

Stettler, P., 1980. *Die Kommunistische Partei der Schweiz 1921–1931. Ein Beitrag zur schweizerischer Parteiforschung und zur Geschichte der schweizerischen Arbeiter-*

bewegung im Rahmen der Kommunistischen Internationalen. Bern: Francke Verlag.

Stinchome, A. L., 1965. *Social Structure and Organisation.* In March (1965: 142–193).

Stjernquist, N., 1966. *Sweden: Stability or Deadlock.* In Dahl (1966a: 116–146).

Stoetzel, J., 1955. Voting Behaviour in France. *British Journal of Sociology* 6: 118–119.

Stråth, B., 1983. Workers' Radicalism in Theory and Practice. *Scandinavian Journal of History* 8: 261–291.

——— 1988a. *Continuity and Discontinuity in Passing from I to II: Swedish 19th Century Civil Society, Culture, Social Formations, and Political Change.* In Stråth (1988b: 21–42).

——— ed., 1988b. *Democratisation in Scandinavia in Comparison.* Gothenburg: Gothenburg University, Department of History.

Strikwerda, C., 1988. The Divided Class: Catholics versus Socialists in Belgium, 1880–1914. *Comparative Studies in Society and History* 31: 333–359.

Studer, B., 1993. Le parti communiste suisse. *Cahiers d'Histoire du Mouvement Ouvrier* n. 9: 5–38.

Suleiman, E. N., 1974. *Politics, Power and Bureaucracy in France. The Administrative Elite.* Princeton: Princeton University Press.

Sundberg, J., 1987. Exploring the Case of Declining Party Membership in Denmark: A Scandinavian Comparison. *Scandinavian Political Studies* 10: 17–38.

Suviranta, A. J., 1987. *Finland.* In Blainpain (1987: para 275).

Svåsand, L., 1978. *On the Formation of Political Parties: Conditions, Causes and Patterns of Development.* Grenoble: ECPR.

——— 1980. *Democratisation and Party Formation in Scandinavia.* In Büsch (1980: 398–411).

Sworatowski, W. S., ed., 1973. *World Communism: A Handbook.* Washington, DC: Hoover Institution Press.

Szabo, E., 1982. *Socialism and Social Science: Selected Writings of Ervin Szabo (1877–1918),* edited by G. Lituàn and J. Back. London: Routledge and Kegan Paul.

Talos, E., 1981. *Staatliche Sozialpolitik in Oesterreich. Rekonstruktion und Analyse.* Vienna: Verlag für Gesellschaftskritik.

Tannahill, R. N., 1976. Leadership as a Determinant of Diversity in Western European Communism. *Studies in Comparative Communism* 9: 349–368.

Tanner, D., 1990. *Political Change and the Labour Party, 1900–1918.* Cambridge: Cambridge University Press.

Tarrow, S. G., 1967. *Peasant Communism in Southern Italy.* New Haven: Yale University Press.

——— 1972. *Partito comunista e contadini nel mezzogiorno.* Turin: Einaudi.

——— 1977. *Between Center and Periphery: Grass-Roots Politicians in Italy and France.* New Haven: Yale University Press.

Tarrow, S. G., and W. Ascher, 1975. The Stability of Communist Electorates: Evidence from a Longitudinal Analysis of French and Italian Aggregate Data. *American Journal of Political Science* 19: 475–499.

Tavernier, Y. M., 1972. *Le Modef.* In Tavernier, Gervais, and Servolin (1972: 467–495).

Tavernier, Y. M., Gervais, and C. Servolin, 1972. *L'univers politique des paysans dans la France contemporaine.* Paris: Colin.

Taylor, C. L., and M. Hudson, 1972. *World Handbook of Political and Social Indicators.* New Haven: Yale University Press.

Taylor, S., 1978. Parkin's Theory of Working Class Conservatism: Two Hypotheses Investigated. *Sociological Review* 26: 827–842.

Tenfelde, K., 1981. Il movimento operaio tedesco nella Prima Guerra Mondiale. *Quellen und Forschungen aus italienischen Archiven und Bibliotheken* 61: 216–247.

     ed., 1986. *Arbeiter und Arbeiterbewegung im Vergleich. Berichte zur internationalen historischen Forschung.* Munich: Oldenburg.

     1990. *Germany.* In Linden and Rojahn (1990: 243–270).

Terjesen, E. A., 1990. *Norway.* In Linden and Rojahn (1990: 103–130).

Therborn, G., 1977. The Rule of Capitalism and the Rise of Democracy. *New Left Review* no.103: 3–41.

Thomas, H., 1977. *Social Democracy in Denmark.* In Paterson and Thomas (1977: 234–271).

Thompson, E. P., 1963. *The Making of the English Working Class.* London: Victor Gollancz.

Thompson, J. G., 1927. *Urbanization: Its Effects on Government and Society.* New York: Dutton.

Thornley, D., 1974. *Historical Introduction.* In Chubb (1974: 1–42).

Tilly, C., ed., 1975. *The Formation of National States in Western Europe.* Princeton: Princeton University Press.

     1978. *From Mobilization to Revolution.* Reading, MA: Addison-Wesley.

Tilly, C., L. Tilly, and R. H. Tilly, 1975. *The Rebellious Century 1830–1930.* Cambridge, MA: Harvard University Press.

Tilly, R. H., 1980. *Kapital, Staat und sozialer Protest in der deutschen Industrialisierung,* Vol. 41. Gottingen: Gesammelte Aufsätze. Kritische Studien zur Geschichtswissenschaft.

     1989. *Comportamento e etica industriale. Indizi di una cultura borghese nella Germania del XIX secolo.* In Kocka (1989a: 325–355).

Tilton, T. A., 1974. The Social Origins of Liberal Democracy: The Swedish Case. *American Political Science Review* 68: 561–571.

Timoten, P., 1973. Sodan Vaikutukset Poliittiseen Käyttäytimiesen. *Politiika* 15: 106–128.

Tingsten, H., 1937. *Political Behavior.* London: P. S. King & Son.

Torgersen, U., 1962. The Trend Toward Political Consensus: The Case of Norway. *Acta Sociologica* 6: 159–172.

Torsvik, P., ed., 1981. *Mobilization, Center–Periphery Structures and Nation Building.* Bergen: Universitetsforlaget.

Tracy, M., 1964. *Agriculture in Western Europe: Challenge and Response 1880–1980.* London: Granada.

Traxler, F., 1992. *Austria: Still the Century of Corporatism.* In Hyman and Ferner (1992: 270–297).

Trebilcock, C., 1981. *The Industrialisation of the Continental Powers, 1780–1914.* London: Longman.

Trede, M., ed., 1992. *Electricité et électrification dans le monde 1880–1980.* Paris: Presses Universitaires de France.

Tucker, A. W., and H. W. Kuhn, eds., 1953. *Contributions to the Theory of Games.* Princeton: Princeton University Press.

Tucker, R. C., 1967. De-Radicalization of Marxist Movements. *American Political Science Review* 61: 341–358.

Tuominen, A., 1955. The Northern European Communist Parties. *Occidente* 11: 193–210.

Työelämän Suhteet – Aikasarjola 1907–1988, 1990. Helsinki: Työministeriö.

Ulam, A. B., 1979. *The Unfinished Revolution: Marxism and Communism in the Modern World,* 2nd ed. London: Longman.

Upton, A. F., ed., 1973. *The Communist Parties of Scandinavia and Finland.* London: Weidenfeld and Nicolson.

Urwin, D. W., 1974. *Germany: Continuity and Change in Electoral Politics.* In R. Rose (1974: 109–170).

   1980. *From Ploughshare to Ballotbox. The Politics of Agrarian Defense in Europe.* Oslo: Universitetsforlaget.

Urwin, D. W., and F. Aarebrot, 1981. *The Socio-Geographic Correlates of Left-Wing Voting in Weimar Germany 1924–1932.* In Torsvik (1981: 241–273).

Valen, H., and S. Rokkan, 1974. *Conflict Structure and Mass Politics in a European Periphery.* In Rose (1974: 315–370).

Valenzuela, J. S., 1981. Uno schema teorico per l'analisi della formazione dei movimenti operai. *Stato e Mercato* 1: 447–482.

   1992. *Labour Movements and Political Systems: Some Variations.* In Regini (1992: 53–101).

Vallier, I., 1970a. *Insulation, and Re-entry: Toward a Theory of Social Religious Change.* In Landsberger (1970: 9–35).

   1970b. *Social Control and Modernization in Latin America.* Englewood Cliffs, NJ: Prentice-Hall.

Vaussard, M., 1956. *Histoire de la démocratie chrétienne. France, Belgique, Italie.* Paris: Seuil.

Veblen, T., 1994 (1st ed., 1915). *Imperial Germany and the Industrial Revolution.* In *The Collected Works of Thorstein Veblen,* Vol. 4. London: Routledge.

Verba, S., N. H. Nie, and J. Kim, 1978. *Participation and Political Equality: A Seven Nation Comparison.* Cambridge: Cambridge University Press.

Vilrokx, J., and J. Leemput, 1992. *Belgium: A New Stability in Industrial Relations.* In Hyman and Ferner (1992: 357–392).

Visser, J., 1987. *In Search of Inclusive Unionism: A Comparative Analysis.* Amsterdam: University of Amsterdam, PhD dissertation.

Vorrink, K., 1945. *Een Halve Eeuw Beginselstrijd: Overdenkingen over verleden en toekomst bij een historische mijlpaal.* Amsterdam: De Arbeiderspers.

Vuilleumier, M., 1988. *Autour de la "fondation" du Parti Socialiste Suisse.* In *Les origines du socialisme en Suisse Romande 1880–1920.* Lausanne: Association pour l'Etude du Mouvement Ouvrier, Cahier no. 5.

INDEX

WITHDRAWN FROM
JUNIATA COLLEGE LIBRARY

Printed in the United States
71270LV00003B/1-15

9 780521 033435